D MAP PAGES

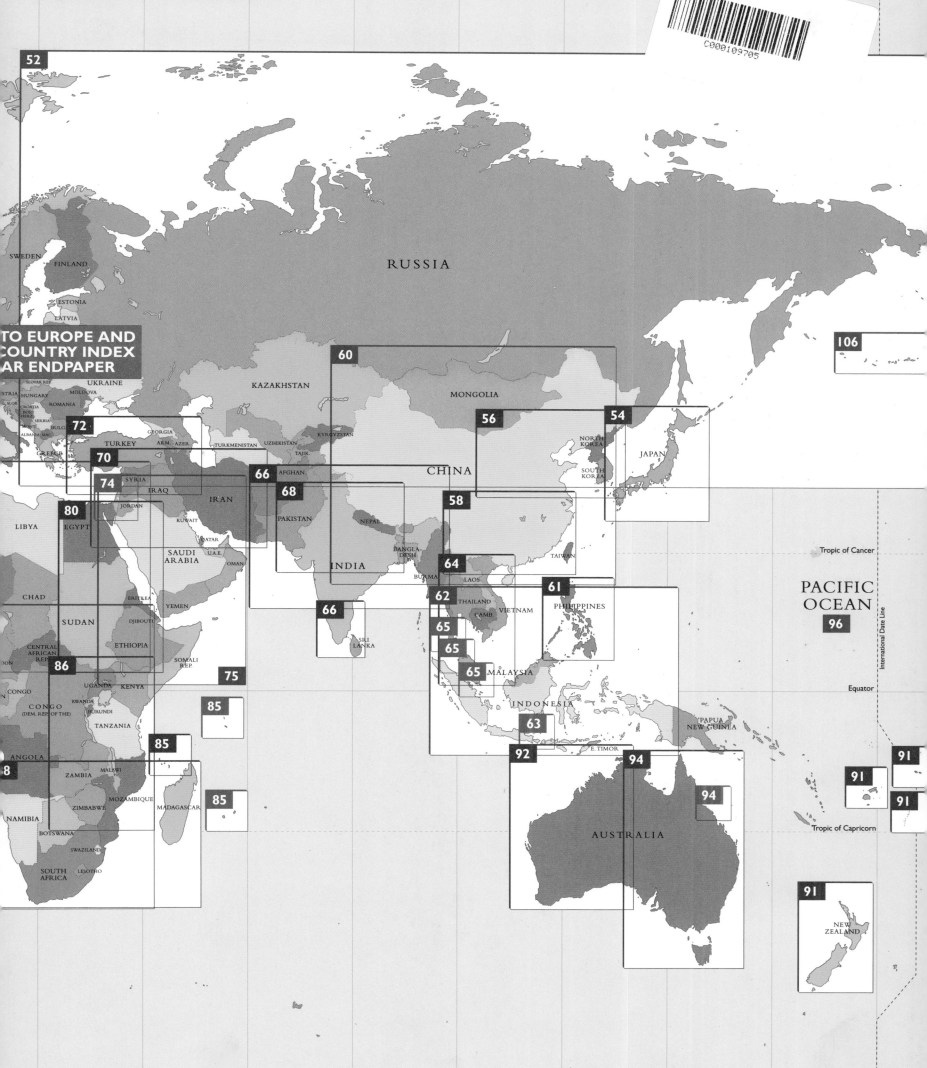

TO EUROPE AND
COUNTRY INDEX
AR ENDPAPER

PHILIP'S

WORLD TRAVELLER'S ATLAS

PHILIP'S

WORLD TRAVELLER'S ATLAS

IN ASSOCIATION WITH
THE ROYAL GEOGRAPHICAL SOCIETY
WITH THE INSTITUTE OF BRITISH GEOGRAPHERS

PICTURE ACKNOWLEDGEMENTS

WORLD EXPLORER:
© *CORBIS* 26 bottom, 27 bottom, /Adam Woolfitt 5 centre right, 30 centre left, /AFP 24 top, 25 bottom, /Angelo Hornak 29 centre left, /Australian Picture Library 13 top, /Bob Krist 14 top, /Bob Winsett 20 top, /Brandon D. Cole 11 bottom, /Buddy Mays 26 centre, 22 bottom, /Catherine Karnow 19 bottom, /Charles and Josette Lenars 30 bottom right, /Charles O'Rear 23 left, /Clem Haagner; Gallo Images 10 centre, /Dave G. Houser 30 top, /David Muench 4 left, /Dean Conger 15 bottom, /Derek Hall; Frank Lane Picture Agency 3 centre, /Douglas Peebles 32 bottom, /Duomo 20 right, /Enzo and Paolo Ragazzini 16 bottom, /Galen Rowell 2 left, 9 bottom, 21 top, /George H. H. Huey 4 top, /George Lepp 12 bottom, /Hans Georg Roth 5 top, /Inge Yspeert 10 bottom right, /James Marshall 6 centre right, /John Dakers; Eye Ubiquitous 25 right, /Kevin Schafer 13 bottom, /Marc Muench 20 left, /Michael and Patricia Fogden 8 /Michael Busselle 3 top, /Michael S. Yamashita 22 top, /Milepost 92½ 15 top, /Mimmo Jodice 29 bottom, /Morton Beebe, S. F. 24 centre right, /Nik Wheeler 19 top, /O. Alamany and E. Vicens 5 bottom, /Patrick Ward 7 bottom, 16 centre right, /Peter Johnson 10 top, /Peter Wilson 28 bottom, /Premium Stock 28 top, /Quadrillion 31 bottom, /Raymond Gehman 2 top, 6 top, /Rick Doyle 23 bottom, /Robert Holmes 16 top, /Roger Ressmeyer 3 bottom, /Roger Tidman 9 left, /Stephanie Maze 24 bottom, /Stephen Frink 12 top, 13 centre, /Steve Kaufman 6 bottom, /Tim Thompson 14 centre right, 14 bottom, /Tiziana and Gianni Baldizzone 7 centre right, /Tom Bean 8 bottom, /Tom Brakefield 11 top, /Tom Nebbia 17 right, /Tony Arruza 23 top, /Vanni Archive 29 top, /W. Cody 18 right, 27 top, /Wild Country 26 top, /Wolfgang Kaehler 17 top, 18 top and bottom, 8 top.
© *ALTON TOWERS* 32 left.

CITY GAZETTEER:
© *CORBIS* /Bettmann 41 right, /Carmen Redondo 44 left, /Charles E. Rotkin 40 right, /Chris Lisle 47 centre, /Hubert Stadler 41 centre, /John Heseltine 42 centre, /Larry Lee 46 right, /Lindsay Hebberd 42 left, /Patrick Ward 44 right, /Paul A. Souders 47 right, /Richard T. Nowitz 43 centre, /Tim Thompson 41 left, /Todd Gipstein 44 centre, /Wolfgang Kaehler 45 right, /Yann Arthus-Bertrand 46 left.
© *MIKE MOULE* 40 left, 42 right, 43 right, 45 left, 46 centre, 48 centre and right.

CITY MAPS
Cartography by Philip's

PAGE 10, DUBLIN: The town plan of Dublin is based on Ordnance Survey Ireland by permission of the Government Permit Number 8097. © Ordnance Survey Ireland and Government of Ireland.

Ordnance Survey PAGE 11, EDINBURGH, and PAGE 15, LONDON:
This product includes mapping data licensed from Ordnance Survey® with the permission of the Controller of Her Majesty's Stationery Office. © Crown copyright 2006. All rights reserved. Licence number 100011710.

VECTOR DATA: Courtesy of Gräfe and Unser Verlag GmbH, München, Germany (city-centre maps of Bangkok, Beijing, Cape Town, Jerusalem, Mexico City, Moscow, Singapore, Sydney, Tokyo and Washington D.C.)

The following city maps utilize base data supplied courtesy of MapQuest.com, Inc. (© MapQuest): Las Vegas, New Orleans, Orlando.

> **NOTE:**
> For reasons of safety or politics, there may be times when it is not advisable, or desirable, to visit one or more of the places described in the World Explorer and City Gazetteer sections. If in doubt, please check with the Foreign Office.

Published in Great Britain in 2006 by Philip's,
a division of Octopus Publishing Group Limited,
2–4 Heron Quays, London E14 4JP

Copyright © 2006 Philip's

Cartography by Philip's

ISBN-13 978-0-540-08896-6
ISBN-10 0-540-08896-X

A CIP catalogue record for this book is available from the British Library.

Printed in Hong Kong

Details of other Philip's titles and services can be found on our website at:
www.philips-maps.co.uk

Philip's World Atlases are published in association with The Royal Geographical Society (with The Institute of British Geographers).

The Society was founded in 1830 and given a Royal Charter in 1859 for 'the advancement of geographical science'. It holds historical collections of national and international importance, many of which relate to the Society's association with and support for scientific exploration and research from the 19th century onwards. It was pivotal in establishing geography as a teaching and research discipline in British universities close to the turn of the century, and has played a key role in geographical and environmental education ever since.

Today the Society is a leading world centre for geographical learning – supporting education, teaching, research and expeditions, and promoting public understanding of the subject.

The Society welcomes those interested in geography as members. For further information, please visit the website at: www.rgs.org

User Guide

The reference maps which form the main body of this atlas have been prepared in accordance with the highest standards of international cartography to provide an accurate and detailed representation of the Earth. The scales and projections used have been carefully chosen to give balanced coverage of the world, while emphasizing the most densely populated and economically significant regions. A hallmark of Philip's mapping is the use of hill shading and relief colouring to create a graphic impression of landforms: this makes the maps exceptionally easy to read. However, knowledge of the key features employed in the construction and presentation of the maps will enable the reader to derive the fullest benefit from the atlas.

MAP SEQUENCE

The atlas covers the Earth continent by continent: first Europe; then its land neighbour Asia (mapped north before south, in a clockwise sequence), then Africa, Australia and Oceania, North America and South America. This is the classic arrangement adopted by most cartographers since the 16th century. For each continent, there are maps at a variety of scales. First, physical relief and political maps

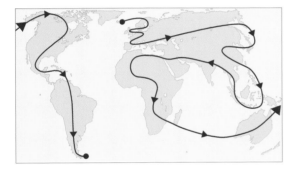

of the whole continent; then a series of larger-scale maps of the regions within the continent, each followed, where required, by still larger-scale maps of the most important or densely populated areas. The governing principle is that by turning the pages of the atlas, the reader moves steadily from north to south through each continent, with each map overlapping its neighbours.

MAP PRESENTATION

With very few exceptions (e.g. for the Arctic and Antarctica), the maps are drawn with north at the top, regardless of whether they are presented upright or sideways on the page. In the borders will be found the map title; a locator diagram showing the area covered; continuation arrows showing the page numbers for maps of adjacent areas; the scale; the projection used; the degrees of latitude and longitude; and the letters and figures used in the index for locating place names and geographical features. Physical relief maps also have a height reference panel identifying the colours used for each layer of contouring.

MAP SYMBOLS

Each map contains a vast amount of detail which can only be conveyed clearly and accurately by the use of symbols. Points and circles of varying sizes locate and identify the relative importance of towns and cities; different styles of type are employed for administrative, geographical and regional place names to aid identification. A variety of pictorial symbols denote landscape features such as glaciers, marshes and coral reefs, and man-made structures including roads, railways, airports, canals and dams. International borders are shown by red lines. Where neighbouring countries are in dispute, for example in parts of the Middle East, the maps show the *de facto* boundary between nations, regardless of the legal or historical situation. The symbols are explained on the first page of the *World Maps* section of the atlas.

MAP SCALES

1:16 000 000
1 inch = 252 statute miles

The scale of each map is given in the numerical form known as the 'representative fraction'. The first figure is always one, signifying one unit of distance on the map; the second figure, usually in millions, is the number by which the map unit must be multiplied to give the equivalent distance on the Earth's surface. Calculations can easily be made in centimetres and kilometres, by dividing the Earth units figure by 100 000 (i.e. deleting the last five 0s). Thus 1:1 000 000 means 1 cm = 10 km. The calculation for inches and miles is more laborious, but 1 000 000 divided by 63 360 (the number of inches in a mile) shows that 1:1 000 000 means approximately 1 inch = 16 miles. The table below provides distance equivalents for scales down to 1:50 000 000.

LARGE SCALE		
1:1 000 000	1 cm = 10 km	1 inch = 16 miles
1:2 500 000	1 cm = 25 km	1 inch = 39.5 miles
1:5 000 000	1 cm = 50 km	1 inch = 79 miles
1:6 000 000	1 cm = 60 km	1 inch = 95 miles
1:8 000 000	1 cm = 80 km	1 inch = 126 miles
1:10 000 000	1 cm = 100 km	1 inch = 158 miles
1:15 000 000	1 cm = 150 km	1 inch = 237 miles
1:20 000 000	1 cm = 200 km	1 inch = 316 miles
1:50 000 000	1 cm = 500 km	1 inch = 790 miles
SMALL SCALE		

MEASURING DISTANCES

Although each map is accompanied by a scale bar, distances cannot always be measured with confidence because of the distortions involved in portraying the curved surface of the Earth on a flat page. As a general rule, the larger the map scale (i.e. the lower the number of Earth units in the representative fraction), the more accurate and reliable will be the distance measured. On small-scale maps such as those of the world and of entire continents, measurement may only

be accurate along the 'standard parallels', or central axes, and should not be attempted without considering the map projection.

MAP PROJECTIONS

Unlike a globe, no flat map can give a true scale representation of the world in terms of area, shape and position of every region. Each of the numerous systems that have been devised for projecting the curved surface of the Earth on to a flat page involves the sacrifice of accuracy in one or more of these elements. The variations in shape and position of landmasses such as Alaska, Greenland and Australia, for example, can be quite dramatic when different projections are compared.

For this atlas, the guiding principle has been to select projections that involve the least distortion of size and distance. The projection used for each map is noted in the border. Most fall into one of three categories – conic, azimuthal or cylindrical – whose basic concepts are shown above. Each involves plotting the forms of the Earth's surface on a grid of latitude and longitude lines, which may be shown as parallels, curves or radiating spokes.

LATITUDE AND LONGITUDE

Accurate positioning of individual points on the Earth's surface is made possible by reference to the geometrical system of latitude and longitude. Latitude *parallels* are drawn west–east around the Earth and numbered by degrees north and south of the Equator, which is designated 0° of latitude. Longitude *meridians* are drawn north–south and numbered by degrees east and west of the *prime meridian*, 0° of longitude, which passes through Greenwich in England. By referring to these co-ordinates and their subdivisions of minutes (1/60th of a degree) and seconds (1/60th of a minute), any place on Earth can be located to within a few hundred metres. Latitude and longitude are indicated by blue lines on the maps; they are straight or curved according to the projection employed. Reference to these lines is the easiest way of determining the relative positions of places on different maps, and for plotting compass directions.

NAME FORMS

For ease of reference, both English and local name forms appear in the atlas. Oceans, seas and countries are shown in English throughout the atlas; country names may be abbreviated to their commonly accepted form (e.g. Germany, not The Federal Republic of Germany). Conventional English forms are also used for place names on the smaller-scale maps of the continents. However, local name forms are used on all large-scale and regional maps, with the English form given in brackets only for important cities – the large-scale map of Russia and Central Asia thus shows Moskva (Moscow). For countries which do not use a Roman script, place names have been transcribed according to the systems adopted by the British and US Geographic Names Authorities. For China, the Pin Yin system has been used, with some more widely known forms appearing in brackets, as with Beijing (Peking). Both English and local names appear in the index, the English form being cross-referenced to the local form.

Contents

WORLD STATISTICS

Countries   x
Cities   xi
Distances   xii
Climate   xiii
Physical Dimensions   xiv–xv
Regions in the News   xvi

WORLD EXPLORER

Mountains and volcanoes   2–3
Deserts and canyons   4–5
Lakes and waterfalls   6–7
Wildlife in the Americas
  and Europe   8–9
Wildlife in Africa, Asia
  and Australasia   10–11
Marine wildlife   12–13
Great railway journeys   14–15
River and canal journeys   16–17
Sea and ocean cruises   18–19
Winter sports   20–21
Great beaches   22–23
Festivals   24–25
Historic sites in the
  Americas   26–27
Historic sites in Europe   28–29
Historic sites in Africa,
  Asia and Australasia   30–31
Theme parks   32

WORLD CITIES

CITY MAPS

Amsterdam   2
Athens   2
Atlanta   3
Baghdad   3
Bangkok   3
Barcelona   4
Beijing   4
Berlin   5
Boston   6
Brussels   6
Budapest   7
Buenos Aires   7
Cairo   7
Cape Town   8
Copenhagen   8
Chicago   9

Delhi   10
Dublin   10
Edinburgh   11
Guangzhou (Canton)   11
Helsinki   11
Hong Kong   12
Istanbul   12
Jakarta   12
Jerusalem   13
Johannesburg   13
Karachi   13
Kolkata (Calcutta)   14
Lagos   14
Las Vegas   14
Lima   14
London   15
Lisbon   16
Los Angeles   16–17
Madrid   17
Manila   17
Melbourne   18
Mexico City   18
Miami   18
Milan   19
Moscow   19
Montréal   20
Mumbai (Bombay)   20
Munich   21
New Orleans   21
New York   22
Orlando   23
Osaka   23
Oslo   23
Paris   24
Prague   25
Rio de Janeiro   25
Rome   26
San Francisco   26
St Petersburg   27
Santiago   27
São Paulo   27
Seoul   27
Shanghai   28
Singapore   28
Stockholm   29
Sydney   29
Tokyo   30
Tehran   31
Toronto   31
Vienna   32
Warsaw   32
Washington   33
Wellington   33

INDEX TO CITY MAPS   34–39

CITY GAZETTEER

Accra, Ghana   40
Agra, India   40
Amsterdam, The Netherlands   40
Antwerp, Belgium   40
Athens, Greece   40
Atlanta, Georgia, USA   40
Auckland, New Zealand   40
Bangkok, Thailand   40
Barcelona, Spain   40
Beijing, China   40
Berlin, Germany   40
Boston, Massachusetts, USA   41
Brisbane, Queensland,
  Australia   41
Brussels, Belgium   41
Budapest, Hungary   41
Buenos Aires, Argentina   41
Cairo, Egypt   41
Cape Town, South Africa   41
Cartagena, Colombia   41
Chicago, Illinois, USA   41
Cologne, Germany   41
Copenhagen, Denmark   41
Delhi, India   42
Dublin, Ireland   42
Edinburgh, Scotland   42
Esfahan, Iran   42
Fès, Morocco   42
Florence, Italy   42
Geneva, Switzerland   42
Guangzhou (Canton), China   42
Hamburg, Germany   42
Hanoi, Vietnam   42
Havana, Cuba   42
Helsinki, Finland   43
Hong Kong, China   43
Istanbul, Turkey   43
Jaipur, India   43
Jakarta, Indonesia   43
Jerusalem, Israel   43
Johannesburg, South Africa   43
Kairouan, Tunisia   43
Karachi, Pakistan   43
Katmandu, Nepal   43
Kolkata (Calcutta), India   43
Kraków, Poland   43
Kuala Lumpur, Malaysia   44
Kyoto, Japan   44
Lagos, Nigeria   44
Lahore, Pakistan   44
Las Vegas, Nevada, USA   44
Lima, Peru   44
Lisbon, Portugal   44
London, England   44

Los Angeles, California, USA   44
Luxembourg City, Luxembourg   44
Madrid, Spain   44
Manila, Philippines   45
Marrakech, Morocco   45
Melbourne, Victoria,
  Australia   45
Mexico City, Mexico   45
Miami, Florida, USA   45
Milan, Italy   45
Montréal, Québec, Canada   45
Moscow, Russia   45
Mumbai (Bombay), India   45
Munich, Germany   45
Nairobi, Kenya   45
New Orleans, Louisiana, USA   45
New York, NY, USA   46
Orlando, Florida, USA   46
Osaka, Japan   46
Oslo, Norway   46
Paris, France   46
Perth, Western Australia,
  Australia   46
Prague, Czech Republic   46
Quito, Ecuador   46
Reykjavik, Iceland   46
Riga, Latvia   46
Rio de Janeiro, Brazil   46
Rome, Italy   46
St Petersburg, Russia   47
San Francisco, California, USA   47
Santiago, Chile   47
São Paulo, Brazil   47
Seattle, Washington, USA   47
Seoul, South Korea   47
Shanghai, China   47
Singapore City, Singapore   47
Stockholm, Sweden   47
Sydney, New South Wales,
  Australia   47
Tehran, Iran   47
Tianjin, China   48
Tokyo, Japan   48
Toronto, Ontario, Canada   48
Vancouver, British Columbia,
  Canada   48
Varanasi, India   48
Venice, Italy   48
Vienna, Austria   48
Warsaw, Poland   48
Washington, DC, USA   48
Wellington, New Zealand   48
Xi'an, China   48
Yangon (Rangoon), Burma
  (Myanmar)   48

WORLD MAPS

Map Symbols   **1**

The World: Political
1:84 000 000   **2–3**

Arctic Ocean
1:31 100 000   **4**

Antarctica
1:31 100 000   **5**

Europe

Europe: Physical
1:17 800 000   **6**

Europe: Political
1:17 800 000   **7**

Scandinavia
1:5 300 000
Iceland 1:5 300 000
Færoe Islands 1:5 300 000

8–9

Denmark and Southern Sweden
1:2 200 000

10–11

Ireland
1:1 800 000

12

Scotland
1:1 800 000
Orkney Islands 1:1 800 000
Shetland Islands 1:1 800 000

13

England and Wales
1:1 800 000
Isles of Scilly 1:1 800 000

14–15

British Isles
1:4 400 000

16

Netherlands, Belgium and Luxembourg
1:2 200 000

17

Northern France
1:2 200 000

18–19

Southern France
1:2 200 000

20–21

Central Europe
1:4 400 000

22–23

Germany and Switzerland
1:2 200 000

24–25

**Austria, Czech Republic and
  Slovak Republic**
1:2 200 000

26–27

**Hungary, Romania and the
  Lower Danube**
1:2 200 000

28–29

Poland and the Southern Baltic
1:2 200 000

30–31

Baltic States, Belarus and Ukraine
1:4 400 000

32–33

The Volga Basin and the Caucasus
1:4 400 000

34–35

Western Spain and Portugal
1:2 200 000

36–37

Eastern Spain
1:2 200 000
Menorca 1:2 200 000

38–39

Northern Italy, Slovenia and Croatia
1:2 200 000

40–41

Southern Italy
1:2 200 000

42–43

The Balkans
1:2 200 000

44–45

Southern Greece and Western Turkey
1:2 200 000

46–47

The Balearics, the Canaries and Madeira
1:900 000 / 1:1 800 000

48

Malta, Crete, Corfu, Rhodes and Cyprus
1:900 000 / 1:1 200 000

49

Asia

Asia: Physical
1:44 400 000

50

Asia: Political
1:44 400 000

51

Russia and Central Asia
1:17 800 000

52–53

Japan
1:4 400 000
Ryukyu Islands 1:4 400 000

54–55

Northern China and Korea
1:5 300 000

56–57

Southern China
1:5 300 000

58–59

China
1:17 800 000

60

The Philippines
1:6 700 000

61

Indonesia and the Philippines
1:11 100 000
Java and Madura 1:6 700 000
Bali 1:1 800 000

62–63

Mainland South-east Asia
1:5 300 000
Ko Phuket 1:900 000
Ko Samui 1:900 000
Pinang 1:900 000
Singapore 1:900 000

64–65

South Asia
1:8 900 000

66–67

Northern India, Pakistan and Nepal
1:5 300 000
Jammu and Kashmir 1:5 300 000

68–69

The Middle East
1:6 200 000

70–71

Turkey and Transcaucasia
1:4 400 000

72–73

The Near East
1:2 200 000

74

Arabia and the Horn of Africa
1:13 300 000

75

Africa

Africa: Physical
1:37 300 000

76

Africa: Political
1: 37 300 000

77

Northern Africa
1:13 300 000
The Azores 1:13 300 000
Cape Verde Islands 1:11 100 000

78–79

The Nile Valley
1:7 100 000
The Nile Delta 1:3 600 000

80–81

West Africa
1:7 100 000

82–83

Central and Southern Africa
1:13 300 000
Seychelles 1:2 200 000
Réunion 1:2 200 000
Mauritius 1:2 200 000
Comoros 1:7 100 000

84–85

East Africa
1:7 100 000

86–87

Southern Africa
1:7 100 000
Madagascar 1:7 100 000

88–89

Australia and Oceania

Australia and Oceania:
 Physical and Political
1:44 400 000   90

New Zealand
1:5 300 000
Fiji 1:5 300 000
Samoan Islands 1:5 300 000
Tonga 1:5 300 000
Tahiti and Moorea 1:1 100 000

91

Western Australia
1:7 100 000

92–93

Eastern Australia
1:7 100 000
Whitsunday Islands 1:2 200 000
Tasmania 1:7 100 000

94–95

Pacific Ocean
1:48 000 000   96–97

North America

North America: Physical
1:31 100 000   98

North America: Political
1:31 100 000   99

Canada
1:13 300 000

100–101

Western Canada
1:6 200 000

102–103

Eastern Canada
1:6 200 000

104–105

United States
1:10 700 000
Hawai'i 1:8 900 000
Alaska 1:26 700 000

106–107

United States – West
1:6 000 000

108–109

Central and Southern California
 and Western Washington
1:2 200 000

110–111

United States Midwest and North-east
1:6 000 000

112–113

North-eastern United States
1:2 200 000

114–115

United States – South
1:6 000 000

116–117

Mexico
1:7 100 000

118–119

Central America and the West Indies
1:7 100 000
Jamaica 1:2 700 000
Guadeloupe 1:1 800 000
Martinique 1:1 800 000
Puerto Rico 1:2 700 000
Virgin Islands 1:1 800 000
St Lucia 1:890 000
Barbados 1:890 000

120–121

South America

South America: Physical
1:31 100 000   122

South America: Political
1:31 100 000   123

South America – North
1:14 200 000
Trinidad and Tobago 1:2 200 000

124–125

Central South America
1:7 100 000

126–127

South America – South
1:14 200 000

128

INDEX TO WORLD MAPS

129–224

World Statistics: Countries

This alphabetical list includes all the countries and territories of the world. If a territory is not completely independent, the country it is associated with is named. The area figures give the total area of land, inland water and ice.

The population figures are 2005 estimates. The annual income is the Gross Domestic Product per capita in US dollars. The figures are the latest available, usually 2005 estimates.

Country/Territory	Area km² Thousands	Area miles² Thousands	Population Thousands	Capital	Annual Income US $
Afghanistan	652	252	29,929	Kabul	800
Albania	28.7	11.1	3,563	Tirana	4,900
Algeria	2,382	920	32,532	Algiers	7,300
American Samoa (US)	0.20	0.08	58	Pago Pago	8,000
Andorra	0.47	0.18	71	Andorra La Vella	26,800
Angola	1,247	481	11,191	Luanda	2,500
Anguilla (UK)	0.10	0.04	13	The Valley	7,500
Antigua & Barbuda	0.44	0.17	69	St John's	11,000
Argentina	2,780	1,074	39,538	Buenos Aires	13,600
Armenia	29.8	11.5	2,983	Yerevan	5,100
Aruba (Netherlands)	0.19	0.07	72	Oranjestad	28,000
Australia	7,741	2,989	20,090	Canberra	32,000
Austria	83.9	32.4	8,185	Vienna	32,900
Azerbaijan	86.6	33.4	7,912	Baku	4,600
Azores (Portugal)	2.2	0.86	236	Ponta Delgada	15,000
Bahamas	13.9	5.4	302	Nassau	18,800
Bahrain	0.69	0.27	688	Manama	20,500
Bangladesh	144	55.6	144,320	Dhaka	2,100
Barbados	0.43	0.17	279	Bridgetown	17,300
Belarus	208	80.2	10,300	Minsk	7,600
Belgium	30.5	11.8	10,364	Brussels	31,800
Belize	23.0	8.9	279	Belmopan	6,800
Benin	113	43.5	7,460	Porto-Novo	1,200
Bermuda (UK)	0.05	0.02	65	Hamilton	36,000
Bhutan	47.0	18.1	2,232	Thimphu	1,400
Bolivia	1,099	424	8,858	La Paz/Sucre	2,700
Bosnia-Herzegovina	51.2	19.8	4,025	Sarajevo	6,800
Botswana	582	225	1,640	Gaborone	10,100
Brazil	8,514	3,287	186,113	Brasília	8,500
Brunei	5.8	2.2	372	Bandar Seri Begawan	23,600
Bulgaria	111	42.8	7,450	Sofia	9,000
Burkina Faso	274	106	13,925	Ouagadougou	1,200
Burma (= Myanmar)	677	261	42,909	Rangoon/Pyinmana	1,800
Burundi	27.8	10.7	6,371	Bujumbura	700
Cambodia	181	69.9	13,607	Phnom Penh	2,100
Cameroon	475	184	16,380	Yaoundé	2,000
Canada	9,971	3,850	32,805	Ottawa	32,800
Canary Is. (Spain)	7.2	2.8	1,682	Las Palmas/Santa Cruz	19,900
Cape Verde Is.	4.0	1.6	418	Praia	6,200
Cayman Is. (UK)	0.26	0.10	44	George Town	32,300
Central African Republic	623	241	3,800	Bangui	1,200
Chad	1,284	496	9,826	Ndjaména	1,900
Chile	757	292	15,981	Santiago	11,300
China	9,597	3,705	1,306,314	Beijing	6,200
Colombia	1,139	440	42,954	Bogotá	7,100
Comoros	2.2	0.86	671	Moroni	600
Congo	342	132	3,039	Brazzaville	800
Congo (Dem. Rep. of the)	2,345	905	60,086	Kinshasa	800
Cook Is. (NZ)	0.24	0.09	21	Avarua	5,000
Costa Rica	51.1	19.7	4,016	San José	10,000
Croatia	56.5	21.8	4,496	Zagreb	11,600
Cuba	111	42.8	11,347	Havana	3,300
Cyprus	9.3	3.6	780	Nicosia	21,600
Czech Republic	78.9	30.5	10,241	Prague	18,100
Denmark	43.1	16.6	5,432	Copenhagen	33,500
Djibouti	23.2	9.0	477	Djibouti	1,300
Dominica	0.75	0.29	69	Roseau	5,500
Dominican Republic	48.5	18.7	8,950	Santo Domingo	6,500
East Timor	14.9	5.7	1,041	Dili	400
Ecuador	284	109	13,364	Quito	3,900
Egypt	1,001	387	77,506	Cairo	4,400
El Salvador	21.0	8.1	6,705	San Salvador	5,100
Equatorial Guinea	28.1	10.8	536	Malabo	2,700
Eritrea	118	45.4	4,562	Asmara	1,000
Estonia	45.1	17.4	1,333	Tallinn	16,400
Ethiopia	1,104	426	73,053	Addis Ababa	800
Faroe Is. (Denmark)	1.4	0.54	47	Tórshavn	22,000
Fiji	18.3	7.1	893	Suva	6,000
Finland	338	131	5,223	Helsinki	30,300
France	552	213	60,656	Paris	29,900
French Guiana (France)	90.0	34.7	196	Cayenne	8,300
French Polynesia (France)	4.0	1.5	270	Papeete	17,500
Gabon	268	103	1,389	Libreville	5,800
Gambia, The	11.3	4.4	1,593	Banjul	1,900
Gaza Strip (OPT)*	0.36	0.14	1,376	–	600
Georgia	69.7	26.9	4,677	Tbilisi	3,400
Germany	357	138	82,431	Berlin	29,700
Ghana	239	92.1	21,030	Accra	2,500
Gibraltar (UK)	0.006	0.002	28	Gibraltar Town	27,900
Greece	132	50.9	10,668	Athens	22,800
Greenland (Denmark)	2,176	840	56	Nuuk (Godthåb)	20,000
Grenada	0.34	0.13	90	St George's	5,000
Guadeloupe (France)	1.7	0.66	449	Basse-Terre	7,900
Guam (US)	0.55	0.21	169	Agana	21,000
Guatemala	109	42.0	14,655	Guatemala City	4,300
Guinea	246	94.9	9,468	Conakry	2,200
Guinea-Bissau	36.1	13.9	1,416	Bissau	800
Guyana	215	83.0	765	Georgetown	3,900
Haiti	27.8	10.7	8,122	Port-au-Prince	1,600
Honduras	112	43.3	6,975	Tegucigalpa	2,900
Hong Kong (China)	1.1	0.42	6,899	–	36,800
Hungary	93.0	35.9	10,007	Budapest	15,900
Iceland	103	39.8	297	Reykjavik	34,600
India	3,287	1,269	1,080,264	New Delhi	3,400
Indonesia	1,905	735	241,974	Jakarta	3,700
Iran	1,648	636	68,018	Tehran	8,100
Iraq	438	169	26,075	Baghdad	3,400
Ireland	70.3	27.1	4,016	Dublin	34,100
Israel	20.6	8.0	6,277	Jerusalem	22,200
Italy	301	116	58,103	Rome	28,300
Ivory Coast (= Côte d'Ivoire)	322	125	17,298	Yamoussoukro	1,400
Jamaica	11.0	4.2	2,732	Kingston	4,300
Japan	378	146	127,417	Tokyo	30,400
Jordan	89.3	34.5	5,760	Amman	4,800
Kazakhstan	2,725	1,052	15,186	Astana	8,700
Kenya	580	224	33,830	Nairobi	1,200
Kiribati	0.73	0.28	103	Tarawa	800
Korea, North	121	46.5	22,912	Pyŏngyang	1,800
Korea, South	99.3	38.3	48,423	Seoul	20,300
Kuwait	17.8	6.9	2,336	Kuwait City	22,100
Kyrgyzstan	200	77.2	5,146	Bishkek	1,800
Laos	237	91.4	6,217	Vientiane	1,900
Latvia	64.6	24.9	2,290	Riga	12,800
Lebanon	10.4	4.0	3,826	Beirut	5,100
Lesotho	30.4	11.7	1,867	Maseru	3,300
Liberia	111	43.0	3,482	Monrovia	700
Libya	1,760	679	5,766	Tripoli	8,400
Liechtenstein	0.16	0.06	34	Vaduz	25,000
Lithuania	65.2	25.2	3,597	Vilnius	13,700
Luxembourg	2.6	1.0	469	Luxembourg	62,700
Macau (China)	0.02	0.007	449	–	19,400
Macedonia (FYROM)	25.7	9.9	2,045	Skopje	7,400
Madagascar	587	227	18,040	Antananarivo	900
Madeira (Portugal)	0.78	0.30	241	Funchal	22,700
Malawi	118	45.7	12,159	Lilongwe	600
Malaysia	330	127	23,953	Kuala Lumpur/Putrajaya	10,400
Maldives	0.30	0.12	349	Malé	3,900
Mali	1,240	479	12,292	Bamako	1,000
Malta	0.32	0.12	399	Valletta	18,800
Marshall Is.	0.18	0.07	59	Majuro	1,600
Martinique (France)	1.1	0.43	433	Fort-de-France	14,400
Mauritania	1,026	396	3,087	Nouakchott	2,000
Mauritius	2.0	0.79	1,231	Port Louis	13,300
Mayotte (France)	0.37	0.14	194	Mamoundzou	2,600
Mexico	1,958	756	106,203	Mexico City	10,000
Micronesia, Fed. States of	0.70	0.27	108	Palikir	2,000
Moldova	33.9	13.1	4,455	Chişinău	2,100
Monaco	0.001	0.0004	32	Monaco	27,000
Mongolia	1,567	605	2,791	Ulan Bator	2,200
Montserrat (UK)	0.10	0.04	9	Plymouth	3,400
Morocco	447	172	32,726	Rabat	4,300
Mozambique	802	309	19,407	Maputo	1,300
Namibia	824	318	2,031	Windhoek	7,800
Nauru	0.02	0.008	13	Yaren District	5,000
Nepal	147	56.8	27,677	Katmandu	1,500
Netherlands	41.5	16.0	16,407	Amsterdam/The Hague	30,500
Netherlands Antilles (Neths)	0.80	0.31	220	Willemstad	11,400
New Caledonia (France)	18.6	7.2	216	Nouméa	15,000
New Zealand	271	104	4,035	Wellington	24,100
Nicaragua	130	50.2	5,465	Managua	2,800
Niger	1,267	489	11,666	Niamey	900
Nigeria	924	357	128,772	Abuja	1,000
Northern Mariana Is. (US)	0.46	0.18	80	Saipan	12,500
Norway	324	125	4,593	Oslo	42,400
Oman	310	119	3,002	Muscat	13,400
Pakistan	796	307	162,420	Islamabad	2,400
Palau	0.46	0.18	20	Koror	9,000
Panama	75.5	29.2	3,039	Panamá	7,300
Papua New Guinea	463	179	5,545	Port Moresby	2,400
Paraguay	407	157	6,348	Asunción	4,900
Peru	1,285	496	27,926	Lima	6,000
Philippines	300	116	87,857	Manila	5,100
Poland	323	125	38,635	Warsaw	12,700
Portugal	88.8	34.3	10,566	Lisbon	18,400
Puerto Rico (US)	8.9	3.4	3,917	San Juan	18,500
Qatar	11.0	4.2	863	Doha	26,000
Réunion (France)	2.5	0.97	777	St-Denis	6,200
Romania	238	92.0	22,330	Bucharest	8,300
Russia	17,075	6,593	143,420	Moscow	10,700
Rwanda	26.3	10.2	8,441	Kigali	1,300
St Kitts & Nevis	0.26	0.10	39	Basseterre	8,800
St Lucia	0.54	0.21	166	Castries	5,400
St Vincent & Grenadines	0.39	0.15	118	Kingstown	2,900
Samoa	2.8	1.1	177	Apia	5,600
San Marino	0.06	0.02	29	San Marino	34,600
São Tomé & Príncipe	0.96	0.37	187	São Tomé	1,200
Saudi Arabia	2,150	830	26,418	Riyadh	12,900
Senegal	197	76.0	11,127	Dakar	1,800
Serbia & Montenegro†	102	39.4	10,829	Belgrade	2,600
Seychelles	0.46	0.18	81	Victoria	7,800
Sierra Leone	71.7	27.7	6,018	Freetown	800
Singapore	0.68	0.26	4,426	Singapore City	29,700
Slovak Republic	49.0	18.9	5,431	Bratislava	15,700
Slovenia	20.3	7.8	2,011	Ljubljana	20,900
Solomon Is.	28.9	11.2	538	Honiara	1,700
Somalia	638	246	8,592	Mogadishu	600
South Africa	1,221	471	44,344	C. Town/Pretoria/Bloem.	11,900
Spain	498	192	40,341	Madrid	25,100
Sri Lanka	65.6	25.3	20,065	Colombo	4,300
Sudan	2,506	967	40,187	Khartoum	2,100
Suriname	163	63.0	438	Paramaribo	4,700
Swaziland	17.4	6.7	1,174	Mbabane	5,300
Sweden	450	174	9,002	Stockholm	29,600
Switzerland	41.3	15.9	7,489	Bern	35,000
Syria	185	71.5	18,449	Damascus	3,500
Taiwan	36.0	13.9	22,894	Taipei	26,700
Tajikistan	143	55.3	7,164	Dushanbe	1,200
Tanzania	945	365	36,766	Dodoma	700
Thailand	513	198	65,444	Bangkok	8,300
Togo	56.8	21.9	5,682	Lomé	1,600
Tonga	0.65	0.25	112	Nuku'alofa	2,300
Trinidad & Tobago	5.1	2.0	1,089	Port of Spain	12,700
Tunisia	164	63.2	10,075	Tunis	7,600
Turkey	775	299	69,661	Ankara	7,900
Turkmenistan	488	188	4,952	Ashkhabad	5,900
Turks & Caicos Is. (UK)	0.43	0.17	21	Cockburn Town	11,500
Tuvalu	0.03	0.01	12	Fongafale	1,100
Uganda	241	93.1	27,269	Kampala	1,700
Ukraine	604	233	47,425	Kiev	6,800
United Arab Emirates	83.6	32.3	2,563	Abu Dhabi	29,100
United Kingdom	242	93.4	60,441	London	30,900
United States of America	9,629	3,718	295,734	Washington, DC	41,800
Uruguay	175	67.6	3,416	Montevideo	10,000
Uzbekistan	447	173	26,851	Tashkent	1,900
Vanuatu	12.2	4.7	206	Port-Vila	2,900
Vatican City	0.0004	0.0002	1	Vatican City	N/A
Venezuela	912	352	25,375	Caracas	6,400
Vietnam	332	128	83,536	Hanoi	3,000
Virgin Is. (UK)	0.15	0.06	23	Road Town	38,500
Virgin Is. (US)	0.35	0.13	109	Charlotte Amalie	17,200
Wallis & Futuna Is. (France)	0.20	0.08	16	Mata-Utu	3,800
West Bank (OPT)*	5.9	2.3	2,386	–	1,100
Western Sahara	266	103	273	El Aaiún	N/A
Yemen	528	204	20,727	Sana'	800
Zambia	753	291	11,262	Lusaka	900
Zimbabwe	391	151	12,747	Harare	1,900

*OPT = Occupied Palestinian Territory   N/A = Not available

† In June 2006, Serbia and Montenegro formally declared their independence and are now separate sovereign states.

World Statistics: Cities

This list shows the principal cities with more than 750,000 inhabitants. The figures are taken from the most recent census or estimate available, usually 2005, and as far as possible are the population of the metropolitan area or urban agglomeration (for example, greater New York, Mexico or Paris). All the figures are in thousands. Local name forms have been used for the smaller cities (for example, Thessaloniki).

AFGHANISTAN	
Kabul	3,288
ALGERIA	
Algiers	3,260
ANGOLA	
Luanda	2,839
ARGENTINA	
Buenos Aires	13,349
Córdoba	1,592
Rosario	1,312
Mendoza	1,072
San Miguel de Tucumán	837
ARMENIA	
Yerevan	1,066
AUSTRALIA	
Sydney	4,388
Melbourne	3,663
Brisbane	1,769
Perth	1,484
Adelaide	1,137
AUSTRIA	
Vienna	2,190
AZERBAIJAN	
Baku	1,830
BANGLADESH	
Dhaka	12,560
Chittagong	4,171
Khulna	1,497
Rajshahi	1,035
BELARUS	
Minsk	1,709
BELGIUM	
Brussels	964
BOLIVIA	
La Paz	1,533
Santa Cruz	1,352
Cochabamba	797
BRAZIL	
São Paulo	18,333
Rio de Janeiro	11,469
Belo Horizonte	5,304
Pôrto Alegre	3,795
Recife	3,527
Brasília	3,341
Salvador	3,331
Fortaleza	3,261
Curitiba	2,871
Campinas	2,640
Belém	2,097
Goiânia	1,878
Manaus	1,673
Santos	1,634
Vitória	1,602
Maceió	1,137
Natal	1,049
São Luís	982
São José dos Campos	972
João Pessoa	931
Teresina	895
Campo Grande	821
BULGARIA	
Sofia	1,045
BURKINA FASO	
Ouagadougou	870
BURMA (MYANMAR)	
Rangoon	4,082
Mandalay	927
CAMBODIA	
Phnom Penh	1,174
CAMEROON	
Douala	1,980
Yaoundé	1,727
CANADA	
Toronto	5,060
Montréal	3,511
Vancouver	2,125
Ottawa	1,120
Calgary	1,074
Edmonton	1,005
CHILE	
Santiago	5,623
CHINA	
Shanghai	12,665
Beijing	10,849
Tianjin	9,346
Hong Kong	7,182
Wuhan	6,003
Chongqing	4,975
Shenyang	4,916
Guangzhou	3,881
Chengdu	3,478
Xi'an	3,256
Changchun	3,092
Harbin	2,898
Nanjing	2,806
Zibo	2,775
Dalian	2,709
Jinan	2,654
Taiyuan	2,516
Guiyang	2,467
Qingdao	2,431
Zhengzhou	2,250
Zaozhuang	2,189
Handan	2,120
Liupanshui	1,118
Changsha	2,051
Linyi	2,035
Lu'an	2,015
Wanxian	1,963
Hangzhou	1,955
Tianmen	1,948
Jinxi	1,850
Heze	1,847
Lanzhou	1,788
Tangshan	1,773
Xiantao	1,758
Kunming	1,748
Nanchang	1,742
Shijiazhuang	1,733
Yantai	1,707
Yulin	1,691
Yancheng	1,678
Xuzhou	1,662
Luoyang	1,594
Xinghua	1,587
Pingxiang	1,562
Ürümqi	1,562
Zhanjiang	1,562
Tai'an	1,550
Suining, Sichuan	1,520
Yiyang	1,510
Jilin	1,496
Changde	1,483
Wenzhou	1,475
Anshan	1,459
Qiqihar	1,452
Neijiang	1,449
Fushun	1,425
Huainan	1,422
Fuzhou	1,398
Nanning	1,395
Baotou	1,367
Weifang	1,360
Shantou	1,356
Xintai	1,334
Hefei	1,320
Huaian	1,297
Yueyang	1,286
Shenzhen	1,285
Tianshui	1,269
Suqian	1,258
Jingmen	1,228
Yuzhou	1,226
Zaoyang	1,210
Suzhou	1,201
Wuxi	1,192
Ningbo	1,188
Yongzhou	1,182
Mianyang	1,174
Leshan	1,172
Dongguan	1,150
Chifeng	1,140
Xiaoshan	1,130
Yixing	1,129
Zigong	1,123
Daqing	1,117
Datong	1,113
Huzhou	1,102
Jining, Shandong	1,101
Nanchong	1,072
Fuyu	1,068
Liuzhou	1,031
Xinyi, Jiangsu	1,022
Jixi	1,012
Linqing	1,009
Jiamusi	1,006
Hohhot	998
Xianyang	988
Changzhou	976
Zhangjiakou	973
Benxi	967
Xiangxiang	936
Zhangjiagang	936
Xinyu	932
Yichun, Heilongjiang	916
Yichun, Jiangxi	890
Jinzhou	888
Zhaotong	879
Yuyao	876
Anshun	864
Hengyang	853
Xuanzhou	851
Tongliao	847
Huaibei	830
Mudanjiang	827
Jiaxing	817
Kaifeng	810
Fuxin	807
Hunjiang	798
COLOMBIA	
Bogotá	7,594
Medellín	3,236
Cali	2,583
Barranquilla	1,918
Bucaramanga	1,069
Cartagena	1,002
Cúcuta	883
CONGO	
Brazzaville	1,153
CONGO (DEM. REP. OF THE)	
Kinshasa	5,717
Lubumbashi	1,102
Mbuji-Mayi	806
COSTA RICA	
San José	1,145
CROATIA	
Zagreb	1,067
CUBA	
Havana	2,192
CZECH REPUBLIC	
Prague	1,164
DENMARK	
Copenhagen	1,091
DOMINICAN REPUBLIC	
Santo Domingo	2,563
Santiago de los Caballeros	804
ECUADOR	
Guayaquil	2,387
Quito	1,514
EGYPT	
Cairo	11,146
Alexandria	3,760
Shubrâ el Kheima	937
EL SALVADOR	
San Salvador	1,472
ETHIOPIA	
Addis Ababa	2,899
FINLAND	
Helsinki	937
FRANCE	
Paris	9,630
Lyons	1,353
Marseilles	1,290
Lille	991
Nice	889
Toulouse	761
Bordeaux	754
GEORGIA	
Tbilisi	1,406
GERMANY	
Berlin	3,387
Hamburg	1,705
Munich	1,195
Cologne	963
GHANA	
Accra	1,970
Kumasi	862
GREECE	
Athens	3,238
Thessaloniki	824
GUATEMALA	
Guatemala City	3,242
GUINEA	
Conakry	1,465
HAITI	
Port-au-Prince	2,090
HONDURAS	
Tegucigalpa	1,061
HUNGARY	
Budapest	1,670
INDIA	
Mumbai	18,336
Delhi	15,334
Kolkata	14,299
Chennai	6,915
Bangalore	6,532
Hyderabad	6,145
Ahmedabad	5,171
Pune	4,485
Surat	3,671
Kanpur	3,040
Jaipur	2,796
Lucknow	2,589
Nagpur	2,359
Patna	2,066
Indore	1,941
Vadodara	1,686
Bhopal	1,656
Coimbatore	1,628
Ludhiana	1,583
Agra	1,526
Visakhapatnam	1,468
Cochin	1,461
Nashik	1,408
Meerut	1,340
Faridabad	1,330
Varanasi	1,300
Ghaziabad	1,277
Asansol	1,272
Jamshedpur	1,246
Madurai	1,245
Jabalpur	1,234
Rajkot	1,205
Dhanbad	1,195
Amritsar	1,162
Allahabad	1,153
Vijayawada	1,093
Srinagar	1,093
Aurangabad	1,065
Bhilainagar-Durg	1,051
Solapur	1,012
Ranchi	999
Jodhpur	954
Guwahati	941
Gwalior	939
Trivandrum	918
Calicut	917
Tiruchchirapalli	913
Chandigarh	896
Hubli-Dharwad	854
Mysore	851
INDONESIA	
Jakarta	13,194
Bandung	4,020
Surabaya	2,735
Medan	2,109
Palembang	1,675
Ujung Pandang	1,205
Bandar Lampung	915
Malang	898
Tegal	898
Semarang	816
Bogor	761
IRAN	
Tehran	7,352
Mashhad	2,147
Esfahan	1,547
Tabriz	1,396
Karaj	1,235
Shiraz	1,230
Qom	1,045
Ahvaz	967
Bakhtaran	771
IRAQ	
Baghdad	5,910
Mosul	1,236
Basra	1,187
Irbil	840
IRELAND	
Dublin	985
ISRAEL	
Tel Aviv-Yafo	3,025
Haifa	948
ITALY	
Rome	2,649
Milan	1,183
Naples	993
Turin	857
Genoa	803
IVORY COAST	
Abidjan	3,516
JAPAN	
Tokyo	12,064
Yokohama	6,427
Osaka	2,599
Nagoya	2,172
Sapporo	1,922
Kobe	1,493
Kyoto	1,468
Fukuoka	1,341
Kawasaki	1,250
Hiroshima	1,126
Kitakyushu	1,011
Sendai	1,008
Chiba	887
Sakai	792
JORDAN	
Amman	1,292
KAZAKHSTAN	
Almaty	1,103
KENYA	
Nairobi	2,818
KOREA, NORTH	
Pyŏngyang	3,124
Hamhung	821
KOREA, SOUTH	
Seoul	9,888
Pusan	3,830
Inch'on	2,884
Taegu	2,675
Taejŏn	1,522
Kwangju	1,379
Sŏngnam	1,353
Ulsan	1,340
Ansan	984
Puch'on	900
Suwŏn	876
P'ohang	790
KUWAIT	
Kuwait City	879
KYRGYZSTAN	
Bishkek	828
LATVIA	
Riga	719
LEBANON	
Beirut	2,070
LIBYA	
Tripoli	1,733
Benghazi	829
MADAGASCAR	
Antananarivo	1,808
MALAYSIA	
Kuala Lumpur	1,392
MALI	
Bamako	1,379
MEXICO	
Mexico City	19,013
Guadalajara	3,905
Monterrey	3,517
Toluca	1,987
Puebla	1,880
Tijuana	1,570
Ciudad Juárez	1,469
León	1,438
Torreón	1,057
San Luis Potosí	927
Mérida	919
Querétaro	913
Mexicali	840
Culiacán	799
MONGOLIA	
Ulan Bator	842
MOROCCO	
Casablanca	3,743
Rabat	1,859
Fès	1,032
Marrakesh	951
MOZAMBIQUE	
Maputo	1,316
NEPAL	
Katmandu	1,176
NETHERLANDS	
Amsterdam	1,157
Rotterdam	1,112
NEW ZEALAND	
Auckland	1,152
NICARAGUA	
Managua	1,159
NIGER	
Niamey	997
NIGERIA	
Lagos	11,135
Kano	2,884
Ibadan	2,375
Kaduna	1,329
Benin City	1,022
Ogbomosho	959
Port Harcourt	942
NORWAY	
Oslo	808
PAKISTAN	
Karachi	11,819
Lahore	6,373
Faisalabad	2,533
Rawalpindi	1,794
Gujranwala	1,466
Multan	1,459
Hyderabad	1,392
Peshawar	1,255
Islamabad	791
PANAMA	
Panamá	1,173
PARAGUAY	
Asunción	1,750
PERU	
Lima	8,180
PHILIPPINES	
Manila	10,677
Davao	1,326
POLAND	
Warsaw	1,626
Lódz	815
PORTUGAL	
Lisbon	1,977
Porto	1,303
PUERTO RICO	
San Juan	2,357
ROMANIA	
Bucharest	1,764
RUSSIA	
Moscow	10,672
Saint Petersburg	5,315
Novosibirsk	1,425
Nizhniy Novgorod	1,288
Yekaterinburg	1,281
Samara	1,140
Omsk	1,132
Kazan	1,108
Rostov	1,081
Chelyabinsk	1,067
Ufa	1,035
Volgograd	1,016
Perm	1,014
Voronezh	918
Saratov	881
Simbirsk	864
Krasnoyarsk	840
Togliatti	771
SAUDI ARABIA	
Riyadh	5,514
Jedda	3,807
Mecca	1,529
Medina	1,044
Dammam	920
SENEGAL	
Dakar	2,313
SERBIA AND MONTENEGRO	
Belgrade	1,116
SIERRA LEONE	
Freetown	1,007
SINGAPORE	
Singapore City	4,372
SOMALIA	
Mogadishu	1,257
SOUTH AFRICA	
Johannesburg	2,950
Cape Town	2,930
Durban / eThekwini	2,391
Pretoria / Tshwane	1,590
Port Elizabeth	1,006
SPAIN	
Madrid	3,017
Barcelona	1,527
SUDAN	
Khartoum	2,742
SWEDEN	
Stockholm	1,729
Gothenburg	829
SWITZERLAND	
Zürich	984
SYRIA	
Aleppo	2,505
Damascus	2,317
Homs	915
TAIWAN	
Taipei	2,473
Kaohsiung	1,506
T'aichung	1,066
TANZANIA	
Dar es Salaam	2,683
THAILAND	
Bangkok	6,604
TUNISIA	
Tunis	2,063
TURKEY	
Istanbul	8,953
Ankara	3,203
Izmir	2,250
Bursa	1,184
Adana	1,133
Gaziantep	862
Konya	761
UGANDA	
Kampala	1,345
UKRAINE	
Kiev	2,621
Kharkov	1,521
Dnepropetrovsk	1,122
Donetsk	1,065
Odessa	1,027
Zaporozhye	863
Lvov	794
UNITED ARAB EMIRATES	
Abu Dhabi	928
Dubai	886
UNITED KINGDOM	
London	8,089
Birmingham	2,373
Manchester	2,353
Liverpool	852
Glasgow	832
UNITED STATES OF AMERICA	
New York	17,800
Los Angeles	11,789
Chicago	8,308
Philadelphia	5,149
Miami	4,919
Dallas–Fort Worth	4,146
Boston	4,032
Washington	3,934
Detroit	3,903
Houston	3,823
Atlanta	3,500
San Francisco	3,229
Phoenix	2,907
Seattle	2,712
San Diego	2,674
Minneapolis–St Paul	2,389
St Louis	2,078
Baltimore	2,076
Tampa–St Petersburg	2,062
Denver	1,985
Cleveland	1,787
Pittsburgh	1,753
Portland	1,583
San Jose	1,538
San Bernardino	1,507
Cincinnati	1,503
Norfolk–Virginia Beach	1,394
Sacramento	1,393
Kansas City	1,362
San Antonio	1,328
Las Vegas	1,314
Milwaukee	1,309
Indianapolis	1,219
Providence	1,175
Orlando	1,157
Columbus	1,133
New Orleans	1,009
Buffalo	977
Memphis	972
Austin	902
Stamford	889
Salt Lake City	888
Jacksonville	882
Louisville	864
Hartford	852
Richmond	819
Charlotte	759
URUGUAY	
Montevideo	1,353
UZBEKISTAN	
Tashkent	2,160
VENEZUELA	
Caracas	3,276
Valencia	2,330
Maracaibo	2,182
Maracay	1,138
Ciudad Guayana	966
Barquisimeto	923
VIETNAM	
Ho Chi Minh City	5,030
Hanoi	4,147
Haiphong	1,817
YEMEN	
Sana'	1,621
ZAMBIA	
Lusaka	1,450
ZIMBABWE	
Harare	1,527
Bulawayo	824

World Statistics: Distances

The table shows air distances in miles and kilometres between 30 major cities. Known as 'Great Circle' distances, these measure the shortest routes between the cities, which aircraft use wherever possible. The maps show the world centred on six cities, and illustrate, for example, why direct flights from Japan to northern America and Europe are across the Arctic regions. The maps have been constructed on an Azimuthal Equidistant projection, on which all distances measured through the centre point are true to scale. The red lines are drawn at 5,000, 10,000 and 15,000 km from the central city.

Distances above the diagonal are in kilometres (km); distances below the diagonal are in miles.

	Beijing	Bombay (Mumbai)	Buenos Aires	Cairo	Calcutta (Kolkata)	Caracas	Chicago	Hong Kong	Honolulu	Johannesburg	Lagos	London	Los Angeles	Mexico City	Moscow	Nairobi	New York	Paris	Rio de Janeiro	Rome	Singapore	Sydney	Tokyo	Wellington
Beijing	Beijing	2956	11972	4688	2031	8947	6588	1220	5070	7276	7119	5057	6251	7742	3600	5727	6828	5106	10773	5049	2783	5561	1304	6700
Bombay (Mumbai)	4757	Bombay (Mumbai)	9275	2706	1034	9024	8048	2683	8024	4334	4730	4467	8700	9728	3126	2816	7793	4356	8332	3837	2432	6313	4189	7686
Buenos Aires	19268	14925	Buenos Aires	7341	10268	3167	5599	11481	7558	5025	4919	6917	6122	4591	8374	6463	5298	6867	1214	6929	9867	7332	11410	6202
Cairo	7544	4355	11814	Cairo	3541	6340	6127	5064	8838	3894	2432	2180	7580	7687	1803	2197	5605	1994	6149	1325	5137	8959	5947	10268
Calcutta (Kolkata)	3269	1664	16524	5699	Calcutta (Kolkata)	9609	7978	1653	7048	5256	5727	4946	8152	9494	3438	3839	7921	4883	9366	4486	1800	5678	3195	7055
Caracas	14399	14522	5096	10203	15464	Caracas	2502	10166	6009	6847	4810	4664	3612	2228	6175	7173	2131	4738	2825	5196	11407	9534	8801	8154
Chicago	10603	12953	9011	3206	12839	4027	Chicago	7783	4247	8689	5973	3949	1742	1694	4971	8005	711	4132	5311	4809	9369	9243	6299	8358
Hong Kong	1963	4317	18478	8150	2659	16360	12526	Hong Kong	5543	6669	7360	5980	7232	8775	4439	5453	8047	5984	11001	5769	1615	4582	1786	5857
Honolulu	8160	12914	12164	14223	11343	9670	6836	8921	Honolulu	11934	10133	7228	2558	3781	7036	10739	4958	7437	8290	8026	6721	5075	3854	4669
Johannesburg	11710	6974	8088	6267	8459	11019	13984	10732	19206	Johannesburg	2799	5637	10362	9063	5692	1818	7979	5426	4420	4811	5381	6860	8418	7308
Lagos	11457	7612	7916	3915	9216	7741	9612	11845	16308	4505	Lagos	3118	7713	6879	3886	2366	5268	2929	3750	2510	6925	9643	8376	9973
London	8138	7190	11131	3508	7961	7507	6356	9623	11632	9071	5017	London	5442	5552	1552	4237	3463	212	5778	889	6743	10558	5942	11691
Los Angeles	10060	14000	9852	12200	13120	5812	2804	11639	4117	16676	12414	8758	Los Angeles	1549	6070	9659	2446	5645	6310	6331	8776	7502	5475	6719
Mexico City	12460	15656	7389	12372	15280	3586	2726	14122	6085	14585	11071	8936	2493	Mexico City	6664	9207	2090	5717	4780	6365	10321	8058	7024	6897
Moscow	5794	5031	13477	2902	5534	9938	8000	7144	11323	9161	6254	2498	9769	10724	Moscow	3942	4666	1545	7184	1477	5237	9008	4651	10283
Nairobi	9216	4532	10402	3536	6179	11544	12883	8776	17282	2927	3807	6819	15544	14818	6344	Nairobi	7358	4029	5548	3350	4635	7552	6996	8490
New York	10988	12541	8526	9020	12747	3430	1145	12950	7980	12841	8477	5572	3936	3264	7510	11842	New York	3626	4832	4280	9531	9935	6741	8951
Paris	8217	7010	11051	3210	7858	7625	6650	9630	11968	8732	4714	342	9085	9200	2486	6485	5836	Paris	5708	687	6671	10539	6038	11798
Rio de Janeiro	17338	13409	1953	9896	15073	4546	8547	17704	13342	7113	6035	9299	10155	7693	11562	8928	7777	9187	Rio de Janeiro	5725	9763	8389	11551	7367
Rome	8126	6175	11151	2133	7219	8363	7739	9284	12916	7743	4039	1431	10188	10243	2376	5391	6888	1105	9214	Rome	6229	10143	6127	11523
Singapore	4478	3914	15879	8267	2897	18359	15078	2599	10816	8660	11145	10852	14123	16610	8428	7460	15339	10737	15712	10025	Singapore	3915	3306	5298
Sydney	8949	10160	11800	14418	9138	15343	14875	7374	8168	11040	15519	16992	12073	12969	14497	12153	15989	16962	13501	16324	6300	Sydney	4861	1383
Tokyo	2099	6742	18362	9571	5141	14164	10137	2874	6202	13547	13480	9562	8811	11304	7485	11260	10849	9718	18589	9861	5321	7823	Tokyo	5762
Wellington	10782	12370	9981	16524	11354	13122	13451	9427	7513	11761	16050	18814	10814	11100	16549	13664	14405	18987	11855	18545	8526	2226	9273	Wellington

Northern Hemisphere

MEXICO CITY
19 26°N 99 4°W

LONDON
51 28°N 0 27°W

TOKYO
35 33°N 139 46°E

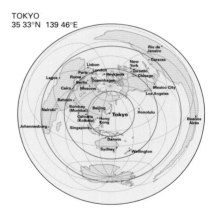

Southern Hemisphere

RIO DE JANEIRO
22 50°S 43 15°W

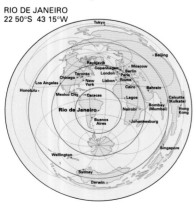

SINGAPORE
1 21°N 103 54°E

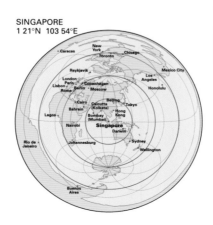

SYDNEY
33 56°S 151 10°E

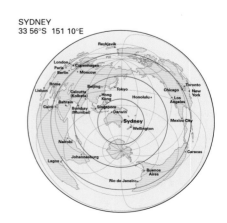

World Statistics: Climate

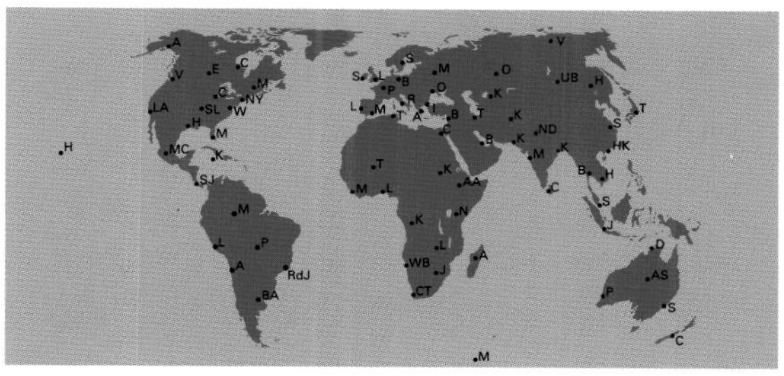

Rainfall and temperature figures are provided for more than 70 cities around the world. As climate is affected by altitude, the height of each city is shown in metres beneath its name. For each location, the top row of figures shows the total rainfall or snow in millimetres, and the bottom row the average temperature in degrees Celsius; the total annual rainfall and average annual temperature are at the end of the rows.

EUROPE	Jan.	Feb.	Mar.	Apr.	May	June	July	Aug.	Sept.	Oct.	Nov.	Dec.	Year
Athens, Greece	62	37	37	23	23	14	6	7	15	51	56	71	402
107 m	10	10	12	16	20	25	28	28	24	20	15	11	18
Berlin, Germany	46	40	33	42	49	65	73	69	48	49	46	43	603
55 m	–1	0	4	9	14	17	19	18	15	9	5	1	9
Istanbul, Turkey	109	92	72	46	38	34	34	30	58	81	103	119	816
14 m	5	6	7	11	16	20	23	23	20	16	12	8	14
Lisbon, Portugal	111	76	109	54	44	16	3	4	33	62	93	103	708
77 m	11	12	14	16	17	20	22	23	21	18	14	12	17
London, UK	54	40	37	37	46	45	57	59	49	57	64	48	593
5 m	4	5	7	9	12	16	18	17	15	11	8	5	11
Málaga, Spain	61	51	62	46	26	5	1	3	29	64	64	62	474
33 m	12	13	16	17	19	29	25	26	23	20	16	13	18
Moscow, Russia	39	38	36	37	53	58	88	71	58	45	47	54	624
156 m	–13	–10	–4	6	13	16	18	17	12	6	–1	–7	4
Odesa, Ukraine	57	62	30	21	34	34	42	37	37	13	35	71	473
64 m	–3	–1	2	9	15	20	22	22	18	12	9	1	10
Paris, France	56	46	35	42	57	54	59	64	55	50	51	50	619
75 m	3	4	8	11	15	18	20	19	17	12	7	4	12
Rome, Italy	71	62	57	51	46	37	15	21	63	99	129	93	744
17 m	8	9	11	14	18	22	25	25	22	17	13	10	16
Shannon, Irish Republic	94	67	56	53	61	57	77	79	86	86	96	117	929
2 m	5	5	7	9	12	14	16	16	14	11	8	6	10
Stockholm, Sweden	43	30	25	31	34	45	61	76	60	48	53	48	554
44 m	–3	–3	–1	5	10	15	18	17	12	7	3	0	7
ASIA													
Bahrain	8	18	13	8	<3	0	0	0	0	0	18	18	81
5 m	17	18	21	25	29	32	33	34	31	28	24	19	26
Bangkok, Thailand	8	20	36	58	198	160	160	175	305	206	66	5	1,397
2 m	26	28	29	30	29	29	28	28	28	28	26	25	28
Beirut, Lebanon	191	158	94	53	18	3	<3	<3	5	51	132	185	892
34 m	14	14	16	18	22	24	27	28	26	24	19	16	21
Colombo, Sri Lanka	89	69	147	231	371	224	135	109	160	348	315	147	2,365
7 m	26	26	27	28	28	27	27	27	27	27	26	26	27
Harbin, China	6	5	10	23	43	94	112	104	46	33	8	5	488
160 m	–18	–15	–5	6	13	19	22	21	14	4	–6	–16	3
Ho Chi Minh, Vietnam	15	3	13	43	221	330	315	269	335	269	114	56	1,984
9 m	26	27	29	30	29	28	28	28	27	27	27	26	28
Hong Kong, China	33	46	74	137	292	394	381	361	257	114	43	31	2,162
33 m	16	15	18	22	26	28	28	28	27	25	21	18	23
Jakarta, Indonesia	300	300	211	147	114	97	64	43	66	112	142	203	1,798
8 m	26	26	27	27	27	27	27	27	27	27	27	26	27
Kabul, Afghanistan	31	36	94	102	20	5	3	3	<3	15	20	10	338
1,815 m	–3	–1	6	13	18	22	25	24	20	14	7	3	12
Karachi, Pakistan	13	10	8	3	3	18	81	41	13	<3	3	5	196
4 m	19	20	24	28	30	31	30	29	28	28	24	20	26
Kazalinsk, Kazakhstan	10	10	13	13	15	5	5	8	8	10	13	15	125
63 m	–12	–11	–3	6	18	23	25	23	16	8	–1	–7	7
Kolkata (Calcutta), India	10	31	36	43	140	297	325	328	252	114	20	5	1,600
6 m	20	22	27	30	30	30	29	29	29	28	23	19	26
Mumbai (Bombay), India	3	3	3	<3	18	485	617	340	264	64	13	3	1,809
11 m	24	24	26	28	30	29	27	27	27	28	27	26	27
New Delhi, India	23	18	13	8	13	74	180	172	117	10	3	10	640
218 m	14	17	23	28	33	34	31	30	29	26	20	15	25
Omsk, Russia	15	8	8	13	31	51	51	51	28	25	18	20	318
85 m	–22	–19	–12	–1	10	16	18	16	10	1	–11	–18	–1
Shanghai, China	48	58	84	94	94	180	147	142	130	71	51	36	1,135
7 m	4	5	9	14	20	24	28	28	23	19	12	7	16
Singapore	252	173	193	188	173	173	170	196	178	208	254	257	2,413
10 m	26	27	28	28	28	28	28	27	27	27	27	27	27
Tehran, Iran	46	38	46	36	13	3	3	3	3	8	20	31	246
1,220 m	2	5	9	16	21	26	30	29	25	18	12	6	17
Tokyo, Japan	48	74	107	135	147	165	142	152	234	208	97	56	1,565
6 m	3	4	7	13	17	21	25	26	23	17	11	6	14
Ulan Bator, Mongolia	<3	<3	3	5	10	28	76	51	23	5	5	3	208
1,325 m	–26	–21	–13	–1	6	14	16	14	8	–1	–13	–22	–3
Verkhoyansk, Russia	5	5	3	5	8	23	28	25	13	8	8	5	134
100 m	–50	–45	–32	–15	0	12	14	9	2	–15	–38	–48	–17
AFRICA													
Addis Ababa, Ethiopia	<3	3	25	135	213	201	206	239	102	28	<3	0	1,151
2,450 m	19	20	20	20	19	18	18	19	21	22	21	20	20
Antananarivo, Madagas.	300	279	178	53	18	8	8	10	18	61	135	287	1,356
1,372 m	21	21	21	19	18	15	14	15	17	19	21	21	19
Cairo, Egypt	5	5	5	3	3	<3	0	0	<3	<3	3	5	28
116 m	13	15	18	21	25	28	28	28	26	24	20	15	22
Cape Town, S. Africa	15	8	18	48	79	84	89	66	43	31	18	10	508
17 m	21	21	20	17	14	13	12	13	14	16	18	19	17
Johannesburg, S. Africa	114	109	89	38	25	8	8	8	23	56	107	125	709
1,665 m	20	20	18	16	13	10	11	13	16	18	19	20	16

	Jan.	Feb.	Mar.	Apr.	May	June	July	Aug.	Sept.	Oct.	Nov.	Dec.	Year
Khartoum, Sudan	<3	<3	<3	<3	3	8	53	71	18	5	<3	0	158
390 m	24	25	28	31	33	34	32	31	32	32	28	25	29
Kinshasa, Congo (D.R.)	135	145	196	196	158	8	3	3	31	119	221	142	1,354
325 m	26	26	27	27	26	24	23	24	25	26	26	26	25
Lagos, Nigeria	28	46	102	150	269	460	279	64	140	206	69	25	1,836
3 m	27	28	29	28	28	26	26	25	26	26	28	28	27
Lusaka, Zambia	231	191	142	18	3	<3	<3	0	<3	10	91	150	836
1,277 m	21	22	21	21	19	16	16	18	22	24	23	22	21
Monrovia, Liberia	31	56	97	216	516	973	996	373	744	772	236	130	5,138
23 m	26	26	27	27	26	25	24	25	25	25	26	26	26
Nairobi, Kenya	38	64	125	211	158	46	15	23	31	53	109	86	958
1,820 m	19	19	19	19	18	16	16	16	18	19	18	18	18
Timbuktu, Mali	<3	<3	3	<3	5	23	79	81	38	3	<3	<3	231
301 m	22	24	28	32	34	35	32	30	32	31	28	23	29
Tunis, Tunisia	64	51	41	36	18	8	3	8	33	51	48	61	419
66 m	10	11	13	16	19	23	26	27	25	20	16	11	18
Walvis Bay, Namibia	<3	5	8	3	3	<3	<3	3	<3	<3	<3	<3	23
7 m	19	19	19	18	17	16	15	14	14	15	17	18	18
AUSTRALIA, NEW ZEALAND AND ANTARCTICA													
Alice Springs, Australia	43	33	28	10	15	13	8	8	8	18	31	38	252
579 m	29	28	25	20	15	12	12	14	18	23	26	28	21
Christchurch, N. Zealand	56	43	48	48	66	66	69	48	46	43	48	56	638
10 m	16	16	14	12	9	6	6	7	9	12	14	16	11
Darwin, Australia	386	312	254	97	15	3	<3	3	13	51	119	239	1,491
30 m	29	29	29	29	28	26	25	26	28	29	30	29	28
Mawson, Antarctica	11	30	20	10	44	180	4	40	3	20	0	0	362
14 m	0	–5	–10	–14	–15	–16	–18	–18	–19	–13	–5	–1	–11
Perth, Australia	8	10	20	43	130	180	170	149	86	56	20	13	881
60 m	23	23	22	19	16	14	13	13	15	16	19	22	18
Sydney, Australia	89	102	127	135	127	117	117	76	73	71	73	73	1,181
42 m	22	22	21	18	15	13	12	13	15	18	19	21	17
NORTH AMERICA													
Anchorage, Alaska, USA	20	18	15	10	13	18	41	66	66	56	25	23	371
40 m	–11	–8	–5	2	7	12	14	13	9	2	–5	–11	2
Chicago, Illinois, USA	51	51	66	71	86	89	84	81	79	66	61	51	836
251 m	–4	–3	2	9	14	20	23	22	19	12	5	–1	10
Churchill, Man., Canada	15	13	18	23	32	44	46	58	51	43	39	21	402
13 m	–28	–26	–20	–10	–2	6	12	11	5	–2	–12	–22	–7
Edmonton, Alta., Canada	25	19	19	22	43	77	89	78	39	17	16	25	466
676 m	–15	–10	–5	4	11	15	17	16	11	6	–4	–10	3
Honolulu, Hawaii, USA	104	66	79	48	25	18	23	28	36	48	64	104	643
12 m	23	18	19	20	22	24	25	26	26	24	22	19	22
Houston, Texas, USA	89	76	84	91	119	117	99	99	104	94	89	109	1,171
12 m	12	13	17	21	24	27	28	29	26	22	16	12	21
Kingston, Jamaica	23	15	23	31	102	89	38	91	99	180	74	36	800
34 m	25	25	25	26	26	28	28	28	27	27	26	26	26
Los Angeles, Calif., USA	79	76	71	25	10	3	<3	<3	5	15	31	66	381
95 m	13	14	14	16	17	19	21	22	21	18	16	14	17
Mexico City, Mexico	13	5	10	20	53	119	170	152	130	51	18	8	747
2,309 m	12	13	16	18	19	19	17	18	18	16	14	13	16
Miami, Florida, USA	71	53	64	81	173	178	155	160	203	234	71	51	1,516
8 m	20	20	22	23	25	27	28	28	27	25	22	21	24
Montréal, Que., Canada	72	65	74	74	66	82	90	92	88	76	81	87	946
57 m	–10	–9	–3	–6	13	18	21	20	15	9	2	–7	6
New York City, NY, USA	94	97	91	81	81	84	107	109	86	89	76	91	1,092
96 m	–1	–1	3	10	16	20	23	23	21	15	7	2	11
St Louis, Mo., USA	58	64	89	97	114	114	89	86	81	74	71	64	1,001
173 m	0	1	7	13	19	24	26	26	22	15	8	2	14
San José, Costa Rica	15	5	20	46	229	241	211	241	305	300	145	41	1,798
1,146 m	19	19	21	21	22	21	21	21	21	20	20	19	20
Vancouver, BC, Canada	154	115	101	60	52	45	32	41	67	114	150	182	1,113
14 m	3	5	6	9	12	15	17	17	14	10	6	4	10
Washington, DC, USA	86	76	91	84	94	99	112	109	94	74	66	79	1,064
22 m	1	2	7	12	18	23	25	24	20	14	8	3	13
SOUTH AMERICA													
Antofagasta, Chile	0	0	0	<3	<3	3	5	3	<3	3	<3	0	13
94 m	21	21	20	18	16	15	14	14	15	16	18	19	17
Buenos Aires, Argentina	79	71	109	89	76	61	56	61	79	86	84	99	950
27 m	23	23	21	17	13	9	10	11	13	15	19	22	16
Lima, Peru	3	<3	<3	<3	5	5	8	8	8	3	3	<3	41
120 m	23	24	24	22	19	17	17	16	17	18	19	21	20
Manaus, Brazil	249	231	262	221	170	84	58	38	46	107	142	203	1,811
44 m	28	28	28	27	28	28	28	28	29	29	29	28	28
Paraná, Brazil	287	236	239	102	13	<3	3	5	28	127	231	310	1,582
260 m	23	23	23	23	23	21	21	22	24	24	24	23	23
Rio de Janeiro, Brazil	125	122	130	107	79	53	41	43	66	79	104	137	1,082
61 m	26	26	25	24	22	21	21	21	21	22	23	25	23

World Statistics: Physical Dimensions

Each topic list is divided into continents and within a continent the items are listed in order of size. The bottom part of many of the lists is selective in order to give examples from as many different countries as possible. The order of the continents is as in the atlas, Europe through to South America. The world top ten are shown in square brackets; in the case of mountains this has not been done because the world top 30 are all in Asia. The figures are rounded as appropriate.

WORLD, CONTINENTS, OCEANS

THE WORLD

THE WORLD	km²	miles²	%
The World	509,450,000	196,672,000	–
Land	149,450,000	57,688,000	29.3
Water	360,000,000	138,984,000	70.7
Asia	44,500,000	17,177,000	29.8
Africa	30,302,000	11,697,000	20.3
North America	24,241,000	9,357,000	16.2
South America	17,793,000	6,868,000	11.9
Antarctica	14,100,000	5,443,000	9.4
Europe	9,957,000	3,843,000	6.7
Australia & Oceania	8,557,000	3,303,000	5.7
Pacific Ocean	155,557,000	60,061,000	46.4
Atlantic Ocean	76,762,000	29,638,000	22.9
Indian Ocean	68,556,000	26,470,000	20.4
Southern Ocean	20,327,000	7,848,000	6.1
Arctic Ocean	14,056,000	5,427,000	4.2

SEAS

PACIFIC	km²	miles²
South China Sea	2,974,600	1,148,500
Bering Sea	2,268,000	875,000
Sea of Okhotsk	1,528,000	590,000
East China & Yellow	1,249,000	482,000
Sea of Japan	1,008,000	389,000
Gulf of California	162,000	62,500
Bass Strait	75,000	29,000

ATLANTIC	km²	miles²
Caribbean Sea	2,766,000	1,068,000
Mediterranean Sea	2,516,000	971,000
Gulf of Mexico	1,543,000	596,000
Hudson Bay	1,232,000	476,000
North Sea	575,000	223,000
Black Sea	462,000	178,000
Baltic Sea	422,170	163,000
Gulf of St Lawrence	238,000	92,000

INDIAN	km²	miles²
Red Sea	438,000	169,000
Persian Gulf	239,000	92,000

MOUNTAINS

EUROPE		m	ft
Elbrus	Russia	5,642	18,510
Mont Blanc	France/Italy	4,807	15,771
Monte Rosa	Italy/Switzerland	4,634	15,203
Dom	Switzerland	4,545	14,911
Liskamm	Switzerland	4,527	14,852
Weisshorn	Switzerland	4,505	14,780
Taschorn	Switzerland	4,490	14,730
Matterhorn/Cervino	Italy/Switzerland	4,478	14,691
Mont Maudit	France/Italy	4,465	14,649
Dent Blanche	Switzerland	4,356	14,291
Nadelhorn	Switzerland	4,327	14,196
Grandes Jorasses	France/Italy	4,208	13,806
Jungfrau	Switzerland	4,158	13,642
Barre des Ecrins	France	4,103	13,461
Gran Paradiso	Italy	4,061	13,323
Piz Bernina	Italy/Switzerland	4,049	13,284
Eiger	Switzerland	3,970	13,025
Monte Viso	Italy	3,841	12,602
Grossglockner	Austria	3,797	12,457
Wildspitze	Austria	3,772	12,382
Monte Disgrazia	Italy	3,678	12,066
Mulhacén	Spain	3,478	11,411
Pico de Aneto	Spain	3,404	11,168
Etna	Italy	3,340	10,958
Zugspitze	Germany	2,962	9,718
Musala	Bulgaria	2,925	9,596
Olympus	Greece	2,917	9,570
Triglav	Slovenia	2,863	9,393
Monte Cinto	France (Corsica)	2,710	8,891
Galdhøpiggen	Norway	2,469	8,100
Ben Nevis	UK	1,342	4,403

ASIA		m	ft
Everest	China/Nepal	8,850	29,035
K2 (Godwin Austen)	China/Kashmir	8,611	28,251
Kanchenjunga	India/Nepal	8,598	28,208
Lhotse	China/Nepal	8,516	27,939
Makalu	China/Nepal	8,481	27,824
Cho Oyu	China/Nepal	8,201	26,906
Dhaulagiri	Nepal	8,167	26,795
Manaslu	Nepal	8,156	26,758
Nanga Parbat	Kashmir	8,126	26,660
Annapurna	Nepal	8,078	26,502
Gasherbrum	China/Kashmir	8,068	26,469
Broad Peak	China/Kashmir	8,051	26,414
Xixabangma	China	8,012	26,286
Gayachung Kang	Nepal	7,897	25,909
Himalchuli	Nepal	7,893	25,896
Disteghil Sar	Kashmir	7,885	25,869
Nuptse	Nepal	7,879	25,849
Kangbachen	Nepal	7,858	25,781
Khunyang Chhish	Kashmir	7,852	25,761
Masherbrum	Kashmir	7,821	25,659
Nanda Devi	India	7,817	25,646
Rakaposhi	Kashmir	7,788	25,551
Batura	Kashmir	7,785	25,541
Namche Barwa	China	7,782	25,531
Kamet	India	7,756	25,447
Soltoro Kangri	Kashmir	7,742	25,400
Gurla Mandhata	China	7,728	25,354
Trivor	Pakistan	7,720	25,328
Kongur Shan	China	7,719	25,324
Jannu	Nepal	7,710	25,295
Tirich Mir	Pakistan	7,690	25,229
K'ula Shan	Bhutan/China	7,543	24,747
Pik Imeni Ismail Samani	Tajikistan	7,495	24,590
Demavend	Iran	5,604	18,386
Ararat	Turkey	5,165	16,945
Gunong Kinabalu	Malaysia (Borneo)	4,101	13,455
Yu Shan	Taiwan	3,997	13,113
Fuji-San	Japan	3,776	12,388

AFRICA		m	ft
Kilimanjaro	Tanzania	5,895	19,340
Mt Kenya	Kenya	5,199	17,057
Ruwenzori (Margherita)	Uganda/Congo (D.R.)	5,109	16,762
Ras Dashen	Ethiopia	4,620	15,157
Meru	Tanzania	4,565	14,977
Karisimbi	Rwanda/Congo (D.R.)	4,507	14,787
Mt Elgon	Kenya/Uganda	4,321	14,176
Batu	Ethiopia	4,307	14,130
Guna	Ethiopia	4,231	13,882
Toubkal	Morocco	4,165	13,665
Irhil Mgoun	Morocco	4,071	13,356
Mt Cameroun	Cameroon	4,070	13,353
Amba Ferit	Ethiopia	3,875	13,042
Pico del Teide	Spain (Tenerife)	3,718	12,198
Thabana Ntlenyana	Lesotho	3,482	11,424
Emi Koussi	Chad	3,415	11,204
Mt aux Sources	Lesotho/South Africa	3,282	10,768
Mt Piton	Réunion	3,069	10,069

OCEANIA		m	ft
Puncak Jaya	Indonesia	5,029	16,499
Puncak Trikora	Indonesia	4,730	15,518
Puncak Mandala	Indonesia	4,702	15,427
Mt Wilhelm	Papua New Guinea	4,508	14,790
Mauna Kea	USA (Hawai'i)	4,205	13,796
Mauna Loa	USA (Hawai'i)	4,169	13,678
Aoraki Mt Cook	New Zealand	3,753	12,313
Mt Balbi	Solomon Is.	2,439	8,002
Orohena	Tahiti	2,241	7,352
Mt Kosciuszko	Australia	2,230	7,316

NORTH AMERICA		m	ft
Mt McKinley (Denali)	USA (Alaska)	6,194	20,321
Mt Logan	Canada	5,959	19,551
Pico de Orizaba	Mexico	5,610	18,405
Mt St Elias	USA/Canada	5,489	18,008
Popocatépetl	Mexico	5,452	17,887
Mt Foraker	USA (Alaska)	5,304	17,401
Iztaccihuatl	Mexico	5,286	17,343
Lucania	Canada	5,226	17,146
Mt Steele	Canada	5,073	16,644
Mt Bona	USA (Alaska)	5,005	16,420
Mt Blackburn	USA (Alaska)	4,996	16,391
Mt Sanford	USA (Alaska)	4,940	16,207
Mt Wood	Canada	4,848	15,905
Nevado de Toluca	Mexico	4,670	15,321
Mt Fairweather	USA (Alaska)	4,663	15,298
Mt Hunter	USA (Alaska)	4,442	14,573
Mt Whitney	USA	4,418	14,495
Mt Elbert	USA	4,399	14,432
Mt Harvard	USA	4,395	14,419
Mt Rainier	USA	4,392	14,409
Blanca Peak	USA	4,372	14,344
Longs Peak	USA	4,345	14,255
Tajumulco	Guatemala	4,220	13,845
Grand Teton	USA	4,197	13,770
Mt Waddington	Canada	3,994	13,104
Mt Robson	Canada	3,954	12,972
Chirripó Grande	Costa Rica	3,837	12,589
Pico Duarte	Dominican Rep.	3,175	10,417

SOUTH AMERICA		m	ft
Aconcagua	Argentina	6,962	22,841
Bonete	Argentina	6,872	22,546
Ojos del Salado	Argentina/Chile	6,863	22,516
Pissis	Argentina	6,779	22,241
Mercedario	Argentina/Chile	6,770	22,211
Huascarán	Peru	6,768	22,205
Llullaillaco	Argentina/Chile	6,723	22,057
Nudo de Cachi	Argentina	6,720	22,047
Yerupaja	Peru	6,632	21,758
N. de Tres Cruces	Argentina/Chile	6,620	21,719
Incahuasi	Argentina/Chile	6,601	21,654
Cerro Galan	Argentina	6,600	21,654
Tupungato	Argentina/Chile	6,570	21,555
Sajama	Bolivia	6,520	21,391
Illimani	Bolivia	6,485	21,276
Coropuna	Peru	6,425	21,079
Ausangate	Peru	6,384	20,945
Cerro del Toro	Argentina	6,380	20,932
Siula Grande	Peru	6,356	20,853
Chimborazo	Ecuador	6,267	20,561
Alpamayo	Peru	5,947	19,511
Cotapaxi	Ecuador	5,896	19,344
Pico Cristóbal Colón	Colombia	5,800	19,029
Pico Bolivar	Venezuela	5,007	16,427

ANTARCTICA		m	ft
Vinson Massif		4,897	16,066
Mt Kirkpatrick		4,528	14,855
Mt Markham		4,349	14,268

OCEAN DEPTHS

ATLANTIC OCEAN	m	ft	
Puerto Rico (Milwaukee) Deep	9,220	30,249	[7]
Cayman Trench	7,680	25,197	[10]
Gulf of Mexico	5,203	17,070	
Mediterranean Sea	5,121	16,801	
Black Sea	2,211	7,254	
North Sea	660	2,165	
Baltic Sea	463	1,519	
Hudson Bay	258	846	

INDIAN OCEAN	m	ft
Java Trench	7,450	24,442
Red Sea	2,635	8,454
Persian Gulf	73	239

PACIFIC OCEAN	m	ft	
Mariana Trench	11,022	36,161	[1]
Tonga Trench	10,882	35,702	[2]
Japan Trench	10,554	34,626	[3]
Kuril Trench	10,542	34,587	[4]
Mindanao Trench	10,497	34,439	[5]
Kermadec Trench	10,047	32,962	[6]

PACIFIC OCEAN (continued)	m	ft	
Peru–Chile Trench	8,050	26,410	[8]
Aleutian Trench	7,822	25,662	[9]

ARCTIC OCEAN	m	ft
Molloy Deep	5,608	18,399

SOUTHERN OCEAN	m	ft
South Sandwich Trench	7,235	23,737

LAND LOWS

		m	ft
Caspian Sea	Europe	−28	−92
Dead Sea	Asia	−418	−1,371
Lake Assal	Africa	−156	−512
Lake Eyre North	Oceania	−16	−52
Death Valley	North America	−86	−282
Valdés Peninsula	South America	−40	−131

RIVERS

EUROPE		km	miles
Volga	Caspian Sea	3,700	2,300
Danube	Black Sea	2,850	1,770
Ural	Caspian Sea	2,535	1,575
Dnepr (Dnipro)	Black Sea	2,285	1,420
Kama	Volga	2,030	1,260
Don	Black Sea	1,990	1,240
Petchora	Arctic Ocean	1,790	1,110
Oka	Volga	1,480	920
Belaya	Kama	1,420	880
Dnister (Dniester)	Black Sea	1,400	870
Vyatka	Kama	1,370	850
Rhine	North Sea	1,320	820
N. Dvina	Arctic Ocean	1,290	800
Desna	Dnepr (Dnipro)	1,190	740
Elbe	North Sea	1,145	710
Wisla	Baltic Sea	1,090	675
Loire	Atlantic Ocean	1,020	635

ASIA		km	miles	
Yangtze	Pacific Ocean	6,380	3,960	[3]
Yenisey–Angara	Arctic Ocean	5,550	3,445	[5]
Huang He	Pacific Ocean	5,464	3,395	[6]
Ob–Irtysh	Arctic Ocean	5,410	3,360	[7]
Mekong	Pacific Ocean	4,500	2,795	[9]
Amur	Pacific Ocean	4,442	2,760	[10]
Lena	Arctic Ocean	4,402	2,735	
Irtysh	Ob	4,250	2,640	
Yenisey	Arctic Ocean	4,090	2,540	
Ob	Arctic Ocean	3,680	2,285	
Indus	Indian Ocean	3,100	1,925	
Brahmaputra	Indian Ocean	2,900	1,800	
Syrdarya	Aral Sea	2,860	1,775	
Salween	Indian Ocean	2,800	1,740	
Euphrates	Indian Ocean	2,700	1,675	
Vilyuy	Lena	2,650	1,645	
Kolyma	Arctic Ocean	2,600	1,615	
Amudarya	Aral Sea	2,540	1,575	
Ural	Caspian Sea	2,535	1,575	
Ganges	Indian Ocean	2,510	1,560	
Si Kiang	Pacific Ocean	2,100	1,305	
Irrawaddy	Indian Ocean	2,010	1,250	
Tarim–Yarkand	Lop Nor	2,000	1,240	
Tigris	Indian Ocean	1,900	1,180	

AFRICA		km	miles	
Nile	Mediterranean	6,670	4,140	[1]
Congo	Atlantic Ocean	4,670	2,900	[8]
Niger	Atlantic Ocean	4,180	2,595	
Zambezi	Indian Ocean	3,540	2,200	
Oubangi/Uele	Congo (D.R.)	2,250	1,400	
Kasai	Congo (D.R.)	1,950	1,210	
Shaballe	Indian Ocean	1,930	1,200	
Orange	Atlantic Ocean	1,860	1,155	
Cubango	Okavango Delta	1,800	1,120	
Limpopo	Indian Ocean	1,770	1,100	
Senegal	Atlantic Ocean	1,640	1,020	
Volta	Atlantic Ocean	1,500	930	

AUSTRALIA		km	miles
Murray–Darling	Southern Ocean	3,750	2,330
Darling	Murray	3,070	1,905
Murray	Southern Ocean	2,575	1,600
Murrumbidgee	Murray	1,690	1,050

NORTH AMERICA		km	miles	
Mississippi–Missouri	Gulf of Mexico	5,971	3,710	[4]
Mackenzie	Arctic Ocean	4,240	2,630	
Missouri	Mississippi	4,088	2,540	

NORTH AMERICA (continued)		km	miles
Mississippi	Gulf of Mexico	3,782	2,350
Yukon	Pacific Ocean	3,185	1,980
Rio Grande	Gulf of Mexico	3,030	1,880
Arkansas	Mississippi	2,340	1,450
Colorado	Pacific Ocean	2,330	1,445
Red	Mississippi	2,040	1,270
Columbia	Pacific Ocean	1,950	1,210
Saskatchewan	Lake Winnipeg	1,940	1,205
Snake	Columbia	1,670	1,040
Churchill	Hudson Bay	1,600	990
Ohio	Mississippi	1,580	980
Brazos	Gulf of Mexico	1,400	870
St Lawrence	Atlantic Ocean	1,170	730

SOUTH AMERICA		km	miles	
Amazon	Atlantic Ocean	6,450	4,010	[2]
Paraná–Plate	Atlantic Ocean	4,500	2,800	
Purus	Amazon	3,350	2,080	
Madeira	Amazon	3,200	1,990	
São Francisco	Atlantic Ocean	2,900	1,800	
Paraná	Plate	2,800	1,740	
Tocantins	Atlantic Ocean	2,750	1,710	
Orinoco	Atlantic Ocean	2,740	1,700	
Paraguay	Paraná	2,550	1,580	
Pilcomayo	Paraná	2,500	1,550	
Araguaia	Tocantins	2,250	1,400	
Juruá	Amazon	2,000	1,240	
Xingu	Amazon	1,980	1,230	
Ucayali	Amazon	1,900	1,180	
Uruguay	Plate	1,610	1,000	

LAKES

EUROPE		km²	miles²
Lake Ladoga	Russia	17,700	6,800
Lake Onega	Russia	9,700	3,700
Saimaa system	Finland	8,000	3,100
Vänern	Sweden	5,500	2,100

ASIA		km²	miles²	
Caspian Sea	Asia	371,000	143,000	[1]
Lake Baikal	Russia	30,500	11,780	[8]
Tonlé Sap	Cambodia	20,000	7,700	
Lake Balqash	Kazakhstan	18,500	7,100	
Aral Sea	Kazakhstan/Uzbekistan	17,160	6,625	
Lake Dongting	China	12,000	4,600	
Lake Ysyk	Kyrgyzstan	6,200	2,400	
Lake Orumiyeh	Iran	5,900	2,300	
Lake Koko	China	5,700	2,200	
Lake Poyang	China	5,000	1,900	
Lake Khanka	China/Russia	4,400	1,700	
Lake Van	Turkey	3,500	1,400	

AFRICA		km²	miles²	
Lake Victoria	East Africa	68,000	26,300	[3]
Lake Tanganyika	Central Africa	33,000	13,000	[6]
Lake Malawi/Nyasa	East Africa	29,600	11,430	[9]
Lake Chad	Central Africa	25,000	9,700	
Lake Turkana	Ethiopia/Kenya	8,500	3,290	
Lake Volta	Ghana	8,480	3,270	
Lake Bangweulu	Zambia	8,000	3,100	
Lake Rukwa	Tanzania	7,000	2,700	
Lake Mai-Ndombe	Congo (D.R.)	6,500	2,500	
Lake Kariba	Zambia/Zimbabwe	5,300	2,000	
Lake Albert	Uganda/Congo (D.R.)	5,300	2,000	
Lake Nasser	Egypt/Sudan	5,200	2,000	
Lake Mweru	Zambia/Congo (D.R.)	4,900	1,900	
Lake Cabora Bassa	Mozambique	4,500	1,700	
Lake Kyoga	Uganda	4,400	1,700	
Lake Tana	Ethiopia	3,630	1,400	

AUSTRALIA		km²	miles²
Lake Eyre	Australia	8,900	3,400
Lake Torrens	Australia	5,800	2,200
Lake Gairdner	Australia	4,800	1,900

NORTH AMERICA		km²	miles²	
Lake Superior	Canada/USA	82,350	31,800	[2]
Lake Huron	Canada/USA	59,600	23,010	[4]
Lake Michigan	USA	58,000	22,400	[5]
Great Bear Lake	Canada	31,800	12,280	[7]
Great Slave Lake	Canada	28,500	11,000	[10]
Lake Erie	Canada/USA	25,700	9,900	
Lake Winnipeg	Canada	24,400	9,400	
Lake Ontario	Canada/USA	19,500	7,500	
Lake Nicaragua	Nicaragua	8,200	3,200	
Lake Athabasca	Canada	8,100	3,100	
Smallwood Reservoir	Canada	6,530	2,520	
Reindeer Lake	Canada	6,400	2,500	
Nettilling Lake	Canada	5,500	2,100	

SOUTH AMERICA		km²	miles²
Lake Titicaca	Bolivia/Peru	8,300	3,200
Lake Poopo	Bolivia	2,800	1,100

ISLANDS

EUROPE		km²	miles²	
Great Britain	UK	229,880	88,700	[8]
Iceland	Atlantic Ocean	103,000	39,800	
Ireland	Ireland/UK	84,400	32,600	
Novaya Zemlya (N.)	Russia	48,200	18,600	
W. Spitzbergen	Norway	39,000	15,100	
Novaya Zemlya (S.)	Russia	33,200	12,800	
Sicily	Italy	25,500	9,800	
Sardinia	Italy	24,000	9,300	
N.E. Spitzbergen	Norway	15,000	5,600	
Corsica	France	8,700	3,400	
Crete	Greece	8,350	3,200	
Zealand	Denmark	6,850	2,600	

ASIA		km²	miles²	
Borneo	South-east Asia	744,360	287,400	[3]
Sumatra	Indonesia	473,600	182,860	[6]
Honshu	Japan	230,500	88,980	[7]
Sulawesi (Celebes)	Indonesia	189,000	73,000	
Java	Indonesia	126,700	48,900	
Luzon	Philippines	104,700	40,400	
Mindanao	Philippines	101,500	39,200	
Hokkaido	Japan	78,400	30,300	
Sakhalin	Russia	74,060	28,600	
Sri Lanka	Indian Ocean	65,600	25,300	
Taiwan	Pacific Ocean	36,000	13,900	
Kyushu	Japan	35,700	13,800	
Hainan	China	34,000	13,100	
Timor	Indonesia	33,600	13,000	
Shikoku	Japan	18,800	7,300	
Halmahera	Indonesia	18,000	6,900	
Ceram	Indonesia	17,150	6,600	
Sumbawa	Indonesia	15,450	6,000	
Flores	Indonesia	15,200	5,900	
Samar	Philippines	13,100	5,100	
Negros	Philippines	12,700	4,900	
Bangka	Indonesia	12,000	4,600	
Palawan	Philippines	12,000	4,600	
Panay	Philippines	11,500	4,400	
Sumba	Indonesia	11,100	4,300	
Mindoro	Philippines	9,750	3,800	

AFRICA		km²	miles²	
Madagascar	Indian Ocean	587,040	226,660	[4]
Socotra	Indian Ocean	3,600	1,400	
Réunion	Indian Ocean	2,500	965	
Tenerife	Atlantic Ocean	2,350	900	
Mauritius	Indian Ocean	1,865	720	

OCEANIA		km²	miles²	
New Guinea	Indonesia/Papua NG	821,030	317,000	[2]
New Zealand (S.)	Pacific Ocean	150,500	58,100	
New Zealand (N.)	Pacific Ocean	114,700	44,300	
Tasmania	Australia	67,800	26,200	
New Britain	Papua New Guinea	37,800	14,600	
New Caledonia	Pacific Ocean	19,100	7,400	
Viti Levu	Fiji	10,500	4,100	
Hawai'i	Pacific Ocean	10,450	4,000	
Bougainville	Papua New Guinea	9,600	3,700	
Guadalcanal	Solomon Is.	6,500	2,500	
Vanua Levu	Fiji	5,550	2,100	
New Ireland	Papua New Guinea	3,200	1,200	

NORTH AMERICA		km²	miles²	
Greenland	Atlantic Ocean	2,175,600	839,800	[1]
Baffin Is.	Canada	508,000	196,100	[5]
Victoria Is.	Canada	212,200	81,900	[9]
Ellesmere Is.	Canada	212,000	81,800	[10]
Cuba	Caribbean Sea	110,860	42,800	
Newfoundland	Canada	110,680	42,700	
Hispaniola	Dominican Rep./Haiti	76,200	29,400	
Banks Is.	Canada	67,000	25,900	
Devon Is.	Canada	54,500	21,000	
Melville Is.	Canada	42,400	16,400	
Vancouver Is.	Canada	32,150	12,400	
Somerset Is.	Canada	24,300	9,400	
Jamaica	Caribbean Sea	11,400	4,400	
Puerto Rico	Atlantic Ocean	8,900	3,400	
Cape Breton Is.	Canada	4,000	1,500	

SOUTH AMERICA		km²	miles²
Tierra del Fuego	Argentina/Chile	47,000	18,100
Falkland Is. (East)	Atlantic Ocean	6,800	2,600
South Georgia	Atlantic Ocean	4,200	1,600
Galapagos (Isabela)	Pacific Ocean	2,250	870

World: Regions in the News

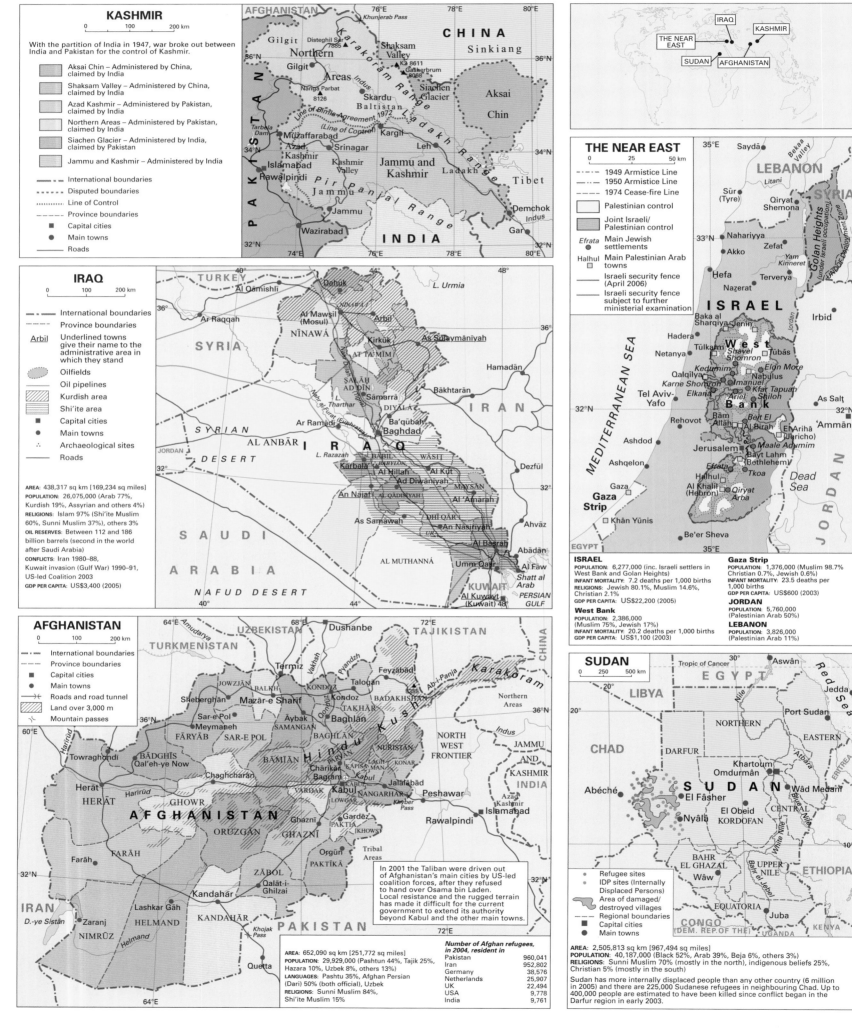

WORLD EXPLORER

CONTENTS

Mountains and volcanoes	2–3	Sea and ocean cruises	18–19
Deserts and canyons	4–5	Winter sports	20–21
Lakes and waterfalls	6–7	Great beaches	22–23
Wildlife in the Americas and Europe	8–9	Festivals	24–25
Wildlife in Africa, Asia and Australasia	10–11	Historic sites in the Americas	26–27
Marine wildlife	12–13	Historic sites in Europe	28–29
Great railway journeys	14–15	Historic sites in Africa, Asia and Australasia	30–31
River and canal journeys	16–17	Theme parks	32

Mountains and volcanoes

The world's mountains provide a huge variety of magnificent scenery, ranging from the tree-covered Blue Mountains of Australia, little more than 1,070 m (3,500 ft) high, to the towering snow-covered Himalayan peaks of Nepal and China, several of which are over 8,000 m (26,000 ft) high. Many are accessible by road, or sometimes by train or cable car, but walking, even if only a short distance, is usually the best way to experience the breathtaking views that they offer.

◄ **Rocky Mountains, Banff National Park, Canada**
Pointed peaks and sheer cliffs contribute to a magnificent landscape. Over 1,600 km (1,000 miles) of trails pass by glaciers, turquoise lakes and forests of pine, fir and spruce. In the town of Banff a cable car rises to the top of Sulfur Mountain, 2,263 m (7,440 ft) high.
Best time to visit: June–September

THE AMERICAS

Mount McKinley, Denali National Park, Alaska, USA
The USA's highest mountain at 6,194 m (20,321 ft) is in a spectacular wilderness of snow-covered peaks and glaciers with wildlife that includes brown bears, caribou, moose and marmots. Activities include river rafting and sightseeing by plane.
Best time to visit: June–August

Popocatepetl Volcano ('Smoking Mountain'), Sierra Nevada, Mexico
A cloud of smoke often hovers above the massive crater of Popocatepetl, which is 5,452 m (17,887 ft) high. It is possible to climb and descend the mountain in one very long day with the aid of a guide.
Best time to climb: November–March

Cotopaxi and Chimborazo Volcanoes, Ecuador
The two highest active volcanoes in the world are in a country where the main road is known as the 'Avenue of the Volcanoes'. Non-mountaineers can climb Cotopaxi (5,896 m/19,344 ft) and get near to the top of Chimborazo (6,267 m/20,561 ft).
Best time to climb: January–April

Cordillera Blanca, Huascaran National Park, Peru
With 663 glaciers, the peaks of the Cordillera Blanca, more than 50 of which rise to heights of between 5,000 and 6,000 m (16,500 and 19,700 ft), are a great attraction for ice climbers. Huaraz is the main climbing centre. An alternative for those who prefer to trek is the richly glaciated Huayhuash range.
Best time to visit: July–September

EUROPE

Landmannalaugar, Iceland
A combination of volcanic and geothermal activity has produced a unique landscape in Landmannalaugar, where mountain peaks (little more than 1,070 m/3,500 ft high) rise above a landscape of convoluted lava fields and blue mountain lakes, and hot springs provide open-air baths.
Best time to visit: July–early September

Mount Vesuvius, Italy
The volcano of Vesuvius dominates the landscape around Naples. Although it lost its plume of smoke after erupting in 1944, it is still active. A bus from Pompeii goes to within 1.5 km (1 mile) of the summit (1,277 m/4,189 ft).
Time to visit: All seasons

AFRICA

Atlas Mountains, Morocco
Canyons with dramatic rock formations are to be found in these rugged mountains that rise to a height of over 3,900 m (13,000 ft). Organized treks pass by numerous isolated Berber villages, far from the road from Marrakech, which winds up to a mountain pass 2,275 m (7,467 ft) high.
Best time to visit: June–October

Mount Kilimanjaro, Tanzania
Africa's highest mountain rises majestically to 5,895 m (19,340 ft) above the plains of Amboseli National Park. It is possible to trek to the top for stunning views over Kenya and Tanzania, along

▲ **Sierra Nevada, Yosemite National Park, USA**
The Californian Yosemite National Park is famous for its sheer-sided granite domes, such as the Half Dome and the 2,307 m (7,569 ft) high El Capitan, which rise above forests and emerald lakes. Among the many species of flowers and trees to be found in the park are ancient giant sequoias over 60 m (200 ft) high, one of which is estimated to be 2,700 years old. An added attraction are the Yosemite Falls which, with a drop of 739 m (2,425 ft), are the highest in North America. Walkers can escape the summer crowds by using the 1,280 km (800 miles) of trails.
Best time to visit: May–September

Town/city with major airport

Denali Nat. Park • Mt McKinley
Anchorage
Banff Nat. Park
Calgary
Yosemite Nat. Park
San Francisco
Albany
Green Mountains
Appalachians
Rocky Mountains
Mexico City • Popocatepetl
Quito • Cotopaxi Chimborazo
Cordillera Blanca
Lima
Andes
Reykjavik • • Landmannalaugar
Mont Blanc Geneva • Alps
Naples • Mt Vesuvius
Casablanca • Atlas Mountains
Karakorams
Islamabad • Himalayas
Katmandu
Mt Kilimanjaro
Dar es Salaam
Durban
Drakensberg
Tokyo Mt Fuji
Hangzhou
Huangshan
Manila
Mayon
Jakarta
Mt Bromo
Blue Mountains
Sydney
Devonport Cradle Mt
Milford Sound
Christchurch
Southern Alps

▲ Mont Blanc, Alps, France
Europe's highest mountain rises to a height of 4,807 m (15,760 ft). A splendid view of it can be had from the peak of the Aiguille de Midi, a granite spear 3,840 m (12,600 ft) high, that is reached by a steep 3 km (2-mile) ascent in a cable car from Chamonix. Below Mont Blanc is the start of a long-distance ski and walking route, which passes ten of the 12 highest peaks in the Alps on its way to the Matterhorn in Switzerland and Italy.
Best time for walking: May–September

▼ Mt Bromo, Java
A crater within a vast outer crater, Bromo emits white smoke, as does Mount Semeru, seen here in the distance. Visitors usually stay overnight in a village at the rim of the outer crater, from where it is possible to walk to Bromo at dawn to watch the sun rise up over the outer crater.
Best time to visit: April–October

routes that pass through farmland and lush forest before reaching alpine-like vegetation and snow-covered rock.
Best time to climb: mid January–late February and late August–September

Drakensberg Mountains, South Africa
Vast pinnacles and blocks of basalt rise to a height of over 3,475 m (11,400 ft) in this range of mountains that also runs through Lesotho. Snowcapped in winter, many of the peaks are an enormous challenge for mountaineers. The Royal Natal National Park has numerous hiking trails.
Best time to visit: April–October

ASIA

Himalayas, Nepal
Within the Himalayas in Nepal are ten of the world's 14 peaks with a height of over 8,000 m (26,000 ft), including Everest (8,850 m/29,035 ft). Far below the snow-capped peaks are terraced hillsides dotted with villages, while above a height of about 2,700 m (9,000 ft) are forests in which rhododendrons bloom between February and April. The most popular base for exploring the mountains is Pokhara. The famous ten-day trek to the mountain town of Jomsom begins here, as does the three- to four-day Annapurna Skyline Trek which provides superb views while being easy enough to be undertaken with children.
Best time to visit: October–April

Karakorams, Pakistan
The jagged peaks of the Karakorams include K2, the world's second highest mountain (8,611 m/28,400 ft). A journey along the Karakoram Highway follows the route of the old Silk Road along the Indus Valley from Rawalpindi to Kashgar in China, sometimes clinging to cliff faces as it winds its way through the mountains up to the Khunjerab Pass at 4,934 m (16,280 ft).
Best time to visit: May–August

Great mountain treks
The following is a selection of great mountain treks that take four or more days. The months given are those in which it is best to undertake each trek.

Long Trail, Vermont, USA (424 km/265 miles; 16–21 days; May–Sept) Easily reached by road, the trail through Vermont's Green Mountains can be walked in sections. It is part of the 3,456 km (2,160-mile) long Appalachian Trail, whose most demanding section is through New Hampshire's White Mountains.
Inca Trail, Peru (4–5 days; April–Sept) By far the best way to approach the spectacular Inca site of Machu Picchu (see *Historic Sites of the Americas*), the Inca Trail begins some distance from Cuzco.
Mont Blanc Circuit, France and Switzerland (10 days; July–Sept) Possibly the finest walk in Europe, it usually starts from Chamonix. With an average altitude of 1,525 m (5,000 ft), it links the seven valleys surrounding Mont Blanc.

Annapurna Circuit, Nepal (17 days; Oct–Nov and March–April) Regarded as Nepal's classic trek, it goes through many types of landscape *(see picture below)*, and reaches a height of 5,416 m (17,765 ft), as well as providing superb views of Annapurna and Dhaulagiri.
Everest Trek, Nepal (14–16 days; Oct–Nov and March–April) A trek from Jiri to the Everest Base Camp on the Khumbu Glacier provides wonderful views of Everest. It is possible to fly back to Katmandu from Lukla, three days' walk away.
Milford Track, New Zealand (54 km/34 miles; 4 days; Oct–April) A walk that is regarded as a must by most New Zealanders ends at the breathtaking Milford Sound (see *Sea and ocean cruises*). The number of walkers is limited and booking well ahead is necessary.

Mayon Volcano, Philippines
Often described as the world's most perfect volcano cone, Mayon (2,462 m/8,075 ft) is still very active. An eruption in 1993 killed 70 people. It can be climbed in two days but it is essential to do so with a guide.
Best time to climb: December–May

Mt Kinabalu, Borneo, Malaysia
It is possible to walk rather than climb to the top of the highest mountain in South-east Asia (4,010 m/13,455 ft). It does, however, take two days and hiring a guide is compulsory. The view from the top sometimes stretches to the Philippines.
Best time to climb: April–September

Huangshan, China
The Chinese regard the 72-peak Huang-shan range as one of the great natural attractions of their country. Some 30 peaks rise to over 1,500 m (4,900 ft). There are two main walking routes up the side of the range, and an eight-minute cable-car ride from Yungusi to the top.
Best time to visit: spring and autumn

Mt Fuji, Japan
The perfectly symmetrical cone of Japan's highest mountain (3,776 m/12,388 ft), which last erupted in 1707, is climbed by people of all ages in the summer. A road goes to the fourth and fifth 'stations', from where it takes four or five hours to climb to the crater. This is best reached at dawn, before the clouds gather.
Best time to climb: July–August

AUSTRALASIA

Blue Mountains, New South Wales, Australia
Reaching a height of just over 1,070 m (3,500 ft), the Blue Mountains – with their densely forested slopes, sandstone chasms, dramatic rock formations and waterfalls – provide a beautiful environment in which to drive and walk. As well as a network of trails there are a number of interesting villages and towns, of which the largest, Katoomba, is served by a railway from Sydney just 80 km (50 miles) away.
Time to visit: All seasons

Cradle Mountain/Lake St Clair National Park, Tasmania, Australia
Australia's best mountain trails and rugged alpine scenery are to be found around Cradle Mountain. Jagged peaks, the highest of which is Mt Ossa (1,617 m/5,300 ft), rise above tarns and lakes in deep valleys.
Best time to visit: November–March

Deserts and canyons

For the adventurous traveller, the stunning landscapes of rock and sand which make up some of the world's most inhospitable environments offer a challenge not to be missed. From the vast sand seas of the Sahara Desert to the deep canyons and distinctive rock formations of the south-western United States, there is an extraordinary range of landforms to explore.

NORTH AMERICA

Bryce Canyon, Utah, USA

On a more human scale than the Grand Canyon, Bryce Canyon is not really a canyon at all but a natural amphitheatre filled with dazzling orange, red and pink rock pinnacles – known as 'hoodoos' – overlooking spectacularly colourful ravines. This surreal landscape can be explored on foot along a network of marked trails, or simply enjoyed from one of the viewpoints along the rim of the amphitheatre.

Monument Valley, Arizona, USA

With its majestic rock pillars towering over a barren, desert landscape, Monument Valley is an awe-inspiring sight. It has been made famous as a backdrop to numerous Hollywood westerns and is now part of the Navajo Reservation. A 27 km (17-mile) road tour of the valley takes two to three hours and offers stunning views of this unforgettable place.

Zion Canyon, Utah, USA

The road through the steep-sided Zion Canyon can become crowded in summer, and it is worth leaving the car to follow one of the short trails to the Emerald Pools or the hanging gardens at Weeping Rock. Longer trails lead from the canyon to the desert plateau above and offer spectacular views of the contrasting landscapes.

SOUTH AMERICA

Colca Canyon, Peru

High in the Andes the River Colca runs through a gorge which is twice the depth of the Grand Canyon, past ancient Inca granaries cut into the rock and green slopes covered by pre-Inca terracing. This astonishingly beautiful landscape, complete with smoking volcano in the background, is home to the Collagua and Cabana people, whose traditional way of life is punctuated with lively festivals.

Atacama Desert, Chile

Overlooked by a ruined pre-Inca fortress, the picturesque oasis village of San Pedro de Atacama, with its adobe buildings and excellent archeological museum, makes a good base for exploring the canyons, saltpans and stark landscapes of the surrounding desert. One of the most beautiful places to visit is the Valle de la Luna, where the multi-coloured desert formations are a magnet for photographers and filmmakers.

EUROPE

Almerían Desert, Spain

The setting for the film *Lawrence of Arabia* as well as many 'spaghetti westerns', the Almerían Desert is an extraordinary, almost lunar landscape of sand dunes dissected by dried-up river beds and littered with sandstone cones. Film sets are open to the public at Mini-Hollywood.

Timanfaya National Park, Lanzarote, Canary Islands

On an island where it rarely rains, a series of volcanic eruptions in the 1730s created an extraordinary apocalyptic landscape. Guided tours go to an area of solidified lava and volcanic cones, aptly called the Mountains of Fire, where a dry bush dropped into a crevice will burst into flames and meals at a solitary restaurant are barbecued on a volcano.

AFRICA

Draa Valley, the Sahara, Morocco

From the town of Ouarzazate, with its dramatic kasbah, the Draa river runs south-east through a rich landscape of dramatic gorges, agricultural land and kasbahs towards the Sahara. After around 160 km (100 miles), the river reaches the former frontier fort of Zagora, which makes a good base for exploring the desert.

▲ **Grand Canyon, Arizona, USA**
Carved by the Colorado River out of the multi-coloured rock of the Arizona Desert, the Grand Canyon is one of North America's most awe-inspiring natural features. Drives and trails around its rim – 443 km (277 miles) in length – provide stunning views. Visitors can walk or ride mules down one of the vertiginous trails to the valley floor, 1.7 km (1 mile) below, or try rafting on the river.

▲ **Sonoran Desert, USA/Mexico**
Almost encircling the Gulf of California and covering 310,000 sq km (120,00 sq miles), the Sonoran Desert is the hottest of North America's deserts. Tucson, Arizona, serves as a base for tours into the desert, including archaeological tours. Nearby are the excellent Arizona-Sonora Desert Museum and the protected desert habitat of Organ Pipe Cactus National Monument where visitors can see the giant saguaro and organ pipe cacti which have come to symbolize the area. There are good trails and scenic drives around the park, and plenty of desert wildlife to watch.

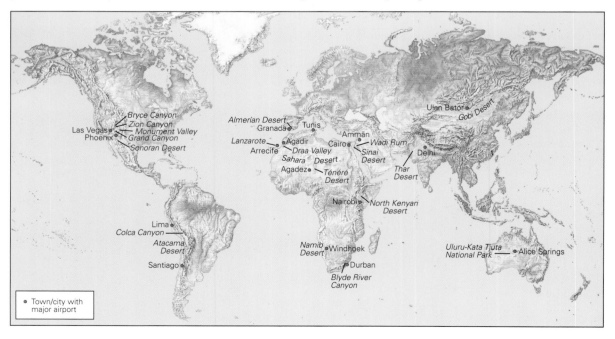

Bryce Canyon
Zion Canyon
Las Vegas
Monument Valley
Phoenix
Grand Canyon
Sonoran Desert

Almerían Desert
Granada
Tunis
Lanzarote
Agadir
Amman
Wadi Rum
Arrecife
Draa Valley
Cairo
Sinai Desert
Delhi
Sahara Desert
Agadez
Ténéré Desert
Thar Desert

Ulan Bator
Gobi Desert

Lima
Colca Canyon
Atacama Desert
Santiago

Nairobi
North Kenyan Desert

Namib Desert
Windhoek
Durban
Blyde River Canyon

Uluru-Kata Tjuta National Park
Alice Springs

• Town/city with major airport

Saharan oases, Tunisia
The shifting sand dunes around the town of Douz are an excellent example of the landscape popularly associated with the Sahara Desert. In fact the desert, which covers an area of 8,600,000 sq km (3,320,000 sq miles), has extensive stony plains, rock-strewn plateaux, mountains and large oasis depressions as well as seas of sand. Douz is

a good base for camel safaris and for exploring the more isolated southern oases. To the north-west the town of Tozeur, with its beautiful 12th-century mosque, is set beside a vast oasis fed by over 200 springs. It serves as an excellent starting point for four-wheel-drive tours into the desert and to the nearby beautiful mountain oases, such as Tamerza, Mides and Chebika.

Guided expeditions of up to a week can include camel riding and stargazing under the immense Saharan sky.

Ténéré Desert, Niger
For desert purists the seemingly endless sea of sand that is the Ténéré Desert is perhaps the most beautiful part of the Sahara. A two-week round trip from the desert city of Agadez might pass through a massive dinosaur cemetery on the way to the classic oasis town of Bilma and the prehistoric cave paintings of the Djado Plateau. Crossing the Ténéré is notoriously challenging and often dangerous, but the experience is unforgettable.

Sinai Desert, Egypt
Inland from the coastal resorts of the Sinai Peninsula is a hot, desolate wilderness sprinkled with oases and ancient settlements. They include the 6th-century monastery of St Catherine, which stands at the foot of Mount Sinai, where Moses is said to have received the Ten Commandments from God. Camel treks and jeep safaris take visitors into the aptly-named Wilderness of Wanderings, in the centre of the peninsula.

North Kenyan Desert
In sharp contrast to the developed south of Kenya, the North Kenyan Desert is a vast tract of scrubland inhabited by ancient nomadic tribes whose way of life has changed little over the centuries. A rich diversity of desert landscapes here includes scrub desert – which bursts into colour after rainfall – and lunar, volcanic areas. There are lush oases and river-cut canyons too, but the reason most people come here is to see the 'Jade Sea', Lake Turkana, with its profusion of birdlife, hippos and Nile crocodiles.

Namib Desert, Namibia
Stretching for 1,930 km (1,200 miles) down the length of the Namibian coastline

to the mouth of the Orange River in South Africa, the Namib is a strip of desert with an average width of 110 km (70 miles). The highest sand dunes in the world – sometimes exceeding 244 m (800 ft) – are to be found at Sossus Vlei, in the Namib-Naukluft National Park. The northern section is known as Skeleton Coast because of the many shipwrecks that lie on the ocean bed nearby.

Blyde River Canyon, South Africa
The view over the canyon from the spot known as God's Window is one of the highlights of any visit to the beautiful Blyde River Nature Reserve, in the Drakensberg. There are two trails down into the canyon – which in some places is over 700 m (2,300 ft) deep – from Bourke's Luck Potholes, where strange natural rock formations can be seen.

ASIA AND AUSTRALASIA

Thar Desert, Rajasthan, India
Within the Rajasthan Desert National Park two areas of interest to tourists can be reached easily from the attractive city of Jaisalmer with its 12th-century fort. One is the Akal Fossil Park where the petrified trunks of 25 trees once covered by the sea lie on a bare hillside. The second is the 3 km (2-mile) long Sam Dunes, just 40 km (25 miles) from Jaisalmer. The dunes are usually crowded with tourists taking camel rides, but it is possible to escape the crowds and go on safaris of several days, by either jeep or camel.

Gobi Desert, Mongolia
For 70 years part of the Soviet Union, the Gobi Desert has only recently become accessible to western travellers. Its greatest attraction is the red sandstone Flaming Cliffs, 80 km (50 miles) north-west of Dalandzadgad, which became famous in the 1920s when the explorer and scientist Roy Chapman Andrews (on whom the character of Indiana Jones was based) discovered fossilized dinosaur remains there. Still rich in dinosaur fossils, the cliffs are just north of the vast Three Beauties National Park with a landscape of mountains, canyons, gravel and sand.

▼ **Wadi Rum, Jordan**
Soaring vertically from the desert floor of Wadi Rum are the massive rock formations known as jebels for which the area is famous. Vehicles and camels can be hired in the Bedouin settlement of Rum, but it is hard to beat the experience of walking through this extraordinary, silent landscape and sleeping out in the desert under the stars.

◄ **Uluru National Park, Northern Territory, Australia**
The largest sandstone monolith in the world, Uluru (Ayers Rock) is a magnificent sight, particularly at sunset when it appears to burn from within. Some 40 km (25 miles) to the west are the Olgas – 36 enormous granite domes – which, like Uluru, are an important Aboriginal site. Access is restricted, but visitors can experience their haunting beauty by following the trail through the Valley of the Winds.

Lakes and waterfalls

From the azure tranquillity of Lake Garda in Italy to the thundering roar of Zimbabwe's Victoria Falls, the great lakes and waterfalls of the world are set amidst dramatically beautiful scenery. Many resorts offer watersports as well as long-distance trails for ramblers and horse-riders.

► Lake Maligne, Jasper National Park, Canada
The glacier-fed Lake Maligne – shown here at dawn – is set among the snow-covered peaks of Jasper National Park, the biggest and wildest of Canada's four Rocky Mountain national parks at 10,400 sq km (4,000 sq miles). Boat and hiking tours, fishing, rafting and riding are available, while the independent explorer can hire a boat or walk along the excellent network of trails.

▼ Lake Argentino, Argentina
The south-western arm of Lake Argentino is periodically dammed by the Moreno Glacier, from which icebergs regularly break off and crash into the channel below. Visitors can see, hear and photograph the glacier in safety from a series of platforms and viewing points. The massive Upsala Glacier on the northern arm of the lake can be reached by boat from Puerto Bandera.

NORTH AMERICA

Niagara Falls, Canada/USA
The most-visited waterfall in the world, Niagara Falls has been developed as a tourist attraction offering every possible viewing experience, including cable cars, helicopter rides, viewing towers, boats and even tunnels in the rockface. Despite the commercialization, this massive, perpetual curtain of falling water lives up to its reputation as one of the wonders of the natural world.

Waterton-Glacier Park, Montana and Alberta, Canada/USA
Silver lakes are a major feature of the landscape of mountain peaks, waterfalls and hanging valleys, carved by glaciers 10,000 years ago, in the Waterton-Glacier Park. There are spectacular trails for walkers of all levels, and the Going-to-the-Sun Road through the park is considered to be one of the USA's driving highlights.

Lake Tahoe, California, USA
High in the Sierra Nevada mountains on the border between California and Nevada, Lake Tahoe is a popular year-round holiday destination. In winter the area is packed with skiers (see *Winter sports*) while summer brings people seeking the cooler temperatures of the mountains and the crystal waters and sandy beaches of the lake. On the California side, there is swimming, boating, fishing and walking, while the Nevada side offers a glittering nightlife of restaurants and casinos.

SOUTH AMERICA

Iguaçu Falls, Brazil
The torrential waters of the Iguaçu River plunge more than 75 m (250 ft) over a huge, crescent-shaped cliff into the gorge below in a series of some 275 separate waterfalls. Surrounded by lush rainforest, the 4 km (2.5-mile) wide cascades can be viewed from platforms and paths on both sides of the Falls.

Lake Titicaca, Bolivia
High in the Altiplano the clear blue waters of Lake Titicaca bring an oasis of life and colour to the parched landscape. At 8,340 sq km (3,220 sq miles), it is the largest lake in South America, with many lakeside settlements. Boat trips can be made to the floating reed islands inhabited by the Uros, and to ancient Inca ruins on the sacred islands of the Sun and Moon.

Lake Llanquihue, Chile
A reflection of the perfect cone of Volcano Osorno can be seen in this immense lake which lies amid gently rolling pastureland. Towns on the shore include Frutillar Bajo, a popular summer resort with black-sand beaches, and Puerto Varas, a centre for 'adventure' activities such as rafting, riding, hiking and climbing.

EUROPE

Lake Siljan, Sweden
In a land of around 96,000 lakes, Siljan is noted as a centre of Swedish folk tradition

▼ Angel Falls, Venezuela
The world's highest waterfall with an uninterrupted drop of 2,650 ft (807 m), Angel Falls are 16 times the height of Niagara Falls. Although often shrouded in mist, the Falls are at their most spectacular during the rainy season (June–November) when the volume of water is greatest and when visitors can travel by motorized canoe along the river to Devil's Canyon at the foot of the Falls.

and art. Locals and visitors arrive in boats reminiscent of Viking longships during midsummer celebrations at the lakeside church of Rättvik, and traditional mystery plays are performed annually in the open-air theatre at Leksand. Visitors can watch traditional painted wooden horses being made at Nusnäs, and visit the studio of the painter Anders Zorn, who lived in the lakeside town of Mora.

Lake District, England
Famous as the haunt of the Romantic Poets, the Lake District is a beautiful and varied landscape of hills, mountains, lakes and rivers, encompassing a wide range of scenery within a relatively small area. The southern lakes – including Windermere, Coniston and Grasmere – are surrounded by gentle green slopes and attract enormous numbers of visitors in summer.

The wilder north, with its sheer, forbidding crags is more spectacular and much less crowded. Boating is popular on the larger lakes, and a network of paths makes the area a haven for walkers and climbers.

Lake Lucerne, Switzerland
The picturesque medieval town of Lucerne with its famous Kapellbrücke bridge makes an excellent base for exploring this beautiful lake and its mountain surroundings. Visitors can go on a lake cruise and stop off at some of the peaceful villages along the shore, or take the oldest mountain railway in Europe to Mount Rigi for wonderful views of the Alpine scenery.

Lake Garda, Italy
The largest of Italy's lakes, Lake Garda is certainly one of its most beautiful. Sheltered from the north-east by the Dolomites, its climate is particularly gentle, with orange and lemon groves flourishing on its banks. Dotted around the lake are many attractive and historic resort towns – some dating back to Roman times – and romantic hillside villas.

AFRICA

Lake Bosumtwi, Ghana
Sacred to the Asante people, the crater lake of Bosumtwi is the deepest natural lake in Ghana, and its waters are still rising. Its beautiful setting among thickly wooded crater walls makes it a relaxing place to go fishing, boating and swimming. Motorboat trips across the lake are available, and walks around the shore can include visits to lakeside villages.

Murchison Falls, Uganda
The sheer force of the Nile as it shoots through a narrow cleft in the rocks and crashes over a 30 m (100 ft) precipice is what makes Murchison Falls so spectacular. A journey up the river from Paraa Camp to the base of the falls is also an excellent way to see some of the wildlife of the Murchison Falls National Park, including crocodiles, elephants, hippos, giraffes, buffalo, waterbucks and many bird species.

Lake Baringo, Kenya
Encircled by mountains and rich in bird and animal life, Lake Baringo is a fascinating and beautiful place to visit. The shoreline is home to crocodiles and herds of hippos and the area is famous for its hundreds of bird species, attracting birdwatchers from all over the world. A resident ornithologist offers guided walks, and there are also horse rides, camel rides and boat trips to the lake's islands.

ASIA

Lake Toba, Sumatra
Encircled by steep crags – once the rim of an enormous ancient volcano – Lake Toba is the largest crater lake in the world. The area is home to the Toba Batak people, whose brightly painted houses with distinctive crescent-shaped roofs can be seen around the lake. The beautiful island of Samosir is a popular tourist destination

with excellent trekking and rafting as well as interesting megalithic tombs to visit.

Lake Batur, Bali
The largest lake in Bali, Lake Batur is a crater lake and is sacred to the Balinese as the home of the goddess Dewi Danu. The hot springs at Toya Bungkah are said to have healing properties, and the lakeside temple of Pura Jati presides over a holy bathing place. From Toyah Bungkah there are trekking routes up to the summit of Gunung Batur, the soaring 1,717 m (5,630 ft) high volcano which dominates the lake.

Lake Karakul, Tajikistan
At a height of 3,600 m (11,800 ft) in the foothills of the Pamir mountains, Lake Karakul's setting is remote and beautiful. Flanked by the massive Mount Kongur to the north and the magnificent Mount Muztaghata to the south, Karakul is the home of the Kirgiz people and their herds of sheep, goats, horses and camels. It takes a day to walk around the lake, after which walkers can stay overnight in a traditional felt-covered *yurt* at the visitors' camp.

Lake Chuzenji-ko and Kegon Waterfall, Japan
Visitors to Lake Chuzenji-ko and the dramatic Kegon Waterfall are well provided for with cable cars and platforms from which to gaze at the spectacular view, especially popular in autumn when the

leaves are changing colour. Beside the lake is a colourful shrine after which both the town and lake are named.

AUSTRALASIA

Lake Rotorua, New Zealand
Bubbling hot springs, vertical jets of steam and scalding geysers make Rotorua an exciting place to visit. There are lakeside bath houses where visitors can sample the waters, as well as cruises and facilities for a wide range of watersports on the lake and nearby rivers. Maoris have lived beside the lake for around 700 years, and there are many cultural attractions on offer, some more authentic than others.

▲ **Keli Mutu, Flores, Indonesia**
An extinct volcano, Keli Mutu has three extraordinary crater lakes. Not only is each lake a different colour, but the colours change over decades from vivid green through to deep red and intense turquoise as mineral layers dissolve.

◀ **Victoria Falls, Zimbabwe**
The 1.7 km (1-mile) wide Victoria Falls are made up of five separate waterfalls which plummet more than 100 m (320 ft) into the gorge below. The Falls are a popular base for adrenaline-boosting activities, such as bungee jumping, white-water rafting and riverboarding, and tours of every description can be taken from operators based in Victoria Falls town.

Wildlife in the Americas and Europe

From the bears and moose of the Alaskan wilderness, to the jaguars and toucans of the Central American forests, to the condors and rheas of Patagonia, the Americas have an amazing variety of wildlife. Europe by contrast is famed for its seabirds, and the vast flocks of migrant wildfowl that gather in its wetlands.

▶ **Torres del Paine National Park, Chile**
An awe-inspiring landscape of forests, glaciers, shimmering lakes, thundering cascades and soaring granite pillars, Torres del Paine National Park in Patagonia is a haven for wildlife, including guanacos, rheas, flamingos, condors and the shy huemul (Chilean deer). There is an excellent network of short- and long-distance trails through the park.

▼ **Wrangell-St Elias National Park, Alaska, USA**
Of all the Alaskan national parks, Wrangell-St Elias is the best for wildlife watching. This vast landscape of mountains and glaciers is home to moose, wolves, wolverines, bears, beavers and herds of caribou. There are several campsites but few other facilities for visitors in this true wilderness park.

NORTH AMERICA

Wood Buffalo National Park, Alberta/NW Territories, Canada
Canada's largest national park, Wood Buffalo is famous for its free-roaming buffalo herd. Among other inhabitants are lynx, bears and hundreds of bird species, including a river rookery of rare white pelicans and the few remaining whooping cranes in the world. Fort Smith has some accommodation, but canoeing along the rivers and camping are perhaps the best ways to explore this wilderness of forest, marsh and grassland.

Yellowstone National Park, Wyoming, USA
Famous for its many geothermal geysers and hot springs, Yellowstone Park is also home to one of the largest and most diverse populations of mammals in North America. Inhabitants include bison, moose, elks, Bighorn sheep, beavers and marmots as well as lynx, bobcats, wolves and coyotes. Millions of visitors flock to Yellowstone every year, but despite the inevitable tourist development, most of the park is still a true wilderness.

Everglades National Park, Florida, USA
The largest sub-tropical wilderness on the North American mainland, Everglades National Park is a vast area of swamps, mangrove forests and grasslands. It is the only place in the world where alligators and crocodiles live side by side, and there are still a few panthers and black bears. Canoe trails and boat tours are the best way to view the abundant wildlife, which includes a huge variety of bird species.

CENTRAL AMERICA

Braulio Carrillo National Park, Costa Rica
Many different habitats exist in Braulio Carrillo, a large area of rainforest covering a range of altitudes from just above sea level to 3,000 m (9,850 ft). Each has its own distinct flora and fauna, although the astonishingly lush vegetation can make spotting animals such as tapirs, sloths, ocelots, jaguars and pumas difficult. The park's abundant birdlife includes toucans, quetzels, umbrella birds, guans and eagles.

Corcovado National Park, Costa Rica
Set on the remote Osa peninsula, Corcovado National Park encompasses coastal mangrove swamps, pristine cloud forests and rocky canyons. Many of Costa Rica's endangered species live here, including tapirs, caymans and jaguars, while crocodiles swim in its waters and turtles lay their eggs on the park's deserted beaches. Ranger stations provide simple accommodation and advice.

Darién National Park, Panama
More than 500 bird species have been seen in the pristine rainforest of Darién National Park, among them many endangered species such as the harpy eagle. Indeed, Cerro Pirre mountain is considered by many birdwatchers to be one of the best sites in the world. Boat trips and forest walks are ideal ways to view the abundant wildlife, although visitors should seek advice on when it is safe to travel because of possible paramilitary activity.

Cockscomb Basin Wildlife Sanctuary, Belize
Beneath the peaks of the Cockscomb mountain range, the dense rainforest of the Cockscomb Basin is home to around 600 jaguars as well as tapirs, anteaters, armadillos and otters. Nearly 300 bird species have been reported in this lush jungle, and a wide variety of reptiles and amphibians are readily visible. Excellent forest trails make this a very rewarding place for wildlife watchers.

SOUTH AMERICA

Podocarpus National Park, Ecuador
Encompassing a wide range of habitats at different altitudes, Podocarpus (near Loja) has many rare plant and animal species, such as the Andean fox, the Andean speckled bear and the mountain tapir. Birdlife is abundant, and it is easy to see many fascinating species. This is, however, a park in peril, with the authorities struggling to protect the environment from poachers, loggers and others. For visitors prepared to rough it, there is much to enjoy in this landscape of lakes, mountains and rainforest.

Manu Biosphere Reserve, Peru
Altitudes range from 200 m (650 ft) to over 4,000 m (13,000 ft) in this area of rainforest near Cuzco. An astonishing 850 bird species are found here, and mammals include jaguars, ocelots, otters and many primate species. The reserve is divided into zones, with restricted visitor access in some areas. A stay in the Reserved Zone, which is set aside for ecotourism and research, must be arranged in advance, but offers the best jungle experience.

▲ **Monteverde Cloud Forest Reserve, Costa Rica**
Festooned with bromeliads and orchids, the towering rainforest trees of Monteverde Cloud Forest provide shelter for an enormous variety of wildlife including tapirs, monkeys, coatimundis and armadillos, as well as more than 400 bird species. The reserve was established in 1950 by a group of Quakers, who have developed a range of unobtrusive facilities for visitors, including simple accommodation and excellent guided walks.

Town/city with major airport

► Handa Island, Scotland

The sea cliffs of Handa Island are one of north-west Europe's largest seabird nesting sites, with the high cliff ledges attracting guillemots, razorbills and kittiwakes in enormous numbers. Fulmars, puffins and shags also nest here, while the island's moorland is home to great and Arctic skuas, red-throated divers, shelducks, ringed plovers, wheatears, meadow pipits and skylarks. The island can be visited for the day by boat from the mainland village of Tarbet, near Loch Laxford.

Pantanal, Brazil

A vast swamp covering an area the size of Great Britain, the Pantanal is perhaps the best place to see wildlife in the Americas. Animals wander freely around the wide open spaces, making it relatively easy for visitors to spot such creatures as alligators, jaguars and anacondas, and birds such as the giant red-necked stork. There are organized tours by boat or jeep and on horseback, with overnight accommodation at converted ranch houses.

Lihué Calel National Park, Argentina

An arid landscape of low, pink granite mountains and scrub forest, Lihué Calel (south-west of Santa Rosa) is home to several wild cat species and other mammals such as guanacos, Patagonian foxes, Patagonian hares and chinchillas. Birdlife is plentiful, too, and includes many species of birds of prey. The park has an excellent campsite and visitor centre.

EUROPE

Lemmenjoki National Park, Lappland, Finland

Lemmenjoki (near Inarijärvi) is one of the most extensive areas of uninhabited, forested wilderness in Europe (2,855 sq km/1,102 sq miles). Wide rivers flow through a landscape of peatland and spruce- and birch-forested hills, home to brown bears, golden eagles, foxes, lynx, wolverines and moose. There are also plenty of semi-domesticated reindeer.

Clear Island, Ireland

Ireland's southernmost inhabited island, tiny Clear Island is famous for its birds. It has breeding populations of chough, black guillemot and rock dove and is visited by many migrant species in August–October, including the rare bee-eater, little bittern, night and purple herons, and great reed warbler, as well as many seabirds. The Bird Observatory has a full-time bird-warden and offers simple accommodation.

Cley Marshes, Norfolk, England

One of Britain's leading birdwatching reserves, Cley Marshes (near Sheringham) has many thatched hides offering excellent views of thousands of water birds. Migrating waders stop in the area on their way to and from their Arctic breeding grounds, and in summer bitterns and avocets breed here. Wildfowl such as teals, widgeons and shovelers are plentiful in winter.

Waddenzee, The Netherlands

Regarded by birdwatchers as the most important intertidal area in Europe, Waddenzee has huge populations of waders and wildfowl. One of the best areas to see the birds is around Schiermonnikoog, particularly at high tide. Among the birds present in summer are avocets, godwits and ruffs, while in winter they include Bewick's swans, barnacle geese, marsh and hen harriers and white-tailed eagles.

Kisbalaton Reserve, Lake Balaton, Hungary

With its reed beds, the Kisbalaton Reserve provides the perfect environment for marsh birds to breed. Night, purple and squacco herons are all to be found here along with little and great white egrets, spoonbills, marsh harriers and several warblers. From October huge flocks of migrating ducks and geese stop in the reserve on their journey south.

Danube Delta, Romania

One of Europe's last unspoiled ecosystems, consisting of forest, lakes, reed beds and marshland, the Danube Delta is home to huge numbers of birds. Due to the lack of tourist facilities, it is probably best-visited in an organized group, ideally from late May–June. Species include bitterns, pygmy cormorants, white pelicans, night, purple and squacco herons, spoonbills, ruddy shelducks, honey buzzards, bee-eaters and white-tailed eagles.

Doñana National Park, Spain

Huge sand dunes and the seasonally flooded plains (*marismas*) behind them provide ideal conditions for a great variety of birdlife in one of Europe's most important wildlife habitats. Peregrines, stone-curlews and short-toed eagles are to be seen in the dunes, while the marismas are feeding grounds for white storks, spoonbills, night and purple herons and colonies of little and cattle egrets.

Galápagos Islands and ecotourism

Lying 960 km (600 miles) off the coast of Ecuador, the fragile wilderness of the Galápagos Islands provides a habitat for a surprising combination of penguins and corals as well as giant tortoises, land and marine iguanas, sperm whales, sea lions, fur seals, orca whales, sharks and a variety of tropical fish. Many of the species living here are found nowhere else in the world, making the Galápagos a vital laboratory for the study of animal and plant life. Access to the islands is strictly controlled and limited to 50 designated visitor sites. The development of ecotourism in the Galápagos Islands aims to ensure the preservation of the habitats and wildlife while enabling tourists to visit and learn about this unique environment.

Wildlife in Africa, Asia and Australasia

An African safari is one of the world's great wildlife-watching experiences. Vast stretches of open savanna are home to the 'big five' – lion, leopard, elephant, rhinoceros and buffalo – as well as herds of zebra and gazelle. The endangered Indian tiger and exotic komodo dragon are just two of the animals that attract visitors to Asia, while Australia has its own unique fauna, including kangaroo, koala and duck-billed platypus.

AFRICA

Abuko Nature Reserve, Gambia
In this small reserve, mangroves, gallery forest and savanna combine to attract over 270 bird species – including the world's largest and smallest kingfishers – making it one of the best birdwatching sites in West Africa. Abuko is also known for its troops of colobus, patas and vervet monkeys.

Niokolo-Koba National Park, Senegal
Some 80 mammal species, including lions, leopards, elephants, waterbucks, bushbucks, baboons and chimpanzees live in Niokolo-Koba, along with around 350 bird species. The best time to see the animals is when they gather at waterholes during the hot season in April and May.

Tsavo (East and West), Kenya
Tsavo East and Tsavo West combine to make one of the world's biggest national parks, covering an area of 21,000 sq km (8,000 sq miles). As well as the 'big five', the animals include cheetahs, giraffes, zebras, crocodiles, hippos, porcupines and mongooses. Tsavo East is a popular safari destination while at Tsavo West the excellent facilities include underwater hides for hippo watching.

Ngorongoro Crater, Tanzania
Protected within a circle of thickly-forested crater walls, Ngorongoro Crater is an expanse of grassland and forest measuring 14 km (9 miles) across and teeming with wildlife. Elephants, leopards, hyenas, bushbucks, buffalo, wildebeest, elands, warthogs, gazelles and ostriches live alongside the rare black rhinoceros and the handsome black-maned lion, while Lake Makat is home to flocks of flamingos and other water birds.

Jozani Reserve, Zanzibar, Tanzania
The largest remaining area of indigenous forest on Zanzibar, Jozani Reserve is home to a variety of birds and butterflies, as well as a number of rare mammals, including the red colobus monkey, which can only be found here.

Bwindi National Park, Uganda
Half of all the world's endangered mountain gorillas live in Bwindi National Park, an area of hilly rainforest. The park supports a rich variety of animal life including chimpanzees, golden cats, civets, leopards, bushpigs and giant forest hogs. Small groups of visitors who have booked several months in advance can go on guided gorilla-tracking expeditions.

Chobe National Park, Botswana
Encompassing habitats that range from marshland to forest, Chobe is home to a great variety of wildlife, including the rare puku and red lechwe antelope. Other inhabitants include lions, cheetahs, buffalo, giraffes, elephants, zebras, jackals, warthogs, hippos, crocodiles, hyenas, antelopes and wildebeest, as well as an abundance of birdlife. The animals can be viewed from boats on the Chobe River.

Kruger National Park, South Africa
A vast game reserve covering almost 20,000 sq km (7,400 sq miles), Kruger Park is home to around 137 mammal species, including lions, elephants, rhinoceros, leopards, buffalo, zebras, giraffes, impalas, wildebeest, hippos and crocodiles, as well as the rare roan and sable antelopes and oribi. The northern part is especially noted for its birdlife, including the highest density of birds of prey anywhere in the world.

Bird Island, Seychelles
Huge colonies of seabirds nest on the tiny, coral Bird Island. The sooty tern, fairy tern and common noddy are everywhere, while passing migrants add to the interest for birdwatchers. The island is also home to large numbers of giant turtles.

▲ Etosha National Park, Namibia
One of the most important wildlife reserves in Africa, Etosha covers a vast 20,000 sq km (7,720 sq miles) of woodland and grassland surrounding the Etosha Pan – an immense saline desert. Animals living here include springboks, impalas, kudu, wildebeest, hartebeest, roan antelopes, elands, zebras, elephants and the rare white rhinoceros, as well as predators such as lions, leopards, cheetahs, caracals, jackals and hyenas. There are around 340 bird species, including eagles, ostriches and secretary birds. Accommodation to suit all budgets is available.

◄ Masai Mara National Reserve, Kenya
Kenya's greatest concentration of wildlife can be seen in Masai Mara, where cheetahs, hyenas, zebras, hartebeest, hippos and crocodiles share the territory with the 'big five'. During the summer enormous herds of wildebeest, zebras and gazelles arrive from the Serengeti on the first stage of their dramatic annual migration.

▼ Serengeti National Park, Tanzania
Covering 14,763 sq km (5,700 sq miles) and including woodland and mountains, as well as huge tracts of open grassland, the Serengeti is home to the 'big five' plus cheetahs, hyenas, zebras, giraffes, gazelles and many others. It also has around 500 bird species. It is most famous for the spectacular summer migration of gazelles, wildebeest and zebras, when around 2 million animals set off on a 800 km (500-mile) trek to fresh feeding grounds.

ASIA

Kaziranga National Park, Assam, India

Famous as the home of the rare one-horned Great Indian Rhinoceros – most of the surviving 1,500 are here – Kaziranga (east of Guwahati) also has tigers, bears, elephants, bison and many bird species. A good way to travel around the tall-grass and swampy terrain is on an elephant. The park is only open from November to April.

Keoladeo Ghana National Park, Rajasthan, India

Formerly known as the Bharatpur Bird Sanctuary, Keoladeo is famous for its breeding populations of native water birds as well as its thousands of migrating birds which arrive every year from China and Siberia, including herons, storks, snake birds and the rare Siberian crane. The best time to visit is from October to February, when the migratory birds are in residence.

Sundarbans Wildlife Sanctuary, India/Bangladesh

Home to one of the largest remaining tiger populations in India, the Sundarbans Wildlife Sanctuary covers 6,695 sq km (2,585 sq miles) of mangrove swamp in the vast Ganges delta. Tigers are not often spotted by visitors, but a boat excursion through the peaceful mangroves will reveal many other animals – monkeys, wild pigs, spotted deer, crocodiles and fishing cats, as well as a profusion of birdlife.

Kanha National Park, Madhya Pradesh, India

Kipling set his *Jungle Book* in this beautiful landscape of forests, rivers and grasslands (near Mandla). Kanha is the only home of the barasingha (swamp deer) and it also plays an important role in the preservation of the tiger, leopard, chital, sambar and gaur (Indian bison). The park is open November–May, with sightings increasing from March onwards as the hot weather brings out the animals in search of water. Excursions are available.

Khao Yai National Park, Thailand

Encompassing a variety of habitats, from mountains clad in evergreen forest to lowland scrub and grassland, Khao Yai (north-east of Bangkok) has an abundance of wildlife, including elephants, gibbons, porcupines, tigers, leopards, Indian munjaks, Malaysian sun bears and several species of deer and monkey. There are over 250 bird species here, too, including the great hornbill and many colourful parrots and parakeets. Visitors can venture deep into the forest on several excellent trails, some of which require guides.

Taman Negara, Malaysia

Covering 4,340 sq km (1,676 sq miles) of ancient tropical rainforest, Taman Negara is a haven for hundreds of species of birds and animals, while its vegetation includes some of the world's rarest orchids. Inhabitants include tapirs, bears, elephants and gibbons. The park, which is the most visited in Pahang, has an elevated canopy walkway, and jungle hides in the trees, where visitors can spend the night.

Komodo National Park, Indonesia

The world's largest lizard, the astonishing 3 m (10 ft) long Komodo dragon, is found only on Komodo and a few neighbouring small islands. Guided treks usually include visits to dragon feeding places, and allow visitors to see some of the other wildlife of the park, such as wild pigs, deer, monkeys, water buffalo and eagles.

Ujung Kulon National Park, Indonesia

The last remaining low-relief forest on Java, in the far west, Ujung Kulon National Park is the only home of the one-horned Javan rhinoceros. Other inhabitants include the Javan gibbon, Javan tiger, muntjac (barking deer), chevrotain (mouse deer), green sea turtle and crocodile.

AUSTRALASIA

Eungella National Park, Queensland, Australia

With its tall, ancient rainforest trees, rocky creeks and spectacular waterfalls, Eungella is an extraordinarily beautiful place to watch wildlife. Among its inhabitants are kangaroos, possums, feathertail gliders, pythons and the native Eungella honey-eater, but the star attraction is the shy duck-billed platypus, which can be seen around the riverbanks at dawn and dusk.

Otago Peninsula, New Zealand

A remarkable variety of wildlife is concentrated on the Otago Peninsula. Seals and other marine life can be seen along the rocky coastline, while the inlets and beaches shelter numerous waders and waterfowl. A protected albatross nesting-site at Taiaroa Head is open to the public once the eggs are laid, and yellow-eyed penguins can be seen at close quarters from an excellent conservation reserve.

Catlins Forest Park, New Zealand

Ancient rainforest runs down to the rocky inlets and estuaries of the coast, offering a variety of habitats for some of New Zealand's rarest plants and animals. There are colonies of Hooker's sea lion and yellow-eyed penguin, and much birdlife. Two- and four-day ecotours are available.

◄ Royal Chitwan National Park, Nepal
With its lush sub-tropical jungle and floodplain swamp, Chitwan National Park is a natural habitat for animals such as the tiger, Indian rhinoceros and leopard. Tours on foot, by jeep or on the back of an elephant are best undertaken between October and March.

▼ Kakadu National Park, Northern Territory, Australia
Australia's largest national park, Kakadu encompasses a spectacular collection of rainforest, ravines and wetlands along the South Alligator River. These varied habitats shelter a vast array of wildlife, including 1,500 species of butterflies and moths, 75 reptile species, including crocodiles, 25 species of frog and one third of all Australia's bird species. Mammals include kangaroos, wallabies, walleroos, dingoes and many species of bat.

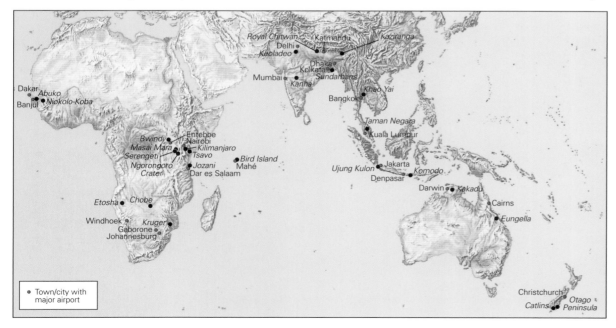

Town/city with major airport

Marine wildlife

With whale numbers recovering strongly following the world ban on hunting, many seaports in North America, South Africa and Australasia offer boat trips to watch whales and other large fish and mammals. In the warm waters of the tropics, coral reefs teeming with vividly coloured sealife can be explored by scuba divers and snorkellers or viewed from the comfort of a glass-bottomed boat.

◄ **Florida Keys, USA**
Among many places in the Caribbean that serve as a base for viewing or swimming with dolphins is Florida Keys. Consisting of 45 islands surrounded by spectacular corals, Florida Keys also provides a perfect environment for scuba diving.

THE AMERICAS

Johnstone Strait, Canada
The sea between Vancouver Island and the mainland is one of the best places in the world to see orcas (killer whales), the largest and most powerful predators on earth, and minke whales.

Hudson Bay, Canada
Beluga whales can be seen in June, July and August in the bay's Arctic waters. Particularly large numbers spend these months in the Churchill River estuary, an area famous for its polar bears.

Cape Breton and Grand Manan Islands, Canada
Whale-watching boat trips take place around both islands. Off Grand Manan, in the Bay of Fundy, up to 20 whale species, including the rare northern right whale and the finback, can be seen.

Massachusetts Bay, USA
Stellwagen Bank in Massachusetts Bay is a feeding ground for humpback, finback and minke whales from April to October. It is a world-renowned whale-watching area, attracting around 1.5 million whale watchers a year. The coastal towns of New England offer a range of boat trips.

Caribbean Sea, Cayman Islands
The islands are famous among scuba divers for their exceptionally clear waters and deep diving with spectacular sponge colonies and a wide range of reef fish. Those interested in larger species can see dolphins, barracudas and sharks – including silky sharks – here.

Caribbean Sea, Belize
The barrier reef of Belize is the largest in the western hemisphere, and second only to Australia's in the world. Between the reef and the mainland lie more than 175 cays and atolls (coral islands and rings) offering some of the best diving opportunities in the world. The extraordinary Blue Hole at the centre of Lighthouse Reef is a circular shaft over 120 m (395 ft) deep which was once a cavern underneath the sea bed. Half Moon Caye offers one of Belize's most spectacular wall dives, with an almost sheer drop overhung with wonderful coral spurs, rich in marine life.

Caribbean Sea, Venezuela
There is good diving to be had around the offshore islands of Venezuela, especially in the archipelago of Los Roques with its white sand beaches and beautiful coral reefs. The Parque Nacional Morrocoy on the north-west coast of Venezuela is very popular for snorkelling.

Paracas National Park, Peru
A boat trip around the offshore islands within this national park provides an opportunity to see dolphins, seals and sea lions, as well as pelicans and the great Andean condors that inhabit the cliffs.

AFRICA AND THE INDIAN OCEAN

Canary Islands
The waters around the islands provide sheltered feeding grounds for pilot whales, not usually seen so close to shore, and there are many boat trips available from Tenerife. Unfortunately, whale watching is not properly regulated here and whales have been injured by the boats.

Red Sea, Egypt
Hurghada is a good base for snorkelling and diving around the coral reefs of the Red Sea. Jolanda Reef, at the tip of the Sinai Peninsula in the Ras Muhammad National Park, is a spectacular column of coral 800 m (2,625 ft) high. The park is best approached from the Sharm el Sheikh resort.

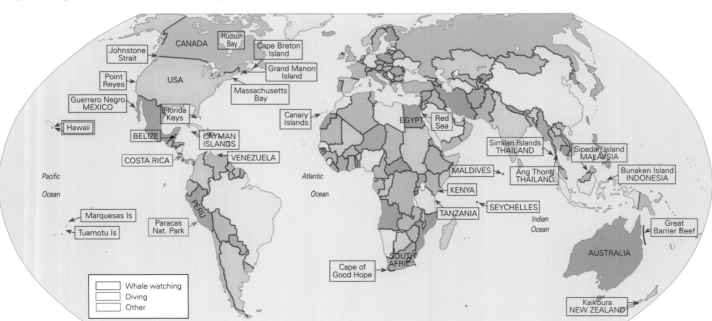

▲ **Point Reyes, California, USA**
Grey whales can be seen from Point Reyes, north of San Francisco, between October and January as they migrate down the coast of Canada and the USA to the Gulf of California. Between December and March they can be found at Guerrero Negro in Mexico, where they gather to calve.

Legend:
◆ Popular diving spot
✈ Airport

(Map showing Great Barrier Reef region with locations: Lizard Island, Cooktown, Cairns, Michaelmas Reef, Dunk Island, Townsville, Hook Reef, Proserpine, Whitsunday Group, Mackay, Swain Reefs, Gt Keppel Island, Rockhampton, Heron Island)

Pemba, Zanzibar and Mafia, Tanzania

The three main islands off the Tanzanian coast are surrounded by spectacular coral reefs which are home to a wide variety of marine species including bat fish, lion fish, turtles and rays. They offer some of the best diving opportunities in the world from August to December. Mafia Island is also a favourite breeding ground for giant turtles.

Cape of Good Hope, South Africa

In a country which has the strictest whale protection laws in the world, most whale watching takes place from the shore. The 'Whale Route' is a spectacularly scenic road along the coast from Cape Town, around the Cape of Good Hope, to the Indian Ocean, with many official whale-viewing sites. The town of Hermanus (the self-proclaimed 'whale capital' of South Africa) makes a good base. From June to October southern right whales, once hunted to near-extinction, can be seen swimming in these waters.

Seychelles

The outlying islands in particular offer world-class diving. The reef-ringed shores are a paradise for snorkellers, with over 150 species of tropical reef fish and 30 species of coral. Dolphins, porpoises, sharks and barracudas can also be seen. There are four marine national parks and diving schools with good facilities.

Maldives

Without doubt the Maldives are the best place in the Indian Ocean for diving. There are hundreds of diving sites, with something for everyone from beginners to experts. The more adventurous can explore shipwrecks as well as spectacular caves and terraces of coral. There is also plenty of scope for snorkellers.

► Tortuguero Park, Costa Rica

In the company of a guide, limited numbers of visitors can watch green turtles at their largest nesting site in the western hemisphere. The turtles lay their eggs on the beach between July and October, the peak time being late August.

Australia's Great Barrier Reef

The Great Barrier Reef is the largest structure on earth made by living organisms. It is a chain of coral reefs 2,000 km (1,200 miles) long, encompassing more than 600 islands and cays. About 20 of these islands have resort facilities, with Heron Island and Lizard Island both especially popular with divers. There are around 2,000 species of fish living on the reef and the area is home to many marine mammals, including the rare dugong and several species of whale. The best time to visit the reef is between April and December. Cairns is the mainland base for most reef activities and offers all kinds of tours.

ASIA

Ang Thong National Marine Park, Thailand

Boat trips around 42 limestone islands, many eroded into fantastic shapes, provide opportunities for seeing a variety of wildlife – including dolphins, turtles and sea otters – and for snorkelling and diving.

Similan Islands, Thailand

The gently sloping coral reefs and deep gorges around the Similan Islands feature a huge variety of marine life, including turtles, manta rays and whale sharks.

Sipadan Island, Sabah, Malaysia

An amazing undersea 'wall', teeming with marine life that includes whale sharks, manta rays, turtles and tuna, makes Sipadan one of the world's great diving destinations. The island is the tip of an underwater mountain, making it possible to dive from the beach.

Bunaken Island, Sulawesi, Indonesia

Perhaps the most famous marine destination in Indonesia, Bunaken Island near Manado serves as the main base for exploring the stunning coral reefs known as the 'sea gardens of Sulawesi'.

AUSTRALASIA AND THE PACIFIC

Kaikoura, New Zealand

A world-famous whale-watching centre, Kaikoura caters for 30,000 whale watchers

a year. The deepwater canyons near the shore are home to sperm whales.

Hawaii, USA

The extraordinary song of the humpback whale can be heard in the waters around Hawaii from November to May, after which these rare animals return to their summer feeding grounds in the near-polar waters of the north Pacific. Whale watching is strictly regulated, but there are plenty of boat trips on offer. Hawaii also has coral reefs, though with fewer species than on other Indo-Pacific reefs. Diving is popular, with lessons being provided in the crater lake of the extinct Molokini volcano. Excursions in submarines down to a depth of 50 m (160 ft) offer superb views of the underwater world through portholes.

Rangiroa, Tuamotu Islands

Among many excellent diving sites in French Polynesia, this is possibly the best, with outstanding coral, sharks, dolphins, barracudas and rays.

Marquesas Islands

The oxygen-rich water around the islands, which is thick with plankton, supports a variety of marine creatures, including hammerhead and white-tipped sharks, leopard and manta rays, tuna and barracudas. There are around 20 dive sites, including some impressive caves.

▲ Malindi and Wasini Island, Kenya

One of a number of good diving and snorkelling spots in Kenya, Malindi also offers excursions in glass-bottomed boats to the nearby coral reef. The Kisite Marine National Park on Wasini Island, in the far south, provides spectacular diving safaris.

Great railway journeys

From the luxury of the Orient-Express to the spartan rigours of the Trans-Siberian Railway, the world's great train journeys exert an irresistible lure for many travellers, passing through spectacular landscapes. Journeys vary in length from a few hours to a fortnight, and the more sought-after trains must be booked well in advance.

NORTH AMERICA

Green Mountain Flyer, Vermont, USA
Distance: 21 km (13 miles)
A vintage train takes passengers through the beautiful Vermont countryside, running alongside the Connecticut River for part of the way. Largely a tourist service, the peak period is during October when the autumn colours are at their best.

Coast Starlight, USA
Distance: 2,235 km (1,389 miles)
A journey from Seattle to Los Angeles, through the magnificent landscapes of the west coast of the USA, includes amongst its highlights the mountains of the Oregon Cascades and the Californian Coast Range. South of Oakland the track runs along the edge of the Pacific Ocean, passing several of California's most popular beaches.

Los Mochis to Chihuahua, Mexico
Distance: 655 km (407 miles)
This 14-hour journey is one of contrasting landscapes, from the tropical Pacific coastlands to the high northern plateau by way of the magnificent Copper Canyon (Barranca del Cobre). Longer and deeper than Arizona's Grand Canyon, this is an area of steeply wooded gorges and spectacular mountain peaks.

SOUTH AMERICA

Guayaquil to Quito, Ecuador
Distance: 463 km (288 miles)
For those who relish danger as well as breathtaking scenery, this line – which has been called 'the world's greatest roller-

► Palace on Wheels
India's most luxurious train, originally hauled by the *Desert Queen*, takes passengers on an eight-day tour that begins and ends in Delhi. It includes Jaipur and the other major cities of Rajasthan, and Agra.

coaster' – is a must. It climbs high into the Andes, zigzagging perilously to an altitude of 3,609 m (11,840 ft) and passing directly under a waterfall. Trains are erratic and often break down.

Central Railway, Peru
Distance: 335 km (208 miles)
The highest railway in the world, this takes passengers on an eight- to nine-hour journey across the Andes, from Lima to Huancayo. Dizzy heights, sheer drops, zigzags, loops and tunnels abound.

EUROPE

Flåm Railway, Norway
Distance: 20 km (12 miles)
Dropping 865 m (2,838 ft) in just 20 km (12 miles), this is one of the steepest non-rack railways in the world. Beginning with a view over the Kjosfossen lake and waterfall, the train weaves its way from Myrdal towards Aurlands Fjord and Flåm through a series of tunnels, with spectacular views between tunnels and snow shelters.

◄ Glacier Express, Switzerland
Distance: 290 km (180 miles)
An exhilarating seven-and-a-half hour journey in the Swiss Alps, between the ski resorts of St Moritz and Zermatt, is provided by this train. Extraordinary feats of engineering are displayed as it weaves its way through the mountains, travelling through 91 tunnels, crossing 291 bridges and negotiating hairpin bends and steep ascents.

West Highland Line, Scotland
Distance: 264 km (164 miles)
Running between Glasgow and Mallaig, this line provides one of the most spectacular railway journeys in Britain. The route is particularly dramatic between Fort William and Mallaig, with a series of viaducts and tunnels through the mountains high above the Atlantic coast.

Venice Simplon-Orient-Express, Europe
Distance: 1,714 km (1,065 miles)
Passengers travel in style on a train that re-creates the romance of the golden age of rail as it crosses Europe from London to Venice, via Paris, Zürich, Innsbruck and Verona, in 32 hours. Orient-Express trains also run to Rome and Istanbul on a variety of routes that go through Venice, Florence, Lucerne, Budapest and Bucharest.

Andalusian Express, Spain
Distance: 740 km (460 miles)
The luxurious *Al Andalus* follows a circular route from Seville through the beautiful Andalusian countryside, with its citrus and olive groves, vineyards and hilltop villages. There are opportunties to stop off and see the sites at Córdoba, Granada, Antequera and Ronda.

▲ Canadian, Canada
Distance: 2,776 miles (4,4467 km)
On a 69-hour journey that begins in Toronto, this train passes through some of the most beautiful scenery on earth. The prairie lands of Manitoba and Saskatchewan give way to the cattle ranches of Alberta, from where the train climbs into the Rockies. Here it passes lakes, glaciers and the dramatic Fraser Canyon before reaching Vancouver.

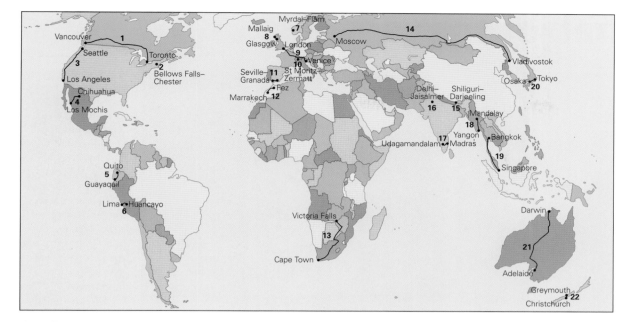

Map legend:
1 Canadian, Canada
2 Green Mountain Flyer, USA
3 Coast Starlight, USA
4 Los Mochis to Chihuahua, Mexico
5 Guayaquil to Quito, Ecuador
6 Central railway, Peru
7 Flåm Railway, Norway
8 West Highland Line, Scotland
9 Venice Simplon-Orient-Express, Europe
10 Glacier Express, Switzerland
11 Andalusian Express, Spain
12 Marrakech Express, Morocco
13 Pride of Africa, Southern Africa
14 Trans-Siberian Railway, Russia
15 Darjeeling Himalayan Railway, India
16 Palace on Wheels, India
17 Madras to Udagamandalam, India
18 Mandalay Express, Burma (Myanmar)
19 Eastern and Oriental Express, Thailand and Malaysia
20 Tokyo to Osaka, Japan
21 The Ghan, Australia
22 TranzAlpine Express, New Zealand

AFRICA

Marrakech Express, Morocco
Distance: 583 km (362 miles)
Passing through Morocco's four imperial cities, this nine-hour journey begins in Marrakech, near the foot of the High Atlas Mountains, and travels north through the desert to Casablanca. From here the line follows the Atlantic coast to Rabat then gradually heads back inland through orchards and olive groves to Meknès and on to Fès.

Pride of Africa, Southern Africa
Distance: 3,2000 km (2,000 miles)
The journey from Cape Town in this luxurious train is full of romance and drama. In the early stages the train travels through a landscape of vineyards and farmland and across the Karoo Desert to Pretoria. Passengers can enjoy watching wildlife as the journey continues through the African bush across Botswana and Zimbabwe to the spectacular Victoria Falls on the Zambian border.

ASIA

Madras to Udagamandalam, India
Distance: 640 km (400 miles)
This 16-hour journey takes travellers from the plains of Madras through a colourful rural landscape and up into the beautiful Nilgiri hills to the famous hill station of Udagamandalam, formerly known as Ootacamund, or Ooty. The train passes through some of the most dramatic scenery India has to offer, climbing steeply on India's only rack railway to the gentler landscapes of the Deccan Plateau.

Darjeeling Himalayan Railway, India
Distance: 88 km (55 miles)
The tiny engine used on this railway, which is a UNESCO heritage site, takes passengers from Shiliguri on the hot Bengal plains to the mountain climate of Darjeeling in the Himalayas. The journey involves steep ascents and precipitous curves, climbing 2,164 m (7,100 ft). On the way the train passes through Ghoom, which is the second highest station in the world at 2,258 m (7,408 ft) above sea level.

Mandalay Express, Burma (Myanmar)
Distance: 616 km (385 miles)
By no means a tourist train, the Express offers the traveller a truly local experience as it makes its way slowly north from Yangon (formerly Rangoon) through a landscape of rice fields and golden-spired pagodas. The crowded train makes numerous – often unscheduled – stops along the way, making it an unpredictable and colourful journey. Best undertaken between November and February, the journey takes around 16 hours.

Eastern and Oriental Express, Thailand and Malaysia
Distance: 1,943 km (1,207 miles)
Starting in Bangkok, this train takes 52 hours to travel south through the terraced farmlands of Thailand and the rubber plantations and jungles of Malaysia to Singapore. It represents the height of luxury in train travel, while International Express trains that follow the same route provide a more down-to-earth experience.

AUSTRALASIA

The Ghan, Australia
Distance: 2,962 km (1,851 miles)
Named after the Afghan camel-drivers who once transported provisions along its route, the Ghan passenger train made its first journey from Adelaide to Darwin in February 2004. In 47 hours the train passes through vine-covered hills to the craggy mountains of the MacDonnell Ranges, the multi-coloured desert of central Australia and the woodland of the north, much to the delight of train enthusiasts who long campaigned for the line north of Alice Springs to be completed.

◄ Tokyo to Osaka, Japan
Distance: 518 km (322 miles)
The Nozomi Express – the fastest scheduled train service in the world – travels at speeds of up to 300 km/h (186 mph) along this line. Not quite as fast, the Hikari Express completes the journey in just over three hours. However, the scenery, which includes Mount Fuji, can best be appreciated from the slower 'bullet' trains.

TranzAlpine Express, New Zealand
Distance: 233 km (154 miles)
Travelling from Christchurch on the South Island's east coast to Greymouth on the west coast, the Express takes passengers on a four-and-a-half hour journey through a variety of landscapes. After crossing the farmlands of the Canterbury Plains it follows the Waimakariri River gorge into the mountainous Arthur's Pass National Park, where it enters the long Otira tunnel. From here the line descends through lush rainforest, passing lakes Poerua and Brunner, to Greymouth.

Trans-Siberian Railway, Russia
Distance: 9,297 km (5,776 miles)
The southern shore of Lake Baikal is on the route of the Trans-Siberian Railway, the world's longest, and possibly most famous, railway. The eight-day journey takes passengers from Moscow to Vladivostok via the Urals, the forested wilderness of Siberia, and the Transbaikalian Mountains.

In the early days of the railway, built between 1891 and 1916, a ferry was used in summer to carry the train across Lake Baikal, while in winter, when the lake froze, temporary rails were laid over the ice. The Siberian landscape is particularly beautiful in winter when it is covered with snow. In the spring there are carpets of wild flowers while in autumn there are the golden colours of the birch forests.

River and canal journeys

The world's great boat journeys give travellers a unique perspective on the countries through which they pass: rivers and canals were the highways of the past, and there are often opportunities to visit historic sites or natural habitats. Whether you are steaming down the Mississippi in a paddleboat, gliding through the French countryside past castles and vineyards or exploring the tributaries of the Amazon, the pace of the journey gives ample time to enjoy the beauty of the surroundings.

NORTH AMERICA

St Lawrence, Canada

From Kingston, where Lake Ontario flows into the majestic St Lawrence River, a six-night journey can be made on a replica steamboat to Montréal (see *World Cities*) and Québec (see *Historic sites in the Americas*). Just east of Kingston the river is dotted with literally a Thousand Islands, many of which have summer houses and opulent mansions set amid forests of yellow birch, silver maple and red and white trillium. In the spring the trillium trees are covered by white blossom.

Upper Mississippi, USA

In the summer months, seven-day cruises by paddleboat run between Minneapolis/St Paul and St Louis. There are also three-day cruises between St Louis and Memphis. The upper river, flowing through relatively flat countryside, is wide, slow moving and dotted with islands, but the stretch immediately below St Louis flows between rocky bluffs. Days spent cruising are alternated with sightseeing tours of such places as the boyhood home of Mark Twain, in Hannibal, Memphis, and a historic Native American site in Burlington, Iowa.

▶ **St Petersburg to Moscow, Russia**
This seven-day cruise passes through a network of rivers, lakes and canals in the richly wooded region of Southern Karelia, and down the upper reaches of the Volga River. Ports of call include the ancient town of Yaroslavl, the attractive Karelian capital of Petrozavodsk, and the Church of the Transfiguration on the island of Kizhi in Lake Onega, with its 22 wooden domes, constructed without a single nail.

CENTRAL AND SOUTH AMERICA

Amazon, Peru and Brazil

Cruises of between three and ten days along the Amazon River, starting from the remote but elegant Peruvian town of Iquitos, or from the brash and bustling Manaus in Brazil, are a relatively comfortable way to see the abundant wildlife of the rainforest. Many companies adopt an educational approach and include lectures on the local flora and fauna. Some include an opportunity to explore smaller tributaries by canoe. For the adventurous independent traveller who is prepared to rough it, a six-day journey by local riverboat from the Atlantic port of Belém to Manaus offers an unforgettable experience of local life and culture.

Orinoco Delta, Venezuela

The vast Orinoco Delta – a maze of channels running between countless forested islands – is one of Venezuela's wildest regions. The area is home to the indigenous Warao people, known for their skilled carving and basketwork, whose houses on stilts can be seen on the

riverbanks. Boat tours into the delta can be arranged from the town of Tucupita, and usually last for between two and four days.

EUROPE

Shropshire Union Canal, UK

From Autherley, a 100 km (60-mile) journey can be taken on a slow-moving barge along the Shropshire Union Canal. Deep wooded cuttings, peaceful rural landscapes, medieval market towns and quiet villages are all passed at little more than walking pace. The ancient city of Chester, with its Roman ruins and medieval city walls, is a highlight of the journey. The canal ends at Ellesmere Port on the River Mersey, where there is an excellent boating museum.

Rhine, Switzerland, Germany and the Netherlands

A ten-day journey down the Rhine from Basel to Arnhem combines stunning scenery with a chance to visit the historic towns and cities along its banks. After flowing through the German Black Forest, the river passes romantic clifftop castles, sloping vineyards and picturesque villages on its way to the cities of the north: Bonn, Cologne and Düsseldorf. A detour up the River Neckar to the historic town of Heidelberg is often included.

◀ **Lower Mississippi, USA**
A seven-day cruise by paddleboat can be taken from Memphis to New Orleans. The Mississippi twists and turns on its way to the marshlands bordering the coast. There are opportunities to visit some of the historic sites of the Deep South, including the Civil War battlefields of Vicksburg, and the elegant mansion at Oak Alley Plantation, and to sample some of the local Creole and Cajun cuisine.

▲ **The Burgundy Canal, France**
Passing through a landscape of wooded valleys and sleepy villages, the six-day journey on a barge from Tonnere to Dijon along the Burgundy Canal provides an opportunity to see the beautiful 16th-century chateaux of Tanlay and Ancy le Franc and the 12th-century Cistercian Abbey of Fontenay. The region is famous for its *grand cru* vineyards and its robust cuisine, and there are plenty of opportunities to enjoy both along the way.

Douro, Portugal

Most cruises on the Douro are round trips of seven to nine days, beginning and ending in Porto. Once the boat leaves the coastal plain, it passes between spectacularly terraced vineyards, in an area unspoilt by major roads. Ports of call include the picturesque towns of Lamego and Vila Real. The region is the centre of Portugal's port wine production, and all cruises include a visit to a vineyard to sample the local produce.

Danube, Hungary, Slovak Republic, Austria and Germany

A Danube cruise of around eight days combines sightseeing tours of some of Central Europe's most historic towns and cities with an opportunity to relax on board, watching rich farmland and terraced slopes slip past. A cruise up-river from Budapest to Regensburg includes frequent stops, enabling passengers to explore Bratislava, Vienna, Linz and Passau, and to visit the sumptuous Baroque palace of Schönbrunn and the Benedictine Abbey in Melk. Since the boat berths overnight, passengers can also enjoy some nightlife ashore, and attend specially organized classical concerts.

AFRICA

River Gambia National Park, Gambia

A day trip on the river from Janjanbureh (Georgetown) or Kuntaur provides an opportunity to view crocodiles and hippos at close range. As the rice fields and coconut trees on the banks give way to dense forest, it may also be possible to glimpse monkeys, baboons and many species of birds.

Niger, Mali

A journey along the River Niger as it curves through the semi-desert of the Sahel is the classic way to see and experience the life of this area. Local passenger boats are scheduled to take seven days, but can take as long as 14 to travel between Gao and Koulikoro. The most popular section is the two days or so between Mopti and Korioumé, the stopping point for visits to the ancient desert city of Timbuktu. Also highly recommended is a detour up the River Bani to the beautiful old town of Djenné, where the mosque is a stunning example of construction using mud bricks and render.

ASIA AND AUSTRALASIA

Backwaters of Kerala, India

The eight-hour journey through the backwaters of Kerala, from Kollam (Quilon) to Alappuzha, is popular with tourists. Passengers are transported along a network of rivers, canals and lagoons, overhung with dense tropical foliage that every so often gives way to open paddy fields. Brightly coloured birds and ancient buildings can be glimpsed on the banks, and the Keralan people can be seen going about their daily lives.

Gorges of the Yangtze, China

Time is running out for those who want to experience the full splendour of a cruise along the Yangtze River as it passes between the rocky pinnacles of the Three Gorges. The controversial Three Gorges Dam project is due to be completed in 2009, and the flooding that will eventually create a 560 km (350-mile) long reservoir is well under way. The dam itself has become a tourist attraction. In the meantime, three- to four-day cruises from Chongqing to Wuhan, through the magnificent Qutang, Wuhang and Xiling gorges, continue to provide stunning views of a dramatic natural landscape. It is also possible to take a longer cruise from Shanghai to Chongqing.

Sepik, Papua New Guinea

The Sepik River twists and turns its way from the central mountains of Papua New Guinea through jungles, swamps and grasslands to the sea. Most cruises start from a remote inland location, to which passengers are transferred from Port Moresby by small plane. There is then a leisurely journey through the rainforest, with stops at riverside villages, some of which are on stilts. The people of the region are renowned for their woodcarving and traditional art, each village having its own distinctive style.

Murray, South Australia

A six-day cruise on a paddleboat, beginning and ending at Mannum, passes through colourful scenery, including verdant wetlands, brick-red plains, sandstone cliffs and deep blue lagoons. The cruise may also include a visit to the old river port of Morgan and an opportunity to hear about Aboriginal customs from elders at the Ngaut Ngaut Conservation Park.

◄ Nile, Egypt

A week-long cruise up the Nile from Luxor to Aswan and back combines visits to magnificent historic sites – such as the huge temple of Karnak and the tombs in the Valley of the Kings at Luxor – with periods of relaxation on board an air-conditioned riverboat. There are also opportunities to take camel rides into the desert that lies beyond the narrow fertile strip on either side of the river. From Aswan, where it is possible to sail on the river in a *felucca* (pictured here), a short flight takes passengers to the splendid temple of Abu Simbel, above the shores of Lake Nasser. Abu Simbel can also be reached by taking a luxury three-day cruise on the lake. Created by the building of the Aswan Dam, the lake itself is an impressive sight.

Useful web addresses
all preceded by www.
rivercruises.com
smallshipcruises.com
burgundy-canal.com
travelchinaguide.com/
   cruise
americanweststeamboat.
   com

▼ Li, China

The 80 km (50-mile) journey down the Li River from Guilin to the beautiful town of Yangshuo passes through a landscape of precipitous peaks, with names such as Paint Brush Hill and Five Tigers Catch a Goat Hill. Gliding past bamboo-lined riverbanks and picturesque villages, the trip and a bus-ride back to Guilin takes one day.

Place of embarkation/ disembarkation

Sea and ocean cruises

Cruises attract all kinds of travellers and cater for an increasingly wide range of tastes. The steep-sided inlets of Alaska, Chile, Norway and New Zealand allow cruise liners to hug the coast, providing matchless views of these dramatic landscapes. Caribbean cruises allow almost daily shore visits, for shopping and exploring. Transatlantic cruises provide lavish on-board entertainment during the long sea passages. Cruise companies also vary in their appeal: some include lectures on the places they visit; others take a far less serious approach!

◄ **The Caribbean**
There are numerous variations on the Caribbean cruise, but virtually all have relatively short sea passages and a visit to a different island almost every day. There are organized trips to the rain-forests of Puerto Rico and sites of European colonial history. Some passengers, however, prefer to spend their time simply enjoying the islands' magnificent beaches.

NORTH AMERICA AND THE ATLANTIC

Alaska/British Columbia
The main attractions of a cruise in this area are the spectacular mountain scenery and the opportunity to see whales and seals, bears and birds of prey at close hand. Ships hug the coastline, entering steep-sided fjords and sailing close to the mouths of glaciers. Ports of call include Juneau, Alaska's capital, the 'gold rush' town of Skagway, and the Russian settlement of Sitka, with its onion domes.

Mexican Riviera
Mexico's west coast is becoming an increasingly popular area for relatively short cruises to catch the late-summer sunshine. For some tourists, the attractions are miles of unspoilt beaches fringed by jungle, such as those at Manzanillo and Zihuatanejo, and being able to go marlin fishing. For others they are the opportunities to experience Mexican culture and to visit the chic resort of Puerto Vallarta.

▼ **Antarctica**
Many of the 'expedition cruises' to the Antarctic use converted research ships or ice breakers, which offer less luxurious accommodation than other cruise ships. Passengers are taken ashore in small inflatable craft, and are thus able to get close to the teeming wildlife. There is always the chance of encountering whales in the surrounding seas, as well as sighting beautifully sculpted icebergs.

Atlantic Isles (Canaries, Madeira)
The Atlantic Isles are a popular cruise destination, particularly in winter and spring, when the lower mountain slopes are brilliant with flowers. Shore visits in Madeira usually include the novelty of a ride in a bullock cart or wicker sled on the mountain roads, while a trip to the summit of Tenerife's Mount Teide (3,718 m/12,000 ft) provides spectacular views of the surrounding islands.

Transatlantic cruises
Cruises link Europe with New York or Boston, with ports further south, such as Miami, and also with various Caribbean islands. The most direct, more northerly, route is for those wishing to enjoy the elaborate onboard entertainment, high standard of cuisine, and formal social life that are typical of the transatlantic liner. On ships plying more southerly waters, passengers can combine a luxury lifestyle with sunbathing, swimming and various other deck activities.

SOUTH AMERICA

Chilean fjords
Cruises along the most southern 1,000 km (625 miles) of Chile's coastline provide magnificent views of mountains and glaciers. The further south, the colder and less predictable the weather becomes, but for many the thrill of travelling the route of Darwin's *Beagle* and visiting Tierra del Fuego outweighs the risk of storms.

EUROPE

Norwegian fjords
Those cruising the fjords of Norway do so primarily to enjoy the majestic mountain scenery. Waterfalls, glaciers and wildlife can all be viewed from the comfort of the ship, while shore visits include a ride on a spectacular mountain railway from Flåm (see *Great railway journeys*). Some cruises extend as far as Europe's most northern point, where passengers can experience the midnight sun.

Western Mediterranean
One of the joys of a cruise in the Western Mediterranean is the opportunity to sample the local cuisine and wines. Most cruises include a day in the vibrant Spanish city of Barcelona. In Italy, there are brief organized trips to view the art treasures of Pisa and Florence, and the Roman remains of Pompeii (see *Historic sites in Europe*). There are also opportunities to enjoy the high-life in some of the fashionable resorts of the French Riviera, such as St Tropez, to visit the casinos of Monte Carlo, and to watch the Spanish flamenco dancers in Cartagena. Some cruises extend as far as the Adriatic, call in at the fortress town of Dubrovnik and include a day's sightseeing in Venice.

Eastern Mediterranean
A region rich in the remains of earlier civilizations, the Eastern Mediterranean provides much of historic interest, and many cruises have on-board experts to give background lectures. Some of the main sites visited include the Roman town of Ephesus in Turkey, the Ancient Greek ruins of Delos, the Crusader castle of Krak des Chevaliers in Syria, and the pyramids in Egypt (see *Historic sites in Africa*). Most cruises also include opportunities for swimming, snorkelling and sunbathing.

▲ **North-east America**
The north-eastern seaboard of America offers areas of great natural beauty such as Acadia National Park in Maine, whose fall colours are the focus of October cruises. There is also an opportunity to see the whales that frequent the waters of Stellwagen Bank off the coast of Massachusetts. Included in a wide variety of shore visits are the Canadian fishing town of Lunenburg, the popular US resort of Martha's Vineyard, and the cities of Boston and New York.

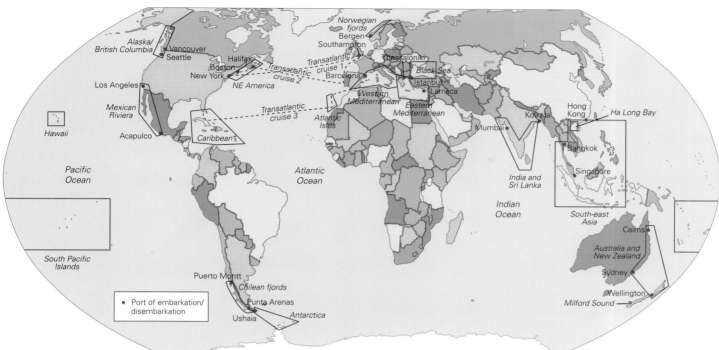

▼ **Black Sea**
A day in Istanbul
(see *World Cities*)
is included in most
cruises of the Black
Sea. The countries
bordering the Black
Sea provide a rich
variety of historic
sites, from the
medieval churches
of Nesebúr in
Bulgaria, to the 19th-
century opera house
in Ukrainian Odessa,
the 18th-century
palace of Tsar
Alexander II on the
Crimean peninsula,
and the abandoned
Byzantine monastery
of Sumela, high
above the Turkish
port of Trabzon.

AFRICA, ASIA AND THE INDIAN OCEAN

India and Sri Lanka

Cruises around the Indian subcontinent provide an opportunity to visit a number of historic sites without the strain of overland travel. A day's sightseeing is followed by a day's relaxation in the relatively cool sea breezes. Many of the sites visited are from India's colonial past – the Dutch fort at Cochin, the former Portuguese colony of Goa, remnants of the British Raj in Madras – but there are also trips to some indigenous sites, such as the Hindu cave temples of Mumbai (Bombay).

South-east Asia

With such a wealth of possible sights and exciting ports of call, there are many varieties of the South-east Asian cruise, which is a popular option for the Christmas break. Most shore visits consist of whistle-stop tours of the port of call, but there are also more adventurous expeditions, such as a visit to an orang-utan

sanctuary in Sarawak, or a trek to catch a glimpse of the famous 'Komodo dragon' (see *Wildlife in Asia*). Many of the cruises visit Bali, with its sandy beaches, terraced rice fields and ornate Hindu temples.

AUSTRALASIA AND THE PACIFIC

Australia and New Zealand

Most cruises of Australia's east coast provide more than one opportunity to stop on the 2,000 km (1,250-mile) long Great Barrier Reef (see *Marine wildlife*). By way of contrast, the natural wonders of New Zealand include the spouting geysers and boiling mud of Rotorua (see *Lakes and waterfalls*), and the dolphins, whales and penguins of the verdant Bay of Islands.

Milford Sound, New Zealand

Milford Sound is perfect for a cruise of just a few hours. It is possible to enjoy lunch while gazing out at towering granite peaks and glaciers, and, on the lower slopes, thick beech forests and waterfalls. There is always the chance of sighting the dolphins, seals, penguins and other sea birds that inhabit the sheltered inlet.

Hawaii, USA

The mountainous Hawaiian island chain was formed by a series of volcanoes, many

of which are still active. Trips to Volcanoes National Park and the world's most active volcano usually include the memorable experience of getting as close as is safe to the actual lava flow. The lower slopes of the mountains are covered in rainforest, home to 20,000 species of orchid and echoing to the sound of waterfalls. Hawaii is a port of call for most Pacific cruises, but it is also possible to take a cruise exclusively of the islands, and so be able to enjoy some of the dramatic beaches and the local culture.

Useful web addresses
all preceded by www.

cruise.com

cruises.about.com

discover-cruises.co.uk

goway.com/cruises

cruiseweb.com

cruisein.co.uk

cruiseinformationservice.
co.uk

◄ **Ha Long Bay, Gulf of Tonkin, Vietnam**
'Ha Long' means 'where the dragon plunged into the sea', and the bay contains around 3,000 islands, famous for their sheer, limestone cliffs with honeycombs of caves. A day trip from Haiphong (by motorboat or slower junk) is included in the itineraries of long-distance cruises as well as being available to the independent traveller.

Where, when and for how long?

	Main season	Duration of cruise (in days)
Alaska	May–Sept	7–14
NE America	Aug–Oct	7–14
Mexican Riviera	Sept–Oct	7–10
Atlantic Islands	Apr–Dec	9–14
Transatlantic	April and Sep–Nov	14
Caribbean	Oct–Dec	3–23
Chilean fjords	Oct–May	3–7
Antarctica	mid-Oct– early March	9–12
Norwegian fjords	May–July	7–14
Western Mediterranean	Apr–Nov	12–14
Eastern Mediterranean	Aug–Dec	10–14
Black Sea	Aug–Oct	14
India/Sri Lanka	Dec–Feb	14
South-east Asia	Dec–Feb	8–17
Ha Long, Vietnam	All year	1
Australia/ New Zealand	Nov–Apr	14
Milford Sound	Nov–Apr	half day
Hawaii	Sept–Oct	7–14

Winter sports

Mountain resorts all over the world are upgrading their facilities: constructing 'ski parks' for snowboarders, installing faster ski-lifts to cut queuing times, and using snow cannons to guarantee good conditions. Now that many of the top resorts can be reached by long-haul flights from either hemisphere, it is possible to enjoy 'winter sports' at any time of year.

THE AMERICAS

Whistler, British Columbia, Canada
Considered one of the top ski resorts in the world, the resort provides access to two mountains with vertical drops of around 1,500 m (5,000 ft). As well as a wide variety of runs, Whistler's crowning glory is its five bowls, which provide plenty of scope for expert skiers and boarders, the latter being well catered for. The base village, which is pedestrian-only, has over 100 restaurants.

Banff, Alberta, Canada
The city of Banff is the gateway to three resorts that are linked by a shuttle bus and share a lift pass. **Lake Louise**, a particularly beautiful resort, is a good choice for families of mixed ability, with a beginners' run from the top of every chair lift. **Sunshine Village** includes 'Delirium Dive', one of the most challenging runs in North America. **Mt Norquay/Mystic Ridge** has a number of runs for the very best skiers and also offers night skiing.

Killington, Vermont, USA
The largest ski area in the eastern USA, Killington spreads over seven mountains. It caters for every level of skier, but is especially suitable for beginners, who have their own network of pistes, and for snowboarders who are provided with their own trail map. Snow cannons ensure good coverage throughout an extended season.

▼ **Jackson Hole, Wyoming, USA**
One of the most spectacular mountain resorts in the United States, Jackson Hole is most suited to the experienced skier or snowboarder. A 60-person cable car transports skiers from Teton Village to Mount Rendezvous, from where the skilled and intrepid can experience some of the most difficult piste skiing in the world. Other attractions include trips into Yellowstone Park, a swim at 2,460 m (8,000 ft) in the Granite Hot Springs, and sleigh rides to view a huge elk herd.

Lake Tahoe (Squaw Valley, Heavenly) California/Nevada, USA
Lake Tahoe is surrounded by ski resorts. **Squaw Valley** comprises six inter-linked mountain areas, some of which are still open in June. It has excellent facilities for children, including a family fun snow park. **Heavenly** has a spectacular setting, with something to suit skiers and snowboarders of all abilities. Snowboarders are further catered for by specially constructed mountainside features and by a dedicated fun park. A single ski pass is available for all resorts in the area.

Aspen, Colorado, USA
Long considered the smartest ski resort in the United States, Aspen provides an enormous range of facilities and entertainment, including opera. A linked ticket gives access to four mountains. Aspen Mountain and Aspen Highlands are most suitable for intermediates and experts, Buttermilk for beginners, and Snowmass for all levels. Snowboarding is allowed on all but Aspen Mountain.

Valle Nevado, Chile
A purpose-built resort in the Andes, at an altitude of 2,900 m (9,500 ft), Valle Nevado has wide, open pistes and spectacular views. It is also possible to heli-ski.

Gran Catedral (Bariloche), Argentina
Perched on Catedral Mountain, overlooking Lake Nahuel Huapi, Gran Catedral (formerly Bariloche) is Argentina's best-known and most extensive resort. Many visitors are attracted to the area in August for the National Snow Party.

EUROPE

Geilo, Norway
On the edge of the Hardanger plateau, Geilo provides uncomplicated downhill skiing as well as extensive cross-country trails. It is an excellent family resort, with ski schools giving tuition (in English) in snowboarding and cross-country skiing, as well as alpine skiing.

Soldeu/El Tarter, Andorra
For those on a budget, Andorra is a good option, and Soldeu/El Tarter the best of its resorts. Its reputable ski school and gentle slopes make it ideal for the beginner. A drag lift linking it with the neighbouring resorts of Pas de la Casa/Grau Roig has expanded the quality and quantity of runs available for the more experienced skier.

◄ **Vail, Colorado, United States**
Vail has runs for all abilities and a special family skiing area. Snowboarders are provided with dedicated pistes, a half-pipe and two fun parks. Numerous winter sports are possible, including dog sledding and snowmobiling.

Three Valleys, France
The vast inter-linked ski area of the Three Valleys can be accessed from several resorts. **Courchevel** provides varied skiing, including wooded slopes, but intrepid skiers can also make their way across the whole Three Valleys system. **Méribel** is conveniently placed in the centre of the system. **Val Thorens**, which at 2,320 m (7,544 ft) is Europe's highest ski resort, has three lifts still open in summer.

Chamonix, France
Chamonix is an attractive town set in a steep-sided valley and dominated by Mont Blanc (see *Mountains and volcanoes*). There is extensive, varied skiing on both sides of the valley, linked by bus services. The most famous run, the Vallée Blanche, involves a cable-car ride up to the Aiguille du Midi, followed by a tough walk to the top of the glacier, and a 20 km (13-mile) run down to the valley. The Mont Blanc Ski Pass includes other resorts, giving access to 1,000 km (625 miles) of piste.

▲ **Val d'Isère/Tignes, France**
Snowboarders and off-piste skiiers are among those well catered for by the huge inter-linked system of L'Espace Killy. The system is served by a number of modern resorts. The largest is **Val d'Isère**, which is better suited to more advanced skiers than to beginners, since its easiest skiing is inconveniently located on the upper slopes. **Tignes**, a collection of villages clustered around a mountain lake, offers skiing for much of the year. The lift pass provides access to the whole Espace Killy, as well as a day's skiing at nearby Les Arcs or La Plagne.

Skiing and snowboarding resorts

Level: B = Beginner I = Intermediate A = Advanced Sb = Snowboarding

Resort	Main season	Skiable area or distance	Best-suited level(s)
THE AMERICAS			
Whistler	Nov–Apr	2,863 ha (7,071 acres)	I/A/Sb
Banff	Dec–Apr	3,059 ha (7,558 acres)	I
Killington	Oct–Apr	489 ha (1,209 acres)	B/Sb
Squaw Valley	Nov–May	1,600 ha (4,000 acres)	I/A/Sb
Heavenly	Nov–May	1,942 ha (4,800 acres)	I/A
Jackson Hole	Dec–Apr	1,011 ha (2,500 acres)	A
Aspen	late Nov–Apr	1,936 ha (4,785 acres)	all
Vail	early Nov–late May	2,140 ha (5,289 acres)	all
Valle Nevado	mid-June–mid-Oct	64 km (40 miles)	I/A
Gran Catedral	mid-June–end Sept	640 ha (1,600 acres)	I
EUROPE			
Geilo	Nov–May	25 km (16 miles) 250 km (156 miles) cross-country	B/I
Soldeu/El Tarter	Dec–Mar	74 km (46 miles)	B/I
Three Valleys	Dec–Apr	600 km (374 miles)	all/Sb
Val d'Isère/Tignes	Dec–Apr	300 km (187 miles)	I/A/Sb
Chamonix	Dec–Apr	140 km (87 miles)	A/Sb
Zermatt	Dec–Apr	150 km (93 miles)	I/A
Cervinia	Dec–Mar	80 km (50 miles)	B/I
Wengen/Grindelwald	Dec–Mar	195 km (121 miles)	B/I
St Moritz	Dec–Mar	80 km (50 miles)	I
St Anton	Dec–Apr	170 km (106 miles)	I/A
Söll, Ski-Welt	Dec–Mar	250 km (156 miles)	B/I
Cortina	Dec–Mar	140 km (87 miles)	all
ASIA AND AUSTRALASIA			
Hakuba	Dec–Apr	c. 500 ha (1,250 acres)	all
Perisher Blue	June–Oct	1,250 ha (3,100 acres)	I
The Remarkables	June–Oct	220 ha (550 acres)	I
Coronet Peak	June–Oct	280 ha (700 acres)	I

◄ **Matterhorn (Zermatt, Cervinia), Switzerland/Italy**
The visitor to the Matterhorn area has the choice of staying in the expensive, car-free, Swiss resort of **Zermatt**, or the cheaper, more lively, Italian resort of **Cervinia**. The lift systems of the two resorts are linked. Zermatt provides a huge variety of skiing, from the wooded slopes immediately above the town to the steep runs below the Kleine Matterhorn. The sunny, south-facing slopes of Cervinia provide plenty of runs of intermediate standard. Summer skiing is possible on the highest slopes.

Jungfrau (Wengen, Grindelwald), Switzerland

The slopes of this famous mountain are served by two of Switzerland's best-known resorts. **Wengen**, which considers itself the 'birthplace of Alpine skiing', is an attractive town whose charm is enhanced by a lack of cars (a mountain railway providing the only access). **Grindelwald** is a larger, livelier town. The two are linked by a lift system that provides access to wonderfully varied skiing.

St Moritz, Switzerland

Famous in particular for its glamorous nightlife, St Moritz serves as a gateway to two major lift systems. Corvatsch/Furtshellas provides an opportunity for glacier skiing in both winter and summer. Corviglia provides varied skiing, interspersed by numerous restaurants in spectacular locations.

St Anton, Austria

St Anton attracts skiers from all over the world to its challenging ski runs, with cannon ensuring a good snow coverage. Dramatic off-piste skiing adds to its attraction for the experienced skier and boarder, but there is little for the beginner.

Söll, Ski-Welt, Austria

Söll provides good family skiing. It is ideal for the beginner and intermediate skier, but is not for the adventurous. Its low altitude results in a short season, although snow cannons have been installed.

Cortina, Italy

Surrounded by the distinctive rocky outcrops of the Dolomites, Cortina provides skiing in five main areas. There are runs for a range of skills, including a difficult descent from the Tofana bowl, and the gentle runs of the Socrepes–Pocol area. Cortina is the smartest of the Italian resorts, with a lively nightlife. Activities off the slopes include ice-skating.

ASIA AND AUSTRALASIA

Hakuba, Japan

The village of Hakuba (near Nagano) is the gateway to seven ski areas, providing runs for different standards of skiers, with beginners and intermediates best served by **Hakuba Goryu-Toomi**, and more advanced skiers by **Happo'one** (where night skiing is possible) and **Hakuba 47**.

Perisher Blue, Australia

This winter sports area comprises four resorts, spread over seven mountain peaks, accessed by an underground alpine railway and covered by one ski pass. There is a Nordic Ski Centre at Guthega, and 90 km (55 miles) of cross-country skiing. The main resort town is Jindabyne.

Queenstown (Coronet Peak, The Remarkables), New Zealand

Queenstown provides a residential base for two winter sports areas, The Remarkables and Coronet Peak, with shuttles operating between them. As well as good skiing, both areas offer facilities for snowboarders, including pipes and a terrain park. Families are well catered for, with good ski schools. Heli-skiing is also available.

Great beaches

▶ **Negril, Jamaica**
Negril beach is 11 km (7 miles) long and fringed by trees that hide low-rise hotels and restaurants. While definitely a tourist resort, it still retains a laid-back Jamaican character. Growing environmentalism has led to planning restrictions and active preservation of the surrounding area, including the creation of the Negril Marine Park. This encompasses the Great Morass swamp behind the beach, and the coral reef, cliffs and grottoes that make Negril so popular with scuba divers and snorkellers.

From California to the Caribbean to Australia, the lure of the beach still has a part in most holiday plans. The range is endless – chic and cosmopolitan in the Mediterranean, wild and rugged along the Atlantic shores or palm-fringed coral in the South Pacific. This small selection highlights some of the great beaches that can be linked into a round-the-world trip – whether for the exhilaration of surfing or sailing, or just to do absolutely nothing.

NORTH AMERICA

Venice Beach, Los Angeles, USA
Venice Beach is famous not so much for its wide stretch of sand as for its curving 'boardwalk'. Here, some of LA's more flamboyant citizens display themselves – on foot, skateboard, rollerblade and cycle. The area was originally developed to imitate its European namesake and, although there is no comparison, it is pleasant to stroll along its canals.

Assateague Island, Maryland/Virginia, USA
Assateague Island National Seashore on the Atlantic coast of the Chesapeake Peninsula consists of 60 km (37 miles) of pristine sandy beach, fringed by pine forest and salt marsh. Only a small area of it is accessible by car and the rest of the beach is deserted, except for the more intrepid campers, many of whom come for the fishing and birdwatching. Herds of wild ponies roam the island.

Sanibel Island, Florida, USA
Sanibel's 19 km (12 miles) of beaches are famous for their seashells. Visitors can be seen scouring the seashore or taking boat trips to more remote locations to find the best shells. Around 40% of the island, which can be toured on rented bicycles, is a wildlife preserve and it is also within striking distance of the Florida Everglades (see *Wildlife in the Americas*).

Puerto Escondido, Mexico
The resort of Puerto Escondido has a beach to suit every taste. 'Playa Zicatela' is considered one of the best surfing beaches in North America, but is suitable only for the strongest swimmers. 'Playa Principal' is a more urban beach, with pleasure craft and waterfront restaurants, while the small coves just out of town provide perfect swimming conditions.

THE CARIBBEAN AND SOUTH AMERICA

Magens Bay, St Thomas, US Virgin Islands
The heart-shaped Magens Bay contains a gently sloping sandy beach, surrounded by overhanging trees that provide welcome shade. Protected from the winds and currents, the bay is safe for bathing. Although nude bathing is not allowed on the main beach, it is permitted on the nearby Little Magens Beach. Interesting rock formations on the fringes of the bay are good for snorkelling. The beach is well served by restaurants and bars, carefully hidden among the trees.

Copacabana Beach, Rio de Janeiro, Brazil
Copacabana's 4 km (2.5 miles) of sand is fringed by a wavy black and white mosaic walkway. The beach is provided with modern amenities, such as public showers, kiosks and restaurants, and the shopping centre is only a short walk away. As well as attracting tourists, the beach is a meeting place for the citizens of Rio, and is the focus of the New Year celebrations. It is framed on one side by a huge granite headland and on the other by an imposing World War I fort, below which is an area from which local fishermen still operate.

Viña del Mar, Chile
Known as 'the Garden City' because of the luscious, tropical foliage that lines its boulevards, Viña del Mar also has a beautiful beach. Visitors who tire of the soft white sand and rolling surf can enjoy a tour of the town by horse-drawn carriage, visit the art museum and the extensive botanical gardens. Evening entertainment comes in the form of gourmet restaurants, casinos, discos and concerts.

▲ **Oahu, Hawaiian Islands, USA**
Most visitors to the island of Oahu flock to the string of connected beaches in the resort of Waikiki, just to the east of Honolulu, where the curving sand, studded with palm trees, is backed by a towering wall of high-rise hotels. Those looking for a more peaceful holiday, however, head further around the coast and seek out Waimanalo Beach (above), with its gently shelving, near-white sand and mountain backdrop. On the north coast the calm waters of Waimea Bay in summer also provide excellent swimming, but in winter months it is the centre of the surfing scene, as 10 m (30 ft) waves roll in across the Pacific.

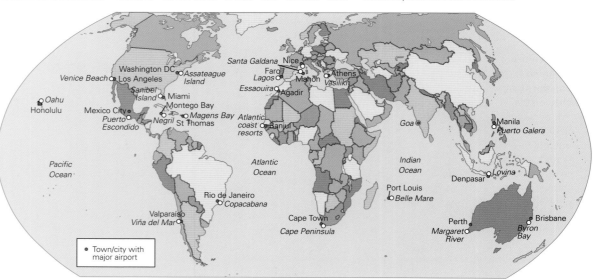

Town/city with major airport

EUROPE

Nice, France

Nice is the largest town on the Côte d'Azur, renowned for the clarity of its light and the colour of its sea. Many famous artists have been inspired by the region, and some are represented in the town's art gallery. The long curved beach is rather pebbly, but its surroundings are attractive, with a wide esplanade on which 'to see and be seen'.

Santa Galdana, Menorca

The Balearic Island least affected by tourism, Menorca is famous for its beaches. The main beach at Santa Galdana can be very crowded in summer, but it is still possible to find relatively unspoilt coves nearby. Just a 1 km (0.5-mile) walk east is the wood-lined sandy beach of Cala Mirjana, where the favourite sport is to jump from rocks into crystal-clear water.

Vasiliki, Levkás, Greece

The small resort of Vasiliki is one of the foremost windsurfing and dinghy sailing centres in the eastern Mediterranean. Set in a bay that provides some shelter for the beginner, it is blessed with reliable winds. The lighter breezes of the morning are followed, after a brief lunchtime lull, by winds strong enough to delight the expert.

AFRICA AND THE INDIAN OCEAN

Essaouira, Morocco

The ancient town of Essaouira provides a fascinating backdrop to 3 km (2 miles) of

▲ Cape Peninsula, South Africa
Among the many beaches on the narrow peninsula south of Cape Town is Boulders Beach, so named because of the huge rocks that provide shelter from the wind. Here, visitors share the sands with a colony of jack-ass penguins. Other resorts on the peninsula, where the ocean water to the west is considerably colder than that of False Bay to the east, include some, such as Fish Hoek, which cater specifically for families, and some, such as the fashionable Clifton area, which attract the young and wealthy. Surfers head for the remote Long Beach at Kommetjie.

sandy shoreline. The commercial life of the town tends to spill over on to the beach, with fishermen offering to cook their catch and camel drivers selling rides, although it is possible to find more secluded areas. The town is the centre of the craft of wood inlay, the local Thuya trees providing the raw material.

Atlantic coast resorts, Gambia

The resorts of Kololi, Kotu, Fajara and Bakau, strung out along a 10 km (6-mile) coastal strip, provide a full range of amenities, including golf courses, equipment for water sports, and swimming pools. Although the sea is relatively safe, there are times when the conditions are unsuitable for all but the strongest swimmer. For those seeking a more authentic African experience, the market town of Serekunda is nearby.

Belle Mare, Mauritius

The coral reef that surrounds much of the island of Mauritius provides a natural breakwater, ensuring calm inshore waters. The beaches are all beautiful, although some have been over-developed or have areas cordoned off by hotels. However, Belle Mare, on the less-developed east coast, still has plenty of public areas. There are also the attractions of a mixed French, Indian and Chinese culture, evident in the island's architecture and cuisine.

ASIA

Goa, India

The dozens of beaches on Goa's 100 km (62-mile) coastline provide plenty of choice. Calangute and Colva, to which young people flocked in the 1970s, are now tourist resorts. However, at both the northern and southern ends of the Goan coast are many relatively unspoilt beaches, including Arambol and Palolem, where beach huts and tree houses provide the main accommodation. At Palolem visitors can take dolphin-watching boat trips.

Puerto Galera, Mindoro, Philippines

A resort area comprising 12 separate coastal districts, Puerto Galera is renowned for its pristine sandy coves, sheltered by a rugged, jungle-covered coastline. Accommodation ranges from bamboo beach huts to air-conditioned bungalows and family-run hotels. The rich marine life of the area attracts scuba-divers, and equipment for underwater and other marine activities is available for hire.

Lovina, Bali

Although second in size only to Kuta, famous for its surf, Lovina manages to retain the relaxed atmosphere its larger rival has long since lost. Situated on Bali's rugged northern coast, the resort comprises six villages, dotted along 8 km (5 miles) of black-sand beach. Those who enjoy some lively nightlife make for the village of Kalibukbuk. Beach-centred activities include snorkelling and dolphin watching. Excursions can be made inland to nearby hot springs and a Buddhist temple, or further afield to the volcanic regions of Bedugul and Batur.

AUSTRALASIA

Byron Bay, New South Wales, Australia

Byron Bay offers a wide range of beaches. Main Beach is ideal for families, with a life-guard patrol and play equipment shaded by trees, while those wishing for more seclusion head for the smaller coves out on Cape Byron. The area also provides some good surfing and the opportunity to watch passing whales and dolphins. The town itself is less commercial, and better suited to those seeking an alternative lifestyle, than the popular resort of Gold Coast, 50 km (30 miles) to the north.

◄ Lagos, Portugal
Lagos is a busy fishing port and one of the Algarve's oldest settlements, with a long maritime tradition. To the east lie miles of sand dunes and the gently sloping Meia beach. West of the town, the dramatically eroded sandstone cliffs typical of the region form numerous small coves, some of which are only accessible from the sea. Lagos is an excellent base for surfers, who can travel the short distance to Portugal's west-facing beaches if local surf fails. The town provides plenty of interest, from seafood restaurants and bars to the curiosities of the local museum.

▼ Margaret River, Western Australia
Margaret River is among the best surfing areas in Australia, providing conditions to suit both beginners and experts. It also has much for the non-surfer to enjoy, including swimming beaches, river canoeing trips, and visits to local vineyards to taste some of Australia's best wines.

Festivals

Whether sacred or profane, festivals throughout the world bring thousands of participants and spectators out on to the streets with grand processions often featuring magnificent costumes and dazzling displays of music and dance, drama and sporting prowess.

THE AMERICAS

Corn Dance Festival, Santa Domingo, New Mexico, USA

At Santa Domingo (near Albuquerque) the Pueblo people honour the harvest goddess, Iyatiko, in the Corn Dance Festival. Celebrants, known as the *koshare*, dress in cornhusks and animal skins to enact the history of their people on a day that is filled with drumming, dancing and feasting. The festival which, unlike many Pueblo ceremonies, is a public event, is always held on 4 August.

Heritage and Jazz Festival, New Orleans, Louisiana, USA

Jazz evolved in New Orleans during the late 19th and early 20th centuries, but the first jazz festival was not until 1968. A major event in the musical calendar and organized by the Heritage and Jazz Festival, it runs over two weekends in April or May. The devastating effects of Hurricane Katrina in 2005 have not stopped the festival being staged, and it continues to feature big-name musicians from all over the world.

Fisherman's Festival, Jamaica

29 June is Saint Peter's day. He is the patron saint of fishermen, and in the fishing ports of Jamaica boats are drawn up to the beach where the owners decorate them with shells and flowers. Long processions follow priests to the edge of the sea where they bless the boats, and the beaches become crowded with steel bands, dancers and family picnics.

Urkupina, Calvario Hill, Bolivia

Early in the 20th century a girl tending her sheep on Calvario Hill had a vision of the Virgin Mary. Now, on 15 August, thousands of pilgrims carrying candles and flowers, and accompanied by musicians, performers and vendors, climb the hill to pay homage to the Virgin. The festivities that follow last for three days.

National Rodeo Festival, Rancagua, Chile

Rodeos take place all over the country and, in late March, the best competitors go to the National Rodeo in Rancagua. This event celebrates the Chilean *huaso* or cowboy. Thousands come to watch as huasos, wearing traditional costume and the heavy spurs unique to Chile, provide exhibitions of horsemanship. The town is given over to feasts of cowboy food and *la cueca*, the erotic folk dance of Chile.

◄ **Palio, Siena, Italy**
Celebrated every year on 2 July and 16 August, the Palio is a bare-back horserace that dates from the 16th century. Ten horses, each representing one of Siena's *contrade*, or districts, race three times around the crowded central piazza, sometimes barging into each other and unseating their riders. Before the race there is a procession in which men dressed in medieval clothes whirl and twist the *palio*, or flag, of their *contrada*, to the accompaniment of drummers.

EUROPE

Puck Fair, Killorglin, Ireland

A billygoat, King Puck – adorned with ribbons and a crown – opens the three-day Puck Fair every year on 2 August. Musicians from all over Europe perform, and Romanies are among those who entertain the crowds with Irish jigs and stories. The billy is honoured because in the 17th century a herd of goats warned the village of an impending English attack.

Oktober Bierfest, Munich, Germany

The Oktober Bierfest has been an annual event since 1835. It is an important festival for most young visitors to the city and is a huge celebration in honour of beer. It lasts for 16 days from 17 October, and vast beer tents that each house 5,000 drinkers are erected. Food stalls and funfairs add to the festive atmosphere.

Lajkonic, Kraków, Poland

Every year, usually in June, a man dressed as a Tartar rides a mock horse through the streets, accompanied by trumpeters and citizens dressed in medieval costume. He does so in memory of Lajkonic, who in the 13th century killed a Tartar and put on the dead man's clothing before riding into the city to warn that the Tartars were about to attack. The resulting defeat of the Tartars is now celebrated with much pageantry.

San Fermin, Pamplona, Spain

Starting on 6 July and running for eight days, the festival is held in honour of Fermin, patron saint of bullfighters. Each day starts with the playing of drums and pipes, and an effigy of the saint is followed by a procession of matadors and horses, dressed and decorated for the occasion. A rocket signals the release of the bulls from their pen to race through the streets to the bullring. Men run and leap ahead of them, a practice that more than once has resulted in someone being killed. Bull fights and parties fill the evenings.

▼ **Chinese New Year, San Francisco, California, USA**
For Chinese communities everywhere, the New Year is a week-long festival. Many celebrations are family-based, but they lead up to a very public grand finale. Chinatown in San Francisco is taken over by the Golden Dragon Parade when hundreds of people, including drummers and other musicians, accompany a 23 m (75 ft) dragon through the streets. The Chinese follow a lunar calendar, which means that their New Year occurs in late January or early February.

Mardi Gras Carnaval, Rio de Janeiro, Brazil

All over the Catholic Christian world, there are festivals at Mardi Gras, the last day before the 40 days of Lenten fasting. The Mardi Gras Carnaval in Rio de Janeiro is the most famous. Over the course of two nights the city's 14 main samba schools compete with each other by dancing and parading down the 1 km (0.5-mile) long Sambadrome, watched by thousands of spectators. Each school's parade consists of around 4,000 people in lavish, often extravagant, costumes, accompanied by enormous and elaborate floats, and a band of over 500 drummers. The judging takes place a few days later. Broadcast live on television, it is followed by great celebrations.

Aksu Black Sea Festival, Turkey

The origins of this July festival are very old, dating back to pre-Christian fertility rites. Cybele, the fertility goddess, wore a pebble in her crown and women still throw pebbles into the Black Sea in the hope that this will help them conceive. The highlight of the festival is a performance by male dancers dressed in black and silver, and other artists – musicians, potters, painters and weavers – flock to the site where they perform or sell their work.

AFRICA

Odwira, Ghana

The Asante calendar is filled with religious days and ceremonies, of which the Odwira, usually in August or September, is one of the most important. The high chiefs and priests are involved for some days in secret and sacred rituals, and then the roll of drums announces the start of feasting. It all ends with a grand procession, in which the chiefs are carried in splendid palanquins.

Abu El-Haggag, Luxor, Egypt

Among the ancient ruins of Luxor is a small mosque dedicated to a 12th-century Muslim saint, El-Haggag. Each year, in October or November, thousands of people crowd into Luxor for the saint's *mulid*, or festival, during which Sufis and floats parade the streets. Three model boats are carried about by groups of men, though whether this is in memory of the Ancient Egyptian journey into the Underworld, or of the time when the pilgrimage to Mecca involved a sea crossing, is uncertain.

Timket, Ethiopia

Ethiopian Christians celebrate the baptism of Christ for three days starting on 19 January. The priests, after all-night prayers, emerge from churches carrying holy tabots – caskets holding sacred texts – followed by singing children. Multi-coloured umbrellas, signifying high office and authority, are held above the priests. After this religious ceremony, a party mood takes over and there are huge communal meals, music, and excited horse races which sometimes lurch into the spectators.

▶ Ganesh Festival, Mumbai, India

Chowpatty Beach is crowded for ten days in August through to September. Families exchange gifts and women decorate shrines to Shiva, mother of the Hindu elephant-headed god Ganesh. On the tenth day a huge effigy of Ganesh is carried through the streets to be cast into the sea. Drummers and pipers announce its passage, which is followed by a large procession of people dancing and singing.

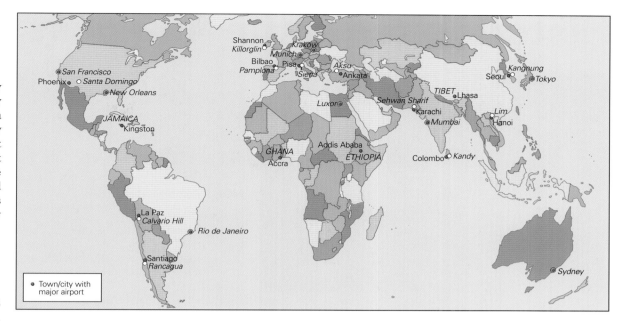

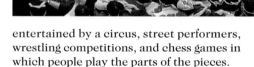

ASIA AND AUSTRALIA

Urs to Lal Shahbaz Qalandar, Sehwan Sharif, Pakistan

All over Pakistan, Muslims celebrate holy men with *urs*, or saints' days. One of the most popular, attracting many thousands of pilgrims, is held in Sehwan Sharif, around the tomb of the 12th-century Iranian scholar-poet Lal Shahbaz Qalandar. For three days, in October or November, Sufis perform their holy, trance-like dances, while drums and gongs beat hour after hour. The entire crowd dances and chants, and many offer votive offerings to the tomb.

Festival of the Tooth, Kandy, Sri Lanka

In the Esala Perhera temple in Kandy is the Tooth Relic of the Buddha. Usually in July, but occasionally in August, there is a spectacular festival in which there are festive meals and dances to celebrate the relic and Buddha. At the festival's climax a great procession of dancers, drummers, temple chieftains, and over 50 elephants in ceremonial attire, goes to the temple, followed by huge crowds of pilgrims.

Ho Lim, Lim, Vietnam

Singers from all over Vietnam pour into the village of Lim (near Bac Ninh) seven days after Tet, the Chinese New Year, in January or February. They participate in a folk-singing contest, and competition is fierce. The crowds who come to listen are also

entertained by a circus, street performers, wrestling competitions, and chess games in which people play the parts of the pieces.

Losar, Tibet

The calendar in Tibet follows the lunar cycle. There are two 'New Year' days, but the significant one is Gyalpo Losar, the King's New Year, which is usually in April. People wear new, decorative clothing; the priests fill the temples with chanting, the beating of gongs and the ringing of bells, and new prayer flags are lifted above the temple roofs. Throughout the city, street theatres and musicians perform while people party and play dice in the parks.

Tano, Kangnung, South Korea

This spring festival, usually in April or May, traditionally involved displays of the Korean form of wrestling, *ssirum*, even in the most remote villages. Now, many Koreans spend the holiday watching *ssirum* on television, except in the village of Kangnung. Here they celebrate for five days, not only with wrestling matches but also with performances of the traditional dance called *nong-ak*. The huge crowds also enjoy a spring drink, *chehotang*.

Gay and Lesbian Mardi Gras, Sydney, Australia

Participants pride themselves on outrageous displays and flamboyant costumes during the annual Mardi Gras parade. The street procession comes at the end of a three- to four-week cultural festival in February–March, and ends in a huge party which is restricted to ticket holders. However, revellers throughout the city regard this as an opportunity to party until dawn and beyond.

▲ **Sanja Matsuri, Tokyo, Japan**
Matsuri – festivals where shrines, or *mikoshi*, believed to contain a god-spirit, are carried through towns and villages – take place all over Japan. However, the biggest event is in Tokyo in April or May. Here the *mikoshi* weigh about 1 tonne each, and 50 men are needed to hoist one through the streets to the Asakusa Temple. Groups of costumed figures, and musicians playing flutes and beating drums, accompany the *mikoshi* on its journey.

Historic sites in the Americas

Amid the rocky canyons of New Mexico, Arizona and Colorado, the dense jungle of Central America and the towering peaks of the Andes lie the spectacular ruins of civilizations that flourished long before 1500 and the arrival of the Europeans. Scattered throughout the continent are the mansions, churches, cathedrals and forts built by European settlers and their descendants since the 16th century.

Mesa Verde and the Anasazi
Mesa Verde National Park in Colorado, USA, contains the ruins of spectacular Anasazi complexes of multi-storey apartments constructed on natural or artificial platforms on the face of canyon cliffs. They are among the remains of hundreds of villages that were built by the Anasazi from the 8th century onwards in south-western USA. Called pueblos by the Spanish, they took various forms. In Chaco Canyon, for example, elaborate complexes of adjoining rooms surrounded circular subterranean ceremonial structures known as *kivas*. The Anasazi began to abandon their pueblos in the 15th century, eventually settling along the Rio Grande. There are many impressive sites worth visiting, but they are usually in remote locations.
Peak season: May–October
Nearest airports: Albuquerque, Santa Fe

NORTH AMERICA

Québec, Canada
Founded by the French in 1608 and now the only walled city in the Americas north of Mexico, Québec has several 17th- and 18th-century buildings. The area by the St Lawrence River has the general appearance of 1759, when the city was captured by the British. On the cliff-top above is the citadel of Cap Diamant, dating from 1820.

Plymouth Plantation, Massachusetts, USA
Costumed actors re-create the life and times of the first permanent colony and a Native American encampment in New England at Plymouth Plantation, a historical theme park. Visitors can go aboard the *Mayflower II*, a reconstruction of the ship that brought the original settlers from England in 1620.

Historic Triangle, Virginia, USA
The colonial towns of Williamsburg, Jamestown and Yorktown comprise the Historic Triangle. **Williamsburg**, Virginia's capital 1699–1780, has a large restored historic district of 17th- and 18th-century buildings with tours led by costumed guides. **Jamestown**, founded in 1607, has some 17th-century ruins, a reconstruction of the 1607 James Fort and full-scale replicas of 17th-century ships. **Yorktown**, the site of the last major battle (1781) in the American Revolution, and besieged during the Civil War, contains fortifications dating from both wars. Other historic sites in Virginia include Thomas Jefferson's house, **Monticello**, George Washington's house, **Mount Vernon**, the plantation house, **Shirley Plantation**, built in the 1660s, and Civil War sites in **Richmond**.

Pueblo de Taos, New Mexico, USA
The largest, multi-storied, adobe (sun-dried brick) structure in the USA, Pueblo de Taos dates from around 1450 and is still inhabited by 1,500 Native Americans. In the town of Taos is the home of Kit Carson, the famous 19th-century mountain man.

Chaco Culture National Historic Park, New Mexico, USA
Impressive Anasazi ruins are to be found in this remote park. Among them is the site of Pueblo Bonito, with remains of a massive plaza surrounded by a semi-circular, five-storey tiered complex of some 200 rooms which once housed up to 1,200 people.

Charleston, South Carolina, USA
A historic centre of Southern culture, Charleston has many colonial buildings. The military relics of the Battery overlook the harbour, while 5 km (3 miles) away is Fort Sumter where the first shot of the Civil War was fired.

San Miguel de Allende, Mexico
An almost totally colonial town, San Miguel de Allende has many attractive houses and churches dating from the 18th century. It is also an important artistic centre, where painting, pottery, sculpture, drama, music and literature all flourish.

Guanajuato, Mexico
A former silver-mining town, founded in the 16th century, Guanajuato has colonial buildings dating from the 17th and 18th centuries among its narrow streets with houses painted in bright colours.

Teotíhuacán, Mexico
Impressive ruins are all that remain of a city which in AD 500 was the sixth largest in the world, with a population of around

▲ Savannah, Georgia, USA
The Cotton Exchange is just one of over 1,000 splendid 18th- and 19th-century buildings that have been restored in the historic downtown district of Savannah. Others include the US Customs House and the gold-domed City Hall. Near the city are the Civil War forts of Old Fort Jackson and Fort Pulaski.

Chichén-Itzá and the Maya
Chichén-Itzá in Mexico is a particularly impressive Mayan site that is unique because it displays many features of the Toltecs who occupied the city in the 10th century. Among them is the reclining sculpture of the Toltec rain god. The magnificent remains of the literate Mayan civilization are scattered throughout southern Mexico, Guatemala, Belize and Honduras. Mayan cities expanded rapidly in the 7th and 8th centuries but were then abandoned between the 9th and 13th centuries. Their ruins often include stone-built pyramids crowned by temples and palaces, and courts used in a ritual ball game that involved the sacrifice of the losing team.

There are numerous Mayan sites worth visiting, and it is possible to spend two to three weeks following a route that links the most important in Mexico, Guatemala and Belize.
Peak season: November–April
Nearest airports: See map of 'Mayan Route'

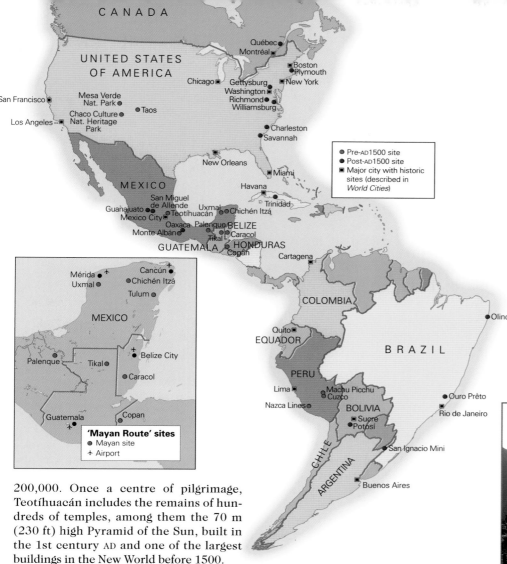

▲ Gettysburg National Cemetery, Pennsylvania, USA
The burial place of 979 Union soldiers killed in the Civil War battle of 1863 is also the site of President Lincoln's famous Gettysburg Address. Tours include the 91 m (300 ft) National Tower and the Cyclorama Centre, where a film about the battle is shown.

Machu Picchu and the Incas
Machu Picchu in Peru is the most spectacular of many Inca sites in the Andes. Tier upon tier of houses, palaces, temples and defensive walls rise up the side of a high mountain ridge overlooked by the granite pinnacle of Huayana Picchu. The Spaniards failed to find the site in the 16th century, and it was mysteriously abandoned and forgotten until the early 20th century. The Incas developed an enormous empire between the 14th and 15th centuries that extended from modern Ecuador, through Peru to southern Chile. It was conquered by the Spaniards in the 1530s.
Peak season: April–October
Nearest airport: Lima

200,000. Once a centre of pilgrimage, Teotíhuacán includes the remains of hundreds of temples, among them the 70 m (230 ft) high Pyramid of the Sun, built in the 1st century AD and one of the largest buildings in the New World before 1500.

Oaxaca and Monte Albán, Mexico
Oaxaca is a well-preserved colonial town with a cathedral and many other buildings dating from the 16th century onwards. Just 10 km (6 miles) away are the impressive ruins of Monte Albán, which from the 7th century BC served as a centre of worship for many different peoples, including the Maya. Surrounding a huge man-made plateau are the remains of pyramids, a ball court, burial chambers with beautiful murals, and carvings of dancers.

Palenque, Mexico
A Mayan site in a clearing in the jungle, Palenque has numerous buildings with particularly beautiful decoration. They include the Temple of Inscriptions, a stepped pyramid with a 25 m (80 ft) tunnel that leads to a crypt containing the sarcophagus of a 7th-century Mayan king.

Uxmal, Mexico
One of the most beautiful pre-1500 sites in Mexico, Uxmal has Classical Maya architecture. The chief building is the smooth-sided El Adivino, or Pyramid of the Soothsayer, up which there is an almost vertical climb to the 35 m (115 ft) high summit that is crowned by a temple. Nearby is the Governor's Palace, which features a frieze with 103 masks.

CENTRAL AMERICA AND THE CARIBBEAN

Caracol, Belize
An amazing Mayan site deep in the rainforest, Caracol is still being excavated. The ruins, whose full extent has only recently become apparent, include a pyramid 42 m (140 ft) high.

Tikal, Guatemala
Possibly the greatest Mayan site, Tikal is surrounded on all sides by jungle. The remains of 3,000 buildings can be seen, some with painted carvings. The pyramid-like Temple of the Great Jaguar, built in AD 700, is considered the world's best example of Mayan temple construction.

Trinidad, Cuba
Cuba's best-preserved colonial town, Trinidad has many buildings that reflect the town's prosperity as a centre of the sugar trade in the 18th and 19th centuries.

SOUTH AMERICA

Cuzco and the Urubumba Valley, Peru
Former capital of the Incas high in the Andes, Cuzco contains extensive Inca ruins mixed with colonial churches, palaces, houses and a 17th-century cathedral. An attractive and lively town, it is the main starting point for people visiting Machu Picchu (by train or a four-day trek) and other Inca ruins in the Urubumba Valley.

Nazca Lines, Peru
People of the Nazca culture (375 BC–AD 650) created gigantic lines by removing stones to expose the desert soil beneath. The lines, which depict geometrical shapes, birds – one with a wing-span of over 100 m (328 ft) – and animals, are best seen from the air, in a local plane.

Potosí, Bolivia
Founded in 1545 as a silver-mining town, Potosí was the largest city in the Americas in the early 17th century. Today it has over 2,000 colonial buildings, including several 18th-century Baroque churches.

Olinda, Brazil
One of the best-preserved colonial cities in Brazil, on a hill overlooking the Atlantic, Olinda has many 16th- to 18th-century buildings. It is a major cultural centre, with art galleries, music and festivals.

Ouro Prêto, Brazil
A beautiful colonial town founded in 1711, Ouro Prêto has cobblestone roads, statues, fountains, churches, a palace and a theatre. It also serves as a base for exploring other colonial towns in Minas Gerais province, such as Diamantina.

San Ignacio Mini, Argentina
The most impressive of the ruins of Jesuit mission villages in the Misiones region, San Ignacio Mini had 4,356 Guarani inhabitants before the Jesuits were expelled from Spanish territory in 1767. The ruins of only three other missions indicate their former splendour: Sao Miguel in Brazil, and Jesús and Trinidad in Paraguay.

Major cities with historic sites
(see *World Cities*)
- Boston
- Buenos Aires
- Cartagena
- Chicago
- Havana
- Lima
- Los Angeles
- Miami
- Mexico City
- Montréal
- New Orleans
- New York
- Quito
- Rio de Janeiro
- San Francisco
- Sucre
- Washington

Historic sites in Europe

There is a huge variety of historic sites in Europe, ranging from prehistoric monuments over 5,000 years old to 19th-century castles. Ruins of the architectural achievements of the Classical Greek and Roman civilizations contrast with what are often perfectly preserved cathedrals, churches, monasteries, castles, palaces and civic buildings dating from the 11th century onwards.

◄ **Neuschwanstein Castle, Germany**
The ultimate fairytale castle, Neuschwanstein (near Fussen) was built in 1869–86 and is the most famous of Ludwig II's castles inspired by Wagner's vision of medieval Germany. It has a wide range of architectural styles, and its tall white marble towers topped by cone-shaped pinnacles, which have been copied by Disneyworld, are instantly recognizable.

Rock of Cashel, Ireland

Poised dramatically above the town of Cashel in County Tipparary stands a limestone outcrop, 109 m (358 ft) high, known as the Rock of Cashel. It is topped by a group of medieval ecclesiastical ruins, which include a bishop's palace, the 13th-century St Patrick's Cathedral, and the adjoining 12th-century Romanesque St Cormac's chapel.

Caernarfon Castle, Wales

Considered to be the finest of the castles built by Edward I of England after his conquest of Wales in 1283, Caernarfon Castle is exceptionally well preserved. Constructed as a royal palace as well as a military stronghold, it dominates the surrounding walled town, which was also founded by Edward.

Stonehenge, England

The most famous prehistoric monument in Europe, Stonehenge is a circular arrangement of massive standing stones, surrounded by earthworks, whose function is a subject of controversy. Built in stages between c. 3100 BC and c. 1000 BC, it may have been an astronomical observatory, a temple or a secular ceremonial centre. Its distinctive stone trilithons – pairs of uprights topped with horizontal lintels – are an impressive landmark on the Salisbury Plain.

Bruges, Belgium

Once one of Europe's greatest trading centres, Bruges is a well-preserved medieval city with narrow streets and canals spanned by picturesque bridges. Within its 13th-century walls are many historic buildings, including the magnificent Gothic Town Hall and the medieval Cloth Hall. The Groeninge Museum contains paintings by the 15th-century Flemish masters.

Mont-St-Michel, France

Rising dramatically out of the Bay of St-Michel is a steep, rocky island with a medieval abbey on its summit. Buildings and fortifications have been added since the 11th century, resulting in a mixture of styles and shapes which culminate in the 19th-century spire of the church.

Versailles, France

Built for Louis XIV, the 'Sun King', the vast Baroque palace of Versailles was the envy of all Europe in the 17th century. Today, visitors flock to see the Hall of Mirrors – where the Treaty of Versailles was signed at the end of World War I – and to wander between the elaborate fountains in the magnificent formal gardens.

Heidelberg, Germany

Majestically set on the banks of the River Neckar and dominated by the romantic ruins of the castle, Heidelberg is one of Germany's most beautiful and best preserved historic towns, with many fascinating buildings. Its 600-year-old university provides a youthful atmosphere on the streets, especially in the evenings.

Petrodvorets, Russia

An imperial palace in the Baroque style, Petrodvorets was built by Peter the Great after he had visited Versailles. It is set in beautiful parkland interwoven by a system of fountains, cascades and waterways connected to the sea.

▼ **Meteora, Greece**
Perched on top of natural rock pinnacles which rise hundreds of metres from the flat plain of Thessaly, near Tríkkala, is a group of Greek orthodox monasteries, some of which are still inhabited today. The highest of these – at 533 m (1,749 ft) is Great Meteoron, which was built from 1356 with a domed church added in the 16th century.

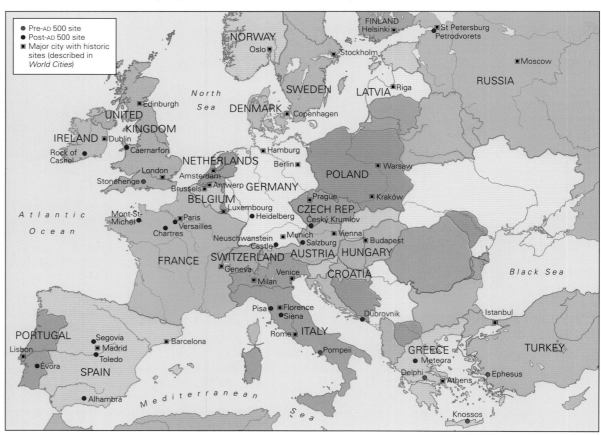

- ● Pre-AD 500 site
- ● Post-AD 500 site
- ■ Major city with historic sites (described in *World Cities*)

Salzburg, Austria
Set in a magnificent subalpine landscape, Salzburg is a picturesque city with many fine Baroque churches and a grand Italianate cathedral, the first of its kind to be built north of the Alps. The simple apartment where Mozart was born is a place of pilgrimage for music lovers.

Český Krumlov, Czech Republic
One of Europe's most picturesque towns, Český Krumlov has hardly changed since the 18th century. Its beautiful medieval and Renaissance buildings are almost

encircled by the Vltava River and overlooked by a magnificent castle. Originally a Gothic fortress, Krumlov Castle was rebuilt in the 16th century as a fortified palace.

Évora, Portugal
An attractive city with a history dating back to Roman times, Évora has a walled medieval centre with a distinctly Moorish atmosphere, and many fine Renaissance buildings from its time as a royal residence. The church of São Francisco is a good example of the Portuguese Manueline style of architecture, combining Gothic and Moorish influences.

Toledo, Spain
An ancient city of steep, winding streets lined with elegant if sombre buildings, Toledo is a splendid monument to the many cultures that have flourished here in the past. Moorish, Jewish and Christian traditions are all represented, and parts of the city walls date from the 6th century, when the Visigoths made Toledo their capital. The cathedral is a particularly fine example of the Spanish Gothic.

Segovia, Spain
Set on a rock, Segovia is a delightful old town with a fairytale castle and a 1st-century Roman aqueduct. Other notable buildings include the palace of La Granja, the 16th-century Gothic cathedral and the 12-sided, 13th-century Templar church of Vera Cruz.

Pisa, Italy
The famous Leaning Tower of Pisa is just one of a quartet of ecclesiastical buildings which make up the beautiful Campo dei

▲ Chartres Cathedral, France
Built in the middle of the 13th century, and almost unaltered since, the great cathedral of Notre Dame at Chartres is an exceptionally fine example of high Gothic architecture, with its flying buttresses, vaulted ceilings, intricate stonework and beautifully detailed stained glass. A rare 13th-century labyrinth design on the floor, a Renaissance choir screen and the glowing stained glass of the rose window all add to the beauty and impact of the building.

Pompeii and the Romans
Pompeii is an exceptional historic site because, when the eruption of Vesuvius in AD 79 engulfed the city in volcanic debris, the life of the people, their homes and streets, public spaces and palaces were preserved as if frozen in time. Excavations have revealed a wealth of detailed information about the everyday life of citizens of the Roman Empire, including their public notices, graffiti, brothels, latrines, furnishings and food. At its greatest extent, in the 1st–4th centuries AD, the Roman Empire encircled the Mediterranean Sea, reaching north as far as Britain and south into Egypt. Remains of Roman theatres, temples, baths, arenas, villas and other buildings can be found at sites throughout Europe and north Africa.

Miracoli (Field of Miracles) in this medieval walled city. The black and white marble facades of the Duomo and Baptistery, decorated by a succession of distinguished sculptors, are perfect examples of the Pisan Romanesque style, while the cloistered cemetery of Camposanto contains 14th-century frescoes.

Siena, Italy
Surrounded by city walls, Siena's medieval centre, with its narrow, winding streets, fine buildings and palaces, is wonderfully preserved. It is dominated by the Piazza del Campo, a large, shell-shaped square where the spectacular horserace known as the Corsa del Palio is held (see *Festivals*).

Delphi, Greece
In a stunning location, at the foot of Mount Parnassós, lie the impressive ruins of a sanctuary dedicated to Apollo, whose oracle was the most important in Classical Greece. The ruins include the 4th-century BC Temple of Apollo, the Doric Treasury of Athens, a theatre restored by the Romans, and a well-preserved stadium where the Pythian games were held.

Knossós, Crete
The ruined palace of Knossós is one of the few remains of the Minoan civilization, which flourished c. 3000–1100 BC. The first palace at Knossós was built around 2000 BC, and was rebuilt after an earthquake in c. 1720 BC. Excavations have revealed workshops, storerooms, dwellings and ceremonial rooms, one of which contains a gypsum throne.

Dubrovnik, Croatia
The fortifications of the ancient port of Dubrovnik rise straight from the Adriatic, and the double line of city walls encompass two palaces, two monasteries and many churches and other historic buildings, mostly dating from the 15th and 16th centuries. The narrow, winding streets of the old city are free from motor vehicles.

Ephesus, Turkey
The extensive and well-preserved ruins of the ancient city of Ephesus are one of Turkey's most popular historic sites, containing buildings from ancient Greek, Roman and Byzantine times. Among those dating from the Roman period are several temples, a theatre, a library, terraced houses, public baths and latrines, as well as some fine mosaics and wall paintings.

▲ The Alhambra, Granada, Spain
The most splendid example of Moorish architecture in Spain is the hilltop Alhambra palace, which was built in the 13th–14th centuries. The unassuming fortress walls contain a richly decorated interior made up of many halls and courtyards, with fountains and pools throughout.

Major cities with historic sites
(see *World Cities*)
• Amsterdam
• Antwerp
• Athens
• Barcelona
• Berlin
• Brussels
• Budapest
• Copenhagen
• Dublin
• Edinburgh
• Florence
• Geneva
• Hamburg
• Helsinki
• Istanbul
• Kraków
• Lisbon
• London
• Luxembourg
• Madrid
• Milan
• Moscow
• Munich
• Oslo
• Paris
• Prague
• Reykjavik
• Riga
• Rome
• St Petersburg
• Stockholm
• Vienna
• Warsaw
• Venice

Historic sites in Africa, Asia and Australasia

Africa is the home of the imposing ruins of ancient Egypt – one of the world's first civilizations. With the Middle East, it also has historic sites that reflect the competing influences of Christianity and Islam. In Asia, vast temple complexes, often adorned with wonderful sculptures, are among the remains of great empires, while in Australia, Aboriginal rock paintings are evidence of a culture that flourished long before the Europeans arrived.

AFRICA AND THE MIDDLE EAST

Dogon cliffside villages, Mali
Built among the rocks at the foot of the Bandiagara escarpment are the picturesque traditional houses, temples, granaries and meeting places of the Dogon people, whose culture has survived since the 14th century. The area can be reached only on foot and conditions can be gruelling. The best time to visit is December, for the harvest celebrations.

Rock churches of Lalibela, Ethiopia
Carved out of the red volcanic rock of the central highlands are 11 extraordinary medieval churches containing rare and beautiful frescoes, elaborate carvings and bas-reliefs. A complex network of tunnels and passageways connects the churches, some of which are hidden in deep trenches while others have been cut into the cliff face. The best time to visit is the Ethiopian Christmas (7 January) and Easter.

Kilwa Kisiwani, Tanzania
Once an Islamic city-state, the island of Kilwa Kisiwani has extensive ruins, which include a 12th-century mosque, several palaces and grand houses, and a 15th-century Portuguese fort. The impressive 14th-century cliff-top palace of Husuni Kubwa has a 30 m (98 ft) high dome and over 100 rooms.

Zanzibar, Tanzania
The buildings of Zanzibar Town's 'old quarter', Stone Town, reflect its colourful history as an important trading centre, particularly in the 19th century. A maze of narrow streets contain a sultan's palace, an ochre-coloured Arab fort, and the home of the notorious slave trader Tippu Tip, as well as numerous bazaars.

Great Zimbabwe, Zimbabwe
The extensive ruins of a major medieval city dating from the 10th century onwards, Great Zimbabwe is made up of curved stone walls and enclosures which incorporate features of the landscape into their design. The Elliptical Building, with an unusual conical tower and a diameter of almost 100 m (328 ft), is the largest ancient structure in sub-Saharan Africa.

Akko, Israel
The ancient walled port of Akko contains many relics of its long and distinguished history, including the underground 12th-century Crusader vaults and halls, the Ottoman Turkish citadel, and the beautiful 18th-century El Jazzar mosque. A remarkable 18th-century Turkish bath-house has been sensitively restored.

Petra, Jordan
Carved out of red sandstone mountains, the majestic remains of the desert city of Petra include two theatres, the High Place of Sacrifice, a temple and many elaborate tombs. The majority date from the period c. 100 BC –AD 150, when Petra was at the height of its prosperity as an important centre of trade. It had strong links with the Greek Hellenistic world, which are reflected in the Classical facades of its tombs.

ASIA

Mohenjodaro, Pakistan
The excavated remains of a city, Mohenjodaro is the most impressive of all the sites relating to the civilization that flourished in the Indus Valley c. 2600–1800 BC. The site consists of a raised citadel, with public buildings that include an assembly hall and a Great Bath, and a lower town containing residential and industrial areas.

◄ **Angkor, Cambodia**
The magnificent ruins at Angkor, capital of the Khmer empire, merit more than one day of sight-seeing. The best-preserved of the buildings is the 12th-century sandstone temple of Angkor Wat, which symbolizes the Hindu universe. Surrounded by pools, it is lavishly decorated with statues and bas-reliefs that are the longest in the world. Around 1.5 km (1 mile) away is the temple complex of Angkor Thom, within which is the Buddhist temple of Bayon with reliefs depicting everyday life.

▼ **Ajanta and Ellora Caves, near Aurangabad, India**
Cut into a spectacular horseshoe-shaped cliff, the Buddhist temples and monasteries of Ajanta are decorated with wall-paintings which are among the greatest examples of early Indian art. The series of rock-cut temples at Ellora includes the 8th-century Hindu Kailasa temple which is renowned for its exceptional sculptures of gods and mythological figures.

The Pyramids and Ancient Egypt
Khafre's Sphinx, 73 m (240 ft) in length and carved from a limestone outcrop, stands near the three pyramids at Giza. The most famous of the Egyptian pyramids, they were built as spectacular royal tombs over 4,500 years ago, during the period of the Old Kingdom. The largest at Giza is nearly 150 m (500 ft) high. The last of the Old Kingdom dynasties collapsed c. 2180 BC, but central government was restored by the dynasties of the Middle Kingdom (c. 2055–1650 BC) and New Kingdom (c. 1550–1070 BC). In the era of the New Kingdom, vast temples and lavishly painted royal tombs were constructed, most notably those either side of the River Nile at Luxor and overlooking Lake Nasser at Abu Simbel (see *River and canal journeys*).

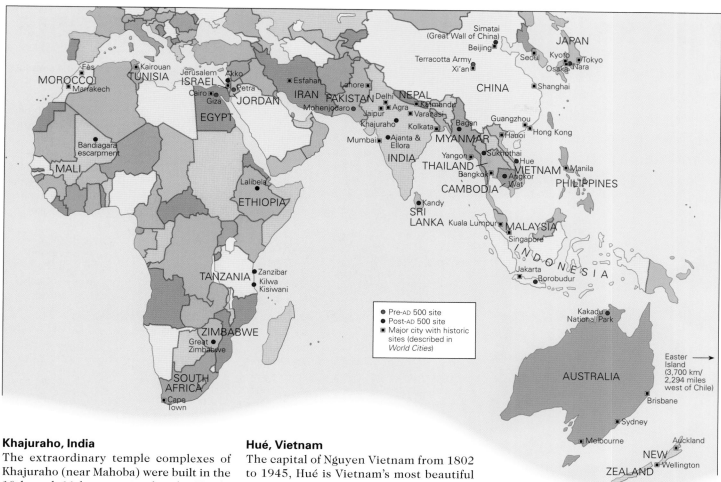

Major cities with historic sites
(see *World Cities*)

AFRICA
• Cairo
• Cape Town
• Fès
• Kairouan
• Marrakech

ASIA
• Agra
• Bangkok
• Beijing
• Delhi
• Esfahan
• Guangzhou
  (Canton)
• Hanoi
• Hong Kong
• Jaipur
• Jakarta
• Jerusalem
• Katmandu
• Kolkata
  (Calcutta)
• Kuala Lumpur
• Kyoto
• Lahore
• Manila
• Mumbai
• Osaka
• Seoul
• Singapore
• Tokyo
• Varanasi
• Xi'an
• Yangon

AUSTRALASIA
• Auckland
• Brisbane
• Melbourne
• Sydney
• Wellington

Legend on map:
• Pre-AD 500 site
• Post-AD 500 site
■ Major city with historic sites (described in *World Cities*)

Khajuraho, India

The extraordinary temple complexes of Khajuraho (near Mahoba) were built in the 10th and 11th centuries by the Hindu Chandela dynasty, but were abandoned in the 14th century. Rediscovered in the jungle in 1838, they were carefully restored and are now famous for their sensual and erotic sculptures depicting human, divine, animal and mythological subjects.

Kandy and the Cultural Triangle, Sri Lanka

Famous for its temple and Festival of the Tooth (see *Festivals*), Kandy is one of three former Sinhalese capitals that together form a 'Cultural Triangle'. The other two are Anuradhapura, a huge site with the remains of palaces and temples dating back to the 3rd century BC, and the more compact and better-preserved Polonnaruwa, around 1,000 years old. Within the triangle is the 1st-century BC cave-temple of Dambulla, with 150 Buddha images, and the impressive 6th-century palace-fortress of Sigiriya. Built on top of 'Lion Rock', this is decorated with frescoes and includes a water garden.

Bagan, Burma (Myanmar)

Built between the 11th and the 13th centuries, Bagan (Pagan, near Pakkoku) became known as 'the city of 4 million pagodas', and was the capital of a vast realm. Today it is an important archeological site covering about 40 sq km (15 sq miles) with over 2,000 structures still standing. Among the most impressive are the Temple of Ananda and the Shwezigon Pagoda, with glazed plaques showing scenes from the life of Buddha.

Old Sukhothai, Thailand

The ruins of the 13th-century capital of the Sukhothai empire have been preserved as a 70 sq km (27 sq mile) historical park. They contain numerous temples set in a landscape of lakes, trees and lawns. The most impressive is Wat Mahathat, with fine stucco work and carved Buddhas.

Hué, Vietnam

The capital of Nguyen Vietnam from 1802 to 1945, Hué is Vietnam's most beautiful city. The magnificent moated citadel with its ten fortified gates contains a palace, a mandarin hall and a museum. In the hills to the south of the city there are seven elaborate royal tombs.

Borobudur, Java, Indonesia

Rising like a squat pyramid from the Kedu Plain, Borobudur (near Yogyakarta) is a colossal 9th-century Buddhist stupa (temple) built by the Sailendra dynasty. The largest monument in the southern hemisphere, it covers 200 sq m (2,153 sq ft) and includes over 500 shrines with seated Buddhas. The walls of the stupa, which has five square and four circular terraces, are decorated with bas-reliefs.

Great Wall of China, Simatai, China

Stretching from the Central Asian desert to the Yellow Sea, the Great Wall is over 2,240 km (1,400 miles) long, averages over 6 m (20 ft) in height, and has a central walkway nearly 4 m (13 ft) wide. Much of what exists today dates from the 14th–16th centuries. The Wall can be visited at Badaling, just 70 km (45 miles) from Beijing. However, a less crowded section is at Simatai, 110 km (68 miles) from Beijing, where there are wonderful views to the distant mountains.

Nara, Japan

The ancient city of Nara has many beautiful pagodas, shrines, gardens and temples, the most famous of which is the 8th-century Eastern Great Temple, the Tadai-Ji. Its Great Buddha Hall houses Japan's largest bronze statue of Buddha; the hall itself is the largest wooden building in the world.

AUSTRALASIA AND THE PACIFIC

Kakadu National Park, Australia

Thousands of Aboriginal rock paintings cover the walls of the caves and cliffs of the ancient Aboriginal lands in Kakadu National Park (see also *Wildlife in Australasia*). The paintings, some of which are estimated to be over 20,000 years old, provide a continuous link with the past for the several hundred Aboriginal people who still live there today.

Easter Island statues, Polynesia

The extraordinary stone statues of Easter Island are the legacy of a lost culture which flourished on the island between around AD 400 and 1600. More than 800 colossal stone heads were erected all around the island's coast. The volcanic crater from which the stone was quarried still contains hundreds of unfinished statues, including the 20 m (65 ft) high El Gigante.

◄ Army of Terracotta Warriors, near Xi'an, China The massive underground mausoleum of China's first emperor, Shi Huang Di, who died in 210 BC, contains an army of around 7,500 life-size terracotta soldiers. Standing in military formation, they are a unique sight.

Theme parks

Inspired by the phenomenon of Disneyland Resort, Los Angeles, the top theme parks around the world are irresistible to children both young and old, as well as adults. The combination of charm and fantasy with white-knuckle rides and superb service guarantees a successful family visit, and since most are located near major cities it is easy to incorporate them into a longer itinerary.

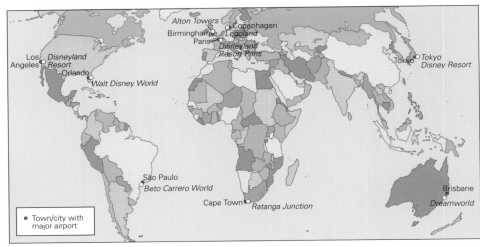

▲ Alton Towers, England
The combination of a ruined stately home, wooded parkland and over 100 rides means that Alton Towers (in Staffordshire) provides entertainment for all tastes. For the benefit of its younger visitors it puts on shows featuring characters from storybooks and songs, such as 'Peter Rabbit and Friends on Ice'. Its more challenging rides have a much darker theme, with names such as Nemesis and Oblivion.

Useful web addresses
preceded by www.

themeparks.about.com

funguide.com/country

disney.go.com

Disneyland Resort, Los Angeles, USA
Disneyland Resort, founded in 1955, is the original Disney theme park, and Mainstreet, Frontierland and Fantasyland – representations of American life and its dreams – have been duplicated in Disney theme parks around the world. Visitors are attracted not only by rides like the runaway train of Big Thunder Mountain, the parade of Disney characters and the famous nightly firework show, but also out of nostalgia and a desire to experience what is itself now a historic site.

Beto Carrero World, Santa Catarina, Brazil
The most extensive theme park in Brazil, Beto Carrero World (near Itajai) combines thrilling rides, shows and a zoo. Its themed areas cover a range of cultures, including a German House complete with beer cellar, a Viking longboat and a Wild West area. Its shows are similarly wide-ranging and feature the legend of Excalibur. Its whiteknuckle rides include the free-falling Tower of Terror, and Star World Mountain, with two 360-degree loops. The animal park includes African wildlife and a large collection of cobras.

Disneyland Resort Paris, France
Although based on the same formula as the Los Angeles theme park, the marketing for Disneyland Resort Paris emphasizes the educational element. There are 'Discovery rides', such as the 'Mississippi Steamboat' which provides information about life in frontier towns, while the Swiss Family Robinson tree-house demonstrates practical survival tips. Most visitors, however, go for the glamour of the shows and parades, and the thrill of the rides. These include being catapulted 'From the Earth to the Moon' on a Jules Verne style rocket.

Legoland, Billund, Denmark
Legoland, in which everything is built out of lego, is divided into themed areas, such as Pirateland and Castleland, where children recognize, and are able to interact with, their favourite lego characters. Although the park is aimed primarily at children, providing them with opportunities to play creatively, adults are also charmed by the intricate scale models of real, if somewhat idealized, scenes.

Ratanga Junction, Cape Town, South Africa
Africa's first theme park opened in the late 1990s. It takes as its theme the wildlife of Africa, with rides such as The Cobra, Monkey Falls, and Crocodile Gorge, in which visitors can experience white-water rafting in controlled conditions. A diamond mine is featured, with an underground runaway mine train providing the thrills. There are also less alarming rides for all the family, and 'interactive play areas' for young children.

Tokyo Disney Resort, Japan
With many of the same attractions as other Disney theme parks, Tokyo Disney Resort is unashamedly American in its culture. Rides range from the gentle Mark Twain Riverboat to the exciting Space Mountain. Around 200 Disney characters, from the earliest cartoons through to the present day, take part in the regular 'Disney's Dreams' parade.

Dreamworld, Queensland, Australia
Thrilling rides and shows are combined with a wildlife park and conservation zone in Dreamworld (near Gold Coast). The Tower of Terror roller coaster reaches speeds of 160 km (100 miles) per hour as it descends from a height of 115 m (375 ft). The Giant Drop uses the same structure to release passengers vertically so that they experience momentary weightlessness. In an 'interactive tiger exhibition' tigers swim with their trainers, while in the Koala Park visitors can handle koalas and watch other native Australian animals.

Walt Disney World, Orlando, Florida, USA
The massive Walt Disney World in Florida encompasses four separate theme parks. At Magic Kingdom there are rides graded for every taste, from those in Fantasyland aimed specifically at younger children, to the Space Mountain rocket trip, which is not for the faint-hearted. The Epcot Centre aims to re-create the atmosphere and architecture of different countries, including Norway, China and Italy. Visitors can eat food typical of the region, and enjoy themed rides, shows and videos. Disney MGM re-creates urban areas, such as New York Street and Hollywood Boulevard, and uses computer technology to enable visitors to come face to face with characters from recent films. The newest of the parks, Animal Kingdom, combines a safari park with typical Disney features, including thrilling rides, exhibitions and shows.

WORLD CITIES

CITY MAPS

Amsterdam	2	Copenhagen	8	Lagos	14	Mumbai	20	São Paulo	27
Athens	2	Chicago	9	Las Vegas	14	Munich	21	Seoul	27
Atlanta	3	Delhi	10	Lima	14	New Orleans	21	Shanghai	28
Baghdad	3	Dublin	10	London	15	New York	22	Singapore	28
Bangkok	3	Edinburgh	11	Lisbon	16	Orlando	23	Stockholm	29
Barcelona	4	Guangzhou	11	Los Angeles	16	Osaka	23	Sydney	29
Beijing	4	Helsinki	11	Madrid	17	Oslo	23	Tokyo	30
Berlin	5	Hong Kong	12	Manila	17	Paris	24	Tehran	31
Boston	6	Istanbul	12	Melbourne	18	Prague	25	Toronto	31
Brussels	6	Jakarta	12	Mexico City	18	Rio de Janeiro	25	Vienna	32
Budapest	7	Jerusalem	13	Miami	18	Rome	26	Warsaw	32
Buenos Aires	7	Johannesburg	13	Milan	19	San Francisco	26	Washington	33
Cairo	7	Karachi	13	Moscow	19	St Petersburg	27	Wellington	33
Cape Town	8	Kolkata	14	Montréal	20	Santiago	27	INDEX	34–39

CITY GAZETTEER 40–48

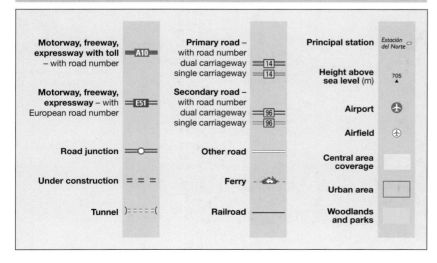

CITY MAPS

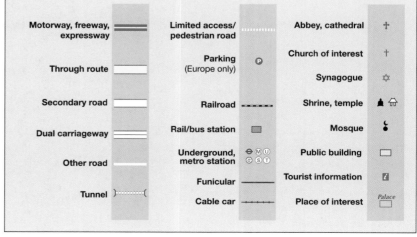

CENTRAL AREA MAPS

AMSTERDAM

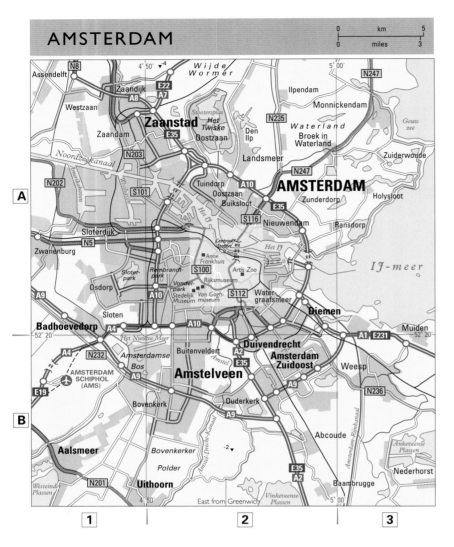

CENTRAL AMSTERDAM

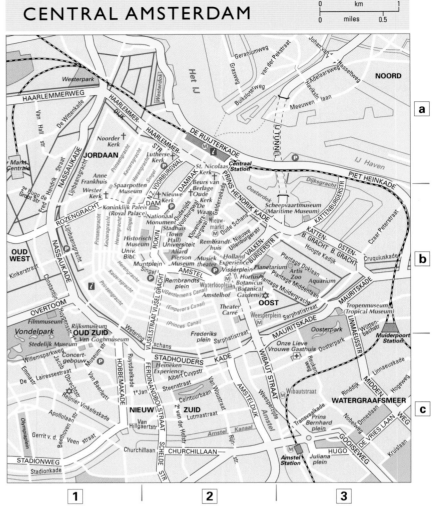

ATHENS

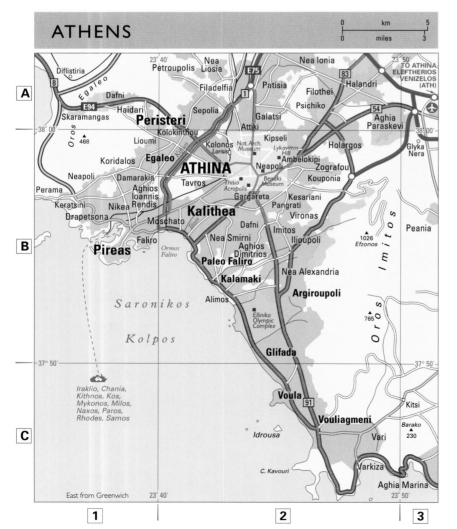

CENTRAL ATHENS

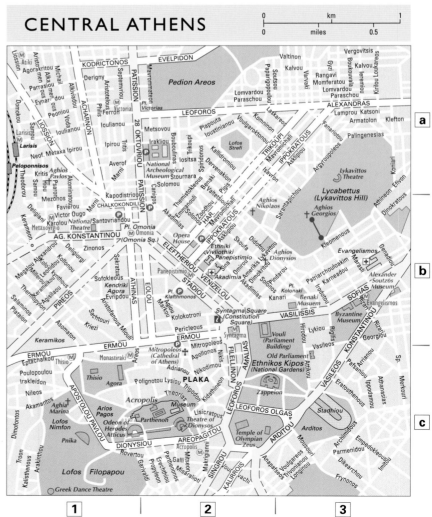

ATLANTA

BAGHDAD

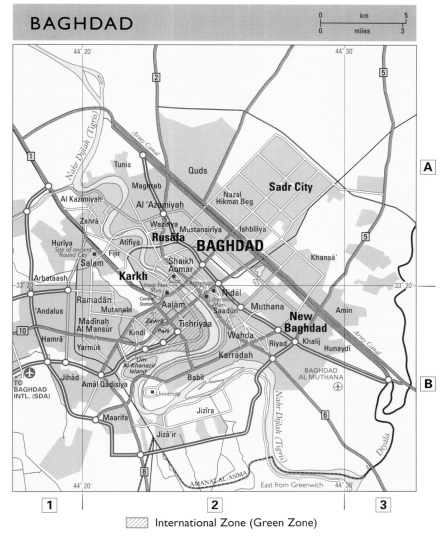

▨▨ International Zone (Green Zone)

BANGKOK

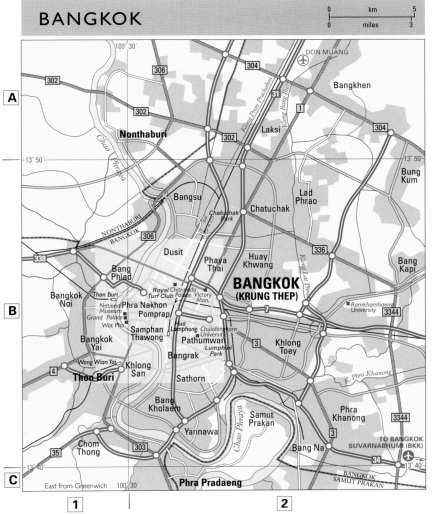

CENTRAL BANGKOK

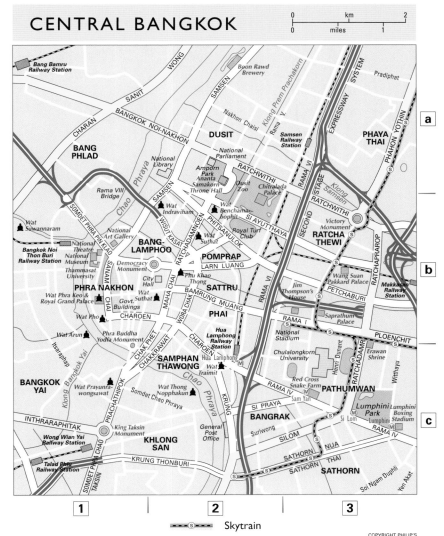

━s━ Skytrain

BARCELONA

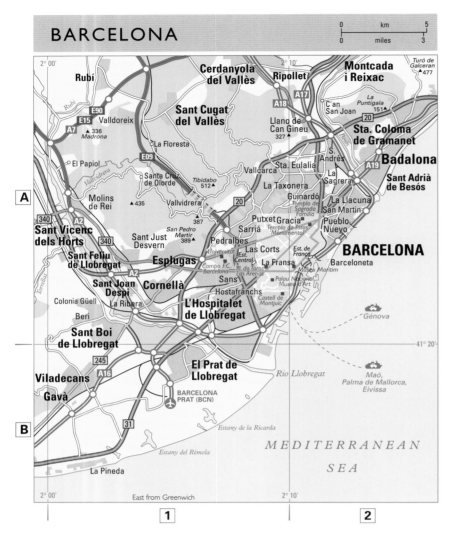

CENTRAL BARCELONA

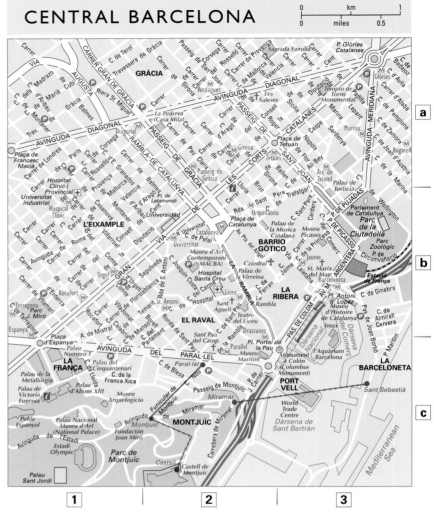

BEIJING

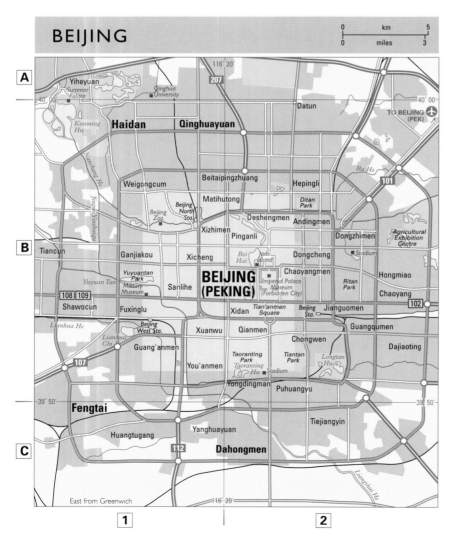

CENTRAL BEIJING

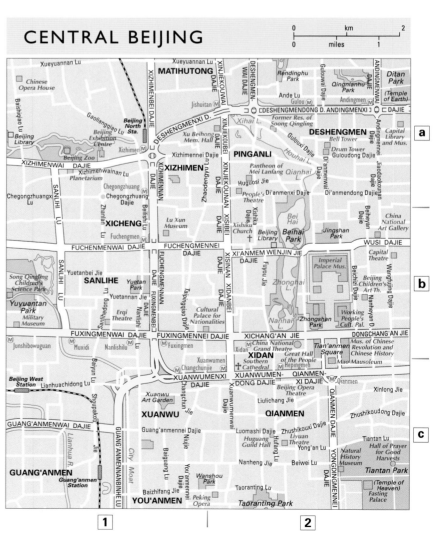

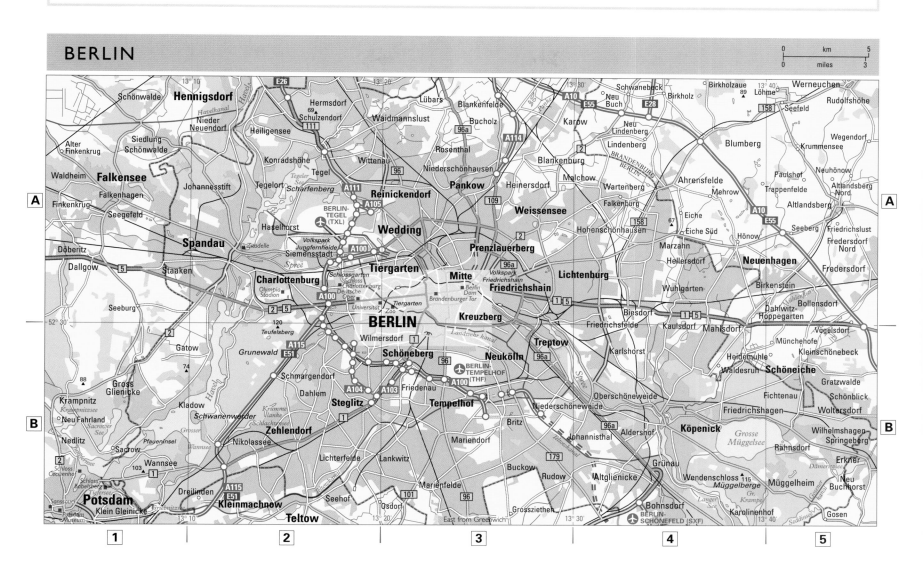

BERLIN

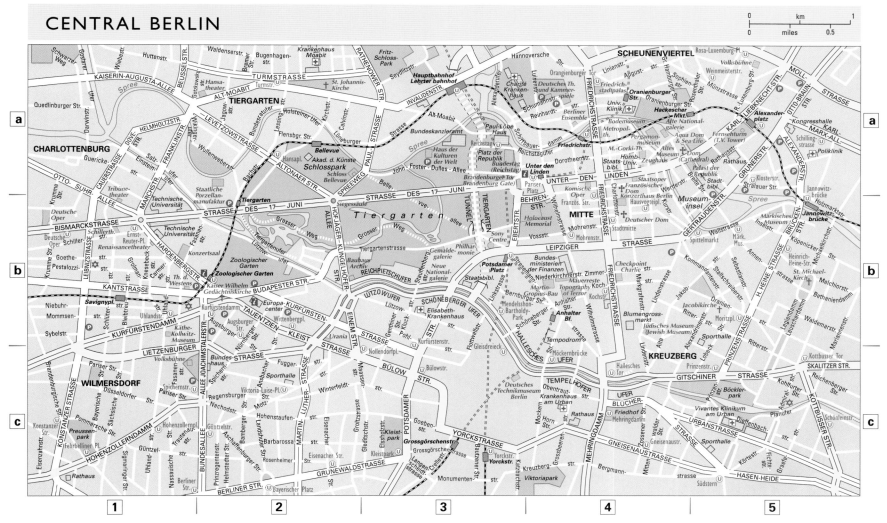

CENTRAL BERLIN

BOSTON

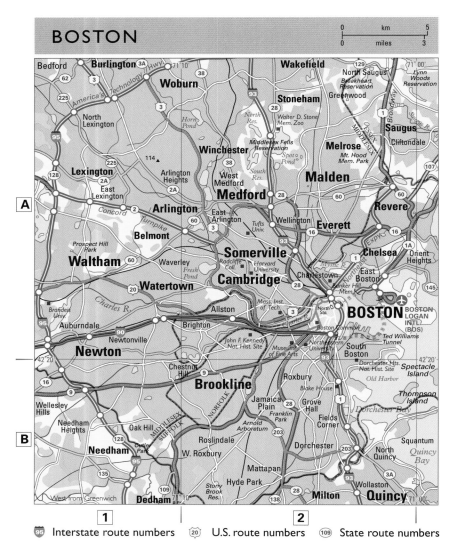

Interstate route numbers 95 U.S. route numbers 20 State route numbers 109

CENTRAL BOSTON

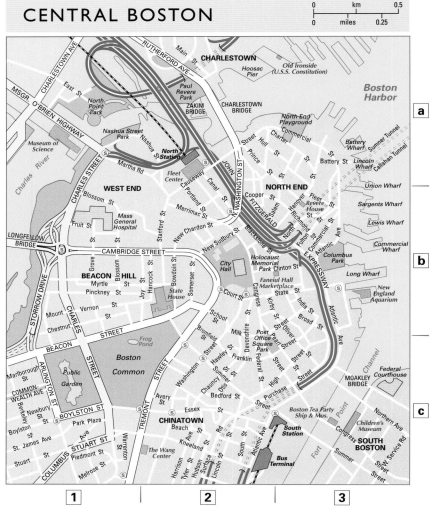

BRUSSELS

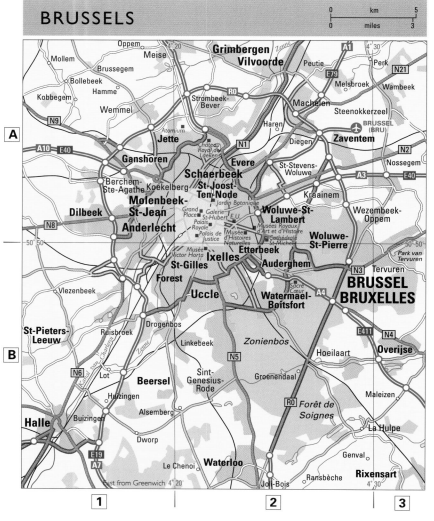

CENTRAL BRUSSELS

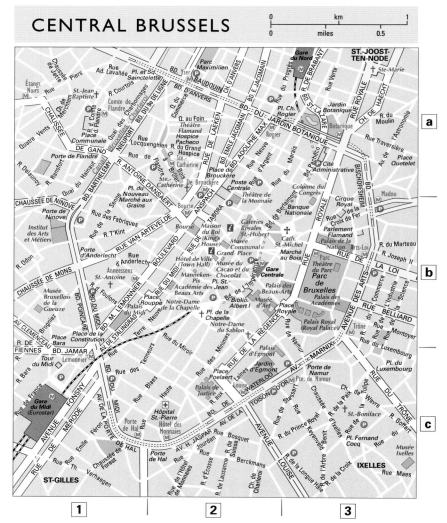

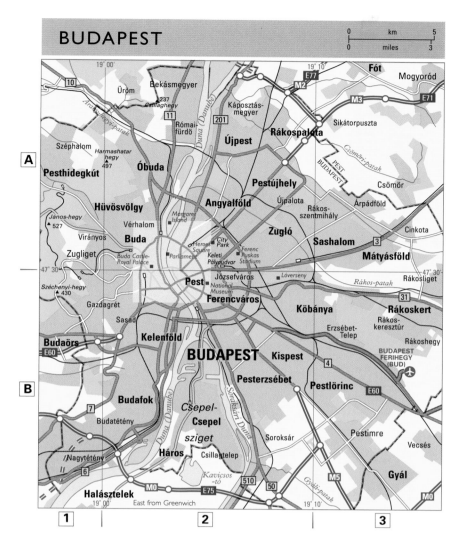

BUDAPEST

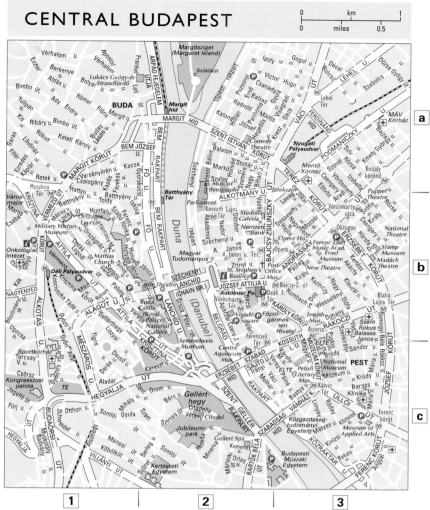

CENTRAL BUDAPEST

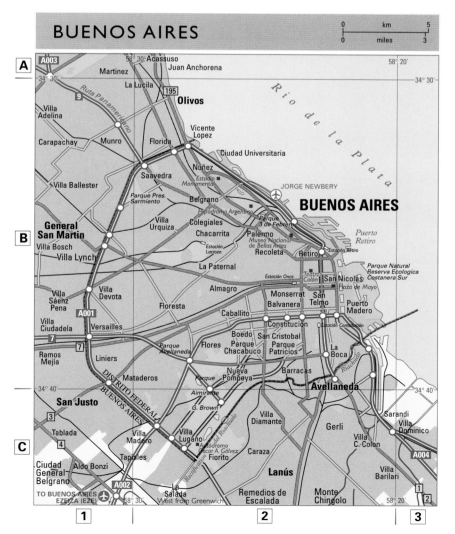

BUENOS AIRES

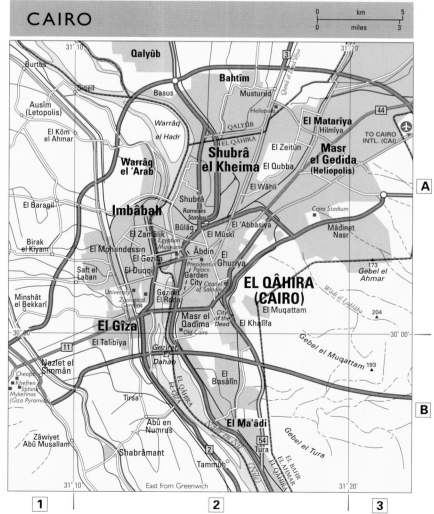

CAIRO

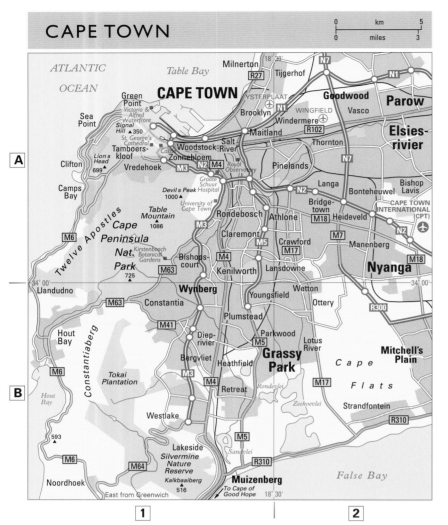

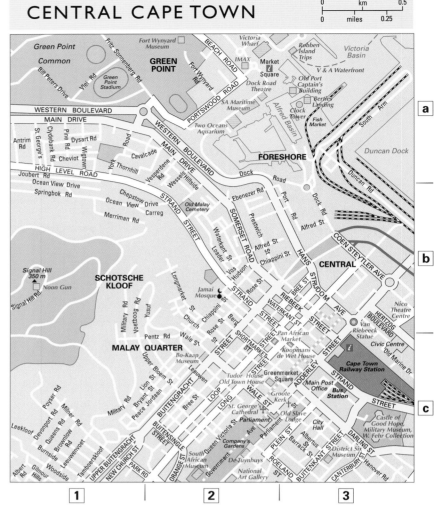

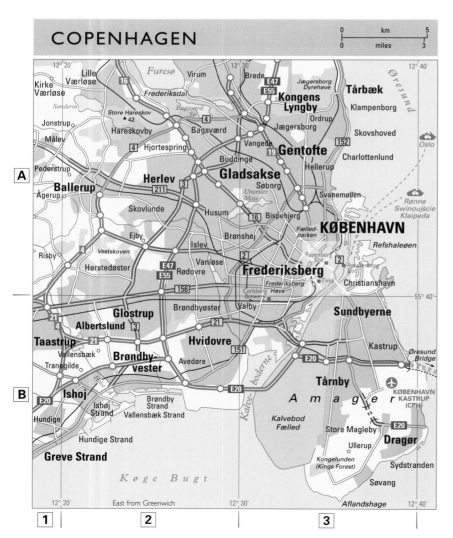

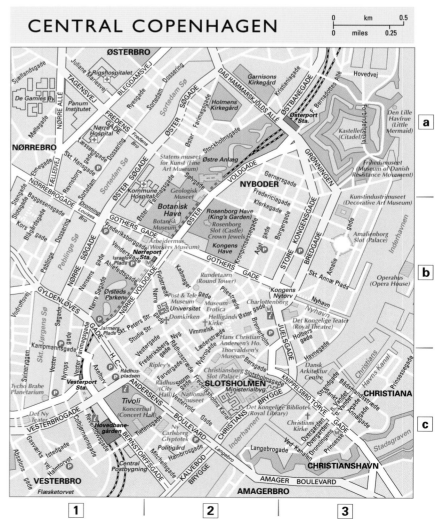

CHICAGO

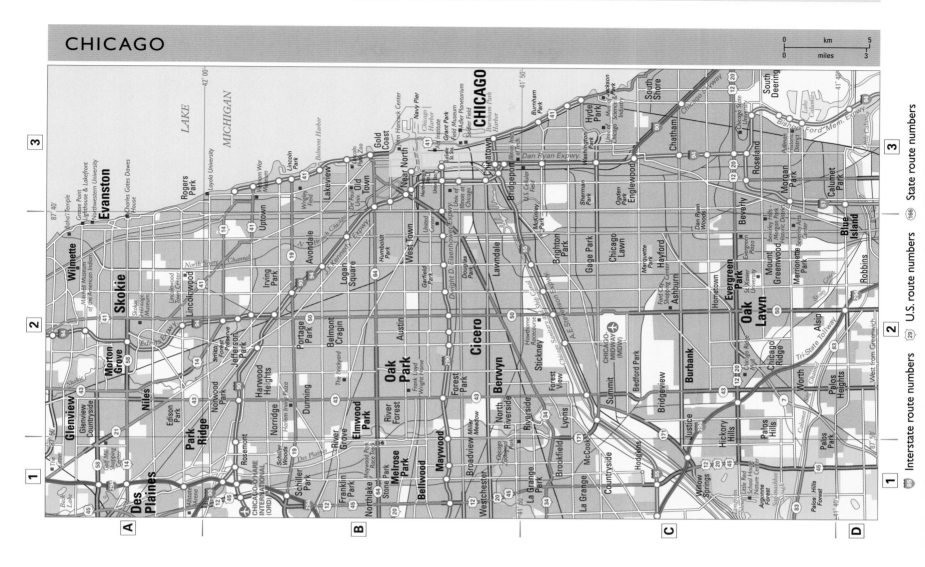

State route numbers
U.S. route numbers
Interstate route numbers

CENTRAL CHICAGO

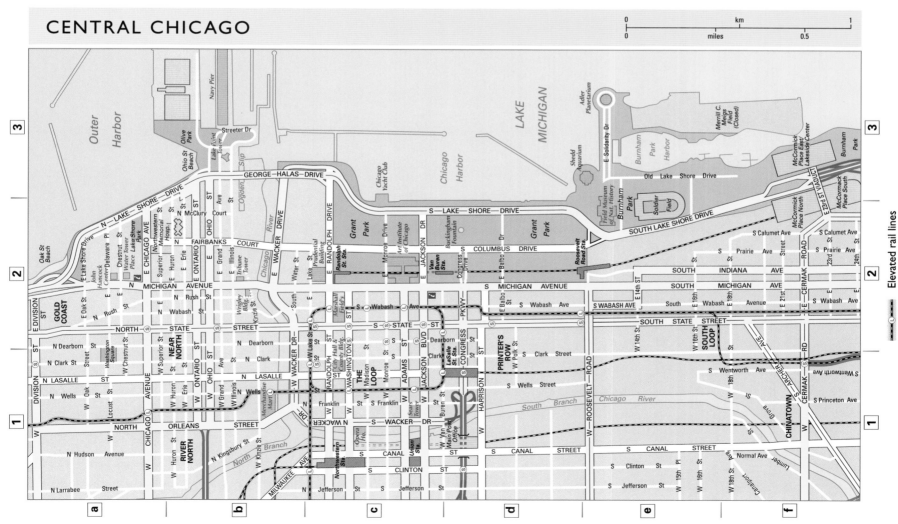

Elevated rail lines

COPYRIGHT PHILIP'S

DELHI

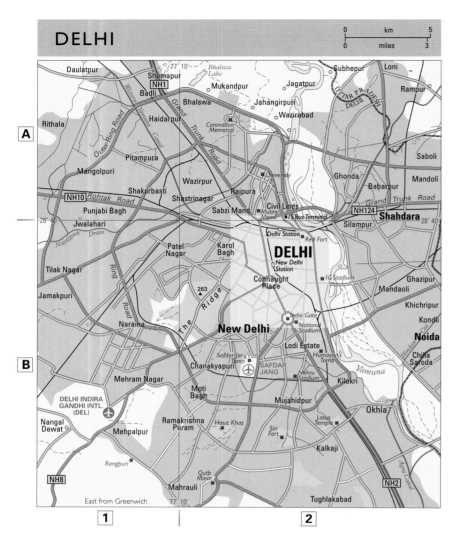

CENTRAL DELHI

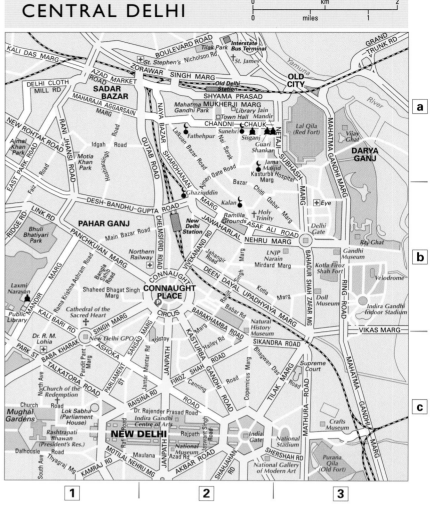

DUBLIN

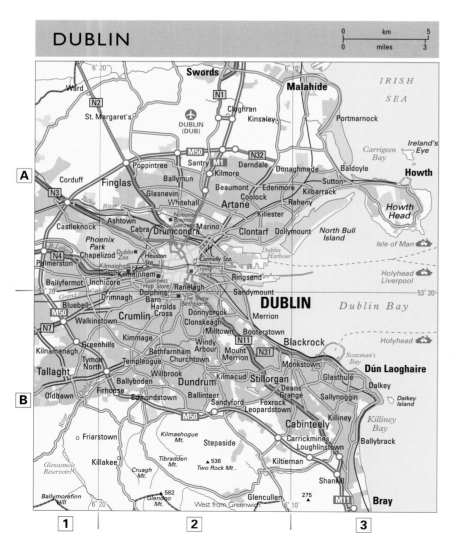

CENTRAL DUBLIN

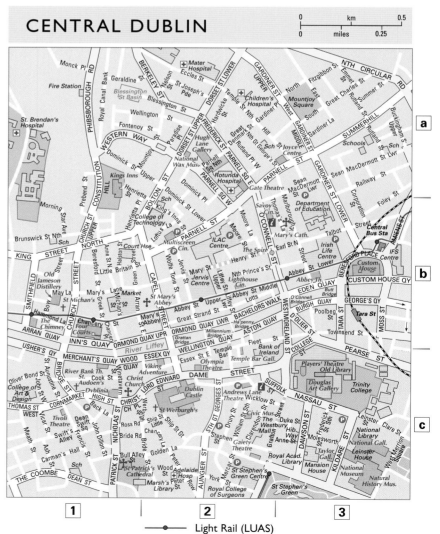

← Light Rail (LUAS) →

EDINBURGH

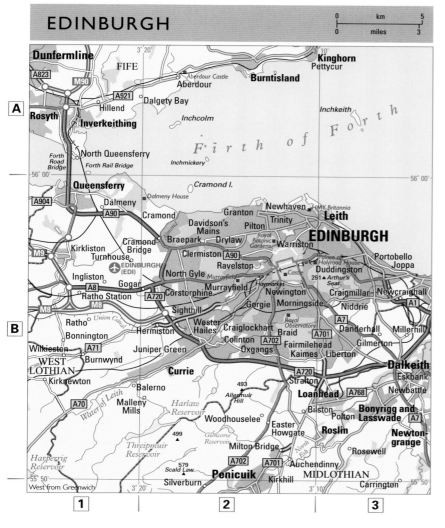

CENTRAL EDINBURGH

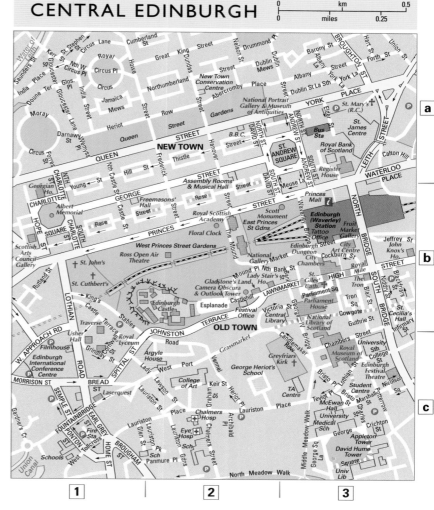

GUANGZHOU

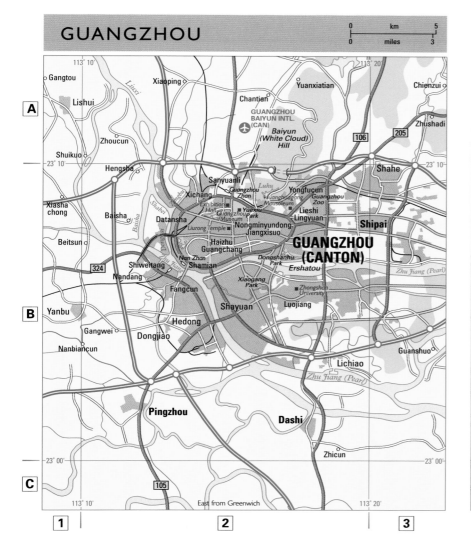

HELSINKI

HONG KONG

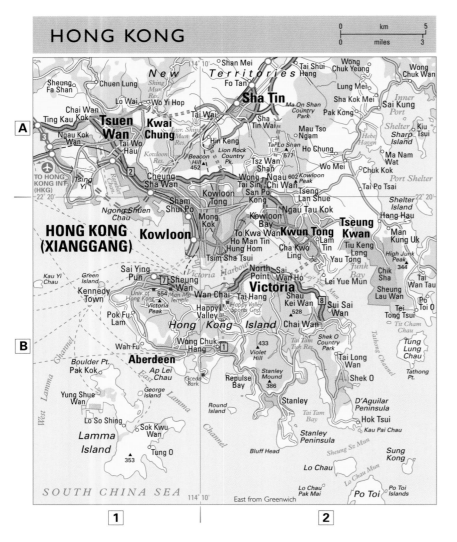

CENTRAL HONG KONG

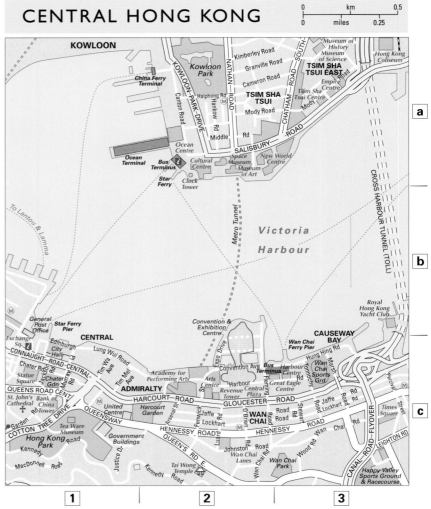

ISTANBUL

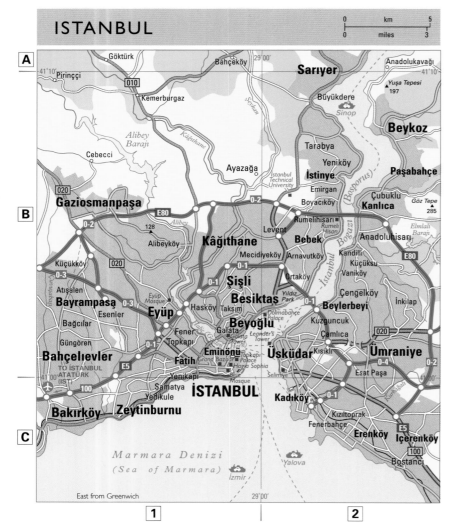

JAKARTA

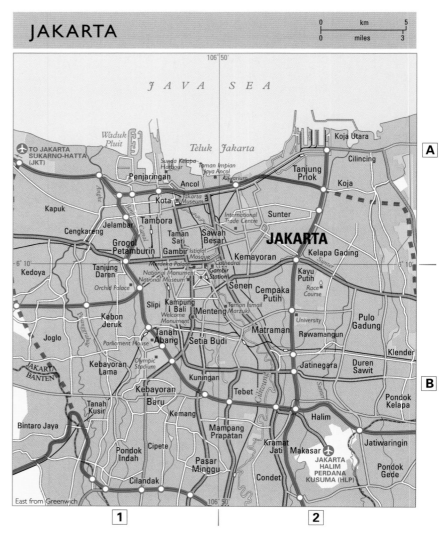

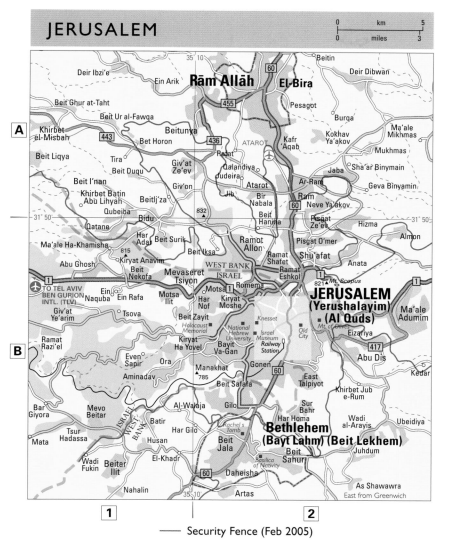

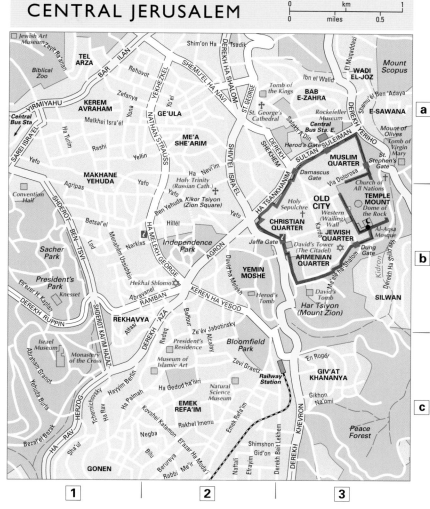

— Security Fence (Feb 2005)

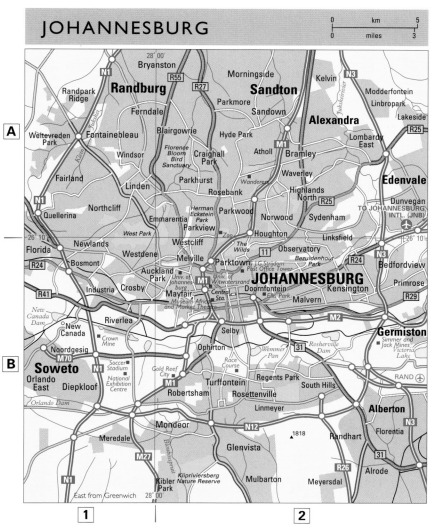

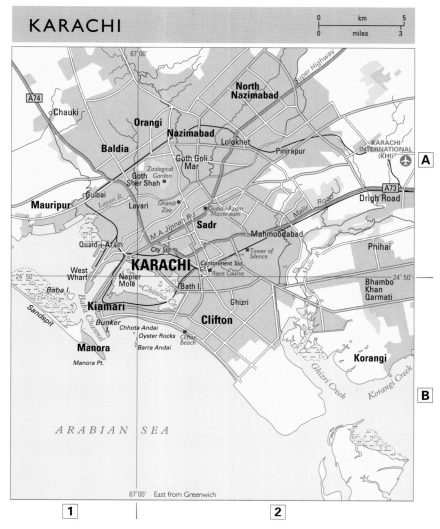

COPYRIGHT PHILIP'S

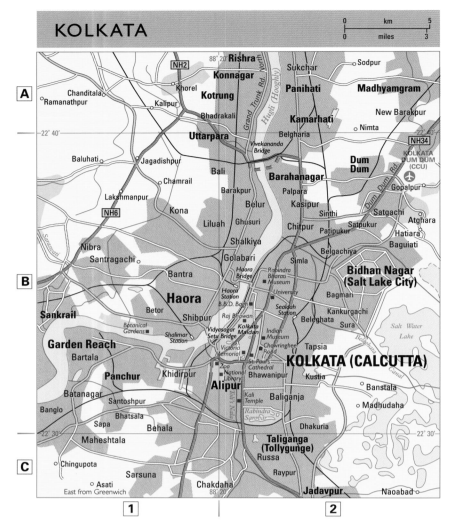

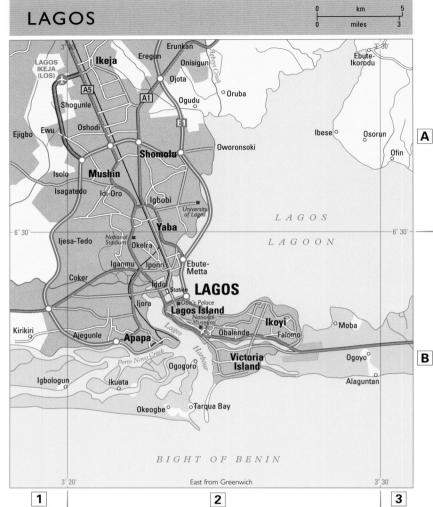

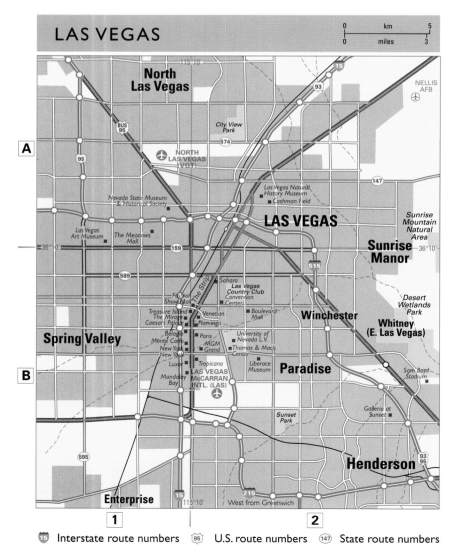

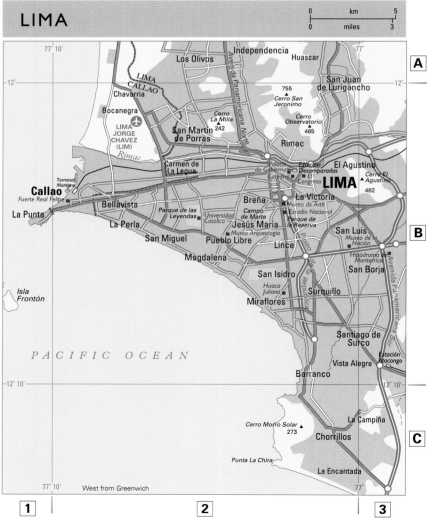

15 Interstate route numbers   95 U.S. route numbers   147 State route numbers

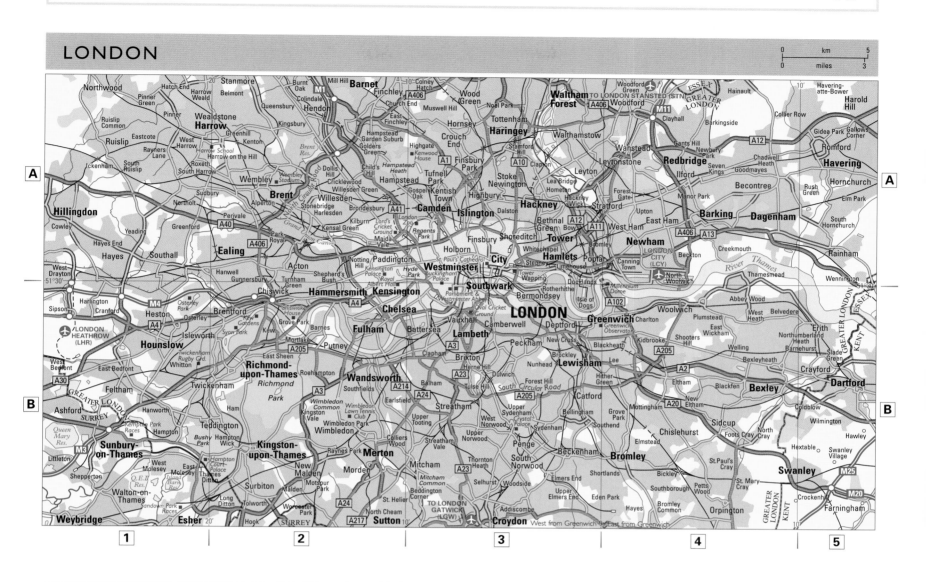

LONDON

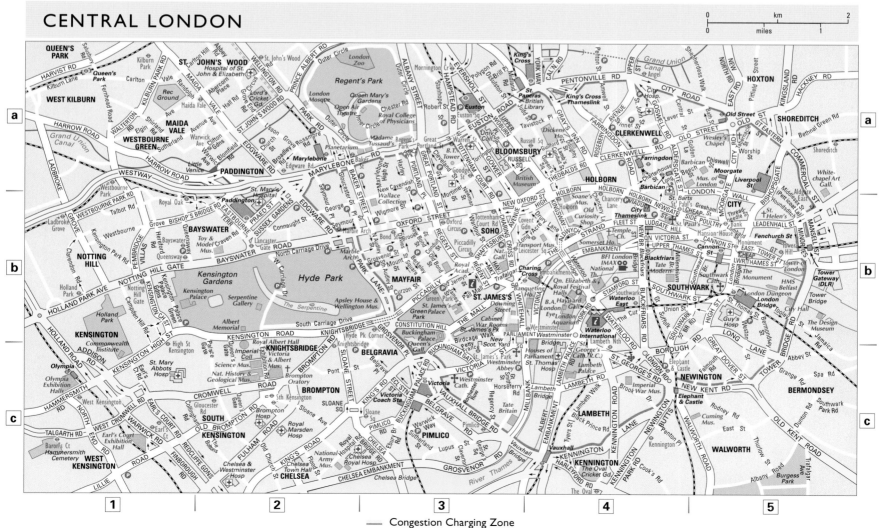

CENTRAL LONDON

— Congestion Charging Zone

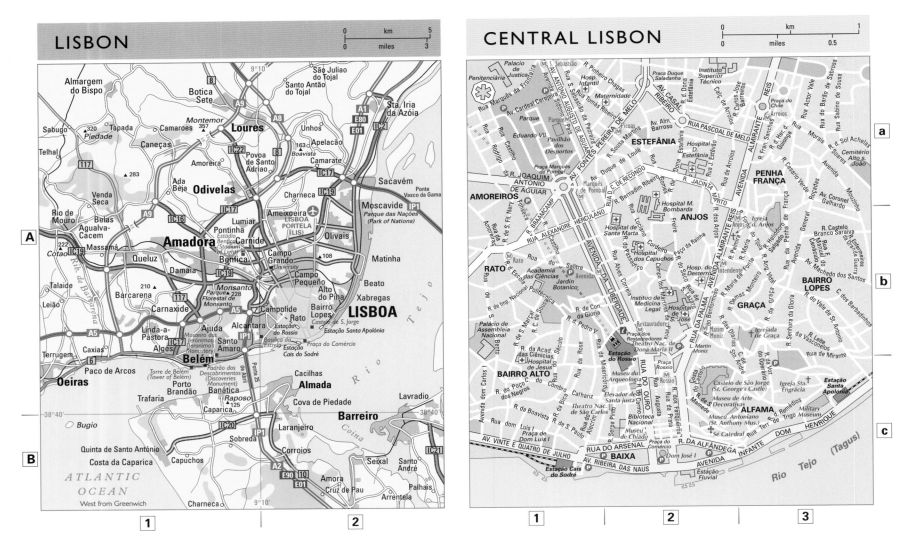

LISBON

CENTRAL LISBON

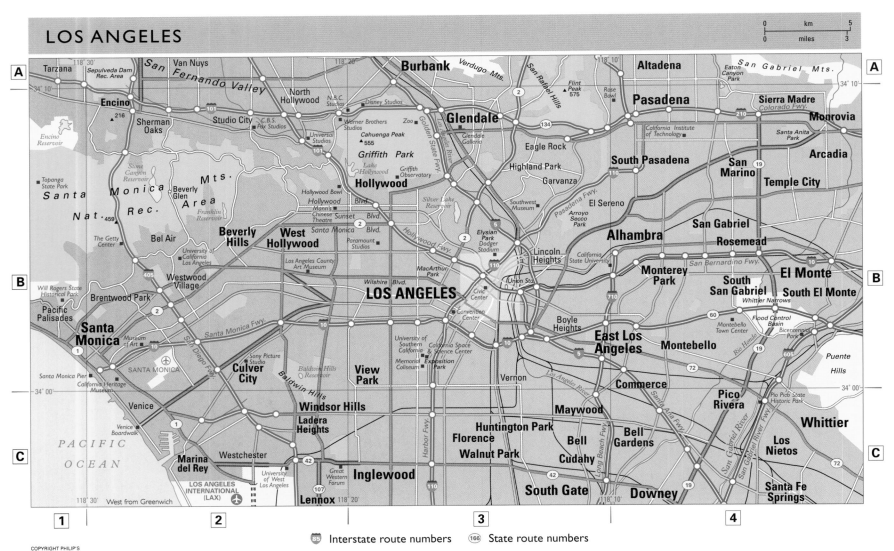

LOS ANGELES

85 Interstate route numbers   166 State route numbers

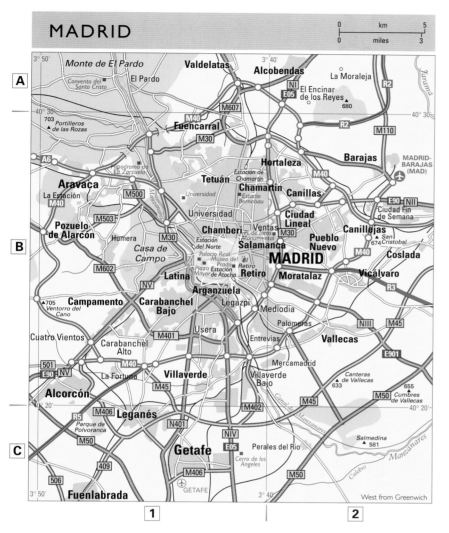

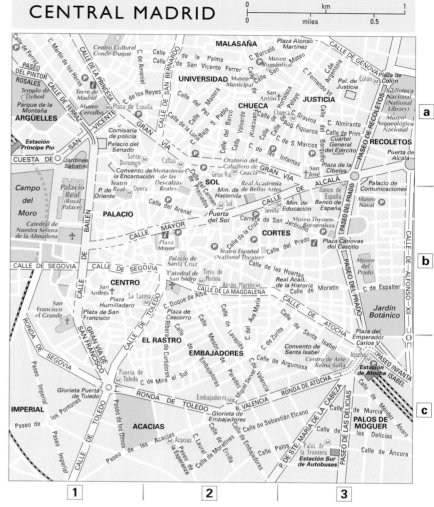

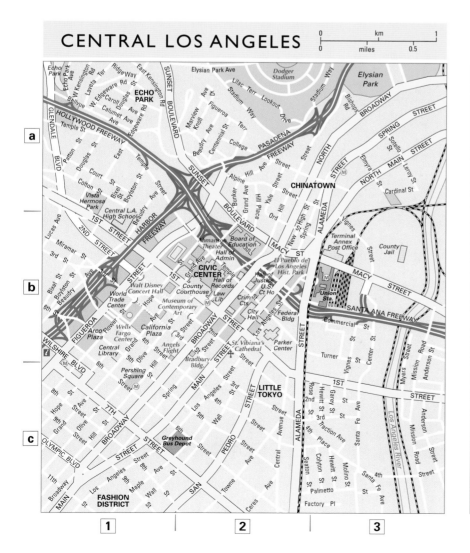

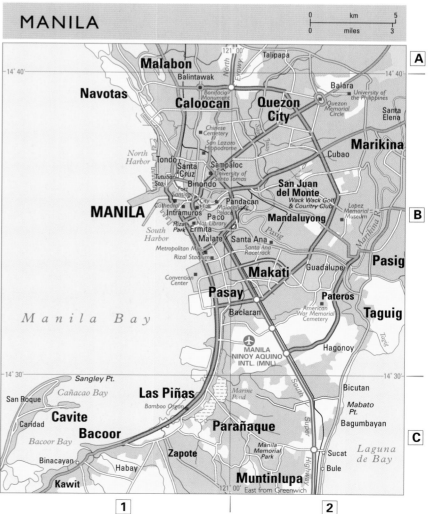

MEXICO CITY

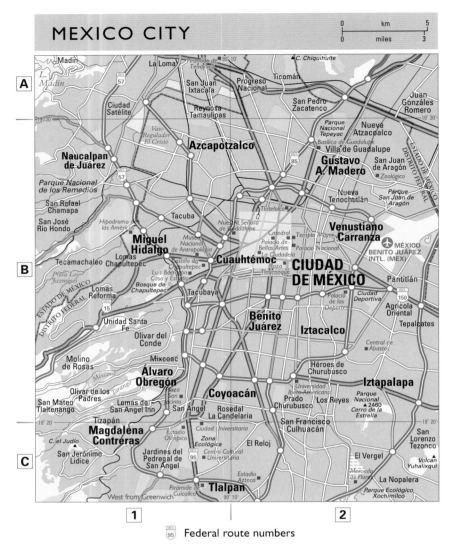

Federal route numbers

CENTRAL MEXICO CITY

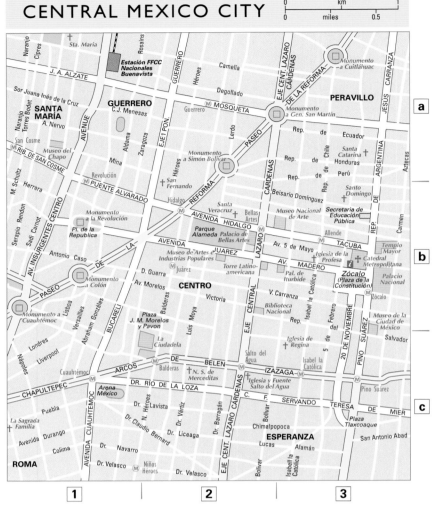

MELBOURNE

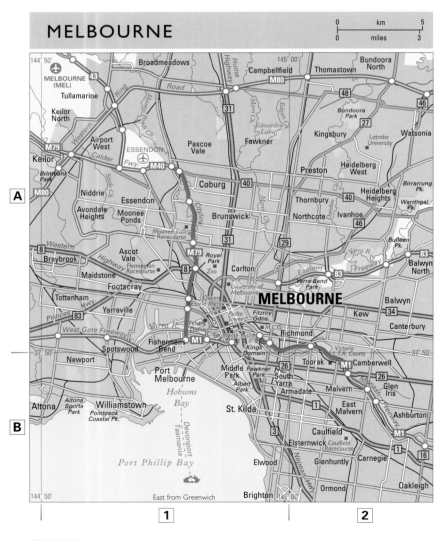

MIAMI

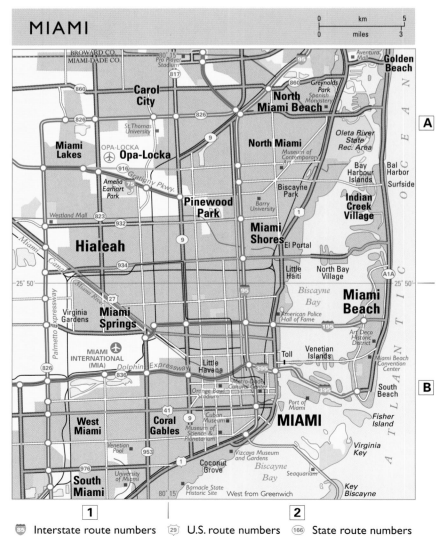

Interstate route numbers   U.S. route numbers   State route numbers

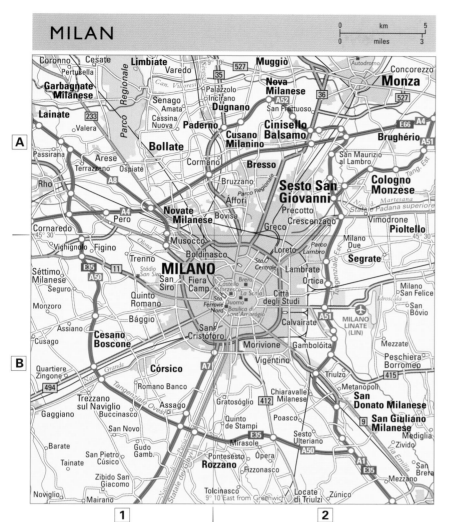

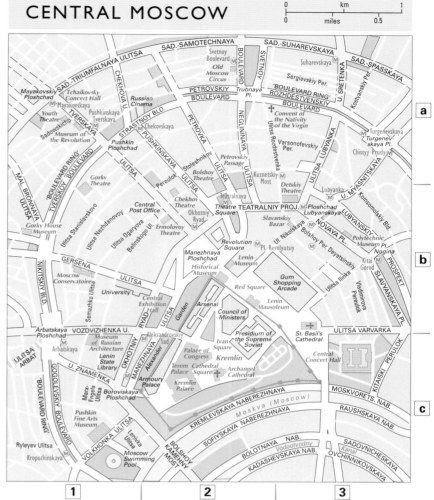

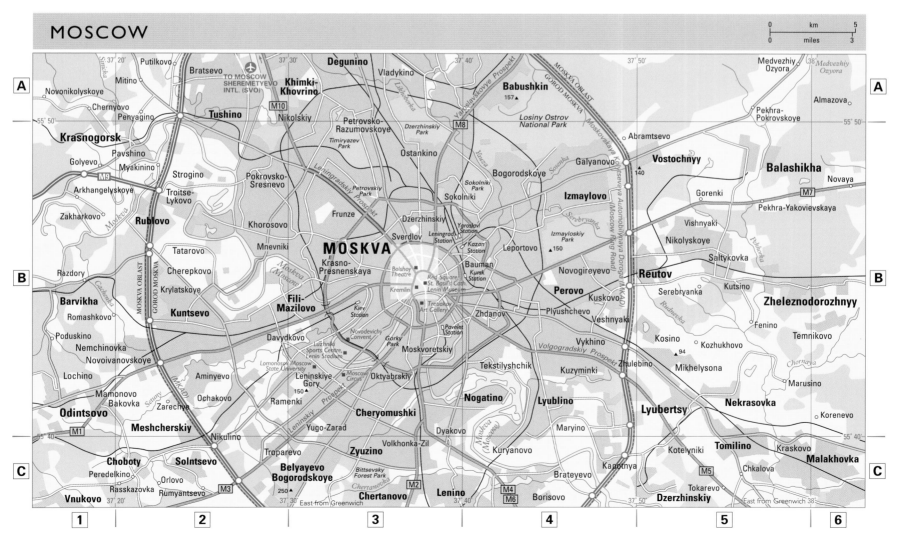

MONTRÉAL

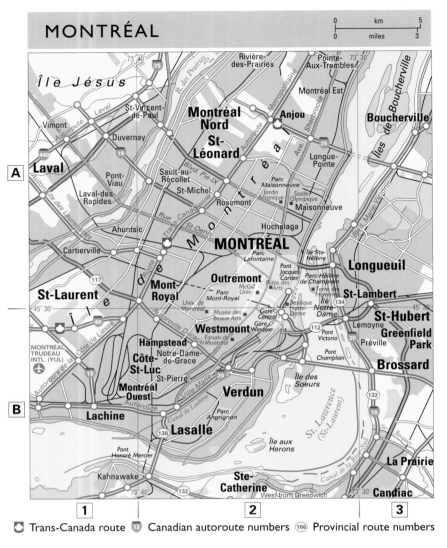

Trans-Canada route   13 Canadian autoroute numbers   166 Provincial route numbers

CENTRAL MONTRÉAL

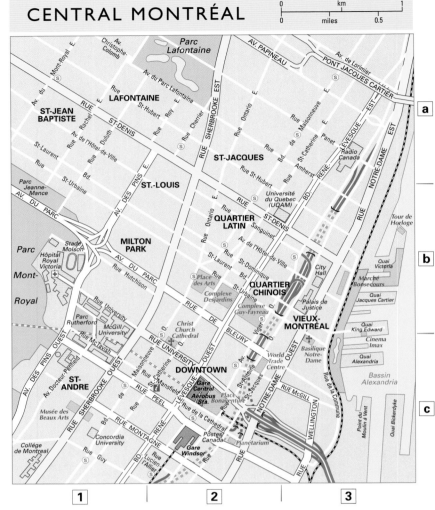

MUMBAI

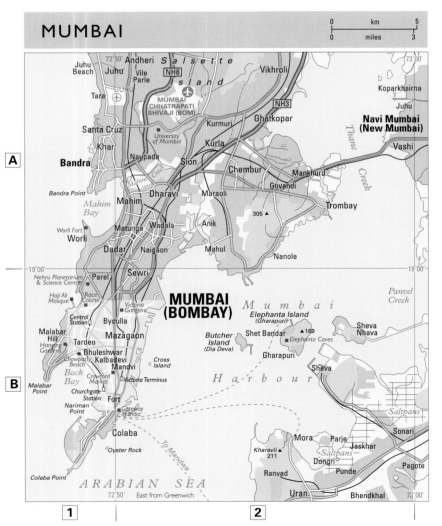

CENTRAL MUMBAI

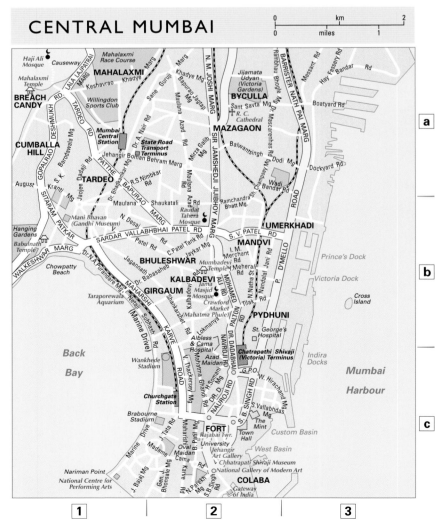

MUNICH

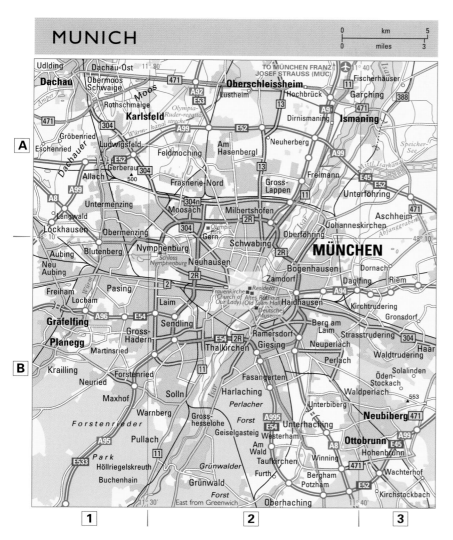

CENTRAL MUNICH

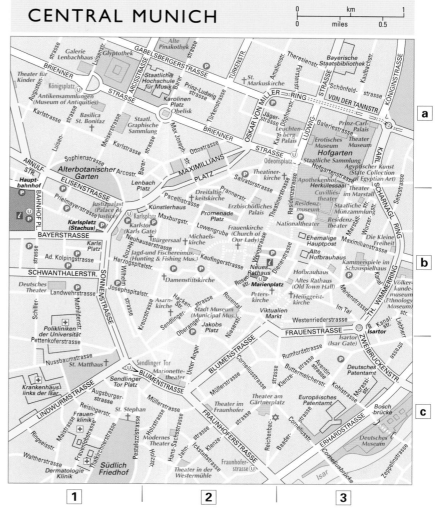

NEW ORLEANS

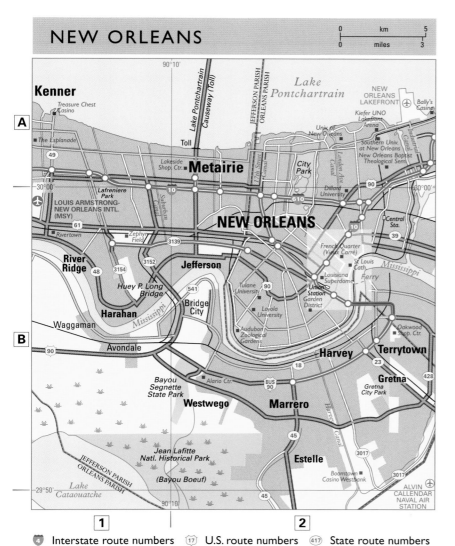

CENTRAL NEW ORLEANS

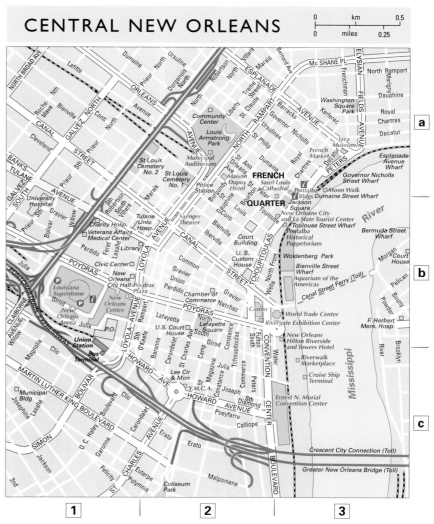

Interstate route numbers   U.S. route numbers   State route numbers

COPYRIGHT PHILIP'S

NEW YORK

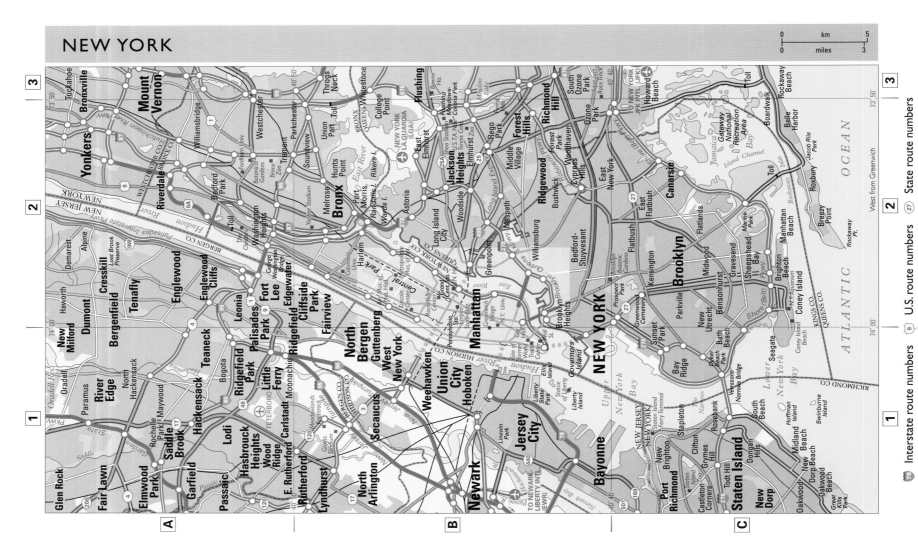

CENTRAL NEW YORK

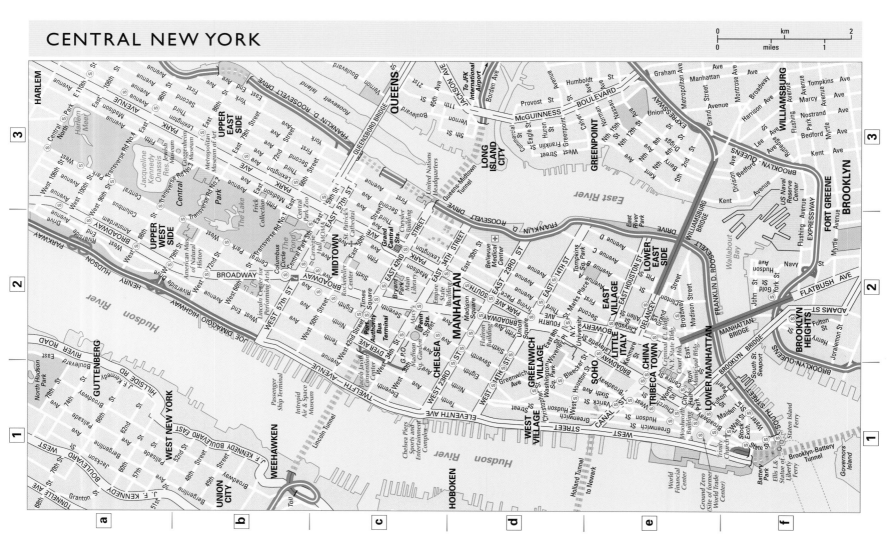

ORLANDO

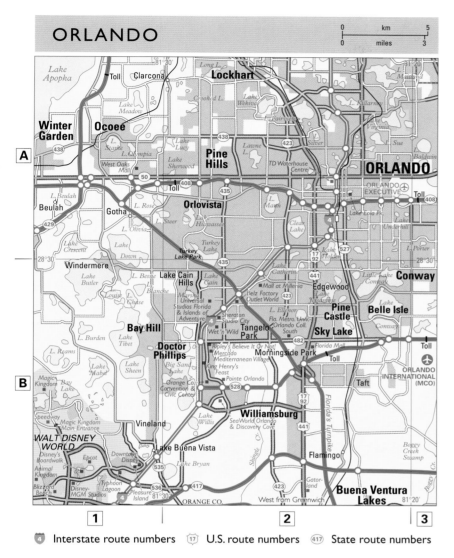

Interstate route numbers ④ · U.S. route numbers ⑰ · State route numbers ④₁₇

OSAKA

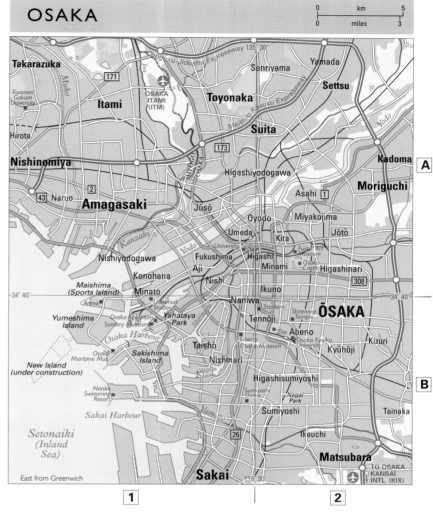

OSLO

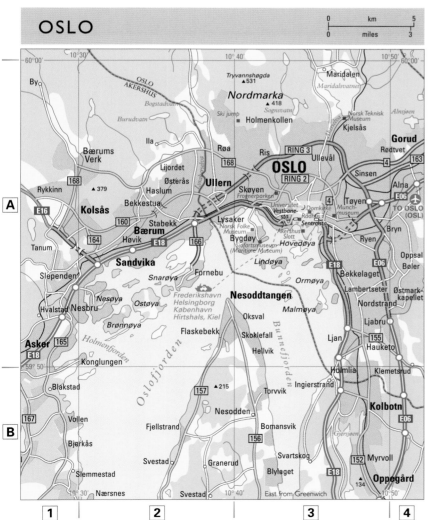

CENTRAL OSLO

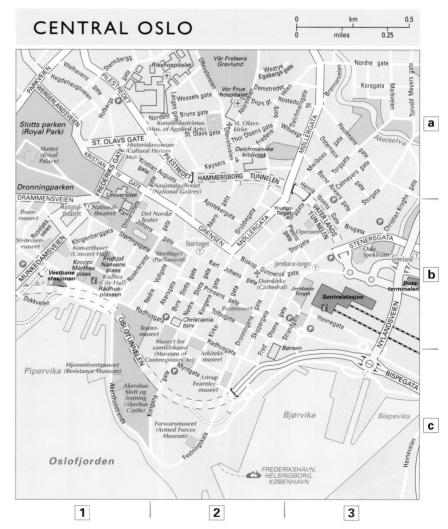

PARIS

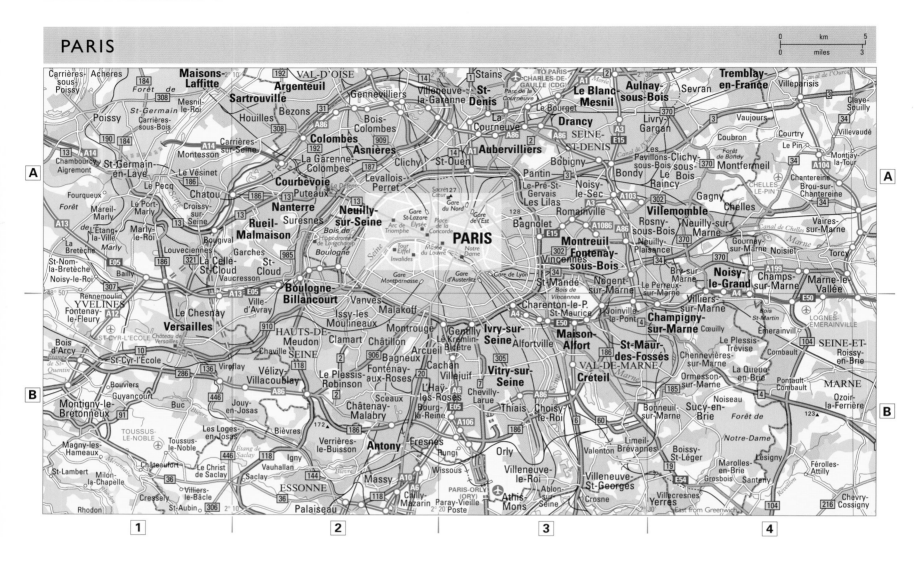

CENTRAL PARIS

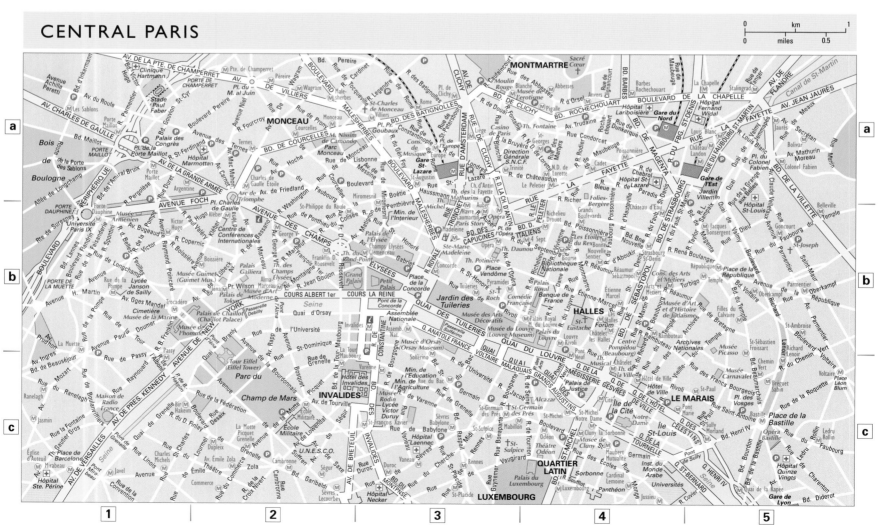

PRAGUE

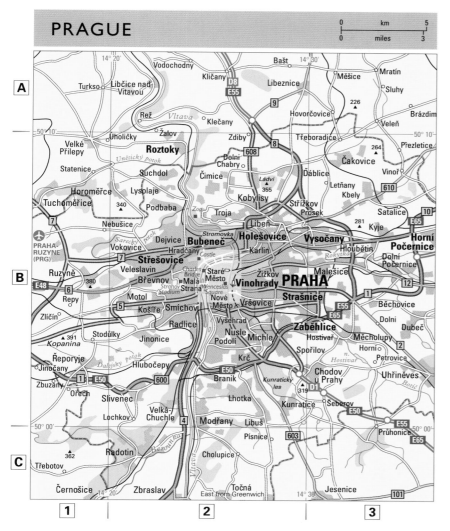

CENTRAL PRAGUE

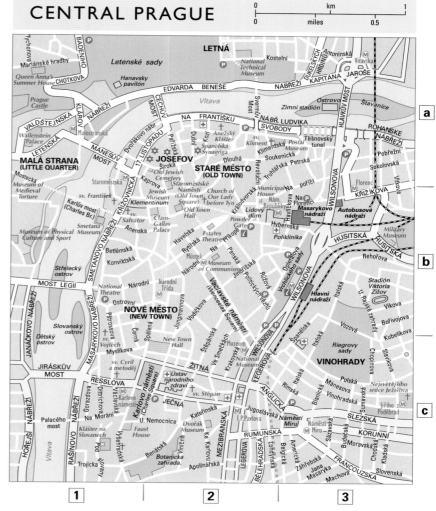

RIO DE JANEIRO

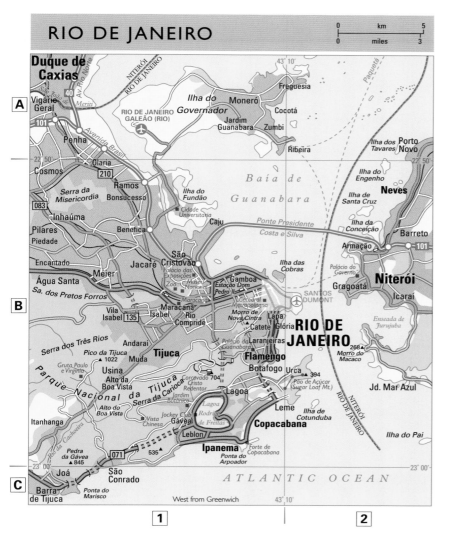

CENTRAL RIO DE JANEIRO

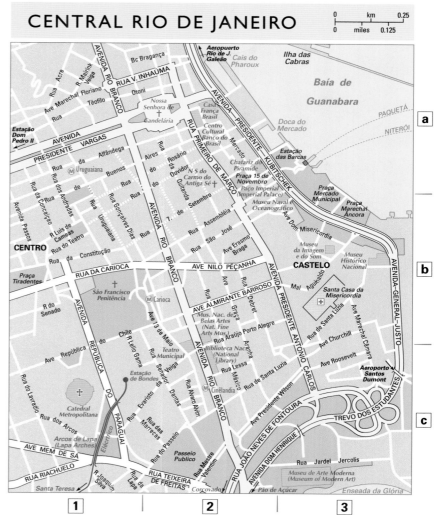

COPYRIGHT PHILIP'S

ROME

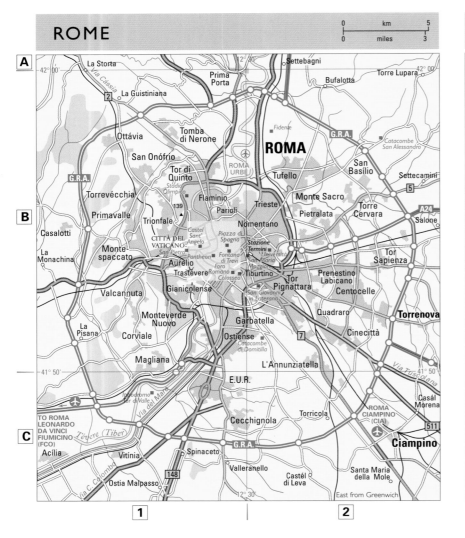

CENTRAL ROME

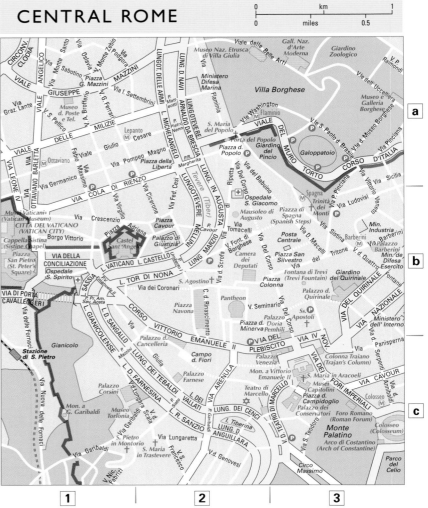

SAN FRANCISCO

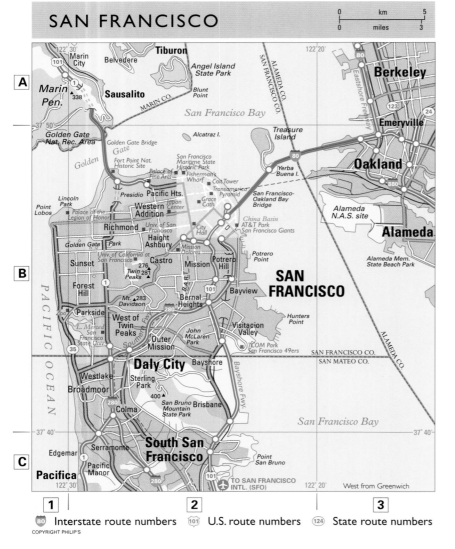

CENTRAL SAN FRANCISCO

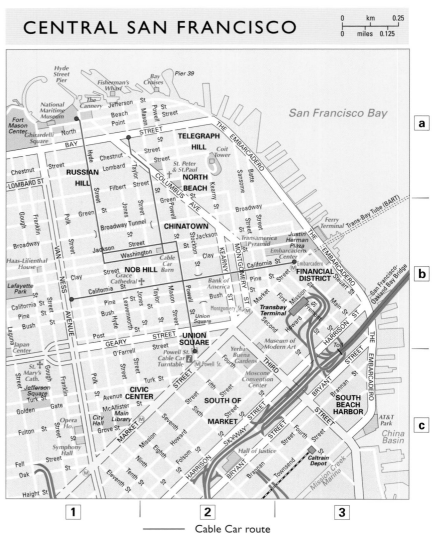

Interstate route numbers   U.S. route numbers   State route numbers

Cable Car route

COPYRIGHT PHILIP'S

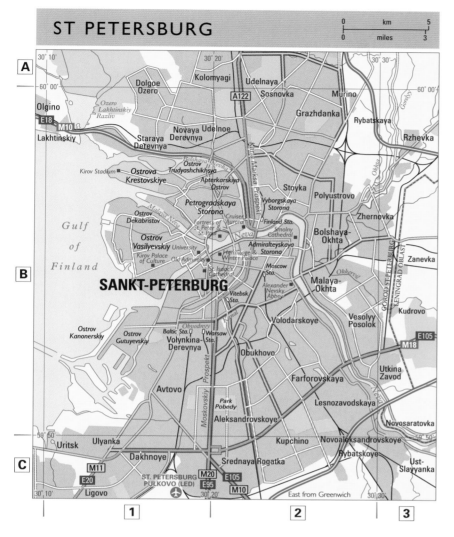

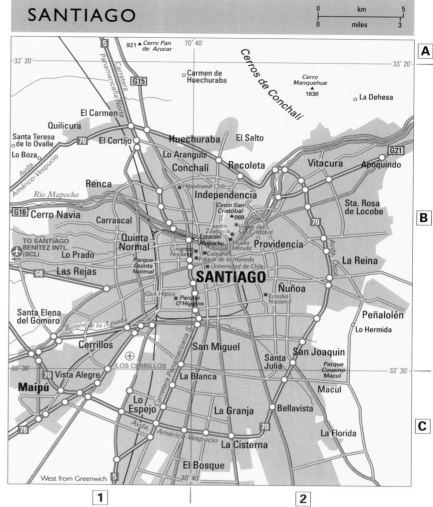

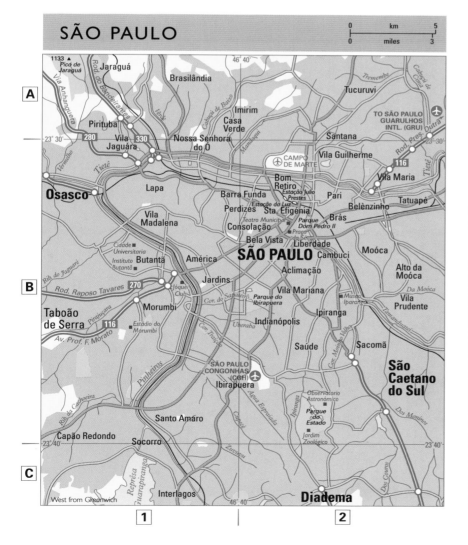

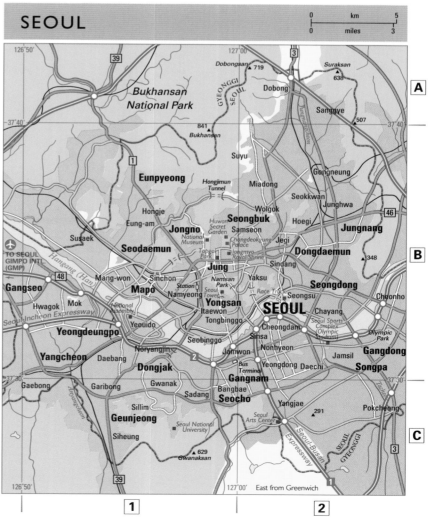

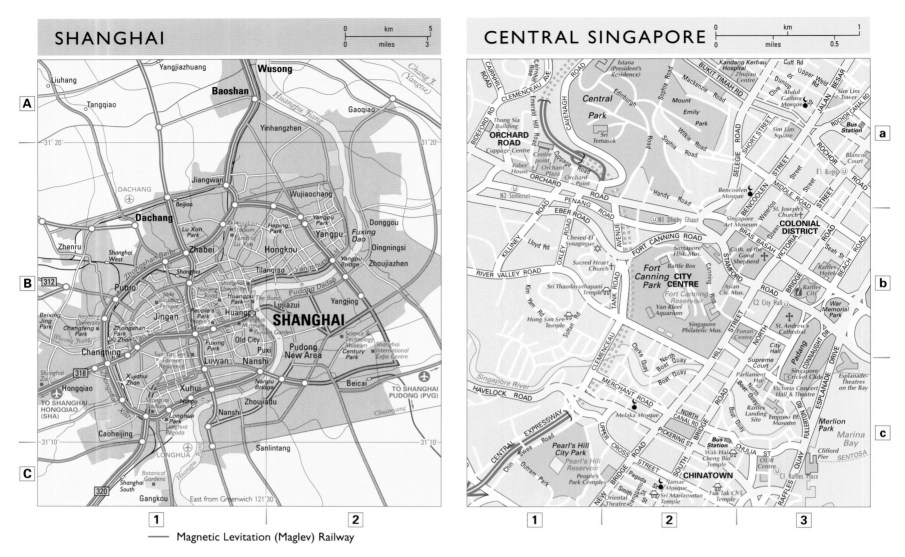

SHANGHAI

km 5
miles 3

A Liuhang
Yangjiazhuang
Wusong
Baoshan
Tangqiao
Gaoqiao
Yinhangzhen
Huangpu Jiang
Chang J. (Yangtse)
31°20'
Jiangwan
DACHANG
Beijiao
Wujiaochang
Dachang
Lu Xun Park
Hongkou Stadium
Heping Park
Yangpu Park
Yangpu
Fuxing Dao
Donggou
Zhenru
Zhabei
Tomb of Lu Xun
Hongkou
Qingningsi
Shanghai West
Shanghai University
Tilanqiao
Zhoujiazhen
Putuo
Jingan
Pudong Dadao
Yangpu Bridge
Yangjing
312
B Beixing Jing Park
Jade Buddha Temple
Nanjing Road
The Bund
Lujiazui
Yangjing
Jiaotong University
Jing'an
Zhongshan Park
People's Park
Huangpu Park
Pudong New Area
Changfeng Park
Yuyuan Garden
SHANGHAI
Changning
Zhongshan
Fuxing Park
Old City
Puxi
Science & Technology Museum
Century Park
Shanghai International Expo Centre
318
Shanghai Zoo
Xujiahui Zhan
Sun Yat-Sen's Former Residence
Shanghai Stadium
Luwan
Nanshi
Hongqiao
Xuhui
Nanpu Bridge
Beicai
TO SHANGHAI HONGQIAO (SHA)
Nanpu
Zhoujiadu
TO SHANGHAI PUDONG (PVG)
Longhua Park
Longhua Pagoda
Nanshi
Chuanyang
C Caoheijing
31°10'
Botanical Gardens
Sanlintang
LONGHUA
Shanghai South
320
Gangkou
East from Greenwich 121°30'

1 | 2

—— Magnetic Levitation (Maglev) Railway

CENTRAL SINGAPORE

km 1
miles 0.5

CAIRNHILL ROAD
CLEMENCEAU ROAD
Istana (President's Residence)
Kandang Kerbau Hospital
BUKIT TIMAH RD
Cuff Rd
Upper Weld Rd
BIDEFORD RD
CAVENAGH ROAD
Central Park
Edinburgh
Sophia
Mackenzie
Dunlop
Clive
Abdul Gaffoor Mosque
Sim Lim Tower
a
Thong Sia Building
Emerald Hill Rd
Sri Temasek
Mount
Emily Park
Wilkie
Rd
Sim Lim Square
ROCHOR CANAL RD
ORCHARD ROAD
Cuppage Centre
Centre point
Orchard Plaza
Sophia
SELEGIE ROAD
SHORT STREET
Blanco Court
Faber House
ORCHARD ROAD
Orchard Point
Handy Road
Bencoolen Mosque
BENCOOLEN STREET
MIDDLE ROAD
E1 Bugis
N2 Somerset
PENANG ROAD
Bencoolen
Waterloo
St. Joseph's Church
b
N1 Dhoby Ghaut
Singapore Art Museum
BRAS BASAH
Cath. of the Good Shepherd
KILLINEY
EBER ROAD
Chesed-El Synagogue
FORT CANNING ROAD
Singapore Hist. Mus.
STAMFORD ROAD
VICTORIA STREET
Seah St
Raffles Hotel
OXLEY RD
Lloyd Rd
Sacred Heart Church
Fort Canning Park
Battle Box
CANNING RISE
Raffles City
RIVER VALLEY ROAD
Kim Yam Rd
Sri Thandayuthapani Temple
TANK ROAD
Fort Canning Reservoir
Van Kleef Aquarium
CITY CENTRE
NORTH BRIDGE ROAD
Cath. Civ. Mus.
St. Andrew's Cathedral
War Memorial Park
Hong San See Temple
Sultan
Singapore Philatelic Mus.
Funan Centre
City Hall
CLEMENCEAU
Clarke Quay
HILL STREET
Supreme Court
City Hall
CONNAUGHT DR
Padang
b
MERCHANT ROAD
North Boat Quay
Parliament Hse.
Singapore Cricket Club
c
Singapore River
HAVELOCK ROAD
Boat Quay
Raffles Landing Site
Victoria Concert Hall & Theatre
Empress Pl. Museum
Esplanade-Theatres on the Bay
CENTRAL EXPRESSWAY
Melaka Mosque
NORTH CANAL RD
Boat Quay
FULLERTON RD
Merlion Park
Marina Bay
Swee Road
UPPER CROSS
PICKERING ST
SOUTH BRIDGE ROAD
Bus Station
CHULIA ST
OUB Centre
Clifford Pier
SENTOSA
Pearl's Hill City Park
Chin
Pearl's Hill Reservoir
Wak Hai Cheng Bio Temple
RAFFLES QUAY
c
People's Park Complex
NEW BRIDGE ROAD
Pagoda St
Smith St
CHINATOWN
Fuk Tak Ch'i Temple
Raffles Place
Oriental Theatre
Jamae Mosque
Sri Mariamman Temple

1 | 2 | 3

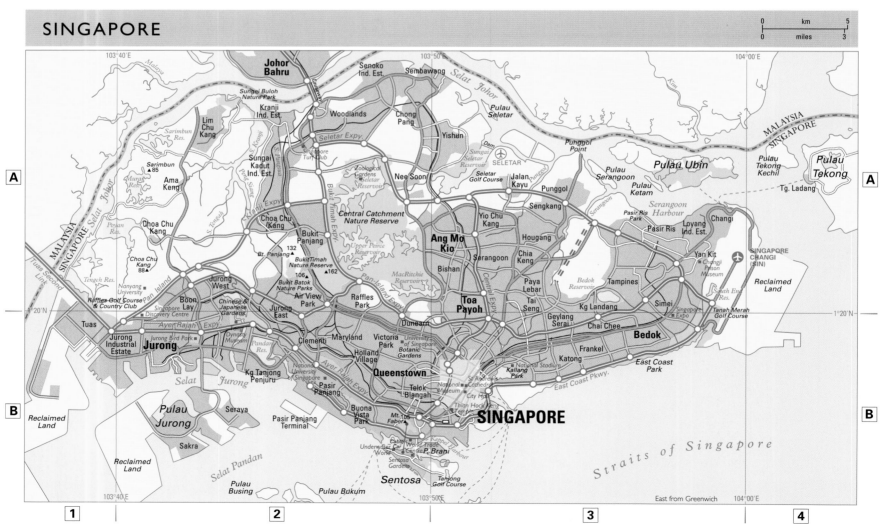

SINGAPORE

km 5
miles 3

103°40'E
Malaysia
Johor Bahru
Senoko Ind. Est.
Sembawang
Selat Johor
103°50'E
104°00'E
Sungai Buloh Nature Park
Causeway
Kranji Ind. Est.
Woodlands
Chong Pang
Yishun
Pulau Seletar
Puhggol Point
MALAYSIA SINGAPORE
A
Sarimbun Res.
Lim Chu Kang
Sungai Kadut Ind. Est.
Seletar Expy.
Singapore Turf Club
Dam
Sungai Seletar Reservoir
SELETAR
Pulau Ubin
Pulau Serangoon
Pulau Tekong Kechil
Pulau Tekong
A
Sarimbun 85
Ama Keng
Zoological Gardens
Seletar Reservoir
Nee Soon
Seletar Golf Course
Jalan Kayu
Punggol
Pulau Ketam
Tg. Ladang
Murai Res.
Poyan Res.
Choa Chu Kang
Bukit Timah Expy.
Upper Peirce Reservoir
Yio Chu Kang
Sengkang
Serangoon Harbour
Pasir Ris Park
Loyang Ind. Est.
Changi
1°20'N
Tengeh Res.
Choa Chu Kang 88
Central Catchment Nature Reserve
Bukit Panjang
Bt. Panjang 132
BukitTimah Nature Reserve 162
MacRitchie Reservoir
Ang Mo Kio
Chia Keng
Bishan
Serangoon
Hougang
Pasir Ris
Yan Kit
Changi Prison Museum
SINGAPORE CHANGI (SIN)
1°20'N
Nanyang University
Pan Island Expy.
106
Bukit Batok Nature Parks
Air View Park
Raffles Park
Toa Payoh
Paya Lebar
Tai Seng
Bedok Reservoir
Tampines
Simei
Tanah Merah Golf Course
Raffles Golf Course & Country Club
Boon Lay
Jurong West
Chinese & Japanese Gardens
Jurong East
Dunearn
Geylang Serai
Chai Chee
Singapore Expo
Discovery Centre
Ayer Rajah Expy.
Clementi
Maryland
Victoria Park
University of Singapore Botanic Gardens
Queenstown
Kg Landang
Bedok
Frankel
East Coast Park
Jurong Industrial Estate
Jurong
Dynasty Museum
Pandan Res.
Holland Village
Telok Blangah
National Museum
Katong
Kallang Park
National Stadium
East Coast Pkwy.
Tuas
Kg Tanjong Penjuru
National University of Singapore
Pasir Panjang
Buona Vista Park
Mt. 105 Faber
St Andrew's Cathedral
City Hall
Thian Hock Keng Temple
SINGAPORE
B
Reclaimed Land
Pulau Jurong
Seraya
Pasir Panjang Terminal
Underwater World
Cable Car
World Trade Centre
P. Brani
Keppel Harbour
B
Reclaimed Land
Sakra
Selat Pandan
Selat Jurong
Sentosa Gardens
Tanjong Golf Course
Straits of Singapore
Pulau Busing
Pulau Bukum
Sentosa
103°40'E
103°50'E
East from Greenwich
104°00'E

1 | 2 | 3 | 4

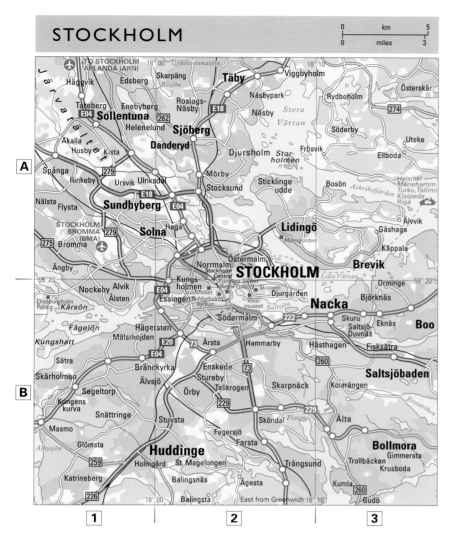

STOCKHOLM

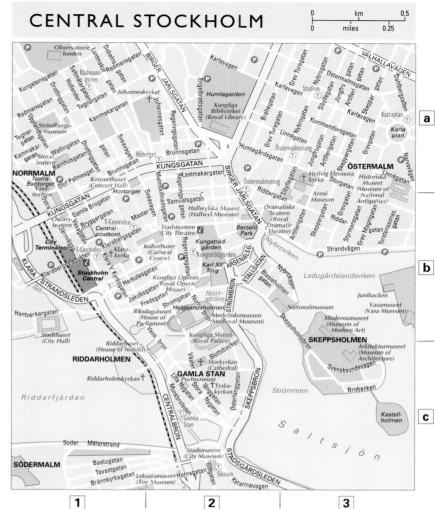

CENTRAL STOCKHOLM

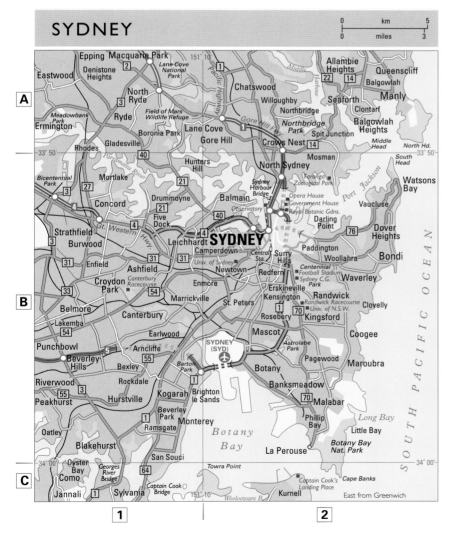

SYDNEY

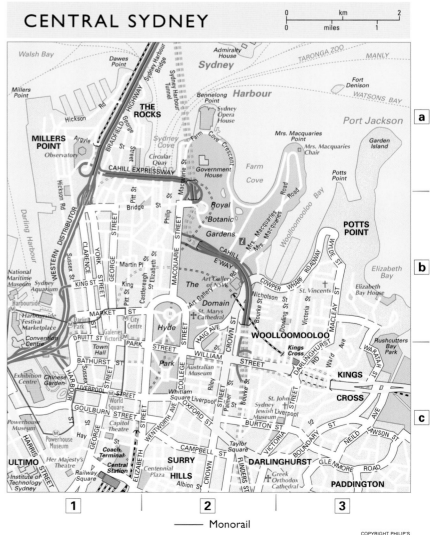

CENTRAL SYDNEY

— Monorail

COPYRIGHT PHILIP'S

CENTRAL TOKYO

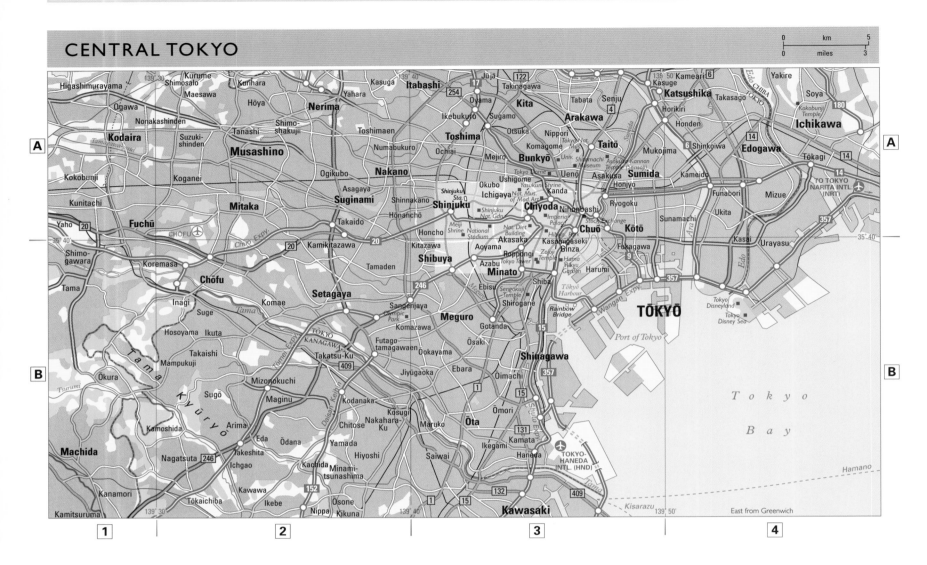

CENTRAL TOKYO

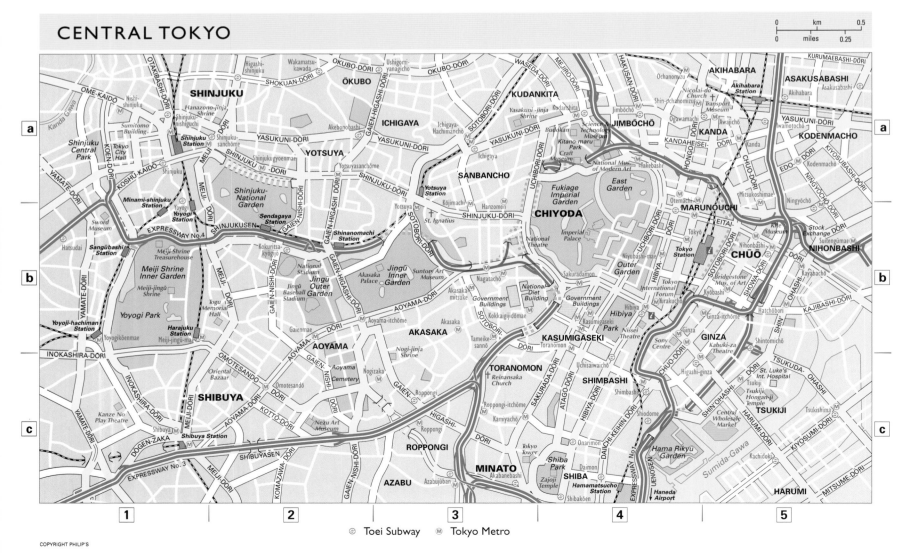

⊖ Toei Subway   Ⓜ Tokyo Metro

TEHRAN

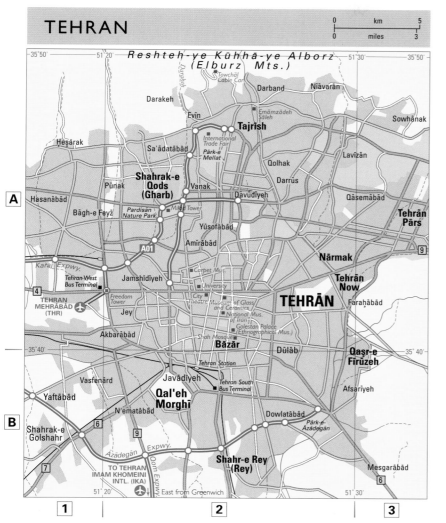

Reshteh-ye Kūhhā-ye Alborz (Elburz Mts.)

Darband · Nīāvārān · Sowhānak · Darakeh · Evīn · Emāmzādeh Ṣāleh · Tajrīsh · Sa'ādatābād · Qolhak · Lavīzān · Hesārak · Shahrak-e Qods (Gharb) · Vanak · Darrūs · Qāsemābād · Tehrān Pärs · Bāgh-e Feyẕ · Pardisān Nature Park · Yūsofābād · Pūnak · Milad Tower · Dāvūdīyeh · Karaj Expwy · Amīrābād · Nārmak · Jamshīdīyeh · Carpet Mus. · University · Tehrān Now · Tehrān West Bus Terminal · Freedom Tower · City Theatre · National Mus. · Museum of Glass and Ceramics · Nat. Iran's · TEHRĀN · Farahābād · TEHRAN MEHRĀBĀD (THR) · Jey · Golestan Palace (Ethnographical Mus.) · Shah Mosque · Akbarābād · Bāzār · Dūlāb · Qaṣr-e Fīrūzeh · Tehran Station · Vasfenārd · Javādīyeh · Tehran South Bus Terminal · Afsarīyeh · Yaftābād · Qal'eh Morghī · N'ematābād · Dowlatābād · Pärk-e Āzādegān · Shahrak-e Golshahr · Āzādegān Expwy · Shahr-e Rey (Rey) · Mesgarābād · TO TEHRAN IMAM KHOMEINI INTL. (IKA) · East from Greenwich

CENTRAL TORONTO

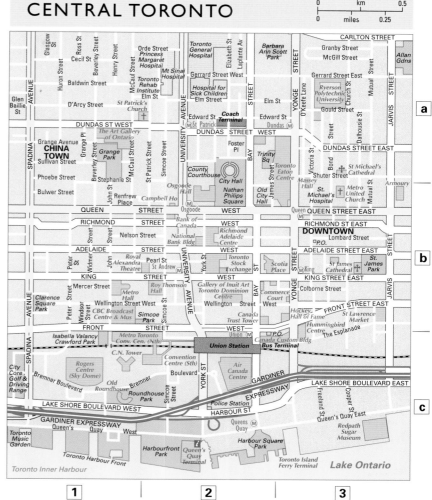

TORONTO

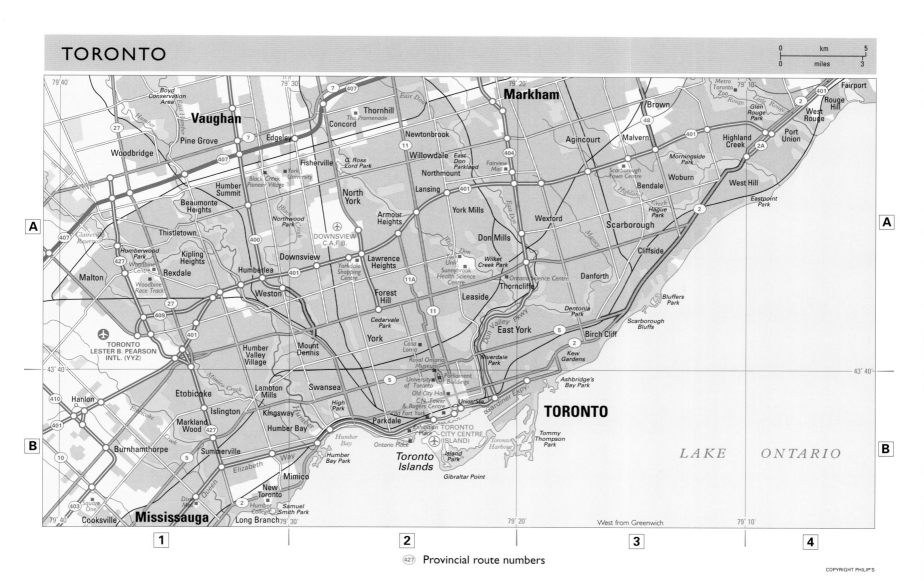

Provincial route numbers

VIENNA

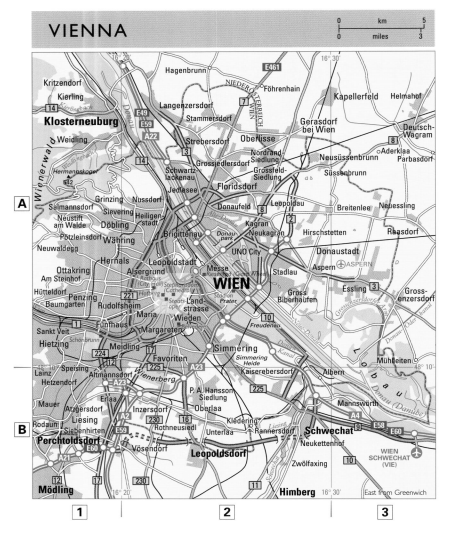

CENTRAL VIENNA

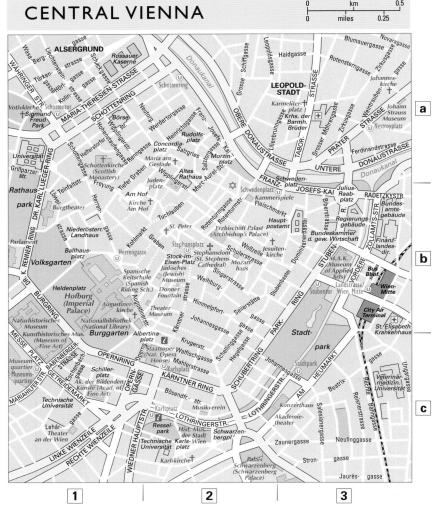

WARSAW

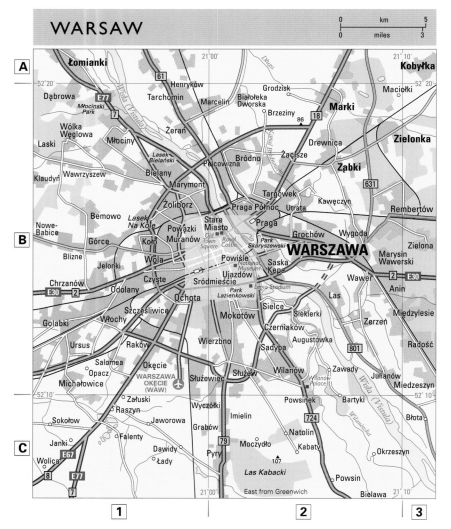

CENTRAL WARSAW

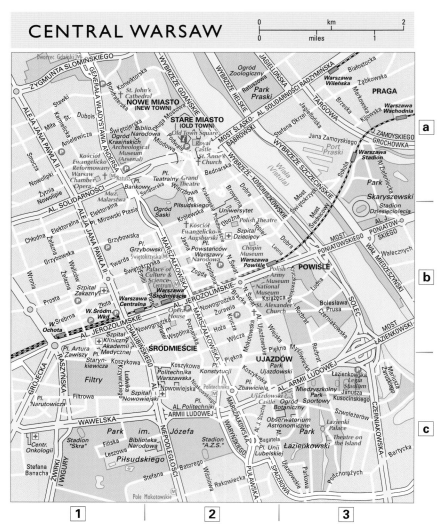

WASHINGTON

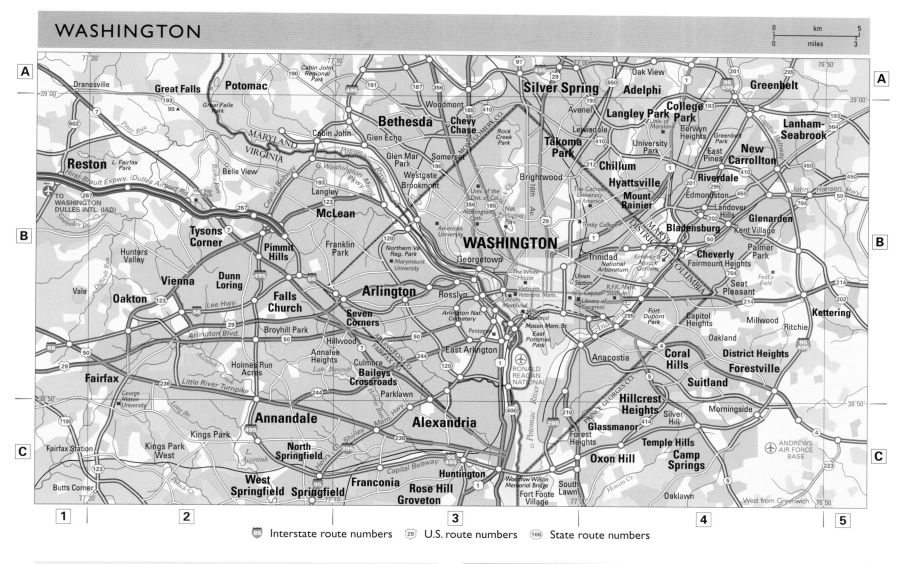

km 0 — 5 / miles 0 — 3

Interstate route numbers (85) U.S. route numbers (29) State route numbers (166)

CENTRAL WASHINGTON

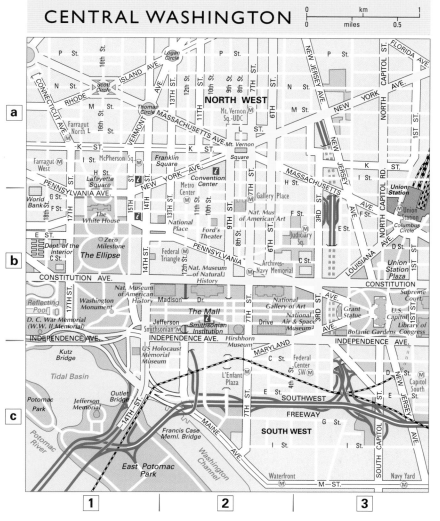

km 0 — / miles 0 — 0.5

WELLINGTON

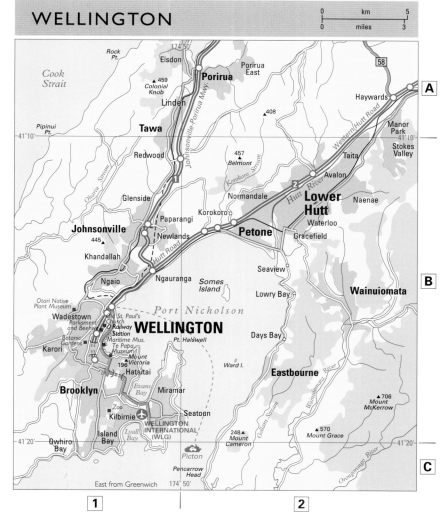

km 0 — 5 / miles 0 — 3

INDEX TO CITY MAPS

The index contains the names of all the principal places and features shown on the City Maps. Each name is followed by an additional entry in italics giving the name of the City Map within which it is located.

The number in bold type which follows each name refers to the number of the City Map page where that feature or place will be found.

The letter and figure which are immediately after the page number give the grid square on the map within which the feature or place is situated.

The letter represents the latitude and the figure the longitude. The full geographic reference is provided in the border of the City Maps.

The location given is the centre of the city, suburb or feature and is not necessarily the name. Rivers, canals and roads are indexed to their name. Rivers carry the symbol → after their name.

An explanation of the alphabetical order rules and a list of the abbreviations used are to be found at the beginning of the World Map Index.

A

Aalām *Baghdad* **3** B2
Abbey Wood *London* **15** B4
Abcoude *Amsterdam* **2** B2
Âbdîn *Cairo* **7** A2
Abeno *Osaka* **23** B2
Aberdeen *Hong Kong* **12** B1
Aberdour *Edinburgh* **11** A2
Aberdour Castle *Edinburgh* **11** A2
Abfanggraben → *Munich* **21** A3
Ablon-sur-Seine *Paris* **24** B3
Abramtsevo *Moscow* **19** B3
Abu Dis *Jerusalem* **13** B2
Abû en Numrus *Cairo* **7** B2
Abu Ghosh *Jerusalem* **13** B1
Acassuso *Buenos Aires* **7** A1
Accotink, L. *Washington* **33** C2
Accotink Cr. → *Washington* **33** B2
Achères *Paris* **24** A1
Acília *Rome* **26** C1
Aclimação *São Paulo* **27** B2
Acropolis *Athens* **2** B2
Acton *London* **15** A2
Açúcar, Pão de *Rio de Janeiro* **25** B2
Ada Beja *Lisbon* **16** A1
Adams Park *Atlanta* **3** B2
Addiscombe *London* **15** B3
Adelphi *Washington* **33** A4
Aderklaa *Vienna* **32** A3
Adler Planetarium *Chicago* **9** B3
Admiralteyskaya Storona *St. Petersburg* **27** B2
Áffori *Milan* **19** A2
Aflandshage *Copenhagen* **8** B3
Afsarīyeh *Tehran* **31** B2
Agboyi Cr. → *Lagos* **14** A2
Ågerup *Copenhagen* **8** A1
Ågesta *Stockholm* **29** B2
Aghia Marina *Athens* **2** C3
Aghia Paraskevi *Athens* **2** A2
Aghios Dimitrios *Athens* **2** B2
Aghios Ioannis Rendis *Athens* **2** B1
Agincourt *Toronto* **31** A3
Agra Canal *Delhi* **10** B2
Agricola Oriental *Mexico City* **18** B2
Agua Espraiada → *São Paulo* **27** B2
Agualva-Cacem *Lisbon* **16** A1
Agustino, Cerro El *Lima* **14** B3
Ahrensfelde *Berlin* **5** A4
Ahuntsic *Montreal* **20** A1
Ai → *Osaka* **23** A2
Aigremont *Paris* **24** A1
Air View Park *Singapore* **28** A2
Airport West *Melbourne* **18** A1
Ajegunle *Lagos* **14** B2
Aji *Osaka* **23** A1
Ajuda *Lisbon* **16** A1
Akalla *Stockholm* **29** A1
Akasaka *Tokyo* **30** A3
Akbarābād *Tehran* **31** A2
Akershus Castle = Akershus Slott *Oslo* **23** A3
Akershus Slott *Oslo* **23** A3
Al 'Azamīyah *Baghdad* **3** A2
Al Quds = Jerusalem *Jerusalem* **13** B2
Al-Walaja *Jerusalem* **13** B1
Alaguntan *Lagos* **14** B2
Alameda *San Francisco* **26** B3
Alameda Memorial State Beach Park *San Francisco* **26** B3
Albern *Vienna* **32** B2
Albert Park *Melbourne* **18** B1
Alberton *Johannesburg* **13** B2
Albertslund *Copenhagen* **8** B2
Albysjön *Stockholm* **29** B1
Alcantara *Lisbon* **16** A1
Alcatraz I. *San Francisco* **26** B2
Alcobendas *Madrid* **17** A2
Alcorcón *Madrid* **17** B1
Aldershof *Berlin* **5** B4
Aldo Bonzi *Buenos Aires* **7** C1
Aleksandrovskoye *St. Petersburg* **27** B2
Alexander Nevsky Abbey *St. Petersburg* **27** B2
Alexandra *Johannesburg* **13** A2
Alexandra *Singapore* **28** B2
Alexandria *Washington* **33** C3
Alfortville *Paris* **24** B3
Algés *Lisbon* **16** A1
Alhambra *Los Angeles* **16** B4
Alibey → *Istanbul* **12** B1
Alibey Barajı *Istanbul* **12** B1
Alibeyköy *Istanbul* **12** B1
Alimos *Athens* **2** B2
Alipur *Kolkata* **14** B1
Allach *Munich* **21** A1
Allambie Heights *Sydney* **29** A2
Allermuir Hill *Edinburgh* **11** B2
Allstate Arena *Chicago* **9** A1
Allston *Boston* **6** A2
Almada *Lisbon* **16** A2
Almagro *Buenos Aires* **7** B2
Almargem do Bispo *Lisbon* **16** A1
Almirante G. Brown, Parque *Buenos Aires* **7** C2
Almon *Jerusalem* **13** B2
Almond → *Edinburgh* **11** B2
Alna *Oslo* **23** A4
Alnsjøen *Oslo* **23** A4
Alperton *London* **15** A2
Alpine *New York* **22** A2
Alrode *Johannesburg* **13** B2
Alsemberg *Brussels* **6** B1
Alsergrund *Vienna* **32** A2
Alsip *Chicago* **9** C2
Ålsten *Stockholm* **29** B1
Älta *Stockholm* **29** B3
Altadena *Los Angeles* **16** A4
Alte-Donau → *Vienna* **32** A2
Alter Finkenkrug *Berlin* **5** A1
Altes Rathaus *Munich* **21** B2
Altglienicke *Berlin* **5** B4
Altlandsberg *Berlin* **5** A5
Altlandsberg Nord *Berlin* **5** A5
Altmannsdorf *Vienna* **32** B1
Alto da Boa Vista *Rio de Janeiro* **25** B1
Alto da Moóca *São Paulo* **27** B2
Alto do Pina *Lisbon* **16** A2
Altona *Melbourne* **18** B1
Alvik *Stockholm* **29** B1
Älvsjo *Stockholm* **29** B2
Älvvik *Stockholm* **29** A3
Am Hasenbergl *Munich* **21** A2
Am Steinhof *Vienna* **32** A1
Am Wald *Munich* **21** B2
Ama Keng *Singapore* **28** A2
Amadora *Lisbon* **16** A1
Amagasaki *Osaka* **23** A1
Amager *Copenhagen* **8** B3
Amāl Qādisiya *Baghdad* **3** B2
Amalienborg Slot *Copenhagen* **8** A3
Amata *Milan* **19** A1
Ambelokipi *Athens* **2** B2
Ameixoeira *Lisbon* **16** A2
América *São Paulo* **27** B1
American Police Hall of Fame *Miami* **18** B2
American University *Washington* **33** B3
Amin *Baghdad* **3** B2
Aminadav *Jerusalem* **13** B1
Amīrābād *Tehran* **31** A2
Amora *Lisbon* **16** B2
Amoreira *Lisbon* **16** A1
Amper → *Munich* **21** A1
Amstel-Drecht-Kanaal *Amsterdam* **2** B2
Amstelveen *Amsterdam* **2** B2
Amsterdam *Amsterdam* **2** A2
Amsterdam ✕ (AMS) *Amsterdam* **2** B1
Amsterdam-Rijnkanaal *Amsterdam* **2** B3
Amsterdam Zuidoost *Amsterdam* **2** B2
Amsterdamse Bos *Amsterdam* **2** B1
Anacosta → *Washington* **33** B4
Anacostia *Washington* **33** B4
Anadoluhisarı *Istanbul* **12** B2
Anadolukavağı *Istanbul* **12** A2
Anata *Jerusalem* **13** B2
Ancol *Jakarta* **12** A1
'Andalus *Baghdad* **3** B1
Andaraí *Rio de Janeiro* **25** B1
Anderlecht *Brussels* **6** A1
Anderson Park *Atlanta* **3** B2
Andingmen *Beijing* **4** B2
Ang Mo Kio *Singapore* **28** A3
Ängby *Stockholm* **29** A1
Angel I. *San Francisco* **26** A2
Angel Island State Park ⌓ *San Francisco* **26** A2
Angke, Kali → *Jakarta* **12** A1
Angyalföld *Budapest* **7** A2
Anik *Mumbai* **20** A2
Anin *Warsaw* **32** B2
Anjou *Montreal* **20** A2
Annalee Heights *Washington* **33** B2
Annandale *Washington* **33** C2
Anne Frankhuis *Amsterdam* **2** A2
Antony *Paris* **24** B2
Aoyama *Tokyo* **30** B3
Ap Lei Chau *Hong Kong* **12** B1
Apapa *Lagos* **14** B2
Apelacão *Lisbon* **16** A2
Apopka, L. *Orlando* **23** A1
Apoquindo *Santiago* **27** B2
Apterkarskiy Ostrov *St. Petersburg* **27** B2
Ar Kazimiyah *Baghdad* **3** B1
Ar Ram *Jerusalem* **13** A2
Ara → *Tokyo* **30** A4
Arakawa *Tokyo* **30** A3
Arany-hegyi-patak → *Budapest* **7** A2
Aravaca *Madrid* **17** B1
Arbataash *Baghdad* **3** A1
Arc de Triomphe *Paris* **24** A2
Arcadia *Los Angeles* **16** B4
Arcueil *Paris* **24** B2
Arese *Milan* **19** A1
Arganzuela *Madrid* **17** B1
Argenteuil *Paris* **24** A2
Argiroupoli *Athens* **2** B2
Argonne Forest *Chicago* **9** C1
Arima *Tokyo* **30** B2
Arlanda ✕ (ARN) *Stockholm* **29** A1
Arlington *Boston* **6** A1
Arlington *Washington* **33** B3
Arlington Heights *Boston* **6** A1
Arlington Nat. Cemetery *Washington* **33** B3
Armação *Rio de Janeiro* **25** B2
Armadale *Melbourne* **18** B2
Armour Heights *Toronto* **31** A2
Arncliffe *Sydney* **29** B1
Arnold Arboretum *Boston* **6** B2
Árpádföld *Budapest* **7** A3
Arrentela *Lisbon* **16** B2
Arroyo Seco Park *Los Angeles* **16** B3
Årsta *Stockholm* **29** B2
Art Institute *Chicago* **9** B3
Artane *Dublin* **10** A2
Artas *Jerusalem* **13** B2
Arthur's Seat *Edinburgh* **11** B3
Arts, Place des *Montreal* **20** A2
As Shawawra *Jerusalem* **13** B2
Asagaya *Tokyo* **30** A2
Asahi *Osaka* **23** A2
Asakusa *Tokyo* **30** A3
Asati *Kolkata* **14** C1
Aschheim *Munich* **21** A3
Ascot Vale *Melbourne* **18** A1
Ashbridge's Bay Park *Toronto* **31** B3
Ashburn *Chicago* **9** C2
Ashburton *Melbourne* **18** B2
Ashfield *Sydney* **29** B1
Ashford *London* **15** B1
Ashtown *Dublin* **10** A2
Askisto *Helsinki* **11** B1
Askrikefjärden *Stockholm* **29** A3
Asnières *Paris* **24** A2
Aspern *Vienna* **32** A2
Aspern ✕ *Vienna* **32** A3
Assago *Milan* **19** B1
Assendelft *Amsterdam* **2** A1
Assiano *Milan* **19** B1
Astoria *New York* **22** B2
Astrolabe Park *Sydney* **29** B2
Atarot *Jerusalem* **13** A2
Atarot ✕ *Jerusalem* **13** A2
Atghara *Kolkata* **14** B2
Athens = Athina *Athens* **2** B2
Athina *Athens* **2** B2
Athina ✕ (ATH) *Athens* **2** A3
Athínai = Athina *Athens* **2** B2
Athis-Mons *Paris* **24** B3
Athlone *Cape Town* **8** A2
Atholl *Johannesburg* **13** A2
Atīfiya *Baghdad* **3** A2
Atişalen *Istanbul* **12** B1
Atlanta *Atlanta* **3** B2
Atlanta Hartsfield Int. ✕ (ATL) *Atlanta* **3** C2
Atlanta Zoo *Atlanta* **3** B2
Atomium *Brussels* **6** A2
Attiki *Athens* **2** A2
Atzgersdorf *Vienna* **32** B1
Aubervilliers *Paris* **24** A3
Aubing *Munich* **21** B1
Auburndale *Boston* **6** A1
Auchendinny *Edinburgh* **11** B2
Auckland Park *Johannesburg* **13** B2
Auderghem *Brussels* **6** B2
Augustówka *Warsaw* **32** B2
Aulnay-sous-Bois *Paris* **24** A3
Aurelio *Rome* **26** B1
Ausîm *Cairo* **7** A1
Austerlitz, Gare d' *Paris* **24** A3
Austin *Chicago* **9** B2
Avalon *Wellington* **33** B2
Avedøre *Copenhagen* **8** B2
Avellaneda *Buenos Aires* **7** C2
Avenel *Washington* **33** B4
Avondale *Chicago* **9** B2
Avondale Heights *Melbourne* **18** A1
Avtovo *St. Petersburg* **27** B1
Ayazağa *Istanbul* **12** B1
Ayer Chawan, Pulau *Singapore* **28** B2
Ayer Merbau, Pulau *Singapore* **28** B2
Azabu *Tokyo* **30** B3
Azcapotzalco *Mexico City* **18** B1
Azteca, Estadia *Mexico City* **18** C2
Azucar, Cerro Pan de *Santiago* **27** A1

B

Baambrugge *Amsterdam* **2** B2
Baba Ch. *Karachi* **13** B1
Baba I. *Karachi* **13** B1
Babarpur *Delhi* **10** A2
Babushkin *Moscow* **19** A3
Back B. *Mumbai* **20** B1
Baclaran *Manila* **17** B2
Bacoor *Manila* **17** C1
Bacoor B. *Manila* **17** C1
Badalona *Barcelona* **4** A2
Badhoevedorp *Amsterdam* **2** A1
Badli *Delhi* **10** A1
Bærum *Oslo* **23** A2
Bağcılar *Istanbul* **12** B1
Bággio *Milan* **19** B1
Bāgh-e-Feyz *Tehran* **31** A1
Baghdād *Baghdad* **3** A2
Baghdad al Muthana ✕ *Baghdad* **3** B2
Baghdad Int. ✕ (SDA) *Baghdad* **3** B1
Bagmari *Kolkata* **14** B2
Bagneux *Paris* **24** B2
Bagnolet *Paris* **24** A3
Bagsværd *Copenhagen* **8** A2
Bagsværd Sø *Copenhagen* **8** A2
Baguiati *Kolkata* **14** B2
Bagumbayan *Manila* **17** C2
Baha'i Temple *Chicago* **9** A2
Bahçeköy *Istanbul* **12** A1
Bahçelievler *Istanbul* **12** B1
Bahtîm *Cairo* **7** A2
Baile Atha Cliath = Dublin *Dublin* **10** A2
Baileys Crossroads *Washington* **33** B3
Bailly *Paris* **24** A1
Bairro Lopes *Lisbon* **16** A2
Baisha *Guangzhou* **11** B2
Baiyun Hill *Guangzhou* **11** B2
Baiyun Int. ✕ (CAN) *Guangzhou* **11** A2
Bakırköy *Istanbul* **12** C1
Bal Harbor *Miami* **18** A2
Balara *Manila* **17** B2
Baldia *Karachi* **13** A1
Baldoyle *Dublin* **10** A3
Baldwin, L. *Orlando* **23** A3
Baldwin Hills *Los Angeles* **16** B2
Baldwin Hills Res. *Los Angeles* **16** B2
Balgowlah *Sydney* **29** A2
Balgowlah Heights *Sydney* **29** A2
Balham *London* **15** B3
Bali *Kolkata* **14** B1
Baliganja *Kolkata* **14** B2
Balingsnäs *Stockholm* **29** B2
Balingsta *Stockholm* **29** B2
Balintawak *Manila* **17** B1
Ballerup *Copenhagen* **8** A2
Ballinteer *Dublin* **10** B2
Ballyboden *Dublin* **10** B2
Ballybrack *Dublin* **10** B3
Ballyfermot *Dublin* **10** A1
Ballymorefinn Hill *Dublin* **10** B1
Ballymun *Dublin* **10** A2
Balmain *Sydney* **29** B2
Baluhati *Kolkata* **14** B1
Balvanera *Buenos Aires* **7** B2
Balwyn *Melbourne* **18** A2
Balwyn North *Melbourne* **18** A2
Banática *Lisbon* **16** A1
Bandra *Mumbai* **20** A1
Bandra Pt. *Mumbai* **20** A1
Bang Kapi *Bangkok* **3** B2
Bang Na *Bangkok* **3** B2
Bangbae *Seoul* **27** C1
Bangkhen *Bangkok* **3** A2
Bangkok *Bangkok* **3** B2
Bangkok Noi *Bangkok* **3** B1
Bangkok Yai *Bangkok* **3** B1
Banglo *Kolkata* **14** B1
Bangrak *Bangkok* **3** B2
Bangsu *Bangkok* **3** B2
Banks, C. *Sydney* **29** C2
Banksmeadow *Sydney* **29** B2
Banstala *Kolkata* **14** B2
Bantra *Kolkata* **14** B1
Baoshan *Shanghai* **28** A1
Bar Giyora *Jerusalem* **13** B1
Barahanagar *Kolkata* **14** B2
Barajas *Madrid* **17** B2
Barajas, Madrid ✕ (MAD) *Madrid* **17** B2
Barakpur *Kolkata* **14** A2
Barcarena *Lisbon* **16** A1
Barcarena, Rib. de → *Lisbon* **16** A1
Barcelona *Barcelona* **4** A2
Barcelona-Prat ✕ (BCN) *Barcelona* **4** B1
Barceloneta *Barcelona* **4** A2
Barcroft, L. *Washington* **33** B3
Barking *London* **15** A4
Barkingside *London* **15** A4
Barnes *London* **15** B2
Barnet *London* **15** A2
Barra Andai *Karachi* **13** B2
Barra Funda *São Paulo* **27** B2
Barracas *Buenos Aires* **7** B2
Barrackpur = Barakpur *Kolkata* **14** A2
Barranco *Lima* **14** B2
Barreiro *Lisbon* **16** B2
Barreto *Rio de Janeiro* **25** B2
Bartala *Kolkata* **14** B1
Barton Park *Sydney* **29** B1
Bartyki *Warsaw* **32** C2
Basus *Cairo* **7** A2
Batanagar *Kolkata* **14** B1
Bath Beach *New York* **22** C1
Bath I. *Karachi* **13** B2
Batir *Jerusalem* **13** B1
Batok, Bukit *Singapore* **28** A2
Battersea *London* **15** B3
Bauman *Moscow* **19** B3
Baumgarten *Vienna* **32** A1
Bay, L. *Orlando* **23** A2
Bay Harbour Islands *Miami* **18** A2
Bay Hill *Orlando* **23** B1
Bay Ridge *New York* **22** C1
Bayit Va-Gan *Jerusalem* **13** B2
Bayonne *New York* **22** B1
Bayrampaşa *Istanbul* **12** B1
Bayshore *San Francisco* **26** B2
Bayt Lahm *Jerusalem* **13** B2
Bayview *San Francisco* **26** B2
Bāzār *Tehran* **31** A2
Beacon Hill *Hong Kong* **12** A2
Beato *Lisbon* **16** A2
Beaumont *Dublin* **10** A2
Beaumonte Heights *Toronto* **31** A1
Bebek *Istanbul* **12** B2
Běchovice *Prague* **25** B3
Beck L. *Chicago* **9** A1
Beckenham *London* **15** B3
Beckton *London* **15** A4
Becontree *London* **15** A4
Beddington Corner *London* **15** B3
Bedford *Boston* **6** A1
Bedford Park *Chicago* **9** C2
Bedford Park *New York* **22** A2
Bedford Stuyvesant *New York* **22** B2
Bedford View *Johannesburg* **13** B2
Bedok *Singapore* **28** B3
Bedok, Res. *Singapore* **28** A3
Beersel *Brussels* **6** B1
Behala *Kolkata* **14** B1
Bei Hai *Beijing* **4** B2
Beicai *Shanghai* **28** B2
Beijing *Beijing* **4** B1
Beit Duqu *Jerusalem* **13** A1
Beit Ghur at-Taht *Jerusalem* **13** A1
Beit Ghur el-Fawqa *Jerusalem* **13** A1
Beit Hanina *Jerusalem* **13** B2
Beit Ij'za *Jerusalem* **13** A1
Beit Iksa *Jerusalem* **13** B2
Beit I'nan *Jerusalem* **13** A1
Beit Jala *Jerusalem* **13** B2
Beit Lekhem = Bayt Lahm *Jerusalem* **13** B2
Beit Liqya *Jerusalem* **13** A1
Beit Nekofa *Jerusalem* **13** B1
Beit Sahur *Jerusalem* **13** B2
Beit Sofafa *Jerusalem* **13** B2
Beit Surik *Jerusalem* **13** B1
Beit Ur al-Fawqa *Jerusalem* **13** A1
Beit Zayit *Jerusalem* **13** B1
Beitaipingzhuan *Beijing* **4** B1
Beitar Ilit *Jerusalem* **13** B1
Beitin *Jerusalem* **13** A2
Beitsun *Guangzhou* **11** B2
Beitunya *Jerusalem* **13** A2
Beixing Jing Park *Shanghai* **28** B1
Békásmegyer *Budapest* **7** A2
Bekkelaget *Oslo* **23** A3
Bekkestua *Oslo* **23** A2
Bel Air *Los Angeles* **16** B2
Bela Vista *São Paulo* **27** B2
Bélanger *Montreal* **20** A1
Belas *Lisbon* **16** A1
Beleghata *Kolkata* **14** B2
Belém *Lisbon* **16** A1
Belém, Torre de *Lisbon* **16** A1
Belènzinho *São Paulo* **27** B2
Belgachiya *Kolkata* **14** B2
Belgharia *Kolkata* **14** B2
Belgrano *Buenos Aires* **7** B2
Bell *Los Angeles* **16** C3
Bell Gardens *Los Angeles* **16** C4
Bellavista *Lima* **14** B2
Bellavista *Santiago* **27** C2
Belle Harbor *New York* **22** C2
Belle Isle *Orlando* **23** B2
Belle View *Washington* **33** B2
Bellingham *London* **15** B3
Bellwood *Chicago* **9** B1
Belmont *Boston* **6** A1
Belmont *London* **15** A2
Belmont, Mt. *Wellington* **33** B2
Belmont Cragin *Chicago* **9** B2
Belmont Harbor *Chicago* **9** B3
Belmore *Sydney* **29** B1
Belur *Kolkata* **14** B2
Belvedere *Atlanta* **3** B3
Belvedere *London* **15** B4
Belvedere *San Francisco* **26** A2
Belyayevo Bogorodskoye *Moscow* **19** C2
Bemowo *Warsaw* **32** B1
Benaki Museum *Athens* **2** B2
Bendale *Toronto* **31** A3
Benefica *Rio de Janeiro* **25** B1
Benfica *Lisbon* **16** A1
Benito Juárez *Mexico City* **18** B2
Benito Juárez, Int. ✕ (MEX) *Mexico City* **18** B2
Bensonhurst *New York* **22** C2
Berchem-Ste-Agathe *Brussels* **6** A1
Berg am Laim *Munich* **21** B2
Bergenfield *New York* **22** A2
Bergham *Munich* **21** B2
Bergvliet *Cape Town* **8** B1
Beri *Barcelona* **4** A1
Berkeley *San Francisco* **26** A3
Berlin *Berlin* **5** A3
Berlin Dom *Berlin* **5** A3
Berlin Tegel ✕ (TXL) *Berlin* **5** A2
Berlin Tempelhof ✕ (THF) *Berlin* **5** B3
Bermondsey *London* **15** B3
Bernabeu, Estadio *Madrid* **17** B1
Bernal Heights *San Francisco* **26** B2
Berwyn *Chicago* **9** B2
Berwyn Heights *Washington* **33** B4
Besiktas *Istanbul* **12** B2
Besós → *Barcelona* **4** A2
Bessie, L. *Orlando* **23** B1
Bet Horon *Jerusalem* **13** A1
Bethesda *Washington* **33** B3
Bethlehem = Bayt Lahm *Jerusalem* **13** B2
Bethnal Green *London* **15** A3
Betor *Kolkata* **14** B1
Beulah *Orlando* **23** A1
Beulah, L. *Orlando* **23** A1
Beverley Hills *Sydney* **29** B1
Beverley Park *Sydney* **29** B1
Beverly *Chicago* **9** C3
Beverly Arts Center *Chicago* **9** C2
Beverly Glen *Los Angeles* **16** B2
Beverly Hills *Los Angeles* **16** B2
Beverly Hills -Morgan Park Historic District *Chicago* **9** C2
Bexley *Sydney* **29** B1
Bexley □ *London* **15** B4
Bexleyheath *London* **15** B4
Beykoz *Istanbul* **12** B2
Beylerbeyi *Istanbul* **12** B2
Beyoğlu *Istanbul* **12** B1
Bezons *Paris* **24** A2
Bezuidenhout Park *Johannesburg* **13** B2
Bhadrakali *Kolkata* **14** A2
Bhalswa *Delhi* **10** A2
Bhambo Khan Qarmati *Karachi* **13** B2
Bhatsala *Kolkata* **14** B1
Bhawanipur *Kolkata* **14** B2
Bhendkhal *Mumbai* **20** B2
Bhuleshwar *Mumbai* **20** B1
Białołeka Dworska *Warsaw* **32** B2
Bicentennial Park *Los Angeles* **16** B4
Bicentennial Park *Sydney* **29** B1
Bickley *London* **15** B4
Bicutan *Manila* **17** C2
Bidhan Nagar *Kolkata* **14** B2
Bidu *Jerusalem* **13** B1
Bielany *Warsaw* **32** B1
Bielawa *Warsaw* **32** C2
Biesdorf *Berlin* **5** A4
Bièvre → *Paris* **24** B1
Bièvres *Paris* **24** B2
Big Sand Lake *Orlando* **23** B2
Bilston *Edinburgh* **11** B2
Binacayan *Manila* **17** C1
Binondo *Manila* **17** B1
Bintaro Jaya *Jakarta* **12** B1
Bir Nabala *Jerusalem* **13** A2
Birak el Kiyam *Cairo* **7** A1
Birch Cliff *Toronto* **31** A3
Birkenstein *Berlin* **5** A5
Birkholz *Berlin* **5** A4
Birkholzaue *Berlin* **5** A4
Birrarrung Park *Melbourne* **18** A2
Biscayne Park *Miami* **18** A2
Bishop Lavis *Cape Town* **8** A2
Bishopscourt *Cape Town* **8** A1
Bispebjerg *Copenhagen* **8** A3
Bittsevsky Forest Park *Moscow* **19** C2
Björknas *Stockholm* **29** B3
Black Cr. → *Toronto* **31** A2
Black Creek Pioneer Village *Toronto* **31** A1
Blackfen *London* **15** B4
Blackheath *London* **15** B4
Blackrock *Dublin* **10** B2
Bladensburg *Washington* **33** B4
Blair Village *Atlanta* **3** C2
Blairgowrie *Johannesburg* **13** A2
Blake House *Boston* **6** B2
Blakehurst *Sydney* **29** B1
Blakstad *Oslo* **23** B1
Blanche, L. *Orlando* **23** B1
Blankenburg *Berlin* **5** A3
Blankenfelde *Berlin* **5** A3
Blizne *Warsaw* **32** B1
Błota *Warsaw* **32** C3
Blue Island *Chicago* **9** D2
Blue Mosque = Sultanahme Camil *Istanbul* **12** B1
Bluebell *Dublin* **10** B1
Bluff Hd. *Hong Kong* **12** B2
Bluffers Park *Toronto* **31** A3
Blumberg *Berlin* **5** A4
Blunt Pt. *San Francisco* **26** A2
Blutenberg *Munich* **21** B1
Blylaget *Oslo* **23** B3
Boa Vista, Alto do *Rio de Janeiro* **25** B1
Boardwalk *New York* **22** C3
Boavista *Lisbon* **16** A2
Bobigny *Paris* **24** A3
Bocanegra *Lima* **14** B2
Boedo *Buenos Aires* **7** B2
Bogenhausen *Munich* **21** B2
Boggy Creek Swamp *Orlando* **23** B2
Bogorodskoye *Moscow* **19** B3
Bogota *New York* **22** A1
Bogstadvatnet *Oslo* **23** A2
Bohnsdorf *Berlin* **5** B4
Bois-Colombes *Paris* **24** A2
Bois-d'Arcy *Paris* **24** B1
Boissy-St-Léger *Paris* **24** B4
Boldinasco *Milan* **19** B1
Bøler *Oslo* **23** A4
Bollate *Milan* **19** A1
Bollebeek *Brussels* **6** A1
Bollensdorf *Berlin* **5** A5
Bollmora *Stockholm* **29** B3
Bolshaya Okhta *St. Petersburg* **27** B2
Bolton *Atlanta* **3** B2
Bom Retiro *São Paulo* **27** B2
Bombay = Mumbai *Mumbai* **20** B2
Bondi *Sydney* **29** B2
Bondy *Paris* **24** A3
Bondy, Forêt de *Paris* **24** A4
Bonifacio Monument *Manila* **17** B1
Bonneuil-sur-Marne *Paris* **24** B4
Bonnington *Edinburgh* **11** B1
Bonnyrigg and Lasswade *Edinburgh* **11** B3
Bonsucesso *Rio de Janeiro* **25** B1
Bonteheuwel *Cape Town* **8** A2
Boo *Stockholm* **29** A3
Booterstown *Dublin* **10** B2
Borisovo *Moscow* **19** C3
Borle *Mumbai* **20** A2
Boronia Park *Sydney* **29** A1
Bosmont *Johannesburg* **13** B1
Bosön *Stockholm* **29** A3
Bosporus = İstanbul Boğazı *Istanbul* **12** B2
Bostancı *Istanbul* **12** C2
Boston *Boston* **6** A2
Boston Common *Boston* **6** A2
Boston Logan Int. ✕ (BOS) *Boston* **6** A2
Botafogo *Rio de Janeiro* **25** B1
Botany *Sydney* **29** B2
Botany B. *Sydney* **29** B2
Botany Bay Nat. Park △ *Sydney* **29** B2
Botič → *Prague* **25** B3
Botica Sete *Lisbon* **16** A1
Boucherville *Montreal* **20** A3
Boucherville, Îs. de *Montreal* **20** A3
Bougival *Paris* **24** A1
Boulder Pt. *Hong Kong* **12** B1
Boulogne, Bois de *Paris* **24** A2
Boulogne-Billancourt *Paris* **24** A2
Bourg-la-Reine *Paris* **24** B2
Bouviers *Paris* **24** B1
Bovenkerk *Amsterdam* **2** B2
Bovenkerker Polder *Amsterdam* **2** B2
Bovisa *Milan* **19** A2
Bow *London* **15** A3
Boyacıköy *Istanbul* **12** B2
Boyd Conservation Area *Toronto* **31** A1
Boyle Heights *Los Angeles* **16** B3
Braepark *Edinburgh* **11** B2
Braid *Edinburgh* **11** B2
Bramley *Johannesburg* **13** A2
Brandeis University *Boston* **6** A1
Brandenburger Tor *Berlin* **5** A3
Brani, Pulau *Singapore* **28** B3
Branik *Prague* **25** B2
Brännkyrka *Stockholm* **29** B2
Brás *São Paulo* **27** B2
Brasilândia *São Paulo* **27** A1
Brateyevo *Moscow* **19** C3
Braybrook *Melbourne* **18** A1
Brázdim *Prague* **25** A3
Breakheart Reservation *Boston* **6** A2
Brede *Copenhagen* **8** A3
Breezy Point *New York* **22** C2
Breitenlee *Vienna* **32** A3
Breña *Lima* **14** B2
Brent □ *London* **15** A2
Brent Res. *London* **15** A2
Brentford *London* **15** B2
Brentwood Park *Los Angeles* **16** B2
Brera *Milan* **19** B2
Bresso *Milan* **19** A2
Brevik *Stockholm* **29** A3
Břevnov *Prague* **25** B2
Brickyard, The *Chicago* **9** B2
Bridgeport *Chicago* **9** B3
Bridgetown *Cape Town* **8** A2
Bridgeview *Chicago* **9** C2
Brighton *Boston* **6** A2
Brighton *Melbourne* **18** B1
Brighton Beach *New York* **22** C2
Brighton le Sands *Sydney* **29** B1
Brighton Park *Chicago* **9** C2
Brightwood *Washington* **33** B3
Brigittenau *Vienna* **32** A2
Brimbank Park *Melbourne* **18** A1
Brisbane *San Francisco* **26** B2
Britz *Berlin* **5** B3
Brixton *London* **15** B3
Broadmeadows *Melbourne* **18** A1
Broadmoor *San Francisco* **26** B2
Broadview *Chicago* **9** B1
Brockley *London* **15** B3
Bródno *Warsaw* **32** B2
Bródnowski, Kanal *Warsaw* **32** B2
Broek *Amsterdam* **2** A2
Bromley □ *London* **15** B4
Bromley Common *London* **15** B4
Bromma *Stockholm* **29** A1
Bromma ✕ *Stockholm* **29** A1
Brøndby Strand *Copenhagen* **8** B2
Brøndbyøster *Copenhagen* **8** B2
Brøndbyvester *Copenhagen* **8** B2
Brondesbury *London* **15** A2
Brønnøya *Oslo* **23** A2
Brønshøj *Copenhagen* **8** A2
Bronxville *New York* **22** A3
Brookfield *Chicago* **9** C1
Brookhaven *Atlanta* **3** A2
Brookline *Boston* **6** B2
Brooklyn *Cape Town* **8** A1
Brooklyn *New York* **22** C2
Brooklyn *Wellington* **33** B1
Brooklyn Heights *New York* **22** B2
Brookmont *Washington* **33** B3
Brossard *Montreal* **20** B3
Brou-sur-Chantereine *Paris* **24** A4
Brown *Toronto* **31** A3
Broyhill Park *Washington* **33** B2
Brughério *Milan* **19** A2
Brunswick *Melbourne* **18** A1
Brussegem *Brussels* **6** A1
Brussel *Brussels* **6** A2
Brussel ✕ (BRU) *Brussels* **6** A2
Brussels = Brussel *Brussels* **6** A2
Bruxelles = Brussel *Brussels* **6** A2
Bruzzano *Milan* **19** A2
Bry-sur-Marne *Paris* **24** A4
Bryan, L. *Orlando* **23** B2
Bryanston *Johannesburg* **13** A1
Bryn *Oslo* **23** A1
Brzeziny *Warsaw* **32** B2
Bubeneč *Prague* **25** B2
Buc *Paris* **24** B1
Buchenhain *Munich* **21** B1
Buchholz *Berlin* **5** A3
Buckhead *Atlanta* **3** A2
Buckingham Palace *London* **15** A3
Buckow *Berlin* **5** B3
Buda *Budapest* **7** A2
Buda Castle = Budaváripalota *Budapest* **7** A2
Budafok *Budapest* **7** B2
Budaörs *Budapest* **7** B1
Budapest *Budapest* **7** B2
Budapest ✕ (BUD) *Budapest* **7** B3
Budatétény *Budapest* **7** B2
Budaváripalota *Budapest* **7** A2
Buddinge *Copenhagen* **8** A3
Buena Ventura Lakes *Orlando* **23** B2
Buena Vista *San Francisco* **26** B2
Buenos Aires *Buenos Aires* **7** B2
Bufalotta *Rome* **26** B2
Bugio *Lisbon* **16** B1
Buiksloot *Amsterdam* **2** A2
Buitenveldert *Amsterdam* **2** B2
Buizingen *Brussels* **6** B1
Bukhansan *Seoul* **27** B1
Bukit Panjang Nature Reserve *Singapore* **28** A2
Bukit Timah Nature Reserve *Singapore* **28** A2
Bukum, Pulau *Singapore* **28** B2
Bûlâq *Cairo* **7** A2
Bule *Manila* **17** C2
Bulim *Singapore* **28** A2
Bullen Park *Melbourne* **18** A2
Bund, The *Shanghai* **28** B1
Bundoora North *Melbourne* **18** A2
Bundoora Park *Melbourne* **18** A2
Bunker Hill Memorial *Boston* **6** A2
Bunker I. *Karachi* **13** B1
Bunkyō *Tokyo* **30** A3
Bunnefjorden *Oslo* **23** A3
Buona Vista Park *Singapore* **28** B2
Burbank *Chicago* **9** C2
Burbank *Los Angeles* **16** A3
Burden, L. *Orlando* **23** B1
Burlington *Boston* **6** A1
Burnham Park *Chicago* **9** C3
Burnham Park Harbor *Chicago* **9** B3
Burnhamthorpe *Toronto* **31** B1
Burnt Oak *London* **15** A2
Burntisland *Edinburgh* **11** A2
Burnwynd *Edinburgh* **11** B1
Burqa *Jerusalem* **13** A2
Burtus *Cairo* **7** A1
Burudvatn *Oslo* **23** A2
Burwood *Sydney* **29** B1
Bushwick *New York* **22** B2
Bushy Park *London* **15** B1
Butantã *São Paulo* **27** B1
Butcher I. *Mumbai* **20** B2
Butler, L. *Orlando* **23** B1
Butts Corner *Washington* **33** C2
Büyükdere *Istanbul* **12** B2
Byculla *Mumbai* **20** B2
Bygdøy *Oslo* **23** A3

C

C.B.S. Fox Studios *Los Angeles* **16** B2
C.N.N. Center *Atlanta* **3** B2
C.N. Tower *Toronto* **31** B2
Caballito *Buenos Aires* **7** B2
Cabin John *Washington* **33** B2
Cabin John Regional Park ⌓ *Washington* **33** A2
Cabinteely *Dublin* **10** B3
Cabra *Dublin* **10** A2
Cabuçú de Baixo → *São Paulo* **27** A1
Cabuçú de Cima → *São Paulo* **27** A2
Cachan *Paris* **24** B2
Cachoeira, Rib. da → *São Paulo* **27** B1
Cacilhas *Lisbon* **16** A2

Cahuenga Park *Los Angeles* 16 B3
Cain, L. *Orlando* 23 B2
Cairo = El Qâhira *Cairo* 7 A2
Cairo Int. ✈ (CAI) *Cairo* 7 A3
Caju *Rio de Janeiro* 25 B1
Čakovice *Prague* 25 B3
Calcutta = Kolkata *Kolkata* 14 B2
California Inst. of Tech.
   Los Angeles 16 B4
California Los Angeles,
   University of *Los Angeles* 16 B2
California State University
   Los Angeles 16 B3
Callao *Lima* 14 B2
Caloocan *Manila* 17 B1
Calumet L. *Chicago* 9 C3
Calumet Park *Chicago* 9 C3
Calumet Sag Channel →
   Chicago 9 C2
Calvairate *Milan* 19 B2
Camarate *Lisbon* 16 A2
Camaroes *Lisbon* 16 A1
Camberwell *London* 15 B3
Camberwell *Melbourne* 18 B2
Cambuci *São Paulo* 27 B2
Cambridge *Boston* 6 A2
Camden ☐ *London* 15 A3
Cameron, Mt. *Wellington* 33 B2
Çamlıca *Istanbul* 12 B2
Camp Springs *Washington* 33 B4
Campamento *Madrid* 17 B1
Campbellfield *Melbourne* 18 A1
Camperdown *Sydney* 29 B2
Campo, Casa de *Madrid* 17 B1
Campo F.C. Barcelona
   Barcelona 4 A1
Campo Grando *Lisbon* 16 A2
Campo Pequeño *Lisbon* 16 A2
Campolide *Lisbon* 16 A2
Camps Bay *Cape Town* 8 A1
C'an San Joan *Barcelona* 4 A2
Cañacao B. *Manila* 17 C1
Canarsie *New York* 22 C2
Candiac *Montreal* 20 B3
Caneças *Lisbon* 16 A1
Canillas *Madrid* 17 B2
Canillejas *Madrid* 17 B2
Canning Town *London* 15 A4
Canteras de Vallecas *Madrid* 17 B2
Canterbury *Melbourne* 18 B2
Canterbury *Sydney* 29 B1
Canton = Guangzhou
   Guangzhou 11 B2
Caoheijing *Shanghai* 28 B1
Capão Redondo *São Paulo* 27 B1
Caparica *Lisbon* 16 A2
Caparica, Costa de *Lisbon* 16 B1
Cape Flats *Cape Town* 8 B2
Cape Peninsula △ *Cape Town* 8 A1
Cape Town *Cape Town* 8 A1
Cape Town Int. ✈ (CPT)
   Cape Town 8 A2
Capitol Heights *Washington* 33 B4
Captain Cook Bridge *Sydney* 29 C1
Captain Cook Landing
   Place Park *Sydney* 29 C2
Capuchos *Lisbon* 16 B1
Carabanchel Alto *Madrid* 17 B1
Carabanchel Bajo *Madrid* 17 B1
Carapachay *Buenos Aires* 7 B1
Caraza *Buenos Aires* 7 C2
Caridad *Manila* 17 C1
Carioca, Sa. da *Rio de Janeiro* 25 B1
Carlstadt *New York* 22 A1
Carlton *Melbourne* 18 A1
Carmen de Huechuraba
   Santiago 27 B1
Carmen de la Legua *Lima* 14 B2
Carnaxide *Lisbon* 16 A1
Carnegie *Melbourne* 18 B2
Carnide *Lisbon* 16 A1
Carol City *Miami* 18 A1
Carrascal *Santiago* 27 B1
Carrickmines *Dublin* 10 B3
Carrières-sous-Bois *Paris* 24 A1
Carrières-sous-Poissy *Paris* 24 A1
Carrières-sur-Seine *Paris* 24 A2
Carrigeen B. *Dublin* 10 A3
Cartierville *Montreal* 20 A1
Casa Loma *Toronto* 31 A2
Casa Verde *São Paulo* 27 A1
Casál Morena *Rome* 26 C2
Casalotti *Rome* 26 B1
Cascade Heights *Atlanta* 3 B2
Castèl di Leva *Rome* 26 C2
Castèl Sant'Angelo *Rome* 26 B1
Castleknock *Dublin* 10 A1
Castleton Corners *New York* 22 C1
Catete *Rio de Janeiro* 25 B1
Catford *London* 15 B3
Catherine, L. *Orlando* 23 B2
Caulfield *Melbourne* 18 B2
Cavite *Manila* 17 C1
Caxias *Lisbon* 16 A1
Cebecci *Istanbul* 12 B1
Cecchignola *Rome* 26 C2
Cecilienhof, Schloss *Berlin* 5 B1
Cedar Grove *Atlanta* 3 C3
Cedarvale Park *Toronto* 31 A2
Cempaka Putih *Jakarta* 12 A1
Çengelköy *Istanbul* 12 B2
Cengkareng *Jakarta* 12 A1
Centennial Olympic Park
   Atlanta 3 B2
Centennial Park *Sydney* 29 B2
Center Hill *Atlanta* 3 B2
Centocelle *Rome* 26 B2
Central, Gare *Montreal* 20 B2
Central Park *New York* 22 B2
Cerdanyola del Vallès
   Barcelona 4 A1
Cerillos *Santiago* 27 B1
Cerro de la Estrella, Parque
   Nacional △ *Mexico City* 18 B2
Cerro de los Angeles *Madrid* 17 C1
Cerro Navia *Santiago* 27 B1
Cesano Boscone *Milan* 19 B1
Cesate *Milan* 19 A1
Cha Kwo Ling *Hong Kong* 12 B2
Chacarrita *Buenos Aires* 7 B2
Chadwell Heath *London* 15 A4
Chai Chee *Singapore* 28 B3
Chai Wan *Hong Kong* 12 B2
Chai Wan Kok *Hong Kong* 12 A1
Chakdaha *Kolkata* 14 C1
Chamartin *Madrid* 17 B1
Chamberi *Madrid* 17 B1
Chambourcy *Paris* 24 A1
Champigny-sur-Marne *Paris* 24 B4
Champlain, Pont *Montreal* 20 B2
Champs-sur-Marne *Paris* 24 A4
Chamrail *Kolkata* 14 B1
Chanakyapuri *Delhi* 10 B2
Chanditala *Kolkata* 14 A1
Changfeng Park *Shanghai* 28 B1

Changhai = Shanghai
   Shanghai 28 B2
Changi *Singapore* 28 A3
Changi, Singapore ✈ (SIN)
   Singapore 28 A3
Changning *Shanghai* 28 B1
Chantereine *Paris* 24 A4
Chantian *Guangzhou* 11 A2
Chaoyang *Beijing* 4 B2
Chaoyangmen *Beijing* 4 B2
Chapelizod *Dublin* 10 A1
Chapultepec, Bosque de
   Mexico City 18 B1
Chapultepec, Castillo de
   Mexico City 18 B1
Charenton-le-Pont *Paris* 24 B3
Charleroi, Kanal de →
   Brussels 6 B1
Charles Bridge = Karlův
   most *Prague* 25 B2
Charles Gates Dawes House
   Chicago 9 A2
Charlestown *Boston* 6 A2
Charlottenburg *Berlin* 5 A2
Charlottenburg, Schloss *Berlin* 5 A2
Charlottenlund *Copenhagen* 8 A3
Charlton *London* 15 B4
Charneca *Lisbon* 16 A2
Chase, L. *Orlando* 23 B1
Châteaufort *Paris* 24 B1
Châtenay-Malabry *Paris* 24 B2
Chatham *Chicago* 9 C3
Châtillon *Paris* 24 B2
Chatou *Paris* 24 A1
Chatpur *Kolkata* 14 B2
Chatswood *Sydney* 29 A2
Chatuchak *Bangkok* 3 B2
Chatuchak Park *Bangkok* 3 B2
Chauki *Karachi* 13 A1
Chavarria *Lima* 14 A2
Chaville *Paris* 24 B2
Chayang *Seoul* 27 B2
Chelles *Paris* 24 A4
Chelles, Canal de *Paris* 24 A4
Chells-le-Pin ✕ *Paris* 24 A4
Chelsea *Rome* 26 B1
Chelsea *London* 15 B3
Chembur *Mumbai* 20 A2
Chennevières-sur-Marne
   Paris 24 B4
Cheongdaem *Seoul* 27 B2
Cheonho *Seoul* 27 B2
Cheops *Cairo* 7 B1
Chertanovka → *Moscow* 19 C2
Chertanovo *Moscow* 19 B2
Cheryomushki *Moscow* 19 B2
Chestnut Hill *Boston* 6 B1
Cheung Sha Wan *Hong Kong* 12 A1
Cheverly *Washington* 33 B4
Chevilly-Larue *Paris* 24 B3
Chevry-Cossigny *Paris* 24 B4
Chevy Chase *Washington* 33 B3
Chhatrapati Shivaji,
   Mumbai ✕ (BOM) *Mumbai* 20 A2
Chia Keng *Singapore* 28 A3
Chiaravalle Milanese *Milan* 19 B2
Chicago *Chicago* 9 C2
Chicago, University of *Chicago* 9 C3
Chicago Harbor *Chicago* 9 B3
Chicago Lawn *Chicago* 9 C2
Chicago-Midway ✕ (MDW)
   Chicago 9 C2
Chicago O'Hare Int. ✕
   (ORD) *Chicago* 9 B1
Chicago Ridge *Chicago* 9 C2
Chicago River, North
   Branch → *Chicago* 9 C2
Chicago Sanitary and Ship
   Canal *Chicago* 9 C1
Chicago State University
   Chicago 9 C3
Chicago Zoo *Chicago* 9 B1
Chienzui *Guangzhou* 11 A3
Chik Sha *Hong Kong* 12 B2
Child's Hill *London* 15 A2
Chilla Saroda *Delhi* 10 B2
Chillum *Washington* 33 B4
Chilly-Mazarin *Paris* 24 B2
China Basin *San Francisco* 26 B2
Chingupota *Kolkata* 14 C1
Chinna Cr. → *Karachi* 13 B2
Chiquihuite, Cerro
   Mexico City 18 A2
Chislehurst *London* 15 B4
Chiswick *London* 15 B2
Chiswick House *London* 15 B2
Chitose *Tokyo* 30 B2
Chitralada Palace *Bangkok* 3 B2
Chiyoda *Tokyo* 30 A3
Choa Chu Kang *Singapore* 28 A2
Chodov u Prahy *Prague* 25 B3
Chōfu *Tokyo* 30 B2
Choisy-le-Roi *Paris* 24 B3
Cholupice *Prague* 25 C2
Chom Thong *Bangkok* 3 B1
Chong Pang *Singapore* 28 A2
Chongwen *Beijing* 4 B2
Chorrillos *Lima* 14 C2
Chowpatty Beach *Mumbai* 20 B1
Christianshavn *Copenhagen* 8 A3
Chrzanów *Warsaw* 32 B1
Chuen Lung *Hong Kong* 12 A1
Chuk Kok *Hong Kong* 12 A2
Chulalongkorn Univ. *Bangkok* 3 B2
Chuō *Tokyo* 30 A3
Church End *London* 15 A2
Churchtown *Dublin* 10 B2
Ciampino *Rome* 26 C2
Ciampino ✕ *Rome* 26 C2
Cicero *Chicago* 9 B2
Cilandak *Jakarta* 12 B1
Cilincing *Jakarta* 12 A2
Ciliwung → *Jakarta* 12 B2
Cimice *Prague* 25 B2
Cinecittà *Rome* 26 B2
Cinisello Bálsamo *Milan* 19 A2
Cipete *Jakarta* 12 B1
Cittá degli Studi *Milan* 19 B2
Città del Vaticano =
   Vatican City ■ *Rome* 26 B1
City, The *London* 15 A3
City of the Dead *Cairo* 7 A2
Ciudad de México *Mexico City* 18 B2
Ciudad Deportiva *Mexico City* 18 B2
Ciudad Fin de Semana *Madrid* 17 B2
Ciudad General Belgrano
   Buenos Aires 7 C1
Ciudad Lineál *Madrid* 17 B2
Ciudad Satélite *Mexico City* 18 A1
Ciudad Universitaria
   Buenos Aires 7 B2
Ciudad Universitaria
   Mexico City 18 C1
Claireville Res. *Toronto* 31 A1

Clamart *Paris* 24 B2
Clapham *London* 15 B3
Clapton *London* 15 A3
Claremont *Cape Town* 8 A1
Clayhall *London* 15 A4
Clear, L. *Orlando* 23 A1
Clermiston *Edinburgh* 11 B2
Clichy *Paris* 24 A2
Clichy-sous-Bois *Paris* 24 A4
Cliffside *Toronto* 31 A3
Cliffside Park *New York* 22 B2
Clifton *Cape Town* 8 A1
Clifton *Karachi* 13 B2
Clifton *New York* 22 C1
Clifton Beach *Karachi* 13 B2
Cliftondale *Boston* 6 A2
Cloghran *Dublin* 10 A2
Clonskeagh *Dublin* 10 B2
Clontarf *Dublin* 10 A2
Clontarf *Sydney* 29 A2
Clovelly *Sydney* 29 B2
Cobras, I. das *Rio de Janeiro* 25 B2
Coburg *Melbourne* 18 A1
Cocotá *Rio de Janeiro* 25 A1
Ceuilly *Paris* 24 B4
Coina *Lisbon* 16 B2
Coker *Lagos* 14 B2
Colaba *Mumbai* 20 B1
Colaba Pt. *Mumbai* 20 B1
Colegiales *Buenos Aires* 7 B2
Colindale *London* 15 A2
Colinton *Edinburgh* 11 B2
College Park *Atlanta* 3 C2
College Park *Washington* 33 B4
College Point *New York* 22 B2
Collégien *Paris* 24 A4
Collier Row *London* 15 A4
Colliers Wood *London* 15 B3
Colma *San Francisco* 26 B2
Colney Hatch *London* 15 A3
Cologno Monzese *Milan* 19 A2
Colombes *Paris* 24 A2
Colonia Güell *Barcelona* 4 A1
Colonial Knob *Wellington* 33 A1
Colosseo *Rome* 26 B1
Colosseum = Colosseo *Rome* 26 B1
Combault *Paris* 24 B4
Comércio, Praça do *Lisbon* 16 A2
Commerce *Los Angeles* 16 B4
Como *Sydney* 29 C1
Conceição, I. da *Rio de Janeiro* 25 B2
Conchali *Santiago* 27 B2
Concord *Sydney* 29 B1
Concord *Toronto* 31 A1
Concorde, Place de la *Paris* 24 A2
Concorezzo *Milan* 19 A2
Condet *Jakarta* 12 B2
Coney Island *New York* 22 C2
Congonhas São Paulo ✕
   (CGH) *São Paulo* 27 B2
Conley → *Atlanta* 3 C3
Connaught Place *Delhi* 10 B2
Consolação *São Paulo* 27 B2
Constantia *Cape Town* 8 A1
Constitución *Buenos Aires* 7 B2
Constitution *Atlanta* 3 B2
Convention Center
   Los Angeles 16 B3
Conway *Orlando* 23 B2
Conway, L. *Orlando* 23 B2
Coogee *Sydney* 29 B2
Cooksville *Toronto* 31 B1
Coolock *Dublin* 10 A2
Copacabana *Rio de Janeiro* 25 B1
Copenhagen = København
   Copenhagen 8 A2
Coral Gables *Miami* 18 B2
Coral Hills *Washington* 33 B4
Corcovado, Cristo Redentor
   Rio de Janeiro 25 B1
Corduff *Dublin* 10 A1
Cormano *Milan* 19 A2
Cornaredo *Milan* 19 B1
Córsico *Milan* 19 B1
Corstorphine *Edinburgh* 11 B2
Corviale *Rome* 26 B1
Coslada *Madrid* 17 B2
Cossigny *Paris* 24 B4
Cotao *Lisbon* 16 A1
Côte-St-Luc *Montreal* 20 B2
Cotunduba, I. de *Rio de Janeiro* 25 B2
Coubron *Paris* 24 A4
Countryside *Chicago* 9 C1
County Art Museum
   Los Angeles 16 B3
Courbevoie *Paris* 24 A2
Courtry *Paris* 24 A4
Cowley *London* 15 A1
Coyoacán *Mexico City* 18 B2
Craighall Park *Johannesburg* 13 B1
Craiglockhart *Edinburgh* 11 B2
Craigmillar *Edinburgh* 11 B3
Cramond *Edinburgh* 11 B2
Cramond Bridge *Edinburgh* 11 B1
Cramond I. *Edinburgh* 11 B2
Cranford *London* 15 B1
Crawford *Cape Town* 8 A2
Crayford *London* 15 B5
Creekmouth *London* 15 A4
Crescent, L. *Orlando* 23 A1
Crescenzago *Milan* 19 A2
Cressely *Paris* 24 B1
Cresskill *New York* 22 A2
Créteil *Paris* 24 B3
Cricklewood *London* 15 A2
Cristo Redentor, Estatua do
   Rio de Janeiro 25 B1
Crockenhill *London* 15 B4
Croissy-Beaubourg *Paris* 24 B4
Croissy-sur-Seine *Paris* 24 A1
Crosby *Johannesburg* 13 B1
Crosne *Paris* 24 B3
Cross I. *Mumbai* 20 A2
Crouch End *London* 15 A3
Crown Mine *Johannesburg* 13 B1
Crows Nest *Sydney* 29 A2
Croydon *London* 15 B3
Croydon Park *Sydney* 29 B1
Cruagh Mt. *Dublin* 10 B2
Crumlin *Dublin* 10 B2
Cruz de Pau *Lisbon* 16 B2
Crystal Palace *London* 15 B3
Csepel *Budapest* 7 B2
Csepelsziget *Budapest* 7 B2
Csillaghegy *Budapest* 7 A2
Csömör *Budapest* 7 A3
Csömöri-patak → *Budapest* 7 A3
Cuatro Vientos *Madrid* 17 B1
Cuauhtémoc *Mexico City* 18 B1
Cuban Museum *Miami* 18 B2
Cubao *Manila* 17 B2
Çubuklu *Istanbul* 12 B2
Cudahy *Los Angeles* 16 C3

Cuicuilco, Pirámido de
   Mexico City 18 C1
Culmore *Washington* 33 B3
Culver City *Los Angeles* 16 B2
Cumbres de Vallecas *Madrid* 17 B2
Cupecê *São Paulo* 27 B1
Currie *Edinburgh* 11 B2
Cusago *Milan* 19 B1
Cusano Milanino *Milan* 19 A2
Cutler Park *Boston* 6 B1
Çuvuşabaşı → *Istanbul* 12 B1
Cypress Hills *New York* 22 B2
Czernników *Warsaw* 32 B2
Cyste *Warsaw* 32 B2

D

Da Moóca → *São Paulo* 27 B2
Ďáblice *Prague* 25 B2
Dąbrowa *Warsaw* 32 B1
Dachang *Shanghai* 28 B1
Dachang ✕ *Shanghai* 28 B1
Dachau *Munich* 21 A1
Dachau-Ost *Munich* 21 A1
Dachauer Moos *Munich* 21 A1
Dadar *Mumbai* 20 A1
Daebang *Seoul* 27 B1
Daechi *Seoul* 27 B2
Dafni *Athens* 2 B1
Dagenham *London* 15 A4
Dagfling *Munich* 21 B2
Dahab, Gezîret el *Cairo* 7 B2
Daheisha *Jerusalem* 13 B2
Dahlem *Berlin* 5 B2
Dahlwitz-Hoppegarten *Berlin* 5 A5
Dahongmen *Beijing* 4 C2
Dajiaoting *Beijing* 4 B2
Dakhnoye *St. Petersburg* 27 C1
Dalejsky potok → *Prague* 25 B2
Dalgety Bay *Edinburgh* 11 A1
Dalkeith *Edinburgh* 11 B3
Dalkey *Dublin* 10 B3
Dalkey I. *Dublin* 10 B3
Dallgow *Berlin* 5 A1
Dalmeny *Edinburgh* 11 B1
Dalston *London* 15 A3
Daly City *San Francisco* 26 B2
Damaia *Lisbon* 16 A1
Damarakia *Athens* 2 B1
Dämeritzsee *Berlin* 5 B5
Dan Ryan Woods *Chicago* 9 C2
Danderhall *Edinburgh* 11 B3
Danderyd *Stockholm* 29 A2
Danforth *Toronto* 31 A2
Darakeh *Tehran* 31 A2
Darband *Tehran* 31 A2
Darling Point *Sydney* 29 B2
Darndale *Dublin* 10 A2
Darrûs *Tehran* 31 A2
Dartford *London* 15 B5
Dashi *Guangzhou* 11 B2
Datansha *Guangzhou* 11 B2
Datun *Beijing* 4 B2
Daulatpur *Delhi* 10 A1
Davidson, Mt. *San Francisco* 26 B2
Davidson's Mains *Edinburgh* 11 B2
Dăvüdiyeh *Tehran* 31 A2
Davydkovo *Moscow* 19 B1
Dawidy *Warsaw* 32 C1
Days Bay *Wellington* 33 B2
Decatur *Atlanta* 3 B3
Dedham *Boston* 6 B1
Deguinino *Moscow* 19 A2
Deir Dibwan *Jerusalem* 13 A2
Deir Ibzi'a *Jerusalem* 13 A1
Dejvice *Prague* 25 B2
Dekabristov, Ostrov
   St. Petersburg 27 B1
Delhi *Delhi* 10 B2
Demarest *New York* 22 A2
Den Ilp *Amsterdam* 2 A2
Denistone Heights *Sydney* 29 A1
Dentonia Park *Toronto* 31 A3
DePaul University *Chicago* 9 B3
Deptford *London* 15 B3
Des Plaines *Chicago* 9 A1
Deshengmen *Beijing* 4 B2
Deutsch-Wagram *Vienna* 32 A3
Deutsche Oper *Berlin* 5 A2
Deutsches Museum *Munich* 21 B2
Devil's Peak *Cape Town* 8 A1
Dhakuria *Kolkata* 14 B2
Dharavi *Mumbai* 20 A2
Diadema *São Paulo* 27 C2
Diegen *Brussels* 6 A2
Diemen *Amsterdam* 2 A2
Diepkloof *Johannesburg* 13 B1
Dieprivier *Cape Town* 8 A1
Difficult Run → *Washington* 33 B2
Dilbeek *Brussels* 6 A1
Dilli *Delhi* 10 B2
Dirnismaning *Munich* 21 A2
Disney-M.G.M. Studios
   Orlando 23 B1
Disney Studios *Los Angeles* 16 B3
District Heights *Washington* 33 B4
Djakarta = Jakarta *Jakarta* 12 A1
Djursholm *Stockholm* 29 A2
Döberitz *Berlin* 5 A1
Döbling *Vienna* 32 A2
Dobong *Seoul* 27 B1
Dobongsan *Seoul* 27 B1
Docklands *London* 15 A3
Doctor Phillips *Orlando* 23 B1
Dodder → *Dublin* 10 B2
Dodger Stadium *Los Angeles* 16 B3
Dogs, Isle of *London* 15 B3
Dolgoe Ozero *St. Petersburg* 27 B1
Dollis Hill *London* 15 A2
Dollymount *Dublin* 10 A2
Dolní *Prague* 25 B3
Dolní Chabry *Prague* 25 B2
Dolní Počernice *Prague* 25 B3
Dolphins Barn *Dublin* 10 B2
Dom Pedro II, Parque
   São Paulo 27 B2
Don Mills *Toronto* 31 A2
Don Muang Int. ✕ (BKK)
   Bangkok 3 A2
Donaghmede *Dublin* 10 A3
Donau-Oder Kanal *Vienna* 32 A3
Donaufeld *Vienna* 32 A2
Donaupark *Vienna* 32 A2
Donaustadt *Vienna* 32 A2
Dongan Hills *New York* 22 C1
Dongcheng *Beijing* 4 B2
Dongdaemung *Seoul* 27 B2
Dongjak *Seoul* 27 B1
Dongjiao *Guangzhou* 11 B2
Dongri *Mumbai* 20 B2
Dongshanhu Park *Guangzhou* 11 B2
Dongzhimen *Beijing* 4 B2
Donnybrook *Dublin* 10 B2

Doornfontein *Johannesburg* 13 B2
Dorchester *Boston* 6 B2
Dorchester B. *Boston* 6 B2
Dorchester Heights Nat.
   Historical Site △ *Boston* 6 B2
Dornach *Munich* 21 B3
Dorval Int., Montréal ✕
   (YUL) *Montreal* 20 B1
Dos Couros → *São Paulo* 27 C2
Dos Moninos → *São Paulo* 27 C2
Douglas Park *Chicago* 9 B2
Dover Heights *Sydney* 29 B2
Down. L. *Orlando* 23 A1
Downey *Los Angeles* 16 C4
Downsview *Toronto* 31 A1
Downsview C.A.F.B. ✕
   Toronto 31 A2
Dragor *Copenhagen* 8 B3
Drancy *Paris* 24 A3
Dranesville *Washington* 33 A1
Drapetsona *Athens* 2 B1
Dreilinden *Berlin* 5 B2
Drewnica *Warsaw* 32 B2
Drigh Road *Karachi* 13 A2
Drimnagh *Dublin* 10 B2
Drogenbos *Brussels* 6 B1
Druid Hills *Atlanta* 3 B2
Drumcondra *Dublin* 10 A2
Drummoyne *Sydney* 29 B1
Drylaw *Edinburgh* 11 B2
Dubeč *Prague* 25 B3
Dublin *Dublin* 10 A2
Dublin ✕ (DUB) *Dublin* 10 A2
Dublin B. *Dublin* 10 A3
Dublin Harbour *Dublin* 10 A2
Duddingston *Edinburgh* 11 B3
Dugnano *Milan* 19 A2
Duivendrecht *Amsterdam* 2 B2
Dülāb *Tehran* 31 A2
Dulwich *London* 15 B3
Dum Dum *Kolkata* 14 B2
Dum Dum Int. ✕ (CCU)
   Kolkata 14 B2
Dumont *New York* 22 A2
Dún Laoghaire *Dublin* 10 B3
Dundrum *Dublin* 10 B2
Dunearn *Singapore* 28 B2
Dúnleary = Dún Laoghaire
   Dublin 10 B3
Dunn Loring *Washington* 33 B2
Dunning *Chicago* 9 B2
Dunvegan *Johannesburg* 13 A2
Duomo *Milan* 19 B2
Duque de Caxias *Rio de Janeiro* 25 A1
Duren Sawit *Jakarta* 12 A2
Dusit *Bangkok* 3 B2
Dworp *Brussels* 6 B1
Dyakovo *Moscow* 19 B2
Dyker Beach Park *New York* 22 C1
Dzerzhinsky *Moscow* 19 C3
Dzerzhinsky Park *Moscow* 19 B2

E

E.U.R. = Esposizione
   Universale di Roma *Rome* 26 C1
Eagle Rock *Los Angeles* 16 B3
Ealing ☐ *London* 15 A2
Earlsfield *London* 15 B2
Earlwood *Sydney* 29 B1
East Arlington *Boston* 6 A2
East Arlington *Washington* 33 B3
East Bedfont *London* 15 B1
East Boston *Boston* 6 A2
East Don → *Toronto* 31 A2
East Don Parkland *Toronto* 31 A2
East Elmhurst *New York* 22 B2
East Finchley *London* 15 A2
East Flatbush *New York* 22 C2
East Ham *London* 15 A4
East Humber → *Toronto* 31 A1
East Lamma Channel
   Hong Kong 12 B1
East Lexington *Boston* 6 A1
East Los Angeles *Los Angeles* 16 B3
East Molesey *London* 15 B1
East New York *New York* 22 B2
East Pines *Washington* 33 B4
East Potomac Park
   Washington 33 B3
East River → *New York* 22 B2
East Rutherford *New York* 22 A1
East Sheen *London* 15 B2
East Talpiyot *Jerusalem* 13 B2
East Wickham *London* 15 B4
East York *Toronto* 31 A2
Eastbourne *Wellington* 33 B2
Eastcote *London* 15 A1
Easter Howgate *Edinburgh* 11 B2
Eastpoint Park *Toronto* 31 A4
Eastwood *Sydney* 29 A1
Eaton Canyon Park
   Los Angeles 16 B4
Ebara *Tokyo* 30 B3
Ebisu *Tokyo* 30 B3
Ebute-Ikorodu *Lagos* 14 A2
Ebute-Metta *Lagos* 14 B2
Eda *Tokyo* 30 B3
Edendale *Johannesburg* 13 A2
Edenmore *Dublin* 10 A2
Edgars Cr. → *Melbourne* 18 A1
Edgeley *Toronto* 31 A1
Edgemar *San Francisco* 26 C2
Edgewater *New York* 22 B2
Edgewood *Orlando* 23 B2
Edinburgh *Edinburgh* 11 B2
Edinburgh ✕ (EDI) *Edinburgh* 11 B1
Edinburgh Castle *Edinburgh* 11 B2
Edison Park *Chicago* 9 B2
Edmondston *Washington* 33 B4
Edmondstown *Dublin* 10 B2
Edo → *Tokyo* 30 B4
Edogawa *Tokyo* 30 A4
Edsberg *Stockholm* 29 A1
Edwards L. *Melbourne* 18 A1
Efzonos *Athens* 2 B2
Egaleo *Athens* 2 B1
Egaleo, Oros *Athens* 2 B1
Eiche *Berlin* 5 A4
Eiche Sud *Berlin* 5 A4
Eiffel, Tour *Paris* 24 A2
Ein Arik *Jerusalem* 13 A1
Ein Naquba *Jerusalem* 13 B1
Ein Rafa *Jerusalem* 13 B1
Eizariya *Jerusalem* 13 B2
Ejby *Copenhagen* 8 A2
Ejigbo *Lagos* 14 A1
Ekeberg *Oslo* 23 A3
Eknäs *Stockholm* 29 B3
El 'Abbasiya *Cairo* 7 A2
El Agustino *Lima* 14 B2
El Baragil *Cairo* 7 A1

El Basâtîn *Cairo* 7 B2
El Bira *Jerusalem* 13 A2
El Bosque *Santiago* 27 C2
El Carmen *Santiago* 27 B1
El Cortijo *Santiago* 27 B1
El Cristo, Vaso Regulador
   Mexico City 18 A1
El Duqqi *Cairo* 7 A2
El Encinar de los Reyes
   Madrid 17 A1
El Gezira *Cairo* 7 A2
El Ghuriya *Cairo* 7 A2
El Gîza *Cairo* 7 A2
El Khadr *Jerusalem* 13 B1
El Khalifa *Cairo* 7 A2
El Kôm el Ahmar *Cairo* 7 A2
El Ma'âdi *Cairo* 7 B2
El Matarîya *Cairo* 7 A2
El Mohandessin *Cairo* 7 A2
El Monte *Los Angeles* 16 B4
El Muqattam *Cairo* 7 A2
El Mûski *Cairo* 7 A2
El Pardo *Madrid* 17 A1
El Portal *Miami* 18 A2
El Prat de Llobregat *Barcelona* 4 B1
El Qâhira *Cairo* 7 A2
El Qubba *Cairo* 7 A2
El Reloj *Mexico City* 18 C2
El Retiro *Madrid* 17 B1
El Salto *Santiago* 27 B2
El Sereno *Los Angeles* 16 B3
El Talibiya *Cairo* 7 B1
El Vergel *Mexico City* 18 C2
El Wâhli *Cairo* 7 A2
El Zeitûn *Cairo* 7 A2
El Zamâlik *Cairo* 7 A2
Elephanta Caves *Mumbai* 20 B2
Elftheria I. *Istanbul* 20 B2
Elsiesrivier *Cape Town* 8 A2
Elsternwick *Melbourne* 18 B2
Eltham *London* 15 B4
Elwood *Melbourne* 18 B1
Élysée *Paris* 24 A2
Elysian Park *Los Angeles* 16 B3
Emämzädeh Sâleh *Tehran* 31 A2
Émerainville *Paris* 24 B4
Emeryville *San Francisco* 26 A3
Eminönü *Istanbul* 12 B1
Emigran *Istanbul* 12 B2
Emmarentia *Johannesburg* 13 A2
Empire State Building
   New York 22 B2
Encantado *Rio de Janeiro* 25 B1
Encino *Los Angeles* 16 B2
Encino Res. *Los Angeles* 16 B1
Enebyberg *Stockholm* 29 A1
Enfield *Sydney* 29 B1
Engenho, I. do *Rio de Janeiro* 25 B2
Englewood *Chicago* 9 C3
Englewood *New York* 22 A2
Englewood Cliffs *New York* 22 A2
Enmore *Sydney* 29 B2
Enskede *Stockholm* 29 B2
Entrevias *Madrid* 17 B1
Epcot *Orlando* 23 B1
Epping *Sydney* 29 A1
Eregun *Lagos* 14 A2
Erenköy *Istanbul* 12 C2
Erith *London* 15 B4
Erlaa *Vienna* 32 B1
Ermington *Sydney* 29 A1
Ermita *Manila* 17 B1
Ershatou *Guangzhou* 11 B2
Erskineville *Sydney* 29 B2
Erunkan *Lagos* 14 A2
Erzsébet-Telep *Budapest* 7 B3
Eschenried *Munich* 21 A1
Esenler *Istanbul* 12 B1
Esher *London* 15 B1
Eskbank *Edinburgh* 11 B3
Esplugues *Barcelona* 4 A1
Esposizione Universale di
   Roma *Rome* 26 C1
Essendon *Melbourne* 18 A1
Essendon ✕ (MEB) *Melbourne* 18 A1
Essingen *Stockholm* 29 B1
Essling *Vienna* 32 A3
Est, Gare de l' *Paris* 24 A3
Estado, Parque do *São Paulo* 27 B2
Estrela, Basílica da *Lisbon* 16 A2
Etobicoke *Toronto* 31 B1
Etobicoke Cr. → *Toronto* 31 B1
Etterbeek *Brussels* 6 B2
Eung-am *Seoul* 27 B1
Eunpyeong *Seoul* 27 B1
Evanston *Chicago* 9 A2
Even Sapir *Jerusalem* 13 B1
Evere *Brussels* 6 A2
Everett *Boston* 6 A2
Evergreen Park *Chicago* 9 C2
Evin *Tehran* 31 A2
Ewu *Lagos* 14 A1
Exhibition Place *Toronto* 31 B2
Exposições, Palácio das
   Rio de Janeiro 25 B1
Eyüp *Istanbul* 12 B1
Ezeiza ✕ (EZE) *Buenos Aires* 7 B2

F

Fabour, Mt. *Singapore* 28 B2
Fælledparken *Copenhagen* 8 A3
Fâgelön *Stockholm* 29 B1
Fagersjö *Stockholm* 29 B2
Fair Lawn *New York* 22 A1
Fairfax *Washington* 33 B2
Fairfax Station *Washington* 33 C2
Fairland *Johannesburg* 13 A1
Fairmilehead *Edinburgh* 11 B2
Fairmount Heights
   Washington 33 B4
Fairport *Toronto* 31 A4
Fairview *New York* 22 B2
Fairview, L. *Orlando* 23 A1
Falenty *Warsaw* 32 C1
Faliro *Athens* 2 B2
Falirn, Órmos *Athens* 2 B2
Falkenberg *Berlin* 5 A4
Falkenhagen *Berlin* 5 A1
Falkensee *Berlin* 5 A1
Falls Church *Washington* 33 B3
Falomo *Lagos* 14 B2

False Bay *Cape Town* 8 B2
Fangcun *Guangzhou* 11 B2
Farahâbâd *Tehran* 31 A2
Farforovskaya *St. Petersburg* 27 B2
Farningham *London* 15 B5
Farsta *Stockholm* 29 B2
Fasanerie-Nord *Munich* 21 A2
Fasangarten *Munich* 21 B2
Fatih *Istanbul* 12 B1
Favoriten *Vienna* 32 B2
Fawkner *Melbourne* 18 A1
FedEx Stadium *Washington* 33 B4
Feijó *Lisbon* 16 B2
Feldkirchen *Munich* 21 B3
Feldmoching *Munich* 21 A2
Feltham *London* 15 B1
Fener *Istanbul* 12 B1
Fenerbahçe *Istanbul* 12 C2
Fengtai *Beijing* 4 C1
Ferencváros *Budapest* 7 B2
Ferihegy, Budapest ✕
   (BUD) *Budapest* 7 B3
Ferndale *Johannesburg* 13 A2
Férolles-Attilly *Paris* 24 B4
Fichtenau *Berlin* 5 B5
Field Museum of Natural
   History *Chicago* 9 B3
Fields Corner *Boston* 6 B2
Fiera Camp *Milan* 19 B1
Figino *Milan* 19 B1
Fijír *Baghdad* 3 A2
Filadelfia *Athens* 2 A2
Fili-Mazilovo *Moscow* 19 B1
Filothei *Athens* 2 A2
Finchley *London* 15 A2
Fine Arts, Museum of *Boston* 6 A2
Finglas *Dublin* 10 A2
Finsbury *London* 15 A3
Finsbury Park *London* 15 A3
Fiorito *Buenos Aires* 7 C2
Firhouse *Dublin* 10 B2
Fischerhäuser *Munich* 21 A3
Fisher Island *Miami* 18 B2
Fisksätra *Stockholm* 29 B3
Fitzroy Gardens *Melbourne* 18 A1
Five Dock *Sydney* 29 B1
Fjellstrand *Oslo* 23 B1
Flamengo *Rio de Janeiro* 25 B1
Flamingo *Orlando* 23 B2
Flaminio *Rome* 26 B1
Flaskebekk *Oslo* 23 A2
Flatbush *New York* 22 C2
Flaten *Stockholm* 29 B2
Flatlands *New York* 22 C2
Flemington Racecourse
   Melbourne 18 A1
Flint Pk. *Los Angeles* 16 B3
Florence *Los Angeles* 16 C3
Florence Bloom Bird
   Sanctuary △ *Johannesburg* 13 A2
Florentia *Johannesburg* 13 B2
Flores *Buenos Aires* 7 B2
Flores, Mercado de
   Mexico City 18 B2
Floresta *Buenos Aires* 7 B2
Florida *Buenos Aires* 7 B2
Florida *Johannesburg* 13 A1
Floridsdorf *Vienna* 32 A2
Flushing *New York* 22 B2
Flushing Meadows Corona
   Park *New York* 22 B2
Flysta *Stockholm* 29 A2
Fo Tan *Hong Kong* 12 A2
Föhrenhain *Vienna* 32 A3
Fontainebleau *Johannesburg* 13 A1
Fontenay-aux-Roses *Paris* 24 B2
Fontenay-le-Fleury *Paris* 24 B1
Fontenay-sous-Bois *Paris* 24 A3
Foots Cray *London* 15 B4
Footscray *Melbourne* 18 B1
Forbidden City = Imperial
   Palace Museum *Beijing* 4 B2
Forest *Brussels* 6 B1
Forest Gate *London* 15 A4
Forest Heights *Washington* 33 C3
Forest Hill *London* 15 B3
Forest Hill *Toronto* 31 A2
Forest Park *Chicago* 9 B2
Forest Park *New York* 22 B2
Forest View *Chicago* 9 C2
Forestville *Washington* 33 B4
Fornebu *Oslo* 23 A2
Foro Romano *Rome* 26 B1
Forstenried *Munich* 21 B1
Forstenrieder Park *Munich* 21 B1
Fort *Mumbai* 20 B2
Fort Dupont Park *Washington* 33 B4
Fort Foote Village *Washington* 33 C3
Fort Lee *New York* 22 B2
Forth, Firth of *Edinburgh* 11 A2
Forth Rail Bridge *Edinburgh* 11 A1
Forth Road Bridge *Edinburgh* 11 A1
Fót *Budapest* 7 A3
Fourqueux *Paris* 24 A1
Foxrock *Dublin* 10 B2
Franconia *Washington* 33 C3
Frank Lloyd Wright Home
   Chicago 9 B2
Frankel *Singapore* 28 B3
Franklin Park *Boston* 6 B2
Franklin Park *Chicago* 9 B1
Franklin Park *Washington* 33 B3
Franklin Res. *Los Angeles* 16 B2
Frauenkirche *Munich* 21 B2
Frederiksberg *Copenhagen* 8 A3
Frederiksdal *Copenhagen* 8 A2
Fredersdof *Berlin* 5 A5
Freguesia *Rio de Janeiro* 25 A1
Freidrichshain, Volkspark
   Berlin 5 A3
Freiham *Munich* 21 B1
Freimann *Munich* 21 A2
French Quarter *New Orleans* 21 B1
Fresh Pond *Boston* 6 A2
Fresnes *Paris* 24 B2
Freudenau *Vienna* 32 A2
Friarstown *Dublin* 10 B1
Friedenau *Berlin* 5 B3
Friedrichsfelde *Berlin* 5 B4
Friedrichshagen *Berlin* 5 B4
Friedrichshain *Berlin* 5 A3
Friedrichslust *Berlin* 5 A5
Friherrs *Helsinki* 11 B1
Frilufts Museum *Helsinki* 11 B3
Frontón, I. *Lima* 14 B1
Frunze *Moscow* 19 B2
Fúchū *Tokyo* 30 A1
Fuencarral *Madrid* 17 B1
Fuenlabrada *Madrid* 17 C1
Fukagawa *Tokyo* 30 A3
Fukushima *Osaka* 23 A1

Fulham *London* 15 B2
Funabori *Tokyo* 30 A4
Fundão, I. do *Rio de Janeiro* 25 B1
Fünfhaus *Vienna* 32 A2
Fureso *Copenhagen* 8 A2
Fürth *Munich* 21 B2
Futago-tamagawaen *Tokyo* 30 B2
Fuxing Dao *Shanghai* 28 B2
Fuxing Park *Shanghai* 28 B1
Fuxinglu *Beijing* 4 B1

G

G. Ross Lord Park *Toronto* 31 A2
Gaebong *Seoul* 27 C1
Gage Park *Chicago* 9 C2
Gagny *Paris* 24 A4
Galata *Istanbul* 12 B1
Galata Tower *Istanbul* 12 B1
Galatsi *Athens* 2 A2
Galeão, Int. de ✕ (GIG)
   Rio de Janeiro 25 B1
Galgánovo *Moscow* 19 B3
Gambir *Jakarta* 12 A1
Gamboa *Rio de Janeiro* 25 B1
Gambolóita *Milan* 19 B2
Gamlebyen *Oslo* 23 A3
Gangdong *Seoul* 27 B2
Gangnam *Seoul* 27 B1
Gangseo *Seoul* 27 B1
Gangtou *Guangzhou* 11 A1
Gangwei *Guangzhou* 11 B2
Ganjiakou *Beijing* 4 B1
Ganshoren *Brussels* 6 A1
Gants Hill *London* 15 A4
Gaoqiao *Shanghai* 28 A2
Garbagnate Milanese *Milan* 19 A1
Garbatella *Rome* 26 B1
Garches *Paris* 24 A2
Garching *Munich* 21 A3
Garden City *Cairo* 7 A2
Garden Reach *Kolkata* 14 B1
Garder *Oslo* 23 B2
Garfield *New York* 22 A1
Garfield Park *Chicago* 9 B2
Gargareta *Athens* 2 B2
Garibong *Seoul* 27 C1
Garvanza *Los Angeles* 16 B3
Gåshaga *Stockholm* 29 A3
Gateway △ *New York* 22 C2
Gateway of India *Mumbai* 20 B2
Gatow *Berlin* 5 B1
Gavà *Barcelona* 4 B1
Gávea *Rio de Janeiro* 25 B1
Gávea, Pedra da *Rio de Janeiro* 25 B1
Gazdagrét *Budapest* 7 B1
Gaziosmanpaşa *Istanbul* 12 B1
Gebel el Ahmar *Cairo* 7 A2
Gebel el Tura *Cairo* 7 B2
Geiselgasteig *Munich* 21 B2
General San Martin
   Buenos Aires 7 B1
Gennevilliers *Paris* 24 A2
Gentilly *Paris* 24 B3
Gentofte *Copenhagen* 8 A3
Genval *Brussels* 6 B2
George I. *Hong Kong* 12 B2
Georges River Bridge *Sydney* 29 C1
Georgetown *Washington* 33 B3
Georgia Dome *Atlanta* 3 B2
Gerasdorf bei Wien *Vienna* 32 A2
Gerberau *Munich* 21 A3
Gerli *Buenos Aires* 7 C2
Germiston *Johannesburg* 13 B2
Gern *Munich* 21 B2
Getafe *Madrid* 17 C1
Getty Center, The *Los Angeles* 16 B2
Geunjeong *Seoul* 27 C1
Geva Binyamin *Jerusalem* 13 A2
Geylang Serai *Singapore* 28 B3
Gharapuri *Mumbai* 20 B2
Gharb = Shahrak-e Qods
   Tehran 31 A2
Ghatkopar *Mumbai* 20 A2
Ghazipur *Delhi* 10 B2
Ghizri *Karachi* 13 B2
Ghizri Cr. → *Karachi* 13 B2
Ghonda *Delhi* 10 A2
Ghusuri *Kolkata* 14 B2
Gianicolense *Rome* 26 B1
Giant Wheel = Riesenrad
   Vienna 32 A2
Gibraltar Pt. *Toronto* 31 B2
Gidea Park *London* 15 A5
Giesing *Munich* 21 B2
Gilmerton *Edinburgh* 11 B3
Gilo *Jerusalem* 13 B2
Gimmersta *Stockholm* 29 B3
Ginza *Tokyo* 30 A3
Giv'at Ram *Jerusalem* 13 B2
Giv'at Ye'arim *Jerusalem* 13 B1
Giv'at Ze'ev *Jerusalem* 13 A2
Giv'on *Jerusalem* 13 A2
Giza = El Gîza *Cairo* 7 A2
Giza Pyramids *Cairo* 7 B1
Gjersjøen *Oslo* 23 B3
Gladesville *Sydney* 29 B1
Gladsakse *Copenhagen* 8 A2
Glasnevin *Dublin* 10 A2
Glassmanor *Washington* 33 C4
Glasthule *Dublin* 10 B3
Glen Iris *Melbourne* 18 B2
Glen Mar Park *Washington* 33 B3
Glen Rock *New York* 22 A1
Glen Rouge Park *Toronto* 31 A4
Glenarden *Washington* 33 B4
Glenasmole Reservoirs *Dublin* 10 B1
Glencorse Res. *Edinburgh* 11 B2
Glencullen *Dublin* 10 B2
Glendale *Los Angeles* 16 B3
Glendoo Mt. *Dublin* 10 B2
Glenhuntly *Melbourne* 18 B2
Glenside *Wellington* 33 B1
Glenview *Chicago* 9 A2
Glenview Countryside *Chicago* 9 A2
Glenvista *Johannesburg* 13 B2
Glifada *Athens* 2 B2
Glinstada *Stockholm* 29 B3
Glostrup *Copenhagen* 8 B2
Gogar *Edinburgh* 11 B2
Göktürk *Istanbul* 12 A1
Golabki *Warsaw* 32 B1
Golabki *Kolkata* 14 B2
Gold Coast *Chicago* 9 B3
Golden Gate *San Francisco* 26 B2
Golden Gate △ *San Francisco* 26 A2
Golden Gate Bridge
   San Francisco 26 B2
Golden Gate Park
   San Francisco 26 B2
Golders Green *London* 15 A2
Goldern Horn = Haliç *Istanbul* 12 B1
Golestan Palace *Tehran* 31 A2

Gollans Stream ➛ *Wellington* 33 B2
Gonen *Jerusalem* 13 B2
Gongneung *Seoul* 27 B2
Goodmayes *London* 15 A4
Goodwood *Cape Town* 8 A2
Gopalpur *Kolkata* 14 B2
Gore Hill *Sydney* 29 A2
Gorelyy ➛ *St. Petersburg* 27 A3
Gorgie *Edinburgh* 11 B2
Gorky Park *Moscow* 19 B2
Gosen *Berlin* 5 B5
Gosener kanal *Berlin* 5 B5
Gospel Oak *London* 15 A3
Gotanda *Tokyo* 30 B3
Goth Goli Mar *Karachi* 13 A2
Goth Sher Shah *Karachi* 13 A1
Gotha *Orlando* 23 B1
Gournay-sur-Marne *Paris* 24 A4
Governador, I. do
    Rio de Janeiro 25 B1
Governors I. *New York* 22 B1
Grabów *Warsaw* 32 C1
Grace, Mt. *Wellington* 33 B2
Gracefield *Wellington* 33 B2
Gracia *Barcelona* 4 A2
Gräfelfing *Munich* 21 B1
Gragoatá *Rio de Janeiro* 25 B2
Grand Bazaar = Kapali
    Carsi *Istanbul* 12 B1
Grand Central Station
    New York 22 B2
Grand Palace *Bangkok* 3 B1
Grande Place *Brussels* 6 A2
Grankulla = Kauniainen
    Helsinki 11 B1
Grant Park *Chicago* 9 B3
Granton *Edinburgh* 11 B2
Grassy Park *Cape Town* 8 B2
Gratosóglio *Milan* 19 B2
Gratzwalde *Berlin* 5 B5
Gravesend *New York* 22 C2
Grazhdanka *St. Petersburg* 27 B2
Great Falls *Washington* 33 B2
Great Falls Park *Washington* 33 B2
Great Western Forum
    Los Angeles 16 C2
Greco *Milan* 19 A2
Green I. *Hong Kong* 12 B1
Green Point *Cape Town* 8 A1
Greenbelt *Washington* 33 A4
Greenbelt Park *Washington* 33 B4
Greenfield Park *Montreal* 20 B3
Greenford *London* 15 A1
Greenhill *London* 15 A2
Greenhills *Dublin* 10 B1
Greenpoint *New York* 22 B2
Greenwich □ *London* 15 B3
Greenwich Observatory
    London 15 B3
Greenwich Village *New York* 22 B2
Greenwood *Boston* 6 A2
Grefsen *Oslo* 23 A3
Gresham Park *Atlanta* 3 B2
Greve Strand *Copenhagen* 8 B1
Griebnitzsee *Berlin* 5 B1
Griffith Park *Los Angeles* 16 B3
Grimbergen *Brussels* 6 A2
Grinzing *Vienna* 32 A2
Gröbenried *Munich* 21 A1
Grochów *Warsaw* 32 C2
Grodzisk *Warsaw* 32 B2
Groenendaal *Brussels* 6 B2
Grogol Petamburin *Jakarta* 12 A1
Gronsdorf *Munich* 21 B3
Grorud *Oslo* 23 A4
Gross-Glienicke *Berlin* 5 B1
Gross-Hadern *Munich* 21 B1
Gross-Lappen *Munich* 21 A2
Grosse Krampe *Berlin* 5 B5
Grosse Müggelsee *Berlin* 5 B4
Grosse Point Lighthouse
    Chicago 9 A2
Grossenzersdorf *Vienna* 32 A3
Grossenzersdorfer Arm ➛
    Vienna 32 A3
Grosser Biberhaufen *Vienna* 32 A2
Grosser Wannsee *Berlin* 5 B2
Grossfeld-Siedlung *Vienna* 32 A2
Grosshesselohe *Munich* 21 B2
Grossjedlersdorf *Vienna* 32 A2
Grossziethen *Berlin* 5 B3
Ground Zero *New York* 22 B1
Grove, The *Chicago* 9 A1
Grove Hall *Boston* 6 B2
Grove Park *Atlanta* 3 B2
Grove Park *Hounslow, London* 15 B2
Grove Park *Lewisham, London* 15 B4
Groveton *Washington* 33 C3
Grünau *Berlin* 5 B4
Grunewald *Berlin* 5 B2
Grünwald *Munich* 21 B2
Grünwalder Forst *Munich* 21 B2
Grymes Hill *New York* 22 C1
Guadalupe *Manila* 17 B2
Guadalupe, Basílica de
    Mexico City 18 B2
Guanabara, B. de
    Rio de Janeiro 25 B1
Guanabara, Jardim
    Rio de Janeiro 25 B1
Guanabara, Palácio da
    Rio de Janeiro 25 B1
Guang'anmen *Beijing* 4 B1
Guangqumen *Beijing* 4 B2
Guangzhou *Guangzhou* 11 B2
Guanshuo *Guangzhou* 11 B3
Gudö *Stockholm* 29 B3
Güell, Parque de *Barcelona* 4 A2
Guinardó *Barcelona* 4 A2
Gulbai *Karachi* 13 A1
Güngören *Istanbul* 12 B1
Gunnersbury *London* 15 B2
Gustavo A. Madero
    Mexico City 18 B2
Guttenberg *New York* 22 B1
Gutuyevskiy, Ostrov
    St. Petersburg 27 B1
Guyancourt *Paris* 24 B1
Gwanak *Seoul* 27 C1
Gwanaksan *Seoul* 27 C1
Gyál *Budapest* 7 B3
Gyáli-patak ➛ *Budapest* 7 B2

H

Haaga *Helsinki* 11 B2
Haar *Munich* 21 B3
Habay *Manila* 17 C1
Hackbridge *London* 15 B3
Hackensack *New York* 22 A1
Hackensack ➛ *New York* 22 B1
Hackney □ *London* 15 A3
Hackney Wick *London* 15 A3
Hadr, Warrâq el *Cairo* 7 A2
Haga *Stockholm* 29 A2
Hagenbrunn *Vienna* 32 A2
Hägersten *Stockholm* 29 B1
Häggvik *Stockholm* 29 A1
Hagonoy *Manila* 17 B2
Hague Park *Toronto* 31 A3
Haidan *Beijing* 4 B1
Haidari *Athens* 2 A1
Haidarpur *Delhi* 10 A1
Haidhausen *Munich* 21 B2
Haight-Ashbury *San Francisco* 26 B2
Hainault *London* 15 A4
Haizhu Guangchang
    Guangzhou 11 B2
Hakunila *Helsinki* 11 B3
Halandri *Athens* 2 A2
Halásztelek *Budapest* 7 B1
Haliç *Istanbul* 12 B1
Halim Perdana Kusuma
    Int. ✈ (HLP) *Jakarta* 12 B2
Halle *Brussels* 6 B1
Haltiala *Helsinki* 11 B2
Haltiavuori *Helsinki* 11 B2
Ham *London* 15 B2
Hämeenkylä *Helsinki* 11 B1
Hammarby *Stockholm* 29 B2
Hamme *Brussels* 6 A1
Hammersmith *London* 15 B2
Hampstead *London* 15 A3
Hampstead *Montreal* 20 B2
Hampstead Garden Suburb
    London 15 A2
Hampstead Heath *London* 15 A2
Hampton *London* 15 B1
Hampton Court Palace
    London 15 B1
Hampton Wick *London* 15 B2
Hamrā' *Baghdad* 3 B1
Hanala *Helsinki* 11 A3
Haneda *Tokyo* 30 B3
Haneda, Tōkyō ✈ (HND)
    Tokyo 30 B3
Hang Hau *Hong Kong* 12 B2
Hanging Gardens *Mumbai* 20 B1
Hanlon *Toronto* 31 B1
Hanwell *London* 15 A1
Hanworth *London* 15 B1
Haora *Kolkata* 14 B2
Hapeville *Atlanta* 3 C2
Happy Valley *Hong Kong* 12 B2
Har Adar *Jerusalem* 13 B1
Har Gilo *Jerusalem* 13 B2
Har Homa *Jerusalem* 13 B2
Har Nof *Jerusalem* 13 B1
Haren *Brussels* 6 A2
Hareskovby *Copenhagen* 8 A2
Haringey □ *London* 15 A3
Harjusuo *Helsinki* 11 B3
Harlaching *Munich* 21 B2
Harlaw Res. *Edinburgh* 11 B2
Harlem *New York* 22 B2
Harlesden *London* 15 A2
Harlington *London* 15 B1
Harmaja *Helsinki* 11 C2
Harmashatar hegy *Budapest* 7 A2
Harolds Cross *Dublin* 10 B2
Háros *Budapest* 7 B2
Harperrig Res. *Edinburgh* 11 B1
Harrow □ *London* 15 A1
Harrow on the Hill *London* 15 A1
Harrow School *London* 15 A1
Harrow Weald *London* 15 A1
Hartsfield-Atlanta Int. ✈
    (ATL) *Atlanta* 3 C2
Harumi *Tokyo* 30 B3
Harvard University *Boston* 6 A2
Harwood Heights *Chicago* 9 B2
Ḥasanābād *Tehran* 31 A1
Hasbrouck Heights *New York* 22 A1
Haselhorst *Berlin* 5 A2
Hasköy *Istanbul* 12 B1
Hasle *Oslo* 23 A4
Haslum *Oslo* 23 A2
Hässelby *Stockholm* 29 A1
Hässhagen *Stockholm* 29 A1
Hataitai *Wellington* 33 B1
Hatch End *London* 15 A1
Hatiara *Kolkata* 14 B2
Hauketo *Oslo* 23 A3
Hauz Khas *Delhi* 10 B2
Havel ➛ *Berlin* 5 A2
Havelkanal *Berlin* 5 A1
Havering □ *London* 15 A5
Havering-atte-Bower *London* 15 A5
Haworth *New York* 22 A2
Hawthorne Racecourse
    Chicago 9 B2
Hayes *Bromley, London* 15 B4
Hayes *Hillingdon, London* 15 A1
Hayes End *London* 15 A1
Hayford *Chicago* 9 C2
Haywards *Wellington* 33 A2
Heathfield *Cape Town* 8 B2
Heathrow, London ✈ (LHR)
    London 15 B1
Hebe Haven *Hong Kong* 12 A2
Hedong *Guangzhou* 11 B2
Heidelberg Heights *Melbourne* 18 A2
Heidelberg West *Melbourne* 18 A2
Heidemühle *Berlin* 5 B5
Heideveld *Cape Town* 8 A2
Heiligensee *Berlin* 5 A2
Heiligenstadt *Vienna* 32 A2
Heinersdorf *Berlin* 5 A3
Hélène de Champlain,
    Parc △ *Montreal* 20 A2
Helenelund *Stockholm* 29 A1
Heliopolis = Masr el Gedida
    Cairo 7 A2
Hellersdorf *Berlin* 5 A4
Hellerup *Copenhagen* 8 A3
Helmahof *Vienna* 32 A3
Helsingfors = Helsinki
    Helsinki 11 B2
Helsinki *Helsinki* 11 B2
Helsinki-Vantaa ✈ (HEL)
    Helsinki 11 B2
Hendon *London* 15 A2
Hengsha *Guangzhou* 11 B2
Hennigsdorf *Berlin* 5 A2
Henryków *Warsaw* 32 B1
Henson Cr. ➛ *Washington* 33 C4
Henttaa *Helsinki* 11 B1
Heping Park *Shanghai* 28 B2
Hepingli *Beijing* 4 B2
Herlev *Copenhagen* 8 A2
Herman Eckstein Park
    Johannesburg 13 A2
Hermannskogel *Vienna* 32 A1
Hermiston *Edinburgh* 11 B2
Hermitage and Winter
    Palace *St. Petersburg* 27 B2
Hermsdorf *Berlin* 5 A3
Hernals *Vienna* 32 A2
Herne Hill *London* 15 B3

Héroes de Churubusco
    Mexico City 18 B2
Herons, Î. aux *Montreal* 20 B2
Herstedøster *Copenhagen* 8 A2
Herttoniemi *Helsinki* 11 B3
Hesārak *Tehran* 31 A1
Heston *London* 15 B1
Hetzendorf *Vienna* 32 B2
Hextable *London* 15 B5
Hialeah *Miami* 18 A1
Hiawassa, L. *Orlando* 23 A2
Hickory Hills *Chicago* 9 C2
Hiekkaharju *Helsinki* 11 B3
Hietaniemi *Helsinki* 11 B2
Hietzing *Vienna* 32 A1
Higashi *Osaka* 23 A2
Higashimurayama *Tokyo* 30 A1
Higashinari *Osaka* 23 A2
Higashisumiyoshi *Osaka* 23 B2
Higashiyodogawa *Osaka* 23 A1
High Park *Toronto* 31 B1
Highbury *London* 15 A3
Highgate *London* 15 A3
Highland Cr. ➛ *Toronto* 31 A3
Highland Creek *Toronto* 31 A3
Highland Park *Los Angeles* 16 B3
Highlands North *Johannesburg* 13 A2
Hillcrest Heights *Washington* 33 C4
Hillend *Edinburgh* 11 A1
Hillingdon □ *London* 15 A1
Hillwood *Washington* 33 B3
Hilmiya *Cairo* 7 A2
Hin Keng *Hong Kong* 12 A2
Hirota *Osaka* 23 A1
Hirschstetten *Vienna* 32 A2
History Centre *Atlanta* 3 B2
Hither Green *London* 15 B3
Hiyoshi *Tokyo* 30 A2
Hizma *Jerusalem* 13 B2
Hjortekær *Copenhagen* 8 A3
Hjortespring *Copenhagen* 8 A2
Hlubočepy *Prague* 25 B2
Ho Chung *Hong Kong* 12 A2
Ho Man Tin *Hong Kong* 12 B2
Hoboken *New York* 22 B1
Hobsons B. *Melbourne* 18 B1
Hochbrück *Munich* 21 A2
Hochelaga *Montreal* 20 A2
Hodgkins *Chicago* 9 C1
Hoegi *Seoul* 27 B2
Hoeilaart *Brussels* 6 B2
Hofburg *Vienna* 32 A2
Hoffman I. *New York* 22 C1
Hohenbrunn *Munich* 21 B3
Hohenschönhausen *Berlin* 5 A4
Holargos *Athens* 2 B2
Holborn *London* 15 A3
Holden, L. *Orlando* 23 B2
Holešovice *Prague* 25 B2
Holland Village *Singapore* 28 B2
Höllriegelskreuth *Munich* 21 B1
Hollywood *Los Angeles* 16 B3
Hollywood Bowl *Los Angeles* 16 B3
Holmenkollen *Oslo* 23 A3
Holmes Run Acres
    Washington 33 B2
Holmgård *Stockholm* 29 B1
Holmlia *Oslo* 23 B3
Holocaust Memorial
    Jerusalem 13 B2
Holyrood House, Palace of
    Edinburgh 11 B3
Holysloot *Amsterdam* 2 A3
Homerton *London* 15 A3
Hometown *Chicago* 9 C2
Hōnanchō *Tokyo* 30 A3
Honcho *Tokyo* 30 A3
Honden *Tokyo* 30 A4
Hondo, Rio ➛ *Los Angeles* 16 B4
Hong Kong *Hong Kong* 12 B2
Hong Kong, Univ. of
    Hong Kong 12 B1
Hong Kong I. *Hong Kong* 12 B2
Hongjae *Seoul* 27 B1
Hongjimun Tunnel *Seoul* 27 B1
Hongkou *Shanghai* 28 B1
Hongmiao *Beijing* 4 B2
Hongqiao *Shanghai* 28 B1
Honjyo *Tokyo* 30 A3
Honoré Mercier, Pont
    Montreal 20 B1
Hönow *Berlin* 5 A4
Hook *London* 15 B2
Horikiri *Tokyo* 30 A4
Horn Pond *Boston* 6 A1
Hornchurch *London* 15 A5
Horni *London* 15 A5
Horni Počernice *Prague* 25 B3
Hornsey *London* 15 A3
Horoměřice *Prague* 25 B1
Hortaleza *Madrid* 17 B2
Hosoyama *Tokyo* 30 B2
Hostafranchs *Barcelona* 4 A1
Hostivař *Prague* 25 B3
Houbětin *Prague* 25 B3
Houghton *Johannesburg* 13 B2
Houilles *Paris* 24 A2
Hounslow □ *London* 15 B1
Hout Bay *Cape Town* 8 B1
Hove Å ➛ *Copenhagen* 8 A1
Hovedoya *Oslo* 23 A2
Hovik *Oslo* 23 A2
Hovorčovice *Prague* 25 A3
Howard Beach *New York* 22 C2
Howrah = Haora *Kolkata* 14 B1
Howth *Dublin* 10 A3
Howth Hd. *Dublin* 10 A3
Hōya *Tokyo* 30 A2
Hradčany *Prague* 25 B2
Huanghuagang
    Mausoleum *Guangzhou* 11 B2
Huangpu *Shanghai* 28 B1
Huangpu Jiang ➛ *Shanghai* 28 B1
Huangpu Park *Shanghai* 28 B1
Huangtugang *Beijing* 4 C1
Huascar *Lima* 14 A2
Huay Khwang *Bangkok* 3 B2
Huddinge *Stockholm* 29 B1
Huechuraba *Santiago* 27 B1
Huertas de San Beltran
    Barcelona 4 A1
Huizingen *Brussels* 6 B1
Humayun's Tomb *Delhi* 10 B2
Humber ➛ *Toronto* 31 A1
Humber B. *Toronto* 31 B2
Humber Bay *Toronto* 31 B2
Humber Bay Park *Toronto* 31 B2
Humber College *Toronto* 31 B1
Humber Summit *Toronto* 31 A1
Humber Valley Village
    Toronto 31 A1
Humberlea *Toronto* 31 A1
Humberwood Park *Toronto* 31 A1
Humboldt Park *Chicago* 9 B2
Humera *Madrid* 17 B1

Hunaydī *Baghdad* 3 B2
Hundige *Copenhagen* 8 B1
Hundige Strand *Copenhagen* 8 B1
Hung Hom *Hong Kong* 12 B2
Hunters Hill *Sydney* 29 B1
Hunters Pt. *San Francisco* 26 B2
Hunters Valley *Washington* 33 B2
Huntington *Washington* 33 C3
Huntington Park *Los Angeles* 16 C3
Huriya *Baghdad* 3 A1
Hurstville *Sydney* 29 B1
Husan *Jerusalem* 13 B1
Husby *Stockholm* 29 A1
Husum *Copenhagen* 8 A2
Hutt ➛ *Wellington* 33 B2
Hüvösvölgy *Budapest* 7 A2
Huwon Secret Garden *Seoul* 27 B1
Hvalstad *Oslo* 23 A1
Hvalstrand *Oslo* 23 A2
Hvidovre *Copenhagen* 8 B2
Hwagok *Seoul* 27 B1
Hwayang *Seoul* 27 B2
Hyattsville *Washington* 33 B4
Hyde Park *Boston* 6 B2
Hyde Park *Chicago* 9 C3
Hyde Park *Johannesburg* 13 A2
Hyde Park *London* 15 A2
Hyde Park *Sydney* 29 B2

I

Ibese *Lagos* 14 A2
Ibirapuera *São Paulo* 27 B1
Ibirapuera, Parque do
    São Paulo 27 B2
Icarai *Rio de Janeiro* 25 B2
Içerenköy *Istanbul* 12 C2
Ichgao *Tokyo* 30 B2
Ichigaya *Tokyo* 30 A3
Ichikawa *Tokyo* 30 A4
Ickenham *London* 15 A1
Iddo *Lagos* 14 B2
Idi-Oro *Lagos* 14 B2
Iganmu *Lagos* 14 B2
Igbobi *Lagos* 14 B2
Igbologun *Lagos* 14 B1
Igny *Paris* 24 B2
Iib *Jerusalem* 13 A2
IJ, Het ➛ *Amsterdam* 2 A2
IJ-meer *Amsterdam* 2 A3
Ijesa-Tedo *Lagos* 14 B1
Ijora *Lagos* 14 B2
Ikebe *Tokyo* 30 B2
Ikebukuro *Tokyo* 30 A3
Ikegami *Tokyo* 30 B3
Ikeja *Lagos* 14 A2
Ikeuchi *Osaka* 23 B2
Ikoyi *Lagos* 14 B2
Ikuata *Lagos* 14 B2
Ikuno *Osaka* 23 A2
Ila *Oslo* 23 A2
Ilford *London* 15 A4
Ilioupoli *Athens* 2 B2
Illinois at Chicago,
    University of *Chicago* 9 B3
Illinois Institute of
    Technology *Chicago* 9 B3
Ilpendam *Amsterdam* 2 A2
Ilsos ➛ *Athens* 2 B2
Imbâbah *Cairo* 7 A2
Imielin *Warsaw* 32 C2
Imirim *São Paulo* 27 A2
Imitos *Athens* 2 B2
Imitos, Oros *Athens* 2 B2
Imperial Palace Museum
    Beijing 4 B2
Inagi *Tokyo* 30 B2
Incheolm *Edinburgh* 11 A2
Inchicore *Dublin* 10 B1
Inchkeith *Edinburgh* 11 A3
Inchmickery *Edinburgh* 11 A2
Incirano *Milan* 19 A1
Independencia *Lima* 14 A2
Independencia *Santiago* 27 B2
India Gate *Delhi* 10 B2
Indian Creek Village *Miami* 18 A2
Indianópolis *São Paulo* 27 B2
Indira Gandhi Int. ✈ (DEL)
    Delhi 10 B1
Industria *Johannesburg* 13 B2
Ingierstrand *Oslo* 23 B3
Inglewood *Los Angeles* 16 C3
Ingliston *Edinburgh* 11 B1
Inhaúma *Rio de Janeiro* 25 B1
Inner Port Shelter *Hong Kong* 12 A2
Interlagos *São Paulo* 27 C1
Intramuros *Manila* 17 B1
Invalides *Paris* 24 A2
Inverkeithing *Edinburgh* 11 A1
Inzersdorf *Vienna* 32 B2
Ipanema *Rio de Janeiro* 25 B1
Ipiranga *São Paulo* 27 B2
Ipiranga ➛ *São Paulo* 27 B2
Iponri *Lagos* 14 B2
Ireland's Eye *Dublin* 10 A3
Irving Park *Chicago* 9 B2
Isabel *Rio de Janeiro* 25 B1
Isagatedo *Lagos* 14 A1
Isar ➛ *Munich* 21 A3
Ishbīliya *Baghdad* 3 A2
Ishoj Strand *Copenhagen* 8 B2
Island Bay *Wellington* 33 B1
Island Park *Toronto* 31 B2
Islev *Copenhagen* 8 A2
Isleworth *London* 15 B2
Islington *Toronto* 31 B1
Islington □ *London* 15 A3
Ismaning *Munich* 21 A3
Israelsky Park *Moscow* 19 B3
Isolo *Lagos* 14 A2
Issy-les-Moulineaux *Paris* 24 A2
Istanbul *Istanbul* 12 B1
İstanbul Boğazı *Istanbul* 12 B2
Istinye *Istanbul* 12 B2
Itä Hakkila *Helsinki* 11 B3
Itaewon *Seoul* 27 B1
Itami *Osaka* 23 A1
Itanhanga *Rio de Janeiro* 25 B1
Ivanhoe *Melbourne* 18 A2
Ivry-sur-Seine *Paris* 24 A3
Ixelles *Brussels* 6 B2
Izmaylovo *Moscow* 19 B3
Iztacalco *Mexico City* 18 B2
Iztapalapa *Mexico City* 18 B2

J

Jaba *Jerusalem* 13 B2
Jacaré *Rio de Janeiro* 25 B1
Jackson Heights *New York* 22 B2
Jackson Park *Chicago* 9 C3
Jacques-Cartier *Montreal* 20 A3
Jacques-Cartier, Pont
    Montreal 20 A2
Jadavpur *Kolkata* 14 C2
Jade Buddha Temple *Shanghai* 28 B1
Jaegersborg *Copenhagen* 8 A3
Jaegersborg Dyrehave
    Copenhagen 8 A3
Jagadishpur *Kolkata* 14 B1
Jagatpur *Delhi* 10 A2
Jaguaré, Rib. do ➛ *São Paulo* 27 B1
Jahangirpur *Delhi* 10 A2
Jakarta *Jakarta* 12 A2
Jakarta, Teluk *Jakarta* 12 A1
Jalan Kayu *Singapore* 28 A3
Jamaica B. *New York* 22 C2
Jamaica Plain *Boston* 6 B2
Jamakpuri *Delhi* 10 B1
Jamshīdiyeh *Tehran* 31 A2
Jamsil *Seoul* 27 B2
Jamwon *Seoul* 27 B2
Janki *Warsaw* 32 C1
Jannali *Sydney* 29 C1
Jaraguá *São Paulo* 27 A1
Jaraguá, Pico de *São Paulo* 27 A1
Jardim Paulista *São Paulo* 27 B1
Järvatältet *Stockholm* 29 A1
Jaskhar *Mumbai* 20 A2
Jatinegara *Jakarta* 12 B2
Javādiyeh *Tehran* 31 A2
Jaworowa *Warsaw* 32 C1
Jedlesee *Vienna* 32 A2
Jefferson Memorial
    Washington 33 B3
Jefferson Park *Chicago* 9 B2
Jegi *Seoul* 27 B2
Jelambar *Jakarta* 12 A1
Jelonki *Warsaw* 32 B1
Jerónimos, Mosteiro dos
    Lisbon 16 A1
Jersey City *New York* 22 B1
Jerusalem *Jerusalem* 13 B2
Jessamine, L. *Orlando* 23 B2
Jésus, Î. *Montreal* 20 A1
Jesús Maria *Lima* 14 B2
Jette *Brussels* 6 A1
Jey *Tehran* 31 B2
Jianguomen *Beijing* 4 B2
Jiangwan *Shanghai* 28 B1
Jiawuomen *Beijing* 4 B2
Jihad *Baghdad* 3 B1
Jingan *Shanghai* 28 B1
Jinočany *Prague* 25 B1
Jinonice *Prague* 25 B2
Jiulong = Kowloon
    Hong Kong 12 B2
Jiyūgaoka *Tokyo* 30 B3
Jizā'ir *Baghdad* 3 B2
Jizīra *Baghdad* 3 A2
Joglo *Jakarta* 12 B1
Johannesburg *Johannesburg* 13 B2
Johannesburg, Univ. of
    Johannesburg 13 B2
Johannesburg Int. ✈ (GCJ)
    Johannesburg 13 B2
Johanneskirchen *Munich* 21 A2
Johannesstift *Berlin* 5 A2
Johannisthal *Berlin* 5 B4
John F. Kennedy Nat.
    Historic Site △ *Boston* 6 A2
John McLaren Park
    San Francisco 26 B2
Johnsonville *Wellington* 33 A1
Joinville-le-Pont *Paris* 24 B3
Joli-Bois *Brussels* 6 B2
Jollas *Helsinki* 11 B3
Jongmyo Royal Shrine *Seoul* 27 B1
Jongno *Seoul* 27 B1
Jonstrup *Copenhagen* 8 A2
Joppa *Edinburgh* 11 B3
Jorge Chavez, Int. ✈ (LIM)
    Lima 14 B2
Jorge Newbery ✈ *Buenos Aires* 7 B2
Jósefa Pilsudskiego Park
    Warsaw 32 B1
Jōtō *Osaka* 23 A2
Jouy-en-Josas *Paris* 24 B2
Juan Anchorena *Buenos Aires* 7 B2
Juan González Romero
    Mexico City 18 A2
Juárez Int. ✈ (MEX)
    Mexico City 18 B2
Judeira *Jerusalem* 13 A2
Juhdum *Jerusalem* 13 B2
Juhu *Mumbai* 20 A2
Jūjā *Tokyo* 30 A3
Jukskeirivier ➛ *Johannesburg* 13 A2
Julianów *Warsaw* 32 B2
Jung *Seoul* 27 B1
Jungfernheide, Volkspark
    Berlin 5 A2
Jungfernsee *Berlin* 5 B1
Junghwa *Seoul* 27 B2
Jungnang *Seoul* 27 B2
Jungnangcheon ➛ *Seoul* 27 B1
Juniper Green *Edinburgh* 11 B2
Junk B. *Hong Kong* 12 B2
Jurong *Singapore* 28 B2
Jurong, Selat *Singapore* 28 B2
Jurong Industrial Estate
    Singapore 28 B2
Jurujuba, Enseada de
    Rio de Janeiro 25 B2
Jūsō *Osaka* 23 A1
Justice *Chicago* 9 C2
Jwalahari *Delhi* 10 B1

K

Kaapstad = Cape Town
    Cape Town 8 A1
Kabaty *Warsaw* 32 C2
Kadıköy *Istanbul* 12 C2
Kadoma *Osaka* 23 A2
Kafr 'Aqab *Jerusalem* 13 A2
Kâğıthane *Istanbul* 12 B1
Kâğıthane ➛ *Istanbul* 12 B1
Kagran *Vienna* 32 A2
Kahnawake *Montreal* 20 B1
Kaimes *Edinburgh* 11 B3
Kaiserebersdorf *Vienna* 32 B2
Kaivoksela *Helsinki* 11 B2
Kalamaki *Athens* 2 B2
Kalbadevi *Mumbai* 20 B1
Kalipur *Kolkata* 14 A2
Kalithea *Athens* 2 B2
Kalkaji *Delhi* 10 B2
Kalvebod Fælled *Copenhagen* 8 B3
Kalveboderne *Copenhagen* 8 B3
Kamarhati *Kolkata* 14 B2
Kamata *Tokyo* 30 B3
Kameari *Tokyo* 30 A4
Kameido *Tokyo* 30 A3
Kami-Itabashi *Tokyo* 30 A3
Kamikitazawa *Tokyo* 30 B2

Kamitsuruma *Tokyo* 30 B1
Kamoshida *Tokyo* 30 B2
Kampong Landang *Singapore* 28 A3
Kampong Tanjong Penjuru
    Singapore 28 B2
Kampung Bali *Jakarta* 12 B2
Kanamori *Tokyo* 30 B1
Kanda *Tokyo* 30 A3
Kandilli *Istanbul* 12 B2
Kankurgachi *Kolkata* 14 B2
Kanlıca *Istanbul* 12 B2
Kanonerskiy, Ostrov
    St. Petersburg 27 B1
Kanzaki ➛ *Osaka* 23 A1
Kapali Carsi *Istanbul* 12 B1
Kapellerfeld *Vienna* 32 A2
Káposztásmegyer *Budapest* 7 A2
Kapotnya *Moscow* 19 C3
Käppala *Stockholm* 29 A2
Kapuk *Jakarta* 12 A1
Kapyla *Helsinki* 11 B2
Karachi *Karachi* 13 A1
Karachi Int. ✈ (KHI) *Karachi* 13 A1
Karkh *Baghdad* 3 B2
Karlin *Prague* 25 B2
Karlsfeld *Munich* 21 A1
Karlshorst *Berlin* 5 B4
Karlův most *Prague* 25 B2
Karol Bagh *Delhi* 10 B2
Karolinenhof *Berlin* 5 B4
Karori *Wellington* 33 B1
Karow *Berlin* 5 A3
Karrādah *Baghdad* 3 B2
Kärsön *Stockholm* 29 B1
Kasai *Tokyo* 30 B4
Kasipur *Kolkata* 14 B2
Kastrup *Copenhagen* 8 B3
Kastrup, København ✈
    (CPH) *Copenhagen* 8 B3
Kasuga *Tokyo* 30 A3
Kasumigaseki *Tokyo* 30 B3
Katsushika *Tokyo* 30 A4
Kau Pai Chau *Hong Kong* 12 B2
Kau Yi Chau *Hong Kong* 12 B1
Kaulsdorf *Berlin* 5 B4
Kauniainen *Helsinki* 11 B1
Kawasaki *Tokyo* 30 B3
Kawawa *Tokyo* 30 B2
Kawęczyn *Warsaw* 32 B2
Kayu Putih *Jakarta* 12 B2
Kbely *Prague* 25 B3
Kebayoran Baru *Jakarta* 12 B1
Kebayoran Lama *Jakarta* 12 B1
Kebon Jeruk *Jakarta* 12 B1
Kedar *Jerusalem* 13 B2
Kedoya *Jakarta* 12 B1
Keilor *Melbourne* 18 A1
Keilor North *Melbourne* 18 A1
Keimola *Helsinki* 11 A2
Kelapa Gading *Jakarta* 12 A2
Kelenföld *Budapest* 7 B2
Kelvin *Johannesburg* 13 A2
Kemang *Jakarta* 12 B2
Kemayoran *Jakarta* 12 B1
Kemerburgaz *Istanbul* 12 B1
Kempton Park Races *London* 15 B1
Kenilworth *Cape Town* 8 B1
Kennedy Town *Hong Kong* 12 B1
Kensal Green *London* 15 A2
Kensington *Johannesburg* 13 B2
Kensington *London* 15 B2
Kensington *New York* 22 C2
Kensington *Sydney* 29 B2
Kensington Palace *London* 15 A2
Kent Village *Washington* 33 B4
Kentish Town *London* 15 A3
Kenton *London* 15 A2
Kenwood House *London* 15 A3
Kepa *Warsaw* 32 B2
Keppel Harbour *Singapore* 28 B2
Kesariani *Athens* 2 B2
Kettering *Washington* 33 B5
Kew *London* 15 B2
Kew *Melbourne* 18 A2
Kew Gardens *London* 15 A2
Kew Gardens *Toronto* 31 B3
Key Biscayne *Miami* 18 B2
Khalij *Baghdad* 3 B2
Khandallah *Wellington* 33 B1
Khansā' *Baghdad* 3 A2
Kharavli *Mumbai* 20 B2
Khefren *Cairo* 7 B1
Khichripur *Delhi* 10 B2
Khidirpur *Kolkata* 14 B2
Khimki-Khovrino *Moscow* 19 A2
Khirbet Batin Abu Lihyah
    Jerusalem 13 B1
Khirbet el-Misbah *Jerusalem* 13 A1
Khirbet Jub el-Rum *Jerusalem* 13 A2
Khlong San *Bangkok* 3 B2
Khlong Toey *Bangkok* 3 B2
Khorel *Karachi* 13 A2
Khorosovo *Moscow* 19 B1
Kiamari *Karachi* 13 B1
Kierling *Vienna* 32 A1
Kierlingbach ➛ *Vienna* 32 A1
Kifisos ➛ *Athens* 2 B2
Kikuna *Tokyo* 30 B2
Kilbarrack *Dublin* 10 A3
Kilbirnie *Wellington* 33 B1
Kilburn *London* 15 A2
Kilkkee *Dublin* 10 B3
Killester *Dublin* 10 A3
Killiney *Dublin* 10 B3
Killiney B. *Dublin* 10 B3
Kilmacud *Dublin* 10 B3
Kilmainham *Dublin* 10 B2
Kilmainham Gaol *Dublin* 10 A2
Kilmashogue Mt. *Dublin* 10 B2
Kilmore *Dublin* 10 A3
Kilnamanagh *Dublin* 10 B1
Kilo *Helsinki* 11 B1
Kilokri *Delhi* 10 B2
Kiltiernan *Dublin* 10 B3
Kimmage *Dublin* 10 B2
Kindi *Baghdad* 3 B2
Kinghorn *Edinburgh* 11 A2
Kings Domain *Melbourne* 18 A1
Kings Forest =
    Kongelunden *Copenhagen* 8 B3
Kings Park *Washington* 33 C2
Kings Park West *Washington* 33 C2
Kingsbury *London* 15 A2
Kingsford *Sydney* 29 B2
Kingsford Smith, Sydney ✈
    (SYD) *Sydney* 29 C2
Kingston-upon-Thames □
    London 15 B2
Kingston Vale *London* 15 B2
Kingsway *Toronto* 31 B1
Kinsaley *Dublin* 10 A2

Kipling Heights *Toronto* 31 A1
Kipseli *Athens* 2 B2
Kirchstockbach *Munich* 21 B3
Kirchruderding *Munich* 21 B3
Kirikiri *Lagos* 14 B1
Kirke Værløse *Copenhagen* 8 A1
Kirkhill *Edinburgh* 11 B2
Kirkliston *Edinburgh* 11 B1
Kirknewton *Edinburgh* 11 B1
Kirov Palace of Culture
    St. Petersburg 27 B1
Kiryat Anavim *Jerusalem* 13 B1
Kiryat Ha Yovel *Jerusalem* 13 B1
Kısıklı *Istanbul* 12 B2
Kispest *Budapest* 7 B2
Kista *Stockholm* 29 A1
Kita *Osaka* 23 A1
Kita *Tokyo* 30 A3
Kitazawa *Tokyo* 30 B3
Kiu Tsiu *Hong Kong* 12 A2
Kiveló *Helsinki* 11 B2
Kiziltoprak *Istanbul* 12 C2
Kizuri *Osaka* 23 B2
Kjelsås *Oslo* 23 A3
Kladow *Berlin* 5 B1
Klampenborg *Copenhagen* 8 A3
Klaudyń *Warsaw* 32 B1
Klečany *Prague* 25 A2
Kledering *Vienna* 32 B2
Klein Jukskei ➛ *Johannesburg* 13 A1
Kleinmachnow *Berlin* 5 B2
Kleinschönebeck *Berlin* 5 B5
Klemetsrud *Oslo* 23 A4
Klender *Jakarta* 12 A2
Klíčany *Prague* 25 A2
Klipriviersberg Nature
    Reserve *Johannesburg* 13 B2
Klosterneuburg *Vienna* 32 A1
Kóbánya *Budapest* 7 B2
Kobbegem *Brussels* 6 A1
København *Copenhagen* 8 B3
København ✈ (CPH)
    Copenhagen 8 B3
Kobylisy *Prague* 25 B2
Kobylka *Warsaw* 32 A3
Kodaira *Tokyo* 30 A1
Kodanaka *Tokyo* 30 B2
Koekelberg *Brussels* 6 A1
Koganei *Tokyo* 30 A2
Kogarah *Sydney* 29 B1
Koivupää *Helsinki* 11 B2
Koja *Jakarta* 12 A2
Koja Utara *Jakarta* 12 A2
Kokhav Ya'akov *Jerusalem* 13 A2
Kokobunji *Tokyo* 30 A1
Kokobunji-Temple *Tokyo* 30 A4
Kolarängen *Stockholm* 29 B2
Kolbotn *Oslo* 23 B3
Kolkata *Kolkata* 14 B2
Kolkata Dum Dum Int. ✈
    (CCU) *Kolkata* 14 B2
Kolkata Maidan *Kolkata* 14 B1
Kolo *Warsaw* 32 B1
Kolokinthou *Athens* 2 B2
Kolomyagi *St. Petersburg* 27 A1
Kolonos *Athens* 2 B2
Kolsås *Oslo* 23 A2
Komae *Tokyo* 30 B2
Komagome *Tokyo* 30 A3
Komazawa *Tokyo* 30 B3
Kon Kolala *Lagos* 14 A1
Konala *Helsinki* 11 B2
Kondli *Delhi* 10 B2
Kongelunden *Copenhagen* 8 B3
Kongens Lyngby *Copenhagen* 8 A3
Kongo *Helsinki* 11 B1
Konnagar *Kolkata* 14 A2
Konohana *Osaka* 23 A1
Konradshöhe *Berlin* 5 A2
Kopanina *Prague* 25 B1
Koparkhairana *Mumbai* 20 A2
Köpenick *Berlin* 5 B4
Koramangala *Karachi* 13 B2
Koramoss *Tokyo* 30 B1
Koridalos *Athens* 2 B1
Korokoro *Wellington* 33 B2
Korokoro Stream ➛
    Wellington 33 B2
Kosino *Moscow* 19 B3
Kosugi *Tokyo* 30 B2
Kota *Jakarta* 12 A1
Kōtō *Tokyo* 30 A3
Kotrung *Kolkata* 14 A2
Kouponia *Athens* 2 B2
Kowloon *Hong Kong* 12 B1
Kowloon Peak *Hong Kong* 12 A2
Kowloon Res. *Hong Kong* 12 A1
Kowloon Tong *Hong Kong* 12 A2
Krainmen *Brussels* 6 A2
Krailling *Munich* 21 B1
Krampnitz *Berlin* 5 B1
Krampnitzsee *Berlin* 5 B1
Kranji, Sungai ➛ *Singapore* 28 A2
Kranji Industrial Estate
    Singapore 28 A2
Krasno-Presnenskaya
    Moscow 19 B2
Krč *Prague* 25 B2
Kremlin *Moscow* 19 B2
Krestovskiye, Ostrov
    St. Petersburg 27 B1
Kreuzberg *Berlin* 5 A3
Kritzendorf *Vienna* 32 A1
Krumme Lanke *Berlin* 5 B2
Krummensee *Berlin* 5 A5
Krung Thep = Bangkok
    Bangkok 3 B2
Krusboda *Stockholm* 29 B3
Kuang'chou = Guangzhou
    Guangzhou 11 B2
Küçükköy *Istanbul* 12 B1
Küçüksu *Istanbul* 12 B2
Kudrovo *St. Petersburg* 27 B3
Kulosaari *Helsinki* 11 B3
Kumla *Stockholm* 29 B3
Kungens kurva *Stockholm* 29 B1
Kungliga Slottet *Stockholm* 29 B2
Kungsholmen *Stockholm* 29 B1
Kuningan *Jakarta* 12 B2
Kunitachi *Tokyo* 30 A1
Kunratice *Prague* 25 B2
Kunratický *Prague* 25 B2
Kupchino *St. Petersburg* 27 B2
Kurbağalı ➛ *Istanbul* 12 C2
Kurihara *Tokyo* 30 A3
Kurmuri *Mumbai* 20 A2
Kurumae *Tokyo* 30 A4
Kuryanovo *Moscow* 19 C3
Kustia *Kolkata* 14 B2

Kwangchow = Guangzhou
    Guangzhou 11 B2
Kwun Tong *Hong Kong* 12 B2
Kyje *Prague* 25 B3
Kyūhōji *Osaka* 23 B2

L

La Blanca *Santiago* 27 C2
La Boca *Buenos Aires* 7 B2
La Brètche *Paris* 24 A1
La Campiña *Lima* 14 C2
La Celle-St-Cloud *Paris* 24 A1
La Cisterna *Santiago* 27 C2
La Courneuve *Paris* 24 A3
La Dehesa *Santiago* 27 B2
La Encantada *Lima* 14 C2
La Estación *Madrid* 17 B1
La Floresta *Barcelona* 4 A1
La Florida *Santiago* 27 C2
La Fortuna *Madrid* 17 B1
La Fransa *Barcelona* 4 A1
La Garenne-Colombes *Paris* 24 A2
La Giustiniana *Rome* 26 B1
La Grange *Chicago* 9 C1
La Grange Park *Chicago* 9 C1
La Guardia, New York ✈
    (LGA) *New York* 22 B2
La Hulpe *Brussels* 6 B2
La Llacuna *Barcelona* 4 A1
La Loma *Mexico City* 18 A1
La Lucila *Buenos Aires* 7 B2
La Maladrerie *Paris* 24 A2
La Milla, Cerro *Lima* 14 B2
La Monachina *Rome* 26 B1
La Moraleja *Madrid* 17 A2
La Nopalera *Mexico City* 18 C2
La Paternal *Buenos Aires* 7 B2
La Perla *Lima* 14 B2
La Perouse *Sydney* 29 B2
La Pineda *Barcelona* 4 A1
La Pisana *Rome* 26 B1
La Prairie *Montreal* 20 B3
La Punta *Lima* 14 B1
La Puntigala *Barcelona* 4 A1
La Queue-en-Brie *Paris* 24 B4
La Reina *Santiago* 27 B2
La Ribera *Barcelona* 4 A1
La Sagrera *Barcelona* 4 A2
La Salada *Buenos Aires* 7 C2
La Scala *Milan* 19 B2
La Storta *Rome* 26 B1
La Taxonera *Barcelona* 4 A2
La Victoria *Lima* 14 B2
Laajalahti *Helsinki* 11 B1
Laajasalo *Helsinki* 11 B3
Laaksolahti *Helsinki* 11 B1
Lablāba, W. ➛ *Cairo* 7 A2
Lachine *Montreal* 20 B1
Lachine, Canal de *Montreal* 20 B2
Lad Phrao *Bangkok* 3 B2
Ladera Heights *Los Angeles* 16 C2
Lādvi *Prague* 25 B2
Łady *Warsaw* 32 C1
Lafontaine, Parc *Montreal* 20 A2
Lagoa *Rio de Janeiro* 25 B2
Lagos *Lagos* 14 B2
Lagos Harbour *Lagos* 14 B2
Lagos-Ikeja ✈ (LOS) *Lagos* 14 A1
Lagos Island *Lagos* 14 B2
Lagos Lagoon *Lagos* 14 B2
Laguna de B. *Manila* 17 C2
Laim *Munich* 21 B2
Lainate *Milan* 19 A1
Lainz *Vienna* 32 B1
Lake Buena Vista *Orlando* 23 B1
Lakemba *Sydney* 29 B1
Lakeside *Cape Town* 8 B1
Lakeside *Johannesburg* 13 A2
Lakeview *Chicago* 9 B3
Lakewood Park *Atlanta* 3 B2
Lakhtinskiy *St. Petersburg* 27 B1
Lakhtinskiy Radiv. Oz.
    St. Petersburg 27 B1
Lakshmanpur *Kolkata* 14 A1
Laksi *Bangkok* 3 A2
Lal Qila *Delhi* 10 B2
Lam Tin *Hong Kong* 12 B2
Lambert *Oslo* 23 A3
Lambeth □ *London* 15 B3
Lambrate *Milan* 19 B2
Lambro, Parco *Milan* 19 A2
Lambton Mills *Toronto* 31 B1
Lamma I. *Hong Kong* 12 B1
Landover Hills *Washington* 33 B4
Landsmeer *Amsterdam* 2 A2
Landstrasse *Vienna* 32 A2
Lane Cove *Sydney* 29 A2
Lane Cove National Park △
    Sydney 29 A1
Langa *Cape Town* 8 A2
Langenzersdorf *Vienna* 32 A2
Langer See *Berlin* 5 B4
Langley *Washington* 33 B2
Langley Park *Washington* 33 B4
Langwald *Munich* 21 A1
Lanham *Washington* 33 B4
Lankwitz *Berlin* 5 B3
Lansdowne Cape *Town* 8 A2
Lansing *Toronto* 31 A2
Lanus *Buenos Aires* 7 C2
Lapa *Rio de Janeiro* 25 B1
Laranjeiras *Rio de Janeiro* 25 B1
Las Corts *Barcelona* 4 A1
Las Kabacki *Warsaw* 32 C2
Las Pinas *Manila* 17 C1
Las Rejas *Santiago* 27 B1
Lasalle *Montreal* 20 B2
LaSalle Street Station *Chicago* 9 B3
Lasek Bielański *Warsaw* 32 B1
Lasek Na Kole *Warsaw* 32 B1
Laski *Warsaw* 32 B1
Latina *Madrid* 17 B1
Lauttasaari *Helsinki* 11 C2
Laval-des-Rapides *Montreal* 20 A1
Lavadero *Lima* 14 A2
Lavradio *Lisbon* 16 A2
Lawndale *Chicago* 9 B2
Lawne L. *Orlando* 23 A2
Lawrence Heights *Toronto* 31 A2
Layari *Karachi* 13 A2
Layari ➛ *Karachi* 13 A1
Łazienkowski Park *Warsaw* 32 B2
Le Blanc-Mesnil *Paris* 24 A3
Le Bourget *Paris* 24 A3
Le Chenoi *Brussels* 6 B2
Le Chesnay *Paris* 24 A1
Le Christ de Saclay *Paris* 24 B1

Le Kremlin-Bicêtre *Paris* 24 B3
Le Mesnil-le-Roi *Paris* 24 A1
Le Pecq *Paris* 24 A1
Le Perreux *Paris* 24 A3
Le Pin *Paris* 24 A4
Le Plessis-Robinson *Paris* 24 B2
Le Plessis-Trévise *Paris* 24 B4
Le Port-Marly *Paris* 24 A1
Le Pré-St-Gervais *Paris* 24 A3
Le Raincy *Paris* 24 A4
Le Vésinet *Paris* 24 A1
Lea Bridge *London* 15 A3
Leaside *Toronto* 31 B1
Leblon *Rio de Janeiro* 25 B1
Lee *London* 15 B4
Leganés *Madrid* 17 C1
Legazpi *Madrid* 17 B1
Lehtisaari *Helsinki* 11 B2
Lei Yue Mun *Hong Kong* 12 B2
Leião *Lisbon* 14 A1
Leichhardt *Sydney* 29 B1
Leith *Edinburgh* 11 B3
Leme *Rio de Janeiro* 25 B1
Lemoyne *Montreal* 20 B3
Lenin *Moscow* 19 B2
Lenino *Moscow* 19 C2
Leninskiye Gory *Moscow* 19 B2
Lennox *Los Angeles* 16 C2
Leonia *New York* 22 A1
Leopardstown *Dublin* 10 B2
Leopoldau *Vienna* 32 A2
Leopoldsdorf *Vienna* 32 B2
Leopoldstadt *Vienna* 32 A2
Leportovo *Moscow* 19 B3
Leppävaara *Helsinki* 11 B1
Les Lilas *Paris* 24 A3
Les Loges-en-Josas *Paris* 24 B1
Les Pavillons-sous-Bois *Paris* 24 A4
Lésigny *Paris* 24 B4
Lesnozavodskaya
      St. Petersburg 27 B2
Lester B. Pearson Int.,
      Toronto ✈ (YYZ) *Toronto* 31 A1
L'Étang-la-Ville *Paris* 24 A1
Letňany *Prague* 26 A2
Letopolis = Ausim *Cairo* 7 A1
Levallois-Perret *Paris* 24 A2
Levent *Istanbul* 12 B2
Lewisdale *Washington* 33 B4
Lewisham ▢ *London* 15 B3
Lexington *Boston* 6 A1
Leyton *London* 15 A3
Leytonstone *London* 15 A4
L'Haÿ-les-Roses *Paris* 24 B3
L'Hospitalet de Llobregat
      Barcelona 4 A1
Lhotka *Prague* 26 B2
Liangshui He ➛ *Beijing* 4 C2
Lianhua Chi *Beijing* 4 B1
Lianhua He ➛ *Beijing* 4 B1
Libčice nad Vltavou *Prague* 26 A2
Libeň *Prague* 26 B2
Liberdade *São Paulo* 27 B2
Liberton *Edinburgh* 11 B3
Liberty I. *New York* 22 B1
Liberty Osaka Museum
      Osaka 23 B1
Liberty State Park =
      New York 22 B1
Libeznice *Prague* 25 A2
Libuš *Prague* 26 B2
Lichiao *Guangzhou* 11 B2
Lichtenburg *Berlin* 5 A4
Lichterfelde *Berlin* 5 B2
Lidingö *Stockholm* 29 A2
Lieshi Lingyuan *Guangzhou* 11 B2
Liesing *Vienna* 32 B1
Liesing ➛ *Vienna* 32 B2
Ligovo *St. Petersburg* 27 C1
Lijordet *Oslo* 23 A2
Likhoborka ➛ *Moscow* 19 A2
Lilla Värtan *Stockholm* 29 A3
Lille Værløse *Copenhagen* 8 A2
Liluah *Kolkata* 14 B1
Lim Chu Kang *Singapore* 28 A2
Lima *Lima* 14 B2
Limbiate *Milan* 19 A1
Limehouse *London* 15 A3
Limeil-Brévannes *Paris* 24 B3
Linate, Milano ✈ (LIN) *Milan* 19 B2
Linbropark *Johannesburg* 13 A2
Lincoln Center for
      Performing Arts *New York* 22 B2
Lincoln Heights *Los Angeles* 16 B3
Lincoln Memorial *Washington* 33 B3
Lincoln Park *Chicago* 9 B3
Lincoln Park *New York* 22 B1
Lincoln Park *San Francisco* 26 B1
Lincoln Park Zoo *Chicago* 9 B3
Lincolnwood *Chicago* 9 A2
Linda-a-Pastora *Lisbon* 16 A1
Linden *Johannesburg* 13 A2
Linden *Wellington* 33 A1
Lindenberg *Berlin* 5 A4
Lindøya *Oslo* 23 A3
Liniers *Buenos Aires* 7 B1
Linkebeek *Brussels* 6 B2
Linksfield *Johannesburg* 13 A2
Linmeyer *Johannesburg* 13 B2
Linna *Helsinki* 11 A2
Lintuvaara *Helsinki* 11 B1
Lion Rock Country Park ▢
      Hong Kong 12 A2
Lion's Head *Cape Town* 8 A1
Lioumi *Athens* 2 B2
Lisbon = Lisboa *Lisbon* 16 A2
Lisboa ✈ (LIS) *Lisbon* 16 A2
Lisbon = Lisboa *Lisbon* 16 A2
Lishui *Guangzhou* 11 A1
Little B. *Sydney* 29 B2
Little Calumet ➛ *Chicago* 9 D3
Little Ferry *New York* 22 A1
Little Lake Conway *Orlando* 23 B2
Little Red Schoolhouse
      Nature Center *Chicago* 9 C1
Little Rouge ➛ *Toronto* 31 A4
Liuhang *Shanghai* 28 A1
Liurong Temple *Guangzhou* 11 B2
Livry-Gargan *Paris* 24 A4
Ljan *Oslo* 23 A3
Llano de Can Gineu *Barcelona* 4 A2
Lo Aranguiz *Santiago* 27 B2
Lo Boza *Santiago* 27 B1
Lo Chau *Hong Kong* 12 B2
Lo Chau Pak Mai *Hong Kong* 12 B2
Lo Espejo *Santiago* 27 C2
Lo Hermida *Santiago* 27 B2
Lo Prado *Santiago* 27 B1
Lo So Shing *Hong Kong* 12 B1
Lo Wai *Hong Kong* 12 A1
Loanhead *Edinburgh* 11 B3
Lobau *Vienna* 32 A3
Lobos, Pt. *San Francisco* 26 B1
Locham *Munich* 21 B1
Lochkov *Prague* 25 B2

Lockhausen *Munich* 21 A1
Lodi *New York* 22 A1
Lodi Estate *Delhi* 10 B2
Logan Int., Boston ✈ (BOS)
      Boston 6 A2
Logan Square *Chicago* 9 B2
Lognes-Émerainville ✈ *Paris* 24 B4
Löhme *Berlin* 5 A5
Lolokhet *Karachi* 13 A2
Lomas Chapultepec
      Mexico City 18 B1
Lomas de San Angel Inn
      Mexico City 18 B1
Lombardy East *Johannesburg* 13 A2
Lomianki *Warsaw* 32 A1
Lomus Reforma *Mexico City* 18 B1
London *London* 15 B3
London City ✈ (LCY) *London* 15 A4
London Heathrow ✈ (LHR)
      London 15 B1
London Zoo *London* 15 A3
Long B. *Sydney* 29 B2
Long Branch *Toronto* 31 B1
Long Brook ➛ *Washington* 33 C2
Long Ditton *London* 15 B2
Long Island City *New York* 22 B2
Longchamp, Hippodrome
      de *Paris* 24 A2
Longhua Pagoda *Shanghai* 28 B1
Longhua Park *Shanghai* 28 B1
Longjohn Slough *Chicago* 9 C1
Longtan Hu ➛ *Beijing* 4 B2
Longue-Pointe *Montreal* 20 A3
Longueuil *Montreal* 20 A3
Longueuil-St-Hubert =
      St-Hubert *Montreal* 20 B3
Loni *Delhi* 10 A2
Loop, The *Chicago* 9 B3
Lord's Cricket Ground *London* 15 A2
Loreto *Milan* 19 B2
Los Angeles *Los Angeles* 16 B3
Los Angeles Int. ✈ (LAX)
      Los Angeles 16 C2
Los Cerrillos ✈ (ULC) *Santiago* 27 B1
Los Nietos *Los Angeles* 16 C4
Los Olivos *Lima* 14 A2
Los Reyes *Mexico City* 18 B2
Losiny Ostrov ▢ *Moscow* 19 A3
Lot *Brussels* 6 B1
Lotus River *Cape Town* 8 B2
Lotus Temple *Delhi* 10 B2
Loughlinstown *Dublin* 10 B3
Louise, L. *Orlando* 23 B1
Louisiana Superdome
      New Orleans 21 B2
Loures *Lisbon* 16 A1
Louveciennes *Paris* 24 A1
Louvre, Musée du *Paris* 24 A3
Lower B. *New York* 22 C1
Lower Hutt *Wellington* 33 B2
Lower New York B. =
      Lower B. *New York* 22 C1
Lower Shing Mun Res.
      Hong Kong 12 A2
Lowry Bay *Wellington* 33 B2
Loyola University *Chicago* 9 B3
Lu Xun, Tomb of *Shanghai* 28 B1
Lu Xun Park *Shanghai* 28 B1
Lübars *Berlin* 5 A3
Lucy, L. *Orlando* 23 A2
Ludwigsfeld *Munich* 21 A1
Luhu *Guangzhou* 11 B2
Lumiar *Lisbon* 16 A1
Lundtofte *Copenhagen* 8 A3
Lung Mei *Hong Kong* 12 A2
Luojiang *Guangzhou* 11 B2
Lustheim *Munich* 21 A2
Luwan *Shanghai* 28 B1
Luzhniki Sports Centre
      Moscow 19 B2
Lyndhurst *New York* 22 B1
Lynn Woods Res. *Boston* 6 A2
Lyon, Gare de *Paris* 24 A3
Lyons *Chicago* 9 C2
Lysaker *Oslo* 23 A2
Lysakerselva ➛ *Oslo* 23 A2
Lysolaje *Prague* 25 B2
Lyublino *Moscow* 19 B3

M

Ma Nam Wat *Hong Kong* 12 A2
Ma On Shan Country
      Park ▢ *Hong Kong* 12 A2
Ma'ale Adumim *Jerusalem* 13 B2
Ma'ale Ha Khamisha
      Jerusalem 13 B1
Ma'ale Mikhmas *Jerusalem* 13 A2
Maantiekylä *Helsinki* 11 A3
Maarifa *Baghdad* 3 B2
Mabato Pt. *Manila* 17 C2
Mabel, L. *Orlando* 23 B1
Macaco, Morro do
      Rio de Janeiro 25 B2
McCook *Chicago* 9 C2
McGill University *Montreal* 20 A2
Machelen *Brussels* 6 A2
Machida *Tokyo* 30 B1
Maciołki *Warsaw* 32 B2
McKerrow, Mt. *Wellington* 33 B2
McKinley Park *Chicago* 9 C2
McLean *Washington* 33 B2
Macopocho ➛ *Santiago* 27 B1
MacRitchie Res. *Singapore* 28 A2
Macul *Santiago* 27 C2
Madhudaha *Kolkata* 14 B2
Madhyamgram *Kolkata* 14 A2
Madin *Mexico City* 18 A1
Madin, L. *Mexico City* 18 A1
Madinah Al Mansûr *Baghdad* 3 B2
Mâdinet Nasr *Cairo* 7 A2
Madrid *Madrid* 17 B1
Madrid Barajas ✈ (MAD)
      Madrid 17 B2
Madrona *Barcelona* 4 A1
Maesawa *Tokyo* 30 A2
Magdalena *Lima* 14 B2
Magdalena Contreras
      Mexico City 18 C1
Maghreb *Baghdad* 3 A2
Maginu *Tokyo* 30 B2
Magliana *Rome* 26 B1
Magny-les-Hameaux *Paris* 24 B1
Maheshtala *Kolkata* 14 C1
Mahim *Mumbai* 20 A2
Mahim B. *Mumbai* 20 A2
Mahlsdorf *Berlin* 5 A4
Mahmoodabad *Karachi* 13 A2
Mahrauli *Delhi* 10 B2
Mahul *Mumbai* 20 A2
Maida Vale *London* 15 A2
Maidstone *Melbourne* 29 A1
Maipú *Santiago* 27 C1
Maisonneuve, Parc *Montreal* 20 A2

Maisons-Alfort *Paris* 24 B3
Maisons-Laffitte *Paris* 24 A1
Maissoneuve *Montreal* 20 A2
Maitland *Cape Town* 8 A1
Makasar *Jakarta* 12 A2
Makati *Manila* 17 B2
Mäkiniitty *Helsinki* 11 A2
Malá Strana *Prague* 25 B2
Malabar *Sydney* 29 B2
Malabar Hill *Mumbai* 20 B1
Malabar Pt. *Mumbai* 20 B1
Malabon *Manila* 17 B1
Malacañang Palace *Manila* 17 B1
Malahide *Dublin* 10 A3
Malakoff *Paris* 24 B2
Målarhöjaen *Stockholm* 29 B1
Malate *Manila* 17 B1
Malaya Neva *St. Petersburg* 27 B1
Malaya Okhta *St. Petersburg* 27 B2
Malchow *Berlin* 5 A3
Malden *Boston* 6 A2
Malden *London* 15 B2
Maleizen *Brussels* 6 B3
Malešice *Prague* 25 B3
Malir ➛ *Karachi* 13 B2
Malleny Mills *Edinburgh* 11 B2
Malmi *Helsinki* 11 B2
Malmøya *Oslo* 23 A3
Målov *Copenhagen* 8 A2
Malton *Toronto* 31 A1
Malvern *Johannesburg* 13 B2
Malvern *Melbourne* 18 B2
Malvern *Toronto* 31 A3
Mampang Prapatan *Jakarta* 12 B1
Mampukuji *Tokyo* 30 B2
Man Budrukh *Mumbai* 20 A2
Man Khurd *Mumbai* 20 A2
Manakhat *Jerusalem* 13 B2
Mandaluyong *Manila* 17 B2
Mandaoli *Delhi* 10 B2
Mandaqui ➛ *São Paulo* 27 A2
Mandoli *Delhi* 10 A2
Mandvi *Mumbai* 20 B2
Manenberg *Cape Town* 8 A2
Mang Kung Uk *Hong Kong* 12 B2
Mang-won *Seoul* 27 B1
Mangolpuri *Delhi* 10 A1
Manguinhos ✈ *Rio de Janeiro* 25 B1
Manhattan *New York* 22 B2
Manhattan Beach *New York* 22 C2
Manila *Manila* 17 B1
Manila Ninoy Aquino
      Int. ✈ (MNL) *Manila* 17 B2
Mankkaa *Helsinki* 11 B1
Manly *Sydney* 29 A2
Mann, L. *Orlando* 23 A2
Mann's Chinese Theatre
      Los Angeles 16 B2
Mannswörth *Vienna* 32 B3
Manor Park *London* 15 A4
Manor Park *Wellington* 33 A2
Manora *Karachi* 13 B1
Manora Pt. *Karachi* 13 B1
Manquehue, Cerro *Santiago* 27 B2
Manzanares, Canal de *Madrid* 17 C2
Mapo *Seoul* 27 B1
Maracanã *Rio de Janeiro* 25 B1
Maraoli *Mumbai* 20 A2
Marcelin *Warsaw* 32 B1
Mareil-Marly *Paris* 24 A1
Margareten *Vienna* 32 A2
Maria *Vienna* 32 A2
Maridalen *Oslo* 23 A3
Maridalsvatnet *Oslo* 23 A3
Mariendorf *Berlin* 5 B3
Marienfelde *Berlin* 5 B3
Marikina *Manila* 17 B2
Marikina ➛ *Manila* 17 B2
Marin City *San Francisco* 26 A2
Marin Pen. *San Francisco* 26 A1
Marina del Rey *Los Angeles* 16 C2
Marino *Dublin* 10 A2
Marisco, Ponta do
      Rio de Janeiro 25 C1
Markham *Toronto* 31 A2
Marki *Warsaw* 32 B2
Markland Wood *Toronto* 31 B1
Marly, Forêt de *Paris* 24 A1
Marly-le-Roi *Paris* 24 A1
Marne-la-Vallée *Paris* 24 A4
Marolles-en-Brie *Paris* 24 B4
Maroubra *Sydney* 29 B2
Marquette Park *Chicago* 9 C2
Marrickville *Sydney* 29 B1
Marsfield *Sydney* 29 A1
Marsha, L. *Orlando* 23 A1
Marte, Campo de *São Paulo* 27 B2
Martesana, Canal della
      Milan 19 A2
Martin Luther King Nat.
      Historic Site ▢ *Atlanta* 3 B2
Martinez *Buenos Aires* 7 A1
Martinkylä *Helsinki* 11 A2
Martinsried *Munich* 21 B1
Maruko *Tokyo* 30 B3
Maryino *Moscow* 19 B3
Maryland *Singapore* 28 B2
Marymont *Warsaw* 32 B2
Marysin Wawerski *Warsaw* 32 B2
Marzahn *Berlin* 5 A4
Mascot *Sydney* 29 B2
Maspeth *New York* 22 B2
Masr el Gedida *Cairo* 7 A2
Masr el Qadîma *Cairo* 7 A2
Massachusetts Inst. of
      Tech. *Boston* 6 A2
Massamá *Lisbon* 16 A1
Massey ➛ *Toronto* 31 A1
Massey *Paris* 24 B2
Mata *Jerusalem* 13 B1
Matinhutong *Beijing* 4 B2
Matinha *Lisbon* 16 A2
Matramam *Jakarta* 12 B2
Matsubara *Osaka* 23 B2
Mattapan *Boston* 6 B2
Mátyásföld *Budapest* 7 A3
Mau Tso Ngam *Hong Kong* 12 A2
Mauer *Vienna* 32 B1
Mauripur *Karachi* 13 A1
Maxhof *Munich* 21 B1
Mayfair *Johannesburg* 13 B2
Mayor, Plaza *Madrid* 17 B1
Maywood *Chicago* 9 B1
Maywood *Los Angeles* 16 C3
Maywood *New York* 22 A1
Maywood Park Race Track
      Chicago 9 B1
Mazagaon *Mumbai* 20 B2
Meadowbank Park *Sydney* 29 A1
Méchoulpy *Paris* 24 B4
Měčice *Prague* 25 A3
Mecidiyeköy *Istanbul* 12 B2
Medford *Boston* 6 A2
Mediodia *Madrid* 17 B2

Meguro *Tokyo* 30 B3
Meguro ➛ *Tokyo* 30 B3
Mehrabpur *Delhi* 10 B1
Mehrābād ✈ (THR) *Tehran* 31 A1
Mehram Nagar *Delhi* 10 B1
Mehrow *Berlin* 5 A4
Meidling *Vienna* 32 A2
Méier *Rio de Janeiro* 25 B1
Meiji Shrine *Tokyo* 30 A3
Meise *Brussels* 6 A1
Mejiro *Tokyo* 30 A3
Melbourne *Melbourne* 18 A1
Melbourne ✈ (MEL)
      Melbourne 18 A1
Melkki *Helsinki* 11 C2
Mellunkylä *Helsinki* 11 B3
Mellunmäki *Helsinki* 11 B3
Melrose *Boston* 6 A2
Melrose *New York* 22 B2
Melrose Park *Chicago* 9 B1
Melsbroek *Brussels* 6 A2
Melville *Johannesburg* 13 B2
Menteng *Jakarta* 12 B1
Mérantaise ➛ *Paris* 24 B1
Mercamadrid *Madrid* 17 B2
Merced, L. *San Francisco* 26 B1
Meredale *Johannesburg* 13 B1
Merlimau, Pulau *Singapore* 28 B2
Merri Cr. ➛ *Melbourne* 18 A1
Merrion *Dublin* 10 A2
Merrionette Park *Chicago* 9 C2
Merton ▢ *London* 15 B2
Mesgarâbâd *Tehran* 31 B3
Messe *Vienna* 32 A2
Metanópoli *Milan* 19 B2
Metro-Dade Cultural
      Centre *Miami* 18 B2
Metro Toronto Zoo *Toronto* 31 A3
Metropolitan Museum of
      Art *New York* 22 B2
Meudon *Paris* 24 B2
Mevaseret Tsiyon *Jerusalem* 13 B1
Mevo Betar *Jerusalem* 13 B1
México *Mexico City* 18 B2
México, Ciudad de
      Mexico City 18 B2
Mexico City Int. ✈ (MEX)
      Mexico City 18 B2
Meyersdal *Johannesburg* 13 B2
Mezzate *Milan* 19 B2
Miadong *Seoul* 27 B2
Miami *Miami* 18 B2
Miami Beach *Miami* 18 B2
Miami Canal *Miami* 18 A1
Miami Int. ✈ (MIA) *Miami* 18 B1
Miami Shores *Miami* 18 A2
Miami Springs *Miami* 18 B1
Miasto *Warsaw* 32 B2
Michalowice *Warsaw* 32 B1
Michle *Prague* 26 B2
Middle Harbour *Sydney* 29 A2
Middle Hd. *Sydney* 29 A2
Middle Park *Melbourne* 18 B1
Middle Village *New York* 22 B2
Middlesex Fells Reservation
      Boston 6 A2
Midland Beach *New York* 22 C1
Midwood *New York* 22 C2
Miedzeszyn *Warsaw* 32 B2
Miedzylesie *Warsaw* 32 B2
Miessaari *Helsinki* 11 C1
Miguel Hidalgo *Mexico City* 18 B1
Milan = Milano *Milan* 19 B1
Milanese, Parco
      Regionale ▢ *Milan* 19 A1
Milano *Milan* 19 B1
Milano Due *Milan* 19 B2
Milano Linate ✈ (LIN) *Milan* 19 B2
Milano San Felice *Milan* 19 B2
Milbertshofen *Munich* 21 A2
Mill Hill *London* 15 A2
Millennium Dome *London* 15 A4
Miller Meadow *Chicago* 9 B2
Millerhill *Edinburgh* 11 B3
Milltown *Dublin* 10 B2
Millwood *Washington* 33 B4
Milnerton *Cape Town* 8 A1
Milon-la-Chapelle *Paris* 24 B1
Milton *Boston* 6 B2
Milton Bridge *Edinburgh* 11 B2
Mimico *Toronto* 31 B2
Mimico Creek ➛ *Toronto* 31 B1
Minami *Osaka* 23 A2
Minamisenju *Tokyo* 30 A4
Minato *Osaka* 23 B1
Minato *Tokyo* 30 B3
Minshât el Bekkarî *Cairo* 7 A2
Miraflores *Lima* 14 B2
Miramar *Wellington* 33 B1
Misericordia, Sa. da
      Rio de Janeiro 25 B2
Mission *San Francisco* 26 B2
Mississauga *Toronto* 31 B1
Mitaka *Tokyo* 30 A2
Mitcham *London* 15 B3
Mitcham Common *London* 15 B3
Mitchell Museum of the
      American Indian *Chicago* 9 A2
Mitchell's Plain *Cape Town* 8 B2
Mitte *Berlin* 5 A3
Mitre Isarkanal ➛ *Munich* 21 A3
Mixcoac *Mexico City* 18 B1
Miyakojima *Osaka* 23 A2
Mizonokuchi *Tokyo* 30 B2
Mizue *Tokyo* 30 A4
Mlocinski Park *Warsaw* 32 B1
Mlociny *Warsaw* 32 B1
Mnevniki *Moscow* 19 B2
Moba *Lagos* 14 B2
Moczydlo *Warsaw* 32 C2
Modderfontein *Johannesburg* 13 A2
Modřany *Prague* 26 B2
Mogyoród *Budapest* 7 A3
Moinho Velho, Cor. ➛
      São Paulo 27 B2
Mok *Seoul* 27 B1
Mokotów *Warsaw* 32 B2
Molenbeek-St-Jean *Brussels* 6 A1
Molino de Rosas *Mexico City* 18 B1
Mollem *Brussels* 6 A1
Mollins de Rey *Barcelona* 4 A1
Mondeor *Johannesburg* 13 B2
Moneda, Palacio de la
      Santiago 27 B2
Monerò *Rio de Janeiro* 25 A1
Mong Kok *Hong Kong* 12 B2
Monkstown *Dublin* 10 B3
Monnickendam *Amsterdam* 2 A3
Monrovia *Los Angeles* 16 B4
Monsanto, Parque Florestal
      de *Lisbon* 16 A1
Mont-Royal *Montreal* 20 A2
Mont-Royal, Parc *Montreal* 20 A2

Montana de Montjuich
      Barcelona 4 A1
Montcada i Reixac *Barcelona* 4 A2
Monte Chingolo *Buenos Aires* 7 C2
Montebello *Los Angeles* 16 B4
Montemor *Lisbon* 16 A1
Monterey Park *Los Angeles* 16 B4
Montespaccato *Rome* 26 B1
Montesverde Nuovo *Rome* 26 B1
Montfermeil *Paris* 24 A4
Montigny-le-Bretonneux
      Paris 24 B1
Montjay-la-Tour *Paris* 24 A4
Montparnasse, Gare *Paris* 24 A2
Montréal *Montreal* 20 A2
Montréal, Í. de *Montreal* 20 A2
Montréal, Université de
      Montreal 20 A2
Montréal Est *Montreal* 20 A2
Montréal-Nord *Montreal* 20 A2
Montréal-Ouest *Montreal* 20 B1
Montréal Trudeau Int. ✈
      (YUL) *Montreal* 20 B2
Montreuil *Paris* 24 A3
Montrouge *Paris* 24 B2
Montserrat *Buenos Aires* 7 B2
Monza *Milan* 19 A2
Monzoro *Milan* 19 B1
Moóca *São Paulo* 27 B2
Moonachie *New York* 22 B1
Moonee Ponds *Melbourne* 18 A1
Moonee Valley Racecourse
      Melbourne 18 A1
Moosach *Munich* 21 A2
Mora *Mumbai* 20 B2
Moratalaz *Madrid* 17 B2
Mörby *Stockholm* 29 A2
Morden *London* 15 B2
Morée ➛ *Paris* 24 A3
Morgan Park *Chicago* 9 C3
Moriguchi *Osaka* 23 A2
Morivione *Milan* 19 B2
Morningside *Edinburgh* 11 B2
Morningside *Johannesburg* 13 A2
Morningside *Washington* 33 C4
Morningside Park *Toronto* 31 A3
Morro Solar, Cerro *Lima* 14 C2
Mortlake *London* 15 B2
Mortlake *Sydney* 29 B1
Morton Grove *Chicago* 9 A2
Morumbi *São Paulo* 27 B1
Moscavide *Lisbon* 16 A2
Moschato *Athens* 2 B1
Moscow = Moskva *Moscow* 19 B2
Moskva *Moscow* 19 B2
Moskvoretskiy *Moscow* 19 B2
Mosman *Sydney* 29 A2
Móstoles *Madrid* 17 C1
Moti Bagh *Delhi* 10 B2
Motol *Prague* 26 B1
Motsa *Jerusalem* 13 B2
Motsa Ilit *Jerusalem* 13 B1
Motspur Park *London* 15 B2
Mottingham *London* 15 B4
Mount Dennis *Toronto* 31 A2
Mount Greenwood *Chicago* 9 C2
Mount Hood Memorial
      Park ▢ *Boston* 6 A2
Mount Merrion *Dublin* 10 B2
Mount Rainier *Washington* 33 B4
Mount Vernon *New York* 22 A3
Müggelberge *Berlin* 5 B4
Müggelheim *Berlin* 5 B5
Muggiò *Milan* 19 A2
Mühleiten *Vienna* 32 A3
Mühlenfliess ➛ *Berlin* 5 A5
Milano Cape Town 8 B1
Muiden *Amsterdam* 2 A3
Muizenberg *Cape Town* 8 B1
Mujahidpur *Delhi* 10 B2
Mukandpur *Delhi* 10 A2
Mukhmas *Jerusalem* 13 A2
Muko ➛ *Osaka* 23 A1
Mukojima *Tokyo* 30 A3
Mulbarton *Johannesburg* 13 B2
Mumbai *Mumbai* 20 B2
Mumbai Chhatrapati
      Shivaji Int. ✈ (BOM)
      Mumbai 20 A2
Mumbai Harbour *Mumbai* 20 B2
Munch Museum *Oslo* 23 A3
Münchehofe *Berlin* 5 B5
München *Munich* 21 B2
Münchener Franz Josef
      Straus ✈ (MUC) *Munich* 21 A2
Munich = München *Munich* 21 B2
Munkkiniemi *Helsinki* 11 B2
Munro *Buenos Aires* 7 B1
Muntinlupa *Manila* 17 C2
Murai Res. *Singapore* 28 A2
Muranów *Warsaw* 32 B1
Murino *St. Petersburg* 27 B2
Murrayfield *Edinburgh* 11 B2
Museu Nacional *Rio de Janeiro* 25 B1
Mushin *Lagos* 14 A2
Musocco *Milan* 19 B1
Mustansiriya *Baghdad* 3 A2
Musturud *Cairo* 7 A2
Muswell Hill *London* 15 A3
Mutanabi *Baghdad* 3 B2
Muthana *Baghdad* 3 A2
Mykerinos *Cairo* 7 B1
Myllypuro *Helsinki* 11 B3
Mystic ➛ *Boston* 6 A2

N

Nacka *Stockholm* 29 B3
Naenae *Wellington* 33 B2
Nærsnes *Oslo* 23 B1
Nagatsuta *Tokyo* 30 B2
Nagytétény *Budapest* 7 B1
Nahalin *Jerusalem* 13 B1
Najafgarh Drain ➛ *Delhi* 10 B1
Nakahara *Tokyo* 30 B2
Nakano *Tokyo* 30 A2
Namsan Park *Seoul* 27 B1
Namyeong *Seoul* 27 B1
Nanbiancun *Guangzhou* 11 B1
Nanchang He ➛ *Beijing* 4 B1
Nangal Dewat *Delhi* 10 B1
Naniwa *Osaka* 23 B1
Nanole *Mumbai* 20 A2
Nanpu Bridge *Shanghai* 28 B2
Nanterre *Paris* 24 A2
Naoabad *Kolkata* 14 B2
Napier Mole *Karachi* 13 B1
Naraina *Delhi* 10 B1
Nariman Point *Mumbai* 20 B1
Nariman Pt. *Mumbai* 20 B1

Närmak *Tehran* 31 A2
Naruo *Osaka* 23 A1
Näsby *Stockholm* 29 A2
Näsbypark *Stockholm* 29 A2
National Arboretum
      Washington 33 B3
National Zoological Park
      Washington 33 B3
Nativity, Basilica of *Jerusalem* 13 B2
Natolin *Warsaw* 32 C2
Naucalpan de Juárez
      Mexico City 18 B1
Naupada *Mumbai* 20 A2
Navi Mumbai *Mumbai* 20 A2
Navíglio di Pavia *Milan* 19 B1
Navíglio Grande *Milan* 19 B1
Navotas *Manila* 17 B1
Navy Pier *Chicago* 9 B3
Nazal Hikmat Beg *Baghdad* 3 A2
Nazimabad *Karachi* 13 A2
Nazlet el Simmân *Cairo* 7 B1
Nea Alexandria *Athens* 2 B2
Nea Ionia *Athens* 2 A2
Nea Liosia *Athens* 2 A2
Nea Smirni *Athens* 2 B2
Neapoli *Athens* 2 B2
Near North *Chicago* 9 B3
Nebušice *Prague* 25 A1
Nederhorst *Amsterdam* 2 B3
Nedlitz *Berlin* 5 B1
Nee Soon *Singapore* 28 A2
Needham *Boston* 6 B1
Needham Heights *Boston* 6 B1
N'ematâbâd *Tehran* 31 B2
Neritna *Tokyo* 30 A3
Nesodden *Oslo* 23 B3
Nesoddtangen *Oslo* 23 A3
Nesoya *Oslo* 23 A2
Neu Aubing *Munich* 21 B1
Neu Buch *Berlin* 5 A4
Neu Buchhorst *Berlin* 5 B5
Neu Fahrland *Berlin* 5 B1
Neu Lindenberg *Berlin* 5 A4
Neubiberg *Munich* 21 B2
Neuenhagen *Berlin* 5 A4
Neuessling *Vienna* 32 A3
Neuhausen *Munich* 21 B2
Neuherberg *Munich* 21 A2
Neuhönow *Berlin* 5 A5
Neuilly-Plaisance *Paris* 24 A4
Neuilly-sur-Marne *Paris* 24 A4
Neuilly-sur-Seine *Paris* 24 A2
Neukagran *Vienna* 32 A3
Neukettenhof *Vienna* 32 B2
Neukölln *Berlin* 5 B3
Neuperlach *Munich* 21 B2
Neuried *Munich* 21 B1
Neustift am Walde *Vienna* 32 A1
Neusüssenbrunn *Vienna* 32 A2
Neuwaldegg *Vienna* 32 A1
Neve Ya'akov *Jerusalem* 13 A2
Neves *Rio de Janeiro* 25 B2
New Bagdâdd *Baghdad* 3 B2
New Barakpur *Kolkata* 14 A2
New Brighton *New York* 22 C1
New Canada *Johannesburg* 13 B1
New Canada Dam
      Johannesburg 13 B1
New Carrollton *Washington* 33 B4
New Cross *London* 15 B3
New Delhi *Delhi* 10 B2
New Dorp *New York* 22 C1
New Dorp Beach *New York* 22 C1
New Malden *London* 15 B2
New Milford *New York* 22 A1
New Mumbai = Navi
      Mumbai *Mumbai* 20 A2
New Territories *Hong Kong* 12 A1
New Toronto *Toronto* 31 B1
New Utrecht *New York* 22 C2
New York *New York* 22 B3
New York La Guardia ✈
      (LGA) *New York* 22 B2
Newark B. *New York* 22 B1
Newbattle *Edinburgh* 11 B3
Newbury Park *London* 15 A4
Newcraighall *Edinburgh* 11 B3
Newham ▢ *London* 15 A4
Newhaven *Edinburgh* 11 B2
Newlands *Johannesburg* 13 B1
Newlands *Wellington* 33 B1
Newport *Melbourne* 18 B1
Newton *Boston* 6 A1
Newtonbrook *Toronto* 31 A2
Newtongrange *Edinburgh* 11 B3
Newtonville *Boston* 6 A1
Newtown *Sydney* 29 B2
Ngaio *Wellington* 33 B1
Ngau Chi Wan *Hong Kong* 12 A2
Ngau Tau Kok *Hong Kong* 12 B2
Ngauranga *Wellington* 33 B1
Ngong Shuen Chau
      Hong Kong 12 B1
Ngua Kok Wan *Hong Kong* 12 A1
Niaväräin *Tehran* 31 A2
Nibra *Kolkata* 14 B1
Nidâl *Baghdad* 3 B2
Niddrie *Edinburgh* 11 B3
Niddrie *Melbourne* 18 A1
Nieder Neuendorf *Berlin* 5 A2
Niederschöneweide *Berlin* 5 B3
Niederschönhausen *Berlin* 5 A3
Niemeyer *Rio de Janeiro* 25 B1
Nieuwendam *Amsterdam* 2 A2
Nihonbashi *Tokyo* 30 A3
Niipperi *Helsinki* 11 B1
Nikea *Athens* 2 B1
Nikolassee *Berlin* 5 B2
Nikolskiy *Moscow* 19 B1
Niles *Chicago* 9 A2
Nimta *Kolkata* 14 A2
Ninoy Aquino Int. ✈ (MNL)
      Manila 17 B2
Nippa *Tokyo* 30 B2
Nippori *Tokyo* 30 A3
Nishi *Osaka* 23 A1
Nishinari *Osaka* 23 B1
Nishinomiya *Osaka* 23 A1
Nishiyodogawa *Osaka* 23 A1
Niterói *Rio de Janeiro* 25 B2
Nockeby *Stockholm* 29 A1
Nogatino *Moscow* 19 B3
Nogent-sur-Marne *Paris* 24 A3
Noida *Delhi* 10 B2
Noiseau *Paris* 24 B4
Noisiel *Paris* 24 A4
Noisy-le-Grand *Paris* 24 A4
Noisy-le-Roi *Paris* 24 A1
Noisy-le-Sec *Paris* 24 A3
Nokkala *Helsinki* 11 C1
Nomentano *Rome* 26 B2
Nonakashimbo *Tokyo* 30 A2
Nongminyundong
      Jiangxisuo *Guangzhou* 11 B2

Nonhyeon *Seoul* 27 B2
Nonthaburi *Bangkok* 3 A1
Noordgesig *Johannesburg* 13 B1
Noordzeekanaal *Amsterdam* 2 A1
Nord, Gare du *Paris* 24 A3
Nordmarka *Oslo* 23 A3
Nordrand-Siedlung *Vienna* 32 A2
Nordstrand *Oslo* 23 A3
Normandale *Wellington* 33 B2
Norridge *Chicago* 9 B2
Norrmalm *Stockholm* 29 A2
North Arlington *New York* 22 B1
North Bay Village *Miami* 18 A2
North Bergen *New York* 22 B1
North Bull I. *Dublin* 10 A3
North Cheam *London* 15 B2
North Cray *London* 15 B4
North Decatur *Atlanta* 3 B3
North Druid Hills *Atlanta* 3 B3
North Esk ➛ *Edinburgh* 11 B3
North Gyle *Edinburgh* 11 B2
North Hackensack *New York* 22 A1
North Harbor *Manila* 17 B1
North Hd. *Sydney* 29 A2
North Hollywood *Los Angeles* 16 B2
North Lexington *Boston* 6 A1
North Miami *Miami* 18 A2
North Miami Beach *Miami* 18 A2
North Nazimabad *Karachi* 13 A2
North Pt. *Hong Kong* 12 B2
North Queensferry *Edinburgh* 11 A1
North Quincy *Boston* 6 B2
North Res. *Boston* 6 A2
North Riverside *Chicago* 9 B2
North Saugus *Boston* 6 A2
North Shore Channel ➛
      Chicago 9 B2
North Springfield *Washington* 33 C2
North Station *Boston* 6 A2
North Sydney *Sydney* 29 B2
North Woolwich *London* 15 A4
North York *Toronto* 31 A2
Northbridge *Sydney* 29 A2
Northbridge Park *Sydney* 29 A2
Northcliff *Johannesburg* 13 A1
Northcote *Melbourne* 18 A1
Northeastern University
      Boston 6 A2
Northern Virginia Regional
      Park ▢ *Washington* 33 B3
Northlake *Chicago* 9 B1
Northmount *Toronto* 31 A2
Northolt *London* 15 A1
Northumberland Heath
      London 15 B5
Northwestern Station *Chicago* 9 B3
Northwestern University
      Chicago 9 A2
Northwood *London* 15 A1
Northwood Park *Toronto* 31 A1
Norwood *Johannesburg* 13 A2
Norwood Park *Chicago* 9 B2
Noryangjin *Seoul* 27 B1
Nossa Senhora do ó *São Paulo* 27 B1
Nossegem *Brussels* 6 A2
Notre-Dame, Basilique
      Montreal 20 A2
Notre-Dame, Bois *Paris* 24 B4
Notre-Dame-de-Grâce
      Montreal 20 B2
Notting Hill *London* 15 A2
Nova Milanese *Milan* 19 A1
Novate Milanese *Milan* 19 A1
Novaya Derevnya
      St. Petersburg 27 B1
Nové Město *Prague* 25 B2
Novoaleksandrovskoye
      St. Petersburg 27 A1
Novodevichy Convent
      Moscow 19 B2
Novogireyevo *Moscow* 19 B3
Novosaratovka *St. Petersburg* 27 B3
Nowe-Babice *Warsaw* 32 B1
Nowe Miasto *Warsaw* 32 B2
Nöykkiö *Helsinki* 11 B1
Nueva Atzacoalco *Mexico City* 18 B2
Nueva Pompeya *Buenos Aires* 7 C2
Nueva Tenochtitlán
      Mexico City 18 B2
Nuijala *Helsinki* 11 B1
Numabukuro *Tokyo* 30 A2
Nuñez *Buenos Aires* 7 B2
Nunhead *London* 15 B3
Ñuñoa *Santiago* 27 B2
Nusle *Prague* 25 B2
Nussdorf *Vienna* 32 A2
Nyanga *Cape Town* 8 A2
Nymphenburg *Munich* 21 B2
Nymphenburg, Schloss
      Munich 21 B2

O

Oak Grove *Atlanta* 3 A3
Oak Hill *Boston* 6 B1
Oak Lawn *Chicago* 9 C2
Oak Park *Chicago* 9 B2
Oak View *Washington* 33 A4
Oakdale *Atlanta* 3 A2
Oakland *San Francisco* 26 B2
Oakland *Washington* 33 B4
Oakleigh *Melbourne* 18 B2
Oakton *Washington* 33 B2
Oakwood Beach *New York* 22 C1
Oatley *Sydney* 29 B1
Obalende *Lagos* 14 B2
Oba's Palace *Lagos* 14 B2
Oberföhring *Munich* 21 B2
Oberhaching *Munich* 21 B2
Oberlaa *Vienna* 32 B2
Oberlisse *Vienna* 32 A2
Obermenzing *Munich* 21 A1
Obermoos Schwaige *Munich* 21 A1
Oberschleissheim *Munich* 21 A2
Oberschöneweide *Berlin* 5 B4
Observatory *Johannesburg* 13 B2
Óbuda *Budapest* 7 A2
Obukhovo *St. Petersburg* 27 C2
Obvodnyy Kanal
      St. Petersburg 27 B2
Ocean Park *Hong Kong* 12 B2
Ochota *Warsaw* 32 B1
Odana *St. Petersburg* 27 B3
Odén-Stockach *Munich* 21 B3
Odilampi *Helsinki* 11 B1
Odivelas *Lisbon* 16 A1
Odolany *Warsaw* 32 B1
Oeiras *Lisbon* 16 A1
Ofin *Lagos* 14 A2
Ogawa *Tokyo* 30 A1
Ogden Park *Chicago* 9 C2

Ogikubo *Tokyo* 30 A2
Ogogoro *Lagos* 14 B2
Ogoyo *Lagos* 14 B2
Ogudu *Lagos* 14 A2
O'Hare Int., Chicago ✈
      (ORD) *Chicago* 9 B1
Ohariu Stream ➛ *Wellington* 33 B1
O'Higgins, Parque *Santiago* 27 B2
Ōimachi *Tokyo* 30 B3
Ojota *Lagos* 14 A2
Okęcie *Warsaw* 32 B1
Okęcie, Warszawa ✈
      (WAW) *Warsaw* 32 B1
Okelra *Lagos* 14 B2
Okeogbe *Lagos* 14 B2
Okhla *Delhi* 10 B2
Okhta ➛ *St. Petersburg* 27 B2
Okkervil ➛ *St. Petersburg* 27 B2
Okrzeszyn *Warsaw* 32 C2
Oksval *Oslo* 23 A3
Oktyabrskiy *Moscow* 19 B2
Okubo *Tokyo* 30 A3
Okura *Tokyo* 30 B1
Olari *Helsinki* 11 B1
Olaria *Rio de Janeiro* 25 B1
Old Admiralty *St. Petersburg* 27 B1
Old City *Jerusalem* 13 B2
Old City *Shanghai* 28 B1
Old City Hall *Toronto* 31 B2
Old Fort York *Toronto* 31 B2
Old Harbor *Boston* 6 B2
Old Town *Chicago* 9 B3
Old Town Hall = Altes
      Rathaus *Munich* 21 B2
Oldbawn *Dublin* 10 B1
Olgino *St. Petersburg* 27 A1
Olímpico, Estadio *Mexico City* 18 C1
Olivais *Lisbon* 16 A2
Olivar de los Padres
      Mexico City 18 C1
Olivar del Conde *Mexico City* 18 C1
Olives, Mt. of *Jerusalem* 13 B2
Olivia, L. *Orlando* 23 A1
Olivos *Buenos Aires* 7 B2
Olona ➛ *Milan* 19 B1
Olympia, L. *Orlando* 23 A1
Olympic Stadium = Turner
      Field *Atlanta* 3 B2
Olympic Stadium *Helsinki* 11 B2
Olympique, Stade *Montreal* 20 A2
Ōmori *Tokyo* 30 B3
Onisigun *Lagos* 14 A2
Ontario Science Centre
      Toronto 31 A2
Ōokayama *Tokyo* 30 B3
Oostzaan *Amsterdam* 2 A2
Opa-Locka *Miami* 18 A1
Opa-Locka ✈ (OPF) *Miami* 18 A1
Opacz *Warsaw* 32 B1
Ophirton *Johannesburg* 13 B2
Oppegård *Oslo* 23 B3
Oppem *Brussels* 6 A1
Oppsal *Oslo* 23 A4
Oradell *New York* 22 A1
Oradell Res. *New York* 22 A1
Orange Bowl Stadium *Miami* 18 B2
Orangi *Karachi* 13 A2
Ordrup *Copenhagen* 8 A3
Orech *Prague* 25 B2
Orient Heights *Boston* 6 A3
Orlando *Orlando* 23 A2
Orlando Dam *Johannesburg* 13 B1
Orlando East *Johannesburg* 13 B1
Orlando Executive ✈ *Orlando* 23 A2
Orlando Int. ✈ (MCO)
      Orlando 23 B3
Orlovista *Orlando* 23 A1
Orly, Paris ✈ (ORY) *Paris* 24 B3
Ormesson-sur-Marne *Paris* 24 B4
Ormond *Melbourne* 18 B2
Ormøya *Oslo* 23 A3
Orpington *London* 15 B4
Ortaköy *Istanbul* 12 B2
Ortica *Milan* 19 B2
Oruba *Lagos* 14 A2
Ōsaka *Osaka* 23 A2
Ōsaka Castle *Osaka* 23 A2
Ōsaka Harbour *Osaka* 23 B1
Ōsaka Itami Int. ✈ (ITM)
      Osaka 23 A1
Ōsaka Kansai ✈ (KIX) *Osaka* 23 B2
Ōsaki *Tokyo* 30 B3
Oasco *São Paulo* 27 B1
Osdorf *Berlin* 5 B1
Osdorp *Amsterdam* 2 A1
Oshodi *Lagos* 14 A2
Oslo *Oslo* 23 A3
Oslo ✈ (OSL) *Oslo* 23 A4
Ōsone *Tokyo* 30 B2
Osorun *Lagos* 14 A2
Ospiate *Milan* 19 A1
Ostankino *Moscow* 19 B2
Osterley *London* 15 B1
Osterley Park *London* 15 B1
Ostersätra *Stockholm* 29 A2
Österskär *Stockholm* 29 A2
Óstia Malpasso *Rome* 26 C1
Ostiense *Rome* 26 B1
Østmarkkapellet *Oslo* 23 A4
Ostøya *Oslo* 23 A2
Østre Aker *Oslo* 23 A3
Ōta *Tokyo* 30 B3
Otaniemi *Helsinki* 11 B1
Otari Open Air Museum
      Wellington 33 B1
Otsuka *Tokyo* 30 A3
Ottakring *Vienna* 32 A1
Ottávia *Rome* 26 B1
Ottery *Cape Town* 8 B2
Ottobrunn *Munich* 21 B2
Ouderkerk *Amsterdam* 2 B2
Oulunkylä *Helsinki* 11 B2
Ourcq, Canal de l' *Paris* 24 A3
Outer Mission *San Francisco* 26 B2
Outremont *Montreal* 20 A2
Overijse *Brussels* 6 B3
Owhiro Bay *Wellington* 33 C1
Oworonsoki *Lagos* 14 A2
Oxgangs *Edinburgh* 11 B2
Oxon Hill *Washington* 33 C4
Oyodo *Osaka* 23 A2
Oyster B. *Sydney* 29 C1
Oyster Rock *Mumbai* 20 B1
Oyster Rocks *Karachi* 13 B2
Ozoir-la-Ferrière *Paris* 24 B4
Ozone Park *New York* 22 B2

P

Pacific Heights *San Francisco* 26 B2
Pacific Manor *San Francisco* 26 C2
Pacific Palisades *Los Angeles* 16 B1

Pacifica *San Francisco* 26 C2
Paco *Manila* 17 B1
Paco de Arcos *Lisbon* 16 A1
Paddington *London* 15 A2
Paddington *Sydney* 29 B2
Paderno *Milan* 19 A1
Pagewood *Sydney* 29 B2
Pagote *Mumbai* 20 B2
Pai, I. do *Rio de Janeiro* 25 B2
Pak Kok *Hong Kong* 12 B1
Pak Kong *Hong Kong* 12 A2
Pakila *Helsinki* 11 B2
Palacio Real *Madrid* 17 B1
Palaiseau *Paris* 24 B2
Palazzolo *Milan* 19 A1
Paleo Faliro *Athens* 2 B2
Palermo *Buenos Aires* 7 B2
Palhais *Lisbon* 16 B2
Palisades Park *New York* 22 A1
Palmerston *Dublin* 10 A1
Paloheinä *Helsinki* 11 B2
Palomeras *Madrid* 17 B2
Palos Heights *Chicago* 9 D2
Palos Hills *Chicago* 9 C1
Palos Hills Forest *Chicago* 9 C1
Palos Park *Chicago* 9 C1
Palpara *Kolkata* 14 B2
Panchur *Kolkata* 14 B1
Pandacan *Manila* 17 B2
Pandan, Selat *Singapore* 28 B2
Pandan Res. *Singapore* 28 B2
Pangrati *Athens* 2 B2
Pangsua, Sungei ➤ *Singapore* 28 A2
Panihati *Kolkata* 14 B2
Panjang, Bukit *Singapore* 28 A2
Panke ➤ *Berlin* 5 A3
Pankow *Berlin* 5 A3
Pantheon *Rome* 26 B1
Panthersville *Atlanta* 3 B3
Pantin *Paris* 24 A3
Pantitlán *Mexico City* 18 B2
Panvel Cr. ➤ *Mumbai* 20 B2
Paparangi *Wellington* 33 B1
Papiol *Barcelona* 4 A1
Paramount Studios
    Los Angeles 16 B2
Paramus *New York* 22 A1
Paranaque *Manila* 17 B2
Paray-Vieille-Poste *Paris* 24 B3
Pardisän Nature Park *Tehran* 31 A2
Parel *Mumbai* 20 B2
Pari *São Paulo* 27 B2
Parioli *Rome* 26 B1
Paris *Paris* 24 A3
Paris Orly ✈ (ORY) *Paris* 24 B3
Parje *Mumbai* 20 B2
Pärk-e Äzädegän *Tehran* 31 B2
Pärk-e Mellat *Tehran* 31 A2
Park Ridge *Chicago* 9 A1
Park Royal *London* 15 A2
Parkchester *New York* 22 B2
Parkdale *Toronto* 31 B2
Parkhurst *Johannesburg* 13 A2
Parklawn *Washington* 33 B3
Parkmore *Johannesburg* 13 A2
Parkside *San Francisco* 26 B2
Parktown *Johannesburg* 13 A2
Parkview *Johannesburg* 13 A2
Parkville *New York* 22 C2
Parkwood *Johannesburg* 13 A2
Parkwood *Cape Town* 8 A2
Parque Chacabuco
    Buenos Aires 7 C2
Parque Patricios *Buenos Aires* 7 B2
Parramatta ➤ *Sydney* 29 A1
Paşabahçe *Istanbul* 12 B2
Pasadena *Los Angeles* 16 B4
Pasar Minggu *Jakarta* 12 B2
Pasay *Manila* 17 B2
Pascoe Vale *Melbourne* 18 A1
Pasig *Manila* 17 B2
Pasig ➤ *Manila* 17 B2
Pasila *Helsinki* 11 B2
Pasing *Munich* 21 B1
Pasir Panjang *Singapore* 28 B2
Pasir Ris *Singapore* 28 A3
Passaic *New York* 22 B1
Passaic ➤ *New York* 22 B1
Passirana *Milan* 19 A1
Patel Nagar *Delhi* 10 B1
Pateros *Manila* 17 B2
Pathumwan *Bangkok* 3 B2
Patipukur *Kolkata* 14 B2
Patisia *Athens* 2 A2
Paulo E. Virginia, Gruta
    Rio de Janeiro 25 B2
Paulshof *Berlin* 5 A5
Paya Lebar *Singapore* 28 A3
Peakhurst *Sydney* 29 B1
Peania *Athens* 2 B2
Pearson Int. Toronto ✈
    (YYZ) *Toronto* 31 A1
Peckham *London* 15 B3
Pederstrup *Copenhagen* 8 A2
Pedralbes *Barcelona* 4 A1
Pedregal de San Angel,
    Jardines del *Mexico City* 18 C1
Peip'ing = Beijing *Beijing* 4 B1
Peking = Beijing *Beijing* 4 B1
Pelcowizna *Warsaw* 32 B2
Peñalolén *Santiago* 27 C2
Pencarrow Hd. *Wellington* 33 C2
Peng Siang ➤ *Singapore* 28 A2
Penge *London* 15 B3
Penha *Rio de Janeiro* 25 B2
Penicuik *Edinburgh* 11 B2
Penjaringan *Jakarta* 12 A1
Pentagon *Washington* 33 B3
Penzing *Vienna* 32 A1
People's Park *Shanghai* 28 B1
People's Square *Shanghai* 28 B1
Perales del Rio *Madrid* 17 C2
Perchtoldsdorf *Vienna* 32 B1
Perdizes *São Paulo* 27 B2
Peristeri *Athens* 2 A2
Perivale *London* 15 A2
Perk *Brussels* 6 A2
Perlach *Munich* 21 B2
Perlacher Forst *Munich* 21 B2
Pero *Milan* 19 A1
Peropok, Bukit *Singapore* 28 B2
Perovo *Moscow* 19 B3
Pertusella *Milan* 19 A1
Pesagot *Jerusalem* 13 A2
Pesanggrahan, Kali ➤
    Jakarta 12 B1
Peschiera Borromeo *Milan* 19 B2
Pesek, Pulau *Singapore* 28 B2
Pest *Budapest* 7 B2
Pesterzsébet *Budapest* 7 B2
Pesthidegkút *Budapest* 7 A1
Pestimre *Budapest* 7 B3
Pestlörinc *Budapest* 7 B3

Pestújhely *Budapest* 7 A2
Petas *Helsinki* 11 B2
Petone *Wellington* 33 B2
Petrogradskaya Storona
    St. Petersburg 27 B2
Petroupoli *Athens* 2 A2
Petrovice *Prague* 25 B3
Petrovsky Park *Moscow* 19 B2
Petrovsko-Razumovskoye
    Moscow 19 B2
Pettycur *Edinburgh* 11 A2
Peutie *Brussels* 6 A2
Pfaueninsel *Berlin* 5 B1
Phaya Thai *Bangkok* 3 B2
Phihai *Karachi* 13 A2
Phillip B. *Sydney* 29 B2
Phoenix Park *Dublin* 10 A2
Phra Khanong *Bangkok* 3 B2
Phra Nakhon *Bangkok* 3 B2
Phra Pradaeng *Bangkok* 3 C2
Phranakhon *Bangkok* 3 B1
Pico Rivera *Los Angeles* 16 C4
Piedade *Lisbon* 16 A1
Piedade *Rio de Janeiro* 25 B1
Piedade, Cova da *Lisbon* 16 A2
Piedmont Park *Atlanta* 3 B2
Pierre Elliott Trudeau ✈
    (YUL) *Montreal* 20 B1
Pietralata *Rome* 26 B1
Pihlajamäki *Helsinki* 11 B2
Pihlajasaari *Helsinki* 11 C2
Pilares *Rio de Janeiro* 25 B1
Pilton *Edinburgh* 11 B2
Pimmit Hills *Washington* 33 B2
Pine Castle *Orlando* 23 B2
Pine Grove *Toronto* 31 A1
Pine Hills *Orlando* 23 A2
Pinewood Park *Miami* 18 A2
Piney Run ➤ *Washington* 33 B2
Pinganli *Beijing* 4 B2
Pingzhou *Guangzhou* 11 B2
Pinheiros ➤ *São Paulo* 27 B1
Pinjrapur *Karachi* 13 A2
Pinner *London* 15 A1
Pinner Green *London* 15 A1
Pioltello *Milan* 19 B2
Pipinui Pt. *Wellington* 33 A1
Piraeus = Pireas *Athens* 2 B1
Piraiévs = Pireas *Athens* 2 B1
Pirajuçara ➤ *São Paulo* 27 B1
Pireas *Athens* 2 B1
Pirinçci *Istanbul* 12 B1
Pirituba *São Paulo* 27 A1
Pirkkola *Helsinki* 11 B2
Pisgat O'mer *Jerusalem* 13 B2
Pisgat Ze'ev *Jerusalem* 13 B2
Pisnice *Prague* 25 C2
Pitampura *Delhi* 10 A1
Pitkäjärvi *Helsinki* 11 B1
Planegg *Munich* 21 B1
Pleasure Island *Orlando* 23 B1
Plumstead *Cape Town* 8 B2
Plumstead *London* 15 B4
Plyushchevo *Moscow* 19 B3
Po Toi *Hong Kong* 12 B2
Po Toi O *Hong Kong* 12 B2
Poasco *Milan* 19 B2
Podbaba *Prague* 25 B2
Podoli *Prague* 25 B2
Pohick Creek ➤ *Washington* 33 C2
Pointe-Aux-Trembles
    Montreal 20 A2
Poissy *Paris* 24 A1
Pok Fu Lam *Hong Kong* 12 B1
Pokcheong *Seoul* 27 C2
Pokrovsko-Sresnevo *Moscow* 19 B1
Polton *Edinburgh* 11 B3
Polvoranca, Parque de
    Madrid 17 C1
Polyustrovo *St. Petersburg* 27 B2
Pomprap *Bangkok* 3 B2
Pondok Gede *Jakarta* 12 A2
Pondok Indah *Jakarta* 12 B1
Pont-Viau *Montreal* 20 A1
Pontault-Combault *Paris* 24 B4
Pontinha *Lisbon* 16 A1
Poplar *London* 15 A3
Poppintree *Dublin* 10 A2
Porirua *Wellington* 33 A2
Porirua East *Wellington* 33 A2
Port Melbourne *Melbourne* 18 B1
Port Nicholson *Wellington* 33 B2
Port Richmond *New York* 22 C1
Port Shelter *Hong Kong* 12 A2
Port Union *Toronto* 31 A4
Portage Park *Chicago* 9 B2
Portela, Lisboa ✈ (LIS) *Lisbon* 16 A2
Porter, L. *Orlando* 23 A3
Portmarnock *Dublin* 10 A3
Porto Brandão *Lisbon* 16 A1
Porto Novo *Rio de Janeiro* 25 B2
Porto Novo Cr. ➤ *Lagos* 14 B2
Portobello *Edinburgh* 11 B3
Portrero *San Francisco* 26 B2
Potomac *Washington* 33 B2
Potrero Pt. *San Francisco* 26 B2
Potsdam *Berlin* 5 B1
Potzham *Munich* 21 B2
Pötzleinsdorf *Vienna* 32 A1
Povoa de Santo Adriao *Lisbon* 16 A2
Powązki *Warsaw* 32 B1
Powisle *Warsaw* 32 B2
Powsin *Warsaw* 32 C2
Powsinek *Warsaw* 32 C2
Poyan Res. *Singapore* 28 A2
Pozuelo de Alarcón *Madrid* 17 B1
Prado, Museo del *Madrid* 17 B1
Prado Churubusco
    Mexico City 18 B2
Praga *Warsaw* 32 B2
Prague = Praha *Prague* 25 B2
Praha *Prague* 25 B2
Praha ✈ (PRG) *Prague* 25 B1
Praires, R. des ➤ *Montreal* 20 A2
Prater *Vienna* 32 A2
Precotto *Milan* 19 A2
Prenestino Labicano *Rome* 26 B2
Prenzlauerberg *Berlin* 5 A3
Preston *Melbourne* 18 A1
Pretos Forros, Sa. dos
    Rio de Janeiro 25 B1
Préville *Montreal* 20 B3
Přezletice *Prague* 25 B3
Prima Porta *Rome* 26 B1
Primavalle *Rome* 26 B1
Primrose *Johannesburg* 13 B2
Primrose Hill *London* 15 A2
Progreso Nacional
    Mexico City 18 A2
Prosek *Prague* 25 B3
Prospect Hill Park *Boston* 6 A2
Providencia *Santiago* 27 B2
Průhonice *Prague* 25 C3
Psichiko *Athens* 2 A2
Pudong New Area *Shanghai* 28 B2
Pueblo Libre *Lima* 14 B2

Pueblo Nuevo *Barcelona* 4 A2
Pueblo Nuevo *Madrid* 17 B2
Puerto Madero *Buenos Aires* 7 B2
Puhuangyu *Beijing* 4 B2
Puistola *Helsinki* 11 B3
Pukinmäki *Helsinki* 11 B3
Pulkovo Int. ✈ (LED)
    St. Petersburg 27 C1
Pullach *Munich* 21 B1
Pullman Historic District
    Chicago 9 C3
Pulo Gadung *Jakarta* 12 B2
Pünak *Tehran* 31 A2
Punchbowl *Sydney* 29 B1
Punde *Mumbai* 20 B2
Punggol *Singapore* 28 A3
Punggol, Sungei ➤ *Singapore* 28 A3
Punggol Pt. *Singapore* 28 A3
Punjabi Bagh *Delhi* 10 A1
Puotila *Helsinki* 11 B3
Puteaux *Paris* 24 A2
Putney *London* 15 B2
Putuo *Shanghai* 28 B1
Putxet *Barcelona* 4 A1
Puxi *Shanghai* 28 B1
Pyramids *Cairo* 7 B1
Pyry *Warsaw* 32 C1

Q

Qalandiya *Jerusalem* 13 A2
Qal'eh Morghi *Tehran* 31 B2
Qanā el Ismā'ilīya *Cairo* 7 A2
Qāsemābād *Tehran* 31 A3
Qasr-e Fīrūzeh *Tehran* 31 B3
Qatane *Jerusalem* 13 B1
Qianmen *Beijing* 4 B2
Qinghuayuan *Beijing* 4 B1
Qingningsi *Shanghai* 28 B2
Qolhak *Tehran* 31 A2
Quadraro *Rome* 26 B2
Quaid-i-Azam *Karachi* 13 A1
Quartiere Zingone *Milan* 19 B1
Queiba *Jerusalem* 13 A1
Quds *Baghdad* 3 A2
Queen Mary Res. *London* 15 B1
Queen Victoria Market
    Melbourne 18 A1
Queensbury *London* 15 A2
Queenscliffe *Sydney* 29 A2
Queensferry *Edinburgh* 11 B1
Queenstown *Singapore* 28 B2
Quellerina *Johannesburg* 13 A1
Queluz *Lisbon* 16 A1
Quezon City *Manila* 17 B2
Quilicura *Santiago* 27 B1
Quincy *Boston* 6 B2
Quincy B. *Boston* 6 B2
Quinta Normal *Santiago* 27 B1
Quinto de Stampi *Milan* 19 B2
Quinto Romano *Milan* 19 B1
Quirinale *Rome* 26 B1

R

R.F.K. Memorial Stadium
    Washington 33 B4
Raasdorf *Vienna* 32 A3
Radcliffe College *Boston* 6 A2
Rådhus *Oslo* 23 A3
Radlice *Prague* 25 B2
Radość *Warsaw* 32 B3
Radotin *Prague* 25 C2
Rafat *Jerusalem* 13 A2
Raffles Park *Singapore* 28 B2
Raheny *Dublin* 10 A3
Rahnsdorf *Berlin* 5 B5
Rainham *London* 15 A5
Rajakylä *Helsinki* 11 B3
Rajpura *Delhi* 10 A2
Rákos-patak ➤ *Budapest* 7 B3
Rákoshegy *Budapest* 7 B3
Rákoskeresztúr *Budapest* 7 B3
Rákoskert *Budapest* 7 B3
Rákosliget *Budapest* 7 B3
Rákospalota *Budapest* 7 A2
Rákosszentmihály *Budapest* 7 A2
Raków *Warsaw* 32 B1
Ram *Jerusalem* 13 A2
Rām Allāh *Jerusalem* 13 A2
Ramadán *Baghdad* 3 A2
Ramakrishna Puram *Delhi* 10 B1
Rāmallāh = Rām Allāh
    Jerusalem 13 A2
Ramanathpur *Kolkata* 14 A1
Ramat Allon *Jerusalem* 13 A2
Ramat Eshkol *Jerusalem* 13 B2
Ramat Razi'el *Jerusalem* 13 B1
Ramat Shafet *Jerusalem* 13 B1
Rambler Channel *Hong Kong* 12 A1
Ramenki *Moscow* 19 B2
Ramersdorf *Munich* 21 B2
Ramses Station *Cairo* 7 A2
Ramos Rio de *Rio de Janeiro* 25 B2
Ramos Mejía *Buenos Aires* 7 B1
Ramot *Jerusalem* 13 B2
Rampur *Delhi* 10 A2
Ramsgate *Sydney* 29 B1
Rand ✈ (QRA) *Johannesburg* 13 B2
Randalls I. *New York* 22 B2
Randburg *Johannesburg* 13 A1
Randhart *Johannesburg* 13 B2
Randpark Ridge *Johannesburg* 13 A1
Randwick *Sydney* 29 B2
Ranelagh *Dublin* 10 A2
Rangpuri *Delhi* 10 B1
Ransbeche *Brussels* 6 B2
Ransdorp *Amsterdam* 2 A2
Ranvad *Mumbai* 20 B2
Raposo *Lisbon* 16 A1
Rastaala *Helsinki* 11 B1
Rastila *Helsinki* 11 B3
Raszyn *Warsaw* 32 C1
Rathfarnham *Dublin* 10 B2
Ratho *Edinburgh* 11 B2
Ratho Station *Edinburgh* 11 B1
Rato *Lisbon* 16 A2
Ravelston *Edinburgh* 11 B2
Rawamangun *Jakarta* 12 B2
Rayners Lane *London* 15 A1
Raynes Park *London* 15 B2
Raypur *Kolkata* 14 C2
Real Felipe, Fuerte *Lima* 14 B2
Reams, L. *Orlando* 23 B1
Recoleta *Buenos Aires* 7 B2
Recoleta *Santiago* 27 B2
Red Fort = Lal Qila *Delhi* 10 B2
Red Square *Moscow* 19 B2
Redbridge □ *London* 15 A4
Redfern *Sydney* 29 B2
Redwood *Wellington* 33 B1

Refshaleøen *Copenhagen* 8 A3
Regents Park *Johannesburg* 13 B2
Regent's Park *London* 15 A3
Rego Park *New York* 22 B2
Reinickendorf *Berlin* 5 A3
Rekola *Helsinki* 11 B3
Rembertów *Warsaw* 32 B3
Rembrandtpark *Amsterdam* 2 A2
Remedios, Parque Nacional
    de los △ *Mexico City* 18 B1
Remedios de Escalada
    Buenos Aires 7 C2
Rémola, Estany del *Barcelona* 4 B1
Renca *Santiago* 27 B1
Rennemoulin *Paris* 24 A1
Řeporyje *Prague* 25 B1
Repulse Bay *Hong Kong* 12 B2
Repy *Prague* 25 B1
Residenz *Munich* 21 B2
Reston *Washington* 33 B2
Retiro *Buenos Aires* 7 B2
Retiro *Madrid* 17 B1
Retiro, Puerto *Buenos Aires* 7 B2
Retreat *Cape Town* 8 B1
Réveillon ➤ *Paris* 24 B4
Revere *Boston* 6 A2
Rexdale *Toronto* 31 A1
Reynosa Tamaulipas
    Mexico City 18 A1
Rho *Milan* 19 A1
Rhodes *Sydney* 29 A2
Rhodon *Paris* 24 B1
Rhodon ➤ *Paris* 24 B1
Rialto Towers *Melbourne* 18 A1
Ribeira *Rio de Janeiro* 25 B2
Ricarda, Estany de la *Barcelona* 4 B1
Richmond *Melbourne* 18 A1
Richmond *San Francisco* 26 B2
Richmond Hill *New York* 22 B2
Richmond Park *London* 15 B2
Richmond-upon-Thames □
    London 15 B2
Ridge, The *Delhi* 10 B2
Ridgefield *New York* 22 A1
Ridgefield Park *New York* 22 A1
Ridgewood *New York* 22 B2
Riem *Munich* 21 B3
Riesenrad *Vienna* 32 A2
Rijksmuseum *Amsterdam* 2 A2
Rikers I. *New York* 22 B2
Rimac *Lima* 14 B2
Ringsend *Dublin* 10 A2
Rinkeby *Stockholm* 29 A1
Rio Compride *Rio de Janeiro* 25 B1
Rio de Janeiro *Rio de Janeiro* 25 B1
Rio de Janeiro Galeão ✈
    (GIG) *Rio de Janeiro* 25 B2
Rio de Mouro *Lisbon* 16 A1
Ripollet *Barcelona* 4 A1
Ris *Oslo* 23 A3
Risby *Copenhagen* 8 A1
Rishra *Kolkata* 14 A2
Ritchie *Washington* 33 B4
Rithala *Delhi* 10 A1
Rive Sud, Canal de la
    Montreal 20 B2
River Edge *New York* 22 A1
River Forest *Chicago* 9 B2
River Grove *Chicago* 9 B2
Riverdale *New York* 22 A2
Riverdale *Washington* 33 B4
Riverdale Park *Toronto* 31 A2
Riverlea *Johannesburg* 13 B1
Riverside *Chicago* 9 C2
Riverwood *Sydney* 29 B1
Rivière-des-Prairies *Montreal* 20 A2
Rixensart *Brussels* 6 B3
Riyad *Baghdad* 3 A2
Rizal Park *Manila* 17 B1
Rizal Stadium *Manila* 17 B1
Roa *Oslo* 23 A2
Robbins *Chicago* 9 D2
Robertsham *Johannesburg* 13 B2
Rochelle Park *New York* 22 A1
Rock Cr. ➤ *Washington* 33 B3
Rock Creek Park *Washington* 33 B3
Rock Pt. *Wellington* 33 A1
Rockaway Beach *New York* 22 C3
Rockaway Pt. *New York* 22 C2
Rockdale *Sydney* 29 B1
Rockefeller Center *New York* 22 B2
Rocky Run ➤ *Washington* 33 B2
Roda, Geziret el *Cairo* 7 A2
Roda I. = Roda, Gezîret el
    Cairo 7 A2
Rodaon *Vienna* 32 B1
Rodovre *Copenhagen* 8 A2
Rodrigo de Freitas, L.
    Rio de Janeiro 25 B1
Roehampton *London* 15 B2
Rogers Park *Chicago* 9 A2
Roihuvuori *Helsinki* 11 B3
Roissy-en-Brie *Paris* 24 B4
Rokytka ➤ *Prague* 25 B3
Roma *Rome* 26 B2
Roma Urbe ✈ *Rome* 26 B2
Római-Fürdõ *Budapest* 7 A2
Romainville *Paris* 24 A3
Roman Forum = Foro
    Romano *Rome* 26 B1
Romano Banco *Milan* 19 B1
Rome = Roma *Rome* 26 B1
Romema *Jerusalem* 13 B2
Romford *London* 15 A5
Ronald Reagan National,
    Washington ✈ (DCA)
    Washington 33 B3
Rondebosch *Cape Town* 8 A1
Roppongi *Tokyo* 30 B3
Rose, L. *Orlando* 23 A3
Rose Bowl *Los Angeles* 16 B4
Rose Hill *Washington* 33 C3
Rosebank *Johannesburg* 13 B2
Rosebank *New York* 22 C1
Rosebery *Sydney* 29 B2
Rosedal La Candelaria
    Mexico City 18 B2
Roseland *Chicago* 9 C3
Rosemead *Los Angeles* 16 B4
Rosemont *Chicago* 9 B1
Rosemont *Montreal* 20 A2
Rosenborg Slot *Copenhagen* 8 A3
Rosenthal *Berlin* 5 A3
Rosettenville *Johannesburg* 13 B2
Rosherville Dam *Johannesburg* 13 B2
Roslags-Näsby *Stockholm* 29 A2
Rösjön *Stockholm* 29 A2
Roslin *Edinburgh* 11 B3
Roslindale *Boston* 6 B3
Rosny-sous-Bois *Paris* 24 A4
Rosslyn *Washington* 33 B3
Rosyth *Edinburgh* 11 A1
Rotherhithe *London* 15 B3

Rothneusiedl *Vienna* 32 B2
Rothschmaige *Munich* 21 A1
Rouge Hill *Toronto* 31 A4
Roxbury *Boston* 6 B2
Roxeth *London* 15 A1
Royal Botanic Gardens
    Edinburgh 11 B2
Royal Observatory *Edinburgh* 11 B2
Royal Palace = Kungliga
    Slottet *Stockholm* 29 B2
Royal Park *Melbourne* 18 A1
Röyla *Helsinki* 11 B3
Rozas, Portilleros de las
    Madrid 17 B1
Roztoky *Prague* 25 B2
Rozzano *Milan* 19 B1
Rubí ➤ *Barcelona* 4 A1
Rudolfsheim *Vienna* 32 A2
Rudolfshöhe *Berlin* 5 A5
Rudow *Berlin* 5 B3
Rueil-Malmaison *Paris* 24 A2
Ruisbroek *Brussels* 6 B1
Ruislip *London* 15 A1
Rumelihisar *Istanbul* 12 B2
Rungis *Paris* 24 B3
Rusäfa *Baghdad* 3 A2
Rush Green *London* 15 A5
Russa *Kolkata* 14 C2
Rutherford *New York* 22 B1
Ružyně *Prague* 25 B1
Ruzyne, Praha ✈ (PRG)
    Prague 25 B1
Rybatskaya *St. Petersburg* 27 B3
Rydboholm *Stockholm* 29 A3
Ryde *Sydney* 29 A2
Ryogoku *Tokyo* 30 A3
Rzhevka *St. Petersburg* 27 B3

S

Sa'ādatābād *Tehran* 31 A2
Saadún *Baghdad* 3 B2
Saavedra *Buenos Aires* 7 B2
Saboli *Delhi* 10 A2
Sabugo *Lisbon* 16 A1
Sabzi Mand *Delhi* 10 A2
Sacavém *Lisbon* 16 A2
Saclay *Paris* 24 B2
Saclay, Étang de *Paris* 24 B2
Sacomã *São Paulo* 27 B2
Sacré Cœur *Paris* 24 A3
Sacrow *Berlin* 5 B1
Sacrower See *Berlin* 5 B1
Sadang *Seoul* 27 C1
Saddle ➤ *New York* 22 A1
Saddle Brook *New York* 22 A1
Sadr *Karachi* 13 A2
Sadr City *Baghdad* 3 A2
Sadyba *Warsaw* 32 C2
Safdar Jang's Tomb *Delhi* 10 B2
Saganashkee Slough *Chicago* 9 C1
Sagene *Oslo* 23 A3
Sagrada Familia, Templo de
    Barcelona 4 A2
Sahar, Mumbai ✈ (BOM)
    Mumbai 20 A2
Sai Kung *Hong Kong* 12 A2
Sai Wan Ho *Hong Kong* 12 B2
Sai Ying Pun *Hong Kong* 12 B1
Saïda *Baghdad* 3 A2
St-Aubin *Paris* 24 B1
St-Cloud *Paris* 24 A2
St-Cyr-l'École *Paris* 24 B1
St-Cyr-l'École ✈ *Paris* 24 B1
St-Denis *Paris* 24 A3
St-Germain, Forêt de *Paris* 24 A1
St-Germain-en-Laye *Paris* 24 A1
St-Gilles *Brussels* 6 B2
St. Helier *London* 15 B2
St-Hubert *Montreal* 20 B3
St. Hubert, Galeries Royales
    Brussels 6 A2
St. Isaac's Cathedral
    St. Petersburg 27 B2
St-Jacques ➤ *Montreal* 20 B1
St-Joost-Ten-Node *Brussels* 6 A2
St. Kilda *Melbourne* 18 B1
St-Lambert *Montreal* 20 A2
St-Lambert *Paris* 24 B1
St-Laurent *Montreal* 20 A1
St-Léonard *Montreal* 20 A2
St. Magelungen *Stockholm* 29 B2
St-Mandé *Paris* 24 A3
St. Margaret's *Dublin* 10 A2
St. Mary Cray *London* 15 B4
St-Maur-des-Fossés *Paris* 24 B3
St-Maurice *Paris* 24 A3
St-Michel *Montreal* 20 A2
St. Nikolaus-Kirken *Prague* 25 B2
St-Ouen *Paris* 24 A3
St. Paul's Cray *London* 15 B4
St. Peters *Sydney* 29 B2
St. Petersburg = Sankt-
    Peterburg *St. Petersburg* 27 B1
St-Pierre *Montreal* 20 B2
St-Pieters Leew *Brussels* 6 B1
St-Quentin, Étang de *Paris* 24 B1
St-Vincent-de-Paul *Montreal* 20 A2
St. Xavier University *Chicago* 9 C2
Ste-Catherine *Montreal* 20 B2
Ste-Hélène, I. *Montreal* 20 A2
Saiwai *Tokyo* 30 B3
Sakai *Osaka* 23 B2
Sakai Harbour *Osaka* 23 B1
Sakra, Pulau *Singapore* 28 B2
Salam *Baghdad* 3 A2
Salamanca *Madrid* 17 B1
Sallynoggin *Dublin* 10 B3
Salmannsdorf *Vienna* 32 A1
Salmedina *Madrid* 17 C2
Salomea *Warsaw* 32 B1
Salsette I. *Mumbai* 20 A2
São Jorge, Castelo de *Lisbon* 16 A2
São Juliao do Tojal *Lisbon* 16 A2
São Paulo Congonhas ✈
    (CGH) *São Paulo* 27 B2
Sapa *Kolkata* 14 B1
Sapateiro, Cor. do ➤
    São Paulo 27 B2
Sarandi *Buenos Aires* 7 C2
Saraswati ➤ *Kolkata* 14 A1
Sarecky potok ➤ *Prague* 25 B2
Saribumbum *Singapore* 28 A2
Sarimbun Res. *Singapore* 28 A2
Sariyer *Istanbul* 12 A2
Sarsuna *Kolkata* 14 C1
Sartrouville *Paris* 24 A2
Sasad *Budapest* 7 B2
Sashalom *Budapest* 7 A3
Saska *Warsaw* 32 B2

Satalice *Prague* 25 B3
Satgachi *Kolkata* 14 B2
Satpukur *Kolkata* 14 B2
Sätra *Stockholm* 29 B1
Saúde *São Paulo* 27 B2
Saugus *Boston* 6 A2
Saugus ➤ *Boston* 6 A2
Sault-au-Récollet *Montreal* 20 A2
Sausalito *San Francisco* 26 B2
Sawah Besar *Jakarta* 12 A1
Scald Law *Edinburgh* 11 B2
Scarborough *Toronto* 31 A3
Scarborough Bluffs *Toronto* 31 A3
Sceaux *Paris* 24 B2
Schaerbeek *Brussels* 6 A2
Scharfenberg *Berlin* 5 A2
Schiller Park *Chicago* 9 B1
Schiller Woods *Chicago* 9 B1
Schiphol, Amsterdam ✈
    (AMS) *Amsterdam* 2 B1
Schlachtensee *Berlin* 5 B2
Schlossgarten *Berlin* 5 A2
Schmargendorf *Berlin* 5 B2
Schönblick *Berlin* 5 A5
Schönbrunn *Vienna* 32 A1
Schöneberg *Berlin* 5 B3
Schönefeld *Berlin* 5 B4
Schöneiche *Berlin* 5 B5
Schönwalde *Berlin* 5 A1
Schulzendorf *Berlin* 5 A2
Schwabing *Munich* 21 B2
Schwanebeck *Berlin* 5 A4
Schwanenwerder *Berlin* 5 B2
Schwarzlackenau *Vienna* 32 A2
Schwechat *Vienna* 32 B2
Schwechat, Wien ✈ (VIE)
    Vienna 32 B2
Science and Industry,
    Museum of *Chicago* 9 C3
Scitrek Museum *Atlanta* 3 B2
Scopus, Mt. *Jerusalem* 13 B2
Scottdale *Atlanta* 3 B3
Scutari = Üsküdar *Istanbul* 12 B2
Sea Point *Cape Town* 8 A1
Seabrook *Washington* 33 B5
Seacliff *San Francisco* 26 B2
Seaforth *Sydney* 29 A2
Seagate *New York* 22 C1
Seat Pleasant *Washington* 33 B4
Seaview *Wellington* 33 B2
SeaWorld *Orlando* 23 B2
Šeberov *Prague* 25 C3
Secaucus *New York* 22 B1
Seddinsee *Berlin* 5 B5
Seeberg *Berlin* 5 A5
Seeburg *Berlin* 5 A1
Seefeld *Berlin* 5 A5
Seegefeld *Berlin* 5 A1
Seehof *Berlin* 5 B2
Segeltorp *Stockholm* 29 B1
Segrate *Milan* 19 A2
Seguro *Milan* 19 A1
Seixal *Lisbon* 16 B2
Selby *Johannesburg* 13 B2
Seletar Hills *Singapore* 28 A3
Seletar Res. *Singapore* 28 A2
Selhurst *London* 15 B3
Sembawang *Singapore* 28 A2
Senago *Milan* 19 A1
Sendling *Munich* 21 B2
Senju *Tokyo* 30 A3
Senriyama *Osaka* 23 A2
Seonan *Singapore* 28 B2
Seobinggo *Seoul* 27 B1
Seocho *Seoul* 27 C1
Seodaemun *Seoul* 27 B1
Seokkwan *Seoul* 27 B2
Seongbuk *Seoul* 27 B2
Seongdong *Seoul* 27 B2
Seongsu *Seoul* 27 B2
Seoul *Seoul* 27 B2
Seoul National University
    Seoul 27 C1
Seoul Tower *Seoul* 27 B1
Sepolia *Athens* 2 A2
Sepulveda Dam Rec.
    Area *Los Angeles* 16 A2
Serangoon *Singapore* 28 A3
Serangoon ➤ *Singapore* 28 A3
Serangoon, Pulau *Singapore* 28 A3
Serangoon, Sungei ➤
    Singapore 28 A3
Serangoon Harbour *Singapore* 28 A3
Seraya, Pulau *Singapore* 28 B3
Serebryanka ➤ *Moscow* 19 B3
Serramonte *San Francisco* 26 C2
Sesto San Giovanni *Milan* 19 A2
Sesto Ulteriano *Milan* 19 B2
Setagaya *Tokyo* 30 B2
Seter *Oslo* 23 A3
Setia Budi *Jakarta* 12 B1
Settebagni *Rome* 26 B2
Settecamini *Rome* 26 B2
Séttimo Milanese *Milan* 19 A1
Settsu *Osaka* 23 A2
Seutula *Helsinki* 11 A2
Seven Corners *Washington* 33 B3
Seven Kings *London* 15 A4
Sévran *Paris* 24 A4
Sèvres *Paris* 24 B2
Sewri *Mumbai* 20 B2
Sfax ➤ *Buenos Aires* 7 C2
Sha Kok Mei *Hong Kong* 12 A2
Sha Tin *Hong Kong* 12 A2
Sha Tin Wai *Hong Kong* 12 A2
Sha'ar Binyamin *Jerusalem* 13 A2
Shabrāmant *Cairo* 7 B1
Shah Mosque *Tehran* 31 A2
Shahdara *Delhi* 10 A2
Shahe *Guangzhou* 11 B2
Shahr-e Rey *Tehran* 31 B2
Shahrak-e Golshahr *Tehran* 31 B1
Shaikh Aomar *Baghdad* 3 A2
Shakurbasti *Delhi* 10 A1
Shalkiya *Kolkata* 14 B1
Sham Shui Po *Hong Kong* 12 A1
Shamapur *Delhi* 10 A1
Shamian *Guangzhou* 11 B2
Shan Mei *Hong Kong* 12 A2
Shanghai *Shanghai* 28 B1
Shanghai Hongqiao ✈
    (SHA) *Shanghai* 28 A1
Shanghai Pudong ✈ (PVG)
    Shanghai 28 B2
Shankill *Dublin* 10 B3
Sharp I. *Hong Kong* 12 A2
Shatin *Hong Kong* 12 A2
Shau Kei Wan *Hong Kong* 12 B2
Shawocun *Beijing* 4 B1
Shayuan *Guangzhou* 11 B2
Sheen, L. *Orlando* 23 B1
Sheepshead Bay *New York* 22 C2
Shek O *Hong Kong* 12 B2

Shelter I. *Hong Kong* 12 B2
Shepherds Bush *London* 15 A2
Shepperton *London* 15 B1
Sheremetyevo ✈ (SVO)
    Moscow 19 B2
Sherman Oaks *Los Angeles* 16 B2
Sherman Park *Chicago* 9 C2
Sherwood, L. *Orlando* 23 B4
Shet Bandar *Mumbai* 20 B2
Sheung Fa Shan *Hong Kong* 12 A1
Sheung Lau Wan *Hong Kong* 12 B2
Sheung Wan *Hong Kong* 12 B1
Sheva *Mumbai* 20 B2
Sheva Nhava *Mumbai* 20 B2
Shiba *Tokyo* 30 B3
Shibpur *Kolkata* 14 B1
Shibuya *Tokyo* 30 B3
Shimoganawa *Tokyo* 30 B1
Shimosalo *Tokyo* 30 A2
Shimoshakujii *Tokyo* 30 A2
Shinagawa *Tokyo* 30 B3
Shing Mun Res. *Hong Kong* 12 A1
Shinjuku *Tokyo* 30 A3
Shinjuku National Garden
    Tokyo 30 A3
Shinkoiwa *Tokyo* 30 A4
Shinnakano *Tokyo* 30 A2
Shipai *Guangzhou* 11 B2
Shirinashi ➤ *Osaka* 23 B1
Shirogane *Tokyo* 30 B3
Shitennoji Temple *Osaka* 23 B2
Shiweitang *Guangzhou* 11 B2
Shogunle *Lagos* 14 A2
Shomolu *Lagos* 14 A2
Shooters Hill *London* 15 B4
Shoreditch *London* 15 A3
Shortlands *London* 15 B4
Shu'afat *Jerusalem* 13 B2
Shubrā *Cairo* 7 A2
Shubrā el Kheima *Cairo* 7 A2
Shuikuo *Guangzhou* 11 B2
Sidcup *London* 15 B4
Siebenhirten *Vienna* 32 B1
Siedlung *Berlin* 5 A5
Siekierki *Warsaw* 32 B2
Sielce *Warsaw* 32 B1
Siemensstadt *Berlin* 5 A2
Sierra Madre *Los Angeles* 16 B4
Sievering *Vienna* 32 A1
Sighthill *Edinburgh* 11 B2
Signal Hill *Cape Town* 8 A1
Siheung *Seoul* 27 C1
Sikátorpuszta *Budapest* 7 A3
Silampur *Delhi* 10 B2
Sillim *Seoul* 27 C1
Silver, L. *Orlando* 23 A2
Silver Hill *Washington* 33 C4
Silver Spring *Washington* 33 A3
Silvermine Nature Reserve
    Cape Town 8 B2
Silvolantekojärvi *Helsinki* 11 B2
Simei *Singapore* 28 A3
Simla *Kolkata* 14 B2
Simmering *Vienna* 32 A2
Simmering Heide *Vienna* 32 A2
Simonkylä *Helsinki* 11 B3
Sinchon *Seoul* 27 B1
Sindang *Seoul* 27 B2
Singapore ■ *Singapore* 28 B3
Singapore, Univ. of *Singapore* 28 B2
Singapore Changi ✈ (SIN)
    Singapore 28 A3
Sinki, Selat *Singapore* 28 B2
Sinsa *Seoul* 27 B2
Sint-Genesius-Rode *Brussels* 6 B2
Sion *Mumbai* 20 A2
Sipson *London* 15 B1
Siqeil *Cairo* 7 A1
Şişli *Istanbul* 12 B1
Site of Former World Trade
    Center = Ground Zero
    New York 22 B1
Skansen *Stockholm* 29 B2
Skärholmen *Stockholm* 29 B1
Skarpäng *Stockholm* 29 A2
Skarpnäck *Stockholm* 29 B2
Skaryszewski, Park *Warsaw* 32 B2
Skokie *Chicago* 9 A2
Skokie ➤ *Chicago* 9 A2
Skokie Heritage Museum
    Chicago 9 A2
Skokiefall *Oslo* 23 A3
Sköndal *Stockholm* 29 B2
Skovlunde *Copenhagen* 8 A2
Skovshoved *Copenhagen* 8 A3
Skuru *Stockholm* 29 B2
Sky Lake *Orlando* 23 B2
Skyland *Atlanta* 3 A3
Slade Green *London* 15 B5
Slemmestad *Oslo* 23 A2
Slependen *Oslo* 23 A2
Slipi *Jakarta* 12 B1
Slivenec *Prague* 25 B2
Sloten *Amsterdam* 2 A1
Sloterdijk *Amsterdam* 2 A1
Sloterpark *Amsterdam* 2 A1
Sluhy *Prague* 25 A3
Służew *Warsaw* 32 C2
Służewiec *Warsaw* 32 B2
Smith Forest Preserve *Chicago* 9 B2
Smolny St. Petersburg *St. Petersburg* 27 B2
Smolny Cathedral
    St. Petersburg 27 B2
Snake Creek Canal *Miami* 18 A2
Snakeden Branch ➤
    Washington 33 B1
Snarøya *Oslo* 23 A2
Snättringe *Stockholm* 29 B1
Søborg *Copenhagen* 8 A3
Sobreda *Lisbon* 16 B1
Söderby *Stockholm* 29 A3
Södermalm *Stockholm* 29 B2
Sodpur *Kolkata* 14 B2
Sœurs, Î. des *Montreal* 20 B2
Sognsvatn *Oslo* 23 A3
Soignes, Forêt de *Brussels* 6 B2
Sok Kwu Wan *Hong Kong* 12 B1
Sokolniki *Moscow* 19 B3
Sokolniki Park *Moscow* 19 B3
Sokołów *Warsaw* 32 C1
Solalinden *Munich* 21 B3
Sollentuna *Stockholm* 29 A1
Solln *Munich* 21 B2
Solna *Stockholm* 29 A1
Solna *Stockholm* 29 A1
Somerset *Washington* 33 B3
Somerville *Boston* 6 A3
Somes I. *Wellington* 33 B2
Sonari *Mumbai* 20 B2
Søndersø *Copenhagen* 8 A2
Songpa *Seoul* 27 B2
Sony Picture Studio
    Los Angeles 16 B2
Soroksár *Budapest* 7 B2

Soroksari Duna → Budapest 7 B2
Sosenka → Moscow 19 B3
Sosnovka St. Petersburg 27 B2
Sŏul = Seoul Seoul 27 B2
Soundview New York 22 C1
South Beach New York 22 C1
South Bend Park Atlanta 3 B2
South Boston 6 A2
South Decatur Atlanta 3 B3
South Deering Chicago 9 C3
South El Monte Los Angeles 16 B4
South Gate Los Angeles 16 C3
South Harbor Manila 17 B1
South Harrow London 15 A1
South Hd. Sydney 29 B2
South Hills Johannesburg 13 B2
South Hornchurch London 15 A5
South Lawn Washington 33 C3
South Miami Miami 25 B1
South Norwood London 15 B3
South of Market San Francisco 26 B2
South Ozone Park New York 22 B3
South Pasadena Los Angeles 16 B4
South Res. Boston 6 A2
South Ruislip London 15 A1
South San Francisco
   San Francisco 26 C2
South San Gabriel Los Angeles 16 B4
South Shore Chicago 9 C3
Southall London 15 A1
Southborough London 15 B4
Southend London 15 B3
Southern California,
   University of Los Angeles 16 B3
Southfields London 15 B2
Southwark □ London 15 B3
Southwest Museum
   Los Angeles 16 B3
Søvang Copenhagen 8 B3
Soweto Johannesburg 13 B1
Sowhānak Tehran 31 A3
Soya Tokyo 30 A4
Spandau Berlin 5 A2
Spånga Stockholm 29 A1
Spanish Monastery Miami 18 A2
Spectacle I. Boston 6 A3
Speicher-See Munich 21 A3
Speising Vienna 32 B1
Sphinx Cairo 7 B1
Spinaceto Rome 26 C1
Spit Junction Sydney 29 A2
Spořilov Prague 25 B3
Spot Pond Boston 6 A2
Spotswood Melbourne 18 B1
Springeberg Berlin 5 B5
Springfield Washington 33 C2
Squantum Boston 6 A2
Srednaya Rogatka
   St. Petersburg 27 C2
Srodmiescie Warsaw 32 B2
Staaken Berlin 5 A1
Stabekk Oslo 23 A2
Stadlau Vienna 32 A2
Stadshuset Stockholm 29 B2
Stains Paris 24 A3
Stamford Hill London 15 A3
Stammersdorf Vienna 32 A2
Stanley Hong Kong 12 B2
Stanley Pen. Hong Kong 12 B2
Stanmore London 15 A1
Stapleton New York 22 C1
Staraya Derevnya
   St. Petersburg 27 B1
Staré Město Prague 25 B2
Stare Miasto Warsaw 32 B2
Starke, L. Orlando 23 A1
Staten Island Zoo New York 22 C1
Staten Islands Ferry
   Terminal New York 22 C1
Statenice Prague 25 B1
Stedelijk Museum Amsterdam 2 A2
Steele Creek Melbourne 18 A1
Steenokkerzeel Brussels 6 A2
Steer, L. Orlando 23 A1
Steglitz Berlin 5 B3
Stepaside Dublin 10 B2
Stephansdom Vienna 32 A2
Stepney London 15 A3
Sterling Park San Francisco 26 B2
Sticklinge udde Stockholm 29 A2
Stickney Chicago 9 C2
Stillorgan Dublin 10 B2
Stockholm Stockholm 29 B2
Stocksund Stockholm 29 A2
Stodůlky Prague 25 B1
Stoke Newington London 15 A3
Stokes Valley Wellington 33 B2
Stone Canyon Res.
   Los Angeles 16 B2
Stone Park Chicago 9 B1
Stonebridge London 15 A2
Stoneham Boston 6 A2
Stony Brook Res. Boston 6 B2
Stony Creek → Chicago 9 C2
Stora Värtan Stockholm 29 A2
Store Hareskov Copenhagen 8 A2
Store Magleby Copenhagen 8 B3
Storholmen Stockholm 29 A2
Stoyka St. Petersburg 27 B2
Straiton Edinburgh 11 B3
Strandfontein Cape Town 8 B2
Strašnice Prague 25 B2
Strasstrudering Munich 21 B3
Stratford London 15 A3
Strathfield Sydney 29 B1
Streatham London 15 B3
Streatham Vale London 15 B3
Strebersdorf Vienna 32 A2
Střešovice Prague 25 B2
Střížkov Prague 25 B2
Strombeek-Bever Brussels 6 A2
Stromovka Prague 25 B2
Studio City Los Angeles 16 B2
Stureby Stockholm 29 B2
Stuvsta Stockholm 29 B2
Subhepur Delhi 10 A2
Sucat Manila 17 C2
Suchdol Prague 25 B1
Sucy-en-Brie Paris 24 B4
Sue, L. Orlando 23 A2
Sugamo Tokyo 30 A3
Sugar Loaf Mt. = Açúcar,
   Pão de Rio de Janeiro 25 B2
Sugie Tokyo 30 B2
Suginami Tokyo 30 A2
Sugō Tokyo 30 B2
Sui Sai Wan Hong Kong 12 B2
Suita Osaka 23 A2
Suitland Washington 33 B4
Sukchar Kolkata 14 A2
Sultanahme Camil Istanbul 12 B1
Sumida → Tokyo 30 A3
Sumida → Tokyo 30 A3
Sumiyoshi Osaka 23 B2

Sumiyoshi Shrine Osaka 23 B1
Summerville Toronto 31 B1
Summit Chicago 9 C2
Sunamachi Tokyo 30 A4
Sunbury-on-Thames London 15 B1
Sundbyberg Stockholm 29 A1
Sundbyerne Copenhagen 8 B3
Sung Kong Hong Kong 12 B2
Sungei Kadut Industrial
   Estate Singapore 28 A2
Sungei Selatar Res. Singapore 28 A3
Sunset Park New York 22 C2
Sunter Jakarta 12 A2
Sunter, Kali → Jakarta 12 B2
Suomenlinna Helsinki 11 C2
Sur Bahr Jerusalem 13 B2
Sura Kolkata 14 B2
Suraksan Seoul 27 A2
Surbiton London 15 B2
Suresnes Paris 24 A2
Surfside Miami 18 A2
Surquillo Lima 17 B2
Surrey Hills Sydney 29 B2
Susaek Seoul 27 B1
Süssenbrunn Vienna 32 A2
Sutton Dublin 10 A3
Sutton London 15 B2
Suyu Seoul 27 A2
Suzukishinden Tokyo 30 A2
Svanemøllen Copenhagen 8 A3
Sveaborg = Suomenlinna
   Helsinki 11 C2
Sverdlov Moscow 19 B2
Svestad Oslo 23 B2
Svinö Helsinki 11 C1
Swanley London 15 B4
Swansea Toronto 31 B2
Swinburne I. New York 22 C1
Swords Dublin 10 A2
Sydenham London 15 B3
Sydenham Johannesburg 13 A2
Sydney Sydney 29 B2
Sydney, Univ. of Sydney 29 B2
Sydney Harbour Bridge
   Sydney 29 B2
Sydney Kingsford Smith ✈
   (SYD) Sydney 29 B2
Sydstranden Copenhagen 8 B3
Sylvania Sydney 29 C1
Syon Park London 15 B2
Szczęśliwice Warsaw 32 B1
Széchnenyi-hegy Budapest 7 B1
Széphalom Budapest 7 A1

T
Taastrup Copenhagen 8 B1
Tabata Tokyo 30 A3
Tablada Buenos Aires 7 C1
Table B. Cape Town 8 A1
Table Mt. Cape Town 8 A1
Taboão da Serra São Paulo 27 B1
Täby Stockholm 29 A2
Tacuba Mexico City 18 B1
Tacubaya Mexico City 18 B1
Tafelbaai = Table B. Cape Town 8 A1
Taft Orlando 23 B2
Tagig → Manila 17 B2
Taguig Manila 17 B2
Tai Hang Hong Kong 12 A2
Tai Lo Shan Hong Kong 12 A2
Tai Po Tsai Hong Kong 12 A2
Tai Seng Singapore 28 A3
Tai Shui Hang Hong Kong 12 A2
Tai Tam B. Hong Kong 12 B2
Tai Tam Tuk Res. Hong Kong 12 B2
Tai Wai Hong Kong 12 A2
Tai Wan Tau Hong Kong 12 A2
Tai Wo Hau Hong Kong 12 A1
Tainaka Osaka 23 B1
Taishō Osaka 23 B1
Taita Wellington 33 B2
Tajrish Tehran 31 A2
Takaido Tokyo 30 A2
Takashi Tokyo 30 A2
Takarazuka Osaka 23 A1
Takasago Tokyo 30 A4
Takatsu Tokyo 30 B2
Takeshita Tokyo 30 B2
Takinegawa Tokyo 30 A3
Takoma Park Washington 33 B3
Taksim Istanbul 12 B1
Talaide Lisbon 16 A1
Taliganga Kolkata 14 B2
Talipapa Manila 17 A2
Tallaght Dublin 10 B1
Tallkrogen Stockholm 29 B2
Tama Tokyo 30 B1
Tama → Tokyo 30 B2
Tama Kyūryō Tokyo 30 B2
Tamaden Tokyo 30 A3
Tamagawa-josui → Tokyo 30 A1
Taman Sari Jakarta 12 A1
Tamanduateí → São Paulo 27 B2
Tamboerskloof Cape Town 8 A1
Tambora Jakarta 12 A1
Tammisalo Helsinki 11 B3
Tammūh Cairo 7 B2
Tampines Singapore 28 A3
Tanah Abang Jakarta 12 B1
Tanah Kusir Jakarta 12 B1
Tangelo Park Orlando 23 B2
Tanjung Duren Jakarta 12 B1
Tanjung Priok Jakarta 12 A1
Tanum Oslo 23 A1
Tapada Lisbon 16 A1
Tapanila Helsinki 11 B3
Tapiales Buenos Aires 7 C1
Tapiola Helsinki 11 B1
Tapsia Kolkata 14 B2
Tara Mumbai 20 A1
Tarabya Istanbul 12 B2
Tårbæk Copenhagen 8 B3
Tarchomin Warsaw 32 B1
Tardeo Mumbai 20 B1
Targówek Warsaw 32 B2
Tärnby Copenhagen 8 B3
Tarqua Bay Lagos 14 B2
Tathong Channel Hong Kong 12 B2
Tathong Pt. Hong Kong 12 B2
Tatuapé São Paulo 27 B2
Taufkirchen Munich 21 B2
Tavares, I. dos Rio de Janeiro 25 B1
Tavros Athens 2 B2
Tawa Wellington 33 A1
Te Papa Museum Wellington 33 B1
Teaneck New York 22 A1
Tebet Jakarta 12 B2
Tecamachalco Mexico City 18 B1
Ted Williams Tunnel Boston 6 A2
Teddington London 15 B1
Tegel, Berlin ✈ (TXL) Berlin 5 A2
Tegeler See Berlin 5 A2

Tegelort Berlin 5 A2
Teheran = Tehrān Tehran 31 A2
Tehrān Tehran 31 A2
Tehrān Pārs Tehran 31 A3
Tei Tong Tsui Hong Kong 12 B2
Tejo, Rio → Lisbon 16 A2
Tekstilyschchik Moscow 19 B3
Telhal Lisbon 16 A1
Telok Blangah Singapore 28 B2
Teltow Berlin 5 B2
Teltow kanal Berlin 5 B3
Tempelhof Berlin 5 B3
Tempelhof, Berlin ✈ (THF)
   Berlin 5 B3
Temple City Los Angeles 16 B4
Temple Hills Washington 33 C4
Templeogue Dublin 10 B2
Temppeliaukio Church
   Helsinki 11 B2
Tenafly New York 22 A2
Tenayuca, Piramide de
   Mexico City 18 A1
Tengah → Singapore 28 A2
Tennoji Osaka 23 B2
Tepalcates Mexico City 18 B2
Tepeyac, Parque
   Nacional △ Mexico City 18 B2
Terrazzano Milan 19 A1
Terre des Hommes Montreal 20 A2
Terrugem Lisbon 16 A1
Tervuren Brussels 6 B3
Tervuren, Park van Brussels 6 B3
Tetuán Madrid 17 B1
Teufelsberg Berlin 5 B2
Thalkirchen Munich 21 B2
Thames Ditton London 15 B1
Thamesmead London 15 A4
Thana Cr. → Mumbai 20 A2
Thiais Paris 24 B3
Thisio Athens 2 B2
Thistletown Toronto 31 A1
Thomastown Melbourne 18 A2
Thompson I. Boston 6 A2
Thon Buri Bangkok 3 B1
Thornbury Melbourne 18 A2
Thorncliffe Toronto 31 A2
Thornhill Toronto 31 A2
Thornton Cape Town 8 A2
Thornton Heath London 15 B3
Threipmuir Res. Edinburgh 11 B2
Throgs Neck New York 22 B3
Tian'anmen Square Beijing 4 B2
Tiancun Beijing 4 B1
Tibet, L. Orlando 23 A1
Tibidabo Barcelona 4 A1
Tibradden Mt. Dublin 10 B2
Tiburon San Francisco 26 A2
Tiburtino Rome 26 B2
Ticomán Mexico City 18 A2
Tiefersee Berlin 5 B5
Tiejiangyin Beijing 4 C2
Tiergarten Berlin 5 A3
Tigerhof Cape Town 8 A2
Tijuca Rio de Janeiro 25 B1
Tijuca, Pico da Rio de Janeiro 25 B1
Tikkurila Helsinki 11 B3
Tilak Nagar Delhi 10 B1
Tilanqiao Shanghai 28 B2
Timah, Bukit Singapore 28 A2
Timiryazev Park Moscow 19 B2
Ting Kau Hong Kong 12 A1
Tira Jerusalem 13 A1
Tirsa Cairo 7 B2
Tishriyaa Baghdad 3 B2
Tiu Keng Leng Hong Kong 12 B2
Tizapán Mexico City 18 C1
Tlalnepantla → Mexico City 18 A1
Tlalpan Mexico City 18 C2
To Kwai Wan Hong Kong 12 B2
Toa Payoh Singapore 28 A3
Točná Prague 25 C2
Toco Hills Atlanta 3 B2
Todt Hill New York 22 C1
Tōkagi Tokyo 30 A4
Tokai Plantation Cape Town 8 B1
Tōkaichiba Tokyo 30 B1
Tōkyō Tokyo 30 B3
Tōkyō B. = Tōkyō-Wan
   Tokyo 30 B4
Tōkyō Disneyland Tokyo 30 B4
Tōkyō Hameda ✈ (HND)
   Tokyo 30 B3
Tōkyō Harbour Tokyo 30 B3
Tōkyō-Wan Tokyo 30 B3
Tolka → Dublin 10 A2
Tollygunge = Taliganga
   Kolkata 14 B2
Tolworth London 15 B2
Tomba di Nerone Rome 26 B1
Tommy Thompson Park
   Toronto 31 B3
Tondo Manila 17 B1
Tongbinggo Seoul 27 B1
Tongqiao Shanghai 28 A1
Toorak Melbourne 18 B2
Topanga State Park △
   Los Angeles 16 B1
Topkapi Istanbul 12 B1
Topkapi Palaca Istanbul 12 B1
Tor di Quinto Rome 26 B1
Tor Pignattara Rome 26 B2
Tor Sapienza Rome 26 B2
Torcy Paris 24 A4
Toronto Toronto 31 B2
Toronto, Univ. of Toronto 31 B2
Toronto City Centre ✈
   (YTZ) Toronto 31 B2
Toronto Harbour Toronto 31 B2
Toronto I. Toronto 31 B2
Toronto Lester B. Pearson
   Int. ✈ (YYZ) Toronto 31 A1
Torre Lupara Rome 26 B2
Torre Nova Rome 26 B2
Torrellas → Barcelona 4 A1
Torrevécchia Rome 26 B1
Toshima Tokyo 30 A3
Toshimaen Tokyo 30 A2
Tottenham London 15 A3
Tottenham Melbourne 18 A1
Toussus-le-Noble Paris 24 B1
Toussus-le-Noble ✈ Paris 24 B1
Towchāl Cable Car Tehran 31 A2
Tower Hamlets □ London 15 A3
Tower of London London 15 A3
Towra Pt. Sydney 29 C2
Töyen Oslo 23 A3
Toyonaka Osaka 23 A1
Trafaria Lisbon 16 A1
Traição, São Paulo 27 B2
Tranegilde Copenhagen 8 B2
Trångsund Stockholm 29 B2
Trappenfelde Berlin 5 A4
Trastévere Rome 26 B1

Treasure I. San Francisco 26 B2
Třeboradice Prague 25 B3
Třebotov Prague 25 C1
Tremblay-en-France Paris 24 A4
Tremembe → São Paulo 27 A2
Tremont New York 22 A2
Trenno Milan 19 A1
Treptow Berlin 5 B3
Trés Rios, Sa. dos
   Rio de Janeiro 25 B1
Trevi, Fontana di Rome 26 B1
Trezzano sul Navíglio Milan 19 B1
Trieste Rome 26 B2
Trinidad Washington 33 B4
Trinity Edinburgh 11 B2
Trinity College Dublin 10 A2
Trionfale Rome 26 B1
Triulzo Milan 19 B2
Troja Prague 25 B2
Trollbäcken Stockholm 29 B3
Trombay Mumbai 20 A2
Troparevo Moscow 19 C1
Trudeau, Montréal ✈ (YUL)
   Montreal 20 B1
Trudyashchikhsya, Ostrov
   St. Petersburg 27 B1
Tryvasshøgda Oslo 23 A3
Tseng Lan Shue Hong Kong 12 A2
Tseung Kwan Hong Kong 12 B2
Tsim Sha Tsui Hong Kong 12 B2
Tsing Yi Hong Kong 12 A1
Tsova Jerusalem 13 B1
Tsuen Wan Hong Kong 12 A1
Tsur Hadassa Jerusalem 13 B1
Tsurumi → Tokyo 30 B3
Tsz Wan Shan Hong Kong 12 A2
Tuas Singapore 28 B1
Tuchoměřice Prague 25 B1
Tuckahoe New York 22 A2
Tucuruvi São Paulo 27 A2
Tufello Rome 26 B2
Tufnell Park London 15 A3
Tufts University Boston 6 A2
Tughlakabad Delhi 10 B2
Tuindorp Amsterdam 2 B1
Tulse Hill London 15 B3
Tung Lung Chau Hong Kong 12 B2
Tung O Hong Kong 12 B1
Tunis Baghdad 3 A2
Tuomarila Helsinki 11 B1
Turffontein Johannesburg 13 B2
Turkey L. Orlando 23 A1
Turkey Lake Park Orlando 23 A2
Turner Field Atlanta 3 B2
Turnham Green London 15 B2
Turnhouse Edinburgh 11 B1
Tuscolana, Via Rome 26 B2
Twelve Apostles Cape Town 8 A1
Twickenham London 15 B1
Twickenham Rugby
   Ground London 15 B1
Twin Peaks San Francisco 26 B2
Two Rock Mt. Dublin 10 B2
Tymon North Dublin 10 B1
Tysons Corner Washington 33 B2

U
U.S. Capitol Washington 33 B3
U.S. Cellular Field Chicago 9 C3
Ubeidiya Jerusalem 13 B2
Uberaba → São Paulo 27 B2
Ubin, Pulau Singapore 28 A3
Uccle Brussels 6 B2
Udelnaya St. Petersburg 27 B1
Udelnoe St. Petersburg 27 B1
Udding Munich 21 A1
Ueno Tokyo 30 A3
Uholičky Prague 25 B1
Uhříněves Prague 25 B3
Uithoorn Amsterdam 2 B1
Ujazdów Warsaw 32 B2
Újpalota Budapest 7 A2
Újpest Budapest 7 A2
Ukita Tokyo 30 A4
Ullerup Copenhagen 8 B3
Ullevål Oslo 23 A3
Ulriksdal Stockholm 29 A1
Ulyanka St. Petersburg 27 B1
Um Al-Khanazir Island
   Baghdad 3 B2
Umeda Osaka 23 A1
Ümraniye Istanbul 12 B2
Underground Atlanta Atlanta 3 B2
Underhill, L. Orlando 23 B2
Unětický potok → Prague 25 B2
Unhos Lisbon 16 A2
Unidad Santa Fe Mexico City 18 B1
Union City New York 22 B1
Union Port New York 22 B2
Union Station Toronto 31 B2
United Center Chicago 9 B2
United Nations
   Headquarters New York 22 B2
Universal Studios Los Angeles 16 B2
Universal Studios Orlando 23 B2
Universidad Madrid 17 B1
Universidad de Chile Santiago 27 B2
University Park Washington 33 B4
Unterbiberg Munich 21 B2
Unterföhring Munich 21 A2
Unterhaching Munich 21 B2
Unterlaa Vienna 32 B2
Untermenzing Munich 21 A1
Upper B. New York 22 C1
Upper Elmers End London 15 B3
Upper New York B. = Upper
   B. New York 22 C1
Upper Norwood London 15 B3
Upper Peirce Res. Singapore 28 A2
Upper Sydenham London 15 B3
Upper Tooting London 15 B3
Upton London 15 A4
Uptown Chicago 9 B2
Uran Mumbai 20 B2
Urayasu Tokyo 30 B4
Urbe ✈ Rome 26 B1
Urca Rio de Janeiro 25 B2
Uritsk St. Petersburg 27 C1
Üröm Budapest 7 A2
Ursus Warsaw 32 B1
Ursvik Stockholm 29 A1
Usera Madrid 17 B1
Ushigome Tokyo 30 A3
Usina Rio de Janeiro 25 B1
Ust-Slavyanka St. Petersburg 27 C3
Uteke Stockholm 29 A2
Utrata Warsaw 32 C1
Uttarpara Kolkata 14 B1
Üsküdar Istanbul 12 B2
Utterslev Mose Copenhagen 8 A2

V
Vaclavské námĕstí Prague 25 B2
Vadaul Mumbai 20 A2
Vaires-sur-Marne Paris 24 A4
Valby Copenhagen 8 B3
Valcannuta Rome 26 B1
Valdelatas Madrid 17 A1
Vale Washington 33 B1
Valenton Paris 24 B3
Valera Milan 19 A1
Vallcarca Barcelona 4 A1
Valldoreix Barcelona 4 A1
Vallecas Madrid 17 B2
Vallensbæk Copenhagen 8 B2
Vallensbæk Strand Copenhagen 8 B2
Vallentunasjön Stockholm 29 A2
Valleranello Rome 26 C1
Vallisaari Helsinki 11 C3
Vallvidrera Barcelona 4 A1
Vallvidrera → Barcelona 4 A1
Van Gogh-museum Amsterdam 2 A2
Vanak Tehran 31 A2
Vanda = Vantaa Helsinki 11 B2
Vangede Copenhagen 8 A3
Vaníköy Istanbul 12 B2
Vanløse Copenhagen 8 A2
Vantaa Helsinki 11 B2
Vantaankoski Helsinki 11 B2
Vantaanpuisto Helsinki 11 B2
Vanves Paris 24 B2
Varedo Milan 19 A1
Varkiza Athens 2 C2
Vartiokylä Helsinki 11 B3
Vartiosaari Helsinki 11 B3
Vasamuseet Stockholm 29 B2
Vasco Cape Town 8 A2
Vasfanärd Tehran 31 A2
Vashi Mumbai 20 A2
Vasilyevskiy, Ostrov
   St. Petersburg 27 B1
Vatican City ■ Rome 26 B1
Vaucluse Sydney 29 B2
Vaucresson Paris 24 A1
Vaughan Toronto 31 A1
Vauhallan Paris 24 B2
Vaujours Paris 24 A4
Vauxhall London 15 B3
Vecsés Budapest 7 B3
Veleň Prague 25 A3
Veleslavin Prague 25 B2
Vélizy-Villacoublay Paris 24 B2
Velka-Chuchle Prague 25 B2
Velké Přílepy Prague 25 B1
Venda Seca Lisbon 16 A1
Venetian Islands Miami 18 B2
Venice Los Angeles 16 C2
Ventas Madrid 17 B1
Ventorro del Cano Madrid 17 B1
Venustiano Carranza
   Mexico City 18 B2
Verde → São Paulo 27 B2
Verdi Athens 2 A2
Verdugo Mts. Los Angeles 16 A3
Verdun Montreal 20 B2
Vérhalom Budapest 7 A2
Vermelho → São Paulo 27 B2
Vernon Los Angeles 16 C3
Verrières-le-Buisson Paris 24 B2
Versailles Buenos Aires 7 B1
Versailles Paris 24 B1
Veshnyaki Moscow 19 B3
Vesolyy Posolok St. Petersburg 27 B2
Vestra Helsinki 11 B1
Vestskoven Copenhagen 8 A2
Vicálvaro Madrid 17 B2
Vicente Lopez Buenos Aires 7 B2
Victoria Hong Kong 12 B2
Victoria, Mt. Wellington 33 B1
Victoria, Pont Montreal 20 B2
Victoria and Alfred
   Waterfront Cape Town 8 A1
Victoria Gardens Mumbai 20 B2
Victoria Harbour Hong Kong 12 B2
Victoria Key Miami 18 B2
Victoria L. Johannesburg 13 B2
Victoria Lawn Tennis
   Courts Melbourne 18 B2
Victoria Park Singapore 28 A2
Victoria Peak Hong Kong 12 B2
Vienna = Wien Vienna 32 A2
Vienna ✈ Wien Vienna 32 A2
Vietnam Veterans
   Memorial Washington 33 B3
Vietnam War Museum
   Chicago 9 B3
View Park Los Angeles 16 B3
Vigário Geral Rio de Janeiro 25 A1
Vigentino Milan 19 B2
Viggbyholm Stockholm 29 A2
Vighignolo Milan 19 B1
Viikki Helsinki 11 B3
Vikhroli Mumbai 20 A2
Vila Guilherme São Paulo 27 B2
Vila Isabel Rio de Janeiro 25 B1
Vila Jaguára São Paulo 27 B1
Vila Madalena São Paulo 27 B1
Vila Maria São Paulo 27 B2
Vila Mariana São Paulo 27 B2
Vila Prudente São Paulo 27 B2
Viladecans Barcelona 4 B1
Vile Parle Mumbai 20 A2
Villa Adelina Buenos Aires 7 B1
Villa Ballester Buenos Aires 7 B1
Villa Barilari Buenos Aires 7 C2
Villa Bosch Buenos Aires 7 B1
Villa C. Colon Buenos Aires 7 B1
Villa Ciudadela Buenos Aires 7 B1
Villa de Guadalupe
   Mexico City 18 A2
Villa Devoto Buenos Aires 7 B1
Villa Diamante Buenos Aires 7 C2
Villa Dominico Buenos Aires 7 C2
Villa Lugano Buenos Aires 7 C2
Villa Lynch Buenos Aires 7 B1
Villa Madero Buenos Aires 7 C1
Villa Sáenz Pena Buenos Aires 7 B1
Villa Urquiza Buenos Aires 7 B1
Villaverde Bajo Madrid 17 B1
Ville-d'Avray Paris 24 B2
Villejuif Paris 24 B3
Villemomble Paris 24 A4
Villeneuve-la-Garenne Paris 24 A2
Villeneuve-le-Roi Paris 24 B3
Villeneuve-St-Georges Paris 24 B3
Villeparisis Paris 24 A4
Villevaudé Paris 24 A4
Villiers-sur-Marne Paris 24 B4
Villinki Helsinki 11 C3

W
Wachterhof Munich 21 B3
Wadala Mumbai 20 A2
Wadestown Wellington 33 B1
Wadi al-Arayis Jerusalem 13 B2
Wadi Fukin Jerusalem 13 B1
Waduk Pluit Jakarta 12 A1
Wah Fu Hong Kong 12 B1
Wahda Baghdad 3 B2
Währing Vienna 32 A2
Waidmannslust Berlin 5 A3
Wainuiomata Wellington 33 B2
Wainuiomata → Wellington 33 B2
Wakefield Boston 6 A2
Waldesruh Berlin 5 B4
Waldperlach Munich 21 B3
Waldtrudering Munich 21 B3
Walkinstown Dublin 10 B1
Wall Street New York 22 B1
Walt Disney World Orlando 23 B1
Walter D. Stone Memorial
   Zoo Boston 6 A2
Waltham Boston 6 A1
Waltham Forest □ London 15 A3
Walthamstow London 15 A3
Walton-on-Thames London 15 B1
Wambeek Brussels 6 A3
Wan Chai Hong Kong 12 B2
Wandsworth □ London 15 B2
Wannsee Berlin 5 B1
Wansdorf Berlin 5 A1
Wanstead London 15 A4
Wapping London 15 A3
Ward Dublin 10 A1
Ward I. Wellington 33 B2
Wards I. New York 22 B2
Warnberg Munich 21 B2
Warner Brothers Studios
   Los Angeles 16 B2
Warrâq el 'Arab Cairo 7 A2
Warringal Park Melbourne 18 A2
Warriston Edinburgh 11 B2
Warsaw = Warszawa
   Warsaw 32 B2
Warszawa Warsaw 32 B2
Warszawa ✈ (WAW)
   Warsaw 32 B2
Washington Washington 33 B3
Washington Heights
   New York 22 B2
Washington Park Chicago 9 C3
Washington Ronald
   Reagan National ✈
   (DCA) Washington 33 B3
Wat Pho Bangkok 3 B1
Water of Leith → Edinburgh 11 B1
Watergraafsmeer Amsterdam 2 A2
Waterland Amsterdam 2 A2
Waterloo Brussels 6 B2
Waterloo Wellington 33 B2
Watermeal-Boitsfort Brussels 6 B2
Watertown Boston 6 A1
Watsonia Melbourne 18 A2
Waverley Boston 6 A1
Waverley Johannesburg 13 A2
Waverley Sydney 29 B2
Wawer Warsaw 32 B2
Wawrzyszew Warsaw 32 B1
Waziabad Delhi 10 A2
Wazirīya Baghdad 3 A2
Wazirpur Delhi 10 A2
Wealdstone London 15 A1
Wedding Berlin 5 A3
Weehawken New York 22 B1
Weesp Amsterdam 2 A3
Weidling Vienna 32 A1
Weidlingbach Vienna 32 A1
Weigongcum Beijing 4 B1
Weissensee Berlin 5 A3
Wellesley Hills Boston 6 B1
Welling London 15 B4
Wellesbourne Edinburgh 11 B2
Wellington Wellington 33 B1
Wellington Int. ✈ (WLE)
   Wellington 33 B1
Weltevreden Park
   Johannesburg 13 A1
Wembley London 15 A2
Wemmel Brussels 6 A1
Wemmer Pan Johannesburg 13 B2
Wenceslas Square =
   Vaclavské námĕstí Prague 25 B2

Wendenschloss Berlin 5 B4
Wennington London 15 A5
Werneuchen Berlin 5 A5
West Don → Toronto 31 A2
West Drayton London 15 A1
West Ham London 15 A4
West Harrow London 15 A1
West Heath London 15 B4
West Hill Toronto 31 A3
West Hollywood Los Angeles 16 B2
West Lamma Channel
   Hong Kong 12 B1
West Los Angeles,
   University of Los Angeles 16 C2
West Medford Boston 6 A2
West Miami Miami 18 B1
West Molesey London 15 B1
West New York New York 22 B1
West of Twin Peaks
   San Francisco 26 B2
West Park Johannesburg 13 A1
West Rouge Toronto 31 A4
West Roxbury Boston 6 B2
West Springfield Washington 33 C2
West Town Chicago 9 B2
West Wharf Karachi 18 B1
Westchester Chicago 9 B1
Westchester Los Angeles 16 C2
Westchester New York 22 A2
Westcliff Johannesburg 13 B1
Westdene Johannesburg 13 B1
Westend London 15 A2
Wester Hailes Edinburgh 11 B2
Westerham Munich 21 B3
Western Addition
   San Francisco 26 B2
Westgate Washington 33 B3
Westlake Cape Town 8 B1
Westlake San Francisco 26 B2
Westminster London 15 A3
Westmount Montreal 20 B2
Weston Boston 6 A1
Westwood Village Los Angeles 16 B2
Westzaan Amsterdam 2 A1
Wetton Cape Town 8 B2
Wexford Toronto 31 A3
Weybridge London 15 B1
Wezembeek-Oppem Brussels 6 A2
White Cloud Hill = Baiyun
   Hill Guangzhou 11 B2
White House, The Washington 33 B3
Whitechapel London 15 A3
Whitehall Dublin 10 A2
Whittier Los Angeles 16 C4
Whitton London 15 B1
Wieden Vienna 32 A2
Wien Vienna 32 A2
Wien-Schwechat ✈ (VIE)
   Vienna 32 B3
Wienerberg Vienna 32 B2
Wierzbno Warsaw 32 B2
Wijde Wormer Amsterdam 2 A2
Wilanów Warsaw 32 C2
Wilanówka → Warsaw 32 C2
Wilds, The Johannesburg 13 B2
Wilhelmshagen Berlin 5 B5
Wilket Creek Park Toronto 31 A2
Wilkieston Edinburgh 11 B1
Will Rogers State Historical
   Park △ Los Angeles 16 B1
Willbrook Dublin 10 B2
Willesden London 15 A2
Willesden Green London 15 A2
Williamsbridge New York 22 A2
Williamsburg New York 22 B2
Williamsdorp Orlando 23 B2
Williamstown Melbourne 18 B1
Willis, L. Orlando 23 B1
Willoughby Sydney 29 A2
Willow Springs Chicago 9 C1
Willowdale Toronto 31 A2
Wilmersdorf Berlin 5 B3
Wilmette Chicago 9 A2
Wilmington London 15 B5
Wimbledon London 15 B2
Wimbledon Common London 15 B2
Wimbledon Park London 15 B2
Wimbledon Tennis Ground
   London 15 B2
Winchester Boston 6 A2
Windermere Cape Town 8 A2
Windermere Orlando 23 B1
Windsor Johannesburg 13 A1
Windsor, Gare Montreal 20 B2
Windsor Hills Los Angeles 16 C2
Windy Arbour Dublin 10 B2
Winning Munich 21 A2
Wissous Paris 24 B2
Wittenau Berlin 5 A2
Witwatersrand, Univ. of
   Johannesburg 13 B2
Wlochy Warsaw 32 B1
Wo Mei Hong Kong 12 A2
Wo Yi Hop Hong Kong 12 A1
Woburn Boston 6 A2
Woburn Toronto 31 A3
Wola Warsaw 32 B2
Wolf Trap Farm Park
   Washington 33 B2
Wolgok Seoul 27 B2
Wolica Warsaw 32 C1
Wólka Weglowa Warsaw 32 B1
Wollaston Boston 6 B2
Woltersdorf Berlin 5 B5
Woluwe-St-Lambert Brussels 6 A2
Woluwe-St-Pierre Brussels 6 A2
Wong Chuk Hang Hong Kong 12 B2
Wong Chuk Wan Hong Kong 12 A2
Wong Chuk Yeung
   Hong Kong 12 A2
Wong Tai Sin Hong Kong 12 A2
Wood Green London 15 A3
Wood Ridge New York 22 A1
Woodbine Race Track
   Toronto 31 A1
Woodbridge Toronto 31 A1
Woodford Bridge London 15 A4
Woodford Green London 15 A4
Woodhaven New York 22 B2
Woodhouselee Edinburgh 11 B2
Woodlands Singapore 28 A2
Woodmont Washington 33 B3
Woodside New York 22 B2
Woodstock Cape Town 8 A1
Woollahra Sydney 29 B2
Woolooware B. Sydney 29 C1
Woolwich London 15 B4
World Trade Center, site of
   former New York 22 B1
Worli Mumbai 20 A1
Worth Chicago 9 C2
Wren's Nest Atlanta 3 B2

Wrigley Field Chicago 9 B3
Wuhlgarten Berlin 5 A5
Wujiaochang Shanghai 28 B2
Würm → Munich 21 B1
Würm-kanal Munich 21 A1
Wusong Shanghai 28 A1
Wyczółki Warsaw 32 C1
Wygoda Warsaw 32 B2
Wynberg Cape Town 8 B1

X
Xabregas Lisbon 16 A2
Xianggang = Hong Kong
   Hong Kong 12 B2
Xiaogang Park Guangzhou 11 B2
Xiaoping Guangzhou 11 A2
Xiasha chong Guangzhou 11 B1
Xichang Guangzhou 11 B2
Xicheng Beijing 4 B1
Xidan Beijing 4 B1
Xizhimen Beijing 4 B1
Xochimilco, Parque
   Ecológico Mexico City 18 C2
Xuanwu Beijing 4 B1
Xuhui Shanghai 28 B1

Y
Yaba Lagos 14 B2
Yaftābād Tehran 31 B1
Yahara Tokyo 30 A2
Yaho Tokyo 30 A1
Yakire Tokyo 30 A4
Yaksu Seoul 27 B2
Yamada Osaka 23 A2
Yamada Tokyo 30 B2
Yamato → Osaka 23 A2
Yan Kit Singapore 28 A3
Yanbu Guangzhou 11 B1
Yangcheon Seoul 27 B1
Yanghuayuan Beijing 4 C1
Yangjae Seoul 27 B2
Yangjiazhuang Shanghai 28 B2
Yangjing Shanghai 28 B2
Yangpu Shanghai 28 B2
Yangpu Park Shanghai 28 B2
Yannawa Bangkok 3 B2
Yarmūk Baghdad 3 A1
Yarra Bend Park Melbourne 18 A2
Yarraville Melbourne 18 A1
Yau Tong Hong Kong 12 B2
Yauza → Moscow 19 B3
Yeading London 15 A1
Yedikule Istanbul 12 C1
Yenikapı Istanbul 12 B1
Yeongdeungpo Seoul 27 B1
Yeongdong Seoul 27 B2
Yeouido Seoul 27 B1
Yerba Buena I. San Francisco 26 B2
Yerres Paris 24 B4
Yerushalayim = Jerusalem
   Jerusalem 13 B2
Yiheyuan Beijing 4 A1
Yıldız Park Istanbul 12 B2
Yinhangzhen Shanghai 28 A2
Yishun Singapore 28 A2
Ylästö Helsinki 11 B2
Yodo → Osaka 23 A2
Yongdingmen Beijing 4 B2
Yongfucun Guangzhou 11 B2
Yongsan Seoul 27 B1
Yonkers New York 22 A2
York Toronto 31 A2
York Mills Toronto 31 A2
York University Toronto 31 A1
You'anmen Beijing 4 B1
Youngsfield Cape Town 8 B1
Yuanxiatian Guangzhou 11 A2
Yuexiu Park Guangzhou 11 B2
Yugo-Zarnal Moscow 19 B2
Yuhaliyazi, Volcan
   Mexico City 18 C1
Yung Shue Wan Hong Kong 12 B1
Yūsofābād Tehran 31 A2

Z
Zaandam Amsterdam 2 A1
Zaandijk Amsterdam 2 A1
Zaanstad Amsterdam 2 A1
Zábĕhlice Prague 25 B2
Zabki Warsaw 32 B2
Żacisze Warsaw 32 B2
Zahrā Baghdad 3 A2
Żalov Prague 25 A1
Zaluski Warsaw 32 C1
Zamdorf Munich 21 B2
Zanevka St. Petersburg 27 B3
Zapote Manila 17 C1
Zaventem Brussels 6 A2
Zawady Warsaw 32 B2
Zâwiyet Abû Musallam Cairo 7 B1
Zawrā' Park Baghdad 3 A2
Zbraslav Prague 25 C2
Zbuzany Prague 25 B1
Zdiby Prague 25 A2
Zeekoevlei Cape Town 8 B2
Zehlendorf Berlin 5 B2
Zenne → Brussels 6 B1
Zerań Warsaw 32 B2
Zerzeń Warsaw 32 B2
Zeytinburnu Istanbul 12 C1
Zhabei Shanghai 28 B1
Zhdanov Moscow 19 B3
Zhenru Shanghai 28 B1
Zhernovka St. Petersburg 27 B2
Zhicun Guangzhou 11 B2
Zhongshan Park Shanghai 28 B1
Zhoucun Guangzhou 11 A2
Zhoujiadu Shanghai 28 B2
Zhoujiazhen Shanghai 28 A1
Zhulebino Moscow 19 B4
Zhushadi Guangzhou 11 A3
Zielona Warsaw 32 B3
Zielonka Warsaw 32 B2
Žižkov Prague 25 B2
Zličín Prague 25 B1
Zografou Athens 2 B2
Zoliborz Warsaw 32 B2
Zonnebloem Cape Town 8 A1
Zugliget Budapest 7 B1
Zugló Budapest 7 A2
Zuiderwoude Amsterdam 2 A3
Zumbi Rio de Janeiro 25 A2
Zuruvuru → São Paulo 27 A1
Zwanenburg Amsterdam 2 A1
Zwölfaxing Vienna 32 B2

CITY GAZETTEER

The entries below provide information on places of interest in cities throughout the world that have particularly large numbers of visitors, whether in a business or tourist capacity. The map page reference at the start of an entry indicates that one or more relevant maps are included in the City Maps section.

Accra, Ghana

Accra is not the most beautiful city in West Africa, but its people are considered to be among the friendliest and best educated. It has several lively markets and a National Museum with displays of West African art and artefacts. Near the city are some beautiful sandy beaches, although visitors should be alert to the powerful undertow. Further along the coast are forts and castles that once served as slave-trading centres, including St George's Castle at Elmina, the oldest European structure in sub-Saharan Africa.

Agra, India

Agra is visited primarily for its architectural wonders, especially the 17th-century Taj Mahal. This magical building, a symbol of Mughal emperor Shah Jahan's love for his favourite wife, Mumtaz Mahal, captures the imagination even when crowded with tourists in the heat of the day. Agra's 16th-century Red Fort contains elaborately decorated royal apartments and gardens that give a vivid impression of life at the Mughal court. Just 40 km (25 miles) away is the Mughal 'ghost city' of Fatehpur Sikri which was abandoned almost immediately after it had been built in the 1570s.

Taj Mahal, Agra

Amsterdam, The Netherlands   Map page 2

In the centre of Amsterdam is a network of canals, crossed by around a thousand bridges and edged with tree-lined streets of 17th- and 18th-century gabled houses. Canal cruises are an excellent way to get to know the city, and visitors can also hire bicycles – a major form of transport in Amsterdam. Among the museums are the Rijksmuseum, with its famous art collection, the Van Gogh Museum, and the Stedelijk Museum, housing modern art. The heart of the city is Dam Square, with the royal palace and Anne Frank's house (now a museum) close by. Rembrandt's house can also be visited in an area full of bars, nightclubs and restaurants.

Antwerp, Belgium

A vibrant city with much to see, Antwerp – on the River Scheldt and Europe's second largest port – deserves to be a highly rated tourist destination. At the heart of its beautiful old town is the Great Market, with a 16th-century town hall. Nearby, among cobbled streets lined with bars, restaurants and shops, is the impressive Gothic cathedral with paintings by Rubens, the city's most famous artist. There is also much to attract those who want a really enjoyable night on the town.

Athens, Greece   Map page 2

Athens is a curious mixture of ancient and modern, where ugly concrete tower blocks rub shoulders with Classical monuments. Dominating the centre of the city are the ruins on the Acropolis, dating from the 5th century BC and crowned by the magnificent Parthenon. Other interesting ruins include the Temple of Olympian Zeus, the largest temple in Greece. The National Archaeological Museum houses gold artefacts from Mycenae and spectacular Minoan frescoes. Nestling beneath the Acropolis is the engaging Pláka quarter, with its small Byzantine churches and bustling tavernas. For most visitors the centre of Athens is Syntagma Square, with its large hotels, banks and open-air cafés. Ferries to the islands depart from the port of Piraeus, 10 km (6 miles) from the square.

Atlanta, Georgia, USA   Map page 3

Beneath the glittering high-rise buildings of Atlanta's modern financial centre lies 'Underground Atlanta' – the revitalized old centre, complete with cobbled, gas-lit streets and packed with shops and restaurants. The piazza above it is filled with street entertainers and flanked by the Coca-Cola Museum. Atlanta is most famously associated with Martin Luther King, and an area of the city is devoted to his memory and to the history of the civil rights movement. The Centennial Olympic Park, with its Fountain of Rings, is an entertaining outdoor venue, and the adjacent CNN Center provides an interesting studio tour.

Auckland, New Zealand

The heart of Auckland is the magnificent Waitemata Harbour, where sailing is a popular pastime. The city is not renowned for its nightlife, but it is pleasant to walk its streets, perhaps following the 13 km (8-mile) Coast-to-Coast Walkway from the Ferry Building to Manukau Harbour. On the route, in an area of parkland known as The Domain, is the Auckland Museum, with a unique collection of Maori and Pacific Island artefacts. Beyond is the inner suburb of Parnell, with its colonial buildings, east of which is Underwater World, a particularly impressive aquarium. There are several city beaches, and surfing beaches beyond the Waitakere Ranges.

Bangkok, Thailand   Map page 3

With its choking traffic, Bangkok can be both a daunting and an exhilarating city for short-stay visitors. Something of the old Siam can be uncovered by using the river-bus service to visit the Royal Grand Palace and the ornate Temple of the Emerald Buddha (Wat Phra Keo). Other Buddhist temples include the Temple of the Dawn (Wat Arun), whose 82 m (266 ft) high gilded stupa is best seen from the Chao Phraya River. At Jim Thompson's House there is an extraordinary private museum of Thai domestic architecture. The network of canals, with their floating markets, is well worth exploring, as are the shops for silk and other textiles, clothes, jewellery and handicrafts. Night-time entertainment includes traditional dancing and Thai boxing.

Floating market, Bangkok

Barcelona, Spain   Map page 4

The capital of Catalonia and Spain's second city, Barcelona is a major port with a fashionable, cosmopolitan cultural life. Particularly enjoyable is strolling along the Ramblas, a broad avenue which bisects central Barcelona, and has a vibrant street life. At the southern end is the renovated harbour area, with shops, restaurants and tapas bars. The district of greatest historic interest is the Barri Gòtic, where medieval houses cluster around the great Gothic cathedral, La Seu. Barcelona has over 50 museums and galleries, including world-class museums dedicated to the works of Picasso and Miró, but it is the buildings of Antonio Gaudí that are most often associated with the city. His incomplete Sagrada Família Cathedral has become a symbol for Barcelona, and is perhaps the most fantastic of all his eccentric creations.

Beijing, China   Map page 4

Despite Beijing's daunting scale, extreme climate and heavy traffic, its sights are well worth visiting. They include the massive Tiananmen Square, the Mao Mausoleum, the Great Hall of the People, the Imperial Palace (Forbidden City), the buildings of the Summer Palace along the shore of Kunming Lake, and the 15th-century Temple of Heaven. Beijing has many interesting parks, including Beihai Park with its historic buildings and exquisite Jade Island. However, perhaps the most famous attraction of all is the Great Wall, which can be visited at Badaling, just 70 km (40 miles) north-west of the city, on a trip that also takes in the Ming tombs in the Shisan Ling Valley.

Berlin, Germany   Map page 5

After decades of being divided into West and East Berlin, the city is once again the capital of a united Germany. From the modern dome on the renovated Reichstag building there are fine views of the new buildings rising in the former no-man's-land between the two sectors, whose distinct character can still be felt. The city's youthful 'alternative' scene also continues to thrive, as does its famous nightlife in and around, for example, Savignyplatz in the west and the Scheunenviertel in the east. To the east of the Brandenburg Gate is an area of grand old squares and streets containing Berlin's main museums, including the Pergamon, with its collection of Ancient, Oriental and Islamic art. To the west is the landscaped Tiergarten, the famous zoo, with its exotic pastiche architecture, and the wealthy, modern heart of former West Berlin.

Boston, Massachusetts, USA
Map page 6

The oldest areas of Boston have a European feel, their street plan based on meandering farm tracks. The Beacon Hill district contains splendid 19th-century brick houses and narrow alleyways, and the Massachusetts State House. A 'Freedom Trail', marked by a line of red bricks, takes the visitor past 17th- and 18th-century buildings, some of which are associated with the American Revolution. There are also guided tours of the USA's oldest surviving battleship – the USS *Constitution*, built in 1797 – moored in Boston Harbour. Across the Charles River lies Cambridge, with Harvard University and Square. Boston is a relatively unthreatening city for visitors, with a lively intellectual and artistic life, and a 'necklace' of city parks and tree-lined streets within a compact central area.

Brisbane, Queensland, Australia

The relaxed atmosphere and compactness of its centre make Brisbane a pleasant place to stroll around. Its historic precinct, next to the Botanic Gardens, contains some fine 19th-century buildings, among them the Treasury. South of the River Brisbane is the State Art Gallery and the Cultural Centre, which includes two theatres and a superb concert hall. Day trips are possible to the beaches of the Gold and Sunshine Coasts.

Brussels, Belgium
Map page 6

The centre of government for the European Union, Brussels is renowned for its excellent restaurants and shops, with everything from flea markets to the designer boutiques in the Galéries St Hubert. The imposing Hôtel de Ville, the gilded 17th-century houses and the Maison du Roi make the Grand-Place one of the world's most beautiful central squares. To the east lies the Gothic cathedral, the Palais Royal and the Royal Art Museums, containing both ancient and modern art. The city is full of fine examples of Art Nouveau architecture, including the museum dedicated to the founder of the movement, Victor Horta. A popular tourist site is the irreverent 17th-century statue, Manneken Pis.

Budapest, Hungary
Map page 7

The Danube and Parliament building, Budapest

Formerly two cities, Buda and Pest, on opposite sides of the Danube, the capital of Hungary is a fascinating destination. The Castle Hill district of Buda includes the cobbled streets and medieval houses of the Old Town, and the Royal Palace (Budavári palota), containing the national art gallery and museum. The Fishermen's Bastion gives sweeping views over the city. A network of grand 19th-century boulevards forms the centre of the larger, more cosmopolitan Pest, with its imposing Parliament building (Orzágház).

There are many elegant spa baths (gyógyfürdo) dotted around the city, and extensive Roman remains, including an amphitheatre, at Óbuda and Rómaifürdo. Famous for its cafés, Budapest has excellent restaurants and offers a huge range of entertainment, including opera, jazz and discos.

Buenos Aires, Argentina
Map page 7

The centre of Buenos Aires is laid out on a grand scale, with wide boulevards, imposing 19th-century buildings, modern tower blocks, and spacious plazas. Around this area, however, are the more intimate districts (*barrios*), each with its distinctive character. San Telmo is the artists' quarter, while La Boca, with its brightly painted houses, is the city's port district. The most fashionable district, Recoleta, houses the National Museum of Art, but is best known for the ornate tombs of its cemetery.

La Boca, Buenos Aires

Cairo, Egypt
Map page 7

The largest city in Africa, Cairo is full of hooting taxis and bustling crowds. Modern buildings have risen next to the minarets of the old mosques, while a maze of markets provide potential bargains. The Pyramids of Giza are visible from the upper storeys of buildings all over the city. Famous worldwide for its unrivalled collection of antiquities, the Egyptian Museum houses the treasures of the Pharaoh Tutankhamun, and more than 100,000 other relics and antiquities from all periods of ancient Egyptian history. Experiences not to be missed include the *Son et Lumière* that takes place daily by the Sphinx at Giza, and drifting on the Nile in a *felucca* while watching the sun sink below the Cairo skyline.

Cape Town, South Africa
Map page 8

South Africa's oldest city, Cape Town has several buildings of historic interest, including the Castle of Good Hope, the Old Town House, the Tuynhuis and the Parliament building. Artefacts from all over Africa are sold at the Saturday market in Greenmarket Square. The city lies below the spectacular Table Mountain, accessible by cable car. There are numerous good beaches, such as those at Clifton and Camps Bay on the cold Atlantic Ocean, and at Muizenberg and Fishoek on the warmer Indian Ocean. The old docks have been developed as the Victoria and Alfred Waterfront, which boasts a range of restaurants. Boat trips run from here to the infamous Robben Island, where Nelson Mandela was imprisoned.

Cartagena, Colombia

Several impressive 16th-century forts overlook the channel leading to the bay of Cartagena, evidence of the city's origins as an imperial

Spanish stronghold. Huge 17th- and 18th-century walls surround narrow streets, palaces, churches, monasteries and plazas. The Palace of the Inquisition is a fine example of colonial architecture, with its magnificent Baroque gateway.

Chicago, Illinois, USA
Map page 9

Built on the shore of Lake Michigan, Chicago played a key role in the economic development of the USA, serving as a railhead for the cattle trade of the Midwest. Its skyline includes skyscrapers dating from the 1890s, buildings in the International Style of the 1950s, and particularly fine examples of more recent architecture. The Sears Tower provides fantastic views of four states from its Space Deck. A closer view can be had on a boat trip up the Chicago River or from 'The Loop', an elevated railway that lends its name to the area it encircles. There are several important museums, including the vast Museum of Science and Industry and the Art Institute of Chicago. For outdoor pursuits, there is the extensive Grant Park, bordering the lake. The city is renowned for its rich musical life and, as well as a world-class symphony orchestra, there is a multitude of clubs offering blues, jazz, rock and folk music.

Skyline with Sears Tower, Chicago

Cologne, Germany

Despite the almost total destruction of central Cologne during World War II, many historic buildings have been restored to their former glory, including the massive and beautiful twin-towered Gothic cathedral (Dom). Among the museums and art galleries are the Roman-Germanic Museum and the Imhoff-Stollwek Museum of Chocolate. The city's unique beer, *kslsch*, can be sampled in the numerous beer halls. Short boat trips on the Rhine provide views of the impressive riverfront, while longer boat excursions go to, for example, Königswinter and Linz.

Copenhagen, Denmark
Map page 8

Scandinavia's largest and liveliest city, Copenhagen has excellent art collections, royal palaces, churches and other historic buildings as well as entertainment late into the night. Punctuated by parks, lakes, fountains and squares, the city is easily explored on foot or bicycle. The old harbour of Nyhavn, with its tall, brightly painted buildings, is packed with pavement cafés and bars, while the Latin Quarter is good for restaurants. From the top of the Round Tower (Rundee Taarn), Europe's oldest functioning observatory, there are magnificent views over the city. The famous Tivoli Gardens is a delightfully varied amusement park dating from 1843. A bridge now links Copenhagen to the attractive Swedish city of Malmö.

Delhi, India
Map page 10

Red Fort, Delhi

The capital of India, Delhi is a city with two centres: New Delhi, which was established by the British in 1911, and Old Delhi, whose present layout dates from the 17th century. The streets of the old town, and in particular Chandni Chauk, are famously frenetic. The massive walls of the Red Fort and the Lahore Gate enclose a host of palace buildings, although many have been stripped of their fine decoration. India's largest mosque, the Jama Masjid, is also in the old town. The new city, with its broad avenues and imposing marble buildings, contains some older sites, including the 16th-century tomb of Humayun and the 12th-century Qutb Minar tower.

Dublin, Ireland
Map page 10

Built on the River Liffey, Ireland's capital contains elegant 18th-century buildings, two Norman cathedrals, a castle, and some fine museums, three of them in Leinster House. One of the oldest books in the world, the 9th-century illuminated Book of Kells, is housed in Trinity College library, while the Writers' Museum pays homage to local literary figures such as W. B. Yeats, James Joyce and Oscar Wilde. Dublin has a relaxed, friendly atmosphere, and plenty of pubs and restaurants. In summer, outdoor events are often held in Phoenix Park. The famous Easter Uprising of 1916 is commemorated at Kilmainham Jail, where many heroes of Irish independence were once incarcerated.

Edinburgh, Scotland
Map page 11

Set on a dramatic rock that soars 76 m (250 ft) from the valley floor, the Old Town of Edinburgh is a collection of historic buildings, towering tenements and narrow passages huddling beneath a romantic castle. The Royal Mile, lined with 16th- and 17th-century buildings, leads from the castle to the royal residence of Holyrood. The Royal Museum lies to its south, as does the lively Grassmarket district with its bars and restaurants. The small but elegant National Gallery sits in Princes Street Gardens to the north. Beyond lie graceful Georgian squares, terraces and crescents of the New Town. Scotland's capital has a rich cultural life, including the world-famous International and Fringe festivals.

Esfahan, Iran

On the four sides of the vast central square of Esfahan, with its formal lawns and pool, are the delicately tiled façades of public buildings. These include the opulent Royal Mosque and the magnificent entrance to the bazaar, whose crowded streets twist and turn towards the steps of the Great Mosque, a complex of buildings spanning a 700-year period. Among other historic sites are the shrine of Imamzadeh Ahmad and several royal palaces. Esfahan's high altitude keeps it relatively cool, making it pleasant to stroll through the streets and parks, and sample the many teahouses.

Fès, Morocco

The old part of Fès – Fès el-Bali – is one of the largest living medieval cities in the world. A fascinating labyrinth of some 94,000 streets and lanes, its covered bazaars are crammed with every conceivable sort of craft workshop, restaurants and market stalls, as well as extensive dye pits and tanneries. On the edge of the old town, the Museum of Moroccan Arts houses a splendid collection of artefacts, including colourful tribal carpets and the city's famous blue pottery.

Florence, Italy

The pedestrianized streets in the beautiful centre of Florence enable visitors to wander about freely, visiting such well-known Renaissance sites as the cathedral, with its red-roofed dome, and the spacious Piazza della Signoria, dominated by the crenellated Palazzo Vecchio. Between the piazza and the River Arno is the Uffizi Gallery, containing famous works by Botticelli and Titian among many others. The 14th-century Ponte Vecchio bridge, lined on both sides with jewellery and gift shops, provides a route to the imposing Pitti Palace. The city's churches range in style from the exquisite San Miniato, through the austere Santo Croce to the classically inspired San Lorenzo. Of the many religious frescoes, those by Fra Angelico in the monastery of San Marco, and by Masaccio in the church of Santa Maria del Carmine, stand out. The Bargello has a fine collection of sculpture, while the Accademia houses Michelangelo's *David*.

Cathedral with Brunelleshci's dome, Florence

Geneva, Switzerland

Geneva enjoys one of the world's most dramatic locations, straddling the Rhône where it leaves Lake Geneva, and overlooked by the Alps on one side and the Jura mountains on the other. A cosmopolitan, French-speaking city, it is a world centre for banking and commerce as well as for international organizations, such as the Red Cross. South of the river, the oldest part has excellent museums, galleries and historic buildings, including St Peter's Cathedral, where John Calvin preached. Geneva lives up to its reputation for efficiency, cleanliness and safety, but all this comes at a price: restaurants, clubs and other entertainments are smart and expensive.

Guangzhou (Canton), China
Map page 11

An economic success but a planning disaster, Guangzhou holds more attraction for the business traveller than for those seeking historic sites. There are, however, numerous decaying French and British colonial buildings on Shamian Island, which provides a haven of peace from the bustle of Guangzhou's streets. A climb to the top of the 11th-century Temple of Six Banyan Trees (Liurong Temple) provides a fine view. Another way of seeing the city is to take a cruise on the Pearl River.

Hamburg, Germany

Germany's largest port (there are daily harbour tours from March to November), Hamburg combines its busy commercial life with a graceful, old-world charm. Situated on the River Elbe and criss-crossed by a network of canals, at its heart is the Alster lake, where boating is a popular pastime in the summer. The city has many extensive parks, stylish shopping arcades, elegant boulevards, museums and art galleries, among them the Kunsthalle with a fine collection of art spanning several centuries. There are numerous café-bars and all-night entertainment, most notably in the St Pauli Quarter, where The Beatles famously performed in the 1960s.

Hanoi, Vietnam

Built on the Red River, around several large lakes, Hanoi has both peaceful tree-lined avenues and parks, and a bustling old city where almost anything can be purchased, including silk, lacquerware, puppets and jewellery. Bikes are the main form of transport. The city's many religious buildings include the One-Pillar Pagoda and the 11th-century Temple of Literature. Ho Chi Minh's mausoleum provides a memorable experience, with visitors being escorted to view the embalmed body. A day trip can be made to the Perfume Pagoda – actually a complex of pagodas and Buddhist shrines carved out of limestone cliffs. A cruise from Haiphong around the limestone islands of Halong Bay is also recommended.

Havana, Cuba

Ironically for a country that is proud of its independence from imperialism, one of the main attractions of Cuba's capital is its colonial past. The vast open space of Plaza de la Revolución and the post-colonial buildings of the Vedado district are worth seeing, but it is the boulevards and squares of Old Havana that are most fascinating. The palaces surrounding the Plaza de Armas, the Baroque cathedral and the elegant thoroughfare 'The Paseo' are all fine examples of colonial architecture. There are few cars on the streets, but many bicycles. There are also many nightclubs, where salsa is the predominant dance style.

Capitol building and Grand Theatre, Havana

Helsinki, Finland
Map page 11

Helsinki is almost surrounded by water and is full of the sounds and scents of the sea. Among its architectural gems are the 19th-century Neo-classical buildings of Senate Square – which also contains the blue-domed Lutheran Cathedral – and the rock-hewn church of Temppeliauko (1969) where many concerts are held. Although its combination of attractive buildings, good restaurants and excellent art galleries and museums make it a year-round tourist destination, Helsinki really comes to life in summer, with open-air cafés, concerts, and boat trips to the ruined fortress on nearby Suomenlinna Island.

Hong Kong, China
Map page 12

Most visitors to Hong Kong take the short ferry ride from Kowloon across the harbour, with its spectacular view of the high-rise buildings on the waterfront of Hong Kong Island. A visit to the Man Mo temple, with its ornate interior, provides a complete contrast. A funicular goes to the top of Victoria Peak where there are shady paths through lush vegetation. The Tsim Sha Tsui area of Kowloon contains a group of modern exhibition buildings, including the Space Museum and the Hong Kong Museum of History, as well as air-conditioned shopping malls. A ferry goes to the islands of Lamma, where there are relatively uncrowded beaches, country walks and seafood restaurants. A hydrofoil goes to Macau.

Istanbul, Turkey
Map page 12

Formerly known as Constantinople, Istanbul has an imperial history dating back to the time of the Roman Empire. Its strategic position straddling the Bosporus Strait makes it both a European and an Asian city. Among the churches built in the 6th century by Emperor Constantine is the domed Hagia Sophia (Aya Sofya), which was converted into a mosque in 1453 and is now a museum. The 17th-century Blue Mosque (Sultanahmet Camii) is a masterpiece of Ottoman architecture, while the Topkapi Palace, with its imperial treasury stuffed with gold and jewels, is on every itinerary. In old Istanbul is the labyrinthine Kapali Carsi (the world's largest covered bazaar) where more than 4,000 shops and stalls sell carpets, jewellery, ceramics, brass and leatherware. A fascinating mixture of both the ancient and modern, Istanbul also has a renowned cuisine.

Jaipur, India

Known as the 'Pink City' because of the salmon-coloured wash applied to many of its buildings, Jaipur is the capital of the colourful state of Rajasthan. It is divided into areas dedicated to specialist activities, such as elephant-handling or the sale of textiles, silver or gems. Within the walled town are the Palace of Winds (Hawa Mahal), with its delicately screened windows, the City Palace – now a museum – and Jai Singh's extraordinary Observatory, with its huge angular stone instruments. Nearby is the hill town and Rajput palace complex of Amber.

Jakarta, Indonesia
Map page 12

Jakarta's glinting high-rise office blocks contrast sharply with the cobbled square at the heart of what was 18th-century Batavia (now known as Kota). Much can be discovered of this colonial period at the dock of Sunda Kelapa, where many magnificent schooners are moored and a maritime museum has been created in an old warehouse. The National Museum has excellent displays on Indonesia's ethnic groups. There is a theme park at Taman Impian Jaya Ancol, and Balinese dancing and traditional music at Taman Ismail Marzuki. Jakarta also offers a fine range of restaurants.

Jerusalem, Israel
Map page 13

Dome of the Rock, Jerusalem

The focus of most visits to Jerusalem is the Old City with its different quarters. The heart of the Christian quarter is the Church of the Holy Sepulchre, the site of Christ's crucifixion. This is reached along the Via Dolorosa, much of which passes through the Muslim quarter, with its impressive Mamluk architecture. The Western (Wailing) Wall is in the Jewish quarter, which also contains the multi-layered Temple Mount Excavations. The Armenian quarter, the centre of the Armenian Church, contains the impressive Citadel. Towering over all these is the golden Dome of the Rock, a sacred Muslim site in the Temple Mount compound.

Johannesburg, South Africa
Map page 13

The richest city in Africa, Johannesburg is also a lively centre of South African culture. Museum-Africa has collections relating to the history and art of all sections of the community, while the nearby Market Theatre Complex, which contains four theatres, is an attractive place in which to eat and drink, and listen to music. Visitors, however, should be aware of the high crime rate in the downtown area, and enjoy instead the restaurants and gardens of northern suburbs such as Rosebank and Melville. Outside the city is Soweto, the vast black township which has a lively music and theatre scene but is best visited on a guided tour.

Kairouan, Tunisia

An important centre for the Muslim faith, Tunisia's holy city has over 130 mosques, including the 9th-century Great Mosque, which once doubled as a fortress. A special permit is required to visit the holy sites. Kairouan's maze of buildings and narrow, winding streets is enclosed by ancient city walls, and it is a fascinating place in which to stroll. Artisans carry out the traditional trades of weaving and carpentry, and carpet sellers try to attract visitors to their stalls in the souk (bazaar).

Karachi, Pakistan
Map page 13

Developed as a city by the British from the 1840s, Karachi is a business rather than a tourist centre. It does, however, have many colourful bazaars in Sadr, the central district, which specialize in such products as jewellery, cloth, dried fruit and bottles. It also has a fascinating coastline which can be viewed on a traditional lateen-sailed boat trip from the harbour. Clifton Beach, with its camel rides and fairground, is well equipped for families, while other, rather less commercialized beaches are a short drive away.

Katmandu, Nepal

Katmandu is an intriguing mixture of modern buildings and narrow, traffic-clogged streets with intricately carved temples and shrines. Many of these ancient buildings are grouped around Durbar Square, including the Jaganath Temple, with its erotic carvings. The Old Royal Palace houses an interesting museum. Jochne, better known as 'Freak Street', is a focal point for many visitors, with its fascinating shops, cheap hotels and restaurants. Outside the city are three huge temples: the Hindu Pashupatinath complex, with its riverside ghats, and the Buddhist stupas of Boudhanath and Swayambunath.

Street scene, Katmandu

Kolkata (Calcutta), India
Map page 14

The capital of West Bengal, Kolkata (Calcutta) is regarded by many as the cultural and intellectual centre of India. It also has a reputation for extreme poverty and squalor. One of the great colonial cities of Asia, its main historic sites date from the days of the British Raj and include the white marble Victoria Memorial, the neo-Gothic St Paul's Cathedral, and the Indian Museum, with sculptures from all over India. These buildings are all in the vicinity of the Maidan, one of the largest city parks in the world, where hundreds of different interests – among them yoga, cricket and riding – are regularly pursued, and live entertainment is provided.

Kraków, Poland

Having come through World War II virtually unscathed, and with not a high-rise building in sight, Kraków's densely packed old centre is full of historic churches and picturesque streets and squares. The central market square, which is reputed to be the largest medieval town square in Europe, contains a number of interesting buildings, among them the largely 16th-century Cloth Hall. The square is also the focus of the city's vigorous cultural life. There are several jazz and cabaret clubs in the Old Town, as well as numerous attractive cafés, bars and restaurants. To the south are the castle and cathedral of Wawel, behind which lies Kazimierz, the gradually reviving Jewish district.

Kuala Lumpur, Malaysia

A city that has sprung up since the 1860s, Kuala Lumpur is short on historic sites but has plenty to offer the visitor. Its colonial, 19th-century heart is Merdeka Square. Nearby is the most spectacular of the city's mosques, Masjid Jamek. Chinatown and Little India provide much of interest, and Malaysian craftwork and antiques can be bought at the Art Deco Central Market. The 'Golden Triangle' business area includes the Petronas Twin Towers, one of the world's tallest buildings. The Lake Gardens contain a Bird Park, Orchid Garden and Butterfly Park. A half-hour drive outside the city are the Batu Caves, used as Hindu temples. Day trips can be made to the historic city of Malacca and the Genting Highlands Casino Complex.

Kyoto, Japan

Japan's capital for over 1,000 years, Kyoto has numerous Buddhist temples, Shinto shrines, palaces and gardens. Despite extensive modern development, there are still traditional wooden houses and craft shops in the back streets. A city that is particularly spectacular when clad in either cherry blossom or autumnal colours, its main sights include the 1,001 gilded statues of Buddha lined up in the Hall of the Thirty-Three Bays, the view from the temple of Kiyomizu-dera, and the intriguing gardens of Ginkaku-ji. Other famous gardens include the lake-garden of Kinkaku-ji, and the 500-year-old garden of Ryoan-ji. The city of Nara, 35 km (22 miles) south, contains the huge bronze Buddha of Todai-ji, and other fine examples of early Japanese art and architecture.

Temple of Kiyomizu-dera, Kyoto

Lagos, Nigeria　　　　　　　　　*Map page 14*

Although no longer the capital of Nigeria, Lagos is by far the largest city in West Africa. At its heart lies Lagos Island, a business centre whose skyline is spiked by skyscrapers. The National Museum provides a fascinating insight into the country's cultural heritage and includes works of art dating back 2,800 years, including beautiful Benin bronzes. The city's main attraction, however, is modern African music, and many of the country's best-known singers have nightclubs here.

Lahore, Pakistan

Lahore is renowned for its Mughal architecture. The most attractive of its many mosques is that of Wazir Kahn, covered in intricate glazed mosaic tiles, but the largest is the Badshahi Mosque. The massive walls of Lahore Fort surround a compound of elegant buildings. Away from the centre is Jahangir's tomb and the Shalimar Garden, with its geometrically arranged terraces, ponds, fountains and, in February and March, its spectacular flowers.

Las Vegas, Nevada, USA　　　　　*Map page 14*

A city whose population grew from 30 to half a million in just 90 years, Las Vegas is continually reinventing itself, with the casinos on The Strip providing ever bigger and better spectacles. The most famous is Caesar's Palace, with staff dressed as centurions and Cleopatra lookalikes. New York, New York entices with its replica skyscrapers and a Statue of Liberty. Treasure Island has a mock sea battle, Mirage an erupting volcano and Circus Circus live fire-eaters. Food and lodging are cheap, particularly midweek, with the real profits being made on the gambling tables and slot machines. Las Vegas is popular for outrageous weddings, with services being conducted in the most unlikely places – in a 'drive-through' chapel, the nearby Grand Canyon, or even in mid-air.

The Strip, Las Vegas

Lima, Peru　　　　　　　　　　*Map page 14*

A once-beautiful city, Lima has suffered badly at the hands of modern developers. It is worth visiting primarily for its fine museums, which provide background information about Peru's Inca sites. It is also a useful base from which to explore the surrounding countryside, including the beautiful beaches to the south, over which towers the temple complex of Pachacamac.

Lisbon, Portugal　　　　　　　*Map page 16*

There are many hills to climb and much to see in Portugal's capital. Stretching north from the Rio Tejo, the Baixa district – rebuilt after the devastating earthquake of 1755 – contains many of the city's museums and theatres. The old Moorish area, the Alfama, survived the earthquake and its warren of narrow streets, stairways and squares leads up to the hilltop Castle of St George, with magnificent views. On the edge of the city the Belém area contains fine examples of 16th-century architecture, including the marvellous Jerônimos Monastery and the famous white Belém Tower. At night the haunting traditional *fado* music is played in bars in, for example, the Bairro Alto district. Day trips can be made to the hill town of Sintra or to the beaches on the Estoril coast.

London, England　　　　　　　*Map page 15*

Europe's largest city, London is a lively, cosmopolitan metropolis, offering a huge range of attractions to the visitor. From the grand squares of Knightsbridge and Belgravia to the business district of the City, central London is made up of a mosaic of areas, each with its own distinctive atmosphere and architectural style. Historic buildings include the Tower of London (containing the Crown Jewels), St Paul's Cathedral, Westminster Abbey, the Houses of Parliament and Buckingham Palace. Among the many art galleries are the Tate Modern, housed in a converted power station on the South Bank of the River Thames,

and The National Gallery, overlooking Trafalgar Square. The British Museum contains a monumental collection of Egyptian, Greek and Roman artefacts. Soho, Piccadilly and Covent Garden form the heart of the theatre district, with numerous restaurants, clubs and bars. Day excursions can be made to Hampton Court Palace, Windsor Castle, Canterbury Cathedral, the Royal Pavilion in Brighton, and the historic university towns of Oxford and Cambridge.

Los Angeles, California, USA　　*Map pages 16–17*

Among the skyscrapers in Los Angeles' downtown area are some notable public buildings, including the Museum of Contemporary Art. To the southwest is Exposition Park, home to three museums, including the interactive California Space and Science Center. Most visitors, however, flock to Hollywood in search of film stars, although the big names have long since left for more salubrious neighbourhoods, such as Beverly Hills and elegant Bel Air. Other attractions include the Warner Bros. Studio Tour, and the thrilling rides at Universal Studios. On the coast, the long sandy beach linking Santa Monica and Venice is a magnet for Los Angeles' more colourful characters.

Luxembourg City, Luxembourg

The picturesque old walled city of Luxembourg perches above the Pétrusse and Alzette valleys, overlooked by the ruins of its ancient fortress with a labyrinth of defensive tunnels and underground chambers (the casemates), which is a UNESCO World Heritage Site. Running between the Citadelle du St Esprit, which provides spectacular views, and the Grand Ducal Palace is the elegant Chemin de la Corniche, one of Europe's most beautiful pedestrian promenades.

Madrid, Spain　　　　　　　　　*Map page 17*

Spain's capital is a huge metropolis with a remarkable collection of museums and art galleries, beautiful parks and a famously vibrant nightlife centred on Plaza de Santa Ana. The city is made up of a number of districts (*barrios*), each with its own distinct character. The area of most interest to visitors is around the 17th-century Plaza Mayor, with the elaborately decorated Royal Palace, the Royal Theatre (Teatro Real) and the famous Prado Museum all within easy reach. The city has a vivacious character and a buzzing street life. Tapas bars are everywhere, and shoppers can explore the busy Gran Via or the atmospheric Rastro flea market centred on Plaza de Cascorro. Excursions can be made to the austere monastery of El Escorial and to the historic towns of Toledo, Segovia, Avila and Aranjuez.

Plaza Mayor, Madrid

Manila, Philippines
Map page 17

Many people visit Manila purely for its bars and nightlife, and the city provides plenty to choose from in the business district of Makati and the streets behind Roxes Boulevard. The walled area known as Intramuros contains the most significant historic sites, including Fort Santiago and the imposing Romanesque cathedral. Rizal Park, projecting out into Manila Bay, contains a lagoon, a spectacular fountain, a replica of Beijing's Summer Palace, a Japanese Garden and planetarium. Manila's Chinatown (on the border of Santa Cruz and Binondo) is the place to go for silk, porcelain and Chinese dumplings.

Marrakech, Morocco

Famous for its lively street life, Marrakech is also known for the pink colour that dominates the city from the earth walls around the old town centre to the flat-roofed houses. Every evening in Djemaa El Fna, the old town's central square, acrobats, snake charmers and storytellers perform. Nearby is the labyrinthine souk (bazaar), with its hundreds of small shops selling jewellery, carpets, metalware and leather. There are several beautiful gardens, and the Museum of Arts contains a magnificent display of carpets. Just an hour's drive away are the spectacular High Atlas mountains.

The souk, Marrakech

Melbourne, Victoria, Australia
Map page 18

Central Melbourne, on the north bank of the River Yarra, is a striking blend of past and present. Ornate 19th-century buildings sit alongside towering skyscrapers, as in Collins Street where the 1980s Rialto Towers provide splendid views from an Observation Deck. Elsewhere, the Old Melbourne Gaol is a major historic attraction and there are many fine parks and gardens, including the outstanding Botanic Gardens. The city's multi-ethnic nature is apparent in the popular Queen Victoria Market and in the huge variety of restaurants. Outside the centre several inner suburbs, each with a distinct character, can be explored by tram. Places of interest nearby include the Yarra Valley with its wineries and wildlife sanctuaries, and Phillip Island with its penguins.

Mexico City, Mexico
Map page 18

It is worth braving the traffic and pollution of Mexico City to see the impressive architecture of the buildings surrounding the main square (Zócalo), including the National Palace, with its murals by Diego Rivera. Nearby are the fascinating excavations of an Aztec temple (Templo Mayor). Bosque de Chapultepec, with its boating lakes, gardens and zoo, provides some relief from the hectic street life. It is also home to the outstanding

Museo de Antropología, whose indoor and outdoor exhibition spaces house the world's greatest collection of Mexican art and artefacts. Just 48 km (30 miles) away from the centre are the splendid ruins of the ancient city of Teotihuacán.

Miami, Florida, USA
Map page 18

Miami is spread out along the fragmented coast-line of Biscayne Bay. The Spanish language pre-dominates and the downtown area, with its modern tower blocks, is greatly enlivened by the Latin American street life. Little Havana and Little Haiti are two areas worth visiting for their strong culture. The city's most elegant neighbourhood is Coral Gables, built as a 'model suburb' in the 1920s. Miami Beach, on an island linked to the mainland by causeways, has many fine examples of Art Deco buildings and miles of sandy beaches, hotels and bars.

Milan, Italy
Map page 19

Famous as a world centre for design and fashion, and for its grand opera house, La Scala, Milan has many historic buildings alongside its modern skyscrapers. The enormous Gothic cathedral dominates the main square, Piazza del Duomo, and the nearby convent of Santa Maria delle Grazie houses Leonardo da Vinci's fresco *The Last Supper*. Italy's most beautiful shopping arcade, the Galleria Vittorio Emanuele II, runs between the cathedral and La Scala. The Castello Sforzesco, a striking red-brick castle which was once the seat of the Dukes of Milan, houses the excellent municipal art collections. Excursions can be made to the old university town of Pavia and to the lake resorts such as Varenna and Bellagio on Lake Como, and Stresa on Lake Maggiore.

Montréal, Québec, Canada
Map page 20

Situated on the St Lawrence River, Montréal is Canada's second-largest city. The multi-ethnic nature of its population, of whom around 60% are French-speaking, is evident in the diversity of its cuisine and cultural festivals. The Parisian-style old city has numerous 17th-, 18th- and 19th-century buildings, among them the Neo-gothic Basilique Notre-Dame. By the river a public space has been created out of the old shipyards, complete with exhibitions and amusements. Boat trips can be taken up and down the St Lawrence, including one through the Lachine Rapids. The collection in the Art Museum is wide-ranging and includes a display of Inuit art. There are also particularly interesting Botanic Gardens.

Moscow, Russia
Map page 19

Moscow radiates outwards from the Kremlin in a series of rings, of which the innermost is of greatest interest to visitors and is small enough to be explored on foot. Among the buildings enclosed by the thick red-brick walls of the Kremlin are three imposing palaces and the Archangel Cathedral. Outside is Red Square, with the exotic, multi-coloured domes of St Basil's Cathedral, the Lenin Mausoleum, the Historical Museum and the magnificent 19th-century state department store, GUM, facing each other across the famous cobbled parade ground. There are also numerous literary museums and art galleries. The palatial metro system with its glittering chandeliers and fabulous marble architecture should not be missed.

St Basil's Cathedral, Moscow

Mumbai (Bombay), India
Map page 20

Home to India's thriving film industry, Mumbai also has the largest slum area of any city in Asia. The influence of the British colonial heritage is apparent in the Victorian Gothic buildings of the Fort district, the triumphal Gateway of India arch, and the red double-decker buses. The frenetic streets and bazaars are, however, pure India. Malabar Hill, with its Hanging Gardens, provides some relief from the crowds, as do the Mahatma Gandhi Museum and an impressive new National Gallery of Modern Art. Most visitors take a boat trip across the large harbour to Elephanta Island, to see the Hindu temples hewn out of the rock.

Munich, Germany
Map page 21

Munich is a cosmopolitan city, close to the Bavarian Alps, with many beautiful buildings and a wide variety of theatres, museums, galleries and restaurants. In the centre of the old town is the Marienplatz with its famous old town hall (Rathaus), and several historic churches. Many visitors shop in the glamorous Maximilianstrasse and spend an evening at the opera or drink in one of the city's many historic beer cellars, such as the famous Hofbräuhaus. Another attraction is the beer festival in October. Just outside the city is the Baroque palace of Nymphenburg.

Nairobi, Kenya

East Africa's most modern city has broad streets lined with jacaranda trees. The compact city centre can be walked in 20 minutes, but visitors should be aware that street robberies are a growing problem. The National Museum details the history of Kenyan tribal groups. Close to the city is the Bomas of Kenya, where traditional dances and songs are performed, and the Nairobi National Park where zebras, giraffes, lions, leopards and rhinos are among the animals that can be seen, particularly from July to September.

New Orleans, Louisiana, USA
Map page 21

Its fantastic mix of cultures – French, Spanish, Native American, African and Caribbean – has traditionally made New Orleans one of America's most stimulating cities. However, it is now only slowly recovering from the enormous damage inflicted by Hurricane Katrina in August 2005, and many neighbourhoods remain abandoned. These do not include the main tourist areas – in particular, the French Quarter, with its elegant architecture – where visitors can enjoy the Creole and Cajun cuisines, both variations on the French, and the music. Known as the 'cradle of jazz', the city continues to stage its annual Jazz Festival in April or May, as well as a Mardi Gras carnival in February or March.

New York, NY, USA
Map page 22

Manhattan and the Statue of Liberty, New York

New York is the ultimate destination for those who love cities, with most of its main attractions on Manhattan Island. However, its famous skyline was changed forever following the destruction of the twin towers of the World Trade Center on 11 September 2001; the 1930s Empire State Building is now the city's tallest building. The dozens of art galleries include the Metropolitan Museum of Art and the Guggenheim Museum of predominantly 20th-century art. The ferry to Staten Island provides panoramic views of Manhattan, while the Circle Line runs ferries across the harbour to the Statue of Liberty and Ellis Island. Districts to be toured on foot include Greenwich Village, with its cafés, SoHo, renowned for its art galleries and boutiques, and Little Italy. Some visitors are drawn to the city by stores such as Bloomingdales, others by its nightlife. Providing a haven from the big-city traffic is Central Park, where there is often live entertainment.

Orlando, Florida, USA
Map page 23

Surrounded by theme parks, and close to Cape Canaveral, Orlando is a thriving tourist centre. It has a lot more than its location to offer, including the excellent restaurants and shops on International Drive, the nightclubs on Orange Avenue, and the scenic boat tours and art museums in Winter Park. Downtown Orlando has a historic district dating from between 1880 and 1940, as well as several good arts centres and museums. The central Lake Eola Park provides a haven from the bustle of the city.

Osaka, Japan
Map page 23

The Japanese city most welcoming to foreign visitors, Osaka is enjoyed mainly for its lively nightlife and varied cuisine. It has some fine historic sites, such as the castle and the red-painted Sumiyoshi Shinto shrine to the gods of the sea. Its museums include the Liberty Osaka Museum of Human Rights and the Suntory Museum of 20th-century graphic art. The spectacular Osaka Aquarium is another attraction.

Oslo, Norway
Map page 23

The oldest of Scandinavia's capitals, Oslo is an attractive city situated at the head of Oslofjord. The impressive medieval Akershus castle contains grand staterooms, dungeons and the Norwegian Resistance Museum. The Munch Museum has over 5,000 drawings and paintings by Edvard Munch, while in the beautiful Vigeland Park, sculptures by Gustav Vigeland are on permanent display. Across the harbour is the Bygdøy peninsula with good beaches, an open-air folk museum and maritime museums containing Viking ships as well as Thor Heyerdahl's raft, Kon-Tiki.

Paris, France
Map page 24

Famously beautiful in springtime, Paris is fascinating at any time of year. Packed with historic buildings, world-famous art collections, fine restaurants and street cafés, it is one of the world's most elegant cities. Compact enough to explore on foot, the centre is made up of a number of distinct areas or quartiers, each with its own character. On a hill crowned by the basilica of Sacré-Coeur is Montmartre, with its village-like atmosphere, street artists, nearby flea markets and a splendid view over the city. The Notre Dame Cathedral and Sainte Chapelle are on the peaceful Île de la Cité, an island in the River Seine. The Picasso Museum is set among the beautiful old houses and courtyards of the Marais. The colourful Pompidou Centre looms above the galleries and cafés of the Beaubourg. The Louvre occupies a vast stretch of the Right Bank of the Seine, and there is a magnificent unbroken view through the Tuileries gardens and along the Champs Elysées to the Arc de Triomphe. Attractions on the Left Bank include the Musée d'Orsay – containing a huge collection of Impressionist art – and the Eiffel Tower. Excursions can be made to the royal palaces of Versailles and Fontainebleu, Monet's house at Giverney, and the beautiful cathedral at Chartres.

The Seine and Notre Dame, Paris

Perth, Western Australia, Australia

Situated on a sweep of the Swan River, Perth has lots of sunshine and an easy-going atmosphere. Its centre is relatively compact and dominated by skyscrapers, among which are scattered some Victorian buildings, such as the ornate Government House and the Old Flour Mill. A few miles to the west lie excellent sandy beaches and opportunities for surfing, while cruise companies offer dolphin- and whale-watching trips. The port of Fremantle, just 20 km (12 miles) away, is worth visiting, as is Rottnest Island.

Prague, Czech Republic
Map page 25

With a centre full of beautiful buildings covering 900 years of architecture it is easy to see why Prague, on the River Vitava, is one of Europe's top tourist attractions. Prague Castle (Prazsky Hrad), encompassing the 10th-century Church of St George and the Gothic St Vitus' Cathedral, is the focus of most visits to the city. Other architectural treasures include Baroque and Rococo palaces and the Neoclassical National Theatre (Náordní divadlo). The Old Jewish Quarter (Josefov) contains the Jewish Cemetery and several synagogues, including the Old-New Synagogue (Staranová). Prague's rich cultural life centres especially on its music – it is home to two fine orchestras. It is also arguably the beer-drinking capital of the world, and has several famous beer halls as well as numerous pubs and bars.

Quito, Ecuador

At a height of 2,850 m (9,350 ft), Quito escapes the oppressive temperature and pollution of many Latin American cities. The historic centre, with its whitewashed buildings and red roofs, is a UNESCO heritage site and includes a 16th-century monastery and cathedral, as well as a number of museums. There is also a fascinating vivarium, with displays of many of Ecuador's reptiles, both living and dead.

Reykjavik, Iceland

The world's northernmost capital, Reykjavik is a small modern city with colourful buildings, fashionable shops and a lively nightlife. The Arni Magnússon Institute houses a famous collection of Icelandic saga manuscripts, while the National Museum in the Old Town displays relics from the earliest days of settlement. The modern church of Hallgrímskirkja is built in the shape of a lava mountain and offers excellent views over the city from its 75 m (246 ft) high tower.

Riga, Latvia

A bustling industrial city, Riga also has a waterfront castle, a medieval centre and a lively cultural life. Places to visit include the cavernous Dome Cathedral, the Riga Motor Museum, an open-air ethnographical museum and St Peter's Church – with a view over Old Riga from the spire, which is reached by a lift. To the west, a string of resort towns known collectively as Jurmala stretches for 20 km (12 miles) along the coast, with peaceful beaches and good restaurants.

Rio de Janeiro, Brazil
Map page 25

With a spectacular location at the entrance to a bay, Rio has two famous landmarks that provide breathtaking views: Corcovado Mountain, topped by a huge statue of Christ, and Sugar Loaf Mountain. There are many museums, including the National Historical and the wide-ranging National. The city is best known, however, for its lively beaches, including Copacabana, and the more upmarket Ipanema. At night, the bars, clubs and discos of Rio resound to jazz and rock. There are samba shows primarily for tourists as well as more authentic dancehalls. A particularly popular time to visit is during the spectacular Mardi Gras Carnaval, in February or March.

View from Sugar Loaf Mountain, Rio de Janeiro

Rome, Italy
Map page 26

The historic capital of the Roman Empire, of Latin Christendom and now of Italy, Rome is exceptionally rich in treasures from many eras. Ancient buildings include the Colosseum, the Arch of Constantine, Trajan's Column, the Roman Forum

and the Pantheon. Among the early Christian sites are the famous catacombs and the basilicas of Santa Maria Maggiore and San Giovanni in Laterano (near the Colosseum). Michelangelo's Piazza del Campidoglio – bordered by three palaces – is a fine example of Renaissance town planning, but Rome is known more for its Baroque buildings and squares, and landmarks such as the Trevi Fountain and the Spanish Steps. In the centre of Rome, the Vatican City is the world's smallest independent state, containing St Peter's Square, St Peter's Basilica, the Sistine Chapel and ten museums. Increased pedestrianization of the centre has made it easier to enjoy the exuberant street life for which the city is famous.

St Petersburg, Russia   *Map page 27*

Situated in the Neva River delta, St Petersburg is a city of canals, bridges and elegant architecture. Founded in 1703 by Peter the Great, its oldest landmark is the massive Peter-Paul Fortress, with the slender spire of the Cathedral of St Peter and St Paul rising above it. At the heart of the city is Palace Square, dominated by the pastel-coloured façade of the Winter Palace. The palace is part of the Hermitage Museum, which contains one of the world's greatest collections of European art. Along the Nevsky Prospekt are the former homes of many famous Russians as well as several palaces, department stores, theatres, restaurants, churches and the richly decorated Kazan Cathedral. Day trips can be taken to several summer palaces, among them Pushkin and Petrodvorets.

San Francisco, California, USA   *Map page 26*

One of the USA's most spectacular cities, San Francisco's trademarks are its elegant suspension bridges (Golden Gate and Oakland Bay Bridge) and the street cars that service the steep streets. It is also famous as America's gay capital, the main focus of the gay community being the Castro district. The city has a thriving Chinatown, and its North Beach area (between Russian and Telegraph hills) has long been associated with alternative culture. The northern waterfront includes the famous and crowded Fisherman's Wharf development, with its numerous restaurants. The Golden Gate Park is home to several specialist gardens, art galleries and museums. A boat takes visitors to Alcatraz, the notorious island prison.

Santiago, Chile   *Map page 27*

Santiago is a sprawling city set on a wide plain at the foot of the Andes. However, its central area is relatively compact, and its tree-lined streets and landscaped parks are pleasant to explore on foot, with diversions to the Museum of Pre-Colombian Art in the Real Casa de Aduana and the Santiago Museum, close to the cathedral. A funicular goes to the peak of San Cristóbal and the Pablo Neruda Museum. Day trips can be made to the beaches of Valparaiso and the ski resort of Valle Nevado.

São Paulo, Brazil   *Map page 27*

Although much of São Paulo is modern, the area around the central square (Praça da Sé) contains several interesting old buildings, such as the whitewashed Palácio do Colégio, (a 19th-century replica of Baroque buildings), the Igreja de Santo Antônio and the Solar da Marquesa de Santos. The city has plenty of nightlife and a varied cuisine,

some of its best bars and restaurants being in the suburb known as the Jardins. The nearby Parque do Ibirapuera is a centre for sporting activities and home to several of the city's museums, as well as providing a haven of peace in its 'reading woods'.

Seattle, Washington, USA

The sparkling skyscrapers of downtown Seattle, including the trademark 'flying saucer' of the Space Needle, rise from the shores of Elliott Bay against the spectacular backdrop of the snowy peak of Mount Rainier. A recent surge in the city's prosperity (Seattle is home to the Microsoft Corporation) has led to much new building and the restoration of the historic centre. The city is a centre for contemporary arts and music, the embodiment of which is the high-tech Experience Music Project building. It also contains the headquarters of the Boeing Corporation, whose out-of-town Museum of Flight is a popular attraction.

Seoul, South Korea   *Map page 27*

Secret Garden of palace of Ch'angdok, Seoul

Selected as the site of the ruling dynasty's capital in 1394, Seoul today consists of a series of linked districts, each with its own centre. The National Assembly and financial institutions are on the small island of Youido. Spread around the old centre is a series of royal palaces, the best preserved of which is Ch'angdok, with its Secret Garden of wooded hills and ponds. T'apkol Park is a good place to meet the locals, while Namsan Park is home to the Botanic Gardens, and also to Seoul Tower, which provides a fine view of the city.

Shanghai, China   *Map page 28*

Rapidly regaining its status as a major trading and commercial centre, Shanghai's colonial past is clearly visible in the massive 1920s Neoclassical buildings of its waterfront trading area, famous as 'The Bund'. The maze of narrow streets in the Old City and the crowded bazaar of Yuyuan Park provide a complete contrast. Chinese culture is celebrated in the impressive collection of paintings, ceramics, calligraphy, and sculpture in the new Shanghai Museum. Just 80 km (50 miles) away are the famous city gardens of Suzhou, some of which are over 1,000 years old.

Singapore City, Singapore   *Map page 28*

Singapore is a popular 'stopover' city because it is relatively compact, has an efficient infrastructure and its shopping malls are a source of bargains. Amid the high-rise developments are colonial, Chinese, Malay and Indian enclaves that have retained their character, and some fine historic buildings, such as Coleman's Parliament building, the Buddhist Temple of Heavenly Happiness (Thian Hock Keng Temple) and the colourful Sri

Mariamman Hindu Temple. On the riverside are the restored old shops of Boat and Clarke Quays, both of which are relatively lively nightspots. To the south a cable car and causeway go to the island of Sentosa, which has beaches and attractions such as the impressive Underwater World, while to the north is the well-designed zoo, which features a night safari park. To the west attractions include the Jurong Bird Park and Tang Dynasty City.

Stockholm, Sweden   *Map page 29*

Built on 14 islands, between Lake Mälaren and the Baltic Sea, Stockholm is a beautiful city with numerous parks. It has an essentially modern feel, with many fine 20th-century buildings, although there is still a medieval Old Town (Gamla Stan), with narrow streets and a 15th-century cathedral (Storkyrkan). A ferry goes to Drottningholm – the royal family's island castle, complete with lakeside gardens and an 18th-century theatre. The island of Djurgarden is home to an open-air museum of Swedish vernacular architecture (Skansen) and the cathedral-like building that covers the *Vasa* – a beautifully restored 17th-century warship.

Sydney, NSW, Australia   *Map page 29*

Australia's oldest and largest city is built around a beautiful harbour that is both a major port and recreational area. Best known for its sail-shaped opera house and striking steel-arched harbour bridge, Sydney also has excellent beaches such as Manly, which can be reached by ferry, and the famous Bondi. In the centre, ferries and harbour cruises set out from Circular Quay, near which is The Rocks, with a restored historic quarter. Another area of waterside redevelopment is Darling Harbour, not far from which is the bustling Sydney Fish Market. Away from the harbour, inner suburbs worth visiting include Glebe, Newtown and Paddington, each with a distinct character and attractive 19th-century terraced houses. With an exciting mix of Asian and European cultures, the city offers a cosmopolitan choice of restaurants, theatres and music. The many museums and art galleries include the Australian Museum, which has a gallery devoted to Aboriginal history. A day trip can be made by train to the spectacular Blue Mountains only 80 km (50 miles) away.

Opera House, Sydney

Tehran, Iran   *Map page 31*

Most visitors to Tehran concentrate on its excellent museums. The National Museum and the Golestan Palace Museum house many ancient objects, including those taken from famous sites such as Persepolis. The Museum of Glass and Ceramics is well designed and organized, and the Reza Abbasis Museum displays Islamic art. For those willing to brave the heat and noise, Iran has an extensive bazaar.

Tianjin, China

The centre of Tianjin, for decades an important trading port, is a mixture of international architectural styles – British, French, German and Japanese – from the late 19th century. The Ancient Culture Street, a major draw for visitors, is an attempt to re-create the feel of ancient China. For a more authentic experience of Chinese culture, it is worth going to the Antiques Market and taking a walk through the Hai River Park.

Tokyo, Japan   *Map page 30*

Visitors to Tokyo, faced with a vast urban sprawl, normally work outwards from the Imperial Palace and the surrounding gardens, which contain the remains of Edo Castle. Immediately to the east is the downtown area, with a wide choice of restaurants and shops and some fine examples of modern architecture, including the Tokyo International Forum, with a 60 m (200 ft) high glass atrium. To the west is the Meijii Shrine, set in attractive gardens. The city centre has many art galleries, exhibiting both Japanese and European art. However, many of the largest museums, including the Tokyo National Museum, are further north, in Ueno. The adjacent Asakusa district reveals a more tranquil world of wooden houses, temples and shrines, including the magnificent temple of Senso-ji.

Toronto, Ontario, Canada   *Map page 31*

Standing on the shore of Lake Ontario, Toronto is Canada's leading commercial city. In its centre is the tallest free-standing structure in the world: the CN Tower. Glass-fronted lifts transport visitors to the Space Deck, 442 m (1,400 ft high), from where it is possible to see as far as Niagara Falls. The city's museums include the Royal Ontario Museum and the Gallery of Inuit Art. Along the waterfront an area of old warehouses has been developed as the Harbourfront Park, with hotels, theatres, shops and restaurants. Toronto's large immigrant population has helped create a vibrant city culture, with a thriving music scene.

Vancouver, British Columbia, Canada

Built around a natural harbour, Vancouver is a major port and city of inlets and green spaces, set against a mountain backdrop. The downtown area contains a cluster of sparkling, glass-fronted skyscrapers. Vancouver has a thriving Chinatown and a dynamic artistic and musical scene that encompasses classical, jazz and rock music. Of the many museums, the Museum of Anthropology is the finest. Stanley Park – a peninsula containing a large area of semi-wilderness – has three of Vancouver's many city beaches and the Vancouver Aquarium. Nearby is Vancouver Island, with its rainforest and glacial mountain peaks.

Varanasi, India

Built on the banks of the sacred River Ganges, Varanasi is famous for the flights of stone steps (ghats), lining 5 km (3 miles) of the river banks, where Hindu pilgrims bathe in the waters and cremate their dead. The old town consists of a maze of narrow alleyways at the heart of which is the Golden Temple, dedicated to the god Shiva. The city is also sacred for Buddhists, and at nearby Sarnath there is a collection of restored temples.

Venice, Italy

Distant view of Church of Santa Maria delle Salute, Venice

Built on a collection of islands and criss-crossed by 177 canals, Venice is a city like no other, where boats are the only means of transport. A journey by gondola or vaporetto along the Grand Canal passes many grand palaces, including the Gothic Ca' d'Oro and Ca' Foscari, the Renaissance Palazzo Grimani and the Baroque Rezzonico. The familiar landmark of the Rialto Bridge presides over the busiest shopping area in Venice. Around St Mark's Square is the stunning 11th-century Byzantine Basilica, the Pala d'Oro, and the Doge's Palace. A lift to the top of the towering Campanile provides exceptional views over the city and the lagoon, across which lies the Lido, with beaches and hotels. The Accademia contains the world's most comprehensive collection of Venetian art, including paintings by Titian, while the Peggy Guggenheim collection is one of the most important of 20th-century art outside the USA.

Vienna, Austria   *Map page 32*

Formerly the capital of the Habsburg and Austro-Hungarian empires, today's Vienna preserves an atmosphere of historic grandeur. A city of cafés, beer cellars, parks and elegant boulevards, it has a centre, the Innere Stadt, that is sufficiently compact to be explored on foot. It contains numerous Baroque churches and palaces, the magnificent Gothic St Stephen's Cathedral, and the Hofburg – the Habsburgs' imperial palace, which is now home to the famous Spanish Riding School. Among the city's many museums are the Kunsthistorisches (Art History Museum), with an unrivalled collection of paintings by Peter Breugel the Elder, and the fine 18th-century Belvedere palace complex which features paintings by Klimt and Schiele among others. Outside the centre is Schönbrunn, the Habsburgs' impressive summer palace, and the Prater (in Leopoldstadt), a vast park featuring Vienna's giant ferris wheel. To the north the hills of Kahlenberg and Leopoldsberg provide magnificent views over the city.

Warsaw, Poland   *Map page 32*

The old centre of Warsaw, on the left bank of the River Vistula, was reduced to rubble during World War II, but it has been meticulously rebuilt and is now a UNESCO World Heritage site. All the buildings appear to date from the 18th century or earlier. They include St John's Cathedral and the Renaissance and Baroque merchants' houses surrounding the Old Market Square (Rynek Starego Miasta). There is also the excellent Historical Museum of Warsaw, many lively cafés and some fine restaurants. Outside the Old Town is the beautiful Lazienki park and palace complex and, 6 km (4 miles) further south, the restored Baroque Wilanów park and palace.

Washington, DC, USA   *Map page 33*

The main public buildings of Washington, DC, are grouped on and around the National Mall – a broad swathe of parkland containing the Washington Monument, the Lincoln and Jefferson memorials, and the V-shaped polished black stone wall incised with thousands of names, which commemorates the Americans who fell in Vietnam. On the north side of the Mall is the White House, and overlooking all from the eastern end is the Capitol building, with its 55 m (180 ft) high rotunda. Home to the House of Representatives and the Senate, it is open to visitors. The National Gallery of Art and the National Air and Space Museum are two of the many museums. Central Washington, DC, can be dangerous at night. Georgetown is more relaxed, with its restaurants, bars and handsome streets. Within easy reach of the city are Chesapeake Bay and several Civil War battle sites.

Wellington, New Zealand   *Map page 33*

Overlooked by Mount Victoria, Wellington is the political and commercial capital of New Zealand. Wooden Victorian houses climb the steep hills surrounding the magnificent harbour of Port Nicholson, and a cable car provides a spectacular view of the city. Among the historic buildings in the centre are the Old Government Buildings, while the city's museums include the recently opened Museum of New Zealand (Te Papa). A lively, cosmopolitan city, Wellington has an exciting cultural scene, as evidenced in February and March by the annual Fringe Festival and the biennial International Festival of the Arts.

View over the harbour, Wellington

Xi'an, China

As well as being a base from which to visit the famous Army of Terracotta Warriors, Xi'an possesses its own historic sites. These include the impressive city walls that all but surround the old town, and the 64 m (200 ft) high Big Goose Pagoda. Xi'an also has a strong Islamic culture and its Great Mosque is the largest in China. The Shaanxi Provincial Museum presents a fascinating history of the Silk Road.

Yangon (Rangoon), Burma (Myanmar)

The main focus of any visit to Yangon will be the magnificent Shwedagon stupa. The stupa is 90 m (290 ft) high and shaped like a bell. Completely covered in gold, it is surrounded by a host of smaller gilded stupas, statues, temples and pavilions. Of the many other Buddhist sites around the city, the huge reclining Buddha at Chaukhtatgyi Paya is the most impressive. Two large lakes provide areas of recreation, and the many tree-lined streets and areas of near-jungle give some parts an almost rural feel.

WORLD MAPS

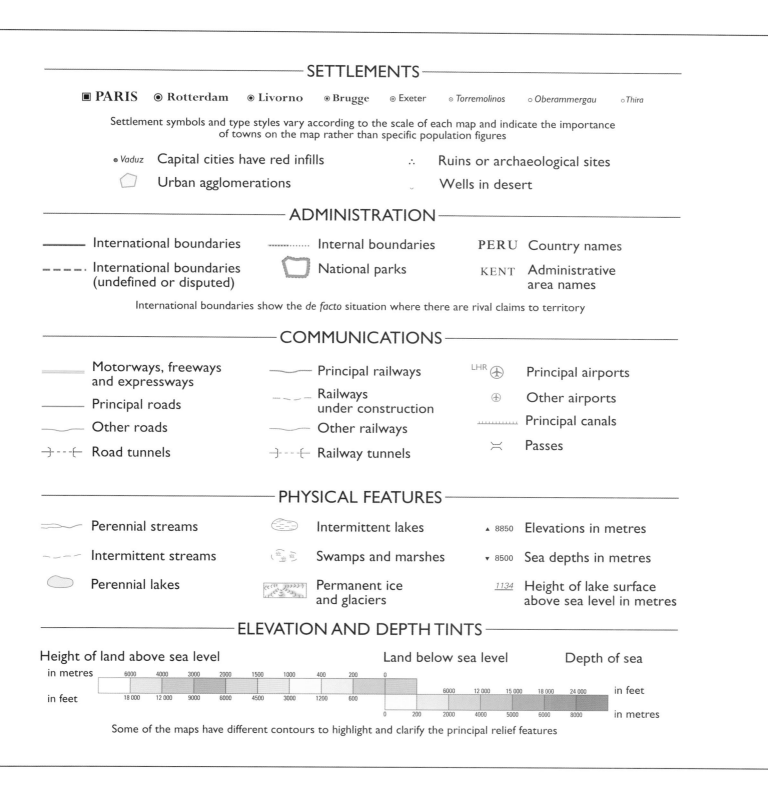

SETTLEMENTS

■ **PARIS**   ◉ Rotterdam   ◉ Livorno   ◉ Brugge   ◉ Exeter   ○ *Torremolinos*   ○ *Oberammergau*   ○ *Thira*

Settlement symbols and type styles vary according to the scale of each map and indicate the importance
of towns on the map rather than specific population figures

• *Vaduz*   Capital cities have red infills   ∴   Ruins or archaeological sites

⬠   Urban agglomerations   ⌄   Wells in desert

ADMINISTRATION

────── International boundaries   ┈┈┈┈┈ Internal boundaries   PERU Country names

─ ─ ─ International boundaries   ⬡ National parks   KENT Administrative
(undefined or disputed)   area names

International boundaries show the *de facto* situation where there are rival claims to territory

COMMUNICATIONS

═════ Motorways, freeways   ───── Principal railways   LHR ✈ Principal airports
and expressways

───── Principal roads   ─ ─ ─ Railways   ⊕ Other airports
under construction

───── Other roads   ───── Other railways   ⊤⊤⊤⊤ Principal canals

┼┈┈┼ Road tunnels   ┼┈┈┼ Railway tunnels   )(Passes

PHYSICAL FEATURES

∿∿ Perennial streams   ⬭ Intermittent lakes   ▲ 8850 Elevations in metres

─ ─ Intermittent streams   ⬭ Swamps and marshes   ▼ 8500 Sea depths in metres

⬭ Perennial lakes   ⬭ Permanent ice   *1134* Height of lake surface
and glaciers   above sea level in metres

ELEVATION AND DEPTH TINTS

Height of land above sea level   Land below sea level   Depth of sea

in metres | 6000 | 4000 | 3000 | 2000 | 1500 | 1000 | 400 | 200 | 0 |

6000 12 000 15 000 18 000 24 000   in feet

in feet | 18 000 | 12 000 | 9000 | 6000 | 4500 | 3000 | 1200 | 600 |

0   200   2000   4000   5000   6000   8000   in metres

Some of the maps have different contours to highlight and clarify the principal relief features

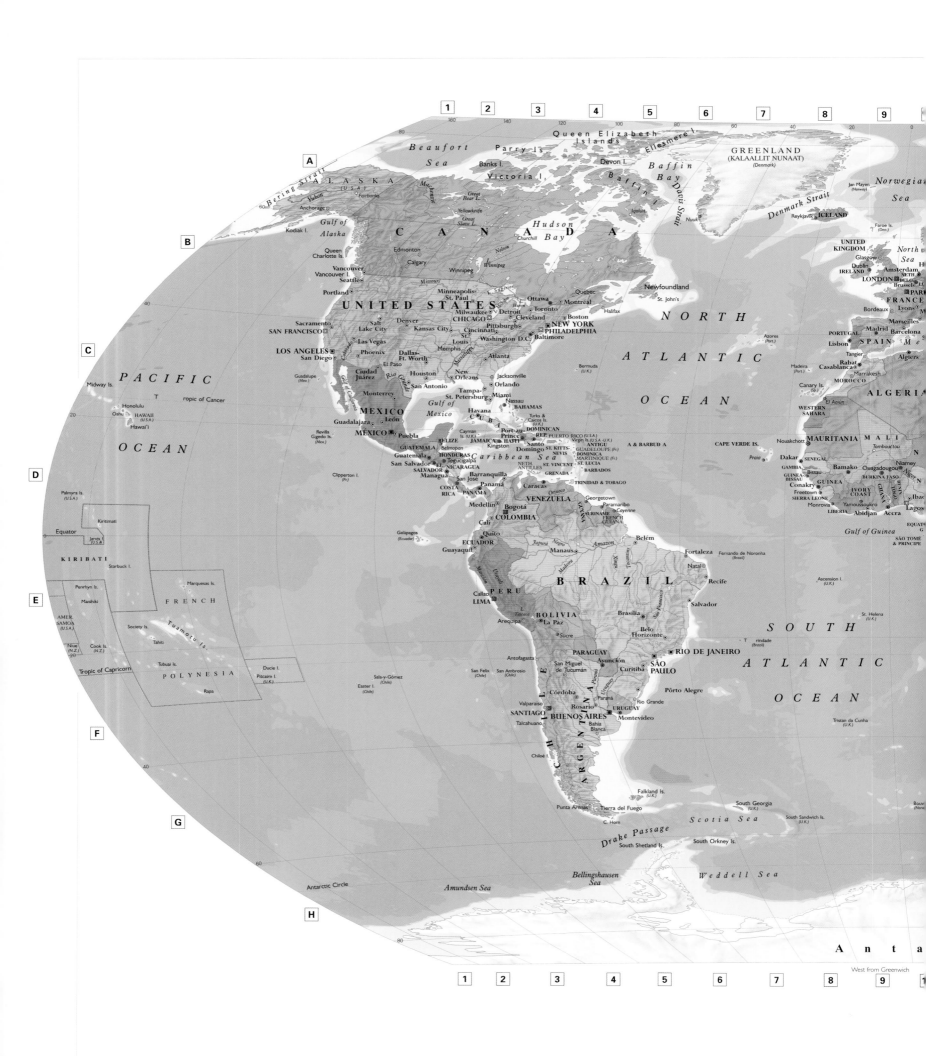

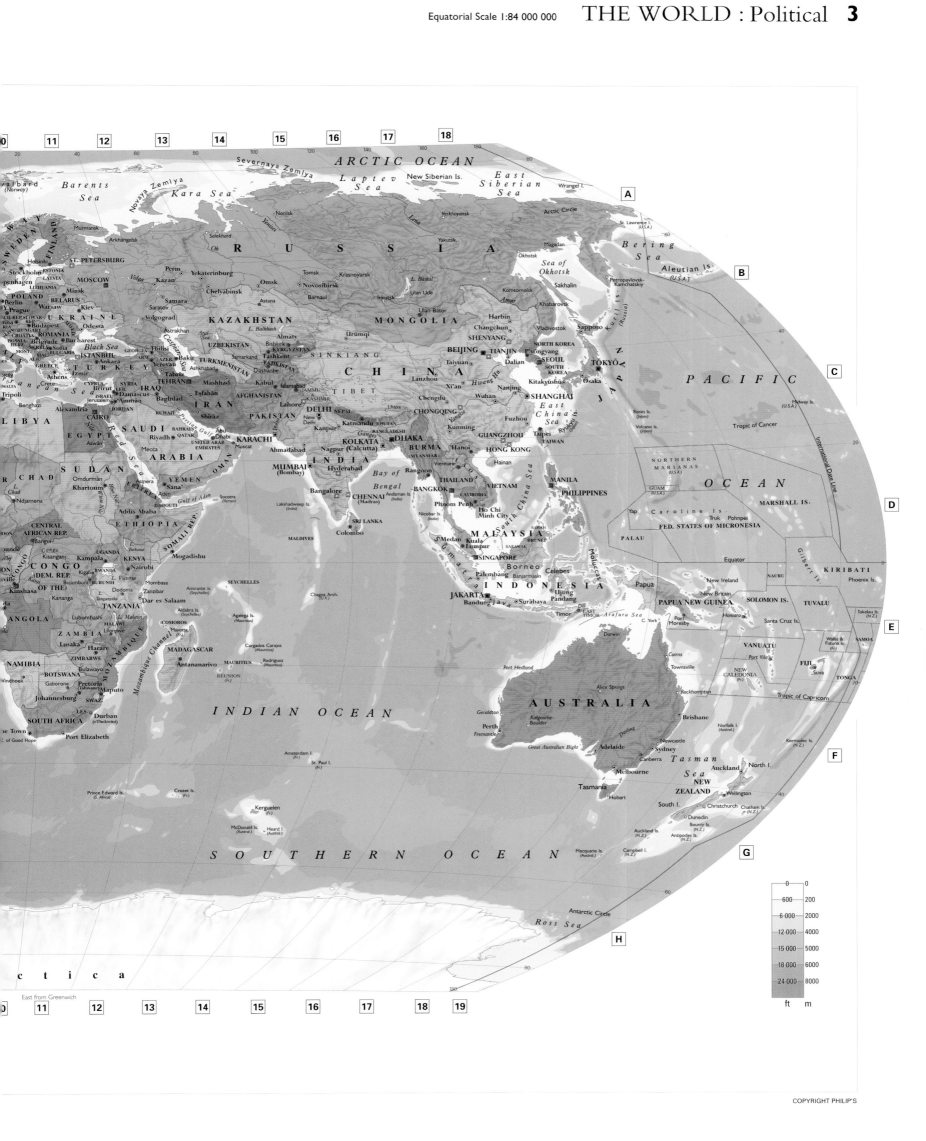

ARCTIC OCEAN

Barents Sea   Novaya Zemlya   *Kara Sea*   Severnaya Zemlya   *Laptev Sea*   New Siberian Is.   *East Siberian Sea*   Wrangel I.

Salbard (Norway)

SWEDEN   FINLAND   Murmansk   Arkhangelsk   Norilsk   Verkhoyansk   Arctic Circle

Helsinki   ST. PETERSBURG   Salekhard   Ob   Yenisey   Lena   Yakutsk   Magadan   St. Lawrence I. (U.S.A.)

Stockholm   ESTONIA   Perm   Yekaterinburg   Tomsk   Krasnoyarsk   Okhotsk   *Bering Sea*

penhagen   LATVIA   MOSCOW   Kazan   Omsk   Novosibirsk   *Sea of Okhotsk*   Petropavlovsk-Kamchatskiy   Aleutian Is. (U.S.A.)

Berlin   LITHUANIA   Minsk   Volga   Samara   Chelyabinsk   Barnaul   Komsomolsk   Sakhalin   Khabarovsk

POLAND   BELARUS   Kiev   Saratov   L. Balkhash   Irkutsk   Ulan Ude   Amur

CH REP. SLOVAK.   UKRAINE   Volgograd   KAZAKHSTAN   MONGOLIA   Harbin   Vladivostok   Sapporo   Kuril Is. (Russia)

Prague   Warsaw   Odessa   Astrakhan   Aral Sea   Astana   Ulan-Bator   Changchun   SHENYANG   NORTH KOREA

anna   HUNGARY   Budapest   Bucharest   Caspian Sea   L. Balkhash   Almaty   Ürümqi   BEIJING   TIANJIN   Dalian   SEOUL   SOUTH KOREA   TŌKYŌ

BOSNIA   ROMANIA   GEORGIA   Tbilisi   UZBEKISTAN   Bishkek   KYRGYZSTAN   SINKIANG   Taiyuan   PYONGYANG   Kitakyūshū   Osaka

CROATIA   SERBIA   Sofia   ISTANBUL   ARM.   AZER.   Baku   Samarkand   Tashkent   TAJIKISTAN   CHINA   Lanzhou   Xi'an   Nanjing   SHANGHAI

MAC. BULGARIA   Ankara   Yerevan   TURKMENISTAN   Ashkhabad   Mashhad   TIBET   Chengdu   Wuhan

ALB.   GREECE   Izmir   TURKEY   Tabriz   Dushanbe   Kābul   Islamabad   Lhasa   CHONGQING   Hwang Ho   East China Sea

Athens   TEHRAN   AFGHANISTAN   JAMMU   Kunming   GUANGZHOU   Fuzhou

Tripoli   CYPRUS   SYRIA   Beirut   Damascus   IRAQ   Baghdad   Esfahān   IRAN   PAKISTAN   Lahore   DELHI   NEPAL   Katmandu   BHUTAN   Taipei   TAIWAN

Benghazi   ISRAEL   LEB.   Jerusalem   JORDAN   Amman   Shīrāz   New Delhi   Kanpur   HONG KONG

Alexandria   KUWAIT   Persian Gulf   Abu   KARACHI   Ahmadābād   INDIA   Nagpur   KOLKATA (Calcutta)   DHAKA   Hanoi   Hainan

CAIRO   SAUDI   BAHRAIN   QATAR   Dhabi   UNITED ARAB   Muscat   BANGLADESH   BURMA (MYANMAR)

LIBYA   EGYPT   Riyadh   EMIRATES   MUMBAI (Bombay)   Hyderabad   *Bay of Bengal*   Rangoon   VIETNAM   MANILA

Aswan   Mecca   ARABIA   OMAN   Ganges   THAILAND   PHILIPPINES

Red Sea   YEMEN   Bangalore   CHENNAI (Madras)   Andaman Is. (India)   BANGKOK   CAMBODIA

CHAD   SUDAN   Omdurman   Asmera   Sana'   Socotra (Yemen)   Lakshadweep Is. (India)   Nicobar Is. (India)   Phnom Penh   Ho Chi Minh City

L. Chad   Khartoum   Blue Nile   ERITREA   DJIBOUTI   *Gulf of Aden*   SRI LANKA

Ndjamena   Addis Ababa   ETHIOPIA   SOMALI REP.   MALDIVES   Colombo   MALAYSIA   Kuala   BRUNEI

CENTRAL AFRICAN REP.   White Nile   UGANDA   Mogadishu   SEYCHELLES   Medan   Lumpur   SARAWAK

Bangui   Kisangani   Kampala   KENYA   Nairobi   SINGAPORE   Borneo   Celebes

CONGO   Kigali   RWANDA   Chagos Arch. (U.K.)   Palembang   Banjarmasin   Moluccas   Papua

CONGO (DEM. REP. OF THE)   Bujumbura   BURUNDI   L. Victoria   Dodoma   Zanzibar   INDONESIA   Ujung   PAPUA NEW GUINEA

Kinshasa   TANZANIA   Dar es Salaam   Amirante Is. (Seychelles)   Aldabra Is. (Seychelles)   JAKARTA   Bandung   Java   Surabaya   Pandang   Dili   EAST TIMOR   Port Moresby

ANGOLA   L. Tanganyika   MALAWI   L. Malawi   COMOROS   Mayotte   Cargados Carajos (Mauritius)   Timor   *Arafura Sea*   C. York

ZAMBIA   Lubumbashi   Lilongwe   MADAGASCAR   Antananarivo   MAURITIUS   Rodriguez (Mauritius)   Darwin

NAMIBIA   Lusaka   Harare   ZIMBABWE   RÉUNION (Fr.)   Cairns

BOTSWANA   Bulawayo   MOZAMBIQUE   Mozambique Channel   Port Hedland   AUSTRALIA   Townsville

Windhoek   Gaborone   Pretoria (Tshwane)   Maputo   SWAZ.   Alice Springs   Rockhampton

Johannesburg   SOUTH AFRICA   LES.   Durban (eThekwini)   Geraldton   Kalgoorlie-Boulder   Brisbane

Cape Town   C. of Good Hope   Port Elizabeth   Prince Edward Is. (S. African)   Crozet Is. (Fr.)   Perth   Fremantle   *Great Australian Bight*   Adelaide   Newcastle   Sydney   Norfolk I. (Austral.)

INDIAN OCEAN

Amsterdam I. (Fr.)   St. Paul I. (Fr.)   Kerguelen (Fr.)   McDonald Is. (Austral.)   Heard I. (Austral.)   Melbourne   Canberra   *Tasman Sea*   Auckland   North I.

Tasmania   Hobart   NEW ZEALAND   Wellington   Christchurch   Chatham Is. (N.Z.)   South I.   Dunedin

PACIFIC OCEAN

Midway Is. (U.S.A.)   Tropic of Cancer   Bonin Is. (Japan)   Volcano Is. (Japan)

International Date Line

NORTHERN MARIANAS   GUAM (U.S.A.)   MARSHALL IS.   Yap   Caroline Is.   Truk   Pohnpei   FED. STATES OF MICRONESIA   PALAU   Equator   Gilbert Is.   KIRIBATI

NAURU   Phoenix Is.   New Ireland   New Britain   SOLOMON IS.   TUVALU   Tokelau (N.Z.)   Honiara   Santa Cruz Is.   Wallis & Futuna Is. (Fr.)   SAMOA

VANUATU   Port Vila   NEW CALEDONIA (Fr.)   FIJI   Suva   TONGA

Tropic of Capricorn   Kermadec Is. (N.Z.)

Auckland Is. (N.Z.)   Bounty Is. (N.Z.)   Antipodes Is. (N.Z.)   Macquarie I. (Austral.)   Campbell I. (N.Z.)

SOUTHERN OCEAN

Antarctic Circle   *Ross Sea*

ctica

East from Greenwich

Depth/height scale (ft / m):

ft	m
0	0
600	200
6 000	2000
12 000	4000
15 000	5000
18 000	6000
24 000	8000

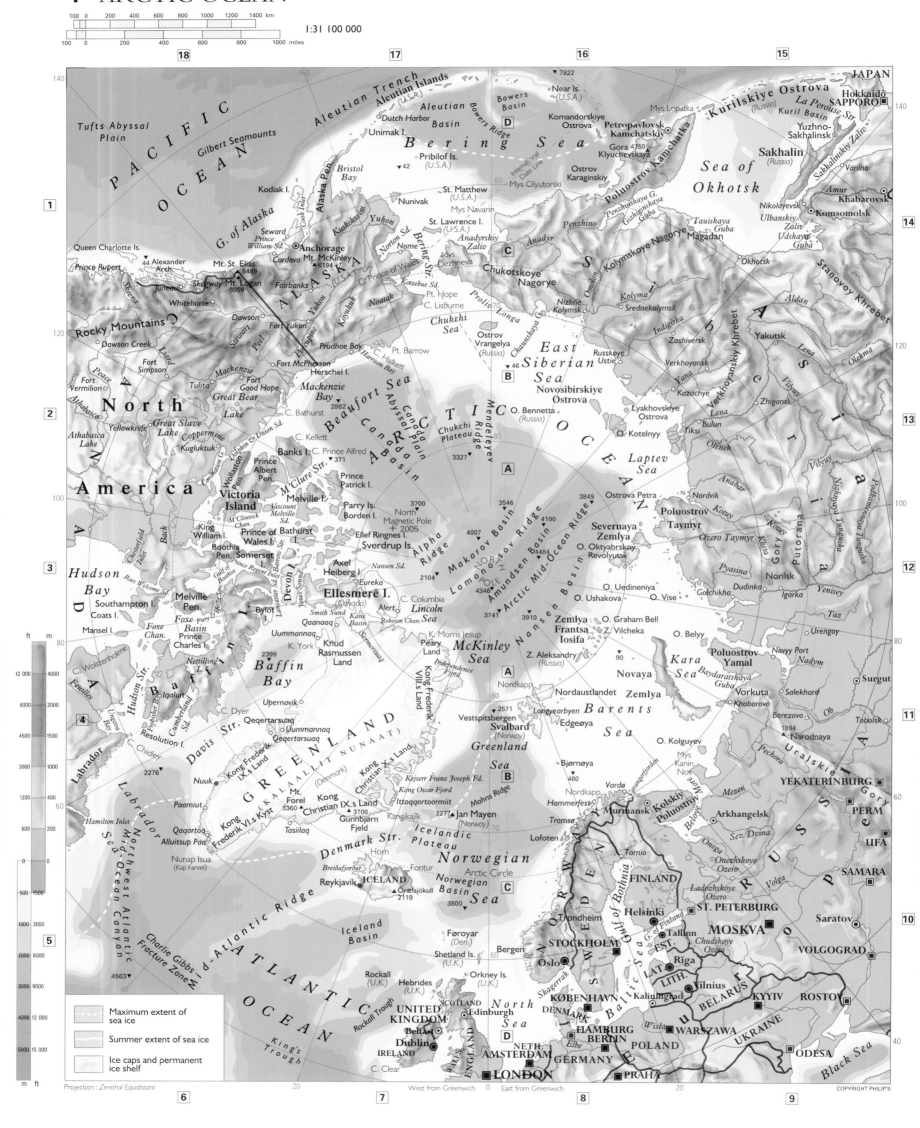

100 0 200 400 600 800 1000 1200 1400 km

1:31 100 000

100 0 200 400 600 800 1000 miles

Maximum extent of sea ice

Summer extent of sea ice

Ice caps and permanent ice shelf

Projection: Zenithal Equidistant

West from Greenwich   East from Greenwich

COPYRIGHT PHILIP'S

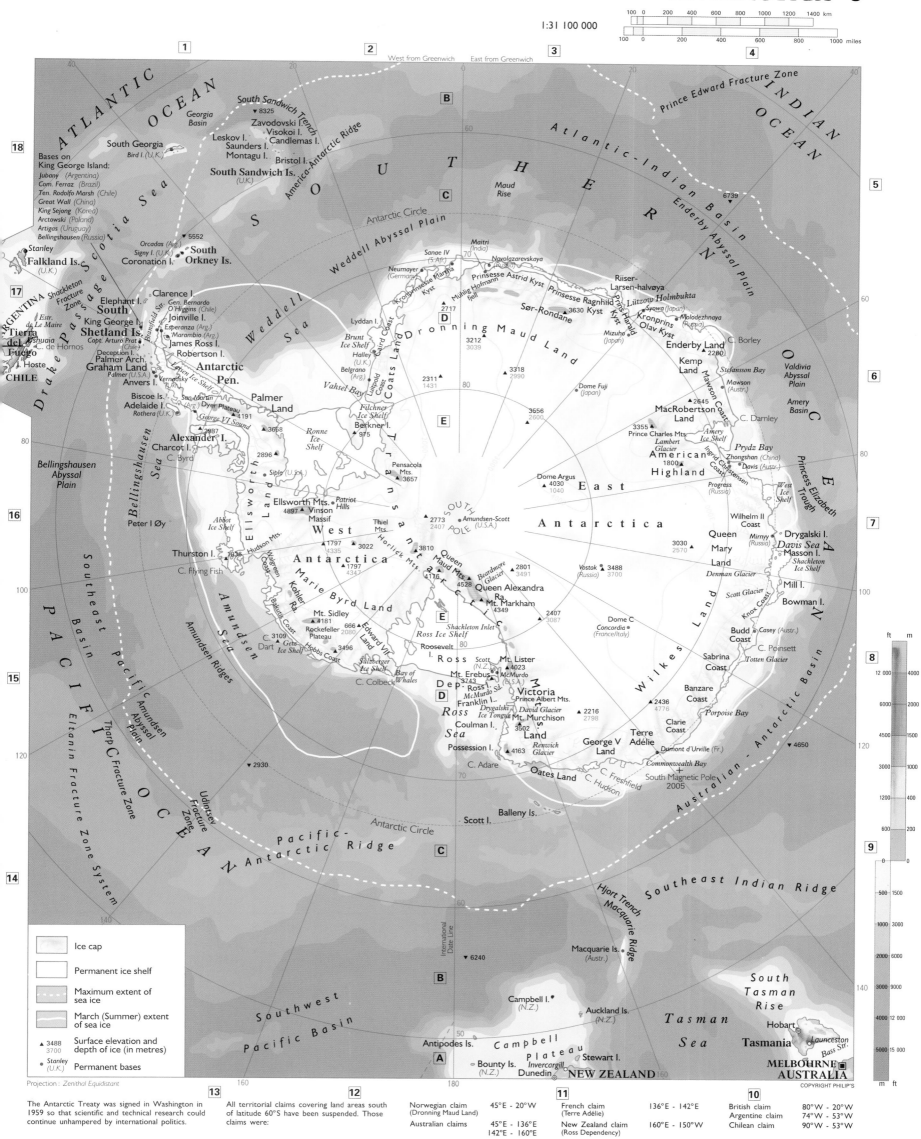

1:31 100 000

100 0 200 400 600 800 1000 1200 1400 km

100 0 200 400 600 800 1000 miles

West from Greenwich   East from Greenwich

ATLANTIC OCEAN

Prince Edward Fracture Zone

INDIAN OCEAN

Georgia Basin

South Sandwich Trench

Zavodovski I.
Visokoi I.
Candlemas I.
Bristol I.

South Sandwich Is. (U.K.)

Leskov I.
Saunders I.
Montagu I.

▼8325

South Georgia
Bird I. (U.K.)

Bases on King George Island:
Jubany (Argentina)
Com. Ferraz (Brazil)
Ten. Rodolfo Marsh (Chile)
Great Wall (China)
King Sejong (Korea)
Arctowski (Poland)
Artigas (Uruguay)
Bellingshausen (Russia)

Atlantic-Antarctic Ridge

America-Antarctic Ridge

Atlantic-Indian Basin

Enderby Abyssal Plain

Maud Rise

6739

Antarctic Circle

SOUTHERN

Weddell Abyssal Plain

Sanae IV (S.Afr.)
Maitri (India)
Novolazarevskaya (Russia)

Neumayer (Germany)
Kronprinsesse Märtha Kyst

Prinsesse Astrid Kyst

Prinsesse Ragnhild Kyst

Riiser-Larsen-halvøya

Lützow Holmbukta

Orcadas (Arg.)
Signy I. (U.K.)
Coronation I.
South Orkney Is.

▼5552

Muhlig Hofmann fjell

Sør-Rondane

3630 Kyst

Prins Harald Kyst

Kronprins Olav Kyst

Syowa (Japan)

Molodezhnaya (Russia)

C. Borley

Clarence I.

Weddell Sea

Lyddan I.

Dronning Maud Land

2717

Mizuho (Japan)

Enderby Land

Kemp Land

2280

Elephant I.
Gen. Bernardo O'Higgins (Chile)
King George I.
Shetland Is.
Joinville I.
Esperanza (Arg.)
Marambio (Arg.)
Capt. Arturo Prat (Chile)
James Ross I.
Robertson I.

Antarctic Pen.

Brunt Ice Shelf
Halley (U.K.)
Belgrano (Arg.)

Coats Land

Caird Coast

3212
3039

Dome Fuji (Japan)

3318
2990

Stefansson Bay

Mawson (Austr.)

2645

Valdivia Abyssal Plain

Deception I.
Palmer Arch.
Graham Land
Palmer (U.S.A.)
Anvers I.
Vernadsky (U.K.)

Larsen Ice Shelf

San Martin (Arg.)

Vahsel Bay

Filchner Ice Shelf

Berkner I.

Luitpold Coast

2311
1431

3656
2600

MacRobertson Land

Prince Charles Mts.

3355
2600

Amery Ice Shelf

C. Darnley

Amery Basin

Biscoe Is.
Adelaide I.
Rothera (U.K.)

Dyer Plateau
George VI Sound
4191

3658

Ronne Ice Shelf

975

Lambert Glacier

American Highland

1800

Prydz Bay
Zhongshan (China)
Davis (Austr.)

Alexander I.
Charcot I.
C. Byrd

2987

2896

Dome Argus
4030
1040

East

Ingrid Christensen Coast

Progress (Russia)

West Ice Shelf

Princess Elizabeth

Bellingshausen Abyssal Plain

Siple (U.S.A.)

Pensacola Mts.
3657

Antarctica

Wilhelm II Coast

Peter I Øy

Ellsworth Land

Ellsworth Mts.
4897 Vinson Massif

Patriot Hills

Thiel Mts.

SOUTH POLE
Amundsen-Scott (U.S.A.)
2773
2407

3810

Vostok (Russia)
3488
3700

3030
2570

Queen Mary Land

Mirnyy (Russia)

Drygalski I.

Davis Sea
Masson I.
Shackleton Ice Shelf

Thurston I.
1936

Hudson Mts.

1797
4335

3022

West Antarctica

Horlick Mts.
1797
4347

Queen Maud Mts.

4116

Denman Glacier

Scott Glacier

Mill I.

C. Flying Fish

Marie Byrd Land

Kohler Ra.

2801
3491

Beardmore Glacier

4528

Queen Alexandra Ra.

Dome C
Concordia (France/Italy)

2407
3087

Knox Coast

Bowman I.

Mt. Sidley
4181

Rockefeller Plateau

666
2080

Edward VII Land

Queen Elizabeth Ra.

Mt. Markham
4349

Budd Coast

Casey (Austr.)

C. Poinsett

Amundsen Sea

Bakutis Coast

Getz Ice Shelf

3109
Dart

3496

Hobbs Coast

Roosevelt I.

Ross Ice Shelf

Shackleton Inlet

Sabrina Coast

Totten Glacier

Amundsen Ridges

Walgreen Coast

Saltzberger Ice Shelf

C. Colbeck

Bay of Whales

Ross Sea

Ross Dep.

Scott (N.Z.)
McMurdo (U.S.A.)
McMurdo Sd.
Franklin I.

Mt. Lister
4023
Mt. Erebus
3743

Victoria

Prince Albert Mts.

Drygalski Ice Tongue
Mt. Murchison

Banzare Coast

2436
4776

Clarie Coast

Porpoise Bay

Terre Adélie

Dumont d'Urville (Fr.)

▼4650

2930

Pacific-Antarctic Ridge

Coulman I.

3502

David Glacier
2216
2798

Renwick Glacier

George V Land

Possession I.

Victoria Land

Oates Land

C. Freshfield

Commonwealth Bay
South Magnetic Pole 2005
C. Hudson

Australian-Antarctic Basin

Southeast Pacific Basin

Eltanin Fracture Zone System

Tharp Fracture Zone

Udintsev Fracture Zone

4163

C. Adare

Balleny Is.

Scott I.

Antarctic Circle

Hjort Trench
Macquarie Ridge

Southeast Indian Ridge

International Date Line

6240

Macquarie Is. (Austr.)

South Tasman Rise

Southwest Pacific Basin

Campbell I. (N.Z.)

Auckland Is. (N.Z.)

Tasman Sea

Hobart

Launceston

Bass Str.

Tasmania

MELBOURNE
AUSTRALIA

COPYRIGHT PHILIP'S

Antipodes Is.
Bounty Is. (N.Z.)
Campbell Plateau
Invercargill
Dunedin
Stewart I.
NEW ZEALAND

ATLANTIC OCEAN

Scotia Sea

Stanley
Falkland Is. (U.K.)

ARGENTINA

Tierra del Fuego

CHILE

Shackleton Fracture Zone

Drake Passage

Estr. de Le Maire
Ushuaia
C. de Hornos
I. Hoste

South Shetland Is.

Bransfield Str.

Palmer Land

PACIFIC OCEAN

ft   m
12 000 4000
9000   3000
6000   2000
4500   1500
3000   1000
1200   400
600   200
0   0
500   1500
1000
2000 6000
3000 9000
4000 12 000
5000 15 000
m   ft

Legend:
- Ice cap
- Permanent ice shelf
- Maximum extent of sea ice
- March (Summer) extent of sea ice
- ▲3488 / 3700 Surface elevation and depth of ice (in metres)
- • Stanley (U.K.) Permanent bases

Projection: Zenithal Equidistant

The Antarctic Treaty was signed in Washington in 1959 so that scientific and technical research could continue unhampered by international politics.

All territorial claims covering land areas south of latitude 60°S have been suspended. Those claims were:

Norwegian claim (Dronning Maud Land)	45°E - 20°W
Australian claims	45°E - 136°E
	142°E - 160°E
French claim (Terre Adélie)	136°E - 142°E
New Zealand claim (Ross Dependency)	160°E - 150°W
British claim	80°W - 20°W
Argentine claim	74°W - 53°W
Chilean claim	90°W - 53°W

1:17 800 000

Projection: Bonne

COPYRIGHT PHILIP'S

1:17 800 000

ICELAND
on same scale

FÆROE
ISLANDS
on same scale

1:5 300

12 IRELAND

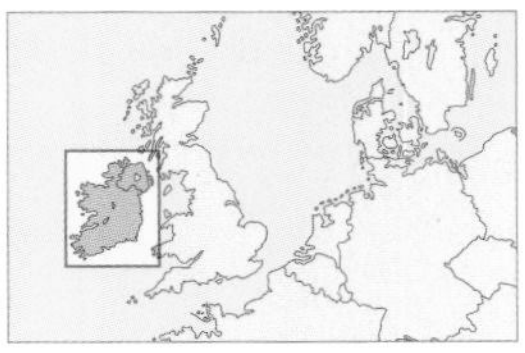

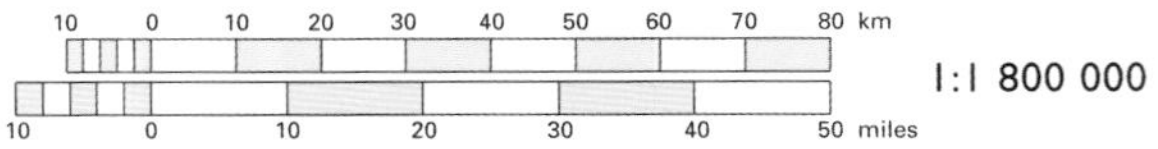

1:1 800 000

10 0 10 20 30 40 50 60 70 80 km
10 0 10 20 30 40 50 miles

ATLANTIC OCEAN

NORTH CHANNEL

IRISH SEA

CELTIC SEA

St. George's Channel

NORTHERN IRELAND

IRELAND

Ulster

Connacht

Leinster

Munster

Londonderry · Belfast · Dublin · Cork · Limerick · Galway · Waterford · Sligo · Dundalk · Drogheda

Donegal · Tyrone · Antrim · Down · Armagh · Fermanagh · Monaghan · Cavan · Leitrim · Sligo · Mayo · Roscommon · Longford · Westmeath · Meath · Louth · Kildare · Offaly · Laois · Wicklow · Carlow · Kilkenny · Wexford · Tipperary · Clare · Galway · Kerry · Cork · Waterford · Limerick

National Parks

Projection : Lambert's Conformal Conic

COPYRIGHT PHILIP'S

West from Greenwich

1:1 800 000

10 0 10 20 30 40 50 60 70 80 km
10 0 10 20 30 40 50 miles

Key to Scottish unitary authorities on map

1 CITY OF ABERDEEN
2 DUNDEE CITY
3 WEST DUNBARTONSHIRE
4 EAST DUNBARTONSHIRE
5 CITY OF GLASGOW
6 INVERCLYDE
7 RENFREWSHIRE
8 EAST RENFREWSHIRE
9 NORTH LANARKSHIRE
10 FALKIRK
11 CLACKMANNANSHIRE
12 WEST LOTHIAN
13 CITY OF EDINBURGH
14 MIDLOTHIAN

ORKNEY IS.
on same scale

ORKNEY

SHETLAND IS.
on same scale

SHETLAND

NORTH SEA

ATLANTIC OCEAN

SCOTLAND

WESTERN ISLES

NORTH CHANNEL

NORTHERN IRELAND

ENGLAND

Projection : Lambert's Conformal Conic

West from Greenwich

COPYRIGHT PHILIP'S

National Parks and Forest Parks in Scotland

1:1 800 000

Key to English unitary authorities on map

25 HARTLEPOOL
26 DARLINGTON
27 STOCKTON-ON-TEES
28 MIDDLESBROUGH
29 REDCAR AND CLEVELAND
30 BLACKPOOL
31 BLACKBURN WITH DARWEN
32 HALTON
33 WARRINGTON
34 KINGSTON UPON HULL
35 NORTH EAST LINCOLNSHIRE
36 STOKE-ON-TRENT
37 TELFORD AND WREKIN
38 DERBY CITY
39 CITY OF NOTTINGHAM
40 LEICESTER CITY
41 RUTLAND
42 PETERBOROUGH
43 MILTON KEYNES
44 LUTON
45 NORTH SOMERSET
46 CITY OF BRISTOL
47 BATH AND NORTH EAST SOMERSET
48 SWINDON
49 READING
50 WOKINGHAM
51 WINDSOR AND MAIDENHEAD
52 SLOUGH
53 BRACKNELL FOREST
54 THURROCK
55 SOUTHEND-ON-SEA
56 MEDWAY
57 PLYMOUTH
58 TORBAY
59 POOLE
60 BOURNEMOUTH
61 SOUTHAMPTON
62 PORTSMOUTH
63 BRIGHTON AND HOVE

Key to Welsh unitary authorities on map

15 SWANSEA
16 NEATH PORT TALBOT
17 BRIDGEND
18 RHONDDA CYNON TAFF
19 MERTHYR TYDFIL
20 CAERPHILLY
21 BLAENAU GWENT
22 TORFAEN
23 CARDIFF
24 NEWPORT

NORTH SEA

IRISH SEA

North Channel

SCOTLAND

NORTHERN IRELAND

ISLE OF MAN

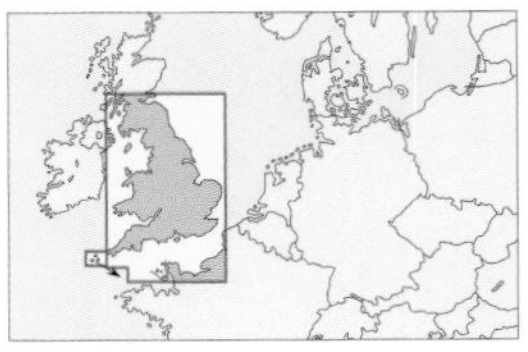

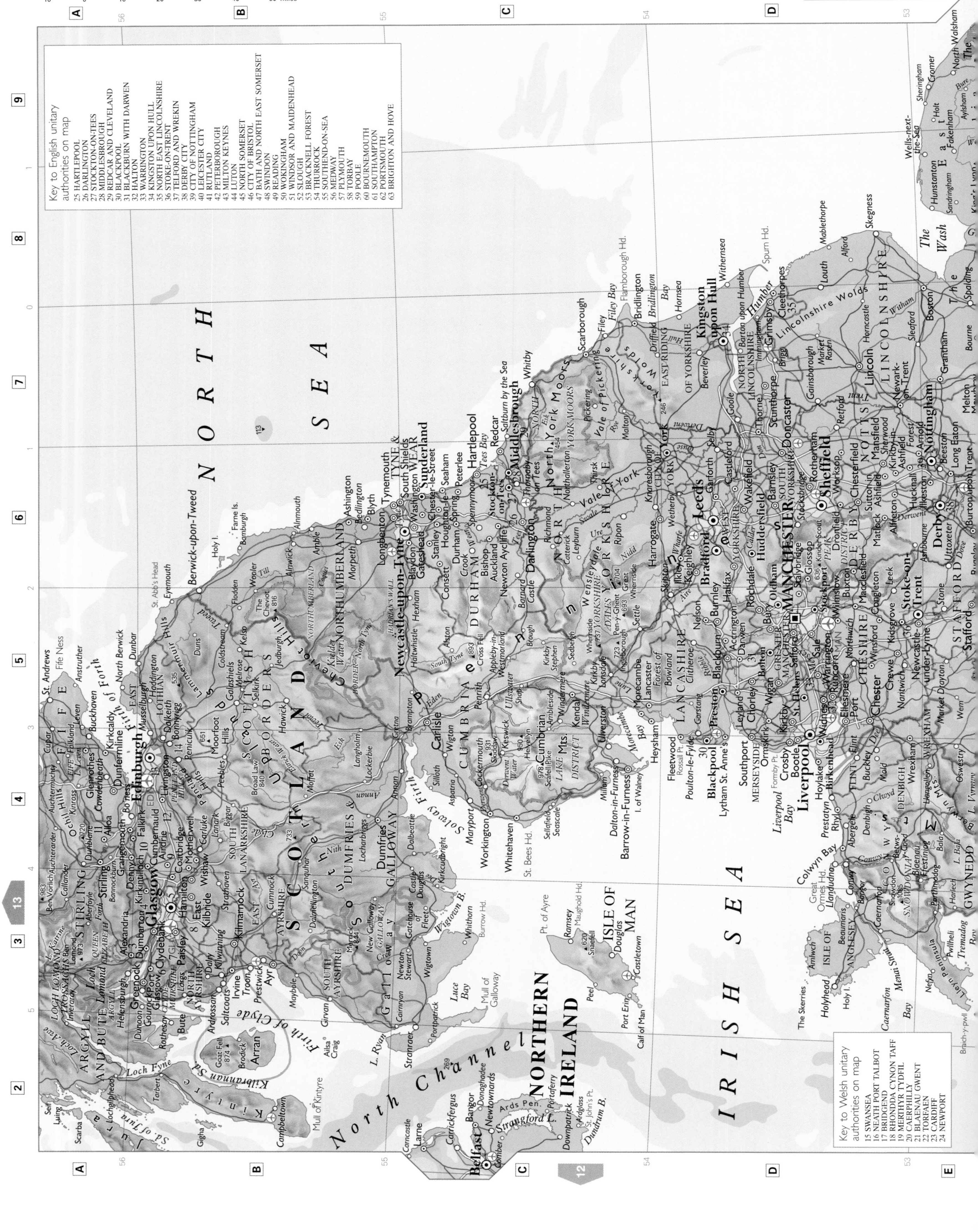

E N G L A N D

W A L E S

F R A N C E

N O R M A N D I E

HAUTE-NORMANDIE

SEINE-MARITIME

CALVADOS

MANCHE

E N G L I S H   C H A N N E L

Bristol Channel

Cardigan Bay

Strait of Dover

Lyme Bay

Baie de la Seine

Baie de la Somme

LONDON
BIRMINGHAM
BRISTOL
Cardiff
Swansea
Southampton
Portsmouth
Bournemouth
Brighton
Plymouth
Le Havre
Rouen
Dieppe
Calais
Boulogne-sur-Mer
Cherbourg
Caen
Bayeux

NORFOLK
SUFFOLK
ESSEX
KENT
EAST SUSSEX
WEST SUSSEX
SURREY
HANTS
BERKSHIRE
WILTSHIRE
DORSET
DEVON
CORNWALL
SOMERSET
GLOUCS
HEREFORD
SHROPSHIRE
POWYS
CEREDIGION
PEMBROKESHIRE
CARMARTHENSHIRE
GLAMORGAN
VALE OF GLAMORGAN
GWENT
WARWICK
OXFORD
BUCKS
HERTS
CAMBRIDGE
BEDFORD
NORTHAMPTON

ISLE OF WIGHT
Newport
Ryde
Cowes

CHANNEL ISLANDS (U.K.)
Jersey · St. Helier
Guernsey · St. Peter Port
Alderney
Sark
Herm

ISLES OF SCILLY
on same scale
Isles of Scilly
St. Mary's
Tresco

Projection: Lambert's Conformal Conic

COPYRIGHT PHILIP'S

East from Greenwich
West from Greenwich

National Parks in England and Wales
Forest Parks in Scotland

ft   m
3000 1000
1500 500
600   200
300   100
0   0
        150
        300
        600
m ft

50   0   25   50   75   100   125   150   175 km
50   0   25   50   75   100   125 miles

1:4 400 000

1 **2** **3** **4** **5** **6** **7** **8** **9**

A ATLANTIC OCEAN Shetland Is. Yell Unst Fetlar Askøyna Bergen

Osøyro

B Orkney Is. Westray Sanday Stronsay Mainland Foula Lerwick NORWA
Mainland Hoy Kirkwall South Ronaldsay Fair Isle Stord Bømlo Haugesund
Pentland Firth Kopervik Åkrahamn Boknafo
C. Wrath Thurso Wick Stavange
Sandnes Bryne Nærbø

C Lewis Stornoway North West Highlands Helmsdale NORTH
Outer Hebrides Harris North Minch Lairg Golspie
St. Kilda Ullapool Tain Moray Firth Buckie Fraserburgh SEA
North Uist 789 Skye Invergordon Inverness Nairn Elgin Banff Peterhead
Benbecula 1182 L. Ness Aviemore CAIRNGORMS Don Huntly Inverurie
South Uist Portree Glen More SCOTLAND Mts. Aberdeen
Barra Rhum Fort William Ben Nevis 1311 Dee Ballater Stonehaven
Eigg 1342 Grampian Forfar Arbroath 238
Coll Tobermory 1214 Tay Montrose

D Mull Oban L. Awe Perth Dundee N. York Moors
Colonsay Tiree L. Lomond Stirling St. Andrews Berwick-upon-Tweed
Jura L. Fyne 973 Dunfermline Glenrothes Southern Uplands Galashiels
Islay Greenock Glasgow Edinburgh 816 Hawick 840 Cheviot Hills Alnwick
Paisley Motherwell Hamilton Jedburgh NORTHUMBERLAND
Campbeltown East Kilbride Kilmarnock Dumfries Hexham Newcastle-upon-Tyne
Arran Irvine Ayr Kirkcudbright Annan Carlisle Gateshead South Shields Sunderland
Malin Hd. Girvan Stranraer Workington 893 Durham Hartlepool Redcar
Buncrana Coleraine Larne Mull of Galloway Whitehaven Cumbrian Darlington Middlesbrough
Aran I. Letterkenny Ballymena Bangor 978 LAKE Stockton-on-Tees Scarborough
GLENVEAGH Londonderry NORTHERN IRELAND Belfast Barrow-in-Furness DISTRICT YORKSHIRE Bridlington
Donegal Omagh Lough Neagh Portadown Lisburn Lurgan Douglas I. of Man Lancaster DALES

E Bundoran Enniskillen Clones Armagh Newry Harrogate York Beverley
Lower L. Erne Cavan Castleblaney Dundalk Blackpool Keighley Leeds Kingston upon Hull
Sligo Leitrim Ceanannus Mor Drogheda Preston Burnley Bradford Huddersfield Barnsley Scunthorpe Grimsby
Ballina L. Corn Longford Boyne Blackburn Halifax Bolton Oldham 636 Doncaster Humber Louth
Achill I. Castlebar Roscommon Lough Ree Mullingar MANCHESTER Rotherham Lincoln
Westport Athlone IRISH Liverpool Warrington Stockport Sheffield
Lough Mask Connemara Lough Corrib Ballinasloe Anglesey Colwyn Bay Chester Chesterfield Mansfield Skegness
Galway B. Galway SEA Holyhead Bangor 926 Wrexham Crewe PEAK Boston The Wash
Aran Is. BURREN Lough Derg Tullamore Dublin Snowdon Stoke- DISTRICT Nottingham Cromer

F Ennis Nenagh Thurles Port Laoise Athy Dun Laoghaire SNOWDONIA Pwllheli on-Trent Derby Grantham King's Lynn THE Great Yarmouth
Limerick Kilkenny Carlow Bray Cardigan Shrewsbury Telford Stafford Trent Leicester Norwich BROADS Lowestoft
Kilrush Tipperary Carrick-on-Suir Wexford Mts. Welshpool Nuneaton Corby Peterborough Thetford
Listowel Clonmel Rosslare Cardigan Aberystwyth Cambrian Mts. Wolverhampton Coventry Rugby Northampton Ely Bury St. Edmunds
Tralee 953 Mallow Waterford Bay BIRMINGHAM Redditch Royal Bedford Cambridge Ipswich
Dingle Killarney Blackwater Dungarvan WALES 886 Worcester Leamington Spa Milton Keynes Felixstowe Harwich
Carrantoohill 1041 Fishguard Brecon Hereford Cheltenham Gloucester Stevenage Colchester
Valencia I. Kinsale 99 Haverfordwest Carmarthen BRECON Cwmbran Oxford Hemel Luton Harlow Chelmsford
Bantry Milford Haven Merthyr Tydfil BEACONS Newport Hempstead Watford Basildon
Bandon PEMBROKESHIRE Pembroke Llanelli Neath Rhondda Bristol Swindon High Wycombe Slough LONDON Southend-on-Sea
C. Clear COAST Swansea Port Talbot Cardiff Bath Newbury Reading Margate 36

G CELTIC Bristol Channel Barry Weston-super-Mare Salisbury Basingstoke Guildford Reigate Chatham Canterbury Dover
SEA EXMOOR Exmoor Taunton Yeovil Winchester Crawley Ashford Folkestone
Barnstaple 618 Southampton Fareham Havant Brighton Hastings Eastbourne
Bude DARTMOOR Dartmoor Exmouth Bournemouth NEW Portsmouth Worthing
Newquay Torquay Weymouth Poole FOREST Isle of Wight Newport
Truro St. Austell Plymouth English Channel
Land's End Penzance Falmouth
Isles of Scilly

Projection: Conical with two standard parallels

West from Greenwich   East from Greenwich

COPYRIGHT PHILIP'S

18 **19**

C. de la Hague Pte. de Barfleur Fécamp FRANCE
Alderney Cherbourg Valognes Le Havre Rouen
Guernsey St. Peter Port Sark Bayeux Trouville-sur-Mer Rolbec Seine Elbeuf
Channel Is. St. Helier Jersey Corentin Lisieux Caen Elbeuf
(U.K.)

NETHERLAND
's-Gravenhage (Den Haag) Hoek van Holland ROTTERDAM Dordrec
Haarlem Alkma Den Helde Tex

BELGIUM Brussel (Bruxelles) Antwerpe Brugge Gent Mechele
Zeebrugge Oostende Vlissingen
Dunkerque Calais St-Omer Béthune Lille Tourcoing Roubaix Tournai
Boulogne-sur-Mer Bruay-la- Buissiere Valenciennes Cambrai
Le Touquet-Paris-Plage 33 Abbeville Picardie Amiens St. Quentin
Le Tréport Dieppe Pays de Caux Laon

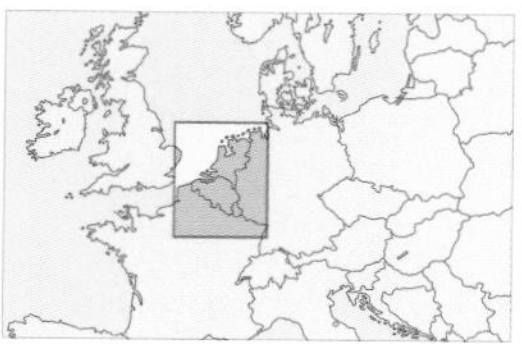

1:2 200 000

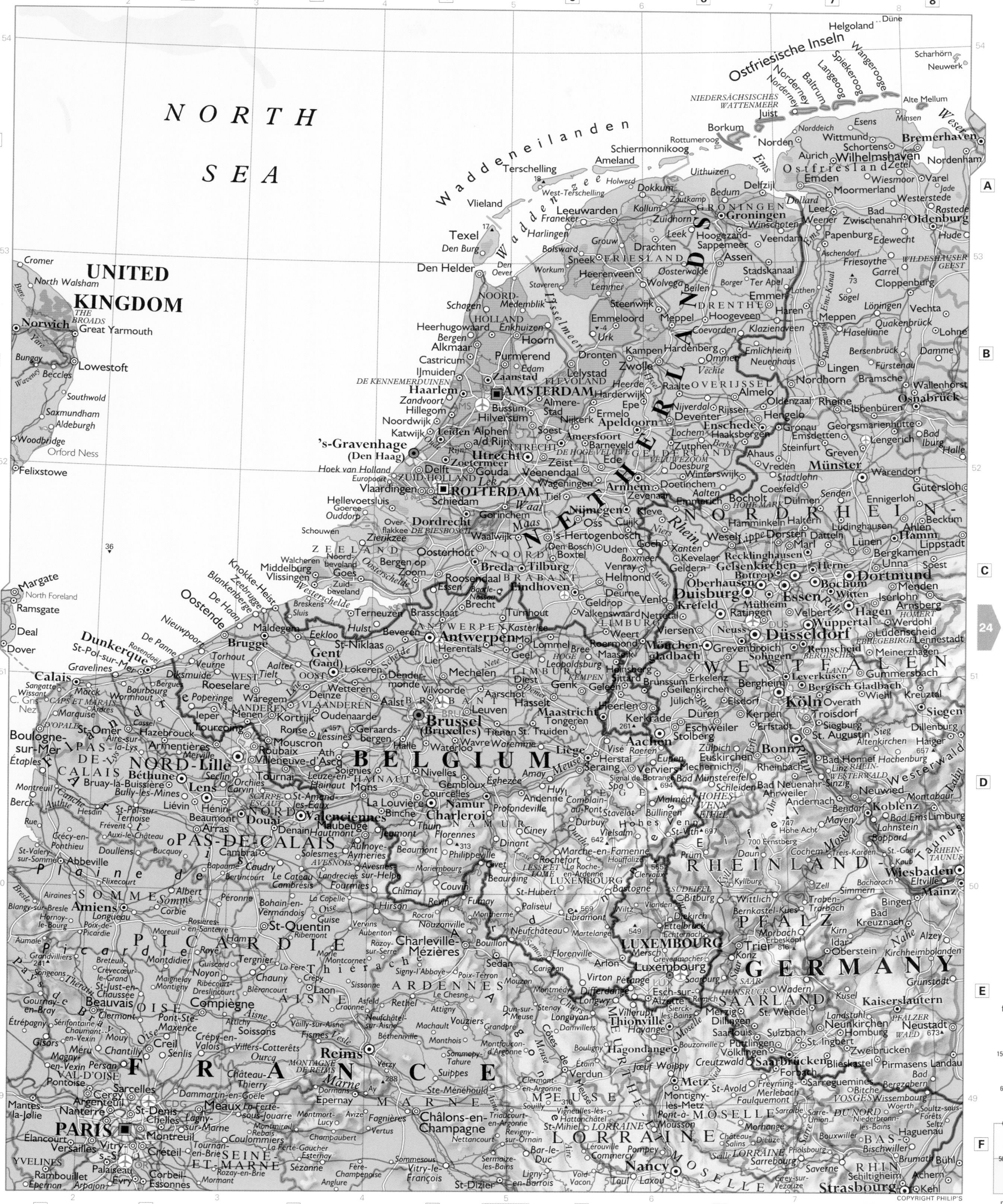

NORTH SEA

UNITED KINGDOM

NETHERLANDS

BELGIUM

GERMANY

FRANCE

LUXEMBOURG

National Parks

Underlined towns give their name to the administrative area in which they stand.

COPYRIGHT PHILIP'S

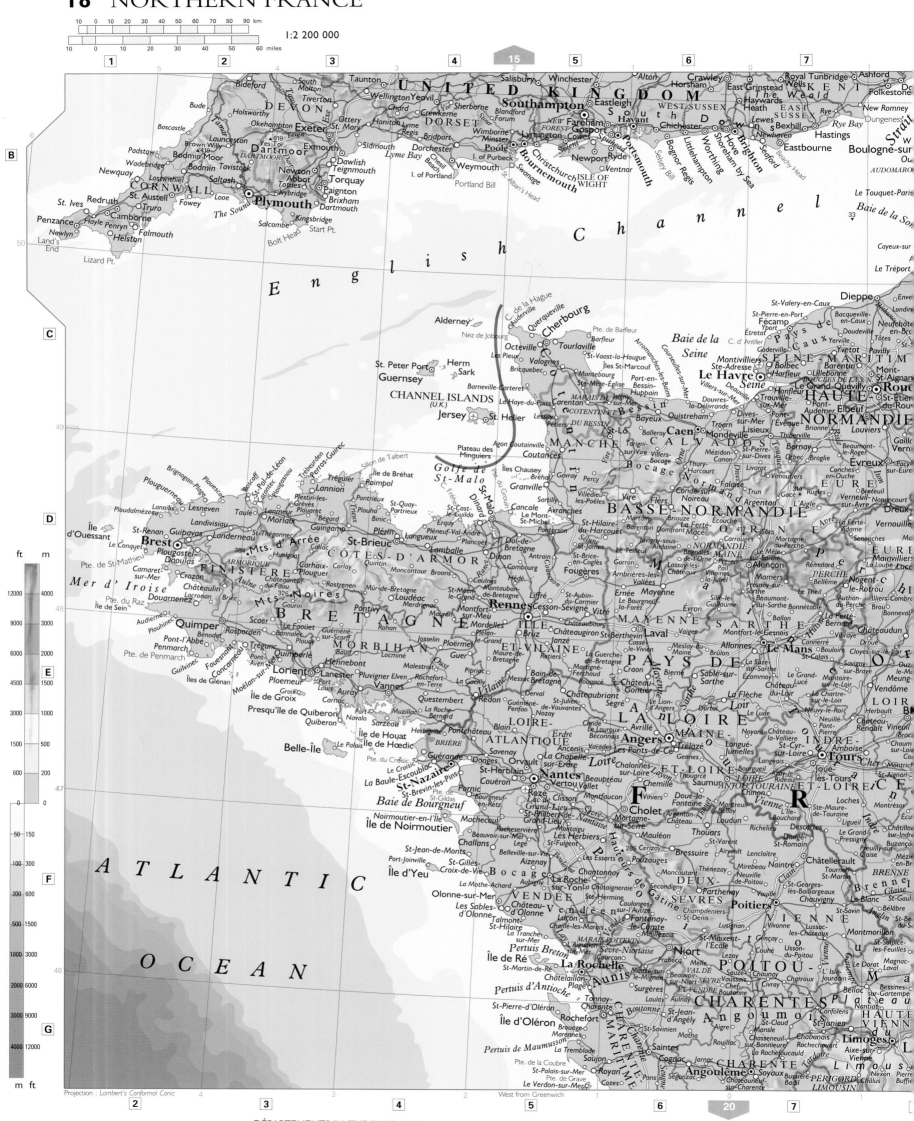

10 0 10 20 30 40 50 60 70 80 90 km

1:2 200 000

10 0 10 20 30 40 50 60 miles

| 1 | 2 | 3 | 4 | 15 | 5 | 6 | 7 |

B

C

D

E

F

G

UNITED KINGDOM

Bideford Taunton Winchester Alton Crawley East Grinstead Royal Tunbridge Wells Ashford
South Molton Yeovil Sherborne Salisbury Southampton Eastleigh Horsham Haywards Heath The Weald KENT Folkestone
Bude Wellington Crewkerne Blandford Forum WEST SUSSEX Lewes EAST SUSSEX Rye New Romney
Boscastle Holsworthy Tiverton Ottery St. Mary Honiton Lyme Regis Bournemouth Fareham Gosport Havant Chichester Bognor Regis Worthing Shoreham-by-Sea Newhaven Bexhill Hastings Boulogne-sur-
Padstow Okehampton Exeter Sidmouth Dorchester Bridport Poole I. of Purbeck Lymington Cowes Portsmouth Littlehampton Brighton Seaford Beachy Head Eastbourne AUDOMARO
Newquay Bodmin Moor DARTMOOR Dawlish Teignmouth Weymouth I. of Portland Swanage ISLE OF WIGHT Ryde Selsey Bill Hove Le Touquet-Plage
Wadebridge Bodmin Tavistock Newton Abbot Torquay Paignton Brixham Dartmouth Portland Bill St. Alban's Head Newport Ventnor Le Tréport
St. Ives Redruth Truro Saltash Totnes Kingsbridge Solent Baie de la So
Penzance Camborne Falmouth Plymouth The Sound Salcombe Start Pt. Cayeux-sur-
Newlyn Helston Land's End Lizard Pt. Bolt Head

ENGLISH CHANNEL

CORNWALL DEVON DORSET

Alderney C. de la Hague Cherbourg St-Valery-en-Caux Dieppe
Nez de Jobourg Querqueville Barfleur Fécamp
St. Peter Port Guernsey Herm Sark Octeville Tourlaville Pte. de Barfleur Étretat Le Havre Rouen
CHANNEL ISLANDS (U.K.) Valognes SEINE-MARITIME
Jersey St Helier Carentan Bayeux Caen HAUTE-NORMANDIE Évreux
Coutances MANCHE CALVADOS BASSE-NORMANDIE EURE
Golfe de St-Malo St-Malo Dinard Granville Avranches Le Mont-St-Michel Falaise Argentan L'Aigle
Île de Bréhat Paimpol St-Brieuc Dinan Fougères Domfront Alençon PERCHE
Brest FINISTÈRE Morlaix Lannion CÔTES-D'ARMOR Rennes Mayenne Le Mans SARTHE Châteaudun
Quimper BRETAGNE Pontivy ILLE-ET-VILAINE Laval MAYENNE PAYS DE LA LOIRE Vendôme
MORBIHAN Vannes Redon Angers MAINE-ET-LOIRE Tours
Lorient Auray Belle-Île Nantes LOIRE-ATLANTIQUE Saumur INDRE-ET-LOIRE Loches
St-Nazaire Baie de Bourgneuf Cholet Chinon
Île de Noirmoutier VENDÉE La Roche-sur-Yon DEUX-SÈVRES Poitiers VIENNE Châtellerault
Île d'Yeu Bocage Niort POITOU-CHARENTES Montmorillon
Les Sables-d'Olonne Fontenay-le-Comte
La Rochelle CHARENTE-MARITIME Angoulême CHARENTE Limoges
Île de Ré Rochefort Saintes Cognac LIMOUSIN
Île d'Oléron

ATLANTIC OCEAN

Mer d'Iroise

Projection: Lambert's Conformal Conic

West from Greenwich

| 2 | 3 | 4 | 5 | 6 | 20 | 7 |

DÉPARTEMENTS IN THE PARIS AREA
1 Ville de Paris   3 Val-de-Marne
2 Seine-St-Denis   4 Hauts-de-Seine

ft m
12000 4000
9000 3000
6000 2000
4500 1500
3000 1000
1500 500
600 200
0 0
50 150
100 300
500 1500
1000 3000
2000 6000
3000 9000
4000 12000
m ft

Underlined towns give their name to the
administrative area in which they stand.

National Parks and Regional Nature Parks in France

East from Greenwich

COPYRIGHT PHILIP'S

National Parks and Regional Nature Parks in France

COPYRIGHT PHILIP'S

1:4 400 000

50   0 25 50 75 100 125 150 175 km
50   0   25   50   75   100   125 miles

Countries: UNITED KINGDOM · NETHERLANDS · BELGIUM · LUXEMBOURG · FRANCE · GERMANY · DENMARK · SWITZERLAND · LIECHTENSTEIN · ITALY · AUSTRIA · CZECH · SLOVENIA · CROATIA · MONACO · SAN MARINO

Seas: NORTH SEA · BALTIC SEA · ADRIATIC SEA · Golfo di Génova · Golfo di Venézia

Selected places (north / Germany / Denmark):
Sylt, Westerland, Föhr, Nordfriesische Inseln, Flensburg, Schleswig, Rendsburg, Kiel, Neumünster, Itzehoe, Lübeck, Travemünde, Wismar, Rostock, Stralsund, Greifswald, Rügen, Sassnitz, Kołobrzeg, Koszalin, Białogard, Szczecin, Świnoujście, Wolin, Wolliński, Stettiner Haff, Police, Goleniów, Stargard Szczeciński, Choszczno, Gorzów Wielkopolski, Berlin, Potsdam, Brandenburg, Magdeburg, Hannover, Braunschweig, Wolfsburg, Salzgitter, Hildesheim, Hamburg, Norderstedt, Bremen, Bremerhaven, Cuxhaven, Wilhelmshaven, Emden, Oldenburg, Delmenhorst, Lüneburg, Celle, Helgoland, Deutsche Bucht, Ostfriesische Inseln, Borkum, Norderney

Amsterdam, 's-Gravenhage (Den Haag), Rotterdam, Dordrecht, Utrecht, Arnhem, Nijmegen, Groningen, Leeuwarden, Assen, Zwolle, Deventer, Enschede, Apeldoorn, Haarlem, Alkmaar, Den Helder, Texel, Terschelling, Ameland, Schiermonnikoog

Antwerpen, Brussel (Bruxelles), Gent, Brugge, Oostende, Charleroi, Namur, Liège, Leuven, Mechelen, Maastricht, Hasselt, Mons, Dunkerque, Calais, Lille, Roubaix, Tourcoing, Valenciennes

Norwich, Ipswich, Felixstowe, Harwich, Great Yarmouth, Lowestoft, Cromer, Margate, Dover, Norwich

Köln (Cologne), Bonn, Aachen, Düsseldorf, Essen, Dortmund, Duisburg, Bochum, Wuppertal, Gelsenkirchen, Mönchengladbach, Krefeld, Solingen, Münster, Osnabrück, Bielefeld, Paderborn, Kassel, Göttingen, Halle, Leipzig, Dresden, Chemnitz, Zwickau, Gera, Jena, Erfurt, Weimar, Gotha, Fulda, Frankfurt, Offenbach, Wiesbaden, Mainz, Darmstadt, Mannheim, Ludwigshafen, Heidelberg, Worms, Speyer, Kaiserslautern, Saarbrücken, Trier, Luxembourg, Metz, Nancy, Strasbourg, Karlsruhe, Pforzheim, Stuttgart, Esslingen, Tübingen, Reutlingen, Ulm, Augsburg, München (Munich), Ingolstadt, Regensburg, Nürnberg, Fürth, Erlangen, Würzburg, Bamberg, Bayreuth, Schweinfurt, Coburg, Hof, Plauen

Praha (Prague), Plzeň, České Budějovice, Karlovy Vary, Kladno, Ústí nad Labem, Liberec, Jablonec nad Nisou, Hradec Králové, Pardubice, Jihlava, Cheb, Chomutov, Most, Děčín

Salzburg, Linz, Innsbruck, Wels, Steyr, Wiener Neustadt, Graz, Klagenfurt, Villach, Bruck an der Mur, Leoben, Kapfenberg

Zürich, Bern, Basel, Genève, Lausanne, Luzern, St. Gallen, Winterthur, Chur, Vaduz, Neuchâtel, Fribourg, Thun, Interlaken, Davos, St. Moritz, Bellinzona, Lugano, Locarno

Paris, Reims, Troyes, Dijon, Besançon, Mulhouse, Belfort, Lyon, St-Étienne, Grenoble, Chambéry, Annecy, Valence, Nîmes, Avignon, Arles, Aix-en-Provence, Marseille, Toulon, Nice, Cannes, Monaco, Fréjus

Milano, Torino, Genova, Bologna, Firenze (Florence), Venézia (Venice), Verona, Pádova, Vicenza, Trento, Bolzano, Trieste, Brescia, Bérgamo, Como, Novara, Varese, Piacenza, Parma, Módena, Reggio nell'Emília, Ferrara, Ravenna, Rímini, Forlì, La Spézia, Livorno, Pisa, San Marino

Ljubljana, Maribor, Zagreb, Rijeka, Pula, Karlovac

Physical / mountains: Alpen, Dolomiti, Böhmerwald, Erzgebirge, Sudety, Schwarzwald, Vogesen, Ardenne, Massif Central, Mont Blanc 4808, Grossglockner 3797, Zugspitze 2962, Piz Bernina, Ortles 3899, Mte. Rosa, Gran Paradiso, Matterhorn, Jungfrau, Rhein, Elbe, Donau, Rhône, Weser, Main, Neckar, Mosel, Oder/Odra, Po

COPYRIGHT PHILIP'S

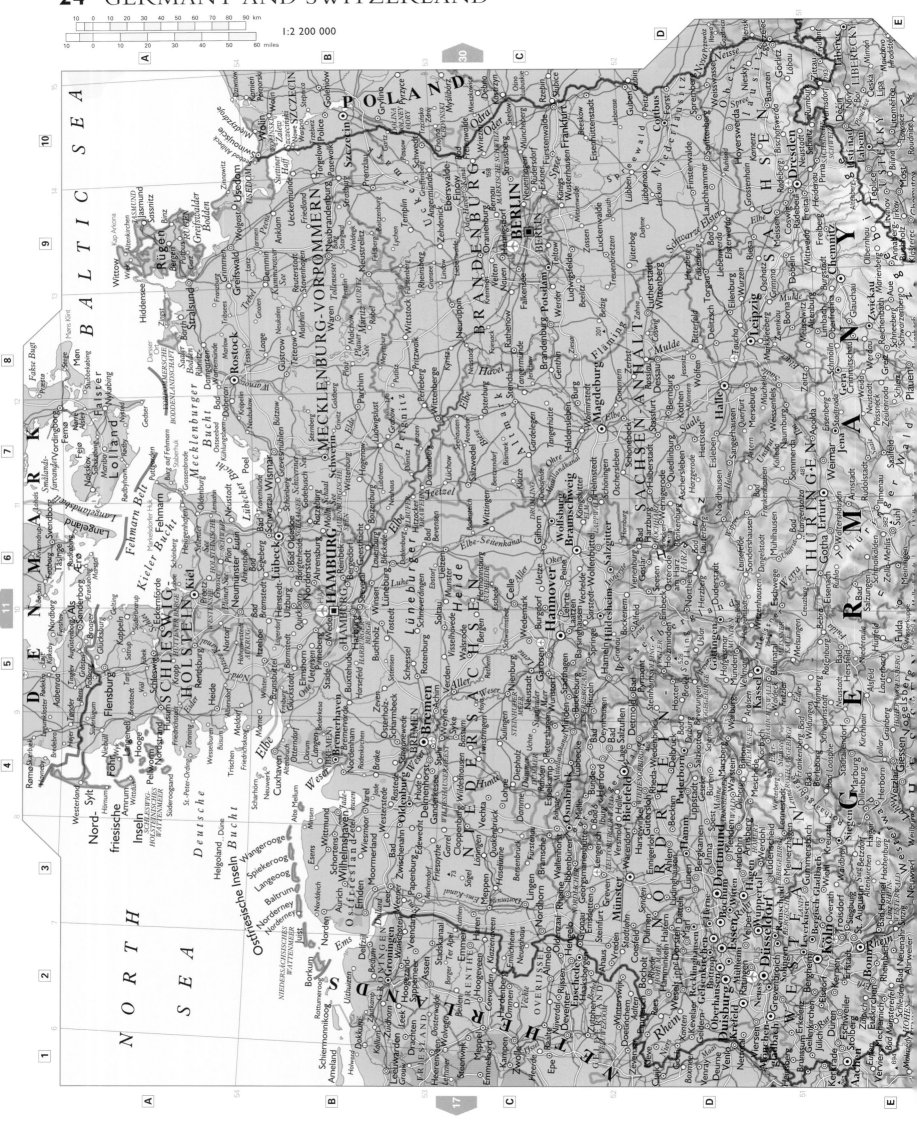

National Parks and Nature Parks in Germany

Underlined towns give their name to the
administrative area in which they stand.

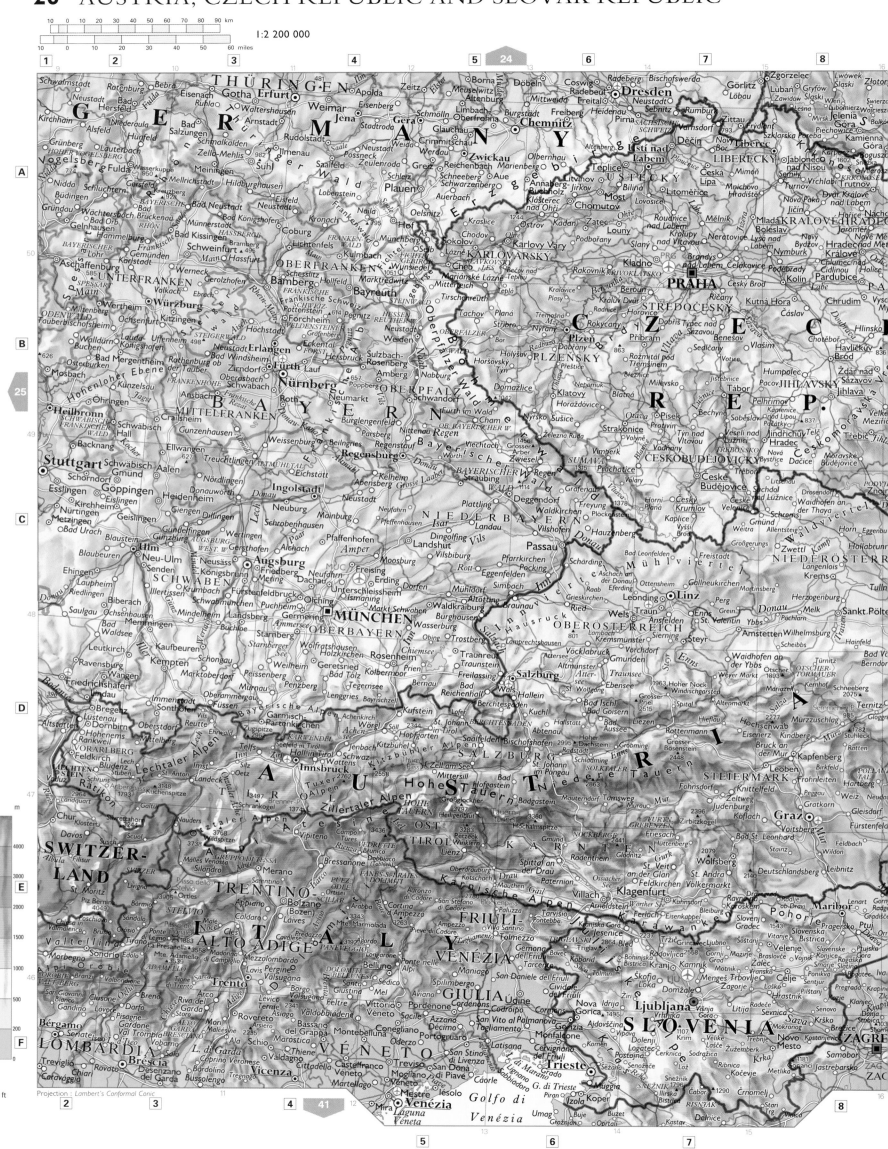

National Parks

East from Greenwich

Underlined towns give their name to the administrative area in which they stand.

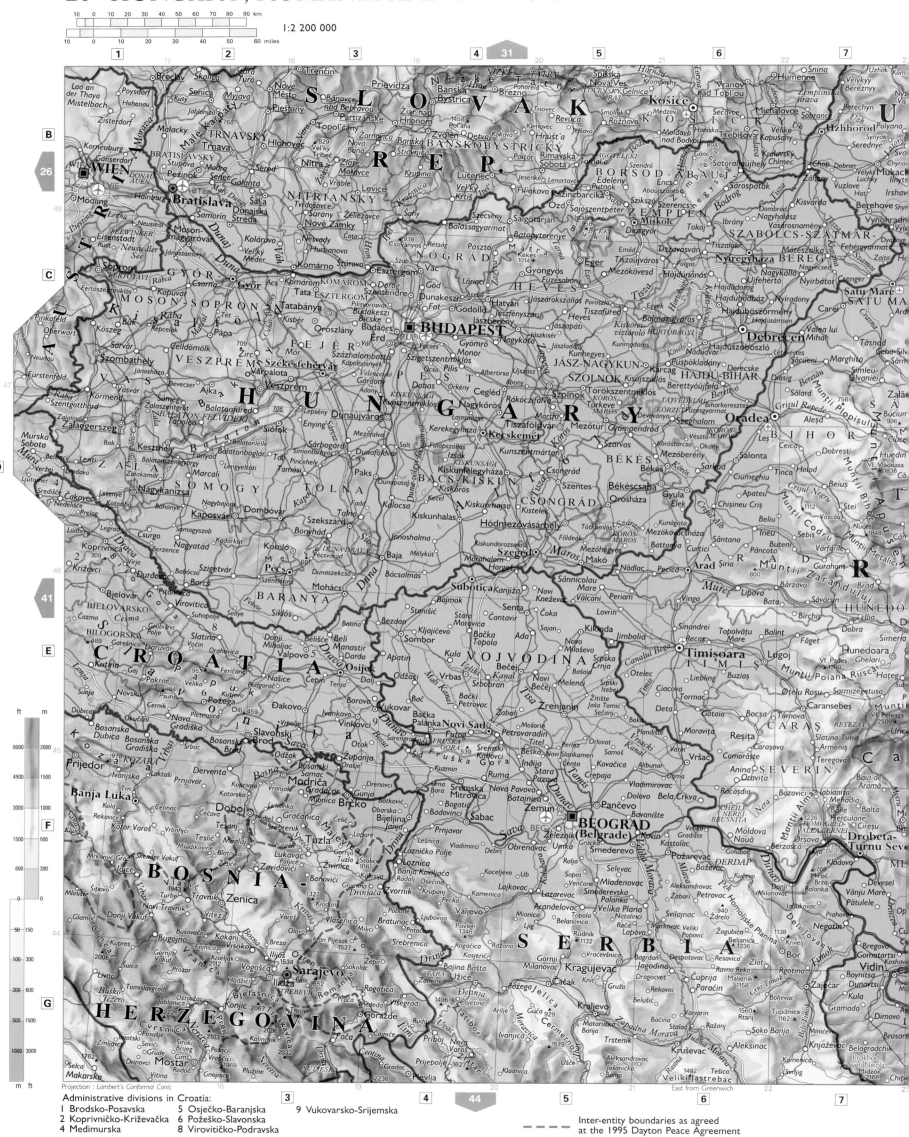

1:2 200 000

Projection : Lambert's Conformal Conic

Administrative divisions in Croatia:
1 Brodsko-Posavska   5 Osječko-Baranjska   9 Vukovarsko-Srijemska
2 Koprivničko-Križevačka   6 Požeško-Slavonska
4 Medimurska   8 Virovitičko-Podravska

Inter-entity boundaries as agreed
at the 1995 Dayton Peace Agreement

National Parks

Underlined towns give their name to the
administrative area in which they stand.

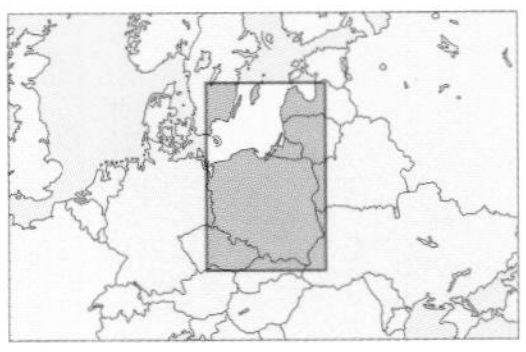

1:2 200 000

10 0 10 20 30 40 50 60 70 80 90 km
10 0 10 20 30 40 50 60 miles

Gulf of Riga

Irbes saurums (Kurų kurk)

LATVIA

LITHUANIA

KALININGRAD (Russia)

Nemunas / Neman

Kuršių Zalio

KURŠIŲ NERIJOS
KURSHSKAYA KOSA

SWEDEN

Gotland (Sweden)

GOTLANDS LÄN

Öland (Sweden)

KALMAR

BLEKINGE LÄN

SMÅLAND

JÖNKÖPINGS LÄN

Bornholm (Denmark)

BORNHOLMS AMT.

Hanöbukten

Bornholmsgattet

B A L T I C   S E A

POMORSKIE

ZACHODNIO-POMORSKIE

WARMIŃSKO-MAZURSKIE

Riga

Jūrmala

Jelgava

JELGAVA

Šiauliai

Kaunas

MARIJAMPOLĖ

Marijampolė

Hrodna

Ventspils

Liepāja

Klaipėda

Palanga

Nida

Neringa

Kaliningrad

Elbląg

Gdańsk

Gdynia

Sopot

Zatoka Gdańska

Mierzeja Helska

Władysławowo

Słupsk

Koszalin

Wisła

Suwałki

Olsztyn

Underlined towns give their name to the administrative area in which they stand.

National Parks

Projection: Lambert's Conformal Conic

East from Greenwich

COPYRIGHT PHILIP'S

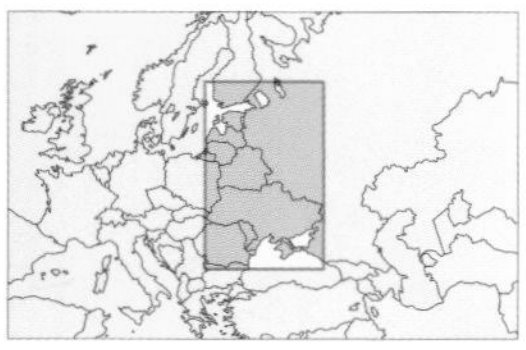

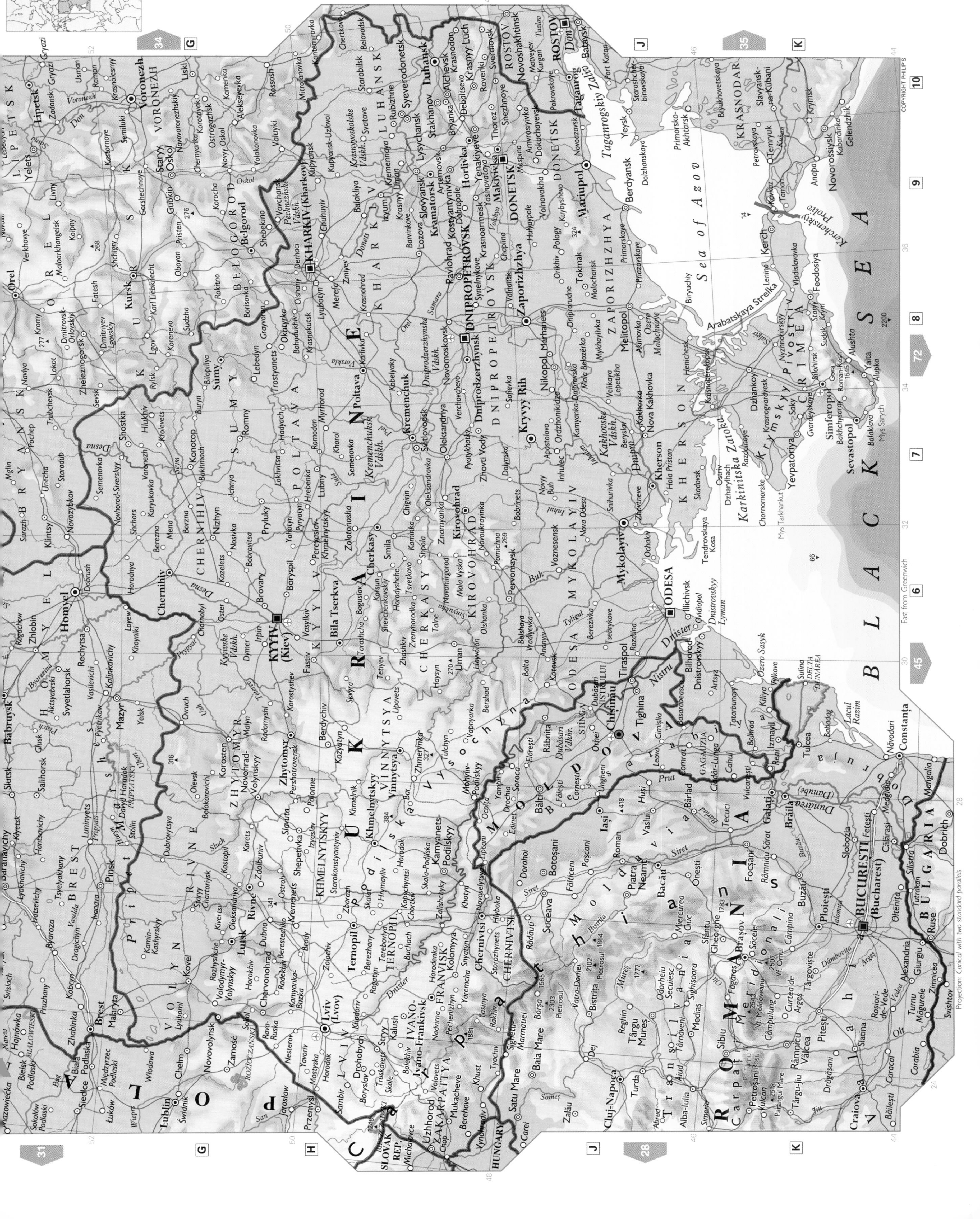

KHARKIV (Kharkiv)

KYYIV (Kiev)

DNIPROPETROVSK

DONETSK

LUHANSK

ROSTOV

VORONEZH

Sea of Azov

BLACK SEA

CRIMEA

KRASNODAR

BULGARIA

ROMANIA

MOLDOVA

BUCUREŞTI (Bucharest)

Constanţa

ODESA

Mykolaïv

Kherson

Zaporizhzhya

Mariupol

Simferopol

Sevastopol

Yalta

Kerch

SLOVAK REP.

HUNGARY

East from Greenwich

Projection: Conical with two standard parallels

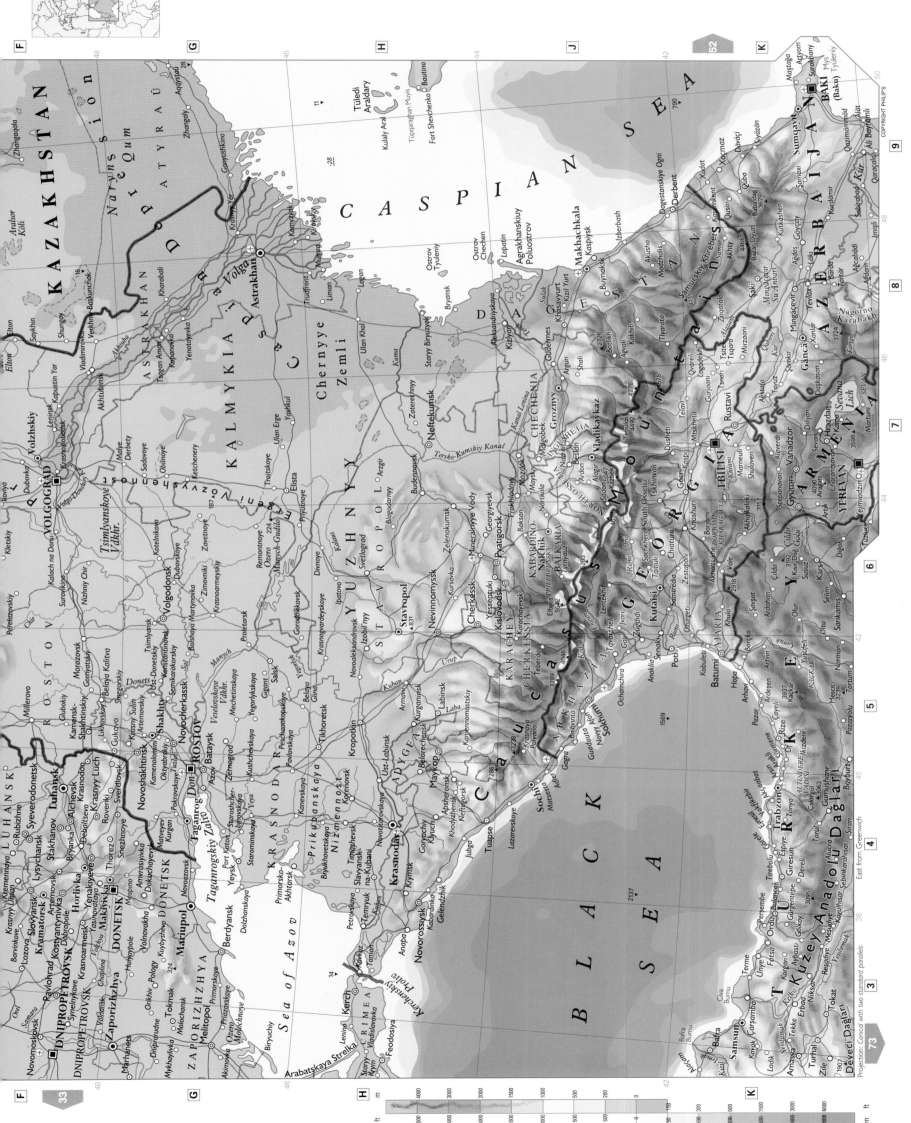

Projection: Conical with two standard parallels

East from Greenwich

COPYRIGHT PHILIP'S

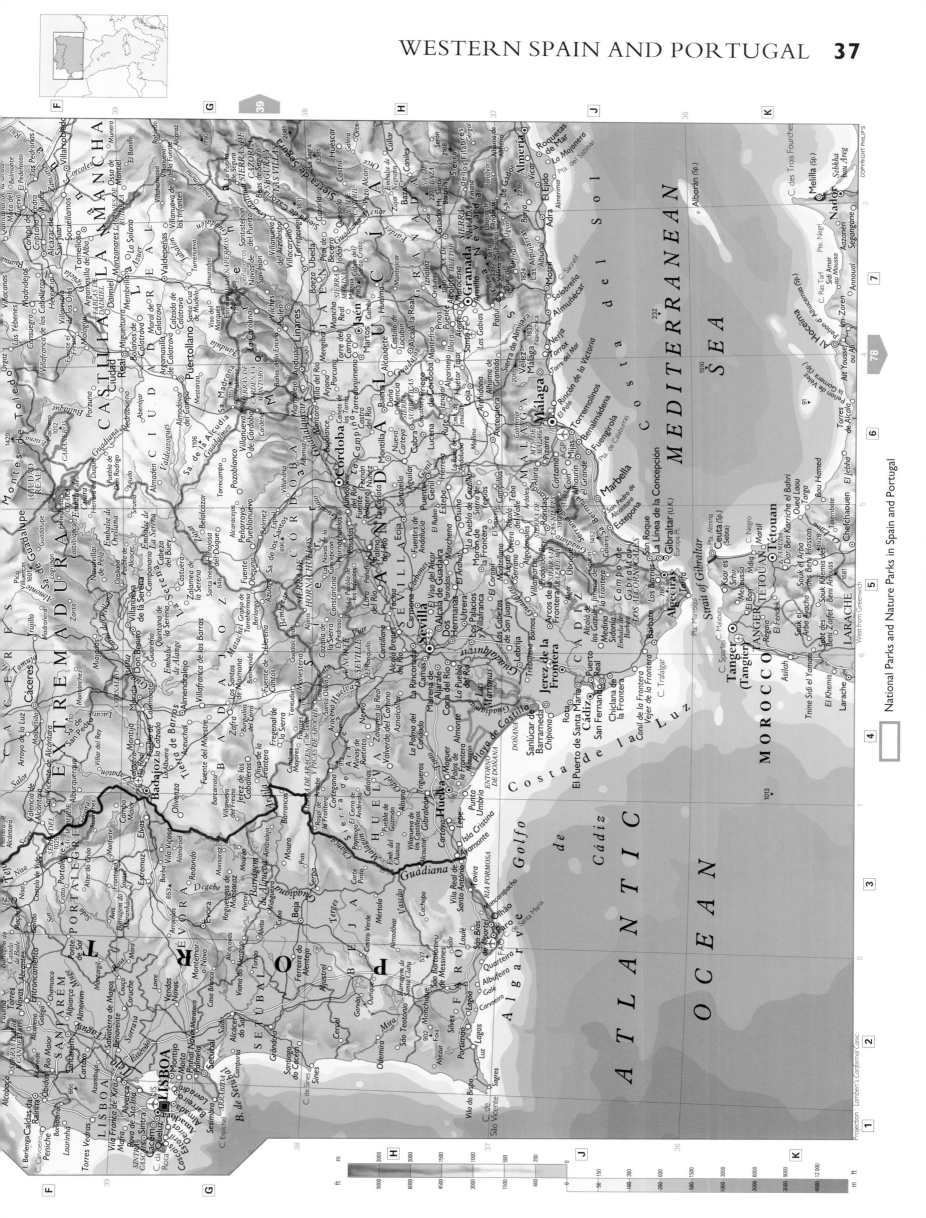

National Parks and Nature Parks in Spain and Portugal

National Parks and Nature Parks in Spain

COPYRIGHT PHILIPS

Projection: Lambert's Conformal Conic

1:2 200 000

Underlined towns give their name to t
administrative area in which they stand

Administrative divisions in Croatia:

Brodsko-Posavska 4 Medimurska   8 Virovitičko-Podravska
Koprivničko-Križevačka 6 Požeško-Slavonska   10 Zagreba čka
Krapinsko-Zagorska 7 Varaždinska

National Parks and Nature Parks in Italy

Inter-entity boundaries as agreed
at the 1995 Dayton Peace Agreement

COPYRIGHT PHILIP'S

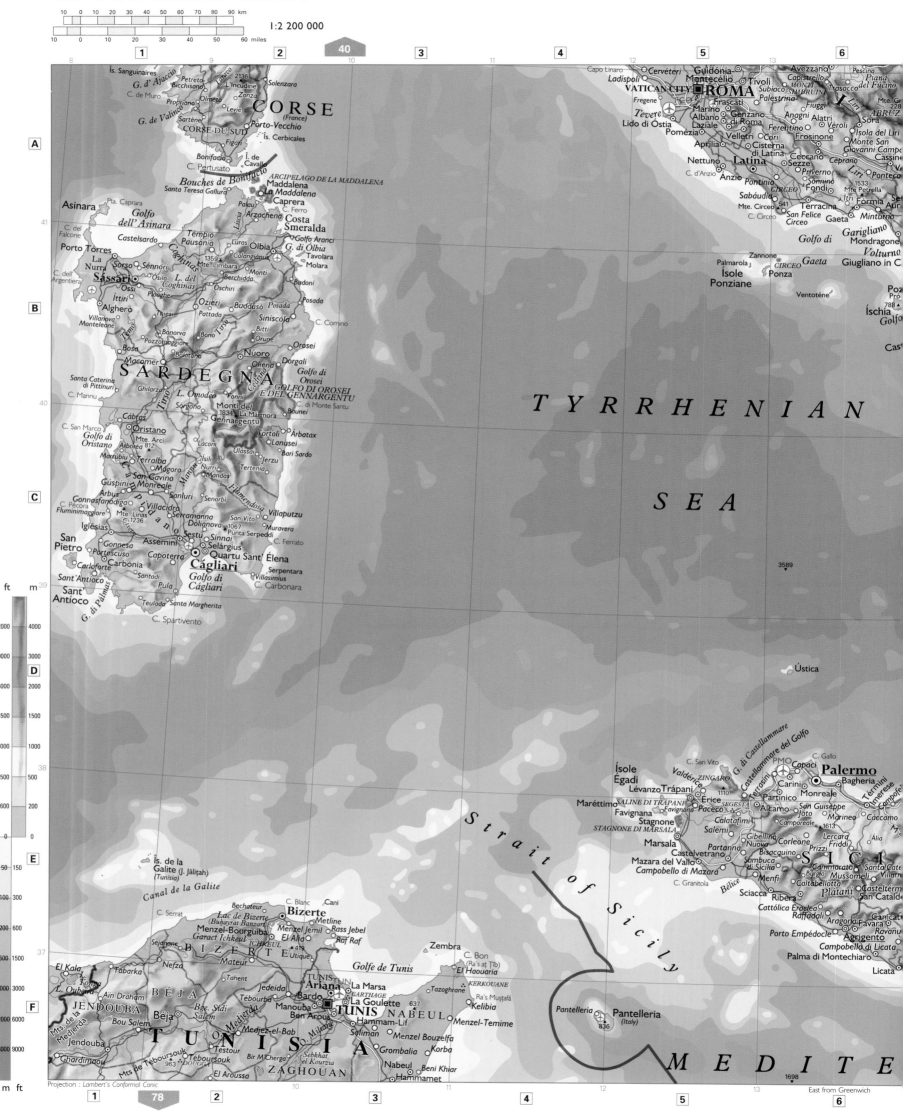

1:2 200 000

Projection : Lambert's Conformal Conic

East from Greenwich

Inter-entity boundaries as agreed
at the 1995 Dayton Peace Agreement

Projection : Lambert's Conformal Conic

East from Greenwich

BLACK SEA

TURKEY

BULGARIA

Marmara Denizi (Sea of Marmara)

Saros Körfezi

Çanakkale Boğazı (Dardanelles)

Major places and features (selected):

Bucureşti (Bucharest), Ploieşti, Buzău, Brăila, Galaţi, Constanţa, Ruse, Giurgiu, Pleven, Veliko Tŭrnovo, Gabrovo, Sliven, Stara Zagora, Yambol, Burgas, Varna, Dobrich, Plovdiv, Pazardzhik, Asenovgrad, Khaskovo, Dimitrovgrad, Kŭrdzhali, Smolyan, Edirne, Kırklareli, Lüleburgaz, Tekirdağ, Çorlu, İstanbul, Üsküdar, Kartal, Pendik, Kocaeli (İzmit), Gebze, Bursa, Bandırma, Çanakkale, Gökçeada, Bozcaada, Limnos, Samothraki, Thasos, Kavala, Xanthi, Komotini, Alexandroupoli, Anatoliki Makedonia, Kai Thraki, Rodopi, Evros

Sea of Thrace

Marmara Denizi (Sea of Marmara)

İstanbul Boğazı (Bosporus)

National Parks

Underlined towns give their name to the administrative area in which they stand.

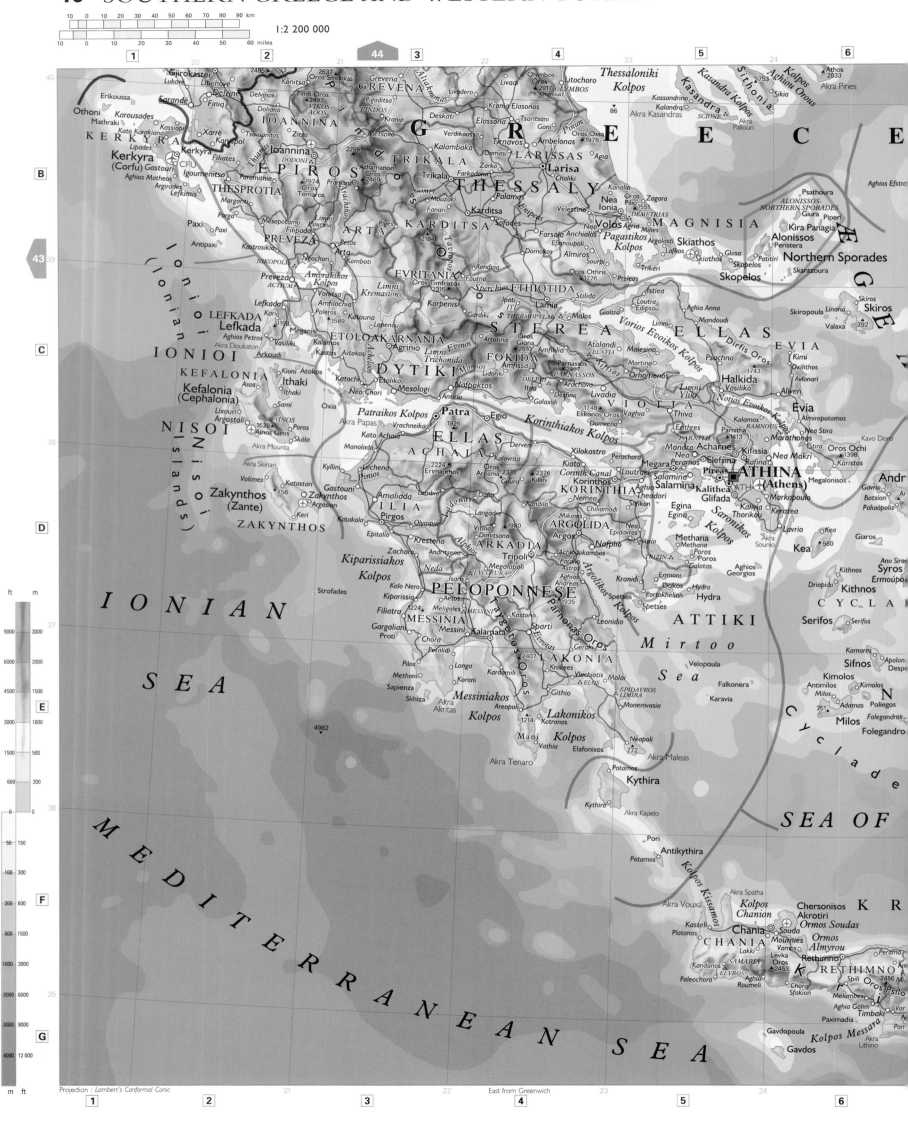

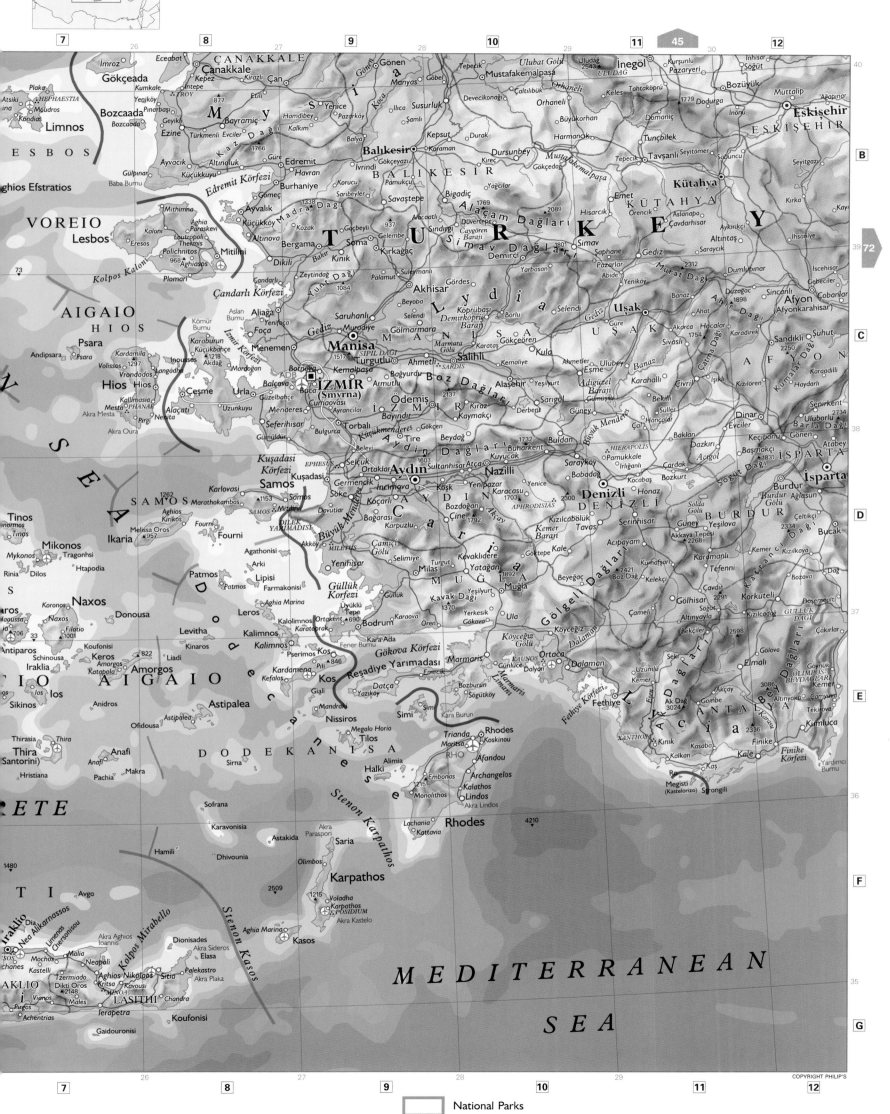

National Parks

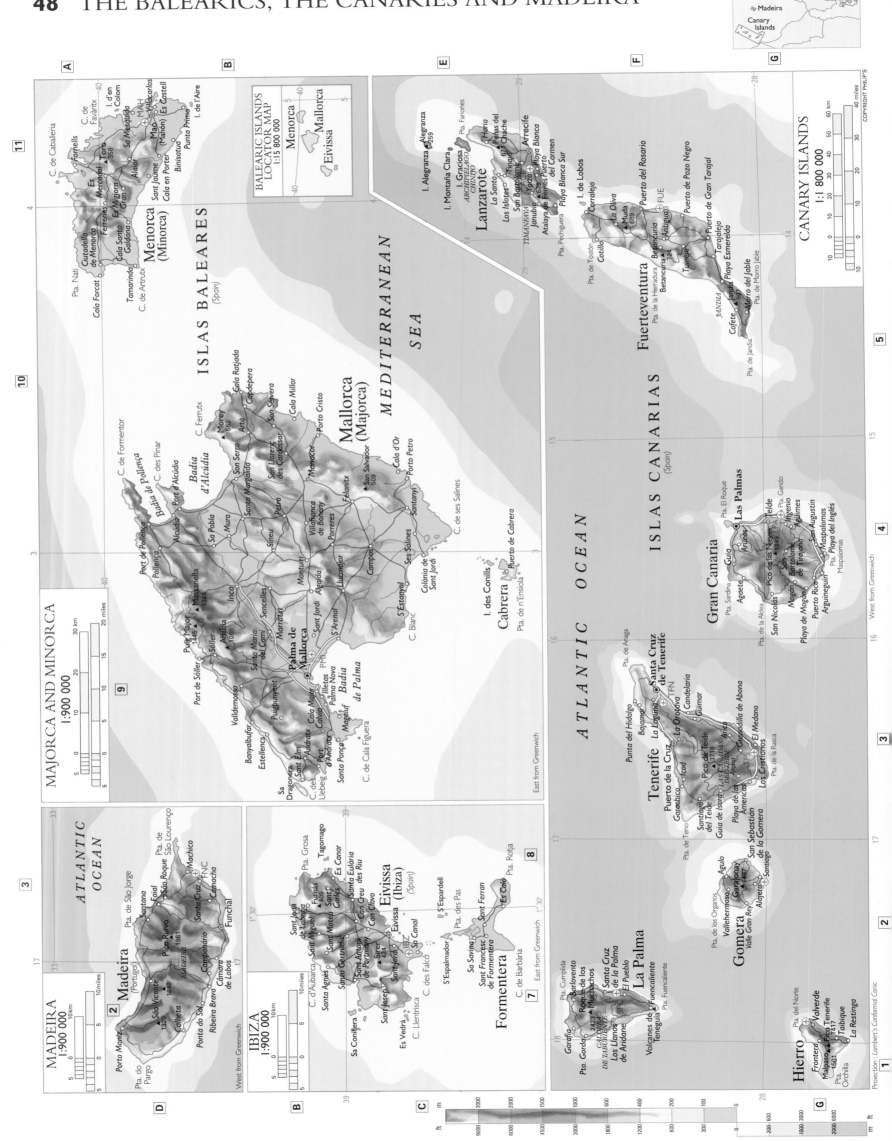

Madeira

Canary Islands

Balearic Islands

BALEARIC ISLANDS
LOCATOR MAP
1:15 800 000

Menorca

Mallorca

Eivissa

MEDITERRANEAN SEA

ISLAS BALEARES
(Spain)

Menorca (Minorca)

C. de Caballeria
Fornells
Ferreríes
Ciutadella de Menorca
Cala Santa Galdana
C. de Arrubx
Pta. Nati
Cala Forcat
Tamarinda
Es Mercadal
Sa Mesquida
Toro 358
Alaior
Binisatuo
Sant Jaume (Mahón)
Cala en Porter
MAH
Mao (Mahón)
Es Castell
Villacarlos
I. de l'Aire
Punta Prima
I. d'en Colom
C. de Favártx
Es Migjorn Gran

Mallorca (Majorca)

C. de Formentor
Port de Pollença
Pollença
C. de Pollença
Alcúdia
Badia de Pollença
C. des Pinar
Port d'Alcúdia
Badia d'Alcúdia
Puig Major 1445
Massanella 1346
Sóller
Port de Sóller
Valldemossa
Banyalbufar
Estellencs
Sa Dragonera
C. des Llebeig
Sant Elm
Port d'Andratx
Andratx
S'Arracó
Santa Ponça
C. de Cala Figuera
Calvià
Magaluf
Palma Nova
Illetas
Cala Major
PM
Palma de Mallorca
Badia de Palma
S'Arenal
Puigpunyent
Alaró 1068
Santa Maria del Camí
Inca
Sa Pobla
Muro
Petra
Sineu
Sencelles
Sa Vileta
Marràtxi
Sant Jordi
Algaida
Llucmajor
Montuïri
Villafranca de Bonany
Porreres
Campos
Ses Salines
C. de ses Salines
Colònia de Sant Jordi
S'Estanyol
Santanyí
C. de ses Salines
Felanitx
San Salvador 509
Cala d'Or
Porto Petro
Porto Cristo
Manacor
Son Servera
Cala Millor
Son Llorenç des Cardassar
Son Serra
Santa Margalida
Sa Pobla
Morey 560
Artà
Capdepera
Cala Ratjada
C. Ferrutx
S'Estanyol
Colònia de Sant Jordi
I. des Conills
Cabrera
Puerto de Cabrera
I. de n'Ensiola
Pta. de n'Ensiola
C. Blanc

MAJORCA AND MINORCA
1:900 000

30 km
20 miles

MADEIRA
1:900 000

Madeira (Portugal)

ATLANTIC OCEAN

Pta. de São Lourenço
Pta. de São Jorge
Porto Monte
Santana
São Vicente 1640
Faial
São Roque
Machico
Camacha
FNC
Santa Cruz
Funchal
Pico Ruivo 1861
MADEIRA
Curral
Câmara de Lobos
Campanário
Ribeira Brava
Ponta do Sol
Colheta
Pargo
Porto do Moniz
Ponta do Pargo

IBIZA
1:900 000

Eivissa (Ibiza) (Spain)

Pta. Grosa
Tagomago
Pta. de sa Mata
Es Canar
Santa Eulària des Riu
Cala Llonga
Pta. des Andreu
Sant Joan de Labritja
Portinatx
Sant Miquel
Sant Mateu
Sant Carles
Sant Rafel
Santa Gertrudis
Sant Antoni de Portmany
Sant Josep
Sant Jordi
Sant Agnès
Sa Talaia 424
IBZ
Eivissa
Sa Canal
S'Espardell
Es Espalmador
Sa Savina
Sant Francesc de Formentera
Es Caló
Pta. Roja
Sant Ferran
Formentera
C. de Barbària
Es Vedrà
C. Llentrisca
Sa Conillera
C. d'Aubarca
S'Espalmador
Pta. des Pas
Pta. de ses Portes
C. des Falcó

MEDITERRANEAN SEA

East from Greenwich

West from Greenwich

CANARY ISLANDS
1:1 800 000

ISLAS CANARIAS
(Spain)

ATLANTIC OCEAN

Lanzarote

I. Alegranza 259
I. Montaña Clara
I. Graciosa
ARCHIPIÉLAGO CHINIJO
Haría
Peñas del Chache 671
La Santa
Los Islotes
San Bartolomé
Tinajo
TIMANFAYA
Arrecife
Playa Blanca
Puerto del Carmen
Playa Blanca Sur
Yaiza
Pta. Pechiguera
I. de Lobos

Fuerteventura

Corralejo
La Oliva
Pta. de Tostón
Cotillo
Pta. de la Herradura
La Muda 689
Betancuria
Antigua
Puerto del Rosario
FUE
Betancuria
Tuineje
Puerto de Pozo Negro
Tarajalejo
Playa Esmerelda
Puerto de Gran Tarajal
JANDÍA
Cofete
Morro del Jable
Pta. de Jandía
Pta. de Morro Jable

Gran Canaria

Pta. El Roque
Las Palmas
Guía
Agaete
Gando
Telde
Ingenio
Arucas
Pico de las Nieves 1949
Aguimes
San Bartolomé de Tirajana
Santa Lucía
Agüimes
San Augustín
Maspalomas
Playa del Inglés
Pta. de Maspalomas
Puerto Rico
Arguineguín
Mogán
Playa de Mogán
San Nicolás
Pta. de la Aldea

Tenerife

Punta del Hidalgo
La Laguna
Santa Cruz de Tenerife
TFN
Bajamar
La Orotava
Puerto de la Cruz
Candelaria
Guimar
Pico de Teide 3718
LAS CAÑADAS
Arico
Icod
Garachico
Guía de Isora
Adeje
Playa de las Américas
Los Cristianos
Granadilla de Abona
El Médano
Pta. de la Rasca
Pta. de Teno
Santiago del Teide

Gomera

Agulo
Vallehermoso
Hermigua
San Sebastián de la Gomera
Garajonay 1487
Alajeró
Santiago
Valle Gran Rey
Pta. de los Órganos

La Palma

Pta. Cumplida
Barlovento
Roque de los Muchachos 2423
Santa Cruz de la Palma
CALDERA DE TABURIENTE
SPC
El Pueblo
Los Llanos de Aridane
Fuencaliente
Pta. de Fuencaliente
Volcanes de Teneguía
Garafía
Pta. Gorda

Hierro

Pta. del Norte
Frontera
Valverde
Malpaso 1501
Pico Tenerife 1417
Taibique
La Restinga
Pta. Orchilla

ISLAS CANARIAS
(Spain)

West from Greenwich

Projection: Lambert's Conformal Conic

COPYRIGHT PHILIP'S

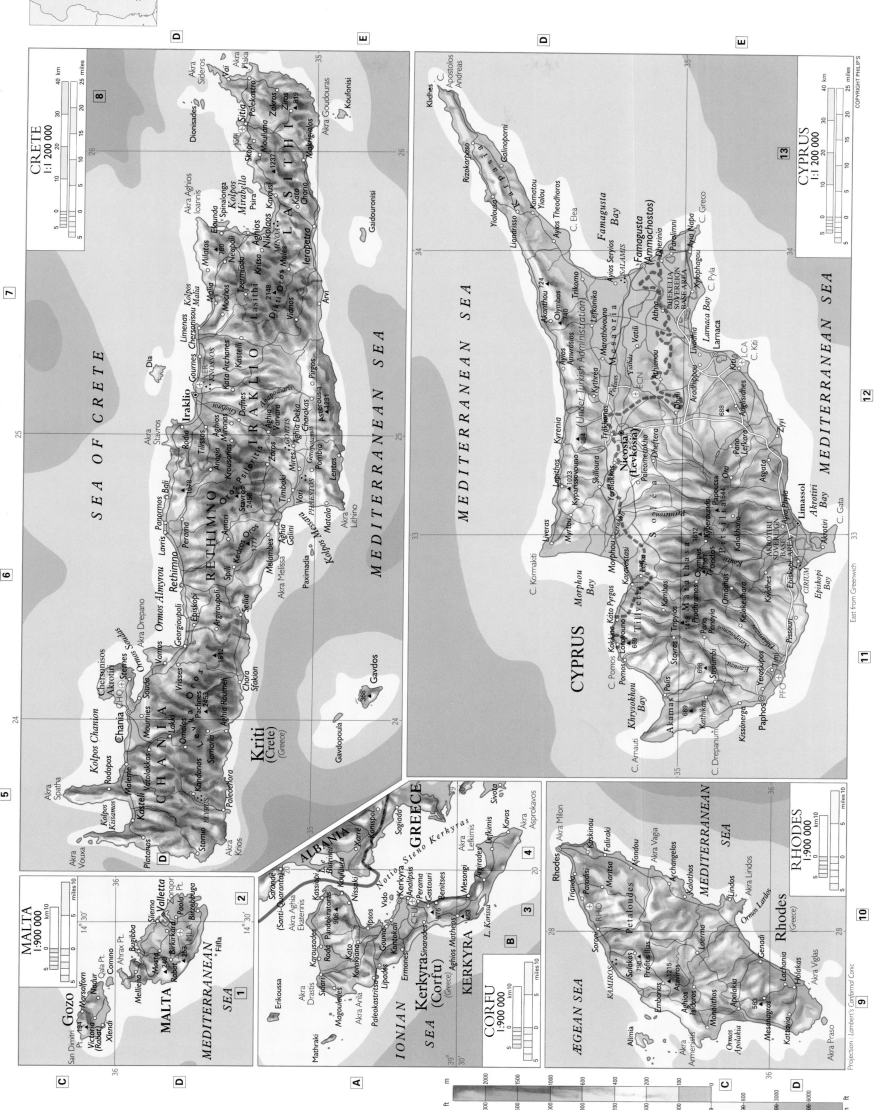

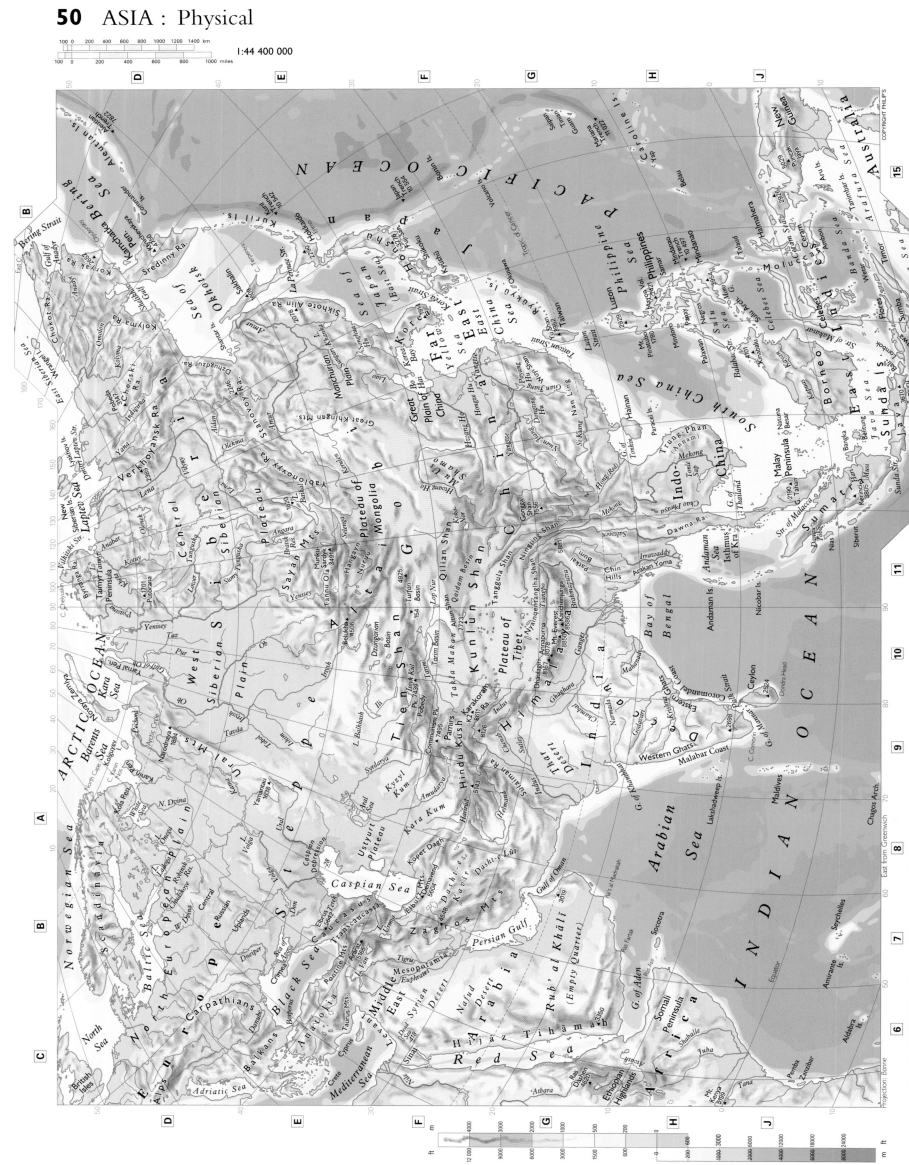

1:44 400 000

Projection: Borrie

COPYRIGHT PHILIP'S

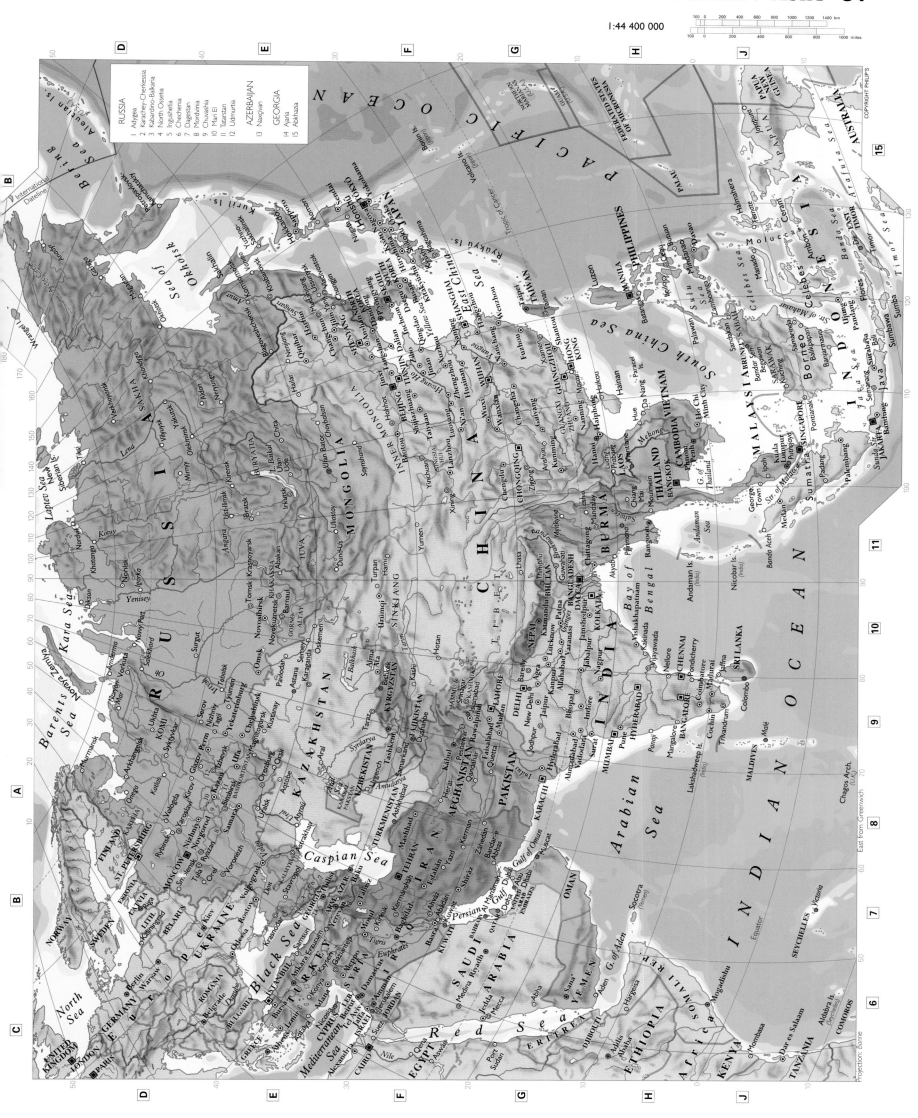

1:44 400 000

RUSSIA
1 Adygea
2 Karachey-Cherkessia
3 Kabardino-Balkaria
4 North Ossetia
5 Ingushetia
6 Chechenia
7 Dagestan
8 Mordovia
9 Chuvashia
10 Mari El
11 Tatarstan
12 Udmurtia

AZERBAIJAN
13 Naxçivan

GEORGIA
14 Ajaria
15 Abkhazia

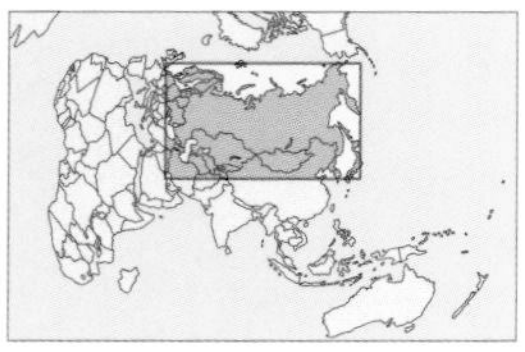

OCEAN

Laptev Sea

East Siberian Sea

Bering Sea

Sea of Okhotsk

Sea of Japan (East Sea)

R U S S I A

MONGOLIA

C H I N A

JAPAN

SOUTH KOREA

NORTH KOREA

Sakhalin

Kamchatka

Poluostrov Kamchatka

Kolymskoye Nagorye

Sredinnyy Khrebet

Sikhote Alin

Stanovoy Khrebet

Yablonovyy Khrebet

Khrebet Cherskogo

Verkhoyanskiy Khrebet

Khrebet Dzhugdzur

Da Hinggan Ling

Dongbei (Manchuria)

Gobi

Hangayn Nuruu

Hentiyn Nuruu

Severnaya Zemlya

Ostrov Vrangelya

Novosibirskiye Ostrova

Kurilskiye Ostrova

Poluostrov Taymyr

Gory Byrranga

Arctic Circle

BEIJING

Ulaanbaatar

Irkutsk

Krasnoyarsk

Bratsk

Angarsk

Ulan Ude

Chita

Yakutsk

Norilsk

Khabarovsk

Vladivostok

Komsomolsk

Blagoveshchensk

HARBIN

CHANGCHUN

SHENYANG

DALIAN

QIQIHAR

DAQING

JILIN

FUSHUN

ANSHAN

CHIFENG

BAOTOU

Hohhot

Zhangjiakou

Chengde

PYONGYANG

SEOUL

INCHEON

DAEJEON

DAEGU

BUSAN

GWANGJU

KYOTO

OSAKA

KOBE

SAPPORO

Hokkaido

Honshu

Petropavlovsk-Kamchatskiy

Magadan

Tiksi

Khatanga

Nordvik

COPYRIGHT PHILIP'S

1:4 400 000

50   0   25   50   75   100   125   150   175 km

50   0   25   50   75   100   125 miles

SEA OF OKHOTSK

Sakhalin (Russia)

La Perouse Strait
(Sōya-Kaikyō)
Sōya-Misaki

Ostrov
Moneron
(Russia)

Wakkanai
RISHIRI-
REBUN
SHIROBETSU
Rebun-Tō
Rishiri-Tō △1721

HOKKAIDŌ

Ostrov Kunashiri
Nemuro-
Kaikyō
Nosappu-Misaki

Shiretoko-
Misaki
Abashiri
Rausu-Dake
1661
Aboshiri
Shari
Kitami
Kitami-Sammyaku
DAISETSU-ZAN
Asahigawa
Ashibetsu
Asahi-Dake
2290
Okan-Dake
2011
Kushiro-Gawa
Nakashibetsu
Neinato
Akkeshi
KUSHIRO
SHITSUGEN
Kushiro
Homboetsu
Hiroo
Erimo-Misaki

Otaru
Ishikari-Wan
(Otaru-Wan)
SAPPORO
Chitose
Iwanizawa
Yūbari
Toka-chi-Gata
Obihiro
Poroshiri-Dake
2052
Hidaka-Sammyaku
Samani
Urakawa

Muroran
Noboribetsu
Shiraoi
Uchiura-Wan
Mori
Hakodate
Tsugaru-Kaikyō

Ō-Shima
Okushiri-Tō
Setana

Honshū

Aomori
Mutsu-Wan
Hachinohe
Misawa
Towada
Morioka
Hachimantai
2041
TŌHOKU
Kitakami
RIKUCHŪ-KAIGAN
Miyako
Kamaishi
AKITA
Akita
Sendai
Sendai-Wan
Fukushima
BANDAI
Sado

SEA OF JAPAN (EAST SEA)

Yamato Rise

RUSSIA

Svetlaya
Amgu
Velikaya Kema
Terney
Plastun
Rudnaya Pristan
Dalnegorsk
Olga
Margaritovo
Valentin
Preobrazheniye
Nakhodka
Partizansk
Artem
Vladivostok
Zaliv
Petra Velikogo
Ussuriysk
Spassk-
Dalniy
Lake Khanka

CHINA
HEILONGJIANG

Jiamusi
Shuangyashan
Boli
Jixi

JILIN

Hunchun
Kraskino
Khasan

NORTH KOREA

Ch'ŏngjin

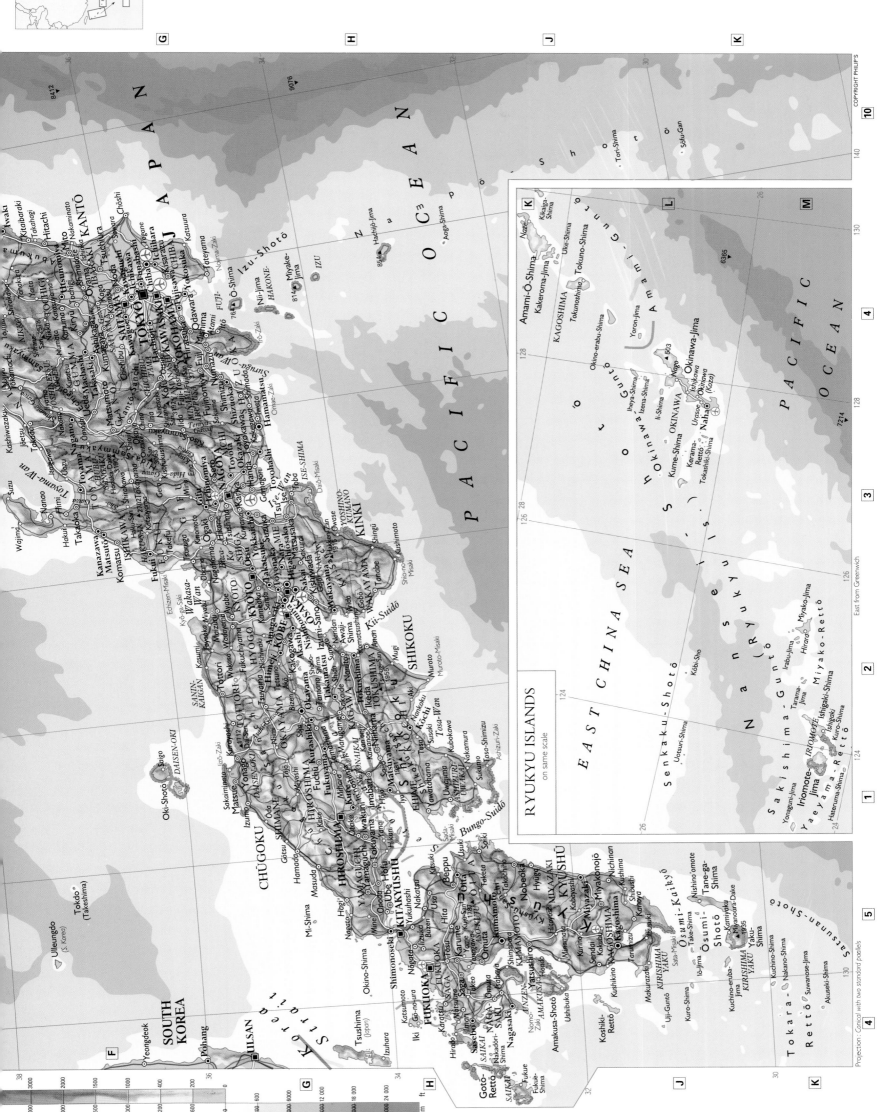

RYUKYU ISLANDS
on same scale

Projection: Conical with two standard parallels

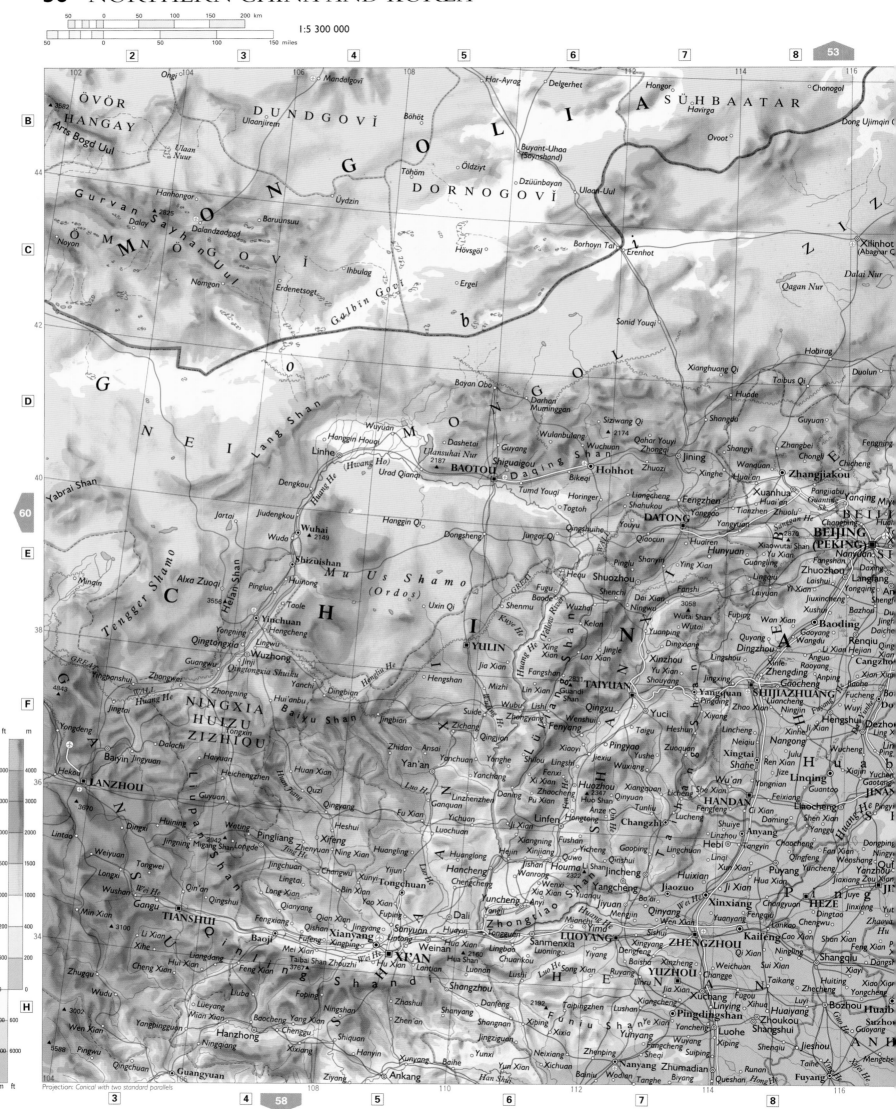

1:5 300 000

Projection: Conical with two standard parallels

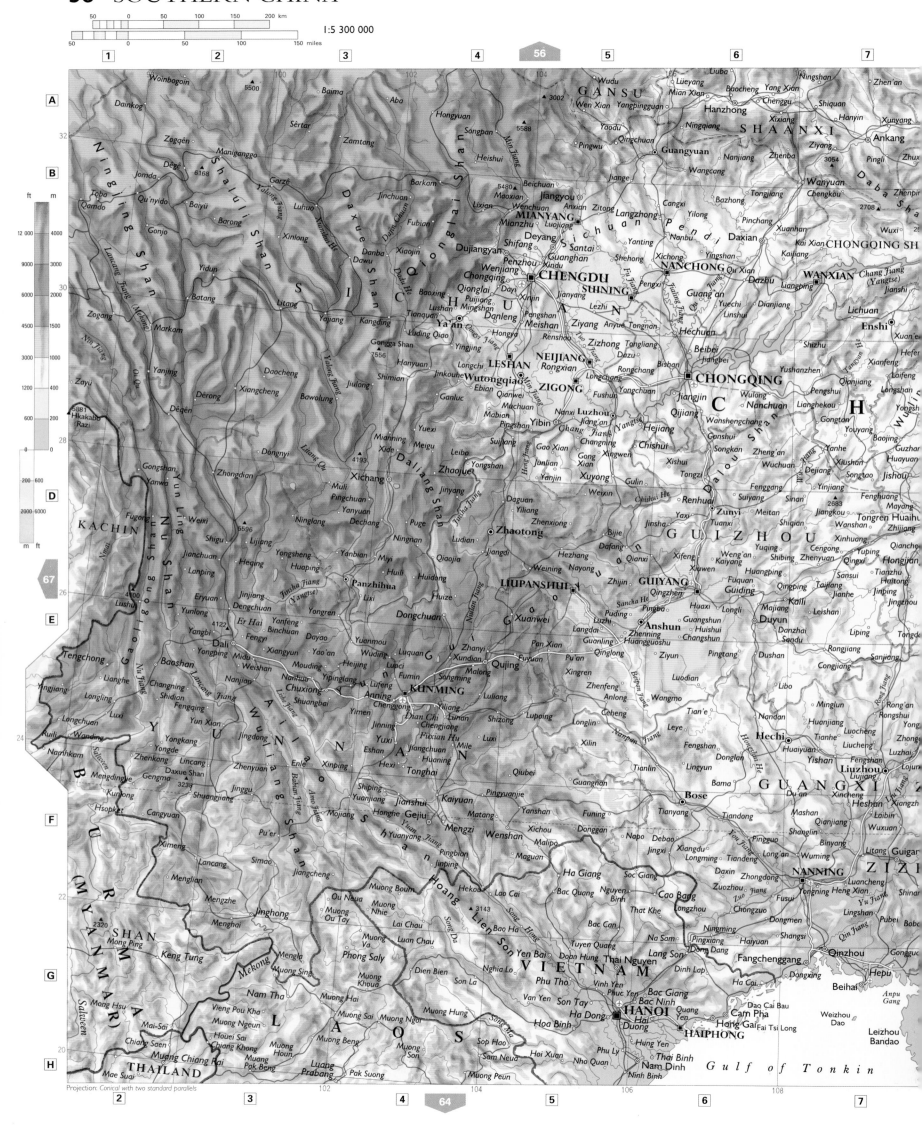

Projection: Conical with two standard parallels

SOUTH CHINA SEA

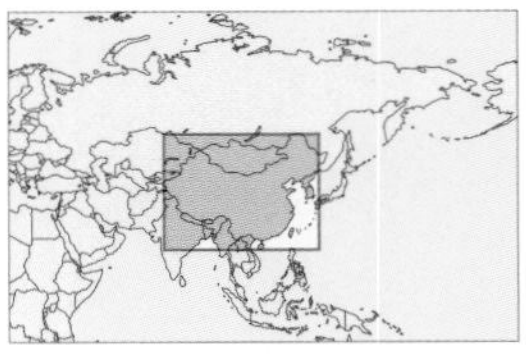

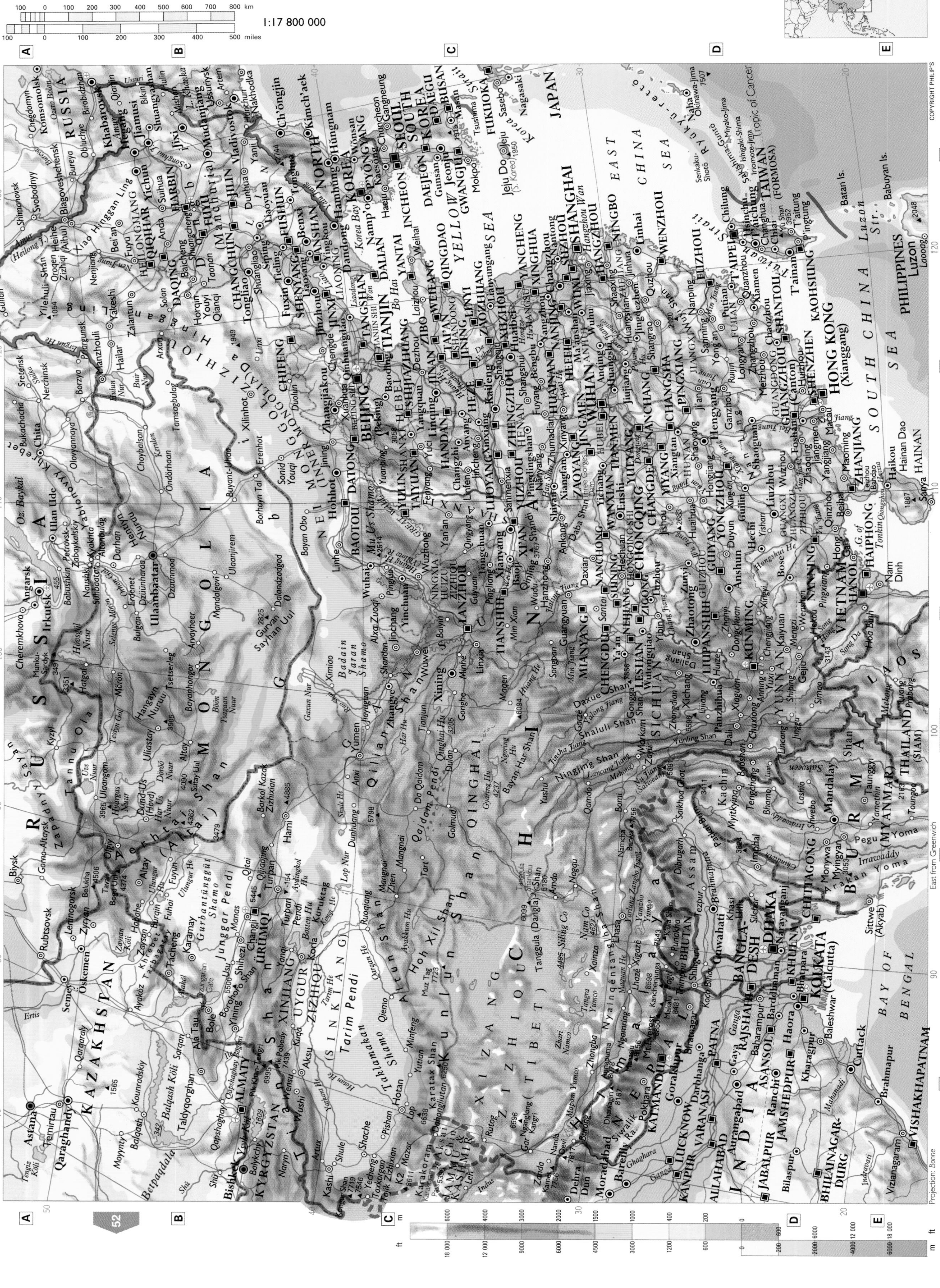

100 0 100 200 300 400 500 600 700 800 km
100 0 100 200 300 400 500 miles

1:17 800 000

COPYRIGHT PHILIP'S

Projection: Bonne

East from Greenwich

Countries and Regions

RUSSIA

KAZAKHSTAN

KYRGYZSTAN

MONGOLIA

CHINA

INDIA

NEPAL

BHUTAN

BANGLADESH

MYANMAR (BURMA)

THAILAND (SIAM)

LAOS

VIETNAM

NORTH KOREA

SOUTH KOREA

JAPAN

PHILIPPINES

TAIWAN (FORMOSA)

Chinese Provinces / Regions

XINJIANG UYGUR ZIZHIQU (SINKIANG)

XIZANG ZIZHIQU (TIBET)

QINGHAI

GANSU

NEI MONGGOL ZIZHIQU (INNER MONGOLIA)

NINGXIA HUIZU ZIZHIQU

SHAANXI

SHANXI

HEBEI

SHANDONG

HENAN

HUBEI

ANHUI

JIANGSU

SICHUAN

YUNNAN

GUIZHOU

HUNAN

JIANGXI

ZHEJIANG

FUJIAN

GUANGXI ZHUANGZU ZIZHIQU

GUANGDONG

HAINAN

HEILONGJIANG

JILIN

LIAONING

Major Cities

BEIJING (Peking)

TIANJIN

SHANGHAI

CHONGQING

WUHAN

GUANGZHOU (Canton)

SHENZHEN

HONG KONG (Xianggang)

Macau

NANJING

XI'AN

CHENGDU

LANZHOU

TAIYUAN

SHENYANG

HARBIN

CHANGCHUN

ULAANBAATAR

SEOUL

PYONGYANG

BUSAN

DAEGU

INCHEON

DAEJEON

FUKUOKA

TAIPEI

KAOHSIUNG

HANOI

HAIPHONG

MANDALAY

DHAKA

KOLKATA (Calcutta)

KATHMANDU

Seas and Bodies of Water

EAST CHINA SEA

SOUTH CHINA SEA

YELLOW SEA

BAY OF BENGAL

Bo Hai

Korea Bay

Hangzhou Wan

Lop Nur

Qinghai Hu

Oz. Baykal

Physical Features

Tarim Pendi

Taklamakan Shamo

Kunlun Shan

Altun Shan

Qilian Shan

Tien Shan

Junggar Pendi

Gobi (desert)

Badain Jaran Shamo

Mu Us Shamo

Tanggula Shan

Nyainqêntanglha Shan

Hengduan Shan

Da Hinggan Ling

Xiao Hinggan Ling

K2 8611

Everest 8848

Tropic of Cancer

1:6 700 000

50 0 100 150 200 250 300 km
50 0 50 100 150 200 miles

Projection: Lambert's Conformal Conic

COPYRIGHT PHILIP'S

National Parks

Dongsha Dao
(China)

A

P A C I F I C

Itbayat I.
Batan Is.
Batan I.

Balintang Channel

Calayan I.
Dalupiri I. Babuyan Babuyan I.
Islands Camiguin I.
Fuga I.

B

O C E A N

Mayraira Pt. *Babuyan Channel*
Bacarra Aparri Santa Ana
San Nicolas Laoag Kabugao Gonzaga
Batac Claveria Gattaran
Cabugao Tuao Tuguegarao
Vigan Bangued 2360 Cagayan Mt. Cresta
Santa Maria Roxas 1685
Candon Lubuagan Ilagan Palanan Pt.
Tagudin Bontoc San Mateo Palanan
Balaoan MT. Santiago
San Fernando DATA Cordon Luzon
Bolinao Mt. Pulog Baguio Bayombong Casiguran
Alaminos 2928 Solano

C

S O U T H

C H I N A

S E A

PHILIPPINE

Lingayen HUNDRED Rosario Mt. Anacuao
Lingayen ISLANDS Dagupan 1852
Gulf San Manuel C. San Ildefonso
San Carlos Bayambang San Jose
Santa Cruz Moncada Cuyapo Baler Bay
Camiling Victoria AURORA Baler
Masinloc Tarlac MEMORIAL
Iba 2037 La Cabanatuan
Concepcion Paz Gapan Dingalan
Angeles

S E A

D

Mt. Pinatubo San Fernando
1780
San Antonio Polillo Is.
Olongapo Orani Malabon Patnanongan I.
Bataan Manila Caloocan Jomalig I.
Bay Cavite Quezon City
Mariveles MANILA Lamon Bay Paracale
Dasmariñas Pasay Santa Cruz Labo
Nasugbu Tagaytay L. de Bay Lucban Alabat I. Daet Pandan
Balayan San QUEZON Atimonan Viga Catanduanes
Lemery Pablo Calauag BICOL Calabanga San Andres
Lubang Batangas Lipa Lucena Catanauan Naga Mt. Isarog Virac
Lobo Boac Nabua 1976
C. Calavite Verde I. Pass Tayabas Bay Iriga 2462 Rapu Rapu I.
Marin- Ligao Mayon Vol. Sorsogon
Mamburao Calapan Victoria duque Tabaco Legazpi
Sablayan LAKE Pinamalayan Burias I. Donsol Gubat
Mt. Baco NAUJAN Magallanes San Bernardino Str.
2487 SIBUYAN Bulan Allen Looaon
Bongabong Romblon Ticao I. Irosin Catarman Mondragon
APO REEF Roxas Tablas I. Aroroy Calbayog Gamay
San Jose Odiongan SEA Mandaon Masbate Arteche
Busuanga I. Ilin I. Semirara Is. Milagros Oras
Culion I. Placer Masbate

E

S E A

Mindoro

Mindoro Strait

Tablas Strait

F

Calamian Pandan Kalibo Cataclogan VISAYAN Sibuyan I. Caibiran Santa Taft
Group Roxas SEA Bilinan I. Rita Borongan
Linapacan Str. Dao Pilar Calubian Cargara Basey General MacArthur
Linapacan I. Tibiao 2117 Bantayan Palompon Leyte Tacloban Guiuan
Bugasong Sara Bogo Ormoc Dulag Homonhon I.
Taytay Cuyo Is. Passi Silay Tuburan Baybay Leyte Gulf
Cuyo Ajuy Camotes Is. Abuyog
Cuyo West Pass Cuyo East Pass San Jose Panay Cadiz Camotes Sogod San Juan
Iloilo Sagay Victorias CENTRAL Sea Maasin Dinagat I.
Guimaras Bacolod Danao CEBU
Dumaran I. Jordan San Carlos Mandaue Dinagat
Hoilo Silay 2450 Cebu Sea Bato Siargao I.
Carlota Guihulngan Argao Bohol
Palawan Higantan Carcar Panaon I. Surigao
ST PAUL Binalbagan Kabankalan Tanon Placer Bucas Grande I.
1593 Himamaylan Bais Oslob RAJAH Tagbilaran Carrascal
Irahuan Honda Bay Sipalay Tanjay SIKATUNA L. Mainit Tandag
Puerto Princesa Hinoba-an Dumaguete BOHOL Cabadbaran 2012 Lanuza
Negros Bayawan Siquijor I. Camiguin I. Butuan Tago
Siaton Zamboanguita SEA Nasipit Marihatag

G

S U L U

TUBBATAHA
REEFS

Mt. Mantalingajan
2085

C. Buliluyan Bugsuk I.
Balabac I.
Balambangan Bangqi
Balambangan

Cagayan Sulu

Cagayan Is.

Dipolog Dapitan Balingasag Esperanza Lianga
Manukan Oroquieta Opol Cagayan de Oro Bislig
Sindangan MT. Iligan Malaybalay Bunawan
Labason Iligan Marawi City Hinatuan
Liloy MALINDANG Bay Iligan 2938 Talacogan
Siocon Kabasalan Pagadian Marawi City Cateel
Kolambugan L. Lanao Baganga
Sicuba Margosatubig Illana Parang 2815
Zamboanga Bay Cotabato Midsayap Panabo Manay
Basilan Str. Pikit Tagum Pantukan Mati
Isabela Datu Piang Mt. Apo DAVAO
Lamitan Talayan 2954 Davao
Basilan Kalamansig Digos Gulf San Isidro
Group Lebak Palimbang Malita
Jolo Group 2083 General C. San Agustin
Jolo Talipao Santos
Parang Siasi I. Kiamba
Tapul Group Tinaca Pt.
Siasi Sarangani Is.
Tapul Group

H

S E A

Zamboanga Moro Gulf Pilas
Group Pangutaran
Group Samales
Group

M i n d a n a o

J

S A B A H

MALAYSIA

Kota Kinabalu Kudat Serasa
Langkon Jembongan
Suba Talan
Tenghilan Kota Belud Telok
Papar G. Kinabulu Labuk Sandakan
4101 Turtle Is.

B o r n e o

Balambangan Semporna

Tawi-tawi
Group

Sibutu
Group

C E L E B E S

S E A

INDONESIA Kep. Talaud

East from Greenwich

ft m
9000 3000
6000 2000
4500 1500
3000 1000
1200 400
600
0
200 600
4000 12 000
8000 24 000
m ft

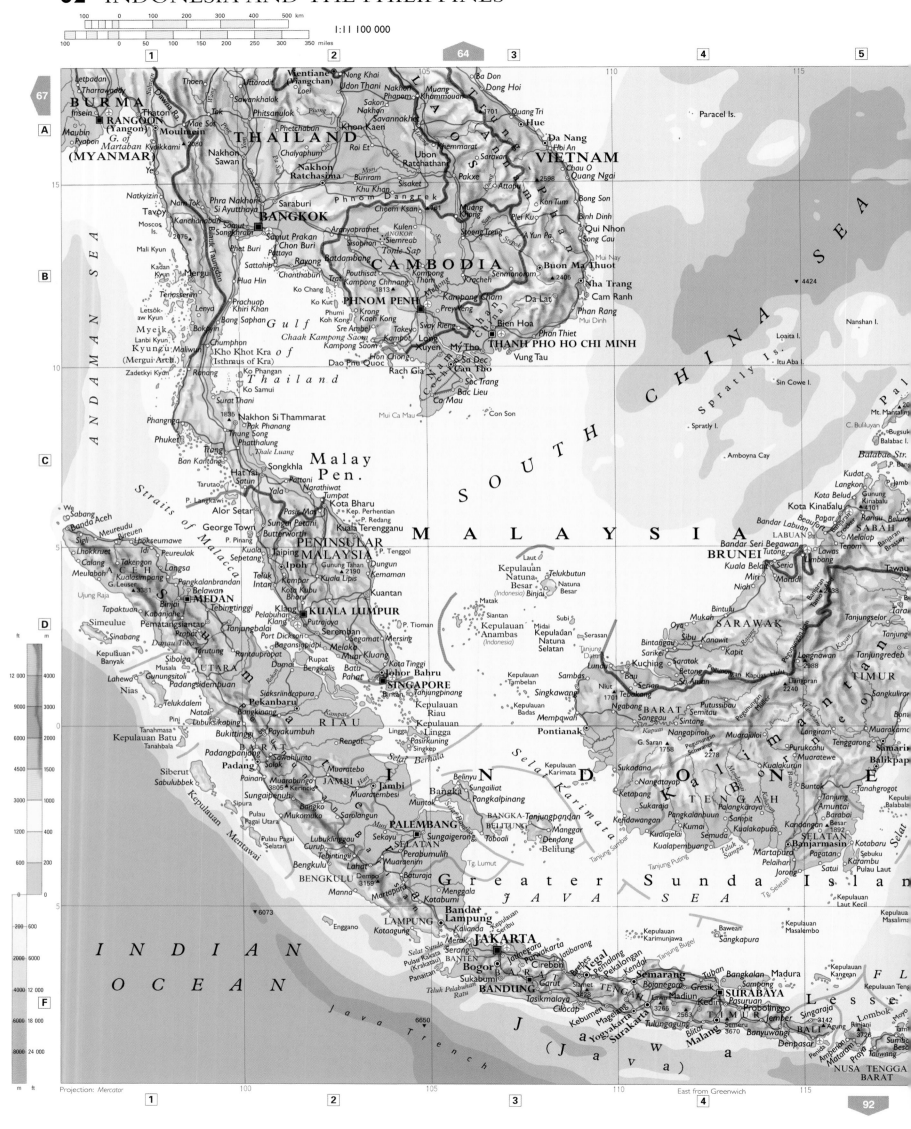

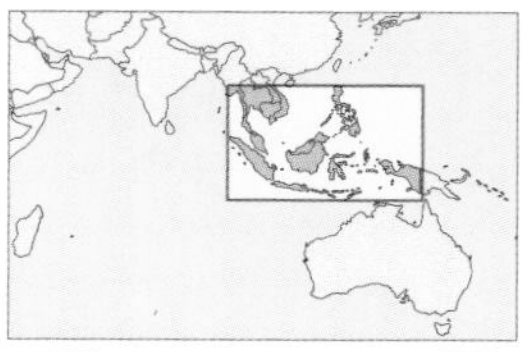

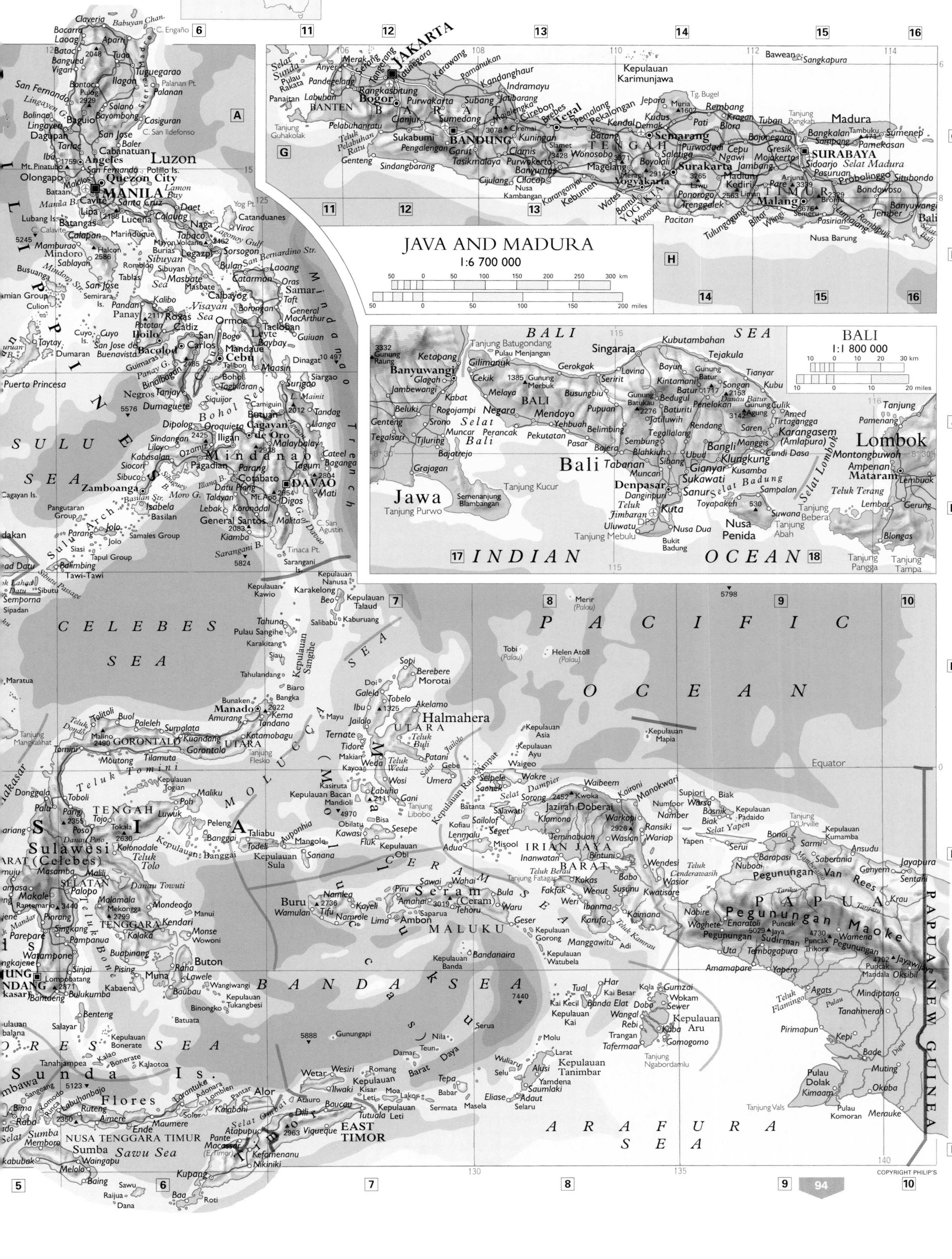

JAVA AND MADURA
1:6 700 000

50   0   50   100   150   200   250   300 km
50   0   50   100   150   200 miles

BALI
1:1 800 000
10   0   10   20   30 km
10   0   10   20 miles

Luzon

MANILA
Quezon City
Cavite

JAKARTA
Bogor · Bandung · Semarang · Surakarta
SURABAYA
Yogyakarta
Malang · Madura

Cebu
Iloilo · Bacolod
Davao
Mindanao
Zamboanga
General Santos

CELEBES SEA
SULU SEA
Manado
GORONTALO
Sulawesi (Celebes)

PACIFIC OCEAN

Halmahera
Ternate · Tidore

Equator

IRIAN JAYA BARAT
PAPUA
Pegunungan Maoke
Jayawijaya
Jayapura

Seram (Ceram)
Ambon
MALUKU

BANDA SEA

BALI SEA
Singaraja
Bali
Denpasar
Kuta
Lombok
Mataram
Ampenan

INDIAN OCEAN

FLORES SEA
Flores
Sumbawa
Sumba

NUSA TENGGARA TIMUR
Kupang
Dili
EAST TIMOR

ARAFURA SEA

PAPUA NEW GUINEA
Merauke

COPYRIGHT PHILIP'S

1:5 300 000

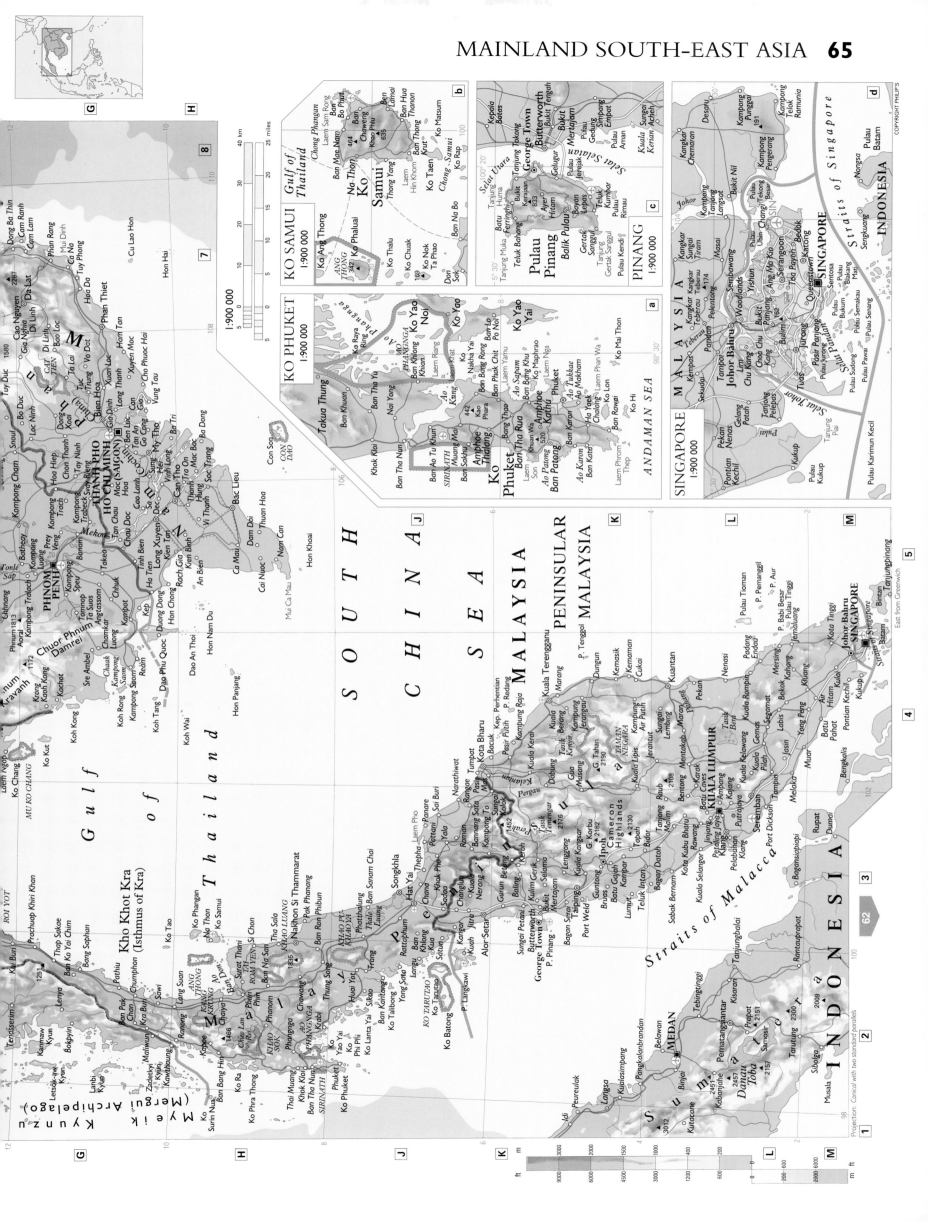

1:8 900 000

Continuation Southwards
on same scale

Projection: Conical with two standard parallels

BAY OF BENGAL

INDIAN OCEAN

1:5 300 000

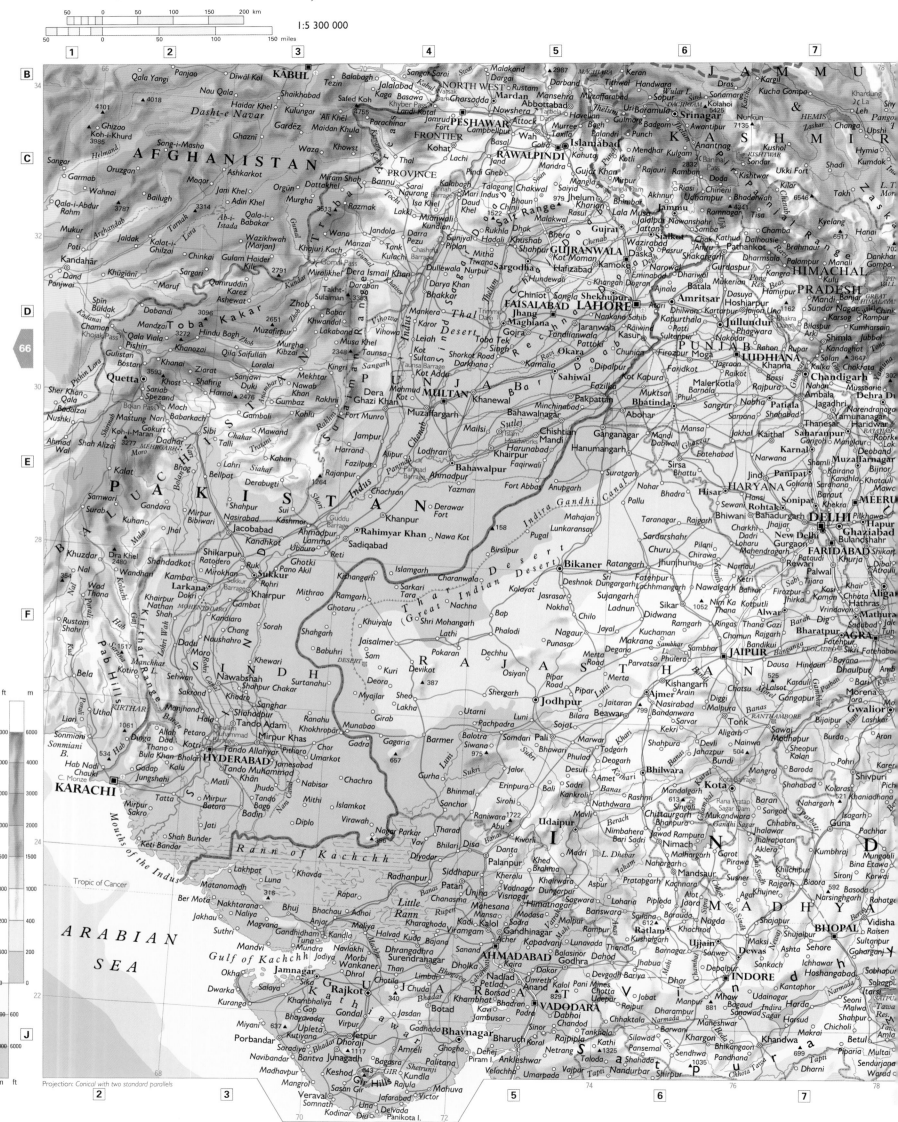

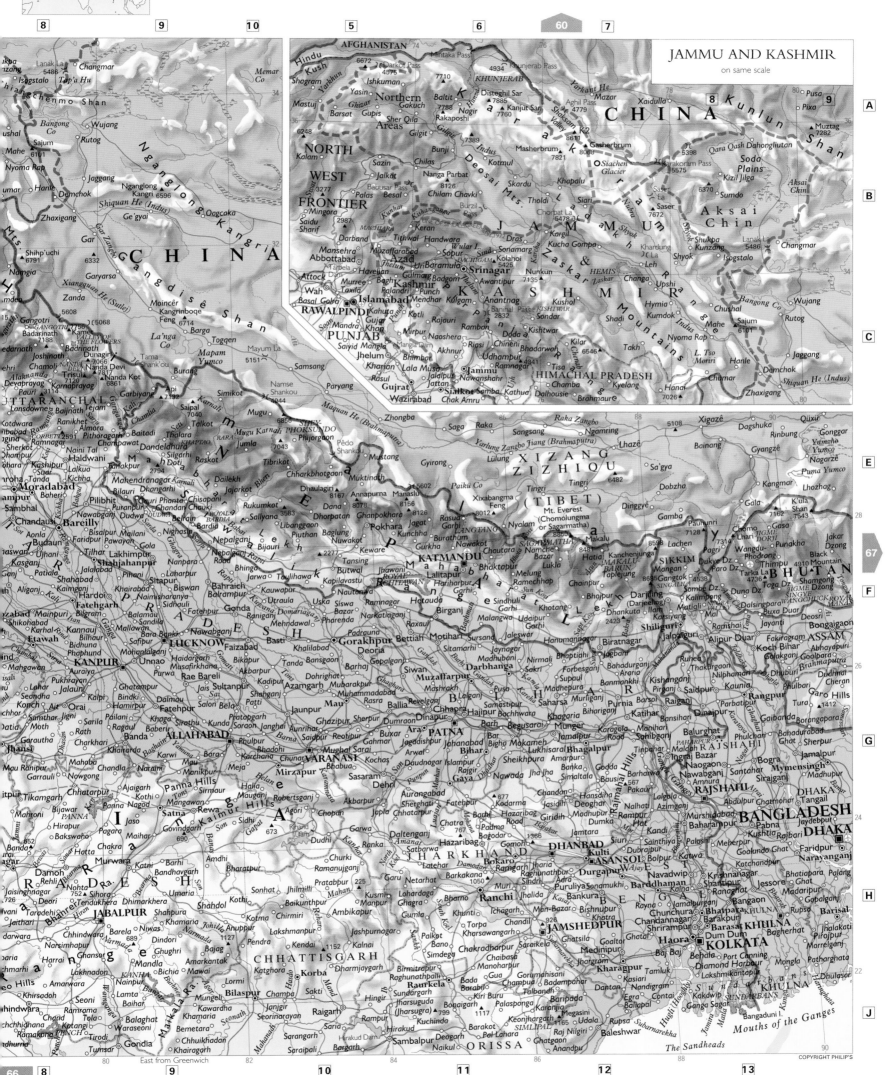

JAMMU AND KASHMIR
on same scale

1:6 200 000

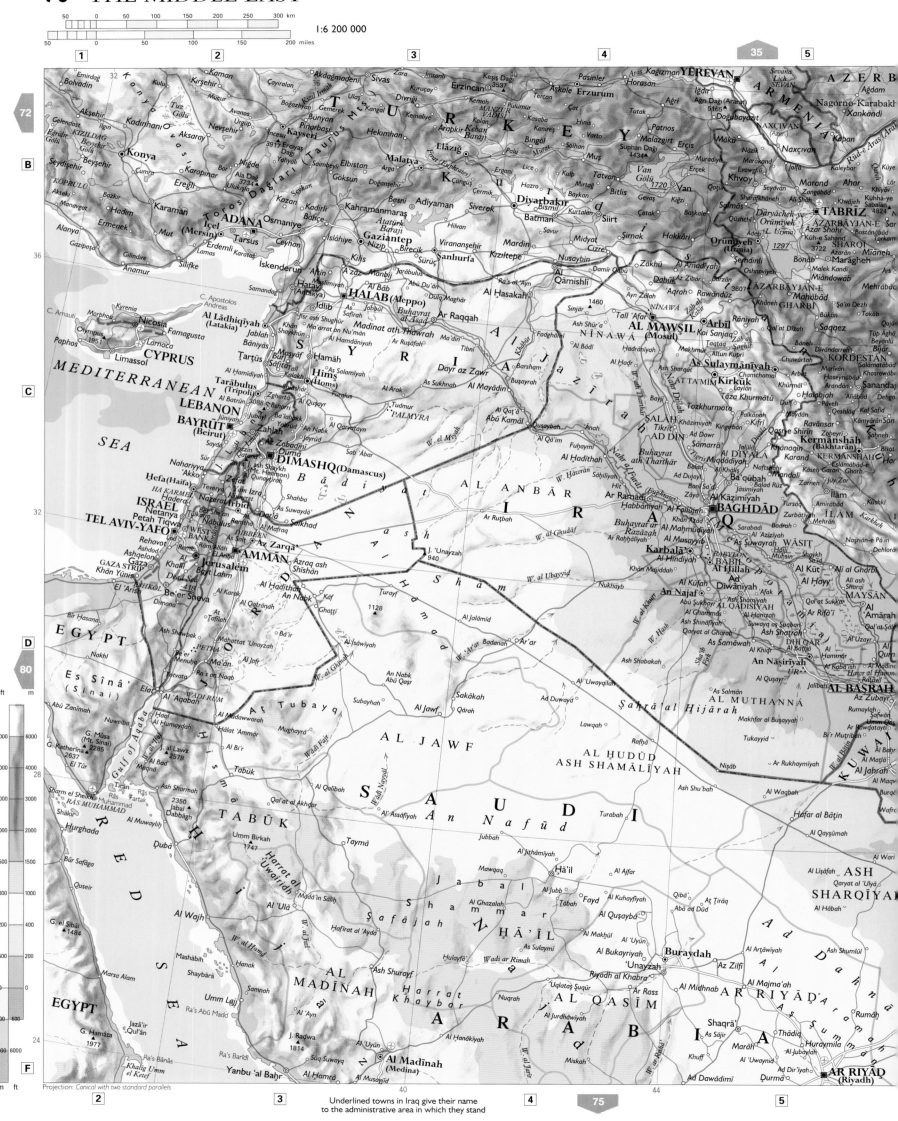

Underlined towns in Iraq give their name
to the administrative area in which they stand

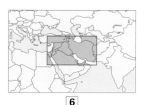

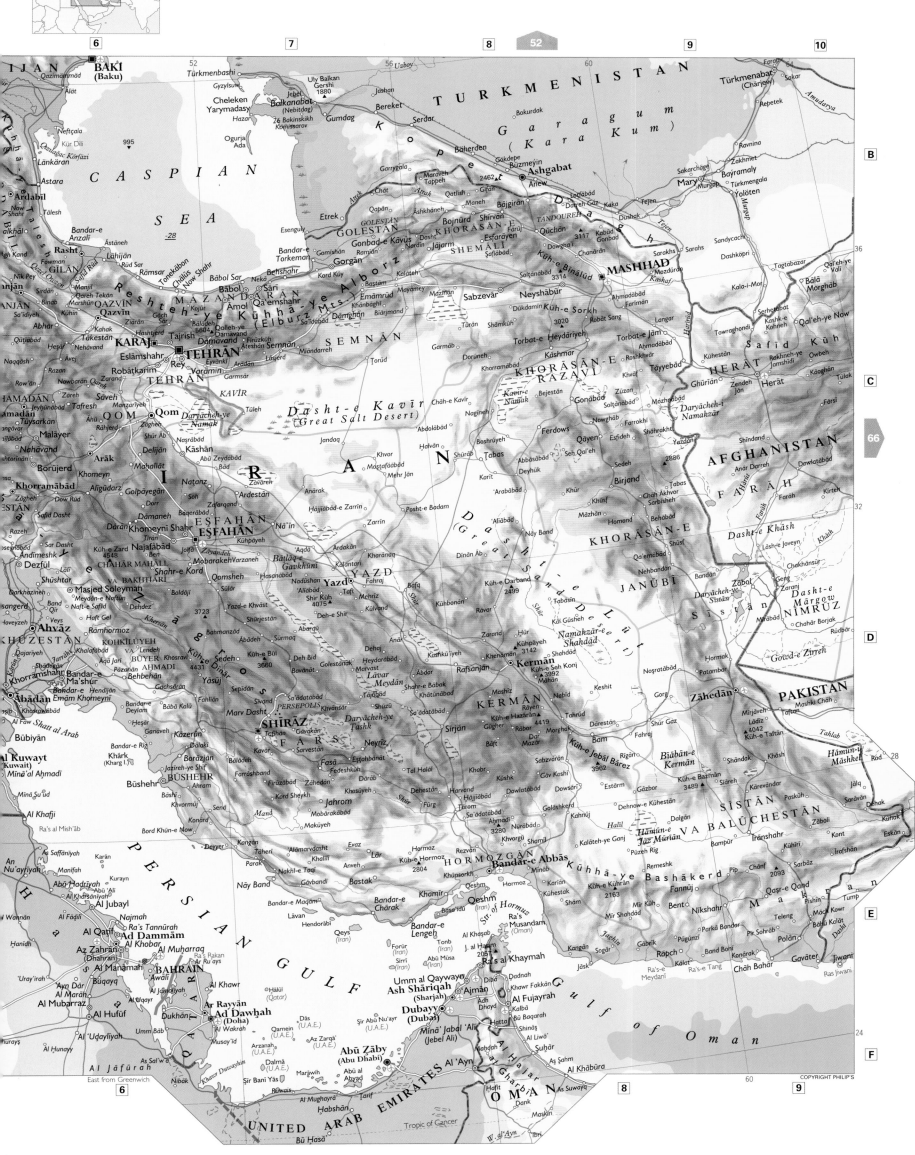

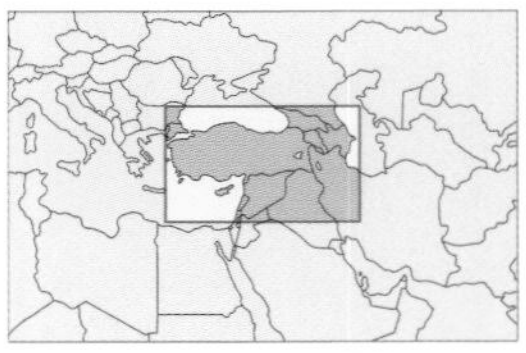

1: 4 400 000

50 0 25 50 75 100 125 150 175 km
50 0 25 50 75 100 125 miles

BLACK SEA

BULGARIA

MEDITERRANEAN SEA

GREECE

CYPRUS

LEBANON

ISRAEL

SYRIA

JORDAN

İSTANBUL
BURSA
İZMİR (Smyrna)
ANKARA
Konya
Adana
Kayseri
Gaziantep
KAHRAMAN-MARAŞ
Sivas
Tokat
SAMSUN
Zonguldak
Kastamonu
Edirne
Tekirdağ
Çanakkale
Balıkesir
Manisa
Denizli
Muğla
Antalya
İçel (Mersin)
Tarsus
İskenderun
HATAY
HALAB (Aleppo)
Al Lādhiqīyah (Latakia)
Ḥamāh
Ḥimş (Homs)
Tarābulus
BAYRŪT (Beirut)
DIMASHQ (Damascus)
AS SUWAYDA'
Nicosia
Famagusta
Kyrenia
Larnaca
Limassol
Paphos
Troodos
Marmara Denizi
İstanbul Boğazı (Bosporus)
Anadolu
Toros Dağları
Tuz Gölü
Rhodes
Karpathos
Lesbos
Hios
Samos

Marmara Denizi

Projection: Conical with two standard parallels

Division between Greeks and Turks
in Cyprus; Turks to the North.

TEL AVIV-YAFO
Hefa (Haifa)
Netanya
AMMĀN
Jerusalem
Az Zarqā

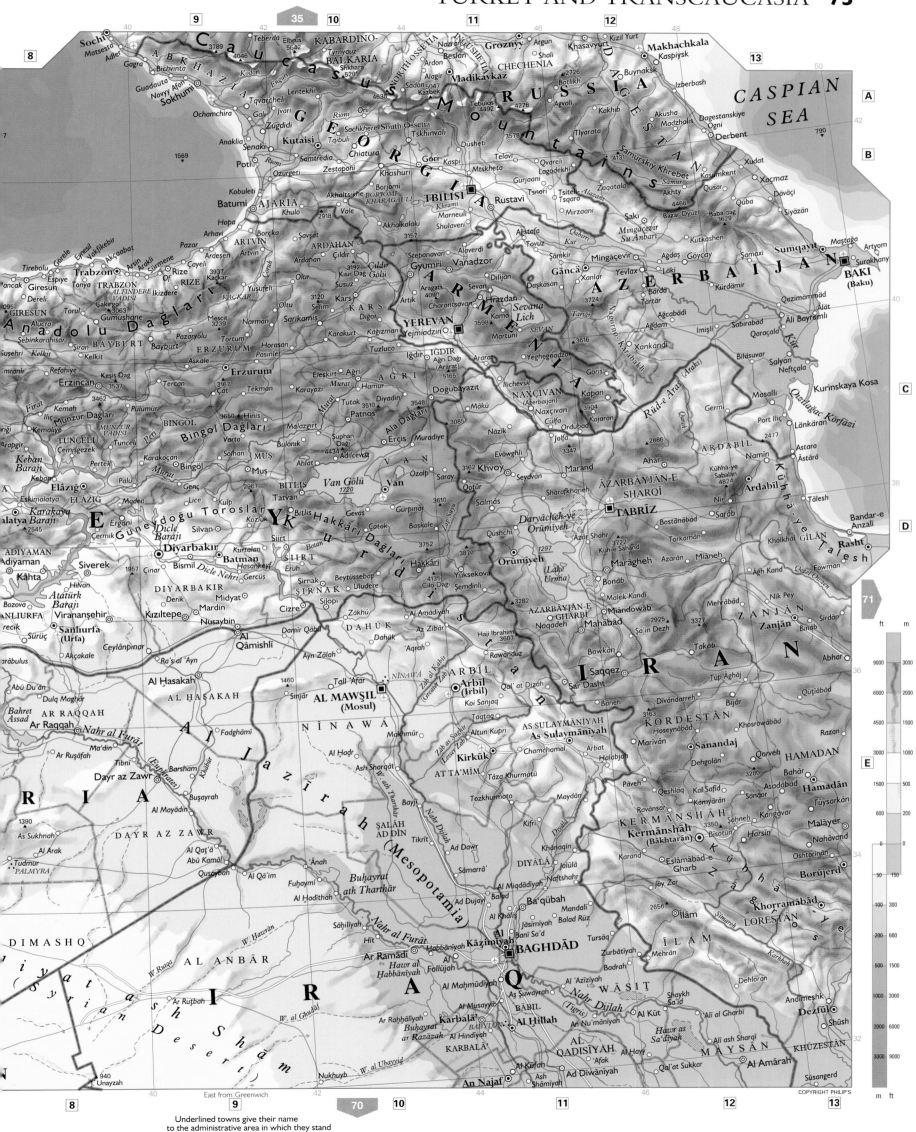

Underlined towns give their name
to the administrative area in which they stand

COPYRIGHT PHILIP'S

1:2 200 000

10 0 10 20 30 40 50 60 70 80 100 km
10 0 10 20 30 40 50 60 miles

CYPRUS

Paphos • Kividhes • Zyyi
Episkopi • Limassol • C. Gata
Episkopi Bay • Akrotiri Bay

Al Hamidiyah • Hims (Homs) • Shinshar • Furqlus
Tall Kalakh
Al Minā' • ASH SHAMĀL • Al Hirmil • Al Qusayr • HIMS
Tarābulus (Tripoli) • Zgharta • Qurnat as Sawdā' 3088 • Al Burayj
Al Batrūn • Bsharri • 2616 • Al Qaryatayn
Jubayl • Qartabā • 2464 • Al Labwan
Ibrāhim • Ba'labakk • Yabrūd • Bi'r Ghadir
Jūniyah • Bikfayyā • 2628 • An Nabk
BAYRŪT (Beirut) • J. Sannin • Zahlah • Yabrūd
Ash Shuwayfat • 'Alayh • Sirghāyā • Khān Abū Shāmat
LEBANON • Ad Dāmūr • JABAL LUBNĀN • Az Zabadāni • Dumayr
Saydā (Sidon) • Jazzin • 1942 • J. al Bārūk • DIMASHQ
An Nabatīyah at Tahta • Ash Shaykh (Mt. Hermon) • Darayyā • DIMASHQ (Damascus)
AL JANŪB • Sūr (Tyre) • 2814 • Qatanā • Jaramānah
Qiryat Shemona • Marj 'Uyūn • Al Kiswah • Al Hājānah
Nahariyya • Me'ona • Al Khiyam • Mas'ada • Buraq
'Akko (Acre) • HA GALIL • 1208 • Zefat • Al Qunaytirah • As Sanamayn
Mifraz Hefa • (Galilee) • Yam Kinneret (Sea of Galilee) • DAR'Ā • AS SUWAYDĀ
Qiryat • Karmi'el • Fiq • Shaykh Miskin • Shahbā
Hefa (Haifa) • Yam HAZAFON • 210 • Sahom al 'Awlan • 1800 • Salah
Qiryat Ata • Teverya (Tiberias) • Ar Rafid • Izra' • As Suwaydā
Daliyat el Karmel • Nazerat (Nazareth) • Dar'ā • Malah
HEFA • Afula • Tayibe • IRBID • Busrā ash Shām • Shalkhad
TEL MEGIDDO • Yarmūk • AT RAMTHĀ • Umm al Qittayn
Umm el Fahm • Bet She'an • AL MAFRAQ
CAESAREA • Jenin • AJLŪN • Jārash • Al Mafraq
Hadera • SHOMRON • J. Umm ad Daraj • Umm al Qittayn
Hanna-Karkur • SAMARIA • DIBBEEN • JARASH
ISRAEL • Tulkarm • Tūbās • 4247 • Jorash
Netanya • Nābulus • N. az Zarqā
HAMERKAZ • Ra'anana • AL BALQĀ • Az Zarqā
Herzliyya • Kefar Sava • SHILOH • As Salt
Benē Beraq • Petah Tiqwa • Wādi as Sir • AMMAN
TEL AVIV-YAFO • Ramat Gan • AL BALQĀ • Karama • AMM
Bat Yam • Lod • WEST BANK • Nā'ur • AZ ZARQĀ
Holon • Ramla • Rām Allāh • El 'Arīha (Jericho)
Rishon le Ziyyon • Yavne • 289
Ashdod • Rehovot • Jerusalem (Yerushalayim) (Al Quds) • Ma'daba • 'AMMAN
Qiryat Mal'akhi • Bet Shemesh • Bayt Lahm (Bethlehem) • MA'DABA
Ashqelon • Qiryat Gat • TEL LAKHISH • Dhibān
Gaza • N. Shiqma • Al Khalil (Hebron) • W. al Haydan • Al Hadithah
GAZA STRIP • Sederot • Az Zāhiriya • 'En Gedi
Khān Yūnis • ESHKOL • MASADA • Al Karak
Rafah • Be'er Sheva (Beersheba) • Arad • Al Mazār • AL KARAK
Būr Sa'īd (Port Said) • Bor Mashash • Sedom • 1305
Būr Fu'ād • El Daheir • Dimona • -333 • W. al Hasa
BŪR SA'ĪD • Sabkhet el Bardawil • HADAROM • At Tafilah • W. Ba'ir
Qanā es Suweis • Rās Burūn • Qezi'ot • Sedé Boqér • AT TAFILAH
Ramāni • Bir el 'Abd • Birein • JORDAN
El Qantara • Bir el Garārāt • -121 • J. ash Shawmari
Bir el Duweidar • Bir Lahfān • SHAMĀL SINĪ • Mizpe Ramon • Nijil • 1072
Ismā'iliya • Bir Kaseiba • Abu 'Aweigila • Mahattat 'Unayzah
Wāhid • Bir Madkūr • Bir el Mālhi • 892 • El Quseima • Rujm Tal'at al Jamā'ah • 1736
Talāta • ISMĀ'ILĪYA • Bir Hasana • Hanegev (Negev Desert) • PETRA • Ma'ān
Khamsa • El Buheirat • G. Yi 'Allaq 1094 • Bir Beiḍa • Wādi Mūsā
el Murrat el Kubra (Great Bitter L.) • El 'Agrūd • N. Paran • Al Jafr • Qa'el Jafr • MA'ĀN
Gineifa • Bir el Thamāda • W. Chdiya • El Agrūd • Ra's an Naqb • Mahattat ash Shidiya
EGYPT • W. el Bruk • N. Hiyyon • Rā's an Naqb
El Suweis (Suez) • Būr Taufiq • ES SINĀ' (Sinai) • El Kuntilla • Yotvata • Al 'Aqabah • 1435
Adabiya • Uyūn Mūsa • Mamarr Mitlā • Ain Sudr • Nakhl • W. Girāfi • 'En Avrona • Bi'r al Butayyihat • Bi'r al Qattar
Sudr • G. el Kabrit 948 • El Thamad • Bir Abu Muhammad • SAUDI
Ghubbet el Būs • JANŪB SINĪ • W. Ruaq • 1592 • Rum 1754 • WADI RUM • Baṭn al Ghūl
Rās Matarma • W. Abu Ga'da • Bir el Biarāt • Elat • Al 'Aqaba • At Tubayq • ARABIA
Bir Abu Sandūq 1272 • Bir Wuseit • Bir el Heisi • 1165 • Bir Tāba • Rum • Al Mudawwarah • Haql

MEDITERRANEAN SEA
2775 • 2089

= = = 1974 Cease Fire Lines

Projection: Polyconic
East from Greenwich
COPYRIGHT PHILIP'S

1:13 300 000

100   0   100   200   300   400   500   600 km
100   0   100   200   300   400 miles

LEBANON BAYRŪT (Beirut)   Sur   **SYRIA** DIMASHQ (Damascus)
ISRAEL TEL AVIV-YAFO   Ḥefa   Jabal ad Durūz 1801
Ashdod   Jerusalem WEST BANK   ‘AMMĀN
Būr Sa‘īd (Port Said) GAZA STRIP   418
Qan‘ es Suweis (Suez Canal)   Ismâ‘îliya   El Suweis (Suez)

IRAQ   Ar Ramādī   **BAGHDĀD**   Khorramābād   Al Kūt
Ar Ruṭbah   Karbalā’   **ESFAHĀN**   4548
Al Ḥillah   Dezfūl
An Najaf   Al ‘Amārah   Yazd
Ar‘ar   An Nāṣirīyah   Ahvāz

JORDAN   Bādiyat   ash Shām
Jabal ad Durūz   1801
Ma‘ān   Al Jawf   Rafḥā   Hafar al Bāṭin
El ‘Aqaba   Al ‘Aqaba   2578

IRAN   Kūhhā-ye Zagros   Khvor   Birjand   **AFGHANISTAN**   Farāh
Dasht-e Lut   Zābol   Daryācheh-ye Sīstān

AL BAṢRAH (Basra)   Ābādān   4431   PERSEPOLIS   Zāhedān
Khorramshahr   Būbiyān   **SHĪRĀZ**   Neyrīz   Sirjan   Kermān   Bam
Al Kuwayt   J. Khārk   Kāzerūn   Deyyer   Jahrom
KUWAIT   Būshehr

Es Sînâ’   G. Mûsa 2285   Al Muwayliḥ   Dubā   **An Nafūd**
Sharm el Sheikh 2187   Tabūk   Tamyā   Ḥā’il
Hurghada   Būr Safāga   Al Wajh
Qena   Quseir   KARNAK   El Uqsur (Luxor) 1977
Isna   Idfû   Kôm Ombo   Aswân   Sadd el ‘Alî
Ras Bânâs   Bîr Shalatein

Al Jubayl   Al Qaṭīf   **Persian Gulf**   Bandar-e ‘Abbās
Ad Dammām   **BAHRAIN**   Al Manāmah   Khamīr   Bampūr
Az Zahrān (Dhahran)   **QATAR**   Ra’s al-Khaymah   Ra’s Musandam (Oman)   Jāsk   Gābrīk
Al Mubarraz   Ash Shāriqah (Sharjah)   **Gulf of Oman**
Al Hufūf   Ad Dawḥah (Doha)   **Dubayy** (Dubai)
Buraydah   Unayzah   Abū Ẓaby (Abu Dhabi)   Al ‘Ayn   Ṣuḥār   As Suwayq

S A U D I   Shaqrā   **AR RIYĀD** (Riyadh)   **UNITED ARAB EMIRATES**
Maṭraḥ   Masqaṭ (Muscat)   Ṣūr
As Sulaymānīyah   Ḥaraḍ   Nizwā   Izki   3019   Ra’s al Ḥadd
A R A B I A   Tropic of Cancer   Ibrī

Al Madīnah (Medina)   Rābigh   **RED SEA**   Layla   Al ‘Ubaylah   **O M A N**
Yanbu‘ al Baḥr   Muhammad Qol   2259
JIDDAH (Jedda)   **MAKKAH** (Mecca)   Aṭ Ṭā’if 2565   As Sulayyil   Khalūf
Ras Abu Shagara   Al Līth   Turabah   Maṣīrah
Būr Sûdân   Suakin   Al Qunfudhah   **Rub‘ al Khālī** (Empty Quarter)   Ḥaymā’   Khalīj Maṣīrah
Sinkat   Trinkitat   **‘Asīr**   Ẓufār   Ra’s al Madrakah

EGYPT   Buheirat en Naser (L. Nasser)   Halaib Triangle   Halaib
ABU SIMBEL   Wadi Halfa   **Es Sahrâ en Nûbîya**
Kosha   Delgo   3rd Cataract   Dongola   4th Cataract   Kareima   Berber   Atbara
Ed Debba   Nahr en Nîl (Nile)   5th Cataract   Adarama

Abu Hamed   Haiya   Karora 2180   Khamīs Mushayṭ
Abhā   Najrān   Ash Sharawrah   Salālah   Mirbāṭ

SUDAN   Wad Hamid   6th Cataract   Shendî   Nakfa
Omdurmân   **EL KHARTÛM** (Khartoum)   Kassalâ   Akordat
Farasān   Jīzān   Ḥajjah   Khamir   **Ḥadramawt**   Rās Fartak   Shibām   2469
El Ei   Wâd Medanî   Khashm el Girba   Gedaref   **Asmera** 3018   Mitsiwa   Zula   Al Luḥayyah   Kamaran
Al Hudaydah   Dhamār   Djebel Manar   **SANA’**   **YEMEN**   Al Mukallā   Sayḥūt

Ed Dueim   Umm Ruwaba   Kôstî   Singa   Nîl el Azraq (Blue Nile)
Ed Damazin   Roseires Res.   **E R I T R E A**   Aksum   Adigrat   Adwa -116-
Aseb   Ḥanīsh   Ibb 3200   Niṣāb   Al Mukallā
Jibalan Nubah   Gezira   Mekele   Ras Dashen 4533   **Danakil Desert**   Ta‘izz   Shaqrā’   Aḥwar
Al Mukhā   Madīnat ash Sha‘b   Al ‘Adan (Aden)
‘Abd al Kūrī (Yemen)   **Gulf of Aden**   Hadīboh   **Socotra** (Yemen)

Ethiopian   Gonder 1830   Lalibela 4190   Bāb el Mandeb
L. Tana   Debre Tabor   **DJIBOUTI**   Tadjoura   L. Assal -156-   **Djibouti**   Zeila   Bereda   Ras Asir
Bahir Dar   Dese   Dikhil   L. Abbé   Berbera   Bosaso   Xaafuun   Ras Xaafuun
Bure   Debre Markos 4000   Karin   El Gal
Highlands   Dire Dawa   **Hargeisa**   Burao   Gardo   Bender Beila

S û d d   Bahr el Jebel (Nile)   Abay (Blue Nile)
Dembidolo   Metu 3302   Nekemte   **ADDIS ABEBA**   Debre Zeyit   Awash   3381   Jijiga   **Somaliland**   2408   Erigavo   Eil
Gore   **ETHIOPIA**   Nazret   Harer   Las Anod   Garoe   Garge
Jima   Asela   **O g a d e n**   Kebri Dehar   Galcaio

INDIAN
Awasa   Shashemene   Ginir   Imi   Sinadogo   Obbia
3686   Yirga Alem   Goba   Mt. Batu 4307   Ferfer
Omo   Dila   Kibre Mengist   Genale   **S O M A L I A**   Dolo   **OCEAN**
L. Abaya   Negele   Scebeli   Belet Uen
Arba Minch   L. Shamo   Chew Bahir   Mega   El Dere
Elemi Triangle   Lokitaung 1794   Dolo   Lugh Ganana

Juba   Mongalla   Kapoeta   L. Turkana   Wajir   Baidoa   Bur Acaba   Giohar   Uanle Uen
Yei   Kajo Kaji 3187   Torit   Lodwar   Marsabit   Moyale   El Wak   Bardera   **MUQDISHO** (Mogadishu)
Tali Post   Bôr   Pibor Post   South Horr 2752   Wabi Scebeli   Merca
UGANDA   Gulu   Liro   Moroto   Kitale   Dif   **KENYA**   Gelib   Merca
2434   Pakwach   3084   Soroti   Mt. Elgon 4321   3206
L. Albert   Masindi   L. Kyoga   Mbale   East from Greenwich

Equator   **Kismayu**   Giamama

ft   m
12 000   4000
9000   3000
6000   2000
4500   1500
3000   1000
1200   400
600   200
0   0
200   600
1000   3000
2000   6000
4000   12 000
m   ft

Projection: Sanson-Flamsteed's Sinusoidal   COPYRIGHT PHILIP'S

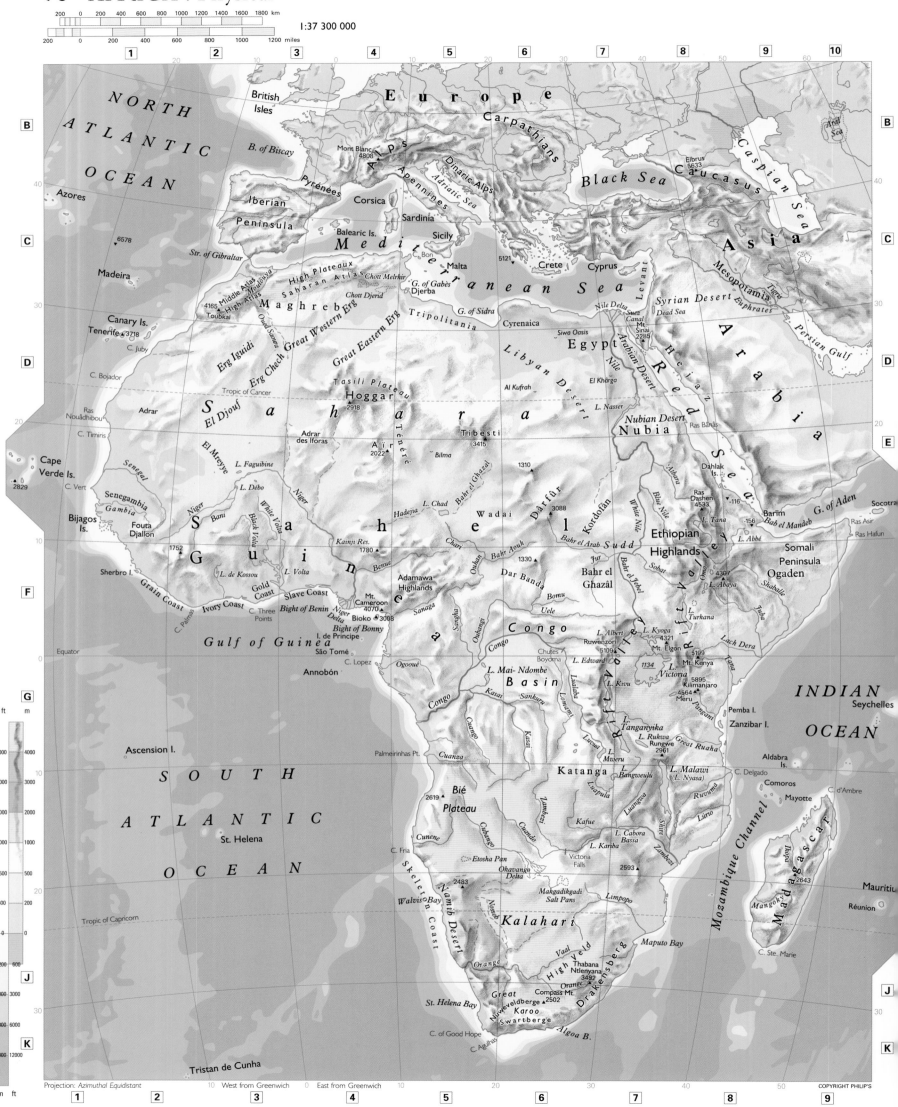

1:37 300 000

Projection: *Azimuthal Equidistant*

West from Greenwich   East from Greenwich

COPYRIGHT PHILIP'S

1:37 300 000

200 0 200 400 600 800 1000 1200 1400 1600 1800 km
200 0 200 400 600 800 1000 1200 miles

1 2 3 4 5 6 7 8 9 10

NORTH ATLANTIC OCEAN

Azores (Port.)
Ponta Delgada

RUSSIA
KAZAKHSTAN

UNITED KINGDOM
LONDON
NETH.
BELG.
GERMANY POLAND
Warsaw
Prague
CZECH REP.
Vienna
SLOVAK REP.
FRANCE
SWITZ.
AUSTRIA
HUNGARY
CROATIA
BOS.-HERZ.
SERBIA
MONT.
MAC.
ROMANIA
BULGARIA
Kiev
UKRAINE
Odessa
Volgograd

B. of Biscay
PARIS

Corsica
Rome
ITALY
Sardinia
Sicily
Adriatic Sea
Black Sea
GEORGIA
Ankara
ARM. AZER.
Baku
TURKMEN.
Caspian Sea
Aral Sea

PORTUGAL
Lisbon
SPAIN
Madrid

GREECE
Athens
Crete
CYPRUS
TURKEY
Aleppo
Mosul
TEHRĀN
Eṣfahān

Madeira (Port.)
Funchal
Rabat
Tétouan
Fès
Casablanca
Algiers
Oran
Annaba
Constantine
Tunis
Sfax
MALTA
Mediterranean Sea
Tripoli
Miṣrātah
Benghazi

MOROCCO
Marrakesh

Santa Cruz de Tenerife
Canary Is. (Sp.)
Las Palmas
El Aaiún

LEB.
Tel Aviv-Jaffa
Damascus
Jerusalem
ISRAEL
JORDAN
Baghdād
Basra
KUWAIT
Syrian Desert
Tigris
Euphrates
IRAQ
IRAN

Alexandria
Port Said
CAIRO
El Faiyûm
Suez
Asyût
EGYPT

SAUDI ARABIA
Medina
Riyadh
BAHRAIN
QATAR
Persian Gulf

Dakhla
Ras Nouâdhibou
Fdérik
WESTERN SAHARA
In Salah
Sabhā
Al Jawf
Aswân
Wadi Halfa
Port Sudan

Sahara
Tropic of Cancer

ALGERIA
LIBYA

Red Sea
Jedda
Mecca

CAPE VERDE IS.
Praia
C. Vert
St-Louis
Dakar
SENEGAL
GAMBIA
Banjul
Nouakchott
MAURITANIA
Tombouctou
NIGER
CHAD
SUDAN
Omdurmân
Khartoum
Wâd Medani
El Obeid
El Fâsher
Abéché
Ndjamena
L. Chad
Agadès
Niamey
Kano
Maiduguri

Atbara
'Atbara
Massawa
ERITREA
Asmera
YEMEN
Socotra (Yemen)
Ras Asir
G. of Aden
DJIBOUTI
Djibouti
Berbera
SOMALILAND

MALI
GUINEA-BISSAU
Bissau
Conakry
Freetown
SIERRA LEONE
GUINEA
Bamako
BURKINA FASO
Ouagadougou
Bobo-Dioulasso
BENIN
NIGERIA
Abuja
Ibadan
Enugu
LAGOS
TOGO
GHANA
IVORY COAST
Yamoussoukro
Bouaké
Kumasi
LIBERIA
Monrovia
Abidjan
Sekondi-Takoradi
Accra
Lomé
Porto Novo

Niger
Benue
Chari
L. Tana
White Nile
Blue Nile
Malakâl
Wâw
Addis Ababa
Harer
ETHIOPIA
Shabelle
SOMALI REP.

CAMEROON
Douala
Yaoundé
Rey Malabo
EQUATORIAL GUINEA
CENTRAL AFRICAN REP.
Bangui
UGANDA
KENYA
Nairobi
L. Turkana
Juba
Mogadishu
Kismayu

Bight of Benin
Port Harcourt
Gulf of Guinea
SÃO TOMÉ & PRÍNCIPE
Libreville
GABON
Annobón
C. Lopez
Equator

CONGO
Mbandaka
Kisangani
L. Albert
L. Edward
RWANDA
Kigali
BURUNDI
Bujumbura
L. Kivu
Kampala
Kisumu
L. Victoria
INDIAN OCEAN
Victoria
SEYCHELLES

SOUTH ATLANTIC OCEAN

Ascension I. (U.K.)
St. Helena (U.K.)

Pointe-Noire
Brazzaville
CABINDA (Angola)
KINSHASA
Matadi
CONGO (DEM. REP. OF THE)
Kananga
Mbuji-Mayi
TANZANIA
Dodoma
Zanzibar
Dar es Salaam
Mombasa
L. Tanganyika
Kasai
Congo

Luanda
Lobito
ANGOLA
Namibe
Huambo
C. Fria
Cunene
Cuango
Cubango
Zambeze
L. Mweru
Likasi
Lubumbashi
Ndola
ZAMBIA
Lusaka
Livingstone
Aldabra Is. (Seychelles)
COMOROS
Moroni
Mamoudzou
Mayotte (Fr.)
Antsiranana
Mahajanga
Toamasina

Malawi
L. Malawi
MALAWI
Lilongwe
Blantyre
MOZAMBIQUE
Moçambique
Mozambique Channel

Namibe
Windhoek
NAMIBIA
BOTSWANA
Gaborone
ZIMBABWE
Harare
Bulawayo
Beira
Limpopo
MADAGASCAR
Antananarivo
Fianarantsoa
St-Denis
Réunion (Fr.)
MAURITIUS
Port Louis

Tropic of Capricorn

SOUTH AFRICA
Johannesburg
Pretoria (Tshwane)
Maputo
Mbabane
SWAZ.
LESOTHO
Maseru
Kimberley
Vaal
Orange
Durban (eThekwini)
East London
Cape Town
C. of Good Hope
C. Agulhas
Port Elizabeth

Tristan da Cunha (U.K.)

Projection: Azimuthal Equidistant
West from Greenwich
East from Greenwich

● Dakar Capital Cities

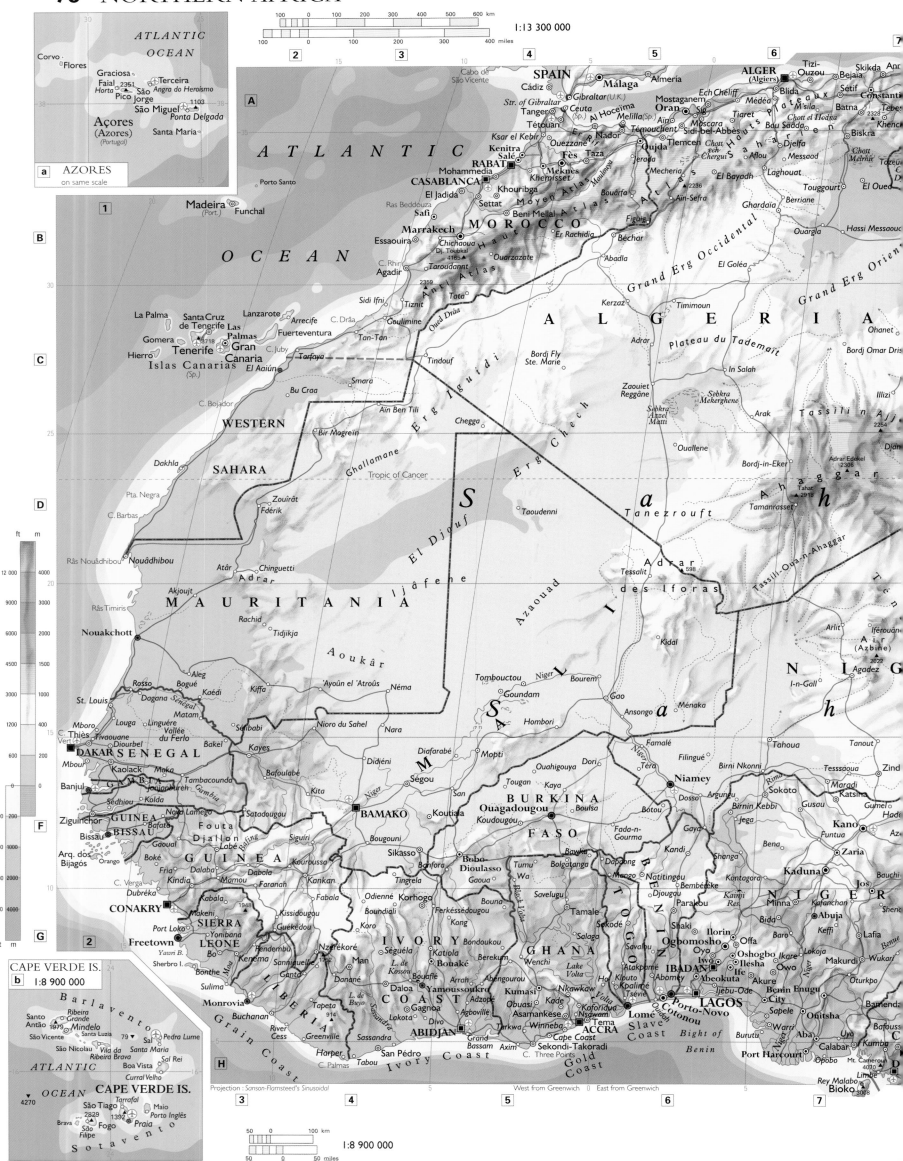

1:13 300 000

100 0 100 200 300 400 500 600 km
100 0 100 200 300 400 miles

AZORES
on same scale

ATLANTIC OCEAN

Corvo · Flores
Graciosa
Faial 2351 · Terceira
Horta · Pico · São Jorge · Angra do Heroismo
São Miguel
Açores 1103
(Azores) · Ponta Delgada
(Portugal) · Santa Maria

a

CAPE VERDE IS.

b 1:8 900 000

Barlavento
Santo · Ribeira
Antão 1979 · Grande
São Vicente · Mindelo · Santa Luzia
São Nicolau · 79 · Sal · Pedra Lume
Vila da · Santa Maria · Sal Rei
Ribeira Brava · Boa Vista

ATLANTIC

OCEAN

CAPE VERDE IS.

4270
São Tiago · Tarrafal
2829 · 1392
Brava · São · Maio · Porto Inglês
Fogo · Praia
São Filipe

Sotavento

1:8 900 000

50 0 100 km
50 0 50 miles

Projection : Sanson-Flamsteed's Sinusoidal

West from Greenwich 0 East from Greenwich

1:7 100 000

50   0   50   100   150   200   250   300 km

50   0   50   100   150   200 miles

THE NILE DELTA
1:3 600 000

MEDITERRANEAN SEA

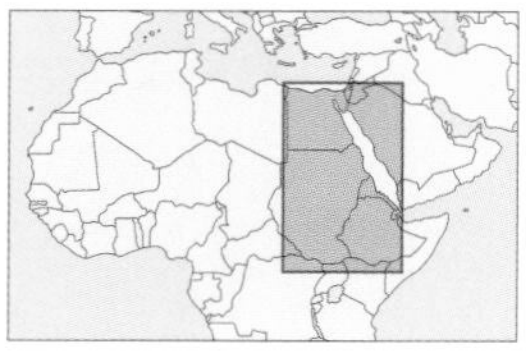

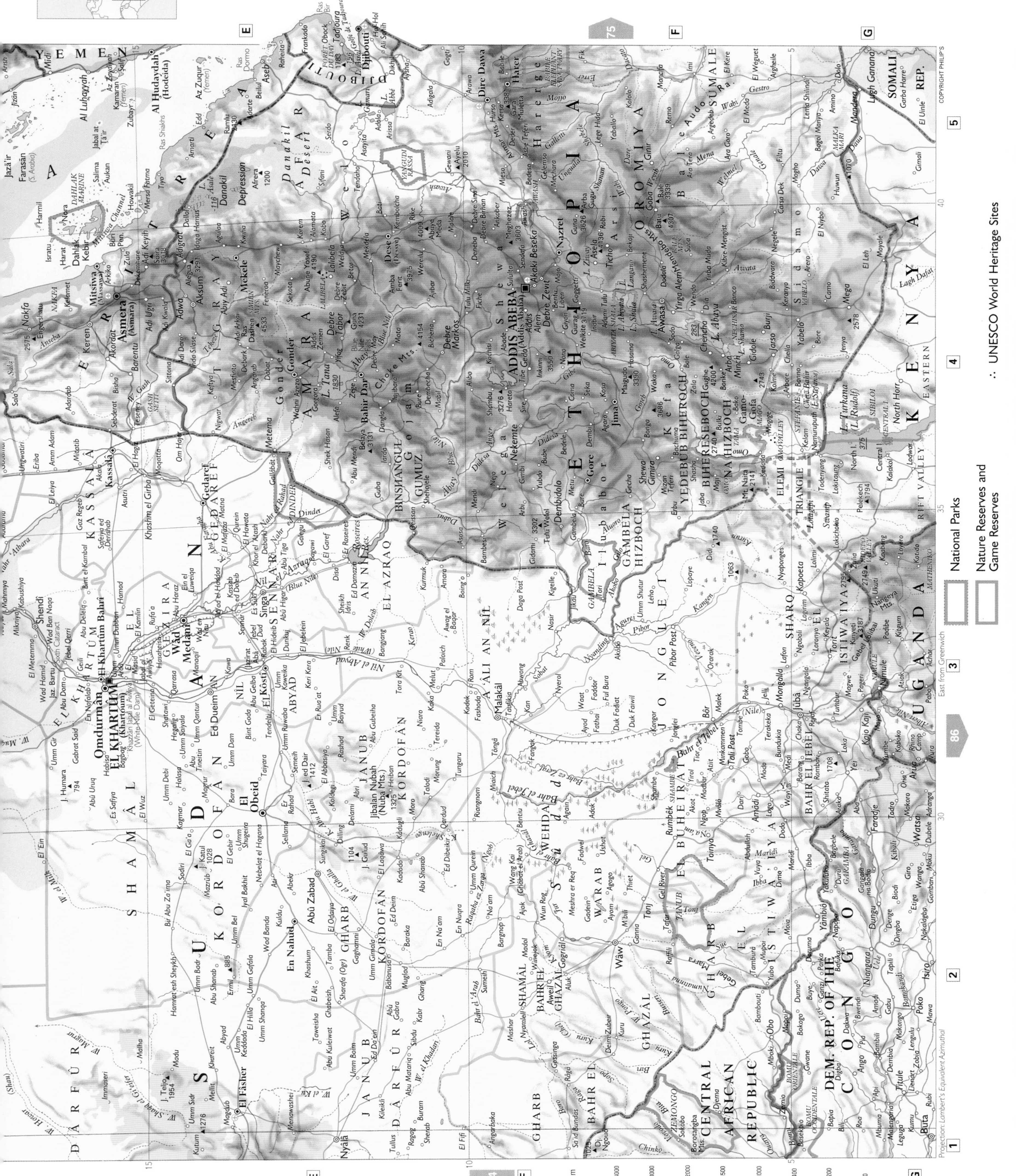

YEMEN
ERITREA
Asmera (Asmara)
Mitsiwa (Massawa)
DJIBOUTI
Djibouti
ETHIOPIA
ADDIS ABEBA (Addis Abeba)
Dire Dawa
Gonder
Bahir Dar
L. Tana
Dese
Jima
Nazret
Awasa
SUDAN
EL KHARTÛM (Khartoum)
Omdurman
Kassala
Gedaref
Wad Medani
Kôsti
El Obeid
En Nahud
El Fâsher
Nyala
Malakâl
Wâw
Juba
KENYA
L. Turkana (L. Rudolf)
UGANDA
CENTRAL AFRICAN REPUBLIC
DEM. REP. OF THE CONGO
SOMALI REP.
Projection: Lambert's Equivalent Azimuthal
East from Greenwich
COPYRIGHT PHILIP'S
84
86
75
National Parks
Nature Reserves and Game Reserves
∴ UNESCO World Heritage Sites

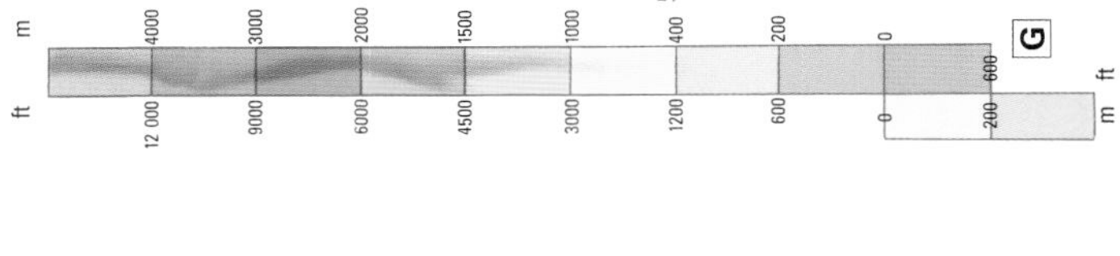

m
4000
3000
2000
1500
1000
400
200
0
200
ft
12 000
9000
6000
4500
3000
1200
600
0
600

Projection : *Lambert's Equivalent Azimuthal*

Underlined towns give their name to the
administrative area in which they stand.

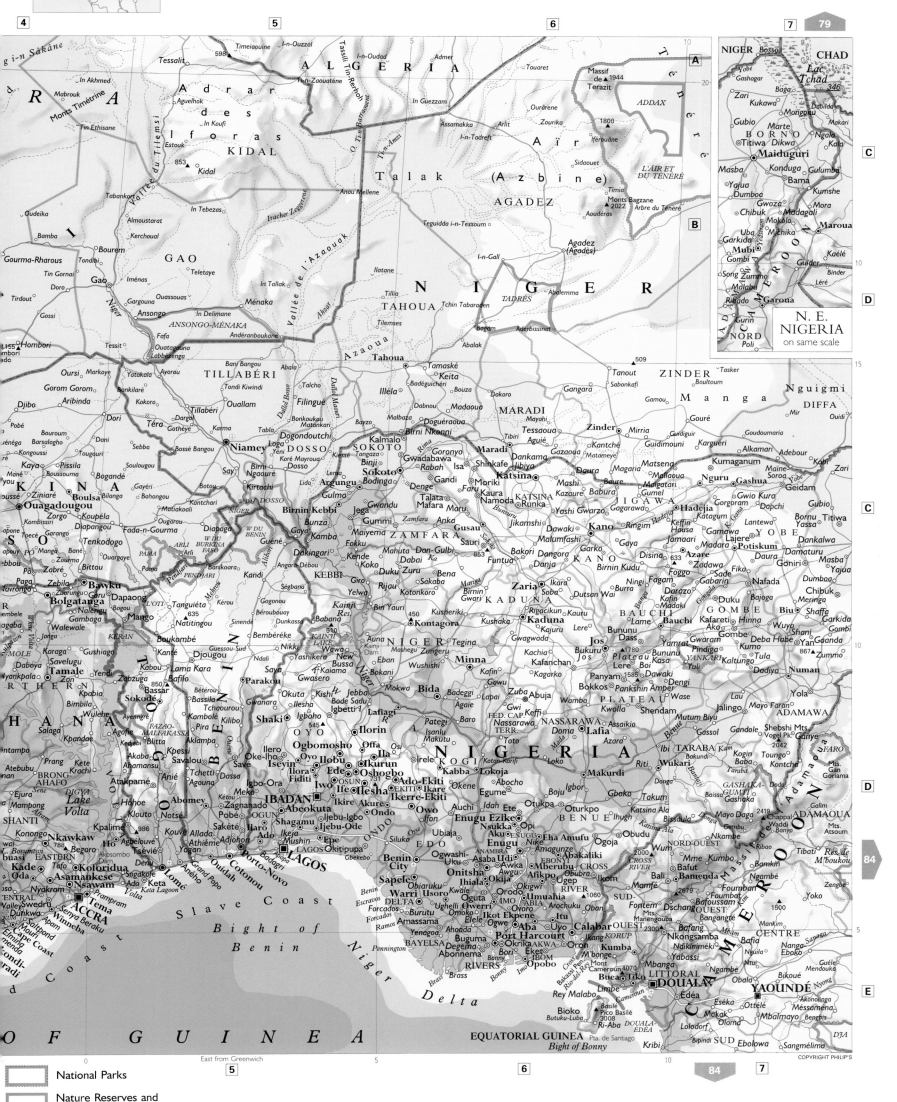

National Parks

Nature Reserves and
Game Reserves

∴ UNESCO World Heritage Sites

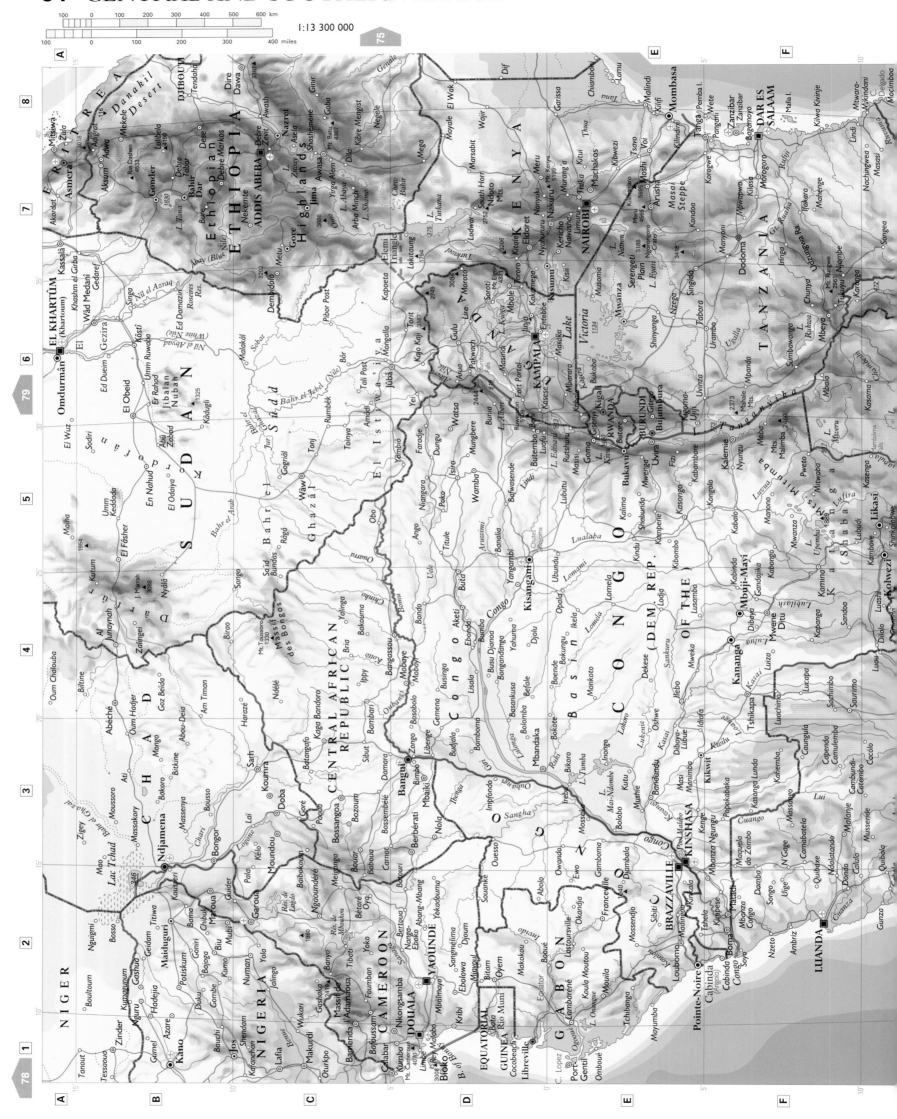

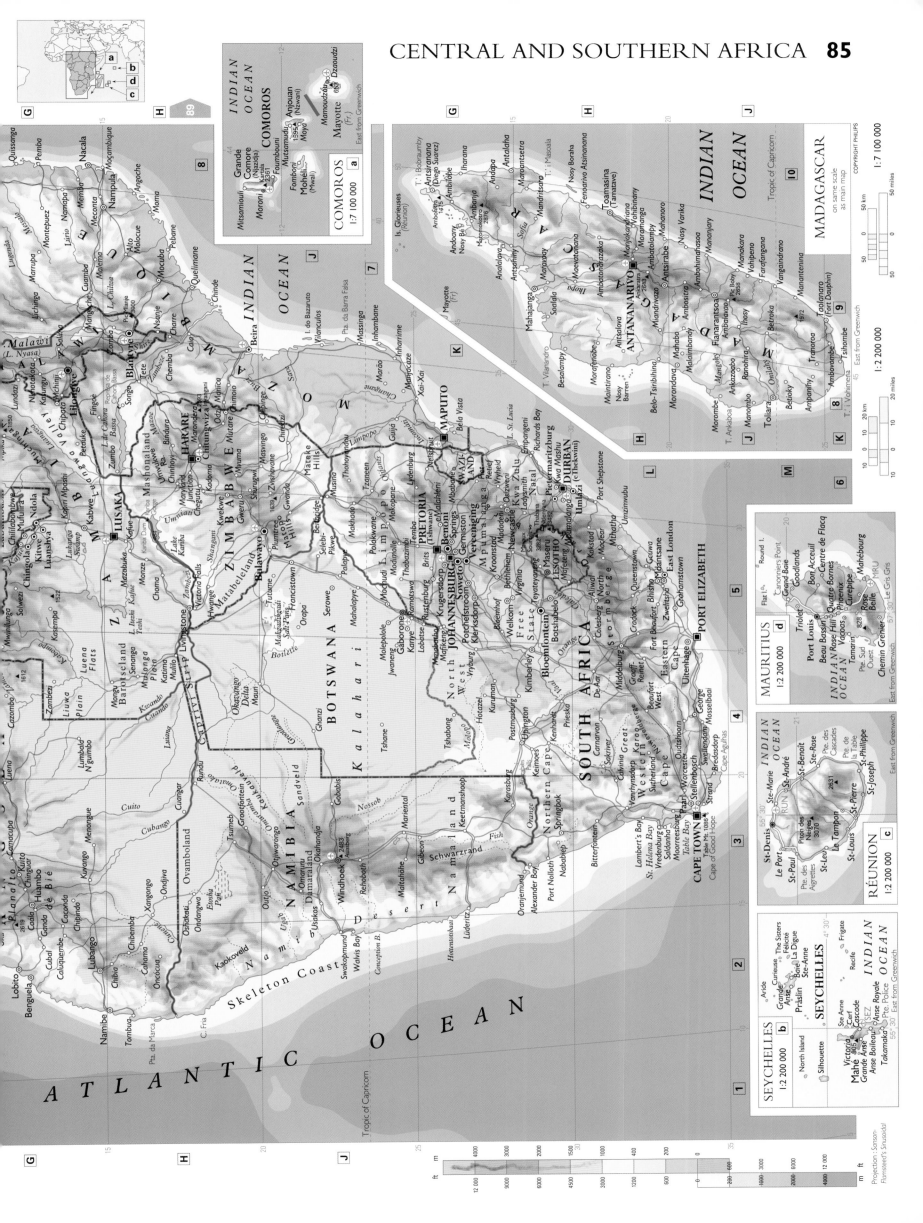

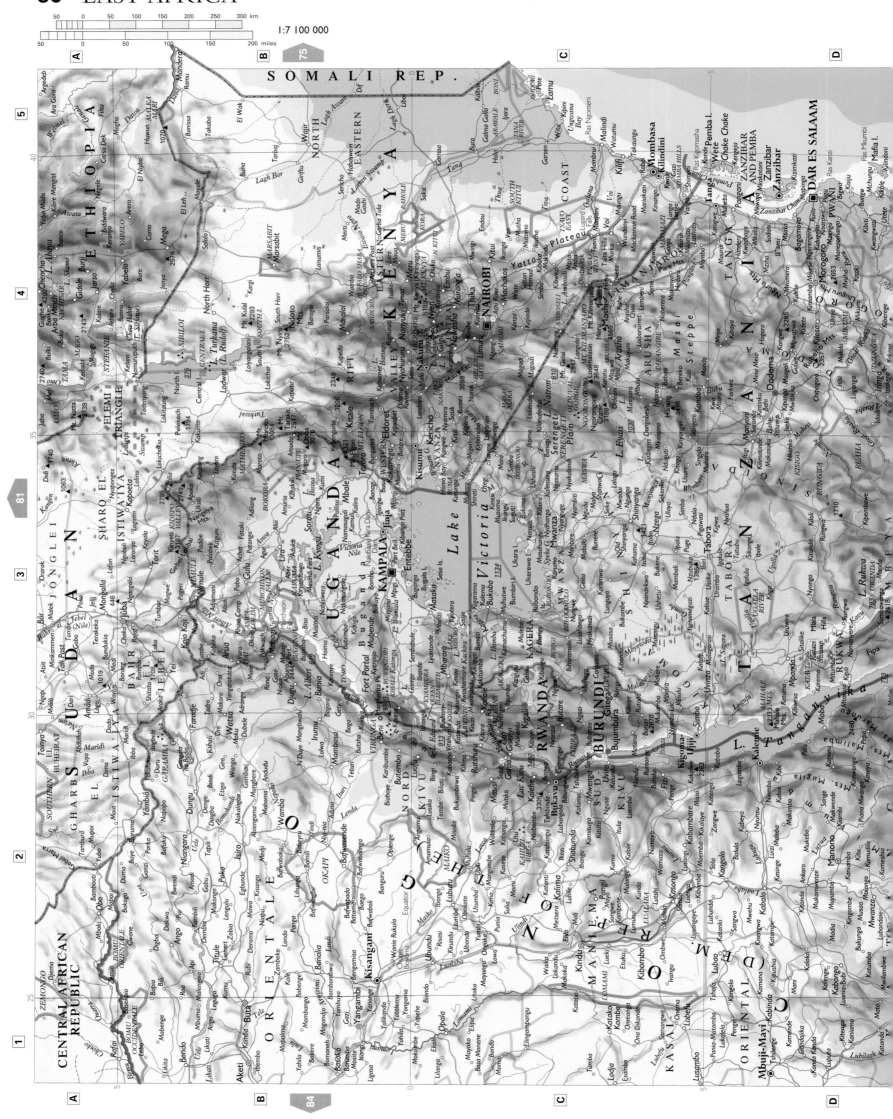

1:7 100 000

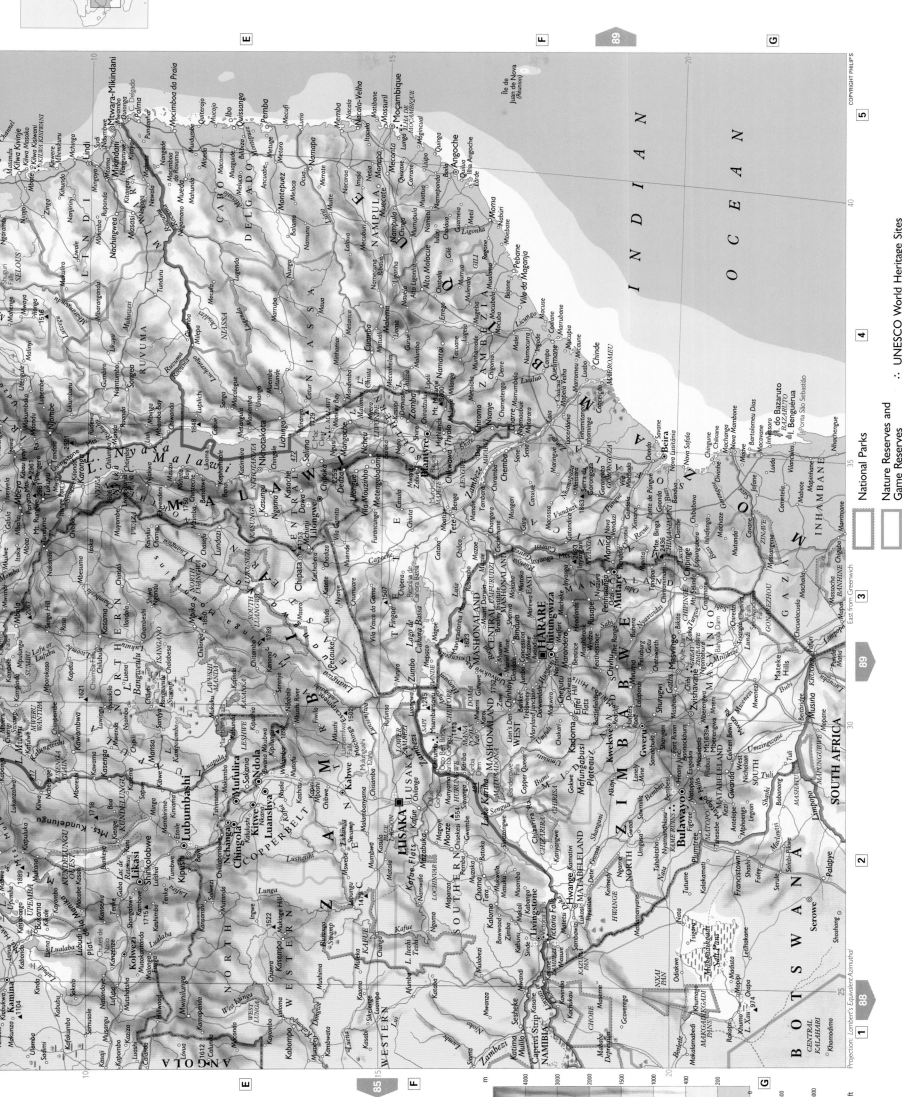

National Parks

Nature Reserves and
Game Reserves

:: UNESCO World Heritage Sites

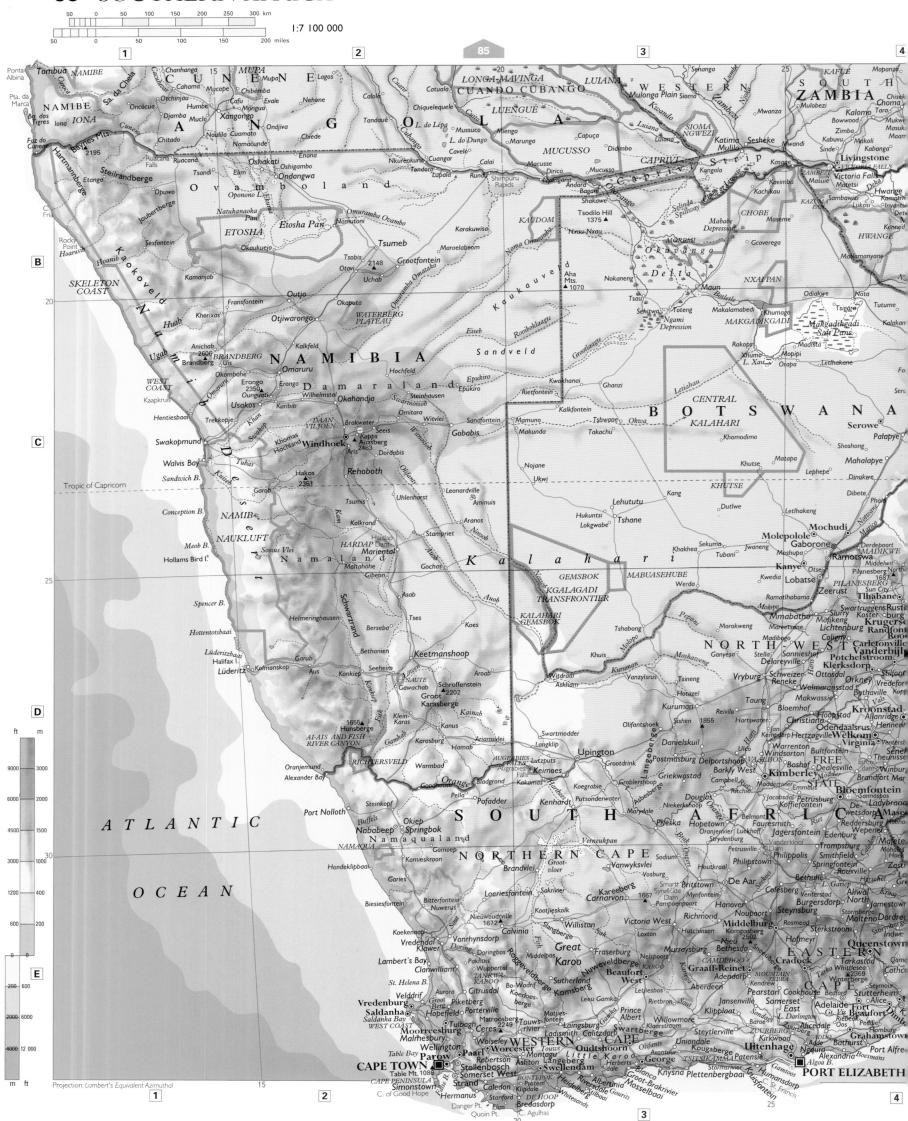

50 0 50 100 150 200 250 300 km

1:7 100 000

50 0 50 100 150 200 miles

Projection: Lambert's Equivalent Azimuthal

National Parks

Nature Reserves and
Game Reserves

∴ UNESCO World Heritage Sites

MADAGASCAR

on same scale

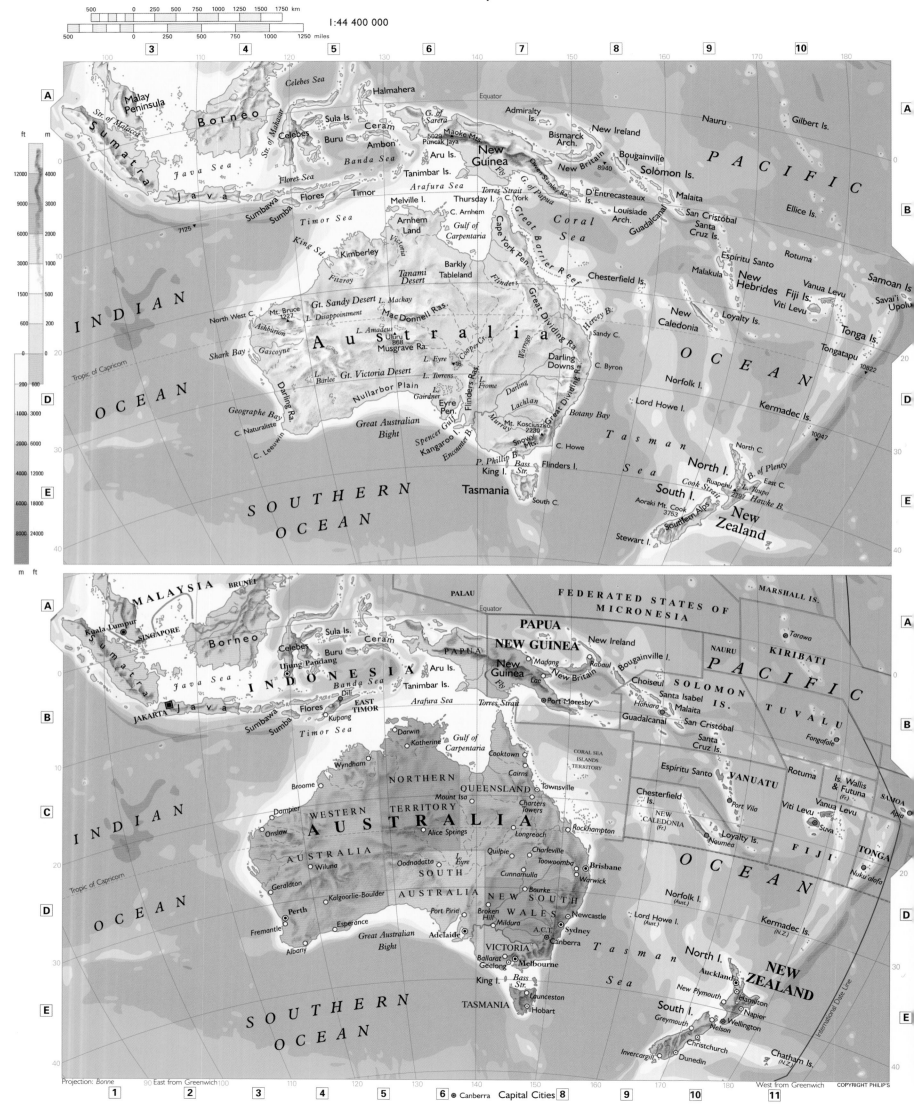

500   0   250   500   750   1000   1250   1500   1750 km
500   0   250   500   750   1000   1250 miles

1:44 400 000

Projection: *Bonne*   90 East from Greenwich 100   West from Greenwich   COPYRIGHT PHILIP'S

⊙ Canberra   Capital Cities

1:5 300 000

50   0   50   100   150   200 km
50   0   50   100   150 miles

4   96   5   6   7

FIJI a
on same scale

178 E   180   Great Sea Reef   Kia   Udu Pt.   Ringgold Is.
Yasawa Group   Yaqaga   Labasa   Natewa Bay   Rabi
Nacula   Yasawa   Yadua   Bua   Savusavu   Qamea   Taveuni
Naviti   Vanua Levu   ▲1031   Buca   Somosomo Str.   Naitaba
Viwa   Nabouwalu   Somosomo   Kanacea   Vanua Balavu
Waya   Nasau   Koro   Vacata   Lomaloma
Vomo   Tavua   ▲1323   Lawaki   Makogai   Wakaya   Northern Lau Group   Tuvuca
Mamanuca Group   KOROYANITU   Ovalau   Batiki   Sawaleke.   Cicia   Lakeba Passage
Lautoka   Tomanivi   Levuka   Nairai   Namuka-i-Lau
Malolo   Nadi   Viti Levu   Korovou   Nayau   Lakeba   Tubou
   Keiyasi   Vunidawa   Southern Lau Group   Moce
Sigatoka   Koroleu   Navua   Suva   Nausori   Yagasa Cluster
Vatulele   Yanuca   Beqa   Moala   Kabara   Fulaga   Ogea Levu
   Kadavu Passage   FIJI   Vanua Vatu   Ogea Driki
Kadavu   Ono   Totoya   Matuku
Tavuki   Yunisea   East from Greenwich   West from Greenwich

PACIFIC OCEAN
KORO SEA
Lau Group

18 S

SAMOAN ISLANDS b
on same scale

Asau   Safune   SAMOA   Pu'apu'a
Falelima   ▲1858   Saleilologa   Falefa   Apia   Falelatai
Savai'i   Taga   Mulifanua   Manono   Amaile
OLE PUPU PUE   Safata Bay   'Upolu
PACIFIC OCEAN
AMERICAN SAMOA (U.S.A.)
Ofu   Olosega
AMERICAN SAMOA   Luma   Ta'u
Tutuila   Pago Pago   Aunu'u   Manu'a Is.   AMERICAN SAMOA
Leone   Vaitogi   West from Greenwich

14 S   170 W   172   172 W

TONGA c
on same scale

Fonualei   Toku
Vava'u   Neiafu
PACIFIC OCEAN   Vava'u Group
Late   Home Reef
Disney Reef
Ofolanga
Tofua   Kao   Foa   Ha'ano   Ha'apai Group
   Lifuka   Uiha
Kotu Group
Fonuafo'ou   Nomuka   Oto Tolu Group
Hunga Ha'apai   Nomuka Group   Mango   Tonumea
TONGA
Nuku'alofa   Tongatapu
Tongatapu Group   'Eua
West from Greenwich

18 S   174 W   170   20 S

New Zealand main map

C. Reinga   North C.
C. Maria van Diemen
Houhora Heads   Rangaunu B.   Doubtless B.
Ahipara B.   Mongonui   Whangaroa Harb.
Kaitaia   Okaihau   B. of Islands
Tauroa Pt.   Kaikohe   Waitangi   C. Brett
Rawene   Opua
Hokianga Harbour   Kaikohe   Hikurangi
Waipoua Forest   Whangarei   Whangarei Harb.
Dargaville   Waipu   Bream Hd.   Bream B.
   Barrier I.
Warkworth   C. Rodney   Great Barrier I.
Kaipara Harbour   Helensville   Cuvier I.
   C. Colville
Takapuna   Coromandel   Whitianga
AUCKLAND   Hauraki Gulf   Mayor I.
Manukau   Papakura   Thames   Whangamata
Waiuku   Pukekohe   Whangamata
Mercer   Waihi   Tauranga Harb.
Waikato   Paeroa   Waihi   Whakaari (White I.)   Runaway
Huntly   Te Aroha   Mount Maunganui   Tauranga
Raglan   Morrinsville   Te Puke   Bay of Plenty
Hamilton   Cambridge   Whakatane   Opotiki   East C.
Kawhia   Te Awamutu   Kawerau   Raukumara Ra.
Kawhia Harbour   Putaruru   Rotorua   Taneatua   Hikurangi ▲1753
Waitomo   Tokoroa   Rotorua   Murupara   Motu   Waipiro
Otorohanga   L. Rotorua   L. Tarawera   Tolaga Bay
Te Kuiti   Kinleith   UREWERA   Ormond
North Taranaki Bight   Mokau   Mangakino   Waikaremoana   Gisborne
Waitara   Ongarue   Taupo   Wairoa   Poverty Bay
New Plymouth   Taumarunui   L. Taupo   Ruatahuna   Nuhaka   Waikokopu
Inglewood   WHANGANUI   Turangi   Kaimanawa Mts.   Mahia Pen.
Mt. Taranaki or Mt. Egmont   Whangamomona   Wairoa
▲2518   EGMONT   Raetihi   Kaimanawa Mts.   Bay View   Hawke Bay
Opunake   Stratford   Ohakune   TONGARIRO ▲2797   Napier
Kaponga   Eltham   Waiouru   Ruahine Ra.   Hastings
Hawera   Taihape   C. Kidnappers
South Taranaki Bight   Waverley   Mangaweka   Waipawa
Patea   Hunterville   Dannevirke   Waipukurau
Wanganui   Marton   Halcombe   Feilding   Woodville   Pahiatua
   Bulls   Palmerston North   Eketahuna
Foxton   Shannon   Masterton   C. Turnagain
Levin   Otaki   Carterton   Greytown
Paraparaumu   Kapiti I.   Featherston   Martinborough   Wairarapa
Upper Hutt   Pelorus Sd.   Wairau
Petone   Lower Hutt   Blenheim
Wellington   Eastbourne   Seddon   Ward
Cook Strait

C. Farewell
Golden B.   D'Urville I.
Collingwood   Takaka   ABEL TASMAN   Tasman B.
KAHURANGI   Tasman Mts.   Motueka   Nelson   Havelock
Karamea   Takaka   Nelson   Richmond   Picton
Karamea Bight   Wakefield
Seddonville   Tadmor   NELSON LAKES   L. Rotoiti
Granity   Lyell   Murchison   L. Rotoroa   ▲2885 Tapuae-o-Uenuku
Westport   Inangahua   Mt. Travers ▲2337   Kaikoura
PAPAROA   Reefton   Spenser Mts.   Clarence
Punakaiki   Lewis Pass   Hanmer Springs
Blackball   Waiau   Waiau
Runanga   Stillwater   Culverden   Waipara
Greymouth   L. Brunner   Jacksons   Amberley
Kumara   ARTHUR'S PASS   Waikari   Oxford   Pegasus Bay
Hokitika   Otira   Springfield   Rangiora   New Brighton
Ross   Coleridge   Whitecliffs   Kaiapoi   Christchurch
Abut Hd.   Riccarton   Lincoln   Lyttelton
Westland Bight   WESTLAND   Methven   Banks Pen.
   Mt. Cook 3753   Staveley   Akaroa
Aoraki   Mount Cook   MT COOK   L. Ellesmere   Little River
   Fairlie   Rakaia
Jackson B.   Tekapo   Ashburton   Canterbury Bight
MOUNT ASPIRING   Pukaki   Temuka
Mt. Aspiring ▲3033   Ohau   Timaru
Mt. Earnslaw ▲2819   L. Wanaka   St. Andrews   Waimate
Milford Sd.   Wanaka   Kurow   Ngapara   Oamaru
Sutherland Falls   Arrowtown   Cromwell   Tokarahi   Maheno
Bligh Sound   Queenstown   Clyde   Naseby   Hampden   Danback
George Sound   Wakatipu   Alexandra   Roxburgh   Palmerston
Secretary I.   FIORDLAND   Garvie Mts.   Waikouaiti
Doubtful Sd.   Manapouri   Umbrella Mts.   Otago Harbour
Breaksea Sd.   Mossburn   Ediovale   Kelso   Port Chalmers
Resolution I.   Lumsden   Waipori   Mosgiel   C. Saunders
Dusky Sd.   Manapouri   Kingston   Milton   Dunedin
Preservation Inlet   Nightcaps   Winton   Clinton
Chalky Inlet   Southland   Gore   Kaitangata   Nugget Pt.
Te Waewae B.   Clifden   Mataura   Wyndham   Owaka
Orepuki   Riverton   Hedgehope   Balclutha   Tahakopa
Solander I.   Invercargill   South Invercargill   Bluff   Ruapuke I.
Foveaux Str.
Halfmoon Bay
Stewart I. (Rakiura)   RAKIURA   Port Pegasus
South West C.

North Island
South Island
South West C.

TASMAN SEA
PACIFIC OCEAN

Projection : Conical with two standard parallels

166   168   170   East from Greenwich   172
1   2   3   4

TAHITI & MOOREA d
1:1 100 000

Pte. Aroa
Papetoai   Pte. Vénus   Mahina
Paopao   B. de Matavai   Arué   Papenoo
Mt. Tohiea ▲1207   Papeete   Pirae   Tiarei   Tahiti (France)
Haapiti   Faaa   Afareaitu   Hitiaa
Moorea (France)   Punaauia   Mt. Aorai ▲2060   Mt. Orohena ▲2241
Pte. Nuupere   Mt. Terufera ▲1793   Faaone   Isthme de Taravao
PACIFIC OCEAN   Paea   Lac Vaihiria   Afaahiti
   Maraa   Papara   Taravao   Pte. Tatatua
   Atimaono   Mataiea   Vairao ▲   Pueu   Tautira
   Teahupoo   Mt. Rooniu ▲1332
Presqu'île de Taiarapu

149°30'W   West from Greenwich   149°15'W
1:900 000
10   0   10 km
10   0   10 miles

COPYRIGHT PHILIP'S

ft   m
9000   3000
6000   2000
3000   1000
1200   400
600   200
0   0
200   600
2000   6000
4000   12000
6000   18000
m   ft

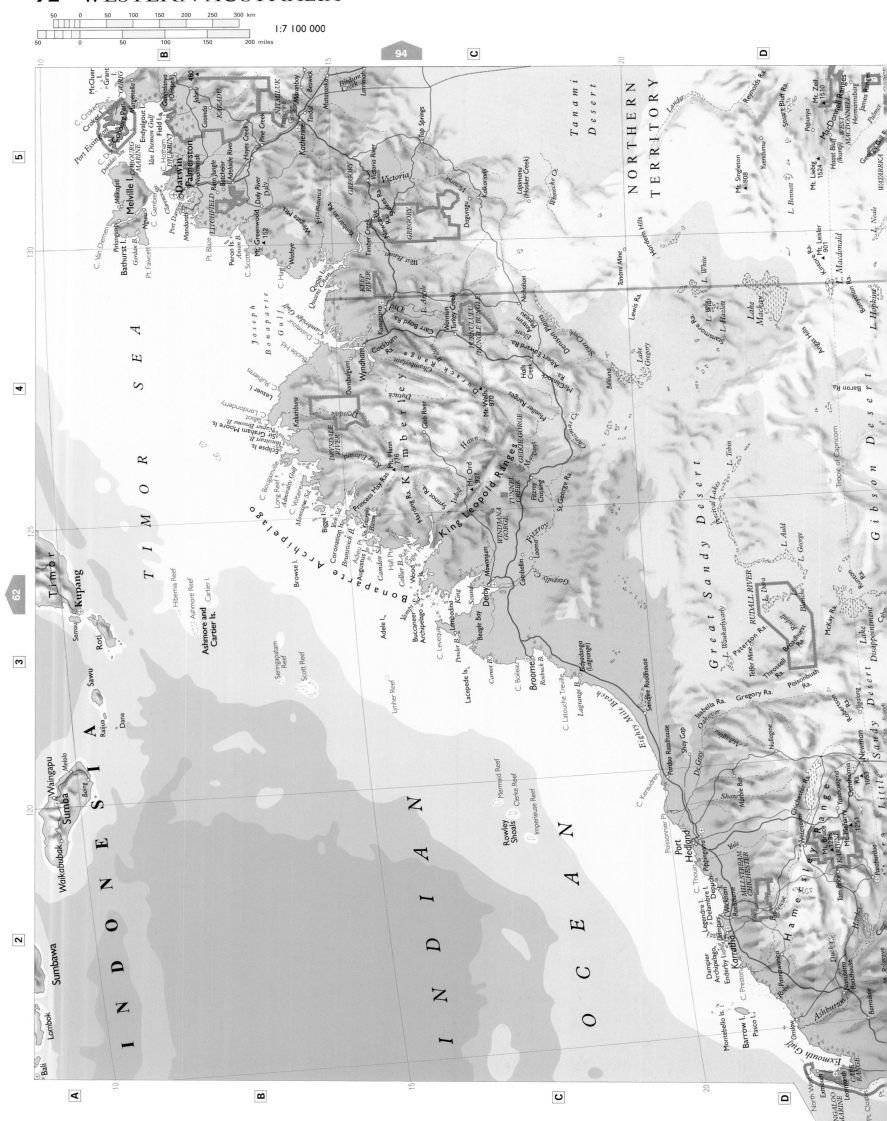

WESTERN AUSTRALIA

SOUTH AUSTRALIA

INDIAN OCEAN

SOUTHERN OCEAN

Great Victoria Desert

Great Australian Bight

Nullarbor Plain

Hampton Tableland

NULLARBOR

Uluru KATA TJUTA
(Ayers Rock) 863
Kata Tjuta 1069
(The Olgas)

Mt. Musgrave Ranges
Mt. Woodroffe 1440
Petermann Ranges

Kalgoorlie-
Boulder

GOONGARRIE

PERTH
Fremantle
Rockingham
Mandurah
Bunbury
Busselton

Geraldton

KALBARRI

Carnarvon

SHARK BAY

Albany

Esperance

Norseman

CAPE ARID

CAPE LE GRAND

Northam
Midland

95

East from Greenwich

COPYRIGHT PHILIP'S

Projection: Bonne

m
1000
400
200
0

ft
3000
1200
600
200-600
0

ft
12 000
6000
2000-6000
0

m

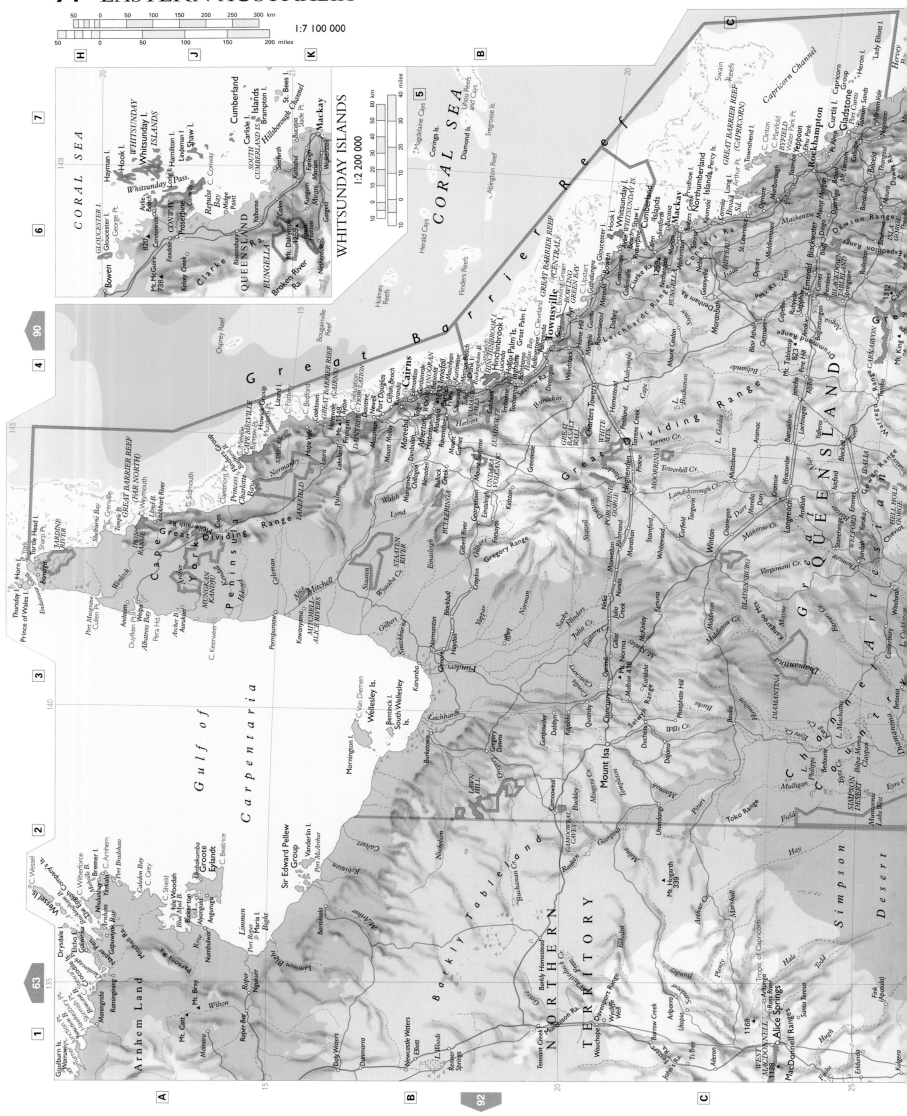

1:7 100 000

WHITSUNDAY ISLANDS

1:2 200 000

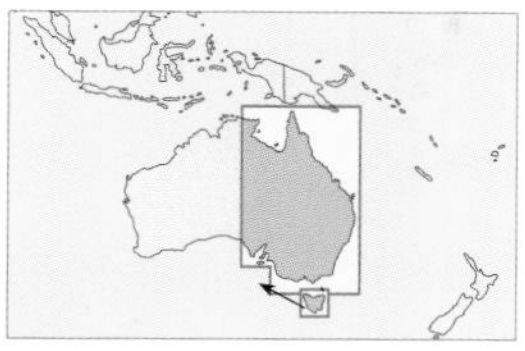

QUEENSLAND

NEW SOUTH WALES

SOUTH AUSTRALIA

VICTORIA

TASMANIA

TASMAN SEA

Bass Strait

BRISBANE
Gold Coast
Sunshine Coast
Toowoomba
Ipswich
Newcastle
SYDNEY
Wollongong
Canberra
MELBOURNE
Geelong
Ballarat
Bendigo
ADELAIDE
Broken Hill
Mildura
Hobart
Launceston

Great Dividing Range
Darling Range
Grey Range
Barrier Range
Flinders Ranges
Gammon Ranges

Lake Eyre
Lake Torrens
Lake Gairdner
Lake Frome
Lake Blanche

Murray R.
Darling R.
Murrumbidgee R.
Cooper Cr.

Kangaroo I.
King Island
Flinders Island
Furneaux Group
Cape Barren I.

Spencer Gulf
Gulf St Vincent

COPYRIGHT, GEORGE PHILIP LTD.

East from Greenwich

RUSSIA

Yekaterinburg
Tomsk
Moskva
Volga
Novosibirsk
Irkutsk
Ob
Lena
Chita
Astana
(Aqmola)
Semey
Ulaanbaatar
Blagoveshchensk
Khabarovsk
Amur
Sea of Okhotsk
Okhotsk
Poluostrov Kamchatka
Komandorskiye Ostrova (Russia)
Near Is. (U.S.A.)
Andreanof
Bering Sea
Shirshov Ridge
Aleutian Basin
KAZAKHSTAN
Aral Sea
Balqash Köl
Almaty
Ürümqi
MONGOLIA
Changchun
Harbin
Sapporo
Petropavlovsk-Kamchatskiy
Vladivostok
Hakodate
Kurilskiye Ostrova (Russia)
La Perouse Str.
Kuril-Kamchatka Trench
10,542
Aleutia
Aleutian Trench
7822

Toshkent
KYRGYZSTAN
Beijing
Tianjin
Taiyuan
Shenyang
Dalian
Seoul
NORTH KOREA
SOUTH KOREA
Sendai
Tōkyō
Nagoya
Yokohama
Sea of Japan
Northwest
Emperor Trough
Emperor Seamount Chain
Chinook Trou

TAJIKISTAN
AFGHANISTAN
Kabul
Srinagar
PAKISTAN
Lahore
Delhi
Kanpur
CHINA
XIZANG
Kunlun Shan
Lanzhou
Xi'an
Nanjing
Qingdao
Yellow Sea
Kitakyushū
Kyūshū
Osaka
Kyōto
Shikoku
JAPAN
Fuji-San 3776
10,554
Japan Trench
Shatsky Rise
Pacific
Midway Is. (U.S.A.)
Lisianski I. (U.S.A.)

Himalaya
Lhasa
Mt. Everest 8848
NEPAL
Ganga
Brahmaputra
Chongqing
Chang J.
Changsha
Wuhan
Hangzhou
Shanghai
East China Sea
Fuzhou
Guangzhou
Taipei
Okinawa
Ryūkyū-retto (Japan)
Kyushu-Palau Ridge
Sirito-Ozima Ridge
Iwo-Jima (Japan)
Ogasawara Gunto (Japan)
Kazan-Rettō (Japan)
Minami-Tori-Shima (Japan)
Mid-Pacific
Wake I. (U.S.A.)
International Date Line
P A

INDIA
Kolkata (Calcutta)
Dhaka
BANGLADESH
Kunming
Mandalay
BURMA
Irrawaddy
Salween
Hanoi
Hainan
LAOS
Macau
Hong Kong
TAIWAN
Philippine Sea
C. Engano
West Mariana Basin
Philippine Basin
NORTHERN MARIANAS (U.S.A.)
Saipan
Tinian
East Mariana Basin
MARSHALL IS.
Bikini
Enewetak Atoll
Ralik Chain
Ratak Chain

Hyderabad
Bay of Bengal
Rangoon
Bangkok
THAILAND
VIETNAM
Mekong
Luzon
Paracel Is.
Manila
GUAM (U.S.A.)
Challenger 11,022 Deep
Mariana Trench
Yap
Caroline Is.
Chuuk
Micronesia
Kwajalein
Majuro

Chennai (Madras)
Andaman Is. (India)
CAMBODIA
Phnom Penh
Thanh Pho Ho Chi Minh
G. of Thailand
Palawan
Mindoro
South China Sea
PHILIPPINES
Samar 10,497
Koror
PALAU
West Caroline Basin
FED. STATES OF MICRONESIA
East Caroline Basin
Palikir
Pohnpei
Jaluit I.

SRI LANKA
Nicobar Is. (India)
Colombo
MALAYSIA
Kuala Lumpur
PEN. MALAYSIA
SARAWAK
BRUNEI
SABAH
Sulu Sea
Mindanao
Davao
Mindanao Trench 4101
Celebes Sea
Eauripik Rise
West Caroline Basin
Melanesia
Solomon Rise
Melanesian Basin
Butaritari
Tarawa
Gilbert Is.
Banaba
Howland I. (U.S.
Baker I. (U.
Pacifi

Singapore
Sumatera
Borneo
Halmahera
Sulawesi
Buru
Seram
Maluku
Puncak Jaya 5029
PAPUA
Admiralty Is.
New Ireland
Bismarck Arch.
PAPUA NEW GUINEA
NAURU
Melanesia
Nauru
Phoenix Is.
Abariringa Enderbury

INDIAN
Palembang
Java Sea
Jakarta
INDONESIA
Ujung Pandang
Banda Sea
Flores Sea
Flores
7440
New Guinea
New Britain
Rabaul 8940
Bougainville
Lae
Port Moresby
SOLOMON IS.
Honiara
Guadalcanal
Santa Cruz I. 9165
TUVALU
Fongafale
KI
Sunda Islands
Selat Sunda
Surabaya
Jawa
Bali
Sumbawa
Sumba
Dili
EAST TIMOR
Timor
Arafura Sea
Torres Strait
C. York
Louisiade Arch.
Ninetyeast Ridge
Java Trench

OCEAN
Cocos Is. (Austral.)
Christmas I. (Austral.)
C. Arnhem
Darwin
Gulf of Carpentaria
Coral Sea Basin
Coral Sea
ESpíritu Santo
VANUATU
Rotuma
Is. Wallis & Futuna (Fr.)
SAMOA
Apia
Wharton Basin
North West C.
North Australian Basin
Broome
Exmouth Plateau
Cairns
Townsville
Great Barrier Reef
Is. Chesterfield
Port Vila
West Fiji Basin
Vanua Levu
Viti Levu
FIJI
Suva
Nuku'alofa
TONGA

Mount Isa
AUSTRALIA
Rockhampton
Coral Sea
NEW CALEDONIA (Fr.)
Nouméa
Is. Loyauté
7570
Lord Howe Rise
Middleton Basin
Brisbane
Norfolk Ridge
New Caledonia Trough
South Fiji Basin
10,822
Tonga Trench

Geraldton
Great Australian Bight
Broken Ridge
Perth Basin
Perth
L. Eyre
Alice Springs
Darling
Norfolk I. (Austral.)
Lord Howe I. (Austral.)
Kermadec Is. (N.Z.)
Kermadec Trench 10,047

Naturaliste Plateau
Albany
Adelaide
Murray
Canberra
Sydney
Mt. Kosciuszko 2230
Tasman Sea
NEW ZEALAND
Auckland
Nouvelle Amsterdam (Fr.)
I. St. Paul (Fr.)
Melbourne
Bass Str.
Tasmania
Hobart
East Tasman Plateau
Aoraki Mt. Cook 3753
Christchurch
Chatham Rise (N.Z.)
Chatham I. (N.Z.)
Wellington
Dunedin
Bounty Trough
Bounty Is. (N.Z.)

Is. Crozet (Fr.)
SOUTHERN
South Australian Basin
South Tasman Rise
Invercargill
Antipodes Is. (N.Z.)
Auckland I. (N.Z.)
Campbell I. (N.Z.)
Campbell Plateau

Kerguelen (Fr.)
Heard I. (Austral.)
OCEAN
Macquarie I. (Austral.)

Indian Ridge
Mid-Indian Ridge

ft m
12 000 4000
6000 3000
6000 2000
3000 1000
1500 500
600 200
0 0
200 600
1000 3000
2000 6000
4000 12 000
6000 18 000
8000 24 000
m ft

Arctic Circle

ALASKA
(U.S.A.)
Anchorage
5959

Juneau

Bristol Bay
Gulf of Alaska
Prince of Wales I.
(U.S.A.) Prince Rupert
Queen Charlotte Is.
(Canada)

ROCKY
CANADA

Edmonton
L. Winnipeg
Calgary
Winnipeg
Regina

Newfoundland
St. Lawrence
NORTH

Vancouver
Vancouver I.
Victoria
Seattle
Portland

Tufts
Abyssal
Plain

Boise
Salt Lake
City

Minneapolis
Missouri
L. Superior
L. Michigan
Detroit
Chicago

Québec
Montréal
Ottawa
Toronto
Buffalo
L. Ontario
L. Erie

Boston
St. John's

Northeast
Mendocino Fracture Zone C. Mendocino

Sacramento
San Francisco

6741

4418

Denver
Kansas City
St. Louis
Cincinnati
Pittsburgh

UNITED STATES

New York
Philadelphia
Baltimore
Washington D.C.

ATLANTIC

Pacific

Murray Fracture Zone

Los Angeles
San Diego

Phoenix

Oklahoma City
Memphis
Dallas
Houston

Atlanta
C. Hatteras

Bermuda
(U.K.)

OCEAN

Guadalupe
(Mex.)
Molokai Fracture Zone

MEXICO

Ciudad
Juárez
San Antonio

New
Orleans
Monterrey

Jacksonville
Tampa
Miami

Sargasso Sea

Tropic of Cancer

Basin

C. San Lucas
Gulf of California
Baja California

Gulf of Mexico

BAHAMAS

OCEAN

Honolulu
Maui
Kauai
Oahu
HAWAIIAN IS.
(U.S.A.)
4205
Hilo Hawaii

Guadalajara
Mexico
5610
Puebla
Acapulco

Mérida
Canal de Yucatán

La Habana
CUBA

West Indies

HAITI
9200
DOMINICAN REP.
Kingston
JAMAICA
PUERTO
RICO
(U.S.A.)
Leeward
Is.

Johnston I.
(U.S.A.)

Clarion Fracture Zone Is. Revilla Gigedo
(Mex.)
7680

BELIZE
GUATEMALA
6662
Guatemala
HONDURAS
Middle America Trench

Caribbean Sea

BARBADOS
Windward Is.

PACIFIC

Palmyra Is.
(U.S.A.)
Teraina
Tabuaeran
Kiritimati

Clipperton Fracture Zone

I. Clipperton
(Fr.)

Guatemala
Basin

San Salvador
EL SALVADOR
NICARAGUA
Managua

Barranquilla
San José
Maracaibo

Cooper Ridge

COSTA
RICA
Colón
Panamá
PANAMA
Panama
Basin

Caracas

VENEZUELA

Cocos Ridge
I. del Coco
(Costa Rica)
Medellín

Bogotá

Equator

Galápagos Fracture Zone

I. de Malpelo
(Colombia)
Cali
COLOMBIA

Jarvis I.
(U.S.A.)
Line Islands

Galápagos
(Ecuador)
Carnegie Ridge

Quito
ECUADOR

Amazonas

KIRIBATI

Malden I.
Starbuck I.

Guayaquil

Iquitos

BRAZIL

Penrhyn
(Tongareva)
Manihiki
Pukapuka
Manihiki
Plateau
Suwarrow Is.

Nuku Hiva
Caroline I.
(Millennium I.)
Vostok I.
Flint I.

Îs. Marquises
Hiva Oa

Marquesas Fracture Zone

East Pacific Ridge

Yupanqui
Basin

Trujillo

6369

PERU
Peru
Basin
Galápagos Rise
Mendaña
Fracture Zone

Lima
Cuzco
L. Titicaca
Nevada Ancohuma
6550

Îs. de la
Société
Bora Bora
Huahine
Raiatea
Papeete
Tahiti
Rangiroa

Îs. Tuamotu

Cook Is.
(N.Z.)
Aitutaki
Rarotonga
Mangaia

Îs. Gambier
Mururoa

FRENCH POLYNESIA

Îs. Tubuaï

Peru-
Chile

6866
Arequipa
Arica
Iquique

La Paz
BOLIVIA

Tropic of Capricorn

Nazca Ridge

Antofagasta

PARAGUAY

Oeno I.
Henderson I.
Pitcairn I.
(U.K.)
Ducie I.
Rapa

Easter Fracture Zone
Sala-y-Gómez
(Chile)
I. de Pascua
(Chile)

Sala y Gómez Ridge

San Felix
(Chile)
San Ambrosio
(Chile)

8050
Trench

San Miguel
de Tucumán

Asunción

Porto
Alegre

Córdoba

Southwest

Roggeveen
Basin

Arch. de
Juan Fernández
(Chile)

Aconcagua
6962
Valparaíso
Santiago
Concepción

Rosario
Buenos
Aires
URUGUAY
Montevideo
Río de la Plata

Pacific

Chile Rise

ARGENTINA

SOUTH

Basin

Pacific-Antarctic Ridge
East Pacific Rise
Challenger Fracture Zone
Menard Fracture Zone

ATLANTIC

6212 OCEAN

Southeast
Pacific Basin

Punta Arenas
Est. de Magallanes
C. de Hornos
Tierra del Fuego

Drake Passage

Falkland Is.
(U.K.)

South Georgia
(U.K.)

1:31 100 000

COPYRIGHT PHILIP'S

Projection: Bonne

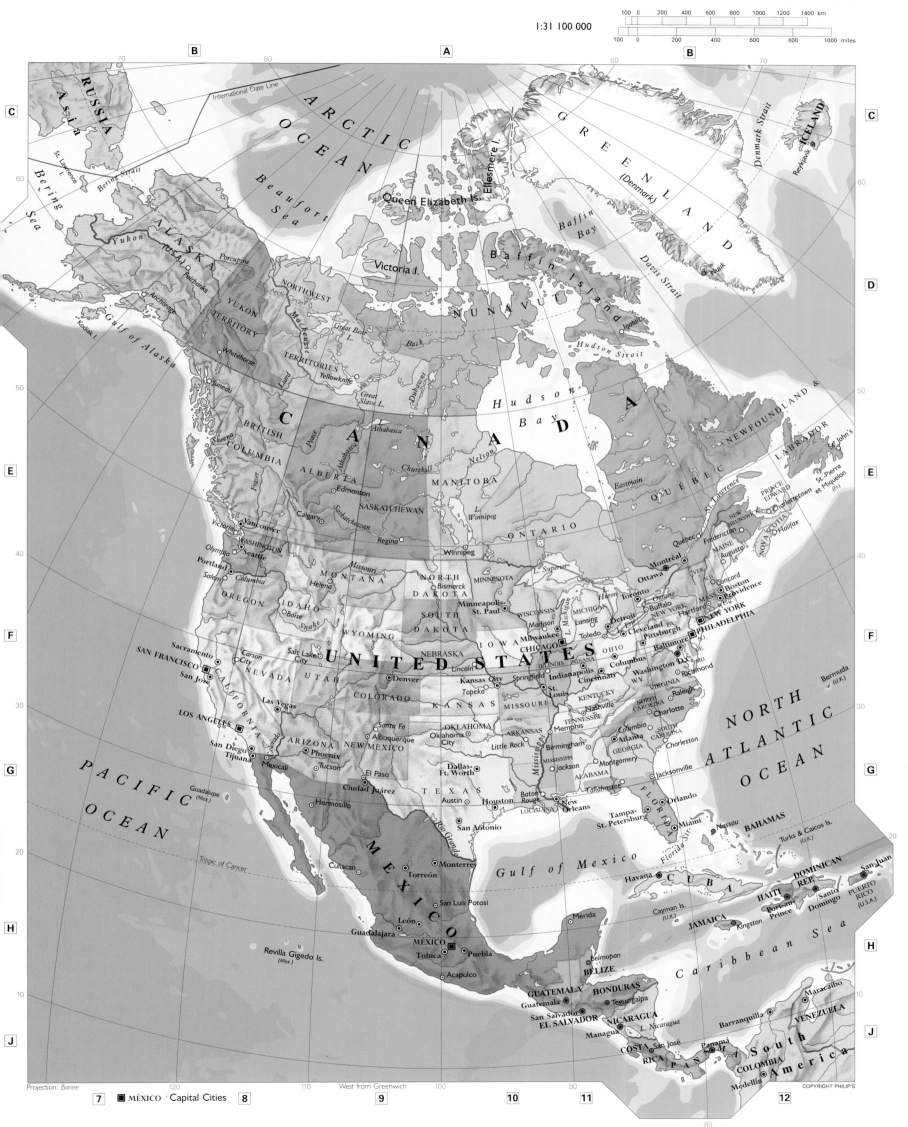

1:31 100 000

100 0 200 400 600 800 1000 1200 1400 km
100 0 200 400 600 800 1000 miles

RUSSIA
Asia
ARCTIC OCEAN
International Date Line
St. Lawrence I.
Bering Strait
Bering Sea
Beaufort Sea
Queen Elizabeth Is.
Ellesmere I.
GREENLAND (Denmark)
Denmark Strait
ICELAND
Reykjavik
Baffin Bay
Victoria I.
Baffin Island
Davis Strait
Nuuk
ALASKA (U.S.A.)
Yukon
Porcupine
Fairbanks
Anchorage
Kodiak I.
Gulf of Alaska
Juneau
Whitehorse
YUKON TERRITORY
Arctic Circle
NORTHWEST TERRITORIES
Great Bear L.
Mackenzie
Back
Yellowknife
NUNAVUT
Iqaluit
Hudson Strait
Great Slave L.
Liard
Dubawnt
BRITISH COLUMBIA
Skeena
Fraser
Peace
CANADA
Athabasca
ALBERTA
L. Athabasca
SASKATCHEWAN
Churchill
Nelson
Hudson Bay
Eastmain
QUÉBEC
NEWFOUNDLAND & LABRADOR
St. John's
Victoria
Vancouver
Edmonton
Calgary
Saskatchewan
Regina
L. Winnipeg
MANITOBA
ONTARIO
St. Lawrence
PRINCE EDWARD I.
Charlottetown
St-Pierre et Miquelon (Fr.)
Olympia
WASHINGTON
Seattle
Portland
Salem
OREGON
Columbia
Snake
MONTANA
Helena
Missouri
Winnipeg
L. Superior
NORTH DAKOTA
Bismarck
MINNESOTA
NEW BRUNSWICK
Fredericton
MAINE
Augusta
NOVA SCOTIA
Halifax
Québec
Montréal
Ottawa
VER.
N.H.
Concord
Boston
Providence
Sacramento
San Francisco
San Jose
CALIFORNIA
IDAHO
Boise
WYOMING
SOUTH DAKOTA
UNITED STATES
IOWA
WISCONSIN
Madison
Minneapolis-St. Paul
L. Michigan
Milwaukee
CHICAGO
MICHIGAN
Lansing
L. Huron
Toronto
Detroit
Toledo
Cleveland
Buffalo
NEW YORK
Pittsburgh
PA.
Hartford
MASS.
CONN.
NEW YORK
PHILADELPHIA
Carson City
Salt Lake City
NEVADA
UTAH
NEBRASKA
Lincoln
ILLINOIS
INDIANA
OHIO
Columbus
Cincinnati
Indianapolis
Springfield
Baltimore
Washington D.C.
MD.
DEL.
W.V.
Richmond
VIRGINIA
Los Angeles
San Diego
Tijuana
Mexicali
Denver
COLORADO
KANSAS
Topeka
Kansas City
St. Louis
MISSOURI
KENTUCKY
Nashville
TENNESSEE
NORTH CAROLINA
Raleigh
Charlotte
Bermuda (U.K.)
Las Vegas
ARIZONA
Phoenix
Tucson
NEW MEXICO
Santa Fe
Albuquerque
OKLAHOMA
Oklahoma City
ARKANSAS
Little Rock
Memphis
Birmingham
Columbia
SOUTH CAROLINA
Charleston
Atlanta
GEORGIA
NORTH ATLANTIC OCEAN
Colorado
El Paso
Ciudad Juárez
TEXAS
Dallas-Ft. Worth
Austin
Mississippi
Jackson
MISSISSIPPI
ALABAMA
Montgomery
Jacksonville
Tallahassee
FLORIDA
Orlando
PACIFIC OCEAN
Guadalupe (Mex.)
Hermosillo
Houston
Baton Rouge
LOUISIANA
New Orleans
Tampa-St. Petersburg
Miami
Nassau
BAHAMAS
Turks & Caicos Is. (U.K.)
Florida Str.
San Antonio
Rio Grande
Tropic of Cancer
Gulf of Mexico
Havana
CUBA
Culiacán
Torreón
Monterrey
MEXICO
San Luis Potosí
Mérida
Cayman Is. (U.K.)
HAITI
Port-au-Prince
DOMINICAN REP.
Santo Domingo
PUERTO RICO (U.S.A.)
San Juan
León
Guadalajara
MÉXICO
Toluca
Puebla
JAMAICA
Kingston
Caribbean Sea
Maracaibo
Revilla Gigedo Is. (Mex.)
Acapulco
Belmopan
BELIZE
Mérida
Barranquilla
VENEZUELA
GUATEMALA
Guatemala
San Salvador
EL SALVADOR
HONDURAS
Tegucigalpa
NICARAGUA
Managua
L. Nicaragua
COSTA RICA
San José
PANAMA
Panamá
COLOMBIA
Medellín
South America

Projection: Bonne
West from Greenwich
COPYRIGHT PHILIP'S

7 ■ MÉXICO ·Capital Cities **8**   **9**   **10**   **11**   **12**

1:13 300 000

Projection : Bonne

NORTHERN CANADA
continuation northwards on same
scale as main map

ARCTIC OCEAN

Baffin Bay

Devon I.
Lancaster Sound

Sverdrup Islands
Queen Elizabeth Is.
Ellesmere Island
Greenland (Denmark)
Alert
Eureka
Grise Fiord
Jones Sound
Devon Island

Banks Island
Melville I.
Victoria Island
Prince Patrick I.
Parry Islands
Viscount Melville Sound
Resolute
Cornwallis
Bathurst
NUNAVUT
NORTHWEST TERRITORIES
Prince of Wales Island
Prince Somerset Island
Baffin Island
Arctic Bay
Nanisivik
Bylot I.
Pond Inlet
Brodeur Peninsula

Baffin Island
Foxe Basin
Foxe Peninsula
Cumberland Peninsula
Pangnirtung
Iqaluit
Hall Peninsula
Frobisher Bay
Cape Dorset
Resolution I.

NUNAVUT
Hudson Strait
Southampton I.
Coral Harbour
Chesterfield Inlet
Repulse Bay
Rae Isthmus

Hudson Bay
James Bay
Sleeper Is.
King George Is.
Belcher Is.
Coats I.
Mansel I.
Nottingham I.

Péninsule d'Ungava
Ungava Bay
Puvirnituq
Inukjuak
Kuujjuaq
Kangiqsualujjuaq
Hebron
Nain
Hopedale

Labrador Sea

NEWFOUNDLAND AND LABRADOR
Labrador
Churchill Falls
Happy Valley-Goose Bay
Smallwood Res.
Schefferville (Kawawachikamach)
Labrador City
Fermont
Gagnon
Port Hope Simpson
Cartwright
St-Augustin
Belle Isle
St. Anthony
Baie Verte
Grand Falls-Windsor
Gander
Lewisporte
Bonavista
Carbonear
St. John's
Placentia
C. Race
Corner Brook
Deer Lake
Stephenville
Channel-Port aux Basques
Newfoundland
I. d'Anticosti

ATLANTIC OCEAN

QUÉBEC
James Bay
Chisasibi
La Grande
Kanaaupscow
Chibougamau
L. Mistassini
Sept-Îles
Baie-Comeau
Havre-St-Pierre
Natashquan
Gaspé
Matane
Rimouski
Rivière-du-Loup
Chicoutimi
Roberval
Jonquière
Dolbeau-Mistassini
La Tuque
Trois-Rivières
Shawinigan
Québec
Lévis
MONTRÉAL
Hull
Sherbrooke
Granby
St-Hyacinthe
St-Jean

ONTARIO
Thunder Bay
Nipigon
Greenstone
Marathon
Wawa
Sault Ste. Marie
Sudbury
Elliot Lake
North Bay
Timmins
Cochrane
Kapuskasing
Hearst
Kirkland Lake
Rouyn-Noranda
Val-d'Or
Amos
Matagami
Moosonee
Fort Albany
Attawapiskat
Winisk
Peawanuck
OTTAWA
Pembroke
Huntsville
Parry Sound
Owen Sound
Barrie
Peterborough
Belleville
Kingston
Cornwall
TORONTO
HAMILTON
Kitchener
London
Sarnia
Windsor
Niagara Falls
Oshawa
L. Ontario
L. Erie

NEW BRUNSWICK
Fredericton
Saint John
Moncton
Edmundston
Woodstock
Miramichi
Bathurst
Campbellton
Grand Falls

NOVA SCOTIA
Halifax
Dartmouth
Sydney
Glace Bay
Truro
New Glasgow
Antigonish
Amherst
Kentville
Bridgewater
Liverpool
Yarmouth
Digby
Port Hawkesbury
Cape Breton I.
Sable I.

PR. EDWARD I.
Charlottetown
Summerside

Gulf of St. Lawrence
Cabot Str.
Northumberland Str.
ST-PIERRE et MIQUELON (Fr.)

MAINE
VERMONT
NEW HAMPSHIRE
MASS.
CONN.
R.I.
NEW YORK
PENNSYLVANIA
OHIO
INDIANA
MICHIGAN
WISCONSIN
ILLINOIS

BOSTON
Providence
New Haven
Bridgeport
Hartford
Springfield
Albany
Syracuse
Rochester
Buffalo
NEW YORK
Newark
Allentown
Trenton
Scranton
Binghamton
Elmira
Jamestown
CLEVELAND
Toledo
DETROIT
CHICAGO
MILWAUKEE
Grand Rapids
Lansing
Flint
Saginaw
Green Bay
Madison
Racine
Kenosha
Rockford
Gary
South Bend
Portland
Augusta
Concord
Manchester
Montpelier
Burlington
Lewiston
Bangor

Lake Superior
Lake Michigan
Lake Huron
Georgian Bay
Lake Erie
Lake Ontario

West from Greenwich

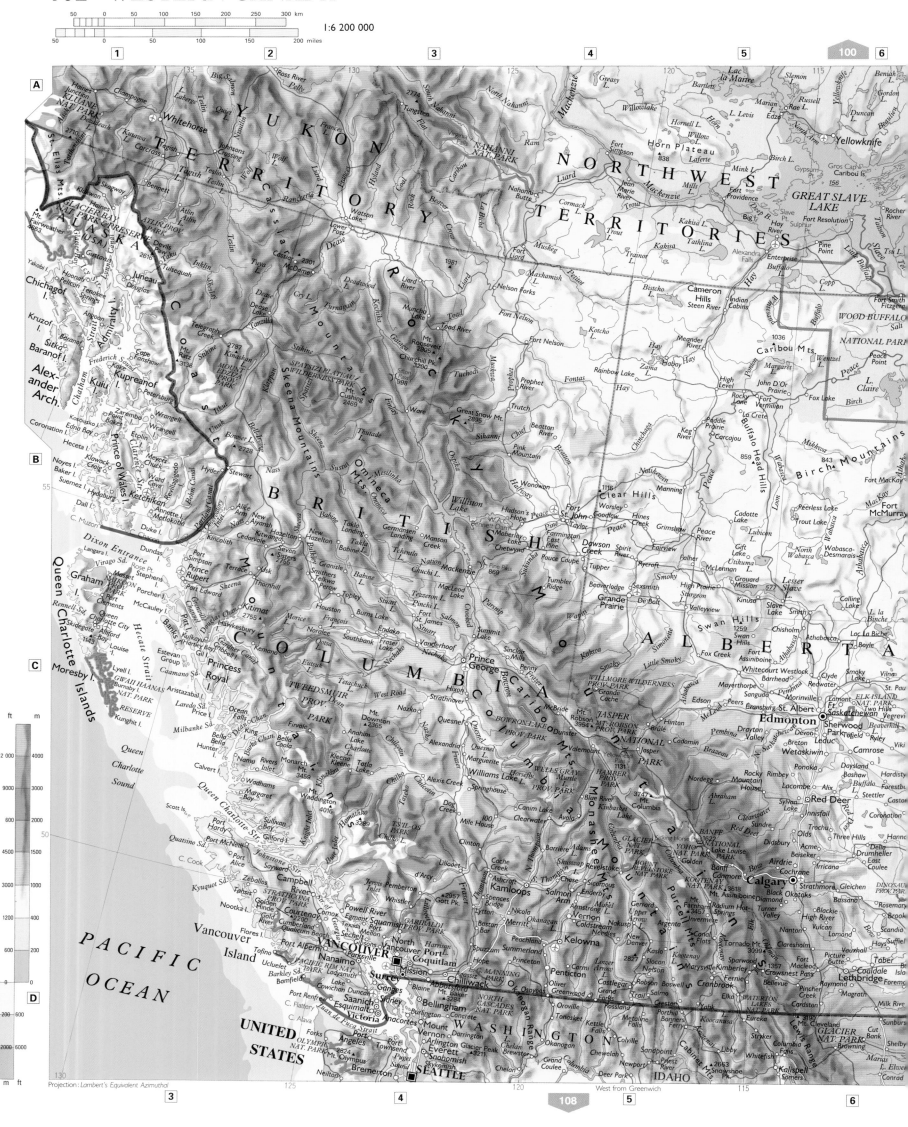

A

B

104

C

D

HUDSON BAY

NUNAVUT

MANITOBA

SASKATCHEWAN

ONTARIO

MINNESOTA

MONTANA

NORTH DAKOTA

Lake Athabasca

Reindeer Lake

LAKE WINNIPEG

Lake Winnipegosis

Winnipeg

Regina

Saskatoon

Prince Albert

Brandon

Moose Jaw

Churchill

Thompson

COPYRIGHT PHILIP'S

1:6 200 000

101

LABRADOR SEA

NEWFOUNDLAND &

Labrador Plateau

LABRADOR

Newfoundland

GULF OF
ST. LAWRENCE

Î. d'Anticosti

Î. de la
Madeleine
(Québec)

Cabot Strait

ST-PIERRE
et MIQUELON
(France)

Long Range Mts.

QUÉBEC

Mts. Chic-Chocs
Pén. de la Gaspésie

NEW
BRUNSWICK

PRINCE EDWARD
ISLAND

Cape Breton
Island

MAINE

NOVA SCOTIA

ATLANTIC

Halifax

Bay of Fundy

Sable I.
(Nova Scotia)

OCEAN

UNITED
STATES

BOSTON

West from Greenwich

COPYRIGHT PHILIP'S

1:10 700 000

Projection: Albers' Equal Area with two standard parallels

ALASKA
1:26 650 000

HAWAI'I
1:8 900 000

Tallahassee ⊛   U.S. State capitals

COPYRIGHT PHILIP'S

1:6 250 000

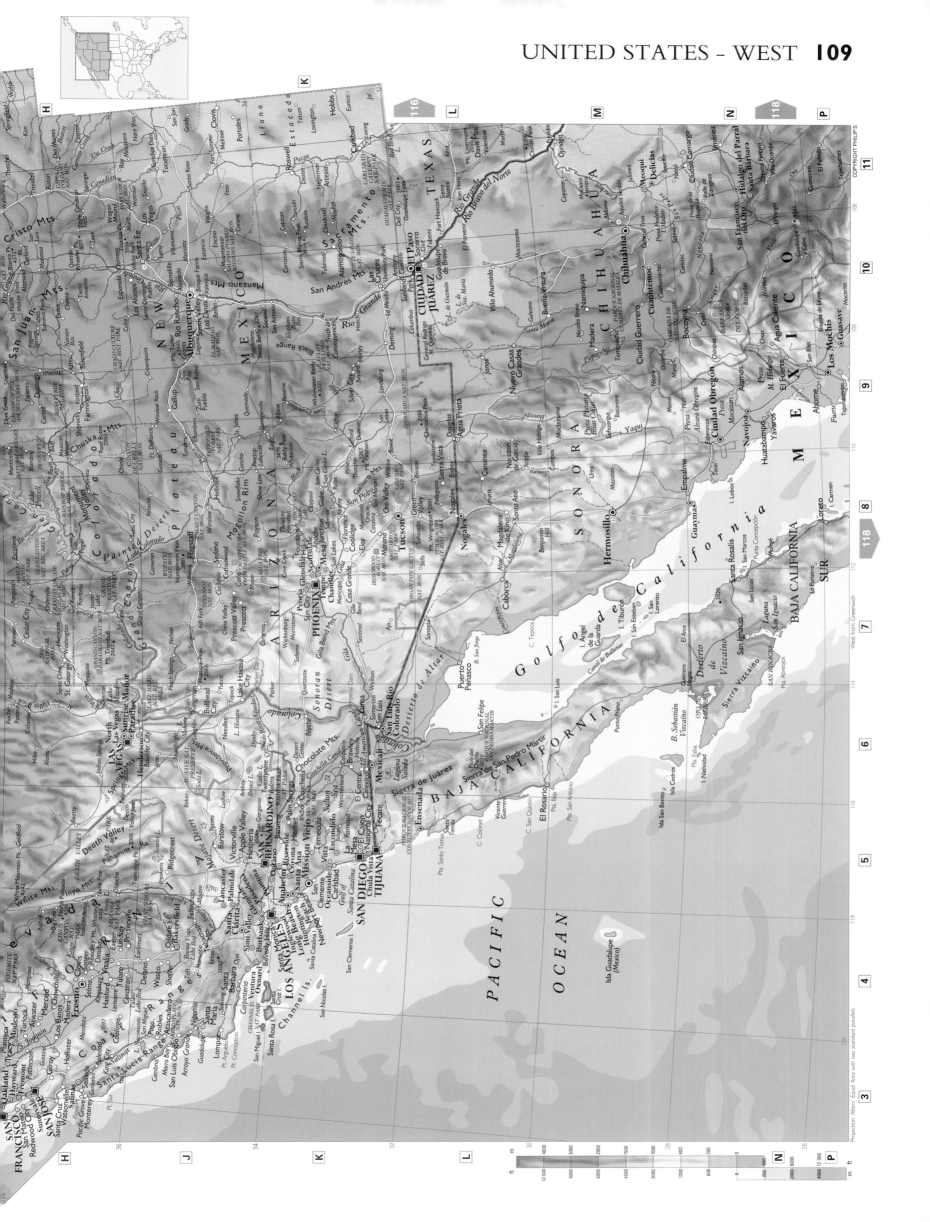

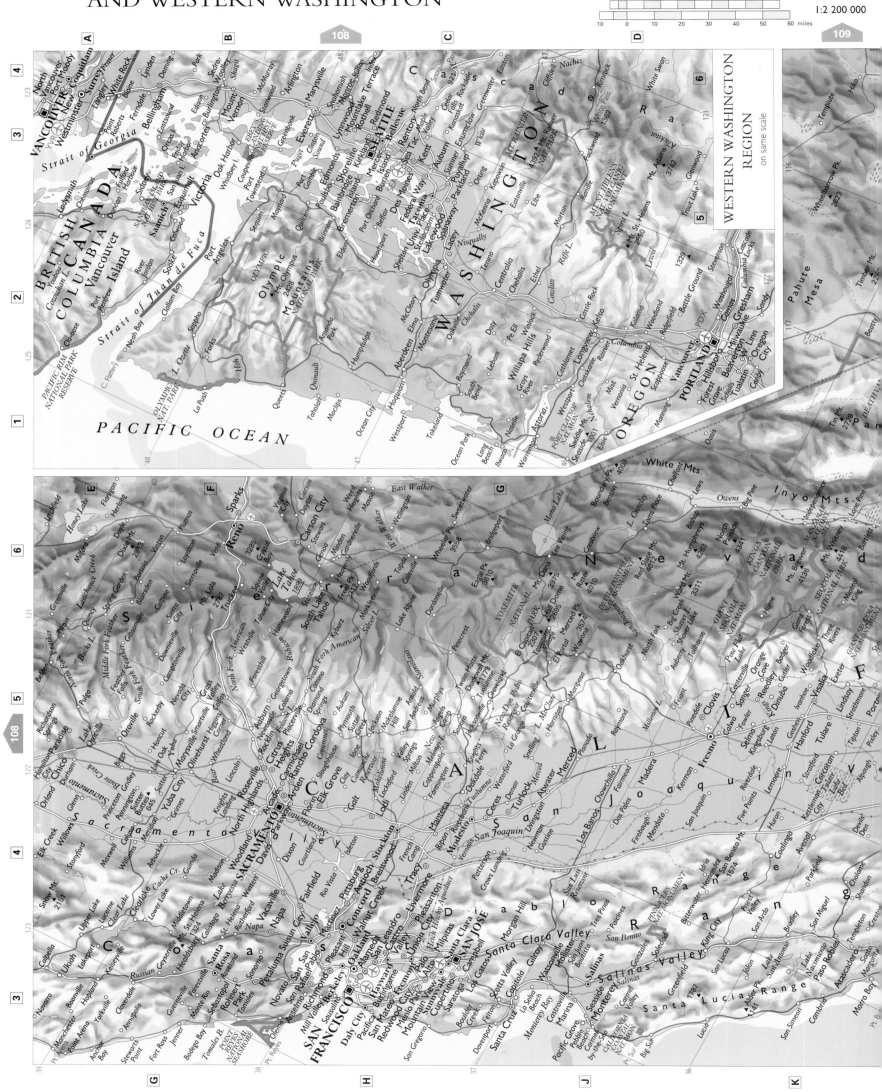

WESTERN WASHINGTON REGION
on same scale

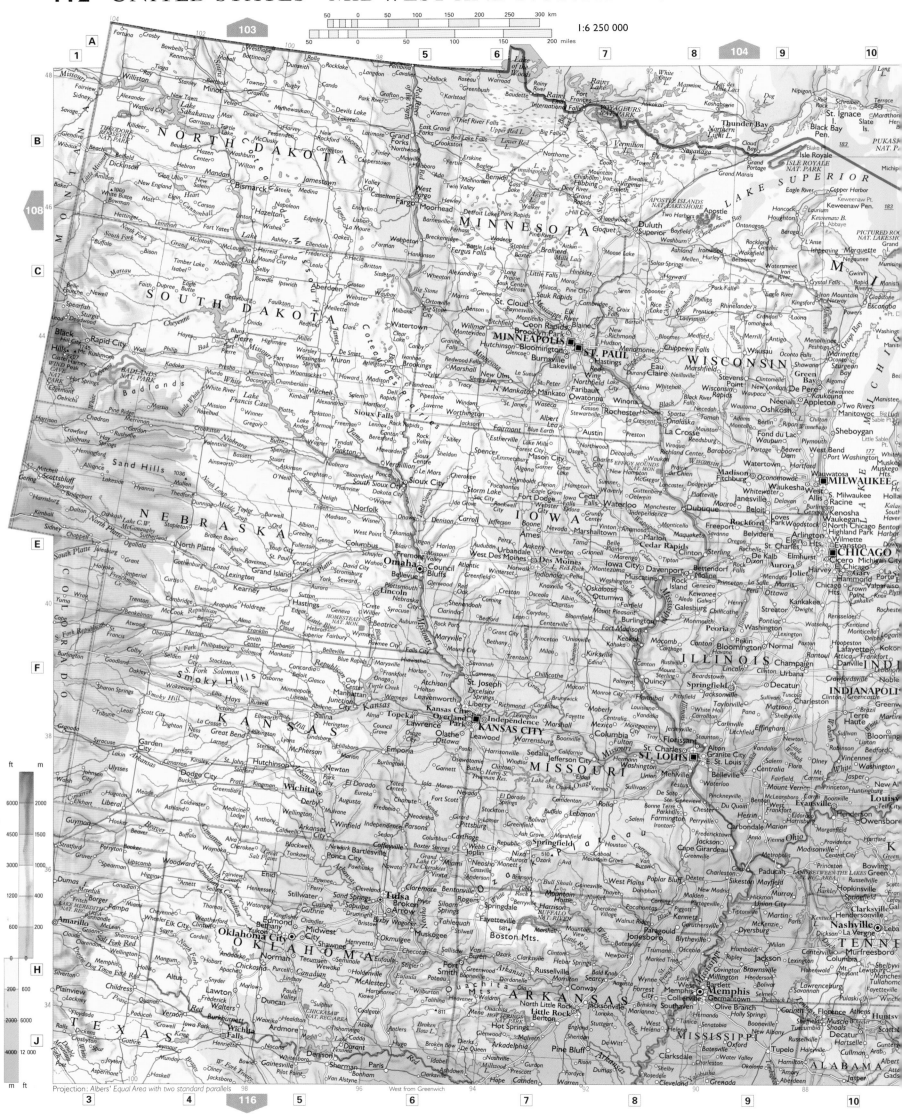

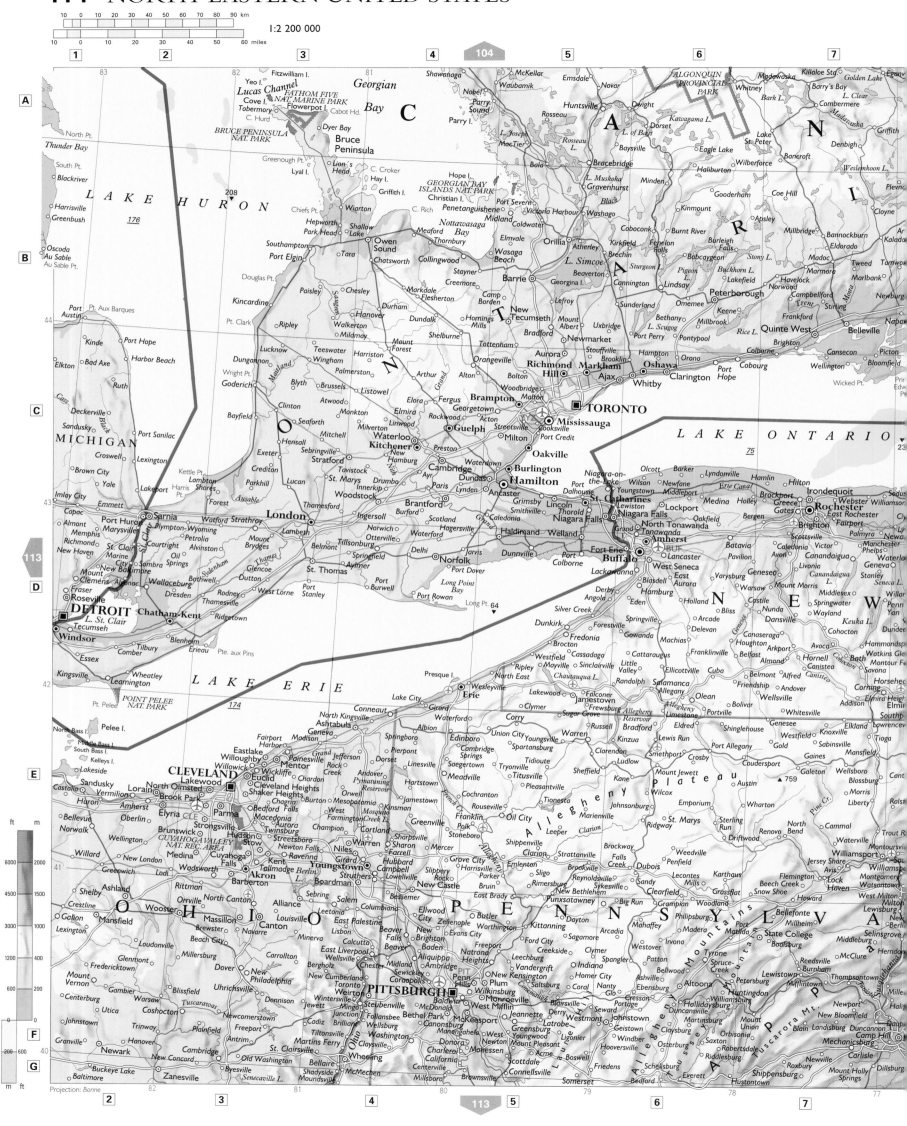

1:2 200 000

Projection: Bonne

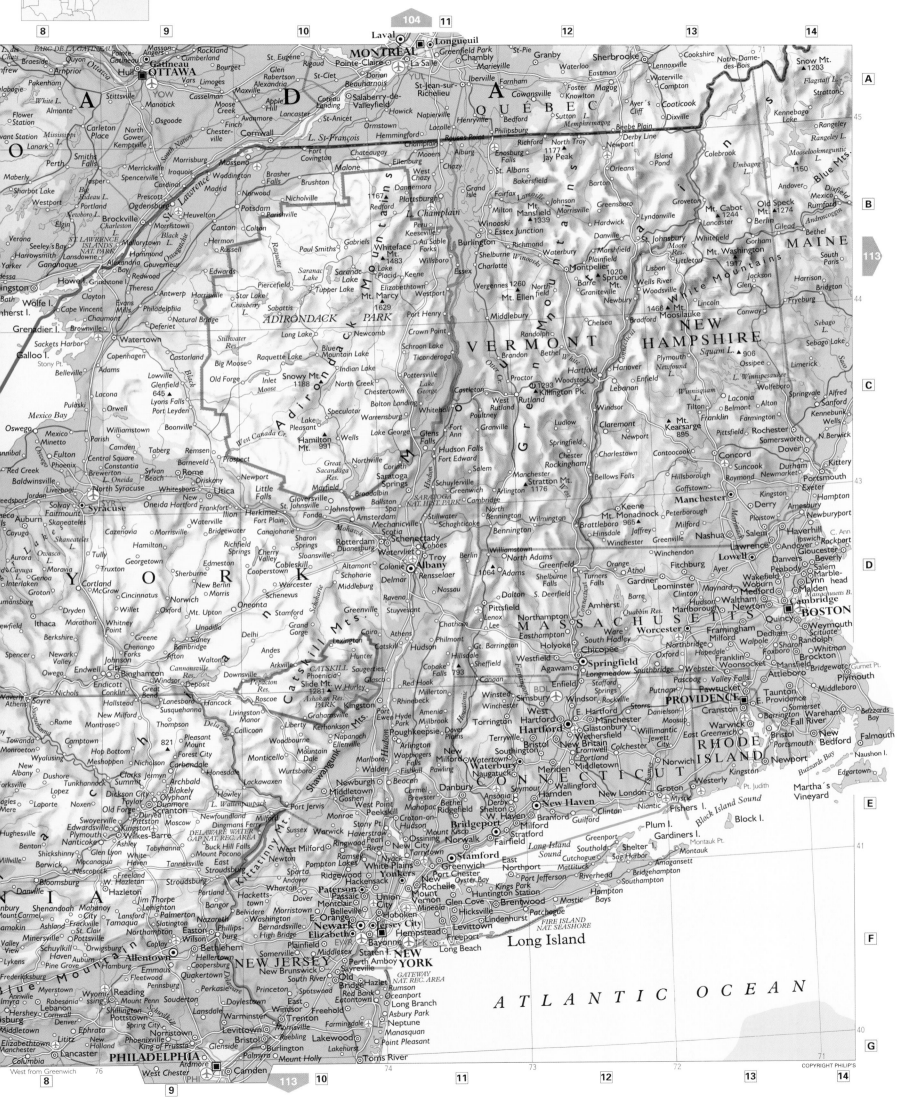

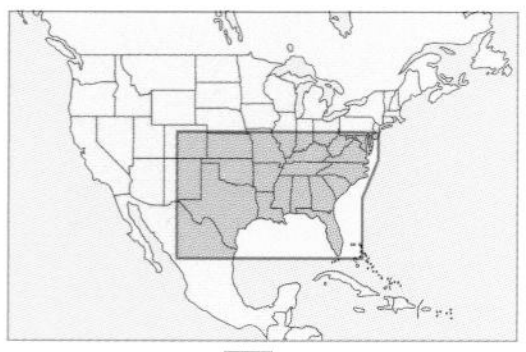

9 10 11 12 113 13 14 15 16 17

B

C

D

E

F

G

H

J

ILLINOIS

INDIANA

OHIO

PENNSYLVANIA

PITTSBURGH

PHILADELPHIA

INDIANAPOLIS

COLUMBUS

CINCINNATI

WEST VIRGINIA

MARYLAND

BALTIMORE

WASHINGTON D.C.

VIRGINIA

Richmond

NORFOLK

Virginia Beach

KENTUCKY

Louisville

Lexington

Nashville

TENNESSEE

Knoxville

Asheville

NORTH CAROLINA

Raleigh

Greensboro

Winston-Salem

Durham

Charlotte

Memphis

Chattanooga

SOUTH CAROLINA

Columbia

Charleston

Myrtle Beach

MISSISSIPPI

Jackson

ALABAMA

Birmingham

Montgomery

Mobile

GEORGIA

ATLANTA

Macon

Columbus

Augusta

Savannah

FLORIDA

Jacksonville

Tallahassee

ORLANDO

Daytona Beach

TAMPA

St. Petersburg

Sarasota

West Palm Beach

Fort Lauderdale

MIAMI

Miami Beach

Key West

New Orleans

GULF OF MEXICO

ATLANTIC OCEAN

BAHAMAS

Freeport

Grand Bahama

New Providence

Nassau

Andros I.

Everglades

Florida Keys

Str. of Florida

90 88 86 84 78

10 11 12 120 15 16

COPYRIGHT PHILIP'S

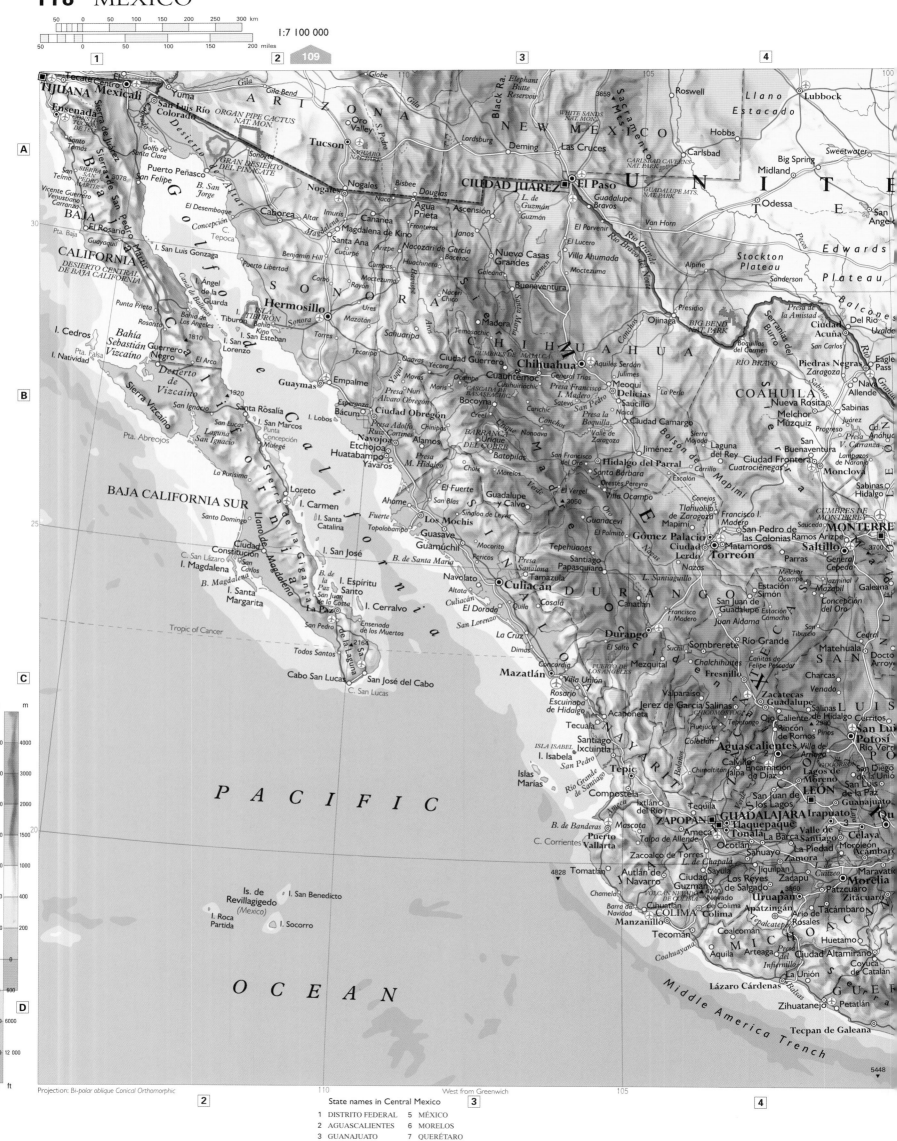

50 0 50 100 150 200 250 300 km
50   0   50   100   150   200 miles
1:7 100 000

PACIFIC

OCEAN

ft   m

12 000   4000

9000   3000

6000   2000

4500   1500

3000   1000

1200   400

600   200

0   0

200   600

2000   6000

4000   12 000

m   ft

Projection: Bi-polar oblique Conical Orthomorphic

West from Greenwich

State names in Central Mexico

1 DISTRITO FEDERAL   5 MÉXICO
2 AGUASCALIENTES   6 MORELOS
3 GUANAJUATO   7 QUERÉTARO
4 HIDALGO   8 TLAXCALA

5448

GULF OF MEXICO

Golfo de Campeche

Banco Campeche

Yucatan Basin

Map labels (partial transcription):

ARKANSAS
MISSISSIPPI
ALABAMA
GEORGIA
LOUISIANA
FLORIDA
STATES

Wichita Falls
Denison
Sherman
Paris
Denton
DALLAS
Fort Worth
Ranger
Cleburne
Tyler
Corsicana
Longview
Marshall
Texarkana
El Dorado
Camden
Greenville
Tuscaloosa
Opelika
Columbus
McRae
Meridian
Montgomery
Phenix City
Americus
Cordele
Troy
Tifton
Waycross
Abilene
Brownwood
Hillsboro
Palestine
Waco
Temple
Bryan
Huntsville
College Station
Navasota
Lufkin
Nacogdoches
Alexandria
Natchez
Vicksburg
Jackson
Laurel
Hattiesburg
Brewton
Dothan
Valdosta
Selma
Monroe
Tallulah
Pearl
Bogalusa
McComb
Mobile
Pensacola
Panama City
Tallahassee
Chattahoochee
Lake City
Albany
Possum Kingdom Lake
Red
Hope
Greenville
Marshall
Toledo Bend Res.
Sam Rayburn Reservoir
Lake Livingston
Trinity
Sabine
Beaumont
Port Arthur
Lake Charles
Lafayette
Baton Rouge
Hammond
L. Pontchartrain
NEW ORLEANS
Gulfport
Biloxi
Mobile Bay
C. San Blas
Apalachee Bay
Suwannee
Clearwater
Austin
San Antonio
Dilley
Houston
Rosenberg
Galveston
Victoria
Breton Sd.
Atchafalaya Bay
Terrebonne Bay
Mississippi River Delta

Nueces
Guadalupe
Colorado
Escarpment
Alice
Kingsville
Corpus Christi
Laredo
Nuevo Laredo
Zapata
McAllen
Harlingen
Brownsville
Camargo
Reynosa
Río Bravo
Matamoros
Valle Hermoso
Santa Teresa
China
Aderreyta Jiménez
Montemorelos
Villa de Méndez
San Fernando
Linares
Villagrán
Villa Hidalgo
Zaragoza
Santander Jiménez
Conchos
Padre Island Nat. Seashore
Laguna Madre
Presa Falcón
Nueva Ciudad Guerrero
General Trevino
Presa M. R. Gómez

Ciudad Victoria
Llera de Canales
Ocampo
González
Aldama
Sierra de Tamaulipas
Soto la Marina
La Pesca
Pta. Jerez
3540
TAMAULIPAS
Ciudad Mante
Ciudad Madero
Altamira
Ebano
Ciudad Valles
Tampico
Pánuco
Cárdenas
Ozuluama
L. de Tamiahua
Naranjos
Tempoal
Naranjos de Sánchez
Tamuín
Tantoyuca
C. Rojo
Chicontepec
Tuxpan
Tamazunchale
POTOSÍ

Querétaro
Zimapán
Zacualtipán
Poza Rica
Papantla
Nautla
San Juan del Río
Huichapan
Pachuca
Tula
El Oro
Zumpango
Tulancingo
Teziutlán
Huauchinango
Misantla
VERACRUZ
Xalapa
ZEMPOALA
Veracruz
Boca del Río
MEXICO
ECATEPEC
Toluca
Tlaxcala
Apizaco
Amecameca
PUEBLA
Popocatépetl 5452
Pico de Orizaba 5610
Malinche 4282
Coatepec
Córdoba
Orizaba
Alvarado
Tlacotalpan
San Andrés Tuxtla
1250
Cuernavaca
Iguala
Taxco
Izúcar de Matamoros
San Gabriel Chilac
Chiautla
Acatlán
Tehuacán
Ajalpan
Tierra Blanca
Cosamaloapan
Tres Valles
Tuxtepec
Acayucan
Minatitlán
Coatzacoalcos
TABASCO
Cárdenas
Comalcalco
Paraíso
Frontera
Villahermosa
Macuspana
Palenque
Tenosique
Ciudad del Carmen
L. de Términos
Champotón
Campeche
Hopelchén
Escárcega
CAMPEGE
CALAKMUL
Balancán
Palizada
PANTANOS DE CENTLA
LA VENTA

Progreso
Dzilam de Bravo
Motul
Temax
Espita
Tizimín
Río Lagartos
El Cuyo
C. Catoche
Isla Mujeres
Cancún
Puerto Morelos
Playa del Carmen
Isla Cozumel
Cozumel
Mérida
YUCATÁN
DZIBILCHALTUN
Izamal
Maxcanú
Ticul
CHICHÉN ITZA
Valladolid
COBA
Sotuta
Peto
UXMAL
Tekax
MAYAPÁN
Bolonchén
Tenabo
Hopelchén
QUINTANA ROO
Felipe Carrillo Puerto
B. de la Ascensión
SIAN KA'AN
B. del Espíritu Santo
Bacalar
Chetumal
B. de Chetumal
Banco Chinchorro
Corozal
Orange Walk
Ambergris Cay
San Pedro
Belize City
Turneffe Is.
Barrier Reef
Is. de la Bahía
Roatán

I. Desterrada
I. Pérez (Mexico)
Pta. Yalkubul
Tropic of Cancer
CUBA
Guane
La Fé
La Esperanza
C. San Antonio
C. Corrientes
Canal de Yucatán
Pta. Yalkubul

OAXACA
Oaxaca
Tlacolula
MONTE ALBÁN
Ejutla
Ocotlán
Tlaxiaco
Taviche
San Jerónimo Ixtepec
Matías Romero
Juchitán de Zaragoza
Tehuantepec
Salina Cruz
Istmo de Tehuantepec
Jesús Carranza
Presa Nezahualcóyotl
Copainalá
Simojovel
Ocosingo
Chiapa de Corzo
Tuxtla Gutiérrez
San Cristóbal de las Casas
La Independencia
Comitán de Domínguez
CHIAPAS
CAÑON DEL SUMIDERO
MONTES AZULES
LACANDON
Palenque
Uaxactún
TIKAL
San Ignacio
Benque Viejo
Belmopan
BLUE HOLE
Belize City
Dangriga
Monkey River
Maya Mts.
CHIQUIBUL
Flores
L. Petén Itzá
La Libertad
Sayaxché
Sierra de Chiapas
GUATEMALA
Acapulco
Chilpancingo
Chilapa
Tlapa
GUERRERO
Ometepec
Pinotepa Nacional
Santiago Jamiltepec
San Pedro Pochutla
Puerto Ángel
Puerto Escondido
Miahuatlán
Golfo de Tehuantepec
LAGUNAS DE CHACAHUA
Salina Cruz
Bahías de Huatulco
Tonalá
Pijijiapan
Mapastepec
Motozintla de Mendoza
Huixtla
Tapachula
Puerto Madero
San Marcos
Huehuetenango
Retalhuleu
Mazatenango
Coatepeque
Quetzaltenango
Sololá
Totonicapán
ATITLÁN
GUATEMALA
Amatitlán
Antigua
Jalapa
Chiquimula
Zacapa
Cobán
Sierra de las Minas
L. de Izabal
RÍO DULCE
Puerto Barrios
Livingston
Punta Gorda
Golfo de Honduras
Puerto Cortés
Choloma
San Pedro Sula
El Progreso
Villanueva
La Ceiba
Tela
Trujillo
Balfate
Puerto Castilla
Iriona
HONDURAS
Santa Rosa de Copán
Santa Bárbara
L. de Yojoa
Siguatepeque
Comayagua
Tegucigalpa
Danlí
Yuscarán
La Esperanza
La Paz
Juticalpa
Catacamas
Olanchito
Yoro
Arenal
Sává
PATUCA
COPÁN

1:7 100 00

50 0 50 100 150 200 250 300 km
0 50 100 150 200 miles

JAMAICA
1:2 700 000
10 0 10 20 30 40 50 km
10 0 10 20 30 miles

CARIBBEAN SEA

Montego Bay · Falmouth · Runaway St. Ann's Bay · Galina Point
Lucea · Wakefield · Ocho Rios · Port Maria
Negril · The Cockpit Country · Mount Denham · Moneague · Annotto Bay
Cambridge · 985▲ · Linstead · Port Antonio
South Negril Pt. · Maggotty · Don Figuero Mts · Spanish Town · The Blue Mountains · 2256▲ · John Crow Mts
Black River · Mandeville · Santa Cruz Mts. · May Pen · Portmore · Blue Mountain Peak · Morant Point
Savanna-la-Mar · KINGSTON · Morant Bay · Port Morant
Great Pedro Bluff · Alligator Pond · Portland Bight · Portland Point

GULF OF MEXICO

Canal de Yucatán

U.S.A. · West Palm Beach · Little Abaco I.
Cape Coral · Fort Myers · Boca Raton · West End · Free port · Grand Bahama · Hope Town · Abaco I.
Naples · Fort Lauderdale · Northwest Providence Channel
MIAMI · Bimini Is. · Berry Is. · Eleuthera
EVERGLADES NAT. PARK · Nassau · New Providence · Governor's
Dry Tortugas (U.S.A.) · Key West · Florida Keys · Andros Island · Great Exuma
Florida Bay · Andros Town

LA HABANA (Havana) · Guanabacoa · Santa Cruz del Norte · Canal Nicholas · Great Guana Cay
Marianao · Matanzas · Cárdenas · Sagua la Grande · Great Exuma
Guanajay · Bahía Honda · Jovellanos · Colón · Caibarién · Canal Viejo de Bahama
Pinar del Río · San Antonio de los Baños · Güines · Jagüey Grande · Santa Clara · Morón · Cayo Romano · Duncan Town
Guane · San Luis · La Esperanza · Cienfuegos · Placetas · Ciego de Ávila · Nuevitas
La Fé · Nueva Gerona · Trinidad · Sancti Spíritus · Júcaro · Florida · Camagüey · Puerto Manatí · Puerto Padre
I. de la Juventud · Arch. de los Canarreos · Tunas de Zaza · Santa Cruz del Sur · Victoria de las Tunas · Holguín
Corrientes · Golfo de Guacanayabo · Bayamo · Manzanillo · Gibara
Arch. de Jardines de la Reina · Sierra Maestra · Santiago de Cuba

Cayman Islands (U.K.) · Cayman Brac · Little Cayman
George Town · Grand Cayman · 7680

Is. Santanilla (Swan Islands) (Honduras)

Montego Bay · Falmouth · St. Ann's Bay · Port Maria
Lucea · Negril · Cambridge · Annotto Bay · Port Antonio
South Negril Pt. · Savanna-la-Mar · Black River · Mandeville · May Pen · Spanish Town · Kingston · Morant
Pedro Cays (Jamaica)

MEXICO
Punta Yalkukul · Río Lagartos · C. Catoche · Isla Mujeres · Cancún
Progreso · Dzilam de Bravo · El Cuyo · Cabo Catoche
Mérida · Motul · Temax · Tizimín
Maxcanú · Izamal · Espita · Puerto Morelos
YUCATÁN · Sotuta · CHICHÉN ITZÁ · Valladolid · Player del Carmen
Campeche · Calkiní · Ticul · Peto · MAYAPÁN · Cozumel · Isla Cozumel
Tenabo · Hopelchén · Bolonchén · TULUM
Champotón · San José Carpizo · Felipe Carrillo Puerto · QUINTANA ROO · B. de la Ascensión · SIAN KA'AN
Ciudad del Carmen · I. de Términos · Bacalar · B. del Espíritu Santo
PANTANOS DE CENTLA · Palizada · Chetumal · Banco Chinchorro
Balancán · CALAKMUL · Orange Walk · B. de Chetumal
Tenosique · Río Hondo · Ambergris Cay
Ocosingo · PALENQUE · MIRADOR-RÍO AZUL · Uaxactún · San Pedro
Comitán de Domínguez · SIERRA DE LACANDÓN · LAGUNA DEL TIGRE · TIKAL · Belize City · Turneffe Is.
LAGUNAS DE MONTEBELLO · L. Petén Itzá · Flores · BLUE HOLE · BELIZE
3784▲ · MONTES AZULES · San Ignacio · Belmopan · Middlesex · Barrier Reef
GUATEMALA · SIERRA DE LOS CUCHUMATANES · La Libertad · CARACOL · Benque Viejo · 1120 · Dangriga
Culco · Cobán · Maya Mts. · Golfo de Honduras · Monkey River
Huehuetenango · Sebol · San Luis · Punta Gorda · Puerto Barrios
Vol. Tajumulco · 4211▲ · UTATLÁN · Totonicapán · Livingston · Puerto Cortés · Tela · Roatán · Is. de la Bahía · Utila
Quezaltenango · Sololá · Sierra de las Minas · San Pedro Sula · La Ceiba · Balfate · Trujillo
San Marcos · Chichicastenango · Guastatoya · Santa Rosa · El Progreso · PICO BONITO · Savá · Iriona · Punta Patuca
Coatepeque · Antigua · Jalapa · Zacapa · Santa Bárbara · Yoro · Olanchito · Brus Laguna
Retalhuleu · GUATEMALA · Chiquimula · Copán · HONDURAS · Arenal · Puerto Castilla
Mazatenango · Escuintla · 2730▲ · Chiquimula de Copán · El Jaral · La Ceiba · RÍO PLÁTANO · Laguna Caratasca
San José · 2849▲ · La Esperanza · L. de Yojoa · Comayagua · Juticalpa · Catacamas · Puerto Lempira
Amatitlán · Santa Ana · La Paz · Tegucigalpa · Mosquitia · Puerto Cabo Gracias á Dios
Ahuachapán · Sonsonate · Cojutepeque · Yuscarán · Danlí · Coco (Segovia) · Kisalaya
SAN SALVADOR · Zacatecoluca · San Vicente · Nacaome · Cholutega · Cayos Miskitos (Nicaragua)
EL SALVADOR · Usulután · San Miguel · La Unión · Choluteca · Somoto · Siuna · Puerto Cabezas
G. de Fonseca · Puerto Morazán · El Sauce · Estelí · Jinotega · Matagalpa · Muy Muy · San Pedro del Norte · Río Grande · Prinzapolca
Chinandega · Corinto · León · Boaco · Santo Domingo · Rama · Bluefields · El Bluff
La Paz Centro · MANAGUA · Masaya · Granada · Juigalpa · Punta de Perlas
NICARAGUA · Diriamba · Jinotepe · Lago de Nicaragua · Cord. de Yolaina · El Bluff · Is. del Maiz (Nicaragua)
Rivas · San Juan del Sur · I. de Ometepe · San Carlos · B. de San Juan del Norte
B. de Salinas · GUANACASTE · La Cruz · San Juan · San Juan del Norte
C. Santa Elena · SANTA ROSA · Los Chiles
G. de Papagayo · Liberia · Cord. Guanacaste · COSTA RICA · Tortuguero
C. Velas · Santa Cruz · PALO VERDE · Cord. Central · Guápiles · Siquirres · Limón
Carmona · Nicoya · Alajuela · San José · Cartago · Bocas del Toro · Almirante
Puntarenas · Pen. de Nicoya · Esparta · Bribri · Panamá Canal · Colón · Portobelo
C. Blanco · San José · RICA · Pandora · Bocas del Toro · Chepo · PANAMÁ
Puerto Quepos · Chirripó · Cord. de Talamanca · AMISTAD · Volcán Barú · G. de los Mosquitos · Balboa
B. de Coronado · Buenos Aires · San Vito · Boquete · L. Gatún · Río Hato · Arch. de las Perlas
CORCOVADO · Puerto Cortés · San Isidro · David · Concepción · Santiago · Penonomé · San Miguel · La Palma
Pen. de Osa · Golfito · Remedios · Aguadulce · I. del Rey · Garachiné · Yaviza
G. Dulce · Puerto Armuelles · Sona · Chitré · Las Tablas · Golfo de Panamá · El Real
Pta. Burica · G. de Chiriquí · COIBA · Pen. de Azuero · Jaqué
I. de Coiba · I. de Cebaco · Tonosí · CERRO HOYA · Punta Mala
I. Jicarón · Punta Manato

Is. de la Bahía · Roatán · Guanaja
Golfo de Honduras · Puerto Cortés · Puerto Castilla
Monkey River

Bajo Nuevo (Colombia)

CARIB

I. de Providencia (Colombia)
Cayos Roncador (Colombia)
I. de San Andrés (Colombia)
Cayos de Albuquerque (Colombia)

Pta. Manzanillo · Nombre de Dios · Archipiélago de San Blas · G. de Morrosquillo
I. de San Bernardo
Serranía del Darién · Golfo del Darién · Cartagena
Serranía de Tabasará · Loric · Cerret · Montería
DARIÉN · CÓRDOBA

PACIFIC OCEAN

Projection: Bi-polar oblique Conical Orthomorphic

GUADELOUPE
Pte. de la Grande Vigie
Port-Louis · Grande-Terre
Petit-Canal
Ste-Rose · Pointe-à-Pitre · Le Moule · La Désirade
Pointe-Noire · Ste-Anne · Pointe des Châteaux
Basse-Terre · GUADELOUPE (Fr.) · Îles de la Petite Terre
Bouillante · Capesterre-Belle-Eau · St-Louis · Marie-Galante
Soufrière · 1467▲ · Trois-Rivières · Grand-Bourg · Capesterre · 204▲
Basse-Terre · Îles des Saintes · Pte. des Basses

MARTINIQUE
Cap St-Martin · Basse-Pointe
Le Prêcheur · 1463▲ · Ste-Marie
Montagne Pelée · Presqu'île de la Caravelle
St-Pierre · La Trinité
Schoelcher · Le Robert
St-Joseph · Le François
Fort-de-France · Le Lamentin · Le St-Esprit
MARTINIQUE (Fr.) · Rivière-Salée · Rivière-Pilote · Le Marin
Ste-Luce · Pte. d'Enfer

GUADELOUPE AND MARTINIQUE
1:1 800 000
10 0 10 20 30 40 50 60 km
10 0 10 20 30 40 miles

ATLANTIC OCEAN

PUERTO RICO d
1:2 700 000
10 0 10 20 30 40 50 km
10 0 10 20 30 miles

PUERTO RICO
(U.S.A.)

Pta. Aguijereada
Isabela
Aguadilla
Arecibo
Barceloneta
Manati
SAN JUAN
Vega
Baja
Bayamón
Carolina
Río Grande
Fajardo
Dewey
Culebra
San Sebastian
Adjuntas
Utuado
Cordillera Central
Cerro
1338
de Punta
Sierra de
Luquillo
Puerca
Mayagüez
Uroyan Mts.
Yauco
Caguas
Cayey
Humacoa
Naguabo
Vieques
Esperanza
San German
Guanica
Ponce
Coamo
Yabucoa
Pta. Aguila
Guayama
I. Caja de Muertos

VIRGIN ISLANDS e
1:1 800 000
10 0 10 20 30 km
10 0 10 20 miles

Ruffing Pt.
The Settlement
Anegada
East Pt.
Virgin Islands
(U.K.)
Jost Van Dyke I.
Guana I.
Great Camanoe
Charlotte Amalie
Haus
Lollik I.
Cruz Bay
Tortola
521
Road Town
Beef I.
Peter I.
Virgin Gorda
Spanish Town
Virgin Is.
(U.S.A.)
St. Thomas I.
St. John I.
VIRGIN IS.

ST. LUCIA f
1:890 000
5 0 5 10 km
5 0 5 10 miles

Cap Point
Gros Islet
Pte. Hardy
Esperance Bay
Castries
Marquis
L'Anse la Raye
Dennery
Canaries
Millet
Sourière
Mt. Gimie
Trou Gras Pt.
750
950
Sourière Bay
Petit Piton
Micoud
Gros Piton Pt.
796
Vierge Pt.
Gros Piton
Choiseul
Laborie
Vieux Fort
C. Moule à Chique
ST. LUCIA

BARBADOS g
1:890 000
5 0 5 10 km
5 0 5 10 miles

Crabhill
North Point
ATLANTIC OCEAN
Fustic
Spring Hall
Boscobelle
Portland
245
Belleplaine
Speightstown
Fustic
BARBADOS
Westmoreland
Alleynes Bay
Bathsheba
340
Hillcrest
Martin's Bay
Holetown
Massiah Street
Ragged Pt.
Black Rock
Jackson
Bridgefield
Ellerton
Six Cross Roads
The Crane
Bridgetown
Ivy
Edey
St. Martins
Worthing
Oistins Bay
Oistins
Chancery Lane
South Point
BGI

ATLANTIC OCEAN

AMAS

arthur's Town
The Bight
Cat I.
San Salvador I.
Conception I.
Rum Cay
Long I.
Tropic of Cancer
Clarence Town
Samana Cay
Crooked I.
Plana Cays
Albert Town
Snug Corner
Mayaguana I.
Cay Verde
Acklins I.
Mira por vos Cay
Turks & Caicos (U.K.)
Hogsty Reef
Caicos Is.
Little Inagua I.
Cockburn Town
Turks Is.
Lake Rose
INAGUA
Turks Island Passage
Great Inagua I.
tilla
Moa
Matthew Town
Baracoa
Pta. de Maisi
Î. de la Tortue
Monte Cristi
LA ISABELA
Santiago de los Caballeros
uantanamo
Cap-Haitien
Puerto Plata
La Vega
Nagua
Samana
GUANTANAMO BAY (U.S.A.)
Jean Rabel
Port-de-Paix
Fort Liberté
San Francisco de Macorís
Milwaukee Deep 9200
Puerto Rico Trench
Cap-à-Foux
G. de la Gonâve
Gonaïves
Hinche
Pico Duarte 3175
Sanchez
Sabana de la Mar
Bayamón
SAN JUAN
Virgin Gorda
Anegada
Sombrero (U.K.)
St-Marc
St. Thomas
Carolina
Tortola
Virgin Is. (U.K.)
Anguilla (U.K.)
Jérémie
Î. de la Gonâve
PORT-AU-PRINCE
DOMINICAN REP.
San Pedro de Macorís
Higüey
Arecibo
1338
Fajardo
Road Town
St-Martin (Fr.)
vassa I. (U.S.A.)
Dame
Massif de la Hotte
Petit
2680
Aguadilla
Ponce
Caguas
Charlotte Amalie
Virgin Is. (U.S.A.)
St. Maarten (Neth.)
St-Barthélemy (Fr.)
C. Carcasse
Les Cayes
Aquin
Jacmel
SIERRA DE BAORUCO
Barahona
Mayagüez
Guayama
Christiansted
St. Croix
Saba (Neth.)
Barbuda
Pointe-à-Gravois
à Vache
Pedernales
L. Enriquillo
Bani
San Cristóbal
SANTO DOMINGO
ESTE
B. de Yuma
I. Saona
Isla Mona
PUERTO RICO (U.S.A.)
Frederiksted
St. Eustatius (Neth.)
ST. KITTS & NEVIS
ANTIGUA & BARBUDA
St. John's
I. Beata
C. Beata
Mona Passage
Basseterre
Nevis
Antigua
Redonda (U.K.)
Montserrat (U.K.)
Hispaniola
Antilles
Lesser Antilles
Ste-Rose
Le Moule
La Désirade
Leeward Islands
Guadeloupe Passage
GUADELOUPE (Fr.)
1467
Pointe-à-Pitre
Marie-Galante (Fr.)
Basse-Terre
Grand-Bourg
I. des Saintes (Fr.)
Dominica Passage
I. de Aves (Venezuela)
Portsmouth
DOMINICA
1447
Roseau
MORNE TROIS PITONS
Martinique Passage
Mt. Pelée
Ste-Marie
1397
Le François
Fort-de-France
Rivière-Pilote
MARTINIQUE (Fr.)
St. Lucia Channel
Castries
ST. LUCIA
Sourière
St. Vincent Passage
Souvière 1234
St. Vincent
Speightstown
Kingstown
Bridgetown
BARBADOS
Grenadines
ST. VINCENT & THE GRENADINES
Hillsborough
St. George's
GRENADA

B E A N
C A R I B B E A N   S E A

Windward Islands
Windward Antilles

COLOMBIA

Pta. Gallinas
Oranjestad
Aruba (Neth.)
Curaçao
Bonaire
Lesser Antilles
I. Blanquilla (Ven.)
Tobago
Scarborough
MACUIRA
C. San Román
Willemstad
NETH. ANTILLES
ARC. LOS ROQUES
Is. Los Hermanos (Ven.)
Port of Spain
Galera Point
Pen. de la Guajira
Pta. Espada
Pen. de Paraguaná
Punto Fijo
Is. Las Aves (Ven.)
I. Orchila (Ven.)
NUEVA ESPARTA
Is. Los Testigos (Ven.)
Trinidad
Arima
Santa Marta
Ríohacha
Uribia
Golfo de Venezuela
Punta Cardón
MÉDANOS DE CORO
Puerto Cumarebo
Is. Los Roques (Ven.)
I. La Tortuga (Ven.)
I. de Margarita
La Asunción
Cerro El Copey
Río Caribe
Güiria
Rio Claro
BARRANQUILLA
TAYRONA
GUAJIRA
San Rafael
Coro
La Vela de Coro
CUEVA DE LA QUEBRADA DEL TORO
Tucacas
FALCÓN
HENRI PITTIER
MARACAY
La Guaira
CARACAS
VARGAS
Porlamar
LAGUNA DE LA RESTINGA
Cumaná
Carúpano
TRINIDAD & TOBAGO
Barano
ISLA DE SALAMANCA
Ciénaga
Sabanalarga
SIERRA NEVADA DE STA. MARTA
Santa Marta 5800
La Concepción
Santa Rita
Baragua
Mene de Mauroa
Puerto Cabello
MIRANDA
Río Chico
Higuerote
Puerto La Cruz
Barcelona
G. de Paria
San Fernando
Serpent's Mouth
LÁNTICO
Soledad
Fundación
Calamar
Valledupar
Cabimas
Machiques
Ciudad Ojeda
Lago de Maracaibo
LARA
CERRO SAROCHE
Carora
San Felipe
YARACUY
CARABOBO
VALENCIA
Los Teques
Ocumare del Tuy
San Juan de los Morros
Aragua de Barcelona
Anaco
Caripito
Maturín
SUCRE
DELTA AMACURO
MAGDALENA
CÉSAR
Agustín Codazzi
Villa del Rosario
ZULIA
Mene Grande
TRUJILLO
COJEDES
GUÁRICO
Valle de la Pascua
El Tigre
MONAGAS
MARIUSA
Carmen
Zambrano
 Sabana
San Marcos
Sincé
Mompos
Magangue
Sahagún
Corozal
El Banco
Ocaña
CIENAGAS DEL CATATUMBO
San Carlos del Zulia
Betijoque
Valera
El Guache
El Baúl
Calabozo
Santa María de Ipire
Los Barrancos
AMACURO
Rica
Ayapel
NORTE
Trujillo
PORTUGUESA
Guanare
El Sombrero
Pariaguán
Ciudad Guayana
BOLÍVAR
Simiti
SANTANDER
MÉRIDA
BARINAS
Barinas
Libertad
Puerto de Nutrias
San Fernando de Apure
Guasipati
El Callao
El Banco
TACHIRA
Cúcuta
V E N E Z U E L A
Achaguas
Apure
Caicara
Ciudad Bolívar
Embalse de Guri
Tumeremo

West from Greenwich

4000 3000 2000 1500 1000 400 200
600
6000 12 000 18 000 24 000 ft
12 000 9000 6000 4500 3000 1500 600
200 1000 2000 4000 6000 8000 m

COPYRIGHT PHILIP'S

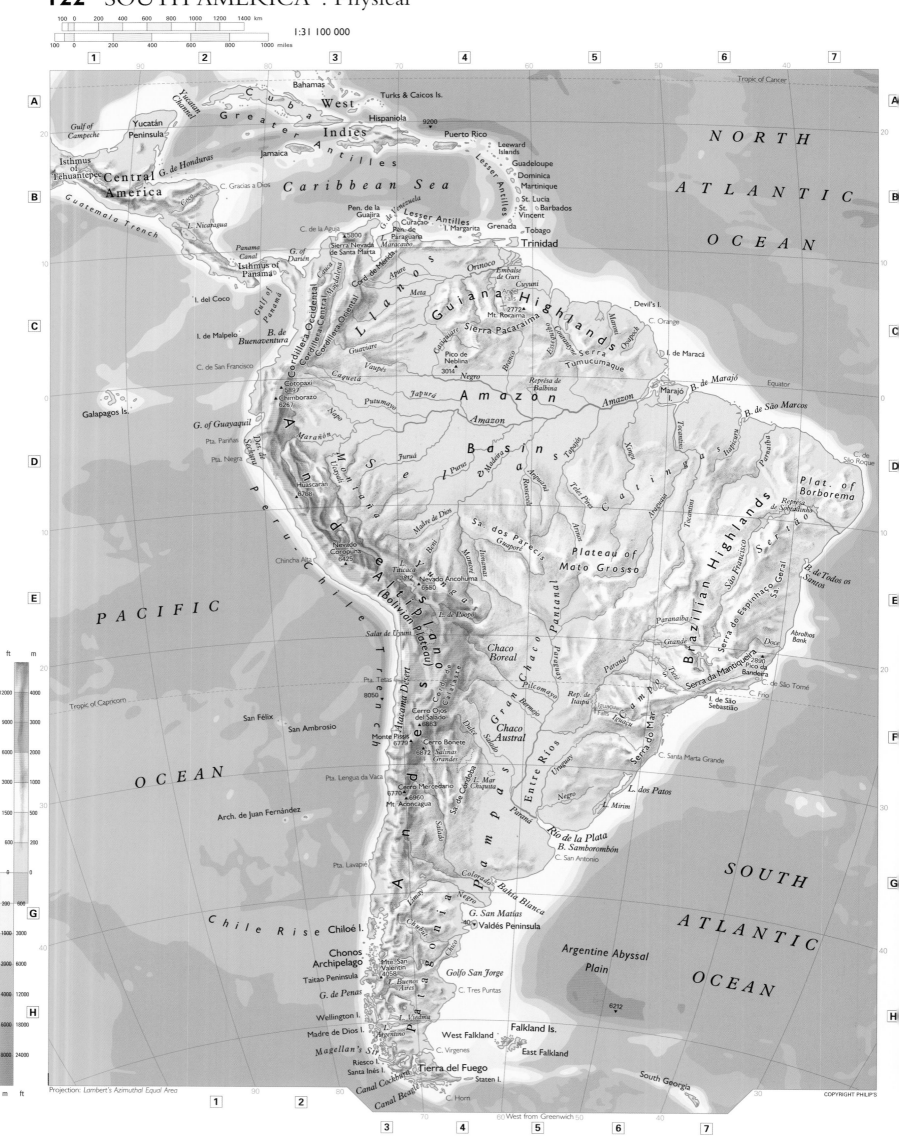

1:31 100 000

Projection: Lambert's Azimuthal Equal Area

COPYRIGHT PHILIP'S

1:31 100 000

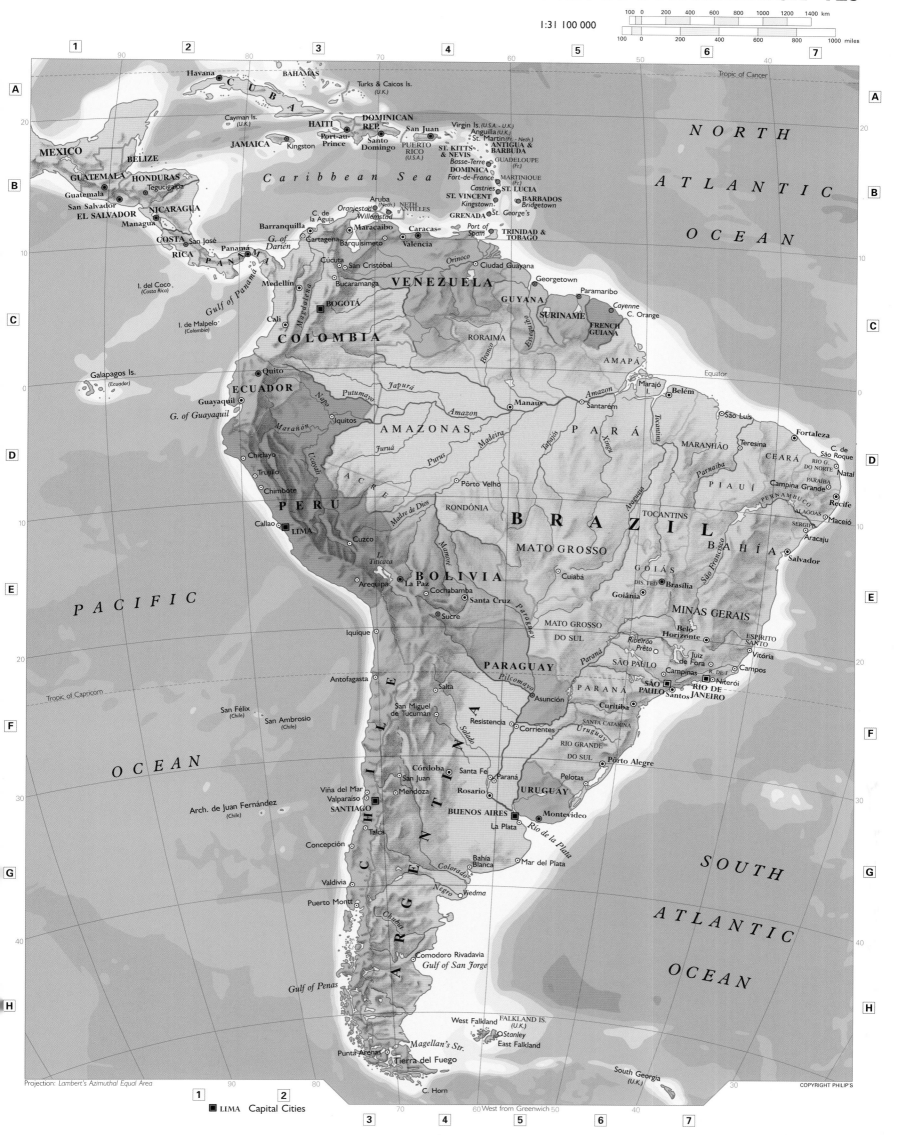

■ LIMA Capital Cities

Projection: Lambert's Azimuthal Equal Area

COPYRIGHT PHILIP'S

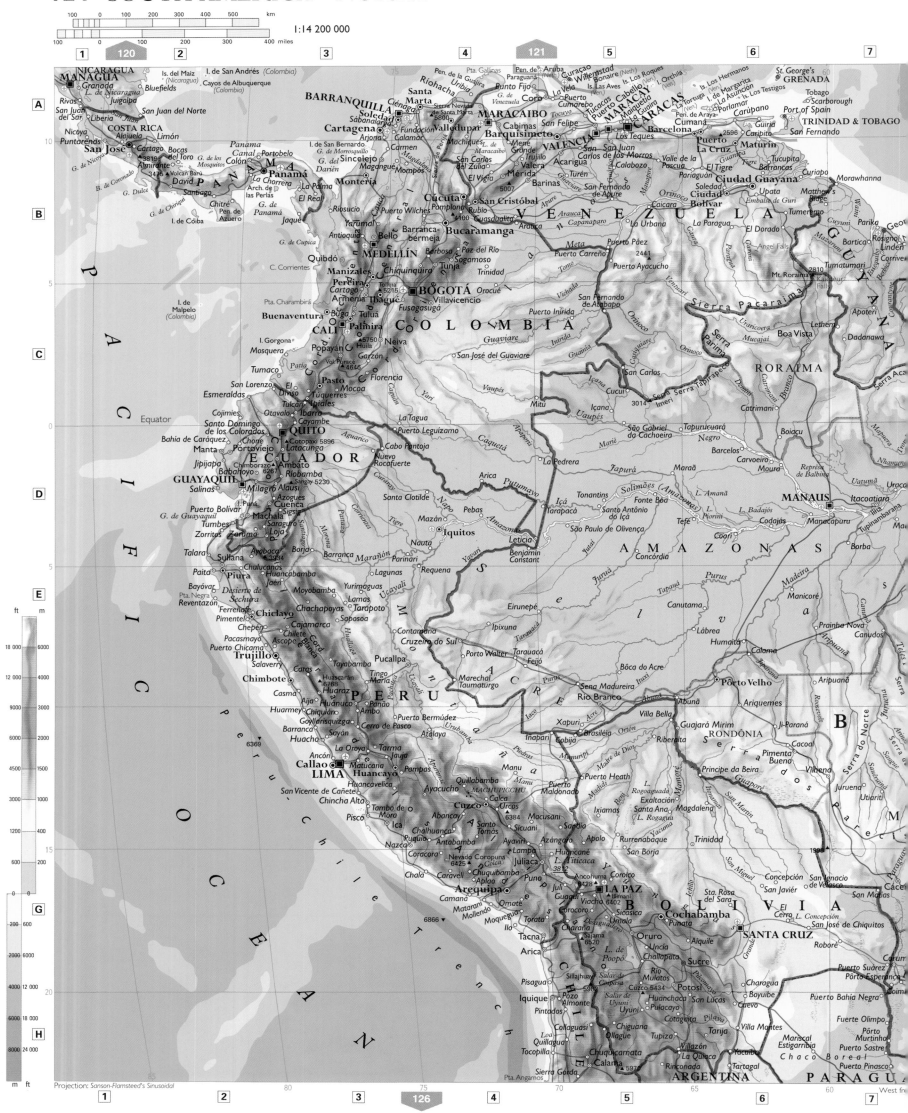

1:14 200 000

Projection: Sanson-Flamsteed's Sinusoidal

ATLANTIC

OCEAN

TRINIDAD AND TOBAGO
1:2 200 000

10   0   10   20   30   40   50 km
10   0   10   20   30 miles

Tobago
Charlotteville   North Pt.
Castara   565   Little
Plymouth   Main Ridge   Tobago
Buccoo Reef   Scarborough   Roxborough
Crown Pt.   Rocky Bay

VENEZUELA   Blanchisseuse   Sans Souci   Toco
Pen. de   La Vache Pt.   Maracas Bay   Galera Pt.
Paria   Corozal   Village   936   940   Redhead
Maracob   Pt.   Maraval   Mt. Aripo   Salybia
Güiria   Monos   Northern Range   Matura
Dragon's   Tunapuna   Valencia   Bay
Mouths   Port   San   Arima   Guaico   ATLANTIC
of   Juan   Sangre   OCEAN
Golfo de Paria   Spain   Caroni   Grande   Talparo   Upper Manzanilla
Chaguanas   Couva   Nariva   Cocos
Point Lisas   Swamp   Bay   Trinidad
Otaheite Bay   Gasparillo   Rio Claro   Guatuaro Pt.
San Fernando   Princes Town   Pierreville
Brighton   La Brea   Penal   Mayaro Bay
Guapo Bay   Pitch   Basse Terre   Guayaguayare
Point Fortin   Lake   Siparia   304   Galeota Pt.
Cedros Bay   Palo Seco   La Lune   Trinity
Bonasse   Erin Pt.   Moruga   Hills
Icacos Pt.
Serpent's Mouth
VENEZUELA   Pta. Bombedor   West from Greenwich

ATLANTIC

OCEAN

Equator

São Pedro &
São Paulo
(Braz.)

SURINAME   FRENCH
GUIANA

Paramaribo   St-Laurent
Nieuw Amsterdam   Cayenne
Nieuw Nickerie   Sinnamary
Totness   Iracoubo   Kourou
Albina   Kaw
Moengo   C. Orange
Prof. Van   Approuague
Blommestein-   St-Georges
meer   Oiapoque
1230   Camopi
matop   Amapá   I. de Maracá

AMAPÁ

Serra Tumucumaque
Meruma   Serra do
Navio   Araguari
Óbidos   Macapá
Monte   Mazagão   I. Caviana
Alegre   I. de Gurupá   I. Mexiana
Alenquer   Afuá   Chaves   C. Maguarinho
Juruti   Prainha   Soure   Curuçá   Salinópolis
Santarém   Almeirim   Marajó   BELÉM
Belterra   Gurupá   Breves   Vigia
Brasília   Pôrto de Móz   Castanhal
Legal   Cametá   Abaetetuba
Altamira   Baião   Bragança
Itaituba   Tucuruí   Viseu
Represa de   Turiaçu
Tucuruí   Curralinho

PARÁ

Marabá
Serra dos Carajás
São João   Carajás
de Araguaia
Tocantinópolis
Conceição do   Pôrto Franco
Araguaia   Estreito
Araguacema   Carolina
Riachão

BRAZIL

Serra do Cachimbo
Serra do Roncador

MATO GROSSO
Planalto do

Cuiabá   Mato Grosso

MATO GROSSO
DO SUL

Coxim
Aquidauana
Miranda

Campo
Grande
Ribas
do Rio
Pardo
Três Lagoas

Dourados
Ponta Porã
Pedro Juan
Caballero

São Luís
Rosário   Barreirinhas
Alcântara   Tutóia
Pinheiro   Parnaíba   Camocim
Viana   Piracuruca   Granja   Itapipoca
Bacabal   Brejo   Ipu   Caucaia   FORTALEZA
Santa Inês   Codó   Piripiri   Sobral   Cascavel
Turiaçu   Coroatá   Campo   Maranguape   Aracati
Pedreiras   Caxias   Maior   Baturité   Russas
Caxias   Oiticica   Quixadá   Areia Branca
Acailândia   Crateús   Macau
MARANHÃO   Senador Pompeu   Ceará Mirim
Teresina   CEARÁ   C. de São Roque
Imperatriz   Mossoró   Natal
Barra   Amarante   RIO GRANDE   Currais
do Corda   Colinas   Valença   DO NORTE   Novos
Floriano   do Piauí   Iguatu   Caraúbas   Canguaretama
Loreto   Nova Iorque   Oeiras   Cedro   Caicó   Mamanguape
Araguaína   Riachão   Picos   Cajàzeiras   Sousa   Alagoa   Cabedelo
PIAUÍ   Uruçuí   Ouricuri   Juazeiro   Patos   Grande   João Pessoa
São João   do Norte   Campina   Olinda
do Piauí   Crato   Salgueiro   Grande   RECIFE
Pedro Afonso   Caracol   Sta. Dois Irmãos   Paulistana   Pesqueira   Caruaru   Jaboatão
Santa   Petrolina   PARAÍBA
Filomena   Novo Remanso   PERNAMBUCO   Garanhuns   Vitória de Santo Antão
Palmas   Nova Casa   Petrolândia   Palmares   Rio Largo
Nova   São Francisco   Palmeira   Maceió
TOCANTINS   Parnaguá   Represa de   Indios   dos   Arapiraca
Pôrto Nacional   Sobradinho   Juàzeiro   Paulo Afonso   ALAGOAS
Gurupi   Barra   Xique-Xique   Senhor do   Propriá   Penedo
Peixe   Bonfim   Capela   SERGIPE
Paranã   Jacobina   Itapicuru   Aracaju
Taguatinga   Mundo   Queimadas   São Cristóvão
BAHIA   Novo   Serrinha   Estância
Barreiras   Feira de   Alagoinhas
Ibotirama   Santana   Santo Amaro
Itaberaba   Cachoeira   SALVADOR
Santa Maria   Bom Jesus   Castro   Santo Amaro
da Vitória   da Lapa   Alves   B. de Todos os Santos
Serra do Sincorá   Valença   Nazaré
Caetité   Jequié
Carinhanha   Brumado   Ubaitaba
Niquelândia   Condeúba   Vitória da   Itabuna
Posse   Conquista   Ilhéus
Aruanã   Uruaçu   1678   Januária   Monte Azul   Canavieiras
Formosa   São Francisco   Pedra Azul   Belmonte
DIST.   BRASÍLIA   Janaúba   Pôrto Seguro
FED.   Luziânia   Salinas   Jequitinhonha   Itamaraju
Anápolis   Vianópolis   Montes   Araçuaí   Prado
GOIÂNIA   Claros   Jequitinhonha   Caravelas
GOIÁS   Ipameri   Piraporá   Teófilo Otoni   Nanuque   Mucuri   Banco
Catalão   Paracatu   Diamantina   Abrolhos
Rio Verde   Itumbiara   Patos de   1340   Governador
Jataí   Araguari   Minas   Corinto   Valadares
Quirinópolis   Ipatinga   Nova   Conceição da Barra
Uberlândia   Araxá   Curvelo   Venécia   São Mateus
Alto Araguaia   Prata   Ibiá   Itabira   Colatina   Linhares
Barra do Garças   Uberaba   Sête Lagoas   Caratinga   ESPÍRITO SANTO
Rondonópolis   MINAS GERAIS   Sabará   Ponte Nova   Cariacica
Santo   BELO HORIZONTE   2890   Vitória
Antônio   Divinópolis   Nova   Vila Velha
Santa Fé   São José do   Igarapava   Lima   Oura   Cachoeiro de Itapemirim
do Sul   Barretos   Franca   Conselheiro   Prêto
Andradina   Passos   Lafaiete   Ubá   Itapetinga
Araçatuba   Ribeirão Prêto   Caldas   Barbacena   Campos
Penápolis   Guaxupé   São   Barra   Juiz de Fora
Presidente   Catanduva   Poços de   Rei do   Três Rios   Nova Friburgo
Prudente   Lins   Araraquara   Caldas   Lourenço
Presidente   São Carlos   São   RIO DE JANEIRO
Epitácio   Marília   Mogi-Mirim   Volta   Petrópolis
Panorama   Bauru   PAULO   Limeira   Redonda   Cabo Frio
Assis   Jaú   Piracicaba   Niterói
Botucatu   RIO DE JANEIRO
CAMPINAS

Trindade
(Braz.)

Rocas
Fernando de Noronha
(Braz.)

6059

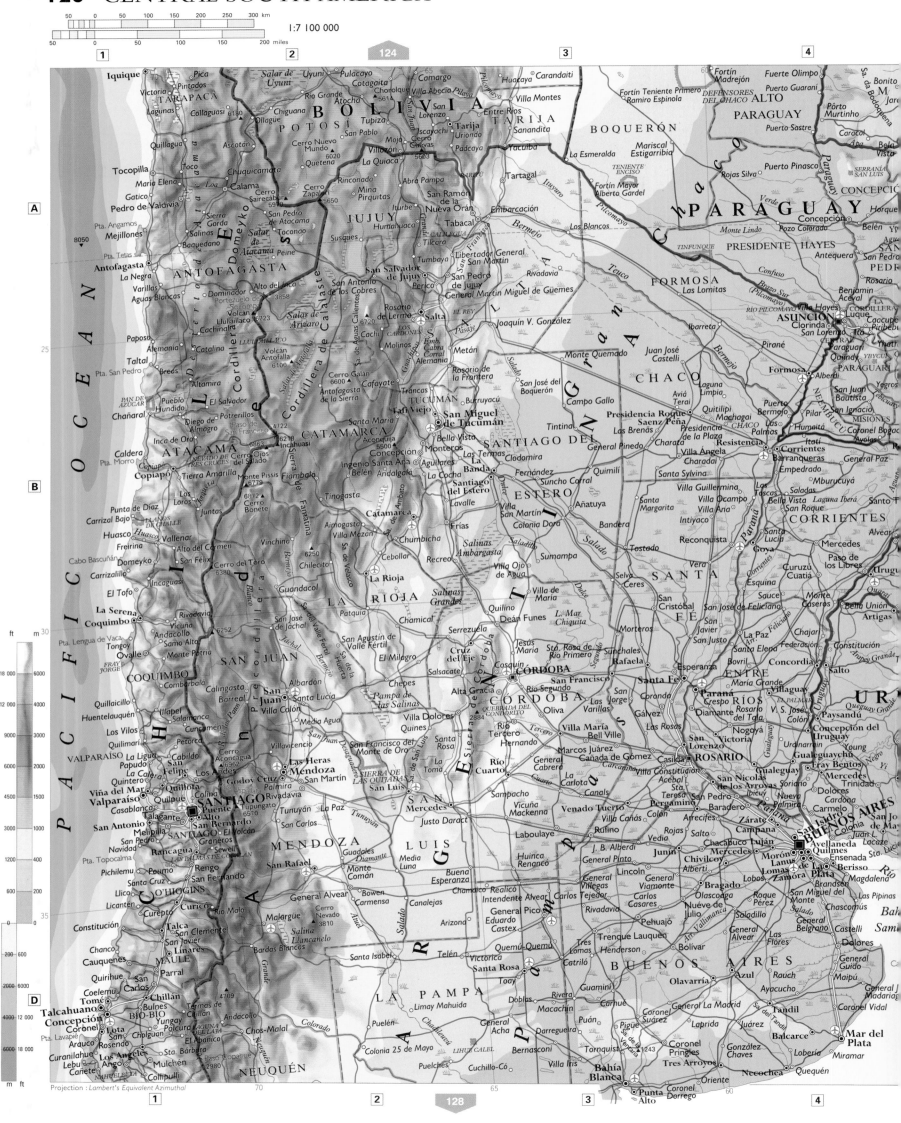

1:7 100 000

Projection : Lambert's Equivalent Azimuthal

BELO
HORIZONTE
Nova Lima
Itabirito

Vitória
Itaquari
Vila
Velha
Guarapari

TO GROSSO
Sidrolândia
Nioaque
uia Lopes
a Laguna
Maracaju
Nova Alvorada
do Sul
Dourados
Rio
Brilhante
Ponto Pora
Pedro Juan Caballero
Xavantina
Panorama
Andradina
Mirandópolis
Aguapei
Araçatuba
Birigui
Mirassol
São José
do Rio Prêto
Olímpia
Catanduva
Bebedouro
Ribeirão
Prêto
Passos
Batatais
Oliveira
Congonhas
Conselheiro Lafaiete
Ouro
Prêto
Ponte Nova
Congonhas
Pico da
Bandeira
2890
Castelo
Cachoeiro
de Itapemirim

D O   S U L

Nova
Andradina
do Sul
Presidente
Epitácio
Adamantina
Santo
Anastácio
Tupã
Penápolis
Lins
Taquaritinga
Novo
Horizonte
Jaboticabal
Guaxupé
Campo Belo
São João
del Rei
Barbacena
Cataguases
Ubá
Muriaé
Carangola
Cambuci
Guarus
Campos

Nova
Andradina
Presidente
Prudente
Martinópolis
Rancharia
Marília
Paraguaçu
Paulista
Bauru
Garça Bariri
Araraquara
São
Carlos
São João
da Boa Vista
Poços de
Caldas
Alfenas
Varginha
Três
Corações
Pouso
Alegre
Lavras
São
Lourenço
Juiz de Fora
Leopoldina
Além Paraíba
Paraíba do Sul
Santos
Dumont
Rio Claro
Limeira

S Ã O
P A U L O

Rosana
Centenário do Sul
Sertanópolis
Assis
Cambará
Ourinhos
Santa Cruz
do Rio Pardo
Piracicaba
CAMPINAS
Americana
Mogi-Mirim
Cruzeiro
Guaratinguetá
Bragança
Paulista
Itajubá
Volta
Redonda
Piraí
Nova
Iguaçu
Petrópolis
Nova Friburgo
Macaé

Paranavaí
Nova
Esperança
Londrina
Rolândia
Arapongas
Joaquim
Távora
Cornélio
Procópio
Jacarèzinho
Botucatu
Itu
Jundiaí
Sorocaba
São José dos C.
Guarulhos
Duque de Caxias
São Gonçalo
Niterói
RIO DE JANEIRO

Umuarama
Cianorte
Mandaguari
Apucarana
Maringá
Ivaí
Tibagi
Itapetininga
SÃO PAULO
São Bernardo
Santo André
São
Vicente
Guarujá
Ilha de São Sebastião
Pta. de Boi
Tropic of Capricorn

BRAZIL
PARANÁ
Guaíra
Pôrto Mendes
Toledo
Ubiratã
Goio-Erê
Campo
Mourão
Cândido de Abreu
Pitanga
Prudentópolis
Ponta
Grossa
Palmeira
CURITIBA
Antonina
Paranaguá
Matinhos
Guaratuba
Ilha do Cardoso
Registro
Iguape
Ilha Comprida

Foz do Iguaçu
Cascavel
Guarapuava
Laranjeiras
do Sul
Irati
Lapa
Rio Negro
Joinville
São Francisco do Sul

Ciudad
del Este
Francisco
Beltrão
União da
Vitória
São
Mateus
do Sul
Mafra
Itajaí

PARANÁ
Bernardo
de Irigoyen
Pato Branco
Palmas
Pôrto União
Xanxerê
Caçador
Chapecó
São Miguel
do Oeste
Clevelândia
Blumenau
Brusque

MISIONES
San
Pedro
Uruguai
Joaçaba
SANTA CATARINA
Santa Cecília
Rio do Sul
Curitibanos
Ilha de Santa Catarina
Florianópolis

Corpus
Frederico
Westphalen
Erechim
Campos
Novos
São
Joaquim
São José
Encarnación
Obera
Monteagudo
Palmeira
das Missões
Lajes
Vacaria
Tubarão
Laguna
Cabo Santa Marta Grande

Candelaria
Santa Rosa
Ijuí
Cruz Alta
Guaporé
São
Joaquim
Criciúma
Ararangúa

Santo
Ângelo
São Luís
Gonzaga
Passo
Fundo
Bento Gonçalves
Torres

RIO   GRANDE
Carazinho
Caxias do Sul
São Borja
Santa
Maria
Santa Cruz
do Sul
Montenegro
Nôvo Hamburgo
São
Leopoldo
Canoas
Osorio

Santiago
Alegrete
sário do Sul
Cachoeira do Sul
Rio Pardo
Viamão
PORTO ALEGRE

D O   S U L
Santana do
Livramento
São
Gabriel
Caçapava
do Sul
Encantadas
Tapes

Rivera
Santana
Dom Pedrito
Camaquã
Camaquã

Bagé
São Lourenço
do Sul
Mostardas
LAGOA DE PEIXE

Tacuarembó
Pinheiro
Machado
Canguçu
Pelotas
Lagoa
dos Patos

UAY
L. Rincón
Bonete
Fraile
Muerto
Melo
Rio Branco
Jaguarão
São José
do Norte
Rio Grande

San Gregorio
Blanquillo
Vergara
Mirim
Lagoa Mangueira

A T L A N T I C

Cerro
Chato
Sarandí del Yi
Treinta y Tres
Santa Vitória do Palmar

José Batlle
y Ordóñez
Lascano
Chuy
SANTA TERESA

Tala
Aigua
Castillos

rida
elones
Minas
las Piedras
Rocha

Pando
San Carlos
Maldonado

ONTEVIDEO
O C E A N

Plata

bón

Antonio

5304

25

30

35

A

B

C

D

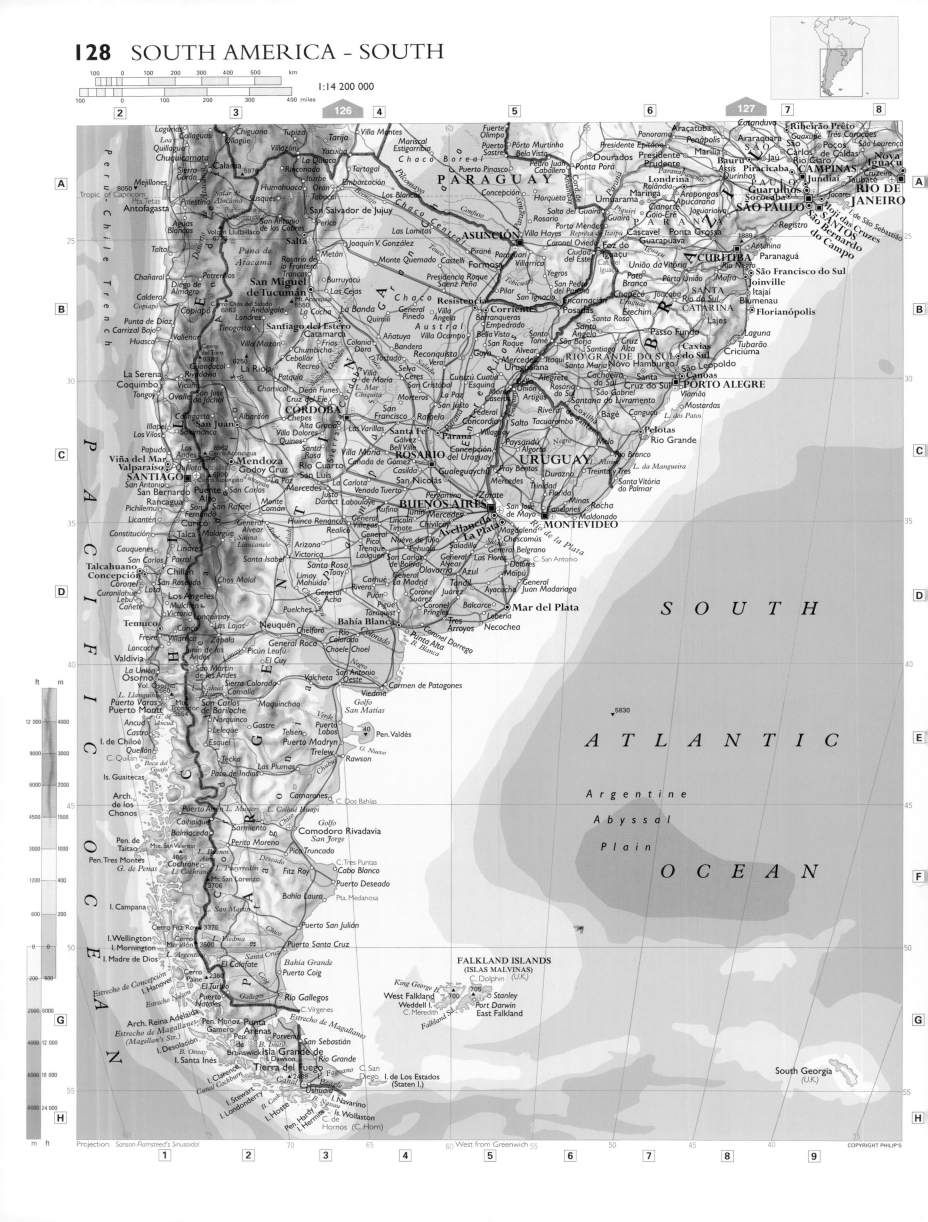

1:14 200 000

South America – South

INDEX TO WORLD MAPS

How to use the index

The index contains the names of all the principal places and features shown on the World Maps. Each name is followed by an additional entry in italics giving the country or region within which it is located. The alphabetical order of names composed of two or more words is governed primarily by the first word and then by the second. This is an example of the rule:

Miquelon *St-P. &M.* **105** C8
Mir *Niger* **83** C7
Mīr Kūh *Iran* **71** E8
Mīr Shahdād *Iran* **71** E8
Mira *Italy* **41** C9

Physical features composed of a proper name (Erie) and a description (Lake) are positioned alphabetically by the proper name. The description is positioned after the proper name and is usually abbreviated:

Erie, L. *N. Amer.* **114** D4

Where a description forms part of a settlement or administrative name however, it is always written in full and put in its true alphabetic position:

Mount Morris *U.S.A.* **114** D7

Names beginning with M' and Mc are indexed as if they were spelled Mac. Names beginning St. are alphabetised under Saint, but Sankt, Sint, Sant', Santa and San are all spelt in full and are alphabetised accordingly. If the same place name occurs two or more times in the index and all are in the same country, each is followed by the name of the administrative subdivision in which it is located. For example:

Jackson *Ky., U.S.A.* **113** G12
Jackson *Mich., U.S.A.* **113** D11
Jackson *Minn., U.S.A.* **112** D6

The number in bold type which follows each name in the index refers to the number of the map page where that feature or place will be found. This is usually the largest scale at which the place or feature appears.

The letter and figure which are in bold type immediately after the page number give the grid square on the map page, within which the feature is situated. The letter represents the latitude and the figure the longitude. A lower case letter immediately after the page number refers to an inset map on that page.

In some cases the feature itself may fall within the specified square, while the name is outside. This is usually the case only with features which are larger than a grid square.

Rivers are indexed to their mouths or confluences, and carry the symbol ➔ after their names. The following symbols are also used in the index: ■ country, ☑ overseas territory or dependency, ☐ first order administrative area, △ national park, ⌂ other park (provincial park, nature reserve or game reserve), ✈ (LHR) principal airport (and location identifier).

How to pronounce place names

English-speaking people usually have no difficulty in reading and pronouncing correctly English place names. However, foreign place name pronunciations may present many problems. Such problems can be minimised by following some simple rules. However, these rules cannot be applied to all situations, and there will be many exceptions.

1. In general, stress each syllable equally, unless your experience suggests otherwise.
2. Pronounce the letter 'a' as a broad 'a' as in 'arm'.
3. Pronounce the letter 'e' as a short 'e' as in 'elm'.
4. Pronounce the letter 'i' as a cross between a short 'i' and long 'e', as the two 'i's in 'California'.
5. Pronounce the letter 'o' as an intermediate 'o' as in 'soft'.
6. Pronounce the letter 'u' as an intermediate 'u' as in 'sure'.
7. Pronounce consonants hard, except in the Romance-language areas where 'g's are likely to be pronounced softly like 'j' in 'jam'; 'j' itself may be pronounced as 'y'; and 'x's may be pronounced as 'h'.
8. For names in mainland China, pronounce 'q' like the 'ch' in 'chin', 'x' like the 'sh' in 'she', 'zh' like the 'j' in 'jam', and 'z' as if it were spelled 'dz'. In general pronounce 'a' as in 'father', 'e' as in 'but', 'i' as in 'keep', 'o' as in 'or', and 'u' as in 'rule'.

Moreover, English has no diacritical marks (accent and pronunciation signs), although some languages do. The following is a brief and general guide to the pronunciation of those most frequently used in the principal Western European languages.

		Pronunciation as in
French	é	day and shows that the e is to be pronounced; e.g. Orléans.
	è	mare
	î	used over any vowel and does not affect pronunciation; shows contraction of the name, usually omission of 's' following a vowel.
	ç	's' before 'a', 'o' and 'u'.
	ë, ï, ü	over 'e', 'i' and 'u' when they are used with another vowel and shows that each is to be pronounced.
German	ä	fate
	ö	fur
	ü	no English equivalent; like French 'tu'
Italian	à, é	over vowels and indicates stress.
Portuguese	ã, õ	vowels pronounced nasally.
	ç	boss
	á	shows stress
	ô	shows that a vowel has an 'i' or 'u' sound combined with it.
Spanish	ñ	canyon
	ü	pronounced as w and separately from adjoining vowels.
	á	usually indicates that this is a stressed vowel.

Abbreviations

A.C.T. – Australian Capital Territory
A.R. – Autonomous Region
Afghan. – Afghanistan
Afr. – Africa
Ala. – Alabama
Alta. – Alberta
Amer. – America(n)
Arch. – Archipelago
Ariz. – Arizona
Ark. – Arkansas
Atl. Oc. – Atlantic Ocean
B. – Baie, Bahía, Bay, Bucht, Bugt
B.C. – British Columbia
Bangla. – Bangladesh
Barr. – Barrage
Bos.-H. – Bosnia-Herzegovina
C. – Cabo, Cap, Cape, Coast
C.A.R. – Central African Republic
C. Prov. – Cape Province
Calif. – California
Cat. – Catarata
Cent. – Central
Chan. – Channel
Colo. – Colorado
Conn. – Connecticut
Cord. – Cordillera
Cr. – Creek
Czech. – Czech Republic
D.C. – District of Columbia
Del. – Delaware
Dem. – Democratic
Dep. – Dependency
Des. – Desert
Dét. – Détroit
Dist. – District
Dj. – Djebel
Domin. – Dominica
Dom. Rep. – Dominican Republic
E. – East

E. Salv. – El Salvador
Eq. Guin. – Equatorial Guinea
Est. – Estrecho
Falk. Is. – Falkland Is.
Fd. – Fjord
Fla. – Florida
Fr. – French
G. – Golfe, Golfo, Gulf, Guba, Gebel
Ga. – Georgia
Gt. – Great, Greater
Guinea-Biss. – Guinea-Bissau
H.K. – Hong Kong
H.P. – Himachal Pradesh
Hants. – Hampshire
Harb. – Harbor, Harbour
Hd. – Head
Hts. – Heights
I.(s). – Île, Ilha, Insel, Isla, Island, Isle
Ill. – Illinois
Ind. – Indiana
Ind. Oc. – Indian Ocean
Ivory C. – Ivory Coast
J. – Jabal, Jebel
Jaz. – Jazīrah
Junc. – Junction
K. – Kap, Kapp
Kans. – Kansas
Kep. – Kepulauan
Ky. – Kentucky
L. – Lac, Lacul, Lago, Lagoa, Lake, Limni, Loch, Lough
La. – Louisiana
Ld. – Land
Liech. – Liechtenstein
Lux. – Luxembourg
Mad. P. – Madhya Pradesh
Madag. – Madagascar
Man. – Manitoba

Mass. – Massachusetts
Md. – Maryland
Me. – Maine
Medit. S. – Mediterranean Sea
Mich. – Michigan
Minn. – Minnesota
Miss. – Mississippi
Mo. – Missouri
Mont. – Montana
Mozam. – Mozambique
Mt.(s) – Mont, Montaña, Mountain
Mte. – Monte
Mti. – Monti
N. – Nord, Norte, North, Northern, Nouveau
N.B. – New Brunswick
N.C. – North Carolina
N. Cal. – New Caledonia
N. Dak. – North Dakota
N.H. – New Hampshire
N.I. – North Island
N.J. – New Jersey
N. Mex. – New Mexico
N.S. – Nova Scotia
N.S.W. – New South Wales
N.W.T. – North West Territory
N.Y. – New York
N.Z. – New Zealand
Nac. – Nacional
Nat. – National
Nebr. – Nebraska
Neths. – Netherlands
Nev. – Nevada
Nfld. & L. – Newfoundland and Labrador
Nic. – Nicaragua
O. – Oued, Ouadi
Occ. – Occidentale
Okla. – Oklahoma

Ont. – Ontario
Or. – Orientale
Oreg. – Oregon
Os. – Ostrov
Oz. – Ozero
P. – Pass, Passo, Pasul, Pulau
P.E.I. – Prince Edward Island
Pa. – Pennsylvania
Pac. Oc. – Pacific Ocean
Papua N.G. – Papua New Guinea
Pass. – Passage
Peg. – Pegunungan
Pen. – Peninsula, Péninsule
Phil. – Philippines
Pk. – Peak
Plat. – Plateau
Prov. – Province, Provincial
Pt. – Point
Pta. – Ponta, Punta
Pte. – Pointe
Qué. – Québec
Queens. – Queensland
R. – Rio, River
R.I. – Rhode Island
Ra. – Range
Raj. – Rajasthan
Recr. – Recreational, Récréatif
Reg. – Region
Rep. – Republic
Res. – Reserve, Reservoir
Rhld-Pfz. – Rheinland-Pfalz
S. – South, Southern, Sur
Si. Arabia – Saudi Arabia
S.C. – South Carolina
S. Dak. – South Dakota
S.I. – South Island
S. Leone – Sierra Leone
Sa. – Serra, Sierra
Sask. – Saskatchewan

Scot. – Scotland
Sd. – Sound
Sev. – Severnaya
Sib. – Siberia
Sprs. – Springs
St. – Saint
Sta. – Santa
Ste. – Sainte
Sto. – Santo
Str. – Strait, Stretto
Switz. – Switzerland
Tas. – Tasmania
Tenn. – Tennessee
Terr. – Territory, Territoire
Tex. – Texas
Tg. – Tanjung
Trin. & Tob. – Trinidad & Tobago
U.A.E. – United Arab Emirates
U.K. – United Kingdom
U.S.A. – United States of America
Ut. P. – Uttar Pradesh
Va. – Virginia
Vdkhr. – Vodokhranilishche
Vdskh. – Vodoskhovyshche
Vf. – Vîrful
Vic. – Victoria
Vol. – Volcano
Vt. – Vermont
W. – Wadi, West
W. Va. – West Virginia
Wall. & F. Is. – Wallis and Futuna Is.
Wash. – Washington
Wis. – Wisconsin
Wlkp. – Wielkopolski
Wyo. – Wyoming
Yorks. – Yorkshire

A

A 'Âli an Nîl □ Sudan 81 F3
A Baña Spain 36 C2
A Cañiza Spain 36 C2
A Coruña Spain 36 B2
A Estrada Spain 36 C2
A Fonsagrada Spain 36 B3
A Guarda Spain 36 D2
A Gudiña Spain 36 C3
A Rúa Spain 36 C3
Aabenraa Denmark 11 J3
Aabybro Denmark 11 G3
Aachen Germany 24 E2
Aalborg Denmark 11 G3
Aalborg Bugt Denmark 11 H4
Aalen Germany 25 G6
Aalestrup Denmark 11 H3
Aalst Belgium 17 D4
Aalten Neths. 17 C6
Aalter Belgium 17 C3
Äänekoski Finland 8 E21
Aarau Switz. 25 H4
Aarberg Switz. 25 H3
Aare → Switz. 25 H4
Aargau □ Switz. 25 H4
Aarhus = Århus Denmark 11 H4
Aars Denmark 11 H3
Aarschot Belgium 17 D4
Aba China 58 A3
Aba Dem. Rep. of the Congo 86 B3
Aba Nigeria 83 D6
Âbâ, Jazîrat Sudan 81 E3
Abaco I. Bahamas 120 A4
Abadab, J. Sudan 80 D4
Ābādān Iran 71 D6
Abade Ethiopia 81 F4
Ābādeh Iran 71 D7
Abadin Spain 36 B3
Abadla Algeria 78 B5
Abaetetuba Brazil 125 D9
Abagnar Qi = Xilinhot China 56 C9
Abah, Tanjung Indonesia 63 K18
Abai Paraguay 127 B4
Abak Nigeria 83 E6
Abakaliki Nigeria 83 D6
Abakan Russia 53 D10
Abala Niger 83 C5
Abalak Niger 83 B6
Abalemma Niger 83 B6
Abana Turkey 72 B6
Abancay Peru 124 F4
Abano Terme Italy 41 C8
Abarán Spain 39 G3
Abariringa Kiribati 96 H10
Abarqū Iran 71 D7
Abashiri Japan 54 B12
Abashiri-Wan Japan 54 C12
Abaújszántó Hungary 28 B6
Abava → Latvia 30 A8
Ābay = Nîl el Azraq → Sudan 81 D3
Abay Kazakhstan 52 E8
Abaya, L. Ethiopia 81 F4
Abaza Russia 52 D9
Abbadia di Fiastra ⌓ Italy 41 E10
Abbadia San Salvatore Italy 41 F8
'Abbāsābād Iran 71 C8
Abbay = Nîl el Azraq → Sudan 81 D3
Abbaye, Pt. U.S.A. 112 B9
Abbé, L. Ethiopia 81 E5
Abbeville France 19 B8
Abbeville Ala., U.S.A. 117 F12
Abbeville La., U.S.A. 116 G8
Abbeville S.C., U.S.A. 117 D13
Abbeyfeale Ireland 12 D2
Abbiategrasso Italy 40 C5
Abbot Ice Shelf Antarctica 5 D16
Abbotsford Canada 102 D4
Abbottabad Pakistan 68 B5
ABC Islands = Netherlands Antilles ⊠ W. Indies 124 A5
Abd al Kūrī Yemen 75 E5
Ābdar Iran 71 D7
'Abdolābād Iran 71 C8
Abdulpur Bangla. 69 G13
Abéché Chad 79 F10
Abejar Spain 38 D2
Abekr Sudan 81 E2
Abel Tasman △ N.Z. 91 D4
Abengourou Ivory C. 82 D4
Abenójar Spain 37 G6
Åbenrå = Aabenraa Denmark 11 J3
Abensberg Germany 25 G7
Abeokuta Nigeria 83 D5
Aber Uganda 86 B3
Aberaeron U.K. 15 E3
Aberayron = Aberaeron U.K. 15 E3
Aberchirder U.K. 13 D6
Abercorn Australia 95 D5
Aberdare U.K. 15 F4
Aberdare △ Kenya 86 C4
Aberdare Ra. Kenya 86 C4
Aberdeen Australia 95 E5
Aberdeen Canada 103 C7
Aberdeen S. Africa 88 E3
Aberdeen U.K. 13 D6
Aberdeen Idaho, U.S.A. 108 E7
Aberdeen Md., U.S.A. 113 F15
Aberdeen Miss., U.S.A. 117 E10
Aberdeen S. Dak., U.S.A. 112 C4
Aberdeen Wash., U.S.A. 110 D3
Aberdeen, City of □ U.K. 13 D6
Aberdeenshire □ U.K. 13 D6
Aberdovey = Aberdyfi U.K. 15 E3
Aberdyfi U.K. 15 E3
Aberfeldy U.K. 13 E5
Aberfoyle U.K. 13 E4
Abergavenny U.K. 15 F4
Abergele U.K. 14 D4
Abernathy U.S.A. 116 E4
Abert, L. U.S.A. 108 E3
Aberystwyth U.K. 15 E3
Abhā Si. Arabia 80 D5
Abhar Iran 73 D13
Abhayapuri India 69 F14
Abia □ Nigeria 83 D6
Abide Turkey 47 C11
Abidiya Sudan 80 D3
Abidjan Ivory C. 82 D4
Abilene Kans., U.S.A. 112 F5
Abilene Tex., U.S.A. 116 E5
Abingdon U.K. 15 F6
Abingdon U.S.A. 113 G13
Abington Reef Australia 94 B4
Abitau → Canada 103 B7
Abitibi → Canada 104 B3
Abitibi, L. Canada 104 C4
Abiy Adi Ethiopia 81 E4
Abiyata-Shala △ Ethiopia 81 F4
Abkhaz Republic = Abkhazia □ Georgia 35 J5
Abkhazia □ Georgia 35 J5
Abminga Australia 95 D1
Abnûb Egypt 80 B3
Åbo = Turku Finland 32 B2
Abocho Nigeria 83 D6
Abohar India 68 D6
Aboisso Ivory C. 82 D4
Abomey Benin 83 D5
Abong-Mbang Cameroon 84 D2
Abonnema Nigeria 83 E6
Abony Hungary 28 C5
Aboso Ghana 82 D4
Abou-Deïa Chad 79 F9
Aboyne U.K. 13 D6
Abra Pampa Argentina 126 A2
Abraham L. Canada 102 C5
Abrantes Portugal 37 F2
Abreojos, Pta. Mexico 118 B2
Abri Esh Shamâliya, Sudan 80 C3
Abri Janub Kordofân, Sudan 81 E3
Abrolhos, Banco Brazil 125 F11
Abrud Romania 28 D8
Abruzzo □ Italy 41 F10
Absaroka Range U.S.A. 108 D9
Abtenau Austria 26 D6
Abu India 68 G5
Abū al Abyad U.A.E. 71 E7
Abū al Khaşīb Iraq 71 D6
Abū 'Alī Si. Arabia 71 E6
Abū 'Alī → Lebanon 74 A4
Abu Ballas Egypt 80 C2
Abu Deleiq Sudan 81 D3
Abu Dhabi = Abū Ẓāby U.A.E. 71 E7
Abu Dis Sudan 80 D3
Abu Dom Sudan 81 D3
Abū Du'ān Syria 73 D8
Abu el Gaīn, W. → Egypt 74 F2
Abu Fatma, Ras Sudan 80 C4
Abû Gabra Sudan 81 E2
Abu Ga'da, W. → Egypt 74 F1
Abu Gelba Sudan 81 E3
Abu Gubeiha Sudan 81 E3
Abu Habl, Khawr → Sudan 81 E3
Abū Ḩadrīyah Si. Arabia 71 E6
Abu Hamed Sudan 80 D3
Abu Haraz An Nîl el Azraq, Sudan 80 D3
Abu Haraz El Gezira, Sudan 81 E3
Abu Haraz Esh Shamâliya, Sudan 80 D3
Abû Higar Sudan 81 E3
Abū Kamāl Syria 73 E9
Abu Kuleiwat Sudan 81 E2
Abū Madd, Ra's Si. Arabia 70 E3
Abu Matariq Sudan 81 E2
Abu Mendi Ethiopia 81 E4
Abū Mūsā U.A.E. 71 E7
Abū Qaşr Si. Arabia 70 D3
Abu Qir Egypt 80 H7
Abu Qireiya Egypt 80 C4
Abu Qurqâs Egypt 80 B3
Abu Shagara, Ras Sudan 80 C4
Abû Shanab Sudan 81 E2
Abu Simbel Egypt 80 C3
Abū Şukhayr Iraq 73 G11
Abu Sultân Egypt 80 H8
Abu Tabari Sudan 80 D2
Abu Tig Egypt 80 B3
Abu Tiga Sudan 81 E3
Abu Tineitin Sudan 81 E3
Abû Uruq Sudan 81 D3
Abû Zabad Sudan 81 E2
Abū Ẓāby U.A.E. 71 E7
Abū Zeydābād Iran 71 C6
Abuja Nigeria 83 D6
Abukuma-Gawa → Japan 54 E10
Abukuma-Sammyaku Japan 54 F10
Abunã Brazil 124 E5
Abunã → Brazil 124 E5
Abune Yosef Ethiopia 81 E4
Aburo Dem. Rep. of the Congo 86 B3
Abut Hd. N.Z. 91 E3
Abuye Meda Ethiopia 81 E4
Abwong Sudan 81 F3
Åby Sweden 11 F10
Aby, Lagune Ivory C. 82 D4
Abyad Sudan 81 E2
Acadia △ U.S.A. 113 C19
Açailândia Brazil 125 D9
Acajutla El Salv. 120 D2
Acámbaro Mexico 118 D4
Acanthus Greece 44 F7
Acaponeta Mexico 118 C3
Acapulco Mexico 119 D5
Acarai, Serra Brazil 124 C7
Acarigua Venezuela 124 B5
Acatlán Mexico 119 D5
Acayucán Mexico 119 D6
Accéglio Italy 40 D4
Accomac U.S.A. 113 G16
Accous France 20 E3
Accra Ghana 83 D4
Accrington U.K. 14 D5
Acebal Argentina 126 C3
Aceh □ Indonesia 62 D1
Acerra Italy 43 B7
Aceuchal Spain 37 G4
Achaia □ Greece 46 C3
Achalpur India 66 J10
Acharnes Greece 46 C5
Acheloos → Greece 46 C3
Acheng China 57 B14
Achenkirch Austria 26 D4
Achensee Austria 26 D4
Achentrias Greece 47 G7
Acher India 68 H5
Achern Germany 25 G4
Achill Hd. Ireland 12 C1
Achill I. Ireland 12 C1
Achim Germany 24 B5
Achinsk Russia 53 D10
Achladokambos Greece 46 D4
Acıgöl Turkey 47 D11
Acıpayam Turkey 47 D11
Acireale Italy 43 E8
Ackerman U.S.A. 117 E10
Acklins I. Bahamas 121 B5
Acme Canada 102 C6
Acme U.S.A. 114 F5
Aconcagua, Cerro Argentina 126 C2
Aconquija, Mt. Argentina 126 B2
Açores, Is. dos Atl. Oc. 78 a
Acornhoek S. Africa 89 C5
Acquapendente Italy 41 F8
Acquasanta Terme Italy 41 F10
Acquasparta Italy 41 F9
Acquaviva delle Fonti Italy 43 B9
Ácqui Terme Italy 40 D5
Acraman, L. Australia 95 E2
Acre = 'Akko Israel 74 C4
Acre □ Brazil 124 E4
Acre → Brazil 124 E5
Acri Italy 43 C9
Acs Hungary 28 C3
Actium Greece 46 C2
Acton Canada 114 C4
Ad Dammām Si. Arabia 71 E6
Ad Dāmūr Lebanon 74 B4
Ad Dawādimī Si. Arabia 70 E5
Ad Dawḩah Qatar 71 E6
Ad Dawr Iraq 73 E10
Ad Dir'īyah Si. Arabia 70 E5
Ad Dīwānīyah Iraq 73 F11
Ad Dujayl Iraq 73 F11
Ad Duwayd Si. Arabia 70 D4
Ada Ghana 83 D5
Ada Serbia 28 E5
Ada Minn., U.S.A. 112 B5
Ada Okla., U.S.A. 116 D6
Adabiya Egypt 74 F1
Adair, C. Canada 101 B12
Adaja → Spain 36 D6
Adak I. U.S.A. 106 a
Adamaoua □ Cameroon 83 D7
Adamaoua, Massif de l' Cameroon 83 D7
Adamawa □ Nigeria 83 D7
Adamawa Highlands = Adamaoua, Massif de l' Cameroon 83 D7
Adamello, Mte. Italy 40 B7
Adamello ⌓ Italy 40 B7
Adami Tulu Ethiopia 81 F4
Adaminaby Australia 95 F4
Adams Mass., U.S.A. 115 D11
Adams N.Y., U.S.A. 115 C8
Adams Wis., U.S.A. 112 D9
Adams, Mt. U.S.A. 110 D5
Adam's Bridge Sri Lanka 66 Q11
Adams L. Canada 102 C5
Adam's Peak Sri Lanka 66 R12
Adamuz Spain 37 G6
Adana Turkey 72 D6
Adana □ Turkey 72 D6
Adanero Spain 36 E6
Adapazarı = Sakarya Turkey 72 B4
Adar Gwagwa, J. Sudan 80 C4
Adarama Sudan 81 D3
Adare, C. Antarctica 5 D11
Adarte Eritrea 81 E5
Adaut Indonesia 63 F8
Adavale Australia 95 D3
Adda → Italy 40 C6
Addis Ababa = Addis Abeba Ethiopia 81 F4
Addis Abeba Ethiopia 81 F4
Addis Alem Ethiopia 81 F4
Addis Zemen Ethiopia 81 E4
Addison U.S.A. 114 D7
Addo S. Africa 88 E4
Addo △ S. Africa 88 E4
Adebour Niger 83 C7
Ādeh Iran 70 B5
Adel U.S.A. 117 F13
Adelaide Australia 95 E2
Adelaide S. Africa 88 E4
Adelaide I. Antarctica 5 C17
Adelaide Pen. Canada 100 C10
Adelaide River Australia 92 B5
Adelaide Village Bahamas 120 A4
Adelanto U.S.A. 111 L9
Adele I. Australia 92 C3
Adélie, Terre Antarctica 5 C10
Adelie Land = Adélie, Terre Antarctica 5 C10
Adelsk Belarus 30 E10
Ademuz Spain 38 E3
Aden = Al 'Adan Yemen 75 E4
Aden, G. of Ind. Oc. 75 E4
Adendorp S. Africa 88 E3
Aderbissinat Niger 83 B6
Adh Dhayd U.A.E. 71 E7
Adhoi India 68 H4
Adi Indonesia 63 E8
Adi Arkai Ethiopia 81 E4
Adi Daro Ethiopia 81 E4
Adi Keyih Eritrea 81 E4
Adi Kwala Eritrea 81 E4
Adi Ugri Eritrea 81 E4
Adieu, C. Australia 93 F5
Adieu Pt. Australia 92 C3
Adigala Ethiopia 81 E5
Adige → Italy 41 C9
Adigrat Ethiopia 81 E4
Adıgüzel Barajı Turkey 47 C11
Adilabad India 66 K11
Adilcevaz Turkey 73 C10
Adirondack ⌓ U.S.A. 115 C10
Adirondack Mts. U.S.A. 115 C10
Adis Abeba = Addis Abeba Ethiopia 81 F4
Adıyaman Turkey 73 D8
Adıyaman □ Turkey 73 D8
Adjohon Benin 83 D5
Adjud Romania 29 D12
Adjumani Uganda 86 B3
Adjuntas Puerto Rico 121 d
Adlavik Is. Canada 105 B8
Adler Russia 35 J4
Admer Algeria 83 A6
Admiralty G. Australia 92 B4
Admiralty I. U.S.A. 102 B2
Admiralty Is. Papua N. G. 90 B7
Adnan Menderes, İzmir ✈ (ADB) Turkey 47 C9
Ado Nigeria 83 D5
Ado-Ekiti Nigeria 83 D6
Adok Sudan 81 F3
Adola Ethiopia 81 E5
Adolfo Ruiz Cortines, Presa Mexico 118 B3
Adonara Indonesia 63 F6
Adoni India 66 M10
Adony Hungary 28 C3
Adour → France 20 E2
Adra India 69 H12
Adra Spain 37 J7
Adrano Italy 43 E7
Adrar Algeria 78 C6
Adrar Mauritania 78 D3
Adrar □ Mauritania 82 A3
Adrar des Iforas Africa 83 B5
Ádria Italy 41 C9
Adrian Mich., U.S.A. 113 E11
Adrian Tex., U.S.A. 116 D3
Adriatic Sea Medit. S. 6 G9
Adua Indonesia 63 E7
Adwa Ethiopia 81 E4
Adygea □ Russia 35 H5
Adzhar Republic = Ajaria □ Georgia 35 K6
Adzopé Ivory C. 82 D4
Ægean Sea Medit. S. 47 C7
Aerhtai Shan Mongolia 60 B4
Ærø Denmark 11 K4
Ærøskøbing Denmark 11 K4
Aetos Greece 46 D3
Afaahiti Tahiti 91 d
'Afak Iraq 73 F11
Afandou Greece 49 C10
Afar □ Ethiopia 81 E5
Afareaitu Moorea 91 d
Afghanistan ■ Asia 66 C4
Afikpo Nigeria 83 D6
Aflou Algeria 78 B6
Afragóla Italy 43 B7
Afram → Ghana 83 D4
Afrera Ethiopia 81 E5
Africa 76 E6
'Afrīn Syria 72 D7
Afşin Turkey 72 C7
Afton N.Y., U.S.A. 115 D9
Afton Wyo., U.S.A. 108 E8
Afuá Brazil 125 D8
'Afula Israel 74 C4
Afyon Turkey 47 C12
Afyon □ Turkey 47 C12
Afyonkarahisar = Afyon Turkey 47 C12
Aga Egypt 80 H7
Agadès = Agadez Niger 83 B6
Agadez Niger 83 B6
Agadir Morocco 78 B4
Agaete Canary Is. 48 F4
Agaie Nigeria 83 D6
Again Sudan 81 F2
Agalega Is. Mauritius 3 E12
Ağapınar Turkey 47 B12
Agar India 68 H7
Agaro Ethiopia 81 F4
Agartala India 67 H17
Agăş Romania 29 D11
Agassiz Canada 102 D4
Agats Indonesia 63 F9
Agawam U.S.A. 115 D12
Agbélouvé Togo 83 D5
Agboville Ivory C. 82 D4
Ağcabädi Azerbaijan 35 K8
Ağdam Azerbaijan 35 L8
Ağdaş Azerbaijan 35 K8
Agde France 20 E7
Agde, C. d' France 20 E7
Agdzhabedi = Ağcabädi Azerbaijan 35 K8
Agen France 20 D4
Agerbæk Denmark 11 J2
Agersø Denmark 11 J5
Ageyevo Russia 32 E9
Aggteleki △ Hungary 28 B5
Āgh Kand Iran 73 D13
Aghathonisi Greece 47 D8
Aghia Anna Greece 46 C5
Aghia Deka Greece 49 D6
Aghia Ekaterinis, Akra Greece 49 A3
Aghia Galini Greece 49 D6
Aghia Marina Kasos, Greece 47 F8
Aghia Marina Leros, Greece 47 D8
Aghia Paraskevi Greece 47 B8
Aghia Roumeli Greece 46 F5
Aghia Varvara Greece 49 D7
Aghiasos Greece 47 B8
Aghio Theodori Greece 46 D5
Aghion Oros □ Greece 45 F8
Aghios Andreas Greece 46 D4
Aghios Efstratios Greece 46 B6
Aghios Georgios Greece 46 D5
Aghios Ioannis, Akra Greece 49 D7
Aghios Isidoros Greece 49 C9
Aghios Kirikos Greece 47 D8
Aghios Matheos Greece 49 B3
Aghios Mironas Greece 47 F7
Aghios Nikolaos Greece 49 D7
Aghios Petros Greece 46 C2
Aghiou Orous, Kolpos Greece 44 F7
Aghireşu Romania 29 D8
Agia Greece 46 B4
Aginskoye Russia 53 D12
Ağlasun Turkey 47 D12
Agly → France 20 F7
Agnew Australia 93 E3
Agnibilékrou Ivory C. 82 D4
Agnita Romania 29 E9
Agnone Italy 41 G11
Agofie Ghana 83 D5
Agogna → Italy 40 C5
Agogo Sudan 81 F2
Agön Sweden 10 C11
Agon Coutainville France 18 C5
Ágordo Italy 41 B9
Agori India 69 G10
Agouna Benin 83 D5
Agout → France 20 E5
Agra India 68 F7
Agrakhanskiy Poluostrov Russia 35 J8
Agramunt Spain 38 D6
Agreda Spain 38 D3
Ağri Turkey 73 C10
Ağri □ Turkey 73 C10
Agri → Italy 43 B9
Ağrı Dağı Turkey 73 C11
Ağri Karakose = Ağri Turkey 73 C10
Agria Greece 46 B5
Agrigento Italy 42 E6
Agrinio Greece 46 C3
Agrópoli Italy 43 B7
Ağstafa Azerbaijan 35 K7
Agua Caliente Mexico 111 N10
Agua Caliente Springs U.S.A. 111 N10
Água Clara Brazil 125 H8
Agua Fria ⌓ U.S.A. 109 J8
Agua Hechicera Mexico 111 N10
Agua Prieta Mexico 118 A3
Aguadilla Puerto Rico 121 d
Aguadulce Panama 120 E3
Aguanga U.S.A. 111 M10
Aguanish Canada 105 B7
Aguanus → Canada 105 B7
Aguapey → Argentina 126 B4
Aguaray Guazú → Paraguay 126 A4
Aguarico → Ecuador 124 D3
Aguaro-Guariquito △ Venezuela 121 E6
Aguas → Spain 38 D4
Aguas Blancas Chile 126 A2
Aguas Calientes, Sierra de Argentina 126 B2
Aguascalientes Mexico 118 C4
Aguascalientes □ Mexico 118 C4
Agudo Spain 37 G6
Águeda Portugal 36 E2
Agueda → Spain 36 D4
Aguelhok Mali 83 B5
Aguié Niger 83 C6
Aguila, Punta Puerto Rico 121 d
Aguilafuente Spain 36 D6
Aguilar Spain 37 H6
Aguilar de Campóo Spain 36 C6
Aguilares Argentina 126 B2
Aguilas Spain 39 H3
Agüimes Canary Is. 48 G4
Aguja, C. de la Colombia 122 B3
Agujereada, Pta. Puerto Rico 121 d
Agulaa Ethiopia 81 E4
Agulhas, C. S. Africa 88 E3
Agulo Canary Is. 48 F2
Agung, Gunung Indonesia 63 J18
Agur Uganda 86 B3
Agusan → Phil. 61 G6
Ağva Turkey 45 E13
Agvali Russia 35 J8
Aha Mts. Botswana 88 B3
Ahaggar Algeria 78 D7
Ahamansu Ghana 83 D5
Ahar Iran 73 C12
Ahat Turkey 47 C11
Ahaus Germany 24 C2
Ahipara B. N.Z. 91 A4
Ahir Dağı Turkey 47 C12
Ahiri India 66 K12
Ahlat Turkey 73 C10
Ahlen Germany 24 D3
Ahmad Wal Pakistan 68 E1
Ahmadabad India 68 H5
Aḩmadābād Khorāsān, Iran 71 C9
Aḩmadābād Khorāsān, Iran 71 C8
Aḩmadī Iran 71 E8
Ahmadnagar India 66 K9
Ahmadpur Pakistan 68 E4
Ahmadpur Lamma Pakistan 68 E4
Ahmar, Mts. Ethiopia 81 F5
Ahmedabad = Ahmadabad India 68 H5
Ahmednagar = Ahmadnagar India 66 K9
Ahmetbey Turkey 45 E11
Ahmetler Turkey 47 C11
Ahmetli Turkey 47 C9
Ahoada Nigeria 83 D6
Ahome Mexico 118 B3
Ahoskie U.S.A. 117 C16
Ahr → Germany 24 E3
Ahram Iran 71 D6
Ahrax Pt. Malta 49 D1
Ahrensbök Germany 24 A6
Ahrensburg Germany 24 B6
Āhū Iran 71 C6
Ahuachapán El Salv. 120 D2
Ahun France 19 F9
Åhus Sweden 11 J8
Ahvāz Iran 71 D6
Ahvenanmaa = Åland Finland 9 F19
Aḩwar Yemen 75 E4
Ahzar → Mali 83 B5
Ai → India 69 F14
Ai-Ais Namibia 88 D2
Ai-Ais and Fish River Canyon △ Namibia 88 C2
Aichach Germany 25 G7
Aichi □ Japan 55 G8
Aigle Switz. 25 J2
Aignay-le-Duc France 19 E11
Aigoual, Mt. France 20 D7
Aigre France 20 C4

Aigrettes, Pte. des *Réunion* **85** c
Aigua *Uruguay* **127** C5
Aigueperse *France* **19** F10
Aigues *France* **21** D8
Aigues → *France* **21** E8
Aigues-Mortes *France* **21** E8
Aigues-Mortes, G. d' *France* **21** E8
Aigües Tortes y Lago San Mauricio △ *Spain* **38** C4
Aiguilles *France* **21** D10
Aiguillon *France* **20** D4
Aigurande *France* **19** F8
Aihui = Heihe *China* **60** A7
Aija *Peru* **124** E3
Aikawa *Japan* **54** E9
Aiken *U.S.A.* **117** E14
Ailao Shan *China* **58** F3
Aileron *Australia* **94** C1
Aillant-sur-Tholon *France* **19** E10
Aillik *Canada* **105** A8
Ailsa Craig *U.K.* **13** F3
Aim *Russia* **53** D14
Aimere *Indonesia* **63** F6
Aimogasta *Argentina* **126** B2
Ain □ *France* **19** F12
Ain → *France* **21** C9
Aïn Ben Tili *Mauritania* **78** C4
Ain Dalla *Egypt* **80** B2
Ain Girba *Egypt* **80** B2
Ain Murr *Sudan* **80** C2
Ain Qeiqab *Egypt* **80** B1
Aïn Sefra *Algeria* **78** B5
Ain Sheikh Murzûk *Egypt* **80** B2
Ain Sudr *Egypt* **74** F2
Ain Sukhna *Egypt* **80** J8
Aïn Témouchent *Algeria* **78** A5
Ain Zeitûn *Egypt* **80** B2
Ainaži *Latvia* **32** D3
Ainos Oros *Greece* **46** C2
Ainsworth *U.S.A.* **112** D4
Aiquile *Bolivia* **124** G5
Aïr *Niger* **83** B6
Air Force I. *Canada* **101** C12
Air Hitam *Malaysia* **65** M4
Airaines *France* **19** C8
Airdrie *Canada* **102** C6
Airdrie *U.K.* **13** F5
Aire → *France* **19** C11
Aire → *U.K.* **14** D7
Aire, I. de l' *Spain* **48** B11
Aire-sur-la-Lys *France* **19** B9
Aire-sur-l'Adour *France* **20** E3
Airlie Beach *Australia* **94** J6
Airvault *France* **18** F6
Aisch → *Germany* **25** F6
Aisne □ *France* **19** C10
Aisne → *France* **19** C9
Ait *India* **69** G8
Aitana, Sierra de *Spain* **39** G4
Aitkin *U.S.A.* **112** B7
Aitutaki *Cook Is.* **97** J12
Aiud *Romania* **29** D8
Aix-en-Provence *France* **21** E9
Aix-la-Chapelle = Aachen *Germany* **24** E2
Aix-les-Bains *France* **21** C9
Aixe-sur-Vienne *France* **20** C5
Aíyina = Egina *Greece* **46** D5
Aizawl *India* **67** H18
Aizenay *France* **18** F5
Aizkraukle *Latvia* **32** D3
Aizpute *Latvia* **30** B8
Aizuwakamatsu *Japan* **54** F9
Ajaccio *France* **21** G12
Ajaccio, G. d' *France* **21** G12
Ajai △ *Uganda* **86** B3
Ajaigarh *India* **69** G9
Ajalpan *Mexico* **119** D5
Ajanta Ra. *India* **66** J10
Ajari Rep. = Ajaria □ *Georgia* **35** K6
Ajaria □ *Georgia* **35** K6
Ajax *Canada* **114** C5
Ajdâbiyâ *Libya* **79** B10
Ajdovščina *Slovenia* **41** C10
Ajibar *Ethiopia* **81** E4
Ajka *Hungary* **28** C7
'Ajlûn *Jordan* **74** C4
'Ajlûn □ *Jordan* **74** C4
'Ajmân *U.A.E.* **71** E7
Ajmer *India* **68** F6
Ajnala *India* **68** D6
Ajo *U.S.A.* **109** K7
Ajo, C. de *Spain* **36** B7
Ajok *Sudan* **81** F2
Ajuy *Phil.* **61** F5
Ak Dağ *Turkey* **47** E11
Ak Dağları *Turkey* **47** E11
Ak Dağları *Sivas, Turkey* **72** C7
Akaba *Togo* **83** D5
Akabira *Japan* **54** C11
Akagera △ *Rwanda* **86** C3
Akaki Beseka *Ethiopia* **81** F4
Akala *Sudan* **81** E3
Akamas *Cyprus* **49** D11
Akan △ *Japan* **54** C12
Akanthou *Cyprus* **49** D12
Akarca *Turkey* **47** C11

Akaroa *N.Z.* **91** E4
Akasha *Sudan* **80** C3
Akashi *Japan* **55** G7
Akbarpur *Bihar, India* **69** G10
Akbarpur *Ut. P., India* **69** F10
Akçaabat *Turkey* **73** B8
Akçadağ *Turkey* **72** C7
Akçakale *Turkey* **73** D8
Akçakoca *Turkey* **72** B4
Akçaova *Turkey* **45** E13
Akçay *Turkey* **47** E11
Akçay → *Turkey* **47** D10
Akdağ *Turkey* **47** C8
Akdağmadeni *Turkey* **72** C6
Akelamo *Indonesia* **63** D7
Åkers styckebruk *Sweden* **10** E11
Åkersberga *Sweden* **10** E12
Aketi *Dem. Rep. of the Congo* **84** D4
Akhalkalaki *Georgia* **35** K6
Akhaltsikhe *Georgia* **35** K6
Akhisar *Turkey* **47** C9
Akhmîm *Egypt* **80** B3
Akhnur *India* **69** C6
Akhtopol *Bulgaria* **45** D11
Akhtuba → *Russia* **35** G8
Akhtubinsk *Russia* **35** F8
Akhty *Russia* **35** K8
Akhtyrka = Okhtyrka *Ukraine* **33** G8
Aki *Japan* **55** H6
Akimiski I. *Canada* **104** B3
Akimovka *Ukraine* **33** J8
Akıncı Burnu *Turkey* **72** D6
Akita *Japan* **54** E10
Akita □ *Japan* **54** E10
Akjoujt *Mauritania* **82** B2
Akka *Morocco* **78** C4
Akkaya Tepesi *Turkey* **47** D11
Akkeshi *Japan* **54** C12
'Akko *Israel* **74** C4
Akköy *Turkey* **47** D9
Aklampa *Benin* **83** D5
Aklavik *Canada* **100** C6
Aklera *India* **68** G7
Akmenė *Lithuania* **30** B9
Akmenrags *Latvia* **30** B8
Akmonte = Almonte *Spain* **37** H4
Akô *Japan* **55** G7
Ako *Nigeria* **83** C7
Akôbô *Sudan* **81** F3
Akobo → *Ethiopia* **81** F3
Akola *India* **66** J10
Akonolinga *Cameroon* **83** E7
Akor *Mali* **82** C3
Akordat *Eritrea* **81** D4
Akosombo Dam *Ghana* **83** D5
Akot *Sudan* **81** F3
Akoupé *Ivory C.* **82** D4
Akpatok I. *Canada* **101** C13
Åkrahamn *Norway* **9** G11
Akranes *Iceland* **8** D2
Akreïjit *Mauritania* **82** B3
Akritas, Akra *Greece* **46** E4
Akron *Colo., U.S.A.* **108** F12
Akron *Ohio, U.S.A.* **114** E3
Akrotiri *Cyprus* **49** E11
Akrotiri, Akra *Greece* **45** F9
Akrotiri Bay *Cyprus* **49** E12
Aksai Chin *China* **69** B8
Aksaray *Turkey* **72** C6
Aksaray □ *Turkey* **72** C5
Aksay = Aqsay *Kazakhstan* **52** D6
Akşehir *Turkey* **72** C4
Akşehir Gölü *Turkey* **72** C4
Akstafa = Ağstafa *Azerbaijan* **35** K7
Aksu *China* **60** B3
Aksu → *Turkey* **72** D4
Aksum *Ethiopia* **81** E4
Aktash *Russia* **34** C11
Aktsyabrski *Belarus* **23** B15
Aktyubinsk = Aqtöbe *Kazakhstan* **52** D6
Aku *Nigeria* **83** D6
Akure *Nigeria* **83** D6
Akureyri *Iceland* **8** D4
Akuseki-Shima *Japan* **55** K4
Akusha *Russia* **35** J8
Akwa-Ibom □ *Nigeria* **83** E6
Akyab = Sittwe *Burma* **67** J18
Akyazı *Turkey* **72** B4
Al 'Adan *Yemen* **75** E4
Al Aḥsā = Hasa *Si. Arabia* **71** E6
Al Ajfar *Si. Arabia* **70** E4
Al Amādīyah *Iraq* **73** D10
Al 'Amārah *Iraq* **73** G12
Al Anbār □ *Iraq* **70** C4
Al 'Aqabah *Jordan* **74** F4
Al 'Aqabah □ *Jordan* **74** F4
Al Arak *Syria* **73** E8
Al 'Aramah *Si. Arabia* **70** E5
Al 'Arṭāwīyah *Si. Arabia* **70** E5
Al 'Aṣimah = 'Ammān □ *Jordan* **74** C4
Al 'Assāfiyah *Si. Arabia* **70** D3
Al 'Ayn *Si. Arabia* **70** E3
Al 'Ayn *U.A.E.* **71** E7
Al 'Azīzīyah *Iraq* **73** F11

Al Bāb *Syria* **72** D7
Al Bad' *Si. Arabia* **70** D2
Al Bādī *Iraq* **70** C4
Al Baḥrah *Kuwait* **70** D5
Al Baḥral Mayyit = Dead Sea *Asia* **74** D4
Al Balqā' □ *Jordan* **74** C4
Al Bārūk, J. *Lebanon* **74** B4
Al Baṣrah *Iraq* **70** D5
Al Baṭḥā *Iraq* **70** D5
Al Batrūn *Lebanon* **74** A4
Al Baydā *Libya* **79** B10
Al Bi'r *Si. Arabia* **70** D3
Al Bukayrīyah *Si. Arabia* **70** E4
Al Burayj *Syria* **74** A5
Al Faḍilī *Si. Arabia* **71** E6
Al Fallūjah *Iraq* **73** F10
Al Fāw *Iraq* **71** D6
Al Fujayrah *U.A.E.* **71** E8
Al Ghadaf, W. → *Jordan* **74** D5
Al Ghammās *Iraq* **70** D5
Al Ghazālah *Si. Arabia* **70** E4
Al Ḥaḍar *Iraq* **73** E9
Al Ḥadīthah *Iraq* **73** E10
Al Ḥadīthah *Si. Arabia* **74** D6
Al Ḥaḍr *Iraq* **73** E9
Al Ḥājānah *Syria* **74** B5
Al Ḥajar al Gharbī *Oman* **71** E8
Al Ḥāmad *Si. Arabia* **70** D3
Al Ḥamdānīyah *Syria* **70** C3
Al Ḥamīdīyah *Syria* **74** A4
Al Ḥammār *Iraq* **70** D5
Al Ḥamrā' *Si. Arabia* **70** E3
Al Ḥanākīyah *Si. Arabia* **70** E4
Al Ḥarīr, W. → *Syria* **74** C4
Al Ḥarūj al Aswad *Libya* **79** C9
Al Ḥasakah *Syria* **73** D9
Al Ḥasakah □ *Syria* **73** D9
Al Ḥayy *Iraq* **73** F12
Al Ḥijarah *Asia* **70** D4
Al Ḥillah *Iraq* **73** F11
Al Ḥillah *Si. Arabia* **75** B4
Al Ḥindīyah *Iraq* **73** F11
Al Hirmil *Lebanon* **74** A5
Al Hoceïma *Morocco* **78** A5
Al Ḥudaydah *Yemen* **75** E3
Al Ḥudūd ash Shamālīyah □ *Si. Arabia* **70** D4
Al Ḥufūf *Si. Arabia* **71** E6
Al Ḥumaydah *Si. Arabia* **70** D2
Al Ḥunayy *Si. Arabia* **71** E6
Al Ḥ¸sāwīyah *Si. Arabia* **70** D3
Al Jafr *Jordan* **74** E5
Al Jāfūrah *Si. Arabia* **71** E7
Al Jaghbūb *Libya* **79** C10
Al Jahrah *Kuwait* **70** D5
Al Jalāmīd *Si. Arabia* **70** D4
Al Jamalīyah *Qatar* **71** E6
Al Janūb □ *Lebanon* **74** B4
Al Jawf *Libya* **79** D10
Al Jawf *Si. Arabia* **70** D3
Al Jawf □ *Si. Arabia* **70** D3
Al Jazair = Algeria ■ *Africa* **78** C6
Al Jazirah *Iraq* **73** E9
Al Jithāmīyah *Si. Arabia* **70** E4
Al Jubayl *Si. Arabia* **70** E6
Al Jubaylah *Si. Arabia* **70** E5
Al Jubb *Si. Arabia* **70** E4
Al Junaynah *Sudan* **79** F10
Al Kabā'ish *Iraq* **70** D5
Al Karak *Jordan* **74** D4
Al Karak □ *Jordan* **74** E5
Al Kāzimīyah *Iraq* **73** F11
Al Khābūra *Oman* **71** F8
Al Khafjī *Si. Arabia* **70** E6
Al Khalīl = Hebron *West Bank* **74** D4
Al Khāliṣ *Iraq* **73** F11
Al Kharsānīyah *Si. Arabia* **71** E6
Al Khaṣab *Oman* **71** E8
Al Khawr *Qatar* **71** E6
Al Khiḍr *Iraq* **70** D5
Al Khiyām *Lebanon* **74** B4
Al Khobar *Si. Arabia* **71** E6
Al Khums *Libya* **79** B8
Al Kiswah *Syria* **74** B5
Al Kūfah *Iraq* **73** F11
Al Kufrah *Libya* **79** D10
Al Kūt *Iraq* **73** F11
Al Kuwayt *Kuwait* **70** D5
Al Labwah *Lebanon* **74** A5
Al Lādhiqīyah *Syria* **72** E6
Al Lādhiqīyah □ *Syria* **72** E6
Al Līth *Si. Arabia* **80** C5
Al Liwā' *Oman* **71** E8
Al Luḥayyah *Yemen* **75** D3
Al Madīnah *Iraq* **70** D5
Al Madīnah *Si. Arabia* **70** E3
Al Mafraq *Jordan* **74** C5
Al Mafraq □ *Jordan* **74** C5
Al Maḥmūdīyah *Iraq* **73** F11
Al Majma'ah *Si. Arabia* **70** E5
Al Makhruq, W. → *Jordan* **74** D6
Al Makhūl *Si. Arabia* **70** E4
Al Manāmah *Bahrain* **71** E6
Al Maqwa' *Kuwait* **70** D5

Al Marāḥ *Si. Arabia* **71** E6
Al Marj *Libya* **79** B10
Al Maṭlā *Kuwait* **70** D5
Al Mawṣil *Iraq* **70** D5
Al Mayādin *Syria* **73** E9
Al Mazār *Jordan* **74** D4
Al Midhnab *Si. Arabia* **70** E5
Al Minā' *Lebanon* **74** A4
Al Miqdādīyah *Iraq* **73** E11
Al Mubarraz *Si. Arabia* **71** E6
Al Mudawwarah *Jordan* **74** F5
Al Mughayrā' *U.A.E.* **71** E7
Al Muḥarraq *Bahrain* **71** E6
Al Mukallā *Yemen* **75** E4
Al Mukhā *Yemen* **75** E3
Al Musayjid *Si. Arabia* **70** E3
Al Musayyib *Iraq* **73** F11
Al Muthanná □ *Iraq* **70** D5
Al Muwayh *Si. Arabia* **80** C5
Al Muwayliḥ *Si. Arabia* **70** E2
Al Owuho = Otukpa *Nigeria* **83** D6
Al Qādisīyah □ *Iraq* **70** D5
Al Qā'im *Iraq* **73** E9
Al Qalībah *Si. Arabia* **70** D3
Al Qāmishlī *Syria* **73** D9
Al Qaryatayn *Syria* **74** A6
Al Qaṣīm □ *Si. Arabia* **70** E4
Al Qaṭ'ā *Syria* **73** E9
Al Qaṭīf *Si. Arabia* **71** E6
Al Qaṭrānah *Jordan* **74** D5
Al Qaṭrūn *Libya* **79** D9
Al Qayṣūmah *Si. Arabia* **70** D5
Al Quds = Jerusalem *Israel/West Bank* **74** D4
Al Qunayṭirah *Syria* **74** C4
Al Qunfudhah *Si. Arabia* **80** D5
Al Qurnah *Iraq* **70** D5
Al Quṣayr *Iraq* **70** D5
Al Quṣayr *Syria* **74** A5
Al Qutayfah *Syria* **74** B5
Al 'Ubaylah *Si. Arabia* **75** C5
Al 'Uḍaylīyah *Si. Arabia* **71** E6
Al 'Ulā *Si. Arabia* **70** E3
Al 'Uqayr *Si. Arabia* **71** E6
Al 'Uwaynid *Si. Arabia* **70** E5
Al 'Uwayqīlah *Si. Arabia* **70** D4
Al 'Uyūn *Ḥijāz, Si. Arabia* **70** E3
Al 'Uyūn *Najd, Si. Arabia* **70** E4
Al 'Uzayr *Iraq* **70** D5
Al Wajh *Si. Arabia* **70** E3
Al Wakrah *Qatar* **71** E6
Al Waqbah *Si. Arabia* **70** D5
Al Wari'āh *Si. Arabia* **70** E5
Al Yaman = Yemen ■ *Asia* **75** E3
Ala *Italy* **40** C8
Ala Dağ *Turkey* **70** B2
Ala Dağları *Turkey* **73** C10
Alabama □ *U.S.A.* **117** E11
Alabama → *U.S.A.* **117** F11
Alabaster *U.S.A.* **117** E11
Alaca *Turkey* **72** B6
Alacaatlı *Turkey* **47** B10
Alaçam *Turkey* **72** B6
Alaçam Dağları *Turkey* **47** B10
Alacant = Alicante *Spain* **39** G4
Alaçatı *Turkey* **47** C8
Alachua *U.S.A.* **117** G13
Alaejos *Spain* **36** D5
Alagna Valsésia *Italy* **40** C4
Alagoa Grande *Brazil* **125** E11
Alagoas □ *Brazil* **125** E11
Alagoinhas *Brazil* **125** F11
Alagón *Spain* **38** D3
Alagón → *Spain* **36** F4
Alaior *Spain* **48** B11
Alajero *Canary Is.* **48** F2
Alajuela *Costa Rica* **120** D3
Alakamisy *Madag.* **89** C8
Alaknanda → *India* **69** D8
Alaköl *Kazakhstan* **60** B3
Alalakeiki Channel *U.S.A.* **106** b
Alamarvdasht *Iran* **71** E7
Alamata *Ethiopia* **81** E4
Alameda *Calif., U.S.A.* **110** H4
Alameda *N. Mex., U.S.A.* **109** J10
Alaminos *Phil.* **61** C3
Alamo *U.S.A.* **111** H11
Alamogordo *U.S.A.* **109** K11
Alamos *Mexico* **118** B3
Alamosa *U.S.A.* **109** H11
Åland *Finland* **9** F19
Ålands hav *Europe* **9** G18
Alange, Embalse d' *Spain* **37** G4
Alania = North Ossetia □ *Russia* **35** J7
Alanís *Spain* **37** G5
Alanya *Turkey* **72** D5
Alaotra, Farihin' *Madag.* **89** B8
Alapayevsk *Russia* **52** D7
Alappuzha = Alleppey *India* **66** Q10
Alar del Rey *Spain* **36** C6
Alaraz *Spain* **36** E5
Alarcón, Embalse de *Spain* **38** F2
Alarobia-Vohiposa *Madag.* **89** C8
Alaşehir *Turkey* **47** C10

Alaska □ *U.S.A.* **106** a
Alaska, G. of *Pac. Oc.* **106** a
Alaska Peninsula *U.S.A.* **106** a
Alaska Range *U.S.A.* **106** a
Alássio *Italy* **40** E5
Älät *Azerbaijan* **35** L9
Alatri *Italy* **41** G10
Alatyr *Russia* **34** C8
Alatyr → *Russia* **34** C8
Alausí *Ecuador* **124** D3
Álava □ *Spain* **38** C2
Alava, C. *U.S.A.* **108** B1
Alaverdi *Armenia* **35** K7
Alavo = Alavus *Finland* **8** E20
Alavus *Finland* **8** E20
Alawoona *Australia* **95** E3
Alba *Italy* **40** D5
Alba □ *Romania* **29** D8
Alba Adriática *Italy* **41** F10
Alba de Tormes *Spain* **36** E5
Alba-Iulia *Romania* **29** D8
Albac *Romania* **28** D7
Albacete *Spain* **39** G3
Albacete □ *Spain* **39** G3
Albacutya, L. *Australia* **95** F3
Albæk *Denmark* **11** G4
Albæk Bugt *Denmark* **11** G4
Albaida *Spain* **39** G4
Albalate de las Nogueras *Spain* **38** E2
Albalate del Arzobispo *Spain* **38** D4
Alban *France* **20** E6
Albanel, L. *Canada* **104** B5
Albania ■ *Europe* **44** E4
Albano Laziale *Italy* **41** G9
Albany *Australia* **93** G2
Albany *Ga., U.S.A.* **117** F12
Albany *N.Y., U.S.A.* **115** D11
Albany *Oreg., U.S.A.* **108** D2
Albany *Tex., U.S.A.* **116** E5
Albany → *Canada* **104** B3
Albardón *Argentina* **126** C2
Albarracín *Spain* **38** E3
Albarracín, Sierra de *Spain* **38** E3
Albatera *Spain* **39** G4
Albatross B. *Australia* **94** A3
Albegna → *Italy* **41** F8
Albemarle *U.S.A.* **117** D14
Albemarle Sd. *U.S.A.* **117** C16
Albenga *Italy* **40** D5
Alberche → *Spain* **36** F6
Alberdi *Paraguay* **126** B4
Albères, Mts. *France* **20** F6
Albert *France* **19** C9
Albert, L. *Africa* **86** B3
Albert, L. *Australia* **95** F2
Albert Edward Ra. *Australia* **92** C4
Albert Lea *U.S.A.* **112** D7
Albert Nile → *Uganda* **86** B3
Albert Town *Bahamas* **121** B5
Alberta □ *Canada* **102** C6
Alberti *Argentina* **126** D3
Albertinia *S. Africa* **88** E3
Albertirsa *Hungary* **28** C4
Alberton *Canada* **105** C7
Albertville *France* **21** C10
Albertville *U.S.A.* **117** D11
Albi *France* **20** E6
Albia *U.S.A.* **112** E7
Albina *Suriname* **125** B8
Albina, Ponta *Angola* **88** B1
Albino *Italy* **40** C6
Albion *Mich., U.S.A.* **113** D11
Albion *Nebr., U.S.A.* **112** E4
Albion *Pa., U.S.A.* **114** E4
Albocácer *Spain* **38** E5
Albolote *Spain* **37** H7
Alborán *Medit. S.* **37** K7
Ålborg = Aalborg *Denmark* **11** G3
Ålborg Bugt = Aalborg Bugt *Denmark* **11** H4
Alborz, Reshteh-ye Kūhhā-ye *Iran* **71** C7
Albox *Spain* **39** H2
Albufeira *Portugal* **37** H2
Albula → *Switz.* **25** J5
Albuñol *Spain* **37** J7
Albuquerque *U.S.A.* **109** J10
Albuquerque, Cayos de *Caribbean* **120** D3
Alburno, Mte. *Italy* **43** B8
Alburquerque *Spain* **37** F4
Albury *Australia* **95** F4
Alcácer do Sal *Portugal* **37** G2
Alcáçovas *Portugal* **37** G2
Alcalá de Chivert *Spain* **38** E5
Alcalá de Guadaira *Spain* **37** H5
Alcalá de Henares *Spain* **36** E7
Alcalá de los Gazules *Spain* **37** J5
Alcalá del Júcar *Spain* **39** F3
Alcalá del Río *Spain* **37** H5

Alcalá del Valle *Spain* **37** J5
Alcalá la Real *Spain* **37** H7
Álcamo *Italy* **42** E5
Alcanadre *Spain* **38** C2
Alcanadre → *Spain* **38** D4
Alcanar *Spain* **38** E5
Alcanede *Portugal* **37** F2
Alcanena *Portugal* **37** F2
Alcañices *Spain* **36** D4
Alcañiz *Spain* **38** D4
Alcântara *Brazil* **125** D10
Alcántara *Spain* **36** F4
Alcántara, Embalse de *Spain* **36** F4
Alcantarilla *Spain* **39** H3
Alcaracejos *Spain* **37** G6
Alcaraz *Spain* **39** G2
Alcaraz, Sierra de *Spain* **39** G2
Alcaudete *Spain* **37** H6
Alcázar de San Juan *Spain* **37** F7
Alchevsk *Ukraine* **33** H10
Alcira = Alzira *Spain* **39** F4
Alcobaça *Portugal* **37** F2
Alcobendas *Spain* **36** E7
Alcolea del Pinar *Spain* **38** D2
Alcora *Spain* **38** E4
Alcorcón *Spain* **36** E7
Alcoutim *Portugal* **37** H3
Alcova *U.S.A.* **108** E10
Alcoy *Spain* **39** G4
Alcubierre, Sierra de *Spain* **38** D4
Alcublas *Spain* **38** F4
Alcúdia *Spain* **48** B10
Alcudia, B. d' *Spain* **48** B10
Alcudia, Sierra de la *Spain* **37** G6
Aldabra Is. *Seychelles* **77** G8
Aldama *Mexico* **119** C5
Aldan *Russia* **53** D13
Aldan → *Russia* **53** C13
Aldea, Pta. de la *Canary Is.* **48** G4
Aldeburgh *U.K.* **15** E9
Alder Pk. *U.S.A.* **110** K5
Alderney *U.K.* **15** H5
Aldershot *U.K.* **15** F7
Åled *Sweden* **11** H6
Aledo *U.S.A.* **112** E8
Alefa *Ethiopia* **81** E4
Aleg *Mauritania* **82** B2
Alegranza *Canary Is.* **48** E6
Alegranza, I. *Canary Is.* **48** E6
Alegre *Brazil* **127** A7
Alegrete *Brazil* **127** B4
Aleksandriya = Oleksandriya *Kirovohrad, Ukraine* **33** H7
Aleksandriya = Oleksandriya *Rivne, Ukraine* **23** C14
Aleksandriyskaya *Russia* **35** J8
Aleksandrov *Russia* **32** D10
Aleksandrov Gay *Russia* **34** E9
Aleksandrovac *Serbia* **44** C5
Aleksandrovac *Serbia* **44** B5
Aleksandrovka = Oleksandrovka *Ukraine* **33** H7
Aleksandrovo *Bulgaria* **45** C8
Aleksandrovsk-Sakhalinskiy *Russia* **53** D15
Aleksandrów Kujawski *Poland* **31** F5
Aleksandrów Łódżki *Poland* **31** G6
Aleksandry, Zemlya *Russia* **4** A10
Alekseyevka *Samara, Russia* **34** D10
Alekseyevka *Voronezh, Russia* **33** G10
Aleksin *Russia* **32** E9
Aleksinac *Serbia* **44** C5
Além Paraíba *Brazil* **127** A7
Alemania *Argentina* **126** B2
Alemania *Chile* **126** B2
Alençon *France* **18** D7
Alenquer *Brazil* **125** D8
'Alenuihähä Channel *U.S.A.* **106** b
Alépé *Ivory C.* **82** D4
Aleppo = Ḥalab *Syria* **72** D7
Aléria *France* **21** F13
Alert *Canada* **101** A13
Alès *France* **21** D8
Aleşd *Romania* **28** C7
Alessándria *Italy* **40** D5
Ålesund *Norway* **8** E12
Alet-les-Bains *France* **20** F6
Aletschhorn *Switz.* **25** J4
Aleutian Basin *Pac. Oc.* **96** B9
Aleutian Is. *Pac. Oc.* **106** b
Aleutian Trench *Pac. Oc.* **4** D17
Alexander *U.S.A.* **112** B2
Alexander, Mt. *Australia* **93** E3
Alexander Arch. *U.S.A.* **100** D6
Alexander Bay *S. Africa* **88** D2
Alexander City *U.S.A.* **117** E12
Alexander I. *Antarctica* **5** C17
Alexandra *Australia* **95** F4
Alexandra *N.Z.* **91** F2
Alexandra Falls *Canada* **102** A5
Alexandria = El Iskandarîya *Egypt* **80** H7
Alexandria *B.C., Canada* **102** C4
Alexandria *Ont., Canada* **115** A10

Alexandria *Romania* **29** G10
Alexandria *S. Africa* **88** E4
Alexandria *U.K.* **13** F4
Alexandria *La., U.S.A.* **116** F8
Alexandria *Minn., U.S.A.* **112** C6
Alexandria *S. Dak., U.S.A.* **112** D5
Alexandria *Va., U.S.A.* **113** F15
Alexandria Bay *U.S.A.* **115** B9
Alexandrina, L. *Australia* **95** F2
Alexandroupoli *Greece* **45** F9
Alexis → *Canada* **105** B8
Alexis Creek *Canada* **102** C4
Aleysk *Russia* **52** D9
Alfabia *Spain* **48** B9
Alfambra *Spain* **38** E3
Alfândega da Fé *Portugal* **36** D4
Alfaro *Spain* **38** C3
Alfatar *Bulgaria* **45** C11
Alfaz del Pi *Spain* **39** G4
Alfeld *Germany* **24** D5
Alfenas *Brazil* **127** A6
Alföld *Hungary* **28** D5
Alfonsine *Italy* **41** D9
Alford *Aberds., U.K.* **13** D6
Alford *Lincs., U.K.* **14** D8
Alfred *Maine, U.S.A.* **115** C14
Alfred *N.Y., U.S.A.* **114** D7
Alfreton *U.K.* **14** D6
Alfta *Sweden* **10** C10
Alga *Kazakhstan* **52** E6
Algaida *Spain* **48** B9
Algar *Spain* **37** J5
Ålgård *Norway* **9** G11
Algarinejo *Spain* **37** H6
Algarve *Portugal* **37** J2
Algeciras *Spain* **37** J5
Algemesí *Spain* **39** F4
Alger *Algeria* **78** A6
Alger □ *Algeria* **39** J8
Alger ✈ (ALG) *Algeria* **39** J8
Algeria ■ *Africa* **78** C6
Alghero *Italy* **42** B1
Älghult *Sweden* **11** G9
Algiers = Alger *Algeria* **78** A6
Algoa B. *S. Africa* **88** E4
Algodonales *Spain* **37** J5
Algodor → *Spain* **36** F7
Algoma *U.S.A.* **112** C10
Algona *U.S.A.* **112** D6
Algonac *U.S.A.* **114** D2
Algonquin △ *Canada* **104** C4
Algorta *Uruguay* **128** C5
Alhama de Almería *Spain* **37** J8
Alhama de Aragón *Spain* **38** D3
Alhama de Granada *Spain* **37** H7
Alhama de Murcia *Spain* **39** H3
Alhambra *U.S.A.* **111** L8
Alhaurín el Grande *Spain* **37** J6
Alhucemas = Al Hoceïma
   Morocco **78** A5
'Alī al Gharbī *Iraq* **73** F12
'Alī ash Sharqī *Iraq* **73** F12
Äli Bayramlı *Azerbaijan* **35** L9
'Alī Khēl *Afghan.* **68** C3
Alī Sahīh *Djibouti* **81** E5
Alī Shāh *Iran* **70** B5
Ália *Italy* **42** E6
'Alīābād *Khorāsān, Iran* **71** C8
'Alīābād *Kordestān, Iran* **70** C5
'Alīābād *Yazd, Iran* **71** D7
Aliaga *Spain* **38** E4
Aliağa *Turkey* **47** C8
Aliakmonas → *Greece* **44** F6
Alibo *Ethiopia* **81** F4
Alibori → *Benin* **83** C5
Alibunar *Serbia* **28** E5
Alicante *Spain* **39** G4
Alicante □ *Spain* **39** G4
Alicante ✈ (ALC) *Spain* **39** G4
Alice *S. Africa* **88** E4
Alice *U.S.A.* **116** H5
Alice → *Queens., Australia* **94** C3
Alice → *Queens., Australia* **94** B3
Alice, Punta *Italy* **43** C10
Alice Arm *Canada* **102** B3
Alice Springs *Australia* **94** C1
Alicedale *S. Africa* **88** E4
Aliceville *U.S.A.* **117** E10
Alicudi *Italy* **43** D7
Aliganj *India* **69** F8
Aligarh *Raj., India* **68** G7
Aligarh *Ut. P., India* **68** F8
Alīgūdarz *Iran* **71** C6
Alijó *Portugal* **36** D3
Alimia *Greece* **49** C9
Alingsås *Sweden* **11** G6
Alipur *Pakistan* **68** E4
Alipur Duar *India* **67** F16
Aliquippa *U.S.A.* **114** F4
Alishan *Taiwan* **59** F13
Aliste → *Spain* **36** D5
Alitus = Alytus *Lithuania* **32** E3
Aliveri *Greece* **46** C6
Aliwal North *S. Africa* **88** E4
Alix *Canada* **102** C6
Aljezur *Portugal* **37** H2
Aljustrel *Portugal* **37** H2
Alkamari *Niger* **83** C7

Alkmaar *Neths.* **17** B4
All American Canal *U.S.A.* **109** K6
Allada *Benin* **83** D5
Allagash → *U.S.A.* **113** B19
Allah Dad *Pakistan* **68** G2
Allahabad *India* **69** G9
Allan *Canada* **103** C7
Allanche *France* **20** C6
Allanridge *S. Africa* **88** D4
Allaqi, Wadi → *Egypt* **80** C3
Allariz *Spain* **36** C3
Allassac *France* **20** C5
Ålleberg *Sweden* **11** F7
Allegany *U.S.A.* **114** D6
Allegheny → *U.S.A.* **114** F5
Allegheny Mts. *U.S.A.* **113** F13
Allegheny Plateau *U.S.A.* **113** E14
Allegheny Res. *U.S.A.* **114** E6
Allègre *France* **20** C7
Allègre, Pte. *Guadeloupe* **120** b
Allen, Bog of *Ireland* **12** C5
Allen, L. *Ireland* **12** B3
Allendale *U.S.A.* **117** E14
Allende *Mexico* **118** B4
Allentown *U.S.A.* **115** F9
Allentsteig *Austria* **26** C8
Alleppey *India* **66** Q10
Allepuz *Spain* **38** E4
Aller → *Germany* **24** C5
Alleynes B. *Barbados* **121** g
Alliance *Nebr., U.S.A.* **112** D2
Alliance *Ohio, U.S.A.* **114** F3
Allier □ *France* **19** F9
Allier → *France* **19** F10
Alliford Bay *Canada* **102** C2
Alligator Pond *Jamaica* **120** a
Allinge *Denmark* **11** J8
Alliston = New Tecumseth
   Canada **114** B5
Alloa *U.K.* **13** E5
Allones *France* **18** D8
Allora *Australia* **95** D5
Allos *France* **21** D10
Alluitsup Paa *Greenland* **4** C5
Alma *Canada* **105** C5
Alma *Ga., U.S.A.* **117** F13
Alma *Kans., U.S.A.* **112** F6
Alma *Mich., U.S.A.* **113** D11
Alma *Nebr., U.S.A.* **112** E4
Alma *Wis., U.S.A.* **112** C8
Alma Ata = Almaty
   Kazakhstan **52** E8
Almacelles *Spain* **38** D5
Almada *Portugal* **37** G1
Almaden *Australia* **94** B3
Almadén *Spain* **37** G6
Almanor, L. *U.S.A.* **108** F3
Almansa *Spain* **39** G3
Almanza *Spain* **36** C6
Almanzor, Pico *Spain* **36** E5
Almanzora → *Spain* **39** H3
Almaş, Munţii *Romania* **28** F7
Almassora *Spain* **38** E4
Almaty *Kazakhstan* **52** E8
Almazán *Spain* **38** D2
Almeirim *Brazil* **125** D8
Almeirim *Portugal* **37** F2
Almelo *Neths.* **17** B6
Almenar de Soria *Spain* **38** D2
Almenara *Spain* **38** F4
Almenara, Sierra de la *Spain* **39** H3
Almendra, Embalse de *Spain* **36** D4
Almendralejo *Spain* **37** G4
Almere-Stad *Neths.* **17** B5
Almería *Spain* **37** J8
Almería □ *Spain* **39** H2
Almería, G. de *Spain* **39** J2
Almetyevsk *Russia* **34** C11
Älmhult *Sweden* **11** H8
Almirante *Panama* **120** E3
Almiropotamos *Greece* **46** C6
Almiros *Greece* **46** B4
Almodôvar *Portugal* **37** H2
Almodóvar del Campo *Spain* **37** G6
Almodóvar del Río *Spain* **37** H5
Almond → *U.S.A.* **114** D7
Almont *U.S.A.* **114** D1
Almonte *Canada* **115** A8
Almonte *Spain* **37** H4
Almora *India* **69** E8
Almoradí *Spain* **39** G4
Almorox *Spain* **36** E6
Almoustarat *Mali* **83** B5
Älmsta *Sweden* **10** E12
Almudévar *Spain* **38** C4
Almuñécar *Spain* **37** J7
Almunge *Sweden* **10** E12
Almuradiel *Spain* **37** G7
Almyrou, Ormos *Greece* **49** D6
Alness *U.K.* **13** D4
Alnmouth *U.K.* **14** B6
Alnwick *U.K.* **14** B6
Aloi *Uganda* **86** B3
Alon *Burma* **67** H19
Alonissos *Greece* **46** B5
Alonissos-Northern
   Sporades △ *Greece* **46** B6
Alor *Indonesia* **63** F6

Alor Setar *Malaysia* **65** J3
Álora *Spain* **37** J6
Alosno *Spain* **37** H3
Alot *India* **68** H6
Aloysius, Mt. *Australia* **93** E4
Alpaugh *U.S.A.* **110** K7
Alpe Apuane △ *Italy* **40** D7
Alpedrinha *Portugal* **36** E3
Alpena *U.S.A.* **113** C12
Alpes-de-Haute-
   Provence □ *France* **21** D10
Alpes-Maritimes □ *France* **21** E11
Alpha *Australia* **94** C4
Alpha Ridge *Arctic* **4** A2
Alphen aan den Rijn *Neths.* **17** B4
Alphios → *Greece* **46** D3
Alpiarça *Portugal* **37** F2
Alpine *Ariz., U.S.A.* **109** K9
Alpine *Calif., U.S.A.* **111** N10
Alpine *Tex., U.S.A.* **116** F3
Alps *Europe* **22** E5
Alpu *Turkey* **72** C4
Alqueta, Barragem do
   Portugal **37** G3
Alrø *Denmark* **11** J4
Als *Denmark* **11** K3
Alsace □ *France* **19** D14
Alsask *Canada* **103** C7
Alsasua *Spain* **38** C2
Alsek → *U.S.A.* **102** B1
Alsfeld *Germany* **24** E5
Alsta *Norway* **8** D15
Alstermo *Sweden* **11** H9
Alston *U.K.* **14** C5
Alta *Norway* **8** B20
Alta, Sierra *Spain* **38** E3
Alta Gracia *Argentina* **126** C3
Alta Sierra *U.S.A.* **111** K8
Altaelva → *Norway* **8** B20
Altafjorden *Norway* **8** A20
Altai = Aerhtai Shan
   Mongolia **60** B4
Altai = Gorno-Altay □
   Russia **52** D9
Altamaha → *U.S.A.* **117** F14
Altamira *Brazil* **125** D8
Altamira *Chile* **126** B2
Altamira *Mexico* **119** C5
Altamira, Cuevas de *Spain* **36** B6
Altamont *U.S.A.* **115** D10
Altamura *Italy* **43** B9
Altanbulag *Mongolia* **60** A5
Altar *Mexico* **118** A2
Altar, Gran Desierto de
   Mexico **118** B2
Altata *Mexico* **118** C3
Altavista *U.S.A.* **113** G14
Altay *China* **60** B3
Altdorf *Switz.* **25** J4
Alte Mellum *Germany* **24** B4
Altea *Spain* **39** G4
Altenberg *Germany* **24** E9
Altenbruch *Germany* **24** B4
Altenburg *Germany* **24** E8
Altenkirchen
   Mecklenburg-Vorpommern,
   Germany **24** A9
Altenkirchen *Rhld-Pfz.,*
   Germany **24** E3
Altenmarkt *Austria* **26** D7
Alter do Chão *Portugal* **37** F3
Altınkaya Baraji *Turkey* **72** B6
Altınoluk *Turkey* **47** B8
Altınova *Turkey* **47** B8
Altıntaş *Turkey* **47** B12
Altınyaka *Turkey* **47** E12
Altınyayla *Turkey* **47** D11
Altiplano *Bolivia* **124** G5
Altkirch *France* **19** E14
Altmühl → *Germany* **25** G7
Altmühltal △ *Germany* **25** G7
Altmark *Germany* **24** C7
Altınlı → *Germany* **24** C7
Altun Kupri *Iraq* **73** E11
Altun Shan *China* **60** C3
Alturas *U.S.A.* **108** F3

Altus *U.S.A.* **116** D5
Alubijid *Phil.* **61** G6
Alucra *Turkey* **73** B8
Aluk *Sudan* **81** F2
Alunda *Sweden* **10** D12
Alunite *U.S.A.* **111** K12
Aluoro → *Ethiopia* **81** F3
Alupka *Ukraine* **33** K8
Alushta *Ukraine* **33** K8
Alusi *Indonesia* **63** F8
Alva *U.S.A.* **116** C5
Alvaiázere *Portugal* **36** F2
Älvängen *Sweden* **11** G6
Alvão △ *Portugal* **36** D3
Alvarado *Mexico* **119** D5
Alvarado *U.S.A.* **116** E6
Alvaro Obregón, Presa
   Mexico **118** B3
Alvear *Argentina* **126** B4
Alverca *Portugal* **37** G1
Alvesta *Sweden* **11** H8
Alvin *U.S.A.* **116** G7
Alvinston *Canada* **114** D3
Alvito *Portugal* **37** G3
Älvkarleby *Sweden* **10** D11
Alvord Desert *U.S.A.* **108** E4
Älvros *Sweden* **10** B8
Älvsbyn *Sweden* **8** D19
Alwar *India* **68** F7
Alxa Zuoqi *China* **56** E3
Alyangula *Australia* **94** A2
Alyata = Älät *Azerbaijan* **35** L9
Alyth *U.K.* **13** E5
Alytus *Lithuania* **32** E3
Alzada *U.S.A.* **108** D11
Alzey *Germany* **25** F4
Alzira *Spain* **39** F4
Am Timan *Chad* **79** F10
Amadeus, L. *Australia* **93** D5
Amâdi *Dem. Rep. of the Congo* **86** B2
Amadi *Sudan* **81** F3
Amadjuak L. *Canada* **101** C12
Amadora *Portugal* **37** G1
Amagansett *U.S.A.* **115** F12
Amagasaki *Japan* **55** G7
Amager *Denmark* **11** J6
Amagunze *Nigeria* **83** D6
Amahai *Indonesia* **63** E7
Amaile *Samoa* **91** b
Amakusa-Shotō *Japan* **55** H5
Åmål *Sweden* **10** E6
Amalfi *Italy* **43** B7
Amaliada *Greece* **46** D3
Amalner *India* **66** J9
Amamapare *Indonesia* **63** E9
Amambaí *Brazil* **127** A4
Amambaí → *Brazil* **127** A5
Amambay □ *Paraguay* **127** A4
Amambay, Cordillera de
   S. Amer. **127** A4
Amami-Guntō *Japan* **55** L4
Amami-Ō-Shima *Japan* **55** K4
Aman, Pulau *Malaysia* **65** c
Amaná, L. *Brazil* **124** D6
Amanat → *India* **69** G11
Amanda Park *U.S.A.* **110** C3
Amankeldi *Kazakhstan* **52** D7
Amantea *Italy* **43** C9
Amapá *Brazil* **125** C8
Amapá □ *Brazil* **125** C8
Amaqjuak → *Canada* —
Amargosa → *U.S.A.* **111** J10
Amargosa Desert *U.S.A.* **111** J10
Amargosa Range *U.S.A.* **111** J10
Amari *Greece* **49** D6
Amarillo *U.S.A.* **116** D4
Amarkantak *India* **69** H9
Amârna, Tell el' *Sudan* **80** B3
Amaro, Mte. *Italy* **41** F11
Amarpur *India* **69** G12
Amarti *Eritrea* **81** E5
Amarwara *India* **69** H8
Amasra *Turkey* **72** B5
Amassama *Nigeria* **83** D6
Amasya *Turkey* **72** B6
Amasya □ *Turkey* **72** B6
Amata *Australia* **93** E5
Amatikulu *S. Africa* **89** D5
Amatitlán *Guatemala* **120** D1
Amatrice *Italy* **41** F10
Amay *Belgium* **17** D5
Amazon = Amazonas →
   S. Amer. **125** D8
Amazonas □ *Brazil* **124** E6
Amazonas □ *S. Amer.* **125** D8
Amba Ferit *Ethiopia* **81** E4
Ambah *India* **68** F8
Ambahakily *Madag.* **89** C7
Ambahita *Madag.* **89** C8
Ambala *India* **68** D7

Ambalavao *Madag.* **89** C8
Ambanja *Madag.* **89** A8
Ambararata *Madag.* **89** B8
Ambarchik *Russia* **53** C17
Ambarijeby *Madag.* **89** A8
Ambaro, Helodranon'
   Madag. **89** A8
Ambato *Ecuador* **124** D3
Ambato *Madag.* **89** A8
Ambato, Sierra de *Argentina* **126** B2
Ambato Boeny *Madag.* **89** B8
Ambatofinandrahana
   Madag. **89** C8
Ambatolampy *Madag.* **89** B8
Ambatomainty *Madag.* **89** B8
Ambatomanoina *Madag.* **89** B8
Ambatondrazaka *Madag.* **89** B8
Ambatosoratra *Madag.* **89** B8
Ambelonas *Greece* **46** B4
Ambenja *Madag.* **89** B8
Amberg *Germany* **25** F7
Ambergris Cay *Belize* **119** D7
Ambérieu-en-Bugey *France* **21** C9
Amberley *N.Z.* **91** E4
Ambert *France* **20** C7
Ambidédi *Mali* **82** C2
Ambikapur *India* **69** H10
Ambikol *Sudan* **80** D3
Ambilobé *Madag.* **89** A8
Amble *U.K.* **14** B6
Ambleside *U.K.* **14** C5
Ambo *Peru* **124** F3
Amboahangy *Madag.* **89** C8
Ambodifototra *Madag.* **89** B8
Ambodilazana *Madag.* **89** B8
Ambodiriana *Madag.* **89** B8
Ambohidratrimo *Madag.* **89** B8
Ambohidray *Madag.* **89** B8
Ambohimahamasina
   Madag. **89** C8
Ambohimahasoa *Madag.* **89** C8
Ambohimanga *Madag.* **89** C8
Ambohimitombo *Madag.* **89** C8
Ambohitra *Madag.* **89** A8
Amboise *France* **18** E8
Ambon *Indonesia* **63** E7
Ambondro *Madag.* **89** D8
Amboseli, L. *Kenya* **86** C4
Amboseli △ *Kenya* **86** C4
Ambositra *Madag.* **89** C8
Ambovombe *Madag.* **89** D8
Amboy *U.S.A.* **111** L11
Amboyna Cay *S. China Sea* **62** C4
Ambridge *U.S.A.* **114** F4
Ambriz *Angola* **84** F2
Amchitka I. *U.S.A.* **106** a
Amderma *Russia* **52** C7
Amdhi *India* **69** H9
Amdo *China* **67** C17
Ameca *Mexico* **118** C4
Ameca → *Mexico* **118** C3
Amecameca de Juárez
   Mexico **119** D5
Ameland *Neths.* **17** A5
Amélia *Italy* **41** F9
Amendolara *Italy* **43** C9
Amenia *U.S.A.* **115** E11
America-Antarctica Ridge
   S. Ocean **5** B2
American Falls *U.S.A.* **108** E7
American Falls Res. *U.S.A.* **108** E7
American Fork *U.S.A.* **108** F8
American Highland
   Antarctica **5** D6
American Samoa ☑ *Pac. Oc.* **91** b
American Samoa △
   Amer. Samoa **91** b
Americana *Brazil* **127** A6
Americus *U.S.A.* **117** E12
Amersfoort *Neths.* **17** B5
Amersfoort *S. Africa* **89** D4
Amery Basin *S. Ocean* **5** C6
Amery Ice Shelf *Antarctica* **5** C6
Ames *Spain* **36** C2
Ames *U.S.A.* **112** D7
Amesbury *U.S.A.* **115** D14
Amet *India* **68** G5
Amfiklia *Greece* **46** C4
Amfilochia *Greece* **46** C3
Amfipoli *Greece* **44** F7
Amfissa *Greece* **46** C4
Amga *Russia* **53** C14
Amga → *Russia* **53** C14
Amgu *Russia* **54** B8
Amgun → *Russia* **53** D14
Amherst *Canada* **105** C7
Amherst *Mass., U.S.A.* **115** D12
Amherst *N.Y., U.S.A.* **114** D6
Amherst *Ohio, U.S.A.* **114** E2
Amherst I. *Canada* **115** B8
Amherstburg *Canada* **104** D3
Amiata, Mte. *Italy* **41** F8
Amidon *U.S.A.* **112** B2

Amiens *France* **19** C9
Amindeo *Greece* **44** F5
Åminne *Sweden* **11** G7
Amino *Ethiopia* **81** G5
Aminuis *Namibia* **88** C2
Amīrābād *Iran* **70** C5
Amirante Is. *Seychelles* **50** J7
Amisk △ *Canada* **103** B9
Amisk L. *Canada* **103** C8
Amistad, Presa de la *Mexico* **118** B4
Amistad △ *U.S.A.* **116** G4
Amite *U.S.A.* **117** F9
Amla *India* **68** J8
Amlapura = Karangasem
   Indonesia **63** J18
Amlia I. *U.S.A.* **106** a
Amlwch *U.K.* **14** D3
Amm Adam *Sudan* **81** D4
'Ammān *Jordan* **74** D4
'Ammān □ *Jordan* **74** D5
'Ammān ✈ (AMM) *Jordan* **74** D5
Ammanford *U.K.* **15** F4
Ammassalik = Tasiilaq
   Greenland **4** C6
Ammerån → *Sweden* **10** A10
Ammersee *Germany* **25** G7
Ammochostos =
   Famagusta *Cyprus* **49** D12
Ammon *U.S.A.* **108** E8
Amnat Charoen *Thailand* **64** E5
Amnura *Bangla.* **69** G13
Amo Jiang → *China* **58** F3
Åmol *Iran* **71** B7
Amorgos *Greece* **47** E7
Amory *U.S.A.* **117** E10
Amos *Canada* **104** C4
Åmot *Norway* **9** G13
Åmotfors *Sweden* **10** E6
Amoy = Xiamen *China* **59** E12
Ampanavoana *Madag.* **89** B9
Ampang *Malaysia* **65** L3
Ampangalana,
   Lakandranon' *Madag.* **89** C8
Ampanihy *Madag.* **89** C7
Amparafaravola *Madag.* **89** B8
Amparihy *Madag.* **89** C8
Ampasindava,
   Helodranon' *Madag.* **89** A8
Ampasindava, Saikanosy
   Madag. **89** A8
Ampenan *Indonesia* **63** K18
Amper *Nigeria* **83** D6
Amper → *Germany* **25** G7
Ampezzo *Italy* **41** B9
Amphoe Kathu *Thailand* **65** a
Amphoe Thalang *Thailand* **65** a
Ampitsikinana *Madag.* **89** A8
Ampombiantambo *Madag.* **89** A8
Amposta *Spain* **38** E5
Ampotaka *Madag.* **89** D7
Ampoza *Madag.* **89** C7
Amqui *Canada* **105** C6
Amravati *India* **66** J10
Amreli *India* **68** J4
Amritsar *India* **68** D6
Amroha *India* **69** E8
Amrum *Germany* **24** A4
Amsterdam *Neths.* **17** B4
Amsterdam *U.S.A.* **115** D10
Amsterdam ✈ (AMS) *Neths.* **17** B4
Amsterdam, I. = Nouvelle
   Amsterdam, Î. *Ind. Oc.* **3** F13
Amstetten *Austria* **26** C7
Amudarya → *Uzbekistan* **52** E6
Amund Ringnes I. *Canada* **101** B10
Amundsen Abyssal Plain
   S. Ocean **5** C14
Amundsen Basin *Arctic* **4** A
Amundsen Gulf *Canada* **100** B7
Amundsen Ridges *S. Ocean* **5** C14
Amundsen-Scott *Antarctica* **5** E
Amundsen Sea *Antarctica* **5** D15
Amungen *Sweden* **10** C9
Amuntai *Indonesia* **62** E5
Amur → *Russia* **53** D15
Amur, W. → *Sudan* **80** D3
Amurang *Indonesia* **63** D6
Amurrio *Spain* **38** B1
Amursk *Russia* **53** D14
Amusco *Spain* **36** C6
Amvrakikos Kolpos *Greece* **46** C4
Amvrosiyivka *Ukraine* **33** J10
Amyderya =
   Amudarya → *Uzbekistan* **52** E6
An Bien *Vietnam* **65** H5
An Hoa *Vietnam* **64** E7
An Nabatīyah at Tahta
   Lebanon **74** B4
An Nabk *Si. Arabia* **70** D3
An Nabk *Syria* **74** A5
An Nafūd *Si. Arabia* **70** D4
An Najaf *Iraq* **73** G11
An Nāşirīyah *Iraq* **70** D5
An Nhon *Vietnam* **64** F7
An Nîl □ *Sudan* **80** D3
An Nîl el Abyad □ *Sudan* **81** E3
An Nîl el Azraq □ *Sudan* **81** E3
An Nu'ayrīyah *Si. Arabia* **71** E6

An Nu'mānīyah *Iraq* **73** F11
An Thoi, Dao *Vietnam* **65** H5
An Uaimh *Ireland* **12** C5
Anabar → *Russia* **53** B12
'Anabtā *West Bank* **74** C4
Anaconda *U.S.A.* **108** C7
Anacortes *U.S.A.* **110** B4
Anacuao, Mt. *Phil.* **61** C4
Anadarko *U.S.A.* **116** D5
Anadia *Portugal* **36** E2
Anadolu *Turkey* **72** C5
Anadyr *Russia* **53** C18
Anadyr → *Russia* **53** C18
Anadyrskiy Zaliv *Russia* **53** C19
Anafi *Greece* **47** E7
Anaga, Pta. de *Canary Is.* **48** F3
Anagni *Italy* **41** G10
'Ānah *Iraq* **73** E10
Anaheim *U.S.A.* **111** M9
Anahim Lake *Canada* **102** C3
Anakapalle *India* **67** L13
Anakie *Australia* **94** C4
Anaklia *Georgia* **35** J5
Analalava *Madag.* **89** A8
Analavoka *Madag.* **89** C8
Analipsis *Greece* **49** A3
Anambar → *Pakistan* **68** D3
Anambas, Kepulauan *Indonesia* **62** D3
Anambas Is. = Anambas, Kepulauan *Indonesia* **62** D3
Anambra □ *Nigeria* **83** D6
Anamosa *U.S.A.* **112** D8
Anamur *Turkey* **72** D5
Anamur Burnu *Turkey* **72** D5
Anan *Japan* **55** H7
Anand *India* **68** H5
Ananes *Greece* **46** E6
Anantapur *India* **66** M10
Anantnag *India* **69** C6
Ananyiv *Ukraine* **29** C14
Anapa *Russia* **33** K9
Anapodiaris → *Greece* **49** E7
Anápolis *Brazil* **125** G9
Anapu → *Brazil* **125** D8
Anār *Iran* **71** D7
Anārak *Iran* **71** C7
Anarisfjällen *Sweden* **10** A7
Anas → *India* **68** H5
Anatolia = Anadolu *Turkey* **72** C5
Anatsogno *Madag.* **89** C7
Añatuya *Argentina* **126** B3
Anauenthad L. *Canada* **103** A8
Anbyŏn *N. Korea* **57** E14
Ancares, Sierra de *Spain* **36** C4
Ancares △ *Spain* **36** C4
Ancaster *Canada* **114** C5
Ancenis *France* **18** E5
Anchor Bay *U.S.A.* **110** G3
Anchorage *U.S.A.* **100** C5
Anci *China* **56** E9
Ancohuma, Nevado *Bolivia* **124** G5
Ancón *Peru* **124** F3
Ancona *Italy* **41** E10
Ancud *Chile* **128** E2
Ancud, G. de *Chile* **128** E2
Ancy-le-Franc *France* **19** E11
Andacollo *Argentina* **126** D1
Andacollo *Chile* **126** C1
Andaingo *Madag.* **89** B8
Andalgalá *Argentina* **126** B2
Åndalsnes *Norway* **8** E12
Andalucía □ *Spain* **37** H6
Andalusia = Andalucía □ *Spain* **37** H6
Andalusia *U.S.A.* **117** F11
Andaman Is. *Ind. Oc.* **3** D14
Andaman Sea *Ind. Oc.* **62** B1
Andamooka *Australia* **95** E2
Andapa *Madag.* **89** A8
Andara *Namibia* **88** B3
Andelot-Blancheville *France* **19** D12
Andenes *Norway* **8** B17
Andenne *Belgium* **17** D5
Andéranboukane *Mali* **83** B5
Andermatt *Switz.* **25** J4
Andernach *Germany* **24** E3
Andernos-les-Bains *France* **20** D2
Anderslöv *Sweden* **11** J7
Anderson *Alaska, U.S.A.* **106** a
Anderson *Calif., U.S.A.* **108** F2
Anderson *Ind., U.S.A.* **113** E11
Anderson *Mo., U.S.A.* **112** G6
Anderson *S.C., U.S.A.* **117** D13
Anderson → *Canada* **100** C7
Anderstorp *Sweden* **11** G7
Andes *U.S.A.* **115** D10
Andes, Cord. de los *S. Amer.* **124** H5
Andfjorden *Norway* **8** B17
Andhra Pradesh □ *India* **66** L11
Andijon *Uzbekistan* **52** E8
Andikíthira = Antikythira *Greece* **46** F5
Andilamena *Madag.* **89** B8
Andímeshk *Iran* **71** C6
Andímilos = Antimilos *Greece* **46** E6
Andíparos = Antiparos *Greece* **47** D7
Andípaxoi = Antipaxi *Greece* **46** B2
Andipsara *Greece* **47** C7
Andizhan = Andijon *Uzbekistan* **52** E8
Andoain *Spain* **38** B2
Andoany *Madag.* **89** A8
Andohahela △ *Madag.* **89** C8
Andong *S. Korea* **57** F15
Andongwei *China* **57** G10
Andoom *Australia* **94** A3
Andorra *Spain* **38** E4
Andorra ■ *Europe* **20** F5
Andorra La Vella *Andorra* **20** F5
Andover *U.K.* **15** F6
Andover *Maine, U.S.A.* **115** B14
Andover *Mass., U.S.A.* **115** D13
Andover *N.J., U.S.A.* **115** F10
Andover *N.Y., U.S.A.* **114** D7
Andover *Ohio, U.S.A.* **114** E4
Andøya *Norway* **8** B16
Andradina *Brazil* **125** H8
Andrahary *Madag.* **89** A8
Andramasina *Madag.* **89** B8
Andranopasy *Madag.* **89** C7
Andranovory *Madag.* **89** C7
Andratx *Spain* **48** B9
Andreanof Is. *U.S.A.* **106** a
Andreapol *Russia* **32** D7
Andrews *S.C., U.S.A.* **117** E15
Andrews *Tex., U.S.A.* **116** E3
Andreyevka *Russia* **34** D10
Ándria *Italy* **43** A9
Andriamena *Madag.* **89** B8
Andriandampy *Madag.* **89** C8
Andriba *Madag.* **89** B8
Andrijevica *Montenegro* **44** D3
Andringitra △ *Madag.* **89** C8
Andritsena *Greece* **46** D3
Androka *Madag.* **89** C7
Andros *Greece* **46** D6
Andros I. *Bahamas* **120** B4
Andros Town *Bahamas* **120** B4
Androscoggin → *U.S.A.* **115** C14
Andrychów *Poland* **31** J6
Andselv *Norway* **8** B18
Andújar *Spain* **37** G6
Andulo *Angola* **84** G3
Aneby *Sweden* **11** G8
Anegada *Br. Virgin Is.* **121** e
Anegada Passage *W. Indies* **121** C7
Aného *Togo* **83** D5
Anenni-Noi *Moldova* **29** D14
Aneto, Pico de *Spain* **38** C5
Anfu *China* **59** D10
Ang Mo Kio *Singapore* **65** d
Ang Thong *Thailand* **64** E3
Ang Thong, Ko *Thailand* **65** b
Ang Thong △ *Thailand* **65** H2
Angamos, Punta *Chile* **126** A1
Angara → *Russia* **53** D10
Angara-Débou *Benin* **83** C5
Angarsk *Russia* **53** D11
Angas Hills *Australia* **92** D4
Angaston *Australia* **95** E2
Ånge *Sweden* **10** B9
Ángel, Salto = Angel Falls *Venezuela* **124** B6
Ángel de la Guarda, I. *Mexico* **118** B2
Angel Falls *Venezuela* **124** B6
Angeles *Phil.* **61** D4
Ängelholm *Sweden* **11** H6
Angels Camp *U.S.A.* **110** G6
Ängelsberg *Sweden* **10** E10
Anger → *Ethiopia* **81** F4
Angereb → *Ethiopia* **81** E4
Ångermanälven → *Sweden* **10** A11
Ångermanland *Sweden* **8** E17
Angermünde *Germany* **24** B9
Angers *Canada* **115** A9
Angers *France* **18** E6
Angerville *France* **19** D9
Ängesån → *Sweden* **8** C20
Angikuni L. *Canada* **103** A9
Anglès *Spain* **38** D7
Anglesey *U.K.* **14** D3
Anglesey, Isle of □ *U.K.* **14** D3
Anglet *France* **20** E2
Angleton *U.S.A.* **116** G7
Anglin → *France* **20** B4
Anglisidhes *Cyprus* **49** E12
Anglure *France* **19** D10
Angmagssalik = Tasiilaq *Greenland* **4** C6
Ango *Dem. Rep. of the Congo* **86** B2
Angoche *Mozam.* **87** F4
Angoche, I. *Mozam.* **87** F4
Angol *Chile* **126** D1
Angola *Ind., U.S.A.* **113** E11
Angola *N.Y., U.S.A.* **114** D5
Angola ■ *Africa* **85** G3
Angoulême *France* **20** C4
Angoumois *France* **20** C4

Angra do Heroismo *Azores* **78** a
Angra dos Reis *Brazil* **127** A7
Angrapa → *Russia* **30** D8
Angren *Uzbekistan* **52** E8
Angtassom *Cambodia* **65** G5
Angu *Dem. Rep. of the Congo* **86** B1
Anguang *China* **57** B12
Anguilla ☑ *W. Indies* **121** C7
Anguo *Mali* **83** D5
Angurugu *Australia* **94** A2
Angus □ *U.K.* **13** E6
Angwa → *Zimbabwe* **89** B5
Anhanduí → *Brazil* **127** A5
Anholt *Denmark* **11** H5
Anhua *China* **59** C8
Anhui □ *China* **59** B11
Anhwei = Anhui □ *China* **59** B11
Anichab *Namibia* **88** C1
Andros *Greece* **47** E7
Anié *Togo* **83** D5
Anima → *U.S.A.* **109** H9
Anina *Romania* **28** E4
Aninoasa *Romania* **29** F9
Anivorano *Madag.* **89** B8
Anjalankoski *Finland* **32** B4
Anjar *India* **68** H4
Anji *China* **59** B12
Anjou *France* **18** E6
Anjouan *Comoros Is.* **85** a
Anjozorobe *Madag.* **89** B8
Anju *N. Korea* **57** E13
Anka *Nigeria* **83** C6
Ankaboa, Tanjona *Madag.* **89** C7
Ankang *China* **56** H5
Ankara *Turkey* **72** C5
Ankara □ *Turkey* **72** C5
Ankarafantsika △ *Madag.* **89** B8
Ankaramena *Madag.* **89** C8
Ankaratra *Madag.* **85** H9
Ankarsrum *Sweden* **11** G10
Ankasakasa *Madag.* **89** B7
Ankavandra *Madag.* **89** B8
Ankazoabo *Madag.* **89** C7
Ankazobe *Madag.* **89** B8
Ankeny *U.S.A.* **112** E7
Ankilimalinika *Madag.* **89** C7
Ankilizato *Madag.* **89** C8
Ankisabe *Madag.* **89** B8
Anklam *Germany* **24** B9
Ankober *Ethiopia* **81** F4
Ankoro *Dem. Rep. of the Congo* **86** D2
Ankororoka *Madag.* **89** D8
Anlong *China* **58** E5
Anlu *China* **59** B9
Anmyeondo *S. Korea* **57** F14
Ånn *Sweden* **10** A6
Ann, C. *U.S.A.* **115** D14
Ann Arbor *U.S.A.* **113** D12
Anna *Russia* **34** E5
Anna *U.S.A.* **112** G9
Annaba *Algeria* **78** A7
Annaberg-Buchholz *Germany* **24** E9
Annalee → *Ireland* **12** B4
Annam *Vietnam* **64** E7
Annamitique, Chaîne *Asia* **64** D6
Annan *U.K.* **13** G5
Annan → *U.K.* **13** G5
Annapolis *U.S.A.* **113** F15
Annapolis Royal *Canada* **105** D6
Annapurna *Nepal* **69** E10
Annean, L. *Australia* **93** E2
Anneberg *Sweden* **11** G8
Annecy *France* **21** C10
Annecy, Lac d' *France* **21** C10
Annemasse *France* **19** F13
Annenskiy Most *Russia* **32** B9
Annette I. *U.S.A.* **102** B2
Anning *China* **58** E4
Anniston *U.S.A.* **117** E12
Annobón *Atl. Oc.* **77** G4
Annonay *France* **21** C8
Annot *France* **21** E10
Annotto B. *Jamaica* **120** a
Annville *U.S.A.* **115** F8
Annweiler *Germany* **25** F3
Ano Poroia *Greece* **44** E7
Ano Siros *Greece* **46** D6
Anogia *Greece* **49** D6
Anorotsangana *Madag.* **89** A8
Anosibe *Madag.* **89** B8
Anou Mellene *Mali* **83** B5
Anoumaba *Ivory C.* **82** D4
Anping *Hebei, China* **56** E8
Anping *Liaoning, China* **57** D12
Anpu Gang *China* **58** G7
Anqing *China* **59** B11
Anqiu *China* **57** F10
Anren *China* **59** D9
Ansager *Denmark* **11** J2
Ansai *China* **56** F5
Ansan *S. Korea* **57** F14
Anse Boileau *Seychelles* **85** b
Anse Royale *Seychelles* **85** b
Anseba → *Eritrea* **81** D4
Ansfelden *Austria* **26** C7

Anshan *China* **57** D12
Anshun *China* **58** D5
Ansião *Portugal* **36** F2
Ansley *U.S.A.* **112** E4
Ansó *Spain* **38** C4
Ansoain *Spain* **38** C3
Anson *U.S.A.* **116** E5
Anson B. *Australia* **92** B5
Ansongo *Mali* **83** B5
Ansongo-Ménaka △ *Mali* **83** B5
Ansonia *U.S.A.* **115** E11
Anstruther *U.K.* **13** E6
Ansudu *Indonesia* **63** E9
Antabamba *Peru* **124** F4
Antakya = Hatay *Turkey* **72** D7
Antalaha *Madag.* **89** A9
Antalya *Turkey* **72** D4
Antalya □ *Turkey* **47** E12
Antalya Körfezi *Turkey* **72** D4
Antambohobe *Madag.* **89** C8
Antanambao-Manampotsy *Madag.* **89** B8
Antanambe *Madag.* **89** B8
Antananarivo *Madag.* **89** B8
Antananarivo □ *Madag.* **89** B8
Antanifotsy *Madag.* **89** B8
Antanimbaribe *Madag.* **89** C7
Antanimora *Madag.* **89** C8
Antarctic Pen. *Antarctica* **5** C18
Antarctica **5** E3
Antelope *Zimbabwe* **87** G2
Antequera *Paraguay* **126** A4
Antequera *Spain* **37** H6
Antero, Mt. *U.S.A.* **108** G10
Antevamena *Madag.* **89** C7
Anthony *Kans., U.S.A.* **112** G4
Anthony *N. Mex., U.S.A.* **109** K10
Anti Atlas *Morocco* **78** C4
Anti-Lebanon = Sharqi, Al Jabal ash *Lebanon* **74** B5
Antibes *France* **21** E11
Antibes, C. d' *France* **21** E11
Anticosti, Î. d' *Canada* **105** C7
Antifer, C. d' *France* **18** C7
Antigo *U.S.A.* **112** C9
Antigonish *Canada* **105** C7
Antigua *Canary Is.* **48** F5
Antigua *Guatemala* **120** D1
Antigua *W. Indies* **121** C7
Antigua & Barbuda ■ *W. Indies* **121** C7
Antikythira *Greece* **46** F5
Antilla *Cuba* **120** B4
Antilles = West Indies *Cent. Amer.* **121** D7
Antimilos *Greece* **46** E6
Antioch *U.S.A.* **110** G5
Antioche, Pertuis d' *France* **20** B2
Antioquia *Colombia* **124** B3
Antiparos *Greece* **47** D7
Antipaxi *Greece* **46** B2
Antipodes Is. *Pac. Oc.* **96** M9
Antirio *Greece* **46** C3
Antler *U.S.A.* **112** A4
Antlers *U.S.A.* **116** D7
Antoetra *Madag.* **89** C8
Antofagasta *Chile* **126** A1
Antofagasta □ *Chile* **126** A2
Antofagasta de la Sierra *Argentina* **126** B2
Antofalla *Argentina* **126** B2
Antofalla, Salar de *Argentina* **126** B2
Anton *U.S.A.* **116** E3
Antongila, Helodrano *Madag.* **89** B8
Antonibé *Madag.* **89** B8
Antonibé, Presqu'île d' *Madag.* **89** A8
Antonina *Brazil* **127** B6
Antrain *France* **18** D5
Antrim *U.K.* **12** B5
Antrim *U.S.A.* **114** F3
Antrim □ *U.K.* **12** B5
Antrim, Mts. of *U.K.* **12** A5
Antrim Plateau *Australia* **92** C4
Antrodoco *Italy* **41** F10
Antropovo *Russia* **34** A6
Antsakabary *Madag.* **89** B8
Antsalova *Madag.* **89** B7
Antsenavolo *Madag.* **89** C8
Antsiafabositra *Madag.* **89** B8
Antsirabe *Antananarivo, Madag.* **89** B8
Antsirabe *Antsiranana, Madag.* **89** A8
Antsirabe *Mahajanga, Madag.* **89** B8
Antsiranana *Madag.* **89** A8
Antsiranana □ *Madag.* **89** A8
Antsohihy *Madag.* **89** A8
Antsohimbondrona Seranana *Madag.* **89** A8
Antu *China* **57** C15
Antwerp = Antwerpen *Belgium* **17** C4
Antwerp *U.S.A.* **115** B9
Antwerpen *Belgium* **17** C4
Antwerpen □ *Belgium* **17** C4
Anupgarh *India* **68** E5

Anuppur *India* **69** H9
Anuradhapura *Sri Lanka* **66** Q12
Anveh *Iran* **71** E7
Anvers = Antwerpen *Belgium* **17** C4
Anvers I. *Antarctica* **5** C17
Anwen *China* **59** C13
Anxi *Fujian, China* **59** E12
Anxi *Gansu, China* **60** B4
Anxian *China* **58** B5
Anxiang *China* **59** C9
Anxious B. *Australia* **95** E1
Anyama *Ivory C.* **82** D4
Anyang *China* **56** F8
Anyang *S. Korea* **57** F14
Anyer *Indonesia* **63** G11
Anyi *Jiangxi, China* **59** C10
Anyi *Shanxi, China* **56** G6
Anyuan *China* **59** E10
Anyue *China* **58** B5
Anza *U.S.A.* **111** M10
Anze *China* **56** F7
Anzhero-Sudzhensk *Russia* **52** D9
Ánzio *Italy* **42** A5
Ao Makham *Thailand* **65** a
Ao Phangnga △ *Thailand* **65** a
Aoga-Shima *Japan* **55** H9
Aoiz *Spain* **38** C3
Aoji *N. Korea* **57** C16
Aomen = Macau *China* **59** F9
Aomori *Japan* **54** D10
Aomori □ *Japan* **54** D10
Aonla *India* **69** E8
Aorai, Mt. *Tahiti* **91** d
Aoraki Mount Cook *N.Z.* **91** E3
Aoral, Phnum *Cambodia* **65** G5
Aosta *Italy* **40** C4
Aotearoa = New Zealand ■ *Oceania* **91** D6
Aoudéras *Niger* **83** B6
Aoukâr *Mauritania* **82** B3
Aozou Strip *Chad* **79** D9
Apa → *S. Amer.* **126** A4
Apache *U.S.A.* **116** D5
Apache Junction *U.S.A.* **109** K8
Apalachee B. *U.S.A.* **117** G13
Apalachicola *U.S.A.* **117** G12
Apalachicola → *U.S.A.* **117** G12
Apam *Ghana* **83** D4
Apapa *Nigeria* **83** D5
Apaporis → *Colombia* **124** D5
Aparados da Serra △ *Brazil* **127** B5
Aparri *Phil.* **61** B4
Apateu *Romania* **28** D6
Apatin *Serbia* **28** E4
Apatity *Russia* **8** C25
Apatula = Finke *Australia* **94** D1
Apatzingán *Mexico* **118** D4
Apeldoorn *Neths.* **17** B5
Apen *Germany* **24** B3
Apennines = Appennini *Italy* **40** D7
Aphrodisias *Turkey* **47** D10
Apia *Samoa* **91** b
Apiacás, Serra dos *Brazil* **124** E7
Apies → *S. Africa* **89** D4
Apizaco *Mexico* **119** D5
Aplao *Peru* **124** G4
Apo, Mt. *Phil.* **63** C7
Apolakia *Greece* **49** C9
Apolakia, Ormos *Greece* **49** C9
Apolda *Germany* **24** D7
Apollonia = Marsá Susah *Libya* **79** B10
Apolo *Bolivia* **124** F5
Apolonia *Greece* **46** E6
Apostle Is. *U.S.A.* **112** B8
Apostle Islands △ *U.S.A.* **112** B8
Apóstoles *Argentina* **127** B4
Apostolos Andreas, C. *Cyprus* **49** D13
Apostolovo *Ukraine* **33** J7
Appalachian Mts. *U.S.A.* **113** G14
Äppelbo *Sweden* **10** D8
Appennini *Italy* **40** D7
Appennino Ligure *Italy* **40** D6
Appenzell-Ausser Rhoden □ *Switz.* **25** H5
Appenzell-Inner Rhoden □ *Switz.* **25** H5
Appiano *Italy* **41** B8
Apple Hill *Canada* **115** A10
Apple Valley *U.S.A.* **111** L9
Appleby-in-Westmorland *U.K.* **14** C5
Appledore *U.K.* **15** F3
Appleton *U.S.A.* **112** C9
Approuague → *Fr. Guiana* **125** C8
Apricena *Italy* **41** G12
Aprília *Italy* **42** A5
Apsheronsk *Russia* **35** H4
Apsley *Canada* **114** B6
Apt *France* **21** E9
Apuane, Alpi *Italy* **40** D7
Apucarana *Brazil* **127** A5
Apulia = Púglia □ *Italy* **43** A9

Apure → *Venezuela* **124** B5
Apurimac → *Peru* **124** F4
Apuseni, Munţii *Romania* **28** D7
Āqā Jarī *Iran* **71** D6
Aqaba = Al 'Aqabah *Jordan* **74** F4
Aqaba, G. of *Red Sea* **70** D2
'Aqabah, Khalīj al = Aqaba, G. of *Red Sea* **70** D2
'Aqdā *Iran* **71** C7
Aqīq *Sudan* **80** D4
Aqīq, Khalīg *Sudan* **80** D4
'Aqrah *Iraq* **73** D10
Aqsay *Kazakhstan* **52** E6
Aqtaū *Kazakhstan* **52** E6
Aqtöbe *Kazakhstan* **52** D6
Aqtoghay *Kazakhstan* **52** E8
Aquidauana *Brazil* **125** H7
Aquila *Mexico* **118** D4
Aquiles Serdán *Mexico* **118** B3
Aquin *Haiti* **121** C5
Aquitaine □ *France* **20** D3
Ar Rachidiya = Er Rachidia *Morocco* **78** B5
Ar Rafid *Syria* **74** C4
Ar Raḩḩālīyah *Iraq* **73** F10
Ar Ramādī *Iraq* **73** F10
Ar Ramthā *Jordan* **74** C5
Ar Raqqah *Syria* **73** E8
Ar Raqqah □ *Syria* **73** E8
Ar Rass *Si. Arabia* **70** E4
Ar Rawshān *Si. Arabia* **80** C5
Ar Rayyān *Qatar* **71** E6
Ar Rifā'ī *Iraq* **70** D5
Ar Riyāḑ *Si. Arabia* **70** E5
Ar Ru'ays *Qatar* **71** E6
Ar Rukhaymīyah *Iraq* **70** D5
Ar Ruşāfah *Syria* **73** E8
Ar Ruţbah *Iraq* **73** F9
Ara *India* **69** G11
Ara Goro *Ethiopia* **81** F5
Ara Tera *Ethiopia* **81** F5
Arab *U.S.A.* **117** D11
'Arab, Bahr el → *Sudan* **81** F2
Arab, Khalīg el *Egypt* **80** A2
Arab, Shatt al → *Asia* **71** D6
'Araba, W. → *Egypt* **80** J8
'Arabābād *Iran* **71** C8
Araban *Turkey* **72** D7
Arabatskaya Strelka *Ukraine* **33** K8
Arabba *Italy* **41** B8
Arabia *Asia* **50** F6
Arabian Desert = Es Sahrā' Esh Sharqīya *Egypt* **80** B3
Arabian Gulf = Persian Gulf *Asia* **71** E6
Arabian Sea *Ind. Oc.* **50** G8
Araç *Turkey* **72** B5
Aracaju *Brazil* **125** F11
Aracati *Brazil* **125** D11
Araçatuba *Brazil* **127** A5
Aracena *Spain* **37** H4
Aracena, Sierra de *Spain* **37** H4
Arachova *Greece* **46** C4
Arachthos → *Greece* **46** B3
Aračinovo *Macedonia* **44** D5
Araçuaí *Brazil* **125** G10
'Arad *Israel* **74** D4
Arad *Romania* **28** D6
Arad □ *Romania* **28** D6
Arādān *Iran* **71** C7
Aradhippou *Cyprus* **49** E12
Arafura Sea *E. Indies* **90** B6
Aragats *Armenia* **35** K7
Aragón □ *Spain* **38** D4
Aragón → *Spain* **38** C3
Aragona *Italy* **42** E6
Araguacema *Brazil* **125** E9
Araguaia → *Brazil* **125** E9
Araguaína *Brazil* **125** E9
Araguari *Brazil* **125** G9
Araguari → *Brazil* **125** C9
Arain *India* **68** F6
Arak *Algeria* **78** C6
Arāk *Iran* **71** C6
Araka *Sudan* **81** G3
Arakan Coast *Burma* **67** K19
Arakan Yoma *Burma* **67** K19
Arakli *Turkey* **73** B9
Araks = Aras, Rūd-e → *Asia* **73** C13
Aral *Kazakhstan* **52** E7
Aral Sea *Asia* **52** E7
Aral Tengizi = Aral Sea *Asia* **52** E7
Aralsk = Aral *Kazakhstan* **52** E7
Aralskoye More = Aral Sea *Asia* **52** E7
Aralsor, Ozero = Aralsor Köli *Kazakhstan* **35** F9
Aralsor Köli *Kazakhstan* **35** F9
Aramac *Australia* **94** C4
Aran I. *Ireland* **12** A3
Aran Is. *Ireland* **12** C2
Aranda de Duero *Spain* **36** D7
Arandān *Iran* **70** C5
Aranđelovac *Serbia* **44** B4
Aranjuez *Spain* **36** E7
Aranos *Namibia* **88** C2
Aransas Pass *U.S.A.* **116** H6

Aranyaprathet *Thailand* **64** F4
Araouane *Mali* **82** B4
Arapahoe *U.S.A.* **112** E4
Arapey Grande ➤ *Uruguay* **126** C4
Arapgir *Turkey* **73** C8
Arapiraca *Brazil* **125** E11
Arapis, Akra *Greece* **45** F8
Arapongas *Brazil* **127** A5
Ar'ar *Si. Arabia* **70** D4
Ararangúa *Brazil* **127** B6
Araraquara *Brazil* **125** H9
Ararás, Serra das *Brazil* **127** B5
Ararat *Armenia* **73** C11
Ararat *Australia* **95** F3
Ararat, Mt. = Ağrı Dağı
   Turkey **73** C11
Araria *India* **69** F12
Araripe, Chapada do *Brazil*
   125 E11
Araruama, L. de *Brazil* **127** A7
Aras, Rūd-e ➤ *Asia* **35** K9
Aratâne *Mauritania* **82** B3
Arauca *Colombia* **124** B4
Arauca ➤ *Venezuela* **124** B5
Arauco *Chile* **126** D1
Arawa *Ethiopia* **81** F5
Arawale △ *Kenya* **86** C5
Araxá *Brazil* **125** G9
Araya, Pen. de *Venezuela* **124** A6
Arba Gugu *Ethiopia* **81** F5
Arba Minch *Ethiopia* **81** F4
Arbat *Iraq* **73** E11
Árbatax *Italy* **42** C2
Arbi *Ethiopia* **81** F4
Arbīl *Iraq* **73** D11
Arbīl □ *Iraq* **73** D11
Arboga *Sweden* **10** E9
Arbois *France* **19** F12
Arbore *Ethiopia* **81** F4
Arboréa *Italy* **42** C1
Arborfield *Canada* **103** C8
Arborg *Canada* **103** C9
Arbre du Ténéré *Niger* **83** B7
Arbroath *U.K.* **13** E6
Arbuckle *U.S.A.* **110** F4
Arbus *Italy* **42** C1
Arc ➤ *France* **21** C10
Arc-lès-Gray *France* **19** E12
Arcachon *France* **20** D2
Arcachon, Bassin d' *France* **20** D2
Arcade *U.S.A.* **114** D6
Arcadia *Fla., U.S.A.* **117** H14
Arcadia *La., U.S.A.* **116** E8
Arcadia *Pa., U.S.A.* **114** F6
Arcata *U.S.A.* **108** F1
Arcévia *Italy* **41** E9
Archanes *Greece* **47** F7
Archangel = Arkhangelsk
   Russia **52** C5
Archangelos *Greece* **49** C10
Archar *Bulgaria* **44** C6
Archbald *U.S.A.* **115** E9
Archena *Spain* **39** G3
Archer ➤ *Australia* **94** A3
Archer B. *Australia* **94** A3
Archer Bend = Mungkan
   Kandju △ *Australia* **94** A3
Archers Post *Kenya* **86** B4
Arches △ *U.S.A.* **108** G9
Archidona *Spain* **37** H6
Archipel-de-Mingan △
   Canada **105** B7
Archipiélago Chinijo △
   Canary Is. **48** E6
Archipiélago Los Roques △
   Venezuela **121** D6
Arci, Mte. *Italy* **42** C1
Arcidosso *Italy* **41** F8
Arcipelago de la
   Maddalena △ *Italy* **42** A2
Arcipelago Toscano △ *Italy* **40** F7
Arcis-sur-Aube *France* **19** D11
Arckaringa Cr. ➤ *Australia* **95** D2
Arco *Italy* **40** C7
Arco *U.S.A.* **108** E7
Arcos de Jalón *Spain* **38** D2
Arcos de la Frontera *Spain* **37** J5
Arcos de Valdevez *Portugal* **36** D2
Arcot *India* **66** N11
Arcozelo *Portugal* **36** E3
Arctic Bay *Canada* **101** B11
Arctic Mid-Ocean Ridge *Arctic* **4** A
Arctic Ocean *Arctic* **4** B18
Arctic Red River =
   Tsiigehtchic *Canada* **100** C6
Arctowski *Antarctica* **5** C18
Arda ➤ *Bulgaria* **45** E10
Arda ➤ *Italy* **40** C7
Ardabīl *Iran* **73** C13
Ardabīl □ *Iran* **71** B6
Ardahan *Turkey* **73** B10
Ardahan □ *Turkey* **73** B10
Ardakān = Sepīdān *Iran* **71** D7
Ardakān *Iran* **71** C7
Ardala *Sweden* **11** F7
Ardales *Spain* **37** J6
Ardara *Ireland* **12** B3
Ardas ➤ *Greece* **45** E10

Ardèche □ *France* **21** D8
Ardèche ➤ *France* **21** D8
Ardee *Ireland* **12** C5
Arden *Canada* **114** B8
Arden *Denmark* **11** H3
Arden *Calif., U.S.A.* **110** G5
Arden *Nev., U.S.A.* **111** J11
Ardenne *Belgium* **17** E5
Ardennes = Ardenne
   Belgium **17** E5
Ardennes □ *France* **19** C11
Ardentes *France* **19** F8
Arderin *Ireland* **12** C4
Ardeşen *Turkey* **73** B9
Ardestān *Iran* **71** C7
Ardfert *Ireland* **12** D2
Ardglass *U.K.* **12** B6
Ardhéa = Aridea *Greece* **44** F6
Ardila ➤ *Portugal* **37** G3
Ardino *Bulgaria* **45** E9
Ardivachar Pt. *U.K.* **13** D1
Ardlethan *Australia* **95** E4
Ardmore *Okla., U.S.A.* **116** D6
Ardmore *Pa., U.S.A.* **115** F9
Ardnamurchan, Pt. of *U.K.* **13** E2
Ardnave Pt. *U.K.* **13** F2
Ardon *Russia* **35** J7
Ardore *Italy* **43** D9
Ardres *France* **19** B8
Ardrossan *Australia* **95** E2
Ardrossan *U.K.* **13** F4
Ards Pen. *U.K.* **12** B6
Arduan *Sudan* **80** D3
Ardud *Romania* **28** C7
Åre *Sweden* **10** A7
Arecibo *Puerto Rico* **121** d
Areia Branca *Brazil* **125** E11
Arena, Pt. *U.S.A.* **110** G3
Arenal *Honduras* **120** C2
Arenas = Las Arenas *Spain* **36** B6
Arenas de San Pedro *Spain* **36** E5
Arendal *Norway* **9** G13
Arendsee *Germany* **24** C7
Arenys de Mar *Spain* **38** D7
Arenzano *Italy* **40** D5
Areópoli *Greece* **46** E4
Arequipa *Peru* **124** G4
Arero *Ethiopia* **81** G4
Arévalo *Spain* **36** D6
Arezzo *Italy* **41** E8
Arga *Turkey* **70** B3
Arga ➤ *Spain* **38** C3
Argalasti *Greece* **46** B5
Argamasilla de Alba *Spain* **37** F7
Argamasilla de Calatrava
   Spain **37** G6
Arganda *Spain* **36** E7
Arganil *Portugal* **36** E2
Argedeb *Ethiopia* **81** F5
Argelès-Gazost *France* **20** E3
Argelès-sur-Mer *France* **20** F7
Argens ➤ *France* **21** E10
Argenta *Canada* **102** C5
Argenta *Italy* **41** D8
Argentan *France* **18** D6
Argentário, Mte. *Italy* **41** F8
Argentat *France* **20** C5
Argentera *Italy* **40** D4
Argenteuil *France* **19** D9
Argentia *Canada* **105** C9
Argentiera, C. dell' *Italy* **42** B1
Argentina ■ *S. Amer.* **126** D3
Argentine Basin *Atl. Oc.* **128** F6
Argentino, L. *Argentina* **128** G2
Argenton-Château *France* **18** F6
Argenton-sur-Creuse *France* **19** F8
Argeş □ *Romania* **29** F9
Argeş ➤ *Romania* **29** F11
Arghandab ➤ *Afghan.* **68** D1
Argheile *Ethiopia* **81** F5
Argirades *Greece* **49** B3
Argiroupoli *Greece* **49** D6
Argo *Sudan* **80** D3
Argolida □ *Greece* **46** D4
Argolikos Kolpos *Greece* **46** D4
Argonne *France* **19** C12
Argos *Greece* **46** D4
Argos Orestiko *Greece* **44** F5
Argostoli *Greece* **46** C2
Arguedas *Spain* **38** C3
Arguello, Pt. *U.S.A.* **111** L6
Arguineguín *Canary Is.* **48** G4
Argun *Russia* **35** J7
Argun ➤ *Russia* **53** D13
Argungu *Nigeria* **83** C5
Argus Pk. *U.S.A.* **111** K9
Argyle, L. *Australia* **92** C4
Argyll □ *U.K.* **13** E4
Argyll & Bute □ *U.K.* **13** E3
Arhavi *Turkey* **73** B9
Århus *Denmark* **11** H4
Ariadnoye *Russia* **54** B7
Ariamsvlei *Namibia* **88** D2
Ariana *Tunisia* **79** A8
Ariano Irpino *Italy* **43** A8
Aribinda *Burkina Faso* **83** C4

Arica *Chile* **124** G4
Arica *Colombia* **124** D4
Arico *Canary Is.* **48** F3
Arid, C. *Australia* **93** F3
Arida *Japan* **55** G7
Aride *Seychelles* **85** b
Aridea *Greece* **44** F6
Ariège □ *France* **20** F5
Ariège ➤ *France* **20** E5
Arieş ➤ *Romania* **29** D8
Arīhā *Israel* **80** A4
Arila, Akra *Greece* **49** A3
Arilje *Serbia* **44** C4
Arima *Trin. & Tob.* **121** D7
Arinos ➤ *Brazil* **124** F7
Ario de Rosales *Mexico* **118** D4
Ariogala *Lithuania* **30** C10
Aripo, Mt. *Trin. & Tob.* **125** K15
Aripuanã *Brazil* **124** E6
Aripuanã ➤ *Brazil* **124** E6
Ariquemes *Brazil* **124** E6
Arisaig *U.K.* **13** E3
Arish, W. el ➤ *Egypt* **80** A3
Arissa *Ethiopia* **81** E5
Aristazabal I. *Canada* **102** C3
Arivonimamo *Madag.* **89** B8
Ariza *Spain* **38** D2
Arizaro, Salar de *Argentina* **126** A2
Arizona *Argentina* **126** D2
Arizona □ *U.S.A.* **109** J8
Arizpe *Mexico* **118** A2
Årjäng *Sweden* **10** E6
Arjeplog *Sweden* **8** C17
Arjepluovve = Arjeplog
   Sweden **8** C17
Arjona *Colombia* **124** A3
Arjona *Spain* **37** H6
Arjuna *Indonesia* **63** G15
Arka *Russia* **53** C15
Arkadak *Russia* **34** E6
Arkadelphia *U.S.A.* **116** D8
Arkadia □ *Greece* **46** D4
Arkaig, L. *U.K.* **13** E3
Arkalyk = Arqalyk
   Kazakhstan **52** D7
Arkansas □ *U.S.A.* **116** D8
Arkansas ➤ *U.S.A.* **116** E9
Arkansas City *U.S.A.* **112** G5
Arkaroola *Australia* **95** E2
Arkhangelsk *Russia* **52** C5
Arkhangelskoye *Russia* **34** E5
Arki *Greece* **47** D8
Arki *India* **68** D7
Arkiko *Eritrea* **81** D4
Arklow *Ireland* **12** D5
Arkona, Kap *Germany* **24** A9
Arkösund *Sweden* **11** F10
Arkoudi *Greece* **46** C2
Arkport *U.S.A.* **114** D7
Arkticheskiy, Mys *Russia* **53** A10
Arkul *Russia* **34** B10
Arkville *U.S.A.* **115** D10
Ärla *Sweden* **10** E10
Arlanda, Stockholm ✈
   (ARN) *Sweden* **10** E11
Arlanza ➤ *Spain* **36** C6
Arlanzón ➤ *Spain* **36** C6
Arlberg-pass *Austria* **26** D3
Arles *France* **21** E8
Arli *Burkina Faso* **83** C5
Arli △ *Burkina Faso* **83** C5
Arlington *S. Africa* **89** D4
Arlington *N.Y., U.S.A.* **115** E11
Arlington *Oreg., U.S.A.* **108** D3
Arlington *S. Dak., U.S.A.* **112** C5
Arlington *Tex., U.S.A.* **116** E6
Arlington *Va., U.S.A.* **113** F15
Arlington *Vt., U.S.A.* **115** C11
Arlington *Wash., U.S.A.* **110** B4
Arlington Heights *U.S.A.* **112** D10
Arlit *Niger* **83** B7
Arlon *Belgium* **17** E5
Arlparra *Australia* **94** C1
Arltunga *Australia* **94** C1
Armagh *U.K.* **12** B5
Armagh □ *U.K.* **12** B5
Armagnac *France* **20** E4
Armançon ➤ *France* **19** E10
Armando Bermudez △
   Dom. Rep. **121** C5
Armavir *Russia* **35** H5
Armenia *Colombia* **124** C3
Armenia ■ *Asia* **35** K7
Armeniş *Romania* **28** E7
Armenistis, Akra *Greece* **49** C9
Armentières *France* **19** B9
Armidale *Australia* **95** E5
Armilla *Spain* **37** H7
Armorique △ *France* **18** D3
Armour *U.S.A.* **112** D4
Armstrong *B.C., Canada* **102** C5
Armstrong *Ont., Canada* **104** B2
Armutlu *Bursa, Turkey* **45** F12
Armutlu *İzmir, Turkey* **47** C9
Arnarfjörður *Iceland* **8** D2
Arnaud ➤ *Canada* **101** D13
Arnauti, C. *Cyprus* **49** D11
Arnay-le-Duc *France* **19** E11

Arnea *Greece* **44** F7
Arnedillo *Spain* **38** C2
Arnedo *Spain* **38** C2
Arnett *U.S.A.* **116** C5
Arnhem *Neths.* **17** C5
Arnhem, C. *Australia* **94** A2
Arnhem B. *Australia* **94** A2
Arnhem Land *Australia* **94** A1
Arnissa *Greece* **44** F6
Arno ➤ *Italy* **40** E7
Arno Bay *Australia* **95** E2
Arnold *U.K.* **14** D6
Arnold *U.S.A.* **110** G6
Arnoldstein *Austria* **26** E6
Arnon ➤ *France* **19** E9
Arnot *Canada* **103** B9
Arnøya *Norway* **8** A19
Arnprior *Canada* **115** A8
Arnsberg *Germany* **24** D4
Arnsberger Wald △
   Germany **24** D4
Arnstadt *Germany* **24** E6
Aroa, Pte. *Moorea* **91** d
Aroab *Namibia* **88** D2
Aroania Oros *Greece* **46** D4
Aroche *Spain* **37** H4
Arochuku *Nigeria* **83** D6
Arolsen *Germany* **24** D5
Aron *India* **68** G6
Aron ➤ *France* **19** F10
Arona *Canary Is.* **48** F3
Arona *Italy* **40** C5
Aroroy *Phil.* **61** E5
Aros ➤ *Mexico* **118** B3
Arosa, Ría de *Spain* **36** C2
Arpajon *France* **19** D9
Arpajon-sur-Cère *France* **20** D6
Arpaşu de Jos *Romania* **29** E9
Arqalyk *Kazakhstan* **52** D7
Arrah = Ara *India* **69** G11
Arrah *Ivory C.* **82** D4
Arraiolos *Portugal* **37** G3
Arran *U.K.* **13** F3
Arras *France* **19** B9
Arrasate *Spain* **38** B2
Arrats ➤ *France* **20** D4
Arreau *France* **20** F4
Arrecife *Canary Is.* **48** F6
Arrecifes *Argentina* **126** C3
Arrée, Mts. d' *France* **18** D3
Arreso *Denmark* **11** J6
Arriaga *Mexico* **119** D6
Arribes del Duero □ *Spain* **36** D4
Arrilalah *Australia* **94** C3
Arrino *Australia* **93** E2
Arriondas *Spain* **36** B5
Arromanches-les-Bains
   France **18** C6
Arronches *Portugal* **37** F3
Arros ➤ *France* **20** E3
Arrow, L. *Ireland* **12** B3
Arrowtown *N.Z.* **91** F2
Arroyo de la Luz *Spain* **37** F4
Arroyo Grande *U.S.A.* **111** K6
Ars *Iran* **73** B11
Ars-sur-Moselle *France* **19** C13
Arsenault L. *Canada* **103** B7
Arsenev *Russia* **54** B6
Arsi *Ethiopia* **81** F4
Arsiero *Italy* **41** C8
Arsin *Turkey* **73** B8
Arsk *Russia* **34** B9
Årsunda *Sweden* **10** D10
Arta *Greece* **46** B3
Artà *Spain* **48** B10
Arta □ *Greece* **46** B3
Arteaga *Mexico* **118** D4
Arteche *Phil.* **61** E6
Arteijo = Arteixo *Spain* **36** B2
Arteixo *Spain* **36** B2
Artem = Artyom *Azerbaijan* **35** K10
Artem *Russia* **54** C6
Artemovsk *Russia* **53** D10
Artemovsk *Ukraine* **33** H9
Artemovskiy *Russia* **35** G5
Artenay *France* **19** D8
Artern *Germany* **24** D7
Artesa de Segre *Spain* **38** D6
Artesia = Mosomane
   Botswana **88** C4
Artesia *U.S.A.* **109** K11
Arthington *Liberia* **82** D2
Arthur ➤ *Australia* **95** G3
Arthur Cr. ➤ *Australia* **94** C2
Arthur Pt. *Australia* **94** C5
Arthur River *Australia* **93** F2
Arthur's Pass *N.Z.* **91** E3
Arthur's Pass △ *N.Z.* **91** E3
Arthur's Town *Bahamas* **121** B4
Artigas *Antarctica* **5** C18
Artigas *Uruguay* **126** C4
Artik *Armenia* **35** K6
Artillery L. *Canada* **103** A7
Artois *France* **19** B9
Artotina *Greece* **46** C4
Artrutx, C. de *Spain* **48** B10
Artsyz *Ukraine* **29** D14

Artvin *Turkey* **73** B9
Artvin □ *Turkey* **73** B9
Artyom *Azerbaijan* **35** K10
Aru, Kepulauan *Indonesia* **63** F8
Aru Is. = Aru, Kepulauan
   Indonesia **63** F8
Arua *Uganda* **86** B3
Aruanã *Brazil* **125** F8
Aruba ☑ *W. Indies* **121** D6
Arucas *Canary Is.* **48** F4
Arué *Tahiti* **91** d
Arun ➤ *Nepal* **69** F12
Arun ➤ *U.K.* **15** G7
Arunachal Pradesh □ *India* **67** F19
Arusha *Tanzania* **86** C4
Arusha □ *Tanzania* **86** C4
Arusha △ *Tanzania* **86** C4
Arusha Chini *Tanzania* **86** C4
Aruwimi ➤
   Dem. Rep. of the Congo **86** B1
Arvada *Colo., U.S.A.* **108** G11
Arvada *Wyo., U.S.A.* **108** D10
Arve ➤ *France* **19** F13
Arvi *Greece* **49** E7
Arviat *Canada* **103** A10
Arvidsjaur *Sweden* **8** D18
Arvika *Sweden* **10** E6
Arvin *U.S.A.* **111** K8
Arwal *India* **69** G11
Arxan *China* **60** B6
Aryd *Sweden* **11** H8
Arys *Kazakhstan* **52** E7
Arzachena *Italy* **42** A2
Arzamas *Russia* **34** C6
Arzanah *U.A.E.* **71** E7
Arzgir *Russia* **35** H7
Arzignano *Italy* **41** C8
Arzúa *Spain* **36** C2
Aš *Czech Rep.* **26** A5
Ås *Sweden* **10** A8
As Pontes de García
   Rodríguez *Spain* **36** B3
Aş Şafā *Syria* **74** B6
As Saffānīyah *Si. Arabia* **71** E6
As Safirah *Syria* **72** D7
Aş Şahm *Oman* **71** E8
As Sājir *Si. Arabia* **70** E5
As Salamīyah *Syria* **72** E7
As Salmān *Iraq* **70** D5
As Salţ *Jordan* **74** C4
As Sal'w'a *Qatar* **71** E6
As Samāwah *Iraq* **70** D5
As Sanamayn *Syria* **74** B5
As Sohar = Şuḩār *Oman* **71** E8
As Sukhnah *Syria* **73** E8
As Sulaymānīyah *Iraq* **73** E11
As Sulaymānīyah □ *Iraq* **73** E11
As Sulaymī *Si. Arabia* **70** E4
As Sulayyil *Si. Arabia* **75** C4
As Summān *Si. Arabia* **70** E5
As Suwaydā' *Syria* **74** C5
As Suwaydā' □ *Syria* **74** C5
As Suwayq *Oman* **71** F8
Aş Şuwayrah *Iraq* **73** F11
Åsa *Sweden* **11** G6
Asaba *Nigeria* **83** D6
Asad, Buḩayrat al *Syria* **73** D8
Asadābād *Iran* **73** E13
Asahi-Gawa ➤ *Japan* **55** G6
Asahigawa *Japan* **54** C11
Asale, L. *Ethiopia* **81** E5
Asamankese *Ghana* **83** D4
Asan ➤ *India* **69** E8
Asansol *India* **69** H12
Åsarna *Sweden* **10** B8
Asau *Samoa* **91** b
Asayita *Ethiopia* **81** E5
Asbe Teferi *Ethiopia* **81** F5
Asbesberge *S. Africa* **88** D3
Asbestos *Canada* **105** C5
Asbury Park *U.S.A.* **115** F10
Ascea *Italy* **43** B8
Ascensión *Mexico* **118** A3
Ascensión, B. de la *Mexico* **119** D7
Ascension I. *Atl. Oc.* **77** G2
Aschach an der Donau
   Austria **26** C7
Aschaffenburg *Germany* **25** F5
Aschendorf *Germany* **24** B3
Aschersleben *Germany* **24** D7
Asciano *Italy* **41** E8
Áscoli Piceno *Italy* **41** F10
Áscoli Satriano *Italy* **43** A8
Ascope *Peru* **124** E3
Ascotán *Chile* **126** A2
Aseb *Eritrea* **81** E5
Åseda *Sweden* **11** G9
Asela *Ethiopia* **81** F4
Åsen *Sweden* **10** C7
Asenovgrad *Bulgaria* **45** D8
Asfeld *France* **19** C11
Asfūn el Matâ'na *Egypt* **80** B3
Aşgabat = Ashgabat
   Turkmenistan **71** B8
Asgata *Cyprus* **49** E12

Ash Fork *U.S.A.* **109** J7
Ash Grove *U.S.A.* **112** G7
Ash Shabakah *Iraq* **70** D4
Ash Shamāl □ *Lebanon* **74** A5
Ash Shāmīyah *Iraq* **73** G11
Ash Shāriqah *U.A.E.* **71** E7
Ash Sharmah *Si. Arabia* **70** D4
Ash Sharqāt *Iraq* **73** E10
Ash Shaţrah *Iraq* **70** D5
Ash Shawbak *Jordan* **70** D2
Ash Shināfīyah *Iraq* **70** D5
Ash Shu'bah *Si. Arabia* **70** D5
Ash Shumlūl *Si. Arabia* **70** E5
Ash Shūr *Iraq* **70** C4
Ash Shurayf *Si. Arabia* **70** E3
Ash Shuwayfāt *Lebanon* **74** B4
Ashanti □ *Ghana* **83** D4
Ashau *Vietnam* **64** D6
Ashbourne *U.K.* **14** D6
Ashburn *U.S.A.* **117** F13
Ashburton *N.Z.* **91** E3
Ashburton ➤ *Australia* **92** D1
Ashcroft *Canada* **102** C4
Ashdod *Israel* **74** D3
Ashdown *U.S.A.* **116** E7
Asheboro *U.S.A.* **117** D15
Ashern *Canada* **103** C9
Asherton *U.S.A.* **116** G5
Asheville *U.S.A.* **117** D13
Ashewat *Pakistan* **68** D3
Asheweig ➤ *Canada* **104** B2
Ashford *Australia* **95** D5
Ashford *U.K.* **15** F8
Ashgabat *Turkmenistan* **71** B8
Ashibetsu *Japan* **54** C11
Ashikaga *Japan* **55** F9
Ashington *U.K.* **14** B6
Ashizuri-Uwakai △ *Japan* **55** H6
Ashizuri-Zaki *Japan* **55** H6
Ashkarkot *Afghan.* **68** C2
Ashkhabad = Ashgabat
   Turkmenistan **71** B8
Āshkhāneh *Iran* **71** B8
Ashland *Kans., U.S.A.* **112** G4
Ashland *Ky., U.S.A.* **113** F12
Ashland *Maine, U.S.A.* **113** B19
Ashland *Mont., U.S.A.* **108** D10
Ashland *Ohio, U.S.A.* **114** F2
Ashland *Oreg., U.S.A.* **108** E2
Ashland *Pa., U.S.A.* **115** F8
Ashland *Va., U.S.A.* **113** G15
Ashland *Wis., U.S.A.* **112** B9
Ashley *N. Dak., U.S.A.* **112** B4
Ashley *Pa., U.S.A.* **115** E9
Ashmore and Cartier Is.
   Ind. Oc. **92** B3
Ashmore Reef *Australia* **92** B3
Ashmûn *Egypt* **80** H7
Ashmyany *Belarus* **23** A13
Ashokan Res. *U.S.A.* **115** E10
Ashqelon *Israel* **74** D3
Ashta *India* **68** H7
Ashtabula *U.S.A.* **114** E4
Ashton *S. Africa* **88** E3
Ashton *U.S.A.* **108** D8
Ashuanipi, L. *Canada* **105** B6
Ashuapmushuan ➤
   Canada **104** C3
Ashville *U.S.A.* **114** F6
'Āşī ➤ *Asia* **72** D6
Asia **50** E9
Asia, Kepulauan *Indonesia* **63** D8
Asiago *Italy* **41** C8
Asifabad *India* **66** K11
Asinara *Italy* **42** A1
Asinara, G. dell' *Italy* **42** A1
Asino *Russia* **52** D9
Asipovichy *Belarus* **23** B15
'Asīr *Si. Arabia* **75** D3
Asir, Ras *Somali Rep.* **75** E5
Aşkale *Turkey* **73** C9
Askersund *Sweden* **11** F8
Askham *S. Africa* **88** D3
Askim *Norway* **9** G14
Askio, Oros *Greece* **44** F5
Askja *Iceland* **8** D5
Askøyna *Norway* **9** F11
Asl *Egypt* **80** B3
Aslan Burnu *Turkey* **47** C8
Aslanapa *Turkey* **47** B11
Asmara = Asmera *Eritrea* **81** D4
Asmera *Eritrea* **81** D4
Asnæs *Denmark* **11** J4
Åsnen *Sweden* **11** H8
Aso Kuju △ *Japan* **55** H5
Ásola *Italy* **40** C7
Asos *Greece* **46** C2
Asosa *Ethiopia* **81** E3
Asoteriba, Jebel *Sudan* **80** C4
Aspatria *U.K.* **14** C4
Aspe *Spain* **39** G4
Aspen *U.S.A.* **108** G10
Aspendos *Turkey* **72** D4
Aspermont *U.S.A.* **116** E4
Aspiring, Mt. *N.Z.* **91** F2
Aspres-sur-Buëch *France* **21** D9
Asprokavos, Akra *Greece* **49** B4

Aspromonte △ *Italy* **43** D8
Aspur *India* **68** H6
Asquith *Canada* **103** C7
Assab = Aseb *Eritrea* **81** E5
Assâba □ *Mauritania* **82** B2
Assâba, Massif de l'
  Mauritania **82** B2
Assagny *Ivory C.* **82** D4
Assaikio *Nigeria* **83** D6
Assam □ *India* **67** G18
Assamakka *Niger* **83** B6
Assal, L. *Djibouti* **81** E5
Assateague Island △ *U.S.A.*
  113 F16
Asse *Belgium* **17** D4
Assémini *Italy* **42** C1
Assen *Neths.* **17** A6
Assens *Denmark* **11** J3
Assini *Ivory C.* **82** D4
Assiniboia *Canada* **103** D7
Assiniboine ➤ *Canada* **103** D9
Assiniboine, Mt. *Canada* **102** C5
Assis *Brazil* **127** A5
Assisi *Italy* **41** E9
Assynt, L. *U.K.* **13** C3
Astaffort *France* **20** D4
Astakida *France* **47** F8
Astakos *Greece* **46** C3
Astana *Kazakhstan* **52** D8
Āstāneh *Iran* **71** B6
Astara *Azerbaijan* **73** C13
Āstārā *Iran* **73** C13
Asterousia *Greece* **49** E7
Asti *Italy* **40** D5
Astipalea *Greece* **47** E8
Astorga *Spain* **36** C4
Astoria *U.S.A.* **110** D3
Åstorp *Sweden* **11** H6
Astrakhan *Russia* **35** G9
Astrakhan □ *Russia* **35** G8
Astudillo *Spain* **36** C6
Asturias □ *Spain* **36** B5
Asturias ✕ *Spain* **36** B5
Asunción *Paraguay* **126** B4
Asunción Nochixtlán
  Mexico **119** D5
Åsunden *Sweden* **11** F9
Asutri *Sudan* **81** D4
Aswa ➤ *Uganda* **86** B3
Aswa-Lolim △ *Uganda* **86** B3
Aswad, Ra's al *Si. Arabia* **80** C4
Aswân *Egypt* **80** C3
Aswan Dam = Sadd el Aali
  Egypt **80** C3
Asyût *Egypt* **80** B3
Asyûti, Wadi ➤ *Egypt* **80** B3
Aszód *Hungary* **28** C4
Aţ Ţafīlah *Jordan* **74** E4
Aţ Ţafīlah □ *Jordan* **74** E4
Aţ Ţā'if *Si. Arabia* **80** C5
Aţ Ta'mīm □ *Iraq* **70** C5
Aţ Ţirāq *Si. Arabia* **70** E5
Aţ Ţubayq *Si. Arabia* **70** D3
Aţ Ţunayb *Jordan* **74** D4
Atabey *Turkey* **47** D12
Atacama □ *Chile* **126** B2
Atacama, Desierto de *Chile* **126** A2
Atacama, Salar de *Chile* **126** A2
Atakpamé *Togo* **83** D5
Atalandi *Greece* **46** C4
Atalaya *Peru* **124** F4
Atalaya de Femes *Canary Is.* **48** F6
Atami *Japan* **55** G9
Atamyrat *Turkmenistan* **52** F7
Atapupu *Indonesia* **63** F6
Atâr *Mauritania* **78** D3
Atarfe *Spain* **37** H7
Atari *Pakistan* **68** D6
Atascadero *U.S.A.* **110** K6
Atasū *Kazakhstan* **52** E8
Atatürk, İstanbul ✕ (IST)
  Turkey **45** F12
Atatürk Barajı *Turkey* **73** D8
Atauro *E. Timor* **63** F7
Ataviros *Greece* **49** C9
Atbara *Sudan* **80** D3
'Atbara, Nahr ➤ *Sudan* **80** D3
Atbasar *Kazakhstan* **52** D7
Atça *Turkey* **47** D10
Atchafalaya B. *U.S.A.* **116** G9
Atchison *U.S.A.* **112** F6
Atebubu *Ghana* **83** D4
Ateca *Spain* **38** D3
Aterno ➤ *Italy* **41** F10
Āteshān *Iran* **71** C7
Atesine, Alpi *Italy* **41** B8
Atessa *Italy* **41** F11
Atfîh *Egypt* **80** J7
Ath *Belgium* **17** D3
Athabasca *Canada* **102** C6
Athabasca ➤ *Canada* **103** B6
Athabasca, L. *Canada* **103** B7
Athabasca Sand Dunes △
  Canada **103** B7
Athamanon Oros *Greece* **46** B3
Athboy *Ireland* **12** C5
Athenry *Ireland* **12** C3
Athens = Athina *Greece* **46** D5

Athens *Ala., U.S.A.* **117** D11
Athens *Ga., U.S.A.* **117** E13
Athens *N.Y., U.S.A.* **115** D11
Athens *Ohio, U.S.A.* **113** F12
Athens *Pa., U.S.A.* **115** E8
Athens *Tenn., U.S.A.* **117** D12
Athens *Tex., U.S.A.* **116** E7
Atherley *Canada* **114** B5
Atherton *Australia* **94** B4
Athi River *Kenya* **86** C4
Athiéme *Benin* **83** D5
Athienou *Cyprus* **49** D12
Athina *Greece* **46** D5
Athina ✕ (ATH) *Greece* **46** D5
Athínai = Athina *Greece* **46** D5
Athlone *Ireland* **12** C4
Athna *Cyprus* **49** D12
Athol *U.S.A.* **115** D12
Atholl, Forest of *U.K.* **13** E5
Atholville *Canada* **105** C6
Athos *Greece* **45** F8
Athy *Ireland* **12** C5
Ati *Chad* **79** F9
Ati *Sudan* **81** E2
Atiak *Uganda* **86** B3
Atienza *Spain* **38** D2
Atiit *Sudan* **81** F3
Atik L. *Canada* **103** B9
Atikaki △ *Canada* **103** C9
Atikameg ➤ *Canada* **104** B3
Atikokan *Canada* **104** C1
Atikonak L. *Canada* **105** B7
Atimaono *Tahiti* **91** d
Atimonan *Phil.* **61** E4
Atitlán △ *Cent. Amer.* **119** E6
Atiu *Cook Is.* **97** J12
Atka *Russia* **53** C16
Atka I. *U.S.A.* **106** a
Atkarsk *Russia* **34** E7
Atkinson *U.S.A.* **112** D4
Atlanta *Ga., U.S.A.* **117** E12
Atlanta *Tex., U.S.A.* **116** E7
Atlantic *U.S.A.* **112** E6
Atlantic City *U.S.A.* **113** F16
Atlantic-Indian Basin
  Antarctica **5** B4
Atlantic Ocean **2** D8
Atlas Mts. = Haut Atlas
  Morocco **78** B4
Atlin *Canada* **102** B2
Atlin, L. *Canada* **102** B2
Atlin △ *Canada* **102** B2
Atmore *U.S.A.* **117** F11
Atoka *U.S.A.* **116** D6
Atokos *Greece* **46** C2
Atolia *U.S.A.* **111** K9
Atrai ➤ *Bangla.* **69** G13
Atrak = Atrek ➤
  Turkmenistan **71** B8
Ätran *Sweden* **11** G6
Ätran ➤ *Sweden* **11** H6
Atrauli *India* **68** E8
Atrek ➤ *Turkmenistan* **71** B8
Atri *Italy* **41** F10
Atsiki *Greece* **47** B7
Atsoum, Mts. *Cameroon* **83** D7
Atsuta *Japan* **54** C10
Attalla *U.S.A.* **117** D11
Attapu *Laos* **64** E6
Attawapiskat *Canada* **104** B3
Attawapiskat ➤ *Canada* **104** B3
Attawapiskat L. *Canada* **104** B2
Attersee *Austria* **26** D6
Attica *Ind., U.S.A.* **112** E10
Attica *Ohio, U.S.A.* **114** E2
Attichy *France* **19** C10
Attigny *France* **19** C11
Attika = Attiki □ *Greece* **46** D5
Attikamagen L. *Canada* **105** B6
Attikí □ *Greece* **46** D5
Attleboro *U.S.A.* **115** E13
Attock *Pakistan* **68** C5
Attopeu = Attapu *Laos* **64** E6
Attu I. *U.S.A.* **106** a
Attur *India* **66** P11
Atuel ➤ *Argentina* **126** D2
Åtvidaberg *Sweden* **11** F10
Atwater *U.S.A.* **110** H6
Atwood *Canada* **114** C3
Atwood *U.S.A.* **112** F3
Atyraū *Kazakhstan* **52** E6
Au Sable ➤ *U.S.A.* **114** B1
Au Sable *U.S.A.* **113** C12
Au Sable Forks *U.S.A.* **115** B11
Au Sable Pt. *U.S.A.* **114** B1
Auasberg *Namibia* **88** C2
Aubagne *France* **21** E9
Aubarca, C. d' *Spain* **48** B7
Aube □ *France* **19** D11
Aube ➤ *France* **19** D10
Aubenas *France* **21** D8
Aubenton *France* **19** C11
Auberry *U.S.A.* **110** H7
Aubigny-sur-Nère *France* **19** E9
Aubin *France* **20** D6
Aubrac, Mts. d' *France* **20** D7
Auburn *Ala., U.S.A.* **117** E12
Auburn *Calif., U.S.A.* **110** G5

Auburn *Ind., U.S.A.* **113** E11
Auburn *Maine, U.S.A.* **113** C18
Auburn *N.Y., U.S.A.* **115** D8
Auburn *Nebr., U.S.A.* **112** E6
Auburn *Pa., U.S.A.* **115** F8
Auburn *Wash., U.S.A.* **110** C4
Auburn Ra. *Australia* **95** D5
Auburndale *U.S.A.* **117** G14
Aubusson *France* **20** C6
Auce *Latvia* **30** B9
Auch *France* **20** E4
Auchi *Nigeria* **83** D6
Auchterarder *U.K.* **13** E5
Auchtermuchty *U.K.* **13** E5
Auckland *N.Z.* **91** B5
Auckland Is. *Pac. Oc.* **96** N8
Aude □ *France* **20** E6
Aude ➤ *France* **20** E7
Auden *Canada* **104** B2
Auderville *France* **18** C5
Audierne *France* **18** D2
Audincourt *France* **19** E13
Audo Ra. *Ethiopia* **81** F5
Audubon *U.S.A.* **112** E6
Aue *Germany* **24** E8
Auerbach *Germany* **24** E8
Augathella *Australia* **95** D4
Aughnacloy *U.K.* **12** B5
Aughrim *Ireland* **12** C3
Augrabies Falls *S. Africa* **88** D3
Augrabies Falls △ *S. Africa* **88** D3
Augsburg *Germany* **25** G6
Augsburg-Westliche
  Wälder △ *Germany* **25** G6
Augusta *Australia* **93** F2
Augusta *Italy* **43** E8
Augusta *Ark., U.S.A.* **116** D9
Augusta *Ga., U.S.A.* **117** E14
Augusta *Kans., U.S.A.* **112** G5
Augusta *Maine, U.S.A.* **113** C19
Augusta *Mont., U.S.A.* **108** C7
Augustenborg *Denmark* **11** K3
Augustów *Poland* **30** E9
Augustus, Mt. *Australia* **93** D2
Augustus I. *Australia* **92** C3
Aujuittuq = Grise Fiord
  Canada **101** B11
Aukan *Eritrea* **81** D5
Aukra *Norway* **10** E3
Aukrug *Germany* **24** A5
Aukštaitija △ *Lithuania* **9** J22
Aukum *U.S.A.* **110** G6
Auld, L. *Australia* **92** D3
Aulla *Italy* **40** D6
Aulnay *France* **20** B3
Aulne ➤ *France* **18** D2
Aulnoye-Aymeries *France* **19** B10
Ault *France* **18** B8
Ault *U.S.A.* **108** F11
Aulus-les-Bains *France* **20** F5
Aumale *France* **19** C8
Aumont-Aubrac *France* **20** D7
Auna *Nigeria* **83** C5
Auning *Denmark* **11** H4
Aunis *France* **20** B3
Aunu'u *Amer. Samoa* **91** b
Auponhia *Indonesia* **63** E7
Aups *France* **21** E10
Aur, Pulau *Malaysia* **65** L5
Auraiya *India* **69** F8
Aurangabad *Bihar, India* **69** G11
Aurangabad *Maharashtra,*
  India **66** K9
Auray *France* **18** E4
Aurich *Germany* **24** B3
Aurillac *France* **20** D6
Auronzo di Cadore *Italy* **41** B9
Aurora *Canada* **114** C5
Aurora *S. Africa* **88** E2
Aurora *Colo., U.S.A.* **108** G11
Aurora *Ill., U.S.A.* **112** E9
Aurora *Mo., U.S.A.* **112** G7
Aurora *N.Y., U.S.A.* **115** D8
Aurora *Nebr., U.S.A.* **112** E5
Aurora *Ohio, U.S.A.* **114** E3
Aurukun *Australia* **94** A3
Aus *Namibia* **88** D2
Ausable ➤ *Canada* **114** C3
Auschwitz = Oświęcim
  Poland **31** H6
Austerlitz = Slavkov u
  Brna *Czech Rep.* **27** B9
Austin *Minn., U.S.A.* **112** D7
Austin *Nev., U.S.A.* **108** G5
Austin *Pa., U.S.A.* **114** E6
Austin *Tex., U.S.A.* **116** F6
Austin, L. *Australia* **93** E2
Austin I. *Canada* **103** A10
Austra *Norway* **8** D14
Austral Is. = Tubuaï, Îs.
  French Polynesia **97** K13
Austral Seamount Chain
  Pac. Oc. **97** K13
Australia ■ *Oceania* **90** D6
Australian-Antarctic Basin
  S. Ocean **5** C9
Australian Capital
  Territory □ *Australia* **95** F4

Australind *Australia* **93** F2
Austria ■ *Europe* **26** E7
Austvågøya *Norway* **8** B16
Auterive *France* **20** E5
Authie ➤ *France* **19** B8
Authon-du-Perche *France* **18** D7
Autlán de Navarro *Mexico* **118** D4
Autun *France* **19** F11
Auvergne □ *France* **20** C7
Auvergne, Mts. d' *France* **20** C6
Auvézère ➤ *France* **20** C4
Auxerre *France* **19** E10
Auxi-le-Château *France* **19** B9
Auxonne *France* **19** E12
Auzances *France* **19** F9
Ava *U.S.A.* **112** G7
Avallon *France* **19** E10
Avalon *U.S.A.* **110** M8
Avalon Pen. *Canada* **105** C9
Avanos *Turkey* **70** B2
Avantas *Greece* **45** F9
Avaré *Brazil* **127** A6
Avawatz Mts. *U.S.A.* **111** K10
Avdan Dağı *Turkey* **45** F13
Aveiro *Brazil* **125** D7
Aveiro *Portugal* **36** E2
Aveiro □ *Portugal* **36** E2
Āvej *Iran* **71** C6
Avellaneda *Argentina* **126** C4
Avellino *Italy* **43** B7
Avenal *U.S.A.* **110** K6
Aversa *Italy* **43** B7
Avery *U.S.A.* **108** C6
Aves, I. de *W. Indies* **121** C7
Aves, Is. las *Venezuela* **121** D6
Avesnes-sur-Helpe *France* **19** B10
Avesnois △ *France* **19** B10
Avesta *Sweden* **10** D10
Avezzano *Italy* **41** F10
Avgo *Greece* **47** F7
Aviá Terai *Argentina* **126** B3
Aviano *Italy* **41** B9
Aviemore *U.K.* **13** D5
Avigliana *Italy* **40** C4
Avigliano *Italy* **43** B8
Avignon *France* **21** E8
Ávila *Spain* **36** E6
Ávila □ *Spain* **36** E6
Ávila, Sierra de *Spain* **36** E5
Avila Beach *U.S.A.* **111** K6
Avilés *Spain* **36** B5
Avintes *Portugal* **36** D2
Avis *Portugal* **37** G3
Avis *U.S.A.* **114** E7
Avísio ➤ *Italy* **40** B8
Aviz = Avis *Portugal* **37** F3
Avize *France* **19** D11
Avlonari *Greece* **46** C6
Avlum *Denmark* **11** H2
Avoca ➤ *Australia* **95** F3
Avoca ➤ *Ireland* **12** D5
Avola *Canada* **102** C5
Avola *Italy* **43** F8
Avon *U.S.A.* **114** D7
Avon ➤ *Australia* **93** F2
Avon ➤ *Bristol, U.K.* **15** F5
Avon ➤ *Dorset, U.K.* **15** G6
Avon ➤ *Warks., U.K.* **15** E5
Avon Park *U.S.A.* **117** H14
Avondale *Zimbabwe* **87** F3
Avonlea *Canada* **103** D8
Avonmore *Canada* **115** A10
Avonmouth *U.K.* **15** F5
Avramov *Bulgaria* **45** D10
Avranches *France* **18** D5
Avre ➤ *France* **18** D8
Avrig *Romania* **29** E9
Avrillé *France* **18** E6
Avtovac *Bos.-H.* **44** C2
Awa-Shima *Japan* **54** E9
Awag el Baqar *Sudan* **81** E3
A'waj ➤ *Syria* **74** B5
Awaji-Shima *Japan* **55** G7
'Awālī *Bahrain* **71** E6
Awantipur *India* **69** C6
Awasa *Ethiopia* **81** F4
Awasa, L. *Ethiopia* **81** F4
Awash *Ethiopia* **81** F5
Awash ➤ *Ethiopia* **81** E5
Awash △ *Ethiopia* **81** F5
Awaso *Ghana* **82** D4
Awatere ➤ *N.Z.* **91** D5
Awbārī *Libya* **79** C8
Awbārī, Idehan *Libya* **79** C8
Awe, L. *U.K.* **13** E3
Aweil *Sudan* **81** F2
Awgu *Nigeria* **83** D6
Awjilah *Libya* **79** C10
Awka *Nigeria* **83** D6
Ax-les-Thermes *France* **20** F5
Axat *France* **20** F6
Axe ➤ *U.K.* **15** G5
Axel Heiberg I. *Canada* **101** B11
Axim *Ghana* **82** E4
Axintele *Romania* **29** F11

Axios ➤ *Greece* **44** F6
Axminster *U.K.* **15** G4
Axvall *Sweden* **11** F7
Ay *France* **19** C11
Ayabaca *Peru* **124** D3
Ayabe *Japan* **55** G7
Ayacucho *Argentina* **126** D4
Ayacucho *Peru* **124** F4
Ayaguz = Ayaköz
  Kazakhstan **52** E9
Ayamé *Ivory C.* **82** D4
Ayamonte *Spain* **37** H3
Ayan *Russia* **53** D14
Ayancık *Turkey* **72** B6
Ayas *Turkey* **72** B5
Ayaviri *Peru* **124** F4
Aybastı *Turkey* **72** B7
Aydın *Turkey* **72** D2
Aydin □ *Turkey* **47** D9
Aydın Dağları *Turkey* **47** D10
Ayelu *Ethiopia* **81** E5
Ayenngré *Togo* **83** D5
Ayer *U.S.A.* **115** D13
Ayer Hitam *Malaysia* **65** c
Ayerbe *Spain* **38** C4
Ayer's Cliff *Canada* **115** A12
Ayers Rock = Uluru
  Australia **93** E5
Ayeyarwady =
  Irrawaddy ➤ *Burma* **67** M19
Áyia Napa *Cyprus* **49** E13
Áyia Phyla *Cyprus* **49** E12
Áyios Amvrósios *Cyprus* **49** D12
Áyios Seryios *Cyprus* **49** D12
Áyios Theodhoros *Cyprus* **49** D13
Áyios Yeóryios = Aghios
  Georgios *Greece* **46** D5
Aykirikçi *Turkey* **47** B12
Aylesbury *U.K.* **15** F7
Aylmer *Canada* **114** D4
Aylmer, L. *Canada* **100** C9
Ayna *Spain* **39** G2
Ayod *Sudan* **81** F3
Ayolas *Paraguay* **126** B4
Ayom *Sudan* **81** F2
Ayon, Ostrov *Russia* **53** C17
Ayora *Spain* **39** F3
Ayorou *Niger* **83** C5
'Ayoûn el 'Atroûs *Mauritania* **82** B3
Ayr *Australia* **94** B4
Ayr *Canada* **114** C4
Ayr *U.K.* **13** F4
Ayr ➤ *U.K.* **13** F4
Ayrancı *Turkey* **72** D5
Ayrancılar *Turkey* **47** C9
Ayre, Pt. of *I. of Man* **14** C3
Aysha *Ethiopia* **81** E5
Ayton *Australia* **94** B4
Aytos *Bulgaria* **45** D11
Ayton *Australia* **94** B4
Ayu, Kepulauan *Indonesia* **63** D8
Ayutla *Guatemala* **120** D1
Ayutla de los Libres *Mexico* **119** D5
Ayvacık *Turkey* **72** C2
Ayvalık *Turkey* **47** B8
Az Zabadānī *Syria* **74** B5
Az̧ Z̧āhirīyah *West Bank* **74** D3
Aẓ Z̧ahrān *Si. Arabia* **71** E6
Az Zarqā *Jordan* **74** C5
Az Zarqā □ *Jordan* **74** D5
Az Zarqā' *U.A.E.* **71** E7
Az Zāwiyah *Libya* **79** B8
Az Zībār *Iraq* **73** D11
Az Zilfī *Si. Arabia* **70** E5
Az Zubayr *Iraq* **70** D5
Az Zuqur *Yemen* **81** E5
Azad Kashmir □ *Pakistan* **69** C5
Azambuja *Portugal* **37** G2
Azamgarh *India* **69** F10
Azangaro *Peru* **124** F4
Azaoua *Niger* **83** B5
Azaouad *Mali* **82** B4
Azaouak, Vallée de l' *Mali* **83** B5
Āz̧ar Shahr *Iran* **73** D11
Azara *Nigeria* **83** D6
Āzārān *Iran* **73** D12
Āzārbāyjān =
  Azerbaijan ■ *Asia* **35** K9
Āz̧arbāyjān-e Gharbī □ *Iran* **70** B5
Āz̧arbāyjān-e Sharqī □ *Iran* **70** B5
Azay-le-Rideau *France* **18** E7
A'zāz *Syria* **72** D7
Azbine = Aïr *Niger* **83** B6
Azerbaijan ■ *Asia* **35** K9
Azezo *Ethiopia* **81** E4
Azimganj *India* **69** G13
Aznā *Iran* **71** C6
Aznalcóllar *Spain* **37** H4
Azogues *Ecuador* **124** D3
Azores = Açores, Is. dos
  Atl. Oc. **78** a
Azov *Russia* **35** G4
Azov, Sea of *Europe* **33** J9

Azovskoye More = Azov,
  Sea of *Europe* **33** J9
Azpeitia *Spain* **38** B2
Azraq ash Shīshān *Jordan* **74** D5
Aztec *U.S.A.* **109** H10
Azúa de Compostela
  Dom. Rep. **121** C5
Azuaga *Spain* **37** G5
Azuara *Spain* **38** D4
Azuer ➤ *Spain* **37** F7
Azuero, Pen. de *Panama* **120** E3
Azuga *Romania* **29** E10
Azul *Argentina* **126** D4
Azusa *U.S.A.* **111** L9
Azzano Décimo *Italy* **41** C9
Azzel Matti, Sebkra *Algeria* **78** C6

B

Ba Be △ *Vietnam* **64** A5
Ba Don *Vietnam* **64** D6
Ba Dong *Vietnam* **65** H6
Ba Ngoi = Cam Lam *Vietnam* **65** G7
Ba Tri *Vietnam* **65** G6
Ba Vi △ *Vietnam* **64** B5
Ba Xian = Bazhou *China* **56** E9
Baa *Indonesia* **63** F6
Baamonde *Spain* **36** B3
Baardeere = Bardera
  Somali Rep. **75** G3
Baarle-Nassau *Belgium* **17** C4
Bab el Mandeb *Red Sea* **75** E3
Baba *Bulgaria* **44** D7
Bābā, Koh-i- *Afghan.* **66** B5
Baba Burnu *Turkey* **47** B8
Baba dag *Azerbaijan* **35** K9
Bābā Kalū *Iran* **71** D6
Babadag *Romania* **29** F13
Babadağ *Turkey* **47** D10
Babaeski *Turkey* **45** E11
Babahoyo *Ecuador* **124** D3
Babai = Sarju ➤ *India* **69** F9
Babana *Nigeria* **83** C5
Babanusa *Sudan* **81** E2
Babar *Indonesia* **63** F7
Babar *Pakistan* **68** D3
Babarkach *Pakistan* **68** E3
Babayevo *Russia* **32** C8
Babb *U.S.A.* **108** B7
Babenhausen *Germany* **25** F4
Baberu *India* **69** G9
Babi Besar, Pulau *Malaysia* **65** L4
Babia Gora *Europe* **31** J6
Babian Jiang ➤ *China* **58** F3
Bābil □ *Iraq* **70** C5
Babile *Ethiopia* **81** F5
Babimost *Poland* **31** F2
Babinda *Australia* **94** B4
Babine *Canada* **102** B3
Babine ➤ *Canada* **102** B3
Babine L. *Canada* **102** C3
Babiogórski △ *Poland* **31** J6
Babo *Indonesia* **63** E8
Babócsa *Hungary* **28** D2
Bābol *Iran* **71** B7
Bābol Sar *Iran* **71** B7
Baborów *Poland* **31** H5
Baboua *C.A.R.* **84** C2
Babruysk *Belarus* **23** B15
Babuhri *India* **68** F3
Babuna *Macedonia* **44** E5
Babura *Nigeria* **83** C6
Babusar Pass *Pakistan* **69** B5
Babušnica *Serbia* **44** C6
Babuyan Chan. *Phil.* **61** B4
Babylon *Iraq* **73** F11
Bač *Serbia* **28** E4
Bâc ➤ *Moldova* **29** D14
Bac Can *Vietnam* **58** F5
Bac Giang *Vietnam* **58** G6
Bac Lieu *Vietnam* **65** H5
Bac Ninh *Vietnam* **58** G6
Bac Phan *Vietnam* **58** B5
Bac Quang *Vietnam* **58** F5
Bacabal *Brazil* **125** D10
Bacalar *Mexico* **119** D7
Bacan, Kepulauan *Indonesia* **63** E7
Bacarra *Phil.* **61** B4
Bacău *Romania* **29** D11
Bacău □ *Romania* **29** D11
Baccarat *France* **19** D13
Bacerac *Mexico* **118** A3
Băceşti *Romania* **29** D12
Bach Long Vi, Dao *Vietnam* **64** B6
Bach Ma △ *Vietnam* **64** D6
Bacharach *Germany* **25** E3
Bachhwara *India* **69** G11
Bachuma *Ethiopia* **81** F4
Bačina *Serbia* **44** C5
Back ➤ *Canada* **100** C9
Bačka Palanka *Serbia* **28** E4
Bačka Topola *Serbia* **28** E4
Bäckebo *Sweden* **11** H10
Bäckefors *Sweden* **11** F6
Bäckhammar *Sweden* **10** E8
Bački Petrovac *Serbia* **28** E4
Backnang *Germany* **25** G5

Baco, Mt. *Phil.* **61** E4
Bacolod *Phil.* **61** F5
Bacqueville-en-Caux *France* **18** C8
Bács-Kiskun □ *Hungary* **28** D4
Bácsalmás *Hungary* **28** D4
Bacuag = Placer *Phil.* **61** G6
Bacuk *Malaysia* **65** J4
Bácum *Mexico* **118** B2
Bād *Iran* **71** C7
Bad → *U.S.A.* **112** C3
Bad Aussee *Austria* **26** D6
Bad Axe *U.S.A.* **114** C2
Bad Bergzabern *Germany* **25** F3
Bad Berleburg *Germany* **24** D4
Bad Bevensen *Germany* **24** B6
Bad Bramstedt *Germany* **24** B5
Bad Brückenau *Germany* **25** E5
Bad Doberan *Germany* **24** A7
Bad Driburg *Germany* **24** D5
Bad Ems *Germany* **25** E3
Bad Frankenhausen
    Germany **24** D7
Bad Freienwalde *Germany* **24** C10
Bad Goisern *Austria* **26** D6
Bad Harzburg *Germany* **24** D6
Bad Hersfeld *Germany* **24** E5
Bad Hofgastein *Austria* **26** D6
Bad Homburg *Germany* **25** E4
Bad Honnef *Germany* **24** E3
Bad Iburg *Germany* **24** C4
Bad Ischl *Austria* **26** D6
Bad Kissingen *Germany* **25** E6
Bad Königshofen *Germany* **25** E6
Bad Kreuznach *Germany* **25** F3
Bad Krozingen *Germany* **25** H3
Bad Laasphe *Germany* **24** E4
Bad Langensalza *Germany* **24** D6
Bad Lauterberg *Germany* **24** D6
Bad Leonfelden *Austria* **26** C7
Bad Liebenwerda *Germany* **24** D9
Bad Mergentheim *Germany* **25** F5
Bad Münstereifel *Germany* **24** E2
Bad Nauheim *Germany* **25** E4
Bad Neuenahr-Ahrweiler
    Germany **24** E3
Bad Neustadt *Germany* **25** E6
Bad Oeynhausen *Germany* **24** C4
Bad Oldesloe *Germany* **24** B6
Bad Orb *Germany* **25** E5
Bad Pyrmont *Germany* **24** D5
Bad Reichenhall *Germany* **25** H8
Bad Säckingen *Germany* **25** H3
Bad St. Leonhard *Austria* **26** E7
Bad Salzuflen *Germany* **24** C4
Bad Salzungen *Germany* **24** E6
Bad Schwartau *Germany* **24** B6
Bad Segeberg *Germany* **24** B6
Bad Tölz *Germany* **25** H7
Bad Urach *Germany* **25** G5
Bad Vöslau *Austria* **27** D9
Bad Waldsee *Germany* **25** H5
Bad Wildungen *Germany* **24** D5
Bad Wimpfen *Germany* **25** F5
Bad Windsheim *Germany* **25** F6
Bad Zwischenahn *Germany* **24** B4
Bada Barabil *India* **69** H11
Badagara *India* **66** P9
Badagri *Nigeria* **83** D5
Badajós, L. *Brazil* **124** D6
Badajoz *Spain* **37** G4
Badajoz □ *Spain* **37** G4
Badakhshān □ *Afghan.* **66** A7
Badalona *Spain* **38** D7
Badalzai *Afghan.* **68** E1
Badampahar *India* **67** H15
Badanah *Si. Arabia* **70** D4
Badarinath *India* **69** D8
Badas, Kepulauan *Indonesia* **62** D3
Baddo → *Pakistan* **66** F4
Bade *Indonesia* **63** F9
Badeggi *Nigeria* **83** D6
Badéguichéri *Niger* **83** C6
Baden *Austria* **27** C9
Baden *Switz.* **25** H4
Baden *U.S.A.* **114** F4
Baden-Baden *Germany* **25** G4
Baden-Württemberg □
    Germany **25** G4
Badgastein *Austria* **26** D6
Badger *Canada* **105** C8
Badger *U.S.A.* **110** J7
Bādghīs □ *Afghan.* **66** B3
Badgingarra △ *Australia* **93** F2
Badgom *India* **69** B6
Badia Polésine *Italy* **41** C8
Badiar △ *Guinea* **82** C2
Badin *Pakistan* **68** G3
Badinka △ *Mali* **82** C3
Badlands *U.S.A.* **112** D2
Badlands △ *U.S.A.* **112** D2
Badogo *Mali* **82** C3
Badoumbé *Mali* **82** C2
Badrah *Iraq* **73** F11
Badrinath *India* **69** D8
Badulla *Sri Lanka* **66** R12
Badung, Selat *Indonesia* **63** K18
Baena *Spain* **37** H6
Baengnyeongdo *S. Korea* **57** F13

Baeza *Spain* **37** H7
Bafang *Cameroon* **83** D7
Bafatá *Guinea-Biss.* **82** C2
Baffin B. *N. Amer.* **101** B13
Baffin I. *Canada* **101** C12
Bafia *Cameroon* **83** E7
Bafilo *Togo* **83** D5
Bafing → *Mali* **82** C2
Bafing △ *Mali* **82** C2
Bafliyūn *Syria* **70** B3
Bafoulabé *Mali* **82** C2
Bafoussam *Cameroon* **83** D7
Bāfq *Iran* **71** D7
Bafra *Turkey* **72** B6
Bafra Burnu *Turkey* **72** B7
Bāft *Iran* **71** D8
Bafut *Cameroon* **83** D7
Bafwasende
    Dem. Rep. of the Congo **86** B2
Bagam *Niger* **83** B6
Bagamoyo *Tanzania* **86** D4
Bagan Datoh *Malaysia* **65** L3
Bagan Serai *Malaysia* **65** K3
Baganga *Phil.* **61** H7
Bagani *Namibia* **88** B3
Bagansiapiapi *Indonesia* **62** D2
Bagasra *India* **68** J4
Bagaud *India* **68** H6
Bagawi *Sudan* **81** E3
Bagbag *Sudan* **81** D3
Bagdad *U.S.A.* **111** L11
Bagdarin *Russia* **53** D12
Bagé *Brazil* **127** C5
Bagenalstown = Muine
    Bheag *Ireland* **12** D5
Baggs *U.S.A.* **108** F10
Bagh *Pakistan* **69** C5
Baghain → *India* **69** G9
Baghdād *Iraq* **73** F11
Bagheria *Italy* **42** D6
Baghlān *Afghan.* **66** A6
Baghlān □ *Afghan.* **66** B6
Bagley *U.S.A.* **112** B6
Bagnara Cálabra *Italy* **43** D8
Bagnasco *Italy* **40** D5
Bagnères-de-Bigorre *France* **20** E4
Bagnères-de-Luchon *France* **20** F4
Bagni di Lucca *Italy* **40** D7
Bagno di Romagna *Italy* **41** E8
Bagnoles-de-l'Orne *France* **18** D6
Bagnols-sur-Cèze *France* **21** D8
Bagnorégio *Italy* **41** F9
Bago = Pegu *Burma* **67** L20
Bagodar *India* **69** G11
Bagrdan *Serbia* **44** B5
Baguio *Phil.* **61** C4
Bağyurdu *Turkey* **47** C9
Bagzane, Monts *Niger* **83** B6
Bah *India* **69** F8
Bahabón de Esgueva *Spain* **36** D7
Bahadurganj *India* **69** F12
Bahadurgarh *India* **68** E7
Bahama, Canal Viejo de
    W. Indies **120** B4
Bahamas ■ *N. Amer.* **121** B5
Bahār *Iran* **73** E13
Baharampur *India* **69** G13
Baharîya, El Wâhât al *Egypt* **80** B2
Baharu Pandan = Pandan
    Malaysia **65** d
Bahawalnagar *Pakistan* **68** E5
Bahawalpur *Pakistan* **68** E4
Bahçe *Turkey* **72** D7
Bahçecik *Turkey* **45** F13
Bäherden *Turkmenistan* **71** B8
Baheri *India* **69** E8
Bahgul → *India* **69** F8
Bahi *Tanzania* **86** D4
Bahi Swamp *Tanzania* **86** D4
Bahía = Salvador *Brazil* **125** F11
Bahía □ *Brazil* **125** F10
Bahía, Is. de la *Honduras* **120** C2
Bahía Blanca *Argentina* **126** D3
Bahía de Caráquez *Ecuador* **124** D2
Bahía Kino *Mexico* **118** B2
Bahía Laura *Argentina* **128** F3
Bahía Negra *Paraguay* **124** H7
Bahir Dar *Ethiopia* **81** E4
Bahmanzād *Iran* **71** D6
Bahr el Ahmar □ *Sudan* **80** D4
Bahr el Jabal □ *Sudan* **81** G3
Bahraich *India* **69** F9
Bahrain ■ *Asia* **71** E6
Bahror *India* **68** F7
Bāhū Kalāt *Iran* **71** E9
Bai *Mali* **82** C4
Bai Bung, Mui = Ca Mau,
    Mui *Vietnam* **65** H5
Bai Duc *Vietnam* **64** C5
Bai Thuong *Vietnam* **64** C5
Baia de Aramă *Romania* **28** E7
Baia Mare *Romania* **29** C8
Baia-Sprie *Romania* **29** C8
Baião *Brazil* **125** D9
Baïbokoum *Chad* **79** G9
Baicheng *China* **57** B12
Băicoi *Romania* **29** E10

Baidoa *Somali Rep.* **75** G3
Baie-Comeau *Canada* **105** C6
Baie-St-Paul *Canada* **105** C5
Baie Ste-Anne *Seychelles* **85** b
Baie-Trinité *Canada* **105** C6
Baie Verte *Canada* **105** C8
Baignes-Ste-Radegonde
    France **20** C3
Baigneux-les-Juifs *France* **19** E11
Baihar *India* **69** H9
Baihe *China* **56** H6
Ba'ijī *Iraq* **73** E10
Baijnath *India* **69** E8
Baikal, L. = Baykal, Oz.
    Russia **53** D11
Baikonur = Bayqongyr
    Kazakhstan **52** E7
Baikunthpur *India* **69** H10
Baile Atha Cliath = Dublin
    Ireland **12** C5
Băile Govora *Romania* **29** E9
Băile Herculane *Romania* **28** F7
Băile Olănești *Romania* **29** E9
Băile Tușnad *Romania* **29** D10
Bailén *Spain* **37** G7
Băilești *Romania* **29** F8
Baima *China* **58** A3
Bain-de-Bretagne *France* **18** E5
Bainbridge *Ga., U.S.A.* **117** F12
Bainbridge *N.Y., U.S.A.* **115** D9
Bainbridge Island *U.S.A.* **110** C4
Baing *Indonesia* **63** F6
Bainiu *China* **56** H7
Baiona *Spain* **36** C2
Bā'ir *Jordan* **74** E5
Bairiki = Tarawa *Kiribati* **96** G9
Bairin Youqi *China* **57** C10
Bairin Zuoqi *China* **57** C10
Bairnsdale *Australia* **95** F4
Bais *Phil.* **61** G5
Baisha *China* **56** G7
Baissa *Nigeria* **83** D7
Baitadi *Nepal* **69** E9
Baixa Limia-Sierra do
    Xurés △ *Spain* **36** C3
Baiyin *China* **56** F3
Baiyü *China* **58** B2
Baiyu Shan *China* **56** F4
Baiyuda *Sudan* **80** D3
Baj Baj *India* **69** H13
Baja *Hungary* **28** D3
Baja, Pta. *Mexico* **118** B1
Baja California *Mexico* **118** A1
Baja California □ *Mexico* **118** B2
Baja California Sur □
    Mexico **118** B2
Bajag *India* **69** H9
Bajamar *Canary Is.* **48** F3
Bajana *India* **68** H4
Bajatrejo *Indonesia* **63** J17
Bajera *Indonesia* **63** J18
Băjgīrān *Iran* **71** B8
Bajimba, Mt. *Australia* **95** D5
Bajina Bašta *Serbia* **44** C3
Bajmok *Serbia* **28** E4
Bajo Nuevo *Caribbean* **120** C4
Bajoga *Nigeria* **83** C7
Bajool *Australia* **94** C5
Bak *Hungary* **28** D1
Bakar *Croatia* **41** C11
Bakassi Pen. *Cameroon* **83** E6
Bakel *Senegal* **82** C2
Baker *Calif., U.S.A.* **111** K10
Baker *Mont., U.S.A.* **108** C11
Baker, L. *Canada* **100** C10
Baker, Mt. *U.S.A.* **108** B3
Baker City *U.S.A.* **108** D5
Baker I. *Pac. Oc.* **96** G10
Baker I. *U.S.A.* **102** B2
Baker L. *Australia* **93** E4
Baker Lake *Canada* **100** C10
Bakers Creek *Australia* **94** C4
Bakers Dozen Is. *Canada* **104** A4
Bakersfield *Calif., U.S.A.* **111** K8
Bakersfield *Vt., U.S.A.* **115** B12
Bakharden = Bäherden
    Turkmenistan **71** B8
Bakhchysaray *Ukraine* **33** K7
Bakhmach *Ukraine* **33** G7
Bäkhtarān = Kermānshāh
    Iran **73** E12
Bäkhtarān =
    Kermānshāh □ *Iran* **70** C5
Bakı *Azerbaijan* **35** K9
Bakır → *Turkey* **47** C9
Bakırdağı *Turkey* **72** C6
Bakkafjörður *Iceland* **8** C6
Baklan *Turkey* **47** C11
Bako *Ethiopia* **81** F4
Bako *Ivory C.* **82** D3
Bakony *Hungary* **28** D2
Bakony Forest = Bakony
    Hungary **28** D2
Bakori *Nigeria* **83** C6
Bakouma *C.A.R.* **84** C4
Baksan *Russia* **35** J6
Bakswaho *India* **69** G8
Baku = Bakı *Azerbaijan* **35** K9

Bakundi *Nigeria* **83** D7
Bakutis Coast *Antarctica* **5** D15
Baky = Bakı *Azerbaijan* **35** K9
Bala *Canada* **114** A5
Bala *Senegal* **82** C2
Bâlâ *Turkey* **72** C5
Bala *U.K.* **14** E4
Bala, L. *U.K.* **14** E4
Balabac I. *Phil.* **62** C5
Balabac Str. *E. Indies* **62** C5
Balabagh *Afghan.* **68** B4
Ba'labakk *Lebanon* **74** B5
Bălăcița *Romania* **29** F8
Balad *Iraq* **73** F11
Balad Rūz *Iraq* **73** F11
Bālādeh *Fārs, Iran* **71** D6
Bālādeh *Māzandaran, Iran* **71** B6
Balaghat *India* **66** J12
Balaghat Ra. *India* **66** K10
Balaguer *Spain* **38** D5
Balakhna *Russia* **34** B6
Balaklava *Ukraine* **33** K7
Balakliya *Ukraine* **33** H9
Balakovo *Russia* **34** D8
Balamau *India* **69** F9
Bălan *Romania* **29** D10
Balancán *Mexico* **119** D6
Balanivka *Ukraine* **29** B14
Balashov *Russia* **34** E6
Balasinor *India* **68** H5
Balasore = Baleshwar *India* **67** J15
Balassagyarmat *Hungary* **28** B4
Balaton *Hungary* **28** D2
Balaton-Felvidéki △
    Hungary **28** D2
Balatonboglár *Hungary* **28** D2
Balatonfüred *Hungary* **28** D2
Balatonszentgyörgy
    Hungary **28** D2
Balayan *Phil.* **61** E4
Balazote *Spain* **39** G2
Balbieriškis *Lithuania* **30** D10
Balbigny *France* **21** C8
Balbina, Reprêsa de *Brazil* **124** D7
Balboa *Panama* **120** E4
Balbriggan *Ireland* **12** C5
Balcarce *Argentina* **126** D4
Balcarres *Canada* **103** C8
Bălcești *Romania* **29** F8
Balchik *Bulgaria* **45** C12
Balclutha *N.Z.* **91** G2
Balcones Escarpment
    U.S.A. **116** G5
Balçova *Turkey* **47** C9
Bald Hd. *Australia* **93** G2
Bald I. *Australia* **93** F2
Bald Knob *U.S.A.* **116** D9
Baldock L. *Canada* **103** B9
Baldwin *Mich., U.S.A.* **113** D11
Baldwin *Pa., U.S.A.* **114** F5
Baldwinsville *U.S.A.* **115** C8
Baldy Peak *U.S.A.* **109** K9
Bale *Croatia* **41** C10
Bale *Oromiya, Ethiopia* **81** F5
Bale *Oromiya, Ethiopia* **81** F5
Bale Mts. △ *Ethiopia* **81** F4
Baleares *Is. Spain* **48** B10
Balearic Is. = Baleares, Is.
    Spain **48** B10
Baleine → Whale → *Canada* **105** A6
Baleine, Petite R. de la →
    Canada **104** A4
Băleni *Romania* **29** E12
Baler *Phil.* **61** D4
Baler Bay *Phil.* **61** D4
Baleshare *U.K.* **13** D1
Baleshwar *India* **67** J15
Balezino *Russia* **34** B11
Balfate *Honduras* **120** C2
Bali *Cameroon* **83** D7
Bali *Greece* **49** D6
Bali *India* **68** G5
Bali □ *Indonesia* **63** J18
Bali □ *Indonesia* **63** J18
Bali, Selat *Indonesia* **63** J17
Bali Sea *Indonesia* **63** J17
Balia *S. Leone* **82** D2
Baliapal *India* **69** J12
Baligród *Poland* **31** J9
Balik Pulau *Malaysia* **65** c
Balıkesir *Turkey* **47** B9
Balıkesir □ *Turkey* **47** B9
Balıklıçeşme *Turkey* **45** F11
Balikpapan *Indonesia* **62** E5
Balimbing *Phil.* **63** C5
Baling *Malaysia* **65** K3
Balingen *Germany* **25** G4
Balinț *Romania* **28** E6
Balintang Channel *Phil.* **61** B4
Balkan Mts. = Stara
    Planina *Bulgaria* **44** C7
Balkanabat *Turkmenistan* **71** B7
Balkash = Balqash
    Kazakhstan **52** E8

Balkhash, Ozero = Balqash
    Köli *Kazakhstan* **52** E8
Ballachulish *U.K.* **13** E3
Balladonia *Australia* **93** F3
Ballarat *Australia* **95** F3
Ballard, L. *Australia* **93** E3
Ballater *U.K.* **13** D5
Ballé *Mali* **82** B3
Ballenas, Canal de *Mexico* **118** B2
Balleny Is. *Antarctica* **5** C11
Balleroy *France* **18** C6
Ballerup *Denmark* **11** J6
Ballı *Turkey* **45** F11
Ballia *India* **69** G11
Ballina *Australia* **95** D5
Ballina *Ireland* **12** B2
Ballinasloe *Ireland* **12** C3
Ballinger *U.S.A.* **116** F5
Ballinrobe *Ireland* **12** C2
Ballinskelligs B. *Ireland* **12** E1
Ballon *France* **18** D7
Ballons des Vosges △
    France **19** E14
Ballsh *Albania* **44** F3
Ballston Spa *U.S.A.* **115** D11
Ballybofil *Ireland* **12** C5
Ballybunion *Ireland* **12** D2
Ballycanew *Ireland* **12** D5
Ballycastle *U.K.* **12** A5
Ballyclare *U.K.* **12** B5
Ballydehob *Ireland* **12** E2
Ballygawley *U.K.* **12** B4
Ballyhaunis *Ireland* **12** C3
Ballyheige *Ireland* **12** D2
Ballymena *U.K.* **12** B5
Ballymoney *U.K.* **12** A5
Ballymote *Ireland* **12** B3
Ballynahinch *U.K.* **12** B6
Ballyquintin Pt. *U.K.* **12** B6
Ballyshannon *Ireland* **12** B3
Balmaceda *Chile* **128** F2
Balmaseda *Spain* **38** B1
Balmazújváros *Hungary* **28** C6
Balmertown *Canada* **103** C10
Balmoral *Australia* **95** F3
Balmorhea *U.S.A.* **116** F3
Balochistan =
    Baluchistan □ *Pakistan* **66** F4
Balonne → *Australia* **95** D4
Balotra *India* **68** G5
Balqash *Kazakhstan* **52** E8
Balqash Köli *Kazakhstan* **52** E8
Balrampur *India* **69** F10
Balranald *Australia* **95** E3
Balsas → *Brazil* **125** E9
Balsas → *Mexico* **118** D4
Balsas del Norte *Mexico* **119** D5
Bålsta *Sweden* **10** E11
Balta *Romania* **28** F7
Balta *Ukraine* **29** B14
Baltanás *Spain* **36** D6
Bălți *Moldova* **29** C12
Baltic Sea *Europe* **9** H18
Baltîm *Egypt* **80** H7
Baltimore *Ireland* **12** E2
Baltimore *Md., U.S.A.* **113** F15
Baltimore *Ohio, U.S.A.* **114** G2
Baltinglass *Ireland* **12** D5
Baltit *Pakistan* **69** A6
Baltiysk *Russia* **30** D6
Baltrum *Germany* **24** B3
Baluchistan □ *Pakistan* **66** F4
Balurghat *India* **69** G13
Balvi *Latvia* **32** D4
Balya *Turkey* **47** B9
Bam *Iran* **71** D8
Bama *China* **58** E6
Bama *Nigeria* **83** C7
Bamaga *Australia* **94** A3
Bamaji L. *Canada* **104** B1
Bamako *Mali* **82** C3
Bamba *Mali* **83** B4
Bambara Maoundé *Mali* **82** B4
Bambari *C.A.R.* **84** C4
Bambaroo *Australia* **94** B4
Bambaya *Guinea* **82** D2
Bamberg *Germany* **25** F6
Bamberg *U.S.A.* **117** E14
Bambesi *Ethiopia* **81** F3
Bambey *Senegal* **82** C1
Bambili *Dem. Rep. of the Congo* **86** B2
Bamboi *Ghana* **82** D4
Bamburgh *U.K.* **14** B6
Bamenda *Cameroon* **83** D7
Bamfield *Canada* **102** D3
Bāmīān □ *Afghan.* **66** B5
Bamkin *Cameroon* **83** D7
Bampūr *Iran* **71** E9
Ban *Burkina Faso* **82** C4
Ban Ao Tu Khun *Thailand* **65** a
Ban Ban *Laos* **64** C4
Ban Bang Hin *Thailand* **65** H2
Ban Bang Khu *Thailand* **65** a
Ban Bang Rong *Thailand* **65** a
Ban Bo Phut *Thailand* **65** b

Ban Chaweng *Thailand* **65** b
Ban Chiang Klang *Thailand* **64** C3
Ban Chik *Laos* **64** D4
Ban Choho *Thailand* **64** E4
Ban Dan Lan Hoi *Thailand* **64** D2
Ban Don = Surat Thani
    Thailand **65** H2
Ban Don *Vietnam* **64** F6
Ban Don, Ao → *Thailand* **65** H2
Ban Dong *Thailand* **64** C2
Ban Hong *Thailand* **64** C2
Ban Hua Thanon *Thailand* **65** b
Ban Kaeng *Thailand* **64** D3
Ban Kantang *Thailand* **65** J2
Ban Karon *Thailand* **65** a
Ban Kata *Thailand* **65** a
Ban Keun *Laos* **64** C4
Ban Khai *Thailand* **64** F3
Ban Kheun *Laos* **64** B3
Ban Khlong Khian *Thailand* **65** a
Ban Khlong Kua *Thailand* **65** J3
Ban Khuan *Thailand* **65** a
Ban Khuan Mao *Thailand* **65** J2
Ban Ko Yai Chim *Thailand* **65** G2
Ban Kok *Thailand* **64** D4
Ban Laem *Thailand* **64** F2
Ban Lamai *Thailand* **65** b
Ban Lao Ngam *Laos* **64** E6
Ban Le Kathe *Thailand* **64** E2
Ban Lo Po Noi *Thailand* **65** a
Ban Mae Chedi *Thailand* **64** C2
Ban Mae Laeng *Thailand* **64** B2
Ban Mae Nam *Thailand* **65** b
Ban Mae Sariang *Thailand* **64** C1
Ban Mê Thuôt = Buon Ma
    Thuot *Vietnam* **64** F7
Ban Mi *Thailand* **64** E3
Ban Muong Mo *Laos* **64** C4
Ban Na Bo *Thailand* **65** b
Ban Na Mo *Laos* **64** D5
Ban Na San *Thailand* **65** H2
Ban Na Tong *Laos* **64** B3
Ban Nam Bac *Laos* **64** B4
Ban Nam Ma *Laos* **64** A3
Ban Ngang *Laos* **64** E6
Ban Nong Bok *Laos* **64** D5
Ban Nong Boua *Laos* **64** E6
Ban Nong Pling *Thailand* **64** E3
Ban Pak Chan *Thailand* **65** G2
Ban Patong *Thailand* **65** a
Ban Phai *Thailand* **64** D4
Ban Phak Chit *Thailand* **65** a
Ban Pong *Thailand* **64** F2
Ban Rawai *Thailand* **65** a
Ban Ron Phibun *Thailand* **65** H2
Ban Sakhu *Thailand* **65** a
Ban Sanam Chai *Thailand* **65** J3
Ban Sangkha *Thailand* **64** E4
Ban Tak *Thailand* **64** D2
Ban Tako *Thailand* **64** E4
Ban Tha Dua *Thailand* **64** D2
Ban Tha Li *Thailand* **64** D3
Ban Tha Nun *Thailand* **65** a
Ban Tha Rua *Thailand* **65** a
Ban Tha Yu *Thailand* **65** a
Ban Thahine *Laos* **64** E5
Ban Thong Krut *Thailand* **65** b
Ban Xien Kok *Laos* **64** B3
Ban Yen Nhan *Vietnam* **64** B6
Banaba *Kiribati* **96** H8
Banalia *Dem. Rep. of the Congo* **86** B2
Banam *Cambodia* **65** G5
Banamba *Mali* **82** C3
Banana *Ivory C.* **82** C3
Banana Is. *S. Leone* **82** D2
Bananal, I. do *Brazil* **125** F8
Banaras = Varanasi *India* **69** G10
Banas → *Gujarat, India* **68** H4
Banas → *Mad. P., India* **69** G9
Bânâs, Ras *Egypt* **80** C4
Banaz *Turkey* **47** C11
Banaz → *Turkey* **47** C11
Banbridge *U.K.* **12** B5
Banbury *U.K.* **15** E6
Banchory *U.K.* **13** D6
Banco *Ethiopia* **81** F4
Bancroft *Canada* **114** A7
Band *Romania* **29** D9
Band Bonī *Iran* **71** E8
Band Qīr *Iran* **71** D6
Banda, Kepulauan *Indonesia* **63** E7
Banda *Mad. P., India* **69** G8
Banda *Ut. P., India* **69** G9
Banda, Kepulauan *Indonesia* **63** E7
Banda Aceh *Indonesia* **62** C1
Banda Banda, Mt. *Australia* **95** E5
Banda Elat *Indonesia* **63** F8
Banda Is. = Banda,
    Kepulauan *Indonesia* **63** E7
Banda Sea *Indonesia* **63** F7
Bandai-Asahi △ *Japan* **54** F10
Bandai-San *Japan* **54** F10
Bandama → *Ivory C.* **82** D3
Bandama Blanc → *Ivory C.* **82** D4
Bandama Rouge → *Ivory C.* **82** D4
Bandān *Iran* **71** D9
Bandanaira *Indonesia* **63** E7
Bandanwara *India* **68** F6
Bandar = Machilipatnam
    India **67** L12

INDEX TO WORLD MAPS

Batuata **137**

Bandar-e Abbās *Iran* **71** E8
Bandar-e Anzalī *Iran* **73** D13
Bandar-e Būshehr =
　Būshehr *Iran* **71** D6
Bandar-e Chārak *Iran* **71** E7
Bandar-e Deylam *Iran* **71** D6
Bandar-e Emām
　Khomeynī *Iran* **71** D6
Bandar-e Lengeh *Iran* **71** E7
Bandar-e Maqām *Iran* **71** E7
Bandar-e Ma'shur *Iran* **71** D6
Bandar-e Rīg *Iran* **71** D6
Bandar-e Torkeman *Iran* **71** B7
Bandar Lampung =
　Tanjungkarang
　Telukbetung *Indonesia* **62** F3
Bandar Maharani = Muar
　Malaysia **65** L4
Bandar Penggaram = Batu
　Pahat *Malaysia* **65** M4
Bandar Seri Begawan *Brunei* **62** D5
Bandar Sri Aman = Sri
　Aman *Malaysia* **62** D4
Bandawe *Malawi* **87** E3
Bande *Spain* **36** C3
Bandeira, Pico da *Brazil* **127** A7
Bandera *Argentina* **126** B3
Banderas, B. de *Mexico* **118** C3
Bandhavgarh *India* **69** H9
Bandi → *India* **68** F6
Bandiagara *Mali* **82** C4
Bandikui *India* **68** F7
Bandırma *Turkey* **45** F11
Bandjarmasin =
　Banjarmasin *Indonesia* **62** E4
Bandol *France* **21** E9
Bandon *Ireland* **12** E3
Bandon → *Ireland* **12** E3
Bandula *Mozam.* **87** F3
Bandundu
　Dem. Rep. of the Congo **84** E3
Bandung *Indonesia* **63** G12
Bané *Burkina Faso* **83** C4
Băneasa *Romania* **29** E12
Bāneh *Iran* **73** E11
Bañeres *Spain* **39** G4
Banes *Cuba* **121** B4
Banff *Canada* **102** C5
Banff *U.K.* **13** D6
Banff △ *Canada* **102** C5
Banfora *Burkina Faso* **82** C4
Bang Fai → *Laos* **64** D5
Bang Hieng → *Laos* **64** D5
Bang Krathum *Thailand* **64** D3
Bang Lamung *Thailand* **64** F3
Bang Mun Nak *Thailand* **64** D3
Bang Pa In *Thailand* **64** E3
Bang Rakam *Thailand* **64** D3
Bang Saphan *Thailand* **65** G2
Bang Thao *Thailand* **65** a
Bangaduni I. *India* **69** J13
Bangala Dam *Zimbabwe* **87** G3
Bangalore *India* **66** N10
Banganga → *India* **68** F6
Bangangté *Cameroon* **83** D7
Bangaon *India* **69** H13
Bangassou *C.A.R.* **84** D4
Banggai *Indonesia* **63** E6
Banggai, Kepulauan
　Indonesia **63** E6
Banggai Arch. = Banggai,
　Kepulauan *Indonesia* **63** E6
Banggi, Pulau *Malaysia* **62** C5
Banghāzī *Libya* **79** B10
Bangjang *Sudan* **81** E3
Bangka *Sulawesi, Indonesia* **63** D7
Bangka *Sumatera, Indonesia* **62** E3
Bangka, Selat *Indonesia* **62** E3
Bangka-Belitung □ *Indonesia* **62** E3
Bangkalan *Indonesia* **63** G15
Bangkinang *Indonesia* **62** D2
Bangko *Indonesia* **62** E2
Bangkok *Thailand* **64** F3
Bangladesh ■ *Asia* **67** H17
Bangli *Indonesia* **63** J18
Bangolo *Ivory C.* **82** D3
Bangong Co *China* **69** B8
Bangor *Down, U.K.* **12** B6
Bangor *Gwynedd, U.K.* **14** D3
Bangor *Maine, U.S.A.* **113** C19
Bangor *Pa., U.S.A.* **115** F9
Bangued *Phil.* **61** C4
Bangui *C.A.R.* **84** D3
Bangui *Phil.* **61** B4
Banguru
　Dem. Rep. of the Congo **86** B2
Bangweulu, L. *Zambia* **87** E3
Bangweulu Swamp *Zambia* **87** E3
Banhine △ *Mozam.* **89** C5
Baní *Dom. Rep.* **121** C5
Bani → *Mali* **82** C4
Bani Bangou *Niger* **83** B5
Banī Sa'd *Iraq* **73** F11
Bania *Ivory C.* **82** D4
Banihal Pass *India* **69** C6
Banikoara *Benin* **83** C5
Banissa *Kenya* **86** B4
Bāniyās *Syria* **72** E6

Banja Luka *Bos.-H.* **28** F2
Banjar *India* **68** D7
Banjar → *India* **69** H9
Banjarmasin *Indonesia* **62** E4
Banjul *Gambia* **82** C1
Banka *India* **69** G12
Bankas *Mali* **82** C4
Bankeryd *Sweden* **11** G8
Banket *Zimbabwe* **87** F3
Bankilaré *Niger* **83** C5
Bankipore *India* **67** G14
Banks I. *B.C., Canada* **102** C3
Banks I. *N.W.T., Canada* **100** B7
Banks Pen. *N.Z.* **91** E4
Banks Str. *Australia* **95** G4
Bankura *India* **69** H12
Bankya *Bulgaria* **44** D7
Banmankhi *India* **69** G12
Bann → *Armagh, U.K.* **12** B5
Bann → *L'derry., U.K.* **12** A5
Bannalec *France* **18** E3
Bannang Sata *Thailand* **65** J3
Banning *U.S.A.* **111** M10
Banno *Ethiopia* **81** G4
Bannockburn *Canada* **114** B7
Bannockburn *U.K.* **13** E5
Bannockburn *Zimbabwe* **87** G2
Bannu *Pakistan* **66** C7
Bano *India* **69** H11
Bañolas = Banyoles *Spain* **38** C7
Banon *France* **21** D9
Baños de la Encina *Spain* **37** G7
Baños de Molgas *Spain* **36** C3
Bánovce nad Bebravou
　Slovak Rep. **27** C11
Banovići *Bos.-H.* **28** F3
Bansgaon *India* **69** F10
Banská Bystrica *Slovak Rep.* **27** C12
Banská Štiavnica
　Slovak Rep. **27** C11
Bansko *Bulgaria* **44** E7
Banskobystrický □
　Slovak Rep. **27** C12
Banswara *India* **68** H6
Bantaeng *Indonesia* **63** F5
Bantaji *Nigeria* **83** D7
Bantayan *Phil.* **61** F5
Banten □ *Indonesia* **63** G11
Bantry *Ireland* **12** E2
Bantry B. *Ireland* **12** E2
Bantul *Indonesia* **63** G14
Bantva *India* **68** J4
Banya *Bulgaria* **45** D8
Banyak, Kepulauan
　Indonesia **62** D1
Banyalbufar *Spain* **48** B9
Banyo *Cameroon* **83** D7
Banyoles *Spain* **38** C7
Banyuls-sur-Mer *France* **20** F7
Banyumas *Indonesia* **63** G13
Banyuwangi *Indonesia* **63** J17
Banzare Coast *Antarctica* **5** C9
Bao Ha *Vietnam* **58** F5
Bao Lac *Vietnam* **64** A5
Bao Loc *Vietnam* **65** G6
Bao'an = Shenzhen *China* **59** F10
Baocheng *China* **56** H4
Baode *China* **56** E6
Baodi *China* **57** E9
Baoding *China* **56** E8
Baoji *China* **56** G4
Baojing *China* **58** C7
Baokang *China* **59** B8
Baoshan *Shanghai, China* **59** B13
Baoshan *Yunnan, China* **58** E2
Baotou *China* **56** D6
Baoxing *China* **58** B4
Baoying *China* **57** H10
Baoyou = Ledong *China* **64** C7
Bap *India* **68** F5
Bapatla *India* **67** M12
Bapaume *France* **19** B9
Bāqerābād *Iran* **71** C6
Ba'qūbah *Iraq* **73** F11
Baquedano *Chile* **126** A2
Bar *Montenegro* **44** D3
Bar *Ukraine* **23** D14
Bar Bigha *India* **69** G11
Bar Harbor *U.S.A.* **113** C19
Bar-le-Duc *France* **19** D12
Bar-sur-Aube *France* **19** D11
Bar-sur-Seine *France* **19** D11
Bara *India* **69** G9
Bâra *Romania* **29** C12
Bara Banki *India* **69** F9
Barabai *Indonesia* **62** E5
Baraboo *U.S.A.* **112** D10
Baracoa *Cuba* **121** B5
Baradā → *Syria* **74** B5
Baradero *Argentina* **126** C4
Baraga *U.S.A.* **112** B9
Bărăganul *Romania* **29** F12
Baragoi *Kenya* **86** B4
Barah → *India* **68** F6
Barahona *Dom. Rep.* **121** C5
Barahona *Spain* **38** D2
Barail Range *India* **67** G18

Barajas, Madrid ✈ (MAD)
　Spain **36** E7
Baraka *Sudan* **81** E2
Baraka → *Sudan* **80** D4
Barakaldo *Spain* **38** B2
Barakar → *India* **69** G12
Barakot *India* **69** J11
Barakpur *India* **69** H13
Baralaba *Australia* **94** C4
Baralla *Spain* **36** C3
Baralzon L. *Canada* **103** B9
Barameiya *Sudan* **80** D4
Baramula *India* **69** B6
Baran *India* **68** G7
Baran → *Pakistan* **68** G3
Barañain *Spain* **38** C3
Baranavichy *Belarus* **23** B14
Barani *Burkina Faso* **82** C4
Baranof *U.S.A.* **102** B2
Baranof I. *U.S.A.* **100** D6
Baranów Sandomierski
　Poland **31** H8
Baranya □ *Hungary* **28** E3
Baraolt *Romania* **29** D10
Barapasi *Indonesia* **63** E9
Barasat *India* **69** H13
Barat Daya, Kepulauan
　Indonesia **63** F7
Barataria B. *U.S.A.* **117** G10
Barauda *India* **68** H6
Baraut *India* **68** E7
Barbacena *Brazil* **127** A7
Barbados ■ *W. Indies* **121** g
Barbària, C. de *Spain* **48** C7
Barbaros *Turkey* **45** F11
Barbas, C. *W. Sahara* **78** D2
Barbastro *Spain* **38** C5
Barbate *Spain* **37** J5
Barberino di Mugello *Italy* **41** E8
Barberton *S. Africa* **89** D5
Barberton *U.S.A.* **114** E3
Barbezieux-St-Hilaire *France* **20** C3
Barbosa *Colombia* **124** B4
Barbourville *U.S.A.* **113** G12
Barbuda *W. Indies* **121** C7
Bârca *Romania* **29** G8
Barcaldine *Australia* **94** C4
Barcarrota *Spain* **37** G4
Barcellona Pozzo di Gotto
　Italy **43** D8
Barcelona *Spain* **38** D7
Barcelona *Venezuela* **124** A6
Barcelona □ *Spain* **38** D7
Barcelona-Prat ✈ (BCN)
　Spain **38** D7
Barceloneta *Puerto Rico* **121** d
Barcelonette *France* **21** D10
Barcelos *Brazil* **124** D6
Barcin *Poland* **31** F4
Barclayville *Liberia* **82** E3
Barcoo → *Australia* **94** D3
Barcs *Hungary* **28** E2
Barczewo *Poland* **30** E7
Bärdä *Azerbaijan* **35** K8
Bardaï *Chad* **79** D9
Bardas Blancas *Argentina* **126** D2
Bardawîl, Sabkhet el *Egypt* **74** D2
Barddhaman *India* **69** H12
Bardejov *Slovak Rep.* **27** B14
Bardera *Somali Rep.* **75** G3
Bardi *Italy* **40** D6
Bardīyah *Libya* **79** B10
Bardolino *Italy* **40** C7
Bardonécchia *Italy* **40** C3
Bardsey I. *U.K.* **14** E3
Bardstown *U.S.A.* **113** G11
Bareilly *India* **69** E8
Barela *India* **69** H9
Barentin *France* **18** C7
Barenton *France* **18** D6
Barents Sea *Arctic* **4** B9
Barentu *Eritrea* **81** D4
Barfleur *France* **18** C5
Barfleur, Pte. de *France* **18** C5
Barga *Italy* **40** D7
Bargara *Australia* **94** C5
Bargas *Spain* **36** F6
Bârgăului Bistrița *Romania* **29** C9
Barge *Italy* **40** D4
Bargnop *Sudan* **81** F2
Bargteheide *Germany* **24** B6
Barguzin *Russia* **53** D11
Barh *India* **69** G11
Barhaj *India* **69** F10
Barharwa *India* **69** G12
Barhi *India* **69** G11
Bari *India* **68** F7
Bari *Italy* **43** A9
Bari Doab *Pakistan* **68** D5
Bari Sadri *India* **68** G6
Bari Sardo *Italy* **42** C2
Barīdī, Ra's *Si. Arabia* **70** E3
Barīm *Yemen* **76** E8
Barinas *Venezuela* **124** B4
Baring, C. *Canada* **100** C8
Baringo, L. *Kenya* **86** B4
Bârîs *Egypt* **80** C3

Barisal *Bangla.* **67** H17
Barisal □ *Bangla.* **67** H17
Barisan, Pegunungan
　Indonesia **62** E2
Barito → *Indonesia* **62** E4
Baritú △ *Argentina* **126** A3
Barjac *France* **21** D8
Barjols *France* **21** E10
Barjūj, Wadi → *Libya* **79** C8
Bark L. *Canada* **114** A7
Barka = Baraka → *Sudan* **80** D4
Barkakana *India* **69** H11
Barkam *China* **58** B4
Barker *U.S.A.* **114** C6
Barkley, L. *U.S.A.* **117** C10
Barkley Sound *Canada* **102** D3
Barkly East *S. Africa* **88** E4
Barkly Homestead *Australia* **94** B2
Barkly Tableland *Australia* **94** B2
Barkly West *S. Africa* **88** D3
Barkol, Wadi → *Sudan* **80** D3
Barla Dağı *Turkey* **47** C12
Bârlad *Romania* **29** D12
Bârlad → *Romania* **29** E12
Barlee, L. *Australia* **93** E2
Barlee, Mt. *Australia* **93** D4
Barletta *Italy* **41** A9
Barlinek *Poland* **31** F2
Barlovento *Canary Is.* **48** F2
Barlovento *C. Verde Is.* **78** b
Barlow L. *Canada* **103** A8
Barmedman *Australia* **95** E4
Barmer *India* **68** G4
Barmera *Australia* **95** E3
Barmouth *U.K.* **14** E3
Barmstedt *Germany* **24** B5
Barna → *India* **69** G10
Barnagar *India* **68** H6
Barnala *India* **68** D6
Barnard Castle *U.K.* **14** C6
Barnaul *Russia* **52** D9
Barnesville *Ga., U.S.A.* **117** E12
Barnesville *Minn., U.S.A.* **112** B5
Barnet □ *U.K.* **15** F7
Barneveld *Neths.* **17** B5
Barneville-Carteret *France* **18** C5
Barnhart *U.S.A.* **116** F4
Barnsley *U.K.* **14** D6
Barnstable *U.S.A.* **113** E18
Barnstaple *U.K.* **15** F3
Barnstaple Bay = Bideford
　Bay *U.K.* **15** F3
Barnwell *U.S.A.* **117** E14
Baro *Nigeria* **83** D6
Baro → *Ethiopia* **81** F3
Baroda = Vadodara *India* **68** H5
Baroda *India* **68** G7
Baroe *S. Africa* **88** E3
Baron Ra. *Australia* **92** D4
Barong *China* **58** B3
Barotseland *Zambia* **85** H4
Barouéli *Mali* **82** C3
Barpeta *India* **67** F17
Barques, Pt. Aux *U.S.A.* **114** B2
Barquísimeto *Venezuela* **124** A5
Barr, Ras al *Egypt* **80** H7
Barr Smith Range *Australia* **93** E3
Barra *Brazil* **125** F10
Barra *U.K.* **13** E1
Barra, Sd. of *U.K.* **13** D1
Barra de Navidad *Mexico* **118** D4
Barra do Corda *Brazil* **125** E9
Barra do Piraí *Brazil* **127** A7
Barra Falsa, Pta. da *Mozam.* **89** C6
Barra Hd. *U.K.* **13** E1
Barra Mansa *Brazil* **127** A7
Barraba *Australia* **95** E5
Barrackpur = Barakpur
　India **69** H13
Barradale *Australia* **92** D1
Barrafranca *Italy* **43** E7
Barraigh = Barra *U.K.* **13** E1
Barranca *Lima, Peru* **124** F3
Barranca *Loreto, Peru* **124** D3
Barranca del Cobre △
　Mexico **118** B3
Barrancabermeja *Colombia* **124** B4
Barrancas *Venezuela* **124** B6
Barrancos *Portugal* **37** G4
Barranqueras *Argentina* **126** B4
Barranquilla *Colombia* **124** A4
Barraute *Canada* **104** C4
Barre *Mass., U.S.A.* **115** D12
Barre *Vt., U.S.A.* **115** B12
Barreal *Argentina* **126** C2
Barreiras *Brazil* **125** F10
Barreirinhas *Brazil* **125** D10
Barreiro *Portugal* **37** G1
Barrême *France* **21** E10
Barren, Nosy *Madag.* **89** B7
Barretos *Brazil* **125** H9
Barrhead *Canada* **102** C6
Barrie *Canada* **114** B5
Barrier Ra. *Australia* **95** E3
Barrière *Canada* **102** C4
Barrington *U.S.A.* **115** E13

Barrington L. *Canada* **103** B8
Barrington Tops *Australia* **95** E5
Barringun *Australia* **95** D4
Barro do Garças *Brazil* **125** G8
Barron *U.S.A.* **112** C8
Barrow *U.S.A.* **106** a
Barrow → *Ireland* **12** D5
Barrow, Pt. *U.S.A.* **98** B4
Barrow Creek *Australia* **94** C1
Barrow I. *Australia* **92** D2
Barrow-in-Furness *U.K.* **14** C4
Barrow Pt. *Australia* **94** A3
Barrow Ra. *Australia* **93** E4
Barrow Str. *Canada* **4** B3
Barruecopardo *Spain* **36** D4
Barruelo de Santullán *Spain* **36** C6
Barry *U.K.* **15** F4
Barry's Bay *Canada* **114** A7
Barsalogho *Burkina Faso* **83** C4
Barsat *Pakistan* **69** A5
Barsham *Syria* **73** E9
Barsi *India* **66** K9
Barsinghausen *Germany* **24** C5
Barsoi *India* **67** G15
Barstow *U.S.A.* **111** L9
Barth *Germany* **24** A8
Barthélemy, Col *Vietnam* **64** C5
Bartica *Guyana* **124** B7
Bartın *Turkey* **72** B5
Bartle Frere *Australia* **94** B4
Bartlesville *U.S.A.* **116** C7
Bartlett *Calif., U.S.A.* **110** J8
Bartlett *Tenn., U.S.A.* **117** D10
Bartlett, L. *Canada* **102** A5
Bartolomeu Dias *Mozam.* **87** G4
Barton *U.S.A.* **115** B12
Barton upon Humber *U.K.* **14** D7
Bartoszyce *Poland* **30** D7
Bartow *U.S.A.* **117** H14
Barú, Volcan *Panama* **120** E3
Barumba
　Dem. Rep. of the Congo **86** B1
Baruth *Germany* **24** C9
Baruunsuu *Mongolia* **56** C3
Barvinkove *Ukraine* **33** H9
Barwani *India* **68** H6
Barwice *Poland* **30** E3
Barycz → *Poland* **31** G3
Barysaw *Belarus* **23** A15
Barysh *Russia* **34** D8
Barzān *Iraq* **70** B5
Bârzava *Romania* **28** D6
Bas-Rhin □ *France* **19** D14
Baša'id *Serbia* **28** E5
Bāsa'idū *Iran* **71** E7
Basal *Pakistan* **68** C5
Basankusa
　Dem. Rep. of the Congo **84** D3
Basarabeasca *Moldova* **29** D13
Basarabi *Romania* **29** F13
Basarabia = Bessarabiya
　Moldova **23** E15
Basauri *Spain* **38** B2
Basawa *Afghan.* **68** B4
Bascuñán, C. *Chile* **126** B1
Basel *Switz.* **25** H3
Basel, Euroairport ✈ (BSL)
　Europe **19** E14
Basel-Landschaft □ *Switz.* **25** H3
Basento → *Italy* **43** B9
Bashākerd, Kūhhā-ye *Iran* **71** E8
Bashaw *Canada* **102** C6
Bāshī *Iran* **71** D6
Bashkir Republic =
　Bashkortostan □ *Russia* **52** D6
Bashkortostan □ *Russia* **52** D6
Bashtanivka *Ukraine* **29** E14
Basibasy *Madag.* **89** C7
Basilan *Phil.* **61** H5
Basilan Str. *Phil.* **61** H5
Basildon *U.K.* **15** F8
Basile *Eq. Guin.* **83** E6
Basile, Pico *Eq. Guin.* **83** E6
Basilicata □ *Italy* **43** B9
Basim = Washim *India* **66** J10
Basin *U.S.A.* **108** D9
Basingstoke *U.K.* **15** F6
Baška *Croatia* **41** D11
Başkale *Turkey* **73** C10
Baskatong, Rés. *Canada* **104** C4
Basle = Basel *Switz.* **25** H3
Başmakçı *Turkey* **47** D12
Basoda *India* **68** H7
Basoko *Dem. Rep. of the Congo* **86** B1
Basque, Pays *France* **20** E2
Basque Provinces = País
　Vasco □ *Spain* **38** C2
Basra = Al Başrah *Iraq* **70** D5
Bass Str. *Australia* **95** F4
Bassano *Canada* **102** C6
Bassano del Grappa *Italy* **41** C8
Bassar *Togo* **83** D5
Bassas da India *Ind. Oc.* **85** J7
Basse-Normandie □ *France* **18** D6
Basse-Pointe *Martinique* **120** c
Basse Santa-Su *Gambia* **82** C2
Basse-Terre *Guadeloupe* **120** b
Basse Terre *Trin. & Tob.* **125** K15

Bassein *Burma* **67** L19
Basses, Pte. des *Guadeloupe* **120** b
Basseterre *St. Kitts & Nevis* **121** C7
Bassett *U.S.A.* **112** D4
Bassi *India* **68** D7
Bassigny *France* **19** E12
Bassikounou *Mauritania* **82** B3
Bassila *Benin* **83** D5
Bassum *Germany* **24** C4
Båstad *Sweden* **11** H6
Bastak *Iran* **71** E7
Baştām *Iran* **71** B7
Bastar *India* **67** K12
Bastelica *France* **21** F13
Basti *India* **69** F10
Bastia *France* **21** F13
Bastogne *Belgium* **17** D5
Bastrop *La., U.S.A.* **116** E9
Bastrop *Tex., U.S.A.* **116** F6
Basuo = Dongfang *China* **64** C7
Bat Yam *Israel* **74** C3
Bata *Eq. Guin.* **84** D1
Bata *Romania* **28** D7
Bataan □ *Phil.* **61** D4
Batabanó *Cuba* **120** B3
Batabanó, G. de *Cuba* **120** B3
Batac *Phil.* **61** B4
Batagai *Russia* **53** C14
Batajnica *Serbia* **44** B4
Batak *Bulgaria* **45** E8
Batala *India* **68** D6
Batalha *Portugal* **36** F2
Batama *Dem. Rep. of the Congo* **86** B2
Batamay *Russia* **53** C13
Batang *China* **58** B3
Batang *Indonesia* **63** G13
Batangafo *C.A.R.* **84** C3
Batangas *Phil.* **61** E4
Batanta *Indonesia* **63** E8
Batatais *Brazil* **127** A6
Batavia *U.S.A.* **114** D6
Bataysk *Russia* **33** J10
Batchelor *Australia* **92** B5
Batdambang *Cambodia* **64** F4
Batemans B. *Australia* **95** F5
Batemans Bay *Australia* **95** F5
Bates Ra. *Australia* **93** E3
Batesburg-Leesville *U.S.A.* **117** E14
Batesville *Ark., U.S.A.* **116** D9
Batesville *Miss., U.S.A.* **117** D10
Batesville *Tex., U.S.A.* **116** G5
Bath *Canada* **115** B8
Bath *U.K.* **15** F5
Bath *Maine, U.S.A.* **113** D19
Bath *N.Y., U.S.A.* **114** D7
Bath & North East
　Somerset □ *U.K.* **15** F5
Batheay *Cambodia* **65** G5
Bathsheba *Barbados* **121** g
Bathurst *Australia* **95** E4
Bathurst *Canada* **105** C6
Bathurst *S. Africa* **88** E4
Bathurst, C. *Canada* **100** B7
Bathurst B. *Australia* **94** A3
Bathurst Harb. *Australia* **95** G4
Bathurst I. *Australia* **92** B5
Bathurst I. *Canada* **101** B11
Bathurst Inlet *Canada* **100** C9
Bati *Ethiopia* **81** E5
Batie *Burkina Faso* **82** D4
Batlow *Australia* **95** F4
Batman *Turkey* **73** D9
Baţn al Ghūl *Jordan* **74** F4
Batna *Algeria* **78** A7
Batobato = San Isidro *Phil.* **61** H7
Batočina *Serbia* **44** B5
Batoka *Zambia* **87** F2
Baton Rouge *U.S.A.* **116** F9
Batong, Ko *Thailand* **65** J2
Bátonyterenye *Hungary* **28** C4
Batopilas *Mexico* **118** B3
Batouri *Cameroon* **84** D2
Båtsfjord *Norway* **8** A23
Battambang =
　Batdambang *Cambodia* **64** F4
Batticaloa *Sri Lanka* **66** R12
Battipáglia *Italy* **43** B7
Battle *U.K.* **15** G8
Battle → *Canada* **103** C7
Battle Creek *U.S.A.* **113** D11
Battle Ground *U.S.A.* **110** E4
Battle Harbour *Canada* **105** B8
Battle Lake *U.S.A.* **112** B6
Battle Mountain *U.S.A.* **108** F5
Battlefields *Zimbabwe* **87** F2
Battleford *Canada* **103** C7
Battonya *Hungary* **28** D6
Batu *Ethiopia* **81** F4
Batu, Kepulauan *Indonesia* **62** E1
Batu Caves *Malaysia* **65** L3
Batu Ferringhi *Malaysia* **65** c
Batu Gajah *Malaysia* **65** K3
Batu Is. = Batu,
　Kepulauan *Indonesia* **62** E1
Batu Pahat *Malaysia* **65** M4
Batuata *Indonesia* **63** F6

Batugondang, Tanjung *Indonesia* 63 J17
Batukau, Gunung *Indonesia* 63 J18
Batumi *Georgia* 35 K5
Batur *Indonesia* 63 J18
Batur, Danau *Indonesia* 63 J18
Batur, Gunung *Indonesia* 63 J18
Baturaja *Indonesia* 62 E2
Baturité *Brazil* 125 D11
Baturiti *Indonesia* 63 J18
Bau *Malaysia* 62 D4
Baubau *Indonesia* 63 F6
Baucau *E. Timor* 63 F7
Bauchi *Nigeria* 83 C6
Bauchi □ *Nigeria* 83 C7
Baud *France* 18 E3
Baudette *U.S.A.* 112 A6
Bauer, C. *Australia* 95 E1
Bauhinia *Australia* 94 C4
Baukau = Baucau *E. Timor* 63 F7
Bauld, C. *Canada* 101 D14
Baume-les-Dames *France* 19 E13
Baunei *Italy* 42 B2
Baure *Nigeria* 83 C6
Bauru *Brazil* 127 A6
Bausi *India* 69 G12
Bauska *Latvia* 30 B11
Bautino *Kazakhstan* 35 H10
Bautzen *Germany* 24 D10
Bauya *S. Leone* 82 D2
Bavănāt *Iran* 71 D7
Bavanište *Serbia* 28 F5
Bavaria = Bayern □ *Germany* 25 G7
Båven *Sweden* 10 E10
Bavispe → *Mexico* 118 B3
Bawdwin *Burma* 67 H20
Bawean *Indonesia* 62 F4
Bawku *Ghana* 83 C4
Bawlake *Burma* 67 K20
Bawolung *China* 58 C3
Baxley *U.S.A.* 117 F4
Baxoi *China* 58 B1
Baxter *U.S.A.* 112 B6
Baxter Springs *U.S.A.* 112 G6
Baxter State △ *U.S.A.* 113 B19
Bay, L. de *Phil.* 61 D4
Bay City Mich., *U.S.A.* 113 D12
Bay City Tex., *U.S.A.* 116 G7
Bay Minette *U.S.A.* 117 F11
Bay Roberts *Canada* 105 C9
Bay St. Louis *U.S.A.* 117 F10
Bay Springs *U.S.A.* 117 F10
Bay View *N.Z.* 91 C6
Baya *Dem. Rep. of the Congo* 87 E2
Bayamo *Cuba* 120 B4
Bayamón *Puerto Rico* 121 d
Bayan Har Shan *China* 60 C4
Bayan Hot = Alxa Zuoqi *China* 56 E3
Bayan Lepas *Malaysia* 65 c
Bayan Obo *China* 56 D5
Bayan-Ovoo = Erdenetsogt *Mongolia* 56 C4
Bayana *India* 68 F7
Bayanaŭyl *Kazakhstan* 52 D8
Bayandalay *Mongolia* 56 C2
Bayanhongor *Mongolia* 60 B5
Bayard N. Mex., *U.S.A.* 109 K9
Bayard Nebr., *U.S.A.* 112 E2
Bayawan *Phil.* 61 G5
Baybay *Phil.* 61 F6
Bayburt *Turkey* 73 B9
Bayburt □ *Turkey* 73 B8
Baydhabo = Baidoa *Somali Rep.* 75 G3
Bayelsa □ *Nigeria* 83 E6
Bayerische Alpen *Germany* 25 H7
Bayerische Rhön *Germany* 25 E6
Bayerischer Spessart △ *Germany* 25 F6
Bayerischer Wald *Germany* 25 G8
Bayern □ *Germany* 25 G7
Bayeux *France* 18 C6
Bayfield *Canada* 114 C3
Bayfield *U.S.A.* 112 B8
Bayındır *Turkey* 47 C9
Baykal, Oz. *Russia* 53 D11
Baykan *Turkey* 70 B4
Baynes Mts. *Namibia* 88 B1
Bayombong *Phil.* 61 C4
Bayon *France* 19 D13
Bayona = Baiona *Spain* 36 C2
Bayonne *France* 20 E2
Bayonne *U.S.A.* 115 F10
Bayovar *Peru* 124 E2
Bayqongyr *Kazakhstan* 52 E7
Bayram-Ali = Baýramaly *Turkmenistan* 71 B9
Baýramaly *Turkmenistan* 71 B9
Bayramiç *Turkey* 47 B8
Bayreuth *Germany* 25 F7
Bayrischzell *Germany* 25 H8
Bayrūt *Lebanon* 74 B4
Bays, L. of *Canada* 114 A5
Baysville *Canada* 114 A5
Bayt Lahm *West Bank* 74 D4

Baytown *U.S.A.* 116 G7
Bayun *Indonesia* 63 J18
Bayzo *Niger* 83 C5
Baza *Spain* 37 H8
Bazar Dyuzi *Russia* 35 K8
Bazardüzü = Bazar Dyuzi *Russia* 35 K8
Bazarny Karabulak *Russia* 34 D8
Bazarnyy Syzgan *Russia* 34 D8
Bazaruto, I. do *Mozam.* 89 C6
Bazaruto △ *Mozam.* 89 C6
Bazas *France* 20 D3
Bazhong *China* 58 B6
Bazhou *China* 56 E9
Bazmān, Kūh-e *Iran* 71 D9
Beach *U.S.A.* 112 B2
Beach City *U.S.A.* 114 F3
Beachport *Australia* 95 F3
Beachy Hd. *U.K.* 15 G8
Beacon *Australia* 93 F2
Beacon *U.S.A.* 115 E11
Beaconsfield *Australia* 95 G4
Beagle, Canal *S. Amer.* 128 H3
Beagle Bay *Australia* 92 C3
Bealanana *Madag.* 89 A8
Beals Cr. → *U.S.A.* 116 E4
Beamsville = Lincoln *Canada* 114 C5
Bear → *Calif., U.S.A.* 110 G5
Bear → *Utah, U.S.A.* 106 B4
Béar, C. *France* 20 F7
Bear I. *Ireland* 12 E2
Bear L. *Canada* 103 B9
Bear L. *U.S.A.* 108 F8
Beardmore *Canada* 104 C2
Beardmore Glacier *Antarctica* 5 E11
Beardstown *U.S.A.* 112 E8
Bearma → *India* 69 G8
Béarn *France* 20 E3
Bearpaw Mts. *U.S.A.* 108 B9
Bearskin Lake *Canada* 104 B1
Beas → *India* 68 D6
Beas de Segura *Spain* 37 G8
Beasain *Spain* 38 B2
Beata, C. *Dom. Rep.* 121 C5
Beata, I. *Dom. Rep.* 121 C5
Beatrice *U.S.A.* 112 E5
Beatrice *Zimbabwe* 87 F3
Beatrice, C. *Australia* 94 A2
Beatton → *Canada* 102 B4
Beatton River *Canada* 102 B4
Beatty *U.S.A.* 110 J10
Beau Bassin *Mauritius* 85 d
Beaucaire *France* 21 E8
Beauce, Plaine de la *France* 19 D8
Beauceville *Canada* 105 C5
Beaudesert *Australia* 95 D5
Beaufort *France* 21 C10
Beaufort *Malaysia* 62 C5
Beaufort N.C., *U.S.A.* 117 D16
Beaufort S.C., *U.S.A.* 117 E14
Beaufort Sea *Arctic* 98 B5
Beaufort West *S. Africa* 88 E3
Beaugency *France* 19 E8
Beauharnois *Canada* 115 A11
Beaujeu *France* 19 F11
Beaujolais *France* 19 F11
Beaulieu → *Canada* 102 A6
Beaulieu-sur-Dordogne *France* 20 D5
Beaulieu-sur-Mer *France* 21 E11
Beauly *U.K.* 13 D4
Beauly → *U.K.* 13 D4
Beaumaris *U.K.* 14 D3
Beaumont *Belgium* 17 D4
Beaumont *France* 20 D4
Beaumont *U.S.A.* 116 F7
Beaumont-de-Lomagne *France* 20 E5
Beaumont-le-Roger *France* 18 C7
Beaumont-sur-Sarthe *France* 18 D7
Beaune *France* 19 E11
Beaune-la-Rolande *France* 19 D9
Beaupré *Canada* 105 C5
Beaupréau *France* 18 E6
Beauraing *Belgium* 17 D4
Beaurepaire *France* 21 C9
Beausejour *Canada* 103 C9
Beauvais *France* 19 C9
Beauval *Canada* 103 B7
Beauvoir-sur-Mer *France* 18 F4
Beauvoir-sur-Niort *France* 20 B3
Beaver Okla., *U.S.A.* 116 C4
Beaver → *B.C., Canada* 102 B4
Beaver → *Ont., Canada* 104 A2
Beaver → *Sask., Canada* 103 B7
Beaver → *U.S.A.* 116 C5
Beaver City *U.S.A.* 112 E4
Beaver Creek *Canada* 100 C6
Beaver Dam *U.S.A.* 112 D10
Beaver Falls *U.S.A.* 114 F4
Beaver Hill L. *Canada* 103 C10
Beaver I. *U.S.A.* 113 C11
Beavercreek *U.S.A.* 113 F11
Beaverhill L. *Canada* 102 C6

Beaverlodge *Canada* 102 B5
Beaverstone → *Canada* 104 B2
Beaverton *Canada* 114 B5
Beaverton *U.S.A.* 110 E4
Beawar *India* 68 F6
Bebedouro *Brazil* 127 A6
Bebera, Tanjung *Indonesia* 63 K18
Beboa *Madag.* 89 B7
Bebra *Germany* 24 E5
Becán *Mexico* 119 D7
Bécancour *Canada* 113 B17
Beccles *U.K.* 15 E9
Bečej *Serbia* 28 E5
Beceni *Romania* 29 E11
Becerreá *Spain* 36 C3
Béchar *Algeria* 78 B5
Bechyně *Czech Rep.* 26 B7
Beckley *U.S.A.* 113 G13
Beckum *Germany* 24 D4
Beclean *Romania* 29 C9
Bečov nad Teplou *Czech Rep.* 26 A5
Bečva → *Czech Rep.* 27 B10
Bédar *Spain* 39 H3
Bédarieux *France* 20 E7
Beddouza, Ras *Morocco* 78 B4
Bedele *Ethiopia* 81 F4
Bederkesa *Germany* 24 B4
Bedeso *Ethiopia* 81 F5
Bedford *Canada* 115 A12
Bedford *S. Africa* 88 E4
Bedford *U.K.* 15 E7
Bedford Ind., *U.S.A.* 112 F10
Bedford Iowa, *U.S.A.* 112 E6
Bedford Ohio, *U.S.A.* 114 E3
Bedford Pa., *U.S.A.* 114 F6
Bedford Va., *U.S.A.* 113 G14
Bedford, C. *Australia* 94 B4
Bedfordshire □ *U.K.* 15 E7
Będków *Poland* 31 G6
Bednja → *Croatia* 41 B13
Bednodemyanovsk *Russia* 34 D6
Bedok *Singapore* 65 d
Bedónia *Italy* 40 D6
Bedourie *Australia* 94 C2
Bedum *Neths.* 17 A6
Będzin *Poland* 31 H6
Beebe Plain *Canada* 115 A12
Beech Creek *U.S.A.* 114 E7
Beechy *Canada* 103 C7
Beef I. *Br. Virgin Is.* 121 e
Beenleigh *Australia* 95 D5
Be'er Menuha *Israel* 70 D2
Be'er Sheva *Israel* 74 D3
Beersheba = Be'er Sheva *Israel* 74 D3
Beeskow *Germany* 24 C10
Beestekraal *S. Africa* 89 D4
Beeston *U.K.* 14 E6
Beetaloo *Australia* 94 B1
Beetzendorf *Germany* 24 C7
Beeville *U.S.A.* 116 G6
Befale *Dem. Rep. of the Congo* 84 D4
Befandriana Mahajanga, *Madag.* 89 B8
Befandriana Toliara, *Madag.* 89 C7
Befasy *Madag.* 89 C7
Befotaka Antsiranana, *Madag.* 89 A8
Befotaka Fianarantsoa, *Madag.* 89 C8
Bega *Australia* 95 F4
Bega, Canalul *Romania* 28 E5
Bégard *France* 18 D3
Behābād *Iran* 71 C8
Behala *India* 69 H13
Behara *Madag.* 89 C8
Behbehān *Iran* 71 D6
Behm Canal *U.S.A.* 102 B2
Behshahr *Iran* 71 B7
Bei Jiang → *China* 59 F9
Bei'an *China* 60 B7
Beibei *China* 58 C6
Beihai *China* 58 G7
Beijing *China* 56 E9
Beijing □ *China* 56 E9
Beilen *Neths.* 17 B6
Beiliu *China* 59 F8
Beilngries *Germany* 25 F7
Beilpajah *Australia* 95 E3
Beilul *Eritrea* 81 E5
Beinn na Faoghla = Benbecula *U.K.* 13 D1
Beipan Jiang → *China* 58 E5
Beipiao *China* 57 D11
Beira *Mozam.* 87 F3
Beirut = Bayrūt *Lebanon* 74 B4
Beiseker *Canada* 102 C6
Beit Lekhem = Bayt Lahm *West Bank* 74 D4
Beitaolaizhao *China* 57 B13
Beitbridge *Zimbabwe* 87 G3
Beiuş *Romania* 28 D7
Beizhen = Binzhou *China* 57 F10
Beizhen *China* 57 D11
Beizhengzhen *China* 57 B12

Beja *Portugal* 37 G3
Béja *Tunisia* 79 A7
Beja □ *Portugal* 37 H3
Bejaïa *Algeria* 78 A7
Béjar *Spain* 36 E5
Bejestān *Iran* 71 C8
Bekaa Valley = Al Biqā *Lebanon* 74 B5
Bekçiler *Turkey* 47 E11
Békés *Hungary* 28 D6
Békés □ *Hungary* 28 D6
Békéscsaba *Hungary* 28 D6
Bekilli *Turkey* 47 C11
Bekily *Madag.* 89 C8
Bekisopa *Madag.* 89 C8
Bekitro *Madag.* 89 C8
Bekodoka *Madag.* 89 B8
Bekoji *Ethiopia* 81 F4
Bekok *Malaysia* 65 L4
Bekopaka *Madag.* 89 B7
Bekuli *Indonesia* 63 J17
Bekwai *Ghana* 83 D4
Bela *India* 69 G10
Bela *Pakistan* 68 F2
Bela Bela *S. Africa* 89 C4
Bela Crkva *Serbia* 28 F6
Bela Palanka *Serbia* 44 C6
Bela Vista *Brazil* 126 A4
Bela Vista *Mozam.* 89 D5
Bélâbre *France* 20 B5
Belalcázar *Spain* 37 G5
Belan → *India* 69 G9
Belanovica *Serbia* 44 B4
Belarus ■ *Europe* 23 B14
Belau = Palau ■ *Palau* 90 A6
Belavenona *Madag.* 89 C8
Belawan *Indonesia* 62 D1
Belaya *Ethiopia* 81 E4
Belaya Glina *Russia* 35 G5
Belaya Kalitva *Russia* 35 F5
Belaya Tserkov = Bila Tserkva *Ukraine* 23 D16
Belceşti *Romania* 29 C12
Belchatów *Poland* 31 G6
Belcher Chan. *Canada* 101 B10
Belcher Is. *Canada* 104 A3
Belchite *Spain* 38 D4
Belden *U.S.A.* 110 E5
Beled Weyne = Belet Uen *Somali Rep.* 75 G4
Belém *Brazil* 125 D9
Belén *Argentina* 126 B2
Belén *Paraguay* 126 A4
Belen *Turkey* 72 D7
Belen *U.S.A.* 109 J10
Belene *Bulgaria* 45 C9
Bélesta *France* 20 F5
Belet Uen *Somali Rep.* 75 G4
Belev *Russia* 32 F9
Belevi *Turkey* 47 C9
Belfair *U.S.A.* 110 C4
Belfast *S. Africa* 89 D5
Belfast *U.K.* 12 B6
Belfast Maine, *U.S.A.* 113 C19
Belfast N.Y., *U.S.A.* 114 D6
Belfast L. *U.K.* 12 B6
Belfield *U.S.A.* 112 B2
Belfort *France* 19 E13
Belfort, Territoire de □ *France* 19 E13
Belfry *U.S.A.* 108 D9
Belgaum *India* 66 M9
Belgioioso *Italy* 40 C6
Belgium ■ *Europe* 17 D4
Belgodère *France* 21 F13
Belgorod *Russia* 33 G9
Belgorod □ *Russia* 33 G9
Belgorod-Dnestrovskiy = Bilhorod-Dnistrovskyy *Ukraine* 33 J9
Belgrade = Beograd *Serbia* 44 B4
Belgrade *U.S.A.* 108 D8
Belgrano *Antarctica* 5 D1
Belhaven *U.S.A.* 117 D16
Beli Drim → *Europe* 44 D4
Beli Manastir *Croatia* 28 E3
Beli Timok → *Serbia* 44 C6
Bélice → *Italy* 42 E5
Belimbing *Indonesia* 63 J18
Belinskiy *Russia* 34 D6
Belinyu *Indonesia* 62 E3
Beliton Is. = Belitung *Indonesia* 62 E3
Belitung *Indonesia* 62 E3
Beliu *Romania* 28 D6
Belize ■ *Cent. Amer.* 119 D7
Belize City *Belize* 119 D7
Beljakovci *Macedonia* 44 D5
Beljanica *Serbia* 44 B5
Belkovskiy, Ostrov *Russia* 53 B14
Bell → *Canada* 104 C4
Bell I. *Canada* 105 B8
Bell Peninsula *Canada* 101 C11
Bell Ville *Argentina* 126 C3
Bella *Italy* 43 B8
Bella Bella *Canada* 102 C3
Bella Coola *Canada* 102 C3

Bella Unión *Uruguay* 126 C4
Bella Vista *Corrientes, Argentina* 126 B4
Bella Vista *Tucuman, Argentina* 126 B2
Bellac *France* 20 B5
Bellágio *Italy* 40 C6
Bellaire *U.S.A.* 114 F4
Bellária *Italy* 41 D9
Bellary *India* 66 M10
Bellata *Australia* 95 D4
Belle Fourche *U.S.A.* 112 C2
Belle Fourche → *U.S.A.* 106 B6
Belle Glade *U.S.A.* 117 H14
Belle-Île *France* 18 E3
Belle Isle *Canada* 105 B8
Belle Isle, Str. of *Canada* 105 B8
Belle Plaine *U.S.A.* 112 E7
Belle Yella *Liberia* 82 D3
Belledonne *France* 21 C10
Bellefontaine *U.S.A.* 113 E12
Bellefonte *U.S.A.* 114 F7
Bellegarde *France* 19 E9
Bellegarde-en-Marche *France* 20 C6
Bellegarde-sur-Valserine *France* 19 F12
Bellême *France* 18 D7
Belleoram *Canada* 105 C8
Belleplaine *Barbados* 121 g
Belleville *Canada* 114 B7
Belleville *France* 19 F11
Belleville Ill., *U.S.A.* 112 F8
Belleville Kans., *U.S.A.* 112 F5
Belleville N.J., *U.S.A.* 115 F10
Belleville N.Y., *U.S.A.* 115 C8
Belleville-sur-Vie *France* 18 F5
Bellevue *Canada* 102 D6
Bellevue Idaho, *U.S.A.* 108 E6
Bellevue Nebr., *U.S.A.* 112 E6
Bellevue Ohio, *U.S.A.* 114 E2
Bellevue Wash., *U.S.A.* 110 C4
Belley *France* 21 C9
Bellin = Kangirsuk *Canada* 101 D13
Bellinge *Denmark* 11 J4
Bellingen *Australia* 95 E5
Bellingham *U.S.A.* 110 B4
Bellingshausen Abyssal Plain *S. Ocean* 5 C16
Bellingshausen Sea *Antarctica* 5 C17
Bellinzona *Switz.* 25 J5
Bello *Colombia* 124 B3
Bellows Falls *U.S.A.* 115 C12
Bellpat *Pakistan* 68 E3
Bellpuig d'Urgell *Spain* 38 D6
Belluno *Italy* 41 B9
Bellwood *U.S.A.* 114 F6
Bélmez *Spain* 37 G5
Belmont *Canada* 114 D3
Belmont *S. Africa* 88 D3
Belmont *U.S.A.* 114 D6
Belmonte *Brazil* 125 G11
Belmonte *Portugal* 36 E3
Belmonte *Spain* 39 F2
Belmopan *Belize* 119 D7
Belmullet *Ireland* 12 B2
Belo Horizonte *Brazil* 125 G10
Belo-sur-Mer *Madag.* 89 C7
Belo-Tsiribihina *Madag.* 89 B7
Belogorsk = Bilohirsk *Ukraine* 33 K8
Belogorsk *Russia* 53 D13
Belogradchik *Bulgaria* 44 C6
Belogradets *Bulgaria* 45 C11
Beloha *Madag.* 89 D8
Beloit Kans., *U.S.A.* 112 F4
Beloit Wis., *U.S.A.* 112 D9
Belokorovichi *Ukraine* 23 C15
Belomorsk *Russia* 52 C4
Belonia *India* 67 H17
Belopolye = Bilopillya *Ukraine* 33 G8
Belorechensk *Russia* 35 H4
Belorussia = Belarus ■ *Europe* 23 B14
Beloslav *Bulgaria* 45 C11
Belovo *Russia* 52 D9
Belovodsk *Ukraine* 33 H10
Beloye, Ozero *Russia* 32 B9
Beloye More *Russia* 8 C25
Belozem *Bulgaria* 45 D9
Belozersk *Russia* 32 B9
Belpasso *Italy* 43 E7
Belpre *U.S.A.* 113 F13
Belrain *India* 69 E9
Belt *U.S.A.* 108 C8
Beltana *Australia* 95 E2
Belterra *Brazil* 125 D8
Belton *U.S.A.* 116 F6
Belton L. *U.S.A.* 116 F6
Beltsy = Bălţi *Moldova* 29 C12
Belturbet *Ireland* 12 B4
Belukha *Russia* 52 E9
Beluša *Slovak Rep.* 27 B11

Belušić *Serbia* 44 C5
Belvedere Maríttimo *Italy* 43 C8
Belvès *France* 20 D5
Belvidere Ill., *U.S.A.* 112 D9
Belvidere N.J., *U.S.A.* 115 F9
Belvis de la Jara *Spain* 36 F6
Belyando → *Australia* 94 C4
Belyy *Russia* 32 E7
Belyy, Ostrov *Russia* 52 B8
Belyy Yar *Russia* 52 D9
Belz *Ukraine* 31 H11
Bełżec *Poland* 31 H10
Belzig *Germany* 24 C8
Belzoni *U.S.A.* 117 E9
Bełżyce *Poland* 31 G9
Bemaraha, Lembalemban' i *Madag.* 89 B7
Bemarivo *Madag.* 89 C7
Bemarivo → Antsiranana, *Madag.* 89 A9
Bemarivo → Mahajanga, *Madag.* 89 B8
Bemavo *Madag.* 89 C8
Bembéréke *Benin* 83 C5
Bembesi *Zimbabwe* 87 G2
Bembesi → *Zimbabwe* 87 F2
Bembézar → *Spain* 37 H5
Bembibre *Spain* 36 C4
Bemetara *India* 69 J9
Bemidji *U.S.A.* 112 B6
Bemolanga *Madag.* 89 B8
Ben *Iran* 71 C6
Ben Cruachan *U.K.* 13 E3
Ben Dearg *U.K.* 13 D4
Ben En △ *Vietnam* 64 C5
Ben Gardane *Tunisia* 79 B8
Ben Hope *U.K.* 13 C4
Ben Lawers *U.K.* 13 E4
Ben Lomond N.S.W., *Australia* 95 E5
Ben Lomond Tas., *Australia* 95 G4
Ben Lomond *U.K.* 13 E4
Ben Lomond △ *Australia* 95 G4
Ben Luc *Vietnam* 65 G6
Ben Macdhui *U.K.* 13 D5
Ben Mhor *U.K.* 13 D1
Ben More Argyll & Bute, *U.K.* 13 E2
Ben More Stirling, *U.K.* 13 E4
Ben More Assynt *U.K.* 13 C4
Ben Nevis *U.K.* 13 E3
Ben Quang *Vietnam* 64 D6
Ben Vorlich *U.K.* 13 E4
Ben Wyvis *U.K.* 13 D4
Bena *Nigeria* 83 C6
Benalla *Australia* 95 F4
Benalmádena *Spain* 37 J6
Benares = Varanasi *India* 69 G10
Bénat, C. *France* 21 E10
Benavente *Portugal* 37 G2
Benavente *Spain* 36 C5
Benavides *U.S.A.* 116 H5
Benavides de Órbigo *Spain* 36 C5
Benbecula *U.K.* 13 D1
Benbonyathe Hill *Australia* 95 E2
Bend *U.S.A.* 108 D3
Bender Beila *Somali Rep.* 75 F5
Bendery = Tighina *Moldova* 29 D14
Bendigo *Australia* 95 F3
Bendorf *Germany* 24 E3
Benĕ Beraq *Israel* 74 C3
Bénéna *Mali* 82 C4
Benenitra *Madag.* 89 C8
Benešov *Czech Rep.* 26 B7
Benevento *Italy* 43 A7
Benfeld *France* 19 D14
Benga *Mozam.* 87 F3
Bengal, Bay of *Ind. Oc.* 67 M17
Bengalūru = Bangalore *India* 66 N10
Bengbis *Cameroon* 83 E7
Bengbu *China* 57 H9
Benghazi = Banghāzī *Libya* 79 B10
Bengkalis *Indonesia* 62 D2
Bengkulu *Indonesia* 62 E2
Bengkulu □ *Indonesia* 62 E2
Bengough *Canada* 103 D7
Bengtsfors *Sweden* 10 E6
Benguela *Angola* 85 G2
Benguérua, I. *Mozam.* 89 C6
Benha *Egypt* 80 H7
Beni *Dem. Rep. of the Congo* 86 B2
Beni → *Bolivia* 124 F5
Beni Mazâr *Egypt* 80 B3
Beni Mellal *Morocco* 78 B4
Beni Suef *Egypt* 80 J7
Beniah L. *Canada* 102 A6
Benicarló *Spain* 38 E5
Benicássim *Spain* 38 E5
Benidorm *Spain* 39 G4
Benin ■ *Africa* 83 D5
Benin → *Nigeria* 83 D6
Benin, Bight of *W. Afr.* 83 E5
Benin City *Nigeria* 83 D6
Benisa *Spain* 39 G5
Benitses *Greece* 49 A3
Benjamin Aceval *Paraguay* 126 A4
Benjamin Constant *Brazil* 124 D4
Benjamín Hill *Mexico* 118 A2

Benkelman *U.S.A.* **112** E3
Benkovac *Croatia* **41** D12
Bennett *Canada* **102** B2
Bennett, L. *Australia* **92** D5
Bennetta, Ostrov *Russia* **53** B15
Bennettsville *U.S.A.* **117** D15
Bennichchâb *Mauritania* **82** B1
Bennington *N.H., U.S.A.* **115** D11
Bennington *Vt., U.S.A.* **115** D11
Bénodet *France* **18** E2
Benoni *S. Africa* **89** D4
Benque Viejo *Belize* **119** D7
Bensheim *Germany* **25** F4
Benson *Ariz., U.S.A.* **109** L8
Benson *Minn., U.S.A.* **112** C6
Bent *Iran* **71** E8
Benteng *Indonesia* **63** F6
Bentinck I. *Australia* **94** B2
Bentiu *Sudan* **81** F2
Bento Gonçalves *Brazil* **127** B5
Benton *Ark., U.S.A.* **116** D8
Benton *Calif., U.S.A.* **110** H8
Benton *Ill., U.S.A.* **112** F9
Benton *Pa., U.S.A.* **115** E8
Benton Harbor *U.S.A.* **112** D10
Bentong *Malaysia* **65** L3
Bentonville *U.S.A.* **116** C7
Bentu Liben *Ethiopia* **81** F4
Benue □ *Nigeria* **83** D6
Benue ➤ *Nigeria* **83** D6
Benxi *China* **57** D12
Beo *Indonesia* **63** D7
Beograd *Serbia* **44** B4
Beograd ✈ (BEG) *Serbia* **44** C4
Beolgyo *S. Korea* **57** G14
Beoumi *Ivory C.* **82** D3
Bepan Jiang ➤ *China* **58** E6
Beppu *Japan* **55** H5
Beqa *Fiji* **91** a
Beqaa Valley = Al Biqâ
    Lebanon **74** A5
Ber Mota *India* **68** H3
Berach ➤ *India* **68** G6
Beraketa *Madag.* **89** C7
Berane *Montenegro* **44** D3
Berat *Albania* **44** F3
Berau, Teluk *Indonesia* **63** E8
Beravina *Madag.* **89** B8
Berber *Sudan* **80** D3
Berbera *Somali Rep.* **75** E4
Berbérati *C.A.R.* **84** D3
Berbice ➤ *Guyana* **124** B7
Berceto *Italy* **40** D6
Berchidda *Italy* **42** B2
Berchtesgaden *Germany* **25** H8
Berchtesgaden △ *Germany* **25** H8
Berck *France* **19** B8
Berdichev = Berdychiv
    Ukraine **23** D15
Berdsk *Russia* **52** D9
Berdyansk *Ukraine* **33** J9
Berdychiv *Ukraine* **23** D15
Berea *U.S.A.* **113** G11
Berebere *Indonesia* **63** D7
Bereda *Somali Rep.* **75** E5
Berehomet *Ukraine* **29** B10
Berehove *Ukraine* **28** B7
Bereket *Turkmenistan* **71** B7
Berekum *Ghana* **82** D4
Berenice *Egypt* **80** C4
Berens ➤ *Canada* **103** C9
Berens I. *Canada* **103** C9
Berens River *Canada* **103** C9
Beresford *U.S.A.* **112** D5
Berestechko *Ukraine* **23** C13
Bereşti *Romania* **29** D12
Beretău ➤ *Romania* **28** C6
Berettyó ➤ *Hungary* **28** D6
Berettyóújfalu *Hungary* **28** C6
Berevo Mahajanga, *Madag.* **89** B7
Berevo Toliara, *Madag.* **89** B7
Bereza = Byaroza *Belarus* **33** F3
Berezhany *Ukraine* **23** D13
Berezina = Byarezina ➤
    Belarus **23** B16
Berezivka *Ukraine* **33** J6
Berezna *Ukraine* **33** G6
Bereznik *Russia* **52** C5
Berezniki *Russia* **52** D6
Berezovo *Russia* **52** C7
Berezyne *Ukraine* **29** D14
Berga *Spain* **38** C6
Berga *Sweden* **11** G10
Bergama *Turkey* **47** B9
Bérgamo *Italy* **40** C6
Bergara *Spain* **38** B2
Bergby *Sweden* **10** D11
Berge *Norway* **10** E2
Bergedorf *Germany* **24** B6
Bergeforsen *Sweden* **10** B11
Bergen
    Mecklenburg-Vorpommern,
    Germany **24** A9
Bergen *Niedersachsen,*
    Germany **24** C5
Bergen *Neths.* **17** B4
Bergen *Norway* **8** F11
Bergen *U.S.A.* **114** C7

Bergen op Zoom *Neths.* **17** C4
Bergerac *France* **20** D4
Bergheim *Germany* **24** E2
Bergholz *Germany* **114** F4
Bergisch Gladbach *Germany* **17** D7
Bergisches Land △ *Germany* **24** E3
Bergkamen *Germany* **24** D3
Bergkvara *Sweden* **11** H10
Bergshamra *Sweden* **10** E12
Bergsjö *Sweden* **10** C11
Bergstrasse-Odenwald △
    Germany **25** F1
Bergues *France* **19** B9
Bergville *S. Africa* **89** D4
Berhala, Selat *Indonesia* **62** E2
Berhampore =
    Baharampur *India* **69** G13
Berhampur = Brahmapur
    India **67** K14
Berheci ➤ *Romania* **29** E12
Bering Sea *Pac. Oc.* **106** a
Bering Strait *Pac. Oc.* **106** a
Beringovskiy *Russia* **53** C18
Berisso *Argentina* **126** C4
Berja *Spain* **37** J8
Berkeley *U.S.A.* **110** H4
Berkner I. *Antarctica* **5** D18
Berkovitsa *Bulgaria* **44** C7
Berkshire *U.S.A.* **115** D8
Berkshire Downs *U.K.* **15** F6
Berlanga *Spain* **37** G5
Berlanga, I. *Portugal* **37** F1
Berlin *Germany* **24** C9
Berlin *Md., U.S.A.* **113** F16
Berlin *N.H., U.S.A.* **115** B13
Berlin *N.Y., U.S.A.* **115** D11
Berlin *Wis., U.S.A.* **112** D9
Berlin □ *Germany* **24** C9
Berlin L. *U.S.A.* **114** E4
Berlin Tegel ✈ (TXL)
    Germany **24** C9
Bermeja, Sierra *Spain* **37** J5
Bermejo ➤ *Formosa,*
    Argentina **126** B4
Bermejo ➤ *San Juan,*
    Argentina **126** C2
Bermejo, Paso = Uspallata,
    P. de *Argentina* **126** C2
Bermen, L. *Canada* **105** B6
Bermeo *Spain* **38** B2
Bermillo de Sayago *Spain* **36** D4
Bermuda ☑ *Atl. Oc.* **99** F13
Bern *Switz.* **25** J3
Bern □ *Switz.* **25** J3
Bernalda *Italy* **43** B9
Bernalillo *U.S.A.* **109** J10
Bernardo de Irigoyen
    Argentina **127** B5
Bernardo O'Higgins □
    Chile **126** C1
Bernardsville *U.S.A.* **115** F10
Bernasconi *Argentina* **126** D3
Bernau *Bayern, Germany* **25** H8
Bernau *Brandenburg, Germany* **24** C9
Bernay *France* **18** C7
Bernburg *Germany* **24** D7
Berndorf *Austria* **26** D9
Berne = Bern *Switz.* **25** J3
Berne = Bern □ *Switz.* **25** J3
Berner Alpen *Switz.* **25** J3
Berneray *U.K.* **13** D1
Bernier I. *Australia* **93** D1
Bernina, Piz *Switz.* **25** J5
Bernkastel-Kues *Germany* **25** F3
Beroroha *Madag.* **89** C8
Béroubouay *Benin* **83** C5
Beroun *Czech Rep.* **26** B7
Berounka ➤ *Czech Rep.* **26** B7
Berovo *Macedonia* **44** E6
Berre, Étang de *France* **21** E9
Berre-l'Étang *France* **21** E9
Berri *Australia* **95** E3
Berriane *Algeria* **78** B6
Berrigan *Australia* **95** E4
Berry *Australia* **95** E5
Berry *France* **19** F8
Berry Is. *Bahamas* **120** A4
Berryessa, L. *U.S.A.* **110** G4
Berryville *U.S.A.* **116** C8
Berseba *Namibia* **88** D2
Bersenbrück *Germany* **24** C3
Bershad *Ukraine* **29** B14
Berthold *U.S.A.* **112** A3
Berthoud *U.S.A.* **108** F11
Bertincourt *France* **19** B9
Bertoua *Cameroon* **84** D2
Bertraghboy B. *Ireland* **12** C2
Berwick *U.S.A.* **115** E8
Berwick-upon-Tweed *U.K.* **14** B6
Berwyn Mts. *U.K.* **14** E4
Beryslav *Ukraine* **33** J7
Berzasca *Romania* **28** F7
Berzence *Hungary* **28** D2
Besal *Pakistan* **69** B5
Besalampy *Madag.* **89** B7
Besançon *France* **19** E13
Besar *Indonesia* **62** E5
Beshenkovichi *Belarus* **32** E5

Beška *Serbia* **28** E5
Beslan *Russia* **35** J7
Besna Kobila *Serbia* **44** D6
Besnard L. *Canada* **103** B7
Besni *Turkey* **72** D7
Besor, ➤ *Egypt* **74** D3
Bessarabiya *Moldova* **23** E15
Bessarabka =
    Basarabeasca *Moldova* **29** D13
Bessèges *France* **21** D8
Bessemer *Ala., U.S.A.* **117** E11
Bessemer *Mich., U.S.A.* **112** B8
Bessemer *Pa., U.S.A.* **114** F4
Bessin *France* **18** C6
Bessines-sur-Gartempe
    France **20** B5
Beswick *Australia* **92** B5
Bet She'an *Israel* **74** C4
Bet Shemesh *Israel* **74** D4
Betafo *Madag.* **89** B8
Betancuria *Canary Is.* **48** F5
Betanzos *Spain* **36** B2
Bétaré Oya *Cameroon* **84** C2
Betatao *Madag.* **89** B8
Bétera *Spain* **39** F4
Bétérou *Benin* **83** D5
Bethal *S. Africa* **89** D4
Bethanien *Namibia* **88** D2
Bethany *Canada* **114** B6
Bethany *Mo., U.S.A.* **112** E6
Bethany *Okla., U.S.A.* **116** D6
Bethel *Alaska, U.S.A.* **106** a
Bethel *Conn., U.S.A.* **115** E11
Bethel *Maine, U.S.A.* **115** B14
Bethel *Vt., U.S.A.* **115** C12
Bethel Park *U.S.A.* **114** F4
Béthenville *France* **19** C11
Bethlehem = Bayt Lahm
    West Bank **74** D4
Bethlehem *S. Africa* **89** D4
Bethlehem *U.S.A.* **115** F9
Bethulie *S. Africa* **88** E4
Béthune *France* **19** B9
Béthune ➤ *France* **18** C8
Betioky *Madag.* **89** C7
Betong *Malaysia* **62** D4
Betong *Thailand* **65** K3
Betoota *Australia* **94** D3
Betor *Ethiopia* **81** E4
Betpaqdala *Kazakhstan* **52** E8
Betroka *Madag.* **89** C8
Betsiamites *Canada* **105** C6
Betsiamites ➤ *Canada* **105** C6
Betsiboka ➤ *Madag.* **89** B8
Bettendorf *U.S.A.* **112** E8
Bettiah *India* **69** F11
Bettna *Sweden* **11** F10
Béttola *Italy* **40** D6
Betul *India* **66** J10
Betws-y-Coed *U.K.* **14** D4
Betxi *Spain* **38** F4
Betzdorf *Germany* **24** E3
Beuil *France* **21** D10
Beulah *Mich., U.S.A.* **112** C10
Beulah *N. Dak., U.S.A.* **112** B3
Beuvron ➤ *France* **18** E8
Beveren *Belgium* **17** C4
Beverley *Australia* **93** F2
Beverley *U.K.* **14** D7
Beverly *U.S.A.* **115** D14
Beverly Hills *Calif., U.S.A.* **111** L8
Beverly Hills *Fla., U.S.A.* **117** G13
Beverungen *Germany* **24** D5
Bevoalavo *Madag.* **89** D7
Bewas ➤ *India* **69** H8
Bex *Switz.* **25** J3
Bexhill *U.K.* **15** G8
Bey Dağları *Turkey* **47** E12
Beyānlū *Iran* **70** C5
Beyazköy *Turkey* **45** E11
Beyçayırı *Turkey* **45** F10
Beydağ *Turkey* **47** C10
Beyeğaç *Turkey* **47** D10
Beyin *Ghana* **82** D4
Beykoz *Turkey* **45** E13
Beyla *Guinea* **82** D3
Beynat *France* **20** C5
Beyneu *Kazakhstan* **52** E6
Beyoba *Turkey* **47** C9
Beyoğlu *Turkey* **45** E12
Beypazarı *Turkey* **72** B4
Beyşehir *Turkey* **72** D4
Beyşehir Gölü *Turkey* **72** D4
Beytüşşebap *Turkey* **73** D10
Bezdan *Serbia* **28** E3
Bezhetsk *Russia* **32** D9
Béziers *France* **20** E7
Bezwada = Vijayawada
    India **67** L12
Bhabua *India* **69** G10
Bhachau *India* **66** H7
Bhadar ➤ *Gujarat, India* **68** H5
Bhadar ➤ *Gujarat, India* **68** J3
Bhadarwah *India* **69** C6
Bhadgaon = Bhaktapur
    Nepal **69** F11
Bhadohi *India* **69** G10
Bhadra *India* **68** E6

Bhadrakh *India* **67** J15
Bhadran *India* **68** H5
Bhadravati *India* **66** N9
Bhag *Pakistan* **68** E2
Bhagalpur *India* **69** G12
Bhagirathi ➤ *Uttaranchal,*
    India **69** D8
Bhagirathi ➤ *W. Bengal,*
    India **69** H13
Bhakkar *Pakistan* **68** D4
Bhakra Dam *India* **68** D7
Bhaktapur *Nepal* **69** F11
Bhamo *Burma* **67** G20
Bhandara *India* **66** J11
Bhanpura *India* **68** G6
Bhanrer Ra. *India* **69** H8
Bhaptiahi *India* **69** F12
Bharat = India ■ *Asia* **66** K11
Bharatpur *Chhattisgarh, India* **69** H9
Bharatpur *Raj., India* **68** F7
Bharno *India* **69** H10
Bharuch *India* **66** J8
Bhatinda *India* **68** D6
Bhatpara *India* **69** H13
Bhattu *India* **68** E6
Bhaun *Pakistan* **68** C5
Bhaunagar = Bhavnagar
    India **68** J8
Bhavnagar *India* **66** J8
Bhawari *India* **68** G5
Bhayavadar *India* **68** J4
Bhera *Pakistan* **68** C5
Bhikangaon *India* **68** J6
Bhilai = Bhilainagar-Durg
    India **67** J12
Bhilainagar-Durg *India* **67** J12
Bhilsa = Vidisha *India* **68** H7
Bhilwara *India* **68** G6
Bhima ➤ *India* **66** L10
Bhimbar *Pakistan* **69** C6
Bhind *India* **69** F8
Bhinga *India* **69** F9
Bhinmal *India* **68** G5
Bhisho *S. Africa* **89** E4
Bhiwandi *India* **66** K8
Bhiwani *India* **68** E6
Bhogava ➤ *India* **68** H5
Bhola *Bangla.* **67** H17
Bholari *Pakistan* **68** G3
Bhopal *India* **68** H7
Bhubaneshwar *India* **67** J14
Bhuj *India* **66** H5
Bhumiphol Res. *Thailand* **64** D2
Bhusawal *India* **66** J9
Bhutan ■ *Asia* **67** F17
Biafra, B. of = Bonny,
    Bight of *Africa* **83** E6
Biak *Indonesia* **63** E9
Biała *Poland* **31** H4
Biała ➤ *Poland* **31** H7
Biała Piska *Poland* **30** E9
Biała Podlaska *Poland* **31** F10
Biała Rawska *Poland* **31** G7
Białobrzegi *Poland* **31** G7
Białogard *Poland* **30** D2
Białowieski △ *Poland* **31** F10
Białowieża *Poland* **31** F10
Biały Bór *Poland* **30** E3
Białystok *Poland* **31** E10
Biancavilla *Italy* **43** E7
Bianco *Italy* **43** D9
Biankouma *Ivory C.* **82** D3
Biaora *India* **68** H7
Biaro *Indonesia* **63** D7
Biarritz *France* **20** E2
Bias *Indonesia* **63** J18
Biasca *Switz.* **25** J4
Biba *Egypt* **80** J7
Bibai *Japan* **54** C10
Bibbiena *Italy* **41** E8
Bibby I. *Canada* **103** A10
Bibel ➤ *Spain* **36** C3
Biberach *Germany* **25** G5
Bibiani *Ghana* **82** D4
Bibungwa
    Dem. Rep. of the Congo **86** C2
Bicaj *Albania* **44** E4
Bicaz *Romania* **29** D11
Bicazu Ardelean *Romania* **29** D10
Bíccari *Italy* **43** A8
Bicester *U.K.* **15** F6
Bichena *Ethiopia* **81** E4
Bicheno *Australia* **95** G4
Bichia *India* **69** H9
Bichvinta *Georgia* **35** J5
Bickerton I. *Australia* **94** A2
Bicske *Hungary* **28** C3
Bida *Nigeria* **83** D6
Bidar *India* **66** L10
Biddeford *U.S.A.* **113** D18
Biddwara *Ethiopia* **81** F4
Bideford *U.K.* **15** F3
Bideford Bay *U.K.* **15** F3
Bidhuna *India* **69** F8
Bidor *Malaysia* **65** K3
Bidyadanga *Australia* **92** C3
Bie *Sweden* **10** E10

Bié, Planalto de *Angola* **85** G3
Bieber *U.S.A.* **108** F3
Biebrza ➤ *Poland* **31** E9
Biebrzański △ *Poland* **30** E9
Biecz *Poland* **31** J8
Biel *Switz.* **25** H3
Bielawa *Poland* **31** H3
Bielefeld *Germany* **24** C4
Bielersee *Switz.* **25** H3
Biella *Italy* **40** C5
Bielsk Podlaski *Poland* **31** F10
Bielsko-Biała *Poland* **31** J6
Bien Hoa *Vietnam* **65** G6
Bienne = Biel *Switz.* **25** H3
Bienvenida *Spain* **37** G4
Bienville, L. *Canada* **104** A5
Bierné *France* **18** E6
Bierun *Poland* **31** H6
Bierutów *Poland* **31** G4
Biescas *Spain* **38** C4
Biese ➤ *Germany* **24** C7
Biesiesfontein *S. Africa* **88** E2
Bieszczadzki △ *Poland* **31** J9
Bietigheim-Bissingen
    Germany **25** G5
Bieżuń *Poland* **31** F6
Biferno ➤ *Italy* **41** G12
Big ➤ *Canada* **105** B8
Big B. *Canada* **105** A7
Big Bear City *U.S.A.* **111** L10
Big Bear Lake *U.S.A.* **111** L10
Big Belt Mts. *U.S.A.* **108** C8
Big Bend *Swaziland* **89** D5
Big Bend △ *U.S.A.* **116** G3
Big Blue ➤ *U.S.A.* **112** F5
Big Creek *U.S.A.* **110** H7
Big Cypress ➤ *U.S.A.* **117** H14
Big Desert *Australia* **95** F3
Big Falls *U.S.A.* **112** A7
Big Fork ➤ *U.S.A.* **112** A7
Big Horn Mts. = Bighorn
    Mts. *U.S.A.* **108** D10
Big I. *Canada* **102** A5
Big Lake *U.S.A.* **116** F4
Big Moose *U.S.A.* **115** C10
Big Muddy Cr. ➤ *U.S.A.* **108** B11
Big Pine *U.S.A.* **110** H8
Big Piney *U.S.A.* **108** E8
Big Rapids *U.S.A.* **113** D11
Big Rideau L. *Canada* **115** B8
Big River *Canada* **103** C7
Big Run *U.S.A.* **114** F6
Big Sable Pt. *U.S.A.* **112** C10
Big Salmon ➤ *Canada* **102** A2
Big Sand L. *Canada* **103** B9
Big Sandy *U.S.A.* **108** B8
Big Sandy ➤ *U.S.A.* **113** F12
Big Sandy Cr. = Sandy
    Cr. ➤ *U.S.A.* **108** F9
Big Sandy Cr. ➤ *U.S.A.* **108** G12
Big Sioux ➤ *U.S.A.* **112** D5
Big South Fork △ *U.S.A.* **117** C12
Big Spring *U.S.A.* **116** E4
Big Stone City *U.S.A.* **112** C5
Big Stone Gap *U.S.A.* **113** G12
Big Stone L. *U.S.A.* **112** C5
Big Sur *U.S.A.* **110** J5
Big Timber *U.S.A.* **108** D9
Big Trout L. *Canada* **104** B2
Big Trout Lake *Canada* **104** B2
Biğa *Turkey* **45** F11
Biga ➤ *Turkey* **45** F11
Bigadiç *Turkey* **47** B10
Biganos *France* **20** D3
Biggar *Canada* **103** C7
Biggar *U.K.* **13** F5
Bigge I. *Australia* **92** B4
Biggenden *Australia* **95** D5
Biggleswade *U.K.* **15** E7
Biggs *U.S.A.* **110** F5
Bighorn *U.S.A.* **108** C10
Bighorn ➤ *U.S.A.* **108** C10
Bighorn Canyon △ *U.S.A.* **108** D10
Bighorn L. *U.S.A.* **108** D9
Bighorn Mts. *U.S.A.* **108** D10
Bignona *Senegal* **82** C1
Bigorre *France* **20** E4
Bigstone L. *Canada* **103** C9
Biguglia, Étang de *France* **21** F13
Bigwa *Tanzania* **86** D4
Bihać *Bos.-H.* **41** D12
Bihar *India* **69** G11
Bihar □ *India* **69** G12
Biharamulo *Tanzania* **86** C3
Biharamulo △ *Tanzania* **86** C3
Bihariganj *India* **69** G12
Biharkeresztes *Hungary* **28** C6
Bihor □ *Romania* **28** D7
Bihor, Munții *Romania* **28** D7
Bijagós, Arquipélago dos
    Guinea-Biss. **82** C1
Bijaipur *India* **68** F7
Bijapur *Chhattisgarh, India* **67** K12
Bijapur *Karnataka, India* **66** L9
Bījār *Iran* **73** E12
Bijawar *India* **69** G8
Bijela *Montenegro* **44** D2
Bijeljina *Bos.-H.* **28** F4

Bijelo Polje *Montenegro* **44** C3
Bijie *China* **58** D5
Bijnor *India* **68** E8
Bikaner *India* **68** E5
Bikapur *India* **69** F10
Bikeqi *China* **56** D6
Bikfayyā *Lebanon* **74** B4
Bikin *Russia* **54** A7
Bikin ➤ *Russia* **54** A7
Bikini Atoll *Marshall Is.* **96** F8
Bikita *Zimbabwe* **89** C5
Bikoué *Cameroon* **83** E7
Bila Tserkva *Ukraine* **23** D16
Bilanga *Burkina Faso* **83** C4
Bilara *India* **68** F5
Bilaspur *Chhattisgarh, India* **69** H10
Bilaspur *Punjab, India* **68** D7
Biläsuvar *Azerbaijan* **73** C13
Bilauk Taungdan *Thailand* **64** F2
Bilbao *Spain* **38** B2
Bilbao ✈ (BIO) *Spain* **38** B2
Bilbeis *Egypt* **80** H7
Bilbo = Bilbao *Spain* **38** B2
Bilbor *Romania* **29** C10
Bilче-Zolote *Ukraine* **29** B10
Bilciureşti *Romania* **29** F10
Bíldudalur *Iceland* **8** D2
Bílé Karpaty *Europe* **27** B11
Bileća *Bos.-H.* **44** D2
Bilecik *Turkey* **72** B4
Bilecik □ *Turkey* **72** B3
Bilećko Jezero *Bos.-H.* **44** D2
Bilgoraj *Poland* **31** H9
Bilgram *India* **69** F9
Bilhaur *India* **69** F9
Bilhorod-Dnistrovskyy
    Ukraine **33** J6
Bilibino *Russia* **53** C17
Bilibiza *Mozam.* **87** E5
Bilisht *Albania* **44** F5
Billdal *Sweden* **11** G5
Billiluna *Australia* **92** C4
Billings *U.S.A.* **108** D9
Billiton Is. = Belitung
    Indonesia **62** E3
Billsta *Sweden* **10** A12
Billund *Denmark* **11** J3
Bilma *Niger* **79** E8
Bilo Gora *Croatia* **28** E2
Biloela *Australia* **94** C5
Bilohirsk *Ukraine* **33** K8
Bilopillya *Ukraine* **33** G8
Biloxi *U.S.A.* **117** F10
Bilpa Morea Claypan
    Australia **94** D3
Biltine *Chad* **79** F10
Bilyarsk *Russia* **34** C10
Bima *Indonesia* **63** F5
Bimban *Egypt* **80** C3
Bimbila *Ghana* **83** D5
Bimbo *C.A.R.* **84** D3
Bimini Is. *Bahamas* **120** A4
Bin Xian *Heilongjiang, China* **57** B14
Bin Xian *Shaanxi, China* **56** G5
Bin Yauri *Nigeria* **83** C5
Bina-Etawah *India* **68** G8
Bināb *Iran* **73** D13
Binalbagan *Phil.* **61** F5
Binalong *Australia* **95** E4
Bīnālūd, Kūh-e *Iran* **71** B8
Binatang = Bintangau
    Malaysia **62** D4
Binche *Belgium* **17** D4
Binchuan *China* **58** E3
Binder *Chad* **83** D7
Bindki *India* **69** F9
Bindslev *Denmark* **11** G4
Bindura *Zimbabwe* **87** F3
Binefar *Spain* **38** D5
Bingara *Australia* **95** D5
Bingen *Germany* **25** F3
Bingerville *Ivory C.* **82** D4
Bingham *U.S.A.* **113** C19
Binghamton *U.S.A.* **115** D9
Bingöl *Turkey* **73** C9
Bingöl □ *Turkey* **73** C9
Bingöl Dağları *Turkey* **73** C9
Bingsjö *Sweden* **10** C9
Binh Dinh = An Nhon
    Vietnam **64** F7
Binh Khe *Vietnam* **64** F7
Binh Son *Vietnam* **64** E7
Binhai *China* **57** G10
Binic *France* **18** D4
Binisatua *Spain* **48** B11
Binjai *Indonesia* **62** D1
Binji *Nigeria* **83** C5
Binnaway *Australia* **95** E4
Binongko *Indonesia* **63** F6
Binscarth *Canada* **103** C8
Binshangul Gumuz □
    Ethiopia **81** E4
Bint Goda *Sudan* **81** F3
Bintan *Indonesia* **62** D2
Bintangau *Malaysia* **62** D4
Bintulu *Malaysia* **62** D4
Bintuni *Indonesia* **63** E8
Binyang *China* **58** F7

Binz *Germany* **24** A9
Binzert = Bizerte *Tunisia* **79** A7
Binzhou *China* **57** F10
Bío Bío □ *Chile* **126** D1
Biograd na Moru *Croatia* **41** E12
Biogradska Gora △ *Montenegro* **44** D3
Bioko *Eq. Guin.* **83** E6
Biokovo *Croatia* **41** E14
Bipindi *Cameroon* **83** E7
Bir *India* **66** K9
Bir, Ras *Djibouti* **81** E5
Bîr Abu Hashim *Egypt* **80** C3
Bîr Abu Minqar *Egypt* **80** B2
Bîr Abu Muḥammad *Egypt* **74** F3
Bi'r ad Dabbāghāt *Jordan* **74** F4
Bîr Adal Deib *Sudan* **80** C4
Bi'r al Butayyihât *Jordan* **74** F4
Bi'r al Mārī *Jordan* **74** E4
Bi'r al Qattār *Jordan* **74** F4
Bîr 'Asal *Egypt* **80** B3
Bir Atrun *Sudan* **80** D2
Bîr Beiḍa *Egypt* **74** E3
Bîr Diqnash *Egypt* **80** A2
Bîr el 'Abd *Egypt* **74** D2
Bîr el Basur *Egypt* **80** B2
Bîr el Biarât *Egypt* **74** F3
Bîr el Duweidar *Egypt* **74** E1
Bîr el Garârât *Egypt* **74** D2
Bîr el Gellaz *Egypt* **80** A2
Bîr el Heisi *Egypt* **74** F3
Bîr el Jafir *Egypt* **74** E1
Bîr el Mâlḥi *Egypt* **74** E2
Bîr el Shaqqa *Egypt* **80** A2
Bîr el Thamâda *Egypt* **74** E2
Bîr Fuad *Egypt* **80** A2
Bîr Gebeil Ḥisn *Egypt* **74** E2
Bi'r Ghadîr *Syria* **74** A6
Bîr Haimur *Egypt* **80** C3
Bîr Ḥasana *Egypt* **74** E2
Bîr Hôoker *Egypt* **80** H7
Bîr Kanayis *Egypt* **80** C3
Bîr Kaseiba *Egypt* **74** D2
Bîr Kerawein *Egypt* **80** B2
Bîr Lahfân *Egypt* **74** E2
Bîr Madkûr *Egypt* **74** E1
Bîr Maql *Egypt* **80** C3
Bîr Mîneiga *Sudan* **80** C4
Bîr Misaha *Egypt* **80** C2
Bîr Mogreïn *Mauritania* **78** C3
Bîr Murr *Egypt* **80** C3
Bi'r Muṭribah *Kuwait* **70** D5
Bîr Nakheila *Egypt* **80** C3
Bîr Qaṭia *Egypt* **74** E1
Bîr Qatrani *Egypt* **80** A2
Bîr Ranga *Egypt* **80** C4
Bîr Sahara *Egypt* **80** C2
Bîr Seiyâla *Egypt* **80** B3
Bîr Shalatein *Egypt* **80** C4
Bîr Shebb *Egypt* **80** C2
Bîr Shût *Egypt* **80** C4
Bîr Terfawi *Egypt* **80** C2
Bîr Umm Qubûr *Egypt* **80** C3
Bîr Ungât *Egypt* **80** C3
Bîr Za'farâna *Egypt* **80** J8
Bîr Zeidûn *Egypt* **80** B3
Birâk *Libya* **79** C8
Biramféro *Guinea* **82** C3
Biratnagar *Nepal* **69** F12
Birawa *Dem. Rep. of the Congo* **86** C2
Birch → *Canada* **102** B6
Birch Hills *Canada* **103** C7
Birch I. *Canada* **103** C9
Birch L. N.W.T., *Canada* **102** A5
Birch L. Ont., *Canada* **104** B1
Birch Mts. *Canada* **102** B6
Birch River *Canada* **103** C8
Birchip *Australia* **95** F3
Birchiş *Romania* **28** E7
Bird *Canada* **103** B10
Bird I. = Aves, I. de *W. Indies* **121** C7
Bird I. *Antarctica* **5** B1
Birdsville *Australia* **94** D2
Birdum Cr. → *Australia* **92** C5
Birecik *Turkey* **73** D8
Birein *Israel* **74** E3
Bireuen *Indonesia* **62** C1
Biri → *Sudan* **81** F2
Birifo *Gambia* **82** C2
Birigui *Brazil* **127** A5
Bîrjand *Iran* **71** C8
Birkenfeld *Germany* **25** F3
Birkenhead *U.K.* **14** D4
Birkerød *Denmark* **11** J6
Birket Qârûn *Egypt* **80** J7
Birkfeld *Austria* **26** D8
Bîrlad = Bârlad *Romania* **29** D12
Birmingham *U.K.* **15** E6
Birmingham *U.S.A.* **117** E11
Birmingham Int. ✈ (BHX) *U.K.* **15** E6
Birmitrapur *India* **67** H14
Birni Ngaouré *Niger* **83** C5
Birni Nkonni *Niger* **83** C6
Birnin Gwari *Nigeria* **83** C6
Birnin Kebbi *Nigeria* **83** C5
Birnin Kudu *Nigeria* **83** C6

Birobidzhan *Russia* **53** E14
Birr *Ireland* **12** C4
Birrie → *Australia* **95** D4
Birsilpur *India* **68** E5
Birsk *Russia* **52** D6
Birštonas *Lithuania* **30** D11
Birtle *Canada* **103** C8
Birur *India* **66** N9
Biryuchiy *Ukraine* **33** J8
Biržai *Lithuania* **32** D3
Birzebbugga *Malta* **49** D2
Bisa *Indonesia* **63** E7
Bisáccia *Italy* **43** A8
Bisacquino *Italy* **42** E6
Bisalpur *India* **69** E8
Bisbee *U.S.A.* **109** L9
Biscarrosse *France* **20** D2
Biscarrosse et de Parentis, Étang de *France* **20** D2
Biscay, B. of *Atl. Oc.* **6** F5
Biscayne B. *U.S.A.* **117** J14
Biscéglie *Italy* **43** A9
Bischheim *France* **19** D14
Bischofshofen *Austria* **26** D6
Bischofswerda *Germany* **24** D10
Bischwiller *France* **19** D14
Biscoe Is. *Antarctica* **5** C17
Biscostaing *Canada* **104** C3
Biševo *Croatia* **41** F13
Bisha *Eritrea* **81** D4
Bishah, W. → *Si. Arabia* **80** C5
Bishan *China* **58** C6
Bishkek *Kyrgyzstan* **52** E8
Bishnupur *India* **69** H12
Bisho = Bhisho *S. Africa* **89** E4
Bishop *Calif., U.S.A.* **110** H8
Bishop *Tex., U.S.A.* **116** M6
Bishop Auckland *U.K.* **14** C6
Bishop's Falls *Canada* **105** C8
Bishop's Stortford *U.K.* **15** F8
Bisignano *Italy* **43** C9
Bisina, L. *Uganda* **86** B3
Biskra *Algeria* **78** B7
Biskupiec *Poland* **30** E7
Bismarck *U.S.A.* **112** B3
Bismarck Arch. *Papua N. G.* **90** B7
Bismark *Germany* **24** C7
Bismil *Turkey* **73** D9
Biso *Uganda* **86** B3
Bison *U.S.A.* **112** C2
Bisotûn *Iran* **73** E12
Bispgården *Sweden* **10** A10
Bissagos = Bijagós, Arquipélago dos *Guinea-Biss.* **82** C1
Bissau *Guinea-Biss.* **82** C1
Bissaula *Nigeria* **83** D7
Bissikrima *Guinea* **82** C2
Bissorã *Guinea-Biss.* **82** C1
Bistcho L. *Canada* **102** B5
Bistreţ *Romania* **29** G8
Bistrica = Ilirska-Bistrica *Slovenia* **41** C11
Bistriţa *Romania* **29** C9
Bistriţa → *Romania* **29** D11
Bistriţa Năsăud □ *Romania* **29** C9
Bistriţei, Munţii *Romania* **29** C10
Biswan *India* **69** F9
Bisztynek *Poland* **30** D7
Bitam *Gabon* **84** D2
Bitburg *Germany* **25** F2
Bitche *France* **19** C14
Bithynia *Turkey* **72** B4
Bitkine *Chad* **79** F9
Bitlis *Turkey* **73** C10
Bitlis □ *Turkey* **73** C10
Bitola *Macedonia* **44** E5
Bitolj = Bitola *Macedonia* **44** E5
Bitonto *Italy* **43** A9
Bitter Creek *U.S.A.* **108** F9
Bitter L. = Buheirat-Murrat-el-Kubra *Egypt* **80** H8
Bitterfeld *Germany* **24** D8
Bitterfontein *S. Africa* **88** E2
Bitterroot → *U.S.A.* **108** C6
Bitterroot Range *U.S.A.* **108** C6
Bitterwater *U.S.A.* **110** J6
Bitti *Italy* **42** B2
Bittou *Burkina Faso* **83** C4
Biu *Nigeria* **83** C7
Bivolari *Romania* **29** C12
Bivolu, Vf. *Romania* **29** C10
Biwa-Ko *Japan* **55** G8
Biwabik *U.S.A.* **112** B7
Bixad *Romania* **29** C8
Bixby *U.S.A.* **116** H7
Biyang *China* **56** H7
Biysk *Russia* **52** D9
Bizana *S. Africa* **89** E4
Bizen *Japan* **55** G7
Bizerte *Tunisia* **79** A7
Bjargtangar *Iceland* **8** D1
Bjärnum *Sweden* **11** H7
Bjästa *Sweden* **10** A12
Bjelašica *Montenegro* **44** D3
Bjelašnica *Bos.-H.* **28** G3
Bjelovar *Croatia* **41** C13
Bjerringbro *Denmark* **11** H3

Björbo *Sweden* **10** D8
Björklinge *Sweden* **10** D11
Björneborg = Pori *Finland* **32** B1
Björneborg *Sweden* **10** E8
Bjørnevatn *Norway* **8** B24
Bjørnøya *Arctic* **4** B8
Bjursås *Sweden* **10** D9
Bjuv *Sweden* **11** H6
Bla *Mali* **82** C3
Blace *Serbia* **44** C5
Blachownia *Poland* **31** H5
Black → *Canada* **114** B5
Black → Da → *Vietnam* **58** G5
Black → *Ariz., U.S.A.* **109** K8
Black → *Ark., U.S.A.* **116** D9
Black → *La., U.S.A.* **116** F9
Black → *Mich., U.S.A.* **114** D2
Black → *N.Y., U.S.A.* **115** C8
Black → *Wis., U.S.A.* **112** D8
Black Bay Pen. *Canada* **104** C2
Black Birch L. *Canada* **103** B7
Black Canyon of the Gunnison △ *U.S.A.* **108** G10
Black Diamond *Canada* **102** C6
Black Duck → *Canada* **104** A2
Black Forest = Schwarzwald *Germany* **25** G4
Black Forest *U.S.A.* **108** G11
Black Hd. *Ireland* **12** C2
Black Hills *U.S.A.* **112** D2
Black I. *Canada* **103** C9
Black L. *Canada* **103** B7
Black L. *Mich., U.S.A.* **113** C11
Black L. *N.Y., U.S.A.* **115** B9
Black Lake *Canada* **103** B7
Black Mesa *U.S.A.* **116** C3
Black Mt. = Mynydd Du *U.K.* **15** F4
Black Mts. *U.K.* **15** F4
Black Range *U.S.A.* **109** K10
Black River *Jamaica* **120** a
Black River Falls *U.S.A.* **112** C8
Black Rock *Barbados* **121** g
Black Sea *Eurasia* **6** G12
Black Tickle *Canada* **105** B8
Black Volta → *Africa* **82** D4
Black Warrior → *U.S.A.* **117** E11
Blackall *Australia* **94** C4
Blackball *N.Z.* **91** E3
Blackbull *Australia* **94** B3
Blackburn *U.K.* **14** D5
Blackburn with Darwen □ *U.K.* **14** D5
Blackdown Tableland △ *Australia* **94** C4
Blackfoot *U.S.A.* **108** E7
Blackfoot → *U.S.A.* **108** C7
Blackfoot Res. *U.S.A.* **108** E8
Blackpool □ *U.K.* **14** D4
Blackpool *U.K.* **14** D4
Blackpool □ *U.K.* **14** D4
Blackriver *U.S.A.* **114** B1
Blacks Harbour *Canada* **105** C6
Blacksburg *U.S.A.* **113** G13
Blacksod B. *Ireland* **12** B1
Blackstairs Mt. *Ireland* **12** D5
Blackstone *U.S.A.* **113** G14
Blackstone Ra. *Australia* **93** E4
Blacktown *Australia* **95** E5
Blackwater = West Road → *Canada* **102** C4
Blackwater *Australia* **94** C4
Blackwater → *Meath, Ireland* **12** C4
Blackwater → *Waterford, Ireland* **12** D4
Blackwater → *U.K.* **12** B5
Blackwell *U.S.A.* **116** C6
Blackwells Corner *U.S.A.* **111** K7
Bladensburg △ *Australia* **94** C3
Blaenau Ffestiniog *U.K.* **14** E4
Blaenau Gwent □ *U.K.* **15** F4
Blagaj *Bos.-H.* **44** C1
Blagnac *France* **20** E5
Blagnac, Toulouse ✈ (TLS) *France* **20** E5
Blagodarnoye = Blagodarnyy *Russia* **35** H6
Blagodarnyy *Russia* **35** H6
Blagoevgrad *Bulgaria* **44** D7
Blagoveshchensk *Russia* **53** D13
Blahkiuh *Indonesia* **63** J18
Blain *France* **18** E5
Blain *U.S.A.* **114** F7
Blaine *Minn., U.S.A.* **112** C7
Blaine *Wash., U.S.A.* **110** B4
Blaine Lake *Canada* **103** C7
Blair *U.S.A.* **112** E5
Blair Athol *Australia* **94** C4
Blair Atholl *U.K.* **13** E5
Blairgowrie *U.K.* **13** E5
Blairsden *U.S.A.* **110** F6
Blairsville *U.S.A.* **114** F5
Blaj *Romania* **29** D8
Blakang Mati, Pulau *Singapore* **65** d
Blake Pt. *U.S.A.* **112** A9
Blakely *Ga., U.S.A.* **117** F12
Blakely *Pa., U.S.A.* **115** E9
Blâmont *France* **19** D13

Blanc, C. *Spain* **48** B9
Blanc, Mont *Europe* **21** C10
Blanca, B. *Argentina* **128** D4
Blanca, C. *Australia* **95** E1
Blanca Peak *U.S.A.* **109** H11
Blanca, Cord. *Peru* **124** E3
Blanche, C. *S. Austral., Australia* **95** E1
Blanche, L. *S. Austral., Australia* **95** D2
Blanche, L. *W. Austral., Australia* **92** D3
Blanchisseuse *Trin. & Tob.* **125** K15
Blanco *S. Africa* **88** E3
Blanco *U.S.A.* **116** F5
Blanco → *Argentina* **126** C2
Blanco, C. *Costa Rica* **120** E2
Blanco, C. *U.S.A.* **108** E1
Blanda → *Iceland* **8** D3
Blandford Forum *U.K.* **15** G5
Blanding *U.S.A.* **109** H9
Blanes *Spain* **38** D7
Blangy-sur-Bresle *France* **19** C8
Blanice → *Czech Rep.* **26** B7
Blankaholm *Sweden* **11** G10
Blankenberge *Belgium* **17** C3
Blankenburg *Germany* **24** D6
Blanquefort *France* **20** D3
Blanquilla *Venezuela* **121** D7
Blanquillo *Uruguay* **127** C4
Blansko *Czech Rep.* **27** B9
Blantyre *Malawi* **87** F4
Blasdell *U.S.A.* **114** D6
Blaskaket *U.S.A.* **114** D6
Blato *Croatia* **41** F13
Blaubeuren *Germany* **25** G5
Blaustein *Germany* **25** G5
Blåvands Huk *Denmark* **11** J2
Blaydon *U.K.* **14** C6
Blaye *France* **20** C3
Blaye-les-Mines *France* **20** D6
Blayney *Australia* **95** E4
Blaze, Pt. *Australia* **92** B5
Blażowa *Poland* **31** J9
Bleckede *Germany* **24** B6
Bled *Slovenia* **41** B11
Bleiburg *Austria* **26** E8
Blejeşti *Romania* **29** F10
Blekinge *Sweden* **9** H16
Blekinge län □ *Sweden* **11** H9
Blenheim *Canada* **114** D3
Blenheim *N.Z.* **91** D4
Bléone → *France* **21** D10
Blérancourt *France* **19** C10
Bletchley *U.K.* **15** F7
Blida *Algeria* **78** A6
Blidö *Sweden* **10** E12
Blidsberg *Sweden* **11** G7
Blieskastel *Germany* **25** F3
Bligh Sound *N.Z.* **91** F1
Bligh Water *Fiji* **91** a
Blind River *Canada* **104** C3
Blinisht *Albania* **44** E3
Bliss *Idaho, U.S.A.* **108** E6
Bliss *N.Y., U.S.A.* **114** D6
Blissfield *U.S.A.* **114** F3
Blitar *Indonesia* **63** H15
Blitta *Togo* **83** D5
Block I. *U.S.A.* **115** E13
Block Island Sd. *U.S.A.* **115** E13
Blockton *Australia* **95** E3
Blockton *U.S.A.* **112** E7
Bloemfontein *S. Africa* **88** D4
Bloemhof *S. Africa* **88** D4
Blois *France* **18** E8
Blomskog *Sweden* **10** E6
Blomstermåla *Sweden* **11** H10
Blönduós *Iceland* **8** D3
Blongas *Indonesia* **63** K19
Blonie *Poland* **31** F7
Bloodvein → *Canada* **103** C9
Bloody Foreland *Ireland* **12** A3
Bloomer *U.S.A.* **112** C8
Bloomfield *Canada* **114** C7
Bloomfield *Iowa, U.S.A.* **112** E7
Bloomfield *N. Mex., U.S.A.* **109** H10
Bloomfield *Nebr., U.S.A.* **112** D5
Bloomington *Ill., U.S.A.* **112** E9
Bloomington *Ind., U.S.A.* **112** F10
Bloomington *Minn., U.S.A.* **112** C7
Bloomsburg *U.S.A.* **115** F8
Bloomsbury *Australia* **94** J6
Blora *Indonesia* **63** G14
Blossburg *U.S.A.* **114** E7
Blouberg *S. Africa* **89** C4
Blountstown *U.S.A.* **117** F12
Bludenz *Austria* **26** D2
Blue Earth *U.S.A.* **112** D6
Blue Hole △ *Belize* **120** C2
Blue Lagoon △ *Zambia* **87** F2
Blue Mesa Res. *U.S.A.* **108** G10
Blue Mountain Lake *U.S.A.* **115** C10
Blue Mountain Pk. *Jamaica* **120** a
Blue Mt. *U.S.A.* **115** F8
Blue Mts. *Jamaica* **120** a
Blue Mts. *Maine, U.S.A.* **115** B14
Blue Mts. *Oreg., U.S.A.* **108** D4
Blue Mud B. *Australia* **94** A2

Blue Nile = Nîl el Azraq → *Sudan* **81** D3
Blue Nile Falls *Ethiopia* **81** E4
Blue Rapids *U.S.A.* **112** F5
Blue Ridge *U.S.A.* **113** G13
Blue River *Canada* **102** C5
Bluefield *U.S.A.* **113** G13
Bluefields *Nic.* **120** D3
Bluff *Australia* **94** C4
Bluff *N.Z.* **91** G2
Bluff *U.S.A.* **109** H9
Bluff Knoll *Australia* **93** F2
Bluff Pt. *Australia* **93** E1
Bluffton *U.S.A.* **113** E11
Blumenau *Brazil* **127** B6
Blunt *U.S.A.* **112** C4
Bly *U.S.A.* **108** E3
Blyde River Canyon △ *S. Africa* **89** C5
Blyth *Canada* **114** C3
Blyth *U.K.* **14** B6
Blythe *U.S.A.* **111** M12
Blytheville *U.S.A.* **117** D10
Bo *S. Leone* **82** D2
Bo Duc *Vietnam* **65** G6
Bo Hai *China* **57** E10
Bo Xian = Bozhou *China* **56** H8
Boa Vista *Brazil* **124** C6
Boa Vista *C. Verde Is.* **78** b
Boac *Phil.* **61** E4
Boaco *Nic.* **120** D2
Bo'ai *China* **56** G7
Boal *Spain* **36** B4
Boalsburg *U.S.A.* **114** F7
Boane *Mozam.* **89** D5
Boardman *U.S.A.* **114** E4
Bobadah *Australia* **95** E4
Bobai *China* **58** F7
Bóbbio *Italy* **40** D6
Bobbili *India* **67** K13
Bobcaygeon *Canada* **114** B6
Böblingen *Germany* **25** G5
Bobo-Dioulasso *Burkina Faso* **82** C4
Bobolice *Poland* **30** E9
Boboshevo *Bulgaria* **44** D7
Bobov Dol *Bulgaria* **44** D6
Bóbr → *Poland* **31** F2
Bobraomby, Tanjon' i *Madag.* **89** A8
Bobrinets *Ukraine* **33** H7
Bobrov *Russia* **34** E5
Bobrovitsa *Ukraine* **33** G6
Bobruysk = Babruysk *Belarus* **23** B15
Boby, Pic *Madag.* **85** J9
Boca de Drago *Venezuela* **125** K15
Boca del Río *Mexico* **119** D5
Bôca do Acre *Brazil* **124** E5
Boca Raton *U.S.A.* **117** H14
Bocanda *Ivory C.* **82** D4
Bocas del Toro *Panama* **120** E3
Boceguillas *Spain* **36** D7
Bochmanivka *Ukraine* **29** C14
Bochnia *Poland* **31** J7
Bocholt *Germany* **24** D2
Bochum *Germany* **24** D3
Bockenem *Germany* **24** C6
Bočki *Poland* **31** F10
Bocognano *France* **21** F13
Bocoyna *Mexico* **118** B3
Bocşa *Romania* **28** E6
Boda *Dalarna, Sweden* **10** C9
Böda *Kalmar, Sweden* **11** G11
Boda *Västernorrland, Sweden* **10** B10
Bodafors *Sweden* **11** G8
Bodaybo *Russia* **53** D12
Boddam *U.K.* **13** B7
Boddington *Australia* **93** F2
Bode Sadu *Nigeria* **83** D5
Bodega Bay *U.S.A.* **110** G3
Boden *Sweden* **8** D19
Bodenteich *Germany* **24** C6
Bodhan *India* **66** K10
Bodinga *Nigeria* **83** C6
Bodmin *U.K.* **15** G3
Bodmin Moor *U.K.* **15** G3
Bodø *Norway* **8** C16
Bodrog → *Hungary* **28** B6
Bodrum *Turkey* **47** D9
Bódva → *Hungary* **28** B5
Boën *France* **21** C8
Boende *Dem. Rep. of the Congo* **84** E4
Boerne *U.S.A.* **116** G5
Boesmans → *S. Africa* **88** E4
Boffa *Guinea* **82** C2
Bogalusa *U.S.A.* **117** F10
Bogan → *Australia* **95** D4
Bogan Gate *Australia* **95** E4
Bogandé *Burkina Faso* **83** C4
Bogantungan *Australia* **94** C4
Bogata *U.S.A.* **116** E7
Bogatić *Serbia* **44** B3
Boğazkale *Turkey* **72** B6
Boğazlıyan *Turkey* **72** C6
Bogen *Sweden* **10** D6
Bogense *Denmark* **11** J4
Bogetići *Montenegro* **44** D2

Boggabilla *Australia* **95** D5
Boggabri *Australia* **95** E5
Boggeragh Mts. *Ireland* **12** D3
Boglan = Solhan *Turkey* **73** C9
Bognor Regis *U.K.* **15** G7
Bogo *Phil.* **61** F6
Bogodukhov = Bohodukhiv *Ukraine* **33** G8
Bogol Manya *Ethiopia* **81** G5
Bogong, Mt. *Australia* **95** F4
Bogor *Indonesia* **63** G12
Bogoroditsk *Russia* **32** F10
Bogorodsk *Russia* **34** B6
Bogoso *Ghana* **82** D4
Bogotá *Colombia* **124** C4
Bogotol *Russia* **52** D9
Bogou *Togo* **83** C5
Bogra *Bangla.* **67** G16
Boguchany *Russia* **53** D10
Boguchar *Russia* **34** F5
Bogué *Mauritania* **82** B2
Boguslav *Ukraine* **33** H6
Boguszów-Gorce *Poland* **31** H3
Bohain-en-Vermandois *France* **19** C10
Bohdan *Ukraine* **29** B9
Bohemian Forest = Böhmerwald *Germany* **25** F9
Bohinjska Bistrica *Slovenia* **41** B11
Böhmerwald *Germany* **25** F9
Bohmte *Germany* **24** C4
Bohodukhiv *Ukraine* **33** G8
Bohol □ *Phil.* **61** G6
Bohol Sea *Phil.* **63** C6
Bohongou *Burkina Faso* **83** C5
Böhönye *Hungary* **28** D2
Bohorodchany *Ukraine* **29** B9
Bohuslän *Sweden* **11** F5
Boi *Nigeria* **83** D6
Boi, Pta. de *Brazil* **127** A6
Boiaçu *Brazil* **124** D6
Boileau, C. *Australia* **92** C3
Boing'o *Sudan* **81** F3
Boiro *Spain* **36** C2
Boise *U.S.A.* **108** E5
Boise City *U.S.A.* **116** C3
Boissevain *Canada* **103** D8
Bóite → *Italy* **41** B9
Boitzenburg *Germany* **24** B9
Boizenburg *Germany* **24** B6
Bojador, C. *W. Sahara* **78** C3
Bojana → *Albania* **44** E3
Bojano *Italy* **43** A7
Bojanowo *Poland* **31** G3
Bøjden *Denmark* **11** J4
Bojnûrd *Iran* **71** B8
Bojonegoro *Indonesia* **63** G14
Boju *Nigeria* **83** D6
Boka *Serbia* **28** E5
Boka Kotorska *Montenegro* **44** D2
Bokala *Ivory C.* **82** D4
Bokani *Nigeria* **83** D6
Bokaro *India* **69** H11
Boké *Guinea* **82** C2
Bokhara → *Australia* **95** D4
Bokkos *Nigeria* **83** D6
Boknafjorden *Norway* **9** G11
Bokora → *Uganda* **86** B3
Bokoro *Chad* **79** F9
Bokpyin *Burma* **65** G2
Boksitogorsk *Russia* **32** C7
Bokungu *Dem. Rep. of the Congo* **84** E4
Bol *Croatia* **41** E13
Bolama *Guinea-Biss.* **82** C1
Bolan → *Pakistan* **68** E2
Bolan Pass *Pakistan* **68** E2
Bolaños → *Mexico* **118** C4
Bolaños de Calatrava *Spain* **37** G7
Bolayır *Turkey* **45** F10
Bolbec *France* **18** C7
Boldājī *Iran* **71** D6
Boldeşti-Scăeni *Romania* **29** E11
Bole *China* **60** B3
Bole *Ethiopia* **81** F4
Bole *Ghana* **82** D4
Bolekhiv *Ukraine* **23** D12
Bolesławiec *Poland* **31** G2
Bolgatanga *Ghana* **83** C4
Bolgrad = Bolhrad *Ukraine* **29** E13
Bolhrad *Ukraine* **29** E13
Bolinao *Phil.* **61** C3
Bolintin-Vale *Romania* **29** F10
Bolívar *Argentina* **126** D3
Bolivar *Mo., U.S.A.* **112** G7
Bolivar *N.Y., U.S.A.* **114** D6
Bolivar *Tenn., U.S.A.* **117** D10
Bolivia ■ *S. Amer.* **124** G6
Bolivian Plateau = Altiplano *Bolivia* **124** G5
Boljevac *Serbia* **44** C5
Bolkhov *Russia* **32** F9
Bolków *Poland* **31** H3
Bollebygd *Sweden* **11** G6
Bollène *France* **21** D8
Bollnäs *Sweden* **10** C10
Bollon *Australia* **95** D4
Bollstabruk *Sweden* **10** B11

Bolmen *Sweden* 11 H7
Bolobo *Dem. Rep. of the Congo* 84 E3
Bologna *Italy* 41 D8
Bologna ✈ (BLQ) *Italy* 41 D8
Bologoye *Russia* 32 D8
Bolomba
  Dem. Rep. of the Congo 84 D3
Bolon, Ozero *Russia* 60 B8
Bolonchén *Mexico* 119 D7
Bolótana *Italy* 42 B1
Boloven, Cao Nguyen *Laos* 64 E6
Bolpur *India* 69 H12
Bolsena *Italy* 41 F8
Bolsena, L. di *Italy* 41 F8
Bolshakovo *Russia* 30 D8
Bolshaya Chernigovka
  Russia 34 D10
Bolshaya Glushitsa *Russia* 34 D10
Bolshaya Martynovka
  Russia 35 G5
Bolshaya Vradiyevka
  Ukraine 33 J6
Bolshevik, Ostrov *Russia* 53 B11
Bolshoy Anyuy → *Russia* 53 C17
Bolshoy Begichev, Ostrov
  Russia 53 B12
Bolshoy Kavkaz =
  Caucasus Mountains
  Eurasia 35 J7
Bolshoy Lyakhovskiy,
  Ostrov *Russia* 53 B15
Bolshoy Tyuters, Ostrov
  Russia 32 C4
Bolsward *Neths.* 17 A5
Bolt Head *U.K.* 15 G4
Boltaña *Spain* 38 C5
Boltigen *Switz.* 25 J3
Bolton *Canada* 114 C5
Bolton *U.K.* 14 D5
Bolton Landing *U.S.A.* 115 C11
Bolu *Turkey* 72 B4
Bolu □ *Turkey* 72 B4
Bolungavík *Iceland* 8 C2
Boluo *China* 59 F10
Bolvadin *Turkey* 72 C4
Bolzano *Italy* 41 B8
Bom Jesus da Lapa *Brazil* 125 F10
Boma *Dem. Rep. of the Congo* 84 F2
Bombala *Australia* 95 F4
Bombarral *Portugal* 37 F1
Bombay = Mumbai *India* 66 K8
Bombedor, Pta. *Venezuela* 125 L15
Bomboma
  Dem. Rep. of the Congo 84 D3
Bombombwa
  Dem. Rep. of the Congo 86 B2
Bomi Hills *Liberia* 82 D2
Bomili *Dem. Rep. of the Congo* 86 B2
Bømlo *Norway* 9 G11
Bomokandi →
  Dem. Rep. of the Congo 86 B2
Bomu → *C.A.R.* 84 D4
Bon, C. *Tunisia* 76 C5
Bon Acceuil *Mauritius* 85 d
Bon Sar Pa *Vietnam* 64 F6
Bonāb *Iran* 73 D12
Bonaigarh *India* 69 J11
Bonaire *Neth. Ant.* 121 D6
Bonampak *Mexico* 119 D6
Bonang *Australia* 95 F4
Bonanza *Nic.* 120 D3
Bonaparte Arch. *Australia* 92 B3
Boñar *Spain* 36 C5
Bonar Bridge *U.K.* 13 D4
Bonasse *Trin. & Tob.* 125 K15
Bonaventure *Canada* 105 C6
Bonavista *Canada* 105 C9
Bonavista, C. *Canada* 105 C9
Bonavista B. *Canada* 105 C9
Bondeno *Italy* 41 D8
Bondo *Dem. Rep. of the Congo* 86 B2
Bondoukou *Ivory C.* 82 D4
Bondowoso *Indonesia* 63 G15
Bone, Teluk *Indonesia* 63 E6
Bonerate *Indonesia* 63 F6
Bonerate, Kepulauan
  Indonesia 63 F6
Bo'ness *U.K.* 13 E5
Bonete, Cerro *Argentina* 126 B2
Bong Son = Hoai Nhon
  Vietnam 64 E7
Bonga *Ethiopia* 81 F4
Bongabong *Phil.* 61 E4
Bongandanga
  Dem. Rep. of the Congo 84 D4
Bongor *Chad* 79 F9
Bongos, Massif des *C.A.R.* 84 C4
Bongouanou *Ivory C.* 82 D4
Bonham *U.S.A.* 116 E6
Boni *Mali* 82 B4
Boni △ *Kenya* 86 C5
Bonifacio *France* 21 G13
Bonifacio, Bouches de
  Medit. S. 42 A2
Bonin Is. = Ogasawara
  Gunto *Pac. Oc.* 96 E6
Bonke *Ethiopia* 81 F4
Bonkoukou *Niger* 83 C5

Bonn *Germany* 24 E3
Bonnat *France* 19 F8
Bonne Terre *U.S.A.* 112 G8
Bonners Ferry *U.S.A.* 108 B5
Bonnétable *France* 18 D7
Bonneval *France* 21 C11
Bonneval-sur-Arc *France* 18 D8
Bonneville *France* 19 F13
Bonney, L. *Australia* 95 F3
Bonnie Rock *Australia* 93 F2
Bonny *Nigeria* 83 E6
Bonny → *Nigeria* 83 E6
Bonny, Bight of *Africa* 83 E6
Bonny-sur-Loire *France* 19 E9
Bonnyrigg *U.K.* 13 F5
Bonnyville *Canada* 103 C6
Bono *Italy* 42 B2
Bonoi *Indonesia* 63 E9
Bonorva *Italy* 42 B1
Bonsall *U.S.A.* 111 M9
Bontang *Indonesia* 62 D5
Bontebok △ *S. Africa* 88 E3
Bonthe *S. Leone* 82 D2
Bontoc *Phil.* 61 C4
Bonyeri *Ghana* 82 D4
Bonyhád *Hungary* 28 D3
Bonython Ra. *Australia* 92 D4
Bookabie *Australia* 93 F5
Booker *U.S.A.* 116 C4
Boola *Guinea* 82 D3
Booligal *Australia* 95 E3
Boonah *Australia* 95 D5
Boone *Iowa, U.S.A.* 112 D7
Boone *N.C., U.S.A.* 117 C14
Booneville *Ark., U.S.A.* 116 D8
Booneville *Miss., U.S.A.* 117 D10
Boonville *Calif., U.S.A.* 110 F3
Boonville *Ind., U.S.A.* 112 F10
Boonville *Mo., U.S.A.* 112 F7
Boonville *N.Y., U.S.A.* 115 C9
Boorabbin △ *Australia* 93 F3
Boorindal *Australia* 95 E4
Boorowa *Australia* 95 E4
Boosaaso = Bosaso
  Somali Rep. 75 E4
Boothia, Gulf of *Canada* 101 B11
Boothia Pen. *Canada* 100 B10
Bootle *U.K.* 14 D4
Booué *Gabon* 84 E2
Boppard *Germany* 25 E3
Boquete *Panama* 120 E3
Boquilla, Presa de la *Mexico* 118 B3
Boquillas del Carmen
  Mexico 118 B4
Bor *Czech Rep.* 26 B5
Bor *Russia* 34 B7
Bor *Serbia* 44 B6
Bôr *Sudan* 81 F3
Bor *Sweden* 11 G8
Bor *Turkey* 72 D6
Bor Mashash *Israel* 74 D3
Bora Bora *French Polynesia* 97 J12
Borah Peak *U.S.A.* 108 D7
Borang *Sudan* 81 G3
Borås *Sweden* 11 G6
Borāzjān *Iran* 71 D6
Borba *Brazil* 124 D7
Borba *Portugal* 37 G3
Borborema, Planalto da
  Brazil 122 D7
Borcea *Romania* 29 F12
Borçka *Turkey* 73 B9
Bord Khūn-e Now *Iran* 71 D6
Borda, C. *Australia* 95 F2
Bordeaux *France* 20 D3
Bordeaux ✈ (BOD) *France* 20 D3
Borden *Australia* 93 F2
Borden-Carleton *Canada* 105 C7
Borden I. *Canada* 101 B8
Borden Pen. *Canada* 101 B11
Border Ranges △ *Australia* 95 D5
Borders = Scottish
  Borders □ *U.K.* 13 F6
Bordertown *Australia* 95 F3
Borðeyri *Iceland* 8 D3
Bordighera *Italy* 40 E4
Bordj Fly Ste. Marie *Algeria* 78 C5
Bordj-in-Eker *Algeria* 78 D7
Bordj Omar Driss *Algeria* 78 C7
Bore *Ethiopia* 81 G4
Borehamwood *U.K.* 15 F7
Borek Wielkopolski *Poland* 31 G4
Borensberg *Sweden* 11 F9
Borgå = Porvoo *Finland* 32 B3
Borgarfjörður *Iceland* 8 D7
Borgarnes *Iceland* 8 D3
Børgefjellet *Norway* 8 D15
Borger *Neths.* 17 B6
Borger *U.S.A.* 116 D4
Borgholm *Sweden* 11 H10
Bórgia *Italy* 43 D9
Borgo San Dalmazzo *Italy* 40 D4
Borgo San Lorenzo *Italy* 41 E8
Borgo Val di Taro *Italy* 40 D6
Borgo Valsugana *Italy* 41 B8
Borgomanero *Italy* 40 C5
Borgorose *Italy* 41 F10
Borgosésia *Italy* 40 C5

Borhoyn Tal *Mongolia* 56 C6
Bori *Nigeria* 83 E6
Borikhane *Laos* 64 C4
Borisoglebsk *Russia* 34 E6
Borisov = Barysaw *Belarus* 23 A15
Borisovka *Russia* 33 G9
Borja *Peru* 124 D3
Borja *Spain* 38 D3
Borjas Blancas = Les
  Borges Blanques *Spain* 38 D5
Borjomi *Georgia* 35 K6
Børkop *Denmark* 11 J3
Borkou *Chad* 79 E9
Borkum *Germany* 24 B2
Borlänge *Sweden* 10 D9
Borley, C. *Antarctica* 5 C5
Borlu *Turkey* 47 C10
Bormida → *Italy* 40 D5
Bórmio *Italy* 40 B7
Borna *Germany* 24 D8
Borne *Neths.* 17 B6
Borne Sulinowo *Poland* 30 E3
Borneo *E. Indies* 62 D5
Bornholm *Denmark* 11 J8
Bornholmsgattet *Europe* 11 J8
Borno □ *Nigeria* 83 C7
Bornos *Spain* 37 J5
Bornova *Turkey* 47 C9
Bornu Yassa *Nigeria* 83 C7
Boro → *Sudan* 81 F2
Borodino *Russia* 32 E8
Borodino *Ukraine* 29 D14
Borogontsy *Russia* 53 C14
Boromo *Burkina Faso* 82 C4
Boron *U.S.A.* 111 L9
Borongan *Phil.* 61 F6
Borotangba Mts. *C.A.R.* 81 F2
Borotou *Ivory C.* 82 D3
Borovan *Bulgaria* 44 C7
Borovichi *Russia* 32 C7
Borovsk *Russia* 32 E9
Borrby *Sweden* 11 J8
Borrego Springs *U.S.A.* 111 M10
Borriol *Spain* 38 E4
Borrisokane *Ireland* 12 D3
Borroloola *Australia* 94 B2
Borşa *Cluj, Romania* 29 D8
Borşa *Maramureş, Romania* 29 C9
Borsad *India* 68 H5
Borsec *Romania* 29 D10
Borshchiv *Ukraine* 29 B11
Borsod-Abaúj-Zemplén □
  Hungary 28 B6
Bort-les-Orgues *France* 20 C6
Borth *U.K.* 15 E3
Börtnan *Sweden* 10 B7
Borūjerd *Iran* 73 F13
Boryeong *S. Korea* 57 F14
Borynya *Ukraine* 31 J10
Boryslav *Ukraine* 31 J10
Boryspil *Ukraine* 33 G6
Borzhomi = Borjomi *Georgia* 35 K6
Borzna *Ukraine* 33 G7
Borzya *Russia* 53 D12
Bosa *Italy* 42 B1
Bosanska Dubica *Bos.-H.* 41 C13
Bosanska Gradiška *Bos.-H.* 28 E2
Bosanska Kostajnica
  Bos.-H. 41 C13
Bosanska Krupa *Bos.-H.* 41 D13
Bosanski Brod *Bos.-H.* 28 E2
Bosanski Novi *Bos.-H.* 41 C13
Bosanski Petrovac *Bos.-H.* 41 D13
Bosanski Šamac *Bos.-H.* 28 E3
Bosansko Grahovo *Bos.-H.* 41 D13
Bosaso *Somali Rep.* 75 E4
Boscastle *U.K.* 15 G3
Boscobelle *Barbados* 121 g
Bose *China* 58 F6
Boseong *S. Korea* 57 G14
Boshan *China* 57 F9
Boshof *S. Africa* 88 D4
Boshrūyeh *Iran* 71 C8
Bosilegrad *Serbia* 44 D6
Boskovice *Czech Rep.* 27 B9
Bosna → *Bos.-H.* 28 E3
Bosna i Hercegovina =
  Bosnia-Herzegovina ■
  Europe 28 G2
Bosnia-Herzegovina ■
  Europe 28 G2
Bosnik *Indonesia* 63 E9
Bosobolo
  Dem. Rep. of the Congo 84 D3
Bosporus = İstanbul
  Boğazı *Turkey* 45 E13
Bossangoa *C.A.R.* 84 C3
Bossé Bangou *Niger* 83 C5
Bossier City *U.S.A.* 116 E8
Bosso *Niger* 83 C7
Bosso, Dallol → *Niger* 83 C5
Bostan *Pakistan* 68 D2
Bostānābād *Iran* 73 D12
Bosten Hu *China* 60 B3
Boston *U.K.* 14 E7
Boston *U.S.A.* 115 D13
Boston Bar *Canada* 102 D4
Boston Mts. *U.S.A.* 116 D8

Bosumtwi, L. *Ghana* 83 D4
Bosut → *Croatia* 28 E3
Boswell *Canada* 102 D5
Boswell *U.S.A.* 114 F5
Botad *India* 68 H4
Botan → *Turkey* 73 D10
Botany B. *Australia* 90 E8
Botene *Laos* 64 D3
Botev *Bulgaria* 45 D8
Botevgrad *Bulgaria* 44 D7
Bothaville *S. Africa* 88 D4
Bothnia, G. of *Europe* 8 F19
Bothwell *Australia* 95 G4
Bothwell *Canada* 114 D3
Boticas *Portugal* 36 D3
Botletle → *Botswana* 88 C3
Botlikh *Russia* 35 J8
Botna → *Moldova* 29 D14
Botoroaga *Romania* 29 F10
Botoşani *Romania* 29 C11
Botoşani □ *Romania* 29 C11
Botou *Burkina Faso* 83 C5
Botricello *Italy* 43 D9
Botro *Ivory C.* 82 D3
Botshabelo *S. Africa* 85 K5
Botswana ■ *Africa* 88 C3
Bottineau *U.S.A.* 112 A3
Bottnaryd *Sweden* 11 G7
Bottrop *Germany* 17 C6
Botucatu *Brazil* 127 A6
Botwood *Canada* 105 C8
Bou Djébéha *Mali* 82 B4
Boû Rjeïmât *Mauritania* 82 B1
Bou Saâda *Algeria* 78 A6
Bouaflé *Ivory C.* 82 D3
Bouaké *Ivory C.* 82 D3
Bouar *C.A.R.* 84 C3
Bouârfa *Morocco* 78 B5
Boucaut B. *Australia* 94 A1
Bouches-du-Rhône □ *France* 21 E9
Boucle de Baoule △ *Mali* 82 C3
Boucles de la Seine
  Normande △ *France* 18 C7
Bouctouche *Canada* 105 C7
Bougainville, C. *Australia* 92 B4
Bougainville I. *Papua N. G.* 90 B8
Bougainville Reef *Australia* 94 B4
Bougie = Bejaïa *Algeria* 78 A7
Bougouni *Mali* 82 C3
Bouillon *Belgium* 17 E5
Boukombé *Benin* 83 C5
Boulal *Mali* 82 B3
Boulazac *France* 20 C4
Boulder *Colo., U.S.A.* 108 F11
Boulder *Mont., U.S.A.* 108 C7
Boulder City *U.S.A.* 111 K12
Boulder Creek *U.S.A.* 110 H4
Boulder Dam = Hoover
  Dam *U.S.A.* 111 K12
Bouli *Mauritania* 82 B2
Boulia *Australia* 94 C2
Bouligny *France* 19 C12
Boulogne → *France* 18 E5
Boulogne-sur-Gesse *France* 20 E4
Boulogne-sur-Mer *France* 19 B8
Bouloire *France* 18 E7
Boulouli *Mali* 82 B3
Boulsa *Burkina Faso* 83 C4
Boultoum *Niger* 83 C7
Bouma △ *Fiji* 91 a
Boûmdeïd *Mauritania* 82 B2
Boun Neua *Laos* 64 B3
Boun Tai *Laos* 64 B3
Bouna *Ivory C.* 82 D4
Boundary Peak *U.S.A.* 110 H8
Boundiali *Ivory C.* 82 D3
Bountiful *U.S.A.* 108 F8
Bounty Is. *Pac. Oc.* 96 M9
Bounty Trough *Pac. Oc.* 96 M9
Boura *Mali* 82 C4
Bourbon-Lancy *France* 19 F10
Bourbon-l'Archambault
  France 19 F10
Bourbonnais *France* 19 F10
Bourbonne-les-Bains
  France 19 E12
Bourbourg *France* 19 B9
Bourdel L. *Canada* 104 A5
Bourem *Mali* 83 B4
Bourg *France* 20 C3
Bourg-Argental *France* 21 C8
Bourgas = Burgas *Bulgaria* 45 D11
Bourges *France* 19 E9
Bourg-de-Péage *France* 21 C9
Bourg-en-Bresse *France* 19 F12
Bourg-Lastic *France* 20 C6
Bourg-Madame *France* 20 F5
Bourg-St-Andéol *France* 21 D8
Bourg-St-Maurice *France* 21 C10
Bourganeuf *France* 20 C5
Bourgneuf, B. de *France* 18 E4
Bourgneuf-en-Retz *France* 18 E5
Bourgogne *France* 19 F11
Bourgoin-Jallieu *France* 21 C9
Bourgueil *France* 18 E7
Bourke *Australia* 95 E4

Bourne *U.K.* 14 E7
Bournemouth *U.K.* 15 G6
Bournemouth □ *U.K.* 15 G6
Bouroum *Burkina Faso* 83 C4
Bouse *U.S.A.* 111 M13
Boussac *France* 19 F9
Boussé *Burkina Faso* 83 C4
Bousso *Chad* 79 F9
Boussouma *Burkina Faso* 83 C4
Boutilimit *Mauritania* 82 B2
Boutonne → *France* 20 C3
Bouvet I. = Bouvetøya
  Antarctica 2 G10
Bouvetøya *Antarctica* 2 G10
Bouxwiller *France* 19 D14
Bouza *Niger* 83 C6
Bouzonville *France* 19 C13
Bova Marina *Italy* 43 E8
Bovalino Marina *Italy* 43 D9
Bovec *Slovenia* 41 B10
Bovill *U.S.A.* 108 C5
Bovino *Italy* 43 A8
Bovril *Argentina* 126 C4
Bow → *Canada* 102 C6
Bow Island *Canada* 108 B8
Bowbells *U.S.A.* 112 A2
Bowdle *U.S.A.* 112 C4
Bowelling *Australia* 93 F2
Bowen *Argentina* 126 D2
Bowen *Australia* 94 J6
Bowen Mts. *Australia* 95 F4
Bowers Basin *Pac. Oc.* 4 D16
Bowers Ridge *Pac. Oc.* 4 D17
Bowie *Ariz., U.S.A.* 109 K9
Bowie *Tex., U.S.A.* 116 E6
Bowland, Forest of *U.K.* 14 D5
Bowling Green *Ky., U.S.A.* 112 G10
Bowling Green *Ohio, U.S.A.*
  113 E12
Bowling Green, C. *Australia* 94 B4
Bowling Green Bay △
  Australia 94 B4
Bowman *U.S.A.* 112 B2
Bowman I. *Antarctica* 5 C8
Bowmanville = Clarington
  Canada 114 C6
Bowmore *U.K.* 13 F2
Bowral *Australia* 95 E5
Bowraville *Australia* 95 E5
Bowron → *Canada* 102 C4
Bowron Lake △ *Canada* 102 C4
Bowser L. *Canada* 102 B3
Bowsman *Canada* 103 C8
Bowwood *Zambia* 87 F2
Box Cr. → *Australia* 95 E3
Boxholm *Sweden* 11 F9
Boxmeer *Neths.* 17 C5
Boxtel *Neths.* 17 C5
Boyabat *Turkey* 72 B6
Boyalıca *Turkey* 45 F13
Boyang *China* 59 C11
Boyani *Ukraine* 29 B11
Boyce *U.S.A.* 116 F8
Boyd L. *Canada* 104 B4
Boyle *Canada* 102 C6
Boyle *Ireland* 12 C3
Boyne → *Ireland* 12 C5
Boyne City *U.S.A.* 113 C11
Boynitsa *Bulgaria* 44 C6
Boynton Beach *U.S.A.* 117 H14
Boyolali *Indonesia* 63 G14
Boyoma, Chutes
  Dem. Rep. of the Congo 86 B2
Boysen Res. *U.S.A.* 108 E9
Boyuibe *Bolivia* 124 G6
Boyup Brook *Australia* 93 F2
Boz Burun *Turkey* 45 F12
Boz Dağ *Turkey* 47 D11
Boz Dağları *Turkey* 47 C10
Bozburun *Turkey* 47 E10
Bozcaada *Turkey* 72 C2
Bozdoğan *Turkey* 47 D10
Bozeman *U.S.A.* 108 D8
Bozen = Bolzano *Italy* 41 B8
Boževac *Serbia* 44 B5
Bozhou *China* 56 H8
Bozkır *Turkey* 72 D5
Bozkurt *Turkey* 47 D11
Bozouls *France* 20 D6
Bozoum *C.A.R.* 84 C3
Bozova *Antalya, Turkey* 47 D12
Bozova *Sanlıurfa, Turkey* 73 D8
Bozovici *Romania* 28 F7
Bozüyük *Turkey* 47 B12
Bra *Italy* 40 D4
Braås *Sweden* 11 G9
Brabant □ *Belgium* 17 C4
Brabant L. *Canada* 103 B8
Brabrand *Denmark* 11 H4
Brač *Croatia* 41 E13
Bracadale, L. *U.K.* 13 D2
Bracciano *Italy* 41 F9
Bracciano, L. di *Italy* 41 F9
Bracebridge *Canada* 114 A5
Bracieux *France* 18 E8
Bräcke *Sweden* 10 B9
Brackettville *U.S.A.* 116 G4
Bracki Kanal *Croatia* 41 E13

Bracknell *U.K.* 15 F7
Bracknell Forest □ *U.K.* 15 F7
Brad *Romania* 28 D7
Brádano → *Italy* 43 B9
Bradenton *U.S.A.* 117 H13
Bradford *Canada* 114 B5
Bradford *U.K.* 14 D6
Bradford *Pa., U.S.A.* 114 E6
Bradford *Vt., U.S.A.* 115 C12
Bradley *Ark., U.S.A.* 116 E8
Bradley *Calif., U.S.A.* 110 K6
Bradley Institute *Zimbabwe* 87 F3
Brady *U.S.A.* 116 F5
Brædstrup *Denmark* 11 J3
Braeside *Canada* 115 A8
Braga *Portugal* 36 D2
Braga □ *Portugal* 36 D2
Bragadiru *Romania* 29 G10
Bragado *Argentina* 126 D3
Bragança *Brazil* 125 D9
Bragança *Portugal* 36 D4
Bragança □ *Portugal* 36 D4
Bragança Paulista *Brazil* 127 A6
Brahestad = Raahe *Finland* 8 D21
Brahmanbaria *Bangla.* 67 H17
Brahmani → *India* 67 J15
Brahmapur *India* 67 K14
Brahmaputra → *Asia* 69 H13
Braich-y-pwll *U.K.* 14 E3
Braidwood *Australia* 95 F4
Brăila *Romania* 29 E12
Brăila □ *Romania* 29 E12
Brainerd *U.S.A.* 112 B6
Braintree *U.K.* 15 F8
Braintree *U.S.A.* 115 D14
Brak → *S. Africa* 88 D3
Brake *Germany* 24 B4
Brakel *Germany* 24 D5
Brakna □ *Mauritania* 82 B2
Bräkne-Hoby *Sweden* 11 H9
Brakwater *Namibia* 88 C2
Brålanda *Sweden* 11 F6
Bramberg *Germany* 25 E6
Bramdrupdam *Denmark* 11 J3
Bramming *Denmark* 11 J2
Brämön *Sweden* 10 B11
Brampton *Canada* 114 C5
Brampton *U.K.* 14 C5
Bramsche *Germany* 24 C3
Bramton I. *Australia* 94 J7
Branco → *Brazil* 124 D6
Brandberg *Namibia* 88 C1
Brandberg △ *Namibia* 88 C1
Brande *Denmark* 11 J3
Brandenburg =
  Neubrandenburg
  Germany 24 B9
Brandenburg *Germany* 24 C8
Brandenburg □ *Germany* 24 C9
Brandfort *S. Africa* 88 D4
Brando *France* 21 F13
Brandon *Canada* 103 D9
Brandon *U.S.A.* 115 C11
Brandon B. *Ireland* 12 D1
Brandon Mt. *Ireland* 12 D1
Brandsen *Argentina* 126 D4
Brandvlei *S. Africa* 88 E3
Brandýs nad Labem
  Czech Rep. 26 A7
Brănești *Romania* 29 F11
Branford *U.S.A.* 115 E12
Braniewo *Poland* 30 D6
Bransfield Str. *Antarctica* 5 C18
Brańsk *Poland* 31 F9
Branson *U.S.A.* 112 G7
Brantford *Canada* 114 C4
Brantôme *France* 20 C4
Branzi *Italy* 40 B6
Bras d'Or L. *Canada* 105 C7
Brasher Falls *U.S.A.* 115 B10
Brasil = Brazil ■ *S. Amer.* 125 F9
Brasil, Planalto *Brazil* 122 E6
Brasiléia *Brazil* 124 F5
Brasília *Brazil* 125 G9
Brasília Legal *Brazil* 125 D7
Braslaw *Belarus* 32 E4
Braslovče *Slovenia* 41 B12
Braşov *Romania* 29 E10
Braşov □ *Romania* 29 E10
Brass *Nigeria* 83 E6
Brass → *Nigeria* 83 E6
Brassac-les-Mines *France* 20 C7
Brasschaat *Belgium* 17 C4
Brassey, Banjaran *Malaysia* 62 D5
Brassey Ra. *Australia* 93 E3
Brasstown Bald *U.S.A.* 117 D13
Brastad *Sweden* 11 F5
Brastavățu *Romania* 29 G9
Bratan = Morozov *Bulgaria* 45 D9
Brateș *Romania* 29 F13
Bratislava *Slovak Rep.* 27 C10
Bratislava M.R. Stefanik ✈
  (BTS) *Slovak Rep.* 27 C10
Bratislavský □ *Slovak Rep.* 27 C10
Bratsigovo *Bulgaria* 45 D8
Bratsk *Russia* 53 D11
Brattleboro *U.S.A.* 115 D12
Bratunac *Bos.-H.* 28 F4

Braunau *Austria* **26 C6**
Braunschweig *Germany* **24 C6**
Braunton *U.K.* **15 F3**
Brava *C. Verde Is.* **78 b**
Bravicea *Moldova* **29 C13**
Båviken *Sweden* **11 F10**
Bravo del Norte, Rio =
Grande, Rio ➤ *N. Amer.* **116 J6**
Brawley *U.S.A.* **111 N11**
Bray *Ireland* **12 C5**
Bray, Mt. *Australia* **94 A1**
Bray-sur-Seine *France* **19 D10**
Brazeau ➤ *Canada* **102 C5**
Brazil *U.S.A.* **112 F10**
Brazil ■ *S. Amer.* **125 F9**
Brazilian Highlands =
Brasil, Planalto *Brazil* **122 E6**
Brazo Sur ➤ *S. Amer.* **126 B4**
Brazos ➤ *U.S.A.* **116 G7**
Brazzaville *Congo* **84 E3**
Brčko *Bos.-H.* **28 F3**
Brda ➤ *Poland* **31 E5**
Brdy *Czech Rep.* **26 B6**
Breaden, L. *Australia* **93 E4**
Breaksea Sd. *N.Z.* **91 F1**
Bream B. *N.Z.* **91 A5**
Bream Hd. *N.Z.* **91 A5**
Breas *Chile* **126 B1**
Breaza *Romania* **29 E10**
Brebes *Indonesia* **63 G13**
Brechin *Canada* **114 B5**
Brechin *U.K.* **13 E6**
Brecht *Belgium* **17 C4**
Breckenridge *Colo., U.S.A.* **108 G10**
Breckenridge *Minn., U.S.A.* **112 B5**
Breckenridge *Tex., U.S.A.* **116 E5**
Breckland *U.K.* **15 E8**
Břeclav *Czech Rep.* **27 C9**
Brecon *U.K.* **15 F4**
Brecon Beacons *U.K.* **15 F4**
Brecon Beacons △ *U.K.* **15 F4**
Breda *Neths.* **17 C4**
Bredaryd *Sweden* **11 G7**
Bredasdorp *S. Africa* **88 E3**
Bredebro *Denmark* **11 J2**
Bredstedt *Germany* **24 A4**
Bree *Belgium* **17 C5**
Bregalnica ➤ *Macedonia* **44 E6**
Bregenz *Austria* **26 D2**
Bregovo *Bulgaria* **44 B6**
Bréhal *France* **18 D5**
Bréhat, Î. de *France* **18 D4**
Breiðafjörður *Iceland* **8 D2**
Breil-sur-Roya *France* **21 E11**
Breisach *Germany* **25 G3**
Brejo *Brazil* **125 D10**
Bremen *Germany* **24 B4**
Bremen □ *Germany* **24 B4**
Bremer Bay *Australia* **93 F2**
Bremer I. *Australia* **94 A2**
Bremerhaven *Germany* **24 B4**
Bremerton *U.S.A.* **110 C4**
Bremervörde *Germany* **24 B5**
Brenes *Spain* **37 H5**
Brenham *U.S.A.* **116 F6**
Brenne *France* **20 B5**
Brenne ➤ *France* **20 B5**
Brennerpass *Austria* **26 D4**
Breno *Italy* **40 C7**
Brent *U.S.A.* **117 E11**
Brenta ➤ *Italy* **41 C9**
Brentwood *U.K.* **15 F8**
Brentwood *Calif., U.S.A.* **110 H5**
Brentwood *N.Y., U.S.A.* **115 F11**
Bréscia *Italy* **40 C7**
Breskens *Neths.* **17 C3**
Breslau = Wrocław *Poland* **31 G4**
Bresle ➤ *France* **18 B8**
Bressanone *Italy* **41 B8**
Bressay *U.K.* **13 A7**
Bresse *France* **19 F12**
Bressuire *France* **18 F6**
Brest *Belarus* **23 B12**
Brest *France* **18 D2**
Brest □ *Belarus* **33 F4**
Brest-Litovsk = Brest
Belarus **23 B12**
Bretagne □ *France* **18 D3**
Bretçu *Romania* **29 D11**
Bretenoux *France* **20 D5**
Breteuil *Eure, France* **18 D7**
Breteuil *Oise, France* **19 C9**
Breton *Canada* **102 C6**
Breton, Pertuis *France* **20 B2**
Breton Sd. *U.S.A.* **117 G10**
Brett, C. *N.Z.* **91 A5**
Bretten *Germany* **25 F4**
Breuil-Cervínia *Italy* **40 C4**
Brevard *U.S.A.* **117 D13**
Breves *Brazil* **125 D8**
Brewarrina *Australia* **95 E4**
Brewer *U.S.A.* **113 C19**
Brewer, Mt. *U.S.A.* **110 J8**
Brewerville *Liberia* **82 D2**
Brewster *N.Y., U.S.A.* **115 E11**
Brewster *Ohio, U.S.A.* **114 F3**
Brewster *Wash., U.S.A.* **108 B4**

Brewster, Kap =
Kangikajik *Greenland* **4 B6**
Brewton *U.S.A.* **117 F11**
Breyten *S. Africa* **89 D5**
Breza *Bos.-H.* **28 F3**
Brežice *Slovenia* **41 C12**
Březnice *Czech Rep.* **26 B6**
Breznik *Bulgaria* **44 D6**
Brezno *Slovak Rep.* **27 C12**
Brezoi *Romania* **29 E9**
Brezovica *Serbia* **44 D5**
Brezovo *Bulgaria* **45 D9**
Bria *C.A.R.* **84 C4**
Briançon *France* **21 D10**
Briare *France* **19 E9**
Briático *Italy* **43 D9**
Bribie I. *Australia* **95 D5**
Bribri *Costa Rica* **120 E3**
Briceni *Moldova* **29 B12**
Bricquebec *France* **18 C5**
Bridgefield *Barbados* **121 g**
Bridgehampton *U.S.A.* **115 F12**
Bridgend *U.K.* **15 F4**
Bridgend □ *U.K.* **15 F4**
Bridgeport *Calif., U.S.A.* **110 G7**
Bridgeport *Conn., U.S.A.* **115 E11**
Bridgeport *Nebr., U.S.A.* **112 E2**
Bridgeport *Tex., U.S.A.* **116 E6**
Bridger *U.S.A.* **108 D9**
Bridgeton *U.S.A.* **113 F16**
Bridgetown *Australia* **93 F2**
Bridgetown *Barbados* **121 g**
Bridgetown *Canada* **105 D6**
Bridgewater *Australia* **95 G4**
Bridgewater *Canada* **105 D7**
Bridgewater *Mass., U.S.A.* **115 E14**
Bridgewater *N.Y., U.S.A.* **115 D9**
Bridgewater, C. *Australia* **95 F3**
Bridgnorth *U.K.* **15 E5**
Bridgton *U.S.A.* **115 B14**
Bridgwater *U.S.A.* **15 F5**
Bridgwater B. *U.K.* **15 F4**
Bridlington *U.K.* **14 C7**
Bridlington B. *U.K.* **14 C7**
Bridport *Australia* **95 G4**
Bridport *U.K.* **15 G5**
Briec *France* **18 D2**
Brienne-le-Château *France* **19 D11**
Brienon-sur-Armançon
France **19 E10**
Brienz *Switz.* **25 J4**
Brienzersee *Switz.* **25 J3**
Brière ➤ *France* **18 E4**
Brig *Switz.* **25 J3**
Brigg *U.K.* **14 D7**
Brigham City *U.S.A.* **108 F7**
Bright *Australia* **95 F4**
Brighton *Australia* **95 F2**
Brighton *Canada* **115 B7**
Brighton *Trin. & Tob.* **125 K15**
Brighton *U.K.* **15 G7**
Brighton *U.S.A.* **108 G2**
Brignogan-Plage *France* **18 D2**
Brignoles *France* **21 E10**
Brihuega *Spain* **38 E2**
Brikama *Gambia* **82 C1**
Brilliant *U.S.A.* **114 F4**
Brilon *Germany* **24 D4**
Bríndisi *Italy* **43 B10**
Brinje *Croatia* **41 D12**
Brinkley *U.S.A.* **116 D9**
Brinnon *U.S.A.* **110 C4**
Brion, Î. *Canada* **105 C7**
Brionne *France* **18 C7**
Brionski *Croatia* **41 D10**
Brioude *France* **20 C7**
Briouze *France* **18 D6**
Brisbane *Australia* **95 D5**
Brisbane ➤ *Australia* **95 D5**
Brisighella *Italy* **41 D8**
Bristol *U.K.* **15 F5**
Bristol *Conn., U.S.A.* **115 E12**
Bristol *Pa., U.S.A.* **115 F10**
Bristol *R.I., U.S.A.* **115 E13**
Bristol *Tenn., U.S.A.* **117 C13**
Bristol, City of □ *U.K.* **15 F5**
Bristol B. *U.S.A.* **106 a**
Bristol Channel *U.K.* **15 F3**
Bristol I. *Antarctica* **5 B1**
Bristol L. *U.S.A.* **111 J6**
Bristow *U.S.A.* **116 D6**
Britain = Great Britain *Europe* **6 E5**
British Columbia □ *Canada* **102 C3**
British Indian Ocean Terr.
= Chagos Arch. ☑ *Ind. Oc.* **50 J9**
British Isles *Europe* **16 D5**
British Virgin Is. ☑ *W. Indies* **121 e**
Brits *S. Africa* **89 D4**
Britstown *S. Africa* **88 E3**
Britt *Canada* **104 C3**
Brittany = Bretagne □
France **18 D3**
Britton *U.S.A.* **112 C5**
Brive-la-Gaillarde *France* **20 C5**
Briviesca *Spain* **36 C7**
Brixham *U.K.* **15 G4**
Brixen = Bressanone *Italy* **41 B8**
Brnaze *Croatia* **41 E13**

Brnenský □ *Czech Rep.* **27 B9**
Brno *Czech Rep.* **27 B9**
Broach = Bharuch *India* **66 J8**
Broad ➤ *U.S.A.* **117 D14**
Broad Arrow *Australia* **93 F3**
Broad B. *U.K.* **13 C2**
Broad Haven *Ireland* **12 B2**
Broad Law *U.K.* **13 F5**
Broad Sd. *Australia* **94 C4**
Broadalbin *U.S.A.* **115 C10**
Broadback ➤ *Canada* **104 B4**
Broadhurst Ra. *Australia* **92 D3**
Broads, The *U.K.* **14 E9**
Broadus *U.S.A.* **108 D11**
Broager *Denmark* **11 K3**
Broby *Sweden* **11 H8**
Brocēni *Latvia* **30 B9**
Brochet *Canada* **103 B8**
Brochet, L. *Canada* **103 B8**
Brock I. *Canada* **101 B8**
Brocken *Germany* **24 D6**
Brockport *U.S.A.* **114 C7**
Brockton *U.S.A.* **115 D13**
Brockville *Canada* **115 B9**
Brockway *Mont., U.S.A.* **108 C11**
Brockway *Pa., U.S.A.* **114 E6**
Brocton *U.S.A.* **114 D5**
Brod *Macedonia* **44 E5**
Brodarevo *Serbia* **44 C3**
Brodeur Pen. *Canada* **101 B11**
Brodick *U.K.* **13 F3**
Brodnica *Poland* **31 E6**
Brogan *U.S.A.* **108 D5**
Broglie *France* **18 C7**
Brok *Poland* **31 F8**
Broken Arrow *U.S.A.* **116 C7**
Broken Bow *Nebr., U.S.A.* **112 E4**
Broken Bow *Okla., U.S.A.* **116 D7**
Broken Bow Lake *U.S.A.* **116 D7**
Broken Hill *Australia* **95 E3**
Broken Ridge *Ind. Oc.* **96 L1**
Broken River Ra. *Australia* **94 K6**
Brokind *Sweden* **11 F9**
Bromley □ *U.K.* **15 F8**
Bromo *Indonesia* **63 G15**
Bromölla *Sweden* **11 H8**
Bromsgrove *U.K.* **15 E5**
Brønderslev *Denmark* **11 G3**
Brønnøysund *Norway* **8 D15**
Bronte *Italy* **43 E7**
Brook Park *U.S.A.* **114 E4**
Brookhaven *U.S.A.* **117 F9**
Brookings *Oreg., U.S.A.* **108 E1**
Brookings *S. Dak., U.S.A.* **112 C5**
Brooklin *Canada* **114 C6**
Brooklyn Park *U.S.A.* **112 C7**
Brooks *Canada* **102 C6**
Brooks Range *U.S.A.* **106 a**
Brooksville *U.S.A.* **117 G13**
Brookton *Australia* **93 F2**
Brookville *U.S.A.* **114 E5**
Broom, L. *U.K.* **13 D3**
Broome *Australia* **92 C3**
Broons *France* **18 D4**
Brora *U.K.* **13 C5**
Brora ➤ *U.K.* **13 C5**
Brørup *Denmark* **11 J2**
Brösarp *Sweden* **11 J8**
Brosna ➤ *Ireland* **12 C4**
Brothers *U.S.A.* **108 E3**
Brou *France* **18 D8**
Brouage *France* **20 C2**
Brough *U.K.* **14 C5**
Brough Hd. *U.K.* **13 B5**
Broughton Island =
Qikiqtarjuaq *Canada* **101 C13**
Broumov *Czech Rep.* **27 A9**
Brovary *Ukraine* **33 G6**
Brovst *Denmark* **11 G3**
Brown, L. *Australia* **93 F2**
Brown, Pt. *Australia* **95 E1**
Brown City *U.S.A.* **114 C2**
Brown Willy *U.K.* **15 G3**
Brownfield *U.S.A.* **116 E3**
Browning *U.S.A.* **108 B7**
Brownsville *Oreg., U.S.A.* **108 D2**
Brownsville *Pa., U.S.A.* **114 F5**
Brownsville *Tenn., U.S.A.* **117 D10**
Brownsville *Tex., U.S.A.* **116 J6**
Brownwood *U.S.A.* **116 F5**
Browse I. *Australia* **92 B3**
Bruas *Malaysia* **65 K3**
Bruay-la-Buissière *France* **19 B9**
Bruce, Mt. *Australia* **92 D2**
Bruce Pen. *Canada* **114 B3**
Bruce Peninsula △ *Canada* **114 A3**
Bruce Rock *Australia* **93 F2**
Bruche ➤ *France* **19 D14**
Bruchsal *Germany* **25 F4**
Bruck an der Leitha *Austria* **27 C9**
Bruck an der Mur *Austria* **26 D8**

Brue ➤ *U.K.* **15 F5**
Bruges = Brugge *Belgium* **17 C3**
Brugg *Switz.* **25 H4**
Brugge *Belgium* **17 C3**
Bruin *U.S.A.* **114 E5**
Brûk, W. ➤ *Egypt* **74 E2**
Brûlé *Canada* **102 C5**
Brûlon *France* **18 E6**
Brumado *Brazil* **125 F10**
Brumath *France* **19 D14**
Brumunddal *Norway* **8 F14**
Bruneau *U.S.A.* **108 E6**
Bruneau ➤ *U.S.A.* **108 E6**
Bruneck = Brunico *Italy* **41 B8**
Brunei = Bandar Seri
Begawan *Brunei* **62 D5**
Brunei ■ *Asia* **62 D5**
Brunflo *Sweden* **10 A8**
Brunico *Italy* **41 B8**
Brunna *Sweden* **10 E11**
Brunnen *Switz.* **25 J4**
Brunner, L. *N.Z.* **91 E3**
Brunsbüttel *Germany* **24 B5**
Brunssum *Neths.* **17 D5**
Brunswick =
Braunschweig *Germany* **24 C6**
Brunswick *Ga., U.S.A.* **117 F14**
Brunswick *Maine, U.S.A.* **113 D19**
Brunswick *Md., U.S.A.* **113 F15**
Brunswick *Mo., U.S.A.* **112 F7**
Brunswick *Ohio, U.S.A.* **114 E3**
Brunswick, Pen. de *Chile* **128 G2**
Brunswick B. *Australia* **92 C3**
Brunswick Junction
Australia **93 F2**
Brunt Ice Shelf *Antarctica* **5 D2**
Bruntál *Czech Rep.* **27 B10**
Brus Laguna *Honduras* **120 C3**
Brusartsi *Bulgaria* **44 C7**
Brush *U.S.A.* **108 F12**
Brushton *U.S.A.* **115 B10**
Brusio *Switz.* **25 J6**
Brusque *Brazil* **127 B6**
Brussel *Belgium* **17 D4**
Brussel ✈ (BRU) *Belgium* **17 D5**
Brussels = Brussel *Belgium* **17 D4**
Brussels *Canada* **114 C3**
Brusy *Poland* **30 E4**
Bruthen *Australia* **95 F4**
Bruxelles = Brussel *Belgium* **17 D4**
Bruyères *France* **19 D13**
Bruz *France* **18 D5**
Bruzual *Venezuela* ...
Bryan *Ohio, U.S.A.* **113 E11**
Bryan *Tex., U.S.A.* **116 F6**
Bryan, Mt. *Australia* **95 E2**
Bryanka *Ukraine* **33 H10**
Bryansk *Bryansk, Russia* **33 F8**
Bryansk *Dagestan, Russia* **35 H8**
Bryansk □ *Russia* **33 F7**
Bryanskoye = Bryansk
Russia **35 H8**
Bryce Canyon △ *U.S.A.* **109 H7**
Bryne *Norway* **9 G11**
Bryson City *U.S.A.* **117 D13**
Bryukhovetskaya *Russia* **35 K10**
Brza Palanka *Serbia* **44 B6**
Brzeg *Poland* **31 H4**
Brzeg Dolny *Poland* **31 G3**
Brześć Kujawski *Poland* **31 F5**
Brzesko *Poland* **31 J7**
Brzeziny *Poland* **31 G6**
Brzozów *Poland* **31 J9**
Bsharri *Lebanon* **74 A5**
Bū Baqarah *U.A.E.* **71 E8**
Bu Craa *W. Sahara* **78 C3**
Bū Ḩasā *U.A.E.* **71 F7**
Bua *Fiji* **91 a**
Bua *Sweden* **11 G6**
Bua Yai *Thailand* **64 E4**
Buan *S. Korea* **57 G14**
Buapinang *Indonesia* **63 E6**
Buba *Guinea-Biss.* **82 C2**
Bubanza *Burundi* **86 C2**
Bubaque *Guinea-Biss.* **82 C1**
Bube *Ethiopia* **81 F4**
Bubi ➤ *Zimbabwe* **87 G3**
Būbiyān *Kuwait* **71 D6**
Buca *Fiji* **91 a**
Buca *Turkey* **47 C9**
Bucak *Turkey* **47 D12**
Bucaramanga *Colombia* **124 B4**
Bucas Grande I. *Phil.* **61 G6**
Bucasia *Australia* **94 K7**
Buccaneer Arch. *Australia* **92 C3**
Buccino *Italy* **43 B8**
Buccoo Reef *Trin. & Tob.* **125 J16**
Bucecea *Romania* **29 C11**
Bucegi △ *Romania* **29 E10**
Buchach *Ukraine* **23 D13**
Buchan *U.K.* **13 D6**
Buchan Ness *U.K.* **13 D7**
Buchanan *Canada* **103 C8**
Buchanan *Liberia* **82 D2**
Buchanan, L. *Queens.,*
Australia **94 C4**

Buchanan, L. *W. Austral.,*
Australia **93 E3**
Buchanan, L. *U.S.A.* **116 F5**
Buchanan Cr. ➤ *Australia* **94 B2**
Buchans *Canada* **105 C8**
Bucharest = Bucureşti
Romania **29 F11**
Buchen *Germany* **25 F5**
Bucheon *S. Korea* **57 F14**
Buchholz *Germany* **24 B5**
Buchloe *Germany* **25 G6**
Buchon, Pt. *U.S.A.* **110 K6**
Buciumi *Romania* **28 C8**
Buck Hill Falls *U.S.A.* **115 E9**
Bückeburg *Germany* **24 C5**
Buckeye Lake *U.S.A.* **114 G2**
Buckhannon *U.S.A.* **113 F13**
Buckhaven *U.K.* **13 E5**
Buckhorn L. *Canada* **114 B6**
Buckie *U.K.* **13 D6**
Buckingham *Canada* **104 C4**
Buckingham *U.K.* **15 F7**
Buckingham B. *Australia* **94 A2**
Buckinghamshire □ *U.K.* **15 F7**
Buckle Hd. *Australia* **92 B4**
Buckleboo *Australia* **95 E2**
Buckley *U.K.* **14 D4**
Buckley ➤ *Australia* **94 C2**
Bucklin *U.S.A.* **112 G4**
Bucquoy *France* **19 B9**
Bucureşti *Romania* **29 F11**
Bucureşti Otopeni ✈ (OTP)
Romania **29 F11**
Bucyrus *U.S.A.* **113 E12**
Budacu, Vf. *Romania* **29 C10**
Budalin *Burma* **67 H19**
Budaörs *Hungary* **28 C4**
Budapest *Hungary* **28 C4**
Budapest □ *Hungary* **28 C4**
Budapest ✈ (BUD) *Hungary* **28 C4**
Budaun *India* **69 E8**
Budd Coast *Antarctica* **5 C8**
Buddusò *Italy* **42 B2**
Bude *U.K.* **15 G3**
Budennovsk *Russia* **35 H7**
Budeşti *Romania* **29 F11**
Budeyi *Ukraine* **29 B14**
Budge Budge = Baj Baj
India **69 H13**
Budgewoi *Australia* **95 E5**
Budia *Spain* **38 E2**
Büdingen *Germany* **25 E5**
Budjala *Dem. Rep. of the Congo* **84 D3**
Budoni *Italy* **42 B2**
Búdrio *Italy* **41 D8**
Budva *Montenegro* **44 D2**
Budzyń *Poland* **31 F3**
Buea *Cameroon* **83 E6**
Buellton *U.S.A.* **111 L6**
Buena Esperanza *Argentina* **126 C2**
Buena Park *U.S.A.* **111 M9**
Buena Vista *Colo., U.S.A.* **108 G10**
Buena Vista *Va., U.S.A.* **113 G14**
Buena Vista Lake Bed
U.S.A. **111 K7**
Buenaventura *Colombia* **124 C3**
Buenaventura *Mexico* **118 B3**
Buendía, Embalse de *Spain* **38 E2**
Buenos Aires *Argentina* **126 C4**
Buenos Aires *Costa Rica* **120 E3**
Buenos Aires □ *Argentina* **126 D4**
Buenos Aires, L. *Argentina* **128 F2**
Buffalo *Mo., U.S.A.* **112 G7**
Buffalo *N.Y., U.S.A.* **114 D6**
Buffalo *Okla., U.S.A.* **116 C5**
Buffalo *S. Dak., U.S.A.* **112 C2**
Buffalo *Wyo., U.S.A.* **108 D10**
Buffalo ➤ *Canada* **102 A5**
Buffalo ➤ *S. Africa* **89 D5**
Buffalo △ *U.S.A.* **116 C5**
Buffalo Head Hills *Canada* **102 B5**
Buffalo L. *Alta., Canada* **102 C6**
Buffalo L. *N.W.T., Canada* **102 A5**
Buffalo Narrows *Canada* **103 B7**
Buffalo Springs △ *Kenya* **86 B4**
Buffels ➤ *S. Africa* **88 D2**
Buford *U.S.A.* **117 D12**
Bug = Buh ➤ *Ukraine* **33 J6**
Bug ➤ *Poland* **31 F8**
Buga *Colombia* **124 C3**
Bugala I. *Uganda* **86 C3**
Buganda *Uganda* **86 C3**
Buganga *Uganda* **86 C3**
Bugasong *Phil.* **61 F5**
Bugeat *France* **20 C5**
Bugel, Tanjung *Indonesia* **63 G14**
Bugojno *Bos.-H.* **28 F2**
Bugsuk I. *Phil.* **62 C5**
Buguma *Nigeria* **83 E6**
Bugun Shara *Mongolia* **60 B5**
Bugungu △ *Uganda* **86 B3**
Buguruslan *Russia* **52 D6**
Buh ➤ *Ukraine* **33 J6**
Buharkent *Turkey* **47 D10**
Buheirat-Murrat-el-Kubra
Egypt **80 H8**

Buhera *Zimbabwe* **89 B5**
Bühl *Germany* **25 G4**
Buhl *U.S.A.* **108 E6**
Buhuşi *Romania* **29 D11**
Bui △ *Ghana* **82 D4**
Builth Wells *U.K.* **15 E4**
Buinsk *Russia* **34 C9**
Buir Nur *Mongolia* **60 B6**
Buis-les-Baronnies *France* **21 D9**
Buitrago del Lozoya *Spain* **36 E7**
Bujalance *Spain* **37 H6**
Bujanovac *Serbia* **44 D5**
Bujaraloz *Spain* **38 D4**
Buje *Croatia* **41 C10**
Bujumbura *Burundi* **86 C2**
Bük *Hungary* **28 C1**
Buk *Poland* **31 F3**
Bukachacha *Russia* **53 D12**
Bukama
Dem. Rep. of the Congo **87 D2**
Būkān *Iran* **73 D12**
Bukavu *Dem. Rep. of the Congo* **86 C2**
Bukene *Tanzania* **86 C3**
Bukhara = Bukhoro
Uzbekistan **52 F7**
Bukhoro *Uzbekistan* **52 F7**
Bukima *Tanzania* **86 C3**
Bukit Badung *Indonesia* **63 K18**
Bukit Kerajaan *Malaysia* **65 c**
Bukit Mertajam *Malaysia* **65 c**
Bukit Ni *Malaysia* **65 d**
Bukit Panjang *Singapore* **65 d**
Bukit Tengah *Malaysia* **65 c**
Bukittinggi *Indonesia* **62 E2**
Bükk *Hungary* **28 B5**
Bükki △ *Hungary* **28 B5**
Bukoba *Tanzania* **86 C3**
Bukum, Pulau *Singapore* **65 d**
Bulan *Phil.* **61 E5**
Bulancak *Turkey* **73 B8**
Bulandshahr *India* **68 E7**
Bulanık *Turkey* **73 C10**
Būlâq *Egypt* **80 B3**
Bulawayo *Zimbabwe* **87 G2**
Buldan *Turkey* **47 C10**
Bulgar *Russia* **34 C9**
Bulgaria ■ *Europe* **45 D9**
Bulgheria, Monte *Italy* **43 B8**
Bulgurca *Turkey* **47 C9**
Buli, Teluk *Indonesia* **63 D7**
Buliluyan, C. *Phil.* **61 G2**
Bulim *Singapore* **65 d**
Bulki *Ethiopia* **81 F4**
Bulkley ➤ *Canada* **102 B3**
Bull Shoals L. *U.S.A.* **116 C8**
Bullaque ➤ *Spain* **37 G6**
Bullas *Spain* **39 G3**
Bulle *Switz.* **25 J3**
Bulleringa △ *Australia* **94 B3**
Bullhead City *U.S.A.* **111 K12**
Büllingen *Belgium* **17 D6**
Bullock Creek *Australia* **94 B3**
Bulloo ➤ *Australia* **95 D3**
Bulloo L. *Australia* **95 D3**
Bulls *N.Z.* **91 D5**
Bully-les-Mines *France* **19 B9**
Bulnes *Chile* **126 D1**
Bulqizë *Albania* **44 E4**
Bulsar = Valsad *India* **66 J8**
Bultfontein *S. Africa* **88 D4**
Bulukumba *Indonesia* **63 F6**
Bulun *Russia* **53 B13**
Bumba *Dem. Rep. of the Congo* **84 D4**
Bumbeşti-Jiu *Romania* **29 E8**
Bumbiri I. *Tanzania* **86 C3**
Bumbuna *S. Leone* **82 D2**
Bumhpa Bum *Burma* **67 F20**
Bumi ➤ *Zimbabwe* **87 F2**
Buna *Kenya* **86 B4**
Bunaken *Indonesia* **63 D6**
Bunawan *Phil.* **61 G6**
Bunazi *Tanzania* **86 C3**
Bunbah, Khalīj *Libya* **79 B10**
Bunbury *Australia* **93 F2**
Bunclody *Ireland* **12 D5**
Buncrana *Ireland* **12 A4**
Bundaberg *Australia* **95 C5**
Bünde *Germany* **24 C4**
Bundey ➤ *Australia* **94 C2**
Bundi *India* **68 G6**
Bundjalung △ *Australia* **95 D5**
Bundoran *Ireland* **12 B3**
Bundukia *Sudan* **81 F3**
Bung Kan *Thailand* **64 C4**
Bunga ➤ *Nigeria* **83 D6**
Bungay *U.K.* **15 E9**
Bungil Cr. ➤ *Australia* **95 D4**
Bungle Bungle =
Purnululu △ *Australia* **92 C4**
Bungo-Suidō *Japan* **55 H6**
Bungoma *Kenya* **86 B3**

Bungotakada *Japan* 55 H5
Bungu *Tanzania* 86 D4
Bunia *Dem. Rep. of the Congo* 86 B3
Bunji *Pakistan* 69 B6
Bunkie *U.S.A.* 116 F8
Bunnell *U.S.A.* 117 G14
Buñol *Spain* 39 F4
Bunsuru *Nigeria* 83 C5
Buntok *Indonesia* 62 E4
Bununu Dass *Nigeria* 83 C6
Bununu Kasa *Nigeria* 83 D6
Bunya Mts. △ *Australia* 95 D5
Bünyan *Turkey* 72 C6
Bunyu *Indonesia* 62 D5
Bunza *Nigeria* 83 C5
Buol *Indonesia* 63 D6
Buon Brieng *Vietnam* 64 F7
Buon Ma Thuot *Vietnam* 64 F7
Buong Long *Cambodia* 64 F6
Buorkhaya, Mys *Russia* 53 B14
Buqayq *Si. Arabia* 71 E6
Buqbuq *Egypt* 80 A2
Bur Acaba *Somali Rep.* 75 G3
Bûr Fuad *Egypt* 80 H8
Bûr Safâga *Egypt* 70 E2
Bûr Sa'îd *Egypt* 80 H8
Bûr Sûdân *Sudan* 80 D4
Bûr Taufiq *Egypt* 80 J8
Bura *Kenya* 86 C4
Burakin *Australia* 93 F2
Buram *Sudan* 81 E2
Burao *Somali Rep.* 75 F4
Burâq *Syria* 74 C4
Buraydah *Si. Arabia* 70 E4
Burbank *U.S.A.* 111 L8
Burda *India* 68 G6
Burdekin → *Australia* 94 B4
Burdur *Turkey* 47 D12
Burdur □ *Turkey* 47 D12
Burdur Gölü *Turkey* 47 D12
Burdwan = Barddhaman *India* 69 H12
Bure *Gojam, Ethiopia* 81 E4
Bure *Ilubabor, Ethiopia* 81 F4
Bure → *U.K.* 14 E9
Büren *Germany* 24 D4
Bureya → *Russia* 53 E13
Burford *Canada* 114 C4
Burg *Germany* 24 C7
Burg auf Fehmarn *Germany* 24 A7
Burg el Arab *Egypt* 80 H6
Burg et Tuyur *Sudan* 80 C2
Burg Stargard *Germany* 24 B9
Burgas *Bulgaria* 45 D11
Burgas □ *Bulgaria* 45 D10
Burgaski Zaliv *Bulgaria* 45 D11
Burgdorf *Germany* 24 C6
Burgdorf *Switz.* 25 H3
Burgenland □ *Austria* 27 D9
Burgeo *Canada* 105 C8
Burgersdorp *S. Africa* 88 E4
Burges, Mt. *Australia* 93 F3
Burghausen *Germany* 25 G8
Burghead *U.K.* 13 D5
Búrgio *Italy* 42 E6
Burglengenfeld *Germany* 25 F8
Burgohondo *Spain* 36 E6
Burgos *Spain* 36 C7
Burgos □ *Spain* 36 C7
Burgstädt *Germany* 24 E8
Burgsvik *Sweden* 11 G12
Burguillos del Cerro *Spain* 37 G4
Burgundy = Bourgogne □ *France* 19 F11
Burhaniye *Turkey* 47 B8
Burhanpur *India* 66 J10
Burhi Gandak → *India* 69 G12
Burhner → *India* 69 H9
Buri Pen. *Eritrea* 81 D4
Burias I. *Phil.* 61 E5
Burica, Pta. *Costa Rica* 120 E3
Burien *U.S.A.* 110 C4
Burigi, L. *Tanzania* 86 C3
Burigi △ *Tanzania* 86 C3
Burin *Canada* 105 C8
Buriram *Thailand* 64 E4
Burji *Ethiopia* 81 F4
Burkburnett *U.S.A.* 116 D5
Burke → *Australia* 94 C2
Burke Chan. *Canada* 102 C3
Burketown *Australia* 94 B2
Burkina Faso ■ *Africa* 82 C4
Burk's Falls *Canada* 104 C4
Burlada *Spain* 38 C3
Burleigh Falls *Canada* 114 B6
Burley *U.S.A.* 108 E7
Burlingame *U.S.A.* 110 H4
Burlington *Canada* 114 C5
Burlington *Colo., U.S.A.* 108 G12
Burlington *Iowa, U.S.A.* 112 E8
Burlington *Kans., U.S.A.* 112 F6
Burlington *N.C., U.S.A.* 117 C15
Burlington *N.J., U.S.A.* 115 F10
Burlington *Vt., U.S.A.* 115 B11
Burlington *Wash., U.S.A.* 110 B4
Burlington *Wis., U.S.A.* 112 D9
Burma ■ *Asia* 67 J20
Burnaby I. *Canada* 102 C2

Burnet *U.S.A.* 116 F5
Burney *U.S.A.* 108 F3
Burnham *U.S.A.* 114 F7
Burnham-on-Sea *U.K.* 15 F5
Burnie *Australia* 95 G4
Burnley *U.K.* 14 D5
Burns *U.S.A.* 108 E4
Burns Junction *U.S.A.* 108 E5
Burns Lake *Canada* 102 C3
Burnside → *Canada* 100 C9
Burnside, L. *Australia* 93 E3
Burnsville *U.S.A.* 112 C7
Burnt, L. *Canada* 105 B7
Burnt River *Canada* 114 B6
Burntwood → *Canada* 103 B9
Burntwood L. *Canada* 103 B8
Burqān *Kuwait* 70 D5
Burra *Australia* 95 E2
Burra *Nigeria* 83 C6
Burray *U.K.* 13 C6
Burrel *Albania* 44 E4
Burren *Ireland* 12 C2
Burren △ *Ireland* 12 C3
Burren Junction *Australia* 95 E4
Burriana *Spain* 38 F4
Burrinjuck Res. *Australia* 95 F4
Burro, Serranías del *Mexico* 118 B4
Burrow Hd. *U.K.* 13 G4
Burrum Coast △ *Australia* 95 D5
Burruyacú *Argentina* 126 B3
Burry Port *U.K.* 15 F3
Bursa *Turkey* 45 F13
Bursa □ *Turkey* 72 B3
Burseryd *Sweden* 11 G7
Burstall *Canada* 103 C7
Burton *Ohio, U.S.A.* 114 E3
Burton *S.C., U.S.A.* 117 E14
Burton, L. *Canada* 104 B4
Burton upon Trent *U.K.* 14 E6
Buru *Indonesia* 63 E7
Burullus, Bahra el *Egypt* 80 H7
Burûn, Râs *Egypt* 74 D2
Burundi ■ *Africa* 86 C3
Bururi *Burundi* 86 C2
Burutu *Nigeria* 83 D6
Burwell *U.S.A.* 112 E4
Burwick *U.K.* 13 C5
Bury *U.K.* 14 D5
Bury St. Edmunds *U.K.* 15 E8
Buryatia □ *Russia* 53 D12
Buryn *Ukraine* 33 G7
Burzenin *Poland* 31 G5
Busalla *Italy* 40 D5
Busango Swamp *Zambia* 87 E2
Buşayrah *Syria* 73 E9
Busca *Italy* 40 D4
Bushat *Albania* 44 E3
Büshehr *Iran* 71 D6
Büshehr □ *Iran* 71 D6
Bushell *Canada* 103 B7
Bushenyi *Uganda* 86 C3
Bushire = Büshehr *Iran* 71 D6
Bushtyna *Ukraine* 29 B8
Busie *Ghana* 82 C4
Businga *Dem. Rep. of the Congo* 84 D4
Busko-Zdrój *Poland* 31 H7
Busovača *Bos.-H.* 28 F2
Buşra ash Shām *Syria* 74 C5
Busselton *Australia* 93 F2
Busseri → *Sudan* 81 F2
Busseto *Italy* 40 D7
Bussière-Badil *France* 20 C4
Bussolengo *Italy* 40 C7
Bussum *Neths.* 17 B5
Buşteni *Romania* 29 E10
Busto, C. *Spain* 36 B4
Busto Arsízio *Italy* 40 C5
Busu Djanoa *Dem. Rep. of the Congo* 84 D4
Busuanga I. *Phil.* 61 E4
Büsum *Germany* 24 A5
Busungbiu *Indonesia* 63 J17
Buta *Dem. Rep. of the Congo* 86 B1
Butare *Rwanda* 86 C2
Butaritari *Kiribati* 96 G9
Bute *U.K.* 13 F3
Bute Inlet *Canada* 102 C4
Butemba *Uganda* 86 B3
Butembo *Dem. Rep. of the Congo* 86 B2
Buteni *Romania* 28 D7
Butera *Italy* 43 E7
Butere *Kenya* 86 B3
Butha Qi *China* 60 B7
Butiaba *Uganda* 86 B3
Butler *Mo., U.S.A.* 112 F6
Butler *Pa., U.S.A.* 114 F5
Buton *Indonesia* 63 E6
Butte *Mont., U.S.A.* 108 C7
Butte *Nebr., U.S.A.* 112 D5
Butte Creek → *U.S.A.* 110 F5
Butterworth = Gcuwa *S. Africa* 89 E4
Butterworth *Malaysia* 65 c
Buttevant *Ireland* 12 D3
Buttfield, Mt. *Australia* 93 D4

Button B. *Canada* 103 B10
Buttonwillow *U.S.A.* 111 K7
Butty Hd. *Australia* 93 F3
Butuan *Phil.* 61 G6
Butuku-Luba *Eq. Guin.* 83 E6
Butung = Buton *Indonesia* 63 E6
Buturlinovka *Russia* 34 E5
Butzbach *Germany* 25 E4
Bützow *Germany* 24 B7
Buur Hakaba = Bur Acaba *Somali Rep.* 75 G3
Buxa Duar *India* 69 F13
Buxar *India* 69 G10
Buxoro = Bukhoro *Uzbekistan* 52 F7
Buxtehude *Germany* 24 B5
Buxton *U.K.* 14 D6
Buxy *France* 19 F11
Buy *Russia* 34 A5
Buyant-Uhaa *Mongolia* 60 B6
Büyük Menderes → *Turkey* 47 D9
Büyükçekmece *Turkey* 45 E12
Büyükkariştiran *Turkey* 45 E11
Büyükkemikli Burnu *Turkey* 45 F10
Büyükkorhan *Turkey* 47 B10
Büyükyoncalı *Turkey* 45 E11
Buzançais *France* 18 F8
Buzău *Romania* 29 E11
Buzău □ *Romania* 29 E11
Buzău → *Romania* 29 E12
Buzău, Pasul *Romania* 29 E11
Buzen *Japan* 55 H5
Buzet *Croatia* 41 C10
Buzi → *Mozam.* 87 F3
Buziaş *Romania* 28 E6
Büzmeyin *Turkmenistan* 71 B8
Buzuluk *Russia* 52 D6
Buzuluk → *Russia* 34 E6
Buzzards Bay *U.S.A.* 115 E14
Bwana Mkubwe *Dem. Rep. of the Congo* 87 E2
Bwindi △ *Uganda* 86 C2
Byala *Ruse, Bulgaria* 45 C9
Byala *Varna, Bulgaria* 45 D11
Byala Slatina *Bulgaria* 44 C7
Byarezina → *Belarus* 23 B16
Byaroza *Belarus* 33 F3
Bychawa *Poland* 31 G9
Byczyna *Poland* 31 G5
Bydgoszcz *Poland* 31 E5
Byelorussia = Belarus ■ *Europe* 23 B14
Byers *U.S.A.* 108 G11
Byesville *U.S.A.* 114 F3
Byfield △ *Australia* 94 C5
Byford *Australia* 93 F2
Bykhaw *Belarus* 23 B16
Bykhov = Bykhaw *Belarus* 23 B16
Bykovo *Russia* 34 F7
Bylas *U.S.A.* 109 K8
Bylot *Canada* 103 B10
Bylot I. *Canada* 101 B12
Byrd, C. *Antarctica* 5 C17
Byrock *Australia* 95 E4
Byron, C. *Australia* 95 D5
Byron Bay *Australia* 95 D5
Byrranga, Gory *Russia* 53 B11
Byrranga Mts. = Byrranga, Gory *Russia* 53 B11
Byrum *Denmark* 11 G5
Byske *Sweden* 8 D19
Byskeälven → *Sweden* 8 D19
Bystrytsya *Ukraine* 29 B9
Bystrzyca → *Dolnośląskie, Poland* 31 G3
Bystrzyca → *Lubelskie, Poland* 31 G9
Bystrzyca Kłodzka *Poland* 31 H3
Bytča *Slovak Rep.* 27 B11
Bytkiv *Ukraine* 29 B9
Bytom *Poland* 31 H5
Bytom Odrzański *Poland* 31 G2
Bytów *Poland* 30 D4
Byumba *Rwanda* 86 C3
Bzenec *Czech Rep.* 27 C10
Bzura → *Poland* 31 F7

C

C.W. McConaughy, L. *U.S.A.* 112 E3
Ca → *Vietnam* 64 C5
Ca Mau *Vietnam* 65 H5
Ca Mau, Mui *Vietnam* 65 H5
Ca Na *Vietnam* 65 G7
Caacupé *Paraguay* 126 B4
Caaguazú *Paraguay* 127 B4
Caála *Angola* 85 G3
Caamaño Sd. *Canada* 102 C3
Caazapá *Paraguay* 126 B4
Caazapá □ *Paraguay* 127 B4
Cabadbaran *Phil.* 61 G6
Cabalian = San Juan *Phil.* 61 F6
Caballeria, C. de *Spain* 48 A11

Cabana *Spain* 36 B2
Cabañaquinta *Spain* 36 B5
Cabanatuan *Phil.* 61 D4
Cabañeros △ *Spain* 37 F6
Cabanes *Spain* 38 E5
Cabano *Canada* 105 C6
Čabar *Croatia* 41 C11
Cabazon *U.S.A.* 111 M10
Cabedelo *Brazil* 125 E12
Cabeza del Buey *Spain* 37 G5
Cabezón de la Sal *Spain* 36 B6
Cabildo *Chile* 126 C1
Cabimas *Venezuela* 124 A4
Cabinda *Angola* 84 F2
Cabinda □ *Angola* 84 F2
Cabinet Mts. *U.S.A.* 108 B6
Cabo Blanco *Argentina* 128 F3
Cabo de Gata-Níjar △ *Spain* 39 J2
Cabo Frio *Brazil* 127 A7
Cabo Pantoja *Peru* 124 D3
Cabo San Lucas *Mexico* 118 C3
Cabo Verde = Cape Verde Is. ■ *Atl. Oc.* 78 b
Cabonga, Réservoir *Canada* 104 C4
Cabool *U.S.A.* 112 G7
Caboolture *Australia* 95 D5
Cabora Bassa Dam = Cahora Bassa, Reprêsa de *Mozam.* 87 F3
Caborca *Mexico* 118 A2
Cabot, Mt. *U.S.A.* 115 B13
Cabot Hd. *Canada* 114 A3
Cabot Str. *Canada* 105 C8
Cabra *Spain* 37 H6
Cabra del Santo Cristo *Spain* 37 H7
Cábras *Italy* 42 C1
Cabrera *Spain* 36 B4
Cabrera, Sierra *Spain* 36 C4
Cabrera △ *Spain* 39 F7
Cabri *Canada* 103 C7
Cabriel → *Spain* 39 F3
Cabugao *Phil.* 61 C4
Cacabelos *Spain* 36 C4
Caçador *Brazil* 127 B5
Čačak *Serbia* 44 C4
Caçapava do Sul *Brazil* 127 C5
Cáccamo *Italy* 42 E6
Cacém *Portugal* 37 G1
Cáceres *Brazil* 124 G7
Cáceres *Spain* 37 F4
Cáceres □ *Spain* 36 F5
Cache Bay *Canada* 104 C4
Cache Cr. → *U.S.A.* 110 G5
Cache Creek *Canada* 102 C4
Cacheu *Guinea-Biss.* 82 C1
Cachi *Argentina* 126 B2
Cachimbo, Serra do *Brazil* 125 E7
Cachinal de la Sierra *Chile* 126 A2
Cachoeira *Brazil* 125 F11
Cachoeira do Sul *Brazil* 127 C5
Cachoeiro de Itapemirim *Brazil* 127 A7
Cachopo *Portugal* 37 H3
Cacine *Guinea-Biss.* 82 C1
Cacoal *Brazil* 124 F6
Cacólo *Angola* 84 G3
Caconda *Angola* 85 G3
Cadca *Slovak Rep.* 27 B11
Caddo *U.S.A.* 116 D6
Cader Idris *U.K.* 15 E4
Cadereyta de Jiménez *Mexico* 118 B5
Cadí, Sierra del *Spain* 38 C6
Cadí-Moixeró △ *Spain* 38 C6
Cadibarrawirracanna, L. *Australia* 95 D2
Cadillac *France* 20 D3
Cadillac *U.S.A.* 113 C11
Cádiz *Phil.* 61 F5
Cádiz *Spain* 37 J4
Cadiz *Calif., U.S.A.* 111 L11
Cadiz *Ohio, U.S.A.* 114 F4
Cádiz □ *Spain* 37 J5
Cádiz, G. de *Spain* 37 J3
Cadiz L. *U.S.A.* 109 J6
Cadney Park *Australia* 95 D1
Cadomin *Canada* 102 C5
Cadotte Lake *Canada* 102 B5
Cadours *France* 20 E5
Cadoux *Australia* 93 F2
Caen *France* 18 C6
Caernarfon *U.K.* 14 D3
Caernarfon B. *U.K.* 14 D3
Caernarvon = Caernarfon *U.K.* 14 D3
Caerphilly *U.K.* 15 F4
Caerphilly □ *U.K.* 15 F4
Caesarea *Israel* 74 C3
Caetité *Brazil* 125 F10
Cafayate *Argentina* 126 B2
Cafu *Angola* 88 B2
Cagayan → *Phil.* 61 B4
Cagayan de Oro *Phil.* 61 G6
Cagayan Is. *Phil.* 61 G4
Cagayan Sulu I. *Phil.* 61 H3
Cagli *Italy* 41 E9
Cágliari *Italy* 42 C2
Cágliari, G. di *Italy* 42 C2

Cagnano Varano *Italy* 41 G12
Cagnes-sur-Mer *France* 21 E11
Caguán → *Colombia* 124 D4
Caguas *Puerto Rico* 121 d
Caha Mts. *Ireland* 12 E2
Cahama *Angola* 88 B1
Caher *Ireland* 12 D4
Cahersiveen *Ireland* 12 E1
Cahora Bassa, L. de *Mozam.* 87 F3
Cahora Bassa, Reprêsa de *Mozam.* 87 F3
Cahore Pt. *Ireland* 12 D5
Cahors *France* 20 D5
Cahul *Moldova* 29 E13
Caì Bau, Dao *Vietnam* 58 G6
Cai Nuoc *Vietnam* 65 H5
Caia *Mozam.* 87 F4
Caianda *Angola* 87 E1
Caibarién *Cuba* 120 B4
Caibiran *Phil.* 61 F6
Caicara *Venezuela* 124 B5
Caicó *Brazil* 125 E11
Caicos Is. *Turks & Caicos* 121 B5
Caicos Passage *W. Indies* 121 B5
Caidian *China* 59 B10
Caird Coast *Antarctica* 5 D1
Cairn Gorm *U.K.* 13 D5
Cairngorm Mts. *U.K.* 13 D5
Cairngorms △ *U.K.* 13 D5
Cairnryan *U.K.* 13 G3
Cairns *Australia* 94 B4
Cairns L. *Canada* 103 C10
Cairo = El Qâhira *Egypt* 80 H7
Cairo *Ga., U.S.A.* 117 F12
Cairo *Ill., U.S.A.* 112 G9
Cairo *N.Y., U.S.A.* 115 D10
Cairo Montenotte *Italy* 40 D5
Caithness *U.K.* 13 C5
Caithness, Ord of *U.K.* 13 C5
Caja de Muertos, I. *Puerto Rico* 121 d
Cajamarca *Peru* 124 E3
Cajarc *France* 20 D5
Cajàzeiras *Brazil* 125 E11
Čajetina *Serbia* 44 C3
Çakırgol *Turkey* 73 B8
Çakırlar *Turkey* 47 E12
Čakovec *Croatia* 41 B13
Çal *Turkey* 47 C11
Cala *Spain* 37 H4
Cala → *Spain* 37 H4
Cala Cadolar, Punta de = Rotja, Pta. *Spain* 39 G6
Cala d'Or *Spain* 48 B10
Cala en Porter *Spain* 48 B11
Cala Figuera, C. de *Spain* 48 B9
Cala Forcat *Spain* 48 B10
Cala Major *Spain* 48 B9
Cala Mezquida = Sa Mesquida *Spain* 48 B11
Cala Millor *Spain* 48 B10
Cala Ratjada *Spain* 48 B10
Cala Santa Galdana *Spain* 48 B10
Calabanga *Phil.* 61 E5
Calabar *Nigeria* 83 E6
Calabogie *Canada* 115 A8
Calabozo *Venezuela* 124 B5
Calábria □ *Italy* 43 C9
Calábria △ *Italy* 43 C9
Calaburras, Pta. de *Spain* 37 J6
Calaceite *Spain* 38 D5
Calacuccia *France* 21 F13
Calafat *Romania* 28 G7
Calafate *Argentina* 128 G2
Calafell *Spain* 38 D6
Calahorra *Spain* 38 C3
Calais *France* 19 B8
Calais *U.S.A.* 113 C20
Calakmul △ *Mexico* 119 D7
Calalaste, Cord. de *Argentina* 126 B2
Calama *Brazil* 124 E6
Calama *Chile* 126 A2
Calamar *Colombia* 124 A4
Calamian Group *Phil.* 61 F3
Calamocha *Spain* 38 E3
Calamonte *Spain* 37 G4
Călan *Romania* 28 E7
Calañas *Spain* 37 H4
Calanda *Spain* 38 E4
Calang *Indonesia* 62 D1
Calangiánus *Italy* 42 B2
Calanscio, Sarīr *Libya* 79 C10
Calapan *Phil.* 61 E4
Călărași *Moldova* 29 C13
Călărași *Romania* 29 F12
Călărași □ *Romania* 29 F12
Calascibetta *Italy* 43 E7
Calasparra *Spain* 39 G3
Calatafimi *Italy* 42 E5
Calatayud *Spain* 38 D3
Călățele *Romania* 28 D8
Calato = Kalathos *Greece* 47 E10
Calauag *Phil.* 61 E5
Calavà, C. *Italy* 43 D7
Calavite, C. *Phil.* 61 E4
Calayan *Phil.* 61 B4
Calbayog *Phil.* 61 E6

Calca *Peru* 124 F4
Calcasieu L. *U.S.A.* 116 G8
Calcutta = Kolkata *India* 69 H13
Calcutta *U.S.A.* 114 F4
Caldaro *Italy* 41 B8
Caldas da Rainha *Portugal* 37 F1
Caldas de Reis *Spain* 36 C2
Calder → *U.K.* 14 D6
Caldera *Chile* 126 B1
Caldera de Taburiente △ *Canary Is.* 48 F2
Caldwell *Idaho, U.S.A.* 108 E5
Caldwell *Kans., U.S.A.* 112 G5
Caldwell *Tex., U.S.A.* 116 F6
Caledon *S. Africa* 88 E2
Caledon → *S. Africa* 88 E4
Caledon B. *Australia* 94 A2
Caledonia *Canada* 114 C5
Caledonia *U.S.A.* 114 D7
Calella *Spain* 38 D7
Calemba *Angola* 88 B2
Calen *Australia* 94 b
Calenzana *France* 21 F12
Caletones *Chile* 126 C1
Calexico *U.S.A.* 111 N11
Calf of Man *I. of Man* 14 C3
Calgary *Canada* 102 C6
Calheta *Madeira* 48 D2
Calhoun *U.S.A.* 117 D12
Cali *Colombia* 124 C3
Calicut *India* 66 P9
Caliente *U.S.A.* 109 H6
California *Mo., U.S.A.* 112 F7
California *Pa., U.S.A.* 114 F5
California □ *U.S.A.* 110 H7
California, Baja, T.N. = Baja California □ *Mexico* 118 B2
California, Baja, T.S. = Baja California Sur □ *Mexico* 118 B2
California, G. de *Mexico* 118 B2
California City *U.S.A.* 111 K9
California Hot Springs *U.S.A.* 111 K8
Calilegua △ *Argentina* 126 B3
Călimănești *Romania* 29 E9
Călimani, Munții *Romania* 29 C10
Calingasta *Argentina* 126 C2
Calipatria *U.S.A.* 111 M11
Calistoga *U.S.A.* 110 G4
Calitri *Italy* 43 B8
Calitzdorp *S. Africa* 88 E3
Callabonna, L. *Australia* 95 D3
Callac *France* 18 D3
Callan *Ireland* 12 D4
Callander *U.K.* 13 E4
Callao *Peru* 124 F3
Callicoon *U.S.A.* 115 E9
Calling Lake *Canada* 102 B6
Calliope *Australia* 94 C5
Callosa de Ensarriá *Spain* 39 G4
Callosa de Segura *Spain* 39 G4
Calne *U.K.* 15 F6
Calola *Angola* 88 B2
Calolbon = San Andres *Phil.* 61 E6
Calonge *Spain* 38 D8
Calore → *Italy* 43 B7
Caloundra *Australia* 95 D5
Calpe *Spain* 39 G5
Calpella *U.S.A.* 110 F3
Calpine *U.S.A.* 110 F6
Calstock *Canada* 104 C3
Caltabellotta *Italy* 42 E6
Caltagirone *Italy* 43 E7
Caltanissetta *Italy* 43 E7
Çaltıbük *Turkey* 45 G12
Caluire-et-Cuire *France* 19 G11
Calulo *Angola* 84 G2
Caluso *Italy* 40 C4
Calvados □ *France* 18 C6
Calvert → *Australia* 94 B2
Calvert I. *Canada* 102 C3
Calvert Ra. *Australia* 92 D3
Calvi *France* 21 F12
Calviá *Spain* 39 F7
Calvillo *Mexico* 118 C4
Calvinia *S. Africa* 88 E2
Calvo, Mte. *Italy* 41 G12
Calwa *U.S.A.* 110 J7
Calzada Almuradiel = Almuradiel *Spain* 37 G7
Calzada de Calatrava *Spain* 37 G7
Cam → *U.K.* 15 E8
Cam Lam *Vietnam* 65 G7
Cam Pha *Vietnam* 58 G6
Cam Ranh *Vietnam* 65 G7
Cam Xuyen *Vietnam* 64 C6
Camabatela *Angola* 84 F3
Camacha *Madeira* 48 D3
Camacupa *Angola* 85 G3
Camagüey *Cuba* 120 B4
Camaiore *Italy* 40 E7
Camaná *Peru* 124 G4
Camanche Res. *U.S.A.* 110 G6
Camaquã *Brazil* 127 C5
Camaquã → *Brazil* 127 C5
Câmara de Lobos *Madeira* 48 D3

Camarat, C. *France* **21** E10
Camarès *France* **20** E6
Camaret-sur-Mer *France* **18** D2
Camargo *Mexico* **119** B5
Camargue *France* **21** E8
Camargue △ *France* **21** E8
Camarillo *U.S.A.* **111** L7
Camariñas *Spain* **36** B1
Camarón, C. *Honduras* **120** C2
Camarones *Argentina* **128** E3
Camas *Spain* **37** H4
Camas *U.S.A.* **110** E4
Camas Valley *U.S.A.* **108** E2
Camballin *Australia* **92** C3
Cambará *Brazil* **127** A5
Cambay = Khambhat *India* **68** H5
Cambay, G. of =
    Khambhat, G. of *India* **66** J8
Cambil *Spain* **37** H7
Cambo-les-Bains *France* **20** E2
Cambodia ■ *Asia* **64** F5
Camborne *U.K.* **15** G2
Cambrai *France* **19** B10
Cambre *Spain* **36** B2
Cambria *U.S.A.* **110** K5
Cambrian Mts. *U.K.* **15** E4
Cambridge *Canada* **114** C4
Cambridge *Jamaica* **120** a
Cambridge *N.Z.* **91** B5
Cambridge *U.K.* **15** E8
Cambridge *Mass., U.S.A.* **115** D13
Cambridge *Minn., U.S.A.* **112** C7
Cambridge *N.Y., U.S.A.* **115** C11
Cambridge *Nebr., U.S.A.* **112** E3
Cambridge *Ohio, U.S.A.* **114** F3
Cambridge Bay =
    Ikaluktutiak *Canada* **100** C9
Cambridge G. *Australia* **92** B4
Cambridge Springs *U.S.A.* **114** E4
Cambridgeshire □ *U.K.* **15** E7
Cambrils *Spain* **38** D6
Cambuci *Brazil* **127** A7
Cambundi-Catembo *Angola* **84** G3
Camden *Ala., U.S.A.* **117** F11
Camden *Ark., U.S.A.* **116** E8
Camden *Maine, U.S.A.* **113** C19
Camden *N.J., U.S.A.* **115** G9
Camden *N.Y., U.S.A.* **115** C9
Camden *S.C., U.S.A.* **117** D14
Camden Sd. *Australia* **92** C3
Camdenton *U.S.A.* **112** F7
Camelford *U.K.* **15** G3
Çameli *Turkey* **47** D11
Camenca *Moldova* **29** B13
Camerino *Italy* **41** E10
Cameron *Ariz., U.S.A.* **109** J8
Cameron *La., U.S.A.* **116** G8
Cameron *Mo., U.S.A.* **112** F6
Cameron *Tex., U.S.A.* **116** F6
Cameron Highlands
    Malaysia **65** K3
Cameron Hills *Canada* **102** B5
Cameroon ■ *Africa* **79** G7
Camerota *Italy* **43** B8
Cameroun → *Cameroon* **83** E6
Cameroun, Mt. *Cameroon* **83** E6
Cametá *Brazil* **125** D9
Çamiçi Gölü *Turkey* **47** D9
Camiguin □ *Phil.* **61** G6
Camiguin I. *Phil.* **61** B4
Camiling *Phil.* **61** D4
Camilla *U.S.A.* **117** F12
Caminha *Portugal* **36** D2
Camino *U.S.A.* **110** G6
Camira Creek *Australia* **95** D5
Cammal *U.S.A.* **114** E7
Cammarata *Italy* **42** E6
Camocim *Brazil* **125** D10
Camooweal *Australia* **94** B2
Camooweal Caves △
    Australia **94** C2
Camopi *Fr. Guiana* **125** C8
Camotes Is. *Phil.* **61** F6
Camotes Sea *Phil.* **61** F6
Camp Borden *Canada* **114** B5
Camp Hill *U.S.A.* **114** F8
Camp Nelson *U.S.A.* **111** J8
Camp Pendleton *U.S.A.* **111** M9
Camp Verde *U.S.A.* **109** J8
Camp Wood *U.S.A.* **116** G4
Campagna *Italy* **43** B8
Campana *Argentina* **126** C4
Campana, I. *Chile* **128** F1
Campanário *Madeira* **48** D2
Campanario *Spain* **37** G5
Campánia □ *Italy* **43** B7
Campbell *S. Africa* **88** D3
Campbell *Calif., U.S.A.* **110** H5
Campbell *Ohio, U.S.A.* **114** E4
Campbell I. *Pac. Oc.* **96** N8
Campbell L. *Canada* **103** A7
Campbell Plateau *S. Ocean* **5** A11
Campbell River *Canada* **102** C3
Campbell Town *Australia* **95** G4
Campbellford *Canada* **114** B7
Campbellpur *Pakistan* **68** C5
Campbellton *Canada* **105** C6

Campbelltown *Australia* **95** E5
Campbeltown *U.K.* **13** F3
Campeche *Mexico* **119** D6
Campeche □ *Mexico* **119** D6
Campeche, Golfo de *Mexico* **119** D6
Campello *Spain* **39** G4
Câmpeni *Romania* **28** D8
Camperdown *Australia* **95** F3
Camperville *Canada* **103** C8
Campi Salentina *Italy* **43** B11
Câmpia Turzii *Romania* **29** D8
Campidano *Italy* **42** C1
Campíglia Maríttima *Italy* **40** E7
Campillo de Altobuey *Spain* **39** F3
Campillos *Spain* **37** H6
Câmpina *Romania* **29** E10
Campina Grande *Brazil* **125** E11
Campinas *Brazil* **127** A6
Campli *Italy* **41** F10
Campo *Spain* **38** C5
Campo de Criptana *Spain* **37** F7
Campo de Gibraltar *Spain* **37** J5
Campo Grande *Brazil* **125** H8
Campo Maior *Brazil* **125** D10
Campo Maior *Portugal* **37** F3
Campo Mourão *Brazil* **127** A5
Campo Túres *Italy* **41** B8
Campobasso *Italy* **43** A7
Campobello di Licata *Italy* **42** E6
Campobello di Mazara *Italy* **42** E5
Campofelice di Roccella *Italy* **42** E6
Campomarino *Italy* **41** G12
Camporeale *Italy* **42** E6
Camporrobles *Spain* **38** F3
Campos *Brazil* **127** A7
Campos *Spain* **48** B10
Campos Belos *Brazil* **125** F9
Campos Novos *Brazil* **127** B5
Camprodón *Spain* **38** C7
Camptonville *U.S.A.* **110** F5
Camptown *U.S.A.* **115** E8
Câmpulung *Argeş, Romania* **29** E10
Câmpulung *Suceava,
    Romania* **29** C11
Câmpuri *Romania* **29** D11
Camrose *Canada* **102** C6
Camsell Portage *Canada* **103** B7
Çamyuva *Turkey* **47** E12
Çan *Turkey* **45** F11
Can Clavo *Spain* **48** C7
Can Creu *Spain* **48** C7
Can Gio *Vietnam* **65** G6
Can Tho *Vietnam* **65** G5
Canaan *U.S.A.* **115** D11
Canada ■ *N. Amer.* **100** D10
Canada Abyssal Plain *Arctic* **4** B18
Canada Basin *Arctic* **4** B18
Cañada de Gómez *Argentina* **126** C3
Canadian *U.S.A.* **116** D4
Canadian → *U.S.A.* **116** D7
Canadian Shield *Canada* **98** D12
Canajoharie *U.S.A.* **115** D10
Çanakkale *Turkey* **45** F10
Çanakkale □ *Turkey* **45** F10
Çanakkale Boğazı *Turkey* **45** F10
Canal Flats *Canada* **102** C5
Canalejas *Argentina* **126** D2
Canals *Argentina* **126** C3
Canals *Spain* **39** G4
Canandaigua *U.S.A.* **114** D7
Canandaigua L. *U.S.A.* **114** D7
Cananea *Mexico* **118** A2
Canarias, Is. *Atl. Oc.* **48** F4
Canaries *St. Lucia* **121** f
Canarreos, Arch. de los
    Cuba **120** B3
Canary Is. = Canarias, Is.
    Atl. Oc. **48** F4
Canaseraga *U.S.A.* **114** D7
Canatlán *Mexico* **118** C4
Canaveral, C. *U.S.A.* **117** G14
Canaveral △ *U.S.A.* **117** G14
Cañaveruelas *Spain* **38** E2
Canavieiras *Brazil* **125** G11
Canberra *Australia* **95** F4
Canby *Calif., U.S.A.* **108** F3
Canby *Minn., U.S.A.* **112** C5
Canby *Oreg., U.S.A.* **110** E4
Cancale *France* **18** D5
Canche → *France* **19** B8
Cancún *Mexico* **119** C7
Candanchu *Spain* **38** C4
Çandarlı *Turkey* **47** C8
Çandarlı Körfezi *Turkey* **47** C8
Candas *Spain* **36** B5
Candé *France* **18** E5
Candela *Italy* **43** A8
Candelaria *Argentina* **127** B4
Candelaria *Canary Is.* **48** F3
Candelario △ *U.S.A.* **111** L7
Candeleda *Spain* **36** E5
Candelo *Australia* **95** F4
Candi Dasa *Indonesia* **63** J18
Candia = Iraklio *Greece* **49** D7
Candia, Sea of = Crete, Sea
    of *Greece* **47** E7
Candle L. *Canada* **103** C7
Candlemas I. *Antarctica* **5** B1

Cando *U.S.A.* **112** A4
Candon *Phil.* **61** C4
Canea = Chania *Greece* **49** D6
Canelli *Italy* **40** D5
Canelones *Uruguay* **127** C4
Canet-Plage *France* **20** F7
Cañete *Chile* **126** D1
Cañete *Peru* **124** F3
Cañete *Spain* **38** E3
Cañete de las Torres *Spain* **37** H6
Cangas *Spain* **36** C2
Cangas de Narcea *Spain* **36** B4
Cangas de Onís *Spain* **36** B5
Cangnan *China* **59** D13
Canguaretama *Brazil* **125** E11
Canguçu *Brazil* **127** C5
Canguçu, Serra do *Brazil* **127** C5
Cangwu *China* **59** F8
Cangxi *China* **58** B5
Cangyuan *China* **58** F2
Cangzhou *China* **56** E9
Caniapiscau → *Canada* **105** A6
Caniapiscau, L. *Canada* **105** B6
Canicattì *Italy* **42** E6
Canicattini Bagni *Italy* **43** E8
Caniles *Spain* **37** H8
Canim Lake *Canada* **102** C4
Canindeyú □ *Paraguay* **127** A5
Canino *Italy* **41** F8
Canisteo *U.S.A.* **114** D7
Canisteo → *U.S.A.* **114** D7
Cañitas de Felipe Pescador
    Mexico **118** C4
Cañizal *Spain* **36** D5
Canjáyar *Spain* **37** H8
Çankırı *Turkey* **72** B5
Çankırı □ *Turkey* **72** B5
Cankuzo *Burundi* **86** C3
Canmore *Canada* **102** C5
Cann River *Australia* **95** F4
Canna *U.K.* **13** D2
Cannannore *India* **66** P9
Cannes *France* **21** E11
Canning Town = Port
    Canning *India* **69** H13
Cannington *Canada* **114** B5
Cannóbio *Italy* **40** B5
Cannock *U.K.* **15** E5
Cannonball → *U.S.A.* **112** B3
Cannondale Mt. *Australia* **94** D4
Cannonsville Res. *U.S.A.* **115** D9
Cannonvale *Australia* **94** J6
Canoas *Brazil* **127** B5
Canoe L. *Canada* **103** B7
Canon City *U.S.A.* **108** G11
Cañón de Río Blanco △
    Mexico **119** D5
Cañón del Río Lobos △ *Spain* **36** D7
Cañón del Sumidero △
    Mexico **119** D5
Canonniers Pt. *Mauritius* **85** d
Canora *Canada* **103** C8
Canosa di Púglia *Italy* **43** A9
Canowindra *Australia* **95** E4
Canso *Canada* **105** C7
Cantabria □ *Spain* **36** B7
Cantabria, Sierra de *Spain* **38** C2
Cantabrian Mts. =
    Cantábrica, Cordillera
    Spain **36** C5
Cantábrica, Cordillera *Spain* **36** C5
Cantal □ *France* **20** C6
Cantal, Plomb du *France* **20** C6
Cantanhede *Portugal* **36** E2
Cantavieja *Spain* **38** E4
Čantavir *Serbia* **28** E4
Cantemir *Moldova* **29** D13
Canterbury *Australia* **94** D3
Canterbury *U.K.* **15** F9
Canterbury Bight *N.Z.* **91** F3
Canterbury Plains *N.Z.* **91** E3
Cantil *U.S.A.* **111** K9
Cantillana *Spain* **37** H5
Canton = Guangzhou *China* **59** F9
Canton *Ga., U.S.A.* **117** D12
Canton *Ill., U.S.A.* **112** E8
Canton *Miss., U.S.A.* **117** E9
Canton *Mo., U.S.A.* **112** E8
Canton *N.Y., U.S.A.* **115** B9
Canton *Ohio, U.S.A.* **114** F3
Canton *Pa., U.S.A.* **114** E8
Canton *S. Dak., U.S.A.* **112** D5
Canton L. *U.S.A.* **116** C5
Cantù *Italy* **40** C6
Canudos *Brazil* **124** E7
Canumã → *Brazil* **124** D7
Canutama *Brazil* **124** E6
Canutillo *U.S.A.* **116** F1
Canvey *U.K.* **15** F8
Canyon *U.S.A.* **116** D4
Canyon De Chelly △ *U.S.A.* **109** H9
Canyonlands △ *U.S.A.* **109** G9
Canyons of the Ancients △
    U.S.A. **109** H9
Canyonville *U.S.A.* **108** E2
Cao Bang *Vietnam* **58** F6
Cao He → *China* **57** D13
Cao Lanh *Vietnam* **65** G5

Cao Xian *China* **56** G8
Cáorle *Italy* **41** C9
Cap-aux-Meules *Canada* **105** C7
Cap-Chat *Canada* **105** C6
Cap-de-la-Madeleine
    Canada **104** C5
Cap-Haïtien *Haiti* **121** C5
Cap Pt. *St. Lucia* **121** f
Capac *U.S.A.* **114** D1
Capaccio *Italy* **43** B8
Capáccio *Italy* **43** B8
Capanaparo → *Venezuela* **124** B5
Capánnori *Italy* **40** E7
Capbreton *France* **20** E2
Capdenac *France* **20** D6
Capdepera *Spain* **48** B10
Cape → *Australia* **94** C4
Cape Arid △ *Australia* **93** F3
Cape Barren I. *Australia* **95** G4
Cape Breton Highlands △
    Canada **105** C7
Cape Breton I. *Canada* **105** C7
Cape Charles *U.S.A.* **113** G15
Cape Coast *Ghana* **83** D4
Cape Cod △ *U.S.A.* **113** E18
Cape Coral *U.S.A.* **117** H14
Cape Dorset *Canada* **101** C12
Cape Fear → *U.S.A.* **117** E15
Cape Girardeau *U.S.A.* **112** G9
Cape Hatteras △ *U.S.A.* **117** D17
Cape Le Grand △ *Australia* **93** F3
Cape Lookout △ *U.S.A.* **117** D16
Cape May *U.S.A.* **113** F16
Cape May Point *U.S.A.* **113** F16
Cape Melville △ *Australia* **94** A3
Cape Mount △ *Liberia* **82** D2
Cape Peninsula △ *S. Africa* **88** E2
Cape Range △ *Australia* **92** D1
Cape Tormentine *Canada* **105** C7
Cape Town *S. Africa* **88** E2
Cape Tribulation △ *Australia* **94** B4
Cape Verde Is. ■ *Atl. Oc.* **78** b
Cape Vincent *U.S.A.* **115** B8
Cape York Peninsula
    Australia **94** A3
Capela *Brazil* **125** F11
Capella *Australia* **94** C4
Capendu *France* **20** E6
Capestang *France* **20** E7
Capesterre-Belle-Eau
    Guadeloupe **120** b
Capesterre-de-Marie-
    Galante *Guadeloupe* **120** b
Capim → *Brazil* **125** D9
Capistrello *Italy* **41** G10
Capitan *U.S.A.* **109** K11
Capitán Arturo Prat
    Antarctica **5** C17
Capitol Reef △ *U.S.A.* **109** G8
Capitola *U.S.A.* **110** J5
Capizzi *Italy* **43** E7
Capoche → *Mozam.* **87** F3
Capodichino, Nápoli ✈
    (NAP) *Italy* **43** B7
Capoterra *Italy* **42** C1
Cappadocia *Turkey* **72** C6
Cappraia *Italy* **40** E6
Caprara, Pta. *Italy* **42** A1
Caprarola *Italy* **41** F9
Capreol *Canada* **104** C3
Caprera *Italy* **42** A2
Capri *Italy* **43** B7
Capricorn Group *Australia* **94** C5
Capricorn Ra. *Australia* **92** D2
Caprino Veronese *Italy* **40** C7
Caprivi □ *Namibia* **88** B3
Caprivi Strip *Namibia* **88** B3
Caps et Marais d'Opale △
    France **19** B9
Captain's Flat *Australia* **95** F4
Captieux *France* **20** D3
Capulin Volcano △ *U.S.A.* **116** C3
Caquetá → *Colombia* **124** D5
Caracal *Romania* **29** F9
Caracas *Venezuela* **124** A5
Caracol *Belize* **120** C2
Caracol *Mato Grosso do Sul,
    Brazil* **126** A4
Caracol *Piauí, Brazil* **125** E10
Carágito *Italy* **40** D4
Carajás *Brazil* **125** E8
Carajás, Serra dos *Brazil* **125** E8
Carangola *Brazil* **127** A7
Caransebeş *Romania* **28** E7
Carantec *France* **18** D3
Caraquet *Canada* **105** C6
Caras *Peru* **124** E3
Caraş Severin □ *Romania* **28** E7
Caraşova *Romania* **28** E6
Caratasca, L. *Honduras* **120** C3
Caratinga *Brazil* **125** G10
Caraúbas *Brazil* **125** E11
Caravaca de la Cruz *Spain* **39** G3
Caravággio *Italy* **40** C6
Caravela *Guinea-Biss.* **82** C1
Caravelas *Brazil* **125** G11
Caraveli *Peru* **124** G4

Caravelle, Presqu'île de la
    Martinique **120** c
Caràzinho *Brazil* **127** B5
Carballino = O Carballiño
    Spain **36** C2
Carballo *Spain* **36** B2
Carberry *Canada* **103** D9
Carbó *Mexico* **118** B2
Carbonara, C. *Italy* **42** C2
Carbondale *Colo., U.S.A.* **108** G10
Carbondale *Ill., U.S.A.* **112** G9
Carbondale *Pa., U.S.A.* **115** E9
Carbonear *Canada* **105** C9
Carboneras *Spain* **39** J3
Carboneras de Guadazaón
    Spain **38** F3
Carbónia *Italy* **42** C1
Carcabuey *Spain* **37** H6
Carcagente = Carcaixent
    Spain **39** F4
Carcaixent *Spain* **39** F4
Carcajou *Canada* **102** B5
Carcar *Phil.* **61** F5
Carcasse, C. *Haiti* **121** C5
Carcassonne *France* **20** E6
Carcross *Canada* **102** A2
Çardak *Çanakkale, Turkey* **45** F10
Çardak *Denizli, Turkey* **47** D11
Cardamon Hills *India* **66** Q10
Cardeña *Spain* **37** G6
Cárdenas *Cuba* **120** B3
Cárdenas *San Luis Potosí,
    Mexico* **119** C5
Cárdenas *Tabasco, Mexico* **119** D6
Cardenete *Spain* **38** F3
Cardiff *U.K.* **15** F4
Cardiff □ *U.K.* **15** F4
Cardiff-by-the-Sea *U.S.A.* **111** M9
Cardigan *U.K.* **15** E3
Cardigan B. *U.K.* **15** E3
Cardinal *Canada* **115** B9
Cardona *Italy* **38** D6
Cardona *Uruguay* **126** C4
Cardoner → *Spain* **38** D6
Cardoso, Ilha do *Brazil* **127** B5
Cardston *Canada* **102** D6
Cardwell *Australia* **94** B4
Careen L. *Canada* **103** B7
Carei *Romania* **28** C7
Careme = Ciremay
    Indonesia **63** G13
Carentan *France* **18** C5
Carey *U.S.A.* **108** E7
Carey, L. *Australia* **93** E3
Carey L. *Canada* **103** A8
Careysburg *Liberia* **82** D2
Cargèse *France* **21** F12
Carhaix-Plouguer *France* **18** D3
Carhué *Argentina* **126** D3
Caria *Turkey* **47** D10
Cariacica *Brazil* **125** H10
Cariati *Italy* **43** C9
Caribbean Sea *W. Indies* **121** D5
Cariboo Mts. *Canada* **102** C4
Caribou *U.S.A.* **113** B19
Caribou → *Man., Canada* **103** B10
Caribou → *N.W.T., Canada* **102** A3
Caribou I. *Canada* **104** C2
Caribou Is. *Canada* **102** A6
Caribou L. *Man., Canada* **103** B9
Caribou L. *Ont., Canada* **104** B2
Caribou Mts. *Canada* **102** B5
Caribou River △ *Canada* **103** B9
Caribrod = Dimitrovgrad
    Serbia **44** C6
Carichíc *Mexico* **118** B3
Carigara *Phil.* **61** F6
Carignan *France* **19** C12
Carignano *Italy* **40** D4
Carinda *Australia* **95** E4
Cariñena *Spain* **38** D3
Carinhanha *Brazil* **125** F10
Carinhanha → *Brazil* **125** F10
Carini *Italy* **42** D6
Cariño *Spain* **36** B3
Carínola *Italy* **42** A6
Carinthia = Kärnten □
    Austria **26** E6
Caripito *Venezuela* **124** A6
Carlet *Spain* **39** F4
Carleton, Mt. *Canada* **105** C6
Carleton Place *Canada* **115** A8
Carletonville *S. Africa* **88** D4
Cârlibaba *Romania* **29** C10
Carlin *U.S.A.* **108** F5
Carlingford L. *U.K.* **12** B5
Carlinville *U.S.A.* **112** F9
Carlisle *U.K.* **14** C5
Carlisle *U.S.A.* **114** F7
Carlisle B. *Barbados* **121** g
Carlisle I. *Australia* **94** J7
Carlit, Pic *France* **20** F5
Carloforte *Italy* **42** C1
Carlos Casares *Argentina* **126** D3
Carlos Tejedor *Argentina* **126** D3
Carlow *Ireland* **12** D5
Carlow □ *Ireland* **12** D5

Carlsbad *Calif., U.S.A.* **111** M9
Carlsbad *N. Mex., U.S.A.* **109** K11
Carlsbad Caverns △ *U.S.A.*
    109 K11
Carluke *U.K.* **13** F5
Carlyle *Canada* **103** D8
Carmacks *Canada* **100** C6
Carmagnola *Italy* **40** D4
Carman *Canada* **103** D9
Carmarthen *U.K.* **15** F3
Carmarthen B. *U.K.* **15** F3
Carmarthenshire □ *U.K.* **15** F3
Carmaux *France* **20** D6
Carmel *U.S.A.* **115** E11
Carmel-by-the-Sea *U.S.A.* **110** J5
Carmel Valley *U.S.A.* **110** J5
Carmelo *Uruguay* **126** C4
Carmen *Colombia* **124** B3
Carmen *Paraguay* **127** B4
Carmen → *Mexico* **118** A3
Carmen, I. *Mexico* **118** B2
Carmen de Patagones
    Argentina **128** E4
Cármenes *Spain* **36** C5
Carmensa *Argentina* **126** D2
Carmi *Canada* **102** D5
Carmi *U.S.A.* **112** F9
Carmichael *U.S.A.* **110** G5
Carmila *Australia* **94** C4
Carmona *Costa Rica* **120** E2
Carmona *Spain* **37** H5
Carn Ban *U.K.* **13** D4
Carn Eige *U.K.* **13** D3
Carnac *France* **18** E3
Carnamah *Australia* **93** E2
Carnarvon *Australia* **93** D1
Carnarvon *S. Africa* **88** E3
Carnarvon △ *Australia* **94** C4
Carnarvon Ra. *Queens.,
    Australia* **94** D4
Carnarvon Ra. *W. Austral.,
    Australia* **93** E3
Carnation *U.S.A.* **110** C5
Carncastle *U.K.* **12** B6
Carndonagh *Ireland* **12** A4
Carnduff *Canada* **103** D8
Carnegie *U.S.A.* **114** F4
Carnegie, L. *Australia* **93** E3
Carnegie Ridge *Pac. Oc.* **97** H19
Carnic Alps = Karnische
    Alpen *Europe* **26** E6
Carniche Alpi = Karnische
    Alpen *Europe* **26** E6
Carnot *C.A.R.* **84** D3
Carnot, C. *Australia* **95** E2
Carnot B. *Australia* **92** C3
Carnoustie *U.K.* **13** E6
Carnsore Pt. *Ireland* **12** D5
Caro *U.S.A.* **113** D12
Carol City *U.S.A.* **117** J14
Carolina *Brazil* **125** E9
Carolina *Puerto Rico* **121** d
Carolina *S. Africa* **89** D5
Caroline I. *Kiribati* **97** H12
Caroline Is. *Micronesia* **96** G6
Caroni *Trin. & Tob.* **125** K15
Caroni → *Venezuela* **124** B6
Caronie = Nébrodi, Monti
    Italy **43** E7
Caroona *Australia* **95** E5
Carpathians *Europe* **23** D11
Cărpineni *Moldova* **29** D13
Carpathians *Europe* **23** D11
Carpaţii Meridionali
    Romania **29** E9
Carpentaria, G. of *Australia* **94** A2
Carpentras *France* **21** D9
Carpi *Italy* **40** D7
Carpinteria *U.S.A.* **111** L7
Carpio *Spain* **36** D5
Carr Boyd Ra. *Australia* **92** C4
Carra, L. *Ireland* **12** C2
Carrabelle *U.S.A.* **117** G12
Carral *Spain* **36** B2
Carranza, Presa V. *Mexico* **118** B4
Carrara *Italy* **40** D7
Carrascal *Phil.* **61** G6
Carrascosa del Campo *Spain* **38** E2
Carrauntoohill *Ireland* **12** D2
Carrick-on-Shannon *Ireland* **12** C3
Carrick-on-Suir *Ireland* **12** D4
Carrickfergus *U.K.* **12** B6
Carrickmacross *Ireland* **12** C5
Carrieton *Australia* **95** E2
Carrillo *Mexico* **118** B4
Carrington *U.S.A.* **112** B4
Carrión → *Spain* **36** D6
Carrión de los Condes *Spain* **36** C6
Carrizal Bajo *Chile* **126** B1
Carrizalillo *Chile* **126** B1
Carrizo Cr. → *U.S.A.* **109** H12
Carrizo Plain △ *U.S.A.* **110** K7
Carrizo Springs *U.S.A.* **116** G5
Carrizozo *U.S.A.* **109** K11
Carroll *U.S.A.* **112** D6
Carrollton *Ga., U.S.A.* **117** E12
Carrollton *Ill., U.S.A.* **112** F8
Carrollton *Ky., U.S.A.* **113** F11
Carrollton *Mo., U.S.A.* **112** F7

Carrollton *Ohio, U.S.A.* **114** F3
Carron ➤ *U.K.* **13** D4
Carron, L. *U.K.* **13** D3
Carrot ➤ *Canada* **103** C8
Carrot River *Canada* **103** C8
Carrouges *France* **18** D6
Carrù *Italy* **40** D4
Carruthers *Canada* **103** C7
Carsa Dek *Ethiopia* **81** F4
Çarşamba *Turkey* **72** B7
Carsóli *Italy* **41** F10
Carson *Calif., U.S.A.* **111** M8
Carson *N. Dak., U.S.A.* **112** B3
Carson ➤ *U.S.A.* **110** F8
Carson City *U.S.A.* **110** F7
Carson Sink *U.S.A.* **108** G4
Cartagena *Colombia* **124** A3
Cartagena *Spain* **39** H4
Cartago *Colombia* **124** C3
Cartago *Costa Rica* **120** E3
Cártama *Spain* **37** J6
Cartaxo *Portugal* **37** F2
Cartaya *Spain* **37** H3
Cartersville *U.S.A.* **117** D12
Carterton *N.Z.* **91** D5
Carthage *Tunisia* **42** F3
Carthage *Ill., U.S.A.* **112** E8
Carthage *Mo., U.S.A.* **112** G6
Carthage *N.Y., U.S.A.* **113** D16
Carthage *Tex., U.S.A.* **116** E7
Cartier I. *Australia* **92** B3
Cartwright *Canada* **105** B8
Caruaru *Brazil* **125** E11
Carúpano *Venezuela* **124** A6
Caruthersville *U.S.A.* **112** G9
Carvin *France* **19** B9
Carvoeiro *Brazil* **124** D6
Carvoeiro, C. *Portugal* **37** F1
Cary *U.S.A.* **117** D15
Casa, Pas de la = Envalira,
  Port d' *Europe* **38** C6
Casa Branca *Portugal* **37** G2
Casa Grande *U.S.A.* **109** K8
Casablanca *Chile* **126** C1
Casablanca *Morocco* **78** B4
Casacalenda *Italy* **41** G11
Casalbordino *Italy* **41** F11
Casale Monferrato *Italy* **40** C5
Casalmaggiore *Italy* **40** D7
Casalpusterlengo *Italy* **40** C6
Casamance ➤ *Senegal* **82** C1
Casarano *Italy* **43** B11
Casares *Spain* **37** J5
Casas Ibáñez *Spain* **39** F3
Casasimarro *Spain* **39** F2
Casatejada *Spain* **36** F5
Casavieja *Spain* **36** E6
Cascada de Basaseachic △
  Mexico **118** B3
Cascade *Seychelles* **85** b
Cascade *Idaho, U.S.A.* **108** D5
Cascade *Mont., U.S.A.* **108** C8
Cascade Locks *U.S.A.* **110** E5
Cascade Ra. *U.S.A.* **110** D5
Cascade Res. *U.S.A.* **108** D5
Cascades, Pte. des *Réunion* **85** c
Cascais *Portugal* **37** G1
Cascavel *Brazil* **127** A5
Cáscina *Italy* **40** E7
Casco B. *U.S.A.* **113** D19
Caselle Torinese *Italy* **40** C4
Caserta *Italy* **43** A7
Casey *Antarctica* **5** C8
Caseyr, Raas = Asir, Ras
  Somali Rep. **75** E5
Cashel *Ireland* **12** D4
Casiguran *Phil.* **61** C5
Casilda *Argentina* **126** C3
Casimcea *Romania* **29** F13
Casino *Australia* **95** D5
Casiquiare ➤ *Venezuela* **124** C5
Casma *Peru* **124** E3
Casmalia *U.S.A.* **111** L6
Cásola Valsénio *Italy* **41** D8
Cásoli *Italy* **41** F11
Caspe *Spain* **38** D4
Casper *U.S.A.* **108** E10
Caspian Depression *Eurasia* **35** G9
Caspian Sea *Eurasia* **52** B6
Cass Lake *U.S.A.* **112** B6
Cassà de la Selva *Spain* **38** D7
Cassadaga *U.S.A.* **114** D5
Cassano allo Iónio *Italy* **43** C9
Cassel *France* **19** B9
Casselman *Canada* **115** A9
Casselton *U.S.A.* **112** B6
Cassiar *Canada* **102** B3
Cassiar Mts. *Canada* **102** B2
Cassino *Italy* **42** A6
Cassis *France* **21** E9
Cassville *U.S.A.* **112** G7
Castagneto Carducci *Italy* **40** E7
Castaic *U.S.A.* **111** L8
Castalia *U.S.A.* **114** E2
Castara *Trin. & Tob.* **125** J16
Castéggio *Italy* **40** C6

Castejón de Monegros *Spain* **38** D4
Castèl di Sangro *Italy* **41** G11
Castèl San Giovanni *Italy* **40** C6
Castèl San Pietro Terme
  Italy **41** D8
Castelbuono *Italy* **43** E7
Castelfidardo *Italy* **41** E10
Castelfiorentino *Italy* **40** E7
Castelfranco Emília *Italy* **41** D8
Castelfranco Véneto *Italy* **41** C8
Casteljaloux *France* **20** D4
Castellabate *Italy* **43** B7
Castellammare, G. di *Italy* **42** D5
Castellammare del Golfo
  Italy **42** D5
Castellammare di Stábia
  Italy **43** B7
Castellamonte *Italy* **40** C4
Castellane *France* **21** E10
Castellaneta *Italy* **43** B9
Castelli *Argentina* **126** D4
Castelló de la Plana *Spain* **38** F4
Castellón de la Plana □
  Spain **38** E4
Castellote *Spain* **38** E4
Castelmáuro *Italy* **41** G11
Castelnau-de-Médoc *France* **20** C3
Castelnau-Magnoac *France* **20** E4
Castelnaudary *France* **20** E5
Castelnovo ne' Monti *Italy* **40** D7
Castelnuovo di Val di
  Cécina *Italy* **40** E7
Castelo *Brazil* **127** A7
Castelo Branco *Portugal* **36** F3
Castelo Branco □ *Portugal* **36** F3
Castelo de Paiva *Portugal* **36** D2
Castelo de Vide *Portugal* **37** F3
Castelsardo *Italy* **42** B1
Castelsarrasin *France* **20** D5
Casteltérmini *Italy* **42** E6
Castelvetrano *Italy* **42** E5
Casterton *Australia* **95** F3
Castets *France* **20** E2
Castiglion Fiorentino *Italy* **41** E8
Castiglione del Lago *Italy* **41** E9
Castiglione della Pescáia
  Italy **40** F7
Castiglione delle Stiviere
  Italy **40** C7
Castilblanco *Spain* **37** F5
Castile *U.S.A.* **114** D6
Castilla, Playa de *Spain* **37** J4
Castilla-La Mancha □ *Spain* **37** F7
Castilla y Leon □ *Spain* **36** D6
Castillo de Locubín *Spain* **37** H7
Castillon-en-Couserans
  France **20** F5
Castillonès *France* **20** D4
Castillos *Uruguay* **127** C5
Castle Dale *U.S.A.* **108** G8
Castle Douglas *U.K.* **13** G5
Castle Rock *Colo., U.S.A.* **108** G11
Castle Rock *Wash., U.S.A.* **110** D4
Castlebar *Ireland* **12** C2
Castlebay *U.K.* **13** E1
Castleblaney *Ireland* **12** B5
Castlederg *U.K.* **12** B4
Castleford *U.K.* **14** D6
Castlegar *Canada* **102** D5
Castlemaine *Australia* **95** F3
Castlemaine *Ireland* **12** D2
Castlepollard *Ireland* **12** C4
Castlerea *Ireland* **12** C3
Castlereagh ➤ *Australia* **95** E4
Castlereagh B. *Australia* **94** A2
Castleton *U.S.A.* **115** C11
Castletown *I. of Man* **14** C3
Castletown Bearhaven
  Ireland **12** E2
Castor *Canada* **102** C6
Castor ➤ *Canada* **104** B4
Castorland *U.S.A.* **115** C9
Castres *France* **20** E6
Castricum *Neths.* **17** B4
Castries *St. Lucia* **121** f
Castril *Spain* **37** H8
Castro *Brazil* **127** A6
Castro *Chile* **128** E2
Castro Alves *Brazil* **125** F11
Castro del Río *Spain* **37** H6
Castro-Urdiales *Spain* **36** B7
Castro Valley *U.S.A.* **110** H4
Castro Verde *Portugal* **37** H2
Castrojeriz *Spain* **36** C6
Castropol *Spain* **36** B4
Castroreale *Italy* **43** D8
Castrovíllari *Italy* **43** C9
Castroville *U.S.A.* **110** J5
Castuera *Spain* **37** G5
Çat *Turkey* **73** C9
Cat Ba, Dao *Vietnam* **64** B6
Cat Ba △ *Vietnam* **64** B6
Cat I. *Bahamas* **121** B4
Cat L. *Canada* **104** B1
Cat Lake *Canada* **104** B1
Cat Tien △ *Vietnam* **65** G6
Čata *Slovak Rep.* **27** D11
Catacamas *Honduras* **120** D2

Cataguases *Brazil* **127** A7
Catak *Turkey* **73** C10
Catalão *Brazil* **125** G9
Çatalca *Turkey* **45** E12
Catalina *Canada* **105** C9
Catalina *Chile* **126** B2
Catalina *U.S.A.* **109** K8
Catalonia = Cataluña □
  Spain **38** D6
Cataluña □ *Spain* **38** D6
Çatalzeytin *Turkey* **72** B6
Catamarca *Argentina* **126** B2
Catamarca □ *Argentina* **126** B2
Catanauan *Phil.* **61** E5
Catanduanes □ *Phil.* **61** E6
Catanduva *Brazil* **127** A6
Catánia *Italy* **43** E8
Catánia, G. di *Italy* **43** E8
Catanzaro *Italy* **43** D9
Catarman *Phil.* **61** E6
Catatumbo-Bari △ *Colombia* **121** E5
Catbalogan *Phil.* **61** F6
Cateel *Phil.* **61** H7
Catembe *Mozam.* **89** D5
Caterham *U.K.* **15** F7
Cathcart *S. Africa* **88** E4
Cathedral City *U.S.A.* **111** M10
Cathlamet *U.S.A.* **110** D3
Catio *Guinea-Biss.* **82** C1
Catlettsburg *U.S.A.* **113** F12
Çatma Dağı *Turkey* **47** C11
Catoche, C. *Mexico* **119** C7
Católica *Italy* **41** E9
Cattólica Eraclea *Italy* **42** E6
Catuala *Angola* **88** B2
Catuane *Mozam.* **89** D5
Catur *Mozam.* **87** E4
Cauca ➤ *Colombia* **124** B4
Caucaia *Brazil* **125** D11
Caucasus Mountains *Eurasia* **35** J7
Caudete *Spain* **39** G3
Caudry *France* **19** B10
Caulnes *France* **18** D4
Caulónia *Italy* **43** D9
Caungula *Angola* **84** F3
Cauquenes *Chile* **126** D1
Caura ➤ *Venezuela* **124** B6
Cauresi ➤ *Mozam.* **87** F3
Căușani *Moldova* **29** D14
Causapscal *Canada* **105** C6
Caussade *France* **20** D5
Causse-Méjean *France* **20** D7
Causses du Quercy △ *France* **20** D5
Cauterets *France* **20** F3
Cauvery ➤ *India* **66** P11
Caux, Pays de *France* **18** C7
Cava de' Tirreni *Italy* **43** B7
Cavaillon *France* **21** E9
Cavalaire-sur-Mer *France* **21** E10
Cavalese *Italy* **41** B8
Cavalier *U.S.A.* **112** A5
Cavalla = Cavally ➤ *Africa* **82** E3
Cavallo, Î. de *France* **21** G13
Cavally ➤ *Africa* **82** E3
Cavan *Ireland* **12** C4
Cavan □ *Ireland* **12** C4
Cavárzere *Italy* **41** C9
Çavdarhisar *Turkey* **47** B11
Çavdır *Turkey* **47** D11
Cave Creek *U.S.A.* **109** K8
Cavenagh Ra. *Australia* **93** E4
Cavendish *Australia* **95** F3
Caviana, I. *Brazil* **125** C8
Cavite *Phil.* **61** D4
Cavnic *Romania* **29** C8
Cavour *Italy* **40** D4
Cavtat *Croatia* **44** D2
Cawndilla L. *Australia* **95** E3
Cawnpore = Kanpur *India* **69** F9
Caxias *Brazil* **125** D10
Caxias do Sul *Brazil* **127** B5
Çay *Turkey* **72** C4
Cay Sal Bank *Bahamas* **120** B4
Cayambe *Ecuador* **124** C3
Çaycuma *Turkey* **72** B5
Çayeli *Turkey* **73** B9
Cayenne *Fr. Guiana* **125** B8
Cayey *Puerto Rico* **121** d
Caygören Barají *Turkey* **47** B10
Cayiralan *Turkey* **72** C6
Caylus *France* **20** D5
Cayman Brac *Cayman Is.* **120** C4
Cayman Is. □ *W. Indies* **120** C3
Cayman Trough *Caribbean* **98** H11
Cayres *France* **20** D7

Cayuga *U.S.A.* **115** D8
Cayuga L. *U.S.A.* **115** D8
Cazalla de la Sierra *Spain* **37** H5
Cazânești *Romania* **29** F12
Cazaubon *France* **20** E3
Cazaux et de Sanguinet,
  Étang de *France* **20** D2
Cazenovia *U.S.A.* **115** D9
Cazombo *Angola* **85** G4
Cazorla *Spain* **37** H7
Cazorla, Sierra de *Spain* **37** G8
Cea ➤ *Spain* **36** C5
Ceamurlia de Jos *Romania* **29** F13
Ceanannus Mor *Ireland* **12** C5
Ceará = Fortaleza *Brazil* **125** D11
Ceará □ *Brazil* **125** E11
Ceará Mirim *Brazil* **125** E11
Ceauru, L. *Romania* **29** F8
Cebaco, I. de *Panama* **120** E3
Cebollar *Argentina* **126** B2
Cebollera, Sierra de *Spain* **38** D2
Cebreros *Spain* **36** E6
Cebu *Phil.* **61** F5
Čečava *Bos.-H.* **28** F2
Ceccano *Italy* **42** A6
Cece *Hungary* **28** D3
Cechi *Ivory C.* **82** D4
Cécina *Italy* **40** E7
Cécina ➤ *Italy* **40** E7
Ceclavín *Spain* **36** F4
Cedar ➤ *U.S.A.* **112** E8
Cedar City *U.S.A.* **109** H7
Cedar Creek Res. *U.S.A.* **116** E6
Cedar Falls *Iowa, U.S.A.* **112** D7
Cedar Falls *Wash., U.S.A.* **110** C5
Cedar Key *U.S.A.* **117** G13
Cedar L. *Canada* **103** C9
Cedar Park *U.S.A.* **116** F6
Cedar Rapids *U.S.A.* **112** E8
Cedartown *U.S.A.* **117** D12
Cedarvale *Canada* **102** B3
Cedarville *S. Africa* **89** E4
Cedeira *Spain* **36** B2
Cedral *Mexico* **118** C4
Cedrino ➤ *Italy* **42** B2
Cedro *Brazil* **125** E11
Cedros B. *Trin. & Tob.* **125** K15
Ceduna *Australia* **95** E1
Cée *Spain* **36** C1
Cefalù *Italy* **43** D7
Cega ➤ *Spain* **36** D6
Cegléd *Hungary* **28** C4
Céglie Messápico *Italy* **43** B10
Cehegín *Spain* **39** G3
Ceheng *China* **58** E5
Cehu-Silvaniei *Romania* **29** C8
Ceica *Romania* **28** D7
Ceira ➤ *Portugal* **36** E2
Cekik *Indonesia* **63** J17
Čelákovice *Czech Rep.* **26** A7
Celano *Italy* **41** F10
Celanova *Spain* **36** C3
Celaque △ *Honduras* **120** D2
Celaya *Mexico* **118** C4
Celebes = Sulawesi *Indonesia* **63** E6
Celebes Sea *Indonesia* **63** D6
Čelić *Bos.-H.* **28** F3
Celina *U.S.A.* **113** E11
Celinac *Bos.-H.* **28** F2
Celje *Slovenia* **41** B12
Celldömölk *Hungary* **28** C2
Celle *Germany* **24** C6
Celorico da Beira *Portugal* **36** E3
Celtic Sea *Atl. Oc.* **16** F2
Çeltikçi *Turkey* **47** D12
Çemişgezek *Turkey* **73** C8
Cenderwasih, Teluk
  Indonesia **63** E9
Cengong *China* **58** D7
Ceno ➤ *Italy* **40** D7
Centallo *Italy* **40** D4
Centelles *Spain* **38** D7
Center *N. Dak., U.S.A.* **112** B3
Center *Tex., U.S.A.* **116** F7
Centerburg *U.S.A.* **114** F2
Centerville *Calif., U.S.A.* **110** J7
Centerville *Iowa, U.S.A.* **112** E7
Centerville *Pa., U.S.A.* **114** F5
Centerville *Tenn., U.S.A.* **117** D11
Centerville *Tex., U.S.A.* **116** F7
Cento *Italy* **41** D8
Central = Tsentralnyy □
  Russia **34** D4
Central □ *Ghana* **83** D4
Central □ *Kenya* **86** C4
Central □ *Malawi* **87** E3
Central □ *Zambia* **87** E2
Central, Cordillera *Colombia* **124** C4
Central, Cordillera
  Costa Rica **120** D3

Central, Cordillera
  Dom. Rep. **121** C5
Central, Cordillera *Phil.* **61** C4
Central, Cordillera
  Puerto Rico **121** d
Central African Rep. ■
  Africa **79** G9
Central America *America* **98** H11
Central Butte *Canada* **103** C7
Central City *Colo., U.S.A.* **108** G11
Central City *Ky., U.S.A.* **112** G10
Central City *Nebr., U.S.A.* **112** E4
Central I. *Kenya* **86** B4
Central Island △ *Kenya* **86** B4
Central Kalahari □
  Botswana **88** C3
Central Makran Range
  Pakistan **66** F4
Central Pacific Basin
  Pac. Oc. **96** G10
Central Patricia *Canada* **104** B1
Central Point *U.S.A.* **108** E2
Central Russian Uplands
  Europe **6** E13
Central Siberian Plateau
  Russia **50** B12
Central Square *U.S.A.* **115** C8
Centralia *Ill., U.S.A.* **112** F9
Centralia *Mo., U.S.A.* **112** F7
Centralia *Wash., U.S.A.* **110** D4
Centre □ *Cameroon* **83** E7
Centre de Flacq *Mauritius* **85** d
Cenxi *China* **59** F8
Ceotina ➤ *Bos.-H.* **44** C2
Cephalonia = Kefalonia
  Greece **46** C2
Čepin *Croatia* **28** E3
Ceprano *Italy* **42** A6
Ceptura *Romania* **29** E11
Cepu *Indonesia* **63** G14
Ceram = Seram *Indonesia* **63** E7
Ceram Sea = Seram Sea
  Indonesia **63** E7
Cerbère *France* **20** F7
Cerbicales, Îs. *France* **21** G13
Cercal *Portugal* **37** H2
Cerdaña *Spain* **38** C6
Cère ➤ *France* **20** D5
Cerea *Italy* **41** C8
Ceredigion □ *U.K.* **15** E3
Ceres *Argentina* **126** B3
Ceres *S. Africa* **88** E2
Ceres *U.S.A.* **110** H6
Céret *France* **20** F6
Cerignola *Italy* **43** A8
Cérilly *France* **19** F9
Cerisiers *France* **19** D10
Cerizay *France* **18** F6
Çerkeş *Turkey* **72** B5
Çerkezköy *Turkey* **45** E12
Cerknica *Slovenia* **41** C11
Cerkovica *Bulgaria* **45** C8
Cermerno *Serbia* **44** C3
Çermik *Turkey* **73** C8
Cerna *Romania* **29** E13
Cerna ➤ *Romania* **29** F8
Cernavodă *Romania* **29** F13
Cernay *France* **19** E14
Cernik *Croatia* **28** E2
Cerralvo, I. *Mexico* **118** C3
Cërrik *Albania* **44** E3
Cerritos *Mexico* **118** C4
Cerro Chato *Uruguay* **127** C4
Cerro Cofre de Perote △
  Mexico **119** D5
Cerro Corá △ *Paraguay* **127** A4
Cerro el Copey △ *Venezuela* **121** D7
Cerro Hoya △ *Panama* **120** E3
Cerro Saroche △ *Venezuela* **121** D6
Certaldo *Italy* **40** E8
Cervaro ➤ *Italy* **43** A8
Cervati, Monte *Italy* **43** B8
Cervera *Spain* **38** D6
Cervera de Pisuerga *Spain* **36** C6
Cervera del Río Alhama
  Spain **38** C3
Cervéteri *Italy* **41** F9
Cérvia *Italy* **41** D9
Cervignano del Friuli *Italy* **41** C10
Cervione *France* **21** F13
Cervo *Spain* **36** B3
Cesar ➤ *Colombia* **124** A4
Cesena *Italy* **41** D9
Cesenático *Italy* **41** D9
Cēsis *Latvia* **32** D3
Česká Lípa *Czech Rep.* **26** A7
Ceská Rep. = Czech Rep. ■
  Europe **26** B8
Ceská Třebová *Czech Rep.* **27** B9
České Budějovice *Czech Rep.* **26** C7
České Velenice *Czech Rep.* **26** C7
Českobudějovický □
  Czech Rep. **26** B7

Českomoravská Vrchovina
  Czech Rep. **26** B8
Český Brod *Czech Rep.* **26** A7
Český Krumlov *Czech Rep.* **26** C7
Český Těšín *Czech Rep.* **27** B11
Cesma ➤ *Croatia* **41** C13
Çeşme *Turkey* **47** C8
Cessnock *Australia* **95** E5
Cesson-Sévigné *France* **18** D5
Cestas *France* **20** D3
Cestos ➤ *Liberia* **82** D3
Cestos Sehnkwehn △ *Liberia* **82** D3
Cetate *Romania* **29** F8
Cetin Grad *Croatia* **41** C12
Cetina ➤ *Croatia* **41** E13
Cetinje *Montenegro* **44** D2
Cetraro *Italy* **43** C8
Ceuta *N. Afr.* **78** A4
Ceva *Italy* **40** D5
Cévennes *France* **20** D7
Cévennes △ *France* **20** D7
Ceyhan *Turkey* **72** D6
Ceyhan ➤ *Turkey* **72** D6
Ceylânpınar *Turkey* **73** D9
Ceylon = Sri Lanka ■ *Asia* **66** R12
Cèze ➤ *France* **21** D8
Cha-am *Thailand* **64** F2
Cha Pa *Vietnam* **64** A4
Chabanais *France* **20** C4
Chabeuil *France* **21** D9
Chablais *France* **19** F13
Chablis *France* **19** E10
Chacabuco *Argentina* **126** C3
Chachapoyas *Peru* **124** E3
Chachoengsao *Thailand* **64** F3
Chachran *Pakistan* **68** E4
Chachro *Pakistan* **68** G4
Chaco □ *Argentina* **126** B3
Chaco □ *Paraguay* **126** A4
Chaco ➤ *U.S.A.* **109** H9
Chaco △ *Argentina* **126** B4
Chaco Austral *S. Amer.* **128** B4
Chaco Boreal *S. Amer.* **124** H6
Chaco Central *S. Amer.* **128** A4
Chaco Culture △ *U.S.A.* **109** H10
Chacon, C. *U.S.A.* **102** C2
Chad ■ *Africa* **79** F8
Chad, L. = Tchad, L. *Chad* **79** F8
Chadan *Russia* **53** D10
Chadileuvú ➤ *Argentina* **126** D2
Chadiza *Zambia* **87** E3
Chadron *U.S.A.* **112** D2
Chadyr-Lunga =
  Ciadâr-Lunga *Moldova* **29** D13
Chae Hom *Thailand* **64** C2
Chae Son △ *Thailand* **64** C2
Chaem ➤ *Thailand* **64** C2
Chaeryŏng *N. Korea* **57** E13
Chagai Hills = Chāh Gay
  Hills *Afghan.* **66** E3
Chagda *Russia* **53** D14
Chaghcharān *Afghan.* **66** B4
Chagny *France* **19** F11
Chagoda *Russia* **32** C9
Chagos Arch. ☑ *Ind. Oc.* **50** J9
Chagres △ *Panama* **120** E4
Chagrin Falls *U.S.A.* **114** E3
Chaguanas *Trin. & Tob.* **125** K15
Chāh Ākhvor *Iran* **71** C8
Chāh Bahar *Iran* **71** E9
Chāh-e Kavīr *Iran* **71** C8
Chāh Gay Hills *Afghan.* **66** E3
Chahār Borjak *Afghan.* **66** D3
Chahār Mahāll va
  Bakhtīarī □ *Iran* **71** C6
Chaibasa *India* **69** H11
Chaillé-les-Marais *France* **20** B2
Chainat *Thailand* **64** E3
Chaiya *Thailand* **65** H2
Chaiyaphum *Thailand* **64** E4
Chaj Doab *Pakistan* **68** C5
Chajari *Argentina* **126** C4
Chak Amru *Pakistan* **68** C6
Chaka *Sudan* **81** G3
Chakar ➤ *Pakistan* **68** E3
Chakari *Zimbabwe* **89** B4
Chake Chake *Tanzania* **86** D4
Chakhānsūr *Afghan.* **66** D3
Chakonipau, L. *Canada* **105** A6
Chakradharpur *India* **69** H11
Chakrata *India* **68** D7
Chakwal *Pakistan* **68** C5
Chala *Peru* **124** G4
Chalais *France* **20** C4
Chalchihuites *Mexico* **118** C4
Chalcis = Halkida *Greece* **46** C5
Châlette-sur-Loing *France* **19** D9
Chaleur B. *Canada* **105** C6
Chalfant *U.S.A.* **110** H8
Chalhuanca *Peru* **124** F4
Chaliki *Greece* **46** B3
Chaling *China* **59** D9
Chalisgaon *India* **66** J9
Chalk River *Canada* **104** C4
Chalky Inlet *N.Z.* **91** G1
Challans *France* **18** F5
Challapata *Bolivia* **124** G5

Challenger Deep *Pac. Oc.* **96 F6**
Challenger Fracture Zone
Pac. Oc. **97 L17**
Challis *U.S.A.* **108 D6**
Chalmette *U.S.A.* **117 G10**
Chalon-sur-Saône *France* **19 F11**
Chalonnes-sur-Loire *France* **18 E6**
Châlons-en-Champagne
France **19 D11**
Cháltén, Cerro = Fitz Roy,
Cerro *Argentina* **128 F2**
Châlus *France* **20 C4**
Chālūs *Iran* **71 B6**
Cham *Germany* **25 F8**
Cham, Cu Lao *Vietnam* **64 E7**
Chama *U.S.A.* **109 H10**
Chamaicó *Argentina* **126 D3**
Chaman *Pakistan* **66 D5**
Chamba *India* **68 C7**
Chamba *Tanzania* **87 E4**
Chambal → *India* **69 F8**
Chamberlain *U.S.A.* **112 D4**
Chamberlain → *Australia* **92 C4**
Chamberlain L. *U.S.A.* **113 B19**
Chambers *U.S.A.* **109 J9**
Chambersburg *U.S.A.* **113 F15**
Chambéry *France* **21 C9**
Chambeshi → *Zambia* **84 G6**
Chambly *Canada* **115 A11**
Chambord *Canada* **105 C5**
Chamboulive *France* **20 C5**
Chamchamal *Iraq* **73 E11**
Chamela *Mexico* **118 D3**
Chamical *Argentina* **126 C2**
Chamkar Luong *Cambodia* **65 G4**
Chamoli *India* **69 D8**
Chamonix-Mont Blanc
France **21 C10**
Champa *India* **69 H10**
Champagne *Canada* **102 A1**
Champagne *France* **19 D11**
Champagnole *France* **19 F12**
Champaign *U.S.A.* **112 E9**
Champassak *Laos* **64 E5**
Champaubert *France* **19 D10**
Champawat *India* **69 E9**
Champdeniers-St-Denis
France **20 B3**
Champdoré, L. *Canada* **105 A6**
Champeix *France* **20 C7**
Champion *U.S.A.* **114 E4**
Champlain *U.S.A.* **115 B11**
Champlain, L. *U.S.A.* **115 B11**
Champlitte *France* **19 E12**
Champotón *Mexico* **119 D6**
Champua *India* **69 H11**
Chamusca *Portugal* **37 F2**
Chana *Thailand* **65 J3**
Chañaral *Chile* **126 B1**
Chanārān *Iran* **71 B8**
Chanasma *India* **68 H5**
Chancery Lane *Barbados* **121 g**
Chanco *Chile* **126 D1**
Chand *India* **69 J8**
Chandan *India* **69 G12**
Chandan Chauki *India* **69 E9**
Chandannagar *India* **69 H13**
Chandausi *India* **69 E8**
Chandeleur Is. *U.S.A.* **117 G10**
Chandeleur Sd. *U.S.A.* **117 G10**
Chandigarh *India* **68 D7**
Chandil *India* **69 H12**
Chandler *Australia* **95 D1**
Chandler *Canada* **105 C7**
Chandler *Ariz., U.S.A.* **109 K8**
Chandler *Okla., U.S.A.* **116 D6**
Chandod *India* **68 J5**
Chandpur *Bangla.* **67 H17**
Chandra *Greece* **49 F8**
Chandrapur *India* **66 K11**
Chānf *Iran* **71 E9**
Chang *Pakistan* **68 F3**
Chang, Ko *Thailand* **65 G4**
Ch'ang Chiang = Chang
Jiang → *China* **59 B13**
Chang Jiang → *China* **59 B13**
Chang-won *S. Korea* **57 G15**
Changa *India* **69 C7**
Changanacheri *India* **66 Q10**
Changane → *Mozam.* **89 C5**
Changbai *China* **57 D15**
Changbai Shan *China* **57 C15**
Changchiak'ou =
Zhangjiakou *China* **56 D8**
Ch'angchun = Changzhou
China **59 B12**
Changchun *China* **57 C13**
Changchunling *China* **57 B13**
Changde *China* **59 C8**
Changdo-ri *N. Korea* **57 E14**
Changfeng *China* **59 A11**
Changhai = Shanghai
China **59 B13**
Changhua *China* **59 B12**
Changhua *Taiwan* **59 E13**
Changhǔngni *N. Korea* **57 D15**
Changi *Singapore* **65 d**

Changi, Singapore ✈ (SIN)
Singapore **65 M4**
Changjiang *China* **64 C7**
Changjin *N. Korea* **57 D14**
Changjin-ho *N. Korea* **57 D14**
Changle *China* **59 E12**
Changli *China* **57 E10**
Changling *China* **57 B12**
Changlun *Malaysia* **65 J3**
Changning *Hunan, China* **59 D9**
Changning *Sichuan, China* **58 C5**
Changning *Yunnan, China* **58 E2**
Changping *China* **56 D9**
Changsha *China* **59 C9**
Changshan *China* **59 C12**
Changshan Qundao *China* **57 E12**
Changshu *China* **59 B13**
Changshun *China* **58 D6**
Changtai *China* **59 E11**
Changting *China* **59 E11**
Changwu *China* **56 G4**
Changxing *China* **59 B12**
Changyang *China* **59 B8**
Changyi *China* **57 F10**
Changyǒn *N. Korea* **57 E13**
Changyuan *China* **56 G8**
Changzhi *China* **56 F7**
Changzhou *China* **59 B12**
Chanhanga *Angola* **88 B1**
Chania *Greece* **49 D6**
Chania □ *Greece* **49 D6**
Chanion, Kolpos *Greece* **49 D5**
Chanlar = Xanlar *Azerbaijan* **35 K8**
Channapatna *India* **66 N10**
Channel Is. *U.K.* **15 H5**
Channel Is. *U.S.A.* **111 M7**
Channel Islands △ *U.S.A.* **111 L7**
Channel-Port aux Basques
Canada **105 C8**
Channel Tunnel *Europe* **15 F9**
Channing *U.S.A.* **116 D3**
Chantada *Spain* **36 C3**
Chanthaburi *Thailand* **64 F4**
Chantilly *France* **19 C9**
Chantonnay *France* **18 F5**
Chantrey Inlet *Canada* **100 C10**
Chanute *U.S.A.* **112 G6**
Chanza → *Spain* **37 H3**
Chao Hu *China* **59 B11**
Chao Phraya → *Thailand* **64 F3**
Chao Phraya Lowlands
Thailand **64 E3**
Chaocheng *China* **56 F8**
Chaohu *China* **59 B11**
Chaoyang *Guangdong, China* **59 F11**
Chaoyang *Liaoning, China* **57 D11**
Chaozhou *China* **59 F11**
Chapais *Canada* **104 C5**
Chapala *Mozam.* **87 F4**
Chapala, L. de *Mexico* **118 C4**
Chapayev *Kazakhstan* **34 E10**
Chapayevsk *Russia* **34 D9**
Chapecó *Brazil* **127 B5**
Chapel Hill *U.S.A.* **117 D15**
Chapleau *Canada* **104 C3**
Chaplin *Canada* **103 C7**
Chaplin L. *Canada* **103 C7**
Chaplino *Ukraine* **33 H9**
Chaplygin *Russia* **32 F11**
Chappell *U.S.A.* **112 E2**
Chapra = Chhapra *India* **69 G11**
Chara *Russia* **53 D12**
Charadai *Argentina* **126 B4**
Charagua *Bolivia* **124 G6**
Charakas *Greece* **49 D7**
Charambirá, Punta
Colombia **124 C3**
Charaña *Bolivia* **124 G5**
Charantsavan *Armenia* **35 K7**
Charanwala *India* **68 F5**
Charata *Argentina* **126 B3**
Charcas *Mexico* **118 C4**
Charcot I. *Antarctica* **5 C17**
Chard *U.K.* **15 G5**
Chardon *U.S.A.* **114 E3**
Chardzhou =
Türkmenabat
Turkmenistan **71 B9**
Charente □ *France* **20 C4**
Charente → *France* **20 C2**
Charente-Maritime □
France **20 C3**
Charenton-du-Cher *France* **19 F9**
Chari → *Chad* **79 F8**
Chārīkār *Afghan.* **66 B6**
Chariton *U.S.A.* **112 E7**
Chariton → *U.S.A.* **112 F7**
Chärjew = Türkmenabat
Turkmenistan **71 B9**
Charkhari *India* **69 G8**
Charkhi Dadri *India* **68 E7**
Charleroi *Belgium* **17 D4**
Charleroi *U.S.A.* **114 F5**
Charles, C. *U.S.A.* **113 G16**
Charles, Peak *Australia* **93 F3**
Charles City *U.S.A.* **112 D7**
Charles de Gaulle, Paris ✈
(CDG) *France* **19 D9**

Charles L. *Canada* **103 B6**
Charles Town *U.S.A.* **113 F15**
Charlesbourg *Canada* **113 B18**
Charleston *Ill., U.S.A.* **112 F9**
Charleston *Miss., U.S.A.* **117 D9**
Charleston *Mo., U.S.A.* **112 G9**
Charleston *S.C., U.S.A.* **117 E15**
Charleston *W. Va., U.S.A.* **113 F13**
Charleston L. *Canada* **115 B9**
Charleston Peak *U.S.A.* **111 J11**
Charlestown *Ireland* **12 C3**
Charlestown *S. Africa* **89 D4**
Charlestown *Ind., U.S.A.* **113 F11**
Charlestown *N.H., U.S.A.* **115 C12**
Charlestown of Aberlour
U.K. **13 D5**
Charleville = Rath Luirc
Ireland **12 D3**
Charleville *Australia* **95 D4**
Charleville-Mézières *France* **19 C11**
Charlevoix *U.S.A.* **113 C11**
Charlieu *France* **19 F11**
Charlotte *Mich., U.S.A.* **113 D11**
Charlotte *N.C., U.S.A.* **117 D14**
Charlotte *Vt., U.S.A.* **115 B11**
Charlotte Amalie
U.S. Virgin Is. **121 e**
Charlotte Harbor *U.S.A.* **117 H13**
Charlotte L. *Canada* **102 C3**
Charlottenberg *Sweden* **10 E6**
Charlottesville *U.S.A.* **113 F14**
Charlottetown *Nfld. & L.,
Canada* **105 B8**
Charlottetown *P.E.I.,
Canada* **105 C7**
Charlotteville *Trin. & Tob.* **125 J16**
Charlton *Australia* **95 F3**
Charlton I. *Canada* **104 B4**
Charmes *France* **19 D13**
Charny *France* **19 F11**
Charolles *France* **19 F11**
Chârost *France* **19 F9**
Charre *Mozam.* **87 F4**
Charroux *France* **20 B4**
Charsadda *Pakistan* **68 B4**
Charters Towers *Australia* **94 C4**
Chartres *France* **18 D8**
Chartreuse △ *France* **21 C9**
Chascomús *Argentina* **126 D4**
Chase *Canada* **102 C5**
Chasefu *Zambia* **87 E3**
Chashma Barrage *Pakistan* **68 C4**
Chasseneuil-sur-
Bonnieure *France* **20 C4**
Chāt *Iran* **71 B7**
Chatal Balkan = Udvoy
Balkan *Bulgaria* **45 D10**
Château-Arnoux-St-
Auban *France* **21 D10**
Château-Chinon *France* **19 E10**
Château-d'Olonne *France* **20 B2**
Château-du-Loir *France* **18 E7**
Château-Gontier *France* **18 E6**
Château-la-Vallière *France* **18 E7**
Château-Landon *France* **19 D9**
Château-Renard *France* **19 E9**
Château-Renault *France* **18 E7**
Château-Salins *France* **19 D13**
Château-Thierry *France* **19 C10**
Châteaubourg *France* **18 D5**
Châteaubriant *France* **18 E5**
Châteaudun *France* **18 D8**
Châteaugiron *France* **18 D5**
Châteauguay, L. *Canada* **105 A5**
Châteaulin *France* **18 D2**
Châteaumeillant *France* **19 F9**
Châteauneuf-du-Faou
France **18 D3**
Châteauneuf-sur-Charente
France **20 C3**
Châteauneuf-sur-Cher
France **19 F9**
Châteauneuf-sur-Loire
France **19 E9**
Châteaurenard *France* **21 E8**
Châteauroux *France* **19 F8**
Châteauvillain *France* **19 D11**
Châteaux, Pte. des
Guadeloupe **120 b**
Châtelaillon-Plage *France* **20 B2**
Châtelguyon *France* **20 C7**
Châtellerault *France* **18 F7**
Châtelus-Malvaleix *France* **19 F9**
Chatham = Chatham-Kent
Canada **114 D2**
Chatham *U.K.* **15 F8**
Chatham *U.S.A.* **115 D11**
Chatham Is. *Pac. Oc.* **96 M10**
Chatham-Kent *Canada* **114 D2**
Chatham Rise *Pac. Oc.* **96 M10**
Châtillon *Italy* **40 C4**
Châtillon-Coligny *France* **19 E9**
Châtillon-en-Diois *France* **21 D9**
Châtillon-sur-Indre *France* **18 F8**

Châtillon-sur-Loire *France* **19 E9**
Châtillon-sur-Seine *France* **19 E11**
Chatmohar *Bangla.* **69 G13**
Chatra *India* **69 G11**
Chatrapur *India* **67 K14**
Chats, L. des *Canada* **115 A8**
Chatsu *India* **68 F6**
Chatsworth *Canada* **114 B4**
Chatsworth *Zimbabwe* **87 F3**
Châttagâm = Chittagong
Bangla. **67 H17**
Chattahoochee *U.S.A.* **117 F12**
Chattahoochee → *U.S.A.* **117 F12**
Chattanooga *U.S.A.* **117 D12**
Chatteris *U.K.* **15 E8**
Chaturat *Thailand* **64 E3**
Chau Doc *Vietnam* **65 G5**
Chaudes-Aigues *France* **20 D7**
Chauffailles *France* **19 F11**
Chaukan Pass *Burma* **67 F20**
Chaumont *France* **19 D12**
Chaumont *U.S.A.* **115 B8**
Chaumont-en-Vexin *France* **19 C8**
Chaumont-sur-Loire *France* **18 E8**
Chaunay *France* **20 B4**
Chaunskaya G. *Russia* **4 C16**
Chauny *France* **19 C10**
Chausey, Îs. *France* **18 D5**
Chaussin *France* **19 F12**
Chautauqua L. *U.S.A.* **114 D5**
Chauvigny *France* **18 F7**
Chauvin *Canada* **103 C6**
Chavanges *France* **19 D11**
Chaves *Brazil* **125 D9**
Chaves *Portugal* **36 D3**
Chawang *Thailand* **65 H2**
Chazelles-sur-Lyon *France* **21 C8**
Chazy *U.S.A.* **115 B11**
Cheb *Czech Rep.* **26 A5**
Cheboksarskoye Vdkhr.
Russia **34 B8**
Cheboksary *Russia* **34 B8**
Cheboygan *U.S.A.* **113 C11**
Chebsara *Russia* **32 C10**
Chech, Erg *Africa* **78 D5**
Chechelnyk *Ukraine* **29 B14**
Chechen, Ostrov *Russia* **35 H8**
Chechenia □ *Russia* **35 J7**
Checheno-Ingush Republic
= Chechenia □ *Russia* **35 J7**
Chechnya = Chechenia □
Russia **35 J7**
Chęciny *Poland* **31 H7**
Checotah *U.S.A.* **116 D7**
Chedabucto B. *Canada* **105 C7**
Cheduba I. *Burma* **67 K18**
Cheepie *Australia* **95 D4**
Chef-Boutonne *France* **20 B3**
Chegdomyn *Russia* **53 D14**
Chegga *Mauritania* **78 C4**
Chegutu *Zimbabwe* **87 F3**
Chehalis *U.S.A.* **110 D4**
Chehalis → *U.S.A.* **110 D3**
Cheile Nerei-Beusnita △
Romania **28 F6**
Cheiron, Mt. *France* **21 E10**
Cheju = Jeju *S. Korea* **57 H14**
Cheju-do = Jeju-do *S. Korea* **57 H14**
Chekalin *Russia* **32 E9**
Chekhov *Russia* **30 D7**
Chekiang = Zhejiang □
China **59 C13**
Chel = Kuru, Bahr el →
Sudan **81 F2**
Chela, Sa. da *Angola* **88 B1**
Chelan *U.S.A.* **108 C3**
Chelan, L. *U.S.A.* **108 B3**
Cheleken = Hazar
Turkmenistan **52 F6**
Cheleken Yarymadasy
Turkmenistan **71 B7**
Chelforó *Argentina* **128 D3**
Chelkar = Shalqar
Kazakhstan **52 E6**
Chella *Ethiopia* **81 F4**
Chelles *France* **19 D9**
Chelm *Poland* **31 G10**
Chelmno *Poland* **31 E5**
Chelmsford *U.K.* **15 F8**
Chełmża *Poland* **31 E5**
Chelsea *Australia* **95 F4**
Chelsea *U.S.A.* **115 C12**
Cheltenham *U.K.* **15 F5**
Chelva *Spain* **38 F4**
Chelyabinsk *Russia* **52 D7**
Chelyuskin, C. =
Chelyuskin, Mys *Russia* **53 B11**
Chelyuskin, Mys *Russia* **53 B11**
Chemainus *Canada* **110 B3**
Chemba *Mozam.* **85 H6**
Chembar = Belinskiy *Russia* **34 D6**
Chemillé *France* **18 E6**
Chemin Grenier *Mauritius* **85 d**
Chemnitz *Germany* **24 E8**
Chemult *U.S.A.* **108 E3**
Chen, Gora *Russia* **53 C15**
Chenab → *Pakistan* **68 D4**
Chenango Forks *U.S.A.* **115 D9**

Chencha *Ethiopia* **81 F4**
Chenchiang = Zhenjiang
China **59 A12**
Cheney *U.S.A.* **108 C5**
Cheng Xian *China* **56 H3**
Chengbu *China* **59 D8**
Chengcheng *China* **56 G5**
Chengchou = Zhengzhou
China **56 G7**
Chengde *China* **57 D9**
Chengdong Hu *China* **59 A11**
Chengdu *China* **58 B5**
Chenggong *China* **58 E4**
Chenggu *China* **58 H4**
Chenghai *China* **59 F11**
Chengjiang *China* **58 E4**
Chengjiang *China* **59 A11**
Chengkou *China* **58 B7**
Chengmai *China* **64 C7**
Chengwu *China* **56 G8**
Chengxi Hu *China* **59 A11**
Chengyang *China* **57 F11**
Chenjiagang *China* **57 G10**
Chennai *India* **66 N12**
Chenôve *France* **19 E12**
Chenxi *China* **59 C8**
Chenzhou *China* **59 E9**
Cheom Ksan *Cambodia* **64 E5**
Cheonan *S. Korea* **57 F14**
Cheongdo *S. Korea* **57 G15**
Cheongju *S. Korea* **57 F14**
Cheorwon *S. Korea* **57 E14**
Chepelare *Bulgaria* **45 E8**
Chepén *Peru* **124 E3**
Chepes *Argentina* **126 C2**
Chepo *Panama* **120 E4**
Chepstow *U.K.* **15 F5**
Chequamegon B. *U.S.A.* **112 B8**
Cher □ *France* **19 E9**
Cher → *France* **18 E7**
Chéradi *Italy* **43 B10**
Cherasco *Italy* **40 D4**
Cheraw *U.S.A.* **117 D15**
Cherbourg *France* **18 C5**
Cherdakly *Russia* **34 C9**
Cherdyn *Russia* **52 C6**
Cheremkhovo *Russia* **53 D11**
Cherepanovo *Russia* **52 D9**
Cherepovets *Russia* **32 C9**
Chergui, Chott ech *Algeria* **78 B6**
Cherikov = Cherykaw
Belarus **23 B16**
Cherkasy *Ukraine* **33 H7**
Cherkasy □ *Ukraine* **33 H6**
Cherkessk *Russia* **35 H6**
Cherlak *Russia* **52 D8**
Chernaya *Russia* **53 B15**
Chernelytsya *Ukraine* **29 B10**
Chernihiv *Ukraine* **33 G6**
Chernihiv □ *Ukraine* **33 G7**
Chernivtsi *Chernivtsi,
Ukraine* **29 B10**
Chernivtsi *Vinnyts'ka,
Ukraine* **29 B13**
Chernivtsi □ *Ukraine* **29 B10**
Chernobyl = Chornobyl
Ukraine **23 C16**
Chernogorsk *Russia* **53 D10**
Chernomorskoye =
Chornomorske *Ukraine* **33 K7**
Chernovtsy = Chernivtsi
Ukraine **29 B10**
Chernyakhovsk *Russia* **30 D8**
Chernyanka *Russia* **33 G9**
Chernysheyskiy *Russia* **53 C12**
Chernyye Zemli *Russia* **35 H8**
Cherokee *Iowa, U.S.A.* **112 D6**
Cherokee *Okla., U.S.A.* **116 C5**
Cherokee Village *U.S.A.* **116 C9**
Cherokees, Grand Lake O'
The *U.S.A.* **116 C7**
Cherrapunji *India* **67 G17**
Cherry Valley *U.S.A.* **115 D10**
Cherskiy *Russia* **53 C17**
Cherskogo Khrebet *Russia* **53 C15**
Chersonisos *Greece* **49 D7**
Chersonisos Akrotiri *Greece* **49 D6**
Chertkovo *Russia* **33 H11**
Cherven *Belarus* **23 B15**
Cherven-Bryag *Bulgaria* **45 C8**
Chervonoarmiyske *Ukraine* **29 E13**
Chervonograd *Russia* **23 C13**
Cherwell → *U.K.* **15 F6**
Cherykaw *Belarus* **23 B16**
Chesapeake *U.S.A.* **113 G15**
Chesapeake B. *U.S.A.* **113 F14**
Cheshire □ *U.K.* **14 D5**
Cheshskaya Guba *Russia* **52 C5**
Cheshunt *U.K.* **15 F7**
Chesil Beach *U.K.* **15 G5**
Chesley *Canada* **114 B3**
Cheste *Spain* **39 F4**
Chester *U.K.* **14 D5**
Chester *Calif., U.S.A.* **108 F3**

Chester *Ill., U.S.A.* **112 G9**
Chester *Mont., U.S.A.* **108 B8**
Chester *Pa., U.S.A.* **113 F16**
Chester *S.C., U.S.A.* **117 D14**
Chester *Vt., U.S.A.* **115 C12**
Chester *W. Va., U.S.A.* **114 F4**
Chester-le-Street *U.K.* **14 C6**
Chesterfield *U.K.* **14 D6**
Chesterfield, Îs. *N. Cal.* **90 C8**
Chesterfield Inlet *Canada* **100 C10**
Chesterton Ra. *Australia* **95 D4**
Chesterton Range △
Australia **95 D4**
Chestertown *U.S.A.* **115 C11**
Chesterville *Canada* **115 A9**
Chesuncook L. *U.S.A.* **113 C19**
Chéticamp *Canada* **105 C7**
Chetrosu *Moldova* **29 B12**
Chetumal *Mexico* **119 D7**
Chetumal, B. de *Cent. Amer.* **119 D7**
Chetwynd *Canada* **102 B4**
Chevanceaux *France* **20 C3**
Cheviot, The *U.K.* **14 B5**
Cheviot Hills *U.K.* **14 B5**
Cheviot Ra. *Australia* **94 D3**
Chew Bahir *Ethiopia* **81 G4**
Chewelah *U.S.A.* **108 B5**
Chewore △ *Zimbabwe* **87 F2**
Cheyenne *Okla., U.S.A.* **116 D5**
Cheyenne *Wyo., U.S.A.* **108 F11**
Cheyenne → *U.S.A.* **112 C3**
Cheyenne Wells *U.S.A.* **108 G12**
Cheyne B. *Australia* **93 F2**
Chhabra *India* **68 G7**
Chhaktala *India* **68 H6**
Chhapra *India* **69 G11**
Chhata *India* **68 F7**
Chhatarpur *Jharkhand, India* **69 G11**
Chhatarpur *Mad. P., India* **69 G8**
Chhattisgarh □ *India* **69 J10**
Chhep *Cambodia* **64 F5**
Chhindwara *Mad. P., India* **69 H8**
Chhindwara *Mad. P., India* **69 H8**
Chhlong *Cambodia* **65 F5**
Chhota Tawa → *India* **68 H7**
Chhoti Kali Sindh → *India* **68 G6**
Chhuikhadan *India* **69 J9**
Chhuk *Cambodia* **65 G5**
Chi → *Thailand* **64 E5**
Chiai *Taiwan* **59 F13**
Chiali *Taiwan* **59 F13**
Chiamboni *Somali Rep.* **84 E8**
Chianciano Terme *Italy* **41 E8**
Chiang Dao *Thailand* **64 C2**
Chiang Kham *Thailand* **64 C3**
Chiang Khan *Thailand* **64 D3**
Chiang Khong *Thailand* **58 G3**
Chiang Mai *Thailand* **64 C2**
Chiang Rai *Thailand* **58 H2**
Chiang Saen *Thailand* **58 G3**
Chianti *Italy* **41 E8**
Chiapa → *Mexico* **119 D6**
Chiapa de Corzo *Mexico* **119 D6**
Chiapas □ *Mexico* **119 D6**
Chiapas, Sa. Madre de
Mexico **119 D6**
Chiaramonte Gulfi *Italy* **43 E7**
Chiaravalle *Italy* **41 E10**
Chiaravalle Centrale *Italy* **43 D9**
Chiari *Italy* **40 C6**
Chiatura *Georgia* **35 J6**
Chiautla de Tapia *Mexico* **119 D5**
Chiávari *Italy* **40 D6**
Chiavenna *Italy* **40 B6**
Chiba *Japan* **55 G10**
Chiba □ *Japan* **55 G10**
Chibabava *Mozam.* **89 C5**
Chibemba *Cunene, Angola* **85 H2**
Chibemba *Huila, Angola* **88 B2**
Chibi *Zimbabwe* **89 C5**
Chibia *Angola* **85 H2**
Chibougamau *Canada* **104 C5**
Chibougamau, L. *Canada* **104 C5**
Chibuk *Nigeria* **83 C7**
Chibuto *Mozam.* **89 C5**
Chic-Chocs, Mts. *Canada* **105 C6**
Chicacole = Srikakulam
India **67 K13**
Chicago *U.S.A.* **112 E10**
Chicago Heights *U.S.A.* **112 E10**
Chichagof I. *U.S.A.* **100 D6**
Chichaoua *Morocco* **78 B4**
Chichén-Itzá *Mexico* **119 C7**
Chicheng *China* **56 D8**
Chichester *U.K.* **15 G7**
Chichester Ra. *Australia* **92 D2**
Chichibu *Japan* **55 F9**
Chichibu-Tama △ *Japan* **55 G9**
Ch'ich'ihaerh = Qiqihar
China **53 E13**
Chicholi *India* **68 H8**
Chickasaw △ *U.S.A.* **116 D6**
Chickasha *U.S.A.* **116 D6**
Chiclana de la Frontera
Spain **37 J4**
Chiclayo *Peru* **124 E3**
Chico *U.S.A.* **110 F5**

Chico → Chubut, Argentina 128 E3
Chico → Santa Cruz, Argentina 128 G3
Chicomo Mozam. 89 C5
Chicomostoc Mexico 118 C4
Chicontepec Mexico 119 C5
Chicopee U.S.A. 115 D12
Chicoutimi Canada 105 C5
Chicualacuala Mozam. 89 C5
Chidambaram India 66 P11
Chidenguele Mozam. 89 C5
Chidley, C. Canada 101 C13
Chiducuane Mozam. 89 C5
Chiede Angola 88 B2
Chiefs Pt. Canada 114 B3
Chiem Hoa Vietnam 64 A5
Chiemsee Germany 25 H8
Chiengi Zambia 87 D2
Chiengmai = Chiang Mai Thailand 64 C2
Chienti → Italy 41 E10
Chieri Italy 40 C4
Chiers → France 19 C11
Chiesa in Valmalenco Italy 40 B6
Chiese → Italy 40 C7
Chieti Italy 41 F11
Chifeng China 57 C10
Chigirin Ukraine 33 H7
Chignecto B. Canada 105 C7
Chiguana Bolivia 126 A2
Chigwell U.K. 15 F8
Chihli, G. of = Bo Hai China 57 E10
Chihuahua Mexico 118 B3
Chihuahua □ Mexico 118 B3
Chiili = Shïeli Kazakhstan 52 E7
Chik Bollapur India 66 N10
Chikmagalur India 66 N9
Chikwawa Malawi 87 F3
Chilam Chavki Pakistan 69 B6
Chilanga Zambia 87 F2
Chilapa Mexico 119 D5
Chilas Pakistan 69 B6
Chilaw Sri Lanka 66 R11
Chilcotin → Canada 102 C4
Childers Australia 95 D5
Childress U.S.A. 116 D4
Chile ■ S. Amer. 128 D2
Chile Rise Pac. Oc. 97 L18
Chilecito Argentina 126 B2
Chilete Peru 124 E3
Chilia, Brațul → Romania 29 E14
Chililabombwe Zambia 87 E2
Chilin = Jilin China 57 C14
Chiliomodi Greece 46 D4
Chilka L. India 67 K14
Chilko → Canada 102 C4
Chilko L. Canada 102 C4
Chillagoe Australia 94 B3
Chillán Chile 126 D1
Chillicothe, Ill., U.S.A. 112 E9
Chillicothe Mo., U.S.A. 112 F7
Chillicothe Ohio, U.S.A. 113 F12
Chilliwack Canada 102 D4
Chilo India 68 F5
Chiloane, I. Mozam. 89 C5
Chiloé, I. de Chile 128 E2
Chilpancingo Mexico 119 D5
Chiltern Hills U.K. 15 F7
Chilton U.S.A. 112 C9
Chilubi Zambia 87 E2
Chilubula Zambia 87 E3
Chilumba Malawi 87 E3
Chilung Taiwan 59 E13
Chilwa, L. Malawi 87 F4
Chimaltitán Mexico 118 C4
Chimán Panama 120 E4
Chimanimani Zimbabwe 89 B5
Chimay Belgium 17 D4
Chimayo U.S.A. 109 J11
Chimbay Uzbekistan 52 E6
Chimborazo Ecuador 124 D3
Chimbote Peru 124 E3
Chimkent = Shymkent Kazakhstan 52 E7
Chimoio Mozam. 87 F3
Chimpembe Zambia 87 D2
Chin □ Burma 67 J18
Chin Hills Burma 67 H18
Chin Ling Shan = Qinling Shandi China 56 H5
China Mexico 119 B5
China ■ Asia 60 D6
China, Great Plain of Asia 50 E13
China Lake U.S.A. 111 K9
Chinan = Jinan China 56 F9
Chinandega Nic. 120 D2
Chinati Peak U.S.A. 116 G2
Chincha Alta Peru 124 F3
Chinchaga → Canada 102 B5
Chinchilla Australia 95 D5
Chinchilla de Monte Aragón Spain 39 G3
Chinchorro, Banco Mexico 119 D7
Chinchou = Jinzhou China 57 D11
Chincoteague U.S.A. 113 G16
Chinde Mozam. 87 F4
Chindwin → Burma 67 J19

Chineni India 69 C6
Chinga Mozam. 87 F4
Chingola Zambia 87 E2
Chingole Malawi 87 E3
Ch'ingtao = Qingdao China 57 F11
Chinguetti Mauritania 78 D3
Chingune Mozam. 89 C5
Chinhanguanine Mozam. 89 D5
Chinhoyi Zimbabwe 87 F3
Chini India 68 D8
Chiniot Pakistan 68 D5
Chínipas Mexico 118 B3
Chinji Pakistan 68 C5
Chinju = Jinju S. Korea 57 G15
Chinko → C.A.R. 84 D4
Chinle U.S.A. 109 H9
Chinmen Taiwan 59 E13
Chinmen Tao Taiwan 59 E12
Chinnampo = Namp'o N. Korea 57 E13
Chino Japan 55 G9
Chino U.S.A. 111 L9
Chino Valley U.S.A. 109 J7
Chinon France 18 E7
Chinook U.S.A. 108 B9
Chinook Trough Pac. Oc. 96 C10
Chinsali Zambia 87 E3
Chióggia Italy 41 C9
Chíos = Hios Greece 47 C8
Chipata Zambia 87 E3
Chiperceni Moldova 29 C13
Chipindo Angola 85 G3
Chipinge Zimbabwe 87 G3
Chipinge △ Zimbabwe 87 G3
Chipiona Spain 37 J4
Chipley U.S.A. 117 F12
Chipman Canada 105 C6
Chipoka Malawi 87 E3
Chippenham U.K. 15 F5
Chippewa → U.S.A. 112 C7
Chippewa Falls U.S.A. 112 C8
Chipping Norton U.K. 15 F6
Chiprovtsi Bulgaria 44 C6
Chiputneticook Lakes N. Amer. 113 C20
Chiquián Peru 124 F3
Chiquibul △ Belize 120 C2
Chiquimula Guatemala 120 D2
Chiquinquira Colombia 124 B4
Chir → Russia 35 F6
Chirala India 66 M12
Chiramba Mozam. 87 F3
Chirawa India 68 E6
Chirchiq Uzbekistan 52 E7
Chiredzi Zimbabwe 89 C5
Chiricahua △ U.S.A. 109 K9
Chiricahua Peak U.S.A. 109 L9
Chiriquí, G. de Panama 120 E3
Chiriquí, L. de Panama 120 E3
Chirisa △ Zimbabwe 87 F2
Chirivira Falls Zimbabwe 87 G3
Chirmiri India 69 H10
Chirnogi Romania 29 F11
Chirpan Bulgaria 45 D9
Chirripó Grande, Cerro Costa Rica 120 E3
Chirundu Zimbabwe 89 B4
Chisamba Zambia 87 E2
Chisapani Nepal 69 E9
Chisasibi Canada 104 B4
Ch'ishan Taiwan 59 F13
Chisholm Canada 102 C6
Chisholm U.S.A. 112 B8
Chishtian Mandi Pakistan 68 E5
Chishui China 58 C5
Chishui He → China 58 C5
Chisimaio Somali Rep. 75 H3
Chisimba Falls Zambia 87 E3
Chişinău Moldova 29 C13
Chişinău ✈ (KIV) Moldova 29 C13
Chişineu Criş Romania 28 D6
Chisone → Italy 40 D4
Chisos Mts. U.S.A. 116 G3
Chistopol Russia 34 C10
Chita Russia 53 D12
Chitipa Malawi 87 D3
Chitose Japan 54 C10
Chitral Pakistan 66 B7
Chitré Panama 120 E3
Chittagong Bangla. 67 H17
Chittagong □ Bangla. 67 G17
Chittaurgarh India 68 G6
Chittoor India 66 N11
Chitungwiza Zimbabwe 87 F3
Chiusi Italy 41 E8
Chiva Spain 39 F4
Chivasso Italy 40 C4
Chivhu Zimbabwe 87 F3
Chivilcoy Argentina 126 C4
Chiwanda Tanzania 87 E3
Chixi China 59 G9
Chizarira Zimbabwe 87 F2
Chizarira △ Zimbabwe 87 F2
Chizela Zambia 87 E2
Chkalov = Orenburg Russia 52 D6
Chkolovsk Russia 34 B6
Chloride U.S.A. 111 K12

Chlumec nad Cidlinou Czech Rep. 26 A8
Chmielnik Poland 31 H7
Cho Bo Vietnam 58 G5
Cho-do N. Korea 57 E13
Cho Phuoc Hai Vietnam 65 G6
Choa Chu Kang Singapore 65 d
Choba Kenya 86 B4
Chobe → Botswana 88 B4
Chocianów Poland 31 G2
Chociwel Poland 30 E2
Chocolate Mts. U.S.A. 111 M11
Choctawhatchee → U.S.A. 117 F11
Chodecz Poland 31 F6
Chodov Czech Rep. 26 A5
Chodziez Poland 31 F3
Choele Choel Argentina 128 D3
Choiseul St. Lucia 121 f
Choiseul Solomon Is. 90 B8
Choix Mexico 118 B3
Chojna Poland 31 F1
Chojnice Poland 30 E4
Chojnów Poland 31 G2
Chōkai-San Japan 54 E10
Choke Canyon Res. U.S.A. 116 G5
Choke Mts. Ethiopia 81 E4
Chokurdakh Russia 53 B15
Cholame U.S.A. 110 K6
Cholet France 18 E6
Cholguan Chile 126 D1
Choluteca Honduras 120 D2
Choluteca → Honduras 120 D2
Chom Bung Thailand 64 F2
Chom Thong Thailand 64 C2
Choma Zambia 87 F2
Chomolungma = Everest, Mt. Nepal 69 E12
Chomun India 68 F6
Chomutov Czech Rep. 26 A6
Chon Buri Thailand 64 F3
Chon Thanh Vietnam 65 G6
Chone Ecuador 124 D3
Chong Kai Cambodia 64 F4
Chong Mek Thailand 64 E5
Chong Phangan Thailand 65 b
Chong Samui Thailand 65 b
Chongde China 59 B13
Chongging China 59 B13
Chongming Dao China 59 B13
Chongqing Chongqing, China 58 C6
Chongqing Sichuan, China 58 B4
Chongqing Shi □ China 58 C6
Chongren China 59 D11
Chonguene Mozam. 89 C5
Chongyi China 59 E10
Chongzuo China 58 F6
Chonos, Arch. de los Chile 128 F2
Chop Ukraine 28 B7
Chopim → Brazil 127 B5
Chor Pakistan 68 G3
Chora Greece 46 D3
Chora Sfakion Greece 49 D6
Chorbat La India 69 B7
Chorley U.K. 14 D5
Chorna Ukraine 29 C14
Chornobyl Ukraine 23 C16
Chornomorske Ukraine 33 K7
Chorolque, Cerro Bolivia 126 A2
Choroszcz Poland 31 E9
Chorregon Australia 94 C3
Chorro el Indio △ Venezuela 121 E5
Chortkiv Ukraine 23 D13
Chorzele Poland 31 E7
Chorzów Poland 31 H5
Chos-Malal Argentina 126 D1
Ch'osan N. Korea 57 D13
Choszczno Poland 31 E2
Choteau U.S.A. 108 C7
Chotěboř Czech Rep. 26 B8
Chotila India 68 H4
Chotta Udepur India 68 H6
Chowchilla U.S.A. 110 H6
Choybalsan Mongolia 60 B6
Christchurch N.Z. 91 E4
Christchurch U.K. 15 G6
Christian I. Canada 114 B4
Christiana S. Africa 88 D4
Christiansfeld Denmark 11 J3
Christiansted U.S. Virgin Is. 121 C7
Christie B. Canada 103 A6
Christina → Canada 103 B6
Christmas Cr. → Australia 92 C4
Christmas I. = Kiritimati Kiribati 97 G12
Christmas I. Ind. Oc. 96 J2
Christopher, L. Australia 93 D4
Chrudim Czech Rep. 26 B8
Chrzanów Poland 31 H6
Chtimba Malawi 87 E3
Chū = Shū Kazakhstan 52 E8
Chu → Vietnam 64 C5
Chu Lai Vietnam 64 E7
Chuak, Ko Thailand 65 b

Ch'uanchou = Quanzhou China 59 E12
Chuanbou China 56 G6
Chubbuck U.S.A. 108 E7
Chūbu □ Japan 55 F8
Chubu-Sangaku △ Japan 55 F8
Chubut → Argentina 128 E3
Chuchi L. Canada 102 B4
Chuda India 68 H4
Chudovo Russia 32 C6
Chudskoye, Ozero Russia 32 C4
Chuguyev = Chuhuyiv Ukraine 33 H9
Chugwater U.S.A. 108 F11
Chuhuyiv Ukraine 33 H9
Chuka Kenya 86 C4
Chukchi Plateau Arctic 4 B17
Chukchi Sea Russia 53 C19
Chukotskoye Nagorye Russia 53 C18
Chula Vista U.S.A. 111 N9
Chulucanas Peru 124 E2
Chulym → Russia 52 D9
Chum Phae Thailand 64 D4
Chum Saeng Thailand 64 E3
Chumar India 69 C8
Chumbicha Argentina 126 B2
Chumerna Bulgaria 45 D9
Chumikan Russia 53 D14
Chumphon Thailand 65 G2
Chumuare Mozam. 87 E3
Chuna → Russia 53 D10
Chun'an China 59 C12
Chuncheon S. Korea 57 F14
Chunchura India 69 H13
Chunga Zambia 87 F2
Chunggang-ǔp N. Korea 57 D14
Chunghwa N. Korea 57 E13
Chungju S. Korea 57 F14
Chungking = Chongqing China 58 C6
Chungli Taiwan 59 E13
Chungt'iaoshan = Zhongtiao Shan China 56 G6
Chungyang Shanmo Taiwan 59 F13
Chunian Pakistan 68 D6
Chunya Tanzania 87 D3
Chunyang China 57 C15
Chupara Pt. Trin. & Tob. 125 K15
Chuquibamba Peru 124 G4
Chuquicamata Chile 126 A2
Chur Switz. 25 J5
Churachandpur India 67 G18
Church Stretton U.K. 15 E5
Churchill Canada 103 B10
Churchill → Man., Canada 103 B10
Churchill → Nfld. & L., Canada 105 B7
Churchill, C. Canada 103 B10
Churchill Falls Canada 105 B7
Churchill L. Canada 103 B7
Churchill Pk. Canada 102 B3
Churki India 69 H10
Churu India 68 E6
Churún Merú = Angel Falls Venezuela 124 B6
Chuska Mts. U.S.A. 109 H9
Chushal India 69 C8
Chusovoy Russia 52 D6
Chute-aux-Outardes Canada 105 C6
Chuuk = Truk Micronesia 96 G7
Chuvash Republic = Chuvashia □ Russia 34 C8
Chuvashia □ Russia 34 C8
Chuwārtah Iraq 70 C5
Chuxiong China 58 E3
Chuy Uruguay 127 C5
Chuzhou China 59 A12
Chynadiyeve Ukraine 28 B7
Ci Xian China 56 F8
Ciacova Romania 28 E6
Ciadâr-Lunga Moldova 29 D13
Ciamis Indonesia 63 G13
Cianjur Indonesia 63 G12
Cianorte Brazil 127 A5
Cibola U.S.A. 111 M12
Cibuk = Zulja → Russia 52 D6
Ciciega Colombia 124 A4
Ciciego de Ávila Cuba 120 B4
Cienfuegos Cuba 120 B3
Cíes, Is. Spain 36 C2
Cieszanów Poland 31 H10
Cieszyn Poland 31 J5
Cieza Spain 39 G3

Çifteler Turkey 72 C4
Cifuentes Spain 38 E2
Cihanbeyli Turkey 72 C5
Cihuatlán Mexico 118 D4
Cijara, Embalse de Spain 37 F6
Cijara △ Spain 37 F6
Cijulang Indonesia 63 G13
Cilacap Indonesia 63 G13
Çıldır Turkey 73 B10
Çıldır Gölü Turkey 73 B10
Cilento e Vallo di Diano △ Italy 43 B8
Cili China 59 C8
Cilibia Romania 29 E12
Cilicia Turkey 72 D5
Cilo Dağı Turkey 73 D10
Cima U.S.A. 111 K11
Cimarron Kans., U.S.A. 112 G3
Cimarron N. Mex., U.S.A. 109 H11
Cimarron → U.S.A. 116 C6
Cimişlia Moldova 29 D13
Cimone, Mte. Italy 40 D7
Çınar Turkey 73 D9
Çınarcık Turkey 45 F13
Cinca → Spain 38 D5
Cincar Bos.-H. 28 G2
Cincinnati U.S.A. 113 F11
Cincinnatus U.S.A. 115 D9
Ciney Belgium 17 D5
Cíngoli Italy 41 E10
Cinigiano Italy 41 F8
Cinto, Mte. France 21 F12
Cintruénigo Spain 38 C3
Ciocile Romania 29 F12
Ciolǎneşti din Deal Romania 29 F10
Ciorani Romania 29 F11
Čiovo Croatia 41 E13
Circeo, Mte. Italy 42 A6
Çırçır Turkey 72 C7
Circle Alaska, U.S.A. 106 a
Circle Mont., U.S.A. 108 C11
Circleville U.S.A. 113 F12
Cirebon Indonesia 63 G13
Ciremay Indonesia 63 G13
Cirencester U.K. 15 F6
Cireşu Romania 28 F7
Cirey-sur-Vezouze France 19 D13
Ciriè Italy 40 C4
Cirium Cyprus 49 E11
Cirò Italy 43 C10
Cirò Marina Italy 43 C10
Ciron → France 20 D3
Cisco U.S.A. 116 E5
Cislău Romania 29 E11
Cisna Poland 31 J9
Cisnădie Romania 29 E9
Cisterna di Latina Italy 42 A5
Cisternino Italy 43 B10
Cistierna Spain 36 C5
Citeli-Ckaro = Tsiteli-Tsqaro Georgia 35 K8
Citlaltépetl = Orizaba, Pico de Mexico 119 D5
Citrus Heights U.S.A. 110 G5
Citrusdal S. Africa 88 E2
Città del Vaticano = Vatican City ■ Europe 41 G9
Città della Pieve Italy 41 F9
Città di Castello Italy 41 E9
Città Sant' Angelo Italy 41 F11
Cittadella Italy 41 C8
Cittaducale Italy 41 F9
Cittanova Italy 43 D9
Ciuc, Munţii Romania 29 D11
Ciucaş, Vf. Romania 29 E10
Ciucea Romania 28 D7
Ciuciulea Moldova 29 C12
Ciuciuleni Moldova 29 C13
Ciudad Acuña Mexico 118 B4
Ciudad Altamirano Mexico 118 D4
Ciudad Anáhuac Mexico 118 B4
Ciudad Bolívar Venezuela 124 B6
Ciudad Camargo Mexico 118 B3
Ciudad de México Mexico 119 D5
Ciudad de Valles Mexico 119 C5
Ciudad del Carmen Mexico 119 D6
Ciudad del Este Paraguay 127 B5
Ciudad Delicias = Delicias Mexico 118 B3
Ciudad Frontera Mexico 118 B4
Ciudad Guayana Venezuela 124 B6
Ciudad Guerrero Mexico 118 B3
Ciudad Guzmán Mexico 118 D4
Ciudad Juárez Mexico 118 A3
Ciudad Lerdo Mexico 118 B4
Ciudad Madero Mexico 119 C5
Ciudad Mante Mexico 119 C5
Ciudad Obregón Mexico 118 B3
Ciudad Real Spain 37 G7
Ciudad Real □ Spain 37 G7
Ciudad Rodrigo Spain 36 E4
Ciudad Victoria Mexico 119 C5
Ciudadela Spain 48 B10
Ciulniţa Romania 29 F12

Ciumeghiu Romania 28 D6
Ciuperceni Romania 28 F8
Civa Burnu Turkey 72 B7
Cividale del Friuli Italy 41 B10
Civita Castellana Italy 41 F9
Civitanova Marche Italy 41 E10
Civitavécchia Italy 41 F8
Civray France 20 B4
Çivril Turkey 47 C11
Cixerri → Italy 42 C1
Cixi China 59 B13
Cizre Turkey 73 D10
Cizur Mayor Spain 38 C3
Clackmannanshire □ U.K. 13 E5
Clacton-on-Sea U.K. 15 F9
Clain → France 18 F7
Claire, L. Canada 102 B6
Clairton U.S.A. 114 F5
Clairvaux-les-Lacs France 19 F12
Claise → France 20 B5
Clallam Bay U.S.A. 110 B2
Clamecy France 19 E10
Clanton U.S.A. 117 E11
Clanwilliam S. Africa 88 E2
Clara Ireland 12 C4
Claraville U.S.A. 111 K8
Clare Australia 95 E2
Clare U.S.A. 113 D11
Clare □ Ireland 12 D3
Clare → Ireland 12 C2
Clare I. Ireland 12 C1
Claremont Calif., U.S.A. 111 L9
Claremont N.H., U.S.A. 115 C12
Claremont Pt. Australia 94 A3
Claremore U.S.A. 116 C7
Claremorris Ireland 12 C3
Clarence → Australia 95 D5
Clarence → N.Z. 91 E4
Clarence, I. Chile 128 G2
Clarence I. Antarctica 5 C18
Clarence Str. Australia 92 B5
Clarence Town Bahamas 121 B5
Clarendon Pa., U.S.A. 114 E5
Clarendon Tex., U.S.A. 116 D4
Clarenville-Shoal Harbour Canada 105 C9
Claresholm Canada 102 D6
Clarie Coast Antarctica 5 C9
Clarinda U.S.A. 112 E6
Clarington Canada 114 C6
Clarion Iowa, U.S.A. 112 D7
Clarion Pa., U.S.A. 114 E5
Clarion → U.S.A. 114 E5
Clarion Fracture Zone Pac. Oc. 98 H7
Clark U.S.A. 112 C5
Clark, Pt. Canada 114 B3
Clark Fork U.S.A. 108 B5
Clark Fork → U.S.A. 108 B5
Clarkdale U.S.A. 109 J7
Clarke City Canada 105 B6
Clarke I. Australia 95 G4
Clarke Ra. Australia 94 J6
Clarks Fork Yellowstone → U.S.A. 108 D9
Clark's Harbour Canada 105 D6
Clarks Hill L. = J. Strom Thurmond L. U.S.A. 117 E13
Clarks Summit U.S.A. 115 E9
Clarksburg U.S.A. 113 F13
Clarksdale U.S.A. 117 D9
Clarkston U.S.A. 108 C5
Clarksville Ark., U.S.A. 116 D8
Clarksville Tenn., U.S.A. 117 C11
Clarksville Tex., U.S.A. 116 E7
Clatskanie U.S.A. 110 D3
Claude U.S.A. 116 D4
Claveria Phil. 61 B4
Clay U.S.A. 110 G5
Clay Center U.S.A. 112 F5
Claypool U.S.A. 109 K8
Claysburg U.S.A. 114 F6
Claysville U.S.A. 114 F4
Clayton N. Mex., U.S.A. 109 H12
Clayton N.Y., U.S.A. 115 B8
Clear, C. Ireland 12 E2
Clear, L. Canada 114 A7
Clear Hills Canada 102 B5
Clear I. Ireland 12 E2
Clear L. U.S.A. 110 F4
Clear Lake Iowa, U.S.A. 112 D7
Clear Lake S. Dak., U.S.A. 112 C5
Clear Lake Res. U.S.A. 108 F3
Clearfield Pa., U.S.A. 114 E6
Clearfield Utah, U.S.A. 108 F7
Clearlake U.S.A. 110 G4
Clearwater Canada 102 C4
Clearwater U.S.A. 117 H13
Clearwater → Alta., Canada 102 C6
Clearwater → Alta., Canada 103 B6
Clearwater L. Canada 103 C9
Clearwater → Canada 103 C8
Clearwater Mts. U.S.A. 108 C6
Clearwater River △ Canada 103 B8
Cleburne U.S.A. 116 E6
Clee Hills U.K. 15 E5
Cleethorpes U.K. 14 D7

Cleeve Cloud *U.K.* **15** F6
Clelles *France* **21** D9
Clemson *U.S.A.* **117** D13
Clerke Reef *Australia* **92** C2
Clermont *Australia* **94** C4
Clermont *France* **19** C9
Clermont *U.S.A.* **117** G14
Clermont-en-Argonne
  France **19** C12
Clermont-Ferrand *France* **20** C7
Clermont-l'Hérault *France* **20** E7
Clerval *France* **19** E13
Clervaux *Lux.* **17** D6
Cles *Italy* **40** B8
Clevedon *U.K.* **15** F5
Cleveland *Miss., U.S.A.* **117** E9
Cleveland *Ohio, U.S.A.* **114** E3
Cleveland *Okla., U.S.A.* **116** C6
Cleveland *Tenn., U.S.A.* **117** D12
Cleveland *Tex., U.S.A.* **116** F7
Cleveland, C. *Australia* **94** B4
Cleveland, Mt. *U.S.A.* **108** B7
Cleveland Heights *U.S.A.* **114** E3
Clevelândia *Brazil* **127** B5
Clew B. *Ireland* **12** C2
Clewiston *U.S.A.* **117** H14
Clifden *Ireland* **12** C1
Clifden *N.Z.* **91** G1
Cliffdell *U.S.A.* **110** D5
Cliffy Hd. *Australia* **93** G2
Clifton *Australia* **95** D5
Clifton *Ariz., U.S.A.* **109** K9
Clifton *Colo., U.S.A.* **108** G9
Clifton *Tex., U.S.A.* **116** F6
Clifton Beach *Australia* **94** B4
Climax *Canada* **103** D7
Clinch → *U.S.A.* **117** D12
Clingmans Dome *U.S.A.* **117** D13
Clint *U.S.A.* **116** F1
Clinton *B.C., Canada* **102** C4
Clinton *Ont., Canada* **114** C3
Clinton *N.Z.* **91** G2
Clinton *Ark., U.S.A.* **116** D8
Clinton *Conn., U.S.A.* **115** E12
Clinton *Ill., U.S.A.* **112** E9
Clinton *Ind., U.S.A.* **112** F10
Clinton *Iowa, U.S.A.* **112** E8
Clinton *Mass., U.S.A.* **115** D13
Clinton *Miss., U.S.A.* **117** E9
Clinton *Mo., U.S.A.* **112** F7
Clinton *N.C., U.S.A.* **117** D15
Clinton *Okla., U.S.A.* **116** D5
Clinton *S.C., U.S.A.* **117** D14
Clinton *Tenn., U.S.A.* **117** C12
Clinton *Wash., U.S.A.* **110** C4
Clinton C. *Australia* **94** C5
Clinton Colden L. *Canada* **100** C9
Clintonville *U.S.A.* **112** C9
Clipperton, I. *Pac. Oc.* **97** F17
Clipperton Fracture Zone
  Pac. Oc. **97** G16
Clisham *U.K.* **13** D2
Clisson *France* **18** E5
Clitheroe *U.K.* **14** D5
Clo-oose *Canada* **110** B2
Cloates, Pt. *Australia* **92** D1
Clocolan *S. Africa* **89** D4
Clodomira *Argentina* **126** B3
Clogher Hd. *Ireland* **12** C5
Clonakilty *Ireland* **12** E3
Clonakilty B. *Ireland* **12** E3
Cloncurry *Australia* **94** C3
Cloncurry *Ireland* **12** C5
Cloncurry → *Australia* **94** B3
Clondalkin *Ireland* **12** C5
Clones *Ireland* **12** B4
Clonmel *Ireland* **12** D4
Cloppenburg *Germany* **24** C4
Cloquet *U.S.A.* **112** B7
Clorinda *Argentina* **126** B4
Cloud Bay *Canada* **104** C2
Cloud Peak *U.S.A.* **108** D10
Cloudcroft *U.S.A.* **109** K11
Cloverdale *U.S.A.* **110** G4
Clovis *Calif., U.S.A.* **110** J7
Clovis *N. Mex., U.S.A.* **109** J12
Cloyes-sur-le-Loir *France* **18** E8
Cloyne *Canada* **114** B7
Cluj □ *Romania* **29** D8
Cluj-Napoca *Romania* **29** D8
Clunes *Australia* **95** F3
Cluny *France* **19** F11
Cluses *France* **19** F13
Clusone *Italy* **40** C6
Clutha → *N.Z.* **91** G2
Clwyd → *U.K.* **14** D4
Clyde *Canada* **102** C6
Clyde *N.Z.* **91** F2
Clyde *U.S.A.* **114** C8
Clyde → *U.K.* **13** F4
Clyde, Firth of *U.K.* **13** F3
Clyde Muirshiel △ *U.K.* **13** F4
Clyde River *Canada* **101** B13
Clydebank *U.K.* **13** F4
Clymer *N.Y., U.S.A.* **114** D5
Clymer *Pa., U.S.A.* **114** D5
Ćmielów *Poland* **31** H8

Côa → *Portugal* **36** D3
Coachella *U.S.A.* **111** M10
Coachella Canal *U.S.A.* **111** N12
Coahoma *U.S.A.* **116** E4
Coahuayana → *Mexico* **118** D4
Coahuila □ *Mexico* **118** B4
Coal → *Canada* **102** B3
Coalane *Mozam.* **87** F4
Coalcomán *Mexico* **118** D4
Coaldale *Canada* **102** D6
Coalgate *U.S.A.* **116** D6
Coalinga *U.S.A.* **110** J6
Coalisland *U.K.* **12** B5
Coalville *U.K.* **14** E6
Coalville *U.S.A.* **108** F8
Coamo *Puerto Rico* **121** d
Coari *Brazil* **124** D6
Coast □ *Kenya* **86** C4
Coast Mts. *Canada* **102** C3
Coast Ranges *U.S.A.* **110** G4
Coatbridge *U.K.* **13** F4
Coatepec *Mexico* **119** D5
Coatepeque *Guatemala* **120** D1
Coatesville *U.S.A.* **113** F16
Coaticook *Canada* **115** A13
Coats I. *Canada* **101** C11
Coats Land *Antarctica* **5** D1
Coatzacoalcos *Mexico* **119** D6
Cobá *Mexico* **119** C7
Cobadin *Romania* **29** F13
Cobalt *Canada* **104** C4
Cobán *Guatemala* **120** C1
Çobanlar *Turkey* **47** C12
Cobar *Australia* **95** E4
Cóbh *Ireland* **12** E3
Cobija *Bolivia* **124** F5
Cobleskill *U.S.A.* **115** D10
Coboconk *Canada* **114** B6
Cobourg *Canada* **114** C6
Cobourg △ *Australia* **92** B5
Cobourg Pen. *Australia* **92** B5
Cobram *Australia* **95** F4
Coburg *Germany* **25** E6
Coca *Spain* **36** D6
Cocanada = Kakinada
  India **67** L13
Cocentaina *Spain* **39** G4
Cochabamba *Bolivia* **124** G5
Cochem *Germany* **25** E3
Cochemane *Mozam.* **87** F3
Cochin *India* **66** Q10
Cochin China =
  Nam-Phan *Vietnam* **65** G6
Cochran *U.S.A.* **117** E13
Cochrane *Alta., Canada* **102** C6
Cochrane *Ont., Canada* **104** C3
Cochrane *Chile* **128** F2
Cochrane → *Canada* **103** B8
Cochrane, L. *Chile* **128** F2
Cochranton *U.S.A.* **114** E4
Cockburn *Australia* **95** E3
Cockburn, Canal *Chile* **128** G2
Cockburn I. *Canada* **104** C3
Cockburn Ra. *Australia* **92** C4
Cockermouth *U.K.* **14** C4
Cocklebiddy *Australia* **93** F4
Cockpit Country, The
  Jamaica **120** a
Coco → *Cent. Amer.* **120** D3
Coco, I. del *Pac. Oc.* **97** G19
Cocoa *U.S.A.* **117** G14
Cocobeach *Gabon* **84** D1
Cocora *Romania* **29** F12
Cocos B. *Trin. & Tob.* **125** K15
Cocos Is. *Ind. Oc.* **96** J1
Cocos Ridge *Pac. Oc.* **97** G19
Cod, C. *U.S.A.* **113** D18
Codajás *Brazil* **124** D6
Codigoro *Italy* **41** D9
Codlea *Romania* **29** E10
Codó *Brazil* **125** D10
Codogno *Italy* **40** C6
Codróipo *Italy* **41** C10
Codru, Munții *Romania* **28** D7
Cody *U.S.A.* **108** D9
Coe Hill *Canada* **114** B7
Coelemu *Chile* **126** D1
Coen *Australia* **94** A3
Coesfeld *Germany* **24** D3
Coeur d'Alene *U.S.A.* **108** C5
Coeur d'Alene L. *U.S.A.* **108** C5
Coevorden *Neths.* **17** B6
Cofete *Canary Is.* **48** F5
Coffeyville *U.S.A.* **112** G6
Coffin B. *Australia* **95** E2
Coffin Bay *Australia* **95** E2
Coffin Bay △ *Australia* **95** E2
Coffin Bay Peninsula
  Australia **95** E2
Coffs Harbour *Australia* **95** E5
Cofrentes *Spain* **39** F3
Cogealnic → *Moldova* **29** E14
Cogealac *Romania* **29** F13
Coghinas → *Italy* **42** B1
Coghinas, L. del *Italy* **42** B2
Cognac *France* **20** C3

Cogne *Italy* **40** C4
Cogolin *France* **21** E10
Cogolludo *Spain* **38** E1
Cohocton *U.S.A.* **114** D7
Cohocton → *U.S.A.* **114** D7
Cohoes *U.S.A.* **115** D11
Cohuna *Australia* **95** F3
Coiba, I. de *Panama* **120** E3
Coig → *Argentina* **128** G3
Coigeach, Rubha *U.K.* **13** D3
Coihaique *Chile* **128** F2
Coimbatore *India* **66** P10
Coimbra *Brazil* **124** G7
Coimbra *Portugal* **36** E2
Coimbra □ *Portugal* **36** E2
Coín *Spain* **37** J6
Coipasa, Salar de *Bolivia* **124** G5
Cojimies *Ecuador* **124** C3
Cojocna *Romania* **29** D8
Cojutepequé *El Salv.* **120** D2
Čoka *Serbia* **28** E5
Coka *India* **69** J12
Colac *Australia* **95** F3
Colatina *Brazil* **125** G10
Colbeck, C. *Antarctica* **5** D13
Colborne *Canada* **114** C7
Colby *U.S.A.* **112** F3
Colca → *Peru* **124** G4
Colchester *U.K.* **15** F8
Colchester *U.S.A.* **115** E12
Cold L. *Canada* **103** C7
Coldstream *Canada* **102** C5
Coldstream *U.K.* **13** F6
Coldwater *Canada* **114** B5
Coldwater *Kans., U.S.A.* **112** G4
Coldwater *Mich., U.S.A.* **113** E11
Colebrook *U.S.A.* **115** B13
Coleman *U.S.A.* **116** F5
Coleman → *Australia* **94** B3
Colenso *S. Africa* **89** D4
Coleraine *Australia* **95** F3
Coleraine *U.K.* **12** A5
Coleridge, L. *N.Z.* **91** E3
Colesberg *S. Africa* **88** E4
Coleville *U.S.A.* **110** G7
Colfax *Calif., U.S.A.* **110** F6
Colfax *La., U.S.A.* **116** F8
Colfax *Wash., U.S.A.* **108** C5
Colhué Huapi, L. *Argentina* **128** F3
Colibași *Moldova* **29** E13
Colibași *Romania* **29** F9
Cólico *Italy* **40** B6
Coligny *France* **19** F12
Coligny *S. Africa* **89** D4
Colima *Mexico* **118** D4
Colima □ *Mexico* **118** D4
Colima, Nevado de *Mexico* **118** D4
Colina *Brazil* **126** C1
Colina do Norte *Guinea-Biss.* **82** C2
Colinas *Brazil* **125** E10
Colindres *Spain* **36** B7
Coll *U.K.* **13** E2
Collaguasi *Chile* **126** A2
Collarada, Peña *Spain* **38** C4
Collarenebri *Australia* **95** D4
Colle di Val d'Elsa *Italy* **40** E8
Colleen Bawn *Zimbabwe* **87** G2
College Park *U.S.A.* **117** E12
College Station *U.S.A.* **116** F6
Collesalvetti *Italy* **40** E7
Colli Euganei △ *Italy* **41** C8
Collie *Australia* **93** F2
Collier B. *Australia* **92** C3
Collier Ra. *Australia* **93** D2
Collier Range △ *Australia* **93** D2
Collierville *U.S.A.* **117** D10
Collina, Passo di *Italy* **40** D7
Collingwood *Canada* **114** B4
Collingwood *N.Z.* **91** D4
Collins *Canada* **104** B2
Collinsville *Australia* **94** C4
Collipulli *Chile* **126** D1
Collooney *Ireland* **12** B3
Colmar *France* **19** D14
Colmars *France* **21** D10
Colmenar *Spain* **37** J6
Colmenar de Oreja *Spain* **36** E7
Colmenar Viejo *Spain* **36** E7
Colo → *Australia* **95** E5
Cologne = Köln *Germany* **24** E2
Colom, I. d'en *Spain* **48** B11
Coloma *U.S.A.* **110** G6
Colomb-Béchar = Béchar
  Algeria **78** B5
Colombey-les-Belles *France* **19** D12
Colombey-les-Deux-Églises
  France **19** D11
Colombia ■ *S. Amer.* **124** C4
Colombian Basin *S. Amer.* **98** H12
Colombo *Sri Lanka* **66** R11
Colomiers *France* **20** E5
Colón *B. Aires, Argentina* **126** C3
Colón *Entre Ríos, Argentina* **126** C4
Colón *Cuba* **120** B3
Colón *Panama* **120** E4
Colón, Arch. de *Ecuador* **122** D1

Colònia de Sant Jordi *Spain* **48** B9
Colonia del Sacramento
  Uruguay **126** C4
Colonia Dora *Argentina* **126** B3
Colonial Beach *U.S.A.* **113** F15
Colonie *U.S.A.* **115** D11
Colonna, C. *Italy* **43** C10
Colonsay *Canada* **103** C7
Colonsay *U.K.* **13** E2
Colorado □ *U.S.A.* **108** G11
Colorado → *Argentina* **128** D4
Colorado → *N. Amer.* **109** L6
Colorado → *U.S.A.* **116** G7
Colorado City *U.S.A.* **116** E4
Colorado Plateau *U.S.A.* **109** H8
Colorado River Aqueduct
  U.S.A. **111** L12
Colorado Springs *U.S.A.* **108** G11
Colorno *Italy* **40** D7
Colotlán *Mexico* **118** C4
Colstrip *U.S.A.* **108** D10
Colton *U.S.A.* **115** B10
Columbia *Ky., U.S.A.* **113** G11
Columbia *La., U.S.A.* **116** E8
Columbia *Miss., U.S.A.* **117** F10
Columbia *Mo., U.S.A.* **112** F7
Columbia *Pa., U.S.A.* **115** F8
Columbia *S.C., U.S.A.* **117** D14
Columbia *Tenn., U.S.A.* **117** D11
Columbia → *N. Amer.* **110** D2
Columbia, District of □
  U.S.A. **113** F15
Columbia, Mt. *Canada* **102** C5
Columbia Basin *U.S.A.* **108** C4
Columbia Falls *U.S.A.* **108** B6
Columbia Mts. *Canada* **102** C5
Columbia Plateau *U.S.A.* **108** E5
Columbiana *U.S.A.* **114** F4
Columbretes, Is. *Spain* **38** F5
Columbus *Ga., U.S.A.* **117** E12
Columbus *Ind., U.S.A.* **113** F11
Columbus *Kans., U.S.A.* **112** G6
Columbus *Miss., U.S.A.* **117** E11
Columbus *Mont., U.S.A.* **108** D9
Columbus *N. Mex., U.S.A.* **109** L10
Columbus *Nebr., U.S.A.* **112** E6
Columbus *Ohio, U.S.A.* **113** F12
Columbus *Tex., U.S.A.* **116** G6
Colunga *Spain* **36** B5
Colusa *U.S.A.* **110** F4
Colville *U.S.A.* **108** B5
Colville → *U.S.A.* **106** a
Colville, C. *N.Z.* **91** B5
Colwood *Canada* **110** B3
Colwyn Bay *U.K.* **14** D4
Coma *Ethiopia* **81** F4
Comácchio *Italy* **41** D9
Comalcalco *Mexico* **119** D6
Comallo *Argentina* **128** E2
Comana *Romania* **29** F11
Comanche *U.S.A.* **116** F5
Comandante Ferraz
  Antarctica **5** C18
Comănești *Romania* **29** D11
Comarnic *Romania* **29** E10
Comayagua *Honduras* **120** D2
Combahee → *U.S.A.* **117** E14
Combarbalá *Chile* **126** C1
Combe Martin *U.K.* **15** F3
Combeaufontaine *France* **19** E12
Comber *Canada* **114** D2
Comber *U.K.* **12** B6
Combermere *Canada* **114** A7
Comblain-au-Pont *Belgium* **17** D5
Combourg *France* **18** D5
Combrailles *France* **19** F9
Combronde *France* **20** C7
Comeragh Mts. *Ireland* **12** D4
Comet *Australia* **94** C4
Comilla *Bangla.* **67** H17
Comino *Malta* **49** C1
Comino, C. *Italy* **42** B2
Cómiso *Italy* **43** F7
Comitán de Domínguez
  Mexico **119** D6
Commentry *France* **19** F9
Commerce *Ga., U.S.A.* **117** D13
Commerce *Tex., U.S.A.* **116** E7
Commercy *France* **19** D12
Committee B. *Canada* **101** C11
Commonwealth B. *Antarctica* **5** C10
Commoron Cr. → *Australia* **95** D5
Communism Pk. = imeni
  Ismail Samani, Pik
  Tajikistan **52** F8
Como *Italy* **40** C6
Como, Lago di *Italy* **40** B6
Comodoro Rivadavia
  Argentina **128** F3
Comorin, C. =
  Kanyakumari *India* **66** Q10
Comoros ■ *Ind. Oc.* **85** a
Comox *Canada* **102** D4
Compiègne *France* **19** C9

Comporta *Portugal* **37** G2
Compostela *Mexico* **118** C4
Comprida, I. *Brazil* **127** A6
Compton *Canada* **115** A13
Compton *U.S.A.* **111** M8
Comrat *Moldova* **29** D13
Con Cuong *Vietnam* **64** C5
Con Dao △ *Vietnam* **65** H6
Con Son *Vietnam* **65** H6
Conakry *Guinea* **82** D2
Conara *Australia* **95** G4
Concarneau *France* **18** E3
Conceição *Mozam.* **87** F4
Conceição da Barra *Brazil* **125** G11
Conceição do Araguaia
  Brazil **125** E9
Concepción *Argentina* **126** B2
Concepción *Bolivia* **124** G6
Concepción *Chile* **126** D1
Concepción *Mexico* **119** D6
Concepción *Paraguay* **126** A4
Concepción □ *Chile* **126** D1
Concepción → *Mexico* **118** A2
Concepción, Est. de *Chile* **128** G2
Concepción, L. *Bolivia* **124** G6
Concepción, Pta. *Mexico* **118** B2
Concepción del Oro *Mexico* **118** C4
Concepción del Uruguay
  Argentina **126** C4
Conception, Pt. *U.S.A.* **111** L6
Conception B. *Canada* **105** C9
Conception B. *Namibia* **88** C1
Conception I. *Bahamas* **121** B4
Concession *Zimbabwe* **87** F3
Conchas Dam *U.S.A.* **109** J11
Conches-en-Ouche *France* **18** D7
Concho *U.S.A.* **109** J9
Concho → *U.S.A.* **116** F5
Conchos → *Chihuahua,*
  Mexico **118** B4
Conchos → *Chihuahua,*
  Mexico **118** B3
Conchos → *Tamaulipas,*
  Mexico **119** B5
Concord *Calif., U.S.A.* **110** H4
Concord *N.C., U.S.A.* **117** D14
Concord *N.H., U.S.A.* **115** C13
Concordia *Antarctica* **5** D17
Concórdia *Argentina* **126** C4
Concórdia *Brazil* **124** D5
Concordia *Mexico* **118** C3
Concordia *U.S.A.* **112** F5
Concrete *U.S.A.* **108** B3
Condamine *Australia* **95** D5
Condat *France* **20** C6
Condé-sur-Noireau *France* **18** D6
Condeúba *Brazil* **125** F10
Condobolin *Australia* **95** E4
Condom *France* **20** E4
Condon *U.S.A.* **108** D3
Conegliano *Italy* **41** C9
Conejera, I. = Conills, I. des
  Spain **48** B9
Conejos *Mexico* **118** B4
Conemaugh → *U.S.A.* **114** F5
Conero △ *Italy* **41** E10
Confolens *France* **20** B4
Confuso → *Paraguay* **126** B4
Congaz *Moldova* **29** D13
Conghua *China* **59** F9
Congjiang *China* **58** E7
Congleton *U.K.* **14** D5
Congo (Brazzaville) =
  Congo ■ *Africa* **84** E3
Congo (Kinshasa) =
  Congo, Dem. Rep. of
  the ■ *Africa* **84** E4
Congo ■ *Africa* **84** E3
Congo → *Africa* **84** F2
Congo, Dem. Rep. of the ■
  Africa **84** E4
Congo Basin *Africa* **84** E4
Congonhas *Brazil* **127** A7
Congress *U.S.A.* **109** J7
Conil de la Frontera *Spain* **37** J4
Conills, I. des *Spain* **48** B9
Coniston *Canada* **104** C3
Conjeeveram =
  Kanchipuram *India* **66** N11
Conklin *Canada* **103** B6
Conklin *U.S.A.* **115** D9
Conn, L. *Ireland* **12** B2
Connacht □ *Ireland* **12** C2
Conneaut *U.S.A.* **114** E4
Connecticut □ *U.S.A.* **115** E12
Connecticut → *U.S.A.* **115** E12
Connell *U.S.A.* **108** C4
Connellsville *U.S.A.* **114** F5
Connemara *Ireland* **12** C2
Connemara △ *Ireland* **12** C2
Connerré *France* **18** D7
Connersville *U.S.A.* **113** F11
Connors Ra. *Australia* **94** C4
Conques *France* **20** D6
Conquest *Canada* **103** C7
Conrad *U.S.A.* **108** B8

Conran, C. *Australia* **95** F4
Conroe *U.S.A.* **116** F7
Consecon *Canada* **114** C7
Conselheiro Lafaiete *Brazil* **127** A7
Conselve *Italy* **41** C8
Consett *U.K.* **14** C6
Consort *Canada* **103** C6
Constance = Konstanz
  Germany **25** H5
Constance, L. = Bodensee
  Europe **25** H5
Constanța *Romania* **29** F13
Constanța □ *Romania* **29** F13
Constantia *U.S.A.* **115** C8
Constantina *Spain* **37** H5
Constantine *Algeria* **78** A7
Constitución *Chile* **126** D1
Constitución *Uruguay* **126** C4
Constitución de 1857 △
  Mexico **118** A1
Consuegra *Spain* **37** F7
Consul *Canada* **103** D7
Contact *U.S.A.* **108** F6
Contai *India* **69** J12
Contamana *Peru* **124** E4
Contarina *Italy* **41** C9
Contas → *Brazil* **125** F11
Contes *France* **21** E11
Contoocook *U.S.A.* **115** C13
Contra Costa *Mozam.* **89** D5
Contres *France* **18** E8
Contrexéville *France* **19** D12
Contwoyto L. *Canada* **100** C8
Conversano *Italy* **43** B10
Conway = Conwy *U.K.* **14** D4
Conway = Conwy → *U.K.* **14** D4
Conway *Australia* **94** J6
Conway *Ark., U.S.A.* **116** D8
Conway *N.H., U.S.A.* **115** C13
Conway *S.C., U.S.A.* **117** E15
Conway, C. *Australia* **94** J6
Conway, L. *Australia* **95** D2
Conwy *U.K.* **14** D4
Conwy □ *U.K.* **14** D4
Conwy → *U.K.* **14** D4
Coober Pedy *Australia* **95** D1
Cooch Behar = Koch Bihar
  India **67** F16
Cooinda *Australia* **92** B5
Cook *Australia* **93** F5
Cook *U.S.A.* **112** B7
Cook, B. *Chile* **128** H3
Cook, C. *Canada* **102** C3
Cook, Mt. = Aoraki Mount
  Cook *N.Z.* **91** E3
Cook Inlet *U.S.A.* **100** D4
Cook Is. *Pac. Oc.* **97** J12
Cook Strait *N.Z.* **91** D5
Cookeville *U.S.A.* **117** C12
Cookhouse *S. Africa* **88** E4
Cookshire *Canada* **115** A13
Cookstown *U.K.* **12** B5
Cooksville *Canada* **114** C5
Cooktown *Australia* **94** B4
Coolabah *Australia* **95** E4
Cooladdi *Australia* **95** D4
Coolah *Australia* **95** E4
Coolamon *Australia* **95** E4
Coolgardie *Australia* **93** F3
Coolidge *U.S.A.* **109** K8
Coolidge Dam *U.S.A.* **109** K8
Cooma *Australia* **95** F4
Coon Rapids *U.S.A.* **112** C7
Coonabarabran *Australia* **95** E4
Coonamble *Australia* **95** E4
Coonana *Australia* **93** F3
Coondapoor *India* **66** N9
Cooninnie, L. *Australia* **95** D2
Cooper *U.S.A.* **116** E7
Cooper Cr. → *Australia* **95** D2
Cooper Ridge *Pac. Oc.* **97** G12
Cooperstown *N. Dak., U.S.A.* **112** B4
Cooperstown *N.Y., U.S.A.* **115** D10
Coorabie *Australia* **93** F5
Coorong, The *Australia* **95** F2
Coorow *Australia* **93** E2
Cooroy *Australia* **95** D5
Coos Bay *U.S.A.* **108** E1
Coosa → *U.S.A.* **117** E11
Cootamundra *Australia* **95** E4
Cootehill *Ireland* **12** B4
Copahue Paso *Argentina* **126** D1
Copainalá *Mexico* **119** D6
Copake *U.S.A.* **115** D11
Copalnic Mănăștur *Romania* **29** C8
Copán *Honduras* **120** D2
Cope *U.S.A.* **108** G12
Cope, C. *Spain* **39** H3
Copenhagen = København
  Denmark **11** J6
Copenhagen *U.S.A.* **115** C9
Copertino *Italy* **43** B11
Copiapó *Chile* **126** B1
Copiapó → *Chile* **126** B1
Coplay *U.S.A.* **115** F9
Copp L. *Canada* **102** A6
Copparo *Italy* **41** D8

Coppename → *Suriname* 125 B7
Copper Canyon =
  Barranca del Cobre △
  Mexico 118 B3
Copper Harbor *U.S.A.* 112 B10
Copper Queen *Zimbabwe* 87 F2
Copperas Cove *U.S.A.* 116 F6
Copperbelt □ *Zambia* 87 E2
Coppermine = Kugluktuk
  Canada 100 C8
Coppermine → *Canada* 100 C8
Copperopolis *U.S.A.* 110 H6
Coquet → *U.K.* 14 B6
Coquille *U.S.A.* 108 E1
Coquimbo *Chile* 126 C1
Coquimbo □ *Chile* 126 C1
Corabia *Romania* 29 G9
Coracora *Peru* 124 G4
Coraki *Australia* 95 D5
Coral *U.S.A.* 114 F5
Coral Gables *U.S.A.* 117 J14
Coral Harbour *Canada* 101 C11
Coral Sea *Pac. Oc.* 90 C8
Coral Sea Basin *Pac. Oc.* 96 J7
Coral Sea Islands Terr. □
  Australia 90 C8
Coral Springs *U.S.A.* 117 H14
Coraopolis *U.S.A.* 114 F4
Corato *Italy* 43 A9
Corbeil-Essonnes *France* 19 D9
Corbett △ *India* 69 E8
Corbie *France* 19 C9
Corbières *France* 20 F6
Corbigny *France* 19 E10
Corbin *U.S.A.* 113 G11
Corbones → *Spain* 37 H5
Corbu *Romania* 29 F13
Corby *U.K.* 15 E7
Corcaigh = Cork *Ireland* 12 E3
Corcoran *U.S.A.* 110 J7
Corcovado △ *Costa Rica* 120 E3
Cordele *U.S.A.* 117 F13
Cordell *U.S.A.* 116 D5
Cordenòns *Italy* 41 C9
Cordes-sur-Ciel *France* 20 D5
Córdoba *Argentina* 126 C3
Córdoba *Mexico* 119 D5
Córdoba *Spain* 37 H6
Córdoba □ *Argentina* 126 C3
Córdoba □ *Spain* 37 G6
Córdoba, Sierra de
  Argentina 126 C3
Cordon *Phil.* 61 C4
Cordova *U.S.A.* 100 C5
Corella *Spain* 38 C3
Corella → *Australia* 94 B3
Corfield *Australia* 94 C3
Corfu = Kerkyra *Greece* 49 A3
Corfu ✈ (CFU) *Greece* 46 B1
Corfu, Str. of = Kerkyras,
  Notio Steno *Greece* 49 A4
Corgo = O Corgo *Spain* 36 C3
Cori *Italy* 42 A5
Coria *Spain* 36 F4
Coria del Río *Spain* 37 H4
Corigliano Cálabro *Italy* 43 C9
Coringa Is. *Australia* 94 B4
Corinth = Korinthos *Greece* 46 D4
Corinth *Miss., U.S.A.* 117 D10
Corinth *N.Y., U.S.A.* 115 C11
Corinth, G. of =
  Korinthiakos Kolpos
  Greece 46 C4
Corinth Canal *Greece* 46 D4
Corinto *Brazil* 125 G10
Corinto *Nic.* 120 D2
Cork *Ireland* 12 E3
Cork □ *Ireland* 12 E3
Cork Harbour *Ireland* 12 E3
Corlay *France* 18 D3
Corleone *Italy* 42 E6
Corleto Perticara *Italy* 43 B9
Cormòns *Italy* 41 C10
Cormack L. *Canada* 102 A4
Cormorant *Canada* 103 C8
Cormorant L. *Canada* 103 C8
Corn Is. = Maíz, Is. del *Nic.* 120 D3
Cornalvo △ *Spain* 37 F4
Cornélio Procópio *Brazil* 127 A5
Corner Brook *Canada* 105 C8
Cornești *Moldova* 29 C13
Corníglio *Italy* 40 D7
Corning *Ark., U.S.A.* 117 C9
Corning *Calif., U.S.A.* 108 G2
Corning *Iowa, U.S.A.* 112 E6
Corning *N.Y., U.S.A.* 114 D7
Corno Grande *Italy* 41 F10
Cornwall *Canada* 115 A10
Cornwall *U.S.A.* 115 F8
Cornwall □ *U.K.* 15 G3
Cornwall I. *Canada* 101 B10
Cornwallis I. *Canada* 101 B10
Corny Pt. *Australia* 95 E2
Coro *Venezuela* 124 A5
Coroatá *Brazil* 125 D10

Corocoro *Bolivia* 124 G5
Coroico *Bolivia* 124 G5
Coromandel *N.Z.* 91 B5
Coromandel Coast *India* 66 N12
Corona *Calif., U.S.A.* 111 M9
Corona *N. Mex., U.S.A.* 109 J11
Coronach *Canada* 103 D7
Coronado *U.S.A.* 111 N9
Coronado, B. de *Costa Rica* 120 E3
Coronados, Is. Los *Mexico* 111 N9
Coronation *Canada* 102 C6
Coronation Gulf *Canada* 100 C9
Coronation I. *Antarctica* 5 C18
Coronation Is. *Australia* 92 B3
Coronda *Argentina* 126 C3
Coronel *Chile* 126 D1
Coronel Bogado *Paraguay* 126 B4
Coronel Dorrego *Argentina* 126 D3
Coronel Oviedo *Paraguay* 126 B4
Coronel Pringles *Argentina* 126 D3
Coronel Suárez *Argentina* 126 D3
Coronel Vidal *Argentina* 126 D4
Coropuna, Nevado *Peru* 124 G4
Çorovodë *Albania* 44 F4
Corowa *Australia* 95 F4
Corozal □ *Belize* 119 D7
Corozal Pt. *Trin. & Tob.* 125 K15
Corps *France* 21 D9
Corpus *Argentina* 127 B4
Corpus Christi *U.S.A.* 116 H6
Corpus Christi, L. *U.S.A.* 116 G6
Corral de Almaguer *Spain* 36 F7
Corralejo *Canary Is.* 48 F6
Corraun Pen. *Ireland* 12 C2
Corréggio *Italy* 40 D7
Correntes, C. das *Mozam.* 89 C6
Corrèze □ *France* 20 C5
Corrèze → *France* 20 C5
Corrib, L. *Ireland* 12 C2
Corridònia *Italy* 41 E10
Corrientes *Argentina* 126 B4
Corrientes □ *Argentina* 126 B4
Corrientes → *Argentina* 126 C4
Corrientes → *Peru* 124 D4
Corrientes, C. *Colombia* 124 B3
Corrientes, C. *Cuba* 120 B3
Corrientes, C. *Mexico* 118 C3
Corrigan *U.S.A.* 116 F7
Corrigin *Australia* 93 F2
Corriverton *Guyana* 124 B7
Corry *U.S.A.* 114 E5
Corse □ *France* 21 G13
Corse, C. *France* 21 E13
Corse △ *France* 21 F13
Corse-du-Sud □ *France* 21 G13
Corsica = Corse □ *France* 21 G13
Corsicana *U.S.A.* 116 E6
Corte *France* 21 F13
Corte Pinto *Portugal* 37 H3
Cortegana *Spain* 37 H4
Cortés, Mar de =
  California, G. de *Mexico* 118 B2
Cortez *U.S.A.* 109 H9
Cortina d'Ampezzo *Italy* 41 B9
Cortland *N.Y., U.S.A.* 115 D8
Cortland *Ohio, U.S.A.* 114 E4
Cortona *Italy* 41 E8
Corubal → *Guinea-Biss.* 82 C2
Coruche *Portugal* 37 G2
Çoruh → *Turkey* 35 K5
Çorum *Turkey* 72 B6
Çorum □ *Turkey* 72 B6
Corumbá *Brazil* 124 G7
Corund *Romania* 29 D10
Corunna = A Coruña *Spain* 36 B2
Corvallis *U.S.A.* 108 D2
Corvette, L. de la *Canada* 104 B5
Corvo *Azores* 78 a
Cosalá *Mexico* 118 C3
Cosamaloapan de Carpio
  Mexico 119 D5
Cosenza *Italy* 43 C9
Coșereni *Romania* 29 F11
Coshocton *U.S.A.* 114 F3
Cosmo Newberry *Australia* 93 E3
Cosne-Cours-sur-Loire
  France 19 E9
Coso Junction *U.S.A.* 111 J9
Coso Pk. *U.S.A.* 111 J9
Cospeito *Spain* 36 B3
Cosquín *Argentina* 126 C3
Cossato *Italy* 40 C5
Cossé-le-Vivien *France* 18 E6
Cosson → *France* 18 E8
Costa Blanca *Spain* 39 G4
Costa Brava *Spain* 38 D8
Costa del Sol *Spain* 37 J6
Costa Dorada *Spain* 38 D6
Costa Mesa *U.S.A.* 111 M9
Costa Rica ■ *Cent. Amer.* 120 E3
Costa Smeralda *Italy* 42 A2
Costești *Romania* 29 F9
Costigliole d'Asti *Italy* 40 D5
Cosumnes → *U.S.A.* 110 G5
Coswig *Sachsen, Germany* 24 D9
Coswig *Sachsen-Anhalt,*
  Germany 24 D8

Cotabato *Phil.* 61 H6
Cotagaita *Bolivia* 126 A2
Côte d'Azur *France* 21 E11
Côte-d'Ivoire = Ivory
  Coast ■ *Africa* 82 D4
Côte d'Or *France* 19 E11
Côte-d'Or □ *France* 19 E11
Coteau des Prairies *U.S.A.* 112 C5
Coteau du Missouri *U.S.A.* 112 B4
Cotentin *France* 18 C5
Côtes de Meuse *France* 19 C12
Côtes-du-Nord =
  Côtes-d'Armor □ *France* 18 D4
Cotiella *Spain* 38 C5
Cotillo *Canary Is.* 48 F5
Cotiujeni *Moldova* 29 C13
Cotonou *Benin* 83 D5
Cotopaxi *Ecuador* 124 D3
Cotronei *Italy* 43 C9
Cotswold Hills *U.K.* 15 F5
Cottage Grove *U.S.A.* 108 E2
Cottbus *Germany* 24 D10
Cottonwood *U.S.A.* 109 J7
Cotulla *U.S.A.* 116 G5
Coubre, Pte. de la *France* 20 C2
Couches *France* 19 F11
Couço *Portugal* 37 G2
Coudersport *U.S.A.* 114 E6
Couedic, C. du *Australia* 95 F2
Couëron *France* 18 E5
Couesnon → *France* 18 D5
Couhé *France* 20 B4
Coulanges-sur-Yonne
  France 19 E10
Coulee City *U.S.A.* 108 C4
Coulee Dam Nat. Recr.
  Area = Lake
  Roosevelt △ *U.S.A.* 108 B4
Coulman I. *Antarctica* 5 D11
Coulommiers *France* 19 D10
Coulon → *France* 21 E9
Coulonge → *Canada* 104 C4
Coulonges-sur-l'Autize
  France 20 B3
Coulounieix-Chamiers
  France 20 C4
Coulterville *U.S.A.* 110 H6
Council *U.S.A.* 108 D5
Council Bluffs *U.S.A.* 112 E6
Council Grove *U.S.A.* 112 F5
Coupeville *U.S.A.* 110 B4
Courantyne → *S. Amer.* 124 B7
Courcelles *Belgium* 17 D4
Courchevel *France* 21 C10
Courçon *France* 20 B3
Courmayeur *Italy* 40 C3
Couronne, C. *France* 21 E9
Cours-la-Ville *France* 19 F11
Coursan *France* 20 E7
Courseulles-sur-Mer *France* 18 C6
Courtenay *Canada* 102 D4
Courtenay *France* 19 D10
Courtland *U.S.A.* 110 G5
Courtrai = Kortrijk *Belgium* 17 D3
Courtright *Canada* 114 D2
Coushatta *U.S.A.* 116 E8
Coutances *France* 18 C5
Coutras *France* 20 C3
Coutts Crossing *Australia* 95 D5
Couva *Trin. & Tob.* 125 K15
Couvin *Belgium* 17 D4
Covarrubias *Spain* 36 C7
Covasna *Romania* 29 E11
Covasna □ *Romania* 29 E10
Cove I. *Canada* 114 A3
Coventry *U.K.* 15 E6
Covilhã *Portugal* 36 E3
Covington *Ga., U.S.A.* 117 E13
Covington *Ky., U.S.A.* 113 F11
Covington *Tenn., U.S.A.* 117 D10
Covington *Va., U.S.A.* 113 G14
Cowal, L. *Australia* 95 E4
Cowan, L. *Australia* 93 F3
Cowan L. *Canada* 103 C7
Cowangie *Australia* 95 F3
Cowansville *Canada* 115 A12
Coward Springs *Australia* 95 D2
Cowcowing Lakes *Australia* 93 F2
Cowdenbeath *U.K.* 13 E5
Cowell *Australia* 95 E2
Cowes *U.K.* 15 G6
Cowichan L. *Canada* 110 B2
Cowlitz → *U.S.A.* 110 D4
Cowra *Australia* 95 E4
Cox *Spain* 39 G4
Coxilha Grande *Brazil* 127 B5
Coxim *Brazil* 125 G8
Cox's Bazar *Bangla.* 67 J17
Coyote Wells *U.S.A.* 111 N11
Coyuca de Benítez *Mexico* 119 D4
Coyuca de Catalán *Mexico* 118 D4
Cozad *U.S.A.* 112 E4
Cozes *France* 20 C3
Cozumel *Mexico* 119 C7
Cozumel, Isla *Mexico* 119 C7
Crab Hill *Barbados* 121 g

Cracow = Kraków *Poland* 31 H6
Cracow *Australia* 95 D5
Cradle Mt.-Lake St. Clair △
  Australia 95 G4
Cradock *Australia* 95 E2
Cradock *S. Africa* 88 E4
Craig *U.S.A.* 108 F10
Craigavon *U.K.* 12 B5
Craigmore *Zimbabwe* 87 G3
Craik *Canada* 103 C7
Craiova *Romania* 29 F8
Cramsie *Australia* 94 C3
Cranberry L. *U.S.A.* 115 B10
Cranberry Portage *Canada* 103 C8
Cranbrook *Australia* 93 F2
Cranbrook *Canada* 102 D5
Crandon *U.S.A.* 112 C9
Crane *Oreg., U.S.A.* 108 E4
Crane *Tex., U.S.A.* 116 F3
Crane, The *Barbados* 121 g
Cranston *U.S.A.* 115 E13
Craon *France* 18 E6
Craonne *France* 19 C10
Craponne-sur-Arzon *France* 20 C7
Crasna *Romania* 29 D12
Crasna → *Romania* 28 C7
Crasnei, Munții *Romania* 29 C8
Crater L. *U.S.A.* 108 E2
Crater Lake △ *U.S.A.* 108 E2
Craters of the Moon △
  U.S.A. 108 E7
Crateús *Brazil* 125 E10
Crati → *Italy* 43 C9
Crato *Brazil* 125 E11
Crato *Portugal* 37 F3
Craven, L. *Canada* 104 B4
Crawford *U.S.A.* 112 D2
Crawfordsville *U.S.A.* 112 E10
Crawley *U.K.* 15 F7
Crazy Mts. *U.S.A.* 108 C8
Crean L. *Canada* 103 C7
Crécy-en-Ponthieu *France* 19 B8
Crediton *Canada* 114 C3
Crediton *U.K.* 15 G4
Cree → *Canada* 103 B7
Cree → *U.K.* 13 G4
Cree L. *Canada* 103 B7
Creede *U.S.A.* 109 H10
Creekside *U.S.A.* 114 F5
Creel *Mexico* 118 B3
Creemore *Canada* 114 B4
Creighton *Canada* 103 C8
Creighton *U.S.A.* 112 D5
Creil *France* 19 C9
Crema *Italy* 40 C6
Cremona *Italy* 40 C7
Crepaja *Serbia* 28 E5
Crépy *France* 19 C10
Crépy-en-Valois *France* 19 C9
Cres *Croatia* 41 D11
Crescent City *U.S.A.* 108 F1
Crescentino *Italy* 40 C5
Crespo *Argentina* 126 C3
Cresson *U.S.A.* 114 F6
Crest *France* 21 D9
Cresta, Mt. *Phil.* 61 C5
Crestline *Calif., U.S.A.* 111 L9
Crestline *Ohio, U.S.A.* 114 F2
Creston *Canada* 102 D5
Creston *Calif., U.S.A.* 110 K6
Creston *Iowa, U.S.A.* 112 E7
Crestview *Calif., U.S.A.* 110 H8
Crestview *Fla., U.S.A.* 117 F11
Crêt de la Neige *France* 19 F12
Crete = Kriti *Greece* 49 D7
Crete *U.S.A.* 112 E5
Crete, Sea of = Kritiko
  Pelagos *Greece* 47 E7
Créteil *France* 19 D9
Creus, C. de *Spain* 38 C8
Creuse □ *France* 19 F9
Creuse → *France* 20 B4
Creuzwald *France* 19 C13
Creutzburg *Germany* 24 D6
Crèvecœur-le-Grand *France* 19 C9
Crevillente *Spain* 39 G4
Crewe *U.K.* 14 D5
Crewkerne *U.K.* 15 G5
Crianlarich *U.K.* 13 E4
Criciúma *Brazil* 127 B6
Cricova *Moldova* 29 C13
Crieff *U.K.* 13 E5
Crikvenica *Croatia* 41 C11
Crimea □ *Ukraine* 33 K8
Crimean Pen. = Krymskyy
  Pivostriv *Ukraine* 33 K8
Crimmitschau *Germany* 24 E9
Cristuru Secuiesc *Romania* 29 D10
Crişul Alb → *Romania* 28 D6
Crişul Negru → *Romania* 28 D6
Crişul Repede → *Romania* 28 D5
Criuleni *Moldova* 29 C14
Crivitz *Germany* 24 B7
Crna → *Macedonia* 44 E5
Crna Gora =
  Montenegro ■ *Europe* 44 D3
Crna Gora *Macedonia* 44 D5

Crna Reka = Crna →
  Macedonia 44 E5
Crna Trava *Serbia* 44 D6
Crni Drim → *Macedonia* 44 E4
Crni Timok → *Serbia* 44 C6
Crnoljeva Planina *Serbia* 44 D5
Črnomelj *Slovenia* 41 C12
Croagh Patrick *Ireland* 12 C2
Croatia ■ *Europe* 41 C13
Crocker, Banjaran *Malaysia* 62 C5
Crockett *U.S.A.* 116 F7
Crocodile = Umgwenya →
  Mozam. 89 D5
Crocodile Is. *Australia* 94 A1
Crocq *France* 20 C6
Crodo *Italy* 40 B5
Crohy Hd. *Ireland* 12 B3
Croisette, C. *France* 21 E9
Croisic, Pte. du *France* 18 E4
Croix, L. la *Canada* 104 C1
Croker, C. *Australia* 92 B5
Croker, C. *Canada* 114 B4
Croker I. *Australia* 92 B5
Cromarty *U.K.* 13 D4
Cromer *U.K.* 14 E9
Cromwell *N.Z.* 91 F2
Cromwell *U.S.A.* 115 E12
Cronat *France* 19 F10
Crook *U.K.* 14 C6
Crooked → *Canada* 102 C4
Crooked → *U.S.A.* 108 D3
Crooked I. *Bahamas* 121 B5
Crooked Island Passage
  Bahamas 121 B5
Crookston *Minn., U.S.A.* 112 B5
Crookston *Nebr., U.S.A.* 112 D3
Crookwell *Australia* 95 E4
Cropane-Micone → *Italy* 43 D9
Crosby *U.K.* 14 D4
Crosby *N. Dak., U.S.A.* 112 A2
Crosby *Pa., U.S.A.* 114 E6
Crosbyton *U.S.A.* 116 E4
Crosía *Italy* 43 C9
Cross → *Nigeria* 83 E6
Cross City *U.S.A.* 117 G13
Cross Fell *U.K.* 14 C5
Cross L. *Canada* 103 C9
Cross Lake *Canada* 103 C9
Cross River □ *Nigeria* 83 D6
Cross River △ *Nigeria* 83 D6
Cross Sound *U.S.A.* 100 D6
Crossett *U.S.A.* 116 E9
Crosshaven *Ireland* 12 E3
Crossmaglen *U.K.* 12 B5
Crossmolina *Ireland* 12 B2
Crossville *U.S.A.* 117 D12
Croswell *U.S.A.* 114 C2
Croton-on-Hudson *U.S.A.* 115 E11
Crotone *Italy* 43 C10
Crow → *Canada* 102 B4
Crow Agency *U.S.A.* 108 D10
Crow Hd. *Ireland* 12 E1
Crowell *U.S.A.* 116 E5
Crowley *U.S.A.* 116 F8
Crowley, L. *U.S.A.* 110 H8
Crown Point *Ind., U.S.A.* 112 E10
Crown Point *N.Y., U.S.A.* 115 C11
Crownpoint *U.S.A.* 109 J9
Crows Landing *U.S.A.* 110 H5
Crows Nest *Australia* 95 D5
Crowsnest Pass *Canada* 102 D6
Croydon *Australia* 94 B3
Croydon □ *U.K.* 15 F7
Crozet, Is. *Ind. Oc.* 3 G12
Crozon *France* 18 D2
Cruden Bay *U.K.* 13 D7
Crumlin *U.K.* 12 B5
Cruz, C. *Cuba* 120 C4
Cruz Alta *Brazil* 127 B5
Cruz Bay *U.S. Virgin Is.* 121 e
Cruz de Incio *Spain* 36 C3
Cruz del Eje *Argentina* 126 C3
Cruzeiro *Brazil* 127 A7
Cruzeiro do Oeste *Brazil* 127 A5
Cruzeiro do Sul *Brazil* 124 E4
Cry L. *Canada* 102 B3
Crystal Bay *U.S.A.* 110 F7
Crystal Brook *Australia* 95 E2
Crystal City *U.S.A.* 116 G5
Crystal Falls *U.S.A.* 112 B9
Crystal River *U.S.A.* 117 G13
Crystal Springs *U.S.A.* 117 F9
Csenger *Hungary* 28 C7
Csongrád *Hungary* 28 D5
Csongrád □ *Hungary* 28 D5
Csorna *Hungary* 28 C2
Csurgo *Hungary* 28 D2
Cu Lao Hon *Vietnam* 65 G7
Cua Rao *Vietnam* 64 C5
Cuácua → *Mozam.* 87 F4
Cuamato *Angola* 88 B2
Cuamba *Mozam.* 87 E4
Cuando → *Angola* 85 H4
Cuando Cubango □ *Angola* 88 B3
Cuangar *Angola* 88 B2
Cuango = Kwango →
  Dem. Rep. of the Congo 84 E3

Cuanza → *Angola* 84 F2
Cuarto → *Argentina* 126 C3
Cuatrociénegas *Mexico* 118 B4
Cuauhtémoc *Mexico* 118 B3
Cuba *Portugal* 37 G3
Cuba *N. Mex., U.S.A.* 109 H10
Cuba *N.Y., U.S.A.* 114 D6
Cuba ■ *W. Indies* 120 B4
Cubango → *Africa* 88 B3
Çubuk *Turkey* 72 B5
Cuc Phuong △ *Vietnam* 64 B5
Cuchumatanes, Sierra de
  los *Guatemala* 120 C1
Cuckfield *U.K.* 15 F7
Cucuí *Brazil* 124 C5
Cucurpé *Mexico* 118 A2
Cúcuta *Colombia* 124 B4
Cudalbi *Romania* 29 E12
Cuddalore *India* 66 P11
Cuddapah *India* 66 M11
Cuddapan, L. *Australia* 94 D3
Cudillero *Spain* 36 B4
Cue *Australia* 93 E2
Cuéllar *Spain* 36 D6
Cuenca *Ecuador* 124 D3
Cuenca *Spain* 38 E2
Cuenca □ *Spain* 38 F3
Cuenca, Serranía de *Spain* 38 F3
Cuenca Alta del
  Manzanares △ *Spain* 36 E7
Cuerdo del Pozo, Embalse
  de la *Spain* 38 D2
Cuernavaca *Mexico* 119 D5
Cuero *U.S.A.* 116 G6
Cuers *France* 21 E10
Cueva de la Quebrada del
  Toro △ *Venezuela* 121 D6
Cuevas del Almanzora *Spain* 39 H3
Cuevo *Bolivia* 124 H6
Cugir *Romania* 29 E8
Cugnaux *France* 20 E5
Cuhai-Bakony → *Hungary* 28 C2
Cuiabá *Brazil* 125 G7
Cuiabá → *Brazil* 125 G7
Cuijk *Neths.* 17 C5
Cuilco *Guatemala* 120 C1
Cuillin Hills *U.K.* 13 D2
Cuillin Sd. *U.K.* 13 D2
Cuilo = Kwilu →
  Dem. Rep. of the Congo 84 E3
Cuiseaux *France* 19 F12
Cuito → *Angola* 88 B3
Cuitzeo, L. de *Mexico* 118 D4
Cujmir *Romania* 28 F7
Cukai *Malaysia* 65 K4
Culbertson *U.S.A.* 108 B11
Culcairn *Australia* 95 F4
Culebra *Puerto Rico* 121 d
Culebra, Sierra de la *Spain* 36 D4
Culfa *Azerbaijan* 73 C11
Culgoa → *Australia* 95 D4
Culgoa Flood Plain △
  Australia 95 D4
Culiacán *Mexico* 118 C3
Culiacán → *Mexico* 118 C3
Culik *Indonesia* 63 J18
Culion *Phil.* 61 F4
Cúllar *Spain* 37 H8
Cullarin Ra. *Australia* 95 E4
Cullen *U.K.* 13 D6
Cullen Pt. *Australia* 94 A3
Cullera *Spain* 39 F4
Cullman *U.S.A.* 117 D11
Cullompton *U.K.* 15 G4
Culoz *France* 21 C9
Culpeper *U.S.A.* 113 F14
Culuene → *Brazil* 125 F8
Culver, Pt. *Australia* 93 F3
Culverden *N.Z.* 91 E4
Cumaná *Venezuela* 124 A6
Cumaovası *Turkey* 47 C9
Cumberland *B.C., Canada* 102 D4
Cumberland *Ont., Canada* 115 A9
Cumberland *U.S.A.* 113 F14
Cumberland → *U.S.A.* 112 G9
Cumberland, L. *U.S.A.* 113 G11
Cumberland Gap △ *U.S.A.* 113 G12
Cumberland I. *U.S.A.* 117 F14
Cumberland Is. *Australia* 94 J7
Cumberland Island △
  U.S.A. 117 F14
Cumberland L. *Canada* 103 C8
Cumberland Pen. *Canada* 101 C13
Cumberland Plateau *U.S.A.*
  117 D12
Cumberland Sd. *Canada* 101 C13
Cumbernauld *U.K.* 13 F5
Cumborah *Australia* 95 D4
Cumbres de Majalca △
  Mexico 118 B3
Cumbres de Monterrey △
  Mexico 118 B4
Cumbres Mayores *Spain* 37 G4
Cumbria □ *U.K.* 14 C5
Cumbrian Mts. *U.K.* 14 C5
Cumbum *India* 66 M11
Cuminá → *Brazil* 125 D7

Cummings Mt. *U.S.A.* **111 K8**
Cummins *Australia* **95 E2**
Cumnock *U.S.A.* **95 E4**
Cumnock *U.K.* **13 F4**
Cumpas *Mexico* **118 B3**
Cumplida, Pta. *Canary Is.* **48 F2**
Çumra *Turkey* **72 D5**
Cunco *Chile* **128 D2**
Cumcumén *Chile* **126 C1**
Cunderdin *Australia* **93 F2**
Cunene → *Angola* **88 B1**
Cúneo *Italy* **40 D4**
Çüngüş *Turkey* **70 B3**
Cunillera, I. = Sa Conillera
  Spain **48 C7**
Cunlhat *France* **20 C7**
Cunnamulla *Australia* **95 D4**
Cuorgnè *Italy* **40 C4**
Cupar *Canada* **103 C8**
Cupar *U.K.* **13 E5**
Cupcini *Moldova* **29 B12**
Cupertino *U.S.A.* **110 H4**
Cupica, G. de *Colombia* **124 B3**
Čuprija *Serbia* **44 C5**
Curaçao *Neth. Ant.* **121 D6**
Curanilahue *Chile* **126 D1**
Curaray → *Peru* **124 D4**
Cure → *France* **19 E10**
Curepipe *Mauritius* **85 d**
Curepto *Chile* **126 D1**
Curiapo *Venezuela* **124 B6**
Curicó *Chile* **126 C1**
Curieuse *Seychelles* **85 b**
Curinga *Italy* **43 D9**
Curitiba *Brazil* **127 B6**
Curitibanos *Brazil* **127 B5**
Currabubula *Australia* **95 E5**
Currais Novos *Brazil* **125 E11**
Curral Velho *C. Verde Is.* **78 b**
Curralinho *Brazil* **125 D9**
Currane, L. *Ireland* **12 E1**
Currant *U.S.A.* **108 G6**
Currawinya △ *Australia* **95 D3**
Current → *U.S.A.* **108 G8**
Currie *Australia* **95 F3**
Currie *U.S.A.* **108 F6**
Curtea de Argeş *Romania* **29 E9**
Curtici *Romania* **28 D6**
Curtis *U.S.A.* **112 E3**
Curtis Group *Australia* **95 F4**
Curtis I. *Australia* **94 C5**
Curuápanema → *Brazil* **125 D7**
Curuçá *Brazil* **125 D9**
Curuguaty *Paraguay* **127 A4**
Curup *Indonesia* **62 E2**
Cururupu *Brazil* **125 D10**
Curuzú Cuatiá *Argentina* **126 B4**
Curvelo *Brazil* **125 G10**
Cusco = Cuzco *Peru* **124 F4**
Cushendall *U.K.* **12 A5**
Cushing *U.S.A.* **116 D6**
Cushing, Mt. *Canada* **102 B3**
Cusihuiríachic *Mexico* **118 B3**
Cusna, Mte. *Italy* **40 D7**
Cusset *France* **19 F10**
Custer *U.S.A.* **112 D2**
Cut Bank *U.S.A.* **108 B7**
Cutchogue *U.S.A.* **115 E12**
Cuthbert *U.S.A.* **117 F12**
Cutler *U.S.A.* **110 J7**
Cutro *Italy* **43 C9**
Cuttaburra → *Australia* **95 D3**
Cuttack *India* **67 J14**
Cuvier, C. *Australia* **93 D1**
Cuvier I. *N.Z.* **91 B5**
Cuxhaven *Germany* **24 B4**
Cuyahoga Falls *U.S.A.* **114 E3**
Cuyahoga Valley △ *U.S.A.* **114 E3**
Cuyapo *Phil.* **61 D4**
Cuyo *Phil.* **61 F4**
Cuyo East Pass *Phil.* **61 F4**
Cuyo West Pass *Phil.* **61 F4**
Cuyuni → *Guyana* **124 B7**
Cuzco *Bolivia* **124 H5**
Cuzco *Peru* **124 F4**
Čvrsnica *Bos.-H.* **28 G2**
Cwmbran *U.K.* **15 F4**
Cyangugu *Rwanda* **86 C2**
Cybinka *Poland* **31 F1**
Cyclades *Greece* **46 E6**
Cyclades □ *Greece* **46 D6**
Cygnet *Australia* **95 G4**
Cynthiana *U.S.A.* **113 F11**
Cypress Hills *Canada* **103 D7**
Cypress Hills △ *Canada* **103 D7**
Cyprus ■ *Asia* **49 E12**
Cyrenaica *Libya* **79 C10**
Cyrene *Libya* **79 B10**
Czaplinek *Poland* **30 E3**
Czar *Canada* **103 C6**
Czarna → *Łódzkie, Poland* **31 G6**
Czarna → *Świętokrzyskie,
  Poland* **31 H5**
Czarna Białostocka *Poland* **31 E10**
Czarna Woda *Poland* **30 E5**
Czarne *Poland* **30 E3**
Czarnków *Poland* **31 F3**

Czech Rep. ■ *Europe* **26 B8**
Czechowice-Dziedzice *Poland* **31 J5**
Czempiń *Poland* **31 F3**
Czeremcha *Poland* **31 F10**
Czerniejewo *Poland* **31 F4**
Czersk *Poland* **30 E4**
Czerwieńsk *Poland* **31 F2**
Czerwionka-Leszczyny
  Poland **31 H5**
Częstochowa *Poland* **31 H6**
Człopa *Poland* **31 E3**
Człuchów *Poland* **30 E4**
Czyżew-Osada *Poland* **31 F9**

D

Da → *Vietnam* **58 G5**
Da Hinggan Ling *China* **60 B7**
Da Lat *Vietnam* **65 G7**
Da Nang *Vietnam* **64 D7**
Da Qaidam *China* **60 C4**
Da Yunhe → *Hopei, China* **57 E9**
Da Yunhe → *Jiangsu, China* **57 G11**
Da'an *China* **57 B13**
Daan Viljoen △ *Namibia* **88 C2**
Dab'a, Ras el *Egypt* **80 H6**
Daba Shan *China* **58 B7**
Dabai *Nigeria* **83 C6**
Dabakala *Ivory C.* **82 D4**
Dabas *Hungary* **28 C4**
Dabat *Ethiopia* **81 E4**
Dabbagh, Jabal *Si. Arabia* **70 E2**
Dabhoi *India* **68 H5**
Dąbie *Poland* **31 F5**
Dabie Shan *China* **59 B10**
Dabilda *Cameroon* **83 C7**
Dabnou *Niger* **83 C6**
Dabo = Pasirkuning
  Indonesia **62 E2**
Dabola *Guinea* **82 C2**
Dabou *Ivory C.* **82 D4**
Daboya *Ghana* **83 D4**
Dabravolya *Belarus* **31 F10**
Dąbrowa Białostocka
  Poland **30 E10**
Dąbrowa Górnicza *Poland* **31 H6**
Dąbrowa Tarnowska *Poland* **31 H7**
Dabu *China* **59 E11**
Dabung *Malaysia* **65 K4**
Dabus → *Ethiopia* **81 E4**
Dacato → *Ethiopia* **81 F5**
Dacca = Dhaka *Bangla.* **69 H14**
Dacca = Dhaka □ *Bangla.* **69 G14**
Dachau *Germany* **25 G7**
Dachigam △ *India* **68 B6**
Dachstein, Hoher *Austria* **26 D6**
Dačice *Czech Rep.* **26 B8**
Dadanawa *Guyana* **124 C7**
Daday *Turkey* **72 B5**
Dade City *U.S.A.* **117 G13**
Dadhar *Pakistan* **68 E2**
Dadiya *Nigeria* **83 D7**
Dadnah *U.A.E.* **71 E8**
Dadra & Nagar Haveli □
  India **66 J8**
Dadri = Charkhi Dadri *India* **68 E7**
Dadu *Pakistan* **68 F2**
Dadu He → *China* **58 C4**
Daegu *S. Korea* **57 G15**
Daejeon *S. Korea* **57 F14**
Daejeong *S. Korea* **57 H14**
Daet *Phil.* **61 D5**
Dafang *China* **58 D5**
Dafnes *Greece* **49 D7**
Dafni *Greece* **46 D4**
Dağ *Turkey* **47 D12**
Dagana *Senegal* **82 B1**
Dagash *Sudan* **80 D3**
Dagestan □ *Russia* **35 J8**
Dagestanskiye Ogni *Russia* **35 J9**
Daggett *U.S.A.* **111 L10**
Daghestan Republic =
  Dagestan □ *Russia* **35 J8**
Daghfeli *Sudan* **80 D3**
Dağlıq Qarabağ =
  Nagorno-Karabakh □
  Azerbaijan **73 C12**
Dagö = Hiiumaa *Estonia* **32 C2**
Dagu *China* **57 E9**
Daguan *China* **58 D4**
Dagupan *Phil.* **61 C4**
Daguragu *Australia* **92 C5**
Dahab *Egypt* **80 B3**
Dahlak *Eritrea* **81 D5**
Dahlak Kebir *Eritrea* **81 D5**
Dahlenburg *Germany* **24 B6**
Dahlonega *U.S.A.* **117 D13**
Dahme *Germany* **24 D9**
Dahod *India* **68 H6**
Dahong Shan *China* **59 B9**
Dahongliutan *China* **69 B8**
Dahra *Libya* **79 C9**
Dahra *Senegal* **82 B1**
Dahshûr *Egypt* **80 J7**
Dahūk *Iraq* **73 D10**
Dahūk □ *Iraq* **73 D10**
Dai Hao *Vietnam* **64 C6**

Dai-Sen *Japan* **55 G6**
Dai Shan *China* **59 B14**
Dai Xian *China* **56 E7**
Daicheng *China* **56 E9**
Daikondi = Day Kundī □
  Afghan. **66 C5**
Daimiel *Spain* **37 F7**
Daingean *Ireland* **12 C4**
Dainkog *China* **58 A1**
Daintree *Australia* **94 B4**
Daintree △ *Australia* **94 B4**
Daiō-Misaki *Japan* **55 G8**
Dair, J. ed *Sudan* **81 E3**
Dairût *Egypt* **80 B3**
Daisen-Oki △ *Japan* **55 G6**
Daisetsu-Zan *Japan* **54 C11**
Daisetsu-Zan △ *Japan* **54 C11**
Dajarra *Australia* **94 C2**
Dajiawa *China* **57 F10**
Dajin Chuan → *China* **58 B3**
Dak Dam *Cambodia* **64 F6**
Dak Nhe *Vietnam* **64 E6**
Dak Pek *Vietnam* **64 E6**
Dak Song *Vietnam* **65 F6**
Dak Sui *Vietnam* **64 E6**
Dakar *Senegal* **82 C1**
Dakar □ *Senegal* **82 C1**
Dakhla *W. Sahara* **78 D2**
Dakhla, El Wâhât el- *Egypt* **80 B2**
Dakingari *Nigeria* **83 C5**
Dakor *India* **68 H5**
Dakoro *Niger* **83 C6**
Dakota City *U.S.A.* **112 D5**
Đakovica *Serbia* **44 D4**
Đakovo *Croatia* **28 E3**
Dalaba *Guinea* **82 C2**
Dalachi *China* **56 F3**
Dalai Nur *China* **56 C9**
Dālakī *Iran* **71 D6**
Dalälven → *Sweden* **10 D10**
Dalaman *Turkey* **47 E10**
Dalaman → *Turkey* **47 E10**
Dalandzadgad *Mongolia* **56 C3**
Dalap-Uliga-Darrit =
  Majuro *Marshall Is.* **96 G9**
Dalarna *Sweden* **10 D8**
Dalarnas län □ *Sweden* **10 C8**
Dālbandīn *Pakistan* **66 E4**
Dalbeattie *U.K.* **13 G5**
Dalbeg *Australia* **94 C4**
Dalby *Australia* **95 D5**
Dalby *Sweden* **11 J7**
Dalby Söderskog △ *Sweden* **11 J7**
Dale City *U.S.A.* **113 F15**
Dale Hollow L. *U.S.A.* **117 C12**
Dalga *Egypt* **80 B3**
Dalgán *Iran* **71 E8**
Dalhart *U.S.A.* **116 C3**
Dalhousie *Canada* **105 C6**
Dalhousie *India* **68 C6**
Dali *Shaanxi, China* **56 G5**
Dali *Yunnan, China* **58 E3**
Dalian *China* **57 E11**
Daliang Shan *China* **58 D4**
Daling He → *China* **57 D11**
Dāliyat el Karmel *Israel* **74 C4**
Dalj *Croatia* **28 E3**
Dalkeith *U.K.* **13 F5**
Dallas *Oreg., U.S.A.* **108 D2**
Dallas *Tex., U.S.A.* **116 E6**
Dalles, The *U.S.A.* **108 D3**
Dallol *Ethiopia* **81 E5**
Dalmā *U.A.E.* **71 E7**
Dalmacija *Croatia* **41 E13**
Dalmas, L. *Canada* **105 B5**
Dalmatia = Dalmacija
  Croatia **41 E13**
Dalmau *India* **69 F9**
Dalmellington *U.K.* **13 F4**
Dalnegorsk *Russia* **54 B7**
Dalnerechensk *Russia* **54 B6**
Dalnevostochnyy □ *Russia* **53 C14**
Daloa *Ivory C.* **82 D3**
Dalou Shan *China* **58 C6**
Dalry *U.K.* **13 F4**
Dalrymple, L. *Australia* **94 C4**
Dalrymple, Mt. *Australia* **94 K6**
Dals Långed *Sweden* **11 F6**
Dalsjöfors *Sweden* **11 G7**
Dalsland *Sweden* **11 F6**
Daltenganj *India* **69 H11**
Dalton *Ga., U.S.A.* **117 D12**
Dalton *Mass., U.S.A.* **115 D11**
Dalton *Nebr., U.S.A.* **112 E2**
Dalton-in-Furness *U.K.* **14 C4**
Dalupiri I. *Phil.* **61 B4**
Dalvík *Iceland* **8 D4**
Dálvvadis = Jokkmokk
  Sweden **8 C18**
Dalwallinu *Australia* **93 F2**
Daly → *Australia* **92 B5**
Daly City *U.S.A.* **110 H4**
Daly L. *Canada* **103 B7**
Daly River *Australia* **92 B5**
Daly Waters *Australia* **94 B1**
Dalyan *Turkey* **47 E10**

Dam Doi *Vietnam* **65 H5**
Dam Ha *Vietnam* **64 B6**
Damachova *Belarus* **31 G10**
Daman *India* **66 J8**
Dāmaneh *Iran* **71 C6**
Damanhûr *Egypt* **80 H7**
Damant L. *Canada* **103 A7**
Damanzhuang *China* **56 E9**
Damar *Indonesia* **63 F7**
Damara *C.A.R.* **84 D3**
Damaraland *Namibia* **88 C2**
Damascus = Dimashq *Syria* **74 B5**
Damasi *Greece* **46 B4**
Damaturu *Nigeria* **83 C7**
Damāvand *Iran* **71 C7**
Damāvand, Qolleh-ye *Iran* **71 C7**
Damba *Angola* **84 F3**
Dame Marie *Haiti* **121 C5**
Dāmghān *Iran* **71 B7**
Damietta = Dumyât *Egypt* **80 H7**
Daming *China* **56 F8**
Damīr Qābū *Syria* **70 B4**
Dammam = Ad Dammām
  Si. Arabia **71 E6**
Dammarie-les-Lys *France* **19 D9**
Dammartin-en-Goële *France* **19 C9**
Damme *Germany* **24 C4**
Damodar → *India* **69 H12**
Damoh *India* **69 H8**
Dampier *Australia* **92 D2**
Dampier, Selat *Indonesia* **63 E8**
Dampier Arch. *Australia* **92 D2**
Damrei, Chuor Phnum
  Cambodia **65 G4**
Damvillers *France* **19 C12**
Damyang *S. Korea* **57 G14**
Dan-Gulbi *Nigeria* **83 C6**
Dana *Indonesia* **63 F6**
Dana, L. *Canada* **104 B4**
Dana, Mt. *U.S.A.* **110 H7**
Danakil Desert *Ethiopia* **81 E5**
Danané *Ivory C.* **82 D3**
Danao *Phil.* **61 F6**
Danau Poso *Indonesia* **63 E6**
Danba *China* **58 B3**
Danbury *U.S.A.* **115 E11**
Danby L. *U.S.A.* **109 J6**
Dand *Afghan.* **68 D1**
Dandeldhura *Nepal* **69 E9**
Dandeli *India* **66 M9**
Dandenong *Australia* **95 F4**
Dandîl *Egypt* **80 J7**
Dandong *China* **57 D13**
Danfeng *China* **56 H6**
Dangan Liedao *China* **59 F10**
Dangé-St-Romain *France* **20 B4**
Dângeni *Romania* **29 C11**
Danger Is. = Pukapuka
  Cook Is. **97 J11**
Danger Pt. *S. Africa* **88 E2**
Danginpuri *Indonesia* **63 K18**
Dangla *Ethiopia* **81 E4**
Dangla Shan = Tanggula
  Shan *China* **60 C4**
Dangora *Nigeria* **83 C6**
Dangouadougou
  Burkina Faso **82 D4**
Dangrek, Phnom *Thailand* **64 E5**
Dangriga *Belize* **119 D7**
Dangshan *China* **56 G9**
Dangtu *China* **59 B12**
Dangyang *China* **59 B8**
Dani *Burkina Faso* **83 C4**
Daniel *U.S.A.* **108 E8**
Daniel's Harbour *Canada* **105 B8**
Danielskuil *S. Africa* **88 D3**
Danielson *U.S.A.* **115 E13**
Danilov *Russia* **32 C11**
Danilovgrad *Montenegro* **44 D3**
Danilovka *Russia* **34 E7**
Daning *China* **56 F6**
Danja *Nigeria* **83 C6**
Danjiangkou *China* **59 A8**
Danjiangkou Shuiku *China* **59 A8**
Đank *Oman* **71 F8**
Dankalwa *Nigeria* **83 C7**
Dankama *Nigeria* **83 C6**
Dankhar Gompa *India* **68 C8**
Dankov *Russia* **32 F10**
Danleng *China* **58 B4**
Danlí *Honduras* **120 D2**
Danmark = Denmark ■
  Europe **11 J3**
Dannemora *U.S.A.* **115 B11**
Dannenberg *Germany* **24 B7**
Dannevirke *N.Z.* **91 D6**
Dannhauser *S. Africa* **89 D5**
Dansville *U.S.A.* **114 D7**
Danta *India* **68 G5**
Dantan *India* **69 J12**
Danube = Dunărea →
  Europe **29 E14**

Danvers *U.S.A.* **115 D14**
Danville *Ill., U.S.A.* **112 E10**
Danville *Ky., U.S.A.* **113 G11**
Danville *Pa., U.S.A.* **115 F8**
Danville *Va., U.S.A.* **113 G14**
Danville *Vt., U.S.A.* **115 B12**
Danyang *China* **59 B12**
Danzhai *China* **58 D6**
Danzhou *China* **64 C7**
Danzig = Gdańsk *Poland* **30 D5**
Dão → *Portugal* **36 E2**
Dao Xian *China* **59 E8**
Daocheng *China* **58 C3**
Daokou *China* **56 E9**
Daoukro *Ivory C.* **82 D4**
Dapaong *Togo* **83 C5**
Dapchi *Nigeria* **83 C7**
Dapitan *Phil.* **61 G5**
Daqing Shan *China* **56 D6**
Daqu Shan *China* **59 B14**
Dar Banda *Africa* **76 F6**
Dar el Beida = Casablanca
  Morocco **78 B4**
Dar es Salaam *Tanzania* **86 D4**
Dar Mazār *Iran* **71 D8**
Dar'ā *Syria* **74 C5**
Dar'ā □ *Syria* **74 C5**
Dārāb *Iran* **71 D7**
Daraban *Pakistan* **68 D4**
Darabani *Romania* **29 B11**
Daraina *Madag.* **89 A8**
Daraj *Libya* **79 B8**
Dārān *Iran* **71 C6**
Daravica *Serbia* **44 D4**
Daraw *Egypt* **80 C3**
Darazo *Nigeria* **83 C7**
Darband *Pakistan* **68 B5**
Darband, Kūh-e *Iran* **71 D8**
Darbhanga *India* **69 F11**
D'Arcy *Canada* **102 C4**
Darda *Croatia* **28 E3**
Dardanelle *Ark., U.S.A.* **116 D8**
Dardanelle *Calif., U.S.A.* **110 G7**
Dardanelles = Çanakkale
  Boğazı *Turkey* **45 F10**
Dare → *Ethiopia* **81 F5**
Darende *Turkey* **72 C7**
Darfo *Italy* **40 C7**
Dârfûr *Sudan* **79 F10**
Dargai *Pakistan* **68 B4**
Dargan Ata = Darganata
  Turkmenistan **52 E6**
Dargaville *N.Z.* **91 A4**
Dargol *Niger* **83 C5**
Darhan *Mongolia* **60 B5**
Darhan Muminggan
  Lianheqi *China* **56 D6**
Dari *Sudan* **81 F3**
Darıca *Turkey* **72 B3**
Darién, G. del *Colombia* **124 B3**
Darién △ *Panama* **120 E4**
Dariganga = Ovoot *Mongolia* **56 B7**
Darinskoye *Kazakhstan* **34 E10**
Darjeeling = Darjiling *India* **69 F13**
Darjiling *India* **69 F13**
Darkan *Australia* **93 F2**
Darkhana *Pakistan* **68 D5**
Darkhazīneh *Iran* **71 D6**
Darkot Pass *Pakistan* **69 A5**
Darling → *Australia* **95 E3**
Darling Downs *Australia* **95 D5**
Darling Ra. *Australia* **93 F2**
Darlington *U.K.* **14 C6**
Darlington *U.S.A.* **117 D15**
Darlington □ *U.K.* **14 C6**
Darlington, L. *S. Africa* **88 E4**
Darlot, L. *Australia* **93 E3**
Darłowo *Poland* **30 D3**
Dărmăneşti *Bacău, Romania* **29 D11**
Dărmăneşti *Suceava,
  Romania* **29 C11**
Darmstadt *Germany* **25 F4**
Darnah *Libya* **79 B10**
Darnall *S. Africa* **89 D5**
Darney *France* **19 D13**
Darnley, C. *Antarctica* **5 C6**
Darnley B. *Canada* **100 C7**
Daroca *Spain* **38 D3**
Darou-Mousti *Senegal* **82 B1**
Darr → *Australia* **94 C3**
Darra Pezu *Pakistan* **68 C4**
Darregueira *Argentina* **126 D3**
Darrington *U.S.A.* **108 B3**
Darssser Ort *Germany* **24 A8**
Dart → *U.K.* **15 G4**
Dart, C. *Antarctica* **5 D14**
Dartford *U.K.* **15 F8**
Dartmoor △ *U.K.* **15 G4**
Dartmouth *Canada* **105 D7**
Dartmouth *U.K.* **15 G4**
Dartmouth Res. *Australia* **95 D4**
Dartuch, C. = Artrutx, C.
  de *Spain* **48 B10**
Daru *Papua N. G.* **96 H6**
Daruvar *Croatia* **28 E2**
Darvaza *Turkmenistan* **52 E6**
Darvel, Teluk = Lahad
  Datu, Telok *Malaysia* **63 D5**

Darwen *U.K.* **14 D5**
Darwendale *Zimbabwe* **89 B5**
Darwha *India* **66 J10**
Darwin *Australia* **92 B5**
Darwin *U.S.A.* **111 J9**
Darya Khan *Pakistan* **68 D4**
Daryoi Amu =
  Amudarya → *Uzbekistan* **52 E6**
Dās *U.A.E.* **71 E7**
Dashen, Ras *Ethiopia* **81 E4**
Dashetai *China* **56 D6**
Dashkesan = Daşkäsän
  Azerbaijan **35 K7**
Dashköpri *Turkmenistan* **71 B9**
Dashoguz *Turkmenistan* **52 E6**
Dasht *Iran* **71 B8**
Dasht → *Pakistan* **66 G2**
Daska *Pakistan* **68 C6**
Daşkäsän *Azerbaijan* **35 K7**
Dassa *Benin* **83 D5**
Dasuya *India* **68 D6**
Datça *Turkey* **47 E9**
Datia *India* **69 G8**
Datian *China* **59 E11**
Datong *Anhui, China* **59 B11**
Datong *Shanxi, China* **56 D7**
Dattakhel *Pakistan* **68 C3**
Datteln *Germany* **24 D3**
Datu, Tanjung *Indonesia* **62 D3**
Datu Piang *Phil.* **61 H6**
Datuk, Tanjong = Datu,
  Tanjung *Indonesia* **62 D3**
Daua = Dawa → *Africa* **81 G5**
Daud Khel *Pakistan* **68 C4**
Daudnagar *India* **69 G11**
Daugava → *Latvia* **32 D3**
Daugavpils *Latvia* **32 E4**
Daulpur *India* **68 F7**
Daun *Germany* **25 E2**
Dauphin *Canada* **103 C8**
Dauphin *U.S.A.* **114 F8**
Dauphin L. *Canada* **103 C9**
Dauphiné *France* **21 C9**
Daura *Borno, Nigeria* **83 C7**
Daura *Katsina, Nigeria* **83 C6**
Dausa *India* **68 F7**
Däväçi *Azerbaijan* **35 K9**
Davangere *India* **66 M9**
Davao *Phil.* **61 H6**
Davao G. *Phil.* **61 H6**
Dāvar Panāh = Sarāvān
  Iran **71 E9**
Davenport *Calif., U.S.A.* **110 H4**
Davenport *Iowa, U.S.A.* **112 E8**
Davenport *Wash., U.S.A.* **108 C4**
Davenport Ra. *Australia* **94 C1**
Daventry *U.K.* **15 E6**
David *Panama* **120 E3**
David City *U.S.A.* **112 E5**
David Glacier *Antarctica* **5 D21**
David Gorodok = Davyd
  Haradok *Belarus* **23 B14**
Davidson *Canada* **103 C7**
Davis *Antarctica* **5 C6**
Davis *U.S.A.* **110 G5**
Davis Dam *U.S.A.* **111 K12**
Davis Inlet *Canada* **105 A7**
Davis Mts. *U.S.A.* **116 F3**
Davis Sea *Antarctica* **5 C7**
Davis Str. *N. Amer.* **98 C14**
Davo → *Ivory C.* **82 D3**
Davos *Switz.* **25 J5**
Davutlar *Turkey* **47 D9**
Davy L. *Canada* **103 B7**
Davyd Haradok *Belarus* **23 B14**
Dawa → *Africa* **81 G5**
Dawaki *Bauchi, Nigeria* **83 D6**
Dawaki *Kano, Nigeria* **83 C6**
Dawei = Tavoy *Burma* **64 E2**
Dawes Ra. *Australia* **94 C5**
Dawlish *U.K.* **15 G4**
Dawna Ra. *Burma* **64 D2**
Dawros Hd. *Ireland* **12 B3**
Dawson *Canada* **100 C6**
Dawson *U.S.A.* **117 F12**
Dawson, I. *Chile* **128 G2**
Dawson B. *Canada* **103 C8**
Dawson Creek *Canada* **102 B4**
Dawson Inlet *Canada* **103 A10**
Dawson Ra. *Australia* **94 C4**
Dawu *Hubei, China* **59 B9**
Dawu *Sichuan, China* **58 B3**
Daxian *China* **58 B6**
Daxin *China* **58 F6**
Daxindian *China* **57 F11**
Daxinggou *China* **57 C15**
Daxue Shan *Sichuan, China* **58 B3**
Daxue Shan *Yunnan, China* **58 F2**
Day Kundī □ *Afghan.* **66 C5**
Dayao *China* **58 D3**
Daye *China* **59 B10**
Dayet en Naharat *Mali* **82 B4**
Dayi *China* **58 B4**
Daylesford *Australia* **95 F3**
Dayong *China* **59 C8**
Dayr az Zawr *Syria* **73 E9**

Dayr az Zawr □ *Syria* **73** E9
Daysland *Canada* **102** C6
Dayton *Nev., U.S.A.* **110** F7
Dayton *Ohio, U.S.A.* **113** F11
Dayton *Pa., U.S.A.* **114** F5
Dayton *Tenn., U.S.A.* **117** D12
Dayton *Wash., U.S.A.* **108** C5
Dayton *Wyo., U.S.A.* **108** D10
Daytona Beach *U.S.A.* **117** G14
Dayu *China* **59** E10
Dayville *U.S.A.* **108** D4
Dazhu *China* **58** B6
Dazkırı *Turkey* **47** D11
Dazu *China* **58** C5
De Aar *S. Africa* **88** E3
De Biesbosch △ *Neths.* **17** C4
De Funiak Springs *U.S.A.* **117** F11
De Grey → *Australia* **92** D2
De Haan *Belgium* **17** C3
De Hoge Veluwe △ *Neths.* **17** B5
De Hoop → *S. Africa* **88** E3
De Kennemerduinen △
   Neths. **17** B4
De Land *U.S.A.* **117** G14
De Leon *U.S.A.* **116** E5
De Panne *Belgium* **17** C2
De Pere *U.S.A.* **112** C9
De Queen *U.S.A.* **116** D7
De Quincy *U.S.A.* **116** F8
De Smet *U.S.A.* **112** C5
De Soto *U.S.A.* **112** F8
De Tour Village *U.S.A.* **113** B12
De Witt *U.S.A.* **116** D9
Dead Sea *Asia* **74** D4
Deadwood *U.S.A.* **112** C2
Deadwood L. *Canada* **102** B3
Deal *U.K.* **15** F9
Deal I. *Australia* **95** F4
Dealesville *S. Africa* **88** D4
De'an *China* **59** C10
Dean → *Canada* **102** C3
Dean, Forest of *U.K.* **15** F5
Dean Chan. *Canada* **102** C3
Deán Funes *Argentina* **126** C3
Dease → *Canada* **102** B3
Dease L. *Canada* **102** B2
Dease Lake *Canada* **102** B2
Death Valley *U.S.A.* **111** J10
Death Valley △ *U.S.A.* **111** J9
Death Valley Junction
   U.S.A. **111** J10
Deauville *France* **18** C7
Deba *Spain* **38** B2
Deba Habe *Nigeria* **83** C7
Debaltsevo *Ukraine* **33** H10
Debao *China* **58** F6
Debar *Macedonia* **44** E4
Debark *Ethiopia* **81** E4
Debden *Canada* **103** C7
Dębica *Poland* **31** H8
Dęblin *Poland* **31** G8
Dębno *Poland* **31** F1
Débo, L. *Mali* **82** B4
DeBolt *Canada* **102** B5
Deborah East, L. *Australia* **93** F2
Deborah West, L. *Australia* **93** F2
Debrc *Serbia* **44** B3
Debre Birhan *Ethiopia* **81** F4
Debre Markos *Ethiopia* **81** E4
Debre May *Ethiopia* **81** E4
Debre Sina *Ethiopia* **81** F4
Debre Tabor *Ethiopia* **81** E4
Debre Zebit *Ethiopia* **81** E4
Debre Zeyit *Ethiopia* **81** F4
Debrecen *Hungary* **28** C6
Debrzno *Poland* **30** E4
Dečani *Serbia* **44** D4
Decatur *Ala., U.S.A.* **117** D11
Decatur *Ga., U.S.A.* **117** E12
Decatur *Ill., U.S.A.* **112** F9
Decatur *Ind., U.S.A.* **113** E11
Decatur *Tex., U.S.A.* **116** E6
Decazeville *France* **20** D6
Deccan *India* **66** L11
Deception Bay *Australia* **95** D5
Deception I. *Antarctica* **5** C17
Deception L. *Canada* **103** B8
Dechang *China* **58** D4
Dechhu *India* **68** F5
Děčín *Czech Rep.* **26** A7
Decize *France* **19** F10
Deckerville *U.S.A.* **114** C2
Decollatura *Italy* **43** C9
Decorah *U.S.A.* **112** D8
Deda *Romania* **29** D9
Dedéagach =
   Alexandroúpoli *Greece* **45** F9
Deder *Ethiopia* **81** F5
Dedham *U.S.A.* **115** D13
Dédougou *Burkina Faso* **82** C4
Dedovichi *Russia* **32** D5
Dedza *Malawi* **87** E3
Dee → *Aberds., U.K.* **13** D6
Dee → *Dumf. & Gall., U.K.* **13** G4
Dee → *Wales, U.K.* **14** D4
Deep B. *Canada* **102** A5
Deepwater *Australia* **95** D5

Deer → *Canada* **103** B10
Deer L. *Canada* **103** C10
Deer Lake *Nfld. & L., Canada* **105** C8
Deer Lake *Ont., Canada* **103** C10
Deer Lodge *U.S.A.* **108** C7
Deer Park *U.S.A.* **108** C5
Deer River *U.S.A.* **112** B7
Deeragun *Australia* **94** B4
Deerdepoort *S. Africa* **88** C4
Deferiet *U.S.A.* **115** B9
Defiance *U.S.A.* **113** E11
Degana *India* **68** F6
Dêgê *China* **58** B2
Degebe → *Portugal* **37** G3
Degeberga *Sweden* **11** J8
Dégelis *Canada* **105** C6
Degema *Nigeria* **83** E6
Degerfors *Sweden* **10** E8
Degerhamn *Sweden* **11** H10
Deggendorf *Germany* **25** G8
Degh → *Pakistan* **68** D5
Değirmendere *Turkey* **45** F13
Deh Bīd *Iran* **71** D7
Deh-e Shīr *Iran* **71** D7
Dehaj *Iran* **71** D7
Dehak *Iran* **71** E9
Dehdez *Iran* **71** D6
Dehej *India* **68** J5
Dehestān *Iran* **71** D7
Dehgolān *Iran* **73** E12
Dehibat *Tunisia* **79** B8
Dehlorān *Iran* **73** F12
Dehnow-e Kūhestān *Iran* **71** E8
Dehra Dun *India* **68** D8
Dehri *India* **69** G11
Dehua *China* **59** E12
Dehui *China* **57** B13
Deim Zubeir *Sudan* **81** F2
Deinze *Belgium* **17** D3
Dej *Romania* **29** C8
Deje *Sweden* **10** E7
Dejiang *China* **58** C7
Deka → *Zimbabwe* **88** B4
DeKalb *U.S.A.* **112** E9
Dekemhare *Eritrea* **81** D4
Dekese *Dem. Rep. of the Congo* **84** E4
Del Mar *U.S.A.* **111** N9
Del Norte *U.S.A.* **109** H10
Del Rio *U.S.A.* **116** G4
Delai *Sudan* **80** D4
Delambre I. *Australia* **92** D2
Delami *Sudan* **81** E3
Delano *U.S.A.* **111** K7
Delano Peak *U.S.A.* **108** G7
Delareyville *S. Africa* **88** D4
Delaronde L. *Canada* **103** C7
Delavan *U.S.A.* **112** D9
Delaware *U.S.A.* **113** E12
Delaware □ *U.S.A.* **113** F16
Delaware → *U.S.A.* **115** G9
Delaware B. *U.S.A.* **113** F16
Delaware Water Gap △
   U.S.A. **115** E10
Delay → *Canada* **105** A5
Delbrück *Germany* **24** D4
Delčevo *Macedonia* **44** E6
Delegate *Australia* **95** F4
Delémont *Switz.* **25** H3
Delevan *U.S.A.* **114** D6
Delft *Neths.* **17** B4
Delfzijl *Neths.* **17** A6
Delgado, C. *Mozam.* **87** E5
Delgerhet *Mongolia* **56** B6
Delgo *Sudan* **80** C3
Delhi *Canada* **114** D4
Delhi *India* **68** E7
Delhi *La., U.S.A.* **116** E9
Delhi *N.Y., U.S.A.* **115** D10
Deli Jovan *Serbia* **44** B6
Delia *Canada* **102** C6
Delice *Turkey* **72** C6
Delicias *Mexico* **118** B3
Delījān *Iran* **71** C6
Déline *Canada* **100** C7
Delisle *Canada* **103** C7
Dell City *U.S.A.* **116** F2
Dell Rapids *U.S.A.* **112** D5
Delle *France* **19** E14
Delmar *U.S.A.* **115** D11
Delmenhorst *Germany* **24** B4
Delnice *Croatia* **41** C11
Delonga, Ostrova *Russia* **53** B15
Deloraine *Australia* **95** G4
Deloraine *Canada* **103** D8
Delphi *Greece* **46** C4
Delphi *U.S.A.* **112** E10
Delphos *U.S.A.* **113** E11
Delportshoop *S. Africa* **88** D3
Delray Beach *U.S.A.* **117** H14
Delsbo *Sweden* **10** C10
Delta *Colo., U.S.A.* **108** G9
Delta *Utah, U.S.A.* **108** G7
Delta □ *Nigeria* **83** D6
Delta del Ebro → *Spain* **38** E5
Delta del Po → *Italy* **41** D9
Deqing *China* **59** F8

Delta Dunărea △ *Romania* **29** E14
Delta Junction *U.S.A.* **100** C5
Deltona *U.S.A.* **117** G14
Delungra *Australia* **95** D5
Delvada *India* **68** J4
Delvinaki *Greece* **46** B2
Delyatyn *Ukraine* **29** B9
Demak *Indonesia* **63** G14
Demanda, Sierra de la *Spain* **38** C2
Demavend = Damāvand,
   Qolleh-ye *Iran* **71** C7
Dembecha *Ethiopia* **81** E4
Dembi *Ethiopia* **81** F4
Dembia *Dem. Rep. of the Congo* **86** B2
Dembidolo *Ethiopia* **81** F3
Demer → *Belgium* **17** D4
Demetrias *Greece* **46** B5
Demidov *Russia* **32** E6
Deming *N. Mex., U.S.A.* **109** K10
Deming *Wash., U.S.A.* **110** B4
Demini → *Brazil* **124** D6
Demirci *Turkey* **47** B10
Demirköprü Barajı *Turkey* **47** C10
Demirköy *Turkey* **45** E11
Demmin *Germany* **24** B9
Demonte *Italy* **40** D4
Demopolis *U.S.A.* **117** E11
Dempo *Indonesia* **62** E2
Demyansk *Russia* **32** D7
Den Bosch =
   's-Hertogenbosch *Neths.* **17** C5
Den Burg *Neths.* **17** A4
Den Chai *Thailand* **64** D3
Den Haag =
   's-Gravenhage *Neths.* **17** B4
Den Helder *Neths.* **17** B4
Den Oever *Neths.* **17** B5
Denain *France* **19** B10
Denair *U.S.A.* **110** H6
Denali = McKinley, Mt.
   U.S.A. **106** a
Denau *Uzbekistan* **52** F7
Denbigh *Canada* **114** A7
Denbigh *U.K.* **14** D4
Denbighshire □ *U.K.* **14** D4
Dendang *Indonesia* **62** E3
Dendermonde *Belgium* **17** C4
Deneba *Ethiopia* **81** F4
Deng Deng *Cameroon* — (see note)
Dengchuan *China* **58** E3
Denge *Nigeria* **83** C6
Dengfeng *China* **56** G7
Dengi *Nigeria* **83** D6
Dengkou *China* **56** D4
Dengzhou *China* **59** A9
Denham *Australia* **93** E1
Denham, Mt. *Jamaica* **120** a
Denham Ra. *Australia* **94** C4
Denham Sd. *Australia* **93** E1
Denholm *Canada* **103** C7
Denia *Spain* **39** G5
Denial B. *Australia* **95** E1
Deniliquin *Australia* **95** F3
Denison *Iowa, U.S.A.* **112** D6
Denison *Tex., U.S.A.* **116** E6
Denison Plains *Australia* **92** C4
Denizli *Turkey* **47** D11
Denizli □ *Turkey* **47** D11
Denman Glacier *Antarctica* **5** C7
Denmark *Australia* **93** F2
Denmark ■ *Europe* **11** J4
Denmark Str. *Atl. Oc.* **98** C17
Dennery *St. Lucia* **121** f
Dennison *U.S.A.* **114** F3
Denny *U.K.* **13** E5
Denpasar *Indonesia* **63** K18
Denpasar ✈ (DPS) *Indonesia* **63** K18
Denton *Mont., U.S.A.* **108** C9
Denton *Tex., U.S.A.* **116** E6
D'Entrecasteaux, Pt.
   Australia **93** F2
D'Entrecasteaux △ *Australia* **93** F2
D'Entrecasteaux Is.
   Papua N. G. **90** B8
Denu *Ghana* **83** D5
Denver *Colo., U.S.A.* **108** G11
Denver *Pa., U.S.A.* **115** F8
Denver City *U.S.A.* **116** E3
Deoband *India* **68** E7
Deogarh *India* **68** G5
Deoghar *India* **69** G12
Deolali *India* **66** K8
Deoli = Devli *India* **68** G6
Déols *France* **19** F8
Deora *India* **68** F4
Deori *India* **69** H8
Deoria *India* **69** F10
Depalpur *India* **68** H6
Deping *China* **57** F9
Deposit *U.S.A.* **115** D9
Depuch I. *Australia* **92** D2
Deputatskiy *Russia* **53** C14
Dêqên *China* **58** C2
Deqing *China* **59** F8

Dera Ghazi Khan *Pakistan* **68** D4
Dera Ismail Khan *Pakistan* **68** D4
Derabugti *Pakistan* **68** E3
Derawar Fort *Pakistan* **68** E4
Derbent *Russia* **35** J9
Derbent *Turkey* **47** C10
Derby *Australia* **92** C3
Derby *U.K.* **14** E6
Derby *Conn., U.S.A.* **115** E11
Derby *Kans., U.S.A.* **112** G5
Derby *N.Y., U.S.A.* **114** D6
Derby City *U.K.* **14** E6
Derby Line *U.S.A.* **115** B12
Derbyshire □ *U.K.* **14** D6
Derdap *Serbia* **44** B6
Derdepoort *S. Africa* **88** C4
Dereham *U.K.* **15** E8
Dereköy *Turkey* **45** E11
Dereli *Turkey* **73** B8
Derg → *U.K.* **12** B4
Derg, L. *Ireland* **12** D3
Dergachi = Derhaci *Ukraine* **33** G9
Derhaci *Ukraine* **33** G9
Deridder *U.S.A.* **116** F8
Derik *Turkey* **73** D9
Derinkuyu *Turkey* **72** C6
Derik *Turkey* — (see note)
Derry = Londonderry *U.K.* **12** B4
Derry = Londonderry □
   U.K. **12** B4
Derry *N.H., U.S.A.* **115** D13
Derry *Pa., U.S.A.* **114** F5
Derryveagh Mts. *Ireland* **12** B3
Derudub *Sudan* **80** D4
Derval *France* **18** E5
Derveni *Greece* **46** C4
Derventa *Bos.-H.* **28** F7
Derwent → *Cumb., U.K.* **14** C4
Derwent → *Derby, U.K.* **14** E6
Derwent → *N. Yorks., U.K.* **14** D7
Derwent Water *U.K.* **14** C4
Des Moines *Iowa, U.S.A.* **112** E7
Des Moines *N. Mex., U.S.A.* **109** H12
Des Moines *Wash., U.S.A.* **110** C4
Des Moines → *U.S.A.* **112** E8
Desa *Romania* **28** G8
Desaguadero → *Argentina* **126** C2
Desaguadero → *Bolivia* **124** G5
Desantne *Ukraine* **29** E14
Desar *Malaysia* **65** d
Descanso, Pta. *Mexico* **111** N9
Descartes *France* **20** B4
Deschaillons-sur-St-
   Laurent *Canada* **105** C5
Deschambault L. *Canada* **103** C8
Deschutes → *U.S.A.* **108** D3
Dese *Ethiopia* **81** E4
Deseado → *Argentina* **128** F3
Desenzano del Garda *Italy* **40** C7
Desert Center *U.S.A.* **111** M11
Desert Hot Springs *U.S.A.* **111** M10
Desfina *Greece* **46** C4
Deshnok *India* **68** F5
Desierto Central de Baja
   California △ *Mexico* **118** B2
Deskati *Greece* **44** G5
Desna → *Ukraine* **23** C16
Desnățui → *Romania* **29** G8
Desolación, I. *Chile* **128** G2
Despeñaperros, Paso *Spain* **37** G7
Despeñaperros △ *Spain* **37** G7
Despotiko *Greece* **46** e
Despotovac *Serbia* **44** B5
Dessau *Germany* **24** D8
Dessye = Dese *Ethiopia* **81** E4
D'Estrees B. *Australia* **95** F2
Desuri *India* **68** G5
Desvres *France* **19** B8
Det Udom *Thailand* **64** E5
Deta *Romania* **28** E6
Dete *Zimbabwe* **88** B4
Detinja → *Serbia* **44** C4
Detmold *Germany* **24** D4
Detour, Pt. *U.S.A.* **112** C10
Detroit *U.S.A.* **114** D1
Detroit Lakes *U.S.A.* **112** B6
Detva *Slovak Rep.* **27** C12
Deua △ *Australia* **95** F4
Deurne *Neths.* **17** C5
Deutsch-
   Luxemburgischer △
   Germany **25** F2
Deutsche Bucht *Germany* **24** A4
Deutschland =
   Germany ■ *Europe* **24** E6
Deutschlandsberg *Austria* **26** E8
Deux-Sèvres □ *France* **18** F6
Deva *Romania* **28** E7
Devakottai *India* **66** Q11
Devaprayag *India* **69** D8
Dévaványa *Hungary* **28** C5
Deveci Dağları *Turkey* **72** B7
Devecikonağı *Turkey* **45** G12
Devecser *Hungary* **28** C2

Develi *Turkey* **72** C6
Deventer *Neths.* **17** B6
Deveron → *U.K.* **13** D6
Devesel *Romania* **28** F7
Devgadh Bariya *India* **68** H5
Devikot *India* **68** F4
Devils Den *U.S.A.* **110** K7
Devils Hole = Death
   Valley = *U.S.A.* **111** J9
Devils Lake *U.S.A.* **112** A4
Devils Paw *Canada* **102** B2
Devils Postpile △ *U.S.A.* **110** H7
Devils Tower *U.S.A.* **108** D11
Devils Tower △ *U.S.A.* **108** D11
Devin *Bulgaria* **45** E8
Devine *U.S.A.* **116** G5
Devizes *U.K.* **15** F6
Devli *India* **68** G6
Devnya *Bulgaria* **45** C11
Devoll → *Albania* **44** F4
Devon *Canada* **102** C6
Devon □ *U.K.* **15** G4
Devon I. *Canada* **101** B11
Devonport *Australia* **95** G4
Devonport *N.Z.* **91** B5
Devrek *Turkey* **72** B4
Devrekâni *Turkey* **72** B5
Devrez → *Turkey* **72** B6
Dewas *India* **68** H7
Dewetsdorp *S. Africa* **88** D4
Dewey *Puerto Rico* **121** d
Dexing *China* **59** C11
Dexter *Maine, U.S.A.* **113** C19
Dexter *Mo., U.S.A.* **112** G9
Dexter *N. Mex., U.S.A.* **109** K11
Dey-Dey, L. *Australia* **93** E5
Deyang *China* **58** B5
Deyhūk *Iran* **71** C8
Deyyer *Iran* **71** E6
Dezadeash L. *Canada* **102** A1
Dezfūl *Iran* **73** F13
Dezhneva, Mys *Russia* **53** C19
Dezhou *China* **56** F9
Dhadhar → *India* **69** G11
Dhahaban *Si. Arabia* **80** C4
Dhahiriya = Aẕ Ẕāhirīyah
   West Bank **74** D3
Dhahran = Aẕ Ẕahrān
   Si. Arabia **71** E6
Dhak *Pakistan* **68** C5
Dhaka *Bangla.* **69** H14
Dhaka □ *Bangla.* **69** G14
Dhali *Cyprus* **49** D12
Dhamār *Yemen* **75** E3
Dhampur *India* **69** E8
Dhamtari *India* **67** J12
Dhanbad *India* **69** H12
Dhangarhi *Nepal* **69** E9
Dhankuta *Nepal* **69** F12
Dhar *India* **68** H6
Dharampur *India* **68** H6
Dharan → *Bangla.* **69** G13
Dharla → *Bangla.* **69** G13
Dharmapuri *India* **66** N11
Dharmjaygarh *India* **69** H10
Dharmsala *India* **68** C7
Dharni *India* **68** J7
Dharwad *India* **66** M9
Dhasan → *India* **69** G8
Dhaulagiri *Nepal* **69** E10
Dhebar, L. *India* **68** G6
Dheftera *Cyprus* **49** D12
Dhenkanal *India* **67** J14
Dherinia *Cyprus* **49** D12
Dheskáti = Deskati *Greece* **44** G5
Dhī Qār □ *Iraq* **70** D5
Dhiarrizos → *Cyprus* **49** E11
Dhībān *Jordan* **74** D4
Dhilwan *India* **68** D6
Dhimarkhera *India* **69** H9
Dhodhekánisos =
   Dodecanese *Greece* **47** E8
Dholka *India* **68** H5
Dhomokós = Domokós
   Greece **46** B4
Dhoraji *India* **68** J4
Dhrangadhra *India* **68** H4
Dhrol *India* **68** H4
Dhuburi *India* **67** F16
Dhule *India* **66** J9
Di-ib, W. → *Sudan* **80** C4
Di Linh *Vietnam* **65** G7
Di Linh, Cao Nguyen
   Vietnam **65** G7
Dia *Greece* **49** D7
Diabakania *Guinea* **82** C2
Diablo Range *U.S.A.* **110** J5
Diafarabé *Mali* **82** C4
Diala *Mali* **82** C3
Dialakoto *Senegal* **82** C2
Diallassagou *Mali* **82** C4
Diamante *Argentina* **126** C3

Diamante *Italy* **43** C8
Diamante → *Argentina* **126** C2
Diamantina *Brazil* **125** G10
Diamantina → *Australia* **95** D2
Diamantina △ *Australia* **94** C3
Diamantino *Brazil* **125** F7
Diamond Bar *U.S.A.* **111** L9
Diamond Harbour *India* **69** H13
Diamond Is. *Australia* **94** B5
Diamond Mts. *U.S.A.* **108** G6
Diamond Springs *U.S.A.* **110** G6
Dian Chi *China* **58** E4
Dianalund *Denmark* **11** J5
Dianbai *China* **59** G8
Diancheng *China* **59** G8
Dianjiang *China* **58** B6
Diano Marina *Italy* **40** E5
Dianra *Ivory C.* **82** D3
Diaoyu Tai = Senkaku-
   Shotō *E. China Sea* **55** M1
Diapaga *Burkina Faso* **83** C5
Diapangou *Burkina Faso* **83** C5
Diariguila *Guinea* **82** C2
Dībā *U.A.E.* **71** E8
Dibai *India* **68** E8
Dibaya *Dem. Rep. of the Congo* **84** F4
Dibaya-Lubue
   Dem. Rep. of the Congo **84** E3
Dibbeen △ *Jordan* **74** C4
Dibete *Botswana* **88** C4
Dibrugarh *India* **67** F19
Dickens *U.S.A.* **116** E4
Dickinson *U.S.A.* **112** B2
Dickson *U.S.A.* **117** C11
Dickson City *U.S.A.* **115** E9
Dicle Barajı *Turkey* **73** C9
Dicle Nehri → *Turkey* **73** D9
Dicomano *Italy* **41** E8
Didesa, W. → *Ethiopia* **81** E4
Didi *Sudan* **81** F3
Didiéni *Mali* **82** C3
Didimotiko *Greece* **45** E10
Didsbury *Canada* **102** C6
Didwana *India* **68** F6
Die *France* **21** D9
Diébougou *Burkina Faso* **82** C4
Diecke *Guinea* **82** D3
Diefenbaker, L. *Canada* **103** C7
Diego de Almagro *Chile* **126** B1
Diego Suarez =
   Antsiranana *Madag.* **89** A8
Diekirch *Lux.* **17** E6
Diéma *Mali* **82** C3
Diembéring *Senegal* **82** C1
Diemelsee △ *Germany* **24** D4
Dien Ban *Vietnam* **64** E7
Dien Bien *Vietnam* **58** G4
Dien Khanh *Vietnam* **65** F7
Diepholz *Germany* **24** C4
Dieppe *France* **18** C8
Dierks *U.S.A.* **116** D7
Diest *Belgium* **17** D5
Dietikon *Switz.* **25** H4
Dieulefit *France* **21** D9
Dieuze *France* **19** D13
Dif *Somali Rep.* **75** G3
Diffa □ *Niger* **83** B7
Differdange *Lux.* **17** E5
Dig *India* **68** F7
Digba *Dem. Rep. of the Congo* **86** B2
Digby *Canada* **105** D6
Diggi *India* **68** F6
Dighinala *Bangla.* **67** H18
Dighton *U.S.A.* **112** F3
Digna *Mali* **82** C3
Digne-les-Bains *France* **21** D10
Digoin *France* **19** F11
Digor *Turkey* **73** B10
Digos *Phil.* **61** H6
Digranes *Iceland* **8** C6
Digul → *Indonesia* **63** F9
Digya △ *Ghana* **83** D5
Dihang = Brahmaputra →
   Asia **69** H13
Dijlah, Nahr → *Asia* **70** D5
Dijon *France* **19** E12
Dikhil *Djibouti* **81** E5
Dikili *Turkey* **47** B8
Dikirnis *Egypt* **80** H7
Dikkil = Dikhil *Djibouti* **81** E5
Dikodougou *Ivory C.* **82** D3
Diksmuide *Belgium* **17** C2
Dikson *Russia* **52** B9
Dikti Oros *Greece* **49** D7
Dikwa *Nigeria* **83** C7
Dila *Ethiopia* **81** F4
Dilek Yarımadısı △ *Turkey* **47** D9
Dili *E. Timor* **63** F7
Dilijan *Armenia* **35** K7
Dilinata *Greece* **46** C2
Dilizhan = Dilijan *Armenia* **35** K7
Dilj *Croatia* **28** E3
Dillenburg *Germany* **24** E4
Dilley *U.S.A.* **116** G5
Dilli = Delhi *India* **68** E7
Dilling *Sudan* **81** E2
Dillingen *Bayern, Germany* **25** G6

Dillingen *Saarland, Germany* **25** F2
Dillingham *U.S.A.* **106** a
Dillon *Canada* **103** B7
Dillon *Mont., U.S.A.* **108** D7
Dillon *S.C., U.S.A.* **117** D15
Dillon = *Canada* **103** B7
Dillsburg *U.S.A.* **114** F7
Dilly *Mali* **82** C3
Dilolo *Dem. Rep. of the Congo* **84** G4
Dilos *Greece* **47** D7
Dimas *Mexico* **118** C3
Dimashq *Syria* **74** B5
Dimashq □ *Syria* **74** B5
Dimbaza *S. Africa* **89** E4
Dimbokro *Ivory C.* **82** D4
Dimboola *Australia* **95** F3
Dîmboviţa =
    Dâmboviţa → *Romania* **29** F11
Dimbulah *Australia* **94** B4
Dimitrovgrad *Bulgaria* **45** D9
Dimitrovgrad *Russia* **34** C9
Dimitrovgrad *Serbia* **44** C6
Dimitrovo = Pernik *Bulgaria* **44** D7
Dimitsana *Greece* **46** D4
Dimmitt *U.S.A.* **116** D3
Dimo *Sudan* **81** F2
Dimona *Israel* **74** D4
Dimovo *Bulgaria* **44** C6
Dinagat *Phil.* **61** F6
Dinajpur *Bangla.* **67** G16
Dinan *France* **18** D4
Dīnān Āb *Iran* **71** C8
Dinant *Belgium* **17** D4
Dinapur *India* **69** G11
Dinar *Turkey* **47** C12
Dīnār, Kūh-e *Iran* **71** D6
Dinara Planina *Croatia* **41** D13
Dinard *France* **18** D4
Dinaric Alps = Dinara
    Planina *Croatia* **41** D13
Dindanko *Mali* **82** C3
Dinder, Nahr ed → *Sudan* **81** E3
Dinder △ *Sudan* **81** E4
Dindigul *India* **66** P11
Dindori *India* **69** H9
Ding Xian = Dingzhou *China* **56** E8
Dinga *Pakistan* **68** G2
Dingalan *Phil.* **61** D4
Ding'an *China* **64** C8
Dingbian *China* **56** F4
Dingelstädt *Germany* **24** D6
Dingle *Ireland* **12** D1
Dingle *Sweden* **11** F5
Dingle B. *Ireland* **12** D1
Dingmans Ferry *U.S.A.* **115** E10
Dingnan *China* **59** E10
Dingo *Australia* **94** C4
Dingolfing *Germany* **25** G8
Dingtao *China* **56** G8
Dingxi *China* **56** G3
Dingxiang *China* **56** E7
Dingyuan *China* **59** A11
Dingzhou *China* **56** E8
Dinh, Mui *Vietnam* **65** G7
Dinh Lap *Vietnam* **58** G6
Dinin → *Ireland* **12** D4
Dinira △ *Venezuela* **121** E6
Dinokwe *Botswana* **88** C4
Dinorwic *Canada* **103** D10
Dinosaur △ *Canada* **102** C6
Dinosaur △ *U.S.A.* **108** F9
Dinuba *U.S.A.* **110** J7
Diö *Sweden* **11** H8
Dioïla *Mali* **82** C3
Dioka *Mali* **82** C2
Diongoï *Mali* **82** C3
Dionisiades *Greece* **49** D8
Diósgyör *Hungary* **28** B5
Diosig *Romania* **28** C7
Diougani *Mali* **82** C3
Diouloulou *Senegal* **82** C1
Dioura *Mali* **82** C3
Diourbel *Senegal* **82** C1
Diourbel □ *Senegal* **82** C1
Dipalpur *Pakistan* **68** D5
Diplo *Pakistan* **68** G3
Dipolog *Phil.* **61** G5
Dipperu △ *Australia* **94** C4
Dir *Pakistan* **66** B7
Diré *Mali* **82** B4
Dire Dawa *Ethiopia* **81** F5
Dirfis Oros *Greece* **46** C5
Diriamba *Nic.* **120** D2
Dirk Hartog I. *Australia* **93** E1
Dirranbandi *Australia* **95** D4
Disa *India* **68** G5
Disa *Sudan* **81** E4
Disappointment, C. *U.S.A.* **108** C1
Disappointment, L. *Australia* **92** D3
Disaster B. *Australia* **95** F4
Discovery B. *Australia* **95** F3
Disentis Muster *Switz.* **25** J4
Dishna *Egypt* **80** B3

Disina *Nigeria* **83** C6
Disko = Qeqertarsuaq
    Greenland **98** C14
Disna = Dzisna → *Belarus* **32** E5
Disney Reef *Tonga* **91** c
Diss *U.K.* **15** E9
Disteghil Sar *Pakistan* **69** A6
District of Columbia □
    U.S.A. **113** F15
Distrito Federal □ *Brazil* **125** G9
Distrito Federal □ *Mexico* **119** D5
Disûq *Egypt* **80** H7
Diu *India* **68** J4
Dīvāndarreh *Iran* **73** E12
Dives → *France* **18** C6
Dives-sur-Mer *France* **18** C6
Divichi = Däväçi *Azerbaijan* **35** K9
Divide *U.S.A.* **108** D7
Dividing Ra. *Australia* **93** E2
Divinópolis *Brazil* **125** H10
Divjake *Albania* **44** F3
Divnoye *Russia* **35** H6
Divo *Ivory C.* **82** D3
Divriği *Turkey* **73** D9
Diwal Kol *Afghan.* **68** B2
Dixie Mt. *U.S.A.* **110** F6
Dixon *Calif., U.S.A.* **110** G5
Dixon *Ill., U.S.A.* **112** E10
Dixon Entrance *U.S.A.* **100** D6
Dixville *Canada* **115** A13
Diyadin *Turkey* **73** C10
Diyālā □ *Iraq* **70** C5
Diyālā → *Iraq* **73** F11
Diyarbakır *Turkey* **73** D9
Diyarbakır □ *Turkey* **73** D9
Diyodar *India* **68** G4
Djakarta = Jakarta
    Indonesia **63** G12
Djamba *Angola* **88** B1
Djambala *Congo* **84** E2
Djanet *Algeria* **78** D7
Djawa = Jawa *Indonesia* **62** F3
Djelfa *Algeria* **78** B6
Djema *C.A.R.* **86** A2
Djenné *Mali* **82** C4
Djerba, Î. de *Tunisia* **79** B8
Djerid, Chott *Tunisia* **78** B7
Djibo *Burkina Faso* **83** C4
Djibouti *Djibouti* **81** E5
Djibouti ■ *Africa* **81** E5
Djolu *Dem. Rep. of the Congo* **84** D4
Djougou *Benin* **83** D5
Djoum *Cameroon* **84** D2
Djourab, Erg du *Chad* **79** E9
Djugu *Dem. Rep. of the Congo* **86** B3
Djukbinj △ *Australia* **92** B5
Djúpivogur *Iceland* **8** D6
Djurås *Sweden* **10** D9
Djurö △ *Sweden* **11** F7
Djursland *Denmark* **11** H4
Dmitriya Lapteva, Proliv
    Russia **53** B15
Dmitriyev Lgovskiy *Russia* **33** F8
Dmitrov *Russia* **32** D9
Dmitrovsk-Orlovskiy *Russia* **33** F8
Dnepr = Dnipro → *Ukraine* **33** J7
Dneprodzerzhinsk =
    Dniprodzerzhynsk
    Ukraine **33** H8
Dneprodzerzhinskoye
    Vdkhr. =
    Dniprodzerzhynske
    Vdskh. *Ukraine* **33** H8
Dnepropetrovsk =
    Dnipropetrovsk *Ukraine* **33** H8
Dneprorudnoye =
    Dniprorudne *Ukraine* **33** J8
Dnestr = Dnister → *Europe* **23** E16
Dniester = Dnister →
    Europe **23** E16
Dnipro → *Ukraine* **33** J7
Dniprodzerzhynsk *Ukraine* **33** H8
Dniprodzerzhynske Vdskh.
    Ukraine **33** H8
Dnipropetrovsk *Ukraine* **33** H8
Dnipropetrovsk □ *Ukraine* **33** H8
Dniprorudne *Ukraine* **33** J8
Dnister → *Europe* **23** E16
Dnistrovskyy Lyman
    Ukraine **33** J6
Dno *Russia* **32** D5
Dnyapro = Dnipro →
    Ukraine **33** J7
Doaktown *Canada* **105** C6
Doan Hung *Vietnam* **58** G5
Doany *Madag.* **89** A8
Doba *Chad* **79** G9
Dobandi *Pakistan* **68** D2
Dobbiaco *Italy* **41** B9
Dobbyn *Australia* **94** B3
Dobczyce *Poland* **31** J7
Dobele *Latvia* **30** B10
Dobele □ *Latvia* **30** B10
Döbeln *Germany* **24** D9
Doberai, Jazirah *Indonesia* **63** E8

Dobiegniew *Poland* **31** F2
Doblas *Argentina* **126** D3
Dobo *Indonesia* **63** F8
Doboj *Bos.-H.* **28** F3
Dobra *Wielkopolskie, Poland* **31** G5
Dobra *Zachodnio-Pomorskie,
    Poland* **30** E2
Dobra *Dâmbovita, Romania* **29** F10
Dobra *Hunedoara, Romania* **28** E7
Dobre Miasto *Poland* **30** E7
Dobreşti *Romania* **28** D7
Dobrich *Bulgaria* **45** C11
Dobrinishta *Bulgaria* **44** E7
Dobruja *Europe* **29** F13
Dobromyl *Ukraine* **31** J9
Dobron *Ukraine* **28** B7
Dobropole *Ukraine* **33** H9
Dobrovolsk *Russia* **30** D9
Dobruja *Europe* **29** F13
Dobrush *Belarus* **33** F6
Dobrzany *Poland* **30** E2
Dobrzyń nad Wisłą *Poland* **31** F6
Doc, Mui *Vietnam* **64** D6
Docker River =
    Kaltukatjara *Australia* **93** D4
Docksta *Sweden* **10** A12
Doctor Arroyo *Mexico* **118** C4
Doda *India* **69** C6
Doda, L. *Canada* **104** C4
Dodecanese *Greece* **47** E8
Dodekanisa = Dodecanese
    Greece **47** E8
Dodekanisa □ *Greece* **47** E8
Dodge City *U.S.A.* **112** G3
Dodge L. *Canada* **103** B7
Dodgeville *U.S.A.* **112** D8
Dodo *Cameroon* **83** D7
Dodo *Sudan* **81** F2
Dodola *Ethiopia* **81** F4
Dodoma *Tanzania* **86** D4
Dodoma □ *Tanzania* **86** D4
Dodoni *Greece* **46** B2
Dodori △ *Kenya* **86** C5
Dodsland *Canada* **103** C7
Dodson *U.S.A.* **108** B9
Dodurga *Turkey* **47** B11
Doesburg *Neths.* **17** B6
Doetinchem *Neths.* **17** C6
Dog Creek *Canada* **102** C4
Dog L. *Man., Canada* **103** C9
Dog L. *Ont., Canada* **104** C2
Doğanşehir *Turkey* **72** C7
Dogliani *Italy* **40** D4
Dogo *Japan* **55** F6
Dogondoutchi *Niger* **83** C5
Dogran *Pakistan* **68** D5
Doğubayazıt *Turkey* **73** C11
Doguéraoua *Niger* **83** C6
Doha = Ad Dawḩah *Qatar* **71** E6
Dohazari *Bangla.* **67** H18
Dohrighat *India* **69** F10
Doi *Indonesia* **63** D7
Doi Inthanon △ *Thailand* **64** C2
Doi Khuntan △ *Thailand* **64** C2
Doi Luang *Thailand* **64** C3
Doi Luang △ *Thailand* **64** C2
Doi Saket *Thailand* **64** C2
Doi Suthep △ *Thailand* **64** C2
Dois Irmãos, Sa. *Brazil* **125** E10
Dojransko Jezero *Macedonia* **44** E6
Dokkum *Neths.* **17** A5
Dokos *Greece* **46** D5
Dokri *Pakistan* **68** F3
Dokuchayevsk *Ukraine* **33** J9
Dol-de-Bretagne *France* **18** D5
Dolac *Serbia* **44** D4
Dolak, Pulau *Indonesia* **63** F9
Dolbeau-Mistassini *Canada* **105** C5
Dole *France* **19** E12
Doleib, Wadi → *Sudan* **81** E3
Dolenji Logatec *Slovenia* **41** C11
Dolgellau *U.K.* **14** E4
Dolgelley = Dolgellau *U.K.* **14** E4
Dolhasca *Romania* **29** C11
Doliana *Greece* **46** B2
Dolianova *Italy* **42** C2
Dolinskaya = Dolynska
    Ukraine **33** H7
Dolj □ *Romania* **29** F8
Dollard *Neths.* **17** A7
Dolna Banya *Bulgaria* **44** D7
Dolni Chiflik *Bulgaria* **45** D11
Dolni Dŭbnik *Bulgaria* **45** C8
Dolnośląskie □ *Poland* **31** G3
Dolný Kubín *Slovak Rep.* **27** B12
Dolo *Ethiopia* **81** G5
Dolo *Italy* **41** C9
Dolomites = Dolomiti *Italy* **41** B8
Dolomiti *Italy* **41** B8
Dolomiti Bellunesi △ *Italy* **41** B9
Dolores *Argentina* **126** D4
Dolores *Uruguay* **126** C4
Dolores *U.S.A.* **109** H9
Dolores → *U.S.A.* **108** G9
Dolovo *Serbia* **28** F5
Dolphin, C. *Falk. Is.* **128** G5
Dolphin and Union Str.
    Canada **100** C8

Dolsk *Poland* **31** G4
Dolyna *Ukraine* **23** B9
Dolynska *Ukraine* **33** H7
Dolynske *Ukraine* **29** C14
Dolzhanskaya *Russia* **33** J9
Dom Pedrito *Brazil* **127** C5
Doma *Nigeria* **83** D6
Doma *Zimbabwe* **87** F3
Domaniç *Turkey* **47** B11
Domariaganj → *India* **69** F10
Domasi *Malawi* **87** F4
Domažlice *Czech Rep.* **26** B5
Dombarovskiy *Russia* **52** D6
Dombås *Norway* **8** E13
Dombasle-sur-Meurthe
    France **19** D13
Dombes *France* **21** C9
Dombóvár *Hungary* **28** D3
Dombrád *Hungary* **28** B6
Dome Argus *Antarctica* **5** E12
Dome C. *Antarctica* **5** D17
Dome Fuji *Antarctica* **5** D5
Domel I. = Letsôk-aw
    Kyun *Burma* **65** G2
Domérat *France* **19** F9
Domeyko *Chile* **126** B1
Domeyko, Cordillera *Chile* **126** A2
Domfront *France* **18** D6
Dominador *Chile* **126** A2
Dominica ■ *W. Indies* **121** C7
Dominica Passage *W. Indies* **121** C7
Dominican Rep. ■
    W. Indies **121** C5
Dömitz *Germany* **24** B7
Domme *France* **20** D5
Domneşti *Romania* **29** E9
Domodóssola *Italy* **40** B5
Domogled-Valea Cernei △
    Romania **28** F7
Domokos *Greece* **46** B4
Dompaire *France* **19** D13
Dompierre-sur-Besbre
    France **19** F10
Dompim *Ghana* **82** D4
Domrémy-la-Pucelle *France*
    19 D12
Domvena *Greece* **46** C4
Domville, Mt. *Australia* **95** D5
Domžale *Slovenia* **41** B11
Don → *Russia* **33** J10
Don → *Aberds., U.K.* **13** D6
Don → *S. Yorks., U.K.* **14** D7
Don, C. *Australia* **92** B5
Don Benito *Spain* **37** G5
Don Figuerero Mts. *Jamaica* **120** a
Don Sak *Thailand* **65** b
Dona Ana = Nhamaabué
    Mozam. **87** F4
Doña Mencía *Spain* **37** H6
Donaghadee *U.K.* **12** B6
Donaghmore *Ireland* **12** D4
Donald *Australia* **95** F3
Donaldsonville *U.S.A.* **116** F9
Donalsonville *U.S.A.* **117** F12
Doñana △ *Spain* **37** J4
Donau = Dunărea →
    Europe **29** E14
Donau → *Austria* **27** C10
Donau Auen △ *Austria* **27** C9
Donaueschingen *Germany* **25** H4
Donauwörth *Germany* **25** G6
Doncaster *U.K.* **14** D6
Dondo *Angola* **84** F2
Dondo *Mozam.* **87** F3
Dondo, Teluk *Indonesia* **63** D6
Dondra Head *Sri Lanka* **66** S12
Donduşeni *Moldova* **29** B11
Donegal *Ireland* **12** B3
Donegal □ *Ireland* **12** B4
Donegal B. *Ireland* **12** B3
Donets → *Russia* **35** G5
Donets Basin *Ukraine* **6** F13
Donetsk *Ukraine* **33** J9
Donetsk □ *Ukraine* **33** J9
Dong Ba Thin *Vietnam* **65** F7
Dong Dang *Vietnam* **58** G6
Dong Giam *Vietnam* **64** C5
Dong Ha *Vietnam* **64** D6
Dong Hene *Laos* **64** D5
Dong Hoi *Vietnam* **64** D6
Dong Jiang → *China* **59** F10
Dong Khe *Vietnam* **64** A6
Dong Ujimqin Qi *China* **56** B9
Dong Van *Vietnam* **58** F5
Dong Xoai *Vietnam* **65** G6
Donga *Nigeria* **83** D7
Donga → *China* **59** D7
Dongara *Australia* **93** E1
Dongbei *China* **57** D13
Dongchuan *China* **58** D4
Dongco *China* **67** C14
Donges *France* **18** E4
Dongfang *China* **64** C7
Dongfeng *China* **57** C13
Donggala *Indonesia* **63** E5
Donggan *China* **58** F5

Donggang *China* **57** E13
Dongguan *China* **59** B9
Dongguang *China* **56** F9
Donghae *S. Korea* **57** F15
Donghai Dao *China* **59** G8
Dongjingcheng *China* **57** B15
Dongkou *China* **59** D8
Donglan *China* **58** E6
Dongliu *China* **59** B11
Dongmen *China* **58** F6
Dongnae *S. Korea* **57** G15
Dongning *China* **57** B16
Dongnyi *China* **58** C3
Dongola *Sudan* **80** D3
Dongping *China* **56** G9
Dongsha Dao *China* **59** G11
Dongshan *China* **59** F11
Dongsheng *China* **56** E6
Dongtai *China* **57** H11
Dongting Hu *China* **59** C9
Dongtou *China* **59** D13
Dongxiang *China* **59** C11
Dongxing *China* **58** G7
Dongyang *China* **59** C13
Dongzhi *China* **59** B11
Donington, C. *Australia* **95** E2
Doniphan *U.S.A.* **113** G9
Donja Stubica *Croatia* **41** C12
Donji Dušnik *Serbia* **44** C6
Donji Miholjac *Croatia* **28** E3
Donji Milanovac *Serbia* **44** B6
Donji Vakuf *Bos.-H.* **28** F2
Dønna *Norway* **8** C15
Donna *U.S.A.* **116** H5
Donnacona *Canada* **105** C5
Donnelly's Crossing *N.Z.* **91** A4
Donnybrook *Australia* **93** F2
Donnybrook *S. Africa* **89** D4
Donora *U.S.A.* **114** F5
Donostia = Donostia-San
    Sebastián *Spain* **38** B3
Donostia-San Sebastián
    Spain **38** B3
Donousa *Greece* **47** D7
Donskoy *Russia* **32** F10
Donsol *Phil.* **61** E5
Donzère *France* **21** D8
Donzy *France* **19** E10
Doon → *U.K.* **13** F4
Doonbeg → *Ireland* **12** D2
Dør *Iran* **71** C6
Dora, L. *Australia* **92** D3
Dora Báltea → *Italy* **40** C5
Dora Ripária → *Italy* **40** C4
Doran L. *Canada* **103** A7
Dorchester *U.K.* **15** G5
Dorchester, C. *Canada* **101** C12
Dordabis *Namibia* **88** C2
Dordogne □ *France* **20** C4
Dordogne → *France* **20** C3
Dordrecht *Neths.* **17** C4
Dordrecht *S. Africa* **88** E4
Dore → *France* **20** C7
Dore, Mts. *France* **20** C6
Doré L. *Canada* **103** C7
Dorfen *Germany* **25** G8
Dorgali *Italy* **42** B2
Dori *Burkina Faso* **83** C4
Doring → *S. Africa* **88** E2
Doringbos *S. Africa* **88** E2
Dorking *U.K.* **15** F7
Dormaa-Ahenkro *Ghana* **82** D4
Dormans *France* **19** C10
Dormo, Ras *Eritrea* **81** E5
Dornbirn *Austria* **26** D2
Dornes *France* **19** F10
Dorneşti *Romania* **29** C11
Dornie *U.K.* **13** D3
Dornoch *U.K.* **13** D4
Dornoch Firth *U.K.* **13** D4
Dornogovĭ □ *Mongolia* **56** C6
Doro *Mali* **83** B4
Doro, Kavo *Greece* **46** C6
Dorog *Hungary* **28** C3
Dorogobuzh *Russia* **32** E7
Dorohoi *Romania* **29** C11
Döröö Nuur *Mongolia* **60** B4
Dorr *Iran* **71** C6
Dorre I. *Australia* **93** E1
Dorrigo *Australia* **95** E5
Dorris *U.S.A.* **108** F3
Dorset *Canada* **114** A6
Dorset *U.S.A.* **114** E4
Dorset □ *U.K.* **15** G5
Dorsten *Germany* **24** D2
Dortmund *Germany* **24** D3
Dortmund-Ems-Kanal →
    Germany **24** D3
Dörtyol *Turkey* **72** D7
Dorum *Germany* **24** B4
Doruma
    Dem. Rep. of the Congo **86** B2
Dorûneh *Iran* **71** C8
Dos Bahías, C. *Argentina* **128** E3
Dos Hermanas *Spain* **37** H5
Dos Palos *U.S.A.* **110** J6
Dosso *Niger* **83** C5
Dosso □ *Niger* **83** C5

Dosso → *Niger* **83** C5
Dothan *U.S.A.* **117** F12
Doty *U.S.A.* **110** D3
Douai *France* **19** B10
Douako *Guinea* **82** D2
Douala *Cameroon* **83** E6
Douarnenez *France* **18** D2
Doubabougou *Mali* **82** C3
Double Island Pt. *Australia* **95** D5
Double Mountain Fork →
    U.S.A. **116** E4
Doubrava → *Czech Rep.* **26** A8
Doubs □ *France* **19** E13
Doubs → *France* **19** F12
Doubtful Sd. *N.Z.* **91** F1
Doubtless B. *N.Z.* **91** A4
Doudeville *France* **18** C7
Doué-la-Fontaine *France* **18** E6
Douentza *Mali* **82** C4
Douentza △ *Mali* **82** B4
Douglas *I. of Man* **14** C3
Douglas *S. Africa* **88** D3
Douglas *Ariz., U.S.A.* **109** L9
Douglas *Ga., U.S.A.* **117** F13
Douglas *Wyo., U.S.A.* **108** E11
Douglas Apsley △ *Australia* **95** G4
Douglas Chan. *Canada* **102** C3
Douglas Pt. *Canada* **114** B3
Douglasville *U.S.A.* **117** E12
Doukaton, Akra *Greece* **46** C2
Doulevant-le-Château
    France **19** D11
Doullens *France* **19** B9
Doumen *China* **59** F9
Douna *Mali* **82** C3
Dounreay *U.K.* **13** C5
Dourada, Serra *Brazil* **125** F9
Dourados *Brazil* **127** A5
Dourados → *Brazil* **127** A5
Dourados, Serra dos *Brazil* **127** A5
Dourdan *France* **19** D9
Douro → *Europe* **36** D2
Douvaine *France* **19** F13
Douvres-la-Délivrande
    France **18** C6
Douze → *France* **20** E3
Dove → *U.K.* **14** E6
Dove Creek *U.S.A.* **109** H9
Dover *Australia* **95** G4
Dover *U.K.* **15** F9
Dover *Del., U.S.A.* **113** F16
Dover *N.H., U.S.A.* **115** C14
Dover *N.J., U.S.A.* **115** F10
Dover *Ohio, U.S.A.* **114** F3
Dover, Pt. *Australia* **93** F4
Dover, Str. of *Europe* **15** G9
Dover-Foxcroft *U.S.A.* **113** C19
Dover Plains *U.S.A.* **115** E11
Dovey = Dyfi → *U.K.* **15** E3
Dovhe *Ukraine* **29** B8
Dovrefjell *Norway* **8** E13
Dow Rūd *Iran* **71** C6
Dowa *Malawi* **87** E3
Dowagiac *U.S.A.* **112** E10
Dowerin *Australia* **93** F2
Dowgha'i *Iran* **71** B8
Dowlatābād *Iran* **71** D8
Down □ *U.K.* **12** B5
Downey *Calif., U.S.A.* **111** M8
Downey *Idaho, U.S.A.* **108** E7
Downham Market *U.K.* **15** E8
Downieville *U.S.A.* **110** F6
Downpatrick *U.K.* **12** B6
Downpatrick Hd. *Ireland* **12** B2
Downsville *U.S.A.* **115** D10
Downton, Mt. *Canada* **102** C4
Dowsārī *Iran* **71** D8
Doxato *Greece* **45** E8
Doyle *U.S.A.* **110** E6
Doylestown *U.S.A.* **115** F9
Dozois, Rés. *Canada* **104** C4
Dra Khel *Pakistan* **68** F2
Drâa, C. *Morocco* **78** C3
Drâa, Oued → *Morocco* **78** C3
Drac → *France* **21** C9
Dračevo *Macedonia* **44** E5
Drachten *Neths.* **17** A6
Drăgănești *Moldova* **29** C13
Drăgănești-Olt *Romania* **29** F9
Drăgănești-Vlașca *Romania* **29** F10
Dragaš *Serbia* **44** D4
Drăgășani *Romania* **29** F9
Dragichyn *Belarus* **23** B13
Dragocvet *Serbia* **44** B5
Dragon's Mouths = Boca
    de Drago *Venezuela* **125** K15
Dragovishtitsa *Bulgaria* **44** D6
Draguignan *France* **21** E10
Drahove *Ukraine* **29** B8
Drain *U.S.A.* **108** E2
Drake *U.S.A.* **112** B3
Drake Passage *S. Ocean* **5** B17
Drakensberg *S. Africa* **89** D4
Drama *Greece* **45** E8
Drama □ *Greece* **45** E8
Drammen *Norway* **9** G14
Drangajökull *Iceland* **8** C2

Dranov, Ostrov *Romania* **29** F14
Dras *India* **69** B6
Drastis, Akra *Greece* **49** A3
Drau = Drava → *Croatia* **28** E3
Drava → *Croatia* **28** E3
Dravograd *Slovenia* **41** B12
Drawa → *Poland* **31** F2
Drawieński △ *Poland* **31** E2
Drawno *Poland* **31** E2
Drawsko Pomorskie *Poland* **30** E2
Drayton Valley *Canada* **102** C6
Dreieich *Germany* **25** E4
Dren *Serbia* **44** C4
Drenthe □ *Neths.* **17** B6
Drepano, Akra *Greece* **49** D6
Drepanum, C. *Cyprus* **49** E11
Dresden *Canada* **114** D2
Dresden *Germany* **24** D9
Dreux *France* **18** D8
Drezdenko *Poland* **31** F2
Driffield *U.K.* **14** C7
Driftwood *U.S.A.* **114** E6
Driggs *U.S.A.* **108** E8
Drin ~ *Albania* **44** D3
Drin i Zi → *Albania* **44** E4
Drina → *Bos.-H.* **44** B3
Drincea → *Romania* **28** F7
Drinjača → *Bos.-H.* **28** F4
Driopida *Greece* **46** D6
Drissa =
    Vyerkhnyadzvinsk
    Belarus **32** E4
Drniš *Croatia* **41** E13
Drøbak *Norway* **9** G14
Drobeta-Turnu Severin
    Romania **28** F7
Drobin *Poland* **31** F6
Drochia *Moldova* **29** B12
Drogichin = Dragichyn
    Belarus **23** B13
Drogheda *Ireland* **12** C5
Drogobych = Drohobych
    Ukraine **31** J10
Drohiczyn *Poland* **31** F9
Drohobych *Ukraine* **31** J10
Droichead Atha =
    Drogheda *Ireland* **12** C5
Droichead Nua *Ireland* **12** C5
Droitwich *U.K.* **15** E5
Drôme □ *France* **21** D9
Drôme → *France* **21** D8
Dromedary, C. *Australia* **95** F5
Drömling △ *Germany* **24** C7
Dromore *U.K.* **12** B4
Dromore West *Ireland* **12** B3
Dronero *Italy* **40** D4
Dronfield *U.K.* **14** D6
Dronne → *France* **20** C3
Dronning Maud Land
    Antarctica **5** D3
Dronninglund *Denmark* **11** G4
Dronten *Neths.* **17** B5
Dropt → *France* **20** D3
Drosendorf *Austria* **26** C8
Droué *France* **18** D8
Druk Yul = Bhutan ■ *Asia* **67** F17
Drumbo *Canada* **114** C4
Drumcliff *Ireland* **12** B3
Drumheller *Canada* **102** C6
Drummond *U.S.A.* **108** C7
Drummond I. *U.S.A.* **113** B12
Drummond Pt. *Australia* **95** E2
Drummond Ra. *Australia* **94** C4
Drummondville *Canada* **104** C5
Drumright *U.S.A.* **116** D6
Druskininkai *Lithuania* **32** E2
Drut → *Belarus* **23** B16
Druya *Belarus* **32** E4
Druzhba *Bulgaria* **45** C12
Druzhina *Russia* **53** C15
Drvar *Bos.-H.* **41** D13
Drvenik *Croatia* **41** E13
Drwęca → *Poland* **31** E5
Dry Harbour Mts. *Jamaica* **120** a
Dry Tortugas *U.S.A.* **117** F13
Dryanovo *Bulgaria* **45** D9
Dryden *Canada* **103** D10
Dryden *U.S.A.* **116** F3
Drygalski I. *Antarctica* **5** C7
Drygalski Ice Tongue
    Antarctica **5** D21
Drysdale → *Australia* **92** B4
Drysdale I. *Australia* **94** A2
Drysdale River △ *Australia* **92** B4
Drzewica *Poland* **31** G7
Drzewiczka → *Poland* **31** G7
Dschang *Cameroon* **83** D7
Du Gué → *Canada* **104** A5
Du He *China* **59** A8
Du Quoin *U.S.A.* **112** F9
Du'an *China* **58** F7
Duanesburg *U.S.A.* **115** D10
Duaringa *Australia* **94** C4
Duarte, Pico *Dom. Rep.* **121** D5
Ḍubā *Si. Arabia* **70** E2
Dubai = Dubayy *U.A.E.* **71** E7
Dubăsari *Moldova* **29** C14

Dubăsari Vdkhr. *Moldova* **29** C13
Dubawnt → *Canada* **103** A8
Dubawnt L. *Canada* **103** A8
Dubayy *U.A.E.* **71** E7
Dubbo *Australia* **95** E4
Dübendorf *Switz.* **25** H4
Dubica *Croatia* **41** C13
Dublin *Ireland* **12** C5
Dublin *Ga., U.S.A.* **117** E13
Dublin *Tex., U.S.A.* **116** E5
Dublin □ *Ireland* **12** C5
Dublin ✈ (DUB) *Ireland* **12** C5
Dubna *Russia* **32** D9
Dubnica nad Váhom
    Slovak Rep. **27** C11
Dubno *Ukraine* **23** C13
Dubois *Idaho, U.S.A.* **108** D7
Dubois *Pa., U.S.A.* **114** E6
Dubossary = Dubăsari
    Moldova **29** C14
Dubossary Vdkhr. =
    Dubăsari Vdkhr. *Moldova* **29** C13
Dubove *Ukraine* **29** B8
Dubovka *Russia* **35** F7
Dubovskoye *Russia* **35** G6
Dubrajpur *India* **69** H12
Dubréka *Guinea* **82** D2
Dubrovitsa = Dubrovytsya
    Ukraine **23** C14
Dubrovnik *Croatia* **44** D2
Dubrovytsya *Ukraine* **23** C14
Dubuque *U.S.A.* **112** D8
Duchang *China* **59** C11
Duchesne *U.S.A.* **108** F8
Duchess *Australia* **94** C2
Ducie I. *Pac. Oc.* **97** K15
Duck → *U.S.A.* **117** C11
Duck Cr. → *Australia* **92** D2
Duck Lake *Canada* **103** C7
Duck Mountain △ *Canada* **103** C8
Duckwall, Mt. *U.S.A.* **110** H6
Duderstadt *Germany* **24** D6
Dudhi *India* **69** G10
Dudinka *Russia* **53** C9
Dudley *U.K.* **15** E5
Dudwa *India* **69** E9
Dudwa △ *India* **69** E9
Duékoué *Ivory C.* **82** D3
Dueñas *Spain* **36** D6
Duero = Douro → *Europe* **36** D2
Dufftown *U.K.* **13** D5
Dufourspitz *Switz.* **25** K3
Dugi Otok *Croatia* **41** D11
Dugo Selo *Croatia* **41** C13
Duisburg *Germany* **24** D2
Duiwelskloof =
    Modjadjiskloof *S. Africa* **89** C5
Dujiangyan *China* **58** B4
Duk Fadiat *Sudan* **81** F3
Duk Faiwil *Sudan* **81** F3
Dukat *Albania* **44** F3
Ḍūkdamīn *Iran* **71** C8
Dukelský Průsmyk
    Slovak Rep. **27** B14
Dukhān *Qatar* **71** E6
Dukhovshchina *Russia* **32** E7
Duki *Pakistan* **66** D6
Dukla *Poland* **31** J8
Duku *Bauchi, Nigeria* **83** C7
Duku *Sokoto, Nigeria* **83** C5
Dulag *Phil.* **61** F6
Dulce *U.S.A.* **109** H10
Dulce → *Argentina* **126** C3
Dulce, G. *Costa Rica* **120** E3
Dulf *Iraq* **70** C5
Dŭlgopol *Bulgaria* **45** C11
Duliu *China* **56** E9
Dullewala *Pakistan* **68** D4
Dullstroom *S. Africa* **89** D5
Dülmen *Germany* **24** D3
Dulovo *Bulgaria* **45** C11
Duluth *U.S.A.* **112** B7
Dum Dum *India* **69** H13
Dum Duma *India* **67** F19
Dūmā *Syria* **74** B5
Dumaguete *Phil.* **61** G5
Dumai *Indonesia* **62** D2
Dumaran *Phil.* **61** F3
Dumas *Ark., U.S.A.* **116** E9
Dumas *Tex., U.S.A.* **116** D4
Ḍumayr *Syria* **74** B5
Dumbarton *U.K.* **13** F4
Ďumbier *Slovak Rep.* **27** C12
Dumbleyung *Australia* **93** F2
Dumboa *Nigeria* **83** C7
Dumbrăveni *Romania* **29** D9
Dumfries *U.K.* **13** F5
Dumfries & Galloway □
    U.K. **13** F5
Dumitreşti *Romania* **29** E11
Dumka *India* **69** G12
Dumlupınar *Turkey* **47** C12
Dümmer *Germany* **24** C4
Dümmer △ *Germany* **24** C4

Dumoine → *Canada* **104** C4
Dumoine, L. *Canada* **104** C4
Dumont d'Urville *Antarctica* **5** C10
Dumraon *India* **69** G11
Dumyât *Egypt* **80** H7
Dumyât, Masabb *Egypt* **80** H7
Dún Dealgan = Dundalk
    Ireland **12** B5
Dún Laoghaire *Ireland* **12** C5
Duna = Dunărea → *Europe* **29** E14
Duna-Drava △ *Hungary* **28** D3
Duna-völgyi-főcsatorna
    Hungary **28** D4
Dunaföldvár *Hungary* **28** D3
Dunagiri *India* **69** D8
Dunaj = Dunărea →
    Europe **29** E14
Dunajec → *Poland* **31** H7
Dunajská Streda *Slovak Rep.* **27** C10
Dunakeszi *Hungary* **28** C4
Dunapataj *Hungary* **28** D4
Dunărea → *Europe* **29** E14
Dunaszekcső *Hungary* **28** D3
Dunaújváros *Hungary* **28** D3
Dunav = Dunărea →
    Europe **29** E14
Dunavaţu de Jos *Romania* **29** F14
Dunavtsi *Bulgaria* **44** C6
Dunay *Russia* **54** C6
Dunayivtsi *Ukraine* **29** B11
Dunback *N.Z.* **91** F3
Dunbar *U.K.* **13** E6
Dunblane *U.K.* **13** E5
Duncan *Canada* **110** B3
Duncan *Ariz., U.S.A.* **109** K9
Duncan *Okla., U.S.A.* **116** D6
Duncan, L. *Canada* **104** B4
Duncan L. *Canada* **102** A6
Duncan Town *Bahamas* **120** B4
Duncannon *U.S.A.* **114** F7
Duncansby Head *U.K.* **13** C5
Duncansville *U.S.A.* **114** F6
Dundaga *Latvia* **30** A9
Dundalk *Canada* **114** B4
Dundalk *Ireland* **12** B5
Dundalk *U.S.A.* **113** F15
Dundalk Bay *Ireland* **12** C5
Dundas = Uummannaq
    Greenland **4** B4
Dundas *Canada* **114** C5
Dundas, L. *Australia* **93** F3
Dundas I. *Canada* **102** C2
Dundas Str. *Australia* **92** B5
Dundee *S. Africa* **89** D5
Dundee *U.K.* **13** E6
Dundee *U.S.A.* **114** D7
Dundee City □ *U.K.* **13** E6
Dundgovĭ □ *Mongolia* **56** B4
Dundrum *U.K.* **12** B6
Dundrum B. *U.K.* **12** B6
Dunedin *N.Z.* **91** F3
Dunedin *U.S.A.* **117** G13
Dunfanaghy *Ireland* **12** A4
Dunfermline *U.K.* **13** E5
Dungannon *Canada* **114** C3
Dungannon *U.K.* **12** B5
Dungarpur *India* **68** H5
Dungarvan *Ireland* **12** D4
Dungarvan Harbour *Ireland* **12** D4
Dungeness *U.K.* **15** G8
Dunglow *Ireland* **12** B3
Dungo, L. do *Angola* **88** B2
Dungog *Australia* **95** E5
Dungu *Dem. Rep. of the Congo* **86** B2
Dungun *Malaysia* **65** K4
Dungunâb *Sudan* **80** C4
Dungunâb, Khalig *Sudan* **80** C4
Dunhua *China* **57** C15
Dunhuang *China* **60** B4
Dunk I. *Australia* **94** B4
Dunkassa *Benin* **83** C5
Dunkeld *Australia* **95** F3
Dunkeld *U.K.* **13** E5
Dunkerque *France* **19** A9
Dunkery Beacon *U.K.* **15** F4
Dunkirk = Dunkerque
    France **19** A9
Dunkirk *U.S.A.* **114** D5
Dunkuj *Sudan* **81** E3
Dunkwa *Central, Ghana* **82** D4
Dunkwa *Central, Ghana* **83** D4
Dúnleary = Dún
    Laoghaire *Ireland* **12** C5
Dunleer *Ireland* **12** C5
Dunmanus B. *Ireland* **12** E2
Dunmanway *Ireland* **12** E2
Dunmarra *Australia* **94** B1
Dunmore *U.S.A.* **115** E9
Dunmore East *Ireland* **12** D5
Dunmore Hd. *Ireland* **12** D1
Dunmore Town *Bahamas* **120** A4
Dunn *U.S.A.* **117** D15
Dunnellon *U.S.A.* **117** G13
Dunnet Hd. *U.K.* **13** C5

Dunning *U.S.A.* **112** E3
Dunnville *Canada* **114** D5
Dunolly *Australia* **95** F3
Dunoon *U.K.* **13** F4
Dunqul *Egypt* **80** C3
Duns *U.K.* **13** F6
Dunseith *U.S.A.* **112** A3
Dunshaughlin *Ireland* **12** C5
Dunsmuir *U.S.A.* **108** F2
Dunstable *U.K.* **15** F7
Dunstan Mts. *N.Z.* **91** F2
Dunster *Canada* **102** C5
Dunvegan *U.K.* **13** D2
Dunvegan L. *Canada* **103** A7
Duolun *China* **56** C9
Duong Dong *Vietnam* **65** G4
Dupree *U.S.A.* **112** C3
Dupuyer *U.S.A.* **108** B7
Duque de Caxias *Brazil* **127** A7
Durack → *Australia* **92** C4
Durack Ra. *Australia* **92** C4
Durağan *Turkey* **72** B6
Durak *Turkey* **47** B10
Ðurðevac *Serbia* **44** B4
Durance → *France* **21** E8
Durand *U.S.A.* **112** C8
Durango *Mexico* **118** C4
Durango *U.S.A.* **109** H10
Durango □ *Mexico* **118** C4
Durankulak *Bulgaria* **45** C12
Durant *Miss., U.S.A.* **117** E10
Durant *Okla., U.S.A.* **116** E6
Duratón → *Spain* **36** D6
Durazno *Uruguay* **126** C4
Durazzo = Durrës *Albania* **44** E3
Durban *France* **20** F6
Durban *S. Africa* **89** D5
Durbuy *Belgium* **17** D5
Ðurðevac *Croatia* **28** D2
Düren *Germany* **24** E2
Durg = Bhilainagar-Durg
    India **67** J12
Durgapur *India* **69** H12
Durham *Canada* **114** B4
Durham *U.K.* **14** C6
Durham *Calif., U.S.A.* **110** F5
Durham *N.C., U.S.A.* **117** D15
Durham *N.H., U.S.A.* **115** C14
Durham □ *U.K.* **14** C6
Durleşti *Moldova* **29** C13
Ḏurmā *Si. Arabia* **70** E5
Durmitor *Montenegro* **44** C2
Durmitor △ *Serbia* **44** C2
Durness *U.K.* **13** C4
Durrës *Albania* **44** E3
Durrow *Ireland* **12** D4
Dursey I. *Ireland* **12** E1
Dursley *U.K.* **15** F5
Dursunbey *Turkey* **47** B10
Durtal *France* **18** E6
Duru *Dem. Rep. of the Congo* **86** B2
Duru Gölü *Turkey* **45** E12
Durusu *Turkey* **45** E12
Durūz, Jabal ad *Jordan* **74** C5
D'Urville, Tanjung *Indonesia* **63** E9
D'Urville I. *N.Z.* **91** D4
Duryea *U.S.A.* **115** E9
Dûsh *Egypt* **80** C3
Dushak *Turkmenistan* **71** B9
Dushan *China* **58** E6
Dushanbe *Tajikistan* **52** F7
Dusheti *Georgia* **35** J7
Dushore *U.S.A.* **115** E8
Dusky Sd. *N.Z.* **91** F1
Dussejour, C. *Australia* **92** B4
Düsseldorf *Germany* **24** D2
Düsseldorf Rhein-Ruhr ✈
    (DUS) *Germany* **24** D2
Duszniki-Zdrój *Poland* **31** H3
Dutch Harbor *U.S.A.* **106** a
Dutlwe *Botswana* **88** C3
Dutsan Wai *Nigeria* **83** C6
Dutton *Canada* **114** D3
Dutton → *Australia* **94** C3
Dutywa *S. Africa* **89** E4
Duved *Sweden* **10** A6
Düvertepe *Turkey* **47** B10
Duwadami, Khawr *U.A.E.* **71** E6
Duyfken Pt. *Australia* **94** A3
Duyun *China* **58** D6
Düzağaç *Turkey* **47** C12
Düzce *Turkey* **72** B4
Düzce □ *Turkey* **72** B4
Dve Mogili *Bulgaria* **45** C9
Dvina, Severnaya → *Russia* **6** C13
Dvinsk = Daugavpils *Latvia* **32** E4
Dvor *Croatia* **41** C13
Dvůr Králové nad Labem
    Czech Rep. **26** A8
Dwarka *India* **68** H3
Dwellingup *Australia* **93** F2
Dwight *Canada* **114** A5
Dwight *U.S.A.* **112** E9
Dyakove *Ukraine* **29** B11
Dyatkovo *Russia* **32** F8
Dyatlovo = Dzyatlava
    Belarus **23** B13

Dyce *U.K.* **13** D6
Dyer, C. *Canada* **101** C13
Dyer Bay *Canada* **114** A3
Dyer Plateau *Antarctica* **5** D17
Dyersburg *U.S.A.* **117** C10
Dyersville *U.S.A.* **112** D8
Dyfi → *U.K.* **15** E3
Dyje → *Czech Rep.* **27** C9
Dymer *Ukraine* **23** C16
Dynów *Poland* **31** J9
Dysart *Australia* **94** C4
Dyviziya *Ukraine* **29** E14
Dzaoudzi *Mayotte* **85** a
Dzerzhinsk *Russia* **34** B6
Dzhalinda *Russia* **53** D13
Dzhambul = Taraz
    Kazakhstan **52** E8
Dzhankoy *Ukraine* **33** K8
Dzhanybek = Zhänibek
    Kazakhstan **34** F8
Dzharylhach, Ostriv *Ukraine* **33** J7
Dzhezkazgan =
    Zhezqazghan *Kazakhstan* **52** E7
Dzhizak = Jizzakh *Uzbekistan* **52** E7
Dzhugdzur, Khrebet *Russia* **53** D14
Dzhulynk *Ukraine* **29** B14
Dzhuryn *Ukraine* **29** B13
Dzhvari = Jvari *Georgia* **35** J6
Działdowo *Poland* **31** E7
Działoszyce *Poland* **31** H7
Działoszyn *Poland* **31** G5
Dzibilchaltún *Mexico* **119** C7
Dzierzgoń *Poland* **30** E6
Dzierżoniów *Poland* **31** H3
Dzilam de Bravo *Mexico* **119** C7
Dzisna *Belarus* **32** E5
Dzisna → *Belarus* **32** E5
Dziwnów *Poland* **30** D1
Dzūkija △ *Lithuania* **9** J21
Dzungaria = Junggar
    Pendi *China* **60** B3
Dzungarian Basin =
    Junggar Pendi *China* **60** B3
Dzüünmod *Mongolia* **60** B5
Dzyarzhynsk *Belarus* **23** B14
Dzyatlava *Belarus* **23** B13

E

E.C. Manning △ *Canada* **102** D4
Eabamet L. *Canada* **104** B2
Eads *U.S.A.* **108** G12
Eagar *U.S.A.* **109** J9
Eagle *Alaska, U.S.A.* **100** C5
Eagle *Colo., U.S.A.* **108** G10
Eagle → *Canada* **105** B8
Eagle Butte *U.S.A.* **112** C3
Eagle Grove *U.S.A.* **112** D7
Eagle L. *Canada* **103** D10
Eagle L. *Calif., U.S.A.* **108** F3
Eagle L. *Maine, U.S.A.* **113** B19
Eagle Lake *Canada* **114** A6
Eagle Lake *Maine, U.S.A.* **113** B19
Eagle Lake *Tex., U.S.A.* **116** E6
Eagle Mountain *U.S.A.* **111** M11
Eagle Nest *U.S.A.* **109** H11
Eagle Pass *U.S.A.* **116** G4
Eagle Pk. *U.S.A.* **110** G7
Eagle Pt. *Australia* **92** C3
Eagle River *Mich., U.S.A.* **112** B9
Eagle River *Wis., U.S.A.* **112** C9
Eaglehawk *Australia* **95** F3
Eagles Mere *U.S.A.* **115** E8
Ealing □ *U.K.* **15** F7
Ear Falls *Canada* **103** C10
Earle *U.S.A.* **117** D9
Earlimart *U.S.A.* **111** K7
Earn → *U.K.* **13** E5
Earn, L. *U.K.* **13** E4
Earnslaw, Mt. *N.Z.* **91** F2
Earth *U.S.A.* **116** D3
Easley *U.S.A.* **117** D13
East Anglia *U.K.* **15** E10
East Angus *Canada* **105** C5
East Antarctica *Antarctica* **5** D7
East Aurora *U.S.A.* **114** D6
East Ayrshire □ *U.K.* **13** F4
East Bengal *Bangla.* **67** G17
East Beskids = Vychodné
    Beskydy *Europe* **27** B15
East Brady *U.S.A.* **114** F5
East C. = Dezhneva, Mys
    Russia **53** C19
East C. *N.Z.* **91** B7
East Caroline Basin *Pac. Oc.* **96** G6
East Chicago *U.S.A.* **114** E2
East China Sea *Asia* **60** C7
East Coulee *Canada* **102** C6
East Dereham = Dereham
    U.K. **15** E8
East Dunbartonshire □ *U.K.* **13** F4
East Falkland *Falk. Is.* **122** G5
East Grand Forks *U.S.A.* **112** B5
East Greenwich *U.S.A.* **115** E13
East Grinstead *U.K.* **15** F8
East Hartford *U.S.A.* **115** E12
East Helena *U.S.A.* **108** C8
East Indies *Asia* **50** J14

East Kilbride *U.K.* **13** F4
East Lansing *U.S.A.* **113** D11
East Liverpool *U.S.A.* **114** F4
East London *S. Africa* **89** E4
East Lothian □ *U.K.* **13** F6
East Main = Eastmain
    Canada **104** B4
East Mariana Basin *Pac. Oc.* **96** F7
East Northport *U.S.A.* **115** F11
East Orange *U.S.A.* **115** F10
East Pacific Rise *Pac. Oc.* **97** J17
East Palestine *U.S.A.* **114** F4
East Pine *Canada* **102** B4
East Point *U.S.A.* **117** E12
East Providence *U.S.A.* **115** E13
East Pt. *Br. Virgin Is.* **121** e
East Pt. *Canada* **105** C7
East Renfrewshire □ *U.K.* **13** F4
East Retford = Retford *U.K.* **14** D7
East Riding of Yorkshire □
    U.K. **14** D7
East Rochester *U.S.A.* **114** C7
East St. Louis *U.S.A.* **112** F8
East Schelde =
    Oosterschelde → *Neths.* **17** C4
East Sea = Japan, Sea of *Asia* **54** E7
East Siberian Sea *Russia* **53** B17
East Stroudsburg *U.S.A.* **115** E9
East Sussex □ *U.K.* **15** G8
East Tasman Plateau
    Pac. Oc. **96** M7
East Tawas *U.S.A.* **113** C12
East Timor ■ *Asia* **63** F7
East Toorale *Australia* **95** E4
East Walker → *U.S.A.* **110** G7
East Windsor *U.S.A.* **115** F10
Eastbourne *N.Z.* **91** D5
Eastbourne *U.K.* **15** G8
Eastend *Canada* **103** D7
Easter Fracture Zone
    Pac. Oc. **97** K16
Easter I. = Pascua, I. de
    Chile **97** K17
Eastern □ *Ghana* **83** D4
Eastern □ *Kenya* **86** C4
Eastern □ *S. Leone* **82** D2
Eastern Cape □ *S. Africa* **88** E4
Eastern Cr. → *Australia* **94** C3
Eastern Ghats *India* **66** N11
Eastern Group = Lau
    Group *Fiji* **91** a
Eastern Group *Australia* **93** F3
Eastern Transvaal =
    Mpumalanga □ *S. Africa* **89** D5
Easterville *Canada* **103** C9
Easthampton *U.S.A.* **115** D12
Eastlake *U.S.A.* **114** E3
Eastland *U.S.A.* **116** E5
Eastleigh *U.K.* **15** G6
Eastmain *Canada* **104** B4
Eastmain → *Canada* **104** B4
Eastman *Canada* **115** A12
Eastman *U.S.A.* **117** E13
Easton *Md., U.S.A.* **113** F15
Easton *Pa., U.S.A.* **115** F9
Easton *Wash., U.S.A.* **110** C5
Eastport *U.S.A.* **113** C20
Eastsound *U.S.A.* **110** B4
Eaton *U.S.A.* **108** F11
Eatonia *Canada* **103** C7
Eatonton *U.S.A.* **117** E13
Eatontown *U.S.A.* **115** F10
Eatonville *U.S.A.* **110** D4
Eau Claire *U.S.A.* **112** C8
Eau Claire, L. à l' *Canada* **104** A5
Eauripik Rise *Pac. Oc.* **96** G6
Eauze *France* **20** E4
Eban *Nigeria* **83** D5
Ebano *Mexico* **119** C5
Ebbegebirge △ *Germany* **24** D3
Ebbw Vale *U.K.* **15** F4
Ebeltoft *Denmark* **11** H4
Ebeltoft Vig *Denmark* **11** H4
Ebensburg *U.S.A.* **114** F6
Ebensee *Austria* **26** D6
Eber Gölü *Turkey* **72** C4
Eberbach *Germany* **25** F4
Eberswalde-Finow *Germany* **24** C9
Ebetsu *Japan* **54** C10
Ebey's Landing △ *U.S.A.* **110** B4
Ebian *China* **58** C4
Ebingen *Germany* **25** G5
Éboli *Italy* **43** B8
Ebolowa *Cameroon* **83** E7
Ebonda *Dem. Rep. of the Congo* **84** D4
Ebonyi □ *Nigeria* **83** D6
Ebrach *Germany* **25** F6
Ébrié, Lagune *Ivory C.* **82** D4
Ebro → *Spain* **38** E5
Ebro, Embalse del *Spain* **36** C7
Ebstorf *Germany* **24** B6
Ecatepec de Morelos *Mexico* **119** D5
Eceabat *Turkey* **45** F10
Ech Chéliff *Algeria* **78** A6
Echigo-Sammyaku *Japan* **55** F9
Echinos *Greece* **45** E9
Échirolles *France* **21** C9

Echizen-Misaki *Japan* **55** G7
Echmiadzin = Yejmiadzin
  Armenia **35** K7
Echo Bay *N.W.T., Canada* **100** C8
Echo Bay *Ont., Canada* **104** C3
Echoing → *Canada* **104** B1
Echterdingen, Stuttgart ✕
  (STR) *Germany* **25** G5
Echternach *Lux.* **17** E6
Echuca *Australia* **95** F3
Ecija *Spain* **37** H5
Eckental *Germany* **25** F7
Eckernförde *Germany* **24** A5
Eclipse I. *Australia* **93** G2
Eclipse Is. *Australia* **92** B4
Eclipse Sd. *Canada* **101** B12
Écommoy *France* **18** E7
Écouché *France* **18** D6
Ecrins △ *France* **21** D10
Ecuador ■ *S. Amer.* **124** D3
Écueillé *France* **18** E8
Ed *Sweden* **11** F5
Ed Dabbura *Sudan* **80** D3
Ed Da'ein *Sudan* **81** E2
Ed Damazin *Sudan* **79** F12
Ed Dâmer *Sudan* **80** D3
Ed Dar el Beida =
  Casablanca *Morocco* **78** B4
Ed Débba *Sudan* **80** D3
Ed Déffa *Egypt* **80** A2
Ed Deim *Sudan* **81** E2
Ed Dueim *Sudan* **81** E3
Edam *Canada* **103** C7
Edam *Neths.* **17** B5
Edane *Sweden* **10** E6
Eday *U.K.* **13** B6
Edd *Eritrea* **81** E5
Eddrachillis B. *U.K.* **13** C3
Eddystone *U.K.* **15** G3
Eddystone Pt. *Australia* **95** G4
Ede *Neths.* **17** B5
Ede *Nigeria* **83** D5
Édéa *Cameroon* **83** E7
Edebäck *Sweden* **10** D7
Edehon L. *Canada* **103** A9
Edekel, Adrar *Algeria* **78** D7
Edelény *Hungary* **28** B5
Eden *Australia* **95** F4
Eden *N.C., U.S.A.* **117** C15
Eden *N.Y., U.S.A.* **114** D6
Eden *Tex., U.S.A.* **116** F5
Eden → *U.K.* **14** C4
Edenburg *S. Africa* **88** D4
Edendale *S. Africa* **89** D5
Edenderry *Ireland* **12** C4
Edenton *U.S.A.* **117** C16
Edenville *S. Africa* **89** D4
Eder → *Germany* **24** D5
Eder-Stausee *Germany* **24** D4
Edessa *Greece* **44** F6
Edewecht *Germany* **24** B3
Edgar *U.S.A.* **112** E5
Edgartown *U.S.A.* **115** E14
Edge Hill *U.K.* **15** E6
Edgefield *U.S.A.* **117** E14
Edgeley *U.S.A.* **112** B4
Edgemont *U.S.A.* **112** D2
Edgeøya *Svalbard* **4** B9
Édhessa = Edessa *Greece* **44** F6
Ediévale *N.Z.* **91** F2
Edina *Liberia* **82** D2
Edina *U.S.A.* **112** E7
Edinboro *U.S.A.* **114** E4
Edinburg *U.S.A.* **116** H5
Edinburgh *U.K.* **13** F5
Edinburgh ✕ (EDI) *U.K.* **13** F5
Edinburgh, City of □ *U.K.* **13** F5
Edineț *Moldova* **29** B12
Edirne *Turkey* **45** E10
Edirne □ *Turkey* **45** E10
Edison *U.S.A.* **110** B4
Edithburgh *Australia* **95** F2
Edmond *U.S.A.* **116** D6
Edmonds *U.S.A.* **110** C4
Edmonton *Australia* **94** B4
Edmonton *Canada* **102** C6
Edmund L. *Canada* **104** B1
Edmundston *Canada* **105** C6
Edna *U.S.A.* **116** G6
Edo □ *Nigeria* **83** D6
Edolo *Italy* **40** B7
Edremit *Turkey* **47** B9
Edremit Körfezi *Turkey* **47** B8
Edsbro *Sweden* **10** E12
Edsbyn *Sweden* **10** C9
Edson *Canada* **102** C5
Eduardo Castex *Argentina* **126** D3
Edward → *Australia* **95** F3
Edward, L. *Africa* **86** C2
Edward VII Land *Antarctica* **5** E13
Edwards *Calif., U.S.A.* **111** L9
Edwards *N.Y., U.S.A.* **115** B9
Edwards Plateau *U.S.A.* **116** F4
Edwardsville *U.S.A.* **115** E9
Edzná *Mexico* **119** D6
Edzo *Canada* **102** A5

Eeklo *Belgium* **17** C3
Eesti = Estonia ■ *Europe* **32** C3
Eferding *Austria* **26** C7
Effigy Mounds △ *U.S.A.* **112** D9
Effingham *U.S.A.* **112** F9
Eforie *Romania* **29** F13
Efxinoupoli *Greece* **46** B4
Ega → *Spain* **38** C3
Égadi, Ísole *Italy* **42** E5
Egan Range *U.S.A.* **108** G6
Eganville *Canada* **114** A7
Eger = Cheb *Czech Rep.* **26** A5
Eger *Hungary* **28** C5
Eger → *Hungary* **28** C5
Egersund *Norway* **9** G12
Egg L. *Canada* **103** B7
Eggegebirge Südlicher
  Teutoburger Wald △
  Germany **24** D4
Eggenburg *Austria* **26** C8
Eggenfelden *Germany* **25** G8
Éghezée *Belgium* **17** D4
Egina *Greece* **46** D5
Eginio *Greece* **44** F6
Egio *Greece* **46** C4
Égletons *France* **20** C6
Eglinton I. *Canada* **101** B8
Egmont *Canada* **102** D4
Egmont, C. *N.Z.* **91** C4
Egmont, Mt. = Taranaki,
  Mt. *N.Z.* **91** C5
Egmont △ *N.Z.* **91** C5
Egra *India* **69** J12
Eğridir *Turkey* **72** D4
Eğridir Gölü *Turkey* **72** D4
Egtved *Denmark* **11** J3
Egume *Nigeria* **83** D6
Éguzon-Chantôme *France* **19** F8
Egvekinot *Russia* **53** C19
Egyek *Hungary* **28** C5
Egypt ■ *Africa* **80** B3
Eha Amufu *Nigeria* **83** D6
Ehime □ *Japan* **55** H6
Ehingen *Germany* **25** G5
Ehrenberg *U.S.A.* **111** M12
Ehrwald *Austria* **26** D3
Eibar *Spain* **38** B2
Eichstätt *Germany* **25** G7
Eider → *Germany* **24** A4
Eidsvold *Australia* **95** D5
Eidsvoll *Norway* **9** F14
Eifel *Germany* **25** E2
Eiffel Flats *Zimbabwe* **87** F3
Eiger *Switz.* **40** B5
Eigg *U.K.* **13** E2
Eighty Mile Beach *Australia* **92** C3
Eil *Somali Rep.* **75** F4
Eil, L. *U.K.* **13** E3
Eildon, L. *Australia* **95** F4
Eilean Sar = Western
  Isles □ *U.K.* **13** D1
Eilenburg *Germany* **24** D8
Ein el Luweiqa *Sudan* **81** E3
Einasleigh *Australia* **94** B3
Einasleigh → *Australia* **94** B3
Einbeck *Germany* **24** D5
Eindhoven *Neths.* **17** C5
Einsiedeln *Switz.* **25** H4
Eire = Ireland ■ *Europe* **12** C4
Eiríksjökull *Iceland* **8** D3
Eirunepé *Brazil* **124** E5
Eiseb → *Namibia* **88** C2
Eisenach *Germany* **24** E6
Eisenberg *Germany* **24** E7
Eisenerz *Austria* **26** D7
Eisenhüttenstadt *Germany* **24** C10
Eisenkappel *Austria* **26** E7
Eisenstadt *Austria* **27** D9
Eisfeld *Germany* **25** E6
Eisleben *Germany* **24** D7
Eislingen *Germany* **25** G5
Eivissa *Spain* **48** C7
Eixe, Serra do *Spain* **36** C4
Ejea de los Caballeros *Spain* **38** C3
Ejeda *Madag.* **89** C7
Ejura *Ghana* **83** D4
Ejutla *Mexico* **119** D5
Ekalaka *U.S.A.* **108** D11
Ekaterinburg =
  Yekaterinburg *Russia* **52** D7
Ekenäs = Tammisaari
  Finland **9** F20
Ekenässjön *Sweden* **11** G9
Ekerö *Sweden* **10** E11
Eket *Nigeria* **83** E6
Eketahuna *N.Z.* **91** D5
Ekibastuz *Kazakhstan* **52** D8
Ekiti □ *Nigeria* **83** D6
Ekoli *Dem. Rep. of the Congo* **86** C1
Ekoln *Sweden* **10** E11
Ekshärad *Sweden* **10** D7
Eksjö *Sweden* **11** G8
Ekuma → *Namibia* **88** B2
Ekwan → *Canada* **104** B3
Ekwan Pt. *Canada* **104** B3
El Aaiún *W. Sahara* **78** C3
El Abanico *Chile* **126** D1

El Abbasiya *Sudan* **81** E3
El 'Agrûd *Egypt* **74** E3
El Ait *Sudan* **81** E2
El 'Aiyat *Egypt* **80** J7
El 'Alamein *Egypt* **80** A2
El 'Aqaba, W. → *Egypt* **74** G2
El 'Arag *Egypt* **80** B2
El Arahal *Spain* **37** H5
El Arīḥā *West Bank* **74** D4
El 'Arîsh *Egypt* **74** D2
El 'Arîsh, W. → *Egypt* **74** D2
El Asnam = Ech Chéliff
  Algeria **78** A6
El Astillero *Spain* **36** B7
El Badâri *Egypt* **80** B3
El Bahrein *Egypt* **80** B2
El Ballâs *Egypt* **80** B3
El Balyana *Egypt* **80** B3
El Baqeir *Sudan* **80** D3
El Barco de Ávila *Spain* **36** E5
El Barco de Valdeorras = O
  Barco *Spain* **36** C4
El Bauga *Sudan* **80** D3
El Bawiti *Egypt* **80** B2
El Bayadh *Algeria* **78** B6
El Bierzo *Spain* **36** C4
El Bluff *Nic.* **120** D3
El Bonillo *Spain* **39** G2
El Buheirat □ *Sudan* **81** F3
El Burgo de Osma *Spain* **38** D1
El Cajon *U.S.A.* **111** N10
El Campo *U.S.A.* **116** G6
El Capitan *U.S.A.* **110** H7
El Centro *U.S.A.* **111** N11
El Cerro *Bolivia* **124** G6
El Cerro de Andévalo *Spain* **37** H4
El Compadre *Mexico* **111** N10
El Coronil *Spain* **37** H5
El Cuy *Argentina* **128** D3
El Cuyo *Mexico* **119** C7
El Dab'a *Egypt* **80** H6
El Daheir *Egypt* **74** D3
El Deir *Egypt* **80** B3
El Dere *Somali Rep.* **75** G4
El Descanso *Mexico* **111** N10
El Desemboque *Mexico* **118** A2
El Dilingat *Egypt* **80** H7
El Diviso *Colombia* **124** C3
El Djouf *Mauritania* **78** D4
El Dorado *Ark., U.S.A.* **116** E8
El Dorado *Kans., U.S.A.* **112** G5
El Dorado *Venezuela* **124** B6
El Dorado Springs *U.S.A.* **112** G6
El 'Ein *Sudan* **81** D2
El Ejido *Spain* **37** J8
El Escorial *Spain* **36** E6
El Espinar *Spain* **36** D6
El Faiyûm *Egypt* **80** J7
El Fâsher *Sudan* **81** E2
El Fashn *Egypt* **80** J7
El Ferrol = Ferrol *Spain* **36** B2
El Fifí *Sudan* **81** E2
El Fuerte *Mexico* **118** B3
El Ga'a *Sudan* **81** E2
El Gal *Somali Rep.* **75** E5
El Garef *Sudan* **81** E3
El Gebir *Sudan* **81** E2
El Gedida *Egypt* **80** B2
El Geneina = Al Junaynah
  Sudan **79** F10
El Geteina *Sudan* **81** E3
El Gezira □ *Sudan* **81** E3
El Gir *Sudan* **80** D2
El Gîza *Egypt* **80** J7
El Gogorrón △ *Mexico* **118** C4
El Goléa *Algeria* **78** B6
El Golfo de Santa Clara
  Mexico **118** A2
El Grau *Spain* **39** G4
El Guácharo △ *Venezuela* **121** D7
El Guache △ *Venezuela* **121** E6
El Hagiz *Sudan* **81** D4
El Hâi *Egypt* **80** J7
El Hammam *Egypt* **80** A2
El Hawata *Sudan* **81** E3
El Heiz *Egypt* **80** B2
El Hideib *Sudan* **81** E3
El Hilla *Sudan* **81** E2
El 'Idisât *Egypt* **80** B3
El Iskandarîya *Egypt* **80** H7
El Istiwa'iya *Sudan* **79** G11
El Jadida *Morocco* **78** B4
El Jardal *Honduras* **120** D2
El Jebelein *Sudan* **81** E3
El Kab *Sudan* **80** D3
El Kafr el Sharqi *Egypt* **80** H7
El Kamlin *Sudan* **81** D3
El Karaba *Sudan* **80** D3
El Kef □ *Tunisia* **79** A7
El Kere *Ethiopia* **81** F5
El Khandaq *Sudan* **80** D3
El Khârga *Egypt* **80** B3
El Khartûm *Sudan* **81** D3
El Khartûm □ *Sudan* **81** D3
El Khartûm Bahrî *Sudan* **81** D3
El Kuntilla *Egypt* **74** E3

El Laqâwa *Sudan* **81** E2
El Leh *Ethiopia* **81** G4
El Leiya *Sudan* **81** D4
El Lucero *Mexico* **118** A3
El Maestrazgo *Spain* **38** E4
El Mafâza *Sudan* **81** E3
El Maghra *Egypt* **80** A2
El Mahalla el Kubra *Egypt* **80** H7
El Mahâriq *Egypt* **80** B3
El Maîmûn *Egypt* **80** J7
El Maks el Bahari *Egypt* **80** C3
El Malpais △ *U.S.A.* **109** J10
El Manshâh *Egypt* **80** B3
El Mansûra *Egypt* **80** H7
El Manzala *Egypt* **80** H8
El Marâgha *Egypt* **80** B3
El Masid *Sudan* **81** D3
El Masnou *Spain* **38** D7
El Matarîya *Egypt* **80** H8
El Meda *Ethiopia* **81** F5
El Medano *Canary Is.* **48** F3
El Metemma *Sudan* **81** D3
El Milagro *Argentina* **126** C2
El Minyâ *Egypt* **80** B3
El Monte *U.S.A.* **111** L8
El Montseny △ *Spain* **38** D7
El Mreyye *Mauritania* **82** B3
El Niybo *Ethiopia* **81** G4
El Obeid *Sudan* **81** E3
El Odaiya *Sudan* **81** E2
El Oro *Mexico* **119** D4
El Oued *Algeria* **78** B7
El Palmar △ *Argentina* **126** C4
El Palmito, Presa *Mexico* **118** B3
El Paso *U.S.A.* **116** F1
El Pedernoso *Spain* **39** F2
El Pedroso *Spain* **37** H5
El Pinacate y Gran
  Desierto de Altar = Gran
  Desierto del Pinacate △
  Mexico **118** A2
El Pobo de Dueñas *Spain* **38** E3
El Portal *U.S.A.* **110** H7
El Porvenir *Mexico* **118** A3
El Prat de Llobregat *Spain* **38** D7
El Progreso *Honduras* **120** C2
El Pueblito *Mexico* **118** B3
El Pueblo *Canary Is.* **48** F2
El Puente del Arzobispo
  Spain **36** F5
El Puerto de Santa María
  Spain **37** J4
El Qâhira *Egypt* **80** H7
El Qantara *Egypt* **74** E1
El Qasr *Egypt* **80** B2
El Qubâbât *Egypt* **80** J7
El Quseima *Egypt* **74** E3
El Qusîya *Egypt* **80** B3
El Râshda *Egypt* **80** B2
El Real *Panama* **124** B3
El Reno *U.S.A.* **116** D6
El Rey △ *Argentina* **126** A3
El Rîdisiya *Egypt* **80** C3
El Rio *U.S.A.* **111** L7
El Ronquillo *Spain* **37** H4
El Roque, Pta. *Canary Is.* **48** F4
El Rosarito *Mexico* **118** B2
El Rubio *Spain* **37** H5
El Saff *Egypt* **80** J7
El Salto *Mexico* **118** C3
El Salvador ■ *Cent. Amer.* **120** D2
El Sauce *Nic.* **120** D2
El Saucejo *Spain* **37** H5
El Shallal *Egypt* **80** C3
El Simbillawein *Egypt* **80** H7
El Sueco *Mexico* **118** B3
El Suweis *Egypt* **80** J8
El Tabbîn *Egypt* **80** J7
El Tamarâni, W. → *Egypt* **74** E3
El Thamad *Egypt* **74** F3
El Tigre *Venezuela* **124** B6
El Tîh, Gebel *Egypt* **74** F2
El Tîna *Egypt* **80** H8
El Tofo *Chile* **126** B1
El Tránsito *Chile* **126** B1
El Tûr *Egypt* **70** D2
El Turbio *Argentina* **128** G2
El Uqsur *Egypt* **80** B3
El Valle △ *Spain* **39** H3
El Vendrell *Spain* **38** D6
El Vergel *Mexico* **118** B3
El Vigía *Venezuela* **124** B4
El Viso del Alcor *Spain* **37** H5
El Wabeira *Egypt* **74** F2
El Wak *Kenya* **86** B5
El Waqf *Egypt* **80** B3
El Weguet *Ethiopia* **81** F5
El Wuz *Sudan* **81** D3
Elafonisos *Greece* **46** E4
Élancourt *France* **19** D8
Elasa *Greece* **47** D8
Elassona *Greece* **46** B4
Elat *Israel* **74** F3
Elatia *Greece* **46** C4
Eláziğ *Turkey* **73** C8
Eláziğ □ *Turkey* **73** C8
Elba *Italy* **40** F7

Elba *U.S.A.* **117** F11
Elbasan *Albania* **44** E4
Elbe *U.S.A.* **110** D4
Elbe → *Europe* **24** B4
Elbe-Seitenkanal *Germany* **24** C6
Elbert, Mt. *U.S.A.* **108** G10
Elberton *U.S.A.* **117** D13
Elbeuf *France* **18** C8
Elbing = Elbląg *Poland* **30** D6
Elbistan *Turkey* **72** C7
Elbląg *Poland* **30** D6
Elbow *Canada* **103** C7
Elbrus *Russia* **35** J6
Elburz Mts. = Alborz,
  Reshteh-ye Kūhhā-ye
  Iran **71** C7
Elche *Spain* **39** G4
Elche de la Sierra *Spain* **39** G2
Elcho I. *Australia* **94** A2
Elda *Spain* **39** G4
Eldama Ravine *Kenya* **86** B4
Elde → *Germany* **24** B7
Eldon *Mo., U.S.A.* **112** F7
Eldon *Wash., U.S.A.* **110** C3
Eldora *U.S.A.* **112** D7
Eldorado *Argentina* **127** B5
Eldorado *Canada* **114** B7
Eldorado *Ill., U.S.A.* **112** G9
Eldorado *Tex., U.S.A.* **116** F4
Eldoret *Kenya* **86** B4
Eldred *U.S.A.* **114** E6
Elea, C. *Cyprus* **49** D13
Eleanora, Pk. *Australia* **93** F3
Elefantes → *Africa* **89** C5
Elefsina *Greece* **46** C5
Eleftherios Venizelos ✕
  (ATH) *Greece* **46** D5
Elektrogorsk *Russia* **32** E10
Elektrostal *Russia* **32** E10
Elele *Nigeria* **83** D6
Elemi Triangle *Africa* **81** G4
Elena *Bulgaria* **45** D9
Elephant Butte Res. *U.S.A.* **109** K10
Elephant I. *Antarctica* **5** C18
Eleshnitsa *Bulgaria* **45** E8
Eleşkirt *Turkey* **73** C10
Eleuthera *Bahamas* **120** B4
Eleutheroupoli *Greece* **45** F8
Elgin *Canada* **115** B8
Elgin *U.K.* **13** D5
Elgin *Ill., U.S.A.* **112** D9
Elgin *N. Dak., U.S.A.* **112** B3
Elgin *Oreg., U.S.A.* **108** D5
Elgin *Tex., U.S.A.* **116** F6
Elgoibar *Spain* **38** B2
Elgon, Mt. *Africa* **86** B3
Eliase *Indonesia* **63** F8
Elikonos Oros *Greece* **46** C4
Elim *Namibia* **88** B2
Elim *S. Africa* **88** E2
Elin Pelin *Bulgaria* **44** D7
Elista *Russia* **35** G7
Elizabeth *Australia* **95** E2
Elizabeth *U.S.A.* **115** F10
Elizabeth City *U.S.A.* **117** C16
Elizabethton *U.S.A.* **117** C13
Elizabethtown *Ky., U.S.A.* **113** G11
Elizabethtown *N.Y., U.S.A.* **115** B11
Elizabethtown *Pa., U.S.A.* **115** F8
Elizondo *Spain* **38** B3
Elk *Poland* **30** E9
Elk → *Canada* **102** C5
Elk → *Poland* **30** E9
Elk → *U.S.A.* **117** D11
Elk City *U.S.A.* **116** D5
Elk Creek *U.S.A.* **110** F4
Elk Grove *U.S.A.* **110** G5
Elk Island △ *Canada* **102** C6
Elk Lake *Canada* **104** C3
Elk Point *Canada* **103** C6
Elk River *Idaho, U.S.A.* **108** C5
Elk River *Minn., U.S.A.* **112** C7
Elkedra → *Australia* **94** C2
Elkhart *Ind., U.S.A.* **113** E11
Elkhart *Kans., U.S.A.* **112** G3
Elkhorn *Canada* **103** D8
Elkhorn → *U.S.A.* **112** E5
Elkhovo *Bulgaria* **45** D10
Elkin *U.S.A.* **117** C5
Elkins *U.S.A.* **113** F14
Elkland *U.S.A.* **114** E7
Elko *Canada* **102** D5
Elko *U.S.A.* **108** F6
Elkton *U.S.A.* **114** C1
Ellas = Greece ■ *Europe* **46** B3
Ellef Ringnes I. *Canada* **101** B9
Ellen, Mt. *U.S.A.* **115** B12
Ellenburg *U.S.A.* **115** B11
Ellendale *U.S.A.* **112** B5
Ellensburg *U.S.A.* **108** C3
Ellenville *U.S.A.* **115** E10
Ellerton *Barbados* **121** g
Ellery, Mt. *Australia* **95** F4
Ellesmere, L. *N.Z.* **91** G4
Ellesmere I. *Canada* **101** B12

Ellesmere Port *U.K.* **14** D5
Ellice Is. = Tuvalu ■
  Pac. Oc. **90** B10
Ellicottville *U.S.A.* **114** D6
Elliot *Australia* **94** B1
Elliot *S. Africa* **89** E4
Elliot Lake *Canada* **104** C3
Elliotdale = Xhora *S. Africa* **89** E4
Ellis *U.S.A.* **112** F5
Elliston *Australia* **95** E1
Ellisville *U.S.A.* **117** F10
Ellon *U.K.* **13** D6
Ellore = Eluru *India* **67** L12
Ellsworth *Kans., U.S.A.* **112** F4
Ellsworth *Maine, U.S.A.* **113** C19
Ellsworth Land *Antarctica* **5** D16
Ellsworth Mts. *Antarctica* **5** D16
Ellwangen *Germany* **25** G6
Ellwood City *U.S.A.* **114** F4
Elm *Switz.* **25** J5
Elm-Lappwald △ *Germany* **24** C6
Elma *Canada* **103** D9
Elma *U.S.A.* **110** D3
Elmadağ *Turkey* **72** C5
Elmalı *Turkey* **47** E11
Elmhurst *U.S.A.* **112** E10
Elmina *Ghana* **83** D4
Elmira *Canada* **114** C4
Elmira *U.S.A.* **114** D8
Elmira Heights *U.S.A.* **114** D8
Elmore *Australia* **95** F3
Elmshorn *Germany* **24** B5
Elmvale *Canada* **114** B5
Elne *France* **20** F6
Elora *Canada* **114** C4
Elos *Greece* **46** E4
Elounda *Greece* **49** D7
Eloy *U.S.A.* **109** K8
Éloyes *France* **19** D13
Elrose *Canada* **103** C7
Elsdorf *Germany* **24** E2
Elsie *U.S.A.* **110** E3
Elsinore = Helsingør
  Denmark **11** H6
Elster → *Germany* **24** D7
Elsterwerda *Germany* **24** D9
Eltanin Fracture Zone
  System *S. Ocean* **5** B14
Eltham *N.Z.* **91** C5
Elton *Russia* **35** F8
Elton, Ozero *Russia* **35** F8
Eltville *Germany* **25** E4
Eluru *India* **67** L12
Elvas *Portugal* **37** G3
Elven *France* **18** E4
Elverum *Norway* **8** F14
Elvire → *Australia* **92** C4
Elvire, Mt. *Australia* **93** E2
Elvo → *Italy* **40** C5
Elwell, L. = Tiber Res.
  U.S.A. **108** B8
Elwood *Ind., U.S.A.* **113** E11
Elwood *Nebr., U.S.A.* **112** E4
Elx = Elche *Spain* **39** G4
Ely *U.K.* **15** E8
Ely *Minn., U.S.A.* **112** B8
Ely *Nev., U.S.A.* **108** G6
Elyria *U.S.A.* **114** E2
Elyros *Greece* **46** F5
Elz → *Germany* **25** G3
Emådalen *Sweden* **10** C8
eMalahleni *S. Africa* **89** D4
Emämrūd *Iran* **71** B7
Emån → *Sweden* **11** G10
Embarcación *Argentina* **126** A3
Embarras Portage *Canada* **103** B6
Embetsu *Japan* **54** B10
Embi *Kazakhstan* **52** E6
Embi → *Kazakhstan* **52** E6
Embonas *Greece* **49** C9
Embrun *France* **21** D10
Embu *Kenya* **86** C4
Emden *Germany* **24** B3
Emecik *Turkey* **47** E9
Emerald *Australia* **94** C4
Emerson *Canada* **103** D9
Emet *Turkey* **47** B11
Emi Koussi *Chad* **79** E9
Emília-Romagna □ *Italy* **40** D4
Eminabad *Pakistan* **68** C6
Emilius, Mte. *Italy* **40** C4
Emine, Nos *Bulgaria* **45** D11
Emirdağ *Turkey* **72** C4
Emissi, Tarso *Chad* **79** D9
Emlenton *U.S.A.* **114** E5
Emlichheim *Germany* **24** C2
Emmaboda *Sweden* **11** H9
Emmaus *S. Africa* **88** D4
Emmaus *U.S.A.* **115** F9
Emme → *Switz.* **25** H3
Emmeloord *Neths.* **17** B5
Emmen *Neths.* **17** B6
Emmen *Switz.* **25** H4
Emmendingen *Germany* **25** G3
Emmental *Switz.* **25** J3
Emmerich *Germany* **24** D2
Emmet *Australia* **94** C3

Emmetsburg *U.S.A.* **112** D6
Emmett *Idaho, U.S.A.* **108** E5
Emmett *Mich., U.S.A.* **114** D2
Emmonak *U.S.A.* **106** a
Emo *Canada* **103** D10
Emőd *Hungary* **28** C5
Emona *Bulgaria* **45** D11
Empalme *Mexico* **118** B2
Empangeni *S. Africa* **89** D5
Emperor Seamount Chain
  Pac. Oc. **96** D9
Emperor Trough *Pac. Oc.* **96** C9
Empoli *Italy* **40** E7
Emporia *Kans., U.S.A.* **112** F5
Emporia *Va., U.S.A.* **113** G15
Emporium *U.S.A.* **114** E6
Empress *Canada* **103** C7
Empty Quarter = Rub' al
  Khālī *Si. Arabia* **75** D4
Ems → *Germany* **24** B3
Emsdale *Canada* **114** A5
Emsdetten *Germany* **24** C3
Emu *China* **57** C15
Emu Park *Australia* **94** C5
eMuziwezinto *S. Africa* **89** E5
'En 'Avrona *Israel* **74** F4
'En Boqeq *Israel* **71** D4
'En Gedi *Israel* **71** D4
En Nahud *Sudan* **81** E2
En Nofalab *Sudan* **81** D3
Ena *Japan* **55** G8
Enana *Namibia* **88** B2
Enånger *Sweden* **10** C11
Enard B. *U.K.* **13** C3
Enare = Inarijärvi *Finland* **8** B23
Enarotali *Indonesia* **63** E9
Encampment *U.S.A.* **108** F10
Encantadas, Serra *Brazil* **127** C5
Encarnación *Paraguay* **127** B4
Encarnación de Díaz
  Mexico **118** C4
Enchi *Ghana* **82** D4
Encinitas *U.S.A.* **111** M9
Encino *U.S.A.* **109** J11
Encounter B. *Australia* **95** F2
Encs *Hungary* **28** B6
Endako *Canada* **102** C3
Endau *Kenya* **86** C4
Ende *Indonesia* **63** F6
Endeavour Str. *Australia* **94** A3
Endelave *Denmark* **11** J4
Enderbury I. *Kiribati* **96** H10
Enderby *Canada* **102** C5
Enderby Abyssal Plain
  S. Ocean **5** C3
Enderby I. *Australia* **92** D2
Enderby Land *Antarctica* **5** C5
Enderlin *U.S.A.* **112** B5
Endicott *U.S.A.* **115** D8
Endwell *U.S.A.* **115** D8
Endyalgout I. *Australia* **92** B5
Eneabba *Australia* **93** E2
Enewetak Atoll *Marshall Is.* **96** F8
Enez *Turkey* **45** F10
Enfer, Pte. d' *Martinique* **120** c
Enfield *Canada* **105** D7
Enfield *Conn., U.S.A.* **115** E12
Enfield *N.C., U.S.A.* **117** C16
Enfield *N.H., U.S.A.* **115** C12
Engadin *Switz.* **25** J6
Engaño, C. *Dom. Rep.* **121** C6
Engaño, C. *Phil.* **63** A6
Engaru *Japan* **54** B11
Engcobo = Ngcobo *S. Africa* **89** E4
Engelberg *Switz.* **25** J4
Engels *Russia* **34** E8
Engemann L. *Canada* **103** B7
Engershatu *Eritrea* **81** D4
Enggano *Indonesia* **62** F2
England *U.S.A.* **116** D9
England □ *U.K.* **15** E5
Englee *Canada* **105** B8
Englehart *Canada* **104** C4
Englewood *U.S.A.* **108** G11
English → *Canada* **103** C10
English Bazar = Ingraj
  Bazar *India* **69** G13
English Channel *Europe* **15** G6
English Company's Is., The
  Australia **94** A2
English River *Canada* **104** C1
Engures ezers *Latvia* **30** A10
Enguri → *Georgia* **35** J5
Enid *U.S.A.* **116** C6
Enipeas → *Greece* **46** B4
Enkhuizen *Neths.* **17** B5
Enköping *Sweden* **10** E11
Enle *China* **58** F3
Enna *Italy* **43** E7
Ennadai *Canada* **103** A8
Ennadai L. *Canada* **103** A8
Ennedi *Chad* **79** E10
Engonia *Australia* **95** D4
Ennigerloh *Germany* **24** D4
Ennis *Ireland* **12** D3
Ennis *Mont., U.S.A.* **108** D8

Ennis *Tex., U.S.A.* **116** E6
Enniscorthy *Ireland* **12** D5
Enniskillen *U.K.* **12** B4
Ennistimon *Ireland* **12** D2
Enns *Austria* **26** C7
Enns → *Austria* **26** C7
Eno *Finland* **8** E24
Enontekiö *Finland* **8** B20
Enosburg Falls *U.S.A.* **115** B12
Enping *China* **59** F9
Enriquillo, L. *Dom. Rep.* **121** C5
Enschede *Neths.* **17** B6
Ensenada *Argentina* **126** C4
Ensenada *Mexico* **118** A1
Ensenada de los Muertos
  Mexico **118** C2
Enshi *China* **58** B7
Ensiola, Pta. de n' *Spain* **48** B9
Ensisheim *France* **19** E14
Entebbe *Uganda* **86** B3
Enterprise *Canada* **102** A5
Enterprise *Ala., U.S.A.* **117** F12
Enterprise *Oreg., U.S.A.* **108** D5
Entorno de Doñana △ *Spain* **37** J4
Entraygues-sur-Truyère
  France **20** D6
Entre Ríos *Bolivia* **126** A3
Entre Ríos □ *Argentina* **126** C4
Entrepeñas, Embalse de
  Spain **38** E2
Entroncamento *Portugal* **37** F2
Enugu *Nigeria* **83** D6
Enugu □ *Nigeria* **83** D6
Enugu Ezike *Nigeria* **83** D6
Enumclaw *U.S.A.* **110** C5
Envalira, Port d' *Europe* **38** C6
Envermeu *France* **18** C8
Enviken *Sweden* **10** D9
Enying *Hungary* **28** D3
Enza → *Italy* **40** D7
Eólie, Ís. *Italy* **43** D7
Epanomi *Greece* **44** F6
Epe *Neths.* **17** B5
Epe *Nigeria* **83** D5
Épernay *France* **19** C10
Épernon *France* **19** D8
Ephesus *Turkey* **47** D9
Ephraim *U.S.A.* **108** G8
Ephrata *Pa., U.S.A.* **115** F8
Ephrata *Wash., U.S.A.* **108** C4
Epidavros Limira *Greece* **46** E5
Épila *Spain* **38** D3
Épinac *France* **19** F11
Épinal *France* **19** D13
Epiros □ *Greece* **46** B2
Episkopi *Cyprus* **49** E11
Episkopi *Greece* **49** D6
Episkopi Bay *Cyprus* **49** E11
Epitalio *Greece* **46** D3
Eppan = Appiano *Italy* **41** B8
Eppingen *Germany* **25** F4
Epsom *U.K.* **15** F7
Epukiro *Namibia* **88** C2
Equatoria = El Istiwa'iya
  Sudan **79** G11
Equatorial Guinea ■ *Africa* **84** D1
Er Hai *China* **58** E3
Er Rachidia *Morocco* **78** B5
Er Rahad *Sudan* **81** E3
Er Rif *Morocco* **78** A5
Er Rogel *Sudan* **80** D4
Er Roseires *Sudan* **81** E3
Er Rua'at *Sudan* **81** E3
Eraclea *Italy* **41** C9
Erāwadī Myit =
  Irrawaddy → *Burma* **67** M19
Erāwadī Myitwanya =
  Irrawaddy, Mouths of
  the *Burma* **67** M19
Erba *Italy* **40** C6
Erba *Sudan* **80** D4
Erba, J. *Sudan* **80** C4
Erbaa *Turkey* **72** B7
Erbeskopf *Germany* **25** F3
Erbil = Arbīl *Iraq* **73** D11
Erbu *Ethiopia* **81** E3
Erçek *Turkey* **70** B4
Erçiş *Turkey* **73** C10
Erciyaş Dağı *Turkey* **70** B2
Érd *Hungary* **28** C3
Erdao Jiang → *China* **57** C14
Erdek *Turkey* **45** F11
Erdemli *Turkey* **72** D6
Erdene = Ulaan-Uul
  Mongolia **56** B6
Erdenetsogt *Mongolia* **56** C4
Erding *Germany* **25** G7
Erdre → *France* **18** E5
Erebus, Mt. *Antarctica* **5** D11
Erechim *Brazil* **127** B5
Ereğli *Konya, Turkey* **72** D6
Ereğli *Zonguldak, Turkey* **72** B4
Erei, Monti *Italy* **43** E7
Erenhot *China* **56** C7
Eresma → *Spain* **36** D6
Eresos *Greece* **47** B7
Erfenisdam *S. Africa* **88** D4

Erfstadt *Germany* **24** E2
Erft → *Germany* **24** D2
Erfurt *Germany* **24** E7
Ergani *Turkey* **73** C8
Ergel *Mongolia* **56** C5
Ergene → *Turkey* **45** E10
Ergeni Vozvyshennost
  Russia **35** G7
Ērgli *Latvia* **32** D3
Erhlin *Taiwan* **59** F13
Eria → *Spain* **36** C5
Eriba *Sudan* **81** D4
Eriboll, L. *U.K.* **13** C4
Érice *Italy* **42** D5
Erie *U.S.A.* **114** D4
Erie, L. *N. Amer.* **114** D4
Erie Canal *U.S.A.* **114** C7
Erieau *Canada* **114** D3
Erigavo *Somali Rep.* **75** E4
Erikoussa *Greece* **49** A3
Eriksdale *Canada* **103** C9
Erimanthos *Greece* **46** D3
Erimo-misaki *Japan* **54** D11
Erin Pt. *Trin. & Tob.* **125** K15
Erinpura *India* **68** G5
Eriskay *U.K.* **13** D1
Erithres *Greece* **46** C5
Eritrea ■ *Africa* **81** E4
Erjas → *Portugal* **36** F3
Erkelenz *Germany* **24** D2
Erkner *Germany* **24** C9
Erlangen *Germany* **25** F6
Erldunda *Australia* **94** D1
Ermelo *Neths.* **17** B5
Ermelo *S. Africa* **89** D4
Ermenek *Turkey* **72** D5
Ermil *Sudan* **81** E2
Ermioni *Greece* **46** D5
Ermones *Greece* **49** A3
Ernakulam *India* **66** Q10
Erne → *Ireland* **12** B3
Erne, Lower L. *U.K.* **12** B4
Erne, Upper L. *U.K.* **12** B4
Ernée *France* **18** D6
Ernest Giles Ra. *Australia* **93** E3
Ernstberg *Germany* **25** E2
Erode *India* **66** P10
Eromanga *Australia* **95** D3
Erongo *Namibia* **88** C2
Erquy *France* **18** D4
Erramala Hills *India* **66** M11
Errer → *Ethiopia* **81** F5
Erri-Nundra △ *Australia* **95** F4
Errigal *Ireland* **12** A3
Erris Hd. *Ireland* **12** B1
Erskine *U.S.A.* **112** B6
Erstein *France* **19** D14
Ertholmene *Denmark* **11** J9
Ertil *Russia* **34** E5
Ertis = Irtysh → *Russia* **52** C7
Eruh *Turkey* **73** D10
Eruwa *Nigeria* **83** D5
Ervy-le-Châtel *France* **19** D10
Erwin *U.S.A.* **117** C13
Eryuan *China* **58** D2
Erzgebirge *Germany* **24** E8
Erzin *Russia* **53** D10
Erzincan *Turkey* **73** C8
Erzincan □ *Turkey* **73** C8
Erzurum *Turkey* **73** C9
Erzurum □ *Turkey* **73** C9
Es Caló *Spain* **48** C8
Es Canar *Spain* **48** B8
Es Mercadal *Spain* **48** B11
Es Migjorn Gran *Spain* **48** B11
Es Safiya *Sudan* **81** D3
Es Sahrâ' Esh Sharqîya
  Egypt **80** B3
Es Sînâ' *Egypt* **74** F3
Es Sûkî *Sudan* **81** E3
Es Vedrà *Spain* **48** C7
Esambo *Dem. Rep. of the Congo* **86** C1
Esan-Misaki *Japan* **54** D10
Esashi *Hokkaidō, Japan* **54** B11
Esashi *Hokkaidō, Japan* **54** D10
Esbjerg *Denmark* **11** J2
Esbo = Espoo *Finland* **32** B3
Escalante *U.S.A.* **109** H8
Escalante → *U.S.A.* **109** H8
Escalón *Mexico* **118** B4
Escambia → *U.S.A.* **117** F11
Escanaba *U.S.A.* **112** C10
Escaut = Schelde → *Belgium* **17** C4
Eschede *Germany* **24** C6
Eschwege *Germany* **24** D6
Eschweiler *Germany* **24** E2
Escondido *U.S.A.* **111** M9
Escuinapa de Hidalgo
  Mexico **118** C3
Escuintla *Guatemala* **120** D1
Eséka *Cameroon* **83** E7
Eşen → *Turkey* **47** E11
Esenguly *Turkmenistan* **52** F6
Esens *Germany* **24** B3
Esenyurt *Turkey* **45** E12

Esera → *Spain* **38** C5
Eşfahān *Iran* **71** C6
Eşfahān □ *Iran* **71** C6
Esfarāyen *Iran* **71** B8
Esfideh *Iran* **71** C8
Esgueva → *Spain* **36** D6
Esh Sham = Dimashq *Syria* **74** B5
Esh Shamâlîya □ *Sudan* **80** D2
Esha Ness *U.K.* **13** A7
Eshan *China* **58** E4
Esher *U.K.* **15** F7
Eshkol △ *Israel* **74** D3
Eshowe *S. Africa* **89** D5
Esiama *Ghana* **82** E4
Esigodini *Zimbabwe* **89** C4
Esil = Ishim → *Russia* **52** D8
Esino → *Italy* **41** E10
Esira *Madag.* **89** C8
Esk → *Dumf. & Gall., U.K.* **13** G5
Esk → *N. Yorks., U.K.* **14** C7
Eskān *Iran* **71** E9
Esker *Canada* **105** B6
Eskifjörður *Iceland* **8** D7
Eskilsäter *Sweden* **11** F7
Eskilstuna *Sweden* **10** E10
Eskimalatya *Turkey* **73** C8
Eskimo Point = Arviat
  Canada **103** A10
Eskişehir *Turkey* **47** B12
Eskişehir □ *Turkey* **47** B12
Esla → *Spain* **36** D4
Eslāmābād-e Gharb *Iran* **73** E12
Eslāmshahr *Iran* **71** C6
Eslöv *Sweden* **11** J7
Eşme *Turkey* **47** C10
Esmeraldas *Ecuador* **124** C3
Esnagi L. *Canada* **104** C3
Espalion *France* **20** D6
Espanola *Canada* **104** C3
Espanola *U.S.A.* **109** J10
Esparraguera *Spain* **38** D6
Esparta *Costa Rica* **120** E3
Esperance *Australia* **93** F3
Esperance B. *Australia* **93** F3
Esperance Harbour *St. Lucia* **121** f
Esperanza *Antarctica* **5** C18
Esperanza *Argentina* **126** C3
Esperanza *Phil.* **61** G6
Esperanza *Puerto Rico* **121** d
Espéraza *France* **20** F6
Espichel, C. *Portugal* **37** G1
Espiel *Spain* **37** G5
Espigão, Serra do *Brazil* **127** B5
Espinazo, Sierra del =
  Espinhaço, Serra do
  Brazil **125** G10
Espinhaço, Serra do *Brazil* **125** G10
Espinho *Portugal* **36** D2
Espinilho, Serra do *Brazil* **127** B4
Espinosa de los Monteros
  Spain **36** B7
Espírito Santo □ *Brazil* **125** H10
Espíritu Santo *Vanuatu* **90** C9
Espíritu Santo, B. del
  Mexico **119** D7
Espíritu Santo, I. *Mexico* **118** C2
Espita *Mexico* **119** C7
Espiye *Turkey* **73** B8
Espluga de Francolí *Spain* **38** D6
Espoo *Finland* **32** B3
Espuña, Sierra de *Spain* **39** H3
Espungabera *Mozam.* **89** C5
Esquel *Argentina* **128** E2
Esquimalt *Canada* **110** B3
Esquina *Argentina* **126** C4
Essaouira *Morocco* **78** B4
Essebie *Dem. Rep. of the Congo* **86** B3
Essen *Belgium* **17** C4
Essen *Germany* **24** D3
Essendon, Mt. *Australia* **93** E3
Essequibo → *Guyana* **124** B7
Essex *Canada* **114** D2
Essex *Calif., U.S.A.* **111** L11
Essex *N.Y., U.S.A.* **115** B11
Essex □ *U.K.* **15** F8
Essex Junction *U.S.A.* **115** B11
Esslingen *Germany* **25** G5
Essonne □ *France* **19** D9
Estaca de Bares, C. de *Spain* **36** B3
Estación Camacho *Mexico* **118** C4
Estación Simón *Mexico* **118** C4
Estadilla *Spain* **38** C5
Estados, I. de Los *Argentina* **128** G4
Estagel *France* **20** F6
Eştahbānāt *Iran* **71** D7
Estância *Brazil* **125** F11
Estancia *U.S.A.* **109** J10
Estārm *Iran* **71** D8
Estarreja *Portugal* **36** E2
Estats, Pic d' *Spain* **38** C6
Estcourt *S. Africa* **89** D4
Este *Italy* **41** C8
Este △ *Dom. Rep.* **121** C6
Estelí *Nic.* **120** D2
Estella *Spain* **38** C2

Estellencs *Spain* **48** B9
Estena → *Spain* **37** F6
Estepa *Spain* **37** H6
Estepona *Spain* **37** J5
Esternay *France* **19** D10
Esterri d'Aneu *Spain* **38** C6
Estevan *Canada* **103** D8
Estevan Group *Canada* **102** C3
Estherville *U.S.A.* **112** D6
Estissac *France* **19** D10
Eston *Canada* **103** C7
Estonia ■ *Europe* **32** C3
Estoril *Portugal* **37** G1
Estrela, Serra da *Portugal* **36** E3
Estrella *Spain* **37** G7
Estremoz *Portugal* **37** G3
Estrondo, Serra do *Brazil* **125** E9
Estreito *Brazil* **125** E9
Esztergom *Hungary* **28** C3
Et Tîdra *Mauritania* **82** B1
Etah *India* **69** F8
Étain *France* **19** C12
Étampes *France* **19** D9
Etanga *Namibia* **88** B1
Étaples *France* **19** B8
Etawah *India* **69** F8
Etawney L. *Canada* **103** B9
Etchojoa *Mexico* **118** B3
Ete *Nigeria* **83** D6
eThekwini = Durban
  S. Africa **89** D5
Ethel *U.S.A.* **110** D4
Ethelbert *Canada* **103** C8
Ethiopia ■ *Africa* **75** F3
Ethiopian Highlands *Ethiopia* **75** F2
Etili *Turkey* **45** C10
Etive, L. *U.K.* **13** E3
Etna *Italy* **43** E7
Etoile *Dem. Rep. of the Congo* **87** E2
Etoliko *Greece* **46** C3
Etosha △ *Namibia* **88** B2
Etosha Pan *Namibia* **88** B2
Etowah *U.S.A.* **117** D12
Étréchy *France* **19** D9
Etrek *Turkmenistan* **71** B7
Étrépagny *France* **19** C8
Étretat *France* **18** C7
Etropole *Bulgaria* **45** D8
Ettelbruck *Lux.* **17** E6
Ettlingen *Germany* **25** G4
Ettrick Water → *U.K.* **13** F6
Etuku *Dem. Rep. of the Congo* **86** C2
Etulia *Moldova* **29** E13
Etzná-Tixmucuy = Edzná
  Mexico **119** D6
Eu *France* **18** B8
Eua *Tonga* **91** c
Euboea = Evia *Greece* **46** C6
Eucla *Australia* **93** F4
Euclid *U.S.A.* **114** E3
Eucumbene, L. *Australia* **95** F4
Eudora *U.S.A.* **116** E9
Eufaula *Ala., U.S.A.* **117** F12
Eufaula *Okla., U.S.A.* **116** D7
Eufaula L. *U.S.A.* **116** D7
Eugene *U.S.A.* **108** D2
Eugowra *Australia* **95** E4
Eulo *Australia* **95** D4
Eungella △ *Australia* **94** C4
Eunice *La., U.S.A.* **116** F8
Eunice *N. Mex., U.S.A.* **109** K12
Eupen *Belgium* **17** D6
Euphrates = Furāt, Nahr
  al → *Asia* **70** D5
Eure □ *France* **18** C8
Eure → *France* **18** C8
Eure-et-Loir □ *France* **18** D8
Eureka *Canada* **101** B11
Eureka *Calif., U.S.A.* **108** F1
Eureka *Kans., U.S.A.* **112** G5
Eureka *Mont., U.S.A.* **108** B6
Eureka *Nev., U.S.A.* **108** G6
Eureka *S. Dak., U.S.A.* **112** C4
Eureka, Mt. *Australia* **93** E3
Euroa *Australia* **95** F4
Europa, Île *Ind. Oc.* **85** J8
Europa, Picos de *Spain* **36** B6
Europa, Pt. *Gib.* **37** J5
Europe *Europe* **7** H5
Europoort *Neths.* **17** C4
Euskirchen *Germany* **24** E2
Eustis *U.S.A.* **117** G14
Eutin *Germany* **24** A6
Eutsuk L. *Canada* **102** C3
Evale *Angola* **88** B2
Evans *U.S.A.* **108** F11
Evans, L. *Canada* **104** B4
Evans City *U.S.A.* **114** F4
Evans Head *Australia* **95** D5
Evansburg *Canada* **102** C5
Evanston *Ill., U.S.A.* **112** D10
Evanston *Wyo., U.S.A.* **108** F8
Evansville *U.S.A.* **112** G10

Évaux-les-Bains *France* **19** F9
Evaz *Iran* **71** E7
Evciler *Afyon, Turkey* **47** C11
Evciler *Çanakkale, Turkey* **47** B8
Eveleth *U.S.A.* **112** B7
Evensk *Russia* **53** C16
Everard, L. *Australia* **95** E2
Everard Ranges *Australia* **93** E5
Everest, Mt. *Nepal* **69** E12
Everett *Pa., U.S.A.* **114** F6
Everett *Wash., U.S.A.* **110** C4
Everglades, The *U.S.A.* **117** J14
Everglades △ *U.S.A.* **117** J14
Everglades City *U.S.A.* **117** J14
Evergreen *Ala., U.S.A.* **117** F11
Evergreen *Mont., U.S.A.* **108** B6
Everöd *Sweden* **11** J8
Evertsberg *Sweden* **10** C7
Evesham *U.K.* **15** E6
Evia *Greece* **46** C5
Evia □ *Greece* **46** C5
Évian-les-Bains *France* **19** F13
Evinos → *Greece* **46** C3
Évisa *France* **21** F12
Evje *Norway* **9** G12
Évora *Portugal* **37** G3
Évora □ *Portugal* **37** G3
Evowghlī *Iran* **73** C11
Évreux *France* **18** C8
Evritania □ *Greece* **46** B3
Évron *France* **18** D6
Evros □ *Greece* **45** E10
Evros → *Greece* **72** B2
Evrotas → *Greece* **46** E4
Évry *France* **19** D9
Évvoia = Evia *Greece* **46** C6
Ewe, L. *U.K.* **13** D3
Ewing *U.S.A.* **112** D4
Ewo *Congo* **84** E2
Exaltación *Bolivia* **124** F5
Excelsior Springs *U.S.A.* **112** F6
Excideuil *France* **20** C5
Exe → *U.K.* **15** G4
Exeter *Canada* **114** C3
Exeter *U.K.* **15** G4
Exeter *Calif., U.S.A.* **110** J7
Exeter *N.H., U.S.A.* **115** D14
Exmoor *U.K.* **15** F4
Exmoor △ *U.K.* **15** F4
Exmouth *Australia* **92** D1
Exmouth *U.K.* **15** G4
Exmouth G. *Australia* **92** D1
Exmouth Plateau *Ind. Oc.* **96** J3
Expedition △ *Australia* **95** D4
Expedition Ra. *Australia* **95** C4
Extremadura □ *Spain* **37** F4
Exuma Sound *Bahamas* **120** B4
Eyasi, L. *Tanzania* **86** C4
Eye Pen. *U.K.* **13** C2
Eyemouth *U.K.* **13** F6
Eygues = Aigues → *France* **21** D8
Eygurande *France* **19** G9
Eyjafjörður *Iceland* **8** C4
Eymet *France* **20** D4
Eymoutiers *France* **20** C5
Eynesil *Turkey* **73** B8
Eyre (North), L. *Australia* **95** D2
Eyre (South), L. *Australia* **95** D2
Eyre, L. *Australia* **90** D6
Eyre Mts. *N.Z.* **91** F2
Eyre Pen. *Australia* **95** E2
Eysturoy *Færoe Is.* **8** E9
Eyvänkī *Iran* **71** C6
Ez Zeidab *Sudan* **80** D3
Ezcaray *Spain* **38** C2
Eżerėlis *Lithuania* **30** D10
Ezhou *China* **59** B10
Ezine *Turkey* **47** B8
Ezouza → *Cyprus* **49** E11

F

F.Y.R.O.M. =
  Macedonia ■ *Europe* **44** E5
Faaa *Tahiti* **91** d
Faaborg *Denmark* **11** J4
Faaone *Tahiti* **91** d
Fabala *Guinea* **82** D3
Fabens *U.S.A.* **116** F1
Fabero *Spain* **36** C4
Fabriano *Italy* **41** E9
Făcăeni *Romania* **29** F12
Fachi *Niger* **79** E8
Fada *Chad* **79** E10
Fada-n-Gourma *Burkina Faso* **83** C5
Fadd *Hungary* **28** D3
Faddeyevskiy, Ostrov
  Russia **53** B15
Faddor *Sudan* **81** F3
Fadghāmī *Syria* **73** E9
Fadlab *Sudan* **80** D3
Faenza *Italy* **41** D8
Færoe Is. = Føroyar ☑ *Atl. Oc.* **8** F9
Fafa *Mali* **83** B5
Fafe *Portugal* **36** D2
Fagam *Nigeria* **83** C7
Făgăraş *Romania* **29** E9

Făgăraș, Munții *Romania* **29** E9
Fågelmara *Sweden* **11** H9
Fagerhult *Sweden* **11** G9
Fagersta *Sweden* **10** D9
Faget *Romania* **28** E7
Făget, Munții *Romania* **29** C8
Fagnano, L. *Argentina* **128** G3
Fagnières *France* **19** D11
Faguibine, L. *Mali* **82** B4
Fahliān *Iran* **71** D6
Fahraj *Kermān, Iran* **71** D8
Fahraj *Yazd, Iran* **71** D7
Fai Tsi Long *Vietnam* **58** G6
Faial *Azores* **78** a
Faial *Madeira* **48** D3
Fair Haven *U.S.A.* **113** D17
Fair Hd. *U.K.* **12** A5
Fair Isle *U.K.* **16** B6
Fair Oaks *U.S.A.* **110** G5
Fairbanks *U.S.A.* **100** C5
Fairbury *U.S.A.* **112** E5
Fairfax *U.S.A.* **115** B11
Fairfield *Ala., U.S.A.* **117** E11
Fairfield *Calif., U.S.A.* **110** G4
Fairfield *Conn., U.S.A.* **115** E11
Fairfield *Idaho, U.S.A.* **108** E6
Fairfield *Ill., U.S.A.* **112** F9
Fairfield *Iowa, U.S.A.* **112** E8
Fairfield *Tex., U.S.A.* **116** F6
Fairford *Canada* **103** C9
Fairhope *U.S.A.* **117** F11
Fairlie *N.Z.* **91** F3
Fairmead *U.S.A.* **110** H6
Fairmont *Minn., U.S.A.* **112** D6
Fairmont *W. Va., U.S.A.* **113** F13
Fairmount *Calif., U.S.A.* **111** L8
Fairmount *N.Y., U.S.A.* **115** C8
Fairplay *U.S.A.* **108** G10
Fairport *U.S.A.* **114** C7
Fairport Harbor *U.S.A.* **114** E3
Fairview *Canada* **102** B5
Fairview *Mont., U.S.A.* **108** C11
Fairview *Okla., U.S.A.* **116** C5
Fairweather, Mt. *U.S.A.* **102** B1
Faisalabad *Pakistan* **68** D5
Faith *U.S.A.* **112** C2
Faizabad *India* **69** F10
Fajardo *Puerto Rico* **121** d
Fajr, W. → *Si. Arabia* **70** D3
Fakenham *U.K.* **14** E8
Fåker *Sweden* **10** A8
Fakfak *Indonesia* **63** E8
Fakiya *Bulgaria* **45** D11
Fakobli *Ivory C.* **82** D3
Fakse *Denmark* **11** J6
Fakse Bugt *Denmark* **11** J6
Fakse Ladeplads *Denmark* **11** J6
Faku *China* **57** C12
Falaba *S. Leone* **82** D2
Falaise *France* **18** D6
Falaise, Mui *Vietnam* **64** C5
Falakro Oros *Greece* **44** E7
Falam *Burma* **67** H18
Falces *Spain* **38** C3
Fălciu *Romania* **29** D13
Falcó, C. des *Spain* **48** C7
Falcón, Presa *Mexico* **119** B5
Falcon Lake *Canada* **103** D9
Falcon Res. *U.S.A.* **116** H5
Falconara Maríttima *Italy* **41** E10
Falcone, C. del *Italy* **42** B1
Falconer *U.S.A.* **114** D5
Faléa *Mali* **82** C2
Falefa *Samoa* **91** b
Falelatai *Samoa* **91** b
Falelima *Samoa* **91** b
Falémé → *Senegal* **82** C2
Falerum *Sweden* **11** F10
Faleshty = Fălești *Moldova* **29** C12
Fălești *Moldova* **29** C12
Falfurrias *U.S.A.* **116** H5
Falher *Canada* **102** B5
Faliraki *Greece* **49** C10
Falkenberg *Germany* **24** D9
Falkenberg *Sweden* **11** H6
Falkensee *Germany* **24** C9
Falkirk *U.K.* **13** F5
Falkirk □ *U.K.* **13** F5
Falkland *U.K.* **13** E5
Falkland Is. ☑ *Atl. Oc.* **128** G5
Falkland Sd. *Falk. Is.* **128** G5
Falkonera *Greece* **46** E5
Falköping *Sweden* **11** F7
Fall River *U.S.A.* **115** E13
Fallbrook *U.S.A.* **111** M9
Fallon *U.S.A.* **108** G4
Falls City *U.S.A.* **112** E6
Falls Creek *U.S.A.* **114** E6
Falmouth *Jamaica* **120** a
Falmouth *U.K.* **15** G2
Falmouth *U.S.A.* **115** E14
Falsa, Pta. *Mexico* **118** B1
False B. *S. Africa* **88** E2
Falso, C. *Honduras* **120** C3
Falster *Denmark* **11** K5
Falsterbo *Sweden* **9** J15
Fălticeni *Romania* **29** C11

Falun *Sweden* **10** D9
Famagusta *Cyprus* **49** D12
Famagusta Bay *Cyprus* **49** D13
Famalé *Niger* **78** F6
Famatina, Sierra de
    Argentina **126** B2
Family L. *Canada* **103** C9
Famoso *U.S.A.* **111** K7
Fan Xian *China* **56** G8
Fana *Mali* **82** C3
Fanad Hd. *Ireland* **12** A4
Fanari *Greece* **46** B3
Fandriana *Madag.* **89** C8
Fánes-Sénnes e Braies △
    Italy **41** B9
Fang *Thailand* **58** H2
Fang Xian *China* **59** A8
Fangaga *Sudan* **80** D4
Fangak *Sudan* **81** F3
Fangchang *China* **59** B12
Fangcheng *China* **56** H7
Fangchenggang *China* **58** G7
Fangliao *Taiwan* **59** F13
Fangzi *China* **57** F10
Fani i Madh → *Albania* **44** E4
Fanjakana *Madag.* **89** C8
Fanjiatun *China* **57** C13
Fannich, L. *U.K.* **13** D4
Fannūj *Iran* **71** E8
Fanø *Denmark* **11** J2
Fano *Italy* **41** E10
Fanshi *China* **56** E7
Fao = Al Fāw *Iraq* **71** D6
Faqirwali *Pakistan* **68** E5
Fâqûs *Egypt* **80** H7
Far East =
    Dalnevostochnyy □
    Russia **53** C14
Far East *Asia* **50** E14
Fara in Sabina *Italy* **41** F9
Faradje *Dem. Rep. of the Congo* **86** B2
Farafangana *Madag.* **89** C8
Farāfra, El Wâhât el- *Egypt* **80** B2
Farāh *Afghan.* **66** C3
Farahalana *Madag.* **89** A9
Faraid, Gebel *Egypt* **80** C4
Farako *Ivory C.* **82** D4
Faramana *Burkina Faso* **82** C4
Faranah *Guinea* **82** C2
Farasān, Jazā'ir *Si. Arabia* **75** D3
Farasan Is. = Farasān,
    Jazā'ir *Si. Arabia* **75** D3
Faratsiho *Madag.* **89** B8
Fardes → *Spain* **37** H7
Fareham *U.K.* **15** G6
Farewell, C. *N.Z.* **91** D4
Farewell C. = Nunap Isua
    Greenland **98** D15
Färgelanda *Sweden* **11** F5
Färghona *Uzbekistan* **52** E8
Fargo *U.S.A.* **112** B5
Fār'iah, W. al → *West Bank* **74** C4
Faribault *U.S.A.* **112** C7
Faridabad *India* **68** E6
Faridkot *India* **68** D6
Faridpur *Bangla.* **69** H13
Faridpur *India* **69** E8
Färila *Sweden* **10** C9
Farim *Guinea-Biss.* **82** C1
Farīmān *Iran* **71** C8
Farina *Australia* **95** E2
Fariones, Pta. *Canary Is.* **48** E6
Fâriskûr *Egypt* **80** H7
Färjestaden *Sweden* **11** H10
Farkadona *Greece* **46** B4
Farleigh *Australia* **94** K7
Farmakonisi *Greece* **47** D9
Farmerville *U.S.A.* **116** E8
Farmington *Canada* **102** B4
Farmington *Calif., U.S.A.* **110** H6
Farmington *Maine, U.S.A.* **113** C18
Farmington *Mo., U.S.A.* **112** G8
Farmington *N.H., U.S.A.* **115** C13
Farmington *N. Mex., U.S.A.* **109** H9
Farmington *Utah, U.S.A.* **108** F8
Farmington → *U.S.A.* **115** E12
Farmville *U.S.A.* **113** G14
Färnäs *Sweden* **10** D8
Farne Is. *U.K.* **14** B6
Färnebofjärden △ *Sweden* **10** D10
Farnham *Canada* **115** A12
Farnham, Mt. *Canada* **102** C5
Faro *Brazil* **125** D7
Faro *Canada* **100** C6
Faro *Portugal* **37** H3
Fårö *Sweden* **9** H18
Faro □ *Portugal* **37** H2
Faro ✈ (FAO) *Portugal* **37** H3
Fårösund *Sweden* **11** G13
Farquhar, C. *Australia* **93** D1
Farrars Cr. → *Australia* **94** D3
Farrāshband *Iran* **71** D7
Farrell *U.S.A.* **114** E4
Farrokhī *Iran* **71** C8

Farruch, C. = Ferrutx, C.
    Spain **48** B10
Färs □ *Iran* **71** D7
Farsala *Greece* **46** B4
Farsø *Denmark* **11** H3
Farson *U.S.A.* **108** E9
Farsund *Norway* **9** G12
Fartak, Râs *Si. Arabia* **70** D2
Fartak, Ra's *Yemen* **75** D5
Fârțănești *Romania* **29** E12
Fartura, Serra da *Brazil* **127** B5
Faru *Nigeria* **83** C6
Fārūj *Iran* **71** B8
Fårup *Denmark* **11** H3
Farvel, Kap = Nunap Isua
    Greenland **98** D15
Farwell *U.S.A.* **116** D3
Fasa *Iran* **71** D7
Fasano *Italy* **43** B10
Fashoda *Sudan* **81** F3
Fassa *Mali* **82** C2
Fastiv *Ukraine* **23** C15
Fastnet Rock *Ireland* **12** E2
Fastov = Fastiv *Ukraine* **23** C15
Fatagar, Tanjung *Indonesia* **63** E8
Fatehabad *Haryana, India* **68** E6
Fatehabad *Ut. P., India* **68** F8
Fatehgarh *India* **69** F8
Fatehpur *Bihar, India* **69** G11
Fatehpur *Raj., India* **68** F6
Fatehpur *Ut. P., India* **69** G9
Fatehpur *Ut. P., India* **69** F9
Fatehpur Sikri *India* **68** F6
Fatesh *Russia* **33** F8
Fathai *Sudan* **81** F3
Fathom Five △ *Canada* **114** A3
Fatick *Senegal* **82** C1
Fatick □ *Senegal* **82** C1
Fatima *Canada* **105** C7
Fátima *Portugal* **37** F2
Fatoya *Guinea* **82** C3
Fatsa *Turkey* **72** B7
Faucille, Col de la *France* **19** F13
Faulkton *U.S.A.* **112** C4
Faulquemont *France* **19** C13
Faure I. *Australia* **93** E1
Fauresmith *S. Africa* **88** D4
Fauske *Norway* **8** C16
Favara *Italy* **42** F6
Faváritx, C. de *Spain* **48** B11
Faverges *France* **21** C10
Favignana *Italy* **42** E5
Favignana, I. *Italy* **42** E5
Fawcett, Pt. *Australia* **92** B5
Fawn → *Canada* **104** A2
Fawnskin *U.S.A.* **111** L10
Faxaflói *Iceland* **8** D2
Faxälven → *Sweden* **10** A10
Faya-Largeau *Chad* **79** E9
Fayd *Si. Arabia* **70** E4
Fayence *France* **21** E10
Fayette *Ala., U.S.A.* **117** E11
Fayette *Mo., U.S.A.* **112** F7
Fayetteville *Ark., U.S.A.* **116** C7
Fayetteville *N.C., U.S.A.* **117** D15
Fayetteville *Tenn., U.S.A.* **117** D11
Fayied *Egypt* **80** H8
Fayón *Spain* **38** D5
Fazao-Malfakassa △ *Togo* **83** D5
Fazilka *India* **68** D6
Fazilpur *Pakistan* **68** E4
Fdérik *Mauritania* **78** D3
Feakle *Ireland* **12** D3
Feale → *Ireland* **12** D2
Fear, C. *U.S.A.* **117** E16
Feather → *U.S.A.* **108** G3
Feather Falls *U.S.A.* **110** F5
Featherston *N.Z.* **91** D5
Featherstone *Zimbabwe* **87** F3
Fécamp *France* **18** C7
Fedala = Mohammedia
    Morocco **78** B4
Federación *Argentina* **126** C4
Féderal *Argentina* **128** C5
Federal Capital Terr. □
    Nigeria **83** D6
Federal Way *U.S.A.* **110** C4
Fedeshküh *Iran* **71** D7
Fehérgyarmat *Hungary* **28** C7
Fehmarn *Germany* **24** A7
Fehmarn Bælt *Europe* **11** K5
Fehmarn Belt = Fehmarn
    Bælt *Europe* **11** K5
Fei Xian *China* **57** G9
Feijó *Brazil* **124** E4
Feilding *N.Z.* **91** D5
Feira de Santana *Brazil* **125** F11
Feixi *China* **59** B11
Feixiang *China* **56** F8
Fejér □ *Hungary* **28** C3
Fejø *Denmark* **11** K5
Feke *Turkey* **72** D6
Fekete → *Hungary* **28** E3
Felanitx *Spain* **48** B10
Feldbach *Austria* **26** E8

Feldberg *Baden-W., Germany* **25** H3
Feldberg
    *Mecklenburg-Vorpommern,
    Germany* **24** B9
Feldkirch *Austria* **26** D2
Feldkirchen *Austria* **26** E7
Félicité *Seychelles* **85** b
Felipe Carrillo Puerto
    Mexico **119** D7
Felixburg *Zimbabwe* **89** B5
Felixstowe *U.K.* **15** F9
Felletin *France* **20** C6
Fellingsbro *Sweden* **10** E9
Felton *U.S.A.* **110** H4
Feltre *Italy* **41** B8
Femer Bælt = Fehmarn
    Bælt *Europe* **11** K5
Femø *Denmark* **11** K5
Femunden *Norway* **8** E14
Fen He → *China* **56** G6
Fene *Spain* **36** B2
Fenelon Falls *Canada* **114** B6
Fener Burnu *Turkey* **47** E9
Feneroa *Ethiopia* **81** E4
Feng Xian *Jiangsu, China* **56** G9
Feng Xian *Shaanxi, China* **56** H4
Fengcheng *Jiangxi, China* **59** C10
Fengcheng *Liaoning, China* **57** D13
Fengfeng *China* **56** F8
Fenggang *China* **58** D6
Fenghua *China* **59** C13
Fenghuang *China* **58** D7
Fengkai *China* **59** F8
Fengkang *Taiwan* **59** F13
Fengle *China* **59** B9
Fenglin *Taiwan* **59** F13
Fengning *China* **56** D9
Fengqing *China* **58** E2
Fengqiu *China* **56** G8
Fengrun *China* **57** E10
Fengshan *Guangxi Zhuangzu,
    China* **58** E7
Fengshan *Guangxi Zhuangzu,
    China* **58** E6
Fengshan *Taiwan* **59** F13
Fengshun *China* **59** F11
Fengtai *Anhui, China* **59** A11
Fengtai *Beijing, China* **56** E9
Fengxian *China* **59** B13
Fengxiang *China* **56** G4
Fengxin *China* **59** C10
Fengyang *China* **57** H9
Fengyi *China* **58** E3
Fengyüan *Taiwan* **59** E13
Fengzhen *China* **56** D7
Feno, C. de *France* **21** G12
Fenoarivo *Fianarantsoa,
    Madag.* **89** C8
Fenoarivo *Fianarantsoa,
    Madag.* **89** C8
Fenoarivo Afovoany *Madag.* **89** B8
Fenoarivo Atsinanana
    Madag. **89** B8
Fens, The *U.K.* **14** E7
Fensmark *Denmark* **11** J5
Fenton *U.S.A.* **113** D12
Fenxi *China* **56** F6
Fenyang *China* **56** F6
Fenyi *China* **59** D10
Feodosiya *Ukraine* **33** K8
Ferbane *Ireland* **12** C4
Ferdows *Iran* **71** C8
Fère-Champenoise *France* **19** D10
Fère-en-Tardenois *France* **19** C10
Ferentino *Italy* **41** G10
Feres *Greece* **45** F10
Ferfer *Somali Rep.* **75** F4
Fergana = Farghona
    Uzbekistan **52** E8
Fergus *Canada* **114** C4
Fergus Falls *U.S.A.* **112** B5
Feričanci *Croatia* **28** E2
Ferland *Canada* **104** B2
Ferlach *Austria* **26** E7
Ferlo, Vallée du *Senegal* **82** B2
Ferlo-Nord △ *Senegal* **82** B2
Ferlo-Sud △ *Senegal* **82** B2
Fermanagh □ *U.K.* **12** B4
Fermo *Italy* **41** E10
Fermont *Canada* **105** B6
Fermoselle *Spain* **36** D4
Fermoy *Ireland* **12** D3
Fernán Nuñez *Spain* **37** H6
Fernández *Argentina* **126** B3
Fernandina Beach *U.S.A.* **117** F14
Fernando de Noronha
    Brazil **125** D12
Fernando Póo = Bioko
    Eq. Guin. **83** E6
Ferndale *U.S.A.* **110** B4
Fernie *Canada* **102** D5
Fernlees *Australia* **94** C4
Fernley *U.S.A.* **108** G4

Ferozepore = Firozpur *India* **68** D6
Ferrandina *Italy* **43** B9
Ferrara *Italy* **41** D8
Ferrato, C. *Italy* **42** C2
Ferreira do Alentejo *Portugal* **37** G2
Ferreñafe *Peru* **124** E3
Ferrerías *Spain* **48** B11
Ferret, C. *France* **20** D2
Ferrette *France* **19** E14
Ferriday *U.S.A.* **116** F9
Ferriere *Italy* **40** D6
Ferrières *France* **19** D9
Ferro, Capo *Italy* **42** A2
Ferrol *Spain* **36** B2
Ferron *U.S.A.* **108** G8
Ferrutx, C. *Spain* **48** B10
Fertile *U.S.A.* **112** B5
Fertőszentmiklós *Hungary* **28** C1
Fertotavi △ *Hungary* **28** C1
Fès *Morocco* **78** B5
Fessenden *U.S.A.* **112** B4
Festus *U.S.A.* **112** F8
Feté Bowé *Senegal* **82** C2
Fetești *Romania* **29** F12
Fethiye *Turkey* **47** E11
Fethiye Körfezi *Turkey* **47** E10
Fetlar *U.K.* **13** A8
Feuilles → *Canada* **101** D12
Feurs *France* **21** C8
Fez = Fès *Morocco* **78** B5
Fezzan *Libya* **79** C8
Fiambalá *Argentina* **126** B2
Fianarantsoa *Madag.* **89** C8
Fianarantsoa □ *Madag.* **89** B8
Fiche *Ethiopia* **81** F4
Fichtelgebirge *Germany* **25** E7
Fichtelgebirge → *Germany* **25** E8
Ficksburg *S. Africa* **89** D4
Fidenza *Italy* **40** D7
Fiditi *Nigeria* **83** D5
Field → *Australia* **94** C2
Field I. *Australia* **92** B5
Fieni *Romania* **29** E10
Fier *Albania* **44** F3
Fierzë *Albania* **44** D4
Fife □ *U.K.* **13** E5
Fife △ *U.K.* **13** E5
Fife Ness *U.K.* **13** E6
Fifth Cataract *Sudan* **80** D3
Figari *France* **21** G13
Figeac *France* **20** D6
Figeholm *Sweden* **11** G10
Figline Valdarno *Italy* **41** E8
Figtree *Zimbabwe* **87** G2
Figueira Castelo Rodrigo
    Portugal **36** E4
Figueira da Foz *Portugal* **36** E2
Figueiró dos Vinhos *Portugal* **36** F2
Figueres *Spain* **38** C7
Figuig *Morocco* **78** B5
Fihaonana *Madag.* **89** B8
Fiherenana *Madag.* **89** B8
Fiherenana → *Madag.* **89** C7
Fiji ■ *Pac. Oc.* **91** a
Fik *Ethiopia* **81** F5
Fika *Nigeria* **83** C7
Filabres, Sierra de los *Spain* **37** H8
Filabusi *Zimbabwe* **89** C4
Filadélfia *Italy* **43** D9
Fil'akovo *Slovak Rep.* **27** C12
Filchner Ice Shelf *Antarctica* **5** D1
Filey *U.K.* **14** C7
Filey B. *U.K.* **14** C7
Filfla *Malta* **49** D1
Filiași *Romania* **29** F8
Filiates *Greece* **46** B2
Filiatra *Greece* **46** D3
Filicudi *Italy* **43** D7
Filingué *Niger* **83** C5
Filiourí = Lissos → *Greece* **45** E9
Filipada *Greece* **46** B2
Filipstad *Sweden* **10** E8
Filisur *Switz.* **25** J5
Fillmore *Calif., U.S.A.* **111** L8
Fillmore *Utah, U.S.A.* **108** G7
Filotio *Greece* **47** D7
Filottrano *Italy* **41** E10
Filtu *Ethiopia* **81** F5
Fina △ *Mali* **82** C3
Finale Emília *Italy* **41** D8
Finale Ligure *Italy* **40** D5
Fiñana *Spain* **37** H8
Finch *Canada* **115** A9
Finch Hatton *Australia* **94** K6
Findhorn → *U.K.* **13** D5
Findlay *U.S.A.* **113** E12
Finger L. *Canada* **104** B1
Finger Lakes *U.S.A.* **115** D8
Fíngoè *Mozam.* **87** E3
Finike *Turkey* **47** E12
Finike Körfezi *Turkey* **47** E12
Finiq *Albania* **44** G4
Finistère □ *France* **18** D3
Finisterre = Fisterra *Spain* **36** C1
Finisterre, C. = Fisterra, C.
    Spain **36** C1

Finke *Australia* **94** D1
Finke Gorge △ *Australia* **92** D5
Finland ■ *Europe* **8** E22
Finland, G. of *Europe* **32** C3
Finlay → *Canada* **102** B3
Finley *Australia* **95** F4
Finley *U.S.A.* **112** B5
Finn → *Ireland* **12** B4
Finnerödja *Sweden* **11** F8
Finnigan, Mt. *Australia* **94** B4
Finniss, C. *Australia* **95** E1
Finnmark *Norway* **8** B20
Finnsnes *Norway* **8** B18
Finspång *Sweden* **11** F9
Finsteraarhorn *Switz.* **25** J4
Finsterwalde *Germany* **24** D9
Fiora → *Italy* **41** F8
Fiordland △ *N.Z.* **91** F1
Fiorenzuola d'Arda *Italy* **40** D6
Fīq *Syria* **74** C4
Firat = Furāt, Nahr al →
    Asia **70** D5
Fire Island △ *U.S.A.* **115** F11
Firebag → *Canada* **103** B6
Firebaugh *U.S.A.* **110** J6
Firedrake L. *Canada* **103** A8
Firenze *Italy* **41** E8
Firenze Amerigo
    Vespucci ✈ (FLR) *Italy* **41** E8
Firenze Pisa ✈ (PSA) *Italy* **40** E7
Firenzuola *Italy* **41** D8
Firk, Sha'ib → *Iraq* **70** D5
Firmi *France* **20** D6
Firminy *France* **21** C8
Firozabad *India* **69** F8
Firozpur-Jhirka *India* **68** F7
Firozpur *India* **68** D6
Firūzābād *Iran* **71** D7
Firūzkūh *Iran* **71** C7
Firvale *Canada* **102** C3
Fish → *Namibia* **88** D2
Fish → *S. Africa* **88** E3
Fish River Canyon *Namibia* **88** D2
Fisher B. *Canada* **103** C9
Fishers I. *U.S.A.* **115** E13
Fishguard *U.K.* **15** E3
Fishing L. *Canada* **103** C9
Fishkill *U.S.A.* **115** E11
Fismes *France* **19** C10
Fisterra *Spain* **36** C1
Fisterra, C. *Spain* **36** C1
Fitchburg *Mass., U.S.A.* **115** D13
Fitchburg *Wis., U.S.A.* **112** D9
Fitz Roy *Argentina* **128** F3
Fitz Roy, Cerro *Argentina* **128** F2
Fitzgerald *Canada* **102** B6
Fitzgerald *U.S.A.* **117** F13
Fitzgerald River △ *Australia* **93** F3
Fitzmaurice → *Australia* **92** B5
Fitzroy → *Queens., Australia* **94** C5
Fitzroy → *W. Austral.,
    Australia* **92** C3
Fitzroy Crossing *Australia* **92** C4
Fitzwilliam I. *Canada* **114** A3
Fiuggi *Italy* **41** G10
Fiume = Rijeka *Croatia* **41** C11
Fiumicino, Roma ✈ (FCO)
    Italy **41** G9
Five Points *U.S.A.* **110** J6
Fivizzano *Italy* **40** D7
Fizi *Dem. Rep. of the Congo* **86** C2
Fjällbacka *Sweden* **11** F5
Fjärdhundra *Sweden* **10** E10
Fjellerup *Denmark* **11** H4
Fjerritslev *Denmark* **11** G3
Fjugesta *Sweden* **10** E8
Flåm *Norway* **8** F12
Flambeau → *U.S.A.* **112** C8
Flamborough Hd. *U.K.* **14** C7
Fläming *Germany* **24** C8
Flaming Gorge △ *U.S.A.* **108** F9
Flaming Gorge Res. *U.S.A.* **108** F9
Flamingo, Teluk *Indonesia* **63** F9
Flanders = Flandre *Europe* **19** B9
Flandre *Europe* **19** B9
Flandre-Occidentale =
    West-Vlaanderen □
    Belgium **17** D2
Flandre-Orientale = Oost-
    Vlaanderen □ *Belgium* **17** C3
Flandreau *U.S.A.* **112** C5
Flanigan *U.S.A.* **110** E7
Flannan Is. *U.K.* **13** C1
Flåsjön *Sweden* **8** D16
Flat → *Canada* **102** A3
Flat I. *Mauritius* **85** d
Flathead L. *U.S.A.* **108** C6
Flattery, C. *Australia* **94** A4
Flattery, C. *U.S.A.* **110** B2
Flatwoods *U.S.A.* **113** F12
Fleetwood *U.K.* **14** D4
Fleetwood *U.S.A.* **115** F9
Flekkefjord *Norway* **9** G12
Flemington *U.S.A.* **114** E7

Flen *Sweden* **10** E10
Flensburg *Germany* **24** A5
Flers *France* **18** D6
Flesherton *Canada* **114** B4
Flesko, Tanjung *Indonesia* **63** D6
Fleurance *France* **20** E4
Fleurier *Switz.* **25** J2
Fleurieu Pen. *Australia* **95** F2
Flevoland ☐ *Neths.* **17** B5
Flin Flon *Canada* **103** C8
Flinders → *Australia* **94** B3
Flinders B. *Australia* **93** F2
Flinders Group *Australia* **94** A3
Flinders I. *S. Austral.,*
Australia **95** F1
Flinders I. *Tas., Australia* **95** G4
Flinders Ranges *Australia* **95** E2
Flinders Reefs *Australia* **94** B4
Flint *U.K.* **14** D4
Flint *U.S.A.* **113** D12
Flint → *U.S.A.* **117** F12
Flint I. *Kiribati* **97** J12
Flintshire ☐ *U.K.* **14** D4
Fliseryd *Sweden* **11** G10
Flix *Spain* **38** D5
Flixecourt *France* **19** B9
Fliseryd *Sweden* **11** G10
Floby *Sweden* **11** F7
Floda *Sweden* **11** G6
Flodden *U.K.* **14** B5
Flogny-la-Chapelle *France* **19** E10
Floodwood *U.S.A.* **112** B7
Flora *U.S.A.* **112** F9
Florac *France* **20** D7
Florala *U.S.A.* **117** F11
Florence = Firenze *Italy* **41** E8
Florence *Ala., U.S.A.* **117** D11
Florence *Ariz., U.S.A.* **109** K8
Florence *Colo., U.S.A.* **108** G11
Florence *Oreg., U.S.A.* **108** D1
Florence *S.C., U.S.A.* **117** D15
Florence, L. *Australia* **95** D2
Florencia *Colombia* **124** C3
Florennes *Belgium* **17** D4
Florensac *France* **20** E7
Florenville *Belgium* **17** E5
Flores *Azores* **78** a
Flores *Guatemala* **120** C2
Flores *Indonesia* **63** F6
Flores I. *Canada* **102** D3
Flores Sea *Indonesia* **63** F6
Floreşti *Moldova* **29** C13
Floresville *U.S.A.* **116** G5
Floriano *Brazil* **125** E10
Florianópolis *Brazil* **127** B6
Florida *Cuba* **120** B4
Florida *Uruguay* **127** C4
Florida ☐ *U.S.A.* **117** G14
Florida, Straits of *U.S.A.* **120** B4
Florida B. *U.S.A.* **120** B3
Florida Keys *U.S.A.* **117** J14
Floridia *Italy* **43** E8
Florin *U.S.A.* **110** G5
Florina *Greece* **44** F5
Flórina ☐ *Greece* **44** F5
Florissant *U.S.A.* **112** F8
Florø *Norway* **8** F11
Flower Station *Canada* **115** A8
Flowerpot I. *Canada* **114** A3
Floydada *U.S.A.* **116** E4
Fluk *Indonesia* **63** E7
Flúmen → *Spain* **38** D4
Flumendosa → *Italy* **42** C2
Fluminimaggiore *Italy* **42** C1
Flushing = Vlissingen *Neths.* **17** C3
Fluviá → *Spain* **38** C8
Fly → *Papua N. G.* **90** B7
Flying Fish, C. *Antarctica* **5** D15
Foa *Tonga* **91** c
Foam Lake *Canada* **103** C8
Foča *Bos.-H.* **44** C2
Foça *Turkey* **47** C8
Fochabers *U.K.* **13** D5
Focşani *Romania* **29** E12
Fodécontéa *Guinea* **82** C2
Fogang *China* **59** F9
Fóggia *Italy* **43** A8
Foggo *Nigeria* **83** C6
Foglia → *Italy* **41** E9
Fogo *Canada* **105** C9
Fogo C. *Verde Is.* **78** b
Fogo I. *Canada* **105** C9
Fohnsdorf *Austria* **26** D7
Föhr *Germany* **24** A4
Foia *Portugal* **37** H2
Foix *France* **20** E5
Fojnica *Bos.-H.* **28** G2
Fokida ☐ *Greece* **46** C4
Fokino *Russia* **32** F8
Fokku *Nigeria* **83** C5
Folda *Nord-Trøndelag, Norway* **8** D14
Folda *Nordland, Norway* **8** C16
Földeák *Hungary* **28** D5
Folegandros *Greece* **46** E6
Foley *Botswana* **88** C4
Foley *U.S.A.* **117** F11
Foleyet *Canada* **104** C3
Folgefonna *Norway* **9** F12

Foligno *Italy* **41** F9
Folkestone *U.K.* **15** F9
Folkston *U.S.A.* **117** F13
Follansbee *U.S.A.* **114** F4
Follónica *Italy* **40** F7
Follónica, G. di *Italy* **40** F7
Folsom L. *U.S.A.* **110** G5
Folteşti *Romania* **29** E13
Fomboni *Comoros Is.* **85** a
Fond-du-Lac *U.S.A.* **112** D9
Fond du Lac *U.S.A.* **112** D9
Fond-du-Lac → *Canada* **103** B7
Fonda *U.S.A.* **115** D10
Fondi *Italy* **42** A6
Fonfría *Spain* **36** D4
Fongafale *Tuvalu* **90** B10
Fongen *Norway* **8** E14
Fonni *Italy* **42** B2
Fonsagrada = A
Fonsagrada *Spain* **36** B3
Fonseca, G. de *Cent. Amer.* **120** D2
Font-Romeu-Odeillo-Via
France **20** F5
Fontaine-Française *France* **19** E12
Fontainebleau *France* **19** D9
Fontana *U.S.A.* **111** L9
Fontas → *Canada* **102** B4
Fonte Boa *Brazil* **124** D5
Fontem *Cameroon* **83** D6
Fontenay-le-Comte *France* **20** B3
Fontenelle Res. *U.S.A.* **108** E8
Fontur *Iceland* **8** C6
Fonuafo'ou *Tonga* **91** c
Fonualei *Tonga* **91** c
Fonyód *Hungary* **28** D2
Foochow = Fuzhou *China* **59** D12
Foping *China* **56** H5
Forbach *France* **19** C13
Forbes *Australia* **95** E4
Forbesganj *India* **69** F12
Forcados *Nigeria* **83** D6
Forcados → *Nigeria* **83** D6
Forcalquier *France* **21** E9
Forchheim *Germany* **25** F7
Ford City *Calif., U.S.A.* **111** K7
Ford City *Pa., U.S.A.* **114** F5
Førde *Norway* **8** F11
Fords Bridge *Australia* **95** D4
Fordyce *U.S.A.* **116** E8
Forécariah *Guinea* **82** D2
Forel, Mt. *Greenland* **98** C16
Foremost *Canada* **102** D6
Forest *Canada* **114** C3
Forest *U.S.A.* **117** E10
Forest City *Iowa, U.S.A.* **112** D7
Forest City *N.C., U.S.A.* **117** D14
Forest City *Pa., U.S.A.* **115** E9
Forest Grove *U.S.A.* **110** E3
Forestburg *Canada* **102** C6
Foreste Casentinesi-Monte
Falterona-Campigna △
Italy **41** E8
Foresthill *U.S.A.* **110** F6
Forestier Pen. *Australia* **95** G4
Forestville *Canada* **105** C6
Forestville *Calif., U.S.A.* **110** G4
Forestville *N.Y., U.S.A.* **114** D5
Forêt d'Orient △ *France* **19** D11
Forez, Mts. du *France* **20** C7
Forfar *U.K.* **13** E6
Forillon △ *Canada* **105** C7
Forks *U.S.A.* **110** C2
Forksville *U.S.A.* **115** E8
Forlì *Italy* **41** D9
Forman *U.S.A.* **112** B5
Formby Pt. *U.K.* **14** D4
Formentera *Spain* **48** C7
Formentor, C. de *Spain* **48** B10
Former Yugoslav Republic
of Macedonia =
Macedonia ■ *Europe* **44** E5
Fórmia *Italy* **42** A6
Formígine *Italy* **40** D7
Formosa = Taiwan ■ *Asia* **59** F13
Formosa *Argentina* **126** B4
Formosa *Brazil* **125** G9
Formosa ☐ *Argentina* **126** B4
Formosa, Serra *Brazil* **125** F8
Formosa B. = Ungwana B.
Kenya **86** C5
Fornells *Spain* **48** A11
Fornos de Algodres *Portugal* **36** E3
Fornovo di Taro *Italy* **40** D7
Føroyar ☑ *Atl. Oc.* **8** F9
Forres *U.K.* **13** D5
Forrest *Australia* **93** F4
Forrest, Mt. *Australia* **93** D4
Fors *Sweden* **10** D10
Forsayth *Australia* **94** B3
Forshaga *Sweden* **10** E8
Förslöv *Sweden* **11** H6
Forsmo *Sweden* **10** A11
Forssa *Finland* **32** B2
Forst *Germany* **24** D10
Forster *Australia* **95** E5
Forsvik *Sweden* **11** F8
Forsyth *U.S.A.* **108** C10

Fort Abbas *Pakistan* **68** E5
Fort Albany *Canada* **104** B3
Fort Ann *U.S.A.* **115** C11
Fort Assiniboine *Canada* **102** C6
Fort Augustus *U.K.* **13** D4
Fort Beaufort *S. Africa* **88** E4
Fort Benton *U.S.A.* **108** C8
Fort Bragg *U.S.A.* **108** G2
Fort Bridger *U.S.A.* **108** F8
Fort Chipewyan *Canada* **103** B6
Fort Clatsop △ *U.S.A.* **110** D3
Fort Collins *U.S.A.* **108** F11
Fort-Coulonge *Canada* **104** C4
Fort Covington *U.S.A.* **115** B10
Fort Dauphin = Taolanaro
Madag. **89** D8
Fort Davis *U.S.A.* **116** F3
Fort-de-France *Martinique* **120** c
Fort Defiance *U.S.A.* **109** J9
Fort Dodge *U.S.A.* **112** D6
Fort Edward *U.S.A.* **115** C11
Fort Erie *Canada* **114** D6
Fort Fairfield *U.S.A.* **113** B20
Fort Frances *Canada* **103** D10
Fort Franklin = Déline
Canada **100** C7
Fort Garland *U.S.A.* **109** H11
Fort George = Chisasibi
Canada **104** B4
Fort Good Hope *Canada* **100** C7
Fort Hancock *U.S.A.* **116** F2
Fort Hope *Canada* **104** B2
Fort Irwin *U.S.A.* **111** K10
Fort Kent *U.S.A.* **113** B19
Fort Klamath *U.S.A.* **108** D3
Fort Laramie *U.S.A.* **108** E11
Fort Lauderdale *U.S.A.* **117** H14
Fort Liard *Canada* **102** A4
Fort Liberté *Haiti* **121** C5
Fort Lupton *U.S.A.* **108** F11
Fort MacKay *Canada* **102** B6
Fort Macleod *Canada* **102** D6
Fort McMurray *Canada* **102** B6
Fort McPherson *Canada* **100** C6
Fort Madison *U.S.A.* **112** E8
Fort Meade *U.S.A.* **117** H14
Fort Morgan *U.S.A.* **108** F12
Fort Myers *U.S.A.* **117** H14
Fort Nelson *Canada* **102** B4
Fort Nelson → *Canada* **102** B4
Fort Norman = Tulita
Canada **100** C7
Fort Payne *U.S.A.* **117** D12
Fort Peck *U.S.A.* **108** B10
Fort Peck Dam *U.S.A.* **108** C10
Fort Peck L. *U.S.A.* **108** C10
Fort Pierce *U.S.A.* **117** H14
Fort Pierre *U.S.A.* **112** C3
Fort Plain *U.S.A.* **115** D10
Fort Portal *Uganda* **86** B3
Fort Providence *Canada* **102** A5
Fort Qu'Appelle *Canada* **103** C8
Fort Resolution *Canada* **102** A6
Fort Rixon *Zimbabwe* **87** G2
Fort Ross *U.S.A.* **110** G3
Fort Rupert =
Waskaganish *Canada* **104** B4
Fort St. James *Canada* **102** C4
Fort St. John *Canada* **102** B4
Fort Saskatchewan *Canada* **102** C6
Fort Scott *U.S.A.* **112** G6
Fort Severn *Canada* **104** A2
Fort Shevchenko
Kazakhstan **35** H10
Fort Simpson *Canada* **102** A4
Fort Smith *Canada* **102** B6
Fort Smith *U.S.A.* **116** D7
Fort Stockton *U.S.A.* **116** F3
Fort Sumner *U.S.A.* **109** J11
Fort Thompson *U.S.A.* **112** C4
Fort Union △ *U.S.A.* **109** J11
Fort Valley *U.S.A.* **117** E13
Fort Vermilion *Canada* **102** B5
Fort Walton Beach *U.S.A.* **117** F11
Fort Wayne *U.S.A.* **113** E11
Fort William *U.K.* **13** E3
Fort Worth *U.S.A.* **116** E6
Fort Yates *U.S.A.* **112** B3
Fort Yukon *U.S.A.* **106** a
Fortaleza *Brazil* **125** D11
Forteau *Canada* **105** B8
Fortescue → *Australia* **92** D2
Forth → *U.K.* **13** E5
Forth, Firth of *U.K.* **13** E6
Fortore → *Italy* **41** G12
Fortrose *U.K.* **13** D4
Fortuna *Spain* **39** G3
Fortuna *Calif., U.S.A.* **108** F1
Fortuna *N. Dak., U.S.A.* **112** A2
Fortune *Canada* **105** C8
Fortune B. *Canada* **105** C8
Forūr *Iran* **71** E7
Fos-sur-Mer *France* **21** E8
Fosen *Norway* **8** E14
Foshan *China* **59** F9
Fosnavåg *Norway* **8** E11
Foso *Ghana* **83** D4

Fossano *Italy* **40** D4
Fossil *U.S.A.* **108** D3
Fossil Butte △ *U.S.A.* **108** F8
Fossombrone *Italy* **41** E9
Foster *Canada* **115** A12
Foster → *Canada* **103** B7
Fosters Ra. *Australia* **94** C1
Fostoria *U.S.A.* **113** E12
Fotadrevo *Madag.* **89** C8
Fouesnant *France* **18** E2
Fougères *France* **18** D5
Foul Pt. *Sri Lanka* **66** Q12
Foula *U.K.* **13** A6
Foulness I. *U.K.* **15** F8
Foulpointe *Madag.* **89** B8
Fouman *Cameroon* **83** D7
Foumbot *Cameroon* **83** D7
Foumbouni *Comoros Is.* **85** a
Foundiougne *Senegal* **82** C1
Fountain *U.S.A.* **108** G11
Fountain Hills *U.S.A.* **109** K8
Fountain Springs *U.S.A.* **111** K8
Fourchambault *France* **19** E10
Fouriesburg *S. Africa* **88** D4
Fourmies *France* **19** B11
Fourna *Greece* **46** B3
Fourni *Greece* **47** D8
Fours *France* **19** F10
Fourth Cataract *Sudan* **79** E12
Fouta Djallon *Guinea* **82** C2
Foux, Cap-à- *Haiti* **121** C5
Foveaux Str. *N.Z.* **91** G2
Fowey *U.K.* **15** G3
Fowler *Calif., U.S.A.* **110** J7
Fowler *Colo., U.S.A.* **108** G11
Fowler, Pt. *Australia* **93** F5
Fowlers B. *Australia* **93** F5
Fowman *Iran* **73** D13
Fox → *Canada* **103** B10
Fox Creek *Canada* **102** C5
Fox Lake *Canada* **102** B6
Fox Valley *Canada* **103** C7
Foxboro *U.S.A.* **115** D13
Foxdale *Australia* **94** J6
Foxe Basin *Canada* **101** C12
Foxe Chan. *Canada* **101** C12
Foxe Pen. *Canada* **101** C12
Foxen *Sweden* **10** E5
Foxford *Ireland* **12** C2
Foxton *N.Z.* **91** D5
Foyle, Lough *U.K.* **12** A4
Foynes *Ireland* **12** D2
Foz *Spain* **36** B3
Foz do Cunene *Angola* **88** B1
Foz do Iguaçu *Brazil* **127** B5
Frackville *U.S.A.* **115** F8
Fraga *Spain* **38** D5
Fraile Muerto *Uruguay* **127** C5
Framingham *U.S.A.* **115** D13
Frampol *Poland* **31** H9
Franca *Brazil* **125** H9
Francavilla al Mare *Italy* **41** F11
Francavilla Fontana *Italy* **43** B10
France ■ *Europe* **7** F6
Frances *Australia* **95** F3
Frances → *Canada* **102** A3
Frances L. *Canada* **102** A3
Franceville *Gabon* **84** E2
Franche-Comté ☐ *France* **19** F12
Francis Case, L. *U.S.A.* **112** D4
Francisco Beltrão *Brazil* **127** B5
Francisco Ignacio Madero
Coahuila, Mexico **118** B4
Francisco Ignacio Madero
Durango, Mexico **118** C4
Francisco Ignacio Madero,
Presa *Mexico* **118** B3
Francistown *Botswana* **89** C4
Francofonte *Italy* **43** E7
François *Canada* **105** C8
François L. *Canada* **102** C3
Francois Peron △ *Australia* **93** E1
Francs Pk. *U.S.A.* **108** E9
Franeker *Neths.* **17** A5
Frank Hann △ *Australia* **93** F3
Frankado *Djibouti* **81** E5
Frankenberg *Germany* **24** D4
Frankenhöhe △ *Germany* **25** F6
Frankenwald △ *Germany* **25** E7
Frankenwald △ *Germany* **25** E7
Frankford *Canada* **114** B7
Frankfort *S. Africa* **89** D4
Frankfort *Ind., U.S.A.* **112** E10
Frankfort *Kans., U.S.A.* **112** F5
Frankfort *Ky., U.S.A.* **113** F11
Frankfort *N.Y., U.S.A.* **115** D9
Frankfurt *Brandenburg,*
Germany **24** C10
Frankfurt *Hessen, Germany* **25** E4
Frankfurt ✈ (FRA) *Germany* **25** E4
Fränkische Alb *Germany* **25** F7
Fränkische Rezat →
Germany **25** F7
Fränkische Saale →
Germany **25** E5
Fränkische Schweiz
Germany **25** F7

Fränkische
Schweiz-Veldensteiner
Forst △ *Germany* **25** F7
Frankland → *Australia* **93** G2
Franklin *Ky., U.S.A.* **112** G10
Franklin *La., U.S.A.* **116** G9
Franklin *Mass., U.S.A.* **115** D13
Franklin *N.H., U.S.A.* **115** C13
Franklin *Nebr., U.S.A.* **112** E4
Franklin *Pa., U.S.A.* **114** E5
Franklin *Va., U.S.A.* **113** G15
Franklin *W. Va., U.S.A.* **113** F14
Franklin B. *Canada* **100** C7
Franklin D. Roosevelt L.
U.S.A. **108** B4
Franklin-Gordon Wild
Rivers △ *Australia* **95** G4
Franklin I. *Antarctica* **5** D11
Franklin L. *U.S.A.* **108** F6
Franklin Mts. *Canada* **100** C7
Franklin Str. *Canada* **100** B10
Franklinton *U.S.A.* **117** F9
Franklinville *U.S.A.* **114** D6
Frankston *Australia* **95** F4
Fränö *Sweden* **10** B11
Fransfontein *Namibia* **88** C2
Fränsta *Sweden* **10** B10
Frantsa Iosifa, Zemlya
Russia **52** A6
Franz *Canada* **104** C3
Franz Josef Land = Frantsa
Iosifa, Zemlya *Russia* **52** A6
Franz Josef Strauss ✈
(MUC) *Germany* **25** G7
Franzburg *Germany* **24** A8
Frascati *Italy* **41** G9
Fraser *U.S.A.* **114** D2
Fraser → *B.C., Canada* **110** A3
Fraser → *Nfld. & L., Canada* **105** A7
Fraser, Mt. *Australia* **93** E2
Fraser I. *Australia* **95** D5
Fraser Lake *Canada* **102** C4
Fraserburg *S. Africa* **88** E3
Fraserburgh *U.K.* **13** D6
Fraserdale *Canada* **104** C3
Frashër *Albania* **44** F4
Frasne *France* **19** F13
Frătești *Romania* **29** G10
Frauenfeld *Switz.* **25** H4
Fray Bentos *Uruguay* **126** C4
Fray Jorge △ *Chile* **126** C1
Frechilla *Spain* **36** C6
Frederick *Md., U.S.A.* **113** F15
Frederick *Okla., U.S.A.* **116** D5
Frederick *S. Dak., U.S.A.* **112** C4
Fredericksburg *Pa., U.S.A.* **115** F8
Fredericksburg *Tex., U.S.A.* **116** F5
Fredericksburg *Va., U.S.A.* **113** F15
Fredericktown *Mo., U.S.A.* **112** G8
Fredericktown *Ohio, U.S.A.* **114** F2
Frederico Westphalen
Brazil **127** B5
Fredericton *Canada* **105** C6
Fredericton Junction
Canada **105** C6
Frederikshåb = Paamiut
Greenland **4** C5
Frederikshamn = Hamina
Finland **32** B4
Frederikshavn *Denmark* **11** G4
Frederikssund *Denmark* **11** J6
Frederiksted *U.S. Virgin Is.* **121** C7
Frederiksværk *Denmark* **11** J6
Fredonia *Ariz., U.S.A.* **109** H7
Fredonia *Kans., U.S.A.* **112** G6
Fredonia *N.Y., U.S.A.* **114** D5
Fredriksberg *Sweden* **10** D8
Fredrikstad *Norway* **9** G14
Free State ☐ *S. Africa* **88** D4
Freehold *U.S.A.* **115** F10
Freeland *U.S.A.* **115** E9
Freels, C. *Canada* **105** C9
Freeman *Calif., U.S.A.* **111** K9
Freeman *S. Dak., U.S.A.* **112** D5
Freeport *Bahamas* **120** A4
Freeport *Ill., U.S.A.* **112** D9
Freeport *N.Y., U.S.A.* **115** F11
Freeport *Ohio, U.S.A.* **114** F3
Freeport *Pa., U.S.A.* **114** F5
Freeport *Tex., U.S.A.* **116** G7
Freetown *S. Leone* **82** D2
Frégate, L. de la *Canada* **104** B5
Fregenal de la Sierra *Spain* **37** G4
Fregene *Italy* **41** G9
Fréhel, C. *France* **18** D4
Freiberg *Germany* **24** E9
Freibourg = Fribourg *Switz.* **25** J3
Freiburg *Baden-W., Germany* **25** H3
Freiburg *Niedersachsen,*
Germany **24** B5
Freilassing *Germany* **25** H8
Freire *Chile* **128** D2
Freirina *Chile* **126** B1
Freising *Germany* **25** G7
Freistadt *Austria* **26** C7
Freital *Germany* **24** D9

Fréjus *France* **21** E10
Fremantle *Australia* **93** F2
Fremont *Calif., U.S.A.* **110** H4
Fremont *Mich., U.S.A.* **113** D11
Fremont *Nebr., U.S.A.* **112** E5
Fremont *Ohio, U.S.A.* **113** E12
Fremont → *U.S.A.* **108** G8
French Camp *U.S.A.* **110** H5
French Cays = Plana Cays
Bahamas **121** B5
French Creek → *U.S.A.* **114** E5
French Guiana ☑ *S. Amer.* **125** C8
French Polynesia ☑ *Pac. Oc.* **97** J13
Frenchman → *N. Amer.* **108** B10
Frenchman Cr. → *U.S.A.* **112** E3
Frenštát pod Radhoštěm
Czech Rep. **27** B11
Fresco *Ivory C.* **82** D3
Fresco → *Brazil* **125** E8
Freshfield, C. *Antarctica* **5** C10
Fresnay-sur-Sarthe *France* **18** D7
Fresnillo *Mexico* **118** C4
Fresno *U.S.A.* **110** J7
Fresno Alhandiga *Spain* **36** E5
Fresno Res. *U.S.A.* **108** B9
Freudenstadt *Germany* **25** G4
Frévent *France* **19** B9
Frew → *Australia* **94** C2
Frewsburg *U.S.A.* **114** D5
Freycinet △ *Australia* **95** G4
Freycinet Pen. *Australia* **95** G4
Freyming-Merlebach
France **19** C13
Freyung *Germany* **25** G9
Fria *Guinea* **82** C2
Fria, C. *Namibia* **88** B1
Friant *U.S.A.* **110** J7
Frías *Argentina* **126** B2
Fribourg *Switz.* **25** J3
Fribourg ☐ *Switz.* **25** J3
Fridafors *Sweden* **11** H8
Friday Harbor *U.S.A.* **110** B3
Friedberg *Bayern, Germany* **25** G6
Friedberg *Hessen, Germany* **25** E4
Friedens *U.S.A.* **114** F6
Friedland *Germany* **24** B9
Friedrichshafen *Germany* **25** H5
Friedrichskoog *Germany* **24** A4
Friedrichstadt *Germany* **24** A5
Friendship *U.S.A.* **114** D6
Friesach *Austria* **26** E7
Friesack *Germany* **24** C8
Friesland ☐ *Neths.* **17** A5
Friesoythe *Germany* **24** B3
Frigate *Seychelles* **85** b
Friggesund *Sweden* **10** C10
Frillesås *Sweden* **11** G6
Frinnaryd *Sweden* **11** G8
Frio → *U.S.A.* **116** G5
Frio, C. *Brazil* **122** F7
Friol *Spain* **36** B3
Friona *U.S.A.* **116** D3
Fristad *Sweden* **11** G6
Fritch *U.S.A.* **116** D4
Fritsla *Sweden* **11** G6
Fritzlar *Germany* **24** D5
Friuli-Venézia Giulia ☐ *Italy* **41** B9
Frobisher B. *Canada* **101** C13
Frobisher Bay = Iqaluit
Canada **101** C13
Frobisher L. *Canada* **103** B7
Frohavet *Norway* **8** E13
Frohnleiten *Austria* **26** D8
Frolovo *Russia* **34** F6
Frombork *Poland* **30** D6
Frome *U.K.* **15** F5
Frome → *U.K.* **15** G5
Frome, L. *Australia* **95** E2
Frómista *Spain* **36** C6
Front Range *U.S.A.* **106** C5
Front Royal *U.S.A.* **113** F14
Fronteira *Portugal* **37** F3
Frontera *Canary Is.* **48** G2
Frontera *Mexico* **119** D6
Fronteras *Mexico* **118** A3
Frontignan *France* **20** E7
Frosinone *Italy* **42** A6
Frostburg *U.S.A.* **113** F14
Frostisen *Norway* **8** B17
Frouard *France* **19** D13
Frövi *Sweden* **10** E9
Frøya *Norway* **8** E13
Frumoasa *Romania* **29** D10
Frunze = Bishkek *Kyrgyzstan* **52** E8
Frunzivka *Ukraine* **29** C14
Fruška Gora *Serbia* **28** E4
Fruška Gora *Serbia* **44** A3
Frutal *Brazil* **125** H9
Frutigen *Switz.* **25** J3
Frýdek-Místek *Czech Rep.* **27** B11
Frýdlant *Czech Rep.* **26** A8
Fryeburg *U.S.A.* **115** B14
Fryvaldov = Jeseník
Czech Rep. **27** A10
Fthiotída ☐ *Greece* **46** C4
Fu Jiang → *China* **58** C6
Fu Xian = Wafangdian
China **57** E11

Fu Xian *China* **56** G5
Fu'an *China* **59** D12
Fubian *China* **58** B4
Fucécchio *Italy* **40** E7
Fucheng *China* **56** F9
Fuchou = Fuzhou *China* **59** D12
Fuchū *Japan* **55** G6
Fuchuan *China* **59** E8
Fuchun Jiang → *China* **59** B13
Fuding *China* **59** D13
Fúcino, Piana del *Italy* **41** F10
Fuencaliente *Canary Is.* **48** F2
Fuencaliente *Spain* **37** G6
Fuencaliente, Pta. *Canary Is.* **48** F2
Fuengirola *Spain* **37** J6
Fuenlabrada *Spain* **36** E7
Fuensalida *Spain* **36** E6
Fuente-Álamo *Spain* **39** G3
Fuente-Álamo de Murcia *Spain* **39** H3
Fuente de Cantos *Spain* **37** G4
Fuente del Maestre *Spain* **37** G4
Fuente el Fresno *Spain* **37** F7
Fuente Obejuna *Spain* **37** G5
Fuente Palmera *Spain* **37** H5
Fuentes de Andalucía *Spain* **37** H5
Fuentes de Ebro *Spain* **38** D4
Fuentes de León *Spain* **37** G4
Fuentes de Oñoro *Spain* **36** E4
Fuentesaúco *Spain* **36** D5
Fuerte → *Mexico* **118** B3
Fuerte Olimpo *Paraguay* **126** A4
Fuerteventura *Canary Is.* **48** F6
Fuerteventura ✈ (FUE) *Canary Is.* **48** F6
Fufeng *China* **56** G5
Fuga I. *Phil.* **61** B4
Fugong *China* **58** D2
Fugou *China* **56** G8
Fugu *China* **56** E6
Fuhai *China* **60** B3
Fuḩaymī *Iraq* **73** E10
Fuhlsbüttel, Hamburg ✈ (HAM) *Germany* **24** B5
Fuji *Japan* **55** G9
Fuji-Hakone-Izu △ *Japan* **55** G9
Fuji-San *Japan* **55** G9
Fuji-Yoshida *Japan* **55** G9
Fujian □ *China* **59** E12
Fujinomiya *Japan* **55** G9
Fujisawa *Japan* **55** G9
Fujiyama, Mt. = Fuji-San *Japan* **55** G9
Fukagawa *Japan* **54** C11
Fukien = Fujian □ *China* **59** E12
Fukuchiyama *Japan* **55** G7
Fukue-Shima *Japan* **55** H4
Fukui *Japan* **55** F8
Fukui □ *Japan* **55** G8
Fukuoka *Japan* **55** H5
Fukuoka □ *Japan* **55** H5
Fukushima *Japan* **54** F10
Fukushima □ *Japan* **54** F10
Fukuyama *Japan* **55** G6
Fulacunda *Guinea-Biss.* **82** C1
Fulaga *Fiji* **91** a
Fulda *Germany* **24** E5
Fulda → *Germany* **24** D5
Fulford Harbour *Canada* **110** B3
Fuliang *China* **59** C11
Fullerton *Calif., U.S.A.* **111** M9
Fullerton *Nebr., U.S.A.* **112** E5
Fulongquan *China* **57** B13
Fülöpszállás *Hungary* **28** D4
Fulton *Mo., U.S.A.* **112** F8
Fulton *N.Y., U.S.A.* **115** C8
Fuluálven → *Sweden* **10** C7
Fulufjället *Sweden* **10** C6
Fumay *France* **19** C11
Fumel *France* **20** D4
Fumin *China* **58** E4
Funabashi *Japan* **55** G10
Funafuti = Fongafale *Tuvalu* **90** B10
Funäsdalen *Sweden* **10** B6
Funchal *Madeira* **48** D3
Funchal ✈ (FNC) *Madeira* **48** D3
Fundación *Colombia* **124** A4
Fundão *Portugal* **36** E3
Fundu Moldovei *Romania* **29** C10
Fundulea *Romania* **29** F11
Fundy, B. of *Canada* **105** D6
Fundy △ *Canada* **105** C6
Funhalouro *Mozam.* **89** C5
Funing *Hebei, China* **57** E10
Funing *Jiangsu, China* **57** H10
Funing *Yunnan, China* **58** F5
Funsi *Ghana* **82** C4
Funtua *Nigeria* **83** C6
Fuping *Hebei, China* **56** E8
Fuping *Shaanxi, China* **56** G5
Fuqing *China* **59** E12
Fuquan *China* **58** D6
Furano *Japan* **54** C11
Furāt, Nahr al → *Asia* **70** D5
Fūrg *Iran* **71** D7

Furmanov *Russia* **34** B5
Furmanovo *Kazakhstan* **34** F9
Furnás *Spain* **48** B8
Furnas, Reprêsa de *Brazil* **127** A6
Furneaux Group *Australia* **95** G4
Furqlus *Syria* **74** A6
Fürstenau *Germany* **24** C3
Fürstenberg *Germany* **24** B9
Fürstenfeld *Austria* **26** D9
Fürstenfeldbruck *Germany* **25** G7
Fürstenwalde *Germany* **24** C10
Fürth *Germany* **25** F6
Fürth im Wald *Germany* **25** F8
Furtwangen *Germany* **25** G4
Furudal *Sweden* **10** C9
Furukawa *Japan* **54** E10
Furulund *Sweden* **11** J7
Fury and Hecla Str. *Canada* **101** C11
Fusagasuga *Colombia* **124** C4
Fuscaldo *Italy* **43** C9
Fushan *Shandong, China* **57** F11
Fushan *Shanxi, China* **56** G6
Fushë Arrëz *Albania* **44** D4
Fushë Krujë *Albania* **44** E3
Fushun *Liaoning, China* **57** D12
Fushun *Sichuan, China* **58** C5
Fusong *China* **57** C14
Füssen *Germany* **25** H6
Fustic *Barbados* **121** g
Fusui *China* **58** F6
Futog *Serbia* **28** E4
Fuwa *Egypt* **80** H7
Fuxian Hu *China* **58** E4
Fuxin *China* **57** C11
Fuyang *Anhui, China* **56** H8
Fuyang *Zhejiang, China* **59** B12
Fuyang He → *China* **56** E9
Fuying Dao *China* **59** D13
Fuyu *China* **57** B13
Fuyuan *China* **58** E5
Füzesgyarmat *Hungary* **28** C6
Fuzhou *China* **59** D12
Fylde *U.K.* **14** D5
Fyn *Denmark* **11** J4
Fyne, L. *U.K.* **13** F3
Fynshav *Denmark* **11** K3

G

Ga *Ghana* **82** D4
Gaanda *Nigeria* **83** C7
Gabarin *Nigeria* **83** C7
Gabas → *France* **20** E3
Gabela *Angola* **84** G2
Gabès *Tunisia* **79** B8
Gabès, G. de *Tunisia* **79** B8
Gabgaba, W. → *Egypt* **80** C3
Gabin *Poland* **31** F6
Gabon ■ *Africa* **84** E2
Gaborone *Botswana* **88** C4
Gabriels *U.S.A.* **115** B10
Gäbrīk *Iran* **71** E8
Gabrovo *Bulgaria* **45** D9
Gacé *France* **18** D7
Gäch Sär *Iran* **71** B6
Gachsārān *Iran* **71** D6
Gacko *Bos.-H.* **44** C2
Gadag *India* **66** M9
Gadamai *Sudan* **81** D4
Gadap *Pakistan* **68** G2
Gadarwara *India* **69** H8
Gadebusch *Germany* **24** B7
Gadein *Sudan* **81** F2
Gadhada *India* **68** J4
Gádor, Sierra de *Spain* **37** J8
Gadra *Pakistan* **68** G4
Gadsden *U.S.A.* **117** D11
Gadwal *India* **66** L10
Gadyach = Hadyach *Ukraine* **33** G8
Găeşti *Romania* **29** F10
Gaeta *Italy* **42** A6
Gaeta, G. di *Italy* **42** A6
Gaffney *U.S.A.* **117** D14
Gafsa *Tunisia* **78** B7
Gagaraula *Nigeria* **83** C6
Gagaria *India* **68** G4
Gagarin *Russia* **32** E8
Găgăuzia □ *Moldova* **29** D13
Gaggenau *Germany* **25** G4
Gaghamni *Sudan* **81** E2
Gagino *Russia* **34** C7
Gagliano del Capo *Italy* **43** C11
Gagnef *Sweden* **10** D9
Gagnoa *Ivory C.* **82** D3
Gagnon *Canada* **105** A6
Gagnon, L. *Canada* **103** A6
Gagra *Georgia* **35** J5
Gahini *Rwanda* **86** C3
Gahmar *India* **69** G10
Gai Xian = Gaizhou *China* **57** D12
Gaïdouronisi *Greece* **49** E7
Gail → *Austria* **26** E6
Gaillac *France* **20** E5
Gaillimh = Galway *Ireland* **12** C2
Gaillon *France* **18** C8

Gaines *U.S.A.* **114** E7
Gainesville *Fla., U.S.A.* **117** G13
Gainesville *Ga., U.S.A.* **117** D13
Gainesville *Mo., U.S.A.* **112** G7
Gainesville *Tex., U.S.A.* **116** E6
Gainsborough *U.K.* **14** D7
Gairdner, L. *Australia* **95** E2
Gairloch *U.K.* **13** D3
Gairloch, L. *U.K.* **13** D3
Gaizhou *China* **57** D12
Gaj *Croatia* **28** E2
Gaj → *Pakistan* **68** F2
Gakuch *Pakistan* **69** A5
Galâla, Gebel el *Egypt* **80** J8
Galán, Cerro *Argentina* **126** B2
Galana → *Kenya* **86** C5
Galanta *Slovak Rep.* **27** C10
Galapagar *Spain* **36** E7
Galápagos = Colón, Arch. de *Ecuador* **122** D1
Galapagos Fracture Zone *Pac. Oc.* **97** G17
Galapagos Rise *Pac. Oc.* **97** J18
Galashiels *U.K.* **13** F6
Galatas *Greece* **46** D5
Galați *Romania* **29** E13
Galați □ *Romania* **29** E12
Galatia *Turkey* **72** C5
Galatina *Italy* **43** B11
Galátone *Italy* **43** B11
Galax *U.S.A.* **113** G13
Galaxidi *Greece* **46** C4
Galcaio *Somali Rep.* **75** F4
Galdhøpiggen *Norway* **8** F13
Galeana *Chihuahua, Mexico* **118** A3
Galeana *Nuevo León, Mexico* **118** A3
Galegu *Sudan* **81** E4
Galela *Indonesia* **63** D7
Galena *U.S.A.* **106** a
Galeota Pt. *Trin. & Tob.* **125** K16
Galera *Spain* **39** H2
Galera Pt. *Trin. & Tob.* **121** D7
Galesburg *U.S.A.* **112** E8
Galestan △ *Iran* **71** B8
Galeton *U.S.A.* **114** E7
Galga *Ethiopia* **81** F4
Gali *Georgia* **35** J5
Galicea Mare *Romania* **29** F8
Galich *Russia* **34** A6
Galiche *Bulgaria* **44** C7
Galicia □ *Spain* **36** C3
Galičica △ *Macedonia* **44** E4
Galilee = Hagalil *Israel* **74** C4
Galilee, L. *Australia* **94** C4
Galilee, Sea of = Yam Kinneret *Israel* **74** C4
Galim *Cameroon* **83** D7
Galina Pt. *Jamaica* **120** a
Galinoporni *Cyprus* **49** D13
Galion *U.S.A.* **114** F2
Galiuro Mts. *U.S.A.* **109** K8
Galiwinku *Australia* **94** A2
Gallâbât *Sudan* **81** E4
Gallan Hd. *U.K.* **13** C1
Gallarate *Italy* **40** C5
Gallatin *U.S.A.* **117** C11
Galle *Sri Lanka* **66** R12
Gállego → *Spain* **38** D4
Gallegos → *Argentina* **128** G3
Galletti *Ethiopia* **81** F5
Galley Hd. *Ireland* **12** E3
Galliate *Italy* **40** C5
Gallinas, Pta. *Colombia* **124** A4
Gallipoli = Gelibolu *Turkey* **45** F10
Gallipoli *Italy* **43** B10
Gallipolis *U.S.A.* **113** F12
Gällivare *Sweden* **8** C19
Gallneukirchen *Austria* **26** C7
Gällö *Sweden* **10** B9
Gallo, L. *Egypt* **42** D6
Gallocanta, L. de *Spain* **38** E3
Galloo I. *U.S.A.* **115** C8
Galloway *U.K.* **13** F4
Galloway, Mull of *U.K.* **13** G4
Galloway △ *U.K.* **13** F4
Gallup *U.S.A.* **109** J9
Gallur *Spain* **38** D3
Galoya *Sri Lanka* **66** Q12
Galt *U.S.A.* **110** G5
Galten *Denmark* **11** H3
Galtür *Austria* **26** E3
Galty Mts. *Ireland* **12** D3
Galtymore *Ireland* **12** D3
Galva *U.S.A.* **112** E8
Galve de Sorbe *Spain* **38** D1
Gálvez *Argentina* **126** C3
Galveston *U.S.A.* **116** G7
Galveston B. *U.S.A.* **116** G7
Galway *Ireland* **12** C2
Galway □ *Ireland* **12** C2
Galway B. *Ireland* **12** C2
Gam → *Vietnam* **64** B5
Gamagōri *Japan* **55** G8
Gamari, L. *Ethiopia* **81** E5
Gamawa *Nigeria* **83** C7
Gamay *Phil.* **61** E6
Gambaga *Ghana* **83** C4

Gambat *Pakistan* **68** F3
Gambela *Ethiopia* **81** F3
Gambela △ *Ethiopia* **81** F3
Gambela Hizboch □ *Ethiopia* **81** F3
Gambhir → *India* **68** F6
Gambia ■ *W. Afr.* **82** C1
Gambia → *W. Afr.* **82** C1
Gambier *U.S.A.* **114** F2
Gambier, C. *Australia* **92** B5
Gambier, Îs. *French Polynesia* **97** K14
Gambier Is. *Australia* **95** F2
Gambo *Canada* **105** C9
Gamboli *Pakistan* **68** E3
Gamboma *Congo* **84** E3
Gamka → *S. Africa* **88** E3
Gamkab → *Namibia* **88** D2
Gamla Uppsala *Sweden* **10** E11
Gamlakarleby = Kokkola *Finland* **8** E20
Gamleby *Sweden* **11** G10
Gammon → *Canada* **103** C9
Gammon Ranges △ *Australia* **95** E2
Gamo-Gofa *Ethiopia* **81** F4
Gamou *Niger* **83** C6
Gamtoos → *S. Africa* **88** E4
Gan *France* **20** E3
Gan Goriama, Mts. *Cameroon* **83** D7
Gan Jiang → *China* **59** C11
Ganado *U.S.A.* **109** J9
Gananita *Sudan* **80** D3
Gananoque *Canada* **115** B8
Ganāveh *Iran* **71** D6
Gäncä *Azerbaijan* **35** K8
Gancheng *China* **64** C7
Ganda *Angola* **85** G2
Gandajika *Dem. Rep. of the Congo* **84** F4
Gandak → *India* **69** G11
Gandava *Pakistan* **68** E2
Gander *Canada* **105** C9
Gander L. *Canada* **105** C9
Ganderkesee *Germany* **24** B4
Ganderowe Falls *Zimbabwe* **87** F2
Gandesa *Spain* **38** D5
Gandhi Sagar *India* **68** G6
Gandhinagar *India* **68** H5
Gandi *Nigeria* **83** C6
Gandía *Spain* **39** G4
Gandino *Italy* **40** C6
Gando, Pta. *Canary Is.* **48** G4
Gandole *Nigeria* **83** D7
Gâneb *Mauritania* **82** B2
Ganedidalem = Gani *Indonesia* **63** E7
Ganetti *Sudan* **80** D3
Ganga → *India* **69** H14
Ganga Sagar *India* **69** J13
Gangan → *India* **69** E8
Ganganagar *India* **68** E5
Gangapur *India* **68** F7
Gangara *Niger* **83** C6
Gangaw *Burma* **67** H19
Gangdisê Shan *China* **69** D9
Ganges = Ganga → *India* **69** H14
Ganges *Canada* **102** D4
Ganges *France* **20** E7
Ganges, Mouths of the *India* **69** J14
Ganggyeong *S. Korea* **57** F14
Gånghester *Sweden* **11** G7
Ganghwa *S. Korea* **57** F14
Gangi *Italy* **43** E7
Gângiova *Romania* **29** G8
Gangneung *S. Korea* **57** F15
Gangoh *India* **68** E7
Gangotri *India* **69** D8
Gangotri △ *India* **69** D8
Gangseong *S. Korea* **57** E15
Gangtok *India* **67** F16
Gangu *China* **56** G3
Gangyao *China* **57** B14
Gani *Indonesia* **63** E7
Ganj *India* **69** F8
Ganluc *China* **58** C4
Ganquan *China* **56** F5
Ganshui *China* **58** C6
Gansu □ *China* **56** G3
Ganta *Liberia* **82** D3
Gantheaume, C. *Australia* **95** F2
Gantheaume B. *Australia* **93** E1
Gantsevichi = Hantsavichy *Belarus* **23** B14
Ganye *Nigeria* **83** D7
Ganyem = Genyem *Indonesia* **63** E10
Ganyu *China* **57** G10
Ganyushkino *Kazakhstan* **35** G9
Ganzhou *China* **59** E10
Gao *Mali* **83** B4
Gao Xian *China* **58** C5
Gao'an *China* **59** C10

Gaochun *China* **59** B12
Gaohe *China* **59** F9
Gaohebu *China* **59** B11
Gaokeng *China* **59** D9
Gaolan Dao *China* **59** G9
Gaoligong Shan *China* **58** E2
Gaomi *China* **57** F10
Gaoping *China* **56** G7
Gaotang *China* **56** F9
Gaotou *China* **59** A12
Gaoyang *China* **56** E8
Gaoyao *China* **59** F9
Gaoyou *China* **57** H10
Gaoyou Hu *China* **57** H10
Gaoyuan *China* **57** F9
Gaozhou *China* **59** G8
Gap *France* **21** D10
Gapan *Phil.* **61** D4
Gapat → *Namibia* **88** D2
Gapuwiyak *Australia* **94** A2
Gar *China* **60** C2
Garabogazköl Aylagy *Turkmenistan* **52** E6
Garachico *Canary Is.* **48** F3
Garachiné *Panama* **120** E4
Garafia *Canary Is.* **48** F2
Garagum *Turkmenistan* **71** B8
Garah *Australia* **95** D4
Garajonay *Canary Is.* **48** F2
Garamba △ *Dem. Rep. of the Congo* **86** B2
Garango *Burkina Faso* **83** C4
Garanhuns *Brazil* **125** E11
Garautha *India* **69** G8
Garawe *Liberia* **82** E3
Garba Tula *Kenya* **86** B4
Garberville *U.S.A.* **108** F2
Garbiyang *India* **69** D9
Garbsen *Germany* **24** C5
Gard □ *France* **21** D8
Gard → *France* **21** E8
Garda, L. di *Italy* **40** C7
Gardanne *France* **21** E9
Garde L. *Canada* **103** A7
Gardelegen *Germany* **24** C7
Garden City *Ga., U.S.A.* **117** E14
Garden City *Kans., U.S.A.* **112** G3
Garden City *Tex., U.S.A.* **116** F4
Garden Grove *U.S.A.* **111** M9
Gardez *Afghan.* **68** C3
Gardiki *Greece* **46** C3
Gardiner *Maine, U.S.A.* **113** C19
Gardiner *Mont., U.S.A.* **108** D8
Gardiners I. *U.S.A.* **115** E12
Gardner *U.S.A.* **115** D13
Gardner Canal *Canada* **102** C3
Gardnerville *U.S.A.* **110** G7
Gardno, Jezioro *Poland* **30** D4
Gardo *Somali Rep.* **75** F4
Gardone Val Trómpia *Italy* **40** C7
Gárdony *Hungary* **28** C3
Garešnica *Croatia* **41** C13
Garéssio *Italy* **40** D5
Garey *U.S.A.* **111** L6
Garfield *U.S.A.* **108** C5
Garforth *U.K.* **14** D6
Gargaliani *Greece* **46** D3
Gargan, Mt. *France* **20** C5
Gargano △ *Italy* **41** G12
Gargantua, C. *Canada* **113** B11
Gargett *Australia* **94** K6
Gargouna *Mali* **83** B5
Gargždai *Lithuania* **30** C8
Garibaldi △ *Canada* **102** D4
Gariep, L. *S. Africa* **88** E4
Garies *S. Africa* **88** E2
Garigliano → *Italy* **42** A6
Garissa *Kenya* **86** C4
Garkida *Nigeria* **83** C7
Garko *Nigeria* **83** C6
Garland *Tex., U.S.A.* **116** E6
Garland *Utah, U.S.A.* **108** F7
Garlasco *Italy* **40** C5
Garliava *Lithuania* **30** D10
Garlin *France* **20** E3
Garm *Tajikistan* **52** F8
Garmāb *Iran* **71** C8
Garmisch-Partenkirchen *Germany* **25** H7
Garmsār *Iran* **71** C7
Garner *U.S.A.* **112** D7
Garnett *U.S.A.* **112** F6
Garo Hills *India* **69** G14
Garoe *Somali Rep.* **75** F4
Garonne → *France* **20** C3
Garonne, Canal Latéral à la *France* **20** D4
Garoowe = Garoe *Somali Rep.* **75** F4
Garot *India* **68** G6
Garoua *Cameroon* **83** D7
Garpenberg *Sweden* **10** D10
Garphyttan *Sweden* **10** E8

Garrauli *India* **69** G8
Garrel *Germany* **24** C4
Garrigues *France* **20** E7
Garrison *Mont., U.S.A.* **108** C7
Garrison *N. Dak., U.S.A.* **112** B3
Garrison Res. = Sakakawea, L. *U.S.A.* **112** B3
Garron Pt. *U.K.* **12** A6
Garrovillas *Spain* **37** F4
Garrucha *Spain* **39** H3
Garry → *U.K.* **13** E5
Garry, L. *Canada* **100** C9
Garrygala *Turkmenistan* **71** B8
Garsen *Kenya* **86** C5
Gärsnäs *Sweden* **11** J8
Garson L. *Canada* **103** B6
Garstang *U.K.* **14** D5
Gartempe → *France* **20** B4
Gartz *Germany* **24** B10
Garu *Ghana* **83** C4
Garu *India* **69** H11
Garub *Namibia* **88** D2
Garut *Indonesia* **63** G12
Garvão *Portugal* **37** H2
Garvie Mts. *N.Z.* **91** F2
Garwa = Garoua *Cameroon* **83** D7
Garwa *India* **69** G10
Garwolin *Poland* **31** G8
Gary *U.S.A.* **112** E10
Garz *Germany* **24** A9
Garzê *China* **58** B3
Garzón *Colombia* **124** C3
Gas-San *Japan* **54** E10
Gasan Kuli = Esenguly *Turkmenistan* **52** F6
Gascogne *France* **20** E4
Gascogne, G. de *Europe* **20** E2
Gascony = Gascogne *France* **20** E4
Gascoyne → *Australia* **93** D1
Gascoyne Junction *Australia* **93** E2
Gascueña *Spain* **38** E2
Gash, Wadi → *Ethiopia* **81** D4
Gash Setit □ *Eritrea* **81** D4
Gashagar *Nigeria* **83** C7
Gashaka *Nigeria* **83** D7
Gashaka-Gumti △ *Nigeria* **83** D7
Gasherbrum *Pakistan* **69** B7
Gashua *Nigeria* **83** C7
Gasparillo *Trin. & Tob.* **125** K15
Gaspé *Canada* **105** C7
Gaspé, C. de *Canada* **105** C7
Gaspé Pen. = Gaspésie, Pén. de la *Canada* **105** C6
Gaspésie, Pén. de la *Canada* **105** C6
Gaspésie △ *Canada* **105** C6
Gassan *Burkina Faso* **82** C4
Gassol *Nigeria* **83** D7
Gasteiz = Vitoria-Gasteiz *Spain* **38** C2
Gastonia *U.S.A.* **117** D14
Gastouni *Greece* **46** D3
Gastouri *Greece* **46** B1
Gastre *Argentina* **128** E3
Gästrikland *Sweden* **10** D10
Gata, C. *Cyprus* **49** E12
Gata, C. de *Spain* **39** J2
Gata, Sierra de *Spain* **36** E4
Gataga → *Canada* **102** B3
Gătaia *Romania* **28** E6
Gatchina *Russia* **32** C6
Gatehouse of Fleet *U.K.* **13** G4
Gates *U.S.A.* **114** C7
Gateshead *U.K.* **14** C6
Gatesville *U.S.A.* **116** F6
Gateway △ *U.S.A.* **115** F11
Gaths *Zimbabwe* **87** G3
Gatico *Chile* **126** A1
Gâtinais *France* **19** D9
Gâtine, Hauteurs de *France* **20** B3
Gatineau *Canada* **115** A9
Gatineau → *Canada* **104** C4
Gatineau △ *Canada* **104** C4
Gattaran *Phil.* **61** B4
Gattinara *Italy* **40** C5
Gatton *Australia* **95** D5
Gatun, L. *Panama* **120** E7
Gatwick, London ✈ (LGW) *U.K.* **15** F7
Gatyana *S. Africa* **89** E4
Gau *Fiji* **91** a
Gaucín *Spain* **37** J5
Gauer L. *Canada* **103** B9
Gauhati = Guwahati *India* **67** F17
Gauja → *Latvia* **30** A11
Gaujas △ *Latvia* **9** H21
Gaula → *Norway* **8** E14
Gauri Phanta *India* **69** E9
Gaustatoppen *Norway* **9** G13
Gauteng □ *S. Africa* **89** D4
Gäv Koshī *Iran* **71** D8
Gävakān *Iran* **71** D7
Gavallai → *Liberia* **82** D3
Gavarnie *France* **20** F3
Gaväter *Iran* **71** E9
Gävbandī *Iran* **71** E7
Gavdopoula *Greece* **49** E6
Gavdos *Greece* **49** E6

Gavi *Italy* **40** D5
Gavião *Portugal* **37** F3
Gaviota *U.S.A.* **111** L6
Gāvkhūnī, Baţlāq-e *Iran* **71** C7
Gävle *Sweden* **10** D11
Gävleborgs län □ *Sweden* **10** C10
Gavorrano *Italy* **40** F7
Gavray *France* **18** D5
Gavrilov Yam *Russia* **32** D10
Gavrio *Greece* **46** D6
Gawachab *Namibia* **88** D2
Gawilgarh Hills *India* **66** J10
Gawler *Australia* **95** E2
Gawler Ranges *Australia* **95** E2
Gawu *Nigeria* **83** D6
Gaxun Nur *China* **60** B5
Gaya *India* **69** G11
Gaya *Niger* **83** C5
Gaya *Nigeria* **83** C6
Gayéri *Burkina Faso* **83** C5
Gaylord *U.S.A.* **113** C11
Gayndah *Australia* **95** D5
Gaysin = Haysyn *Ukraine* **29** B14
Gayvoron = Hayvoron
    Ukraine **29** B14
Gaza *Gaza Strip* **74** D3
Gaza □ *Mozam.* **89** C5
Gaza Strip ■ *Asia* **74** D3
Gazanjyk = Bereket
    Turkmenistan **71** B7
Gazaoua *Niger* **83** C6
Gāzbor *Iran* **71** D8
Gazi *Dem. Rep. of the Congo* **86** B1
Gaziantep *Turkey* **72** D7
Gaziantep □ *Turkey* **72** D7
Gazimağosa = Famagusta
    Cyprus **49** D12
Gazipaşa *Turkey* **72** D5
Gbarnga *Liberia* **82** D3
Gbekebo *Nigeria* **83** D5
Gboko *Nigeria* **83** D6
Gbongan *Nigeria* **83** D5
Gcoverega *Botswana* **88** B3
Gcuwa *S. Africa* **89** E4
Gdańsk *Poland* **30** D5
Gdańsk ✈ (GDN) *Poland* **30** D5
Gdańska, Zatoka *Poland* **30** D6
Gdov *Russia* **32** C4
Gdynia *Poland* **30** D5
Geba → *Guinea-Biss.* **82** C1
Gebe *Indonesia* **63** D7
Gebeciler *Turkey* **47** C12
Gebeit Mine *Sudan* **80** C4
Gebel Abyad *Sudan* **80** D2
Gebel Iweibid *Egypt* **80** H8
Gebze *Turkey* **45** F13
Gecha *Ethiopia* **81** F4
Gedaref *Sudan* **81** E4
Gedaref □ *Sudan* **81** E4
Gediz *Turkey* **47** B11
Gediz → *Turkey* **47** C8
Gedo *Ethiopia* **81** F4
Gèdre *France* **20** F4
Gedser *Denmark* **11** K5
Gedung, Pulau *Malaysia* **65** c
Geegully Cr. → *Australia* **92** C3
Geel *Belgium* **17** C4
Geelong *Australia* **95** F3
Geelvink B. =
    Cenderwasih, Teluk
    Indonesia **63** E9
Geelvink Chan. *Australia* **93** E1
Geesthacht *Germany* **24** B6
Geidam *Nigeria* **83** C7
Geikie → *Canada* **103** B8
Geikie Gorge △ *Australia* **92** C4
Geilenkirchen *Germany* **24** E2
Geili *Sudan* **81** D3
Geisingen *Germany* **25** H4
Geislingen *Germany* **25** G5
Geistown *U.S.A.* **114** F6
Geita *Tanzania* **86** C3
Gejiu *China* **58** F4
Gel → *Sudan* **81** F2
Gel, Meydān-e *Iran* **71** D7
Gel River *Sudan* **81** F2
Gela *Italy* **43** E7
Gela, G. di *Italy* **43** F7
Gelahun *Liberia* **82** D2
Gelang Patah *Malaysia* **65** d
Gelderland □ *Neths.* **17** B6
Geldern *Germany* **24** D2
Geldrop *Neths.* **17** C5
Geleen *Neths.* **17** D5
Gelehun *S. Leone* **82** D2
Gelembe *Turkey* **47** B9
Gelemso *Ethiopia* **81** F5
Gelendost *Turkey* **72** C4
Gelendzhik *Russia* **33** K10
Gelib *Somali Rep.* **75** G3
Gelibolu *Turkey* **45** F10
Gelibolu Yarımadası *Turkey* **45** F10
Gelidonya Burnu *Turkey* **72** D4
Gelnhausen *Germany* **25** E5
Gelnica *Slovak Rep.* **27** C13
Gelsenkirchen *Germany* **24** D3

Gelting *Germany* **24** A5
Gelugur *Malaysia* **65** c
Gemas *Malaysia* **65** L4
Gembloux *Belgium* **17** D4
Gembu *Nigeria* **83** D7
Gemena
    Dem. Rep. of the Congo **84** D3
Gemerek *Turkey* **72** C7
Gemla *Sweden* **11** H8
Gemlik *Turkey* **45** F13
Gemlik Körfezi *Turkey* **45** F12
Gemona del Friuli *Italy* **41** B10
Gemsa *Egypt* **80** B3
Gemsbok △ *Botswana* **88** D3
Gemünden *Germany* **25** E5
Genadi *Greece* **49** C9
Genale → *Ethiopia* **81** F4
Genç *Turkey* **73** C9
Gençay *France* **20** B4
Geneina, Gebel *Egypt* **80** B3
Genemuiden *Neths.* **17** B6
General Acha *Argentina* **126** D3
General Alvear *B. Aires,*
    Argentina **126** D4
General Alvear *Mendoza,*
    Argentina **126** D2
General Artigas *Paraguay* **126** B4
General Belgrano *Argentina* **126** D4
General Bernardo
    O'Higgins *Antarctica* **5** C18
General Cabrera *Argentina* **126** C3
General Cepeda *Mexico* **118** B4
General Guido *Argentina* **126** D4
General Juan Madariaga
    Argentina **126** D4
General La Madrid
    Argentina **126** D3
General MacArthur *Phil.* **61** F6
General Martín Miguel de
    Güemes *Argentina* **126** A3
General Paz *Argentina* **126** B4
General Pico *Argentina* **126** D3
General Pinedo *Argentina* **126** B3
General Pinto *Argentina* **126** C3
General Roca *Argentina* **128** D3
General Santos *Phil.* **61** H6
General Toshevo *Bulgaria* **45** C12
General Treviño *Mexico* **119** B5
General Trías *Mexico* **118** B3
General Viamonte
    Argentina **126** D3
General Villegas *Argentina* **126** D3
Genesee *Idaho, U.S.A.* **108** C5
Genesee *Pa., U.S.A.* **114** E7
Genesee → *U.S.A.* **114** C7
Geneseo *Ill., U.S.A.* **112** E8
Geneseo *N.Y., U.S.A.* **114** D7
Geneva = Genève *Switz.* **25** J2
Geneva *Ala., U.S.A.* **117** F12
Geneva *N.Y., U.S.A.* **114** D8
Geneva *Nebr., U.S.A.* **112** E5
Geneva *Ohio, U.S.A.* **114** E4
Geneva, L. = Léman, L.
    Europe **19** F13
Genève *Switz.* **25** J2
Gengenbach *Germany* **25** G4
Gengma *China* **58** F2
Genichesk = Henichesk
    Ukraine **33** J8
Genil → *Spain* **37** H5
Genisea *Greece* **45** E8
Genk *Belgium* **17** D5
Genlis *France* **19** E12
Gennargentu, Mti. del *Italy* **42** B2
Gennes *France* **18** E6
Genoa = Génova *Italy* **40** D5
Genoa *Australia* **95** F4
Genoa *N.Y., U.S.A.* **115** D8
Genoa *Nebr., U.S.A.* **112** E5
Genoa *Nev., U.S.A.* **110** F7
Génova *Italy* **40** D5
Génova ✈ (GOA) *Italy* **40** D5
Génova, G. di *Italy* **40** E6
Genriyetty, Ostrov *Russia* **53** B16
Gent *Belgium* **17** C3
Genteng *Bali, Indonesia* **63** J17
Genteng *Jawa Barat,*
    Indonesia **63** G12
Genthin *Germany* **24** C8
Genyem *Indonesia* **63** E10
Genzano di Lucánia *Italy* **43** B9
Genzano di Roma *Italy* **41** G9
Geoagiu *Romania* **29** E8
Geochang *S. Korea* **57** G14
Geographe B. *Australia* **93** F2
Geographe Chan. *Australia* **93** D1
Geokchay = Göyçay
    Azerbaijan **35** K8
Georga, Zemlya *Russia* **52** A5
George *S. Africa* **88** E3
George → *Canada* **105** A6
George, L. *N.S.W., Australia* **95** F4
George, L. *S. Austral.,*
    Australia **95** F3
George, L. *W. Austral.,*
    Australia **93** F3
George, L. *Uganda* **86** B3
George, L. *Fla., U.S.A.* **117** G14

George, L. *N.Y., U.S.A.* **115** C11
George Gill Ra. *Australia* **92** D5
George Pt. *Australia* **94** J6
George River =
    Kangiqsualujjuaq *Canada*
    101 D13
George Sound *N.Z.* **91** F1
George Town *Australia* **95** G4
George Town *Bahamas* **120** B4
George Town *Cayman Is.* **120** C
George Town *Malaysia* **65** c
George V Land *Antarctica* **5** C10
George VI Sound *Antarctica* **5** D17
George West *U.S.A.* **116** G5
Georgetown =
    Janjanbureh *Gambia* **82** C2
Georgetown *Australia* **94** B3
Georgetown *Ont., Canada* **114** C5
Georgetown *P.E.I., Canada* **105** C7
Georgetown *Guyana* **124** B7
Georgetown *Calif., U.S.A.* **110** G6
Georgetown *Colo., U.S.A.* **108** G11
Georgetown *Ky., U.S.A.* **113** F11
Georgetown *N.Y., U.S.A.* **115** D9
Georgetown *Ohio, U.S.A.* **113** F12
Georgetown *S.C., U.S.A.* **117** E15
Georgetown *Tex., U.S.A.* **116** F6
Georgia □ *U.S.A.* **117** E13
Georgia ■ *Asia* **35** J6
Georgia, Str. of *N. Amer.* **110** A3
Georgia Basin *S. Ocean* **5** B1
Georgian B. *Canada* **114** A4
Georgian Bay Islands △
    Canada **114** B5
Georgina → *Australia* **94** C2
Georgina I. *Canada* **114** B5
Georgioupoli *Greece* **49** D6
Georgiyevsk *Russia* **35** H6
Georgsmarienhütte *Germany* **24** C4
Gera *Germany* **24** E8
Geraardsbergen *Belgium* **17** D3
Geraki *Greece* **46** D4
Geral, Serra *Brazil* **127** B6
Geral de Goiás, Serra *Brazil* **125** F9
Geraldine *U.S.A.* **108** C8
Geraldton *Australia* **93** E1
Geraldton *Canada* **104** C2
Gérardmer *France* **19** D13
Gercüş *Turkey* **73** D9
Gerede *Turkey* **72** B5
Gerês, Sierra do *Portugal* **36** D3
Gereshk *Afghan.* **66** D4
Geretsried *Germany* **25** H7
Gérgal *Spain* **39** H2
Gerik *Malaysia* **65** K3
Gering *U.S.A.* **112** E2
Gerlach *U.S.A.* **108** F4
Gerlachovský štit
    Slovak Rep. **27** B13
German Planina *Macedonia* **44** D6
Germansen Landing *Canada*
    102 B4
Germantown *U.S.A.* **117** D10
Germany ■ *Europe* **24** E6
Germencik *Turkey* **47** D9
Germering *Germany* **25** G7
Germersheim *Germany* **25** F4
Germī *Iran* **73** C13
Germiston *S. Africa* **89** D4
Gernika-Lumo *Spain* **38** B2
Gernsheim *Germany* **25** F4
Gero *Japan* **55** G8
Gerokgak *Indonesia* **63** J17
Gerolzhofen *Germany* **25** F6
Gerona = Girona *Spain* **38** D7
Geropotamos → *Greece* **49** D6
Gerrard *Canada* **102** C5
Gers □ *France* **20** E4
Gers → *France* **20** D4
Gersfeld *Germany* **24** E5
Gersthofen *Germany* **25** G6
Gertak Sanggul *Malaysia* **65** c
Gertak Sanggul, Tanjung
    Malaysia **65** c
Gerung *Indonesia* **63** K19
Gerzat *France* **20** C7
Gerze *Turkey* **72** B6
Geseke *Germany* **24** D4
Geser *Indonesia* **63** E8
Gesso → *Italy* **40** D4
Gestro, Wabi → *Ethiopia* **81** G5
Getafe *Spain* **36** E7
Getinge *Sweden* **11** H6
Gettysburg *Pa., U.S.A.* **113** F15
Gettysburg *S. Dak., U.S.A.* **112** C4
Getxo *Spain* **38** B2
Getz Ice Shelf *Antarctica* **5** D14
Gevaş *Turkey* **73** C10
Gévaudan *France* **20** D7
Gevgelija *Macedonia* **44** E6
Gévora → *Spain* **37** G4
Gewani *Ethiopia* **81** E5
Gex *France* **19** F13
Geyikli *Turkey* **47** B8
Geyser *U.S.A.* **108** C8
Geyserville *U.S.A.* **110** G4
Geyve *Turkey* **72** B4

George, L. *N.Y., U.S.A.* **115** C11
Ghâbat el Arab = Wang
    Kai *Sudan* **81** F2
Ghabeish *Sudan* **81** E2
Ghadāmis *Libya* **79** B8
Ghaggar → *India* **68** E6
Ghaghara → *India* **69** G11
Ghaghat → *Bangla.* **69** G13
Ghagra *India* **69** H11
Ghagra → *India* **69** F9
Ghalla, Wadi el → *Sudan* **81** E2
Ghallamane *Mauritania* **78** D4
Ghana ■ *W. Afr.* **83** D4
Ghansor *India* **69** H9
Ghanzi *Botswana* **88** C3
Gharb Bahr el Ghazâl □
    Sudan **81** F2
Gharb el Istiwa'iya □ *Sudan* **81** G3
Gharb Kordofân □ *Sudan* **81** E2
Gharbîya, Es Sahrâ el □ *Egypt* **80** B2
Ghardaïa *Algeria* **78** B6
Ghârib, G. *Egypt* **80** B3
Gharig *Sudan* **81** E2
Gharyān *Libya* **79** B8
Ghat *Libya* **79** D8
Ghatal *India* **69** H12
Ghatampur *India* **69** F9
Ghats, Eastern *India* **66** N11
Ghats, Western *India* **66** N9
Ghatsila *India* **69** H12
Ghaţţi *Si. Arabia* **70** D3
Ghawdex = Gozo *Malta* **49** C1
Ghazal, Bahr el → *Chad* **79** F9
Ghazâl, Bahr el → *Sudan* **81** F3
Ghaziabad *India* **68** E7
Ghazipur *India* **69** G10
Ghazni *Afghan.* **68** C3
Ghazni □ *Afghan.* **66** C6
Ghedi *Italy* **40** C7
Ghelari *Romania* **28** E7
Ghent = Gent *Belgium* **17** C3
Gheorghe Gheorghiu-
    Dej = Oneşti *Romania* **29** D11
Gheorgheni *Romania* **29** D10
Gherla *Romania* **29** C8
Ghidigeni *Romania* **29** D12
Ghilarza *Italy* **42** B1
Ghimeş-Făget *Romania* **29** D11
Ghīnah, Wādī al →
    Si. Arabia **70** D3
Ghisonaccia *France* **21** F13
Ghisoni *France* **21** F13
Ghizar → *Pakistan* **69** A5
Ghot Ogrein *Egypt* **80** A2
Ghotaru *India* **68** F4
Ghotki *Pakistan* **68** E3
Ghowr □ *Afghan.* **66** C4
Ghudāf, W. al → *Iraq* **73** F10
Ghughri *India* **69** H9
Ghugus *India* **66** K11
Ghulam Mohammad
    Barrage *Pakistan* **68** G3
Ghūrīān *Afghan.* **66** B2
Gia Dinh *Vietnam* **65** G6
Gia Lai = Plei Ku *Vietnam* **64** F7
Gia Nghia *Vietnam* **65** G6
Gia Ngoc *Vietnam* **64** E7
Gia Vuc *Vietnam* **64** E7
Giali *Greece* **47** E9
Gialtra *Greece* **46** C4
Giamama *Somali Rep.* **75** G3
Gianitsa *Greece* **44** F6
Giannutri *Italy* **40** F8
Giant Forest *U.S.A.* **110** J8
Giant Sequoia △ *U.S.A.* **110** K8
Giants Causeway *U.K.* **12** A5
Gianyar *Indonesia* **63** K18
Giarabub = Al Jaghbûb
    Libya **79** C10
Giaros *Greece* **46** D6
Giarre *Italy* **43** E8
Giaveno *Italy* **40** C4
Gibara *Cuba* **120** B4
Gibb River *Australia* **92** C4
Gibbon *U.S.A.* **112** E5
Gibe → *Ethiopia* **81** F4
Gibellina Nuova *Italy* **42** E5
Gibeon *Namibia* **88** D2
Gibraléon *Spain* **37** H4
Gibraltar ☒ *Europe* **37** J5
Gibraltar, Str. of *Medit. S.* **37** K5
Gibraltar Range △ *Australia* **95** D5
Gibson Desert *Australia* **92** D4
Gibsons *Canada* **102** D4
Gibsonville *U.S.A.* **110** F6
Giddings *U.S.A.* **116** F6
Gidole *Ethiopia* **81** F4
Giebnegáisi = Kebnekaise
    Sweden **8** C18
Gien *France* **19** E9
Giengen *Germany* **25** G6
Giessen *Germany* **24** E4
Gifān *Iran* **71** B8
Gifatin, Geziret *Egypt* **80** B3
Gifhorn *Germany* **24** C6
Gift Lake *Canada* **102** B5

Gifu *Japan* **55** G8
Gifu □ *Japan* **55** G8
Gigant *Russia* **35** G5
Giganta, Sa. de la *Mexico* **118** B2
Gigen *Bulgaria* **45** C8
Gigha *U.K.* **13** F3
Gíglio *Italy* **40** F7
Gignac *France* **20** E7
Gigüela → *Spain* **37** F7
Gijón *Spain* **36** B5
Gil I. *Canada* **102** C3
Gila → *U.S.A.* **109** K6
Gila Bend *U.S.A.* **109** K7
Gila Bend Mts. *U.S.A.* **109** K7
Gila Cliff Dwellings △
    U.S.A. **109** K9
Gīlān □ *Iran* **71** B6
Gilău *Romania* **29** D8
Gilbert → *Australia* **94** B3
Gilbert Is. *Kiribati* **90** A10
Gilbert River *Australia* **94** B3
Gilbert Seamounts *Pac. Oc.* **4** D18
Gilead *U.S.A.* **115** B14
Gilford I. *Canada* **102** C3
Gilgandra *Australia* **95** E4
Gilgil *Kenya* **86** C4
Gilgit *India* **69** B6
Gilgit → *Pakistan* **69** B6
Gili △ *Mozam.* **87** F3
Gilimanuk *Indonesia* **63** J17
Giljeva Planina *Europe* **44** C3
Gillam *Canada* **103** B10
Gilleleje *Denmark* **11** H6
Gillen, L. *Australia* **93** E3
Gilles, L. *Australia* **95** E2
Gillette *U.S.A.* **108** D11
Gilliat *Australia* **94** C3
Gillingham *U.K.* **15** F8
Gilmer *U.S.A.* **116** E7
Gilmore, L. *Australia* **93** F3
Gilo → *Ethiopia* **81** F3
Gilort → *Romania* **29** F8
Gilroy *U.S.A.* **110** H5
Gimbi *Ethiopia* **81** F4
Gimcheon *S. Korea* **57** F15
Gimhae *S. Korea* **57** G15
Gimhwa *S. Korea* **57** E14
Gimie, Mt *St. Lucia* **121** f
Gimje *S. Korea* **57** G14
Gimli *Canada* **103** C9
Gimo *Sweden* **10** D12
Gimone → *France* **20** E5
Gimont *France* **20** E4
Gin Gin *Australia* **95** D5
Ginâh *Egypt* **80** B3
Gineifa *Egypt* **80** H9
Gingin *Australia* **93** F2
Gingindlovu *S. Africa* **89** D5
Ginir *Ethiopia* **81** F5
Ginosa *Italy* **43** B9
Ginzo de Limia = Xinzo de
    Limia *Spain* **36** C3
Giofyros → *Greece* **49** D7
Giohar *Somali Rep.* **75** G4
Gióia, G. di *Italy* **43** D8
Gióia del Colle *Italy* **43** B9
Gióia Táuro *Italy* **43** D8
Gioiosa Iónica *Italy* **43** D9
Gioiosa Marea *Italy* **43** D7
Giona, Oros *Greece* **46** C4
Giovi, Passo dei *Italy* **40** D5
Giovinazzo *Italy* **43** A9
Gir △ *India* **68** J4
Gir Hills *India* **68** J4
Girab *India* **68** F4
Girâfi, W. → *Egypt* **74** F3
Giraltovce *Slovak Rep.* **27** B14
Girard *Kans., U.S.A.* **112** G6
Girard *Ohio, U.S.A.* **114** E4
Girard *Pa., U.S.A.* **114** E4
Girdle Ness *U.K.* **13** D6
Giresun *Turkey* **73** B8
Giresun □ *Turkey* **73** B8
Girga *Egypt* **80** B3
Giri → *India* **68** D7
Giridih *India* **69** G12
Girifalco *Italy* **43** D9
Giriftu *Kenya* **86** B5
Girne = Kyrenia *Cyprus* **49** D12
Giro *Nigeria* **83** C5
Giromagny *France* **19** E13
Giron = Kiruna *Sweden* **8** C19
Girona *Spain* **38** D7
Girona □ *Spain* **38** D7
Gironde □ *France* **20** D3
Gironde → *France* **20** C2
Gironella *Spain* **38** C6
Girraween △ *Australia* **95** D5
Giru *Australia* **94** B4
Girvan *U.K.* **13** F4
Gisborne *N.Z.* **91** C7
Gisenyi *Rwanda* **86** C2
Gislaved *Sweden* **11** G7
Gisors *France* **19** C8
Gitega *Burundi* **86** C2

Githio *Greece* **46** E4
Giuba → *Somali Rep.* **75** G3
Giugliano in Campania *Italy* **43** B7
Giulianova *Italy* **41** F10
Giura *Greece* **46** B6
Giurgeni *Romania* **29** F12
Giurgiu *Romania* **29** G10
Giurgiu □ *Romania* **29** F10
Giurgiuleşti *Moldova* **29** E13
Give *Denmark* **11** J3
Givet *France* **19** B11
Givors *France* **21** C8
Givry *France* **19** F11
Giyon *Ethiopia* **81** F4
Giza = El Gîza *Egypt* **80** J7
Giza Pyramids *Egypt* **80** J7
Gizab *Afghan.* **68** C1
Gizhiga *Russia* **53** C17
Gizhiginskaya Guba *Russia* **53** C16
Giżycko *Poland* **30** D8
Gizzeria *Italy* **43** D9
Gjalicë e Lumës, Mal.
    Albania **44** D4
Gjegjan *Albania* **44** E4
Gjirokastër *Albania* **44** F4
Gjoa Haven *Canada* **100** C10
Gjøvik *Norway* **8** F14
Gjuhës, Kep i *Albania* **44** F3
Glace Bay *Canada* **105** C8
Glacier △ *Canada* **102** C5
Glacier △ *U.S.A.* **108** B7
Glacier Bay △ *U.S.A.* **102** B1
Glacier Peak *U.S.A.* **108** B3
Gladewater *U.S.A.* **116** E7
Gladstone *Queens., Australia* **94** C5
Gladstone *S. Austral.,*
    Australia **95** E2
Gladstone *Canada* **103** C9
Gladstone *U.S.A.* **112** C10
Gladwin *U.S.A.* **113** D11
Glafsfjorden *Sweden* **10** E6
Glagah *Indonesia* **63** J17
Głagów Małopolski *Poland* **31** H8
Glâma = Glomma →
    Norway **9** G14
Gláma *Iceland* **8** D2
Glamis *U.S.A.* **111** N11
Glamoč *Bos.-H.* **41** D13
Glamorgan, Vale of □ *U.K.* **15** F4
Glamsbjerg *Denmark* **11** J4
Glarus *Switz.* **25** H5
Glarus □ *Switz.* **25** J5
Glasco *Kans., U.S.A.* **112** F5
Glasco *N.Y., U.S.A.* **115** D11
Glasgow *U.K.* **13** F4
Glasgow *Ky., U.S.A.* **113** G11
Glasgow *Mont., U.S.A.* **108** B10
Glasgow, City of □ *U.K.* **13** F4
Glasgow Int. ✈ (GLA) *U.K.* **13** F4
Glaslyn *Canada* **103** C7
Glastonbury *U.K.* **15** F5
Glastonbury *U.S.A.* **115** E12
Glauchau *Germany* **24** E8
Glava *Sweden* **10** E6
Glavice *Croatia* **41** E13
Glazov *Russia* **34** A11
Gleichen *Canada* **102** C6
Gleisdorf *Austria* **26** D8
Gleiwitz = Gliwice *Poland* **31** H5
Glen *U.S.A.* **115** B13
Glen Affric *U.K.* **13** D3
Glen Canyon *U.S.A.* **109** H8
Glen Canyon △ *U.S.A.* **109** H8
Glen Canyon Dam *U.S.A.* **109** H8
Glen Coe *U.K.* **13** E3
Glen Cove *U.S.A.* **115** F11
Glen Garry *U.K.* **13** D3
Glen Innes *Australia* **95** D5
Glen Lyon *U.S.A.* **115** E8
Glen Mor *U.K.* **13** D4
Glen More △ *U.K.* **13** D5
Glen Moriston *U.K.* **13** D4
Glen Robertson *Canada* **115** A10
Glen Spean *U.K.* **13** E4
Glen Ullin *U.S.A.* **112** B3
Glenallen *U.S.A.* **100** C5
Glénan, Îs. de *France* **18** E3
Glenariff △ *Ireland* **12** A5
Glenarm *Ireland* **12** B6
Glenbeigh *Ireland* **12** D2
Glencoe *Canada* **114** D3
Glencoe *S. Africa* **89** D5
Glencoe *U.S.A.* **112** C6
Glencolumbkille *Ireland* **12** B3
Glendale *Ariz., U.S.A.* **109** K7
Glendale *Calif., U.S.A.* **111** L8
Glendive *U.S.A.* **108** C11
Glendo *U.S.A.* **108** E11
Glenelg → *Australia* **95** F3
Glenfield *U.S.A.* **115** C9
Glengad Hd. *Ireland* **12** A4
Glengarriff *Ireland* **12** E2
Glenmont *U.S.A.* **114** F2
Glenmorgan *Australia* **95** D4
Glenn *U.S.A.* **110** F4
Glennamaddy *Ireland* **12** C3
Glenns Ferry *U.S.A.* **108** E6

Glenorchy *Australia* **95** G4
Glenore *Australia* **94** B3
Glenreagh *Australia* **95** E5
Glenrock *U.S.A.* **108** E11
Glenrothes *U.K.* **13** E5
Glens Falls *U.S.A.* **115** C11
Glenside *U.S.A.* **115** F9
Glenties *Ireland* **12** B3
Glenveagh △ *Ireland* **12** A3
Glenville *U.S.A.* **113** F13
Glenwood *Canada* **105** C9
Glenwood *Ark., U.S.A.* **116** D8
Glenwood *Iowa, U.S.A.* **112** E6
Glenwood *Minn., U.S.A.* **112** C6
Glenwood *Wash., U.S.A.* **110** D5
Glenwood Springs *U.S.A.* **108** G10
Glettinganes *Iceland* **8** D7
Glifada *Greece* **46** D5
Glimåkra *Sweden* **11** H8
Glin *Ireland* **12** D2
Glina *Croatia* **41** C13
Glinojeck *Poland* **31** F7
Gliwice *Poland* **31** H5
Globe *U.S.A.* **109** K8
Glodeanu Siliştea *Romania* **29** F11
Glodeni *Moldova* **29** C12
Glödnitz *Austria* **26** E7
Gloggnitz *Austria* **26** D8
Głogów *Poland* **31** G3
Głogówek *Poland* **31** H4
Glomma → *Norway* **9** G14
Glorieuses, Îs. *Ind. Oc.* **89** A8
Glosa *Greece* **46** B5
Glossop *U.K.* **14** D6
Gloucester *Australia* **95** E5
Gloucester *U.K.* **15** F5
Gloucester *U.S.A.* **115** D14
Gloucester I. *Australia* **94** J6
Gloucester Island △ *Australia* **94** J6
Gloucester Point *U.S.A.* **113** G15
Gloucestershire □ *U.K.* **15** F5
Gloversville *U.S.A.* **115** C10
Glovertown *Canada* **105** C9
Głowno *Poland* **31** G6
Głubczyce *Poland* **31** H4
Glubokiy *Russia* **35** F5
Glubokoye = Hlybokaye
　Belarus **32** E4
Głuchołazy *Poland* **31** H4
Glücksburg *Germany* **24** A5
Glückstadt *Germany* **24** B5
Glukhov = Hlukhiv *Ukraine* **33** G7
Glusk *Belarus* **23** B15
Głuszyca *Poland* **31** H3
Glyngøre *Denmark* **11** H2
Gmünd *Kärnten, Austria* **26** E6
Gmünd *Niederösterreich,*
　Austria **26** C8
Gmunden *Austria* **26** D6
Gnarp *Sweden* **10** B11
Gnesta *Sweden* **10** E11
Gniew *Poland* **30** E5
Gniewkowo *Poland* **31** F5
Gniezno *Poland* **31** F4
Gnjilane *Serbia* **44** D5
Gnoien *Germany* **24** B8
Gnosjö *Sweden* **11** G7
Gnowangerup *Australia* **93** F2
Go Cong *Vietnam* **65** G6
Gō-no-ura *Japan* **55** H4
Goa *India* **66** M8
Goa □ *India* **66** M8
Goalen Hd. *Australia* **95** F5
Goalpara *India* **67** F17
Goaltor *India* **69** H12
Goalundo Ghat *Bangla.* **69** H13
Goaso *Ghana* **82** D4
Goat Fell *U.K.* **13** F3
Goba *Ethiopia* **81** F4
Goba *Mozam.* **89** D5
Gobabis *Namibia* **88** C2
Göbel *Turkey* **45** F12
Goch *Germany* **24** D2
Gochas *Namibia* **88** C2
Göçbeyli *Turkey* **47** B9
Godavari → *India* **67** L13
Godavari Pt. *India* **67** L13
Godbout *Canada* **105** C6
Godda *India* **69** G12
Godech *Bulgaria* **44** C7
Goderich *Canada* **114** C3
Goderville *France* **18** C7
Godfrey Ra. *Australia* **93** D2
Godhavn = Qeqertarsuaq
　Greenland **4** C5
Godhra *India* **68** H5
Gödöllő *Hungary* **28** C4
Godoy Cruz *Argentina* **126** C2
Gods → *Canada* **104** A1
Gods L. *Canada* **104** B1
Gods River *Canada* **103** C10
Godthåb = Nuuk *Greenland* **99** C14
Goeie Hoop, Kaap die =
　Good Hope, C. of *S. Africa* **88** E2

Goéland, L. au *Canada* **104** C4
Goélands, L. aux *Canada* **105** A7
Goeree *Neths.* **17** C3
Goes *Neths.* **17** C3
Goffstown *U.S.A.* **115** C13
Gogama *Canada* **104** C3
Gogebic, L. *U.S.A.* **112** B10
Goggetti *Ethiopia* **81** F4
Gogolin *Poland* **31** H5
Gogonou *Benin* **83** C5
Gogra = Ghaghara → *India*
　69 G11
Gogrial *Sudan* **81** F2
Gogti *Ethiopia* **81** E5
Gohana *India* **68** E7
Goharganj *India* **68** H7
Goi → *India* **68** H6
Goiânia *Brazil* **125** G9
Goiás *Brazil* **125** G8
Goiás □ *Brazil* **125** F9
Goio-Erê *Brazil* **127** A5
Góis *Portugal* **36** E2
Gojam *Ethiopia* **81** E4
Gojeb, Wabi → *Ethiopia* **81** F4
Gojō *Japan* **55** G7
Gojra *Pakistan* **68** D5
Gökçeada *Turkey* **45** F9
Gökçedağ *Turkey* **47** B10
Gökçen *Turkey* **47** C9
Gökçeören *Turkey* **47** C10
Gökçeyazı *Turkey* **47** B9
Gökırmak → *Turkey* **72** B6
Gökova *Turkey* **47** D10
Gökova Körfezi *Turkey* **47** E9
Göksu → *Turkey* **72** D6
Göksun *Turkey* **72** C7
Gokteik *Burma* **67** H20
Göktepe *Turkey* **47** D10
Gokurt *Pakistan* **68** E2
Gokwe *Zimbabwe* **89** B4
Gola *India* **69** E9
Golakganj *India* **69** F13
Golan Heights = Hagolan
　Syria **74** C4
Gołańcz *Poland* **31** F4
Goläshkerd *Iran* **71** E8
Golaya Pristen = Hola
　Pristan *Ukraine* **33** J7
Gölbaşı *Adiyaman, Turkey* **72** D7
Gölbaşı *Ankara, Turkey* **72** C5
Golchikha *Russia* **4** B12
Golconda *U.S.A.* **108** F5
Gölcük *Kocaeli, Turkey* **45** F13
Gölcük *Niğde, Turkey* **72** C6
Gold *U.S.A.* **114** E7
Gold Beach *U.S.A.* **108** E1
Gold Coast *W. Afr.* **83** E4
Gold Hill *U.S.A.* **108** E2
Gold River *Canada* **102** D3
Gołdap *Poland* **30** D9
Goldberg *Germany* **24** B8
Golden *Canada* **102** C5
Golden B. *N.Z.* **91** D4
Golden Gate *U.S.A.* **109** H2
Golden Gate Highlands △
　S. Africa **89** D4
Golden Hinde *Canada* **102** D3
Golden Lake *Canada* **114** A7
Golden Spike △ *U.S.A.* **108** F7
Golden Vale *Ireland* **12** D3
Goldendale *U.S.A.* **108** D3
Goldfield *U.S.A.* **109** H5
Goldsand L. *Canada* **103** B8
Goldsboro *U.S.A.* **117** D16
Goldsmith *U.S.A.* **116** F3
Goldthwaite *U.S.A.* **116** F5
Golęga *Portugal* **37** F2
Goleniów *Poland* **30** E1
Golestān □ *Iran* **71** B7
Golestānak *Iran* **71** D7
Goleta *U.S.A.* **111** L7
Golfito *Costa Rica* **120** E3
Golfo Aranci *Italy* **42** B1
Golfo di Orosei e del
　Gennargentu △ *Italy* **42** B2
Gölgeli Dağları *Turkey* **47** D10
Gölhisar *Turkey* **47** D11
Goliad *U.S.A.* **116** G6
Golija *Montenegro* **44** C2
Golija *Serbia* **44** C4
Golina *Poland* **31** F5
Gölköy *Turkey* **72** B7
Göllersdorf *Austria* **26** C9
Gölmarmara *Turkey* **47** C9
Golo → *France* **21** F13
Gölova *Turkey* **47** E12
Golpāyegān *Iran* **71** C6
Gölpazarı *Turkey* **72** B4
Golra *Pakistan* **68** C5
Golspie *U.K.* **13** D5
Golub-Dobrzyń *Poland* **31** E6
Golubac *Serbia* **44** B5
Golyam Perelik *Bulgaria* **45** E8
Golyama Kamchiya →
　Bulgaria **45** C11
Goma *Dem. Rep. of the Congo* **86** C2
Gomal Pass *Pakistan* **68** D3

Gomati → *India* **69** G10
Gombari
　Dem. Rep. of the Congo **86** B2
Gombe *Nigeria* **83** C7
Gömbe *Turkey* **47** E11
Gombe □ *Nigeria* **83** C7
Gombe → *Tanzania* **86** C3
Gombi *Nigeria* **83** C7
Gomel = Homyel *Belarus* **23** B16
Gomera *Canary Is.* **48** F2
Gómez Palacio *Mexico* **118** B4
Gomfi *Greece* **46** B3
Gomīshān *Iran* **71** B7
Gommern *Germany* **24** C7
Gomogomo *Indonesia* **63** F8
Gomoh *India* **69** H12
Gomotartsi *Bulgaria* **44** B6
Gompa = Ganta *Liberia* **82** D3
Gonābād *Iran* **71** C8
Gonaïves *Haiti* **121** C5
Gonarezhou △ *Zimbabwe* **87** G3
Gonâve, G. de la *Haiti* **121** C5
Gonâve, Île de la *Haiti* **121** C5
Gonbad-e Kāvūs *Iran* **71** B7
Gönc *Hungary* **28** B6
Gonda *India* **69** F9
Gondal *India* **68** J4
Gondia *India* **66** J12
Gondola *Mozam.* **87** F3
Gonder *Ethiopia* **81** E4
Gondomar *Portugal* **36** D2
Gondrecourt-le-Château
　France **19** D12
Gönen *Balıkesir, Turkey* **45** F11
Gönen *Isparta, Turkey* **47** D12
Gönen → *Turkey* **45** F11
Gong Xian *China* **58** C5
Gong'an *China* **59** B9
Gongcheng *China* **59** E8
Gongguan *China* **58** G7
Gonghe *China* **60** C5
Gongju *S. Korea* **57** F14
Gongola → *Nigeria* **83** D7
Gongolgon *Australia* **95** E4
Gongshan *China* **58** D2
Gongtan *China* **58** C7
Gongzhuling *China* **57** C13
Goni *Greece* **46** B4
Goniadz *Poland* **30** E9
Goniri *Nigeria* **83** C7
Gonjo *China* **58** B2
Gonnesa *Italy* **42** C1
Gonnosfanádiga *Italy* **42** C1
Gonzaga *Phil.* **61** B5
Gonzales *Calif., U.S.A.* **110** J5
Gonzales *Tex., U.S.A.* **116** G6
González *Mexico* **119** C5
González Chaves *Argentina* **126** D3
Good Hope, C. of *S. Africa* **88** E2
Gooderham *Canada* **114** B6
Goodhouse *S. Africa* **88** D2
Gooding *U.S.A.* **108** E6
Goodland *U.S.A.* **112** F3
Goodlands *Mauritius* **85** d
Goodlow *Canada* **102** B4
Goodooga *Australia* **95** D4
Goodsprings *U.S.A.* **111** K11
Goole *U.K.* **14** D7
Goolgowi *Australia* **95** E4
Goomalling *Australia* **93** F2
Goomeri *Australia* **95** D5
Goonda *Mozam.* **87** F3
Goondiwindi *Australia* **95** D5
Goongarrie, L. *Australia* **93** F3
Goongarrie △ *Australia* **93** F3
Goonyella *Australia* **94** C4
Goose → *Canada* **105** B7
Goose Creek *U.S.A.* **117** E14
Goose L. *U.S.A.* **108** F3
Gop *India* **68** H3
Gopalganj *India* **69** F11
Göppingen *Germany* **25** G5
Gor *Spain* **37** H8
Góra *Dolnośląskie, Poland* **31** G3
Góra *Mazowieckie, Poland* **31** F7
Góra Kalwaria *Poland* **31** G8
Gorakhpur *India* **69** F10
Goražde *Bos.-H.* **28** G3
Gorbatov *Russia* **34** B6
Gorbea, Peña *Spain* **38** B2
Gorczański △ *Poland* **31** J7
Gorda, Pta. *Canary Is.* **48** F2
Gorda, Pta. *Nic.* **120** D3
Gordan B. *Australia* **92** B5
Gordon *U.S.A.* **112** D2
Gordon → *Australia* **95** G4
Gordon L. *Alta., Canada* **103** B6
Gordon L. *N.W.T., Canada* **102** A6
Gordonvale *Australia* **94** B4
Goré *Chad* **79** G9
Gore *Ethiopia* **81** F4
Gore *N.Z.* **91** G2
Gore Bay *Canada* **104** C3
Görele *Turkey* **73** B8
Goreme *Turkey* **72** C6

Gorey *Ireland* **12** D5
Gorg *Iran* **71** D8
Gorgān *Iran* **71** B7
Gorgol □ *Mauritania* **82** B2
Gorgona *Italy* **40** E6
Gorgona, I. *Colombia* **124** C3
Gorgora *Ethiopia* **81** E4
Gorgoram *Nigeria* **83** C7
Gorham *U.S.A.* **115** B13
Gori *Georgia* **35** J7
Goriganga → *India* **69** E9
Gorinchem *Neths.* **17** C4
Goris *Armenia* **73** C12
Goritsy *Russia* **32** D9
Gorízia *Italy* **41** C10
Gorj □ *Romania* **29** E8
Gorki = Horki *Belarus* **32** E6
Gorkiy = Nizhniy
　Novgorod *Russia* **34** B7
Gorkovskoye Vdkhr. *Russia* **34** B6
Gorleston *U.K.* **15** E9
Gorlice *Poland* **31** J8
Görlitz *Germany* **24** D10
Gorlovka = Horlivka
　Ukraine **33** H10
Gorman *U.S.A.* **111** L8
Gorna Dzhumayo =
　Blagoevgrad *Bulgaria* **44** D7
Gorna Oryahovitsa
　Bulgaria **45** C9
Gornja Radgona *Slovenia* **41** B13
Gornja Tuzla *Bos.-H.* **28** F3
Gornji Grad *Slovenia* **41** B11
Gornji Milanovac *Serbia* **44** B4
Gornji Vakuf *Bos.-H.* **28** G2
Gorno Ablanovo *Bulgaria* **45** C9
Gorno-Altay □ *Russia* **52** D9
Gorno-Altaysk *Russia* **52** D9
Gornyatskiy *Russia* **35** F5
Gornyy *Saratov, Russia* **34** E9
Gornyy *Sib., Russia* **54** B6
Gorodenka = Horodenka
　Ukraine **29** B10
Gorodets *Russia* **34** B6
Gorodishche =
　Horodyshche *Ukraine* **33** H6
Gorodishche *Russia* **34** D7
Gorodnya = Horodnya
　Ukraine **33** G6
Gorodok = Haradok *Belarus* **32** E6
Gorodok = Horodok
　Ukraine **23** D12
Gorodovikovsk *Russia* **35** G5
Gorokhov = Horokhiv
　Ukraine **23** C13
Gorokhovets *Russia* **34** B6
Gorom Gorom *Burkina Faso* **83** C4
Goromonzi *Zimbabwe* **87** F3
Gorong, Kepulauan
　Indonesia **63** E8
Gorongosa △ *Mozam.* **89** B5
Gorongose → *Mozam.* **89** C5
Gorongoza *Mozam.* **87** F3
Gorongoza, Sa. da *Mozam.* **87** F3
Gorontalo *Indonesia* **63** D6
Gorontalo □ *Indonesia* **63** D6
Goronyo *Nigeria* **83** C6
Górowo Iławeckie *Poland* **30** D7
Gorron *France* **18** D6
Gort *Ireland* **12** C3
Gortis *Greece* **49** D6
Góry Bystrzyckie *Poland* **31** H3
Gorzkowice *Poland* **31** G6
Górzno *Poland* **31** E6
Gorzów Śląski *Poland* **31** G5
Gorzów Wielkopolski *Poland* **31** F2
Gosford *Australia* **95** E5
Goshen *Calif., U.S.A.* **110** J7
Goshen *Ind., U.S.A.* **113** E11
Goshen *N.Y., U.S.A.* **115** E10
Goshogawara *Japan* **54** D10
Goslar *Germany* **24** D6
Gospič *Croatia* **41** D12
Gosport *U.K.* **15** G6
Gossas *Senegal* **82** C1
Gosse → *Australia* **94** B1
Gossi *Mali* **83** B4
Gossinga *Sudan* **81** F2
Gostivar *Macedonia* **44** E4
Gostyń *Poland* **31** G4
Gostynin *Poland* **31** F6
Göta älv → *Sweden* **11** G5
Göta kanal *Sweden* **11** F9
Götene *Sweden* **11** F7
Goteşti *Moldova* **29** D13
Gotha *Germany* **24** E6
Gothenburg = Göteborg
　Sweden **11** G5
Gothenburg *U.S.A.* **112** E4
Gothèye *Niger* **83** C5
Gotland *Sweden* **11** G12
Gotlands län □ *Sweden* **11** G12

Gotō-Rettō *Japan* **55** H4
Gotse Delchev *Bulgaria* **44** E7
Gotska Sandön *Sweden* **9** G18
Gōtsu *Japan* **55** G6
Gott Pk. *Canada* **102** C4
Góttero, Monte *Italy* **40** D6
Göttingen *Germany* **24** D5
Gottwald = Zmiyev *Ukraine* **33** H9
Gottwaldov = Zlín
　Czech Rep. **27** B10
Goubangzi *China* **57** D11
Gouda *Neths.* **17** B4
Goudiry *Senegal* **82** C2
Goudoumaria *Niger* **83** C7
Gouéké *Guinea* **82** D3
Gouin, Rés. *Canada* **104** C5
Gouitafla *Ivory C.* **82** D3
Goulburn *Australia* **95** E4
Goulburn Is. *Australia* **94** A1
Goulia *Ivory C.* **82** D3
Goulimine *Morocco* **78** C3
Goumbou *Mali* **82** B3
Goumenissa *Greece* **44** F6
Goundam *Mali* **82** B4
Goura *Greece* **46** D4
Gourbassi *Mali* **82** C2
Gourdon *France* **20** D5
Gouré *Niger* **83** C7
Gourin *France* **18** D3
Gourits → *S. Africa* **88** E3
Gourma-Rharous *Mali* **83** B4
Gournay-en-Bray *France* **19** C8
Gournes *Greece* **49** D7
Gourock *U.K.* **13** F4
Gourou *U.S.A.* **115** B9
Goursi *Burkina Faso* **82** C4
Gourits *S. Africa* **88** E3
Gouverneur *U.S.A.* **115** B9
Gouvia *Greece* **49** A3
Gouzon *France* **19** F9
Governador Valadares
　Brazil **125** G10
Governor's Harbour
　Bahamas **120** A4
Govindgarh *India* **69** G9
Gowan Ra. *Australia* **94** D4
Gowanda *U.S.A.* **114** D6
Gower *U.K.* **15** F3
Gowna, L. *Ireland* **12** C4
Goya *Argentina* **126** B4
Göyçay *Azerbaijan* **35** K8
Goyder Lagoon *Australia* **95** D2
Goyllarisquisga *Peru* **124** F3
Göynük *Antalya, Turkey* **47** E12
Göynük *Bolu, Turkey* **72** B4
Goz Beïda *Chad* **79** F10
Goz Regeb *Sudan* **81** D4
Gozdnica *Poland* **31** G2
Gozo *Malta* **49** C1
Graaff-Reinet *S. Africa* **88** E3
Grabo *Ivory C.* **82** E3
Grabow *Germany* **24** B7
Grabów nad Prosną *Poland* **31** G5
Gračac *Croatia* **41** D12
Gračanica *Bos.-H.* **28** F3
Graçay *France* **19** E8
Gracias a Dios, C. *Honduras* **120** D3
Graciosa *Azores* **78** a
Graciosa, I. *Canary Is.* **48** E6
Grad Sofiya □ *Bulgaria* **44** D7
Gradac *Montenegro* **44** C3
Gradačac *Bos.-H.* **28** F3
Gradeška Planina *Macedonia* **44** E6
Gradets *Bulgaria* **45** D10
Gradište *Slovenia* **41** B12
Grădiştea de Munte *Romania* **29** E8
Grado *Italy* **41** C10
Grado *Spain* **36** B4
Grady *U.S.A.* **109** J12
Graeca, Lacul *Romania* **29** F11
Grafenau *Germany* **25** G9
Gräfenberg *Germany* **25** F7
Grafham Water *U.K.* **15** E7
Grafton *Australia* **95** D5
Grafton *N. Dak., U.S.A.* **112** A5
Grafton *W. Va., U.S.A.* **113** F13
Graham *Canada* **104** C1
Graham *U.S.A.* **116** E5
Graham, Mt. *U.S.A.* **109** K9
Graham Bell, Ostrov =
　Greem-Bell, Ostrov *Russia* **52** A7
Graham I. *Canada* **102** C2
Graham Land *Antarctica* **5** C17
Grahamstown *S. Africa* **88** E4
Grahamsville *U.S.A.* **115** E10
Grahovo *Montenegro* **44** D2
Graie, Alpi *Europe* **21** C11
Grain Coast *W. Afr.* **82** E3
Grajagan *Indonesia* **63** K17
Grajagan, Teluk *Indonesia* **63** K17
Grajaú *Brazil* **125** E9
Grajaú → *Brazil* **125** D10
Grajewo *Poland* **30** E9
Gramada *Bulgaria* **44** C6
Gramat *France* **20** D5
Grammichele *Italy* **43** E7
Grámmos, Óros *Greece* **44** F4
Grampian *U.S.A.* **114** F6

Grampian Highlands =
　Grampian Mts. *U.K.* **13** E5
Grampian Mts. *U.K.* **13** E5
Grampians, The *Australia* **95** F3
Gramsh *Albania* **44** F4
Gran Canaria *Canary Is.* **48** G4
Gran Chaco *S. Amer.* **126** B3
Gran Desierto del
　Pinacate △ *Mexico* **118** A2
Gran Paradiso *Italy* **40** C4
Gran Sasso d'Itália *Italy* **41** F10
Gran Sasso e Monti Della
　Laga △ *Italy* **41** F10
Granada *Nic.* **120** D2
Granada *Spain* **37** H7
Granada *U.S.A.* **108** G12
Granada □ *Spain* **37** H7
Granadilla de Abona
　Canary Is. **48** F3
Granard *Ireland* **12** C4
Granbury *U.S.A.* **116** E6
Granby *Canada* **115** A12
Granby *U.S.A.* **108** F11
Grand → *Canada* **114** D5
Grand → *Mo., U.S.A.* **112** F7
Grand → *S. Dak., U.S.A.* **112** C3
Grand Bahama I. *Bahamas* **120** A4
Grand Baie *Mauritius* **85** d
Grand Bank *Canada* **105** C8
Grand Bassam *Ivory C.* **82** D4
Grand Béréby *Ivory C.* **82** E3
Grand-Bourg *Guadeloupe* **120** b
Grand Canal = Da
　Yunhe → *China* **57** E9
Grand Canyon *U.S.A.* **109** H7
Grand Canyon △ *U.S.A.* **109** H7
Grand Canyon-
　Parashant △ *U.S.A.* **109** H7
Grand Cayman *Cayman Is.* **120** C3
Grand Centre *Canada* **103** C6
Grand Cess *Liberia* **82** E3
Grand Coulee *U.S.A.* **108** C4
Grand Coulee Dam *U.S.A.* **108** C4
Grand Erg de Bilma *Niger* **79** E8
Grand Falls *Canada* **105** C6
Grand Falls-Windsor
　Canada **105** C8
Grand Forks *Canada* **102** D5
Grand Forks *U.S.A.* **112** B5
Grand Gorge *U.S.A.* **115** D10
Grand Haven *U.S.A.* **112** D10
Grand I. *Mich., U.S.A.* **112** B10
Grand I. *N.Y., U.S.A.* **114** D6
Grand Island *U.S.A.* **112** E4
Grand Isle *La., U.S.A.* **117** G9
Grand Isle *Vt., U.S.A.* **115** B11
Grand Junction *U.S.A.* **108** G9
Grand L. *N.B., Canada* **105** C6
Grand L. *Nfld. & L., Canada* **105** C8
Grand L. *Nfld. & L., Canada* **105** B7
Grand L. *U.S.A.* **116** G8
Grand Lahou *Ivory C.* **82** D3
Grand Lake *U.S.A.* **108** F11
Grand-Lieu, L. de *France* **18** E5
Grand Manan I. *Canada* **105** C6
Grand Marais *Mich., U.S.A.*
　113 B11
Grand Marais *Minn., U.S.A.* **104** C1
Grand-Mère *Canada* **104** C5
Grand Popo *Benin* **83** D5
Grand Portage *U.S.A.* **112** B9
Grand Prairie *U.S.A.* **116** E6
Grand Rapids *Canada* **103** C9
Grand Rapids *Mich., U.S.A.* **113** D11
Grand Rapids *Minn., U.S.A.* **112** B7
Grand St-Bernard, Col du
　Europe **25** K3
Grand Staircase-
　Escalante △ *U.S.A.* **109** H8
Grand Teton *U.S.A.* **108** E8
Grand Teton △ *U.S.A.* **108** E8
Grand Union Canal *U.K.* **15** E7
Grandas de Salime *Spain* **36** B4
Grande → *Jujuy, Argentina* **126** A2
Grande → *Mendoza,*
　Argentina **126** D2
Grande → *Bolivia* **124** G6
Grande → *Bahia, Brazil* **125** F10
Grande → *Minas Gerais,*
　Brazil **125** H8
Grande, B. *Argentina* **128** G3
Grande, Rio → *N. Amer.* **116** J5
Grande Anse *Seychelles* **85** b
Grande Baleine, R. de la →
　Canada **104** A4
Grande Cache *Canada* **102** C5
Grande Casse, Pte. de la
　France **21** C10
Grande Comore *Comoros Is.* **85** a
Grande-Entrée *Canada* **105** C7
Grande Prairie *Canada* **102** B5
Grande-Rivière *Canada* **105** C7
Grande-Terre *Guadeloupe* **120** b
Grande-Vallée *Canada* **105** C6
Grande Vigie, Pte. de la
　Guadeloupe **120** b
Grandfalls *U.S.A.* **116** F3

Grândola *Portugal* 37 G2
Grandpré *France* 19 C11
Grands Causses △ *France* 20 D6
Grands-Jardins △ *Canada* 105 C5
Grandview *Canada* 103 C8
Grandview *U.S.A.* 108 C4
Grandvilliers *France* 19 C8
Graneros *Chile* 126 C1
Grangemouth *U.K.* 13 E5
Granger *U.S.A.* 108 F9
Grängesberg *Sweden* 10 D9
Grangeville *U.S.A.* 108 D5
Granisle *Canada* 102 C3
Granite City *U.S.A.* 112 F8
Granite Falls *U.S.A.* 112 C6
Granite L. *Canada* 105 C8
Granite Mt. *U.S.A.* 111 M10
Granite Pk. *U.S.A.* 108 D9
Graniteville *U.S.A.* 115 B12
Granity *N.Z.* 91 D3
Granja *Brazil* 125 D10
Granja de Moreruela *Spain* 36 D5
Granja de Torrehermosa
    Spain 37 G5
Gränna *Sweden* 11 F8
Granollers *Spain* 38 D7
Gransee *Germany* 24 B9
Grant *U.S.A.* 112 E3
Grant, Mt. *U.S.A.* 108 G4
Grant City *U.S.A.* 112 E6
Grant I. *Australia* 92 B5
Grant Range *U.S.A.* 108 G6
Grantham *U.K.* 14 E7
Grantown-on-Spey *U.K.* 13 D5
Grants *U.S.A.* 109 J10
Grants Pass *U.S.A.* 108 E2
Grantsville *U.S.A.* 108 F7
Granville *France* 18 D5
Granville N. Dak., *U.S.A.* 112 A3
Granville N.Y., *U.S.A.* 115 C11
Granville Ohio, *U.S.A.* 114 F2
Granville L. *Canada* 103 B8
Graskop *S. Africa* 89 C5
Gräsö *Sweden* 10 D12
Grass ➤ *Canada* 103 B9
Grass Range *U.S.A.* 108 C9
Grass River △ *Canada* 103 C8
Grass Valley Calif., *U.S.A.* 110 F6
Grass Valley Oreg., *U.S.A.* 108 D3
Grassano *Italy* 43 B9
Grasse *France* 21 E10
Grassflat *U.S.A.* 114 E6
Grasslands △ *Canada* 103 D7
Grassy *Australia* 95 G3
Gråsten *Denmark* 11 K3
Grästorp *Sweden* 11 F6
Gratkorn *Austria* 26 D8
Graubünden □ *Switz.* 25 J5
Graulhet *France* 20 E5
Graus *Spain* 38 C5
Grave, Pte. de *France* 20 C2
Gravelbourg *Canada* 103 D7
Gravelines *France* 19 A9
's-Gravenhage *Neths.* 17 B4
Gravenhurst *Canada* 114 B5
Gravesend *Australia* 95 D5
Gravesend *U.K.* 15 F8
Gravina in Púglia *Italy* 43 B9
Gravois, Pointe-à- *Haiti* 121 C5
Gravone ➤ *France* 21 G12
Gray *France* 19 E12
Grayling *U.S.A.* 113 C11
Grays *U.K.* 15 F8
Grays Harbor *U.S.A.* 108 C1
Grays L. *U.S.A.* 108 E8
Grays River *U.S.A.* 110 D3
Grayvoron *Russia* 33 G8
Graz *Austria* 26 D8
Grdelica *Serbia* 44 D6
Greasy L. *Canada* 102 A4
Great Abaco I. = Abaco I.
    Bahamas 120 A4
Great Artesian Basin
    Australia 94 C3
Great Australian Bight
    Australia 93 F5
Great Bahama Bank
    Bahamas 120 B4
Great Barrier I. *N.Z.* 91 B5
Great Barrier Reef *Australia* 94 B4
Great Barrier Reef △
    Australia 94 B4
Great Barrington *U.S.A.* 115 D11
Great Basalt Wall △
    Australia 94 B4
Great Basin *U.S.A.* 108 G5
Great Basin △ *U.S.A.* 108 G6
Great Bear ➤ *Canada* 100 C7
Great Bear L. *Canada* 100 C8
Great Belt = Store Bælt
    Denmark 11 J4
Great Bend Kans., *U.S.A.* 112 F4
Great Bend Pa., *U.S.A.* 115 E10
Great Blasket I. *Ireland* 12 D1
Great Camanoe *Br. Virgin Is.* 121 e

Great Codroy *Canada* 105 C8
Great Divide, The = Great
    Dividing Ra. *Australia* 94 C4
Great Divide Basin *U.S.A.* 108 E9
Great Dividing Ra. *Australia* 94 C4
Great Driffield = Driffield
    U.K. 14 C7
Great Exuma I. *Bahamas* 120 B4
Great Falls *U.S.A.* 108 C8
Great Fish = Groot-Vis ➤
    S. Africa 88 E4
Great Guana Cay *Bahamas* 120 B4
Great Harbour Deep *Canada* 105 B8
Great Himalayan △ *India* 68 D7
Great Inagua I. *Bahamas* 121 B5
Great Indian Desert = Thar
    Desert *India* 68 F5
Great Karoo *S. Africa* 88 E3
Great Khingan Mts. = Da
    Hinggan Ling *China* 60 B7
Great Lake *Australia* 95 G4
Great Lakes *N. Amer.* 98 E11
Great Malvern *U.K.* 15 E5
Great Miami ➤ *U.S.A.* 113 F11
Great Ormes Head *U.K.* 14 D4
Great Ouse ➤ *U.K.* 14 E8
Great Palm I. *Australia* 94 B4
Great Pedro Bluff *Jamaica* 120 a
Great Pee Dee ➤ *U.S.A.* 117 E15
Great Plains *N. Amer.* 98 E9
Great Ruaha ➤ *Tanzania* 86 D4
Great Sacandaga L. *U.S.A.* 115 C10
Great Saint Bernard Pass =
    Grand St-Bernard, Col
    du *Europe* 25 K3
Great Salt Desert = Kavīr,
    Dasht-e *Iran* 71 C7
Great Salt L. *U.S.A.* 108 F7
Great Salt Lake Desert
    U.S.A. 108 F7
Great Salt Plains L. *U.S.A.* 116 C5
Great Sand Dunes △ *U.S.A.*
    109 H11
Great Sandy △ *Australia* 95 D5
Great Sandy Desert *Australia* 92 D3
Great Sandy Desert *U.S.A.* 106 B2
Great Sangi = Sangihe,
    Pulau *Indonesia* 63 D7
Great Scarcies ➤ *S. Leone* 82 D2
Great Sea Reef *Fiji* 91 a
Great Skellig *Ireland* 12 E1
Great Slave L. *Canada* 102 A5
Great Smoky Mts. △ *U.S.A.*
    117 D13
Great Snow Mt. *Canada* 102 B4
Great Stour = Stour ➤ *U.K.* 15 F9
Great Victoria Desert
    Australia 93 E4
Great Wall *Antarctica* 5 C18
Great Wall *China* 56 E5
Great Whernside *U.K.* 14 C6
Great Yarmouth *U.K.* 15 E9
Great Zab = Zāb al
    Kabīr ➤ *Iraq* 73 D10
Great Zimbabwe *Zimbabwe* 87 G3
Greater Antilles *W. Indies* 121 D5
Greater London □ *U.K.* 15 F7
Greater Manchester □ *U.K.* 14 D5
Greater St. Lucia
    Wetlands △ *S. Africa* 89 D5
Greater Sudbury =
    Sudbury *Canada* 104 C3
Greater Sunda Is. *Indonesia* 62 F4
Grebbestad *Sweden* 11 F5
Grebenka = Hrebinka
    Ukraine 33 G7
Greco, C. *Cyprus* 49 E13
Greco, Mte. *Italy* 41 G7
Gredos, Sierra de *Spain* 36 E6
Greece *U.S.A.* 114 C7
Greece ■ *Europe* 46 B3
Greeley Colo., *U.S.A.* 108 F11
Greeley Nebr., *U.S.A.* 112 E4
Greely Fd. *Canada* 101 A11
Greem-Bell, Ostrov *Russia* 52 A7
Green ➤ Ky., *U.S.A.* 112 G10
Green ➤ Utah, *U.S.A.* 108 G9
Green B. *U.S.A.* 112 C10
Green Bay *U.S.A.* 112 C9
Green C. *Australia* 95 F5
Green Cove Springs *U.S.A.* 117 G14
Green I. = Lü Tao *Taiwan* 59 F13
Green Lake *Canada* 103 C7
Green Mts. *U.S.A.* 115 C12
Green River Utah, *U.S.A.* 108 G8
Green River Wyo., *U.S.A.* 108 F9
Green Valley *U.S.A.* 109 L8
Greenbank *U.S.A.* 110 B4
Greenbush Mich., *U.S.A.* 114 B1
Greenbush Minn., *U.S.A.* 112 A5
Greencastle *U.S.A.* 112 F10
Greene *U.S.A.* 115 D9
Greeneville *U.S.A.* 117 C13
Greenfield Calif., *U.S.A.* 110 J5
Greenfield Calif., *U.S.A.* 111 K8
Greenfield Ind., *U.S.A.* 113 F11
Greenfield Iowa, *U.S.A.* 112 E6

Greenfield Mass., *U.S.A.* 115 D12
Greenfield Mo., *U.S.A.* 112 G7
Greenfield Park *Canada* 115 A11
Greenland ☑ *N. Amer.* 99 C15
Greenland Sea *Arctic* 4 B7
Greenock *U.K.* 13 F4
Greenore *Ireland* 12 B5
Greenore Pt. *Ireland* 12 D5
Greenough *Australia* 93 E1
Greenough ➤ *Australia* 93 E1
Greenough Pt. *Canada* 114 B3
Greenport *U.S.A.* 115 E12
Greensboro Ga., *U.S.A.* 117 E13
Greensboro N.C., *U.S.A.* 117 C15
Greensboro Vt., *U.S.A.* 115 B12
Greensburg Ind., *U.S.A.* 113 F11
Greensburg Kans., *U.S.A.* 112 G4
Greensburg Pa., *U.S.A.* 114 F5
Greenstone Pt. *U.K.* 13 D3
Greenvale *Australia* 94 B4
Greenville *Liberia* 82 D3
Greenville Ala., *U.S.A.* 117 F11
Greenville Calif., *U.S.A.* 110 E6
Greenville Maine, *U.S.A.* 113 C19
Greenville Mich., *U.S.A.* 113 D11
Greenville Mo., *U.S.A.* 112 G8
Greenville N.C., *U.S.A.* 117 D16
Greenville N.H., *U.S.A.* 115 D13
Greenville N.Y., *U.S.A.* 115 D10
Greenville Ohio, *U.S.A.* 113 E11
Greenville Pa., *U.S.A.* 114 E4
Greenville S.C., *U.S.A.* 117 D13
Greenville Tex., *U.S.A.* 116 E6
Greenwater Lake △ *Canada* 103 C8
Greenwich Conn., *U.S.A.* 115 E11
Greenwich N.Y., *U.S.A.* 115 C11
Greenwich Ohio, *U.S.A.* 114 E2
Greenwich □ *U.K.* 15 F8
Greenwood *Canada* 102 D5
Greenwood Ark., *U.S.A.* 116 D7
Greenwood Ind., *U.S.A.* 112 F10
Greenwood Miss., *U.S.A.* 117 E9
Greenwood S.C., *U.S.A.* 117 D13
Greenwood, Mt. *Australia* 92 B5
Gregbe *Ivory C.* 82 D3
Gregory *U.S.A.* 112 D4
Gregory ➤ *Australia* 94 B2
Gregory, L. S. Austral.,
    Australia 95 D2
Gregory, L. W. Austral.,
    Australia 92 D4
Gregory, L. W. Austral.,
    Australia 93 E2
Gregory △ *Australia* 92 C5
Gregory Downs *Australia* 94 B2
Gregory Ra. Queens.,
    Australia 94 B3
Gregory Ra. W. Austral.,
    Australia 92 D3
Greiffenberg *Germany* 24 B9
Greifswald *Germany* 24 A9
Greifswalder Bodden
    Germany 24 A9
Grein *Austria* 26 C7
Greiz *Germany* 24 E8
Gremikha *Russia* 52 C4
Grenaa *Denmark* 11 H4
Grenada *U.S.A.* 117 E10
Grenada ■ *W. Indies* 121 D7
Grenade *France* 20 E5
Grenadier I. *U.S.A.* 115 B8
Grenadines, The *St. Vincent* 121 D7
Grenchen *Switz.* 25 H3
Grenen *Denmark* 11 G4
Grenfell *Australia* 95 E4
Grenfell *Canada* 103 C8
Grenoble *France* 21 C9
Grenville, C. *Australia* 94 A3
Grenville Chan. *Canada* 102 C3
Gréoux-les-Bains *France* 21 E9
Gresham *U.S.A.* 110 E4
Gresik *Indonesia* 63 G15
Gretna *U.K.* 13 F5
Gretna *U.S.A.* 117 G9
Greve Strand *Denmark* 11 J6
Greven *Germany* 24 C3
Grevena *Greece* 44 F5
Grevená □ *Greece* 44 F5
Grevenbroich *Germany* 24 D2
Grevenmacher *Lux.* 17 E6
Grevesmühlen *Germany* 24 B7
Grey ➤ *Canada* 105 C8
Grey ➤ *N.Z.* 91 E3
Grey, C. *Australia* 94 A2
Grey Ra. *Australia* 95 D3
Greybull *U.S.A.* 108 D9
Greymouth *N.Z.* 91 E3
Greystones *Ireland* 12 C5
Greytown *N.Z.* 91 D5
Greytown *S. Africa* 89 D5
Gribanovsky *Russia* 34 E5
Gribbell I. *Canada* 102 C3
Gridley *U.S.A.* 110 F5
Griekwastad *S. Africa* 88 D3
Griesheim *Germany* 25 F4
Grieskirchen *Austria* 26 C6

Griffin *U.S.A.* 117 E12
Griffith *Australia* 95 E4
Griffith *Canada* 114 A7
Griffith I. *Canada* 114 B4
Grignols *France* 20 D3
Grigoriopol *Moldova* 29 C14
Grimaylov = Hrymayliv
    Ukraine 23 D14
Grimes *U.S.A.* 110 F5
Grimsay *U.K.* 13 D1
Grimsby *Canada* 114 C5
Grimsby *U.K.* 14 D7
Grimsey *Iceland* 8 C5
Grimshaw *Canada* 102 B5
Grimslöv *Sweden* 11 H8
Grimstad *Norway* 9 G13
Grindelwald *Switz.* 25 J4
Grindsted *Denmark* 11 J2
Grindstone I. *Canada* 115 B8
Grindu *Romania* 29 F11
Grinnell *U.S.A.* 112 E7
Grintavec *Slovenia* 41 B11
Gris-Nez, C. *France* 19 B8
Grise Fiord *Canada* 101 B11
Grisolles *France* 20 E5
Grisons = Graubünden □
    Switz. 25 J5
Grisslehamn *Sweden* 10 D12
Grmeč Planina *Bos.-H.* 41 D13
Groais I. *Canada* 105 B8
Grobiņa *Latvia* 30 B8
Groblersdal *S. Africa* 89 D4
Grobming *Austria* 26 D6
Grocka *Serbia* 44 B4
Gródek *Poland* 31 E1
Grodków *Poland* 31 H4
Grodno = Hrodna *Belarus* 30 E10
Grodzisk Mazowiecki *Poland* 31 F7
Grodzisk Wielkopolski
    Poland 31 F3
Grodzyanka =
    Hrodzyanka *Belarus* 23 B15
Groesbeck *U.S.A.* 116 F6
Groix *France* 18 E3
Groix, Î. de *France* 18 E3
Grójec *Poland* 31 G7
Gronau Niedersachsen,
    Germany 24 C4
Gronau Nordrhein-Westfalen,
    Germany 24 C3
Grong *Norway* 8 D15
Grönhögen *Sweden* 11 H10
Groningen *Neths.* 17 A6
Groningen □ *Neths.* 17 A6
Groom *U.S.A.* 116 D4
Groot ➤ *S. Africa* 88 E3
Groot-Berg ➤ *S. Africa* 88 E2
Groot-Brakrivier *S. Africa* 88 E3
Groot Karasberge *Namibia* 88 D2
Groot-Kei ➤ *S. Africa* 89 E4
Groot-Vis ➤ *S. Africa* 88 E4
Grootdrink *S. Africa* 88 D3
Groote Eylandt *Australia* 94 A2
Grootfontein *Namibia* 88 B2
Grootlaagte ➤ *Africa* 88 C3
Grootvloer ➤ *S. Africa* 88 E3
Gros C. *Canada* 102 A6
Gros Islet *St. Lucia* 121 f
Gros Morne △ *Canada* 105 C8
Gros Piton *St. Lucia* 121 f
Gros Piton Pt. *St. Lucia* 121 f
Grosa, Pta. *Spain* 48 B8
Grossenbrode *Germany* 24 A7
Grossenhain *Germany* 24 D9
Grosser Arber *Germany* 25 F9
Grosser Plöner See *Germany* 24 A6
Grosseto *Italy* 41 F8
Grossgerungs *Austria* 26 C7
Grossglockner *Austria* 26 D5
Groswater B. *Canada* 105 B8
Groton Conn., *U.S.A.* 115 E12
Groton N.Y., *U.S.A.* 115 D8
Groton S. Dak., *U.S.A.* 112 C4
Grottáglie *Italy* 43 B10
Grottaminarda *Italy* 43 A8
Grottammare *Italy* 41 F10
Grouard Mission *Canada* 102 B5
Grouin, Pte. du *France* 18 D5
Grouw *Neths.* 17 A5
Grove City *U.S.A.* 114 E4
Grove Hill *U.S.A.* 117 F11
Groveland *U.S.A.* 110 H6
Grover Beach *U.S.A.* 111 K6
Groveton *U.S.A.* 115 B13
Groves *U.S.A.* 116 G8
Groznjan *Croatia* 41 C10
Groznyy *Russia* 35 J7
Grubišno Polje *Croatia* 28 E2
Grudovo *Bulgaria* 45 D11
Grudusk *Poland* 31 E7
Grudziądz *Poland* 30 E5
Gruinard B. *U.K.* 13 D3

Gruissan *France* 20 E7
Grumo Áppula *Italy* 43 A9
Grums *Sweden* 10 E7
Grünberg *Germany* 24 E4
Gründau *Germany* 25 E5
Grundy Center *U.S.A.* 112 D7
Grünstadt *Germany* 25 F4
Gruppo di Tessa △ *Italy* 40 B8
Gruvberget *Sweden* 10 C10
Gruver *U.S.A.* 116 C4
Gruyères *Switz.* 25 J3
Gruža *Serbia* 44 C4
Gryazi *Russia* 33 F10
Gryazovets *Russia* 32 C11
Grybów *Poland* 31 J7
Grycksbo *Sweden* 10 D9
Gryfice *Poland* 30 E2
Gryfino *Poland* 31 E1
Gryfów Śląski *Poland* 31 G2
Grythyttan *Sweden* 10 E8
Gstaad *Switz.* 25 J3
Gua *India* 69 H11
Gua Musang *Malaysia* 65 K3
Guacanayabo, G. de *Cuba* 120 B4
Guachípas ➤ *Argentina* 126 B2
Guadajoz ➤ *Spain* 37 H6
Guadalajara *Mexico* 118 C4
Guadalajara *Spain* 38 E1
Guadalajara □ *Spain* 38 E2
Guadalcanal *Solomon Is.* 90 B9
Guadalcanal *Spain* 37 G5
Guadalén ➤ *Spain* 37 G7
Guadales *Argentina* 126 C2
Guadalete ➤ *Spain* 37 J4
Guadalimar ➤ *Spain* 37 G7
Guadalmena ➤ *Spain* 37 G8
Guadalmez ➤ *Spain* 37 G5
Guadalope ➤ *Spain* 38 D4
Guadalquivir ➤ *Spain* 37 J4
Guadalupe =
    Guadeloupe ☑ *W. Indies* 120 b
Guadalupe *Mexico* 111 N10
Guadalupe Zacatecas, Mexico 118 C4
Guadalupe *Spain* 37 F5
Guadalupe *U.S.A.* 111 L6
Guadalupe ➤ *Mexico* 111 N10
Guadalupe ➤ *U.S.A.* 116 G6
Guadalupe, Sierra de *Spain* 37 F5
Guadalupe Bravos *Mexico* 118 A3
Guadalupe I. *Pac. Oc.* 98 G8
Guadalupe Mts. △ *U.S.A.* 116 F2
Guadalupe Peak *U.S.A.* 116 F2
Guadalupe y Calvo *Mexico* 118 B3
Guadarrama, Sierra de *Spain* 36 E7
Guadauta *Georgia* 35 J5
Guadeloupe ☑ *W. Indies* 120 b
Guadeloupe ➤ *Guadeloupe* 120 b
Guadeloupe Passage
    W. Indies 121 C7
Guadiamar ➤ *Spain* 37 J4
Guadiana ➤ *Portugal* 37 H3
Guadiana Menor ➤ *Spain* 37 H7
Guadiaro ➤ *Spain* 37 J5
Guadiato ➤ *Spain* 37 H5
Guadiela ➤ *Spain* 38 E2
Guadix *Spain* 37 H7
Guafo, Boca del *Chile* 128 E2
Guaico *Trin. & Tob.* 125 K15
Guainía ➤ *Colombia* 124 C5
Guaíra *Brazil* 127 A5
Guaíra □ *Paraguay* 126 B4
Guaitecas, Is. *Chile* 128 E2
Guajará-Mirim *Brazil* 124 F5
Guajira, Pen. de la *Colombia* 124 A4
Gualán *Guatemala* 120 C2
Gualdo Tadino *Italy* 41 E9
Gualeguay *Argentina* 126 C4
Gualeguaychú *Argentina* 126 C4
Gualequay ➤ *Argentina* 126 C4
Guam ☑ *Pac. Oc.* 96 F6
Guaminí *Argentina* 126 D3
Guamúchil *Mexico* 118 B3
Guana I. *Br. Virgin Is.* 121 e
Guanabacoa *Cuba* 120 B3
Guanacaste, Cordillera del
    Costa Rica 120 D2
Guanacaste △ *Costa Rica* 120 D2
Guanaceví *Mexico* 118 B3
Guanahani = San
    Salvador I. *Bahamas* 121 B5
Guanajay *Cuba* 120 B3
Guanajuato *Mexico* 118 C4
Guanajuato □ *Mexico* 118 C4
Guandacol *Argentina* 126 B2
Guane *Cuba* 120 B3
Guang'an *China* 58 B6
Guangchang *China* 59 D11
Guangde *China* 59 B12
Guangdong □ *China* 59 F9
Guangfeng *China* 59 C12
Guanghan *China* 58 B5
Guangling *China* 56 E8
Guangnan *China* 58 E5
Guangning *China* 59 F9
Guangrao *China* 57 F10
Guangshui *China* 59 B9
Guangshun *China* 58 D6

Guangwu *China* 56 F3
Guangxi Zhuangzu
    Zizhiqu □ *China* 58 F7
Guangyuan *China* 58 A5
Guangze *China* 59 D11
Guangzhou *China* 59 F9
Guanica *Puerto Rico* 121 d
Guanling *China* 58 E5
Guannan *China* 57 G10
Guantánamo *Cuba* 121 B4
Guantánamo B. *Cuba* 121 C4
Guantao *China* 56 F8
Guanyang *China* 59 E8
Guanyun *China* 57 G10
Guápiles *Costa Rica* 120 D3
Guapo B. *Trin. & Tob.* 125 K15
Guaporé *Brazil* 127 B5
Guaporé ➤ *Brazil* 124 F5
Guaqui *Bolivia* 124 G5
Guara, Sierra de *Spain* 38 C4
Guaramacal △ *Venezuela* 121 E5
Guarapari *Brazil* 127 A7
Guarapuava *Brazil* 127 B5
Guaratinguetá *Brazil* 127 A6
Guaratuba *Brazil* 127 B6
Guarda *Portugal* 36 E3
Guarda □ *Portugal* 36 E3
Guardafui, C. = Asir, Ras
    Somali Rep. 75 E5
Guardamar del Segura *Spain* 39 G4
Guardavalle *Italy* 43 D9
Guárdia Sanframondi *Italy* 43 A7
Guardiagrele *Italy* 41 F11
Guardo *Spain* 36 C6
Guareña *Spain* 37 G5
Guareña ➤ *Spain* 36 D5
Guárico □ *Venezuela* 124 B5
Guarujá *Brazil* 127 A6
Guarulhos *Brazil* 127 A6
Guarus *Brazil* 127 A7
Guasave *Mexico* 118 B3
Guasdualito *Venezuela* 124 B4
Guastalla *Italy* 40 D7
Guatemala *Guatemala* 120 D1
Guatemala ■ *Cent. Amer.* 120 C1
Guatemala Basin *Pac. Oc.* 97 F18
Guatemala Trench *Pac. Oc.* 98 H10
Guatopo △ *Venezuela* 121 D6
Guatuaro Pt. *Trin. & Tob.* 125 K16
Guaviare ➤ *Colombia* 124 C5
Guaxupé *Brazil* 127 A6
Guayaguayare *Trin. & Tob.* 125 K15
Guayama *Puerto Rico* 121 d
Guayaquil *Ecuador* 124 D3
Guayaquil *Mexico* 118 B1
Guayaquil, G. de *Ecuador* 124 D2
Guaymas *Mexico* 118 B2
Guba *Dem. Rep. of the Congo* 87 E2
Guba *Ethiopia* 81 E4
Gûbâl, Madîq *Egypt* 80 B3
Gubat *Phil.* 61 E6
Gúbbio *Italy* 41 E9
Guben *Germany* 24 D10
Gubin *Poland* 31 G1
Gubio *Nigeria* 83 C7
Gubkin *Russia* 33 G9
Gučukolak, Tanjung
    Indonesia 63 G11
Guča *Serbia* 44 C4
Gucheng *China* 59 A8
Gudata = Guadauta *Georgia* 35 J5
Gudbrandsdalen *Norway* 8 F14
Guddu Barrage *Pakistan* 68 E3
Gudenå ➤ *Denmark* 11 H4
Gudermes *Russia* 35 J8
Gudhjem *Denmark* 11 J8
Gudur *India* 66 M11
Guebwiller *France* 19 E14
Guecho = Getxo *Spain* 38 B2
Guékédou *Guinea* 82 D2
Guéle Mendouka *Cameroon* 83 E7
Guelmine = Goulimine
    Morocco 78 C3
Guelph *Canada* 114 C4
Guémené-Penfao *France* 18 E5
Guémené-sur-Scorff *France* 18 D3
Guéné *Benin* 83 C5
Guer *France* 18 E4
Guérande *France* 18 E4
Guéret *France* 19 F8
Guérigny *France* 19 E10
Guerneville *U.S.A.* 110 G4
Guernica = Gernika-Lumo
    Spain 38 B2
Guernsey *U.K.* 15 H5
Guernsey *U.S.A.* 108 E11
Guerrero □ *Mexico* 119 D5
Guessou-Sud *Benin* 83 C5
Gueugnon *France* 19 F11
Guéyo *Ivory C.* 82 D3
Gughe *Ethiopia* 81 F4
Gügher *Iran* 71 D8
Guglionesi *Italy* 41 G11
Guhakolak, Tanjung
    Indonesia 63 G11
Gui Jiang ➤ *China* 59 F8
Guia *Canary Is.* 48 F4
Guia de Isora *Canary Is.* 48 F3

Guia Lopes da Laguna
  Brazil **127** A4
Guiana Highlands *S. Amer.* **122** C4
Guibéroua *Ivory C.* **82** D3
Guichi *China* **59** B11
Guider *Cameroon* **83** D7
Guidiguir *Niger* **83** C6
Guidimaka □ *Mauritania* **82** B2
Guidimouni *Niger* **83** C6
Guiding *China* **58** D6
Guidong *China* **59** D9
Guidónia-Montecélio *Italy* **41** F9
Guiers, L. de *Senegal* **82** B1
Guigang *China* **58** F7
Guiglo *Ivory C.* **82** D3
Guihulñgan *Phil.* **61** F5
Guijá *Mozam.* **89** C5
Guijuelo *Spain* **36** E5
Guildford *U.K.* **15** F7
Guilford *U.S.A.* **115** E12
Guilin *China* **59** E8
Guillaume-Delisle, L.
  Canada **104** A4
Guillaumes *France* **21** D10
Guillestre *France* **21** D10
Guilvinec *France* **18** E2
Güimar *Canary Is.* **48** F3
Guimarães *Portugal* **36** D2
Guimaras □ *Phil.* **61** F5
Guinda *U.S.A.* **110** G4
Guinea *Africa* **76** F4
Guinea ■ *W. Afr.* **82** C2
Guinea, Gulf of *Atl. Oc.* **83** E5
Guinea-Bissau ■ *Africa* **82** C2
Güines *Cuba* **120** B3
Guingamp *France* **18** D3
Guinguinéo *Senegal* **82** C1
Guipavas *France* **18** D2
Guiping *China* **59** F8
Guipúzcoa □ *Spain* **38** B2
Guir *Mali* **82** B4
Guirel *Mauritania* **82** B3
Güiria *Venezuela* **124** A6
Guiscard *France* **19** C10
Guise *France* **19** C10
Guitiriz *Spain* **36** B3
Guitri *Ivory C.* **82** D3
Guiuan *Phil.* **61** F6
Guixi *China* **59** C11
Guiyang *Guizhou, China* **58** D6
Guiyang *Hunan, China* **59** E9
Guizhou □ *China* **58** D6
Gujan-Mestras *France* **20** D2
Gujar Khan *Pakistan* **68** C5
Gujarat □ *India* **68** H4
Gujiang *China* **59** D10
Gujranwala *Pakistan* **68** C6
Gujrat *Pakistan* **68** C6
Gukovo *Russia* **35** F5
Gulbarga *India* **66** L10
Gulbene *Latvia* **32** D4
Gulf, The = Persian Gulf
  Asia **71** E6
Gulf Islands △ *U.S.A.* **117** F11
Gulfport *U.S.A.* **117** F10
Gulgong *Australia* **95** E4
Gulin *China* **58** C5
Gulistan *Pakistan* **68** D2
Gull Lake *Canada* **103** C7
Gullbrandstorp *Sweden* **11** H6
Gullspång *Sweden* **11** F8
Güllük *Turkey* **47** D9
Güllük Daği *Turkey* **47** E12
Güllük Korfezi *Turkey* **47** D9
Gulma *Nigeria* **83** C5
Gulmarg *India* **69** B6
Gülnar *Turkey* **72** D5
Gülpınar *Turkey* **47** B8
Gülşehir *Turkey* **72** C6
Gülshat *Kazakhstan* **52** C8
Gulu *Uganda* **86** B3
Gülübovo *Bulgaria* **45** D9
Gulud, J. *Sudan* **81** E2
Gulwe *Tanzania* **86** D4
Gulyaypole = Hulyaypole
  Ukraine **33** J9
Gumal ➤ *Pakistan* **68** D4
Gumbaz *Pakistan* **68** D3
Gumel *Nigeria* **83** C6
Gumi *S. Korea* **57** F15
Gumla *India* **69** H11
Gumlu *Australia* **94** B4
Gumma □ *Japan* **55** F9
Gummersbach *Germany* **24** D3
Gummi *Nigeria* **83** C6
Gümüldür *Turkey* **47** C9
Gümüşçay *Turkey* **45** F11
Gümüşhacıköy *Turkey* **72** B6
Gümüşhane *Turkey* **73** B8
Gümüşsu *Turkey* **47** C11
Gumzai *Indonesia* **63** F8
Guna *Ethiopia* **81** F4
Guna *India* **68** G7
Gunbalanya *Australia* **92** B5
Gundabooka △ *Australia* **95** E4
Gundelfingen *Germany* **25** G6

Güney *Burdur, Turkey* **47** D11
Güney *Denizli, Turkey* **47** C11
Güneydoğu Toroslar *Turkey* **73** C9
Gunisao ➤ *Canada* **103** C9
Gunisao L. *Canada* **103** C9
Gunjyal *Pakistan* **68** C4
Günlüce *Turkey* **47** E10
Gunnarskog *Sweden* **10** E6
Gunnbjørn Fjeld *Greenland* **4** C6
Gunnebo *Sweden* **11** G10
Gunnedah *Australia* **95** E5
Gunnewin *Australia* **95** D4
Gunningbar Cr. ➤ *Australia* **95** E4
Gunnison *Colo., U.S.A.* **108** G10
Gunnison *Utah, U.S.A.* **108** G8
Gunnison ➤ *U.S.A.* **108** G9
Gunpowder *Australia* **94** B2
Gunsan *S. Korea* **57** G14
Guntakal *India* **66** M10
Guntersville *U.S.A.* **117** D11
Guntong *Malaysia* **65** K3
Guntur *India* **67** L12
Gunungapi *Indonesia* **63** F7
Gunungsitoli *Indonesia* **62** D1
Günz ➤ *Germany* **25** G6
Gunza *Angola* **84** G2
Günzburg *Germany* **25** G6
Gunzenhausen *Germany* **25** F6
Guo He ➤ *China* **57** H9
Guoyang *China* **56** H9
Gupis *Pakistan* **69** A5
Gura Humorului *Romania* **29** C10
Gura-Teghii *Romania* **29** E11
Gurag *Ethiopia* **81** F4
Gurahonţ *Romania* **28** D7
Gurdaspur *India* **68** C6
Gurdon *U.S.A.* **116** E8
Güre *Balıkesir, Turkey* **47** B8
Güre *Uşak, Turkey* **47** C11
Gurgaon *India* **68** E7
Gürgentep *Turkey* **72** B7
Gurghiu, Munţii *Romania* **29** D10
Gurgueia ➤ *Brazil* **125** E10
Gurha *India* **68** G4
Guri, Embalse de *Venezuela* **124** B6
Gurin *Nigeria* **83** D7
Gurjaani *Georgia* **35** K7
Gurk ➤ *Austria* **26** E7
Gurkha *Nepal* **69** E11
Gurley *Australia* **95** D4
Gurnet Point *U.S.A.* **115** D14
Guro *Mozam.* **87** F3
Gürpınar *İstanbul, Turkey* **45** F12
Gürpınar *Van, Turkey* **73** C10
Gürsu *Turkey* **45** F13
Gurué *Mozam.* **87** F4
Gurun *Malaysia* **65** K3
Gürün *Turkey* **72** C7
Gurupá *Brazil* **125** D8
Gurupá, I. Grande de *Brazil* **125** D8
Gurupi *Brazil* **125** F9
Gurupi ➤ *Brazil* **125** D9
Guruwe *Zimbabwe* **89** B5
Guryev = Atyraū *Kazakhstan* **52** E6
Guryevsk *Russia* **30** D7
Gus-Khrustalnyy *Russia* **34** C5
Gusau *Nigeria* **83** C6
Gusev *Russia* **30** D9
Gushan *China* **57** E12
Gushgy = Serhetabat
  Turkmenistan **71** C9
Gushi *China* **59** A10
Gushiago *Ghana* **83** D4
Gusinje *Montenegro* **44** D3
Gusinoozersk *Russia* **53** D11
Gúspini *Italy* **42** C1
Güssing *Austria* **27** D9
Gustavsberg *Sweden* **10** E12
Gustavus *U.S.A.* **102** B1
Gustine *U.S.A.* **110** H6
Güstrow *Germany* **24** B8
Gusum *Sweden* **11** F10
Guta = Kolárovo
  Slovak Rep. **27** D10
Gütersloh *Germany* **24** D4
Gutha *Australia* **93** E2
Guthalungra *Australia* **94** B4
Guthrie *Okla., U.S.A.* **116** D6
Guthrie *Tex., U.S.A.* **116** E4
Gutian *China* **59** D12
Guttenberg *U.S.A.* **112** D8
Gutu *Zimbabwe* **89** B5
Guwahati *India* **67** F17
Guy Fawkes River △
  Australia **95** D5
Guyana ■ *S. Amer.* **124** C7
Guyane française = French
  Guiana ☒ *S. Amer.* **125** C8
Guyang *China* **56** D6
Guyenne *France* **20** D4
Guymon *U.S.A.* **116** C4
Guyra *Australia* **95** E5
Guyuan *Hebei, China* **56** D8
Guyuan *Ningxia Huizu, China* **56** G4
Güzelbahçe *Turkey* **47** C8
Güzelyurt = Morphou
  Cyprus **49** D11

Guzhang *China* **58** C7
Guzhen *China* **57** H9
Guzmán, L. de *Mexico* **118** A3
Gvardeysk *Russia* **30** D8
Gvardeyskoye *Ukraine* **33** K8
Gwa *Burma* **67** L19
Gwaai *Zimbabwe* **87** F2
Gwaai ➤ *Zimbabwe* **87** F2
Gwabegar *Australia* **95** E4
Gwadabawa *Nigeria* **83** C6
Gwādar *Pakistan* **66** G3
Gwagwada *Nigeria* **83** C6
Gwaii Haanas △ *Canada* **102** C2
Gwalior *India* **68** F8
Gwanara *Nigeria* **83** D5
Gwanda *Zimbabwe* **87** G2
Gwandu *Nigeria* **83** C5
Gwane *Dem. Rep. of the Congo* **86** B2
Gwangju *S. Korea* **57** G14
Gwanju = Gwangju
  S. Korea **57** G14
Gwaram *Nigeria* **83** C7
Gwarzo *Nigeria* **83** C6
Gwasero *Nigeria* **83** D5
Gwda ➤ *Poland* **31** B3
Gweebarra B. *Ireland* **12** B3
Gweedore *Ireland* **12** A3
Gweru *Zimbabwe* **87** F2
Gwi *Nigeria* **83** D6
Gwinn *U.S.A.* **112** B10
Gwio Kura *Nigeria* **83** C7
Gwoza *Nigeria* **83** C7
Gwydir ➤ *Australia* **95** D4
Gwynedd □ *U.K.* **14** E3
Gyandzha = Gäncä
  Azerbaijan **35** K8
Gyaring Hu *China* **60** C4
Gydanskiy Poluostrov
  Russia **52** C8
Gyeongju *S. Korea* **57** G15
Gympie *Australia* **95** D5
Gyomaendrőd *Hungary* **28** D5
Gyöngyös *Hungary* **28** C4
Győr *Hungary* **28** C2
Győr-Moson-Sopron □
  Hungary **28** C2
Gypsum Pt. *Canada* **102** A6
Gypsumville *Canada* **103** C9
Gyueshevo *Bulgaria* **44** D6
Gyula *Hungary* **28** D6
Gyumri *Armenia* **35** K6
Gyzylarbat = Serdar
  Turkmenistan **71** B8
Gyzyletrek = Etrek
  Turkmenistan **71** B7
Gzhatsk = Gagarin *Russia* **32** E8

H

Ha 'Arava ➤ *Israel* **74** E4
Ha Coi *Vietnam* **58** G6
Ha Dong *Vietnam* **58** G5
Ha Giang *Vietnam* **58** G5
Ha Karmel △ *Israel* **74** C4
Ha Long, Vinh *Vietnam* **64** B6
Ha Tien *Vietnam* **65** G5
Ha Tinh *Vietnam* **64** C5
Ha Trung *Vietnam* **64** C5
Ha Yaek Chalong *Thailand* **65** a
Haaksbergen *Neths.* **17** B6
Ha'ano *Tonga* **91** c
Ha'apai Group *Tonga* **91** c
Haapiti *Moorea* **91** d
Haapsalu *Estonia* **32** C2
Haarby *Denmark* **11** J4
Haarlem *Neths.* **17** B4
Haast ➤ *N.Z.* **91** E2
Haast Bluff *Australia* **92** D5
Hab ➤ *Pakistan* **68** G2
Hab Nadi Chauki *Pakistan* **68** G2
Habahe *China* **60** B3
Habaswein *Kenya* **86** B4
Habay *Canada* **102** B5
Ḥabbānīyah *Iraq* **73** F10
Ḥabbānīyah, Hawr al *Iraq* **73** F10
Habichtswald △ *Germany* **24** D5
Habo *Sweden* **11** G8
Haboro *Japan* **54** B10
Ḥabshān *U.A.E.* **71** F7
Hachenburg *Germany* **24** E3
Hachijō-Jima *Japan* **55** H9
Hachinohe *Japan* **54** D10
Hachiōji *Japan* **55** G9
Hacıbektaş *Turkey* **72** C6
Hacılar *Turkey* **72** C6
Hackås *Sweden* **10** B8
Hackensack *U.S.A.* **115** F10
Hackettstown *U.S.A.* **115** F10
Hadali *Pakistan* **68** C5
Hadarba, Ras *Sudan* **80** C4
Hadarom □ *Israel* **74** E4
Ḥadd, Ra's al *Oman* **75** C6
Haddington *U.K.* **13** F6
Hadejia *Nigeria* **83** C7
Hadejia ➤ *Nigeria* **83** C7
Ḥadera *Israel* **74** C3
Ḥadera, N. ➤ *Israel* **74** C3

Haderslev *Denmark* **11** J3
Hadhramaut =
  Ḥaḍramawt *Yemen* **75** D4
Ḥadiboh *Yemen* **75** E5
Hadım *Turkey* **72** D5
Hadong *S. Korea* **57** G14
Ḥaḍramawt *Yemen* **75** D4
Ḥadrānīyah *Iraq* **70** C4
Hadrian's Wall *U.K.* **14** B5
Hadsten *Denmark* **11** H4
Hadsund *Denmark* **11** H4
Hadyach *Ukraine* **33** G8
Haeju *N. Korea* **57** E13
Haenam *S. Korea* **57** G14
Haenertsburg *S. Africa* **89** C4
Hälat 'Ammār *Si. Arabia* **70** D3
Haerhpin = Harbin *China* **57** B14
Hafar al Bāṭin *Si. Arabia* **70** D5
Hafik *Turkey* **72** C7
Hafirat al 'Aydā *Si. Arabia* **70** E3
Ḥafit *Oman* **71** F7
Hafizabad *Pakistan* **68** C5
Haflong *India* **67** G18
Hafnarfjörður *Iceland* **8** D3
Haft Gel *Iran* **71** D6
Hagalil *Israel* **74** C4
Hagby *Sweden* **11** H10
Hagen *Germany* **24** D3
Hagenow *Germany* **24** B7
Hagerman *U.S.A.* **108** E6
Hagerman Fossil Beds △
  U.S.A. **108** E6
Hagerstown *U.S.A.* **113** F15
Hagersville *Canada* **114** D4
Hagetmau *France* **20** E3
Hagfors *Sweden* **10** D7
Hagi *Japan* **55** G5
Hagolan *Syria* **74** C4
Hagondange *France* **19** C13
Hags Hd. *Ireland* **12** D2
Hague, C. de la *France* **18** C5
Hague, The =
  's-Gravenhage *Neths.* **17** B4
Haguenau *France* **19** D14
Hai Duong *Vietnam* **58** G6
Hai'an *Guangdong, China* **59** G8
Hai'an *Jiangsu, China* **59** A13
Haicheng *Fujian, China* **59** E11
Haicheng *Liaoning, China* **57** D12
Haidar Khel *Afghan.* **68** C3
Haidarâbâd = Hyderabad
  India **66** L11
Haidargarh *India* **69** F9
Haifa = Ḥefa *Israel* **74** C4
Haifeng *China* **59** F10
Haiger *Germany* **24** E4
Haikou *China* **64** B8
Ḥā'il *Si. Arabia* **70** E4
Ḥā'il □ *Si. Arabia* **70** E4
Hailar *China* **60** B6
Hailey *U.S.A.* **108** E6
Haileybury *Canada* **104** C4
Hailin *China* **57** B15
Hailing Dao *China* **59** G8
Hailuoto *Finland* **8** D21
Haimen *Guangdong, China* **59** F11
Haimen *Jiangsu, China* **59** B13
Hainan □ *China* **64** C7
Hainan Dao *China* **64** C7
Hainan Str. = Qiongzhou
  Haixia *China* **64** B8
Hainaut □ *Belgium* **17** D4
Hainburg *Austria* **27** C9
Haines *Alaska, U.S.A.* **102** B1
Haines *Oreg., U.S.A.* **108** D5
Haines City *U.S.A.* **117** G14
Haines Junction *Canada* **102** A1
Hainfeld *Austria* **26** C8
Haining *China* **59** B13
Haiphong *Vietnam* **58** G6
Haitan Dao *China* **59** E12
Haiti ■ *W. Indies* **121** C5
Haiya *Sudan* **80** D4
Haiyan *China* **59** B13
Haiyang *China* **57** F11
Haiyuan *Guangxi Zhuangzu,*
  China **58** F6
Haiyuan *Ningxia Huizu, China* **56** F3
Haizhou *China* **57** G10
Haizhou Wan *China* **57** G10
Hajdú-Bihar □ *Hungary* **28** C6
Hajdúböszörmény *Hungary* **28** C6
Hajdúdorog *Hungary* **28** C6
Hajdúhadház *Hungary* **28** C6
Hajdúnánás *Hungary* **28** C6
Hajdúsámson *Hungary* **28** C6
Hajdúszoboszló *Hungary* **28** C6
Haji Ibrahim *Iraq* **73** D11
Hajipur *India* **69** G11
Ḥajjah *Yemen* **75** D3
Ḥajjiābād *Iran* **71** D7
Ḥajjiābād-e Zarrīn *Iran* **71** C7
Hajnówka *Poland* **31** F10
Hakansson, Mts.
  Dem. Rep. of the Congo **87** D2
Ḥakkâri *Turkey* **73** D10
Ḥakkâri Dağları *Turkey* **73** C10

Hakken-Zan *Japan* **55** G7
Hakodate *Japan* **54** D10
Hakos *Namibia* **88** C2
Håksberg *Sweden* **10** D9
Haku-San *Japan* **55** F8
Haku-San △ *Japan* **55** F8
Hakui *Japan* **55** F8
Hala *Pakistan* **66** G3
Ḥalab *Syria* **72** D7
Ḥalab □ *Syria* **72** D7
Halabjah *Iraq* **73** E11
Halaib *Sudan* **80** C4
Halaib Triangle *Africa* **80** C4
Halasa *Sudan* **81** E3
Halba *Lebanon* **74** A5
Halberstadt *Germany* **24** D7
Halcombe *N.Z.* **91** D5
Halcon *Phil.* **63** B6
Halden *Norway* **9** G14
Haldensleben *Germany* **24** C7
Haldimand *Canada* **114** D5
Haldwani *India* **69** E8
Hale ➤ *Australia* **94** C2
Halesowen *U.K.* **15** E5
Halesworth *U.K.* **15** E9
Haleyville *U.S.A.* **117** D11
Half Assini *Ghana* **82** D4
Half Dome *U.S.A.* **110** H7
Halfmoon Bay *N.Z.* **91** G2
Halfway ➤ *Canada* **102** B4
Halia *India* **69** G10
Haliburton *Canada* **114** A6
Halifax *Australia* **94** B4
Halifax *Canada* **105** D7
Halifax *U.K.* **14** D6
Halifax *U.S.A.* **114** F8
Halifax B. *Australia* **94** B4
Halifax I. *Namibia* **88** D2
Ḥalīl ➤ *Iran* **71** E8
Halki *Greece* **47** E9
Halkida *Greece* **46** C5
Halkidiki □ *Greece* **44** F7
Halkirk *U.K.* **13** C5
Hall Beach = Sanirajak
  Canada **101** C11
Hall in Tirol *Austria* **26** D4
Hall Pen. *Canada* **101** C13
Hall Pt. *Australia* **92** C3
Hallabro *Sweden* **11** H9
Halland *Sweden* **9** H15
Hallands län □ *Sweden* **11** H6
Hallands Väderö *Sweden* **11** H6
Hallandsås *Sweden* **11** H7
Hallāniyat, Jazā'ir al *Oman* **75** D6
Hallasan *S. Korea* **57** H14
Hallbro *Sweden* **11** H9
Hällbybrunn *Sweden* **10** E10
Halle *Belgium* **17** D4
Halle *Nordrhein-Westfalen,*
  Germany **24** C4
Halle *Sachsen-Anhalt, Germany* **24** D7
Hällefors *Sweden* **10** E8
Hälleforsnäs *Sweden* **10** E10
Hallein *Austria* **26** D6
Hällekis *Sweden* **11** F7
Hallen *Sweden* **10** A8
Hallett *Australia* **95** E2
Hallettsville *U.S.A.* **116** G6
Hallim *S. Korea* **57** H14
Hallingdalselva ➤ *Norway* **8** F13
Hallock *U.S.A.* **112** A5
Halls Creek *Australia* **92** C4
Halls Gap *Australia* **95** F3
Hallsberg *Sweden* **10** E9
Hallstahammar *Sweden* **10** E10
Hallstatt *Austria* **26** D6
Hallstavik *Sweden* **10** D12
Hallstead *U.S.A.* **115** E9
Halmahera *Indonesia* **63** D7
Halmeu *Romania* **28** B7
Halmstad *Sweden* **11** H6
Hals *Denmark* **11** H4
Hälsingborg = Helsingborg
  Sweden **11** H6
Hälsingland *Sweden* **10** C10
Halstead *U.K.* **15** F8
Haltern *Germany* **24** D3
Haltiatunturi *Finland* **8** B19
Halton □ *U.K.* **14** D5
Haltwhistle *U.K.* **14** C5
Ḥālūl *Qatar* **71** E7
Halvad *India* **68** H4
Halvān *Iran* **71** C8
Ham *France* **19** C10
Ham Tan *Vietnam* **65** G6
Ham Yen *Vietnam* **64** A5
Hamab *Namibia* **88** D2
Hamad *Sudan* **81** D3
Hamada *Japan* **55** G6
Hamadān *Iran* **73** E13
Hamadān □ *Iran* **71** C6
Ḥamāh *Syria* **72** D7
Ḥamāh □ *Syria* **72** E7
Hamamatsu *Japan* **55** G8
Hamar *Norway* **8** F14

Hamâta, Gebel *Egypt* **70** E2
Hambantota *Sri Lanka* **66** R12
Hamber △ *Canada* **102** C5
Hamburg *Germany* **24** B5
Hamburg *Ark., U.S.A.* **116** E9
Hamburg *N.Y., U.S.A.* **114** D6
Hamburg *Pa., U.S.A.* **115** F9
Hamburg □ *Germany* **24** B5
Hamburg Fuhlsbüttel ✈
  (HAM) *Germany* **24** B5
Ḥamd, W. al ➤ *Si. Arabia* **70** E3
Hamden *U.S.A.* **115** E12
Hamdibey *Turkey* **47** B9
Häme *Finland* **32** B2
Hämeenlinna *Finland* **32** B3
Hamélé *Ghana* **82** C4
Hamelin Pool *Australia* **93** E1
Hameln *Germany* **24** C5
Hamerkaz □ *Israel* **74** C3
Hamersley Ra. *Australia* **92** D2
Hamhŭng *N. Korea* **57** E14
Hami *China* **60** B4
Hamili *Greece* **47** F8
Hamilton *Australia* **95** F3
Hamilton *Canada* **114** C5
Hamilton *N.Z.* **91** B5
Hamilton *U.K.* **13** F4
Hamilton *Ala., U.S.A.* **117** D11
Hamilton *Mont., U.S.A.* **108** C6
Hamilton *N.Y., U.S.A.* **115** D9
Hamilton *Ohio, U.S.A.* **113** F11
Hamilton *Tex., U.S.A.* **116** F5
Hamilton ➤ *Queens.,*
  Australia **94** C2
Hamilton ➤ *S. Austral.,*
  Australia **95** D2
Hamilton City *U.S.A.* **110** F4
Hamilton I. *Australia* **94** J6
Hamilton Inlet *Canada* **105** B8
Hamilton Mt. *U.S.A.* **115** C10
Hamina *Finland* **32** B4
Hamirpur *H.P., India* **68** D7
Hamirpur *Ut. P., India* **69** G9
Hamitabat *Turkey* **45** E11
Hamju *N. Korea* **57** E14
Hamlet *U.S.A.* **117** D15
Hamley Bridge *Australia* **95** E2
Hamlin = Hameln *Germany* **24** C5
Hamlin *N.Y., U.S.A.* **114** C7
Hamlin *Tex., U.S.A.* **116** E4
Hamm *Germany* **24** D3
Ḥammār, Hawr al *Iraq* **70** D5
Hammarstrand *Sweden* **10** A10
Hammelburg *Germany* **25** E5
Hammeren *Denmark* **11** J8
Hammerfest *Norway* **8** A20
Hammerum *Denmark* **11** H3
Hamminkeln *Germany* **24** D2
Hammond *Ind., U.S.A.* **112** E10
Hammond *La., U.S.A.* **117** F9
Hammond *N.Y., U.S.A.* **115** B9
Hammondsport *U.S.A.* **114** D7
Hammonton *U.S.A.* **113** F16
Hamneda *Sweden* **11** H7
Hampden *N.Z.* **91** F3
Hampshire □ *U.K.* **15** F6
Hampshire Downs *U.K.* **15** F6
Hampton *N.B., Canada* **105** D6
Hampton *Ont., Canada* **114** C6
Hampton *Ark., U.S.A.* **116** E8
Hampton *Iowa, U.S.A.* **112** D7
Hampton *N.H., U.S.A.* **115** D14
Hampton *S.C., U.S.A.* **117** E14
Hampton *Va., U.S.A.* **113** G15
Hampton Bays *U.S.A.* **115** F12
Hampton Tableland
  Australia **93** F4
Hamra *Sweden* **10** C8
Hamrat esh Sheykh *Sudan* **81** E2
Hamur *Turkey* **73** C10
Hamyang *S. Korea* **57** G14
Han i Hotit *Albania* **44** D3
Han Jiang ➤ *China* **59** F11
Han Shui ➤ *China* **59** B10
Hanak *Si. Arabia* **70** E3
Hanamaki *Japan* **54** E10
Hanang *Tanzania* **86** C4
Hanau *Germany* **25** E4
Hanbogd = Ihbulag
  Mongolia **56** C4
Hançalar *Turkey* **47** C11
Hâncești *Moldova* **29** D13
Hancheng *China* **56** G6
Hanchuan *China* **59** B9
Hancock *Mich., U.S.A.* **112** B9
Hancock *N.Y., U.S.A.* **115** E9
Handa *Japan* **55** G8
Handa I. *U.K.* **13** C3
Handan *China* **56** F8
Handeni *Tanzania* **86** D4
Handlová *Slovak Rep.* **27** C11
Handub *Sudan* **80** D4
Handwara *India* **69** B6
Hanegev *Israel* **74** E4
Hanford *U.S.A.* **110** J7
Hanford Reach △ *U.S.A.* **108** C4

Hang Chat *Thailand* **64** C2
Hang Dong *Thailand* **64** C2
Hangang → *S. Korea* **57** F14
Hangayn Nuruu *Mongolia* **60** B4
Hangchou = Hangzhou
    China **59** B13
Hanggin Houqi *China* **56** D4
Hanggin Qi *China* **56** E5
Hangu *China* **57** E9
Hangzhou *China* **59** B13
Hangzhou Wan *China* **59** B13
Hanhongor *Mongolia* **56** C3
Hania = Chania *Greece* **49** D6
Ḥanīdh *Si. Arabia* **71** E6
Ḥanīsh *Yemen* **75** E3
Haniska *Slovak Rep.* **27** C14
Hanjiang *China* **59** E12
Hankinson *U.S.A.* **112** B5
Hankö *Finland* **32** C2
Hankou *China* **59** B10
Hanksville *U.S.A.* **108** G8
Hanle *India* **69** C8
Hanmer Springs *N.Z.* **91** E4
Hann → *Australia* **92** C4
Hann, Mt. *Australia* **92** C4
Hanna *Canada* **102** C6
Hanna *U.S.A.* **108** F10
Hannah B. *Canada* **104** B4
Hannibal *Mo., U.S.A.* **112** F8
Hannibal *N.Y., U.S.A.* **115** C8
Hannik *Sudan* **80** D3
Hannover *Germany* **24** C5
Hanö *Sweden* **11** H8
Hanöbukten *Sweden* **11** J8
Hanoi *Vietnam* **58** G5
Hanover = Hannover
    Germany **24** C5
Hanover *Canada* **114** B3
Hanover *S. Africa* **88** E3
Hanover *N.H., U.S.A.* **115** C12
Hanover *Ohio, U.S.A.* **114** F2
Hanover, I. *Chile* **128** G2
Hans Lollik I. *U.S. Virgin Is.* **121** e
Hansdiha *India* **69** G12
Hanshou *China* **59** C8
Hansi *India* **68** E6
Hanson, L. *Australia* **95** E2
Hanstholm *Denmark* **11** G2
Hantsavichy *Belarus* **23** B14
Hanumangarh *India* **68** E6
Hanyin *China* **58** A7
Hanyuan *China* **58** C4
Hanzhong *China* **56** H4
Hanzhuang *China* **57** G9
Haora *India* **69** H13
Haoxue *China* **59** B9
Haparanda *Sweden* **8** D21
Happy *U.S.A.* **116** D4
Happy Camp *U.S.A.* **108** F2
Happy Valley-Goose Bay
    Canada **105** B7
Hapsu *N. Korea* **57** D15
Hapur *India* **68** E7
Ḥaql *Si. Arabia* **74** F3
Har *Indonesia* **63** F8
Har-Ayrag *Mongolia* **56** B5
Har Hu *China* **60** C4
Har Us Nuur *Mongolia* **60** B4
Har Yehuda *Israel* **74** D3
Ḥarad *Si. Arabia* **75** C4
Haradok *Belarus* **32** E6
Häradsbäck *Sweden* **11** H8
Haranomachi *Japan* **54** F10
Harare *Zimbabwe* **87** F3
Harat *Eritrea* **81** D4
Harazé *Chad* **79** G10
Harbin *China* **57** B14
Harbiye *Turkey* **72** D7
Harbo *Sweden* **10** D11
Harboøre *Denmark* **11** H2
Harbor Beach *U.S.A.* **114** C2
Harbour Breton *Canada* **105** C8
Harburg *Germany* **24** B5
Harburger Berge → *Germany* **24** B5
Harda *India* **68** H7
Hardangerfjorden *Norway* **9** F12
Hardangervidda *Norway* **8** F12
Hardap □ *Namibia* **88** C2
Hardap Dam *Namibia* **88** C2
Hardenberg *Neths.* **17** B6
Harderwijk *Neths.* **17** B5
Hardey → *Australia* **92** D2
Hardin *U.S.A.* **108** D10
Harding *S. Africa* **89** E4
Harding Ra. *Australia* **92** C3
Hardisty *Canada* **102** C6
Hardoi *India* **69** F9
Hardwar = Haridwar *India* **68** E8
Hardwick *U.S.A.* **115** B12
Hardy, Pen. *Chile* **128** H3
Hardy, Pte. *St. Lucia* **121** f
Hare B. *Canada* **105** B8
Hareid *Norway* **8** E12
Haren *Germany* **24** C3
Harer *Ethiopia* **81** F5
Harerge *Ethiopia* **81** F5

Hareto *Ethiopia* **81** F4
Harfleur *France* **18** C7
Hargeisa *Somali Rep.* **75** F3
Harghita □ *Romania* **29** D10
Harghita, Munții *Romania* **29** D10
Hargshamn *Sweden* **10** D12
Hari → *Indonesia* **62** E2
Haria *Canary Is.* **48** E6
Haridwar *India* **68** E8
Harim, Jabal al *Oman* **71** E8
Haringhata → *Bangla.* **67** J16
Harīr, W. al → *Syria* **74** C4
Harīrūd → *Asia* **71** B9
Härjedalen *Sweden* **10** B7
Harlan *Iowa, U.S.A.* **112** E7
Harlan *Ky., U.S.A.* **113** G12
Hârlău *Romania* **29** C11
Harlech *U.K.* **14** E3
Harlem *U.S.A.* **108** B9
Harlingen *Neths.* **17** A5
Harlingen *U.S.A.* **116** H6
Harlow *U.K.* **15** F8
Harlowton *U.S.A.* **108** C9
Harmancık *Turkey* **47** B11
Harmånger *Sweden* **10** C11
Harmil *Eritrea* **81** D5
Harnai *Pakistan* **68** D2
Harney Basin *U.S.A.* **108** E4
Harney L. *U.S.A.* **108** E4
Harney Peak *U.S.A.* **112** D2
Härnön *Sweden* **10** B12
Härnösand *Sweden* **10** B11
Haro *Spain* **38** C2
Haroldswick *U.K.* **13** A8
Harp L. *Canada* **105** A7
Harper *Liberia* **82** E3
Harplinge *Sweden* **11** H6
Harrai *India* **69** H8
Harrand *Pakistan* **68** E4
Harricana → *Canada* **104** B4
Harriman *U.S.A.* **117** D12
Harrington Harbour
    Canada **105** B8
Harris *U.K.* **13** D2
Harris, L. *Australia* **95** E2
Harris, Sd. of *U.K.* **13** D1
Harris Pt. *Canada* **114** C2
Harrisburg *Ill., U.S.A.* **112** G9
Harrisburg *Nebr., U.S.A.* **112** E2
Harrisburg *Pa., U.S.A.* **114** F8
Harrismith *S. Africa* **89** D4
Harrison *Ark., U.S.A.* **116** C8
Harrison *Maine, U.S.A.* **115** B14
Harrison *Nebr., U.S.A.* **112** D2
Harrison, C. *Canada* **105** B8
Harrison L. *Canada* **102** D4
Harrisonburg *U.S.A.* **113** F14
Harrisonville *U.S.A.* **112** F6
Harriston *Canada* **114** C4
Harrisville *Mich., U.S.A.* **114** B1
Harrisville *N.Y., U.S.A.* **115** B9
Harrisville *Pa., U.S.A.* **114** E5
Harrodsburg *U.S.A.* **113** G11
Harrogate *U.K.* **14** C6
Harrow → *U.K.* **15** F7
Harrowsmith *Canada* **115** B8
Harry S. Truman Res.
    U.S.A. **112** F7
Harsefeld *Germany* **24** B5
Harsewinkel *Germany* **24** D4
Harsīn *Iran* **73** E12
Hârșova *Romania* **29** F12
Harstad *Norway* **8** B17
Harsud *India* **68** H7
Hart *U.S.A.* **112** D10
Hart, L. *Australia* **95** E2
Hartbees → *S. Africa* **88** D3
Hartberg *Austria* **26** D8
Hartford *Conn., U.S.A.* **115** E12
Hartford *Ky., U.S.A.* **112** G10
Hartford *S. Dak., U.S.A.* **112** D6
Hartford *Vt., U.S.A.* **115** C12
Hartford *Wis., U.S.A.* **112** D9
Hartford City *U.S.A.* **113** E11
Hartland *Canada* **105** C6
Hartland Pt. *U.K.* **15** F3
Hartlepool *U.K.* **14** C6
Hartlepool □ *U.K.* **14** C6
Hartley Bay *Canada* **102** C3
Hartmannberge *Namibia* **88** B1
Hartney *Canada* **103** D8
Hârtop *Moldova* **29** D13
Harts → *S. Africa* **88** D3
Havârna *Romania* **29** B11
Havasor = Kızız *Turkey* **70** B4
Havasu, L. *U.S.A.* **111** L12
Havdhem *Sweden* **11** G12
Havel → *Germany* **24** C8
Havelian *Pakistan* **68** B5
Havelock *Canada* **114** B7
Havelock *N.Z.* **91** D4
Havelock *U.S.A.* **117** D16
Haverfordwest *U.K.* **15** F3
Haverhill *U.K.* **15** E8

Harts → *S. Africa* **88** D3
Hartselle *U.S.A.* **117** D11
Hartshorne *U.S.A.* **116** D7
Hartstown *U.S.A.* **114** E4
Hartsville *U.S.A.* **117** D14
Hartswater *S. Africa* **88** D3
Hartwell *U.S.A.* **117** D13
Harunabad *Pakistan* **68** E5
Harvand *Iran* **71** D7
Harvey *Australia* **93** F2
Harvey *Ill., U.S.A.* **112** E10

Harvey *N. Dak., U.S.A.* **112** B4
Harwich *U.K.* **15** F9
Haryana □ *India* **68** E7
Haryn → *Belarus* **23** B14
Harz *Germany* **24** D6
Harz △ *Germany* **24** D6
Harzgerode *Germany* **24** D7
Hasa *Si. Arabia* **71** E6
Ḥasa, W. al → *Jordan* **74** D4
Hasaheisa *Sudan* **81** E3
Hasanābād *Iran* **71** C7
Hasankeyf *Turkey* **73** D9
Hasdo → *India* **69** J10
Haselünne *Germany* **24** C3
Hashimoto *Japan* **55** G7
Hashtjerd *Iran* **71** C6
Haskell *U.S.A.* **116** E5
Haskovo = Khaskovo
    Bulgaria **45** E9
Hasköy *Turkey* **45** E10
Haslach *Germany* **25** G4
Hasle *Denmark* **11** J8
Haslemere *U.K.* **15** F7
Haslev *Denmark* **11** J5
Hasparren *France* **20** E2
Hassa *Turkey* **72** D7
Hassberge → *Germany* **25** E6
Hassela *Sweden* **10** B10
Hasselt *Belgium* **17** D5
Hassfurt *Germany* **25** E6
Hassi Messaoud *Algeria* **78** B7
Hässleholm *Sweden* **11** H7
Hassloch *Germany* **25** F4
Hästholmen *Sweden* **11** F8
Hastings *N.Z.* **91** C6
Hastings *U.K.* **15** G8
Hastings *Mich., U.S.A.* **113** D11
Hastings *Minn., U.S.A.* **112** C7
Hastings *Nebr., U.S.A.* **112** E4
Hastings Ra. *Australia* **95** E5
Hästveda *Sweden* **11** H7
Hatay *Turkey* **72** D7
Hatay □ *Turkey* **72** D7
Hatch *U.S.A.* **109** K10
Hatchet L. *Canada* **103** B8
Hațeg *Romania* **28** E7
Hateruma-Shima *Japan* **55** M1
Hatfield P.O. *Australia* **95** E3
Hatgal *Mongolia* **60** A5
Hathras *India* **68** F8
Hatia *Bangla.* **67** H17
Hato Mayor *Dom. Rep.* **121** C6
Hatta *India* **69** G8
Hatta *U.A.E.* **71** E8
Hattah *Australia* **95** E3
Hattah Kulkyne △ *Australia* **95** E3
Hatteras, C. *U.S.A.* **117** D17
Hattiesburg *U.S.A.* **117** F10
Hatvan *Hungary* **28** C4
Hau Duc *Vietnam* **64** E7
Haugesund *Norway* **9** G11
Haukipudas *Finland* **8** D21
Haultain → *Canada* **103** B7
Hauraki G. *N.Z.* **91** B5
Hausruck *Austria* **26** C6
Haut Atlas *Morocco* **78** B4
Haut-Jura ○ *France* **19** F9
Haut-Niger △ *Guinea* **82** C2
Haut-Languedoc ○ *France* **20** E6
Haut-Rhin □ *France* **19** E14
Haute-Corse □ *France* **21** F13
Haute-Garonne □ *France* **20** E5
Haute-Loire □ *France* **20** C7
Haute-Marne □ *France* **19** D12
Haute-Normandie □ *France* **18** C7
Haute-Saône □ *France* **19** E13
Haute-Savoie □ *France* **21** C10
Haute-Vienne □ *France* **20** C5
Hautes-Alpes □ *France* **21** D10
Hautes Fagnes = Hohes
    Venn *Belgium* **17** D6
Hautes-Pyrénées □ *France* **20** F4
Hauteville-Lompnès *France* **21** C9
Hautmont *France* **19** B10
Hauts-de-Seine □ *France* **19** D9
Hauts Plateaux *Algeria* **78** B6
Hauzenberg *Germany* **25** G9
Havana = La Habana *Cuba* **120** B3
Havana *U.S.A.* **112** E8
Havant *U.K.* **15** G7

Haverhill *U.S.A.* **115** D13
Haverstraw *U.S.A.* **115** E11
Håverud *Sweden* **11** F6
Havirga *Mongolia* **56** B7
Havířov *Czech Rep.* **27** B11
Havlíčkův Brod *Czech Rep.* **26** B8
Havneby *Denmark* **11** J2
Havran *Turkey* **47** B9
Havre *U.S.A.* **108** B9
Havre-Aubert *Canada* **105** C7
Havre-St.-Pierre *Canada* **105** B7
Havsa *Turkey* **45** E10
Havza *Turkey* **72** B6
Haw → *U.S.A.* **117** D15
Hawai'i *U.S.A.* **106** b
Hawai'i □ *U.S.A.* **106** b
Hawaiian Is. *Pac. Oc.* **106** b
Hawaiian Ridge *Pac. Oc.* **97** E11
Hawarden *U.S.A.* **112** D5
Hawea, L. *N.Z.* **91** F2
Hawera *N.Z.* **91** C5
Hawick *U.K.* **13** F6
Hawk Junction *Canada* **104** C3
Hawke B. *N.Z.* **91** C6
Hawker *Australia* **95** E2
Hawke's Bay *Canada* **105** B8
Hawkesbury *Canada* **104** C5
Hawkesbury I. *Canada* **102** C3
Hawkesbury Pt. *Australia* **94** A1
Hawkinsville *U.S.A.* **117** E13
Hawley *Minn., U.S.A.* **112** B6
Hawley *Pa., U.S.A.* **115** E9
Ḥawrān, W. → *Iraq* **73** F10
Hawsh Mūssá *Lebanon* **74** B4
Hawthorne *U.S.A.* **108** G4
Hay *Australia* **95** E3
Hay → *Australia* **94** C2
Hay → *Canada* **102** A5
Hay, C. *Australia* **92** B4
Hay I. *Canada* **114** B4
Hay L. *Canada* **102** B5
Hay-on-Wye *U.K.* **15** E4
Hay River *Canada* **102** A5
Hay Springs *U.S.A.* **112** D2
Haya = Tehoru *Indonesia* **63** E7
Hayachine-San *Japan* **54** E10
Hayange *France* **19** C13
Hayastan = Armenia ■ *Asia* **35** K7
Haydān, W. al → *Jordan* **74** D4
Haydarlı *Turkey* **47** C12
Hayden *U.S.A.* **108** F10
Haydon *Australia* **94** B3
Hayes *U.S.A.* **112** C3
Hayes → *Canada* **104** A1
Hayes Creek *Australia* **92** B5
Hayle *U.K.* **15** G2
Hayling I. *U.K.* **15** G7
Haymana *Turkey* **72** C5
Haymen I. *Australia* **94** J6
Hayrabolu *Turkey* **45** E11
Hays *Canada* **102** C6
Hays *U.S.A.* **112** F4
Haysyn *Ukraine* **29** B14
Hayvoron *Ukraine* **29** B14
Hayward *Calif., U.S.A.* **110** H4
Hayward *Wis., U.S.A.* **112** B8
Haywards Heath *U.K.* **15** G7
Hazafon □ *Israel* **74** C4
Hazar *Turkmenistan* **52** F6
Hazārān, Kūh-e *Iran* **71** D8
Hazard *U.S.A.* **113** G12
Hazaribag *India* **69** H11
Hazaribag Road *India* **69** G11
Hazebrouck *France* **19** B9
Hazelton *Canada* **102** B3
Hazelton *U.S.A.* **112** B3
Hazen *U.S.A.* **112** B3
Hazlehurst *Ga., U.S.A.* **117** F13
Hazlehurst *Miss., U.S.A.* **117** F9
Hazlet *U.S.A.* **115** F10
Hazleton *U.S.A.* **115** F9
Hazlett, L. *Australia* **92** D4
Hazro *Turkey* **70** B4
He Xian *Anhui, China* **59** B12
He Xian *Guangxi Zhuangzu,*
    China **59** E8
Head of Bight *Australia* **93** F5
Headlands *Zimbabwe* **87** F3
Healdsburg *U.S.A.* **110** G4
Healdton *U.S.A.* **116** D6
Healesville *Australia* **95** F4
Heany Junction *Zimbabwe* **89** C4
Heard I. *Ind. Oc.* **3** G13
Hearne *U.S.A.* **116** F6
Hearst *Canada* **104** C3
Heart → *U.S.A.* **112** B3
Heart's Content *Canada* **105** C9
Heath, Pte. *Canada* **105** C7
Heathrow, London ✈
    (LHR) *U.K.* **15** F7
Heavener *U.S.A.* **116** D7
Hebbronville *U.S.A.* **116** H5
Hebei □ *China* **56** E9
Hebel *Australia* **95** D4
Heber *U.S.A.* **111** N11
Heber Springs *U.S.A.* **116** D8
Hebgen L. *U.S.A.* **108** D8

Hebi *China* **56** G8
Hebrides *U.K.* **6** D4
Hebrides, Sea of the *U.K.* **13** D2
Hebron = Al Khalīl
    West Bank **74** D4
Hebron *Canada* **101** D13
Hebron *N. Dak., U.S.A.* **112** B2
Hebron *Nebr., U.S.A.* **112** E5
Heby *Sweden* **10** D10
Hecate Str. *Canada* **102** C2
Hechi *China* **58** E7
Hechingen *Germany* **25** G4
Hechuan *China* **58** B6
Hecla *U.S.A.* **112** C4
Hecla I. *Canada* **103** C9
Hedal *Norway* **10** D3
Hédé *France* **18** D5
Hede *Sweden* **10** B7
Hedemora *Sweden* **10** D9
Hedensted *Denmark* **11** J3
Hedesunda *Sweden* **10** D10
Heerde *Neths.* **17** B6
Heerenveen *Neths.* **17** B5
Heerhugowaard *Neths.* **17** B4
Heerlen *Neths.* **17** D5
Ḥefa *Israel* **74** C4
Ḥefa □ *Israel* **74** C4
Hefei *China* **59** B11
Hefeng *China* **59** C8
Hegalig *Sudan* **81** E3
Hegang *China* **60** B8
Heiban *Sudan* **81** E3
Heichengzhen *China* **56** F4
Heide *Germany* **24** A5
Heidelberg *Germany* **25** F4
Heidelberg *S. Africa* **88** E3
Heidenau *Germany* **24** E9
Heidenheim *Germany* **25** G6
Heihe *China* **60** A7
Heijing *China* **58** E3
Heilbad Heiligenstadt
    Germany **24** D6
Heilbron *S. Africa* **89** D4
Heilbronn *Germany* **25** F5
Heiligenblut *Austria* **26** D5
Heiligenhafen *Germany* **24** A6
Heilongjiang □ *China* **60** B7
Heilunkiang =
    Heilongjiang □ *China* **60** B7
Heimaey *Iceland* **8** E3
Heinola *Finland* **32** B4
Heinsberg *Germany* **24** D2
Heinze Kyun *Burma* **64** E1
Heishan *China* **57** D12
Heishui *Liaoning, China* **57** C10
Heishui *Sichuan, China* **58** A4
Hejaz = Ḥijāz *Si. Arabia* **70** E3
Hejian *China* **56** E9
Hejiang *China* **58** C5
Hejin *China* **56** G6
Hekimhan *Turkey* **72** C7
Hekla *Iceland* **8** E4
Hekou *Guangdong, China* **59** F9
Hekou *Yunnan, China* **58** F4
Hel *Poland* **30** D5
Helagsfjället *Sweden* **10** B6
Helan Shan *China* **56** E4
Helechosa *Spain* **37** F6
Helen Atoll *Pac. Oc.* **63** D8
Helena *Ark., U.S.A.* **117** D9
Helena *Mont., U.S.A.* **108** C7
Helendale *U.S.A.* **111** L9
Helensburgh *U.K.* **13** E4
Helensville *N.Z.* **91** B5
Helenvale *Australia* **94** B4
Helgasjön *Sweden* **11** H8
Helgeland *Norway* **8** C15
Helgoland *Germany* **24** A3
Heligoland = Helgoland
    Germany **24** A3
Heligoland B. = Deutsche
    Bucht *Germany* **24** A4
Heliopolis = Masr el
    Gedida *Egypt* **80** H7
Hell Hole Gorge △ *Australia* **94** D3
Hella *Iceland* **8** E3
Hellas = Greece ■ *Europe* **46** B3
Hellertown *U.S.A.* **115** F9
Hellespont = Çanakkale
    Boğazı *Turkey* **45** F10
Hellevoetsluis *Neths.* **17** C4
Hellín *Spain* **39** G3
Hells Canyon △ *U.S.A.* **108** D5
Hell's Gate △ *Kenya* **86** C4
Helmand □ *Afghan.* **66** D4
Helmand → *Afghan.* **66** D2
Helme → *Germany* **24** D7
Helmeringhausen *Namibia* **88** D2
Helmond *Neths.* **17** C5
Helmsdale *U.K.* **13** C5
Helmsdale → *U.K.* **13** C5
Helmstedt *Germany* **24** C7
Helong *China* **57** C15
Helper *U.S.A.* **108** G8
Helsingborg *Sweden* **11** H6
Helsinge *Denmark* **11** H6

Helsingfors = Helsinki
    Finland **32** B3
Helsingør *Denmark* **11** H6
Helsinki *Finland* **32** B3
Helska, Mierzeja *Poland* **30** D5
Helston *U.K.* **15** G2
Helvellyn *U.K.* **14** C4
Helwân *Egypt* **80** J7
Hemel Hempstead *U.K.* **15** F7
Hemet *U.S.A.* **111** M10
Hemingford *U.S.A.* **112** D2
Hemis △ *India* **68** B7
Hemmingford *Canada* **115** A11
Hempstead *N.Y., U.S.A.* **115** F11
Hempstead *Tex., U.S.A.* **116** F6
Hemse *Sweden* **11** G12
Hemsön *Sweden* **10** B12
Henån *Sweden* **11** F5
Henan □ *China* **56** H8
Henares → *Spain* **36** E7
Henashi-Misaki *Japan* **54** D9
Hendaye *France* **20** E2
Hendek *Turkey* **72** B4
Henderson *Argentina* **126** D3
Henderson *Ky., U.S.A.* **112** G10
Henderson *N.C., U.S.A.* **117** C15
Henderson *Nev., U.S.A.* **111** J12
Henderson *Tenn., U.S.A.* **117** D10
Henderson *Tex., U.S.A.* **116** E7
Henderson I. *Pac. Oc.* **97** K15
Hendersonville *N.C., U.S.A.*
    117 D13
Hendersonville *Tenn., U.S.A.*
    117 C11
Hendījān *Iran* **71** D6
Hendorābī *Iran* **71** E7
Heng Jiang *China* **58** C5
Heng Xian *China* **58** F7
Hengcheng *China* **56** E4
Hěngch'un *Taiwan* **59** F13
Hengdaohezi *China* **57** B15
Hengelo *Neths.* **17** B6
Hengfeng *China* **59** C10
Hengshan *Hunan, China* **59** D9
Hengshan *Shaanxi, China* **56** F5
Hengshui *China* **56** F8
Hengyang *China* **59** D9
Henichesk *Ukraine* **33** J8
Hénin-Beaumont *France* **19** B9
Henley-on-Thames *U.K.* **15** F7
Henlopen, C. *U.S.A.* **113** F16
Hennan *Sweden* **10** B9
Hennebont *France* **18** E3
Hennenman *S. Africa* **88** D4
Hennessey *U.S.A.* **116** C6
Hennigsdorf *Germany* **24** C9
Henri Pittier △ *Venezuela* **121** D6
Henrietta *U.S.A.* **116** E5
Henrietta, Ostrov =
    Genriyetty, Ostrov *Russia*
    53 B16
Henrietta Maria, C. *Canada* **104** A3
Henry *U.S.A.* **112** E9
Henryetta *U.S.A.* **116** D7
Henryville *Canada* **115** A11
Hensall *Canada* **114** C3
Henstedt-Ulzburg *Germany* **24** B6
Hentiesbaai *Namibia* **88** C1
Hentiyn Nuruu *Mongolia* **60** B5
Henty *Australia* **95** F4
Henzada *Burma* **67** L19
Hephaestia *Greece* **47** B7
Heping *China* **59** E10
Heppner *U.S.A.* **108** D4
Hepu *China* **58** G7
Hepworth *Canada* **114** B3
Heqing *China* **58** D3
Hequ *China* **56** E6
Héraðsflói *Iceland* **8** D6
Héraðsvötn → *Iceland* **8** D4
Heraklion = Iraklio *Greece* **49** D7
Herald Cays *Australia* **94** B4
Herāt *Afghan.* **66** B3
Herāt □ *Afghan.* **66** B3
Hérault □ *France* **20** E7
Hérault → *France* **20** E7
Herbault *France* **18** E8
Herbert *Canada* **103** C7
Herbert → *Australia* **94** B4
Herberton *Australia* **94** B4
Herbertsdale *S. Africa* **88** E3
Herbignac *France* **18** E4
Herborn *Germany* **24** E4
Herby *Poland* **31** H5
Herceg-Novi *Montenegro* **44** D2
Herchmer *Canada* **103** B10
Herðubreið *Iceland* **8** D5
Hereford *U.K.* **15** E5
Hereford *U.S.A.* **116** D3
Herefordshire □ *U.K.* **15** E5
Hereke *Turkey* **45** F13
Herencia *Spain* **37** F7
Herentals *Belgium* **17** C4
Herford *Germany* **24** C4
Héricourt *France* **19** E13
Herington *U.S.A.* **112** F5
Herisau *Switz.* **25** H5

Hérisson *France* **19** F9
Herkimer *U.S.A.* **115** D10
Herlong *U.S.A.* **110** E6
Herm *U.K.* **15** H5
Hermakivka *Ukraine* **29** B11
Hermann *U.S.A.* **112** F8
Hermannsburg *Australia* **92** D5
Hermannsburg *Germany* **24** C6
Hermanus *S. Africa* **88** E2
Herment *France* **20** C6
Hermidale *Australia* **95** E4
Hermiston *U.S.A.* **108** D4
Hermite, I. *Chile* **128** H3
Hermon *U.S.A.* **115** B9
Hermon, Mt. = Shaykh, J.
  ash *Lebanon* **74** B4
Hermosillo *Mexico* **118** B2
Hernád → *Hungary* **28** C6
Hernandarias *Paraguay* **127** B5
Hernandez *U.S.A.* **110** J5
Hernando *Argentina* **126** C3
Hernando *U.S.A.* **117** D10
Hernani *Spain* **38** B3
Herndon *U.S.A.* **114** F8
Herne *Germany* **17** C7
Herne Bay *U.K.* **15** F9
Herning *Denmark* **11** H2
Heroica Caborca =
  Caborca *Mexico* **118** A2
Heroica Nogales = Nogales
  Mexico **118** A2
Heron Bay *Canada* **104** C2
Heron I. *Australia* **94** C5
Herradura, Pta. de la
  Canary Is. **48** F5
Herreid *U.S.A.* **112** C3
Herrenberg *Germany* **25** G4
Herrera *Spain* **37** H6
Herrera de Alcántara *Spain* **37** F3
Herrera de Pisuerga *Spain* **36** C6
Herrera del Duque *Spain* **37** F5
Herrestad *Sweden* **11** F5
Herrin *U.S.A.* **112** G9
Herriot *Canada* **103** B8
Herrljunga *Sweden* **11** F7
Hersbruck *Germany* **25** F7
Herschel I. *Canada* **4** C1
Hershey *U.S.A.* **115** F8
Herso *Greece* **44** E6
Herstal *Belgium* **17** D5
Hertford *U.K.* **15** F7
Hertfordshire □ *U.K.* **15** F7
's-Hertogenbosch *Neths.* **17** C5
Hertsa *Ukraine* **29** B11
Hertzogville *S. Africa* **88** D4
Hervás *Spain* **36** E5
Hervey B. *Australia* **94** C5
Herzberg *Brandenburg,*
  Germany **24** D9
Herzberg *Niedersachsen,*
  Germany **24** D6
Herzliyya *Israel* **74** C3
Herzogenburg *Austria* **26** C8
Ḥeşār *Fārs, Iran* **71** D6
Ḥeşār *Markazī, Iran* **71** C6
Hesdin *France* **19** B9
Heshan *China* **58** F7
Heshui *China* **56** G5
Heshun *China* **56** F7
Hesperia *U.S.A.* **111** L9
Hesse = Hessen □ *Germany* **24** E4
Hessen □ *Germany* **24** E4
Hessenreuther und
  Manteler Wald △
  Germany **25** F8
Hestra *Sweden* **11** G7
Hetauda *Nepal* **68** F11
Hetch Hetchy Aqueduct
  U.S.A. **110** H5
Hettinger *U.S.A.* **112** B2
Hettstedt *Germany* **24** D7
Heuksando *S. Korea* **57** G13
Heunghae *S. Korea* **57** F15
Heuvelton *U.S.A.* **115** B9
Heves *Hungary* **28** C5
Heves □ *Hungary* **28** C5
Hewitt *U.S.A.* **116** F6
Hexham *U.K.* **14** C5
Hexi *Yunnan, China* **58** E4
Hexi *Zhejiang, China* **59** D12
Hexigten Qi *China* **57** C9
Ḥeydarābād *Iran* **71** D7
Heysham *U.K.* **14** C5
Heyuan *China* **59** F10
Heywood *Australia* **95** F3
Heze *China* **56** G8
Hezhang *China* **58** D5
Hi, Ko *Thailand* **65** a
Hi Vista *U.S.A.* **111** L9
Hialeah *U.S.A.* **117** J14
Hiawatha *U.S.A.* **112** F6
Hibbing *U.S.A.* **112** B7
Hibbs B. *Australia* **95** G4
Hibernia Reef *Australia* **92** B3
Hickman *U.S.A.* **112** G9
Hickory *U.S.A.* **117** D14
Hicks, Pt. *Australia* **95** F4

Hicks L. *Canada* **103** A9
Hicksville *U.S.A.* **115** F11
Hida *Romania* **29** C8
Hida-Gawa → *Japan* **55** G8
Hida-Sammyaku *Japan* **55** F8
Hidaka-Sammyaku *Japan* **54** C11
Hidalgo □ *Mexico* **119** C5
Hidalgo, Presa M. *Mexico* **118** B3
Hidalgo del Parral *Mexico* **118** B3
Hiddensee *Germany* **24** A9
Hieflau *Austria* **26** D7
Hiendelaencina *Spain* **38** D2
Hierro *Canary Is.* **48** G1
Higashiajima-San *Japan* **54** F10
Higashiōsaka *Japan* **55** G7
Higgins *U.S.A.* **116** C4
Higgins Corner *U.S.A.* **110** F5
High Bridge *U.S.A.* **115** F10
High Level *Canada* **102** B5
High Point *U.S.A.* **117** D15
High Prairie *Canada* **102** B5
High River *Canada* **102** C6
High Tatra = Tatry
  Slovak Rep. **27** B13
High Veld *Africa* **76** J6
High Wycombe *U.K.* **15** F7
Highland □ *U.K.* **13** D4
Highland Park *U.S.A.* **112** D10
Highmore *U.S.A.* **112** C4
Highrock L. *Man., Canada* **103** B8
Highrock L. *Sask., Canada* **103** B7
Higüey *Dom. Rep.* **121** C6
Hihya *Egypt* **80** H7
Hiiumaa *Estonia* **32** C2
Híjar *Spain* **38** D4
Ḥijāz *Si. Arabia* **70** E3
Hijo = Tagum *Phil.* **61** H6
Hikari *Japan* **55** H5
Hikmak, Ras el *Egypt* **80** A2
Hiko *U.S.A.* **110** H11
Hikone *Japan* **55** G8
Hikurangi *Gisborne, N.Z.* **91** C6
Hikurangi *Northland, N.Z.* **91** A5
Hildburghausen *Germany* **24** E6
Hildesheim *Germany* **24** C5
Hill → *Australia* **93** F2
Hill City *Idaho, U.S.A.* **108** E6
Hill City *Kans., U.S.A.* **112** F4
Hill City *Minn., U.S.A.* **112** B7
Hill City *S. Dak., U.S.A.* **112** D2
Hill Island L. *Canada* **103** A7
Hillaby, Mt. *Barbados* **121** g
Hillared *Sweden* **11** G7
Hillcrest *Barbados* **121** g
Hillcrest Center *U.S.A.* **111** K8
Hillegom *Neths.* **17** B4
Hillerød *Denmark* **11** J6
Hillerstorp *Sweden* **11** G7
Hillsboro *Kans., U.S.A.* **112** F5
Hillsboro *N. Dak., U.S.A.* **112** B5
Hillsboro *Ohio, U.S.A.* **113** F12
Hillsboro *Oreg., U.S.A.* **110** E4
Hillsboro *Tex., U.S.A.* **116** E6
Hillsborough *Grenada* **121** D7
Hillsborough *U.S.A.* **115** C13
Hillsborough Channel
  Australia **94** J7
Hillsdale *Mich., U.S.A.* **113** E11
Hillsdale *N.Y., U.S.A.* **115** D11
Hillsport *Canada* **104** C2
Hillston *Australia* **95** E4
Hilo *U.S.A.* **106** b
Hilton *U.S.A.* **114** C7
Hilvan *Turkey* **73** D8
Hilversum *Neths.* **17** B5
Himachal Pradesh □ *India* **68** D7
Himalaya *Asia* **69** E11
Himamaylan *Phil.* **61** F5
Himarë *Albania* **44** F3
Himatnagar *India* **68** H5
Himeji *Japan* **55** G7
Himi *Japan* **55** F8
Himmerland *Denmark* **11** H3
Ḥimş *Syria* **74** A5
Ḥimş □ *Syria* **74** A6
Hinche *Haiti* **121** C5
Hinchinbrook I. *Australia* **94** B4
Hinchinbrook Island △
  Australia **94** B4
Hinckley *U.K.* **15** E6
Hinckley *U.S.A.* **112** B7
Hindaun *India* **68** F7
Hindmarsh, L. *Australia* **95** F3
Hindsholm *Denmark* **11** J4
Hindu Bagh *Pakistan* **68** D2
Hindu Kush *Asia* **66** B7
Hindupur *India* **66** N10
Hines Creek *Canada* **102** B5
Hinesville *U.S.A.* **117** F14
Hinganghat *India* **66** J11
Hingham *U.S.A.* **108** B8
Hingir *India* **69** J10
Hingoli *India* **66** K10
Hinigaran *Phil.* **61** F5
Hinis *Turkey* **73** C9
Hinna = Imi *Ethiopia* **81** F5

Hinna *Nigeria* **83** C7
Hinnerup *Denmark* **11** H4
Hinnøya *Norway* **8** B16
Hinojosa del Duque *Spain* **37** G5
Hinsdale *U.S.A.* **115** D12
Hinterrhein → *Switz.* **25** J5
Hinthada = Henzada
  Burma **67** L19
Hinton *Canada* **102** C5
Hinton *U.S.A.* **113** G13
Hios *Greece* **47** C8
Hios □ *Greece* **47** C8
Hirado *Japan* **55** H4
Hirakud Dam *India* **67** J13
Hiran → *India* **69** H5
Hirapur *India* **69** G8
Hirara *Japan* **55** M2
Hiratsuka *Japan* **55** G9
Hirfanlı Barajı *Turkey* **72** C5
Hiroo *Japan* **54** C11
Hirosaki *Japan* **54** D10
Hiroshima *Japan* **55** G6
Hiroshima □ *Japan* **55** G6
Hirson *France* **19** C11
Hirtshals *Denmark* **11** G3
Hisar *India* **68** E6
Hisarcık *Turkey* **47** B11
Hisaria *Bulgaria* **45** D8
Hisb, Sha'ib → *W.*
  Iraq **70** D5
Ḥismá *Si. Arabia* **70** D3
Hispaniola *W. Indies* **121** C5
Ḥīt *Iraq* **73** F10
Hita *Japan* **55** H5
Hitachi *Japan* **55** F10
Hitchin *U.K.* **15** F7
Hitiaa *Tahiti* **91** d
Hitoyoshi *Japan* **55** H5
Hitra *Norway* **8** E13
Hitzacker *Germany* **24** B7
Hiva Oa *French Polynesia* **97** H14
Hixon *Canada* **102** C4
Ḥiyyon, N. → *Israel* **74** E4
Hjalmar L. *Canada* **103** A7
Hjälmaren *Sweden* **10** E9
Hjältevad *Sweden* **11** G9
Hjo *Sweden* **11** F8
Hjørring *Denmark* **11** G3
Hjort Trench *S. Ocean* **5** B10
Hjortkvarn *Sweden* **11** F9
Hkakabo Razi *Burma* **67** E20
Hlinsko *Czech Rep.* **26** B8
Hlobane *S. Africa* **89** D5
Hlohovec *Slovak Rep.* **27** C10
Hlučín *Czech Rep.* **27** B11
Hluhluwe *S. Africa* **89** D5
Hluhluwe △ *S. Africa* **89** C5
Hlukhiv *Ukraine* **33** G7
Hlyboka *Ukraine* **29** B10
Hlybokaye *Belarus* **32** E4
Hnúšť'a *Slovak Rep.* **27** C12
Ho *Ghana* **83** D5
Ho Chi Minh City = Thanh
  Pho Ho Chi Minh *Vietnam* **65** G6
Ho Thuong *Vietnam* **64** C5
Hoa Binh *Vietnam* **58** B5
Hoa Da *Vietnam* **65** G7
Hoa Hiep *Vietnam* **65** G5
Hoai Nhon *Vietnam* **64** E7
Hoang Lien Son *Vietnam* **58** F4
Hoanib → *Namibia* **88** B2
Hoare B. *Canada* **101** C13
Hoarusib → *Namibia* **88** B2
Hobart *Australia* **95** G4
Hobart *U.S.A.* **116** D5
Hobbs *U.S.A.* **109** K12
Hobbs Coast *Antarctica* **5** D14
Hobe Sound *U.S.A.* **117** H14
Hoboken *U.S.A.* **115** F10
Hobro *Denmark* **11** H3
Hoburgen *Sweden* **11** H12
Hocalar *Turkey* **47** C11
Hochfeld *Namibia* **88** C2
Hochharz △ *Germany* **24** D6
Hochschwab *Austria* **26** D8
Höchstadt *Germany* **25** F6
Hochtaunus △ *Germany* **25** E4
Hockenheim *Germany* **25** F4
Hodaka-Dake *Japan* **55** F8
Hodeida = Al Ḥudaydah
  Yemen **75** E3
Hodgeville *Canada* **103** C7
Hodgson *Canada* **103** C9
Hodh El Gharbi □ *Mauritania* **82** B3
Hódmezővásárhely *Hungary* **28** D5
Hodna, Chott el *Algeria* **78** A6
Hodonín *Czech Rep.* **27** C10
Hœdic, Î. de *France* **18** E4
Hoek van Holland *Neths.* **17** C4
Hoengseong *S. Korea* **57** F14
Hoeryong *N. Korea* **57** C15
Hoeyang *N. Korea* **57** E14
Hof *Germany* **25** E7
Hofgeismar *Germany* **24** D5
Hofheim *Germany* **25** E4
Hofmeyr *S. Africa* **88** E4
Höfn *Iceland* **8** D6

Hofors *Sweden* **10** D10
Hofsjökull *Iceland* **8** D4
Hōfu *Japan* **55** G5
Hogan Group *Australia* **95** F4
Höganäs *Sweden* **11** H6
Hogarth, Mt. *Australia* **94** C2
Hoge Kempen △ *Belgium* **17** C5
Hoggar = Ahaggar *Algeria* **78** D7
Högsäter *Sweden* **11** F6
Högsby *Sweden* **11** G10
Högsjö *Sweden* **10** E9
Hogsty Reef *Bahamas* **121** B5
Hoh → *U.S.A.* **110** C2
Hohd ech Chargui □
  Mauritania **82** B3
Hohe Acht *Germany* **25** E3
Hohe Tauern *Austria* **26** D5
Hohe Tauern △ *Austria* **26** D5
Hohenau *Austria* **27** C9
Hohenems *Austria* **26** D2
Hohenloher Ebene *Germany* **25** F5
Hohenwald *U.S.A.* **117** D11
Hohenwestedt *Germany* **24** A5
Hoher Rhön = Rhön
  Germany **24** E5
Hoher Vogelsberg △
  Germany **24** D5
Hohes Venn = Hohe → *Belgium* **17** D6
Hohes Venn-Eifel △ *Europe* **24** E2
Hohhot *China* **56** D6
Hohoe *Ghana* **83** D5
Hoi An *Vietnam* **64** E7
Hoi Xuan *Vietnam* **58** G5
Hoisington *U.S.A.* **112** F4
Højer *Denmark* **11** K2
Hōjō *Japan* **55** H6
Hok *Sweden* **11** G8
Hok, Río → *Belize* **119** D7
Hökensås *Sweden* **11** G8
Hökerum *Sweden* **11** G7
Hokianga Harbour *N.Z.* **91** A4
Hokitika *N.Z.* **91** E3
Hokkaidō □ *Japan* **54** C11
Hol-Hol *Djibouti* **81** E5
Hola *Kenya* **86** B4
Hola Pristan *Ukraine* **33** J7
Holakas *Greece* **49** D9
Holbæk *Denmark* **11** J5
Holbrook *Australia* **95** F4
Holbrook *U.S.A.* **109** J8
Holden *U.S.A.* **108** G7
Holdenville *U.S.A.* **116** D6
Holdrege *U.S.A.* **112** E4
Holešov *Czech Rep.* **27** B10
Holetown *Barbados* **121** g
Holguín *Cuba* **120** B4
Holíč *Slovak Rep.* **27** C10
Holice *Czech Rep.* **26** A8
Höljes *Sweden* **10** D6
Hollabrunn *Austria* **26** C9
Hollams Bird I. *Namibia* **88** C1
Holland *Mich., U.S.A.* **112** D10
Holland *N.Y., U.S.A.* **114** D6
Holley *U.S.A.* **114** C6
Hollfeld *Germany* **25** F7
Hollidaysburg *U.S.A.* **114** F6
Hollis *U.S.A.* **116** D5
Hollister *Calif., U.S.A.* **110** J5
Hollister *Idaho, U.S.A.* **108** E6
Höllviken = Höllviksnäs
  Sweden **11** J6
Höllviksnäs *Sweden* **11** J6
Holly Hill *U.S.A.* **117** G14
Holly Springs *U.S.A.* **117** D10
Hollywood *U.S.A.* **117** J14
Holman *Canada* **100** B8
Hólmavík *Iceland* **8** D3
Holmen *U.S.A.* **112** D8
Holmes Reefs *Australia* **94** B4
Holmsjö *Sweden* **11** H9
Holmsjön *Västernorrland,*
  Sweden **10** B10
Holmsjön *Västernorrland,*
  Sweden **10** B9
Holmsland Klit *Denmark* **11** J2
Holmsund *Sweden* **8** E19
Holod *Romania* **28** D7
Holovne *Ukraine* **31** G11
Holroyd → *Australia* **94** A3
Holstebro *Denmark* **11** H2
Holsteinische Schweiz △
  Germany **24** A6
Holsworthy *U.K.* **15** G3
Holton *Canada* **105** B8
Holton *U.S.A.* **112** F6
Holtville *U.S.A.* **111** N11
Holwerd *Neths.* **17** A5
Holy I. *Anglesey, U.K.* **14** D3
Holy I. *Northumberland, U.K.* **14** B6
Holyhead *U.K.* **14** D3
Holyoke *Colo., U.S.A.* **108** F12
Holyoke *Mass., U.S.A.* **115** D12
Holyrood *Canada* **105** C9
Holzkirchen *Germany* **25** H7
Holzminden *Germany* **24** D5
Homa Bay *Kenya* **86** C3
Homalin *Burma* **67** G19
Hope, L. *S. Austral., Australia* **95** D2

Homand *Iran* **71** C8
Homathko → *Canada* **102** C4
Homberg *Germany* **24** D5
Hombori *Mali* **83** B4
Hombori Tondo *Mali* **83** B4
Homburg *Germany* **25** F3
Home B. *Canada* **101** C13
Home Hill *Australia* **94** B4
Home Reef *Tonga* **91** c
Homedale *U.S.A.* **108** E5
Homer *Alaska, U.S.A.* **100** D4
Homer *La., U.S.A.* **116** E8
Homer City *U.S.A.* **114** F5
Homert △ *Germany* **24** D4
Homestead *Australia* **94** C4
Homestead *U.S.A.* **117** J14
Homestead △ *U.S.A.* **112** E5
Homoine *Mozam.* **89** C6
Homoljske Planina *Serbia* **44** B5
Homorod *Romania* **29** D10
Homs = Ḥimş *Syria* **74** A5
Homyel *Belarus* **23** B16
Homyel □ *Belarus* **33** F6
Hon Chong *Vietnam* **65** G5
Hon Hai *Vietnam* **65** H7
Hon Me *Vietnam* **64** C5
Honan = Henan □ *China* **56** H8
Honaz *Turkey* **47** D11
Honbetsu *Japan* **54** C11
Honda, Bahía *Colombia* **120** B3
Honda Bay *Phil.* **61** G3
Hondeklipbaai *S. Africa* **88** E2
Hondo *Japan* **55** H5
Hondo *U.S.A.* **116** G5
Hondo, Río → *Belize* **119** D7
Honduras ■ *Cent. Amer.* **120** D2
Honduras, G. de *Caribbean* **120** C2
Hønefoss *Norway* **9** F14
Honesdale *U.S.A.* **115** E9
Honey L. *U.S.A.* **110** E6
Honfleur *France* **18** C7
Høng *Denmark* **11** J5
Hong Gai *Vietnam* **58** G6
Hong He → *China* **56** H8
Hong Hu *China* **59** C9
Hong Kong □ *China* **59** F10
Hong'an *China* **59** B10
Hongcheon *S. Korea* **57** F14
Honghai Wan *China* **59** F10
Honghe *China* **58** F4
Honghu *China* **59** C9
Hongjiang *China* **58** D7
Hongliu He → *China* **56** F5
Hongor *Mongolia* **56** B7
Hongsa *Laos* **64** C3
Hongseong *S. Korea* **57** F14
Hongshui He → *China* **58** F7
Hongtong *China* **56** F6
Honguedo, Détroit d'
  Canada **105** C7
Hongwon *N. Korea* **57** E14
Hongya *China* **58** C4
Hongyuan *China* **58** A4
Hongze Hu *China* **57** H10
Honiara *Solomon Is.* **90** B8
Honingsvåg *Norway* **8** A21
Honiton *U.K.* **15** G4
Honjō *Japan* **54** E10
Honkorâb, Ras *Egypt* **80** C4
Honningsvåg *Norway* **8** A21
Hönö *Sweden* **11** G5
Honolulu *U.S.A.* **106** b
Honshū *Japan* **55** G9
Hontoria del Pinar *Spain* **38** D1
Hood, Mt. *U.S.A.* **108** D3
Hood, Pt. *Australia* **93** F2
Hood River *U.S.A.* **108** D3
Hoodsport *U.S.A.* **110** C3
Hooge *Germany* **24** A4
Hoogeveen *Neths.* **17** B6
Hoogezand-Sappemeer
  Neths. **17** A6
Hooghly = Hugli → *India* **69** J13
Hooghly-Chinsura =
  Chunchura *India* **69** H13
Hook Hd. *Ireland* **12** D5
Hook I. *Australia* **94** J6
Hook of Holland = Hoek
  van Holland *Neths.* **17** C4
Hooker *U.S.A.* **116** C4
Hooker Creek = Lajamanu
  Australia **92** C5
Hoonah *U.S.A.* **102** B1
Hooper Bay *U.S.A.* **106** a
Hoopeston *U.S.A.* **112** E10
Hoopstad *S. Africa* **88** D4
Höör *Sweden* **11** J7
Hoorn *Neths.* **17** B5
Hoover *U.S.A.* **117** E11
Hoover Dam *U.S.A.* **111** K12
Hooversville *U.S.A.* **114** F6
Hop Bottom *U.S.A.* **115** E9
Hopa *Turkey* **73** B9
Hope *Canada* **102** D4
Hope *Ariz., U.S.A.* **111** M13
Hope *Ark., U.S.A.* **116** E8

Hope, L. *W. Austral., Australia* **93** F3
Hope, Pt. *U.S.A.* **98** C3
Hope I. *Canada* **114** B4
Hope Town *Bahamas* **120** A4
Hope Vale *Australia* **94** B4
Hopedale *Canada* **105** A7
Hopedale *U.S.A.* **115** D13
Hopefield *S. Africa* **88** E2
Hopei = Hebei □ *China* **56** E9
Hopelchén *Mexico* **119** D7
Hopetoun *Vic., Australia* **95** F3
Hopetoun *W. Austral.,*
  Australia **93** F3
Hopetown *S. Africa* **88** D3
Hopewell *U.S.A.* **113** G15
Hopfgarten *Austria* **26** D5
Hopkins, L. *Australia* **92** D4
Hopkinsville *U.S.A.* **112** G10
Hopland *U.S.A.* **110** G3
Hoquiam *U.S.A.* **110** D3
Hora Hoverla *Ukraine* **29** B9
Horasan *Turkey* **73** B10
Horaždovice *Czech Rep.* **26** B6
Horb *Germany* **25** G4
Hörby *Sweden* **11** J7
Horcajo de Santiago *Spain* **38** F1
Hordern Hills *Australia* **92** D5
Horezu *Romania* **29** E8
Horgen *Switz.* **25** H4
Horgoš *Serbia* **28** D4
Hořice *Czech Rep.* **26** A8
Horinchove *Ukraine* **29** B8
Horinger *China* **56** D6
Horki *Belarus* **32** G4
Horlick Mts. *Antarctica* **5** E15
Horlivka *Ukraine* **33** H10
Hormak *Iran* **71** D9
Hormoz *Iran* **71** E7
Hormoz, Jaz.-ye *Iran* **71** E8
Hormozgān □ *Iran* **71** E8
Hormuz, Kūh-e *Iran* **71** E7
Hormuz, Str. of *The Gulf* **71** E8
Horn *Austria* **26** C8
Horn *Sweden* **11** G9
Horn → *Canada* **102** A5
Horn, Cape = Hornos, C. de
  Chile **128** H3
Horn Head *Ireland* **12** A3
Horn I. *Australia* **94** A3
Horn Plateau *Canada* **102** A5
Hornachuelos *Spain* **37** H5
Hornavan *Sweden* **8** C17
Hornbeck *U.S.A.* **116** F8
Hornbrook *U.S.A.* **108** F2
Hornburg *Germany* **24** C6
Horncastle *U.K.* **14** D7
Horndal *Sweden* **10** D10
Hornell *U.S.A.* **114** D7
Hornell L. *Canada* **102** A5
Hornepayne *Canada* **104** C3
Horní Planá *Czech Rep.* **26** C7
Hornings Mills *Canada* **114** B4
Hornitos *U.S.A.* **110** H6
Hornos, C. de *Chile* **128** H3
Hornoy-le-Bourg *France* **19** C8
Hornsea *U.K.* **14** D7
Hornslandet *Sweden* **10** C11
Hörnum *Germany* **24** A4
Horobetsu = Noboribetsu
  Japan **54** C10
Horodenka *Ukraine* **29** B10
Horodnya *Ukraine* **33** G6
Horodok *Khmelnytskyy,*
  Ukraine **23** D14
Horodok *Lviv, Ukraine* **23** D12
Horodyshche *Ukraine* **33** H6
Horokhiv *Ukraine* **23** C13
Horovice *Czech Rep.* **26** B6
Horqin Youyi Qianqi *China* **57** A12
Horqueta *Paraguay* **126** A4
Horred *Sweden* **11** G6
Horse Cr. → *U.S.A.* **108** F12
Horse I. *Canada* **103** C9
Horse Is. *Canada* **105** B8
Horsefly L. *Canada* **102** C4
Horseheads *U.S.A.* **114** D8
Horsens *Denmark* **11** J3
Horsham *Australia* **95** F3
Horsham *U.K.* **15** F7
Horšovský Týn *Czech Rep.* **26** B5
Horta *Azores* **78** a
Horten *Norway* **9** G14
Hortobágy → *Hungary* **28** C6
Hortobágyi △ *Hungary* **28** C6
Horton *U.S.A.* **112** F6
Horton → *Canada* **100** C7
Horwood L. *Canada* **104** C3
Hosaina *Ethiopia* **81** F4
Ḥoseynābād *Khuzestān, Iran* **71** C6
Ḥoseynābād *Kordestān, Iran* **73** E12
Hoshangabad *India* **68** H7
Hoshiarpur *India* **68** D6
Hospet *India* **66** M10
Hoste, I. *Chile* **128** H3
Hostens *France* **20** D3
Hot *Thailand* **64** C2
Hot Creek Range *U.S.A.* **108** G5

Hot Springs *Ark., U.S.A.* **116** D8
Hot Springs *S. Dak., U.S.A.* **112** D2
Hot Springs △ *U.S.A.* **116** D8
Hotagen *Sweden* **8** E16
Hotan *China* **60** C2
Hotazel *S. Africa* **88** D3
Hotchkiss *U.S.A.* **108** G10
Hotham, C. *Australia* **92** B5
Hoting *Sweden* **8** D17
Hotolisht *Albania* **44** E4
Hotte, Massif de la *Haiti* **121** C5
Hottentotsbaai *Namibia* **88** D1
Houat, Î. de *France* **18** E4
Houdan *France* **19** D8
Houei Sai *Laos* **58** G3
Houeillès *France* **20** D4
Houffalize *Belgium* **17** D5
Houghton *Mich., U.S.A.* **112** B9
Houghton *N.Y., U.S.A.* **114** D6
Houghton L. *U.S.A.* **113** C11
Houghton-le-Spring *U.K.* **14** C6
Houhora Heads *N.Z.* **91** A4
Houlton *U.S.A.* **113** B20
Houma *U.S.A.* **117** G9
Houndé *Burkina Faso* **82** C4
Hourtin *France* **20** C2
Hourtin-Carcans, Étang d' *France* **20** C2
Housatonic → *U.S.A.* **115** E11
Houston *Canada* **102** C3
Houston *Mo., U.S.A.* **112** G8
Houston *Tex., U.S.A.* **116** G7
Hout = Mogwadi → *S. Africa* **89** C4
Houtkraal *S. Africa* **88** E3
Houtman Abrolhos *Australia* **93** E1
Hovd □ *Mongolia* **60** B4
Hove *U.K.* **15** G7
Hovedstaden □ *Denmark* **11** J6
Hovenweep △ *U.S.A.* **109** H9
Hoveyzeh *Iran* **71** D6
Hovmantorp *Sweden* **11** H9
Hövsgöl *Mongolia* **56** C5
Hövsgöl Nuur *Mongolia* **60** A5
Hovsta *Sweden* **10** E9
Howakil *Eritrea* **81** D5
Howar, Wadi → *Sudan* **81** D2
Howard *Australia* **95** D5
Howard *Pa., U.S.A.* **114** F7
Howard *S. Dak., U.S.A.* **112** C5
Howe *U.S.A.* **108** E7
Howe, C. *Australia* **95** F5
Howe, West Cape *Australia* **93** G2
Howe I. *Canada* **115** B8
Howell *U.S.A.* **113** D12
Howick *Canada* **115** A11
Howick *S. Africa* **89** D5
Howick Group *Australia* **94** A4
Howitt, L. *Australia* **95** D2
Howland I. *Pac. Oc.* **96** G10
Howrah = Haora *India* **69** H13
Howth *Ireland* **12** C5
Howth Hd. *Ireland* **12** C5
Höxter *Germany* **24** D5
Hoy *U.K.* **13** C5
Hoya *Germany* **24** B5
Høyanger *Norway* **8** F12
Hoyerswerda *Germany* **24** D10
Hoylake *U.K.* **14** D4
Hoyos *Spain* **36** E4
Hpa-an = Pa-an *Burma* **67** L20
Hpunan Pass *Burma* **67** F20
Hradec Králové *Czech Rep.* **26** A8
Hrádek *Czech Rep.* **27** C9
Hranice *Czech Rep.* **27** B10
Hrazdan *Armenia* **35** K7
Hrebenka *Ukraine* **33** G7
Hrisoupoli *Greece* **45** F8
Hristiana *Greece* **47** E7
Hrodna *Belarus* **30** E10
Hrodna □ *Belarus* **32** F3
Hrodzyanka *Belarus* **23** B15
Hron → *Slovak Rep.* **27** D11
Hrubieszów *Poland* **31** H10
Hrubý Jeseník *Czech Rep.* **27** A10
Hrvatska = Croatia ■ *Europe* **41** C13
Hrymayliv *Ukraine* **23** D14
Hrynyava *Ukraine* **29** C9
Hsenwi *Burma* **67** H20
Hsiamen = Xiamen *China* **59** E12
Hsian = Xi'an *China* **56** G5
Hsinchu *Taiwan* **59** E13
Hsinhailien = Lianyungang *China* **57** G10
Hsinying *Taiwan* **59** F13
Hsopket *Burma* **58** F2
Hsüchou = Xuzhou *China* **57** G9
Htapodia *Greece* **47** D7
Hu Xian *China* **56** G5
Hua Hin *Thailand* **64** F2
Hua Xian *Henan, China* **56** G8
Hua Xian *Shaanxi, China* **56** G5
Hua'an *China* **59** E11
Huab → *Namibia* **88** B2
Huacheng *China* **59** E10
Huachinera *Mexico* **118** A3

Huacho *Peru* **124** F3
Huade *China* **56** D7
Huadian *China* **57** C14
Huadu *China* **59** F9
Huahine, Î. *French Polynesia* **97** J12
Huai Had △ *Thailand* **64** D5
Huai He → *China* **59** A12
Huai Nam Dang △ *Thailand* **64** C2
Huai Yot *Thailand* **65** J2
Huai'an *Hebei, China* **56** D8
Huai'an *Jiangsu, China* **57** H10
Huaibei *China* **56** G9
Huaibin *China* **59** A10
Huaide = Gongzhuling *China* **57** C13
Huaidezhen *China* **57** C13
Huaihua *China* **58** D7
Huaiji *China* **59** F9
Huainan *China* **59** A11
Huaining *China* **59** B11
Huairen *China* **56** E7
Huairou *China* **56** D9
Huaiyang *China* **56** H8
Huaiyin *China* **57** H10
Huaiyuan *Anhui, China* **57** H9
Huaiyuan *Guangxi Zhuangzu, China* **58** E7
Huajuapán de León *Mexico* **119** D5
Hualapai Peak *U.S.A.* **109** J7
Hualien *Taiwan* **59** E13
Huallaga → *Peru* **124** E3
Huambo *Angola* **85** G3
Huan Jiang → *China* **56** G5
Huan Xian *China* **56** F4
Huancabamba *Peru* **124** E3
Huancane *Peru* **124** G5
Huancavelica *Peru* **124** F3
Huancayo *Peru* **124** F3
Huanchaca *Bolivia* **124** H5
Huang Hai = Yellow Sea *China* **57** G12
Huang He → *China* **57** F10
Huang Xian *China* **57** F11
Huangchuan *China* **59** A10
Huanggang *China* **59** B10
Huangguoshu *China* **58** E5
Huangling *China* **56** G5
Huanglong *China* **56** G5
Huanglongtan *China* **59** A8
Huangmei *China* **59** B10
Huangpi *China* **59** B10
Huangping *China* **58** D6
Huangshan *Anhui, China* **59** B12
Huangshan *Anhui, China* **59** C12
Huangshi *China* **59** B10
Huangsongdian *China* **57** C14
Huangyan *China* **59** C13
Huangyangsi *China* **59** D8
Huaning *China* **58** E4
Huanjiang *China* **58** E7
Huanren *China* **57** D13
Huantai *China* **57** F9
Huánuco *Peru* **124** E3
Huaping *China* **58** D3
Huaraz *Peru* **124** E3
Huarmey *Peru* **124** F3
Huarong *China* **59** C9
Huascarán, Nevado *Peru* **124** E3
Huasco *Chile* **126** B1
Huasco → *Chile* **126** B1
Huasna *U.S.A.* **111** K6
Huatabampo *Mexico* **118** B3
Huauchinango *Mexico* **119** C5
Huautla de Jiménez *Mexico* **119** D5
Huaxi *China* **58** D6
Huayin *China* **56** G6
Huayuan *China* **58** C7
Huayun *China* **58** B6
Huazhou *China* **59** G8
Hubbard *Ohio, U.S.A.* **114** E4
Hubbard *Tex., U.S.A.* **116** F6
Hubbart Pt. *Canada* **103** B10
Hubei □ *China* **59** B9
Hubli *India* **66** M9
Huch'ang *N. Korea* **57** D14
Hucknall *U.K.* **14** D6
Huddersfield *U.K.* **14** D6
Hude *Germany* **24** B4
Hudi *Sudan* **80** D3
Hudiksvall *Sweden* **10** C11
Hudson *Canada* **104** B1
Hudson *Mass., U.S.A.* **115** D13
Hudson *N.Y., U.S.A.* **115** D11
Hudson *Wis., U.S.A.* **112** C7
Hudson *Wyo., U.S.A.* **108** E9
Hudson → *U.S.A.* **115** F10
Hudson, C. *Antarctica* **5** C20
Hudson Bay *Nunavut, Canada* **101** D11
Hudson Bay *Sask., Canada* **103** C8
Hudson Falls *U.S.A.* **115** C11
Hudson Mts. *Antarctica* **5** D16
Hudson Str. *Canada* **101** C13
Hudson's Hope *Canada* **102** B4
Hue *Vietnam* **64** D6
Huebra → *Spain* **36** D4
Huedin *Romania* **28** D8

Huehuetenango *Guatemala* **120** C1
Huejúcar *Mexico* **118** C4
Huélamo *Spain* **38** E3
Huelgoat *France* **18** D3
Huelma *Spain* **37** H7
Huelva *Spain* **37** H4
Huelva □ *Spain* **37** H4
Huelva → *Spain* **37** H5
Huentelauquén *Chile* **126** C1
Huércal-Overa *Spain* **39** H3
Huerta, Sa. de la *Argentina* **126** C2
Huertas, C. de las *Spain* **39** G4
Huerva → *Spain* **38** D4
Huesca *Spain* **38** C4
Huesca □ *Spain* **38** C5
Huéscar *Spain* **39** H2
Huetamo *Mexico* **118** D4
Huete *Spain* **38** E2
Hugh → *Australia* **94** D1
Hughenden *Australia* **94** C3
Hughesville *U.S.A.* **115** E8
Hugli → *India* **69** J13
Hugo *Colo., U.S.A.* **108** G12
Hugo *Okla., U.S.A.* **116** D7
Hugoton *U.S.A.* **112** G3
Hui Xian = Huixian *China* **56** G7
Hui Xian *China* **56** H4
Hui'an *China* **59** E12
Hui'anbu *China* **56** F4
Huichang *China* **59** E10
Huichapan *Mexico* **119** C5
Huichon *N. Korea* **57** D14
Huidong *Guangdong, China* **59** F10
Huidong *Sichuan, China* **58** D4
Huifa He → *China* **57** C14
Huila, Nevado del *Colombia* **124** C3
Huilai *China* **59** F11
Huili *China* **58** D4
Huimin *China* **57** F9
Huinan *China* **57** C14
Huinca Renancó *Argentina* **126** C3
Huining *China* **56** G3
Huinong *China* **56** E4
Huishui *China* **58** D6
Huisne → *France* **18** E7
Huiting *China* **56** G9
Huitong *China* **58** D7
Huixian *China* **56** H4
Huixtla *Mexico* **119** D6
Huize *China* **58** D4
Huizhou *China* **59** F10
Hukawng Valley *Burma* **67** F20
Hukou *China* **59** C11
Hukuntsi *Botswana* **88** C3
Ḥulayfā' *Si. Arabia* **70** E4
Hulin He → *China* **57** B12
Hull = Kingston upon Hull *U.K.* **14** D7
Hull *Canada* **115** A9
Hull → *U.K.* **14** D7
Hulst *Neths.* **17** C4
Hultsfred *Sweden* **11** G9
Hulun Nur *China* **60** B6
Hulyaypole *Ukraine* **33** J9
Huma, Tanjung *Malaysia* **65** c
Humacao *Puerto Rico* **121** d
Humahuaca *Argentina* **126** A2
Humaitá *Brazil* **124** E6
Humaitá *Paraguay* **126** B4
Humansdorp *S. Africa* **88** E3
Humara, J. *Sudan* **81** D3
Humbe *Angola* **88** B1
Humber → *U.K.* **14** D7
Humboldt *Canada* **103** C7
Humboldt *Iowa, U.S.A.* **112** D6
Humboldt *Tenn., U.S.A.* **117** D8
Humboldt → *U.S.A.* **108** G4
Humboldt Gletscher = Sermersuaq *Greenland* **4** B4
Hume *U.S.A.* **110** J8
Hume, L. *Australia* **95** F4
Humenné *Slovak Rep.* **27** C14
Hummelsta *Sweden* **10** E10
Humphreys, Mt. *U.S.A.* **110** H8
Humphreys Peak *U.S.A.* **109** J8
Humpolec *Czech Rep.* **26** B8
Humptulips *U.S.A.* **110** C3
Hūn *Libya* **79** C9
Hun Jiang → *China* **57** D13
Húnaflói *Iceland* **8** D3
Hunan □ *China* **59** D9
Hunchun *China* **57** C16
Hundested *Denmark* **11** J5
Hundewali *Pakistan* **68** D5
Hundred Mile House *Canada* **102** C4
Hunedoara *Romania* **28** E7
Hunedoara □ *Romania* **28** E7
Hünfeld *Germany* **24** E5
Hung Yen *Vietnam* **58** G6
Hunga Ha'apai *Tonga* **91** c
Hungary ■ *Europe* **27** D10
Hungary, Plain of *Europe* **6** F10
Hungerford *Australia* **95** D3
Húngnam *N. Korea* **57** E14
Hungt'ou Hsü = Lan Yü *Taiwan* **59**

Huni Valley *Ghana* **82** D4
Hunjiang *China* **57** D14
Hunneberg *Sweden* **11** F6
Hunnebostrand *Sweden* **11** F5
Hunsberge *Namibia* **88** D2
Hunsrück *Germany* **25** F3
Hunstanton *U.K.* **14** E8
Hunte → *Germany* **24** B4
Hunter *U.S.A.* **115** D10
Hunter I. *Australia* **95** G3
Hunter I. *Canada* **102** C3
Hunter Ra. *Australia* **95** E5
Hunters Road *Zimbabwe* **87** F2
Hunterville *N.Z.* **91** C5
Huntingburg *U.S.A.* **112** F10
Huntingdon *Canada* **104** C5
Huntingdon *U.K.* **15** E7
Huntingdon *U.S.A.* **114** F6
Huntington *Ind., U.S.A.* **113** E11
Huntington *N.Y., U.S.A.* **115** F11
Huntington *Oreg., U.S.A.* **108** D5
Huntington *Utah, U.S.A.* **108** G8
Huntington *W. Va., U.S.A.* **113** F12
Huntington Beach *U.S.A.* **111** M9
Huntly *N.Z.* **91** B5
Huntly *U.K.* **13** D6
Huntsville *Canada* **114** A5
Huntsville *Ala., U.S.A.* **117** D11
Huntsville *Tex., U.S.A.* **116** F7
Hunyani → *Zimbabwe* **87** F3
Hunyuan *China* **56** E7
Hunza → *India* **69** B6
Huo Xian = Huozhou *China* **56** F6
Huong Khe *Vietnam* **64** C5
Huonville *Australia* **95** G4
Huoqiu *China* **59** A11
Huoshan *Anhui, China* **59** A12
Huoshan *Anhui, China* **59** B11
Huoshao Dao = Lü Tao *Taiwan* **59** F13
Huozhou *China* **56** F6
Hupeh = Hubei □ *China* **59** B9
Hūr *Iran* **71** D8
Ḥuraymīla *Si. Arabia* **70** E5
Hurbanovo *Slovak Rep.* **27** D11
Hurd, C. *Canada* **114** A3
Hure Qi *China* **57** C11
Hurezani *Romania* **29** F8
Hurghada *Egypt* **80** B3
Hurley *N. Mex., U.S.A.* **109** K9
Hurley *Wis., U.S.A.* **112** B8
Huron *Calif., U.S.A.* **110** J6
Huron *Ohio, U.S.A.* **114** E2
Huron *S. Dak., U.S.A.* **112** C4
Huron, L. *U.S.A.* **114** B2
Huron East *Canada* **114** C3
Hurricane *U.S.A.* **109** H7
Hurso *Ethiopia* **81** F5
Hurungwe △ *Zimbabwe* **87** F2
Hurunui → *N.Z.* **91** E4
Hurup *Denmark* **11** H2
Húsavík *Iceland* **8** C5
Huși *Romania* **29** D13
Huskvarna *Sweden* **11** G8
Hustadvika *Norway* **8** E12
Hustontown *U.S.A.* **114** F6
Hustopeče *Czech Rep.* **27** C9
Husum *Germany* **24** A5
Husum *Sweden* **10** A13
Hutchinson *Kans., U.S.A.* **112** F5
Hutchinson *Minn., U.S.A.* **112** C6
Hutte Sauvage, L. de la *Canada* **105** A7
Hüttenberg *Austria* **26** E7
Hüttener Berge △ *Germany* **24** A5
Hutton, Mt. *Australia* **95** D4
Huwun *Ethiopia* **81** G5
Huy *Belgium* **17** D5
Huzhou *China* **59** B13
Hvalpsund *Denmark* **11** H3
Hvammstangi *Iceland* **8** D3
Hvar *Croatia* **41** E13
Hvarski Kanal *Croatia* **41** E13
Hvítá → *Iceland* **8** D3
Hvizdets *Ukraine* **29** B10
Hwachang-Cheosuji *S. Korea* **57** E14
Hwang Ho = Huang He → *China* **57** F10
Hwange *Zimbabwe* **87** F2
Hwange △ *Zimbabwe* **88** B4
Hyannis *Mass., U.S.A.* **113** E18
Hyannis *Nebr., U.S.A.* **112** E3
Hyargas Nuur *Mongolia* **60** B4
Hybo *Sweden* **10** C10
Hydaburg *U.S.A.* **102** B2
Hyde Park *U.S.A.* **115** E11
Hyden *Australia* **93** F2
Hyder *U.S.A.* **102** B2
Hyderabad *India* **66** L11
Hyderabad *Pakistan* **68** G3
Hydra *Greece* **46** D5
Hyères *France* **21** E10
Hyères, Îs. d' *France* **21** F10
Hyesan *N. Korea* **57** D15
Hyland → *Canada* **102** B3
Hyltebruk *Sweden* **11** H7

Hymia *India* **69** C8
Hyndman Peak *U.S.A.* **108** E6
Hyōgo □ *Japan* **55** G7
Hyrum *U.S.A.* **108** F8
Hysham *U.S.A.* **108** C10
Hythe *U.K.* **15** F9
Hyūga *Japan* **55** H5
Hyvinge = Hyvinkää *Finland* **32** B3
Hyvinkää *Finland* **32** B3

I

I-n-Gall *Niger* **83** B6
I-n-Oudad *Algeria* **83** A5
I-n-Ouzzal *Algeria* **83** A5
I-n-Tadreft *Niger* **83** B6
Iablaniţa *Romania* **28** F7
Iaco → *Brazil* **124** E5
Iacobeni *Romania* **29** C10
Iakora *Madag.* **89** C8
Ialomiţa □ *Romania* **29** F12
Ialomiţa → *Romania* **29** F12
Ialoveni *Moldova* **29** D13
Ialpug → *Moldova* **29** E13
Ianca *Romania* **29** E12
Iara *Romania* **29** D8
Iarda *Ethiopia* **81** E4
Iargara *Moldova* **29** D13
Iaşi *Romania* **29** C12
Iaşi □ *Romania* **29** C12
Iasmos *Greece* **45** E9
Ib → *India* **69** J10
Iba *Phil.* **61** D4
Ibadan *Nigeria* **83** D5
Ibagué *Colombia* **124** C3
Iballë *Albania* **44** D4
Ibănești, *Botoșani, Romania* **29** B11
Ibănești *Mureș, Romania* **29** D9
Ibar → *Serbia* **44** C4
Ibaraki □ *Japan* **55** F10
Ibarra *Ecuador* **124** C3
Ibb *Yemen* **75** E3
Ibba *Sudan* **81** G2
Ibba, Bahr el → *Sudan* **81** F2
Ibbenbüren *Germany* **24** C3
Ibembo *Dem. Rep. of the Congo* **86** B1
Ibenga → *Congo* **84** D3
Ibera, L. *Argentina* **126** B4
Iberian Peninsula *Europe* **6** H5
Iberville *Canada* **115** A11
Iberville, Lac d' *Canada* **104** A5
Ibi *Indonesia* **63** D6
Ibi *Spain* **39** G4
Ibiá *Brazil* **125** G9
Ibiapaba, Sa. da *Brazil* **125** D10
Ibicuí → *Brazil* **127** B4
Ibicuy *Argentina* **126** C4
Ibiza = Eivissa *Spain* **48** C7
Ibiza *Spain* **39** G6
Ibiza ✈ (IBZ) *Spain* **39** G6
Íblei, Monti *Italy* **43** E7
Ibo *Mozam.* **87** E5
Ibonma *Indonesia* **63** E8
Ibotirama *Brazil* **125** F10
Ibrāhīm → *Lebanon* **74** A4
'Ibrī *Oman* **71** F8
Ibshawāi *Egypt* **80** J7
Ibu *Indonesia* **63** D7
Ibusuki *Japan* **55** J5
Ica *Peru* **124** F3
Iça → *Brazil* **124** D5
Icacos Pt. *Trin. & Tob.* **125** K15
Içana *Brazil* **124** C5
Içana → *Brazil* **124** C5
İçel *Turkey* **72** D6
İçel □ *Turkey* **72** D5
Iceland ■ *Europe* **8** D4
Iceland Basin *Atl. Oc.* **4** C7
Icelandic Plateau *Arctic* **4** C7
Ich'ang = Yichang *China* **59** B8
Ichchapuram *India* **67** K14
Icheon *S. Korea* **57** F14
Ichhawar *India* **68** H7
Ichihara *Japan* **55** G10
Ichikawa *Japan* **55** G9
Ichilo → *Bolivia* **124** G6
Ichinohe *Japan* **54** D10
Ichinomiya *Japan* **55** G8
Ichinoseki *Japan* **54** E10
Ichnya *Ukraine* **33** G7
Icod *Canary Is.* **48** F3
Icy C. *U.S.A.* **98** B3
Ida Grove *U.S.A.* **112** D6
Idabel *U.S.A.* **116** E7
Idaga Hamus *Ethiopia* **81** E4
Idah *Nigeria* **83** D6
Idaho □ *U.S.A.* **108** D6
Idaho City *U.S.A.* **108** E6
Idaho Falls *U.S.A.* **108** E7
Idalia △ *Australia* **94** C3
Idanha-a-Nova *Portugal* **36** F3
Idar-Oberstein *Germany* **25** F3
Idensalmi = Iisalmi *Finland* **8** E22
Idfû *Egypt* **80** J7
Ídhra = Hydra *Greece* **46** D5
Idi *Indonesia* **62** C1
Idi, Oros = Psiloritis, Oros *Greece* **49** D6
Idiofa *Dem. Rep. of the Congo* **84** E3

Idkerberget *Sweden* **10** D9
Idku, Bahra el *Egypt* **80** H7
Idlib *Syria* **72** E7
Idlib □ *Syria* **72** E7
Idre *Sweden* **10** C6
Idria *U.S.A.* **110** J6
Idrija *Slovenia* **41** C11
Idritsa *Russia* **32** D5
Idutywa = Dutywa *S. Africa* **89** E4
Ieper *Belgium* **17** D2
Ierapetra *Greece* **49** E7
Ierissos *Greece* **44** F7
Ierissos Kolpos *Greece* **44** F7
Iernut *Romania* **29** D9
Iesi *Italy* **41** E10
Iésolo *Italy* **41** C9
Ifach, Peñón de *Spain* **39** G5
Ifakara *Tanzania* **84** F7
Ifanadiana *Madag.* **89** C8
Ife *Nigeria* **83** D5
Iférouâne *Niger* **83** B6
Iffley *Australia* **94** B3
Ifon *Nigeria* **83** D6
Iforas, Adrar des *Africa* **83** B5
Ifould, L. *Australia* **93** F5
Igalo *Montenegro* **44** D2
Iganga *Uganda* **86** B3
Igarapava *Brazil* **125** H9
Igarka *Russia* **52** C9
Igatimi *Paraguay* **127** A4
Igbetti *Nigeria* **83** D5
Igbo-Ora *Nigeria* **83** D5
Igboho *Nigeria* **83** D5
Igbor *Nigeria* **83** D6
Iğdır *Turkey* **73** C11
Igelfors *Sweden* **11** F9
Iggesund *Sweden* **10** C11
Iglésias *Italy* **42** C1
Igloolik *Canada* **101** C11
Igluligaarjuk = Chesterfield Inlet *Canada* **100** C10
Iglulik = Igloolik *Canada* **101** C11
'Igma, Gebel el *Egypt* **80** B3
Ignace *Canada* **104** C1
İğneada *Turkey* **45** E11
İğneada Burnu *Turkey* **45** E12
Igoumenitsa *Greece* **46** B2
Igra *Russia* **34** B11
Iguaçu → *Brazil* **127** B5
Iguaçu, Cat. del *Brazil* **127** B5
Iguaçu △ *Brazil* **127** B5
Iguaçu Falls = Iguaçu, Cat. del *Brazil* **127** B5
Iguala *Mexico* **119** D5
Igualada *Spain* **38** D6
Iguassu = Iguaçu → *Brazil* **127** B5
Iguatu *Brazil* **125** E11
Iguazú △ *Argentina* **127** B5
Iguidi, Erg *Africa* **78** C4
Iharana *Madag.* **89** A9
Ihbulag *Mongolia* **56** C4
Iheya-Shima *Japan* **55** L3
Ihiala *Nigeria* **83** D6
Ihosy *Madag.* **89** C8
Ihotry, Farihy *Madag.* **89** C7
Ihugh *Nigeria* **83** D6
Ii *Finland* **8** D21
Ii-Shima *Japan* **55** L3
Iida *Japan* **55** G8
Iijoki → *Finland* **8** D21
Iisalmi *Finland* **8** E22
Iiyama *Japan* **55** F9
Iizuka *Japan* **55** H5
Ijâfene *Mauritania* **78** D4
Ijebu-Igbo *Nigeria* **83** D5
Ijebu-Ode *Nigeria* **83** D5
IJmuiden *Neths.* **17** B4
Ijo älv = Iijoki → *Finland* **8** D21
IJssel → *Neths.* **17** B5
IJsselmeer *Neths.* **17** B5
Ijuí *Brazil* **127** B5
Ijuí → *Brazil* **127** B4
Ikalamavony *Madag.* **89** C8
Ikale *Nigeria* **83** D6
Ikang *Nigeria* **83** E6
Ikanga *Kenya* **86** C4
Ikara *Nigeria* **83** C6
Ikare *Nigeria* **83** D6
Ikaria *Greece* **47** D8
Ikast *Denmark* **11** H3
Ikeda *Japan* **55** G6
Ikeja *Nigeria* **83** D5
Ikela *Dem. Rep. of the Congo* **84** E4
Ikerre-Ekiti *Nigeria* **83** D6
Ikhtiman *Bulgaria* **44** D7
Iki *Japan* **55** H4
Ikimba L. *Tanzania* **86** C3
Ikire *Nigeria* **83** D5
İkizdere *Turkey* **73** B9
Ikom *Nigeria* **83** D6
Ikongo *Madag.* **89** C8
Ikopa → *Madag.* **89** B8
Ikorongo △ *Tanzania* **86** C3
Ikot Ekpene *Nigeria* **83** D6
Ikparjuk = Arctic Bay *Canada* **101** B11

Iksan S. Korea 57 G14
Ikungu Tanzania 86 C3
Ikuntji = Haast Bluff Australia 92 D5
Ikurun Nigeria 83 D5
Ila Nigeria 83 D5
Ilagan Phil. 61 C4
Ilaka Madag. 89 B8
Īlām Iran 73 F12
Ilam Nepal 69 F12
Īlām □ Iran 70 C5
Ilan Taiwan 59 E13
Ilanskiy Russia 53 D10
Ilaro Nigeria 83 D5
Ilatane Niger 83 B5
Iława Poland 30 E6
Ile → Kazakhstan 52 E8
Île-à-la-Crosse Canada 103 B7
Île-à-la-Crosse, Lac Canada 103 B7
Île-de-France □ France 19 D9
Ileanda Romania 29 C8
Ilebo Dem. Rep. of the Congo 84 E4
Ilek Russia 52 D6
Ilero Nigeria 83 D5
Ilesha Kwara, Nigeria 83 D5
Ilesha Oyo, Nigeria 83 D5
Ilford Canada 103 B9
Ilfracombe Australia 94 C3
Ilfracombe U.K. 15 F3
Ilgaz Turkey 72 B5
Ilgaz Dağları Turkey 72 B5
Ilgın Turkey 72 C4
Ilha de Moçambique Mozam. 87 F5
Ílhavo Portugal 36 E2
Ilhéus Brazil 125 F11
Ili = Ile → Kazakhstan 52 E8
Ilia Romania 28 E7
Ilía □ Greece 46 D3
Iliamna L. U.S.A. 106 a
Ilias, Profitis Greece 49 C9
Iliç Turkey 73 C8
Ilıca Turkey 47 B9
Ilichevsk Azerbaijan 73 C11
Iligan Phil. 61 G6
Iligan Bay Phil. 61 G6
Ilin I. Phil. 61 E4
Ilion U.S.A. 115 D9
Ilirska-Bistrica Slovenia 41 C11
Ilkeston U.K. 14 E6
Ilkley U.K. 14 D6
Illampu = Ancohuma, Nevado Bolivia 124 G5
Illana B. Phil. 61 H5
Illapel Chile 126 C1
Ille-et-Vilaine □ France 18 D5
Ille-sur-Têt France 20 F6
Illéla Niger 83 C6
Iller → Germany 25 G5
Illertissen Germany 25 G6
Illescas Spain 36 E7
Illetas Spain 48 B9
Illichivsk Ukraine 33 J6
Illiers-Combray France 18 D8
Illimani, Nevado Bolivia 124 G5
Illinois □ U.S.A. 112 E9
Illinois → U.S.A. 112 F8
Illizi Algeria 78 C7
Illkirch-Graffenstaden France 19 D14
Íllora Spain 37 H7
Ilm → Germany 24 D7
Ilma, L. Australia 93 E4
Ilmajoki Finland 8 E20
Ilmen, Ozero Russia 32 C6
Ilmenau Germany 24 E6
Ilnytsya Ukraine 28 B8
Ilo Peru 124 G4
Ilobu Nigeria 83 D5
Iloilo Phil. 61 F5
Ilomantsi Finland 8 E24
Ilora Nigeria 83 D5
Ilorin Nigeria 83 D5
Ilovatka Russia 34 E7
Ilovlya Russia 35 F7
Ilovlya → Russia 35 F7
Iłowa Poland 31 G2
Ilubabor Ethiopia 81 F4
Ilva Mică Romania 29 C9
Ilwaco U.S.A. 110 D2
Ilwaki Indonesia 63 F7
Ilyichevsk = Illichivsk Ukraine 33 J6
Iłża Poland 31 G8
Ilzanka → Poland 31 G8
Imabari Japan 55 G6
Imaloto → Madag. 89 C8
İmamoğlu Turkey 72 D6
Imandra, Ozero Russia 8 C25
Imanombo Madag. 89 C8
Imari Japan 55 H4
Imasa Sudan 80 D4
Imathia □ Greece 44 F6
Imatra Finland 32 B5
Iménas Mali 83 B5
imeni 26 Bakinskikh Komissarov = Neftçala Azerbaijan 73 C13

imeni 26 Bakinskikh Komissarov Turkmenistan 71 B7
imeni Ismail Samani, Pik Tajikistan 52 F8
Imeri, Serra Brazil 124 C5
Imerimandroso Madag. 89 B8
Imfolozi △ S. Africa 89 D5
Imi Ethiopia 81 F5
Imishly = Imişli Azerbaijan 35 L9
Imişli Azerbaijan 35 L9
Imlay U.S.A. 108 F4
Imlay City U.S.A. 114 D1
Immaseri Sudan 81 D2
Immenstadt Germany 25 H6
Immingham U.K. 14 D7
Immokalee U.S.A. 117 H14
Imo □ Nigeria 83 D6
Imo → Nigeria 83 E6
Ímola Italy 41 D8
Imotski Croatia 41 E14
Imperatriz Brazil 125 E9
Impéria Italy 40 E5
Imperial Canada 103 C7
Imperial Calif., U.S.A. 111 N11
Imperial Nebr., U.S.A. 112 E3
Imperial Beach U.S.A. 111 N9
Imperial Dam U.S.A. 111 N12
Imperial Res. U.S.A. 111 N12
Imperial Valley U.S.A. 111 N11
Imperieuse Reef Australia 92 C2
Impfondo Congo 84 D3
Imphal India 67 G18
Imphy France 19 F10
İmranlı Turkey 73 C8
İmroz = Gökçeada Turkey 45 F9
İmroz Turkey 45 F9
Imst Austria 26 D3
Imuris Mexico 118 A2
Imuruan B. Phil. 63 B5
In Akhmed Mali 83 B4
In Aleï Mali 82 B4
In Delimane Mali 83 B5
In Guezzam Algeria 83 B6
In Koufi Mali 83 B5
In Salah Algeria 78 C6
In Tallak Mali 83 B5
In Tebezas Mali 83 B5
Ina Japan 55 G8
Inagua △ Bahamas 121 B5
Inangahua N.Z. 91 D3
Inanwatan Indonesia 63 E8
Iñapari Peru 124 F5
Inari Finland 8 B22
Inarijärvi Finland 8 B23
Inawashiro-Ko Japan 54 F10
Inca Spain 48 B9
Inca de Oro Chile 126 B2
Incaguasi Chile 126 B1
Incahuasi Argentina 126 B2
İnce Burun Turkey 72 A6
İncekum Burnu Turkey 72 D5
İncesu Turkey 70 B2
Incheon S. Korea 57 F14
Inchiri □ Mauritania 82 B2
Incio = Cruz de Incio Spain 36 C3
İncirliova Turkey 47 D9
Incline Village U.S.A. 108 G4
Incomáti → Mozam. 89 D5
Incudine, Mte. France 21 G13
Inda Silase Ethiopia 81 E4
Indal Sweden 10 B11
Indalsälven → Sweden 10 B11
Indaw Burma 67 G20
Indbir Ethiopia 81 F4
Independence Calif., U.S.A. 110 J8
Independence Iowa, U.S.A. 112 D8
Independence Kans., U.S.A. 112 G6
Independence Ky., U.S.A. 113 F11
Independence Mo., U.S.A. 112 F6
Independence Fjord Greenland 4 A6
Independence Mts. U.S.A. 108 F5
Independenţa Romania 29 E12
Index U.S.A. 110 C5
India ■ Asia 66 K11
Indian → U.S.A. 117 H14
Indian Cabins Canada 102 B5
Indian Harbour Canada 105 B8
Indian Head Canada 103 C8
Indian Lake U.S.A. 115 C10
Indian Springs U.S.A. 111 J11
Indiana U.S.A. 114 F5
Indiana □ U.S.A. 113 F11
Indianapolis U.S.A. 112 F10
Indianola Iowa, U.S.A. 112 E7
Indianola Miss., U.S.A. 117 E9
Indigirka → Russia 53 B15
Indija Serbia 28 E5
Indio U.S.A. 111 M10
Indira Gandhi Canal India 68 F5
Indira Sagar India 68 H7
Indo-China Asia 50 G12
Indonesia ■ Asia 62 F5
Indore India 68 H6
Indramayu Indonesia 63 G13
Indravati → India 67 K12
Indre □ France 19 F8
Indre → France 18 E7

Indre-et-Loire □ France 18 E7
Indulkana Australia 95 D1
Indura Belarus 30 E10
Indus → Pakistan 68 G2
Indus, Mouths of the Pakistan 68 H3
İnebolu Turkey 72 B5
İnecik Turkey 45 F11
İnegöl Turkey 45 F13
Ineu Romania 28 D6
Infantes = Villanueva de los Infantes Spain 37 G7
Infiernillo, Presa del Mexico 118 D4
Infiesto Spain 36 B5
Ingelstad Sweden 11 H8
Ingersoll Canada 114 C4
Ingham Australia 94 B4
Ingleborough U.K. 14 C5
Inglewood Queens., Australia 95 D5
Inglewood Vic., Australia 95 F3
Inglewood N.Z. 91 C5
Inglewood U.S.A. 111 M8
Ingólfshöfði Iceland 8 E5
Ingolstadt Germany 25 G7
Ingomar U.S.A. 108 C10
Ingonish Canada 105 C7
Ingore Guinea-Biss. 82 C1
Ingraj Bazar India 69 G13
Ingrid Christensen Coast Antarctica 5 C6
Ingul = Inhul → Ukraine 33 J7
Ingulec = Inhulec Ukraine 33 J7
Ingulets = Inhulets → Ukraine 33 J7
Inguri = Enguri → Georgia 35 J5
Ingushetia □ Russia 35 J7
Ingwavuma S. Africa 89 D5
Inhaca Mozam. 89 D5
Inhafenga Mozam. 89 C5
Inhambane Mozam. 89 C6
Inhambane □ Mozam. 89 C6
Inhaminga Mozam. 87 F4
Inharrime Mozam. 89 C6
Inharrime → Mozam. 89 C6
Inhisar Turkey 47 A12
Inhul → Ukraine 33 J7
Inhulec Ukraine 33 J7
Inhulets → Ukraine 33 J7
Iniesta Spain 39 F3
Ining = Yining China 52 E9
Inírida → Colombia 124 C5
Inishbofin Ireland 12 C1
Inisheer Ireland 12 C2
Inishfree B. Ireland 12 A3
Inishkea North Ireland 12 B1
Inishkea South Ireland 12 B1
Inishmaan Ireland 12 C2
Inishmore Ireland 12 C2
Inishmurray I. Ireland 12 B3
Inishowen Pen. Ireland 12 A4
Inishshark Ireland 12 C1
Inishturk Ireland 12 C1
Inishvickillane Ireland 12 D1
Injibara Ethiopia 81 E4
Injune Australia 95 D4
Inklin → N. Amer. 102 B2
Inland Kaikoura Ra. N.Z. 91 D4
Inland Sea = Setonaikai Japan 55 G6
Inle L. Burma 67 J20
Inlet U.S.A. 115 C10
Inn → Austria 26 C6
Innamincka Australia 95 D3
Inner Hebrides U.K. 13 E2
Inner Mongolia = Nei Monggol Zizhiqu □ China 56 D7
Inner Sound U.K. 13 D3
Innerkip Canada 114 C4
Innetalling I. Canada 104 A4
Innisfail Australia 94 B4
Innisfail Canada 102 C6
In'noshima Japan 55 G6
Innsbruck Austria 26 D4
Innviertel Austria 26 C6
Inny → Ireland 12 C4
Inongo Dem. Rep. of the Congo 84 E3
İnönü Turkey 47 B12
Inoucdjouac = Inukjuak Canada 101 D12
Inousses Greece 47 C8
Inowrocław Poland 31 F5
Inscription, C. Australia 93 E1
Insein Burma 67 L20
Insjön Sweden 10 D9
Ińsko Poland 30 E2
İnsurăţei Romania 29 F12
Inta Russia 52 C6
Intendente Alvear Argentina 126 D3
İntepe Turkey 47 A8
Interlaken Switz. 25 J3
Interlaken U.S.A. 115 D8
International Falls U.S.A. 112 A7
Intiyaco Argentina 126 B3

Întorsura Buzăului Romania 29 E11
Inukjuak Canada 101 D12
Inútil, B. Chile 128 G2
Inuvik Canada 100 B6
Inveraray U.K. 13 E3
Inverbervie U.K. 13 E6
Invercargill N.Z. 91 G2
Inverclyde □ U.K. 13 F4
Inverell Australia 95 D5
Invergordon U.K. 13 D4
Inverloch Australia 95 F4
Invermere Canada 102 C5
Inverness Canada 105 C7
Inverness U.K. 13 D4
Inverness U.S.A. 117 G13
Inverurie U.K. 13 D6
Investigator Group Australia 95 E1
Investigator Str. Australia 95 F2
Inya Russia 52 D9
Inyanga Zimbabwe 87 F3
Inyangani Zimbabwe 87 F3
Inyantue Zimbabwe 88 B4
Inyo Mts. U.S.A. 110 J9
Inyokern U.S.A. 111 K9
Inza Russia 34 D8
Inzhavino Russia 34 D6
Iō-Jima Japan 55 J5
Ioannina Greece 46 B2
Ioannina □ Greece 46 B2
Iola U.S.A. 112 G6
Ion Corvin Romania 29 F12
Iona U.K. 13 E2
Ione U.S.A. 110 G6
Ionia U.S.A. 113 D11
Ionian Is. = Ionioi Nisoi Greece 46 C2
Ionian Sea Medit. S. 6 H9
Ionioi Nisoi Greece 46 C2
Ionioi Nisoi □ Greece 46 C2
Ios Greece 47 E7
Iowa □ U.S.A. 112 D7
Iowa → U.S.A. 112 E8
Iowa City U.S.A. 112 E8
Iowa Falls U.S.A. 112 D7
Iowa Park U.S.A. 116 E5
Ipala Tanzania 86 C3
Ipameri Brazil 125 G9
Ipati Greece 46 C4
Ipatinga Brazil 125 G10
Ipatovo Russia 35 H6
Ipel' → Europe 27 D11
Ipiales Colombia 124 C3
Ipin = Yibin China 58 C5
Ipixuna Brazil 124 E4
Ipoh Malaysia 65 K3
Ippy C.A.R. 84 C4
Ípsala Turkey 45 F10
Ipsario, Oros Greece 45 F8
Ipswich Australia 95 D5
Ipswich U.K. 15 E9
Ipswich Mass., U.S.A. 115 D14
Ipswich S. Dak., U.S.A. 112 C4
Ipu Brazil 125 D10
Iqaluit Canada 101 C13
Iquique Chile 124 H4
Iquitos Peru 124 D4
Irabu-Jima Japan 55 M2
Iracoubo Fr. Guiana 125 B8
Iráfshān Iran 71 E9
Irahuan Phil. 61 G3
Iraklia Cyclades, Greece 47 E7
Iraklia Serres, Greece 44 E7
Iráklio Greece 49 D7
Iráklio □ Greece 49 D7
Iráklion = Iráklio Greece 49 D7
Irala Paraguay 127 B5
Iran ■ Asia 71 C7
Iran, Pegunungan Malaysia 62 D4
Iran Ra. = Iran, Pegunungan Malaysia 62 D4
Īrānshahr Iran 71 E9
Irapuato Mexico 118 C4
Iraq ■ Asia 73 F10
Irati Brazil 127 B5
Irbes saurums Latvia 30 A9
Irbid Jordan 74 C4
Irbid □ Jordan 74 C5
Irebu Dem. Rep. of the Congo 84 E3
Iregua → Spain 38 C2
Ireland ■ Europe 12 C4
Irele Nigeria 83 D6
Irgiz, Bolshaya → Russia 34 D9
Iri = Iksan S. Korea 57 G14
Irian Jaya = Papua □ Indonesia 63 E9
Irian Jaya Barat □ Indonesia 63 E8
Irié Guinea 82 D3
Iringa Tanzania 86 D4
Iringa □ Tanzania 86 D4
Iriomote △ Japan 55 M1
Iriomote-Jima Japan 55 M1
Iriona Honduras 120 C2
Iriri → Brazil 125 D8
Irish Republic ■ Europe 12 C4
Irish Sea Europe 14 D3
Irkutsk Russia 53 D11

Îrlãhanlı Turkey 47 D11
Irma Canada 103 C6
Irõ-Zaki Japan 55 G9
Iroise, Mer d' France 18 D2
Iron Baron Australia 95 E2
Iron Gate = Portile de Fier Europe 27 F10
Iron Knob Australia 95 E2
Iron Mountain U.S.A. 112 C9
Iron Range △ Australia 94 A3
Iron River U.S.A. 112 B9
Irondequoit U.S.A. 114 C7
Ironton Mo., U.S.A. 112 G9
Ironton Ohio, U.S.A. 113 F12
Ironwood U.S.A. 112 B8
Ironwood Forest △ U.S.A. 109 K8
Iroquois Canada 115 B9
Iroquois Falls Canada 104 C3
Irpin Ukraine 23 C16
Irrara Cr. → Australia 95 D4
Irrawaddy □ Burma 67 L19
Irrawaddy → Burma 67 M19
Irrawaddy, Mouths of the Burma 67 M19
Irricana Canada 102 C6
Irshava Ukraine 28 B8
Irsina Italy 43 B9
Irtysh → Russia 52 C7
Irumu Dem. Rep. of the Congo 86 B2
Irún Spain 38 B3
Irunea = Pamplona Spain 38 C3
Irurzun Spain 38 C3
Irvine Canada 103 D6
Irvine U.K. 13 F4
Irvine Calif., U.S.A. 111 M9
Irvine Ky., U.S.A. 113 G12
Irvinestown U.K. 12 B4
Irving U.S.A. 116 E6
Irvona U.S.A. 114 F6
Irwin → Australia 93 E1
Irymple Australia 95 E3
Is, Jebel Sudan 80 C4
Is-sur-Tille France 19 E12
Isa Nigeria 83 C6
Isa Khel Pakistan 68 C4
Isaac → Australia 94 C4
Isabel U.S.A. 112 C3
Isabel, I. Mexico 118 C3
Isabela Phil. 61 H5
Isabela Puerto Rico 121 d
Isabella, Cord. Nic. 120 D2
Isabella Ra. Australia 92 D3
Isaccea Romania 29 E13
Ísafjarðardjúp Iceland 8 C2
Ísafjörður Iceland 8 C2
Isagarh India 68 G7
Isahaya Japan 55 H5
Isaka Tanzania 86 C3
Işalniţa Romania 29 F8
Isalo △ Madag. 89 C8
Isan → India 69 F9
Isana = Içana → Brazil 124 C5
Isangano △ Zambia 87 E3
Isanlu Makutu Nigeria 83 D6
Isar → Germany 25 G8
Isarco → Italy 41 B8
Isarog, Mt. Phil. 61 E5
Ísari Greece 46 D3
Íscar Spain 36 D6
Íscehisar Turkey 47 C12
Íschia Italy 42 B6
Isdell → Australia 92 C3
Ise Japan 55 G8
Ise-Shima △ Japan 55 G8
Ise-Wan Japan 55 G8
Isefjord Denmark 11 J5
Isel → Austria 26 E5
Iseo Italy 40 C7
Iseo, L. d' Italy 40 C7
Iseramagazi Tanzania 86 C3
Isère □ France 21 C9
Isère → France 21 D8
Iserlohn Germany 24 D3
Isérnia Italy 43 A7
Iseyin Nigeria 83 D5
Isfahan = Eşfahān Iran 71 C6
Ishëm Albania 44 E3
Ishigaki Japan 55 M2
Ishigaki-Shima Japan 55 M2
Ishikari-Gawa → Japan 54 C10
Ishikari-Sammyaku Japan 54 C11
Ishikari-Wan Japan 54 C10
Ishikawa Japan 55 L3
Ishikawa □ Japan 55 F8
Ishim Russia 52 D7
Ishim → Russia 52 D8
Ishinomaki Japan 54 E10
Ishioka Japan 55 F10
Ishkuman Pakistan 69 A5
Ishpeming U.S.A. 112 B10
Isigny-sur-Mer France 18 C5
Isil Kul Russia 52 D8
Isili Italy 42 C2
Isiolo Kenya 86 B4
Isiro Dem. Rep. of the Congo 86 B2

Isisford Australia 94 C3
İskenderun Turkey 72 D7
İskenderun Körfezi Turkey 72 D6
İskilip Turkey 72 B6
Iskŭr → Bulgaria 45 C8
Iskŭr, Yazovir Bulgaria 44 D7
Iskut → Canada 102 B2
Isla → U.K. 13 E5
Isla Coiba △ Panama 120 E3
Isla Cristina Spain 37 H3
Isla de Salamanca △ Colombia 121 D5
Isla Gorge △ Australia 94 D4
Isla Isabel △ Mexico 118 C3
Isla Tiburón y San Esteban △ Mexico 118 B2
Isla Vista U.S.A. 111 L7
İslâhiye Turkey 72 D7
Islam Headworks Pakistan 68 E5
Islamabad Pakistan 68 C5
Islamgarh Pakistan 68 F4
Islamkot Pakistan 68 G4
Islampur India 69 G11
Island = Iceland ■ Europe 8 D4
Island L. Canada 103 C10
Island Lagoon Australia 95 E2
Island Pond U.S.A. 115 B13
Islands, B. of Canada 105 C8
Islands, B. of N.Z. 91 A5
Islay U.K. 13 F2
Isle → France 20 D3
Isle aux Morts Canada 105 C8
Isle of Wight □ U.K. 15 G6
Isle Royale △ U.S.A. 112 B9
Isleton U.S.A. 110 G5
Ismail = Izmayil Ukraine 29 E14
Ismâ'iliya Egypt 80 H8
Ismaning Germany 25 G7
Isna Egypt 80 B3
Isoanala Madag. 89 C8
Isogstalo India 69 B8
Ísola del Liri Italy 41 G10
Ísola della Scala Italy 40 C7
Ísola di Capo Rizzuto Italy 43 D10
Ísparta Turkey 47 D12
Ísparta □ Turkey 72 D4
Isperikh Bulgaria 45 C10
Íspica Italy 43 F7
Israel ■ Asia 74 D3
Isratu Eritrea 81 D4
Issakly Russia 34 C10
Issia Ivory C. 82 D3
Issoire France 20 C7
Issoudun France 19 F8
Issyk-Kul, Ozero = Ysyk-Köl Kyrgyzstan 52 E8
Ist Croatia 41 D11
Istállós-kő Hungary 28 B5
İstanbul Turkey 45 E12
İstanbul □ Turkey 45 E12
İstanbul ✈ (IST) Turkey 45 F12
İstanbul Boğazı Turkey 45 E13
Istiea Greece 46 C5
Istok Serbia 44 D4
Istokpoga, L. U.S.A. 117 H14
Istra Croatia 41 C10
Istres France 21 E8
Istria = Istra Croatia 41 C10
Itá Paraguay 126 B4
Itaberaba Brazil 125 F10
Itabira Brazil 125 G10
Itabirito Brazil 127 A7
Itabuna Brazil 125 F11
Itacaunas → Brazil 125 E9
Itacoatiara Brazil 124 D7
Itaipú, Reprêsa de Brazil 127 B5
Itaituba Brazil 125 D7
Itajaí Brazil 127 B6
Itajubá Brazil 127 A6
Itaka Tanzania 87 D3
Itala △ S. Africa 89 D5
Italy ■ Europe 7 G8
Itamaraju Brazil 125 G11
Itampolo Madag. 89 C7
Itandrano Madag. 89 C8
Itapecuru-Mirim Brazil 125 D10
Itaperuna Brazil 127 A7
Itapetininga Brazil 127 A6
Itapeva Brazil 127 A6
Itapicuru → Bahia, Brazil 125 F11
Itapicuru → Maranhão, Brazil 125 D10
Itapipoca Brazil 125 D11
Itapuá □ Paraguay 127 B4
Itaquari Brazil 127 A7
Itaquí Brazil 126 B4
Itararé Brazil 127 A6
Itarsi India 68 H7
Itati Argentina 126 B4
Itatiaia △ Brazil 127 A7
Itbayat Phil. 61 A4
Itchen → U.K. 15 G6
Itea Greece 46 C4
Itezhi Tezhi, L. Zambia 87 F2
Ithaca = Itháki Greece 46 C2
Ithaca U.S.A. 115 D8
Itháki Greece 46 C2

Iti △ *Greece* **46** C4
Itiquira → *Brazil* **125** G7
Itō *Japan* **55** G9
Itoigawa *Japan* **55** F8
Iton → *France* **18** C8
Itonamas → *Bolivia* **124** F6
Itri *Italy* **42** A6
Itsa *Egypt* **80** J7
Íttiri *Italy* **42** B1
Ittoqqortoormiit *Greenland* **4** B6
Itu *Brazil* **127** A6
Itu *Nigeria* **83** D6
Itu Aba I. *S. China Sea* **62** B4
Ituiutaba *Brazil* **125** G9
Itumbiara *Brazil* **125** G9
Ituna *Canada* **103** C8
Itunge Port *Tanzania* **87** D3
Iturbe *Argentina* **126** A2
Ituri → *Dem. Rep. of the Congo* **86** B2
Iturup, Ostrov *Russia* **53** E15
Ituxi → *Brazil* **124** E6
Ituyuro → *Argentina* **126** A3
Itzehoe *Germany* **24** B5
Ivahona *Madag.* **89** C8
Ivaí → *Brazil* **127** A5
Ivaló *Finland* **8** B22
Ivalojoki → *Finland* **8** B22
Ivanava *Belarus* **23** B13
Ivančice *Czech Rep.* **27** B9
Ivane-Puste *Ukraine* **29** B11
Ivăneşti *Romania* **29** D12
Ivangorod *Russia* **32** C5
Ivanhoe *Australia* **95** E3
Ivanhoe *Calif., U.S.A.* **110** J7
Ivanhoe *Minn., U.S.A.* **112** C5
Ivanhorod *Ukraine* **29** B14
Ivanić Grad *Croatia* **41** C13
Ivanjica *Serbia* **44** C4
Ivanjska *Bos.-H.* **28** F2
Ivankoyskoye Vdkhr.
   Russia **32** D9
Ivano-Frankivsk *Ukraine* **29** B9
Ivano-Frankivsk □ *Ukraine* **29** B9
Ivanovo = Ivanava *Belarus* **23** B13
Ivanovo *Russia* **32** D11
Ivanovo □ *Russia* **34** B5
Ivanšćica *Croatia* **41** B13
Ivato *Madag.* **89** C8
Ivatsevichy *Belarus* **23** B13
Ivaylovgrad *Bulgaria* **45** E10
Ivinheima → *Brazil* **127** A5
Ivinhema *Brazil* **127** A5
Ivohibe *Madag.* **89** C8
Ivory Coast *W. Afr.* **82** E4
Ivory Coast ■ *Africa* **82** D4
Ivösjön *Sweden* **11** H8
Ivrea *Italy* **40** C4
Ívrindi *Turkey* **47** B9
Ivujivik *Canada* **101** C12
Ivybridge *U.K.* **15** G4
Iwaizumi *Japan* **54** E10
Iwaki *Japan* **55** F10
Iwakuni *Japan* **55** G6
Iwamizawa *Japan* **54** C10
Iwanai *Japan* **54** C10
Iwata *Japan* **55** G8
Iwate □ *Japan* **54** E10
Iwate-San *Japan* **54** E10
Iwo *Nigeria* **83** D5
Iwŏn *N. Korea* **57** D15
Iwonicz-Zdrój *Poland* **31** J8
Ixiamas *Bolivia* **124** F5
Ixopo *S. Africa* **89** E5
Ixtepec *Mexico* **119** D5
Ixtlán del Río *Mexico* **118** C4
Iyal Bakhit *Sudan* **81** E2
Iyo *Japan* **55** H6
Izabal, L. de *Guatemala* **120** C2
Izamal *Mexico* **119** C7
Izberbash *Russia* **35** J8
Izbica *Poland* **31** H10
Izbica Kujawska *Poland* **31** F5
Izbiceni *Romania* **29** G9
Izena-Shima *Japan* **55** L3
Izgrev *Bulgaria* **45** C10
Izhevsk *Russia* **52** D6
Izmayil *Ukraine* **29** E13
İzmir *Turkey* **47** C9
İzmir □ *Turkey* **47** C9
İzmir Adnan Menderes ✈
   (ADB) *Turkey* **47** C9
İzmir Körfezi *Turkey* **47** C8
İzmit = Kocaeli *Turkey* **45** F13
Iznájar *Spain* **37** H6
Iznalloz *Spain* **37** H7
İznik *Turkey* **72** B3
İznik Gölü *Turkey* **45** F13
Izobil'nyy *Russia* **35** H5
Izola *Slovenia* **41** C10
Izra *Syria* **74** C5
Iztochni Rodopi *Bulgaria* **45** E9
Izu-Shotō *Japan* **55** G10
Izúcar de Matamoros
   Mexico **119** D5
Izumi-Sano *Japan* **55** G7
Izumo *Japan* **55** G6
Izyaslav *Ukraine* **23** C14
Izyum *Ukraine* **33** H9

J

J.F.K. Int. ✈ (JFK) *U.S.A.* **115** F11
J. Strom Thurmond L.
   U.S.A. **117** E13
Jaba *Ethiopia* **81** F4
Jabal at Ţā'ir *Red Sea* **81** D5
Jabalón → *Spain* **37** G6
Jabalpur *India* **69** H8
Jabbūl *Syria* **70** B3
Jabiru *Australia* **92** B5
Jablah *Syria* **72** E6
Jablanac *Croatia* **41** D11
Jablanica *Bos.-H.* **28** G2
Jablonec nad Nisou
   Czech Rep. **26** A6
Jablonica *Slovak Rep.* **27** C10
Jabłonowo Pomorskie
   Poland **30** E6
Jablunkov *Czech Rep.* **27** B11
Jaboatão *Brazil* **125** E11
Jaboticabal *Brazil* **127** A6
Jabukovac *Serbia* **44** B6
Jaca *Spain* **38** C4
Jacareí *Brazil* **127** A6
Jacarèzinho *Brazil* **127** A6
Jackman *U.S.A.* **113** C18
Jacksboro *U.S.A.* **116** E5
Jackson *Barbados* **121** g
Jackson *Ala., U.S.A.* **117** F11
Jackson *Calif., U.S.A.* **110** G6
Jackson *Ky., U.S.A.* **113** G12
Jackson *Mich., U.S.A.* **113** D11
Jackson *Minn., U.S.A.* **112** D6
Jackson *Miss., U.S.A.* **117** E9
Jackson *Mo., U.S.A.* **112** G9
Jackson *N.H., U.S.A.* **115** B13
Jackson *Ohio, U.S.A.* **113** F12
Jackson *Tenn., U.S.A.* **117** D10
Jackson *Wyo., U.S.A.* **108** E8
Jackson B. *N.Z.* **91** E2
Jackson L. *U.S.A.* **108** E8
Jacksons *N.Z.* **91** E3
Jackson's Arm *Canada* **105** C8
Jacksonville *Ala., U.S.A.* **117** E12
Jacksonville *Ark., U.S.A.* **116** D8
Jacksonville *Calif., U.S.A.* **110** H6
Jacksonville *Fla., U.S.A.* **117** F14
Jacksonville *Ill., U.S.A.* **112** F8
Jacksonville *N.C., U.S.A.* **117** D16
Jacksonville *Tex., U.S.A.* **116** F7
Jacksonville Beach *U.S.A.* **117** F14
Jacmel *Haiti* **121** C5
Jacob Lake *U.S.A.* **109** H7
Jacobabad *Pakistan* **68** E3
Jacobina *Brazil* **125** F10
Jacques-Cartier, Dét. de
   Canada **105** C7
Jacques-Cartier, Mt. *Canada* **105** C6
Jacques-Cartier △ *Canada* **105** C5
Jacqueville *Ivory C.* **82** D4
Jacuí → *Brazil* **127** C5
Jacumba *U.S.A.* **111** N10
Jacundá → *Brazil* **125** D8
Jade *Germany* **24** B4
Jade Mt. = Yü Shan *Taiwan* **59** F13
Jadebusen *Germany* **24** B4
Jadovnik *Serbia* **44** C3
Jadraque *Spain* **38** E2
Jaén *Peru* **124** E3
Jaén *Spain* **37** H7
Jaén □ *Spain* **37** H7
Jafarabad *India* **68** J4
Jaffa = Tel Aviv-Yafo *Israel* **74** C3
Jaffa, C. *Australia* **95** F2
Jaffna *Sri Lanka* **66** Q12
Jaffray *Canada* **103** D10
Jaffrey *U.S.A.* **115** D12
Jagadhri *India* **68** D7
Jagadishpur *India* **69** G11
Jagdalpur *India* **67** K13
Jagdaqi *China* **60** B7
Jagersfontein *S. Africa* **88** D4
Jaghīn → *Iran* **71** E8
Jagodina *Serbia* **44** B5
Jagraon *India* **68** D6
Jagst → *Germany* **25** F5
Jagtial *India* **66** K11
Jaguariaíva *Brazil* **127** A6
Jaguaribe → *Brazil* **125** D11
Jagüey Grande *Cuba* **120** B3
Jahanabad *India* **69** G11
Jahazpur *India* **68** G6
Jahrom *Iran* **71** D7
Jaijon *India* **68** D7
Jailolo *Indonesia* **63** D7
Jailolo, Selat *Indonesia* **63** D7
Jaipur *India* **68** F6
Jais *India* **69** F9
Jaisalmer *India* **68** F4
Jaisinghnagar *India* **69** H8
Jaitaran *India* **68** F5
Jaithari *India* **69** H8
Jājarm *Iran* **71** B8
Jajce *Bos.-H.* **28** F2
Jakam → *India* **68** H6
Jakarta *Indonesia* **63** G12
Jakhal *India* **68** E6

Jakhau *India* **68** H3
Jakobstad = Pietarsaari
   Finland **8** E20
Jakupica *Macedonia* **44** E5
Jal *U.S.A.* **109** K12
Jalālābād *Afghan.* **68** B4
Jalalabad *India* **69** F8
Jalalpur Jattan *Pakistan* **68** C6
Jalama *Brazil* **125** L6
Jalapa *Guatemala* **120** D2
Jalapa Enríquez = Xalapa
   Mexico **119** D5
Jalasjärvi *Finland* **8** E20
Jalaun *India* **69** F8
Jaldhaka → *Bangla.* **69** F13
Jalesar *India* **68** F8
Jaleswar *Nepal* **69** F11
Jalgaon *India* **66** J9
Jalībah *Iraq* **70** D5
Jalingo *Nigeria* **83** D7
Jalisco □ *Mexico* **118** D4
Jalkot *Pakistan* **69** B5
Jallas → *Spain* **36** C1
Jalna *India* **66** K9
Jalón → *Spain* **38** D3
Jalor *India* **68** G5
Jalpa *Mexico* **118** C4
Jalpaiguri *India* **67** F16
Jalpan *Mexico* **119** C5
Jaluit I. *Marshall Is.* **96** G8
Jalūlā *Iraq* **73** E11
Jamaame = Giamama
   Somali Rep. **75** G3
Jamaari *Nigeria* **83** C6
Jamaica ■ *W. Indies* **120** a
Jamalpur *Bangla.* **67** G16
Jamalpur *India* **69** G12
Jamalpurganj *India* **69** H13
Jamanxim → *Brazil* **125** D7
Jambewangi *Indonesia* **63** J17
Jambi *Indonesia* **62** E2
Jambi □ *Indonesia* **62** E2
Jambongan, Pulau *Malaysia* **62** C5
Jambusar *India* **68** H5
James → *S. Dak., U.S.A.* **112** D5
James → *Va., U.S.A.* **113** G15
James B. *Canada* **104** B3
James Ranges *Australia* **92** D5
James Ross I. *Antarctica* **5** C18
Jamesabad *Pakistan* **68** G3
Jamestown *Australia* **95** E2
Jamestown *S. Africa* **88** E4
Jamestown *N. Dak., U.S.A.* **112** B4
Jamestown *N.Y., U.S.A.* **114** D5
Jamestown *N.Y., U.S.A.* **114** E4
Jamīlābād *Iran* **71** C6
Jamira → *India* **69** J13
Jämjö *Sweden* **11** H9
Jamkhandi *India* **66** L9
Jammerbugten *Denmark* **11** G3
Jammu *India* **68** C6
Jammu & Kashmir □ *India* **69** B7
Jamnagar *India* **68** H4
Jamni → *India* **69** G8
Jampur *Pakistan* **68** E4
Jamrud *Pakistan* **68** C4
Jämsä *Finland* **32** B3
Jamshedpur *India* **69** H12
Jamtara *India* **69** H12
Jämtland *Sweden* **8** E16
Jämtlands län □ *Sweden* **10** B7
Jan L. *Canada* **103** C8
Jan Mayen *Arctic* **4** B7
Janakkala *Finland* **32** B3
Janaúba *Brazil* **125** G10
Jand *Pakistan* **68** C5
Jandaq *Iran* **71** C7
Jandía *Canary Is.* **48** F5
Jandía, Pta. de *Canary Is.* **48** F5
Jandía △ *Canary Is.* **48** F5
Jandola *Pakistan* **68** C4
Jandowae *Australia* **95** D5
Jándula → *Spain* **37** G6
Janesville *U.S.A.* **112** D9
Janga *Ghana* **83** C4
Jangamo *Mozam.* **89** C6
Janghai *India* **69** G10
Jangheung *S. Korea* **57** G14
Janikowo *Poland* **31** F5
Janín = Ioannina □ *Greece* **46** B2
Janja *Bos.-H.* **28** F4
Janjanbureh *Gambia* **82** C2
Janjevo *Serbia* **44** D5
Janjgir *India* **69** J10
Janjina *Croatia* **41** F14
Janjina *Madag.* **89** C8
Janos *Mexico* **118** A3
Jánoshalma *Hungary* **28** D4
Jánosháza *Hungary* **28** C2
Jánossomorja *Hungary* **28** C2
Janów *India* **31** H6
Janów Lubelski *Poland* **31** H9
Janów Podlaski *Poland* **31** F10
Janowiec Wielkopolski
   Poland **31** F4
Januária *Brazil* **125** G10
Janub △ *Sudan* **81** F2

Janub Dârfûr □ *Sudan* **81** E2
Janub Kordofân □ *Sudan* **81** E3
Janūb Sīnî □ *Egypt* **74** F2
Janubio *Canary Is.* **48** F6
Janville *France* **19** D8
Janzé *France* **18** E5
Jaora *India* **68** H6
Japan ■ *Asia* **55** G8
Japan, Sea of *Asia* **54** E7
Japan Trench *Pac. Oc.* **96** D6
Japen = Yapen *Indonesia* **63** E9
Japla *India* **69** G11
Japurá → *Brazil* **124** D5
Jaquarão *Brazil* **127** C5
Jaqué *Panama* **120** E4
Jaraicejo *Spain* **37** F5
Jaraíz de la Vera *Spain* **36** E5
Jarama → *Spain* **36** E7
Jaramānah *Syria* **72** E7
Jarandilla *Spain* **36** E5
Jaranwala *Pakistan* **68** D5
Jarash *Jordan* **74** C4
Jarash □ *Jordan* **74** C4
Järbo *Sweden* **10** D10
Jardim *Brazil* **126** A4
Jardín → *Spain* **39** G2
Jardine River △ *Australia* **94** A3
Jardines de la Reina, Arch.
   de los *Cuba* **120** B4
Jargalang *China* **57** C12
Jari → *Brazil* **125** D8
Jarīr, W. al → *Si. Arabia* **70** E4
Järlåsa *Sweden* **10** E11
Jarmen *Germany* **24** B9
Järna *Dalarna, Sweden* **10** D8
Järna *Stockholm, Sweden* **10** E11
Jarnac *France* **20** C3
Jarny *France* **19** C12
Jarocin *Poland* **31** G4
Jaroměř *Czech Rep.* **26** A8
Jarosław *Poland* **31** H9
Järpås *Sweden* **11** F6
Järpen *Sweden* **10** A7
Jarrahdale *Australia* **93** F2
Jarrahi → *Iran* **71** D6
Jarres, Plaine des *Laos* **64** C4
Jarso *Ethiopia* **81** F4
Jartai *China* **56** E3
Jarud Qi *China* **57** B11
Järvenpää *Finland* **32** B3
Jarvis *Canada* **114** D4
Jarvis I. *Pac. Oc.* **97** H12
Jarvorník *Czech Rep.* **27** A10
Järvsö *Sweden* **10** C10
Jarwa *India* **69** F10
Jaša Tomić *Serbia* **28** E5
Jasdan *India* **68** H4
Jashpurnagar *India* **69** H11
Jasidih *India* **69** G12
Jasień *Poland* **31** G2
Jāsimīyah *Iraq* **73** F11
Jasin *Malaysia* **65** L4
Jāsk *Iran* **71** E8
Jasło *Poland* **31** J8
Jasmund *Germany* **24** A9
Jasmund △ *Germany* **24** A9
Jaso *India* **69** G9
Jasper *Alta., Canada* **102** C5
Jasper *Ont., Canada* **115** B9
Jasper *Ala., U.S.A.* **117** E11
Jasper *Fla., U.S.A.* **117** F13
Jasper *Ind., U.S.A.* **112** F10
Jasper *Tex., U.S.A.* **116** F7
Jasper △ *Canada* **102** C5
Jasrasar *India* **68** F5
Jastarnia *Poland* **30** D5
Jastrebarsko *Croatia* **41** C12
Jastrowie *Poland* **31** E3
Jastrzębie Zdrój *Poland* **31** J5
Jász-Nagykun-Szolnok □
   Hungary **28** C5
Jászapáti *Hungary* **28** C5
Jászárokszállás *Hungary* **28** C4
Jászberény *Hungary* **28** C4
Jászkisér *Hungary* **28** C5
Jászladány *Hungary* **28** C5
Jataí *Brazil* **125** G8
Jati *Pakistan* **68** G3
Jatibarang *Indonesia* **63** G13
Jatiluwih *Indonesia* **63** J18
Jatinegara *Indonesia* **63** G12
Játiva = Xàtiva *Spain* **39** G4
Jaú *Brazil* **127** A6
Jauja *Peru* **124** F3
Jaunpur *India* **69** G10
Java = Jawa *Indonesia* **62** F3
Java Sea *Indonesia* **62** E3
Java Trench *Ind. Oc.* **62** F3
Javalambre, Sa. de *Spain* **38** E4
Jávea *Spain* **39** G5
Javron *France* **18** D6
Jawa *Indonesia* **62** F3
Jawa Barat □ *Indonesia* **63** G12
Jawa Tengah □ *Indonesia* **63** G14
Jawa Timur □ *Indonesia* **63** G15
Jawad *India* **68** G6

Jawor *Poland* **31** G3
Jaworzno *Poland* **31** H6
Jaworzyna Śląska *Poland* **31** H3
Jay Peak *U.S.A.* **115** B12
Jaya, Puncak *Indonesia* **63** E9
Jayanti *India* **67** F16
Jayapura *Indonesia* **63** E10
Jaynagar *India* **69** F12
Jayrūd *Syria* **72** F7
Jayton *U.S.A.* **116** E4
Jāz Mūriān, Hāmūn-e *Iran* **71** E8
Jazīreh-ye Shīf *Iran* **71** D6
Jazminal *Mexico* **118** C4
Jazzīn *Lebanon* **74** B4
Jean *U.S.A.* **111** K11
Jean Marie River *Canada* **102** A4
Jean-Rabel *Haiti* **121** C5
Jeanerette *U.S.A.* **116** G9
Jeanette, Ostrov =
   Zhannetty, Ostrov *Russia* **53** B16
Jeannette *U.S.A.* **114** F5
Jebāl Bārez, Kūh-e *Iran* **71** D8
Jebba *Nigeria* **83** D5
Jebel, Bahr el → *Sudan* **81** F3
Jebel Ali = Minā' Jabal 'Alī
   U.A.E. **71** E7
Jebel Dud *Sudan* **81** E3
Jebel Qerri *Sudan* **81** D3
Jecheon *S. Korea* **57** F15
Jedburgh *U.K.* **13** F6
Jedda = Jiddah *Si. Arabia* **75** C2
Jeddore L. *Canada* **105** C8
Jedlicze *Poland* **31** J8
Jędrzejów *Poland* **31** H7
Jedwabne *Poland* **31** E9
Jeetzel → *Germany* **24** B7
Jefferson *Iowa, U.S.A.* **112** D6
Jefferson *Ohio, U.S.A.* **114** E4
Jefferson *Tex., U.S.A.* **116** E7
Jefferson, Mt. *Nev., U.S.A.* **108** G5
Jefferson, Mt. *Oreg., U.S.A.* **108** D3
Jefferson City *Mo., U.S.A.* **112** F8
Jefferson City *Tenn., U.S.A.* **117** C13
Jeffersontown *U.S.A.* **113** F11
Jeffersonville *U.S.A.* **113** F11
Jeffrey City *U.S.A.* **108** E10
Jega *Nigeria* **83** C5
Jeju *S. Korea* **57** H14
Jeju-do *S. Korea* **57** H14
Jēkabpils *Latvia* **32** D3
Jekyll I. *U.S.A.* **117** F14
Jelcz-Laskowice *Poland* **31** G4
Jelenia Góra *Poland* **31** H2
Jelgava *Latvia* **30** B10
Jelgava □ *Latvia* **30** B10
Jelica *Serbia* **44** C4
Jelli *Sudan* **81** F3
Jelšava *Slovak Rep.* **27** C13
Jemaja *Indonesia* **65** L5
Jemaluang *Malaysia* **65** L4
Jember *Indonesia* **63** H15
Jena *Germany* **24** E7
Jena *U.S.A.* **116** F8
Jenbach *Austria* **26** D4
Jenin *West Bank* **74** C4
Jenkins *U.S.A.* **113** G12
Jenner *Canada* **110** G3
Jennings *U.S.A.* **116** F8
Jeong-eup *S. Korea* **57** G14
Jeonju *S. Korea* **57** G14
Jepara *Indonesia* **63** G14
Jeparit *Australia* **95** F3
Jequié *Brazil* **125** F10
Jequitinhonha *Brazil* **125** G10
Jequitinhonha → *Brazil* **125** G11
Jerada *Morocco* **78** B5
Jerantut *Malaysia* **65** L4
Jerejak, Pulau *Malaysia* **65** c
Jérémie *Haiti* **121** C5
Jerez, Pta. *Mexico* **119** C5
Jerez de García Salinas
   Mexico **118** C4
Jerez de la Frontera *Spain* **37** J4
Jerez de los Caballeros *Spain* **37** G4
Jericho = El Arīḩā *West Bank* **74** D4
Jericho *Australia* **94** C4
Jerichow *Germany* **24** C8
Jerid, Chott el = Djerid,
   Chott *Tunisia* **78** B7
Jerilderie *Australia* **95** F4
Jermyn *U.S.A.* **115** E9
Jerome *U.S.A.* **108** E6
Jerramungup *Australia* **93** F2
Jersey *U.K.* **15** H5
Jersey City *U.S.A.* **115** F10
Jersey Shore *U.S.A.* **114** E7
Jerseyville *U.S.A.* **112** F8
Jerusalem *Israel/West Bank* **74** D4
Jervis B. *Australia* **95** F5
Jervis Inlet *Canada* **102** C4

Jessnitz *Germany* **24** D8
Jessore *Bangla.* **67** H16
Jesup *U.S.A.* **117** F14
Jesús Carranza *Mexico* **119** D5
Jesús María *Argentina* **126** C3
Jetmore *U.S.A.* **112** F4
Jetpur *India* **68** J4
Jeumont *France* **19** B11
Jevnaker *Norway* **9** F14
Jewett *U.S.A.* **114** F3
Jewett City *U.S.A.* **115** E13
Jeyḩūnābād *Iran* **71** C6
Jeypore *India* **67** K13
Jeziorak, Jezioro *Poland* **30** E6
Jeziorany *Poland* **30** E7
Jeziorka → *Poland* **31** F8
Jha Jha *India* **69** G12
Jhaarkand = Jharkhand □
   India **69** H11
Jhabua *India* **68** H6
Jhajjar *India* **68** E7
Jhal *Pakistan* **68** E2
Jhal Jhao *Pakistan* **66** F4
Jhalawar *India* **68** G7
Jhalida *India* **69** H11
Jhalrapatan *India* **68** G7
Jhang Maghiana *Pakistan* **68** D5
Jhansi *India* **69** G8
Jhargram *India* **69** H12
Jharia *India* **69** H12
Jharkhand □ *India* **69** H11
Jharsuguda *India* **67** J14
Jhelum *Pakistan* **68** C5
Jhelum → *Pakistan* **68** D5
Jhilmilli *India* **69** H10
Jhudo *Pakistan* **68** G3
Jhunjhunu *India* **68** E6
Ji-Paraná *Brazil* **124** F6
Ji Xian *Hebei, China* **56** F8
Ji Xian *Henan, China* **56** G8
Ji Xian *Shanxi, China* **56** F6
Jia Xian *Henan, China* **56** H7
Jia Xian *Shaanxi, China* **56** E6
Jiading *China* **59** B13
Jiahe *China* **59** E9
Jiaji = Qionghai *China* **64** C8
Jialing Jiang → *China* **58** C6
Jiamusi *China* **60** B8
Ji'an *Jiangxi, China* **59** D10
Ji'an *Jilin, China* **57** D14
Jianchang *China* **57** D11
Jianchangying *China* **57** D10
Jianchuan *China* **58** D2
Jiande *China* **59** C12
Jiang'an *China* **58** C5
Jiangbei *China* **58** C6
Jiangcheng *China* **58** F3
Jiangchuan *China* **58** E4
Jiangdi *China* **58** D4
Jiangdu *China* **59** A12
Jiange *China* **58** A5
Jianghua *China* **59** E8
Jiangjin *China* **58** C6
Jiangkou *China* **58** D7
Jiangle *China* **59** D11
Jiangling *China* **59** B9
Jiangmen *China* **59** F9
Jiangning *China* **59** B12
Jiangshan *China* **59** C12
Jiangsu □ *China* **57** H11
Jiangxi □ *China* **59** D11
Jiangyan *China* **59** A13
Jiangyin *China* **59** B13
Jiangyong *China* **59** E8
Jiangyou *China* **58** B5
Jianhe *China* **58** D7
Jianli *China* **59** C9
Jianning *China* **59** D11
Jian'ou *China* **59** D12
Jianshi *China* **58** B7
Jianshui *China* **58** F4
Jianyang *Fujian, China* **59** D12
Jianyang *Sichuan, China* **58** B5
Jiao Xian = Jiaozhou *China* **57** F11
Jiaohe *Hebei, China* **56** E9
Jiaohe *Jilin, China* **57** C14
Jiaojiang *China* **59** C13
Jiaoling *China* **59** E11
Jiaozhou *China* **57** F11
Jiaozhou Wan *China* **57** F11
Jiaozuo *China* **56** G7
Jiashan *China* **59** B13
Jiawang *China* **57** G9
Jiaxiang *China* **56** G9
Jiaxing *China* **59** B13
Jiayi = Chiai *Taiwan* **59** F13
Jiayu *China* **59** C9
Jibiya *Nigeria* **83** C6
Jibou *Romania* **29** C8
Jibuti = Djibouti ■ *Africa* **81** E5
Jicarón, I. *Panama* **120** E3
Jičín *Czech Rep.* **26** A8
Jiddah *Si. Arabia* **75** C2
Jido *India* **67** E19
Jieshou *China* **56** H8
Jiexiu *China* **56** F6
Jieyang *China* **59** F11

Jigalong Australia 92 D3
Jigawa □ Nigeria 83 C6
Jigni India 69 G8
Jihlava Czech Rep. 26 B8
Jihlava → Czech Rep. 27 C9
Jihlavský □ Czech Rep. 26 B8
Jihočeský □ Czech Rep. 26 B7
Jihomoravský □ Czech Rep. 27 B9
Jijiga Ethiopia 75 F3
Jikamshi Nigeria 83 C6
Jikau Sudan 81 F3
Jilib = Gelib Somali Rep. 75 G3
Jilin China 57 C14
Jilin □ China 57 C14
Jiloca → Spain 38 D3
Jilong = Chilung Taiwan 59 E13
Jim Thorpe U.S.A. 115 F9
Jima Ethiopia 81 F4
Jimbaran, Teluk Indonesia 63 K18
Jimbolia Romania 28 E5
Jimena de la Frontera Spain 37 J5
Jiménez Mexico 118 B4
Jimo China 57 F11
Jin Jiang → China 59 C10
Jin Xian = Jinzhou Hebei,
    China 56 E8
Jin Xian = Jinzhou Liaoning,
    China 57 E11
Jinan China 56 F9
Jinchang China 60 C5
Jincheng China 56 G7
Jinchuan China 58 B4
Jind India 68 E7
Jindabyne Australia 95 F4
Jindo S. Korea 57 G14
Jindřichův Hradec Czech Rep. 26 B8
Jing He → China 56 G5
Jing Shan China 59 B8
Jing Xian China 59 B12
Jingbian China 56 F5
Jingchuan China 56 G4
Jingde China 59 B12
Jingdezhen China 59 C11
Jingdong China 58 E3
Jinggangshan China 59 D10
Jinggu China 58 F3
Jinghai China 56 E9
Jinghong China 58 G3
Jingjiang China 59 A13
Jingle China 56 E6
Jingmen China 59 B9
Jingning China 56 G3
Jingpo Hu China 57 C15
Jingshan China 59 B9
Jingtai China 56 F3
Jingxi China 58 F6
Jingxing China 56 E8
Jingyang China 56 G5
Jingyu China 57 C14
Jingyuan China 56 F3
Jingziguan China 56 H6
Jinhua China 59 C12
Jining Nei Monggol Zizhiqu,
    China 56 D7
Jining Shandong, China 56 G9
Jinja Uganda 86 B3
Jinjang Malaysia 65 L3
Jinji China 56 F4
Jinjiang Fujian, China 59 E12
Jinjiang Yunnan, China 58 D3
Jinjini Ghana 82 D4
Jinju S. Korea 57 G15
Jinkou China 59 B10
Jinkouhe China 58 C4
Jinmen Dao China 59 E12
Jinning China 58 E4
Jinotega Nic. 120 D2
Jinotepe Nic. 120 D2
Jinping Guizhou, China 58 D7
Jinping Yunnan, China 58 F4
Jinsha China 58 D6
Jinsha Jiang → China 58 C5
Jinshan China 59 B13
Jinshi China 59 C8
Jintan China 59 B12
Jinxi Jiangxi, China 59 D11
Jinxi Liaoning, China 57 D11
Jinxian China 59 C11
Jinxiang China 56 G9
Jinyang China 58 D4
Jinyun China 59 C13
Jinzhai China 59 B10
Jinzhou Hebei, China 56 E8
Jinzhou Liaoning, China 57 E11
Jiparaná → Brazil 124 E6
Jipijapa Ecuador 124 D2
Jiquilpan Mexico 118 D4
Jirisan S. Korea 57 G14
Jishan China 56 G6
Jishou China 58 C7
Jishui China 59 D10
Jisr ash Shughūr Syria 72 E7
Jitarning Australia 93 F2

Jitra Malaysia 65 J3
Jiu → Romania 29 G8
Jiudengkou China 56 E4
Jiujiang Guangdong, China 59 F9
Jiujiang Jiangxi, China 59 C10
Jiuling Shan China 59 C10
Jiulong = Kowloon China 59 F10
Jiulong China 58 C3
Jiutai China 57 B13
Jiuxincheng China 56 E8
Jiuyuhang China 59 B12
Jiwani Pakistan 66 G2
Jixi Anhui, China 59 B12
Jixi Heilongjiang, China 57 B16
Jiyang China 57 F9
Jiyuan China 56 G7
Jīzān Si. Arabia 75 D3
Jize China 56 F8
Jizera → Czech Rep. 26 A7
Jizl, Wādī al → Si. Arabia 70 E3
Jizō-Zaki Japan 55 G6
Jizzakh Uzbekistan 52 E7
Joaçaba Brazil 127 B5
Joal Fadiout Senegal 82 C1
João Pessoa Brazil 125 E12
Joaquín V. González
    Argentina 126 B3
Jobat India 68 H6
Jobourg, Nez de France 18 C5
Jódar Spain 37 H7
Jodhpur India 68 F5
Jodiya India 68 H4
Joensuu Finland 8 E23
Jōetsu Japan 55 F9
Jœuf France 19 C12
Jofane Mozam. 89 C5
Jogbani India 69 F12
Jõgeva Estonia 32 C4
Jogjakarta = Yogyakarta
    Indonesia 63 G14
Johannesburg S. Africa 89 D4
Johannesburg U.S.A. 111 K9
Johansfors Sweden 11 H9
John Crow Mts. Jamaica 120 a
John Day U.S.A. 108 D4
John Day → U.S.A. 108 D3
John Day Fossil Beds △
    U.S.A. 108 D4
John D'Or Prairie Canada 102 B5
John H. Kerr Res. U.S.A. 117 C15
John o' Groats U.K. 13 C5
John's Ra. Australia 94 C1
Johnnie U.S.A. 111 J10
Johnson U.S.A. 115 B12
Johnson City Kans., U.S.A. 112 G3
Johnson City N.Y., U.S.A. 115 D9
Johnson City Tenn., U.S.A. 117 C13
Johnson City Tex., U.S.A. 116 F5
Johnsonburg U.S.A. 114 E6
Johnsondale U.S.A. 111 K8
Johnsons Crossing Canada 102 A2
Johnston, L. Australia 93 F3
Johnston Falls =
    Mambilima Falls Zambia 87 E2
Johnston I. Pac. Oc. 97 F11
Johnstone Str. Canada 102 C3
Johnstown Ireland 12 D4
Johnstown N.Y., U.S.A. 115 C10
Johnstown Ohio, U.S.A. 114 F2
Johnstown Pa., U.S.A. 114 F6
Johor, Selat Asia 65 d
Johor Bahru Malaysia 65 d
Jõhvi Estonia 32 C4
Joigny France 19 E10
Joinville Brazil 127 B6
Joinville France 19 D12
Joinville I. Antarctica 5 C18
Jojutla Mexico 119 D5
Jokkmokk Sweden 8 C18
Jökulsá á Bru → Iceland 8 D6
Jökulsá á Fjöllum → Iceland 8 C5
Jolfā Āzarbājān-e Sharqī, Iran 73 C11
Jolfā Eşfahan, Iran 71 C6
Joliet U.S.A. 112 E9
Joliette Canada 104 C5
Jolo Phil. 61 J4
Jolon U.S.A. 110 K5
Jomalig I. Phil. 61 D5
Jombang Indonesia 63 G15
Jomda China 58 B2
Jones Sound Canada 101 B11
Jonesboro Ark., U.S.A. 117 D9
Jonesboro La., U.S.A. 116 E8
Jong → S. Leone 82 D2
Jonglei Sudan 81 F3
Jonglei □ Sudan 81 F3
Joniškis Lithuania 30 B10
Jönköping Sweden 11 G8
Jönköpings län □ Sweden 11 G8
Jonquière Canada 105 C5
Jonzac France 20 C3
Joplin U.S.A. 112 G6
Jora India 68 F6
Jordan Mont., U.S.A. 108 C10

Jordan N.Y., U.S.A. 115 C8
Jordan ■ Asia 74 E5
Jordan → Asia 74 D4
Jordan Valley U.S.A. 108 E5
Jordanów Poland 31 J6
Jorhat India 67 F19
Jori → Norway 10 B3
Jörn Sweden 8 D19
Jorong Indonesia 62 E4
Jørpeland Norway 9 G12
Jorquera → Chile 126 B2
Jos Nigeria 83 D6
Jos Plateau Nigeria 83 D6
Jošanička Banja Serbia 44 C4
José Batlle y Ordóñez
    Uruguay 127 C4
Joseni Romania 29 D10
Joseph, L. Nfld. & L., Canada 105 B6
Joseph, L. Ont., Canada 114 A5
Joseph Bonaparte G.
    Australia 92 B4
Joshinath India 69 D8
Joshinetsu-Kōgen △ Japan 55 F9
Joshua Tree U.S.A. 111 L10
Joshua Tree △ U.S.A. 111 M10
Josselin France 18 E4
Jost Van Dyke I. Br. Virgin Is. 121 e
Jostedalsbreen Norway 8 F12
Jotunheimen Norway 8 F13
Joubertberge Namibia 88 B1
Joué-lès-Tours France 18 E7
Jourdanton U.S.A. 116 G5
Joutseno Finland 32 B5
Jovellanos Cuba 120 B3
Juan Aldama Mexico 118 C4
Juan Bautista Alberdi
    Argentina 126 C3
Juan de Fuca, Str of.
    N. Amer. 110 B3
Juán de Nova Ind. Oc. 89 B7
Juan Fernández, Arch. de
    Pac. Oc. 122 G2
Juan José Castelli Argentina 126 B3
Juan L. Lacaze Uruguay 126 C4
Juankoski Finland 8 E23
Juárez Argentina 126 D4
Juárez Mexico 111 N11
Juárez Coahuila, Mexico 118 B4
Juárez, Sierra de Mexico 118 A1
Juàzeiro Brazil 125 E10
Juàzeiro do Norte Brazil 125 E11
Juba = Giuba → Somali Rep. 75 G3
Juba → Giuba → Somali Rep. 75 G3
Jūbâ Sudan 81 G3
Jubany Antarctica 5 C18
Jubayl Lebanon 74 A4
Jubbah Si. Arabia 70 D4
Jubbal India 68 D7
Jubbulpore = Jabalpur India 69 H8
Jübek Germany 24 A5
Jubga Russia 35 H4
Jubilee L. Australia 93 E4
Juby, C. Morocco 78 C3
Júcar = Xúquer → Spain 39 F4
Júcaro Cuba 120 B4
Juchitán de Zaragoza
    Mexico 119 D5
Judea = Har Yehuda Israel 74 D3
Judenburg Austria 26 D7
Judith → U.S.A. 108 C9
Judith, Pt. U.S.A. 115 E13
Judith Gap U.S.A. 108 C9
Juelsminde Denmark 11 J4
Jugoslavia = Serbia ■
    Europe 44 C4
Juigalpa Nic. 120 D2
Juillac France 20 C5
Juist Germany 24 B2
Juiz de Fora Brazil 127 A7
Jujuy □ Argentina 126 A2
Julesburg U.S.A. 108 F12
Juli Peru 124 G5
Julia Cr. → Australia 94 C3
Julia Creek Australia 94 C3
Juliaca Peru 124 G4
Julian U.S.A. 111 M10
Julian, L. Canada 104 B4
Julian Alps = Julijske Alpe
    Slovenia 41 B11
Julianatop Suriname 125 C7
Julianehåb = Qaqortoq
    Greenland 4 C5
Jülich Germany 24 E2
Julijske Alpe Slovenia 41 B11
Julimes Mexico 118 B3
Jullundur India 68 D6
Julu China 56 F8
Jumbo Zimbabwe 87 F3
Jumbo Pk. U.S.A. 111 J12
Jumentos Cays Bahamas 120 B4
Jumilla Spain 39 G3
Jumla Nepal 69 E10
Jumna = Yamuna → India 69 G9

Jumunjin S. Korea 57 F15
Junagadh India 68 J4
Junction Tex., U.S.A. 116 F5
Junction Utah, U.S.A. 109 G7
Junction B. Australia 94 A1
Junction City Kans., U.S.A. 112 F5
Junction City Oreg., U.S.A. 108 D2
Junction Pt. Australia 94 A1
Jundah Australia 94 C3
Jundiaí Brazil 127 A6
Junee Australia 95 E4
Jungfrau Switz. 25 J3
Junggar Pendi China 60 B3
Jungshahi Pakistan 68 G2
Juniata → U.S.A. 114 F7
Junín Argentina 126 C3
Junín de los Andes
    Argentina 128 D2
Jūniyah Lebanon 74 B4
Junlian China 58 C5
Juntas Chile 126 B2
Juntura U.S.A. 108 E4
Jur, Nahr el → Sudan 81 F2
Jura U.K. 13 F3
Jura = Jura, Mts. du Europe 19 F13
Jura = Schwäbische Alb
    Germany 25 G5
Jura □ France 19 F12
Jura □ Switz. 25 H3
Jūra → Lithuania 30 C9
Jura, Mts. du Europe 19 F13
Jura, Sd. of U.K. 13 F3
Jurbarkas Lithuania 30 C9
Jurien Australia 93 F2
Jurilovca Romania 29 F13
Jūrmala Latvia 30 B10
Jurong China 59 B12
Jurong Singapore 65 d
Juruá → Brazil 124 D5
Juruena Brazil 124 F7
Juruena → Brazil 124 E7
Juruti Brazil 125 D7
Jussey France 19 E12
Justo Daract Argentina 126 C2
Jutaí → Brazil 124 D5
Jüterbog Germany 24 D9
Juticalpa Honduras 120 D2
Jutland = Jylland Denmark 11 H3
Juuka Finland 8 E23
Juventud, I. de la Cuba 120 B3
Juvigny-sous-Andaine
    France 18 D6
Jūy Zar Iran 73 F12
Juye China 56 G9
Juzennecourt France 19 D11
Jvari Georgia 35 J6
Jwaneng Botswana 85 J4
Jyderup Denmark 11 J5
Jylland Denmark 11 H3
Jyväskylä Finland 32 A3

K

K2 Pakistan 69 B7
Ka → Nigeria 83 C5
Kaakha = Kaka
    Turkmenistan 71 B8
Kaap Plateau S. Africa 88 D3
Kaapkruis Namibia 88 C1
Kaapstad = Cape Town
    S. Africa 88 E2
Kaba Guinea 82 C2
Kabaena Indonesia 63 F6
Kabala S. Leone 82 D2
Kabale Uganda 86 C3
Kabalo Dem. Rep. of the Congo 86 D2
Kabambare
    Dem. Rep. of the Congo 86 C2
Kabango
    Dem. Rep. of the Congo 87 D2
Kabankalan Phil. 61 G5
Kabara Fiji 91 a
Kabara Mali 82 B4
Kabardinka Russia 33 K10
Kabardino-Balkar
    Republic = Kabardino-
    Balkaria □ Russia 35 J6
Kabardino-Balkaria □
    Russia 35 J6
Kabarega Falls =
    Murchison Falls Uganda 86 B3
Kabarnet Kenya 86 B4
Kabasalan Phil. 61 H5
Kabat Indonesia 63 J17
Kabba Nigeria 83 D6
Kabi Niger 83 C7
Kabin Buri Thailand 64 F3
Kabinakagami L. Canada 104 C3
Kabinda
    Dem. Rep. of the Congo 84 F4
Kabna Sudan 80 D3
Kabompo Zambia 87 E1
Kabompo → Zambia 85 G4
Kabondo
    Dem. Rep. of the Congo 87 D2

Kabongo
    Dem. Rep. of the Congo 86 D2
Kabot Guinea 82 C2
Kabou Togo 83 D5
Kabr Sudan 81 E2
Kabrît, G. el Egypt 74 F2
Kabrousse Senegal 82 C1
Kabūd Gonbad Iran 71 B8
Kabugao Phil. 61 B4
Kābul Afghan. 68 B3
Kābul □ Afghan. 66 B6
Kābul → Pakistan 68 C5
Kabunga
    Dem. Rep. of the Congo 86 C2
Kaburuang Indonesia 63 D7
Kabushiya Sudan 81 D3
Kabwe Zambia 87 E2
Kačanik Serbia 44 D5
Kačergine Lithuania 30 D10
Kachchh, Gulf of India 68 H3
Kachchh, Rann of India 68 H4
Kachchhidhana India 69 J8
Kachebera Zambia 87 E3
Kachia Nigeria 83 D6
Kachikau Botswana 88 B3
Kachin □ Burma 58 D1
Kachira, L. Uganda 86 C3
Kachiry Kazakhstan 52 D8
Kachisi Ethiopia 81 F4
Kachnara India 68 H6
Kachot Cambodia 65 G4
Kaçkar Turkey 73 B9
Kadan Czech Rep. 26 A6
Kadan Kyun Burma 64 F2
Kadanai → Afghan. 68 D1
Kadavu Fiji 91 a
Kadavu Passage Fiji 91 a
Kade Ghana 83 D4
Kadhimain = Al
    Kāzimīyah Iraq 73 F11
Kadi India 68 H5
Kadina Australia 95 E2
Kadinhanı Turkey 72 C5
Kadiolo Mali 82 C3
Kadipur India 69 F10
Kadirli Turkey 72 D7
Kadiyevka = Stakhanov
    Ukraine 33 H10
Kadodo Sudan 81 E2
Kadoka U.S.A. 112 D3
Kadoma Zimbabwe 87 F2
Kâdugli Sudan 81 E2
Kaduna Nigeria 83 C6
Kaduna □ Nigeria 83 C6
Kaduy Russia 32 C9
Kaédi Mauritania 82 B2
Kaélé Cameroon 83 C7
Kaeng Khoï Thailand 64 E3
Kaeng Kra Chan △ Thailand 64 F2
Kaeng Tana △ Thailand 64 E5
Kaesŏng N. Korea 57 F14
Kāf Si. Arabia 70 D3
Kafan = Kapan Armenia 73 C12
Kafanchan Nigeria 83 D6
Kafarati Nigeria 83 C7
Kaffrine Senegal 82 C1
Kafin Nigeria 83 D6
Kafin Madaki Nigeria 83 C6
Kafinda Zambia 87 E3
Kafr el Battikh Egypt 80 H7
Kafr el Dauwâr Egypt 80 H7
Kafr el Sheikh Egypt 80 H7
Kafue Zambia 87 F2
Kafue → Zambia 85 H5
Kafue △ Zambia 87 F2
Kafue Flats Zambia 87 F2
Kafulwe Zambia 87 D2
Kaga Afghan. 68 B4
Kaga Bandoro C.A.R. 84 C3
Kagan Uzbekistan 52 F7
Kagarko Nigeria 83 D6
Kagawa □ Japan 55 G7
Kagera □ Tanzania 86 C3
Kagera → Uganda 86 C3
Kağızman Turkey 73 B10
Kagmar Sudan 81 E3
Kagoshima Japan 55 J5
Kagoshima □ Japan 55 J5
Kagul = Cahul Moldova 29 E13
Kahak Iran 71 B6
Kahama Tanzania 86 C3
Kahan Pakistan 68 E3
Kahang Malaysia 65 L4
Kahayan → Indonesia 62 E4
Kahe Tanzania 86 C4
Kahemba
    Dem. Rep. of the Congo 84 F3
Kahnūj Iran 71 E8
Kahoka U.S.A. 112 E8
Kaho'olawe U.S.A. 106 b
Kahramanmaraş Turkey 72 D7
Kahramanmaraş □ Turkey 72 D7
Kâhta Turkey 73 D8
Kahul, Ozero Ukraine 29 E13
Kahului U.S.A. 106 b

Kahurangi △ N.Z. 91 D4
Kahuta Pakistan 68 C5
Kahuzi-Biega △
    Dem. Rep. of the Congo 86 C2
Kai, Kepulauan Indonesia 63 F8
Kai Besar Indonesia 63 F8
Kai Is. = Kai, Kepulauan
    Indonesia 63 F8
Kai Kecil Indonesia 63 F8
Kai Xian China 58 B7
Kaiama Nigeria 83 D5
Kaiapoi N.Z. 91 E4
Kaieteur Falls Guyana 124 B7
Kaifeng China 56 G8
Kaihua China 59 C12
Kaijiang China 58 B6
Kaikohe N.Z. 91 A4
Kaikoura N.Z. 91 E4
Kailahun S. Leone 82 D2
Kailash = Kangrinboqe
    Feng China 69 D9
Kaili China 58 D6
Kailu China 57 C11
Kailua U.S.A. 106 b
Kaimaktsalan Oros =
    Voras Oros Greece 44 F5
Kaimana Indonesia 63 E8
Kaimanawa Mts. N.Z. 91 C5
Kaimganj India 69 F8
Kaimur Hills India 69 G10
Kainab → Namibia 88 D2
Kainji Dam Nigeria 83 D5
Kainji Lake △ Nigeria 83 C5
Kainji Res. Nigeria 83 D5
Kainuu Finland 8 D23
Kaipara Harbour N.Z. 91 B5
Kaiping China 59 F9
Kaipokok B. Canada 105 B8
Kaira India 68 H5
Kairana India 68 E7
Kaironi Indonesia 63 E8
Kairouan Tunisia 79 A8
Kaiserslautern Germany 25 F3
Kaiserstuhl Germany 25 G3
Kaitaia N.Z. 91 A4
Kaitangata N.Z. 91 G2
Kaithal India 68 E7
Kaitu → Pakistan 68 C4
Kaiyang China 58 D6
Kaiyuan Liaoning, China 57 C13
Kaiyuan Yunnan, China 58 F4
Kajaani Finland 8 D22
Kajabbi Australia 94 C3
Kajana = Kajaani Finland 8 D22
Kajang Malaysia 65 L3
Kajaran Armenia 73 C12
Kajiado Kenya 86 C4
Kajo Kaji Sudan 81 G3
Kajuru Nigeria 83 C6
Kaka Sudan 81 E3
Kaka Turkmenistan 71 B8
Kakabeka Falls Canada 104 C2
Kakadu △ Australia 92 B5
Kakamas S. Africa 88 D3
Kakamega Kenya 86 B3
Kakamega □ Kenya 86 B3
Kakanui Mts. N.Z. 91 F3
Kakanj Bos.-H. 28 F3
Kakata Liberia 82 D2
Kakdwip India 69 J13
Kake Japan 55 G6
Kake U.S.A. 102 B2
Kakegawa Japan 55 G9
Kakeroma-Jima Japan 55 K4
Kakhib Russia 35 J8
Kakhovka Ukraine 33 J7
Kakhovske Vdskh. Ukraine 33 J7
Kakinada India 67 L13
Kakisa Canada 102 A5
Kakisa L. Canada 102 A5
Kakogawa Japan 55 G7
Kakum △ Ghana 83 D4
Kakuma Kenya 86 B3
Kakwa → Canada 102 C5
Kāl Gūsheh Iran 71 D8
Kal Safid Iran 73 E12
Kala Nigeria 83 C7
Kalaallit Nunaat =
    Greenland ☒ N. Amer. 99 C15
Kalabagh Pakistan 68 C4
Kalabahi Indonesia 63 F6
Kalabana Mali 82 C3
Kalach Russia 34 E5
Kalach na Donu Russia 35 F6
Kaladan → Burma 67 J18
Kaladar Canada 114 B7
Kalahari Africa 88 C3
Kalahari Gemsbok △
    S. Africa 88 D3
Kalajoki Finland 8 D21
Kalakamati Botswana 89 C4
Kalakan Russia 53 D12
K'alak'unlun Shank'ou =
    Karakoram Pass Asia 69 B7
Kalam Pakistan 69 B5
Kalama Dem. Rep. of the Congo 86 C2
Kalama U.S.A. 110 E4
Kalamaria Greece 44 F6

Kalamata *Greece* **46** D4
Kalamazoo *U.S.A.* **113** D11
Kalamazoo → *U.S.A.* **112** D10
Kalambaka *Greece* **46** B3
Kalambo Falls *Tanzania* **87** D3
Kalamos *Attiki, Greece* **46** C5
Kalamos *Lefkada, Greece* **46** C2
Kalan *Turkey* **70** B3
Kalankalan *Guinea* **82** C3
Kalannie *Australia* **93** F2
Kalāntarī *Iran* **71** C7
Kalao *Indonesia* **63** F6
Kalaotoa *Indonesia* **63** F6
Kälarne *Sweden* **10** B10
Kalasin *Thailand* **64** D4
Kālat *Iran* **71** E8
Kalat *Pakistan* **66** E5
Kalāteh *Iran* **71** B7
Kalāteh-ye Ganj *Iran* **71** E8
Kalathos *Greece* **47** E10
Kalaus → *Russia* **35** H7
Kalavrita *Greece* **46** C4
Kalbā *U.A.E.* **71** E8
Kalbarri *Australia* **93** E1
Kalbarri △ *Australia* **93** E1
Kalce *Slovenia* **22** F8
Kale *Antalya, Turkey* **47** E12
Kale *Denizli, Turkey* **47** D10
Kalecik *Turkey* **72** B5
Kalegauk Kyun *Burma* **64** E1
Kalehe *Dem. Rep. of the Congo* **86** C2
Kalema *Tanzania* **86** C3
Kalemie
    Dem. Rep. of the Congo **86** D2
Kalety *Poland* **31** H5
Kalewa *Burma* **67** H19
Kaleybar *Iran* **70** B5
Kalgoorlie-Boulder *Australia* **93** F3
Kali → *India* **69** F8
Kali Sindh → *India* **68** G6
Kaliakra, Nos *Bulgaria* **45** C12
Kalianda *Indonesia* **62** F3
Kalibo *Phil.* **61** F5
Kalima *Dem. Rep. of the Congo* **86** C2
Kalimantan *Indonesia* **62** E4
Kalimantan Barat □
    Indonesia **62** E4
Kalimantan Selatan □
    Indonesia **62** E5
Kalimantan Tengah □
    Indonesia **62** E4
Kalimantan Timur □
    Indonesia **62** D5
Kálimnos *Greece* **47** D8
Kalimpong *India* **69** F13
Kaliningrad *Russia* **30** D7
Kaliningrad ✈ (KGD) *Russia* **30** D7
Kalininsk *Russia* **34** E7
Kalinkavichy *Belarus* **23** B15
Kalinkovichi =
    Kalinkavichy *Belarus* **23** B15
Kalinovik *Bos.-H.* **44** C2
Kalipetrovo *Bulgaria* **45** B11
Kalirachi *Greece* **45** F8
Kaliro *Uganda* **86** B3
Kalispell *U.S.A.* **108** B6
Kalisz *Poland* **31** G5
Kalisz Pomorski *Poland* **31** E2
Kalithea *Greece* **46** D5
Kaliua *Tanzania* **86** D3
Kalivia Thorikou *Greece* **46** D5
Kalix = Kalixälven →
    Sweden **8** D20
Kalix *Sweden* **8** D20
Kalixälven → *Sweden* **8** D20
Kalka *India* **68** D7
Kalkan *Turkey* **47** E11
Kalkarindji *Australia* **92** C5
Kalkaska *U.S.A.* **113** C11
Kalkfeld *Namibia* **88** C2
Kalkfontein *Botswana* **88** C3
Kalkım *Turkey* **47** B9
Kalkrand *Namibia* **88** C2
Kållandsö *Sweden* **11** F7
Kallavesi *Finland* **8** E22
Källby *Sweden* **11** F7
Kållered *Sweden* **11** G6
Kallimasia *Greece* **47** C8
Kallinge *Sweden* **11** H9
Kallmet *Albania* **44** E3
Kallsjön *Sweden* **8** E15
Kalmalo *Nigeria* **83** C6
Kalmar *Sweden* **11** H10
Kalmar län □ *Sweden* **11** G10
Kalmar sund *Sweden* **11** H10
Kalmyk Republic =
    Kalmykia □ *Russia* **35** G8
Kalmykia □ *Russia* **35** G8
Kalna *India* **69** H13
Kalnai *India* **69** H10
Kalo Nero *Greece* **46** D3
Kalocsa *Hungary* **28** D4
Kalofer *Bulgaria* **45** D8
Kalokhorio *Cyprus* **49** E12
Kaloko *Dem. Rep. of the Congo* **86** D2
Kalol *Gujarat, India* **68** H5
Kalol *Gujarat, India* **68** H5

Kalolimnos *Greece* **47** D9
Kalomo *Zambia* **87** F2
Kaloni *Greece* **47** B8
Kaloni, Kolpos *Greece* **47** B8
Kalpi *India* **69** F8
Kaltern = Caldaro *Italy* **41** B8
Kaltukatjara *Australia* **93** D4
Kaltungo *Nigeria* **83** D7
Kalu *Pakistan* **68** G2
Kaluga *Russia* **32** E9
Kaluga □ *Russia* **32** E8
Kalulushi *Zambia* **87** E2
Kalumburu *Australia* **92** B4
Kalundborg *Denmark* **11** J5
Kalush *Ukraine* **23** D13
Kałuszyn *Poland* **31** F8
Kalutara *Sri Lanka* **66** R12
Kalvarija *Lithuania* **30** D10
Kalyan *India* **66** K8
Kalyazin *Russia* **32** D9
Kam *Albania* **44** D4
Kam → *Nigeria* **83** D7
Kama *Dem. Rep. of the Congo* **86** C2
Kama → *Russia* **6** D16
Kamachumu *Tanzania* **86** C3
Kamaishi *Japan* **54** E10
Kamalia *Pakistan* **68** D5
Kaman *India* **68** F6
Kaman *Turkey* **72** C5
Kamanjab *Namibia* **88** B2
Kamapanda *Zambia* **87** E1
Kamarān *Yemen* **75** D3
Kamativi *Zimbabwe* **88** B4
Kamba *Nigeria* **83** C5
Kambalda West *Australia* **93** F3
Kambar *Pakistan* **68** F3
Kambia *S. Leone* **82** D2
Kambolé *Togo* **83** D5
Kambolé *Zambia* **87** D3
Kambos *Cyprus* **49** D11
Kambove
    Dem. Rep. of the Congo **87** E2
Kamchatka, Poluostrov
    Russia **53** D17
Kamchatka Pen. =
    Kamchatka, Poluostrov
    Russia **53** D17
Kamchiya → *Bulgaria* **45** C11
Kame Ruins *Zimbabwe* **87** G2
Kamen *Russia* **52** D9
Kamen-Rybolov *Russia* **54** B6
Kamenica *Serbia* **44** C6
Kamenica *Serbia* **44** B3
Kamenice nad Lipou
    Czech Rep. **26** B8
Kamenjak, Rt *Croatia* **41** D10
Kamenka = Kaminka
    Ukraine **33** H7
Kamenka *Kazakhstan* **34** E10
Kamenka *Penza, Russia* **34** D6
Kamenka *Voronezh, Russia* **33** G10
Kamenka Bugskaya =
    Kamyanka-Buzka
    Ukraine **23** C13
Kamenka Dneprovskaya
    = Kamyanka-
    Dniprovska *Ukraine* **33** J8
Kamennomostskiy *Russia* **35** H5
Kameno *Bulgaria* **45** D11
Kamenolomini *Russia* **35** G5
Kamensk-Shakhtinskiy
    Russia **35** F5
Kamensk Uralskiy *Russia* **52** D7
Kamenskiy *Russia* **34** E7
Kamenskoye *Russia* **53** C17
Kamenyak *Bulgaria* **45** C10
Kamenz *Germany* **24** D10
Kameoka *Japan* **55** G7
Kamet *India* **69** D8
Kamiah *U.S.A.* **108** C5
Kamień Krajeński *Poland* **30** E4
Kamień Pomorski *Poland* **30** E1
Kamieńsk *Poland* **31** G6
Kamieskroon *S. Africa* **88** E2
Kamilukuak L. *Canada* **103** A8
Kamin-Kashyrskyy *Ukraine*
    23 C13
Kamina
    Dem. Rep. of the Congo **87** D2
Kaminak L. *Canada* **103** A10
Kaministiquia *Canada* **104** C1
Kaminka *Ukraine* **33** H7
Kaminoyama *Japan* **54** E10
Kamiros *Greece* **49** C9
Kamituga
    Dem. Rep. of the Congo **86** C2
Kamla → *India* **69** G12
Kamloops *Canada* **102** C4
Kamnik *Slovenia* **41** B11
Kamo *Armenia* **35** K7
Kamo *Japan* **54** F9
Kamoke *Pakistan* **68** D6
Kamp → *Austria* **26** C8
Kampala *Uganda* **86** B3
Kampar *Malaysia* **65** K3

Kampar → *Indonesia* **62** D2
Kampen *Neths.* **17** B5
Kampene
    Dem. Rep. of the Congo **84** E5
Kamphaeng Phet *Thailand* **64** D2
Kampinoski △ *Poland* **31** F7
Kampolombo, L. *Zambia* **87** E2
Kampong Chhnang
    Cambodia **65** F5
Kampong Pengerang
    Malaysia **65** d
Kampong Punggai *Malaysia* **65** d
Kampong Saom *Cambodia* **65** G4
Kampong Saom, Chaak
    Cambodia **65** G4
Kampong Tanjong
    Langsat *Malaysia* **65** d
Kampong Telok Ramunia
    Malaysia **65** d
Kampong To *Thailand* **65** J3
Kampot *Cambodia* **65** G5
Kampti *Burkina Faso* **82** C4
Kampuchea =
    Cambodia ■ *Asia* **64** F5
Kampung Air Putih
    Malaysia **65** K4
Kampung Jerangau
    Malaysia **65** K4
Kampung Raja *Malaysia* **65** K4
Kampungbaru = Tolitoli
    Indonesia **63** D6
Kamrau, Teluk *Indonesia* **63** E8
Kamsack *Canada* **103** C8
Kamsai *Guinea* **82** C2
Kamskoye Ustye *Russia* **34** C9
Kamuchawie L. *Canada* **103** B8
Kamuela *U.S.A.* **106** b
Kamui-Misaki *Japan* **54** C10
Kamyanets-Podilskyy
    Ukraine **29** B11
Kamyanka-Buzka *Ukraine* **23** C13
Kamyanka-Dniprovska
    Ukraine **33** J8
Kamyanyets *Belarus* **31** F10
Kamyanyuki *Belarus* **31** F10
Kāmyārān *Iran* **73** E12
Kamyshin *Russia* **34** E7
Kamyzyak *Russia* **35** G9
Kan *Sudan* **81** F3
Kanaaupscow *Canada* **101** D12
Kanaaupscow → *Canada* **104** B4
Kanab *U.S.A.* **109** H7
Kanab Cr. → *U.S.A.* **109** H7
Kanacea *Lau Group, Fiji* **91** a
Kanacea *Taveuni, Fiji* **91** a
Kanagi *Japan* **54** D10
Kanairiktok → *Canada* **105** A7
Kanalia *Greece* **46** B4
Kananga
    Dem. Rep. of the Congo **84** F4
Kanash *Russia* **34** C8
Kanaskat *U.S.A.* **110** C5
Kanastraíon, Ákra =
    Paliouri, Akra *Greece* **44** G7
Kanawha → *U.S.A.* **113** F12
Kanazawa *Japan* **55** F8
Kanchanaburi *Thailand* **64** E2
Kanchenjunga *Nepal* **69** F13
Kanchipuram *India* **66** N11
Kańczuga *Poland* **31** J9
Kandaghat *India* **68** D7
Kandahār *Afghan.* **66** D4
Kandahār □ *Afghan.* **66** D4
Kandalaksha *Russia* **8** C25
Kandangan *Indonesia* **62** E5
Kandanghaur *Indonesia* **63** G13
Kandanos *Greece* **49** D5
Kandava *Latvia* **30** A9
Kandavu = Kadavu *Fiji* **91** a
Kandavu Passage =
    Kadavu Passage *Fiji* **91** a
Kandhkot *Pakistan* **68** E3
Kandhla *India* **68** E7
Kandi *Benin* **83** C5
Kandi *India* **69** H13
Kandiaro *Pakistan* **68** F3
Kandila *Greece* **46** D4
Kandıra *Turkey* **72** B4
Kandla *India* **68** H4
Kandos *Australia* **95** E4
Kandreho *Madag.* **89** B8
Kandy *Sri Lanka* **66** R12
Kane *U.S.A.* **114** E6
Kane Basin *Greenland* **98** B12
Kanel *Senegal* **82** B2
Käne'ohe *U.S.A.* **106** b
Kanevskaya *Russia* **35** G4
Kanfanar *Croatia* **41** C10
Kang *Botswana* **88** C3
Kang Krung △ *Thailand* **65** H2
Kangaba *Mali* **82** C3
Kangal *Turkey* **72** C7
Kangān *Fārs, Iran* **71** E7
Kangān *Hormozgan, Iran* **71** E8
Kangar *Malaysia* **65** J3
Kangaré *Mali* **82** C3
Kangaroo I. *Australia* **95** F2

Kangaroo Mts. *Australia* **94** C3
Kangasala *Finland* **32** B3
Kangāvar *Iran* **73** E12
Kangding *China* **58** B3
Kangdong *N. Korea* **57** E14
Kangean, Kepulauan
    Indonesia **62** F5
Kangean Is. = Kangean,
    Kepulauan *Indonesia* **62** F5
Kangen → *Sudan* **81** F3
Kanggye *N. Korea* **57** D14
Kangikajik *Greenland* **4** B6
Kangiqliniq = Rankin Inlet
    Canada **100** C10
Kangiqsualujjuaq *Canada* **101** D13
Kangiqsujuaq *Canada* **101** C12
Kangiqtugaapik = Clyde
    River *Canada* **101** B13
Kangirsuk *Canada* **101** D13
Kangkar Chemaran *Malaysia* **65** d
Kangkar Sungai Tiram
    Malaysia **65** d
Kangkar Teberau *Malaysia* **65** d
Kangping *China* **57** C12
Kangra *India* **68** C7
Kangrinboqe Feng *China* **69** D9
Kangto *China* **67** F18
Kanha △ *India* **69** H9
Kanhar → *India* **69** G10
Kani *Ivory C.* **82** D3
Kaniama
    Dem. Rep. of the Congo **86** D1
Kaniapiskau =
    Caniapiscau → *Canada* **105** A6
Kaniapiskau, L. =
    Caniapiscau, L. *Canada* **105** B6
Kanin, Poluostrov *Russia* **6** B14
Kanin Nos, Mys *Russia* **52** C5
Kanin Pen. = Kanin,
    Poluostrov *Russia* **6** B14
Kaninë *Albania* **44** F3
Kaniva *Australia* **95** F3
Kanjiža *Serbia* **28** D5
Kanjut Sar *Pakistan* **69** A6
Kankaanpää *Finland* **32** B2
Kankakee *U.S.A.* **112** E10
Kankakee → *U.S.A.* **112** E9
Kankan *Guinea* **82** C3
Kankendy = Xankändi
    Azerbaijan **73** C12
Kanker *India* **67** J12
Kankossa *Mauritania* **82** B2
Kankroli *India* **68** G5
Kannapolis *U.S.A.* **117** D14
Kannauj *India* **69** F8
Kannod *India* **66** H10
Kano *Japan* **55** G6
Kano □ *Nigeria* **83** C6
Kan'onji *Japan* **55** G6
Kanor, Ras *India* **68** J3
Kanoya *Japan* **55** J5
Kanpetlet *Burma* **67** J18
Kanpur *India* **69** F9
Kansas □ *U.S.A.* **112** F4
Kansas → *U.S.A.* **112** F6
Kansas City *Kans., U.S.A.* **112** F6
Kansas City *Mo., U.S.A.* **112** F6
Kansenia
    Dem. Rep. of the Congo **87** E2
Kansk *Russia* **53** D10
Kansu = Gansu □ *China* **56** G3
Kantaphor *India* **68** H7
Kantchari *Burkina Faso* **83** C5
Kanté *Niger* **83** C6
Kanté *Togo* **83** D5
Kantemirovka *Russia* **33** H10
Kantharalak *Thailand* **64** E5
Kantli → *India* **68** E6
Kantō □ *Japan* **55** F9
Kantō-Sanchi *Japan* **55** G9
Kanturk *Ireland* **12** D3
Kanuma *Japan* **55** F9
Kanus *Namibia* **88** D2
Kanyakumari *India* **66** Q10
Kanye *Botswana* **88** C4
Kanzenze
    Dem. Rep. of the Congo **87** E2
Kanzi, Ras *Tanzania* **86** D4
Kao *Tonga* **91** c
Kao Phara *Thailand* **65** a
Kaohsiung *Taiwan* **59** F13
Kaokoveld *Namibia* **88** B1
Kaolack *Senegal* **82** C1
Kaolack □ *Senegal* **82** C1
Kaoshan *China* **57** B13
Kapaa *U.S.A.* **106** b
Kapadvanj *India* **68** H5
Kapaklı *Turkey* **45** E11
Kapan *Armenia* **73** C12
Kapanga
    Dem. Rep. of the Congo **84** F4
Kapchagai = Qapshaghay
    Kazakhstan **52** E8
Kapedo *Kenya* **86** B4
Kapela = Velika Kapela
    Croatia **41** C12

Kapelo, Akra *Greece* **46** E5
Kapema
    Dem. Rep. of the Congo **87** E2
Kapenguria *Kenya* **86** B4
Kapfenberg *Austria* **26** D8
Kapı Dağı *Turkey* **45** F11
Kapiri Mposhi *Zambia* **87** E2
Kāpīsā □ *Afghan.* **66** B6
Kapiskau → *Canada* **104** B3
Kapit *Malaysia* **62** D4
Kapiti I. *N.Z.* **91** D5
Kaplan *U.S.A.* **116** F8
Kaplice *Czech Rep.* **26** C7
Kapoe *Thailand* **65** H2
Kapoeta *Sudan* **81** G3
Kápolnásnyék *Hungary* **28** C3
Kapos → *Hungary* **28** D3
Kaposvár *Hungary* **28** D2
Kapowsin *U.S.A.* **110** D4
Kappeln *Germany* **24** A5
Kappelshamn *Sweden* **11** G12
Kapps *Namibia* **88** C2
Kaprije *Croatia* **41** E12
Kapsabet *Kenya* **86** B4
Kapsan *N. Korea* **57** D15
Kapsukas = Marijampolė
    Lithuania **30** D10
Kapuas → *Indonesia* **62** E3
Kapuas Hulu,
    Pegunungan *Malaysia* **62** D4
Kapuas Hulu Ra. =
    Kapuas Hulu,
    Pegunungan *Malaysia* **62** D4
Kapulo *Dem. Rep. of the Congo* **87** D2
Kapunda *Australia* **95** E2
Kapuni *N.Z.* **91** C5
Kapurthala *India* **68** D6
Kapuskasing *Canada* **104** C3
Kapuskasing → *Canada* **104** C3
Kaputar, Mt. *Australia* **95** E5
Kaputir *Kenya* **86** B4
Kapuvár *Hungary* **28** C2
Kara *Russia* **52** C7
Karā, W. → *Si. Arabia* **80** C5
Kara *Adaa Turkey* **47** F9
Kara Bogaz Gol, Zaliv =
    Garabogazköl Aylagy
    Turkmenistan **52** E6
Kara Burun *Turkey* **47** E9
Kara-Kala = Garrygala
    Turkmenistan **71** B8
Kara Kalpak Republic =
    Qoraqalpoghiston □
    Uzbekistan **52** E6
Kara Kum = Garagum
    Turkmenistan **71** B8
Kara Sea *Russia* **52** B8
Karaadilli *Turkey* **47** C13
Karabiğa *Turkey* **45** F11
Karabük *Turkey* **72** B5
Karabük □ *Turkey* **72** B5
Karaburun *Albania* **44** F3
Karaburun *Turkey* **47** C8
Karabutak = Qarabutaq
    Kazakhstan **52** E7
Karacabey *Turkey* **45** F12
Karacakılavuz *Turkey* **45** E11
Karacaköy *Turkey* **45** E12
Karacasu *Turkey* **47** D10
Karachala = Qaraçala
    Azerbaijan **35** L9
Karachayevsk *Russia* **35** J5
Karachev *Russia* **33** F8
Karachey-Cherkessia □
    Russia **35** J5
Karachi *Pakistan* **68** G2
Karad *India* **66** L9
Karadirek *Turkey* **47** C12
Karaga *Ghana* **83** D4
Karaganda = Qaraghandy
    Kazakhstan **52** E8
Karagayly = Qaraghayly
    Kazakhstan **52** E8
Karaginskiy, Ostrov *Russia* **53** D17
Karagola Road *India* **69** G12
Karagüney Dağları *Turkey* **72** B6
Karahallı *Turkey* **47** C11
Karaikal *India* **66** P11
Karaikkudi *India* **66** P11
Karaisalı *Turkey* **72** D6
Karaj *Iran* **71** C6
Karak *Malaysia* **65** L4
Karakalpakstan =
    Qoraqalpoghiston □
    Uzbekistan **52** E6
Karakelong *Indonesia* **63** D7
Karakitang *Indonesia* **63** D7
Karakoçan *Turkey* **73** C9
Karakol *Kyrgyzstan* **52** E8
Karakoram Pass *Asia* **69** B7
Karakoram Ra. *Pakistan* **69** B7
Karakurt *Turkey* **73** B10
Karakuwisa *Namibia* **88** B2
Karalon *Russia* **53** D12

Karama *Jordan* **74** D4
Karaman *Balıkesir, Turkey* **47** B9
Karaman *Konya, Turkey* **72** D5
Karamanlı *Turkey* **47** D11
Karamay *China* **60** B3
Karambu *Indonesia* **62** E5
Karamea Bight *N.Z.* **91** D3
Karamnasa → *India* **69** G10
Karamürsel *Turkey* **45** F13
Kārān *Si. Arabia* **71** E6
Karand *Iran* **73** E12
Karangana *Mali* **82** C3
Karanganyar *Indonesia* **63** G13
Karangasem *Indonesia* **63** J18
Karanjia *India* **69** J11
Karankasso *Burkina Faso* **82** C4
Karaova *Turkey* **47** D9
Karapınar *Turkey* **72** D5
Karasburg *Namibia* **88** D2
Karasino *Russia* **52** C9
Karasjok *Norway* **8** B21
Karasu → *Turkey* **72** B4
Karasu → *Turkey* **47** E12
Karasuk *Russia* **52** D8
Karasuyama *Japan* **55** F10
Karataş *Adana, Turkey* **72** D6
Karataş *Manisa, Turkey* **47** C10
Karataş Burnu *Turkey* **72** D6
Karatau, Khrebet =
    Qarataū *Kazakhstan* **52** E7
Karatoprak *Turkey* **47** D9
Karatsu *Japan* **55** H5
Karaul *Russia* **52** B9
Karauli *India* **68** F7
Karavastasë, L. e *Albania* **44** F3
Karavia *Greece* **46** E5
Karawang *Indonesia* **62** F5
Karawanken *Europe* **26** E7
Karayazı *Turkey* **73** C10
Karazhal = Qarazhal
    Kazakhstan **52** E8
Karbalā' *Iraq* **73** F11
Karbalā' □ *Iraq* **73** F11
Kårböle *Sweden* **10** C9
Karcag *Hungary* **28** C5
Karcha → *Pakistan* **69** B7
Karchana *India* **69** G9
Karczew *Poland* **31** F8
Kardam *Bulgaria* **45** C12
Kardamaila *Greece* **47** C8
Kardamili *Greece* **46** E4
Kardeljovo = Ploče *Croatia* **41** E14
Karditsa *Greece* **46** B3
Karditsa □ *Greece* **46** B3
Kärdla *Estonia* **32** C2
Kareeberge *S. Africa* **88** E3
Kareha → *India* **69** G12
Kareima *Sudan* **80** D3
Karelia □ *Russia* **8** D25
Karelian Republic =
    Karelia □ *Russia* **8** D25
Karera *India* **68** G8
Kārevāndar *Iran* **71** E9
Kargasok *Russia* **52** D9
Kargat *Russia* **52** D9
Kargi *Kenya* **86** B4
Kargı *Turkey* **72** B6
Kargil *India* **69** B7
Kargopol *Russia* **32** B10
Kargowa *Poland* **31** F2
Karguéri *Niger* **83** C7
Karhal *India* **69** F8
Karia *Greece* **46** C2
Kariān *Iran* **71** E8
Karianga *Madag.* **89** C8
Kariba *Zimbabwe* **87** F2
Kariba, L. *Zimbabwe* **87** F2
Kariba Dam *Zimbabwe* **87** F2
Kariba Gorge *Zambia* **87** F2
Karibib *Namibia* **88** C2
Karies *Greece* **45** F8
Karijini △ *Australia* **92** D2
Karimata, Kepulauan
    Indonesia **62** E3
Karimata, Selat *Indonesia* **62** E3
Karimata Is. = Karimata,
    Kepulauan *Indonesia* **62** E3
Karimnagar *India* **66** K11
Karimun Kecil, Pulau
    Indonesia **65** d
Karimunjawa, Kepulauan
    Indonesia **62** F4
Karin *Somali Rep.* **75** E4
Karistos *Greece* **46** C6
Karīt *Iran* **71** C8
Kariya *Japan* **55** G8
Kariyangwe *Zimbabwe* **89** B4
Karjala *Finland* **32** A5
Karkaralinsk = Qarqaraly
    Kazakhstan **52** E8
Karkheh → *Iran* **70** D5
Karkinitska Zatoka *Ukraine* **33** K7
Karkinitskiy Zaliv =
    Karkinitska Zatoka
    Ukraine **33** K7
Karkuk = Kirkūk *Iraq* **73** E11

Karkur Tohl *Egypt* **80** C2
Karl Liebknecht *Russia* **33** G8
Karla, L. = Volvi, L. *Greece* **44** F7
Karleby = Kokkola *Finland* **8** E20
Karlholmsbruk *Sweden* **10** D11
Karlino *Poland* **30** D2
Karlivka *Ukraine* **33** H8
Karlobag *Croatia* **41** D12
Karlovac *Croatia* **41** C12
Karlovarský □ *Czech Rep.* **26** A5
Karlovasi *Greece* **47** D8
Karlovka = Karlivka
  Ukraine **33** H8
Karlovo *Bulgaria* **45** D8
Karlovy Vary *Czech Rep.* **26** A5
Karlsbad = Karlovy Vary
  Czech Rep. **26** A5
Karlsborg *Sweden* **11** F8
Karlshamn *Sweden* **11** H8
Karlskoga *Sweden* **10** E8
Karlskrona *Sweden* **11** H9
Karlsruhe *Germany* **25** F4
Karlstad *Sweden* **10** E7
Karlstad *U.S.A.* **112** A5
Karlstadt *Germany* **25** F5
Karma *Niger* **83** C5
Karmėlava *Lithuania* **30** D11
Karmi'el *Israel* **74** C4
Karnak *Egypt* **80** B3
Karnal *India* **68** E7
Karnali → *Nepal* **69** E9
Karnaphuli Res. = Kaptai
  L. *Bangla.* **67** H18
Karnaprayag *India* **69** D8
Karnataka □ *India* **66** N10
Karnes City *U.S.A.* **116** G6
Karnische Alpen *Europe* **26** E6
Karnobat *Bulgaria* **45** D10
Kärnten □ *Austria* **26** E6
Karo *Mali* **82** C4
Karoi *Zimbabwe* **87** F2
Karon, Ao *Thailand* **65** a
Karonga *Malawi* **87** D3
Karoo △ *S. Africa* **88** E3
Karoonda *Australia* **95** F2
Karor *Pakistan* **68** D4
Karora *Sudan* **80** D4
Karounga *Mali* **82** B3
Karousades *Greece* **46** B1
Karpacz *Poland* **31** H2
Karpasia *Cyprus* **49** D13
Karpathos *Greece* **47** F9
Karpathos, Stenon *Greece* **47** F9
Karpatsky △ *Ukraine* **29** B9
Karpenisi *Greece* **46** C4
Karpuz Burnu = Apostolos
  Andreas, C. *Cyprus* **49** D13
Karpuzlu *Turkey* **47** D9
Karratha *Australia* **92** D2
Kars *Turkey* **73** B10
Kars □ *Turkey* **73** B10
Karsakpay *Kazakhstan* **52** E7
Karsha *Kazakhstan* **34** F7
Karshi = Qarshi *Uzbekistan* **52** F7
Karsiyang *India* **69** F13
Karsog *India* **68** D7
Karst = Kras *Croatia* **41** C10
Kartal *Turkey* **45** F13
Kartala *Comoros Is.* **85** a
Kartaly *Russia* **52** D7
Kartapur *India* **68** D6
Karthaus *U.S.A.* **114** E6
Kartuzy *Poland* **30** D5
Karufa *Indonesia* **63** E8
Karuma △ *Uganda* **86** B3
Karumba *Australia* **94** B3
Karumo *Tanzania* **86** C3
Karumwa *Tanzania* **86** C3
Kārūn → *Iran* **71** D6
Karungu *Kenya* **86** C3
Karup *Denmark* **11** H3
Karviná *Czech Rep.* **27** B11
Karwan → *India* **68** F8
Karwar *India* **66** M9
Karwendel △ *Austria* **26** D4
Karwi *India* **69** G9
Kaş *Turkey* **47** E11
Kasaba *Turkey* **47** E11
Kasache *Malawi* **87** E3
Kasai →
  Dem. Rep. of the Congo **84** E3
Kasai-Oriental □
  Dem. Rep. of the Congo **86** D1
Kasaji *Dem. Rep. of the Congo* **87** E1
Kasama *Zambia* **87** E3
Kasan *N. Korea* **57** D14
Kasandra *Greece* **44** F7
Kasandra Kolpos *Greece* **44** F7
Kasandras, Akra *Greece* **44** G7
Kasane *Namibia* **88** B3
Kasanga *Tanzania* **87** E3
Kasanka △ *Zambia* **87** E3
Kasar, Ras *Sudan* **80** D4
Kasaragod *India* **66** N9
Kasba L. *Canada* **103** A8
Kāseh Garān *Iran* **70** C5
Kasempa *Zambia* **87** E2

Kasenga
  Dem. Rep. of the Congo **87** E2
Kasese *Uganda* **86** B3
Kasewa *Zambia* **87** E2
Kashabowie *Canada* **104** C1
Kashaf *Iran* **71** C9
Kāshān *Iran* **71** C6
Kashechewan *Canada* **104** B3
Kashgar = Kashi *China* **60** C2
Kashi *China* **60** C2
Kashimbo
  Dem. Rep. of the Congo **87** E2
Kashin *Russia* **32** D9
Kashipur *India* **69** E8
Kashira *Russia* **32** E10
Kashiwazaki *Japan* **55** F9
Kashk-e Kohneh *Afghan.* **66** B3
Kashkū'īyeh *Iran* **71** D7
Kāshmar *Iran* **71** C8
Kashmir *Asia* **69** C7
Kashmor *Pakistan* **68** E3
Kashpirovka *Russia* **34** D9
Kashun Noerh = Gaxun
  Nur *China* **60** B5
Kasiari *India* **69** H12
Kasimov *Russia* **34** C5
Kasinge
  Dem. Rep. of the Congo **86** D2
Kasiruta *Indonesia* **63** E7
Kaskaskia → *U.S.A.* **112** G9
Kaskattama → *Canada* **103** B10
Kaskinen *Finland* **8** E19
Kaskö = Kaskinen *Finland* **8** E19
Kaslo *Canada* **102** D5
Kasmere L. *Canada* **103** B8
Kasongo
  Dem. Rep. of the Congo **86** C2
Kasongo Lunda
  Dem. Rep. of the Congo **84** F3
Kasos *Greece* **47** F8
Kasos, Stenon *Greece* **47** F8
Kaspi *Georgia* **35** K7
Kaspichan *Bulgaria* **45** C11
Kaspiysk *Russia* **35** J8
Kaspiyskiy *Russia* **35** H8
Kassab ed Doleib *Sudan* **81** E3
Kassaba *Egypt* **80** C2
Kassalâ *Sudan* **81** D4
Kassalâ □ *Sudan* **81** D4
Kassandreio *Greece* **44** F7
Kassel *Germany* **24** D5
Kassinger *Sudan* **80** D3
Kassiopi *Greece* **49** A3
Kasson *U.S.A.* **112** C7
Kastamonu *Turkey* **72** B5
Kastamonu □ *Turkey* **72** B5
Kastav *Croatia* **41** C11
Kasteli *Greece* **49** D5
Kastelli *Greece* **49** D7
Kastellórizon = Megisti
  Greece **47** E11
Kastelo, Akra *Greece* **47** F9
Kasterlee *Belgium* **17** C4
Kastlösa *Sweden* **11** H10
Kastoria *Greece* **44** F5
Kastoria □ *Greece* **44** F5
Kastorias, L. *Greece* **44** F5
Kastorio *Greece* **46** D5
Kastornoye *Russia* **33** G10
Kastos *Greece* **46** C2
Kastrosikia *Greece* **46** B2
Kastrup, København ✈
  (CPH) *Denmark* **11** J6
Kastsyukovichy *Belarus* **32** F7
Kasulu *Tanzania* **86** C3
Kasumi *Japan* **55** G7
Kasungu *Malawi* **87** E3
Kasungu △ *Malawi* **87** E3
Kasur *Pakistan* **68** D6
Kata Archanes *Greece* **49** D7
Kata Tjuta *Australia* **93** E5
Kataba *Zambia* **87** F2
Katagum *Nigeria* **83** C7
Katahdin, Mt. *U.S.A.* **113** C19
Katako Kombe
  Dem. Rep. of the Congo **86** C1
Katakolo *Greece* **46** D3
Katale *Tanzania* **86** C3
Katanda *Katanga,*
  Dem. Rep. of the Congo **86** D1
Katanda *Nord-Kivu,*
  Dem. Rep. of the Congo **86** C2
Katanga □
  Dem. Rep. of the Congo **86** D2
Katangi *India* **69** J11
Katanning *Australia* **93** F2
Katastari *Greece* **46** D2
Katavi △ *Tanzania* **86** D3
Katavi Swamp *Tanzania* **86** D3
Katerini *Greece* **44** F6
Katghora *India* **69** H10
Katha *Burma* **67** G20
Katherîna, Gebel *Egypt* **70** D3
Katherine *Australia* **92** B5
Katherine Gorge *Australia* **92** B5

Kathi *India* **68** J6
Kathiawar *India* **68** H4
Kathikas *Cyprus* **49** E11
Kathmandu = Katmandu
  Nepal **69** F11
Kathua *India* **68** C6
Kati *Mali* **82** C3
Katihar *India* **69** G12
Katima Mulilo *Zambia* **88** B3
Katimbira *Malawi* **87** E3
Katingan = Mendawai →
  Indonesia **62** E4
Katiola *Ivory C.* **82** D3
Katlabukh, Ozero *Ukraine* **29** E14
Katlanovo *Macedonia* **44** E5
Katmandu *Nepal* **69** F11
Katni *India* **69** H9
Kato Achaia *Greece* **46** C3
Kato Chorio *Greece* **49** D7
Kato Korakiana *Greece* **49** A3
Káto Pyrgos *Cyprus* **49** D11
Katochi *Greece* **46** C3
Katompe
  Dem. Rep. of the Congo **86** D2
Katong *Singapore* **65** d
Katonga → *Uganda* **86** B3
Katoomba *Australia* **95** E5
Katouna *Greece* **46** C3
Katowice *Poland* **31** H6
Katrancı Dağı *Turkey* **47** D12
Katrine, L. *U.K.* **13** E4
Katrineholm *Sweden* **10** E10
Katsepe *Madag.* **89** B8
Katsina *Nigeria* **83** C6
Katsina □ *Nigeria* **83** C6
Katsina Ala *Nigeria* **83** D6
Katsina Ala → *Nigeria* **83** D6
Katsumoto *Japan* **55** H4
Katsuura *Japan* **55** G10
Katsuyama *Japan* **55** F8
Kattavia *Greece* **49** D9
Kattegat *Denmark* **11** H5
Katthammarsvik *Sweden* **11** G12
Katul, J. *Sudan* **81** E2
Katumba
  Dem. Rep. of the Congo **86** D2
Katwa *India* **69** H13
Katwijk *Neths.* **17** B4
Kąty Wrocławskie *Poland* **31** G3
Kaua'i *U.S.A.* **106** b
Kauai Channel *U.S.A.* **106** b
Kaub *Germany* **25** E3
Kaudom △ *Namibia* **88** B3
Kaufbeuren *Germany* **25** H6
Kaufman *U.S.A.* **116** E6
Kauhajoki *Finland* **8** E20
Kaukauna *U.S.A.* **112** C9
Kaukauveld *Namibia* **88** C3
Kaunakakai *U.S.A.* **106** b
Kaunas *Lithuania* **30** D10
Kaunas ✈ (KUN) *Lithuania* **30** D11
Kaunia *Bangla.* **69** G13
Kaunos *Turkey* **47** E10
Kaura Namoda *Nigeria* **83** C6
Kauru *Nigeria* **83** C6
Kautokeino *Norway* **8** B20
Kauwapur *India* **69** F10
Kavacha *Russia* **53** C17
Kavadarci *Macedonia* **44** E6
Kavajë *Albania* **44** E3
Kavak *Turkey* **72** B7
Kavak Dağı *Turkey* **47** D10
Kavaklı *Turkey* **45** E11
Kavaklıdere *Turkey* **47** D10
Kavala *Greece* **45** F8
Kavala □ *Greece* **45** E8
Kavala Kolpos *Greece* **45** F8
Kavalerovo *Russia* **54** B7
Kavali *India* **66** M12
Kavār *Iran* **71** D7
Kavarna *Bulgaria* **45** C12
Kavi *India* **68** H5
Kavimba *Botswana* **88** B3
Kavīr, Dasht-e *Iran* **71** C7
Kavīr △ *Iran* **71** C7
Kavkaz *Russia* **33** K9
Kävlinge *Sweden* **11** J7
Kavos *Greece* **49** B4
Kavousi *Greece* **47** F7
Kaw *Fr. Guiana* **125** C8
Kawa *Sudan* **81** E3
Kawagama L. *Canada* **114** A6
Kawagoe *Japan* **55** G9
Kawaguchi *Japan* **55** G9
Kawambwa *Zambia* **87** D2
Kawanoe *Japan* **55** G6
Kawardha *India* **69** J9
Kawasaki *Japan* **55** G9
Kawasi *Indonesia* **63** E7
Kawawachikamach
  Canada **105** B6
Kawerau *N.Z.* **91** C6
Kawhia *N.Z.* **91** C5
Kawhia Harbour *N.Z.* **91** C5
Kawio, Kepulauan *Indonesia* **63** D7
Kawthaung *Burma* **65** H2
Kawthoolei = Kayin □
  Burma **67** L20

Kawthule = Kayin □
  Burma **67** L20
Kaxholmen *Sweden* **11** G8
Kaya *Burkina Faso* **83** C4
Kayah □ *Burma* **67** K20
Kayalıköy Barajı *Turkey* **45** E11
Kayan → *Indonesia* **62** D5
Kaycee *U.S.A.* **108** E10
Kayeli *Indonesia* **63** E7
Kayenta *U.S.A.* **109** H8
Kayes *Mali* **82** C2
Kayes □ *Mali* **82** C2
Kayı *Turkey* **47** B12
Kayima *S. Leone* **82** D2
Kayin □ *Burma* **67** L20
Kaymakçı *Turkey* **47** C10
Kayoa *Indonesia* **63** D7
Kayomba *Zambia* **87** E1
Kaysatskoye *Russia* **34** F8
Kayseri *Turkey* **72** C6
Kayseri □ *Turkey* **72** C7
Kaysville *U.S.A.* **108** F8
Kaz Dağı *Turkey* **47** B8
Kazachye *Russia* **53** B14
Kazakhstan ■ *Asia* **52** E8
Kazan *Russia* **34** C9
Kazan → *Canada* **103** A9
Kazan-Rettō *Pac. Oc.* **96** E6
Kazanlŭk *Bulgaria* **45** D9
Kazanskaya *Russia* **34** F5
Kazatin = Kozyatyn
  Ukraine **23** D15
Kazaure *Nigeria* **83** C6
Kazbek *Russia* **35** J7
Kāzerūn *Iran* **71** D6
Kazi Magomed =
  Qazimämmäd *Azerbaijan* **35** K9
Kazimierz Dolny *Poland* **31** G8
Kazimierza Wielka *Poland* **31** H7
Kazincbarcika *Hungary* **28** B5
Kazlų Rūda *Lithuania* **30** D10
Kaztalovka *Kazakhstan* **34** F9
Kazuma Pan △ *Zimbabwe* **87** F2
Kazuno *Japan* **54** D10
Kazym → *Russia* **52** C7
Kcynia *Poland* **31** F4
Ké-Macina *Mali* **82** C3
Kea *Greece* **46** D6
Keady *U.K.* **12** B5
Kearney *U.S.A.* **112** E4
Kearny *U.S.A.* **109** K8
Kearsarge, Mt. *U.S.A.* **115** C13
Keban *Turkey* **73** C8
Keban Baraji *Turkey* **73** C8
Kebbi □ *Nigeria* **83** C5
Kébi *Ivory C.* **82** D3
Kebnekaise *Sweden* **8** C18
Kebri Dehar *Ethiopia* **75** F3
Kebumen *Indonesia* **63** G13
Kecel *Hungary* **28** D4
Kechika → *Canada* **102** B3
Keçiborlu *Turkey* **47** D12
Kecskemét *Hungary* **28** D4
Kedada *Ethiopia* **81** F4
Kėdainiai *Lithuania* **30** C11
Kedarnath *India* **69** D8
Kedgwick *Canada* **105** C6
Kediri *Indonesia* **63** G15
Kedjebi *Ghana* **83** D5
Kédougou *Senegal* **82** C2
Kedros Oros *Greece* **49** D6
Kędzierzyn-Koźle *Poland* **31** H5
Keeler *U.S.A.* **110** J9
Keeley L. *Canada* **103** C7
Keeling Is. = Cocos Is.
  Ind. Oc. **96** J1
Keelung = Chilung *Taiwan* **59** E13
Keene *Canada* **114** B6
Keene *Calif., U.S.A.* **111** K8
Keene *N.H., U.S.A.* **115** D12
Keene *N.Y., U.S.A.* **115** B11
Keep River △ *Australia* **92** C4
Keeper Hill *Ireland* **12** D3
Keerweer, C. *Australia* **94** A3
Keeseville *U.S.A.* **115** B11
Keetmanshoop *Namibia* **88** D2
Keewatin *Canada* **103** D10
Keewatin → *Canada* **103** B8
Kefa *Ethiopia* **81** F4
Kefalonia *Greece* **46** C2
Kefalonia □ *Greece* **46** C2
Kefalos *Greece* **47** E8
Kefamenanu *Indonesia* **63** F6
Kefar Sava *Israel* **74** C3
Keffi *Nigeria* **83** D6
Keffin Hausa *Nigeria* **83** C6
Keflavík *Iceland* **8** D2
Keftya *Ethiopia* **81** E4
Keg River *Canada* **102** B5
Kegaska *Canada* **105** B7
Kehancha *Kenya* **86** C3
Keheili *Sudan* **80** D3
Kehl *Germany* **25** G3
Keighley *U.K.* **14** D6
Keila *Estonia* **32** C3
Keimoes *S. Africa* **88** D3
Keita *Niger* **83** C6

Keitele *Finland* **8** E22
Keith *Australia* **95** F3
Keith *U.K.* **13** D6
Keiyasi *Fiji* **91** a
Keizer *U.S.A.* **108** D2
Kejimkujik △ *Canada* **105** D6
Kekri *India* **68** G6
Kelam *Ethiopia* **81** G4
Kelamet *Eritrea* **81** D4
Kelan *China* **56** E6
Kelang = Klang *Malaysia* **65** L3
Kelantan → *Malaysia* **65** J4
Kelberrin *Australia* **93** F2
Kelchsau *Turkey* **45** G13
Këlcyrë *Albania* **44** F4
Kelekçi *Turkey* **47** D11
Keles *Turkey* **45** G13
Kelheim *Germany* **25** G7
Kelibia *Tunisia* **79** A8
Kelkit *Turkey* **73** B8
Kelkit → *Turkey* **72** B7
Kellerberrin *Australia* **93** F2
Kellett, C. *Canada* **101** B7
Kelleys I. *U.S.A.* **114** E2
Kellogg *U.S.A.* **108** C6
Kells = Ceanannus Mor
  Ireland **12** C5
Kelmė *Lithuania* **30** C9
Kelmentsi *Ukraine* **29** B11
Kelokedhara *Cyprus* **49** E11
Kelowna *Canada* **102** D5
Kelsey Creek *Australia* **94** J6
Kelseyville *U.S.A.* **110** G4
Kelso *N.Z.* **91** F2
Kelso *U.K.* **13** F6
Kelso *U.S.A.* **110** D4
Keluang = Kluang *Malaysia* **65** L4
Kelvington *Canada* **103** C8
Kem *Russia* **52** C4
Kema *Indonesia* **63** D7
Kemah *Turkey* **73** C8
Kemaliye *Erzincan, Turkey* **73** C8
Kemaliye *Manisa, Turkey* **47** C10
Kemalpaşa *Turkey* **47** C9
Kemano *Canada* **102** C3
Kemasik *Malaysia* **65** K4
Kembolcha *Ethiopia* **81** E4
Kemer *Antalya, Turkey* **47** E12
Kemer *Burdur, Turkey* **47** D12
Kemer *Muğla, Turkey* **47** E11
Kemer Baraji *Turkey* **47** D10
Kemerovo *Russia* **52** D9
Ķemeru △ *Latvia* **30** B10
Kemi *Finland* **8** D21
Kemi älv = Kemijoki →
  Finland **8** D21
Kemi träsk = Kemijärvi
  Finland **8** C22
Kemijärvi *Finland* **8** C22
Kemijoki → *Finland* **8** D21
Kemmerer *U.S.A.* **108** F8
Kemmuna = Comino *Malta* **49** C1
Kemp, L. *U.S.A.* **116** E5
Kemp Land *Antarctica* **5** C5
Kempas *Malaysia* **65** d
Kempsey *Australia* **95** E5
Kempt, L. *Canada* **104** C5
Kempten *Germany* **25** H6
Kempton *Australia* **95** G4
Kemptville *Canada* **115** B9
Ken → *India* **69** G9
Kenai *U.S.A.* **100** C4
Kendai *India* **69** H10
Kendal *Indonesia* **63** G14
Kendal *U.K.* **14** C5
Kendall *Australia* **95** E5
Kendall *U.S.A.* **117** J14
Kendall → *Australia* **94** A3
Kendallville *U.S.A.* **113** E11
Kendari *Indonesia* **63** E6
Kendawangan *Indonesia* **62** E4
Kende *Nigeria* **83** C5
Kendi, Pulau *Malaysia* **65** c
Kendrapara *India* **67** J15
Kendrew *S. Africa* **88** E3
Kene Thao *Laos* **64** D3
Kenedy *U.S.A.* **116** G6
Kenema *S. Leone* **82** D2
Keng Kok *Laos* **64** D5
Keng Tawng *Burma* **67** J21
Keng Tung *Burma* **58** G2
Kengeja *Tanzania* **86** D4
Kenhardt *S. Africa* **88** D3
Kenitra *Morocco* **78** B4
Kenli *China* **57** F10
Kenmare *Ireland* **12** E2
Kenmare *U.S.A.* **112** A2
Kenmare River *Ireland* **12** E2
Kennabago Lake *U.S.A.* **115** A14
Kennebago Lake *U.S.A.* **115** A14
Kennebec → *U.S.A.* **113** D19
Kennebunk *U.S.A.* **115** C14
Kennedy *Zimbabwe* **88** B4

Kennedy Ra. *Australia* **93** D2
Kennedy Range △ *Australia* **93** D2
Kenner *U.S.A.* **117** G9
Kenneth Ra. *Australia* **93** D2
Kennett *U.S.A.* **112** G8
Kennewick *U.S.A.* **108** C4
Kenogami → *Canada* **104** B3
Kenora *Canada* **103** D10
Kenosha *U.S.A.* **112** D10
Kensington *Canada* **105** C7
Kent *Ohio, U.S.A.* **114** E3
Kent *Tex., U.S.A.* **116** F2
Kent *Wash., U.S.A.* **110** C4
Kent □ *U.K.* **15** F8
Kent Group *Australia* **95** F4
Kent Pen. *Canada* **100** C9
Kentaū *Kazakhstan* **52** E7
Kentland *U.S.A.* **112** E10
Kenton *U.S.A.* **113** E12
Kentucky □ *U.S.A.* **113** G11
Kentucky → *U.S.A.* **113** F11
Kentucky L. *U.S.A.* **112** G9
Kentville *Canada* **105** C7
Kentwood *U.S.A.* **117** F9
Kenya ■ *Africa* **86** B4
Kenya, Mt. *Kenya* **86** C4
Keo Neua, Deo *Vietnam* **64** C5
Keokuk *U.S.A.* **112** E8
Keoladeo △ *India* **68** F7
Keonjhargarh *India* **69** J11
Kep *Cambodia* **65** G5
Kep *Vietnam* **64** B6
Kepala Batas *Malaysia* **65** c
Kepez *Turkey* **45** F10
Kepi *Indonesia* **63** F9
Kępice *Poland* **30** D3
Kępno *Poland* **31** G4
Kepsut *Turkey* **47** B10
Kerala □ *India* **66** P10
Kerama-Rettō *Japan* **55** L3
Keran *Pakistan* **69** B5
Keran △ *Togo* **83** C5
Kerang *Australia* **95** F3
Keranyo *Ethiopia* **81** F4
Kerao → *Sudan* **81** E3
Keratea *Greece* **46** D5
Keraudren, C. *Australia* **92** D2
Kerava *Finland* **32** B3
Kerch *Ukraine* **33** K9
Kerchenskiy Proliv *Black Sea* **33** K9
Kerchoual *Mali* **83** B5
Kerempe Burnu *Turkey* **72** A5
Keren *Eritrea* **81** D4
Kerewan *Gambia* **82** C1
Kerguelen *Ind. Oc.* **3** G13
Keri *Greece* **46** D2
Keri Kera *Sudan* **81** E3
Kericho *Kenya* **86** C4
Kerinci *Indonesia* **62** E2
Kerki = Atamyrat
  Turkmenistan **52** F7
Kerkini, L. *Greece* **44** E7
Kerkouane *Tunisia* **82** F4
Kerkrade *Neths.* **17** D6
Kerkyra *Greece* **49** A3
Kerkyra □ *Greece* **46** B1
Kerkyra ✈ (CFU) *Greece* **46** B1
Kerkyras, Notio Steno
  Greece **49** A4
Kerma *Sudan* **80** D3
Kermadec Is. *Pac. Oc.* **90** E11
Kermadec Trench *Pac. Oc.* **96** L10
Kermān *Iran* **71** D8
Kerman *U.S.A.* **110** J6
Kermān □ *Iran* **71** D8
Kermān, Bīābān-e *Iran* **71** D8
Kermānshāh *Iran* **73** E12
Kermānshāh □ *Iran* **70** C5
Kermen *Bulgaria* **45** D10
Kermit *U.S.A.* **116** F3
Kern → *U.S.A.* **111** K7
Kernhof *Austria* **26** D8
Kernow = Cornwall □ *U.K.* **15** G3
Kernville *U.S.A.* **111** K8
Keroh *Malaysia* **65** K3
Keros *Greece* **47** E7
Kérou *Benin* **83** C5
Kérouane *Guinea* **82** D3
Kerrera *U.K.* **13** E3
Kerrobert *Canada* **103** C7
Kerrville *U.S.A.* **116** F5
Kerry □ *Ireland* **12** D2
Kerry Hd. *Ireland* **12** D2
Kersa *Ethiopia* **81** F5
Kerulen → *Asia* **60** B6
Kervo = Kerava *Finland* **32** B3
Kerzaz *Algeria* **78** C5
Kesagami → *Canada* **104** B4
Kesagami L. *Canada* **104** B3
Keşan *Turkey* **45** F10
Kesennuma *Japan* **54** E10
Keshit *Iran* **71** D8
Keşiş Dağ *Turkey* **73** C8
Keskin *Turkey* **72** C5
Kestell *S. Africa* **89** D4

Kestenga *Russia* **8** D24
Keswick *U.K.* **14** C4
Keszthely *Hungary* **28** D2
Ket → *Russia* **52** D9
Keta *Ghana* **83** D5
Keta Lagoon *Ghana* **83** D5
Ketapang *Bali, Indonesia* **63** J17
Ketapang *Kalimantan, Indonesia* **62** E4
Ketchenery *Russia* **35** G7
Ketchikan *U.S.A.* **102** B2
Ketchum *U.S.A.* **108** E6
Kete Krachi *Ghana* **83** D4
Ketef, Khalîg Umm el *Egypt* **70** F2
Kétou *Benin* **83** D5
Ketri *India* **68** E6
Kętrzyn *Poland* **30** D8
Kettering *U.K.* **15** E7
Kettering *U.S.A.* **113** F11
Kettle → *Canada* **103** B11
Kettle Falls *U.S.A.* **108** B4
Kettle Pt. *Canada* **114** C2
Kettleman City *U.S.A.* **110** J7
Kęty *Poland* **31** J6
Keuka L. *U.S.A.* **114** D7
Keuruu *Finland* **32** A3
Kevelaer *Germany* **24** D2
Kewanee *U.S.A.* **112** E9
Kewaunee *U.S.A.* **112** C10
Keweenaw B. *U.S.A.* **112** B9
Keweenaw Pen. *U.S.A.* **112** B9
Keweenaw Pt. *U.S.A.* **112** B10
Key, L. *Ireland* **12** C3
Key Largo *U.S.A.* **117** J14
Key West *U.S.A.* **120** B3
Keyala *Sudan* **81** G3
Keynsham *U.K.* **15** F5
Keyser *U.S.A.* **113** F14
Kezhma *Russia* **53** D11
Kezi *Zimbabwe* **89** C4
Kežmarok *Slovak Rep.* **27** B13
Kgalagadi Transfrontier △ *Africa* **88** D3
Khabarovsk *Russia* **53** E14
Khabr *Iran* **71** D8
Khābūr → *Syria* **73** E9
Khachmas = Xaçmaz *Azerbaijan* **35** K9
Khachrod *India* **68** H6
Khadari, W. el → *Sudan* **81** E2
Khadro *Pakistan* **68** F3
Khadyzhensk *Russia* **35** H4
Khadzhilyangar = Dahongliutan *China* **69** B8
Khaga *India* **69** G9
Khagaria *India* **69** G12
Khaipur *Pakistan* **68** E5
Khair *India* **68** F7
Khairabad *India* **69** F9
Khairagarh *India* **69** J9
Khairpur *Pakistan* **68** F3
Khairpur Nathan Shah *Pakistan* **68** F2
Khairwara *India* **68** H5
Khaisor → *Pakistan* **68** D3
Khajuri Kach *Pakistan* **68** C3
Khakassia □ *Russia* **52** D9
Khakhea *Botswana* **88** C3
Khalafābād *Iran* **71** D6
Khalilabad *India* **69** F10
Khalīlī *Iran* **71** E7
Khalkhāl *Iran* **73** D13
Khalkís = Halkida *Greece* **46** C5
Khalmer Yu *Russia* **52** C7
Khalūf *Oman* **75** C6
Kham Keut *Laos* **64** C5
Khamaria *India* **69** H9
Khambhaliya *India* **68** H3
Khambhat *India* **68** H5
Khambhat, G. of *India* **66** J8
Khamīr *Iran* **71** E7
Khamir *Yemen* **75** D3
Khamīs Mushayṭ *Si. Arabia* **75** D3
Khamsa *Egypt* **74** E1
Khan → *Namibia* **88** C2
Khān Abū Shāmat *Syria* **74** B5
Khān Azād *Iraq* **70** C5
Khān Mujiddah *Iraq* **70** C4
Khān Shaykhūn *Syria* **72** E7
Khān Yūnis *Gaza Strip* **74** D3
Khanai *Pakistan* **68** D2
Khānaqīn *Iraq* **73** E11
Khānbāghī *Iran* **71** B7
Khandwa *India* **66** J10
Khandyga *Russia* **53** C14
Khāneh *Iran* **70** B5
Khanewal *Pakistan* **68** D4
Khangah Dogran *Pakistan* **68** D5
Khanh Duong *Vietnam* **64** F7
Khaniá = Chania *Greece* **49** D6
Khaniadhana *India* **68** G8
Khanka, L. *Asia* **54** B6
Khankendy = Xankändi *Azerbaijan* **73** C12
Khanna *India* **68** D7
Khanozai *Pakistan* **68** D2

Khanpur *Pakistan* **68** E4
Khanty-Mansiysk *Russia* **52** C7
Khao Laem △ *Thailand* **64** E2
Khao Laem Res. *Thailand* **64** E2
Khao Luang △ *Thailand* **65** H2
Khao Phlu *Thailand* **65** b
Khao Pu-Khao Ya △ *Thailand* **65** J2
Khao Sam Roi Yot △ *Thailand* **65** J2
Khao Sok △ *Thailand* **65** H2
Khao Yai △ *Thailand* **64** E3
Khaoen Si Nakarin △ *Thailand* **64** E2
Khapalu *Pakistan* **69** B7
Khapcheranga *Russia* **53** E12
Khaptao △ *Nepal* **69** E9
Kharabali *Russia* **35** G8
Kharaghoda *India* **68** H4
Kharagpur *India* **69** H12
Kharan Kalat *Pakistan* **66** E4
Kharānaq *Iran* **71** C7
Kharda *India* **66** K9
Khardung La *India* **69** B7
Kharg = Khārk, Jazīreh-ye *Iran* **71** D6
Khārga, El Wâhât-el *Egypt* **80** B3
Khargon *India* **66** J9
Khari → *India* **68** G6
Kharian *Pakistan* **68** C5
Kharit, Wadi el → *Egypt* **80** C3
Khārk, Jazīreh-ye *Iran* **71** D6
Kharkiv *Ukraine* **33** H9
Kharkiv □ *Ukraine* **33** H9
Kharkov = Kharkiv *Ukraine* **33** H9
Kharmanli *Bulgaria* **45** E9
Kharovsk *Russia* **32** C11
Kharsawangarh *India* **69** H11
Kharta *Turkey* **72** B3
Khartoum = El Khartûm *Sudan* **81** D3
Khasan *Russia* **54** C5
Khasavyurt *Russia* **35** J8
Khāsh *Iran* **71** D9
Khashm el Girba *Sudan* **81** E4
Khashum *Sudan* **81** E2
Khashuri *Georgia* **35** J6
Khaskovo *Bulgaria* **45** E9
Khaskovo □ *Bulgaria* **45** E9
Khatanga *Russia* **53** B11
Khatanga → *Russia* **53** B11
Khatauli *India* **68** E7
Khatra *India* **69** H12
Khātūnābād *Iran* **71** D7
Khatyrka *Russia* **53** C18
Khavda *India* **68** H3
Khawr Fakkān *U.A.E.* **71** E8
Khaybar, Ḥarrat *Si. Arabia* **70** E4
Khāzimiyah *Iraq* **70** C4
Khazzân Jabal al Awliyâ *Sudan* **81** D3
Khe Bo *Vietnam* **64** C5
Khe Long *Vietnam* **64** B5
Khe Sanh *Vietnam* **64** D6
Khed Brahma *India* **68** G5
Khekra *India* **68** E7
Khemarak Phouminville = Krong Kaoh Kong *Cambodia* **65** G4
Khemisset *Morocco* **78** B4
Khemmarat *Thailand* **64** D5
Khenāmān *Iran* **71** D8
Khenchela *Algeria* **78** A7
Khersān → *Iran* **71** D6
Kherson *Ukraine* **33** J7
Kherson □ *Ukraine* **33** J7
Kheta → *Russia* **53** B11
Khewari *Pakistan* **68** F3
Khilchipur *India* **68** G7
Khilok *Russia* **53** D12
Khimki *Russia* **32** E9
Khíos = Hios *Greece* **47** C8
Khirsadoh *India* **69** H8
Khiuma = Hiiumaa *Estonia* **32** C2
Khiva *Uzbekistan* **52** E7
Khīyāv *Iran* **70** B5
Khlebarovo *Bulgaria* **45** C10
Khlong Khlung *Thailand* **64** D2
Khmelnik *Ukraine* **23** D14
Khmelnitskiy = Khmelnytskyy *Ukraine* **23** D14
Khmelnytskyy *Ukraine* **23** D14
Khmelnytskyy □ *Ukraine* **33** H4
Khmer Rep. = Cambodia ■ *Asia* **64** F5
Khoai, Hon *Vietnam* **65** H5
Khodoriv *Ukraine* **23** D13
Khodzent = Khŭjand *Tajikistan* **52** E7
Khojak Pass *Afghan.* **68** D2
Khok Kloi *Thailand* **65** a
Khok Pho *Thailand* **65** J3
Kholm *Russia* **32** D6
Kholmsk *Russia* **53** E15
Khomas Hochland *Namibia* **88** C2
Khombole *Senegal* **82** C1
Khomeyn *Iran* **71** C6

Khomeynī Shahr *Iran* **71** C6
Khomodino *Botswana* **88** C3
Khon Kaen *Thailand* **64** D4
Khong → *Cambodia* **64** F5
Khong Sedone *Laos* **64** E5
Khonuu *Russia* **53** C15
Khoper → *Russia* **34** F6
Khor el 'Atash *Sudan* **81** E3
Khorāsān □ *Iran* **71** C8
Khorat = Nakhon Ratchasima *Thailand* **64** E4
Khorat, Cao Nguyen *Thailand* **64** E4
Khorixas *Namibia* **88** C1
Khorol *Ukraine* **33** H7
Khorramābād *Khorāsān, Iran* **71** C8
Khorramābād *Lorestān, Iran* **73** F13
Khorrāmshahr *Iran* **71** D6
Khorugh *Tajikistan* **52** F8
Khosravī *Iran* **71** D6
Khosrowābād *Khuzestān, Iran* **71** D6
Khosrowābād *Kordestān, Iran* **73** E12
Khost *Pakistan* **68** D2
Khosūyeh *Iran* **71** D7
Khotyn *Ukraine* **29** B11
Khouribga *Morocco* **78** B4
Khowst *Afghan.* **68** C3
Khowst □ *Afghan.* **66** C6
Khoyniki *Belarus* **23** C15
Khrami → *Georgia* **35** K7
Khrenovoye *Russia* **34** E5
Khrysokhou B. *Cyprus* **49** D11
Khu Khan *Thailand* **64** E5
Khuan Wa *Thailand* **65** a
Khudzhand = Khŭjand *Tajikistan* **52** E7
Khuff *Si. Arabia* **70** E5
Khūgīānī *Afghan.* **68** D2
Khuis *Botswana* **88** D3
Khuiyala *India* **68** F4
Khŭjand *Tajikistan* **52** E7
Khujner *India* **68** H7
Khulna *Bangla.* **67** H16
Khulna □ *Bangla.* **67** H16
Khulo *Georgia* **35** K6
Khumago *Botswana* **88** C3
Khunjerab △ *Pakistan* **69** A6
Khunjerab Pass = Kinjirap Daban *Asia* **69** A6
Khŭnsorkh *Iran* **71** E8
Khūr *Iran* **71** C8
Khurai *India* **68** G8
Khurayş *Si. Arabia* **71** E6
Khureit *Sudan* **81** E2
Khurja *India* **68** E7
Khūrmāl *Iraq* **70** C5
Khurr, Wādī al *Iraq* **70** C4
Khūsf *Iran* **71** C8
Khushab *Pakistan* **68** C5
Khust *Ukraine* **29** B8
Khutse △ *Botswana* **88** C3
Khuzdar *Pakistan* **68** F2
Khūzestān □ *Iran* **71** D6
Khvāf *Iran* **71** C9
Khvājeh *Iran* **70** B5
Khvalynsk *Russia* **34** D9
Khvānsār *Iran* **71** D7
Khvatovka *Russia* **34** D8
Khvor *Iran* **71** C7
Khvorgū *Iran* **71** E8
Khvormūj *Iran* **71** D6
Khvoy *Iran* **73** C11
Khvoynaya *Russia* **32** C8
Khyber Pass *Afghan.* **68** B4
Khyriv *Ukraine* **31** J9
Kia *Fiji* **91** a
Kiabukwa *Dem. Rep. of the Congo* **87** D1
Kiama *Australia* **95** E5
Kiamba *Phil.* **61** H6
Kiambi *Dem. Rep. of the Congo* **86** D2
Kiambu *Kenya* **86** C4
Kiang West △ *Gambia* **82** C1
Kiangara *Madag.* **89** B8
Kiangsi = Jiangxi □ *China* **59** D11
Kiangsu = Jiangsu □ *China* **57** H11
Kiato *Greece* **46** C4
Kibæk *Denmark* **11** H2
Kibale △ *Uganda* **86** B3
Kibanga Port *Uganda* **86** B3
Kibara *Tanzania* **86** C3
Kibare, Mts. *Dem. Rep. of the Congo* **86** D2
Kibira △ *Burundi* **86** C3
Kibombo *Dem. Rep. of the Congo* **86** C2
Kibondo *Tanzania* **86** C3
Kibre Mengist *Ethiopia* **81** F4
Kibris = Cyprus ■ *Asia* **49** E12
Kibumbu *Burundi* **86** C2
Kibungo *Rwanda* **86** C3
Kibuye *Burundi* **86** C2
Kibuye *Rwanda* **86** C2
Kibwesa *Tanzania* **86** D2

Kibwezi *Kenya* **86** C4
Kicasalih *Turkey* **45** E10
Kičevo *Macedonia* **44** E4
Kichha *India* **69** E8
Kichha → *India* **69** E8
Kicking Horse Pass *Canada* **102** C5
Kidal *Mali* **83** B5
Kidal □ *Mali* **83** B5
Kidderminster *U.K.* **15** E5
Kidepo Valley △ *Uganda* **86** B3
Kidete *Tanzania* **86** D4
Kidira *Senegal* **82** C2
Kidnappers, C. *N.Z.* **91** C6
Kidsgrove *U.K.* **14** D5
Kidston *Australia* **94** B3
Kidugallo *Tanzania* **86** D4
Kiel *Germany* **24** A6
Kiel Canal = Nord-Ostsee-Kanal *Germany* **24** A5
Kielce *Poland* **31** H7
Kielder Water *U.K.* **14** B5
Kieler Bucht *Germany* **24** A7
Kiembara *Burkina Faso* **82** C4
Kien Binh *Vietnam* **65** H5
Kien Tan *Vietnam* **65** H5
Kienge *Dem. Rep. of the Congo* **87** E2
Kiessé *Niger* **83** C5
Kiev = Kyyiv *Ukraine* **23** C16
Kifaya *Guinea* **82** C2
Kiffa *Mauritania* **82** B2
Kifisos → *Greece* **46** C5
Kifissia *Greece* **46** C5
Kifrī *Iraq* **73** E11
Kigali *Rwanda* **86** C3
Kigarama *Tanzania* **86** C3
Kigelle *Sudan* **81** F3
Kigezi △ *Uganda* **86** C2
Kigoma □ *Tanzania* **86** D3
Kigoma-Ujiji *Tanzania* **86** C2
Kigomasha, Ras *Tanzania* **86** C4
Kihnu *Estonia* **32** C3
Kii-Sanchi *Japan* **55** G8
Kii-Suidō *Japan* **55** H7
Kiira Dam *Uganda* **86** B3
Kikaiga-Shima *Japan* **55** K4
Kikinda *Serbia* **28** E5
Kikládhes = Cyclades *Greece* **46** E6
Kikwit *Dem. Rep. of the Congo* **84** F3
Kil *Sweden* **10** E7
Kilafors *Sweden* **10** C10
Kilar *India* **68** C7
Kīlauea Caldera *U.S.A.* **106** b
Kilbeggan *Ireland* **12** C4
Kilbrannan Sd. *U.K.* **13** F3
Kilchu *N. Korea* **57** D15
Kilcoy *Australia* **95** D5
Kildare *Ireland* **12** C5
Kildare □ *Ireland* **12** C5
Kildinstroy *Russia* **8** B25
Kileikli *Sudan* **81** E2
Kilfinnane *Ireland* **12** D3
Kilgarvan *Ireland* **12** E2
Kilgore *U.S.A.* **116** E7
Kilgoris *Kenya* **86** C3
Kilibo *Benin* **83** D5
Kilifi *Kenya* **86** C4
Kilimanjaro *Tanzania* **86** C4
Kilimanjaro □ *Tanzania* **86** C4
Kilimli *Turkey* **72** B4
Kilindini *Kenya* **86** C4
Kilis *Turkey* **72** D7
Kilis □ *Turkey* **72** D7
Kiliya *Ukraine* **29** E14
Kilkee *Ireland* **12** D2
Kilkeel *U.K.* **12** B5
Kilkenny *Ireland* **12** D4
Kilkenny □ *Ireland* **12** D4
Kilkieran B. *Ireland* **12** C2
Kilkis *Greece* **44** F6
Kilkis □ *Greece* **44** E6
Killala *Ireland* **12** B2
Killala B. *Ireland* **12** B2
Killaloe *Canada* **114** A7
Killaloe *Ireland* **12** D3
Killarney *Australia* **95** D5
Killarney *Canada* **103** D9
Killarney *Ireland* **12** D2
Killary Harbour *Ireland* **12** C2
Killdeer *U.S.A.* **112** B2
Killeberg *Sweden* **11** H8
Killeen *U.S.A.* **116** F6
Killin *U.K.* **13** E4
Killiney *Ireland* **12** C5
Killington Pk. *U.S.A.* **115** C12
Killíni = Kyllini *Greece* **46** D3
Killini *Greece* **46** D4
Killorglin *Ireland* **12** D2
Killybegs *Ireland* **12** B3
Kilmarnock *U.K.* **13** F4
Kilmez *Russia* **34** B10
Kilmez → *Russia* **34** B10
Kilmore *Australia* **95** F3
Kilmore Quay *Ireland* **12** D5
Kilondo *Tanzania* **87** D3
Kilosa *Tanzania* **86** D4

Kilrush *Ireland* **12** D2
Kilwa Kisiwani *Tanzania* **87** D4
Kilwa Kivinje *Tanzania* **87** D4
Kilwa Masoko *Tanzania* **87** D4
Kilwinning *U.K.* **13** F4
Kim *U.S.A.* **109** H12
Kim → *Cameroon* **83** D7
Kimaam *Indonesia* **63** F9
Kimamba *Tanzania* **86** D4
Kimba *Australia* **95** E2
Kimball *Nebr., U.S.A.* **112** E2
Kimball *S. Dak., U.S.A.* **112** D4
Kimberley *Canada* **102** D5
Kimberley *S. Africa* **88** D3
Kimberly *U.S.A.* **108** E6
Kimch'aek *N. Korea* **57** D15
Kimhae = Gimhae *S. Korea* **57** G15
Kimi *Greece* **46** C6
Kimmirut *Canada* **101** C13
Kimolos *Greece* **46** E6
Kimovsk *Moskva, Russia* **32** E9
Kimovsk *Tula, Russia* **32** E10
Kimparana *Mali* **82** C4
Kimpese *Dem. Rep. of the Congo* **84** F2
Kimry *Russia* **32** D9
Kimstad *Sweden* **11** F9
Kinabalu, Gunung *Malaysia* **62** C5
Kinango *Kenya* **86** C4
Kinaros *Greece* **47** E8
Kinaskan L. *Canada* **102** B2
Kinbasket L. *Canada* **102** C5
Kincardine *Canada* **114** B3
Kincolith *Canada* **102** C3
Kinda *Dem. Rep. of the Congo* **87** D2
Kindberg *Austria* **26** D8
Kinde *U.S.A.* **114** C2
Kinder Scout *U.K.* **14** D6
Kindersley *Canada* **103** C7
Kindia *Guinea* **82** D2
Kindu *Dem. Rep. of the Congo* **86** C2
Kinel *Russia* **34** D10
Kineshma *Russia* **34** B6
Kinesi *Tanzania* **86** C3
King, L. *Australia* **93** F2
King, Mt. *Australia* **94** D4
King City *U.S.A.* **110** J5
King Cr. → *Australia* **94** C2
King Edward → *Australia* **92** B4
King Frederick VI Land = Kong Frederik VI Kyst *Greenland* **4** C5
King George B. *Falk. Is.* **128** G4
King George I. *Antarctica* **5** C18
King George Is. *Canada* **101** D11
King I. = Kadan Kyun *Burma* **64** F2
King I. *Australia* **95** F3
King I. *Canada* **102** C3
King Leopold Ranges *Australia* **92** C4
King of Prussia *U.S.A.* **115** F9
King Sd. *Australia* **92** C3
King Sejong *Antarctica* **5** C18
King William I. *Canada* **100** C10
King William's Town *S. Africa* **88** E4
Kingait = Cape Dorset *Canada* **101** C12
Kingaok = Bathurst Inlet *Canada* **100** C9
Kingaroy *Australia* **95** D5
Kingfisher *U.S.A.* **116** D6
Kingirbān *Iraq* **70** C5
Kingisepp = Kuressaare *Estonia* **32** C2
Kingisepp *Russia* **32** C5
Kingman *Ariz., U.S.A.* **111** K12
Kingman *Kans., U.S.A.* **112** G4
Kingoonya *Australia* **95** E2
Kingri *Pakistan* **68** D3
Kings → *U.S.A.* **110** J7
Kings Canyon △ *U.S.A.* **110** J8
Kings Park *U.S.A.* **115** F11
Kings Peak *U.S.A.* **108** F8
Kingsbridge *U.K.* **15** G4
Kingsburg *U.S.A.* **110** J7
Kingscote *Australia* **95** F2
Kingscourt *Ireland* **12** C5
Kingsford *U.S.A.* **112** C9
Kingsland *U.S.A.* **117** F14
Kingsport *U.S.A.* **117** C13
Kingston *Canada* **115** B8
Kingston *Jamaica* **120** a
Kingston *N.Z.* **91** F2
Kingston *N.H., U.S.A.* **115** D13
Kingston *N.Y., U.S.A.* **115** E11
Kingston *Pa., U.S.A.* **115** E9
Kingston *R.I., U.S.A.* **115** E13
Kingston Pk. *U.S.A.* **111** K11
Kingston South East *Australia* **95** F2
Kingston upon Hull *U.K.* **14** D7
Kingston-upon-Thames □ *U.K.* **15** F7

Kingstown *St. Vincent* **121** D7
Kingstree *U.S.A.* **117** E15
Kingsville *Canada* **114** D2
Kingsville *U.S.A.* **116** H6
Kingussie *U.K.* **13** D4
Kingwood *U.S.A.* **116** F7
Kınık *Antalya, Turkey* **47** E11
Kınık *Izmir, Turkey* **47** B9
Kinistino *Canada* **103** C7
Kinjirap Daban *Asia* **66** A9
Kinkala *Congo* **84** E2
Kinki □ *Japan* **55** H8
Kinleith *N.Z.* **91** C5
Kinlochleven *U.K.* **13** E4
Kinmount *Canada* **114** B6
Kinna *Sweden* **11** G6
Kinnairds Hd. *U.K.* **13** D6
Kinnared *Sweden* **11** G7
Kinnarp *Sweden* **11** F7
Kinneviken *Sweden* **11** F7
Kino Nuevo *Mexico* **118** B2
Kinoje → *Canada* **104** B3
Kinomoto *Japan* **55** G8
Kinoni *Uganda* **86** C3
Kinoosao *Canada* **103** B8
Kinross *U.K.* **13** E5
Kinsale *Ireland* **12** E3
Kinsale, Old Hd. of *Ireland* **12** E3
Kinsha = Chang Jiang → *China* **59** B13
Kinshasa *Dem. Rep. of the Congo* **84** E3
Kinsley *U.S.A.* **112** G4
Kinsman *U.S.A.* **114** E4
Kinston *U.S.A.* **117** D16
Kintamani *Indonesia* **63** J18
Kintampo *Ghana* **83** D4
Kintore *U.K.* **13** D6
Kintore Ra. *Australia* **92** D4
Kintyre *U.K.* **13** F3
Kintyre, Mull of *U.K.* **13** F3
Kinushseo → *Canada* **104** A3
Kinuso *Canada* **102** B5
Kinvarra *Ireland* **12** C3
Kinyangiri *Tanzania* **86** C3
Kinyeti *Sudan* **81** G3
Kinzig → *Germany* **25** G3
Kinzua *U.S.A.* **114** E6
Kioni *Greece* **46** C2
Kiosk *Canada* **104** C4
Kiowa *Kans., U.S.A.* **112** G4
Kiowa *Okla., U.S.A.* **116** D7
Kipahigan L. *Canada* **103** B8
Kipanga *Tanzania* **86** D4
Kiparissia *Greece* **46** D3
Kiparissiakos Kolpos *Greece* **46** D3
Kipawa, L. *Canada* **104** C4
Kipembawe *Tanzania* **86** D3
Kipengere Ra. *Tanzania* **87** D3
Kipili *Tanzania* **86** D3
Kipini *Kenya* **86** C5
Kipling *Canada* **103** C8
Kippure *Ireland* **12** C5
Kipushi *Dem. Rep. of the Congo* **87** E2
Kira Panagia *Greece* **46** B6
Kirane *Mali* **82** B2
Kiranomena *Madag.* **89** B8
Kiraz *Turkey* **47** C10
Kirazlı *Turkey* **45** F10
Kirchhain *Germany* **24** E5
Kirchheim *Germany* **25** G5
Kirchheimbolanden *Germany* **25** F3
Kirchschlag *Austria* **27** D9
Kireç *Turkey* **47** B10
Kirensk *Russia* **53** D11
Kirghizia = Kyrgyzstan ■ *Asia* **52** E8
Kiribati ■ *Pac. Oc.* **90** B10
Kırıkhan *Turkey* **72** D7
Kırıkkale *Turkey* **72** C5
Kirillov *Russia* **32** C10
Kirin = Jilin *China* **57** C14
Kirinyaga = Kenya, Mt. *Kenya* **86** C4
Kirishi *Russia* **32** C7
Kirishima Yaku △ *Japan* **55** J5
Kiritimati *Kiribati* **97** G12
Kırka *Turkey* **47** B12
Kirkağaç *Turkey* **47** B9
Kirkby *U.K.* **14** D5
Kirkby-in-Ashfield *U.K.* **14** D6
Kirkby Lonsdale *U.K.* **14** C5
Kirkby Stephen *U.K.* **14** C5
Kirkcaldy *U.K.* **13** E5
Kirkcudbright *U.K.* **13** G4
Kirkee *India* **66** K8
Kirkenes *Norway* **8** B24
Kirkfield *Canada* **114** B6
Kirkintilloch *U.K.* **13** F4
Kirkjubæjarklaustur *Iceland* **8** E4
Kirkkonummi *Finland* **32** B3
Kirkland *U.S.A.* **110** C4
Kirkland Lake *Canada* **104** C3
Kırklareli *Turkey* **45** E11
Kırklareli □ *Turkey* **45** E11
Kirksville *U.S.A.* **112** E7

Kirkūk *Iraq* **73** E11
Kirkwall *U.K.* **13** C6
Kirkwood *S. Africa* **88** E4
Kirn *Germany* **25** F3
Kirov *Kaluga, Russia* **32** E8
Kirov *Kirov, Russia* **52** D5
Kirovabad = Gäncä
　Azerbaijan **35** K8
Kirovograd = Kirovohrad
　Ukraine **33** H7
Kirovohrad *Ukraine* **33** H7
Kirovohrad □ *Ukraine* **33** H6
Kirovskiy *Astrakhan, Russia* **35** H9
Kirovskiy *Kamchatka, Russia* **53** D16
Kirovskiy *Primorsk, Russia* **54** B6
Kirriemuir *U.K.* **13** E5
Kirsanov *Russia* **34** D6
Kırşehir *Turkey* **72** C6
Kirtachi *Niger* **83** C5
Kirthar △ *Pakistan* **68** F2
Kirthar Range *Pakistan* **68** F2
Kirtland *U.S.A.* **109** H9
Kiruna *Sweden* **8** C19
Kirundu
　Dem. Rep. of the Congo **86** C2
Kirya *Russia* **34** C8
Kiryū *Japan* **55** F9
Kisa *Sweden* **11** G9
Kisaga *Tanzania* **86** C3
Kisalaya *Nic.* **120** D3
Kisalföld *Hungary* **28** C2
Kisanga
　Dem. Rep. of the Congo **86** B2
Kisangani
　Dem. Rep. of the Congo **86** B2
Kisar *Indonesia* **63** F7
Kisarawe *Tanzania* **86** D4
Kisarazu *Japan* **55** G9
Kisbér *Hungary* **28** C3
Kishanganga → *Pakistan* **69** B5
Kishanganj *India* **69** F13
Kishangarh *Raj., India* **68** F6
Kishangarh *Raj., India* **68** F4
Kishi *Nigeria* **83** D5
Kishinev = Chişinău
　Moldova **29** C13
Kishiwada *Japan* **55** G7
Kishtwar *India* **68** C6
Kisielice *Poland* **30** E6
Kisigo → *Tanzania* **86** D3
Kisii *Kenya* **86** C3
Kisiju *Tanzania* **86** D4
Kisir *Turkey* **73** B10
Kisizi *Uganda* **86** C2
Kiskomárom = Zalakomár
　Hungary **28** D2
Kiskörei-víztároló *Hungary* **28** C5
Kiskőrös *Hungary* **28** D4
Kiskundorozsma *Hungary* **28** D5
Kiskunfélegyháza *Hungary* **28** D4
Kiskunhalas *Hungary* **28** D4
Kiskunmajsa *Hungary* **28** D4
Kiskunsági △ *Hungary* **28** D4
Kislovodsk *Russia* **35** J6
Kismayu = Chisimaio
　Somali Rep. **75** H3
Kiso-Gawa → *Japan* **55** G8
Kiso-Sammyaku *Japan* **55** G8
Kisofukushima *Japan* **55** G8
Kisoro *Uganda* **86** C2
Kissamos = Kasteli *Greece* **49** D5
Kissamos, Kolpos *Greece* **49** D5
Kissidougou *Guinea* **82** D2
Kissimmee *U.S.A.* **117** G14
Kissimmee → *U.S.A.* **117** H14
Kississing L. *Canada* **103** B8
Kissónerga *Cyprus* **49** E11
Kissu, J. *Sudan* **80** C2
Kistanje *Croatia* **41** E12
Kisújszállás *Hungary* **28** C5
Kisumu *Kenya* **86** C3
Kisvárda *Hungary* **28** B7
Kiswani *Tanzania* **86** C4
Kiswere *Tanzania* **87** D4
Kit Carson *U.S.A.* **108** G12
Kita *Mali* **82** C3
Kitaibaraki *Japan* **55** F10
Kitakami *Japan* **54** E10
Kitakami-Gawa → *Japan* **54** E10
Kitakami-Sammyaku *Japan* **54** E10
Kitakata *Japan* **54** F9
Kitakyūshū *Japan* **55** H5
Kitale *Kenya* **86** B4
Kitami *Japan* **54** C11
Kitami-Sammyaku *Japan* **54** B11
Kitangiri, L. *Tanzania* **86** C3
Kitaya *Tanzania* **87** E5
Kitchener *Canada* **114** C4
Kitee *Finland* **32** A6
Kitega = Gitega *Burundi* **86** C2
Kitgum *Uganda* **86** B3
Kithira = Kythira *Greece* **46** E5
Kithnos *Greece* **46** D6
Kiti *Cyprus* **49** E12
Kiti, C. *Cyprus* **49** E12
Kitima *Canada* **102** C3

Kitinen → *Finland* **8** C22
Kitiyab *Sudan* **81** D3
Kitros *Greece* **44** F6
Kitsman *Ukraine* **29** B10
Kitsuki *Japan* **55** H5
Kittakittaooloo, L. *Australia* **95** D2
Kittanning *U.S.A.* **114** F5
Kittatinny Mt. *U.S.A.* **115** F10
Kittery *U.S.A.* **115** C14
Kittilä *Finland* **8** C21
Kitui *Kenya* **86** C4
Kitwanga *Canada* **102** B3
Kitwe *Zambia* **87** E2
Kitzbühel *Austria* **26** D5
Kitzbühler Alpen *Austria* **26** D5
Kitzingen *Germany* **25** F6
Kivarli *India* **68** G5
Kivertsi *Ukraine* **23** C13
Kividhes *Cyprus* **49** E11
Kivik *Sweden* **11** J8
Kivotos *Greece* **44** F5
Kivu, L. *Dem. Rep. of the Congo* **86** C2
Kiyev = Kyyiv *Ukraine* **23** C16
Kiyevskoye Vdkhr. =
　Kyyivske Vdskh. *Ukraine* **23** C16
Kıyıköy *Turkey* **45** E12
Kizhi, Ostrov *Russia* **32** A8
Kiziguru *Rwanda* **86** C3
Kızıl Adalar *Turkey* **45** F13
Kizil Jilga *China* **69** B8
Kizil Yurt *Russia* **35** J8
Kızılcabölük *Turkey* **47** D11
Kızılcadağ *Turkey* **47** D11
Kızılcahamam *Turkey* **72** B5
Kızıldağ △ *Turkey* **70** B1
Kızılhisar *Turkey* **72** D3
Kızılırmak *Turkey* **72** B5
Kızılkaya *Turkey* **47** D12
Kızılören *Turkey* **47** C12
Kızıltepe *Turkey* **73** D9
Kizimkazi *Tanzania* **86** D4
Kizlyar *Russia* **35** J8
Kizyl-Arvat = Serdar
　Turkmenistan **71** B8
Kjellerup *Denmark* **11** H3
Kjölur *Iceland* **8** D4
Kladanj *Bos.-H.* **28** F3
Kladnica *Serbia* **44** C4
Kladno *Czech Rep.* **26** A7
Kladovo *Serbia* **44** B6
Klaeng *Thailand* **64** F3
Klagenfurt *Austria* **26** E7
Klaipėda *Lithuania* **30** C8
Klaipėda □ *Lithuania* **30** C8
Klaksvík *Faroe Is.* **8** E9
Klamath → *U.S.A.* **108** F1
Klamath Falls *U.S.A.* **108** E3
Klamath Mts. *U.S.A.* **108** F2
Klamono *Indonesia* **63** E8
Klang *Malaysia* **65** L3
Klanjec *Croatia* **41** B12
Klappan → *Canada* **102** B3
Klarälven → *Sweden* **10** E7
Klässbol *Sweden* **10** E6
Klatovy *Czech Rep.* **26** B6
Klawer *S. Africa* **88** E2
Klazienaveen *Neths.* **17** B6
Klé *Mali* **82** C3
Klecko *Poland* **31** F4
Kleczew *Poland* **31** F5
Kleena Kleene *Canada* **102** C4
Klein-Karas *Namibia* **88** D2
Klekovača *Bos.-H.* **41** D13
Klembivka *Ukraine* **29** B13
Klenoec *Macedonia* **44** E4
Klenovec *Slovak Rep.* **27** C12
Klerksdorp *S. Africa* **88** D4
Kleszczele *Poland* **31** F10
Kletnya *Russia* **32** F7
Kletsk = Klyetsk *Belarus* **23** B14
Kletskiy *Russia* **35** F6
Kleve *Germany* **24** D2
Klickitat *U.S.A.* **108** D3
Klickitat → *U.S.A.* **110** E5
Klidhes *Cyprus* **49** D13
Klimovichi *Belarus* **32** F6
Klin *Russia* **32** D9
Klina *Serbia* **44** D4
Klinaklini → *Canada* **102** C3
Klintehamn *Sweden* **11** G12
Klintsy *Russia* **33** F7
Klip → *S. Africa* **89** D4
Klipdale *S. Africa* **88** E2
Klippan *Sweden* **11** H7
Klipplaat *S. Africa* **88** E3
Klishkivtsi *Ukraine* **29** B11
Klisura *Bulgaria* **45** D8
Kljajićevo *Serbia* **28** E4
Ključ *Bos.-H.* **41** D13
Klobuck *Poland* **31** H5
Klockestrand *Sweden* **10** B11
Klodawa *Poland* **31** F5
Kłodzko *Poland* **31** H3
Klong Wang Chao △
　Thailand **64** D2
Klos *Albania* **44** E4

Klosterneuburg *Austria* **27** C9
Klosters *Switz.* **25** J5
Klötze *Germany* **24** C7
Klouto *Togo* **83** D5
Kluane △ *Canada* **102** A1
Kluane L. *Canada* **100** C6
Kluang *Malaysia* **65** L4
Kluczbork *Poland* **31** H5
Klukwan *U.S.A.* **102** B1
Klukhori Estonia* **32** C4
Klundert *Neths.* [not present]
Klutlan → *Canada* **102** A1
Klyetsk *Belarus* **23** B14
Knäred *Sweden* **11** H7
Knaresborough *U.K.* **14** C6
Knee L. *Man., Canada* **104** A1
Knee L. *Sask., Canada* **103** B7
Knezha *Bulgaria* **45** C8
Knight Inlet *Canada* **102** C3
Knighton *U.K.* **15** E4
Knights Ferry *U.S.A.* **110** H6
Knights Landing *U.S.A.* **110** G5
Knin *Croatia* **41** D13
Knislinge *Sweden* **11** H8
Knittelfeld *Austria* **26** D7
Knivsta *Sweden* **10** E11
Knjaževac *Serbia* **44** C6
Knob, C. *Australia* **93** F2
Knock *Ireland* **12** C3
Knockmealdown Mts.
　Ireland **12** D4
Knokke-Heist *Belgium* **17** C3
Knossos *Greece* **49** D7
Knowlton *Canada* **115** A12
Knox *U.S.A.* **112** E10
Knox Coast *Antarctica* **5** C8
Knoxville *Iowa, U.S.A.* **112** E7
Knoxville *Pa., U.S.A.* **114** E7
Knoxville *Tenn., U.S.A.* **117** D13
Knud Rasmussen Land
　Greenland **4** A5
Knysna *S. Africa* **88** E3
Knyszyn *Poland* **30** E9
Ko Kha *Thailand* **64** C2
Ko Tarutao △ *Thailand* **65** J2
Ko Yao *Thailand* **65** a
Koartac = Quaqtaq *Canada* **101** C13
Koba *Indonesia* **63** F8
Kobarid *Slovenia* **41** B10
Kobayashi *Japan* **55** J5
Kōbe *Japan* **55** G7
Kobelyaky *Ukraine* **33** H8
København *Denmark* **11** J6
København ✈ (CPH)
　Denmark **11** J6
Kobenni *Mauritania* **82** B3
Kōbi-Sho *Japan* **55** M1
Koblenz *Germany* **25** E3
Kobo *Ethiopia* **81** E4
Kobryn *Belarus* **23** B13
Kobuleti *Georgia* **35** K5
Kobylin *Poland* **31** G4
Kobyłka *Poland* **31** F8
Kobylkino *Russia* **34** C6
Koca → *Turkey* **45** F11
Kocabaş *Turkey* **47** D11
Kocaeli *Turkey* **45** F13
Kocaeli □ *Turkey* **45** F13
Kočane *Serbia* **44** C5
Kočani *Macedonia* **44** E6
Koçarlı *Turkey* **47** D9
Koceljevo *Serbia* **44** B3
Kočevje *Slovenia* **41** C11
Koch Bihar *India* **67** F16
Kochas *India* **69** G10
Kocher → *Germany* **25** F5
Kochi = Cochin *India* **66** Q10
Kōchi *Japan* **55** H6
Kōchi □ *Japan* **55** H6
Kochiu = Gejiu *China* **58** F4
Kock *Poland* **31** G9
Kodarma *India* **69** G11
Kode *Sweden* **11** G5
Kodiak *U.S.A.* **106** a
Kodiak I. *U.S.A.* **106** a
Kodinar *India* **68** J4
Kodok *Sudan* **81** F3
Kodori → *Georgia* **35** J5
Kodyma *Ukraine* **29** B14
Koedoesberge *S. Africa* **88** E3
Koes *Namibia* **88** D2
Kofçaz *Turkey* **45** E11
Koffiefontein *S. Africa* **88** D4
Kofiau *Indonesia* **63** E8
Köflach *Austria* **26** D8
Koforidua *Ghana* **83** D4
Kōfu *Japan* **55** G9
Koga *Japan* **55** F9
Kôm Hamâda *Egypt* **80** H7
Kôm Ombo *Egypt* **80** C3
Komadugu Gana → *Nigeria* **83** C7
Komandorskie Is. =
　Komandorskiye Ostrova
　Russia **53** D17
Komandorskiye Ostrova
　Russia **53** D17

Kohat *Pakistan* **68** C4
Kohima *India* **67** G19
Kohkīlūyeh va Būyer
　Aḥmadī □ *Iran* **71** D6
Kohler Ra. *Antarctica* **5** D15
Kohlu *Pakistan* **68** E3
Kohtla-Järve *Estonia* **32** C4
Kohylnyk → *Ukraine* **29** E14
Koi Sanjaq *Iraq* **73** D11
Koillismaa *Finland* **8** D23
Koin *N. Korea* **57** D14
Koinare *Bulgaria* **45** C8
Koindu *S. Leone* **82** D2
Kojetín *Czech Rep.* **27** B10
Kojonup *Australia* **93** F2
Kojūr *Iran* **71** B6
Koka *Sudan* **80** C3
Kokand = Qŭqon *Uzbekistan* **52** E8
Kokas *Indonesia* **63** E8
Kokava *Slovak Rep.* **27** C12
Kokchetav = Kökshetaŭ
　Kazakhstan **52** D7
Kokemäenjoki → *Finland* **32** B1
Kokhma *Russia* **34** B5
Koki *Senegal* **82** B1
Kokkola *Finland* **8** E20
Koko *Nigeria* **83** C5
Koko Kyunzu *Burma* **67** M18
Kokolopozo *Ivory C.* **82** D3
Kokomo *U.S.A.* **112** E10
Kokoro *Niger* **83** C5
Koksan *N. Korea* **57** E14
Kökshetaŭ *Kazakhstan* **52** D7
Koksoak → *Canada* **101** D13
Kokstad *S. Africa* **89** E4
Kokubu *Japan* **55** J5
Kola *Indonesia* **63** F8
Kola *Russia* **8** B25
Kola Pen. = Kolskiy
　Poluostrov *Russia* **6** B13
Kolachi → *Pakistan* **68** F2
Kolahoi *India* **69** B6
Kolahun *Liberia* **82** D2
Kolaka *Indonesia* **63** E6
Kolar *India* **66** N11
Kolar Gold Fields *India* **66** N11
Kolaras *India* **68** G6
Kolari *Finland* **8** C20
Kolárovo *Slovak Rep.* **27** D10
Kolašin *Montenegro* **44** D3
Kolayat *India* **68** F5
Kolbäck *Sweden* **10** E10
Kolbäcksån → *Sweden* **10** E10
Kolbermoor *Germany* **25** H8
Kolbuszowa *Poland* **31** H8
Kolchugino *Russia* **32** D10
Kolda *Senegal* **82** C2
Kolda □ *Senegal* **82** C2
Koldegi *Sudan* **81** E3
Kolding *Denmark* **11** J3
Kolepom = Dolak, Pulau
　Indonesia **63** F9
Kolguyev, Ostrov *Russia* **52** C5
Kolhapur *India* **66** L9
Kolia *Ivory C.* **82** D3
Kolín *Czech Rep.* **26** A8
Kolind *Denmark* **11** H4
Kolkas rags *Latvia* **30** A9
Kolkata *India* **69** H13
Kollam = Quilon *India* **66** Q10
Kölleda *Germany* **24** D7
Kollum *Neths.* **17** A6
Kolmanskop *Namibia* **88** D2
Köln *Germany* **24** E2
Kolno *Poland* **30** E8
Koło *Poland* **31** F5
Kołobrzeg *Poland* **30** D2
Kolochava *Ukraine* **29** B8
Kolokani *Mali* **82** C3
Kokoko *Burkina Faso* **82** C3
Kolomna *Russia* **32** E10
Kolomyya *Ukraine* **29** B10
Kolondiéba *Mali* **82** C3
Kolonodale *Indonesia* **63** E6
Kolonowskie *Poland* **31** H5
Kolosib *India* **67** G18
Kolpashevo *Russia* **52** D9
Kolpino *Russia* **32** C6
Kolpny *Russia* **33** G9
Kolskiy Poluostrov *Russia* **6** B13
Kolskiy Zaliv *Russia* **8** B26
Kolsva *Sweden* **10** E9
Kolubara → *Serbia* **44** B4
Koluszki *Poland* **31** G6
Kolwezi *Dem. Rep. of the Congo* **87** E2
Kolyma → *Russia* **53** C17
Kolymskoye Nagorye
　Russia **53** C16
Kôm Hamâda *Egypt* **80** H7
Komandorskiye Ostrova
　Russia **53** D17

Kómarno *Slovak Rep.* **27** D11
Komarnyky *Ukraine* **28** B8
Komárom *Hungary* **28** C3
Komárom-Esztergom □
　Hungary **28** C3
Komatipoort *S. Africa* **89** D5
Komatou Yialou *Cyprus* **49** D13
Komatsu *Japan* **55** F8
Komatsushima *Japan* **55** H7
Kombissiri *Burkina Faso* **83** C4
Kombori *Burkina Faso* **82** C4
Komboti *Greece* **46** B3
Komen *Slovenia* **41** C10
Komenda *Ghana* **83** D4
Komi □ *Russia* **52** C6
Komiža *Croatia* **41** E13
Komló *Hungary* **28** D3
Kommunarsk = Alchevsk
　Ukraine **33** H10
Kommunizma, Pik =
　imeni Ismail Samani,
　Pik *Tajikistan* **52** F8
Komodo *Indonesia* **63** F5
Komoé → *Ivory C.* **82** D4
Komoran, Pulau *Indonesia* **63** F9
Komoro *Japan* **55** F9
Komotini *Greece* **45** E9
Komovi *Montenegro* **44** D3
Kompasberg *S. Africa* **88** E3
Kompong Bang *Cambodia* **65** F5
Kompong Cham *Cambodia* **65** G5
Kompong Chhnang =
　Kampong Chhnang
　Cambodia **65** F5
Kompong Chikreng
　Cambodia **65** F5
Kompong Kleang *Cambodia* **64** F5
Kompong Luong *Cambodia* **65** G5
Kompong Pranak *Cambodia* **64** F5
Kompong Saom =
　Kampong Saom *Cambodia* **65** G4
Kompong Saom, Chhung =
　Kampong Saom, Chaak
　Cambodia **65** G4
Kompong Speu *Cambodia* **65** G5
Kompong Sralau *Cambodia* **64** E5
Kompong Thom *Cambodia* **64** F5
Kompong Trabeck *Cambodia* **64** F5
Kompong Trabeck *Cambodia* **65** G5
Kompong Trach *Cambodia* **65** G5
Kompong Tralach *Cambodia* **65** G5
Komrat = Comrat *Moldova* **29** D13
Komsberg *S. Africa* **88** E3
Komsomolets, Ostrov
　Russia **53** A10
Komsomolsk *Amur, Russia* **53** D14
Komsomolsk *Ivanovo, Russia* **32** D11
Komsomolskiy *Russia* **34** C7
Kömür Burnu *Turkey* **47** C8
Kon Tum *Vietnam* **64** E7
Kon Tum, Plateau du
　Vietnam **64** E7
Kona *Mali* **82** C4
Konakovo *Russia* **32** D9
Konar □ *Afghan.* **66** B7
Konārī *Iran* **71** D6
Konch *India* **69** G8
Konde *Tanzania* **86** D4
Kondias *Greece* **47** B7
Kondinin *Australia* **93** F2
Kondoa *Tanzania* **86** C4
Kondopaga *Russia* **32** A8
Kondratyevo *Russia* **53** D10
Kondrovo *Russia* **32** E8
Konduga *Nigeria* **83** C7
Köneürgench *Turkmenistan* **52** E6
Konevo *Russia* **32** B10
Kong *Ivory C.* **82** D4
Kong, Koh *Cambodia* **65** G4
Kong Christian IX Land
　Greenland **4** C6
Kong Christian X Land
　Greenland **4** B6
Kong Frederik IX Land
　Greenland **4** C5
Kong Frederik VI Kyst
　Greenland **4** C5
Kong Frederik VIII Land
　Greenland **4** B6
Kong Oscar Fjord *Greenland* **4** B6
Kongeå → *Denmark* **11** J2
Kongelsev *Denmark* **11** H4
Konglu *Burma* **67** F20
Kongola *Namibia* **88** B3
Kongolo *Kasai-Or.,*
　Dem. Rep. of the Congo **86** D1
Kongolo *Katanga,*
　Dem. Rep. of the Congo **86** D2
Kongor *Sudan* **81** F3
Kongoussi *Burkina Faso* **83** C4
Kongsberg *Norway* **9** G13
Kongsvinger *Norway* **9** F15
Kongwa *Tanzania* **86** D4
Koni *Dem. Rep. of the Congo* **87** E2
Koni, Mts.
　Dem. Rep. of the Congo **87** E2

Koniakari *Mali* **82** C2
Koniecpol *Poland* **31** H6
Königs Wusterhausen
　Germany **24** C9
Königsbrunn *Germany* **25** G6
Königslutter *Germany* **24** C6
Konin *Poland* **31** F5
Konispol *Albania* **44** G4
Kónitsa *Greece* **46** A2
Konjic *Bos.-H.* **28** G2
Konkiep *Namibia* **88** D2
Können *Germany* **24** D7
Konkouré → *Guinea* **82** D2
Kono *S. Leone* **82** D2
Konongo *Ghana* **83** D4
Konosha *Russia* **32** B11
Kōnosu *Japan* **55** F9
Konotop *Ukraine* **33** G7
Konsankoro *Guinea* **82** D3
Końskie *Poland* **31** G7
Konstancin-Jeziorna *Poland* **31** F8
Konstantinovka =
　Kostyantynivka *Ukraine* **33** H9
Konstantinovsk *Russia* **35** G5
Konstantynów Łódzki
　Poland **31** G6
Konstanz *Germany* **25** H5
Kont *Iran* **71** E9
Kontagora *Nigeria* **83** C6
Kontcha *Cameroon* **83** D7
Kontiolahti *Finland* **8** E23
Kontokali *Greece* **49** A3
Konya *Turkey* **72** D5
Konya □ *Turkey* **72** D5
Konya Ovası *Turkey* **72** C5
Konz *Germany* **25** F2
Konza *Kenya* **86** C4
Koocanusa, L. *Canada* **108** B6
Kookynie *Australia* **93** E3
Koolyanobbing *Australia* **93** F2
Koonibba *Australia* **95** E1
Koorawatha *Australia* **95** E4
Koorda *Australia* **93** F2
Kooskia *U.S.A.* **108** C6
Kootenay → *U.S.A.* **102** D5
Kootenay △ *Canada* **102** C5
Kootenay L. *Canada* **108** B5
Kootjieskolk *S. Africa* **88** E3
Kopanovka *Russia* **35** G8
Kopaonik *Serbia* **44** C4
Kopaonik △ *Serbia* **44** C4
Kópavogur *Iceland* **8** D3
Kopayhorod *Ukraine* **29** B12
Koper *Slovenia* **41** C10
Kopervik *Norway* **9** G11
Kopet Dagh *Asia* **71** B8
Kopi *Australia* **95** E2
Köping *Sweden* **10** E10
Köpingsvik *Sweden* **11** H10
Kopište *Croatia* **41** F13
Koplik *Albania* **44** D3
Köpmanholmen *Sweden* **10** A12
Kopparberg *Sweden* **10** E9
Koppeh Dāgh = Kopet
　Dagh *Asia* **71** B8
Koppies *S. Africa* **89** D4
Koppom *Sweden* **10** E6
Koprivlen *Bulgaria* **44** E7
Koprivnica *Croatia* **41** B13
Kopřivnice *Czech Rep.* **27** B11
Koprivshtitsa *Bulgaria* **45** D8
Köprübaşı *Turkey* **47** C10
Köprülü □ *Turkey* **70** B1
Kopychyntsi *Ukraine* **23** D13
Kora △ *Kenya* **86** C4
Korab *Macedonia* **44** E4
Koral *India* **68** J5
Korarou, L. *Mali* **82** B4
Korba *India* **69** H10
Korbach *Germany* **24** D4
Korbu, G. *Malaysia* **65** K3
Korçë *Albania* **44** F4
Korčula *Croatia* **41** F13
Korčulanski Kanal *Croatia* **41** E13
Kord Kūy *Iran* **71** B7
Kord Sheykh *Iran* **71** D7
Kordestan = Kurdistan
　Asia **73** D10
Kordestān □ *Iran* **70** C5
Kordofân *Sudan* **79** F11
Koré Mayroua *Niger* **83** C5
Korea, North ■ *Asia* **57** E14
Korea, South ■ *Asia* **57** G15
Korea Bay *Korea* **57** E13
Korea Strait *Asia* **57** H15
Korem *Ethiopia* **81** E4
Korenevo *Russia* **33** G8
Korenovsk *Russia* **35** H4
Korets *Ukraine* **23** C14
Korfantów *Poland* **31** H4
Korgan *Turkey* **72** B7
Korgus *Sudan* **80** D3
Korhogo *Ivory C.* **82** D3
Koribundu *S. Leone* **82** D2
Korienzé *Mali* **82** B4
Korinthía □ *Greece* **46** D4
Korinthiakos Kolpos *Greece* **46** C4

Korinthos *Greece* **46** D4
Korioumé *Mali* **82** B4
Korissa, L. *Greece* **49** B3
Kōriyama *Japan* **54** F10
Korkuteli *Turkey* **47** D12
Kormakiti, C. *Cyprus* **49** D11
Körmend *Hungary* **28** C1
Kornat *Croatia* **41** E12
Kornat △ *Croatia* **41** E12
Korneshty = Corneşti
  Moldova **29** C13
Korneuburg *Austria* **27** C9
Kórnik *Poland* **31** F4
Koro *Fiji* **91** a
Koro *Ivory C.* **82** D3
Koro *Mali* **82** C4
Koro Sea *Fiji* **91** a
Korocha *Russia* **33** G9
Köroğlu Dağları *Turkey* **72** B5
Korogwe *Tanzania* **86** D4
Koroleve *Ukraine* **29** B8
Korolevu *Fiji* **91** a
Koronadal *Phil.* **61** H6
Koroni *Greece* **46** E3
Koronia, L. *Greece* **44** F7
Koronos *Greece* **47** D7
Koronowo *Poland* **31** E4
Koropets *Ukraine* **29** B10
Koror *Palau* **96** G5
Körös → *Hungary* **28** D5
Körös Maros △ *Hungary* **28** C5
Köröstarcsa *Hungary* **28** D6
Korosten *Ukraine* **23** C15
Korostyshev *Ukraine* **23** C15
Korotoyak *Russia* **33** G10
Korovou *Fiji* **91** a
Koroyanitu △ *Fiji* **91** a
Korraraika, Helodranon' i
  Madag. **89** B7
Korsakov *Russia* **53** E15
Korsberga *Sweden* **11** G9
Korshiv *Ukraine* **29** B10
Korshunovo *Russia* **53** D12
Korsør *Denmark* **11** J5
Korsun Shevchenkovskiy
  Ukraine **33** H6
Korsze *Poland* **30** D8
Korti *Sudan* **80** D3
Kortrijk *Belgium* **17** D3
Korucu *Turkey* **47** B9
Korwai *India* **68** G8
Koryakskoye Nagorye
  Russia **53** C18
Koryukovka *Ukraine* **33** G7
Kos *Greece* **47** E9
Kosa *Ethiopia* **81** F4
Kosan *N. Korea* **57** E14
Kosaya Gora *Russia* **32** E9
Kościan *Poland* **31** F3
Kościerzyna *Poland* **30** D4
Kosciusko *U.S.A.* **117** E10
Kosciuszko, Mt. *Australia* **95** F4
Kösély → *Hungary* **28** C6
Kosha *Sudan* **80** C3
Koshava *Bulgaria* **44** B7
K'oshih = Kashi *China* **60** C2
Koshiki-Rettō *Japan* **55** J4
Kosi *India* **68** F7
Kosi → *India* **69** E8
Košice *Slovak Rep.* **27** C14
Košický □ *Slovak Rep.* **27** C14
Kosiv *Ukraine* **29** B10
Kosjerić *Serbia* **44** B3
Köşk *Turkey* **47** D10
Koskinou *Greece* **49** C10
Koslan *Russia* **52** C5
Kosmach *Ukraine* **29** B9
Kosŏng *N. Korea* **57** E15
Kosovo □ *Serbia* **44** D4
Kosovo Polje *Serbia* **44** D5
Kosovska Kamenica *Serbia* **44** D5
Kosovska Mitrovica *Serbia* **44** D4
Kossou, L. de *Ivory C.* **82** D3
Kosta *Sweden* **11** H9
Kostajnica *Croatia* **41** C13
Kostanjevica *Slovenia* **41** C12
Kostenets *Bulgaria* **44** D7
Koster *S. Africa* **88** D4
Kôsti *Sudan* **81** E3
Kostinbrod *Bulgaria* **44** D7
Kostolac *Serbia* **44** B5
Kostopil *Ukraine* **23** C14
Kostroma *Russia* **32** D11
Kostromo □ *Russia* **34** A6
Kostromskaya Vdkhr.
  Russia **32** D11
Kostryzhivka *Ukraine* **29** B10
Kostrzyn *Lubuskie, Poland* **31** F1
Kostrzyn *Wielkopolskie, Poland* **31** F4
Kostyukovichi =
  Kastsyukovichy *Belarus* **32** F7
Koszalin *Poland* **30** D3
Kőszeg *Hungary* **28** C1
Kot Addu *Pakistan* **68** D4
Kot Kapura *India* **68** D6
Kot Moman *Pakistan* **68** C5

Kot Sultan *Pakistan* **68** D4
Kota *India* **68** G6
Kota Barrage *India* **68** G6
Kota Belud *Malaysia* **62** C5
Kota Bharu *Malaysia* **65** J4
Kota Kinabalu *Malaysia* **62** C5
Kota Kubu Bharu *Malaysia* **65** L3
Kota Tinggi *Malaysia* **65** M4
Kotaagung *Indonesia* **62** F3
Kotabaru *Indonesia* **62** E5
Kotabumi *Indonesia* **62** E2
Kotamobagu *Indonesia* **63** D6
Kotcho L. *Canada* **102** B4
Kotdwara *India* **69** E8
Kotel *Bulgaria* **45** D10
Kotelnich *Russia* **34** A9
Kotelnikovo *Russia* **35** G6
Kotelnyy, Ostrov *Russia* **53** B14
Kothari → *India* **68** G6
Köthen *Germany* **24** D7
Kothi *Chhattisgarh, India* **69** H10
Kothi *Mad. P., India* **69** G9
Kotiro *Pakistan* **68** F2
Kotka *Finland* **32** B4
Kotlas *Russia* **52** C5
Kotlenska Planina *Bulgaria* **45** D10
Kotli *Pakistan* **68** C5
Kotma *India* **69** H9
Kotmul *Pakistan* **69** B6
Koton-Karifi *Nigeria* **83** D6
Kotonkoro *Nigeria* **83** C6
Kotor *Montenegro* **44** D2
Kotor Varoš *Bos.-H.* **28** F2
Kotoriba *Croatia* **41** B13
Kotovo *Russia* **34** E7
Kotovsk *Russia* **34** D5
Kotovsk *Ukraine* **23** E15
Kotputli *India* **68** F7
Kotri *Pakistan* **68** G3
Kotronas *Greece* **46** E4
Kötschach-Mauthen *Austria* **26** E6
Kotto → *C.A.R.* **84** D4
Kotturu *India* **66** M10
Kotu Group *Tonga* **91** c
Kotuy → *Russia* **53** B11
Kotyuzhany *Ukraine* **29** B12
Kotzebue *U.S.A.* **106** a
Kotzebue Sound *U.S.A.* **98** C3
Kouchibouguac △ *Canada* **105** C6
Koudougou *Burkina Faso* **82** C4
Koufonisi *Iraklio, Greece* **49** E8
Koufonisi *Notio Aigaio, Greece* **47** E7
Kougaberge *S. Africa* **88** E3
Kouibli *Ivory C.* **82** D3
Kouilou → *Congo* **84** E2
Koula *Greece* **45** E8
Koula Moutou *Gabon* **84** E2
Koulen = Kulen *Cambodia* **64** F5
Koulikoro *Mali* **82** C3
Koulikoro □ *Mali* **82** C3
Kouloura *Greece* **49** A3
Koumala *Australia* **94** C4
Koumankou *Mali* **82** C3
Koumbia *Burkina Faso* **82** C4
Koumbia *Guinea* **82** C2
Koumboum *Guinea* **82** C2
Koumpenntoum *Senegal* **82** C2
Koumra *Chad* **79** G9
Koun-Fao *Ivory C.* **82** D4
Koundara *Guinea* **82** C2
Koundian *Guinea* **82** C3
Koungheul *Senegal* **82** C2
Kountze *U.S.A.* **116** F7
Koupéla *Burkina Faso* **83** C4
Kourémalé *Mali* **82** C3
Kouris → *Cyprus* **49** E11
Kourou *Fr. Guiana* **125** B8
Kourouba *Mali* **82** C2
Kouroukoto *Mali* **82** C2
Kouroussa *Guinea* **82** C2
Kourouma *Burkina Faso* **82** C4
Kourouninkoto *Mali* **82** C3
Koussanar *Senegal* **82** C2
Koussané *Mali* **82** C2
Koussane *Senegal* **82** C2
Kousseri *Cameroon* **79** F8
Koutiala *Mali* **82** C3
Kouto *Ivory C.* **82** D3
Kouvé *Togo* **83** D5
Kouvola *Finland* **32** B4
Kovačica *Serbia* **28** E5
Kovdor *Russia* **8** C4
Kovel *Ukraine* **23** C13
Kovin *Serbia* **28** F5
Kovrov *Russia* **34** B5
Kowal *Poland* **31** F6
Kowalewo Pomorskie
  Poland **31** E5
Kowanyama *Australia* **94** B3
Kowloon *China* **59** F10
Kowŏn *N. Korea* **57** E14
Koyampattur =
  Coimbatore *India* **66** P10
Köyceğiz *Turkey* **47** E10
Köyceğiz Gölü *Turkey* **47** E10
Koyukuk → *U.S.A.* **98** C4
Koyulhisar *Turkey* **72** B7

Koyunyeri *Turkey* **45** F10
Koza = Okinawa *Japan* **55** L3
Kozak *Turkey* **47** B9
Kozan *Turkey* **72** D6
Kozani *Greece* **44** F5
Kozani □ *Greece* **44** F5
Kozara *Bos.-H.* **41** D14
Kozara △ *Bos.-H.* **28** F2
Kozarac *Bos.-H.* **41** D13
Kozelets *Ukraine* **33** G6
Kozelsk *Russia* **32** E8
Kozhikode = Calicut *India* **66** P9
Koziegłowy *Poland* **31** H6
Kozienice *Poland* **31** G8
Kozje *Slovenia* **41** B12
Kozloduy *Bulgaria* **44** C7
Kozlovets *Bulgaria* **45** C9
Kozlovka *Russia* **34** C9
Kozlu *Turkey* **72** B4
Kozluk *Turkey* **73** C9
Koźmin *Poland* **31** G4
Kozmodemyansk *Russia* **34** B8
Kożuchów *Poland* **31** G2
Kozyatyn *Ukraine* **23** D15
Kpabia *Ghana* **83** D4
Kpalimé *Togo* **83** D5
Kpandae *Ghana* **83** D4
Kpessi *Togo* **83** D5
Kra, Isthmus of = Kra,
  Kho Khot *Thailand* **65** G2
Kra, Kho Khot *Thailand* **65** G2
Kra Buri *Thailand* **65** G2
Kraai → *S. Africa* **88** E4
Krabi *Thailand* **65** H2
Kracheh *Cambodia* **64** F6
Kragan *Indonesia* **63** G14
Kragerø *Norway* **9** G13
Kragujevac *Serbia* **44** B4
Krajenka *Poland* **31** E3
Krakatau = Rakata, Pulau
  Indonesia **62** F3
Krakatoa = Rakata, Pulau
  Indonesia **62** F3
Krakor *Cambodia* **64** F5
Kraków *Poland* **31** H6
Kraków ✈ (KRK) *Poland* **31** H6
Kralanh *Cambodia* **64** F4
Králíky *Czech Rep.* **27** A9
Kraljevo *Serbia* **44** C4
Kralovéhradecký □
  Czech Rep. **26** A8
Kráľovský Chlmec
  Slovak Rep. **27** C14
Kralupy nad Vltavou
  Czech Rep. **26** A7
Kramatorsk *Ukraine* **33** H9
Kramfors *Sweden* **10** B11
Krania *Greece* **44** G5
Krania Elasonas *Greece* **46** B4
Kranidi *Greece* **46** D5
Kranj *Slovenia* **41** B11
Kranjska Gora *Slovenia* **41** B10
Krankskop *S. Africa* **89** D5
Krapina *Croatia* **41** B12
Krapina → *Croatia* **41** C12
Krapkowice *Poland* **31** H4
Kras *Croatia* **41** C10
Kraskino *Russia* **54** C5
Kráslava *Latvia* **32** E4
Kraslice *Czech Rep.* **26** A5
Krasnaya Gorbatka *Russia* **34** C5
Krasnaya Polyana *Russia* **35** J5
Krasne *Ukraine* **29** D14
Krasni Okny *Ukraine* **29** C14
Kraśnik *Poland* **31** H9
Krasnoarmeisk *Ukraine* **33** H9
Krasnoarmeysk *Russia* **34** E7
Krasnoarmeyskiy *Russia* **35** G6
Krasnobród *Poland* **31** H10
Krasnodar *Russia* **35** H4
Krasnodar □ *Russia* **35** G4
Krasnodon *Ukraine* **33** H10
Krasnogorskiy *Russia* **34** B9
Krasnograd = Krasnohrad
  Ukraine **33** H8
Krasnogvardeysk *Ukraine* **33** K8
Krasnogvardeyskoye *Russia* **35** H5
Krasnohrad *Ukraine* **33** H8
Krasnokutsk *Ukraine* **33** G8
Krasnolesnyy *Russia* **33** G10
Krasnoperekopsk *Ukraine* **33** J7
Krasnorechenskiy *Russia* **54** B7
Krasnoselkup *Russia* **52** C9
Krasnoslobodsk *Mordvinia,
  Russia* **34** C6
Krasnoslobodsk *Volgograd,
  Russia* **35** F7
Krasnoturinsk *Russia* **52** D7
Krasnoufimsk *Russia* **53** D10
Krasnoyarsk *Russia* **53** D10
Krasnoye = Krasnyy *Russia* **32** E6
Krasnoyilsk *Ukraine* **29** C10
Krasnozavodsk *Russia* **32** D10
Krasnoznamensk *Russia* **30** D9
Krasny Sulin *Russia* **33** J11
Krasnystaw *Poland* **31** H10
Krasnyy *Russia* **32** E6

Krasnyy Kholm *Russia* **32** C9
Krasnyy Kut *Russia* **34** E8
Krasnyy Liman *Ukraine* **33** H9
Krasnyy Luch *Ukraine* **33** H10
Krasnyy Profintern *Russia* **32** D11
Krasnyy Yar *Astrakhan,
  Russia* **35** G9
Krasnyy Yar *Samara, Russia* **34** D10
Krasnyy Yar *Volgograd,
  Russia* **34** E7
Krasnyye Baki *Russia* **34** B7
Krasnyyoskolske Vdskh.
  Ukraine **33** H9
Kraszna → *Hungary* **28** B7
Kratie = Kracheh *Cambodia* **64** F6
Kratovo *Macedonia* **44** D6
Krau *Indonesia* **63** E10
Kravanh, Chuor Phnum
  Cambodia **65** G4
Krefeld *Germany* **24** D2
Kremaston, L. *Greece* **46** C3
Kremen *Croatia* **41** D12
Kremenchuk *Ukraine* **33** H7
Kremenchuksk Vdskh.
  Ukraine **33** H7
Kremenets *Ukraine* **23** C13
Kremennaya *Ukraine* **33** H10
Kremges = Svitlovodsk
  Ukraine **33** H7
Kremmen *Germany* **24** C9
Kremmling *U.S.A.* **108** F10
Kremnica *Slovak Rep.* **27** C11
Krems *Austria* **26** C8
Kremsmünster *Austria* **26** C7
Krestena *Greece* **46** D3
Krestena *Greece* **46** D3
Krettsy *Russia* **32** C7
Kreuzberg *Germany* **25** E5
Kreuztal *Germany* **24** E4
Kria Vrisi *Greece* **44** F6
Kribi *Cameroon* **83** E6
Krichem *Bulgaria* **45** D8
Krichev = Krychaw *Belarus* **23** B16
Krim *Slovenia* **41** C11
Krios, Akra *Greece* **49** D5
Krishna → *India* **67** M12
Krishnanagar *India* **69** H13
Kristdala *Sweden* **11** G10
Kristiansand *Norway* **9** G13
Kristianstad *Sweden* **11** H8
Kristiansund *Norway* **8** E12
Kristiinankaupunki *Finland* **8** E19
Kristinehamn *Sweden* **10** E8
Kristinestad =
  Kristiinankaupunki
  Finland **8** E19
Kriti *Greece* **49** D7
Kritsa *Greece* **49** D7
Kriva → *Macedonia* **44** D5
Kriva Palanka *Macedonia* **44** D6
Krivaja → *Bos.-H.* **28** F3
Krivelj *Serbia* **44** B5
Krivoy Rog = Kryvyy Rih
  Ukraine **33** J7
Križevci *Croatia* **41** B13
Krk *Croatia* **41** C11
Krka → *Slovenia* **41** C12
Krka △ *Croatia* **41** E12
Krkonoše *Czech Rep.* **26** A8
Krkonoše △ *Czech Rep.* **26** A8
Krnov *Czech Rep.* **27** A10
Krobia *Poland* **31** G3
Krokees *Greece* **46** E4
Krokek *Sweden* **11** F10
Krokodil = Umgwenya →
  Mozam. **89** D5
Krokom *Sweden* **10** A8
Krokowa *Poland* **30** D5
Krolevets *Ukraine* **33** G7
Kroměříž *Czech Rep.* **27** B10
Kromy *Russia* **33** F8
Kronach *Germany* **25** E7
Krong Kaoh Kong *Cambodia* **65** G4
Kronobergs län □ *Sweden* **11** H8
Kronprins Olav Kyst
  Antarctica **5** C5
Kronprinsesse Märtha
  Kyst *Antarctica* **5** D2
Kronshtadt *Russia* **32** C5
Kroonstad *S. Africa* **88** D4
Kröpelin *Germany* **24** A7
Kropotkin *Russia* **35** H5
Kropp *Germany* **24** A5
Krosna *Lithuania* **30** D10
Krośniewice *Poland* **31** F6
Krosno *Poland* **31** J8
Krosno Odrzańskie *Poland* **31** F2
Krotoszyn *Poland* **31** G4
Krotovka *Russia* **34** D10
Krousonas *Greece* **49** D6
Krrabë *Albania* **44** E3
Krško *Slovenia* **41** C12
Krstača *Serbia* **44** D4
Kruger △ *S. Africa* **89** C5
Krugersdorp *S. Africa* **89** D4
Kruisfontein *S. Africa* **88** E3

Krujë *Albania* **44** E3
Krulevshchina =
  Krulyewshchyna *Belarus* **32** E4
Krulyewshchyna *Belarus* **32** E4
Krumbach *Germany* **25** G6
Krumë *Albania* **44** D4
Krumovgrad *Bulgaria* **45** E9
Krung Thep = Bangkok
  Thailand **64** F3
Krupanj *Serbia* **44** B3
Krupina *Slovak Rep.* **27** C12
Krupinica → *Slovak Rep.* **27** C11
Krupki *Belarus* **23** A15
Krupol *Belarus* **23** A15
Kruševac *Serbia* **44** C5
Kruševo *Macedonia* **44** E5
Krushelnyksya *Ukraine* **31** J10
Kruszwica *Poland* **31** F5
Krychaw *Belarus* **23** B16
Krymsk *Russia* **33** K8
Krymskiy Poluostrov =
  Krymskyy Pivostriv
  Ukraine **33** K8
Krymskyy Pivostriv *Ukraine* **33** K8
Krynica *Poland* **31** J7
Krynica Morska *Poland* **30** D6
Krynki *Poland* **31** E10
Krynychne *Ukraine* **29** E13
Kryvyy Rih *Ukraine* **33** J7
Kryzhopil *Ukraine* **29** B13
Krzepice *Poland* **31** H5
Krzeszów *Poland* **31** G2
Krzna → *Poland* **31** F10
Krzywiń *Poland* **31** G3
Krzyż Wielkopolski *Poland* **31** F2
Ksar el Kebir *Morocco* **78** B4
Ksar es Souk = Er Rachidia
  Morocco **78** B5
Ksiąz Wielkopolski *Poland* **31** F4
Kstovo *Russia* **34** B7
Ku, W. el → *Sudan* **81** E2
Kuah *Malaysia* **65** J2
Kuala Belait *Malaysia* **62** D4
Kuala Berang *Malaysia* **65** K4
Kuala Dungun = Dungun
  Malaysia **65** K4
Kuala Kangsar *Malaysia* **65** K3
Kuala Kelawang *Malaysia* **65** L4
Kuala Kerai *Malaysia* **65** K4
Kuala Kerian *Malaysia* **65** c
Kuala Lipis *Malaysia* **65** K4
Kuala Lumpur *Malaysia* **65** L3
Kuala Nerang *Malaysia* **65** J3
Kuala Pilah *Malaysia* **65** L4
Kuala Rompin *Malaysia* **65** L4
Kuala Selangor *Malaysia* **65** L3
Kuala Sepetang *Malaysia* **65** K3
Kuala Terengganu *Malaysia* **65** K4
Kualajelai *Indonesia* **62** E4
Kualakapuas *Indonesia* **62** E4
Kualakurun *Indonesia* **62** E4
Kualapembuang *Indonesia* **62** E4
Kualasimpang *Indonesia* **62** D1
Kuancheng *China* **57** D10
Kuandang *Indonesia* **63** D6
Kuandian *China* **57** D13
Kuangchou = Guangzhou
  China **59** F9
Kuanshan *Taiwan* **59** F13
Kuantan *Malaysia* **65** L4
Kuba = Quba *Azerbaijan* **35** K9
Kuban → *Russia* **33** K9
Kuban Depression =
  Prikubanskaya
  Nizmennost *Russia* **35** H4
Kubenskoye, Ozero *Russia* **32** C10
Kubokawa *Japan* **55** H6
Kubrat *Bulgaria* **45** C10
Kubu *Indonesia* **63** J18
Kubutambahan *Indonesia* **63** J18
Kučevo *Serbia* **44** B5
Kucha Gompa *India* **69** B7
Kuchaman *India* **68** F6
Kuchenspitze *Austria* **26** D3
Kuchinda *India* **69** J11
Kuchino-eruba-Jima *Japan* **55** J5
Kuchino-Shima *Japan* **55** K4
Kuchinotsu *Japan* **55** H5
Kuchl *Austria* **26** D6
Kuchurhan → *Ukraine* **29** D14
Kucing = Kuching *Malaysia* **62** D4
Küçükbahçe *Turkey* **47** C8
Küçükköy *Turkey* **47** B8
Küçükkuyu *Turkey* **47** B8
Küçükmenderes → *Turkey* **47** D9
Kud → *Pakistan* **68** F2
Kuda *India* **68** H4
Kudat *Malaysia* **62** C5
Kudirkos Naumiestis
  Lithuania **30** D9
Kudowa-Zdrój *Poland* **31** H3
Kudus *Indonesia* **63** G14
Kudymkar *Russia* **52** D6
Kueiyang = Guiyang *China* **58** D6
Kufra Oasis = Al Kufrah
  Libya **79** D10

Kufstein *Austria* **26** D5
Kugaaruk = Pelly Bay
  Canada **101** C11
Kugluktuk *Canada* **100** C8
Kugong I. *Canada* **104** A4
Kūh-e-Jebāl Bārez *Iran* **71** D8
Kūhak *Iran* **71** E9
Kuhan *Pakistan* **68** E2
Kūhbonān *Iran* **71** D8
Kūhestak *Iran* **71** E8
Kuhin *Iran* **71** B6
Kūhīrī *Iran* **71** E9
Kuhmo *Finland* **8** D23
Kuhnsdorf *Austria* **26** E7
Kūhpāyeh *Eşfahan, Iran* **71** C7
Kūhpāyeh *Kermān, Iran* **71** D8
Kūhrān, Kūh-e *Iran* **71** E8
Kui Buri *Thailand* **65** F2
Kuiseb → *Namibia* **88** C1
Kuito *Angola* **85** G3
Kuiu I. *U.S.A.* **102** B2
Kujang *N. Korea* **57** E14
Kujawsko-Pomorskie □
  Poland **30** E5
Kuji *Japan* **54** D10
Kujū-San *Japan* **55** H5
Kukava *Ukraine* **29** B12
Kukavica *Serbia* **44** D5
Kukawa *Nigeria* **83** C7
Kukës *Albania* **44** D4
Kukmor *Russia* **34** B10
Kukup *Malaysia* **65** d
Kukup, Pulau *Malaysia* **65** d
Kukvidze *Russia* **34** E6
Kula *Bulgaria* **44** C6
Kula *Serbia* **28** E4
Kula *Turkey* **47** C10
Kulachi *Pakistan* **68** D4
Kulai *Malaysia* **65** M4
Kulaly, Ostrov = Kulaly
  Aral *Kazakhstan* **35** H10
Kulaly Aral *Kazakhstan* **35** H10
Kulasekarappattinam *India* **66** Q11
Kulautuva *Lithuania* **30** D10
Kuldīga *Latvia* **30** B8
Kuldīga □ *Latvia* **30** B8
Kuldu *Sudan* **81** E2
Kulebaki *Russia* **34** C6
Kulen *Cambodia* **64** F5
Kulen Vakuf *Bos.-H.* **41** D13
Kulgam *India* **69** C6
Kulgera *Australia* **94** D1
Kulim *Malaysia* **65** K3
Kulin *Australia* **93** F2
Kulkayu = Hartley Bay
  Canada **102** C3
Kullen *Sweden* **11** H6
Kulmbach *Germany* **25** E7
Kŭlob *Tajikistan* **52** F7
Kulp *Turkey* **73** C9
Kulpawn → *Ghana* **83** D4
Kulsary *Kazakhstan* **52** E6
Kulti *India* **69** H12
Kulu *India* **68** D7
Kulu *Turkey* **72** C5
Kulunda *Russia* **52** D8
Kulungar *Afghan.* **68** C3
Kŭlvand *Iran* **71** D7
Kulwin *Australia* **95** F3
Kulyab = Kŭlob *Tajikistan* **52** F7
Kuma → *Russia* **35** H8
Kumafşarı *Turkey* **47** D11
Kumaganum *Nigeria* **83** C7
Kumagaya *Japan* **55** F9
Kumai *Indonesia* **62** E4
Kumalar Dağı *Turkey* **47** C12
Kumamba, Kepulauan
  Indonesia **63** E9
Kumamoto *Japan* **55** H5
Kumamoto □ *Japan* **55** H5
Kumanovo *Macedonia* **44** D5
Kumara *N.Z.* **91** E3
Kumarina Roadhouse
  Australia **93** D2
Kumasi *Ghana* **82** D4
Kumba *Cameroon* **83** E6
Kumbağ *Turkey* **45** F11
Kumbakonam *India* **66** P11
Kumbarilla *Australia* **95** D5
Kumbhraj *India* **68** G7
Kumbia *Australia* **95** D5
Kumbo *Cameroon* **83** D7
Kŭmch'ŏn *N. Korea* **57** E14
Kumdok *India* **69** C8
Kumeny *Russia* **34** A9
Kumharsain *India* **68** D7
Kumi *Uganda* **86** B3
Kumkale *Turkey* **45** G10
Kumla *Sweden* **10** E9
Kumluca *Turkey* **47** E12
Kummerower See *Germany* **24** B8
Kumo *Nigeria* **83** C7
Kumo älv =
  Kokemäenjoki → *Finland* **32** B1
Kumon Bum *Burma* **67** F20
Kumylzhenskaya *Russia* **34** F6
Kunágota *Hungary* **28** D6

Kunashir, Ostrov *Russia* **53** E15
Kunda *Estonia* **32** C4
Kunda *India* **69** G9
Kundar → *Pakistan* **68** D3
Kundelungu △
Dem. Rep. of the Congo **87** E2
Kundelungu Ouest △
Dem. Rep. of the Congo **87** D2
Kundian *Pakistan* **68** C4
Kundla *India* **68** J4
Kung, Ao *Thailand* **65** a
Kunga → *Bangla.* **69** J13
Kungälv *Sweden* **11** G5
Kunghit I. *Canada* **102** C2
Kungrad = Qŭnghirot
Uzbekistan **52** E6
Kungsängen *Sweden* **10** E11
Kungsbacka *Sweden* **11** G6
Kungsgården *Sweden* **10** D10
Kungshamn *Sweden* **11** F5
Kungsör *Sweden* **10** E10
Kungur *Russia* **52** D6
Kungurri *Australia* **94** K6
Kunhar → *Pakistan* **69** B5
Kunhegyes *Hungary* **28** C5
Kuningan *Indonesia* **63** G13
Kunlong *Burma* **58** F2
Kunlun Shan *Asia* **60** C3
Kunmadaras *Hungary* **28** C5
Kunming *China* **58** E4
Kunów *Poland* **31** H8
Kunshan *China* **59** B13
Kunszentmárton *Hungary* **28** D5
Kunszentmiklós *Hungary* **28** C4
Kuntaur *Senegal* **82** C2
Kununurra *Australia* **92** C4
Kunwari → *India* **69** F8
Kunya-Urgench =
Köneürgench
Turkmenistan **52** E6
Künzelsau *Germany* **25** F5
Kuopio *Finland* **8** E22
Kupa → *Croatia* **41** C13
Kupang *Indonesia* **63** F6
Kupreanof I. *U.S.A.* **102** B2
Kupres *Bos.-H.* **28** C2
Kupyansk *Ukraine* **33** H9
Kupyansk-Uzlovoi *Ukraine* **33** H9
Kuqa *China* **60** B3
Kür → *Azerbaijan* **73** C13
Kür Dili *Azerbaijan* **73** C13
Kura = Kür → *Azerbaijan* **73** C13
Kuranda *Australia* **94** B4
Kuranga *India* **68** H3
Kurashiki *Japan* **55** G6
Kurayn *Si. Arabia* **71** E6
Kurayoshi *Japan* **55** G6
Kürdämir *Azerbaijan* **35** K9
Kurdistan *Asia* **73** D10
Kŭrdzhali *Bulgaria* **45** E9
Kure *Japan* **55** G6
Küre *Turkey* **72** B5
Küre Dağları *Turkey* **72** B6
Kuressaare *Estonia* **32** C2
Kurgan *Russia* **52** D7
Kurganinsk *Russia* **35** H5
Kurgannaya =
Kurganinsk *Russia* **35** H5
Kuri *India* **68** F4
Kuria Maria Is. =
Ḩallāniyat, Jazā'ir al
Oman **75** D6
Kuridala *Australia* **94** C3
Kurigram *Bangla.* **67** G16
Kurikka *Finland* **8** E20
Kuril Basin *Pac. Oc.* **4** E15
Kuril Is. = Kurilskiye
Ostrova *Russia* **53** E16
Kuril-Kamchatka Trench
Pac. Oc. **96** C7
Kurilsk *Russia* **53** E15
Kurilskiye Ostrova *Russia* **53** E16
Kurino *Japan* **55** J5
Kurinskaya Kosa = Kür
Dili *Azerbaijan* **73** C13
Kurkur *Egypt* **80** C3
Kurlovskiy *Russia* **34** C5
Kurmuk *Sudan* **81** E3
Kurnool *India* **66** M11
Kuro-Shima *Kagoshima, Japan* **55** J4
Kuro-Shima *Okinawa, Japan* **55** M2
Kuror, J. *Sudan* **80** C3
Kurow *N.Z.* **91** F3
Kurów *Poland* **31** G9
Kurram → *Pakistan* **68** C4
Kurri Kurri *Australia* **95** E5
Kurrimine *Australia* **94** B4
Kursavka *Russia* **35** H6
Kurshskaya Kosa △ *Russia* **30** C7
Kurshskiy Zaliv *Russia* **30** C8
Kuršių Nerijos △ *Lithuania* **30** C8
Kursk *Russia* **33** G9
Kursk □ *Russia* **33** G9
Kuršumlija *Serbia* **44** C5
Kuršumlijska Banja *Serbia* **44** C5
Kurşunlu *Bursa, Turkey* **45** F13
Kurşunlu *Çankırı, Turkey* **72** B5

Kurtbey *Turkey* **45** E10
Kuru *Sudan* **81** F2
Kuru, Bahr el → *Sudan* **81** F2
Kurucaşile *Turkey* **72** B5
Kuruçay *Turkey* **70** B3
Kuruktag *China* **60** B3
Kuruman *S. Africa* **88** D3
Kuruman → *S. Africa* **88** D3
Kurume *Japan* **55** H5
Kurun → *Sudan* **81** F3
Kurunegala *Sri Lanka* **66** R12
Kurya *Russia* **52** C6
Kus Gölü *Turkey* **45** F11
Kusadası *Turkey* **72** D2
Kuşadası Körfezi *Turkey* **47** D8
Kusamba *Indonesia* **63** K18
Kusatsu *Japan* **55** F9
Kusel *Germany* **25** F3
Kushaka *Nigeria* **83** C6
Kushalgarh *India* **68** H6
Kushchevskaya *Russia* **35** G4
Kusheriki *Nigeria* **83** C6
Kushikino *Japan* **55** J5
Kushima *Japan* **55** J5
Kushimoto *Japan* **55** H7
Kushiro *Japan* **54** C12
Kushiro-Gawa → *Japan* **54** C12
Kushiro Shitsugen △ *Japan* **54** C12
Kūshk *Iran* **71** D8
Kushka = Serhetabat
Turkmenistan **71** C9
Kūshkī *Iran* **70** C5
Kushnytsya *Ukraine* **29** B8
Kushol *India* **69** C7
Kushtia *Bangla.* **67** H16
Kushum → *Kazakhstan* **34** F10
Kuskokwim → *U.S.A.* **98** C3
Kuskokwim B. *U.S.A.* **106** a
Kusmi *India* **69** H10
Kusŏng *N. Korea* **57** E13
Kussharo-Ko *Japan* **54** C12
Kustanay = Qostanay
Kazakhstan **52** D7
Kut, Ko *Thailand* **65** G4
Kuta *Indonesia* **63** K18
Kütahya *Turkey* **47** B12
Kütahya □ *Turkey* **47** B11
Kutaisi *Georgia* **35** J6
Kutaraja = Banda Aceh
Indonesia **62** C1
Kutch, Gulf of = Kachchh,
Gulf of *India* **68** H3
Kutch, Rann of =
Kachchh, Rann of *India* **68** H4
Kutina *Croatia* **41** C13
Kutiyana *India* **68** J4
Kutjevo *Croatia* **28** E2
Kutkashen *Azerbaijan* **35** K8
Kutná Hora *Czech Rep.* **26** B8
Kutno *Poland* **31** F6
Kutse *Botswana* **88** C3
Kuttabul *Australia* **94** K6
Kutu *Dem. Rep. of the Congo* **84** E3
Kutum *Sudan* **81** E1
Kúty *Slovak Rep.* **27** C10
Kuty *Ukraine* **29** B10
Kuujjuaq *Canada* **101** D13
Kuujjuarapik *Canada* **104** A4
Kuusamo *Finland* **8** D23
Kuusankoski *Finland* **32** B4
Kuvshinovo *Russia* **32** B8
Kuwait = Al Kuwayt *Kuwait* **70** D5
Kuwait ■ *Asia* **70** D5
Kuwana *Japan* **55** G8
Kuwana → *India* **69** F10
Kuybyshev = Samara
Russia **34** D10
Kuybyshev *Russia* **52** D8
Kuybyshevo *Ukraine* **33** J9
Kuybyshevskoye Vdkhr.
Russia **34** C9
Kuye He → *China* **56** E6
Küyeh *Iran* **70** B5
Kuyto, Ozero *Russia* **8** D24
Kuyucak *Turkey* **47** D10
Kuyumba *Russia* **53** C10
Kuzey Anadolu Dağları
Turkey **72** B7
Kuzmin *Serbia* **28** E4
Kuznetsk *Russia* **34** D8
Kuzomen *Russia* **52** C4
Kvænangen *Norway* **8** A19
Kværndrup *Denmark* **11** J4
Kvaløya *Norway* **8** B18
Kvänum *Sweden* **11** F7
Kvareli = Qvareli *Georgia* **35** K7
Kvarner *Croatia* **41** D11
Kvarnerič *Croatia* **41** D11
Kvicksund *Sweden* **10** E10
Kvillsfors *Sweden* **11** G9
Kvissleby *Sweden* **10** B11
Kwabhaca *S. Africa* **89** E4
Kwakhanai *Botswana* **88** C3
Kwakoegron *Suriname* **125** B7
Kwale *Kenya* **86** C4

Kwale *Nigeria* **83** D6
KwaMashu *S. Africa* **89** D5
Kwando → *Africa* **88** B3
Kwangchow = Guangzhou
China **59** F9
Kwango →
Dem. Rep. of the Congo **84** E3
Kwangsi-Chuang =
Guangxi Zhuangzu
Zizhiqu □ *China* **58** F7
Kwangtung =
Guangdong □ *China* **59** F9
Kwara □ *Nigeria* **83** D6
Kwataboahegan → *Canada* **104** B3
Kwatisore *Indonesia* **63** E8
KwaZulu Natal □ *S. Africa* **89** D5
Kwekwe *Zimbabwe* **87** F2
Kwidzyn *Poland* **30** E5
Kwiha *Ethiopia* **81** E4
Kwilu →
Dem. Rep. of the Congo **84** E3
Kwinana *Australia* **93** F2
Kwisa → *Poland* **31** G2
Kwoka *Indonesia* **63** E8
Kwolla *Nigeria* **83** D6
Kyabra Cr. → *Australia* **95** D3
Kyabram *Australia* **95** F4
Kyaikto *Burma* **64** D1
Kyakhta *Russia* **53** D11
Kyancutta *Australia* **95** E2
Kyaukpadaung *Burma* **67** J19
Kyaukpyu *Burma* **67** K18
Kyaukse *Burma* **67** J20
Kybartai *Lithuania* **30** D9
Kyburz *U.S.A.* **110** G6
Kyelang *India* **68** C7
Kyenjojo *Uganda* **86** B3
Kyjov *Czech Rep.* **27** B10
Kyle *Canada* **103** C7
Kyle Dam *Zimbabwe* **87** G3
Kyle of Lochalsh *U.K.* **13** D3
Kyll → *Germany* **25** F2
Kyllburg *Germany* **25** E2
Kyllini *Greece* **46** D3
Kymijoki → *Finland* **32** B4
Kymmene älv =
Kymijoki → *Finland* **32** B4
Kyneton *Australia* **95** F3
Kynuna *Australia* **94** C3
Kyō-ga-Saki *Japan* **55** G7
Kyoga, L. *Uganda* **86** B3
Kyogle *Australia* **95** D5
Kyom → *Sudan* **81** F2
Kyŏngju = Gyeongju
S. Korea **57** G15
Kyŏngsŏng *N. Korea* **57** D15
Kyonpyaw *Burma* **67** L19
Kyōto *Japan* **55** G7
Kyōto □ *Japan* **55** G7
Kyparissovouno *Cyprus* **49** D12
Kyperounda *Cyprus* **49** E11
Kypros = Cyprus ■ *Asia* **49** E12
Kyrenia *Cyprus* **49** D12
Kyrgyzstan ■ *Asia* **52** E8
Kyritz *Germany* **24** C8
Kyrkhult *Sweden* **11** H8
Kyrnasivka *Ukraine* **29** B13
Kyrnychky *Ukraine* **29** E14
Kyro älv = Kyrönjoki →
Finland **8** E19
Kyrönjoki → *Finland* **8** E19
Kystatyam *Russia* **53** C13
Kysucké Nové Mesto
Slovak Rep. **27** B11
Kytay, Ozero *Ukraine* **29** E14
Kythira *Greece* **46** E5
Kythréa *Cyprus* **49** D12
Kyunhla *Burma* **67** H19
Kyuquot Sound *Canada* **102** D3
Kyurdamir = Kürdämir
Azerbaijan **35** K9
Kyūshū *Japan* **55** H5
Kyūshū □ *Japan* **55** H5
Kyushu-Palau Ridge *Pac. Oc.* **96** E5
Kyūshū-Sanchi *Japan* **55** H5
Kyustendil *Bulgaria* **44** D6
Kyusyur *Russia* **53** B13
Kyyiv *Ukraine* **23** C16
Kyyiv □ *Ukraine* **23** C16
Kyyivske Vdskh. *Ukraine* **23** C16
Kyzyl *Russia* **53** D10
Kyzyl Kum *Uzbekistan* **52** E7
Kyzyl-Kyya *Kyrgyzstan* **52** E8
Kyzyl-Orda = Qyzylorda
Kazakhstan **52** E7

L

La Albuera *Spain* **37** G4
La Alcarria *Spain* **38** E2
La Almarcha *Spain* **38** F2
La Almunia de Doña
Godina *Spain* **38** D3
La Amistad △ *Cent. Amer.* **120** E3

La Asunción *Venezuela* **124** A6
La Baie *Canada* **105** C5
La Banda *Argentina* **126** B3
La Bañeza *Spain* **36** C5
La Barca *Mexico* **118** C4
La Barge *U.S.A.* **108** E8
La Bastide-Puylaurent
France **20** D7
La Baule *France* **18** E4
La Belle *U.S.A.* **117** H14
La Biche → *Canada* **102** B4
La Biche, L. *Canada* **102** C6
La Bisbal d'Empordà *Spain* **38** D8
La Brea *Trin. & Tob.* **125** K15
La Brède *France* **20** D3
La Bresse *France* **19** D13
La Bureba *Spain* **36** C7
La Calera *Chile* **126** C1
La Campana △ *Chile* **126** C1
La Campiña *Spain* **37** H6
La Canal = Sa Canal *Spain* **48** C7
La Cañiza = A Cañiza *Spain* **36** C2
La Canourgue *France* **20** D7
La Capelle *France* **19** C10
La Carlota *Argentina* **126** C3
La Carlota *Phil.* **61** F5
La Carlota *Spain* **37** H6
La Carolina *Spain* **37** G7
La Cavalerie *France* **20** D7
La Ceiba *Honduras* **120** C2
La Chaise-Dieu *France* **20** C7
La Chapelle d'Angillon
France **19** E9
La Chapelle-St-Luc *France* **19** D11
La Chapelle-sur-Erdre *France* **18** E5
La Charité-sur-Loire *France* **19** E10
La Chartre-sur-le-Loir *France* **18** E7
La Châtaigneraie *France* **20** B3
La Châtre *France* **19** F9
La Chaux-de-Fonds *Switz.* **25** H2
La Chorrera *Panama* **120** E4
La Ciotat *France* **21** E9
La Clayette *France* **19** F11
La Cocha *Argentina* **126** B2
La Concepción *Panama* **120** E3
La Concordia *Mexico* **119** D6
La Coruña = A Coruña *Spain* **36** B2
La Coruña □ *Spain* **36** B2
La Côte-St-André *France* **21** C9
La Courtine *France* **20** C6
La Crau *Bouches-du-Rhône,*
France **21** E8
La Crau *Var, France* **21** E10
La Crescent *U.S.A.* **112** D8
La Crete *Canada* **102** B5
La Crosse *Kans., U.S.A.* **112** F4
La Crosse *Wis., U.S.A.* **112** D8
La Cruz *Costa Rica* **120** D2
La Cruz *Mexico* **118** C3
La Désirade *Guadeloupe* **120** b
La Digue *Seychelles* **85** b
La Esmeralda *Paraguay* **126** A3
La Esperanza *Cuba* **120** B3
La Esperanza *Honduras* **120** D2
La Estrada = A Estrada *Spain* **36** C2
La Faouët *France* **18** D3
La Fayette *U.S.A.* **117** D12
La Fé *Cuba* **120** B3
La Fère *France* **19** C10
La Ferté-Bernard *France* **18** D7
La Ferté-Gaucher *France* **19** D10
La Ferté-Macé *France* **18** D6
La Ferté-St-Aubin *France* **19** E8
La Ferté-sous-Jouarre
France **19** D10
La Ferté-Vidame *France* **18** D7
La Flèche *France* **18** E6
La Follette *U.S.A.* **117** C12
La Fregeneda *Spain* **36** E4
La Fuente de San Esteban
Spain **36** E4
La Gacilly *France* **18** E4
La Gineta *Spain* **39** F2
La Grand'Combe *France* **21** D8
La Grande *U.S.A.* **108** D4
La Grande → *Canada* **104** B5
La Grande Deux, Rés.
Canada **104** B4
La Grande Quatre, Rés.
Canada **104** B5
La Grande Trois, Rés.
Canada **104** B5
La Grange *Calif., U.S.A.* **110** H6
La Grange *Ga., U.S.A.* **117** E12
La Grange *Ky., U.S.A.* **113** F11
La Grange *Tex., U.S.A.* **116** G6
La Grave *France* **21** C10
La Guaira *Venezuela* **124** A5
La Guardia = A Guarda
Spain **36** D2
La Gudiña = A Gudiña *Spain* **36** C3
La Guerche-de-Bretagne
France **18** E5
La Guerche-sur-l'Aubois
France **19** F10
La Habana *Cuba* **120** B3

La Haute Vallée de
Chevreuse △ *France* **19** D8
La Haye-du-Puits *France* **18** C5
La Horra *Spain* **36** D7
La Independencia *Mexico* **119** D6
La Isabela *Dom. Rep.* **121** C5
La Jonquera *Spain* **38** C7
La Junta *U.S.A.* **108** H12
La Laguna *Canary Is.* **48** F3
La Libertad = Puerto
Libertad *Mexico* **118** B2
La Libertad *Guatemala* **120** C1
La Ligua *Chile* **126** C1
La Línea de la Concepción
Spain **37** J5
La Loche *Canada* **103** B7
La Londe-les-Maures
France **21** E10
La Lora *Spain* **36** C7
La Loupe *France* **18** D8
La Louvière *Belgium* **17** D4
La Lune *Trin. & Tob.* **125** K15
La Machine *France* **19** F10
La Maddalena *Italy* **42** A2
La Malbaie *Canada* **105** C5
La Malinche △ *Mexico* **119** D5
La Mancha *Spain* **39** F2
La Mariña *Spain* **36** B3
La Martre, L. *Canada* **102** A5
La Mesa *Mexico* **111** N10
La Mesa *U.S.A.* **111** N9
La Mesilla *U.S.A.* **109** K10
La Misión *Mexico* **118** A1
La Mothe-Achard *France* **18** F5
La Motte-Chalançon *France* **21** D9
La Motte-du-Caire *France* **21** D10
La Motte-Servolex *France* **21** C9
La Moure *U.S.A.* **112** B4
La Muela *Spain* **38** D3
La Mure *France* **21** D9
La Negra *Chile* **126** A1
La Oliva *Canary Is.* **48** F6
La Orotava *Canary Is.* **48** F3
La Oroya *Peru* **124** F3
La Pacaudière *France* **19** F10
La Palma *Canary Is.* **48** F2
La Palma *Panama* **120** E4
La Palma del Condado *Spain* **37** H4
La Paloma *Chile* **126** C1
La Pampa □ *Argentina* **126** D2
La Paragua *Venezuela* **124** B6
La Paz *Entre Ríos, Argentina* **126** C4
La Paz *San Luis, Argentina* **126** C2
La Paz *Bolivia* **124** G5
La Paz *Honduras* **120** D2
La Paz *Mexico* **118** C2
La Paz *Phil.* **61** D4
La Paz Centro *Nic.* **120** D2
La Pedrera *Colombia* **124** D5
La Pérade *Canada* **105** C5
La Perla *Mexico* **118** B4
La Perouse Str. *Asia* **54** B11
La Pesca *Mexico* **119** C5
La Piedad *Mexico* **118** C4
La Pine *U.S.A.* **108** E3
La Plata *Argentina* **126** D4
La Pobla de Lillet *Spain* **38** C6
La Pocatière *Canada* **105** C5
La Pola de Gordón *Spain* **36** C5
La Porta *France* **21** F13
La Porte *U.S.A.* **116** G7
La Presanella *Italy* **40** B7
La Puebla = Sa Pobla *Spain* **38** F8
La Puebla de Cazalla *Spain* **37** H5
La Puebla de los Infantes
Spain **37** H5
La Puebla de Montalbán
Spain **36** F6
La Puebla del Río *Spain* **37** H4
La Puerta de Segura *Spain* **37** G8
La Purísima *Mexico* **118** B2
La Push *U.S.A.* **110** C2
La Quiaca *Argentina* **126** A2
La Réole *France* **20** D3
La Restinga *Canary Is.* **48** G2
La Rioja *Argentina* **126** B2
La Rioja □ *Argentina* **126** B2
La Rioja □ *Spain* **38** C2
La Robla *Spain* **36** C5
La Roche-Bernard *France* **18** E4
La Roche-Canillac *France* **20** C5
La Roche-en-Ardenne
Belgium **17** D5
La Roche-sur-Foron *France* **19** F13
La Roche-sur-Yon *France* **18** F5
La Rochefoucauld *France* **20** C4
La Rochelle *France* **20** B2
La Roda *Spain* **39** F2
La Roda de Andalucía *Spain* **37** H6
La Romaine *Canada* **105** B7
La Romana *Dom. Rep.* **121** C6
La Ronge *Canada* **103** B7
La Rumorosa *Mexico* **111** N10
La Sabina = Sa Savina *Spain* **48** C7
La Sagra *Spain* **39** H2
La Salle *U.S.A.* **112** E9
La Sanabria *Spain* **36** C4

La Santa *Canary Is.* **48** E6
La Sarre *Canada* **104** C4
La Scie *Canada* **105** C8
La Selva *Spain* **38** C7
La Selva Beach *U.S.A.* **110** J5
La Selva del Camp *Spain* **38** D6
La Serena *Chile* **126** B1
La Serena *Spain* **37** G5
La Seu d'Urgell *Spain* **38** C6
La Seyne-sur-Mer *France* **21** E9
La Sila *Italy* **43** C9
La Solana *Spain* **37** G7
La Soufrière *St. Vincent* **121** D7
La Souterraine *France* **19** F8
La Spézia *Italy* **40** D6
La Suze-sur-Sarthe *France* **18** E7
La Tagua *Colombia* **124** C4
La Teste-de-Buch *France* **20** D2
La Tortuga *Venezuela* **121** D6
La Tour-du-Pin *France* **21** C9
La Tranche-sur-Mer *France* **18** F5
La Tremblade *France* **20** C2
La Trinité *Martinique* **120** c
La Tuque *Canada* **104** C5
La Unión *Chile* **128** E2
La Unión *El Salv.* **120** D2
La Unión *Mexico* **118** D4
La Unión *Spain* **39** H4
La Urbana *Venezuela* **124** B5
La Vache Pt. *Trin. & Tob.* **125** K15
La Vall d'Uixó *Spain* **38** F4
La Vecilla de Curveño *Spain* **36** C5
La Vega *Dom. Rep.* **121** C5
La Vela de Coro *Venezuela* **124** A5
La Veleta *Spain* **37** H7
La Venta *Mexico* **119** D6
La Vergne *U.S.A.* **117** C11
La Voulte-sur-Rhône *France* **21** D8
Laa an der Thaya *Austria* **27** C9
Laaber, Grosse → *Germany* **25** G8
Laage *Germany* **24** B8
Laas Caanood = Las Anod
Somali Rep. **75** F4
Laatzen *Germany* **24** C5
Laba → *Russia* **35** H4
Labasa *Fiji* **91** a
Labason *Phil.* **61** G5
Labastide-Murat *France* **20** D5
Labastide-Rouairoux *France* **20** E6
Labbézenga *Mali* **83** B5
Labdah = Leptis Magna
Libya **79** B8
Labe = Elbe → *Europe* **24** B4
Labé *Guinea* **82** C2
Laberge, L. *Canada* **102** A1
Labin *Croatia* **41** C11
Labinsk *Russia* **35** H5
Labis *Malaysia* **65** L4
Labo *Phil.* **61** D5
Laboe *Germany* **24** A6
Laborec → *Slovak Rep.* **27** C14
Laborie *St. Lucia* **121** f
Labouheyre *France* **20** D3
Laboulaye *Argentina* **126** C3
Labrador *Canada* **105** B7
Labrador City *Canada* **105** B6
Labrador Sea *Atl. Oc.* **101** D14
Lábrea *Brazil* **124** E6
Labruguière *France* **20** E6
Labuan *Malaysia* **62** C5
Labuan, Pulau *Malaysia* **62** C5
Labuha *Indonesia* **63** E7
Labuhan *Indonesia* **63** G11
Labuhanbajo *Indonesia* **63** F6
Labuk, Telok *Malaysia* **62** C5
Labyrinth, L. *Australia* **95** E2
Labytnangi *Russia* **52** C7
Laç *Albania* **44** E3
Lac-Bouchette *Canada* **105** C5
Lac Édouard *Canada* **104** C5
Lac La Biche *Canada* **102** C6
Lac la Martre = Wha Ti
Canada **100** C8
Lac La Ronge △ *Canada* **103** B7
Lac-Mégantic *Canada* **105** C5
Lac Thien *Vietnam* **64** F7
Lacanau *France* **20** D2
Lacanau, Étang de *France* **20** D2
Lacantún → *Mexico* **119** D6
Lacara → *Spain* **37** G4
Lacaune *France* **20** E6
Lacaune, Mts. de *France* **20** E6
Laccadive Is. =
Lakshadweep Is. *India* **3** D13
Lacepede B. *Australia* **95** F2
Lacepede Is. *Australia* **92** C3
Lacerdónia *Mozam.* **87** F4
Lacey *U.S.A.* **110** C4
Lachania *Greece* **49** D9
Lachhmangarh *India* **68** F6
Lachi *Pakistan* **68** C4
Lachine *Canada* **104** C5
Lachute *Canada* **104** C5
Lackagh Hills *Ireland* **12** B3
Lackawanna *U.S.A.* **114** D6

Lackawaxen *U.S.A.* **115** E10
Lacolle *Canada* **115** A11
Lacombe *Canada* **102** C6
Lácona *U.S.A.* **115** C8
Láconi *Italy* **42** C2
Laconia *U.S.A.* **115** C13
Lacq *France* **20** E3
Ladakh Ra. *India* **69** C8
Lądek-Zdrój *Poland* **31** H3
Ladik *Turkey* **72** B6
Ladismith *S. Africa* **88** E3
Ladíspoli *Italy* **41** G9
Lādīz *Iran* **71** D9
Ladnun *India* **68** F6
Ladoga, L. = Ladozhskoye
    Ozero *Russia* **32** B6
Ladonas → *Greece* **46** D3
Ladozhskoye Ozero *Russia* **32** B6
Ladushkin *Russia* **30** D7
Lady Elliott I. *Australia* **94** C5
Lady Grey *S. Africa* **88** E4
Ladybrand *S. Africa* **88** D4
Ladysmith *Canada* **110** B3
Ladysmith *S. Africa* **88** D4
Ladysmith *U.S.A.* **112** C8
Ladyznyn *Ukraine* **29** B14
Lae *Papua N. G.* **90** B7
Laem Hin Khom *Thailand* **65** b
Laem Khat *Thailand* **65** a
Laem Nga *Thailand* **65** a
Laem Ngop *Thailand* **65** F4
Laem Phan Wa *Thailand* **65** a
Laem Pho *Thailand* **65** J3
Laem Phrom Thep *Thailand* **65** a
Laem Riang *Thailand* **65** a
Laem Sam Rong *Thailand* **65** b
Laem Son *Thailand* **65** a
Laem Yamu *Thailand* **65** a
Laerma *Greece* **49** C9
Læsø *Denmark* **11** G5
Læsø Rende *Denmark* **11** G4
Lafayette *Ind., U.S.A.* **112** E10
Lafayette *La., U.S.A.* **116** F8
Lafayette *Tenn., U.S.A.* **117** C11
Laferte → *Canada* **102** A5
Lafia *Nigeria* **83** D6
Lafiagi *Nigeria* **83** D6
Lafkos *Greece* **46** B5
Laflèche *Canada* **103** D7
Lafon *Sudan* **81** F3
Lagan *Sweden* **11** H7
Lagan → *Sweden* **11** H6
Lagan → *U.K.* **12** B6
Lagarfljót → *Iceland* **8** D6
Lagdo, Rés. de *Cameroon* **79** G8
Lage *Germany* **24** D4
Lågen → *Oppland, Norway* **8** F14
Lågen → *Vestfold, Norway* **9** G14
Lägerdorf *Germany* **24** B5
Laghouat *Algeria* **78** B6
Lagnieu *France* **21** C9
Lagny-sur-Marne *France* **19** D9
Lago *Italy* **43** C9
Lago de Sanabria y
    Entorno △ *Spain* **36** C4
Lagôa *Portugal* **37** H2
Lagoa do Peixe △ *Brazil* **127** C5
Lagoa Vermelha *Brazil* **127** B5
Lagoaça *Portugal* **36** D4
Lagodekhi *Georgia* **35** K8
Lagónegro *Italy* **43** B8
Lagonoy G. *Phil.* **61** E5
Lagos *Greece* **45** E9
Lagos *Nigeria* **83** D5
Lagos *Portugal* **37** H2
Lagos □ *Nigeria* **83** D5
Lagos de Moreno *Mexico* **118** C4
Lagrange = Bidyadanga
    Australia **92** C3
Lagrange B. *Australia* **92** C3
Laguardia *Spain* **38** C2
Laguépie *France* **20** D5
Laguna *Brazil* **127** B6
Laguna *U.S.A.* **109** J10
Laguna, Sa. de la *Mexico* **118** C3
Laguna Beach *U.S.A.* **111** M9
Laguna de Duera *Spain* **36** D6
Laguna de la Restinga △
    Venezuela **121** D6
Laguna del Laja △ *Chile* **126** D1
Laguna del Tigre △
    Guatemala **120** C1
Laguna Limpia *Argentina* **126** B4
Lagunas *Chile* **126** A2
Lagunas *Peru* **124** E3
Lagunas de Chacahua △
    Mexico **119** D5
Lagunas de Montebello △
    Mexico **119** D6
Lagunas de Ruidera △ *Spain* **39** G2
Lahad Datu *Malaysia* **63** D5
Lahad Datu, Telok *Malaysia* **63** D5
Lahan Sai *Thailand* **64** E4
Lahanam *Laos* **64** D5
Lahar *India* **69** F8
Laharpur *India* **69** F9
Lahat *Indonesia* **62** E2

Lahewa *Indonesia* **62** D1
Lāhījān *Iran* **71** B6
Lahn → *Germany* **25** E3
Lahnstein *Germany* **25** E3
Laholm *Sweden* **11** H7
Laholmsbukten *Sweden* **11** H6
Lahore *Pakistan* **68** D6
Lahr *Germany* **25** G3
Lahri *Pakistan* **68** E3
Lahti *Finland* **32** B3
Lahtis = Lahti *Finland* **32** B3
Laï *Chad* **79** G9
Lai Chau *Vietnam* **58** F4
Lai'an *China* **59** A12
Laibin *China* **58** F7
Laifeng *China* **58** C7
L'Aigle *France* **18** D7
Laignes *France* **19** E11
L'Aiguillon-sur-Mer *France* **20** B2
Laila = Layla *Si. Arabia* **75** C4
Laingsburg *S. Africa* **88** E3
Lainioälven → *Sweden* **8** C20
Lairg *U.K.* **13** C4
Laisamis *Kenya* **86** B4
Laishui *China* **56** E8
Laissac *France* **20** D6
Láives *Italy* **41** B8
Laiwu *China* **57** F9
Laixi *China* **57** F11
Laiyang *China* **57** F11
Laiyuan *China* **56** E8
Laizhou *China* **57** F10
Laizhou Wan *China* **57** F10
Laja → *Mexico* **118** C4
Lajamanu *Australia* **92** C5
Lajere *Nigeria* **83** C7
Lajes *Brazil* **127** B5
Lajkovac *Serbia* **44** B4
Lajosmizse *Hungary* **28** C4
Lak Sao *Laos* **64** C5
Lakaband *Pakistan* **68** D3
Lakamané *Mali* **82** C3
Lake *U.S.A.* **108** D8
Lake Alpine *U.S.A.* **110** G7
Lake Andes *U.S.A.* **112** D4
Lake Arthur *U.S.A.* **116** F8
Lake Bindegolly △ *Australia* **95** D3
Lake Cargelligo *Australia* **95** E4
Lake Charles *U.S.A.* **116** F8
Lake City, *Colo., U.S.A.* **108** G10
Lake City, *Fla., U.S.A.* **117** F13
Lake City, *Mich., U.S.A.* **113** C11
Lake City, *Minn., U.S.A.* **112** C7
Lake City, *Pa., U.S.A.* **114** D4
Lake City, *S.C., U.S.A.* **117** E15
Lake Cowichan *Canada* **102** D4
Lake District △ *U.K.* **14** C4
Lake Elsinore *U.S.A.* **111** M9
Lake Eyre △ *Australia* **95** D2
Lake Gairdner △ *Australia* **95** E2
Lake George *U.S.A.* **115** C11
Lake Grace *Australia* **93** F2
Lake Harbour = Kimmirut
    Canada **101** C13
Lake Havasu City *U.S.A.* **111** L12
Lake Hughes *U.S.A.* **111** L8
Lake Isabella *U.S.A.* **111** K8
Lake Jackson *U.S.A.* **116** G7
Lake King *Australia* **93** F2
Lake Lenore *Canada* **103** C8
Lake Louise *Canada* **102** C5
Lake Malawi = Malawi ■ *Africa* **87** E3
Lake Mburo △ *Uganda* **86** C3
Lake Mead △ *U.S.A.* **111** K12
Lake Meredith △ *U.S.A.* **116** D4
Lake Mills *U.S.A.* **112** D7
Lake Nakura △ *Kenya* **86** C4
Lake Placid *U.S.A.* **115** B11
Lake Pleasant *U.S.A.* **115** C10
Lake Providence *U.S.A.* **116** E9
Lake Roosevelt △ *U.S.A.* **108** B4
Lake St. Peter *Canada* **114** A6
Lake Superior △ *Canada* **104** C3
Lake Torrens △ *Australia* **95** E2
Lake Village *U.S.A.* **116** E9
Lake Wales *U.S.A.* **117** H14
Lake Worth *U.S.A.* **117** H14
Lakeba *Fiji* **91** a
Lakeba Passage *Fiji* **91** a
Lakefield *Canada* **114** B6
Lakefield △ *Australia* **94** B3
Lakehurst *U.S.A.* **115** F10
Lakeland *Australia* **94** B3
Lakeland *U.S.A.* **117** G14
Lakemba = Lakeba *Fiji* **91** a
Lakeport *Calif., U.S.A.* **110** F4
Lakeport *Mich., U.S.A.* **114** C2
Lakes Entrance *Australia* **95** F4
Lakeside *Calif., U.S.A.* **111** N10
Lakeside *Nebr., U.S.A.* **112** D2
Lakeside *Ohio, U.S.A.* **114** E2
Lakeview *U.S.A.* **108** E3
Lakeville *U.S.A.* **112** C7
Lakewood *Colo., U.S.A.* **108** G11
Lakewood *N.J., U.S.A.* **115** F10
Lakewood *N.Y., U.S.A.* **114** D5
Lakewood *Ohio, U.S.A.* **114** E3

Lakewood *Wash., U.S.A.* **110** C4
Lakha *India* **68** F4
Lakhimpur *India* **69** F9
Lakhnadon *India* **69** H8
Lakhnau = Lucknow *India* **69** F9
Lakhonpheng *Laos* **64** E5
Lakhpat *India* **68** H3
Läki *Azerbaijan* **35** K8
Lakin *U.S.A.* **112** G3
Lakitusaki → *Canada* **104** B3
Lakki *Greece* **49** D5
Lakki *Pakistan* **68** C4
Lakonia □ *Greece* **46** E4
Lakonikos Kolpos *Greece* **46** E4
Lakor *Indonesia* **63** F7
Lakota *Ivory C.* **82** D3
Lakota *U.S.A.* **112** A4
Laksar *India* **68** E8
Laksefjorden *Norway* **8** A22
Lakselv *Norway* **8** A21
Lakshadweep Is. *India* **3** D13
Lakshmanpur *India* **69** H10
Lakshmikantapur *India* **69** H13
Lala Musa *Pakistan* **68** C5
Lalaghat *India* **67** G18
Lalago *Tanzania* **86** C3
Lalapanzi *Zimbabwe* **87** F3
Lalapaşa *Turkey* **45** E10
Lalbenque *France* **20** D5
L'Albufera *Spain* **39** F4
Lalganj *India* **69** G11
Lalgola *India* **69** G13
Lālī *Iran* **71** C6
Lalibela *Ethiopia* **81** E4
Lalín *China* **57** B14
Lalín *Spain* **36** C2
Lalin He → *China* **57** B13
Lalinde *France* **20** D4
Lalitapur *Nepal* **69** F11
Lalitpur *India* **69** G8
Lalkua *India* **69** E8
Lalsot *India* **68** F7
Lam *Vietnam* **64** B6
Lam Pao Res. *Thailand* **64** D4
Lamaing *Burma* **64** E1
Lamar *Colo., U.S.A.* **108** G12
Lamar *Mo., U.S.A.* **112** G6
Lamas *Peru* **124** E3
Lamastre *France* **21** D8
Lambach *Austria* **26** C6
Lamballe *France* **18** D4
Lambaréné *Gabon* **84** E2
Lambasa = Labasa *Fiji* **91** a
Lambay I. *Ireland* **12** C5
Lambert's Bay *S. Africa* **88** E2
Lambesc *France* **21** E9
Lambeth *Canada* **114** D3
Lambía *Greece* **46** D3
Lambomakondro △ *Madag.* **89** C7
Lambro → *Italy* **40** C6
Lambton Shores *Canada* **114** C3
Lame *Nigeria* **83** C6
Lame Deer *U.S.A.* **108** D10
Lamego *Portugal* **36** D3
Lamèque *Canada* **105** C7
Lameroo *Australia* **95** F3
Lamesa *U.S.A.* **116** E4
Lamía *Greece* **46** C4
Lamington △ *Australia* **95** D5
Lamitan *Phil.* **61** H5
Lammermuir Hills *U.K.* **13** F6
Lammhult *Sweden* **11** G8
Lamoille → *U.S.A.* **115** B11
Lamon B. *Phil.* **61** D5
Lamont *Canada* **102** C6
Lamont *Calif., U.S.A.* **111** K8
Lamont *Wyo., U.S.A.* **108** E10
Lamotte-Beuvron *France* **19** E9
Lampa *Peru* **124** G4
Lampang *Thailand* **64** C2
Lampasas *U.S.A.* **116** F5
Lampazos de Naranjo
    Mexico **118** B4
Lampertheim *Germany* **25** F4
Lampeter *U.K.* **15** E3
Lampman *Canada* **103** D8
Lamprechtshausen *Austria* **26** D5
Lampung □ *Indonesia* **62** F2
Lamta *India* **69** H9
Lamu *Kenya* **86** C5
Lamy *U.S.A.* **109** J11
Lan Xian *China* **56** E6
Lan Yü *Taiwan* **59**
Lanak La *China* **69** B8
Lanak'o Shank'ou =
    Lanak La *China* **69** B8
Lanao, L. *Phil.* **61** H6
Lanark *Canada* **115** A8
Lanark □ *U.K.* **13** F5
Lanbi Kyun *Burma* **65** G2
Lancang *China* **58** F2
Lancang Jiang → *China* **58** G3
Lancashire □ *U.K.* **14** D5
Lancaster *Canada* **115** A10
Lancaster *U.K.* **14** C5

Lakewood *Wash., U.S.A.* **110** C4
Lancaster *Calif., U.S.A.* **111** L8
Lancaster *Ky., U.S.A.* **113** G11
Lancaster *N.H., U.S.A.* **115** B13
Lancaster *N.Y., U.S.A.* **114** D6
Lancaster *Ohio, U.S.A.* **113** F12
Lancaster *Pa., U.S.A.* **115** F8
Lancaster *S.C., U.S.A.* **117** D14
Lancaster *Wis., U.S.A.* **112** D8
Lancaster Sd. *Canada* **101** B11
Lancelin *Australia* **93** F2
Lanchow = Lanzhou *China* **56** F2
Lanchyn *Ukraine* **29** B9
Lanciano *Italy* **41** F11
Lancun *China* **57** F11
Łańcut *Poland* **31** H9
Land Between the Lakes △
    U.S.A. **117** C11
Landau *Bayern, Germany* **25** G8
Landau *Rhld.-Pfz., Germany* **25** F4
Landeck *Austria* **26** D3
Lander *U.S.A.* **108** E9
Lander → *Australia* **92** D5
Landerneau *France* **18** D2
Landeryd *Sweden* **11** G7
Landes *France* **20** D2
Landes □ *France* **20** E3
Landes de Gascogne △
    France **20** D3
Landete *Spain* **38** F3
L'Albufera → *Spain* **39** F4
Landi Kotal *Pakistan* **68** B4
Landisburg *U.S.A.* **114** F7
Landivisiau *France* **18** D2
Landmannalaugar *Iceland* **8** E4
Landquart *Switz.* **25** J5
Landrecies *France* **19** B10
Land's End *U.K.* **15** G2
Landsberg *Germany* **25** G6
Landsborough Cr. →
    Australia **94** C3
Landsbro *Sweden* **11** G8
Landshut *Germany* **25** G8
Landskrona *Sweden* **11** J6
Landstuhl *Germany* **25** F3
Landvetter *Sweden* **11** G6
Lanesboro *U.S.A.* **115** E9
Lanester *France* **18** E3
Lanett *U.S.A.* **117** E12
Lang Qua *Vietnam* **64** A5
Lang Shan *China* **56** D4
Lang Son *Vietnam* **58** G6
Lang Suan *Thailand* **65** H2
Langå *Denmark* **11** H3
La'nga Co *China* **69** D9
Langadás *Greece* **44** F7
Langadhia *Greece* **46** D4
Langan → *Sweden* **10** A8
Langano, L. *Ethiopia* **81** F4
Langar *Iran* **71** C9
Langara I. *Canada* **102** C2
Langdai *China* **58** D5
Langdon *U.S.A.* **112** A4
Länge Jan = Ölands södra
    udde *Sweden* **11** H10
Langeac *France* **20** C7
Langeais *France* **18** E7
Langeb Baraka → *Sudan* **80** D4
Langeberg *S. Africa* **88** E3
Langeberge *S. Africa* **88** D3
Langeland *Denmark* **11** K4
Langelands Bælt *Denmark* **11** K4
Langen *Hessen, Germany* **25** F4
Langen *Niedersachsen,*
    Germany **24** B4
Langenburg *Canada* **103** C8
Langeneß *Germany* **24** A4
Langenlois *Austria* **26** C8
Langeoog *Germany* **24** B3
Langeskov *Denmark* **11** J4
Länghem *Sweden* **11** G7
Langhirano *Italy* **40** D7
Langholm *U.K.* **13** F5
Langjökull *Iceland* **8** D3
Langkawi, Pulau *Malaysia* **65** J2
Langklip *S. Africa* **88** D3
Langkon *Malaysia* **62** C5
Langlade *St-P. & M.* **105** C8
Langley *Canada* **110** A4
Langnau *Switz.* **25** J3
Langogne *France* **20** D7
Langon *France* **20** D3
Langøya *Norway* **8** B16
Langres *France* **19** E12
Langres, Plateau de *France* **19** E12
Langsa *Indonesia* **62** D1
Långsele *Sweden* **10** A11
Långshyttan *Sweden* **10** D10
Langtang △ *Nepal* **69** E11
Langtry *U.S.A.* **116** G4
Langu *Thailand* **65** J2
Langue de Barbarie △
    Senegal **82** C1
Languedoc *France* **20** E7
Languedoc-Roussillon □
    France **20** E6
Langxi *China* **59** B12

Langxiangzhen *China* **56** E9
Langzhong *China* **58** B5
Lanigan *Canada* **103** C7
Lankao *China* **56** G8
Länkäran *Azerbaijan* **73** C13
Lanmeur *France* **18** D3
Lannemezan *France* **20** E4
Lannilis *France* **18** D2
Lannion *France* **18** D3
L'Annonciation *Canada* **104** C5
Lanouaille *France* **20** C5
Lanping *China* **58** D2
Lansdale *U.S.A.* **115** F9
Lansdowne *Australia* **95** E5
Lansdowne *Canada* **115** B8
Lansdowne *India* **69** E8
Lansdowne House *Canada* **104** B2
L'Anse *U.S.A.* **112** B9
L'Anse au Loup *Canada* **105** B8
L'Anse aux Meadows
    Canada **105** B8
L'Anse à la Raye *St. Lucia* **121** f
Lansford *U.S.A.* **115** F9
Lanshan *China* **59** E9
Lansing *U.S.A.* **113** D11
Lanslebourg-Mont-Cenis
    France **21** C10
Lanta Yai, Ko *Thailand* **65** J2
Lantewa *Nigeria* **83** C7
Lantian *China* **56** G5
Lanus *Argentina* **126** C4
Lanusei *Italy* **42** C2
Lanuza *Phil.* **61** G7
Lanxi *China* **59** C12
Lanzarote *Canary Is.* **48** F6
Lanzarote ✈ (ACE) *Canary Is.* **48** F6
Lanzhou *China* **56** F2
Lanzo Torinese *Italy* **40** C4
Lao → *Italy* **43** C8
Lao Bao *Laos* **64** D6
Lao Cai *Vietnam* **58** F4
Laoag *Phil.* **61** B4
Laoang *Phil.* **61** E6
Laoha He → *China* **57** C11
Laohekou *China* **59** A8
Laois □ *Ireland* **12** D4
Laon *France* **19** C10
Laona *U.S.A.* **112** C9
Laos ■ *Asia* **64** D5
Lapa *Brazil* **127** B6
Lapai *Nigeria* **83** D6
Lapalisse *France* **19** F10
Lapapisai *Argentina* **126** D3
Lapeer *U.S.A.* **113** D12
Lapeyrade *France* **20** D3
Lapithos *Cyprus* **49** D12
Lapland = Lappland *Europe* **8** B21
LaPorte *Ind., U.S.A.* **112** E10
Laporte *Pa., U.S.A.* **115** E8
Lapovo *Serbia* **44** B5
Lappeenranta *Finland* **32** B5
Lappland *Europe* **8** B21
Lappo = Lapua *Finland* **8** E20
Laprida *Argentina* **126** D3
Lapseki *Turkey* **45** F10
Laptev Sea *Russia* **53** B13
Lapua *Finland* **8** E20
Lăpuş → *Romania* **29** C8
Lăpuş, Munţii *Romania* **29** C8
Lăpuşna *Moldova* **29** D13
Łapy *Poland* **31** F9
Laqiya Arba'in *Sudan* **80** C2
Laqiya Umran *Sudan* **80** D2
L'Áquila *Italy* **41** F10
Lār *Āzarbāijān-e Sharqī, Iran* **70** B5
Lār *Fārs, Iran* **71** E7
Larabanga *Ghana* **82** D4
Laragne-Montéglin *France* **21** D9
Laramie *U.S.A.* **108** F11
Laramie Mts. *U.S.A.* **108** F11
Laranjeiras do Sul *Brazil* **127** B5
Larantuka *Indonesia* **63** F6
Larat *Indonesia* **63** F8
L'Arbresle *France* **21** C8
Lärbro *Sweden* **11** G12
Larde *Mozam.* **87** F4
Larder Lake *Canada* **104** C4
Lardos, Akra = Lindos,
    Akra *Greece* **49** C10
Lardos, Ormos *Greece* **49** C10
Lare *Kenya* **86** C4
Laredo *Spain* **36** B7
Laredo *U.S.A.* **116** H5
Laredo Sd. *Canada* **102** C3
Largentière *France* **21** D8
L'Argentière-la-Bessée
    France **21** D10
Largo *U.S.A.* **117** H13
Largs *U.K.* **13** F4
Lari *Italy* **40** E7
Lariang *Indonesia* **63** E5
Larimore *U.S.A.* **112** B5
Larino *Italy* **41** G11
Larisa *Greece* **46** B4
Larissa □ *Greece* **46** B4
Larkana *Pakistan* **68** F3
Larnaca *Cyprus* **49** E12
Larnaca Bay *Cyprus* **49** E12

Larne *U.K.* **12** B6
Larned *U.S.A.* **112** F4
Laroquebrou *France* **20** D6
Larose *U.S.A.* **117** G9
Larrimah *Australia* **92** C5
Larsen Ice Shelf *Antarctica* **5** C17
Laruns *France* **20** F3
Larvik *Norway* **9** G14
Larzac, Causse du *France* **20** E7
Las Alpujarras *Spain* **39** J1
Las Animas *U.S.A.* **108** G12
Las Anod *Somali Rep.* **75** F4
Las Arenas *Spain* **36** B6
Las Batuecas △ *Spain* **36** E4
Las Breñas *Argentina* **126** B3
Las Cabezas de San Juan
    Spain **37** J5
Las Cañadas del Teide △
    Canary Is. **48** F3
Las Cejas *Argentina* **128** B4
Las Chimeneas *Mexico* **111** N10
Las Cruces *U.S.A.* **109** K10
Las Flores *Argentina* **126** D4
Las Heras *Argentina* **126** C2
Las Lajas *Argentina* **128** D2
Las Lomitas *Argentina* **126** A3
Las Marismas *Spain* **37** H4
Las Minas *Spain* **39** G3
Las Navas de la
    Concepción *Spain* **37** H5
Las Navas del Marqués *Spain* **36** E6
Las Palmas *Argentina* **126** B4
Las Palmas *Canary Is.* **48** F4
Las Palmas → *Mexico* **111** N10
Las Palmas ✈ (LPA)
    Canary Is. **48** G4
Las Palmas de Cocalán △
    Chile **126** C1
Las Pedroñas *Spain* **39** F2
Las Piedras *Uruguay* **127** C4
Las Pipinas *Argentina* **126** D4
Las Plumas *Argentina* **128** E3
Las Rosas *Argentina* **126** C3
Las Rozas *Spain* **36** E7
Las Tablas *Panama* **120** E3
Las Termas *Argentina* **126** B3
Las Toscas *Argentina* **126** B4
Las Truchas *Mexico* **118** D4
Las Tunas *Cuba* **120** B4
Las Varillas *Argentina* **126** C3
Las Vegas *N. Mex., U.S.A.* **109** J11
Las Vegas *Nev., U.S.A.* **111** J11
Las Vegas McCarran Int. ✈
    (LAS) *U.S.A.* **111** J11
Lasarte *Spain* **38** B2
Lascano *Uruguay* **127** C5
Lash-e Joveyn *Afghan.* **66** D2
Lashburn *Canada* **103** C7
Lashio *Burma* **67** H20
Lashkar *India* **68** F8
Łasin *Poland* **30** E6
Lasithi *Greece* **49** D7
Lasithi □ *Greece* **49** D7
Lāsjerd *Iran* **71** C7
Łask *Poland* **31** G6
Łaskarzew *Poland* **31** G8
Laško *Slovenia* **41** B12
Lassay-les-Châteaux *France* **18** D6
Lassen Pk. *U.S.A.* **108** F3
Lassen Volcanic △ *U.S.A.* **108** F3
Last Mountain L. *Canada* **103** C7
Lastchance Cr. → *U.S.A.* **110** E5
Lastoursville *Gabon* **84** E2
Lastovo *Croatia* **41** F13
Lastovski Kanal *Croatia* **41** F14
Lat Yao *Thailand* **64** E2
Latacunga *Ecuador* **124** D3
Latakia = Al Lādhiqīyah
    Syria **72** E6
Latchford *Canada* **104** C4
Late *Tonga* **91** c
Latehar *India* **69** H11
Laterza *Italy* **43** B9
Latham *Australia* **93** E2
Lathen *Germany* **24** C3
Lathi *India* **68** F4
Lathrop Wells *U.S.A.* **111** J10
Latiano *Italy* **43** B10
Latina *Italy* **42** A5
Latisana *Italy* **41** C10
Latium = Lazio □ *Italy* **41** F9
Laton *U.S.A.* **110** J7
Latorytsya → *Slovak Rep.* **27** C14
Latouche Treville, C.
    Australia **92** C3
Latrobe *Australia* **95** G4
Latrobe *U.S.A.* **114** F5
Latrónico *Italy* **43** B9
Latvia ■ *Europe* **32** C3
Lau *Nigeria* **83** D7
Lau Group *Fiji* **91** a
Lauchhammer *Germany* **24** D9
Lauda-Königshofen *Germany* **25** F5
Lauenburg *Germany* **24** B6
Lauenburgische Seen △
    Germany **24** B6
Lauf *Germany* **25** F7

Laughlin *U.S.A.* **109** J6
Laujar de Andarax *Spain* **39** H2
Laukaa *Finland* **8** E21
Launceston *Australia* **95** G4
Launceston *U.K.* **15** G3
Laune → *Ireland* **12** D2
Launglon Bok *Burma* **64** F1
Laupheim *Germany* **25** G5
Laura *Australia* **94** B3
Laureana di Borrello *Italy* **43** D9
Laurel *Miss., U.S.A.* **117** F10
Laurel *Mont., U.S.A.* **108** D9
Laurel Hill *U.S.A.* **114** F5
Laurencekirk *U.K.* **13** E6
Laurens *U.S.A.* **117** D13
Laurentian Plateau *Canada* **105** B6
Lauria *Italy* **43** B8
Laurie L. *Canada* **103** B8
Laurinburg *U.S.A.* **117** D15
Laurium *U.S.A.* **112** B9
Lausanne *Switz.* **25** J2
Laut *Indonesia* **62** D3
Laut, Pulau *Indonesia* **62** E5
Laut Kecil, Kepulauan *Indonesia* **62** E5
Lauterbach *Germany* **24** E5
Lauterecken *Germany* **25** F3
Lautoka *Fiji* **91** a
Lauzès *France* **20** D5
Lava → *Russia* **30** D8
Lava Beds △ *U.S.A.* **108** F3
Lavagh More *Ireland* **12** B3
Lavagna *Italy* **40** D6
Laval *France* **18** D6
Laval-des-Rapides *Canada* **104** C5
Lavalle *Argentina* **126** B2
Lavant Station *Canada* **115** A8
Lāvar Meydān *Iran* **71** D7
Lavara *Greece* **45** E10
Lavardac *France* **20** D4
Lavaur *France* **20** E5
Lavelanet *France* **20** F5
Lavello *Italy* **43** A8
Laverton *Australia* **93** E3
Lavis *Italy* **40** B8
Lavos *Portugal* **36** E2
Lavradio *Portugal* **37** G1
Lavras *Brazil* **127** A7
Lavre *Portugal* **37** G2
Lavrio *Greece* **46** D6
Lavris *Greece* **46** D6
Lavumisa *Swaziland* **89** D5
Lawaki *Fiji* **91** a
Lavushi Manda △ *Zambia* **87** E3
Lawas *Malaysia* **62** D5
Lawele *Indonesia* **63** F6
Lawn Hill △ *Australia* **94** B2
Lawqah *Si. Arabia* **70** D4
Lawra *Ghana* **82** C4
Lawrence *N.Z.* **91** F2
Lawrence *Ind., U.S.A.* **112** F10
Lawrence *Kans., U.S.A.* **112** F6
Lawrence *Mass., U.S.A.* **115** D13
Lawrenceburg *Ind., U.S.A.* **113** F11
Lawrenceburg *Tenn., U.S.A.* **117** D11
Lawrenceville *Ga., U.S.A.* **117** E13
Lawrenceville *Pa., U.S.A.* **114** E7
Laws *U.S.A.* **110** H4
Lawton *U.S.A.* **116** D5
Lawu *Indonesia* **63** G14
Lawz, J. al *Si. Arabia* **80** B4
Laxå *Sweden* **11** F8
Laxford, L. *U.K.* **13** C3
Laxou *France* **19** D13
Lay → *France* **20** B2
Layla *Si. Arabia* **75** C4
Laylān *Iraq* **70** C5
Layon → *France* **18** E6
Layton *U.S.A.* **108** F8
Laytonville *U.S.A.* **108** G2
Lazarevac *Serbia* **44** B4
Lazarevskoye *Russia* **35** J4
Lazarivo *Madag.* **89** C8
Lázaro Cárdenas *Mexico* **118** D4
Lazdijai *Lithuania* **30** D10
Lazio □ *Italy* **41** F9
Lazo *Moldova* **29** C13
Lazo *Russia* **54** C6
Le Beausset *France* **21** E9
Le Bic *Canada* **105** C6
Le Blanc *France* **20** B5
Le Bleymard *France* **20** D7
Le Bourgneuf-la-Fôret *France* **18** D6
Le Bugue *France* **20** D4
Le Cateau Cambrésis *France* **19** B10
Le Caylar *France* **20** E7
Le Chambon-Feugerolles *France* **21** C8
Le Châtelet *France* **19** F9
Le Chesne *France* **19** C11
Le Cheylard *France* **21** D8
Le Conquet *France* **18** D2
Le Creusot *France* **19** F11
Le Croisic *France* **18** E4
Le Donjon *France* **19** F10

Le Dorat *France* **20** B5
Le François *Martinique* **120** c
Le Gosier *Guadeloupe* **120** b
Le Grand-Lucé *France* **18** E7
Le Grand-Pressigny *France* **18** F7
Le Grand-Quevilly *France* **18** C8
Le Gris Gris *Mauritius* **85** d
Le Havre *France* **18** C7
Le Lamentin *Martinique* **120** c
Le Lavandou *France* **21** E10
Le Lion-d'Angers *France* **18** E6
Le Louroux-Béconnais *France* **18** E6
Le Luc *France* **21** E10
Le Lude *France* **18** E7
Le Mans *France* **18** E7
Le Marin *Martinique* **120** c
Le Mars *U.S.A.* **112** D5
Le Mayet-de-Montagne *France* **19** F10
Le Mêle-sur-Sarthe *France* **18** D7
Le Monastier-sur-Gazeille *France* **20** D7
Le Monêtier-les-Bains *France* **21** D10
Le Mont-Dore *France* **20** C6
Le Mont-St-Michel *France* **18** D5
Le Moule *Guadeloupe* **120** b
Le Muy *France* **21** E10
Le Palais *France* **18** E3
Le Perthus *France* **20** F6
Le Port *Réunion* **85** c
Le Prêcheur *Martinique* **120** c
Le Puy-en-Velay *France* **20** C7
Le Robert *Martinique* **120** c
Le St-Esprit *Martinique* **120** c
Le Sueur *U.S.A.* **112** C7
Le Tampon *Réunion* **85** c
Le Teil *France* **21** D8
Le Teilleul *France* **18** D6
Le Theil *France* **18** D7
Le Thillot *France* **19** E13
Le Thuy *Vietnam* **64** D6
Le Touquet-Paris-Plage *France* **19** B8
Le Tréport *France* **18** B8
Le Val-d'Ajol *France* **19** E13
Le Verdon-sur-Mer *France* **20** C2
Le Vigan *France* **20** E7
Lea → *U.K.* **15** F8
Leach *Cambodia* **65** F4
Lead *U.S.A.* **112** C2
Leader *Canada* **103** C7
Leadville *U.S.A.* **108** G10
Leaf → *U.S.A.* **117** F10
Leaf Rapids *Canada* **103** B9
Leamington *Canada* **114** D2
Leamington *U.S.A.* **108** G7
Leamington Spa = Royal Leamington Spa *U.K.* **15** E6
Le'an *China* **59** D10
Leandro Norte Alem *Argentina* **127** B4
Leane, L. *Ireland* **12** D2
Leask *Canada* **103** C7
Leatherhead *U.K.* **15** F7
Leavenworth *Kans., U.S.A.* **112** F6
Leavenworth *Wash., U.S.A.* **108** C3
Leawood *U.S.A.* **112** F6
Łeba *Poland* **30** D4
Łeba → *Poland* **30** D4
Lebach *Germany* **25** F2
Lebak *Phil.* **61** H6
Lebane *Serbia* **44** D5
Lebanon *Ind., U.S.A.* **112** E10
Lebanon *Kans., U.S.A.* **112** F4
Lebanon *Ky., U.S.A.* **113** G11
Lebanon *Mo., U.S.A.* **112** G7
Lebanon *N.H., U.S.A.* **115** C12
Lebanon *Oreg., U.S.A.* **108** D2
Lebanon *Pa., U.S.A.* **115** F8
Lebanon *Tenn., U.S.A.* **117** C11
Lebanon ■ *Asia* **74** B5
Lebec *U.S.A.* **111** L8
Lebedyan *Russia* **33** F10
Lebedyn *Ukraine* **33** G8
Lebel-sur-Quévillon *Canada* **104** C4
Lebomboberge *S. Africa* **89** C5
Lębork *Poland* **30** D4
Lebrija *Spain* **37** J4
Łebsko, Jezioro *Poland* **30** D4
Lebu *Chile* **126** D1
Leca da Palmeira *Portugal* **36** D2
Lecce *Italy* **43** B11
Lecco *Italy* **40** C6
Lecco, L. di *Italy* **40** C6
Lécera *Spain* **38** D4
Lech *Austria* **26** D3
Lech → *Germany* **25** G6
Lechang *China* **59** E9
Lechena *Greece* **46** D3
Lechtaler Alpen *Austria* **26** D3
Lecontes Mills *U.S.A.* **114** E6
Lectoure *France* **20** E4
Łęczna *Poland* **31** G9

Łęczyca *Poland* **31** F6
Ledesma *Spain* **36** D5
Ledong *China* **64** C7
Leduc *Canada* **102** C6
Lee *U.S.A.* **115** D11
Lee → *Ireland* **12** E3
Lee Vining *U.S.A.* **110** H7
Leech L. *U.S.A.* **112** B6
Leechburg *U.S.A.* **114** F5
Leeds *U.K.* **14** D6
Leeds *U.S.A.* **117** E11
Leek *Neths.* **17** A6
Leek *U.K.* **14** D5
Leeman *Australia* **93** E1
Leeper *U.S.A.* **114** E5
Leer *Germany* **24** B3
Leesburg *U.S.A.* **117** G14
Leesville *U.S.A.* **116** F8
Leeton *Australia* **95** E4
Leetonia *U.S.A.* **114** F4
Leeu Gamka *S. Africa* **88** E3
Leeuwarden *Neths.* **17** A5
Leeuwin, C. *Australia* **93** F2
Leeuwin Naturaliste △ *Australia* **93** F2
Leeward Is. *Atl. Oc.* **121** C7
Lefka *Cyprus* **49** D11
Lefkada *Greece* **46** C2
Lefkimis *Greece* **49** B4
Lefkimis, Akra *Greece* **49** B4
Lefkímmi = Lefkimis *Greece* **49** B4
Lefkoniko *Cyprus* **49** D12
Lefroy *Canada* **114** B5
Lefroy, L. *Australia* **93** F3
Łeg → *Poland* **31** H8
Leganés *Spain* **36** E7
Legazpi *Phil.* **61** E5
Lège-Cap-Ferret *France* **20** D2
Lege Hida *Ethiopia* **81** F5
Legendre I. *Australia* **92** D2
Leghorn = Livorno *Italy* **40** E7
Legionowo *Poland* **31** F7
Legnago *Italy* **41** C8
Legnano *Italy* **40** C5
Legnica *Poland* **31** G3
Legrad *Croatia* **41** B13
Leh *India* **69** B7
Lehigh Acres *U.S.A.* **117** H14
Lehighton *U.S.A.* **115** F9
Lehliu *Romania* **29** F11
Leho *Sudan* **81** F3
Lehrte *Germany* **24** C5
Lehututu *Botswana* **88** C3
Lei Shui → *China* **59** D9
Leiah *Pakistan* **68** D4
Leibnitz *Austria* **26** E8
Leibo *China* **58** C4
Leicester *U.K.* **15** E6
Leicester City □ *U.K.* **15** E6
Leicestershire □ *U.K.* **15** E6
Leichhardt → *Australia* **94** B2
Leichhardt Ra. *Australia* **94** C4
Leiden *Neths.* **17** B4
Leie → *Belgium* **17** C3
Leifers = Láives *Italy* **41** B8
Leimen *Germany* **25** F4
Leine → *Germany* **24** C5
Leinefelde *Germany* **24** D6
Leinster *Australia* **93** E3
Leinster □ *Ireland* **12** C4
Leinster, Mt. *Ireland* **12** D5
Leipalingis *Lithuania* **30** D10
Leipzig *Germany* **24** D8
Leiria *Portugal* **36** F2
Leiria □ *Portugal* **36** F2
Leirvik *Norway* **9** G11
Leishan *China* **58** D7
Leisler, Mt. *Australia* **92** D4
Leith *U.K.* **13** F5
Leith Hill *U.K.* **15** F7
Leitha → *Europe* **27** D10
Leitrim *Ireland* **12** B3
Leitrim □ *Ireland* **12** B4
Leitza *Spain* **38** B3
Leiyang *China* **59** D9
Leizhou *China* **59** G8
Leizhou Bandao *China* **58** G7
Leizhou Wan *China* **59** G8
Lek → *Neths.* **17** C4
Leka *Norway* **8** D14
Lekani *Greece* **45** E8
Lekbibaj *Albania* **44** D3
Lekeitio *Spain* **38** B2
Lekoui *Burkina Faso* **82** C4
Leksand *Sweden* **10** D9
Leland *U.S.A.* **113** C11
Lelång *Sweden* **10** E6
Leleque *Argentina* **128** E2
Lelystad *Neths.* **17** B5
Lema *Nigeria* **83** C5
Lema Shilindi *Ethiopia* **81** G5
Léman, L. *Europe* **19** F13
Lembar *Indonesia* **63** K19
Lembuak *Indonesia* **63** K19
Lemera *Dem. Rep. of the Congo* **86** C2
Lemery *Phil.* **61** E4

Lemhi Ra. *U.S.A.* **108** D7
Lemmer *Neths.* **17** B5
Lemnos = Limnos *Greece* **47** B8
Lemon *U.S.A.* **112** C2
Lemon Grove *U.S.A.* **111** N9
Lemoore *U.S.A.* **110** J7
Lempdes *France* **20** C7
Lemvig *Denmark* **11** H2
Lena → *Russia* **53** B13
Lenadoon Pt. *Ireland* **12** B2
Lenart *Slovenia* **41** B12
Lenartovce *Slovak Rep.* **27** C13
Lenclôitre *France* **18** F7
Lendava *Slovenia* **41** B13
Lendeh *Iran* **71** D6
Lendinara *Italy* **41** C8
Lengerich *Germany* **24** C3
Lenggong *Malaysia* **65** K3
Lenggries *Germany* **25** H7
Lengshuijiang *China* **59** D8
Lengshuitan *China* **59** D8
Lengua de Vaca, Pta. *Chile* **126** C1
Lengwe △ *Malawi* **87** F3
Lengyeltóti *Hungary* **28** D2
Lenhovda *Sweden* **11** G9
Lenina, Kanal → *Russia* **35** J7
Leningrad □ *Russia* **32** C7
Lenino *Ukraine* **33** K8
Leninogorsk *Kazakhstan* **52** D9
Leninsk *Russia* **35** F7
Leninsk-Kuznetskiy *Russia* **52** D9
Leninskoye *Russia* **34** A8
Lenk *Switz.* **25** J3
Lenkoran = Länkäran *Azerbaijan* **73** C13
Lenmalu *Indonesia* **63** E8
Lenne → *Germany* **24** D3
Lennestadt *Germany* **24** D4
Lennox *U.S.A.* **112** D5
Lennoxville *Canada* **115** A13
Leno *Italy* **40** C7
Lenoir *U.S.A.* **117** D14
Lenoir City *U.S.A.* **117** D12
Lenore L. *Canada* **103** C8
Lenox *U.S.A.* **115** D11
Lens *France* **19** B9
Lensahn *Germany* **24** A6
Lensk *Russia* **53** C12
Lentas *Greece* **49** E6
Lenti *Hungary* **28** D1
Lentini *Italy* **43** E8
Lenwood *U.S.A.* **111** L9
Lenya *Burma* **65** G2
Lenzen *Germany* **24** B7
Léo *Burkina Faso* **82** C4
Leoben *Austria* **26** D8
Leodhas = Lewis *U.K.* **13** C2
Leola *U.S.A.* **112** C4
Leominster *U.K.* **15** E5
Leominster *U.S.A.* **115** D13
Léon *France* **20** E2
León *Mexico* **118** C4
León *Nic.* **120** D2
León *Spain* **36** C5
Leon *U.S.A.* **112** E7
León □ *Spain* **36** C5
Leon → *U.S.A.* **116** F6
León, Montes de *Spain* **36** C4
Leonardo da Vinci, Roma ✈ (FCO) *Italy* **41** G9
Leonardtown *U.S.A.* **113** F15
Leonardville *Namibia* **88** C2
Leonberg *Germany* **25** G5
Leonding *Austria* **26** C7
Leone *Amer. Samoa* **91** b
Leonessa *Italy* **41** F9
Leonforte *Italy* **43** E7
Leongatha *Australia* **95** F4
Leonidio *Greece* **46** D4
Leonora *Australia* **93** E3
Leopoldina *Brazil* **127** A7
Leopoldsburg *Belgium* **17** C5
Leoti *U.S.A.* **112** F4
Leova *Moldova* **29** D13
Lepe *Spain* **37** H3
Lepel = Lyepyel *Belarus* **32** E5
Lepenou *Greece* **46** C3
Leping *China* **59** C11
Lépo, L. do *Angola* **88** B2
Lepontine, Alpi *Italy* **40** B5
Leppävirta *Finland* **8** E22
Lepsény *Hungary* **28** D3
Leptis Magna *Libya* **79** B8
Lequeitio = Lekeitio *Spain* **38** B2
Lercara Friddi *Italy* **42** E6
Léré *Chad* **83** D7
Léré *Mali* **82** B4
Lere *Bauchi, Nigeria* **83** D6
Lere *Kaduna, Nigeria* **83** C6
Leribe *Lesotho* **89** D4
Lérici *Italy* **40** D6
Lérins, Îs. de *France* **21** E11
Lerma *Spain* **36** C7
Léros *Greece* **47** D8
Lérouville *France* **19** D12

Lerum *Sweden* **11** G6
Lerwick *U.K.* **13** A7
Leş *Romania* **28** D6
Les Abrets *France* **21** C9
Les Andelys *France* **18** C8
Les Borges Blanques *Spain* **38** D5
Les Cayes *Haiti* **121** C5
Les Coteaux *Canada* **115** A10
Les Escoumins *Canada* **105** C6
Les Essarts *France* **18** F5
Les Herbiers *France* **18** F5
Les Minquiers, Plateau des Chan. Is. **18** D4
Les Pieux *France* **18** C5
Les Ponts-de-Cé *France* **18** E6
Les Riceys *France* **19** E11
Les Sables-d'Olonne *France* **20** B2
Les Vans *France* **21** D8
Lesbos *Greece* **47** B8
L'Escala *Spain* **38** C8
Leshan *China* **58** C4
Leshwe △ *Dem. Rep. of the Congo* **87** E2
Lésina *Italy* **41** G12
Lésina, L. di *Italy* **41** G12
Lesjöfors *Sweden* **10** E8
Lesko *Poland* **31** J9
Leskov I. *Antarctica* **5** B1
Leskovac *Serbia* **44** C5
Leskovik *Albania* **44** F4
Leśna *Poland* **31** G2
Lesneven *France* **18** D2
Leśnica *Poland* **31** H5
Lešnica *Serbia* **44** B3
Lesnoye *Russia* **32** C8
Lesopilnoye *Russia* **54** A7
Lesosibirsk *Russia* **53** D10
Lesotho ■ *Africa* **89** D4
Lesozavodsk *Russia* **54** B6
Lesparre-Médoc *France* **20** C3
Lessay *France* **18** C5
Lesse → *Belgium* **17** D4
Lesse et Lomme △ *Belgium* **17** D5
Lessebo *Sweden* **11** H9
Lesser Antilles *W. Indies* **121** D7
Lesser Slave L. *Canada* **102** B5
Lesser Sunda Is. *Indonesia* **63** F6
Lessines *Belgium* **17** D3
Lester B. Pearson Int., Toronto ✈ (YYZ) *Canada* **114** C5
Lestock *Canada* **103** C8
Lesuer L. *Australia* **92** B4
Lesueur △ *Australia* **93** F2
Lesuk, → *Belgium* **17** D4
Letaba *S. Africa* **89** C5
Letälven → *Sweden* **10** E8
Létavértes *Hungary* **28** C6
Letchworth *U.K.* **15** F7
Letea, Ostrov *Romania* **29** E14
Lethbridge *Canada* **102** D6
Lethem *Guyana* **124** C7
Leti, Kepulauan *Indonesia* **63** F7
Leti Is. = Leti, Kepulauan *Indonesia* **63** F7
Letiahau → *Botswana* **88** C3
Leticia *Colombia* **124** D5
Leting *China* **57** E10
Letjiesbos *S. Africa* **88** E3
Letlhakane *Botswana* **88** C4
Letlhakeng *Botswana* **88** C3
Letpadan *Burma* **67** L19
Letpan *Burma* **67** K19
Letsôk-aw Kyun *Burma* **65** G2
Letterkenny *Ireland* **12** B4
Leu *Romania* **29** F9
Leucadia *U.S.A.* **111** M9
Leucate *France* **20** F7
Leucate, Étang de *France* **20** F7
Leuchars *U.K.* **13** E6
Leuk *Switz.* **25** J3
Leuşeni *Moldova* **29** D13
Leuser, G. *Indonesia* **62** D1
Leutkirch *Germany* **25** H6
Leuven *Belgium* **17** D4
Leuze-en-Hainaut *Belgium* **17** D3
Lev Tolstoy *Russia* **32** F10
Levan *Albania* **44** F3
Levanger *Norway* **8** E14
Levant, Î. du *France* **21** E10
Levanto *Italy* **40** D6
Lévanzo *Italy* **42** D5
Levelland *U.S.A.* **116** E3
Leven *U.K.* **13** E6
Leven, L. *U.K.* **13** E5
Leven, Toraka *Madag.* **89** A8
Leveque C. *Australia* **92** C3
Leverano *Italy* **43** B10
Leverkusen *Germany* **24** D3
Levice *Slovak Rep.* **27** C11
Lévico Terme *Italy* **41** C8
Levie *France* **21** G13
Levier *France* **19** F13
Levin *N.Z.* **91** D5
Lévis *Canada* **105** C5
Levis, L. *Canada* **102** A5
Levitha *Greece* **47** D8
Levittown *N.Y., U.S.A.* **115** F11

Levittown *Pa., U.S.A.* **115** F10
Levka *Bulgaria* **45** E10
Levka Oros *Greece* **49** D6
Levkada □ *Greece* **46** C2
Levkás = Lefkada *Greece* **46** C2
Levkôsia = Nicosia *Cyprus* **49** D12
Levoča *Slovak Rep.* **27** C13
Levroux *France* **19** F8
Levski *Bulgaria* **45** C9
Levskigrad = Karlovo *Bulgaria* **45** D8
Levuka *Fiji* **91** a
Lewes *U.K.* **15** G8
Lewes *U.S.A.* **113** F16
Lewin Brzeski *Poland* **31** H4
Lewis *U.K.* **13** C2
Lewis → *U.S.A.* **110** E4
Lewis, Butt of *U.K.* **13** C2
Lewis Ra. *Australia* **92** D4
Lewis Range *U.S.A.* **108** B7
Lewis Run *U.S.A.* **114** E6
Lewisburg *Pa., U.S.A.* **114** F8
Lewisburg *Tenn., U.S.A.* **117** D11
Lewisburg *W. Va., U.S.A.* **113** G13
Lewisporte *Canada* **105** C8
Lewiston *Idaho, U.S.A.* **108** C5
Lewiston *Maine, U.S.A.* **113** C18
Lewiston *N.Y., U.S.A.* **114** C5
Lewistown *Mont., U.S.A.* **108** C9
Lewistown *Pa., U.S.A.* **114** F7
Lexington *Ill., U.S.A.* **112** E9
Lexington *Ky., U.S.A.* **113** F11
Lexington *Mich., U.S.A.* **114** C2
Lexington *Mo., U.S.A.* **112** F7
Lexington *N.C., U.S.A.* **117** D10
Lexington *N.Y., U.S.A.* **115** D10
Lexington *Nebr., U.S.A.* **112** E5
Lexington *Ohio, U.S.A.* **114** F2
Lexington *Tenn., U.S.A.* **117** D10
Lexington *Va., U.S.A.* **113** G14
Lexington Park *U.S.A.* **113** F15
Leyburn *U.K.* **14** C6
Leye *China* **58** E6
Leyland *U.K.* **14** D5
Leyre → *France* **20** D2
Leyte □ *Phil.* **61** F6
Leyte Gulf *Phil.* **61** F6
Leżajsk *Poland* **31** H9
Lezay *France* **20** B3
Lezha *Albania* **44** E3
Lezhi *China* **58** B5
Lézignan-Corbières *France* **20** E6
Lezoux *France* **20** C7
Lgov *Russia* **33** G8
Lhasa *China* **60** D4
Lhazê *China* **60** D3
Lhokkruet *Indonesia* **62** D1
Lhokseumawe *Indonesia* **62** C1
L'Hospitalet de Llobregat *Spain* **38** D7
Li *Thailand* **64** D2
Li Jiang → *China* **59** E8
Li Shui → *China* **59** C9
Li Xian *Gansu, China* **56** G3
Li Xian *Hebei, China* **56** E8
Li Xian *Hunan, China* **59** C9
Liadi *Greece* **47** E8
Liancheng *China* **59** E11
Liancourt Rocks = Tok-do *Asia* **55** F5
Lianga *Phil.* **61** G7
Liangcheng *Nei Monggol Zizhiqu, China* **56** D7
Liangcheng *Shandong, China* **57** G10
Liangdang *China* **56** H4
Lianghe *China* **58** E2
Lianghekou *China* **58** C7
Liangping *China* **58** B6
Liangpran *Indonesia* **62** D4
Lianhua *China* **59** D9
Lianjiang *Fujian, China* **59** D12
Lianjiang *Guangdong, China* **59** G8
Lianping *China* **59** E10
Lianshan *China* **59** E9
Lianshanguan *China* **57** D12
Lianshui *China* **57** H10
Lianyuan *China* **59** D8
Lianyungang *China* **57** G10
Lianzhou *China* **59** E9
Liao He → *China* **57** D11
Liaocheng *China* **56** F8
Liaodong Bandao *China* **57** E12
Liaodong Wan *China* **57** D11
Liaoning □ *China* **57** D12
Liaotung, G. of = Liaodong Wan *China* **57** D11
Liaoyang *China* **57** D12
Liaoyuan *China* **57** C13
Liaozhong *China* **57** D12
Liard → *Canada* **102** A4
Liard River *Canada* **102** B3
Liari *Pakistan* **68** G2
Libau = Liepāja *Latvia* **30** B8
Libby *U.S.A.* **108** B6
Libenge *Dem. Rep. of the Congo* **84** D3
Liberal *U.S.A.* **112** G3
Liberec *Czech Rep.* **26** A8

Liberecký □ *Czech Rep.* **26** A8
Liberia *Costa Rica* **120** D2
Liberia ■ *W. Afr.* **82** D3
Liberty *Mo., U.S.A.* **112** F6
Liberty *N.Y., U.S.A.* **115** E10
Liberty *Pa., U.S.A.* **114** E7
Liberty *Tex., U.S.A.* **116** F7
Liberty-Newark Int. ✈
   (EWR) *U.S.A.* **115** F10
Libiąż *Poland* **31** H6
Lîbîya, Sahrâ' *Africa* **79** C10
Libo *China* **58** E6
Libobo, Tanjung *Indonesia* **63** E7
Libode *S. Africa* **89** E4
Libohovë *Albania* **44** F4
Libourne *France* **20** D3
Libramont *Belgium* **17** E5
Librazhd *Albania* **44** E4
Libreville *Gabon* **84** D1
Libya ■ *N. Afr.* **79** C9
Libyan Desert = Lîbîya,
   Sahrâ' *Africa* **79** C10
Libyan Plateau = Ed Déffa
   Egypt **80** A2
Licantén *Chile* **126** D1
Licata *Italy* **42** E6
Lice *Turkey* **73** C9
Licheng *China* **56** F7
Lichfield *U.K.* **15** E6
Lichinga *Mozam.* **87** E4
Lichtenburg *S. Africa* **88** D4
Lichtenfels *Germany* **25** E7
Lichuan *Hubei, China* **58** B7
Lichuan *Jiangxi, China* **59** D11
Licking → *U.S.A.* **113** F11
Licosa, Punta *Italy* **43** B7
Licungo → *Mozam.* **87** F4
Lida *Belarus* **23** B13
Liden *Sweden* **10** B10
Lidhult *Sweden* **11** H7
Lidköping *Sweden* **11** F7
Lido *Italy* **41** C9
Lido *Niger* **83** C5
Lido di Roma = Óstia, Lido
   di *Italy* **41** G9
Lidoríki *Greece* **46** C4
Lidzbark *Poland* **31** E6
Lidzbark Warmiński *Poland* **30** D7
Liebenwalde *Germany* **24** C9
Lieberose *Germany* **24** D10
Liebig, Mt. *Australia* **92** D5
Liebling *Romania* **28** E6
Liechtenstein ■ *Europe* **25** H5
Liège *Belgium* **17** D5
Liège □ *Belgium* **17** D5
Liegnitz = Legnica *Poland* **31** G3
Lieksa *Finland* **8** E24
Lienart *Dem. Rep. of the Congo* **86** B2
Lienyünchiangshih =
   Lianyungang *China* **57** G10
Lienz *Austria* **26** E5
Liepāja *Latvia* **30** B8
Liepāja □ *Latvia* **30** B8
Liepājas ezers *Latvia* **30** B8
Lier *Belgium* **17** C4
Liernais *France* **19** E11
Lieşti *Romania* **29** E12
Lietuva = Lithuania ■
   Europe **32** E2
Liévin *France* **19** B9
Lièvre → *Canada* **104** C4
Liezen *Austria* **26** D7
Liffey → *Ireland* **12** C5
Lifford *Ireland* **12** B4
Liffré *France* **18** D5
Lifudzin *Russia* **54** B7
Ligao *Phil.* **61** E5
Lightning Ridge *Australia* **95** D4
Lignano Sabbiadoro *Italy* **41** C10
Ligny-en-Barrois *France* **19** D12
Ligonha → *Mozam.* **87** F4
Ligonier *U.S.A.* **114** F5
Ligourio *Greece* **46** D5
Ligueil *France* **18** E7
Liguria □ *Italy* **40** D5
Ligurian Sea *Medit.* **40** E5
Lihou Reefs and Cays
   Australia **94** B5
Lihue *U.S.A.* **106** b
Lihué Calel △ *Argentina* **126** D2
Lijiang *China* **58** D3
Likasi *Dem. Rep. of the Congo* **87** E2
Likenäs *Sweden* **10** D7
Likhoslavl *Russia* **32** D8
Likhovskoy *Russia* **33** H11
Likoma I. *Malawi* **87** E3
Likumburu *Tanzania* **87** D4
L'Île-Bouchard *France* **18** E7
L'Île-Rousse *France* **21** F12
Liling *China* **59** D9
Lilla Edet *Sweden* **11** F6
Lille *France* **19** B10
Lille Bælt *Denmark* **11** J3
Lillebonne *France* **18** C7
Lillehammer *Norway* **8** F14
Lillesand *Norway* **9** G13
Lillhärdal *Sweden* **10** C8

Lillian Pt. *Australia* **93** E4
Lillo *Spain* **36** F7
Lillooet *Canada* **102** C4
Lillooet → *Canada* **102** D4
Lilongwe *Malawi* **87** E3
Liloy *Phil.* **63** C6
Lim → *Europe* **44** C3
Lim Chu Kang *Singapore* **65** d
Lima *Indonesia* **63** E7
Lima *Peru* **124** F3
Lima *Mont., U.S.A.* **108** D7
Lima *Ohio, U.S.A.* **113** E11
Lima → *Portugal* **36** D2
Liman *Indonesia* **63** G14
Liman *Russia* **35** H8
Limanowa *Poland* **31** J7
Limassol *Cyprus* **49** E12
Limavady *U.K.* **12** A5
Limay → *Argentina* **128** D3
Limay Mahuida *Argentina* **126** D2
Limbach-Oberfrohna
   Germany **24** E8
Limbang *Brunei* **62** D5
Limbara, Mte. *Italy* **42** B2
Limbaži *Latvia* **32** D3
Limbdi *India* **68** H4
Limbe *Cameroon* **83** E6
Limburg *Germany* **25** E4
Limburg □ *Belgium* **17** C5
Limburg □ *Neths.* **17** C5
Limedsforsen *Sweden* **10** D7
Limeira *Brazil* **127** A6
Limenaria *Greece* **45** F8
Limenas Chersonisou *Greece* **47** F7
Limerick *Ireland* **12** D3
Limerick *U.S.A.* **115** C14
Limerick □ *Ireland* **12** D3
Limestone *U.S.A.* **114** D6
Limestone → *Canada* **103** B10
Limfjorden *Denmark* **11** H3
Limia = Lima → *Portugal* **36** D2
Limingen *Norway* **8** D15
Limmared *Sweden* **11** G7
Limmen Bight *Australia* **94** A2
Limmen Bight → *Australia* **94** B2
Limni *Greece* **46** C5
Límnos *Greece* **47** B7
Limoges *Canada* **115** A9
Limoges *France* **20** C5
Limón *Costa Rica* **120** E3
Limon *U.S.A.* **108** G12
Limone Piemonte *Italy* **40** D4
Limousin □ *France* **20** C5
Limousin, Plateaux du
   France **20** C5
Limoux *France* **20** E6
Limpopo → *S. Africa* **89** C4
Limpopo → *Africa* **89** D5
Limuru *Kenya* **86** C4
Lin Xian *China* **56** F6
Lin'an *China* **59** B12
Linapacan I. *Phil.* **61** F3
Linapacan Str. *Phil.* **61** F3
Linares *Chile* **126** D1
Linares *Mexico* **119** C5
Linares *Spain* **37** G7
Linaro, Capo *Italy* **41** F8
Línas Mte. *Italy* **42** C1
Linate, Milano ✈ (LIN) *Italy* **40** C6
Lincang *China* **58** F3
Lincheng *China* **56** F8
Linchuan *China* **59** D11
Lincoln *Argentina* **126** C3
Lincoln *Canada* **114** C5
Lincoln *N.Z.* **91** E4
Lincoln *U.K.* **14** D7
Lincoln *Calif., U.S.A.* **110** G5
Lincoln *Ill., U.S.A.* **112** E9
Lincoln *Kans., U.S.A.* **112** F5
Lincoln *Maine, U.S.A.* **113** C19
Lincoln *N.H., U.S.A.* **115** B13
Lincoln *N. Mex., U.S.A.* **109** K11
Lincoln *Nebr., U.S.A.* **112** E5
Lincoln City *U.S.A.* **108** D1
Lincoln Hav = Lincoln Sea
   Arctic **98** A14
Lincoln Sea *Arctic* **98** A14
Lincolnshire □ *U.K.* **14** D7
Lincolnshire Wolds *U.K.* **14** D7
Lincolnton *U.S.A.* **117** D14
Lind *U.S.A.* **108** C4
Linda *U.S.A.* **110** F5
Lindau *Germany* **25** H5
Lindeman I. *Australia* **94** J7
Linden *Guyana* **124** B7
Linden *Ala., U.S.A.* **117** E11
Linden *Calif., U.S.A.* **110** G5
Linden *Tex., U.S.A.* **116** E7
Lindenhurst *U.S.A.* **115** F11
Lindesberg *Sweden* **10** E9
Lindesnes *Norway* **9** H12
Líndi *Tanzania* **87** D4
Lindi □ *Tanzania* **87** D4
Lindi →
   Dem. Rep. of the Congo **86** B2
Lindö *Sweden* **11** F10
Lindome *Sweden* **11** G6

Lindos *Greece* **49** C10
Lindos, Ákra *Greece* **49** C10
Lindoso *Portugal* **36** D2
Lindow *Germany* **24** C8
Lindsay *Canada* **114** B6
Lindsay *Calif., U.S.A.* **110** J7
Lindsay *Okla., U.S.A.* **116** D6
Lindsborg *U.S.A.* **112** F5
Lindsdal *Sweden* **11** H10
Line Islands *Pac. Oc.* **97** H12
Linesville *U.S.A.* **114** E4
Linfen *China* **56** F6
Ling Xian *Hunan, China* **59** D9
Ling Xian *Shandong, China* **56** F9
Lingao *China* **64** C7
Lingayen *Phil.* **61** C4
Lingayen G. *Phil.* **61** C4
Lingbi *China* **57** H9
Lingbo *Sweden* **10** C10
Lingchuan
   Guangxi Zhuangzu, China **59** E8
Lingchuan *Shanxi, China* **56** G7
Lingen *Germany* **24** C3
Lingga *Indonesia* **62** E2
Lingga, Kepulauan *Indonesia* **62** E2
Lingga Arch. = Lingga,
   Kepulauan *Indonesia* **62** E2
Linghem *Sweden* **11** F9
Lingle *U.S.A.* **108** E11
Lingqiu *China* **56** E8
Lingshan *China* **58** F7
Lingshi *China* **56** F6
Lingshou *China* **56** E8
Lingshui *China* **64** C8
Lingtai *China* **56** G4
Linguère *Senegal* **82** B1
Lingui *China* **59** E8
Lingwu *China* **56** E4
Lingyuan *China* **57** D10
Lingyun *China* **58** E6
Linhai *China* **59** C13
Linhares *Brazil* **125** G10
Linhe *China* **56** D4
Linjiang *China* **57** D14
Linköping *Sweden* **11** F9
Linkou *China* **57** B16
Linli *China* **59** C8
Linnhe, L. *U.K.* **13** E3
Linqi *China* **56** G7
Linqing *China* **56** F8
Linqu *China* **57** F10
Linru *China* **56** G7
Lins *Brazil* **127** A6
Linshui *China* **58** B6
Linstead *Jamaica* **120** a
Linta → *Madag.* **89** D7
Linth → *Switz.* **25** H5
Linthal *Switz.* **25** J5
Linton *Ind., U.S.A.* **112** F10
Linton *N. Dak., U.S.A.* **112** B3
Lintong *China* **56** G5
Linwood *Canada* **114** C4
Linwu *China* **59** E9
Linxi *China* **57** C10
Linxia *China* **60** C5
Linxiang *China* **59** C9
Linyanti → *Africa* **88** B4
Linyi *China* **57** G10
Linz *Austria* **26** C7
Linz *Germany* **24** E3
Linzhenzhen *China* **56** F5
Linzi *China* **57** F10
Lion, G. du *France* **20** E7
Lionárisso *Cyprus* **49** D13
Lioni *Italy* **43** B8
Lions, G. of = Lion, G. du
   France **20** E7
Lion's Den *Zimbabwe* **87** F3
Lion's Head *Canada* **114** B3
Liozno = Lyozna *Belarus* **32** E6
Lipa *Phil.* **61** E4
Lipali *Mozam.* **87** F4
Lipany *Slovak Rep.* **27** B13
Lípari *Italy* **43** D7
Lípari, I. *Italy* **43** D7
Lípari, Is. = Éolie, Ís. *Italy* **43** D7
Lipcani *Moldova* **29** B11
Lipeni *Finland* **8** E23
Lipetsk *Russia* **33** F10
Lipetsk □ *Russia* **34** D4
Lipiany *Poland* **31** E1
Liping *China* **58** D7
Lipisi *Greece* **47** D8
Lipkany = Lipcani *Moldova* **29** B11
Lipník nad Bečvou
   Czech Rep. **27** B10
Lipno *Poland* **31** F6
Lipova *Romania* **28** D6
Lipovets *Ukraine* **23** D15
Lippe → *Germany* **24** D2
Lippstadt *Germany* **24** D4
Lipscomb *U.S.A.* **116** C4
Lipsk *Poland* **30** E10
Lipsko *Poland* **31** G8
Liptovský Hrádok
   Slovak Rep. **27** B12

Liptovský Milkuláš
   Slovak Rep. **27** B12
Liptrap, C. *Australia* **95** F4
Lipu *China* **59** E8
Lira *Uganda* **86** B3
Liri → *Italy* **42** A6
Liria = Llíria *Spain* **39** F4
Lisala *Dem. Rep. of the Congo* **84** D4
Lisboa *Portugal* **37** G1
Lisboa □ *Portugal* **37** F1
Lisboa ✈ (LIS) *Portugal* **37** G1
Lisbon = Lisboa *Portugal* **37** G1
Lisbon *N. Dak., U.S.A.* **112** B5
Lisbon *N.H., U.S.A.* **115** B13
Lisbon *Ohio, U.S.A.* **114** F4
Lisbon Falls *U.S.A.* **113** D18
Lisburn *U.K.* **12** B5
Lisburne, C. *U.S.A.* **4** C17
Liscannor B. *Ireland* **12** D2
Liscia → *Italy* **42** A2
Lisdoonvarna *Ireland* **12** C2
Lishe Jiang → *China* **58** E3
Lishi *China* **56** F6
Lishu *China* **57** C13
Lishui *Jiangsu, China* **59** B12
Lishui *Zhejiang, China* **59** C12
Lisianski I. *U.S.A.* **96** E10
Lisichansk = Lysychansk
   Ukraine **33** H10
Lisieux *France* **18** C7
Liski *Russia* **33** G10
L'Isle-Jourdain *Gers, France* **20** E5
L'Isle-Jourdain *Vienne, France* **20** B4
L'Isle-sur-la-Sorgue *France* **21** E9
Lisle-sur-Tarn *France* **20** E5
Lismore *Australia* **95** D5
Lismore *Ireland* **12** D4
Lisos → *Greece* **45** E9
Lista *Norway* **9** G12
Lister, Mt. *Antarctica* **5** D11
Liston *Australia* **95** D5
Listowel *Canada* **114** C4
Listowel *Ireland* **12** D2
Lit *Sweden* **10** A8
Lit-et-Mixe *France* **20** D2
Litang *Guangxi Zhuangzu,
   China* **58** F7
Litang *Sichuan, China* **58** B3
Litang Qu → *China* **58** C3
Litani → *Lebanon* **74** B4
Litchfield *Calif., U.S.A.* **110** E6
Litchfield *Conn., U.S.A.* **115** E11
Litchfield *Ill., U.S.A.* **112** F9
Litchfield *Minn., U.S.A.* **112** C6
Litchfield △ *Australia* **92** B5
Liteni *Romania* **29** C11
Lithgow *Australia* **95** E5
Líthino, Ákra *Greece* **49** E6
Lithuania ■ *Europe* **32** E2
Litija *Slovenia* **41** B11
Lititz *U.S.A.* **115** F8
Litoměřice *Czech Rep.* **26** A7
Litomyšl *Czech Rep.* **27** B9
Litschau *Austria* **26** C8
Little Abaco *Bahamas* **120** A4
Little Barrier I. *N.Z.* **91** B5
Little Belt Mts. *U.S.A.* **108** C8
Little Bighorn Battlefield △
   U.S.A. **108** D10
Little Blue → *U.S.A.* **112** F5
Little Buffalo → *Canada* **102** A6
Little Cayman *Cayman Is.* **120** C3
Little Churchill → *Canada* **103** B9
Little Colorado → *U.S.A.* **109** H8
Little Current *Canada* **104** C3
Little Current → *Canada* **104** B3
Little Falls *Minn., U.S.A.* **112** C6
Little Falls *N.Y., U.S.A.* **115** C10
Little Fork → *U.S.A.* **112** A7
Little Grand Rapids *Canada* **103** C9
Little Humboldt → *U.S.A.* **108** F5
Little Inagua I. *Bahamas* **121** B5
Little Karoo *S. Africa* **88** E3
Little Khingan Mts. = Xiao
   Hinggan Ling *China* **60** B7
Little Lake *U.S.A.* **111** K9
Little Laut Is. = Laut Kecil,
   Kepulauan *Indonesia* **62** E5
Little Mecatina = Petit-
   Mécatina → *Canada* **105** B8
Little Minch *U.K.* **13** D2
Little Missouri → *U.S.A.* **112** B2
Little Ouse → *U.K.* **15** E9
Little Rann *India* **68** H4
Little Red → *U.S.A.* **116** D9
Little River *N.Z.* **91** E4
Little Rock *U.S.A.* **116** D8
Little Ruaha → *Tanzania* **86** D4
Little Sable Pt. *U.S.A.* **112** D10
Little Scarcies → *S. Leone* **82** D2
Little Sioux → *U.S.A.* **112** E5
Little Smoky → *Canada* **102** C5
Little Snake → *U.S.A.* **108** F9
Little Tobago *Trin. & Tob.* **125** J16
Little Valley *U.S.A.* **114** D6
Little Wabash → *U.S.A.* **112** G9

Little White → *U.S.A.* **112** D3
Little Zab = Zāb aş
   Şaghīr → *Iraq* **73** E10
Littlefield *U.S.A.* **116** E3
Littlehampton *U.K.* **15** G7
Littleton *U.S.A.* **115** B13
Liu He → *China* **57** D11
Liu Jiang → *China* **58** F7
Liuba *China* **56** H4
Liucheng *China* **58** E7
Liugou *China* **57** D10
Liuhe *China* **57** C13
Liuheng Dao *China* **59** C14
Liujiang *China* **58** E7
Liukang Tenggaja =
   Sabalana, Kepulauan
   Indonesia **63** F5
Liuli *Tanzania* **87** E3
Liupanshui *China* **58** D5
Liuwa Plain *Zambia* **85** G4
Liuyang *China* **59** C10
Liuzhou *China* **58** E7
Liuzhuang *China* **57** H11
Livada *Romania* **28** C8
Livadero *Greece* **44** F5
Livadhia *Cyprus* **49** E12
Livadi *Greece* **46** A4
Livadia *Greece* **46** C4
Livarot *France* **18** D7
Live Oak *Calif., U.S.A.* **110** F5
Live Oak *Fla., U.S.A.* **117** F13
Lively *Canada* **113** B13
Liveras *Cyprus* **49** D11
Livermore *U.S.A.* **110** H5
Livermore, Mt. *U.S.A.* **116** F2
Livermore Falls *U.S.A.* **113** C18
Liverpool *Canada* **105** D7
Liverpool *U.K.* **14** D4
Liverpool *U.S.A.* **115** C8
Liverpool Bay *U.K.* **14** D4
Liverpool Ra. *Australia* **95** E5
Livigno *Italy* **40** B7
Livingston *Guatemala* **120** C2
Livingston *U.K.* **13** F5
Livingston *Ala., U.S.A.* **117** E10
Livingston *Calif., U.S.A.* **110** H6
Livingston *Mont., U.S.A.* **108** D8
Livingston *S.C., U.S.A.* **117** E14
Livingston *Tenn., U.S.A.* **117** C12
Livingston *Tex., U.S.A.* **116** F7
Livingston Manor *U.S.A.* **115** E10
Livingston, L. *U.S.A.* **116** F7
Livingstone *Zambia* **87** F2
Livingstone Mts. *Tanzania* **87** D3
Livingstonia *Malawi* **87** E3
Livingtsi *Ukraine* **29** B11
Livny *Russia* **33** F9
Livonia *Mich., U.S.A.* **113** D12
Livonia *N.Y., U.S.A.* **114** D7
Livorno *Italy* **40** E7
Livradois-Forez △ *France* **20** E7
Livramento *Brazil* **127** C4
Livron-sur-Drôme *France* **21** D8
Liwale *Tanzania* **87** D4
Liwiec → *Poland* **31** F8
Liwonde △ *Malawi* **87** E4
Lixi *China* **58** D4
Lixian *China* **58** B4
Lixouri *Greece* **46** C2
Liyang *China* **59** B12
Lizard I. *Australia* **94** A4
Lizard Pt. *U.K.* **15** H2
Lizzano *Italy* **43** B10
Ljig *Serbia* **44** B4
Ljubija *Bos.-H.* **41** D13
Ljubinje *Bos.-H.* **44** D2
Ljubišnja *Europe* **44** C3
Ljubljana *Slovenia* **41** B11
Ljubljana ✈ (LJU) *Slovenia* **41** B11
Ljubno *Slovenia* **41** B11
Ljubovija *Serbia* **44** B3
Ljugarn *Sweden* **11** G12
Ljung *Sweden* **11** G7
Ljungan → *Sweden* **10** B11
Ljungaverk *Sweden* **10** B10
Ljungby *Sweden* **11** H7
Ljungbyholm *Sweden* **11** H10
Ljungdalen *Sweden* **10** B6
Ljungsbro *Sweden* **11** F9
Ljungskile *Sweden* **11** F5
Ljusdal *Sweden* **10** C10
Ljusfallshammar *Sweden* **11** F9
Ljusnan → *Sweden* **10** C11
Ljusne *Sweden* **10** C11

Llangollen *U.K.* **14** E4
Llanidloes *U.K.* **15** E4
Llano *U.S.A.* **116** F5
Llano → *U.S.A.* **116** F5
Llano Estacado *U.S.A.* **116** E3
Llanos *S. Amer.* **124** C4
Llanos de Challe △ *Chile* **126** B1
Llanquihue, L. *Chile* **128** E1
Llanwrtyd Wells *U.K.* **15** E4
Llebeig, C. des *Spain* **48** B9
Lleida *Spain* **38** D5
Lleida □ *Spain* **38** C6
Llentrisca, C. *Spain* **48** C7
Llera de Canales *Mexico* **119** C5
Llerena *Spain* **37** G5
Lleyn Peninsula *U.K.* **14** E3
Llico *Chile* **126** C1
Llíria *Spain* **39** F4
Llívia *Spain* **20** F5
Llobregat → *Spain* **38** D7
Llodio *Spain* **38** B2
Lloret de Mar *Spain* **38** D7
Lloyd B. *Australia* **94** A3
Lloyd L. *Canada* **103** B7
Lloydminster *Canada* **103** C7
Llucena del Cid *Spain* **38** E4
Llucmajor *Spain* **48** B9
Llullaillaco, Volcán
   S. Amer. **126** A2
Llullaillaco △ *Chile* **126** A2
Lo → *Vietnam* **64** B5
Loa *U.S.A.* **108** G8
Loa → *Chile* **126** A1
Loaita I. *S. China Sea* **62** B4
Loange →
   Dem. Rep. of the Congo **84** E4
Loano *Italy* **40** D5
Lobatse *Botswana* **88** D4
Löbau *Germany* **24** D10
Lobenstein *Germany* **24** E7
Lobería *Argentina* **126** D4
Löberöd *Sweden* **11** J7
Łobez *Poland* **30** E2
Lobito *Angola* **85** G2
Lobo → *Ivory C.* **82** D3
Lobos *Argentina* **126** D4
Lobos, I. *Mexico* **118** B2
Lobos, I. de *Canary Is.* **48** F6
Łobżenica *Poland* **31** E4
Loc Binh *Vietnam* **64** B6
Loc Ninh *Vietnam* **65** G6
Locarno *Switz.* **25** J4
Loch Baghasdail =
   Lochboisdale *U.K.* **13** D1
Loch Garman = Wexford
   Ireland **12** D5
Loch Lomond and the
   Trossachs △ *U.K.* **13** E4
Loch Nam Madadh =
   Lochmaddy *U.K.* **13** D1
Lochaber *U.K.* **13** E3
Locharbriggs *U.K.* **13** F5
Lochboisdale *U.K.* **13** D1
Loche, L. La *Canada* **103** B7
Lochem *Neths.* **17** B6
Loches *France* **18** E7
Lochgilphead *U.K.* **13** E3
Lochinvar △ *Zambia* **87** F2
Lochinver *U.K.* **13** C3
Lochmaddy *U.K.* **13** D1
Lochnagar *Australia* **94** C4
Lochnagar *U.K.* **13** E5
Lochów *Poland* **31** F8
Lochy, L. *U.K.* **13** E4
Lock *Australia* **95** E2
Lock Haven *U.S.A.* **114** E7
Lockeford *U.S.A.* **110** G5
Lockeport *Canada* **105** D6
Lockerbie *U.K.* **13** F5
Lockhart *U.S.A.* **116** G6
Lockhart, L. *Australia* **93** F2
Lockhart River *Australia* **94** A3
Lockney *U.S.A.* **116** D4
Lockport *U.S.A.* **114** C6
Locminé *France* **18** E4
Locri *Italy* **43** D9
Locronan *France* **18** D2
Lod *Israel* **74** D3
Lodeïnoye Pole *Russia* **32** B7
Lodève *France* **20** E7
Lodge Bay *Canada* **105** B8
Lodge Grass *U.S.A.* **108** D10
Lodhran *Pakistan* **68** E4
Lodi *Italy* **40** C6
Lodi *Calif., U.S.A.* **110** G5
Lodi *Ohio, U.S.A.* **114** E3
Lodja *Dem. Rep. of the Congo* **86** C1
Lodosa *Spain* **38** C2
Lödöse *Sweden* **11** F6
Lodwar *Kenya* **86** B4
Łódź *Poland* **31** G6
Łódzkie □ *Poland* **31** G6
Loei *Thailand* **64** D3
Loengo *Dem. Rep. of the Congo* **86** C2
Loeriesfontein *S. Africa* **88** E2
Lofa □ *Liberia* **82** D2
Lofa Mano △ *Liberia* **82** D2

Lofer *Austria* **26** D5
Lofoten *Norway* **8** B16
Lofsdalen *Sweden* **10** B7
Lofsen ➤ *Sweden* **10** B7
Loftahammar *Sweden* **11** G10
Loga *Niger* **83** C5
Logan *Iowa, U.S.A.* **112** E6
Logan *Ohio, U.S.A.* **113** F12
Logan *Utah, U.S.A.* **108** F8
Logan *W. Va., U.S.A.* **113** G13
Logan, Mt. *Canada* **100** C5
Logandale *U.S.A.* **111** J12
Logansport *Ind., U.S.A.* **112** E10
Logansport *La., U.S.A.* **116** F8
Logirim *Sudan* **81** G3
Logo *Sudan* **81** F3
Logone ➤ *Chad* **79** F9
Logone *Sudan* **81** G3
Logroño *Spain* **38** C2
Logrosán *Spain* **37** F5
Løgstør *Denmark* **11** H3
Løgumkloster *Denmark* **11** J2
Lohals *Denmark* **11** J4
Lohardaga *India* **69** H11
Loharia *India* **68** H6
Loharu *India* **68** E6
Lohja *Finland* **32** B3
Löhne *Germany* **24** C4
Lohr *Germany* **25** F5
Lohri Wah ➤ *Pakistan* **68** F2
Loi-kaw *Burma* **67** K20
Loimaa *Finland* **32** B2
Loir ➤ *France* **18** E6
Loir-et-Cher □ *France* **18** E8
Loire □ *France* **21** C8
Loire ➤ *France* **18** E4
Loire Anjou Touraine △
   France **18** E6
Loire-Atlantique □ *France* **18** E5
Loiret □ *France* **19** E10
Loitz *Germany* **24** B9
Loja *Ecuador* **124** D3
Loja *Spain* **37** H6
Loji = Kawasi *Indonesia* **63** E7
Lojo = Lohja *Finland* **32** B3
Lojung *China* **58** E7
Loka *Sudan* **81** G3
Lokandu
   Dem. Rep. of the Congo **86** C2
Lokeren *Belgium* **17** C3
Lokgwabe *Botswana* **88** C3
Lokhvitsa *Ukraine* **33** G7
Lokichar *Kenya* **86** B4
Lokichokio *Kenya* **86** B3
Lokitaung *Kenya* **86** B4
Lokkan tekojärvi *Finland* **8** C22
Løkken *Denmark* **11** G3
Loknya *Russia* **32** D6
Loko *Nigeria* **83** D6
Lokoja *Nigeria* **83** D6
Lokoro ➤
   Dem. Rep. of the Congo **84** E3
Lokot *Russia* **33** F8
Lol ➤ *Sudan* **81** F2
Lola *Guinea* **82** D3
Lola, Mt. *U.S.A.* **110** F6
Lolgorien *Kenya* **86** C3
Lolibai, Gebel *Sudan* **81** G3
Lolimi *Sudan* **81** G3
Loliondo *Tanzania* **86** C4
Lolland *Denmark* **11** K5
Lollar *Germany* **24** E4
Lolo *U.S.A.* **108** C6
Lolodorf *Cameroon* **83** E7
Lom *Bulgaria* **44** C7
Lom ➤ *Bulgaria* **44** C7
Lom Kao *Thailand* **64** D3
Lom Sak *Thailand* **64** D3
Loma *U.S.A.* **108** C8
Loma Linda *U.S.A.* **111** L9
Loma Mansa *S. Leone* **82** D2
Lomaloma *Fiji* **91** a
Lomami ➤
   Dem. Rep. of the Congo **86** B1
Lomas de Zamóra *Argentina* **126** C4
Lombadina *Australia* **92** C3
Lombárdia □ *Italy* **40** C6
Lombardy = Lombárdia □
   Italy **40** C6
Lombez *France* **20** E4
Lomblen *Indonesia* **63** F6
Lombok *Indonesia* **62** F5
Lombok, Selat *Indonesia* **63** K18
Lomé *Togo* **83** D5
Lomela *Dem. Rep. of the Congo* **84** E4
Lomela ➤
   Dem. Rep. of the Congo **84** E4
Lomianki *Poland* **31** F7
Lomma *Sweden* **11** J7
Lommel *Belgium* **17** C5
Lomond *Canada* **102** C6
Lomond, L. *U.K.* **13** E4
Lomonosov Ridge *Arctic* **4** A
Lomphat *Cambodia* **64** F6
Lompobatang *Indonesia* **63** F5
Lompoc *U.S.A.* **111** L6
Łomża *Poland* **31** E9

Lon, Ko *Thailand* **65** a
Loncoche *Chile* **128** D2
Londa *India* **66** M9
Londiani *Kenya* **86** C4
Londinières *France* **18** C8
London *Canada* **114** D3
London *U.K.* **15** F7
London *Ky., U.S.A.* **113** G11
London *Ohio, U.S.A.* **113** F12
London, Greater □ *U.K.* **15** F7
London Gatwick ✈ (LGW)
   U.K. **15** F7
London Heathrow ✈
   (LHR) *U.K.* **15** F7
London Stansted ✈ (STN)
   U.K. **15** F5
Londonderry *U.K.* **12** B4
Londonderry □ *U.K.* **12** B4
Londonderry, C. *Australia* **92** B4
Londonderry, I. *Chile* **128** H2
Londres *Argentina* **128** B3
Londrina *Brazil* **127** A5
Lone Pine *U.S.A.* **110** J8
Lonely Mine *Zimbabwe* **89** B4
Long B. *U.S.A.* **117** E15
Long Beach *Calif., U.S.A.* **111** M8
Long Beach *N.Y., U.S.A.* **115** F11
Long Beach *Wash., U.S.A.* **110** D2
Long Branch *U.S.A.* **115** F11
Long Creek *U.S.A.* **108** D4
Long Eaton *U.K.* **14** E6
Long I. *Australia* **94** J6
Long I. *Bahamas* **121** B4
Long I. *Canada* **104** B4
Long I. *Ireland* **12** E2
Long I. *U.S.A.* **115** F11
Long Island Sd. *U.S.A.* **115** E12
Long L. *Canada* **104** C2
Long Lake *U.S.A.* **115** C10
Long Point B. *Canada* **114** D4
Long Prairie *U.S.A.* **112** C6
Long Pt. ➤ *U.S.A.* **112** B6
Long Pt. *Canada* **114** D4
Long Range Mts. *Canada* **105** C8
Long Reef *Australia* **92** B4
Long Spruce *Canada* **103** B10
Long Str. = Longa, Proliv
   Russia **4** C16
Long Thanh *Vietnam* **65** G6
Long Xian *China* **56** G4
Long Xuyen *Vietnam* **65** G5
Longa *Greece* **46** E3
Longa, Proliv *Russia* **4** C16
Long'an *China* **58** F6
Longarone *Italy* **41** B9
Longbenton *U.K.* **14** B6
Longboat Key *U.S.A.* **117** H13
Longchang *China* **58** C5
Longchi *China* **58** C4
Longchuan *Guangdong,*
   China **59** E10
Longchuan *Yunnan, China* **58** E1
Longde *China* **56** G4
Longeau *France* **19** E12
Longford *Australia* **95** G4
Longford *Ireland* **12** C4
Longford □ *Ireland* **12** C4
Longhai *China* **59** E11
Longhua *China* **57** D9
Longhui *China* **59** D8
Longido *Tanzania* **86** C4
Longiram *Indonesia* **62** E5
Longkou *Jiangxi, China* **59** D10
Longkou *Shandong, China* **57** F11
Longlac *Canada* **104** C2
Longli *China* **58** D6
Longlin *China* **58** E5
Longling *China* **58** E2
Longmeadow *U.S.A.* **115** D12
Longmen *China* **59** F10
Longming *China* **58** F6
Longmont *U.S.A.* **108** F11
Longnan *China* **59** E10
Longnawan *Indonesia* **62** D4
Longobucco *Italy* **43** C9
Longquan *China* **59** C12
Longreach *Australia* **94** C3
Longshan *China* **58** C7
Longsheng *China* **59** E8
Longué-Jumelles *France* **18** E6
Longueau *France* **19** C9
Longueuil *Canada* **115** A11
Longuyon *France* **19** C12
Longvic *France* **19** E12
Longview *Tex., U.S.A.* **116** E7
Longview *Wash., U.S.A.* **110** D4
Longwy *France* **19** C12
Łosice *Poland* **31** F9
Lošinj *Croatia* **41** D11
Loskop Dam *S. Africa* **89** D4
Losning *Denmark* **11** J3
Lossiemouth *U.K.* **13** D5
Lossnen △ *Sweden* **10** B6
Lostwithiel *U.K.* **15** G3
Lot □ *France* **20** D5
Lot ➤ *France* **20** D4
Lot-et-Garonne □ *France* **20** D4
Lota *Chile* **126** D1

Lons-le-Saunier *France* **19** F12
Lönsboda *Sweden* **11** H8
Looe *U.K.* **15** G3
Lookout, C. *Canada* **104** A3
Lookout, C. *U.S.A.* **117** D16
Loolmalasin *Tanzania* **86** C4
Loon ➤ *Alta., Canada* **102** B5
Loon ➤ *Man., Canada* **103** B8
Loon Lake *Canada* **103** C7
Loongana *Australia* **93** F4
Loop Hd. *Ireland* **12** D2
Lop Buri *Thailand* **64** E3
Lop Nor = Lop Nur *China* **60** B4
Lop Nur *China* **60** B4
Lopare *Bos.-H.* **28** F3
Lopatin *Russia* **35** J8
Lopatina, Gora *Russia* **53** D15
Lopaye *Sudan* **81** F3
Lopez *Phil.* **61** E5
Lopez *U.S.A.* **115** E8
Lopez, C. *Gabon* **84** E1
Lopphavet *Norway* **8** A19
Loppi *Finland* **32** B3
Lora ➤ *Afghan.* **66** D4
Lora, Hāmūn-i- *Pakistan* **66** E4
Lora Cr. ➤ *Australia* **95** D2
Lora del Río *Spain* **37** H5
Lorain *U.S.A.* **114** E2
Loralai *Pakistan* **68** D3
Lorca *Spain* **39** H3
Lord Howe I. *Pac. Oc.* **90** E8
Lord Howe Rise *Pac. Oc.* **96** L8
Lordsburg *U.S.A.* **109** K9
Lorestān □ *Iran* **71** C6
Loreto *Brazil* **125** E9
Loreto *Italy* **41** E10
Loreto *Mexico* **118** B2
Lorgues *France* **21** E10
Lorhosso *Burkina Faso* **82** C4
Lorient *France* **18** E3
Lőrinci *Hungary* **28** C4
Loris *U.S.A.* **117** C15
Lorn, Firth of *U.K.* **13** E3
Lorne *Australia* **95** F3
Loronyo *Sudan* **81** G3
Lorovouno *Cyprus* **49** D11
Lörrach *Germany* **25** H3
Lorraine □ *France* **19** D13
Lorraine □ *France* **19** D12
Los *Sweden* **10** C9
Los, Îles de *Guinea* **82** D2
Los Alamos *Calif., U.S.A.* **111** L6
Los Alamos *N. Mex., U.S.A.* **109** J10
Los Alcornocales △ *Spain* **37** J5
Los Altos *U.S.A.* **110** H5
Los Andes *Chile* **126** C1
Los Angeles *Chile* **126** D1
Los Angeles *U.S.A.* **111** M8
Los Angeles, Bahia de
   Mexico **118** B2
Los Angeles Aqueduct
   U.S.A. **111** K9
Los Angeles Int. ✈ (LAX)
   U.S.A. **111** M8
Los Banos *U.S.A.* **110** H6
Los Barrios *Spain* **37** J5
Los Blancos *Argentina* **126** A3
Los Cardones △ *Argentina* **126** B2
Los Chiles *Costa Rica* **120** D3
Los Corrales de Buelna *Spain* **36** B6
Los Cristianos *Canary Is.* **48** F3
Los Gallardos *Spain* **39** H3
Los Gatos *U.S.A.* **110** H5
Los Haïtises △ *Dom. Rep.* **121** C6
Los Hermanos Is. *Venezuela* **121** D7
Los Islotes *Canary Is.* **48** E6
Los Llanos de Aridane
   Canary Is. **48** F2
Los Loros *Chile* **126** B1
Los Lunas *U.S.A.* **109** J10
Los Mochis *Mexico* **118** B3
Los Monegros *Spain* **38** D4
Los Nietos *Spain* **39** H4
Los Olivos *U.S.A.* **111** L6
Los Palacios *Cuba* **120** B3
Los Palacios y Villafranca
   Spain **37** H5
Los Reyes de Salgado
   Mexico **118** D4
Los Roques Is. *Venezuela* **121** D6
Los Santos de Maimona
   Spain **37** G4
Los Teques *Venezuela* **124** A5
Los Testigos, Is. *Venezuela* **124** A6
Los Vilos *Chile* **126** C1
Los Yébenes *Spain* **37** F7

Lotagipi Swamp *Sudan* **81** G3
Loṭfābād *Iran* **71** B8
Lothair *S. Africa* **89** D5
Lotorp *Sweden* **11** F9
Lötschbergtunnel *Switz.* **25** J3
Lotta ➤ *Europe* **8** B24
Löttorp *Sweden* **11** H11
Lotung *Taiwan* **59** E13
Loubomo *Congo* **84** E2
Loudéac *France* **18** D4
Loudi *China* **59** D8
Loudonville *U.S.A.* **114** F2
Loudun *France* **18** E7
Loue ➤ *France* **19** E12
Louga *Senegal* **82** B1
Louga □ *Senegal* **82** B1
Loughborough *U.K.* **14** E6
Lougheed I. *Canada* **101** B9
Loughrea *Ireland* **12** C3
Loughros More B. *Ireland* **12** B3
Louhans *France* **19** F12
Louis Trichardt *S. Africa* **89** C4
Louis XIV, Pte. *Canada* **104** B4
Louisa *U.S.A.* **113** F12
Louisbourg *Canada* **105** C8
Louisburgh *Ireland* **12** C2
Louise I. *Canada* **102** C2
Louiseville *Canada* **104** C5
Louisiade Arch. *Papua N. G.* **90** C8
Louisiana *U.S.A.* **112** F8
Louisiana □ *U.S.A.* **116** F9
Louisville *Ky., U.S.A.* **113** F11
Louisville *Miss., U.S.A.* **117** E10
Louisville *Ohio, U.S.A.* **114** F3
Louisville Ridge *Pac. Oc.* **96** L10
Loulay *France* **20** B3
Loulé *Portugal* **37** H3
Louny *Czech Rep.* **26** A6
Loup City *U.S.A.* **112** E5
Loup ➤ *U.S.A.* **112** E5
Loups Marins, Lacs des
   Canada **104** A5
Lourdes *France* **20** E3
Lourdes-de-Blanc-Sablon
   Canada **105** B8
Lourinhã *Portugal* **37** F1
Lousã *Portugal* **36** E2
Louta *Burkina Faso* **82** C4
Louth *Australia* **95** E4
Louth *Ireland* **12** C5
Louth □ *Ireland* **12** C5
Louth *U.K.* **14** D7
Louth □ *Ireland* **12** C5
Loutra Edipsou *Greece* **46** C5
Loutraki *Greece* **46** D4
Loutropoli Thermis *Greece* **47** B8
Louvain = Leuven *Belgium* **17** D4
Louviers *France* **18** C8
Louwsburg *S. Africa* **89** D5
Lovat ➤ *Russia* **32** C6
Lovćen *Montenegro* **44** D2
Lovčen △ *Serbia* **44** D2
Lovech *Bulgaria* **45** C8
Lovech □ *Bulgaria* **45** C8
Loveland *U.S.A.* **108** F11
Lovell *U.S.A.* **108** D9
Lovelock *U.S.A.* **108** F4
Lovere *Italy* **40** C7
Lóvestad *Sweden* **11** J7
Loviisa *Finland* **32** B4
Loving *U.S.A.* **109** K11
Lovington *U.S.A.* **109** K12
Lovisa = Loviisa *Finland* **32** B4
Lovosice *Czech Rep.* **26** A7
Lovran *Croatia* **41** C11
Lovrin *Romania* **28** E5
Lövstabruk *Sweden* **10** D11
Lövstabukten *Sweden* **11** D11
Low, L. *Canada* **104** B4
Low Pt. *Australia* **93** F4
Low Tatra = Nízké Tatry
   Slovak Rep. **27** C12
Lowa *Dem. Rep. of the Congo* **86** C2
Lowa ➤
   Dem. Rep. of the Congo **86** C2
Lowell *U.S.A.* **115** D13
Lowellville *U.S.A.* **114** E4
Löwen ➤ *Namibia* **88** D2
Lower Alkali L. *U.S.A.* **108** F3
Lower Arrow L. *Canada* **102** D5
Lower Austria =
   Niederösterreich □
   Austria **26** C8
Lower California = Baja
   California *Mexico* **118** A1
Lower Hutt *N.Z.* **91** D5
Lower Lake *U.S.A.* **110** G4
Lower Manitou L. *Canada* **103** D10
Lower Post *Canada* **102** B3
Lower Red L. *U.S.A.* **112** B6
Lower Saxony =
   Niedersachsen □ *Germany* **24** C4
Lower Tunguska =
   Tunguska,
   Nizhnyaya ➤ *Russia* **53** C9
Lower Zambezi △ *Zambia* **87** F2
Lowestoft *U.K.* **15** E9
Lowgar □ *Afghan.* **66** B6
Łowicz *Poland* **31** F6

Lowville *U.S.A.* **115** C9
Loxton *Australia* **95** E3
Loxton *S. Africa* **88** E3
Loyalton *U.S.A.* **110** F6
Loyalty Is. = Loyauté, Îs.
   N. Cal. **90** D9
Loyang = Luoyang *China* **56** G7
Loyev = Loyew *Belarus* **23** C16
Loyew *Belarus* **23** C16
Loyoro *Uganda* **86** B3
Lož *Slovenia* **41** C11
Lozère □ *France* **20** D7
Loznica *Serbia* **44** B3
Lozova *Ukraine* **33** H9
Lü Shan *China* **59** C11
Lü Tao *Taiwan* **59** F13
Luachimo *Angola* **84** F4
Luajan ➤ *India* **69** G11
Lualaba ➤
   Dem. Rep. of the Congo **86** B2
Luampa *Zambia* **87** F1
Lu'an *China* **59** B11
Luan Chau *Vietnam* **58** G4
Luan He ➤ *China* **57** E10
Luan Xian *China* **57** E10
Luancheng
   Guangxi Zhuangzu, China **58** F7
Luancheng *Hebei, China* **56** F8
Luanco *Spain* **36** B5
Luanda *Angola* **84** F2
Luang, Thale *Thailand* **65** J3
Luang Prabang *Laos* **58** H4
Luangwa *Zambia* **87** F3
Luangwa ➤ *Zambia* **87** E3
Luangwa Valley *Zambia* **87** E3
Luanne *China* **57** D9
Luanping *China* **57** D9
Luanshya *Zambia* **87** E2
Luapula □ *Zambia* **87** E2
Luapula ➤ *Africa* **87** D2
Luarca *Spain* **36** B4
Luashi *Dem. Rep. of the Congo* **87** E1
Luau *Angola* **84** G4
Lubaczów *Poland* **31** H10
Lubań *Poland* **31** G2
Lubana, Ozero = Lubānas
   Ezers *Latvia* **32** D4
Lubānas Ezers *Latvia* **32** D4
Lubang *Phil.* **61** E4
Lubang Is. *Phil.* **63** B6
Lubango *Angola* **85** G2
Lubao *Dem. Rep. of the Congo* **86** D2
Lubartów *Poland* **31** G9
Lubawa *Poland* **30** E6
Lübbecke *Germany* **24** C4
Lübben *Germany* **24** D9
Lübbenau *Germany* **24** D9
Lubbock *U.S.A.* **116** E4
Lübeck *Germany* **24** B6
Lübecker Bucht *Germany* **24** A6
Lubefu *Dem. Rep. of the Congo* **86** C1
Lubefu ➤
   Dem. Rep. of the Congo **86** C1
Lubelskie □ *Poland* **31** G9
Lubero = Luofu
   Dem. Rep. of the Congo **86** C2
Luberon □ *France* **21** E9
Lubersac *France* **20** C5
Lubicon L. *Canada* **102** B5
Lubień Kujawski *Poland* **31** F6
Lubilash ➤
   Dem. Rep. of the Congo **84** F4
Lubin *Poland* **31** G3
Lublin *Poland* **31** G9
Lubliniec *Poland* **31** H5
Lubnān = Lebanon ■ *Asia* **74** B5
Lubnān, Jabal *Lebanon* **74** B4
Lubniewice *Poland* **31** F2
Lubny *Ukraine* **33** G7
Lubomierz *Poland* **31** G2
Lubon *Poland* **31** F3
Lubongola
   Dem. Rep. of the Congo **86** C2
L'ubotín *Slovak Rep.* **27** B13
Lubraniec *Poland* **31** F5
Lubsko *Poland* **31** G1
Lubtheen *Germany* **24** B7
Lubuagan *Phil.* **61** C4
Lubudi *Dem. Rep. of the Congo* **84** F5
Lubudi ➤
   Dem. Rep. of the Congo **87** D2
Lubuklinggau *Indonesia* **62** E2
Lubuksikaping *Indonesia* **62** D2
Lubumbashi
   Dem. Rep. of the Congo **87** E2
Lubunda
   Dem. Rep. of the Congo **86** D2
Lubungu *Zambia* **87** E2
Lubuskie □ *Poland* **31** F2
Lubutu *Dem. Rep. of the Congo* **86** C2
Luc An Chau *Vietnam* **64** A5
Luc-en-Diois *France* **21** D9
Lucan *Canada* **114** C3
Lucania, Mt. *Canada* **100** C5
Lucas Channel *Canada* **114** A3

Lucca *Italy* **40** E7
Lucé *France* **18** D8
Luce Bay *U.K.* **13** G4
Lucea *Jamaica* **120** a
Lucedale *U.S.A.* **117** F10
Lucena *Phil.* **61** E4
Lucena *Spain* **37** H6
Lučenec *Slovak Rep.* **27** C12
Lucera *Italy* **43** A8
Lucerne = Luzern *Switz.* **25** H4
Lucerne *U.S.A.* **110** F4
Lucerne Valley *U.S.A.* **111** L10
Lucero *Mexico* **118** A3
Luchena ➤ *Spain* **39** H3
Lucheng *China* **56** F7
Lucheringo ➤ *Mozam.* **87** E4
Lüchow *Germany* **24** C7
Luchuan *China* **59** F8
Lucia *U.S.A.* **110** J5
Lucinda *Australia* **94** B4
Luckau *Germany* **24** D9
Luckenwalde *Germany* **24** C9
Luckhoff *S. Africa* **88** D3
Lucknow *Canada* **114** C3
Lucknow *India* **69** F9
Luçon *France* **20** B2
Lüda = Dalian *China* **57** E11
Luda Kamchiya ➤
   Bulgaria **45** C11
Ludbreg *Croatia* **41** B13
Lüdenscheid *Germany* **24** D3
Lüderitz *Namibia* **88** D2
Lüderitzbaai *Namibia* **88** D2
Ludhiana *India* **68** D6
Ludian *China* **58** D4
Luding Qiao *China* **58** C4
Lüdinghausen *Germany* **24** D3
Ludington *U.S.A.* **112** D10
Ludlow *U.K.* **15** E5
Ludlow *Calif., U.S.A.* **111** L10
Ludlow *Pa., U.S.A.* **114** E6
Ludlow *Vt., U.S.A.* **115** C12
Ludus *Romania* **29** D9
Ludvika *Sweden* **10** D9
Ludwigsburg *Germany* **25** G5
Ludwigsfelde *Germany* **24** C9
Ludwigshafen *Germany* **25** F4
Ludwigslust *Germany* **24** B7
Ludza *Latvia* **32** D4
Lueki *Dem. Rep. of the Congo* **86** C2
Luena *Dem. Rep. of the Congo* **87** D2
Luena *Zambia* **87** E3
Luena Flats *Zambia* **85** G4
Luenha = Ruenya ➤ *Africa* **87** F3
Lüeyang *China* **56** H4
Lufeng *Guangdong, China* **59** F10
Lufeng *Yunnan, China* **58** E4
Lufira ➤
   Dem. Rep. of the Congo **87** D2
Lufkin *U.S.A.* **116** F7
Lufupa *Dem. Rep. of the Congo* **87** E1
Luga *Russia* **32** C5
Luga ➤ *Russia* **32** C5
Lugano *Switz.* **25** J4
Lugano, L. di *Switz.* **40** C6
Lugansk = Luhansk
   Ukraine **33** H10
Lugard's Falls *Kenya* **86** C4
Lugela *Mozam.* **87** F4
Lugenda ➤ *Mozam.* **87** E4
Lugh Ganana *Somali Rep.* **75** G3
Lugnaquillia *Ireland* **12** D5
Lugo *Italy* **41** D8
Lugo *Spain* **36** B3
Lugo □ *Spain* **36** C3
Lugoj *Romania* **28** E6
Lugovoy = Qulan *Kazakhstan* **52** E8
Luhansk *Ukraine* **33** H10
Luhansk □ *Ukraine* **33** H10
Luhe *China* **59** A12
Luhe ➤ *Germany* **24** B6
Luhuo *China* **58** B3
Lui ➤ *Angola* **84** F3
Luiana *Angola* **88** B3
Luiana ➤ *Angola* **85** H4
Luichow Pen. = Leizhou
   Bandao *China* **58** G7
Luimneach = Limerick
   Ireland **12** D3
Luing *U.K.* **13** E3
Luino *Italy* **40** C5
Luís Correia *Brazil* **125** D10
Luitpold Coast *Antarctica* **5** D1
Luiza *Dem. Rep. of the Congo* **84** F4
Luizi *Dem. Rep. of the Congo* **86** D2
Luján *Argentina* **126** C4
Lujiang *China* **59** B11
Lukang *Taiwan* **59** E13
Lukanga Swamp *Zambia* **87** E2
Lukenie ➤
   Dem. Rep. of the Congo **84** E3
Lukhisaral *India* **69** G12
Lŭki *Bulgaria* **45** E8
Lukolela
   Dem. Rep. of the Congo **86** D1
Lukosi *Zimbabwe* **87** F2

Lukovë *Albania* **44** G3
Lukovit *Bulgaria* **45** C8
Łuków *Poland* **31** G9
Lukoyanov *Russia* **34** C7
Lukusuzi △ *Zambia* **87** E3
Luleå *Sweden* **8** D20
Luleälven ➤ *Sweden* **8** D20
Lüleburgaz *Turkey* **45** E11
Luliang *China* **58** E4
Luling *U.S.A.* **116** G6
Lulong *China* **57** E10
Lulonga ➤
  Dem. Rep. of the Congo **84** D3
Lulua ➤
  Dem. Rep. of the Congo **84** E4
Luma *Amer. Samoa* **91** b
Lumajang *Indonesia* **63** H15
Lumbala N'guimbo *Angola* **85** G4
Lumberton *U.S.A.* **117** D15
Lumholtz △ *Australia* **94** B4
Lumsden *Canada* **103** C8
Lumsden *N.Z.* **91** F2
Lumut *Malaysia* **65** K3
Lumut, Tanjung *Indonesia* **62** E3
Luna *India* **68** H3
Lunan *China* **58** E4
Lunavada *India* **68** H5
Lunca *Romania* **29** C10
Lunca Corbului *Romania* **29** F9
Lund *Sweden* **11** J7
Lundazi *Zambia* **87** E3
Lunderskov *Denmark* **11** J3
Lundi ➤ *Zimbabwe* **87** G3
Lundu *Malaysia* **62** D3
Lundy *U.K.* **15** F3
Lune ➤ *U.K.* **14** C5
Lüneburg *Germany* **24** B6
Lüneburg Heath =
  Lüneburger Heide
  Germany **24** B6
Lüneburger Heide *Germany* **24** B6
Lunel *France* **21** E8
Lünen *Germany* **24** D3
Lunenburg *Canada* **105** D7
Lunéville *France* **19** D13
Lunga ➤ *Zambia* **87** E2
Lunga Lunga *Kenya* **86** C4
Lungi Airport *S. Leone* **82** D2
Lunglei *India* **67** H18
Luni *India* **68** G5
Luni ➤ *India* **68** G4
Luninets = Luninyets
  Belarus **23** B14
Luning *U.S.A.* **108** G4
Lunino *Russia* **34** D7
Luninyets *Belarus* **23** B14
Lunkaransar *India* **68** E5
Lunsemfwa ➤ *Zambia* **87** E3
Lunsemfwa Falls *Zambia* **87** E2
Luo He ➤ *China* **56** G6
Luocheng *China* **58** E7
Luochuan *China* **56** G5
Luoci *China* **58** E4
Luodian *China* **58** E6
Luoding *China* **59** F8
Luofu *Dem. Rep. of the Congo* **86** C2
Luohe *China* **56** H8
Luojiang *China* **58** B5
Luoning *China* **56** G6
Luoshan *China* **59** A10
Luotian *China* **59** B10
Luoxiao Shan *China* **59** D10
Luoyang *China* **56** G7
Luoyuan *China* **59** D12
Luozigou *China* **57** C16
Lupeni *Romania* **29** E8
Lupilichi *Mozam.* **87** E4
Łupków *Poland* **31** J9
Luping *China* **58** E5
Luquan *China* **58** E4
Luque *Paraguay* **126** B4
Luquillo, Sierra de
  Puerto Rico **121** d
Lúras *Italy* **42** B2
Luray *U.S.A.* **113** F14
Lure *France* **19** E13
Lurgan *U.K.* **12** B5
Lusaka *Zambia* **87** F2
Lusaka □ *Zambia* **87** F2
Lusambo
  Dem. Rep. of the Congo **86** C1
Lusangaye
  Dem. Rep. of the Congo **86** C2
Luseland *Canada* **103** C7
Lusenga Plain △ *Zambia* **87** D2
Lushan *Henan, China* **56** H7
Lushan *Sichuan, China* **58** B4
Lushi *China* **56** G6
Lushnjë *Albania* **44** F3
Lushui *China* **58** E2
Lüshun *China* **57** E11

Lustenau *Austria* **26** D2
Lūt, Dasht-e *Iran* **71** D8
Luta = Dalian *China* **57** E11
Lutherstadt Wittenberg
  Germany **24** D8
Luton *U.K.* **15** F7
Luton □ *U.K.* **15** F7
Lutselk'e *Canada* **103** A6
Lutsk *Ukraine* **23** C13
Lutto = Lotta ➤ *Europe* **8** B24
Lützow Holmbukta *Antarctica* **5** C4
Lutzputs *S. Africa* **88** D3
Luuq = Lugh Ganana
  Somali Rep. **75** G3
Luverne *Ala., U.S.A.* **117** F11
Luverne *Minn., U.S.A.* **112** D6
Luvua *Dem. Rep. of the Congo* **87** D2
Luvua ➤
  Dem. Rep. of the Congo **86** D2
Luvuvhu ➤ *S. Africa* **89** C5
Luwegu ➤ *Tanzania* **87** D4
Luwuk *Indonesia* **63** E6
Luxembourg *Lux.* **17** E6
Luxembourg □ *Belgium* **17** E5
Luxembourg ■ *Europe* **17** E5
Luxembourg ✈ (LUX) *Lux.* **17** E6
Luxeuil-les-Bains *France* **19** E13
Luxi *Hunan, China* **59** C8
Luxi *Yunnan, China* **58** E4
Luxi *Yunnan, China* **58** E2
Luxor = El Uqsur *Egypt* **80** B3
Luy-de-Béarn ➤ *France* **20** E3
Luy-de-France ➤ *France* **20** E3
Luyi *China* **56** H8
Luz-St-Sauveur *France* **20** F4
Luzern *Switz.* **25** H4
Luzern □ *Switz.* **25** H3
Luzhai *China* **58** E7
Luzhany *Ukraine* **29** B10
Luzhi *China* **58** D5
Luzhou *China* **58** C5
Luziânia *Brazil* **125** G9
Lužnice ➤ *Czech Rep.* **26** B7
Luzon *Phil.* **61** D4
Luzon Strait *Asia* **59** G13
Luzy *France* **19** F10
Luzzi *Italy* **43** C9
Lviv *Ukraine* **23** D13
Lviv □ *Ukraine* **33** H2
Lvov = Lviv *Ukraine* **23** D13
Lwówek *Poland* **31** F3
Lwówek Śląski *Poland* **31** G2
Lyakhavichy *Belarus* **23** B14
Lyakhovskiye, Ostrova
  Russia **53** B15
Lyaki = Läki *Azerbaijan* **35** K8
Lyal I. *Canada* **114** B3
Lyaskovets *Bulgaria* **45** C9
Lyasnaya *Belarus* **31** F10
Lyaki = Läki *Azerbaijan* **35** K8
Lybster *U.K.* **13** C5
Lycaonia *Turkey* **72** D5
Lychen *Germany* **24** B9
Lychkova *Russia* **32** D7
Lycia *Turkey* **47** E11
Lyckebyån ➤ *Sweden* **11** H9
Lycksele *Sweden* **8** D18
Lycosura *Greece* **46** D4
Lydda = Lod *Israel* **74** D3
Lyddan I. *Antarctica* **5** D2
Lydenburg *S. Africa* **89** D5
Lydia *Turkey* **47** C10
Łydynia ➤ *Poland* **31** F7
Lyell *N.Z.* **91** D4
Lyell I. *Canada* **102** C2
Lyepyel *Belarus* **32** E5
Lygnern *Sweden* **11** G6
Lykens *U.S.A.* **115** F8
Lyman *Ukraine* **29** E14
Lyman *U.S.A.* **108** F8
Lymanske *Ukraine* **29** D14
Lyme B. *U.K.* **15** G4
Lyme Regis *U.K.* **15** G5
Lymington *U.K.* **15** G6
Łyna ➤ *Poland* **30** D8
Lynchburg *U.S.A.* **113** G14
Lynd ➤ *Australia* **94** B3
Lynd Ra. *Australia* **95** D4
Lynden *Canada* **114** C4
Lynden *U.S.A.* **110** B4
Lyndhurst *Australia* **95** E4
Lyndon ➤ *Australia* **93** D1
Lyndonville *N.Y., U.S.A.* **114** C6
Lyndonville *Vt., U.S.A.* **115** B12
Lyngen *Norway* **8** B19
Lynher Reef *Australia* **92** C3
Lynn *U.S.A.* **115** D14
Lynn Haven *U.S.A.* **117** F12
Lynn Lake *Canada* **103** B8
Lynnwood *U.S.A.* **110** C4
Lynton *U.K.* **15** F4
Lyntupy *Belarus* **32** E4
Lynx L. *Canada* **103** A7
Lyon *France* **21** C8
Lyon St-Exupery ✈ (LYS)
  France **21** C9
Lyonnais *France* **21** C8
Lyons = Lyon *France* **21** C8

Lyons *Ga., U.S.A.* **117** E13
Lyons *Kans., U.S.A.* **112** F4
Lyons *N.Y., U.S.A.* **114** C8
Lyons ➤ *Australia* **93** E2
Lyons Falls *U.S.A.* **115** C9
Lyozna *Belarus* **32** E6
Lys = Leie ➤ *Belgium* **17** C3
Lysá nad Labem *Czech Rep.* **26** A7
Lysekil *Sweden* **11** F5
Lyskovo *Russia* **34** B7
Lystrup *Denmark* **11** H4
Lysvik *Sweden* **10** D7
Lysychansk *Ukraine* **33** H10
Lytham St. Anne's *U.K.* **14** D4
Lytton *Canada* **102** C4
Lyuban *Russia* **32** C6
Lyubim *Russia* **32** C11
Lyubimets *Bulgaria* **45** E10
Lyuboml *Ukraine* **31** G11
Lyubotyn *Ukraine* **33** H8
Lyubytino *Russia* **32** C7
Lyudinovo *Russia* **32** F8

M

M.R. Stefanik,
  Bratislava ✈ (BTS)
  Slovak Rep. **27** (C10)
Ma ➤ *Vietnam* **58** H5
Ma'adaba *Jordan* **74** E4
Maamba *Zambia* **88** B4
Ma'ān *Jordan* **74** E4
Ma'ān □ *Jordan* **74** F5
Maanselkä *Finland* **8** E23
Ma'anshan *China* **59** B12
Maarianhamina =
  Mariehamn *Finland* **9** F18
Ma'arrat an Nu'mān *Syria* **72** E7
Maas ➤ *Neths.* **17** C4
Maaseik *Belgium* **17** C5
Maasin *Phil.* **63** B6
Maastricht *Neths.* **17** D5
Maave *Mozam.* **89** C5
Mababe Depression
  Botswana **88** B3
Mabalane *Mozam.* **89** C5
Mabel L. *Canada* **102** C5
Mabenge
  Dem. Rep. of the Congo **86** B1
Maberly *Canada* **115** B8
Mabian *China* **58** C4
Mabil *Ethiopia* **81** E4
Mablethorpe *U.K.* **14** D8
Mably *France* **19** F11
Maboma
  Dem. Rep. of the Congo **86** B2
Mabonto *S. Leone* **82** D2
Mabrouk *Mali* **83** B4
Mabuasehube △ *Botswana* **88** D3
Mac Bac *Vietnam* **65** H6
Macachín *Argentina* **126** D3
Macaé *Brazil* **127** A7
Macael *Spain* **39** H2
Macalester *U.S.A.* **116** D7
McAllen *U.S.A.* **116** H5
MacAlpine L. *Canada* **100** C9
Macamic *Canada* **104** C4
Macao = Macau *China* **59** F9
Macão *Portugal* **37** F3
Macapá *Brazil* **125** C8
Macarao △ *Venezuela* **121** D6
McArthur ➤ *Australia* **94** B2
McArthur, Port *Australia* **94** B2
Macau *Brazil* **125** E11
Macau *China* **59** F9
McBride *Canada* **102** C4
McCall *U.S.A.* **108** D5
McCamey *U.S.A.* **116** F3
McCammon *U.S.A.* **108** E7
McCarran Int., Las
  Vegas ✈ (LAS) *U.S.A.* **111** J11
McCauley I. *Canada* **102** C2
McCleary *U.S.A.* **110** C3
McClenny *U.S.A.* **117** F13
Macclesfield *U.K.* **14** D5
M'Clintock Chan. *Canada* **100** B9
McClintock Ra. *Australia* **92** C4
McCloud *U.S.A.* **108** F2
McCluer I. *Australia* **92** B5
McClure *U.S.A.* **114** F7
McClure, L. *U.S.A.* **110** H6
M'Clure Str. *Canada* **101** B8
McClusky *U.S.A.* **112** B3
McComb *U.S.A.* **117** F9
McCook *U.S.A.* **112** E3
McCreary *Canada* **103** C9
McCullough Mt. *U.S.A.* **111** K11
McCusker ➤ *Canada* **103** B7
McDame *Canada* **102** B3
McDermitt *U.S.A.* **108** F5
McDonald *U.S.A.* **114** F4
McDonald Is. *Ind. Oc.* **3** G13
MacDonnell Ranges
  Australia **92** D5

MacDowell L. *Canada* **104** B1
Macduff *U.K.* **13** D6
Maceda *Spain* **36** C3
Macedonia △ *U.S.A.* **114** E3
Macedonia ■ *Europe* **44** E5
Maceió *Brazil* **125** E11
Macenta *Guinea* **82** D3
Macerata *Italy* **41** E10
McFarland *U.S.A.* **111** K7
McFarlane ➤ *Canada* **103** B7
Macfarlane, L. *Australia* **95** E2
McGehee *U.S.A.* **116** E9
McGill *U.S.A.* **108** G6
Macgillycuddy's Reeks
  Ireland **12** E2
McGraw *U.S.A.* **115** D8
McGregor *U.S.A.* **112** D8
McGregor Ra. *Australia* **95** D3
McGuire, Mt. *Australia* **94** D4
Mach *Pakistan* **68** E2
Māch Kowr *Iran* **71** E9
Machado = Jiparaná ➤
  Brazil **124** E6
Machagai *Argentina* **126** B3
Machakos *Kenya* **86** C4
Machala *Ecuador* **124** D3
Machanga *Mozam.* **89** C6
Machattie, L. *Australia* **94** C2
Machault *France* **19** C11
Machava *Mozam.* **89** D5
Machece *Mozam.* **87** F4
Machecoul *France* **18** F5
Macheke *Zimbabwe* **89** B5
Macheng *China* **59** B10
Machero *Spain* **37** F6
Machhu ➤ *India* **68** H4
Machiara △ *Pakistan* **68** B5
Machias *Maine, U.S.A.* **113** C20
Machias *N.Y., U.S.A.* **114** D6
Machichi ➤ *Canada* **103** B10
Machico *Madeira* **48** D3
Machilipatnam *India* **67** L12
Machiques *Venezuela* **124** A4
Machupicchu *Peru* **124** F4
Machynlleth *U.K.* **15** E4
Macia *Mozam.* **89** D5
Maciejowice *Poland* **31** G8
McIlwraith Ra. *Australia* **94** A3
Măcin *Romania* **29** E13
Macina *Mali* **82** C4
McInnes L. *Canada* **103** C10
McIntosh *U.S.A.* **112** C3
McIntosh L. *Canada* **103** B8
Macintosh Ra. *Australia* **93** E4
Macintyre ➤ *Australia* **95** D5
Macizo Galaico *Spain* **36** C3
Mackay *Australia* **94** K7
Mackay *U.S.A.* **108** E7
MacKay ➤ *Canada* **102** B6
Mackay, L. *Australia* **92** D4
McKay Ra. *Australia* **92** D3
McKeesport *U.S.A.* **114** F5
McKellar *Canada* **114** A5
McKenna *U.S.A.* **110** D4
Mackenzie *Canada* **102** B4
McKenzie *U.S.A.* **117** C10
Mackenzie ➤ *Australia* **94** C4
Mackenzie ➤ *Canada* **100** C6
McKenzie ➤ *U.S.A.* **108** D2
Mackenzie Bay *Canada* **98** C6
Mackenzie City = Linden
  Guyana **124** B7
Mackenzie King I. *Canada* **101** B8
Mackenzie Mts. *Canada* **100** C7
Mackinaw City *U.S.A.* **113** C11
McKinlay *Australia* **94** C3
McKinlay ➤ *Australia* **94** C3
McKinley, Mt. *U.S.A.* **106** a
McKinley Sea *Arctic* **4** A7
McKinney *U.S.A.* **116** E6
Mackinnon Road *Kenya* **86** C4
McKittrick *U.S.A.* **111** K7
Macklin *Canada* **103** C7
Macksville *Australia* **95** E5
McLaughlin *U.S.A.* **112** C3
Maclean *Australia* **95** D5
McLean *U.S.A.* **116** D4
McLeansboro *U.S.A.* **112** F10
Maclear *S. Africa* **89** E4
Maclear, C. *Malawi* **87** E3
Macleay ➤ *Australia* **95** E5
McLennan *Canada* **102** B5
McLeod ➤ *Canada* **102** C5
McLeod, L. *Australia* **93** D1
MacLeod B. *Canada* **103** A7
MacLeod Lake *Canada* **102** C4
McLoughlin, Mt. *U.S.A.* **108** E2
McMechen *U.S.A.* **114** G4
McMinnville *Oreg., U.S.A.* **108** D2
McMinnville *Tenn., U.S.A.* **117** D12
McMurdo *U.S.A.* **112** F9
McMurdo Sd. *Antarctica* **5** D11
McMurray = Fort
  McMurray *Canada* **102** B6
McMurray *U.S.A.* **110** B4
Macodoene *Mozam.* **89** C6

Macomb *U.S.A.* **112** E8
Macomer *Italy* **42** B1
Mâcon *France* **19** F11
Macon *Ga., U.S.A.* **117** E13
Macon *Miss., U.S.A.* **117** E10
Macon *Mo., U.S.A.* **112** F7
Macossa *Mozam.* **87** F3
Macoun L. *Canada* **103** B8
Macovane *Mozam.* **89** C6
Macquarie ➤ *Australia* **95** E4
Macquarie Harbour
  Australia **95** G4
Macquarie Is. *Pac. Oc.* **96** N7
Macquarie Ridge *S. Ocean* **5** B10
MacRobertson Land
  Antarctica **5** D6
Macroom *Ireland* **12** E3
MacTier *Canada* **114** A5
Macubela *Mozam.* **87** F4
Macugnaga *Italy* **40** C4
Macuira △ *Colombia* **121** D5
Macuiza *Mozam.* **87** F3
Macumba ➤ *Australia* **95** D2
Macuro *Venezuela* **125** K15
Macusani *Peru* **124** F4
Macuse *Mozam.* **87** F4
Macuspana *Mexico* **119** D6
Macusse *Angola* **88** B3
Mada ➤ *Nigeria* **83** D6
Madadeni *S. Africa* **89** D5
Madagali *Nigeria* **83** C7
Madagascar ■ *Africa* **89** C8
Madā'in Sālih *Si. Arabia* **70** E3
Madama *Niger* **79** D8
Madame, I. *Canada* **105** C7
Madan *Bulgaria* **45** E8
Madang *Papua N. G.* **90** B7
Madaoua *Niger* **83** C6
Madara *Nigeria* **83** C7
Madaripur *Bangla.* **67** H17
Madauk *Burma* **67** L20
Madawaska *Canada* **114** A7
Madawaska ➤ *Canada* **114** A7
Madaya *Burma* **67** H20
Madbar *Sudan* **81** F3
Maddalena *Italy* **42** A2
Maddaloni *Italy* **43** A7
Madeira *Atl. Oc.* **48** D3
Madeira ➤ *Brazil* **124** D7
Madeleine, Îs. de la *Canada* **105** C7
Maden *Turkey* **73** C8
Madera *Mexico* **118** B3
Madera *Calif., U.S.A.* **110** J6
Madera *Pa., U.S.A.* **114** F6
Madha *India* **66** L9
Madhavpur *India* **68** J3
Madhepura *India* **69** F12
Madhubani *India* **69** F12
Madhupur *India* **69** G12
Madhya Pradesh □ *India* **68** J8
Madidi ➤ *Bolivia* **124** F5
Madikeri *India* **66** N9
Madikwe △ *S. Africa* **89** D5
Madill *U.S.A.* **116** D6
Madimba
  Dem. Rep. of the Congo **84** E3
Ma'din *Syria* **73** E8
Madinani *Ivory C.* **82** D3
Madingou *Congo* **84** E2
Madirovalo *Madag.* **89** B8
Madison *Calif., U.S.A.* **110** G5
Madison *Fla., U.S.A.* **117** F13
Madison *Ind., U.S.A.* **113** F11
Madison *Nebr., U.S.A.* **112** E5
Madison *Ohio, U.S.A.* **114** E3
Madison *S. Dak., U.S.A.* **112** C5
Madison *Wis., U.S.A.* **112** D9
Madison ➤ *U.S.A.* **108** D8
Madison Heights *U.S.A.* **113** G14
Madisonville *Ky., U.S.A.* **112** G10
Madisonville *Tex., U.S.A.* **116** F7
Madista *Botswana* **88** C4
Madiun *Indonesia* **63** G14
Mado Gashi *Kenya* **86** B4
Madoc *Canada* **114** B7
Madol *Sudan* **81** F2
Madon ➤ *France* **19** D13
Madona *Latvia* **32** D4
Madonie *Italy* **42** E6
Madonna di Campíglio *Italy* **40** B7
Madra Dağı *Turkey* **47** B9
Madrakah, Ra's al *Oman* **75** D6
Madras = Chennai *India* **66** N12
Madras = Tamil Nadu □
  India **66** P10
Madras *U.S.A.* **108** D3
Madre, L. *U.S.A.* **116** J6
Madre, Sierra *Phil.* **61** C5
Madre de Dios ➤ *Bolivia* **124** F5
Madre de Dios, I. *Chile* **128** G1
Madre del Sur, Sierra
  Mexico **119** D5

Madre Occidental, Sierra
  Mexico **118** B3
Madre Oriental, Sierra
  Mexico **118** C5
Madri *India* **68** G5
Madrid *U.S.A.* **115** B9
Madrid □ *Spain* **36** E7
Madrid *Spain* **36** E7
Madrid Barajas ✈ (MAD)
  Spain **36** E7
Madridejos *Spain* **37** F7
Madrigal de las Altas
  Torres *Spain* **36** D6
Madrona, Sierra *Spain* **37** G6
Madroñera *Spain* **37** F5
Madu *Sudan* **81** E2
Madura *Australia* **93** F4
Madura *Indonesia* **63** G15
Madura, Selat *Indonesia* **63** G15
Madurai *India* **66** Q11
Madurantakam *India* **66** N11
Madzhalis *Russia* **35** J8
Mae Chan *Thailand* **64** B2
Mae Hong Son *Thailand* **64** C2
Mae Khlong ➤ *Thailand* **64** F3
Mae Phrik *Thailand* **64** D2
Mae Ping △ *Thailand* **64** D2
Mae Ramat *Thailand* **64** D2
Mae Rim *Thailand* **64** C2
Mae Sot *Thailand* **64** D2
Mae Suai *Thailand* **58** H2
Mae Tha *Thailand* **64** C2
Mae Wong △ *Thailand* **64** E2
Mae Yom △ *Thailand* **64** C3
Maebashi *Japan* **55** F9
Maella *Spain* **38** D5
Maesteg *U.K.* **15** F4
Maestra, Sierra *Cuba* **120** B4
Maevatanana *Madag.* **89** B8
Mafeking = Mafikeng
  S. Africa **88** D4
Mafeking *Canada* **103** C8
Maféré *Ivory C.* **82** D4
Mafeteng *Lesotho* **88** D4
Maffra *Australia* **95** F4
Mafia I. *Tanzania* **86** D4
Mafikeng *S. Africa* **88** D4
Mafra *Brazil* **127** B6
Mafra *Portugal* **37** G1
Mafungabusi Plateau
  Zimbabwe **87** F2
Magadan *Russia* **53** D16
Magadi *Kenya* **86** C4
Magadi, L. *Kenya* **86** C4
Magaliesburg *S. Africa* **89** D4
Magallanes, Estrecho de
  Chile **128** G2
Magaluf *Spain* **39** F7
Magangué *Colombia* **124** B4
Magaria *Niger* **83** C6
Magburaka *S. Leone* **82** D2
Magdalen Is. = Madeleine,
  Îs. de la *Canada* **105** C7
Magdalena *Argentina* **126** D4
Magdalena *Bolivia* **124** F6
Magdalena *U.S.A.* **109** J10
Magdalena ➤ *Colombia* **124** A4
Magdalena ➤ *Mexico* **118** A2
Magdalena, B. *Mexico* **118** C2
Magdalena, I. *Mexico* **118** C2
Magdalena, Llano de
  Mexico **118** C2
Magdalena de Kino *Mexico* **118** A2
Magdeburg *Germany* **24** C7
Magdelaine Cays *Australia* **94** B5
Magdub *Sudan* **81** E2
Magee *U.S.A.* **117** F10
Magelang *Indonesia* **63** G14
Magellan's Str. =
  Magallanes, Estrecho de
  Chile **128** G2
Magenta *Italy* **40** C5
Magenta, L. *Australia* **93** F2
Magerøya *Norway* **8** A21
Maggia ➤ *Switz.* **25** J4
Maggiorasca, Mte. *Italy* **40** D6
Maggiore, Lago *Italy* **40** B5
Maggotty *Jamaica* **120** a
Maghâgha *Egypt* **80** B3
Maghama *Mauritania* **82** B2
Magherafelt *U.K.* **12** B5
Maghreb *N. Afr.* **78** B5
Magione *Italy* **41** E9
Magistralnyy *Russia* **53** D11
Maglaj *Bos.-H.* **28** F3
Magliano in Toscana *Italy* **41** F8
Máglie *Italy* **43** B11
Magnac-Laval *France* **20** B5
Magnetic Pole (North)
  Canada **101** B9
Magnetic Pole (South)
  Antarctica **5** C9
Magnisia □ *Greece* **46** B5
Magnitogorsk *Russia* **52** D6
Magnolia *Ark., U.S.A.* **116** E8
Magnolia *Miss., U.S.A.* **117** F9
Magny-en-Vexin *France* **19** C8

Mago *Fiji* **91** a
Mago △ *Ethiopia* **81** F4
Magog *Canada* **115** A12
Magoro *Uganda* **86** B3
Magoša = Famagusta
  Cyprus **49** D12
Magoulades *Greece* **49** A3
Magoye *Zambia* **87** F2
Magpie, L. *Canada* **105** B7
Magrath *Canada* **102** D6
Magre ➤ *Spain* **39** F4
Magrur *Sudan* **81** E3
Magrur, Wadi ➤ *Sudan* **81** D2
Magta Lahjar *Mauritania* **82** B2
Maguan *China* **58** F5
Maguarinho, C. *Brazil* **125** D9
Magude *Mozam.* **89** D5
Magurski △ *Poland* **31** J8
Maguse L. *Canada* **103** A9
Maguse Pt. *Canada* **103** A10
Magvana *India* **68** H3
Magwe *Burma* **67** J19
Magwe *Sudan* **81** G3
Magyarország =
  Hungary ■ *Europe* **27** D12
Maha Sarakham *Thailand* **64** D4
Mahābād *Iran* **73** D11
Mahabharat Lekh *Nepal* **69** E10
Mahabo *Madag.* **89** C7
Mahadeo Hills *India* **69** H8
Mahaffey *U.S.A.* **114** F6
Mahagi *Dem. Rep. of the Congo* **86** B3
Mahajamba ➤ *Madag.* **89** B8
Mahajamba, Helodranon' i
  Madag. **89** B8
Mahajan *India* **68** E5
Mahajanga *Madag.* **89** B8
Mahajanga □ *Madag.* **89** B8
Mahajilo ➤ *Madag.* **89** B8
Mahakam ➤ *Indonesia* **62** E5
Mahalapye *Botswana* **88** C4
Mahale Mts. *Tanzania* **86** D3
Mahale Mts. △ *Tanzania* **86** D2
Maḥallāt *Iran* **71** C6
Māhān *Iran* **71** D8
Mahan ➤ *India* **69** H10
Mahanadi ➤ *India* **67** J15
Mahananda ➤ *India* **69** G12
Mahanoro *Madag.* **89** B8
Mahanoy City *U.S.A.* **115** F8
Maharashtra □ *India* **66** J9
Mahasham, W. ➤ *Egypt* **74** E3
Mahasoa *Madag.* **89** C8
Mahasolo *Madag.* **89** B8
Mahattat ash Shīdīyah
  Jordan **74** F4
Mahattat 'Unayzah *Jordan* **74** E4
Mahavavy ➤ *Madag.* **89** B8
Mahaxay *Laos* **64** D5
Mahbubnagar *India* **66** L10
Maḥḍah *Oman* **71** E7
Mahdia *Tunisia* **79** A8
Mahe *India* **69** C8
Mahé *Seychelles* **85** b
Mahé ✈ (SEZ) *Seychelles* **85** b
Mahébourg *Mauritius* **85** d
Mahendragarh *India* **68** E7
Mahendranagar *Nepal* **69** E9
Mahenge *Tanzania* **87** D4
Maheno *N.Z.* **91** F3
Mahesana *India* **68** H5
Maheshwar *India* **68** H6
Mahgawan *India* **69** F8
Mahi ➤ *India* **68** H5
Mahia Pen. *N.Z.* **91** C6
Mahilyow *Belarus* **23** B16
Mahilyow □ *Belarus* **32** E6
Mahina *Tahiti* **91** d
Mahinerangi, L. *N.Z.* **91** F2
Mahmiya *Sudan* **81** D3
Mahmud Kot *Pakistan* **68** D4
Mahmudia *Romania* **29** E14
Mahmudiye *Turkey* **47** B12
Mahmutbey *Turkey* **45** E12
Mahnomen *U.S.A.* **112** B6
Mahoba *India* **69** G8
Mahón = Maó *Spain* **48** B11
Mahon, Menorca ✈
  (MAH) *Spain* **38** F9
Mahone Bay *Canada* **105** D7
Mahopac *U.S.A.* **115** E11
Mahuta *Nigeria* **83** C5
Mahuva *India* **68** J4
Mahya Daği *Turkey* **45** E11
Mai-Ndombe, L.
  Dem. Rep. of the Congo **84** E3
Mai-Sai *Thailand* **58** G2
Mai Thon, Ko *Thailand* **65** a
Maia *Portugal* **36** D2
Maia *Spain* **38** B3
Maials *Spain* **38** D5
Maîche *France* **19** E13
Maicurú ➤ *Brazil* **125** D8
Máida *Italy* **43** D9
Maidan Khula *Afghan.* **68** C3

Maidenhead *U.K.* **15** F7
Maidstone *Canada* **103** C7
Maidstone *U.K.* **15** F8
Maiduguri *Nigeria* **83** C7
Maiella △ *Italy* **41** F11
Măieruş *Romania* **29** E10
Maigatari *Nigeria* **83** C7
Maignelay Montigny *France* **19** C9
Maigo *Phil.* **61** G5
Maigudo *Ethiopia* **81** F4
Maihar *India* **69** G9
Maijdi *Bangla.* **67** H17
Maikala Ra. *India* **67** J12
Maiko △
  Dem. Rep. of the Congo **86** C2
Mailani *India* **69** E9
Maillezais *France* **20** B3
Mailsi *Pakistan* **68** E5
Main ➤ *Germany* **25** F4
Main ➤ *U.K.* **12** B5
Main Range △ *Australia* **95** D5
Main Ridge *Trin. & Tob.* **125** J16
Mainburg *Germany* **25** G7
Maine *France* **18** D6
Maine □ *U.S.A.* **113** C19
Maine ➤ *Ireland* **12** D2
Maine, G. of *U.S.A.* **113** D19
Maine-et-Loire □ *France* **18** E6
Maïne-Soroa *Niger* **83** C7
Maingkwan *Burma* **67** F20
Mainit, L. *Phil.* **61** G6
Mainland *Orkney, U.K.* **13** C5
Mainland *Shet., U.K.* **13** A7
Mainoru *Australia* **94** A1
Mainpuri *India* **69** F8
Maintal *Germany* **25** E4
Maintenon *France* **19** D8
Maintirano *Madag.* **89** B7
Mainz *Germany* **25** E4
Maio *C. Verde Is.* **78** b
Maipú *Argentina* **126** D4
Maiquetía *Venezuela* **124** A5
Máira ➤ *Italy* **40** D4
Mairabari *India* **67** F18
Maisí *Cuba* **121** B5
Maisí, Pta. de *Cuba* **121** B5
Maitland *N.S.W., Australia* **95** E5
Maitland *S. Austral., Australia* **95** E2
Maitland ➤ *Canada* **114** C3
Maitri *Antarctica* **5** D3
Maiyema *Nigeria* **83** C5
Maiyuan *China* **59** E11
Maiz, Is. del *Nic.* **120** D3
Maizuru *Japan* **55** G7
Majalengka *Indonesia* **63** G13
Majene *Indonesia* **63** E5
Majete *Malawi* **87** F3
Majevica *Bos.-H.* **28** F3
Maji *Ethiopia* **81** F4
Majiang *China* **58** D6
Majorca = Mallorca *Spain* **48** B10
Majuro *Marshall Is.* **96** G9
Maka *Senegal* **82** C2
Makaha *Zimbabwe* **89** B5
Makak *Cameroon* **83** E7
Makalamabedi *Botswana* **88** C3
Makale *Indonesia* **63** E5
Makalu-Barun △ *Nepal* **69** F12
Makamba *Burundi* **86** C2
Makari *Cameroon* **83** C7
Makarikari =
  Makgadikgadi Salt Pans
  Botswana **88** C4
Makarov Basin *Arctic* **4** A
Makarovo *Russia* **53** D11
Makarska *Croatia* **41** E14
Makaryev *Russia* **34** B6
Makasar = Ujung
  Pandang *Indonesia* **63** F5
Makasar, Selat *Indonesia* **63** E5
Makasar, Str. of =
  Makasar, Selat *Indonesia* **63** E5
Makat = Maqat *Kazakhstan* **52** E6
Makedonija =
  Macedonia ■ *Europe* **44** E5
Makeni *S. Leone* **82** D2
Makeyevka = Makiyivka
  Ukraine **33** H9
Makgadikgadi △ *Botswana* **88** C3
Makgadikgadi Salt Pans
  Botswana **88** C4
Makhachkala *Russia* **35** J8
Makhado = Louis
  Trichardt *S. Africa* **89** C4
Makharadze = Ozurgeti
  Georgia **35** K5
Makhfar al Buşayyah *Iraq* **70** D5
Makhmūr *Iraq* **73** E10
Makian *Indonesia* **63** D7
Makindu *Kenya* **86** C4
Makīnsk *Kazakhstan* **52** D8
Makira = San Cristóbal
  Solomon Is. **90** C9
Makiv *Ukraine* **29** B11
Makiyivka *Ukraine* **33** H9
Makkah *Si. Arabia* **80** C4
Makkovik *Canada* **105** A8

Makó *Hungary* **28** D5
Mako *Senegal* **82** C2
Makogai *Fiji* **91** a
Makokou *Gabon* **84** D2
Makongo
  Dem. Rep. of the Congo **86** B2
Makoro *Dem. Rep. of the Congo* **86** B2
Maków Mazowiecki *Poland* **31** F8
Maków Podhalański *Poland* **31** J6
Makra *Greece* **47** E7
Makrai *India* **68** H7
Makran Coast Range
  Pakistan **66** G4
Makrana *India* **68** F6
Makrany *Belarus* **31** G11
Makri *Greece* **45** E9
Makrigialos *Greece* **49** D7
Mākū *Iran* **73** C11
Makunda *Botswana* **88** C3
Makung *Taiwan* **59** F12
Makurazaki *Japan* **55** J5
Makurdi *Nigeria* **83** D6
Makūyeh *Iran* **71** D7
Makwassie *S. Africa* **88** D4
Makwiro *Zimbabwe* **89** B5
Mål ➤ *Sweden* **11** G9
Mal B. *Ireland* **12** D2
Mala, Pta. *Panama* **120** E3
Mala Belozërka *Ukraine* **33** J8
Malá Fatra △ *Slovak Rep.* **27** B12
Mala Kapela *Croatia* **41** D12
Mała Panew ➤ *Poland* **31** H5
Mala Vyska *Ukraine* **33** H6
Malabang *Phil.* **61** H6
Malabar Coast *India* **66** P9
Malabon *Phil.* **61** D4
Malabu *Nigeria* **83** D7
Malacca, Straits of *Indonesia* **65** L3
Malacky *Slovak Rep.* **27** C10
Malad City *U.S.A.* **108** E7
Maladeta *Spain* **38** C5
Maladzyechna *Belarus* **23** A14
Málaga *Spain* **37** J6
Málaga □ *Spain* **37** J6
Malagarasi *Tanzania* **86** D3
Malagarasi ➤ *Tanzania* **86** D2
Malagasy Rep. =
  Madagascar ■ *Africa* **89** C8
Malagón *Spain* **37** F7
Malagón ➤ *Spain* **37** H3
Malahide *Ireland* **12** C5
Malaimbandy *Madag.* **89** C8
Malaita *Solomon Is.* **90** B9
Malakāl *Sudan* **81** F3
Malakand *Pakistan* **68** B4
Malakula *Vanuatu* **90** C9
Malakwal *Pakistan* **68** C5
Malamala *Indonesia* **63** E6
Malanda *Australia* **94** B4
Malang *Indonesia* **63** G15
Malangen *Norway* **8** B18
Malanje *Angola* **84** F3
Mälaren *Sweden* **10** E11
Malargüe *Argentina* **126** D2
Malartic *Canada* **104** C4
Malaryta *Belarus* **31** G11
Malatya *Turkey* **73** C8
Malatya □ *Turkey* **72** C7
Malawi ■ *Africa* **87** E3
Malawi, L. *Africa* **87** E3
Malay Pen. *Asia* **65** J3
Malaya Belozërka = Mala
  Belozërka *Ukraine* **33** J8
Malaya Vishera *Russia* **32** C7
Malaya Viska = Mala
  Vyska *Ukraine* **33** H6
Malaybalay *Phil.* **61** G6
Malāyer *Iran* **73** E13
Malaysia ■ *Asia* **65** K4
Malazgirt *Turkey* **73** C10
Malbaza *Niger* **83** C6
Malbon *Australia* **94** C3
Malbooma *Australia* **95** E1
Malbork *Poland* **30** D6
Malcésine *Italy* **40** C7
Malchin *Germany* **24** B8
Malchow *Germany* **24** B8
Malcolm *Australia* **93** E3
Malcolm, Pt. *Australia* **93** F3
Malczyce *Poland* **31** G3
Maldah *India* **69** G13
Maldegem *Belgium* **17** C3
Malden *Mass., U.S.A.* **115** D13
Malden *Mo., U.S.A.* **112** G9
Malden I. *Kiribati* **97** H12
Maldives ■ *Ind. Oc.* **50** H9
Maldon *U.K.* **15** F8
Maldonado *Uruguay* **127** C5
Maldonado, Pta. *Mexico* **119** D5
Malè *Italy* **40** B7
Malé *Maldives* **50** H9
Malé Karpaty *Slovak Rep.* **27** C10
Maleas, Akra *Greece* **46** E5
Malebo, Pool *Africa* **84** E3
Malegaon *India* **66** J9
Malei *Mozam.* **87** F4
Malek *Sudan* **81** F3
Malek Kandī *Iran* **73** D12

Malela *Dem. Rep. of the Congo* **86** C2
Malema *Mozam.* **87** E4
Maleme *Ghana* **82** D4
Maleme *Ghana* **49** D5
Mälerås *Sweden* **11** H9
Malerkotla *India* **68** D6
Males *Greece* **49** D7
Malesherbes *France* **19** D9
Malesina *Greece* **46** C5
Malestroit *France* **18** E4
Malfa *Italy* **43** D7
Malgobek *Russia* **35** J7
Malgomaj *Sweden* **8** D17
Malgrat de Mar *Spain* **38** D7
Malha *Sudan* **81** D2
Malhargarh *India* **68** G6
Malheur ➤ *U.S.A.* **108** D5
Malheur L. *U.S.A.* **108** E4
Mali *Guinea* **82** C2
Mali ■ *Africa* **82** B4
Mali ➤ *Burma* **67** G20
Mali Kanal *Serbia* **28** E4
Mali Kyun *Burma* **64** F2
Malia *Greece* **49** D7
Malia, Kolpos *Greece* **49** D7
Malibu *U.S.A.* **111** L8
Maliku *Indonesia* **63** E6
Malili *Indonesia* **63** E6
Målilla *Sweden* **11** G9
Malimba, Mts.
  Dem. Rep. of the Congo **86** D2
Malin Hd. *Ireland* **12** A4
Malin Pen. *Ireland* **12** A4
Malines = Mechelen *Belgium* **17** C4
Malino *Indonesia* **63** D6
Malinyi *Tanzania* **87** D4
Maliq *Albania* **44** F4
Malita *Phil.* **63** C7
Maliya *India* **68** H4
Maljenik *Serbia* **44** C5
Malka Mari △ *Kenya* **86** B5
Malkara *Turkey* **45** F10
Malkinia Górna *Poland* **31** F9
Malko Tŭrnovo *Bulgaria* **45** E11
Mallacoota Inlet *Australia* **95** F4
Mallaig *U.K.* **13** D3
Mallaoua *Niger* **83** C6
Mallawan *India* **69** F9
Mallawi *Egypt* **80** B3
Mallemort *France* **21** E9
Málles Venosta *Italy* **40** B7
Mallicolo = Malakula
  Vanuatu **90** C9
Mallorca *Spain* **48** B10
Mallorytown *Canada* **115** B9
Mallow *Ireland* **12** D3
Malmbäck *Sweden* **11** G8
Malmberget *Sweden* **8** C19
Malmédy *Belgium* **17** D6
Malmesbury *S. Africa* **88** E2
Malmivaara =
  Malmberget *Sweden* **8** C19
Malmköping *Sweden* **10** E10
Malmö *Sweden* **11** J7
Malmslätt *Sweden* **11** F9
Malmyzh *Russia* **34** B10
Malnaş *Romania* **29** D10
Malo *Fiji* **91** a
Malolos *Phil.* **63** B6
Malolotja △ *Swaziland* **89** D5
Malombe L. *Malawi* **87** E4
Malomice *Poland* **31** G2
Malomir *Bulgaria* **45** D10
Malone *U.S.A.* **115** B10
Malong *China* **58** E4
Małopolskie □ *Poland* **31** J7
Malorad *Bulgaria* **45** C8
Maloyaroslovets *Russia* **32** E9
Malpartida *Spain* **37** F4
Malpaso *Canary Is.* **48** G1
Malpaso, Presa =
  Netzahualcóyotl, Presa
  Mexico **119** D6
Malpelo, I. de *Colombia* **124** C2
Malpica de Bergantiños
  Spain **36** B2
Malpur *India* **68** H5
Malpura *India* **68** F6
Malta *Idaho, U.S.A.* **108** E7
Malta *Mont., U.S.A.* **108** B10
Malta ■ *Europe* **49** D2
Maltahöhe *Namibia* **88** C2
Maltepe *Turkey* **45** F13
Malton *Canada* **114** C5
Malton *U.K.* **14** C7
Maluku *Indonesia* **63** E7
Maluku □ *Indonesia* **63** E7
Maluku Sea = Molucca
  Sea *Indonesia* **63** E6
Malumfashi *Nigeria* **83** C6

Malung *Sweden* **10** D7
Malungsfors *Sweden* **10** D7
Maluwe *Ghana* **82** D4
Malvan *India* **66** L8
Malvern *U.S.A.* **116** D8
Malvern Hills *U.K.* **15** E5
Malvinas, Is. = Falkland
  Is. ☑ *Atl. Oc.* **128** G5
Malý Dunaj ➤ *Slovak Rep.* **27** D11
Malya *Tanzania* **86** C3
Malye Derbety *Russia* **35** G7
Malyy Lyakhovskiy,
  Ostrov *Russia* **53** B15
Mama *Russia* **53** D12
Mamadysh *Russia* **34** C10
Mamanguape *Brazil* **125** E11
Mamanuca Group *Fiji* **91** a
Mamarr Mitlā *Egypt* **74** E1
Mamasa *Indonesia* **63** E5
Mambasa
  Dem. Rep. of the Congo **86** B2
Mamberamo ➤ *Indonesia* **63** E9
Mambilima Falls *Zambia* **87** E2
Mambirima
  Dem. Rep. of the Congo **87** E2
Mambo *Tanzania* **86** C4
Mambrui *Kenya* **86** C5
Mamburao *Phil.* **61** E4
Mameigwess L. *Canada* **104** B2
Mamers *France* **18** D7
Mamfé *Cameroon* **83** D6
Mammoth *U.S.A.* **109** K8
Mammoth Cave △ *U.S.A.* **112** G10
Mamonovo *Russia* **30** D6
Mamoré ➤ *Bolivia* **124** F5
Mamou *Guinea* **82** C2
Mamoudzou *Mayotte* **85** a
Mampaté *Guinea-Biss.* **82** C2
Mampikony *Madag.* **89** B8
Mampong *Ghana* **83** D4
Mamry, Jezioro *Poland* **30** D8
Mamuju *Indonesia* **63** E5
Mamuno *Botswana* **88** C3
Mamuras *Albania* **44** E3
Man *Ivory C.* **82** D3
Man, I. of *U.K.* **14** C3
Man-Bazar *India* **69** H12
Man Na *Burma* **67** H20
Mana ➤ *Fr. Guiana* **125** B8
Mana Pools △ *Zimbabwe* **87** F2
Manaar, G. of = Mannar,
  G. of *Asia* **66** Q11
Manacapuru *Brazil* **124** D6
Manacor *Spain* **48** B10
Manado *Indonesia* **63** D6
Managua *Nic.* **120** D2
Managua, L. de *Nic.* **120** D2
Manakara *Madag.* **89** C8
Manali *India* **68** C7
Manama = Al Manāmah
  Bahrain **71** E6
Manambao ➤ *Madag.* **89** B7
Manambato ➤ *Madag.* **89** A8
Manambolo ➤ *Madag.* **89** B7
Manambolosy *Madag.* **89** B8
Mananara *Madag.* **89** B8
Mananara ➤ *Madag.* **89** C8
Mananara △ *Madag.* **89** B8
Mananjary *Madag.* **89** C8
Manankoro *Mali* **82** C3
Manantenina *Madag.* **89** C8
Manaos = Manaus *Brazil* **124** D7
Manapire ➤ *Venezuela* **124** B5
Manapouri *N.Z.* **91** F1
Manapouri, L. *N.Z.* **91** F1
Manaqil *Sudan* **81** E3
Manār, Jabal *Yemen* **75** E3
Manaravolo *Madag.* **89** C8
Manas *China* **60** B3
Manas ➤ *India* **67** F17
Manaslu *Nepal* **69** E11
Manasquan *U.S.A.* **115** F10
Manassa *U.S.A.* **109** H11
Manati *Puerto Rico* **121** d
Manaung *Burma* **67** K18
Manaus *Brazil* **124** D7
Manavgat *Turkey* **72** D4
Manawan L. *Canada* **103** B8
Manay *Phil.* **61** H7
Manbij *Syria* **72** D7
Mancha Real *Spain* **37** H7
Manche □ *France* **18** C5
Manchegorsk *Russia* **52** C4
Manchester *U.K.* **14** D5
Manchester *Calif., U.S.A.* **110** G3
Manchester *Conn., U.S.A.* **115** E12
Manchester *Ga., U.S.A.* **117** E12
Manchester *Iowa, U.S.A.* **112** D8
Manchester *Ky., U.S.A.* **113** G12
Manchester *N.H., U.S.A.* **115** D13
Manchester *N.Y., U.S.A.* **114** D7
Manchester *Pa., U.S.A.* **115** F8
Manchester *Tenn., U.S.A.* **117** D11
Manchester *Vt., U.S.A.* **115** C11
Manchester Int. ✈ (MAN)
  U.K. **14** D5

Manchester L. *Canada* **103** A7
Manchhar L. *Pakistan* **68** F2
Manchuria = Dongbei
  China **57** D13
Manciano *Italy* **41** F8
Mancifa *Ethiopia* **81** F5
Mand ➤ *India* **69** J10
Mand ➤ *Iran* **71** D7
Manda *Ludewe, Tanzania* **87** E3
Manda *Mbeya, Tanzania* **86** D3
Manda *Mbeya, Tanzania* **87** D3
Mandabé *Madag.* **89** C7
Mandaguari *Brazil* **127** A5
Mandah = Töhöm *Mongolia* **56** B5
Mandal *Norway* **9** G12
Mandala, Puncak *Indonesia* **63** E10
Mandalay *Burma* **67** J20
Mandale = Mandalay
  Burma **67** J20
Mandalgarh *India* **68** G6
Mandalgovĭ *Mongolia* **56** B4
Mandalī *Iraq* **73** F11
Mandan *U.S.A.* **112** B3
Mandaon *Phil.* **61** E5
Mandar, Teluk *Indonesia* **63** E5
Mándas *Italy* **42** C2
Mandaue *Phil.* **61** F5
Mandelieu-la-Napoule
  France **21** E11
Mandera *Kenya* **86** B5
Mandeville *Jamaica* **120** a
Mandi *India* **68** D7
Mandi Dabwali *India* **68** E6
Mandiana *Guinea* **82** C3
Mandimba *Mozam.* **87** E4
Mandioli *Indonesia* **63** E7
Mandla *India* **69** H9
Mandø *Denmark* **11** J2
Mandorah *Australia* **92** B5
Mandoto *Madag.* **89** B8
Mandoudi *Greece* **46** C5
Mandra *Greece* **46** C5
Mandra *Pakistan* **68** C5
Mandraki *Greece* **47** E9
Mandrare ➤ *Madag.* **89** D8
Mandritsara *Madag.* **89** B8
Mandronarivo *Madag.* **89** C8
Mandsaur *India* **68** G6
Mandurah *Australia* **93** F2
Mandúria *Italy* **43** B10
Mandvi *India* **68** H3
Mandya *India* **66** N10
Mandzai *Pakistan* **68** D2
Mané *Burkina Faso* **83** C4
Maneh *Iran* **71** B8
Manengouba, Mts. *Cameroon* **83** E6
Manera *Madag.* **89** C7
Manérbio *Italy* **40** C7
Maneroo Cr. ➤ *Australia* **94** C3
Manfalût *Egypt* **80** B3
Manfredónia *Italy* **41** G12
Manfredónia, G. di *Italy* **41** G13
Manga *Burkina Faso* **83** C4
Manga *Niger* **83** C7
Mangabeiras, Chapada das
  Brazil **125** F9
Mangaia *Cook Is.* **97** K12
Mangalia *Romania* **29** G13
Mangalore *India* **66** N9
Mangan *India* **69** F13
Mangawan *India* **69** G9
Mangaweka *N.Z.* **91** C5
Manggar *Indonesia* **62** E3
Manggawitu *Indonesia* **63** E8
Mangghystaū Tübegi
  Kazakhstan **52** F5
Manggis *Indonesia* **63** J18
Mangindrano *Madag.* **89** A8
Mangkalihat, Tanjung
  Indonesia **63** D5
Mangla *Pakistan* **68** C5
Mangla Dam *Pakistan* **69** C5
Manglaur *India* **68** E7
Mangnai *China* **60** C4
Mango *Togo* **83** C5
Mango *Tonga* **91** c
Mangoche *Malawi* **87** E4
Mangoky ➤ *Madag.* **89** C7
Mangole *Indonesia* **63** E6
Mangombe
  Dem. Rep. of the Congo **86** C2
Mangonui *N.Z.* **91** A4
Mangoro ➤ *Madag.* **89** B8
Mangrol *Mad. P., India* **68** J4
Mangrol *Raj., India* **68** G6
Mangualde *Portugal* **36** E3
Mangueira, L. da *Brazil* **127** C5
Mangum *U.S.A.* **116** D5
Mangyshlak, Poluostrov =
  Mangghystaū Tübegi
  Kazakhstan **52** E6
Manhattan *U.S.A.* **112** F5
Manhiça *Mozam.* **89** D5
Mania ➤ *Madag.* **89** B8
Maniago *Italy* **41** B9
Manica *Mozam.* **89** B5

Manica □ Mozam. 89 B5
Manicaland □ Zimbabwe 87 F3
Manicoré Brazil 124 E6
Manicouagan → Canada 105 C6
Manicouagan, Rés. Canada 105 B6
Maniema □ Dem. Rep. of the Congo 86 C2
Manīfah Si. Arabia 71 E6
Manifold, C. Australia 94 C5
Maniganggo China 58 B2
Manigotagan Canada 103 C9
Manigotagan → Canada 103 C9
Manihari India 69 G12
Manihiki Cook Is. 97 J11
Manihiki Plateau Pac. Oc. 97 J11
Manika, Plateau de la Dem. Rep. of the Congo 87 E2
Manikpur India 69 G9
Manila Phil. 61 D4
Manila U.S.A. 108 F9
Manila B. Phil. 61 D4
Manilla Australia 95 E5
Manimpé Mali 82 C3
Maningrida Australia 94 A1
Maninian Ivory C. 82 C3
Manipur □ India 67 G19
Manipur → Burma 67 H19
Manisa Turkey 47 C9
Manisa □ Turkey 47 C9
Manistee U.S.A. 112 C10
Manistee → U.S.A. 112 C10
Manistique U.S.A. 112 C10
Manitoba □ Canada 103 B9
Manitoba, L. Canada 103 C9
Manitou Canada 103 D9
Manitou, L. Canada 105 B6
Manitou Is. U.S.A. 113 C10
Manitou L. Canada 103 C7
Manitou Springs U.S.A. 108 G11
Manitoulin I. Canada 104 C3
Manitouwadge Canada 104 C2
Manitowoc U.S.A. 112 C10
Manizales Colombia 124 B3
Manja Madag. 89 C7
Manjacaze Mozam. 89 C5
Manjakandriana Madag. 89 B8
Manjhand Pakistan 68 G3
Manjil Iran 71 B6
Manjimup Australia 93 F2
Manjra → India 66 K10
Mankato Kans., U.S.A. 112 F4
Mankato Minn., U.S.A. 112 C6
Mankayane Swaziland 89 D5
Mankera Pakistan 68 D4
Mankim Cameroon 83 D7
Mankono Ivory C. 82 D3
Mankota Canada 103 D7
Manlay = Üydzin Mongolia 56 B4
Manlleu Spain 38 C7
Manmad India 66 J9
Mann Ranges Australia 93 E5
Manna Indonesia 62 E2
Mannahill Australia 95 E3
Mannar Sri Lanka 66 Q11
Mannar, G. of Asia 66 Q11
Mannar I. Sri Lanka 66 Q11
Mannheim Germany 25 F4
Manning Canada 102 B5
Manning Oreg., U.S.A. 110 E3
Manning S.C., U.S.A. 117 E14
Mannu → Italy 42 C2
Mannu, C. Italy 42 B1
Mannum Australia 95 E2
Mano S. Leone 82 D2
Mano → Liberia 82 D2
Mano River Liberia 82 D2
Manoharpur India 69 H11
Manokwari Indonesia 63 E8
Manolada Greece 46 C3
Manombo Madag. 89 C7
Manono Dem. Rep. of the Congo 86 D2
Manono Samoa 91 b
Manoppello Italy 41 F11
Manorhamilton Ireland 12 B3
Manosque France 21 E9
Manotick Canada 115 A9
Manouane → Canada 105 C5
Manouane, L. Canada 105 B5
Manp'o N. Korea 57 D14
Manpojin = Manp'o N. Korea 57 D14
Manpur Chhattisgarh, India 69 H10
Manpur Mad. P., India 68 H6
Manresa Spain 38 D6
Mansa Gujarat, India 68 H5
Mansa Punjab, India 68 E6
Mansa Zambia 87 E2
Månsåsen Sweden 10 A8
Mansehra Pakistan 68 B5
Mansel I. Canada 101 C12
Mansfield Australia 95 F4
Mansfield U.K. 14 D6
Mansfield La., U.S.A. 116 E8
Mansfield Mass., U.S.A. 115 D13
Mansfield Ohio, U.S.A. 114 F2
Mansfield Pa., U.S.A. 114 E7
Mansfield Tex., U.S.A. 116 E6
Mansfield, Mt. U.S.A. 115 B12
Mansilla de las Mulas Spain 36 C5
Mansle France 20 C4
Mansoa Guinea-Biss. 82 C1
Manson Creek Canada 102 B4
Manta Ecuador 124 D2
Mantadia △ Madag. 89 B8
Mantalingajan, Mt. Phil. 61 G2
Mantare Tanzania 86 C3
Manteca U.S.A. 110 H5
Manteo U.S.A. 117 D17
Mantes-la-Jolie France 19 D8
Manthani India 66 K11
Manti U.S.A. 108 G8
Mantiqueira, Serra da Brazil 127 A7
Manton U.S.A. 113 C11
Mantorp Sweden 11 F9
Mántova Italy 40 C7
Mänttä Finland 32 A3
Mantua = Mántova Italy 40 C7
Manturovo Russia 34 A7
Manu Peru 124 F4
Manu → Peru 124 F4
Manu'a Is. Amer. Samoa 91 b
Manuel Alves → Brazil 125 F9
Manui Indonesia 63 E6
Manukau N.Z. 91 B5
Manuripi → Bolivia 124 F5
Many U.S.A. 116 F8
Manyani Kenya 86 C4
Manyara, L. Tanzania 86 C4
Manyas Turkey 45 F11
Manyava Ukraine 29 B9
Manych → Russia 35 G5
Manych-Gudilo, Ozero Russia 35 G6
Manyonga → Tanzania 86 C3
Manyoni Tanzania 86 D3
Manzai Pakistan 68 C4
Manzala, Bahra el Egypt 80 H7
Manzanar ⌓ U.S.A. 110 J7
Manzanares Spain 37 F7
Manzaneda Spain 36 C3
Manzanillo Cuba 120 B4
Manzanillo Mexico 118 D4
Manzanillo, Pta. Panama 120 E4
Manzano Mts. U.S.A. 109 J10
Manzarīyeh Iran 71 C6
Manzhouli China 60 B6
Manzini Swaziland 89 D5
Manzur Vadisi △ Turkey 70 B3
Mao Chad 79 F9
Maó Spain 48 B11
Maoke, Pegunungan Indonesia 63 E9
Maolin China 57 C12
Maoming China 59 G8
Maopi T'ou China 59 G13
Maouri, Dallol → Niger 83 C5
Maoxian China 58 B4
Maoxing China 57 B13
Mapam Yumco China 69 D9
Mapastepec Mexico 119 D6
Maphrao, Ko Thailand 65 a
Mapia, Kepulauan Indonesia 63 D8
Mapimí Mexico 118 B4
Mapimí, Bolsón de Mexico 118 B4
Maping China 59 B9
Mapinga Tanzania 86 D4
Mapinhane Mozam. 89 C6
Maple Creek Canada 103 D7
Maple Valley U.S.A. 110 C4
Mapleton U.S.A. 108 D2
Mapuera → Brazil 124 D7
Mapulanguene Mozam. 89 C5
Mapungubwe △ S. Africa 87 G2
Maputo Mozam. 89 D5
Maputo □ Mozam. 89 D5
Maputo, B. de Mozam. 89 D5
Maputo ⌓ Mozam. 89 D5
Maqat Kazakhstan 52 E6
Maqiaohe China 57 B16
Maqnā Si. Arabia 70 D2
Maquan He = Brahmaputra → Asia 69 H13
Maqueda Spain 36 E6
Maquela do Zombo Angola 84 F3
Maquinchao Argentina 128 E3
Maquoketa U.S.A. 112 D8
Mar, Serra do Brazil 127 B6
Mar Chiquita, L. Argentina 126 C3
Mar del Plata Argentina 126 D4
Mar Menor Spain 39 H4
Mara Tanzania 86 C3
Mara □ Tanzania 86 C3
Maraã Brazil 124 D5
Maraa Tahiti 91 d
Marabá Brazil 125 E9
Maracá, I. de Brazil 125 C8
Maracaibo Venezuela 124 A4
Maracaibo, L. de Venezuela 124 B4
Maracaju Brazil 127 A4
Maracas Bay Village Trin. & Tob. 125 K15
Maracay Venezuela 124 A5
Maracena Spain 37 H7
Maradi Niger 83 C6
Maradi □ Niger 83 C6
Marāgheh Iran 73 D12
Marāh Si. Arabia 70 E5
Marahoue △ Ivory C. 82 D3
Marais du Cotentin et du Bessin ⌓ France 18 C5
Marais Poitevin, Val de Sèvre et Vendée ⌓ France 20 B3
Marajó, I. de Brazil 125 D9
Marākand Iran 70 B5
Marakele △ S. Africa 89 E4
Maralal Kenya 86 B4
Maralinga Australia 93 F5
Maramaraereğlisi Turkey 45 F11
Marambio Antarctica 5 C18
Marampa S. Leone 82 D2
Maramureş □ Romania 29 C9
Maran Malaysia 65 L4
Marana U.S.A. 109 K8
Maranboy Australia 92 B5
Maranchón Spain 38 D2
Marand Iran 73 C11
Marang Malaysia 65 K4
Maranguape Brazil 125 D11
Maranhão = São Luís Brazil 125 D10
Maranhão □ Brazil 125 E9
Marano, L. di Italy 41 C10
Maranoa → Australia 95 D4
Marañón → Peru 124 D4
Marão Mozam. 89 C5
Maraş = Kahramanmaraş Turkey 72 D7
Mărăşeşti Romania 29 E12
Maratea Italy 43 C8
Marateca Portugal 37 G2
Marathasa Cyprus 49 E11
Marathokambos Greece 47 D8
Marathon Australia 94 C3
Marathon Canada 104 C2
Marathon N.Y., U.S.A. 115 D8
Marathon Tex., U.S.A. 116 F3
Marathonas Greece 46 C5
Marathóvouno Cyprus 49 D12
Maratua Indonesia 63 D5
Maraval Trin. & Tob. 125 K15
Maravatío Mexico 118 D4
Marawi City Phil. 61 H6
Marāwih U.A.E. 71 E7
Marazliyivka 29 D15
Marbella Spain 37 J6
Marble Bar Australia 92 D2
Marble Falls U.S.A. 116 F5
Marblehead U.S.A. 115 D14
Marburg Germany 24 E4
Marca, Pta. Da Angola 85 H2
Marcal → Hungary 28 C2
Marcali Hungary 28 D2
Marcaria Italy 40 C7
Mărcăuţi Moldova 29 B12
March U.K. 15 E8
Marche France 20 B5
Marche □ Italy 41 E10
Marche-en-Famenne Belgium 17 D5
Marchena Spain 37 H5
Marches = Marche □ Italy 41 E10
Marchesale ⌓ Italy 43 D9
Marciana Marina Italy 40 F7
Marcianise Italy 43 A7
Marcigny France 19 F11
Marcillat-en-Combraille France 19 F9
Marck France 19 B8
Marckolsheim France 19 D14
Marco Island U.S.A. 117 J14
Marcos Juárez Argentina 126 C3
Mărculeşti Moldova 29 C13
Marcus I. = Minami-Tori-Shima Pac. Oc. 96 E7
Marcy, Mt. U.S.A. 115 B11
Mardan Pakistan 68 B5
Mardarivka Ukraine 29 C14
Mardin Turkey 73 D9
Mårdsjö Sweden 10 A9
Marécchia → Italy 41 D9
Maree, L. U.K. 13 D3
Mareeba Australia 94 B4
Mareetsane S. Africa 88 D4
Maremma Italy 41 F8
Maremma ⌓ Italy 40 F8
Marèna Kayes, Mali 82 C2
Maréna Koulikouro, Mali 82 C3
Marengo U.S.A. 112 E7
Marennes France 20 C2
Marerano Madag. 89 C7
Maréttimo Italy 42 E5
Mareuil France 20 C4
Marfa U.S.A. 116 F2
Marfa Pt. Malta 49 D1
Marganets = Marhanets Ukraine 33 J8
Margaret → Australia 92 C4
Margaret Bay Canada 102 C3
Margaret L. Canada 102 B5
Margaret River Australia 93 F2
Margarita, I. de Venezuela 124 A6
Margariti Greece 46 B2
Margaritovo Russia 54 C7
Margate S. Africa 89 E5
Margate U.K. 15 F9
Margeride, Mts. de la France 20 D7
Margherita di Savóia Italy 43 A9
Margherita Pk. Uganda 86 B3
Marghita Romania 28 C7
Margonin Poland 31 F4
Margosatubig Phil. 61 H5
Mārgow, Dasht-e Afghan. 66 D3
Marguerite Canada 102 C4
Marhanets Ukraine 33 J8
Mari El □ Russia 34 B8
Mari Indus Pakistan 68 C4
Mari Republic = Mari El □ Russia 34 B8
María, Sa. de Spain 39 H2
María Elena Chile 126 A2
María Grande Argentina 126 C4
Maria I. N. Terr., Australia 94 A2
Maria I. Tas., Australia 95 G4
Maria Island △ Australia 95 G4
Maria van Diemen, C. N.Z. 91 A4
Mariager Denmark 11 H3
Mariager Fjord Denmark 11 H4
Mariakani Kenya 86 C4
Mariala △ Australia 95 D4
Marian Australia 94 K6
Marian L. Canada 102 A5
Mariana Trench Pac. Oc. 96 F6
Marianna U.S.A. 117 F12
Mariannelund Sweden 11 G9
Mariánské Lázně Czech Rep. 26 B5
Marias → U.S.A. 108 C8
Marías, Islas Mexico 118 C3
Mariato, Punta Panama 120 E3
Mariazell Austria 26 D8
Maribo Denmark 11 K5
Maribor Slovenia 41 B12
Marico → Africa 88 C4
Maricopa Ariz., U.S.A. 109 K7
Maricopa Calif., U.S.A. 111 K7
Marîdî Sudan 81 G2
Marîdî, Wadi → Sudan 81 F2
Marié → Brazil 124 D5
Marie Byrd Land Antarctica 5 D14
Marie-Galante Guadeloupe 120 b
Mariecourt = Kangiqsujuaq Canada 101 C12
Mariefred Sweden 10 E11
Mariehamn Finland 9 F18
Marieholm Sweden 11 J7
Mariembourg Belgium 17 D4
Marienbad = Mariánské Lázně Czech Rep. 26 B5
Marienberg Germany 24 E9
Mariental Namibia 88 C2
Marienville U.S.A. 114 E5
Mariestad Sweden 11 F7
Marietta Ga., U.S.A. 117 E12
Marietta Ohio, U.S.A. 113 F13
Marieville Canada 115 A11
Mariga → Nigeria 83 C6
Marignane France 21 E9
Marihatag Phil. 61 G7
Mariinsk Russia 52 D9
Mariinskiy Posad Russia 34 B8
Marijampolė Lithuania 30 D10
Marijampolės □ Lithuania 30 D10
Marília Brazil 127 A6
Marín Spain 36 C2
Marina U.S.A. 110 J5
Marinduque Phil. 63 B6
Marine City U.S.A. 114 D2
Marineo Italy 42 E6
Marinette U.S.A. 112 C10
Maringá Brazil 127 A5
Marinha Grande Portugal 36 F2
Marino Italy 41 G9
Marion Ala., U.S.A. 117 E11
Marion Ill., U.S.A. 112 G9
Marion Ind., U.S.A. 113 E11
Marion Iowa, U.S.A. 112 D8
Marion Kans., U.S.A. 112 F5
Marion N.C., U.S.A. 117 D13
Marion Ohio, U.S.A. 113 E12
Marion S.C., U.S.A. 117 D15
Marion Va., U.S.A. 113 G13
Marion, L. U.S.A. 117 E14
Mariposa U.S.A. 110 H7
Mariscal Estigarribia Paraguay 126 A3
Maritime Alps = Maritimes, Alpes Europe 21 D11
Maritimes, Alpes Europe 21 D11
Maritsa = Evros → Greece 72 B2
Maritsa Greece 49 C10
Mariupol Ukraine 33 J9
Mariusa △ Venezuela 121 E7
Marīvān Iran 73 E12
Marj 'Uyūn Lebanon 74 B4
Marka = Merca Somali Rep. 75 G3
Marka Si. Arabia 80 D5
Markam China 58 C2
Markaryd Sweden 11 H7
Markdale Canada 114 B4
Marked Tree U.S.A. 117 D9
Markelsdorfer Huk Germany 24 A7
Market Drayton U.K. 14 E5
Market Harborough U.K. 15 E7
Market Rasen U.K. 14 D7
Markham Canada 114 C5
Markham, Mt. Antarctica 5 E11
Marki Poland 31 F8
Märkische Schweiz ⌓ Germany 24 C10
Markkleeberg Germany 24 D8
Markleeville U.S.A. 110 G7
Markopoulo Greece 46 D5
Markovac Serbia 44 B5
Markovo Russia 53 C17
Markoye Burkina Faso 83 C5
Marks Russia 34 E8
Marksville U.S.A. 116 F8
Markt Schwaben Germany 25 G7
Marktoberdorf Germany 25 H6
Marktredwitz Germany 25 E8
Marl Germany 24 D3
Marla Australia 95 D1
Marlbank Canada 114 B7
Marlboro U.S.A. 115 E11
Marlborough Australia 94 C4
Marlborough U.K. 15 F6
Marlborough U.S.A. 115 D13
Marlborough Downs U.K. 15 F6
Marle France 19 C10
Marlin U.S.A. 116 F6
Marlow Germany 24 A8
Marlow U.K. 15 F7
Marlow U.S.A. 116 D6
Marmagao India 66 M8
Marmande France 20 D4
Marmara Turkey 45 F11
Marmara, Sea of = Marmara Denizi Turkey 45 F12
Marmara Denizi Turkey 45 F12
Marmara Gölü Turkey 47 C10
Marmaris Turkey 47 E10
Marmaris Limanı Turkey 47 E10
Marmion, Mt. Australia 93 E2
Marmion L. Canada 104 C1
Marmolada, Mte. Italy 41 B8
Marmolejo Spain 37 G6
Marmora Canada 114 B7
Mármora, La Italy 42 C2
Marnay France 19 E12
Marne Germany 24 B5
Marne □ France 19 D11
Marne → France 19 D9
Marneuli Georgia 35 K7
Maroala Madag. 89 B8
Maroantsetra Madag. 89 B8
Maroelaboom Namibia 88 B2
Marofandilia Madag. 89 C7
Marojejy ⌓ Madag. 89 A8
Marolambo Madag. 89 C8
Maromandia Madag. 89 A8
Maromokotro Madag. 89 A8
Marondera Zimbabwe 87 F3
Maroni → Fr. Guiana 125 B8
Maronia Greece 45 F9
Maronne → France 20 C5
Maroochydore Australia 95 D5
Maroona Australia 95 F3
Maros → Hungary 28 D5
Marosakoa Madag. 89 B8
Maroseranana Madag. 89 B8
Maróstica Italy 41 C8
Marotandrano Madag. 89 B8
Marotaolano Madag. 89 A8
Maroua Cameroon 83 C7
Marovato Madag. 89 B8
Marovoay Madag. 89 B8
Marquard S. Africa 88 D4
Marquesas Fracture Zone Pac. Oc. 97 H15
Marquesas Is. = Marquises, Îs. French Polynesia 97 H14
Marquette U.S.A. 112 B10
Marquis St. Lucia 121 f
Marquise France 19 B8
Marquises, Îs. French Polynesia 97 H14
Marra, Djebel Sudan 79 F10
Marra, Gebel Sudan 81 F2
Marracuene Mozam. 89 D5
Marradi Italy 41 D8
Marrakech Morocco 78 B4
Marratxi Spain 38 F7
Marrawah Australia 95 G3
Marree Australia 95 D2
Marrero U.S.A. 117 G9
Marrimane Mozam. 89 C5
Marromeu Mozam. 89 B6
Marromeu ⌓ Mozam. 89 B6
Marroquí, Punta Spain 37 K5
Marrowie Cr. → Australia 95 E4
Marrubane Mozam. 87 F4
Marrúbiu Italy 42 C1
Marrupa Mozam. 87 E4
Mars Hill U.S.A. 113 B20
Marsá 'Alam Egypt 80 B3
Marsá Matrûh Egypt 80 A2
Marsá Sha'b Sudan 80 C4
Marsá Susah Libya 79 B10
Marsabit Kenya 86 B4
Marsabit △ Kenya 86 B4
Marsala Italy 42 E5
Marsalforn Malta 49 C1
Mârşani Romania 29 F9
Marsberg Germany 24 D4
Marsciano Italy 41 F9
Marsden Australia 95 E4
Marseillan France 20 E7
Marseille France 21 E9
Marseille-Marignane ✈ (MRS) France 21 E9
Marseilles = Marseille France 21 E9
Marsh I. U.S.A. 116 G9
Marshall Liberia 82 D2
Marshall Ark., U.S.A. 116 D8
Marshall Mich., U.S.A. 113 D11
Marshall Minn., U.S.A. 112 C6
Marshall Mo., U.S.A. 112 F7
Marshall Tex., U.S.A. 116 E7
Marshall → Australia 94 C2
Marshall Is. ■ Pac. Oc. 90 A10
Marshalltown U.S.A. 112 D7
Marshbrook Zimbabwe 89 B5
Marshfield Mo., U.S.A. 112 G7
Marshfield Vt., U.S.A. 115 B12
Marshfield Wis., U.S.A. 112 C8
Marshūn Iran 71 B6
Mársico Nuovo Italy 43 B8
Märsta Sweden 10 E11
Marstal Denmark 11 K4
Marstrand Sweden 11 G5
Mart U.S.A. 116 F6
Marta → Italy 41 F8
Martaban Burma 67 L20
Martaban, G. of Burma 67 L20
Martano Italy 43 B11
Martapura Kalimantan, Indonesia 62 E4
Martapura Sumatera, Indonesia 62 E2
Marte Nigeria 83 C7
Marte R. Gómez, Presa Mexico 119 B5
Martel France 20 D5
Martelange Belgium 17 E5
Martellago Italy 41 C9
Martés, Sierra Spain 39 F4
Martfű Hungary 28 C5
Martha's Vineyard U.S.A. 115 E14
Martigné-Ferchaud France 18 E5
Martigny Switz. 25 J3
Martigues France 21 E9
Martin Slovak Rep. 27 B11
Martin S. Dak., U.S.A. 112 D3
Martin Tenn., U.S.A. 117 C10
Martín → Spain 38 D4
Martin L. U.S.A. 117 E12
Martina Franca Italy 43 B10
Martinborough N.Z. 91 D5
Martinez Calif., U.S.A. 110 G4
Martinez Ga., U.S.A. 117 E13
Martinique ☒ W. Indies 120 c
Martinique Passage W. Indies 121 C7
Martino Greece 46 C5
Martinópolis Brazil 127 A5
Martin's Bay Barbados 121 g
Martins Ferry U.S.A. 114 F4
Martinsberg Austria 26 C8
Martinsburg Pa., U.S.A. 114 F6
Martinsburg W. Va., U.S.A. 113 F15
Martinsicuro Italy 41 F10
Martinsville Ind., U.S.A. 112 F10
Martinsville Va., U.S.A. 113 G14
Marton N.Z. 91 D5
Martorell Spain 38 D6
Martos Spain 37 H7
Martuni Armenia 35 K7
Maru Nigeria 83 C6
Marudi Malaysia 62 D4
Maruf Afghan. 66 D5
Marugame Japan 55 G6
Marunga Angola 88 B3
Marungu, Mts. Dem. Rep. of the Congo 86 D3
Marv Dasht Iran 71 D7
Marvast Iran 71 D7
Marvejols France 20 D7
Marvel Loch Australia 93 F2
Marwar India 68 G5
Mary Turkmenistan 71 B9
Maryborough = Port Laoise Ireland 12 C4
Maryborough Queens., Australia 95 D5
Maryborough Vic., Australia 95 F3
Maryfield Canada 103 D8
Maryland □ U.S.A. 113 F15
Maryland Junction Zimbabwe 87 F3
Maryport U.K. 14 C4

Mary's Harbour *Canada* **105** B8
Marystown *Canada* **105** C8
Marysville *Canada* **102** D5
Marysville *Calif., U.S.A.* **110** F5
Marysville *Kans., U.S.A.* **112** F5
Marysville *Mich., U.S.A.* **114** D2
Marysville *Ohio, U.S.A.* **113** E12
Marysville *Wash., U.S.A.* **110** B4
Maryville *Mo., U.S.A.* **112** E6
Maryville *Tenn., U.S.A.* **117** D13
Marzūq *Libya* **79** C8
Marzūq, Idehān *Libya* **79** D8
Masada *Israel* **74** D4
Masahunga *Tanzania* **86** C3
Masai *Malaysia* **65** d
Masai Mara △ *Kenya* **86** C4
Masai Steppe *Tanzania* **86** C4
Masaka *Uganda* **86** C3
Masalembo, Kepulauan
    Indonesia **62** F4
Masalima, Kepulauan
    Indonesia **62** F5
Masallı *Azerbaijan* **73** C13
Masamba *Indonesia* **63** E6
Masan *S. Korea* **57** G15
Masandam, Ra's *Oman* **71** E8
Masasa *Nic.* **120** D2
Masasi *Tanzania* **87** E4
Masaya *Nic.* **120** D2
Masba *Nigeria* **83** C7
Masbate *Phil.* **61** E5
Máscali *Italy* **43** E8
Mascara *Algeria* **78** A6
Mascota *Mexico* **118** C4
Masela *Indonesia* **63** F7
Maseru *Lesotho* **88** D4
Mashaba *Zimbabwe* **87** G3
Mashābih *Si. Arabia* **70** E3
Mashan *China* **58** F7
Mashar *Sudan* **81** F2
Mashegu *Nigeria* **83** D6
Masherbrum *Pakistan* **69** B7
Mashhad *Iran* **71** B8
Mashi *Nigeria* **83** C6
Mashiz *Iran* **71** D8
Māshkel, Hāmūn-i- *Pakistan* **71** D9
Mashki Chāh *Pakistan* **66** E3
Mashonaland *Zimbabwe* **85** H6
Mashonaland Central □
    Zimbabwe **89** B5
Mashonaland East □
    Zimbabwe **89** B5
Mashonaland West □
    Zimbabwe **89** B4
Mashrakh *India* **69** F11
Mashtaga = Maştağa
    Azerbaijan **35** K10
Masi Manimba
    Dem. Rep. of the Congo **84** E3
Masindi *Uganda* **86** B3
Masindi Port *Uganda* **86** B3
Maşīrah *Oman* **75** C6
Maşīrah, Khalīj *Oman* **75** C6
Masisi *Dem. Rep. of the Congo* **86** C2
Masjed Soleyman *Iran* **71** D6
Mask, L. *Ireland* **12** C2
Maskin *Oman* **71** F8
Maslen Nos *Bulgaria* **45** D11
Maslinica *Croatia* **41** E13
Masnou = El Masnou *Spain* **38** D7
Masoala, Tanjon' i *Madag.* **89** B9
Masoala △ *Madag.* **89** B9
Masoarivo *Madag.* **89** B7
Masohi = Amahai *Indonesia* **63** E7
Masomeloka *Madag.* **89** C8
Mason *Nev., U.S.A.* **110** G7
Mason *Tex., U.S.A.* **116** F5
Mason City *U.S.A.* **112** D8
Maspalomas *Canary Is.* **48** G4
Maspalomas, Pta. *Canary Is.* **48** G4
Masqat *Oman* **75** C6
Masr el Gedida *Egypt* **80** H7
Massa *Italy* **40** D7
Massa Maríttima *Italy* **40** E7
Massachusetts □ *U.S.A.* **115** D13
Massachusetts B. *U.S.A.* **115** D14
Massafra *Italy* **43** B10
Massakory *Chad* **79** F9
Massanella *Spain* **48** B9
Massangena *Mozam.* **89** C5
Massango *Angola* **84** F3
Massat *France* **20** F5
Massawa = Mitsiwa *Eritrea* **81** D4
Massena *U.S.A.* **115** B10
Massénya *Chad* **79** F9
Masset *Canada* **102** C2
Masseube *France* **20** E4
Massiac *France* **20** C7
Massiah Street *Barbados* **121** g
Massif Central *France* **20** D7
Massif des Bauges △ *France* **19** G13
Massigui *Mali* **82** C3
Massillon *U.S.A.* **114** F3
Massinga *Mozam.* **89** C6
Massingir *Mozam.* **89** C5
Masson-Angers *Canada* **115** A9
Masson I. *Antarctica* **5** C7

Maştağa *Azerbaijan* **35** K10
Mastanli = Momchilgrad
    Bulgaria **45** E9
Masterton *N.Z.* **91** D5
Mastic *U.S.A.* **115** F12
Mastuj *Pakistan* **69** A5
Mastung *Pakistan* **66** E5
Mastūrah *Si. Arabia* **80** C4
Masty *Belarus* **23** B13
Masuda *Japan* **55** G5
Masvingo *Zimbabwe* **87** G3
Masvingo □ *Zimbabwe* **87** G3
Maswa △ *Tanzania* **86** C3
Maşyāf *Syria* **72** E7
Maszewo *Poland* **30** E2
Mat → *Albania* **44** E3
Mata-au = Clutha → *N.Z.* **91** G2
Matabeleland North □
    Zimbabwe **87** F2
Matabeleland South □
    Zimbabwe **87** G2
Matachel → *Spain* **37** G4
Matachewan *Canada* **104** C3
Matadi *Dem. Rep. of the Congo* **84** F2
Matagalpa *Nic.* **120** D2
Matagami *Canada* **104** C4
Matagami, L. *Canada* **104** C4
Matagorda B. *U.S.A.* **116** G6
Matagorda I. *U.S.A.* **116** G6
Mataiea *Tahiti* **91** d
Matak *Indonesia* **62** D3
Matala *Greece* **49** E6
Matam *Senegal* **82** B2
Matameye *Niger* **83** C6
Matamoros *Campeche,
    Mexico* **119** D6
Matamoros *Coahuila, Mexico* **118** B4
Matamoros *Tamaulipas,
    Mexico* **119** B5
Matandu → *Tanzania* **87** D3
Matane *Canada* **105** C6
Matang *China* **58** F5
Matankari *Niger* **83** C5
Matanomadh *India* **68** H3
Matanzas *Cuba* **120** B3
Matapa *Botswana* **88** C3
Matapan, C. = Ténaro,
    Akra *Greece* **46** E4
Matapédia *Canada* **105** C6
Matapo △ *Zimbabwe* **87** G2
Matara *Sri Lanka* **66** S12
Mataram *Indonesia* **63** K19
Matarani *Peru* **124** G4
Mataranka *Australia* **92** B5
Matarma, Râs *Egypt* **74** E1
Mataró *Spain* **38** D7
Matarraña → *Spain* **38** D5
Mataruška Banja *Serbia* **44** C4
Matatiele *S. Africa* **89** E4
Mataura *N.Z.* **91** G2
Matavai, B. de *Tahiti* **91** d
Matehuala *Mexico* **118** C4
Mateke Hills *Zimbabwe* **87** G3
Matelot *Trin. & Tob.* **125** K15
Matera *Italy* **43** B9
Matese, Monti del *Italy* **43** A7
Matese △ *Italy* **43** A7
Mátészalka *Hungary* **28** C7
Matetsi *Zimbabwe* **87** F2
Matfors *Sweden* **10** B11
Matha *France* **20** C3
Matheniko △ *Uganda* **86** B3
Mathis *U.S.A.* **116** G6
Mathraki *Greece* **49** A3
Mathura *India* **68** F7
Mati *Phil.* **61** H7
Matiakoali *Burkina Faso* **83** C5
Matiali *India* **69** F13
Matías Romero *Mexico* **119** D5
Matibane *Mozam.* **87** E5
Matiri Ra. *N.Z.* **91** D4
Matjiesfontein *S. Africa* **88** E3
Matla → *India* **69** J13
Matlamanyane *Botswana* **88** B4
Matli *Pakistan* **68** G3
Matlock *U.K.* **14** D6
Matna *Sudan* **81** E4
Mato Grosso □ *Brazil* **125** F8
Mato Grosso, Planalto do
    Brazil **125** G8
Mato Grosso do Sul □
    Brazil **125** G8
Matobo = Matapo △
    Zimbabwe **87** G2
Matochkin Shar *Russia* **52** B6
Matopo Hills *Zimbabwe* **87** G2
Matopos *Zimbabwe* **87** G2
Matosinhos *Portugal* **36** D2
Matour *France* **19** F11
Matroosberg *S. Africa* **88** E2
Matsena *Nigeria* **83** C7
Matsesta *Russia* **35** J4
Matsu Tao *Taiwan* **59** E13
Matsue *Japan* **55** G6

Matsum, Ko *Thailand* **65** b
Matsumae *Japan* **54** D10
Matsumoto *Japan* **55** F9
Matsusaka *Japan* **55** G8
Matsuura *Japan* **55** H4
Matsuyama *Japan* **55** H6
Mattagami → *Canada* **104** B3
Mattancheri *India* **66** Q10
Mattawa *Canada* **104** B4
Matterhorn *Switz.* **25** K3
Mattersburg *Austria* **27** D9
Matthew Town *Bahamas* **121** B5
Matthews Ridge *Guyana* **124** B6
Mattice *Canada* **104** C3
Mattituck *U.S.A.* **115** F12
Mattò *Japan* **55** F8
Mattoon *U.S.A.* **112** F9
Matuba *Mozam.* **89** C5
Matucana *Peru* **124** F3
Matuku *Fiji* **91** a
Matūn = Khowst *Afghan.* **68** C3
Matura *Trin. & Tob.* **125** K15
Maturín *Venezuela* **124** B6
Matusadona △ *Zimbabwe* **87** F2
Matveyev Kurgan *Russia* **33** J10
Matxitxako, C. *Spain* **38** B2
Mau *Mad. P., India* **69** F8
Mau *Ut. P., India* **69** G9
Mau *Ut. P., India* **69** G9
Mau Escarpment *Kenya* **86** C4
Mau Ranipur *India* **69** G8
Maua *Kenya* **86** C4
Maubeuge *France* **19** B10
Maubin *Burma* **67** L19
Maubourguet *France* **20** E4
Maud, Pt. *Australia* **92** D1
Maud Rise *S. Ocean* **5** C3
Maude *Australia* **95** E3
Maudin Sun *Burma* **67** M19
Maués *Brazil* **124** D7
Mauganj *India* **69** G9
Maughold Hd. *I. of Man* **14** C3
Mauguio *France* **20** E7
Maui *U.S.A.* **106** b
Maulamyaing =
    Moulmein *Burma* **67** L20
Maule □ *Chile* **126** D1
Mauléon-Licharre *France* **20** E3
Maumee *U.S.A.* **113** E12
Maumee → *U.S.A.* **113** E12
Maumere *Indonesia* **63** F6
Maumusson, Pertuis de
    France **20** C2
Maun *Botswana* **88** C3
Mauna Kea *U.S.A.* **106** b
Mauna Loa *U.S.A.* **106** b
Maungmagan Kyunzu
    Burma **64** E1
Maungu *Kenya* **86** C4
Maupin *U.S.A.* **108** D3
Maure-de-Bretagne *France* **18** E5
Maurepas, L. *U.S.A.* **117** F9
Maures *France* **21** E10
Mauriac *France* **20** C6
Maurice, L. *Australia* **93** E5
Mauricie △ *Canada* **104** C5
Maurienne *France* **21** C10
Mauritania ■ *Africa* **78** E3
Mauritius ■ *Ind. Oc.* **85** d
Mauron *France* **18** D4
Maurs *France* **20** D6
Mauston *U.S.A.* **112** D8
Mauterndorf *Austria* **26** D6
Mauthen *Austria* **26** E6
Mauvezin *France* **20** E4
Mauzé-sur-le-Mignon
    France **20** B3
Mavli *India* **68** G5
Mavrovë *Albania* **44** F3
Mavrovo △ *Macedonia* **44** E4
Mavuradonha Mts.
    Zimbabwe **87** F3
Mawa *Dem. Rep. of the Congo* **86** B2
Mawai *India* **69** H9
Mawana *India* **68** E7
Mawand *Pakistan* **68** E3
Mawjib, W. al → *Jordan* **74** D4
Mawk Mai *Burma* **67** J20
Mawlaik *Burma* **67** H19
Mawlamyine = Moulmein
    Burma **67** L20
Mawqaq *Si. Arabia* **70** E4
Mawson Base *Antarctica* **5** C6
Mawson Coast *Antarctica* **5** C6
Max *U.S.A.* **112** B3
Maxcanú *Mexico* **119** C6
Maxesibeni *S. Africa* **89** E4
Maxhamish L. *Canada* **102** B4
Maxixe *Mozam.* **89** C6
Maxville *Canada* **115** A10
Maxwell *U.S.A.* **110** F4
Maxwelton *Australia* **94** C3
May, C. *U.S.A.* **113** F16
May Pen *Jamaica* **120** a
Maya → *Russia* **53** D14
Maya Mts. *Belize* **119** D7
Mayaguana *Bahamas* **121** B5

Mayagüez *Puerto Rico* **121** d
Mayahi *Niger* **83** C6
Mayaky *Ukraine* **29** C14
Mayals = Maials *Spain* **38** D5
Mayang *China* **58** D7
Mayanup *Australia* **93** F2
Mayapán *Mexico* **119** C7
Mayarí *Cuba* **121** B4
Mayaro B. *Trin. & Tob.* **125** K16
Maybell *U.S.A.* **108** F9
Maybole *U.K.* **13** F4
Maychew *Ethiopia* **81** E4
Maydān *Iraq* **73** E11
Maydan *Ukraine* **29** B8
Maydena *Australia* **95** G4
Mayen *Germany* **25** E3
Mayenne *France* **18** D6
Mayenne □ *France* **18** D6
Mayenne → *France* **18** E6
Mayer *U.S.A.* **109** J7
Mayerthorpe *Canada* **102** C5
Mayfield *Ky., U.S.A.* **112** G9
Mayfield *N.Y., U.S.A.* **115** C10
Mayhill *U.S.A.* **109** K11
Maykop *Russia* **35** H5
Maymyo *Burma* **64** A1
Maynard *Mass., U.S.A.* **115** D13
Maynard *Wash., U.S.A.* **110** C4
Maynard Hills *Australia* **93** E2
Mayne → *Australia* **94** C3
Maynooth *Ireland* **12** C5
Mayo *Canada* **100** C6
Mayo □ *Ireland* **12** C2
Mayo Daga *Nigeria* **83** D7
Mayo Faran *Nigeria* **83** D7
Mayon Volcano *Phil.* **61** E5
Mayor I. *N.Z.* **91** B6
Mayorga *Spain* **36** C5
Mayotte ☑ *Ind. Oc.* **85** a
Mayraira Pt. *Phil.* **61** B4
Maysān □ *Iraq* **70** D5
Mayskiy *Russia* **35** J7
Maysville *U.S.A.* **113** F12
Mayu *Indonesia* **63** D7
Mayville *N. Dak., U.S.A.* **112** B5
Mayville *N.Y., U.S.A.* **114** D5
Mayya *Russia* **53** C14
Mazabuka *Zambia* **87** F2
Mazagán = El Jadida
    Morocco **78** B4
Mazagão *Brazil* **125** D8
Mazamet *France* **20** E6
Mazán *Peru* **124** D4
Māzandarān □ *Iran* **71** B7
Mazapil *Mexico* **118** C4
Mazara del Vallo *Italy* **42** E5
Mazarrón *Spain* **39** H3
Mazarrón, G. de *Spain* **39** H3
Mazaruni → *Guyana* **124** B7
Mazatán *Mexico* **118** B2
Mazatenango *Guatemala* **120** D1
Mazatlán *Mexico* **118** C3
Mažeikiai *Lithuania* **30** B9
Māzhān *Iran* **71** C8
Mazīnān *Iran* **71** B8
Mazoe *Mozam.* **87** F3
Mazoe → *Mozam.* **87** F3
Mazowe *Zimbabwe* **87** F3
Mazowieckie □ *Poland* **31** F8
Mazrûb *Sudan* **81** E2
Mazu Dao *China* **59** D12
Mazurian Lakes =
    Mazurski, Pojezierze
    Poland **30** E7
Mazurski, Pojezierze *Poland* **30** E7
Mazyr *Belarus* **23** B15
Mba *Fiji* **91** a
Mbaba *Senegal* **82** C1
Mbabane *Swaziland* **89** D5
Mbagne *Mauritania* **82** B2
M'bahiakro *Ivory C.* **82** D4
Mbaïki *C.A.R.* **84** D3
Mbala *Zambia* **87** D3
Mbalabala *Zimbabwe* **89** C4
Mbale *Uganda* **86** B3
Mbalmayo *Cameroon* **83** E7
Mbam → *Cameroon* **83** E7
Mbamba Bay *Tanzania* **87** E3
Mbandaka
    Dem. Rep. of the Congo **84** D3
Mbanga *Cameroon* **83** E6
Mbanza Congo *Angola* **84** F2
Mbanza Ngungu
    Dem. Rep. of the Congo **84** F2
Mbarangandu *Tanzania* **87** D4
Mbarara *Uganda* **86** C3
Mbatto *Ivory C.* **82** D4
Mbengga = Beqa *Fiji* **91** a
Mbenkuru → *Tanzania* **87** D4
Mberengwa *Zimbabwe* **87** G2
Mberengwa, Mt. *Zimbabwe* **87** G2
Mberubu *Nigeria* **83** D6
Mbesuma *Zambia* **87** E3
Mbeya *Tanzania* **87** D3
Mbeya □ *Tanzania* **86** D3
Mbhashe → *S. Africa* **89** E4

M'bili *Sudan* **81** F2
Mbinga *Tanzania* **87** E4
Mbini = Río Muni □
    Eq. Guin. **84** D2
Mboki *C.A.R.* **81** F2
M'bonge *Cameroon* **83** E6
Mboro *Senegal* **82** B1
M'boukou, Rés. de *Cameroon* **83** D7
Mboune *Senegal* **82** C2
Mbour *Senegal* **82** C1
Mbout *Mauritania* **82** B2
Mbuji-Mayi
    Dem. Rep. of the Congo **86** D1
Mbulu *Tanzania* **86** C4
Mburucuyá *Argentina* **126** B4
Mchinja *Tanzania* **87** D4
Mchinji *Malawi* **87** E3
Mdantsane *S. Africa* **89** L5
Mead, L. *U.S.A.* **111** J12
Meade *U.S.A.* **112** G3
Meadow Lake *Canada* **103** C7
Meadow Lake △ *Canada* **103** C7
Meadow Valley Wash →
    U.S.A. **111** J12
Meadville *U.S.A.* **114** E4
Mealy Mts. *Canada* **105** B8
Meander River *Canada* **102** B5
Meares, C. *U.S.A.* **108** D1
Mearim → *Brazil* **125** D10
Meath □ *Ireland* **12** C5
Meath Park *Canada* **103** C7
Meaulne *France* **19** F9
Meaux *France* **19** D9
Mebechi-Gawa → *Japan* **54** D10
Mebulu, Tanjung *Indonesia* **63** K18
Mecanhelas *Mozam.* **87** F4
Mecca = Makkah *Si. Arabia* **80** C4
Mecca *U.S.A.* **111** M10
Mechanicsburg *U.S.A.* **114** F8
Mechanicville *U.S.A.* **115** D11
Mechara *Ethiopia* **81** F5
Mechelen *Belgium* **17** C4
Mecheria *Algeria* **78** B5
Mechernich *Germany* **24** E2
Mechetinskaya *Russia* **35** G5
Mecidiye *Turkey* **45** F10
Mecitözü *Turkey* **72** B6
Mecklenburg *Germany* **22** B7
Mecklenburg-
    Vorpommern □ *Germany* **24** B8
Mecklenburger Bucht
    Germany **24** A7
Meconta *Mozam.* **87** E4
Mecsek *Hungary* **28** D3
Meda *Portugal* **36** E3
Medan *Indonesia* **62** D1
Médanos de Coro △
    Venezuela **121** D6
Medanosa, Pta. *Argentina* **128** F3
Mede *Italy* **40** C5
Médéa *Algeria* **78** A6
Mededa *Bos.-H.* **28** C4
Medellín *Colombia* **124** B3
Medelpad *Sweden* **10** B10
Medemblik *Neths.* **17** B5
Medford *Mass., U.S.A.* **115** D13
Medford *Oreg., U.S.A.* **108** E2
Medford *Wis., U.S.A.* **112** C8
Medgidia *Romania* **29** F13
Medi *Sudan* **81** F3
Media Agua *Argentina* **126** C2
Media Luna *Argentina* **126** C2
Medianeira *Brazil* **127** B5
Mediaş *Romania* **29** D9
Medicina *Italy* **41** D8
Medicine Bow *U.S.A.* **108** F10
Medicine Bow Mts. *U.S.A.* **108** F10
Medicine Bow Pk. *U.S.A.* **108** F10
Medicine Hat *Canada* **103** D6
Medicine Lake *U.S.A.* **108** B11
Medicine Lodge *U.S.A.* **112** G4
Medina = Al Madīnah
    Si. Arabia **80** C4
Medina *N. Dak., U.S.A.* **112** B5
Medina *N.Y., U.S.A.* **114** C6
Medina *Ohio, U.S.A.* **114** E3
Medina → *U.S.A.* **116** G5
Medina de Pomar *Spain* **36** C7
Medina de Ríoseco *Spain* **36** D5
Medina del Campo *Spain* **36** D6
Medina L. *U.S.A.* **116** G5
Medina Sidonia *Spain* **37** J5
Medinaceli *Spain* **38** D2
Medinipur *India* **69** H12
Mediterranean Sea *Europe* **6** H7
Médoc *France* **20** C3
Medulin *Croatia* **41** D10
Medveda *Serbia* **44** D5
Medvedevo *Russia* **34** B8
Medveditsa → *Tver, Russia* **32** D9
Medveditsa →
    *Volgograd,
    Russia* **34** F6
Medvedok *Russia* **34** B10
Medvezhi, Ostrava *Russia* **53** B17

Medvezhyegorsk *Russia* **52** C4
Medway □ *U.K.* **15** F8
Medway → *U.K.* **15** F8
Medzev *Slovak Rep.* **27** C13
Medzilaborce *Slovak Rep.* **27** B14
Medžitlija *Macedonia* **44** F5
Meekatharra *Australia* **93** E2
Meeker *U.S.A.* **108** F10
Meelpaeg L. *Canada* **105** C8
Meersburg *Germany* **25** H5
Meerut *India* **68** E7
Meeteetse *U.S.A.* **108** D9
Mega *Ethiopia* **81** G4
Megalo Horio *Greece* **47** E9
Megalonisos *Greece* **46** D5
Megalopoli *Greece* **46** D4
Meganisi *Greece* **46** C2
Megara *Greece* **46** D5
Megasini *India* **69** J12
Megdovas = Tavropos →
    Greece **46** B3
Megève *France* **21** C10
Meghalaya □ *India* **67** G17
Meghezez *Ethiopia* **81** F4
Meghna → *Bangla.* **67** H17
Mégiscane, L. *Canada* **104** C4
Megisti *Greece* **47** E11
Megra *Russia* **32** B9
Mehadia *Romania* **28** F7
Meharry, Mt. *Australia* **92** D2
Mehedeby *Sweden* **10** D11
Mehedinţi □ *Romania* **28** F7
Meheisa *Sudan* **80** D3
Mehlville *U.S.A.* **112** F8
Mehndawal *India* **69** F10
Mehr Jān *Iran* **71** C7
Mehrābād *Iran* **73** D12
Mehrān *Iran* **73** F12
Mehrgarh *Pakistan* **68** E2
Mehrīz *Iran* **71** D7
Mehun-sur-Yèvre *France* **19** E9
Mei Jiang → *China* **59** E11
Mei Xian *China* **56** G4
Meicheng *China* **59** C12
Meichengzhen *China* **59** C8
Meichuan *China* **59** B10
Meighen I. *Canada* **101** B10
Meigu *China* **58** C4
Meihekou *China* **57** C13
Meiktila *Burma* **67** J19
Meinerzhagen *Germany* **24** D3
Meiningen *Germany* **24** E6
Meira, Serra de *Spain* **36** B3
Meiringen *Switz.* **25** J4
Meishan *China* **58** B4
Meissen *Germany* **24** D9
Meissner *Germany* **24** D5
Meissner-Kaufunger
    Wald △ *Germany* **24** D5
Meitan *China* **58** D6
Meizhou *China* **59** E11
Meja *India* **69** G10
Mejillones *Chile* **126** A1
Mekdela *Ethiopia* **81** E4
Mekerghene, Sebkra *Algeria* **78** C6
Mekhtar *Pakistan* **66** D6
Meko *Nigeria* **83** D5
Mekong → *Asia* **65** H6
Mekongga *Indonesia* **63** E6
Mekrou → *Benin* **83** C5
Mekvari = Kür →
    Azerbaijan **73** C13
Mel *Italy* **41** B9
Melagiri Hills *India* **66** N10
Melaka *Malaysia* **65** L4
Melalap *Malaysia* **62** C5
Melambes *Greece* **49** D6
Melanesia *Pac. Oc.* **96** H7
Melanesian Basin *Pac. Oc.* **96** G8
Melaya *Indonesia* **63** J17
Melbourne *Australia* **95** F4
Melbourne *U.S.A.* **117** G14
Melchor Múzquiz *Mexico* **118** B4
Melchor Ocampo *Mexico* **118** C4
Méldola *Italy* **41** D9
Meldorf *Germany* **24** A5
Melegnano *Italy* **40** C6
Melenci *Serbia* **28** E5
Melenki *Russia* **34** C5
Mélèzes → *Canada* **104** A5
Melfi *Italy* **43** B8
Melfort *Canada* **103** C8
Melfort *Zimbabwe* **87** F3
Melgaço *Portugal* **36** C2
Melgar de Fernamental
    Spain **36** C6
Melhus *Norway* **8** E14
Melide *Spain* **36** C2
Meligalas *Greece* **46** D3
Melilla *N. Afr.* **78** A5
Melilli *Italy* **43** E8
Melipilla *Chile* **126** C1
Melissa, Akra *Greece* **49** D6
Melissa Oros *Greece* **47** D8
Melita *Canada* **103** D8

Mélito di Porto Salvo *Italy* **43** E8
Melitopol *Ukraine* **33** J8
Melk *Austria* **26** C8
Mellan Fryken *Sweden* **10** E7
Mellansel *Sweden* **8** E18
Mellbystrand *Sweden* **11** H6
Melle *France* **20** B3
Melle *Germany* **24** C4
Mellen *U.S.A.* **112** B8
Mellette *U.S.A.* **112** C4
Mellid = Melide *Spain* **36** C2
Mellieha *Malta* **49** D1
Mellit *Sudan* **81** E2
Mellrichstadt *Germany* **24** E6
Melnik *Bulgaria* **44** E7
Mělník *Czech Rep.* **26** A7
Melnytsya Podilska *Ukraine* **29** B11
Melo *Uruguay* **127** C5
Melolo *Indonesia* **63** F6
Melouprey *Cambodia* **64** F5
Melrhir, Chott *Algeria* **78** B7
Melrose *Australia* **95** E4
Melrose *U.K.* **13** F6
Melrose *Minn., U.S.A.* **112** C6
Melrose *N. Mex., U.S.A.* **109** J12
Melstone *U.S.A.* **108** C10
Melsungen *Germany* **24** D5
Melton Mowbray *U.K.* **14** E7
Melun *France* **19** D9
Melut *Sudan* **81** E3
Melville *Canada* **103** C8
Melville, C. *Australia* **94** A3
Melville, L. *Canada* **105** B8
Melville B. *Australia* **94** A2
Melville I. *Australia* **92** B5
Melville I. *Canada* **101** B8
Melville Pen. *Canada* **101** C11
Melvin, Lough *Ireland* **12** B3
Mélykút *Hungary* **28** D4
Memaliaj *Albania* **44** F3
Memba *Mozam.* **87** E5
Memboro *Indonesia* **63** F5
Membrilla *Spain* **37** G7
Memel = Klaipeda *Lithuania* **30** C8
Memel *S. Africa* **89** D4
Memmingen *Germany* **25** H6
Mempawah *Indonesia* **62** D3
Memphis *Egypt* **80** J7
Memphis *Mich., U.S.A.* **114** D2
Memphis *Tenn., U.S.A.* **117** D9
Memphis *Tex., U.S.A.* **116** D4
Memphrémagog, L.
  N. Amer. **115** B12
Mena *Ukraine* **33** G7
Mena *U.S.A.* **116** D7
Mena → *Ethiopia* **81** F5
Menai Strait *U.K.* **14** D3
Ménaka *Mali* **83** B5
Menan = Chao Phraya →
  Thailand **64** F3
Menarandra → *Madag.* **89** D7
Menard *U.S.A.* **116** F5
Menard Fracture Zone
  Pac. Oc. **97** M18
Menawashei *Sudan* **81** E1
Mendaña Fracture Zone
  Pac. Oc. **97** J18
Mendawai → *Indonesia* **62** E4
Mende *France* **20** D7
Mendebo Mts. *Ethiopia* **81** F4
Mendeleyev Ridge *Arctic* **4** B17
Menden *Germany* **24** D3
Menderes *Turkey* **47** C9
Mendhar *India* **69** C6
Mendi *Ethiopia* **81** F4
Mendip Hills *U.K.* **15** F5
Mendocino *U.S.A.* **108** G2
Mendocino, C. *U.S.A.* **108** F1
Mendocino Fracture Zone
  Pac. Oc. **97** D13
Mendota *Calif., U.S.A.* **110** J6
Mendota *Ill., U.S.A.* **112** E9
Mendoyo *Indonesia* **63** J17
Mendoza *Argentina* **126** C2
Mendoza □ *Argentina* **126** C2
Mene Grande *Venezuela* **124** B4
Menemen *Turkey* **47** C9
Menen *Belgium* **17** D3
Menfi *Italy* **42** E5
Mengdingjie *China* **58** F2
Mengeš *Slovenia* **41** B11
Menggala *Indonesia* **62** E3
Menghai *China* **58** G3
Mengíbar *Spain* **37** H7
Mengjin *China* **56** G7
Mengla *China* **58** G3
Menglian *China* **58** F2
Mengshan *China* **59** E8
Mengyin *China* **57** G9
Mengzhe *China* **58** F3
Mengzi *China* **58** F4
Menihek *Canada* **105** B6
Menihek L. *Canada* **105** B6
Menin = Menen *Belgium* **17** D3
Menindee *Australia* **95** E3
Menindee L. *Australia* **95** E3

Meningie *Australia* **95** F2
Menjangan, Pulau
  Indonesia **63** J17
Menlo Park *U.S.A.* **110** H4
Menominee *U.S.A.* **112** C10
Menominee → *U.S.A.* **112** C10
Menomonie *U.S.A.* **112** C8
Menongue *Angola* **85** G3
Menorca *Spain* **48** B11
Menorca ✈ (MAH) *Spain* **38** F9
Mentakab *Malaysia* **65** L4
Mentawai, Kepulauan
  Indonesia **62** E1
Menton *France* **21** E11
Mentor *U.S.A.* **114** E3
Menzies *Australia* **93** E3
Meob B. *Namibia* **88** C1
Me'ona *Israel* **74** B4
Meoqui *Mexico* **118** B3
Mepaco *Mozam.* **87** F3
Meppel *Neths.* **17** B6
Meppen *Germany* **24** C4
Mequinenza *Spain* **38** D5
Mequinenza, Embalse de
  Spain **38** D5
Mer *France* **18** E8
Merak *Indonesia* **63** F12
Meramangye, L. *Australia* **93** E5
Meran = Merano *Italy* **41** B8
Merano *Italy* **41** B8
Merate *Italy* **40** C6
Merauke *Indonesia* **63** F10
Merbein *Australia* **95** E3
Merbuk, Gunung *Indonesia* **63** J17
Merca = Marca *Somali Rep.* **75** G3
Mercato Saraceno *Italy* **41** E9
Merced *U.S.A.* **110** H6
Merced → *U.S.A.* **110** H6
Merced Pk. *U.S.A.* **110** H7
Mercedes *B. Aires, Argentina* **126** C4
Mercedes *Corrientes,*
  Argentina **126** B4
Mercedes *San Luis, Argentina* **126** C2
Mercedes *Uruguay* **126** C4
Merceditas *Chile* **126** B1
Mercer *N.Z.* **91** B5
Mercer *U.S.A.* **114** E4
Mercer Island *U.S.A.* **110** C4
Mercury *U.S.A.* **111** J11
Mercy, C. *Canada* **101** C13
Merdrignac *France* **18** D4
Mere *U.K.* **15** F5
Meredith, C. *Falk. Is.* **128** G4
Meredith, L. *U.S.A.* **116** D4
Merefa *Ukraine* **33** H9
Merei *Romania* **29** E11
Merga = Nukheila *Sudan* **80** D2
Mergui = Myeik *Burma* **65** G1
Mergui Arch. = Myeik
  Kyunzu *Burma* **65** G1
Metabetchouan *Canada* **105** C5
Méribel-les-Allues *France* **21** C10
Meriç *Turkey* **45** E10
Meriç → *Turkey* **45** F10
Mérida *Mexico* **119** C7
Mérida *Spain* **37** G4
Mérida *Venezuela* **124** B4
Mérida, Cord. de *Venezuela* **124** B4
Meriden *U.K.* **15** E6
Meriden *U.S.A.* **115** E12
Meridian *Calif., U.S.A.* **110** F5
Meridian *Idaho, U.S.A.* **108** E5
Meridian *Miss., U.S.A.* **117** E10
Mérignac *France* **20** D3
Mérinaghène *Senegal* **82** B1
Merinda *Australia* **94** C4
Mering *Germany* **25** G6
Meringa *Nigeria* **83** C7
Merir *Pac. Oc.* **63** D8
Merirumã *Brazil* **125** C8
Merkel *U.S.A.* **116** E4
Mermaid Reef *Australia* **92** C2
Merowe *Sudan* **80** D3
Merowe Dam *Sudan* **80** D3
Merredin *Australia* **93** F2
Merrick *U.K.* **13** F4
Merrickville *Canada* **115** B9
Merrill *Oreg., U.S.A.* **108** E3
Merrill *Wis., U.S.A.* **112** C9
Merrimack → *U.S.A.* **115** D14
Merriman *U.S.A.* **112** D3
Merritt *Canada* **102** C4
Merritt Island *U.S.A.* **117** G14
Merriwa *Australia* **95** E5
Merry I. *Canada* **104** A4
Merryville *U.S.A.* **116** F8
Mersa Fatma *Eritrea* **81** E5
Mersch *Lux.* **17** E6
Merse → *Italy* **41** E8
Mersea I. *U.K.* **15** F8
Merseburg *Germany* **24** D7
Mersey → *U.K.* **14** D4
Merseyside □ *U.K.* **14** D4
Mersin = İçel *Turkey* **72** D6
Mersing *Malaysia* **65** L4
Merta *India* **68** F6
Merta Road *India* **68** F5

Merthyr Tydfil *U.K.* **15** F4
Merthyr Tydfil □ *U.K.* **15** F4
Merti *Kenya* **86** B4
Mértola *Portugal* **37** H3
Mertzon *U.S.A.* **116** F4
Méru *France* **19** C9
Meru *Kenya* **86** B4
Meru *Tanzania* **86** C4
Meru △ *Kenya* **86** B4
Merville *France* **19** B9
Méry-sur-Seine *France* **19** D10
Merzifon *Turkey* **72** B6
Merzig *Germany* **25** F2
Mesa *U.S.A.* **109** K8
Mesa Verde △ *U.S.A.* **109** H9
Mesagne *Italy* **43** B10
Mesanagros *Greece* **49** C9
Mesaoría *Cyprus* **49** D12
Meschede *Germany* **24** D4
Mescit *Turkey* **73** B9
Mesfinto *Ethiopia* **81** E4
Mesgouez, L. *Canada* **104** B5
Meshchovsk *Russia* **32** E8
Meshed = Mashhad *Iran* **71** B8
Meshoppen *U.S.A.* **115** E8
Meshra er Req *Sudan* **81** F2
Mesilinka → *Canada* **102** B4
Meslay-du-Maine *France* **18** E6
Mesocco *Switz.* **25** J5
Mesologi *Greece* **46** C3
Mesongi *Greece* **49** B3
Mesopotamia = Al Jazirah
  Iraq **73** E10
Mesopotamia *U.S.A.* **114** E4
Mesopotamo *Greece* **46** B2
Mesoraca *Italy* **43** C9
Mésou Volimais = Volimes
  Greece **46** D2
Mesquite *U.S.A.* **109** H6
Messaad *Algeria* **78** B6
Messac *France* **18** E5
Messalo → *Mozam.* **87** E4
Méssamena *Cameroon* **83** E7
Messara, Kolpos *Greece* **49** D6
Messina = Musina *S. Africa* **89** C5
Messina *Italy* **43** D8
Messina, Str. di *Italy* **43** D8
Messini *Greece* **46** D4
Messinia □ *Greece* **46** D3
Messiniakos Kolpos *Greece* **46** E4
Messkirch *Germany* **25** H5
Messlingen *Sweden* **10** B6
Mesta → *Bulgaria* **44** E7
Mesta, Akra *Greece* **47** C7
Mestanza *Spain* **37** G6
Mestre *Italy* **41** C9
Mesudiye *Turkey* **72** B7
Meta → *S. Amer.* **124** B5
Meta Incognita Pen. *Canada*
  101 C13
Metabetchouan *Canada* **105** C5
Metairie *U.S.A.* **117** F9
Metalici, Munții *Romania* **28** D7
Metaline Falls *U.S.A.* **108** B5
Metallifere, Colline *Italy* **40** E8
Metán *Argentina* **126** B3
Metangula *Mozam.* **87** E3
Metauro → *Italy* **41** E10
Metema *Ethiopia* **81** E4
Metengobalame *Mozam.* **87** E3
Methana *Greece* **46** D5
Methoni *Greece* **46** E3
Methven *N.Z.* **91** E3
Metil *Mozam.* **87** F4
Metlakatla *U.S.A.* **100** D6
Metković *Croatia* **41** E14
Metlika *Slovenia* **41** C12
Metropolis *U.S.A.* **112** G9
Metsovo *Greece* **46** B3
Metu *Ethiopia* **81** F4
Metz *France* **19** C13
Metzingen *Germany* **25** G5
Meulaboh *Indonesia* **62** D1
Meung-sur-Loire *France* **19** E8
Meureudu *Indonesia* **62** C1
Meurthe → *France* **19** D13
Meurthe-et-Moselle □
  France **19** D13
Meuse □ *France* **19** C12
Meuse → *Europe* **17** D5
Meuselwitz *Germany* **24** D8
Mexia *U.S.A.* **116** F6
Mexiana, I. *Brazil* **125** D9
Mexicali *Mexico* **111** N11
Mexican Plateau *Mexico* **98** G9
Mexican Water *U.S.A.* **109** H9
México *Mexico* **119** D5
Mexico *Maine, U.S.A.* **115** B14
Mexico *Mo., U.S.A.* **112** F8
Mexico *N.Y., U.S.A.* **115** C8
México □ *Mexico* **119** D5
Mexico ■ *Cent. Amer.* **118** C4
México, Ciudad de *Mexico* **119** D5
Mexico, G. of *Cent. Amer.* **119** C7
Mexico B. *U.S.A.* **115** C8
Meydān-e Naftūn *Iran* **71** D6

Meydani, Ra's-e *Iran* **71** E8
Meyenburg *Germany* **24** B8
Meyers Chuck *U.S.A.* **102** B2
Meymac *France* **20** C6
Meymaneh *Afghan.* **66** B4
Meyrueis *France* **20** D7
Meyssac *France* **20** C5
Meyzieu *France* **21** C8
Mezdra *Bulgaria* **44** C7
Mezen *Russia* **52** C5
Mezen → *Russia* **6** B14
Mezen *Russia* **52** C5
Mézenc, Mt. *France* **21** D8
Mezeș, Munții *Romania* **28** C8
Mezha → *Russia* **32** E6
Mezhdurechenskiy *Russia* **52** D7
Mézidon-Canon *France* **18** C6
Mézières-en-Brenne *France* **20** B5
Mézilhac *France* **21** D8
Mézin *France* **20** D4
Mézőberény *Hungary* **28** D6
Mezőfalva *Hungary* **28** D3
Mezőhegyes *Hungary* **28** D5
Mezőkövácsháza *Hungary* **28** D5
Mezőkövesd *Hungary* **28** C5
Mézos *France* **20** D2
Mezőtúr *Hungary* **28** C5
Mezquital *Mexico* **118** C4
Mezzolombardo *Italy* **40** B8
Mfolozi → *S. Africa* **89** D5
Mgeta *Tanzania* **87** D4
Mglin *Russia* **33** F7
Mhlaba Hills *Zimbabwe* **87** F3
Mhow *India* **68** H6
Miahuatlán *Mexico* **119** D5
Miajadas *Spain* **37** F5
Miami *Fla., U.S.A.* **117** J14
Miami *Okla., U.S.A.* **116** C7
Miami *Tex., U.S.A.* **116** D4
Miami Beach *U.S.A.* **117** J14
Mian Xian *China* **56** H4
Mianchi *China* **56** G6
Miandarreh *Iran* **71** C7
Miandowāb *Iran* **73** D12
Miandrivazo *Madag.* **89** B8
Mīāneh *Iran* **73** D12
Mianning *China* **58** C4
Mianwali *Pakistan* **68** C4
Mianyang *China* **58** B5
Mianzhu *China* **58** B5
Miaoli *Taiwan* **59** E13
Miarinarivo *Antananarivo,*
  Madag. **89** B8
Miarinarivo *Toamasina,*
  Madag. **89** B8
Miariravaratra *Madag.* **89** C8
Miass *Russia* **52** D7
Miastko *Poland* **30** E3
Mica *S. Africa* **89** C5
Micăsasa *Romania* **29** D9
Michalovce *Slovak Rep.* **27** C14
Michigan □ *U.S.A.* **113** C11
Michigan, L. *U.S.A.* **112** D10
Michigan City *U.S.A.* **112** E10
Michika *Nigeria* **83** C7
Michipicoten I. *Canada* **104** C2
Michoacán □ *Mexico* **118** D4
Michurin *Bulgaria* **45** D11
Michurinsk *Russia* **34** D5
Mico, Pta. *Nic.* **120** D3
Micoud *St. Lucia* **121** f
Micronesia *Pac. Oc.* **96** G7
Micronesia, Federated
  States of ■ *Pac. Oc.* **90** A8
Mid-Pacific Seamounts
  Pac. Oc. **96** F10
Midai *Indonesia* **62** D3
Midale *Canada* **103** D8
Middelburg *Neths.* **17** C3
Middelburg *Eastern Cape,*
  S. Africa **88** E4
Middelburg *Mpumalanga,*
  S. Africa **89** D4
Middelfart *Denmark* **11** J3
Middelpos *S. Africa* **88** E3
Middelwit *S. Africa* **88** C4
Middle Alkali L. *U.S.A.* **108** F3
Middle America Trench =
  Guatemala Trench
  Pac. Oc. **98** H10
Middle Bass I. *U.S.A.* **114** E2
Middle East *Asia* **50** E5
Middle Fork Feather →
  U.S.A. **110** F5
Middle I. *Australia* **93** F3
Middle Loup → *U.S.A.* **112** E4
Middle Sackville *Canada* **105** D7
Middleboro *U.S.A.* **115** E14
Middleburg *Fla., U.S.A.* **117** F14
Middleburg *Pa., U.S.A.* **114** F7
Middleburgh *U.S.A.* **115** D10
Middlebury *U.S.A.* **115** B11
Middlemount *Australia* **94** C4
Middleport *N.Y., U.S.A.* **114** C6
Middleport *Ohio, U.S.A.* **113** F12

Middlesboro *U.S.A.* **113** G12
Middlesbrough *U.K.* **14** C6
Middlesbrough □ *U.K.* **14** C6
Middlesex *Belize* **120** C2
Middlesex *N.J., U.S.A.* **115** F10
Middlesex *N.Y., U.S.A.* **114** D7
Middleton *Australia* **94** C3
Middleton *Canada* **105** D6
Middleton Cr. → *Australia* **94** C3
Middletown *U.K.* **12** B5
Middletown *Calif., U.S.A.* **110** G4
Middletown *Conn., U.S.A.* **115** E12
Middletown *N.Y., U.S.A.* **115** E10
Middletown *Ohio, U.S.A.* **113** F11
Middletown *Pa., U.S.A.* **115** F8
Midge Point *Australia* **94** J6
Midhurst *U.K.* **15** G7
Mīdī *Yemen* **81** D5
Midi, Canal du → *France* **20** E5
Midi d'Ossau, Pic du *France* **20** F3
Midi-Pyrénées □ *France* **20** E5
Midland *Australia* **93** F2
Midland *Canada* **114** B5
Midland *Calif., U.S.A.* **111** M12
Midland *Mich., U.S.A.* **113** D11
Midland *Pa., U.S.A.* **114** F4
Midland *Tex., U.S.A.* **116** F3
Midlands □ *Zimbabwe* **87** F2
Midleton *Ireland* **12** E3
Midlothian *U.S.A.* **116** E6
Midlothian □ *U.K.* **13** F5
Midongy,
  Tangorombohitr' i *Madag.* **89** C8
Midongy Atsimo *Madag.* **89** C8
Midou → *France* **20** E3
Midouze → *France* **20** E3
Midsayap *Phil.* **61** H6
Midtjylland □ *Denmark* **11** H2
Midu *China* **58** E3
Midway Is. *Pac. Oc.* **96** E10
Midway Wells *U.S.A.* **111** N11
Midwest *U.S.A.* **107** B9
Midwest *Wyo., U.S.A.* **108** E10
Midwest City *U.S.A.* **116** D6
Midyat *Turkey* **73** D9
Midzŏr *Bulgaria* **44** C6
Mie □ *Japan* **55** G8
Miechów *Poland* **31** H7
Miedwie, Jezioro *Poland* **31** E1
Międzybórz *Poland* **31** G4
Międzychód *Poland* **31** F2
Międzylesie *Poland* **31** H3
Międzyrzec Podlaski *Poland* **31** G9
Międzyrzecz *Poland* **31** F2
Międzyzdroje *Poland* **30** E9
Miejska Górka *Poland* **31** G3
Miélan *France* **20** E4
Mielec *Poland* **31** H8
Mienga *Angola* **88** B2
Miercurea-Ciuc *Romania* **29** D10
Miercurea Sibiului *Romania* **29** E8
Mieres *Spain* **36** B5
Mieroszów *Poland* **31** H3
Mieso *Ethiopia* **81** F5
Mieszkowice *Poland* **31** F1
Mifflintown *U.S.A.* **114** F7
Mifraz Ḥefa *Israel* **74** C4
Migennes *France* **19** E10
Migliarino *Italy* **41** D8
Migliarino-San Rossore-
  Massaciuccoli △ *Italy* **40** E7
Migori *Kenya* **86** C3
Miguel Alemán, Presa
  Mexico **119** D5
Miguelturra *Spain* **37** G7
Mihăileni *Romania* **29** C10
Mihăileşti *Romania* **29** F10
Mihailovca *Moldova* **29** D13
Mihalgazi *Turkey* **47** A12
Mihaliçcik *Turkey* **72** B4
Mihara *Japan* **55** G6
Mikha-Tskhakaya =
  Senaki *Georgia* **35** J6
Mikhailovka =
  Mykhaylivka *Ukraine* **33** J8
Mikhaylov *Russia* **32** E10
Mikhaylovgrad =
  Montana *Bulgaria* **44** C7
Mikhaylovka *Russia* **34** E6
Mikhnevo *Russia* **32** E10
Mikines *Greece* **46** D4
Mikkeli *Finland* **32** B5
Mikkwa → *Canada* **102** B6
Míkonos = Mykonos *Greece* **47** D7
Mikri Prespa, L. *Greece* **44** F5
Mikro Derio *Greece* **45** E10
Mikstat *Poland* **31** G4
Mikulov *Czech Rep.* **27** C9
Mikumi *Tanzania* **86** D4
Mikumi △ *Tanzania* **86** D4
Milaca *U.S.A.* **112** C7
Milagro *Ecuador* **124** D3
Milagros *Phil.* **61** E5

Milan = Milano *Italy* **40** C6
Milan *Mo., U.S.A.* **112** E7
Milan *Tenn., U.S.A.* **117** D10
Milange *Mozam.* **87** F4
Milano *Italy* **40** C6
Milano Linate ✈ (LIN) *Italy* **40** C6
Milanoa *Madag.* **89** A8
Milâs *Turkey* **47** D9
Milatos *Greece* **49** D7
Milazzo *Italy* **43** D8
Milbank *U.S.A.* **112** C5
Milbanke Sd. *Canada* **102** C3
Milden *Canada* **103** C7
Mildenhall *U.K.* **15** E8
Mildmay *Canada* **114** B3
Mildura *Australia* **95** E3
Mile *China* **58** E4
Miles *Australia* **95** D5
Miles City *U.S.A.* **108** C11
Milești *Moldova* **29** C13
Milestone *Canada* **103** D8
Mileto *Italy* **43** D9
Miletto, Mte. *Italy* **43** A7
Miletus *Turkey* **47** D9
Milford *Calif., U.S.A.* **110** E6
Milford *Conn., U.S.A.* **115** E11
Milford *Del., U.S.A.* **113** F16
Milford *Mass., U.S.A.* **115** D13
Milford *N.H., U.S.A.* **115** D13
Milford *Pa., U.S.A.* **115** E10
Milford *Utah, U.S.A.* **108** G7
Milford Haven *U.K.* **15** F2
Milford Sd. *N.Z.* **91** F1
Milford Sound *N.Z.* **91** F1
Milḥ, Baḥr al = Razāzah,
  Buḥayrat ar *Iraq* **73** F10
Milicz *Poland* **31** G4
Milies *Greece* **46** B5
Milikapiti *Australia* **92** B5
Miling *Australia* **93** F2
Militello in Val di Catánia
  Italy **43** E7
Milk, Wadi el → *Sudan* **80** D3
Milk River *Canada* **102** D6
Mill I. *Antarctica* **5** C8
Mill Valley *U.S.A.* **110** H4
Millárs → *Spain* **38** F4
Millau *France* **20** D7
Millbridge *Canada* **114** B7
Millbrook *Canada* **114** B6
Millbrook *Ala., U.S.A.* **117** E11
Millbrook *N.Y., U.S.A.* **115** E11
Mille Lacs, L. des *Canada* **104** C1
Mille Lacs L. *U.S.A.* **112** B7
Milledgeville *U.S.A.* **117** E13
Millen *U.S.A.* **117** E14
Millennium I. = Caroline I.
  Kiribati **97** H12
Miller *U.S.A.* **112** C4
Millerovo *Russia* **35** F5
Millersburg *Ohio, U.S.A.* **114** F3
Millersburg *Pa., U.S.A.* **114** F8
Millerton *U.S.A.* **115** E11
Millerton L. *U.S.A.* **110** J7
Millet *St. Lucia* **121** f
Millevaches, Plateau de
  France **20** C6
Millheim *U.S.A.* **114** F7
Millicent *Australia* **95** F3
Millington *U.S.A.* **117** D10
Millinocket *U.S.A.* **113** C19
Millmerran *Australia* **95** D5
Millom *U.K.* **14** C4
Mills L. *Canada* **102** A5
Millsboro *U.S.A.* **114** G5
Millstream Chichester △
  Australia **92** D2
Millstreet *Ireland* **12** D2
Milltown Malbay *Ireland* **12** D2
Millville *N.J., U.S.A.* **113** F16
Millville *Pa., U.S.A.* **115** E8
Millwood L. *U.S.A.* **116** E8
Milna *Croatia* **41** E13
Milne → *Australia* **94** C2
Milo → *U.S.A.* **113** C19
Milon, Akra *Greece* **49** C10
Milos *Greece* **46** E6
Milosław *Poland* **31** F4
Milot *Albania* **44** E3
Milparinka *Australia* **95** D3
Milpitas *U.S.A.* **110** H5
Miltenberg *Germany* **25** F5
Milton *N.S., Canada* **105** D7
Milton *Ont., Canada* **114** C5
Milton *N.Z.* **91** G2
Milton *Calif., U.S.A.* **110** G6
Milton *Fla., U.S.A.* **117** F11
Milton *Pa., U.S.A.* **114** F8
Milton *Vt., U.S.A.* **115** B11
Milton-Freewater *U.S.A.* **108** D4
Milton Keynes *U.K.* **15** E7
Milton Keynes □ *U.K.* **15** E7
Miluo *China* **59** C9
Milverton *Canada* **114** C4
Milwaukee *U.S.A.* **112** D10
Milwaukee Deep *Atl. Oc.* **121** C6

Milwaukie *U.S.A.* **110** E4
Mim *Ghana* **82** D4
Mimizan *France* **20** D2
Mimoň *Czech Rep.* **26** A7
Min Jiang → *Fujian, China* **59** E12
Min Jiang → *Sichuan, China* **58** C5
Min Xian *China* **56** G3
Mīnā' Jabal 'Alī *U.A.E.* **71** E7
Mina Pirquitas *Argentina* **126** A2
Mina Gerais □ *Brazil* **125** G9
Mīnā Su'ud *Si. Arabia* **71** D6
Minago → *Canada* **103** C9
Minaki *Canada* **103** D10
Minamata *Japan* **55** H5
Minami-Arapusa △ *Japan* **55** G9
Minami-Tori-Shima *Pac. Oc.* **96** E7
Minas *Uruguay* **127** C4
Minas, Sierra de las
　Guatemala **120** C2
Minas Basin *Canada* **105** C7
Minas de Riotinto *Spain* **37** H4
Minas Gerais □ *Brazil* **125** G9
Minatitlán *Mexico* **119** D6
Minbu *Burma* **67** J19
Minchinabad *Pakistan* **68** D5
Mincio → *Italy* **40** C7
Minčol *Slovak Rep.* **27** B13
Mindanao *Phil.* **61** H6
Mindanao Sea = Bohol Sea
　Phil. **63** C6
Mindanao Trench *Pac. Oc.* **61** F7
Mindel → *Germany* **25** G6
Mindelheim *Germany* **25** G6
Mindelo *C. Verde Is.* **78** b
Minden *Canada* **114** B6
Minden *Germany* **24** C4
Minden *La., U.S.A.* **116** E8
Minden *Nev., U.S.A.* **110** G7
Mindiptana *Indonesia* **63** F10
Mindoro *Phil.* **61** E4
Mindoro Str. *Phil.* **61** E4
Mine *Japan* **55** G5
Minehead *U.K.* **15** F4
Mineola *N.Y., U.S.A.* **115** F11
Mineola *Tex., U.S.A.* **116** E7
Mineral King *U.S.A.* **110** J8
Mineral Wells *U.S.A.* **116** E5
Mineralnyye Vody *Russia* **35** H6
Minersville *U.S.A.* **115** F8
Minerva *U.S.A.* **114** F3
Minervino Murge *Italy* **43** A9
Minetto *U.S.A.* **115** C8
Mingäçevir *Azerbaijan* **35** K8
Mingäçevir Su Anbarı
　Azerbaijan **35** K8
Mingan *Canada* **105** B7
Mingechaur = Mingäçevir
　Azerbaijan **35** K8
Mingechaurskoye
　Vdkhr. = Mingäçevir Su
　Anbarı *Azerbaijan* **35** K8
Mingela *Australia* **94** B4
Mingenew *Australia* **93** E2
Mingera Cr. → *Australia* **94** C2
Minggang *China* **59** A10
Mingguang *China* **59** A11
Mingin *Burma* **67** H19
Mingir *Moldova* **29** D13
Minglanilla *Spain* **39** F3
Minglun *China* **58** E7
Mingo Junction *U.S.A.* **114** F4
Mingora *Pakistan* **68** B5
Mingorria *Spain* **36** E6
Mingshan *China* **58** B4
Mingteke Daban =
　Mintaka Pass *Pakistan* **69** A6
Mingxi *China* **59** D11
Mingyuegue *China* **57** C15
Minho = Miño → *Spain* **36** D2
Minho *China* **59** E12
Minićevo *Serbia* **28** G7
Minidoka *U.S.A.* **108** E7
Minigwal, L. *Australia* **93** E3
Minilya → *Australia* **93** D1
Minilya Roadhouse *Australia* **93** D1
Minipi L. *Canada* **105** B7
Mink L. *Canada* **102** A5
Minkammen *Sudan* **81** F3
Minna *Nigeria* **83** D6
Minneapolis *Kans., U.S.A.* **112** F5
Minneapolis *Minn., U.S.A.* **112** C7
Minnedosa *Canada* **103** C9
Minnesota □ *U.S.A.* **112** B6
Minnesota → *U.S.A.* **112** C7
Minnewaukan *U.S.A.* **112** A4
Minnipa *Australia* **95** E2
Minnitaki L. *Canada* **104** C1
Mino *Japan* **55** G8
Miño *Spain* **36** B2
Miño → *Spain* **36** D2
Minoa *Greece* **47** F7
Minorca = Menorca *Spain* **48** B11
Minot *U.S.A.* **112** A3
Minqin *China* **56** C5
Minqing *China* **59** D12
Minsen *Germany* **24** B3
Minsk *Belarus* **23** B14

Minsk □ *Belarus* **32** F4
Mińsk Mazowiecki *Poland* **31** F8
Mintabie *Australia* **95** D1
Mintaka Pass *Pakistan* **69** A6
Minto *Canada* **105** C6
Minto, L. *Canada* **104** A5
Minton *Canada* **103** D8
Minturn *U.S.A.* **108** G10
Minturno *Italy* **42** A6
Minûf *Egypt* **80** H7
Minusinsk *Russia* **53** D10
Minutang *India* **67** E20
Minvoul *Gabon* **84** D2
Minya el Qamh *Egypt* **80** H7
Minya Konka = Gongga
　Shan *China* **58** C5
Mionica *Bos.-H.* **28** F3
Mionica *Serbia* **44** B4
Miquelon *Canada* **104** C4
Miquelon *St-P. & M.* **105** C8
Mir *Niger* **83** C7
Mīr Kūh *Iran* **71** E8
Mīr Shahdād *Iran* **71** E8
Mira *Italy* **41** C9
Mira *Portugal* **36** E2
Mira → *Portugal* **37** H2
Mira por vos Cay *Bahamas* **121** B5
Mirabella Eclano *Italy* **43** A7
Mirabello, Kolpos *Greece* **49** D7
Mirador-Río Azul △
　Guatemala **120** C2
Miraj *India* **66** L9
Miram Shah *Pakistan* **68** C4
Miramar *Argentina* **126** D4
Miramar *Mozam.* **89** C6
Miramas *France* **21** E8
Mirambeau *France* **20** C3
Miramichi *Canada* **105** C6
Miramichi B. *Canada* **105** C7
Miramont-de-Guyenne
　France **20** D4
Miranda *Brazil* **125** H7
Miranda → *Brazil* **124** D7
Miranda de Ebro *Spain* **38** C2
Miranda do Corvo *Portugal* **36** E2
Miranda do Douro *Portugal* **36** D4
Mirande *France* **20** E4
Mirandela *Portugal* **36** D3
Mirándola *Italy* **40** D8
Mirandópolis *Brazil* **127** A5
Mirango *Malawi* **87** E3
Mirani *Australia* **94** K6
Mirano *Italy* **41** C9
Miras *Albania* **44** F4
Mirassol *Brazil* **127** A6
Mirbāṭ *Oman* **75** D5
Mirear *Egypt* **80** C4
Mirebeau *France* **18** F7
Mirebeau-sur-Bèze *France* **19** E12
Mirecourt *France* **19** D13
Mires *Greece* **49** D6
Mirgorod = Myrhorod
　Ukraine **33** H7
Miri *Malaysia* **62** D4
Miriam Vale *Australia* **94** C5
Miribel *France* **19** G11
Mirim, L. *S. Amer.* **127** C5
Mīrjāveh *Iran* **71** D9
Mirnyy *Antarctica* **5** C14
Mirnyy *Russia* **53** C12
Miroč *Serbia* **44** B6
Mirokhan *Pakistan* **68** F3
Mirond L. *Canada* **103** B8
Mirosławiec *Poland* **30** E3
Mirpur *Pakistan* **69** C5
Mirpur Batoro *Pakistan* **68** G3
Mirpur Bibiwari *Pakistan* **68** E2
Mirpur Khas *Pakistan* **68** G3
Mirpur Sakro *Pakistan* **68** G2
Mirria *Niger* **83** C6
Mirsk *Poland* **31** H2
Mirtağ *Turkey* **70** B4
Mirtoo Sea *Greece* **46** D5
Miryang *S. Korea* **57** G15
Mirzaani *Georgia* **35** K8
Mirzapur *India* **69** G10
Mirzapur-cum-
　Vindhyachal =
　Mirzapur *India* **69** G10
Misantla *Mexico* **119** D5
Misawa *Japan* **54** D10
Miscou I. *Canada* **105** C7
Mish'āb, Ra's al *Si. Arabia* **71** D6
Mishan *China* **60** B8
Mishawaka *U.S.A.* **112** E10
Mishbih, Gebel *Egypt* **80** C3
Mishima *Japan* **55** G9
Misión *Mexico* **111** N10
Misiones □ *Argentina* **127** B5
Misiones □ *Paraguay* **126** B4
Miskah *Si. Arabia* **70** E4
Miskitos, Cayos *Nic.* **120** D3
Miskolc *Hungary* **28** B5
Misoke *Dem. Rep. of the Congo* **86** C2
Misool *Indonesia* **63** E8
Miṣr = Egypt ■ *Africa* **80** B3
Miṣrātah *Libya* **79** B9

Missanabie *Canada* **104** C3
Missinaibi → *Canada* **104** B3
Missinaibi L. *Canada* **104** C3
Mission *Canada* **102** D4
Mission *S. Dak., U.S.A.* **112** D3
Mission *Tex., U.S.A.* **116** H5
Mission Beach *Australia* **94** B4
Mission Viejo *U.S.A.* **111** M9
Missira *Senegal* **82** C1
Missisa L. *Canada* **104** B2
Missisicabi → *Canada* **104** B4
Mississagi → *Canada* **104** C3
Mississauga *Canada* **114** C5
Mississippi □ *U.S.A.* **117** E10
Mississippi → *U.S.A.* **117** G10
Mississippi L. *Canada* **115** A8
Mississippi River Delta
　U.S.A. **117** G10
Mississippi Sd. *U.S.A.* **117** F10
Missoula *U.S.A.* **108** C6
Missouri □ *U.S.A.* **112** F7
Missouri → *U.S.A.* **112** F8
Missouri City *U.S.A.* **116** G7
Missouri Valley *U.S.A.* **112** E6
Mist *U.S.A.* **110** E3
Mistassibi → *Canada* **105** B5
Mistassini → *Canada* **105** C5
Mistassini, L. *Canada* **104** B5
Mistastin L. *Canada* **105** A7
Mistelbach *Austria* **27** C9
Misterbianco *Italy* **43** E8
Mistinibi, L. *Canada* **105** A7
Mistissini *Canada* **105** C5
Mistretta *Italy* **43** E7
Misty L. *Canada* **103** B8
Misurata = Miṣrātah *Libya* **79** B9
Mît Ghamr *Egypt* **80** H7
Mitatib *Sudan* **81** D4
Mitchell *Australia* **95** D4
Mitchell *Canada* **114** C3
Mitchell *Nebr., U.S.A.* **112** E2
Mitchell *Oreg., U.S.A.* **108** D3
Mitchell *S. Dak., U.S.A.* **112** D4
Mitchell → *Australia* **94** B3
Mitchell, Mt. *U.S.A.* **117** D13
Mitchell-Alice Rivers △
　Australia **94** B3
Mitchell Ra. *Australia* **94** A2
Mitchelstown *Ireland* **12** D3
Mitha Tiwana *Pakistan* **68** C5
Mithi *Pakistan* **68** G3
Mithimna *Greece* **47** B8
Mithrao *Pakistan* **68** F3
Mitilíni *Greece* **47** B8
Mitilínii *Greece* **47** D8
Mitla Pass = Mamarr
　Mitlā *Egypt* **74** E1
Mito *Japan* **55** F10
Mitrofanovka *Russia* **33** H10
Mitrovica = Kosovska
　Mitrovica *Serbia* **44** D4
Mitsamiouli *Comoros Is.* **85** a
Mitsinjo *Madag.* **89** B8
Mitsiwa *Eritrea* **81** D4
Mitsiwa Channel *Eritrea* **81** D5
Mitsukaidō *Japan* **55** F9
Mittagong *Australia* **95** E5
Mittelberg *Austria* **26** D3
Mittelfranken □ *Germany* **25** F6
Mittellandkanal → *Germany* **24** C4
Mittenwalde *Germany* **24** C9
Mittersill *Austria* **26** D5
Mitterteich *Germany* **25** F8
Mittimatalik = Pond Inlet
　Canada **101** B12
Mittweida *Germany* **24** E8
Mitú *Colombia* **124** C4
Mitumba *Tanzania* **86** D3
Mitumba, Mts.
　Dem. Rep. of the Congo **86** D2
Mitwaba
　Dem. Rep. of the Congo **87** D2
Mityana *Uganda* **86** B3
Mixteco → *Mexico* **119** D5
Miyagi □ *Japan* **54** E10
Miyāh, W. el → *Egypt* **80** C3
Miyāh, W. el → *Syria* **70** C3
Miyake-Jima *Japan* **55** G9
Miyako *Japan* **54** E10
Miyako-Jima *Japan* **55** M2
Miyako-Rettō *Japan* **55** M2
Miyakonojō *Japan* **55** J5
Miyani *India* **68** J3
Miyanoura-Dake *Japan* **55** J5
Miyazaki *Japan* **55** J5
Miyazaki □ *Japan* **55** H5
Miyazu *Japan* **55** G7
Miyet, Bahr el = Dead Sea
　Asia **74** D4
Miyi *China* **58** D3
Miyoshi *Japan* **55** G6
Miyun *China* **56** D9
Miyun Shuiku *China* **57** D9
Mizan Teferi *Ethiopia* **81** F4
Mizdah *Libya* **79** B8
Mizen Hd. *Cork, Ireland* **12** E2
Mizen Hd. *Wicklow, Ireland* **12** D5

Mizhhirya *Ukraine* **29** B8
Mizhi *China* **56** F6
Mizil *Romania* **29** F11
Mizpe Ramon *Israel* **74** E3
Mizuho *Antarctica* **5** D7
Mizusawa *Japan* **54** E10
Mjällby *Sweden* **11** H8
Mjöbäck *Sweden* **11** G6
Mjölby *Sweden* **11** F9
Mjörn *Sweden* **11** G6
Mjøsa *Norway* **8** F14
Mkata *Tanzania* **86** D4
Mkhaya △ *Swaziland* **89** D5
Mkhuze △ *S. Africa* **89** D5
Mkokotoni *Tanzania* **86** D4
Mkomazi *Tanzania* **86** C4
Mkomazi → *S. Africa* **89** E5
Mkomazi △ *Tanzania* **86** C3
Mkulwe *Tanzania* **87** D3
Mkumbi, Ras *Tanzania* **86** D4
Mkushi *Zambia* **87** E2
Mkushi River *Zambia* **87** E2
Mkuze *S. Africa* **89** D5
Mladá Boleslav *Czech Rep.* **26** A7
Mladenovac *Serbia* **44** B4
Mlala Hills *Tanzania* **86** D3
Mlange = Mulanje *Malawi* **87** F4
Mlava → *Serbia* **44** B5
Mława *Poland* **31** E7
Mlawula △ *Swaziland* **89** D5
Mlinište *Bos.-H.* **41** D13
Mljet *Croatia* **41** F14
Mljet △ *Croatia* **41** F14
Mljetski Kanal *Croatia* **41** F14
Młynary *Poland* **30** D6
Mmabatho *S. Africa* **88** D4
Mmeda *Sweden* **11** G8
Mme *Cameroon* **83** D7
Mnichovo Hradiště
　Czech Rep. **26** A7
Mo i Rana *Norway* **8** C16
Moa *Cuba* **121** B4
Moa *Indonesia* **63** F7
Moa → *S. Leone* **82** D2
Moab *U.S.A.* **108** G9
Moala *Fiji* **91** a
Moama *Australia* **95** F3
Moamba *Mozam.* **89** D5
Moapa *U.S.A.* **111** J12
Moate *Ireland* **12** C4
Moba *Dem. Rep. of the Congo* **86** D2
Mobārakābād *Iran* **71** D7
Mobaye *C.A.R.* **84** D4
Mobayi *Dem. Rep. of the Congo* **84** D4
Moberley Lake *Canada* **102** B4
Moberly *U.S.A.* **112** F7
Mobile *U.S.A.* **117** F10
Mobile B. *U.S.A.* **117** F11
Mobridge *U.S.A.* **112** C3
Moc Chau *Vietnam* **64** B5
Moc Hoa *Vietnam* **65** G5
Mocabe Kasari
　Dem. Rep. of the Congo **87** D2
Moçambique =
　Mozambique ■ *Africa* **87** F4
Moçambique *Mozam.* **87** F5
Mocanaqua *U.S.A.* **115** E9
Moce *Fiji* **91** a
Mochima △ *Venezuela* **121** D7
Mochos *Greece* **49** D7
Mochudi *Botswana* **88** C4
Mocimboa da Praia *Mozam.* **87** E5
Mociu *Romania* **29** D9
Möckeln *Sweden* **11** H8
Mockfjärd *Sweden* **10** D8
Moclips *U.S.A.* **110** C2
Mocoa *Colombia* **124** C3
Mococa *Brazil* **127** A6
Mocorito *Mexico* **118** B3
Moctezuma *Mexico* **118** B3
Moctezuma → *Mexico* **119** C5
Mocuba *Mozam.* **87** F4
Modane *France* **21** C10
Modasa *India* **68** H5
Modder → *S. Africa* **88** D3
Modderrivier *S. Africa* **88** D3
Módena *Italy* **40** D7
Modena *U.S.A.* **109** H7
Modesto *U.S.A.* **110** H6
Módica *Italy* **43** F7
Modimolle *S. Africa* **89** C4
Modjadjiskloof *S. Africa* **89** C5
Mödling *Austria* **27** C9
Modo *Sudan* **81** F3
Modra *Slovak Rep.* **27** C10
Modračka *Bos.-H.* **28** F3
Modran → *Australia* **95** F4
Moe *Australia* **95** F4
Moebase *Mozam.* **87** F4
Moëlan-sur-Mer *France* **18** E3
Moengo *Suriname* **125** B8
Moffat *U.K.* **13** F5
Moga *India* **68** D6
Mogadishu = Muqdisho
　Somali Rep. **75** G4
Mogador = Essaouira
　Morocco **78** B4
Mogadouro *Portugal* **36** D4

Mogalakwena → *S. Africa* **89** C4
Mogami-Gawa → *Japan* **54** E10
Mogán *Canary Is.* **48** G4
Mogaung *Burma* **67** G20
Mogente = Moixent *Spain* **39** G4
Mogho *Ethiopia* **81** G5
Mogi das Cruzes *Brazil* **127** A6
Mogi-Guaçu → *Brazil* **127** A6
Mogi-Mirim *Brazil* **127** A6
Mogielnica *Poland* **31** G7
Mogige *Ethiopia* **81** F4
Mogilev = Mahilyow
　Belarus **23** B16
Mogilev-Podolskiy =
　Mohyliv-Podilskyy
　Ukraine **29** B12
Mogilno *Poland* **31** F4
Mogincual *Mozam.* **87** F5
Mogliano Véneto *Italy* **41** C9
Mogocha *Russia* **53** D12
Mogok *Burma* **67** H20
Mogollon Rim *U.S.A.* **109** J8
Mógoro *Italy* **42** C1
Mograt *Sudan* **80** D3
Moguer *Spain* **37** H4
Mogumber *Australia* **93** F2
Mogwadi → *S. Africa* **89** C4
Mohács *Hungary* **28** E3
Mohales Hoek *Lesotho* **88** E4
Mohall *U.S.A.* **112** A3
Moḥammadābād *Iran* **71** B8
Mohammedia *Morocco* **78** B4
Mohana → *India* **69** G11
Mohanlalganj *India* **69** F9
Mohave, L. *U.S.A.* **111** K12
Mohawk → *U.S.A.* **115** D11
Moheda *Sweden* **11** G8
Mohéli *Comoros Is.* **85** a
Moher, Cliffs of *Ireland* **12** D2
Mohicanville Res. *U.S.A.* **114** F2
Möhne → *Germany* **24** D3
Mohns Ridge *Arctic* **4** B7
Mohoro *Tanzania* **86** D4
Mohyliv-Podilskyy *Ukraine* **29** B12
Moia *Sudan* **81** F2
Moidart, L. *U.K.* **13** E3
Moineşti *Romania* **29** D11
Moira → *Canada* **114** B7
Moirans *France* **21** C9
Moirans-en-Montagne
　France **19** F12
Moisaküla *Estonia* **32** C3
Moisie *Canada* **105** B6
Moisie → *Canada* **105** B6
Moissac *France* **20** D5
Moita *Portugal* **37** G2
Moixent *Spain* **39** G4
Mojácar *Spain* **39** H3
Mojados *Spain* **36** D6
Mojave *U.S.A.* **111** K8
Mojave △ *U.S.A.* **111** K11
Mojave Desert *U.S.A.* **111** L10
Mojiang *China* **58** F3
Mojo → *Ethiopia* **81** F5
Mojkovac *Montenegro* **44** D3
Mojo *Bolivia* **126** A2
Mojo *Ethiopia* **81** F4
Mojokerto *Indonesia* **63** G15
Mokai *N.Z.* **91** C5
Mokameh *India* **69** G11
Mokau *N.Z.* **91** C5
Mokelumne → *U.S.A.* **110** G5
Mokelumne Hill *U.S.A.* **110** G6
Mokhotlong *Lesotho* **89** D4
Möklinta *Sweden* **10** D10
Mokokchung *India* **67** F19
Mokolo *Cameroon* **83** C7
Mokolo → *S. Africa* **89** C4
Mokopane *S. Africa* **89** C4
Mokpo *S. Korea* **57** G14
Mokra Gora *Europe* **44** D4
Mokronog *Slovenia* **41** C12
Moksha → *Russia* **34** C6
Mokwa *Nigeria* **83** D6
Mol *Belgium* **17** C5
Mola di Bari *Italy* **43** A10
Molai *Greece* **46** E4
Molala *Ethiopia* **81** E4
Molara *Italy* **42** B2
Molat *Croatia* **41** D11
Molchanovo *Russia* **52** D9
Mold *U.K.* **14** D4
Moldava nad Bodvou
　Slovak Rep. **27** C14
Moldavia = Moldova ■
　Europe **29** C13
Moldavia *Romania* **29** D12
Molde *Norway* **8** E12
Moldova ■ *Europe* **29** C13
Moldova Nouă *Romania* **28** F6
Moldoveanu, Vf. *Romania* **29** E9
Moldoviţa *Romania* **29** C10

Mole → *U.K.* **15** F7
Mole △ *Ghana* **83** D4
Mole Creek *Australia* **95** G4
Molepolole *Botswana* **88** C4
Molfetta *Italy* **43** A9
Molina de Aragón *Spain* **38** E3
Molina de Segura *Spain* **39** G3
Moline *U.S.A.* **112** E8
Molinella *Italy* **41** D8
Molinos *Argentina* **126** B2
Moliro *Dem. Rep. of the Congo* **86** D3
Moliterno *Italy* **43** B8
Molkom *Sweden* **10** E7
Mölle *Sweden* **11** H6
Molledo *Spain* **36** B6
Mollendo *Peru* **124** G4
Mollerin, L. *Australia* **93** F2
Mollerussa *Spain* **38** D5
Mollina *Spain* **37** H6
Mölln *Germany* **24** B6
Mölltorp *Sweden* **11** F8
Mölnlycke *Sweden* **11** G6
Molo *Kenya* **86** C4
Molochansk *Ukraine* **33** J8
Molochnoye, Ozero *Ukraine* **33** J8
Molodechno =
　Maladzyechna *Belarus* **23** A14
Molodove *Ukraine* **29** D14
Molodezhnaya *Antarctica* **5** C9
Moloka'i *U.S.A.* **106** b
Molokai Fracture Zone
　Pac. Oc. **97** E15
Molong *Australia* **95** E4
Molopo → *Africa* **88** D3
Molos *Greece* **46** C4
Molsheim *France* **19** D14
Molson L. *Canada* **103** C9
Molteno *S. Africa* **88** E4
Molu *Indonesia* **63** F8
Molucca Sea *Indonesia* **63** E6
Moluccas = Maluku
　Indonesia **63** E7
Moma *Dem. Rep. of the Congo* **86** C1
Moma *Mozam.* **87** F4
Mombasa *Kenya* **86** C4
Mombetsu *Japan* **54** B11
Mombuey *Spain* **36** C4
Momchilgrad *Bulgaria* **45** E9
Momi *Dem. Rep. of the Congo* **86** C2
Mompós *Colombia* **124** B4
Møn *Denmark* **11** K6
Mon □ *Burma* **67** L20
Mona, Canal de la = Mona
　Passage *W. Indies* **121** C6
Mona, Isla *Puerto Rico* **121** C6
Mona, Pta. *Costa Rica* **120** E3
Mona Passage *W. Indies* **121** C6
Monaca *U.S.A.* **114** F4
Monaco ■ *Europe* **21** E11
Monadhliath Mts. *U.K.* **13** D4
Monadnock, Mt. *U.S.A.* **115** D12
Monaghan *Ireland* **12** B5
Monaghan □ *Ireland* **12** B5
Monahans *U.S.A.* **116** F3
Monapo *Mozam.* **87** E5
Monar, L. *U.K.* **13** D3
Monarch Mt. *Canada* **102** C3
Monashee Mts. *Canada* **102** C5
Monasterevin *Ireland* **12** C4
Monastir = Bitola *Macedonia* **44** E5
Monastir *Tunisia* **79** A8
Moncada *Spain* **38** F4
Moncalieri *Italy* **40** D4
Moncalvo *Italy* **40** C5
Monção *Portugal* **36** C2
Moncarapacho *Portugal* **37** H3
Moncayo, Sierra del *Spain* **38** D3
Monchegorsk *Russia* **8** C25
Mönchengladbach *Germany* **24** D2
Monchique *Portugal* **37** H2
Moncks Corner *U.S.A.* **117** E14
Monclova *Mexico* **118** B4
Moncontour *France* **18** D4
Moncton *Canada* **105** C7
Mondariz *Spain* **36** C2
Mondego → *Portugal* **36** E2
Mondego, C. *Portugal* **36** E2
Mondeodo *Indonesia* **63** E6
Mondeville *France* **18** C6
Mondolfo *Italy* **41** E10
Mondoñedo *Spain* **36** B3
Mondovì *Italy* **40** D4
Mondragon *Phil.* **61** E6
Mondragone *Italy* **42** A6
Mondrain I. *Australia* **93** F3
Moneague *Jamaica* **120** a
Monemvasia *Greece* **46** E5
Moneron, Ostrov *Russia* **54** A10
Monessen *U.S.A.* **114** F5
Monesterio *Spain* **37** G4
Monestier-de-Clermont
　France **21** D9
Monett *U.S.A.* **112** G7
Moneymore *U.K.* **12** B5
Monfalcone *Italy* **41** C10
Monflanquin *France* **20** D4
Monforte *Portugal* **37** F3

Monforte de Lemos *Spain* **36** C3
Mong Cai *Vietnam* **64** B6
Mong Hsu *Burma* **58** G2
Mong Kung *Burma* **67** J20
Mong Nai *Burma* **67** J20
Mong Pawk *Burma* **67** H21
Mong Ping *Burma* **58** G2
Mong Ton *Burma* **67** J21
Mong Wa *Burma* **67** J20
Mong Yai *Burma* **67** H21
Mongalla *Sudan* **81** F3
Mongers, L. *Australia* **93** E2
Monghyr = Munger *India* **69** G12
Mongibello = Etna *Italy* **43** E7
Mongo *Chad* **79** F9
Mongo → *S. Leone* **82** D2
Mongolia ■ *Asia* **53** E10
Mongolia, Plateau of *Asia* **50** D12
Mongonu *Nigeria* **83** C7
Mongu *Zambia* **85** H4
Môngua *Angola* **88** B2
Monifieth *U.K.* **13** E6
Monistrol-sur-Loire *France* **21** C8
Monkey Bay *Malawi* **87** E4
Monkey Mia *Australia* **93** E1
Monkey River *Belize* **119** D7
Mońki *Poland* **30** E9
Monkoto
  Dem. Rep. of the Congo **84** E4
Monkton *Canada* **114** C3
Monmouth *U.K.* **15** F5
Monmouth *Ill., U.S.A.* **112** E8
Monmouth *Oreg., U.S.A.* **108** D2
Monmouthshire □ *U.K.* **15** F5
Mono L. *U.S.A.* **110** H7
Monolith *U.S.A.* **111** K8
Monolithos *Greece* **49** C9
Monongahela *U.S.A.* **114** F5
Monópoli *Italy* **43** B10
Monor *Hungary* **28** C4
Monos I. *Trin. & Tob.* **125** K15
Monóvar *Spain* **39** G4
Monreal del Campo *Spain* **38** E3
Monreale *Italy* **42** D6
Monroe *Ga., U.S.A.* **117** E13
Monroe *La., U.S.A.* **116** E8
Monroe *Mich., U.S.A.* **113** E12
Monroe *N.C., U.S.A.* **117** D14
Monroe *N.Y., U.S.A.* **115** E10
Monroe *Utah, U.S.A.* **108** G7
Monroe *Wash., U.S.A.* **110** C5
Monroe *Wis., U.S.A.* **112** D9
Monroe City *U.S.A.* **112** F8
Monroeton *U.S.A.* **115** E8
Monroeville *Ala., U.S.A.* **117** F11
Monroeville *Pa., U.S.A.* **114** F5
Monrovia *Liberia* **82** D2
Mons *Belgium* **17** D3
Møns Klint *Denmark* **11** K6
Monsaraz *Portugal* **37** G3
Monse *Indonesia* **63** E6
Monségur *France* **20** D4
Monsélice *Italy* **41** C8
Mönsterås *Sweden* **11** G10
Mont Cenis, Col du *France* **21** C10
Mont-de-Marsan *France* **20** E3
Mont-Joli *Canada* **105** C6
Mont-Laurier *Canada* **104** C4
Mont-Louis *Canada* **105** C6
Mont Peko △ *Ivory C.* **82** D3
Mont-roig del Camp *Spain* **38** D5
Mont-St-Michel, Le *France* **18** D5
Mont Sangbe △ *Ivory C.* **82** D3
Mont-Tremblant △ *Canada* **104** C5
Montabaur *Germany* **24** E3
Montagnac *France* **20** E7
Montagnana *Italy* **41** C8
Montagne d'Ambre △
  Madag. **89** A8
Montagne de Reims △
  France **19** C11
Montagu *S. Africa* **88** E3
Montagu I. *Antarctica* **5** B1
Montague *Canada* **105** C7
Montague, I. *Mexico* **118** A2
Montague Ra. *Australia* **93** E2
Montague Sd. *Australia* **92** B4
Montaigu *France* **18** F5
Montalbán *Spain* **38** E4
Montalbano Iónico *Italy* **43** B9
Montalbo *Spain* **38** F2
Montalcino *Italy* **41** E8
Montalegre *Portugal* **36** D3
Montalto *Italy* **43** D8
Montalto di Castro *Italy* **41** F8
Montalto Uffugo *Italy* **43** C9
Montalvo *U.S.A.* **111** L7
Montamarta *Spain* **36** D5
Montana *Bulgaria* **44** C7
Montaña *Peru* **124** E4
Montana □ *Bulgaria* **44** C7
Montana □ *U.S.A.* **108** C9
Montaña Clara, I. *Canary Is.* **48** E6
Montañas de Malaga △
  Spain **37** J6
Montánchez *Spain* **37** F4
Montargil *Portugal* **37** F2

Montargis *France* **19** E9
Montauban *France* **20** D5
Montauk *U.S.A.* **115** E13
Montauk Pt. *U.S.A.* **115** E13
Montbard *France* **19** E11
Montbarrey *France* **19** E12
Montbéliard *France* **19** E13
Montblanc *Spain* **38** D6
Montbrison *France* **21** C8
Montcalm, Pic de *France* **20** F5
Montceau-les-Mines *France* **19** F11
Montcenis *France* **21** B8
Montclair *U.S.A.* **115** F10
Montcornet *France* **19** C11
Montcuq *France* **20** D5
Montdidier *France* **19** C9
Monte Albán *Mexico* **119** D5
Monte Alegre *Brazil* **125** D8
Monte Azul *Brazil* **125** G10
Monte-Carlo *Monaco* **21** E11
Monte Caseros *Argentina* **126** C4
Monte Comán *Argentina* **126** C2
Monte Cristi *Dom. Rep.* **121** C5
Monte Cucco △ *Italy* **41** E9
Monte Lindo → *Paraguay* **126** A4
Monte Patria *Chile* **126** C1
Monte Quemado *Argentina* **126** B3
Monte Redondo *Portugal* **36** F2
Monte Rio *U.S.A.* **110** G4
Monte San Giovanni
  Campano *Italy* **42** A6
Monte San Savino *Italy* **41** E8
Monte Sant' Ángelo *Italy* **41** G12
Monte Santu, C. di *Italy* **42** B6
Monte Sibillini △ *Italy* **41** F10
Monte Subasio △ *Italy* **41** E9
Monte Vista *U.S.A.* **109** H10
Monteagudo *Argentina* **127** B5
Montealegre del Castillo
  Spain **39** G3
Montebello *Canada* **104** C5
Montebello Iónico *Italy* **43** E8
Montebello Is. *Australia* **92** D2
Montebelluna *Italy* **41** C9
Montebourg *France* **18** C5
Montecastrilli *Italy* **41** F9
Montecatini Terme *Italy* **40** E7
Montecito *U.S.A.* **111** L7
Montecristo *Italy* **40** F7
Montefalco *Italy* **41** F9
Montefiascone *Italy* **41** F9
Montefrío *Spain* **37** H7
Montegiórgio *Italy* **41** E10
Montego Bay *Jamaica* **120** a
Montehermoso *Spain* **36** E4
Montejicar *Spain* **37** H7
Montélimar *France* **21** D8
Montella *Italy* **43** B8
Montellano *Spain* **37** J5
Montello *U.S.A.* **112** D9
Montemor-o-Novo *Portugal* **37** G2
Montemor-o-Velho *Portugal* **36** F2
Montemorelos *Mexico* **119** B5
Montendre *France* **20** C3
Montenegro *Brazil* **127** B5
Montenegro ■ *Europe* **44** D3
Montenero di Bisáccia *Italy* **41** G11
Montepuez *Mozam.* **87** E4
Montepuez → *Mozam.* **87** E5
Montepulciano *Italy* **41** E8
Montereale *Italy* **41** F10
Montereau-Faut-Yonne
  France **19** D9
Monterey *U.S.A.* **110** J5
Monterey B. *U.S.A.* **110** J5
Montería *Colombia* **124** B3
Monteros *Argentina* **126** B2
Monterotondo *Italy* **41** F9
Monterrey *Mexico* **118** B4
Montes Azules △ *Mexico* **119** D6
Montes Claros *Brazil* **125** G10
Montesano *U.S.A.* **110** D3
Montesano sulla
  Marcellana *Italy* **43** B8
Montesárchio *Italy* **43** A7
Montescaglioso *Italy* **43** B9
Montesilvano *Italy* **41** F11
Montesinho △ *Portugal* **36** D4
Montevarchi *Italy* **41** E8
Montevideo *Uruguay* **127** C4
Montevideo *U.S.A.* **112** C6
Montezuma *U.S.A.* **112** E7
Montezuma Castle △
  U.S.A. **109** J8
Montfaucon *France* **18** E5
Montfaucon-d'Argonne
  France **19** C12
Montfaucon-en-Velay
  France **21** C8
Montfort-le-Gesnois *France* **18** D7
Montfort-sur-Meu *France* **18** D5
Montfragüe △ *Spain* **36** F5
Montgenèvre *France* **21** D10
Montgomery *U.K.* **15** E4
Montgomery *Ala., U.S.A.* **117** E11
Montgomery *Pa., U.S.A.* **114** E8
Montgomery *W. Va., U.S.A.*
  113 F13

Montgomery City *U.S.A.* **112** F8
Montguyon *France* **20** C3
Monthermé *France* **19** C11
Monthey *Switz.* **25** J2
Monthois *France* **19** C11
Monti *Italy* **42** B2
Monti Lucrétili △ *Italy* **41** F9
Monti Picentini △ *Italy* **43** B8
Monti Simbruini △ *Italy* **41** G10
Monticelli d'Ongina *Italy* **40** C6
Monticello *Ark., U.S.A.* **116** E9
Monticello *Fla., U.S.A.* **117** F13
Monticello *Ind., U.S.A.* **112** E10
Monticello *Iowa, U.S.A.* **112** D8
Monticello *Ky., U.S.A.* **113** G11
Monticello *Minn., U.S.A.* **112** C7
Monticello *Miss., U.S.A.* **117** F9
Monticello *N.Y., U.S.A.* **115** E10
Monticello *Utah, U.S.A.* **109** H9
Montichiari *Italy* **40** C7
Montier-en-Der *France* **19** D11
Montignac *France* **20** C5
Montigny-les-Metz *France* **19** C13
Montigny-sur-Aube *France* **19** E11
Montijo *Portugal* **37** G2
Montijo *Spain* **37** G4
Montilla *Spain* **37** H6
Montivilliers *France* **18** C7
Montluçon *France* **19** F9
Montmagny *Canada* **105** C5
Montmarault *France* **19** F9
Montmartre *Canada* **103** C8
Montmédy *France* **19** C12
Montmélian *France* **21** C10
Montmirail *France* **19** D10
Montmoreau-St-Cybard
  France **20** C4
Montmorillon *France* **20** B4
Montmort-Lucy *France* **19** D10
Monto *Australia* **94** C5
Montoire-sur-le-Loir *France* **18** E7
Montongbuwoh *Indonesia* **63** K19
Montoro *Spain* **37** G6
Montour Falls *U.S.A.* **114** D8
Montoursville *U.S.A.* **114** E8
Montpelier *Idaho, U.S.A.* **108** E8
Montpelier *Vt., U.S.A.* **115** B12
Montpellier *France* **20** E7
Montpezat-de-Quercy
  France **20** D5
Montpon-Ménestérol *France* **20** D4
Montréal *Canada* **115** A11
Montréal *Aude, France* **20** E6
Montréal *Gers, France* **20** E4
Montreal → *Canada* **104** C3
Montreal L. *Canada* **103** C7
Montreal Lake *Canada* **103** C7
Montredon-Labessonnié
  France **20** E6
Montrésor *France* **18** E8
Montret *France* **19** F12
Montreuil *Pas-de-Calais,*
  France **19** B8
Montreuil *Seine-St-Denis,*
  France **19** D9
Montreuil-Bellay *France* **18** E6
Montreux *Switz.* **25** J2
Montrevel-en-Bresse *France* **19** F12
Montrichard *France* **18** E8
Montroe *U.K.* **13** E6
Montrose *Colo., U.S.A.* **108** G10
Montrose *Pa., U.S.A.* **115** E9
Monts, Pte. des *Canada* **105** C6
Montsalvy *France* **20** D6
Montsant, Serra de *Spain* **38** D6
Montsauche-les-Settons
  France **19** E11
Montsec, Serra del *Spain* **38** C5
Montseny △ *Spain* **38** D2
Montserrat *Spain* **38** D6
Montserrat ☑ *W. Indies* **121** C7
Montuenga *Spain* **36** D6
Montuiri *Spain* **48** B9
Monywa *Burma* **67** H19
Monza *Italy* **40** C6
Monze *Zambia* **87** F2
Monze, C. *Pakistan* **68** G2
Monzón *Spain* **38** D5
Mooers *U.S.A.* **115** B11
Mooi → *S. Africa* **89** D5
Mooi River *S. Africa* **89** D4
Moonah → *Australia* **94** C2
Moonda, L. *Australia* **94** D3
Moonie *Australia* **95** D5
Moonie → *Australia* **95** D4
Moonta *Australia* **95** E2
Moora *Australia* **93** F2
Moorcroft *U.S.A.* **108** D11
Moore → *Australia* **93** F2
Moore, L. *Australia* **93** E2
Moore Park *Australia* **94** C5
Moore Res. *U.S.A.* **115** B13
Moore River △ *Australia* **93** F2
Moorea *French Polynesia* **91** d
Moorefield *U.S.A.* **113** F14
Moorfoot Hills *U.K.* **13** F5

Moorhead *U.S.A.* **112** B5
Moormerland *Germany* **24** B3
Moorpark *U.S.A.* **111** L8
Moorreesburg *S. Africa* **88** E2
Moorrinya △ *Australia* **94** C3
Moose → *Canada* **104** B3
Moose → *U.S.A.* **115** C10
Moose Creek *Canada* **115** A10
Moose Factory *Canada* **104** B3
Moose Jaw *Canada* **103** C7
Moose Jaw → *Canada* **103** C7
Moose Lake *Canada* **103** C8
Moose Lake *U.S.A.* **112** B7
Moose Mountain △ *Canada* **103** D8
Moosehead L. *U.S.A.* **113** C19
Mooselookmeguntic L.
  U.S.A. **115** B14
Moosilauke, Mt. *U.S.A.* **115** B13
Moosomin *Canada* **103** C8
Moosonee *Canada* **104** B3
Moosup *U.S.A.* **115** E13
Mopane *S. Africa* **89** C4
Mopeia Velha *Mozam.* **87** F4
Mopipi *Botswana* **88** C3
Mopoi *C.A.R.* **86** A2
Mopti *Mali* **82** C4
Mopti □ *Mali* **82** C4
Moqatta *Sudan* **81** E4
Moqor *Afghan.* **68** C2
Moquegua *Peru* **124** G4
Mór *Hungary* **28** C3
Mora *Cameroon* **83** C7
Móra *Portugal* **37** G2
Mora *Spain* **37** F7
Mora *Sweden* **10** C8
Mora *Minn., U.S.A.* **112** C7
Mora *N. Mex., U.S.A.* **109** J11
Mora de Rubielos *Spain* **38** E4
Mòra d'Ebre *Spain* **38** D5
Mòra la Nova *Spain* **38** D5
Moraça → *Montenegro* **44** D3
Moradabad *India* **69** E8
Morafenobe *Madag.* **89** B7
Morag *Poland* **30** E6
Moral de Calatrava *Spain* **37** G7
Moraleja *Spain* **36** E4
Moramanga *Madag.* **89** B8
Moran *Kans., U.S.A.* **112** G6
Moran *Wyo., U.S.A.* **108** E8
Moranbah *Australia* **94** C4
Morano Cálabro *Italy* **43** C9
Morant Bay *Jamaica* **120** a
Morant Cays *Jamaica* **120** C4
Morant Pt. *Jamaica* **120** a
Morar *India* **68** F8
Morar, L. *U.K.* **13** E3
Moratalla *Spain* **39** G3
Moratuwa *Sri Lanka* **66** R11
Morava → *Slovak Rep.* **27** C9
Moravia *U.S.A.* **115** D8
Moravian Hts. =
  Českomoravská
  Vrchovina *Czech Rep.* **26** B8
Moravica → *Serbia* **44** C4
Moraviţa *Romania* **28** E6
Moravská Třebová
  Czech Rep. **27** B9
Moravské Budějovice
  Czech Rep. **26** B8
Morawa *Australia* **93** E2
Morawhanna *Guyana* **124** B7
Moray □ *U.K.* **13** D5
Moray Firth *U.K.* **13** D5
Morbach *Germany* **25** F3
Morbegno *Italy* **40** B6
Morbi *India* **68** H4
Morbihan □ *France* **18** E4
Mörbylånga *Sweden* **11** H10
Morcenx *France* **20** D3
Morcone *Italy* **43** A7
Mordelles *France* **18** D5
Morden *Canada* **103** D9
Mordoğan *Turkey* **47** C8
Mordovian Republic =
  Mordvinia □ *Russia* **34** C7
Mordovo *Russia* **34** D5
Mordvinia □ *Russia* **34** C7
Mordy *Poland* **31** F9
Moreau → *U.S.A.* **112** C3
Morebeng *S. Africa* **89** C4
Morecambe *U.K.* **14** C5
Morecambe B. *U.K.* **14** C5
Moree *Australia* **95** D4
Morehead *U.S.A.* **113** F12
Morehead City *U.S.A.* **117** D16
Morel → *India* **68** F7
Morelia *Mexico* **118** D4
Morella *Australia* **94** C3
Morella *Spain* **38** E4
Morelos *Mexico* **118** B3
Morelos □ *Mexico* **119** D5
Moremi △ *Botswana* **88** B3
Morena *Australia* **95** D4
Morena, Sierra *Spain* **37** G7
Moreni *Romania* **29** F10
Moreno Valley *U.S.A.* **111** M10

Moresby I. *Canada* **102** C2
Morestel *France* **21** C9
Moreton I. *Australia* **95** D5
Moreton Island △ *Australia* **95** D5
Moreuil *France* **19** C9
Morey *Spain* **48** B10
Morez *France* **19** F13
Morgan *U.S.A.* **108** F8
Morgan City *U.S.A.* **116** G9
Morgan Hill *U.S.A.* **110** H5
Morganfield *U.S.A.* **112** G10
Morganton *U.S.A.* **117** D14
Morgantown *U.S.A.* **113** F14
Morgenzon *S. Africa* **89** D4
Morges *Switz.* **25** J2
Morghak *Iran* **71** D8
Morgongåva *Sweden* **10** E10
Morhange *France* **19** D13
Morhar → *India* **69** G11
Mori *Italy* **40** C7
Mori *Japan* **54** C10
Moriarty *U.S.A.* **109** J10
Moribaya *Guinea* **82** D3
Morice L. *Canada* **102** C3
Moriki *Nigeria* **83** C6
Morinville *Canada* **102** C6
Morioka *Japan* **54** E10
Moris *Mexico* **118** B3
Morlaàs *France* **20** E3
Morlaix *France* **18** D3
Mörlunda *Sweden* **11** H9
Mormanno *Italy* **43** C8
Mormant *France* **19** D9
Mornington *Australia* **95** F4
Mornington, I. *Chile* **128** C3
Mornington I. *Australia* **94** B2
Mornos → *Greece* **46** C3
Moro *Pakistan* **68** F2
Moro *Sudan* **81** E3
Moro → *Phil.* **61** H5
Moro G. *Phil.* **61** H5
Morocco ■ *N. Afr.* **78** B4
Morogoro *Tanzania* **86** D4
Morogoro □ *Tanzania* **86** D4
Moroleón *Mexico* **118** C4
Morombe *Madag.* **89** C7
Moron *Argentina* **126** C4
Morón *Cuba* **120** B4
Morón de Almazán *Spain* **38** D2
Morón de la Frontera *Spain* **37** H5
Morona → *Peru* **124** D3
Morondava *Madag.* **89** C7
Morondo *Ivory C.* **82** D3
Morongo Valley *U.S.A.* **111** L10
Moroni *Comoros Is.* **85** a
Moroni *U.S.A.* **108** G8
Moronou *Ivory C.* **82** D4
Morotai *Indonesia* **63** D7
Moroto *Uganda* **86** B3
Moroto, Mt. *Uganda* **86** B3
Morozov *Bulgaria* **45** D9
Morozovsk *Russia* **35** F5
Morpeth *U.K.* **14** B6
Morphou *Cyprus* **49** D11
Morphou Bay *Cyprus* **49** D11
Morrilton *U.S.A.* **116** D8
Morrinhos *Brazil* **125** G9
Morrinsville *N.Z.* **91** B5
Morris *Canada* **103** D9
Morris *Ill., U.S.A.* **112** E9
Morris *Minn., U.S.A.* **112** C6
Morris *N.Y., U.S.A.* **115** D9
Morris *Pa., U.S.A.* **114** E7
Morris, Mt. *Australia* **93** E5
Morris Jesup, Kap *Greenland* **98** A16
Morrisburg *Canada* **115** B9
Morristown *Ariz., U.S.A.* **109** K7
Morristown *N.J., U.S.A.* **115** F10
Morristown *N.Y., U.S.A.* **115** B9
Morristown *Tenn., U.S.A.* **117** C13
Morrisville *N.Y., U.S.A.* **115** D9
Morrisville *Pa., U.S.A.* **115** F10
Morrisville *Vt., U.S.A.* **115** B12
Morro, Pta. *Chile* **126** B1
Morro Bay *U.S.A.* **110** K6
Morro del Jable *Canary Is.* **48** F5
Morro Jable, Pta. de
  Canary Is. **48** F5
Morrocoy △ *Venezuela* **121** D6
Morrosquillo, G. de
  Colombia **120** E4
Mörrum *Sweden* **11** H8
Morrumbene *Mozam.* **89** C6
Mörsil *Sweden* **10** A7
Mortagne → *France* **19** D13
Mortagne-au-Perche *France* **18** D7
Mortagne-sur-Gironde
  France **20** C3
Mortagne-sur-Sèvre *France* **18** F6
Mortain *France* **18** D6
Mortara *Italy* **40** C5
Morteau *France* **19** E13
Morteros *Argentina* **126** C3
Mortlach *Canada* **103** C7

Mortlake *Australia* **95** F3
Morton *Tex., U.S.A.* **116** E3
Morton *Wash., U.S.A.* **110** D4
Moruga *Trin. & Tob.* **125** K15
Morundah *Australia* **95** E4
Moruya *Australia* **95** F5
Morvan *France* **19** E11
Morvan □ *France* **19** E11
Morven *Australia* **95** D4
Morvern *U.K.* **13** E3
Morwell *Australia* **95** F4
Moryń *Poland* **31** F1
Morzine *France* **19** F13
Mosalsk *Russia* **32** E8
Mosbach *Germany* **25** F5
Moščenice *Croatia* **41** C11
Mosciano Sant' Ángelo
  Italy **41** F10
Moscos Is. *Burma* **64** F1
Moscow = Moskva *Russia* **32** E9
Moscow *Idaho, U.S.A.* **108** C5
Moscow *Pa., U.S.A.* **115** E9
Mosel → *Europe* **19** B14
Moselle = Mosel → *Europe* **19** B14
Moselle □ *France* **19** D13
Moses Lake *U.S.A.* **108** C4
Mosgiel *N.Z.* **91** F3
Moshaweng → *S. Africa* **88** D3
Moshchnyy, Ostrov *Russia* **9** F22
Moshi *Tanzania* **86** C4
Moshupa *Botswana* **88** C4
Mosina *Poland* **31** F3
Mosjøen *Norway* **8** D15
Moskenesøya *Norway* **8** C15
Moskenstraumen *Norway* **8** C15
Moskva *Russia* **32** E9
Moskva □ *Russia* **32** D9
Moskva → *Russia* **32** E10
Moslavačka Gora *Croatia* **41** C13
Mosomane *Botswana* **88** C4
Mosonmagyaróvár *Hungary* **28** C2
Mošorin *Serbia* **28** E5
Mospino *Ukraine* **33** J9
Mosquera *Colombia* **124** C3
Mosquero *U.S.A.* **109** J12
Mosqueruela *Spain* **38** E4
Mosquitia *Honduras* **120** C3
Mosquito Coast =
  Mosquitia *Honduras* **120** C3
Mosquito Creek L. *U.S.A.* **114** E4
Mosquito L. *Canada* **103** A8
Mosquitos, G. de los
  Panama **120** E3
Moss *Norway* **9** G14
Moss Vale *Australia* **95** E5
Mossaka *Congo* **84** E3
Mossbank *Canada* **103** D7
Mossburn *N.Z.* **91** F2
Mosselbaai *S. Africa* **88** E3
Mossendjo *Congo* **84** E2
Mossgiel *Australia* **95** E3
Mossingen *Germany* **25** G5
Mossman *Australia* **94** B4
Mossoró *Brazil* **125** E11
Mossuril *Mozam.* **87** E5
Most *Czech Rep.* **26** A6
Mosta *Malta* **49** D1
Mostaganem *Algeria* **78** A6
Mostar *Bos.-H.* **28** G2
Mostardas *Brazil* **127** C5
Mostiska = Mostyska
  Ukraine **31** J10
Móstoles *Spain* **36** E7
Mosty = Masty *Belarus* **23** B13
Mostyska *Ukraine* **31** J10
Mosul = Al Mawşil *Iraq* **73** D10
Mota *Ethiopia* **81** E4
Mota del Cuervo *Spain* **39** F2
Mota del Marqués *Spain* **36** D5
Motagua → *Guatemala* **120** C2
Motala *Sweden* **11** F9
Motaze *Mozam.* **89** C5
Moţca *Romania* **29** C11
Moth *India* **69** G8
Motherwell *U.K.* **13** F5
Motihari *India* **69** F11
Motilla del Palancar *Spain* **39** F3
Motnik *Slovenia* **41** B11
Motovun *Croatia* **41** C10
Motozintla de Mendoza
  Mexico **119** D6
Motril *Spain* **37** J7
Motru *Romania* **28** F7
Motru → *Romania* **29** F8
Mott *U.S.A.* **112** B2
Móttola *Italy* **43** B10
Motueka *N.Z.* **91** D4
Motueka → *N.Z.* **91** D4
Motul *Mexico* **119** C7
Mouchalagane → *Canada* **105** B6
Mouding *China* **58** E3
Moudjeria *Mauritania* **82** B2
Moudon *Switz.* **25** J2
Moudros *Greece* **47** B7
Mouila *Gabon* **84** E2
Moulamein *Australia* **95** F3
Moule à Chique, C. *St. Lucia* **121** f

Mouliana *Greece* **49** D7
Moulins *France* **19** F10
Moulmein *Burma* **67** L20
Moulouya, O. → *Morocco* **78** B5
Moultrie *U.S.A.* **117** F13
Moultrie, L. *U.S.A.* **117** E14
Mound City *Mo., U.S.A.* **112** E6
Mound City *S. Dak., U.S.A.* **112** C3
Moundou *Chad* **79** G9
Moundsville *U.S.A.* **114** G4
Moung *Cambodia* **64** F4
Mount Airy *U.S.A.* **117** C14
Mount Albert *Canada* **114** B5
Mount Aspiring △ *N.Z.* **91** F2
Mount Barker *S. Austral., Australia* **95** F2
Mount Barker *W. Austral., Australia* **93** F2
Mount Bellew Bridge *Ireland* **12** C3
Mount Brydges *Canada* **114** D3
Mount Burr *Australia* **95** F3
Mount Carmel = Ha Karmel △ *Israel* **74** C4
Mount Carmel *Ill., U.S.A.* **112** F10
Mount Carmel *Pa., U.S.A.* **115** F8
Mount Clemens *U.S.A.* **114** D2
Mount Coolon *Australia* **94** C4
Mount Darwin *Zimbabwe* **87** F3
Mount Desert I. *U.S.A.* **113** C19
Mount Dora *U.S.A.* **117** G14
Mount Edziza △ *Canada* **102** B2
Mount Elgon △ *E. Afr.* **86** B3
Mount Field △ *Australia* **95** G4
Mount Fletcher *S. Africa* **89** E4
Mount Forest *Canada* **114** C4
Mount Frankland △ *Australia* **92** F2
Mount Gambier *Australia* **95** F3
Mount Garnet *Australia* **94** B4
Mount Holly *U.S.A.* **115** G10
Mount Holly Springs *U.S.A.* **114** F7
Mount Hope *N.S.W., Australia* **95** E4
Mount Hope *S. Austral., Australia* **95** E2
Mount Isa *Australia* **94** C2
Mount Jewett *U.S.A.* **114** E6
Mount Kaputar △ *Australia* **95** E5
Mount Kenya △ *Kenya* **86** C4
Mount Kilimanjaro △ *Tanzania* **86** C4
Mount Kisco *U.S.A.* **115** E11
Mount Laguna *U.S.A.* **111** N10
Mount Larcom *Australia* **94** C5
Mount Lofty Ranges *Australia* **95** E2
Mount Magnet *Australia* **93** E2
Mount Maunganui *N.Z.* **91** B6
Mount Molloy *Australia* **94** B4
Mount Morgan *Australia* **94** C5
Mount Morris *U.S.A.* **114** D7
Mount Pearl *Canada* **105** C9
Mount Penn *U.S.A.* **115** F9
Mount Perry *Australia* **95** D5
Mount Pleasant *Iowa, U.S.A.* **112** E8
Mount Pleasant *Mich., U.S.A.* **113** D11
Mount Pleasant *Pa., U.S.A.* **114** F5
Mount Pleasant *S.C., U.S.A.* **117** E15
Mount Pleasant *Tenn., U.S.A.* **117** D11
Mount Pleasant *Tex., U.S.A.* **116** E7
Mount Pleasant *Utah, U.S.A.* **108** G8
Mount Pocono *U.S.A.* **115** E9
Mount Rainier △ *U.S.A.* **110** D5
Mount Revelstoke △ *Canada* **102** C5
Mount Robson △ *Canada* **102** C5
Mount St. Helens △ *U.S.A.* **110** D4
Mount Selinda *Zimbabwe* **89** C5
Mount Shasta *U.S.A.* **108** F2
Mount Signal *U.S.A.* **111** N11
Mount Sterling *Ill., U.S.A.* **112** F8
Mount Sterling *Ky., U.S.A.* **113** F12
Mount Surprise *Australia* **94** B3
Mount Union *U.S.A.* **114** F7
Mount Upton *U.S.A.* **115** D9
Mount Vernon *Ill., U.S.A.* **112** F9
Mount Vernon *Ind., U.S.A.* **112** G10
Mount Vernon *N.Y., U.S.A.* **115** F11
Mount Vernon *Ohio, U.S.A.* **114** F2
Mount Vernon *Wash., U.S.A.* **110** B4
Mount William △ *Australia* **95** G4
Mounta, Akra *Greece* **46** C2
Mountain Ash *U.K.* **15** F4
Mountain Center *U.S.A.* **111** M10
Mountain City *Nev., U.S.A.* **108** F6
Mountain City *Tenn., U.S.A.* **117** C14
Mountain Dale *U.S.A.* **115** E10
Mountain Grove *U.S.A.* **112** G7
Mountain Home *Ark., U.S.A.* **116** C8

Mountain Home *Idaho, U.S.A.* **108** E6
Mountain Iron *U.S.A.* **112** B7
Mountain Pass *U.S.A.* **111** K11
Mountain View *Ark., U.S.A.* **116** D8
Mountain View *Calif., U.S.A.* **110** H4
Mountain View *Hawai'i, U.S.A.* **106** b
Mountain Zebra △ *S. Africa* **88** E4
Mountainair *U.S.A.* **109** J10
Mountlake Terrace *U.S.A.* **110** C4
Mountmellick *Ireland* **12** C4
Mountrath *Ireland* **12** D4
Moura *Australia* **94** C4
Moura *Brazil* **124** D6
Moura *Portugal* **37** G3
Mourão *Portugal* **37** G3
Mourdi, Dépression du *Chad* **79** E10
Mourdiah *Mali* **82** C3
Mourenx *France* **20** E3
Mouri *Ghana* **83** D4
Mourilyan *Australia* **94** B4
Mourmelon-le-Grand *France* **19** C11
Mourne → *U.K.* **12** B4
Mourne Mts. *U.K.* **12** B5
Mournies *Greece* **49** D6
Mouscron *Belgium* **17** D3
Moussoro *Chad* **79** F9
Mouthe *France* **19** F13
Moûtiers *France* **21** C10
Moutong *Indonesia* **63** D6
Mouy *France* **19** C9
Mouzaki *Greece* **46** B3
Mouzon *France* **19** C12
Movas *Mexico* **118** B3
Moville *Ireland* **12** A4
Mowandjum *Australia* **92** C3
Moy → *Ireland* **12** B2
Moya *Comoros Is.* **85** a
Moyale *Kenya* **81** G4
Moyamba *S. Leone* **82** D2
Moyen Atlas *Morocco* **78** B4
Moyne, L. Le *Canada* **105** A6
Moyo *Indonesia* **62** F5
Moyobamba *Peru* **124** E3
Moyyero → *Russia* **53** C11
Moyynqum *Kazakhstan* **52** E8
Moyynty *Kazakhstan* **52** E8
Mozambique = Moçambique *Mozam.* **87** F5
Mozambique ■ *Africa* **87** F4
Mozambique Chan. *Africa* **89** B7
Mozdok *Russia* **35** J7
Mozdūrān *Iran* **71** B9
Mozhaysk *Russia* **32** E9
Mozhga *Russia* **34** B11
Mozhnābād *Iran* **71** C9
Mozirje *Slovenia* **41** B11
Mozyr = Mazyr *Belarus* **23** B15
Mpanda *Tanzania* **86** D3
Mpésoba *Mali* **82** C3
Mphoengs *Zimbabwe* **89** C4
Mpika *Zambia* **87** E3
Mpulungu *Zambia* **87** D3
Mpumalanga *S. Africa* **89** D5
Mpumalanga □ *S. Africa* **89** D5
Mpwapwa *Tanzania* **86** D4
Mqanduli *S. Africa* **89** E4
Mqinvartsveri = Kazbek *Russia* **35** J7
Mrągowo *Poland* **30** E8
Mramor *Serbia* **44** C5
Mrkonjić Grad *Bos.-H.* **28** F2
Mrkopalj *Croatia* **41** C11
Mrocza *Poland* **31** E4
Msaken *Tunisia* **79** A8
Msambansovu *Zimbabwe* **87** F3
M'sila → *Algeria* **78** A6
Msoro *Zambia* **87** E3
Msta → *Russia* **32** C6
Mstislavl = Mstsislaw *Belarus* **23** A16
Mstsislaw *Belarus* **23** A16
Mszana Dolna *Poland* **31** J7
Mszczonów *Poland* **31** G7
Mtama *Tanzania* **87** E4
Mtamvuna = Mthamvuna → *S. Africa* **89** E5
Mthamvuna → *S. Africa* **89** E5
Mthatha *S. Africa* **89** E4
Mtilikwe → *Zimbabwe* **87** G3
Mtito Andei *Kenya* **86** C4
Mtsensk *Russia* **32** F9
Mtskheta *Georgia* **35** K7
Mtubatuba *S. Africa* **89** D5
Mtwalume *S. Africa* **89** E5
Mtwara-Mikindani *Tanzania* **87** E5
Mu Gia, Deo *Vietnam* **64** D5
Mu Ko Chang △ *Thailand* **65** G4
Mu Us Shamo *China* **56** E5
Muang Chiang Rai = Chiang Rai *Thailand* **58** H2
Muang Khong *Laos* **64** E5

Muang Lamphun *Thailand* **64** C2
Muang Mai *Thailand* **65** a
Muang Pak Beng *Laos* **58** H3
Muar *Malaysia* **65** L4
Muarabungo *Indonesia* **62** E2
Muaraenim *Indonesia* **62** E2
Muarajuloi *Indonesia* **62** E4
Muarakaman *Indonesia* **62** E5
Muaratebo *Indonesia* **62** E2
Muaratembesi *Indonesia* **62** E2
Muaratewe *Indonesia* **62** E4
Mubarakpur *India* **69** F10
Mubarraz = Al Mubarraz *Si. Arabia* **71** E6
Mubende *Uganda* **86** B3
Mubi *Nigeria* **83** C7
Mucajaí → *Brazil* **124** C6
Muchachos, Roque de los *Canary Is.* **48** F2
Müchein *Germany* **24** D7
Muchinga Mts. *Zambia* **87** E3
Muchkapskiy *Russia* **34** E6
Muchuan *China* **58** C5
Muck *U.K.* **13** E2
Muckadilla *Australia* **95** D4
Muckle Flugga *U.K.* **13** A8
Mucojo *Mozam.* **87** E5
Mucondo *China* **58** D3
Mudanjiang *China* **57** B15
Mudanya *Turkey* **45** F12
Muddy Cr. → *U.S.A.* **108** G8
Mudgee *Australia* **95** E4
Mudjatik → *Canada* **103** B7
Mudurnu *Turkey* **72** B4
Muecate *Mozam.* **87** E4
Mueda *Mozam.* **87** E4
Mueller Ranges *Australia* **92** C4
Muende *Mozam.* **87** E3
Muerto, Mar *Mexico* **119** D6
Mufu Shan *China* **59** C10
Mufulira *Zambia* **87** E2
Mufumbiro Range *Africa* **86** C2
Mugardos *Spain* **36** B2
Muge → *Portugal* **37** F2
Múggia *Italy* **41** C10
Mughal Sarai *India* **69** G10
Mughayrā' *Si. Arabia* **70** D3
Mugi *Japan* **55** H7
Mugia = Muxía *Spain* **36** B1
Mugila, Mts. *Dem. Rep. of the Congo* **86** D2
Muğla *Turkey* **47** D10
Muğla □ *Turkey* **47** D10
Muglad *Sudan* **81** E2
Muğlizh *Bulgaria* **45** D9
Mugu *Nepal* **69** E10
Muhammad, Râs *Egypt* **70** E2
Muhammad Qol *Sudan* **80** C4
Muhammadabad *India* **69** F10
Muhesi → *Tanzania* **86** D4
Mühlacker *Germany* **25** G4
Mühldorf *Germany* **25** G8
Mühlhausen *Germany* **24** D6
Mühlig Hofmann fjell *Antarctica* **5** D3
Mühlviertel *Austria* **26** C7
Muhos *Finland* **8** D21
Muhu *Estonia* **32** C2
Muhutwe *Tanzania* **86** C3
Muine Bheag *Ireland* **12** D5
Muir, L. *Australia* **93** F2
Muir of Ord *U.K.* **13** D4
Mujnak = Muynak *Uzbekistan* **52** E6
Muka, Tanjung *Malaysia* **65** c
Mukacheve *Ukraine* **28** B7
Mukachevo = Mukacheve *Ukraine* **28** B7
Mukah *Malaysia* **62** D4
Mukandwara *India* **68** G6
Mukawwa, Geziret *Egypt* **80** C4
Mukawwar *Sudan* **80** C4
Mukdahan *Thailand* **64** D5
Mukden = Shenyang *China* **57** D12
Mukerian *India* **68** D6
Mukhavyets *Belarus* **31** F10
Mukhtolovo *Russia* **34** C6
Mukinbudin *Australia* **93** F2
Mukishi *Dem. Rep. of the Congo* **87** D1
Mukomuko *Indonesia* **62** E2
Mukomwenze *Dem. Rep. of the Congo* **86** D2
Muktsar *India* **68** D6
Mukur = Moqor *Afghan.* **68** C2
Mukutawa → *Canada* **103** C9
Mukwela *Zambia* **87** F2
Mula *Spain* **39** G3
Mula → *Pakistan* **68** F2
Mulange *Dem. Rep. of the Congo* **86** C2
Mulanje *Malawi* **87** F4
Mulanje, Mt. *Malawi* **87** F4
Mulchén *Chile* **126** D1
Mulde → *Germany* **24** D8

Mule Creek Junction *U.S.A.* **108** E11
Muleba *Tanzania* **86** C3
Mulegé *Mexico* **118** B2
Muleshoe *U.S.A.* **116** D3
Muletta, Gara *Ethiopia* **81** F5
Mulgrave *Canada* **105** C7
Mulhacén *Spain* **37** H7
Mülheim *Germany* **24** D2
Mulhouse *France* **19** E14
Muli *China* **58** D3
Mulifanua *Samoa* **91** b
Muling *China* **57** B16
Mull *U.K.* **13** E3
Mull, Sound of *U.K.* **13** E3
Mullaittivu *Sri Lanka* **66** Q12
Mullen *U.S.A.* **112** D3
Mullens *U.S.A.* **113** G13
Muller, Pegunungan *Indonesia* **62** D4
Mullet Pen. *Ireland* **12** B1
Mullewa *Australia* **93** E2
Müllheim *Germany* **25** H3
Mulligan → *Australia* **94** D2
Mullingar *Ireland* **12** C4
Mullins *U.S.A.* **117** D15
Mullsjö *Sweden* **11** G7
Mullumbimby *Australia* **95** D5
Mulobezi *Zambia* **87** F2
Mulonga Plain *Zambia* **85** H4
Mulroy B. *Ireland* **12** A4
Multan *Pakistan* **68** D4
Mulumbe, Mts. *Dem. Rep. of the Congo* **87** D2
Mulungushi Dam *Zambia* **87** E2
Mulvane *U.S.A.* **112** G5
Mulwad *Sudan* **80** D3
Mumbai *India* **66** K8
Mumbwa *Zambia* **87** F2
Mumias *Kenya* **86** C4
Mumra *Russia* **35** H8
Mun → *Thailand* **64** E5
Muna *Indonesia* **63** F6
Munabao *India* **68** G4
Munamagi *Estonia* **32** D4
Muncan *Indonesia* **63** K18
Muncar *Indonesia* **63** J17
Münchberg *Germany* **25** E7
Müncheberg *Germany* **24** C10
München *Germany* **25** G7
München Franz Josef Strauss Int. ✈ (MUC) *Germany* **25** G7
Munchen-Gladbach = Mönchengladbach *Germany* **24** D2
Muncho Lake *Canada* **102** B3
Munch'ŏn *N. Korea* **57** E14
Muncie *U.S.A.* **113** E11
Muncoonie L. West *Australia* **94** D2
Mundabbera *Australia* **95** D5
Munday *U.S.A.* **116** E5
Münden *Germany* **24** D5
Münden = Germany **24** D5
Mundiwindi *Australia* **92** D3
Mundo → *Spain* **39** G2
Mundo Novo *Brazil* **125** F10
Mundra *India* **68** H3
Mundrabilla *Australia* **93** F4
Munera *Spain* **39** F2
Mungallala *Australia* **95** D4
Mungallala Cr. → *Australia* **95** D4
Mungana *Australia* **94** B3
Mungaoli *India* **68** G8
Mungari *Mozam.* **87** F3
Mungbere *Dem. Rep. of the Congo* **86** B2
Mungeli *India* **69** H9
Munger *India* **69** G12
Mungkan Kandju △ *Australia* **94** A3
Munich = München *Germany* **25** G7
Munising *U.S.A.* **112** B10
Munka-Ljungby *Sweden* **11** H6
Munkebo *Denmark* **11** J4
Munkedal *Sweden* **11** F5
Munkfors *Sweden* **10** E7
Munku-Sardyk *Russia* **53** D11
Münnerstadt *Germany* **25** E6
Muñoz Gamero, Pen. *Chile* **128** G2
Munroe L. *Canada* **103** B9
Munsan *S. Korea* **57** F14
Munster *France* **19** D14
Münster *Niedersachsen, Germany* **24** C6
Münster *Nordrhein-Westfalen, Germany* **24** D3
Munster □ *Ireland* **12** D3
Muntadgin *Australia* **93** F2
Muntele Mare, Vf. *Romania* **29** D8
Muntok *Indonesia* **62** E3
Munyama *Zambia* **87** F2
Munzur Dağları *Turkey* **73** C8
Muong Beng *Laos* **58** G3
Muong Boum *Vietnam* **58** F4

Muong Et *Laos* **64** B5
Muong Hai *Laos* **58** G3
Muong Hiem *Laos* **64** B4
Muong Houn *Laos* **58** G3
Muong Hung *Vietnam* **58** G4
Muong Kau *Laos* **64** E5
Muong Khao *Laos* **58** G4
Muong Khoua *Laos* **58** G4
Muong Liep *Laos* **64** C3
Muong May *Laos* **64** E6
Muong Ngeun *Laos* **58** G3
Muong Ngoi *Laos* **58** G4
Muong Nhie *Vietnam* **58** F4
Muong Nong *Laos* **64** D6
Muong Ou Tay *Laos* **58** F3
Muong Oua *Laos* **64** C3
Muong Peun *Laos* **58** G4
Muong Phalane *Laos* **64** D5
Muong Phieng *Laos* **64** C3
Muong Phine *Laos* **64** D6
Muong Sai *Laos* **58** G3
Muong Saiapoun *Laos* **64** C3
Muong Sen *Vietnam* **64** C5
Muong Sing *Laos* **58** G3
Muong Son *Laos* **58** G4
Muong Soui *Laos* **64** C4
Muong Va *Laos* **58** G4
Muong Xia *Vietnam* **64** B5
Muonio *Finland* **8** C20
Muonio älv = Muonionjoki → *Finland* **8** C20
Muonioälven = Muonionjoki → *Finland* **8** C20
Muonionjoki → *Finland* **8** C20
Muping *China* **57** F11
Mupoi *Sudan* **81** F2
Muqaddam, Wadi → *Sudan* **80** D3
Muqdisho *Somali Rep.* **75** G4
Mur → *Austria* **27** E9
Mûr-de-Bretagne *France* **18** D4
Muradiye *Manisa, Turkey* **47** C9
Muradiye *Van, Turkey* **73** C10
Murakami *Japan* **54** E9
Murallón, Cerro *Chile* **128** F2
Muranda *Rwanda* **86** C2
Murang'a *Kenya* **86** C4
Murashi *Russia* **52** D5
Murat *France* **20** C6
Murat → *Turkey* **73** C9
Murat Dağı *Turkey* **47** C11
Murato *France* **21** F13
Murau *Austria* **26** D7
Murava *Belarus* **31** F11
Muravera *Italy* **42** C2
Murayama *Japan* **54** E10
Murça *Portugal* **36** D3
Murchison → *Australia* **93** E1
Murchison, Mt. *Antarctica* **5** D11
Murchison Falls *Uganda* **86** B3
Murchison Falls △ *Uganda* **86** B3
Murchison Ra. *Australia* **94** C1
Murchison Rapids *Malawi* **87** F3
Murcia *Spain* **39** G3
Murcia □ *Spain* **39** H3
Murdo *U.S.A.* **112** D3
Murdoch Pt. *Australia* **94** A3
Mürefte *Turkey* **45** F11
Mureş □ *Romania* **29** D9
Mureş → *Romania* **28** D5
Mureşul = Mureş → *Romania* **28** D5
Muret *France* **20** E5
Murewa *Zimbabwe* **89** B5
Murfreesboro *N.C., U.S.A.* **117** C16
Murfreesboro *Tenn., U.S.A.* **117** D11
Murgap *Tajikistan* **52** F8
Murgap → *Turkmenistan* **71** B9
Murgenella *Australia* **92** B5
Murgeni *Romania* **29** D13
Murgha Kibzai *Pakistan* **68** D3
Murghob = Murgap *Tajikistan* **52** F8
Murgon *Australia* **95** D5
Muri *India* **69** H11
Muria *Indonesia* **63** G14
Muriaé *Brazil* **127** A7
Murias de Paredes *Spain* **36** C4
Muriel Mine *Zimbabwe* **87** F3
Müritz *Germany* **24** B8
Müritz □ *Germany* **24** B8
Murliganj *India* **69** G12
Murmansk *Russia* **8** B25
Murmashi *Russia* **8** B25
Murnau *Germany* **25** H7
Muro *France* **21** F12
Muro *Spain* **48** B10
Muro, C. de *France* **21** G12
Muro de Alcoy *Spain* **39** G4
Muro Lucano *Italy* **43** B8
Murom *Russia* **34** C6
Muros *Spain* **36** C1
Muros y de Noya, Ría de *Spain* **36** C1
Muroto *Japan* **55** H7
Muroto-Misaki *Japan* **55** H7

Murovani Kurylivtsi *Ukraine* **29** B12
Murowana Goślina *Poland* **31** F3
Murphy *U.S.A.* **108** E5
Murphys *U.S.A.* **110** G6
Murrat *Sudan* **80** D2
Murrat Wells *Sudan* **80** C3
Murray *Ky., U.S.A.* **112** G9
Murray *Utah, U.S.A.* **108** F8
Murray → *Australia* **95** F2
Murray, L. *U.S.A.* **117** D14
Murray Bridge *Australia* **95** F2
Murray Fracture Zone *Pac. Oc.* **97** D14
Murray Harbour *Canada* **105** C7
Murray River △ *Australia* **95** F3
Murraysburg *S. Africa* **88** E3
Murree *Pakistan* **68** C5
Murrieta *U.S.A.* **111** M9
Murro di Porco, Capo *Italy* **43** F8
Murrumbidgee → *Australia* **95** E3
Murrumburrah *Australia* **95** E4
Murrurundi *Australia* **95** E5
Murshid *Sudan* **80** C3
Murshidabad *India* **69** G13
Murska Sobota *Slovenia* **41** B13
Murtle L. *Canada* **102** C5
Murtoa *Australia* **95** F3
Murtosa *Portugal* **36** E2
Murungu *Tanzania* **86** C3
Mururoa *French Polynesia* **97** K14
Murwara *India* **69** H9
Murwillumbah *Australia* **95** D5
Mürz → *Austria* **26** D8
Mürzzuschlag *Austria* **26** D8
Muş *Turkey* **73** C9
Muş □ *Turkey* **73** C9
Mûsa, Gebel *Egypt* **70** D2
Musa Khel *Pakistan* **68** D3
Mūsa Qal'eh *Afghan.* **66** C4
Musafirkhana *India* **69** F9
Musala *Bulgaria* **44** D7
Musala *Indonesia* **62** D1
Musan *N. Korea* **57** C15
Musangu *Dem. Rep. of the Congo* **87** E1
Musasa *Tanzania* **86** C3
Musay'īd *Qatar* **71** E6
Muscat = Masqat *Oman* **75** C6
Muscatine *U.S.A.* **112** E8
Muscle Shoals *U.S.A.* **117** D11
Musengezi = Unsengedsi → *Zimbabwe* **87** F3
Musgrave Harbour *Canada* **105** C9
Musgrave Ranges *Australia* **93** E5
Mushie *Dem. Rep. of the Congo* **84** E3
Mushin *Nigeria* **83** D5
Musi → *Indonesia* **62** E2
Musina *S. Africa* **89** C5
Muskeg → *Canada* **102** A4
Muskegon *U.S.A.* **112** D10
Muskegon → *U.S.A.* **112** D10
Muskegon Heights *U.S.A.* **112** D10
Muskogee *U.S.A.* **116** D7
Muskoka, L. *Canada* **114** B5
Muskwa → *Canada* **102** B4
Muslīmiyah *Syria* **70** B3
Musmar *Sudan* **80** D4
Musofu *Zambia* **87** E2
Musoma *Tanzania* **86** C3
Musquaro, L. *Canada* **105** B7
Musquodoboit Harbour *Canada* **105** D7
Musselburgh *U.K.* **13** F5
Musselshell → *U.S.A.* **108** C10
Mussende *Angola* **84** G3
Mussidan *France* **20** C4
Mussomeli *Italy* **42** E6
Mussoorie *India* **68** D8
Mussuco *Angola* **88** B2
Mustafakemalpaşa *Turkey* **45** F12
Mustang *Nepal* **69** E10
Musters, L. *Argentina* **128** F3
Musudan *N. Korea* **57** D15
Muswellbrook *Australia* **95** E5
Muszyna *Poland* **31** J7
Mût *Egypt* **80** B2
Mut *Turkey* **72** D5
Mutanda *Mozam.* **89** C5
Mutanda *Zambia* **87** E2
Mutare *Zimbabwe* **87** F3
Mutawintji △ *Australia* **95** E3
Mutha *Kenya* **86** C4
Muting *Indonesia* **63** F10
Mutki = Mirtağ *Turkey* **70** B4
Mutoko *Zimbabwe* **89** B5
Mutomo *Kenya* **86** C4
Mutoray *Russia* **53** C11
Mutsamudu *Comoros Is.* **85** a
Mutshatsha *Dem. Rep. of the Congo* **87** E1
Mutsu *Japan* **54** D10
Mutsu-Wan *Japan* **54** D10
Muttaburra *Australia* **94** C3
Muttalip *Turkey* **47** B12
Mutton I. *Ireland* **12** D2
Mutuáli *Mozam.* **87** E4

Mutum Biyu *Nigeria* **83** D7
Muweilih *Egypt* **74** E3
Muxía *Spain* **36** B1
Muy Muy *Nic.* **120** D2
Muyinga *Burundi* **86** C3
Muynak *Uzbekistan* **52** E6
Muyunkum, Peski =
   Moyynqum *Kazakhstan* **52** E8
Muzaffarabad *Pakistan* **69** B5
Muzaffargarh *Pakistan* **68** D4
Muzaffarnagar *India* **68** E7
Muzaffarpur *India* **69** F11
Muzafirpur *Pakistan* **68** D3
Muzhi *Russia* **52** C7
Muzillac *France* **18** E4
Muzūra *Egypt* **80** J7
Mvôlô *Sudan* **81** F2
Mvuma *Zimbabwe* **87** F3
Mvurwi *Zimbabwe* **87** F3
Mwabvi △ *Malawi* **87** F3
Mwadui *Tanzania* **86** C3
Mwali = Mohéli *Comoros Is.* **85** a
Mwambo *Tanzania* **87** E5
Mwandi *Zambia* **87** F1
Mwanza
   Dem. Rep. of the Congo **86** D2
Mwanza *Tanzania* **86** C3
Mwanza *Zambia* **87** F1
Mwanza □ *Tanzania* **86** C3
Mwaya *Tanzania* **87** D3
Mweelrea *Ireland* **12** C2
Mweka *Dem. Rep. of the Congo* **84** E4
Mwene-Ditu
   Dem. Rep. of the Congo **84** F4
Mwenezi *Zimbabwe* **87** G3
Mwenezi → *Mozam.* **87** G3
Mwenga
   Dem. Rep. of the Congo **86** C2
Mweru, L. *Zambia* **87** D2
Mweru Wantipa △ *Zambia* **87** D2
Mweza Range *Zimbabwe* **87** G3
Mwilambwe
   Dem. Rep. of the Congo **86** D2
Mwimbi *Tanzania* **87** D3
Mwingi *Kenya* **86** C4
Mwinilunga *Zambia* **87** E1
My Tho *Vietnam* **65** G6
Myajlar *India* **68** F4
Myanaung *Burma* **67** K19
Myanmar = Burma ■ *Asia* **67** J20
Myaungmya *Burma* **67** L19
Mycenæ = Mikines *Greece* **46** D4
Myedna *Belarus* **31** G10
Myeik Kyunzu *Burma* **65** G1
Myerstown *U.S.A.* **115** F8
Myingyan *Burma* **67** J19
Myitkyina *Burma* **67** G20
Myjava *Slovak Rep.* **27** C10
Mykhaylivka *Ukraine* **33** J8
Mykines *Færoe Is.* **8** E9
Mykolayiv *Ukraine* **33** J7
Mykolayiv □ *Ukraine* **33** J6
Mykonos *Greece* **47** D7
Mymensingh *Bangla.* **67** G17
Mynydd Du *U.K.* **15** F4
Mýrdalsjökull *Iceland* **8** E4
Myrhorod *Ukraine* **33** H7
Myrtle Beach *U.S.A.* **117** E15
Myrtle Creek *U.S.A.* **108** E2
Myrtle Point *U.S.A.* **108** E1
Myrtou *Cyprus* **49** D12
Mysia *Turkey* **45** G11
Myślenice *Poland* **31** J6
Myślibórz *Poland* **31** F1
Mysłowice *Poland* **31** H6
Mysore = Karnataka □
   India **66** N10
Mysore *India* **66** N10
Mystic *U.S.A.* **115** E13
Myszków *Poland* **31** H6
Myszyniec *Poland* **30** E8
Mytishchi *Russia* **32** B9
Mývatn *Iceland* **8** D5
Mže → *Czech Rep.* **26** B6
Mzimba *Malawi* **87** E3
Mzimkulu → *S. Africa* **89** E5
Mzimvubu → *S. Africa* **89** E4
Mzuzu *Malawi* **87** E3

N

Na Hearadh = Harris *U.K.* **13** D2
Na Noi *Thailand* **64** C3
Na Phao *Laos* **64** D5
Na Sam *Vietnam* **58** F6
Na San *Vietnam* **64** B5
Na Thon *Thailand* **65** b
Naab → *Germany* **25** F8
Na'am *Sudan* **81** F2
Na'am → *Sudan* **81** F2
Naantali *Finland* **32** B1
Naas *Ireland* **12** C5
Nababeep *S. Africa* **88** D2
Nabadwip = Navadwip
   India **69** H13
Nabawa *Australia* **93** E1
Nabberu, L. *Australia* **93** E3

Nabburg *Germany* **25** F8
Naberezhnyye Chelny
   Russia **34** C11
Nabeul *Tunisia* **79** A8
Nabha *India* **68** D7
Nabid *Iran* **71** D8
Nabire *Indonesia* **63** E9
Nabisar *Pakistan* **68** G3
Nabisipi → *Canada* **105** B7
Nabiswera *Uganda* **86** B3
Nāblus = Nābulus *West Bank* **74** C4
Naboomspruit *S. Africa* **89** C4
Nabou *Burkina Faso* **82** C4
Nabouwalu *Fiji* **91** a
Nabua *Phil.* **61** E5
Nābulus *West Bank* **74** C4
Nacala *Mozam.* **87** E5
Nacala-Velha *Mozam.* **87** E5
Nacaome *Honduras* **120** D2
Nacaroa *Mozam.* **87** E4
Naches *U.S.A.* **108** C3
Naches → *U.S.A.* **110** D6
Nachicapau, L. *Canada* **105** A6
Nachingwea *Tanzania* **87** E4
Nachna *India* **68** F4
Náchod *Czech Rep.* **26** A9
Nacimiento, L. *U.S.A.* **110** K6
Naco *Mexico* **118** A3
Nacogdoches *U.S.A.* **116** F7
Nácori Chico *Mexico* **118** B3
Nacozari de García *Mexico* **118** A3
Nacula *Fiji* **91** a
Nādendal = Naantali *Finland* **32** B1
Nadi *Fiji* **91** a
Nadi *Sudan* **80** D3
Nadiad *India* **68** H5
Nādlac *Romania* **28** D5
Nador *Morocco* **78** B5
Nadur *Malta* **49** C1
Nadūshan *Iran* **71** C7
Nadvirna *Ukraine* **29** B9
Nadvornaya = Nadvirna
   Ukraine **29** B9
Nadym *Russia* **52** C8
Nadym → *Russia* **52** C8
Nærbø *Norway* **9** G11
Næstved *Denmark* **11** J5
Nafada *Nigeria* **83** C7
Nafpaktos *Greece* **46** C3
Nafplio *Greece* **46** D4
Naft-e Safīd *Iran* **71** D6
Naftshahr *Iran* **73** E11
Nafud Desert = An Nafūd
   Si. Arabia **70** D4
Nag Hammâdi *Egypt* **80** B3
Naga *Phil.* **61** E5
Nagagami → *Canada* **104** B3
Nagahama *Japan* **55** G8
Nagai *Japan* **54** E10
Nagaland □ *India* **67** G19
Nagano *Japan* **55** F9
Nagano □ *Japan* **55** F9
Nagaoka *Japan* **55** F9
Nagappattinam *India* **66** P11
Nagar → *Bangla.* **69** G13
Nagar Parkar *Pakistan* **68** G4
Nagasaki *Japan* **55** H4
Nagasaki □ *Japan* **55** H4
Nagato *Japan* **55** G5
Nagaur *India* **68** F5
Nagda *India* **68** H6
Nagercoil *India* **66** Q10
Nagina *India* **69** E8
Nagīneh *Iran* **71** C8
Nagir *Pakistan* **69** A6
Naglarby *Sweden* **10** D9
Nagles Mts. *Ireland* **12** D3
Nagod *India* **69** G9
Nagold *Germany* **25** G4
Nagold → *Germany* **25** G4
Nagoorin *Australia* **94** C5
Nagorno-Karabakh □
   Azerbaijan **73** C12
Nagornyy *Russia* **53** D13
Nagoya *Japan* **55** G8
Nagpur *India* **66** J11
Nagua *Dom. Rep.* **121** C6
Naguabo *Puerto Rico* **121** d
Nagyatád *Hungary* **28** D2
Nagyecsed *Hungary* **28** C7
Nagykálló *Hungary* **28** C6
Nagykanizsa *Hungary* **28** D2
Nagykáta *Hungary* **28** C4
Nagykőrös *Hungary* **28** C4
Naha *Japan* **55** L3
Nahan *India* **68** D7
Nahanni △ *Canada* **102** A4
Nahanni Butte *Canada* **102** A4
Nahargarh *Mad. P., India* **68** G6
Nahargarh *Raj., India* **68** G7
Nahariyya *Israel* **72** F6
Nahāvand *Iran* **73** E13
Nahe → *Germany* **25** F3
Nahîrne *Ukraine* **29** E13
Nahîya, W. → *Egypt* **80** B3
Nahuel Huapi, L. *Argentina* **128** E2
Nahuelbuta △ *Chile* **126** D1

Nai Yong *Thailand* **65** a
Naicá *Mexico* **118** B3
Naicam *Canada* **103** C8
Naikoon △ *Canada* **102** C2
Naila *Germany* **25** E7
Naimisharanya *India* **69** F9
Nain *Canada* **105** A7
Nā'īn *Iran* **71** C7
Naini Tal *India* **69** E8
Nainpur *India* **69** H9
Nainwa *India* **68** G6
Naipu *Romania* **29** F11
Nairai *Fiji* **91** a
Nairn *U.K.* **13** D5
Nairobi *Kenya* **86** C4
Nairobi △ *Kenya* **86** C4
Naissaar *Estonia* **32** C3
Naita, Mt. *Ethiopia* **81** F4
Naitaba *Fiji* **91** a
Naivasha *Kenya* **86** C4
Naivasha, L. *Kenya* **86** C4
Najac *France* **20** D5
Najaf = An Najaf *Iraq* **73** G11
Najafābād *Iran* **71** C6
Najd *Si. Arabia* **75** B3
Nájera *Spain* **38** C2
Najerilla → *Spain* **38** C2
Najibabad *India* **68** E8
Najin *N. Korea* **57** C16
Najmah *Si. Arabia* **71** E6
Najrān *Si. Arabia* **75** D3
Naju *S. Korea* **57** G14
Nakadōri-Shima *Japan* **55** H4
Nakalagba
   Dem. Rep. of the Congo **86** B2
Nakaminato *Japan* **55** F10
Nakamura *Japan* **55** H6
Nakano *Japan* **55** F9
Nakano-Shima *Japan* **55** K4
Nakashibetsu *Japan* **54** C12
Nakfa *Eritrea* **81** D4
Nakfa △ *Eritrea* **81** D4
Nakha Yai, Ko *Thailand* **65** a
Nakhichevan = Naxçıvan
   Azerbaijan **73** C11
Nakhichevan Rep. =
   Naxçıvan □ *Azerbaijan* **73** C11
Nakhl *Egypt* **74** F2
Nakhl-e Taqī *Iran* **71** E7
Nakhodka *Russia* **54** C6
Nakhon Nayok *Thailand* **64** E3
Nakhon Pathom *Thailand* **64** F3
Nakhon Phanom *Thailand* **64** D5
Nakhon Ratchasima
   Thailand **64** E4
Nakhon Sawan *Thailand* **64** E3
Nakhon Si Thammarat
   Thailand **65** H3
Nakhon Thai *Thailand* **64** D3
Nakhtarana *India* **68** H3
Nakina *Canada* **104** B2
Nakło nad Notecią *Poland* **31** E4
Nako *Burkina Faso* **82** C4
Nakodar *India* **68** D6
Nakskov *Denmark* **11** K5
Naktong → *S. Korea* **57** G15
Nakuru *Kenya* **86** C4
Nakuru, L. *Kenya* **86** C4
Nakusp *Canada* **102** C5
Nal *Pakistan* **68** F2
Nal → *Pakistan* **68** G1
Nalázi *Mozam.* **89** C5
Nalchik *Russia* **35** J6
Nałęczów *Poland* **31** G9
Nalerigu *Ghana* **83** C4
Nalgonda *India* **66** L11
Nalhati *India* **69** G12
Naliya *India* **68** H3
Nallamalai Hills *India* **66** M11
Nallıhan *Turkey* **72** B4
Nalón → *Spain* **36** B4
Nalubaale Dam *Uganda* **86** B3
Nam Can *Vietnam* **65** H5
Nam-ch'on *N. Korea* **57** E14
Nam Co *China* **60** C4
Nam Dinh *Vietnam* **58** G6
Nam Du, Hon *Vietnam* **65** H5
Nam Nao △ *Thailand* **64** D3
Nam Ngum Res. *Laos* **64** C4
Nam-Phan *Vietnam* **65** G6
Nam Phong *Thailand* **64** D4
Nam Tha *Laos* **58** G3
Nam Tok *Thailand* **64** E2
Namacunde *Angola* **88** B2
Namacurra *Mozam.* **89** B6
Namak, Daryācheh-ye *Iran* **71** C7
Namak, Kavir-e *Iran* **71** C8
Namakzār, Daryācheh-ye
   Iran **71** C9
Namaland *Namibia* **88** C2
Namanga *Kenya* **86** C4
Namangan *Uzbekistan* **52** E8
Namapa *Mozam.* **87** E4
Namaqualand *S. Africa* **88** E2
Namasagali *Uganda* **86** B3
Namber *Indonesia* **63** E8

Nambour *Australia* **95** D5
Nambouwalu =
   Nabouwalu *Fiji* **91** a
Nambucca Heads *Australia* **95** E5
Nambung △ *Australia* **93** F2
Namche Bazar *Nepal* **69** F12
Namchonjŏm =
   Nam-ch'on *N. Korea* **57** E14
Namecunda *Mozam.* **87** E4
Namenalala *Fiji* **91** a
Nameponda *Mozam.* **87** F4
Náměšt' nad Oslavou
   Czech Rep. **27** B9
Námestovo *Slovak Rep.* **27** B12
Nametil *Mozam.* **87** F4
Namew L. *Canada* **103** C8
Namgia *India* **69** D8
Namhkam *Burma* **58** E1
Namib Desert *Namibia* **88** C2
Namib-Naukluft △ *Namibia* **88** C2
Namibe *Angola* **85** H2
Namibe □ *Angola* **88** B1
Namibia ■ *Africa* **88** C2
Namibwoestyn = Namib
   Desert *Namibia* **88** C2
Namīn *Iran* **73** C13
Namlea *Indonesia* **63** E7
Namoi → *Australia* **95** E4
Nampa *U.S.A.* **108** E5
Nampala *Mali* **82** B3
Namp'o *N. Korea* **57** E13
Nampō-Shotō *Japan* **55** J10
Nampula *Mozam.* **87** F4
Namrole *Indonesia* **63** E7
Namse Shankou *China* **69** E10
Namsen → *Norway* **8** D14
Namsos *Norway* **8** D14
Namtok Chat Trakan △
   Thailand **64** D3
Namtok Mae Surin △
   Thailand **64** C2
Namtsy *Russia* **53** C13
Namtu *Burma* **67** H20
Namtumbo *Tanzania* **87** E4
Namu *Canada* **102** C3
Namuka-i-Lau *Fiji* **91** a
Namur *Belgium* **17** D4
Namur □ *Belgium* **17** D4
Namuruputh *Kenya* **86** B4
Namutoni *Namibia* **88** B2
Namwala *Zambia* **87** F2
Namwon *S. Korea* **57** G14
Namyang *N. Korea* **57** C15
Namysłów *Poland* **31** G4
Nan *Thailand* **64** C3
Nan → *Thailand* **64** E3
Nan-ch'ang = Nanchang
   China **59** C10
Nan Ling *China* **59** E8
Nan Xian *China* **59** C9
Nana *Romania* **29** F11
Nana Kru *Liberia* **82** E3
Nanaimo *Canada* **102** D4
Nanam *N. Korea* **57** D15
Nanan *China* **59** E12
Nanango *Australia* **95** D5
Nan'ao *China* **59** F11
Nanao *Japan* **55** F8
Nanbu *China* **58** B6
Nanchang *China* **59** C10
Nancheng *China* **59** D11
Nanching = Nanjing *China* **59** A12
Nanchong *China* **58** B6
Nanchuan *China* **58** C6
Nancy *France* **19** D13
Nanda Devi *India* **69** D8
Nanda Devi △ *India* **69** D8
Nanda Kot *India* **69** D9
Nandan *China* **58** E6
Nandan *Japan* **55** G7
Nanded *India* **66** K10
Nandewar Ra. *Australia* **95** E5
Nandi = Nadi *Fiji* **91** a
Nandigram *India* **69** H12
Nandurbar *India* **66** J9
Nandyal *India* **66** M11
Nanfeng *Guangdong, China* **59** F8
Nanfeng *Jiangxi, China* **59** D11
Nanga-Eboko *Cameroon* **83** E7
Nanga Parbat *Pakistan* **69** B6
Nangade *Mozam.* **87** E4
Nangapinoh *Indonesia* **62** E4
Nangarhār □ *Afghan.* **66** B7
Nangatayap *Indonesia* **62** E4
Nangeya Mts. *Uganda* **86** B3
Nangis *France* **19** D10
Nangong *China* **56** F8
Nanhua *China* **58** D3
Nanhuang *China* **57** F11
Nanhui *China* **59** B13
Nanjeko *Zambia* **87** F1
Nanji Shan *China* **59** D13
Nanjian *China* **58** E3
Nanjiang *China* **58** A6
Nanjing *Fujian, China* **59** E11
Nanjing *Jiangsu, China* **59** A12
Nanjirinji *Tanzania* **87** D4

Nankana Sahib *Pakistan* **68** D5
Nankang *China* **59** E10
Nanking = Nanjing *China* **59** A12
Nankoku *Japan* **55** H6
Nanling *China* **59** B12
Nanning *China* **58** F7
Nannup *Australia* **93** F2
Nanpi *China* **56** E9
Nanping *Fujian, China* **59** D12
Nanping *Henan, China* **59** C9
Nanri Dao *China* **59** E12
Nanripe *Mozam.* **87** E4
Nansei-Shotō =
   Ryūkyū-rettō *Japan* **55** M3
Nansen Basin *Arctic* **4** A10
Nansen Sd. *Canada* **101** A10
Nanshan I. *S. China Sea* **62** B5
Nansio *Tanzania* **86** C3
Nant *France* **20** D7
Nanterre *France* **19** D9
Nantes *France* **18** E5
Nantiat *France* **20** B5
Nanticoke *U.S.A.* **115** E8
Nanton *Canada* **102** C6
Nantong *China* **59** A13
Nant'ou *Taiwan* **59** F13
Nantua *France* **19** F12
Nantucket *U.S.A.* **113** E18
Nantucket I. *U.S.A.* **113** E18
Nantwich *U.K.* **14** D5
Nanty Glo *U.S.A.* **114** F6
Nanuku Passage *Fiji* **91** a
Nanuque *Brazil* **125** G10
Nanusa, Kepulauan
   Indonesia **63** D7
Nanutarra Roadhouse
   Australia **92** D2
Nanxi *China* **58** C5
Nanxiong *China* **59** E10
Nanyang *China* **56** H7
Nanyi Hu *China* **59** B12
Nanyuki *Kenya* **86** B4
Nanzhang *China* **59** B8
Nao, C. de la *Spain* **39** G5
Naococane, L. *Canada* **105** B5
Naoussa *Cyclades, Greece* **47** D7
Naoussa *Imathia, Greece* **44** F6
Naozhou Dao *China* **59** G8
Napa *U.S.A.* **110** G4
Napa → *U.S.A.* **110** G4
Napanee *Canada* **114** B8
Napanook *U.S.A.* **115** E10
Nape *Laos* **64** C5
Nape Pass = Keo Neua,
   Deo *Vietnam* **64** C5
Napier *N.Z.* **91** C6
Napier Broome B. *Australia* **92** B4
Napier Pen. *Australia* **94** A2
Napierville *Canada* **115** A11
Naples = Nápoli *Italy* **43** B7
Naples *U.S.A.* **117** H14
Napo *China* **58** F5
Napo → *Peru* **124** D4
Napoleon *N. Dak., U.S.A.* **112** B4
Napoleon *Ohio, U.S.A.* **113** E11
Nápoli *Italy* **43** B7
Nápoli, G. di *Italy* **43** B7
Nápoli Capodichino ✈
   (NAP) *Italy* **43** B7
Napopo *Dem. Rep. of the Congo* **86** B2
Naqâda *Egypt* **80** B3
Naqadeh *Iran* **73** D11
Naqb, Ra's an *Jordan* **74** F4
Naqqāsh *Iran* **71** C6
Nara *Japan* **55** G7
Nara *Mali* **82** B3
Nara □ *Japan* **55** G7
Nara Canal *Pakistan* **68** G3
Nara Visa *U.S.A.* **109** J12
Naracoorte *Australia* **95** F3
Naradhan *Australia* **95** E4
Naraini *India* **69** G9
Naranjos *Mexico* **119** C5
Narasapur *India* **67** L12
Narathiwat *Thailand* **65** J3
Narayanganj *Bangla.* **67** H17
Narayanpet *India* **66** L10
Narberth *U.K.* **15** F3
Narbonne *France* **20** E7
Narcea → *Spain* **36** B4
Nardīn *Iran* **71** B7
Nardò *Italy* **43** B11
Narembeen *Australia* **93** F2
Narendranagar *India* **68** D8
Nares Str. *Arctic* **98** A13
Naretha *Australia* **93** F3
Narew → *Poland* **31** F7
Nari → *Pakistan* **68** F2
Narin *Afghan.* **66** A6
Narindra, Helodranon' i
   Madag. **89** A8
Narita *Japan* **55** G10
Nariva Swamp *Trin. & Tob.* **125** K15
Närke *Sweden* **10** E8
Narmada → *India* **68** J5

Narman *Turkey* **73** B9
Narnaul *India* **68** E7
Narni *Italy* **41** F9
Naro *Ghana* **82** C4
Naro Fominsk *Russia* **32** E9
Narodnaya *Russia* **6** B17
Narok *Kenya* **86** C4
Narón *Spain* **36** B2
Narooma *Australia* **95** F5
Narowal *Pakistan* **68** C6
Narrabri *Australia* **95** E4
Narran → *Australia* **95** D4
Narrandera *Australia* **95** E4
Narrogin *Australia* **93** F2
Narromine *Australia* **95** E4
Narrow Hills △ *Canada* **103** C8
Narsimhapur *India* **69** H8
Narsinghgarh *India* **68** H7
Nartes, L. e *Albania* **44** F3
Nartkala *Russia* **35** J6
Naruto *Japan* **55** G7
Narva *Estonia* **32** C5
Narva → *Russia* **32** C4
Narva Bay = Narva Laht
   Estonia **9** G22
Narva Laht *Estonia* **9** G22
Narvik *Norway* **8** B17
Narvskoye Vdkhr. *Russia* **32** C5
Narwana *India* **68** E7
Narwiański △ *Poland* **31** F9
Naryan-Mar *Russia* **52** C6
Narym *Russia* **52** D9
Naryn *Kyrgyzstan* **52** E8
Naryn Qum *Kazakhstan* **35** G9
Nasa *Norway* **8** C16
Nasau *Fiji* **91** a
Năsăud *Romania* **29** C9
Nasca = Nazca *Peru* **124** F4
Naseby *N.Z.* **91** F3
Naselle *U.S.A.* **110** D3
Naser, Buheirat en *Egypt* **80** C3
Nashua *Mont., U.S.A.* **108** B10
Nashua *N.H., U.S.A.* **115** D13
Nashville *Ark., U.S.A.* **116** E8
Nashville *Ga., U.S.A.* **117** F13
Nashville *Tenn., U.S.A.* **117** C11
Našice *Croatia* **28** E3
Nasielsk *Poland* **31** F7
Nasik *India* **66** K8
Nasipit *Phil.* **61** G6
Nasir *Sudan* **81** F3
Nasirabad *India* **68** F6
Nasirabad *Pakistan* **68** E3
Nasiriyah = An Nāşirīyah
   Iraq **70** D5
Naskaupi → *Canada* **105** B7
Naso *Italy* **43** D7
Naşrābād *Iran* **71** C6
Naşrīān-e Pā'īn *Iran* **70** C5
Nass → *Canada* **102** C3
Nassarawa *Nigeria* **83** D6
Nassarawa □ *Nigeria* **83** D6
Nassau *Bahamas* **120** A4
Nassau *U.S.A.* **115** D11
Nassau, B. *Chile* **128** H3
Nasser, L. = Naser,
   Buheirat en *Egypt* **80** C3
Nassian *Ivory C.* **82** D4
Nässjö *Sweden* **11** G8
Nastapoka → *Canada* **104** A4
Nastapoka, Is. *Canada* **104** A4
Nasugbu *Phil.* **61** D4
Näsum *Sweden* **11** H8
Näsviken *Sweden* **10** C10
Nata *Botswana* **88** C4
Nata → *Botswana* **88** C4
Natal *Brazil* **125** E12
Natal *Indonesia* **62** D1
Natal Drakensberg △
   S. Africa **89** D4
Natalinci *Serbia* **28** F5
Naţanz *Iran* **71** C6
Natashquan *Canada* **105** B7
Natashquan → *Canada* **105** B7
Natchez *U.S.A.* **116** F9
Natchitoches *U.S.A.* **116** F8
Natewa B. *Fiji* **91** a
Nathalia *Australia* **95** F4
Nathdwara *India* **68** G5
Nati, Pta. *Spain* **48** A10
Natimuk *Australia* **95** F3
Nation → *Canada* **102** B4
National City *U.S.A.* **111** N9
Natitingou *Benin* **83** C5
Natkyizin *Burma* **64** E1
Natron, L. *Tanzania* **86** C4
Natrona Heights *U.S.A.* **114** F5
Natrûn, W. el → *Egypt* **80** H7
Nättraby *Sweden* **11** H9
Natukanaoka Pan *Namibia* **88** B2
Natuna Besar, Kepulauan
   Indonesia **62** D3
Natuna Is. = Natuna
   Besar, Kepulauan
   Indonesia **62** D3
Natuna Selatan,
   Kepulauan *Indonesia* **62** D3

Natural Bridge *U.S.A.* 115 B9
Natural Bridges △ *U.S.A.* 109 H9
Naturaliste, C. *Tas., Australia* 95 G4
Naturaliste, C. *W. Austral.,*
  Australia 90 E4
Naturaliste Plateau *Ind. Oc.* 96 L3
Nau Qala *Afghan.* 68 B3
Naucelle *France* 20 D6
Nauders *Austria* 26 E3
Nauen *Germany* 24 C8
Naugatuck *U.S.A.* 115 E11
Naujaat = Repulse Bay
  Canada 101 C11
Naujoji Akmenė *Lithuania* 30 B9
Naumburg *Germany* 24 D7
Nauru ■ *Pac. Oc.* 90 B9
Naushahra = Nowshera
  Pakistan 66 C8
Naushahro *Pakistan* 68 F3
Naushon I. *U.S.A.* 115 E14
Nausori *Fiji* 91 a
Nauta *Peru* 124 D4
Nautanwa *India* 69 F10
Naute △ *Namibia* 88 D2
Nautla *Mexico* 119 C5
Nava *Mexico* 118 B4
Nava *Spain* 36 B5
Nava del Rey *Spain* 36 D5
Navadwip *India* 69 H13
Navahermosa *Spain* 37 F6
Navahrudak *Belarus* 23 B13
Navajo Res. *U.S.A.* 109 H10
Navalcarnero *Spain* 36 E6
Navalmoral de la Mata *Spain* 36 F5
Navalvillar de Pela *Spain* 37 F5
Navan = An Uaimh *Ireland* 12 C5
Navapolatsk *Belarus* 32 E5
Navarin, Mys *Russia* 4 C16
Navarino, I. *Chile* 128 H3
Navarra □ *Spain* 38 C3
Navarre *U.S.A.* 114 F3
Navarro → *U.S.A.* 110 F3
Navas de San Juan *Spain* 37 G7
Navasota *U.S.A.* 116 G7
Navassa I. *W. Indies* 121 C5
Nävekvarn *Sweden* 11 F10
Naver → *U.K.* 13 C4
Navia *Spain* 36 B4
Navia → *Spain* 36 B4
Navia de Suarna *Spain* 36 C3
Navibandar *India* 68 J3
Navidad *Chile* 126 C1
Naviraí *Brazil* 127 A5
Naviti *Fiji* 91 a
Navlakhi *India* 68 H4
Navlya *Russia* 33 F8
Năvodari *Romania* 29 F13
Navoi = Nawoiy *Uzbekistan* 52 E7
Navojoa *Mexico* 118 B3
Navolato *Mexico* 118 C3
Navrongo *Ghana* 83 C4
Navsari *India* 66 J8
Navua *Fiji* 91 a
Nawa Kot *Pakistan* 68 E4
Nawab Khan *Pakistan* 68 D3
Nawabganj *Ut. P., India* 69 F9
Nawabganj *Ut. P., India* 69 E8
Nawabshah *Pakistan* 68 F3
Nawada *India* 69 G11
Nawakot *Nepal* 69 F11
Nawalgarh *India* 68 F6
Nawanshahr *India* 69 C6
Nawar, Dasht-i- *Afghan.* 68 C3
Nawi *Sudan* 80 D3
Nawoiy *Uzbekistan* 52 E7
Naxçıvan *Azerbaijan* 73 C11
Naxçıvan □ *Azerbaijan* 73 C11
Naxos *Greece* 47 D7
Nay *France* 20 E3
Nay, Mui *Vietnam* 62 B3
Nāy Band *Būshehr, Iran* 71 E7
Nāy Band *Khorāsān, Iran* 71 C8
Nayakhan *Russia* 53 C16
Nayarit □ *Mexico* 118 C4
Nayau *Fiji* 91 a
Nayé *Senegal* 82 C2
Nayong *China* 58 D5
Nayoro *Japan* 54 B11
Nayyāl, W. → *Si. Arabia* 70 D3
Nazaré *Brazil* 125 F11
Nazaré *Portugal* 37 F1
Nazareth = Nazerat *Israel* 74 C4
Nazareth *U.S.A.* 115 F9
Nazas *Mexico* 118 B4
Nazas → *Mexico* 118 B4
Nazca *Peru* 124 F4
Nazca Ridge *Pac. Oc.* 97 K19
Naze *Japan* 55 K4
Naze, The *U.K.* 15 F9
Nazerat *Israel* 74 C4
Nāzīk *Iran* 73 C11
Nazilli *Turkey* 47 D10
Nazko *Canada* 102 C4
Nazko → *Canada* 102 C4
Nazret *Ethiopia* 81 F4
Nchanga *Zambia* 87 E2
Ncheu *Malawi* 87 E3

Ndala *Tanzania* 86 C3
Ndalatando *Angola* 84 F2
Ndali *Benin* 83 D5
Ndareda *Tanzania* 86 C4
Ndélé *C.A.R.* 84 C4
Ndiael → *Senegal* 82 B1
N'Dioum *Senegal* 82 B2
Ndikinimeki *Cameroon* 83 E7
Ndjamena *Chad* 79 F8
Ndola *Zambia* 87 E2
Ndomo △ *S. Africa* 89 D5
Ndoto Mts. *Kenya* 86 B4
Nduguti *Tanzania* 86 C3
Nea Alikarnassos *Greece* 47 F7
Nea Anchialos *Greece* 46 B4
Nea Epidavros *Greece* 46 D5
Nea Ionia *Greece* 46 B4
Nea Kalikratia *Greece* 44 F7
Nea Makri *Greece* 46 C5
Nea Moudania *Greece* 44 F7
Nea Peramos *Attiki, Greece* 46 C5
Nea Peramos *Kavala, Greece* 45 F8
Nea Visa *Greece* 45 E10
Nea Zichni *Greece* 44 E7
Neagh, Lough *U.K.* 12 B5
Neah Bay *U.S.A.* 110 B2
Neale, L. *Australia* 92 D5
Neales → *Australia* 95 D2
Neamţ □ *Romania* 29 C11
Neapoli *Kozani, Greece* 44 F5
Neapoli *Kriti, Greece* 49 D7
Neapoli *Lakonia, Greece* 46 E5
Near Is. *U.S.A.* 106 a
Neath *U.K.* 15 F4
Neath Port Talbot □ *U.K.* 15 F4
Nebbou *Burkina Faso* 83 C4
Nebelat el Hagana *Sudan* 81 E2
Nebine Cr. → *Australia* 95 D4
Nebitdag = Balkanabat
  Turkmenistan 71 B7
Nebo *Australia* 94 C4
Nebolchy *Russia* 32 C7
Nebraska □ *U.S.A.* 112 E4
Nebraska City *U.S.A.* 112 E6
Nébrodi, Monti *Italy* 43 E7
Necedah *U.S.A.* 112 C8
Nechako → *Canada* 102 C4
Neches → *U.S.A.* 116 G8
Nechisar △ *Ethiopia* 81 F4
Neckar → *Germany* 25 F4
Neckartal-Odenwald △
  Germany 25 F5
Necochea *Argentina* 126 D4
Neda *Spain* 36 B2
Neda → *Greece* 46 D3
Nedelino *Bulgaria* 45 E9
Nedelišče *Croatia* 41 B13
Nederland =
  Netherlands ■ *Europe* 17 C5
Nedoboyivtsi *Ukraine* 29 B11
Needles *Canada* 102 D5
Needles *U.S.A.* 111 L12
Needles, The *U.K.* 15 G6
Neembucú □ *Paraguay* 126 B4
Neemuch = Nimach *India* 68 G6
Neenah *U.S.A.* 112 C9
Neepawa *Canada* 103 C9
Neftçala *Azerbaijan* 73 C13
Neftegorsk *Russia* 35 H4
Neftekumsk *Russia* 35 H7
Nefyn *U.K.* 14 E3
Négala *Mali* 82 C3
Negapatam =
  Nagappattinam *India* 66 P11
Negara *Indonesia* 63 J17
Negaunee *U.S.A.* 112 B10
Negele *Ethiopia* 81 F4
Negev Desert = Hanegev
  Israel 74 E4
Negoiul, Vf. *Romania* 29 E9
Negombo *Sri Lanka* 66 R11
Negotin *Serbia* 44 B6
Negotino *Macedonia* 44 E6
Negra, Peña *Spain* 36 C4
Negra, Pta. *Mauritania* 78 D2
Negra, Pta. *Peru* 124 E2
Negrais, C. = Maudin Sun
  Burma 67 M19
Negreşti *Romania* 29 D12
Negreşti-Oaş *Romania* 29 C8
Negril *Jamaica* 120 a
Negro → *Argentina* 128 E4
Negro → *Brazil* 124 D7
Negro → *Uruguay* 126 C4
Negros *Phil.* 61 G5
Negru Vodă *Romania* 29 G13
Neguac *Canada* 105 C6
Nehalem → *U.S.A.* 110 E3
Nehāvand *Iran* 71 C6
Nehbandān *Iran* 71 D9
Nehoiu *Romania* 29 E11
Nei Monggol Zizhiqu □
  China 56 D7
Neiafu *Tonga* 91 c
Neiges, Piton des *Réunion* 85 c
Neijiang *China* 58 C5
Neillsville *U.S.A.* 112 C8

Neilton *U.S.A.* 108 C2
Neiqiu *China* 56 F8
Neiva *Colombia* 124 C3
Neixiang *China* 56 H6
Nejanilini L. *Canada* 103 B9
Nejd = Najd *Si. Arabia* 75 B3
Nejo *Ethiopia* 81 F4
Nekā *Iran* 71 B7
Nekemte *Ethiopia* 81 F4
Nêkheb *Egypt* 80 B3
Neksø *Denmark* 11 J9
Nelas *Portugal* 36 E3
Nelia *Australia* 94 C3
Nelidovo *Russia* 32 D7
Neligh *U.S.A.* 112 D4
Nelkan *Russia* 53 D14
Nellore *India* 66 M11
Nelson *Canada* 102 D5
Nelson *N.Z.* 91 D4
Nelson *U.K.* 14 D5
Nelson *Ariz., U.S.A.* 109 J7
Nelson *Nev., U.S.A.* 111 K12
Nelson → *Canada* 103 C9
Nelson, C. *Australia* 95 F3
Nelson, Estrecho *Chile* 128 G2
Nelson Forks *Canada* 102 B4
Nelson House *Canada* 103 B9
Nelson L. *Canada* 103 B8
Nelson Lakes △ *N.Z.* 91 D4
Nelspoort *S. Africa* 88 E3
Nelspruit *S. Africa* 89 D5
Néma *Mauritania* 82 B3
Neman = Nemunas →
  Lithuania 30 C8
Neman *Russia* 30 C9
Nemea *Greece* 46 D4
Nemeiben L. *Canada* 103 B7
Nemërçkë, Mal *Albania* 44 F4
Nemira, Vf. *Romania* 29 D11
Nemiscau *Canada* 104 B4
Nemiscau, L. *Canada* 104 B4
Nemours *France* 19 D9
Nemšová *Slovak Rep.* 27 C11
Nemunas → *Lithuania* 30 C8
Nemuro *Japan* 54 C12
Nemuro-Kaikyō *Japan* 54 C12
Nemyriv *Ukraine* 31 H10
Nen Jiang → *China* 57 B13
Nenagh *Ireland* 12 D3
Nenasi *Malaysia* 65 L4
Nene → *U.K.* 15 E8
Nenita *Greece* 47 C8
Nenjiang *China* 60 B7
Neno *Malawi* 87 F3
Neo Chori *Greece* 46 C3
Neochori *Greece* 46 B2
Neodesha *U.S.A.* 112 G6
Neon Petritsi *Greece* 44 E7
Neora Valley △ *India* 69 F13
Neosho *U.S.A.* 112 G6
Neosho → *U.S.A.* 116 C7
Nepal ■ *Asia* 69 F11
Nepalganj *Nepal* 69 E9
Nepalganj Road *India* 69 E9
Nephi *U.S.A.* 108 G8
Nephin *Ireland* 12 B2
Nephin Beg Range *Ireland* 12 C2
Nepi *Italy* 41 F9
Nepomuk *Czech Rep.* 26 B6
Neptune *U.S.A.* 115 F10
Nera → *Italy* 41 F9
Nera → *Romania* 28 F6
Nérac *France* 20 D4
Nerang *Australia* 95 D5
Nerastro, Sarīr *Libya* 79 D10
Neratovice *Czech Rep.* 26 A7
Nerchinsk *Russia* 53 D12
Nereju *Romania* 29 E11
Nerekhta *Russia* 32 D11
Neresnytsya *Ukraine* 29 B8
Néret, L. *Canada* 105 B5
Neretvanski Kanal *Croatia* 41 E14
Neringa *Lithuania* 30 C8
Neris → *Lithuania* 32 E3
Nerja *Spain* 37 J7
Nerpio *Spain* 39 G2
Nerva *Spain* 37 H4
Nervi *Italy* 40 D6
Neryungri *Russia* 53 D13
Nescopeck *U.S.A.* 115 E8
Nesebŭr *Bulgaria* 45 D11
Ness, L. *U.K.* 13 D4
Ness City *U.S.A.* 112 F4
Nesterov *Russia* 30 D9
Nesterov *Ukraine* 23 C12
Nestorio *Greece* 44 F5
Nestos → *Greece* 45 E8
Nesvady *Slovak Rep.* 27 D11
Nesvizh = Nyasvizh *Belarus* 23 B14
Netanya *Israel* 74 C3
Netarhat *India* 69 H11
Nete → *Belgium* 17 C4
Netherdale *Australia* 94 K6
Netherlands ■ *Europe* 17 C5
Netherlands Antilles ☑
  W. Indies 124 A5

Neto → *Italy* 43 C10
Netrang *India* 68 J5
Nettancourt *France* 19 D11
Nettetal *Germany* 24 D2
Nettilling L. *Canada* 101 C12
Nettuno *Italy* 42 A5
Netzahualcóyotl, Presa
  Mexico 119 D6
Neu-Isenburg *Germany* 25 E4
Neu-Ulm *Germany* 25 G6
Neubrandenburg *Germany* 24 B9
Neubukow *Germany* 24 A7
Neuburg *Germany* 25 G7
Neuchâtel *Switz.* 25 J2
Neuchâtel □ *Switz.* 25 J2
Neuchâtel, Lac de *Switz.* 25 J2
Neudau *Austria* 26 D9
Neuenhagen *Germany* 24 C9
Neuenhaus *Germany* 24 C2
Neuf-Brisach *France* 19 D14
Neufahrn *Bayern, Germany* 25 G6
Neufahrn *Bayern, Germany* 25 G7
Neufchâteau *Belgium* 17 E5
Neufchâteau *France* 19 D12
Neufchâtel-en-Bray *France* 18 C8
Neufchâtel-sur-Aisne
  France 19 C11
Neuhaus *Germany* 24 B6
Neuillé-Pont-Pierre *France* 18 E7
Neuilly-St-Front *France* 19 C10
Neukalen *Germany* 24 B8
Neumarkt *Germany* 25 F7
Neumayer *Antarctica* 5 D17
Neumünster *Germany* 24 A5
Neung-sur-Beuvron *France* 19 E8
Neunkirchen *Austria* 26 D9
Neunkirchen *Germany* 25 F3
Neuquén *Argentina* 128 D3
Neuquén □ *Argentina* 126 D2
Neuruppin *Germany* 24 C8
Neusäss *Germany* 25 G6
Neuse → *U.S.A.* 117 D16
Neusiedl *Austria* 27 D9
Neusiedler See *Austria* 27 D9
Neusiedler
  See-Seewinkel △ *Austria* 27 D9
Neuss *Germany* 24 D2
Neussargues-Moissac *France* 20 C7
Neustadt *Bayern, Germany* 25 F8
Neustadt *Bayern, Germany* 25 G7
Neustadt *Bayern, Germany* 25 F6
Neustadt *Bayern, Germany* 25 G7
Neustadt *Brandenburg,*
  Germany 24 C8
Neustadt *Hessen, Germany* 24 E5
Neustadt *Niedersachsen,*
  Germany 24 C5
Neustadt *Rhld.-Pfz., Germany* 25 F4
Neustadt *Sachsen, Germany* 24 D10
Neustadt *Schleswig-Holstein,*
  Germany 24 A6
Neustadt *Thüringen, Germany* 24 E7
Neustrelitz *Germany* 24 B9
Neuvic *France* 20 C6
Neuville-sur-Saône *France* 21 C9
Neuvy-le-Roi *France* 18 E7
Neuvy-St-Sépulchre *France* 19 F8
Neuvy-sur-Barangeon
  France 19 E9
Neuwerk *Germany* 24 B4
Neuwied *Germany* 24 E3
Neva → *Russia* 32 C6
Nevada *Iowa, U.S.A.* 112 D7
Nevada *Mo., U.S.A.* 112 G6
Nevada □ *U.S.A.* 108 G5
Nevada City *U.S.A.* 110 F6
Nevado, Cerro *Argentina* 126 D2
Nevado de Colima =
  Volcán de Colima △
  Mexico 118 D4
Nevado de Tres Cruces △
  Chile 126 B2
Nevel *Russia* 32 D5
Nevers *France* 19 F10
Nevertire *Australia* 95 E4
Nevesinje *Bos.-H.* 44 C2
Neville *Canada* 103 D7
Nevinnomyssk *Russia* 35 H6
Nevis *St. Kitts & Nevis* 121 C7
Nevrokop = Gotse Delchev
  Bulgaria 44 E7
Nevşehir *Turkey* 72 C6
Nevşehir □ *Turkey* 72 C6
Nevskoye *Russia* 30 D9
New → *U.S.A.* 113 F13
New Aiyansh *Canada* 102 B3
New Albany *Ind., U.S.A.* 113 F11
New Albany *Miss., U.S.A.* 117 D10
New Albany *Pa., U.S.A.* 115 E8
New Amsterdam *Guyana* 124 B7
New Angledool *Australia* 95 D4
New Baltimore *U.S.A.* 114 D2
New Bedford *U.S.A.* 115 E14
New Berlin *N.Y., U.S.A.* 115 D9
New Berlin *Pa., U.S.A.* 114 F8
New Bern *U.S.A.* 117 D16
New Bethlehem *U.S.A.* 114 F5

New Bight *Bahamas* 121 B4
New Bloomfield *U.S.A.* 114 F7
New Boston *U.S.A.* 116 E7
New Braunfels *U.S.A.* 116 G5
New Brighton *N.Z.* 91 E4
New Brighton *U.S.A.* 114 F4
New Britain *Papua N. G.* 90 B8
New Britain *U.S.A.* 115 E12
New Brunswick *U.S.A.* 115 F10
New Brunswick □ *Canada* 105 C6
New Bussa *Nigeria* 83 D5
New Caledonia ☑ *Pac. Oc.* 90 D9
New Caledonia Trough
  Pac. Oc. 96 L8
New Castile = Castilla-La
  Mancha □ *Spain* 37 F7
New Castle *Ind., U.S.A.* 113 F11
New Castle *Pa., U.S.A.* 114 F4
New City *U.S.A.* 115 E11
New Concord *U.S.A.* 114 G3
New Cumberland *U.S.A.* 114 F4
New Cuyama *U.S.A.* 111 L7
New Delhi *India* 68 E7
New Denver *Canada* 102 D5
New Don Pedro Res. *U.S.A.* 110 H6
New England *U.S.A.* 107 B12
New England *N. Dak.,*
  U.S.A. 112 B3
New England Ra. *Australia* 95 E5
New Forest △ *U.K.* 15 G6
New Galloway *U.K.* 13 F4
New Glasgow *Canada* 105 C7
New Guinea *Oceania* 90 B6
New Hamburg *Canada* 114 C4
New Hampshire □ *U.S.A.* 115 C13
New Hampton *U.S.A.* 112 D7
New Hanover *S. Africa* 89 D5
New Hartford *U.S.A.* 115 C9
New Haven *Conn., U.S.A.* 115 E12
New Haven *Mich., U.S.A.* 114 D2
New Hazelton *Canada* 102 B3
New Hebrides =
  Vanuatu ■ *Pac. Oc.* 90 C9
New Holland *U.S.A.* 115 F8
New Iberia *U.S.A.* 116 F9
New Ireland *Papua N. G.* 90 B8
New Jersey □ *U.S.A.* 113 F16
New Kensington *U.S.A.* 114 F5
New Lexington *U.S.A.* 113 F12
New Liskeard *Canada* 104 C4
New London *Conn., U.S.A.* 115 E12
New London *Ohio, U.S.A.* 114 E2
New London *Wis., U.S.A.* 112 C9
New Madrid *U.S.A.* 112 G9
New Martinsville *U.S.A.* 113 F13
New Meadows *U.S.A.* 108 D5
New Melones L. *U.S.A.* 110 H6
New Mexico □ *U.S.A.* 109 J11
New Milford *Conn., U.S.A.* 115 E11
New Milford *Pa., U.S.A.* 115 E9
New Norcia *Australia* 93 F2
New Norfolk *Australia* 95 G4
New Orleans *U.S.A.* 117 G9
New Philadelphia *U.S.A.* 114 F3
New Plymouth *N.Z.* 91 C5
New Plymouth *U.S.A.* 108 E5
New Port Richey *U.S.A.* 117 G13
New Providence *Bahamas* 120 A4
New Quay *U.K.* 15 E3
New Radnor *U.K.* 15 E4
New Richmond *Canada* 105 C6
New Richmond *U.S.A.* 112 C7
New River Gorge △ *U.S.A.* 113 G13
New Roads *U.S.A.* 116 F9
New Rochelle *U.S.A.* 115 F11
New Rockford *U.S.A.* 112 B4
New Romney *U.K.* 15 G8
New Ross *Ireland* 12 D5
New Salem *U.S.A.* 112 B3
New Scone = Scone *U.K.* 13 E5
New Siberian I. = Novaya
  Sibir, Ostrov *Russia* 53 B16
New Siberian Is. =
  Novosibirskiye Ostrova
  Russia 53 B15
New Smyrna Beach *U.S.A.* 117 G14
New South Wales □
  Australia 95 E4
New Tecumseth *Canada* 114 B5
New Town *U.S.A.* 112 B2
New Tredegar *U.K.* 15 F4
New Ulm *U.S.A.* 112 C6
New Waterford *Canada* 105 C7
New-Wes-Valley *Canada* 105 C9
New Westminster *Canada* 110 A4
New York *U.S.A.* 115 F11
New York □ *U.S.A.* 115 D9
New York J.F. Kennedy
  Int. ✈ (JFK) *U.S.A.* 115 F11
New Zealand ■ *Oceania* 91 D6
Newaj → *India* 68 G7
Newala *Tanzania* 87 E4
Newark *Del., U.S.A.* 113 F16
Newark *N.J., U.S.A.* 115 F10
Newark *N.Y., U.S.A.* 114 C7
Newark *Ohio, U.S.A.* 114 F2
Newark Liberty Int. ✈
  (EWR) *U.S.A.* 115 F10

Newark-on-Trent *U.K.* 14 D7
Newark Valley *U.S.A.* 115 D8
Newberg *U.S.A.* 108 D2
Newberry *Mich., U.S.A.* 113 B11
Newberry *S.C., U.S.A.* 117 D14
Newberry Springs *U.S.A.* 111 L10
Newboro L. *Canada* 115 B8
Newbridge = Droichead
  Nua *Ireland* 12 C5
Newburgh *Canada* 114 B8
Newburgh *U.S.A.* 115 E10
Newbury *U.K.* 15 F6
Newbury *N.H., U.S.A.* 115 C12
Newbury *Vt., U.S.A.* 115 B12
Newburyport *U.S.A.* 115 C14
Newcastle *Australia* 95 E5
Newcastle *N.B., Canada* 105 C6
Newcastle *Ont., Canada* 104 D4
Newcastle *S. Africa* 89 D4
Newcastle *U.K.* 12 B6
Newcastle *Calif., U.S.A.* 110 G5
Newcastle *Wyo., U.S.A.* 108 D2
Newcastle Emlyn *U.K.* 15 E3
Newcastle Ra. *Australia* 92 C5
Newcastle-under-Lyme *U.K.* 14 D5
Newcastle-upon-Tyne *U.K.* 14 C6
Newcastle Waters *Australia* 94 B1
Newcastle West *Ireland* 12 D2
Newcomb *U.S.A.* 115 C10
Newcomerstown *U.S.A.* 114 F3
Newdegate *Australia* 93 F2
Newell *Australia* 94 B4
Newell *U.S.A.* 112 C2
Newfane *U.S.A.* 114 C6
Newfield *U.S.A.* 115 D8
Newfound L. *U.S.A.* 115 C13
Newfoundland *Canada* 105 C8
Newfoundland *U.S.A.* 115 E9
Newfoundland &
  Labrador □ *Canada* 105 B8
Newhaven *U.K.* 15 G8
Newkirk *U.S.A.* 116 C6
Newlyn *U.K.* 15 G2
Newman *Australia* 92 D2
Newman *U.S.A.* 110 H5
Newmarket *Canada* 114 B5
Newmarket *Ireland* 12 D2
Newmarket *U.K.* 15 E8
Newmarket *U.S.A.* 115 C14
Newnan *U.S.A.* 117 E12
Newport *Ireland* 12 C2
Newport *I. of W., U.K.* 15 G6
Newport *Newport, U.K.* 15 F5
Newport *Ark., U.S.A.* 116 D9
Newport *Ky., U.S.A.* 113 F11
Newport *N.H., U.S.A.* 115 C12
Newport *N.Y., U.S.A.* 115 C9
Newport *Oreg., U.S.A.* 108 D1
Newport *Pa., U.S.A.* 114 F7
Newport *R.I., U.S.A.* 115 E13
Newport *Tenn., U.S.A.* 117 D13
Newport *Vt., U.S.A.* 115 B12
Newport *Wash., U.S.A.* 108 B5
Newport □ *U.K.* 15 F4
Newport Beach *U.S.A.* 111 M9
Newport News *U.S.A.* 113 G15
Newport Pagnell *U.K.* 15 E7
Newquay *U.K.* 15 G2
Newry *U.K.* 12 B5
Newton *Ill., U.S.A.* 112 F9
Newton *Iowa, U.S.A.* 112 E7
Newton *Kans., U.S.A.* 112 F5
Newton *Mass., U.S.A.* 115 D13
Newton *Miss., U.S.A.* 117 E10
Newton *N.C., U.S.A.* 117 D14
Newton *N.J., U.S.A.* 115 E10
Newton *Tex., U.S.A.* 116 F8
Newton Abbot *U.K.* 15 G4
Newton Aycliffe *U.K.* 14 C6
Newton Falls *U.S.A.* 114 E4
Newton Stewart *U.K.* 13 G4
Newtonmore *U.K.* 13 D4
Newtown *U.K.* 15 E4
Newtownabbey *U.K.* 12 B6
Newtownards *U.K.* 12 B6
Newtownbarry =
  Bunclody *Ireland* 12 D5
Newtownstewart *U.K.* 12 B4
Newville *U.S.A.* 114 F7
Nexon *France* 20 C5
Neya *Russia* 34 A6
Neyrīz *Iran* 71 D7
Neyshābūr *Iran* 71 B8
Nezhin = Nizhyn *Ukraine* 33 G6
Nezperce *U.S.A.* 108 C5
Nezvysko *Ukraine* 29 B10
Ngabang *Indonesia* 62 D3
Ngabordamlu, Tanjung
  Indonesia 63 F8
Ngambé *Centre, Cameroon* 83 D7
Ngambé *Littoral, Cameroon* 83 E7
Ngami Depression *Botswana* 88 C3
Ngamo *Zimbabwe* 87 F2
Ngangala *Sudan* 81 G3
Nganglong Kangri *China* 69 C9

Ngao *Thailand* 64 C2
Ngaoundéré *Cameroon* 84 C2
Ngapara *N.Z.* 91 F3
Ngara *Tanzania* 86 C3
Ngawi *Indonesia* 63 G14
Ngcobo *S. Africa* 89 E4
Nghia Lo *Vietnam* 58 G5
Ngoboli *Sudan* 81 G3
Ngoma *Malawi* 87 E3
Ngomahura *Zimbabwe* 87 G3
Ngomba *Tanzania* 87 D3
Ngomeni, Ras *Kenya* 86 C5
Ngong *Kenya* 86 C4
Ngop *Sudan* 81 F3
Ngoring Hu *China* 60 C4
Ngorkou *Mali* 82 B4
Ngorongoro *Tanzania* 86 C4
Ngorongoro △ *Tanzania* 86 C4
Ngozi *Burundi* 86 C2
Ngudu *Tanzania* 86 C3
Nguigmi *Niger* 79 F8
Nguila *Cameroon* 83 E7
Nguiu *Australia* 92 B5
Ngukurr *Australia* 94 A1
Ngunga *Tanzania* 86 C3
Nguru *Nigeria* 83 C7
Nguru Mts. *Tanzania* 86 D4
Ngusi *Malawi* 87 E3
Nguyen Binh *Vietnam* 58 F5
Nha Trang *Vietnam* 65 F7
Nhacoongo *Mozam.* 89 C6
Nhamaabué *Mozam.* 87 F4
Nhamundá → *Brazil* 125 D7
Nhangulaze, L. *Mozam.* 89 C5
Nhill *Australia* 95 F3
Nho Quan *Vietnam* 58 G5
Nhulunbuy *Australia* 94 A2
Nia-nia *Dem. Rep. of the Congo* 86 B2
Niafounké *Mali* 82 B4
Niagara Falls *Canada* 114 C5
Niagara Falls *U.S.A.* 114 C6
Niagara-on-the-Lake
    Canada 114 C5
Niah *Malaysia* 62 D4
Niamey *Niger* 83 C5
Niandan-Koro *Guinea* 82 C3
Nianforando *Guinea* 82 D2
Niangara
    Dem. Rep. of the Congo 86 B2
Niangbo *Ivory C.* 82 D3
Niangoloko *Burkina Faso* 82 C4
Niantic *U.S.A.* 115 E12
Niaro *Sudan* 81 E3
Nias *Indonesia* 62 D1
Niassa □ *Mozam.* 87 E4
Niassa △ *Mozam.* 87 E4
Nibāk *Si. Arabia* 71 E7
Nibe *Denmark* 11 H3
Nicaragua ■ *Cent. Amer.* 120 D2
Nicaragua, L. de *Nic.* 120 D2
Nicastro *Italy* 43 D9
Nice *France* 21 E11
Nice-Côte-d'Azur ✈ (NCE)
    France 21 E11
Niceville *U.S.A.* 117 F11
Nichicun, L. *Canada* 105 B5
Nichinan *Japan* 55 J5
Nicholás, Canal *W. Indies* 120 B3
Nicholasville *U.S.A.* 113 G11
Nichols *U.S.A.* 115 D8
Nicholson *Australia* 92 C4
Nicholson *U.S.A.* 115 E9
Nicholson → *Australia* 94 B2
Nicholson L. *Canada* 103 A8
Nicholson Ra. *Australia* 93 E2
Nicholville *U.S.A.* 115 B10
Nicobar Is. *Ind. Oc.* 3 D14
Nicola *Canada* 102 C4
Nicolls Town *Bahamas* 120 A4
Nicosia *Cyprus* 49 D12
Nicosia *Italy* 43 E7
Nicótera *Italy* 43 D8
Nicoya *Costa Rica* 120 D2
Nicoya, G. de *Costa Rica* 120 E3
Nicoya, Pen. de *Costa Rica* 120 E2
Nida *Lithuania* 30 C8
Nidd → *U.K.* 14 D6
Nidda *Germany* 25 E5
Nidda → *Germany* 25 E4
Nidwalden □ *Switz.* 25 J4
Nidzica *Poland* 31 E7
Niebüll *Germany* 24 A4
Nied → *Germany* 19 C13
Niederaula *Germany* 24 E5
Niederbayern □ *Germany* 25 G8
Niederbronn-les-Bains
    France 19 D14
Niedere Tauern *Austria* 26 D7
Niederlausitz *Germany* 24 D9
Niederösterreich □ *Austria* 26 C8
Niedersachsen □ *Germany* 24 C4
Niedersächsisches
    Wattenmeer △ *Germany* 24 B3
Niederbayern □ *Germany* 25 G8
Niekerkshoop *S. Africa* 88 D3
Niellé *Ivory C.* 82 C3
Niemba *Dem. Rep. of the Congo* 86 D2
Niemen = Nemunas →
    Lithuania 30 C8

Niemodlin *Poland* 31 H4
Nienburg *Germany* 24 C5
Niepołomice *Poland* 31 H7
Niers → *Germany* 24 D1
Niesky *Germany* 24 D10
Nieszawa *Poland* 31 F5
Nieu Bethesda *S. Africa* 88 E3
Nieuw Amsterdam
    Suriname 125 B7
Nieuw Nickerie *Suriname* 125 B7
Nieuwoudtville *S. Africa* 88 E2
Nieuwpoort *Belgium* 17 C2
Nieves, Pico de las *Canary Is.* 48 G4
Nièvre □ *France* 19 E10
Niga *Mali* 82 C3
Niğde *Turkey* 72 D6
Niğde □ *Turkey* 72 D6
Nigel *S. Africa* 89 D4
Niger □ *Nigeria* 83 D6
Niger ■ *W. Afr.* 83 B7
Niger → *W. Afr.* 83 D6
Niger Delta *Africa* 83 E6
Nigeria ■ *W. Afr.* 83 D6
Nighasin *India* 69 E9
Nightcaps *N.Z.* 91 F2
Nigrita *Greece* 44 F7
Nihon = Japan ■ *Asia* 55 G8
Nii-Jima *Japan* 55 G9
Niigata *Japan* 54 F9
Niigata □ *Japan* 55 F9
Niihama *Japan* 55 H6
Ni'ihau *U.S.A.* 106 b
Niimi *Japan* 55 G6
Niitsu *Japan* 54 F9
Níjar *Spain* 39 J2
Nijil *Jordan* 74 E4
Nijkerk *Neths.* 17 B5
Nijmegen *Neths.* 17 C5
Nijverdal *Neths.* 17 B6
Nīk Pey *Iran* 73 D13
Nike *Nigeria* 83 D6
Nikel *Russia* 8 B24
Nikiniki *Indonesia* 63 F6
Nikisiani *Greece* 45 F8
Nikiti *Greece* 44 F7
Nikki *Benin* 83 D5
Nikkō *Japan* 55 F9
Nikkō △ *Japan* 55 F9
Nikolayev = Mykolayiv
    Ukraine 33 J7
Nikolayevsk *Russia* 34 E7
Nikolayevsk-na-Amur
    Russia 53 D15
Nikolsk *Russia* 34 D8
Nikolskoye *Russia* 53 D17
Nikopol *Bulgaria* 45 C8
Nikopol *Ukraine* 33 J8
Nikopolis *Greece* 46 B2
Niksar *Turkey* 72 B7
Nīkshahr *Iran* 71 E9
Nikšić *Montenegro* 44 D2
Nîl, Nahr en → *Africa* 80 H7
Nîl el Abyad → *Sudan* 81 D3
Nîl el Azraq → *Sudan* 81 D3
Nila *Indonesia* 63 F7
Niland *U.S.A.* 111 M11
Nile = Nîl, Nahr en → *Africa* 80 H7
Nile Delta *Egypt* 80 H7
Niles *Mich., U.S.A.* 112 E10
Niles *Ohio, U.S.A.* 114 E4
Nilüfer → *Turkey* 45 F12
Nim Ka Thana *India* 68 F6
Nimach *India* 68 G6
Nimba, Mt. *Guinea* 82 D3
Nimbahera *India* 68 G6
Nîmes *France* 21 E8
Nimfaíon, Ákra = Pines,
    Akra *Greece* 45 F8
Nimmitabel *Australia* 95 F4
Nimule *Sudan* 81 G3
Nimule △ *Sudan* 81 G3
Nin *Croatia* 41 D12
Nīnawá *Iraq* 73 D10
Nīnawá □ *Iraq* 70 B4
Nindigully *Australia* 95 D4
Nineveh = Nīnawá *Iraq* 73 D10
Ning Xian *China* 56 G4
Ning'an *China* 57 B15
Ningbo *China* 59 C13
Ningcheng *China* 57 D10
Ningde *China* 59 D12
Ningdu *China* 59 D10
Ninggang *China* 59 D9
Ningguo *China* 59 C12
Ninghai *China* 59 C13
Ninghua *China* 59 D11
Ningi *Nigeria* 83 C6
Ningjin *China* 56 F8
Ningjing Shan *China* 58 C2
Ninglang *China* 58 D3
Ningling *China* 56 G8
Ningming *China* 58 F6
Ningnan *China* 58 D4
Ningpo = Ningbo *China* 59 C13
Ningqiang *China* 56 H4
Ningshan *China* 56 H5

Ningsia Hui A.R. =
    Ningxia Huizu
    Zizhiqu □ *China* 56 F4
Ningwu *China* 56 E7
Ningxia Huizu Zizhiqu □
    China 56 F4
Ningxiang *China* 59 C9
Ningyang *China* 56 G9
Ningyuan *China* 59 E8
Ninh Binh *Vietnam* 58 G5
Ninh Giang *Vietnam* 64 B6
Ninh Hoa *Vietnam* 64 F7
Ninh Ma *Vietnam* 64 F7
Nini-Suhien △ *Ghana* 82 D4
Ninove *Belgium* 17 D4
Nioaque *Brazil* 127 A4
Niobrara *U.S.A.* 112 D4
Niobrara → *U.S.A.* 112 D4
Niokolo-Koba △ *Senegal* 82 C2
Niono *Mali* 82 C3
Nionsamoridougou *Guinea* 82 D3
Nioro du Rip *Senegal* 82 C1
Nioro du Sahel *Mali* 82 B3
Niort *France* 20 B3
Nipawin *Canada* 103 C8
Nipfjället *Sweden* 10 C6
Nipigon *Canada* 104 C2
Nipigon, L. *Canada* 104 C2
Nipishish L. *Canada* 105 B7
Nipissing, L. *Canada* 104 C4
Nipomo *U.S.A.* 111 K6
Nippon = Japan ■ *Asia* 55 G8
Nipton *U.S.A.* 111 K11
Niquelândia *Brazil* 125 F9
Nīr *Iran* 73 C12
Nirasaki *Japan* 55 G9
Nirmal *India* 66 K11
Nirmali *India* 69 F12
Niš *Serbia* 44 C5
Nisa *Portugal* 37 F3
Nišava → *Serbia* 44 C5
Niscemi *Italy* 43 E7
Nishinomiya *Japan* 55 G7
Nishino'omote *Japan* 55 J5
Nishiwaki *Japan* 55 G7
Niška Banja *Serbia* 44 C6
Niskibi → *Canada* 104 A2
Nisko *Poland* 31 H9
Nisporeni *Moldova* 29 C13
Nisqually → *U.S.A.* 110 C4
Nissaki *Greece* 49 A3
Nissan → *Sweden* 11 H6
Nissiros *Greece* 47 E5
Nissum Bredning *Denmark* 11 H2
Nissum Fjord *Denmark* 11 H2
Nistru = Dnister → *Europe* 23 E16
Nisutlin → *Canada* 102 A2
Nitchequon *Canada* 105 B5
Niterói *Brazil* 127 A7
Nith → *Canada* 114 C4
Nith → *U.K.* 13 F5
Nitmiluk △ *Australia* 92 B5
Nitra *Slovak Rep.* 27 C11
Nitra → *Slovak Rep.* 27 D11
Nitriansky □ *Slovak Rep.* 27 C11
Nittenau *Germany* 25 F8
Niue *Pac. Oc.* 97 J11
Niulan Jiang → *China* 58 D4
Niut *Indonesia* 62 D4
Niuzhuang *China* 57 D12
Nivala *Finland* 8 E21
Nivelles *Belgium* 17 D4
Nivernais *France* 19 E10
Niverville *Canada* 103 D9
Niwas *India* 69 H9
Nixa *U.S.A.* 112 G7
Nixon *U.S.A.* 116 G6
Nizamabad *India* 66 K11
Nizamghat *India* 67 E19
Nizhne Kolymsk *Russia* 53 C17
Nizhneangarsk *Russia* 53 D11
Nizhnegorskiy =
    Nyzhnohirskyy *Ukraine* 33 K8
Nizhnekamsk *Russia* 34 C10
Nizhneudinsk *Russia* 53 D10
Nizhnevartovsk *Russia* 52 C8
Nizhniy Chir *Russia* 35 F6
Nizhniy Lomov *Russia* 34 D6
Nizhniy Novgorod *Russia* 34 B7
Nizhniy Novgorod □ *Russia* 34 B7
Nizhniy Tagil *Russia* 52 D6
Nizhyn *Ukraine* 33 G6
Nizina Mazowiecka *Poland* 31 F8
Nizip *Turkey* 72 D7
Nízké Tatry *Slovak Rep.* 27 C12
Nízke Tatry △ *Slovak Rep.* 27 C12
Nízký Jeseník *Czech Rep.* 27 B10
Nizwá *Oman* 75 C6
Nizza Monferrato *Italy* 40 D5
Njakwa *Malawi* 87 E3
Njanji *Zambia* 87 E3
Njazidja = Grande Comore
    Comoros Is. 85 a
Njegoš *Montenegro* 44 D2

Njinjo *Tanzania* 87 D4
Njombe *Tanzania* 87 D3
Njombe → *Tanzania* 86 D4
Njurundabommen *Sweden* 10 B11
Nkambe *Cameroon* 83 D7
Nkana *Zambia* 87 E2
Nkandla *S. Africa* 89 D5
Nkawkaw *Ghana* 83 D4
Nkayi *Zimbabwe* 87 F2
Nkhotakota *Malawi* 87 E3
Nkhotakota △ *Malawi* 87 E3
Nkongsamba *Cameroon* 83 E6
Nkurenkuru *Namibia* 88 B2
Nkwanta *Ghana* 82 D4
Nmai → *Burma* 58 F2
Noakhali = Maijdi *Bangla.* 67 H17
Nobel *Canada* 114 A4
Nobeoka *Japan* 55 H5
Noblejas *Spain* 36 F7
Noblesville *U.S.A.* 112 E10
Noboribetsu *Japan* 54 C10
Noccundra *Australia* 95 D3
Noce → *Italy* 40 B7
Nocera Inferiore *Italy* 43 B7
Nocera Umbra *Italy* 41 E9
Noci *Italy* 43 B10
Nocona *U.S.A.* 116 E6
Nocrich *Romania* 29 E9
Noda *Japan* 55 D9
Nogales *Mexico* 118 A2
Nogales *U.S.A.* 109 L8
Nogaro *France* 20 E3
Nogat → *Poland* 30 D6
Nōgata *Japan* 55 H5
Nogent *France* 19 D12
Nogent-le-Rotrou *France* 18 D7
Nogent-sur-Seine *France* 19 D10
Noggerup *Australia* 93 F2
Noginsk *Moskva, Russia* 32 E10
Noginsk *Tunguska, Russia* 53 C10
Nogoa → *Australia* 94 C4
Nogoyá *Argentina* 126 C4
Nógrád □ *Hungary* 28 C4
Noguera Pallaresa → *Spain* 38 D5
Noguera Ribagorzana →
    Spain 38 D5
Nohar *India* 68 E6
Nohfelden *Germany* 25 F3
Nohta *India* 69 H8
Noia *Spain* 36 C2
Noire, Montagne *France* 20 E6
Noires, Mts. *France* 18 D3
Noirétable *France* 20 C7
Noirmoutier, Î. de *France* 18 F4
Noirmoutier-en-l'Île *France* 18 F4
Nojane *Botswana* 88 C3
Nojima-Zaki *Japan* 55 G9
Nok Kundi *Pakistan* 66 E3
Nok Ta Phao, Ko *Thailand* 65 b
Nokaneng *Botswana* 88 B3
Nokia *Finland* 32 B2
Nokomis *Canada* 103 C8
Nokomis L. *Canada* 103 B8
Nola *C.A.R.* 84 D3
Nola *Italy* 43 B7
Nolay *France* 19 F11
Noli, C. di *Italy* 40 D5
Nolinsk *Russia* 34 B9
Noma Omuramba →
    Namibia 88 B3
Nombre de Dios *Panama* 120 E4
Nome *U.S.A.* 106 a
Nomo-Zaki *Japan* 55 H4
Nomuka *Tonga* 91 c
Nomuka Group *Tonga* 91 c
Nonacho L. *Canada* 103 A7
Nonancourt *France* 18 D8
Nonda *Australia* 94 C3
None *Italy* 40 D4
Nong Chang *Thailand* 64 E2
Nong Het *Laos* 64 C4
Nong Khai *Thailand* 64 D4
Nong'an *China* 57 B13
Nongoma *S. Africa* 89 D5
Nongsa *Indonesia* 65 d
Nonoava *Mexico* 118 B3
Nonsan *S. Korea* 57 F14
Nonthaburi *Thailand* 64 F3
Nontron *France* 20 C4
Nonza *France* 21 F13
Noonamah *Australia* 92 B5
Noondie, L. *Australia* 93 E2
Noord Brabant □ *Neths.* 17 C5
Noord Holland □ *Neths.* 17 B4
Noordbeveland *Neths.* 17 C3
Noordoostpolder *Neths.* 17 B5
Noordwijk *Neths.* 17 B4
Noosa Heads *Australia* 95 D5
Nootka I. *Canada* 102 D3
Nopiming △ *Canada* 103 C9
Nora *Eritrea* 81 D5
Nora *Sweden* 10 E9
Noralee *Canada* 102 C3
Noranda =
    Rouyn-Noranda *Canada* 104 C4
Norberg *Sweden* 10 D9
Nórcia *Italy* 41 F10

Norco *U.S.A.* 111 M9
Nord □ *Cameroon* 83 D7
Nord □ *France* 19 B10
Nord-Kivu □
    Dem. Rep. of the Congo 86 C2
Nord-Ostsee-Kanal *Germany* 24 A5
Nord-Ouest □ *Cameroon* 83 D7
Nord-Pas-de-Calais □ *France* 19 B9
Nordaustlandet *Svalbard* 4 B9
Nordborg *Denmark* 11 J3
Nordby *Denmark* 11 J2
Norddeich *Germany* 24 B3
Nordegg *Canada* 102 C5
Norden *Germany* 24 B3
Nordenham *Germany* 24 B4
Norderney *Germany* 24 B3
Norderstedt *Germany* 24 B6
Nordfjord *Norway* 8 F11
Nordfriesische Inseln
    Germany 24 A4
Nordhausen *Germany* 24 D6
Nordhorn *Germany* 24 C3
Norðoyar *Færoe Is.* 8 E9
Nördingrå *Sweden* 10 B12
Nordjylland □ *Denmark* 11 G3
Nordkapp *Norway* 8 A21
Nordkapp *Svalbard* 4 A9
Nordkinnhalvøya *Norway* 8 A22
Nördlicher Teutoburger
    Wald-Wiehengebirge △
    Germany 24 C4
Nördlingen *Germany* 25 G6
Nordrhein-Westfalen □
    Germany 24 D3
Nordstrand *Germany* 24 A4
Nordvik *Russia* 53 B12
Nore → *Ireland* 12 D4
Norfolk *Canada* 114 D4
Norfolk *Nebr., U.S.A.* 112 D5
Norfolk *Va., U.S.A.* 113 G15
Norfolk □ *U.K.* 15 E8
Norfolk Broads △ *U.K.* 15 E9
Norfolk I. *Pac. Oc.* 90 D9
Norfolk Ridge *Pac. Oc.* 96 K8
Norfork L. *U.S.A.* 116 C8
Norge = Norway ■ *Europe* 8 E14
Norilsk *Russia* 53 C9
Norma, Mt. *Australia* 94 C3
Normal *U.S.A.* 112 E9
Norman *U.S.A.* 116 D6
Norman → *Australia* 94 B3
Norman Wells *Canada* 100 C7
Normanby → *Australia* 94 A3
Normandie-Maine △ *France* 18 D6
Normandin *Canada* 104 C5
Normanhurst, Mt. *Australia* 93 E3
Normanton *Australia* 94 B3
Normétal *Canada* 104 C4
Norquay *Canada* 103 C8
Norquinco *Argentina* 128 E2
Norra Dellen *Sweden* 10 C10
Norra Kvill △ *Sweden* 11 G9
Norra Ulvön *Sweden* 10 A12
Norrahammar *Sweden* 11 G8
Norrbottens län □ *Sweden* 8 C19
Nørre Åby *Denmark* 11 J3
Nørre Alslev *Denmark* 11 K5
Nørresundby *Denmark* 11 G3
Norrhult-Klavreström
    Sweden 11 G9
Norris Point *Canada* 105 C8
Norristown *U.S.A.* 115 F9
Norrköping *Sweden* 11 F10
Norrland *Sweden* 8 E16
Norrsundet *Sweden* 10 D11
Norrtälje *Sweden* 10 E12
Norseman *Australia* 93 F3
Norsk *Russia* 53 D14
Norte, Pta. del *Canary Is.* 48 G2
Norte, Serra do *Brazil* 124 F7
North, C. *Canada* 105 C7
North Adams *U.S.A.* 115 D11
North America *98 F10*
North Arm *Canada* 102 A5
North Augusta *U.S.A.* 117 E14
North Australian Basin
    Ind. Oc. 96 J3
North Ayrshire □ *U.K.* 13 F4
North Bass I. *U.S.A.* 114 E2
North Battleford *Canada* 103 C7
North Bay *Canada* 104 C4
North Belcher Is. *Canada* 104 A4
North Bend *Oreg., U.S.A.* 108 E1
North Bend *Pa., U.S.A.* 114 E7
North Bend *Wash., U.S.A.* 110 C4
North Bennington *U.S.A.* 115 D11
North Berwick *U.K.* 13 E6
North Berwick *U.S.A.* 115 C14
North C. *Canada* 105 C7
North C. *N.Z.* 91 A4
North Canadian → *U.S.A.* 116 D7
North Canton *U.S.A.* 114 F3
North Cape = Nordkapp
    Norway 8 A21
North Carolina □ *U.S.A.* 117 D15

North Cascades △ *U.S.A.* 108 B3
North Channel *Canada* 104 C3
North Channel *U.K.* 13 F3
North Charleston *U.S.A.* 117 E15
North Chicago *U.S.A.* 112 D10
North Creek *U.S.A.* 115 C11
North Dakota □ *U.S.A.* 112 B3
North Downs *U.K.* 15 F8
North East *U.S.A.* 114 D5
North East Frontier
    Agency = Arunachal
    Pradesh □ *India* 67 F19
North East Lincolnshire □
    U.K. 14 D7
North Eastern □ *Kenya* 86 B5
North Esk → *U.K.* 13 E6
North European Plain
    Europe 6 E10
North Foreland *U.K.* 15 F9
North Fork *U.S.A.* 110 H7
North Fork American →
    U.S.A. 110 G5
North Fork Feather →
    U.S.A. 110 F5
North Fork Grand →
    U.S.A. 112 C3
North Fork Red → *U.S.A.* 116 D5
North Frisian Is. =
    Nordfriesische Inseln
    Germany 24 A4
North Gower *Canada* 115 A9
North Hd. *Australia* 93 F1
North Henik L. *Canada* 103 A9
North Highlands *U.S.A.* 110 G5
North Horr *Kenya* 86 B4
North I. *Kenya* 86 B4
North I. *N.Z.* 91 C5
North I. *Seychelles* 85 b
North Kingsville *U.S.A.* 114 E4
North Kitui △ *Kenya* 86 C4
North Knife → *Canada* 103 B10
North Koel → *India* 69 G10
North Korea ■ *Asia* 57 E14
North Lakhimpur *India* 67 F19
North Lanarkshire □ *U.K.* 13 F5
North Las Vegas *U.S.A.* 111 J11
North Lincolnshire □ *U.K.* 14 D7
North Little Rock *U.S.A.* 116 D8
North Loup → *U.S.A.* 112 E4
North Luangwa △ *Zambia* 87 E3
North Magnetic Pole
    Canada 101 B9
North Mankato *U.S.A.* 112 C6
North Minch *U.K.* 13 C3
North Moose L. *Canada* 103 C8
North Myrtle Beach *U.S.A.* 117 E15
North Nahanni → *Canada* 102 A4
North Olmsted *U.S.A.* 114 E3
North Ossetia □ *Russia* 35 J7
North Pagai, I. = Pagai
    Utara, Pulau *Indonesia* 62 E2
North Palisade *U.S.A.* 110 H8
North Platte *U.S.A.* 112 E3
North Platte → *U.S.A.* 112 E3
North Pole *Arctic* 4 A
North Portal *Canada* 103 D8
North Powder *U.S.A.* 108 D5
North Pt. *Barbados* 121 g
North Pt. *Trin. & Tob.* 125 J16
North Pt. *U.S.A.* 114 A1
North Rhine Westphalia =
    Nordrhein-Westfalen □
    Germany 24 D3
North River *Canada* 105 B8
North Ronaldsay *U.K.* 13 B6
North Saskatchewan →
    Canada 103 C7
North Sea *Europe* 6 D6
North Seal → *Canada* 103 B9
North Somerset □ *U.K.* 15 F5
North Sydney *Canada* 105 C7
North Syracuse *U.S.A.* 115 C8
North Taranaki Bight *N.Z.* 91 C5
North Thompson →
    Canada 102 C4
North Tonawanda *U.S.A.* 114 D6
North Troy *U.S.A.* 115 B12
North Twin I. *Canada* 104 B4
North Tyne → *U.K.* 14 B5
North Uist *U.K.* 13 D1
North Vancouver *Canada* 110 A3
North Vernon *U.S.A.* 113 F11
North Wabasca L. *Canada* 102 B6
North Walsham *U.K.* 14 E9
North West = Severo-
    Zapadnyy □ *Russia* 52 C4
North-West □ *S. Africa* 88 D4
North West *Australia* 92 D1
North West Frontier □
    Pakistan 66 C4
North West Highlands *U.K.* 13 D4
North West River *Canada* 105 B7
North Western □ *Zambia* 87 E2
North Wildwood *U.S.A.* 113 F16
North York Moors *U.K.* 14 C7
North York Moors △ *U.K.* 14 C7
North Yorkshire □ *U.K.* 14 C6

Northallerton *U.K.* **14 C6**
Northam *Australia* **93 F2**
Northam *S. Africa* **88 C4**
Northampton *Australia* **93 E1**
Northampton *U.K.* **15 E7**
Northampton *Mass., U.S.A.*
  115 D12
Northampton *Pa., U.S.A.* **115 F9**
Northamptonshire □ *U.K.* **15 E7**
Northbridge *U.S.A.* **115 D13**
Northcliffe *Australia* **93 F2**
Northeast Pacific Basin
  Pac. Oc. **97 D13**
Northeast Providence
  Chan. *W. Indies* **120 A4**
Northeim *Germany* **24 D6**
Northern = Limpopo □
  S. Africa **89 C4**
Northern □ *Ghana* **83 D4**
Northern □ *Malawi* **87 E3**
Northern □ *S. Leone* **82 D2**
Northern □ *Zambia* **87 E3**
Northern Areas □ *Pakistan* **69 A5**
Northern Cape □ *S. Africa* **88 D3**
Northern Circars *India* **67 L13**
Northern Indian L. *Canada* **103 B9**
Northern Ireland □ *U.K.* **12 B5**
Northern Lau Group *Fiji* **91 a**
Northern Light L. *Canada* **104 C1**
Northern Marianas ☑
  Pac. Oc. **96 F6**
Northern Province □
  S. Africa **89 C4**
Northern Range
  Trin. & Tob. **125 K15**
Northern Sporades *Greece* **46 B5**
Northern Territory □
  Australia **92 D5**
Northfield *Minn., U.S.A.* **112 C7**
Northfield *Vt., U.S.A.* **115 B12**
Northland □ *N.Z.* **91 A4**
Northome *U.S.A.* **112 B6**
Northport *Ala., U.S.A.* **117 E11**
Northport *Wash., U.S.A.* **108 B5**
Northumberland □ *U.K.* **14 B6**
Northumberland, C.
  Australia **95 F3**
Northumberland Is.
  Australia **94 C4**
Northumberland Str.
  Canada **105 C7**
Northville *U.S.A.* **115 C10**
Northwest Pacific Basin
  Pac. Oc. **96 D8**
Northwest Providence
  Channel *W. Indies* **120 A4**
Northwest Territories □
  Canada **100 C8**
Northwich *U.K.* **14 D5**
Northwood *Iowa, U.S.A.* **112 D7**
Northwood *N. Dak., U.S.A.* **112 B5**
Norton *U.S.A.* **112 F4**
Norton *Zimbabwe* **87 F3**
Norton Sd. *U.S.A.* **106 a**
Nortorf *Germany* **24 A5**
Norwalk *Calif., U.S.A.* **111 M8**
Norwalk *Conn., U.S.A.* **115 E11**
Norwalk *Iowa, U.S.A.* **112 E7**
Norwalk *Ohio, U.S.A.* **114 E2**
Norway *Maine, U.S.A.* **113 C18**
Norway *Mich., U.S.A.* **112 C10**
Norway ■ *Europe* **8 E14**
Norway House *Canada* **103 C9**
Norwegian B. *Canada* **101 B11**
Norwegian Basin *Atl. Oc.* **4 C7**
Norwegian Sea *Atl. Oc.* **6 B6**
Norwich *Canada* **114 D4**
Norwich *U.K.* **15 E9**
Norwich *Conn., U.S.A.* **115 E12**
Norwich *N.Y., U.S.A.* **115 D9**
Norwood *Canada* **114 B7**
Norwood *U.S.A.* **115 B10**
Nosappu-Misaki *Japan* **54 C12**
Noshiro *Japan* **54 D10**
Nosivka *Ukraine* **33 G6**
Nosovka = Nosivka *Ukraine* **33 G6**
Noşratābād *Iran* **71 D8**
Noss Hd. *U.K.* **13 C5**
Nossebro *Sweden* **11 F6**
Nossob → *S. Africa* **88 D3**
Nossombougou *Mali* **82 C3**
Nosy Barren *Madag.* **85 H8**
Nosy Bé *Madag.* **85 G9**
Nosy Boraha *Madag.* **89 B8**
Nosy Lava *Madag.* **89 A8**
Nosy Varika *Madag.* **89 C8**
Noteć → *Poland* **31 F2**
Notikewin → *Canada* **102 B5**
Notio Aigaio = Notios
  Aiyaíon □ **47 E7**
Notios Aiyaíon □ **47 E7**
Notios Evvoïkos Kólpos
  Greece **46 C5**
Noto *Italy* **43 F8**
Noto, G. di *Italy* **43 F8**
Notodden *Norway* **9 G13**
Notre Dame B. *Canada* **105 C8**

Notre-Dame-de-Koartac =
  Quaqtaq *Canada* **101 C13**
Notre-Dame-des-Bois
  Canada **115 A13**
Notre-Dame-d'Ivugivic =
  Ivujivik *Canada* **101 C12**
Notre-Dame-du-Nord
  Canada **104 C4**
Notsé *Togo* **83 D5**
Nottawasaga B. *Canada* **114 B4**
Nottaway → *Canada* **104 B4**
Nottingham *U.K.* **14 E6**
Nottingham, City of □ *U.K.* **14 E6**
Nottingham I. *Canada* **101 C12**
Nottinghamshire □ *U.K.* **14 D6**
Nottoway → *U.S.A.* **113 G15**
Notwane → *Botswana* **88 C4**
Nouâdhibou *Mauritania* **78 D2**
Nouâdhibou, Râs *Mauritania* **78 D2**
Nouakchott *Mauritania* **82 B1**
Nouâmghâr *Mauritania* **82 B1**
Nouméa *N. Cal.* **90 D9**
Nouna *Burkina Faso* **82 C4**
Noupoort *S. Africa* **88 E3**
Nouveau Comptoir =
  Wemindji *Canada* **104 B4**
Nouvelle Amsterdam, Î.
  Ind. Oc. **3 F13**
Nouvelle-Calédonie = New
  Caledonia ☑ *Pac. Oc.* **90 D9**
Nouzonville *France* **19 C11**
Nová Baňa *Slovak Rep.* **27 C11**
Nová Bystřice *Czech Rep.* **26 B8**
Nova Casa Nova *Brazil* **125 E10**
Nova Esperança *Brazil* **127 A5**
Nova Friburgo *Brazil* **127 A7**
Nova Gorica *Slovenia* **41 C10**
Nova Gradiška *Croatia* **28 E2**
Nova Iguaçu *Brazil* **127 A7**
Nova Iorque *Brazil* **125 E10**
Nova Kakhovka *Ukraine* **33 J7**
Nova Lamego *Guinea-Biss.* **82 C2**
Nova Lima *Brazil* **127 A7**
Nova Lusitânia *Mozam.* **87 F3**
Nova Mambone *Mozam.* **89 C6**
Nova Odesa *Ukraine* **33 J6**
Nová Paka *Czech Rep.* **26 A8**
Nova Pavova *Serbia* **28 F5**
Nova Scotia □ *Canada* **105 C7**
Nova Siri *Italy* **43 B9**
Nova Sofala *Mozam.* **89 C5**
Nova Ushytsya *Ukraine* **29 B12**
Nova Varoš *Serbia* **44 C3**
Nova Venécia *Brazil* **125 G10**
Nova Zagora *Bulgaria* **45 D10**
Novaci *Macedonia* **44 E5**
Novaci *Romania* **29 E8**
Novaféltria *Italy* **41 E9**
Novannenskiy =
  Novoannenskiy *Russia* **34 E6**
Novar *Canada* **114 A5**
Novara *Italy* **40 C5**
Novato *U.S.A.* **110 G4**
Novaya Kakhovka = Nova
  Kakhovka *Ukraine* **33 J7**
Novaya Kazanka =
  Zhangaqala *Kazakhstan* **35 F9**
Novaya Ladoga *Russia* **32 B7**
Novaya Lyalya *Russia* **52 D7**
Novaya Sibir, Ostrov *Russia* **53 B16**
Novaya Zemlya *Russia* **52 B6**
Nové Město *Slovak Rep.* **27 C10**
Nové Město na Moravě
  Czech Rep. **26 B9**
Nové Město nad Metují
  Czech Rep. **27 A9**
Nové Zámky *Slovak Rep.* **27 C11**
Novelda *Spain* **39 G4**
Novellara *Italy* **40 D7**
Noventa Vicentina *Italy* **41 C8**
Novgorod *Russia* **32 C6**
Novgorod □ *Russia* **32 C7**
Novgorod-Severskiy =
  Novhorod-Siverskyy
  Ukraine **33 G7**
Novhorod-Siverskyy *Ukraine* **33 G7**
Novi Bečej *Serbia* **28 E5**
Novi Iskar *Bulgaria* **44 D7**
Novi Knežević *Serbia* **28 D5**
Novi Lígure *Italy* **40 D5**
Novi Pazar *Bulgaria* **45 C11**
Novi Pazar *Serbia* **44 C4**
Novi Sad *Serbia* **28 E4**
Novi Slankamen *Serbia* **28 E5**
Novi Travnik *Bos.-H.* **28 F2**
Novi Vinodolski *Croatia* **41 C11**
Novigrad *Istra, Croatia* **41 C10**
Novigrad *Zadar, Croatia* **41 D12**
Novigradsko More *Croatia* **41 D12**
Novo Hamburgo *Brazil* **127 B5**
Novo Ivanivka *Ukraine* **29 E14**
Novo Mesto *Slovenia* **41 C12**
Novo Miloševo *Serbia* **28 E5**
Novo Remanso *Brazil* **125 E10**
Novoaleksandrovsk *Russia* **35 H5**
Novoaleksandrovskaya =
  Novoaleksandrovsk
  Russia **35 H5**

Novoaltaysk *Russia* **52 D9**
Novoannenskiy *Russia* **34 E6**
Novoazovsk *Ukraine* **33 J10**
Novocheboksarsk *Russia* **34 B8**
Novocherkassk *Russia* **35 G5**
Novodevichye *Russia* **34 D9**
Novogrudok =
  Navahrudak *Belarus* **23 B13**
Novohrad-Volynskyy
  Ukraine **23 C14**
Novokachalinsk *Russia* **54 B5**
Novokhopersk *Russia* **34 E5**
Novokuybyshevsk *Russia* **34 D9**
Novokuznetsk *Russia* **52 D9**
Novolazarevskaya *Antarctica* **5 D3**
Novomirgorod *Ukraine* **33 H6**
Novomoskovsk *Russia* **32 E10**
Novomoskovsk *Ukraine* **33 H8**
Novopolotsk =
  Navapolatsk *Belarus* **32 E5**
Novorossiysk *Russia* **33 K9**
Novorybnoye *Russia* **53 B11**
Novorzhev *Russia* **32 D5**
Novosej *Albania* **44 E4**
Novoselytsya *Ukraine* **29 B11**
Novoshakhtinsk *Russia* **33 J10**
Novosibirsk *Russia* **52 D9**
Novosibirskiye Ostrova
  Russia **53 B15**
Novosil *Russia* **33 F9**
Novosokolniki *Russia* **32 D6**
Novotitarovskaya *Russia* **35 H4**
Novotroitsk *Russia* **52 D6**
Novoukrayinka *Ukraine* **33 H6**
Novoulyanovsk *Russia* **34 C9**
Novouzensk *Russia* **34 E9**
Novovolynsk *Ukraine* **31 H11**
Novovoronezhskiy *Russia* **33 G10**
Novoyavoriske *Ukraine* **31 J10**
Novozybkov *Russia* **33 F6**
Novska *Croatia* **41 C14**
Novvy Urengoy *Russia* **52 C8**
Nový Bor *Czech Rep.* **26 A7**
Novy Bug = Novyy Buh
  Ukraine **33 J7**
Nový Bydžov *Czech Rep.* **26 A8**
Novy Dvor *Belarus* **31 F11**
Novy Dwór Mazowiecki
  Poland **31 F7**
Nový Jičín *Czech Rep.* **27 B11**
Novyy Afon *Georgia* **35 J5**
Novyy Buh *Ukraine* **33 J7**
Novyy Oskol *Russia* **33 G9**
Novyy Port *Russia* **52 C8**
Now Shahr *Iran* **71 B6**
Nowa Deba *Poland* **31 H8**
Nowa Ruda *Poland* **31 H3**
Nowa Sarzyna *Poland* **31 H9**
Nowa Sól *Poland* **31 G2**
Nowata *U.S.A.* **116 C7**
Nowbarān *Iran* **71 C6**
Nowe *Poland* **30 E5**
Nowe Miasteczko *Poland* **31 G2**
Nowe Miasto *Poland* **31 G7**
Nowe Miasto Lubawskie
  Poland **30 E6**
Nowe Skalmierzyce *Poland* **31 G4**
Nowe Warpno *Poland* **30 E1**
Nowghāb *Iran* **71 C8**
Nowgong *Assam, India* **67 F18**
Nowgong *Mad. P., India* **69 G8**
Nowogard *Poland* **30 E2**
Nowogród *Poland* **31 E8**
Nowogród Bobrzanski
  Poland **31 G2**
Nowogrodziec *Poland* **31 G2**
Nowra *Australia* **95 E5**
Nowshera *Pakistan* **66 C8**
Nowy Dwór Gdański *Poland* **30 D6**
Nowy Sącz *Poland* **31 J7**
Nowy Staw *Poland* **30 D6**
Nowy Targ *Poland* **31 J7**
Nowy Tomyśl *Poland* **31 F3**
Nowy Wiśnicz *Poland* **31 J7**
Noxen *U.S.A.* **115 E8**
Noyabr'sk *Russia* **52 C8**
Noyant *France* **18 E7**
Noyers *France* **19 E10**
Noyon *France* **19 C9**
Noyon *Mongolia* **56 C2**
Nozay *France* **18 E5**
Nqutu *S. Africa* **89 D5**
Nsanje *Malawi* **87 F4**
Nsawam *Ghana* **83 D4**
Nsomba *Zambia* **87 E2**
Nsukka *Nigeria* **83 D6**
Ntui *Cameroon* **83 E7**
Nu Jiang → *China* **58 E2**
Nu Shan *China* **58 E2**
Nuba Mts. = Nubah,
  Jibalan *Sudan* **81 E3**
Nubah, Jibalan *Sudan* **81 E3**
Nubia *Africa* **76 D7**
Nubian Desert = Nûbîya,
  Es Sahrâ en *Sudan* **80 C3**
Nûbîya, Es Sahrâ en *Sudan* **80 C3**
Nubledo *Spain* **36 B5**

Nuboai *Indonesia* **63 E9**
Nubra → *India* **69 B7**
Nucet *Romania* **28 D7**
Nueces → *U.S.A.* **116 H6**
Nueltin L. *Canada* **103 A9**
Nueva Carteya *Spain* **37 H6**
Nueva Ciudad Guerrero
  Mexico **119 B5**
Nueva Gerona *Cuba* **120 B3**
Nueva Palmira *Uruguay* **126 C4**
Nueva Rosita *Mexico* **118 B4**
Nueva San Salvador
  El Salv. **120 D2**
Nueva Tabarca *Spain* **39 G4**
Nuéve de Julio *Argentina* **126 D3**
Nuevitas *Cuba* **120 B4**
Nuevo, G. *Argentina* **128 E4**
Nuevo Casas Grandes
  Mexico **118 A3**
Nuevo Laredo *Mexico* **119 B5**
Nuevo León □ *Mexico* **118 C5**
Nuevo Rocafuerte *Ecuador* **124 D3**
Nugget Pt. *N.Z.* **91 G2**
Nugrus, Gebel *Egypt* **80 C3**
Nuhaka *N.Z.* **91 C6**
Nuhayb *Iraq* **73 F10**
Nukey Bluff *Australia* **95 E2**
Nukhayb *Iraq* **73 F10**
Nukheila *Sudan* **80 D3**
Nuku Hiva *French Polynesia* **97 H13**
Nuku'alofa *Tonga* **91 c**
Nukus *Uzbekistan* **52 E6**
Nules *Spain* **38 F4**
Nullagine *Australia* **92 D3**
Nullagine → *Australia* **92 D3**
Nullarbor *Australia* **93 F5**
Nullarbor △ *Australia* **93 F2**
Nullarbor Plain *Australia* **93 F4**
Numalla, L. *Australia* **95 D3**
Numan *Nigeria* **83 D7**
Numata *Japan* **55 F9**
Numatinna → *Sudan* **81 F2**
Numazu *Japan* **55 G9**
Numbulwar *Australia* **94 A2**
Numfoor *Indonesia* **63 E8**
Numurkah *Australia* **95 F4**
Nunaksaluk I. *Canada* **105 A7**
Nunap Isua *Greenland* **98 D15**
Nunavut □ *Canada* **101 C11**
Nunda *U.S.A.* **114 D7**
Nuneaton *U.K.* **15 E6**
Nungarin *Australia* **93 F2**
Nungo *Mozam.* **87 E4**
Nungwe *Tanzania* **86 C3**
Nunivak I. *U.S.A.* **106 a**
Nunkun *India* **69 C7**
Núoro *Italy* **42 B2**
Nūrābād *Iran* **71 E8**
Nure → *Italy* **40 C6**
Nuremberg = Nürnberg
  Germany **25 F7**
Nuri *Mexico* **118 B3**
Nuri *Sudan* **80 D3**
Nuriootpa *Australia* **95 E2**
Nuristān □ *Afghan.* **66 B7**
Nurlat *Russia* **34 C10**
Nurmes *Finland* **8 E23**
Nürnberg *Germany* **25 F7**
Nurpur *Pakistan* **68 D4**
Nurra, La *Italy* **42 B1**
Nurran, L. = Terewah, L.
  Australia **95 D4**
Nurrari Lakes *Australia* **93 E5**
Nurri *Italy* **42 C2**
Nürtingen *Germany* **25 G5**
Nurzec → *Poland* **31 F9**
Nus *Italy* **40 C4**
Nusa Barung *Indonesia* **63 H15**
Nusa Dua *Indonesia* **63 K18**
Nusa Kambangan *Indonesia* **63 G13**
Nusa Tenggara Barat □
  Indonesia **62 F5**
Nusa Tenggara Timur □
  Indonesia **63 F6**
Nusaybin *Turkey* **73 D9**
Nushki *Pakistan* **68 E2**
Nuuk *Greenland* **98 C14**
Nuupere, Pte. *Moorea* **91 d**
Nuwakot *Nepal* **69 E10**
Nuwayb'ī, W. an →
  Si. Arabia **74 F3**
Nuweiba' *Egypt* **70 D2**
Nuwerus *S. Africa* **88 E2**
Nuweveldberge *S. Africa* **88 E3**
Nuyts, Pt. *Australia* **93 G2**
Nuyts Arch. *Australia* **95 E1**
Nxai Pan △ *Botswana* **88 B3**
Nxau-Nxau *Botswana* **88 B3**
Nyaake *Liberia* **82 E3**
Nyabing *Australia* **93 F2**
Nyack *U.S.A.* **115 E11**
Nyagan *Russia* **52 C7**
Nyahanga *Tanzania* **86 C3**
Nyahua *Tanzania* **86 D3**
Nyahururu *Kenya* **86 B4**
Nyaingêntanglha Shan
  China **60 C4**

Nyakanazi *Tanzania* **86 C3**
Nyakrom *Ghana* **83 D4**
Nyâlâ *Sudan* **81 E1**
Nyamandhlovu *Zimbabwe* **87 F2**
Nyambiti *Tanzania* **86 C3**
Nyamlell *Sudan* **81 F2**
Nyamwaga *Tanzania* **86 C3**
Nyandekwa *Tanzania* **86 C3**
Nyanding → *Sudan* **81 F3**
Nyandoma *Russia* **32 B11**
Nyanga △ *Zimbabwe* **87 F3**
Nyangana *Namibia* **88 B3**
Nyanguge *Tanzania* **86 C3**
Nyankpala *Ghana* **83 D4**
Nyanza *Rwanda* **86 C2**
Nyanza □ *Kenya* **86 C3**
Nyanza-Lac *Burundi* **86 C2**
Nyaponges *Sudan* **81 F3**
Nyasa, L. = Malawi, L. *Africa* **87 E3**
Nyasvizh *Belarus* **23 B14**
Nyazura *Zimbabwe* **87 F3**
Nyazwidzi → *Zimbabwe* **87 G3**
Nyborg *Denmark* **11 J4**
Nybro *Sweden* **11 H9**
Nyda *Russia* **52 C8**
Nyeri *Kenya* **86 C4**
Nyerol *Sudan* **81 F3**
Nyhammar *Sweden* **10 D8**
Nyika △ *Malawi* **87 E3**
Nyinahin *Ghana* **82 D4**
Nyíradony *Hungary* **28 C6**
Nyírbátor *Hungary* **28 C7**
Nyíregyháza *Hungary* **28 C6**
Nyiru, Mt. *Kenya* **86 B4**
Nykarleby =
  Uusikaarlepyy *Finland* **8 E20**
Nykøbing *Nordjylland,*
  Denmark **11 H2**
Nykøbing *Sjælland, Denmark* **11 K5**
Nykøbing *Sjælland, Denmark* **11 J5**
Nyköping *Sweden* **11 F11**
Nykroppa *Sweden* **10 E8**
Nykvarn *Sweden* **10 E11**
Nyland *Sweden* **10 A11**
Nylstroom = Modimolle
  S. Africa **89 C4**
Nymagee *Australia* **95 E4**
Nymboida → *Australia* **95 D5**
Nymburk *Czech Rep.* **26 A8**
Nynäshamn *Sweden* **11 F11**
Nyngan *Australia* **95 E4**
Nyoma Rap *India* **69 C8**
Nyoman = Nemunas →
  Lithuania **30 C8**
Nyon *Switz.* **25 J2**
Nyong → *Cameroon* **83 E6**
Nyons *France* **21 D9**
Nyou *Burkina Faso* **83 C4**
Nýrsko *Czech Rep.* **26 B6**
Nysa *Poland* **31 H4**
Nysa → *Europe* **24 C10**
Nysa Kłodzka → *Poland* **31 H4**
Nysäter *Sweden* **10 E6**
Nyssa *U.S.A.* **108 E5**
Nyslott = Savonlinna
  Finland **32 B5**
Nystad = Uusikaupunki
  Finland **32 B1**
Nysted *Denmark* **11 K5**
Nyunzu *Dem. Rep. of the Congo* **86 D2**
Nyurba *Russia* **53 C12**
Nyzhankovychi *Ukraine* **31 J9**
Nyzhnohirskyy *Ukraine* **33 K8**
Nyzhny Vorota *Ukraine* **28 B8**
Nzébéla *Guinea* **82 D3**
Nzega *Tanzania* **86 C3**
Nzérékoré *Guinea* **82 D3**
Nzeto *Angola* **84 F2**
Nzilo, Chutes de
  Dem. Rep. of the Congo **87 E2**
N'zo → *Ivory C.* **82 D3**
N'zo → *Ivory C.* **82 D3**
Nzubuka *Tanzania* **86 C3**
Nzwani = Anjouan
  Comoros Is. **85 a**

O

O Barco *Spain* **36 C4**
O Carballiño *Spain* **36 C2**
O Corgo *Spain* **36 C3**
O Le Pupū Pu'e △ *Samoa* **91 b**
O Pino *Spain* **36 C2**
O Porriño *Spain* **36 C2**
Ō-Shima *Hokkaidō, Japan* **54 D9**
Ō-Shima *Shizuoka, Japan* **55 G9**
Oa, Mull of *U.K.* **13 F2**
Oacoma *U.S.A.* **112 D4**
Oahe, L. *U.S.A.* **112 C3**
Oahe Dam *U.S.A.* **112 C3**
O'ahu *U.S.A.* **106 b**
Oak Harbor *U.S.A.* **110 B4**
Oak Hill *U.S.A.* **113 G13**
Oak Island *U.S.A.* **117 E15**
Oak Ridge *U.S.A.* **117 C12**
Oak View *U.S.A.* **111 L7**

Oakan-Dake *Japan* **54 C12**
Oakdale *Calif., U.S.A.* **110 H6**
Oakdale *La., U.S.A.* **116 F8**
Oakes *U.S.A.* **112 B4**
Oakesdale *U.S.A.* **108 C5**
Oakey *Australia* **95 D5**
Oakfield *U.S.A.* **114 C6**
Oakham *U.K.* **15 E7**
Oakhurst *U.S.A.* **110 H7**
Oakland *U.S.A.* **110 H4**
Oakley *Idaho, U.S.A.* **108 E7**
Oakley *Kans., U.S.A.* **112 F3**
Oakover → *Australia* **92 D3**
Oakridge *U.S.A.* **108 E2**
Oakville *Canada* **114 C5**
Oakville *U.S.A.* **110 D3**
Oamaru *N.Z.* **91 F3**
Oancea *Romania* **29 E12**
Oasi Faunistica di
  Vendicari △ *Italy* **43 F8**
Oasis *Calif., U.S.A.* **110 H9**
Oasis *Calif., U.S.A.* **111 M10**
Oates Land *Antarctica* **5 C11**
Oatlands *Australia* **95 G4**
Oatman *U.S.A.* **111 K12**
Oaxaca *Mexico* **119 D5**
Oaxaca □ *Mexico* **119 D5**
Ob → *Russia* **52 C7**
Oba *Canada* **104 C3**
Obala *Cameroon* **83 E7**
Obama *Japan* **55 G7**
Oban *Nigeria* **83 D6**
Oban *U.K.* **13 E3**
Obbia *Somali Rep.* **75 F4**
Obera *Argentina* **127 B4**
Oberammergau *Germany* **25 H7**
Oberasbach *Germany* **25 F6**
Oberbayern □ *Germany* **25 G7**
Oberdrauburg *Austria* **26 E5**
Obere Donau △ *Germany* **25 G5**
Oberer Bayerischer
  Wald → *Germany* **25 F8**
Oberfranken □ *Germany* **25 E7**
Oberhausen *Germany* **24 D2**
Oberkirch *Germany* **25 G4**
Oberlausitz *Germany* **24 D10**
Oberlin *Kans., U.S.A.* **112 F3**
Oberlin *La., U.S.A.* **116 F8**
Oberlin *Ohio, U.S.A.* **114 E2**
Obernai *France* **19 D14**
Oberndorf *Germany* **25 G4**
Oberon *Australia* **95 E4**
Oberösterreich □ *Austria* **26 C7**
Oberpfalz □ *Germany* **25 F8**
Oberpfälzer Wald *Germany* **25 F8**
Oberpfälzer Wald △
  Germany **25 F8**
Oberstdorf *Germany* **25 H6**
Obertyn *Ukraine* **29 B10**
Oberursel *Germany* **25 E4**
Oberwart *Austria* **27 D9**
Obi, Kepulauan *Indonesia* **63 E7**
Obiaruku *Nigeria* **83 D6**
Óbidos *Brazil* **125 D7**
Óbidos *Portugal* **37 F1**
Obihiro *Japan* **54 C11**
Obilatu *Indonesia* **63 E7**
Obilnoye *Russia* **35 G7**
Obing *Germany* **25 G8**
Objat *France* **20 C5**
Obluchye *Russia* **53 E14**
Obninsk *Russia* **32 E9**
Obo *C.A.R.* **86 A2**
Oboa, Mt. *Uganda* **86 B3**
Obock *Djibouti* **81 E5**
Obodivka *Ukraine* **29 B14**
Oborniki *Poland* **31 F3**
Oborniki Śląskie *Poland* **31 G3**
Oboyan *Russia* **33 G9**
Obozerskaya = Obozerskiy
  Russia **52 C5**
Obozerskiy *Russia* **52 C5**
Obrenovac *Serbia* **44 B4**
Obrovac *Croatia* **41 D12**
Obruk *Turkey* **72 C5**
Obrzycko *Poland* **31 F3**
Observatory Inlet *Canada* **102 C3**
Obshchi Syrt *Russia* **6 E16**
Obskaya Guba *Russia* **52 C8**
Obuasi *Ghana* **83 D4**
Obubra *Nigeria* **83 D6**
Obudu *Nigeria* **83 D6**
Obwalden □ *Switz.* **25 J4**
Obzor *Bulgaria* **45 D11**
Ocala *U.S.A.* **117 G13**
Ocampo *Chihuahua, Mexico* **118 B3**
Ocampo *Tamaulipas, Mexico* **119 C5**
Ocaña *Spain* **36 F7**
Occidental, Cordillera
  Colombia **124 C3**
Occidental, Grand Erg
  Algeria **78 B6**
Ocean City *Md., U.S.A.* **113 F16**
Ocean City *N.J., U.S.A.* **113 F16**
Ocean City *Wash., U.S.A.* **110 C2**
Ocean Falls *Canada* **102 C3**
Ocean I. = Banaba *Kiribati* **96 H8**

Ocean Park *U.S.A.* **110** D2
Oceano *U.S.A.* **111** K6
Oceanport *U.S.A.* **115** F10
Oceanside *U.S.A.* **111** M9
Ochagavía *Spain* **38** C3
Ochakiv *Ukraine* **33** J6
Ochamchira *Georgia* **35** J5
Ochi, Oros *Greece* **46** C6
Ochil Hills *U.K.* **13** E5
Ocho Rios *Jamaica* **120** a
Ochsenfurt *Germany* **25** F6
Ochsenhausen *Germany* **25** G5
Ocilla *U.S.A.* **117** F13
Ockelbo *Sweden* **10** D10
Ocmulgee → *U.S.A.* **117** F13
Ocna Mureş *Romania* **29** D8
Ocna Sibiului *Romania* **29** E9
Ocnele Mari *Romania* **29** E9
Ocniţa *Moldova* **29** B12
Oconee → *U.S.A.* **117** F13
Oconomowoc *U.S.A.* **112** D9
Oconto *U.S.A.* **112** C10
Oconto Falls *U.S.A.* **112** C9
Ocosingo *Mexico* **119** D6
Ocotal *Nic.* **120** D2
Ocotlán *Jalisco, Mexico* **118** C4
Ocotlán *Oaxaca, Mexico* **119** D5
Ocreza → *Portugal* **37** F3
Ócsa *Hungary* **28** C4
Octeville *France* **18** C5
Oda *Ghana* **83** D4
Ōda *Japan* **55** G6
Oda, J. *Sudan* **80** C4
Ódáðahraun *Iceland* **8** D5
Ódaejin *N. Korea* **57** D15
Ódákra *Sweden* **11** H6
Odate *Japan* **54** D10
Odawara *Japan* **55** G9
Odda *Norway* **9** F12
Odder *Denmark* **11** J4
Odei → *Canada* **103** B9
Odemira *Portugal* **37** H2
Ödemiş *Turkey* **47** C9
Odendaalsrus *S. Africa* **88** D4
Odensbacken *Sweden* **10** E9
Odense *Denmark* **11** J4
Odenwald = Neckartal-
   Odenwald △ *Germany* **25** F5
Odenwald *Germany* **25** F5
Oder → *Europe* **24** B10
Oder-Havel Kanal *Germany* **24** C10
Oderzo *Italy* **41** C9
Odesa *Ukraine* **33** J6
Odesa □ *Ukraine* **33** J5
Ödeshög *Sweden* **11** F8
Odessa = Odesa *Ukraine* **33** J6
Odessa *Canada* **115** B8
Odessa *Tex., U.S.A.* **116** F3
Odessa *Wash., U.S.A.* **108** C4
Odiakwe *Botswana* **88** C4
Odiel → *Spain* **37** H4
Odienné *Ivory C.* **82** D3
Odintsovo *Russia* **32** E9
Odiongan *Phil.* **61** E4
Odobeşti *Romania* **29** E12
Odolanów *Poland* **31** G4
O'Donnell *U.S.A.* **116** E4
Odorheiu Secuiesc *Romania* **29** D10
Odoyevo *Russia* **32** F9
Odra = Oder → *Europe* **24** B10
Odra → *Spain* **36** C6
Odžaci *Serbia* **28** E4
Odžak *Bos.-H.* **28** E3
Odzi *Zimbabwe* **89** B5
Odzi → *Zimbabwe* **89** B5
Oebisfelde *Germany* **24** C6
Oeiras *Brazil* **125** E10
Oeiras *Portugal* **37** G1
Oelrichs *U.S.A.* **112** D2
Oelsnitz *Germany* **25** E8
Oelwein *U.S.A.* **112** D8
Oeno I. *Pac. Oc.* **97** K14
Oenpelli = Gunbalanya
   Australia **92** B5
Oetz *Austria* **26** D3
Of *Turkey* **73** B9
Ofanto → *Italy* **43** A9
Offa *Nigeria* **83** D5
Offaly □ *Ireland* **12** C4
Offenbach *Germany* **25** E4
Offenburg *Germany* **25** G3
Officer Cr. → *Australia* **93** E5
Offida *Italy* **41** F10
Ofidousa *Greece* **47** E8
Ofolanga *Tonga* **91** c
Ofotfjorden *Norway* **8** B17
Ofu *Amer. Samoa* **91** b
Ōfunato *Japan* **54** E10
Oga *Japan* **54** E9
Oga-Hantō *Japan* **54** E9
Ogaden *Ethiopia* **75** F3
Ōgaki *Japan* **55** G8
Ogallala *U.S.A.* **112** E3
Ogasawara Gunto *Pac. Oc.* **96** E6
Ogbomosho *Nigeria* **83** D5
Ogden *U.S.A.* **108** F8
Ogdensburg *U.S.A.* **115** B9

Ogea Driki *Fiji* **91** a
Ogea Levu *Fiji* **91** a
Ogeechee → *U.S.A.* **117** F14
Ogilby *U.S.A.* **111** N12
Oglio → *Italy* **40** C7
Óglio Nord △ *Italy* **40** C6
Óglio Sud △ *Italy* **40** C7
Ogmore *Australia* **94** C4
Ognon → *France* **19** E12
Ogoja *Nigeria* **83** D6
Ogoki *Canada* **104** B2
Ogoki → *Canada* **104** B2
Ogoki L. *Canada* **104** B2
Ogoki Res. *Canada* **104** B2
Ogooué → *Gabon* **84** E1
Ogosta → *Bulgaria* **44** C7
Ogowe = Ogooué → *Gabon* **84** E1
Ogr = Sharafa *Sudan* **81** E2
Ograżden *Macedonia* **44** E6
Ogre *Latvia* **32** H3
Ogrein *Sudan* **80** D3
Ogulin *Croatia* **41** C12
Ogun □ *Nigeria* **83** D5
Ogurchinskiy, Ostrov
   Turkmenistan **71** B7
Oguta *Nigeria* **83** D6
Ogwashi-Uku *Nigeria* **83** D6
Ogwe *Nigeria* **83** E6
Ohai *N.Z.* **91** F2
Ohakune *N.Z.* **91** C5
Ohata *Japan* **54** D10
Ohau, L. *N.Z.* **91** F2
Ohio □ *U.S.A.* **114** F2
Ohio → *U.S.A.* **112** G9
Ohře → *Czech Rep.* **26** A7
Ohre → *Germany* **24** C7
Ohrid *Macedonia* **44** E4
Ohridsko Jezero *Macedonia* **44** E4
Ohrigstad *S. Africa* **89** C5
Öhringen *Germany* **25** F5
Oi Qu *China* **58** C2
Oiapoque *Brazil* **125**
Oikou *China* **57** E9
Oil City *U.S.A.* **114** E5
Oil Springs *Canada* **114** D2
Oildale *U.S.A.* **111** K7
Oinousa = Inousses *Greece* **47** C8
Oise □ *France* **19** C9
Oise → *France* **19** C9
Oiseaux du Djoudj △ *Senegal* **82** B1
Oistins *Barbados* **121** g
Oistins B. *Barbados* **121** g
Ōita *Japan* **55** H5
Ōita □ *Japan* **55** H5
Oiticica *Brazil* **125** E10
Ojai *U.S.A.* **111** L7
Ojcowski △ *Poland* **31** H6
Ojinaga *Mexico* **118** B4
Ojiya *Japan* **55** F9
Ojo Caliente *Mexico* **118** C4
Ojos del Salado, Cerro
   Argentina **126** B3
Oka → *Russia* **34** B7
Okaba *Indonesia* **63** F9
Okahandja *Namibia* **88** C2
Okandja *Gabon* **84** E2
Okanagan L. *Canada* **102** D5
Okanogan *U.S.A.* **108** B4
Okanogan → *U.S.A.* **108** B4
Okanogan Range *N. Amer.* **102** D5
Okány *Hungary* **28** D6
Okapi △
   Dem. Rep. of the Congo **86** B2
Okaputa *Namibia* **88** C2
Okara *Pakistan* **68** D5
Okaukuejo *Namibia* **88** B2
Okavango Delta *Botswana* **88** B3
Okavango Swamp =
   Okavango Delta *Botswana* **88** B3
Okaya *Japan* **55** F9
Okayama *Japan* **55** G6
Okayama □ *Japan* **55** G6
Okazaki *Japan* **55** G8
Oke-Iho *Nigeria* **83** D5
Okęcie, Warszawa ✈
   (WAW) *Poland* **31** F7
Okeechobee *U.S.A.* **117** H14
Okeechobee, L. *U.S.A.* **117** H14
Okefenokee △ *U.S.A.* **117** F13
Okefenokee Swamp *U.S.A.*
   117 F13
Okehampton *U.K.* **15** G4
Okene *Nigeria* **83** D6
Oker → *Germany* **24** C6
Okha *India* **68** H3
Okha *Russia* **53** D15
Okhotsk *Russia* **53** D15
Okhotsk, Sea of *Asia* **53** D15
Okhotskiy Perevoz *Russia* **53** C14
Okhtyrka *Ukraine* **33** G8
Oki-Shotō *Japan* **55** F6
Okiep *S. Africa* **88** D2
Okigwi *Nigeria* **83** D6
Okija *Nigeria* **83** D6
Okinawa *Japan* **55** L4
Okinawa □ *Japan* **55** L4
Okinawa-Guntō *Japan* **55** L4

Okinawa-Jima *Japan* **55** L4
Okino-erabu-Shima *Japan* **55** L4
Okitipupa *Nigeria* **83** D5
Oklahoma □ *U.S.A.* **116** D6
Oklahoma City *U.S.A.* **116** D6
Okmulgee *U.S.A.* **116** D7
Oknitsa = Ocniţa *Moldova* **29** B12
Oko, W. → *Sudan* **80** C4
Okolo *Uganda* **86** B3
Okolona *U.S.A.* **117** E10
Okombahe *Namibia* **88** C2
Okonek *Poland* **30** E3
Okotoks *Canada* **102** C6
Okrika *Nigeria* **83** E6
Oksibil *Indonesia* **63** E10
Oktabrsk = Oktyabrsk
   Kazakhstan **52** E6
Oktyabrsk *Kazakhstan* **52** E6
Oktyabrsk *Russia* **34** D9
Oktyabrskiy =
   Aktsyabrski *Belarus* **23** B15
Oktyabrskiy *Russia* **35** G5
Oktyabrskoy Revolyutsii,
   Ostrov *Russia* **53** B10
Oktyabrskoye =
   Zhovtneve *Ukraine* **33** J7
Okulovka *Russia* **32** C7
Okuru *N.Z.* **91** E2
Okushiri-Tō *Japan* **54** C9
Okuta *Nigeria* **83** D5
Okwa → *Botswana* **88** C3
Ola *U.S.A.* **116** D8
Ólafsfjörður *Iceland* **8** C4
Ólafsvík *Iceland* **8** D2
Olancha *U.S.A.* **111** J8
Olancha Pk. *U.S.A.* **111** J8
Olanchito *Honduras* **120** C2
Öland *Sweden* **11** H10
Ölands norra udde *Sweden* **11** G11
Ölands södra udde *Sweden* **11** H10
Olargues *France* **20** E6
Olary *Australia* **95** E3
Olascoaga *Argentina* **126** D3
Olathe *U.S.A.* **112** F6
Olavarría *Argentina* **126** D3
Oława *Poland* **31** H4
Olbernhau *Germany* **24** E9
Ólbia *Italy* **42** B2
Ólbia, G. di *Italy* **42** B2
Olching *Germany* **25** G7
Olcott *U.S.A.* **114** C6
Old Bahama Chan. =
   Bahama, Canal Viejo de
   W. Indies **120** B4
Old Baldy Pk. = San
   Antonio, Mt. *U.S.A.* **111** L9
Old Bridge *U.S.A.* **115** F10
Old Castile = Castilla y
   Leon □ *Spain* **36** D6
Old Crow *Canada* **100** C6
Old Dale *U.S.A.* **111** L11
Old Forge *N.Y., U.S.A.* **115** C10
Old Forge *Pa., U.S.A.* **115** E9
Old Perlican *Canada* **105** C9
Old Shinyanga *Tanzania* **86** C3
Old Speck Mt. *U.S.A.* **115** B14
Old Town *U.S.A.* **113** C19
Old Washington *U.S.A.* **114** F3
Old Wives L. *Canada* **103** C7
Oldbury *U.K.* **15** F5
Oldcastle *Ireland* **12** C4
Oldeani *Tanzania* **86** C4
Oldenburg *Niedersachsen,*
   Germany **24** B4
Oldenburg
   Schleswig-Holstein, Germany **24** A6
Oldenzaal *Neths.* **17** B6
Oldham *U.K.* **14** D5
Oldman → *Canada* **102** D6
Oldmeldrum *U.K.* **13** D6
Olds *Canada* **102** C6
Oldziyt *Mongolia* **56** B5
Olean *U.S.A.* **114** D6
Olecko *Poland* **30** D9
Oléggio *Italy* **40** C5
Oleiros *Portugal* **36** F3
Oleiros *Spain* **36** B2
Olekma → *Russia* **53** C13
Olekminsk *Russia* **53** C13
Oleksandriya *Kirovohrad,*
   Ukraine **33** H7
Oleksandriya *Rivne, Ukraine* **23** C14
Oleksandrovka *Ukraine* **33** H7
Olema *U.S.A.* **110** G4
Olenegorsk *Russia* **8** B25
Olenek *Russia* **53** C12
Olenek → *Russia* **53** B13
Olenino *Russia* **32** D7
Oléron, Î. d' *France* **20** C2
Oleśnica *Poland* **31** G4
Olesno *Poland* **31** H5
Olevsk *Ukraine* **23** C14
Olga *Russia* **53** E14
Olga, L. *Canada* **104** C4

Olgas, The = Kata Tjuta
   Australia **93** E5
Ølgod *Denmark* **11** J2
Olhão *Portugal* **37** H3
Olhopil *Ukraine* **29** B14
Olhovatka *Russia* **30** D9
Olib *Croatia* **41** D11
Oliena *Italy* **42** B2
Oliete *Spain* **38** D4
Olifants = Elefantes →
   Africa **89** C5
Olifants → *Namibia* **88** C2
Olifantshoek *S. Africa* **88** D3
Olimbos *Greece* **47** F6
Ólimbos, Óros = Olymbos
   Oros *Greece* **44** F6
Olímpia *Brazil* **127** A6
Olimpos-Beydaglari △
   Turkey **47** E12
Olinda *Brazil* **125** E12
Olite *Spain* **38** C3
Oliva *Argentina* **126** C3
Oliva *Spain* **39** G4
Oliva, Punta del *Spain* **36** B5
Oliva de la Frontera *Spain* **37** G4
Olivares *Spain* **38** F2
Olive Branch *U.S.A.* **117** D10
Olivehurst *U.S.A.* **110** F5
Oliveira de Azeméis *Portugal* **36** E2
Oliveira do Douro *Portugal* **36** D2
Olivenza *Spain* **37** G3
Oliver *Canada* **102** D5
Oliver L. *Canada* **103** B8
Olivet *France* **19** E8
Olkhovka *Russia* **34** F7
Olkusz *Poland* **31** H6
Ollagüe *Chile* **126** A2
Olmedo *Spain* **36** D6
Olmeto *France* **21** G12
Olmos *Peru* — (not present; check)
Olney *Ill., U.S.A.* **112** F9
Olney *Tex., U.S.A.* **116** E5
Olofström *Sweden* **11** H8
Oloitokitok *Kenya* **86** C4
Oloma *Cameroon* **83** E7
Olomane → *Canada* **105** B7
Olomouc *Czech Rep.* **27** B10
Olomoucký □ *Czech Rep.* **27** B10
Olonets *Russia* **32** B7
Olongapo *Phil.* **61** D4
Olonne-sur-Mer *France* **20** B2
Oloron, Gave d' → *France* **20** E2
Oloron-Ste-Marie *France* **20** E3
Olosega *Amer. Samoa* **91** b
Olosenga = Swains I.
   Amer. Samoa **91** J11
Olot *Spain* **38** C7
Olovo *Bos.-H.* **28** F3
Olovyannaya *Russia* **53** D12
Oloy → *Russia* **53** C16
Olsberg *Germany* **24** D4
Olshammar *Sweden* **11** F8
Olshanka *Ukraine* **33** H6
Olshany *Ukraine* **33** G8
Olsztyn *Poland* **30** E7
Olsztynek *Poland* **30** E7
Olt □ *Romania* **29** F9
Olt → *Romania* **29** G9
Olten *Switz.* **25** H3
Olteniţa *Romania* **29** F11
Olton *U.S.A.* **116** D3
Oltu *Turkey* **73** B9
Oluan Pi *Taiwan* **59** G13
Olula del Rio *Spain* **39** H2
Olur *Turkey* **73** B10
Olutanga *Phil.* **61** H5
Olvega *Spain* **38** D2
Olvera *Spain* **37** J5
Olymbos *Cyprus* **49** D12
Olymbos Oros *Greece* **44** F6
Olympia *Greece* **46** D3
Olympia *U.S.A.* **110** D4
Olympic △ *U.S.A.* **110** C3
Olympic Dam *Australia* **95** E2
Olympic Mts. *U.S.A.* **110** C3
Olympus *Cyprus* **49** E11
Olympus, Mt. = Olymbos
   Oros *Greece* **44** F6
Olympus, Mt. = Uludağ
   Turkey **45** F13
Olympus, Mt. *U.S.A.* **110** C3
Olyphant *U.S.A.* **115** E9
Om → *Russia* **52** D8
Om Hajer *Eritrea* **81** E4
Om Koi *Thailand* **64** D2
Ōma *Japan* **54** D10
Ōmachi *Japan* **55** F8
Omae-Zaki *Japan* **55** G9
Ōmagari *Japan* **54** E10
Omagh *U.K.* **12** B4
Omagh □ *U.K.* **12** B4
Omaha *U.S.A.* **112** E6
Omak *U.S.A.* **108** B4
Omalos *Greece* **49** D5
Oman ■ *Asia* **75** C6
Oman, G. of *Asia* **71** E8
Omaruru *Namibia* **88** C2
Omaruru → *Namibia* **88** C1

Omate *Peru* **124** G4
Ombai, Selat *Indonesia* **63** F6
Ombone → *Italy* **40** F8
Omboué *Gabon* **84** E1
Omdurmân *Sudan* **81** D3
Omegna *Italy* **40** C5
Omemee *Canada* **114** B6
Omeonga
   Dem. Rep. of the Congo **86** C1
Ometepe, I. de *Nic.* **120** D2
Ometepec *Mexico* **119** D5
Ominato *Japan* **54** D10
Omineca → *Canada* **102** B4
Omineca Mts. *Canada* **102** B3
Omiš *Croatia* **41** E13
Omišalj *Croatia* **41** C11
Ōmiya = Saitama *Japan* **55** G9
Omme Å → *Denmark* **11** J2
Ommen *Neths.* **17** B6
Ömnögovi □ *Mongolia* **56** C3
Omo → *Ethiopia* **81** F4
Omo □ *Ethiopia* **81** F4
Omo Valley *Ethiopia* **81** F4
Omodeo, L. *Italy* **42** B1
Omodhos *Cyprus* **49** E11
Omoko *Nigeria* **83** D6
Omolon → *Russia* **53** C16
Omono-Gawa → *Japan* **54** E10
Omsk *Russia* **52** D8
Omsukchan *Russia* **53** C16
Ōmu *Japan* **54** B11
Omul, Vf. *Romania* **29** E10
Omulew → *Poland* **31** E8
Ōmura *Japan* **55** H4
Omuramba Omatako →
   Namibia **88** B2
Omuramba Ovambo →
   Namibia **88** B2
Omurtag *Bulgaria* **45** C10
Ōmuta *Japan* **55** H5
Oña *Spain* **36** C7
Onaga *U.S.A.* **112** F5
Onalaska *U.S.A.* **112** D8
Onancock *U.S.A.* **113** G8
Onang *Indonesia* **63** E5
Onangue, L. *Gabon* **84** E2
Onaping L. *Canada* **104** C3
Oñati *Spain* **38** B2
Onavas *Mexico* **118** B3
Onawa *U.S.A.* **112** D5
Oncócua *Angola* **88** B1
Onda *Spain* **38** F4
Ondangwa *Namibia* **88** B2
Ondarroa *Spain* **38** B2
Ondava → *Slovak Rep.* **27** C14
Ondjiva *Angola* **88** B2
Ondo *Nigeria* **83** D5
Ondo □ *Nigeria* **83** D6
Öndörshil *Mongolia* **56** B5
Öndverðarnes *Iceland* **8** D2
One Tree *Australia* **95** E3
Oneata *Fiji* **91** a
Onega *Russia* **52** C4
Onega → *Russia* **52** C4
Onega, L. = Onezhskoye
   Ozero *Russia* **32** B8
Oneida *U.S.A.* **115** C9
Oneida L. *U.S.A.* **115** C9
O'Neill *U.S.A.* **112** D4
Onekotan, Ostrov *Russia* **53** E16
Onema *Dem. Rep. of the Congo* **86** C1
Oneonta *U.S.A.* **115** D9
Oneşti *Romania* **29** D11
Onezhskoye Ozero *Russia* **32** B8
Ongarue *N.Z.* **91** C5
Ongea Levu = Ogea Levu *Fiji* **91** a
Ongers → *S. Africa* **88** E3
Ongerup *Australia* **93** F2
Ongjin *N. Korea* **57** F13
Ongkharak *Thailand* **64** E3
Ongniud Qi *China* **57** C10
Ongoka
   Dem. Rep. of the Congo **86** C2
Ongole *India* **66** M12
Ongon = Havirga *Mongolia* **56** B7
Oni *Georgia* **35** J6
Onida *U.S.A.* **112** C3
Onilahy → *Madag.* **89** C7
Onitsha *Nigeria* **83** D6
Ono *Fiji* **91** a
Onoda *Japan* **55** G5
Ons, I. de *Spain* **36** C2
Onsala *Sweden* **11** G6
Onslow *Australia* **92** D2
Onslow B. *U.S.A.* **117** D16
Ontake-San *Japan* **55** G8
Ontario *Calif., U.S.A.* **111** L9
Ontario *Oreg., U.S.A.* **108** D5
Ontario □ *Canada* **104** B2
Ontario, L. *N. Amer.* **114** C7
Ontinyent *Spain* **39** G4
Ontonagon *U.S.A.* **112** B9
Ontur *Spain* **39** G3
Onyx *U.S.A.* **111** K8
Oodnadatta *Australia* **95** D2
Ooldea *Australia* **93** F5

Oombulgurri *Australia* **92** C4
Oorindi *Australia* **94** C3
Oost-Vlaanderen □ *Belgium* **17** C3
Oostende *Belgium* **17** C2
Oosterhout *Neths.* **17** C4
Oosterschelde → *Neths.* **17** C4
Oosterwolde *Neths.* **17** B6
Ootacamund =
   Udagamandalam *India* **66** P10
Ootsa L. *Canada* **102** C3
Op Luang △ *Thailand* **64** C2
Opaka *Bulgaria* **45** C10
Opala *Dem. Rep. of the Congo* **86** C1
Opalenica *Poland* **31** F3
Opan *Bulgaria* **45** D9
Opanake *Sri Lanka* **66** R12
Opasatika *Canada* **104** C3
Opasquia △ *Canada* **104** B1
Opatija *Croatia* **41** C11
Opatów *Poland* **31** H8
Opava *Czech Rep.* **27** B10
Opelika *U.S.A.* **117** E12
Opelousas *U.S.A.* **116** F8
Opémisca, L. *Canada* **104** C5
Opheim *U.S.A.* **108** B10
Ophthalmia Ra. *Australia* **92** D2
Opi *Nigeria* **83** D6
Opinaca → *Canada* **104** B4
Opinaca, Rés. *Canada* **104** B4
Opinnagau → *Canada* **104** B3
Opiscotéo, L. *Canada* **105** B6
Opobo *Nigeria* **83** E6
Opochka *Russia* **32** D5
Opoczno *Poland* **31** G7
Opole *Poland* **31** H4
Opole Lubelskie *Poland* **31** G8
Opolskie □ *Poland* **31** H5
Opononi L. *Namibia* **88** B2
Oporto = Porto *Portugal* **36** D2
Opotiki *N.Z.* **91** C6
Opp *U.S.A.* **117** F11
Oppdal *Norway* **8** E13
Óppido Mamertina *Italy* **43** D8
Opportunity *U.S.A.* **108** C5
Oprişor *Romania* **28** F8
Oprtalj *Croatia* **41** C10
Opua *N.Z.* **91** A5
Opunake *N.Z.* **91** C4
Opuwo *Namibia* **88** B1
Opuzen *Croatia* **41** E14
Ora *Cyprus* **49** E12
Oracle *U.S.A.* **109** K8
Oradea *Romania* **28** C6
Öræfajökull *Iceland* **8** D5
Orahovac *Serbia* **44** D4
Orahovica *Croatia* **28** E2
Orai *India* **69** G8
Oraison *France* **21** E9
Oral = Zhayyq →
   Kazakhstan **34** F9
Oral *Kazakhstan* **34** E10
Oran *Algeria* **78** A5
Orange *Australia* **95** E4
Orange *France* **21** D8
Orange *Calif., U.S.A.* **111** M9
Orange *Mass., U.S.A.* **115** D12
Orange *Tex., U.S.A.* **116** F8
Orange *Va., U.S.A.* **113** F14
Orange → *S. Africa* **88** D2
Orange, C. *Brazil* **125** C8
Orange Cove *U.S.A.* **110** J7
Orange Free State = Free
   State □ *S. Africa* **88** D4
Orange Grove *U.S.A.* **116** H6
Orange Walk *Belize* **119** D7
Orangeburg *U.S.A.* **117** E14
Orangeville *Canada* **114** C4
Orango *Guinea-Biss.* **82** C1
Orani *Phil.* **61** D4
Oranje = Orange →
   S. Africa **88** D2
Oranjemund *Namibia* **88** D2
Oranjerivier *S. Africa* **88** D3
Oranjestad *Aruba* **121** D5
Orapa *Botswana* **85** J5
Orarak *Sudan* **81** F3
Oras *Phil.* **61** D4
Orašje *Bos.-H.* **28** E3
Orăştie *Romania* **29** E8
Orava → *Slovak Rep.* **27** B12
Orava, Vodna nádrž
   Slovak Rep. **27** B12
Oraviţa *Romania* **28** E6
Orb → *France* **20** E7
Orba → *Italy* **40** D5
Ørbæk *Denmark* **11** J4
Orbe *Switz.* **25** J2
Orbec *France* **18** C7
Orbetello *Italy* **41** F8
Órbigo → *Spain* **36** C5
Orbisonia *U.S.A.* **114** F7
Ørbyhus *Sweden* **10** D11
Orcadas *Antarctica* **5** C18
Orcas I. *U.S.A.* **110** B4

Orce *Spain* **39 H2**
Orce → *Spain* **39 H2**
Orchard City *U.S.A.* **108 G10**
Orchard Homes *U.S.A.* **108 C6**
Orchid I. = Lan Yü *Taiwan* **59**
Orchies *France* **19 B10**
Orchila, I. *Venezuela* **121 D6**
Orchilla, Pta. *Canary Is.* **48 G1**
Órcia → *Italy* **41 F8**
Orco → *Italy* **40 C4**
Orcutt *U.S.A.* **111 L6**
Ord *U.S.A.* **112 E4**
Ord → *Australia* **92 C4**
Ord, Mt. *Australia* **92 C4**
Ord Mts. *U.S.A.* **111 L10**
Ordenes = Ordes *Spain* **36 B2**
Orderville *U.S.A.* **109 H7**
Ordes *Spain* **36 B2**
Ordesa y Monte Perido △
   Spain **38 C4**
Ording = St-Peter-Ording
   Germany **24 A4**
Ordos = Mu Us Shamo *China* **56 E5**
Ordu *Turkey* **72 B7**
Ordu □ *Turkey* **72 B7**
Ordubad *Azerbaijan* **73 C12**
Orduña *Álava, Spain* **38 C2**
Orduña *Granada, Spain* **37 H7**
Ordway *U.S.A.* **108 G12**
Ordzhonikidze *Ukraine* **33 J8**
Ore *Dem. Rep. of the Congo* **86 B2**
Ore Mts. = Erzgebirge
   Germany **24 E8**
Orebić *Croatia* **41 F14**
Örebro *Sweden* **10 E9**
Örebro □ *Sweden* **10 E8**
Orecchiella △ *Italy* **40 D7**
Oregon *U.S.A.* **112 D9**
Oregon □ *U.S.A.* **108 E3**
Oregon City *U.S.A.* **110 E4**
Oregon Dunes △ *U.S.A.* **108 E1**
Öregrund *Sweden* **10 D12**
Öregrundsgrepen *Sweden* **10 D12**
Orekhov = Orikhiv *Ukraine* **33 J8**
Orekhovo-Zuyevo *Russia* **32 E10**
Orel *Russia* **33 F9**
Orel □ *Russia* **33 F9**
Orel → *Ukraine* **33 H8**
Orellana *Spain* **37 F5**
Orellana, Canal de *Spain* **37 F5**
Orellana, Embalse de *Spain* **37 F5**
Orem *U.S.A.* **108 F8**
Ören *Turkey* **47 D9**
Orenburg *Russia* **52 D6**
Örencik *Turkey* **47 D11**
Orense = Ourense *Spain* **36 C3**
Orense □ *Spain* **36 C3**
Orepuki *N.Z.* **91 G1**
Orestes Pereyra *Mexico* **118 B3**
Orestiada *Greece* **45 E10**
Øresund *Europe* **11 J6**
Orfanos Kolpos *Greece* **44 F7**
Orford Ness *U.K.* **15 E9**
Organ Pipe Cactus △
   U.S.A. **109 K7**
Organos, Pta. de los
   Canary Is. **48 F2**
Organyà *Spain* **38 C6**
Orgaz *Spain* **37 F7**
Orgeyev = Orhei *Moldova* **29 C13**
Ørsted *Denmark* **11 H4**
Órhaneli *Turkey* **45 G12**
Orhaneli → *Turkey* **45 G12**
Orhangazi *Turkey* **45 F13**
Orhei *Moldova* **29 C13**
Orhon Gol → *Mongolia* **60 A5**
Ória *Italy* **43 B10**
Oriental, Cordillera
   Colombia **124 B4**
Oriental, Grand Erg *Algeria* **78 B7**
Orientale □
   Dem. Rep. of the Congo **86 B2**
Oriente *Argentina* **126 D3**
Orihuela *Spain* **39 G4**
Orihuela del Tremedal *Spain* **38 E3**
Orikhiv *Ukraine* **33 J8**
Orikum *Albania* **44 F3**
Orillia *Canada* **114 B5**
Orinoco → *Venezuela* **124 B6**
Orion *Canada* **103 D6**
Oriskany *U.S.A.* **115 C9**
Orissa □ *India* **67 K14**
Orissaare *Estonia* **32 C2**
Oristano *Italy* **42 C1**
Oristano, G. di *Italy* **42 C1**
Orizaba *Mexico* **119 D5**
Orizaba, Pico de *Mexico* **119 D5**
Orizare *Bulgaria* **45 D11**
Orjen *Bos.-H.* **44 D2**
Orjiva *Spain* **37 J7**
Orkanger *Norway* **8 E13**
Örkelljunga *Sweden* **11 H7**
Örken *Sweden* **11 G9**
Örkény *Hungary* **28 C4**
Orkla → *Norway* **8 E13**
Orkney *S. Africa* **88 D4**
Orkney □ *U.K.* **13 B5**
Orkney Is. *U.K.* **13 B6**

Orland *U.S.A.* **110 F4**
Orlando *U.S.A.* **117 G14**
Orlando, C. d' *Italy* **43 D7**
Orléanais *France* **19 E9**
Orléans *France* **19 E8**
Orleans *U.S.A.* **115 B12**
Orléans, Î. d' *Canada* **105 C5**
Orlice → *Czech Rep.* **26 A8**
Orlivka *Ukraine* **29 E13**
Orlov *Slovak Rep.* **27 B13**
Orlov Gay *Russia* **34 E9**
Orlová *Czech Rep.* **27 B11**
Orlovat *Serbia* **28 E5**
Orly, Paris ✈ (ORY) *France* **19 D9**
Ormara *Pakistan* **66 G4**
Ormea *Italy* **40 D4**
Ormília *Greece* **44 F7**
Ormoc *Phil.* **61 F6**
Ormond *N.Z.* **91 C6**
Ormond Beach *U.S.A.* **117 G14**
Ormož *Slovenia* **41 B13**
Ormskirk *U.K.* **14 D5**
Ormstown *Canada* **115 A11**
Ornans *France* **19 E13**
Orne □ *France* **18 D7**
Orne → *France* **18 C6**
Orneta *Poland* **30 D7**
Ornö *Sweden* **10 E12**
Örnsköldsvik *Sweden* **10 A12**
Oro *N. Korea* **57 D14**
Oro → *Mexico* **118 B3**
Oro Grande *U.S.A.* **111 L9**
Oro Valley *U.S.A.* **109 K8**
Orobie, Alpi *Italy* **40 B6**
Orobie Bergamasche △ *Italy* **40 C6**
Orobie Valtellinesi △ *Italy* **40 B6**
Orocué *Colombia* **124 C4**
Orodara *Burkina Faso* **82 C4**
Orodo *Nigeria* **83 D6**
Orofino *U.S.A.* **108 C5**
Orohena, Mt. *Tahiti* **91 d**
Orol Dengizi = Aral Sea *Asia* **52 E7**
Oromíya □ *Ethiopia* **81 F5**
Oromocto *Canada* **105 C6**
Oron *Nigeria* **83 E6**
Orono *Canada* **114 C6**
Orono *U.S.A.* **113 C19**
Oronsay *U.K.* **13 E2**
Oropesa *Spain* **36 F5**
Oroquieta *Phil.* **61 G5**
Orosei *Italy* **42 B2**
Orosei, G. di *Italy* **42 B2**
Orosháza *Hungary* **28 D5**
Oroszlány *Hungary* **28 C3**
Orotukan *Russia* **53 C16**
Oroville *Calif., U.S.A.* **110 F5**
Oroville *Wash., U.S.A.* **108 B4**
Oroville, L. *U.S.A.* **110 F5**
Orrefors *Sweden* **11 H9**
Orroroo *Australia* **95 E2**
Orrviken *Sweden* **10 A8**
Orrville *U.S.A.* **114 F3**
Orsa *Sweden* **10 C8**
Orsara di Púglia *Italy* **43 A8**
Orsasjön *Sweden* **10 C8**
Orsha *Belarus* **32 E6**
Örsjö *Sweden* **11 H9**
Orsk *Russia* **52 D6**
Orşova *Romania* **28 F7**
Ørsted *Denmark* **11 H4**
Örsundsbro *Sweden* **10 E11**
Orta, L. d' *Italy* **40 C5**
Orta Nova *Italy* **43 A8**
Ortaca *Turkey* **47 E10**
Ortakent *Turkey* **47 D9**
Ortaklar *Turkey* **47 D9**
Ortaköy *Çorum, Turkey* **72 B6**
Ortaköy *Niğde, Turkey* **72 C6**
Orte *Italy* **41 F9**
Ortegal, C. *Spain* **36 B3**
Orthez *France* **20 E3**
Ortigueira *Spain* **36 B3**
Orting *U.S.A.* **110 C4**
Ortisei *Italy* **41 B8**
Ortles *Italy* **40 B7**
Ortón → *Bolivia* **124 F5**
Ortona *Italy* **41 F11**
Ortonville *U.S.A.* **112 C5**
Orūmīyeh *Iran* **73 D11**
Orūmīyeh, Daryācheh-ye
   Iran **73 D11**
Orune *Italy* **42 B2**
Oruro *Bolivia* **124 G5**
Orust *Sweden* **11 F5**
Oruzgān □ *Afghan.* **66 C5**
Orvault *France* **18 E5**
Orvieto *Italy* **41 F9**
Orwell *N.Y., U.S.A.* **115 C9**
Orwell *Ohio, U.S.A.* **114 E4**
Orwell → *U.K.* **15 F9**
Orwigsburg *U.S.A.* **115 F8**
Oryakhovo *Bulgaria* **44 C7**
Orynyn *Ukraine* **29 B11**
Orzinuovi *Italy* **40 C6**
Oryol *Russia* **31 F8**
Orzysz *Poland* **30 E8**
Osa → *Poland* **30 E5**

Osa, Pen. de *Costa Rica* **120 E3**
Osage *U.S.A.* **112 D7**
Osage → *U.S.A.* **112 F8**
Osage City *U.S.A.* **112 F6**
Ōsaka *Japan* **55 G7**
Osan *S. Korea* **57 F14**
Osawatomie *U.S.A.* **112 F6**
Osborne *U.S.A.* **112 F4**
Osby *Sweden* **11 H7**
Osceola *Ark., U.S.A.* **117 D10**
Osceola *Iowa, U.S.A.* **112 E7**
Oschatz *Germany* **24 D9**
Oschersleben *Germany* **24 C7**
Óschiri *Italy* **42 B2**
Oscoda *U.S.A.* **114 B1**
Osečina *Serbia* **44 B3**
Ösel = Saaremaa *Estonia* **32 C2**
Osery *Russia* **32 E10**
Osgoode *Canada* **115 A9**
Osh *Kyrgyzstan* **52 E8**
Oshakati *Namibia* **85 H3**
Oshawa *Canada* **114 C6**
Oshigambo *Namibia* **88 B2**
Oshkosh *Nebr., U.S.A.* **112 E2**
Oshkosh *Wis., U.S.A.* **112 C9**
Oshmyany = Ashmyany
   Belarus **23 A13**
Oshnovīyeh *Iran* **70 B5**
Oshogbo *Nigeria* **83 D5**
Oshtorīnān *Iran* **73 E13**
Oshwe *Dem. Rep. of the Congo* **84 E3**
Osi *Nigeria* **83 D6**
Osięczna *Poland* **31 G3**
Osijek *Croatia* **28 E3**
Ósilo *Italy* **42 B1**
Ósimo *Italy* **41 E10**
Osintorf *Belarus* **32 E6**
Osipenko = Berdyansk *Ukraine* **33 J8**
Osipovichi = Asipovichy
   Belarus **B15**
Osiyan *India* **68 F5**
Osizweni *S. Africa* **89 D5**
Oskaloosa *U.S.A.* **112 E7**
Oskarshamn *Sweden* **11 H10**
Oskarström *Sweden* **11 H6**
Oskélanéo *Canada* **104 C4**
Öskemen *Kazakhstan* **52 E9**
Oskol → *Ukraine* **33 H9**
Oslo *Norway* **9 G14**
Oslob *Phil.* **61 G5**
Oslofjorden *Norway* **9 G14**
Osmanabad *India* **66 K10**
Osmancık *Turkey* **72 B6**
Osmaniye *Turkey* **72 D7**
Osmanlı *Turkey* **45 E10**
Ōsmo *Sweden* **10 F11**
Osnabrück *Germany* **24 C4**
Ośno Lubuskie *Poland* **31 F1**
Osobłaha *Czech Rep.* **27 A10**
Osogovska Planina
   Macedonia **44 D6**
Osor *Italy* **41 D11**
Osório *Brazil* **127 B5**
Osorno *Chile* **128 E2**
Osorno *Spain* **36 C6**
Osorno, Vol. *Chile* **128 D2**
Osoyoos *Canada* **102 D5**
Osoyro *Norway* **8 F11**
Ospika → *Canada* **102 B4**
Osprey Reef *Australia* **94 A4**
Oss *Neths.* **17 C5**
Ossa, Mt. *Australia* **95 G4**
Ossa, Oros *Greece* **46 B4**
Ossa de Montiel *Spain* **39 G2**
Ossabaw I. *U.S.A.* **117 F14**
Osse → *France* **20 D4**
Osse → *Nigeria* **83 D6**
Ossi *Italy* **42 B1**
Ossining *U.S.A.* **115 E11**
Ossipee *U.S.A.* **115 C13**
Ossokmanuan L. *Canada* **105 B7**
Ossora *Russia* **53 D17**
Ostashkov *Russia* **32 D7**
Östavall *Sweden* **10 B9**
Oste → *Germany* **24 B5**
Ostend = Oostende *Belgium* **17 C2**
Oster *Ukraine* **23 C16**
Österbotten = Pohjanmaa
   Finland **8 E20**
Osterburg *Germany* **24 C7**
Osterburg *U.S.A.* **114 F6**
Osterburken *Germany* **25 F5**
Österbybruk *Sweden* **10 D11**
Österbymo *Sweden* **11 G9**
Österdalälven *Sweden* **10 C7**
Østerdalen *Norway* **10 C4**
Österfärnebo *Sweden* **10 D10**
Österfärnebo *Sweden* **10 A11**
Östergötlands län □ *Sweden* **11 F9**
Osterholz-Scharmbeck
   Germany **24 B4**
Østerild *Denmark* **11 G2**
Östermyra = Seinäjoki
   Finland **8 E20**
Osterode *Germany* **24 D6**
Österreich = Austria ■
   Europe **26 E7**
Östersund *Sweden* **10 A8**

Östervåla *Sweden* **10 D11**
Ostfriesische Inseln *Germany* **24 B3**
Ostfriesland *Germany* **24 B3**
Osthammar *Sweden* **10 D12**
Óstia, Lido di *Italy* **41 G9**
Ostíglia *Italy* **41 C8**
Ostmark *Sweden* **10 D6**
Östra Husby *Sweden* **11 F10**
Ostrava *Czech Rep.* **27 B11**
Ostróda *Poland* **30 E6**
Ostrogozhsk *Russia* **33 G10**
Ostroh *Ukraine* **23 C14**
Ostrołęka *Poland* **31 E8**
Ostrov *Bulgaria* **45 C8**
Ostrov *Czech Rep.* **26 A5**
Ostrov *Romania* **29 F12**
Ostrov *Russia* **32 D5**
Ostrów Lubelski *Poland* **31 G9**
Ostrów Mazowiecka *Poland* **31 F8**
Ostrów Wielkopolski *Poland* **31 G4**
Ostrowiec-Świętokrzyski
   Poland **31 H8**
Ostrožac *Bos.-H.* **28 G2**
Ostrzeszów *Poland* **31 G4**
Ostseebad Kühlungsborn
   Germany **24 A7**
Osttirol □ *Austria* **26 E5**
Ostuni *Italy* **43 B10**
Osum → *Albania* **44 F4**
Osŭm → *Bulgaria* **45 C8**
Ōsumi-Kaikyō *Japan* **55 J5**
Ōsumi-Shotō *Japan* **55 J5**
Osun □ *Nigeria* **83 D5**
Osuna *Spain* **37 H5**
Oswegatchie → *U.S.A.* **115 B9**
Oswego *U.S.A.* **115 C8**
Oswego → *U.S.A.* **115 C8**
Oswestry *U.K.* **14 E4**
Oświęcim *Poland* **31 H6**
Otaci *Moldova* **29 B12**
Otago □ *N.Z.* **91 F2**
Otago Harbour *N.Z.* **91 F3**
Otaheite B. *Trin. & Tob.* **125 K15**
Ōtake *Japan* **55 G6**
Otaki *N.Z.* **91 D5**
Otaru *Japan* **54 C10**
Otaru-Wan =
   Ishikari-Wan *Japan* **54 C10**
Otava → *Czech Rep.* **26 B7**
Otavalo *Ecuador* **124 C3**
Otavi *Namibia* **88 B2**
Otchinjau *Angola* **88 B1**
Otelec *Romania* **28 E5**
Otelnuk, L. *Canada* **105 A6**
Oţelu Roşu *Romania* **28 E7**
Otero de Rey = Outeiro de
   Rei *Spain* **36 B3**
Othello *U.S.A.* **108 C4**
Othoni *Greece* **46 B1**
Othris, Oros *Greece* **46 B4**
Oti → *Togo* **83 C5**
Otjiwarongo *Namibia* **88 C2**
Otmuchów *Poland* **31 H4**
Oto Tolu Group *Tonga* **91 c**
Otočac *Croatia* **41 D12**
Otoineppu *Japan* **54 B11**
Otok *Croatia* **41 E13**
Otopeni, Bucureşti ✈
   (OTP) *Romania* **29 F11**
Otorohanga *N.Z.* **91 C5**
Otoskwin → *Canada* **104 B2**
Otra → *Norway* **9 G13**
Otradnyy *Russia* **34 D10**
Otranto *Italy* **43 B11**
Otranto, C. d' *Italy* **43 B11**
Otranto, Str. of *Italy* **43 B11**
Otrokovice *Czech Rep.* **27 B10**
Otse *S. Africa* **88 D4**
Ōtsu *Japan* **55 G7**
Ōtsuki *Japan* **55 G9**
Ottawa = Outaouais →
   Canada **104 C5**
Ottawa *Canada* **115 A9**
Ottawa *Ill., U.S.A.* **112 E9**
Ottawa *Kans., U.S.A.* **112 F6**
Ottawa Is. *Canada* **101 D11**
Ottélé *Cameroon* **83 E7**
Ottensheim *Austria* **26 C7**
Otter Cr. → *U.S.A.* **115 B11**
Otter L. *Canada* **103 B8**
Otterndorf *Germany* **24 B4**
Otterville *Canada* **114 D4**
Ottery St. Mary *U.K.* **15 G4**
Otto Beit Bridge *Zimbabwe* **87 F2**
Ottosdal *S. Africa* **88 D4**
Ottumwa *U.S.A.* **112 E7**
Otu *Nigeria* **83 D5**
Otukpa *Nigeria* **83 D6**
Oturkpo *Nigeria* **83 D6**
Otway, B. *Chile* **128 G2**
Otway, C. *Australia* **95 F3**
Otwock *Poland* **31 F8**
Otynia *Ukraine* **29 B9**
Ötztaler Ache → *Austria* **26 D3**
Ötztaler Alpen *Austria* **26 E3**

Ou → *Laos* **64 B4**
Ou Neua *Laos* **58 F3**
Ou-Sammyaku *Japan* **54 E10**
Ouachita → *U.S.A.* **116 F9**
Ouachita, L. *U.S.A.* **116 D8**
Ouachita Mts. *U.S.A.* **116 D7**
Ouagadougou *Burkina Faso* **83 C4**
Ouahigouya *Burkina Faso* **82 C4**
Ouahran = Oran *Algeria* **78 A5**
Oualâta *Mauritania* **82 B3**
Ouallam *Niger* **83 C5**
Ouallene *Algeria* **78 D6**
Ouargaye *Burkina Faso* **83 C5**
Ouargla *Algeria* **78 B7**
Ouarkoye *Burkina Faso* **82 C4**
Ouarra → *C.A.R.* **84 C4**
Ouarzazate *Morocco* **78 B4**
Ouassouas *Mali* **83 B5**
Ouatagouna *Mali* **83 B5**
Oubangi →
   Dem. Rep. of the Congo **84 E3**
Ouche → *France* **19 E12**
Ouddorp *Neths.* **17 C3**
Oude Rijn → *Neths.* **17 B4**
Oudenaarde *Belgium* **17 D3**
Oudon → *France* **18 E6**
Oudtshoorn *S. Africa* **88 E3**
Oueïka *Mali* **83 B4**
Ouellé *Ivory C.* **82 D4**
Ouéme → *Benin* **83 D5**
Ouessa *Burkina Faso* **82 C4**
Ouessant, Î. d' *France* **18 D1**
Ouesso *Congo* **84 D3**
Ouest □ *Cameroon* **83 D7**
Ouest, Pte. de l' *Canada* **105 C7**
Ouezzane *Morocco* **78 B4**
Ougarou *Burkina Faso* **83 C5**
Oughter, L. *Ireland* **12 B4**
Oughterard *Ireland* **12 C2**
Ouidah *Benin* **83 D5**
Ouidi *Niger* **83 C7**
Ouistreham *France* **18 C6**
Oujda *Morocco* **78 B5**
Oujeft *Mauritania* **82 A2**
Oulainen *Finland* **8 D21**
Ould Yenjé *Mauritania* **82 B2**
Oullins *France* **21 C8**
Oulu *Finland* **8 D21**
Oulujärvi *Finland* **8 D22**
Oulujoki → *Finland* **8 D21**
Oulx *Italy* **40 C3**
Oum Chalouba *Chad* **79 E10**
Oum Hadjer *Chad* **79 F9**
Oumé *Ivory C.* **82 D3**
Ounasjoki → *Finland* **8 C21**
Ounguati *Namibia* **88 C2**
Ounianga Sérir *Chad* **79 E10**
Our → *Lux.* **17 E6**
Oura, Akra *Greece* **47 C8**
Ouranoupoli *Greece* **44 F7**
Ourârene *Niger* **83 B6**
Ouray *U.S.A.* **109 G10**
Ourcq → *France* **19 C10**
Ourense *Spain* **36 C3**
Ouricuri *Brazil* **125 E11**
Ourinhos *Brazil* **127 A6**
Ourique *Portugal* **37 H2**
Ouro Fino *Brazil* **127 A6**
Ouro-Ndia *Mali* **82 B4**
Ouro Prêto *Brazil* **127 A7**
Ouro Sogui *Senegal* **82 B2**
Oursi *Burkina Faso* **83 C4**
Ourthe → *Belgium* **17 D5**
Ouse → *E. Sussex, U.K.* **15 G8**
Ouse → *N. Yorks., U.K.* **14 D7**
Oust *France* **20 F5**
Oust → *France* **18 E4**
Outamba-Kilimi △ *S. Leone* **82 D2**
Outaouais → *Canada* **104 C5**
Outardes → *Canada* **105 C6**
Outeiro de Rei *Spain* **36 B3**
Outer Hebrides *U.K.* **13 D1**
Outes = Serra de Outes
   Spain **36 C2**
Outjo *Namibia* **88 C2**
Outlook *Canada* **103 C7**
Outokumpu *Finland* **8 E23**
Outreau *France* **19 B8**
Ouvèze → *France* **21 E8**
Ouyen *Australia* **95 F3**
Ouzouer-le-Marché *France* **19 E8**
Ovada *Italy* **40 D5**
Ovalau *Fiji* **91 a**
Ovalle *Chile* **126 C1**
Ovamboland *Namibia* **88 B2**
Ovar *Portugal* **36 E2**
Overath *Germany* **24 E3**
Overflakkee *Neths.* **17 C4**
Overijssel □ *Neths.* **17 B6**
Overland Park *U.S.A.* **112 F6**
Overton *U.S.A.* **111 J12**
Övertorneå *Sweden* **8 C20**
Överum *Sweden* **11 F10**
Ovid *U.S.A.* **115 D8**
Ovidiopol *Ukraine* **33 J6**
Ovidiu *Romania* **29 F13**
Oviedo *Spain* **36 B5**

Ou → *Laos* **64 B4**
Oviksfjällen *Sweden* **10 A7**
Oviši *Latvia* **30 A8**
Ovoot *Mongolia* **56 B7**
Övör Hangay □ *Mongolia* **56 B2**
Ovoro *Nigeria* **83 D6**
Øvre Årdal *Norway* **8 F12**
Övre Fryken *Sweden* **10 E7**
Ovruch *Ukraine* **23 C15**
Owaka *N.Z.* **91 G2**
Owambo = Ovamboland
   Namibia **88 B2**
Owasco L. *U.S.A.* **115 D8**
Owase *Japan* **55 G8**
Owatonna *U.S.A.* **112 C7**
Owbeh *Afghan.* **66 B3**
Owego *U.S.A.* **115 D8**
Owen Falls Dam =
   Nalubaale Dam *Uganda* **86 B3**
Owen Sound *Canada* **114 B4**
Owen Stanley Ra.
   Papua N. G. **90 B7**
Oweniny → *Ireland* **12 B2**
Owens → *U.S.A.* **110 J9**
Owens L. *U.S.A.* **111 J9**
Owensboro *U.S.A.* **112 G10**
Owerri *Nigeria* **83 D6**
Owl → *Canada* **103 B10**
Owo *Nigeria* **83 D6**
Owosso *U.S.A.* **113 D11**
Owyhee *U.S.A.* **108 F5**
Owyhee → *U.S.A.* **108 E5**
Owyhee, L. *U.S.A.* **108 E5**
Ox Mts. = Slieve Gamph
   Ireland **12 B3**
Öxarfjörður *Iceland* **8 C5**
Oxbow *Canada* **103 D8**
Oxelösund *Sweden* **11 F11**
Oxford *N.Z.* **91 E4**
Oxford *U.K.* **15 F6**
Oxford *Mass., U.S.A.* **115 D13**
Oxford *Miss., U.S.A.* **117 D10**
Oxford *N.C., U.S.A.* **117 C15**
Oxford *N.Y., U.S.A.* **115 D9**
Oxford *Ohio, U.S.A.* **113 F11**
Oxford L. *Canada* **103 C9**
Oxfordshire □ *U.K.* **15 F6**
Oxia *Greece* **46 C3**
Oxie *Sweden* **11 J7**
Oxilithos *Greece* **46 C6**
Oxnard *U.S.A.* **111 L7**
Oxsjövålen *Sweden* **10 B7**
Oxus = Amudarya →
   Uzbekistan **52 E6**
Oya *Malaysia* **62 D4**
Oyama *Japan* **55 F9**
Oyambre △ *Spain* **36 B6**
Oyem *Gabon* **84 D2**
Oyen *Canada* **103 C6**
Oykel → *U.K.* **13 D4**
Oymyakon *Russia* **53 C15**
Oyo *Nigeria* **83 D5**
Oyo □ *Nigeria* **83 D5**
Oyonnax *France* **19 F12**
Oyster Bay *U.S.A.* **115 F11**
Ōyūbari *Japan* **54 C11**
Ozalp *Turkey* **73 C10**
Ozamiz *Phil.* **61 G5**
Ozark *Ala., U.S.A.* **117 F12**
Ozark *Ark., U.S.A.* **116 D8**
Ozark *Mo., U.S.A.* **112 G7**
Ozark Plateau *U.S.A.* **112 G8**
Ozarks, L. of the *U.S.A.* **112 F8**
Ożarów *Poland* **31 H8**
Ózd *Hungary* **28 B5**
Ozernoye *Russia* **34 E10**
Ozero Svityaz *Ukraine* **31 G10**
Ozersk *Russia* **30 D8**
Ozette, L. *U.S.A.* **110 B2**
Ozieri *Italy* **42 B2**
Ozimek *Poland* **31 H5**
Ozinki *Russia* **34 E10**
Ozona *U.S.A.* **116 F4**
Ozorków *Poland* **31 G6**
Ozren *Bos.-H.* **28 G3**
Ozuluama *Mexico* **119 C5**
Ozun *Romania* **29 E10**
Ozurgeti *Georgia* **35 K5**

P

Pa *Burkina Faso* **82 C4**
Pa-an *Burma* **67 L20**
Pa Mong Dam *Thailand* **64 D4**
Pa Sak → *Thailand* **64 E3**
Paamiut *Greenland* **4 C5**
Paar → *Germany* **25 G7**
Paarl *S. Africa* **88 E2**
Pab Hills *Pakistan* **68 F2**
Pabbay *U.K.* **13 D1**
Pabianice *Poland* **31 G6**
Pabna *Bangla.* **67 G16**
Pabo *Uganda* **86 B3**
Pacaja → *Brazil* **125 D8**
Pacaraima, Sa. *S. Amer.* **124 C6**
Pacasmayo *Peru* **124 E3**
Paceco *Italy* **42 E5**
Pachhar *India* **68 G7**

Pachia *Greece* **47** E7
Pachino *Italy* **43** F8
Pachitea = *Peru* **124** E4
Pachmarhi *India* **69** H8
Pachnes *Greece* **49** D6
Pachpadra *India* **68** G5
Pachuca *Mexico* **119** C5
Pacific Antarctic Ridge
  Pac. Oc. **5** B13
Pacific Grove *U.S.A.* **110** J5
Pacific Ocean **97** G14
Pacific Rim △ *Canada* **110** B2
Pacifica *U.S.A.* **110** H4
Pacitan *Indonesia* **63** H14
Packwood *U.S.A.* **110** D5
Pacov *Czech Rep.* **26** B8
Pacy-sur-Eure *France* **18** C8
Padaido, Kepulauan
  Indonesia **63** E9
Padang *Indonesia* **62** E2
Padang Endau *Malaysia* **65** L4
Padangpanjang *Indonesia* **62** E2
Padangsidempuan *Indonesia* **62** D1
Padborg *Denmark* **11** K3
Paddle Prairie *Canada* **102** B5
Paddockwood *Canada* **103** C7
Paderborn *Germany* **24** D4
Padeş, Vf. *Romania* **28** E7
Padina *Romania* **29** F12
Padma *India* **69** G11
Pádova *Italy* **41** C8
Padra *India* **68** H5
Padrauna *India* **69** F10
Padre I. *U.S.A.* **116** H6
Padre Island △ *U.S.A.* **116** H6
Padrón *Spain* **36** C2
Padstow *U.K.* **15** G3
Padua = Pádova *Italy* **41** C8
Paducah *Ky., U.S.A.* **112** G9
Paducah *Tex., U.S.A.* **116** D4
Padul *Spain* **37** H7
Paea *Tahiti* **91** d
Paeroa *N.Z.* **91** B5
Paesana *Italy* **40** D4
Pafúri *Mozam.* **89** C5
Pag *Croatia* **41** D12
Paga *Ghana* **83** C4
Pagadian *Phil.* **61** H5
Pagai Selatan, Pulau
  Indonesia **62** E2
Pagai Utara, Pulau *Indonesia* **62** E2
Pagalu = Annobón *Atl. Oc.* **77** G4
Pagara *India* **69** G9
Pagastikos Kolpos *Greece* **46** B5
Pagatan *Indonesia* **62** E5
Page *U.S.A.* **109** H8
Pagėgiai *Lithuania* **30** C8
Pago Pago *Amer. Samoa* **91** b
Pagosa Springs *U.S.A.* **109** H10
Pagwa River *Canada* **104** B2
Pāhala *U.S.A.* **106** b
Pahang → *Malaysia* **65** L4
Pahiatua *N.Z.* **91** D5
Pahokee *U.S.A.* **117** H14
Pahute Mesa *U.S.A.* **110** H10
Pai *Thailand* **64** C2
Paicines *U.S.A.* **110** J5
Paide *Estonia* **32** C3
Paignton *U.K.* **15** G4
Paiho *Taiwan* **59** F13
Päijänne *Finland* **32** B3
Pailani *India* **69** G9
Pailin *Cambodia* **64** F4
Paimpol *France* **18** D3
Painan *Indonesia* **62** E2
Painesville *U.S.A.* **114** E3
Paint Hills = Wemindji
  Canada **104** B4
Paint L. *Canada* **103** B9
Painted Desert *U.S.A.* **109** H8
Paintsville *U.S.A.* **113** G12
Paisley *Canada* **114** B3
Paisley *U.K.* **13** F4
Paisley *U.S.A.* **108** E3
Paita *Peru* **124** E2
Paiva → *Portugal* **36** D2
Paizhou *China* **59** B9
Pajares *Spain* **36** B5
Pajares, Puerto de *Spain* **36** C5
Pajęczno *Poland* **31** G5
Pak Lay *Laos* **64** C3
Pak Phanang *Thailand* **65** H3
Pak Sane *Laos* **64** C4
Pak Song *Laos* **64** E6
Pak Suong *Laos* **58** H4
Pakaur *India* **69** G12
Pakch'ŏn *N. Korea* **57** E13
Pakenham *Canada* **115** A8
Pakhuis *S. Africa* **88** E2
Pakistan ■ *Asia* **68** E4
Pakkading *Laos* **64** C4
Paklenica △ *Croatia* **41** D12
Pakokku *Burma* **67** J19
Pakość *Poland* **31** F5
Pakowki L. *Canada* **103** D6

Pakpattan *Pakistan* **68** D5
Pakrac *Croatia* **28** E2
Pakruojis *Lithuania* **30** C10
Paks *Hungary* **28** D3
Paktiā □ *Afghan.* **66** C6
Paktīkā □ *Afghan.* **66** C6
Pakwach *Uganda* **86** B3
Pakxe *Laos* **64** E5
Pal Lahara *India* **69** J11
Pala *Chad* **79** G9
Pala *Dem. Rep. of the Congo* **86** D2
Pala *U.S.A.* **111** M9
Palabek *Uganda* **86** B3
Palacios *U.S.A.* **116** G6
Palafrugell *Spain* **38** D8
Palagiano *Italy* **43** B10
Palagonía *Italy* **43** E7
Palagruža *Croatia* **41** F13
Palaiseau *France* **19** D9
Palam *India* **66** K10
Palamas *Greece* **46** B4
Palamòs *Spain* **38** D8
Palampur *India* **68** C7
Palamut *Turkey* **47** C9
Palana *Australia* **95** F4
Palana *Russia* **53** D16
Palanan *Phil.* **61** C5
Palanan Pt. *Phil.* **61** C5
Palandri *Pakistan* **69** C5
Palanga *Lithuania* **30** C8
Palangkaraya *Indonesia* **62** E4
Palani Hills *India* **66** P10
Palanpur *India* **68** G5
Palapye *Botswana* **88** C4
Palas *Pakistan* **69** B5
Palashi *India* **69** H13
Palasponga *India* **69** J11
Palatka *Russia* **53** C16
Palatka *U.S.A.* **117** G14
Palau *Italy* **42** A2
Palau ■ *Palau* **90** A6
Palauk *Burma* **64** F2
Palawan *Phil.* **61** G3
Palayankottai *India* **66** Q10
Palazzo, Pte. *France* **21** F12
Palazzo San Gervásio *Italy* **43** B8
Palazzolo Acréide *Italy* **43** E7
Paldiski *Estonia* **32** C3
Pale *Bos.-H.* **28** G3
Palekastro *Greece* **49** D8
Paleleh *Indonesia* **63** D6
Palembang *Indonesia* **62** E2
Palencia *Spain* **36** C6
Palencia □ *Spain* **36** C6
Palenque *Mexico* **119** D6
Paleochora *Greece* **49** D5
Paleokastritsa *Greece* **49** A3
Paleometokho *Cyprus* **49** D12
Palermo *Italy* **42** D6
Palermo *U.S.A.* **108** G3
Palermo ✈ (PMO) *Italy* **42** D6
Paleros *Greece* **46** C2
Palestina *Chile* **128** A3
Palestine *Asia* **74** D4
Palestine *U.S.A.* **116** F7
Palestrina *Italy* **41** G9
Paletwa *Burma* **67** J18
Palghat *India* **66** P10
Palgrave, Mt. *Australia* **92** D2
Pali *India* **68** G5
Palikir *Micronesia* **96** G7
Palinuro *Italy* **43** B8
Palinuro, C. *Italy* **43** B8
Paliouri, Akra *Greece* **44** G7
Palisades Res. *U.S.A.* **108** E8
Paliseul *Belgium* **17** E5
Palitana *India* **68** J4
Palizada *Mexico* **119** D6
Palk Bay *Asia* **66** Q11
Palk Strait *Asia* **66** Q11
Palkānah *Iraq* **70** C5
Palkot *India* **69** H11
Pallanza = Verbánia *Italy* **40** C5
Pallarenda *Australia* **94** B4
Pallasovka *Russia* **34** E8
Pallës, Bishti i *Albania* **44** E3
Pallinup → *Australia* **93** F2
Pallisa *Uganda* **86** B3
Pallu *India* **68** E6
Palm Bay *U.S.A.* **117** G14
Palm Beach *U.S.A.* **117** H14
Palm Coast *U.S.A.* **117** G14
Palm Desert *U.S.A.* **111** M10
Palm Is. *Australia* **94** B4
Palm Springs *U.S.A.* **111** M10
Palma *Mozam.* **87** E5
Palma, B. de *Spain* **48** B9
Palma de Mallorca *Spain* **48** B9
Palma de Mallorca ✈
  (PMI) *Spain* **39** F7
Palma del Río *Spain* **37** H5
Palma di Montechiaro *Italy* **42** E6
Palma Soriano *Cuba* **120** B4
Palmares *Brazil* **125** E11
Palmarola *Italy* **42** B5
Palmas *Brazil* **127** B5

Palmas, C. *Liberia* **82** E3
Pálmas, G. di *Italy* **42** D1
Palmdale *U.S.A.* **111** L8
Palmeira das Missões *Brazil* **127** B5
Palmeira dos Índios *Brazil* **125** E11
Palmela *Portugal* **37** G2
Palmer *Antarctica* **5** C17
Palmer *U.S.A.* **100** C5
Palmer → *Australia* **94** B3
Palmer Arch. *Antarctica* **5** C17
Palmer Land *Antarctica* **5** D18
Palmerston *Australia* **92** B5
Palmerston *Canada* **114** C4
Palmerston *N.Z.* **91** F3
Palmerston North *N.Z.* **91** D5
Palmerton *U.S.A.* **115** F9
Palmetto *U.S.A.* **117** H13
Palmi *Italy* **43** D8
Palmira *Argentina* **126** C2
Palmira *Colombia* **124** C3
Palmyra = Tudmur *Syria* **73** E8
Palmyra *Mo., U.S.A.* **112** F8
Palmyra *N.J., U.S.A.* **115** F9
Palmyra *N.Y., U.S.A.* **114** C7
Palmyra *Pa., U.S.A.* **115** F8
Palmyra Is. *Pac. Oc.* **97** G11
Palo Alto *U.S.A.* **110** H4
Palo Seco *Trin. & Tob.* **125** K15
Palo Verde *U.S.A.* **111** M12
Palo Verde △ *Costa Rica* **120** D2
Paloich *Sudan* **81** E3
Palomar Mt. *U.S.A.* **111** M10
Palompon *Phil.* **61** F6
Palopo *Indonesia* **63** E6
Palos, C. de *Spain* **39** H4
Palos de la Frontera *Spain* **37** H4
Palos Verdes, Pt. *U.S.A.* **111** M8
Palos Verdes Estates *U.S.A.* **111** M8
Pålsboda *Sweden* **10** E9
Palu *Indonesia* **63** E5
Palu *Turkey* **73** C9
Paluke *Liberia* **82** D3
Paluzza *Italy* **41** B10
Palwal *India* **68** E7
Pama *Burkina Faso* **83** C5
Pama △ *Burkina Faso* **83** C5
Pamanukan *Indonesia* **63** G12
Pamekasan *Indonesia* **63** G15
Pamenang *Indonesia* **63** J19
Pamiers *France* **20** E5
Pamir *Tajikistan* **52** F8
Pamlico → *U.S.A.* **117** D16
Pamlico Sd. *U.S.A.* **117** D17
Pampa *U.S.A.* **116** D4
Pampa de las Salinas
  Argentina **126** C2
Pampanua *Indonesia* **63** E6
Pampas *Argentina* **126** D3
Pampas *Peru* **124** F4
Pamphylia *Turkey* **72** D4
Pamplona *Colombia* **124** B4
Pamplona *Spain* **38** C3
Pampoenpoort *S. Africa* **88** E3
Pamukçu *Turkey* **47** B9
Pamukkale *Turkey* **47** D11
Pan de Azúcar △ *Chile* **126** B1
Pan Xian *China* **58** E5
Pana *U.S.A.* **112** F9
Panabo *Phil.* **61** H6
Panaca *U.S.A.* **109** H6
Panagyurishte *Bulgaria* **45** D8
Panaitan *Indonesia* **63** G11
Panaji *India* **66** M8
Panamá *Panama* **120** E4
Panama ■ *Cent. Amer.* **120** E4
Panamá, G. de *Panama* **120** E4
Panama, Isthmus of
  Cent. Amer. **98** J12
Panama Basin *Pac. Oc.* **97** G19
Panama Canal *Panama* **120** E4
Panama City *U.S.A.* **117** F12
Panamint Range *U.S.A.* **111** J9
Panamint Springs *U.S.A.* **111** J9
Panão *Peru* **124** E3
Panaon I. *Phil.* **61** F6
Panare *Thailand* **65** J3
Panarea *Italy* **43** B6
Panaro → *Italy* **41** D8
Panay *Phil.* **61** F5
Panay, G. *Phil.* **61** F5
Pančevo *Serbia* **28** F5
Panch'iao *Taiwan* **59** E13
Panciu *Romania* **29** E12
Pancorbo, Desfiladero *Spain* **36** C7
Pâncota *Romania* **28** D6
Panda *Mozam.* **89** C5
Pandan *Antique, Phil.* **61** F5
Pandan *Catanduanes, Phil.* **61** D6
Pandan, Selat *Singapore* **65** d
Pandan Tampoi = Tampoi
  Malaysia **65** d
Pandegelang *Indonesia* **63** G12
Pandhana *India* **68** J7
Pandharpur *India* **66** L9
Pando *Uruguay* **127** C4

Pando, L. = Hope, L.
  Australia **95** D2
Pandokratoras *Greece* **49** A3
Pandora *Costa Rica* **120** E3
Pandrup *Denmark* **11** G3
Panevéggio-Pale di San
  Martino △ *Italy* **41** B8
Panevėžys *Lithuania* **32** E3
Panfilovo *Russia* **34** E6
Pang-Long *Burma* **67** H21
Pang Sida △ *Thailand* **64** E4
Pang-Yang *Burma* **67** H21
Panga *Dem. Rep. of the Congo* **86** B2
Pangáion Óros *Greece* **45** F8
Pangalanes, Canal des =
  Ampangalana,
  Lakandranon' *Madag.* **89** C8
Pangani *Tanzania* **86** D4
Pangani → *Tanzania* **86** D4
Pangfou = Bengbu *China* **57** H9
Pangil *Dem. Rep. of the Congo* **86** C2
Pangkah, Tanjung
  Indonesia **63** G15
Pangkajene *Indonesia* **63** E5
Pangkalanbrandan
  Indonesia **62** D1
Pangkalanbuun *Indonesia* **62** E4
Pangkalpinang *Indonesia* **62** E3
Pangnirtung *Canada* **101** C13
Pangong Tso *India* **68** B8
Panguitch *U.S.A.* **109** H7
Pangutaran Group *Phil.* **61** H4
Panhandle *U.S.A.* **116** D4
Pani Mines *India* **68** H5
Pania-Mutombo
  Dem. Rep. of the Congo **86** D1
Panikota I. *India* **68** J4
Panipat *India* **68** E7
Panjal Range = Pir Panjal
  Range *India* **68** C7
Panjang, Hon *Vietnam* **65** H4
Panjgur *Pakistan* **66** F4
Panjim = Panaji *India* **66** M8
Panjin *China* **57** D12
Panjnad → *Pakistan* **68** E4
Panjnad Barrage *Pakistan* **68** E4
Panjwai *Afghan.* **68** D1
Pankshin *Nigeria* **83** D6
Panmunjŏm *N. Korea* **57** F14
Panna *India* **69** G9
Panna △ *India* **69** G8
Panna Hills *India* **69** G9
Pannawonica *Australia* **92** D2
Panngа, Tanjung *Indonesia* **63** K19
Pannirtuuq =
  Pangnirtung *Canada* **101** C13
Pano Akil *Pakistan* **68** F3
Pano Lefkara *Cyprus* **49** E12
Pano Panayia *Cyprus* **49** E11
Panorama *Brazil* **127** A5
Panormos *Greece* **49** D6
Pansemal *India* **68** J6
Panshan = Panjin *China* **57** D12
Panshi *China* **57** C14
Pantanal *Brazil* **124** H7
Pantano de Centla △
  Mexico **119** D6
Pantar *Indonesia* **63** F6
Pante Macassar *E. Timor* **63** F6
Pante Makasar = Pante
  Macassar *E. Timor* **63** F6
Pantelleria *Italy* **42** F5
Pantón *Spain* **36** C3
Pánuco *Mexico* **119** C5
Panyam *Nigeria* **83** D6
Panyu *China* **59** F9
Panzhihua *China* **58** D3
Páola *Italy* **43** C9
Paola *Malta* **49** D2
Paola *U.S.A.* **112** F6
Paonia *U.S.A.* **108** G10
Paopao *Moorea* **91** d
Paoting = Baoding *China* **56** E8
Paot'ou = Baotou *China* **56** D6
Paoua *C.A.R.* **79** G9
Pápa *Hungary* **28** C2
Papa Stour *U.K.* **13** A7
Papa Westray *U.K.* **13** B6
Papagayo → *Mexico* **119** D5
Papagayo, G. de *Costa Rica* **120** D2
Papakura *N.Z.* **91** B5
Papantla *Mexico* **119** C5
Papar *Malaysia* **62** C5
Papara *Tahiti* **91** d
Paparoa *N.Z.* **91** E3
Papas, Akra *Greece* **46** C3
Papeete *Tahiti* **91** d
Papenburg *Germany* **24** B3
Papenoo *Tahiti* **91** d
Papenoo → *Tahiti* **91** d
Papetoai *Moorea* **91** d
Paphlagonia *Turkey* **72** B5
Paphos *Cyprus* **49** E11
Papigochic → *Mexico* **118** B3
Papikion Oros *Greece* **45** E9
Paposo *Chile* **126** B1
Papoutsa *Cyprus* **49** E12
Papua □ *Indonesia* **63** E9

Papua, G. of *Papua N. G.* **90** B7
Papua New Guinea ■
  Oceania **90** B7
Papudo *Chile* **126** C1
Papuk *Croatia* **28** E2
Papun *Burma* **67** K20
Papunya *Australia* **92** D5
Pará = Belém *Brazil* **125** D9
Pará □ *Brazil* **125** D8
Paraburdoo *Australia* **92** D2
Paracale *Phil.* **61** D5
Paracatu *Brazil* **125** G9
Paracel Is. *S. China Sea* **62** A4
Parachilna *Australia* **95** E2
Parachinar *Pakistan* **68** C4
Paracin *Serbia* **44** C5
Paradas *Spain* **37** H5
Paradela *Spain* **36** C3
Paradip *India* **67** J15
Paradise *Calif., U.S.A.* **110** F5
Paradise *Nev., U.S.A.* **111** J11
Paradise → *Canada* **105** B8
Paradise Hill *Canada* **103** C7
Paradise River *Canada* **105** B8
Paradise Valley *U.S.A.* **108** F5
Paradisi *Greece* **49** C10
Paragould *U.S.A.* **117** C9
Paragua → *Venezuela* **124** B6
Paraguaçu → *Brazil* **125** F11
Paraguaçu Paulista *Brazil* **127** A5
Paraguaná, Pen. de
  Venezuela **124** A5
Paraguarí *Paraguay* **126** B4
Paraguarí □ *Paraguay* **126** B4
Paraguay ■ *S. Amer.* **126** A4
Paraguay → *Paraguay* **126** B4
Paraíba □ *Brazil* **125** E11
Paraíba do Sul → *Brazil* **127** A7
Parainen *Finland* **32** B2
Paraíso *Mexico* **119** D6
Paraíso, Cero *Venezuela* **124** B7
Páramos del Batallón y La
  Negra △ *Venezuela* **121** E5
Paramushir, Ostrov *Russia* **53** D16
Paran → *Israel* **74** E4
Paraná *Argentina* **126** C3
Paraná *Brazil* **125** F9
Paraná □ *Brazil* **127** A5
Paraná → *Argentina* **126** C4
Paranaguá *Brazil* **127** B6
Paranaíba *Brazil* **125** G8
Paranaíba → *Brazil* **125** H8
Paranapanema → *Brazil* **127** A5
Paranapiacaba, Serra do
  Brazil **127** A6
Paranas *Phil.* **61** F6
Paranavaí *Brazil* **127** A5
Parang *Maguindanao, Phil.* **63** C6
Parang *Sulu, Phil.* **61** J4
Parângul Mare, Vf. *Romania* **29** E8
Paraparaumu *N.Z.* **91** D5
Parapóri, Akra *Greece* **47** F9
Paray-le-Monial *France* **19** F11
Parbati → *Mad. P., India* **68** G7
Parbati → *Raj., India* **68** F7
Parbhani *India* **66** K10
Parchim *Germany* **24** B7
Parczew *Poland* **31** G9
Pardes Hanna-Karkur *Israel* **74** C3
Pardilla *Spain* **36** D7
Pardo → *Bahia, Brazil* **125** G11
Pardo → *Mato Grosso, Brazil* **127** A5
Pardoo Roadhouse *Australia* **92** D2
Pardubice *Czech Rep.* **26** A8
Pardubický □ *Czech Rep.* **26** B8
Pare *Indonesia* **63** G15
Pare Mts. *Tanzania* **86** C4
Parecis, Serra dos *Brazil* **124** F7
Paredes de Nava *Spain* **36** C6
Paren *Russia* **53** C17
Parent *Canada* **104** C5
Parent, L. *Canada* **104** C4
Parentis-en-Born *France* **20** D2
Parepare *Indonesia* **63** E5
Parfino *Russia* **32** D6
Parga *Greece* **46** B2
Pargas = Parainen *Finland* **32** B2
Pargo, Pta. do *Madeira* **48** D2
Paria → *U.S.A.* **109** H8
Paria, G. de *Venezuela* **125** K14
Pariaguán *Venezuela* **124** B6
Paricutín, Cerro *Mexico* **118** D4
Parigi *Indonesia* **63** E6
Parika *Guyana* **124** B7
Parikia *Greece* **47** D7
Parikkala *Finland* **32** B5
Parima, Serra *Brazil* **124** C6
Parinari *Peru* **124** D4

Pariñas, Pta. *S. Amer.* **122** D2
Parincea *Romania* **29** D12
Parintins *Brazil* **125** D7
Pariparit Kyun *Burma* **67** M18
Paris *Canada* **114** C4
Paris *France* **19** D9
Paris *Idaho, U.S.A.* **108** E8
Paris *Ky., U.S.A.* **113** F11
Paris *Tenn., U.S.A.* **117** C10
Paris *Tex., U.S.A.* **116** E7
Paris, Ville de □ *France* **19** D9
Paris Charles de Gaulle ✈
  (CDG) *France* **19** D9
Paris Orly ✈ (ORY) *France* **19** D9
Parish *U.S.A.* **115** C8
Parishville *U.S.A.* **115** B10
Park *U.S.A.* **110** B4
Park City *U.S.A.* **112** G5
Park Falls *U.S.A.* **112** C8
Park Head *Canada* **114** B3
Park Hills *U.S.A.* **112** G8
Park Range *U.S.A.* **108** F10
Park Rapids *U.S.A.* **112** B6
Park River *U.S.A.* **112** A5
Park Rynie *S. Africa* **89** E5
Parkā Bandar *Iran* **71** E8
Parkano *Finland* **32** A2
Parker *Ariz., U.S.A.* **111** L12
Parker *Pa., U.S.A.* **114** E5
Parker Dam *U.S.A.* **111** L12
Parkersburg *U.S.A.* **113** F13
Parkes *Australia* **95** E4
Parkfield *U.S.A.* **110** K6
Parkhill *Canada* **114** C3
Parkland *U.S.A.* **110** C4
Parkston *U.S.A.* **112** D5
Parksville *Canada* **102** D4
Parkway *U.S.A.* **110** G5
Parla *Spain* **36** E7
Pârlița *Moldova* **29** C12
Parma *Italy* **40** D7
Parma *Idaho, U.S.A.* **108** E5
Parma *Ohio, U.S.A.* **114** E3
Parma → *Italy* **40** D7
Parnaguá *Brazil* **125** F10
Parnaíba *Brazil* **125** D10
Parnaíba → *Brazil* **125** D10
Parnassos *Greece* **46** C4
Parnitha *Greece* **46** C5
Parnitha △ *Greece* **46** C5
Parnonas Oros *Greece* **46** D4
Pärnu *Estonia* **32** C3
Paro Dzong *Bhutan* **69** F13
Paroo → *Australia* **95** E3
Paroo-Darling △ *Australia* **95** E3
Paros *Greece* **47** D7
Parowan *U.S.A.* **109** H7
Parpaillon *France* **21** D10
Parral *Chile* **126** D1
Parras *Mexico* **118** B4
Parrett → *U.K.* **15** F4
Parris I. *U.S.A.* **117** E14
Parrsboro *Canada* **105** C7
Parry I. *Canada* **114** A4
Parry Is. *Canada* **101** B9
Parry Sound *Canada* **114** A5
Parsaloi *Kenya* **86** B4
Parsberg *Germany* **25** F7
Parseta → *Poland* **30** D2
Parsnip → *Canada* **102** B4
Parsons *U.S.A.* **112** G6
Parsons Ra. *Australia* **94** A2
Partanna *Italy* **42** E5
Partenio △ *Italy* **43** B7
Parthenay *France* **18** F6
Partinico *Italy* **42** D6
Partizansk *Russia* **54** C6
Partizánske *Slovak Rep.* **27** C11
Partridge I. *Canada* **104** A2
Partry Mts. *Ireland* **12** C3
Paru → *Brazil* **125** D8
Parvān □ *Afghan.* **66** B6
Parvatipuram *India* **67** K13
Parvatsar *India* **68** F6
Pâryd *Sweden* **11** H9
Parys *S. Africa* **88** D4
Pas, Pta. des *Spain* **48** C7
Pas, The *Canada* **103** C8
Pas-de-Calais □ *France* **19** B9
Pasada *Spain* **36** B5
Pasadena *Canada* **105** C8
Pasadena *Calif., U.S.A.* **111** L8
Pasadena *Tex., U.S.A.* **116** G7
Pasaje → *Argentina* **126** B3
Paşalimanı *Turkey* **45** F11
Pasar *Indonesia* **63** J17
Pasay *Phil.* **61** D4
Pascagoula *U.S.A.* **117** F10
Pascagoula → *U.S.A.* **117** F10
Paşcani *Romania* **29** C11
Pasco *U.S.A.* **108** C4
Pasco, Cerro de *Peru* **124** F3
Pasco I. *Australia* **92** D2
Pascoag *U.S.A.* **115** E13
Pascua, I. de *Chile* **97** K17
Pasewalk *Germany* **24** B9
Pasfield L. *Canada* **103** B7

Pasha → Russia 32 B7
Pasinler Turkey 73 C9
Pasir Mas Malaysia 65 J4
Pasir Panjang Singapore 65 d
Pasir Putih Malaysia 65 K4
Pasirian Indonesia 63 H15
Pasirkuning Indonesia 62 E2
Påskallavik Sweden 11 G10
Paskūh Iran 71 E9
Paslęk Poland 30 D6
Paslęka → Poland 30 D6
Pasley, C. Australia 93 F3
Pašman Croatia 41 E12
Pasni Pakistan 66 G3
Paso Cantinela Mexico 111 N11
Paso de Indios Argentina 128 E3
Paso de los Libres Argentina 126 B4
Paso de los Toros Uruguay 126 C4
Paso Robles U.S.A. 110 K6
Paspébiac Canada 105 C6
Pasrur Pakistan 68 C6
Passage East Ireland 12 D5
Passage West Ireland 12 E3
Passaic U.S.A. 115 F10
Passau Germany 25 G9
Passero, C. Italy 43 F8
Passo Fundo Brazil 127 B5
Passos Brazil 125 H9
Passow Germany 24 B10
Passy France 21 C10
Pastavy Belarus 32 E4
Pastaza → Peru 124 D3
Pasto Colombia 124 C3
Pastrana Spain 38 E2
Pasuruan Indonesia 63 G15
Pasym Poland 30 E7
Pásztó Hungary 28 C4
Patagonia Argentina 128 F3
Patagonia U.S.A. 109 L8
Patambar Iran 71 D9
Patan = Lalitapur Nepal 69 F11
Patan India 68 H5
Patani Indonesia 63 D7
Pătârlagele Romania 29 E11
Patchewollock Australia 95 F3
Patchogue U.S.A. 115 F11
Pate Kenya 86 C5
Patea N.Z. 91 C5
Pategi Nigeria 83 D6
Patensie S. Africa 88 E3
Paterna Spain 39 F4
Paternion Austria 26 E6
Paternò Italy 43 E7
Pateros U.S.A. 108 B4
Paterson U.S.A. 115 F10
Paterson Ra. Australia 92 D3
Pathankot India 68 C6
Pathein = Bassein Burma 67 L19
Pathfinder Res. U.S.A. 108 E10
Pathiu Thailand 65 G2
Pathum Thani Thailand 64 E3
Pati Indonesia 63 G14
Patía → Colombia 124 C3
Patiala Punjab, India 68 D7
Patiala Ut. P., India 69 F8
Patine Kouka Senegal 82 C2
Patitiri Greece 46 B5
Patkai Bum India 67 F19
Patmos Greece 47 D8
Patna India 69 G11
Patnos Turkey 73 C10
Pato Branco Brazil 127 B5
Patong, Ao Thailand 65 a
Patonga Uganda 86 B3
Patos Albania 44 F3
Patos Brazil 125 E11
Patos, L. dos Brazil 127 C5
Patos, Río de los →
   Argentina 126 C2
Patos de Minas Brazil 125 G9
Patquía Argentina 126 C2
Patra Greece 46 C3
Patraikos Kolpos Greece 46 C3
Patras = Patra Greece 46 C3
Patriot Hills Antarctica 5 E16
Patrocínio Brazil 125 G9
Pattada Italy 42 B2
Pattani Thailand 65 J3
Pattaya Thailand 64 F3
Patten U.S.A. 113 B19
Patterson Calif., U.S.A. 110 H5
Patterson La., U.S.A. 116 G9
Patterson, Mt. U.S.A. 110 G7
Pattoki Pakistan 68 D5
Patton U.S.A. 114 F6
Patuakhali Bangla. 67 H17
Patuanak Canada 103 B7
Patuca → Honduras 120 C3
Patuca, Punta Honduras 120 C3
Patuca △ Honduras 120 D2
Pătulele Romania 28 F7
Patvinsuo △ Finland 8 E24
Pátzcuaro Mexico 118 D4

Pau France 20 E3
Pau, Gave de → France 20 E2
Pauillac France 20 C3
Pauk Burma 67 J19
Paul I. Canada 105 A7
Paul Smiths U.S.A. 115 B10
Paulatuk Canada 100 C7
Paulhan France 20 E7
Paulistana Brazil 125 E10
Paulo Afonso Brazil 125 E11
Paulpietersburg S. Africa 89 D5
Pauls Valley U.S.A. 116 D6
Pauma Valley U.S.A. 111 M10
Pauri India 69 D8
Pāveh Iran 73 E12
Pavelets Russia 32 F10
Pavia Italy 40 C6
Pavilion U.S.A. 114 D6
Pavilly France 18 C7
Pāvilosta Latvia 30 B8
Pavlikeni Bulgaria 45 C9
Pavlodar Kazakhstan 52 D8
Pavlograd = Pavlohrad
   Ukraine 33 H8
Pavlohrad Ukraine 33 H8
Pavlovo Russia 34 C6
Pavlovsk Russia 34 E5
Pavlovskaya Russia 35 G4
Pavlovskiy-Posad Russia 32 E10
Pavullo nel Frignano Italy 40 D7
Pawai, Pulau Singapore 65 d
Pawayan India 69 E9
Pawhuska U.S.A. 116 C6
Pawling U.S.A. 115 E11
Pawnee U.S.A. 116 C6
Pawnee City U.S.A. 112 E5
Pawtucket U.S.A. 115 E13
Paxi Greece 46 B2
Paximadia Greece 49 E6
Paxton U.S.A. 112 E9
Payakumbuh Indonesia 62 E2
Payerne Switz. 25 J2
Paymogo Spain 37 H3
Payne Bay = Kangirsuk
   Canada 101 D13
Payne L. Canada 101 D12
Paynes Find Australia 93 E2
Paynesville Liberia 82 D2
Paynesville U.S.A. 112 C6
Pays de la Loire □ France 18 E6
Paysandú Uruguay 126 C4
Payson Ariz., U.S.A. 109 J8
Payson Utah, U.S.A. 108 F8
Paz → Guatemala 120 D1
Paz, B. de la Mexico 118 C2
Pāzanān Iran 71 D6
Pazar Turkey 73 B9
Pazarcık Turkey 72 D7
Pazardzhik Bulgaria 45 D8
Pazarköy Turkey 47 B9
Pazarlar Turkey 47 C11
Pazaryeri Turkey 47 B11
Pazaryolu Turkey 73 B9
Pazin Croatia 41 C10
Pčinja → Macedonia 44 E5
Pe Ell U.S.A. 110 D3
Peabody U.S.A. 115 D14
Peace → Canada 102 B6
Peace Point Canada 102 B6
Peace River Canada 102 B5
Peach Springs U.S.A. 109 J7
Peachland Canada 102 D5
Peachtree City U.S.A. 117 E12
Peak, The = Kinder Scout
   U.K. 14 D6
Peak Charles △ Australia 93 F3
Peak District △ U.K. 14 D6
Peak Hill N.S.W., Australia 95 E4
Peak Hill W. Austral.,
   Australia 93 E2
Peak Ra. Australia 94 C4
Peake Cr. → Australia 95 D2
Peal de Becerro Spain 37 H7
Peale, Mt. U.S.A. 108 G9
Pearblossom U.S.A. 111 L9
Pearl → U.S.A. 117 F10
Pearl City U.S.A. 106 b
Pearl Harbor U.S.A. 106 b
Pearl River = Zhu Jiang →
   China 59 F9
Pearl River U.S.A. 115 E10
Pearsall U.S.A. 116 G5
Pearson Int. Toronto ✈
   (YYZ) Canada 114 C5
Peary Land Greenland 4 A6
Pease → U.S.A. 116 D5
Peawanuck Canada 101 D11
Pebane Mozam. 87 F4
Pebas Peru 124 D4
Pebble Beach U.S.A. 110 J5
Peć Serbia 44 D4
Péccioli Italy 40 E7
Pechea Romania 29 E12
Pechenga Russia 8 B24
Pechenizhyn Ukraine 29 B9

Pechnezhskoye Vdkhr.
   Ukraine 33 G9
Pechora Russia 52 C6
Pechora → Russia 6 B16
Pechorskaya Guba Russia 52 C6
Pechory Russia 32 D4
Pecica Romania 28 D6
Pecka Serbia 44 B3
Pécora, C. Italy 42 C1
Pecos N. Mex., U.S.A. 109 J11
Pecos Tex., U.S.A. 116 F3
Pecos → U.S.A. 116 G4
Pécs Hungary 28 D3
Pedder, L. Australia 95 G4
Peddie S. Africa 89 E4
Pedernales Dom. Rep. 121 C5
Pedies → Cyprus 49 D12
Pedirka Australia 95 D2
Pedra Azul Brazil 125 G10
Pedra Lume C. Verde Is. 78 b
Pedreguer Spain 39 G5
Pedreiras Brazil 125 D10
Pedro Afonso Brazil 125 E9
Pedro Cays Jamaica 120 C4
Pedro de Valdivia Chile 126 A2
Pedro Juan Caballero
   Paraguay 127 A4
Pedro Muñoz Spain 37 F8
Pedrógão Grande Portugal 36 F2
Pee Dee = Great Pee
   Dee → U.S.A. 117 E15
Peebinga Australia 95 E3
Peebles U.K. 13 F5
Peekskill U.S.A. 115 E11
Peel I. of Man 14 C3
Peel → Australia 95 E5
Peel → Canada 100 C6
Peel Sd. Canada 100 B10
Peene → Germany 24 A9
Peera Peera Poolanna L.
   Australia 95 D2
Peerless Lake Canada 102 B6
Peers Canada 102 C5
Pegasus B. N.Z. 91 E4
Peggau Austria 26 D8
Pegnitz Germany 25 F7
Pegnitz → Germany 25 F6
Pego Spain 39 G4
Pegu Burma 67 L20
Pegu Yoma Burma 67 K20
Pehčevo Macedonia 44 E6
Pehlivanköy Turkey 45 E10
Pehuajó Argentina 126 D3
Pei Xian = Pizhou China 56 G9
Peikang Taiwan 59 F13
Peine Chile 126 A2
Peine Germany 24 C6
Peip'ing = Beijing China 56 E9
Peipus, L. = Chudskoye,
   Ozero Russia 32 C4
Peissenberg Germany 25 H7
Peitz Germany 24 D10
Peixe Brazil 125 F9
Peixe → Brazil 125 H8
Pek → Serbia 44 B5
Pekalongan Indonesia 63 G13
Pekan Malaysia 65 L4
Pekan Nenas Malaysia 65 d
Pekanbaru Indonesia 62 D2
Pekin U.S.A. 112 E9
Pekutatan Indonesia 63 J17
Pela Greece 44 F6
Péla Guinea 82 D3
Pelabuhan Klang Malaysia 65 L3
Pelabuhan Ratu, Teluk
   Indonesia 63 G12
Pelabuhanratu Indonesia 63 G12
Pélagos = Kira Panagia
   Greece 46 B6
Pelaihari Indonesia 62 E4
Pelat, Mt. France 21 D10
Pelée, Mt. Martinique 120 c
Pelee, Pt. Canada 104 D3
Pelee I. Canada 114 E2
Pelekech Kenya 86 B4
Peleng Indonesia 63 E6
Pelentong Malaysia 65 d
Pélézi Ivory C. 82 D3
Pelham U.S.A. 117 F10
Pelican U.S.A. 102 B1
Pelican L. Canada 103 C8
Pelican Narrows Canada 103 B8
Pelister △ Macedonia 44 F5
Pelješac Croatia 41 F14
Pelkosenniemi Finland 8 C22
Pella S. Africa 88 D2
Pella U.S.A. 112 E7
Pella △ Greece 44 F6
Pello Finland 8 C20
Pelly → Canada 102 A1
Pelly Bay Canada 101 C11
Peloponnese □ Greece 46 D4
Peloritani, Monti Italy 43 D8

Pelorus Sd. N.Z. 91 D4
Pelotas Brazil 127 C5
Pelotas → Brazil 127 B5
Pelovo Bulgaria 45 C8
Pelplin Poland 30 E5
Pelvoux, Massif du France 21 D10
Pemalang Indonesia 63 G13
Pemanggil, Pulau Malaysia 65 L5
Pematangsiantar Indonesia 62 D1
Pemba Mozam. 87 E5
Pemba Zambia 87 F2
Pemba Channel Tanzania 86 D4
Pemba I. Tanzania 86 D4
Pemberton Australia 93 F2
Pemberton Canada 102 C4
Pembina → Canada 102 C4
Pembine U.S.A. 112 C2
Pembroke Canada 104 C4
Pembroke U.K. 15 F3
Pembrokeshire □ U.K. 15 F3
Pembrokeshire Coast △
   U.K. 15 F2
Pen-y-Ghent U.K. 14 C5
Peña, Sierra de la Spain 38 C4
Peña de Francia, Sierra de
   la Spain 36 E4
Peñafiel Portugal 36 D2
Peñafiel Spain 36 D6
Peñaflor Spain 37 H5
Penal Trin. & Tob. 125 K15
Penalva Brazil 125 D9
Penamacôr Portugal 36 E3
Penang = Pinang Malaysia 65 c
Penápolis Brazil 127 A6
Peñaranda de Bracamonte
   Spain 36 E5
Peñarroya Spain 38 E4
Peñarroya-Pueblonuevo
   Spain 37 G5
Penarth U.K. 15 F4
Peñas, C. de Spain 36 B5
Peñas, G. de Chile 128 F2
Peñas de San Pedro Spain 39 G3
Peñas del Chache Canary Is. 48 E6
Peñausende Spain 36 D4
Pench △ India 69 J8
Pench'i = Benxi China 57 D12
Pend Oreille → U.S.A. 108 B5
Pend Oreille, L. U.S.A. 108 B5
Pendalofos Greece 44 F5
Pendembu Eastern, S. Leone 82 D2
Pendembu Northern, S. Leone 82 D2
Pender B. Australia 92 C3
Pendik Turkey 45 F13
Pendjari → Benin 83 C5
Pendjari △ Benin 83 C5
Pendleton U.S.A. 108 D4
Pendra India 69 H9
Peneda-Gerês △ Portugal 36 D2
Penedo Brazil 125 F11
Penelokan Indonesia 63 J18
Penetanguishene Canada 114 B5
Penfield U.S.A. 114 E6
Pengalengan Indonesia 63 G12
Penge Kasai-Or.,
   Dem. Rep. of the Congo 86 D1
Penge Sud-Kivu,
   Dem. Rep. of the Congo 86 C2
P'enghu Ch'üntou Taiwan 59 F12
Penglai China 57 F11
Pengshan China 58 B4
Pengshui China 58 C7
Penguin Australia 95 G4
Pengxi China 58 B5
Pengze China 59 C11
Penhalonga Zimbabwe 87 F3
Peniche Portugal 37 F1
Penicuik U.K. 13 F5
Penida, Nusa Indonesia 63 K18
Peninnes, Alpes =
   Pennine, Alpi Alps 25 J3
Peninsular Malaysia □
   Malaysia 65 L4
Peñíscola Spain 38 E5
Penitente, Serra do Brazil 125 E9
Penkridge U.K. 14 E5
Penmarch France 18 E2
Penmarch, Pte. de France 18 E2
Penn Hills U.S.A. 114 F5
Penn Yan U.S.A. 114 D7
Penna, Punta della Italy 41 F11
Pennant Canada 103 C7
Penne Italy 41 F10
Penner → India 66 M12
Pennine, Alpi Alps 25 J3
Pennines U.K. 14 C5
Pennington U.S.A. 110 F5
Pennington → Nigeria 83 E6
Pennino, Mte. Italy 41 E9
Pennsburg U.S.A. 115 F9
Pennsylvania □ U.S.A. 113 E15
Penny Canada 102 C4
Penny Str. Canada 101 B8
Peno Russia 32 D7
Penobscot → U.S.A. 113 C19
Penobscot B. U.S.A. 113 C19
Penola Australia 95 F3
Penong Australia 93 F5

Penonomé Panama 120 E3
Penrhyn Cook Is. 97 H12
Penrith Australia 95 E5
Penrith U.K. 14 C5
Penryn U.K. 15 G2
Pensacola U.S.A. 117 F11
Pensacola Mts. Antarctica 5 E1
Pense Canada 103 C8
Penshurst Australia 95 F3
Penticton Canada 102 D5
Pentland Australia 94 C4
Pentland Firth U.K. 13 C5
Pentland Hills U.K. 13 F5
Pentland Hills △ U.K. 13 F5
Penza Russia 34 D7
Penza □ Russia 34 D7
Penzance U.K. 15 G2
Penzberg Germany 25 H7
Penzhino Russia 53 C17
Penzhinskaya Guba Russia 53 C17
Penzhou China 58 B4
Penzlin Germany 24 B9
Peoria Ariz., U.S.A. 109 K7
Peoria Ill., U.S.A. 112 E9
Pepacton Res. U.S.A. 115 D10
Pepani → S. Africa 88 D3
Pepel S. Leone 82 D2
Peqin Albania 44 E3
Pera Hd. Australia 94 A3
Perabumulih Indonesia 62 E2
Perachora Greece 46 C4
Perak → Malaysia 65 K3
Perales de Alfambra Spain 38 E4
Perales del Puerto Spain 36 E4
Perama Kerkyra, Greece 49 A3
Perama Kriti, Greece 49 D6
Perancak Indonesia 63 J17
Peräpohjola Finland 8 C22
Perast Montenegro 44 D2
Percé Canada 105 C7
Perche France 18 D8
Perche △ France 18 D7
Perchtoldsdorf Austria 27 C9
Percival Lakes Australia 92 D4
Percy France 18 D5
Percy Is. Australia 94 C5
Perdido, Mte. Spain 38 C5
Perdido, Mte. = Perdido, Mte.
   Spain 38 C5
Perdu, Mt. = Perdido, Mte.
   Spain 38 C5
Perechyn Ukraine 28 B7
Pereira Colombia 124 C3
Perelazovskiy Russia 35 F6
Perenjori Australia 93 E2
Peresecina Moldova 29 C13
Pereslavl-Zalesskiy Russia 32 D10
Pereyaslav-Khmelnytskyy
   Ukraine 33 G6
Pereyma Ukraine 29 B14
Pérez, I. Mexico 119 C7
Perg Austria 26 C7
Pergamino Argentina 126 C3
Pérgine Valsugana Italy 41 B8
Pérgola Italy 41 E9
Perham U.S.A. 112 B6
Perhentian, Kepulauan
   Malaysia 65 K4
Peri → Turkey 73 C8
Periam Romania 28 D5
Péribonka → Canada 105 C5
Péribonka, L. Canada 105 B5
Perico Argentina 126 A2
Pericos Mexico 118 B3
Périers France 18 C5
Périgord France 20 D4
Périgord-Limousin △ France 20 C4
Périgueux France 20 C4
Perijá, Sierra de Colombia 124 B4
Perijá △ Venezuela 121 E5
Peristera Greece 46 B5
Peristerona → Cyprus 49 D12
Perito Moreno Argentina 128 F2
Perivol = Dragovishtitsa
   Bulgaria 44 D6
Perkasie U.S.A. 115 F9
Perković Croatia 41 E13
Perlas, Arch. de las Panama 120 E4
Perlas, Punta de Nic. 120 D3
Perleberg Germany 24 B7
Perlez Serbia 28 E5
Perm Russia 52 D6
Përmet Albania 44 F4
Pernambuco = Recife
   Brazil 125 E12
Pernambuco □ Brazil 125 E11
Pernatty Lagoon Australia 95 E2
Pernik Bulgaria 44 D7
Peron Is. Australia 92 B5
Peron Pen. Australia 93 E1
Péronne France 19 C9
Perosa Argentina Italy 40 D4
Perow Canada 102 C3
Perpignan France 20 F6
Perris U.S.A. 111 M9
Perros-Guirec France 18 D3

Perry Fla., U.S.A. 117 F13
Perry Ga., U.S.A. 117 E13
Perry Iowa, U.S.A. 112 E7
Perry Okla., U.S.A. 116 C6
Perryton U.S.A. 116 C4
Perryville U.S.A. 112 G9
Persan France 19 C9
Persberg Sweden 10 E8
Persembe Turkey 72 B7
Persepolis Iran 71 D7
Pershotravensk Ukraine 23 C14
Persia = Iran ■ Asia 71 C7
Persian Gulf Asia 71 E6
Perstorp Sweden 11 H7
Pertek Turkey 73 C8
Perth Australia 93 F2
Perth Canada 115 B8
Perth U.K. 13 E5
Perth □ U.K. 13 E5
Perth & Kinross □ U.K. 13 E5
Perth Amboy U.S.A. 115 F10
Perth-Andover Canada 105 C6
Perth Basin Oc. 96 L2
Pertuis France 21 E9
Pertusato, C. France 21 G13
Peru Ind., U.S.A. 112 E10
Peru N.Y., U.S.A. 115 B11
Peru ■ S. Amer. 124 D4
Peru Basin Pac. Oc. 97 J18
Peru-Chile Trench Pac. Oc. 124 G3
Perúgia Italy 41 E9
Perušic Croatia 41 D12
Pervomaysk Russia 34 C6
Pervomaysk Ukraine 33 H6
Pervouralsk Russia 52 D6
Pésaro Italy 41 E9
Pescadores = P'enghu
   Ch'üntou Taiwan 59 F12
Pescara Italy 41 F11
Pescara → Italy 41 F11
Péscia Italy 40 E7
Pescina Italy 41 F10
Peshawar Pakistan 68 B4
Peshkopi Albania 44 E4
Peshtera Bulgaria 45 D8
Peshtigo U.S.A. 112 C10
Peski Russia 34 E6
Pêso da Régua Portugal 36 D3
Pesqueira Brazil 125 E11
Pessac France 20 D3
Pest □ Hungary 28 C4
Pestovo Russia 32 C8
Pestravka Russia 34 D9
Petah Tiqwa Israel 74 C3
Petalidi Greece 46 E3
Petaling Jaya Malaysia 65 L3
Petaloudes Greece 49 C10
Petaluma U.S.A. 110 G4
Pétange Lux. 17 E5
Petaro Canada 105 C5
Petas Greece 46 B3
Petatlán Mexico 118 D4
Petauke Zambia 87 E3
Petawawa Canada 104 C4
Petén Itzá, L. Guatemala 120 C2
Peter I. Br. Virgin Is. 121 e
Peter I. Øy Antarctica 5 C16
Peter Pond L. Canada 103 B7
Peterbell Canada 104 C3
Peterborough Australia 95 E2
Peterborough Canada 114 B6
Peterborough U.K. 15 E7
Peterborough U.S.A. 115 D13
Peterborough □ U.K. 15 E7
Peterculter U.K. 13 D6
Peterhead U.K. 13 D7
Peterlee U.K. 14 C6
Petermann Ranges Australia 93 E5
Petersburg Alaska, U.S.A. 100 D6
Petersburg Pa., U.S.A. 114 F6
Petersburg Va., U.S.A. 113 G15
Petersburg W. Va., U.S.A. 113 F14
Petersfield U.K. 15 F7
Petershagen Germany 24 C4
Petília Policastro Italy 43 C9
Petit-Canal Guadeloupe 120 b
Petit Goâve Haiti 121 C5
Petit Jardin Canada 105 C8
Petit Lac Manicouagan
   Canada 105 B6
Petit-Mécatina → Canada 105 B8
Petit-Mécatina, Î. du
   Canada 105 B8
Petit Piton St. Lucia 121 f
Petit-Saguenay Canada 105 C5
Petit Saint Bernard, Col du
   Italy 21 C10
Petitcodiac Canada 105 C6
Petite Terre, Îles de la
   Guadeloupe 120 b
Petitot → Canada 102 A4
Petitsikapau L. Canada 105 B6
Petlad India 68 H5
Peto Mexico 119 C7
Petone N.Z. 91 D5
Petorca Chile 126 C1
Petoskey U.S.A. 113 C11

Petra *Jordan* **74** E4
Petra *Spain* **48** B10
Petra, Ostrova *Russia* **4** B13
Petrel = Petrer *Spain* **39** G4
Petrella, Monte *Italy* **42** A6
Petrer *Spain* **39** G4
Petreto-Bicchisano *France* **21** G12
Petrich *Bulgaria* **44** E7
Petrified Forest △ *U.S.A.* **109** J9
Petrijanec *Croatia* **41** B13
Petrikov = Pyetrikaw
  Belarus **23** B15
Petrila *Romania* **29** E8
Petrinja *Croatia* **41** C13
Petrodvorets *Russia* **32** C5
Petrolândia *Brazil* **125** E11
Petrolia *Canada* **114** D2
Petrolina *Brazil* **125** E10
Petropavl *Kazakhstan* **52** D7
Petropavlovsk = Petropavl
  Kazakhstan **52** D7
Petropavlovsk-
  Kamchatskiy *Russia* **53** D16
Petropavlovskiy =
  Akhtubinsk *Russia* **35** F8
Petrópolis *Brazil* **127** A7
Petroşani *Romania* **29** E8
Petrova Gora *Croatia* **41** C12
Petrovac *Montenegro* **44** D2
Petrovac *Serbia* **44** B5
Petrovsk *Russia* **34** D7
Petrovsk-Zabaykalskiy
  Russia **53** D11
Petrovskaya *Russia* **33** K9
Petrozavodsk *Russia* **32** B8
Petrus Steyn *S. Africa* **89** D4
Petrusburg *S. Africa* **88** D4
Petzeck *Austria* **26** E5
Peumo *Chile* **126** C1
Peureulak *Indonesia* **62** D1
Pevek *Russia* **53** C18
Peveragno *Italy* **40** D4
Peyrehorade *France* **20** E2
Peyruis *France* **21** D9
Pézenas *France* **20** E7
Pezinok *Slovak Rep.* **27** C10
Pfaffenhofen *Germany* **25** G7
Pfälzerwald △ *Germany* **25** F5
Pfarrkirchen *Germany* **25** G8
Pfeffenhausen *Germany* **25** G7
Pforzheim *Germany* **25** G4
Pfullendorf *Germany* **25** H5
Pfungstadt *Germany* **25** F4
Pha Taem △ *Thailand* **64** E5
Phaestos *Greece* **49** D6
Phagwara *India* **68** D6
Phala *Botswana* **88** C4
Phalera = Phulera *India* **68** F6
Phalodi *India* **68** F5
Phalsbourg *France* **19** D14
Phaluai, Ko *Thailand* **65** b
Phan *Thailand* **64** C2
Phan Rang *Vietnam* **65** G7
Phan Ri = Hoa Da *Vietnam* **65** G7
Phan Thiet *Vietnam* **65** G7
Phanae *Greece* **47** C7
Phanat Nikhom *Thailand* **64** F3
Phangan, Ko *Thailand* **65** H3
Phangnga *Thailand* **65** H2
Phangnga, Ao *Thailand* **65** a
Phanom Sarakham *Thailand* **64** F3
Phaphund *India* **69** F8
Pharenda *India* **69** F10
Pharr *U.S.A.* **116** H5
Phatthalung *Thailand* **65** J3
Phayao *Thailand* **64** C2
Phelps *U.S.A.* **114** D7
Phelps L. *Canada* **103** B8
Phenix City *U.S.A.* **117** E12
Phet Buri *Thailand* **64** F2
Phetchabun *Thailand* **64** D3
Phetchabun, Thiu Khao
  Thailand **64** E3
Phetchaburi = Phet Buri
  Thailand **64** F2
Phi Phi, Ko *Thailand* **65** J2
Phiafay *Laos* **64** E6
Phibun Mangsahan *Thailand* **64** E5
Phichai *Thailand* **64** D3
Phichit *Thailand* **64** D3
Philadelphia *Miss., U.S.A.* **117** E10
Philadelphia *N.Y., U.S.A.* **115** B9
Philadelphia *Pa., U.S.A.* **115** G9
Philip *U.S.A.* **112** C3
Philip *Greece* **45** E8
Philippeville *Belgium* **17** D4
Philippi *U.S.A.* **113** F13
Philippi L. *Australia* **94** C2
Philippine Basin *Pac. Oc.* **96** F5
Philippine Sea *Pac. Oc.* **96** F4
Philippine Trench =
  Mindanao Trench *Pac. Oc.* **61** F7
Philippines ■ *Asia* **61** F5
Philippolis *S. Africa* **88** E4
Philippopolis = Plovdiv
  Bulgaria **45** D8

Philipsburg *Canada* **115** A11
Philipsburg *Mont., U.S.A.* **108** C7
Philipsburg *Pa., U.S.A.* **114** F6
Philipstown = Daingean
  Ireland **12** C4
Philipstown *S. Africa* **88** E3
Phillip I. *Australia* **95** F4
Phillips *U.S.A.* **112** C8
Phillipsburg *Kans., U.S.A.* **112** F4
Phillipsburg *N.J., U.S.A.* **115** F9
Philmont *U.S.A.* **115** D11
Philomath *U.S.A.* **108** D2
Phimai *Thailand* **64** E4
Phitsanulok *Thailand* **64** D3
Phnom Dangrek *Thailand* **64** E5
Phnom Penh *Cambodia* **65** G5
Phnum Penh = Phnom
  Penh *Cambodia* **65** G5
Phoenicia *U.S.A.* **115** D10
Phoenix *Mauritius* **85** d
Phoenix *Ariz., U.S.A.* **109** K7
Phoenix *N.Y., U.S.A.* **115** C8
Phoenix Is. *Kiribati* **96** H10
Phoenixville *U.S.A.* **115** F9
Phon *Thailand* **64** E4
Phon Tiou *Laos* **64** D5
Phong ➤ *Thailand* **64** D4
Phong Saly *Laos* **58** G4
Phong Tho *Vietnam* **64** A4
Phonhong *Laos* **64** C4
Phonum *Thailand* **65** H2
Phosphate Hill *Australia* **94** C2
Photharam *Thailand* **64** F2
Phra Nakhon Si
  Ayutthaya *Thailand* **64** E3
Phra Thong, Ko *Thailand* **65** H2
Phrae *Thailand* **64** C3
Phrom Phiram *Thailand* **64** D3
Phrygia *Turkey* **72** C4
Phu Bia *Laos* **64** C4
Phu Chong-Na Yoi △
  Thailand **64** E5
Phu Dien *Vietnam* **64** C5
Phu Hin Rang Kla △
  Thailand **64** D3
Phu Krading △ *Thailand* **64** D3
Phu Loi *Laos* **64** B4
Phu Luang △ *Thailand* **64** D3
Phu Ly *Vietnam* **58** G5
Phu Phan △ *Thailand* **64** D4
Phu Quoc, Dao *Vietnam* **65** G4
Phu Tho *Vietnam* **58** G5
Phuc Yen *Vietnam* **58** G5
Phuket *Thailand* **65** a
Phuket, Ko *Thailand* **65** a
Phul *India* **68** D6
Phulad *India* **68** G5
Phulchari *Bangla.* **69** G13
Phulera *India* **68** F6
Phulpur *India* **69** G10
Phun Phin *Thailand* **65** H2
Piacenza *Italy* **40** C6
Piai, Tanjung *Malaysia* **65** d
Pian Cr. ➤ *Australia* **95** E4
Pian-Upe △ *Uganda* **86** B3
Piana *France* **21** F12
Pianella *Italy* **41** F11
Pianosa *Puglia, Italy* **41** F12
Pianosa *Toscana, Italy* **40** F7
Piapot *Canada* **103** D7
Pias *Portugal* **37** G3
Piaseczno *Poland* **31** F8
Piaski *Poland* **31** G9
Piastów *Poland* **31** F7
Piatra *Romania* **29** G10
Piatra Craiului △ *Romania* **29** E10
Piatra Neamţ *Romania* **29** D11
Piatra Olt *Romania* **29** F9
Piauí □ *Brazil* **125** E10
Piauí ➤ *Brazil* **125** E10
Piave ➤ *Italy* **41** C9
Piazza Ármerina *Italy* **43** E7
Pibor ➤ *Sudan* **81** F3
Pibor Post *Sudan* **81** F3
Picardie □ *France* **19** C10
Picardie, Plaine de *France* **19** C9
Picardy = Picardie □
  France **19** C10
Picayune *U.S.A.* **117** F10
Picerno *Italy* **43** B8
Pichhor *India* **69** G8
Pichilemu *Chile* **126** C1
Pichor *India* **68** G8
Pickerel L. *Canada* **104** C1
Pickering *U.K.* **14** C7
Pickering, Vale of *U.K.* **14** C7
Pickle Lake *Canada* **104** B1
Pickwick L. *U.S.A.* **117** D10
Pico *Azores* **78** a
Pico Bonito △ *Honduras* **120** C2
Pico Truncado *Argentina* **128** F3
Picos *Brazil* **125** E10
Picos de Europa △ *Spain* **36** B6
Picton *Australia* **95** E5
Picton *Canada* **114** B7
Picton *N.Z.* **91** D5
Pictou *Canada* **105** C7

Picture Butte *Canada* **102** D6
Pictured Rocks △ *U.S.A.* **112** B10
Picún Leufú *Argentina* **128** D3
Pidbuzh *Ukraine* **31** J10
Pidurutalagala *Sri Lanka* **66** R12
Piechowice *Poland* **31** H2
Piedimonte Matese *Italy* **43** A7
Piedmont = Piemonte □
  Italy **40** D5
Piedmont *Ala., U.S.A.* **117** E12
Piedmont *S.C., U.S.A.* **107** D10
Piedra ➤ *Spain* **38** D3
Piedrabuena *Spain* **37** G6
Piedrahita *Spain* **36** E5
Piedralaves *Spain* **36** E6
Piedras Blancas *Spain* **36** B5
Piedras Negras *Mexico* **118** B4
Piekary Śląskie *Poland* **31** H5
Pieksämäki *Finland* **32** A4
Pielinen *Finland* **8** E23
Piemonte □ *Italy* **40** D5
Pienaarsrivier *S. Africa* **89** D4
Pieniężno *Poland* **30** D7
Pieninský △ *Europe* **27** B13
Pieńsk *Poland* **31** G2
Piercefield *U.S.A.* **115** B10
Pierceland *Canada* **103** C7
Pieria □ *Greece* **44** F6
Pierpont *U.S.A.* **114** E4
Pierre *U.S.A.* **112** C3
Pierre-Buffière *France* **20** C5
Pierre-de-Bresse *France* **19** F12
Pierrefontaine-les-Varans
  France **19** E13
Pierrefort *France* **20** D6
Pierrelatte *France* **21** D8
Pierreville *Trin. & Tob.* **125** K16
Pies(➤ *Austria* **27** C9
Pieštany *Slovak Rep.* **27** C10
Piesting ➤ *Austria* **27** C9
Pieszyce *Poland* **31** H3
Piet Retief *S. Africa* **89** D5
Pietarsaari *Finland* **8** E20
Pietermaritzburg *S. Africa* **89** D5
Pietersburg = Polokwane
  S. Africa **89** C4
Pietragalla *Italy* **43** B8
Pietrasanta *Italy* **40** E7
Pietroşiţa *Romania* **29** E10
Pietrosul, Vf. *Maramureş,*
  Romania **29** C9
Pietrosul, Vf. *Suceava,*
  Romania **29** C10
Pieve di Cadore *Italy* **41** B9
Pieve di Teco *Italy* **40** D4
Pievepélago *Italy* **40** D7
Pigadítsa *Greece* **44** G5
Pigeon L. *Canada* **114** B6
Piges *Greece* **46** B3
Piggott *U.S.A.* **117** C9
Pigna *Italy* **40** E4
Pigüe *Argentina* **126** D3
Pihani *India* **69** F9
Pihlajavesi *Finland* **32** B5
Pijijiapan *Mexico* **119** D6
Pikalevo *Russia* **32** C8
Pikangikum *Canada* **103** C10
Pikes Peak *U.S.A.* **108** G11
Piketberg *S. Africa* **88** E2
Pikeville *U.S.A.* **113** G12
Pikou *China* **57** E12
Pikwitonei *Canada* **103** B9
Piła *Poland* **31** E3
Pila *Spain* **39** G3
Pilanesberg △ *S. Africa* **88** D4
Pilani *India* **68** E6
Pilar *Paraguay* **126** B4
Pilar de la Horadada *Spain* **39** H4
Pilat △ *France* **21** C8
Pilawa *Poland* **31** G8
Pilaya ➤ *Bolivia* **124** H6
Pilbara *Australia* **92** D2
Pilcomayo ➤ *Paraguay* **126** B4
Pilea *Greece* **44** F6
Pilgrim's Rest *S. Africa* **89** C5
Pilgrimstad *Sweden* **10** B9
Pili *Greece* **47** E9
Pilibhit *India* **69** E8
Pilica ➤ *Poland* **31** G8
Pilio, Oros *Greece* **46** B5
Pilipinas = Philippines ■
  Asia **61** F5
Pilis *Hungary* **28** C4
Pilisvörösvár *Hungary* **28** C3
Pilkhawa *India* **68** E7
Pilliga *Australia* **95** E4
Pilos *Greece* **46** E3
Pilot Mound *Canada* **103** D9
Pilot Point *U.S.A.* **116** E6
Pilot Rock *U.S.A.* **108** D4
Pilštanj *Slovenia* **41** B12
Piltene *Latvia* **30** A8
Pilzno *Poland* **31** J8
Pima *U.S.A.* **109** K9
Pimba *Australia* **95** E2
Pimenta Bueno *Brazil* **124** F6
Pimentel *Peru* **124** E3
Pin Valley △ *India* **68** D7

Pina de Ebro *Spain* **38** D4
Pinamalayan *Phil.* **61** E4
Pinang *Malaysia* **65** c
Pinar, C. des *Spain* **48** B10
Pinar del Río *Cuba* **120** B3
Pınarbaşı *Çanakkale, Turkey* **47** B8
Pınarbaşı *Kayseri, Turkey* **72** C7
Pınarhisar *Turkey* **45** E11
Pinatubo, Mt. *Phil.* **61** D3
Pinawa *Canada* **103** C9
Pincehely *Hungary* **28** D3
Pinchang *China* **58** B6
Pincher Creek *Canada* **102** D6
Pinchi L. *Canada* **102** C4
Pind Dadan Khan *Pakistan* — [not present]
Pindar ➤ *Australia* **93** E2
Pindi Gheb *Pakistan* **68** C5
Pindiga *Nigeria* **83** D7
Pindos △ *Greece* **46** B3
Pindos Oros *Greece* **46** B3
Pindus Mts. = Pindos Oros
  Greece **46** B3
Pine ➤ *B.C., Canada* **102** B4
Pine ➤ *Sask., Canada* **103** B7
Pine, C. *Canada* **105** C9
Pine Bluff *U.S.A.* **116** D8
Pine Bluffs *U.S.A.* **108** F11
Pine City *U.S.A.* **112** C8
Pine Cr. ➤ *U.S.A.* **114** E7
Pine Creek *Australia* **92** B5
Pine Falls *Canada* **103** C9
Pine Flat L. *U.S.A.* **110** J7
Pine Grove *U.S.A.* **115** F8
Pine Hill *Australia* **94** C4
Pine Pass *Canada* **102** B4
Pine Point *Canada* **102** A6
Pine Ridge *U.S.A.* **112** D2
Pine River *Canada* **103** C8
Pine River *U.S.A.* **112** B6
Pine Valley *U.S.A.* **111** N10
Pinecrest *U.S.A.* **110** G6
Pineda de Mar *Spain* **38** D7
Pinedale *Calif., U.S.A.* **110** J7
Pinedale *Wyo., U.S.A.* **108** E9
Pinega ➤ *Russia* **52** C5
Pinehouse L. *Canada* **103** B7
Pineimuta ➤ *Canada* **104** B1
Pinerolo *Italy* **40** D4
Pines, Akra *Greece* **45** F8
Pineto *Italy* **41** F11
Pinetop-Lakeside *U.S.A.* **109** J9
Pinetown *S. Africa* **89** D5
Pineville *U.S.A.* **116** F7
Piney *France* **19** D11
Ping ➤ *Thailand* **64** E3
Pingaring *Australia* **93** F2
Pingba *China* **58** D6
Pingbian *China* **58** F4
Pingchuan *China* **58** D3
Pingding *China* **56** F7
Pingdingshan *China* **56** H7
Pingdong *Taiwan* **59** F13
Pingdu *China* **57** F10
Pingelly *Australia* **93** F2
Pingguo *China* **58** F6
Pinghe *China* **59** E11
Pinghu *China* **59** B13
Pingjiang *China* **59** C9
Pingle *China* **59** E8
Pingli *China* **58** A7
Pingliang *China* **56** G4
Pinglu *China* **56** E7
Pingluo *China* **56** E4
Pingnan *Fujian, China* **59** D12
Pingnan *Guangxi Zhuangzu,*
  China **59** F8
Pingquan *China* **57** D10
Pingrup *Australia* **93** F2
Pingshan *China* **58** C5
Pingtan *China* **59** E12
Pingtang *China* **58** E6
P'ingtung *Taiwan* **59** F13
Pingwu *China* **56** H3
Pingxiang
  Guangxi Zhuangzu, China **58** F6
Pingxiang *Jiangxi, China* **59** D9
Pingyao *China* **56** F7
Pingyi *China* **57** G9
Pingyin *China* **56** F9
Pingyuan *Guangdong, China* **59** E10
Pingyuan *Shandong, China* **56** F9
Pingyuanjie *China* **58** F4
Pinhal *Brazil* **127** A6
Pinhal Novo *Portugal* **37** G2
Pinhel *Portugal* **36** E3
Pini *Indonesia* **62** D1
Pinios ➤ *Ilia, Greece* **46** D3
Pinios ➤ *Trikala, Greece* **46** B4
Pinjarra *Australia* **93** F2
Pink Mountain *Canada* **102** B4
Pinkafeld *Austria* **27** D9
Pinnacles △ *U.S.A.* **110** J5
Pinnaroo *Australia* **95** F3
Pinneberg *Germany* **24** B5

Pinon Hills *U.S.A.* **111** L9
Pinos *Mexico* **118** C4
Pinos, Mt. *U.S.A.* **111** L7
Pinos Pt. *U.S.A.* **109** H3
Pinos Puente *Spain* **37** H7
Pinrang *Indonesia* **63** E5
Pins, Pte. aux *Canada* **114** D3
Pinsk *Belarus* **23** B14
Pintados *Chile* **124** H5
Pinyang *China* **59** D13
Pinyug *Russia* **52** C5
Pioche *U.S.A.* **109** H6
Piombino *Italy* **40** F7
Piombino, Canale di *Italy* **40** F7
Pioner, Ostrov *Russia* **53** B10
Pionerskiy *Russia* **30** D7
Pionki *Poland* **31** G8
Piopiotaki = Milford Sd. *N.Z.* **91** F1
Piorini, L. *Brazil* **124** D6
Piotrków Trybunalski
  Poland **31** G6
Piove di Sacco *Italy* **41** C9
Pip *Iran* **71** E9
Pipar *India* **68** F5
Pipar Road *India* **68** F5
Piparia *Mad. P., India* **68** H8
Piparia *Mad. P., India* **68** J7
Piperi *Greece* **46** B6
Pipestone *U.S.A.* **112** D5
Pipestone ➤ *Canada* **104** B2
Pipestone Cr. ➤ *Canada* **103** D8
Piplan *Pakistan* **68** C4
Piploda *India* **68** H6
Pipmuacan, Rés. *Canada* **105** C5
Pippingarra *Australia* **92** D2
Pipriac *France* **18** E5
Piqua *U.S.A.* **113** E11
Piquiri ➤ *Brazil* **127** A5
Pir Panjal Range *India* **68** C7
Pir Sohrāb *Iran* **71** E9
Pīr Sohrāb *Iran* **71** E9
Pira *Benin* **83** D5
Piracicaba *Brazil* **127** A6
Piracuruca *Brazil* **125** D10
Pirae *Tahiti* **91** d
Piræus = Pireas *Greece* **46** D5
Piraiévs = Pireas *Greece* **46** D5
Pirajuí *Brazil* **127** A6
Piram I. *India* **68** J5
Piran *Slovenia* **41** C10
Pirané *Argentina* **126** B4
Pirano = Piran *Slovenia* **41** C10
Pirapora *Brazil* **125** G10
Pirawa *India* **68** G7
Pirdop *Bulgaria* **45** D8
Pireas *Greece* **46** D5
Pirgi *Greece* **47** C7
Pirgos *Ilia, Greece* **46** D3
Pirgos *Kriti, Greece* **47** F7
Pirgovo *Bulgaria* **45** C9
Piribebuy *Paraguay* **126** B4
Pirimapun *Indonesia* **63** F9
Pirin △ *Bulgaria* **44** E7
Pirin Planina *Bulgaria* **44** E7
Pirineos = Pyrénées *Europe* **20** F4
Piripiri *Brazil* **125** D10
Pirlangimpi *Australia* **92** B5
Pirmasens *Germany* **25** F3
Pirna *Germany* **24** E9
Pirot *Serbia* **44** C6
Piru *Indonesia* **63** E7
Piru *U.S.A.* **111** L8
Piryatin = Pyryatyn *Ukraine* **33** G7
Pisa *Italy* **40** E7
Pisa ➤ *Poland* **31** E8
Pisa, Firenze ✈ (PSA) *Italy* **40** E7
Pisagne *Italy* **40** C7
Pisagua *Chile* **124** G4
Pisarovina *Croatia* **41** C12
Pisco *Peru* **124** F3
Piscu *Romania* **29** E12
Písek *Czech Rep.* **26** B7
Pishan *China* **60** C2
Pishcha *Ukraine* **31** G10
Pishchanka *Ukraine* **29** B13
Pīshīn *Iran* **71** E9
Pishin *Pakistan* **68** D2
Pishin Lora ➤ *Pakistan* **68** E1
Pisidia *Turkey* **72** D4
Pising *Indonesia* **63** F6
Pismo Beach *U.S.A.* **111** K6
Piso, L. *Liberia* **82** D2
Pissila *Burkina Faso* **83** C4
Pissos *France* **20** D3
Pissouri *Cyprus* **49** E11
Pisticci *Italy* **43** B9
Pístóia *Italy* **40** E7
Pistol B. *Canada* **103** A10
Pisuerga ➤ *Spain* **36** D6
Pisz *Poland* **30** E8
Pit ➤ *U.S.A.* **108** F2
Pita *Guinea* **82** C2
Pitapunga L. *Australia* **95** E3
Pitcairn I. *Pac. Oc.* **97** K14
Pitch L. *Trin. & Tob.* **125** K15
Piteå *Sweden* **8** D19
Piteälven ➤ *Sweden* **8** D19

Piterka *Russia* **34** E8
Piteşti *Romania* **29** F9
Pithapuram *India* **67** L13
Pithara *Australia* **93** F2
Pithio *Greece* **45** E10
Pithiviers *France* **19** D9
Pithoragarh *India* **69** E9
Pithoro *Pakistan* **68** G3
Pitigliano *Italy* **41** F8
Pitkyaranta *Russia* **32** B6
Pitlochry *U.K.* **13** E5
Pitsilia *Cyprus* **49** E12
Pitt I. *Canada* **102** C3
Pittsburg *Calif., U.S.A.* **110** G5
Pittsburg *Kans., U.S.A.* **112** G6
Pittsburg *Tex., U.S.A.* **116** E7
Pittsburgh *U.S.A.* **114** F5
Pittsfield *Ill., U.S.A.* **112** F8
Pittsfield *Maine, U.S.A.* **113** C19
Pittsfield *Mass., U.S.A.* **115** D11
Pittsfield *N.H., U.S.A.* **115** C13
Pittston *U.S.A.* **115** E9
Pittsworth *Australia* **95** D5
Pituri ➤ *Australia* **94** C2
Piura *Peru* **124** E2
Piva ➤ *Montenegro* **44** C2
Piwniczna *Poland* **31** J7
Pixley *U.S.A.* **110** K7
Pizarra *Spain* **37** J6
Pizhou *China* **56** G9
Pizzo *Italy* **43** D9
Placentia *Canada* **105** C9
Placentia B. *Canada* **105** C9
Placer *Masbate, Phil.* **61** F6
Placer *Surigao N., Phil.* **61** G6
Placerville *U.S.A.* **110** G6
Placetas *Cuba* **120** B4
Plačkovica *Macedonia* **44** E6
Plainfield *N.J., U.S.A.* **115** F10
Plainfield *Ohio, U.S.A.* **114** F3
Plainfield *Vt., U.S.A.* **115** B12
Plains *Mont., U.S.A.* **108** C6
Plains *Tex., U.S.A.* **116** E3
Plainview *Nebr., U.S.A.* **112** D6
Plainview *Tex., U.S.A.* **116** D4
Plainwell *U.S.A.* **113** D11
Plaisance *France* **20** E4
Plaistow *U.S.A.* **115** D13
Plaka *Greece* **47** B7
Plaka, Akra *Greece* **49** D8
Plakenska Planina
  Macedonia **44** E5
Planá *Czech Rep.* **26** B5
Plana Cays *Bahamas* **121** B5
Planada *U.S.A.* **110** H6
Plancoët *France* **18** D4
Plandište *Serbia* **28** E6
Plano *U.S.A.* **116** E6
Plant City *U.S.A.* **117** G13
Plaquemine *U.S.A.* **116** F9
Plasencia *Spain* **36** E4
Plaški *Croatia* **41** C12
Plaster City *U.S.A.* **111** N11
Plaster Rock *Canada* **105** C6
Plastun *Russia* **54** B8
Plasy *Czech Rep.* **26** B6
Plata, Río de la ➤ *S. Amer.* **126** C4
Plátano ➤ *Italy* **42** E6
Platanos *Greece* **49** D5
Plateau □ *Nigeria* **83** D6
Platte *U.S.A.* **112** D4
Platte ➤ *Mo., U.S.A.* **112** F6
Platte ➤ *Nebr., U.S.A.* **112** E6
Platteville *U.S.A.* **112** D8
Plattling *Germany* **25** G8
Plattsburgh *U.S.A.* **115** B11
Plattsmouth *U.S.A.* **112** E6
Plau *Germany* **24** B8
Plauen *Germany* **24** E8
Plauer See *Germany* **24** B8
Plav *Montenegro* **44** D3
Plavinas *Latvia* **32** D3
Plavnica *Montenegro* **44** D3
Plavno *Croatia* **41** D13
Plavsk *Russia* **32** F9
Playa Blanca *Canary Is.* **48** F6
Playa Blanca Sur *Canary Is.* **48** F6
Playa de las Americas
  Canary Is. **48** F3
Playa de Mogán *Canary Is.* **48** G4
Playa del Carmen *Mexico* **119** C7
Playa del Inglés *Canary Is.* **48** G4
Playa Esmerelda *Canary Is.* **48** F5
Playgreen L. *Canada* **103** C9
Pleasant Bay *Canada* **105** C7
Pleasant Hill *U.S.A.* **110** H4
Pleasant Mount *U.S.A.* **115** E9
Pleasanton *Calif., U.S.A.* **110** H5
Pleasanton *Tex., U.S.A.* **116** G5
Pleasantville *N.J., U.S.A.* **113** F16
Pleasantville *Pa., U.S.A.* **114** E5
Pléaux *France* **20** C6
Plei Ku *Vietnam* **64** F7
Plélan-le-Grand *France* **18** D4
Pléneuf-Val-André *France* **18** D4
Plenița *Romania* **29** F8
Plenty ➤ *Australia* **94** C2

Plenty, B. of *N.Z.* **91** B6
Plentywood *U.S.A.* **108** B11
Plérin *France* **18** D4
Plessisville *Canada* **105** C5
Plestin-les-Grèves *France* **18** D3
Pleszew *Poland* **31** G4
Pleternica *Croatia* **28** E2
Plétipi, L. *Canada* **105** B5
Pleven *Bulgaria* **45** C8
Plevlja *Montenegro* **44** C3
Plevna *Canada* **114** B8
Plitvička Jezera △ *Croatia* **41** D12
Plješevica *Croatia* **41** D12
Ploaghe *Italy* **42** B1
Ploče *Croatia* **41** E14
Płock *Poland* **31** F6
Plöckenpass *Italy* **41** B9
Plöckenstein *Germany* **25** G9
Ploemeur *France* **18** E3
Ploërmel *France* **18** E4
Ploiești *Romania* **29** F11
Plomari *Greece* **47** C8
Plombières-les-Bains *France* **19** E13
Plomin *Croatia* **41** C11
Plön *Germany* **24** A6
Plonge, Lac la *Canada* **103** B7
Płońsk *Poland* **31** F7
Plopeni *Romania* **29** E10
Plopișului, Munții *Romania* **28** C7
Ploty *Poland* **30** E2
Plouaret *France* **18** D3
Plouay *France* **18** E3
Ploučnice → *Czech Rep.* **26** A7
Ploudalmézeau *France* **18** D2
Plouescat *France* **18** D2
Plougasnou *France* **18** D3
Plougastel-Daoulas *France* **18** D2
Plouguerneau *France* **18** D2
Plouha *France* **18** D4
Plouhinec *France* **18** E2
Plovdiv *Bulgaria* **45** D8
Plovdiv □ *Bulgaria* **45** D8
Plum *U.S.A.* **114** F5
Plum I. *U.S.A.* **115** E12
Plumas *U.S.A.* **110** F6
Plummer *U.S.A.* **108** C5
Plumtree *Zimbabwe* **87** G2
Plunge *Lithuania* **30** C8
Plužine *Montenegro* **44** C2
Plymouth *Trin. & Tob.* **125** J16
Plymouth *U.K.* **15** G3
Plymouth *Calif., U.S.A.* **110** G6
Plymouth *Ind., U.S.A.* **112** E10
Plymouth *Mass., U.S.A.* **115** E14
Plymouth *N.C., U.S.A.* **117** D16
Plymouth *N.H., U.S.A.* **115** C13
Plymouth *Pa., U.S.A.* **115** E9
Plymouth *Wis., U.S.A.* **112** D10
Plympton-Wyoming
    Canada **114** D2
Plynlimon = Pumlumon
    Fawr *U.K.* **15** E4
Plyusa *Russia* **32** C5
Plyusa → *Russia* **32** C5
Plzeň *Czech Rep.* **26** B6
Plzeňský □ *Czech Rep.* **26** B6
Pniewy *Poland* **31** F3
Pô *Burkina Faso* **83** C4
Po → *Italy* **41** D9
Po, Foci del *Italy* **41** D9
Pô △ *Burkina Faso* **83** C4
Po Hai = Bo Hai *China* **57** E10
Pobé *Benin* **83** D5
Pobé *Burkina Faso* **83** C4
Pobeda *Russia* **53** C15
Pobedy, Pik *Kyrgyzstan* **52** E8
Pobiedziska *Poland* **31** F4
Pobla de Segur *Spain* **38** C5
Pobra de Trives *Spain* **36** C3
Pocahontas *U.S.A.* **112** D6
Pocatello *U.S.A.* **108** E7
Počátky *Czech Rep.* **26** B8
Pochep *Russia* **33** F7
Pochinki *Russia* **34** C7
Pochinok *Russia* **32** E7
Pöchlarn *Austria* **26** C8
Pocking *Germany* **25** G9
Pocomoke City *U.S.A.* **113** F16
Poços de Caldas *Brazil* **127** A6
Podbořany *Czech Rep.* **26** A6
Poddębice *Poland* **31** G5
Poděbrady *Czech Rep.* **26** A8
Podensac *France* **20** D3
Podenzano *Italy* **40** D6
Podgorač *Croatia* **28** E3
Podgorica *Montenegro* **44** D3
Podgorie *Albania* **44** F4
Podilska Vysochyna
    Ukraine **29** B13
Podkova *Bulgaria* **45** F9
Podlapača *Croatia* **41** D12
Podlaskie □ *Poland* **31** E10
Podoleni *Romania* **29** D11
Podolínec *Slovak Rep.* **27** B13

Podolsk *Russia* **32** E9
Podor *Senegal* **82** B1
Podporozhye *Russia* **32** B8
Podu Iloaiei *Romania* **29** C12
Podu Turcului *Romania* **29** D12
Podujevo *Serbia* **44** D5
Podyji △ *Czech Rep.* **26** C8
Poel *Germany* **24** B6
Pofadder *S. Africa* **88** D2
Poggiardo *Italy* **43** B11
Poggibonsi *Italy* **40** E8
Póggio Mirteto *Italy* **41** F9
Pogoanele *Romania* **29** F12
Pogorzela *Poland* **31** G4
Pogradec *Albania* **44** F4
Pogranichnyy *Russia* **54** B5
Poh *Indonesia* **63** E6
Pohang *S. Korea* **57** F15
Pohjanmaa *Finland* **8** E20
Pohnpei *Micronesia* **96** G7
Pohorelá *Slovak Rep.* **27** C13
Pohořelice *Czech Rep.* **27** C9
Pohorje *Slovenia* **41** B12
Pohri *India* **68** G6
Poiana Mare *Romania* **28** G8
Poiana Ruscăi, Munții
    Romania **28** E7
Poiana Stampei *Romania* **29** C10
Poinsett, C. *Antarctica* **5** C8
Point Arena *U.S.A.* **110** G3
Point Baker *U.S.A.* **102** B2
Point Edward *Canada* **104** D3
Point Fortin *Trin. & Tob.* **125** K15
Point Hope *U.S.A.* **106** a
Point L. *Canada* **100** C3
Point Lisas Industrial
    Estate *Trin. & Tob.* **125** K15
Point Pedro *Sri Lanka* **66** Q12
Point Pelee △ *Canada* **114** E2
Point Pleasant *N.J., U.S.A.* **115** F10
Point Pleasant *W. Va.,
    U.S.A.* **113** F12
Point Reyes △ *U.S.A.* **110** G2
Pointe-à-Pitre *Guadeloupe* **120** b
Pointe-au-Pic = La
    Malbaie *Canada* **105** C5
Pointe-Claire *Canada* **115** A11
Pointe-Gatineau *Canada* **115** A9
Pointe-Noire *Congo* **84** E2
Pointe-Noire *Guadeloupe* **120** b
Poio *Spain* **36** C2
Poirino *Italy* **40** D4
Poisonbush Ra. *Australia* **92** D3
Poissonnier Pt. *Australia* **92** C2
Poitiers *France* **18** F7
Poitou *France* **20** B3
Poitou-Charentes □ *France* **20** B4
Poix-de-Picardie *France* **19** C8
Poix-Terron *France* **19** C11
Pojoaque *U.S.A.* **109** J10
Pokaran *India* **68** F4
Pokataroo *Australia* **95** D4
Pokhara *Nepal* **69** E10
Pokhvistnevo *Russia* **34** D11
Poko *Dem. Rep. of the Congo* **86** B2
Poko *Sudan* **81** F3
Pokrov *Russia* **32** E10
Pokrovsk *Russia* **53** C13
Pokrovskoye *Russia* **33** J10
Pola = Pula *Croatia* **41** D10
Pola *Russia* **32** D7
Pola de Allande *Spain* **36** B4
Pola de Lena *Spain* **36** B5
Pola de Siero *Spain* **36** B5
Pola de Somiedo *Spain* **36** B4
Polacca *U.S.A.* **109** J8
Polan *Iran* **71** E9
Pol'ana *Slovak Rep.* **27** C12
Poland ■ *Europe* **31** G3
Polanica-Zdrój *Poland* **31** H3
Polaniec *Poland* **31** H8
Polanów *Poland* **30** D3
Polar Bear △ *Canada* **104** A2
Polatlı *Turkey* **72** C5
Polatsk *Belarus* **32** E5
Polcura *Chile* **126** D1
Polczyn-Zdrój *Poland* **30** E3
Poleski △ *Poland* **31** G10
Polessk *Russia* **30** D8
Polesye = Pripet Marshes
    Europe **23** B15
Polgar *Hungary* **28** C6
Poli *Cameroon* **83** D7
Policastro, G. di *Italy* **43** C8
Police *Poland* **30** E1
Police, Pte. *Seychelles* **85** b
Polichnitos *Greece* **47** B8
Polička *Czech Rep.* **27** B9
Policoro *Italy* **43** B9
Poliegos *Greece* **46** E6
Poligiros *Greece* **44** F7
Polignano a Mare *Italy* **43** A9
Poligny *France* **19** F12
Polillo Is. *Phil.* **61** D5
Polillo Strait *Phil.* **61** D4
Polis *Cyprus* **49** D11
Polístena *Italy* **43** D9

Polk *U.S.A.* **114** E5
Polkowice *Poland* **31** G3
Polla *Italy* **43** B8
Pollachi *India* **66** P10
Pollença *Spain* **48** B10
Pollença, B. de *Spain* **48** B10
Póllica *Italy* **43** B8
Pollino, Mte. *Italy* **43** C9
Pollino △ *Italy* **43** C9
Polna *Russia* **32** C5
Polnovat *Russia* **52** C7
Polokwane *S. Africa* **89** C4
Polokwane → *S. Africa* **89** C5
Polonne *Ukraine* **23** C14
Polonnoye = Polonne
    Ukraine **23** C14
Polski Trümbesh *Bulgaria* **45** C9
Polsko Kosovo *Bulgaria* **45** C9
Polson *U.S.A.* **108** C6
Poltár *Slovak Rep.* **27** C12
Poltava *Ukraine* **33** H8
Poltava □ *Ukraine* **33** G7
Põltsamaa *Estonia* **32** C3
Polunochnoye *Russia* **52** C7
Põlva *Estonia* **32** C4
Polyana *Ukraine* **28** B7
Polyarny *Russia* **8** B25
Polyarnyye Zori *Russia* **8** C25
Polynesia *Pac. Oc.* **97** F11
Polynésie française =
    French Polynesia ☑
    Pac. Oc. **97** J13
Pomarance *Italy* **40** E7
Pombal *Portugal* **36** F2
Pombia *Greece* **49** E6
Pomene *Mozam.* **89** C6
Pomeroy *Ohio, U.S.A.* **113** F12
Pomeroy *Wash., U.S.A.* **108** C5
Pomézia *Italy* **42** A5
Pomichna *Ukraine* **33** H6
Pomona *Australia* **95** D5
Pomona *U.S.A.* **111** L9
Pomorie *Bulgaria* **45** D11
Pomorskie □ *Poland* **30** D5
Pomorskie, Pojezierze *Poland* **30** E3
Pomos *Cyprus* **49** D11
Pomos, C. *Cyprus* **49** D11
Pompano Beach *U.S.A.* **117** H14
Pompei *Italy* **43** B7
Pompey *France* **19** D13
Pompeys Pillar *U.S.A.* **108** D10
Pompeys Pillar △ *U.S.A.* **108** D10
Pompton Lakes *U.S.A.* **115** F10
Ponape = Pohnpei
    Micronesia **96** G7
Ponask L. *Canada* **104** B1
Ponca *U.S.A.* **112** D5
Ponca City *U.S.A.* **116** C6
Ponce *Puerto Rico* **121** d
Ponchatoula *U.S.A.* **117** F9
Poncheville, L. *Canada* **104** B4
Pond *U.S.A.* **111** K7
Pond Inlet *Canada* **101** B12
Pondicherry = Puducherry
    India **66** P11
Ponds, I. of *Canada* **105** B8
Ponferrada *Spain* **36** C4
Pongo, Wadi → *Sudan* **81** F2
Poniatowa *Poland* **31** G9
Poniec *Poland* **31** G3
Ponikva *Slovenia* **41** B12
Ponnani *India* **66** P9
Ponoka *Canada* **102** C6
Ponorogo *Indonesia* **63** G14
Pons = Ponts *Spain* **38** D6
Pons *France* **20** C3
Ponsul → *Portugal* **36** F3
Pont-à-Mousson *France* **19** D13
Pont-Audemer *France* **18** C7
Pont-Aven *France* **18** E3
Pont Canavese *Italy* **40** C4
Pont-d'Ain *France* **19** F12
Pont-de-Roide *France* **19** E13
Pont-de-Salars *France* **20** D6
Pont-de-Vaux *France* **19** F11
Pont-de-Veyle *France* **19** F11
Pont-du-Château *France* **19** G10
Pont-l'Abbé *France* **18** E2
Pont-l'Évêque *France* **18** C7
Pont-St-Esprit *France* **21** D8
Pont-St-Martin *Italy* **40** C4
Pont-Ste-Maxence *France* **19** C9
Pont-sur-Yonne *France* **19** D10
Ponta Delgada *Azores* **78** a
Ponta do Sol *Madeira* **48** D2
Ponta Grossa *Brazil* **127** B5
Ponta Pora *Brazil* **127** A4
Pontacq *France* **20** E3
Pontailler-sur-Saône *France* **19** E12
Pontarlier *France* **19** F13
Pontassieve *Italy* **41** E8
Pontaumur *France* **20** C6
Pontcharra *France* **21** C10
Pontchartrain, L. *U.S.A.* **117** F9
Pontchâteau *France* **18** E4
Ponte da Barca *Portugal* **36** D2

Ponte de Sor *Portugal* **37** F2
Ponte dell'Ólio *Italy* **40** D6
Ponte di Legno *Italy* **40** B7
Ponte do Lima *Portugal* **36** D2
Ponte do Pungué *Mozam.* **87** F3
Ponte-Leccia *France* **21** F13
Ponte nelle Alpi *Italy* **41** B9
Ponte Nova *Brazil* **127** A7
Ponteareas *Spain* **36** C2
Pontebba *Italy* **41** B10
Ponteceso *Spain* **36** B2
Pontecorvo *Italy* **42** A6
Pontedeume *Spain* **36** B2
Ponteix *Canada* **103** D7
Pontevedra *Spain* **36** C2
Pontevedra □ *Spain* **36** C2
Pontevedra, R. de → *Spain* **36** C2
Pontevico *Italy* **40** C7
Pontiac *Ill., U.S.A.* **112** E9
Pontiac *Mich., U.S.A.* **113** D12
Pontian Kechil *Malaysia* **65** d
Pontianak *Indonesia* **62** E3
Pontine Is. = Ponziane,
    Ísole *Italy* **42** B5
Pontine Mts. = Kuzey
    Anadolu Dağları *Turkey* **72** B7
Pontínia *Italy* **42** A6
Pontivy *France* **18** D3
Pontoise *France* **19** C9
Ponton → *Canada* **102** B5
Pontorson *France* **18** D5
Pontrémoli *Italy* **40** D6
Pontrieux *France* **18** D3
Ponts *Spain* **38** D6
Pontypool *Canada* **114** B6
Pontypool *U.K.* **15** F4
Ponza *Italy* **42** B5
Ponziane, Ísole *Italy* **42** B5
Poochera *Australia* **95** E1
Poole *U.K.* **15** G6
Poole □ *U.K.* **15** G6
Poona = Pune *India* **66** K8
Pooncarie *Australia* **95** E3
Poopelloe L. *Australia* **95** E3
Poopó, L. de *Bolivia* **124** G5
Popayán *Colombia* **124** C3
Poperinge *Belgium* **17** D2
Popiltah L. *Australia* **95** E3
Popina *Bulgaria* **45** B10
Popio L. *Australia* **95** E3
Poplar *U.S.A.* **108** B11
Poplar → *Canada* **103** C9
Poplar Bluff *U.S.A.* **112** G9
Poplarville *U.S.A.* **117** F10
Popocatépetl, Volcán
    Mexico **119** D5
Popokabaka
    Dem. Rep. of the Congo **84** F3
Pópoli *Italy* **41** F10
Popovača *Croatia* **41** C13
Popovo *Bulgaria* **45** C10
Poppberg *Germany* **25** F7
Poppi *Italy* **41** E8
Poprad *Slovak Rep.* **27** B13
Poprad → *Slovak Rep.* **27** B13
Porali → *Pakistan* **68** G2
Porbandar *India* **68** J3
Porcher I. *Canada* **102** C2
Porcuna *Spain* **37** H6
Porcupine → *Canada* **103** B8
Porcupine → *U.S.A.* **106** a
Porcupine Gorge △ *Australia* **94** C3
Pordenone *Italy* **41** C9
Pordim *Bulgaria* **45** C8
Poreč *Croatia* **41** C10
Poretskoye *Russia* **34** C8
Pori *Finland* **32** B1
Pori *Greece* **46** D5
Porkhov *Russia* **32** D5
Porlamar *Venezuela* **124** A6
Porlezza *Italy* **40** B6
Porma → *Spain* **36** C5
Pormpuraaw *Australia* **94** A3
Pornic *France* **18** E4
Poronaysk *Russia* **53** E15
Poros *Greece* **46** D5
Poroshiri-Dake *Japan* **54** C11
Poroszló *Hungary* **28** C5
Poroto Mts. *Tanzania* **87** D3
Porpoise B. *Antarctica* **5** C9
Porquerolles, Î. de *France* **21** F10
Porrentruy *Switz.* **25** H3
Porreres *Spain* **48** B10
Porsangerfjorden *Norway* **8** A21
Porsgrunn *Norway* **9** G13
Port Alberni *Canada* **102** D4
Port Alfred *S. Africa* **88** E4
Port Alice *Canada* **102** C3
Port Allegany *U.S.A.* **114** E6
Port Allen *U.S.A.* **117** F9
Port Alma *Australia* **94** C5
Port Angeles *U.S.A.* **110** B3
Port Antonio *Jamaica* **120** a
Port Aransas *U.S.A.* **116** H6
Port Arthur *Australia* **95** G4
Port Arthur *U.S.A.* **116** G8
Port au Choix *Canada* **105** B8

Port au Port B. *Canada* **105** C8
Port-au-Prince *Haiti* **121** C5
Port Augusta *Australia* **95** E2
Port Austin *U.S.A.* **114** B2
Port Bell *Uganda* **86** B3
Port Bergé Vaovao *Madag.* **89** B8
Port Blandford *Canada* **105** C9
Port Bradshaw *Australia* **94** A2
Port Broughton *Australia* **95** E2
Port Burwell *Canada* **114** D4
Port Canning *India* **69** H13
Port-Cartier *Canada* **105** B6
Port Chalmers *N.Z.* **91** F3
Port Charlotte *U.S.A.* **117** H13
Port Chester *U.S.A.* **115** F11
Port Clements *Canada* **102** C2
Port Clinton *U.S.A.* **113** E12
Port Colborne *Canada* **114** D5
Port Coquitlam *Canada* **110** A4
Port Credit *Canada* **114** C5
Port-Cros △ *France* **21** F10
Port Curtis *Australia* **94** C5
Port d'Alcúdia *Spain* **48** B10
Port Dalhousie *Canada* **114** C5
Port d'Andratx *Spain* **48** B9
Port Darwin *Australia* **92** B5
Port Darwin *Falk. Is.* **128** G5
Port Davey *Australia* **95** G4
Port-de-Bouc *France* **21** E8
Port-de-Paix *Haiti* **121** C5
Port de Pollença *Spain* **48** B10
Port de Sóller *Spain* **48** B9
Port Dickson *Malaysia* **65** L3
Port Douglas *Australia* **94** B4
Port Dover *Canada* **114** D4
Port Edward *Canada* **102** C2
Port Elgin *Canada* **114** B3
Port Elizabeth *S. Africa* **88** E4
Port Ellen *U.K.* **13** F2
Port-en-Bessin-Huppain
    France **18** C6
Port Erin *I. of Man* **14** C3
Port Essington *Australia* **92** B5
Port Ewen *U.S.A.* **115** E11
Port Fairy *Australia* **95** F3
Port Fouâd = Bûr Fuad
    Egypt **80** H8
Port Gamble *U.S.A.* **110** C4
Port-Gentil *Gabon* **84** E1
Port Germein *Australia* **95** E2
Port Gibson *U.S.A.* **116** F9
Port Glasgow *U.K.* **13** F4
Port Harcourt *Nigeria* **83** E6
Port Hardy *Canada* **102** C3
Port Harrison = Inukjuak
    Canada **101** D12
Port Hawkesbury *Canada* **105** C7
Port Hedland *Australia* **92** D2
Port Henry *U.S.A.* **115** B11
Port Hood *Canada* **105** C7
Port Hope *Canada* **114** C6
Port Hope *U.S.A.* **114** C2
Port Hope Simpson *Canada* **105** B8
Port Hueneme *U.S.A.* **111** L7
Port Huron *U.S.A.* **114** D2
Port Iliç *Azerbaijan* **73** C13
Port Jefferson *U.S.A.* **115** F11
Port Jervis *U.S.A.* **115** E10
Port Katon *Russia* **33** J10
Port Kelang = Pelabuhan
    Klang *Malaysia* **65** L3
Port Kenny *Australia* **95** E1
Port Laoise *Ireland* **12** C4
Port Lavaca *U.S.A.* **116** G6
Port Leyden *U.S.A.* **115** C9
Port Lincoln *Australia* **95** E2
Port Loko *S. Leone* **82** D2
Port Louis *France* **18** E3
Port-Louis *Guadeloupe* **120** b
Port Louis *Mauritius* **85** d
Port MacDonnell *Australia* **95** F3
Port McNeill *Canada* **102** C3
Port Macquarie *Australia* **95** E5
Port Maria *Jamaica* **120** a
Port Matilda *U.S.A.* **114** F6
Port Mellon *Canada* **102** D4
Port-Menier *Canada* **105** C7
Port Moody *Canada* **110** A4
Port Morant *Jamaica* **120** a
Port Moresby *Papua N. G.* **90** B7
Port Musgrave *Australia* **94** A3
Port-Navalo *France* **18** E4
Port Neches *U.S.A.* **116** G8
Port Nolloth *S. Africa* **88** D2
Port Nouveau-Québec =
    Kangiqsualujjuaq *Canada*
    101 D13
Port of Spain *Trin. & Tob.* **121** D7
Port Orange *U.S.A.* **117** G14
Port Orchard *U.S.A.* **110** C4
Port Orford *U.S.A.* **108** E1
Port Pegasus *N.Z.* **91** G1

Port Perry *Canada* **114** B6
Port Phillip B. *Australia* **95** F3
Port Pirie *Australia* **95** E2
Port Renfrew *Canada* **110** B2
Port Roper *Australia* **94** A2
Port Rowan *Canada* **114** D4
Port Safaga = Bûr Safâga
    Egypt **70** E2
Port Said = Bûr Sa'îd *Egypt* **80** H8
Port St. Joe *U.S.A.* **117** G12
Port St. Johns =
    Umzimvubu *S. Africa* **89** E4
Port-St-Louis-du-Rhône
    France **21** E8
Port St. Lucie *U.S.A.* **117** H14
Port-Ste-Marie *France* **20** D4
Port Sanilac *U.S.A.* **114** C2
Port Severn *Canada* **114** B5
Port Shepstone *S. Africa* **89** E5
Port Simpson *Canada* **102** C2
Port Stanley = Stanley
    Falk. Is. **128** G5
Port Stanley *Canada* **114** D3
Port Sudan = Bûr Sûdân
    Sudan **80** D4
Port Sulphur *U.S.A.* **117** G10
Port-sur-Saône *France* **19** E13
Port Talbot *U.K.* **15** F4
Port Taufiq = Bûr Taufiq
    Egypt **80** J8
Port Townsend *U.S.A.* **110** B4
Port-Vendres *France* **20** F7
Port Vila *Vanuatu* **90** C9
Port Vladimir *Russia* **8** B25
Port Wakefield *Australia* **95** E2
Port Washington *U.S.A.* **112** D10
Porta Orientalis *Romania* **23** F12
Portacloy *Ireland* **12** B2
Portadown *U.K.* **12** B5
Portaferry *U.K.* **12** B6
Portage *Pa., U.S.A.* **114** F6
Portage *Wis., U.S.A.* **112** D9
Portage la Prairie *Canada* **103** D9
Portageville *U.S.A.* **112** G9
Portalegre *Portugal* **37** F3
Portalegre □ *Portugal* **37** F3
Portales *U.S.A.* **109** J12
Portarlington *Ireland* **12** C4
Portbou *Spain* **38** C8
Portel *Portugal* **37** G3
Portela, Lisboa ✈ (LIS)
    Portugal **37** G1
Porter L. *N.W.T., Canada* **103** A7
Porter L. *Sask., Canada* **103** B7
Porterville *S. Africa* **88** E2
Porterville *U.S.A.* **110** J8
Portes-lès-Valence *France* **21** D8
Porthcawl *U.K.* **15** F4
Porthill *U.S.A.* **108** B5
Porthmadog *U.K.* **14** E3
Portile de Fier *Europe* **28** F6
Portimão *Portugal* **37** H2
Portishead *U.K.* **15** F5
Portiței, Gura *Romania* **29** F14
Portknockie *U.K.* **13** D6
Portland *N.S.W., Australia* **95** E4
Portland *Vic., Australia* **95** F3
Portland *Canada* **115** B8
Portland *Conn., U.S.A.* **115** E12
Portland *Maine, U.S.A.* **113** D18
Portland *Mich., U.S.A.* **113** D11
Portland *Oreg., U.S.A.* **110** E4
Portland *Pa., U.S.A.* **115** F9
Portland *Tex., U.S.A.* **116** H6
Portland, I. of *U.K.* **15** G5
Portland B. *Australia* **95** F3
Portland Bight *Jamaica* **120** a
Portland Bill *U.K.* **15** G5
Portland Canal *U.S.A.* **102** B2
Portland Int. ✈ (PDX)
    U.S.A. **110** E4
Portland Pt. *Jamaica* **120** a
Portmadoc = Porthmadog
    U.K. **14** E3
Portmore *Jamaica* **120** a
Porto *France* **21** F12
Porto *Portugal* **36** D2
Porto □ *Portugal* **36** D2
Porto, G. de *France* **21** F12
Pôrto Alegre *Brazil* **127** C5
Porto Azzurro *Italy* **40** F7
Porto Cristo *Spain* **48** B10
Pôrto de Móz *Brazil* **125** D8
Porto Empédocle *Italy* **42** E6
Pôrto Esperança *Brazil* **124** G7
Pôrto Franco *Brazil* **125** E9
Porto Inglês *C. Verde Is.* **78** b
Pôrto Mendes *Brazil* **127** A5
Pôrto Moniz *Madeira* **48** D2
Pôrto Murtinho *Brazil* **124** H7
Pôrto Nacional *Brazil* **125** F9
Porto-Novo *Benin* **83** D5
Porto Petro *Spain* **48** B10
Porto San Giórgio *Italy* **41** E10
Porto Sant' Elpídio *Italy* **41** E10
Porto Santo, I. de *Madeira* **78** B2
Porto Santo Stéfano *Italy* **40** F8

Pôrto São José *Brazil* **127** A5
Pôrto Seguro *Brazil* **125** G11
Porto Tolle *Italy* **41** D9
Porto Tórres *Italy* **42** B1
Pôrto União *Brazil* **127** B5
Pôrto Vâlter *Brazil* **124** E4
Porto-Vecchio *France* **21** G13
Pôrto Velho *Brazil* **124** E6
Portobelo *Panama* **120** E4
Portoferráio *Italy* **40** F7
Portogruaro *Italy* **41** C9
Portola *U.S.A.* **110** F6
Portomaggiore *Italy* **41** D8
Portoscuso *Italy* **42** C1
Portovénere *Italy* **40** D6
Portoviejo *Ecuador* **124** D2
Portpatrick *U.K.* **13** G3
Portree *U.K.* **13** D2
Portrush *U.K.* **12** A5
Portsmouth *Dominica* **121** C7
Portsmouth *U.K.* **15** G6
Portsmouth *N.H., U.S.A.* **115** C14
Portsmouth *Ohio, U.S.A.* **113** F12
Portsmouth *R.I., U.S.A.* **115** E13
Portsmouth *Va., U.S.A.* **113** G15
Portsmouth □ *U.K.* **15** G6
Portsoy *U.K.* **13** D6
Portstewart *U.K.* **12** A5
Porttipahdan tekojärvi
     Finland **8** B22
Portugal ■ *Europe* **36** F3
Portugalete *Spain* **38** B1
Portumna *Ireland* **12** C3
Portville *U.S.A.* **114** D6
Porvenir *Chile* **128** G2
Porvoo *Finland* **32** B3
Porzuna *Spain* **37** F6
Posada *Italy* **42** B2
Posada → *Italy* **42** B2
Posadas *Argentina* **127** B4
Posadas *Spain* **37** H5
Poschiavo *Switz.* **25** J6
Posets *Spain* **38** C5
Posht-e Badam *Iran* **71** C7
Posidium *Greece* **47** F9
Poso *Indonesia* **63** E6
Posse *Brazil* **125** F9
Possession I. *Antarctica* **5** D11
Pössneck *Germany* **24** E7
Possum Kingdom L. *U.S.A.* **116** E5
Post *U.S.A.* **116** E4
Post Falls *U.S.A.* **108** C5
Postavy = Pastavy *Belarus* **32** E4
Poste-de-la-Baleine =
     Kuujjuarapik *Canada* **104** A4
Postmasburg *S. Africa* **88** D3
Postojna *Slovenia* **41** C11
Poston *U.S.A.* **111** M12
Postville *Canada* **105** B8
Potamos *Antikythira, Greece* **46** F5
Potamos *Kythira, Greece* **46** E4
Potchefstroom *S. Africa* **88** D4
Potcoava *Romania* **29** F9
Poteau *U.S.A.* **116** D7
Poteet *U.S.A.* **116** G5
Potenza *Italy* **43** B8
Potenza → *Italy* **41** E10
Potenza Picena *Italy* **41** E10
Poteriteri, L. *N.Z.* **91** G1
Potgietersrus = Mokopane
     S. Africa **89** C4
Poti *Georgia* **35** J5
Potiskum *Nigeria* **83** C7
Potlogi *Romania* **29** F10
Potomac → *U.S.A.* **113** F14
Potosí *Bolivia* **124** G5
Potosi Mt. *U.S.A.* **111** K11
Pototan *Phil.* **61** F5
Potrerillos *Chile* **126** B2
Potsdam *Germany* **24** C9
Potsdam *U.S.A.* **115** B10
Pottenstein *Germany* **25** F7
Pottersville *U.S.A.* **115** C11
Pottsville *U.S.A.* **115** F8
Pottuvil *Sri Lanka* **66** R12
P'otzu *Taiwan* **59** F13
Pouancé *France* **18** E5
Pouce Coupé *Canada* **102** B4
Poughkeepsie *U.S.A.* **115** E11
Pouilly-sur-Loire *France* **19** E9
Poulaphouca Res. *Ireland* **12** C5
Poulsbo *U.S.A.* **110** C4
Poultney *U.S.A.* **115** C11
Poulton-le-Fylde *U.K.* **14** D5
Pouso Alegre *Brazil* **127** A6
Pout *Senegal* **82** C1
Pouthisat *Cambodia* **64** F4
Pouzauges *France* **18** F6
Pova de Santa Iria *Portugal* **37** G1
Považská Bystrica
     Slovak Rep. **27** B11
Poverty B. *N.Z.* **91** C7
Povlen *Serbia* **44** B3
Póvoa de Lanhosa *Portugal* **36** D2
Póvoa de Varzim *Portugal* **36** D2
Povorino *Russia* **34** E6

Povungnituk = Puvirnituq
     Canada **101** C12
Powassan *Canada* **104** C4
Poway *U.S.A.* **111** N9
Powder → *U.S.A.* **108** C11
Powder River *U.S.A.* **108** E10
Powell *U.S.A.* **108** D9
Powell, L. *U.S.A.* **109** H8
Powell River *Canada* **102** D4
Powers *U.S.A.* **112** C10
Powys □ *U.K.* **15** E4
Poyang Hu *China* **59** C11
Poyarkovo *Russia* **53** E13
Poysdorf *Austria* **27** C9
Poza de la Sal *Spain* **36** C7
Poza Rica *Mexico* **119** C5
Pozanti *Turkey* **72** D6
Požarevac *Serbia* **44** B5
Pozazal, Puerto *Spain* **36** C6
Požega *Croatia* **28** E2
Požega *Serbia* **44** C4
Poznań *Poland* **31** F3
Poznań ✕ (POZ) *Poland* **31** F3
Pozo *U.S.A.* **111** K6
Pozo Alcón *Spain* **37** H8
Pozo Almonte *Chile* **124** H5
Pozo Colorado *Paraguay* **126** A4
Pozoblanco *Spain* **37** G6
Pozzallo *Italy* **43** F7
Pozzomaggiore *Italy* **42** B1
Pozzuoli *Italy* **43** B7
Pra → *Ghana* **83** D4
Prabuty *Poland* **30** E6
Prača *Bos.-H.* **28** G3
Prachatice *Czech Rep.* **26** B6
Prachin Buri *Thailand* **64** F3
Prachuap Khiri Khan
     Thailand **65** G2
Pradelles *France* **20** D7
Prades *France* **20** F6
Prado *Brazil* **125** G11
Prado del Rey *Spain* **37** J5
Præstø *Denmark* **11** J6
Pragersko *Slovenia* **41** B12
Prague = Praha *Czech Rep.* **26** A7
Praha *Czech Rep.* **26** A7
Praha ✕ (PRG) *Czech Rep.* **26** A7
Prahecq *France* **20** B3
Prahova □ *Romania* **29** E10
Prahova → *Romania* **29** F10
Prahovo *Serbia* **44** B6
Praia *C. Verde Is.* **78** b
Praia a Mare *Italy* **43** C8
Praid *Romania* **29** D10
Prainha *Amazonas, Brazil* **124** E6
Prainha *Pará, Brazil* **125** D8
Prairie *Australia* **94** C3
Prairie City *U.S.A.* **108** D4
Prairie Dog Town Fork
     Red → *U.S.A.* **116** D5
Prairie du Chien *U.S.A.* **112** D8
Prairies, L. of the *Canada* **103** C8
Pramanda *Greece* **46** B3
Prampram *Ghana* **83** D5
Pran Buri *Thailand* **64** F2
Prang *Ghana* **83** D4
Prapat *Indonesia* **62** D1
Praslin *Seychelles* **85** b
Praso, Akra *Greece* **49** D9
Prästmon *Sweden* **10** A11
Praszka *Poland* **31** G5
Prata *Brazil* **125** E9
Pratabpur *India* **69** H10
Pratapgarh *Raj., India* **68** G6
Pratapgarh *Ut. P., India* **69** G9
Pratas Is. = Dongsha Dao
     China **59** G11
Prato *Italy* **40** E8
Prátola Peligna *Italy* **41** F10
Prats-de-Mollo-la-Preste
     France **20** F6
Pratt *U.S.A.* **112** G4
Prattville *U.S.A.* **117** E11
Pravdinsk *Kaliningrad, Russia* **30** D8
Pravdinsk *Nizhniy Novgorod,*
     Russia **34** B6
Pravets *Bulgaria* **44** D7
Pravia *Spain* **36** B4
Praya *Indonesia* **62** F5
Pré-en-Pail *France* **18** D6
Precipice △ *Australia* **95** D5
Precordillera *Argentina* **126** C2
Predáppio *Italy* **41** D8
Predazzo *Italy* **41** B8
Predeal *Romania* **29** E10
Predejane *Serbia* **44** D6
Preeceville *Canada* **103** C8
Preetz *Germany* **24** A6
Pregolya → *Russia* **30** D7
Pregrada *Croatia* **41** B12
Preili *Latvia* **32** D4
Preko *Croatia* **41** D12
Prelog *Croatia* **41** B13
Prémery *France* **19** E10
Premià de Mar *Spain* **38** D7
Premont *U.S.A.* **116** H5
Premuda *Croatia* **41** D11

Prentice *U.S.A.* **112** C8
Prenzlau *Germany* **24** B9
Preobrazheniye *Russia* **54** C6
Preparis North Channel
     Ind. Oc. **67** M18
Preparis South Channel
     Ind. Oc. **67** M18
Přerov *Czech Rep.* **27** B10
Prescott *Canada* **115** B9
Prescott *Ariz., U.S.A.* **109** J7
Prescott *Ark., U.S.A.* **116** E8
Prescott Valley *U.S.A.* **109** J7
Preservation Inlet *N.Z.* **91** G1
Preševo *Serbia* **44** D5
Presho *U.S.A.* **112** D3
Presicce *Italy* **43** C11
Presidencia de la Plaza
     Argentina **126** B4
Presidencia Roque Sáenz
     Peña *Argentina* **126** B3
Presidente Epitácio *Brazil* **125** H8
Presidente Hayes □
     Paraguay **126** A4
Presidente Prudente *Brazil* **127** A5
Presidio *Mexico* **118** B4
Presidio *U.S.A.* **116** G2
Preslav *Bulgaria* **45** C10
Preslavska Planina
     Bulgaria **45** C10
Prešov *Slovak Rep.* **27** B14
Prešovský □ *Slovak Rep.* **27** B14
Prespa *Bulgaria* **45** E8
Prespa, L. = Prespansko
     Jezero *Macedonia* **44** F5
Prespa △ *Greece* **44** F5
Prespansko Jezero *Macedonia* **44** F5
Presque I. *U.S.A.* **114** D4
Presque Isle *U.S.A.* **113** B19
Prestatyn *U.K.* **14** D4
Prestea *Ghana* **82** D4
Presteigne *U.K.* **15** E5
Přeštice *Czech Rep.* **26** B6
Preston *Canada* **114** C4
Preston *U.K.* **14** D5
Preston *Idaho, U.S.A.* **108** E8
Preston *Minn., U.S.A.* **112** D7
Preston, C. *Australia* **92** D2
Prestonsburg *U.S.A.* **113** G12
Prestranda *Norway* **10** E3
Prestwick *U.K.* **13** F4
Pretoria *S. Africa* **89** D4
Preuilly-sur-Claise *France* **18** F7
Preveza *Greece* **46** C2
Préveza □ *Greece* **46** B2
Prey Veng *Cambodia* **65** G5
Priazovskoye *Ukraine* **33** J8
Pribilof Is. *U.S.A.* **106** a
Priboj *Serbia* **44** C3
Příbram *Czech Rep.* **26** B7
Price *U.S.A.* **108** G8
Price I. *Canada* **102** C3
Prichard *U.S.A.* **117** F10
Priego *Spain* **38** E2
Priego de Córdoba *Spain* **37** H6
Priekule *Latvia* **30** B8
Priekule *Lithuania* **30** C8
Prien *Germany* **25** H8
Prienai *Lithuania* **30** D10
Prieska *S. Africa* **88** D3
Priest L. *U.S.A.* **108** B5
Priest River *U.S.A.* **108** B5
Priest Valley *U.S.A.* **110** J6
Prievidza *Slovak Rep.* **27** C11
Prignitz *Germany* **24** B7
Prijedor *Bos.-H.* **41** D13
Prijepolje *Serbia* **44** C3
Prikaspiyskaya
     Nizmennost = Caspian
     Depression *Eurasia* **35** G9
Prikro *Ivory C.* **82** D4
Prikubanskaya
     Nizmennost *Russia* **35** H4
Prilep *Macedonia* **44** E5
Priluki = Pryluky *Ukraine* **33** G7
Prime Seal I. *Australia* **95** G4
Primo Tapia *Mexico* **111** N10
Primorsk *Kaliningrad, Russia* **30** D6
Primorsk *St. Petersburg,*
     Russia **32** B5
Primorsko *Bulgaria* **45** D11
Primorsko-Akhtarsk
     Russia **33** J10
Primorskoye *Ukraine* **33** J9
Primrose L. *Canada* **103** C7
Prince Albert *Canada* **103** C7
Prince Albert *S. Africa* **88** E3
Prince Albert △ *Canada* **103** C7
Prince Albert Mts. *Antarctica* **5** D11
Prince Albert Pen. *Canada* **100** B8
Prince Albert Sd. *Canada* **100** B8
Prince Alfred, C. *Canada* **101** B7
Prince Charles I. *Canada* **101** C12
Prince Charles Mts. *Antarctica* **5** D6
Prince Edward Fracture
     Zone *Ind. Oc.* **5** A4
Prince Edward I. □ *Canada* **105** C7
Prince Edward Is. *Ind. Oc.* **3** G11

Prince Edward Pt. *Canada* **114** C8
Prince George *Canada* **102** C4
Prince Gustaf Adolf Sea
     Canada **101** B9
Prince of Wales, C. *U.S.A.* **98** C3
Prince of Wales I. *Australia* **94** A3
Prince of Wales I. *Canada* **100** B10
Prince of Wales I. *U.S.A.* **100** D6
Prince Patrick I. *Canada* **101** B8
Prince Regent Inlet *Canada* **4** B3
Prince Rupert *Canada* **102** C2
Princes Town *Trin. & Tob.* **125** K15
Princess Charlotte B.
     Australia **94** A3
Princess Elizabeth Trough
     S. Ocean **5** C7
Princess May Ranges
     Australia **92** C4
Princess Royal I. *Canada* **102** C3
Princeton *Canada* **102** D4
Princeton *Calif., U.S.A.* **110** F4
Princeton *Ill., U.S.A.* **112** E9
Princeton *Ind., U.S.A.* **112** F10
Princeton *Ky., U.S.A.* **112** G10
Princeton *Mo., U.S.A.* **112** E7
Princeton *N.J., U.S.A.* **115** F10
Princeton *W. Va., U.S.A.* **113** G13
Príncipe *São Tomé & Príncipe* **76** F4
Principe da Beira *Brazil* **124** F6
Prineville *U.S.A.* **108** D3
Prins Harald Kyst *Antarctica* **5** D4
Prinsesse Astrid Kyst
     Antarctica **5** D3
Prinsesse Ragnhild Kyst
     Antarctica **5** D3
Prinzapolca *Nic.* **120** D3
Prior, C. *Spain* **36** B2
Priozersk *Russia* **32** B6
Pripet = Prypyat → *Europe* **23** C16
Pripet Marshes *Europe* **23** B15
Pripyat Marshes = Pripet
     Marshes *Europe* **23** B15
Pripyats = Prypyat →
     Europe **23** C16
Prislop, Pasul *Romania* **29** C9
Pristen *Russia* **33** G9
Priština *Serbia* **44** D5
Pritzwalk *Germany* **24** B8
Privas *France* **21** D8
Priverno *Italy* **42** A6
Privolzhsk *Russia* **34** B5
Privolzhskaya
     Vozvyshennost *Russia* **34** E7
Privolzhskiy *Russia* **34** E8
Privolzhskiy □ *Russia* **34** B10
Privolzhye *Russia* **34** D9
Priyutnoye *Russia* **35** G6
Prizren *Serbia* **44** D4
Prizzi *Italy* **42** E6
Prnjavor *Bos.-H.* **28** F2
Probolinggo *Indonesia* **63** G15
Prochowice *Poland* **31** G3
Proctor *U.S.A.* **115** C11
Proddatur *India* **66** M11
Prodhromos *Cyprus* **49** E11
Proença-a-Nova *Portugal* **36** F3
Profondeville *Belgium* **17** D4
Progreso *Coahuila, Mexico* **118** B4
Progreso *Yucatán, Mexico* **119** C7
Progress *Antarctica* **5** C12
Prokhladnyy *Russia* **35** J7
Prokletije *Albania* **44** D3
Prokopyevsk *Russia* **52** D9
Prokuplje *Serbia* **44** C5
Proletarsk *Russia* **35** G5
Proletarskaya = Proletarsk
     Russia **35** G5
Prome = Pyay *Burma* **67** K19
Prophet → *Canada* **102** B4
Prophet River *Canada* **102** B4
Propriá *Brazil* **125** F11
Propriano *France* **21** G12
Proserpine *Australia* **94** J6
Prosna → *Poland* **31** F4
Prospect *U.S.A.* **115** C9
Prosser *U.S.A.* **108** C4
Prostějov *Czech Rep.* **27** B10
Prostki *Poland* **30** E9
Proston *Australia* **95** D5
Proszowice *Poland* **31** H7
Proti *Greece* **46** D3
Provadiya *Bulgaria* **45** C11
Provence *France* **21** E9
Provence-Alpes-Côte
     d'Azur □ *France* **21** D10
Providence *Ky., U.S.A.* **112** G10
Providence *R.I., U.S.A.* **115** E13
Providence Bay *Canada* **104** C3
Providence Mts. *U.S.A.* **111** K11
Providencia, I. de *Colombia* **120** D3
Providenya *Russia* **53** C19
Provincetown *U.S.A.* **113** D18
Provins *France* **19** D10
Provo *U.S.A.* **108** F8
Provost *Canada* **103** C6
Prozor *Bos.-H.* **28** G2
Prrenjas *Albania* **44** E4

Prudhoe Bay *U.S.A.* **106** a
Prudhoe I. *Australia* **94** C4
Prud'homme *Canada* **103** C7
Prudnik *Poland* **31** H4
Prüm *Germany* **25** E2
Prundu *Romania* **29** F11
Pruszcz Gdański *Poland* **30** D5
Pruszków *Poland* **31** F7
Prut → *Romania* **29** E13
Pruzhany *Belarus* **23** B13
Prvič *Croatia* **41** D11
Prydz B. *Antarctica* **5** C6
Pryluky *Ukraine* **33** G7
Pryor *U.S.A.* **116** C7
Prypyat → *Europe* **23** C16
Przasnysz *Poland* **31** E7
Przedbórz *Poland* **31** G6
Przedecz *Poland* **31** F5
Przemków *Poland* **31** G3
Przemyśl *Poland* **31** J9
Przeworsk *Poland* **31** H9
Przewóz *Poland* **31** G2
Przhevalsk = Karakol
     Kyrgyzstan **52** E8
Przysucha *Poland* **31** G7
Psachna *Greece* **46** C5
Psara *Greece* **47** C7
Psathoura *Greece* **46** B6
Psel → *Ukraine* **33** G7
Pserimos *Greece* **47** E9
Psira *Greece* **49** D7
Pskov *Russia* **32** D5
Pskov □ *Russia* **32** D5
Pskovskoye, Ozero *Russia* **32** D5
Psunj *Croatia* **28** E2
Pteleos *Greece* **46** B4
Ptich = Ptsich → *Belarus* **23** B15
Ptichia = Vido *Greece* **49** A3
Ptolemaida *Greece* **44** F5
Ptsich → *Belarus* **23** B15
Ptuj *Slovenia* **41** B12
Ptujska Gora *Slovenia* **41** B12
Pu Xian *China* **56** F6
Pua *Thailand* **64** C3
Puán *Argentina* **126** D3
Pu'an *China* **58** E5
Pu'apu'a *Samoa* **91** b
Pubei *China* **58** F7
Pucallpa *Peru* **124** E4
Pucheng *China* **59** D12
Pucheni *Romania* **29** E10
Puchheim *Germany* **25** G7
Puch'on = Bucheon
     S. Korea **57** F14
Púchov *Slovak Rep.* **27** B11
Pucioasa *Romania* **29** E10
Pučišća *Croatia* **41** E13
Puck *Poland* **30** D5
Pucka, Zatoka *Poland* **30** D5
Puçol *Spain* **39** F4
Pudasjärvi *Finland* **8** D22
Pudozh *Russia* **32** B9
Puducherry *India* **66** P11
Pudukkottai *India* **66** P11
Puebla *Mexico* **119** D5
Puebla □ *Mexico* **119** D5
Puebla de Alcocer *Spain* **37** G5
Puebla de Don Fadrique
     Spain **39** H2
Puebla de Don Rodrigo *Spain* **37** F6
Puebla de Guzmán *Spain* **37** H3
Puebla de la Calzada *Spain* **37** G4
Puebla de Sanabria *Spain* **36** C4
Puebla de Trives = Pobra
     de Trives *Spain* **36** C3
Pueblo *U.S.A.* **108** G11
Pueblo Hundido *Chile* **126** B1
Puelches *Argentina* **126** D2
Puelén *Argentina* **126** D2
Puente Alto *Chile* **126** C1
Puente-Genil *Spain* **37** H6
Puente la Reina *Spain* **38** C3
Puenteareas = Ponteareas
     Spain **36** C2
Puentedeume =
     Pontedeume *Spain* **36** B2
Puentes de Garcia
     Rodriguez = As Pontes
     de García Rodríguez *Spain* **36** B3
Pu'er *China* **58** F3
Puerca, Pta. *Puerto Rico* **121** d
Puerco → *U.S.A.* **109** J10
Puerto Aisén *Chile* **128** F2
Puerto Ángel *Mexico* **119** D5
Puerto Arista *Mexico* **119** D6
Puerto Armuelles *Panama* **120** E3
Puerto Ayacucho *Venezuela* **124** B5
Puerto Barrios *Guatemala* **120** C2
Puerto Bermejo *Argentina* **126** B4
Puerto Bermúdez *Peru* **124** F4
Puerto Bolívar *Ecuador* **124** D3
Puerto Cabello *Venezuela* **124** A5
Puerto Cabezas *Nic.* **120** D3
Puerto Cabo Gracias á Dios
     Nic. **120** D3

Puerto Carreño *Colombia* **124** B5
Puerto Castilla *Honduras* **120** C2
Puerto Chicama *Peru* **124** E3
Puerto Coig *Argentina* **128** G3
Puerto Cortés *Costa Rica* **120** E3
Puerto Cortés *Honduras* **120** C2
Puerto Cumarebo *Venezuela* **124** A5
Puerto de Alcudia = Port
     d'Alcúdia *Spain* **48** B10
Puerto de Cabrera *Spain* **48** B9
Puerto de Gran Tarajal
     Canary Is. **48** F5
Puerto de la Cruz *Canary Is.* **48** F3
Puerto de los Angeles △
     Mexico **118** C3
Puerto de Mazarrón *Spain* **39** H3
Puerto de Pozo Negro
     Canary Is. **48** F6
Puerto de Sóller = Port de
     Sóller *Spain* **48** B9
Puerto de Somosierra *Spain* **36** D7
Puerto del Carmen *Canary Is.* **48** F6
Puerto del Rosario *Canary Is.* **48** F6
Puerto Deseado *Argentina* **128** F3
Puerto Escondido *Mexico* **119** D5
Puerto Heath *Bolivia* **124** F5
Puerto Inírida *Colombia* **124** C5
Puerto Juárez *Mexico* **119** C7
Puerto La Cruz *Venezuela* **124** A6
Puerto Leguízamo *Colombia* **124** D4
Puerto Libertad *Mexico* **118** B2
Puerto Limón *Colombia* **124** C4
Puerto Lobos *Argentina* **128** E3
Puerto Lumbreras *Spain* **39** H3
Puerto Madryn *Argentina* **128** E3
Puerto Maldonado *Peru* **124** F5
Puerto Manatí *Cuba* **120** B4
Puerto Montt *Chile* **128** E2
Puerto Morazán *Nic.* **120** D2
Puerto Morelos *Mexico* **119** C7
Puerto Natales *Chile* **128** G2
Puerto Padre *Cuba* **120** B4
Puerto Páez *Venezuela* **124** B5
Puerto Peñasco *Mexico* **118** A2
Puerto Pinasco *Paraguay* **126** A4
Puerto Plata *Dom. Rep.* **121** C5
Puerto Pollensa = Port de
     Pollença *Spain* **48** B10
Puerto Princesa *Phil.* **61** G3
Puerto Quepos *Costa Rica* **120** E3
Puerto Real *Spain* **37** J4
Puerto Rico *Canary Is.* **48** G4
Puerto Rico ☒ *W. Indies* **121** d
Puerto Rico Trench *Atl. Oc.* **121** C6
Puerto San Julián *Argentina* **128** F3
Puerto Sastre *Paraguay* **126** A4
Puerto Serrano *Spain* **37** J5
Puerto Suárez *Bolivia* **124** G7
Puerto Vallarta *Mexico* **118** C3
Puerto Varas *Chile* **128** E2
Puerto Wilches *Colombia* **124** B4
Puertollano *Spain* **37** G6
Pueu *Tahiti* **91** d
Pueyrredón, L. *Argentina* **128** F2
Púez Odle △ *Italy* **41** B8
Puffin I. *Ireland* **12** E1
Pugachev *Russia* **34** D9
Pugal *India* **68** E5
Puge *China* **58** D4
Puge *Tanzania* **86** C3
Puget Sound *U.S.A.* **108** C2
Puget-Théniers *France* **21** E10
Púglia □ *Italy* **43** B9
Pugŏdong *N. Korea* **57** C16
Pugu *Tanzania* **86** D4
Pūgūnzī *Iran* **71** E8
Pui *Romania* **28** E8
Puieşti *Romania* **29** D12
Puig Major *Spain* **48** B9
Puigcerdà *Spain* **38** C6
Puigmal *Spain* **38** C7
Puigpunyent *Spain* **48** B9
Puijiang *China* **58** B4
Puisaye, Collines de la
     France **19** E10
Puiseaux *France* **19** D9
Pujehun *S. Leone* **82** D2
Pujiang *China* **59** C12
Pujols *France* **20** D3
Pujon-ho *N. Korea* **57** D14
Pukaki, L. *N.Z.* **91** F3
Pukapuka *Cook Is.* **97** J11
Pukaskwa △ *Canada* **104** C2
Pukatawagan *Canada* **103** B8
Pukchin *N. Korea* **57** D13
Pukch'ŏng *N. Korea* **57** D15
Pukë *Albania* **44** D3
Pukekohe *N.Z.* **91** B5
Pukhrayan *India* **69** F8
Pukou *China* **59** A12
Pula *Croatia* **41** D10
Pula *Italy* **42** C1
Pulacayo *Bolivia* **124** H5
Pulai *Malaysia* **65** d
Pulandian *China* **57** E11
Pulaski *N.Y., U.S.A.* **115** C8
Pulaski *Tenn., U.S.A.* **117** D11

Pulaski *Va., U.S.A.* **113** G13
Pulau → *Indonesia* **63** F9
Puławy *Poland* **31** G8
Pulga *U.S.A.* **110** F5
Pulicat L. *India* **66** N12
Pullman *U.S.A.* **108** C5
Pulog, Mt. *Phil.* **61** C4
Pułtusk *Poland* **31** F8
Pülümür *Turkey* **73** C8
Pumlumon Fawr *U.K.* **15** E4
Puná, I. *Ecuador* **124** D2
Punaauia *Tahiti* **91** d
Punakaiki *N.Z.* **91** E3
Punakha Dzong *Bhutan* **67** F16
Punasar *India* **68** F5
Punata *Bolivia* **124** G5
Punch *India* **69** C6
Punch → *Pakistan* **68** C5
Punda Maria *S. Africa* **89** C5
Pune *India* **66** K8
P'ungsan *N. Korea* **57** D15
Pungue, Ponte de *Mozam.* **87** F3
Puning *China* **59** F11
Punjab □ *India* **68** D7
Punjab □ *Pakistan* **68** E6
Puno *Peru* **124** G4
Punpun → *India* **69** G11
Punta, Cerro de *Puerto Rico* **121** d
Punta Alta *Argentina* **128** D4
Punta Arenas *Chile* **128** G2
Punta de Díaz *Chile* **126** B1
Punta del Hidalgo *Canary Is.* **48** F3
Punta Gorda *Belize* **119** D7
Punta Gorda *U.S.A.* **117** H13
Punta Prieta *Mexico* **118** B2
Punta Prima *Spain* **48** B11
Punta Umbria *Spain* **37** H4
Puntarenas *Costa Rica* **120** E3
Punto Fijo *Venezuela* **124** A4
Punxsatawney *U.S.A.* **114** F6
Pupuan *Indonesia* **63** J18
Puqi *China* **59** C9
Puquio *Peru* **124** F4
Pur → *Russia* **52** C8
Puracé, Vol. *Colombia* **124** C3
Puračić *Bos.-H.* **28** F3
Puralia = Puruliya *India* **69** H12
Puranpur *India* **69** E9
Purbeck, Isle of *U.K.* **15** G5
Purcell *U.S.A.* **116** D6
Purcell Mts. *Canada* **102** D5
Puri *India* **67** K14
Purmerend *Neths.* **17** B4
Purnia *India* **69** G12
Purnululu △ *Australia* **92** C4
Pursat = Pouthisat *Cambodia* **64** F4
Purukcahu *Indonesia* **62** E4
Puruliya *India* **69** H12
Purus → *Brazil* **124** D6
Puruvesi *Finland* **8** B5
Purvis *U.S.A.* **117** F10
Pŭrvomay *Bulgaria* **45** D9
Purwa *India* **69** F9
Purwakarta *Indonesia* **63** G12
Purwo, Tanjung *Indonesia* **63** K18
Purwodadi *Indonesia* **63** G14
Purwokerto *Indonesia* **63** G13
Puryŏng *N. Korea* **57** C15
Pusa *India* **69** G11
Pusan = Busan *S. Korea* **57** G15
Pushkin *Russia* **32** C6
Pushkino *Moskva, Russia* **32** D9
Pushkino *Saratov, Russia* **34** E8
Püspökladány *Hungary* **28** C6
Pustoshka *Russia* **32** D5
Puszczykowo *Poland* **31** F3
Putahow L. *Canada* **103** B8
Putao *Burma* **67** F20
Putaruru *N.Z.* **91** C5
Putbus *Germany* **24** A9
Putian *China* **59** E12
Putignano *Italy* **43** B10
Puting, Tanjung *Indonesia* **62** E4
Putlitz *Germany* **24** B8
Putna *Romania* **29** C10
Putna → *Romania* **29** E12
Putnam *U.S.A.* **115** E13
Putnok *Hungary* **28** B5
Putorana, Gory *Russia* **53** C10
Putrajaya *Malaysia* **65** L3
Puttalam *Sri Lanka* **66** Q11
Puttgarden *Germany* **24** A7
Püttlingen *Germany* **25** F2
Putumayo → *S. Amer.* **124** D5
Putuo *China* **59** C14
Putussibau *Indonesia* **62** D4
Putyla *Ukraine* **29** B10
Puvirnituq *Canada* **101** C12
Puy-de-Dôme *France* **20** C6
Puy-de-Dôme □ *France* **20** C7
Puy-l'Évêque *France* **20** D5
Puyallup *U.S.A.* **110** C4
Puyang *China* **56** G8
Puylaurens *France* **20** E6
Pŭzeh Rīg *Iran* **71** E8
Puzhaykove *Ukraine* **29** B14
Pwani □ *Tanzania* **86** D4

Pweto *Dem. Rep. of the Congo* **87** D2
Pwllheli *U.K.* **14** E3
Pya-ozero *Russia* **8** C24
Pyana → *Russia* **34** C8
Pyapon *Burma* **67** L19
Pyasina → *Russia* **53** B9
Pyatigorsk *Russia* **35** H6
Pyatykhatky *Ukraine* **33** H7
Pydna *Greece* **44** F6
Pye = Prome *Burma* **67** K19
Pyeongtaek *S. Korea* **57** F14
Pyetrikaw *Belarus* **23** B15
Pyhäjoki *Finland* **8** D21
Pyinmana *Burma* **67** K20
Pyla, C. *Cyprus* **49** E12
Pymatuning Res. *U.S.A.* **114** E4
Pyŏktong *N. Korea* **57** D13
Pyŏnggang *N. Korea* **57** E14
P'yŏngsong *N. Korea* **57** E13
P'yŏngyang *N. Korea* **57** E13
Pyote *U.S.A.* **116** F3
Pyramid L. *U.S.A.* **108** F4
Pyramid Pk. *U.S.A.* **111** J10
Pyramids *Egypt* **80** J7
Pyrénées *Europe* **20** F4
Pyrénées △ *France* **20** F3
Pyrénées-Atlantiques □ *France* **20** E3
Pyrénées-Orientales □ *France* **20** F6
Pyryatyn *Ukraine* **33** G7
Pyrzyce *Poland* **31** E1
Pyskowice *Poland* **31** H5
Pytalovo *Russia* **32** D4
Pyu *Burma* **67** K20
Pyzdry *Poland* **31** F4

Q

Qaanaaq *Greenland* **4** B4
Qabirri → *Azerbaijan* **35** K8
Qachasnek *S. Africa* **89** E4
Qa'el Jafr *Jordan* **74** E5
Qa'emābād *Iran* **71** D9
Qā'emshahr *Iran* **71** B7
Qagan Nur *China* **56** C8
Qahar Youyi Zhongqi *China* **56** D7
Qahremānshahr = Kermānshāh *Iran* **73** E12
Qaidam Pendi *China* **60** C4
Qajarīyeh *Iran* **71** D6
Qala, Ras il *Malta* **49** C1
Qala-i-Jadid = Spīn Būldak *Afghan.* **68** D2
Qala Point = Qala, Ras il *Malta* **49** C1
Qala Viala *Pakistan* **68** D2
Qala Yangi *Afghan.* **68** B2
Qal'at al Akhḍar *Si. Arabia* **70** E3
Qal'at Dīzah *Iraq* **73** D11
Qal'at Ṣāliḥ *Iraq* **70** D5
Qal'at Sukkar *Iraq* **73** G12
Qalyûb *Egypt* **80** H7
Qamani'tuaq = Baker Lake *Canada* **100** C10
Qamdo *China* **58** B1
Qamea *Fiji* **91** a
Qamruddin Karez *Pakistan* **68** D3
Qandahār = Kandahār *Afghan.* **66** D4
Qandahār = Kandahār □ *Afghan.* **66** D4
Qapān *Iran* **71** B7
Qapshaghay *Kazakhstan* **52** E8
Qaqortoq *Greenland* **4** C5
Qâra *Egypt* **80** B2
Qara Qash → *China* **69** B8
Qarabutaq *Kazakhstan* **52** E7
Qaraçala *Azerbaijan* **35** L9
Qaraghandy *Kazakhstan* **52** E8
Qaraghayly *Kazakhstan* **52** E8
Qārah *Si. Arabia* **70** D4
Qaratau *Kazakhstan* **52** E7
Qaratau *Zhambyl, Kazakhstan* **52** E8
Qarazhal *Kazakhstan* **52** E8
Qardho = Gardo *Somali Rep.* **75** F4
Qardud *Sudan* **81** E2
Qareh → *Iran* **73** D6
Qareh Tekān *Iran* **71** B6
Qarnein *U.A.E.* **71** E7
Qarqan He → *China* **60** C3
Qarqaraly *Kazakhstan* **52** E8
Qarrasa *Sudan* **81** E3
Qarshi *Uzbekistan* **52** F7
Qartabā *Lebanon* **74** A4
Qaryat al Gharab *Iraq* **70** D5
Qaryat al 'Ulyā *Si. Arabia* **70** E5
Qasr 'Amra *Jordan* **70** D4
Qaşr-e Qand *Iran* **71** E9
Qaşr-e Shīrīn *Iran* **70** C5
Qasr Farâfra *Egypt* **80** B2
Qatanā *Syria* **74** B5
Qatar ■ *Asia* **71** E6
Qaţlīsh *Iran* **71** B8
Qattâra *Egypt* **80** A2
Qattâra, Munkhafed el *Egypt* **80** B2

Qattâra Depression = Qattâra, Munkhafed el *Egypt* **80** B2
Qausuittuq = Resolute *Canada* **101** B10
Qawām al Ḥamzah = Al Ḥamzah *Iraq* **70** D5
Qāyen *Iran* **71** C8
Qazaqstan = Kazakhstan ■ *Asia* **52** E8
Qazimämmäd *Azerbaijan* **35** K9
Qazvīn *Iran* **71** B6
Qazvīn □ *Iran* **71** B6
Qeissan *Sudan* **81** E3
Qena *Egypt* **80** B3
Qena, W. → *Egypt* **80** B3
Qeqertarsuaq *Greenland* **4** C5
Qeqertarsuaq *Greenland* **98** C14
Qeshlāq *Iran* **73** E12
Qeshm *Iran* **71** E8
Qeys *Iran* **71** E7
Qezel Owzen → *Iran* **71** B6
Qezi'ot *Israel* **74** E3
Qi Xian *China* **56** G8
Qian Gorlos *China* **57** B13
Qian Xian *China* **56** G5
Qiancheng *China* **58** D7
Qianjiang *Guangxi Zhuangzu, China* **58** F7
Qianjiang *Hubei, China* **59** B9
Qianjiang *Sichuan, China* **58** C7
Qianshan *China* **59** B11
Qianwei *China* **58** C4
Qianxi *China* **58** D6
Qianyang *Hunan, China* **59** D8
Qianyang *Shaanxi, China* **56** G4
Qianyang *Zhejiang, China* **59** B12
Qiaojia *China* **58** D4
Qichun *China* **59** B10
Qidong *Hunan, China* **59** D9
Qidong *Jiangsu, China* **59** B13
Qijiang *China* **58** C6
Qikiqtarjuaq *Canada* **101** C13
Qila Saifullāh *Pakistan* **68** D3
Qilian Shan *China* **60** C4
Qimen *China* **59** C11
Qin He → *China* **56** G7
Qin Jiang → *Guangxi Zhuangzu, China* **58** F7
Qin Jiang → *Jiangxi, China* **59** D10
Qin Ling = Qinling Shandi *China* **56** H5
Qin'an *China* **56** G3
Qing Xian *China* **56** E9
Qingcheng *China* **57** F9
Qingdao *China* **57** F11
Qingfeng *China* **56** G8
Qinghai □ *China* **60** C4
Qinghai Hu *China* **60** C5
Qinghecheng *China* **57** D13
Qinghemen *China* **57** D11
Qingjian *China* **56** F6
Qingjiang = Huaiyin *China* **57** H10
Qingliu *China* **59** D11
Qinglong *China* **58** E5
Qingping *China* **58** D6
Qingpu *China* **59** B13
Qingshui *China* **56** G4
Qingshuihe *China* **56** E6
Qingtian *China* **59** C13
Qingtongxia Shuiku *China* **56** F3
Qingxi *China* **58** D7
Qingxu *China* **56** F7
Qingyang *Anhui, China* **59** B11
Qingyang *Gansu, China* **56** F4
Qingyi Jiang → *China* **58** C4
Qingyuan *Guangdong, China* **59** F9
Qingyuan *Liaoning, China* **57** C13
Qingyuan *Zhejiang, China* **59** D12
Qingyun *China* **57** F9
Qingzhen *China* **58** D6
Qinhuangdao *China* **57** E10
Qinling Shandi *China* **56** H5
Qinshui *China* **56** G7
Qinyang = Jiyuan *China* **56** G7
Qinyuan *China* **56** F7
Qinzhou *China* **58** G7
Qionghai *China* **64** C8
Qionglai *China* **58** B4
Qionglai Shan *China* **58** B4
Qiongzhou Haixia *China* **64** B8
Qiqihar *China* **53** E13
Qiraïya, W. → *Egypt* **74** E3
Qiryat Ata *Israel* **74** C4
Qiryat Gat *Israel* **74** D3
Qiryat Mal'akhi *Israel* **74** D3
Qiryat Shemona *Israel* **74** B4
Qiryat Yam *Israel* **74** C4
Qishan *China* **56** G4
Qiubei *China* **58** E5
Qixia *China* **57** F11
Qiyang *China* **59** D8
Qızılağac Körfäzi *Azerbaijan* **73** C13
Qojūr *Iran* **70** B5
Qom *Iran* **71** C6
Qom □ *Iran* **71** C6

Qomolangma Feng = Everest, Mt. *Nepal* **69** E12
Qomsheh *Iran* **71** D6
Qoqon = Qŭqon *Uzbekistan* **52** E8
Qorveh *Iran* **73** E12
Qostanay *Kazakhstan* **52** D7
Qoţūr *Iran* **73** C11
Qu Jiang → *China* **58** B6
Qu Xian *China* **58** B6
Quabbin Res. *U.S.A.* **115** D12
Quairading *Australia* **93** F2
Quakenbrück *Germany* **24** C3
Quakertown *U.S.A.* **115** F9
Qualicum Beach *Canada* **102** D4
Quambatook *Australia* **95** F3
Quambone *Australia* **95** E4
Quamby *Australia* **94** C3
Quan Long = Ca Mau *Vietnam* **65** H5
Quanah *U.S.A.* **116** D5
Quang Ngai *Vietnam* **64** E7
Quang Tri *Vietnam* **64** D6
Quang Yen *Vietnam* **58** G6
Quannan *China* **59** E10
Quantock Hills *U.K.* **15** F4
Quanzhou *Fujian, China* **59** E12
Quanzhou *Guangxi Zhuangzu, China* **59** E8
Qu'Appelle → *Canada* **103** C8
Quaqtaq *Canada* **101** C13
Quaraí *Brazil* **126** C4
Quarré-les-Tombes *France* **19** E11
Quarteira *Portugal* **37** H2
Quartu Sant'Elena *Italy* **42** C2
Quartzsite *U.S.A.* **111** M12
Quatre Bornes *Mauritius* **85** d
Quatsino Sd. *Canada* **102** C2
Quba *Azerbaijan* **35** K9
Qūchān *Iran* **71** B8
Queanbeyan *Australia* **95** F4
Québec *Canada* **105** C5
Québec □ *Canada* **105** C6
Quebrada del Condorito △ *Argentina* **126** C3
Quedlinburg *Germany* **24** D7
Queen Alexandra Ra. *Antarctica* **5** E11
Queen Charlotte City *Canada* **102** C2
Queen Charlotte Is. *Canada* **102** C2
Queen Charlotte Sd. *Canada* **102** C3
Queen Charlotte Strait *Canada* **102** C3
Queen Elizabeth △ *Uganda* **86** C3
Queen Elizabeth △ *U.K.* **13** E5
Queen Elizabeth Is. *Canada* **101** B10
Queen Mary Land *Antarctica* **5** D7
Queen Maud G. *Canada* **100** C9
Queen Maud Land = Dronning Maud Land *Antarctica* **5** D3
Queen Maud Mts. *Antarctica* **5** E13
Queens Channel *Australia* **92** C4
Queenscliff *Australia* **95** F3
Queensland □ *Australia* **94** C3
Queenstown *Australia* **95** G4
Queenstown *N.Z.* **91** F2
Queenstown *Singapore* **65** d
Queenstown *S. Africa* **88** E4
Queets *U.S.A.* **110** C2
Queguay Grande → *Uruguay* **126** C4
Queimadas *Brazil* **125** F11
Quelimane *Mozam.* **87** F4
Quellón *Chile* **128** E2
Quelpart = Jeju-do *S. Korea* **57** H14
Queluz *Portugal* **37** G1
Quemado *N. Mex., U.S.A.* **109** J9
Quemado *Tex., U.S.A.* **116** G4
Quemoy = Chinmen *Taiwan* **59** E13
Quemú-Quemú *Argentina* **126** D3
Quequén *Argentina* **126** D4
Querétaro *Mexico* **118** C4
Querétaro □ *Mexico* **118** C5
Querfurt *Germany* **24** D7
Quérigut *France* **20** F5
Querqueville *France* **18** C5
Quesada *Spain* **37** H7
Queshan *China* **56** H8
Quesnel *Canada* **102** C4
Quesnel → *Canada* **102** C4
Quesnel L. *Canada* **102** C4
Questa *U.S.A.* **109** H11
Questembert *France* **18** E4
Quetico *Canada* **104** C1
Quetta *Pakistan* **68** D2
Queyras △ *France* **21** D10
Quezaltenango *Guatemala* **120** D1
Quezon City *Phil.* **61** D4
Qufār *Si. Arabia* **70** E4
Qui Nhon *Vietnam* **64** F7
Quibala *Angola* **84** G2
Quibaxe *Angola* **84** F2
Quibdo *Colombia* **124** B3

Quiberon *France* **18** E3
Quiberon, Presqu'île de *France* **18** E3
Quickborn *Germany* **24** B5
Quiindy *Paraguay* **126** B4
Quilá *Mexico* **118** C3
Quilán, C. *Chile* **128** E2
Quilcene *U.S.A.* **110** C4
Quilimari *Chile* **126** C1
Quilino *Argentina* **126** C3
Quill Lakes *Canada* **103** C8
Quillabamba *Peru* **124** F4
Quillagua *Chile* **126** A2
Quillaicillo *Chile* **126** C1
Quillan *France* **20** F6
Quillota *Chile* **126** C1
Quilon *India* **66** Q10
Quilpie *Australia* **95** D3
Quilpué *Chile* **126** C1
Quilua *Mozam.* **87** F4
Quimilí *Argentina* **126** B3
Quimper *France* **18** E2
Quimperlé *France* **18** E3
Quinault → *U.S.A.* **110** C2
Quincy *Calif., U.S.A.* **110** F6
Quincy *Fla., U.S.A.* **117** F12
Quincy *Ill., U.S.A.* **112** F8
Quincy *Mass., U.S.A.* **115** D14
Quincy *Wash., U.S.A.* **108** C4
Quines *Argentina* **126** C2
Quinga *Mozam.* **87** F5
Quingey *France* **19** E12
Quinta de la Serena *Spain* **37** G5
Quintana Roo □ *Mexico* **119** D7
Quintanar de la Orden *Spain* **37** F7
Quintanar de la Sierra *Spain* **38** D2
Quintanar del Rey *Spain* **39** F3
Quintero *Chile* **126** C1
Quintin *France* **18** D4
Quinto *Spain* **38** D4
Quípar → *Spain* **39** G3
Quirihue *Chile* **126** D1
Quirindi *Australia* **95** E5
Quirinópolis *Brazil* **125** G8
Quiroga *Spain* **36** C3
Quissac *France* **21** E8
Quissanga *Mozam.* **87** E5
Quissico *Mozam.* **89** C5
Quitilipi *Argentina* **126** B3
Quitman *U.S.A.* **117** F13
Quito *Ecuador* **124** D3
Quixadá *Brazil* **125** D11
Quixaxe *Mozam.* **87** F5
Qujing *China* **58** E4
Qulan *Kazakhstan* **52** E8
Qul'ân, Jazâ'ir *Egypt* **70** E2
Qumbu *S. Africa* **89** E4
Quneitra *Syria* **74** B4
Qŭnghirot *Uzbekistan* **52** E6
Qu'nyido *China* **58** B2
Quoin I. *Australia* **92** B4
Quoin Pt. *S. Africa* **88** E2
Quorn *Australia* **95** E2
Qŭqon *Uzbekistan* **52** E8
Qurein *Sudan* **81** E3
Qurnat as Sawdā' *Lebanon* **74** A5
Qûs *Egypt* **80** B3
Qusar *Azerbaijan* **35** K9
Quşaybā' *Si. Arabia* **70** E4
Qusaybah *Iraq* **73** E9
Quseir *Egypt* **70** E2
Qūshchī *Iran* **73** D11
Qūţīābād *Iran* **73** E13
Quthing *Lesotho* **89** E4
Quwo *China* **56** G6
Quwū Nhai *Vietnam* **64** B4
Quyon *Canada* **115** A8
Quzhou *China* **59** C12
Quzi *China* **56** F4
Qvareli *Georgia* **35** K7
Qyzylorda *Kazakhstan* **52** E7

R

Ra, Ko *Thailand* **65** H2
Raab *Austria* **26** C6
Raahe *Finland* **8** D21
Raalte *Neths.* **17** B6
Raasay *U.K.* **13** D2
Raasay, Sd. of *U.K.* **13** D2
Rab *Croatia* **41** D11
Raba *Indonesia* **63** F5
Rába → *Hungary* **28** C2
Rabaçal → *Portugal* **36** D3
Rabah *Nigeria* **83** C6
Rabai *Kenya* **86** C4
Rabak *Sudan* **81** E3
Rabastens *France* **20** E5
Rabastens-de-Bigorre *France* **20** E4
Rabat = Victoria *Malta* **49** C1
Rabat *Malta* **49** D1
Rabat *Morocco* **78** B4

Rabaul *Papua N. G.* **90** B8
Rabi *Fiji* **91** a
Rābigh *Si. Arabia* **75** C2
Rabka *Poland* **31** J6
Râbniţa *Moldova* **29** C14
Rābor *Iran* **71** D8
Rača *Serbia* **44** B4
Răcăciuni *Romania* **29** D11
Răcășdia *Romania* **28** F6
Racconigi *Italy* **40** D4
Race, C. *Canada* **105** C9
Rach Gia *Vietnam* **65** G5
Rachid *Mauritania* **82** B2
Raciąż *Poland* **31** F7
Racibórz *Poland* **31** H5
Racichy *Belarus* **30** E10
Racine *U.S.A.* **112** D10
Rackerby *U.S.A.* **110** F5
Radama, Nosy *Madag.* **89** A8
Radama, Saikanosy *Madag.* **89** A8
Radan *Serbia* **44** D5
Rădăuţi *Romania* **29** C10
Rădăuţi-Prut *Romania* **29** B11
Radbuza → *Czech Rep.* **26** B6
Radcliff *U.S.A.* **113** G11
Radeberg *Germany* **24** D9
Radebeul *Germany* **24** D9
Radeče *Slovenia* **41** B12
Radekhiv *Ukraine* **23** C13
Radekhov = Radekhiv *Ukraine* **23** C13
Radenthein *Austria* **26** E6
Radew → *Poland* **30** D2
Radford *U.S.A.* **113** G13
Radhanpur *India* **68** H4
Radhwa, Jabal *Si. Arabia* **70** E3
Radika → *Macedonia* **44** E4
Radisson *Qué., Canada* **104** B4
Radisson *Sask., Canada* **103** C7
Radium Hot Springs *Canada* **102** C5
Radlje ob Dravi *Slovenia* **41** B12
Radnevo *Bulgaria* **45** D9
Radnor Forest *U.K.* **15** E4
Radolfzell *Germany* **25** H4
Radom *Poland* **31** G8
Radomir *Bulgaria* **44** D6
Radomka → *Poland* **31** G8
Radomsko *Poland* **31** G6
Radomyshl *Ukraine* **23** C15
Radomyśl Wielki *Poland* **31** H8
Radoszyce *Poland* **31** G7
Radoviš *Macedonia* **44** E6
Radovljica *Slovenia* **41** B11
Radstadt *Austria* **26** D6
Radstock, C. *Australia* **95** E1
Răducăneni *Romania* **29** D12
Raduša *Macedonia* **44** D5
Radvanichy *Belarus* **31** F11
Radviliškis *Lithuania* **30** C10
Radville *Canada* **103** D8
Raḍwā, J. *Si. Arabia* **80** C4
Radymno *Poland* **31** J9
Radzanów *Poland* **31** F7
Radziejów *Poland* **31** F5
Radzyń Chełmiński *Poland* **30** E5
Radzyń Podlaski *Poland* **31** G9
Rae *Canada* **102** A5
Rae Bareli *India* **69** F9
Rae Isthmus *Canada* **101** C11
Raeren *Belgium* **17** D6
Raeside, L. *Australia* **93** E3
Raetihi *N.Z.* **91** C5
Rafaela *Argentina* **126** C3
Rafah *Gaza Strip* **74** D3
Rafai *C.A.R.* **86** B1
Raffadali *Italy* **42** E6
Raffili *Sudan* **81** F2
Rafḥā *Si. Arabia* **70** D4
Rafsanjān *Iran* **71** D8
Raft Pt. *Australia* **92** C3
Râgâ *Sudan* **81** F2
Raga → *Sudan* **81** F2
Ragachow *Belarus* **23** B16
Ragag *Sudan* **81** E1
Ragama *Sri Lanka* **66** R11
Ragged, Mt. *Australia* **93** F3
Ragged Pt. *Barbados* **121** g
Raghunathpalli *India* **69** H11
Raghunathpur *India* **69** H12
Raglan *N.Z.* **91** B5
Ragusa *Italy* **43** F7
Raha *Indonesia* **63** E6
Rahad, Nahr ed → *Sudan* **81** E3
Rahaeng = Tak *Thailand* **64** D2
Rahatgarh *India* **69** H8
Rahden *Germany* **24** C4
Raheita *Eritrea* **81** E5
Rahimyar Khan *Pakistan* **68** E4
Rāhjerd *Iran* **71** C6
Rahole △ *Kenya* **86** B4
Rahon *India* **68** D7
Raiatéa, Î. *French Polynesia* **97** J12
Raichur *India* **66** L10
Raiganj *India* **69** G13
Raigarh *India* **67** J13
Raijua *Indonesia* **63** F6

Raikot India 68 D6
Railton Australia 95 G4
Rainbow Bridge △ U.S.A. 109 H8
Rainbow Lake Canada 102 B5
Rainier U.S.A. 110 D4
Rainier, Mt. U.S.A. 110 D5
Rainy L. Canada 103 D10
Rainy River Canada 103 D10
Raippaluoto Finland 8 E19
Raipur India 67 J12
Ra'is Si. Arabia 80 C4
Raisen India 68 H8
Raisio Finland 32 B2
Raj Nandgaon India 67 J12
Raj Nilgiri India 69 J12
Raja, Ujung Indonesia 62 D1
Raja Ampat, Kepulauan
   Indonesia 63 E8
Rajahmundry India 67 L12
Rajaji △ India 68 D8
Rajang → Malaysia 62 D4
Rajanpur Pakistan 68 E4
Rajapalaiyam India 66 Q10
Rajasthan □ India 68 F5
Rajasthan Canal = Indira
   Gandhi Canal India 68 F5
Rajauri India 69 C6
Rajgarh Mad. P., India 68 G7
Rajgarh Raj., India 68 F7
Rajgarh Raj., India 68 E6
Rajgir India 69 G11
Rajgród Poland 30 E9
Rajkot India 68 H4
Rajmahal Hills India 69 G12
Rajpipla India 66 J8
Rajpur India 68 H6
Rajpura India 68 D7
Rajshahi Bangla. 67 G16
Rajshahi □ Bangla. 69 G13
Rajula India 68 J4
Rakaia N.Z. 91 E4
Rakaia → N.Z. 91 E4
Rakan, Ra's Qatar 71 E6
Rakaposhi Pakistan 69 A6
Rakata, Pulau Indonesia 62 F3
Rakhiv Ukraine 29 B9
Rakhni Pakistan 68 D3
Rakhni → Pakistan 68 E3
Rakhny-Lisovi Ukraine 29 B13
Rakiraki Fiji 91 a
Rakitnoye Russia 54 B7
Rakitovo Bulgaria 45 E8
Rakiura △ N.Z. 91 G2
Rakoniewice Poland 31 F3
Rakops Botswana 88 C3
Rakovica Croatia 41 D12
Rakovník Czech Rep. 26 A6
Rakovski Bulgaria 45 D8
Rakvere Estonia 32 C4
Raleigh U.S.A. 117 D15
Ralik Chain Pac. Oc. 96 G8
Ralja Serbia 44 B4
Ralls U.S.A. 116 E4
Ralston U.S.A. 114 E8
Ram → Canada 102 A4
Rām Allāh West Bank 74 D4
Rama Nic. 120 D3
Ramacca Italy 43 E7
Ramakona India 69 J8
Ramales de la Victoria Spain 36 B7
Rāmallāh = Rām Allāh
   West Bank 74 D4
Raman Thailand 65 J3
Ramanathapuram India 66 Q11
Ramanetaka, B. de Madag. 89 A8
Ramanujganj India 69 H10
Ramat Gan Israel 74 C3
Ramatlhabama S. Africa 88 D4
Ramban India 69 C6
Rambervillers France 19 D13
Rambi = Rabi Fiji 91 a
Rambipuji Indonesia 63 H15
Rambouillet France 19 D8
Rame Hd. Australia 95 F4
Ramechhap Nepal 69 F12
Ramenskoye Russia 32 E10
Ramganga → India 69 F8
Ramgarh Jharkhand, India 69 H11
Ramgarh Raj., India 68 F6
Ramgarh Raj., India 68 F4
Rāmhormoz Iran 71 D6
Ramīān Iran 71 B7
Ramingining Australia 94 A2
Ramla Israel 74 D3
Ramlu Eritrea 81 E5
Ramm = Rum Jordan 74 F4
Ramm, Jabal Jordan 74 F4
Râmna → Romania 29 E12
Ramnad =
   Ramanathapuram India 66 Q11
Ramnagar
   Jammu & Kashmir, India 69 C6
Ramnagar Uttaranchal, India 69 E8
Ramnäs Sweden 10 E10
Râmnicu Sărat Romania 29 E12
Râmnicu Vâlcea Romania 29 E9

Ramon Russia 33 G10
Ramona U.S.A. 111 M10
Ramonville-St-Agne France 20 E5
Ramore Canada 104 C3
Ramos → Nigeria 83 D6
Ramotswa Botswana 88 C4
Rampur H.P., India 68 D7
Rampur Mad. P., India 68 H5
Rampur Ut. P., India 69 E8
Rampur Hat India 69 G12
Rampura India 68 G6
Ramrama Tola India 69 J8
Ramree I. Burma 67 K19
Rāmsar Iran 71 B6
Ramsey I. of Man 14 C3
Ramsey U.S.A. 115 E10
Ramsey L. Canada 104 C3
Ramsgate U.K. 15 F9
Ramsjö Sweden 10 B9
Ramstein Germany 25 F3
Ramtek India 66 J11
Ramu Kenya 86 B5
Ramvik Sweden 10 B11
Rana Pratap Sagar Dam
   India 68 G6
Ranaghat India 69 H13
Ranahu Pakistan 68 G3
Ranau Malaysia 62 C5
Rancagua Chile 126 C1
Rance → France 18 D5
Rancheria → Canada 102 A3
Ranchester U.S.A. 108 D10
Ranchi India 69 H11
Rancho Cordova U.S.A. 110 G5
Rancho Cucamonga U.S.A. 111 L9
Randalstown U.K. 12 B5
Randan France 19 F10
Randazzo Italy 43 E7
Randers Denmark 11 H4
Randers Fjord Denmark 11 H4
Randfontein S. Africa 89 D4
Randle U.S.A. 110 D5
Randolph Mass., U.S.A. 115 D13
Randolph N.Y., U.S.A. 114 D6
Randolph Utah, U.S.A. 108 F8
Randolph Vt., U.S.A. 115 C12
Randsburg U.S.A. 111 K9
Rânealven → Sweden 8 D20
Rangae Thailand 65 J3
Rangaunu B. N.Z. 91 A4
Range, The Zimbabwe 87 F3
Rangeley U.S.A. 115 B14
Rangeley L. U.S.A. 115 B14
Rangely U.S.A. 108 F9
Ranger U.S.A. 116 E5
Rangia India 67 F17
Rangiora N.Z. 91 E4
Rangitaiki → N.Z. 91 B6
Rangitata → N.Z. 91 E3
Rangitoto ke te tonga =
   D'Urville I. N.Z. 91 D4
Rangkasbitung Indonesia 63 G12
Rangon → Burma 67 L20
Rangoon Burma 67 L20
Rangpur Bangla. 67 G16
Rangsit Thailand 64 F3
Ranibennur India 66 M9
Raniganj Ut. P., India 69 F9
Raniganj W. Bengal, India 67 H15
Ranikhet India 69 E8
Raniwara India 68 G5
Rāniyah Iraq 70 B5
Ranka India 69 H10
Ranken → Australia 94 C2
Rankin U.S.A. 116 F4
Rankin Inlet Canada 100 C10
Rankins Springs Australia 95 E4
Rankweil Austria 26 D2
Rannoch, L. U.K. 13 E4
Rannoch Moor U.K. 13 E4
Ranobe, Helodrano' i
   Madag. 89 C7
Ranohira Madag. 89 C8
Ranomafana Toamasina,
   Madag. 89 B8
Ranomafana Toliara, Madag. 89 C8
Ranomafana △ Madag. 89 C8
Ranomena Madag. 89 C8
Ranong Thailand 65 H2
Ranotsara Nord Madag. 89 C8
Ränsa Iran 71 C6
Ransiki Indonesia 63 E8
Rantabe Madag. 89 B8
Rantauprapat Indonesia 62 D1
Rantemario Indonesia 63 E5
Ranthambore △ India 68 F7
Rantoul U.S.A. 112 E9
Ranum Denmark 11 H3
Ranyah, W. → Si. Arabia 80 C5
Raon l'Étape France 19 D13
Raoping China 59 F11
Raoyang China 56 E8
Rap, Ko Thailand 65 b
Rapa French Polynesia 97 K13
Rapa Nui = Pascua, I. de
   Chile 97 K17
Rapallo Italy 40 D6

Rapar India 68 H4
Rāpch Iran 71 E8
Raper, C. Canada 101 C13
Rapid City U.S.A. 112 C2
Rapid River U.S.A. 112 C10
Rapla Estonia 32 C3
Rapti → India 69 F10
Rapu Rapu I. Phil. 61 E6
Raqaba ez Zarqa → Sudan 81 F2
Raquette → U.S.A. 115 B10
Raquette Lake U.S.A. 115 C10
Rara △ Nepal 69 E10
Rarotonga Cook Is. 97 K12
Ra's al 'Ayn Syria 73 D9
Ra's al Khaymah U.A.E. 71 E7
Râs el Mâ Mali 82 B4
Râs Ghârib Egypt 80 B3
Râs Mallap Egypt 80 B3
Râs Muhammad △ Egypt 80 B3
Rasca, Pta. de la Canary Is. 48 G3
Rāşcani Moldova 29 C12
Raseiniai Lithuania 30 C10
Rashad Sudan 81 E3
Rashîd Egypt 80 H7
Rashîd, Masabb Egypt 80 H7
Rashmi India 68 G6
Rasht Iran 73 D13
Rasi Salai Thailand 64 E5
Raška Serbia 44 C4
Râsnov Romania 29 E10
Rason L. Australia 93 E3
Raşova Romania 29 F12
Rasovo Bulgaria 44 C7
Rasra India 69 G10
Rasskazovo Russia 34 D5
Rast Romania 29 G8
Rastatt Germany 25 G4
Rastede Germany 24 B4
Rāstoliţa Romania 29 D9
Rasul Pakistan 68 C5
Raszków Poland 31 G4
Rat → Canada 103 D9
Rat Buri Thailand 64 F2
Rat Islands U.S.A. 106 a
Rat L. Canada 103 B9
Ratak Chain Pac. Oc. 96 G8
Rätan Sweden 10 B8
Ratangarh India 68 E6
Rath India 69 G8
Rath Luirc Ireland 12 D3
Rathangan Ireland 12 C4
Rathdrum Ireland 12 D5
Rathenow Germany 24 C8
Rathkeale Ireland 12 D3
Rathlin I. U.K. 12 A5
Rathmelton Ireland 12 A4
Ratibor = Racibórz Poland 31 H5
Rätikon Austria 26 D2
Ratingen Germany 24 D2
Ratlam India 68 H6
Ratnagiri India 66 L8
Ratodero Pakistan 68 F3
Raton U.S.A. 109 H11
Rattaphum Thailand 65 J3
Ratten Austria 26 D8
Rattray Hd. U.K. 13 D7
Rättvik Sweden 10 D9
Ratz, Mt. Canada 102 B2
Ratzeburg Germany 24 B6
Raub Malaysia 65 L3
Rauch Argentina 126 D4
Raudales Mexico 119 D6
Raufarhöfn Iceland 8 C6
Raufoss Norway 8 F14
Raukumara Ra. N.Z. 91 C6
Rauma Finland 32 B1
Raumo = Rauma Finland 32 B1
Raung, Gunung Indonesia 63 J17
Raurkela India 69 H11
Rausu-Dake Japan 54 B12
Rāut → Moldova 29 C14
Rava-Ruska Ukraine 31 H10
Rava Russkaya =
   Rava-Ruska Ukraine 31 H10
Ravalli U.S.A. 108 C6
Ravānsar Iran 73 E12
Ravanusa Italy 42 E6
Rāvar Iran 71 D8
Ravena U.S.A. 115 D11
Ravenna Italy 41 D9
Ravenna Nebr., U.S.A. 112 E4
Ravenna Ohio, U.S.A. 114 E3
Ravensburg Germany 25 H5
Ravenshoe Australia 94 B4
Ravensthorpe Australia 93 F3
Ravenswood Australia 94 C4
Ravenswood U.S.A. 113 F13
Ravi → Pakistan 68 D4
Ravna Gora Croatia 41 C11
Ravna Reka Serbia 44 B5
Ravne na Koroškem
   Slovenia 41 B11
Rawa Mazowiecka Poland 31 G7
Rawalpindi Pakistan 68 C5
Rawang Malaysia 65 L3
Rawene N.Z. 91 A4

Rawicz Poland 31 G3
Rawka → Poland 31 F7
Rawlinna Australia 93 F4
Rawlins U.S.A. 108 F10
Rawlinson Ra. Australia 93 D4
Rawson Argentina 128 E3
Raxaul India 69 F11
Ray U.S.A. 112 A2
Ray, C. Canada 105 C8
Raya Ring, Ko Thailand 65 a
Rayadurg India 66 M10
Rayagada India 67 K13
Raychikhinsk Russia 53 E13
Rāyen Iran 71 D8
Rayleigh U.K. 15 F8
Raymond Canada 102 D6
Raymond Calif., U.S.A. 110 H7
Raymond N.H., U.S.A. 115 C13
Raymond Wash., U.S.A. 110 D3
Raymondville U.S.A. 116 H6
Raymore Canada 103 C8
Rayón Mexico 118 B2
Rayong Thailand 64 F3
Rayville U.S.A. 116 E9
Raz, Pte. du France 18 D2
Razan Iran 73 E13
Ražana Serbia 44 B3
Ražanj Serbia 44 C5
Razāzah, Buḥayrat ar Iraq 73 F10
Razāzah, L. = Razāzah,
   Buḥayrat ar Iraq 73 F10
Razdelna Bulgaria 45 C11
Razdel'naya = Rozdilna
   Ukraine 29 D15
Razdolnoye Russia 54 C5
Razdolnoye Ukraine 33 K7
Razeh Iran 71 C6
Razgrad Bulgaria 45 C10
Razim, Lacul Romania 29 F14
Razlog Bulgaria 44 E7
Razmak Pakistan 68 C3
Ré, Î. de France 20 B2
Reading U.K. 15 F7
Reading U.S.A. 115 F9
Reading □ U.K. 15 F7
Realicó Argentina 126 D3
Réalmont France 20 E6
Ream Cambodia 65 G4
Reay Forest U.K. 13 C4
Rebais France 19 D10
Rebi Indonesia 63 F8
Rebiana Libya 79 D10
Rebiana, Sahrâ' Libya 79 D10
Reboly Russia 8 E24
Rebun-Tō Japan 54 B10
Recanati Italy 41 E10
Recaş Romania 28 D6
Recco Italy 40 D6
Recherche, Arch. of the
   Australia 93 F3
Rechna Doab Pakistan 68 D5
Rechytsa Belarus 23 B16
Recife Brazil 125 E12
Recife Seychelles 85 b
Recklinghausen Germany 17 C7
Reconquista Argentina 126 B4
Recreo Argentina 126 B2
Recz Poland 31 E2
Red → U.S.A. 116 F9
Red Bank U.S.A. 115 F10
Red Bay Canada 105 B8
Red Bluff U.S.A. 108 F2
Red Bluff Res. U.S.A. 109 L12
Red Cliffs Australia 95 E3
Red Cloud U.S.A. 112 E5
Red Creek U.S.A. 115 C8
Red Deer Canada 102 C6
Red Deer → Alta., Canada 103 C7
Red Deer → Man., Canada 103 C8
Red Deer L. Canada 103 C8
Red Hook U.S.A. 115 E11
Red Indian L. Canada 105 C8
Red L. Canada 103 C10
Red Lake Canada 103 C10
Red Lake Falls U.S.A. 112 B5
Red Lake Road Canada 103 C10
Red Lodge U.S.A. 108 D9
Red Mountain U.S.A. 111 K9
Red Oak U.S.A. 112 E6
Red River of the North →
   N. Amer. 112 A5
Red Rock Canada 104 C2
Red Rock, L. U.S.A. 112 E7
Red Rocks Pt. Australia 93 F4
Red Sea Asia 75 C2
Red Slate Mt. U.S.A. 110 H8
Red Sucker L. Canada 104 B1
Red Tower Pass = Turnu
   Roşu, P. Romania 29 E9
Red Wing U.S.A. 112 C7
Reda Poland 30 D5
Redang Malaysia 65 K4
Redange Lux. 17 E5
Redcar U.K. 14 C6
Redcar & Cleveland □ U.K. 14 C7
Redcliff Canada 108 A8
Redcliff Australia 95 D5

Redcliffe, Mt. Australia 93 E3
Reddersburg S. Africa 88 D4
Redding U.S.A. 108 F2
Redditch U.K. 15 E6
Redfield U.S.A. 112 C4
Redford U.S.A. 115 B11
Redhead Trin. & Tob. 125 K16
Redkino Russia 32 D9
Redlands U.S.A. 111 M9
Redmond Oreg., U.S.A. 108 D3
Redmond Wash., U.S.A. 110 C4
Redon France 18 E4
Redonda Antigua & B. 121 C7
Redondela Spain 36 C2
Redondo Portugal 37 G3
Redondo Beach U.S.A. 111 M8
Redruth U.K. 15 G2
Redvers Canada 103 D8
Redwater Canada 102 C6
Redwood U.S.A. 115 B9
Redwood △ U.S.A. 108 F1
Redwood City U.S.A. 110 H4
Redwood Falls U.S.A. 112 C6
Ree, L. Ireland 12 C3
Reed City U.S.A. 113 D11
Reed L. Canada 103 C8
Reedley U.S.A. 110 J7
Reedsburg U.S.A. 112 D8
Reedsport U.S.A. 108 E1
Reedsville U.S.A. 114 F7
Reefton N.Z. 91 E3
Rees Germany 24 D2
Reese → U.S.A. 108 F5
Refahiye Turkey 73 C8
Reftele Sweden 11 G7
Refugio U.S.A. 116 G6
Rega → Poland 30 D2
Regalbuto Italy 43 E7
Regen Germany 25 G9
Regen → Germany 25 F8
Regensburg Germany 25 F8
Regenstauf Germany 25 F8
Reggâne = Zaouiet
   Reggâne Algeria 78 C6
Reggello Italy 41 E8
Réggio di Calábria Italy 43 D8
Réggio nell'Emília Italy 40 D7
Reghin Romania 29 D9
Regina Canada 103 C8
Regina Beach Canada 103 C8
Registro Brazil 127 A6
Reguengos de Monsaraz
   Portugal 37 G3
Rehar → India 69 H10
Rehli India 69 H8
Rehoboth Namibia 88 C2
Rehovot Israel 74 D3
Reichenbach Germany 24 E8
Reid Australia 93 F4
Reidsville U.S.A. 117 C15
Reigate U.K. 15 F7
Reillo Spain 38 F3
Reims France 19 C11
Reina Adelaida, Arch. Chile 128 G2
Reina Sofía, Tenerife ✈
   (TFS) Canary Is. 48 F3
Reinbek Germany 24 B6
Reindeer → Canada 103 B8
Reindeer I. Canada 103 C9
Reindeer L. Canada 103 B8
Reinga, C. N.Z. 91 A4
Reinosa Spain 36 B6
Reitz S. Africa 89 D4
Reivilo S. Africa 88 D3
Rejaf Sudan 81 F3
Rejmyre Sweden 11 F9
Rejowiec Fabryczny Poland 31 G10
Reka → Slovenia 41 C11
Rekovac Serbia 44 C5
Reliance Canada 103 A7
RemADAle → Canada 103 C7
Reka → Slovenia 41 C11
Remarkable, Mt. Australia 95 E2
Rembang Indonesia 63 G14
Remedios Panama 120 E3
Remeshk Iran 71 E8
Remetea Romania 29 D10
Remich Lux. 17 E6
Remiremont France 19 D13
Remo Ethiopia 81 F5
Remontnoye Russia 35 G6
Remoulins France 21 E8
Remscheid Germany 17 C7
Ren Xian China 56 F8
Rendang Indonesia 63 J18
Rende Italy 43 C9
Rendina Greece 46 B3
Rendsburg Germany 24 A5
Renfrew Canada 115 A8
Renfrew □ U.K. 13 F4
Rengat Indonesia 62 E2
Rengo Chile 126 C1
Renhua China 59 E9
Renhuai China 58 D6
Reni Ukraine 29 E13
Renk Sudan 81 E3
Renmark Australia 95 E3
Rennell Sd. Canada 102 C2

Renner Springs Australia 94 B1
Rennes France 18 D5
Rennick Glacier Antarctica 5 D21
Rennie L. Canada 103 A7
Reno U.S.A. 110 F7
Reno → Italy 41 D9
Renovo U.S.A. 114 E7
Renqiu China 56 E9
Rens Denmark 11 K3
Renshou China 58 C5
Rensselaer Ind., U.S.A. 112 E10
Rensselaer N.Y., U.S.A. 115 D11
Rentería Spain 38 B3
Renton U.S.A. 110 C4
Réo Burkina Faso 82 C4
Reocín Spain 36 B6
Reotipur India 69 G10
Répcelak Hungary 28 C2
Republic Mo., U.S.A. 112 G7
Republic Wash., U.S.A. 108 B4
Republican → U.S.A. 112 F5
Repulse B. Australia 94 A4
Repulse Bay Canada 101 C11
Requena Peru 124 E4
Requena Spain 39 F3
Réquista France 20 D6
Reşadiye = Datça Turkey 47 E9
Reşadiye Turkey 72 B7
Reşadiye Yarımadası Turkey 47 E9
Resavica Serbia 44 B5
Resen Macedonia 44 E5
Reserve U.S.A. 109 K9
Resht = Rasht Iran 73 D13
Resistencia Argentina 126 B4
Reşiţa Romania 28 E6
Resko Poland 30 E2
Reso = Raisio Finland 32 B2
Resolute Canada 101 B2
Resolution I. Canada 101 C13
Resolution I. N.Z. 91 F1
Ressano Garcia Mozam. 89 D5
Reston Canada 103 D8
Reszel Poland 30 D8
Retalhuleu Guatemala 120 D1
Retenue, L. de
   Dem. Rep. of the Congo 87 E2
Retezat, Munţii Romania 28 E7
Retezat △ Romania 28 E7
Retford U.K. 14 D7
Rethel France 19 C11
Rethem Germany 24 C5
Rethimno Greece 49 D6
Rethimno □ Greece 49 D6
Reti Pakistan 68 E3
Retiche, Alpi Switz. 25 J6
Retiers France 18 E5
Retortillo Spain 36 E4
Retournac France 21 C8
Rétság Hungary 28 C4
Réunion ☑ Ind. Oc. 85 c
Reus Spain 38 D6
Reuterstadt Stavenhagen
   Germany 24 B8
Reutlingen Germany 25 G5
Reutte Austria 26 D3
Reval = Tallinn Estonia 32 C3
Revel France 20 E6
Revelganj India 69 G11
Revelstoke Canada 102 C5
Reventazón Peru 124 E2
Revigny-sur-Ornain France 19 D11
Revillagigedo, Is. de Pac. Oc.
   118 D2
Revin France 19 C11
Revúca Slovak Rep. 27 C13
Revuè → Mozam. 87 F3
Rewa India 69 G9
Rewari India 68 E7
Rexburg U.S.A. 108 E8
Rey Iran 71 C6
Rey, I. del Panama 120 E4
Rey, L. del Mexico 118 B4
Rey Malabo Eq. Guin. 83 E6
Reyðarfjörður Iceland 8 D6
Reyes, Pt. U.S.A. 110 H3
Reyhanlı Turkey 72 D7
Reykjahlíð Iceland 8 D5
Reykjanes Iceland 8 E2
Reykjavík Iceland 8 D3
Reynolds Ra. Australia 92 D5
Reynoldsville U.S.A. 114 E6
Reynosa Mexico 119 B5
Rēzekne Latvia 32 D4
Rezina Moldova 29 C13
Rezovo Bulgaria 45 D12
Rezvān Iran 71 E8
Rgotina Serbia 44 B6
Rhayader U.K. 15 E4
Rheda-Wiedenbrück
   Germany 24 D4
Rhede Germany 24 D2
Rhein → Europe 17 C6
Rhein-Main-Donau-Kanal
   Germany 25 F7
Rhein-Ruhr, Düsseldorf ✈
   (DUS) Germany 24 D2
Rhein-Taunus △ Germany 25 E4

Rhein-Westerwald △
  Germany **24** E3
Rheinbach Germany **24** E2
Rheine Germany **24** C3
Rheinfelden Germany **25** H3
Rheinhessen-Pfalz □
  Germany **25** F3
Rheinland-Pfalz □ Germany **25** E2
Rheinsberg Germany **24** B8
Rhin = Rhein → Europe **17** C6
Rhine = Rhein → Europe **17** C6
Rhinebeck U.S.A. **115** E11
Rhineland-Palatinate =
  Rheinland-Pfalz □
  Germany **25** E2
Rhinelander U.S.A. **112** C9
Rhinns Pt. U.K. **13** F2
Rhino Camp Uganda **86** B3
Rhir, Cap Morocco **78** B4
Rho Italy **40** C6
Rhode Island □ U.S.A. **115** E13
Rhodes Greece **49** D7
Rhodes ✈ (RHO) Greece **47** E10
Rhodope Mts. = Rhodopi
  Planina Bulgaria **45** E8
Rhodopi Planina Bulgaria **45** E8
Rhön Germany **24** E5
Rhondda U.K. **15** F4
Rhondda Cynon Taff □ U.K. **15** F4
Rhône □ France **21** C8
Rhône → France **21** E8
Rhône-Alpes □ France **21** C9
Rhum U.K. **13** E2
Rhyl U.K. **14** D4
Ri-Aba Eq. Guin. **83** E6
Ria Formosa △ Portugal **37** H3
Riachão Brazil **125** D7
Riangnom Sudan **81** F3
Riaño Spain **36** C6
Rians France **21** E9
Riansáres → Spain **37** F7
Riasi India **69** C6
Riau □ Indonesia **62** E2
Riau, Kepulauan Indonesia **62** D2
Riau Arch. = Riau,
  Kepulauan Indonesia **62** D2
Riaza Spain **36** D7
Riaza → Spain **36** D7
Riba de Saelices Spain **38** E2
Riba-Roja de Turia Spain **39** F4
Ribadavia Spain **36** C2
Ribadeo Spain **36** B3
Ribadesella Spain **36** B5
Ribado Nigeria **83** D7
Ribao Cameroon **83** D7
Ribas = Ribes de Freser
  Spain **38** C7
Ribas do Rio Pardo Brazil **125** H8
Ribauè Mozam. **87** E4
Ribble → U.K. **14** D5
Ribe Denmark **11** J2
Ribeauvillé France **19** D14
Ribécourt-Dreslincourt
  France **19** C9
Ribeira = Santa Uxía Spain **36** C2
Ribeira Brava Madeira **48** D2
Ribeira Grande C. Verde Is. **78** b
Ribeirão Prêto Brazil **127** A6
Ribemont France **19** C10
Ribera Italy **42** E6
Ribérac France **20** C4
Riberalta Bolivia **124** F5
Ribes de Freser Spain **38** C7
Ribnica Slovenia **41** C11
Ribnitz-Damgarten Germany **24** A8
Ričany Czech Rep. **26** B7
Riccarton N.Z. **91** E4
Ríccia Italy **43** A7
Riccione Italy **41** E9
Rice U.S.A. **111** L12
Rice L. Canada **114** B6
Rice Lake U.S.A. **112** C8
Rich, C. Canada **114** B4
Richard Toll Senegal **82** B1
Richards Bay S. Africa **89** D5
Richardson → Canada **103** B6
Richardson Lakes U.S.A. **113** C18
Richardson Springs U.S.A. **110** F5
Riche, C. Australia **93** F2
Richelieu France **18** E7
Richey U.S.A. **108** C11
Richfield U.S.A. **108** G7
Richfield Springs U.S.A. **115** D10
Richford U.S.A. **115** B12
Richibucto Canada **105** C7
Richland Ga., U.S.A. **117** E12
Richland Wash., U.S.A. **108** C4
Richland Center U.S.A. **112** D8
Richlands U.S.A. **113** G13
Richmond Australia **94** C3
Richmond N.Z. **91** D4
Richmond U.K. **14** C6
Richmond Calif., U.S.A. **110** H4
Richmond Ind., U.S.A. **113** F11
Richmond Ky., U.S.A. **113** G11
Richmond Mich., U.S.A. **114** D4
Richmond Mo., U.S.A. **112** F7

Richmond Tex., U.S.A. **116** G7
Richmond Utah, U.S.A. **108** F8
Richmond Va., U.S.A. **113** G15
Richmond Vt., U.S.A. **115** B12
Richmond Hill Canada **114** C5
Richmond Ra. Australia **95** D5
Richtersveld △ S. Africa **88** D2
Richwood U.S.A. **113** F13
Ricla Spain **38** D3
Ridder = Leninogorsk
  Kazakhstan **52** D9
Riddlesburg U.S.A. **114** F6
Ridgecrest U.S.A. **111** K9
Ridgefield Conn., U.S.A. **115** E11
Ridgefield Wash., U.S.A. **110** E4
Ridgeland Miss., U.S.A. **117** E9
Ridgeland S.C., U.S.A. **117** E14
Ridgetown Canada **114** D3
Ridgewood U.S.A. **115** F10
Ridgway U.S.A. **114** E6
Riding Mountain △ Canada **103** C9
Ridley, Mt. Australia **93** F3
Riebeek-Oos S. Africa **88** E4
Ried Austria **26** C6
Riedlingen Germany **25** G5
Riesa Germany **24** D9
Riesi Italy **43** E7
Riet → S. Africa **88** D3
Rietavas Lithuania **30** C10
Rietbron S. Africa **88** E3
Rietfontein Namibia **88** C3
Rieti Italy **41** F9
Rieupeyroux France **20** D6
Riez France **21** E10
Rīga Latvia **30** B11
Rīga ✈ (RIX) Latvia **30** B10
Riga, G. of Latvia **30** A10
Rigacikun Nigeria **83** C6
Rīgān Iran **71** D8
Rīgas Jūras Līcis = Riga, G.
  of Latvia **30** A10
Rigaud Canada **115** A10
Rigby U.S.A. **108** E8
Rīgestān Afghan. **66** D4
Riggins U.S.A. **108** D5
Rignac France **20** D6
Rigolet Canada **105** B8
Rihand Dam India **69** G10
Riihimäki Finland **32** B3
Riiser-Larsen-halvøya
  Antarctica **5** C4
Rijau Nigeria **83** C6
Rijeka Croatia **41** C11
Rijeka Crnojevića
  Montenegro **44** D3
Rijssen Neths. **17** B6
Rika → Ukraine **29** B8
Rike Ethiopia **81** E4
Rikuchū-Kaigan △ Japan **54** E11
Rikuzentakada Japan **54** E10
Rila Bulgaria **44** D7
Rila Planina Bulgaria **44** D7
Riley U.S.A. **108** E4
Rima → Nigeria **83** C6
Rimah, Wadi ar → Si. Arabia **70** E4
Rimau, Pulau Malaysia **65** c
Rimavská Sobota
  Slovak Rep. **27** C13
Rimbey Canada **102** C6
Rimbo Sweden **10** E12
Rimersburg U.S.A. **114** E5
Rimforsa Sweden **11** F9
Rimi Nigeria **83** C6
Rímini Italy **41** D9
Rimouski Canada **105** C6
Rimrock U.S.A. **110** D5
Rinca Indonesia **63** F5
Rincón de la Victoria Spain **37** J6
Rincón de Romos Mexico **118** C4
Rinconada Argentina **126** A2
Rind → India **69** G9
Ringarum Sweden **11** F10
Ringas India **68** F6
Ringe Denmark **11** J4
Ringgold Is. Fiji **91** a
Ringim Nigeria **83** C6
Ringkøbing Denmark **11** H2
Ringkøbing Fjord Denmark **11** H2
Ringsjön Sweden **11** J7
Ringsted Denmark **11** J5
Ringvassøya Norway **8** B18
Ringwood U.S.A. **115** E10
Rinia Greece **47** D7
Rinjani Indonesia **62** F5
Rinteln Germany **24** C5
Río, Punta del Spain **39** J2
Río Branco Brazil **124** E5
Río Branco Uruguay **127** C5
Río Bravo Mexico **119** B5
Río Bravo △ N. Amer. **118** B4

Río Bravo del Norte →
  Mexico **119** B5
Rio Brilhante Brazil **127** A5
Rio Claro Brazil **127** A6
Rio Claro Trin. & Tob. **121** D7
Río Colorado Argentina **128** D4
Río Cuarto Argentina **126** C3
Rio das Pedras Mozam. **89** C6
Rio de Janeiro Brazil **127** A7
Rio de Janeiro □ Brazil **127** A7
Rio do Sul Brazil **127** B6
Río Dulce △ Guatemala **120** C2
Río Gallegos Argentina **128** G3
Río Grande Argentina **128** G3
Río Grande Brazil **127** C5
Río Grande Mexico **118** C4
Río Grande Nic. **120** D3
Río Grande Puerto Rico **121** d
Río Grande → N. Amer. **116** A3
Río Grande City U.S.A. **116** H5
Río Grande de Santiago →
  Mexico **118** C3
Rio Grande do Norte □
  Brazil **125** E11
Rio Grande do Sul □ Brazil **127** C5
Río Hato Panama **120** E3
Río Lagartos Mexico **119** C7
Río Largo Brazil **125** E11
Rio Maior Portugal **37** F2
Rio Marina Italy **40** F7
Río Mulatos Bolivia **124** G5
Río Muni □ Eq. Guin. **84** D2
Rio Negro Brazil **127** B6
Río Pardo Brazil **127** C5
Río Pilcomayo △ Argentina **126** B4
Río Platano △ Honduras **120** C3
Río Rancho U.S.A. **109** J10
Río Segundo Argentina **126** C3
Río Tercero Argentina **126** C3
Rio Tinto Portugal **36** D2
Rio Verde Brazil **125** G8
Rio Verde Mexico **119** C5
Rio Vista U.S.A. **110** G5
Ríobamba Ecuador **124** D3
Ríohacha Colombia **124** A4
Riom France **20** C7
Riom-ès-Montagnes France **20** C6
Rion-des-Landes France **20** E3
Rionero in Vúlture Italy **43** B8
Rioni → Georgia **35** J5
Ríos Spain **36** D3
Ríosucio Colombia **124** B3
Riou L. Canada **103** B7
Rioz France **19** E13
Ripatransone Italy **41** F10
Ripley Canada **114** B3
Ripley Calif., U.S.A. **111** M12
Ripley N.Y., U.S.A. **114** D5
Ripley Tenn., U.S.A. **117** D10
Ripley W. Va., U.S.A. **113** F13
Ripoll Spain **38** C7
Ripon U.K. **14** C6
Ripon Calif., U.S.A. **110** H5
Ripon Wis., U.S.A. **112** D9
Riposto Italy **43** E8
Risan Montenegro **44** D2
Riscle France **20** E3
Rishā', W. ar → Si. Arabia **70** E5
Rishiri-Rebun-
  Sarobetsu △ Japan **54** B10
Rishiri-Tō Japan **54** B10
Rishon le Ziyyon Israel **74** D3
Risle → France **18** C7
Risnjak △ Croatia **41** C11
Rison U.S.A. **116** E8
Risør Norway **9** G13
Rita Blanca Cr. → U.S.A. **116** D3
Riti Nigeria **83** D6
Ritter, Mt. U.S.A. **110** H7
Rittman U.S.A. **114** F3
Ritzville U.S.A. **108** C4
Riva del Garda Italy **40** C7
Riva Lígure Italy **40** E4
Rivadavia B. Aires, Argentina
  126 D3
Rivadavia Mendoza,
  Argentina **126** C2
Rivadavia Salta, Argentina **126** A3
Rivadavia Chile **126** B1
Rivarolo Canavese Italy **40** C4
Rivas Nic. **120** D2
Rive-de-Gier France **21** C8
River Cess Liberia **82** D3
River Jordan Canada **110** B2
Rivera Argentina **126** D3
Rivera Uruguay **127** C4
Riverbank U.S.A. **110** H6
Riverdale U.S.A. **110** J7
Riverhead U.S.A. **115** F12
Riverhurst Canada **103** C7
Rivers Canada **103** C8
Rivers □ Nigeria **83** E6
Rivers Inlet Canada **102** C3
Riversdale S. Africa **88** E3
Riverside U.S.A. **111** M9
Riverton Australia **95** E2
Riverton Canada **103** C9

Riverton N.Z. **91** G2
Riverton U.S.A. **108** E9
Rives France **21** C9
Rivesaltes France **20** F6
Riviera U.S.A. **111** K12
Riviera di Levante Italy **40** D6
Riviera di Ponente Italy **40** D5
Rivière-au-Renard Canada **105** C7
Rivière-du-Loup Canada **105** C6
Rivière-Pentecôte Canada **105** C6
Rivière-Pilote Martinique **120** c
Rivière St-Paul Canada **105** B8
Rivière-Salée Martinique **120** c
Rivne Odesa, Ukraine **29** D14
Rivne Rivne, Ukraine **23** C14
Rivne □ Ukraine **33** G4
Rívoli Italy **40** C4
Rivoli B. Australia **95** F3
Rixheim France **19** E14
Riyadh = Ar Riyāḍ Si. Arabia **70** E5
Riyadh al Khabrā' Si. Arabia **70** E4
Riza Greece **44** F7
Rize Turkey **73** B9
Rize □ Turkey **73** B9
Rizhao China **57** G10
Rizokarpaso Cyprus **49** D13
Rizzuto, C. Italy **43** D10
Rjukan Norway **9** G13
Ro Greece **47** E11
Roa Spain **36** D7
Road Town Br. Virgin Is. **121** e
Roan Plateau U.S.A. **108** G9
Roanne France **19** F11
Roanoke Ala., U.S.A. **117** E12
Roanoke Va., U.S.A. **113** G14
Roanoke → U.S.A. **117** D16
Roanoke I. U.S.A. **117** D17
Roanoke Rapids U.S.A. **117** C16
Roatán Honduras **120** C2
Robāṭ Sang Iran **71** C8
Robāṭkarīm Iran **71** C6
Robāṭkarīm □ Iran **71** B6
Robbins I. Australia **95** G4
Robe → Australia **92** D2
Róbbio Italy **40** C5
Robe → Australia **92** D2
Robert Lee U.S.A. **116** F4
Robertsdale U.S.A. **114** F6
Robertsganj India **69** G10
Robertson S. Africa **88** E2
Robertson I. Antarctica **5** C18
Robertson Ra. Australia **92** D3
Robertsport Liberia **82** D2
Robertstown Australia **95** E2
Roberval Canada **105** C5
Robeson Chan. N. Amer. **4** A4
Robesonia U.S.A. **115** F8
Robi Ethiopia **81** F4
Robinson U.S.A. **112** F10
Robinson → Australia **94** B2
Robinson Ra. Australia **93** E2
Robinvale Australia **95** E3
Robledo Spain **39** G2
Roblin Canada **103** C8
Roboré Bolivia **124** G7
Robson Canada **102** D5
Robson, Mt. Canada **102** C5
Robstown U.S.A. **116** H6
Roca, C. da Portugal **37** G1
Roca Partida, I. Mexico **118** D2
Rocamadour France **20** D5
Rocas, I. Brazil **125** D12
Rocca San Casciano Italy **41** D8
Roccadáspide Italy **43** B8
Roccastrada Italy **41** F8
Roccella Iónica Italy **43** D9
Rocciamelone, Monte =
  Roche Melon Italy **21** C11
Rocha Uruguay **127** C5
Rochdale U.K. **14** D5
Roche Melon Italy **21** C11
Rochechouart France **20** C4
Rochefort Belgium **17** D5
Rochefort France **20** C3
Rochefort-en-Terre France **18** E4
Rochelle U.S.A. **112** E9
Rocher River Canada **102** A6
Rocheservière France **18** F5
Rochester U.K. **15** F8
Rochester Ind., U.S.A. **112** E10
Rochester Minn., U.S.A. **112** C7
Rochester N.H., U.S.A. **115** C14
Rochester N.Y., U.S.A. **114** C7
Rociu Romania **29** F10
Rock → Canada **102** A3
Rock, The Australia **95** F4
Rock Creek U.S.A. **114** E4
Rock Falls U.S.A. **112** E9
Rock Hill U.S.A. **117** D14
Rock Island U.S.A. **112** E9
Rock Port U.S.A. **112** E6
Rock Rapids U.S.A. **112** D5
Rock Sound Bahamas **120** B4
Rock Springs Mont., U.S.A. **108** C10
Rock Springs Wyo., U.S.A. **108** F9
Rock Valley U.S.A. **112** D5
Rockall Atl. Oc. **6** D3

Rockdale Tex., U.S.A. **116** F6
Rockdale Wash., U.S.A. **110** C5
Rockeby = Mungkan
  Kandju △ Australia **94** A3
Rockefeller Plateau
  Antarctica **5** E14
Rockford U.S.A. **112** D9
Rockglen Canada **103** D7
Rockhampton Australia **94** C5
Rockingham Australia **93** F2
Rockingham N.C., U.S.A. **117** D15
Rockingham Vt., U.S.A. **115** C12
Rockingham B. Australia **94** B4
Rocklake U.S.A. **112** A4
Rockland Canada **115** A9
Rockland Idaho, U.S.A. **108** E7
Rockland Maine, U.S.A. **113** C19
Rockland Mich., U.S.A. **112** B9
Rocklin U.S.A. **110** G5
Rockmart U.S.A. **117** D12
Rockport Mass., U.S.A. **115** D14
Rockport Tex., U.S.A. **116** G6
Rocksprings U.S.A. **116** F4
Rockville Conn., U.S.A. **115** E12
Rockville Md., U.S.A. **113** F15
Rockwall U.S.A. **116** E6
Rockwell City U.S.A. **112** D6
Rockwood Canada **114** C4
Rockwood Maine, U.S.A. **113** C19
Rockwood Tenn., U.S.A. **117** D12
Rocky Ford U.S.A. **108** G12
Rocky Gully Australia **93** F2
Rocky Harbour Canada **105** C8
Rocky Island L. Canada **104** C3
Rocky Lane Canada **102** B5
Rocky Mount U.S.A. **117** D16
Rocky Mountain △ U.S.A. **108** F11
Rocky Mountain House
  Canada **102** C6
Rocky Mts. N. Amer. **108** B6
Rocky Point Namibia **88** B2
Rocroi France **19** C11
Rod Pakistan **66** E3
Roda Greece **49** A3
Röbel Germany **24** B8
Rødby Denmark **11** K5
Rødbyhavn Denmark **11** K5
Roddickton Canada **105** B8
Rødding Denmark **11** J3
Rödeby Sweden **11** H9
Rødekro Denmark **11** J3
Rodenkirchen Germany **24** B4
Rodez France **20** D6
Ródhos = Rhodes Greece **49** C10
Rodi Gargánico Italy **41** G12
Rodna Romania **29** C9
Rodnei, Munții Romania **29** C9
Rodney Canada **114** D3
Rodney, C. N.Z. **91** B5
Rodniki Russia **34** B5
Rodolivos Greece **44** F7
Rodonit, Kepi i Albania **44** E3
Rodopi □ Greece **45** E9
Rodopos Greece **49** D5
Rodríguez Ind. Oc. **3** E13
Roe → U.K. **12** A5
Roebling U.S.A. **115** F10
Roebourne Australia **92** D2
Roebuck B. Australia **92** C3
Roermond Neths. **17** C6
Roes Welcome Sd. Canada **101** C11
Roeselare Belgium **17** D3
Rogachev = Ragachow
  Belarus **23** B16
Rogaška Slatina Slovenia **41** B12
Rogagua, L. Bolivia **124** F5
Rogatec Slovenia **41** B12
Rogatica Bos.-H. **28** G4
Rogatyn Ukraine **23** D13
Rogers U.S.A. **116** C7
Rogers City U.S.A. **113** C12
Rogersville Canada **105** C6
Roggan → Canada **104** B4
Roggan L. Canada **104** B4
Roggeveen Basin Pac. Oc. **97** L18
Roggeveldberge S. Africa **88** E3
Roggiano Gravina Italy **43** C9
Rogliano France **21** F13
Rogliano Italy **43** C9
Rogoaguado, L. Bolivia **124** F5
Rogojampi Indonesia **63** J17
Rogoźno Poland **31** F3
Rogue → U.S.A. **108** E1
Rohan France **18** D4
Rohnert Park U.S.A. **110** G4
Rohri Pakistan **68** F3
Rohri Canal Pakistan **68** F3
Rohtak India **68** E7
Roi Et Thailand **64** D4
Roja Latvia **30** A9
Rojas Argentina **126** C3
Rojo, C. Mexico **119** C5
Rokan → Indonesia **62** D2
Rokel → S. Leone **82** D2

Rokiškis Lithuania **32** E3
Rokitno Russia **33** G8
Rokycany Czech Rep. **26** B6
Rolândia Brazil **127** A5
Rolla Mo., U.S.A. **112** G8
Rolla N. Dak., U.S.A. **112** A4
Rolleston Australia **94** C4
Rollingstone Australia **94** B4
Rom Sudan **81** F3
Roma Australia **95** D4
Roma Italy **41** G9
Roma Sweden **11** G12
Roma Fiumicino ✈ (FCO)
  Italy **41** G9
Roma-Los Saenz U.S.A. **116** H5
Romain, C. U.S.A. **117** E15
Romaine → Canada **105** B7
Roman Bulgaria **44** C7
Roman Romania **29** D11
Roman-Kosh, Gora Ukraine **33** K8
Romanche → France **21** C9
Romang Indonesia **63** F7
Români Egypt **74** E1
Romania ■ Europe **29** D10
Romanija Bos.-H. **28** G4
Romano, Cayo Cuba **120** B4
Romans-sur-Isère France **21** C9
Romanshorn Switz. **25** H5
Rombari Sudan **81** G3
Romblon Phil. **61** E5
Rome = Roma Italy **41** G9
Rome Ga., U.S.A. **117** D12
Rome N.Y., U.S.A. **115** C9
Rome Pa., U.S.A. **115** E8
Rometta Italy **43** D8
Romilly-sur-Seine France **19** D10
Romney U.S.A. **113** F14
Romney Marsh U.K. **15** F8
Romny Ukraine **33** G7
Rømø Denmark **11** J2
Romodan Ukraine **33** G7
Romodanovo Russia **34** C7
Romont Switz. **25** J2
Romorantin-Lanthenay
  France **19** E8
Romsdalen Norway **8** E12
Romsey U.K. **15** G6
Ron Vietnam **64** D6
Rona U.K. **13** D3
Ronan U.S.A. **108** C6
Roncador, Cayos Colombia **120** D3
Roncador, Serra do Brazil **125** F8
Ronciglione Italy **41** F9
Ronco → Italy **41** D9
Ronda Spain **37** J5
Ronda, Serranía de Spain **37** J5
Rondane Norway **8** F13
Rondônia □ Brazil **124** F6
Rondonópolis Brazil **125** G8
Rong, Koh Cambodia **65** G4
Rong Jiang → China **58** E7
Rong Xian
  Guangxi Zhuangzu, China **59** F8
Rong Xian Sichuan, China **58** C5
Rong'an China **58** E7
Rongchang China **58** C5
Ronge, L. la Canada **103** B7
Rongjiang China **58** E7
Rongshui China **58** E7
Rønne Denmark **11** J8
Ronne Ice Shelf Antarctica **5** D18
Ronneby Sweden **11** H9
Ronneby ✈ Sweden **11** H9
Rönneshytta Sweden **11** F9
Ronsard, C. Australia **93** D1
Ronse Belgium **17** D3
Roodepoort S. Africa **89** D4
Roof Butte U.S.A. **109** H9
Rooiboklaagte → Namibia **88** C3
Rooniu, Mt. Tahiti **91** d
Roorkee India **68** E7
Roosendaal Neths. **17** C4
Roosevelt U.S.A. **108** F9
Roosevelt → Brazil **124** E6
Roosevelt, Mt. Canada **102** B3
Roosevelt I. Antarctica **5** D12
Ropczyce Poland **31** H8
Roper → Australia **94** A2
Roper Bar Australia **94** A1
Roque Pérez Argentina **126** D4
Roquefort France **20** D3
Roquemaure France **21** D8
Roquetas de Mar Spain **39** J2
Roquetes Spain **38** E5
Roquevaire France **21** E9
Roraima □ Brazil **124** C6
Roraima, Mt. Venezuela **124** B6
Røros Norway **8** E14
Rorschach Switz. **25** H5
Rosa Zambia **87** D3
Rosa, Monte Europe **40** C4
Rosal de la Frontera Spain **37** H3
Rosalia U.S.A. **108** C5
Rosamond U.S.A. **111** L8
Rosans France **21** D9
Rosario Argentina **126** C3
Rosário Brazil **125** D10

Rosario Baja Calif., Mexico 118 B1
Rosario Sinaloa, Mexico 118 C3
Rosario Paraguay 126 A4
Rosario de la Frontera
  Argentina 126 B3
Rosario de Lerma Argentina 126 A2
Rosario del Tala Argentina 126 C4
Rosário do Sul Brazil 127 C5
Rosarito Mexico 111 N9
Rosarno Italy 43 D8
Rosas = Roses Spain 38 C8
Roscoe U.S.A. 115 E10
Roscoff France 18 D3
Roscommon Ireland 12 C3
Roscommon □ Ireland 12 C3
Roscrea Ireland 12 D4
Rose → Australia 94 A2
Rose, L. Bahamas 121 B5
Rose Belle Mauritius 85 d
Rose Blanche-Harbour Le
  Cou Canada 105 C8
Rose Hill Mauritius 85 d
Rose Pt. Canada 102 C2
Rose Valley Canada 103 C8
Roseau Dominica 121 C7
Roseau U.S.A. 112 A6
Rosebery Australia 95 G4
Rosebud S. Dak., U.S.A. 112 D3
Rosebud Tex., U.S.A. 116 F6
Roseburg U.S.A. 108 E2
Rosehearty U.K. 13 D6
Roseires Res. Sudan 79 F12
Roseland U.S.A. 110 G4
Rosemary Canada 102 C6
Rosenberg U.S.A. 116 G7
Rosendaël France 19 A9
Rosenheim Germany 25 H8
Roses Spain 38 C8
Roses, G. de Spain 38 C8
Roseto degli Abruzzi Italy 41 F11
Rosetown Canada 103 C7
Rosetta = Rashîd Egypt 80 H7
Roseville Calif., U.S.A. 110 G5
Roseville Mich., U.S.A. 114 D2
Rosewood Australia 95 D5
Roshkhvär Iran 71 C8
Rosières-en-Santerre France 19 C9
Rosignol Guyana 124 B7
Roșiori de Vede Romania 29 F10
Rositsa Bulgaria 45 C11
Rositsa → Bulgaria 45 C9
Roskilde Denmark 11 J6
Roskovec Albania 44 F3
Roslavl Russia 32 F7
Rosmaninhal Portugal 36 F3
Rosmead S. Africa 88 E4
Røsnæs Denmark 11 J4
Rosolini Italy 43 F7
Rosporden France 18 E3
Ross Australia 95 G4
Ross N.Z. 91 E3
Ross Béthio Mauritania 82 B1
Ross Dependency Antarctica 5 D12
Ross I. Antarctica 5 D11
Ross Ice Shelf Antarctica 5 E12
Ross L. U.S.A. 108 B3
Ross-on-Wye U.K. 15 F5
Ross River Australia 94 C1
Ross River Canada 102 A2
Ross Sea Antarctica 5 D11
Rossall Pt. U.K. 14 D4
Rossan Pt. Ireland 12 B3
Rossano Italy 43 C9
Rossburn Canada 103 C8
Rosseau Canada 114 A5
Rosseau, L. Canada 114 A5
Rosses, The Ireland 12 A3
Rossignol, L. Canada 104 B5
Rossignol L. Canada 105 D6
Rossiya = Russia ■ Eurasia 53 C11
Rossland Canada 102 D5
Rosslare Ireland 12 D5
Rosslare Harbour Ireland 12 D5
Rosslau Germany 24 D8
Rosso Mauritania 82 B1
Rosso, C. France 21 F12
Rossosh Russia 33 G10
Røssvatnet Norway 8 D16
Rosthern Canada 103 C7
Rostock Germany 24 A8
Rostov Don, Russia 33 J10
Rostov Sverdlovsk, Russia 32 D10
Rostov Russia 35 F5
Rostrenen France 18 D3
Roswell Ga., U.S.A. 117 D12
Roswell N. Mex., U.S.A. 109 K11
Rota Spain 37 J4
Rotan U.S.A. 116 E4
Rotenburg Hessen, Germany 24 E5
Rotenburg Niedersachsen,
  Germany 24 B5
Roth Germany 25 F7
Rothaargebirge △ Germany 24 D4
Rothaargebirge ⌒ Germany 24 E4
Rothenburg ob der Tauber
  Germany 25 F6

Rother → U.K. 15 G8
Rothera Antarctica 5 C17
Rotherham U.K. 14 D6
Rothes U.K. 13 D5
Rothesay Canada 105 C6
Rothesay U.K. 13 F3
Roti Indonesia 63 F6
Rotja, Pta. Spain 39 G6
Roto Australia 95 E4
Rotondo, Mte. France 21 F13
Rotoroa, L. N.Z. 91 D4
Rotorua N.Z. 91 C6
Rotorua, L. N.Z. 91 C6
Rott → Germany 25 G9
Rottenburg Germany 25 G4
Rottenmann Austria 26 D7
Rotterdam Neths. 17 C4
Rotterdam U.S.A. 115 D10
Rottne Sweden 11 G8
Rottnest I. Australia 93 F2
Rottumeroog Neths. 17 A6
Rottweil Germany 25 G4
Rotuma Fiji 90 C10
Roubaix France 19 B10
Roudnice nad Labem
  Czech Rep. 26 A7
Rouen France 18 C8
Rouergue France 20 D5
Rouillac France 20 C3
Rouleau Canada 103 C8
Round I. Mauritius 85 d
Round Mountain U.S.A. 108 G5
Round Mt. Australia 95 E5
Round Rock U.S.A. 116 F6
Roundup U.S.A. 108 C9
Rousay U.K. 13 B5
Rouses Point U.S.A. 115 B11
Rouseville U.S.A. 114 E5
Rousse = Ruse Bulgaria 45 C9
Roussennois Lom △ Bulgaria 45 C10
Roussillon Isère, France 21 C8
Roussillon Pyrénées-Or.,
  France 20 F6
Rouxville S. Africa 88 E4
Rouyn-Noranda Canada 104 C4
Rovaniemi Finland 8 C21
Rovato Italy 40 C7
Rovenki Ukraine 33 H10
Rovereto Italy 40 C8
Rovigo Italy 41 C8
Rovinj Croatia 41 C10
Rovno = Rivne Ukraine 23 C14
Rovnoye Russia 34 E8
Rovuma = Ruvuma →
  Tanzania 87 E5
Row'ān Iran 71 C6
Rowena Australia 95 D4
Rowley Shoals Australia 92 C2
Roxa Guinea-Biss. 82 C1
Roxas Capiz, Phil. 61 F5
Roxas Isabela, Phil. 61 C4
Roxas Mind. Or., Phil. 61 E4
Roxboro U.S.A. 117 C15
Roxborough Trin. & Tob. 125 J16
Roxburgh N.Z. 91 F2
Roxbury U.S.A. 114 F7
Roxby Downs Australia 95 E2
Roxen Sweden 11 F9
Roy Mont., U.S.A. 108 C9
Roy N. Mex., U.S.A. 109 J11
Roy Utah, U.S.A. 108 F7
Royal Bardia △ Nepal 69 E9
Royal Canal Ireland 12 C4
Royal Chitawan △ Nepal 69 F11
Royal Leamington Spa U.K. 15 E6
Royal Natal △ S. Africa 89 D4
Royal Tunbridge Wells U.K. 15 F8
Royale, Isle U.S.A. 112 B9
Royan France 20 C2
Roye France 19 C9
Royston U.K. 15 E7
Rožaj Montenegro 44 D4
Różan Poland 31 F8
Rozay-en-Brie France 19 D9
Rozdilna Ukraine 29 D15
Rozhnyativ Ukraine 29 B9
Rozhyshche Ukraine 23 C13
Rožmitál pod Třemšínem
  Czech Rep. 26 B6
Rožňava Slovak Rep. 27 C13
Rozogi Poland 30 E8
Rozoy-sur-Serre France 19 C11
Roztoczański △ Poland 31 H10
Rozzano Italy 40 C6
Rrëshen Albania 44 E3
Rrogozhinë Albania 44 E3
Rtanj Serbia 44 C5
Rtishchevo Russia 34 D6
Rúa = A Rúa Spain 36 C3
Ruacaná Namibia 88 B1
Ruaha △ Tanzania 86 D3
Ruahine Ra. N.Z. 91 C6
Ruapehu N.Z. 91 C5
Ruapuke I. N.Z. 91 G2
Ruâq, W. → Egypt 74 F2
Rub' al Khālī Si. Arabia 75 D4
Rubeho Mts. Tanzania 86 D4

Rubezhnoye = Rubizhne
  Ukraine 33 H10
Rubh a' Mhail U.K. 13 F2
Rubha Hunish U.K. 13 D2
Rubha Robhanais = Lewis,
  Butt of U.K. 13 C2
Rubi Spain 38 D7
Rubicon → U.S.A. 110 G5
Rubicone → Italy 41 D9
Rubik Albania 44 E3
Rubino Ivory C. 82 D4
Rubio Venezuela 124 B4
Rubizhne Ukraine 33 H10
Rubondo △ Tanzania 86 C3
Rubtsovsk Russia 52 D9
Ruby L. U.S.A. 108 F6
Ruby Mts. U.S.A. 108 F6
Rubyvale Australia 94 C4
Rucheng China 59 E9
Ruciane-Nida Poland 30 E8
Rūd Sar Iran 71 B6
Ruda Sweden 11 G9
Ruda Śląska Poland 31 H5
Rudall Australia 95 E2
Rudall → Australia 92 D3
Rudall River △ Australia 92 D3
Rüdersdorf Germany 24 C9
Rudewa Tanzania 87 E3
Rudkøbing Denmark 11 K4
Rudky Ukraine 31 J10
Rudna Poland 31 G9
Rudnik Bulgaria 45 D11
Rudnik Poland 31 H9
Rudnik Serbia 44 B4
Rudnya Russia 32 E6
Rudnytsa Ukraine 29 B13
Rudnyy Kazakhstan 52 D7
Rudo Bos.-H. 28 G4
Rudolfa, Ostrov Russia 52 A6
Rudolstadt Germany 24 E7
Rudong China 59 A13
Rudozem Bulgaria 45 E8
Rudyard U.S.A. 113 B11
Rue France 19 B8
Ruenya → Africa 87 F3
Rufa'a Sudan 81 E3
Ruffling Pt. Br. Virgin Is. 121 e
Rufiji → Tanzania 86 D4
Rufino Argentina 126 C3
Rufisque Senegal 82 C1
Rufunsa Zambia 87 F2
Rugao China 59 A13
Rugby U.K. 15 E6
Rugby U.S.A. 112 A4
Rügen Germany 24 A9
Rügen □ Germany 24 A9
Rugles France 18 D7
Ruhengeri Rwanda 86 C2
Ruhla Germany 24 E6
Ruhland Germany 24 D9
Ruhnu Estonia 30 A10
Ruhr → Germany 24 D2
Ruhuhu → Tanzania 87 E3
Rui'an China 59 D13
Ruichang China 59 C10
Ruidoso U.S.A. 109 K11
Ruijin China 59 E10
Ruili China 58 E1
Ruivo, Pico Madeira 48 D3
Ruj Bulgaria 44 D6
Rujen Macedonia 44 D6
Rujm Tal'at al Jamā'ah
  Jordan 74 E4
Ruk Pakistan 68 F3
Rukhla Pakistan 68 C4
Ruki →
  Dem. Rep. of the Congo 84 E3
Rukwa □ Tanzania 86 D3
Rukwa, L. Tanzania 86 D3
Rulhieres, C. Australia 92 B4
Rum = Rhum U.K. 13 E2
Rum Jordan 74 F4
Rum Cay Bahamas 121 B5
Rum Jungle Australia 92 B5
Ruma Serbia 28 E4
Ruma △ Kenya 86 C3
Rumāḥ Si. Arabia 70 E5
Rumania = Romania ■
  Europe 29 D10
Rumaylah Iraq 70 D5
Rumbêk Sudan 81 F2
Rumburk Czech Rep. 26 A7
Rumford U.S.A. 115 B14
Rumia Poland 30 D8
Rumilly France 21 C9
Rumoi Japan 54 C10
Rumonge Burundi 86 C2
Rumson U.S.A. 115 F11
Rumuruti Kenya 86 B4
Runan China 56 H8
Runanga N.Z. 91 E3
Runaway, C. N.Z. 91 B6
Runaway Bay Jamaica 120 a
Runcorn U.K. 14 D5
Rundu Namibia 88 B2
Rungwa Tanzania 86 D3
Rungwa → Tanzania 86 D3

Rungwa △ Tanzania 86 D3
Rungwe Tanzania 87 D3
Rungwe, Mt. Tanzania 84 F6
Runka Nigeria 83 C6
Runn Sweden 10 D9
Runton Ra. Australia 92 D3
Ruokolahti Finland 32 B5
Ruoqiang China 60 C3
Rupa India 67 F18
Rupar India 68 D7
Rupat Indonesia 62 D2
Rupea Romania 29 D10
Rupen → India 68 H4
Rupert U.S.A. 108 E7
Rupert → Canada 104 B4
Rupert B. Canada 104 B4
Rupert House =
  Waskaganish Canada 104 B4
Rupsa India 69 J12
Rur → Germany 24 D1
Rurrenabaque Bolivia 124 F5
Rus → Spain 39 F7
Rusambo Zimbabwe 87 F3
Rusape Zimbabwe 87 F3
Ruschuk = Ruse Bulgaria 45 C9
Ruse Bulgaria 45 C9
Ruse □ Bulgaria 45 C10
Ruşeţu Romania 29 F12
Rush Ireland 12 C5
Rushan China 57 F11
Rushden U.K. 15 E7
Rushmore, Mt. U.S.A. 112 D2
Rushville Ill., U.S.A. 112 E8
Rushville Ind., U.S.A. 113 F11
Rushville Nebr., U.S.A. 112 D2
Russas Brazil 125 D11
Russell Canada 103 C8
Russell Kans., U.S.A. 112 F4
Russell N.Y., U.S.A. 115 B9
Russell Pa., U.S.A. 114 E5
Russell Cave △ U.S.A. 117 D12
Russell L. Man., Canada 103 B8
Russell L. N.W.T., Canada 102 A5
Russellkonda India 67 K14
Russellville Ala., U.S.A. 117 D11
Russellville Ark., U.S.A. 116 D8
Russellville Ky., U.S.A. 117 G11
Rüsselsheim Germany 25 F4
Russi Italy 41 D9
Russia ■ Eurasia 53 C11
Russian → U.S.A. 110 G3
Russkoye Ustie Russia 4 B15
Rust Austria 27 D9
Rustam Pakistan 68 B5
Rustam Shahr Pakistan 68 F2
Rustavi Georgia 35 K7
Rustenburg S. Africa 88 D4
Ruston U.S.A. 116 E8
Rutana Burundi 86 C3
Rute Spain 37 H6
Ruteng Indonesia 63 F6
Ruth U.S.A. 114 C4
Rutherford U.S.A. 110 G4
Rutland U.S.A. 115 C12
Rutland □ U.K. 15 E7
Rutland Water U.K. 15 E7
Rutledge → Canada 103 A6
Rutledge L. Canada 103 A6
Rutqa, W. → Syria 73 E9
Rutshuru
  Dem. Rep. of the Congo 86 C2
Ruvo di Púglia Italy 43 A9
Ruvu Tanzania 86 D4
Ruvu → Tanzania 86 D4
Ruvuma □ Tanzania 87 E4
Ruvuma → Tanzania 87 E5
Ruwais U.A.E. 71 E7
Ruwenzori Africa 86 B2
Ruwenzori △ Uganda 86 B2
Ruya → Zimbabwe 89 B5
Ruyigi Burundi 86 C3
Ruyuan China 59 E9
Ruzayevka Russia 34 C7
Rūzhevo Konare Bulgaria 45 D8
Ružomberok Slovak Rep. 27 B12
Ruzyne, Praha ✈ (PRG)
  Czech Rep. 26 A6
Rwanda ■ Africa 86 C3
Ryakhovo Bulgaria 45 C10
Ryan, L. U.K. 13 G3
Ryazan Russia 32 E10
Ryazan □ Russia 34 C4
Ryazhsk Russia 32 F11
Rybachiy Russia 30 C7
Rybachiy Poluostrov Russia 8 B25
Rybinsk Russia 32 D10
Rybinskoye Vdkhr. Russia 32 C10
Rybnik Poland 31 H5
Rybnitsa = Râbniţa
  Moldova 29 C14
Rybnoye Russia 32 E10
Rychnov nad Kněžnou
  Czech Rep. 27 A9
Rychwał Poland 31 F5
Rycroft Canada 102 B5
Ryd Sweden 11 H8

Rydaholm Sweden 11 H8
Ryde U.K. 15 G6
Ryderwood U.S.A. 110 D3
Rydzyna Poland 31 G3
Rye U.K. 15 G8
Rye → U.K. 14 C7
Rye Bay U.K. 15 G8
Rye Patch Res. U.S.A. 108 F4
Ryegate U.S.A. 108 C9
Ryki Poland 31 G8
Ryley Canada 102 C6
Rylsk Russia 33 G8
Rylstone Australia 95 E4
Rymanów Poland 31 J8
Ryn Poland 30 E8
Ryn Peski = Naryn Qum
  Kazakhstan 35 G9
Ryōtsu Japan 54 E9
Rypin Poland 31 E6
Ryssby Sweden 11 H8
Ryūgasaki Japan 55 G10
Ryukyu Is. =
  Ryūkyū-rettō Japan 55 M3
Ryūkyū-rettō Japan 55 M3
Rzepin Poland 31 F1
Rzeszów Poland 31 H8
Rzhev Russia 32 D8

S

Sa Thailand 64 C3
Sa Canal Spain 48 C7
Sa Conillera Spain 48 C7
Sa Dec Vietnam 65 G5
Sa Dragonera Spain 48 B9
Sa Mesquida Spain 48 B11
Sa Pobla Spain 48 B10
Sa Savina Spain 48 C7
Sa'ādatābād Fārs, Iran 71 D7
Sa'ādatābād Hormozgān, Iran 71 D7
Sa'ādatābād Kermān, Iran 71 D7
Saale → Germany 24 D7
Saaler Bodden Germany 24 A8
Saalfeld Germany 24 E7
Saalfelden Austria 26 D5
Saane → Switz. 25 H3
Saanich Canada 110 B3
Saar → Europe 17 E6
Saar-Hunsrück △ Germany 25 F2
Saarbrücken Germany 25 F2
Saarburg Germany 25 F2
Saaremaa Estonia 32 C1
Saarijärvi Finland 8 E21
Saariselkä Finland 8 B23
Saarland □ Germany 25 F2
Saarlouis Germany 25 F2
Sab 'Abar Syria 72 F7
Saba W. Indies 121 C7
Šabac Serbia 44 B3
Sabadell Spain 38 D7
Sabah □ Malaysia 62 C5
Sabak Bernam Malaysia 65 L3
Sabalān, Kūhhā-ye Iran 73 C12
Sabalana, Kepulauan
  Indonesia 63 F5
Sábana de la Mar Dom. Rep. 121 C6
Sábanalarga Colombia 124 A4
Sabang Indonesia 62 C1
Săbăoani Romania 29 C11
Sabará Brazil 125 G10
Sabarmati → India 68 H5
Sabattis U.S.A. 115 B10
Sabáudia Italy 42 A6
Saberania Indonesia 63 E9
Sabhā Libya 79 C8
Sabi → India 68 E7
Sabidana, J. Sudan 80 D4
Sabie S. Africa 89 D5
Sabinal Mexico 118 A3
Sabinal U.S.A. 116 G5
Sabiñánigo Spain 38 C4
Sabinar, Punta del Spain 39 J2
Sabinas Mexico 118 B4
Sabinas → Mexico 118 B4
Sabinas Hidalgo Mexico 118 B4
Sabine → U.S.A. 116 G8
Sabine L. U.S.A. 116 G8
Sabine Pass U.S.A. 116 G8
Sabinov Slovak Rep. 27 B14
Sabinsville U.S.A. 114 E7
Sabirabad Azerbaijan 35 K9
Sablayan Phil. 61 E4
Sable Canada 105 D6
Sable, C. Canada 105 D6
Sable, C. U.S.A. 120 A3
Sable I. Canada 105 D8
Sablé-sur-Sarthe France 18 E6
Sabonkafi Niger 83 C6
Sabor → Portugal 36 D3
Sabou Burkina Faso 82 C4
Sabres France 20 D3
Sabrina Coast Antarctica 5 C9
Sabugal Portugal 36 E3
Sabulubbek Indonesia 62 E1
Sabuncu Turkey 47 B12
Sabzevār Iran 71 B8

Sabzvārān Iran 71 D8
Sac City U.S.A. 112 D6
Sacedón Spain 38 E2
Săcele Romania 29 E10
Sacheon S. Korea 57 G15
Sachigo → Canada 104 A2
Sachigo, L. Canada 104 B1
Sachimbo Angola 84 F4
Sachkhere Georgia 35 J6
Sachsen □ Germany 24 E9
Sachsen-Anhalt □ Germany 24 D7
Sächsische Schweiz △
  Germany 24 E10
Sacile Italy 41 C9
Sackets Harbor U.S.A. 115 C8
Sackville Canada 105 C7
Saco Maine, U.S.A. 115 C14
Saco Mont., U.S.A. 108 B10
Sacramento U.S.A. 110 G5
Sacramento → U.S.A. 110 G5
Sacramento Mts. U.S.A. 109 K11
Sacramento Valley U.S.A. 110 G5
Sacratif, C. Spain 37 J7
Săcueni Romania 28 C7
Sada Spain 36 B2
Sada-Misaki Japan 55 H6
Sádaba Spain 38 C3
Sadabad India 68 F8
Sadani Tanzania 86 D4
Sadao Thailand 65 J3
Sadd el Aali Egypt 80 C3
Saddle Mt. U.S.A. 110 E3
Sade Nigeria 83 C7
Sadimi Dem. Rep. of the Congo 87 D1
Sadiola Mali 82 C2
Sa'dīyah, Hawr as Iraq 73 F12
Sado Japan 54 F9
Sado → Portugal 37 G2
Sadon Russia 35 J6
Sadra India 68 H5
Sadri India 68 G5
Sæby Denmark 11 G4
Saegertown U.S.A. 114 E4
Saelices Spain 38 F2
Safaalan Turkey 45 E12
Safaga Egypt 80 B3
Safājah Si. Arabia 70 E3
Šafárikovo = Tornaľa
  Slovak Rep. 27 C13
Safata B. Samoa 91 b
Säffle Sweden 10 E6
Safford U.S.A. 109 K9
Saffron Walden U.K. 15 E8
Safi Morocco 78 B4
Şafiābād Iran 71 B8
Safid Dasht Iran 71 C6
Safid Kūh Afghan. 66 B3
Safid Rūd → Iran 71 B6
Safipur India 69 F9
Safonovo Russia 32 E7
Safranbolu Turkey 72 B5
Saft Rashîn Egypt 80 J7
Safune Samoa 91 b
Sag Harbor U.S.A. 115 F12
Saga Japan 55 H5
Saga □ Japan 55 H5
Saga Japan 54 E10
Sagaing Burma 67 J19
Sagala Mali 82 C3
Sagamore U.S.A. 114 F5
Saganaga L. Canada 112 A8
Sagar Karnataka, India 66 M9
Sagar Mad. P., India 69 H8
Sagara, L. Tanzania 86 D3
Sagarmatha = Everest, Mt.
  Nepal 69 E12
Sagarmatha △ Nepal 69 F12
Sagay Phil. 61 F5
Saginaw U.S.A. 113 D12
Saginaw B. U.S.A. 113 D12
Sagleipie Liberia 82 D3
Saglouc = Salluit Canada 101 C12
Sagone France 21 F12
Sagone, G. de France 21 F12
Sagres Portugal 37 J2
Sagua la Grande Cuba 120 B3
Saguache U.S.A. 108 G10
Saguaro △ U.S.A. 109 K8
Saguenay → Canada 105 C5
Sagunt Spain 38 F4
Sagunto = Sagunt Spain 38 F4
Sagwara India 68 H6
Sahaba Sudan 80 D3
Sahagún Spain 36 C6
Saham al Jawlān Syria 74 C4
Sahamandrevo Madag. 89 C8
Sahand, Kūh-e Iran 73 D12
Sahara Africa 78 D6
Saharan Atlas = Saharien,
  Atlas Algeria 78 B6
Saharanpur India 68 E7
Sahārsa India 69 G12
Sahasinaka Madag. 89 C8

Sahaswan *India* **69** E8
Saheira, W. el ⇢ *Egypt* **74** E2
Sahel *Africa* **78** E5
Sahel, Canal du *Mali* **82** C3
Sahibganj *India* **69** G12
Sāḥilīyah *Iraq* **73** F10
Sahiwal *Pakistan* **68** D5
Ṣaḥneh *Iran* **73** E12
Sahrawi = Western
  Sahara ■ *Africa* **78** D3
Sahuaripa *Mexico* **118** B3
Sahuarita *U.S.A.* **109** L8
Sahuayo de Díaz *Mexico* **118** C4
Šahy *Slovak Rep.* **27** C11
Sai ⇢ *India* **69** G10
Sai Buri *Thailand* **65** J3
Sa'id Bundâs *Sudan* **79** G10
Sa'īdābād = Sīrjān *Iran* **71** D7
Sa'īdābād *Iran* **71** B7
Sa'īdīyeh *Iran* **71** B6
Saidpur *Bangla.* **67** G16
Saidpur *India* **69** G10
Saidu Sharif *Pakistan* **69** B5
Saignes *France* **20** C6
Saigō *Japan* **55** F6
Saigon = Thanh Pho Ho
  Chi Minh *Vietnam* **65** G6
Saijō *Japan* **55** H6
Saikai △ *Japan* **55** H4
Saikanosy Masoala *Madag.* **89** B9
Saikhoa Ghat *India* **67** F19
Saiki *Japan* **55** H5
Sailana *India* **68** H6
Saillans *France* **21** D9
Sailolof *Indonesia* **63** E8
Saimaa *Finland* **32** B5
Saimbeyli *Turkey* **72** D7
Saimen = Saimaa *Finland* **32** B5
Ṣa'in Dezh *Iran* **73** D12
St. Abb's Head *U.K.* **13** F6
St-Affrique *France* **20** E6
St-Agrève *France* **21** C8
St-Aignan *France* **18** E8
St. Alban's *Canada* **105** C8
St. Albans *U.K.* **15** F7
St. Albans *Vt., U.S.A.* **115** B11
St. Albans *W. Va., U.S.A.* **113** F13
St. Alban's Head *U.K.* **15** G5
St. Albert *Canada* **102** C6
St-Amand-en-Puisaye
  France **19** E10
St-Amand-les-Eaux *France* **19** B10
St-Amand-Montrond *France* **19** F9
St-Amarin *France* **19** E14
St-Amour *France* **19** F12
St-André *Réunion* **85** c
St-André-de-Cubzac *France* **20** D3
St-André-les-Alpes *France* **21** E10
St. Andrew's *Canada* **105** C8
St. Andrews *U.K.* **13** E6
St-Anicet *Canada* **115** A10
St. Annes *Canada* **103** D9
St. Anns B. *Canada* **105** C7
St. Ann's Bay *Jamaica* **120** a
St. Anthony *Canada* **105** B8
St. Anthony *U.S.A.* **108** E8
St-Antoine *Canada* **105** C7
St-Antonin-Noble-Val
  France **20** D5
St. Arnaud *Australia* **95** F3
St-Astier *France* **20** C4
St-Aubin-du-Cormier *France* **18** D5
St-Augustin *Canada* **105** B8
St-Augustin ⇢ *Canada* **105** B8
St. Augustine *U.S.A.* **117** G14
St-Aulaye *France* **20** C4
St. Austell *U.K.* **15** G3
St-Avold *France* **19** C13
St. Barbe *Canada* **105** B8
St-Barthélemy *W. Indies* **121** C7
St-Béat *France* **20** F4
St. Bees Hd. *U.K.* **14** C4
St. Bees I. *Australia* **94** J7
St-Benoît *Réunion* **85** c
St-Benoît-du-Sault *France* **20** B5
St-Bonnet-en-Champsaur
  France **21** D10
St-Brevin-les-Pins *France* **18** E4
St-Brice-en-Coglès *France* **18** D5
St. Bride's *Canada* **105** C9
St. Brides B. *U.K.* **15** F2
St-Brieuc *France* **18** D4
St-Calais *France* **18** E7
St-Cast-le-Guildo *France* **18** D4
St. Catharines *Canada* **114** C5
St. Catherines I. *U.S.A.* **117** F14
St. Catherine's Pt. *U.K.* **15** G6
St-Céré *France* **20** D5
St-Cergue *Switz.* **25** J2
St-Cernin *France* **20** C6
St-Chamond *France* **21** C8
St. Charles *Ill., U.S.A.* **112** E9
St. Charles *Md., U.S.A.* **113** F15
St. Charles *Mo., U.S.A.* **112** F8
St. Charles *Va., U.S.A.* **113** G12
St-Chély-d'Apcher *France* **20** D7
St-Chinian *France* **20** E6

St. Christopher-Nevis = St.
  Kitts & Nevis ■ *W. Indies* **121** C7
St-Ciers-sur-Gironde *France* **20** C3
St. Clair *Mich., U.S.A.* **114** D2
St. Clair *Pa., U.S.A.* **115** F8
St. Clair ⇢ *U.S.A.* **114** D2
St. Clair, L. *N. Amer.* **114** D2
St. Clairsville *U.S.A.* **114** F4
St-Claud *France* **20** C4
St-Claude *Canada* **103** D9
St-Claude *France* **19** F12
St. Clears *U.K.* **15** F3
St-Clet *Canada* **115** A10
St. Cloud *Fla., U.S.A.* **117** G14
St. Cloud *Minn., U.S.A.* **112** C6
St. Cricq, C. *Australia* **93** E1
St. Croix *U.S. Virgin Is.* **121** C7
St. Croix ⇢ *U.S.A.* **112** C7
St. Croix Falls *U.S.A.* **112** C7
St-Cyprien *France* **20** F7
St-Cyr-sur-Mer *France* **21** E9
St. David's *Canada* **105** C8
St. David's *U.K.* **15** F2
St. David's Head *U.K.* **15** F2
St-Denis *France* **19** D13
St-Denis *Réunion* **85** c
St-Denis ✈ (RUN) *Réunion* **85** c
St-Dié *France* **19** D13
St-Dizier *France* **19** D11
St-Égrève *France* **21** C9
St. Elias, Mt. *U.S.A.* **100** C5
St. Elias Mts. *N. Amer.* **102** A1
St-Eloy-les-Mines *France* **19** F9
St-Émilion *France* **20** D3
St-Étienne *France* **21** C8
St-Étienne-de-Tinée *France* **21** D10
St-Étienne-du-Rouvray
  France **18** C8
St. Eugène *Canada* **115** A10
St. Eustatius *W. Indies* **121** C7
St-Exupery, Lyon ✈ (LYS)
  France **21** C9
St-Fargeau *France* **19** E10
St-Félicien *Canada* **104** C5
St-Florent *France* **21** F13
St-Florent, G. de *France* **21** F13
St-Florent-sur-Cher *France* **19** F9
St-Florentin *France* **19** E10
St-Flour *France* **20** C7
St. Francis *U.S.A.* **112** F3
St. Francis ⇢ *U.S.A.* **117** D9
St. Francis, C. *S. Africa* **88** E3
St. Francisville *U.S.A.* **116** F9
St-François, L. *Canada* **115** A10
St-Fulgent *France* **18** F5
St-Gabriel *Canada* **104** C5
St. Gallen = Sankt Gallen
  Switz. **25** H5
St-Galmier *France* **19** G11
St-Gaudens *France* **20** E4
St-Gaultier *France* **18** F8
St-Gengoux-le-National
  France **19** F11
St-Geniez-d'Olt *France* **20** D6
St. George *Australia* **95** D4
St. George *Canada* **105** C6
St. George *S.C., U.S.A.* **117** E14
St. George *Utah, U.S.A.* **109** H7
St. George, C. *Canada* **105** C8
St. George, C. *U.S.A.* **117** G12
St. George Ra. *Australia* **92** C4
St. George's *Canada* **105** C8
St. George's *Grenada* **121** D7
St. George's B. *Canada* **105** C8
St. Georges Basin *N.S.W.,
  Australia* **95** F5
St. Georges Basin
  W. Austral., Australia **92** C4
St. George's Channel *Europe* **12** E6
St. Georges Hd. *Australia* **95** F5
St-Georges-lès-
  Baillargeaux *France* **20** B4
St-Germain-de-Calberte
  France **20** D7
St-Germain-en-Laye *France* **19** D9
St-Germain-Lembron *France* **20** C7
St-Gervais-d'Auvergne
  France **19** F9
St-Gervais-les-Bains *France* **21** C10
St-Gildas, Pte. de *France* **18** E4
St-Gilles *France* **21** E8
St-Girons *Ariège, France* **20** F5
St-Girons *Landes, France* **20** E2
St. Gotthard P. = San
  Gottardo, P. del *Switz.* **25** J4
St. Helena *Atl. Oc.* **76** H3
St. Helena *U.S.A.* **108** G2
St. Helena, Mt. *U.S.A.* **110** G4
St. Helena B. *S. Africa* **88** E2
St. Helens *Australia* **95** G4
St. Helens *U.K.* **14** D5
St. Helens *U.S.A.* **110** E4
St. Helens, Mt. *U.S.A.* **110** D4
St. Helier *U.K.* **15** H5
St-Herblain *France* **18** E5
St-Hilaire-du-Harcouët
  France **18** D5

St-Hippolyte *France* **19** E13
St-Hippolyte-du-Fort *France* **20** E7
St-Honoré-les-Bains *France* **19** F10
St-Hubert *Belgium* **17** D5
St-Hyacinthe *Canada* **104** C5
St. Ignace *U.S.A.* **113** C11
St. Ignace I. *Canada* **104** C2
St. Ignatius *U.S.A.* **108** C6
St-Imier *Switz.* **25** H2
St. Ives *Cambs., U.K.* **15** E7
St. Ives *Corn., U.K.* **15** G2
St-James *France* **18** D5
St. James *U.S.A.* **112** D6
St-Jean ⇢ *Canada* **105** B7
St-Jean, L. *Canada* **105** C5
St-Jean-d'Angély *France* **20** C3
St-Jean-de-Braye *France* **19** E8
St-Jean-de-Luz *France* **20** E2
St-Jean-de-Maurienne
  France **21** C10
St-Jean-de-Monts *France* **18** F4
St-Jean-du-Gard *France* **20** D7
St-Jean-en-Royans *France* **21** C9
St-Jean-Pied-de-Port *France* **20** E2
St-Jean-Port-Joli *Canada* **105** C5
St-Jean-sur-Richelieu
  Canada **115** A11
St-Jérôme *Canada* **104** C5
St. John *Canada* **105** C6
St. John *U.S.A.* **112** F4
St. John ⇢ *Liberia* **82** D2
St. John ⇢ *N. Amer.* **113** C20
St. John, C. *Canada* **105** C8
St. John I. *U.S. Virgin Is.* **121** e
St. John's *Antigua & B.* **121** C7
St. John's *Canada* **105** C9
St. Johns *Ariz., U.S.A.* **109** J9
St. Johns *Mich., U.S.A.* **113** D11
St. Johns ⇢ *U.S.A.* **117** F14
St. John's Pt. *Ireland* **12** B3
St. Johnsbury *U.S.A.* **115** B12
St. Johnsville *U.S.A.* **115** C10
St-Joseph *Martinique* **120** c
St-Joseph *Réunion* **85** c
St. Joseph *La., U.S.A.* **116** F9
St. Joseph *Mo., U.S.A.* **112** F6
St. Joseph ⇢ *U.S.A.* **112** D10
St. Joseph, I. *Canada* **104** C3
St. Joseph, L. *Canada* **104** B1
St-Jovite *Canada* **104** C5
St-Juéry *France* **20** E6
St-Julien-Chapteuil *France* **21** C8
St-Julien-de-Vouvantes
  France **18** E5
St-Julien-en-Genevois
  France **19** F13
St-Junien *France* **20** C4
St-Just-en-Chaussée *France* **19** C9
St-Just-en-Chevalet *France* **20** C7
St. Kilda *U.K.* **16** C2
St. Kitts & Nevis ■
  W. Indies **121** C7
St. Laurent *Canada* **103** C9
St-Laurent-de-la-Salanque
  France **20** F6
St-Laurent-du-Pont *France* **21** C9
St-Laurent-en-Grandvaux
  France **19** F12
St-Laurent-Médoc *France* **20** C3
St. Lawrence *Australia* **94** C4
St. Lawrence *Canada* **105** C8
St. Lawrence ⇢ *Canada* **105** C6
St. Lawrence, Gulf of
  Canada **105** C7
St. Lawrence I. *U.S.A.* **106** a
St. Lawrence Islands △
  Canada **115** B9
St. Leonard *Canada* **105** C6
St-Léonard-de-Noblat *France* **20** C5
St-Leu *Réunion* **85** c
St. Lewis ⇢ *Canada* **105** B8
St-Lô *France* **18** C5
St-Louis *France* **19** E14
St-Louis *Guadeloupe* **120** b
St-Louis *Réunion* **85** c
St. Louis *Senegal* **82** B1
St. Louis *U.S.A.* **112** F8
St. Louis □ *Senegal* **82** B2
St. Louis ⇢ *U.S.A.* **112** B7
St-Loup-sur-Semouse
  France **19** E13
St. Lucia ■ *W. Indies* **121** f
St. Lucia, L. *S. Africa* **89** D5
St. Lucia Channel *W. Indies* **121** D7
St. Maarten ☑ *W. Indies* **121** C7
St. Magnus B. *U.K.* **13** A7
St-Maixent-l'École *France* **20** B3
St-Malo *France* **18** D4
St-Malo, G. de *France* **18** D4
St-Mandrier-sur-Mer *France* **21** E9
St-Marc *Haiti* **121** C5
St-Marcellin *France* **21** C9
St-Marcouf, Îs. *France* **18** C5
St. Maries *U.S.A.* **108** C5
St-Martin ☑ *W. Indies* **121** C7
St. Martin, C. *Martinique* **120** c
St. Martin, L. *Canada* **103** C9

St-Martin-de-Crau *France* **21** E8
St-Martin-de-Ré *France* **20** B2
St-Martin-d'Hères *France* **21** C9
St-Martin-Vésubie *France* **21** D11
St. Martins *Barbados* **121** g
St. Martory *France* **20** E4
St. Mary Pk. *Australia* **95** E2
St. Marys *Australia* **95** G4
St. Marys *Canada* **114** C3
St. Mary's *Corn., U.K.* **15** H1
St. Mary's *Orkney, U.K.* **13** C6
St. Marys *Ga., U.S.A.* **117** F14
St. Marys *Pa., U.S.A.* **114** E6
St. Mary's, C. *Canada* **105** C9
St. Mary's B. *Canada* **105** C9
St. Marys Bay *Canada* **105** D6
St-Mathieu, Pte. *France* **18** D2
St. Matthew I. *U.S.A.* **106** a
St-Maurice ⇢ *Canada* **104** C5
St. Mawes *U.K.* **15** G2
St-Maximin-la-Ste-Baume
  France **21** E9
St-Médard-en-Jalles *France* **20** D3
St-Méen-le-Grand *France* **18** D4
St-Mihiel *France* **19** D12
St-Nazaire *France* **18** E4
St. Neots *U.K.* **15** E7
St-Nicolas-de-Port *France* **19** D13
St-Niklaas *Belgium* **17** C4
St-Omer *France* **19** B9
St-Palais-sur-Mer *France* **20** C2
St-Pamphile *Canada* **105** C6
St-Pardoux-la-Rivière
  France **20** C4
St-Pascal *Canada* **105** C6
St. Paul *Canada* **102** C6
St-Paul *France* **21** D10
St-Paul *Réunion* **85** c
St. Paul *Minn., U.S.A.* **112** C7
St. Paul *Nebr., U.S.A.* **112** E4
St-Paul ⇢ *Canada* **105** B8
St. Paul ⇢ *Liberia* **82** D2
St. Paul, I. *Ind. Oc.* **3** F13
St-Paul-de-Fenouillet *France* **20** F6
St. Paul I. *Canada* **105** C7
St-Paul-lès-Dax *France* **20** E2
St-Péray *France* **21** D8
St. Peter *U.S.A.* **112** C7
St-Peter-Ording *Germany* **24** A4
St. Peter Port *U.K.* **15** H5
St. Peters *N.S., Canada* **105** C7
St. Peters *P.E.I., Canada* **105** C7
St. Petersburg =
  Sankt-Peterburg *Russia* **32** C6
St. Petersburg *U.S.A.* **117** H13
St-Philbert-de-Grand-Lieu
  France **18** E5
St-Phillippe *Réunion* **85** c
St-Pie *Canada* **115** A12
St-Pierre *Martinique* **120** c
St-Pierre *Réunion* **85** c
St-Pierre *St-P. & M.* **105** C8
St-Pierre, L. *Canada* **104** C5
St-Pierre-d'Oléron *France* **20** C2
St-Pierre-en-Port *France* **18** C7
St-Pierre-et-Miquelon ☑
  N. Amer. **105** C8
St-Pierre-le-Moûtier *France* **19** F10
St-Pierre-sur-Dives *France* **18** C6
St-Pol-de-Léon *France* **18** D3
St-Pol-sur-Mer *France* **19** A9
St-Pol-sur-Ternoise *France* **19** B9
St-Pons *France* **20** E6
St-Pourçain-sur-Sioule
  France **19** F10
St-Priest *France* **21** C8
St-Quay-Portrieux *France* **18** D4
St-Quentin *Canada* **105** C6
St-Quentin *France* **19** C10
St-Rambert-d'Albon *France* **21** C8
St-Raphaël *France* **21** E10
St. Regis *U.S.A.* **108** C6
St-Renan *France* **18** D2
St-Saëns *France* **18** C8
St-Savin *France* **20** B4
St-Savinien *France* **20** C3
St. Sebastien, Tanjon' i
  Madag. **89** A8
St-Seine-l'Abbaye *France* **19** E11
St-Sernin-sur-Rance *France* **20** E6
St-Sever *France* **20** E3
St-Siméon *Canada* **105** C6
St. Simons I. *U.S.A.* **117** F14
St. Simons Island *U.S.A.* **117** F14
St. Stephen *Canada* **105** C6
St-Sulpice *France* **20** E5
St-Sulpice-Laurière *France* **20** B5
St-Sulpice-les-Feuilles *France* **20** B5
St-Syprien = St-Cyprien
  France **20** F7
St-Thégonnec *France* **18** D3
St. Thomas *Canada* **114** D3
St. Thomas I. *U.S. Virgin Is.* **121** e
St-Tite *Canada* **104** C5
St-Tropez *France* **21** E10
St-Troud = St. Truiden
  Belgium **17** D5

St. Truiden *Belgium* **17** D5
St-Vaast-la-Hougue *France* **18** C5
St-Valery-en-Caux *France* **18** C7
St-Valéry-sur-Somme *France* **19** B8
St-Vallier *France* **19** F11
St-Vallier-de-Thiey *France* **21** E10
St-Varent *France* **18** F6
St-Vaury *France* **20** B5
St. Vincent = São Vicente
  C. Verde Is. **78** b
St. Vincent *Italy* **40** C4
St. Vincent, G. *Australia* **95** F2
St. Vincent & the
  Grenadines ■ *W. Indies* **121** D7
St-Vincent-de-Tyrosse
  France **20** E2
St. Vincent Passage
  W. Indies **121** D7
St-Vith *Belgium* **17** D6
St-Vivien-de-Médoc *France* **20** C2
St. Walburg *Canada* **103** C7
St-Yrieix-la-Perche *France* **20** C5
Ste-Adresse *France* **18** C7
Ste-Agathe-des-Monts
  Canada **104** C5
Ste-Anne *Guadeloupe* **120** b
Ste-Anne *Seychelles* **85** b
Ste-Anne, L. *Canada* **105** B6
Ste-Anne-des-Monts-
  Tourelle *Canada* **105** C6
Ste-Croix *Switz.* **25** J2
Ste-Enimie *France* **20** D7
Ste-Foy-la-Grande *France* **20** D4
Ste. Genevieve *U.S.A.* **112** G8
Ste-Hermine *France* **20** B2
Ste-Livrade-sur-Lot *France* **20** D4
Ste-Marguerite ⇢ *Canada* **105** B6
Ste-Marie *Canada* **105** C5
Ste-Marie *Martinique* **120** c
Ste-Marie *Réunion* **85** c
Ste-Marie, Ile = Nosy
  Boraha *Madag.* **89** B8
Ste-Marie-aux-Mines
  France **19** D14
Ste-Maure-de-Touraine
  France **18** E7
Ste-Maxime *France* **21** E10
Ste-Menehould *France* **19** C11
Ste-Mère-Église *France* **18** C5
Ste-Rose *Guadeloupe* **120** b
Ste-Rose *Réunion* **85** c
Ste. Rose du Lac *Canada* **103** C9
Ste-Savine *France* **19** D11
Ste-Sigolène *France* **21** C8
Saintes *France* **20** C3
Saintes, Îs. des *Guadeloupe* **120** b
Stes-Maries-de-la-Mer
  France **21** E8
Saintfield *U.K.* **12** B6
Saintonge *France* **20** C3
Saipan *N. Marianas* **96** F6
Sairang *India* **67** H18
Sairecábur, Cerro *Bolivia* **126** A2
Saitama *Japan* **55** G9
Saitama □ *Japan* **55** F9
Saiteli = Kadınhanı *Turkey* **72** C5
Saitī *Moldova* **29** D14
Saiyid *Pakistan* **68** C5
Saja-Besaya ⇢ *Spain* **36** B6
Sajama *Bolivia* **124** G5
Sajan *Serbia* **28** E5
Sajó ⇢ *Hungary* **28** C6
Sajószentpéter *Hungary* **28** B5
Sajum *India* **69** C8
Sak ⇢ *S. Africa* **88** E3
Saka *Kenya* **86** C5
Sakaba *Nigeria* **83** C6
Sakai *Japan* **55** G7
Sakaide *Japan* **55** G6
Sakaiminato *Japan* **55** G6
Sakākah *Si. Arabia* **70** D4
Sakakawea, L. *U.S.A.* **112** B3
Sakami ⇢ *Canada* **104** B4
Sakami, L. *Canada* **104** B4
Sâkâne, 'Erg i-n *Mali* **83** A4
Sakania
  Dem. Rep. of the Congo **87** E2
Sakaraha *Madag.* **89** C7
Sakartvelo = Georgia ■ *Asia* **35** J6
Sakarya *Turkey* **72** B4
Sakarya □ *Turkey* **72** B4
Sakarya ⇢ *Turkey* **72** B4
Sakashima-Guntō *Japan* **55** M2
Sakassou *Ivory C.* **82** D3
Sakata *Japan* **54** E9
Sakchu *N. Korea* **57** D13
Sakeny ⇢ *Madag.* **89** C8
Sakété *Benin* **83** D5
Sakha □ *Russia* **53** C14
Sakhalin *Russia* **53** D15
Sakhalinskiy Zaliv *Russia* **53** D15
Ṣāki *Azerbaijan* **35** K8
Šakiai *Lithuania* **30** D10
Sakon Nakhon *Thailand* **64** D5
Sakrand *Pakistan* **68** F3
Sakri *India* **69** F12
Sakrivier *S. Africa* **88** E3

Sakskøbing *Denmark* **11** K5
Sakti *India* **69** H10
Sakuma *Japan* **55** G8
Sakurai *Japan* **55** G7
Saky *Ukraine* **33** K7
Sal *C. Verde Is.* **78** b
Sal ⇢ *Russia* **35** G5
Sal Rei *C. Verde Is.* **78** b
Sala *Eritrea* **81** D4
Sala *Sweden* **10** E10
Sala ⇢ *Eritrea* **81** D4
Sala Consilina *Italy* **43** B8
Sala-y-Gómez *Pac. Oc.* **97** K17
Sala y Gómez Ridge *Pac. Oc.* **97** K16
Salaberry-de-Valleyfield
  Canada **115** A10
Salacgrīva *Latvia* **30** A11
Salada, L. *Mexico* **109** K6
Saladas *Argentina* **126** B4
Saladillo *Argentina* **126** D4
Salado ⇢ *B. Aires, Argentina*
  126 D4
Salado ⇢ *La Pampa,
  Argentina* **128** D3
Salado ⇢ *Santa Fe,
  Argentina* **126** C3
Salado ⇢ *Mexico* **116** H5
Salaga *Ghana* **83** D4
Sālah *Syria* **74** C4
Ṣalāḥ ad Dīn □ *Iraq* **70** C4
Sălaj □ *Romania* **28** C8
Salakos *Greece* **49** C9
Salala *Liberia* **82** D2
Salala *Sudan* **80** C4
Salālah *Oman* **75** D5
Salamanca *Chile* **126** C1
Salamanca *Spain* **36** E5
Salamanca *U.S.A.* **114** D6
Salamanca □ *Spain* **36** E5
Salāmatābād *Iran* **70** C5
Salamina *Greece* **49** C7
Salamis *Cyprus* **49** D12
Salar de Atacama *Chile* **126** A2
Salar de Uyuni *Bolivia* **124** H5
Sălard *Romania* **28** C7
Salas *Spain* **36** B4
Salas de los Infantes *Spain* **36** C7
Salatiga *Indonesia* **63** G14
Salaverry *Peru* **124** E3
Salawati *Indonesia* **63** E8
Salaya *India* **68** H3
Salayar *Indonesia* **63** F6
Salazar ⇢ *Spain* **38** C3
Salbris *France* **19** E9
Salcia *Romania* **29** F8
Sălciua *Romania* **29** D8
Salcombe *U.K.* **15** G4
Saldaña *Spain* **36** C6
Saldanha *S. Africa* **88** E2
Saldanha B. *S. Africa* **88** E2
Saldus *Latvia* **30** B9
Saldus □ *Latvia* **30** B9
Sale *Australia* **95** F4
Salé *Morocco* **78** B4
Sale *U.K.* **14** D5
Salekhard *Russia* **52** C7
Salelologa *Samoa* **91** b
Salem *India* **66** P11
Salem *Ill., U.S.A.* **112** F9
Salem *Ind., U.S.A.* **112** F10
Salem *Mass., U.S.A.* **115** D14
Salem *Mo., U.S.A.* **112** G8
Salem *N.H., U.S.A.* **115** D13
Salem *N.J., U.S.A.* **113** F16
Salem *N.Y., U.S.A.* **115** C11
Salem *Ohio, U.S.A.* **114** F4
Salem *Oreg., U.S.A.* **108** D2
Salem *S. Dak., U.S.A.* **112** D5
Salem *Va., U.S.A.* **113** G13
Salemi *Italy* **42** F5
Sälen *Sweden* **10** C7
Salernes *France* **21** E10
Salerno *Italy* **43** B7
Salerno, G. di *Italy* **43** B7
Salford *U.K.* **14** D5
Salgir ⇢ *Ukraine* **33** K8
Salgótarján *Hungary* **28** B4
Salgueiro *Brazil* **125** E11
Salibabu *Indonesia* **63** D7
Salibea = Salybia
  Trin. & Tob. **125** K15
Salida *U.S.A.* **108** C5
Salies-de-Béarn *France* **20** E3
Salihli *Turkey* **72** C3
Salihorsk *Belarus* **23** B14
Salima *Malawi* **85** G6
Salina *Italy* **43** D7
Salina *Kans., U.S.A.* **112** F5
Salina *Utah, U.S.A.* **108** G8
Salina Cruz *Mexico* **119** D5
Salina di Margherita di
  Savoia ⇢ *Italy* **43** A9
Salinas *Brazil* **125** G10
Salinas *Chile* **126** A2
Salinas *Ecuador* **124** D2

Salinas *U.S.A.* **110** J5
Salinas → *Guatemala* **119** D6
Salinas → *U.S.A.* **110** J5
Salinas, B. de *Nic.* **120** D2
Salinas, Pampa de las
  Argentina **126** C2
Salinas Ambargasta
  Argentina **126** B3
Salinas de Hidalgo *Mexico* **118** C4
Salinas Grandes *Argentina* **126** C3
Salinas Pueblo Missions △
  U.S.A. **111** J10
Salinas Valley *U.S.A.* **110** J5
Saline → *Ark., U.S.A.* **116** E8
Saline → *Kans., U.S.A.* **112** F5
Saline di Trapani e
  Paceco △ *Italy* **42** E5
Salines, C. de ses *Spain* **48** B10
Salinópolis *Brazil* **125** D9
Salins-les-Bains *France* **19** F12
Salir *Portugal* **37** H2
Salisbury *Australia* **95** E2
Salisbury *U.K.* **15** F6
Salisbury *Md., U.S.A.* **113** F16
Salisbury *N.C., U.S.A.* **117** D14
Salisbury I. *Canada* **101** C12
Salisbury Plain *U.K.* **15** F6
Săliște *Romania* **29** E8
Salka *Nigeria* **83** C5
Salkove *Ukraine* **29** B14
Salla *Finland* **8** C23
Sallanches *France* **21** C10
Sallent *Spain* **38** D6
Salles *France* **20** D3
Salles-Curan *France* **20** D6
Salling *Denmark* **11** H2
Salliq = Coral Harbour
  Canada **101** C11
Sallisaw *U.S.A.* **116** D7
Sallom *Sudan* **80** D4
Salluit *Canada* **101** C12
Salmās *Iran* **73** C11
Salmerón *Spain* **38** E2
Salmo *Canada* **102** D5
Salmon *U.S.A.* **108** D7
Salmon → *Canada* **102** C4
Salmon → *U.S.A.* **108** D5
Salmon Arm *Canada* **102** C5
Salmon Gums *Australia* **93** F3
Salmon River Mts. *U.S.A.* **108** D6
Salo *Finland* **32** B2
Salò *Italy* **40** C7
Salobreña *Spain* **37** J7
Salome *U.S.A.* **111** M13
Salon *India* **69** F9
Salon-de-Provence *France* **21** E9
Salonica = Thessaloniki
  Greece **44** F6
Salonta *Romania* **28** D6
Salor → *Spain* **37** F3
Salou *Spain* **38** D6
Salou, C. de *Spain* **38** D6
Saloum → *Senegal* **82** C1
Salpausselkä *Finland* **32** B4
Salsacate *Argentina* **126** C2
Salses *France* **20** F6
Salsk *Russia* **35** G5
Salso → *Italy* **42** E6
Salsomaggiore Terme *Italy* **40** D6
Salt *Spain* **38** D7
Salt → *Canada* **102** B6
Salt → *U.S.A.* **109** K7
Salt Fork Red → *U.S.A.* **116** D5
Salt L. *Australia* **95** E3
Salt Lake City *U.S.A.* **108** F8
Salt Range *Pakistan* **68** C5
Salta *Argentina* **126** A2
Salta □ *Argentina* **126** A2
Saltara *Italy* **41** E9
Saltash *U.K.* **15** G3
Saltburn by the Sea *U.K.* **14** C7
Saltcoats *U.K.* **13** F4
Saltee Is. *Ireland* **12** D5
Saltfjellet *Norway* **8** C16
Saltfjorden *Norway* **8** C16
Saltholm *Denmark* **11** J6
Saltillo *Mexico* **118** B4
Salto *Argentina* **126** C3
Salto *Uruguay* **126** C4
Salto del Guaíra *Paraguay* **127** A5
Salton City *U.S.A.* **111** M11
Salton Sea *U.S.A.* **111** M11
Saltpond *Ghana* **83** D4
Saltsburg *U.S.A.* **114** F5
Saltsjöbaden *Sweden* **10** E12
Saluda → *U.S.A.* **117** D14
Salûm *Egypt* **80** A2
Salûm, Khâlig el *Egypt* **80** A2
Salur *India* **67** K13
Saluzzo *Italy* **40** D4
Salvador *Brazil* **125** F11
Salvador *Canada* **103** C7
Salvador, El ■ *Cent. Amer.* **120** D2
Salvador, L. *U.S.A.* **117** G9
Salvaterra de Magos
  Portugal **37** F2

Sálvora, I. de *Spain* **36** C2
Salween → *Burma* **67** L20
Salyan *Azerbaijan* **73** C13
Salybia *Trin. & Tob.* **125** K15
Salza → *Austria* **26** D7
Salzach → *Austria* **26** C5
Salzburg *Austria* **26** D6
Salzburg □ *Austria* **26** D6
Salzgitter *Germany* **24** C6
Salzkotten *Germany* **24** D4
Salzwedel *Germany* **24** C7
Sam *India* **68** F4
Sam Neua *Laos* **58** G5
Sam Ngao *Thailand* **64** D2
Sam Rayburn Res. *U.S.A.* **116** F7
Sam Son *Vietnam* **64** C5
Sam Teu *Laos* **64** C5
Sama de Langreo =
  Langreo *Spain* **36** B5
Samagaltay *Russia* **53** D10
Samales Group *Phil.* **61** J5
Samâlût *Egypt* **80** B3
Samana *India* **68** D7
Samana Cay *Bahamas* **121** B5
Samandağ *Turkey* **72** D6
Samandra *Turkey* **45** F13
Samanga *Tanzania* **87** D4
Samangān □ *Afghan.* **66** B5
Samangwa
  Dem. Rep. of the Congo **86** C1
Samani *Japan* **54** C11
Samanli Dağları *Turkey* **45** F13
Samar *Phil.* **61** F6
Samara *Russia* **34** D9
Samara → *Russia* **34** D10
Samara → *Ukraine* **33** H8
Samaria = Shōmrōn
  West Bank **74** C4
Samaria *Greece* **49** D5
Samaria △ *Greece* **46** F5
Samarinda *Indonesia* **62** E5
Samarkand = Samarqand
  Uzbekistan **52** F7
Samarqand *Uzbekistan* **52** F7
Sāmarrā' *Iraq* **73** E10
Samastipur *India* **69** G11
Şamaxı *Azerbaijan* **35** K9
Samba *Dem. Rep. of the Congo* **86** C2
Samba *India* **69** C6
Sambalpur *India* **67** J14
Sambar, Tanjung *Indonesia* **62** E4
Sambas *Indonesia* **62** D3
Sambava *Madag.* **89** A9
Sambawizi *Zimbabwe* **87** F2
Sambhal *India* **69** E8
Sambhar *India* **68** F6
Sambhar L. *India* **68** F6
Sambiase *Italy* **43** D9
Sambir *Ukraine* **31** J10
Sambor *Cambodia* **64** F6
Samborombón, B. *Argentina* **126** D4
Sambuca di Sicília *Italy* **42** E6
Samburu △ *Kenya* **86** B4
Samcheok *S. Korea* **57** F15
Same *Tanzania* **86** C4
Samer *France* **19** B8
Samfya *Zambia* **87** E2
Sami *Greece* **46** C2
Şämkir *Azerbaijan* **35** K8
Şamlı *Turkey* **47** B9
Samnah *Si. Arabia* **70** E3
Samo Alto *Chile* **126** C1
Samoa ■ *Pac. Oc.* **91** b
Samobor *Croatia* **41** C12
Samoëns *France* **21** C10
Samokov *Bulgaria* **44** D7
Šamorín *Slovak Rep.* **27** C10
Samorogouan *Burkina Faso* **82** C4
Samos *Greece* **47** D8
Samoš *Serbia* **28** E5
Samos *Spain* **36** C3
Samos □ *Greece* **47** D8
Samothráki = Mathraki
  Greece **49** A3
Samothraki *Greece* **45** F9
Samoylovka *Russia* **34** E6
Sampa *Ghana* **82** D4
Sampacho *Argentina* **126** C3
Sampalan *Indonesia* **63** K18
Sampang *Indonesia* **63** G15
Samper de Calanda *Spain* **38** D4
Sampéyre *Italy* **40** D4
Sampit *Indonesia* **62** E4
Sampit, Teluk *Indonesia* **62** E4
Samrong *Cambodia* **64** E4
Samrong *Thailand* **64** E3
Samsø *Denmark* **11** J4
Samsø Bælt *Denmark* **11** J4
Samsun *Turkey* **72** B7
Samsun □ *Turkey* **72** B7
Samtredia *Georgia* **35** J6
Samui, Ko *Thailand* **65** b
Samur → *Russia* **35** K9
Samurskiy Khrebet *Russia* **35** K8
Samusole
  Dem. Rep. of the Congo **87** E1
Samut Prakan *Thailand* **64** F3

Samut Songkhram *Thailand* **64** F3
Samwari *Pakistan* **68** E2
San *Mali* **82** C4
San → *Cambodia* **64** F5
San → *Poland* **31** H8
San Adrián *Spain* **38** C3
San Adrián, C. de *Spain* **36** B2
San Agustin, C. *Phil.* **61** H7
San Agustín de Valle Fértil
  Argentina **126** C2
San Ambrosio *Pac. Oc.* **122** F3
San Andreas *U.S.A.* **110** G6
San Andres *Phil.* **61** E6
San Andrés, I. de *Caribbean* **120** D3
San Andres del Rabanedo
  Spain **36** C5
San Andres Mts. *U.S.A.* **109** K10
San Andrés Tuxtla *Mexico* **119** D5
San Angelo *U.S.A.* **116** F4
San Anselmo *U.S.A.* **110** H4
San Antonio *Belize* **119** D7
San Antonio *Chile* **126** C1
San Antonio *Phil.* **61** D4
San Antonio *N. Mex., U.S.A.*
  109 K10
San Antonio *Tex., U.S.A.* **116** G5
San Antonio → *U.S.A.* **116** G6
San Antonio, C. *Argentina* **126** D4
San Antonio, C. de *Cuba* **120** B3
San Antonio, C. de *Spain* **39** G5
San Antonio, Mt. *U.S.A.* **111** L9
San Antonio de los Baños
  Cuba **120** B3
San Antonio de los Cobres
  Argentina **126** A2
San Antonio Oeste
  Argentina **128** E4
San Arcángelo *Italy* **43** B9
San Ardo *U.S.A.* **110** J6
San Augustín *Canary Is.* **48** G4
San Augustine *U.S.A.* **116** F7
San Bartolomé *Canary Is.* **48** F6
San Bartolomé de Tirajana
  Canary Is. **48** G4
San Bartolomeo in Galdo
  Italy **43** A8
San Benedetto del Tronto
  Italy **41** F10
San Benedetto Po *Italy* **40** C7
San Benedicto, I. *Mexico* **118** D2
San Benito *U.S.A.* **116** H6
San Benito → *U.S.A.* **110** J5
San Benito Mt. *U.S.A.* **110** J6
San Bernardino *U.S.A.* **111** L9
San Bernardino Mts. *U.S.A.*
  111 L10
San Bernardino Str. *Phil.* **61** E6
San Bernardo *Chile* **126** C1
San Bernardo, I. de
  Colombia **124** B3
San Blas *Mexico* **118** B3
San Blas, Arch. de *Panama* **120** E4
San Blas, C. *U.S.A.* **117** G12
San Bonifacio *Italy* **41** C8
San Borja *Bolivia* **124** F5
San Buenaventura =
  Ventura *U.S.A.* **111** L7
San Buenaventura *Mexico* **118** B4
San Carlos = Sant Carles
  Spain **48** B8
San Carlos *Argentina* **126** C2
San Carlos *Chile* **126** D1
San Carlos *Baja Calif. S.,*
  Mexico **118** C2
San Carlos *Coahuila, Mexico* **118** B4
San Carlos *Nic.* **120** D3
San Carlos *Neg. Occ., Phil.* **61** F5
San Carlos *Pangasinan, Phil.* **61** D4
San Carlos *Uruguay* **127** C5
San Carlos *U.S.A.* **109** K8
San Carlos *Venezuela* **124** B5
San Carlos de Bariloche
  Argentina **128** E2
San Carlos de Bolívar
  Argentina **128** D4
San Carlos de la Rápita =
  Sant Carles de la Ràpita
  Spain **38** E5
San Carlos del Zulia
  Venezuela **124** B4
San Carlos L. *U.S.A.* **109** K8
San Cataldo *Italy* **42** E6
San Celoni = Sant Celoni
  Spain **38** D7
San Clemente *Chile* **126** D1
San Clemente *Spain* **39** F2
San Clemente *U.S.A.* **111** M9
San Clemente I. *U.S.A.* **111** N8
San Cristóbal = Es Migjorn
  Gran *Spain* **48** B11
San Cristóbal *Argentina* **126** C3
San Cristóbal *Dom. Rep.* **121** C5
San Cristóbal *Solomon Is.* **90** C9
San Cristóbal *Venezuela* **124** B4
San Cristóbal de las Casas
  Mexico **119** D6
San Damiano d'Asti *Italy* **40** D5

San Daniele del Friuli *Italy* **41** B10
San Diego *Calif., U.S.A.* **111** N9
San Diego *Tex., U.S.A.* **116** H5
San Diego, C. *Argentina* **128** G3
San Diego de la Unión
  Mexico **118** C4
San Diego Int. ✈ (SAN)
  U.S.A. **111** N9
San Dimitri, Ras *Malta* **49** C1
San Dimitri Point = San
  Dimitri, Ras *Malta* **49** C1
San Donà di Piave *Italy* **41** C9
San Esteban de Gormaz
  Spain **38** D1
San Felice Circeo *Italy* **42** A6
San Felice sul Panaro *Italy* **41** D8
San Felipe *Chile* **126** C1
San Felipe *Mexico* **118** A2
San Felipe *Venezuela* **124** A5
San Felipe → *U.S.A.* **111** M11
San Félix *Chile* **126** B1
San Félix *Pac. Oc.* **122** F2
San Fernando = Sant
  Ferran *Spain* **48** C7
San Fernando *Chile* **126** C1
San Fernando *Mexico* **119** C5
San Fernando *La Union, Phil.* **61** C4
San Fernando *Pampanga,*
  Phil. **61** D4
San Fernando *Spain* **37** J4
San Fernando *Trin. & Tob.* **121** D7
San Fernando *U.S.A.* **111** L8
San Fernando de Apure
  Venezuela **124** B5
San Fernando de Atabapo
  Venezuela **124** C5
San Fernando di Púglia *Italy* **43** A9
San Francisco *Argentina* **126** C3
San Francisco *U.S.A.* **110** H4
San Francisco → *U.S.A.* **109** K9
San Francisco, C. de
  Colombia **122** C3
San Francisco, Paso de
  S. Amer. **126** B2
San Francisco de Macorís
  Dom. Rep. **121** C5
San Francisco del Monte
  de Oro *Argentina* **126** C2
San Francisco del Oro
  Mexico **118** B3
San Francisco Int. ✈ (SFO)
  U.S.A. **110** H4
San Francisco Javier =
  Sant Francesc de
  Formentera *Spain* **48** C7
San Fratello *Italy* **43** D7
San Gabriel *Chile* **126** C1
San Gabriel Chilac *Mexico* **119** D5
San Gabriel Mts. *U.S.A.* **111** L9
San Gavino Monreale *Italy* **42** C1
San German *Puerto Rico* **121** d
San Gimignano *Italy* **40** E8
San Giórgio di Nogaro *Italy* **41** C10
San Giórgio Iónico *Italy* **43** B10
San Giovanni Bianco *Italy* **40** C6
San Giovanni in Fiore *Italy* **43** C9
San Giovanni in Persiceto
  Italy **41** D8
San Giovanni Rotondo
  Italy **41** G12
San Giovanni Valdarno *Italy* **41** E8
San Giuliano Terme *Italy* **40** E7
San Gorgonio Mt. *U.S.A.* **111** L10
San Gottardo, P. del *Switz.* **25** J4
San Gregorio *Uruguay* **127** C4
San Gregorio *U.S.A.* **110** H4
San Guiseppe Jato *Italy* **42** E6
San Ignacio *Belize* **119** D7
San Ignacio *Bolivia* **124** G6
San Ignacio *Mexico* **118** B2
San Ignacio *Paraguay* **126** B4
San Ignacio, L. *Mexico* **118** B2
San Ildefonso, C. *Phil.* **61** D5
San Isidro *Argentina* **126** C4
San Isidro *Phil.* **61** H7
San Jacinto *U.S.A.* **111** M10
San Jaime = Sant Jaume
  Spain **48** B11
San Javier *Misiones,*
  Argentina **127** B5
San Javier *Santa Fe,*
  Argentina **126** C4
San Javier *Bolivia* **124** G6
San Javier *Chile* **126** D1
San Javier *Spain* **39** H4
San Jerónimo Taviche
  Mexico **119** D5
San Joaquin *U.S.A.* **110** J6
San Joaquin → *U.S.A.* **110** G5
San Joaquin Valley *U.S.A.* **110** J6
San Jon *U.S.A.* **109** J12
San Jordi = Sant Jordi *Spain* **48** B9
San Jorge *Argentina* **126** C3
San Jorge, B. *Mexico* **118** A2
San Jorge, G. *Argentina* **128** F3
San José = San Josep *Spain* **48** C7

San José *Costa Rica* **120** E3
San José *Guatemala* **120** D1
San Jose *Mind. Occ., Phil.* **61** E4
San Jose *Nueva Ecija, Phil.* **61** D4
San Jose *U.S.A.* **110** H5
San Jose → *U.S.A.* **109** J10
San José, I. *Mexico* **118** C2
San José de Buenavista *Phil.* **63** B6
San José de Chiquitos
  Bolivia **124** G6
San José de Feliciano
  Argentina **126** C4
San José de Jáchal *Argentina* **126** C2
San José de Mayo *Uruguay* **126** C4
San José del Cabo *Mexico* **118** C3
San José del Guaviare
  Colombia **124** C4
San Josep *Spain* **48** C7
San Juan *Argentina* **126** C2
San Juan *Phil.* **61** F6
San Juan *Puerto Rico* **121** d
San Juan *Trin. & Tob.* **125** K15
San Juan □ *Argentina* **126** C2
San Juan □ *Argentina* **126** C2
San Juan → *Nic.* **120** D3
San Juan → *U.S.A.* **109** H8
San Juan Bautista = Sant
  Joan de Labritja *Spain* **48** B8
San Juan Bautista *Paraguay* **126** B4
San Juan Bautista *U.S.A.* **110** J5
San Juan Capistrano *U.S.A.*
  111 M9
San Juan Cr. → *U.S.A.* **110** J5
San Juan de Alicante *Spain* **39** G4
San Juan de Guadalupe
  Mexico **118** C4
San Juan de la Costa *Mexico*
  118 C2
San Juan de los Lagos
  Mexico **118** C4
San Juan de los Morros
  Venezuela **124** B5
San Juan del Norte *Nic.* **120** D3
San Juan del Norte, B. de
  Nic. **120** D3
San Juan del Río *Mexico* **119** C5
San Juan del Sur *Nic.* **120** D2
San Juan I. *U.S.A.* **110** B3
San Juan Island △ *U.S.A.* **110** B4
San Juan Mts. *U.S.A.* **109** H10
San Just, Sierra de *Spain* **38** E4
San Justo *Argentina* **126** C3
San Kamphaeng *Thailand* **64** C2
San Lázaro, C. *Mexico* **118** C2
San Leandro *U.S.A.* **110** H4
San Leonardo de Yagüe
  Spain **38** D1
San Lorenzo = Sant
  Llorenç des Cardassar
  Spain **48** B10
San Lorenzo *Argentina* **126** C3
San Lorenzo *Ecuador* **124** C3
San Lorenzo *Paraguay* **126** B4
San Lorenzo → *Mexico* **118** C3
San Lorenzo, I. *Mexico* **118** B2
San Lorenzo, Mte. *Argentina* **128** F2
San Lorenzo de la Parrilla
  Spain **38** F2
San Lorenzo de Morunys =
  Sant Llorenç de
  Morunys *Spain* **38** C6
San Lucas = Cabo San
  Lucas *Mexico* **118** C3
San Lucas *Bolivia* **124** H5
San Lucas *Mexico* **118** B2
San Lucas *U.S.A.* **110** J5
San Lucas, C. *Mexico* **118** C3
San Lúcido *Italy* **43** C9
San Luis *Argentina* **126** C2
San Luis *Cuba* **120** B3
San Luis *Guatemala* **120** C2
San Luis *Ariz., U.S.A.* **109** K6
San Luis *Colo., U.S.A.* **109** H11
San Luis □ *Argentina* **126** C2
San Luis, I. *Mexico* **118** B2
San Luis, Sierra de
  Argentina **126** C2
San Luis de la Paz *Mexico* **118** C4
San Luis Obispo *U.S.A.* **111** K6
San Luis Potosí *Mexico* **118** C4
San Luis Potosí □ *Mexico* **118** C4
San Luis Res. *U.S.A.* **110** H5
San Luis Río Colorado
  Mexico **118** A2
San Manuel *U.S.A.* **109** K8
San Marco, C. *Italy* **42** C1
San Marco Argentano *Italy* **43** C9
San Marco in Lámis *Italy* **41** G12
San Marcos *Guatemala* **120** D1
San Marcos *Calif., U.S.A.* **111** M9
San Marcos *Tex., U.S.A.* **116** G6
San Marcos, I. *Mexico* **118** B2
San Marino *San Marino* **41** E9
San Marino ■ *Europe* **41** E9
San Martín *Antarctica* **5** C17
San Martín *Argentina* **126** C2
San Martín → *Bolivia* **124** F6

San Martín, L. *Argentina* **128** F2
San Martín de la Vega *Spain* **36** E7
San Martín de los Andes
  Argentina **128** E2
San Martín de
  Valdeiglesias *Spain* **36** E6
San Mateo = Sant Mateu
  Baleares, Spain **48** B7
San Mateo = Sant Mateu
  Valencia, Spain **38** E5
San Mateo *Phil.* **61** C4
San Mateo *U.S.A.* **110** H4
San Matías *Bolivia* **124** G7
San Matías, G. *Argentina* **128** E4
San Miguel = Sant Miquel
  Spain **48** B7
San Miguel *El Salv.* **120** D2
San Miguel *Panama* **120** E4
San Miguel *U.S.A.* **110** K6
San Miguel → *Bolivia* **124** F6
San Miguel de Tucumán
  Argentina **126** B2
San Miguel del Monte
  Argentina **126** D4
San Miguel I. *U.S.A.* **111** L6
San Miniato *Italy* **40** E7
San Nicolás *Canary Is.* **48** G4
San Nicolas *Phil.* **61** B4
San Nicolás de los Arroyas
  Argentina **126** C3
San Nicolas I. *U.S.A.* **111** M7
San Onofre *U.S.A.* **111** M9
San Pablo *Bolivia* **126** A2
San Pablo *Phil.* **61** D4
San Pablo *U.S.A.* **110** H4
San Páolo di Civitate *Italy* **41** G12
San Pedro *B. Aires, Argentina*
  126 C4
San Pedro *Misiones,*
  Argentina **127** B5
San Pedro *Chile* **126** C1
San Pedro *Ivory C.* **82** E3
San Pedro *Mexico* **118** C2
San Pedro □ *Paraguay* **126** A4
San Pedro → *Chihuahua,*
  Mexico **118** B3
San Pedro → *Nayarit,*
  Mexico **118** C3
San Pedro → *U.S.A.* **109** K8
San Pedro, Pta. *Chile* **126** B1
San Pedro, Sierra de *Spain* **37** F4
San Pedro Channel *U.S.A.* **111** M8
San Pedro de Atacama
  Chile **126** A2
San Pedro de Jujuy
  Argentina **126** A3
San Pedro de las Colonias
  Mexico **118** B4
San Pedro de Macorís
  Dom. Rep. **121** C6
San Pedro del Norte *Nic.* **120** D3
San Pedro del Paraná
  Paraguay **126** B4
San Pedro del Pinatar *Spain* **39** H4
San Pedro Mártir, Sierra
  Mexico **118** A1
San Pedro Mártir △ *Mexico* **118** A1
San Pedro Ocampo =
  Melchor Ocampo *Mexico* **118** C4
San Pedro Pochutla *Mexico* **119** D5
San Pedro Sula *Honduras* **120** C2
San Pedro Tututepec
  Mexico **119** D5
San Pietro *Italy* **42** C1
San Pietro Vernótico *Italy* **43** B11
San Rafael *Argentina* **126** C2
San Rafael *Calif., U.S.A.* **110** H4
San Rafael *N. Mex., U.S.A.* **109** J10
San Rafael Mt. *U.S.A.* **111** L7
San Rafael Mts. *U.S.A.* **111** L7
San Ramón de la Nueva
  Orán *Argentina* **126** A3
San Remo *Italy* **40** E4
San Roque *Argentina* **126** B4
San Roque *Spain* **37** J5
San Rosendo *Chile* **126** D1
San Saba *U.S.A.* **116** F5
San Salvador *El Salv.* **120** D2
San Salvador *Spain* **48** B10
San Salvador de Jujuy
  Argentina **126** A3
San Salvador I. *Bahamas* **121** B5
San Salvo *Italy* **41** F11
San Sebastián = Donostia-
  San Sebastián *Spain* **38** B3
San Sebastián *Argentina* **128** G3
San Sebastián *Puerto Rico* **121** d
San Sebastián de la
  Gomera *Canary Is.* **48** F2
San Serra = Son Serra
  Spain **48** B10
San Serverino Marche *Italy* **41** E10
San Severo *Italy* **41** G12
San Simeon *U.S.A.* **110** K5
San Simon *U.S.A.* **109** K9
San Stéfano di Cadore *Italy* **41** B9
San Stino di Livenza *Italy* **41** C9

San Telmo = Sant Elm *Spain* 48 B9
San Telmo *Mexico* 118 A1
San Tiburcio *Mexico* 118 C4
San Valentin, Mte. *Chile* 128 F2
San Vicente de Alcántara *Spain* 37 F3
San Vicente de la Barquera *Spain* 36 B6
San Vincente del Raspeig *Spain* 39 G4
San Vincenzo *Italy* 40 E7
San Vito *Costa Rica* 120 E3
San Vito *Italy* 42 C2
San Vito, C. *Italy* 42 D5
San Vito al Tagliamento *Italy* 41 C9
San Vito Chietino *Italy* 41 F11
San Vito dei Normanni *Italy* 43 B10
Sana' *Yemen* 75 D3
Sana → *Bos.-H.* 41 C13
Sanaba *Burkina Faso* 82 C4
Sanae IV *Antarctica* 5 D2
Şanāfir *Si. Arabia* 80 B3
Sanaga → *Cameroon* 83 E6
Sanaloa, Presa *Mexico* 118 C3
Sanana *Indonesia* 63 E7
Sanand *India* 68 H5
Sanandaj *Iran* 73 E12
Sanandita *Bolivia* 126 A3
Sanary-sur-Mer *France* 21 E9
Sanawad *India* 68 H7
Sancellas = Sencelles *Spain* 48 B9
Sancergues *France* 19 E9
Sancerre *France* 19 E9
Sancerrois, Collines du *France* 19 E9
Sancha He → *China* 58 D6
Sanchahe *China* 57 B14
Sánchez *Dom. Rep.* 121 C6
Sanchor *India* 68 G4
Sancoins *France* 19 F9
Sancti Spíritus *Cuba* 120 B4
Sancy, Puy de *France* 20 C6
Sand = Polokwane → *S. Africa* 89 C5
Sand Hills *U.S.A.* 112 D3
Sand Lakes ⌓ *Canada* 103 B9
Sand Springs *U.S.A.* 116 C6
Sanda *Japan* 55 G7
Sandakan *Malaysia* 62 C5
Sandan = Sambor *Cambodia* 64 F6
Sandanski *Bulgaria* 44 E7
Sandaré *Mali* 82 C2
Sandared *Sweden* 11 G6
Sandarne *Sweden* 10 C11
Sanday *U.K.* 13 B6
Sande *Norway* 10 E4
Sandefjord *Norway* 9 G14
Sanders *U.S.A.* 109 J9
Sanderson *U.S.A.* 116 F3
Sandersville *U.S.A.* 117 E13
Sandfire Roadhouse *Australia* 92 C3
Sandfly L. *Canada* 103 B7
Sandfontein *Namibia* 88 C2
Sandhammaren *Sweden* 11 J8
Sandheads, The *India* 69 J13
Sandía *Peru* 124 F5
Sandıklı *Turkey* 47 C12
Sandila *India* 69 F9
Sandnes *Norway* 9 G11
Sandnessjøen *Norway* 8 C15
Sandoa *Dem. Rep. of the Congo* 84 F4
Sandomierz *Poland* 31 H8
Sândominic *Romania* 29 D10
Sandover → *Australia* 94 C2
Sandoway = Thandwe *Burma* 67 K19
Sandoy *Færoe Is.* 8 F9
Sandpoint *U.S.A.* 108 B5
Sandray *U.K.* 13 E1
Sandringham *U.K.* 14 E8
Sandstone *Australia* 93 E2
Sandu *China* 58 E6
Sandusky *Mich., U.S.A.* 114 C2
Sandusky *Ohio, U.S.A.* 114 E2
Sandveld *Namibia* 88 C3
Sandvig *Denmark* 11 J8
Sandviken *Sweden* 10 D10
Sandwich, C. *Australia* 94 B4
Sandwich B. *Canada* 105 B8
Sandwich B. *Namibia* 88 C1
Sandy *Oreg., U.S.A.* 110 E4
Sandy *Pa., U.S.A.* 114 E6
Sandy *Utah, U.S.A.* 108 F8
Sandy Bay *Canada* 103 B8
Sandy Bight *Australia* 93 F3
Sandy C. *Queens., Australia* 94 C5
Sandy C. *Tas., Australia* 95 G3
Sandy Cay *Bahamas* 121 B4
Sandy Cr. → *U.S.A.* 108 F9
Sandy L. *Canada* 104 B1
Sandy Lake *Canada* 104 B1
Sandy Valley *U.S.A.* 111 K11
Sånfjällets △ *Sweden* 10 B7
Sanford *Fla., U.S.A.* 117 G14
Sanford *Maine, U.S.A.* 115 C14
Sanford *N.C., U.S.A.* 117 D15
Sanford → *Australia* 93 E2
Sanford, Mt. *U.S.A.* 100 C5
Sang-i-Masha *Afghan.* 68 C2
Sanga *Mozam.* 87 E4
Sanga → *Congo* 84 E3
Sangamner *India* 66 K9
Sanganeb Atoll △ *Sudan* 80 D4
Sangar *Afghan.* 68 C1
Sangar *Russia* 53 C13
Sangar Sarai *Afghan.* 68 B4
Sangaredi *Guinea* 82 C2
Sangarh → *Pakistan* 68 D4
Sangasso *Mali* 82 C3
Sangatte *France* 19 B8
Sangay *Ecuador* 124 D3
Sange *Dem. Rep. of the Congo* 86 D2
Sangeang *Indonesia* 63 F5
Sângeorz-Băi *Romania* 29 C9
Sanger *U.S.A.* 110 J7
Sângera *Moldova* 29 D13
Sangerhausen *Germany* 24 D7
Sanggan He → *China* 56 E9
Sanggau *Indonesia* 62 D4
Sanghar *Pakistan* 68 F3
Sangihe, Kepulauan *Indonesia* 63 D7
Sangihe, Pulau *Indonesia* 63 D7
Sangju *S. Korea* 57 F15
Sangkapura *Indonesia* 62 F4
Sangkhla *Thailand* 64 E2
Sangkulirang *Indonesia* 62 D5
Sangla *Pakistan* 68 D5
Sangli *India* 66 L9
Sangmélima *Cameroon* 83 E7
Sangod *India* 68 G7
Sangre de Cristo Mts. *U.S.A.* 109 H11
Sangre Grande *Trin. & Tob.* 125 K15
Sangro → *Italy* 41 F11
Sangrur *India* 68 D6
Sangudo *Canada* 102 C6
Sangue → *Brazil* 124 F7
Sangüesa *Spain* 38 C3
Sanguinaires, Îs. *France* 21 G12
Sangzhi *China* 59 C8
Sanhala *Ivory C.* 82 C3
Sanibel *U.S.A.* 117 H13
Sanikiluaq *Canada* 104 A4
Sanin-Kaigan △ *Japan* 55 G7
Sanirajak *Canada* 101 C11
Sanjawi *Pakistan* 68 D3
Sanje *Uganda* 86 C3
Sanjiang *China* 58 E7
Sanjo *Japan* 54 F9
Sankh → *India* 69 H11
Sankt Andrä *Austria* 26 E7
Sankt Anton *Austria* 25 H6
Sankt Augustin *Germany* 24 E3
Sankt Blasien *Germany* 25 H4
Sankt Gallen *Switz.* 25 H5
Sankt Gallen □ *Switz.* 25 H5
Sankt Goar *Germany* 25 E3
Sankt Ingbert *Germany* 25 F3
Sankt Johann im Pongau *Austria* 26 D6
Sankt Johann in Tirol *Austria* 26 D5
Sankt Michel = Mikkeli *Finland* 32 B4
Sankt Moritz *Switz.* 25 J5
Sankt-Peterburg *Russia* 32 C6
Sankt Pölten *Austria* 26 C8
Sankt Ulrich = Ortisei *Italy* 41 B8
Sankt Valentin *Austria* 26 C7
Sankt Veit an der Glan *Austria* 26 E7
Sankt Wendel *Germany* 25 F3
Sankt Wolfgang *Austria* 26 D6
Sankuru → *Dem. Rep. of the Congo* 84 E4
Sanliurfa *Turkey* 73 D8
Sanliurfa □ *Turkey* 73 D8
Sanlúcar de Barrameda *Spain* 37 J4
Sanluri *Italy* 42 C1
Sânmartin *Romania* 29 D10
Sanmen *China* 59 C13
Sanmenxia *China* 56 G6
Sanming *China* 59 D11
Sannaspos *S. Africa* 88 D4
Sannicandro Gargánico *Italy* 41 G12
Sânnicolau Mare *Romania* 28 D5
Sannieshof *S. Africa* 88 D4
Sannīn, J. *Lebanon* 74 B4
Sanniquellie *Liberia* 82 D3
Sannûr, W. → *Egypt* 80 B3
Sanok *Poland* 31 J9
Sanquhar *U.K.* 13 F5
Sans Souci *Trin. & Tob.* 125 K16
Sansanding *Mali* 82 C3
Sansepolcro *Italy* 41 E9
Sansha *China* 59 D13
Sanshui *China* 59 F9
Sanski Most *Bos.-H.* 41 D13
Sansui *China* 58 D7
Sant Antoni de Portmany *Spain* 48 C7
Sant Boi de Llobregat *Spain* 38 D7
Sant Carles *Spain* 48 B8
Sant Carles de la Ràpita *Spain* 38 E5
Sant Celoni *Spain* 38 D7
Sant Elm *Spain* 48 B9
Sant Feliu de Guíxols *Spain* 38 D8
Sant Feliu de Llobregat *Spain* 38 D7
Sant Ferran *Spain* 48 C7
Sant Francesc de Formentera *Spain* 48 C7
Sant Jaume *Spain* 48 B11
Sant Joan de Labritja *Spain* 48 B8
Sant Jordi *Ibiza, Spain* 48 C7
Sant Jordi *Mallorca, Spain* 48 B9
Sant Jordi, G. de *Spain* 38 E6
Sant Llorenç de Morunys *Spain* 38 C6
Sant Llorenç del Munt y l'Obac ⌂ *Spain* 38 D3
Sant Llorenç des Cardassar *Spain* 48 B10
Sant Mateu *Baleares, Spain* 48 B7
Sant Mateu *Valencia, Spain* 38 E5
Sant Miquel *Spain* 48 B7
Sant' Ágata Militello *Italy* 43 D7
Santa Agnés *Spain* 48 B7
Santa Ana *Bolivia* 124 F5
Santa Ana *El Salv.* 120 D2
Santa Ana *Mexico* 118 A2
Santa Ana *U.S.A.* 111 M9
Sant' Ángelo Lodigiano *Italy* 40 C6
Sant' Antíoco *Italy* 42 C1
Santa Bárbara *Chile* 126 D1
Santa Bárbara *Honduras* 120 D2
Santa Bárbara *Mexico* 118 B3
Santa Bárbara *Spain* 38 E5
Santa Barbara *U.S.A.* 111 L7
Santa Bárbara, Mt. *Spain* 39 H2
Santa Barbara Channel *U.S.A.* 111 L7
Santa Barbara I. *U.S.A.* 111 M7
Santa Catalina, Gulf of *U.S.A.* 111 N9
Santa Catalina, I. *Mexico* 118 B2
Santa Catalina I. *U.S.A.* 111 M8
Santa Catarina □ *Brazil* 127 B6
Santa Catarina, I. de *Brazil* 127 B6
Santa Caterina di Pittinuri *Italy* 42 B1
Santa Caterina Villarmosa *Italy* 43 E7
Santa Cecília *Brazil* 127 B5
Santa Clara *Cuba* 120 B4
Santa Clara *Calif., U.S.A.* 110 H5
Santa Clara *Utah, U.S.A.* 109 H7
Santa Clara de Olimar *Uruguay* 127 C5
Santa Clara Valley *U.S.A.* 110 J5
Santa Clarita *U.S.A.* 111 L8
Santa Clotilde *Peru* 124 D4
Santa Coloma de Farners *Spain* 38 D7
Santa Coloma de Gramenet *Spain* 38 D7
Santa Comba *Spain* 36 B2
Santa Croce Camerina *Italy* 43 F7
Santa Croce di Magliano *Italy* 41 G11
Santa Cruz *Argentina* 128 G3
Santa Cruz *Bolivia* 124 G6
Santa Cruz *Chile* 126 C1
Santa Cruz *Costa Rica* 120 D2
Santa Cruz *Madeira* 48 D3
Santa Cruz *Phil.* 61 D4
Santa Cruz *U.S.A.* 110 J4
Santa Cruz → *Argentina* 128 G3
Santa Cruz de la Palma *Canary Is.* 48 F2
Santa Cruz de la Palma ✈ (SPC) *Canary Is.* 48 F2
Santa Cruz de Mudela *Spain* 37 G7
Santa Cruz de Tenerife *Canary Is.* 48 F3
Santa Cruz del Norte *Cuba* 120 B3
Santa Cruz del Retamar *Spain* 36 E6
Santa Cruz del Sur *Cuba* 120 B4
Santa Cruz do Rio Pardo *Brazil* 127 A6
Santa Cruz do Sul *Brazil* 127 B5
Santa Cruz I. *U.S.A.* 111 M7
Santa Cruz Is. *Solomon Is.* 90 C9
Santa Cruz Mts. *Jamaica* 120 a
Santa Domingo, Cay *Bahamas* 120 B4
Sant' Egídio alla Vibrata *Italy* 41 F10
Santa Elena *Argentina* 126 C4
Santa Elena, C. *Costa Rica* 120 D2
Sant' Eufémia, G. di *Italy* 43 D9
Santa Eulària des Riu *Spain* 48 C8
Santa Fé *Argentina* 126 C3
Santa Fé *Spain* 37 H7
Santa Fe *U.S.A.* 109 J11
Santa Fé □ *Argentina* 126 C3
Santa Fé do Sul *Brazil* 125 H8
Santa Filomena *Brazil* 125 E9
Santa Fiora *Italy* 41 F8
Santa Gertrudis *Spain* 48 C7
Santa Giustina *Italy* 41 B9
Santa Inês *Brazil* 125 F11
Santa Inés *Spain* 37 G5
Santa Inés, I. *Chile* 128 G2
Santa Isabel *Argentina* 126 D2
Santa Isabel do Morro *Brazil* 125 F8
Santa Lucía *Corrientes, Argentina* 126 B4
Santa Lucía *San Juan, Argentina* 126 C2
Santa Lucía *Spain* 39 H4
Santa Lucía *Uruguay* 126 C4
Santa Lucia Range *U.S.A.* 110 K5
Santa Luzia *C. Verde Is.* 78 b
Santa Margalida *Spain* 48 B10
Santa Margarita *Argentina* 126 D3
Santa Margarita *U.S.A.* 110 K6
Santa Margarita → *U.S.A.* 111 M9
Santa Margarita, I. *Mexico* 118 C2
Santa Margherita *Italy* 42 D1
Santa Margherita Ligure *Italy* 40 D6
Santa María *Argentina* 126 B2
Santa Maria *Azores* 78 a
Santa Maria *Brazil* 127 B5
Santa Maria *C. Verde Is.* 78 b
Santa Maria *Phil.* 61 C4
Santa Maria *U.S.A.* 111 L6
Santa María → *Mexico* 118 A3
Santa María, B. de *Mexico* 118 B3
Santa Maria, C. de *Portugal* 37 J3
Santa Maria Cápua Vétere *Italy* 43 A7
Santa Maria da Feira *Portugal* 36 E2
Santa Maria da Vitória *Brazil* 125 F10
Santa María del Camí *Spain* 48 B9
Santa Maria di Léuca, C. *Italy* 43 C11
Santa María la Real de Nieva *Spain* 36 D6
Santa Marinella *Italy* 41 F8
Santa Marta *Colombia* 124 A4
Santa Marta, Sierra Nevada de *Colombia* 124 A4
Santa Marta de Tormes *Spain* 36 E5
Santa Marta Grande, C. *Brazil* 127 B6
Santa Marta Ortigueira, Ría de *Spain* 36 B3
Santa Maura = Lefkada *Greece* 46 C2
Santa Monica *U.S.A.* 111 M8
Santa Monica Mts. ⌂ *U.S.A.* 111 L8
Santa Olalla *Huelva, Spain* 37 H4
Santa Olalla *Toledo, Spain* 36 E6
Santa Paula *U.S.A.* 111 L7
Santa Pola *Spain* 39 G4
Santa Ponça *Spain* 48 B9
Santa Rosa *La Pampa, Argentina* 126 D3
Santa Rosa *San Luis, Argentina* 126 C2
Santa Rosa *Brazil* 127 B5
Santa Rosa *Calif., U.S.A.* 110 G4
Santa Rosa *N. Mex., U.S.A.* 109 J11
Santa Rosa and San Jacinto Mts. ⌂ *U.S.A.* 111 M10
Santa Rosa de Copán *Honduras* 120 D2
Santa Rosa de Río Primero *Argentina* 126 C3
Santa Rosa del Sara *Bolivia* 124 G6
Santa Rosa I. *Calif., U.S.A.* 111 M6
Santa Rosa I. *Fla., U.S.A.* 117 F11
Santa Rosa Range *U.S.A.* 108 F5
Santa Rosalía *Mexico* 118 B2
Santa Sylvina *Argentina* 126 B3
Santa Tecla = Nueva San Salvador *El Salv.* 120 D2
Santa Teresa *Argentina* 126 C3
Santa Teresa *Australia* 94 C1
Santa Teresa *Mexico* 119 B5
Santa Teresa △ *Uruguay* 127 C5
Santa Teresa di Riva *Italy* 43 E8
Santa Teresa Gallura *Italy* 42 A2
Santa Uxía *Spain* 36 C2
Santa Vitória do Palmar *Brazil* 127 C5
Santa Ynez → *U.S.A.* 111 L6
Santa Ynez Mts. *U.S.A.* 111 L6
Santa Ysabel *U.S.A.* 111 M10
Santadi *Italy* 42 C1
Santaella *Spain* 37 H6
Santai *China* 58 B5
Santana *Madeira* 48 D3
Sântana *Romania* 28 D6
Santana, Coxilha de *Brazil* 127 C4
Santana do Livramento *Brazil* 127 C4
Santander *Spain* 36 B7
Santander Jiménez *Mexico* 119 C5
Santanilla, Is. *Honduras* 120 C3
Santanyí *Spain* 48 B10
Santaquin *U.S.A.* 108 G8
Santarcángelo di Romagna *Italy* 41 D9
Santarém *Brazil* 125 D8
Santarém *Portugal* 37 F2
Santarém □ *Portugal* 37 F2
Santaren Channel *W. Indies* 120 B4
Santee *U.S.A.* 111 N10
Santee → *U.S.A.* 117 E15
Santéramo in Colle *Italy* 43 B9
Santerno → *Italy* 41 D8
Santhià *Italy* 40 C5
Santi-Quaranta = Sarandë *Albania* 44 G3
Santiago = Río Grande de Santiago → *Mexico* 118 C3
Santiago = São Tiago *C. Verde Is.* 78 b
Santiago *Brazil* 127 B5
Santiago *Canary Is.* 48 F2
Santiago *Chile* 126 C1
Santiago *Panama* 120 E3
Santiago *Phil.* 61 C4
Santiago □ *Chile* 126 C1
Santiago → *Peru* 124 D3
Santiago, Punta de *Eq. Guin.* 83 E6
Santiago de Compostela *Spain* 36 C2
Santiago de Cuba *Cuba* 120 C4
Santiago de los Caballeros *Dom. Rep.* 121 C5
Santiago del Estero *Argentina* 126 B3
Santiago del Estero □ *Argentina* 126 B3
Santiago del Teide *Canary Is.* 48 F3
Santiago do Cacém *Portugal* 37 G2
Santiago Ixcuintla *Mexico* 118 C3
Santiago Jamiltepec *Mexico* 119 D5
Santiago Papasquiaro *Mexico* 118 C3
Santiago Pinotepa Nacional *Mexico* 119 D5
Santiaguillo, L. de *Mexico* 118 C4
Santiguila *Mali* 82 C3
Santillana *Spain* 36 B6
Santisteban del Puerto *Spain* 37 G7
Santo Amaro *Brazil* 125 F11
Santo Anastácio *Brazil* 127 A5
Santo André *Brazil* 127 A6
Santo Ângelo *Brazil* 127 B5
Santo Antão *C. Verde Is.* 78 b
Santo Antônio do Içá *Brazil* 124 D5
Santo Antônio do Leverger *Brazil* 125 G7
Santo Domingo *Dom. Rep.* 121 C6
Santo Domingo *Baja Calif., Mexico* 118 A1
Santo Domingo *Baja Calif. S., Mexico* 118 B2
Santo Domingo *Nic.* 120 D3
Santo Domingo de la Calzada *Spain* 38 C2
Santo Domingo de los Colorados *Ecuador* 124 D3
Santo Domingo Pueblo *U.S.A.* 109 J10
Santo Stéfano di Camastro *Italy* 43 D7
Santo Tirso *Portugal* 36 D2
Santo Tomás *Mexico* 118 A1
Santo Tomás *Peru* 124 F4
Santo Tomé *Argentina* 127 B4
Santo Tomé de Guayana = Ciudad Guayana *Venezuela* 124 B6
Santomera *Spain* 39 G3
Santoña *Spain* 36 B7
Santorini *Greece* 47 E7
Santos *Brazil* 127 A6
Santos, Sierra de los *Spain* 37 G5
Santos Dumont *Brazil* 127 A7
Sanur *Indonesia* 63 K18
Sanwer *India* 68 H6
Sanxenxo *Spain* 36 C2
Sanya *China* 64 C7
Sanyuan *China* 56 G5
São Bartolomeu de Messines *Portugal* 37 H2
São Bernardo do Campo *Brazil* 127 A6
São Borja *Brazil* 127 B4
São Brás de Alportel *Portugal* 37 H3
São Carlos *Brazil* 127 A6
São Cristóvão *Brazil* 125 F11
São Domingos *Brazil* 125 F9
São Domingos *Guinea-Biss.* 82 C1
São Filipe *C. Verde Is.* 78 b
São Francisco *Brazil* 125 G10
São Francisco → *Brazil* 125 F11
São Francisco do Sul *Brazil* 127 B6
São Gabriel *Brazil* 127 C5
São Gonçalo *Brazil* 127 A7
Sao Hill *Tanzania* 87 D4
São João *Guinea-Biss.* 82 C1
São João da Boa Vista *Brazil* 127 A6
São João da Madeira *Portugal* 36 E2
São João da Pesqueira *Portugal* 36 D3
São João del Rei *Brazil* 127 A7
São João do Araguaia *Brazil* 125 E9
São João do Piauí *Brazil* 125 E10
São Joaquim *Brazil* 127 B6
São Joaquim △ *Brazil* 127 B6
São Jorge *Azores* 78 a
São Jorge, Pta. de *Madeira* 48 D3
São José *Brazil* 127 B5
São José do Norte *Brazil* 127 C5
São José do Rio Prêto *Brazil* 127 A6
São José dos Campos *Brazil* 127 A6
São Leopoldo *Brazil* 127 B5
São Lourenço *Brazil* 127 A6
São Lourenço → *Brazil* 125 G7
São Lourenço, Pta. de *Madeira* 48 D3
São Lourenço do Sul *Brazil* 127 C5
São Luís *Brazil* 125 D10
São Luís Gonzaga *Brazil* 127 B5
São Marcos → *Brazil* 125 G9
São Marcos, B. de *Brazil* 125 D10
São Martinho da Cortiça *Portugal* 36 E2
São Mateus *Brazil* 125 G11
São Mateus do Sul *Brazil* 127 B5
São Miguel *Azores* 78 a
São Miguel do Oeste *Brazil* 127 B5
São Nicolau *C. Verde Is.* 78 b
São Paulo *Brazil* 127 A6
São Paulo □ *Brazil* 127 A6
São Paulo de Olivença *Brazil* 124 D5
São Pedro do Sul *Portugal* 36 E2
São Roque *Madeira* 48 D3
São Roque, C. de *Brazil* 125 E11
São Sebastião, I. de *Brazil* 127 A6
São Sebastião do Paraíso *Brazil* 127 A6
São Teotónio *Portugal* 37 H2
São Tiago *C. Verde Is.* 78 b
São Tomé *São Tomé & Príncipe* 76 F4
São Tomé, C. de *Brazil* 127 A7
São Tomé & Príncipe ■ *Africa* 77 F4
São Vicente *Brazil* 127 A6
São Vicente *C. Verde Is.* 78 b
São Vicente *Madeira* 48 D2
São Vicente, C. de *Portugal* 37 H1
Saona, I. *Dom. Rep.* 121 C6
Saône → *France* 19 G11
Saône-et-Loire □ *France* 19 F11
Saonek *Indonesia* 63 E8
Sapam, Ao *Thailand* 65 a
Sapanca *Turkey* 72 B4
Saparua *Indonesia* 63 E7
Sapele *Nigeria* 83 D6
Sapelo I. *U.S.A.* 117 F14
Sapes *Greece* 45 E9
Şaphane *Turkey* 47 B11
Sapi ⌂ *Zimbabwe* 87 F2
Sapienza *Greece* 46 E3
Sapo △ *Liberia* 82 D3
Sapone *Burkina Faso* 83 C4
Saposoa *Peru* 124 E3
Sapotskina *Belarus* 30 E10
Sapouy *Burkina Faso* 83 C4
Sapozhok *Russia* 34 D5
Sapphire *Australia* 94 C4
Sappho *U.S.A.* 110 B2
Sapporo *Japan* 54 C10
Sapri *Italy* 43 B8
Sapulpa *U.S.A.* 116 D6
Saqqez *Iran* 73 D12
Sar Dasht *Āzarbāyjān-e Gharbī, Iran* 73 D11
Sar Dasht *Khuzestān, Iran* 71 C6
Sar-e Pol □ *Afghan.* 66 B4
Sar Gachīneh = Yāsūj *Iran* 71 D6
Sar Planina *Macedonia* 44 E4
Sara *Burkina Faso* 82 C4
Sara *Phil.* 61 F5
Šara △ *Serbia* 44 D5
Sara Buri = Saraburi *Thailand* 64 E3
Sarāb *Iran* 73 D12
Sarabadi *Iraq* 70 C5
Saraburi *Thailand* 64 E3
Saradiya *India* 68 J4
Saraféré *Mali* 82 B4
Saragossa = Zaragoza *Spain* 38 D4
Saraguro *Ecuador* 124 D3
Sarahs *Turkmenistan* 71 B9
Sarai Naurang *Pakistan* 68 C4
Saraikela *India* 69 H11

Saraiu *Romania* **29** F13
Sarajevo *Bos.-H.* **28** G3
Sarakhs = Sarahs
  Turkmenistan **71** B9
Saran, Gunung *Indonesia* **62** E4
Saranac Lake *U.S.A.* **115** B10
Saranac Lakes *U.S.A.* **115** B10
Saranda *Tanzania* **86** D3
Sarandë *Albania* **44** G3
Sarandí del Yi *Uruguay* **127** C4
Sarandí Grande *Uruguay* **126** C4
Sarangani B. *Phil.* **61** J6
Sarangani Is. *Phil.* **61** J6
Sarangarh *India* **67** J13
Saransk *Russia* **34** C7
Sarapul *Russia* **52** D6
Sarasota *U.S.A.* **117** H13
Sarata *Ukraine* **29** D14
Sarata → *Ukraine* **29** E14
Saratoga *Calif., U.S.A.* **110** H4
Saratoga *Wyo., U.S.A.* **108** F10
Saratoga △ *U.S.A.* **115** D11
Saratoga Springs *U.S.A.* **115** C11
Saratok *Malaysia* **62** D4
Saratov *Russia* **34** E7
Saratov □ *Russia* **34** E8
Sarāvān *Iran* **71** E9
Saravane *Laos* **64** E6
Sarawak □ *Malaysia* **62** D4
Saray *Tekirdağ, Turkey* **45** E11
Saray *Van, Turkey* **73** C11
Saraya *Senegal* **82** C2
Saraycık *Turkey* **47** B11
Sarayköy *Turkey* **47** D10
Saraylar *Turkey* **45** F11
Sarayönü *Turkey* **72** C5
Sarbāz *Iran* **71** E9
Sarbīsheh *Iran* **71** C8
Sárbogárd *Hungary* **28** D3
Sarca → *Italy* **40** C7
Sarcelles *France* **19** D9
Sarda → *India* **69** F9
Sardarshahr *India* **68** E6
Sardegna □ *Italy* **42** B1
Sardhana *India* **68** E7
Sardina, Pta. *Canary Is.* **48** F4
Sardinia = Sardegna □ *Italy* **42** B1
Sardis *Turkey* **47** C10
Sārdūyeh = Dar Mazār *Iran* **71** D8
Saren *Indonesia* **63** J18
S'Arenal *Spain* **48** B9
Sarentino *Italy* **41** B8
Sarera, G. of *Indonesia* **90** B6
Saréyamou *Mali* **82** B4
Sargasso Sea *Atl. Oc.* **98** G13
Sargodha *Pakistan* **68** C5
Sarh *Chad* **79** G9
Sarhala *Ivory C.* **82** D3
Sārī *Iran* **71** B7
Sari d'Orcino *France* **21** F12
Saria *Greece* **47** F9
Saria *India* **69** J10
Sariab *Pakistan* **68** D2
Sarıbeyler *Turkey* **47** B9
Sarıgöl *Turkey* **72** C3
Sarikamiş *Turkey* **73** B10
Sarıkaya *Turkey* **72** C6
Sarikei *Malaysia* **62** D4
Sarıköy *Turkey* **45** F11
Sarila *India* **69** G8
Sarina *Australia* **94** C4
Sariñena *Spain* **38** D4
Sarita *U.S.A.* **116** H6
Sariwŏn *N. Korea* **57** E13
Sariyar Baraji *Turkey* **72** B4
Sarıyer *Turkey* **45** E13
Sarju → *India* **69** F9
Sark *U.K.* **15** H5
Sarkad *Hungary* **28** D6
Sarkari Tala *India* **68** F4
Şarkışla *Turkey* **72** C7
Şarköy *Turkey* **45** F11
Sarlat-la-Canéda *France* **20** D5
Şărmăşag *Romania* **28** C7
Şărmaşu *Romania* **29** D9
Sarmi *Indonesia* **63** E9
Sarmiento *Argentina* **128** F3
Sarmizegetusa *Romania* **28** E7
Särna *Sweden* **10** C7
Sarnano *Italy* **41** E10
Sarnen *Switz.* **25** J4
Sarnia *Canada* **114** D2
Sarno *Italy* **43** B7
Sarnthein = Sarentino *Italy* **41** B8
Sarolangun *Indonesia* **62** E2
Saronikos Kolpos *Greece* **46** D5
Saronno *Italy* **40** C6
Saros Körfezi *Turkey* **45** F10
Sárospatak *Hungary* **28** B6
Sarpsborg *Norway* **9** G14
Sarqan *Kazakhstan* **52** E8
Sarracín *Spain* **36** C7
Sarralbe *France* **19** D14
Sarre = Saar → *Europe* **17** E6
Sarre *Italy* **40** C4
Sarre-Union *France* **19** D14

Sarrebourg *France* **19** D14
Sarreguemines *France* **19** C14
Sarria *Spain* **36** C3
Sarrión *Spain* **38** E4
Sarro *Mali* **82** C3
Sarstedt *Germany* **24** C5
Sartène *France* **21** G12
Sarthe □ *France* **18** D7
Sarthe → *France* **18** E6
Sartilly *France* **18** D5
Saruhanlı *Turkey* **47** C9
Săruleşti *Romania* **29** F11
Saruna → *Pakistan* **68** F2
Sárvár *Hungary* **28** C1
Sarvar *India* **68** F6
Sarvestān *Iran* **71** D7
Sárvíz → *Hungary* **28** D3
Sarzana *Italy* **40** D6
Sarzeau *France* **18** E4
Sasan Gir *India* **68** J4
Sasaram *India* **69** G11
Sasebo *Japan* **55** H4
Saser *India* **69** B7
Saskatchewan □ *Canada* **103** C7
Saskatchewan → *Canada* **103** C8
Saskatoon *Canada* **103** C7
Saskylakh *Russia* **53** B12
Saslaya △ *Nic.* **120** D2
Sasovo *Russia* **34** C5
Sassandra *Ivory C.* **82** E3
Sassandra → *Ivory C.* **82** E3
Sássari *Italy* **42** B1
Sassnitz *Germany* **24** A9
Sasso Marconi *Italy* **41** D8
Sassocorvaro *Italy* **41** E9
Sassoferrato *Italy* **41** E9
Sasstown *Liberia* **82** E3
Sassuolo *Italy* **40** D7
Sástago *Spain* **38** D4
Sasyk, Ozero *Ukraine* **29** E14
Sata-Misaki *Japan* **55** J5
Satadougou *Mali* **82** C2
Satakunda = Satakunta
  Finland **32** B2
Satakunta *Finland* **32** B2
Satama-Soukoura *Ivory C.* **82** D4
Satara *India* **66** L8
Satara *S. Africa* **89** C5
Satbarwa *India* **69** H11
Såtenäs *Sweden* **11** F6
Säter *Sweden* **10** D9
Satevó *Mexico* **118** B3
Satilla → *U.S.A.* **117** F14
Satmala Hills
  Andhra Pradesh, India **66** K11
Satmala Hills *Maharashtra,*
  India **66** J9
Satna *India* **69** G9
Šator *Bos.-H.* **41** D13
Sátoraljaújhely *Hungary* **28** B6
Satpura △ *India* **68** H8
Satpura Ra. *India* **66** J10
Satrup *Germany* **24** A5
Satsuna-Shotō *Japan* **55** K5
Sattahip *Thailand* **64** F3
Satu Mare *Romania* **28** C7
Satu Mare □ *Romania* **28** C8
Satui *Indonesia* **62** E5
Satun *Thailand* **65** J3
Satupa'itea *Samoa* **91** b
Saturnina → *Brazil* **124** F7
Sauce *Argentina* **126** C4
Sauceda *Mexico* **118** B4
Saucillo *Mexico* **118** B3
Sauda *Norway* **9** G12
Sauðarkrókur *Iceland* **8** D4
Saudi Arabia ■ *Asia* **70** B3
Sauerland *Germany* **22** C4
Saugeen → *Canada* **114** B3
Saugerties *U.S.A.* **115** D11
Saugues *France* **20** D7
Saugus *U.S.A.* **111** L8
Saujon *France* **20** C3
Sauk Centre *U.S.A.* **112** C6
Sauk Rapids *U.S.A.* **112** C6
Saulgau *Germany* **25** G5
Saulieu *France* **19** E11
Sault *France* **21** D9
Sault Ste. Marie *Canada* **104** C3
Sault Ste. Marie *U.S.A.* **113** B11
Saumlaki *Indonesia* **63** F8
Saumur *France* **18** E6
Saunders, C. *N.Z.* **91** F3
Saunders I. *Antarctica* **5** B1
Saunders Pt. *Australia* **93** E4
Sauri *Nigeria* **83** C6
Saurimo *Angola* **84** F4
Sausalito *U.S.A.* **110** H4
Sauveterre-de-Béarn *France* **20** E3
Sauzé-Vaussais *France* **20** B4
Savá *Honduras* **120** C2
Sava *Italy* **43** B10

Sava → *Serbia* **28** F5
Savage *U.S.A.* **108** C11
Savage I. = Niue *Pac. Oc.* **97** J11
Savage River *Australia* **95** G4
Savai'i *Samoa* **91** b
Savalou *Benin* **83** D5
Savane *Mozam.* **87** F4
Savanna *U.S.A.* **112** D8
Savanna-la-Mar *Jamaica* **120** a
Savannah *Ga., U.S.A.* **117** E14
Savannah *Mo., U.S.A.* **112** F6
Savannah *Tenn., U.S.A.* **117** D10
Savannah → *U.S.A.* **117** E14
Savannakhet *Laos* **64** D5
Savant L. *Canada* **104** B1
Savant Lake *Canada* **104** B1
Savanur *India* **66** M9
Savaştepe *Turkey* **47** B9
Savé *Benin* **83** D5
Save → *France* **20** E5
Save → *Mozam.* **89** C5
Sāveh *Iran* **71** C6
Savelugu *Ghana* **83** D4
Savenay *France* **18** E5
Săveni *Romania* **29** C11
Saverdun *France* **20** E5
Saverne *France* **19** D14
Savigliano *Italy* **40** D6
Savigny-sur-Braye *France* **18** E7
Sávio → *Italy* **41** D9
Šavnik *Montenegro* **44** D3
Savo *Finland* **8** E22
Savoie □ *France* **21** C10
Savolax = Savo *Finland* **8** E22
Savona *Italy* **40** D5
Savona *U.S.A.* **114** D7
Savonlinna *Finland* **32** B5
Savoy = Savoie □ *France* **21** C10
Savsat *Turkey* **73** B10
Sävsjö *Sweden* **11** G8
Savur *Turkey* **70** B4
Savusavu *Fiji* **91** a
Savusavu B. *Fiji* **91** a
Sawahlunto *Indonesia* **62** E2
Sawai *Indonesia* **63** E7
Sawai Madhopur *India* **68** G7
Sawakele *Fiji* **91** a
Sawang Daen Din *Thailand* **64** D4
Sawankhalok *Thailand* **64** D2
Sawara *Japan* **55** G10
Sawatch Range *U.S.A.* **108** G10
Sawel Mt. *U.K.* **12** B4
Sawi *Thailand* **65** G2
Sawla *Ghana* **82** D4
Sawmills *Zimbabwe* **87** F2
Sawtooth △ *U.S.A.* **108** D6
Sawtooth Range *U.S.A.* **108** D6
Sawu *Indonesia* **63** F6
Sawu Sea *Indonesia* **63** F6
Saxby → *Australia* **94** B3
Saxmundham *U.K.* **15** E9
Saxony = Sachsen □
  Germany **24** E9
Saxony, Lower =
  Niedersachsen □ *Germany* **24** C4
Saxton *U.S.A.* **114** F6
Say *Mali* **82** C4
Say *Niger* **83** C5
Saya *Nigeria* **83** D5
Sayabec *Canada* **105** C6
Sayaboury *Laos* **64** C3
Sayán *Peru* **124** F3
Sayan, Vostochnyy *Russia* **53** D10
Sayan, Zapadnyy *Russia* **53** D10
Saydā *Lebanon* **74** B4
Sayhandulaan = Oldziyt
  Mongolia **56** B5
Sayḩūt *Yemen* **75** D5
Saykhin *Kazakhstan* **35** F8
Saylac = Zeila *Somali Rep.* **75** E3
Saynshand =
  Buyant-Uhaa *Mongolia* **60** B6
Sayre *Okla., U.S.A.* **116** D5
Sayre *Pa., U.S.A.* **115** E8
Sayreville *U.S.A.* **115** F10
Sayula *Mexico* **118** D4
Sayward *Canada* **102** C3
Sazanit *Albania* **44** F7
Sázava → *Czech Rep.* **26** B7
Sazin *Pakistan* **69** B5
Sazlika → *Bulgaria* **45** E9
Scaër *France* **18** D3
Scafell Pike *U.K.* **14** C4
Scalea *Italy* **43** C8
Scalloway *U.K.* **13** A7
Scalpay *U.K.* **13** D3
Scandia *Canada* **102** C6
Scandiano *Italy* **40** D7
Scandicci *Italy* **41** E8
Scandinavia *Europe* **8** E15
Scansano *Italy* **41** F8
Scapa Flow *U.K.* **13** C5
Scappoose *U.S.A.* **110** E4
Scarámia, Capo *Italy* **43** F7
Scarba *U.K.* **13** E3
Scarborough *Trin. & Tob.* **121** D7
Scarborough *U.K.* **14** C7

Scariff I. *Ireland* **12** E1
Scarp *U.K.* **13** C1
Scarpe-Escaut △ *France* **19** B10
Scebeli, Wabi → *Somali Rep.* **75** G3
Ščedro *Croatia* **41** E13
Schaal See *Germany* **24** B6
Schaalsee *Germany* **24** B6
Schaffhausen *Switz.* **25** H4
Schagen *Neths.* **17** B4
Schaghticoke *U.S.A.* **115** D11
Schärding *Austria* **26** C6
Scharhörn *Germany* **24** B4
Scheessel *Germany* **24** B5
Schefferville =
  Kawawachikamach
  Canada **105** B6
Scheibbs *Austria* **26** C8
Schelde → *Belgium* **17** C4
Schell Creek Ra. *U.S.A.* **108** G6
Schellsburg *U.S.A.* **114** F6
Schenectady *U.S.A.* **115** D11
Schenevus *U.S.A.* **115** D10
Scherfede *Germany* **24** D5
Schesslitz *Germany* **25** F7
Schiedam *Neths.* **17** C4
Schiermonnikoog *Neths.* **17** A6
Schiltigheim *France* **19** D14
Schinousa *Greece* **47** E7
Schio *Italy* **41** C8
Schiphol, Amsterdam ✈
  (AMS) *Neths.* **17** B4
Schladming *Austria* **26** D6
Schlanders = Silandro *Italy* **40** B7
Schlei → *Germany* **24** A5
Schleiden *Germany* **24** E2
Schleiz *Germany* **24** E7
Schleswig *Germany* **24** A5
Schleswig-Holstein □
  Germany **24** A5
Schlüchtern *Germany* **25** E5
Schmalkalden *Germany* **24** E6
Schmölln *Germany* **24** E8
Schneeberg *Austria* **26** D8
Schneeberg *Germany* **24** E8
Schneverdingen *Germany* **24** B5
Schœlcher *Martinique* **120** c
Schoharie *U.S.A.* **115** D10
Schoharie Cr. → *U.S.A.* **115** D10
Scholls *U.S.A.* **110** E4
Schönberg
  Mecklenburg-Vorpommern,
  Germany **24** B6
Schönberg
  Schleswig-Holstein, Germany **24** A6
Schönbuch △ *Germany* **25** G5
Schönebeck *Germany* **24** C7
Schöneberg *Germany* **25** H6
Schöningen *Germany* **24** C6
Schopfheim *Germany* **25** H3
Schorndorf *Germany* **25** G5
Schortens *Germany* **24** B3
Schouten I. *Australia* **95** G4
Schouten Is. = Supiori
  Indonesia **63** E9
Schouwen *Neths.* **17** C3
Schramberg *Germany* **25** G4
Schrankogel *Austria* **26** D4
Schreiber *Canada* **104** C2
Schrems *Austria* **26** C8
Schrobenhausen *Germany* **25** G7
Schroffenstein *Namibia* **88** D2
Schroon Lake *U.S.A.* **115** C11
Schruns *Austria* **26** D2
Schuler *Canada* **103** C6
Schumacher *Canada* **104** C3
Schurz *U.S.A.* **108** G4
Schuyler *U.S.A.* **112** E5
Schuylerville *U.S.A.* **115** C11
Schuylkill → *U.S.A.* **115** G9
Schuylkill Haven *U.S.A.* **115** F8
Schwabach *Germany* **25** F7
Schwaben □ *Germany* **25** G6
Schwäbisch-Fränkischer
  Wald △ *Germany* **25** G5
Schwäbisch Gmünd
  Germany **25** G5
Schwäbisch Hall *Germany* **25** F5
Schwäbische Alb *Germany* **25** G5
Schwabmünchen *Germany* **25** G6
Schwalmstadt *Germany* **24** E5
Schwandorf *Germany* **25** F8
Schwaner, Pegunungan
  Indonesia **62** E4
Schwanewede *Germany* **24** B4
Schwarmstedt *Germany* **24** C5
Schwarze Elster → *Germany* **24** D8
Schwarzenberg *Germany* **24** E8
Schwarzrand *Namibia* **88** D2
Schwarzwald *Germany* **25** G4
Schwaz *Austria* **26** D4
Schwechat *Austria* **27** C9
Schwechat, Wien ✈ (VIE)
  Austria **27** C9
Schwedt *Germany* **24** B10
Schweinfurt *Germany* **25** E6
Schweiz = Switzerland ■
  Europe **25** J4

Schweizer-Reneke *S. Africa* **88** D4
Schwenningen =
  Villingen-
  Schwenningen *Germany* **25** G4
Schwerin *Germany* **24** B7
Schweriner See *Germany* **24** B7
Schwetzingen *Germany* **25** F4
Schwyz *Switz.* **25** H4
Schwyz □ *Switz.* **25** H4
Sciacca *Italy* **42** E6
Scicli *Italy* **43** F7
Sciliar △ *Italy* **41** B8
Scilla *Italy* **43** D8
Scilly, Isles of *U.K.* **15** H1
Ścinawa *Poland* **31** G3
Scione *Greece* **44** G7
Scioto → *U.S.A.* **113** F12
Scituate *U.S.A.* **115** D14
Scobey *U.S.A.* **108** B11
Scone *Australia* **95** E5
Scone *U.K.* **13** E5
Scordia *Italy* **43** E7
Scoresbysund =
  Ittoqqortoormiit *Greenland* **4** B6
Scornicești *Romania* **29** F9
Scotia *Calif., U.S.A.* **108** F1
Scotia *N.Y., U.S.A.* **115** D11
Scotia Sea *Antarctica* **5** B18
Scotland *Canada* **114** C4
Scotland □ *U.K.* **13** E5
Scott *Antarctica* **5** D11
Scott, C. *Australia* **92** B4
Scott City *U.S.A.* **112** F4
Scott Glacier *Antarctica* **5** C8
Scott I. *Antarctica* **5** C11
Scott Is. *Canada* **102** C3
Scott L. *Canada* **103** B7
Scott Reef *Australia* **92** B3
Scottburgh *S. Africa* **89** E5
Scottdale *U.S.A.* **114** F5
Scottish Borders □ *U.K.* **13** F6
Scotts Valley *U.S.A.* **110** H4
Scottsbluff *U.S.A.* **112** E2
Scottsboro *U.S.A.* **117** D11
Scottsburg *U.S.A.* **113** F11
Scottsdale *Australia* **95** G4
Scottsdale *U.S.A.* **109** K8
Scottsville *Ky., U.S.A.* **112** G10
Scottsville *N.Y., U.S.A.* **114** C7
Scottville *U.S.A.* **112** D10
Scranton *U.S.A.* **115** E9
Scugog, L. *Canada* **114** B6
Sculeni *Moldova* **29** C12
Scunthorpe *U.K.* **14** D7
Scuol Schuls *Switz.* **25** J6
Sea Is. *U.S.A.* **117** F14
Seabrook, L. *Australia* **93** F2
Seaford *U.K.* **15** G8
Seaford *U.S.A.* **113** F16
Seaforth *Australia* **94** J6
Seaforth *Canada* **114** C3
Seaforth, L. *U.K.* **13** D2
Seagraves *U.S.A.* **116** E3
Seaham *U.K.* **14** C6
Seal → *Canada* **103** B10
Seal L. *Canada* **105** B7
Sealy *U.S.A.* **116** G6
Searchlight *U.S.A.* **111** K12
Searcy *U.S.A.* **116** D9
Searles L. *U.S.A.* **111** K9
Seascale *U.K.* **14** C4
Seaside *Calif., U.S.A.* **110** J5
Seaside *Oreg., U.S.A.* **110** E3
Seaspray *Australia* **95** F4
Seattle *U.S.A.* **110** C4
Seattle-Tacoma Int. ✈
  (SEA) *U.S.A.* **110** C4
Sebago L. *U.S.A.* **115** C14
Sebago Lake *U.S.A.* **115** C14
Sebastián Vizcaíno, B.
  Mexico **118** B2
Sebastopol = Sevastopol
  Ukraine **33** K7
Sebastopol *U.S.A.* **110** G4
Sebba *Burkina Faso* **83** C5
Sebderat *Eritrea* **81** D4
Sébékoro *Mali* **82** C3
Seben *Turkey* **72** B4
Sebeş *Romania* **29** E8
Sebeşului, Munţii *Romania* **29** E8
Sebewaing *U.S.A.* **113** D12
Sebezh *Russia* **32** D5
Sebha = Sabhā *Libya* **79** C8
Sébi *Mali* **82** B4
Şebinkarahisar *Turkey* **73** B8
Sebiş *Romania* **28** D7
Sebnitz *Germany* **24** E10
Sebring *Fla., U.S.A.* **117** H14
Sebring *Ohio, U.S.A.* **114** F3
Sebringville *Canada* **114** C3
Sebta = Ceuta *N. Afr.* **78** A4
Sebuku *Indonesia* **62** E5
Sebuku, Teluk *Malaysia* **62** D5

Secchia → *Italy* **40** C8
Sechelt *Canada* **102** D4
Sechura, Desierto de *Peru* **124** E2
Seclin *France* **19** B10
Secondigny *France* **18** F6
Sečovce *Slovak Rep.* **27** C14
Secretary I. *N.Z.* **91** F1
Secunderabad *India* **66** L11
Security *U.S.A.* **108** G11
Sedalia *U.S.A.* **112** F7
Sedan *France* **19** C11
Sedan *U.S.A.* **112** G5
Sedano *Spain* **36** C7
Sedbergh *U.K.* **14** C5
Seddon *N.Z.* **91** D5
Seddonville *N.Z.* **91** D4
Sedé Boqér *Israel* **74** E3
Sedeh *Fārs, Iran* **71** D7
Sedeh *Khorāsān, Iran* **71** C8
Séderon *France* **21** D9
Sederot *Israel* **74** D3
Sédhiou *Senegal* **82** C1
Sedico *Italy* **41** B9
Sedley *Canada* **103** C8
Sedona *U.S.A.* **109** J8
Sedova, Pik *Russia* **52** B6
Sedro-Woolley *U.S.A.* **110** B4
Šeduva *Lithuania* **30** C10
Sędziszów *Poland* **31** H7
Sędziszów Małopolski *Poland* **31** H8
Seebad Ahlbeck *Germany* **24** B10
Seefeld in Tirol *Austria* **26** D4
Seehausen *Germany* **24** C7
Seeheim *Namibia* **88** D2
Seeheim-Jugenheim
  Germany **25** F4
Seeis *Namibia* **88** C2
Seekoei → *S. Africa* **88** E4
Seeley's Bay *Canada* **115** B8
Seelow *Germany* **24** C10
Sées *France* **18** D7
Seesen *Germany* **24** D6
Seevetal *Germany* **24** B6
Seewinkel = Neusiedler
  See-Seewinkel △ *Austria* **27** D9
Sefadu *S. Leone* **82** D2
Seferihisar *Turkey* **47** C8
Séfeto *Mali* **82** C3
Sefwi Bekwai *Ghana* **82** D4
Segamat *Malaysia* **65** L4
Şegarcea *Romania* **29** F8
Ségbana *Benin* **83** C5
Segbwema *S. Leone* **82** D2
Segesta *Italy* **42** E5
Seget *Indonesia* **63** E8
Segonzac *France* **20** C3
Segorbe *Spain* **38** F4
Ségou *Mali* **82** C3
Ségou □ *Mali* **82** C3
Segovia = Coco →
  Cent. Amer. **120** D3
Segovia *Spain* **36** E6
Segovia □ *Spain* **36** E6
Segré *France* **18** E6
Segre → *Spain* **38** D5
Séguéla *Ivory C.* **82** D3
Seguin *U.S.A.* **116** G6
Segundo → *Argentina* **126** C3
Segura → *Spain* **39** G4
Segura, Sierra de *Spain* **39** G2
Seh Konj, Kūh-e *Iran* **71** D8
Seh Qal'eh *Iran* **71** C8
Sehitwa *Botswana* **88** C3
Sehlabathebe △ *Lesotho* **89** D4
Sehore *India* **68** H7
Sehwan *Pakistan* **68** F2
Şeica Mare *Romania* **29** D9
Seikan Tunnel *Japan* **54** D10
Seil *U.K.* **13** E3
Seiland *Norway* **8** A20
Seilhac *France* **20** C5
Seiling *U.S.A.* **116** C5
Seille → *Moselle, France* **19** C13
Seille → *Saône-et-Loire,*
  France **19** F11
Sein, Î. de *France* **18** D2
Seinäjoki *Finland* **8** E20
Seine → *France* **18** C7
Seine, B. de la *France* **18** C6
Seine-et-Marne □ *France* **19** D10
Seine-Maritime □ *France* **18** C7
Seine-St-Denis □ *France* **19** D9
Seini *Romania* **29** C8
Seirijai *Lithuania* **30** D10
Seistan = Sīstān *Asia* **71** D9
Seistan, Daryācheh-ye =
  Sīstān, Daryācheh-ye
  Iran **71** D9
Sejerø *Denmark* **11** J5
Sejerø Bugt *Denmark* **11** J5
Sejny *Poland* **30** D10
Seka *Ethiopia* **81** F4
Sekayu *Indonesia* **62** E2
Seke *Tanzania* **86** C3
Sekenke *Tanzania* **86** C3

Seki *Turkey* **47** E11
Sekondi-Takoradi *Ghana* **82** E4
Sekota *Ethiopia* **81** E4
Seksna *Russia* **32** C10
Sekudai *Malaysia* **65** d
Sekuma *Botswana* **88** C3
Selah *U.S.A.* **108** C3
Selama *Malaysia* **65** K3
Selaru *Indonesia* **63** F8
Selatan, Selat *Malaysia* **65** c
Selb *Germany* **25** E8
Selby *U.K.* **14** D6
Selby *U.S.A.* **112** C3
Selca *Croatia* **41** E13
Selçuk *Turkey* **47** D9
Selden *U.S.A.* **112** F3
Sele ➤ *Italy* **43** B7
Selebi-Pikwe *Botswana* **89** C4
Selemdzha ➤ *Russia* **53** D13
Selendi *Manisa, Turkey* **47** C10
Selendi *Manisa, Turkey* **47** C9
Selenga = Selenge
  Mörön ➤ *Asia* **60** A5
Selenge Mörön ➤ *Asia* **60** A5
Selenicë *Albania* **44** F3
Selenter See *Germany* **24** A6
Sélestat *France* **19** D14
Seletan, Tanjung *Indonesia* **62** E4
Seletar *S. Africa* **89** D4
Selevac *Serbia* **44** B4
Sélibabi *Mauritania* **82** B2
Seliger, Ozero *Russia* **32** D7
Seligman *U.S.A.* **109** J7
Şelim *Turkey* **73** B10
Selîma, El Wâhât el *Sudan* **80** C2
Selimiye *Turkey* **47** D9
Selinda Spillway ➤
  Botswana **88** B3
Selinsgrove *U.S.A.* **114** F8
Selizharovo *Russia* **32** D7
Selkirk *Canada* **103** C9
Selkirk *U.K.* **13** F6
Selkirk I. = Horse I. *Canada* **103** C9
Selkirk Mts. *Canada* **100** D8
Sellafield *U.K.* **14** C4
Sellama *Sudan* **81** E2
Sellía *Greece* **49** D6
Sellières *France* **19** F12
Sells *U.S.A.* **109** L8
Sellye *Hungary* **28** E2
Selma *Ala., U.S.A.* **117** E11
Selma *Calif., U.S.A.* **110** J7
Selma *N.C., U.S.A.* **117** D15
Selmer *U.S.A.* **117** D10
Selongey *France* **19** E12
Selous △ *Tanzania* **87** D4
Selowandoma Falls
  Zimbabwe **87** G3
Selpele *Indonesia* **63** E8
Selsey Bill ➤ *U.K.* **15** G7
Seltso *Russia* **32** F8
Seltz *France* **19** D15
Selu *Indonesia* **63** F8
Sélune ➤ *France* **18** D5
Selva = La Selva del Camp
  Spain **38** D6
Selva *Argentina* **126** B3
Selva Lancandona =
  Montes Azules △ *Mexico* **119** D6
Selvas *Brazil* **124** E5
Selwyn L. *Canada* **103** B8
Selwyn Mts. *Canada* **100** C6
Selwyn Ra. *Australia* **94** C3
Selyatyn *Ukraine* **29** C10
Seman ➤ *Albania* **44** F3
Semarang *Indonesia* **63** G14
Sembabule *Uganda* **86** C3
Sembawang *Singapore* **65** d
Sembung *Indonesia* **63** J18
Şemdinli *Turkey* **73** D11
Sémé *Senegal* **82** B2
Semeih *Sudan* **81** E3
Semenanjung
  Blambangan *Indonesia* **63** K17
Semenov *Russia* **34** B7
Semenovka *Chernihiv,
  Ukraine* **33** F7
Semenovka *Kremenchuk,
  Ukraine* **33** H7
Semeru *Indonesia* **63** H15
Semey *Kazakhstan* **52** D9
Semikarakorskiy *Russia* **35** G5
Semiluki *Russia* **33** G10
Seminoe Res. *U.S.A.* **108** E10
Seminole *Okla., U.S.A.* **116** D6
Seminole *Tex., U.S.A.* **116** E3
Seminole Draw ➤ *U.S.A.* **116** E3
Semipalatinsk = Semey
  Kazakhstan **52** D9
Semirara Is. *Phil.* **61** F4
Semitau *Indonesia* **62** D4
Semiyarka *Kazakhstan* **52** D8
Semiyarskoye =
  Semiyarka *Kazakhstan* **52** D8
Semmering P. *Austria* **26** D8
Semnān *Iran* **71** C7
Semnān □ *Iran* **71** C7

Semporna *Malaysia* **63** D5
Semuda *Indonesia* **62** E4
Semur-en-Auxois *France* **19** E11
Sen ➤ *Cambodia* **64** F5
Senā *Iran* **71** D6
Sena *Mozam.* **87** F4
Sena Madureira *Brazil* **124** E5
Senador Pompeu *Brazil* **125** E11
Senaki *Georgia* **35** J6
Senanga *Zambia* **85** H4
Senang, Pulau *Singapore* **65** d
Senatobia *U.S.A.* **117** D10
Sencelles *Spain* **48** B9
Sendafa *Ethiopia* **81** F4
Sendai *Kagoshima, Japan* **55** J5
Sendai *Miyagi, Japan* **54** E10
Sendai-Wan *Japan* **54** E10
Senden *Bayern, Germany* **25** G6
Senden *Nordrhein-Westfalen,
  Germany* **24** D3
Sendhwa *India* **68** J6
Sene ➤ *Ghana* **83** D4
Senec *Slovak Rep.* **27** C10
Seneca *U.S.A.* **117** D13
Seneca Falls *U.S.A.* **115** D8
Seneca L. *U.S.A.* **114** D8
Senecaville L. *U.S.A.* **114** G3
Senegal ■ *W. Afr.* **82** C2
Senegal ➤ *W. Afr.* **82** C2
Senegambia *Africa* **76** E2
Senekal *S. Africa* **89** D4
Senftenberg *Germany* **24** D10
Senga Hill *Zambia* **87** D3
Senge Khambab =
  Indus ➤ *Pakistan* **68** G2
Sengiley *Russia* **34** D9
Sengua ➤ *Zimbabwe* **87** F2
Senhor-do-Bonfim *Brazil* **125** F10
Senica *Slovak Rep.* **27** C10
Senigállia *Italy* **41** E10
Senio ➤ *Italy* **41** D9
Senirkent *Turkey* **47** C12
Senise *Italy* **43** B9
Senj *Croatia* **41** D11
Senja *Norway* **8** B17
Senkaku-Shotō *E. China Sea* **55** M1
Senkuang *Indonesia* **65** d
Senlis *France* **19** C9
Senmonorom *Cambodia* **64** F6
Sennâr *Sudan* **81** E3
Sennâr □ *Sudan* **81** E3
Senneterre *Canada* **104** C4
Senno *Belarus* **32** E5
Sénnori *Italy* **42** B1
Seno *Laos* **64** D5
Senonches *France* **18** D8
Senorbì *Italy* **42** C2
Senožeče *Slovenia* **41** C11
Sens *France* **19** D10
Senta *Serbia* **28** E5
Sentani *Indonesia* **63** E10
Sentery = Lubao
  Dem. Rep. of the Congo **86** D2
Sentinel *U.S.A.* **109** K7
Šentjur *Slovenia* **41** B12
Sentosa *Singapore* **65** d
Senya Beraku *Ghana* **83** D4
Seo de Urgel = La Seu
  d'Urgell *Spain* **38** C6
Seogwipo *S. Korea* **57** H14
Seohara *India* **69** E8
Seonath ➤ *India* **69** J10
Seondha *India* **69** F8
Seongnam *S. Korea* **57** F14
Seoni *India* **69** H8
Seoni Malwa *India* **68** H8
Seonsan *S. Korea* **57** F15
Seosan *S. Korea* **57** F14
Seoul *S. Korea* **57** F14
Sepīdān *Iran* **71** D7
Sep'o *N. Korea* **57** E14
Sępólno Krajeńskie *Poland* **30** E4
Sepone *Laos* **64** D6
Sępopol *Poland* **30** D8
Sept-Îles *Canada* **105** B6
Septemvri *Bulgaria* **45** D8
Sepúlveda *Spain* **36** D7
Sequeros *Spain* **36** E4
Sequim *U.S.A.* **110** B3
Sequoia △ *U.S.A.* **110** J8
Serafimovich *Russia* **34** F6
Seraing *Belgium* **17** D5
Serakhis ➤ *Cyprus* **49** D11
Seram *Indonesia* **63** E7
Seram Sea *Indonesia* **63** E7
Seranantsara *Madag.* **89** B8
Serang *Indonesia* **63** G12
Serangoon *Singapore* **65** d
Serasan *Indonesia* **62** D3
Seravezza *Italy* **40** E7
Şerbettar *Turkey* **45** E10
Serbia □ *Serbia* **44** C5
Serbia ■ *Europe* **44** C4
Şercaia *Romania* **29** E10
Serdar *Turkmenistan* **71** B8
Serdo *Ethiopia* **81** E5
Serdobsk *Russia* **34** D7

Sered' *Slovak Rep.* **27** C10
Seredka *Russia* **32** C5
Serednye *Ukraine* **28** B7
Şereflikoçhisar *Turkey* **72** C5
Seregno *Italy* **40** C6
Seremban *Malaysia* **65** L3
Serengeti △ *Tanzania* **86** C3
Serengeti Plain *Tanzania* **86** C4
Serenje *Zambia* **87** E3
Seret ➤ *Ukraine* **29** B10
Sereth = Siret ➤ *Romania* **29** E12
Sergach *Russia* **34** C7
Sergen *Turkey* **45** E11
Sergino *Russia* **52** C7
Sergipe □ *Brazil* **125** F11
Sergiyev Posad *Russia* **32** D10
Serhetabat *Turkmenistan* **71** C9
Seria *Brunei* **62** D4
Serian *Malaysia* **62** D4
Seriate *Italy* **40** C6
Seribu, Kepulauan *Indonesia* **62** F3
Sericho *Kenya* **86** B4
Sérifontaine *France* **19** C8
Serifos *Greece* **46** D6
Sérignan *France* **20** E7
Sérigny ➤ *Canada* **105** A6
Serik *Turkey* **72** D4
Seringapatam Reef *Australia* **92** B3
Serinhisar *Turkey* **47** D11
Seririt *Indonesia* **63** J17
Sermaize-les-Bains *France* **19** D11
Sermata *Indonesia* **63** F7
Sermersuaq *Greenland* **4** B4
Sérmide *Italy* **41** D8
Sernovodsk *Russia* **34** D10
Sernur *Russia* **34** B9
Serock *Poland* **31** F8
Serón *Spain* **39** H2
Seròs *Spain* **38** D5
Serov *Russia* **52** D7
Serowe *Botswana* **88** C4
Serpa *Portugal* **37** H3
Serpeddí, Punta *Italy* **42** C2
Serpentara *Italy* **42** C2
Serpentine Lakes *Australia* **93** E4
Serpent's Mouth = Sierpe,
  Bocas de la *Venezuela* **125** L15
Serpis ➤ *Spain* **39** G4
Serpneve *Ukraine* **29** D14
Serpukhov *Russia* **32** E9
Serra da Estrela △ *Portugal* **36** E3
Serra de Outes *Spain* **36** C2
Serra do Navio *Brazil* **125** C8
Serra San Bruno *Italy* **43** D9
Serradilla *Spain* **36** F4
Serramanna *Italy* **42** C1
Serranía San Luís △
  Paraguay **126** A4
Serras d'Aire e
  Candeeiros △ *Portugal* **37** F2
Serravalle Scrívia *Italy* **40** D5
Serre-Ponçon, L. de *France* **21** D10
Serres *France* **21** D9
Serres *Greece* **44** E7
Serres □ *Greece* **44** E7
Serrezuela *Argentina* **126** C2
Serrinha *Brazil* **125** F11
Sersale *Italy* **43** C9
Sertã *Portugal* **36** F2
Sertanópolis *Brazil* **127** A5
Sêrtar *China* **58** A3
Serua *Indonesia* **63** F8
Serui *Indonesia* **63** E9
Serule *Botswana* **88** C4
Servia *Greece* **44** F6
Serzedelo *Portugal* **36** D2
Ses Salines *Spain* **48** B10
Sese Is. *Uganda* **86** C3
Sesepe *Indonesia* **63** E7
Sesfontein *Namibia* **88** B1
Sesheke *Zambia* **88** B3
Sésia ➤ *Italy* **40** C5
Sesimbra *Portugal* **37** G1
Seskin, L. *Ireland* —
Sessa Aurunca *Italy* **42** A6
S'Espalmador *Spain* **48** C7
S'Espardell *Spain* **48** C7
S'Estanyol *Spain* **48** B9
Sestao *Spain* **38** B2
Sesto Calende *Italy* **40** C5
Sesto San Giovanni *Italy* **40** C6
Sestri Levante *Italy* **40** D6
Sestriere *Italy* **40** D3
Sestroretsk *Russia* **32** B6
Sestrunj *Croatia* **41** D11
Sestu *Italy* **42** C2
Setana *Japan* **54** C9
Sète *France* **20** E7
Sete Lagôas *Brazil* **125** G10
Sétif *Algeria* **78** A7
Seto *Japan* **55** G8
Setonaikai *Japan* **55** G6
Setonaikai △ *Japan* **55** G6
Settat *Morocco* **78** B4
Séttimo Torinese *Italy* **40** C4
Setting L. *Canada* **103** C9
Settle *U.K.* **14** C5
Settlement, The *Br. Virgin Is.* **121** e

Settlers *S. Africa* **89** C4
Setúbal *Portugal* **37** G2
Setúbal □ *Portugal* **37** G2
Setúbal, B. de *Portugal* **37** G2
Seugne ➤ *France* **20** C3
Seul, Lac *Canada* **104** B1
Seurre *France* **19** F12
Sevan *Armenia* **35** K7
Sevan, Ozero = Sevana
  Lich *Armenia* **35** K7
Sevana Lich *Armenia* **35** K7
Sevastopol *Ukraine* **33** K7
Seven Sisters *Canada* **102** C3
Sever ➤ *Spain* **37** F3
Sévérac-le-Château *France* **20** D7
Severn ➤ *Canada* **104** A2
Severn ➤ *U.K.* **15** F5
Severn L. *Canada* **104** B1
Severnaya Zemlya *Russia* **53** B11
Severo-Kurilsk *Russia* **53** D16
Severo-Yeniseyskiy *Russia* **53** C10
Severo-Zapadnyy □ *Russia* **52** C4
Severočeský □
  Czech Rep. **26** A7
Severodonetsk =
  Syeverodonetsk *Ukraine* **33** H10
Severodvinsk *Russia* **52** C4
Severomoravský □
  Czech Rep. **27** B10
Severomorsk *Russia* **8** B25
Sevier ➤ *U.S.A.* **108** G7
Sevier Desert *U.S.A.* **108** G7
Sevier L. *U.S.A.* **108** G7
Sevilla *Spain* **37** H5
Sevilla □ *Spain* **37** H5
Seville = Sevilla *Spain* **37** H5
Sevlievo *Bulgaria* **45** C9
Sevnica *Slovenia* **41** B12
Sèvre-Nantaise ➤ *France* **18** E5
Sèvre-Niortaise ➤ *France* **20** B3
Sevsk *Russia* **33** F8
Sewa ➤ *S. Leone* **82** D2
Sewani *India* **68** E6
Seward *Alaska, U.S.A.* **100** C5
Seward *Nebr., U.S.A.* **112** E6
Seward *Pa., U.S.A.* **114** F5
Seward Peninsula *U.S.A.* **106** a
Sewell *Chile* **126** C1
Sewer *Indonesia* **63** F8
Sewickley *U.S.A.* **114** F4
Sexsmith *Canada* **102** B5
Seychelles ■ *Ind. Oc.* **85** b
Seyðisfjörður *Iceland* **8** D7
Seydişehir *Turkey* **72** D4
Seydvān *Iran* **73** C11
Seyhan ➤ *Turkey* **72** D6
Seyhan Barajı *Turkey* **72** D6
Seyitgazi *Turkey* **47** B12
Seyitömer *Turkey* **47** B11
Seym ➤ *Ukraine* **33** G7
Seymen *Turkey* **45** E11
Seymour *Australia* **95** F4
Seymour *S. Africa* **89** E4
Seymour *Conn., U.S.A.* **115** E11
Seymour *Ind., U.S.A.* **113** F11
Seymour *Tex., U.S.A.* **116** E5
Seyne *France* **21** D10
Seyssel *France* **21** C9
Sézanne *France* **19** D10
Sezze *Italy* **42** A6
Sfântu Gheorghe *Covasna,
  Romania* **29** E10
Sfântu Gheorghe *Tulcea,
  Romania* **29** F14
Sfântu Gheorghe,
  Braţul ➤ *Romania* **29** F14
Sfax *Tunisia* **79** B8
Sha Xi ➤ *China* **59** D12
Sha Xian *China* **59** D11
Shaanxi □ *China* **56** G5
Shaba = Katanga □
  Dem. Rep. of the Congo **86** D2
Shaba △ *Kenya* **86** B4
Shaballe = Scebeli,
  Wabi ➤ *Somali Rep.* **75** G3
Shabla *Bulgaria* **45** C12
Shabogamo L. *Canada* **105** B6
Shabunda
  Dem. Rep. of the Congo **86** C2
Shache *China* **60** C2
Shackleton Fracture Zone
  S. Ocean **5** B18
Shackleton Ice Shelf
  Antarctica **5** C8
Shackleton Inlet *Antarctica* **5** E11
Shādegān *Iran* **71** D6
Shadi *China* **59** D10
Shadi *India* **69** F8
Shadrinsk *Russia* **52** D7
Shadyside *U.S.A.* **114** G4
Shaffa *Nigeria* **83** C7
Shafter *U.S.A.* **111** K7
Shaftesbury *U.K.* **15** F5
Shagamu *Nigeria* **83** D5
Shagram *Pakistan* **69** A5
Shah Alizai *Pakistan* **68** E2
Shah Bunder *Pakistan* **68** G2

Shahabad *Punjab, India* **68** D7
Shahabad *Raj., India* **68** G7
Shahabad *Ut. P., India* **69** F8
Shahadpur *Pakistan* **68** G3
Shahba' *Syria* **74** C5
Shahdād *Iran* **71** D8
Shahdād, Namakzār-e *Iran* **71** D8
Shahdadkot *Pakistan* **68** F2
Shahdol *India* **69** H9
Shahe *China* **56** F8
Shahganj *India* **69** F10
Shahgarh *India* **68** F3
Shahjahanpur *India* **69** F8
Shahpur *India* **68** H7
Shahpur *Baluchistan, Pakistan* **68** E3
Shahpur *Punjab, Pakistan* **68** C5
Shahpur *Mad. P., India* **69** H9
Shahpura *Mad. P., India* **69** H9
Shahpura *Raj., India* **68** G6
Shahr-e Bābak *Iran* **71** D7
Shahr-e Kord *Iran* **71** C6
Shāhrakht *Iran* **71** C9
Shahrig *Pakistan* **68** D2
Shahukou *China* **56** D7
Shaikhabad *Afghan.* **68** B2
Shajapur *India* **68** H7
Shakargarh *Pakistan* **68** C6
Shakawe *Botswana* **88** B3
Shaker Heights *U.S.A.* **114** E3
Shakhty *Russia* **35** G5
Shakhunya *Russia* **34** B8
Shaki *Nigeria* **83** C5
Shākir *Egypt* **80** B3
Shaksam Valley *Asia* **69** A7
Shala, L. *Ethiopia* **81** F4
Shali *Russia* **35** J7
Shallow Lake *Canada* **114** B3
Shalqar *Kazakhstan* **52** E6
Shalskiy *Russia* **32** B8
Shaluli Shan *China* **58** B2
Shām *Iran* **71** E8
Shām, Bādiyat ash *Asia* **70** C3
Shamāl Bahr el Ghazal □
  Sudan **81** F2
Shamāl Dârfûr □ *Sudan* **81** E2
Shamāl Kordofân □ *Sudan* **81** E3
Shamāl Sînî □ *Egypt* **74** D2
Shamattawa *Canada* **104** A1
Shamattawa ➤ *Canada* **104** A2
Shambe *Sudan* **81** F3
Shambe △ *Sudan* **81** F3
Shambu *Ethiopia* **81** F4
Shamil *Iran* **71** E8
Shamkhor = Şämkir
  Azerbaijan **35** K8
Shāmkūh *Iran* **71** C8
Shamli *India* **68** E7
Shammar, Jabal *Si. Arabia* **70** E4
Shamo = Gobi *Asia* **56** C6
Shamo, L. *Ethiopia* **81** F4
Shamokin *U.S.A.* **115** F8
Shamrock *U.S.A.* **116** D4
Shamva *Zimbabwe* **87** F3
Shan □ *Burma* **67** J21
Shan Xian *China* **56** G9
Shanan ➤ *Ethiopia* **81** F5
Shanchengzhen *China* **57** C13
Shandak *Iran* **71** D9
Shandon *U.S.A.* **110** K6
Shandong □ *China* **57** G10
Shandong Bandao *China* **57** F11
Shang Xian = Shangzhou
  China **56** H5
Shanga *Nigeria* **78** F6
Shangalowe
  Dem. Rep. of the Congo **87** E2
Shangani *Zimbabwe* **89** B4
Shangani ➤ *Zimbabwe* **87** F2
Shangbancheng *China* **57** D10
Shangcheng *China* **59** B10
Shangchuan Dao *China* **59** G9
Shangdu *China* **56** D7
Shanggao *China* **59** C10
Shanghai *China* **59** B13
Shanghai Shi □ *China* **59** B13
Shanghang *China* **59** E11
Shanghe *China* **57** F9
Shanglin *China* **58** F7
Shangnan *China* **56** H6
Shangqiu *China* **56** G8
Shangrao *China* **59** C11
Shangshui *China* **60** C6
Shangsi *China* **58** F6
Shangyou *China* **59** E10
Shangyu *China* **59** B13
Shangzhi *China* **57** B14
Shangzhou *China* **56** H5
Shanhetun *China* **57** B14
Shani *Nigeria* **83** C7
Shanklin *U.K.* **15** G6
Shannon *N.Z.* **91** D5
Shannon ➤ *Ireland* **12** D2
Shannon ✈ (SNN) *Ireland* **12** D3
Shannon, Mouth of the
  Ireland **12** D2
Shannon △ *Australia* **93** F2
Shannonbridge *Ireland* **12** C3

Shansi = Shanxi □ *China* **56** F7
Shantar, Ostrov Bolshoy
  Russia **53** D14
Shantipur *India* **69** H13
Shantou *China* **59** F11
Shantung = Shandong □
  China **57** G10
Shanwei *China* **59** F10
Shanxi □ *China* **56** F7
Shanyang *China* **56** H5
Shanyin *China* **56** E7
Shaodong *China* **59** D8
Shaoguan *China* **59** E9
Shaoshan *China* **59** D8
Shaowu *China* **59** D11
Shaoxing *China* **59** C13
Shaoyang *Hunan, China* **59** D8
Shaoyang *Hunan, China* **59** D8
Shap *U.K.* **14** C5
Shapinsay *U.K.* **13** B6
Shaqq el Gi'eifer ➤ *Sudan* **81** D2
Shaqra' *Si. Arabia* **70** E5
Shaqrā' *Yemen* **75** E4
Sharafa *Sudan* **81** E2
Sharafkhāneh *Iran* **73** C11
Sharashova *Belarus* **31** F11
Sharbot Lake *Canada* **115** B8
Sharhorod *Ukraine* **29** B13
Shari *Japan* **54** C12
Sharjah = Ash Shāriqah
  U.A.E. **71** E7
Shark B. *Australia* **93** E1
Shark Bay △ *Australia* **93** E1
Sharm el Sheikh *Egypt* **80** B3
Sharon *Mass., U.S.A.* **115** D13
Sharon *Pa., U.S.A.* **114** E4
Sharon Springs *Kans.,
  U.S.A.* **112** F3
Sharon Springs *N.Y., U.S.A.*
  115 D10
Sharp Pt. *Australia* **94** A3
Sharpe L. *Canada* **104** B1
Sharpsville *U.S.A.* **114** E4
Sharq el Istiwa'iya □ *Sudan* **81** G3
Sharqi, Al Jabal ash *Lebanon* **74** B5
Sharya *Russia* **34** A7
Shasha *Ethiopia* **81** F4
Shashemene *Ethiopia* **81** F4
Shashi *Botswana* **89** C4
Shashi *China* **59** B9
Shashi ➤ *Africa* **87** G2
Shasta, Mt. *U.S.A.* **108** F2
Shasta L. *U.S.A.* **108** F2
Shatawi *Sudan* **81** E3
Shatsk *Russia* **34** C5
Shatsk *Ukraine* **31** G10
Shatsky Rise *Pac. Oc.* **96** D7
Shatskyi □ *Ukraine* **31** G10
Shatt al Arab *Asia* **71** D6
Shatura *Russia* **32** E10
Shaumyani = Shulaveri
  Georgia **35** K7
Shaunavon *Canada* **103** D7
Shaver L. *U.S.A.* **110** H7
Shaw ➤ *Australia* **92** D2
Shaw I. *Australia* **94** J7
Shawanaga *Canada* **114** A4
Shawangunk Mts. *U.S.A.* **115** E10
Shawano *U.S.A.* **112** C9
Shawinigan *Canada* **104** C5
Shawmari, J. ash *Jordan* **74** E5
Shawnee *U.S.A.* **116** D6
Shay Gap *Australia* **92** D3
Shayang *China* **59** B9
Shaybārā *Si. Arabia* **70** E3
Shayib el Banat, Gebel *Egypt* **80** B3
Shaykh, J. ash *Lebanon* **74** B4
Shaykh Miskīn *Syria* **74** C5
Shaykh Sa'īd *Iraq* **73** C11
Shchekino *Russia* **32** E9
Shchigry *Russia* **33** G9
Shchors *Ukraine* **33** G6
Shchūchīnsk *Kazakhstan* **52** D8
She Xian *Anhui, China* **59** C12
She Xian *Hebei, China* **56** F7
Shebekino *Russia* **33** G9
Shebele = Scebeli, Wabi ➤
  Somali Rep. **75** G3
Shebshi Mts. *Nigeria* **83** D7
Shediac *Canada* **105** C7
Sheelin, L. *Ireland* **12** C4
Sheep Haven *Ireland* **12** A4
Sheep Range *U.S.A.* **111** J11
Sheerness *U.K.* **15** F8
Sheet Harbour *Canada* **105** D7
Sheffield *U.K.* **14** D6
Sheffield *Ala., U.S.A.* **117** D11
Sheffield *Mass., U.S.A.* **115** D11
Sheffield *Pa., U.S.A.* **114** E5
Shehojele *Ethiopia* **81** E4
Shehong *China* **58** B5
Sheikh Idris *Sudan* **81** E3
Sheikh Zayed Canal *Egypt* **80** C3
Sheikhpura *India* **69** G11
Shek Hasan *Ethiopia* **81** E4
Shekhupura *Pakistan* **68** D5

Sheki = Şaki *Azerbaijan* **35** K8
Shelburne N.S., *Canada* **105** D6
Shelburne Ont., *Canada* **114** B4
Shelburne *U.S.A.* **115** B11
Shelburne B. *Australia* **94** A3
Shelburne Falls *U.S.A.* **115** D12
Shelby Mich., *U.S.A.* **112** D10
Shelby Mont., *U.S.A.* **108** B8
Shelby N.C., *U.S.A.* **117** D14
Shelby Ohio, *U.S.A.* **114** F2
Shelbyville Ill., *U.S.A.* **112** F9
Shelbyville Ind., *U.S.A.* **113** F11
Shelbyville Ky., *U.S.A.* **113** F11
Shelbyville Tenn., *U.S.A.* **117** D11
Sheldon *U.S.A.* **112** D6
Sheldrake *Canada* **105** B7
Shelengo, Khawr → *Sudan* **81** E2
Shelikhova, Zaliv *Russia* **53** D16
Shell Lakes *Australia* **93** E4
Shellbrook *Canada* **103** C7
Shellharbour *Australia* **95** E5
Shelon → *Russia* **32** C6
Shelter I. *U.S.A.* **115** E12
Shelton Conn., *U.S.A.* **115** E11
Shelton Wash., *U.S.A.* **110** C3
Shemakha = Şamaxi
    Azerbaijan **35** K9
Shēmri *Albania* **44** D4
Shemsi *Sudan* **80** D2
Shen Xian *China* **56** F8
Shenandoah Iowa, *U.S.A.* **112** E6
Shenandoah Pa., *U.S.A.* **115** F8
Shenandoah Va., *U.S.A.* **113** F14
Shenandoah → *U.S.A.* **113** F15
Shenandoah △ *U.S.A.* **113** F14
Shenchi *China* **56** E7
Shendam *Nigeria* **83** D6
Shendī *Sudan* **81** D3
Shenge S. *Leone* **82** D2
Shengfang *China* **56** E9
Shēngjergj *Albania* **44** E4
Shēngjin *Albania* **44** E3
Shengzhou *China* **59** C13
Shenjingzi *China* **57** B13
Shenmu *China* **56** E6
Shennongjia *China* **59** B8
Shenqiu *China* **56** H8
Shensi = Shaanxi □ *China* **56** G5
Shenyang *China* **57** D12
Shenzhen *China* **59** F10
Sheo *India* **68** F4
Sheopur Kalan *India* **68** G7
Shepetivka *Ukraine* **23** C14
Shepetovka = Shepetivka
    Ukraine **23** C14
Shepparton *Australia* **95** F4
Sheppey, I. of *U.K.* **15** F8
Shepton Mallet *U.K.* **15** F5
Sheqi *China* **56** H7
Sher Qila *Pakistan* **69** A6
Sherab *Sudan* **81** E1
Sherborne *U.K.* **15** G5
Sherbro → S. *Leone* **82** D2
Sherbro I. S. *Leone* **82** D2
Sherbrooke N.S., *Canada* **105** C7
Sherbrooke Qué., *Canada* **115** A13
Sherburne *U.S.A.* **115** D9
Shereik *Sudan* **80** D3
Shergarh *India* **68** F5
Sherghati *India* **69** G11
Sheridan Ark., *U.S.A.* **116** D8
Sheridan Wyo., *U.S.A.* **108** D10
Sheringham *U.K.* **14** E9
Sherkin I. *Ireland* **12** E2
Sherkot *India* **69** E8
Sherman *U.S.A.* **116** E6
Sherpur *India* **69** G10
Sherridon *Canada* **103** B8
Sherwood Forest *U.K.* **14** D6
Sherwood Park *Canada* **102** C6
Sheslay → *Canada* **102** B2
Shethanei L. *Canada* **103** B9
Shetland □ *U.K.* **13** A7
Shetland Is. *U.K.* **13** A7
Shetrunji → *India* **68** J5
Shevchenkovo *Ukraine* **29** E14
Shewa *Ethiopia* **81** F4
Shewa Gimira *Ethiopia* **81** F4
Shey-Phoksundo △ *Nepal* **69** E10
Sheyenne → *U.S.A.* **112** B5
Shibām *Yemen* **75** D4
Shibata *Japan* **54** F9
Shibecha *Japan* **54** C12
Shibetsu *Japan* **54** B11
Shibīn el Kôm *Egypt* **80** H7
Shibīn el Qanâtir *Egypt* **80** H7
Shibing *China* **58** D7
Shibogama L. *Canada* **104** B2
Shibushi *Japan* **55** J5
Shicheng *China* **59** D11
Shickshinny *U.S.A.* **115** E8
Shickshock Mts. =
    Chic-Chocs, Mts. *Canada* **105** C6
Shidao *China* **57** F12
Shidian *China* **58** E2
Shido *Japan* **55** G7
Shiel, L. *U.K.* **13** E3

Shield, C. *Australia* **94** A2
Shīeli *Kazakhstan* **52** E7
Shifang *China* **58** B5
Shiga □ *Japan* **55** G8
Shigu *China* **58** D2
Shiguaigou *China* **56** D6
Shihezi *China* **60** B3
Shijak *Albania* **44** E3
Shijiazhuang *China* **56** E8
Shijiu Hu *China* **59** B12
Shikarpur *India* **68** E8
Shikarpur *Pakistan* **68** F3
Shikohabad *India* **69** F8
Shikoku □ *Japan* **55** H6
Shikoku-Sanchi *Japan* **55** H6
Shikotsu-Ko *Japan* **54** C10
Shikotsu-Tōya △ *Japan* **54** C10
Shiliguri *India* **67** F16
Shiliu = Changjiang *China* **64** C7
Shilka *Russia* **53** D12
Shilka → *Russia* **53** D13
Shillelagh *Ireland* **12** D5
Shillington *U.S.A.* **115** F9
Shillong *India* **67** G17
Shilong *China* **59** F9
Shilou *China* **56** F6
Shilovo *Russia* **34** C5
Shimabara *Japan* **55** H5
Shimada *Japan* **55** G9
Shimane □ *Japan* **55** G6
Shimanovsk *Russia* **53** D13
Shimba Hills △ *Kenya* **86** C4
Shimen *China* **59** C8
Shimenjie *China* **59** C11
Shimian *China* **58** C4
Shimizu *Japan* **55** G9
Shimla *India* **68** D7
Shimodate *Japan* **55** F9
Shimoga *India* **66** N9
Shimoni *Kenya* **86** C4
Shimonoseki *Japan* **55** H5
Shimpuru Rapids *Namibia* **88** B2
Shimsk *Russia* **32** C6
Shin, L. *U.K.* **13** C4
Shinan *China* **58** F7
Shinano-Gawa → *Japan* **55** F9
Shinās *Oman* **71** E8
Shīndand *Afghan.* **66** C3
Shinglehouse *U.S.A.* **114** E6
Shingū *Japan* **55** H7
Shingwidzi S. *Africa* **89** C5
Shinjō *Japan* **54** E10
Shinkafe *Nigeria* **83** C6
Shinkolobwe
    Dem. Rep. of the Congo **84** G5
Shinshār *Syria* **74** A5
Shinyanga *Tanzania* **86** C3
Shinyanga □ *Tanzania* **86** C3
Shio-no-Misaki *Japan* **55** H7
Shiogama *Japan* **54** E10
Shiojiri *Japan* **55** F8
Shipchenski Prokhod
    Bulgaria **45** D9
Shiping *China* **58** F4
Shippagan *Canada* **105** C7
Shippensburg *U.S.A.* **114** F7
Shippenville *U.S.A.* **114** E5
Shiprock *U.S.A.* **109** H9
Shiqian *China* **58** D7
Shiqma, N. → *Israel* **74** D3
Shiquan *China* **56** H5
Shiquan He = Indus →
    Pakistan **68** G2
Shīr Kūh *Iran* **71** D7
Shiragami-Misaki *Japan* **54** D10
Shirakawa Fukushima, *Japan* **55** F10
Shirakawa Gifu, *Japan* **55** F8
Shirane-San *Gumma, Japan* **55** F9
Shirane-San *Yamanashi,
    Japan* **55** G9
Shiraoi *Japan* **54** C10
Shīrāz *Iran* **71** D7
Shirbīn *Egypt* **80** H7
Shire → *Africa* **87** F4
Shiretoko-Misaki *Japan* **54** B12
Shirinab → *Pakistan* **68** D2
Shiriya-Zaki *Japan* **54** D10
Shiroishi *Japan* **54** F10
Shirol *India* **69** B8
Shirshov Ridge *Pac. Oc.* **96** B8
Shīrvān *Iran* **71** B8
Shirwa, L. = Chilwa, L.
    Malawi **87** F4
Shishi *China* **59** E12
Shishou *China* **59** C9
Shitai *China* **59** B11
Shivpuri *India* **68** G7
Shixian *China* **57** C15
Shixing *China* **59** E10
Shiyan *China* **59** A8
Shiyata *Egypt* **80** B2
Shizhu *China* **58** C7
Shizong *China* **58** E5
Shizuishan *China* **56** E4
Shizuoka *Japan* **55** G9

Shizuoka □ *Japan* **55** G9
Shkhara *Georgia* **73** A10
Shklov = Shklow *Belarus* **23** A16
Shklow *Belarus* **23** A16
Shkodër *Albania* **44** D3
Shkumbini → *Albania* **44** E3
Shmidta, Ostrov *Russia* **53** A10
Shō-Gawa → *Japan* **55** F8
Shoal L. *Canada* **103** D9
Shoal Lake *Canada* **103** C8
Shōdo-Shima *Japan* **55** G7
Sholapur = Solapur *India* **66** L9
Shōmrōn *West Bank* **74** C4
Shoreham by Sea *U.K.* **15** G7
Shori → *Pakistan* **68** E3
Shorkot Road *Pakistan* **68** D5
Shoshone Calif., *U.S.A.* **111** K10
Shoshone Idaho, *U.S.A.* **108** E6
Shoshone L. *U.S.A.* **108** D8
Shoshone Mts. *U.S.A.* **108** G5
Shoshong *Botswana* **88** C4
Shoshoni *U.S.A.* **108** E9
Shostka *Ukraine* **33** G7
Shou Xian *China* **59** A11
Shouchang *China* **59** C12
Shouguang *China* **57** F10
Shouning *China* **59** D12
Shouyang *China* **56** F7
Show Low *U.S.A.* **109** J8
Shpola *Ukraine* **33** H6
Shpykiv *Ukraine* **29** B13
Shqipēria = Albania ■
    Europe **44** E4
Shreveport *U.S.A.* **116** E8
Shrewsbury *U.K.* **15** E5
Shri Mohangarh *India* **68** F4
Shrirampur *India* **69** H13
Shropshire □ *U.K.* **15** E5
Shū *Kazakhstan* **52** E8
Shuangbai *China* **58** E3
Shuangcheng *China* **57** B14
Shuangfeng *China* **59** D9
Shuanggou *China* **57** G9
Shuangjiang *China* **58** F2
Shuangliao *China* **57** C12
Shuangshanzi *China* **57** D10
Shuangyang *China* **57** C13
Shuangyashan *China* **60** B8
Shubrā el Kheima *Egypt* **80** H7
Shubrā Khīt *Egypt* **80** H7
Shucheng *China* **59** B11
Shugozero *Russia* **32** C8
Shuguri Falls *Tanzania* **87** D4
Shuiji *China* **59** D12
Shuiye *China* **56** F8
Shujalpur *India* **68** H7
Shukpa Kunzang *India* **69** B8
Shulan *China* **57** B14
Shulaveri *Georgia* **35** K7
Shule *China* **60** C2
Shumagin Is. *U.S.A.* **106** a
Shumen *Bulgaria* **45** C10
Shumerlya *Russia* **34** C8
Shumikha *Russia* **52** D7
Shunchang *China* **59** D11
Shunde *China* **59** F9
Shungay *Kazakhstan* **35** F8
Shuo Xian = Shuozhou
    China **56** E7
Shuozhou *China* **56** E7
Shūr → *Fārs, Iran* **71** D7
Shūr → *Kermān, Iran* **71** D8
Shūr → *Yazd, Iran* **71** D7
Shūr Āb *Iran* **71** C6
Shūr Gaz *Iran* **71** D8
Shūrāb *Iran* **71** C8
Shūrjestān *Iran* **71** D7
Shurugwi *Zimbabwe* **87** F3
Shūsf *Iran* **71** D9
Shūsh *Iran* **73** F13
Shūshtar *Iran* **71** D6
Shuswap L. *Canada* **102** C5
Shuya *Russia* **34** B5
Shuyang *China* **57** G10
Shūzū *Iran* **71** D7
Shwebo *Burma* **67** H19
Shwegu *Burma* **67** G20
Shweli → *Burma* **67** H20
Siem Pang *Cambodia* **64** E6
Siem Reap = Siemreab
    Cambodia **64** F4
Siemiatycze *Poland* **31** F9
Siemreab *Cambodia* **64** F4
Siena *Italy* **41** E8
Sieniawa *Poland* **31** H9
Sieradz *Poland* **31** G5
Sieraków *Poland* **31** F3
Sierck-les-Bains *France* **19** C13
Sierning *Austria* **26** C7
Sierpc *Poland* **31** F6
Sierpe, Bocas de la
    Venezuela **125** L15
Sierra Blanca *U.S.A.* **116** F2
Sierra Blanca Peak *U.S.A.* **109** K11
Sierra City *U.S.A.* **110** F6
Sierra Colorada *Argentina* **128** E3
Sierra de Aracena y Picas
    de Aroche △ *Spain* **37** H4

Sian Ka'an △ *Mexico* **119** D7
Sianów *Poland* **30** D3
Siantan *Indonesia* **62** D3
Sīāreh *Iran* **71** D9
Siargao I. *Phil.* **61** G7
Siari *Pakistan* **69** B7
Siasi *Phil.* **63** C6
Siasi I. *Phil.* **61** J4
Siau *Indonesia* **63** D7
Siatista *Greece* **44** F5
Siau *Indonesia* **63** D7
Šiauliai *Lithuania* **30** C10
Šiauliai □ *Lithuania* **30** C10
Siazan = Siyäzän *Azerbaijan* **35** K9
Sibā, Gebel el *Egypt* **70** E2
Sibang *Indonesia* **63** K18
Sibayi, L. S. *Africa* **89** D5
Sibdu *Sudan* **81** E1
Sibenik *Croatia* **41** E12
Siberia = Sibirskiy □ *Russia* **53** D10
Siberia *Russia* **4** D13
Siberut *Indonesia* **62** E1
Sibi *Pakistan* **68** E2
Sibil = Oksibil *Indonesia* **63** E10
Sibiloi △ *Kenya* **86** B4
Sibirskiy □ *Russia* **53** D10
Sibirtsevo *Russia* **54** B5
Sibiti *Congo* **84** E2
Sibiu *Romania* **29** E9
Sibiu □ *Romania* **29** E9
Sibley *U.S.A.* **112** D6
Sibolga *Indonesia* **62** D1
Sibsagar *India* **67** F19
Sibu *Malaysia* **62** D4
Sibuco *Phil.* **61** H5
Sibuguey B. *Phil.* **61** H5
Sibut *C.A.R.* **84** C3
Sibutu *Phil.* **61** J3
Sibutu Group *Phil.* **61** J3
Sibutu Passage E. *Indies* **63** D6
Sibuyan I. *Phil.* **61** E5
Sibuyan Sea *Phil.* **61** E5
Sic *Romania* **29** D8
Sicamous *Canada* **102** C5
Siccus → *Australia* **95** E2
Sichuan □ *China* **58** B5
Sichuan Pendi *China* **58** B5
Sicilia *Italy* **43** E7
Sicily = Sicilia *Italy* **43** E7
Sicily, Str. of = Sicilia, C. △ *Italy* **42** E4
Sicuani *Peru* **124** F4
Šid *Serbia* **28** E4
Sidamo *Ethiopia* **81** G4
Sidaouet *Niger* **83** B6
Sidari *Greece* **49** A3
Siddhapur *India* **68** H5
Siddipet *India* **66** K11
Sidensjö *Sweden* **10** A12
Sidéradougou *Burkina Faso* **82** C4
Siderno *Italy* **43** D9
Sideros, Akra *Greece* **49** D8
Sidhauli *India* **69** F9
Sidhi *India* **69** G9
Sîdi Abd el Rahmân *Egypt* **80** A2
Sîdi Barrâni *Egypt* **80** A2
Sidi-bel-Abbès *Algeria* **78** A5
Sîdi Haneish *Egypt* **80** A2
Sidi Ifni *Morocco* **78** C3
Sîdi Omar *Egypt* **80** A1
Sidirokastro *Greece* **44** E7
Sidlaw Hills *U.K.* **13** E5
Sidley, Mt. *Antarctica* **5** D14
Sidmouth *U.K.* **15** G4
Sidmouth, C. *Australia* **94** A3
Sidney *Canada* **110** B3
Sidney Mont., *U.S.A.* **108** C11
Sidney N.Y., *U.S.A.* **115** D9
Sidney Nebr., *U.S.A.* **112** E2
Sidney Ohio, *U.S.A.* **113** E11
Sidney Lanier, L. *U.S.A.* **117** D12
Sido *Mali* **82** C3
Sidoarjo *Indonesia* **63** G15
Sidon = Saydā *Lebanon* **74** B4
Sidra, G. of = Surt, Khalīj
    Libya **79** B9
Siedlce *Poland* **31** F9
Sieg → *Germany* **24** E3
Siegburg *Germany* **24** E3
Siegen *Germany* **24** E4

Sierra de Bahoruco △
    Dom. Rep. **121** C5
Sierra de Baza △ *Spain* **39** H2
Sierra de Castril △ *Spain* **39** H2
Sierra de Espuña △ *Spain* **39** H3
Sierra de Grazalema △ *Spain* **37** J5
Sierra de Gredos △ *Spain* **36** E5
Sierra de Hornachuelos △
    Spain **37** H5
Sierra de Huétor △ *Spain* **37** H7
Sierra de La Culata △
    Venezuela **121** E5
Sierra de Lancandón △
    Guatemala **120** C1
Sierra de las Nieves △ *Spain* **37** J6
Sierra de las Quijadas △
    Argentina **126** C2
Sierra de María-Los
    Vélez △ *Spain* **39** H2
Sierra de San Luis △
    Venezuela **121** D6
Sierra de San Pedro Mártir,
    Parque Nacional △
    Mexico **118** A1
Sierra de Yeguas *Spain* **37** H6
Sierra del São Mamede △
    Portugal **37** F3
Sierra Gorda *Chile* **126** A2
Sierra Leone ■ *W. Afr.* **82** D2
Sierra Madre *Mexico* **119** D6
Sierra Madre Occidental
    Mexico **118** B3
Sierra Madre Oriental
    Mexico **118** C5
Sierra Mágina △ *Spain* **37** H7
Sierra Mojada *Mexico* **118** B4
Sierra Nevada *Spain* **37** H7
Sierra Nevada △ *U.S.A.* **110** H8
Sierra Nevada △ *Spain* **37** H7
Sierra Nevada △ *Venezuela* **121** E5
Sierra Nevada de Santa
    Marta △ *Colombia* **121** D5
Sierra Norte de Seville △
    Spain **37** H5
Sierra Subbéticas △ *Spain* **37** H6
Sierra Vista *U.S.A.* **109** L8
Sierras de Cardeña y
    Montoro △ *Spain* **37** G6
Sierras de Cazorla, Segura
    y las Villas △ *Spain* **39** J2
Sierraville *U.S.A.* **110** F6
Sierre *Switz.* **25** J3
Sifané *Ethiopia* **81** E5
Sifié *Ivory C.* **82** D3
Sifnos *Greece* **46** E6
Sifton *Canada* **103** C8
Sifton Pass *Canada* **102** B3
Sig *Algeria* **78** A5
Sigatoka *Fiji* **91** a
Sigean *France* **20** E6
Sighetu-Marmaţiei *Romania* **29** C8
Sighişoara *Romania* **29** D9
Sigli *Indonesia* **62** C1
Siglufjörður *Iceland* **8** C4
Sigmaringen *Germany* **25** G5
Signa *Italy* **40** E8
Signakhi = Tsnori *Georgia* **35** K7
Signal de Botrang *Belgium* **17** D6
Signal Pk. *U.S.A.* **111** M12
Signy I. *Antarctica* **5** C18
Signy-l'Abbaye *France* **19** C11
Sigsig *Ecuador* **124** D3
Sigüenza *Spain* **38** D2
Siguiri *Guinea* **82** C3
Sigulda *Latvia* **32** D3
Sihora *India* **69** H9
Sihui *China* **59** F9
Siikajoki → *Finland* **8** D21
Siilinjärvi *Finland* **8** E22
Siirt *Turkey* **73** D9
Siirt □ *Turkey* **73** D9
Sijarira Ra. = Chizarira
    Zimbabwe **87** F2
Sika *India* **68** H3
Sikanni Chief → *Canada* **102** B4
Sikao *Thailand* **65** J2
Sikar *India* **68** F6
Sikasso *Mali* **82** C3
Sikasso □ *Mali* **82** C3
Sikeston *U.S.A.* **112** G9
Sikhote Alin, Khrebet *Russia* **54** B8
Sikhote Alin Ra. = Sikhote
    Alin, Khrebet *Russia* **54** B8
Sikia *Greece* **44** F7
Sikinos *Greece* **47** E7
Sikkim □ *India* **67** F16
Siklós *Hungary* **28** E3
Sil → *Spain* **36** C3
Silacayoapan *Mexico* **119** D5
Šilalė *Lithuania* **30** C8
Silandro *Italy* **40** B7
Silawad *India* **68** J6
Silay *Phil.* **61** F5
Silba *Croatia* **41** D11
Silchar *India* **67** G18
Şile *Turkey* **45** E13
Siler City *U.S.A.* **117** D15

Silesia = Śląsk *Poland* **22** C9
Silgarhi Doti *Nepal* **69** E9
Silghat *India* **67** F18
Silhouette *Seychelles* **85** b
Sili *Burkina Faso* **82** C4
Silifke *Turkey* **72** D5
Siliguri = Shiliguri *India* **67** F16
Siling Co *China* **60** C3
Silistea Nouă *Romania* **29** F10
Silistra *Bulgaria* **45** B11
Silivri *Turkey* **45** E12
Siljan *Sweden* **10** D8
Siljansnäs *Sweden* **10** D8
Silkeborg *Denmark* **11** H3
Silkwood *Australia* **94** B4
Silla *Spain* **39** F4
Sillajhuay, Cordillera *Chile* **124** G5
Sillamäe *Estonia* **32** C4
Sillé-le-Guillaume *France* **18** D6
Silleda *Spain* **36** C2
Silloth *U.K.* **14** C4
Silo *Greece* **46** D5
Siloam Springs *U.S.A.* **116** C7
Silopi *Turkey* **73** D10
Silsbee *U.S.A.* **116** F7
Siluko *Nigeria* **83** D6
Silvan *Turkey* **73** C9
Silvani *India* **69** H8
Silver City *U.S.A.* **109** K9
Silver Cr. → *U.S.A.* **108** E4
Silver Creek *U.S.A.* **114** D5
Silver L. *U.S.A.* **110** G6
Silver Lake Calif., *U.S.A.* **111** K10
Silver Lake Oreg., *U.S.A.* **108** E3
Silverdalen *Sweden* **11** G9
Silvermine Mts. *Ireland* **12** D3
Silverton Colo., *U.S.A.* **109** H10
Silverton Tex., *U.S.A.* **116** D4
Silves *Portugal* **37** H2
Silvi Marina *Italy* **41** F11
Silvies → *U.S.A.* **108** E4
Silvrettahorn *Switz.* **40** B7
Silwa Bahari *Egypt* **80** C3
Silz *Austria* **26** D3
Simaltala *India* **69** G12
Simanggang = Sri Aman
    Malaysia **62** D4
Simao *China* **58** F3
Simard, L. *Canada* **104** C4
Şīmareh → *Iran* **73** F12
Simav *Turkey* **47** B10
Simav → *Turkey* **45** F12
Simav Dağları *Turkey* **47** B10
Simba *Tanzania* **86** C4
Simbach *Germany* **25** G9
Simbirsk *Russia* **34** C9
Simbo *Tanzania* **86** C2
Simcoe *Canada* **114** D4
Simcoe, L. *Canada* **114** B5
Simdega *India* **69** H11
Simeonovgrad *Bulgaria* **45** D9
Simeria *Romania* **28** E8
Simeto → *Italy* **43** E8
Simeulue *Indonesia* **62** D1
Simferopol *Ukraine* **33** K8
Simi *Greece* **47** E9
Simi Valley *U.S.A.* **111** L8
Simien Mts. △ *Ethiopia* **81** E4
Simikot *Nepal* **69** E9
Simitli *Bulgaria* **44** E7
Simla = Shimla *India* **68** D7
Simla *U.S.A.* **108** G2
Simlångsdalen *Sweden* **11** H7
Simleu-Silvaniei *Romania* **28** C7
Simlipal △ *India* **69** J12
Simmern *Germany* **25** F3
Simmie *Canada* **103** D7
Simmler *U.S.A.* **111** K7
Simnas *Lithuania* **30** D10
Simo älv = Simojoki →
    Finland **8** D21
Simojoki → *Finland* **8** D21
Simojovel *Mexico* **119** D6
Simonette → *Canada* **102** B5
Simonstown S. *Africa* **88** E2
Simontornya *Hungary* **28** D3
Simpang Empat *Malaysia* **65** c
Simplonpass *Switz.* **25** J4
Simplontunnel *Switz.* **25** J4
Simpson Desert *Australia* **94** D2
Simpson Pen. *Canada* **101** C11
Simrishamn *Sweden* **11** J8
Simsbury *U.S.A.* **115** E12
Simushir, Ostrov *Russia* **53** E16
Sin Cowe I. *S. China Sea* **62** C4
Sinabang *Indonesia* **62** D1
Sinadogo *Somali Rep.* **75** F4
Sinai = Es Sînâ' *Egypt* **74** F3
Sinai, Mt. = Mûsa, Gebel
    Egypt **70** D2
Sinaia *Romania* **29** E10
Sinaloa □ *Mexico* **118** C3
Sinaloa de Leyva *Mexico* **118** B3
Sinalunga *Italy* **41** E8
Sinan *China* **58** D7
Sînandrei *Romania* **28** E6

Sinarades *Greece* **49** A3
Sincan *Turkey* **72** B5
Sincanlı *Turkey* **47** C12
Sincelejo *Colombia* **124** B3
Sinch'ang *N. Korea* **57** D15
Sinch'ŏn *N. Korea* **57** E13
Sinclair *U.S.A.* **108** F10
Sinclair Mills *Canada* **102** C4
Sinclair's B. *U.K.* **13** C5
Sinclairville *U.S.A.* **114** D5
Sincorá, Serra do *Brazil* **125** F10
Sind = Sindh □ *Pakistan* **68** G3
Sind *Pakistan* **68** G3
Sind → *Jammu & Kashmir, India* **69** B6
Sind → *Mad. P., India* **69** F8
Sind Sagar Doab *Pakistan* **68** D4
Sindal *Denmark* **11** G4
Sindangan *Phil.* **61** G5
Sindangbarang *Indonesia* **63** G12
Sinde *Zambia* **87** F2
Sindelfingen *Germany* **25** G4
Sindh □ *Pakistan* **68** G3
Sındırgı *Turkey* **47** B10
Sindou *Burkina Faso* **82** C3
Sindri *India* **69** H12
Sine → *Senegal* **82** C1
Sinegorskiy *Russia* **35** G5
Sinekli *Turkey* **45** E12
Sinelnikovo = Synelnykove *Ukraine* **33** H8
Sinendé *Benin* **83** C5
Sines *Portugal* **37** H2
Sines, C. de *Portugal* **37** H2
Sineu *Spain* **48** B10
Sinfra *Ivory C.* **82** D3
Sing Buri *Thailand* **64** E3
Singa *Sudan* **81** E3
Singalila △ *India* **69** F13
Singapore ■ *Asia* **65** d
Singapore, Straits of *Asia* **65** d
Singapore Changi ✈ (SIN) *Singapore* **65** M4
Singaraja *Indonesia* **63** J18
Singatoka = Sigatoka *Fiji* **91** a
Singen *Germany* **25** H4
Singida *Tanzania* **86** C3
Singida □ *Tanzania* **86** D3
Singkaling Hkamti *Burma* **67** G19
Singkang *Indonesia* **63** E6
Singkawang *Indonesia* **62** D3
Singkep *Indonesia* **62** E2
Singleton *Australia* **95** E5
Singleton, Mt. *N. Terr., Australia* **92** D5
Singleton, Mt. *W. Austral., Australia* **93** E2
Singö *Sweden* **10** D12
Singoli *India* **68** G6
Singora = Songkhla *Thailand* **65** J3
Sinhüng *N. Korea* **57** D14
Siniscóla *Italy* **42** B2
Sinj *Croatia* **41** E13
Sinjai *Indonesia* **63** F6
Sinjajevina *Montenegro* **44** D3
Sinjär *Iraq* **73** D9
Sinkat *Sudan* **80** D4
Sinkiang = Xinjiang Uygur Zizhiqu □ *China* **60** B3
Sinmak *N. Korea* **57** E14
Sinmi-do *N. Korea* **57** E13
Sinnai *Italy* **42** C2
Sinnamary *Fr. Guiana* **125** B8
Sinni → *Italy* **43** B9
Sinnuris *Egypt* **80** J7
Sinoie, Lacul *Romania* **29** F13
Sinop *Turkey* **72** A6
Sinop □ *Turkey* **72** B6
Sinor *India* **68** J5
Sinp'o *N. Korea* **57** E15
Sinsheim *Germany* **25** F4
Sinsk *Russia* **53** C13
Sintang *Indonesia* **62** D4
Sinton *U.S.A.* **116** G6
Sintra *Portugal* **37** G1
Sintra-Cascais △ *Portugal* **37** G1
Sinüiju *N. Korea* **57** D13
Sinyukha → *Ukraine* **33** H6
Sinzig *Germany* **24** E3
Sio → *Hungary* **28** D3
Siocon *Phil.* **61** H5
Siófok *Hungary* **28** D3
Sion *Switz.* **25** J3
Sion Mills *U.K.* **12** B4
Sioux Center *U.S.A.* **112** D5
Sioux City *U.S.A.* **112** D5
Sioux Falls *U.S.A.* **112** D5
Sioux Lookout *Canada* **104** B1
Sioux Narrows *Canada* **103** D10
Sipadan *Malaysia* **63** D5
Sipalay *Phil.* **61** G5
Sipan *Croatia* **44** D1
Siparia *Trin. & Tob.* **125** K15
Sipil Daği △ *Turkey* **47** C9
Siping *China* **57** C13
Sipiwesk L. *Canada* **103** B9
Siple *Antarctica* **5** D7

Šipovo *Bos.-H.* **28** F2
Sipra → *India* **68** H6
Sipura *Indonesia* **62** E1
Siquia → *Nic.* **120** D3
Siquijor *Phil.* **61** G5
Siquirres *Costa Rica* **120** D3
Şīr Abu Nu'ayr *U.A.E.* **71** E7
Şīr Banī Yās *U.A.E.* **71** E7
Sir Edward Pellew Group *Australia* **94** B2
Sir Graham Moore Is. *Australia* **92** B4
Sir James MacBrien, Mt. *Canada* **100** C7
Sira → *Norway* **9** G12
Siracusa *Italy* **43** E8
Sirajganj *Bangla.* **69** G13
Sirakoro *Mali* **82** C3
Şiran *Turkey* **73** B8
Sirasso *Ivory C.* **82** D3
Sirathu *India* **69** G9
Sīrdān *Iran* **73** D13
Sire *Ethiopia* **81** F4
Siren *U.S.A.* **112** C7
Sirente-Velino △ *Italy* **41** F10
Sirer *Spain* **48** C7
Siret *Romania* **29** C11
Siret → *Romania* **29** E12
Sirghāyā *Syria* **74** B5
Şiria *Romania* **28** D6
Sirinath △ *Thailand* **65** a
Sirino, Mte. *Italy* **43** B8
Sīrjān *Iran* **71** D7
Sirmaur *India* **69** G9
Sirna *Greece* **47** E8
Şırnak *Turkey* **73** D10
Sirohi *India* **68** G5
Sironj *India* **68** G7
Síros = Syros *Greece* **46** D6
Sirretta Pk. *U.S.A.* **111** K8
Sīrrī *Iran* **71** E7
Sirsa *India* **68** E6
Sirsa → *India* **69** F8
Siruela *Spain* **37** G5
Sisak *Croatia* **41** C13
Sisaket *Thailand* **64** E5
Sisante *Spain* **39** F2
Sisargas, Is. *Spain* **36** B2
Sishen *S. Africa* **88** D3
Sishui *Henan, China* **56** G7
Sishui *Shandong, China* **57** G9
Sisipuk L. *Canada* **103** B8
Sisophon *Cambodia* **64** F4
Sisseton *U.S.A.* **112** C5
Sissonne *France* **19** C10
Sīstān *Asia* **71** D9
Sīstān, Daryācheh-ye *Iran* **71** D9
Sīstān va Balūchestān □ *Iran* **71** E9
Sisteron *France* **21** D9
Sisters *U.S.A.* **108** D3
Sisters, The *Seychelles* **85** b
Siswa Bazar *India* **69** F10
Sitakili *Mali* **82** C2
Sitamarhi *India* **69** F11
Sitampiky *Madag.* **89** B8
Sitapur *India* **69** F9
Siteki *Swaziland* **89** D5
Sitges *Spain* **38** D6
Sithonia *Greece* **44** F7
Sitia *Greece* **49** D8
Sitito-Ozima Ridge *Pac. Oc.* **96** E6
Sitka *U.S.A.* **102** B1
Sitoti *Botswana* **88** C3
Sitra *Egypt* **80** B2
Sittang Myit → *Burma* **67** L20
Sittard *Neths.* **17** C5
Sittensen *Germany* **24** B5
Sittingbourne *U.K.* **15** F8
Sittona *Eritrea* **81** E4
Sittoung = Sittang Myit → *Burma* **67** L20
Sittwe *Burma* **67** J18
Situbondo *Indonesia* **63** G16
Si'umu *Samoa* **91** b
Siuna *Nic.* **120** D3
Siuri *India* **69** H12
Siutghiol, Lacul *Romania* **29** F13
Sīvand *Iran* **71** D7
Sivas *Turkey* **72** C7
Sivas □ *Turkey* **72** C7
Sivash *Turkey* **47** C11
Siverek *Turkey* **73** D8
Sivrihisar *Turkey* **72** C4
Sīwa *Egypt* **80** B2
Sīwa, El Wâhât es *Egypt* **80** B2
Sīwa Oasis = Sīwa, El Wâhât es *Egypt* **80** B2
Siwalik Range *Nepal* **69** F10
Siwan *India* **69** F11
Siwana *India* **68** G5
Six Cross Roads *Barbados* **121** g
Sixmilebridge *Ireland* **12** D3
Sixth Cataract *Sudan* **81** D3
Siyâl, Jazâ'ir *Egypt* **80** C4
Siyäzän *Azerbaijan* **35** K9
Siziwang Qi *China* **56** D6

Sjælland *Denmark* **11** J5
Sjælland □ *Denmark* **11** J5
Sjællands Odde *Denmark* **11** J5
Sjenica *Serbia* **44** C3
Sjöbo *Sweden* **11** J7
Sjötofta *Sweden* **11** G7
Sjötorp *Sweden* **11** F8
Sjumen = Shumen *Bulgaria* **45** C10
Sjuntorp *Sweden* **11** F6
Skadarsko Jezero *Europe* **44** D3
Skadovsk *Ukraine* **33** J7
Skælskør *Denmark* **11** J5
Skærbæk *Denmark* **11** J2
Skaftafell *Iceland* **8** D5
Skaftafell △ *Iceland* **8** D5
Skagafjörður *Iceland* **8** D4
Skagaströnd *Iceland* **8** D3
Skagen *Denmark* **11** G4
Skagern *Sweden* **10** E8
Skagerrak *Denmark* **11** G2
Skagit → *U.S.A.* **110** B4
Skagway *U.S.A.* **100** D6
Skala-Podilska *Ukraine* **29** B11
Skala-Podolskaya = Skala-Podilska *Ukraine* **29** B11
Skalat *Ukraine* **23** D13
Skalbmierz *Poland* **31** H7
Skälderviken *Sweden* **11** H6
Skalica *Slovak Rep.* **27** C10
Skallingen *Denmark* **11** J2
Skalni Dol = Kamenyak *Bulgaria* **45** C10
Skanderborg *Denmark* **11** H3
Skåne *Sweden* **11** J7
Skåne län □ *Sweden* **11** H7
Skaneateles *U.S.A.* **115** D8
Skaneateles L. *U.S.A.* **115** D8
Skänninge *Sweden* **11** F9
Skanör med Falsterbo *Sweden* **11** J6
Skantzoura *Greece* **46** B6
Skara *Sweden* **11** F7
Skärblacka *Sweden* **11** F9
Skardu *Pakistan* **69** B6
Skåre *Sweden* **10** E7
Skärhamn *Sweden* **11** G5
Skarszewy *Poland* **30** D5
Skaryszew *Poland* **31** G8
Skarżysko-Kamienna *Poland* **31** G7
Skattkärr *Sweden* **10** E7
Skattungbyn *Sweden* **10** C8
Skawina *Poland* **31** J6
Skebobruk *Sweden* **10** E12
Skeena → *Canada* **102** C2
Skeena Mts. *Canada* **102** B3
Skegness *U.K.* **14** D8
Skeldon = Corriverton *Guyana* **124** B7
Skeleton Coast *Namibia* **85** J2
Skeleton Coast △ *Namibia* **88** C1
Skellefteå *Sweden* **8** D19
Skellefteälven → *Sweden* **8** D19
Skelleftehamn *Sweden* **8** D19
Skender Vakuf *Bos.-H.* **28** F2
Skerries, The *U.K.* **14** D3
Skhidnytsya *Ukraine* **31** J10
Skhíza *Greece* **46** E3
Ski *Norway* **9** G14
Skiathos *Greece* **46** B5
Skibbereen *Ireland* **12** E2
Skiddaw *U.K.* **14** C4
Skidegate *Canada* **102** C2
Skidra *Greece* **44** F6
Skien *Norway* **9** G13
Skierniewice *Poland* **31** G7
Skikda *Algeria* **78** A7
Skillingaryd *Sweden* **11** G8
Skillinge *Sweden* **11** J8
Skilloura *Cyprus* **49** D12
Skinari, Akra *Greece* **46** D2
Skinnskatteberg *Sweden* **10** E9
Skipton *U.K.* **14** D5
Skiring, C. *Senegal* **82** C1
Skirmish Pt. *Australia* **94** A1
Skiropoula *Greece* **46** C6
Skiros *Greece* **46** C6
Skivarp *Sweden* **11** J7
Skive *Denmark* **11** H3
Skjálfandafljót → *Iceland* **8** D5
Skjálfandi *Iceland* **8** C5
Skjern *Denmark* **11** J2
Skoczów *Poland* **31** J5
Škofja Loka *Slovenia* **41** B11
Skoghall *Sweden* **10** E7
Skogstorp *Sweden* **10** E10
Skoki *Poland* **31** F4
Skole *Ukraine* **23** D12
Skopelos *Greece* **46** B5
Skopi *Greece* **49** D8
Skopin *Russia* **32** F10
Skopje *Macedonia* **44** D5
Skopje ✈ (SKP) *Macedonia* **44** E5
Skórcz *Poland* **30** E5
Skørping *Denmark* **11** H3
Skövde *Sweden* **11** F7

Skovorodino *Russia* **53** D13
Skowhegan *U.S.A.* **113** C19
Skradin *Croatia* **41** E12
Skrea *Sweden* **11** H6
Skrunda *Latvia* **30** B9
Skrwa → *Poland* **31** F6
Skuleskogen △ *Sweden* **10** A12
Skull *Ireland* **12** E2
Skultorp *Sweden* **11** F7
Skultuna *Sweden* **10** E10
Skunk → *U.S.A.* **112** E8
Skuodas *Lithuania* **30** B8
Skurup *Sweden* **11** J7
Skutskär *Sweden* **10** D11
Skvyra *Ukraine* **23** D15
Skwierzyna *Poland* **31** F2
Skye *U.K.* **13** D2
Skykomish *U.S.A.* **108** C3
Skyros = Skiros *Greece* **46** C6
Skyttorp *Sweden* **10** D11
Slade Pt. *Australia* **94** K7
Slættaratindur *Færoe Is.* **8** E9
Slagelse *Denmark* **11** J5
Slamet *Indonesia* **63** G13
Slane *Ireland* **12** C5
Slaney → *Ireland* **12** D5
Slangberge *S. Africa* **88** E3
Slânic *Romania* **29** E10
Slano *Croatia* **44** D1
Slantsy *Russia* **32** C5
Slaný *Czech Rep.* **26** A7
Śląsk *Poland* **22** C9
Śląskie □ *Poland* **31** H6
Slatina *Croatia* **28** E2
Slatina *Romania* **29** F9
Slatina Timiş *Romania* **28** E7
Slatington *U.S.A.* **115** F9
Slaton *U.S.A.* **116** E4
Slave → *Canada* **102** A6
Slave Coast *W. Afr.* **83** D5
Slave Lake *Canada* **102** B6
Slave Pt. *Canada* **102** A5
Slavgorod *Russia* **52** D8
Slavinja *Serbia* **44** C6
Slavkov u Brna *Czech Rep.* **27** B9
Slavkovský Les △ *Czech Rep.* **26** A5
Slavonija *Europe* **28** E2
Slavonski Brod *Croatia* **28** E3
Slavsk *Russia* **30** C8
Slavska *Ukraine* **29** B8
Slavskoye *Russia* **30** D7
Slavuta *Ukraine* **23** C14
Slavyanka *Russia* **54** C5
Slavyanovo *Bulgaria* **45** C8
Slavyansk = Slovyansk *Ukraine* **33** H9
Slavyansk-na-Kubani *Russia* **33** K10
Slawa *Poland* **31** G3
Slawharad *Belarus* **23** B16
Sławno *Poland* **30** D3
Slawoborze *Poland* **30** E2
Sleaford *U.K.* **14** D7
Sleaford B. *Australia* **95** E2
Sleat, Sd. of *U.K.* **13** D3
Sleeper Is. *Canada* **101** D11
Sleeping Bear Dunes △ *U.S.A.* **112** C10
Sleepy Eye *U.S.A.* **112** C6
Slemon L. *Canada* **102** A5
Ślesin *Poland* **31** F5
Slide Mt. *U.S.A.* **115** E10
Slidell *U.S.A.* **117** F10
Sliema *Malta* **49** D2
Slieve Aughty *Ireland* **12** C3
Slieve Bloom *Ireland* **12** C4
Slieve Donard *U.K.* **12** B6
Slieve Gamph *Ireland* **12** B3
Slieve Gullion *U.K.* **12** B5
Slieve League *Ireland* **12** B3
Slieve Mish *Ireland* **12** D2
Slievenamon *Ireland* **12** D4
Sligeach = Sligo *Ireland* **12** B3
Sligo *Ireland* **12** B3
Sligo *U.S.A.* **114** E5
Sligo □ *Ireland* **12** B3
Sligo B. *Ireland* **12** B3
Slippery Rock *U.S.A.* **114** E4
Slite *Sweden* **11** G12
Sliven *Bulgaria* **45** D10
Slivnitsa *Bulgaria* **44** C7
Sljeme *Croatia* **41** C12
Sloan *U.S.A.* **111** K11
Sloansville *U.S.A.* **115** D10
Slobidka *Ukraine* **29** C14
Slobozia *Moldova* **29** D14
Slobozia *Argeș, Romania* **29** F10
Slobozia *Ialomiţa, Romania* **29** F12
Slocan *Canada* **102** D5
Slomniki *Poland* **31** H7
Slonim *Belarus* **23** B13
Slough *U.K.* **15** F7
Slough □ *U.K.* **15** F7
Sloughhouse *U.S.A.* **110** G5

Slovak Rep. ■ *Europe* **27** C13
Slovakia = Slovak Rep. ■ *Europe* **27** C13
Slovakian Ore Mts. = Slovenské Rudohorie *Slovak Rep.* **27** C13
Slovenia ■ *Europe* **41** C11
Slovenija = Slovenia ■ *Europe* **41** C11
Slovenj Gradec *Slovenia* **41** B12
Slovenska = Slovak Rep. ■ *Europe* **27** C13
Slovenska Bistrica *Slovenia* **41** B12
Slovenske Konjice *Slovenia* **41** B12
Slovenské Rudohorie *Slovak Rep.* **27** C13
Slovenský Raj △ *Slovak Rep.* **27** C13
Slovyansk *Ukraine* **33** H9
Slowiński △ *Poland* **30** D4
Slubice *Poland* **31** F1
Sluch → *Ukraine* **23** C14
Sluis *Neths.* **17** C3
Slunchev Bryag *Bulgaria* **45** D11
Slunj *Croatia* **41** C12
Slupca *Poland* **31** F4
Slupia → *Poland* **30** D3
Slupsk *Poland* **30** D4
Slurry *S. Africa* **88** D4
Slutsk *Belarus* **23** B14
Slyne Hd. *Ireland* **12** C1
Slyudyanka *Russia* **53** D11
Småland *Sweden* **11** G9
Smålandsfarvandet *Denmark* **11** J5
Smålandsstenar *Sweden* **11** G7
Smalltree L. *Canada* **103** A8
Smallwood Res. *Canada* **105** B7
Smarhon *Belarus* **23** A14
Smartt Syndicate Dam *S. Africa* **88** E3
Smartville *U.S.A.* **110** F5
Smeaton *Canada* **103** C8
Smederevo *Serbia* **44** B4
Smederevska Palanka *Serbia* **44** B4
Smedjebacken *Sweden* **10** D9
Smela = Smila *Ukraine* **33** H6
Smerwick Harbour *Ireland* **12** D1
Smethport *U.S.A.* **114** E6
Smidovich *Russia* **53** E14
Śmigiel *Poland* **31** F3
Smila *Ukraine* **33** H6
Smilyan *Bulgaria* **45** E8
Smith *Canada* **102** B6
Smith Center *U.S.A.* **112** F4
Smith River △ *U.S.A.* **108** F2
Smithburne → *Australia* **94** B3
Smithers *Canada* **102** C3
Smithfield *S. Africa* **89** E4
Smithfield *N.C., U.S.A.* **117** D15
Smithfield *Utah, U.S.A.* **108** F8
Smiths Falls *Canada* **115** B9
Smithton *Australia* **95** G4
Smithville *Canada* **114** C5
Smithville *U.S.A.* **116** F6
Smoky → *Canada* **102** B5
Smoky Bay *Australia* **95** E1
Smoky Hill → *U.S.A.* **112** F5
Smoky Hills *U.S.A.* **112** F4
Smoky Lake *Canada* **102** C6
Smøla *Norway* **8** E13
Smolensk *Russia* **32** E7
Smolensk □ *Russia* **32** E7
Smolikas, Oros *Greece* **44** F4
Smolník *Slovak Rep.* **27** C13
Smolyan *Bulgaria* **45** E8
Smooth Rock Falls *Canada* **104** C3
Smoothstone L. *Canada* **103** C7
Smorgon = Smarhon *Belarus* **23** A14
Smotrych *Ukraine* **29** B11
Smotrych → *Ukraine* **29** B11
Smulţi *Romania* **29** E12
Smyadovo *Bulgaria* **45** C11
Smygehamn *Sweden* **11** J7
Smyrna = İzmir *Turkey* **47** C9
Smyrna *U.S.A.* **113** F16
Snæfell *Iceland* **8** D6
Snaefell *I. of Man* **14** C3
Snæfellsjökull *Iceland* **8** D2
Snake → *U.S.A.* **108** C4
Snake I. *Australia* **95** F4
Snake Range *U.S.A.* **108** G6
Snake River Plain *U.S.A.* **108** E7
Snåsavatnet *Norway* **8** D15
Sneek *Neths.* **17** A5
Sneem *Ireland* **12** E2
Sneeuberge *S. Africa* **88** E3
Snejbjerg *Denmark* **11** H2
Snelling *U.S.A.* **110** H6
Snezhnoye *Ukraine* **33** J10
Snežnik *Slovenia* **41** C11
Sniardwy, Jezioro *Poland* **30** E8

Śnieżka *Europe* **26** A8
Snigirevka = Snihurivka *Ukraine* **33** J7
Snihurivka *Ukraine* **33** J7
Snina *Slovak Rep.* **27** C15
Snizort, L. *U.K.* **13** D2
Snøhetta *Norway* **8** E13
Snohomish *U.S.A.* **110** C4
Snoqualmie Pass *U.S.A.* **110** C5
Snoul *Cambodia* **65** F6
Snow Hill *U.S.A.* **113** F16
Snow Lake *Canada* **103** C8
Snow Mt. *Calif., U.S.A.* **110** F4
Snow Mt. *Maine, U.S.A.* **115** A14
Snow Shoe *U.S.A.* **114** E7
Snowbird L. *Canada* **103** A8
Snowdon *U.K.* **14** D3
Snowdonia △ *U.K.* **14** D4
Snowdrift = Łutselk'e *Canada* **103** A6
Snowdrift → *Canada* **103** A6
Snowflake *U.S.A.* **109** J8
Snowshoe Pk. *U.S.A.* **108** B6
Snowtown *Australia* **95** E2
Snowville *U.S.A.* **108** F7
Snowy → *Australia* **95** F4
Snowy Mt. *U.S.A.* **115** C10
Snowy Mts. *Australia* **95** F4
Snug Corner *Bahamas* **121** B5
Snyatyn *Ukraine* **29** B10
Snyder *Okla., U.S.A.* **116** D5
Snyder *Tex., U.S.A.* **116** E4
Soahanina *Madag.* **89** B7
Soalala *Madag.* **89** B8
Soaloka *Madag.* **89** B8
Soamanonga *Madag.* **89** C7
Soan → *Pakistan* **68** C4
Soanierana-Ivongo *Madag.* **89** B8
Soanindraniny *Madag.* **89** B8
Şoarş *Romania* **29** E9
Soavina *Madag.* **89** C8
Soavinandriana *Madag.* **89** B8
Sob → *Ukraine* **29** B14
Soba *Nigeria* **83** C6
Sobat, Nahr → *Sudan* **81** F3
Soběslav *Czech Rep.* **26** B7
Sobhapur *India* **68** H8
Sobinka *Russia* **32** E11
Sobótka *Poland* **31** H3
Sobra *Croatia* **41** F14
Sobradinho, Reprêsa de *Brazil* **125** E10
Sobral *Brazil* **125** D10
Sobrance *Slovak Rep.* **27** C15
Sobreira Formosa *Portugal* **36** F3
Soc Giang *Vietnam* **58** F6
Soc Trang *Vietnam* **65** H5
Soča → *Europe* **26** E6
Socastee *U.S.A.* **117** E15
Sochaczew *Poland* **31** F7
Soch'e = Shache *China* **60** C2
Sochi *Russia* **35** J4
Sochos *Greece* **44** F7
Société, Îs. de la *French Polynesia* **97** J12
Society Is. = Société, Îs. de la *French Polynesia* **97** J12
Socompa, Portezuelo de *Chile* **126** A2
Socorro *N. Mex., U.S.A.* **109** J10
Socorro *Tex., U.S.A.* **116** F1
Socorro, I. *Mexico* **118** D2
Socotra *Yemen* **75** E5
Socovos *Spain* **39** G3
Socuéllamos *Spain* **39** F2
Soda L. *U.S.A.* **109** J5
Soda Plains *India* **69** B8
Soda Springs *U.S.A.* **108** E8
Sodankylä *Finland* **8** C22
Soddy-Daisy *U.S.A.* **117** D12
Söderala *Sweden* **10** C10
Söderåsen △ *Sweden* **11** H7
Söderbärke *Sweden* **10** D9
Söderfors *Sweden* **10** D11
Söderhamn *Sweden* **10** C11
Söderköping *Sweden* **11** F10
Södermanland *Sweden* **9** G17
Södermanlands län □ *Sweden* **10** E11
Södertälje *Sweden* **10** E11
Sodiri *Sudan* **81** E2
Sodo *Ethiopia* **81** F4
Södra Dellen *Sweden* **10** C10
Södra Finnskoga *Sweden* **10** D6
Södra Sandby *Sweden* **11** J7
Södra Ulvön *Sweden* **10** B12
Södra Vi *Sweden* **11** G9
Sodražica *Slovenia* **41** C11
Sodus *U.S.A.* **114** C7
Sodwana Bay △ *S. Africa* **89** D5
Soekmekaar = Morebeng *S. Africa* **89** C4
Soest *Germany* **24** D4
Soest *Neths.* **17** B5
Sofades *Greece* **46** B4
Sofala □ *Mozam.* **89** B5
Sofara *Mali* **82** C4

Sofia = Sofiya *Bulgaria* **44** D7
Sofia ➤ *Madag.* **89** B8
Sofievka *Ukraine* **33** H7
Sofiko *Greece* **46** D5
Sofiya *Bulgaria* **44** D7
Sofiya □ *Bulgaria* **44** D7
Sofiya ✈ (SOF) *Bulgaria* **44** D7
Sofrana *Greece* **47** E8
Sōfu-Gan *Japan* **55** K10
Sogakofe *Ghana* **83** D5
Sogamoso *Colombia* **124** B4
Sogār *Iran* **71** E8
Sögel *Germany* **24** C3
Sogndalsfjøra *Norway* **8** F12
Søgne *Norway* **9** G12
Sognefjorden *Norway* **8** F11
Söğüt *Bilecik, Turkey* **47** A12
Söğüt *Burdur, Turkey* **47** D11
Söğüt Dağı *Turkey* **47** D11
Söğütköy *Turkey* **47** E10
Soh *Iran* **71** C6
Sohâg *Egypt* **80** B3
Sohagpur *India* **68** H8
Soignies *Belgium* **17** D4
Soin *Burkina Faso* **82** C4
Soira *Eritrea* **81** E4
Soissons *France* **19** C10
Sōja *Japan* **55** G6
Sojat *India* **68** G5
Sok ➤ *Russia* **34** D10
Sokal *Ukraine* **23** C13
Sokcho *S. Korea* **57** E15
Söke *Turkey* **47** D9
Sokelo *Dem. Rep. of the Congo* **87** D1
Sokhumi *Georgia* **35** J5
Soko Banja *Serbia* **44** C5
Sokodé *Togo* **83** D5
Sokol *Russia* **32** C11
Sokolac *Bos.-H.* **28** G3
Sokółka *Poland* **30** E10
Sokolo *Ségou, Mali* **82** C3
Sokolo *Sikasso, Mali* **82** C3
Sokolov *Czech Rep.* **26** A5
Sokołów Małpolski *Poland* **31** H9
Sokołów Podlaski *Poland* **31** F9
Sokoły *Poland* **31** F9
Sokoto *Nigeria* **83** C6
Sokoto □ *Nigeria* **83** C6
Sokoto ➤ *Nigeria* **83** C5
Sokyrnytsya *Ukraine* **29** B8
Sokyryany *Ukraine* **29** B12
Sol Iletsk *Russia* **52** D6
Sola ➤ *Poland* **31** H6
Solai *Kenya* **86** B4
Solan *India* **68** D7
Solana Beach *U.S.A.* **111** N9
Solander I. *N.Z.* **91** G1
Solano *Phil.* **61** C4
Solapur *India* **66** L9
Solca *Romania* **29** C10
Solda Gölü *Turkey* **47** D11
Soldăneşti *Moldova* **29** C13
Soldeu *Andorra* **38** C6
Soldotna *U.S.A.* **100** C4
Soléa *Cyprus* **49** D12
Solec Kujawski *Poland* **31** E5
Soledad *Colombia* **124** A4
Soledad *U.S.A.* **110** J5
Soledad *Venezuela* **124** B6
Solent, The *U.K.* **15** G6
Solenzara *France* **21** G13
Solesmes *France* **19** B10
Solfonntaggen *Norway* **9** F12
Solhan *Turkey* **73** C9
Soligorsk = Salihorsk
   Belarus **23** B14
Solihull *U.K.* **15** E6
Solikamsk *Russia* **52** D6
Solila *Madag.* **89** C8
Solimões = Amazonas ➤
   S. Amer. **125** D8
Solin *Croatia* **41** E13
Solingen *Germany* **24** D3
Söll *Austria* **25** H8
Sollebrunn *Sweden* **11** F6
Sollefteå *Sweden* **10** A11
Sollentuna *Sweden* **10** E11
Sóller *Spain* **48** B9
Sollerön *Sweden* **10** D8
Solling *Germany* **24** D5
Solling-Vogler △ *Germany* **24** D5
Solnechnogorsk *Russia* **32** D9
Solo ➤ *Indonesia* **63** G15
Solofra *Italy* **43** B7
Sologne *France* **19** E8
Solok *Indonesia* **62** E2
Sololá *Guatemala* **120** D1
Sololo *Kenya* **86** B4
Solomon, N. Fork ➤ *U.S.A.* **112** F4
Solomon, S. Fork ➤ *U.S.A.* **112** F4
Solomon Is. ■ *Pac. Oc.* **90** B8
Solomon Rise *Pac. Oc.* **96** G7
Solon *China* **60** B7
Solon Springs *U.S.A.* **112** B8
Solor *Indonesia* **63** F6
Solotcha *Russia* **32** E10
Solothurn *Switz.* **25** H3

Solothurn □ *Switz.* **25** H3
Solotvyn *Ukraine* **29** B9
Solsona *Spain* **38** C6
Solt *Hungary* **28** D4
Šolta *Croatia* **41** E13
Soltānābād *Khorāsān, Iran* **71** C8
Soltānābād *Khorāsān, Iran* **71** B8
Soltau *Germany* **24** C5
Soltsy *Russia* **32** C6
Solunska Glava *Macedonia* **44** E5
Solvang *U.S.A.* **111** L6
Solvay *U.S.A.* **111** L6
Sölvesborg *Sweden* **11** H8
Solway Firth *U.K.* **14** C4
Solwezi *Zambia* **87** E2
Sōma *Japan* **54** F10
Soma *Turkey* **47** B9
Somabhula *Zimbabwe* **89** B4
Somali Pen. *Africa* **76** F3
Somali Rep. ■ *Africa* **75** F4
Somalia = Somali Rep. ■
   Africa **75** F4
Somaliland □ *Somali Rep.* **75** F4
Sombernon *France* **19** E11
Sombor *Serbia* **28** E4
Sombra *Canada* **114** D2
Sombrerete *Mexico* **118** C4
Sombrero *Anguilla* **121** C7
Şomcuta Mare *Romania* **29** C8
Somdari *India* **68** G5
Someido △ *Spain* **36** B4
Somers *U.S.A.* **108** B6
Somerset *Ky., U.S.A.* **113** G11
Somerset *Mass., U.S.A.* **115** E13
Somerset *Pa., U.S.A.* **114** F5
Somerset □ *U.K.* **15** F5
Somerset East *S. Africa* **88** E4
Somerset I. *Canada* **100** B10
Somerset West *S. Africa* **88** E2
Somersworth *U.S.A.* **115** C14
Somerton *U.S.A.* **109** K6
Somerville *U.S.A.* **115** F10
Someş ➤ *Romania* **28** C7
Someşul Mare ➤ *Romania* **29** C8
Somme □ *France* **19** C9
Somme ➤ *France* **19** B8
Somme, B. de la *France* **18** B8
Sommen *Jönköping, Sweden* **11** F8
Sommen *Östergötland, Sweden* **11** F9
Sommepy-Tahure *France* **19** C11
Sömmerda *Germany* **24** D7
Sommesous *France* **19** D11
Sommières *France* **21** E8
Somnath *India* **68** J4
Somogy □ *Hungary* **28** D2
Somogyszob *Hungary* **28** D2
Somosomo *Fiji* **91** a
Somosomo Str. *Fiji* **91** a
Somoto *Nic.* **120** D2
Sompolno *Poland* **31** F5
Somport, Puerto de *Spain* **38** C4
Son ➤ *India* **69** G11
Son Ha *Vietnam* **64** E7
Son Hoa *Vietnam* **64** F7
Son La *Vietnam* **58** G4
Son Serra *Spain* **48** B10
Son Servera *Spain* **38** F8
Soná *Panama* **120** E3
Sonamarg *India* **69** B6
Sonamukhi *India* **69** H12
Sonar ➤ *India* **69** G8
Sŏnch'ŏn *N. Korea* **57** E13
Sondags ➤ *S. Africa* **88** E4
Sóndalo *Italy* **40** B7
Sondar *India* **69** C6
Sønder Felding *Denmark* **11** J2
Sønder Omme *Denmark* **11** J2
Sønderborg *Denmark* **11** K3
Sondershausen *Germany* **24** D6
Sóndrio *Italy* **40** B6
Sone *Mozam.* **87** F3
Sonepur *India* **67** J13
Song *Nigeria* **83** D7
Song *Thailand* **64** C3
Song Cau *Vietnam* **64** F7
Song Hong ➤ *Vietnam* **58** F5
Song Xian *China* **56** G7
Songan *Indonesia* **63** J18
Songea *Tanzania* **87** E4
Songeons *France* **19** C8
Songhua Hu *China* **57** C14
Songhua Jiang ➤ *China* **60** B8
Songimvelo △ *S. Africa* **89** D5
Songjiang *China* **59** B13
Sŏngjin = Kimch'aek
   N. Korea **57** D15
Songkan *China* **58** C6
Songkhla *Thailand* **65** J3
Songming *China* **58** E4
Songnim *N. Korea* **57** E13
Songo *Mozam.* **85** H6
Songo *Sudan* **79** G10
Songpan *China* **58** A4
Songtao *China* **58** C7
Songwe *Dem. Rep. of the Congo* **86** C2
Songwe ➤ *Africa* **87** D3

Songxi *China* **59** D12
Songzi *China* **59** B8
Sonhat *India* **69** H10
Sonid Youqi *China* **56** C7
Sonipat *India* **68** E7
Sonkach *India* **68** H7
Sonkovo *Russia* **32** D9
Sonmiani *Pakistan* **68** G2
Sonmiani B. *Pakistan* **68** G2
Sonnino *Italy* **42** A6
Sono ➤ *Brazil* **125** E9
Sonoma *U.S.A.* **110** G4
Sonora *Calif., U.S.A.* **110** H6
Sonora *Tex., U.S.A.* **116** F4
Sonora □ *Mexico* **118** B2
Sonora ➤ *Mexico* **118** B2
Sonoran Desert *U.S.A.* **111** L12
Sonoyta *Mexico* **118** A2
Sonqor *Iran* **73** E12
Sonseca *Spain* **37** F7
Sonsonate *El Salv.* **120** D2
Sonstorp *Sweden* **11** F9
Sonthofen *Germany* **25** H6
Soochow = Suzhou *China* **59** B13
Sooke *Canada* **110** B3
Soomaaliya = Somali
   Rep. ■ *Africa* **75** F4
Sop Hao *Laos* **58** G5
Sop Prap *Thailand* **64** D2
Sopelana *Spain* **38** B2
Sopi *Indonesia* **63** D7
Sopo, Nahr ➤ *Sudan* **81** F2
Sopot *Bulgaria* **45** D8
Sopot *Poland* **30** D5
Sopot *Serbia* **44** B4
Sopotnica *Macedonia* **44** E5
Sopron *Hungary* **28** C1
Sopur *India* **69** B6
Sør-Rondane *Antarctica* **5** D4
Sora *Italy* **41** G10
Sorah *Pakistan* **68** F3
Söråker *Sweden* **10** B11
Sorano *Italy* **41** F8
Soraon *India* **69** G9
Sorbas *Spain* **39** H2
Sörbygden *Sweden* **10** B10
Sore *France* **20** D3
Sorel-Tracy *Canada* **104** C5
Soresina *Italy* **40** C6
Sörforsa *Sweden* **10** C10
Sórgono *Italy* **42** B2
Sorgues *France* **21** D8
Sorgun *Turkey* **72** C6
Soria *Spain* **38** D2
Soria □ *Spain* **38** D2
Soriano *Uruguay* **126** C4
Soriano nel Cimino *Italy* **41** F9
Sorkh, Kuh-e *Iran* **71** C8
Sorø *Denmark* **11** J5
Soro *Guinea* **82** C3
Soroca *Moldova* **29** B13
Sorocaba *Brazil* **127** A6
Soroki = Soroca *Moldova* **29** B13
Sorong *Indonesia* **63** E8
Soroni *Greece* **49** C10
Soroti *Uganda* **86** B3
Sørøya *Norway* **8** A20
Sørøysundet *Norway* **8** A20
Sorraia ➤ *Portugal* **37** G2
Sorrell *Australia* **95** G4
Sorrento *Italy* **43** B7
Sorsele *Sweden* **8** D17
Sörsjön *Sweden* **10** C7
Sorso *Italy* **42** B1
Sorsogon *Phil.* **61** E6
Sortavala *Russia* **32** B6
Sortino *Italy* **43** E8
Sortland *Norway* **8** B16
Sorvizhi *Russia* **34** B9
Sos del Rey Católico *Spain* **38** C3
Soscumica, L. *Canada* **104** B4
Sösdala *Sweden* **11** H7
Sosna ➤ *Russia* **33** F10
Sosnovka *Kirov, Russia* **34** B10
Sosnovka *Tambov, Russia* **34** D5
Sosnovyy Bor *Russia* **32** C5
Sosnowiec *Poland* **31** H6
Sospel *France* **21** E11
Sossus Vlei *Namibia* **88** C2
Šoštanj *Slovenia* **41** B12
Sōsura *N. Korea* **57** C16
Sot ➤ *India* **69** F8
Sotavento *C. Verde Is.* **78** b
Sotik *Kenya* **86** C4
Soto del Barco *Spain* **36** B4
Soto la Marina *Mexico* **119** C5
Soto la Marina ➤ *Mexico* **119** C5
Soto y Amío *Spain* **36** C5
Sotrondio *Spain* **36** B5
Sotuta *Mexico* **119** C7
Souanké *Congo* **84** D2
Soubré *Ivory C.* **82** D3
Souda *Greece* **49** D6
Soudas, Ormos *Greece* **49** D6
Souderton *U.S.A.* **115** F9
Soufli *Greece* **45** E10

Soufrière *Guadeloupe* **120** b
Soufrière *St. Lucia* **121** f
Soufrière Bay *Dominica* **121** f
Souillac *France* **20** D5
Souilly *France* **19** C12
Soukhouma *Laos* **64** E5
Soukougou *Burkina Faso* **83** C5
Sŏul = Seoul *S. Korea* **57** F14
Soulac-sur-Mer *France* **20** C2
Soulougou *Burkina Faso* **83** C5
Soultz-sous-Forêts *France* **19** D14
Sound, The = Øresund
   Europe **11** J6
Sound, The *U.K.* **15** G3
Sounio, Akra *Greece* **46** D6
Sources, Mt. aux *Lesotho* **89** D4
Soure *Brazil* **125** D9
Soure *Portugal* **36** E2
Souris *Man., Canada* **103** D8
Souris *P.E.I., Canada* **105** C7
Souris ➤ *N. Amer.* **112** A4
Sourou ➤ *Africa* **82** C4
Sourpi *Greece* **46** B4
Sousa *Brazil* **125** E11
Sousel *Portugal* **37** G3
Sousse *Tunisia* **79** A8
Soustons *France* **20** E2
Sout ➤ *S. Africa* **88** E2
South Africa ■ *Africa* **88** E3
South America **122** E5
South Aulatsivik I. *Canada* **105** A7
South Australia □ *Australia* **95** E2
South Australian Basin
   Ind. Oc. **96** L4
South Ayrshire □ *U.K.* **13** F4
South Baldy Pk. *U.S.A.* **109** J10
South Bass I. *U.S.A.* **114** E2
South Bend *Ind., U.S.A.* **112** E10
South Bend *Wash., U.S.A.* **110** D3
South Boston *U.S.A.* **113** G14
South Branch *Canada* **105** C8
South Brook *Canada* **105** C8
South Bruny I. *Australia* **95** G4
South C. *Australia* **90** F7
South Carolina □ *U.S.A.* **117** E14
South Charleston *U.S.A.* **113** F13
South China Sea *Asia* **62** C4
South Cumberland Is. △
   Australia **94** J7
South Dakota □ *U.S.A.* **112** C4
South Deerfield *U.S.A.* **115** D12
South Downs *U.K.* **15** G7
South East C. *Australia* **95** G4
South East Is. *Australia* **93** F3
South Esk ➤ *U.K.* **13** E6
South Fiji Basin *Pac. Oc.* **96** K9
South Foreland *U.K.* **15** F9
South Fork American ➤
   U.S.A. **110** G5
South Fork Feather ➤
   U.S.A. **110** F5
South Fork Grand ➤
   U.S.A. **112** C2
South Fork Milk ➤ *U.S.A.*
   108 B10
South Fork Republican ➤
   U.S.A. **112** E3
South Georgia *Antarctica* **128** G9
South Gloucestershire □
   U.K. **15** F5
South Hadley *U.S.A.* **115** D12
South Haven *U.S.A.* **112** D10
South Henik L. *Canada* **103** A9
South Horr *Kenya* **86** B4
South I. *Kenya* **86** B4
South I. *N.Z.* **91** F3
South Indian Lake *Canada* **103** B9
South Invercargill *N.Z.* **91** G2
South Island △ *Kenya* **86** B4
South Kitui △ *Kenya* **86** C4
South Knife ➤ *Canada* **103** B10
South Koel ➤ *India* **69** H11
South Korea ■ *Asia* **57** G15
South Lake Tahoe *U.S.A.* **110** G6
South Lanarkshire □ *U.K.* **13** F5
South Loup ➤ *U.S.A.* **112** E5
South Luangwa △ *Zambia* **87** E3
South Magnetic Pole
   Antarctica **5** C9
South Milwaukee *U.S.A.* **112** D10
South Molton *U.K.* **15** F4
South Moose L. *Canada* **103** C8
South Nahanni ➤ *Canada* **102** A4
South Nation ➤ *Canada* **115** A9
South Natuna Is. =
   Natuna Selatan,
   Kepulauan *Indonesia* **62** D3
South Negril Pt. *Jamaica* **120** a
South Orkney Is. *Antarctica* **5** C18
South Ossetia □ *Georgia* **35** J7
South Pagai, I. = Pagai
   Selatan, Pulau *Indonesia* **62** E2
South Paris *U.S.A.* **115** B14
South Pittsburg *U.S.A.* **117** D12
South Platte ➤ *U.S.A.* **112** E4
South Pole *Antarctica* **5** E
South Porcupine *Canada* **104** C3
South Portland *U.S.A.* **113** D18

South Pt. *Barbados* **121** g
South Pt. *U.S.A.* **114** B1
South River *Canada* **104** C4
South River *U.S.A.* **115** F10
South Ronaldsay *U.K.* **13** C6
South Sandwich Is. *Antarctica* **5** B1
South Sandwich Trench
   Atl. Oc. **5** B1
South Saskatchewan ➤
   Canada **103** C7
South Seal ➤ *Canada* **103** B9
South Shetland Is. *Antarctica* **5** C18
South Shields *U.K.* **14** C6
South Sioux City *U.S.A.* **112** D5
South Sister *U.S.A.* **108** D3
South Taranaki Bight *N.Z.* **91** C5
South Tasman Rise *S. Ocean* **5** A10
South Thompson ➤
   Canada **102** C4
South Twin I. *Canada* **104** B4
South Tyne ➤ *U.K.* **14** C5
South Uist *U.K.* **13** D1
South Valley *U.S.A.* **109** J10
South Wellesley Is. *Australia* **94** B2
South West C. *Australia* **95** G4
South West C. *N.Z.* **91** G1
South Williamsport *U.S.A.* **114** E8
South Yorkshire □ *U.K.* **14** D6
Southampton *Canada* **114** B3
Southampton *U.K.* **15** G6
Southampton *U.S.A.* **115** F12
Southampton □ *U.K.* **15** G6
Southampton I. *Canada* **101** C11
Southaven *U.S.A.* **117** D9
Southbank *Canada* **102** C3
Southbridge *N.Z.* **91** E4
Southbridge *U.S.A.* **115** D12
Southend *Canada* **103** B8
Southend-on-Sea *U.K.* **15** F8
Southend-on-Sea □ *U.K.* **15** F8
Southern = Janub □
   Sudan **81** F2
Southern = Yedebub
   Biheroch Bihereseboch
   na Hizboch □ *Ethiopia* **81** F4
Southern = Yuzhnyy □
   Russia **35** H5
Southern □ *Malawi* **87** F4
Southern □ *S. Leone* **82** D2
Southern □ *Zambia* **87** F2
Southern Alps *N.Z.* **91** E3
Southern Cross *Australia* **93** F2
Southern Indian L. *Canada* **103** B9
Southern Lau Group *Fiji* **91** a
Southern Ocean *Antarctica* **5** C6
Southern Pines *U.S.A.* **117** D15
Southern Uplands *U.K.* **13** F5
Southington *U.S.A.* **115** E12
Southland □ *N.Z.* **91** F1
Southold *U.S.A.* **115** E12
Southport *Australia* **95** D5
Southport *U.K.* **14** D4
Southport *U.S.A.* **114** D8
Southwest ➤ *Australia* **95** G4
Southwest Pacific Basin
   Pac. Oc. **5** A12
Southwold *U.K.* **15** E9
Southwood △ *Australia* **95** D5
Soutpansberg *S. Africa* **89** C4
Souvigny *France* **19** F10
Sovata *Romania* **29** D10
Soverato *Italy* **43** D9
Sovetsk *Kaliningrad, Russia* **30** C8
Sovetsk *Kirov, Russia* **34** B9
Sovicille *Italy* **41** E8
Soweto *S. Africa* **89** D4
Sōya-Kaikyō = La Perouse
   Str. *Asia* **54** B11
Sōya-Misaki *Japan* **54** B10
Soyaux *France* **20** C4
Soyo *Angola* **84** F2
Sozh ➤ *Belarus* **23** B16
Sozopol *Bulgaria* **45** D11
Spa *Belgium* **17** D5
Spain ■ *Europe* **7** H5
Spalding *Australia* **95** E2
Spalding *U.K.* **14** E7
Spanaway *U.S.A.* **110** C4
Spangler *U.S.A.* **114** F6
Spanish *Canada* **104** C3
Spanish Fork *U.S.A.* **108** F8
Spanish Town *Br. Virgin Is.* **121** e
Spanish Town *Jamaica* **120** a
Sparks *U.S.A.* **110** F7
Sparreholm *Sweden* **10** E10
Sparta = Sparti *Greece* **46** D4
Sparta *Mich., U.S.A.* **113** D11
Sparta *N.J., U.S.A.* **115** E10
Sparta *Wis., U.S.A.* **112** D8
Spartanburg *U.S.A.* **117** D14
Spartansburg *U.S.A.* **114** E5
Sparti *Greece* **46** D4
Spartivento, C. *Calabria, Italy* **43** E9
Spartivento, C. *Sard., Italy* **42** D1
Sparwood *Canada* **102** D6
Spas-Demensk *Russia* **32** E7
Spas-Klepiki *Russia* **32** E11
Spassk Dalniy *Russia* **54** B6

Spassk-Ryazanskiy *Russia* **32** E11
Spatha, Akra *Greece* **49** D5
Spatsizi ➤ *Canada* **102** B3
Spatsizi Plateau
   Wilderness △ *Canada* **102** B3
Spean ➤ *U.K.* **13** E4
Spearfish *U.S.A.* **112** C2
Spearman *U.S.A.* **116** C4
Speculator *U.S.A.* **115** C10
Speia *Moldova* **29** D14
Speightstown *Barbados* **121** g
Speke Gulf *Tanzania* **86** C3
Spello *Italy* **41** F9
Spence Bay = Taloyoak
   Canada **100** C10
Spencer *Idaho, U.S.A.* **108** D7
Spencer *Iowa, U.S.A.* **112** D6
Spencer *N.Y., U.S.A.* **115** D8
Spencer *Nebr., U.S.A.* **112** D5
Spencer, C. *Australia* **95** F2
Spencer B. *Namibia* **88** D1
Spencer G. *Australia* **95** E2
Spencerville *Canada* **115** B9
Spences Bridge *Canada* **102** C4
Spennymoor *U.K.* **14** C6
Spenser Mts. *N.Z.* **91** E4
Spentrup *Denmark* **11** H4
Sperchios ➤ *Greece* **46** C4
Sperrin Mts. *U.K.* **12** B5
Spessart *Germany* **25** F5
Spetses *Greece* **46** D5
Spey ➤ *U.K.* **13** D5
Speyer *Germany* **25** F4
Spezand *Pakistan* **68** E2
Spezzano Albanese *Italy* **43** C9
Spiddle *Ireland* **12** C2
Spiekeroog *Germany* **24** B3
Spiez *Switz.* **25** J3
Spili *Greece* **49** D6
Spilimbergo *Italy* **41** B9
Spin Būldak *Afghan.* **68** D2
Spinalonga *Greece* **49** D7
Spineni *Romania* **29** F9
Spirit Lake *U.S.A.* **110** D4
Spirit River *Canada* **102** B5
Spiritwood *Canada* **103** C7
Spišská Nová Ves
   Slovak Rep. **27** C13
Spišské Podhradie
   Slovak Rep. **27** B13
Spital *Austria* **26** D7
Spithead *U.K.* **15** G6
Spittal an der Drau *Austria* **26** E6
Spitzbergen = Svalbard *Arctic* **4** B8
Spjelkavik *Norway* **8** E12
Split *Croatia* **41** E13
Split ✈ (SPU) *Croatia* **41** E13
Split L. *Canada* **103** B9
Split Lake *Canada* **103** B9
Splitski Kanal *Croatia* **41** E13
Splügenpass *Switz.* **25** J5
Spofford *U.S.A.* **116** G4
Spokane *U.S.A.* **108** C5
Spoleto *Italy* **41** F9
Spooner *U.S.A.* **112** C8
Sporyy Navolok, Mys *Russia* **52** B7
Sprague *U.S.A.* **108** C5
Spratly I. *S. China Sea* **62** C4
Spratly Is. *S. China Sea* **62** C4
Spray *U.S.A.* **108** D4
Spreča ➤ *Bos.-H.* **28** F3
Spree ➤ *Germany* **24** C9
Spreewald *Germany* **24** D9
Spremberg *Germany* **24** D10
Sprengisandur *Iceland* **8** D4
Spring City *U.S.A.* **115** F9
Spring Creek *U.S.A.* **108** F6
Spring Garden *U.S.A.* **110** F6
Spring Hall *Barbados* **121** g
Spring Hill *U.S.A.* **117** G13
Spring Mts. *U.S.A.* **111** J11
Spring Valley *Calif., U.S.A.* **111** N10
Spring Valley *Nev., U.S.A.* **111** J11
Springbok *S. Africa* **88** D2
Springboro *U.S.A.* **114** E4
Springdale *Canada* **105** C8
Springdale *U.S.A.* **116** G7
Springe *Germany* **24** C5
Springer *U.S.A.* **109** H11
Springerville *U.S.A.* **109** J9
Springfield *Canada* **114** D4
Springfield *N.Z.* **91** E3
Springfield *Colo., U.S.A.* **109** H12
Springfield *Ill., U.S.A.* **112** F7
Springfield *Mass., U.S.A.* **115** D12
Springfield *Mo., U.S.A.* **112** G7
Springfield *Ohio, U.S.A.* **113** F12
Springfield *Oreg., U.S.A.* **108** D2
Springfield *Tenn., U.S.A.* **117** C11
Springfield *Vt., U.S.A.* **115** C12
Springfontein *S. Africa* **88** E4
Springhill *Canada* **105** C7
Springhill *U.S.A.* **116** E8
Springhouse *Canada* **102** C4
Springs *S. Africa* **89** D4
Springsure *Australia* **94** C4

Springvale *U.S.A.* **115** C14
Springville *Calif., U.S.A.* **110** J8
Springville *N.Y., U.S.A.* **114** D6
Springville *Utah, U.S.A.* **108** F8
Springwater *U.S.A.* **114** D7
Spruce-Creek *U.S.A.* **114** F6
Spruce Knob-Seneca
  Rocks △ *U.S.A.* **113** F14
Spruce Mt. *U.S.A.* **115** B12
Spur *U.S.A.* **116** E4
Spurn Hd. *U.K.* **14** D8
Spuž *Montenegro* **44** D3
Spuzzum *Canada* **102** D4
Squam L. *U.S.A.* **115** C13
Squamish *Canada* **102** D4
Square Islands *Canada* **105** B8
Squillace, G. di *Italy* **43** D9
Squinzano *Italy* **43** B11
Squires, Mt. *Australia* **93** E4
Srbac *Bos.-H.* **28** E2
Srbica *Serbia* **44** D4
Srbija = Serbia ■ *Europe* **44** C4
Srbobran *Serbia* **28** E4
Sre Ambel *Cambodia* **65** G4
Sre Khtum *Cambodia* **65** F6
Sre Umbell = Sre Ambel
  Cambodia **65** G4
Srebrenica *Bos.-H.* **28** F4
Sredinny Ra. = Sredinnyy
  Khrebet *Russia* **53** D17
Sredinnyy Khrebet *Russia* **53** D17
Središče *Slovenia* **41** B13
Sredna Gora *Bulgaria* **45** D8
Srednekolymsk *Russia* **53** C16
Sredni Rodopi *Bulgaria* **45** E8
Srednogorie *Bulgaria* **45** D8
Śrem *Poland* **31** F4
Sremska Mitrovica *Serbia* **28** F4
Sremski Karlovci *Serbia* **28** E4
Srepok → *Cambodia* **64** F6
Sretensk *Russia* **53** D12
Sri Aman *Malaysia* **62** D4
Sri Lanka ■ *Asia* **66** R12
Srikakulam *India* **67** K13
Srinagar *India* **69** B6
Srinagarind Res. *Thailand* **64** E2
Środa Śląska *Poland* **31** G3
Środa Wielkopolski *Poland* **31** F4
Srono *Indonesia* **63** J17
Srpska Crnja *Serbia* **28** E5
Srpski Itebej *Serbia* **28** E5
Staaten → *Australia* **94** B3
Staaten River △ *Australia* **94** B3
Staberhuk *Germany* **24** A7
Stade *Germany* **24** B5
Stadskanaal *Neths.* **17** A6
Stadtallendorf *Germany* **24** E5
Stadthagen *Germany* **24** C5
Stadtlohn *Germany* **24** D2
Stadtroda *Germany* **24** E7
Staffa *U.K.* **13** E2
Staffanstorp *Sweden* **11** J7
Stafford *U.K.* **14** E5
Stafford *U.S.A.* **112** G4
Stafford Springs *U.S.A.* **115** E12
Staffordshire □ *U.K.* **14** E5
Stagnone *Italy* **42** E5
Stagnone di Marsala △ *Italy* **42** E5
Staines *U.K.* **15** F7
Stainz *Austria* **26** E8
Stakhanov *Ukraine* **33** H10
Stalać *Serbia* **44** C5
Stalida *Greece* **49** D7
Stallarholmen *Sweden* **10** E11
Ställdalen *Sweden* **10** E8
Stalowa Wola *Poland* **31** H9
Stalybridge *U.K.* **14** D5
Stamford *Australia* **94** C3
Stamford *U.K.* **15** E7
Stamford *Conn., U.S.A.* **115** E11
Stamford *N.Y., U.S.A.* **115** D10
Stamford *Tex., U.S.A.* **116** E5
Stampriet *Namibia* **88** C2
Stamps *U.S.A.* **116** E8
Stančevo = Kalipetrovo
  Bulgaria **45** B11
Standerton *S. Africa* **89** D4
Standish *U.S.A.* **113** D12
Stanford *S. Africa* **88** E2
Stanford *U.S.A.* **108** C8
Stånga *Sweden* **11** G12
Stanger *S. Africa* **89** D5
Stängselåsen =
  Salpausselkä *Finland* **32** B4
Stanišić *Serbia* **28** E4
Stanislaus → *U.S.A.* **110** H5
Stanisławów *Poland* **31** F8
Stanley *Australia* **95** G4
Stanley *Falk. Is.* **128** G5
Stanley *U.K.* **14** C6
Stanley *Idaho, U.S.A.* **108** D6
Stanley *N. Dak., U.S.A.* **112** A2
Stanley *N.Y., U.S.A.* **114** D7
Stanley Mission *Canada* **103** B8
Stanovoy Khrebet *Russia* **53** D14
Stanovoy Ra. = Stanovoy
  Khrebet *Russia* **53** D14

Stansmore Ra. *Australia* **92** D4
Stansted, London ✈ (STN)
  U.K. **15** F8
Stanthorpe *Australia* **95** D5
Stanton *U.S.A.* **116** E4
Stanwood *U.S.A.* **110** B4
Staples *U.S.A.* **112** B6
Stapleton *U.S.A.* **112** E3
Stąporków *Poland* **31** G7
Star City *Canada* **103** C8
Star Lake *U.S.A.* **115** B9
Stará Ľubovňa *Slovak Rep.* **27** B13
Stara Moravica *Serbia* **28** E4
Stara Pazova *Serbia* **28** F5
Stara Planina *Bulgaria* **44** C7
Stara Sil *Ukraine* **31** J9
Stará Turá *Slovak Rep.* **27** C10
Stara Ushytsya *Ukraine* **29** B12
Stara Zagora *Bulgaria* **45** D9
Starachowice *Poland* **31** G8
Staraya Russa *Russia* **32** D6
Starbuck I. *Kiribati* **97** H12
Starchiojd *Romania* **29** E11
Starcke △ *Australia* **94** A4
Stargard Szczeciński *Poland* **30** E2
Stari Bar *Montenegro* **44** D3
Stari Trg *Slovenia* **41** C12
Staritsa *Russia* **32** D8
Starke *U.S.A.* **117** G13
Starkville *U.S.A.* **117** E10
Starnberg *Germany* **25** H7
Starnberger See *Germany* **25** H7
Starobilsk *Ukraine* **33** H10
Starodub *Russia* **33** F7
Starogard Gdański *Poland* **30** E5
Starokonstantinov =
  Starokonstyantyniv
  Ukraine **23** D14
Starokonstyantyniv
  Ukraine **23** D14
Starokozache *Ukraine* **29** D14
Starominskaya *Russia* **33** J10
Staroshcherbinovskaya
  Russia **33** J10
Start Pt. *U.K.* **15** G4
Stary Sącz *Poland* **31** J7
Staryy Biryuzyak *Russia* **35** H8
Staryy Chartoriysk *Ukraine* **23** C13
Staryy Krym *Ukraine* **33** K8
Staryy Oskol *Russia* **33** G9
Staryy Sambir *Ukraine* **31** J9
Stassfurt *Germany* **24** D7
Staszów *Poland* **31** H8
State College *U.S.A.* **114** F7
Stateline *U.S.A.* **110** G7
Staten, I. = Estados, I. de
  Los *Argentina* **128** G4
Staten I. *U.S.A.* **115** F10
Statesboro *U.S.A.* **117** E14
Statesville *U.S.A.* **117** D14
Statia = St. Eustatius
  W. Indies **121** C7
Stauffer *U.S.A.* **111** L7
Staunton *Ill., U.S.A.* **112** F9
Staunton *Va., U.S.A.* **113** F14
Stavanger *Norway* **9** G11
Staveley *N.Z.* **91** E3
Stavelot *Belgium* **17** D5
Stavern *Norway* **9** G14
Stavoren *Neths.* **17** B5
Stavropol *Russia* **35** H6
Stavropol □ *Russia* **35** G6
Stavros *Cyprus* **49** D11
Stavros *Kriti, Greece* **49** D6
Stavros *Thessaloniki, Greece* **44** F7
Stavros, Akra *Greece* **49** D6
Stavroupoli *Greece* **45** E8
Stawell *Australia* **95** F3
Stawell → *Australia* **94** C3
Stawiski *Poland* **30** E9
Stawiszyn *Poland* **31** G5
Stayner *Canada* **114** B4
Stayton *U.S.A.* **108** D2
Steamboat Springs *U.S.A.* **108** F10
Steblevë *Albania* **44** E4
Steele *U.S.A.* **112** B4
Steelton *U.S.A.* **114** F8
Steen River *Canada* **102** B5
Steens Mt. *U.S.A.* **108** E4
Steenwijk *Neths.* **17** B6
Steep Pt. *Australia* **93** E1
Steep Rock *Canada* **103** C9
Ştefan Vodă *Moldova* **29** D14
Ştefăneşti *Romania* **29** C12
Stefanie △ *Ethiopia* **81** G4
Stefanie L. = Chew Bahir
  Ethiopia **81** G4
Stefansson Bay *Antarctica* **5** C5
Stege *Denmark* **11** K6
Ştei *Romania* **28** D7
Steiermark □ *Austria* **26** D8
Steigerwald *Germany* **25** F6
Steigerwald △ *Germany* **25** F6
Steilacoom *U.S.A.* **110** C4
Steilrandberge *Namibia* **88** B1
Steinbach *Canada* **103** D9
Steinfurt *Germany* **24** C3

Steinhausen *Namibia* **88** C2
Steinheim *Germany* **24** D5
Steinhuder Meer *Germany* **24** C5
Steinhuder Meer △ *Germany* **24** C5
Steinkjer *Norway* **8** D14
Steinkopf *S. Africa* **88** D2
Steinwald △ *Germany* **25** F8
Stellarton *Canada* **105** C7
Stellenbosch *S. Africa* **88** E2
Stelvio, Paso dello *Italy* **40** B7
Stenay *France* **19** C12
Stendal *Germany* **24** C7
Stende *Latvia* **30** A9
Stenhamra *Sweden* **10** E11
Stenshuvud △ *Sweden* **11** J8
Stenstorp *Sweden* **11** F7
Stenungsund *Sweden* **11** F5
Stepanavan *Armenia* **35** K7
Stephens Creek *Australia* **95** E3
Stephens I. *Canada* **102** C2
Stephens L. *Canada* **103** B9
Stephenville *Canada* **105** C8
Stephenville *U.S.A.* **116** E5
Stepnica *Poland* **30** E1
Steppe *Asia* **50** C7
Sterea Ellas □ *Greece* **46** C4
Sterkstroom *S. Africa* **88** E4
Sterling *Colo., U.S.A.* **108** F12
Sterling *Ill., U.S.A.* **112** E9
Sterling *Kans., U.S.A.* **112** F4
Sterling City *U.S.A.* **116** F4
Sterling Heights *U.S.A.* **113** D12
Sterling Run *U.S.A.* **114** E6
Sterlitamak *Russia* **52** D6
Sternberg *Germany* **24** B7
Šternberk *Czech Rep.* **27** B10
Sternes *Greece* **49** D6
Sterzing = Vipiteno *Italy* **41** B8
Stettin = Szczecin *Poland* **30** E1
Stettiner Haff *Germany* **24** B10
Stettler *Canada* **102** C6
Steubenville *U.S.A.* **114** F4
Stevenage *U.K.* **15** F7
Stevens Point *U.S.A.* **112** C9
Stevenson *U.S.A.* **110** E5
Stevenson → *Australia* **95** D2
Stevenson L. *Canada* **103** C9
Stevensville *U.S.A.* **108** C6
Stevns Klint *Denmark* **11** J6
Stewart *Canada* **102** B3
Stewart *U.S.A.* **110** F7
Stewart → *Canada* **100** C6
Stewart, C. *Australia* **94** A1
Stewart, I. *Chile* **128** G2
Stewarts Point *U.S.A.* **110** G3
Stewartville *U.S.A.* **112** D7
Stewiacke *Canada* **105** C7
Steynsburg *S. Africa* **88** E4
Steyr *Austria* **26** C7
Steyr → *Austria* **26** C7
Steytlerville *S. Africa* **88** E3
Stia *Italy* **41** E8
Stigler *U.S.A.* **116** D7
Stigliano *Italy* **43** B9
Stigtomta *Sweden* **11** F10
Stikine → *Canada* **102** B2
Stilfontein *S. Africa* **88** D4
Stilida *Greece* **46** C4
Stillwater *N.Z.* **91** E3
Stillwater *N.Y., U.S.A.* **115** D11
Stillwater *Okla., U.S.A.* **116** C6
Stillwater Range *U.S.A.* **108** G4
Stillwater Res. *U.S.A.* **115** C9
Stilo, Pta. *Italy* **43** D9
Stilwell *U.S.A.* **116** D7
Stînga Nistrului □ *Moldova* **29** C14
Ştip *Macedonia* **44** E6
Stira *Greece* **46** C6
Stirling *Canada* **114** B7
Stirling *U.K.* **13** E5
Stirling □ *U.K.* **13** E4
Stirling Ra. *Australia* **93** F2
Stirling Range △ *Australia* **93** F2
Stittsville *Canada* **115** A9
Stjernøya *Norway* **8** A20
Stjørdalshalsen *Norway* **8** E14
Stockach *Germany* **25** H5
Stockaryd *Sweden* **11** G8
Stockerau *Austria* **27** C9
Stockholm *Sweden* **10** E12
Stockholm Arlanda ✈
  (ARN) *Sweden* **10** E11
Stockholms län □ *Sweden* **10** E12
Stockport *U.K.* **14** D5
Stocksbridge *U.K.* **14** D6
Stockton *Calif., U.S.A.* **110** H5
Stockton *Kans., U.S.A.* **112** F4
Stockton *Mo., U.S.A.* **112** G7
Stockton-on-Tees *U.K.* **14** C6
Stockton-on-Tees □ *U.K.* **14** C6
Stockton Plateau *U.S.A.* **116** F3
Stoczek Łukowski *Poland* **31** G8

Stöde *Sweden* **10** B10
Stoeng Treng *Cambodia* **64** F5
Stoer, Pt. of *U.K.* **13** C3
Stogovo *Macedonia* **44** E4
Stoholm *Denmark* **11** H3
Stoke-on-Trent *U.K.* **14** D5
Stoke-on-Trent □ *U.K.* **14** D5
Stokes △ *Australia* **93** F3
Stokes Pt. *Australia* **95** G3
Stokes Ra. *Australia* **92** C5
Stokksnes *Iceland* **8** D6
Stokmarknes *Norway* **8** B16
Stolac *Bos.-H.* **44** C1
Stolberg *Germany* **24** E2
Stolbovoy, Ostrov *Russia* **53** B14
Stolbtsy = Stowbtsy *Belarus* **23** B14
Stolin *Belarus* **23** C14
Stolnici *Romania* **29** F9
Stöllet *Sweden* **10** D7
Stomio *Greece* **49** D5
Ston *Croatia* **41** F14
Stone *U.S.A.* **14** E5
Stoneboro *U.S.A.* **114** E4
Stonehaven *U.K.* **13** E6
Stonehenge *Australia* **94** C3
Stonehenge *U.K.* **15** F6
Stonewall *Canada* **103** C9
Stony L. *Man., Canada* **103** B9
Stony L. *Ont., Canada* **114** B6
Stony Point *U.S.A.* **115** E11
Stony Pt. *U.S.A.* **115** C8
Stony Rapids *Canada* **103** B7
Stony Tunguska =
  Tunguska,
  Podkamennaya →
  Russia **53** C10
Stonyford *U.S.A.* **110** F4
Stopnica *Poland* **31** H7
Storå *Sweden* **10** E9
Storå → *Denmark* **11** H2
Stora Gla *Sweden* **10** E5
Stora Le *Sweden* **10** E5
Stora Lulevatten *Sweden* **8** C18
Storavan *Sweden* **8** D18
Stord *Norway* **9** G11
Store Bælt *Denmark* **11** J4
Store Heddinge *Denmark* **11** J6
Store Mosse □ *Sweden* **11** G7
Storebro *Sweden* **11** G9
Storfors *Sweden* **10** E8
Storlien *Sweden* **10** A6
Storm B. *Australia* **95** G4
Storm Lake *U.S.A.* **112** D6
Stormberge *S. Africa* **88** E4
Stormsrivier *S. Africa* **88** E3
Stornoway *U.K.* **13** C2
Storo *Italy* **40** C7
Storozhinets =
  Storozhynets *Ukraine* **29** B10
Storozhynets *Ukraine* **29** B10
Storrs *U.S.A.* **115** E12
Storsjön *Gävleborg, Sweden* **10** D10
Storsjön *Jämtland, Sweden* **10** B7
Storsjön *Jämtland, Sweden* **10** A8
Storuman *Sweden* **8** D17
Storuman, L. *Sweden* **8** D17
Storvätteshågna *Sweden* **10** B6
Storvik *Sweden* **10** D10
Storvreta *Sweden* **10** E11
Stouffville *Canada* **114** C5
Stoughton *Canada* **103** D8
Stour → *Dorset, U.K.* **15** G6
Stour → *Kent, U.K.* **15** F9
Stour → *Suffolk, U.K.* **15** F9
Stourbridge *U.K.* **15** E5
Stout L. *Canada* **103** C10
Stove Pipe Wells Village
  U.S.A. **111** J9
Støvring *Denmark* **11** H3
Stow *U.S.A.* **114** E3
Stowbtsy *Belarus* **23** B14
Stowmarket *U.K.* **15** E9
Strabane *U.K.* **12** B4
Stracin *Macedonia* **44** D6
Stradella *Italy* **40** C6
Strahan *Australia* **95** G4
Strajitsa *Bulgaria* **45** C9
Strakonice *Czech Rep.* **26** B6
Straldzha *Bulgaria* **45** D10
Stralsund *Germany* **24** A9
Stranda *Møre og Romsdal,*
  Norway **8** E12
Stranda *Nord-Trøndelag,*
  Norway **8** D14
Strandby *Denmark* **11** G4
Strangford L. *U.K.* **12** B6
Strängnäs *Sweden* **10** E11
Stranorlar *Ireland* **12** B4
Stranraer *U.K.* **13** G3
Strasbourg *Canada* **103** C8
Strasbourg *France* **19** D14
Strasburg *Germany* **24** B9
Strășeni *Moldova* **29** C13
Strässa *Sweden* **10** E9
Stratford *Canada* **114** C4
Stratford *N.Z.* **91** C5

Stratford *Calif., U.S.A.* **110** J7
Stratford *Conn., U.S.A.* **115** E11
Stratford *Tex., U.S.A.* **116** C3
Stratford-upon-Avon *U.K.* **15** E6
Strath Spey *U.K.* **13** D5
Strathalbyn *Australia* **95** F2
Strathaven *U.K.* **13** F4
Strathcona △ *Canada* **102** D3
Strathmore *Canada* **102** C6
Strathmore *U.K.* **13** E5
Strathmore *U.S.A.* **110** J7
Strathnaver *Canada* **102** C4
Strathpeffer *U.K.* **13** D4
Strathroy *Canada* **114** D3
Strathy Pt. *U.K.* **13** C4
Strattanville *U.S.A.* **114** E5
Stratton *U.S.A.* **115** A14
Stratton Mt. *U.S.A.* **115** C12
Straubing *Germany* **25** G8
Straumnes *Iceland* **8** C2
Strausberg *Germany* **24** C9
Strawberry → *U.S.A.* **108** F8
Strážnice *Czech Rep.* **27** C10
Streaky B. *Australia* **95** E1
Streaky Bay *Australia* **95** E1
Streator *U.S.A.* **112** E9
Středočeský □ *Czech Rep.* **26** B7
Streetsboro *U.S.A.* **114** E3
Streetsville *U.S.A.* **114** C5
Strehaia *Romania* **29** F8
Strelcha *Bulgaria* **45** D8
Strelka *Russia* **53** D10
Streng → *Cambodia* **64** F4
Stresa *Italy* **40** C5
Streymoy *Færoe Is.* **8** E9
Strezhevoy *Russia* **52** C8
Stříbro *Czech Rep.* **26** A6
Strilky *Ukraine* **31** J9
Strimonas → *Greece* **44** E7
Strofades *Greece* **46** D3
Strokestown *Ireland* **12** C3
Stroma *U.K.* **13** C5
Stromberg-Heuchelberg △
  Germany **25** F4
Strómboli *Italy* **43** D8
Stromeferry *U.K.* **13** D3
Stromness *U.K.* **13** C5
Strömsbruk *Sweden* **10** C11
Strömsnäsbruk *Sweden* **11** H7
Strömstad *Sweden* **11** F5
Strömsund *Sweden* **8** E16
Strongili *Greece* **47** E11
Stróngoli *Italy* **43** C10
Strongsville *U.S.A.* **114** E3
Stronie Śląskie *Poland* **31** H3
Stronsay *U.K.* **13** C6
Stropkov *Slovak Rep.* **27** B14
Stroud *U.K.* **15** F5
Stroud Road *Australia* **95** E5
Stroudsburg *U.S.A.* **115** F9
Stroumbi *Cyprus* **49** E11
Struer *Denmark* **11** H2
Struga *Macedonia* **44** E4
Strugi Krasnyye *Russia* **32** C5
Struma → *Europe* **44** E7
Strumica *Macedonia* **44** E6
Strumica → *Europe* **44** E7
Strumok *Ukraine* **29** E14
Struthers *Canada* **104** C2
Struthers *U.S.A.* **114** E4
Stryama *Bulgaria* **45** D8
Stryker *U.S.A.* **108** B6
Stryków *Poland* **31** G6
Stryy *Ukraine* **23** D12
Strzegom *Poland* **31** H3
Strzelce Krajeńskie *Poland* **31** F2
Strzelce Opolskie *Poland* **31** H5
Strzelecki Cr. → *Australia* **95** D2
Strzelecki Desert *Australia* **95** D3
Strzelin *Poland* **31** H4
Strzelno *Poland* **31** F5
Strzybnica *Poland* **31** H5
Strzyżów *Poland* **31** J8
Stuart *Fla., U.S.A.* **117** H14
Stuart *Nebr., U.S.A.* **112** D5
Stuart → *Canada* **102** C4
Stuart Bluff Ra. *Australia* **92** D5
Stuart L. *Canada* **102** C4
Stuart Ra. *Australia* **95** D1
Stubbekøbing *Denmark* **11** K6
Stuben *Austria* **26** D3
Studen Kladenets, Yazovir
  Bulgaria **45** E9
Studenka *Czech Rep.* **27** B11
Stugun *Sweden* **10** B9
Stuhr *Germany* **24** B4
Stull L. *Canada* **104** B1
Stupava *Slovak Rep.* **27** C10
Stupino *Russia* **32** E10
Sturgeon → *Canada* **103** C9
Sturgeon B. *Canada* **103** C9
Sturgeon Bay *U.S.A.* **112** C10
Sturgeon Falls *Canada* **104** C4
Sturgeon L. *Alta., Canada* **102** B5
Sturgeon L. *Ont., Canada* **104** C1

Sturgeon L. *Ont., Canada* **114** B6
Sturgis *Canada* **103** C8
Sturgis *Mich., U.S.A.* **113** E11
Sturgis *S. Dak., U.S.A.* **112** C2
Šturovo *Slovak Rep.* **27** D11
Sturt △ *Australia* **95** D3
Sturt Cr. → *Australia* **92** C4
Sturt Stony Desert *Australia* **95** D3
Stutterheim *S. Africa* **88** E4
Stuttgart *Germany* **25** G5
Stuttgart *U.S.A.* **116** D9
Stuttgart Echterdingen ✈
  (STR) *Germany* **25** G5
Stuyvesant *U.S.A.* **115** D11
Stykkishólmur *Iceland* **8** D2
Styria = Steiermark □
  Austria **26** D8
Styrsö *Sweden* **11** G5
Su Xian = Suzhou *China* **56** H9
Suakin *Sudan* **80** D4
Suan *N. Korea* **57** E14
Suar *India* **69** E8
Subang *Indonesia* **63** G12
Subansiri → *India* **67** F18
Subarnarekha → *India* **69** H12
Subayhah *Si. Arabia* **70** D3
Subcetate *Romania* **28** E8
Subi *Indonesia* **62** D3
Subiaco *Italy* **41** G10
Subotica *Serbia* **28** D4
Suca *Ethiopia* **81** F4
Suceava *Romania* **29** C11
Suceava □ *Romania* **29** C10
Suceava → *Romania* **29** C11
Sucha-Beskidzka *Poland* **31** J6
Suchan = Partizansk *Russia* **54** C6
Suchań *Poland* **31** E2
Suchedniów *Poland* **31** G7
Suchil *Mexico* **118** C4
Suchitoto *El Salv.* **120** D2
Suchou = Suzhou *China* **59** B13
Suchowola *Poland* **30** E10
Süchow = Xuzhou *China* **57** G9
Suck → *Ireland* **12** C3
Sucre *Bolivia* **124** G5
Sućuraj *Croatia* **41** E14
Sucuriú → *Brazil* **125** H8
Sud □ *Cameroon* **83** E7
Sud, Pte. du *Canada* **105** C7
Sud-Kivu □
  Dem. Rep. of the Congo **86** C2
Sud-Ouest □ *Cameroon* **83** D6
Sud-Ouest, Pte. *Canada* **105** C7
Sud Ouest, Pte. *Mauritius* **85** d
Suda → *Russia* **32** C9
Sudak *Ukraine* **33** K8
Sudan *U.S.A.* **116** D3
Sudan ■ *Africa* **81** E3
Sudbury *Canada* **104** C3
Sudbury *U.K.* **15** E8
Sûdd *Sudan* **81** F3
Sudeifel = Deutsch-
  Luxemburgischer △
  Germany **25** F2
Süderbrarup *Germany* **24** A5
Süderlügum *Germany* **24** A4
Süderoogsand *Germany* **24** A4
Sudeten Mts. = Sudety
  Europe **27** A9
Sudety *Europe* **27** A9
Südheide □ *Germany* **24** C6
Suðuroy *Færoe Is.* **8** F9
Sudi *Tanzania* **87** E4
Sudirman, Pegunungan
  Indonesia **63** E5
Sudiţi *Romania* **29** F12
Sudogda *Russia* **34** C5
Sudong, Pulau *Singapore* **65** d
Sudova Vyshnya *Ukraine* **31** J10
Sudr *Egypt* **80** B3
Sudzha *Russia* **33** G8
Sue → *Sudan* **81** F2
Sueca *Spain* **39** F4
Süedinenie *Bulgaria* **45** D8
Suemez I. *U.S.A.* **102** B2
Suez = El Suweis *Egypt* **80** J8
Suez, G. of = Suweis,
  Khalîg el *Egypt* **80** J8
Suez Canal = Suweis,
  Qanâ es *Egypt* **80** H8
Suffield *Canada* **102** C6
Suffolk *U.S.A.* **113** G15
Suffolk □ *U.K.* **15** E9
Şugag *Romania* **29** E8
Sugar Grove *U.S.A.* **114** E5
Sugarive → *India* **69** F12
Suğla Gölü *Turkey* **72** D5
Sugluk = Salluit *Canada* **101** C12
Suhaia, Lacul *Romania* **29** G10
Şuḩār *Oman* **71** E8
Sühbaatar □ *Mongolia* **56** B8
Suhl *Germany* **24** E6
Şuhut *Turkey* **47** C12
Sui *Pakistan* **68** E3
Sui Xian *China* **56** G8
Šuica *Bos.-H.* **28** G2

Suichang *China* 59 C12
Suichuan *China* 59 D10
Suide *China* 56 F6
Suifenhe *China* 57 B16
Suihua *China* 60 B7
Suijiang *China* 58 C4
Suining *Hunan, China* 59 D8
Suining *Jiangsu, China* 57 H9
Suining *Sichuan, China* 58 B5
Suiping *China* 56 H7
Suippes *France* 19 C11
Suir → *Ireland* 12 D4
Suisse = Switzerland ■
   Europe 25 J4
Suisun City *U.S.A.* 110 G4
Suixi *China* 59 G8
Suiyang *Guizhou, China* 58 D6
Suiyang *Heilongjiang, China* 57 B16
Suizhong *China* 57 D11
Suizhou *China* 59 B9
Sujangarh *India* 68 F6
Sukabumi *Indonesia* 63 G12
Sukadana *Indonesia* 62 E4
Sukagawa *Japan* 55 F10
Sukaraja *Indonesia* 62 E4
Sukawati *Indonesia* 63 K18
Sukch'ŏn *N. Korea* 57 E13
Sukhindol *Bulgaria* 45 C9
Sukhinichi *Russia* 32 E8
Sukhona → *Russia* 52 D4
Sukhothai *Thailand* 64 D2
Sukhumi = Sokhumi *Georgia* 35 J5
Sukkur *Pakistan* 68 F3
Sukkur Barrage *Pakistan* 68 F3
Sukovo *Serbia* 44 C6
Sukri → *India* 68 G4
Sukumo *Japan* 55 H6
Sukunka → *Canada* 102 B4
Sula → *Ukraine* 33 H7
Sula, Kepulauan *Indonesia* 63 E7
Sulaco → *Honduras* 120 C2
Sulaiman Range *Pakistan* 68 D3
Sulak → *Russia* 35 J8
Sūlār *Iran* 71 D6
Sulawesi *Indonesia* 63 E6
Sulawesi Barat □ *Indonesia* 63 E5
Sulawesi Sea = Celebes Sea
   Indonesia 63 D6
Sulawesi Selatan □ *Indonesia* 63 E6
Sulawesi Tengah □ *Indonesia* 63 E6
Sulawesi Tenggara □
   Indonesia 63 E6
Sulawesi Utara □ *Indonesia* 63 D6
Sulechów *Poland* 31 F2
Sulęcin *Poland* 31 F2
Sulejów *Poland* 31 G6
Sulejówek *Poland* 31 F8
Süleymanlı *Turkey* 47 C9
Sulima *S. Leone* 82 D2
Sulina *Romania* 29 E14
Sulina, Brațul → *Romania* 29 E14
Sulingen *Germany* 24 C4
Sulița *Romania* 29 C11
Sulitjelma *Norway* 8 C17
Sułkowice *Poland* 31 J6
Sullana *Peru* 124 D2
Süller *Turkey* 47 C11
Sullivan *Ill., U.S.A.* 112 F9
Sullivan *Ind., U.S.A.* 112 F10
Sullivan *Mo., U.S.A.* 112 F8
Sullivan Bay *Canada* 102 C3
Sullivan I. = Lanbi Kyun
   Burma 65 G2
Sullom Voe *U.K.* 13 A7
Sully-sur-Loire *France* 19 E9
Sulmierzyce *Poland* 31 G4
Sulmona *Italy* 41 F10
Süloğlu *Turkey* 45 E10
Sulphur *La., U.S.A.* 116 F8
Sulphur *Okla., U.S.A.* 116 D6
Sulphur Pt. *Canada* 102 A6
Sulphur Springs *U.S.A.* 116 E7
Sultan *Canada* 104 C3
Sultan *U.S.A.* 110 C5
Sultan Dağları *Turkey* 72 C4
Sultan Hamud *Kenya* 86 C4
Sultanhisar *Turkey* 47 D10
Sultaniça *Turkey* 45 F10
Sultaniye *Turkey* 45 F12
Sultanpur *Mad. P., India* 68 H8
Sultanpur *Punjab, India* 68 D6
Sultanpur *Ut. P., India* 69 F10
Sulu Arch. *Phil.* 61 J4
Sulu Sea *E. Indies* 61 H4
Sülüklü *Turkey* 72 C5
Sululta *Ethiopia* 81 F4
Suluova *Turkey* 72 B6
Suluq *Libya* 79 B10
Sulzbach *Germany* 25 F3
Sulzbach-Rosenberg
   Germany 25 F7
Sulzberger Ice Shelf
   Antarctica 5 E13
Sumalata *Indonesia* 63 D6
Sumampa *Argentina* 126 B3
Sumatera *Indonesia* 62 D2
Sumatera Barat □ *Indonesia* 62 E2

Sumatera Utara □ *Indonesia* 62 D1
Sumatra = Sumatera
   Indonesia 62 D2
Sumava △ *Czech Rep.* 26 C6
Sumba *Indonesia* 63 F5
Sumba, Selat *Indonesia* 63 F5
Sumbawa *Indonesia* 62 F5
Sumbawa Besar *Indonesia* 62 F5
Sumbawanga □ *Tanzania* 84 F6
Sumbe *Angola* 84 G2
Sumbu △ *Zambia* 87 D3
Sumburgh Hd. *U.K.* 13 B7
Sumdeo *India* 69 D8
Sumdo *China* 69 B8
Sumedang *Indonesia* 63 G12
Sümeg *Hungary* 28 D2
Sumeih *Sudan* 81 F2
Šumen = Shumen *Bulgaria* 45 C10
Sumenep *Indonesia* 63 G15
Sumgait = Sumqayıt
   Azerbaijan 35 K9
Summer L. *U.S.A.* 108 E3
Summerland *Canada* 102 D5
Summerside *Canada* 105 C7
Summersville *U.S.A.* 113 F13
Summerville *Ga., U.S.A.* 117 D12
Summerville *S.C., U.S.A.* 117 E14
Summit Lake *Canada* 102 C4
Summit Peak *U.S.A.* 109 H10
Sumner *Iowa, U.S.A.* 112 D7
Sumner *Wash., U.S.A.* 110 C4
Sumoto *Japan* 55 G7
Šumperk *Czech Rep.* 27 B9
Sumqayıt *Azerbaijan* 35 K9
Sumter *U.S.A.* 117 E14
Sumy *Ukraine* 33 G8
Sumy □ *Ukraine* 33 G7
Sun City *S. Africa* 88 D4
Sun City *Ariz., U.S.A.* 109 K7
Sun City *Calif., U.S.A.* 111 M9
Sun City Center *U.S.A.* 117 H13
Sun Lakes *U.S.A.* 109 K8
Sun Valley *U.S.A.* 108 E6
Sunagawa *Japan* 54 C10
Sunan *N. Korea* 57 E13
Sunart, L. *U.K.* 13 E3
Sunburst *U.S.A.* 108 B8
Sunbury *Australia* 95 F3
Sunbury *U.S.A.* 115 F8
Sunchales *Argentina* 126 C3
Suncheon *S. Korea* 57 G14
Suncho Corral *Argentina* 126 B3
Sunch'on *N. Korea* 57 E13
Suncook *U.S.A.* 115 C13
Sunda, Selat *Indonesia* 62 F3
Sunda Is. *Indonesia* 96 H2
Sunda Str. = Sunda, Selat
   Indonesia 62 F3
Sunda Trench = Java
   Trench *Ind. Oc.* 52 F3
Sundance *Canada* 103 B10
Sundance *U.S.A.* 108 D11
Sundar Nagar *India* 68 D7
Sundarbans *Asia* 67 J16
Sundarbans △ *India* 69 J13
Sundargarh *India* 67 H14
Sundays = Sondags →
   S. Africa 88 E4
Sunderland *Canada* 114 B5
Sunderland *U.K.* 14 C6
Sundown △ *Australia* 95 D5
Sundre *Canada* 102 C6
Sunds *Denmark* 11 H3
Sundsvall *Sweden* 10 B11
Sundsvallsbukten *Sweden* 10 B11
Sung Hei *Vietnam* 65 G6
Sungai Acheh *Malaysia* 65 c
Sungai Kolok *Thailand* 65 J3
Sungai Lembing *Malaysia* 65 L4
Sungai Petani *Malaysia* 65 K3
Sungaigerong *Indonesia* 62 E2
Sungailiat *Indonesia* 62 E3
Sungaipenuh *Indonesia* 62 E2
Sungari = Songhua
   Jiang → *China* 60 B8
Sunghua Chiang =
   Songhua Jiang → *China* 60 B8
Sungikai *Sudan* 81 E2
Sungurlu *Turkey* 72 B6
Sunja *Croatia* 41 C13
Sunland Park *U.S.A.* 109 L10
Sunnansjö *Sweden* 10 D8
Sunndalsøra *Norway* 8 E13
Sunne *Sweden* 10 E7
Sunnemo *Sweden* 10 E7
Sunnyside *U.S.A.* 108 C4
Sunnyvale *U.S.A.* 110 H4
Sunrise Manor *U.S.A.* 111 J11
Suntar *Russia* 53 C12
Sunyani *Ghana* 82 D4
Suomenselkä *Finland* 8 E21
Suomi = Finland ■ *Europe* 8 E22
Suomussalmi *Finland* 8 D23
Suoyarvi *Russia* 32 A7
Supai *U.S.A.* 109 H7
Supaul *India* 69 F12
Superior *Ariz., U.S.A.* 109 K8

Superior *Mont., U.S.A.* 108 C6
Superior *Nebr., U.S.A.* 112 E4
Superior *Wis., U.S.A.* 112 B7
Superior, L. *N. Amer.* 104 C2
Supetar *Croatia* 41 E13
Suphan Buri *Thailand* 64 E3
Suphan Dağı *Turkey* 73 C10
Supiori *Indonesia* 63 E9
Supraśl *Poland* 31 E10
Supraśl → *Poland* 31 E9
Supung Shuiku *China* 57 D13
Sūq Suwayq *Si. Arabia* 70 E3
Suqian *China* 57 H10
Suquţra = Socotra *Yemen* 75 E5
Sūr *Lebanon* 74 B4
Şūr *Oman* 75 C6
Sur, Pt. *U.S.A.* 110 J5
Sura → *Russia* 34 C8
Surab *Pakistan* 68 E2
Surabaja = Surabaya
   Indonesia 63 G15
Surabaya *Indonesia* 63 G15
Surahammar *Sweden* 10 E10
Suraia *Romania* 29 E12
Surakarta *Indonesia* 63 G14
Surakhany *Azerbaijan* 35 K10
Šurany *Slovak Rep.* 27 C11
Surat *Australia* 95 D4
Surat *India* 66 J8
Surat Thani *Thailand* 65 H2
Suratgarh *India* 68 E5
Suraż *Poland* 31 F9
Surazh *Belarus* 32 E6
Surazh *Russia* 33 F7
Surduc *Romania* 29 C8
Surduc Pasul *Romania* 29 E8
Surdulica *Serbia* 44 D6
Surendranagar *India* 68 H4
Surf *U.S.A.* 111 L6
Surfers Paradise *Australia* 95 D5
Surgères *France* 20 B3
Surgut *Russia* 52 C8
Sùria *Spain* 38 D6
Suriapet *India* 66 L11
Surigao *Phil.* 61 G6
Surigao Strait *Phil.* 61 F6
Surin *Thailand* 64 E4
Surin Nua, Ko *Thailand* 65 H1
Surinam = Suriname ■
   S. Amer. 125 C7
Suriname ■ *S. Amer.* 125 C7
Suriname → *Suriname* 125 B7
Sûrmaq *Iran* 71 D7
Sürmene *Turkey* 73 B9
Surovikino *Russia* 35 F6
Surrey *Canada* 110 A4
Surrey □ *U.K.* 15 F7
Sursand *India* 69 F11
Sursar → *India* 69 F12
Sursee *Switz.* 25 H4
Sursk *Russia* 34 D8
Surskoye *Russia* 34 C8
Surt *Libya* 79 B9
Surt, Khalij *Libya* 79 B9
Surte *Sweden* 11 G6
Surtanahu *Pakistan* 68 F4
Surtsey *Iceland* 8 E3
Süruç *Turkey* 73 D8
Suruga-Wan *Japan* 55 G9
Susa *Italy* 40 C4
Susà → *Denmark* 11 J5
Sušac *Croatia* 41 F13
Susak *Croatia* 41 D11
Susaki *Japan* 55 H6
Susangerd *Iran* 71 D6
Susanville *U.S.A.* 108 F3
Susch *Switz.* 25 J6
Suşehri *Turkey* 73 B8
Susleni *Moldova* 29 C13
Susner *India* 68 H7
Susong *China* 59 B11
Susquehanna *U.S.A.* 115 E9
Susquehanna → *U.S.A.* 115 G8
Susques *Argentina* 126 A2
Sussex *Canada* 105 C6
Sussex *U.S.A.* 115 E10
Sussex, E. □ *U.K.* 15 G8
Sussex, W. □ *U.K.* 15 G7
Sustut → *Canada* 102 B3
Susuman *Russia* 53 C15
Susunu *Indonesia* 63 E8
Susurluk *Turkey* 47 B10
Susuz *Turkey* 73 B10
Susz *Poland* 30 E6
Sutherland *S. Africa* 88 E3
Sutherland *U.K.* 13 C4
Sutherland *U.S.A.* 112 E3
Sutherland Falls *N.Z.* 91 F1
Sutherlin *U.S.A.* 108 E2
Suthri *India* 68 H3
Sutjeska △ *Bos.-H.* 28 G3
Sutlej → *Pakistan* 68 E4
Sutter *U.S.A.* 110 F5
Sutter Buttes *U.S.A.* 110 F5

Sutter Creek *U.S.A.* 110 G6
Sutton *Canada* 115 A12
Sutton *Nebr., U.S.A.* 112 E5
Sutton *W. Va., U.S.A.* 113 F13
Sutton → *Canada* 104 A3
Sutton Coldfield *U.K.* 15 E6
Sutton in Ashfield *U.K.* 14 D6
Sutton L. *Canada* 104 B3
Suttor → *Australia* 94 C4
Suttsu *Japan* 54 C10
Suva *Fiji* 91 a
Suva Gora *Macedonia* 44 E5
Suva Planina *Serbia* 44 C6
Suva Reka *Serbia* 44 D4
Suvorov *Russia* 32 E9
Suvorov Is. = Suwarrow
   Is. *Cook Is.* 97 J11
Suvorove *Ukraine* 29 E13
Suvorovo *Bulgaria* 45 C11
Suwałki *Poland* 30 D9
Suwana *Indonesia* 63 K18
Suwannaphum *Thailand* 64 E4
Suwannee → *U.S.A.* 117 G13
Suwanose-Jima *Japan* 55 K4
Suwarrow Is. *Cook Is.* 97 J11
Suwayq aş Şuqban *Iraq* 70 D5
Suweis, Khalig el *Egypt* 80 J8
Suweis, Qanâ es *Egypt* 80 H8
Suwon *S. Korea* 57 F14
Suzdal *Russia* 32 D11
Suzhou *Anhui, China* 56 H9
Suzhou *Jiangsu, China* 59 B13
Suzu *Japan* 55 F8
Suzu-Misaki *Japan* 55 F8
Suzuka *Japan* 55 G8
Suzzara *Italy* 40 D7
Svalbard *Arctic* 4 B8
Svalbard Radio =
   Longyearbyen *Svalbard* 4 B8
Svalöv *Sweden* 11 J7
Svalyava *Ukraine* 28 B7
Svaneke *Denmark* 11 J9
Svängsta *Sweden* 11 H8
Svanskog *Sweden* 10 E6
Svappavaara *Sweden* 8 C19
Svärdsjö *Sweden* 10 D9
Svartå *Sweden* 10 E8
Svartisen *Norway* 8 C15
Svartvik *Sweden* 10 B11
Svatove *Ukraine* 33 H10
Svatovo = Svatove *Ukraine* 33 H10
Svay Chek *Cambodia* 64 F4
Svay Rieng *Cambodia* 65 G5
Svealand *Sweden* 10 D9
Sveg *Sweden* 10 B8
Svendborg *Denmark* 11 J4
Svenljunga *Sweden* 11 G7
Svenstavik *Sweden* 10 B8
Svenstrup *Denmark* 11 H3
Sverdlovsk *Ukraine* 33 H10
Sverdrup Chan. *Canada* 101 B10
Sverdrup Is. *Canada* 101 B10
Sverige = Sweden ■ *Europe* 9 H16
Svetac *Croatia* 41 E12
Sveti Nikola, Prokhod
   Europe 44 C6
Sveti Nikole *Macedonia* 44 E5
Sveti Rok *Croatia* 41 D12
Svetlaya *Russia* 54 A9
Svetlogorsk =
   Svyetlahorsk *Belarus* 23 B15
Svetlogorsk *Russia* 30 D7
Svetlograd *Russia* 35 H6
Svetlovodsk = Svitlovodsk
   Ukraine 33 H7
Svetlyy *Russia* 30 D7
Svidník *Slovak Rep.* 27 B14
Svilaja Planina *Croatia* 41 E13
Svilajnac *Serbia* 44 B5
Svilengrad *Bulgaria* 45 E10
Svir → *Russia* 32 B7
Sviritsa *Russia* 32 B7
Svishtov *Bulgaria* 45 C9
Svislach *Belarus* 31 F11
Svitava → *Czech Rep.* 27 B9
Svitavy *Czech Rep.* 27 B9
Svitlovodsk *Ukraine* 33 H7
Svizzera = Switzerland ■
   Europe 25 J4
Svobodnyy *Russia* 53 D13
Svoge *Bulgaria* 44 D7
Svolvær *Norway* 8 B16
Svratka → *Czech Rep.* 27 B9
Svrljig *Serbia* 44 C6
Svyetlahorsk *Belarus* 23 B15
Swabian Alps =
   Schwäbische Alb *Germany* 25 G5
Swaffham *U.K.* 15 E8
Swains I. *Amer. Samoa* 97 J11
Swainsboro *U.S.A.* 117 E13
Swakop → *Namibia* 88 C2
Swakopmund *Namibia* 88 C1
Swale → *U.K.* 14 C6
Swan → *Australia* 93 F2
Swan → *Canada* 103 C8
Swan Hill *Australia* 95 F3

Swan Hills *Canada* 102 C5
Swan Is. = Santanilla, Is.
   Honduras 120 C3
Swan L. *Canada* 103 C8
Swan Ra. *U.S.A.* 108 C7
Swan River *Canada* 103 C8
Swanage *U.K.* 15 G6
Swansea *Australia* 95 G4
Swansea *Canada* 114 C5
Swansea *U.K.* 15 F4
Swansea □ *U.K.* 15 F3
Swar → *Pakistan* 69 B5
Swartberg *S. Africa* 88 E3
Swartmodder *S. Africa* 88 D3
Swartnossob → *Namibia* 88 C2
Swartruggens *S. Africa* 88 D4
Swarzędz *Poland* 31 F4
Swastika *Canada* 104 C3
Swatow = Shantou *China* 59 F11
Swaziland ■ *Africa* 89 D5
Sweden ■ *Europe* 9 H16
Swedru *Ghana* 83 D4
Sweet Grass *U.S.A.* 108 B8
Sweet Home *U.S.A.* 108 D2
Sweetwater *Nev., U.S.A.* 110 G7
Sweetwater *Tenn., U.S.A.* 117 D12
Sweetwater *Tex., U.S.A.* 116 E4
Sweetwater → *U.S.A.* 108 E10
Swellendam *S. Africa* 88 E3
Swider → *Poland* 31 F8
Świdnica *Poland* 31 H3
Świdnik *Poland* 31 G9
Świdwin *Poland* 30 E2
Świebodzice *Poland* 31 H3
Świebodzin *Poland* 31 F2
Świecie *Poland* 30 E5
Swierzawa *Poland* 31 G2
Świętokrzyski △ *Poland* 31 H7
Świętokrzyskie □ *Poland* 31 H7
Świętokrzyskie, Góry *Poland* 31 H7
Swift → *Canada* 103 C7
Swift Current *Canada* 103 C7
Swiftcurrent → *Canada* 103 C7
Swilly, L. *Ireland* 12 A4
Swindon *U.K.* 15 F6
Swindon □ *U.K.* 15 F6
Swinemünde =
   Świnoujście *Poland* 30 E1
Świnoujście *Poland* 30 E1
Switzerland ■ *Europe* 25 J4
Swords *Ireland* 12 C5
Swoyerville *U.S.A.* 115 E9
Syasstroy *Russia* 32 B7
Sychevka *Russia* 32 E8
Sycόw *Poland* 31 G4
Syddanmark □ *Denmark* 11 J2
Sydenham → *Canada* 114 D2
Sydney *Australia* 95 E5
Sydney *Canada* 105 C7
Sydney L. *Canada* 103 C10
Sydney Mines *Canada* 105 C7
Sydprøven = Alluitsup Paa
   Greenland 4 C5
Sydra, G. of = Surt, Khalij
   Libya 79 B9
Syeverodonetsk *Ukraine* 33 H10
Syke *Germany* 24 C4
Sykesville *U.S.A.* 114 E6
Syktyvkar *Russia* 52 C6
Sylacauga *U.S.A.* 117 E11
Sylarna *Sweden* 8 E15
Sylhet *Bangla.* 67 G17
Sylhet □ *Bangla.* 67 G17
Sylt *Germany* 24 A4
Sylvan Beach *U.S.A.* 115 C9
Sylvan Lake *Canada* 102 C6
Sylvania *Ga., U.S.A.* 117 E13
Sylvania *Ohio, U.S.A.* 113 E12
Sylvester *U.S.A.* 117 F13
Sym → *Russia* 52 C9
Synelnykove *Ukraine* 33 H8
Synevyr △ *Ukraine* 29 B8
Synevyrska Polyana *Ukraine* 29 B8
Synnot Ra. *Australia* 92 C4
Synyak *Ukraine* 28 B7
Syowa *Antarctica* 5 C5
Syracuse *Kans., U.S.A.* 112 G3
Syracuse *N.Y., U.S.A.* 115 C8
Syracuse *Nebr., U.S.A.* 112 E5
Syrdarya → *Kazakhstan* 52 E7
Syria ■ *Asia* 73 E8
Syrian Desert = Shām,
   Bādiyat ash *Asia* 70 C5
Syros *Greece* 46 D6
Sysslebäck *Sweden* 10 D6
Syzran *Russia* 34 D9
Szabolcs-Szatmár-Bereg □
   Hungary 28 B6
Szadek *Poland* 31 G5
Szamocin *Poland* 31 E4
Szamos → *Hungary* 28 B7
Szamotuly *Poland* 31 F3
Száraz → *Hungary* 28 D6
Szarvas *Hungary* 28 D5
Százhalombatta *Hungary* 28 C3
Szczawnica *Poland* 31 J7
Szczebrzeszyn *Poland* 31 H9

Szczecin *Poland* 30 E1
Szczecinek *Poland* 30 E3
Szczeciński, Zalew =
   Stettiner Haff *Germany* 24 B10
Szczekociny *Poland* 31 H6
Szczucin *Poland* 31 H8
Szczuczyn *Poland* 30 E9
Szczyrk *Poland* 31 J6
Szczytna *Poland* 31 H3
Szczytno *Poland* 30 E7
Szechuan = Sichuan □
   China 58 B5
Szechwan = Sichuan □
   China 58 B5
Szécsény *Hungary* 28 B4
Szeged *Hungary* 28 D5
Szeghalom *Hungary* 28 C6
Székesfehérvár *Hungary* 28 C3
Szekszárd *Hungary* 28 D3
Szendrő *Hungary* 28 B5
Szentendre *Hungary* 28 C4
Szentes *Hungary* 28 D5
Szentgotthárd *Hungary* 28 D1
Szentlőrinc *Hungary* 28 D3
Szerencs *Hungary* 28 B6
Szigetszentmiklós *Hungary* 28 C4
Szigetvár *Hungary* 28 D2
Szikszó *Hungary* 28 B5
Szklarska Poreba *Poland* 31 H2
Szkwa → *Poland* 31 E8
Szob *Hungary* 28 C3
Szolnok *Hungary* 28 C5
Szombathely *Hungary* 28 C1
Szprotawa *Poland* 31 G2
Sztum *Poland* 30 E6
Sztutowo *Poland* 30 D6
Szubin *Poland* 31 E4
Szydłowiec *Poland* 31 G7
Szypliszki *Poland* 30 D10

T

Ta Khli Khok *Thailand* 64 E3
Ta Lai *Vietnam* 65 G6
Tab *Hungary* 28 D3
Tabacal *Argentina* 126 A3
Tabaco *Phil.* 61 E5
Tabagné *Ivory C.* 82 D4
Ṭābah *Si. Arabia* 70 E4
Tabanan *Indonesia* 63 K18
Tabankort *Niger* 83 B5
Ṭabas *Khorāsān, Iran* 71 C9
Ṭabas *Yazd, Iran* 71 C8
Tabasará, Serranía de
   Panama 120 E3
Tabasco □ *Mexico* 119 D6
Tabāsīn *Iran* 71 D8
Tabatinga, Serra da *Brazil* 125 F10
Taber *Canada* 102 D6
Taberg *Sweden* 11 G8
Taberg *U.S.A.* 115 C9
Tabla *Niger* 83 C5
Tablas *Phil.* 61 E5
Tablas de Daimiel △ *Spain* 37 F7
Tablas Strait *Phil.* 61 E4
Table, Pte. de la *Réunion* 85 c
Table B. *Canada* 105 B8
Table B. *S. Africa* 88 E2
Table Mt. *S. Africa* 88 E2
Table Rock L. *U.S.A.* 112 G7
Tabletop, Mt. *Australia* 94 C4
Tábor *Czech Rep.* 26 B7
Tabora *Tanzania* 84 D3
Tabora □ *Tanzania* 86 D3
Tabou *Ivory C.* 82 E3
Tabrīz *Iran* 73 C12
Tabuaeran *Kiribati* 97 G12
Tabuenca *Spain* 38 D3
Tabūk *Si. Arabia* 70 D3
Tabūk □ *Si. Arabia* 70 E3
Taburno-Camposauro △
   Italy 43 A7
Täby *Sweden* 10 E12
Tacámbaro de Codallos
   Mexico 118 D4
Tacheng *China* 60 B3
Tach'i *Taiwan* 59 E13
Tachia *Taiwan* 59 E13
Tach'ing Shan = Daqing
   Shan *China* 56 D6
Tachov *Czech Rep.* 26 B5
Tácina → *Italy* 43 D9
Tacloban *Phil.* 61 F6
Tacna *Peru* 124 G4
Tacoma *U.S.A.* 110 C4
Tacuarembó *Uruguay* 127 C4
Tademaït, Plateau du *Algeria* 78 C6
Tadio, L. *Ivory C.* 82 D3
Tadjoura *Djibouti* 81 E5
Tadjoura, Golfe de *Djibouti* 81 E5
Tadmor *N.Z.* 91 D4
Tadoule L. *Canada* 103 B9
Tadoussac *Canada* 105 C6
Tadrés △ *Niger* 83 B6
Tadzhikistan =
   Tajikistan ■ *Asia* 52 F8

Taegu = Daegu *S. Korea* **57** G15
Taegwan *N. Korea* **57** D13
Taejŏn = Daejeon *S. Korea* **57** F14
Taen, Ko *Thailand* **65** b
Tafalla *Spain* **38** C3
Tafar *Sudan* **81** F2
Tafelbaai = Table B. *S. Africa* **88** E2
Tafermaar *Indonesia* **63** F8
Tafí Viejo *Argentina* **126** B2
Tafīhān *Iran* **71** D7
Tafiré *Ivory C.* **82** D4
Tafo *Ghana* **83** D4
Tafresh *Iran* **71** C6
Taft *Iran* **71** D7
Taft *Phil.* **61** F6
Taft *U.S.A.* **111** K7
Taftan *Pakistan* **66** E2
Taftān, Kūh-e *Iran* **71** D9
Taga *Samoa* **91** b
Taga Dzong *Bhutan* **67** F16
Taganrog *Russia* **33** J10
Taganrogskiy Zaliv *Russia* **33** J10
Tagânt □ *Mauritania* **82** B3
Tagatay *Phil.* **61** D4
Tagbilaran *Phil.* **61** G5
Tággia *Italy* **40** E4
Tagish *Canada* **102** A2
Tagish L. *Canada* **102** A2
Tagliacozzo *Italy* **41** F10
Tagliamento → *Italy* **41** C10
Táglio di Po *Italy* **41** D9
Tago *Phil.* **61** G7
Tagomago *Spain* **48** B8
Tagourâret *Mauritania* **82** B3
Taguatinga *Brazil* **125** F10
Tagudin *Phil.* **61** C4
Tagum *Phil.* **61** H6
Tagus = Tejo → *Europe* **37** F2
Tahakopa *N.Z.* **91** G2
Tahan, Gunung *Malaysia* **65** K4
Tahat *Algeria* **78** D7
Tāherī *Iran* **71** E7
Tahiti *French Polynesia* **91** d
Tahiti, I. *Tahiti* **91** d
Tahlequah *U.S.A.* **116** D7
Tahoe, L. *U.S.A.* **110** G6
Tahoe City *U.S.A.* **110** F6
Tahoka *U.S.A.* **116** E4
Taholah *U.S.A.* **110** C2
Tahoua *Niger* **83** C6
Tahrūd *Iran* **71** D8
Tahsis *Canada* **102** D3
Tahta *Egypt* **80** B3
Tahtaköprü *Turkey* **45** G13
Tahtalı Dağları *Turkey* **72** C7
Tahulandang *Indonesia* **63** D7
Tahuna *Indonesia* **63** D7
Taï *Ivory C.* **82** D3
Taï △ *Ivory C.* **82** D3
Tai Hu *China* **59** B12
Tai Rom Yen △ *Thailand* **65** H2
Tai Shan *China* **57** F9
Tai'an *China* **57** F9
Taiarapu, Presqu'île de *Tahiti* **91** d
Taibei = T'aipei *Taiwan* **59** E13
Taibique *Canary Is.* **48** G2
Taibus Qi *China* **56** D8
Taicang *China* **59** B13
T'aichung *Taiwan* **59** E13
Taieri → *N.Z.* **91** G3
Taigu *China* **56** F7
Taihang Shan *China* **56** G7
Taihape *N.Z.* **91** C5
Taihe *Anhui, China* **56** H8
Taihe *Jiangxi, China* **59** D10
Taihu *China* **59** B11
Taijiang *China* **58** D7
Taikang *China* **56** G8
Tailem Bend *Australia* **95** F2
Tailfingen *Germany* **25** G5
T'ailuko *Taiwan* **59** E13
Taimyr Peninsula =
    Taymyr, Poluostrov
    Russia **53** B11
Tain *U.K.* **13** D4
T'ainan *Taiwan* **59** F13
Taining *China* **59** D11
T'aipei *Taiwan* **59** E13
Taiping *China* **59** B12
Taiping *Malaysia* **65** K3
Taipingzhen *China* **56** H6
Tairbeart = Tarbert *U.K.* **13** D2
Taishan *China* **59** F9
Taishun *China* **59** D12
Taita Hills *Kenya* **86** C4
Taitao, Pen. de *Chile* **128** F2
T'aitung *Taiwan* **59** F13
Taivalkoski *Finland* **8** D23
Taiwan ■ *Asia* **59** F13
Taiwan Strait *Asia* **59** E12
Taixing *China* **59** A13
Taiyara *Sudan* **81** E3
Taiyiba *Israel* **74** C4
Taiyuan *China* **56** F7
Taizhong = T'aichung
    Taiwan **59** E13
Taizhou *China* **59** A12

Taizhou Liedao *China* **59** C13
Ta'izz *Yemen* **75** E3
Tájābād *Iran* **71** D7
Tajikistan ■ *Asia* **52** F8
Tajima *Japan* **55** F9
Tajo = Tejo → *Europe* **37** F2
Tajrīsh *Iran* **71** C6
Tak *Thailand* **64** D2
Takāb *Iran* **73** D12
Takachiho *Japan* **55** H5
Takachu *Botswana* **88** C3
Takada *Japan* **55** F9
Takahagi *Japan* **55** F10
Takaka *N.Z.* **91** D4
Takamaka *Seychelles* **85** b
Takamatsu *Japan* **55** G7
Takaoka *Japan* **55** F8
Takapuna *N.Z.* **91** B5
Takasaki *Japan* **55** F9
Takatsuki *Japan* **55** G7
Takaungu *Kenya* **86** C4
Takayama *Japan* **55** F8
Take-Shima *Japan* **55** J5
Takefu *Japan* **55** G8
Takengon *Indonesia* **62** D1
Takeo *Japan* **55** H5
Tåkern *Sweden* **11** F8
Takeshima = Tok-do *Asia* **55** F5
Tākestān *Iran* **71** C6
Taketa *Japan* **55** H5
Takev *Cambodia* **65** G5
Takh *India* **69** C7
Takht-Sulaiman *Pakistan* **68** D3
Takikawa *Japan* **54** C10
Takla L. *Canada* **102** B3
Takla Landing *Canada* **102** B3
Takla Makan *China* **60** C3
Taklamakan Shamo =
    Takla Makan *China* **60** C3
Taku → *Canada* **102** B2
Takua Thung *Thailand* **65** a
Takum *Nigeria* **83** D6
Tal Halāl *Iran* **71** D7
Tala *Uruguay* **127** C4
Talachyn *Belarus* **32** E5
Talacogan *Phil.* **61** G6
Talagang *Pakistan* **68** C5
Talagante *Chile* **126** C1
Talak *Niger* **83** B6
Talamanca, Cordillera de
    Cent. Amer. **120** E3
Talant *France* **19** E11
Talara *Peru* **124** D2
Talas *Kyrgyzstan* **52** E8
Talas *Turkey* **72** C6
Talâta *Egypt* **74** E1
Talata Mafara *Nigeria* **83** C6
Talaud, Kepulauan *Indonesia* **63** D7
Talaud Is. = Talaud,
    Kepulauan *Indonesia* **63** D7
Talavera de la Reina *Spain* **36** F6
Talavera la Real *Spain* **37** G4
Talayan *Phil.* **61** H6
Talayuela *Spain* **36** F5
Talbandh *India* **69** H12
Talbert, Sillon de *France* **18** D3
Talbot, C. *Australia* **92** B4
Talbragar → *Australia* **95** E4
Talca *Chile* **126** D1
Talcahuano *Chile* **126** D1
Talcher *India* **67** J14
Talcho *Niger* **83** C5
Taldy Kurgan =
    Taldyqorghan *Kazakhstan* **52** E8
Taldyqorghan *Kazakhstan* **52** E8
Tālesh *Iran* **73** D13
Tālesh, Kūhhā-ye *Iran* **73** D13
Talguharai *Sudan* **80** D4
Tali Post *Sudan* **81** F3
Taliabu *Indonesia* **63** E6
Talibon *Phil.* **63** B6
Talibong, Ko *Thailand* **65** J2
Talihina *U.S.A.* **116** D7
Talisayan *Phil.* **61** G6
Taliwang *Indonesia* **62** F5
Tall 'Afar *Iraq* **73** D10
Tall Kalakh *Syria* **74** A5
Talla *Egypt* **80** J7
Talladega *U.S.A.* **117** E11
Tallahassee *U.S.A.* **117** F12
Tallangatta *Australia* **95** F4
Tallard *France* **21** D10
Tållberg *Sweden* **10** D9
Tallering Pk. *Australia* **93** E2
Talli *Pakistan* **68** E3
Tallinn *Estonia* **32** C3
Tallmadge *U.S.A.* **114** E3
Tallulah *U.S.A.* **116** E9
Tălmaciu *Romania* **29** E9
Talmont-St-Hilaire *France* **20** B2
Talne *Ukraine* **33** H6
Talnoye = Talne *Ukraine* **33** H6
Talodi *Sudan* **81** E3
Talovaya *Russia* **34** E5
Taloyoak *Canada* **100** C10
Talpa de Allende *Mexico* **118** C4
Talparo *Trin. & Tob.* **125** K15

Talsi *Latvia* **30** A9
Talsi □ *Latvia* **30** A9
Taltal *Chile* **126** B1
Taltson → *Canada* **102** A6
Talwood *Australia* **95** D4
Talyawalka Cr. → *Australia* **95** E3
Tam Ky *Vietnam* **64** E7
Tam Quan *Vietnam* **64** E7
Tama *U.S.A.* **112** E7
Tama △ *Ethiopia* **81** F4
Tama-ga-Shima *Japan* **55** J5
Tamale *Ghana* **83** D4
Taman *Russia* **33** K9
Taman Negara △ *Malaysia* **65** K4
Tamani *Mali* **82** C3
Tamano *Japan* **55** G6
Tamanrasset *Algeria* **78** D7
Tamaqua *U.S.A.* **115** F9
Tamar → *U.K.* **15** G3
Tamarin *Mauritius* **85** d
Tamarinda *Spain* **48** B10
Tamarite de Litera *Spain* **38** D5
Tamashima *Japan* **55** G6
Tamási *Hungary* **28** D3
Tamaské *Niger* **83** C6
Tamatave = Toamasina
    Madag. **89** B8
Tamaulipas □ *Mexico* **119** C5
Tamaulipas, Sierra de
    Mexico **119** C5
Tamazula *Mexico* **118** C3
Tamazunchale *Mexico* **119** C5
Tamba-Dabatou *Guinea* **82** C2
Tambach *Kenya* **86** B4
Tambacounda *Senegal* **82** C2
Tambacounda □ *Senegal* **82** C2
Tambelan, Kepulauan
    Indonesia **62** D3
Tambellup *Australia* **93** F2
Tambo *Australia* **94** C4
Tambo de Mora *Peru* **124** F3
Tambohorano *Madag.* **89** B7
Tambora *Indonesia* **62** F5
Tamboril *Indonesia* **63** G15
Tambov *Russia* **34** D5
Tambov □ *Russia* **34** D5
Tambre → *Spain* **36** C2
Tambuku *Indonesia* **63** G15
Tambura *Sudan* **81** F2
Tâmchekket *Mauritania* **82** B2
Tâmega → *Portugal* **36** D2
Tamenglong *India* **67** G18
Tamgué, Massif du *Guinea* **82** C2
Tamiahua, L. de *Mexico* **119** C5
Tamil Nadu □ *India* **66** P10
Tamis → *Serbia* **28** F5
Tamluk *India* **69** H12
Tammerfors = Tampere
    Finland **32** B2
Tammisaari *Finland* **32** B2
Tämnaren *Sweden* **10** D11
Tamo Abu, Banjaran
    Malaysia **62** D5
Tampa *U.S.A.* **117** H13
Tampa, Tanjung *Indonesia* **63** K19
Tampa B. *U.S.A.* **117** H13
Tampere *Finland* **32** B2
Tampico *Mexico* **119** C5
Tampin *Malaysia* **65** L4
Tampoi *Malaysia* **65** d
Tamsweg *Austria* **26** D6
Tamu *Burma* **67** G19
Tamuja → *Spain* **37** F4
Tamworth *Australia* **95** E5
Tamworth *Canada* **114** B8
Tamworth *U.K.* **15** E6
Tan An *Vietnam* **65** G6
Tan Chau *Vietnam* **65** G5
Tan-Tan *Morocco* **78** C3
Tana → *Kenya* **86** C5
Tana → *Norway* **8** A23
Tana, L. *Ethiopia* **81** E4
Tana River Primate △ *Kenya* **86** C5
Tanabe *Japan* **55** H7
Tanafjorden *Norway* **8** A23
Tanahbala *Indonesia* **62** E1
Tanahgrogot *Indonesia* **62** E5
Tanahjampea *Indonesia* **63** F6
Tanahmasa *Indonesia* **62** E1
Tanahmerah *Indonesia* **63** F10
Tanakpur *India* **69** E9
Tanakura *Japan* **55** F10
Tanami Desert *Australia* **92** C5
Tanami Mine *Australia* **92** C4
Tananarive =
    Antananarivo *Madag.* **89** B8
Tánaro → *Italy* **40** D5
Tancheng *China* **57** G10
Tanch'ŏn *N. Korea* **57** D15
Tanda *Ut. P., India* **69** F9
Tanda *Ut. P., India* **69** E8
Tanda *Ivory C.* **82** D4
Tandag *Phil.* **61** G7
Tandaia *Tanzania* **87** D3
Tăndărei *Romania* **29** F12
Tandaué *Angola* **88** B2
Tandil *Argentina* **126** D4
Tandil, Sa. del *Argentina* **126** D4
Tandlianwala *Pakistan* **68** D5

Tando Adam *Pakistan* **68** G3
Tando Allahyar *Pakistan* **68** G3
Tando Bago *Pakistan* **68** G3
Tando Mohomed Khan
    Pakistan **68** G3
Tandou L. *Australia* **95** E3
Tandoureh △ *Iran* **70** B8
Tandragee *U.K.* **12** B5
Tandsjöborg *Sweden* **10** C8
Tane-ga-Shima *Japan* **55** J5
Taneatua *N.Z.* **91** C6
Tanen Tong Dan = Dawna
    Ra. *Burma* **64** D2
Tanew → *Poland* **31** H9
Tanezrouft *Algeria* **78** D6
Tang, Koh *Cambodia* **65** G4
Tang, Ra's-e *Iran* **71** E8
Tang Krasang *Cambodia* **64** F5
Tanga *Tanzania* **86** D4
Tanga □ *Tanzania* **86** D4
Tanganyika, L. *Africa* **86** D3
Tangaza *Nigeria* **83** C5
Tanger *Morocco* **78** A4
Tangerang *Indonesia* **63** G12
Tangerhütte *Germany* **24** C7
Tangermünde *Germany* **24** C7
Tanggu *China* **57** E9
Tanggula Shan *China* **60** C4
Tanghe *China* **56** H7
Tanghla Range =
    Tanggula Shan *China* **60** C4
Tangier = Tanger *Morocco* **78** A4
Tangorin *Australia* **94** C3
Tangorombohitr'i Makay
    Madag. **89** C8
Tangshan *China* **57** E10
Tangtou *China* **57** G10
Tanguiéta *Benin* **83** C5
Tangxi *China* **59** C12
Tangyan He → *China* **58** C7
Tanimbar, Kepulauan
    Indonesia **63** F8
Tanimbar Is. = Tanimbar,
    Kepulauan *Indonesia* **63** F8
Taninthari = Tenasserim
    Burma **65** F2
Tanjay *Phil.* **61** G5
Tanjong Malim *Malaysia* **65** L3
Tanjong Pelepas *Malaysia* **65** d
Tanjore = Thanjavur *India* **66** P11
Tanjung *Indonesia* **62** E5
Tanjung *Phil.* **62** E5
Tanjung Tokong *Malaysia* **65** c
Tanjungbalai *Indonesia* **62** D1
Tanjungbatu *Indonesia* **62** D5
Tanjungkarang
    Telukbetung *Indonesia* **62** F3
Tanjungpandan *Indonesia* **62** E3
Tanjungpinang *Indonesia* **62** D2
Tanjungredeb *Indonesia* **62** D5
Tanjungselor *Indonesia* **62** D5
Tank *Pakistan* **68** C4
Tankhala *India* **68** J5
Tankwa-Karoo △ *S. Africa* **88** E2
Tännäs *Sweden* **10** B6
Tannersville *U.S.A.* **115** E9
Tannis Bugt *Denmark* **11** G4
Tannu Ola *Asia* **53** D10
Tannum Sands *Australia* **94** C5
Tano → *Ghana* **82** D4
Tanon Str. *Phil.* **61** G5
Tanout *Niger* **83** C6
Tanshui *Taiwan* **59** E13
Tansilla *Burkina Faso* **82** C4
Tanta *Egypt* **80** H7
Tantoyuca *Mexico* **119** C5
Tantung = Dandong *China* **57** D13
Tanumshede *Sweden* **11** F5
Tanunda *Australia* **95** E2
Tanus *France* **20** D6
Tanzania ■ *Africa* **86** D3
Tanzilla → *Canada* **102** B2
Tao, Ko *Thailand* **65** G2
Tao'an = Taonan *China* **57** B12
Tao'er He → *China* **57** B13
Taohua Dao *China* **59** C14
Taolanaro *Madag.* **89** D8
Taole *China* **56** E4
Taonan *China* **57** B12
Taormina *Italy* **43** E8
Taos *U.S.A.* **109** H11
Taoudenni *Mali* **78** D5
Taoyuan *China* **59** C8
T'aoyüan *Taiwan* **59** E13
Tapa *Estonia* **32** C3
Tapa Shan = Daba Shan
    China **58** B7
Tapachula *Mexico* **119** E6
Tapah *Malaysia* **65** K3
Tapajós → *Brazil* **125** D8
Tapaktuan *Indonesia* **62** D1
Tapanahoni → *Suriname* **125** C8
Tapanui *N.Z.* **91** F2
Tapauá → *Brazil* **124** E6
Tapes *Brazil* **127** C5
Tapeta *Liberia* **82** D3
Taphan Hin *Thailand* **64** D3

Tapia de Casariego *Spain* **36** B4
Tapirapecó, Serra *Venezuela* **124** C6
Tapo-Capara △ *Venezuela* **121** E5
Tapolca *Hungary* **28** D2
Tapti → *India* **66** J8
Tapuae-o-Uenuku *N.Z.* **91** E4
Tapul Group *Phil.* **61** J4
Tapurucuará *Brazil* **124** D5
Taquara *Brazil* **127** B5
Taquari → *Brazil* **124** G7
Tara *Australia* **95** D5
Tara *Canada* **114** B3
Tara *Russia* **52** D8
Tara *Zambia* **87** F2
Tara → *Montenegro* **44** C2
Tara △ *Serbia* **44** C3
Taraba □ *Nigeria* **83** D7
Taraba → *Nigeria* **83** D7
Tarābulus *Lebanon* **74** A4
Tarābulus *Libya* **79** B8
Taraclia *Taraclia, Moldova* **29** E13
Taraclia *Tighina, Moldova* **29** D14
Taradehi *India* **69** H8
Tarajalejo *Canary Is.* **48** F5
Tarakan *Indonesia* **62** D5
Tarakit, Mt. *Kenya* **86** B4
Tarama-Jima *Japan* **55** M2
Taran, Mys *Russia* **30** D6
Taranagar *India* **68** E6
Taranaki □ *N.Z.* **91** C5
Taranaki, Mt. *N.Z.* **91** C5
Tarancón *Spain* **38** E1
Tarangire △ *Tanzania* **86** C4
Taransay *U.K.* **13** D1
Táranto *Italy* **43** B10
Táranto, G. di *Italy* **43** B10
Tarapacá *Colombia* **124** D5
Tarapacá □ *Chile* **126** A2
Tarapoto *Peru* **124** E3
Tarare *France* **21** C8
Tararua Ra. *N.Z.* **91** D5
Tarascon *France* **21** E8
Tarascon-sur-Ariège *France* **20** F5
Tarashcha *Ukraine* **23** D16
Tarauacá *Brazil* **124** E4
Tarauacá → *Brazil* **124** E5
Taravao *Tahiti* **91** d
Taravao, Isthme de *Tahiti* **91** d
Taravo → *France* **21** G12
Tarawa *Kiribati* **96** G9
Tarawera *N.Z.* **91** C6
Tarawera, L. *N.Z.* **91** C6
Taraz *Kazakhstan* **52** E8
Tarazona *Spain* **38** D3
Tarazona de la Mancha
    Spain **39** F3
Tarbagatay, Khrebet
    Kazakhstan **52** E9
Tarbat Ness *U.K.* **13** D5
Tarbela Dam *Pakistan* **68** B5
Tarbert *Ireland* **12** D2
Tarbert *Argyll & Bute, U.K.* **13** F3
Tarbert *W. Isles, U.K.* **13** D2
Tarbes *France* **20** E4
Tarboro *U.S.A.* **117** D16
Tărcău, Munții *Romania* **29** D11
Tarcento *Italy* **41** B10
Tarcoola *Australia* **95** E1
Tarcoon *Australia* **95** E4
Tardets-Sorholus *France* **20** E3
Tardoire → *France* **20** C4
Taree *Australia* **95** E5
Tarfa, W. el → *Egypt* **80** B3
Tarfaya *Morocco* **78** C3
Târgoviște *Romania* **29** F10
Târgu Bujor *Romania* **29** E12
Târgu Cărbunești *Romania* **29** F8
Târgu Frumos *Romania* **29** C12
Târgu Jiu *Romania* **29** E8
Târgu Lăpuș *Romania* **29** C8
Târgu Mureș *Romania* **29** D9
Târgu Neamț *Romania* **29** C11
Târgu Ocna *Romania* **29** D11
Târgu Secuiesc *Romania* **29** E11
Târgușor *Romania* **29** F13
Tărhăus, Vf. *Romania* **29** D11
Tarif *U.A.E.* **71** E7
Tarifa *Spain* **37** J5
Tarija *Bolivia* **126** A3
Tarija □ *Bolivia* **126** A3
Tariku → *Indonesia* **63** E9
Tarim He → *China* **60** C3
Tarim Pendi *China* **60** C3
Taritatu → *Indonesia* **63** E9
Tarka → *S. Africa* **88** E4
Tarka La *Bhutan* **69** F13
Tarkastad *S. Africa* **88** E4
Tarkhankut, Mys *Ukraine* **33** K7
Tarko Sale *Russia* **52** C8
Tarkwa *Ghana* **82** D4
Tarlac *Phil.* **61** D4
Tarma *Peru* **124** F3
Tarn □ *France* **20** E6

Tarn → *France* **20** D5
Tarn-et-Garonne □ *France* **20** D5
Tarna → *Hungary* **28** C4
Târnava Mare → *Romania* **29** D8
Târnava Mică → *Romania* **29** D8
Târnăveni *Romania* **29** D9
Tarnica *Poland* **31** J9
Tarnobrzeg *Poland* **31** H8
Tarnogród *Poland* **31** H9
Tarnos *France* **20** E2
Târnova *Moldova* **29** B12
Târnova *Romania* **28** E6
Tarnów *Poland* **31** H8
Tarnowskie Góry *Poland* **31** H5
Tärnsjö *Sweden* **10** D10
Táro → *Italy* **40** C7
Țărom *Iran* **71** D7
Taroom *Australia* **95** D4
Taroudannt *Morocco* **78** B4
Tarp *Germany* **24** A5
Tarpon Springs *U.S.A.* **117** G13
Tarquínia *Italy* **41** F8
Tarrafal *C. Verde Is.* **78** b
Tarragona *Spain* **38** D6
Tarragona □ *Spain* **38** D6
Tarraleah *Australia* **95** G4
Tarrasa = Terrassa *Spain* **38** D7
Tàrrega *Spain* **38** D6
Tarrytown *U.S.A.* **115** E11
Tårs *Denmark* **11** G4
Tarshiha = Me'ona *Israel* **74** B4
Tarsus *Turkey* **72** D6
Tartagal *Argentina* **126** A3
Tärtär *Azerbaijan* **35** K8
Tärtär → *Azerbaijan* **35** K8
Tartas *France* **20** E3
Tartu *Estonia* **32** C4
Ţarţūs *Syria* **72** E7
Ţarţūs □ *Syria* **72** E7
Tarumizu *Japan* **55** J5
Tarussa *Russia* **32** E9
Tarutao = Ko Tarutao △
    Thailand **65** J2
Tarutao, Ko *Thailand* **65** J2
Tarutung *Indonesia* **62** D1
Tarutyne *Ukraine* **29** D14
Tarvísio *Italy* **41** B10
Taseko → *Canada* **102** C4
Tash-Kömür *Kyrgyzstan* **52** E8
Tash-Kumyr =
    Tash-Kömür *Kyrgyzstan* **52** E8
Tashauz = Dashoguz
    Turkmenistan **52** E6
Tashi Chho Dzong =
    Thimphu *Bhutan* **67** F16
Tashk, Daryācheh-ye *Iran* **71** D7
Tashkent = Toshkent
    Uzbekistan **52** E7
Tashtagol *Russia* **52** D9
Tasiilaq *Greenland* **4** C6
Tasik Kenyir *Malaysia* **65** K4
Tasikmalaya *Indonesia* **63** G13
Tåsinge *Denmark* **11** J4
Tåsjön *Sweden* **8** D16
Taskan *Russia* **53** C16
Tasker *Niger* **83** C7
Taşköprü *Turkey* **72** B6
Tasman B. *N.Z.* **91** D4
Tasman Basin *Pac. Oc.* **96** M7
Tasman Mts. *N.Z.* **91** D4
Tasman Pen. *Australia* **95** G4
Tasman Sea *Pac. Oc.* **90** G9
Tasmania □ *Australia* **95** G4
Tasmanian Wilderness
    World Heritage Area △
    Australia **95** G4
Tăşnad *Romania* **28** C7
Tassili n'Ajjer △ *Algeria* **78** C7
Tassili-Oua-n-Ahaggar
    Algeria **78** D7
Tassili Tin-Rerhoh *Algeria* **83** A5
Tata *Hungary* **28** C3
Tata *Morocco* **78** C4
Tatabánya *Hungary* **28** C3
Tatahouine *Tunisia* **79** B8
Tataouine *Tunisia* **79** B8
Tatar Republic =
    Tatarstan □ *Russia* **34** C10
Tatarbunary *Ukraine* **29** E14
Tatarsk *Russia* **52** D8
Tatarstan □ *Russia* **34** C10
Tatatua, Pte. *Tahiti* **91** d
Tateyama *Japan* **55** G9
Tathlina L. *Canada* **102** A5
Tathra *Australia* **95** F4
Tatinnai L. *Canada* **103** A9
Tatla Lake *Canada* **102** C4
Tatlısu *Turkey* **45** F11
Tatnam, C. *Canada* **103** B10
Tatra = Tatry *Slovak Rep.* **27** B13
Tatranský △ *Slovak Rep.* **27** B13
Tatry *Slovak Rep.* **27** B13
Tatshenshini → *Canada* **102** B1
Tatsuno *Japan* **55** G7
Tatta *Pakistan* **68** G2
Tatuī *Brazil* **127** A6

Tatum *U.S.A.* **109** K12
Tat'ung = Datong *China* **56** D7
Tatvan *Turkey* **73** C10
Ta'ū *Amer. Samoa* **91** b
Taubaté *Brazil* **127** A6
Tauberbischofsheim
 Germany **25** F5
Taucha *Germany* **24** D8
Tauern *Austria* **22** E7
Tauern-tunnel *Austria* **26** D6
Taufikia *Sudan* **81** F3
Taulé *France* **18** D3
Taumarunui *N.Z.* **91** C5
Taumaturgo *Brazil* **124** E4
Taung *S. Africa* **88** D3
Taungdwingyi *Burma* **67** J19
Taunggyi *Burma* **67** J20
Taungup *Burma* **67** K19
Taunsa *Pakistan* **68** D4
Taunsa Barrage *Pakistan* **68** D4
Taunton *U.K.* **15** F4
Taunton *U.S.A.* **115** E13
Taunus *Germany* **25** E4
Taupo *N.Z.* **91** C6
Taupo, L. *N.Z.* **91** C5
Tauragé *Lithuania* **30** C9
Tauragė □ *Lithuania* **30** C9
Tauranga *N.Z.* **91** B6
Tauranga Harb. *N.Z.* **91** B6
Taureau, Rés. *Canada* **104** C5
Taurianova *Italy* **43** D9
Taurus Mts. = Toros
 Dağları *Turkey* **72** D5
Tauste *Spain* **38** D3
Tautira *Tahiti* **91** d
Tauz = Tovuz *Azerbaijan* **35** K7
Tavas *Turkey* **47** D11
Tavastehus =
 Hämeenlinna *Finland* **32** B3
Tavda *Russia* **52** D7
Tavda → *Russia* **52** D7
Tavernes de la Valldigna
 Spain **39** F4
Taveta *Kenya* **86** C4
Taveuni *Fiji* **91** a
Taviano *Italy* **43** C11
Tavignano → *France* **21** F13
Tavira *Portugal* **37** H3
Tavistock *Canada* **114** C4
Tavistock *U.K.* **15** G3
Tavolara *Italy* **42** B2
Távora → *Portugal* **36** D3
Tavoy *Burma* **64** E2
Tavropos → *Greece* **46** B3
Tavşanlı *Turkey* **47** B11
Tavua *Fiji* **91** a
Tavuki *Fiji* **91** a
Taw → *U.K.* **15** F3
Tawa → *India* **68** H8
Tawas City *U.S.A.* **113** C12
Tawau *Malaysia* **62** D5
Taweisha *Sudan* **81** E2
Tawi-Tawi *Phil.* **63** C6
Tawu *Taiwan* **59** F13
Taxco *Mexico* **119** D5
Taxila *Pakistan* **68** C5
Tay → *U.K.* **13** E5
Tay, Firth of *U.K.* **13** E5
Tay, L. *Australia* **93** F3
Tay, L. *U.K.* **13** E4
Tay △ *U.K.* **13** E5
Tay Ninh *Vietnam* **65** G6
Tayabamba *Peru* **124** E3
Tayabas Bay *Phil.* **61** E4
Taygetos Oros *Greece* **46** D4
Taylakova *Russia* **52** D8
Taylakovy = Taylakova
 Russia **52** D8
Taylor *Canada* **102** B4
Taylor *Nebr., U.S.A.* **112** E4
Taylor *Pa., U.S.A.* **115** E9
Taylor *Tex., U.S.A.* **116** F6
Taylor, Mt. *U.S.A.* **109** J10
Taylorville *U.S.A.* **112** F9
Taymā *Si. Arabia* **70** E3
Taymyr, Oz. *Russia* **53** B11
Taymyr, Poluostrov *Russia* **53** B11
Tayport *U.K.* **13** E6
Tayrona △ *Colombia* **121** D5
Tayshet *Russia* **53** D10
Taytay *Phil.* **61** F3
Tāyyebād *Iran* **71** C9
Tāyyebād □ *Iran* **71** C9
Taz → *Russia* **52** C8
Taza *Morocco* **78** B5
Tāza Khurmātū *Iraq* **73** E11
Tazawa-Ko *Japan* **54** E10
Tazin → *Canada* **103** B7
Tazin L. *Canada* **103** B7
Tazovskiy *Russia* **52** C8
Tbilisi *Georgia* **35** K7
Tchad = Chad ■ *Africa* **79** F8
Tchad, L. *Chad* **79** F8
Tchaourou *Benin* **83** D5
Tch'eng-tou = Chengdu
 China **58** B5
Tchentlo L. *Canada* **102** B4

Tchetti *Benin* **83** D5
Tchibanga *Gabon* **84** E2
Tchien *Liberia* **82** D3
Tchin Tabaraden *Niger* **83** B6
Tch'ong-k'ing =
 Chongqing *China* **58** C6
Tczew *Poland* **30** D5
Te Anau, L. *N.Z.* **91** F1
Te Aroha *N.Z.* **91** B5
Te Awamutu *N.Z.* **91** C5
Te Ika a Maui = North I.
 N.Z. **91** C5
Te Kuiti *N.Z.* **91** C5
Te-n-Dghâmcha, Sebkhet
 Mauritania **82** B1
Te Puke *N.Z.* **91** B6
Te Waewae B. *N.Z.* **91** G1
Te Wai Pounamu = South
 I. *N.Z.* **91** F3
Teaca *Romania* **29** D9
Teague *U.S.A.* **116** F6
Teahupoo *Tahiti* **91** d
Teano *Italy* **43** A7
Teapa *Mexico* **119** D6
Teba *Spain* **37** J6
Tebakang *Malaysia* **62** D4
Teberda *Russia* **35** J5
Teberu *Malaysia* **65** d
Tébessa *Algeria* **78** A7
Tebicuary → *Paraguay* **126** B4
Tebingtinggi *Riau, Indonesia* **62** E2
Tebingtinggi
 Sumatera Utara, Indonesia **62** D1
Tebulos *Georgia* **35** J7
Tecate *Mexico* **111** N10
Tecer Dağları *Turkey* **72** C7
Tech → *France* **20** F7
Techiman *Ghana* **82** D4
Techirghiol *Romania* **29** F13
Tecka *Argentina* **128** E2
Tecomán *Mexico* **118** D4
Tecopa *U.S.A.* **111** K10
Tecoripa *Mexico* **118** B3
Tecuala *Mexico* **118** C3
Tecuci *Romania* **29** E12
Tecumseh *Canada* **114** D2
Tecumseh *Mich., U.S.A.* **113** D12
Tecumseh *Okla., U.S.A.* **116** D6
Tedzhen = Tejen
 Turkmenistan **52** F7
Tees → *U.K.* **14** C6
Tees B. *U.K.* **14** C6
Teeswater *Canada* **114** C3
Tefé *Brazil* **124** D6
Tefenni *Turkey* **47** D11
Tegal *Indonesia* **63** G13
Tegallalang *Indonesia* **63** J18
Tegalsari *Indonesia* **63** J17
Tegel, Berlin ✈ (TXL)
 Germany **24** C9
Tegernsee *Germany* **25** H7
Teggiano *Italy* **43** B8
Tegid, L. = Bala, L. *U.K.* **14** E4
Tegina *Nigeria* **83** C6
Tegucigalpa *Honduras* **120** D2
Teguidda i-n-Tessoum *Niger* **83** B6
Tehachapi *U.S.A.* **111** K8
Tehachapi Mts. *U.S.A.* **111** L8
Tehamiyam *Sudan* **80** D4
Teheran = Tehrān *Iran* **71** C6
Tehilla *Sudan* **80** D4
Téhini *Ivory C.* **82** D4
Tehoru *Indonesia* **63** E7
Tehrān *Iran* **71** C6
Tehrān □ *Iran* **71** C6
Tehri *India* **69** D8
Tehuacán *Mexico* **119** D5
Tehuantepec *Mexico* **119** D5
Tehuantepec, G. de *Mexico* **119** D5
Tehuantepec, Istmo de
 Mexico **119** D6
Teide, Pico de *Canary Is.* **48** F3
Teifi → *U.K.* **15** E3
Teigebyen *Norway* **10** D5
Teign → *U.K.* **15** G4
Teignmouth *U.K.* **15** G4
Teiuş *Romania* **29** D8
Teixeira Pinto *Guinea-Biss.* **82** C1
Tejakula *Indonesia* **63** J18
Tejam *India* **69** E9
Tejen *Turkmenistan* **52** F7
Tejen → *Turkmenistan* **71** B9
Tejo → *Europe* **37** F2
Tejon Pass *U.S.A.* **111** L8
Tekamah *U.S.A.* **112** E5
Tekapo, L. *N.Z.* **91** E3
Tekax *Mexico* **119** C7
Teke *Turkey* **45** E13
Tekeli *Kazakhstan* **52** E8
Tekeze → *Ethiopia* **81** E4
Tekija *Serbia* **44** B6
Tekirdağ *Turkey* **45** F11
Tekirdağ □ *Turkey* **45** E11
Tekirova *Turkey* **47** E12
Tekkali *India* **67** K14
Tekke *Turkey* **72** B7
Tekman *Turkey* **73** C9

Tekoa *U.S.A.* **108** C5
Tekong Besar, Pulau
 Singapore **65** d
Tel Aviv ✈ (TLV) *Israel* **74** C3
Tel Aviv-Yafo *Israel* **74** C3
Tel Lakhish *Israel* **74** D3
Tel Megiddo *Israel* **74** C4
Tela *Honduras* **120** C2
Telanaipura = Jambi
 Indonesia **62** E2
Telašćica △ *Croatia* **41** E12
Telavi *Georgia* **35** J7
Telč *Czech Rep.* **26** B8
Telciu *Romania* **29** C9
Telde *Canary Is.* **48** G4
Telegraph Creek *Canada* **102** B2
Telekhany =
 Tsyelyakhany *Belarus* **23** B13
Telemark *Norway* **9** G12
Telén *Argentina* **126** D2
Teleneşti *Moldova* **29** C13
Teleng *Iran* **71** E9
Teleño *Spain* **36** C4
Teleorman □ *Romania* **29** G10
Teleorman → *Romania* **29** G10
Teles Pires → *Brazil* **124** E7
Telescope Pk. *U.S.A.* **111** J9
Teletaye *Mali* **83** B5
Telfer Mine *Australia* **92** C3
Telford *U.K.* **15** E5
Telford and Wrekin □ *U.K.* **14** E5
Telfs *Austria* **26** D4
Télimélé *Guinea* **82** C2
Teljo, J. *Sudan* **81** E2
Telkwa *Canada* **102** C3
Tell City *U.S.A.* **112** G10
Tellicherry *India* **66** P9
Telluride *U.S.A.* **109** H10
Teloloapán *Mexico* **119** D5
Telpos Iz *Russia* **6** C17
Telsen *Argentina* **128** E3
Telšiai *Lithuania* **30** C9
Telšiai □ *Lithuania* **30** C9
Teltow *Germany* **24** C9
Teluk Anson = Teluk
 Intan *Malaysia* **65** K3
Teluk Bahang *Malaysia* **65** c
Teluk Betung =
 Tanjungkarang
 Telukbetung *Indonesia* **62** F3
Teluk Intan *Malaysia* **65** K3
Teluk Kumbar *Malaysia* **65** c
Telukbutun *Indonesia* **62** D3
Telukdalem *Indonesia* **62** D1
Tema *Ghana* **83** D5
Temagami, L. *Canada* **104** C3
Temax *Mexico* **119** C7
Temba *S. Africa* **89** D4
Tembagapura *Indonesia* **63** E9
Tembe, Dem. Rep. of the Congo* **86** C2
Tembe △ *S. Africa* **89** D5
Tembleque *Spain* **36** F7
Temblor Range *U.S.A.* **111** K7
Teme → *U.K.* **15** E5
Temecula *U.S.A.* **111** M9
Temerloh *Malaysia* **62** D2
Teminabuan *Indonesia* **63** E8
Temir *Kazakhstan* **52** E6
Temirtau *Kazakhstan* **52** D8
Temirtau *Russia* **52** D9
Témiscamie → *Canada* **105** B5
Témiscaming *Canada* **104** C4
Témiscamingue, L. *Canada* **104** C4
Temnikov *Russia* **34** C6
Temo → *Italy* **42** B1
Temora *Australia* **95** E4
Témpio Pausánia *Italy* **42** B2
Tempiute *U.S.A.* **110** H11
Temple *U.S.A.* **116** F6
Temple B. *Australia* **94** A3
Templemore *Ireland* **12** D4
Templeton *U.S.A.* **110** K6
Templeton → *Australia* **94** C2
Templin *Germany* **24** B9
Tempoal de Sánchez *Mexico*
 119 C5
Temryuk *Russia* **33** K9
Temska → *Serbia* **44** C6
Temuco *Chile* **128** D2
Temuka *N.Z.* **91** F3
Tenabo *Mexico* **119** C6
Tenaha *U.S.A.* **116** F7
Tenakee Springs *U.S.A.* **102** B1
Tenali *India* **67** L12
Tenancingo de Degollado
 Mexico **119** D5
Tenango del Valle *Mexico* **119** D5
Tenaro, Akra *Greece* **46** E4
Tenasserim *Burma* **65** F2
Tenasserim □ *Burma* **64** F2
Tenby *U.K.* **15** F3
Tenda, Colle di *France* **21** D11
Tendaho *Ethiopia* **81** E5
Tende *France* **21** D11
Tendelti *Sudan* **81** E3
Tendrovskaya Kosa *Ukraine* **33** J6

Tendukhera *India* **69** H8
Teneguía, Volcanes de
 Canary Is. **48** F2
Teneida *Egypt* **80** B2
Tenenkou *Mali* **82** C4
Ténéré *Niger* **83** B7
Tenerife *Canary Is.* **48** F3
Tenerife, Pico *Canary Is.* **48** G1
Tenerife Norte ✈ (TFN)
 Canary Is. **48** F3
Tenerife Sur ✈ (TFS)
 Canary Is. **48** F3
Teng Xian
 Guangxi Zhuangzu, China **59** F8
Teng Xian *Shandong, China* **57** G9
Tengah, Kepulauan
 Indonesia **62** F5
Tengchong *China* **58** E2
Tengchowfu = Penglai
 China **57** F11
Tenggarong *Indonesia* **62** E5
Tenggol, Pulau *Malaysia* **65** K4
Tengiz Köli *Kazakhstan* **52** D7
Tenhult *Sweden* **11** G8
Tenino *U.S.A.* **110** D4
Tenkasi *India* **66** Q10
Tenke *Katanga,*
 Dem. Rep. of the Congo **87** E2
Tenke *Katanga,*
 Dem. Rep. of the Congo **87** E2
Tenkodogo *Burkina Faso* **83** C4
Tenna → *Italy* **41** E10
Tennant Creek *Australia* **94** B1
Tennessee □ *U.S.A.* **117** D11
Tennessee → *U.S.A.* **117** C10
Teno, Pta. de *Canary Is.* **48** F3
Tenom *Malaysia* **62** C5
Tenosique *Mexico* **119** D6
Tenryū-Gawa → *Japan* **55** G8
Tenterden *U.K.* **15** F8
Tenterfield *Australia* **95** D5
Teo *Spain* **36** C2
Teófilo Otoni *Brazil* **125** G10
Tepa *Indonesia* **63** F7
Tepalcatepec → *Mexico* **118** D4
Tepecik *Bursa, Turkey* **45** F12
Tepecik *Kütahya, Turkey* **47** B11
Tepehuanes *Mexico* **118** B3
Tepelenë *Albania* **44** F4
Tepetongo *Mexico* **118** C4
Tepic *Mexico* **118** C4
Teplá *Czech Rep.* **26** B5
Teplice *Czech Rep.* **26** A6
Teplyk *Ukraine* **29** B14
Tepoca, C. *Mexico* **118** A2
Tequila *Mexico* **118** C4
Ter → *Spain* **38** C8
Ter Apel *Neths.* **17** B7
Téra *Niger* **83** C5
Tera → *Spain* **36** D5
Teraina *Kiribati* **97** G12
Terakeka *Sudan* **81** F3
Téramo *Italy* **41** F10
Terang *Australia* **95** F3
Terang, Teluk *Indonesia* **63** K19
Terazit, Massif de *Niger* **83** A6
Tercan *Turkey* **73** C9
Terceira *Azores* **78** a
Tercero → *Argentina* **126** C3
Terebovlya *Ukraine* **23** D13
Teregova *Romania* **28** E7
Tereida *Sudan* **81** E3
Terek → *Russia* **35** J8
Terepaima △ *Venezuela* **121** E6
Tereshka → *Russia* **34** E8
Teresina *Brazil* **125** E10
Teresva *Ukraine* **29** B8
Terewah, L. *Australia* **95** D4
Terges → *Portugal* **37** H3
Tergnier *France* **19** C10
Teridgerie Cr. → *Australia* **95** E4
Terlizzi *Italy* **43** A9
Terme *Turkey* **72** B7
Termez = Termiz *Uzbekistan* **52** F7
Términi Imerese *Italy* **42** E6
Términos, L. de *Mexico* **119** D6
Termiz *Uzbekistan* **52** F7
Térmoli *Italy* **41** F12
Ternate *Indonesia* **63** D7
Terneuzen *Neths.* **17** C3
Terney *Russia* **54** B4
Terni *Italy* **41** F9
Ternitz *Austria* **26** D9
Ternivka *Ukraine* **29** B14
Ternopil *Ukraine* **23** D13
Ternopil □ *Ukraine* **33** H3
Ternopol = Ternopil
 Ukraine **23** D13
Terowie *Australia* **95** E2
Terpni *Greece* **44** F7
Terra Bella *U.S.A.* **111** K7
Terra Nova △ *Canada* **105** C9
Terrace *Canada* **102** C3

Terrace Bay *Canada* **104** C2
Terracina *Italy* **42** A6
Terralba *Italy* **42** C1
Terrasini *Italy* **42** D6
Terrassa *Spain* **38** D7
Terrasson-la-Villedieu
 France **20** C5
Terre Haute *U.S.A.* **112** F10
Terrebonne B. *U.S.A.* **117** G9
Terrell *U.S.A.* **116** E6
Terrenceville *Canada* **105** C9
Terry *U.S.A.* **108** C11
Terryville *U.S.A.* **115** E11
Tersko-Kumskiy Kanal
 Russia **35** H7
Tertenía *Italy* **42** C2
Terter = Tärtär → *Azerbaijan* **35** K8
Teruel *Spain* **38** E3
Teruel □ *Spain* **38** E4
Tervel *Bulgaria* **45** C11
Tervola *Finland* **8** C21
Teryaweynya L. *Australia* **95** E3
Tešanj *Bos.-H.* **28** F3
Teseney *Eritrea* **81** D4
Tesha → *Russia* **34** C7
Teshio *Japan* **54** B10
Teshio-Gawa → *Japan* **54** B10
Tešica *Serbia* **44** C5
Tesiyn Gol → *Mongolia* **60** A4
Teslić *Bos.-H.* **28** F2
Teslin *Canada* **102** A2
Teslin → *Canada* **102** A2
Teslin L. *Canada* **102** A2
Tessalit *Mali* **83** A5
Tessaoua *Niger* **83** C6
Tessin *Germany* **24** A8
Tessit *Mali* **83** B5
Test → *U.K.* **15** G6
Testa del Gargano *Italy* **41** G13
Testigos, Is. Los *Venezuela* **121** D7
Tét *Hungary* **28** C2
Têt → *France* **20** F7
Tetachuck L. *Canada* **102** C3
Tetas, Pta. *Chile* **126** A1
Tete *Mozam.* **87** F3
Tete □ *Mozam.* **87** F3
Teterev → *Ukraine* **23** C16
Teterow *Germany* **24** B8
Teteven *Bulgaria* **45** D8
Tethul → *Canada* **102** A6
Teton → *U.S.A.* **108** C8
Tétouan *Morocco* **78** A4
Tetovo *Macedonia* **44** D4
Tetufera, Mt. *Tahiti* **91** d
Tetyushi *Russia* **34** C9
Teuco → *Argentina* **126** B3
Teulada *Italy* **42** D1
Teulon *Canada* **103** C9
Teun *Indonesia* **63** F7
Teuri-Tō *Japan* **54** B10
Teutoburger Wald *Germany* **24** C4
Tevere → *Italy* **41** G9
Tevere △ *Italy* **41** F9
Teverya *Israel* **74** C4
Teviot → *U.K.* **13** F6
Tewantin *Australia* **95** D5
Tewkesbury *U.K.* **15** F5
Texada I. *Canada* **102** D4
Texarkana *Ark., U.S.A.* **116** E7
Texarkana *Tex., U.S.A.* **116** E7
Texas *Australia* **95** D5
Texas □ *U.S.A.* **116** F5
Texas City *U.S.A.* **116** G7
Texel *Neths.* **17** A4
Texline *U.S.A.* **116** C3
Texoma, L. *U.S.A.* **116** E6
Teyateyaneng *Lesotho* **85** K5
Teykovo *Russia* **32** D11
Teza → *Russia* **34** B5
Tezin *Afghan.* **68** B3
Teziutlán *Mexico* **119** D5
Tezpur *India* **67** F18
Tezzeron L. *Canada* **102** C4
Tha-anne → *Canada* **103** A10
Tha Deua *Laos* **64** D4
Tha Deua *Laos* **64** C3
Tha Pla *Thailand* **64** D3
Tha Rua *Thailand* **64** E3
Tha Sala *Thailand* **65** H2
Tha Song Yang *Thailand* **64** D1
Thaba Putsoa *Lesotho* **89** D4
Thabana Ntlenyana *Lesotho* **89** D4
Thabazimbi *S. Africa* **89** C4
Thādiq *Si. Arabia* **70** E5
Thai Binh *Vietnam* **58** G6
Thai Muang *Thailand* **65** H2
Thai Nguyen *Vietnam* **58** G5
Thailand ■ *Asia* **64** E4
Thailand, G. of *Asia* **65** G3
Thakhek *Laos* **64** D5
Thal *Pakistan* **68** C4
Thal Desert *Pakistan* **68** D4
Thala La = Hkakabo Razi
 Burma **67** E20

Thallon *Australia* **95** D4
Thalu, Ko *Thailand* **65** b
Thalwil *Switz.* **25** H4
Thames *N.Z.* **91** B5
Thames → *Canada* **114** D2
Thames → *U.K.* **15** F8
Thames → *U.S.A.* **115** E12
Thames Estuary *U.K.* **15** F8
Thamesford *Canada* **114** C4
Thamesville *Canada* **114** D3
Than *India* **68** H4
Than Uyen *Vietnam* **64** B4
Thana Gazi *India* **68** F7
Thandla *India* **68** H6
Thandwe *Burma* **67** K19
Thane *India* **66** K8
Thanesar *India* **68** D7
Thanet, I. of *U.K.* **15** F9
Thangool *Australia* **94** C5
Thanh Hoa *Vietnam* **64** C5
Thanh Hung *Vietnam* **65** H5
Thanh Pho Ho Chi Minh
 Vietnam **65** G6
Thanh Thuy *Vietnam* **64** A5
Thanjavur *India* **66** P11
Thann *France* **19** E14
Thano Bula Khan *Pakistan* **68** G2
Thaolintoa L. *Canada* **103** A9
Thaon-les-Vosges *France* **19** D13
Thap Lan △ *Thailand* **64** E4
Thap Sakae *Thailand* **65** G2
Thap Than *Thailand* **64** E2
Thar Desert *India* **68** F5
Tharad *India* **68** G4
Thargomindah *Australia* **95** D3
Tharp Fracture Zone
 S. Ocean **5** B14
Tharrawaddy *Burma* **67** L19
Tharthar, Buḥayrat ath
 Iraq **73** E10
Tharthar, L. = Tharthār,
 Buḥayrat ath *Iraq* **73** E10
Tharthār, W. ath → *Iraq* **73** E10
Thasopoula *Greece* **45** F8
Thasos *Greece* **45** F8
That Khe *Vietnam* **58** F6
Thatcher *Ariz., U.S.A.* **109** K9
Thatcher *Colo., U.S.A.* **109** H11
Thaton *Burma* **67** L20
Thau, Bassin de *France* **20** E7
Thaungdut *Burma* **67** G19
Thayer *U.S.A.* **112** G8
Thayetmyo *Burma* **67** K19
Thazi *Burma* **67** J20
The Broads *U.K.* **14** E9
The Everglades *U.S.A.* **117** J14
The Gulf = Persian Gulf *Asia* **71** E6
The Hague =
 's-Gravenhage *Neths.* **17** B4
The Pas *Canada* **103** C8
The Wash *U.K.* **14** E8
The Weald *U.K.* **15** F8
Thebes = Thíva *Greece* **46** C5
Thebes *Egypt* **80** B3
Thedford *U.S.A.* **112** E3
Theebine *Australia* **95** D5
Thekulthili L. *Canada* **103** A7
Thelon → *Canada* **103** A8
Thénezay *France* **18** F6
Thenon *France* **20** C5
Theodore *Australia* **94** C5
Theodore *Canada* **103** C8
Theodore *U.S.A.* **117** F10
Theodore Roosevelt △
 U.S.A. **112** B3
Theodore Roosevelt L.
 U.S.A. **109** K8
Thepha *Thailand* **65** J3
Thérain → *France* **19** C9
Theresa *U.S.A.* **115** B9
Thermopolis *U.S.A.* **108** E9
Thermopylae *Greece* **46** C4
Thesprotia □ *Greece* **46** B2
Thessalon *Canada* **104** C3
Thessaloníki *Greece* **44** F7
Thessaloníki □ *Greece* **44** F7
Thessaloníki ✈ (SKG) *Greece* **44** F7
Thessaloniki, Gulf of =
 Thessaloniki Kolpos
 Greece **44** F6
Thessaloniki Kolpos *Greece* **44** F6
Thessaly □ *Greece* **46** B4
Thetford *U.K.* **15** E8
Thetford Mines *Canada* **105** C5
Theun → *Laos* **64** C5
Theunissen *S. Africa* **88** D4
Thevenard *Australia* **95** E1
Thiamis → *Greece* **46** B2
Thiberville *France* **18** C7
Thicket Portage *Canada* **103** B9
Thief River Falls *U.S.A.* **112** A5
Thiel Mts. *Antarctica* **5** E16
Thiene *Italy* **41** C8
Thiérache *France* **19** C10
Thiers *France* **20** C7
Thiès *Senegal* **82** C1
Thiès □ *Senegal* **82** C1

Thiesi *Italy* **42** B1
Thiet *Sudan* **81** F2
Thika *Kenya* **86** C4
Thille-Boubacar *Senegal* **82** B1
Thimphu *Bhutan* **67** F16
Thina → *S. Africa* **89** E4
Þingvallavatn *Iceland* **8** D3
Thionville *France* **19** C13
Thira = Santorini *Greece* **47** E7
Thirasia *Greece* **47** E7
Third Cataract *Sudan* **80** D3
Thirsk *U.K.* **14** C6
Thiruvananthapuram = Trivandrum *India* **66** Q10
Thisted *Denmark* **11** H2
Thistle I. *Australia* **95** F2
Thithia = Cicia *Fiji* **91** a
Thiva *Greece* **46** C5
Thiviers *France* **20** C4
Thizy *France* **19** F11
Þjórsá → *Iceland* **8** E3
Thlewiaza → *Canada* **103** A10
Thmar Puok *Cambodia* **64** F4
Tho Vinh *Vietnam* **64** C5
Thoa → *Canada* **103** A7
Thoen *Thailand* **64** D2
Thoeng *Thailand* **64** C3
Thohoyandou *S. Africa* **85** J6
Tholdi *Pakistan* **69** B7
Thomas *U.S.A.* **116** D5
Thomas, L. *Australia* **95** D2
Thomaston *U.S.A.* **117** E12
Thomasville *U.S.A.* **117** E9
Thomasville *Ala., U.S.A.* **117** F11
Thomasville *Ga., U.S.A.* **117** F13
Thomasville *N.C., U.S.A.* **117** D14
Thompson *Canada* **103** B9
Thompson *U.S.A.* **115** E9
Thompson → *Canada* **102** C4
Thompson → *U.S.A.* **112** F7
Thompson Falls *U.S.A.* **108** C6
Thompson Pk. *U.S.A.* **108** F2
Thompson Springs *U.S.A.* **108** G9
Thompsontown *U.S.A.* **114** F7
Thomson *U.S.A.* **117** E13
Thomson → *Australia* **94** C3
Thônes *France* **21** C10
Thong Yang *Thailand* **65** b
Thonon-les-Bains *France* **19** F13
Thorez *Ukraine* **33** H10
Þórisvatn *Iceland* **8** D4
Thornaby on Tees *U.K.* **14** C6
Thornbury *Canada* **114** B4
Thorne *U.K.* **14** D7
Thornhill *Canada* **102** C3
Thornton *U.S.A.* **108** G11
Thorold *Canada* **114** C5
Þórshöfn *Iceland* **8** C6
Thouarcé *France* **18** E6
Thouars *France* **18** F6
Thouet → *France* **18** E6
Thouin, C. *Australia* **92** D2
Thousand Oaks *U.S.A.* **111** L8
Thrace *Turkey* **45** F10
Thrace, Sea of *Greece* **45** F8
Three Forks *U.S.A.* **108** D8
Three Gorges Dam *China* **59** B8
Three Hills *Canada* **102** C6
Three Hummock I. *Australia* **95** G3
Three Pagodas Pass *Asia* **64** E2
Three Points, C. *Ghana* **82** E4
Three Rivers *Calif., U.S.A.* **110** J8
Three Rivers *Tex., U.S.A.* **116** G5
Three Springs *Australia* **93** E2
Throssell, L. *Australia* **93** E3
Throssell Ra. *Australia* **92** D3
Thrushton △ *Australia* **95** D4
Thua → *Kenya* **86** C4
Thuan Hoa *Vietnam* **65** H5
Thubun Lakes *Canada* **103** A6
Thueyts *France* **21** D8
Thuin *Belgium* **17** D4
Thuir *France* **20** F6
Thule = Qaanaaq *Greenland* **4** B4
Thule Air Base = Uummannaq *Greenland* **4** B4
Thun *Switz.* **25** J3
Thunder B. *U.S.A.* **114** B1
Thunder Bay *Canada* **104** C2
Thunersee *Switz.* **25** J3
Thung Salaeng Luang △ *Thailand* **64** D3
Thung Song *Thailand* **65** H2
Thunkar *Bhutan* **67** F17
Thuong Tra *Vietnam* **64** D6
Thur → *Switz.* **25** H5
Thurgau □ *Switz.* **25** H5
Thüringen □ *Germany* **24** E6
Thüringer Wald *Germany* **24** E6
Thurles *Ireland* **12** D4
Thurn P. *Austria* **26** D5
Thurrock □ *U.K.* **15** F8
Thursday I. *Australia* **94** A3
Thurso *Canada* **104** C4
Thurso *U.K.* **13** C5
Thurso → *U.K.* **13** C5
Thurston I. *Antarctica* **5** D16
Thury-Harcourt *France* **18** D6

Thutade L. *Canada* **102** B3
Thy *Denmark* **11** H2
Thyborøn *Denmark* **11** H2
Thyolo *Malawi* **87** F4
Ti-n-Amzi → *Niger* **83** B5
Ti-n-Barraouene, O. → *Africa* **83** B5
Ti-n-Zaouatene *Algeria* **83** B5
Ti-Tree *Australia* **94** C1
Tiadiaye *Senegal* **82** C1
Tian Shan *Asia* **60** B3
Tianchang *China* **59** A12
Tiandeng *China* **58** F6
Tiandong *China* **58** F6
Tian'e *China* **58** E6
Tianhe *China* **58** E7
Tianjin *China* **57** E9
Tiankoura *Burkina Faso* **82** C4
Tianlin *China* **58** E6
Tianmen *China* **59** B9
Tianquan *China* **58** B4
Tianshifu *China* **57** D13
Tianshui *China* **56** G3
Tiantai *China* **59** C13
Tianyang *China* **58** F6
Tianyar *Indonesia* **63** J18
Tianzhen *China* **56** D8
Tianzhu *China* **58** D7
Tianzhuangtai *China* **57** D12
Tiarei *Tahiti* **91** d
Tiaret *Algeria* **78** A6
Tiassalé *Ivory C.* **82** D4
Tibagi *Brazil* **127** A5
Tibagi → *Brazil* **127** A5
Tibastî, Sarîr *Libya* **79** D9
Tibati *Cameroon* **83** D7
Tibe *Ethiopia* **81** F4
Tiber = Tevere → *Italy* **41** G9
Tiber Res. *U.S.A.* **108** B8
Tiberias = Teverya *Israel* **74** C4
Tiberias, L. = Yam Kinneret *Israel* **74** C4
Tibesti *Chad* **79** D9
Tibet = Xizang Zizhiqu □ *China* **60** C3
Tibet, Plateau of *Asia* **50** E10
Tibiao *Phil.* **61** F5
Tibiri *Niger* **83** C6
Tibooburra *Australia* **95** D3
Tibro *Sweden* **11** F8
Tiburón, I. *Mexico* **118** B2
Ticao I. *Phil.* **61** E5
Tîchît *Mauritania* **82** B3
Ticho *Ethiopia* **81** F4
Ticino □ *Switz.* **25** J4
Ticino → *Italy* **25** J4
Ticleni *Romania* **29** F8
Ticonderoga *U.S.A.* **115** C11
Ticul *Mexico* **119** C7
Tidaholm *Sweden* **11** F7
Tidan *Sweden* **11** F8
Tiddim *Burma* **67** H18
Tidioute *U.S.A.* **114** E5
Tidjikja *Mauritania* **82** B2
Tidore *Indonesia* **63** D7
Tiébissou *Ivory C.* **82** D3
Tiefa *China* **57** C12
Tiel *Neths.* **17** C5
Tiel *Senegal* **82** C1
Tieling *China* **57** C12
Tielt *Belgium* **17** C3
Tien Shan = Tian Shan *Asia* **60** B3
Tien-tsin = Tianjin *China* **57** E9
Tien Yen *Vietnam* **64** B6
T'ienching = Tianjin *China* **57** E9
Tienen *Belgium* **17** D4
Tiénigbé *Ivory C.* **82** D3
Tientsin = Tianjin *China* **57** E9
Tieri *Australia* **94** C4
Tierp *Sweden* **10** D11
Tierra Amarilla *Chile* **126** B1
Tierra Amarilla *U.S.A.* **109** H10
Tierra Colorada *Mexico* **119** D5
Tierra de Barros *Spain* **37** G4
Tierra de Campos *Spain* **36** C6
Tierra del Fuego, I. Gr. de *Argentina* **128** G3
Tiétar → *Spain* **36** F4
Tietê → *Brazil* **127** A5
Tiffin *U.S.A.* **113** E12
Tifton *U.S.A.* **117** F13
Tifu *Indonesia* **63** E7
Tighina *Moldova* **29** D14
Tigil *Russia* **53** D16
Tignish *Canada* **105** C7
Tigray □ *Ethiopia* **81** E4
Tigre → *Peru* **124** D4
Tigre → *Venezuela* **124** B6
Tigris = Dijlah, Nahr → *Asia* **70** D5
Tigveni *Romania* **29** E9
Tigyaing *Burma* **67** H20
Tîh, Gebel el *Egypt* **80** B3
Tijara *India* **68** F7

Tijuana *Mexico* **111** N9
Tikal *Guatemala* **120** C2
Tikal △ *Guatemala* **120** C2
Tikamgarh *India* **69** G8
Tikaré *Burkina Faso* **83** C4
Tikhoretsk *Russia* **35** H5
Tikhvin *Russia* **32** C7
Tikiraqjuaq = Whale Cove *Canada* **103** A10
Tiko *Cameroon* **83** E6
Tikrît *Iraq* **73** E10
Tiksi *Russia* **53** B13
Tilamuta *Indonesia* **63** D6
Tilburg *Neths.* **17** C5
Tilbury *Canada* **114** D2
Tilbury *U.K.* **15** F8
Tilcara *Argentina* **126** A2
Tilden *U.S.A.* **112** D5
Tilemses *Niger* **83** B5
Tilemsi, Vallée du *Mali* **83** B5
Tilhar *India* **69** F8
Tilichiki *Russia* **53** C17
Tilissos *Greece* **49** D7
Till → *U.K.* **14** B5
Tillabéri *Niger* **83** C5
Tillamook *U.S.A.* **108** D2
Tillberga *Sweden* **10** E10
Tillia *Niger* **83** B5
Tillsonburg *Canada* **114** D4
Tillyeria *Cyprus* **49** D11
Tilogne *Senegal* **82** B2
Tilos *Greece* **47** E9
Tilpa *Australia* **95** E3
Tilt → *U.K.* **13** E5
Tilton *U.S.A.* **115** C13
Tiltonsville *U.S.A.* **114** F4
Tim *Denmark* **11** H2
Timanfaya △ *Canary Is.* **48** F6
Timaru *N.Z.* **91** F3
Timashevo *Russia* **34** D10
Timashevsk *Russia* **35** H4
Timau *Kenya* **86** B4
Timbaki *Greece* **49** D6
Timbedgha *Mauritania* **82** B3
Timber Creek *Australia* **92** C5
Timber Lake *U.S.A.* **112** C3
Timber Mt. *U.S.A.* **110** H10
Timbo *Guinea* **82** C2
Timbo *Liberia* **82** D3
Timbuktu = Tombouctou *Mali* **82** B4
Timeiaouine *Algeria* **83** A5
Timétrine, Mts. *Mali* **83** B4
Timfi Oros *Greece* **46** B2
Timfristos, Oros *Greece* **46** C3
Timi *Cyprus* **49** E11
Timia *Niger* **83** B6
Timimoun *Algeria* **78** C6
Timiris, Râs *Mauritania* **82** B1
Timiş = Tamiš → *Serbia* **28** F5
Timiş □ *Romania* **28** E6
Timiskaming, L. = Témiscamingue, L. *Canada* **104** C4
Timişoara *Romania* **28** E6
Timmersdala *Sweden* **11** F7
Timmins *Canada* **104** C3
Timok → *Serbia* **44** B6
Timoleague *Ireland* **12** E3
Timor *Asia* **63** F7
Timor Leste = East Timor ■ *Asia* **63** F7
Timor Sea *Ind. Oc.* **92** B4
Timrå *Sweden* **10** B11
Tin Can Bay *Australia* **95** D5
Tin Ethisane *Mali* **83** B4
Tin Gornai *Mali* **83** B4
Tin Mt. *U.S.A.* **110** J9
Tina = Thina → *S. Africa* **89** E4
Tîna, Khalîg el *Egypt* **74** D1
Tinaca Pt. *Phil.* **61** J6
Tinajo *Canary Is.* **48** F6
Tinca *Romania* **28** D6
Tindal *Australia* **92** B5
Tindouf *Algeria* **78** C4
Tinée → *France* **21** E11
Tineo *Spain* **36** B4
Tinfunque △ *Paraguay* **126** A3
Ting Jiang → *China* **59** E11
Tinggi, Pulau *Malaysia* **65** L5
Tinglev *Denmark* **11** K3
Tingo Maria *Peru* **124** E3
Tingrela *Ivory C.* **82** C3
Tingsryd *Sweden* **11** H9
Tingstäde *Sweden* **11** G12
Tinh Bien *Vietnam* **65** G5
Tinian *N. Marianas* **96** F6
Tinnevelly = Tirunelveli *India* **66** Q10
Tinogasta *Argentina* **126** B2
Tinos *Greece* **47** D7
Tiñoso, C. *Spain* **39** H3
Tinpahar *India* **69** G12
Tintagel *Argentina* **126** B3
Tintina *Argentina* **126** B3
Tintinara *Australia* **95** F3
Tintioulé *Guinea* **82** C3
Tinto → *Spain* **37** H4

Tioga *N. Dak., U.S.A.* **112** A2
Tioga *Pa., U.S.A.* **114** E7
Tioman, Pulau *Malaysia* **65** L5
Tione di Trento *Italy* **40** B7
Tionesta *U.S.A.* **114** E5
Tior *Sudan* **81** F3
Tipperary *Ireland* **12** D3
Tipperary □ *Ireland* **12** D4
Tipton *Calif., U.S.A.* **110** J7
Tipton *Iowa, U.S.A.* **112** E9
Tipton *Ind., U.S.A.* **112** E10
Tipton Mt. *U.S.A.* **111** K12
Tiptonville *U.S.A.* **117** C10
Tîrân *Iran* **71** C6
Tîrân *Si. Arabia* **80** B3
Tiranë *Albania* **44** E3
Tiranë ✈ (TIA) *Albania* **44** E3
Tirano *Italy* **40** B7
Tirari Desert *Australia* **95** D2
Tiraspol *Moldova* **29** D14
Tirdout *Mali* **83** B4
Tire *Turkey* **47** C9
Tirebolu *Turkey* **73** B8
Tiree *U.K.* **13** E2
Tiree, Passage of *U.K.* **13** E2
Tîrgovişte = Târgovişte *Romania* **29** F10
Tîrgu Jiu = Târgu Jiu *Romania* **29** F8
Tîrgu Mureş = Târgu Mureş *Romania* **29** D9
Tirich Mir *Pakistan* **66** A7
Tiriolo *Italy* **43** D9
Tiriro *Guinea* **82** C3
Tiritiri o te Moana = Southern Alps *N.Z.* **91** E3
Tirodi *India* **66** J11
Tirol □ *Austria* **26** D3
Tirso → *Italy* **42** C1
Tirstrup *Denmark* **11** H4
Tiruchchirappalli *India* **66** P11
Tirunelveli *India* **66** Q10
Tirupati *India* **66** N11
Tiruppur *India* **66** P10
Tiruvannamalai *India* **66** N11
Tisa → *Serbia* **28** E5
Tisa → *Serbia* **28** E5
Tisdale *Canada* **103** C8
Tishomingo *U.S.A.* **116** D6
Tisjön *Sweden* **10** D7
Tisnaren *Sweden* **11** F9
Tišnov *Czech Rep.* **27** B9
Tisovec *Slovak Rep.* **27** C12
Tisza = Tisa → *Serbia* **28** E5
Tiszaföldvár *Hungary* **28** D5
Tiszafüred *Hungary* **28** C5
Tiszalök *Hungary* **28** B6
Tiszavasvári *Hungary* **28** C6
Tit-Ary *Russia* **53** B13
Titaguas *Spain* **38** F3
Titao *Burkina Faso* **83** C4
Titel *Serbia* **28** E5
Tithwal *Pakistan* **69** B5
Titicaca, L. *S. Amer.* **124** G5
Titisee *Germany* **25** H4
Titiwa *Nigeria* **83** C7
Tito *Italy* **43** B8
Titova Korenica *Croatia* **41** D12
Titu *Romania* **29** F10
Titule *Dem. Rep. of the Congo* **86** B2
Titusville *Fla., U.S.A.* **117** G14
Titusville *Pa., U.S.A.* **114** E5
Tivaouane *Senegal* **82** C1
Tivat *Montenegro* **44** D2
Tivedens △ *Sweden* **11** F8
Tiverton *U.K.* **15** G4
Tívoli *Italy* **41** G9
Tiyo *Eritrea* **81** E5
Tizi-Ouzou *Algeria* **78** A6
Tizimín *Mexico* **119** C7
Tiznit *Morocco* **78** C4
Tjæreborg *Denmark* **11** J2
Tjällmo *Sweden* **11** F9
Tjeggelvas = Tjeggelvas *Sweden* **8** C17
Tjeggelvas = Tjeggelvas *Sweden* **8** C17
Tjirebon = Cirebon *Indonesia* **63** G13
Tjluring *Indonesia* **63** J17
Tjörn *Sweden* **11** G6
Tkibuli = Tqibuli *Georgia* **35** J6
Tkvarcheli = Tqvarcheli *Georgia* **35** J5
Tlacotalpan *Mexico* **119** D5
Tlahualilo de Zaragoza *Mexico* **118** B4
Tlaquepaque *Mexico* **118** C4
Tlaxcala *Mexico* **119** D5
Tlaxcala □ *Mexico* **119** D5
Tlaxiaco *Mexico* **119** D5
Tlemcen *Algeria* **78** B5
Tlumach *Ukraine* **29** B10
Tluszcz *Poland* **31** F8
Tlyarata *Russia* **35** J8
To Bong *Vietnam* **64** F7
Toa Payoh *Singapore* **65** d

Toad → *Canada* **102** B4
Toad River *Canada* **102** B3
Toamasina *Madag.* **89** B8
Toamasina □ *Madag.* **89** B8
Toay *Argentina* **126** D3
Toba *China* **58** B1
Toba *Japan* **55** G8
Toba, Danau *Indonesia* **62** D1
Toba Kakar *Pakistan* **68** D3
Toba Tek Singh *Pakistan* **68** D5
Tobago *Trin. & Tob.* **121** D7
Tobarra *Spain* **39** G3
Tobelo *Indonesia* **63** D7
Tobermory *Canada* **114** A3
Tobermory *U.K.* **13** E2
Tobi *Pac. Oc.* **63** D8
Tobi-Shima *Japan* **54** D9
Tobin, L. *Australia* **92** D4
Tobin, L. *Canada* **103** C8
Toblach = Dobbiaco *Italy* **41** B9
Toboali *Indonesia* **62** E3
Tobol → *Russia* **52** D7
Toboli *Indonesia* **63** E6
Tobolsk *Russia* **52** D7
Tobor *Senegal* **82** C1
Tobruk = Tubruq *Libya* **79** B10
Tobyhanna *U.S.A.* **115** E9
Tobyl = Tobol → *Russia* **52** D7
Tocantinópolis *Brazil* **125** E9
Tocantins □ *Brazil* **125** F9
Tocantins → *Brazil* **125** D9
Toccoa *U.S.A.* **117** D13
Toce → *Italy* **40** C5
Tochi → *Pakistan* **68** C4
Tochigi *Japan* **55** F9
Tochigi □ *Japan* **55** F9
Tocina *Spain* **37** H5
Töcksfors *Sweden* **10** E5
Toco *Trin. & Tob.* **125** K16
Toconao *Chile* **126** A2
Tocopilla *Chile* **126** A1
Tocumwal *Australia* **95** F4
Tocuyo → *Venezuela* **124** A5
Todd → *Australia* **94** C2
Todeli *Indonesia* **63** E6
Todenyang *Kenya* **86** B4
Todgarh *India* **68** G5
Todi *Italy* **41** F9
Todos os Santos, B. de *Brazil* **125** F11
Todos Santos *Mexico* **118** C2
Todtnau *Germany* **25** H3
Toe Hd. *U.K.* **13** D1
Toecé *Burkina Faso* **83** C4
Tofield *Canada* **102** C6
Tofino *Canada* **102** D3
Töfsingdalens △ *Sweden* **10** B6
Tofua *Tonga* **91** c
Togane *Japan* **55** G10
Togba *Mauritania* **82** B2
Togian, Kepulauan *Indonesia* **63** E6
Togliatti *Russia* **34** D9
Togo ■ *W. Afr.* **83** D5
Togtoh *China* **56** D6
Tohiea, Mt. *Moorea* **91** d
Tohma → *Turkey* **72** C8
Tôhoku □ *Japan* **54** E10
Töhöm *Mongolia* **56** B5
Toinya *Sudan* **81** F2
Toiyabe Range *U.S.A.* **108** G5
Tojikiston = Tajikistan ■ *Asia* **52** F8
Tojo *Indonesia* **63** E6
Tôjô *Japan* **55** G6
Tok *U.S.A.* **100** C5
Tok-do *Asia* **55** F5
Tokachi-Dake *Japan* **54** C11
Tokachi-Gawa → *Japan* **54** C11
Tokaj *Hungary* **28** B6
Tokala *Indonesia* **63** E6
Tôkamachi *Japan* **55** F9
Tokanui *N.Z.* **91** G2
Tokar *Sudan* **80** D4
Tokara-Rettō *Japan* **55** K4
Tokarahi *N.Z.* **91** F3
Tokashiki-Shima *Japan* **55** L3
Tokat *Turkey* **72** B7
Tokat □ *Turkey* **72** B7
Tôkch'ŏn *N. Korea* **57** E14
Tokelau Is. *Pac. Oc.* **96** H10
Tokmak *Kyrgyzstan* **52** E8
Tokmak *Ukraine* **33** J8
Toko Ra. *Australia* **94** C2
Tokoro-Gawa → *Japan* **54** B12
Toku *Tonga* **91** c
Tokuno-Shima *Japan* **55** L4
Tokushima *Japan* **55** G7
Tokushima □ *Japan* **55** H7
Tokuyama *Japan* **55** G5
Tôkyô *Japan* **55** G9
Tolaga Bay *N.Z.* **91** C7
Tolbukhin = Dobrich *Bulgaria* **45** C11
Toledo *Brazil* **127** A5
Toledo *Spain* **36** F6
Toledo *Ohio, U.S.A.* **113** E12

Toledo *Oreg., U.S.A.* **108** D2
Toledo *Wash., U.S.A.* **108** C2
Toledo, Montes de *Spain* **37** F6
Toledo Bend Res. *U.S.A.* **116** F8
Tolentino *Italy* **41** E10
Tolfa *Italy* **41** F8
Tolga *Australia* **94** B4
Toliara *Madag.* **89** C7
Toliara □ *Madag.* **89** C8
Tolima *Colombia* **124** C3
Tolitoli *Indonesia* **63** D6
Tolkmicko *Poland* **30** D6
Tollarp *Sweden* **11** J7
Tollensesee *Germany* **24** B9
Tollhouse *U.S.A.* **110** H7
Tolmachevo *Russia* **32** C5
Tolmezzo *Italy* **41** B10
Tolmin *Slovenia* **41** B10
Tolna *Hungary* **28** D3
Tolna □ *Hungary* **28** D3
Tolo, Teluk *Indonesia* **63** E6
Tolochin = Talachyn *Belarus* **32** E5
Tolosa *Spain* **38** B2
Tolox *Spain* **37** J6
Toluca *Mexico* **119** D5
Tom Burke *S. Africa* **89** C4
Tom Price *Australia* **92** D2
Toma *Burkina Faso* **82** C4
Tomah *U.S.A.* **112** D8
Tomahawk *U.S.A.* **112** C9
Tomai *Moldova* **29** D13
Tomakomai *Japan* **54** C10
Tomales *U.S.A.* **110** G4
Tomales B. *U.S.A.* **110** G3
Tomanivi *Fiji* **91** a
Tomar *Portugal* **37** F2
Tomaros, Oros *Greece* **46** B2
Tomarza *Turkey* **72** C6
Tomashevka *Belarus* **31** G10
Tomashpil *Ukraine* **29** B13
Tomaszów Lubelski *Poland* **31** H10
Tomaszów Mazowiecki *Poland* **31** G7
Tomatlán *Mexico* **118** D3
Tombador, Serra do *Brazil* **124** F7
Tombe *Sudan* **81** F3
Tombigbee → *U.S.A.* **117** F11
Tombouctou *Mali* **82** B4
Tombouctou □ *Mali* **82** B4
Tombstone *U.S.A.* **109** L8
Tombua *Angola* **88** B1
Tomé *Chile* **126** D1
Tomelilla *Sweden* **11** J7
Tomelloso *Spain* **37** F7
Tomini *Indonesia* **63** D6
Tomini, Teluk *Indonesia* **63** E6
Tominian *Mali* **82** C4
Tomiño *Spain* **36** D2
Tomintoul *U.K.* **13** D5
Tomislavgrad *Bos.-H.* **28** G2
Tomkinson Ranges *Australia* **93** E4
Tommot *Russia* **53** D13
Tomnop Ta Suos *Cambodia* **65** G3
Tomo → *Colombia* **124** B5
Toms Place *U.S.A.* **110** H8
Toms River *U.S.A.* **115** G10
Tomsk *Russia* **52** D9
Tomtabacken *Sweden* **11** G8
Tona *Spain* **38** D7
Tonalá *Chiapas, Mexico* **119** D6
Tonalá *Jalisco, Mexico* **118** C4
Tonale, Passo del *Italy* **40** B7
Tonantins *Brazil* **124** D5
Tonasket *U.S.A.* **108** B4
Tonawanda *U.S.A.* **114** D6
Tonb *Iran* **71** E7
Tonbridge *U.K.* **15** F8
Tondano *Indonesia* **63** D6
Tondela *Portugal* **36** E2
Tønder *Denmark* **11** K2
Tondi Kiwindi *Niger* **83** C5
Tondibi *Mali* **83** B4
Tondoro *Namibia* **88** B2
Tone → *Australia* **93** F2
Tone-Gawa → *Japan* **55** F9
Tonekābon *Iran* **71** B6
Tong Xian *China* **56** E9
Tong-Yeong *S. Korea* **57** G15
Tônga *Sudan* **81** F3
Tonga ■ *Pac. Oc.* **91** c
Tonga Trench *Pac. Oc.* **96** J10
Tongaat *S. Africa* **89** D5
Tong'an *China* **59** E12
Tongareva = Penrhyn *Cook Is.* **97** H12
Tongariro △ *N.Z.* **91** C5
Tongatapu *Tonga* **91** c
Tongatapu Group *Tonga* **91** c
Tongbai *China* **59** A9
Tongcheng *Anhui, China* **59** B11
Tongcheng *Hubei, China* **59** C9
Tongchuan *China* **56** G5
Tongdao *China* **58** D7
Tongeren *Belgium* **17** D5
Tonggu *China* **59** C10
Tongguan *China* **56** G6

Tonghai *China* **58** E4
Tonghua *China* **57** D13
Tongjiang *China* **58** B6
Tongjosŏn Man *N. Korea* **57** E15
Tongking, G. of = Tonkin,
    G. of *Asia* **64** C7
Tongliang *China* **58** C6
Tongliao *China* **57** C12
Tongling *China* **59** B11
Tonglu *China* **59** C12
Tongnan = Anyue *China* **58** B5
Tongobory *Madag.* **89** C7
Tongoy *Chile* **126** C1
Tongren *China* **58** D7
Tongres = Tongeren
    Belgium **17** D5
Tongsa Dzong *Bhutan* **67** F17
Tongshi *China* **64** C7
Tongue *U.K.* **13** C4
Tongue ➤ *U.S.A.* **108** C11
Tongwei *China* **56** G3
Tongxiang *China* **59** B13
Tongxin *China* **56** F3
Tongyang *N. Korea* **57** E14
Tongyu *China* **57** B12
Tongzi *China* **58** C6
Tonj *Sudan* **81** F2
Tonj ➤ *Sudan* **81** F2
Tonk *India* **68** F6
Tonkawa *U.S.A.* **116** C6
Tonkin = Bac Phan *Vietnam* **64** B5
Tonkin, G. of *Asia* **64** C7
Tonle Sap *Cambodia* **65** F5
Tonnay-Charente *France* **20** C3
Tonneins *France* **20** D4
Tonnerre *France* **19** E10
Tönning *Germany* **24** A4
Tono *Japan* **54** E10
Tonopah *U.S.A.* **109** G5
Tonosí *Panama* **120** E3
Tons ➤ *Haryana, India* **68** D7
Tons ➤ *Ut. P., India* **69** F10
Tønsberg *Norway* **9** G14
Tonto ➤ *U.S.A.* **109** K8
Tonumea *Tonga* **91** c
Tonya *Turkey* **73** B8
Toobanna *Australia* **94** B4
Toodyay *Australia* **93** F2
Tooele *U.S.A.* **108** F7
Toompine *Australia* **95** D3
Toora *Australia* **95** F4
Toora-Khem *Russia* **53** D10
Toowoomba *Australia* **95** D5
Top-ozero *Russia* **8** D25
Top Springs *Australia* **92** C5
Topalu *Romania* **29** F13
Topaz *U.S.A.* **110** G7
Topeka *U.S.A.* **112** F6
Topl'a ➤ *Slovak Rep.* **27** C14
Topley *Canada* **102** C3
Toplica ➤ *Serbia* **44** C5
Topliţa *Romania* **29** D10
Topocalma, Pta. *Chile* **126** C1
Topock *U.S.A.* **111** L12
Topola *Serbia* **44** B4
Topolčani *Macedonia* **44** E5
Topol'čany *Slovak Rep.* **27** C11
Topolnitsa ➤ *Bulgaria* **45** D8
Topolobampo *Mexico* **118** B3
Topoloveni *Romania* **29** F10
Topolovgrad *Bulgaria* **45** D10
Topolváţu Mare *Romania* **28** E6
Toppenish *U.S.A.* **108** C3
Topusko *Croatia* **41** C12
Torà *Spain* **38** D6
Tora Kit *Sudan* **81** E3
Toraka Vestale *Madag.* **89** B7
Torata *Peru* **124** G4
Torbalı *Turkey* **47** C9
Torbat-e Ḩeydārīyeh *Iran* **71** C8
Torbat-e Jām *Iran* **71** C9
Torbay *Canada* **105** C9
Torbay □ *U.K.* **15** G4
Torbjörntorp *Sweden* **11** F7
Tordesillas *Spain* **36** D6
Töreboda *Sweden* **11** F8
Torekov *Sweden* **11** H6
Torelló *Spain* **38** C7
Toreno *Spain* **36** C4
Torfaen □ *U.K.* **15** F4
Torgau *Germany* **24** D8
Torgelow *Germany* **24** B10
Torhamn *Sweden* **11** H9
Torhout *Belgium* **17** C3
Torhovtsya *Ukraine* **29** B10
Tori *Ethiopia* **81** F3
Tori-Shima *Japan* **55** J10
Torigni-sur-Vire *France* **18** C6
Torija *Spain* **38** E1
Torino *Italy* **40** C4
Torit *Sudan* **81** G3
Torkamān *Iran* **73** D12
Torkovichi *Russia* **32** C6
Tormac *Romania* **28** E6
Tormes ➤ *Spain* **36** D4
Tornado Mt. *Canada* **102** D6

Tornal'a *Slovak Rep.* **27** C13
Torneå = Tornio *Finland* **8** D21
Torneälven ➤ *Europe* **8** D21
Torneträsk *Sweden* **8** B18
Tornio *Finland* **8** D21
Tornionjoki =
    Torneälven ➤ *Europe* **8** D21
Tornquist *Argentina* **126** D3
Toro *Baleares, Spain* **48** B11
Toro *Zamora, Spain* **36** D5
Torö *Sweden* **11** F11
Toro, Cerro del *Chile* **126** B2
Toro △ *Uganda* **86** C3
Toro Pk. *U.S.A.* **111** M10
Törökszentmiklós *Hungary* **28** C5
Toronto *Canada* **114** C5
Toronto *U.S.A.* **114** F4
Toronto Lester B. Pearson
    Int. ✈ (YYZ) *Canada* **114** C5
Toropets *Russia* **32** D6
Tororo *Uganda* **86** B3
Toros Dağları *Turkey* **72** D5
Torpa *India* **69** H11
Torquay *U.K.* **15** G4
Torquemada *Spain* **36** C6
Torrance *U.S.A.* **111** M8
Torrão *Portugal* **37** G2
Torre Annunziata *Italy* **43** B7
Torre de Moncorvo *Portugal* **36** D3
Torre del Campo *Spain* **37** H7
Torre del Greco *Italy* **43** B7
Torre del Mar *Spain* **37** J6
Torre-Pacheco *Spain* **39** H4
Torre Péllice *Italy* **40** D4
Torreblanca *Spain* **38** E5
Torrecampo *Spain* **37** G6
Torrecilla en Cameros *Spain* **38** C2
Torredembarra *Spain* **38** D6
Torredonjimeno *Spain* **37** H7
Torrejón de Ardoz *Spain* **36** E7
Torrejoncillo *Spain* **36** F4
Torrelaguna *Spain* **36** E7
Torrelavega *Spain* **36** B6
Torremaggiore *Italy* **41** G12
Torremolinos *Spain* **37** J6
Torrens, L. *Australia* **95** E2
Torrens Cr. ➤ *Australia* **94** C4
Torrens Creek *Australia* **94** C4
Torrent *Spain* **39** F4
Torrenueva *Spain* **37** G7
Torreón *Mexico* **118** B4
Torreperogil *Spain* **37** G7
Torres *Brazil* **127** B5
Torres *Mexico* **118** B2
Torres Novas *Portugal* **37** F2
Torres Strait *Australia* **90** B7
Torres Vedras *Portugal* **37** F1
Torrevieja *Spain* **39** H4
Torrey *U.S.A.* **108** G8
Torridge ➤ *U.K.* **15** G3
Torridon, L. *U.K.* **13** D3
Torrijos *Spain* **36** F6
Tørring *Denmark* **11** J3
Torrington *Conn., U.S.A.* **115** E11
Torrington *Wyo., U.S.A.* **108** E11
Torroella de Montgrì *Spain* **38** C8
Torrox *Spain* **37** J7
Torsås *Sweden* **11** H9
Torsby *Sweden* **10** E10
Torshälla *Sweden* **10** E10
Tórshavn *Færoe Is.* **8** E9
Torslanda *Sweden* **11** G5
Torsö *Sweden* **11** F7
Tortola *Br. Virgin Is.* **121** e
Tórtoles de Esgueva *Spain* **36** D6
Tortolì *Italy* **42** C2
Tortona *Italy* **40** D5
Tortorici *Italy* **43** D7
Tortosa *Spain* **38** E5
Tortosa, C. *Spain* **38** E5
Tortosendo *Portugal* **36** E3
Tortue, Î. de la *Haiti* **121** B5
Tortuguero △ *Costa Rica* **120** D3
Tortum *Turkey* **73** B9
Ţorūd *Iran* **71** C7
Torul *Turkey* **73** B8
Toruń *Poland* **31** E5
Torun *Ukraine* **29** B8
Tory I. *Ireland* **12** A3
Torysa ➤ *Slovak Rep.* **27** C14
Torzhok *Russia* **32** D8
Torzym *Poland* **31** F2
Tosa *Japan* **55** H6
Tosa-Shimizu *Japan* **55** H6
Tosa-Wan *Japan* **55** H6
Toscana □ *Italy* **40** E8
Toscano, Arcipelago *Italy* **40** F7
Toshka, Egypt *80** D3
Toshka Lakes *Egypt* **80** C3
Toshkent *Uzbekistan* **52** E7
Tosno *Russia* **32** C6
Tossa de Mar *Spain* **38** D7
Tösse *Sweden* **11** F6
Tostado *Argentina* **126** B3
Tostedt *Germany* **24** B5
Tostón, Pta. de *Canary Is.* **48** F5
Tosu *Japan* **55** H5

Tosya *Turkey* **72** B6
Toszek *Poland* **31** H5
Totana *Spain* **39** H3
Totebo *Sweden* **11** G10
Tôtes *France* **18** C8
Tótkomlós *Hungary* **28** D5
Totma *Russia* **52** D5
Totnes *U.K.* **15** G4
Totness *Suriname* **125** B7
Toto *Nigeria* **83** D6
Totonicapán *Guatemala* **120** D1
Totoya, I. *Fiji* **91** a
Totten Glacier *Antarctica* **5** C8
Tottenham *Australia* **95** E4
Tottenham *Canada* **114** B5
Tottori *Japan* **55** G7
Tottori □ *Japan* **55** G7
Touamotou *Niger* **79** D8
Touba *Ivory C.* **82** D3
Touba *Senegal* **82** C1
Toubkal, Djebel *Morocco* **78** B4
Toucy *France* **19** E10
Tougan *Burkina Faso* **82** C4
Touggourt *Algeria* **78** B7
Tougouri *Burkina Faso* **83** C4
Tougué *Guinea* **82** C2
Toukoto *Mali* **82** C3
Toul *France* **19** D12
Toulepleu *Ivory C.* **82** D3
Touliu *Taiwan* **59** F13
Toulon *France* **21** E9
Toulouse *France* **20** E5
Toulouse Blagnac ✈ (TLS)
    France **20** E5
Toummo *Niger* **79** D8
Toumodi *Ivory C.* **82** D3
Tounan *Taiwan* **59** F13
Toungo *Nigeria* **83** D7
Toungoo *Burma* **67** K20
Touques ➤ *France* **18** C7
Touraine *France* **18** E7
Tourcoing *France* **19** B10
Tourinán, C. *Spain* **36** B1
Tournai *Belgium* **17** D3
Tournan-en-Brie *France* **19** D9
Tournay *France* **20** E4
Tournon-St-Martin *France* **18** F7
Tournon-sur-Rhône *France* **21** C8
Tournus *France* **19** F11
Tours *France* **18** E7
Toussoro, Mt. *C.A.R.* **84** C4
Touws ➤ *S. Africa* **88** E3
Touwsrivier *S. Africa* **88** E3
Tovarkovskiy *Russia* **32** F10
Tovste *Ukraine* **29** B10
Tovuz *Azerbaijan* **35** K7
Towada *Japan* **54** D10
Towada-Hachimantai △
    Japan **54** D10
Towada-Ko *Japan* **54** D10
Towanda *U.S.A.* **115** E8
Tower *U.S.A.* **112** B7
Towerhill Cr. ➤ *Australia* **94** C3
Towner *U.S.A.* **112** A3
Townsend *U.S.A.* **108** C8
Townshend I. *Australia* **94** C5
Townsville *Australia* **94** B4
Towraghondī *Afghan.* **66** B3
Towson *U.S.A.* **113** F15
Towuti, Danau *Indonesia* **63** E6
Toya-Ko *Japan* **54** C10
Toyama *Japan* **55** F8
Toyama □ *Japan* **55** F8
Toyama-Wan *Japan* **55** F8
Toyapakeh *Indonesia* **63** K18
Toyohashi *Japan* **55** G8
Toyokawa *Japan* **55** G8
Toyonaka *Japan* **55** G7
Toyooka *Japan* **55** G7
Toyota *Japan* **55** G8
Tozeur *Tunisia* **78** B7
Tozkhurmato *Iraq* **73** E11
Tqibuli *Georgia* **35** J6
Tqvarcheli *Georgia* **35** J5
Trá Li = Tralee *Ireland* **12** D2
Tra On *Vietnam* **65** H5
Trabancos ➤ *Spain* **36** D5
Traben-Trarbach *Germany* **25** F3
Trabzon *Turkey* **73** B8
Trabzon □ *Turkey* **73** B8
Tracadie-Sheila *Canada* **105** C7
Tracy *Calif., U.S.A.* **110** H5
Tracy *Minn., U.S.A.* **112** C6
Tradate *Italy* **40** C5
Trade Town *Liberia* **82** D3
Trafalgar, C. *Spain* **37** J4
Tragonhsi *Greece* **47** D7
Traian *Brăila, Romania* **29** E12
Traian *Tulcea, Romania* **29** E13
Trail *Canada* **102** D5
Trainor L. *Canada* **102** A4
Trakai △ *Lithuania* **9** J21
Trákhonas *Cyprus* **49** D12
Tralee *Ireland* **12** D2
Tralee B. *Ireland* **12** D2
Tramore *Ireland* **12** D4

Tramore B. *Ireland* **12** D4
Tran Ninh, Cao Nguyen
    Laos **64** C4
Tranås *Sweden* **11** F8
Tranbjerg *Denmark* **11** H4
Trancas *Argentina* **126** B2
Trancoso *Portugal* **36** E3
Tranebjerg *Denmark* **11** J4
Tranemo *Sweden* **11** G7
Trang *Thailand* **65** J2
Trangahy *Madag.* **89** B7
Trangan *Indonesia* **63** F8
Trangie *Australia* **95** E4
Trångsviken *Sweden* **10** A7
Trani *Italy* **43** A9
Tranoroa *Madag.* **89** C8
Tranqueras *Uruguay* **127** C4
Trans Nzoia □ *Kenya* **86** B3
Transantarctic Mts.
    Antarctica **5** E12
Transcarpathia =
    Zakarpattya □ *Ukraine* **29** B8
Transilvania *Romania* **29** D9
Transilvanian Alps =
    Carpaţii Meridionali
    Romania **29** E9
Transnistria = Stînga
    Nistrului □ *Moldova* **29** C14
Transtrand *Sweden* **10** C7
Transtrandsfjällen *Sweden* **10** C6
Transylvania =
    Transilvania *Romania* **29** D9
Trápani *Italy* **42** D5
Trapper Pk. *U.S.A.* **108** D6
Traralgon *Australia* **95** F4
Trarza □ *Mauritania* **82** B2
Trasacco *Italy* **41** G10
Trascău, Munţii *Romania* **29** D8
Trasimeno, L. *Italy* **41** E9
Träslövsläge *Sweden* **11** G6
Trasvase Tajo-Segura,
    Canal de *Spain* **38** E2
Trat *Thailand* **65** F4
Tratani ➤ *Pakistan* **68** E3
Traun *Austria* **26** C7
Traun ➤ *Germany* **25** H8
Traunreut *Germany* **25** H8
Traunsee *Austria* **26** D6
Traunstein *Germany* **25** H8
Travellers L. *Australia* **95** E3
Travemünde *Germany* **24** B6
Travers, Mt. *N.Z.* **91** E4
Traverse City *U.S.A.* **113** C11
Travis, L. *U.S.A.* **116** F6
Travnik *Bos.-H.* **28** F2
Trawbreaga B. *Ireland* **12** A4
Trbovlje *Slovenia* **41** B12
Trbušani ➤ *Italy* **40** C6
Trebbia ➤ *Italy* **40** C6
Trebel ➤ *Germany* **24** B9
Trébeurden *France* **18** D3
Trebević △ *Bos.-H.* **28** G3
Třebíč *Czech Rep.* **26** B8
Trebinje *Bos.-H.* **44** D2
Trebisacce *Italy* **43** C9
Trebišnjica ➤ *Bos.-H.* **44** D2
Trebišov *Slovak Rep.* **27** C14
Trebižat ➤ *Bos.-H.* **41** E14
Trebnje *Slovenia* **41** C12
Třeboň *Czech Rep.* **26** B7
Trebonne *Australia* **94** B4
Třeboňsko △ *Czech Rep.* **26** B7
Trebujena *Spain* **37** J4
Trecate *Italy* **40** C5
Tregaron *U.K.* **15** E4
Tregnago *Italy* **41** C8
Tregrosse Is. *Australia* **94** B5
Tréguier *France* **18** D3
Trégunc *France* **18** E3
Treherne *Canada* **103** D9
Tréia *Italy* **41** E10
Treignac *France* **20** C5
Treinta y Tres *Uruguay* **127** C5
Treis-karden *Germany* **25** E3
Treklyano *Bulgaria* **44** D6
Trelawney *Zimbabwe* **89** B5
Trélazé *France* **18** E6
Trelew *Argentina* **128** E3
Trélissac *France* **20** C4
Trelleborg *Sweden* **11** J7
Tremadog Bay *U.K.* **14** E3
Tremiti *Italy* **41** F12
Tremonton *U.S.A.* **108** F7
Tremp *Spain* **38** C5
Trenche ➤ *Canada* **104** C5
Trenčiansky □ *Slovak Rep.* **27** C11
Trenčín *Slovak Rep.* **27** C11
Trenggalek *Indonesia* **63** H14
Trent ➤ *Canada* **114** B7
Trent ➤ *U.K.* **14** D7
Trentino-Alto Adige □ *Italy* **41** B8
Trento *Italy* **40** B8
Trenton = Quinte West
    Canada **114** B7
Trenton *Mo., U.S.A.* **112** E7
Trenton *N.J., U.S.A.* **115** F10
Trenton *Nebr., U.S.A.* **112** E3
Trepassey *Canada* **105** C9
Trepuzzi *Italy* **43** B11

Tres Arroyos *Argentina* **126** D3
Três Corações *Brazil* **127** A6
Três Lagoas *Brazil* **125** H8
Tres Lomas *Argentina* **126** D3
Tres Pinos *U.S.A.* **110** J5
Três Pontas *Brazil* **127** A6
Tres Puentes *Chile* **126** B1
Tres Puntas, C. *Argentina* **128** F3
Três Rios *Brazil* **127** A7
Tres Valles *Mexico* **119** D5
Tresco *U.K.* **15** H1
Treska ➤ *Macedonia* **44** E5
Treskavica *Bos.-H.* **28** G3
Trespaderne *Spain* **36** C7
Tresticklan △ *Sweden* **11** F5
Trets *France* **21** E9
Treuchtlingen *Germany* **25** G6
Treuenbrietzen *Germany* **24** C8
Trevi *Italy* **41** F9
Trevíglio *Italy* **40** C6
Trevínca, Peña *Spain* **36** C4
Treviso *Italy* **41** C9
Trévoux *France* **21** C8
Trgovište *Serbia* **44** D6
Triabunna *Australia* **95** G4
Trianda *Greece* **49** C10
Triangle *Zimbabwe* **89** C5
Triaucourt-en-Argonne
    France **19** D12
Tribal Areas □ *Pakistan* **68** C4
Tribsees *Germany* **24** A8
Tribulation, C. *Australia* **94** B4
Tribune *U.S.A.* **112** F3
Tricárico *Italy* **43** B9
Tricase *Italy* **43** C11
Trichinopoly =
    Tiruchchirappalli *India* **66** P11
Trichonida, L. *Greece* **46** C3
Trichur *India* **66** P10
Trida *Australia* **95** E4
Trier *Germany* **25** F2
Trieste *Italy* **41** C10
Trieste, G. di *Italy* **41** C10
Trieux ➤ *France* **18** D3
Triggiano *Italy* **43** A9
Triglav *Slovenia* **41** B10
Triglavski △ *Slovenia* **41** B10
Trigno ➤ *Italy* **41** F11
Trigueros *Spain* **37** H4
Trikala *Greece* **46** B3
Trikala □ *Greece* **46** B3
Trikeri *Greece* **46** B5
Trikomo *Cyprus* **49** D12
Trikora, Puncak *Indonesia* **63** E9
Trilj *Croatia* **41** E13
Trillo *Spain* **38** E2
Trim *Ireland* **12** C5
Trimmu Dam *Pakistan* **68** D5
Trincomalee *Sri Lanka* **66** Q12
Trindade *Brazil* **125** G9
Trindade, I. *Atl. Oc.* **2** F8
Třinec *Czech Rep.* **27** B11
Trinidad *Bolivia* **124** F6
Trinidad *Cuba* **120** B4
Trinidad *Uruguay* **126** C4
Trinidad *U.S.A.* **109** H11
Trinidad ➤ *Mexico* **119** D5
Trinidad & Tobago ■
    W. Indies **121** D7
Trinitápoli *Italy* **43** A9
Trinity *Canada* **105** C9
Trinity *U.S.A.* **116** F7
Trinity ➤ *Calif., U.S.A.* **108** F2
Trinity ➤ *Tex., U.S.A.* **116** G7
Trinity B. *Canada* **105** C9
Trinity Hills *Trin. & Tob.* **125** K15
Trinity Is. *U.S.A.* **106** a
Trinity Range *U.S.A.* **108** F4
Trinkitat *Sudan* **80** D4
Trino *Italy* **40** C5
Trinway *U.S.A.* **114** F2
Triolet *Mauritius* **85** d
Trionto, C. *Italy* **43** C9
Triora *Italy* **40** D4
Tripoli = Tarābulus *Lebanon* **74** A4
Tripoli = Tarābulus *Libya* **79** B8
Tripoli *Greece* **46** D4
Tripolitania *N. Afr.* **79** B8
Tripura □ *India* **67** H18
Tripylos *Cyprus* **49** E11
Trischen *Germany* **24** A4
Trisul *India* **69** D8
Trivandrum *India* **66** Q10
Trivento *Italy* **41** G11
Trizin *Greece* **46** D5
Trnava *Slovak Rep.* **27** C10
Trnavský □ *Slovak Rep.* **27** C10
Troarn *France* **18** C6
Trochu *Canada* **102** C6
Trodely I. *Canada* **104** B4
Trogir *Croatia* **41** E13
Troglav *Croatia* **41** E13
Tróia *Italy* **43** A8
Troilus, L. *Canada* **104** B5

Troina *Italy* **43** E7
Trois-Pistoles *Canada* **105** C6
Trois-Rivières *Canada* **104** C5
Trois-Rivières *Guadeloupe* **120** b
Troisdorf *Germany* **24** E3
Troitsk *Russia* **52** D7
Troitsko Pechorsk *Russia* **52** C6
Troitskoye *Russia* **35** G7
Trölladyngja *Iceland* **8** D5
Trollhättan *Sweden* **11** F6
Trollheimen *Norway* **8** E13
Trombetas ➤ *Brazil* **125** D7
Tromsø *Norway* **8** B18
Trona *U.S.A.* **111** K9
Tronador, Mte. *Argentina* **128** E2
Trøndelag *Norway* **8** D14
Trondheim *Norway* **8** E14
Trondheimsfjorden *Norway* **8** E14
Trönninge *Sweden* **11** H6
Tronto ➤ *Italy* **41** F10
Troodos *Cyprus* **49** E11
Troon *U.K.* **13** F4
Tropea *Italy* **43** D8
Tropic *U.S.A.* **109** H7
Tropojë *Albania* **44** D4
Trosa *Sweden* **11** F11
Trostan *U.K.* **12** A5
Trostberg *Germany* **25** G8
Trostyanets *Sumy, Ukraine* **33** G8
Trostyanets *Vinnyts'ka,
    Ukraine* **29** B14
Trou Gras Pt. *St. Lucia* **121** f
Trout ➤ *Canada* **102** A5
Trout L. *N.W.T., Canada* **102** A4
Trout L. *Ont., Canada* **103** C10
Trout Lake *Canada* **102** B6
Trout Lake *U.S.A.* **110** E5
Trout River *Canada* **105** C8
Trout Run *U.S.A.* **114** E7
Trouville-sur-Mer *France* **18** C7
Trowbridge *U.K.* **15** F5
Troy *Turkey* **47** B8
Troy *Ala., U.S.A.* **117** F12
Troy *Kans., U.S.A.* **112** F6
Troy *Mo., U.S.A.* **112** F8
Troy *Mont., U.S.A.* **108** B6
Troy *N.Y., U.S.A.* **115** D11
Troy *Ohio, U.S.A.* **113** E11
Troy *Pa., U.S.A.* **115** E8
Troyan *Bulgaria* **45** D9
Troyes *France* **19** D11
Trpanj *Croatia* **41** E14
Trstenik *Serbia* **44** C5
Trubchevsk *Russia* **33** F7
Truchas Pk. *U.S.A.* **109** J11
Trucial States = United
    Arab Emirates ■ *Asia* **71** F7
Truckee *U.S.A.* **110** F6
Trudfront *Russia* **35** H8
Trudovoye *Russia* **54** C6
Trujillo *Honduras* **120** C2
Trujillo *Peru* **124** E3
Trujillo *Spain* **37** F5
Trujillo *U.S.A.* **109** J11
Trujillo *Venezuela* **124** B4
Truk *Micronesia* **96** G7
Trumann *U.S.A.* **117** D9
Trumansburg *U.S.A.* **115** D8
Trumbull, Mt. *U.S.A.* **109** H7
Trun *France* **18** D7
Trundle *Australia* **95** E4
Trung-Phan = Annam
    Vietnam **64** E7
Truro *Canada* **105** C7
Truro *U.K.* **15** G2
Truskavets *Ukraine* **23** D12
Trůstenik *Bulgaria* **45** C8
Trustrup *Denmark* **11** H4
Trutch *Canada* **102** B4
Truth or Consequences
    U.S.A. **109** K10
Trutnov *Czech Rep.* **26** A8
Truxton *U.S.A.* **115** D8
Truyère ➤ *France* **20** D6
Tryavna *Bulgaria* **45** D9
Tryonville *U.S.A.* **114** E5
Trzcianka *Poland* **31** E3
Trzciel *Poland* **31** F2
Trzcińsko Zdrój *Poland* **31** F1
Trzebiatów *Poland* **30** D2
Trzebiez *Poland* **30** E1
Trzebnica *Poland* **31** G4
Trzemeszno *Poland* **31** F4
Tržič *Slovenia* **41** B11
Tsagan Aman *Russia* **35** G8
Tsamandas *Greece* **46** B2
Tsandi *Namibia* **88** B1
Tsaratanana *Madag.* **89** B8
Tsaratanana, Mt. de =
    Maromokotro *Madag.* **89** A8
Tsaratanana △ *Madag.* **89** A8
Tsarevo *Bulgaria* **45** D9
Tsaritsani *Greece* **46** B4
Tsau *Botswana* **88** C3
Tsavo *Kenya* **86** C4
Tsavo East △ *Kenya* **86** C4

Tsavo West △ *Kenya* **86** C4
Tsebrykove *Ukraine* **33** J6
Tsentralnyy □ *Russia* **34** D4
Tses *Namibia* **88** D2
Tsetserleg *Mongolia* **60** B5
Tsévié *Togo* **83** D5
Tshabong *Botswana* **88** D3
Tshane *Botswana* **88** C3
Tshela *Dem. Rep. of the Congo* **84** E2
Tshesebe *Botswana* **89** C4
Tshibeke
  Dem. Rep. of the Congo **86** C2
Tshibinda
  Dem. Rep. of the Congo **86** C2
Tshikapa
  Dem. Rep. of the Congo **84** F4
Tshilenge
  Dem. Rep. of the Congo **86** D1
Tshinsenda
  Dem. Rep. of the Congo **87** E2
Tshofa *Dem. Rep. of the Congo* **86** D2
Tshwane = Pretoria *S. Africa* **89** D4
Tshwane *Botswana* **88** C3
Tsigara *Botswana* **88** C4
Tsihombe *Madag.* **89** D8
Tsiigehtchic *Canada* **100** C6
Ts'il-os △ *Canada* **102** C4
Tsimlyansk *Russia* **35** G6
Tsimlyansk Res. =
  Tsimlyanskoye Vdkhr.
  Russia **35** F6
Tsimlyanskoye Vdkhr.
  Russia **35** F6
Tsinan = Jinan *China* **56** F9
Tsineng *S. Africa* **88** D3
Tsinghai = Qinghai □ *China* **60** C4
Tsingtao = Qingdao *China* **57** F11
Tsingy de Bemaraha △
  Madag. **89** B8
Tsingy de Namoraka △
  Madag. **89** B8
Tsinjoarivo *Madag.* **89** B8
Tsinjomitondraka *Madag.* **89** B8
Tsirigo = Kythira *Greece* **46** E5
Tsiroanomandidy *Madag.* **89** B8
Tsiteli-Tsqaro *Georgia* **35** K8
Tsitondroana *Madag.* **89** C8
Tsitsikamma △ *S. Africa* **88** E3
Tsivilsk *Russia* **34** C8
Tsivory *Madag.* **89** C8
Tskhinvali *Georgia* **35** J7
Tsna → *Russia* **34** C6
Tsnori *Georgia* **35** K7
Tso Moriri, L. *India* **69** C8
Tsobis *Namibia* **88** B2
Tsodilo Hill *Botswana* **88** B3
Tsogttsetsiy = Baruunsuu
  Mongolia **56** C3
Tsolo *S. Africa* **89** E4
Tsomo *S. Africa* **89** E4
Tsu *Japan* **55** G8
Tsu L. *Canada* **102** A6
Tsuchiura *Japan* **55** F10
Tsuen Wan *China* **59** F10
Tsugaru-Kaikyō *Japan* **54** D10
Tsumeb *Namibia* **88** B2
Tsumis *Namibia* **88** C2
Tsuruga *Japan* **55** G8
Tsurugi-San *Japan* **55** H7
Tsuruoka *Japan* **54** E9
Tsushima *Gifu, Japan* **55** G8
Tsushima *Nagasaki, Japan* **55** G4
Tsuyama *Japan* **55** G7
Tsvetkovo *Ukraine* **33** H6
Tsyelyakhany *Belarus* **23** B13
Tua → *Portugal* **36** D3
Tual *Indonesia* **63** F8
Tualatin *U.S.A.* **110** E4
Tuam *Ireland* **12** C3
Tuamotu, Îs.
  French Polynesia **97** J13
Tuamotu Arch. =
  Tuamotu, Îs.
  French Polynesia **97** J13
Tuamotu Ridge *Pac. Oc.* **97** K14
Tuanfeng *China* **59** B10
Tuanxi *China* **58** D6
Tuao *Phil.* **61** C4
Tuapse *Russia* **35** H4
Tuas *Singapore* **65** d
Tuatapere *N.Z.* **91** G1
Tuba City *U.S.A.* **109** H8
Tuban *Indonesia* **63** G15
Tubani *Botswana* **88** C3
Tubarão *Brazil* **127** B6
Tûbâs *West Bank* **74** C4
Tubas → *Namibia* **88** C2
Tübingen *Germany* **25** G5
Tubou *Fiji* **91** a
Tubruq *Libya* **79** B10
Tubuaï, Îs. *French Polynesia* **97** K13
Tuc Trung *Vietnam* **65** G6
Tucacas *Venezuela* **124** A5
T'uch'ang *Taiwan* **59** E13
Tuchodi → *Canada* **102** B4
Tuchola *Poland* **30** E4
Tuchów *Poland* **31** J8

Tuckanarra *Australia* **93** E2
Tucson *U.S.A.* **109** K8
Tucumán *Argentina* **126** B2
Tucumcari *U.S.A.* **109** J12
Tucupita *Venezuela* **124** B6
Tucuruí *Brazil* **125** D9
Tucuruí, Reprêsa de *Brazil* **125** D9
Tuczno *Poland* **31** E3
Tudela *Spain* **38** C3
Tudmur *Syria* **73** E8
Tudor, L. *Canada* **105** A6
Tudora *Romania* **29** C11
Tuella → *Portugal* **36** D3
Tugela → *S. Africa* **89** D5
Tuguegarao *Phil.* **61** C4
Tugur *Russia* **53** D14
Tui *Spain* **36** C2
Tuineje *Canary Is.* **48** F5
Tukangbesi, Kepulauan
  Indonesia **63** F6
Tukarak I. *Canada* **104** A4
Tukayyid *Iraq* **70** D5
Tûkh *Egypt* **80** H7
Tukhlya *Ukraine* **29** B8
Tukkae, Ao *Thailand* **65** a
Tukobo *Ghana* **82** D4
Tuktoyaktuk *Canada* **100** C6
Tukums *Latvia* **30** B10
Tukums □ *Latvia* **30** B10
Tukuyu *Tanzania* **87** D3
Tula *Hidalgo, Mexico* **119** C5
Tula *Tamaulipas, Mexico* **119** C5
Tula *Nigeria* **83** D7
Tula *Russia* **32** E9
Tula □ *Russia* **32** F9
Tulancingo *Mexico* **119** C5
Tulare *Serbia* **44** D5
Tulare *U.S.A.* **110** J7
Tulare Lake Bed *U.S.A.* **110** K7
Tularosa *U.S.A.* **109** K10
Tulbagh *S. Africa* **88** E2
Tulcán *Ecuador* **124** C3
Tulcea *Romania* **29** E13
Tulcea □ *Romania* **29** E13
Tulchyn *Ukraine* **29** B13
Tüledi Araldary *Kazakhstan* **35** H10
Tüleh *Iran* **71** C7
Tulemalu L. *Canada* **103** A9
Tulghes *Romania* **29** D10
Tuli *Zimbabwe* **87** G2
Tulia *U.S.A.* **116** D4
Tuliszków *Poland* **31** F5
Tulita *Canada* **100** C7
Tulla *Ireland* **12** D3
Tullahoma *U.S.A.* **117** D11
Tullamore *Australia* **95** E4
Tullamore *Ireland* **12** C4
Tulle *France* **20** C5
Tulln *Austria* **26** C9
Tullow *Ireland* **12** D5
Tullus *Sudan* **81** E1
Tully *Australia* **94** B4
Tully *U.S.A.* **115** D8
Tulnici *Romania* **29** E11
Tulovo *Bulgaria* **45** D9
Tulsa *U.S.A.* **116** C7
Tulsequah *Canada* **102** B2
Tulu Milki *Ethiopia* **81** F4
Tulu Welel *Ethiopia* **81** F3
Tulua *Colombia* **124** C3
Tuluceşti *Romania* **29** E13
Tulun *Russia* **53** D11
Tulungagung *Indonesia* **63** H14
Tuma *Russia* **32** E11
Tuma → *Nic.* **120** D3
Tumacacori △ *U.S.A.* **109** L8
Tumaco *Colombia* **124** C3
Tumatumari *Guyana* **124** B7
Tumba *Sweden* **10** E11
Tumba, L.
  Dem. Rep. of the Congo **84** E3
Tumbarumba *Australia* **95** F4
Tumbaya *Argentina* **126** A2
Tumbes *Peru* **124** D2
Tumbler Ridge *Canada* **102** B4
Tumbur *Sudan* **81** G3
Tumbwe
  Dem. Rep. of the Congo **87** E2
Tumby Bay *Australia* **95** E2
Tumd Youqi *China* **56** D6
Tumen *China* **57** C15
Tumen Jiang → *China* **57** C16
Tumeremo *Venezuela* **124** B6
Tumkur *India* **66** N10
Tump *Pakistan* **66** F3
Tumpat *Malaysia* **65** J4
Tumu *Ghana* **82** C4
Tumucumaque, Serra
  Brazil **125** C8
Tumut *Australia* **95** F4
Tumwater *U.S.A.* **110** C4
Tuna *India* **68** H4
Tunadal *Sweden* **10** B11
Tunapuna *Trin. & Tob.* **125** K15
Tunas de Zaza *Cuba* **120** B4
Tunbridge Wells = Royal
  Tunbridge Wells *U.K.* **15** F8

Tunçbilek *Turkey* **47** B11
Tunceli *Turkey* **73** C8
Tunceli □ *Turkey* **73** C8
Tuncurry *Australia* **95** E5
Tundla *India* **68** F8
Tundubai *Sudan* **80** D2
Tunduru *Tanzania* **87** E4
Tundzha → *Bulgaria* **45** E10
Tungaru *Sudan* **81** E3
Tungabhadra → *India* **66** M11
Tungla *Nic.* **120** D3
Tungsha Tao = Dongsha
  Dao *China* **59** G11
Tungshih *Taiwan* **59** E13
Tungsten *Canada* **102** A3
Tunguska, Nizhnyaya →
  Russia **53** C9
Tunguska,
  Podkamennaya →
  Russia **53** C10
Tunica *U.S.A.* **117** D9
Tunis *Tunisia* **78** A7
Tunis ✈ (TUN) *Tunisia* **42** F3
Tunisia ■ *Africa* **79** A7
Tunja *Colombia* **124** B4
Tunkhannock *U.S.A.* **115** E9
Tunliu *China* **56** F7
Tunnel Creek △ *Australia* **92** C4
Tunnsjøen *Norway* **8** D15
Tunø *Denmark* **11** J4
Tunungayualok I. *Canada* **105** A7
Tunuyán *Argentina* **126** C2
Tunuyán → *Argentina* **126** C2
Tuo Jiang → *China* **58** C5
Tuolumne *U.S.A.* **110** H6
Tuolumne → *U.S.A.* **110** H5
Tüp Ăghăl *Iran* **73** D12
Tupã *Brazil* **127** A5
Tupelo *U.S.A.* **117** D10
Tupik *Russia* **32** E7
Tupinambaranas *Brazil* **124** D7
Tupiza *Bolivia* **126** A2
Tupižnica *Serbia* **44** C6
Tupman *U.S.A.* **111** K7
Tupper *Canada* **102** B4
Tupper Lake *U.S.A.* **115** B10
Tüpqarghan Muyis
  Kazakhstan **35** H10
Tupungato, Cerro *S. Amer.* **126** C2
Tuquan *China* **57** B11
Túquerres *Colombia* **124** C3
Tura *Russia* **53** C11
Turabah *Ḥā'il, Si. Arabia* **70** D4
Turabah *Makkah, Si. Arabia* **80** C5
Tūrān *Iran* **71** C8
Turan *Russia* **53** D10
Ţurayf *Si. Arabia* **70** D3
Turbacz *Poland* **31** J7
Turbe *Bos.-H.* **28** F2
Turčianske Teplice
  Slovak Rep. **27** C11
Turcoaia *Romania* **29** E13
Turda *Romania* **29** D8
Turek *Poland* **31** F5
Turén *Venezuela* **124** B5
Turgeon → *Canada* **104** C4
Türgovishte *Bulgaria* **45** C10
Turgut *Turkey* **47** D10
Turgutlu *Turkey* **47** C9
Turgwe → *Zimbabwe* **89** C5
Turhal *Turkey* **72** B7
Turia → *Spain* **39** F4
Turiaçu *Brazil* **125** D9
Turiaçu → *Brazil* **125** D9
Turiec → *Slovak Rep.* **27** B11
Turka *Ukraine* **31** J10
Turkana, L. *Africa* **86** B4
Türkeli *Turkey* **45** F11
Turkestan = Türkistan
  Kazakhstan **52** E7
Túrkeve *Hungary* **28** C5
Turkey ■ *Eurasia* **72** C7
Turkey Creek = Warmun
  Australia **92** C4
Turki *Russia* **34** D6
Türkistan *Kazakhstan* **52** E7
Türkmenabat *Turkmenistan* **71** B9
Türkmenbashi *Turkmenistan* **71** A7
Turkmenistan ■ *Asia* **52** F6
Türkmenli *Turkey* **45** F10
Türkoğlu *Turkey* **72** D7
Turks & Caicos Is. ☑
  W. Indies **121** B5
Turks Island Passage
  W. Indies **121** B5
Turku *Finland* **32** B2
Turkwel → *Kenya* **86** B4
Turlock *U.S.A.* **110** H6
Turnagain → *Canada* **102** B3
Turnagain, C. *N.Z.* **91** D6
Turneffe Is. *Belize* **119** D7
Turner → *U.S.A.* **108** A9
Turner Pt. *Australia* **94** A1
Turner Valley *Canada* **102** C6
Turners Falls *U.S.A.* **115** D12

Turnhout *Belgium* **17** C4
Turnor L. *Canada* **103** B7
Turnov *Czech Rep.* **26** A8
Tûrnovo = Veliko Tûrnovo
  Bulgaria **45** C9
Turnu Măgurele *Romania* **29** G9
Turnu Roşu, P. *Romania* **29** E9
Turobin *Poland* **31** H9
Turpan *China* **60** B3
Turrës, Kala e *Albania* **44** E3
Turriff *U.K.* **13** D6
Tursāq *Iraq* **73** F11
Tursi *Italy* **43** B9
Turtle Head I. *Australia* **94** A3
Turtle Is. *S. Leone* **82** D2
Turtle L. *Canada* **103** C7
Turtle Lake *U.S.A.* **112** B3
Turtleford *Canada* **103** C7
Turuépano △ *Venezuela* **121** D7
Turukhansk *Russia* **53** C9
Turzovka *Slovak Rep.* **27** B11
Tuscaloosa *U.S.A.* **117** E11
Tuscarawas → *U.S.A.* **114** F3
Tuscarora Mt. *U.S.A.* **114** F7
Tuscola *Ill., U.S.A.* **112** F9
Tuscola *Tex., U.S.A.* **116** E5
Tuscumbia *U.S.A.* **117** D11
Tuskegee *U.S.A.* **117** E12
Tuszyn *Poland* **31** G6
Tutak *Turkey* **73** C10
Tutayev *Russia* **32** D10
Tuticorin *India* **66** Q11
Tutin *Serbia* **44** D4
Tutóia *Brazil* **125** D10
Tutong *Brunei* **62** D4
Tutova → *Romania* **29** D12
Tutrakan *Bulgaria* **45** B10
Tuttle Creek L. *U.S.A.* **112** F5
Tuttlingen *Germany* **25** H4
Tutuala *E. Timor* **63** F7
Tutuila *Amer. Samoa* **91** b
Tutume *Botswana* **85** J5
Tutun *Egypt* **80** J7
Tuva □ *Russia* **53** D10
Tuvalu ■ *Pac. Oc.* **90** J7
Tuvuca *Fiji* **91** a
Tuxer Alpen *Austria* **26** D4
Tuxpan *Mexico* **119** C5
Tuxtla Gutiérrez *Mexico* **119** D6
Tuy = Tui *Spain* **36** C2
Tuy An *Vietnam* **64** F7
Tuy Duc *Vietnam* **65** F6
Tuy Hoa *Vietnam* **64** F7
Tuy Phong *Vietnam* **65** G7
Tuya L. *Canada* **102** B2
Tuyen Hoa *Vietnam* **64** D6
Tuyen Quang *Vietnam* **58** G5
Tüysarkän *Iran* **73** E13
Tuz Gölü *Turkey* **72** C5
Ţūz Khurmātū =
  Tozkhurmato *Iraq* **73** E11
Tuzi *Montenegro* **44** D3
Tuzigoot △ *U.S.A.* **109** J7
Tuzla *Bos.-H.* **28** F3
Tuzluca *Turkey* **73** B10
Tuzly *29* E15
Tvååker *Sweden* **11** G6
Tvardiţa *Moldova* **29** D13
Tver *Russia* **32** D8
Tver □ *Russia* **32** D8
Tvrdošin *Slovak Rep.* **27** B12
Tvrdošovce *Slovak Rep.* **27** C11
Tvûrditsa *Bulgaria* **45** D9
Twain *U.S.A.* **110** E5
Twain Harte *U.S.A.* **110** G6
Twardogóra *Poland* **31** G4
Tweed *Canada* **114** B7
Tweed → *U.K.* **13** F6
Tweed Heads *Australia* **95** D5
Tweedsmuir △ *Canada* **102** C3
Twentynine Palms *U.S.A.* **111** L10
Twillingate *Canada* **105** C9
Twin Bridges *U.S.A.* **108** D7
Twin Falls *Canada* **105** B7
Twin Falls *U.S.A.* **108** E6
Twin Valley *U.S.A.* **112** B5
Twinsburg *U.S.A.* **114** E3
Twistringen *Germany* **24** C4
Twitchell Res. *U.S.A.* **111** L6
Two Harbors *U.S.A.* **112** B8
Two Hills *Canada* **102** C6
Two Rivers *U.S.A.* **112** C10
Two Rocks *Australia* **93** F2
Twofold B. *Australia* **95** F4
Tyachiv *Ukraine* **23** D12
Tychy *Poland* **31** H5
Tyczyn *Poland* **31** J9
Tyler *Minn., U.S.A.* **112** C5
Tyler *Tex., U.S.A.* **116** E7
Tyligul → *Ukraine* **33** J6
Tymanivka *Ukraine* **29** B13
Týn nad Vltavou *Czech Rep.* **26** B7

Tynda *Russia* **53** D13
Tyndall *U.S.A.* **112** D5
Tyne → *U.K.* **14** C6
Tyne & Wear □ *U.K.* **14** B6
Tynemouth *U.K.* **14** B6
Tynec nad Sázavou
  Czech Rep. **26** B7
Tyre = Sūr *Lebanon* **74** B4
Tyresta △ *Sweden* **10** E12
Tyrifjorden *Norway* **9** F14
Tyringe *Sweden* **11** H7
Tyrnyauz *Russia* **35** J6
Tyrol = Tirol □ *Austria* **26** D3
Tyrone *U.S.A.* **114** F6
Tyrone □ *U.K.* **12** B4
Tyrrell → *Australia* **95** F3
Tyrrell, L. *Australia* **95** F3
Tyrrell L. *Canada* **103** A7
Tyrrhenian Sea *Medit. S.* **6** G8
Tysfjorden *Norway* **8** B17
Tysmenytsya *Ukraine* **29** B9
Tystberga *Sweden* **11** F11
Tytuvėnai *Lithuania* **30** C10
Tyub Karagan, Mys =
  Tüpqarghan Muyis
  Kazakhstan **35** H10
Tyuleni, Ostrova = Tüledi
  Araldary *Kazakhstan* **35** H10
Tyuleniy *Russia* **35** H8
Tyuleniy, Mys *Azerbaijan* **35** K10
Tyumen *Russia* **52** D7
Tywi → *U.K.* **15** F3
Tywyn *U.K.* **15** E3
Tzaneen *S. Africa* **89** C5
Tzermiado *Greece* **49** D7
Tzoumérka, Óros =
  Athamanon Oros *Greece* **46** B3
Tzukong = Zigong *China* **58** C5

U

U Taphao *Thailand* **64** F3
U.S.A. = United States of
  America ■ *N. Amer.* **106** C7
U.S. Virgin Is. ☑ *W. Indies* **121** e
Uanle Uen *Somali Rep.* **75** G3
Uatumã → *Brazil* **124** D7
Uaupés *Brazil* **124** D5
Uaupés → *Brazil* **124** C5
Uaxactún *Guatemala* **120** C2
Ub *Serbia* **44** B4
Ubá *Brazil* **127** A7
Uba *Nigeria* **83** C7
Ubaitaba *Brazil* **125** F11
Ubangi = Oubangi →
  Dem. Rep. of the Congo **84** E3
Ubauro *Pakistan* **68** E3
Ubayyiḍ, W. al → *Iraq* **73** F10
Ube *Japan* **55** H5
Úbeda *Spain* **37** G7
Uberaba *Brazil* **125** G9
Uberlândia *Brazil* **125** G9
Überlingen *Germany* **25** H5
Ubiaja *Nigeria* **83** D6
Ubin, Pulau *Singapore* **65** d
Ubolratna Res. *Thailand* **64** D4
Ubombo *S. Africa* **89** D5
Ubon Ratchathani *Thailand* **64** E5
Ubondo *Dem. Rep. of the Congo* **86** C2
Ubort → *Belarus* **23** B15
Ubrique *Spain* **37** J5
Ubud *Indonesia* **63** J18
Ubundu
  Dem. Rep. of the Congo **86** C2
Ucayali → *Peru* **124** D4
Uchab *Namibia* **88** B2
Uchiura-Wan *Japan* **54** C10
Uchquduq *Uzbekistan* **52** E7
Uchte *Germany* **24** C4
Uchur → *Russia* **53** D14
Uckermark *Germany* **24** B9
Ucluelet *Canada* **102** D3
Uda → *Russia* **53** D14
Udagamandalam *India* **66** P10
Udainagar *India* **68** H7
Udaipur *India* **68** G5
Udaipur Garhi *Nepal* **69** F12
Udala *India* **69** J12
Udbina *Croatia* **41** D12
Uddeholm *Sweden* **10** D7
Uddevalla *Sweden* **11** F5
Uddjaure *Sweden* **8** D17
Uden *Neths.* **17** C5
Udgir *India* **66** K10
Udhampur *India* **69** C6
Udi *Nigeria* **83** D6
Údine *Italy* **41** B10
Udintsev Fracture Zone
  S. Ocean **5** B13
Udmurtia □ *Russia* **52** D6
Udon Thani *Thailand* **64** D4
Udu Pt. *Fiji* **91** a
Udupi *India* **66** N9
Udvoy Balkan *Bulgaria* **45** D10
Udzungwa △ *Tanzania* **86** D4
Udzungwa Range *Tanzania* **87** D4

Ueckermünde *Germany* **24** B10
Ueda *Japan* **55** F9
Uedineniya, Os. *Russia* **4** B12
Uele → *Dem. Rep. of the Congo* **84** D4
Uelen *Russia* **53** C19
Uelzen *Germany* **24** C6
Uetersen *Germany* **24** B5
Uetze *Germany* **24** C6
Ufa *Russia* **52** D6
Uffenheim *Germany* **25** F6
Ugab → *Namibia* **88** C1
Ugalla → *Tanzania* **86** D3
Ugalla River △ *Tanzania* **86** D3
Uganda ■ *Africa* **86** B3
Ugento *Italy* **43** C11
Ugep *Nigeria* **83** D6
Ughelli *Nigeria* **83** D6
Ugie *S. Africa* **89** E4
Ugíjar *Spain* **37** J7
Ugine *France* **21** C10
Uglegorsk *Russia* **53** E15
Uglich *Russia* **32** D10
Ugljan *Croatia* **41** D12
Ugljane *Croatia* **41** E13
Ugra → *Russia* **32** E9
Uğurchin *Bulgaria* **45** C8
Uh → *Slovak Rep.* **27** C15
Uherské Hradiště *Czech Rep.* **27** B10
Uherský Brod *Czech Rep.* **27** B10
Úhlava → *Czech Rep.* **26** B6
Uhniv *Ukraine* **31** H10
Uhrichsville *U.S.A.* **114** F3
Uibhist a Deas = South
  Uist *U.K.* **13** D1
Uibhist a Tuath = North
  Uist *U.K.* **13** D1
Uig *U.K.* **13** D2
Uíge *Angola* **84** F2
Uiha *Tonga* **91** c
Uijeongbu *S. Korea* **57** F14
Ûiju *N. Korea* **57** D13
Uinta Mts. *U.S.A.* **108** F8
Uis *Namibia* **88** C1
Uiseong *S. Korea* **57** F15
Uitenhage *S. Africa* **88** E4
Uithuizen *Neths.* **17** A6
Ujazd *Poland* **31** H5
Újfehértó *Hungary* **28** C6
Ujh → *India* **68** C6
Ujhani *India* **69** F8
Uji-guntō *Japan* **55** J4
Ujjain *India* **68** H6
Ujście *Poland* **31** E3
Újszász *Hungary* **28** C5
Ujung Pandang *Indonesia* **63** F5
Uka *Russia* **53** D17
Ukara I. *Tanzania* **86** C3
Uke-Shima *Japan* **55** K4
Ukerewe I. *Tanzania* **86** C3
Ukholovo *Russia* **34** D5
Ukhrul *India* **67** G19
Ukhta *Russia* **52** C6
Ukiah *U.S.A.* **110** F3
Ukmergė *Lithuania* **32** E5
Ukraine ■ *Europe* **33** H7
Ukwi *Botswana* **88** C3
Ulaan-Uul *Mongolia* **56** B6
Ulaanbaatar *Mongolia* **53** E11
Ulaangom *Mongolia* **60** A4
Ulaanjirem *Mongolia* **56** B3
Ulamba *Dem. Rep. of the Congo* **87** D2
Ulan Bator = Ulaanbaatar
  Mongolia **53** E11
Ulan Erge *Russia* **35** J7
Ulan Khol *Russia* **35** H8
Ulan Ude *Russia* **53** D11
Ulanów *Poland* **31** H9
Ulaş *Sivas, Turkey* **72** C7
Ulaş *Tekirdağ, Turkey* **45** E11
Ulaya *Morogoro, Tanzania* **86** D4
Ulaya *Tabora, Tanzania* **86** C3
Ulcinj *Montenegro* **44** E3
Ulco *S. Africa* **88** D3
Ule älv = Oulujoki →
  Finland **8** D21
Ule träsk = Oulujärvi
  Finland **8** D22
Uleåborg = Oulu *Finland* **8** D21
Ulefoss *Norway* **9** G13
Ulëz *Albania* **44** E3
Ulfborg *Denmark* **11** H2
Ulhasnagar *India* **66** K8
Uliastay *Mongolia* **60** B4
Uljin *S. Korea* **57** F15
Uljma *Serbia* **28** E6
Ulla → *Spain* **36** C2
Ulladulla *Australia* **95** F5
Ullapool *U.K.* **13** D3
Ullared *Sweden* **11** G6
Ulldecona *Spain* **38** E5
Ulleungdo *S. Korea* **55** F5
Ullswater *U.K.* **14** C5
Ulm *Germany* **25** G5
Ulmarra *Australia* **95** D5
Ulmeni *Buzău, Romania* **29** E11
Ulmeni *Maramureş, Romania* **29** C8

Ulonguè *Mozam.* **87** E3
Ulricehamn *Sweden* **11** G7
Ulrika *Sweden* **11** F9
Ulsan *S. Korea* **57** G15
Ulsta *U.K.* **13** A7
Ulster □ *U.K.* **12** B5
Ulstrem *Bulgaria* **45** D10
Ulubat Gölü *Turkey* **45** F12
Ulubey *Turkey* **47** C11
Uluborlu *Turkey* **47** C12
Uluçinar *Turkey* **72** D6
Uludağ *Turkey* **45** F13
Uludağ △ *Turkey* **45** F13
Uludere *Turkey* **73** D10
Uluguru Mts. *Tanzania* **86** D4
Ulukışla *Turkey* **72** D6
Ulungur He → *China* **60** B3
Uluru *Australia* **93** E5
Uluru-Kata Tjuta △
  Australia **93** E5
Ulutau *Kazakhstan* **52** E7
Uluwatu *Indonesia* **63** K18
Ulva *U.K.* **13** E2
Ulverston *U.K.* **14** C4
Ulverstone *Australia* **95** G4
Ulya *Russia* **53** D15
Ulyanovo *Russia* **30** D9
Ulyanovsk = Simbirsk
  Russia **34** C9
Ulyanovsk □ *Russia* **34** C9
Ulyasutay = Uliastay
  Mongolia **60** B4
Ulysses *U.S.A.* **112** G3
Umag *Croatia* **41** C10
Umala *Bolivia* **124** G5
'Umān = Oman ■ *Asia* **75** C6
Uman *Ukraine* **23** D16
Umaria *India* **69** H9
Umarkot *Pakistan* **68** G3
Umarpada *India* **68** J5
Umatilla *U.S.A.* **108** D4
Umbagog L. *U.S.A.* **115** B13
Umbértide *Italy* **41** E9
Umbrella Mts. *N.Z.* **91** F2
Umbria □ *Italy* **41** F9
Umeå *Sweden* **8** E19
Umeälven → *Sweden* **8** E19
Umera *Indonesia* **63** E7
Umfuli → *Zimbabwe* **87** F2
Umfurudzi △ *Zimbabwe* **87** F3
Umgusa *Zimbabwe* **87** F2
Umgwenya → *Mozam.* **89** D5
Umim Urūmah *Si. Arabia* **80** B4
Umiujaq *Canada* **104** A4
Umka *Serbia* **44** B4
Umkomaas *S. Africa* **89** E5
Umlazi *S. Africa* **85** L6
Umm ad Daraj, J. *Jordan* **74** C4
Umm al Qaywayn *U.A.E.* **71** E7
Umm al Qittayn *Jordan* **74** C5
Umm Arda *Sudan* **81** D3
Umm Bāb *Qatar* **71** E6
Umm Badr *Sudan* **81** E2
Umm Baiyud *Sudan* **81** E3
Umm Bel *Sudan* **81** E2
Umm Birkah *Si. Arabia* **80** B4
Umm Boim *Sudan* **81** E2
Umm Dam *Sudan* **81** E3
Umm Debi *Sudan* **81** E3
Umm Dubban *Sudan* **81** D3
Umm Durman =
  Omdurmân *Sudan* **81** D3
Umm el Fahm *Israel* **74** C4
Umm Gafala *Sudan* **81** E2
Umm Gimala *Sudan* **81** E2
Umm Inderaba *Sudan* **80** D3
Umm Keddada *Sudan* **81** E2
Umm Koweika *Sudan* **81** E3
Umm Lajj *Si. Arabia* **70** E3
Umm Merwa *Sudan* **80** D3
Umm Qantur *Sudan* **81** E3
Umm Qasr *Iraq* **70** D5
Umm Qurein *Sudan* **81** F2
Umm Ruwaba *Sudan* **81** E3
Umm Saiyala *Sudan* **81** E3
Umm Shanqa *Sudan* **81** E2
Umm Shutur *Sudan* **81** F3
Umm Sidr *Sudan* **81** E2
Umm Zehetir *Egypt* **80** J8
Umnak I. *U.S.A.* **106** a
Umniati → *Zimbabwe* **87** F2
Umpqua → *U.S.A.* **108** E1
Umreth *India* **68** H5
Umtata = Mthatha *S. Africa* **89** E4
Umuahia *Nigeria* **83** D6
Umuarama *Brazil* **127** A5
Umurbey *Turkey* **45** F10
Umvukwe Ra. *Zimbabwe* **87** F3
Umzimvubu *S. Africa* **89** E4
Umzingwane → *Zimbabwe* **87** G2
Umzinto = eMuziwezinto
  S. Africa **89** E5
Una *India* **68** J4
Una → *Bos.-H.* **41** D13
Unac → *Bos.-H.* **41** D13
Unadilla *U.S.A.* **115** D9

Unalakleet *U.S.A.* **106** a
Unalaska *U.S.A.* **106** a
Unalaska I. *U.S.A.* **106** a
'Unayzah *Si. Arabia* **70** E4
'Unayzah, J. *Asia* **73** F8
Uncastillo *Spain* **38** C3
Uncía *Bolivia* **124** G5
Uncompahgre Peak *U.S.A.*
  108 G10
Uncompahgre Plateau
  U.S.A. **108** G9
Undara Volcanic △ *Australia* **94** B3
Unden *Sweden* **11** F8
Underbool *Australia* **95** F3
Undersaker *Sweden* **10** A7
Unecha *Russia* **33** F7
Ungarie *Australia* **95** E4
Ungarra *Australia* **95** E2
Ungava, Pén. d' *Canada* **101** D12
Ungava B. *Canada* **101** D13
Ungeny = Ungheni *Moldova* **29** C12
Unggi *N. Korea* **57** C16
Ungheni *Moldova* **29** C12
Unguala → *Ethiopia* **81** F5
Ungwana B. *Kenya* **86** C5
Ungwatiri *Sudan* **81** D4
Uni *Russia* **34** B10
União da Vitória *Brazil* **127** B5
Uničov *Czech Rep.* **27** B10
Uniejów *Poland* **31** G5
Unije *Croatia* **41** D11
Unimak I. *U.S.A.* **106** a
Union *Miss., U.S.A.* **117** E10
Union *Mo., U.S.A.* **112** F8
Union *S.C., U.S.A.* **117** D14
Union City *Calif., U.S.A.* **110** H4
Union City *N.J., U.S.A.* **115** F10
Union City *Pa., U.S.A.* **114** E5
Union City *Tenn., U.S.A.* **117** C10
Union Gap *U.S.A.* **108** C3
Union Springs *U.S.A.* **117** E12
Uniondale *S. Africa* **88** E3
Uniontown *U.S.A.* **113** F14
Unionville *U.S.A.* **112** E7
Unirea *Romania* **29** F12
United Arab Emirates ■ *Asia* **71** F7
United Kingdom ■ *Europe* **16** E6
United States of America ■
  N. Amer. **106** C7
Unity *Canada* **103** C7
Universales, Mtes. *Spain* **38** E3
University Park *U.S.A.* **109** K10
University Place *U.S.A.* **110** C4
Unjha *India* **68** H5
Unna *Germany* **24** D3
Unnao *India* **69** F9
Uno, Ilha *Guinea-Biss.* **82** C1
Unsengedsi → *Zimbabwe* **87** F3
Unst *U.K.* **13** A8
Unstrut → *Germany* **24** D7
Unterfranken □ *Germany* **25** F5
Unterschleissheim *Germany* **25** G7
Unuk → *Canada* **102** B2
Ünye *Turkey* **72** B7
Unzen-Amakusa △ *Japan* **55** H5
Unzha *Russia* **34** A7
Unzha → *Russia* **34** B6
Uozu *Japan* **55** F8
Upata *Venezuela* **124** B6
Upemba, L.
  Dem. Rep. of the Congo **87** D2
Upemba △
  Dem. Rep. of the Congo **87** D2
Upernavik *Greenland* **4** B5
Upington *S. Africa* **88** D3
Upleta *India* **68** J4
'Upolu *Samoa* **91** b
Upper □ *Ghana* **83** C4
Upper Alkali L. *U.S.A.* **108** F3
Upper Arrow L. *Canada* **102** C5
Upper Darby *U.S.A.* **113** F16
Upper Foster L. *Canada* **103** B7
Upper Hutt *N.Z.* **91** D5
Upper Klamath L. *U.S.A.* **108** E3
Upper Lake *U.S.A.* **110** F4
Upper Manzanilla
  Trin. & Tob. **125** K15
Upper Missouri Breaks △
  U.S.A. **108** C9
Upper Musquodoboit
  Canada **105** C7
Upper Red L. *U.S.A.* **112** A6
Upper Sandusky *U.S.A.* **113** E12
Upper Volta = Burkina
  Faso ■ *Africa* **82** C4
Upphärad *Sweden* **11** F6
Uppland *Sweden* **10** D12
Upplands-Väsby *Sweden* **10** E11
Uppsala *Sweden* **10** E11
Uppsala län □ *Sweden* **10** D11
Upshi *India* **69** C7
Upstart, C. *Australia* **94** B4
Upton *U.S.A.* **108** D11
Uqsuqtuuq = Gjoa Haven
  Canada **100** C10
Ur *Iraq* **70** D5
Urad Qianqi *China* **56** D5

Urakawa *Japan* **54** C11
Ural = Uralskiy □ *Russia* **52** C7
Ural = Zhayyq → *Kazakhstan* **6** F16
Ural *Australia* **95** E4
Ural Mts. = Uralskie Gory
  Eurasia **6** C17
Uralla *Australia* **95** E5
Uralsk = Oral *Kazakhstan* **34** E10
Uralskie Gory *Eurasia* **6** C17
Uralskiy □ *Russia* **52** C7
Urambo *Tanzania* **86** D3
Urandangi *Australia* **94** C2
Uranium City *Canada* **103** B7
Uraricoera → *Brazil* **124** C6
Urasoe *Japan* **55** L3
Urawa = Saitama *Japan* **55** G9
Uray *Russia* **52** C7
'Uray'irah *Si. Arabia* **71** E6
Urbana *Ill., U.S.A.* **112** E9
Urbana *Ohio, U.S.A.* **113** E12
Urbandale *U.S.A.* **112** E7
Urbánia *Italy* **41** E9
Urbel → *Spain* **36** C7
Urbino *Italy* **41** E9
Urbión, Picos de *Spain* **38** C2
Urcos *Peru* **124** F4
Urdinarrain *Argentina* **126** C4
Urdos *France* **20** F3
Ure → *U.K.* **14** C6
Uren *Russia* **34** B7
Ures *Mexico* **118** B2
Urewera △ *N.Z.* **91** C6
Urfa = Sanlıurfa *Turkey* **73** D8
Urganch *Uzbekistan* **52** E7
Urgench = Urganch
  Uzbekistan **52** E7
Ürgüp *Turkey* **70** B2
Uri *India* **69** B6
Uri □ *Switz.* **25** J4
Uribia *Colombia* **124** A4
Uricani *Romania* **28** E7
Uriondo *Bolivia* **126** A3
Urique *Mexico* **118** B3
Urique → *Mexico* **118** B3
Urk *Neths.* **17** B5
Urkiola △ *Spain* **38** B3
Urla *Turkey* **47** C8
Urlați *Romania* **29** F11
Urmia = Orūmīyeh *Iran* **73** D11
Uroševac *Serbia* **44** D5
Uroyan, Montanas de
  Puerto Rico **121** d
Urshult *Sweden* **11** H8
Uruaçu *Brazil* **125** F9
Uruapan *Mexico* **118** D4
Urubamba → *Peru* **124** F4
Uruçara *Brazil* **124** D7
Uruçuí *Brazil* **125** E10
Uruguai → *Brazil* **127** B5
Uruguaiana *Brazil* **126** B4
Uruguay ■ *S. Amer.* **126** C4
Uruguay → *S. Amer.* **126** C4
Urumchi = Ürümqi *China* **52** E9
Ürümqi *China* **52** E9
Urup → *Russia* **35** H5
Urup, Ostrov *Russia* **53** E16
Uryupinsk *Russia* **34** E5
Ürzhar *Kazakhstan* **52** E9
Urzhum *Russia* **34** B9
Urziceni *Romania* **29** F11
Usa → *Russia* **52** C6
Uşak *Turkey* **47** C11
Uşak □ *Turkey* **47** C11
Usakos *Namibia* **88** C2
Ušće *Serbia* **44** C4
Usedom *Germany* **24** B10
Usedom △ *Germany* **24** B10
Useless Loop *Australia* **93** E1
'Usfān *Si. Arabia* **80** C4
Ushakova, Ostrov *Russia* **4** A12
Ushakovo *Russia* **30** D7
Ushant = Ouessant, Î. d'
  France **18** D1
Ushashi *Tanzania* **86** C3
Ushat *Sudan* **81** F2
'Ushayrah *Si. Arabia* **80** C5
Ushibuka *Japan* **55** H5
Üshtöbe *Kazakhstan* **52** E8
Ushuaia *Argentina* **128** G3
Ushumun *Russia* **53** D13
Ushytsya → *Ukraine* **29** B12
Usk *Canada* **102** C3
Usk → *U.K.* **15** F5
Uska *India* **69** F10
Üsküdar *Turkey* **45** F13
Uslar *Germany* **24** D5
Usman *Russia* **33** F10
Usoke *Tanzania* **86** D3
Usolye-Sibirskoye *Russia* **53** D11
Usoro *Nigeria* **83** D6
Uspallata, P. de *Argentina* **126** C2
Ussel *France* **20** C6
Usson-du-Poitou *France* **20** B4
Ussuriysk *Russia* **54** B6
Ussurka *Russia* **54** B6
Ust-Bolsheretsk *Russia* **53** D16
Ust-Buzulukskaya *Russia* **34** E6

Ust-Chaun *Russia* **53** C18
Ust-Chorna *Ukraine* **29** B8
Ust-Donetskiy *Russia* **35** G5
Ust-Ilimsk *Russia* **53** D11
Ust-Ishim *Russia* **52** D8
Ust-Kamchatsk *Russia* **53** D17
Ust-Kamenogorsk =
  Öskemen *Kazakhstan* **52** E9
Ust-Khayryuzovo *Russia* **53** D16
Ust-Kut *Russia* **53** D11
Ust-Kuyga *Russia* **53** B14
Ust-Labinsk *Russia* **35** H4
Ust-Luga *Russia* **32** C5
Ust-Maya *Russia* **53** C14
Ust-Mil *Russia* **53** D14
Ust-Nera *Russia* **53** C15
Ust-Nyukzha *Russia* **53** D13
Ust-Olenek *Russia* **53** B12
Ust-Omchug *Russia* **53** C15
Ust-Port *Russia* **52** C9
Ust-Tsilma *Russia* **52** C6
Ust-Urt = Ustyurt Plateau
  Asia **52** E6
Ustaritz *France* **20** E2
Ústecký □ *Czech Rep.* **26** A7
Ústí nad Labem *Czech Rep.* **26** A7
Ústí nad Orlicí *Czech Rep.* **27** B9
Ústica *Italy* **42** D6
Ustinov = Izhevsk *Russia* **52** D6
Ustka *Poland* **30** D3
Ustron *Poland* **31** J5
Ustrzyki Dolne *Poland* **31** J9
Ustyluh *Ukraine* **31** H11
Ustyurt Plateau *Asia* **52** E6
Ustyuzhna *Russia* **32** C9
Usu *China* **60** B3
Usuki *Japan* **55** H5
Usulután *El Salv.* **120** D2
Usumacinta → *Mexico* **119** D6
Usumbura = Bujumbura
  Burundi **86** C2
Usure *Tanzania* **86** C3
Usutuo → *Mozam.* **89** D5
Uta *Indonesia* **63** E9
Utah □ *U.S.A.* **108** G8
Utah L. *U.S.A.* **108** F8
Utansjö *Sweden* **10** B11
Utara, Selat *Malaysia* **65** c
Utarni *India* **68** F4
Utatlan *Guatemala* **120** C1
Ute Creek → *U.S.A.* **109** J12
Utebo *Spain* **38** D3
Utena *Lithuania* **32** E3
Utete *Tanzania* **86** D4
Uthai Thani *Thailand* **64** E3
Uthal *Pakistan* **68** G2
Utiariti *Brazil* **124** F7
Utica *N.Y., U.S.A.* **115** C9
Utica *Ohio, U.S.A.* **114** F2
Utiel *Spain* **39** F3
Utikuma L. *Canada* **102** B5
Utö *Sweden* **10** F12
Utopia *Australia* **94** C1
Utraula *India* **69** F10
Utrecht *Neths.* **17** B5
Utrecht *S. Africa* **89** D5
Utrecht □ *Neths.* **17** B5
Utrera *Spain* **37** H5
Utsjoki → *Finland* **8** B22
Utsunomiya *Japan* **55** F9
Uttar Pradesh □ *India* **69** F9
Uttaradit *Thailand* **64** D3
Uttaranchal □ *India* **69** D8
Uttoxeter *U.K.* **14** E6
Utuado *Puerto Rico* **121** d
Uummannaq *Greenland* **4** B4
Uummannaq *Greenland* **4** B5
Uummannarsuaq =
  Nunap Isua *Greenland* **98** D15
Uusikaarlepyy *Finland* **8** E20
Uusikaupunki *Finland* **32** B1
Uva *Russia* **34** B11
Uvac → *Serbia* **44** C3
Uvalde *U.S.A.* **116** G5
Uvarovo *Russia* **34** E6
Uvat *Russia* **52** D7
Uvinza *Tanzania* **86** D3
Uvira *Dem. Rep. of the Congo* **86** C2
Uvs Nuur *Mongolia* **60** A4
'Uwairidh, Ḥarrat al
  Si. Arabia **80** C5
Uwajima *Japan* **55** H6
Uwanda △ *Tanzania* **86** D3
Uweinat, Jebel *Sudan* **80** C1
Uxbridge *Canada* **114** B5
Uxin Qi *China* **56** E5
Uxmal *Mexico* **119** C7
Üydzin *Mongolia* **56** B4
Uyo *Nigeria* **83** D6
Üyüklü Tepe *Turkey* **47** D9
Uyûn Mûsa *Egypt* **74** F1
Uyuni *Bolivia* **124** H5
Uzbekistan ■ *Asia* **52** E7
Uzboy → *Turkmenistan* **71** B7
Uzen, Bolshoi = Uzen,
  Mal → *Kazakhstan* **35** F9

Uzen, Mal → *Kazakhstan* **35** F9
Uzerche *France* **20** C5
Uzès *France* **21** D8
Uzh → *Ukraine* **23** C16
Uzhgorod = Uzhhorod
  Ukraine **28** B7
Uzhhorod *Ukraine* **28** B7
Uzhok *Ukraine* **28** B7
Užice *Serbia* **44** C3
Uzlovaya *Russia* **32** F10
Üzümlü *Turkey* **47** E11
Uzunköprü *Turkey* **45** E10
Uzunkuyu *Turkey* **47** C8

V

Vaal → *S. Africa* **88** D3
Vaal Dam *S. Africa* **89** D4
Vaalbos △ *S. Africa* **88** D3
Vaalwater *S. Africa* **89** C4
Vaasa *Finland* **8** E19
Vabre *France* **20** E6
Vác *Hungary* **28** C4
Vacaria *Brazil* **127** B5
Vacata *Fiji* **91** a
Vacaville *U.S.A.* **110** G5
Vaccarès, Étang de *France* **21** E8
Vach = Vakh → *Russia* **52** C8
Vache, Î. à *Haiti* **121** C5
Vacoas *Mauritius* **85** d
Väddö *Sweden* **10** D12
Väderstad *Sweden* **11** F8
Vadnagar *India* **68** H5
Vado Lígure *Italy* **40** D5
Vadodara *India* **68** H5
Vadsø *Norway* **8** A23
Vadstena *Sweden* **11** F8
Vaduz *Liech.* **25** H5
Værøy *Norway* **8** C15
Vágar *Færoe Is.* **8** E9
Vaggeryd *Sweden* **11** G8
Vaghia *Greece* **46** C5
Vagia, Akra *Greece* **49** C10
Vagney *France* **19** D13
Vagnhärad *Sweden* **11** F11
Vagos *Portugal* **36** E2
Vågsfjorden *Norway* **8** B17
Váh → *Slovak Rep.* **27** D11
Vahsel B. *Antarctica* **5** D1
Váhtjer = Gällivare *Sweden* **8** C19
Vaï *Greece* **49** D8
Vaigach *Russia* **52** B6
Vaiges *France* **18** D6
Vaihingen *Germany* **25** G4
Vaihiria, L. *Tahiti* **91** d
Vail *U.S.A.* **106** C5
Vailly-sur-Aisne *France* **19** C10
Vairao *Tahiti* **91** d
Vaisali → *India* **69** F8
Vaison-la-Romaine *France* **21** D9
Vaitogi *Amer. Samoa* **91** b
Vakarel *Bulgaria* **44** D7
Vakfikebir *Turkey* **73** B8
Vakh → *Russia* **52** C8
Vakhtan *Russia* **34** B8
Vál *Hungary* **28** C3
Val-de-Marne □ *France* **19** D9
Val-d'Isère *France* **21** C10
Val-d'Oise □ *France* **19** C9
Val-d'Or *Canada* **104** C4
Val Grande △ *Italy* **40** B5
Val Marie *Canada* **103** D7
Val Thorens *France* **21** C10
Valaam *Russia* **32** B6
Valadares *Portugal* **36** D2
Valahia *Romania* **29** F9
Valais □ *Switz.* **25** J3
Valais, Alpes du *Switz.* **25** J3
Valandovo *Macedonia* **44** E6
Valaxa *Greece* **46** C6
Vålberg *Sweden* **10** E7
Valbo *Sweden* **10** D10
Valbondione *Italy* **40** B7
Vălcani *Romania* **28** D5
Vâlcea □ *Romania* **29** F9
Valcheta *Argentina* **128** E3
Valdagno *Italy* **41** C8
Valdahon *France* **19** E13
Valdai Hills = Valdayskaya
  Vozvyshennost *Russia* **32** D7
Valday *Russia* **32** D7
Valdayskaya
  Vozvyshennost *Russia* **32** D7
Valdeazogues → *Spain* **37** G6
Valdecañas, Embalse de
  Spain **36** F5
Valdemarsvik *Sweden* **11** F10
Valdemoro *Spain* **36** E7
Valdepeñas *Spain* **37** G7
Valderaduey → *Spain* **36** D5
Valdérice *Italy* **42** D5
Valderrobres *Spain* **38** E5
Valdés, Pen. *Argentina* **128** E4
Valdez *U.S.A.* **100** C5
Valdivia *Chile* **128** D2

Valdivia Abyssal Plain
  S. Ocean **5** C6
Valdobbiádene *Italy* **41** C8
Valdosta *U.S.A.* **117** F13
Valdoviño *Spain* **36** B2
Valdres *Norway* **8** F13
Vale *Georgia* **35** K6
Vale *U.S.A.* **108** E5
Vale of Glamorgan □ *U.K.* **15** F4
Valea lui Mihai *Romania* **28** C6
Valea Mărului *Romania* **29** E12
Valemount *Canada* **102** C5
Valença *Brazil* **125** F11
Valença *Portugal* **36** C2
Valença do Piauí *Brazil* **125** E10
Valençay *France* **19** E8
Valence *France* **21** D8
Valence d'Agen *France* **20** D4
Valencia *Spain* **39** F4
Valencia *Trin. & Tob.* **125** K15
Valencia *U.S.A.* **109** J10
Valencia *Venezuela* **124** A5
Valencia □ *Spain* **39** F4
Valencia ✈ (VLC) *Spain* **39** F4
Valencia, G. de *Spain* **39** F5
Valencia de Alcántara *Spain* **37** F3
Valencia de Don Juan *Spain* **36** C5
Valencia I. *Ireland* **12** E1
Valenciennes *France* **19** B10
Văleni *Romania* **29** F9
Vălenii de Munte *Romania* **29** E11
Valensole *France* **21** E9
Valentigney *France* **19** E13
Valentim, Sa. do *Brazil* **125** E10
Valentin *Russia* **54** C7
Valentine *Nebr., U.S.A.* **112** D3
Valentine *Tex., U.S.A.* **116** F2
Valenza *Italy* **40** C5
Valera *Venezuela* **124** B4
Valga *Estonia* **32** D4
Valguarnera Caropepe *Italy* **43** E7
Valier *U.S.A.* **108** B7
Valjevo *Serbia* **44** B3
Valka *Latvia* **32** D3
Valkeakoski *Finland* **32** B2
Valkenswaard *Neths.* **17** C5
Vall de la Vall
  d'Uixó *Spain* **38** F4
Valla *Sweden* **10** E10
Valladolid *Mexico* **119** C7
Valladolid *Spain* **36** D6
Valladolid □ *Spain* **36** D6
Vallata *Italy* **43** A8
Valldemossa *Spain* **48** B9
Valle d'Aosta □ *Italy* **40** C4
Valle de Arán *Spain* **38** C5
Valle de la Pascua *Venezuela* **124** B5
Valle de las Palmas *Mexico* **111** N10
Valle de Santiago *Mexico* **118** C4
Valle de Zaragoza *Mexico* **118** B3
Valle del Ticino △ *Italy* **40** C6
Valle Fértil, Sierra del
  Argentina **126** C2
Valle Gran Rey *Canary Is.* **48** F2
Valle Hermoso *Mexico* **119** B5
Valle Nacional *Mexico* **119** D5
Valledupar *Colombia* **124** A4
Vallehermoso *Canary Is.* **48** F2
Vallejo *U.S.A.* **110** G4
Vallenar *Chile* **126** B1
Vallentuna *Sweden* **10** E12
Valleraugue *France* **20** D7
Vallet *France* **18** E5
Valletta *Malta* **49** D2
Valley Center *U.S.A.* **111** M9
Valley City *U.S.A.* **112** B5
Valley Falls *Oreg., U.S.A.* **108** E3
Valley Falls *R.I., U.S.A.* **115** E13
Valley of Flowers △ *India* **69** D8
Valley of the Kings *Egypt* **80** B3
Valley Springs *U.S.A.* **110** G6
Valley View *U.S.A.* **115** F8
Valley Wells *U.S.A.* **111** K11
Valleyview *Canada* **102** B5
Valli di Comácchio *Italy* **41** D9
Vallimanca, Arroyo
  Argentina **126** D4
Vallo della Lucánia *Italy* **43** B8
Vallon-Pont-d'Arc *France* **21** D8
Vallorbe *Switz.* **25** J2
Valls *Spain* **38** D6
Valmaseda = Balmaseda
  Spain **38** B1
Valmiera *Latvia* **32** D3
Valnera *Spain* **36** B7
Valognes *France* **18** C5
Valona = Vlorë *Albania* **44** F3
Valongo *Portugal* **36** D2
Valozhyn *Belarus* **23** A14
Valpaços *Portugal* **36** D3
Valparaíso *Chile* **126** C1
Valparaíso *Mexico* **118** C4
Valparaíso *U.S.A.* **114** E2
Valparaíso □ *Chile* **126** C1
Valpovo *Croatia* **28** E3
Valréas *France* **21** D9

Vals *Switz.* **25** J5
Vals → *S. Africa* **88** D4
Vals, Tanjung *Indonesia* **63** F9
Vals-les-Bains *France* **21** D8
Valsad *India* **66** J8
Valtellina *Italy* **40** B6
Valuyki *Russia* **33** G10
Valverde *Canary Is.* **48** G2
Valverde del Camino *Spain* **37** H4
Valverde del Fresno *Spain* **36** E4
Vama *Romania* **29** C10
Vamdrup *Denmark* **11** J3
Våmhus *Sweden* **10** C8
Vammala *Finland* **32** B2
Vamos *Greece* **49** D6
Van *Turkey* **73** C10
Van □ *Turkey* **73** C10
Van, L. = Van Gölü *Turkey* **73** C10
Van Alstyne *U.S.A.* **116** E6
Van Blommestein Meer
   Suriname **125** C7
Van Buren *Canada* **105** C6
Van Buren *Ark., U.S.A.* **116** D7
Van Buren *Maine, U.S.A.* **113** B20
Van Buren *Mo., U.S.A.* **112** G8
Van Canh *Vietnam* **64** F7
Van Diemen, C. *N. Terr.,*
   Australia **92** B5
Van Diemen, C. *Queens.,*
   Australia **94** B2
Van Diemen G. *Australia* **92** B5
Van Gölü *Turkey* **73** C10
Van Horn *U.S.A.* **116** F2
Van Ninh *Vietnam* **64** F7
Van Rees, Pegunungan
   Indonesia **63** E9
Van Wert *U.S.A.* **113** E11
Van Yen *Vietnam* **58** G5
Vanadzor *Armenia* **35** K7
Vanavara *Russia* **53** C11
Vancouver *Canada* **110** A3
Vancouver *U.S.A.* **110** E4
Vancouver, C. *Australia* **93** G2
Vancouver I. *Canada* **110** D3
Vancouver Int. ✈ (YVR)
   Canada **110** A3
Vanda = Vantaa *Finland* **32** B3
Vandalia *Ill., U.S.A.* **112** F9
Vandalia *Mo., U.S.A.* **112** F8
Vandenberg Village *U.S.A.* **111** L6
Vandergrift *U.S.A.* **114** F5
Vanderhoof *Canada* **102** C4
Vanderkloof Dam *S. Africa* **88** E3
Vanderlin I. *Australia* **94** B2
Vänern *Sweden* **11** F7
Vänersborg *Sweden* **11** F6
Vang Vieng *Laos* **64** C4
Vanga *Kenya* **86** C4
Vangaindrano *Madag.* **89** C8
Vanguard *Canada* **103** D7
Vanino *Russia* **53** E15
Vânju Mare *Romania* **28** F7
Vännäs *Sweden* **8** E18
Vannes *France* **18** E4
Vannøya *Norway* **8** A18
Vanoise, Massif de la *France*
   21 C10
Vanrhynsdorp *S. Africa* **88** E2
Vansbro *Sweden* **10** D8
Vansittart B. *Australia* **92** B4
Vantaa *Finland* **32** B3
Vanua Balavu *Fiji* **91** a
Vanua Levu *Fiji* **91** a
Vanua Vatu *Fiji* **91** a
Vanuatu ■ *Pac. Oc.* **90** C9
Vanwyksvlei *S. Africa* **88** E3
Vanzylsrus *S. Africa* **88** D3
Vapnyarka *Ukraine* **29** B13
Var □ *France* **21** E10
Var → *France* **21** E11
Vara *Sweden* **11** F6
Varades *France* **18** E5
Varáita → *Italy* **40** D4
Varallo *Italy* **40** C5
Varāmīn *Iran* **71** C6
Varāmīn □ *Iran* **71** B6
Varanasi *India* **69** G10
Varangerfjorden *Norway* **8** A23
Varangerhalvøya *Norway* **8** A23
Varano, Lago di *Italy* **41** G12
Varaždin *Croatia* **41** B13
Varazze *Italy* **40** D5
Varberg *Sweden* **11** H6
Vardak □ *Afghan.* **66** B6
Vardar = Axios → *Greece* **44** F6
Varde *Denmark* **11** J2
Varde Å → *Denmark* **11** J2
Vardø *Norway* **8** A24
Varel *Germany* **24** B4
Varella, Mui *Vietnam* **64** F7
Varéna *Lithuania* **32** E3
Varennes-sur-Allier *France* **19** F10
Varennes-Vauzelles *France* **19** E10
Vareš *Bos.-H.* **28** F3
Varese *Italy* **40** C5
Vårfurile *Romania* **28** D7

Vårgårda *Sweden* **11** F6
Varginha *Brazil* **127** A6
Vargön *Sweden* **11** F6
Varillas *Chile* **126** A1
Varkaus *Finland* **32** A4
Värmdölandet *Sweden* **10** E12
Värmeln *Sweden* **10** E6
Värmlands län □ *Sweden* **10** E6
Värmlandsbro *Sweden* **10** E7
Varna *Bulgaria* **45** C11
Varna □ *Bulgaria* **45** C11
Värnamo *Sweden* **11** G8
Varnsdorf *Czech Rep.* **26** A7
Várpalota *Hungary* **28** C3
Vars *Canada* **115** A9
Vars *France* **21** D10
Varsyburg *U.S.A.* **114** D6
Varzaneh *Iran* **71** C7
Varzi *Italy* **40** D6
Varzo *Italy* **40** B5
Varzy *France* **19** E10
Vas □ *Hungary* **28** C1
Vasa = Vaasa *Finland* **8** E19
Vasa Barris → *Brazil* **125** F11
Vascão → *Portugal* **37** H3
Vaşcău *Romania* **28** D7
Vascongadas = País
   Vasco □ *Spain* **38** C2
Vashkivtsi *Ukraine* **29** B10
Vasht = Khāsh *Iran* **71** D9
Vasilevichi *Belarus* **23** B15
Vasiliki *Greece* **46** C2
Vasiliko *Greece* **46** C5
Vasilkov = Vasylkiv
   Ukraine **23** C16
Vaslui *Romania* **29** D12
Vaslui □ *Romania* **29** D12
Väsman *Sweden* **10** D9
Vassar *Canada* **103** D9
Vassar *U.S.A.* **113** D12
Västerås *Sweden* **10** E10
Västerbotten *Sweden* **8** D19
Västerdalälven → *Sweden* **10** D8
Västergötland *Sweden* **11** F7
Västerhaninge *Sweden* **10** E12
Vastervik *Sweden* **11** G10
Västmanland *Sweden* **9** G17
Västmanlands län □
   Sweden **10** E10
Vasto *Italy* **41** F11
Västra Götalands Län □
   Sweden **11** F6
Vasvár *Hungary* **28** C1
Vasylivka *Ukraine* **29** E13
Vasylkiv *Ukraine* **23** C16
Vatan *France* **19** E8
Vatersay *U.K.* **13** E1
Vathia *Greece* **46** E4
Vatican City ■ *Europe* **41** G9
Vaticano, C. *Italy* **43** D8
Vatili *Cyprus* **49** D12
Vatin *Serbia* **28** E6
Vatiu = Atiu *Cook Is.* **97** J12
Vatnajökull *Iceland* **8** D5
Vatolakkos *Greece* **49** D5
Vatoloha *Madag.* **89** B8
Vatomandry *Madag.* **89** B8
Vatra-Dornei *Romania* **29** C10
Vatrak → *India* **68** H5
Vättern *Sweden* **11** F8
Vatu Vara *Fiji* **91** a
Vatulele *Fiji* **91** a
Vaucluse □ *France* **21** E9
Vaucouleurs *France* **19** D12
Vaud □ *Switz.* **25** J2
Vaudreuil-Dorion *Canada* **115** A10
Vaughn *Mont., U.S.A.* **108** C8
Vaughn *N. Mex., U.S.A.* **109** J11
Vaujours L. *Canada* **104** A5
Vaupés = Uaupés → *Brazil* **124** C4
Vaupes □ *Colombia* **124** C4
Vauvert *France* **21** E8
Vauxhall *Canada* **102** C6
Vav *India* **68** G4
Vavatenina *Madag.* **89** B8
Vava'u *Tonga* **91** c
Vava'u Group *Tonga* **91** c
Vavoua *Ivory C.* **82** D3
Vawkavysk *Belarus* **23** B13
Vaxholm *Sweden* **10** E12
Växjö *Sweden* **11** H8
Våxtorp *Sweden* **11** H7
Vaygach, Ostrov *Russia* **52** C7
Veaikevárri =
   Svappavaara *Sweden* **8** C19
Vechelde *Germany* **24** C6
Vechta *Germany* **24** C4
Vechte → *Neths.* **17** B6
Vecsés *Hungary* **28** C4
Veddige *Sweden* **11** G6
Vedea → *Romania* **29** G10
Vedia *Argentina* **126** C3
Vedrette di Ries-Aurina △
   Italy **41** B9

Vedum *Sweden* **11** F7
Veendam *Neths.* **17** A6
Veenendaal *Neths.* **17** B5
Vefsna → *Norway* **8** D15
Vega *Norway* **8** D14
Vega *U.S.A.* **116** D3
Vega Baja *Puerto Rico* **121** d
Vegadeo *Spain* **36** B3
Vegorítida, L. *Greece* **44** F5
Vegreville *Canada* **102** C6
Veinge *Sweden* **11** H7
Veisiejai *Lithuania* **30** D10
Vejbystrand *Sweden* **11** H6
Vejen *Denmark* **11** J3
Vejer de la Frontera *Spain* **37** J5
Vejle *Denmark* **11** J3
Vejle Fjord *Denmark* **11** J3
Vela, C. *Costa Rica* **120** D2
Vela Luka *Croatia* **41** F13
Velas, C. *Costa Rica* **120** D2
Velasco, Sierra de *Argentina* **126** B2
Velay, Mts. du *France* **20** D7
Velbert *Germany* **24** D3
Velddrif *S. Africa* **88** E2
Velebit *Croatia* **41** D12
Velebit Planina *Croatia* **41** D12
Velebitski Kanal *Croatia* **41** D11
Veleka → *Bulgaria* **45** D11
Velencei-tó *Hungary* **28** C3
Velenje *Slovenia* **41** B12
Veles *Macedonia* **44** E5
Velestíno *Greece* **46** C4
Vélez-Málaga *Spain* **37** J6
Vélez Rubio *Spain* **39** H2
Velhas → *Brazil* **125** G10
Velika *Croatia* **28** E2
Velika Gorica *Croatia* **41** C13
Velika Kapela *Croatia* **41** C12
Velika Kladuša *Bos.-H.* **41** C12
Velika Kruša *Serbia* **44** D4
Velika Morava → *Serbia* **44** B5
Velika Plana *Serbia* **44** B5
Velikaya → *Russia* **32** D5
Velikaya Kema *Russia* **54** B8
Velikaya Lepetikha *Ukraine* **33** J7
Veliké Kapušany
   Slovak Rep. **27** C15
Velike Lašče *Slovenia* **41** C11
Veliki Jastrebac *Serbia* **44** C5
Veliki Kanal *Serbia* **28** E4
Veliki Popović *Serbia* **44** B5
Velikiye Luki *Russia* **32** D6
Veliko Gradište *Serbia* **44** B5
Veliko Tŭrnovo *Bulgaria* **45** C9
Velikonda Range *India* **66** M11
Vélingara *Kolda, Senegal* **82** C2
Vélingara *Louga, Senegal* **82** B2
Velingrad *Bulgaria* **44** D7
Velino, Mte. *Italy* **41** F10
Velizh *Russia* **32** E6
Velké Karlovice *Czech Rep.* **27** B11
Velké Meziříčí *Czech Rep.* **26** B9
Vel'ký Javorník *Slovak Rep.* **27** B11
Vel'ký Krtíš *Slovak Rep.* **27** C12
Vel'ký Meder *Slovak Rep.* **27** D10
Vel'ký Tribeč *Slovak Rep.* **27** C11
Velletri *Italy* **42** A5
Vellinge *Sweden* **11** J6
Vellmar *Germany* **24** D5
Vellore *India* **66** N11
Velopoula *Greece* **46** E5
Velsk *Russia* **32** B11
Velten *Germany* **24** C9
Veluwezoom △ *Neths.* **17** B6
Velva *U.S.A.* **112** A3
Velvendos *Greece* **44** F5
Velyka Mykhaylivka
   Ukraine **29** C14
Velyki Luchky *Ukraine* **28** B7
Velykyy Bereznyy *Ukraine* **28** B7
Velykyy Bychkiv *Ukraine* **29** C9
Vemb *Denmark* **11** H2
Vemdalen *Sweden* **10** B7
Ven *Sweden* **11** J6
Venaco *France* **21** F13
Venado *Mexico* **118** C4
Venado Tuerto *Argentina* **126** C3
Venafro *Italy* **43** A7
Venarey-les-Laumes *France* **19** E11
Venaría *Italy* **40** C4
Venčane *Serbia* **44** B4
Vence *France* **21** E11
Vendas Novas *Portugal* **37** G2
Vendée □ *France* **18** F5
Vendée → *France* **18** F5
Vendéen, Bocage *France* **20** B2
Vendeuvre-sur-Barse
   France **19** D11
Vendôme *France* **18** E8
Vendrell = El Vendrell *Spain* **38** D6
Vendsyssel *Denmark* **11** G4
Vendychany *Ukraine* **29** B12
Venelles *France* **21** E9
Véneta, L. *Italy* **41** C9
Véneto □ *Italy* **41** C9
Venev *Russia* **32** E10
Venézia *Italy* **41** C9
Venézia, G. di *Italy* **41** C10

Venezuela ■ *S. Amer.* **124** B5
Venezuela, G. de *Venezuela* **124** A4
Vengurla *India* **66** M8
Venice = Venézia *Italy* **41** C9
Venice *U.S.A.* **117** H13
Vénissieux *France* **21** C8
Venjansjön *Sweden* **10** D8
Venkatapuram *India* **67** K12
Venlo *Neths.* **17** C6
Vennesla *Norway* **9** G12
Venosa *Italy* **43** B8
Venray *Neths.* **17** C6
Venta → *Latvia* **30** A8
Venta de Baños *Spain* **36** D6
Venta de Cardeña =
   Cardeña *Spain* **37** G6
Ventana, Punta de la
   Mexico **118** C3
Ventana, Sa. de la *Argentina* **126** D3
Ventersburg *S. Africa* **88** D4
Venterstad *S. Africa* **88** E4
Ventimíglia *Italy* **40** E4
Ventnor *U.K.* **15** G6
Ventoténe *Italy* **42** B6
Ventoux, Mt. *France* **21** D9
Ventspils *Latvia* **30** A8
Ventspils □ *Latvia* **30** A8
Ventuarí → *Venezuela* **124** C5
Ventucopa *U.S.A.* **111** L7
Ventura *U.S.A.* **111** L7
Vénus, Pte. *Tahiti* **91** d
Venus B. *Australia* **95** F4
Venustiano Carranza
   Mexico **118** A1
Vera *Argentina* **126** B3
Vera *Spain* **39** H3
Veracruz *Mexico* **119** D5
Veracruz □ *Mexico* **119** D5
Veraval *India* **68** J4
Verbánia *Italy* **40** C5
Verbicaro *Italy* **43** C8
Vercelli *Italy* **40** C5
Verchovchevo *Ukraine* **33** H8
Vercors △ *France* **21** D9
Verdalsøra *Norway* **8** E14
Verde → *Argentina* **128** E3
Verde → *Goiás, Brazil* **125** G8
Verde → *Mato Grosso do Sul,
   Brazil* **125** H8
Verde → *Chihuahua, Mexico* **118** B3
Verde → *Oaxaca, Mexico* **119** D5
Verde → *Veracruz, Mexico* **118** C4
Verde → *Paraguay* **126** A4
Verde → *U.S.A.* **106** D4
Verde, Cay *Bahamas* **120** B4
Verde Island Pass *Phil.* **61** E4
Verden *Germany* **24** C5
Verdi *U.S.A.* **110** F7
Verdikoussa *Greece* **46** B3
Verdon → *France* **21** E9
Verdon □ *France* **21** E10
Verdun *France* **19** C12
Verdun-sur-le-Doubs
   France **19** F12
Vereeniging *S. Africa* **89** D4
Verga, C. *Guinea* **82** C2
Vergara *Uruguay* **127** C5
Vergato *Italy* **40** D8
Vergemont Cr. → *Australia* **94** C3
Vergennes *U.S.A.* **115** B11
Vergt *France* **20** C4
Veria *Greece* **44** F6
Verín *Spain* **36** D3
Verkhnedvinsk =
   Vyerkhnyadzvinsk
   Belarus **32** E5
Verkhnetulomskoye
   Vdkhr. *Russia* **8** B24
Verkhniy Baskunchak
   Russia **35** F8
Verkhovye *Russia* **33** F9
Verkhovyna *Ukraine* **29** B9
Verkhoyansk *Russia* **53** C14
Verkhoyansk Ra. =
   Verkhoyanskiy Khrebet
   Russia **53** C13
Verkhoyanskiy Khrebet
   Russia **53** C13
Vermenton *France* **19** E10
Vermilion *Canada* **103** C6
Vermilion *U.S.A.* **114** E2
Vermilion → *Canada* **103** C6
Vermilion B. *U.S.A.* **116** G9
Vermilion Bay *Canada* **103** D10
Vermilion L. *U.S.A.* **112** B7
Vermillion *U.S.A.* **112** D5
Vermillion → *Canada* **104** C5
Vermont *U.S.A.* **115** C12
Vermont □ *U.S.A.* **115** C12
Vermosh *Albania* **44** D3
Vernadsky *Antarctica* **5** C17
Vernal *U.S.A.* **108** F9
Vernalis *U.S.A.* **110** H5
Vernazza *Italy* **40** D6
Verner *Canada* **104** C3

Verneuil-sur-Avre *France* **18** D7
Verneukpan *S. Africa* **88** E3
Vernier *Switz.* **35** J2
Vérnio *Italy* **40** D8
Vernon *Canada* **102** C5
Vernon *France* **18** C8
Vernon *U.S.A.* **116** D5
Vernonia *U.S.A.* **110** E3
Vero Beach *U.S.A.* **117** H14
Véroia = Veria *Greece* **44** F6
Véroli *Italy* **41** G10
Verona *Canada* **115** B8
Verona *Italy* **40** C7
Verrès *Italy* **40** C4
Versailles *France* **19** D9
Versmold *Germany* **24** C4
Vert, C. *Senegal* **82** C1
Vertou *France* **18** E5
Vertus *France* **19** D11
Verulam *S. Africa* **89** D5
Verviers *Belgium* **17** D5
Vervins *France* **19** C10
Veržej *Slovenia* **41** B13
Verzy *France* **19** C11
Vescovato *France* **21** F13
Veselí nad Lužnicí *Czech Rep.* **26** B7
Veselie *Bulgaria* **45** D11
Veselovskoye Vdkhr. *Russia* **35** G5
Veshenskaya *Russia* **34** F5
Vesle → *France* **19** C10
Vesoul *France* **19** E13
Vessigebro *Sweden* **11** H6
Vesterålen *Norway* **8** B16
Vestfjorden *Norway* **8** C16
Vestmannaeyjar *Iceland* **8** E3
Vestspitsbergen *Svalbard* **4** B8
Vestvågøya *Norway* **8** B15
Vesúvio *Italy* **43** B7
Vesuvius, Mt. = Vesúvio
   Italy **43** B7
Vetlanda *Sweden* **11** G9
Vetlugu → *Russia* **34** B8
Vetluga *Russia* **34** B7
Vetluzhskiy *Kostroma, Russia* **34** A7
Vetluzhskiy
   Nizhniy Novgorod, Russia **34** B7
Vetovo *Bulgaria* **45** C10
Vetralla *Italy* **41** F9
Vetren *Bulgaria* **45** D8
Vettore, Mte. *Italy* **41** F10
Veurne *Belgium* **17** C2
Veveno → *Sudan* **81** F3
Vevey *Switz.* **25** J2
Vévi *Greece* **44** F5
Veynes *France* **21** D9
Veys *Iran* **71** D6
Vézelay *France* **19** E10
Vézelise *France* **19** D13
Vézère → *France* **20** D4
Vezhen *Bulgaria* **45** D8
Vezirköprü *Turkey* **72** B6
Vezzani *France* **21** F13
Vi Thanh *Vietnam* **65** H5
Viacha *Bolivia* **124** G5
Viadana *Italy* **40** D7
Viamão *Brazil* **127** C5
Viana *Brazil* **125** D10
Viana *Spain* **38** C2
Viana do Alentejo *Portugal* **37** G3
Viana do Bolo *Spain* **36** C3
Viana do Castelo *Portugal* **36** D2
Viana do Castelo □ *Portugal* **36** D2
Vianden *Lux.* **17** E6
Viangchan = Vientiane *Laos* **64** D4
Vianópolis *Brazil* **125** G9
Vianos *Greece* **49** D7
Viar → *Spain* **37** H5
Viaréggio *Italy* **40** E7
Viaur → *France* **20** D5
Vibble *Sweden* **11** G12
Vibo Valéntia *Italy* **43** D9
Viborg *Denmark* **11** H3
Vibraye *France* **18** D7
Vic *Spain* **38** D7
Vic, Étang de *France* **20** E7
Vic-en-Bigorre *France* **20** E4
Vic-Fezensac *France* **20** E4
Vic-le-Comte *France* **19** G10
Vic-sur-Cère *France* **20** D6
Vícar *Spain* **39** J2
Vicenza *Italy* **41** C8
Vich = Vic *Spain* **38** D7
Vichada → *Colombia* **124** C5
Vichuga *Russia* **34** B5
Vichy *France* **19** F10
Vicksburg *U.S.A.* **111** M13
Vico *France* **21** F12
Vico, L. di *Italy* **41** F9
Vico del Gargano *Italy* **41** G12
Vicovu de Sus *Romania* **29** C10
Victor *India* **68** J4
Victor *U.S.A.* **114** D7
Victor Harbor *Australia* **95** F2

Victoria *Argentina* **126** C3
Victoria *Canada* **110** B3
Victoria *Chile* **128** D2
Victoria *Guinea* **82** C2
Victoria *Malta* **49** C1
Victoria *Phil.* **61** D4
Victoria *Romania* **29** E9
Victoria *Seychelles* **85** b
Victoria *Kans., U.S.A.* **112** F4
Victoria *Tex., U.S.A.* **116** G6
Victoria □ *Australia* **95** F3
Victoria → *Australia* **92** C4
Victoria, Grand L. *Canada* **104** C4
Victoria, L. *Africa* **86** C3
Victoria, L. *Australia* **95** E3
Victoria, Mt. *Burma* **67** J18
Victoria Beach *Canada* **103** C9
Victoria de Durango =
   Durango *Mexico* **118** C4
Victoria de las Tunas = Las
   Tunas *Cuba* **120** B4
Victoria Falls *Zimbabwe* **87** F2
Victoria Harbour *Canada* **114** B5
Victoria I. *Canada* **100** B8
Victoria L. *Canada* **105** C8
Victoria Ld. *Antarctica* **5** D11
Victoria Nile → *Uganda* **86** B3
Victoria Pk. *Belize* **119** D7
Victoria River *Australia* **92** C4
Victoria Str. *Canada* **100** C9
Victoria West *S. Africa* **88** E3
Victórias *Phil.* **61** F5
Victoriaville *Canada* **105** C5
Victorica *Argentina* **126** D2
Victorville *U.S.A.* **111** L9
Vicuña *Chile* **126** C1
Vicuña Mackenna
   Argentina **126** C3
Vidal *U.S.A.* **111** L12
Vidal Junction *U.S.A.* **111** L12
Vidalia *U.S.A.* **117** E13
Vidamlya *Belarus* **31** F10
Vidauban *France* **21** E10
Videbæk *Denmark* **11** H2
Videle *Romania* **29** F10
Vidigueira *Portugal* **37** G3
Vidin *Bulgaria* **44** C6
Vidio, C. *Spain* **36** B4
Vidisha *India* **68** H7
Vido *Greece* **49** A3
Vidra *Romania* **29** E11
Viduša *Bos.-H.* **44** D2
Vidzy *Belarus* **32** E4
Viechtach *Germany* **25** F8
Viedma *Argentina* **128** E4
Viedma, L. *Argentina* **128** F2
Vieira do Minho *Portugal* **36** D2
Vielha *Spain* **38** C5
Viella = Vielha *Spain* **38** C5
Vielsalm *Belgium* **17** D5
Vienenburg *Germany* **24** D6
Vieng Pou Kha *Laos* **58** G3
Vienna = Wien *Austria* **27** C9
Vienna *Ill., U.S.A.* **112** G9
Vienna *Mo., U.S.A.* **112** F8
Vienne *France* **21** C8
Vienne □ *France* **20** B4
Vienne → *France* **18** E7
Vientiane *Laos* **64** D4
Vientos, Paso de los
   Caribbean **121** C5
Vieques *Puerto Rico* **121** d
Vierge Pt. *St. Lucia* **121** f
Viernheim *Germany* **25** F4
Viersen *Germany* **24** D2
Vierwaldstättersee *Switz.* **25** J4
Vierzon *France* **19** E9
Vieste *Italy* **41** G13
Vietnam ■ *Asia* **64** C6
Vieux-Boucau-les-Bains
   France **20** E2
Vieux Fort *St. Lucia* **121** f
Vif *France* **21** C9
Vigan *Phil.* **61** C4
Vigévano *Italy* **40** C5
Vigia *Brazil* **125** D9
Vigía *Brazil* **125** D9
Viglas, Akra *Greece* **49** D9
Vignemale *France* **20** F3
Vigneulles-lès-
   Hattonchâtel *France* **19** D12
Vignola *Italy* **40** D8
Vigo *Spain* **36** C2
Vigo, Ría de *Spain* **36** C2
Vigsø Bugt *Denmark* **11** G2
Vihiers *France* **18** E6
Vihowa *Pakistan* **68** D4
Vihowa → *Pakistan* **68** D4
Vijayawada *India* **67** L12
Vijosë → *Albania* **44** F3
Vík *Iceland* **8** E4
Vika *Sweden* **10** D8
Vikarbyn *Sweden* **10** D9
Vikeke = Viqueque *E. Timor* **63** F7
Viken *Skåne, Sweden* **11** H6
Viken *Västra Götaland, Sweden* **11** F8
Viking *Canada* **102** C6
Vikmanshyttan *Sweden* **10** D9

Vikna *Norway* **8** D14
Vikos-Aóös △ *Greece* **46** B2
Vila da Maganja *Mozam.* **87** F4
Vila da Ribeira Brava
    C. Verde Is. **78** b
Vila de Rei *Portugal* **36** F2
Vila do Bispo *Portugal* **37** H2
Vila do Conde *Portugal* **36** D2
Vila Franca de Xira *Portugal* **37** G2
Vila Gamito *Mozam.* **87** E3
Vila Gomes da Costa *Mozam.* **89** C5
Vila Machado *Mozam.* **87** F3
Vila Mouzinho *Mozam.* **87** E3
Vila Nova de Famalicão
    Portugal **36** D2
Vila Nova de Fos Côa
    Portugal **36** D3
Vila Nova de Gaia *Portugal* **36** D2
Vila Nova de Ourém *Portugal* **36** F2
Vila Pouca de Aguiar
    Portugal **36** D3
Vila Real *Portugal* **36** D3
Vila Real □ *Portugal* **36** D3
Vila-real de los Infantes
    Spain **38** F4
Vila Real de Santo António
    Portugal **37** H3
Vila Vasco da Gama *Mozam.* **87** E3
Vila Velha *Brazil* **127** A7
Vila Viçosa *Portugal* **37** G3
Vilafranca del Maestrat
    Spain **38** E4
Vilafranca del Penedès *Spain* **38** D6
Vilagarcía de Arousa *Spain* **36** C2
Vilaine ➤ *France* **18** E4
Vilanandro, Tanjona *Madag.* **89** B7
Vilanculos *Mozam.* **89** C6
Vilanova de Castelló *Spain* **39** F4
Vilanova i la Geltrú *Spain* **38** D6
Vilar Formoso *Portugal* **36** E4
Vilaseca *Spain* **38** D6
Vilaseca-Salou = Vilaseca
    Spain **38** D6
Vilbjerg *Denmark* **11** H2
Vilcheka, Zemlya *Russia* **4** A11
Vilches *Spain* **37** G7
Vileyka *Belarus* **23** A14
Vilhelmina *Sweden* **8** D17
Vilhena *Brazil* **124** F6
Viliya = Neris ➤ *Lithuania* **32** E3
Viljandi *Estonia* **32** C3
Vilkaviškis *Lithuania* **30** D10
Vilkija *Lithuania* **30** C10
Vilkitskogo, Proliv *Russia* **53** B11
Vilkovo = Vylkove *Ukraine* **29** E14
Villa Abecia *Bolivia* **126** A2
Villa Ana *Argentina* **126** B4
Villa Ángela *Argentina* **126** B3
Villa Bella *Bolivia* **124** F5
Villa Cañás *Argentina* **126** C3
Villa Colón *Argentina* **126** C2
Villa Constitución *Argentina* **126** C3
Villa de Arriaga *Mexico* **118** C4
Villa de María *Argentina* **126** B3
Villa de Méndez *Mexico* **119** B5
Villa del Rio *Spain* **37** H6
Villa Dolores *Argentina* **126** C2
Villa Frontera *Mexico* **118** B4
Villa Guillermina *Argentina* **126** B4
Villa Hayes *Paraguay* **126** B4
Villa Hidalgo *Mexico* **119** C5
Villa Iris *Argentina* **126** D3
Villa María *Argentina* **126** C3
Villa Mazán *Argentina* **126** B2
Villa Minozzo *Italy* **40** D7
Villa Montes *Bolivia* **126** A3
Villa Ocampo *Argentina* **126** B4
Villa Ocampo *Mexico* **118** B3
Villa Ojo de Agua *Argentina* **126** B3
Villa San Giovanni *Italy* **43** D8
Villa San José *Argentina* **126** C4
Villa San Martín *Argentina* **126** B3
Villa Santina *Italy* **41** B9
Villa Unión *Mexico* **118** C3
Villablino *Spain* **36** C4
Villacarlos *Spain* **48** B11
Villacarriedo *Spain* **36** B7
Villacarrillo *Spain* **37** G7
Villacastín *Spain* **36** E6
Villach *Austria* **26** E6
Villacidro *Italy* **42** C1
Villada *Spain* **36** C6
Villadiego *Spain* **36** C6
Villadóssola *Italy* **40** B5
Villafeliche *Spain* **38** D3
Villafranca *Spain* **38** C2
Villafranca de los
    Caballeros *Baleares, Spain* **48** B10
Villafranca de los
    Caballeros *Toledo, Spain* **37** F7
Villafranca del Cid =
    Vilafranca del Maestrat
    Spain **38** E4
Villafranca del Panadés =
    Vilafranca del Penedès
    Spain **38** D6

Villafranca di Verona *Italy* **40** C7
Villafranca Tirrena *Italy* **43** D8
Villagrán *Mexico* **119** C5
Villaguay *Argentina* **126** C4
Villaharta *Spain* **37** G6
Villahermosa *Mexico* **119** D6
Villahermosa *Spain* **39** G2
Villaines-la-Juhel *France* **18** D6
Villajoyosa *Spain* **39** G4
Villalba *Spain* **36** B3
Villalba de Guardo *Spain* **36** C6
Villalón de Campos *Spain* **36** C5
Villalpando *Spain* **36** D5
Villaluenga *Spain* **36** E7
Villamanán *Spain* **36** C5
Villamartín *Spain* **37** J5
Villamayor de Santiago
    Spain **38** F2
Villamblard *France* **20** C4
Villanova Monteleone *Italy* **42** B1
Villanueva *U.S.A.* **109** J11
Villanueva de Castellón =
    Vilanova de Castelló *Spain* **39** F4
Villanueva de Córdoba *Spain* **37** G6
Villanueva de la Fuente
    Spain **39** G2
Villanueva de la Serena
    Spain **37** G5
Villanueva de la Sierra *Spain* **36** E4
Villanueva de los
    Castillejos *Spain* **37** H3
Villanueva de los Infantes
    Spain **37** G7
Villanueva del Arzobispo
    Spain **39** G2
Villanueva del Fresno *Spain* **37** G3
Villanueva y Geltrú =
    Vilanova i la Geltrú *Spain* **38** D6
Villaputzu *Italy* **42** C2
Villaquilambre *Spain* **36** C5
Villar del Arzobispo *Spain* **38** F4
Villar del Rey *Spain* **37** F4
Villard-de-Lans *France* **21** C9
Villarramiel *Spain* **36** C6
Villarreal = Vila-real de los
    Infantes *Spain* **38** F4
Villarrica *Chile* **128** D2
Villarrica *Paraguay* **126** B4
Villarrobledo *Spain* **39** F2
Villarroya de la Sierra *Spain* **38** D3
Villarrubia de los Ojos *Spain* **37** F7
Villars-les-Dombes *France* **19** F12
Villasayas *Spain* **38** D2
Villaseca de los Gamitos =
    Villaseco de los Gamitos
    Spain **36** D4
Villaseco de los Gamitos
    Spain **36** D4
Villasimíus *Italy* **42** C2
Villastar *Spain* **38** E3
Villatobas *Spain* **36** F7
Villavicencio *Argentina* **126** C2
Villavicencio *Colombia* **124** C4
Villaviciosa *Spain* **36** B5
Villazón *Bolivia* **126** A2
Ville-Marie *Canada* **104** C4
Ville Platte *U.S.A.* **116** F8
Villedieu-les-Poêles *France* **18** D5
Villefort *France* **20** D7
Villefranche-de-Lauragais
    France **20** E5
Villefranche-de-Rouergue
    France **20** D6
Villefranche-du-Périgord
    France **20** D5
Villefranche-sur-Saône
    France **21** C8
Villel *Spain* **38** E3
Villemur-sur-Tarn *France* **20** E5
Villena *Spain* **39** G4
Villenauxe-la-Grande
    France **19** D10
Villenave-d'Ornon *France* **20** D3
Villeneuve-d'Ascq *France* **19** B10
Villeneuve-l'Archevêque
    France **19** D10
Villeneuve-lès-Avignon
    France **21** E8
Villeneuve-sur-Allier
    France **19** F10
Villeneuve-sur-Lot *France* **20** D4
Villeneuve-sur-Yonne
    France **19** D10
Villeréal *France* **20** D4
Villers-Bocage *France* **18** C6
Villers-Cotterêts *France* **19** C10
Villers-sur-Mer *France* **18** C6
Villersexel *France* **19** E13
Villerupt *France* **19** C12
Villeurbanne *France* **21** C8
Villiers *S. Africa* **89** D4
Villingen-Schwenningen
    Germany **25** G4
Villmanstrand =
    Lappeenranta *Finland* **32** B5
Vilna *Canada* **102** C6
Vilnius *Lithuania* **32** E3

Vils *Austria* **26** D3
Vils ➤ *Bayern, Germany* **25** G9
Vils ➤ *Bayern, Germany* **25** F7
Vilsbiburg *Germany* **25** G8
Vilshofen *Germany* **25** G9
Vilusi *Montenegro* **44** D2
Vilvoorde *Belgium* **17** D4
Vilyuy ➤ *Russia* **53** C13
Vilyuysk *Russia* **53** C13
Vimianzo *Spain* **36** B1
Vimioso *Portugal* **36** D4
Vimmerby *Sweden* **11** G9
Vimoutiers *France* **18** D7
Vimperk *Czech Rep.* **26** B6
Viña del Mar *Chile* **126** C1
Vinarós *Spain* **38** E5
Vincennes *U.S.A.* **112** F10
Vincent *U.S.A.* **111** L8
Vinchina *Argentina* **126** B2
Vindelälven ➤ *Sweden* **8** E18
Vindeln *Sweden* **8** D18
Vinderup *Denmark* **11** H2
Vindhya Ra. *India* **68** H7
Vineland *U.S.A.* **113** F16
Vineuil *France* **18** E8
Vinga *Romania* **28** D6
Vingåker *Sweden* **10** E9
Vinh *Vietnam* **64** C5
Vinh Linh *Vietnam* **64** D6
Vinh Long *Vietnam* **65** G5
Vinh Yen *Vietnam* **58** G5
Vinhais *Portugal* **36** D4
Vinica *Croatia* **41** B13
Vinica *Macedonia* **44** E6
Vinica *Slovenia* **41** C12
Vinita *U.S.A.* **116** C7
Vinkovci *Croatia* **28** E3
Vinnitsa = Vinnytsya
    Ukraine **23** D15
Vinnytsya *Ukraine* **23** D15
Vinnytsya □ *Ukraine* **33** H5
Vinslöv *Sweden* **11** H7
Vinson Massif *Antarctica* **5** D16
Vintjärn *Sweden* **10** D10
Vinton *Calif., U.S.A.* **110** F6
Vinton *Iowa, U.S.A.* **112** D7
Vinton *La., U.S.A.* **116** F8
Vințu de Jos *Romania* **29** D8
Viöl *Germany* **24** A5
Viotia □ *Greece* **46** C5
Vipava *Slovenia* **41** C10
Vipiteno *Italy* **41** B8
Viqueque *E. Timor* **63** F7
Vir *Croatia* **41** D12
Virac *Phil.* **61** E6
Virachey *Cambodia* **64** F6
Virachey ➤ *Cambodia* **64** F6
Virago Sd. *Canada* **102** C2
Viramgam *India* **68** H5
Virananşehir *Turkey* **73** D8
Virawah *Pakistan* **68** G4
Virbalis *Lithuania* **30** D9
Virden *Canada* **103** D8
Vire *France* **18** D6
Vire ➤ *France* **18** C5
Vírgenes, C. *Argentina* **128** G3
Virgin ➤ *U.S.A.* **109** H6
Virgin Gorda *Br. Virgin Is.* **121** e
Virgin Is. (British) ☑
    W. Indies **121** e
Virgin Is. (U.S.) ☑ *W. Indies* **121** e
Virgin Islands △
    U.S. Virgin Is. **121** C7
Virginia *S. Africa* **88** D4
Virginia *U.S.A.* **112** B7
Virginia □ *U.S.A.* **113** G14
Virginia Beach *U.S.A.* **113** F16
Virginia City *Mont., U.S.A.* **108** D8
Virginia City *Nev., U.S.A.* **110** F7
Virginia Falls *Canada* **102** A3
Virginiatown *Canada* **104** C4
Virje *Croatia* **41** B13
Viroqua *U.S.A.* **112** D8
Virovitica *Croatia* **28** E2
Virpazar *Montenegro* **44** D3
Virpur *India* **68** J4
Virserum *Sweden* **11** G9
Virton *Belgium* **17** E5
Virudunagar *India* **66** Q10
Virunga △
    Dem. Rep. of the Congo **86** B2
Vis *Croatia* **41** E13
Visalia *U.S.A.* **110** J7
Visayan Sea *Phil.* **61** F5
Visby *Sweden* **11** G12
Viscount Melville Sd.
    Canada **101** B9
Visé *Belgium* **17** D5
Višegrad *Bos.-H.* **28** G4
Viseu *Brazil* **125** D9
Viseu *Portugal* **36** E3
Viseu □ *Portugal* **36** E3
Vișeu de Sus *Romania* **29** C9
Vishakhapatnam *India* **67** L13
Vișina *Romania* **29** G9
Vișinești *Moldova* **29** D13
Visingsö *Sweden* **11** F8

Viskafors *Sweden* **11** G6
Viskan ➤ *Sweden* **11** G6
Viški Kanal *Croatia* **41** E13
Vislanda *Sweden* **11** H8
Visnagar *India* **68** H5
Višnja Gora *Slovenia* **41** C11
Viso, Mte. *Italy* **40** D4
Viso del Marqués *Spain* **37** G7
Visoko *Bos.-H.* **28** G3
Visokoi I. *Antarctica* **5** B1
Visp *Switz.* **25** J3
Vissefjärda *Sweden* **11** H9
Visselhövede *Germany* **24** C5
Vissenbjerg *Denmark* **11** J4
Vista *U.S.A.* **111** M9
Vistonida, L. *Greece* **45** E9
Vistonikos, Ormos =
    Vistonida, L. *Greece* **45** E9
Vistula = Wisła ➤ *Poland* **30** D5
Vit ➤ *Bulgaria* **45** C8
Vitanje *Slovenia* **41** B12
Vitebsk = Vitsyebsk *Belarus* **32** E6
Viterbo *Italy* **41** F9
Vitez *Bos.-H.* **28** F2
Viti Levu *Fiji* **91** a
Vitigudino *Spain* **36** D4
Vitim *Russia* **53** D12
Vitim ➤ *Russia* **53** D12
Vitina *Bos.-H.* **41** E14
Vitina *Greece* **46** D4
Vítkov *Czech Rep.* **27** B10
Vitória *Brazil* **125** H10
Vitória da Conquista *Brazil*
    125 F10
Vitória de São Antão *Brazil*
    125 E11
Vitoria-Gasteiz *Spain* **38** C2
Vitosha △ *Bulgaria* **44** D7
Vitré *France* **18** D5
Vitry-le-François *France* **19** D11
Vitry-sur-Seine *France* **19** D9
Vitsand *Sweden* **10** D7
Vitsi, Oros *Greece* **44** F5
Vitsyebsk *Belarus* **32** E6
Vitsyebsk □ *Belarus* **32** E5
Vittaryd *Sweden* **11** H7
Vitteaux *France* **19** E11
Vittel *France* **19** D12
Vittória *Italy* **43** F7
Vittório Véneto *Italy* **41** C9
Vittsjö *Sweden* **11** H7
Viveiro *Spain* **36** B3
Vivian *U.S.A.* **116** E8
Viviers *France* **21** D8
Vivonne *France* **20** B4
Viwa *Fiji* **91** a
Vizcaíno, Desierto de
    Mexico **118** B2
Vizcaíno, Sierra *Mexico* **118** B2
Vizcaya □ *Spain* **38** B2
Vize *Turkey* **45** E11
Vizianagaram *India* **67** K13
Vizille *France* **21** C9
Viziñada *Croatia* **41** C10
Viziru *Romania* **29** E12
Vizzini *Italy* **43** F7
Vlaardingen *Neths.* **17** C4
Vlachiotis *Greece* **46** E4
Vlădeasa, Vf. *Romania* **28** D7
Vladičin Han *Serbia* **44** D6
Vladikavkaz *Russia* **35** J7
Vladimir *Russia* **32** D11
Vladimir □ *Russia* **34** B5
Vladimir Volynskiy =
    Volodymyr-Volynskyy
    Ukraine **23** C13
Vladimirci *Serbia* **44** B3
Vladimirovac *Serbia* **28** E5
Vladimirovka *Russia* **35** F8
Vladimirovo *Bulgaria* **44** C7
Vladimorvka *Kazakhstan* **34** E10
Vladislavovka *Ukraine* **33** K8
Vladivostok *Russia* **54** C5
Vlăhița *Romania* **29** D10
Vlasenica *Bos.-H.* **28** F3
Vlašić *Bos.-H.* **28** F2
Vlašim *Czech Rep.* **26** B7
Vlasinsko Jezero *Serbia* **44** D6
Vlasotince *Serbia* **44** D6
Vlieland *Neths.* **17** A4
Vlissingen *Neths.* **17** C3
Vlorë *Albania* **44** F3
Vlorës, Gjiri i *Albania* **44** F3
Vltava ➤ *Czech Rep.* **26** A7
Vo Dat *Vietnam* **65** G6
Vobarno *Italy* **40** C7
Voćin *Croatia* **28** E2
Vöcklabruck *Austria* **26** C6
Vodice *Croatia* **41** E12
Vodňany *Czech Rep.* **26** B7
Vodnjan *Croatia* **41** D10
Voe *U.K.* **13** A7
Vogel Pk. *Nigeria* **83** D7
Vogelkop = Doberai,
    Jazirah *Indonesia* **63** E8
Vogelsberg *Germany* **24** E5
Voghera *Italy* **40** D6

Vohibinany *Madag.* **89** B8
Vohilava *Madag.* **89** C8
Vohimarina = Iharana
    Madag. **89** A9
Vohimena, Tanjon' i *Madag.* **89** D8
Vohipeno *Madag.* **89** C8
Voi *Kenya* **86** C4
Void-Vacon *France* **19** D12
Voinești *Iași, Romania* **29** C12
Voinești *Prahova, Romania* **29** E10
Voiron *France* **21** C9
Voisey B. *Canada* **105** A7
Voitsberg *Austria* **26** D8
Vojens *Denmark* **11** J3
Vojmsjön *Sweden* **8** D17
Vojnić *Croatia* **41** C12
Vojnik *Italy* **41** B12
Vojvodina □ *Serbia* **28** E5
Vokhtoga *Russia* **32** C10
Volary *Czech Rep.* **26** C6
Volborg *U.S.A.* **108** D11
Volcán de Colima △ *Mexico* **118** D4
Volcano Is. = Kazan-Rettō
    Pac. Oc. **96** E6
Volcans △ *Rwanda* **86** C2
Volcans d'Auvergne ○
    France **20** C6
Volchansk = Vovchansk
    Ukraine **33** H8
Volchya ➤ *Ukraine* **33** H8
Volda *Norway* **8** E12
Volga ➤ *Russia* **35** G9
Volga = Privolzhskiy □
    Russia **34** B10
Volga Hts. =
    Privolzhskaya
    Vozvyshennost *Russia* **34** E7
Volga-Baltiyskiy Kanal
    Russia **32** B9
Volgo-Donskoy Kanal
    Russia **35** F7
Volgodonsk *Russia* **35** G6
Volgograd *Russia* **35** F7
Volgograd □ *Russia* **34** F7
Volgogradskoye Vdkhr.
    Russia **34** B5
Volgorechensk *Russia* **34** B5
Volimes *Greece* **46** D2
Volintiri *Moldova* **29** D14
Volissos *Greece* **47** C7
Volkach *Germany* **25** F6
Völkermarkt *Austria* **26** E7
Volkhov *Russia* **32** C7
Volkhov ➤ *Russia* **32** B7
Völklingen *Germany* **25** F2
Volkovysk = Vawkavysk
    Belarus **23** B13
Volksrust *S. Africa* **89** D4
Volnansk *Ukraine* **33** H8
Volnovakha *Ukraine* **33** J9
Volochanka *Russia* **53** B10
Volodarsk *Russia* **34** B6
Volodymyr-Volynskyy
    Ukraine **23** C13
Vologda *Russia* **32** C10
Vologda □ *Russia* **32** B10
Volokolamsk *Russia* **32** D8
Volokonovka *Russia* **33** G9
Volos *Greece* **46** B4
Volosovo *Russia* **32** C5
Volovets *Ukraine* **29** B8
Volovo *Russia* **32** F10
Volozhin = Valozhyn
    Belarus **23** A14
Volsk *Russia* **34** D8
Volta □ *Ghana* **83** D5
Volta ➤ *Ghana* **83** D5
Volta, L. *Ghana* **83** D5
Volta Blanche = White
    Volta ➤ *Ghana* **83** D4
Volta Redonda *Brazil* **127** A7
Voltaire, C. *Australia* **92** B4
Volterra *Italy* **40** E7
Voltri *Italy* **40** D5
Volturno ➤ *Italy* **42** A6
Volvi, L. *Greece* **44** F7
Volvo *Fiji* **91** a
Volzhsk *Russia* **34** C9
Volzhskiy *Russia* **35** F7
Vomo *Fiji* **91** a
Vondrozo *Madag.* **89** C8
Vonitsa *Greece* **46** C2
Vopnafjörður *Iceland* **8** D6
Vorarlberg □ *Austria* **26** D2
Voras Oros *Greece* **44** F5
Vorbasse *Denmark* **11** J3
Vorchdorf *Austria* **26** C6
Vorderrhein ➤ *Switz.* **25** J5
Vordingborg *Denmark* **11** J5
Vorë *Albania* **44** E3
Voreio Aigaio □ *Greece* **47** C7
Voreppe *France* **21** C9
Vori *Greece* **46** F6
Vorios Evoikos Kolpos
    Greece **46** C5

Vorkuta *Russia* **52** C7
Vormsi *Estonia* **32** C2
Vorona ➤ *Russia* **34** E6
Voronezh *Russia* **33** G10
Voronezh *Ukraine* **33** G7
Voronezh □ *Russia* **34** E4
Voronezh ➤ *Russia* **33** G10
Vorontsovo-
    Aleksandrovskoye =
    Zelenokumsk *Russia* **35** H6
Vorpommersche
    Boddenlandschaft △
    Germany **24** A9
Vorskla ➤ *Ukraine* **33** H8
Võrts Järv *Estonia* **32** C4
Võru *Estonia* **32** D4
Vosges *France* **19** D14
Vosges □ *France* **19** D13
Vosges du Nord ○ *France* **19** D14
Voskopojë *Albania* **44** F4
Voskresensk *Russia* **32** E10
Voskresenskoye *Russia* **34** B7
Voss *Norway* **8** F12
Vostok *Antarctica* **5** D8
Vostok I. *Kiribati* **97** J12
Votice *Czech Rep.* **26** B7
Votsuri-Shima *Japan* **55** M1
Vouga ➤ *Portugal* **36** E2
Vouillé *France* **18** F7
Vouxa, Akra *Greece* **49** D5
Vouzela *Portugal* **36** E2
Vouziers *France* **19** C11
Vovchansk *Ukraine* **33** G9
Vowchyn *Belarus* **31** F10
Voyageurs △ *U.S.A.* **112** A7
Voynitsa *Russia* **8** D24
Vozhe, Ozero *Russia* **32** B10
Vozhega *Russia* **32** B10
Voznesensk *Ukraine* **33** J6
Voznesenye *Russia* **32** B8
Vrå *Denmark* **11** G3
Vráble *Slovak Rep.* **27** C11
Vračevšnica *Serbia* **44** B4
Vrachneika *Greece* **46** C3
Vrancea □ *Romania* **29** E11
Vrancei, Munții *Romania* **29** E11
Vrangelya, Ostrov *Russia* **53** B19
Vranica *Bos.-H.* **28** G2
Vranje *Serbia* **44** D5
Vranjska Banja *Serbia* **44** D6
Vranov nad Topľou
    Slovak Rep. **27** C14
Vransko *Slovenia* **41** B11
Vransko Jezero *Croatia* **41** E12
Vrapčište *Macedonia* **44** E4
Vratsa *Bulgaria* **44** C7
Vrbas *Serbia* **28** E4
Vrbas ➤ *Bos.-H.* **28** E2
Vrbnik *Croatia* **41** C11
Vrbovec *Croatia* **41** C13
Vrbovsko *Croatia* **41** C12
Vrchlabí *Czech Rep.* **26** A8
Vrede *S. Africa* **89** D4
Vredefort *S. Africa* **88** D4
Vreden *Germany* **24** C2
Vredenburg *S. Africa* **88** E2
Vredendal *S. Africa* **88** E2
Vretstorp *Sweden* **10** E8
Vrgorac *Croatia* **41** E14
Vrhnika *Slovenia* **41** C11
Vridi *Ivory C.* **82** D4
Vrigstad *Sweden* **11** G8
Vrindavan *India* **68** F7
Vrisses *Greece* **49** D6
Vrnograč *Bos.-H.* **41** C12
Vrondados *Greece* **47** C7
Vrpolje *Croatia* **28** E3
Vršac *Serbia* **28** E6
Vrsacki Kanal *Serbia* **28** E5
Vrútky *Slovak Rep.* **27** B11
Vryburg *S. Africa* **88** D3
Vryheid *S. Africa* **89** D5
Vsetín *Czech Rep.* **27** B11
Vu Liet *Vietnam* **64** C5
Vúcha ➤ *Bulgaria* **45** D8
Vučitrn *Serbia* **44** D4
Vukovar *Croatia* **28** E3
Vulcan *Canada* **102** C6
Vulcan *Romania* **29** E9
Vulcănești *Moldova* **29** E13
Vulcano *Italy* **43** D7
Vúlchedruma *Bulgaria* **44** C7
Vulkaneshty = Vulcănești
    Moldova **29** E13
Vunduzi ➤ *Mozam.* **87** F3
Vung Tau *Vietnam* **65** G6
Vunidawa *Fiji* **91** a
Vunisea *Fiji* **91** a
Vúrbitsa *Bulgaria* **45** D10
Vurshets *Bulgaria* **44** C7
Vutcani *Romania* **29** D13
Vuya *Sudan* **81** F2
Vuzlove *Ukraine* **28** B7
Vwaza △ *Malawi* **87** E3
Vyartsilya *Russia* **32** A6
Vyatka = Kirov *Russia* **52** D5
Vyatka ➤ *Russia* **34** C10

Vyatskiye Polyany *Russia* **34** B10
Vyazemskiy *Russia* **53** E14
Vyazma *Russia* **32** E8
Vyazniki *Russia* **34** B6
Vyborg *Russia* **32** B5
Vychegda ➔ *Russia* **52** C5
Vychodné Beskydy *Europe* **27** B15
Vyerkhnyadzvinsk *Belarus* **32** E4
Vyhoda *Ukraine* **29** B8
Vyksa *Russia* **34** C6
Vylkove *Ukraine* **29** E14
Vylok *Ukraine* **28** B7
Vynohradiv *Ukraine* **28** B8
Vyrnwy, L. *U.K.* **14** E4
Vyshkiv *Ukraine* **29** B8
Vyshkove *Ukraine* **29** B8
Vyshniy Volochek *Russia* **32** D8
Vyshzha = imeni 26
  Bakinskikh Komissarov
  Turkmenistan **71** B7
Vyškov *Czech Rep.* **27** B9
Vysokaye *Belarus* **31** F10
Vysoké Mýto *Czech Rep.* **27** B9
Vysokovsk *Russia* **32** D9
Vytegra *Russia* **34** B6
Vyzhnytsya *Ukraine* **29** B10
Vyzhnytsya ➔ *Ukraine* **29** B10

W

W du Benin △ *Benin* **83** C5
W du Burkina Faso △
  Burkina Faso **83** C4
W du Niger △ *Niger* **83** C5
W.A.C. Bennett Dam
  Canada **102** B4
Wa *Ghana* **82** C4
Waal ➔ *Neths.* **17** C5
Waalwijk *Neths.* **17** C5
Waat *Sudan* **81** F3
Wabakimi △ *Canada* **104** B2
Wabana *Canada* **105** C9
Wabasca ➔ *Canada* **102** B5
Wabasca-Desmarais
  Canada **102** B6
Wabash *U.S.A.* **113** E11
Wabash ➔ *U.S.A.* **112** G9
Wabi ➔ *Ethiopia* **81** F5
Wabigoon L. *Canada* **103** D10
Wabowden *Canada* **103** C9
Wąbrzeźno *Poland* **31** E5
Wabu Hu *China* **59** A11
Wabuk Pt. *Canada* **104** A2
Wabush *Canada* **105** B6
Wąchock *Poland* **31** G8
Wächtersbach *Germany* **25** E5
Waco *U.S.A.* **116** F6
Waconichi, L. *Canada* **104** B5
Wad Ban Naqa *Sudan* **81** D3
Wad Banda *Sudan* **81** E2
Wad el Haddad *Sudan* **81** E3
Wad en Nau *Sudan* **81** E3
Wad Hamid *Sudan* **81** D3
Wad Medanî *Sudan* **81** E3
Wad Thana *Pakistan* **68** F2
Wadai *Africa* **76** E5
Wadayama *Japan* **55** G7
Waddeneilanden *Neths.* **17** A5
Waddenzee *Neths.* **17** A5
Waddi, Chappal *Nigeria* **83** D7
Waddington *U.S.A.* **115** B9
Waddington, Mt. *Canada* **102** C3
Waddy Pt. *Australia* **95** C5
Wadebridge *U.K.* **15** G3
Wadena *Canada* **103** C8
Wadena *U.S.A.* **112** B6
Wädenswil *Switz.* **25** H4
Wadern *Germany* **25** F2
Wadeye *Australia* **92** B4
Wadhams *Canada* **102** C3
Wādī as Sīr *Jordan* **74** D4
Wâdi Gemâl *Egypt* **80** C4
Wadi Halfa *Sudan* **80** C3
Wadi Rum △ *Jordan* **74** F4
Wadian *China* **59** A9
Wadlew *Poland* **31** G6
Wadowice *Poland* **31** J6
Wadsworth *Nev., U.S.A.* **108** G4
Wadsworth *Ohio, U.S.A.* **114** E3
Waegwan *S. Korea* **57** G15
Wafangdian *China* **57** E11
Wafrah *Si. Arabia* **70** D5
Wageningen *Neths.* **17** C5
Wager B. *Canada* **101** C11
Wagga Wagga *Australia* **95** F4
Waghete *Indonesia* **63** E9
Wagin *Australia* **93** F2
Wagner *U.S.A.* **112** D4
Wagoner *U.S.A.* **116** D7
Wagon Mound *U.S.A.* **109** H11
Wągrowiec *Poland* **31** F4
Wah *Pakistan* **68** C5
Wahai *Indonesia* **63** E7
Wahiawā *U.S.A.* **106** b
Wāḩid *Egypt* **74** E1
Wahnai *Afghan.* **68** C1

Wahni *Ethiopia* **81** E4
Wahoo *U.S.A.* **112** E5
Wahpeton *U.S.A.* **112** B5
Waiau ➔ *N.Z.* **91** E4
Waibeem *Indonesia* **63** E8
Waiblingen *Germany* **25** G5
Waidhofen an der Thaya
  Austria **26** C8
Waidhofen an der Ybbs
  Austria **26** D7
Waigeo *Indonesia* **63** E8
Waihi *N.Z.* **91** B5
Waihou ➔ *N.Z.* **91** B5
Waika *Dem. Rep. of the Congo* **86** C2
Waikabubak *Indonesia* **63** F5
Waikaremoana, L. *N.Z.* **91** C6
Waikari *N.Z.* **91** E4
Waikato ➔ *N.Z.* **91** B5
Waikerie *Australia* **95** E3
Waikokopu *N.Z.* **91** C6
Waikouaiti *N.Z.* **91** F3
Wailuku *U.S.A.* **106** b
Waimakariri ➔ *N.Z.* **91** E4
Waimate *N.Z.* **91** F3
Wainganga ➔ *India* **66** K11
Waingapu *Indonesia* **63** F6
Waini ➔ *Guyana* **124** B7
Wainwright *Canada* **103** C6
Waiouru *N.Z.* **91** C6
Waipara *N.Z.* **91** E4
Waipawa *N.Z.* **91** C6
Waipiro *N.Z.* **91** C7
Waipoua Forest *N.Z.* **91** A4
Waipu *N.Z.* **91** A5
Waipukurau *N.Z.* **91** D6
Wairakei *N.Z.* **91** C6
Wairarapa, L. *N.Z.* **91** D5
Wairoa ➔ *N.Z.* **91** C6
Waitaki ➔ *N.Z.* **91** F3
Waitangi *N.Z.* **91** A5
Waitara *N.Z.* **91** C5
Waitomo Caves *N.Z.* **91** C5
Waitsburg *U.S.A.* **108** C4
Waiuku *N.Z.* **91** B5
Wajima *Japan* **55** F8
Wajir *Kenya* **86** B5
Waka *Ethiopia* **81** F4
Wakasa *Japan* **55** G7
Wakasa-Wan *Japan* **55** G7
Wakaw *Canada* **103** C7
Wakaya *Fiji* **91** a
Wakayama *Japan* **55** G7
Wakayama □ *Japan* **55** H7
Wake Forest *U.S.A.* **117** D15
Wake I. *Pac. Oc.* **96** F8
WaKeeney *U.S.A.* **112** F4
Wakefield *Jamaica* **120** a
Wakefield *N.Z.* **91** D4
Wakefield *U.K.* **14** D6
Wakefield *Mass., U.S.A.* **115** D13
Wakefield *Mich., U.S.A.* **112** B9
Wakkanai *Japan* **54** B10
Wakkerstroom *S. Africa* **89** D5
Wakool *Australia* **95** F3
Wakool ➔ *Australia* **95** F3
Wakre *Indonesia* **63** E8
Wakuach, L. *Canada* **105** A6
Walamba *Zambia* **87** E2
Wałbrzych *Poland* **31** H3
Walbury Hill *U.K.* **15** F6
Walcha *Australia* **95** E5
Walcheren *Neths.* **17** C3
Walcott *U.S.A.* **108** F10
Walcz *Poland* **31** E3
Waldbröl *Germany* **24** E3
Waldburg Ra. *Australia* **93** D2
Waldeck *Germany* **24** D5
Walden *Colo., U.S.A.* **108** F10
Walden *N.Y., U.S.A.* **115** E10
Waldkirch *Germany* **25** G3
Waldkirchen *Germany* **25** G9
Waldkraiburg *Germany* **25** G8
Waldport *U.S.A.* **108** D1
Waldron *U.S.A.* **116** D7
Waldviertel *Austria* **26** C8
Walebing *Australia* **93** F2
Walembele *Ghana* **82** C4
Walensee *Switz.* **25** H5
Wales □ *U.K.* **15** E3
Walewale *Ghana* **83** C4
Walgett *Australia* **95** E4
Walgreen Coast *Antarctica* **5** D15
Walker *U.S.A.* **112** B6
Walker, L. *Canada* **105** B6
Walker L. *Canada* **103** C9
Walker L. *U.S.A.* **108** G4
Walkerston *Australia* **94** K7
Walkerton *Canada* **114** B3
Wall *U.S.A.* **112** C2
Walla Walla *U.S.A.* **108** C4
Wallace *Idaho, U.S.A.* **108** C6
Wallace *N.C., U.S.A.* **117** D16
Wallaceburg *Canada* **114** D2
Wallachia = Valahia
  Romania **29** F9
Wallal *Australia* **95** D4

Wallam Cr. ➔ *Australia* **95** D4
Wallambin, L. *Australia* **93** F2
Wallangarra *Australia* **95** D5
Wallaroo *Australia* **95** E2
Walldürn *Germany* **25** F5
Wallenhorst *Germany* **24** C4
Wallenpaupack, L. *U.S.A.* **115** E9
Wallingford *U.S.A.* **115** E12
Wallis & Futuna, Is.
  Pac. Oc. **90** C11
Wallowa *U.S.A.* **108** D5
Wallowa Mts. *U.S.A.* **108** D5
Walls *U.K.* **13** A7
Walls of Jerusalem △
  Australia **95** G4
Wallula *U.S.A.* **108** C4
Wallumbilla *Australia* **95** D4
Walmsley L. *Canada* **103** A7
Walney, I. of *U.K.* **14** C4
Walnut Canyon △ *U.S.A.* **109** J8
Walnut Creek *U.S.A.* **110** H4
Walpole *Australia* **93** F2
Walpole *U.S.A.* **115** D13
Walpole-Nornalup △
  Australia **93** G2
Wals *Austria* **26** D5
Walsall *U.K.* **15** E6
Walsenburg *U.S.A.* **109** H11
Walsh *U.S.A.* **109** H12
Walsh ➔ *Australia* **94** B3
Walsrode *Germany* **24** C5
Walter F. George Res.
  U.S.A. **117** F12
Walterboro *U.S.A.* **117** E14
Walters *U.S.A.* **116** D5
Waltershausen *Germany* **24** E6
Waltham *U.S.A.* **115** D13
Waltman *U.S.A.* **108** E10
Walton *U.S.A.* **115** D9
Walton-on-the-Naze *U.K.* **15** F9
Walvis Bay *Namibia* **88** C1
Walvisbaai = Walvis Bay
  Namibia **88** C1
Wamba *Dem. Rep. of the Congo* **86** B2
Wamba *Kenya* **86** B4
Wamba *Nigeria* **83** D6
Wamego *U.S.A.* **112** F5
Wamena *Indonesia* **63** E9
Wamsutter *U.S.A.* **108** F10
Wamulan *Indonesia* **63** E7
Wan Xian *China* **56** E8
Wana *Pakistan* **68** C3
Wanaaring *Australia* **95** D3
Wanaka *N.Z.* **91** F2
Wanaka, L. *N.Z.* **91** F2
Wan'an *China* **59** D10
Wanapitei L. *Canada* **104** C3
Wandel Sea = McKinley
  Sea *Arctic* **4** A7
Wandérama *Ivory C.* **82** D4
Wanderer *Zimbabwe* **87** F3
Wandhari *Pakistan* **68** F2
Wanding *China* **58** E2
Wandoan *Australia* **95** D4
Wanfu *China* **57** D12
Wang ➔ *Thailand* **64** D2
Wang Kai *Sudan* **81** F2
Wang Noi *Thailand* **64** E3
Wang Saphung *Thailand* **64** D3
Wang Thong *Thailand* **64** D3
Wanga *Dem. Rep. of the Congo* **86** B2
Wangal *Indonesia* **63** F8
Wanganella *Australia* **95** F3
Wanganui *N.Z.* **91** C5
Wangaratta *Australia* **95** F4
Wangary *Australia* **95** E2
Wangcang *China* **58** A6
Wangcheng *China* **59** C9
Wangdu *China* **56** E8
Wangen *Germany* **25** H5
Wangerooge *Germany* **24** B3
Wangiwangi *Indonesia* **63** F6
Wangjiang *China* **59** B11
Wangmo *China* **58** E6
Wangqing *China* **57** C15
Wankaner *India* **68** H4
Wanlaweyne = Uanle Uen
  Somali Rep. **75** G3
Wanless *Canada* **103** C8
Wanneroo *Australia* **93** F2
Wannian *China* **59** C11
Wanning *China* **64** C8
Wannoo Billabong
  Roadhouse *Australia* **93** E2
Wanon Niwat *Thailand* **64** D4
Wanquan *China* **56** D8
Wanrong *China* **56** G6
Wanshan *China* **58** D7
Wanshengchang *China* **58** C6
Wantage *U.K.* **15** F6
Wanxian *China* **58** B7
Wanzai *China* **59** C10
Wapakoneta *U.S.A.* **113** E11
Wapato *U.S.A.* **108** C3
Wapawekka L. *Canada* **103** C8

Wapikopa L. *Canada* **104** B2
Wapiti ➔ *Canada* **102** B5
Wappingers Falls *U.S.A.* **115** E11
Wapsipinicon ➔ *U.S.A.* **112** E8
Wapusk △ *Canada* **103** B10
Warab □ *Sudan* **81** F2
Warangal *India* **66** L11
Waraseoni *India* **69** J9
Waratah *Australia* **95** G4
Waratah B. *Australia* **95** F4
Warburg *Germany* **24** D5
Warburton *Vic., Australia* **95** F4
Warburton *W. Austral.,*
  Australia **93** E4
Warburton ➔ *Australia* **95** D2
Warburton Ra. *Australia* **93** E4
Ward *N.Z.* **91** D5
Ward ➔ *Australia* **95** D4
Ward Mt. *U.S.A.* **110** H8
Warden *S. Africa* **89** D4
Wardha *India* **66** J11
Wardha ➔ *India* **66** K11
Ware *Canada* **102** B3
Ware *U.K.* **15** F8
Ware *U.S.A.* **115** D12
Waregem *Belgium* **17** D3
Wareham *U.S.A.* **115** E14
Waremme *Belgium* **17** D5
Waren *Germany* **24** B8
Warendorf *Germany* **24** D4
Warialda *Australia* **95** D5
Wariap *Indonesia* **63** E8
Warin Chamrap *Thailand* **64** E5
Warka *Poland* **31** G8
Warkopi *Indonesia* **63** E8
Warm Springs *U.S.A.* **109** G5
Warman *Canada* **103** C7
Warmbad = Bela Bela
  S. Africa **89** C4
Warmbad *Namibia* **88** D2
Warmińsko-Mazurskie □
  Poland **30** D8
Warminster *U.K.* **15** F5
Warminster *U.S.A.* **115** F9
Warmun *Australia* **92** C4
Warnemünde *Germany* **24** A8
Warner Mts. *U.S.A.* **108** F3
Warner Robins *U.S.A.* **117** E13
Warnow ➔ *Germany* **24** A8
Waroona *Australia* **93** F2
Warracknabeal *Australia* **95** F3
Warragul *Australia* **95** F4
Warrego ➔ *Australia* **95** E4
Warrego Ra. *Australia* **94** C4
Warren *Australia* **95** E4
Warren *Ark., U.S.A.* **116** E8
Warren *Mich., U.S.A.* **113** D12
Warren *Minn., U.S.A.* **112** A5
Warren *Ohio, U.S.A.* **114** E4
Warren *Pa., U.S.A.* **114** E5
Warrenpoint *U.K.* **12** B5
Warrensburg *Mo., U.S.A.* **112** F7
Warrensburg *N.Y., U.S.A.* **115** C11
Warrenton *S. Africa* **88** D3
Warrenton *U.S.A.* **110** D3
Warri *Nigeria* **83** D6
Warrina *Australia* **95** D2
Warrington *U.K.* **14** D5
Warrington *U.S.A.* **117** F11
Warrnambool *Australia* **95** F3
Warroad *U.S.A.* **112** A6
Warruwi *Australia* **94** A1
Warsa *Indonesia* **63** E9
Warsak Dam *Pakistan* **68** B4
Warsaw = Warszawa *Poland* **31** F8
Warsaw *Ind., U.S.A.* **113** E11
Warsaw *N.Y., U.S.A.* **114** D6
Warsaw *Ohio, U.S.A.* **114** F3
Warstein *Germany* **24** D4
Warszawa *Poland* **31** F8
Warszawa ✈ (WAW) *Poland* **31** F7
Warta *Poland* **31** G5
Warta ➔ *Poland* **31** F1
Warthe = Warta ➔ *Poland* **31** F1
Waru *Indonesia* **63** E8
Warwick *Australia* **95** D5
Warwick *U.K.* **15** E6
Warwick *N.Y., U.S.A.* **115** E10
Warwick *R.I., U.S.A.* **115** E13
Warwickshire □ *U.K.* **15** E6
Wasaga Beach *Canada* **114** B4
Wasagaming *Canada* **103** C9
Wasatch Ra. *U.S.A.* **108** F8
Wasbank *S. Africa* **89** D5
Wasco *Calif., U.S.A.* **111** K7
Wasco *Oreg., U.S.A.* **108** D3
Waseca *U.S.A.* **112** C7
Wasekamio L. *Canada* **103** B7
Wash, The *U.K.* **14** E8
Washago *Canada* **114** B5
Washburn *N. Dak., U.S.A.* **112** B3
Washburn *Wis., U.S.A.* **112** B8
Washim *India* **66** J10
Washington *U.K.* **14** C6
Washington *D.C., U.S.A.* **113** F15

Washington *Ga., U.S.A.* **117** E13
Washington *Ind., U.S.A.* **112** F10
Washington *Iowa, U.S.A.* **112** E9
Washington *Mo., U.S.A.* **112** F8
Washington *N.C., U.S.A.* **117** D16
Washington *N.J., U.S.A.* **115** F10
Washington *Pa., U.S.A.* **114** F4
Washington *Utah, U.S.A.* **109** H7
Washington □ *U.S.A.* **108** C3
Washington, Mt. *U.S.A.* **115** B13
Washington Court House
  U.S.A. **113** F12
Washington I. *U.S.A.* **112** C10
Washougal *U.S.A.* **110** E4
Washpool △ *Australia* **95** D5
Wasian *Indonesia* **63** E8
Wasilków *Poland* **31** E10
Wasilla *U.S.A.* **100** C5
Wasior *Indonesia* **63** E8
Wāsiṭ □ *Iraq* **73** F11
Waskaganish *Canada* **104** B4
Waskaiowaka L. *Canada* **103** B9
Waskesiu Lake *Canada* **103** C7
Wasserburg *Germany* **25** G8
Wasserkuppe *Germany* **24** E5
Wassy *France* **19** D11
Waswanipi *Canada* **104** C4
Waswanipi, L. *Canada* **104** C4
Watampone *Indonesia* **63** E6
Watamu *Kenya* **86** C5
Watarrka △ *Australia* **92** D5
Water Park Pt. *Australia* **94** C5
Water Valley *U.S.A.* **117** D10
Waterberg Plateau △
  Namibia **88** C2
Waterberge *S. Africa* **89** C4
Waterbury *Conn., U.S.A.* **115** E11
Waterbury *Vt., U.S.A.* **115** B12
Waterbury L. *Canada* **103** B8
Waterdown *Canada* **114** C5
Waterford *Canada* **114** D4
Waterford *Ireland* **12** D4
Waterford *Calif., U.S.A.* **110** H6
Waterford *Pa., U.S.A.* **114** E5
Waterford □ *Ireland* **12** D4
Waterford Harbour *Ireland* **12** D5
Waterhen L. *Canada* **103** C9
Waterloo *Belgium* **17** D4
Waterloo *Ont., Canada* **114** C4
Waterloo *Qué., Canada* **115** A12
Waterloo *S. Leone* **82** D2
Waterloo *Ill., U.S.A.* **112** F8
Waterloo *Iowa, U.S.A.* **112** D7
Waterloo *N.Y., U.S.A.* **114** D8
Watersmeet *U.S.A.* **112** B9
Waterton Lakes △ *Canada* **102** D6
Watertown *Conn., U.S.A.* **115** E11
Watertown *N.Y., U.S.A.* **115** C9
Watertown *S. Dak., U.S.A.* **112** C5
Watertown *Wis., U.S.A.* **112** D9
Waterval-Boven *S. Africa* **89** D5
Waterville *Canada* **115** A13
Waterville *Maine, U.S.A.* **113** C19
Waterville *N.Y., U.S.A.* **115** D9
Waterville *Pa., U.S.A.* **114** E7
Waterville *Wash., U.S.A.* **108** C3
Watervliet *U.S.A.* **115** D11
Wates *Indonesia* **63** G14
Watford *Canada* **114** D3
Watford *U.K.* **15** F7
Watford City *U.S.A.* **112** B2
Wathaman ➔ *Canada* **103** B8
Wathaman L. *Canada* **103** B8
Watheroo *Australia* **93** F2
Watheroo △ *Australia* **93** F2
Wating *China* **56** G4
Watkins Glen *U.S.A.* **114** D8
Watling I. = San Salvador
  I. *Bahamas* **121** B5
Watonga *U.S.A.* **116** D5
Watrous *Canada* **103** C7
Watrous *U.S.A.* **109** J11
Watsa *Dem. Rep. of the Congo* **86** B2
Watseka *U.S.A.* **112** E10
Watson *Canada* **103** C8
Watson Lake *Canada* **102** A3
Watsontown *U.S.A.* **114** E8
Watsonville *U.S.A.* **110** J5
Wattiwarriganna Cr. ➔
  Australia **95** D2
Wattwil *Switz.* **25** H5
Watuata = Batuata *Indonesia* **63** F6
Watubela, Kepulauan
  Indonesia **63** E8
Watubela Is. = Watubela,
  Kepulauan *Indonesia* **63** E8
Wau = Wâw *Sudan* **81** F2
Waubamik *Canada* **114** A4
Waubay *U.S.A.* **112** C5
Wauchope *N.S.W., Australia* **95** E5
Wauchope *N. Terr., Australia* **94** C1
Wauchula *U.S.A.* **117** H14
Waukarlycarly, L. *Australia* **92** D3
Waukegan *U.S.A.* **112** D10
Waukesha *U.S.A.* **112** D9
Waukon *U.S.A.* **112** D8
Waupaca *U.S.A.* **112** C9

Waupun *U.S.A.* **112** D9
Waurika *U.S.A.* **116** D6
Wausau *U.S.A.* **112** C9
Wautoma *U.S.A.* **112** C9
Wauwatosa *U.S.A.* **112** D9
Waveney ➔ *U.K.* **15** E9
Waverley *N.Z.* **91** C5
Waverly *Iowa, U.S.A.* **112** D7
Waverly *N.Y., U.S.A.* **115** E8
Wavre *Belgium* **17** D4
Wâw *Sudan* **81** F2
Wâw al Kabîr *Libya* **79** C9
Wawa *Canada* **104** C3
Wawa *Nigeria* **83** D5
Wawa *Sudan* **80** C3
Wawanesa *Canada* **103** D9
Wawona *U.S.A.* **110** H7
Waxahachie *U.S.A.* **116** E6
Way, L. *Australia* **93** E3
Waya *Fiji* **91** a
Waycross *U.S.A.* **117** F13
Wayi *Sudan* **81** F3
Wayland *U.S.A.* **114** D7
Wayne *Nebr., U.S.A.* **112** D5
Wayne *W. Va., U.S.A.* **113** F12
Waynesboro *Ga., U.S.A.* **117** E13
Waynesboro *Miss., U.S.A.* **117** F10
Waynesboro *Pa., U.S.A.* **113** F15
Waynesboro *Va., U.S.A.* **113** F14
Waynesburg *U.S.A.* **113** F13
Waynesville *U.S.A.* **117** D13
Waynoka *U.S.A.* **116** C5
Wazirabad *Pakistan* **68** C6
Wda ➔ *Poland* **30** E5
We *Indonesia* **62** C1
Weald, The *U.K.* **15** F8
Wear ➔ *U.K.* **14** C6
Weatherford *Okla., U.S.A.* **116** D5
Weatherford *Tex., U.S.A.* **116** E6
Weaverville *U.S.A.* **108** F2
Webb City *U.S.A.* **112** G6
Webequie *Canada* **104** B2
Webo = Nyaake *Liberia* **82** E3
Webster *Mass., U.S.A.* **115** D13
Webster *N.Y., U.S.A.* **114** C7
Webster *S. Dak., U.S.A.* **112** C5
Webster City *U.S.A.* **112** D7
Webster Springs *U.S.A.* **113** F13
Weda *Indonesia* **63** D7
Weda, Teluk *Indonesia* **63** D7
Weddell Abyssal Plain
  S. Ocean **5** C2
Weddell I. *Falk. Is.* **128** G4
Weddell Sea *Antarctica* **5** D1
Wedderburn *Australia* **95** F3
Wedel *Germany* **24** B5
Wedemark *Germany* **24** C5
Wedgeport *Canada* **105** D6
Wedza *Zimbabwe* **87** F3
Wee Waa *Australia* **95** E4
Weed *U.S.A.* **108** F2
Weed Heights *U.S.A.* **110** G7
Weedsport *U.S.A.* **115** C8
Weedville *U.S.A.* **114** E6
Weenen *S. Africa* **89** D5
Weener *Germany* **24** B3
Weert *Neths.* **17** C5
Węgierska-Górka *Poland* **31** J6
Węgliniec *Poland* **31** G2
Węgorzewo *Poland* **30** D8
Węgorzyno *Poland* **30** E2
Węgrów *Poland* **31** F9
Wehda □ *Sudan* **81** F3
Wei He ➔ *Hebei, China* **56** F8
Wei He ➔ *Shaanxi, China* **56** G6
Weichang *China* **57** D9
Weichuan *China* **56** G7
Weida *Germany* **24** E8
Weiden *Germany* **25** F8
Weifang *China* **57** F10
Weihai *China* **57** F12
Weil *Germany* **25** H3
Weilburg *Germany* **24** E4
Weilheim *Germany* **25** H7
Weimar *Germany* **24** E7
Weinan *China* **56** G5
Weingarten *Germany* **25** F4
Weinheim *Germany* **25** F4
Weining *China* **58** D5
Weipa *Australia* **94** A3
Weir ➔ *Australia* **95** D4
Weir ➔ *Canada* **103** B10
Weir River *Canada* **103** B10
Weirton *U.S.A.* **114** F4
Weiser *U.S.A.* **108** D5
Weishan *Shandong, China* **57** G9
Weishan *Yunnan, China* **58** E3
Weissenburg *Germany* **25** F6
Weissenfels *Germany* **24** D7
Weisswasser *Germany* **24** D10
Wéitra *Austria* **26** C7
Weixi *China* **58** D2
Weixin *China* **58** D5
Weiyuan *China* **56** G3
Weiz *Austria* **26** D8
Weizhou Dao *China* **58** G7
Wejherowo *Poland* **30** D5

Wekusko L. *Canada* **103** C9
Welch *U.S.A.* **113** G13
Weldya *Ethiopia* **81** E4
Welega *Ethiopia* **81** F3
Welford △ *Australia* **94** D3
Welkite *Ethiopia* **81** F4
Welkom *S. Africa* **88** D4
Welland *Canada* **114** D5
Welland → *U.K.* **15** E7
Wellesley Is. *Australia* **94** B2
Wellingborough *U.K.* **15** E7
Wellington *Australia* **95** E4
Wellington *Canada* **114** C7
Wellington *N.Z.* **91** D5
Wellington *S. Africa* **88** E2
Wellington *Somst., U.K.* **15** G4
Wellington *Telford & Wrekin, U.K.* **15** E5
Wellington *Colo., U.S.A.* **108** F11
Wellington *Kans., U.S.A.* **112** G5
Wellington *Nev., U.S.A.* **110** G7
Wellington *Ohio, U.S.A.* **114** E2
Wellington *Tex., U.S.A.* **113** H4
Wellington, I. *Chile* **128** F2
Wellington, L. *Australia* **95** F4
Wellington Chan. *Canada* **101** B10
Wells *U.K.* **15** F5
Wells *Maine, U.S.A.* **115** C14
Wells *N.Y., U.S.A.* **115** C10
Wells *Nev., U.S.A.* **108** F6
Wells, L. *Australia* **93** E3
Wells, Mt. *Australia* **92** C4
Wells Gray △ *Canada* **102** C4
Wells River *U.S.A.* **115** B12
Wellsboro *U.S.A.* **114** E7
Wellsburg *U.S.A.* **114** F4
Wellsville *N.Y., U.S.A.* **114** D7
Wellsville *Ohio, U.S.A.* **114** F4
Wellsville *Utah, U.S.A.* **108** F8
Wellton *U.S.A.* **109** K6
Welmel, Wabi → *Ethiopia* **81** F5
Welo *Ethiopia* **81** E4
Wels *Austria* **26** C7
Welshpool *U.K.* **15** E4
Welwyn Garden City *U.K.* **15** F7
Wem *U.K.* **14** E5
Wembere → *Tanzania* **86** C3
Wemindji *Canada* **104** B4
Wen Xian *China* **56** G7
Wenatchee *U.S.A.* **108** C3
Wenchang *China* **64** C8
Wencheng *China* **59** D13
Wenchi *Ghana* **82** D4
Wenchow = Wenzhou *China* **59** D13
Wenchuan *China* **58** B4
Wenden *U.S.A.* **111** M13
Wendeng *China* **57** F12
Wendesi *Indonesia* **63** E8
Wendo *Ethiopia* **81** F4
Wendover *U.S.A.* **108** F6
Weng'an *China* **58** D6
Wengcheng *China* **59** E9
Wengen *Switz.* **19** F14
Wengyuan *China* **59** E10
Wenjiang *China* **58** B4
Wenling *China* **59** C13
Wenlock → *Australia* **94** A3
Wenshan *China* **58** F5
Wenshang *China* **56** G9
Wenshui *China* **56** F7
Wensleydale *U.K.* **14** C6
Wensu *China* **60** B3
Wensum → *U.K.* **14** E8
Wentworth *Australia* **95** E3
Wentzel L. *Canada* **102** B6
Wenut *Indonesia* **63** E8
Wenxi *China* **56** G6
Wenxian *China* **56** H3
Wenzhou *China* **59** D13
Weott *U.S.A.* **108** F2
Wepener *S. Africa* **88** D4
Werda *Botswana* **88** D3
Werdau *Germany* **24** E8
Werder *Germany* **24** C8
Werdohl *Germany* **24** D3
Wereilu *Ethiopia* **81** E4
Weri *Indonesia* **63** E8
Werneck *Germany* **25** F6
Wernigerode *Germany* **24** D6
Werra → *Germany* **24** D5
Werrimull *Australia* **95** E3
Werris Creek *Australia* **95** E5
Wertach → *Germany* **25** G6
Wertheim *Germany* **25** F5
Wertingen *Germany* **25** G6
Wesel *Germany* **24** D2
Weser → *Germany* **24** B4
Weser-Ems □ *Germany* **24** C3
Weserbergland *Germany* **24** C5
Weserbergland Schaumburg Hameln △ *Germany* **24** C5
Wesiri *Indonesia* **63** F7
Weslaco *U.S.A.* **116** H6
Weslemkoon L. *Canada* **114** A7

Wesleyville *U.S.A.* **114** D4
Wessel, C. *Australia* **94** A2
Wessel Is. *Australia* **94** A2
Wesselburen *Germany* **24** A4
Wessington Springs *U.S.A.* **112** C4
West *U.S.A.* **116** F6
West → *U.S.A.* **115** D12
West Allis *U.S.A.* **112** D9
West Antarctica *Antarctica* **5** D15
West Baines → *Australia* **92** C4
West Bank ■ *Asia* **74** C4
West Bend *U.S.A.* **112** D9
West Bengal □ *India* **69** H13
West Berkshire □ *U.K.* **15** F6
West Beskids = Západné Beskydy *Europe* **27** B12
West Branch *U.S.A.* **113** C11
West Branch Susquehanna → *U.S.A.* **115** F8
West Bromwich *U.K.* **15** E6
West Burra *U.K.* **13** A7
West Canada Cr. → *U.S.A.* **115** C10
West Caroline Basin *Pac. Oc.* **96** G5
West Chazy *U.S.A.* **115** B11
West Chester *U.S.A.* **115** G9
West Coast △ *Namibia* **88** C1
West Coast △ *S. Africa* **88** E2
West Columbia *U.S.A.* **116** G7
West Covina *U.S.A.* **111** L9
West Des Moines *U.S.A.* **112** E7
West Dunbartonshire □ *U.K.* **13** F4
West End *Bahamas* **120** A4
West Falkland *Falk. Is.* **128** G4
West Fargo *U.S.A.* **112** B5
West Farmington *U.S.A.* **114** E4
West Fiji Basin *Pac. Oc.* **96** J9
West Fjord = Vestfjorden *Norway* **8** C16
West Fork Trinity → *U.S.A.* **116** E6
West Frankfort *U.S.A.* **112** G9
West Grand L. *U.S.A.* **113** C20
West Hartford *U.S.A.* **115** E12
West Haven *U.S.A.* **115** E12
West Hazleton *U.S.A.* **115** F9
West Helena *U.S.A.* **117** D9
West Hurley *U.S.A.* **115** E10
West Ice Shelf *Antarctica* **5** C7
West Indies *Cent. Amer.* **121** D7
West Jordan *U.S.A.* **108** F8
West Linn *U.S.A.* **110** E4
West Lorne *Canada* **114** D3
West Lothian □ *U.K.* **13** F5
West Lunga → *Zambia* **87** E1
West MacDonnell △ *Australia* **92** D5
West Mariana Basin *Pac. Oc.* **96** F5
West Memphis *U.S.A.* **117** D9
West Midlands □ *U.K.* **15** E6
West Mifflin *U.S.A.* **114** F5
West Milford *U.S.A.* **115** E10
West Milton *U.S.A.* **114** E8
West Monroe *U.S.A.* **116** E8
West Newton *U.S.A.* **114** F5
West Nicholson *Zimbabwe* **87** G2
West Odessa *U.S.A.* **116** F3
West Palm Beach *U.S.A.* **117** H14
West Plains *U.S.A.* **112** G8
West Point *Miss., U.S.A.* **117** E10
West Point *N.Y., U.S.A.* **115** E11
West Point *Nebr., U.S.A.* **112** E5
West Point *Va., U.S.A.* **113** G15
West Point L. *U.S.A.* **117** E12
West Pt. = Ouest, Pte. de l' *Canada* **105** C7
West Pt. *Australia* **95** F2
West Road → *Canada* **102** C4
West Rutland *U.S.A.* **115** C11
West Schelde = Westerschelde → *Neths.* **17** C3
West Seneca *U.S.A.* **114** D6
West Siberian Plain *Russia* **50** B9
West Sussex □ *U.K.* **15** G7
West-Terschelling *Neths.* **17** A5
West-Valley City *U.S.A.* **108** F8
West Virginia □ *U.S.A.* **113** F13
West-Vlaanderen □ *Belgium* **17** D2
West Walker → *U.S.A.* **110** G7
West Wyalong *Australia* **95** E4
West Yellowstone *U.S.A.* **108** D8
West Yorkshire □ *U.K.* **14** D6
Westall, Pt. *Australia* **95** E1
Westbrook *U.S.A.* **113** D18
Westbury *Australia* **95** G4
Westby *U.S.A.* **108** B11
Westend *U.S.A.* **111** K9
Westerland *Germany* **24** A4
Westerly *U.S.A.* **115** E13
Western □ *Ghana* **82** D4
Western □ *Kenya* **86** B3
Western □ *S. Leone* **82** D2
Western □ *Zambia* **87** F1
Western Australia □ *Australia* **93** E2
Western Cape □ *S. Africa* **88** E3

Western Dvina = Daugava → *Latvia* **32** D3
Western Ghats *India* **66** N9
Western Isles □ *U.K.* **13** D1
Western Sahara ■ *Africa* **78** D3
Western Samoa = Samoa ■ *Pac. Oc.* **91** b
Western Sierra Madre = Madre Occidental, Sierra *Mexico* **118** B3
Westernport *U.S.A.* **113** F14
Westerschelde → *Neths.* **17** C3
Westerstede *Germany* **24** B3
Westerwald *Germany* **24** E3
Westfield *Mass., U.S.A.* **115** D12
Westfield *N.Y., U.S.A.* **114** D5
Westfield *Pa., U.S.A.* **114** E7
Westhill *U.K.* **13** D6
Westhope *U.S.A.* **112** A3
Westland → *N.Z.* **91** E2
Westland Bight *N.Z.* **91** E3
Westlock *Canada* **102** C6
Westmar *U.S.A.* **95** D4
Westmeath □ *Ireland* **12** C4
Westminster *Calif., U.S.A.* **111** M8
Westminster *Colo., U.S.A.* **108** G11
Westminster *Md., U.S.A.* **113** F15
Westmont *U.S.A.* **114** F6
Westmoreland *Barbados* **121** g
Westmorland *U.S.A.* **111** M11
Weston *Oreg., U.S.A.* **108** D4
Weston *W. Va., U.S.A.* **113** F13
Weston I. *Canada* **104** B4
Weston-super-Mare *U.K.* **15** F5
Westover *U.S.A.* **114** F6
Westport *Canada* **115** B8
Westport *Ireland* **12** C2
Westport *N.Z.* **91** D3
Westport *N.Y., U.S.A.* **115** B11
Westport *Oreg., U.S.A.* **110** D3
Westport *Wash., U.S.A.* **110** D2
Westray *Canada* **103** C8
Westray *U.K.* **13** B5
Westree *Canada* **104** C3
Westville *U.S.A.* **110** F6
Westwood *U.S.A.* **108** F3
Wetar *Indonesia* **63** F7
Wetaskiwin *Canada* **102** C6
Wete *Tanzania* **84** F7
Wetherby *U.K.* **14** D6
Wethersfield *U.S.A.* **115** E12
Wetteren *Belgium* **17** D3
Wetzlar *Germany* **24** E4
Wewoka *U.S.A.* **116** H6
Wexford *Ireland* **12** D5
Wexford □ *Ireland* **12** D5
Wexford Harbour *Ireland* **12** D5
Weyburn *Canada* **103** D8
Weyer Markt *Austria* **26** D7
Weyhe *Germany* **24** C4
Weyib → *Ethiopia* **81** F5
Weymouth *Canada* **105** D6
Weymouth *U.K.* **15** G5
Weymouth *U.S.A.* **115** D14
Weymouth, C. *Australia* **94** A3
Wha Ti *Canada* **100** C8
Whakaari = White I. *N.Z.* **91** B6
Whakatane *N.Z.* **91** B6
Whale → *Canada* **105** A6
Whale Cove *Canada* **103** A10
Whales, B. of *Antarctica* **5** D12
Whalsay *U.K.* **13** A8
Whangamata *N.Z.* **91** B5
Whangamomona *N.Z.* **91** C5
Whanganui △ *N.Z.* **91** C5
Whangarei *N.Z.* **91** A5
Whangarei Harb. *N.Z.* **91** A5
Wharekauri = Chatham Is. *Pac. Oc.* **96** M10
Wharfe → *U.K.* **14** D6
Wharfedale *U.K.* **14** C5
Wharton *N.J., U.S.A.* **115** F10
Wharton *Pa., U.S.A.* **114** E6
Wharton *Tex., U.S.A.* **116** G6
Wharton Basin *Ind. Oc.* **96** J2
Wheatland *Calif., U.S.A.* **110** F5
Wheatland *Wyo., U.S.A.* **108** E11
Wheatley *Canada* **114** D2
Wheaton *Md., U.S.A.* **113** F15
Wheaton *Minn., U.S.A.* **112** C5
Wheelbarrow Pk. *U.S.A.* **110** H10
Wheeler *Oreg., U.S.A.* **108** D2
Wheeler *Tex., U.S.A.* **116** D4
Wheeler → *Canada* **105** A6
Wheeler L. *U.S.A.* **117** D11
Wheeler Pk. *N. Mex., U.S.A.* **109** H11
Wheeler Pk. *Nev., U.S.A.* **108** G6
Wheeler Ridge *U.S.A.* **111** L8
Wheelersburg *U.S.A.* **113** F12
Wheeling *U.S.A.* **114** F4
Whernside *U.K.* **14** C5
Whiddy I. *Ireland* **12** E2
Whiskey Jack L. *Canada* **103** B8
Whiskeytown-Shasta-Trinity △ *U.S.A.* **108** F2
Whistleduck Cr. → *Australia* **94** C2

Whistler *Canada* **102** C4
Whitby *Canada* **114** C6
Whitby *U.K.* **14** C7
White → *Ark., U.S.A.* **116** E9
White → *Ind., U.S.A.* **112** F10
White → *S. Dak., U.S.A.* **112** D4
White → *Tex., U.S.A.* **116** E4
White → *Utah, U.S.A.* **108** F9
White → *Vt., U.S.A.* **115** C12
White → *Wash., U.S.A.* **110** C4
White, L. *Australia* **92** D4
White B. *Canada* **105** C8
White Bird *U.S.A.* **108** D5
White Butte *U.S.A.* **112** B2
White City *U.S.A.* **108** E2
White Cliffs *Australia* **95** E3
White Hall *U.S.A.* **112** F8
White Haven *U.S.A.* **115** E9
White Horse, Vale of *U.K.* **15** F6
White I. *N.Z.* **91** B6
White L. *Canada* **115** A8
White L. *U.S.A.* **116** G8
White Mountain Peak *U.S.A.* **109** H4
White Mts. *Calif., U.S.A.* **110** H8
White Mts. *N.H., U.S.A.* **115** B13
White Mts. △ *Australia* **94** C4
White Nile = Nîl el Abyad → *Sudan* **81** D3
White Nile Dam = Khazzân Jabal al Awliyâ *Sudan* **81** D3
White Otter L. *Canada* **104** C1
White Pass *U.S.A.* **110** D5
White Plains *U.S.A.* **115** E11
White River *Canada* **104** C2
White River *S. Africa* **89** D5
White River *U.S.A.* **112** D3
White Rock *Canada* **110** A4
White Rock *U.S.A.* **109** J10
White Russia = Belarus ■ *Europe* **23** B14
White Sands △ *U.S.A.* **109** K10
White Sea = Beloye More *Russia* **8** C25
White Sulphur Springs *Mont., U.S.A.* **108** C8
White Sulphur Springs *W. Va., U.S.A.* **113** G13
White Swan *U.S.A.* **110** D6
White Volta → *Ghana* **83** D4
Whitecliffs *N.Z.* **91** E3
Whitecourt *Canada* **102** C5
Whiteface Mt. *U.S.A.* **115** B11
Whitefield *U.S.A.* **115** B13
Whitefish *U.S.A.* **108** B6
Whitefish L. *Canada* **104** C3
Whitefish L. *Canada* **103** A7
Whitefish Pt. *U.S.A.* **113** B11
Whitegull, L. = Goélands, L. aux *Canada* **105** A7
Whitehall *Mich., U.S.A.* **112** D10
Whitehall *Mont., U.S.A.* **108** D7
Whitehall *N.Y., U.S.A.* **115** C11
Whitehall *Wis., U.S.A.* **112** C8
Whitehaven *U.K.* **14** C4
Whitehorse *Canada* **102** A1
Whitemark *Australia* **95** G4
Whiteplains *Liberia* **82** D2
Whiteriver *U.S.A.* **109** K9
Whitesand → *Canada* **102** A5
Whitesands *S. Africa* **88** E3
Whitesboro *N.Y., U.S.A.* **115** C9
Whitesboro *Tex., U.S.A.* **116** E6
Whiteshell △ *Canada* **103** D9
Whitesville *U.S.A.* **114** D7
Whiteville *U.S.A.* **117** D15
Whitewater *U.S.A.* **112** D9
Whitewater Baldy *U.S.A.* **109** K9
Whitewater L. *Canada* **104** B2
Whitewood *Australia* **94** C3
Whitewood *Canada* **103** C8
Whithorn *U.K.* **13** G4
Whitianga *N.Z.* **91** B5
Whitman *U.S.A.* **115** D14
Whitney *Canada* **114** A6
Whitney, Mt. *U.S.A.* **110** J8
Whitney Point *U.S.A.* **115** D9
Whitstable *U.K.* **15** F9
Whitsunday I. *Australia* **94** J7
Whitsunday Islands △ *Australia* **94** J7
Whitsunday Passage *Australia* **94** J6
Whittier *U.S.A.* **111** M8
Whittlesea *Australia* **95** F4
Wholdaia L. *Canada* **103** A8
Whyalla *Australia* **95** E2
Wiang Kosai △ *Thailand* **64** D2
Wiarton *Canada* **114** B3
Wiawso *Ghana* **82** D4
Wiay *U.K.* **13** D1
Wiazów *Poland* **31** H4
Wibaux *U.S.A.* **108** C11
Wichian Buri *Thailand* **64** E3
Wichita *U.S.A.* **112** G5
Wichita Falls *U.S.A.* **116** E5

Wick *U.K.* **13** C5
Wicked Pt. *Canada* **114** C7
Wickenburg *U.S.A.* **109** K7
Wickepin *Australia* **93** F2
Wickham *Australia* **92** D2
Wickham, C. *Australia* **95** F3
Wickliffe *U.S.A.* **114** E3
Wicklow *Ireland* **12** D5
Wicklow □ *Ireland* **12** D5
Wicklow Hd. *Ireland* **12** D6
Wicklow Mts. *Ireland* **12** C5
Wicklow Mts. △ *Ireland* **12** C5
Widawa *Poland* **31** G5
Widawka → *Poland* **31** G5
Widgeegoara Cr. → *Australia* **95** D4
Widgiemooltha *Australia* **93** F3
Widnes *U.K.* **14** D5
Więcbork *Poland* **31** E4
Wiehengebirge = Nördlicher Teutoburger Wald-Wiehengebirge △ *Germany* **24** C4
Wiehl *Germany* **24** E3
Wiek *Germany* **24** A9
Wielbark *Poland* **30** E7
Wieleń *Poland* **31** F3
Wielichowo *Poland* **31** F3
Wieliczka *Poland* **31** J7
Wielkopolski △ *Poland* **31** F3
Wielkopolskie □ *Poland* **31** F4
Wieluń *Poland* **31** G5
Wien *Austria* **27** C9
Wien-Schwechat ✈ (VIE) *Austria* **27** C9
Wiener Neustadt *Austria* **27** D9
Wieprz → *Poland* **31** G8
Wieprza → *Poland* **30** D3
Wieruszów *Poland* **31** G5
Wiesbaden *Germany* **25** E4
Wiesental *Germany* **25** F4
Wiesloch *Germany* **25** F4
Wiesmoor *Germany* **24** B3
Wieżyca *Poland* **30** D5
Wigan *U.K.* **14** D5
Wiggins *Colo., U.S.A.* **108** F11
Wiggins *Miss., U.S.A.* **117** F10
Wight, I. of *U.K.* **15** G6
Wigierski △ *Poland* **30** D10
Wigry, Jezioro *Poland* **30** D10
Wigston *U.K.* **15** E6
Wigton *U.K.* **14** C4
Wigtown *U.K.* **13** G4
Wigtown B. *U.K.* **13** G4
Wil *Switz.* **25** H5
Wilber *U.S.A.* **112** E5
Wilberforce *Canada* **114** A6
Wilberforce, C. *Australia* **94** A2
Wilburton *U.S.A.* **116** D7
Wilcannia *Australia* **95** E3
Wilcox *U.S.A.* **114** E6
Wildbad *Germany* **25** G4
Wildeshausen *Germany* **24** C4
Wildeshauser Geest △ *Germany* **24** C4
Wildon *Austria* **26** E8
Wildrose *U.S.A.* **111** J9
Wildspitze *Austria* **26** E3
Wilga → *Poland* **31** G8
Wilge → *S. Africa* **89** D4
Wilhelm II Coast *Antarctica* **5** C7
Wilhelmsburg *Austria* **26** C8
Wilhelmshaven *Germany* **24** B4
Wilhelmstal *Namibia* **88** C2
Wilkes-Barre *U.S.A.* **115** E9
Wilkes Land *Antarctica* **5** D9
Wilkie *Canada* **103** C7
Wilkinsburg *U.S.A.* **114** F5
Wilkinson Lakes *Australia* **93** E5
Willandra Creek → *Australia* **95** E4
Willapa B. *U.S.A.* **108** C1
Willapa Hills *U.S.A.* **110** D3
Willard *N.Y., U.S.A.* **114** D8
Willard *Ohio, U.S.A.* **114** E2
Willcox *U.S.A.* **109** K9
Willemstad *Neth. Ant.* **121** D6
Willet *U.S.A.* **115** F9
William → *Canada* **103** B7
William 'Bill' Dannelly Res. *U.S.A.* **117** E11
William Creek *Australia* **95** D2
Williams *Australia* **93** F2
Williams *Ariz., U.S.A.* **109** J7
Williams *Calif., U.S.A.* **110** F4
Williams Harbour *Canada* **105** B8
Williams Lake *Canada* **102** C4
Williamsburg *Ky., U.S.A.* **113** G11
Williamsburg *Pa., U.S.A.* **114** F6
Williamsburg *Va., U.S.A.* **113** G15
Williamson *N.Y., U.S.A.* **114** C7
Williamson *W. Va., U.S.A.* **113** G12
Williamsport *U.S.A.* **114** E8
Williamston *U.S.A.* **117** D16
Williamstown *Australia* **95** F3
Williamstown *Ky., U.S.A.* **113** F11

Williamstown *Mass., U.S.A.* **115** D11
Williamstown *N.Y., U.S.A.* **115** C9
Willimantic *U.S.A.* **115** E12
Willingboro *U.S.A.* **113** E16
Williston *S. Africa* **88** E3
Williston *Fla., U.S.A.* **117** G13
Williston *N. Dak., U.S.A.* **112** A2
Willits *U.S.A.* **108** G2
Willmar *U.S.A.* **112** C6
Willmore Wilderness △ *Canada* **102** C5
Willoughby *U.S.A.* **114** E3
Willow Bunch *Canada* **103** D7
Willow L. *Canada* **102** A5
Willow Wall, The *China* **57** C12
Willowlake → *Canada* **102** A4
Willowmore *S. Africa* **88** E3
Willows *U.S.A.* **110** F4
Willowvale = Gatyana *S. Africa* **89** E4
Wills, L. *Australia* **92** D4
Wills Cr. → *Australia* **94** C3
Willsboro *U.S.A.* **115** B11
Willunga *Australia* **95** F2
Wilmette *U.S.A.* **112** D10
Wilmington *Australia* **95** E2
Wilmington *Del., U.S.A.* **113** F16
Wilmington *N.C., U.S.A.* **117** D16
Wilmington *Ohio, U.S.A.* **113** F12
Wilmington *Vt., U.S.A.* **115** D12
Wilmslow *U.K.* **14** D5
Wilpena Cr. → *Australia* **95** E2
Wilsall *U.S.A.* **108** D8
Wilson *N.C., U.S.A.* **117** D16
Wilson *N.Y., U.S.A.* **114** C6
Wilson *Pa., U.S.A.* **115** F9
Wilson → *Australia* **92** C4
Wilson Bluff *Australia* **93** F4
Wilson Inlet *Australia* **93** G2
Wilsons Promontory *Australia* **95** F4
Wilster *Germany* **24** B5
Wilton *U.S.A.* **112** B3
Wilton → *Australia* **94** A1
Wiltshire □ *U.K.* **15** F6
Wiltz *Lux.* **17** E5
Wiluna *Australia* **93** E3
Wimborne Minster *U.K.* **15** G6
Wimereux *France* **19** B8
Wimmera → *Australia* **95** F3
Winam G. *Kenya* **86** C3
Winburg *S. Africa* **88** D4
Winchendon *U.S.A.* **115** D12
Winchester *U.K.* **15** F6
Winchester *Conn., U.S.A.* **115** E11
Winchester *Idaho, U.S.A.* **108** C5
Winchester *Ind., U.S.A.* **113** E11
Winchester *Ky., U.S.A.* **113** G11
Winchester *N.H., U.S.A.* **115** D12
Winchester *Nev., U.S.A.* **111** J11
Winchester *Tenn., U.S.A.* **117** D11
Winchester *Va., U.S.A.* **113** F14
Wind → *U.S.A.* **108** E9
Wind Cave △ *U.S.A.* **112** D2
Wind River Range *U.S.A.* **108** E9
Windau = Ventspils *Latvia* **30** A8
Windber *U.S.A.* **114** F6
Winder *U.S.A.* **117** D14
Windermere *U.K.* **14** C5
Windhoek *Namibia* **88** C2
Windischgarsten *Austria* **26** D7
Windom *U.S.A.* **112** D6
Windorah *Australia* **94** D3
Window Rock *U.S.A.* **109** J9
Windrush → *U.K.* **15** F6
Windsor *Australia* **95** E5
Windsor *N.S., Canada* **105** D7
Windsor *Ont., Canada* **114** D2
Windsor *U.K.* **15** F7
Windsor *Calif., U.S.A.* **108** G2
Windsor *Colo., U.S.A.* **108** F11
Windsor *Conn., U.S.A.* **115** E12
Windsor *Mo., U.S.A.* **112** F7
Windsor *N.Y., U.S.A.* **115** D9
Windsor *Vt., U.S.A.* **115** C12
Windsor & Maidenhead □ *U.K.* **15** F7
Windsorton *S. Africa* **88** D3
Windward Is. *W. Indies* **121** D7
Windward Passage = Vientos, Paso de los *Caribbean* **121** C5
Winefred L. *Canada* **103** B6
Winejok *Sudan* **81** F2
Winfield *U.S.A.* **112** G5
Wingate Mts. *Australia* **92** B5
Wingham *Australia* **95** E5
Wingham *Canada* **114** C3
Winisk *Canada* **104** A2
Winisk → *Canada* **104** A2
Winisk L. *Canada* **104** B2
Wink *U.S.A.* **116** F3
Winkler *Canada* **103** D9

Winklern *Austria* **26** E5
Winlock *U.S.A.* **110** D4
Winneba *Ghana* **83** D4
Winnebago, L. *U.S.A.* **112** D9
Winnecke Cr. → *Australia* **92** C5
Winnemucca *U.S.A.* **108** F5
Winnemucca L. *U.S.A.* **108** F4
Winner *U.S.A.* **112** D4
Winnett *U.S.A.* **108** C9
Winnfield *U.S.A.* **116** F8
Winnibigoshish, L. *U.S.A.* **112** B6
Winnipeg *Canada* **103** D9
Winnipeg → *Canada* **103** C9
Winnipeg, L. *Canada* **103** C9
Winnipeg Beach *Canada* **103** C9
Winnipegosis *Canada* **103** C8
Winnipegosis L. *Canada* **103** C9
Winnipesaukee, L. *U.S.A.* **115** C13
Winnisquam L. *U.S.A.* **115** C13
Winnsboro *La., U.S.A.* **116** E9
Winnsboro *S.C., U.S.A.* **117** D14
Winnsboro *Tex., U.S.A.* **116** E7
Winokapau, L. *Canada* **105** B7
Winona *Minn., U.S.A.* **112** C8
Winona *Miss., U.S.A.* **117** E10
Winooski *U.S.A.* **115** B11
Winooski → *U.S.A.* **115** B11
Winschoten *Neths.* **17** A7
Winsen *Germany* **24** B6
Winsford *U.K.* **14** D5
Winslow = Bainbridge
   Island *U.S.A.* **110** C4
Winslow *U.S.A.* **109** J8
Winsted *U.S.A.* **115** E11
Winston-Salem *U.S.A.* **117** C14
Winter Garden *U.S.A.* **117** G14
Winter Haven *U.S.A.* **117** G14
Winter Park *U.S.A.* **117** G14
Winterberg *Germany* **24** D4
Winterhaven *U.S.A.* **111** N12
Winters *U.S.A.* **110** G5
Winterset *U.S.A.* **112** E6
Wintersville *U.S.A.* **114** F4
Winterswijk *Neths.* **17** C6
Winterthur *Switz.* **25** H4
Winthrop *U.S.A.* **108** B3
Winton *Australia* **94** C3
Winton *N.Z.* **91** G2
Wipper → *Germany* **24** D7
Wirrulla *Australia* **95** E1
Wisbech *U.K.* **15** E8
Wisconsin □ *U.S.A.* **112** C9
Wisconsin → *U.S.A.* **112** D8
Wisconsin Rapids *U.S.A.* **112** C9
Wisdom *U.S.A.* **108** D7
Wishaw *U.K.* **13** F5
Wishek *U.S.A.* **112** B4
Wisła *Poland* **31** J5
Wisła → *Poland* **30** D5
Wisłok → *Poland* **31** H9
Wisłoka → *Poland* **31** H8
Wismar *Germany* **24** B7
Wisner *U.S.A.* **112** E5
Wissant *France* **19** B8
Wissembourg *France* **19** C14
Wisznice *Poland* **31** G10
Witbank = eMalahleni
   S. Africa **89** D4
Witdraai *S. Africa* **88** D3
Witham *U.K.* **15** F8
Witham → *U.K.* **14** E7
Withernsea *U.K.* **14** D8
Witjira △ *Australia* **95** D2
Witkowo *Poland* **31** F4
Witless Bay *Canada* **105** C9
Witney *U.K.* **15** F6
Witnica *Poland* **31** F1
Witnossob → *Namibia* **88** D3
Wittdün *Germany* **24** A4
Witten *Germany* **24** D3
Wittenberge *Germany* **24** B7
Wittenburg *Germany* **24** B7
Wittenheim *France* **19** E14
Wittenoom *Australia* **92** D2
Wittingen *Germany* **24** C6
Wittlich *Germany* **25** F2
Wittmund *Germany* **24** B3
Wittow *Germany* **24** A9
Wittstock *Germany* **24** B8
Witu *Kenya* **86** C5
Witvlei *Namibia* **88** C2
Witzenhausen *Germany* **24** D5
Wiwon *N. Korea* **57** D14
Wkra → *Poland* **31** F7
Władysławowo *Poland* **30** D5
Wleń *Poland* **31** G2
Wlingi *Indonesia* **63** H15
Włocławek *Poland* **31** F6
Włodawa *Poland* **31** G10
Włoszczowa *Poland* **31** H6
Woburn *U.S.A.* **115** D13
Wodian *China* **56** H7
Wodonga *Australia* **95** F4
Wodzisław Śląski *Poland* **31** H5
Wœrth *France* **19** D14
Woinbogoin *China* **58** A2
Woippy *France* **19** C13

Wojcieszow *Poland* **31** H2
Wokam *Indonesia* **63** F8
Woking *U.K.* **15** F7
Wokingham *U.K.* **15** F7
Wokingham □ *U.K.* **15** F7
Wolbrom *Poland* **31** H6
Wołczyn *Poland* **31** G5
Woldegk *Germany* **24** B9
Wolf → *Canada* **102** A2
Wolf Creek *U.S.A.* **108** C7
Wolf L. *Canada* **102** A2
Wolf Point *U.S.A.* **108** B11
Wolfe I. *Canada* **115** B8
Wolfeboro *U.S.A.* **115** C13
Wolfen *Germany* **24** D8
Wolfenbüttel *Germany* **24** C6
Wolfratshausen *Germany* **25** H7
Wolfsberg *Austria* **26** E7
Wolfsburg *Germany* **24** C6
Wolgast *Germany* **24** A9
Wolhusen *Switz.* **25** H4
Wolin *Poland* **30** E1
Woliński △ *Poland* **30** E1
Wollaston, Is. *Chile* **128** H3
Wollaston L. *Canada* **103** B8
Wollaston Lake *Canada* **103** B8
Wollaston Pen. *Canada* **100** C8
Wollongong *Australia* **95** E5
Wolmaransstad *S. Africa* **88** D4
Wolmirstedt *Germany* **24** C7
Wołomin *Poland* **31** F8
Wołów *Poland* **31** G3
Wolseley *S. Africa* **88** E2
Wolsey *U.S.A.* **112** C4
Wolstenholme, C. *Canada* **98** C12
Wolsztyn *Poland* **31** F3
Wolvega *Neths.* **17** B6
Wolverhampton *U.K.* **15** E5
Wondai *Australia* **95** D5
Wongalarroo L. *Australia* **95** E3
Wongan Hills *Australia* **93** F2
Wonju *S. Korea* **57** F14
Wonosari *Indonesia* **63** G14
Wonosobo *Indonesia* **63** G13
Wonowon *Canada* **102** B4
Wŏnsan *N. Korea* **57** E14
Wonthaggi *Australia* **95** F4
Wood Buffalo △ *Canada* **102** B6
Wood Is. *Australia* **92** C3
Wood L. *Canada* **103** B8
Woodah, I. *Australia* **94** A2
Woodbourne *U.S.A.* **115** E10
Woodbridge *Canada* **114** C5
Woodbridge *U.K.* **15** E9
Woodburn *U.S.A.* **108** D2
Woodenbong *Australia* **95** D5
Woodend *Australia* **95** F3
Woodford *Australia* **95** D5
Woodfords *U.S.A.* **110** G7
Woodlake *U.S.A.* **110** J7
Woodland *Calif., U.S.A.* **110** G5
Woodland *Maine, U.S.A.* **113** C20
Woodland *Pa., U.S.A.* **114** F6
Woodland *Wash., U.S.A.* **110** E4
Woodland Caribou △
   Canada **103** C10
Woodlands *Singapore* **65** d
Woodlands, The *U.S.A.* **116** F7
Woodonga *Australia* **95** F4
Woodridge *Canada* **103** D9
Woodroffe, Mt. *Australia* **93** E5
Woods, L. *Australia* **94** B1
Woods, L. of the *Canada* **103** D10
Woodstock *Australia* **94** B4
Woodstock *N.B., Canada* **105** C6
Woodstock *Ont., Canada* **114** C4
Woodstock *U.K.* **15** F6
Woodstock *Ill., U.S.A.* **112** D9
Woodstock *Vt., U.S.A.* **115** C12
Woodsville *U.S.A.* **115** B13
Woodville *N.Z.* **91** D5
Woodville *Miss., U.S.A.* **116** F9
Woodville *Tex., U.S.A.* **116** F7
Woodward *U.S.A.* **116** C5
Woody *U.S.A.* **111** K8
Woody → *Canada* **103** C8
Woolacombe *U.K.* **15** F3
Woolamai, C. *Australia* **95** F4
Woolgoolga *Australia* **95** E5
Woomera *Australia* **95** E2
Woonsocket *R.I., U.S.A.* **115** E13
Woonsocket *S. Dak., U.S.A.* **112** C4
Wooramel → *Australia* **93** E1
Wooramel Roadhouse
   Australia **93** E1
Wooroonooran △ *Australia* **94** B4
Wooster *U.S.A.* **114** F3
Worcester *S. Africa* **88** E2
Worcester *U.K.* **15** E5
Worcester *Mass., U.S.A.* **115** D13
Worcester *N.Y., U.S.A.* **115** D10
Worcestershire □ *U.K.* **15** E5
Wörgl *Austria* **26** D5
Workington *U.K.* **14** C4
Worksop *U.K.* **14** D6
Workum *Neths.* **17** B5

Worland *U.S.A.* **108** D10
Wormhout *France* **19** B9
Worms *Germany* **25** F4
Worsley *Canada* **102** B5
Wortham *U.S.A.* **116** F6
Worth *Germany* **25** F8
Wörther See *Austria* **26** E7
Worthing *Barbados* **121** g
Worthing *U.K.* **15** G7
Worthington *Minn., U.S.A.* **112** D6
Worthington *Pa., U.S.A.* **114** F5
Wosi *Indonesia* **63** E7
Wote *Kenya* **86** C4
Wou-han = Wuhan *China* **59** B10
Wousi = Wuxi *China* **59** B13
Wowoni *Indonesia* **63** E6
Wrangel I. = Vrangelya,
   Ostrov *Russia* **53** B19
Wrangell *U.S.A.* **102** B2
Wrangell Mts. *U.S.A.* **100** C5
Wrath, C. *U.K.* **13** C3
Wray *U.S.A.* **108** F12
Wrekin, The *U.K.* **15** E5
Wrens *U.S.A.* **117** E13
Wrexham *U.K.* **14** D4
Wrexham □ *U.K.* **14** D5
Wriezen *Germany* **24** C10
Wright = Paranas *Phil.* **61** F6
Wright *Fla., U.S.A.* **117** F11
Wright *Wyo., U.S.A.* **108** E11
Wright Pt. *Canada* **114** C3
Wrightson, Mt. *U.S.A.* **109** L8
Wrightwood *U.S.A.* **111** L9
Wrigley *Canada* **100** C7
Wrocław *Poland* **31** G4
Wronki *Poland* **31** F3
Września *Poland* **31** F4
Wschowa *Poland* **31** G3
Wu Jiang → *China* **58** C6
Wu'an *China* **56** F8
Wubin *Australia* **93** F2
Wubu *China* **56** F6
Wuchang *China* **57** B14
Wucheng *China* **56** F9
Wuchuan *Guangdong, China* **59** G8
Wuchuan *Guizhou, China* **58** C7
Wuchuan
   Nei Monggol Zizhiqu, China **56** D6
Wudi *China* **57** F9
Wuding *China* **58** E4
Wuding He → *China* **56** F6
Wudinna *Australia* **95** E2
Wudu *China* **56** H3
Wufeng *China* **59** B8
Wugang *China* **59** D8
Wugong Shan *China* **59** D9
Wuhan *China* **59** B10
Wuhe *China* **57** H9
Wuhsi = Wuxi *China* **59** B13
Wuhu *China* **59** B12
Wujiang *China* **59** B13
Wukari *Nigeria* **83** D6
Wulajie *China* **57** B14
Wulanbulang *China* **56** D6
Wular L. *India* **69** B6
Wulehe *Ghana* **83** D5
Wulian *China* **57** G10
Wuliang Shan *China* **58** E3
Wuliaru *Indonesia* **63** F8
Wuling Shan *China* **58** C7
Wulong *China* **58** C6
Wulumuchi = Ürümqi *China* **52** E9
Wum *Cameroon* **83** D7
Wuming *China* **58** F7
Wun Rog *Sudan* **81** F2
Wundanyi *Kenya* **86** C4
Wuning *China* **59** C10
Wunnummin L. *Canada* **104** B2
Wunsiedel *Germany* **25** E8
Wunstorf *Germany* **24** C5
Wuntho *Burma* **67** H19
Wupatki △ *U.S.A.* **109** J8
Wuppertal *Germany* **24** D3
Wuppertal *S. Africa* **88** E2
Wuqing *China* **57** E9
Wurtsboro *U.S.A.* **115** E10
Würzburg *Germany* **25** F5
Wurzen *Germany* **24** D8
Wushan *China* **56** G3
Wushishi *Nigeria* **83** D6
Wutach → *Germany* **25** H4
Wutai *China* **56** E7
Wuting = Huimin *China* **57** F9
Wutong *China* **59** E8
Wutongbaolai *China* **57** C11
Wutongqiao *China* **58** C4
Wuwei *Anhui, China* **59** B11
Wuwei *Gansu, China* **60** C5
Wuxi *Jiangsu, China* **59** B13
Wuxi *Sichuan, China* **58** B7
Wuxiang *China* **56** F7
Wuxue *China* **59** C10
Wuyang *China* **56** H7
Wuyi *Hebei, China* **56** F8
Wuyi *Zhejiang, China* **59** C12

Wuyi Shan *China* **59** D11
Wuyishan *China* **59** D12
Wuyo *Nigeria* **83** C7
Wuyuan *Jiangxi, China* **59** C11
Wuyuan
   Nei Monggol Zizhiqu, China **56** D5
Wuzhai *China* **56** E6
Wuzhi Shan *China* **64** C7
Wuzhong *China* **56** E4
Wuzhou *China* **59** F8
Wyaaba Cr. → *Australia* **94** B3
Wyalkatchem *Australia* **93** F2
Wyalusing *U.S.A.* **115** E8
Wyandotte *U.S.A.* **113** D12
Wyandra *Australia* **95** D4
Wyangala, L. *Australia* **95** E4
Wyara, L. *Australia* **95** D3
Wycheproof *Australia* **95** F3
Wycliffe Well *Australia* **94** C1
Wye → *U.K.* **15** F5
Wyemandoo *Australia* **93** E2
Wyk *Germany* **24** A4
Wymondham *U.K.* **15** E9
Wymore *U.S.A.* **112** E5
Wyndham *Australia* **92** C4
Wyndham *N.Z.* **91** G2
Wynyard *Australia* **95** G4
Wynyard *Canada* **103** C8
Wyola L. *Australia* **93** E4
Wyoming = Plympton-
   Wyoming *Canada* **114** D2
Wyoming □ *U.S.A.* **108** E10
Wyomissing *U.S.A.* **115** F9
Wyong *Australia* **95** E5
Wyrzysk *Poland* **31** E4
Wysoka *Poland* **31** E4
Wysokie *Poland* **31** H9
Wysokie Mazowieckie
   Poland **31** F9
Wyszków *Poland* **31** F8
Wyszogród *Poland* **31** F7
Wytheville *U.S.A.* **113** G13
Wyżyna Małopolska *Poland* **31** H7

X

Xaafuun *Somali Rep.* **75** E5
Xaafuun, Ras *Somali Rep.* **75** E5
Xaçmaz *Azerbaijan* **35** K9
Xai-Xai *Mozam.* **89** D5
Xainza *China* **60** C3
Xalapa *Mexico* **119** D5
Xangongo *Angola* **88** B2
Xankändi *Azerbaijan* **73** C12
Xanlar *Azerbaijan* **35** K8
Xanten *Germany* **24** D2
Xanthi *Greece* **45** E8
Xanthi □ *Greece* **45** E8
Xanthos *Turkey* **47** E11
Xanxerê *Brazil* **127** B5
Xapuri *Brazil* **124** F5
Xar Moron He → *China* **57** C11
Xarrë *Albania* **44** G3
Xátiva *Spain* **39** G4
Xau, L. *Botswana* **88** C3
Xavantina *Brazil* **127** A5
Xenia *U.S.A.* **113** F12
Xeropotamos → *Cyprus* **49** E11
Xertigny *France* **19** D13
Xhora *S. Africa* **89** E4
Xhumo *Botswana* **88** C3
Xi Jiang → *China* **59** F9
Xi Xian *Henan, China* **59** A10
Xi Xian *Shanxi, China* **56** F6
Xia Xian *China* **56** G6
Xiachengzi *China* **57** B16
Xiachuan Dao *China* **59** G9
Xiaguan *China* **60** D5
Xiajiang *China* **59** D10
Xiajin *China* **56** F9
Xiamen *China* **59** E12
Xi'an *China* **56** G5
Xian Xian *China* **56** E9
Xianfeng *China* **58** C7
Xiang Jiang → *China* **59** C9
Xiangcheng *Henan, China* **56** H8
Xiangcheng *Henan, China* **56** H7
Xiangcheng *Sichuan, China* **58** C2
Xiangdu *China* **58** F6
Xiangfan *China* **59** A9
Xianggang = Hong
   Kong □ *China* **59** F10
Xianghuang Qi *China* **56** C7
Xiangning *China* **56** G6
Xiangquan *China* **56** F7
Xiangquan He = Sutlej →
   Pakistan **68** E4
Xiangshan *China* **59** C13
Xiangshui *China* **57** G10
Xiangtan *China* **59** D9
Xiangxiang *China* **59** D9
Xiangyin *China* **59** C9
Xiangyun *China* **58** E3
Xiangzhou *China* **58** F7
Xianju *China* **59** C13
Xianning *China* **59** C10

Xianshui He → *China* **58** B3
Xiantao *China* **59** B9
Xianyang *China* **56** G5
Xianyou *China* **59** E12
Xiao Hinggan Ling *China* **60** B7
Xiao Xian *China* **56** G9
Xiaofeng *China* **59** B12
Xiaogan *China* **59** B9
Xiaojin *China* **58** B4
Xiaolan *China* **59** F9
Xiaoshan *China* **59** B13
Xiaoyi *China* **56** F6
Xiapu *China* **59** D12
Xiawa *China* **57** C11
Xiayi *China* **56** G9
Xichang *China* **58** D4
Xichong *China* **58** B5
Xichou *China* **58** E5
Xichuan *China* **56** H6
Xide *China* **58** C4
Xiemahe *China* **59** B8
Xieng Khouang *Laos* **64** C4
Xifei He → *China* **56** H9
Xifeng *Gansu, China* **56** G4
Xifeng *Guizhou, China* **58** D6
Xifeng *Liaoning, China* **57** C13
Xifengzhen = Xifeng *China* **56** G4
Xigazê *China* **60** D3
Xihe *China* **56** G3
Xihua *China* **56** H8
Xilagani *Greece* **45** F9
Xiliao He → *China* **57** C12
Xilin *China* **58** E5
Xilinhot *China* **56** C9
Xilokastro *Greece* **46** C4
Ximana *Mozam.* **87** F3
Xime *Guinea-Biss.* **82** C2
Ximeng *China* **58** F2
Xin Jiang → *China* **59** C11
Xin Xian = Xinzhou *China* **56** E7
Xinavane *Mozam.* **89** D5
Xinbin *China* **57** D13
Xincai *China* **59** A10
Xinchang *China* **59** C13
Xincheng *Guangxi Zhuangzu,
   China* **58** E7
Xincheng *Jiangxi, China* **59** D10
Xincun *China* **59** F8
Xindu *China* **58** B5
Xinfeng *Guangdong, China* **59** E10
Xinfeng *Jiangxi, China* **59** D11
Xinfeng *Jiangxi, China* **59** E10
Xinfengjiang Skuiku *China* **59** F10
Xing Xian *China* **56** E6
Xing'an *Guangxi Zhuangzu,
   China* **59** E8
Xingan *Jiangxi, China* **59** D10
Xingcheng *China* **57** D11
Xingguo *China* **59** D10
Xinghe *China* **56** D7
Xinghua *China* **57** H10
Xinghua Wan *China* **59** E12
Xinglong *China* **57** D9
Xingning *China* **59** E10
Xingping *China* **56** G5
Xingren *China* **58** E5
Xingshan *China* **59** B8
Xingtai *China* **56** F8
Xingu → *Brazil* **125** D8
Xingwen *China* **58** C5
Xingyang *China* **56** G7
Xinhe *China* **56** F8
Xinhua *China* **59** D8
Xinhuang *China* **58** D7
Xinhui *China* **59** F9
Xining *China* **60** C5
Xinjian *China* **59** C10
Xinjiang *China* **56** G6
Xinjiang Uygur Zizhiqu □
   China **60** B3
Xinjie *China* **58** D3
Xinjin = Pulandian *China* **57** E11
Xinjin *China* **58** B4
Xinkai He → *China* **57** C12
Xinle *China* **56** E8
Xinlitun *China* **57** D12
Xinlong *China* **58** B3
Xinmin *China* **57** D12
Xinning *China* **59** D8
Xinping *China* **58** E3
Xinshao *China* **59** D8
Xintai *China* **57** G9
Xintian *China* **59** E9
Xinxian *China* **59** B10
Xinxiang *China* **56** G7
Xinxing *China* **59** F9
Xinyang *China* **59** A10
Xinye *China* **59** A9
Xinyi *China* **59** F8
Xinyu *China* **59** D10
Xinzhan *China* **57** C14
Xinzheng *China* **56** G7
Xinzhou *Hainan, China* **64** C7
Xinzhou *Shanxi, China* **56** E7
Xinzo de Limia *Spain* **36** C3
Xiongyuecheng *China* **57** D12

Xiping *Henan, China* **56** H8
Xiping *Henan, China* **56** H6
Xiping *Zhejiang, China* **59** C12
Xique-Xique *Brazil* **125** F10
Xisha Qundao = Paracel
   Is. *S. China Sea* **62** A4
Xishui *Guizhou, China* **58** C6
Xishui *Hubei, China* **59** B10
Xitole *Guinea-Biss.* **82** C2
Xiu Shui → *China* **59** C10
Xiuning *China* **59** C12
Xiuren *China* **59** E8
Xiushan *China* **58** C7
Xiushui *China* **59** C10
Xiuwen *China* **58** D6
Xiuyan *China* **57** D12
Xixabangma Feng *China* **69** E11
Xixia *China* **56** H6
Xixiang *China* **56** H4
Xixón = Gijón *Spain* **36** B5
Xiyang *China* **56** F7
Xizang Zizhiqu □ *China* **60** C3
Xlendi *Malta* **49** C1
Xochob *Mexico* **119** D7
Xu Jiang → *China* **59** D11
Xuan Loc *Vietnam* **65** G6
Xuan'en *China* **58** C7
Xuanhan *China* **58** B6
Xuanhua *China* **56** D8
Xuanwei *China* **58** C5
Xuanzhou *China* **59** B12
Xuchang *China* **56** G7
Xudat *Azerbaijan* **35** K9
Xuefeng Shan *China* **59** D8
Xuejiaping *China* **59** B8
Xun Jiang → *China* **59** F8
Xun Xian *China* **56** G8
Xundian *China* **58** E4
Xunwu *China* **59** E10
Xunyang *China* **56** H5
Xunyi *China* **56** G5
Xupu *China* **59** D8
Xúquer → *Spain* **39** F4
Xushui *China* **56** E8
Xuwen *China* **59** G8
Xuyen Moc *Vietnam* **65** G6
Xuyong *China* **58** C5
Xuzhou *China* **57** G9
Xylophagou *Cyprus* **49** E12

Y

Ya Xian = Sanya *China* **64** C7
Yaamba *Australia* **94** C5
Ya'an *China* **58** C4
Yaapeet *Australia* **95** F3
Yabassi *Cameroon* **83** E6
Yabelo *Ethiopia* **81** G4
Yabelo △ *Ethiopia* **81** F4
Yablanitsa *Bulgaria* **45** C8
Yablonovyy Khrebet *Russia* **53** D12
Yablonovyy Ra. =
   Yablonovyy Khrebet
   Russia **53** D12
Yabluniv *Ukraine* **29** B9
Yablunytsya *Ukraine* **29** B9
Yabrai Shan *China* **56** E2
Yabrūd *Syria* **74** B5
Yabucoa *Puerto Rico* **121** d
Yacambú △ *Venezuela* **121** E6
Yacheng *China* **64** C7
Yacuiba *Bolivia* **126** A3
Yacuma → *Bolivia* **124** F5
Yadgir *India* **66** L10
Yadkin → *U.S.A.* **117** D14
Yadrin *Russia* **34** C8
Yadua *Fiji* **91** a
Yaeyama-Rettō *Japan* **55** M1
Yagaba *Ghana* **83** C4
Yagasa Cluster *Fiji* **91** a
Yağcılar *Turkey* **47** B10
Yagodnoye *Russia* **53** C15
Yahila *Dem. Rep. of the Congo* **86** B1
Yahk *Canada* **102** D5
Yahotyn *Ukraine* **33** G6
Yahuma
   Dem. Rep. of the Congo **84** D4
Yahyalı *Turkey* **72** C6
Yaita *Japan* **55** F9
Yaiza *Canary Is.* **48** F6
Yajiang *China* **58** B3
Yajua *Nigeria* **83** C7
Yakima *U.S.A.* **108** C3
Yakima → *U.S.A.* **108** C4
Yakishiri-Jima *Japan* **54** B10
Yako *Burkina Faso* **82** C4
Yakobi I. *U.S.A.* **102** B1
Yakoruda *Bulgaria* **45** D7
Yakovlevka *Russia* **54** B6
Yaku-Shima *Japan* **55** J5
Yakumo *Japan* **54** C10
Yakutat *U.S.A.* **100** D6
Yakutia = Sakha □ *Russia* **53** C14
Yakutsk *Russia* **53** C13
Yala *Thailand* **65** J3
Yalboroo *Australia* **94** J6
Yale *U.S.A.* **114** C2

Yalgoo *Australia* **93** E2
Yalgorup △ *Australia* **93** F2
Yalinga *C.A.R.* **84** C4
Yalkabul, Pta. *Mexico* **119** C7
Yalleroi *Australia* **94** C4
Yalobusha ➤ *U.S.A.* **117** E9
Yalong Jiang ➤ *China* **58** D3
Yalova *Turkey* **45** F13
Yalpuh, Ozero *Ukraine* **29** E13
Yalta *Ukraine* **33** K8
Yalvaç *Turkey* **72** C4
Yam Ha Melah = Dead Sea
  Asia **74** D4
Yam Kinneret *Israel* **74** C4
Yamada *Japan* **55** H5
Yamagata *Japan* **54** E10
Yamagata □ *Japan* **54** E10
Yamaguchi *Japan* **55** G5
Yamaguchi □ *Japan* **55** G5
Yamal, Poluostrov *Russia* **52** B8
Yamal Pen. = Yamal,
  Poluostrov *Russia* **52** B8
Yamanashi □ *Japan* **55** G9
Yamanie Falls △ *Australia* **94** B4
Yamato Ridge *Sea of Japan* **54** E7
Yamba *Australia* **95** D5
Yambarran Ra. *Australia* **92** C5
Yámbé ring *Guinea* **82** C2
Yâmbiô *Sudan* **81** G2
Yambol *Bulgaria* **45** D10
Yamdena *Indonesia* **63** F8
Yame *Japan* **55** H5
Yamethin *Burma* **67** J20
Yamma Yamma, L. *Australia* **95** D3
Yamoussoukro *Ivory C.* **82** D3
Yampa ➤ *U.S.A.* **108** F9
Yampi Sd. *Australia* **92** C3
Yampil *Moldova* **23** D15
Yampol = Yampil *Moldova* **23** D15
Yamrat *Nigeria* **83** D6
Yamrukchal = Botev
  Bulgaria **45** D8
Yamuna ➤ *India* **69** G9
Yamunanagar *India* **68** D7
Yamzho Yumco *China* **60** D4
Yan ➤ *Nigeria* **83** C7
Yana ➤ *Russia* **53** B14
Yanagawa *Japan* **55** H5
Yanai *Japan* **55** H6
Yan'an *China* **56** F5
Yanbian *China* **58** D3
Yanbu 'al Baḥr *Si. Arabia* **70** F3
Yanchang *China* **56** F6
Yancheng *Henan, China* **56** H8
Yancheng *Jiangsu, China* **57** H11
Yanchep *Australia* **93** F2
Yanchi *China* **56** F4
Yanchuan *China* **56** F6
Yanco Cr. ➤ *Australia* **95** F4
Yandicoogina *Australia* **92** D2
Yandoon *Burma* **67** L19
Yanfeng *China* **58** E3
Yanfolila *Mali* **82** C3
Yang Xian *China* **56** H4
Yang-yang *S. Korea* **57** E15
Yang-Yang *Senegal* **82** B1
Yangambi
  Dem. Rep. of the Congo **86** B1
Yangbi *China* **58** E2
Yangcheng *China* **56** G7
Yangch'ü = Taiyuan *China* **56** F7
Yangchun *China* **59** F8
Yanggao *China* **56** D7
Yanggu *China* **56** F8
Yangjiang *China* **59** G8
Yangliuqing *China* **57** E9
Yangon = Rangoon *Burma* **67** L20
Yangping *China* **59** B8
Yangpingguan *China* **56** H4
Yangquan *China* **56** F7
Yangshan *China* **59** E9
Yangshuo *China* **59** E8
Yangtse = Chang Jiang ➤
  China **59** B13
Yangtze Kiang = Chang
  Jiang ➤ *China* **59** B13
Yangudi Rassa △ *Ethiopia* **81** E5
Yangxin *China* **59** C10
Yangyuan *China* **56** D8
Yangzhong *China* **59** A12
Yangzhou *China* **59** A12
Yanhe *China* **58** C7
Yanji *China* **57** C15
Yanjin *China* **58** C5
Yanjing *China* **58** C2
Yankari △ *Nigeria* **83** D7
Yankton *U.S.A.* **112** D5
Yanonge
  Dem. Rep. of the Congo **86** B1
Yanqi *China* **60** B3
Yanqing *China* **56** D8
Yanshan *Hebei, China* **57** E9
Yanshan *Jiangxi, China* **59** C11
Yanshan *Yunnan, China* **58** F5
Yanshou *China* **57** B15
Yantabulla *Australia* **95** D4

Yantai *China* **57** F11
Yantarnyy *Russia* **30** D6
Yanting *China* **58** B5
Yantra ➤ *Bulgaria* **45** C9
Yanuca *Fiji* **91** a
Yanwa *China* **58** D2
Yanyuan *China* **58** D3
Yanzhou *China* **56** G9
Yao Noi, Ko *Thailand* **65** a
Yao Xian *China* **56** G5
Yao Yai, Ko *Thailand* **65** a
Yao'an *China* **58** E3
Yaodu *China* **58** A5
Yaoundé *Cameroon* **83** E7
Yaowan *China* **57** G10
Yap *Pac. Oc.* **96** G5
Yapen *Indonesia* **63** E9
Yapen, Selat *Indonesia* **63** E9
Yapero *Indonesia* **63** E9
Yappar ➤ *Australia* **94** B3
Yaqaga *Fiji* **91** a
Yaqui ➤ *Mexico* **118** B2
Yar-Sale *Russia* **52** C8
Yaraka *Australia* **94** C3
Yaransk *Russia* **34** B8
Yarbasan *Turkey* **47** C10
Yardımcı Burnu *Turkey* **47** E12
Yare ➤ *U.K.* **15** E9
Yaremcha *Ukraine* **29** B9
Yarensk *Russia* **52** C5
Yarfa *Si. Arabia* **80** C4
Yarí ➤ *Colombia* **124** D4
Yarker *Canada* **115** B8
Yarkhun ➤ *Pakistan* **69** A5
Yarkand = Shache *China* **60** C2
Yarlung Ziangbo Jiang =
  Brahmaputra ➤ *Asia* **69** H13
Yarmouth *Canada* **105** D6
Yarmūk ➤ *Syria* **74** C4
Yaroslavl *Russia* **32** D10
Yaroslavl □ *Russia* **32** C10
Yarqa, W. ➤ *Egypt* **74** F2
Yarra Yarra Lakes *Australia* **93** E2
Yarram *Australia* **95** F4
Yarraman *Australia* **95** D5
Yarras *Australia* **95** E5
Yartsevo *Sib., Russia* **53** C10
Yartsevo *Smolensk, Russia* **32** E7
Yarumal *Colombia* **124** B3
Yasawa *Fiji* **91** a
Yasawa Group *Fiji* **91** a
Yaselda *Belarus* **23** B14
Yasen *Ukraine* **29** B9
Yashi *Nigeria* **83** C6
Yashikera *Nigeria* **83** D5
Yashkul *Russia* **35** G7
Yasin *Pakistan* **69** A5
Yasinovataya *Ukraine* **33** H9
Yasinski, L. *Canada* **104** B4
Yasinya *Ukraine* **29** B9
Yasothon *Thailand* **64** E5
Yass *Australia* **95** E4
Yāsūj *Iran* **71** D6
Yatağan *Turkey* **47** D10
Yatakala *Niger* **83** C5
Yates Center *U.S.A.* **112** G6
Yathkyed L. *Canada* **103** A9
Yatsushiro *Japan* **55** H5
Yatta Plateau *Kenya* **86** C4
Yauco *Puerto Rico* **121** d
Yavari ➤ *Peru* **124** D4
Yávaros *Mexico* **118** B3
Yavatmal *India* **66** J11
Yavne *Israel* **74** D3
Yavoriv *Ukraine* **31** J10
Yavorov = Yavoriv *Ukraine* **31** J10
Yavuzeli *Turkey* **72** D7
Yawatahama *Japan* **55** H6
Yawri B. *S. Leone* **82** D2
Yaxi *China* **58** D6
Yaxian = Sanya *China* **64** C7
Yazd *Iran* **71** D7
Yazd □ *Iran* **71** D7
Yazd-e Khvāst *Iran* **71** D7
Yazıköy *Turkey* **47** E9
Yazman *Pakistan* **68** E4
Yazoo City *U.S.A.* **117** E9
Ybbs *Austria* **26** C8
Ybycuí △ *Paraguay* **126** B4
Ybytyruzú △ *Paraguay* **127** B4
Ye *Burma* **64** E1
Ye Xian *China* **56** H7
Yebyu *Burma* **64** E2
Yecheon *S. Korea* **57** F15
Yecla *Spain* **39** G3
Yécora *Mexico* **118** B3
Yedebub Biheroch
  Bihereseboch na
  Hizboch □ *Ethiopia* **81** F4
Yedintsy = Edineț *Moldova* **29** B12
Yedseram ➤ *Nigeria* **83** C7
Yefremov *Russia* **32** F10
Yeghegnadzor *Armenia* **73** C11
Yegorlyk ➤ *Russia* **35** G5
Yegorlykskaya *Russia* **35** G5
Yegoryevsk *Russia* **32** E10
Yegros *Paraguay* **126** B4
Yehbuah *Indonesia* **63** J17

Yehuda, Midbar *Israel* **74** D4
Yei *Sudan* **81** G3
Yei, Nahr ➤ *Sudan* **81** F3
Yejmiadzin *Armenia* **35** K7
Yekaterinburg *Russia* **52** D7
Yelabuga *Russia* **34** C11
Yelan *Russia* **34** E6
Yelarbon *Australia* **95** D5
Yelatma *Russia* **34** C5
Yelets *Russia* **33** F10
Yélimané *Mali* **82** B2
Yelizavetgrad =
  Kirovohrad *Ukraine* **33** H7
Yell *U.K.* **13** A7
Yell Sd. *U.K.* **13** A7
Yellow = Huang He ➤
  China **57** F10
Yellow Sea *China* **57** G12
Yellowhead Pass *Canada* **102** C5
Yellowknife *Canada* **102** A6
Yellowknife ➤ *Canada* **102** A6
Yellowstone △ *U.S.A.* **108** C12
Yellowstone ➤ *U.S.A.* **108** D8
Yellowstone L. *U.S.A.* **108** D8
Yelnya *Russia* **32** E7
Yelsk *Belarus* **23** C15
Yelwa *Nigeria* **83** C5
Yemen ■ *Asia* **75** E3
Yen Bai *Vietnam* **58** G5
Yenagoa *Nigeria* **83** E6
Yenakiyeve *Ukraine* **33** H10
Yenakiyevo = Yenakiyeve
  Ukraine **33** H10
Yenangyaung *Burma* **67** J19
Yenda *Australia* **95** E4
Yende Millimou *Guinea* **82** D2
Yendéré *Burkina Faso* **82** C4
Yendi *Ghana* **83** D4
Yéni *Niger* **83** C5
Yenice *Ankara, Turkey* **72** C5
Yenice *Aydın, Turkey* **47** D10
Yenice *Çanakkale, Turkey* **47** B9
Yenice *Edirne, Turkey* **45** F10
Yenice ➤ *Turkey* **72** D6
Yenifoça *Turkey* **47** C8
Yenihisar *Turkey* **47** D9
Yeniköy *Bursa, Turkey* **45** F13
Yeniköy *Çanakkale, Turkey* **47** B8
Yeniköy *Kütahya, Turkey* **47** C11
Yenipazar *Turkey* **47** D10
Yenişehir *Turkey* **45** F13
Yenisey ➤ *Russia* **52** B9
Yeniseysk *Russia* **53** D10
Yeniseyskiy Zaliv *Russia* **52** B9
Yenne *France* **21** C9
Yenotayevka *Russia* **35** G8
Yenyuka *Russia* **53** D13
Yeo ➤ *U.K.* **15** G5
Yeo, L. *Australia* **93** E3
Yeo I. *Canada* **114** A3
Yeoju *S. Korea* **57** F14
Yeola *India* **66** J9
Yeong-wol *S. Korea* **57** F15
Yeongcheon *S. Korea* **57** G15
Yeongdeok *S. Korea* **57** F15
Yeongdeungpo *S. Korea* **57** F14
Yeongdong *S. Korea* **57** F14
Yeongju *S. Korea* **57** F15
Yeosu *S. Korea* **57** G14
Yeovil *U.K.* **15** G5
Yepes *Spain* **36** F7
Yeppoon *Australia* **94** C5
Yerbent *Turkmenistan* **52** F6
Yerbogachen *Russia* **53** C11
Yerevan *Armenia* **35** K7
Yerington *U.S.A.* **108** G4
Yerkesik *Turkey* **47** D10
Yerköy *Turkey* **72** C6
Yermak *Kazakhstan* **52** D8
Yermo *U.S.A.* **111** L10
Yerólakkos *Cyprus* **49** D12
Yeropol *Russia* **53** C17
Yeroskipos *Cyprus* **49** E11
Yershov *Russia* **34** E9
Yerushalayim = Jerusalem
  Israel/West Bank **74** D4
Yerville *France* **18** C7
Yes Tor *U.K.* **15** G4
Yesan *S. Korea* **57** F14
Yeşilhisar *Turkey* **72** C6
Yeşilırmak ➤ *Turkey* **72** B7
Yeşilkent *Turkey* **72** D7
Yeşilköy *Turkey* **45** F12
Yeşilova *Turkey* **47** D11
Yeşilyurt *Manisa, Turkey* **47** C10
Yeşilyurt *Muğla, Turkey* **47** D10
Yesnogorsk *Russia* **32** E9
Yeso *U.S.A.* **109** J11
Yessentuki *Russia* **35** H6
Yessey *Russia* **53** C11
Yeste *Spain* **39** G2
Yetman *Australia* **95** D5
Yeu, Î. d' *France* **18** F4
Yevlakh = Yevlax *Azerbaijan* **35** K8
Yevlax *Azerbaijan* **35** K8
Yevpatoriya *Ukraine* **33** K7

Yeya ➤ *Russia* **33** J10
Yeysk *Russia* **33** J10
Yezd = Yazd *Iran* **71** D7
Yezerishche *Belarus* **32** E5
Yhati *Paraguay* **126** B4
Yhú *Paraguay* **127** B4
Yi ➤ *Uruguay* **126** C4
Yi 'Allaq, G. *Egypt* **74** E2
Yi He ➤ *China* **57** G10
Yi Xian *Anhui, China* **59** C11
Yi Xian *Hebei, China* **56** E8
Yi Xian *Liaoning, China* **57** D11
Yialiás ➤ *Cyprus* **49** D12
Yialousa *Cyprus* **49** D13
Yibin *China* **58** C5
Yichang *China* **59** B8
Yicheng *Henan, China* **59** B9
Yicheng *Shanxi, China* **56** G6
Yichuan *China* **56** F6
Yichun *Heilongjiang, China* **60** B7
Yichun *Jiangxi, China* **59** D10
Yidu *China* **57** F10
Yidun *China* **58** B2
Yifag *Ethiopia* **81** E4
Yifeng *China* **59** C10
Yihuang *China* **59** D11
Yijun *China* **56** G5
Yilan *China* **60** B7
Yıldız Dağları *Turkey* **45** E11
Yıldızeli *Turkey* **72** C7
Yiliang *Yunnan, China* **58** D5
Yiliang *Yunnan, China* **58** E4
Yilong *China* **58** B6
Yimen *China* **58** E4
Yimianpo *China* **57** B15
Yinchuan *China* **56** E4
Yindarlgooda, L. *Australia* **93** F3
Ying He ➤ *China* **56** H9
Ying Xian *China* **56** E7
Yingcheng *China* **59** B9
Yingde *China* **59** E9
Yingjiang *China* **58** E1
Yingjing *China* **58** C4
Yingkou *China* **57** D12
Yingshan *Henan, China* **59** B9
Yingshan *Hubei, China* **59** B10
Yingshan *Sichuan, China* **58** B6
Yingshang *China* **59** A11
Yingtan *China* **59** C11
Yining *China* **52** E9
Yinjiang *China* **58** C7
Yinmabin *Burma* **67** H19
Yioúra = Giaros *Greece* **46** D6
Yipinglang *China* **58** E3
Yirba Muda *Ethiopia* **81** F4
Yirga Alem *Ethiopia* **81** F4
Yirol *Sudan* **81** F3
Yirrkala *Australia* **94** A2
Yishan *China* **58** E7
Yishui *China* **57** G10
Yishun *Singapore* **65** d
Yitong *China* **57** C13
Yiwu *China* **59** C13
Yixing *China* **59** B12
Yiyang *Henan, China* **56** G7
Yiyang *Hunan, China* **59** C9
Yiyang *Jiangxi, China* **59** C11
Yizhang *China* **59** E9
Yizheng *China* **59** A12
Yli-Kitka *Finland* **8** C23
Yliki, L. *Greece* **46** C5
Ylitornio *Finland* **8** C20
Ylivieska *Finland* **8** D21
Yngaren *Sweden* **11** F10
Yoakum *U.S.A.* **116** G6
Yob △ *Eritrea* **81** D4
Yobe □ *Nigeria* **83** C7
Yog Pt. *Phil.* **63** B6
Yogan *Togo* **83** D5
Yoğuntaş *Turkey* **45** E11
Yogyakarta *Indonesia* **63** G14
Yogyakarta □ *Indonesia* **63** G14
Yoho △ *Canada* **102** C5
Yojoa, L. de *Honduras* **120** D2
Yok Don △ *Vietnam* **64** F6
Yokadouma *Cameroon* **84** D2
Yokkaichi *Japan* **55** G8
Yoko *Cameroon* **83** D7
Yokohama *Japan* **55** G9
Yokosuka *Japan* **55** G9
Yokote *Japan* **54** E10
Yola *Nigeria* **83** D7
Yolaina, Cordillera de *Nic.* **120** D3
Yólöten *Turkmenistan* **71** B9
Yom ➤ *Thailand* **64** E3
Yonago *Japan* **55** G6
Yonaguni-Jima *Japan* **55** M1
Yonan *N. Korea* **57** F14
Yonezawa *Japan* **54** F10
Yong Peng *Malaysia* **65** M4
Yong Sata *Thailand* **65** J2
Yongamp'o *N. Korea* **57** E13
Yong'an *China* **59** E11
Yongcheng *China* **56** H9
Yongchuan *China* **58** C5
Yongchun *China* **59** E12
Yongde *China* **58** E2
Yongdeng *China* **56** F2
Yongding *China* **59** E11

Yongfeng *China* **59** D10
Yongfu *China* **58** E7
Yonghe *China* **56** F6
Yǒnghǔng *N. Korea* **57** E14
Yongji *China* **56** G6
Yongjia *China* **59** C13
Yongkang *Yunnan, China* **58** E2
Yongkang *Zhejiang, China* **59** C13
Yongnian *China* **56** F8
Yongning *Guangxi Zhuangzu,*
  China **58** F7
Yongning *Ningxia Huizu,*
  China **56** E4
Yongping *China* **58** E2
Yongqing *China* **56** E9
Yongren *China* **58** D3
Yongshan *China* **58** C4
Yongsheng *China* **58** D3
Yongshun *China* **58** C7
Yongtai *China* **59** E12
Yongxin = Jinggangshan
  China **59** D10
Yongxing *China* **59** D9
Yongxiu *China* **59** C10
Yongzhou *China* **59** D8
Yonibana *S. Leone* **82** D2
Yonkers *U.S.A.* **115** F11
Yonne □ *France* **19** E10
Yonne ➤ *France* **19** D9
York *Australia* **93** F2
York *U.K.* **14** D6
York *Ala., U.S.A.* **117** E10
York *Nebr., U.S.A.* **112** E5
York *Pa., U.S.A.* **113** F15
York, C. *Australia* **94** A3
York, City of □ *U.K.* **14** D6
York, Kap *Greenland* **4** B4
York, Vale of *U.K.* **14** C6
York Sd. *Australia* **92** C4
Yorke Pen. *Australia* **95** E2
Yorkshire Dales △ *U.K.* **14** C5
Yorkshire Wolds *U.K.* **14** C7
Yorkton *Canada* **103** C8
Yorkville *U.S.A.* **110** G3
Yoro *Honduras* **120** C2
Yoron-Jima *Japan* **55** L4
Yorosso *Mali* **82** C4
Yos Sudarso, Pulau =
  Dolak, Pulau *Indonesia* **63** F9
Yosemite △ *U.S.A.* **110** H7
Yosemite Village *U.S.A.* **110** H7
Yoshino-Kumano △ *Japan* **55** H8
Yoshkar Ola *Russia* **34** B8
Yotvata *Israel* **74** F4
You Jiang ➤ *China* **58** F6
You Xian *China* **59** D9
Youbou *Canada* **110** B2
Youghal *Ireland* **12** E4
Youghal B. *Ireland* **12** E4
Youkounkoun *Guinea* **82** C2
Young *Australia* **95** E4
Young *Canada* **103** C7
Young *Uruguay* **126** C4
Younghusband, L. *Australia* **95** E2
Younghusband Pen.
  Australia **95** F2
Youngstown *Canada* **103** C6
Youngstown *N.Y., U.S.A.* **114** C5
Youngstown *Ohio, U.S.A.* **114** E4
Youngsville *U.S.A.* **114** E5
Youngwood *U.S.A.* **114** F5
Youxi *China* **59** D12
Youyang *China* **58** C7
Youyu *China* **56** D7
Yozgat *Turkey* **72** C6
Yozgat □ *Turkey* **72** C6
Ypacaraí △ *Paraguay* **126** B4
Ypané ➤ *Paraguay* **126** A4
Yport *France* **18** C7
Ypres = Ieper *Belgium* **17** D2
Yreka *U.S.A.* **108** F2
Yssingeaux *France* **21** C8
Ystad *Sweden* **11** J7
Ysyk-Köl *Kyrgyzstan* **52** E8
Ythan ➤ *U.K.* **13** D7
Ytterhogdal *Sweden* **10** B8
Ytyk-Kuyuel *Russia* **53** C14
Yu Jiang ➤ *China* **58** F7
Yü Shan *Taiwan* **59** F13
Yu Xian = Yuzhou *China* **56** G7
Yu Xian *Hebei, China* **56** E8
Yu Xian *Shanxi, China* **56** E7
Yuan Jiang ➤ *Hunan, China* **59** C8
Yuan Jiang ➤ *Yunnan, China* **58** F3
Yuan'an *China* **59** B8
Yuanjiang *Hunan, China* **59** C9
Yuanjiang *Yunnan, China* **58** F4
Yuanli *Taiwan* **59** E13
Yuanlin *Taiwan* **59** F13
Yuanling *China* **59** C8
Yuanmou *China* **58** E3
Yuanqu *China* **56** G6
Yuanyang *Henan, China* **56** G7
Yuanyang *Yunnan, China* **58** F4
Yuba ➤ *U.S.A.* **110** F5
Yuba City *U.S.A.* **110** F5
Yūbari *Japan* **54** C10
Yubdo *Ethiopia* **81** F4

Yūbetsu *Japan* **54** B11
Yubo *Sudan* **81** F2
Yucatán □ *Mexico* **119** C7
Yucatán, Canal de
  Caribbean **120** B2
Yucatán, Península de
  Mexico **98** H11
Yucatan Basin *Cent. Amer.* **119** D7
Yucatan Channel =
  Yucatán, Canal de
  Caribbean **120** B2
Yucca *U.S.A.* **111** L12
Yucca Valley *U.S.A.* **111** L10
Yucheng *China* **56** F9
Yuci *China* **56** F7
Yudu *China* **59** E10
Yuechi *China* **58** B6
Yuendumu *Australia* **92** D5
Yueqing *China* **59** C13
Yueqing Wan *China* **59** D13
Yuexi *Anhui, China* **59** B11
Yuexi *Sichuan, China* **58** C4
Yueyang *China* **59** C9
Yugan *China* **59** C11
Yugoslavia = Serbia ■
  Europe **44** C4
Yuhuan *China* **59** C13
Yühuan Dao *China* **59** C13
Yujiang *China* **59** C11
Yukhnov *Russia* **32** E8
Yukon *U.S.A.* **116** D6
Yukon ➤ *U.S.A.* **106** a
Yukon Territory □ *Canada* **100** C6
Yüksekova *Turkey* **73** D11
Yukta *Russia* **53** C11
Yukuhashi *Japan* **55** H5
Yulara *Australia* **93** E5
Yule ➤ *Australia* **92** D2
Yuleba *Australia* **95** D4
Yuli *Nigeria* **83** D7
Yüli *Taiwan* **59** F13
Yulin *Guangxi Zhuangzu, China* **59** F8
Yulin *Hainan, China* **64** C7
Yulin *Shaanxi, China* **56** E5
Yuma *Ariz., U.S.A.* **111** N12
Yuma *Colo., U.S.A.* **108** F12
Yuma, B. de *Dom. Rep.* **121** C6
Yumbe *Uganda* **86** B3
Yumbi *Dem. Rep. of the Congo* **86** C2
Yumen *China* **60** C4
Yumurtalık *Turkey* **72** D6
Yun Gui Gaoyuan *China* **58** E3
Yun Ling *China* **58** D2
Yun Xian *Hubei, China* **59** A8
Yun Xian *Yunnan, China* **58** E3
Yuna *Australia* **93** E2
Yunak *Turkey* **72** C4
Yunan *China* **59** F9
Yuncheng *Henan, China* **56** G8
Yuncheng *Shanxi, China* **56** G6
Yunfu *China* **59** F9
Yungas *Bolivia* **124** G5
Yungay *Chile* **126** D1
Yunhe *China* **59** C12
Yunkai Dashan *China* **59** F8
Yunlong *China* **58** E2
Yunmeng *China* **59** B9
Yunnan □ *China* **58** E4
Yunquera de Henares *Spain* **38** E1
Yunt Dağı *Turkey* **47** C9
Yunta *Australia* **95** E3
Yunxi *China* **59** A8
Yunxiao *China* **59** F11
Yupanqui Basin *Pac. Oc.* **97** J17
Yuping *China* **58** D7
Yuqing *China* **58** D6
Yuraygir △ *Australia* **95** D5
Yurga *Russia* **52** D9
Yurimaguas *Peru* **124** E3
Yurkiyka *Ukraine* **29** B13
Yurubí △ *Venezuela* **121** D6
Yuryev-Polskiy *Russia* **32** D10
Yuryevets *Russia* **34** B6
Yuscarán *Honduras* **120** D2
Yûsef, Bahr ➤ *Egypt* **80** B3
Yushan *China* **59** C12
Yushanzhen *China* **58** C7
Yushe *China* **56** F7
Yushu *Jilin, China* **57** B14
Yushu *Qinghai, China* **60** C4
Yusufeli *Turkey* **73** B9
Yutai *China* **56** G9
Yutian *China* **57** C9
Yuxarı Qarabāğ =
  Nagorno-Karabakh □
  Azerbaijan **73** C12
Yuxi *China* **58** E4
Yuyao *China* **59** B13
Yuzawa *Japan* **54** E10
Yuzha *Russia* **34** B6
Yuzhno-Sakhalinsk *Russia* **53** E15
Yuzhnyy □ *Russia* **35** H5
Yuzhou *China* **56** G7
Yvelines □ *France* **19** D8
Yverdon-les-Bains *Switz.* **25** J2
Yvetot *France* **18** C7
Yzeure *France* **19** F10

Z

Zaanstad *Neths.* 17 B4
Zāb al Kabīr → *Iraq* 73 D10
Zāb aş Şaghīr → *Iraq* 73 E10
Žabalj *Serbia* 28 E5
Žabari *Serbia* 44 B5
Zabarjad *Egypt* 80 C4
Žabljak *Montenegro* 44 C3
Zabki *Poland* 31 F8
Ząbkowice Śląskie *Poland* 31 H3
Žabljak *Montenegro* 44 C3
Żabno *Poland* 31 H7
Zābol *Iran* 71 D9
Zābol □ *Afghan.* 66 D5
Zābolī *Iran* 71 E9
Zabolotiv *Ukraine* 29 B10
Zabolottya *Ukraine* 31 G11
Zabré *Burkina Faso* 83 C4
Zábřeh *Czech Rep.* 27 B9
Zabrze *Poland* 31 H5
Zabuzhzhya *Ukraine* 31 G10
Zabzuga *Ghana* 83 D5
Zacapa *Guatemala* 120 D2
Zacapu *Mexico* 118 D4
Zacatecas *Mexico* 118 C4
Zacatecas □ *Mexico* 118 C4
Zacatecoluca *El Salv.* 120 D2
Zacharo *Greece* 46 D3
Zachary *U.S.A.* 116 F9
Zachodnio-Pomorskie □
      Poland 30 E2
Zacoalco de Torres *Mexico* 118 C4
Zacualtipán *Mexico* 119 C5
Zadar *Croatia* 41 D12
Zadawa *Nigeria* 83 C7
Zadetkyi Kyun *Burma* 65 G2
Zadonsk *Russia* 33 F10
Zafarqand *Iran* 71 C7
Zafra *Spain* 37 G4
Żagań *Poland* 31 G2
Zagaoua *Chad* 79 E10
Žagarė *Lithuania* 30 B10
Zagazig *Egypt* 80 H7
Zāgheh *Iran* 71 C6
Zagnanado *Benin* 83 D5
Zagora *Greece* 46 B5
Zagorje *Slovenia* 41 B11
Zagórów *Poland* 31 F4
Zagórz *Poland* 31 J9
Zagreb *Croatia* 41 C12
Zagreb ✈ (ZAG) *Croatia* 41 C13
Zāgros, Kūhhā-ye *Iran* 71 C6
Zagros Mts. = Zāgros,
      Kūhhā-ye *Iran* 71 C6
Žagubica *Serbia* 44 B5
Zaguinaso *Ivory C.* 82 C3
Zagyva → *Hungary* 28 C5
Zahamena △ *Madag.* 89 B8
Zāhedān *Fārs, Iran* 71 D7
Zāhedān
      Sīstān va Balūchestān, Iran 71 D9
Zahlah *Lebanon* 74 B4
Zahna *Germany* 24 D8
Zainsk *Russia* 34 C11
Zaïre = Congo → *Africa* 84 F2
Zaječar *Serbia* 44 C6
Zaka *Zimbabwe* 89 C5
Zakamensk *Russia* 53 D11
Zakarpattya □ *Ukraine* 29 B8
Zakataly = Zaqatala
      Azerbaijan 35 K8
Zakhodnaya Dzvina =
      Daugava → *Latvia* 32 D3
Zākhū *Iraq* 73 D10
Zakinthos = Zakynthos
      Greece 46 D2
Zakopane *Poland* 31 J6
Zakroczym *Poland* 31 F7
Zakros *Greece* 49 D8
Zakynthos *Greece* 46 D2
Zakynthos □ *Greece* 46 D2
Zala *Ethiopia* 81 F4
Zala □ *Hungary* 28 D1
Zala → *Hungary* 28 D2
Zalaegerszeg *Hungary* 28 D1
Zalakomár *Hungary* 28 D1
Zalalövö *Hungary* 28 D1
Zalamea de la Serena *Spain* 37 G5
Zalamea la Real *Spain* 37 H4
Zalău *Romania* 28 C8
Žalec *Slovenia* 41 B12
Zaleshchiki = Zalishchyky
      Ukraine 29 B9
Zalesye *Russia* 30 D8
Zalew Wiślany *Poland* 30 D6
Zalewo *Poland* 30 E6
Zalingei *Sudan* 79 F10
Zalishchyky *Ukraine* 29 B10
Zama L. *Canada* 102 B3
Zambeke
      Dem. Rep. of the Congo 86 B2
Zambeze → *Africa* 87 F4
Zambezi = Zambeze →
      Africa 87 F4

Zambezi *Zambia* 85 G4
Zambezi △ *Zimbabwe* 87 F2
Zambezia □ *Mozam.* 87 F4
Zambia ■ *Africa* 87 F2
Zamboanga *Phil.* 61 H5
Zambrów *Poland* 31 F9
Zametchino *Russia* 34 D6
Zamfara □ *Nigeria* 83 C6
Zamfara → *Nigeria* 83 C5
Zamora *Mexico* 118 D4
Zamora *Spain* 36 D5
Zamora □ *Spain* 36 D5
Zamość *Poland* 31 H10
Zamtang *China* 58 A3
Zan *Ghana* 83 D4
Záncara → *Spain* 39 F1
Zandvoort *Neths.* 17 B4
Zangābād *Iran* 70 B5
Zangliveri *Greece* 44 F7
Zangue → *Mozam.* 87 F4
Zanjān *Iran* 73 D13
Zanjān □ *Iran* 71 B6
Zanjān → *Iran* 71 B6
Zannone *Italy* 42 B6
Zante = Zakynthos *Greece* 46 D2
Zanthus *Australia* 93 F3
Zanzibar *Tanzania* 86 D4
Zaouiet El-Kala = Bordj
      Omar Driss *Algeria* 78 C7
Zaouiet Reggâne *Algeria* 78 C6
Zaoyang *China* 59 A9
Zaozhuang *China* 57 G9
Zap Suyu = Zāb al
      Kabīr → *Iraq* 73 D10
Zapadna Morava → *Serbia* 44 C5
Zapadnaya Dvina =
      Daugava → *Latvia* 32 D3
Zapadnaya Dvina *Russia* 32 D7
Západné Beskydy *Europe* 27 B12
Zapadni Rodopi *Bulgaria* 44 E7
Západočeský □ *Czech Rep.* 26 B6
Zapala *Argentina* 128 D2
Zapaleri, Cerro *Bolivia* 126 A2
Zapata *U.S.A.* 116 H5
Zapatón → *Spain* 37 F4
Zapolyarnyy *Russia* 8 B24
Zapopán *Mexico* 118 D4
Zaporizhzhya *Ukraine* 33 J8
Zaporizhzhya □ *Ukraine* 33 J8
Zaporozhye =
      Zaporizhzhya *Ukraine* 33 J8
Zaqatala *Azerbaijan* 35 K8
Zara *Turkey* 72 C7
Zaragoza *Coahuila, Mexico* 118 B4
Zaragoza *Nuevo León, Mexico* 119 C5
Zaragoza *Spain* 38 D4
Zaragoza □ *Spain* 38 D4
Zarand *Kermān, Iran* 71 D8
Zarand *Markazī, Iran* 71 C6
Zărandului, Munţii *Romania* 28 D7
Zaranj *Afghan.* 66 D2
Zarasai *Lithuania* 32 E4
Zárate *Argentina* 126 C4
Zarautz *Spain* 38 B2
Zaraysk *Russia* 32 E10
Zard, Kūh-e *Iran* 71 C6
Zāreh *Iran* 71 C6
Zari *Nigeria* 83 C7
Zaria *Nigeria* 83 C6
Żarki *Poland* 31 H6
Zarko *Greece* 46 B4
Zarneh *Iran* 70 C5
Zărneşti *Romania* 29 E10
Zaros *Greece* 49 D6
Żarów *Poland* 31 H3
Zarqā', Nahr az → *Jordan* 74 C4
Zarrīn *Iran* 71 C7
Zaruma *Ecuador* 124 D3
Żary *Poland* 31 G2
Zarza de Granadilla *Spain* 36 E4
Zarzis *Tunisia* 79 B8
Zas *Spain* 36 B2
Zaskar → *India* 69 B7
Zaskar Mts. *India* 69 C7
Zastavna *Ukraine* 29 B10
Zastron *S. Africa* 88 E4
Zavala *Bos.-H.* 44 D1
Zaväreh *Iran* 71 C7
Zave *Zimbabwe* 89 B5
Zavetnoye *Russia* 35 G6
Zavidovići *Bos.-H.* 28 F3
Zavitinsk *Russia* 53 D13
Zavodovski, I. *Antarctica* 5 B1
Zavolzhsk *Russia* 34 B6
Zavolzhye *Russia* 34 B6
Zawadzkie *Poland* 31 H5
Zawichost *Poland* 31 H8
Zawidów *Poland* 31 G2
Zawiercie *Poland* 31 H6
Zāwiyat al Baydā = Al
      Baydā *Libya* 79 B10
Zâwyet Shammas *Egypt* 80 A2

Zâwyet Um el Rakham
      Egypt 80 A2
Zâwyet Ungeîla *Egypt* 80 A2
Zāyā *Iraq* 70 C5
Zāyandeh → *Iran* 71 C7
Zaysan *Kazakhstan* 52 E9
Zaysan Köli *Kazakhstan* 52 E9
Zayü *China* 58 C1
Zazafotsy *Madag.* 89 C8
Zázrivá *Slovak Rep.* 27 B12
Zbarazh *Ukraine* 23 D13
Zbąszyń *Poland* 31 F2
Zbąszynek *Poland* 31 F2
Zblewo *Poland* 30 E5
Zbruch → 29 B11
Ždár nad Sázavou *Czech Rep.* 26 B8
Zdolbuniv *Ukraine* 23 C14
Ždrelo *Serbia* 44 B5
Zduńska Wola *Poland* 31 G5
Zduny *Poland* 31 G4
Zeballos *Canada* 102 D3
Zebediela *S. Africa* 89 C4
Zebila *Ghana* 83 C4
Zeebrugge *Belgium* 17 C3
Zeehan *Australia* 95 G4
Zeeland *Neths.* 17 C3
Zeeland □ *Neths.* 17 C3
Zeerust *S. Africa* 88 D4
Zefat *Israel* 74 C4
Zege *Ethiopia* 81 E4
Zeggerene, Iracher *Mali* 83 B5
Zégoua *Mali* 82 C3
Zehdenick *Germany* 24 C9
Zeil, Mt. *Australia* 92 D5
Zeila *Somali Rep.* 75 E3
Zeist *Neths.* 17 B5
Zeitz *Germany* 24 D8
Żelechów *Poland* 31 G8
Zelena *Ukraine* 29 B9
Zelengora *Bos.-H.* 44 C2
Zelenodolsk *Ukraine* 33 J7
Zelenodolsk *Russia* 34 C9
Zelenogorsk *Russia* 32 B5
Zelenograd *Russia* 32 D9
Zelenogradsk *Russia* 30 D7
Zelenokumsk *Russia* 35 H6
Železná Ruda *Czech Rep.* 26 B6
Železnik *Serbia* 44 B4
Zelienople *U.S.A.* 114 F4
Železovce *Slovak Rep.* 27 C11
Zelina *Croatia* 41 C13
Zell *Baden-W., Germany* 25 H3
Zell *Rhld-Pfz., Germany* 25 F3
Zell am See *Austria* 26 D5
Zella-Mehlis *Germany* 24 E6
Zelów *Poland* 31 G6
Zeltweg *Austria* 26 D7
Žemaitijos △ *Lithuania* 30 B8
Zémio *C.A.R.* 86 A2
Zempléni-hegység *Hungary* 28 B6
Zemplínska šírava
      Slovak Rep. 27 C15
Zempoala *Mexico* 119 D5
Zemun *Serbia* 44 B4
Zengbé *Cameroon* 83 D7
Zengcheng *China* 59 F9
Zenica *Bos.-H.* 28 F2
Žepče *Bos.-H.* 28 F3
Zeraf, Bahr ez → *Sudan* 81 F3
Zerbst *Germany* 24 D8
Żerków *Poland* 31 F4
Zermatt *Switz.* 25 J3
Zernez *Switz.* 25 J6
Zernograd *Russia* 35 G5
Zerqan *Albania* 44 E4
Zestaponi *Georgia* 35 J6
Zetel *Germany* 24 B3
Zeulenroda *Germany* 24 E7
Zeven *Germany* 24 B5
Zevenaar *Neths.* 17 C6
Zévio *Italy* 40 C8
Zeya *Russia* 53 D13
Zeya → *Russia* 53 D13
Zeytinbaği *Turkey* 45 F12
Zeytindağ *Turkey* 47 C9
Zghartâ *Lebanon* 74 A4
Zgierz *Poland* 31 G6
Zgorzelec *Poland* 31 G2
Zguriţa *Moldova* 29 B13
Zhabinka *Belarus* 31 F11
Zhabokrych *Ukraine* 29 B13
Zhailma *Kazakhstan* 52 D7
Zhambyl = Taraz *Kazakhstan* 52 E8
Zhangaly *Kazakhstan* 35 G10
Zhangaqala *Kazakhstan* 35 F9
Zhangaqazaly *Kazakhstan* 52 E7
Zhangbei *China* 56 D8
Zhangguangcai Ling *China* 57 B15
Zhangjiabian *China* 59
Zhangjiagang *China* 63 B13
Zhangjiakou *China* 56 D8
Zhangping *China* 59 E11
Zhangpu *China* 59 E11
Zhangshu *China* 59 C10
Zhangwu *China* 57 C12
Zhangye *China* 60 C5
Zhangzhou *China* 59 E11
Zhanhua *China* 57 F10

Zhanjiang *China* 59 G8
Zhannetty, Ostrov *Russia* 53 B16
Zhanyi *China* 58 D5
Zhanyu *China* 57 B12
Zhao Xian *China* 56 F8
Zhao'an *China* 59 F11
Zhaocheng *China* 56 F6
Zhaojue *China* 58 C4
Zhaoping *China* 59 E8
Zhaoqing *China* 59 F9
Zhaotong *China* 58 D4
Zhaoyuan *Heilongjiang,*
      China 57 B13
Zhaoyuan *Shandong, China* 57 F11
Zharkent *Kazakhstan* 52 E9
Zharkovskiy *Russia* 32 E7
Zhashkiv *Ukraine* 23 D16
Zhashui *China* 56 H5
Zhayyq → *Kazakhstan* 6 F16
Zhdanov = Mariupol *Ukraine* 33 J9
Zhecheng *China* 56 G8
Zhegao *China* 59 B11
Zhejiang □ *China* 59 C13
Zheleznodorozhnyy *Russia* 30 D8
Zheleznogorsk *Russia* 33 F8
Zheleznogorsk-Ilimskiy
      Russia 53 D11
Zheltyye Vody = Zhovti
      Vody *Ukraine* 33 H7
Zhen'an *China* 56 H5
Zhenba *China* 58 A6
Zhenfeng *China* 58 E5
Zheng'an *China* 58 C6
Zhengding *China* 56 E8
Zhenghe *China* 59 D12
Zhengyang *China* 59 A10
Zhengyangguan *China* 59 A11
Zhengzhou *China* 56 G7
Zhenhai *China* 59 C13
Zhenjiang *China* 59 A12
Zhenkang *China* 58 F2
Zhenlai *China* 57 B12
Zhenning *China* 58 D5
Zhenping *Henan, China* 56 H7
Zhenping *Shaanxi, China* 58 B7
Zhenxiong *China* 58 D5
Zhenyuan *Gansu, China* 56 G4
Zhenyuan *Guizhou, China* 58 D7
Zherdevka *Russia* 34 E5
Zherebkove *Ukraine* 29 C14
Zherong *China* 59 D12
Zhetiqara *Kazakhstan* 52 D7
Zhezqazghan *Kazakhstan* 52 E7
Zhicheng *China* 59 B8
Zhidan *China* 56 F5
Zhigansk *Russia* 53 C13
Zhigulevsk *Russia* 34 D9
Zhijiang *Hubei, China* 59 B8
Zhijiang *Hunan, China* 58 D7
Zhijin *China* 58 D5
Zhilinda *Russia* 53 C12
Zhilino *Russia* 30 D8
Zhirnovsk *Russia* 34 E7
Zhitomir = Zhytomyr
      Ukraine 23 C15
Zhizdra *Russia* 32 F8
Zhlobin *Belarus* 23 B16
Zhmerinka = Zhmerynka
      Ukraine 23 D15
Zhmerynka *Ukraine* 23 D15
Zhob *Pakistan* 68 D3
Zhob → *Pakistan* 68 C3
Zhodino = Zhodzina
      Belarus 23 A15
Zhodzina *Belarus* 23 A15
Zhokhova, Ostrov *Russia* 53 B16
Zhongdian *China* 58 D2
Zhongdong *China* 58 F6
Zhongdu *China* 58 E7
Zhongning *China* 56 F3
Zhongshan *Antarctica* 5 C6
Zhongshan *Guangdong, China* 59 F9
Zhongshan
      Guangxi Zhuangzu, China 59 E8
Zhongtiao Shan *China* 56 G6
Zhongwei *China* 56 F3
Zhongxiang *China* 59 B9
Zhongyang *China* 56 F6
Zhorany *Ukraine* 31 G10
Zhoucun *China* 57 F9
Zhouning *China* 59 D12
Zhoushan *China* 59 B13
Zhoushan Dao *China* 59 C14
Zhouzhi *China* 56 G5
Zhovti Vody *Ukraine* 33 H7
Zhovtneve *Lubelskie, Ukraine* 31 H11
Zhovtneve *Mykolayiv, Ukraine* 33 J7
Zhovtnevoye = Zhovtneve
      Ukraine 33 J7
Zhu Jiang → *China* 59 F9
Zhuanghe *China* 57 E12
Zhucheng *China* 57 G10
Zhugqu *China* 56 H3
Zhuhai *China* 59 F9
Zhuji *China* 59 C13
Zhukovka *Russia* 32 F7
Zhumadian *China* 56 H8

Zhuo Xian = Zhuozhou
      China 56 E8
Zhuolu *China* 56 D8
Zhuozhou *China* 56 E8
Zhuozi *China* 56 D7
Zhushan *China* 59 A8
Zhuxi *China* 58 A7
Zhuzhou *China* 59 D9
Zhvanets *Ukraine* 29 B11
Zhytomyr *Ukraine* 23 C15
Zhytomyr □ *Ukraine* 33 G5
Ži Shui → *China* 59 C9
Žiar nad Hronom
      Slovak Rep. 27 C11
Ziārān *Iran* 71 B6
Ziarat *Pakistan* 68 D2
Zibo *China* 57 F10
Zichang *China* 56 F5
Zidarovo *Bulgaria* 45 D11
Zidi = Wandhari *Pakistan* 68 F2
Ziębice *Poland* 31 H4
Zielona Góra *Poland* 31 G2
Zierikzee *Neths.* 17 C3
Ziesar *Germany* 24 C8
Zifta *Egypt* 80 H7
Zigey *Chad* 79 F9
Zigong *China* 58 C5
Ziguinchor *Senegal* 82 C1
Ziguinchor □ *Senegal* 82 C1
Zihuatanejo *Mexico* 118 D4
Zijin *China* 59 F10
Zile *Turkey* 72 B6
Žilina *Slovak Rep.* 27 B11
Žilinský □ *Slovak Rep.* 27 B12
Zillah *China* 79 C9
Zillertaler Alpen *Austria* 26 D4
Zima *Russia* 53 D11
Zimapán *Mexico* 119 C5
Zimba *Zambia* 87 F2
Zimbabwe *Zimbabwe* 87 G3
Zimbabwe ■ *Africa* 87 F3
Zimi *S. Leone* 82 D2
Zimnicea *Romania* 29 G10
Zimovniki *Russia* 35 G6
Zinave △ *Mozam.* 89 C5
Zinder *Niger* 83 C6
Zinder □ *Niger* 83 C7
Zinga *Tanzania* 87 D4
Zingaro △ *Italy* 42 D5
Zingst *Germany* 24 A8
Ziniaré *Burkina Faso* 83 C4
Zinnowitz *Germany* 24 A9
Zion △ *U.S.A.* 109 H7
Zirbitzkogel *Austria* 26 D7
Zirc *Hungary* 28 C2
Žiri *Slovenia* 41 B11
Žirje *Croatia* 41 E12
Zirl *Austria* 26 D4
Zirndorf *Germany* 25 F6
Ziros *Greece* 49 D8
Zirreh, Gowd-e *Afghan.* 66 E3
Zisterdorf *Austria* 27 C9
Zitácuaro *Mexico* 118 D4
Žitava → *Slovak Rep.* 27 C11
Zitong *China* 58 B5
Zitsa *Greece* 46 B2
Zittau *Germany* 24 E10
Zitundo *Mozam.* 89 D5
Živinice *Bos.-H.* 28 F3
Ziwa Maghariba =
      Kagera □ *Tanzania* 86 C3
Ziway, L. *Ethiopia* 81 F4
Zixi *China* 59 D11
Zixing *China* 59 E9
Ziyang *Shaanxi, China* 56 H5
Ziyang *Sichuan, China* 58 B5
Ziyuan *China* 59 D8
Ziyun *China* 58 E6
Zizhong *China* 58 C5
Zlarin *Croatia* 41 E12
Zlatar *Croatia* 41 B13
Zlatar *Serbia* 44 C3
Zlataritsa *Bulgaria* 45 C9
Zlatibor *Serbia* 44 C3
Zlatitsa *Bulgaria* 45 D8
Zlatna *Romania* 29 D8
Zlatna Panega *Bulgaria* 45 C8
Zlatni Pyasŭtsi *Bulgaria* 45 C12
Zlatograd *Bulgaria* 45 E9
Zlatoust *Russia* 52 D6
Zletovo *Macedonia* 44 E6
Zlín *Czech Rep.* 27 B10
Zlínský □ *Czech Rep.* 27 B10
Złocieniec *Poland* 31 E3
Złoczew *Poland* 31 G5
Zlot *Serbia* 44 B5
Złotoryja *Poland* 31 G2
Złotów *Poland* 30 E4
Zmeinogorsk *Kazakhstan* 52 D9
Żmigród *Poland* 31 G3
Zmiyev *Ukraine* 33 H9
Znamenka = Znamyanka
      Ukraine 33 H7
Znamensk *Russia* 30 D8
Znamyanka *Ukraine* 33 H7

Žnin *Poland* 31 F4
Znojmo *Czech Rep.* 26 C9
Zobeyrī *Iran* 70 C5
Zobia *Dem. Rep. of the Congo* 86 B2
Zoetermeer *Neths.* 17 B4
Zogang *China* 58 C1
Zogno *Italy* 40 C6
Zogqên *China* 58 A2
Zolochev = Zolochiv
      Ukraine 23 D13
Zolochiv *Ukraine* 23 D13
Zolotonosha *Ukraine* 33 H7
Zolotyy Potik *Ukraine* 29 B10
Zomba *Malawi* 87 F4
Zongo *Dem. Rep. of the Congo* 84 D3
Zonguldak *Turkey* 72 B4
Zonguldak □ *Turkey* 72 B4
Zongyang *China* 59 B11
Zonqor Pt. *Malta* 49 D2
Zonza *France* 21 G13
Zorgo *Burkina Faso* 83 C4
Zorita *Spain* 37 F5
Zorleni *Romania* 29 D12
Zornitsa *Bulgaria* 45 D10
Zorritos *Peru* 124 D2
Zorzor *Liberia* 82 D3
Zossen *Germany* 24 C9
Zou Xiang *China* 56 G9
Zouan-Hounien *Ivory C.* 82 D3
Zouar *Chad* 79 D9
Zouérate = Zouîrât
      Mauritania 78 D3
Zouîrât *Mauritania* 78 D3
Zourika *Niger* 83 B6
Zourma *Burkina Faso* 83 C4
Zoutkamp *Neths.* 17 A6
Zrenjanin *Serbia* 28 E5
Zuarungu *Ghana* 83 C4
Zuba *Nigeria* 83 D6
Zubayr *Yemen* 81 D5
Zubtsov *Russia* 32 D8
Zuénoula *Ivory C.* 82 D3
Zuera *Spain* 38 D4
Zufār *Oman* 75 D5
Zug *Switz.* 25 H4
Zugdidi *Georgia* 35 J5
Zugersee *Switz.* 25 H4
Zugspitze *Germany* 25 H6
Zuid-Holland □ *Neths.* 17 C4
Zuidbeveland *Neths.* 17 C3
Zuidhorn *Neths.* 17 A6
Zújar *Spain* 37 H8
Zújar → *Spain* 37 G5
Żukowo *Poland* 30 D5
Zula *Eritrea* 81 D4
Zülpich *Germany* 24 E2
Zumaia *Spain* 38 B2
Zumárraga *Spain* 38 B2
Zumbo *Mozam.* 87 F3
Zummo *Nigeria* 83 D7
Zumpango *Mexico* 119 D5
Zungeru *Nigeria* 83 D6
Zunhua *China* 57 D9
Zuni Pueblo *U.S.A.* 109 J9
Zunyi *China* 58 D6
Zuo Jiang → *China* 58 F6
Zuozhou *China* 58 F6
Županja *Croatia* 28 E3
Žur *Serbia* 44 D4
Zurbāṭīyah *Iraq* 73 F12
Zürich *Switz.* 25 H4
Zürich □ *Switz.* 25 H4
Zürichsee *Switz.* 25 H4
Żuromin *Poland* 31 E6
Zutphen *Neths.* 17 B6
Zuurberg △ *S. Africa* 88 E4
Zuwārah *Libya* 79 B8
Zūzan *Iran* 71 C8
Žužemberk *Slovenia* 41 C11
Zvenigorodka =
      Zvenyhorodka *Ukraine* 33 H6
Zvenyhorodka *Ukraine* 33 H6
Zvezdets *Bulgaria* 45 D11
Zvishavane *Zimbabwe* 87 G3
Zvolen *Slovak Rep.* 27 C12
Zvonce *Serbia* 44 D6
Zvornik *Bos.-H.* 28 F4
Zwedru = Tchien *Liberia* 82 D3
Zweibrücken *Germany* 25 F3
Zwelitsha *S. Africa* 85 L5
Zwenkau *Germany* 24 D8
Zwettl *Austria* 26 C8
Zwickau *Germany* 24 E8
Zwierzyniec *Poland* 31 H9
Zwiesel *Germany* 25 F9
Zwoleń *Poland* 31 G8
Zwolle *Neths.* 17 B6
Zwolle *U.S.A.* 116 F8
Żychlin *Poland* 31 F6
Żyrardów *Poland* 31 F7
Zyryan *Kazakhstan* 52 E9
Zyryanka *Russia* 53 C16
Zyryanovsk = Zyryan
      Kazakhstan 52 E9
Żywiec *Poland* 31 J6
Zyyi *Cyprus* 49 E12

KEY TO EUROPEAN MAP PAGES

 **Large scale maps**
(>1:2 500 000)

 **Medium scale maps**
(1:2 800 000 – 1:9 900 000)

 **Small scale maps**
(<1:10 000 000)

8

ICELAND

WORLD COUNTRY INDEX

Afghanistan	66	**G**ermany	24–25	**P**akistan	66, 68
Albania	44	Ghana	82–83	Panama	120
Algeria	78	Greece	44–47	Papua New Guinea	96
Angola	84–85	Greenland	4	Paraguay	126–127
Argentina	126, 128	Guadeloupe	120	Peru	124
Armenia	73	Guatemala	120	Philippines	61
Australia	92–95	Guinea	82	Poland	30–31
Austria	26–27	Guinea-Bissau	82	Portugal	36–37
Azerbaijan	73	Guyana	124	Puerto Rico	121
Bahamas	120–121	**H**aiti	121	**Q**atar	71
Bahrain	71	Honduras	120		
Bangladesh	67	Hungary	28	**R**omania	28–29
Barbados	121			Russia	32–35, 52–53
Belarus	32–33	**I**celand	8	Rwanda	86
Belgium	17	India	66–69		
Belize	120	Indonesia	62–63	**S**t. Lucia	121
Benin	83	Iran	70–71, 73	Samoa	91
Bhutan	67	Iraq	70–71, 73	Saudi Arabia	70–71, 75
Bolivia	124	Irish Republic	12	Scotland	13
Bosnia-Herzegovina	41, 44	Israel	74	Senegal	82
Botswana	88	Italy	40–43	Serbia	28, 44
Brazil	124–125, 127	Ivory Coast	82	Sierra Leone	82
Brunei	62			Singapore	65
Bulgaria	44–45	**J**amaica	120	Slovak Republic	27
Burkina Faso	82–83	Japan	54–55	Slovenia	41
Burma (Myanmar)	67	Jordan	74	Solomon Is.	96
Burundi	86			Somali Republic	75
		Kazakhstan	52	South Africa	88–89
Cambodia	64–65	Kenya	86	Spain	36–39
Canary Is.	48	Korea, North	57	Sri Lanka	66
Cameroon	83, 84	Korea, South	57	Sudan	80–81
Canada	100–105	Kuwait	70–71	Suriname	124–125
Central African Republic	84	Kyrgyzstan	52	Swaziland	89
Chad	79			Sweden	8–9
Chile	126, 128	**L**aos	64	Switzerland	25
China	56–60	Latvia	32	Syria	70, 72–73
Colombia	124	Lebanon	74		
Congo	84	Lesotho	89	**T**aiwan	59
Congo, Dem. Rep.		Liberia	82	Tajikistan	52
of the	84–85, 86–87	Libya	79	Tanzania	86–87
Costa Rica	120	Lithuania	32	Thailand	64–65
Croatia	41	Luxembourg	17	Togo	83
Cuba	120–121			Tonga	91
Cyprus	49	**M**acedonia	44	Trinidad and Tobago	125
Czech Republic	26–27	Madagascar	89	Tunisia	78–79
		Malawi	87	Turkey	72–73
Denmark	11	Malaysia	62–63, 65	Turkmenistan	52
Djibouti	81	Mali	78, 82–83		
Dominican Republic	121	Malta	49	**U**ganda	86
		Martinique	120	Ukraine	33
East Timor	63	Mauritania	78, 82	United Arab Emirates	75
Ecuador	124	Mexico	118–119	United Kingdom	12–16
Egypt	80	Moldova	29	USA	106–117
El Salvador	120	Mongolia	60	Uruguay	126–127
England	14–15	Montenegro	44	Uzbekistan	52
Equatorial Guinea	84	Morocco	78		
Eritrea	80–81	Mozambique	87, 89	**V**anuatu	96
Estonia	32			Venezuela	124
Ethiopia	75, 81	**N**amibia	88	Vietnam	64–65
		Nepal	69		
Fiji	91	Netherlands	17	**W**ales	14–15
Finland	8–9	New Zealand	91		
France	18–21	Nicaragua	120	**Y**emen	75
French Guiana	125	Niger	78–79, 83		
		Nigeria	83	**Z**ambia	85, 87
Gabon	84	Northern Ireland	12	Zimbabwe	87
Gambia	82	Norway	8–9		
Georgia	35				
		Oman	75		

Arctic Circle

8

16   13

13

13

14

12   22

17

18

20   FRAN

36   38

ANDORRA

PORTUGAL   SPAIN   48

MOROCCO   AL